ENCYCLOPEDIA OF

OCCULTISM & PARAPSYCHOLOGY

ENCYCLOPEDIA OF OCCULTISM & PARAPSYCHOLOGY

A Compendium of Information on the Occult Sciences, Magic, Demonology, Superstitions, Spiritism, Mysticism, Metaphysics, Psychical Science, and Parapsychology, with Biographical and Bibliographical Notes and Comprehensive Indexes

FIFTH EDITION

In Two Volumes

VOLUME TWO
M-Z

Edited by J. Gordon Melton

Detroit
New York
San Francisco
London
Boston
Woodbridge, CT

J. Gordon Melton

Gale Group Staff

Jolen Marya Gedridge, *Editor*
Christy Wood, *Associate Editor*
Pamela A. Dear, *Contributing Associate Editor*
Jason Everett, *Contributing Assistant Editor*
Rita Runchock, *Managing Editor*

Mary Beth Trimper, *Production Director*
Evi Seoud, *Production Manager*
Rita Wimberley, *Buyer*

Kenn Zorn, *Manager, Production Design*
Barbara J. Yarrow, *Manager, Imaging and Multimedia Content*
Tracey Rowens, *Senior Art Director*
Michael Logusz, *Graphic Artist*

Datapage Technologies International, Inc., *Typesetting*

ISBN 0-8103-8570-8 (Complete Set)
ISBN 0-8103-9488-X (Volume 1)
ISBN 0-8103-9489-8 (Volume 2)
Printed in the United States of America
10 9 8 7 6 5 4 3 2 1

Contents

ENCYCLOPEDIA OF
OCCULTISM & PARAPSYCHOLOGY

M

M. A., Oxon

Pseudonym of **William Stainton Moses,** prominent British Spiritualist, author of *Spirit Teachings* (1833) and other books.

Maa-Kheru

According to Egyptologist Gaston Maspero, Maa-Kheru is the Egyptian name of the true intonation with which the dead must recite those magic incantations that would give them power in Amenti, the Egyptian Hades. (See also **Egypt**)

Mabinogion

A collection of ancient Welsh legends translated into English by Lady Charlotte Guest (1812–1895) and published 1838–49. The title is the plural form of the Welsh *maginogi,* originally indicating stories of a hero's childhood, but is here used in the wider sense of "hero tale." The stories in this collection are from various manuscript sources, originally part of the oral tradition of professional minstrels known as *cyvarwyddon.*

In this collection, the section entitled the *Four Branches of the Mabinogi* derives from a manuscript ca. 1060 C.E., dealing with pre-Christian myths that have affinities with traditional Irish folklore. *Kilhwch and Olwen* is from a manuscript ca. 1100 C.E. and is an early Arthurian romance. *The Dream of Rhonabwy* is another Arthurian story, related to the French recension of *Didot Perceval.* The *Lady of the Fountain, Geraint,* and *Peredur* are also Arthurian, ca. 1200 C.E., colored by Breton and French culture, although Celtic in origin. *The Dream of Maxen,* dating from the twelfth century, is a literary work rather than folk tale, the plot resembling the Irish *Dream of Oengus. Taliesin* dates from a sixteenth-century manuscript; it concerns a famous bard of the sixth century and has affinities with Irish legends.

In addition to the translation by Lady Charlotte Guest, there is also a later translation by Gwyn Jones and Thomas Jones (1949). (See also **Wales**)

Machell, Reginald Willoughby (1854–1927)

Artist and theosophist, born on June 20, 1854, in Crackenthorpe, Westmoreland, England. His father was the canon at York Cathedral. Machell attended Owen's College, Manchester, where he was an outstanding student in the classics and in art. In 1875 he moved to London and then Paris to pursue artistic endeavors and won prizes at the Academy de Juliens. In 1880 he settled in London as a professional painter, successfully specializing in portraits.

In 1887 Machell encountered Theosophy and found himself immediately drawn to it. He soon met **Helena Petrovona Blavatsky,** cofounder of the **Theosophical Society,** and joined that organization. He redecorated the facilities at 19 Avenue Rd., Regents Park, where Blavatsky moved in 1890, and she invited him to move his studio into the same building. He designed the urn that held Blavatsky's ashes following her death and cremation in 1891.

Machell's art took on a mystical/Gnostic cast and realism gave way to symbolism. He soon produced some of his most famous paintings, including *Dweller on the Threshold, The Birth of the Planet* and *Lead Kindly Light.* In 1900 he moved to the United States and joined the theosophical community at Point Loma, San Diego, California, established by the independent American branch of the Theosophical Society by **Katherine Tingley.** Over the next years he worked on the decor of the buildings, wrote articles for the community's periodical, *The Theosophical Path,* and did numerous illustrations for the *Path.* His painting "The Path" was used as the cover art of the journal for many years.

Machell died at Point Loma on October 9, 1927.

Machen, Arthur (Llewellyn) (1863–1947)

British novelist born March 3, 1863, at Carleon-on-Usk, Wales, who became one of the leading authors of English occult **fiction,** but was undeservedly neglected during his lifetime. He was a close friend of **Arthur Edward Waite,** one of Britain's greatest authorities on **occult** literature. His books include: *The Great God Pan* (1894), *The House of Souls* (1906), *The Hill of Dreams* (1907), *The Great Return* (1915), and *The Terror* (1917). In addition to his powerful stories on occult themes, he also published a number of volumes of essays and translations.

One of Machen's short stories brought a legend to real life. On September 29, 1914, his story "The Bowmen" appeared in the London *Evening News.* The story describes how British troops, hopelessly outnumbered in the French trenches of World War I, are miraculously rescued by phantom English archers from Agincourt, led by St. George. Many people read it as a factual account of what had happened, and a few months after publication, a number of eyewitness accounts of the **Angels of Mons** began to appear. Throughout the twentieth century people have believed the events actually occurred.

Machen reiterated that his story was fiction in the introduction to the later publication of his story in the book *The Bowmen and Other Legends of the War* (London, 1915), but the actual semi-miraculous retreat of the British from Mons had such an overpowering effect on the British public that they seemed to want to believe in divine intervention.

He died December 15, 1947, at Beaconsfield, England.

Sources:

Machen, Arthur. *The Great God Pan.* 1894. Reprint, London: M. Secker, 1926.

———. *The Great Return.* London: Faith Press, 1915.

———. *The Hill of Dreams.* 1907. Reprint, New York: Dover, 1986.

———. *The House of Souls.* 1906. Reprint, Freeport, N.Y.: Books for Libraries Press, 1971.

———. *The Terror.* 1917. Reprint, New York: W. W. Norton, 1965.

Reynolds, Aidan, and William Charlton. *Arthur Machen: A Short Account of His Life and Work.* London, 1963.

Sullivan, Jack, ed. *The Penguin Encyclopedia of Horror and the Supernatural.* New York: Viking, 1986.

Macionica

Slavonic name for a witch. (See **Slavs**)

Mackenzie, Kenneth R(obert) H(enderson) (1833–1886)

Prominent British occultist, an honorary magus of the **Societas Rosicruciana in Anglia,** and a member of the Hermetic Society of the **Golden Dawn.** During 1858–59 he edited four issues of *Biological Review,* devoted to **Spiritualism,** homeopathy, and electro-dentistry.

Mackenzie was born on October 31, 1833, in London. The following year his family lived in Vienna, where his father, Dr. Rowland H. Mackenzie, was assistant surgeon in the midwifery department at Imperial Hospital. Mackenzie and his wife returned to England about 1840, but it is probable that Kenneth Mackenzie was educated abroad. According to **William Wynn Westcott,** Mackenzie received a Rosicrucian initiation in Austria while living with Count Apponyi as an English tutor. Mackenzie returned to London by 1851 and contributed a series of learned notes to *Notes and Queries.*

As a young man he had an impressive knowledge of German, French, Latin, Greek, and Hebrew and had a precocious talent for antiquarian studies. He had ambitions to follow a literary career, and as early as 1852 he translated K. R. Lepsius's *Briefe aus Aegypten, Aethiopen, 1842–45* into English. He also contributed articles on Peking, America, and Scandinavia to Theodore Alois Buckley's work *Great Cities of the Ancient World* (1852). The next year he assisted Walter Savage Landor in a new edition of *Imaginary Conversations.* In 1870 Mackenzie married Alexandrina Aydon, daughter of a Freemason. His marriage became the occasion of his joining the craft in the same year.

He was author of the *Royal Masonic Cyclopaedia* (1877) and also planned a work called *The Game of Tarot: Archaeologically and Symbolically Considered,* which was announced but not published. In 1861 Mackenzie visited the famous French occultist **Éliphas Lévi** (Alphonse Louis Constant) in Paris and published vivid personal recollections of the man and his outlook in the *Rosicrucian,* the journal of the Societas Rosicruciana in Anglia. He also studied occultism with **Frederick Hockley** (1808–1885).

Mackenzie's other literary publications include *Burmah and the Burmese* (1853), *Zythogala; or, Borne by the Sea* (a novel, 1872), and the *Fundamental Constitutions of Freemasonry* (1877).

In addition he translated and/or edited *Schamyl and Circassia* by F. Wagner (1854), *Fairy Tales* by J. W. Wolf (1855), *The Marvellous Adventures . . . of Tyll Owlglass* by T. Eulenspiegel (1859), *The Life of Bismarck* by J. G. L. Hesekiel (1870), and *Bismarck: His Authentic Biography* by G. E. L. von Bismarck-Schoenhausen. He also edited early issues of a Masonic periodical titled *Kneph* in 1881.

On April 21, 1873, Mackenzie read a paper on Éliphas Lévi to the Rosicrucian Society (**Societas Rosicruciana in Anglia**), of which he became a member. He subsequently contributed papers to their journal, the *Rosicrucian.* He resigned from the society in 1875 while preparing his *Royal Masonic Cyclopaedia.* In subsequent years, he seems to have lived precariously on a modest income from journalism. He developed a system of astrological prediction of horse race winners and also became involved with the promotion of fringe Masonic orders, such as Sat B'Hai.

He died July 3, 1886, before the formation of the Hermetic Order of the **Golden Dawn,** but was claimed posthumously as an adept of the order (together with Lévi and Hockley) by W. W. Westcott, one of the founding chiefs, presuming a continuity of **occult** tradition through Rosicrucianism.

Sources:

Mackenzie, Kenneth. *Royal Masonic Cyclopaedia.* 1877. Reprint, New York: Sterling Publishing, 1987.

Mackenzie, William (1877– ?)

British biologist and writer, living in **Italy,** who played a prominent part in the scientific study of **parapsychology.** Mackenzie, born March 25, 1877, in Genoa, Italy, studied at the University of Turin (Ph.D., 1900). In 1905 he founded the first Marine Biological Laboratory at the University of Genoa and during 1912–13 conducted research in Germany on the phenomenon of "thinking animals." During World War I he was a volunteer in the Italian Army; during World War II (1939–45), he lectured on biological philosophy at the University of Geneva and was a consultant on foreign scientific literature to publishers in Florence beginning in 1960.

He was president of the Second International Congress of Psychical Research, held in Warsaw in 1923, then served as president of the Italian Society for Parapsychology, 1951–54, and honorary president beginning in 1954. He was president of the Third National Congress of Parapsychology, held at the University of Rome in 1956, and honorary member of the **Institut Métapsychique International,** Paris, and the Institut Francais de Florence.

Mackenzie edited *Parapsicologia* (quarterly journal of parapsychology) from 1955 to 1956. He conducted a special study of psychobiology (parapsychology in living organisms) and investigated psychic animals and mathematical mediumship. He published many articles on parapsychology in English and Italian journals such as *Psiche, Archives de Psycholgie, Proceedings of the Italian Society for the Advancement of Science, Quaderni di Psichiatria, Journal of the ASPR, Revue Métapsychique,* and *Uomini e Idee.*

Mackey, Albert Gallatin (1807–1881)

American authority on **Freemasonry** and editor of numerous books on the subject, including *Encyclopedia of Freemasonry* (1874). Mackey was born in Charleston, South Carolina, on March 12, 1807. He was a disciple of the great nineteenth-century Masonic leader Albert Pike (1809–1891), one of those falsely charged by fictitious Satanic priestess **Diana Vaughan** and others with the practice of **devil worship** and **sorcery.** The whole campaign proved to be a conspiracy on the part of journalist **Gabriel Jogand-Pagés** to discredit and embarrass both the Roman Catholic Church and Freemasonry. One of the earliest writers to throw doubt on the revelations of Jogand-Pagès was British occultist and mystic **Arthur E. Waite** in his book *Devil-Worship in France* (1896).

He died on June 20, 1881, in Virginia.

Sources:

Mackey, Albert Gallatin. *Encyclopedia of Freemasonry.* 1874. Reprint, Chicago: Masonic History, 1927.

Stein, Gordon. *Encyclopedia of Hoaxes.* Detroit: Gale Research, 1993.

MacLaine, Shirley (Shirley MacLean Beatty) (1934–)

World-famous actress, dancer, movie star, and writer, whose books on her search for spiritual fulfillment have created widespread popular interest in psychic phenomena, **channeling** of **spirit guides,** and **New Age** teachings. She was born on April 24, 1934, in Richmond, Virginia, and attended high school in Washington, D.C. She began taking dancing lessons before she was three years old; by the time she was 16 she was a chorus girl in New York in a City Center revival of *Oklahoma!* Four years later, she was dancing in the chorus of *Pajama Game* and acting as understudy to Carol Haney, the show's leading dancer. When Haney injured her ankle soon after the show's opening, MacLaine replaced her in the lead. After enthusiastic reviews, the Hollywood producer Hal B. Wallis signed her for a long-term film contract.

Her first motion picture role was in *The Trouble with Harry,* directed by Alfred Hitchcock. Later, her performance in *Irma la douce* earned her a Golden Globe Award and the third of four Academy Award nominations. Honors for her acting have continued into the 1990s.

Apart from her acting, MacLaine has gained a considerable reputation as an outspoken political and humanitarian activist, notably for civil rights, women's rights, and environmental protection. During the Vietnam War, she supported George McGovern's 1972 presidential campaign. She was the first woman ever to speak at the National Democratic Club, where she addressed the dangers of overpopulation. MacLaine's extensive travels have included such remote parts of the world as East Africa, where she lived among the Masai tribe, and the Himalayan kingdom of Bhutan, where she was detained by border guards during a political crisis. When traveling in **India,** she became sympathetic to the plight of the "gutter babies" and helped to establish an orphanage for them in Calcutta. Her best-selling autobiography *Don't Fall Off the Mountain* (1970), which detailed her experiences in **Africa,** India, the Far East, and Hollywood, was translated into eight languages.

In 1973 MacLaine led a delegation of 12 American women, including filmmaker Claudia Weill, on a six-week tour of the People's Republic of **China.** With Weill acting as her co-director, MacLaine produced and wrote the narration for the film *The Other Half of the Sky: A China Memoir,* a documentary of the trip broadcast by Public Broadcasting Service (1975). Her second autobiographical book, *You Can Get There from Here* (1975), discussed her China trip and her involvement with George McGovern's presidential campaign. In 1976, after a 20-year hiatus as an entertainer, she returned to the theatrical stage in *A Gypsy in My Soul,* which attracted rave reviews. By 1983 she had appeared in some 35 movies.

Her third autobiographical book, *Out on a Limb* (1983), described a spiritual odyssey that developed from her world travels. It is a heady exploration of New Age beliefs, including **meditation,** psychic **healing,** channeling of spirit guides, **reincarnation, UFOs,** extraterrestrials, and **out-of-the-body travel.** If at times the book appears naive, it is redeemed by its transparent honesty and sincerity and a deep desire for a spiritual framework to life. The book became the basis for a five-hour prime-time ABC-TV mini-series. Her inner search continued in her book *Dancing in the Light* (1985), in which she stated:

"I like to think of *Dancing in the Light* as a celebration of all my 'selves.' It was a fulfilling and satisfying exploration of the promises I made to myself in *Out on a Limb.* In it I look with pleasure, humor and some contentment upon my experiences as a daughter, a mother, a lover, a friend, a seeker of spiritual destiny and a voice calling for peace in the world."

The book cites several channels from whom she received guidance, but her kindest words are reserved for **J. Z. Knight,** who channels an entity named "Ramtha" and has since attracted a large following.

In the late 1980s MacLaine emerged as a New Age teacher and leader of Higher Life Seminars. Profits from the seminars have funded several New Age centers. MacLaine has continued to write New Age books.

Sources:

MacLaine, Shirley. *Dancing in the Light.* New York: Bantam Books, 1985.

———. *Don't Fall Off the Mountain.* New York: W. W. Norton, 1970.

———. *It's All in the Playing.* New York: Bantam Books, 1987.

———. *Out on a Limb.* New York: Bantam Books, 1983.

———. *You Can Get There from Here.* New York: W. W. Norton, 1975.

Melton, J. Gordon, Jerome Clark, and Aidan Kelly. *New Age Encyclopedia.* Detroit: Gale Research, 1990.

MacLeod, Fiona

Pseudonym of Scottish writer **William Sharp** (1856–1905), virtually a secondary personality who authored mystical writings on Celtic lore, which played a large part in the Scottish Celtic Revival. These works were the product of **automatic writing** by Sharp.

MacRobert, Russell Galbraith (1890–1967)

Psychiatrist and neurologist with a special interest in **parapsychology.** MacRobert was born June 4, 1890, at London, Ontario, Canada, and studied at the University of Western Ontario (M.D., 1912) and the University of Toronto (M.D., 1916). He was an associate neuropsychiatrist at Lenox Hill Hospital, New York (1922–41), a captain in the USNR Medical Corps during World War II, and afterward returned to Lenox Hill (1946–55). In 1955 he entered private practice and became an instructor in clinical neurology at New York University, Bellevue Hospital Medical Center, New York.

He was a member of the American Medical Association, American Academy of Neurology, American Board of Psychiatry and Neurology, and Academy of Religion and Mental Health, and a fellow of the American Psychiatric Association and the American Society of Clinical Hypnosis. His interest in **intuition, clairvoyance,** and mediumship prompted him to join the **American Society for Psychical Research.**

MacRobert published many articles on medical, psychiatric, and neurological subjects, as well as articles in parapsychology, including the chapter "Something Better than Reincarnation" in the book *Reincarnation* (1956) and the preface to **R. DeWitt Miller**'s book *You Do Take It with You* (1956).

He died on July 10, 1967, of cancer.

Sources:

MacRobert, Russell G. "Current Attitudes of American Neuropsychiatrists towards Parapsychology." *Journal of Parapsychology* (November 1948).

———. "Hallucinations of the Sane." *Journal of Insurance Medicine* 5, no. 3 (1950).

———. "Psychiatry and Intuition." *Journal of Insurance Medicine* 4, no. 3 (1949).

———. "Science Studies Intuition." *Tomorrow* (May 1950).

———. "When Is Healing 'Psychic'?" *Tomorrow* (spring 1955).

———. "Where Is Bridey Murphy?" *Tomorrow* (spring 1956).

Pleasants, Helene, ed. *Biographical Dictionary of Parapsychology.* New York: Helix Press, 1964.

The Macrocosm

The whole universe—from the Greek words *macros* (long) and *kosmos* (the world)—symbolized by a six-pointed star, formed of two triangles. This is the sacred symbol of Solomon's seal. It represents the infinite and the absolute—that is, the most simple and complete abridgment of the science of all things. **Paracelsus** stated that all magical figures may be reduced to two: the macrocosm and the **microcosm** (world in miniature). (See also **magical diagrams**)

Macro-PK

Term used to denote the effects of **psychokinesis** (paranormal movements) that, like **table turning,** are large enough to be observed by the naked eye. In contrast, **Micro-PK** refers to psychokinetic effects so minute that they require statistical analysis or special methods to detect.

The Macroprosopus

Representing one of the four magical elements in the **Kabala** and probably representing one of the four simple elements—air, water, earth, or fire. Macroprosopus means "creator of the great world."

Macumba

African-derived Brazilian religions that have spirit **possession** as a central feature.

Madonna Ministry

The Madonna Ministry is a **New Thought** metaphysical ministry founded by Bishop Arnold Michael, formerly a minister with the **United Church of Religious Science.** As a young man, in 1947 he had written a book, *Blessed Among Women,* on the life of the Virgin Mary published in 1948. The writing of the book became a life-altering event and Michael left his job managing a restaurant and studied for the Religious Science ministry. He served Religious Science churches for the next 35 years. In 1980, he returned to his consideration of the Virgin Mary and began writing a series of newsletters under the title *Madonna Ministry* that explored Mary's role as a consciousness of unconditioned love who represents the feminine-mothering aspect of God.

In the mid-1980s he retired from the Religious Science ministry and accepted consecration as a bishop by Archbishop Warren Watters of the Independent Church of Antioch, a church that combines a Gnostic theosophical approach to Christianity with an apostolic lineage through the non- Chalcedonian churches in the Middle East. Michael founded the Church of the Talking Pines before he died in 1987. Two years later he was succeeded by Bishop Charles Sommers, who had also been consecrated by Archbishop Watters. In 1990, the Church of the Talking Pines changed its name to Madonna Ministry.

The church continues a major focus on spiritual healing, as does Religious Science, but includes a wide diversity of healers who represent the broad spectrum of **holistic** health practices. The healing emphasis led it into a relationship with the World Federation of Healing and the Creative Health Network as cosponsors of the annual international Healing Summit. The first summit was held in 1997 in Monterey, California; subsequent summits included meetings at **Glastonbury** (1999) and **Australia** (2000).

The Madonna Ministry is headquartered at 237 W. Ave. Alessandro, San Clemente, CA 92672-4334. It maintains two Internet sites, http://www.madonnaministry.org/, and http://www.paradigm-sys.com/madionnanews/.

Sources:

Madonna Ministry. http://www.madonnaministry.org/. April 4, 2000.

Madre Natura

An old and powerful secret society of Italy whose members worshiped and idealized nature. It seems to have been founded by members of the ancient Italian priesthood. It had a tradition that one of the popes became a member of the fraternity, and there appears to be some documentary evidence for this claim. The society accepted the allegorical interpretation that the Neoplatonists placed upon the pagan creeds during the first ages of Christianity.

Maeterlinck, Maurice (1862–1949)

Famous Belgian writer and poet and winner of the Nobel Prize in literature in 1911. He was born in Ghent, Belgium, on August 29, 1862, and educated at the Collège Sainte-Barbe and the University of Ghent. For a time he lived in Paris, where he became associated with the symbolist school of French poetry. His first publication was *Serres Chaudes,* a volume of poems, in 1889. His play *La Princesse Maleine,* which appeared the following year, was praised by novelist Octave Mirbeau. Although Maeterlinck had already qualified for the legal profession, he decided to follow a literary life.

From the very beginning of his great literary career, he was attracted by the problems of the inner life. His early plays were dominated by the grim specter of death as the destroyer of life. In his later works, his interest in psychic phenomena developed, and the fearful mystery gave place to wondrous fascination.

The Unknown Guest, Our Eternity and *The Wrack of the Storm* disclosed a familiarity with all the prevailing ideas on the paranormal, and he showed no doubt whatever as to the genuineness of phenomena. He wrote:

"The question of fraud and imposture are naturally the first that suggest themselves when we begin the study of these phenomena. But the slightest acquaintance with the life, habits and proceedings of the three or four leading mediums is enough to remove even the faintest shadow of suspicion. Of all the explanations conceivable, the one which attributes everything to imposture and trickery is unquestionably the most extraordinary and the least probable. . . . From the moment that one enters upon this study, all suspicions are dispelled without leaving a trace behind them; and we are soon convinced that the key to the riddle is not to be found in imposture. . . . Less than fifty years ago most of the hypnotic phenomena which are now scientifically classified were likewise looked upon as fraudulent. It seems that man is loathe to admit that there lie within him many more things than he imagined."

Maeterlinck considered **survival** proved but was uncertain as to the possibility of communication with the dead. Between the telepathic and spirit hypotheses, he could not make a choice in favor of the latter. He admitted that:

"the survival of the spirit is no more improbable than the prodigious faculties which we are obliged to attribute to the medium if we deny them to the dead; but the existence of the medium, contrary to that of the spirit, is unquestionable, and therefore it is for the spirit, or for those who make use of its name, first to prove that it exists."

He added that in his view there were five imaginable solutions of the great problem: the religious solution, annihilation, survival with our consciousness of today, survival without any sort of consciousness, and survival with a modified consciousness.

The religious solution he ruled out definitely, because it occupied "a citadel without doors or windows into which human reason does not penetrate." Annihilation he considered unthinkable and impossible: "We are the prisoners of an infinity without outlet, wherein nothing perishes, wherein everything is dispersed but nothing lost." Survival without consciousness of today is inconceivable, as the change of death and the casting aside of the body must bring about an enlarged understanding and an expansion of the intellectual horizon. Survival without any consciousness amounted to the same thing as annihilation.

The only solution that appealed to him was survival with a modified consciousness. He argued that since we have been able to acquire our present consciousness, why should it be impossible for us to acquire another in which our present consciousness is a mere speck, a negligible quantity: "Let us accustom ourselves to regard death as a form of life which we do not as yet understand; let us learn to look upon it with the same eye that looks upon birth; and soon our minds will be accompanied to the steps of the tomb with the same glad expectation that greets a birth."

Maeterlinck died May 6, 1949.

Sources:

Berger, Arthur S., and Joyce Berger. *The Encyclopedia of Parapsychology and Psychical Research.* New York: Paragon House, 1991.

Ebon, Martin. *They Knew the Unknown.* New York: New American Library, 1971.

Maeterlinck, Maurice. *The Great Secret.* New Hyde Park, N.Y.: University Books, 1969.

———. *The Unknown Guest.* New Hyde Park, N.Y.: University Books, 1975.

"Mafu"

"Mafu," the entity said to speak through channel Penny Torres, emerged in the mid-1980s during the growing popularity of **"Ramtha,"** the entity said to speak through **J. Z. Knight.** In the process of developing as a channel, Torres had visited Knight, and as "Mafu" emerged, many people noted the similarity between his speech characteristics and gestures and those of "Ramtha."

Mafu described himself as a 32,000-year-old being who had incarnated on earth 17 different times. He began to manifest through Torres in 1986. Torres's attention had been occupied by some poltergeist activity, in which objects spontaneously flew around the room. She was then told by another channel, Pam Davis, that a master named Mafu wished to speak through her. The very next day "Mafu" first spoke to Torres and instructed her how to use a crystal to heal her son, who was sick with pneumonia. Later that year, in Davis's home, Torres began to channel, though it was not "Mafu" who spoke.

Then a month later "Mafu" again spoke through Torres and began to train her as a trance channel. She gave her first public **channeling** sessions in Santa Barbara, California, and within a short time was regularly conducting channeling sessions in Los Angeles and Santa Barbara. As her popularity grew, she organized Mafu Seminars and began to give weekend programs around the country. In 1988 "Mafu" launched a more advanced study opportunity for people serious about his teachings, developing a course called "Advanced Realization Training Beyond the Human Potential." The course introduced people to a macrobiotic diet, meditation, and other advanced teachings.

The direction of the movement around "Mafu" took a new turn in 1989 when Torres visited **India** and had an intense religious experience. She took the vows of a renounced life (as a sanyassi) and accepted the mission as the "ordained leader of spirituality" for the present age. She also received her new name, Swami Paramananda Saraswati. Torres returned to the United States and established the Foundation for the Realization of Inner Divinity to supersede Mafu Seminars. The subsidiary, the Center for God Realization, now disseminates "Mafu's" teaching materials (tapes and books).

The foundation is headquartered at a campground near Ashland, Oregon, which serves as a retreat center. Mafu's continued teachings, most of which are disseminated in cassette tapes, are seen as forming a distinct path to realization. The foundation may be contacted at P.O. Box 458, White City, OR 97524.

Sources:

"Interview: Penny Torres on Mafu." *Life Times* 1, no. 2 (winter 1986–87): 74–79.

L'Ecuyer, Michele. "Mafu." *Life Times* 1, no. 2 (winter 1986–87): 80–82.

Torres, Penny [Mafu]. *And What Be God?* Vacaville, Calif.: Mafu Seminars, 1989.

———. *Reflections on Yeshua Ben Joseph.* Vacaville, Calif.: Mafu Seminars, 1989.

Magi

Priests of ancient Persia and cultivators of the wisdom of Zoroaster (or Zarathustra) (possibly 1500 B.C.E.). They were instituted by Cyrus when he founded the new Persian empire and are supposed to have been of the Median race.

The German scholar K. W. F. von Schlegel stated in his *Lectures on the Philosophy of History* (2 vols., 1829): "They were not so much a hereditary sacerdotal caste as an order or association, divided into various and successive ranks and grades, such as existed in the mysteries—the grade of apprenticeship—that of mastership—that of perfect mastership." In short, they were a theosophical college; and either its professors were indifferently "magi," or **magicians,** and "wise men" or they were distinguished into two classes by those names.

Their name, pronounced "Mogh" by later Persians, and "Magh" by the ancients, signified "wise," which was the interpretation of it given by the Greek and Roman writers. Stobaeus expressly called the science of the magi, the "service of the gods," as did Plato. According to Joseph Ennemoser in his book *The History of Magic* (1847), "Magiusiah, Madschusie" signified the office and knowledge of the priest, who was called "Mag, Magius, Magiusi," and afterward magi and "Magician." The philosopher J. J. Brucker maintained that the primitive meaning of the word was "fire worshiper" and "worship of the light," an erroneous opinion. In modern Persian, the word is "Mog"; "Mogbed" signifies high priest. The high priest of the Parsees at Surat was called "Mobed." Others derive the word from "Megh," "Meh-ab" signifying something that is great and noble; Zoroaster's disciples were called "Meghestom."

Eusèbe Salverte, author of *Des sciences occulte* (1829), stated that these Mobeds were named in the Pehivi dialect "Magoi." They were divided into three classes: those who abstained from all animal food; those who never ate of the flesh of any tame animals; and those who made no scruple to eat any kind of meat. A belief in the transmigration of the soul was the foundation of this abstinence.

They professed the science of **divination** and for that purpose met together and consulted in their temples. They professed to make truth the great object of their study, for that alone, they said, can make man like God "whose body resembles light, as his soul or spirit resembles truth."

They condemned all images and those who said that the gods were male and female; they had neither temples nor altars, but worshiped the sky, as a representative of the deity, on the tops of mountains; they also sacrificed to the sun, **moon,** earth, fire, water, and winds, said Herodotus, meaning no doubt that they adored the heavenly bodies and the elements. This was probably before the time of Zoroaster, when the religion of Persia seems to have resembled that of ancient India. Their hymns in praise of the Most High exceeded (according to Dio Chrysostom) the sublimity of anything in Homer or Hesiod. They exposed their dead bodies to wild beasts.

Schlegel maintained that it was an open question "whether the old Persian doctrine and wisdom or tradition of light did not undergo material alterations in the hand of its Median restorer, Zoroaster, or whether this doctrine was preserved in all its purity by the order of the magi." He then remarked that on them devolved the important trust of the monarch's education, which must necessarily have given them great weight and influence in the state. They were in high credit at the "Persian gates" (the Oriental name given to the capital of the empire, and the abode of the prince) and they took the most active part in all the factions that encompassed the throne, or that were formed in the vicinity of the court.

In **Greece,** and even in **Egypt,** the sacerdotal fraternities and associations of the initiated, formed by the mysteries, had in general an indirect, although not unimportant, influence on affairs of state, but in the Persian monarchy they acquired a complete political ascendency. Religion, philosophy, and the sciences were all in their hands. They were the universal physicians who healed the sick in body and in spirit, and, in strict consistency with that character, ministered to the state, which is only the individual in a larger sense. The three grades of the magi alluded to were called the "disciples," the "professed," and the "masters."

They were originally from Bactria, where they governed a little state by laws of their own choice, and by their incorporation in the Persian empire, they greatly promoted the consolidation of the conquests of Cyrus.

Their decline dates from the reign of Darius Hystaspes, about 500 B.C.E., by whom they were fiercely persecuted. This produced an emigration that extended from Cappadocia to India, but they were still of so much consideration at a later period as to provoke the jealousy of Alexander the Great.

"Magia Posthuma" (of C. F. de Schertz)

A short treatise on the **vampire** published at Olmutz (now in the Czech Republic) in 1706 and written by Charles Ferdinand de Schertz. Reviewing it, **Dom Antoine Augustin Calmet** stated in his *Dissertation sur les apparitions, des anges . . . et sur les revenaus et vampires* (1746; trans. *The Phantom World,* 2. vols., 1850) that the author related a story of a woman that died in a certain village, after having received all the sacraments, and was buried with the usual ceremonies in the churchyard. About four days after her death and for several months, the inhabitants of the village were frightened by unusual noises and many saw a specter, sometimes shaped like a dog and sometimes like a man, who tried to choke or suffocate them. Several were bruised all over and utterly weak, pale, lean, and disfigured. The specter took his fury out even on the beasts: cows were frequently found beaten to the earth, half dead, at other times with their tails tied to one another, lowing hideously. Horses were found foaming with sweat and out of breath, as if they had been running a long and tiresome race.

Schertz examined the subject in the capacity of a lawyer and was clearly of the opinion that if the suspected person were really the source of these noises, disturbances, and acts of cruelty, the law would justify the burning of the body, as is practiced in the case of other specters that come again and molest the living.

He related several stories of apparitions of this sort and the mischief done by them. One was of a herdsman of the village of Blow near the town of Kadam in Bohemia, who appeared for a considerable time and called upon several persons, who all died within eight days. The inhabitants of Blow dug up the herdsman's body and fixed it in the ground with a stake driven through it. The man, even in this condition, laughed at the people that were employed about him, and told them they were very obliging to furnish him with a stick to defend himself from the dogs.

The same night, he extricated himself from the stake, frightened several persons by appearing to them, and occasioned the death of many more than he had hitherto done. He was then delivered into the hands of the hangman, who put him into a cart in order to burn him outside the town. As they went along, the carcass shrieked in the most hideous manner and threw its arms and legs about as if it had been alive. Upon being again run through with a stake, it gave a loud cry, and a great quantity of fresh, florid blood issued from the wound. At last the body was burnt to ashes, and this execution put a final stop to the specter's appearing and infesting the village.

The same method was practiced in other places where these apparitions were seen, and upon taking them out of the ground, their bodies seemed fresh and florid, their limbs pliant and flexible, without any worms or putrefaction, but not without a great stench.

The author quoted several other writers, who attested to what he related concerning these specters, which, he stated, still appeared in the mountains of Silesia and Moravia. They were seen, it seems, both by day and night, and the things that formerly belonged to them were observed to stir and change their place without any person being seen to touch them. And the only remedy in these cases, he claimed, was to cut off the head and burn the body of the persons supposed to appear.

Sources:

Calmet, Augustine. *The Phantom World.* 2 vols. London: Richard Bentley, 1850.

Magic

General term for "magic art," believed to derive from the Greek *magein,* the science and religion of the priests of Zoroaster (see **Magi**), or, according to philologist Skeat, from Greek *megas* (great), thus signifying "the great science." It commonly refers to the ability to cause change to occur by supernatural or mysterious powers and abilities. In the twentieth century, magic has been more stringently defined as the ability to create change by an act of the will and the use of the cosmic power believed to underpin physical existence. Contemporary magicians also distinguish between high magic and low magic. The latter refers to using magic to make changes in the mundane world, from concocting love potions to drawing money to oneself. The former refers to disciplined change of the self, and practitioners of high magic compare it to **yoga.**

Early History

Until a few centuries ago, most people lived in what they considered a magical universe, and evidence of the practice of magic is found as far back as human prehistory. Among the earliest traces of magic practice are paintings found in the European caves of the middle Paleolithic period. These belong to the last interglacial period of the Pleistocene epoch, named the Aurignacian after the cave dwellers of Aurignac (southern **France**), whose skeletons, artifacts, and drawings link them with the Bushmen of South **Africa.**

In the cave of Gargas, near Bagnères de Luchon, there are, in addition to spirited and realistic drawings of animals, numerous imprints of human hands in various stages of mutilation. Some hands were apparently first smeared with a sticky substance and then pressed onto the rock; others were held in position to be dusted around with red ocher or black pigment. Most of the imprinted hands have mutilated fingers; in some cases the first and second joints of one or more fingers are missing; in others only the stumps of all fingers remain.

A close study of the hand imprints shows that they are not those of lepers. There can be little doubt that the joints were removed for a specific purpose; on this point there is general agreement among anthropologists.

A clue to the mystery is provided by a similar custom among the Bushmen. G. W. Stow, in his book *The Native Races of South Africa* (1905), refers to this strange form of sacrifice. He once came into contact with a number of Bushmen who "had all lost the first joint of the little finger," which had been removed with a "stone knife" for the purpose of ensuring a safe journey to the spirit world. Another writer told of an old Bushman woman whose little fingers of both hands had been mutilated, three joints in all having been removed. She explained that each joint had been sacrificed to express her sorrow as each one of three daughters died.

In his *Report on the Northwestern Tribes of the Dominion of Canada* (1889), Franz Boas gives evidence of the custom among these peoples. When many deaths resulted from disease, the Canadian Indians sacrificed the joints of their little fingers in order to (they explained) "cut off the deaths."

Among the Indian Madigas (Telugu pariahs), the **evil eye** was averted by sacrificers who dipped their hands in the blood of goats or sheep and impressed them on either side of a house door. This custom was also known to the Brahmans of **India.**

Impressions of hands were also occasionally seen on the walls of Muslim mosques in India. As among the northwest Canadian tribes, the hand ceremony was most frequently practiced in India when epidemics took a heavy toll of lives. The Bushmen also removed finger joints when stricken with sickness. In Australia, where during initiation ceremonies the young Aborigine men had teeth knocked out and bodies scarred, the women of some tribes mutilated the little fingers of daughters in order to influence their future lives.

Apparently the finger-chopping customs of Paleolithic times had a magical significance. On some of the paintings in the Aurignacian caves appear symbols that suggest the slaying and butchering of animals. Other symbols are enigmatic. Of special interest are the figures of animal-headed demons, some with hands upraised in the Egyptian posture of adoration; others posed like the animal-headed dancing gods of the Bushmen.

In the Marsonlas Paleolithic cave, there are humanlike faces of angry demons with staring eyes and monstrous noses. In the Spanish Cave at Cogul, several figures of women wearing half-length skirts and shoulder shawls are represented dancing around a nude male. These females so closely resemble those of Bushman paintings that they might, if not for their location, be credited to this interesting people. Religious dances among the Bushman tribes were associated with marriage, birth, and burial ceremonies; they were also performed to exorcise demons in cases of sickness. "Dances are to us what prayers are to you," an elderly Bushman once informed a European.

Whether the cave drawings and wood, bone, and ivory carvings of the Magdalenian or late Paleolithic period at the close of the last ice age are related to magic is a question on which there is no general agreement. It is significant, however, that several carved ornaments bearing animal figures or enigmatic symbols are perforated as if worn as charms. On a piece of horn found at Lorthet, Hautes-Pyrénées, are beautiful, incised drawings of reindeer and salmon, above which appear mystical symbols.

An ape-like demon carved on bone was found at Mas d'Azil. Etched on a reindeer horn from Laugerie Basse is a prostrate man with a tail, creeping on all fours toward a grazing bison. These artifacts strengthen the theory that late Paleolithic art had its origin in magic beliefs and practices—that hunters carved on the handles of weapons and implements, or scratched on cave walls, the images of the animals they desired to capture—sometimes with the secured cooperation of demons and sometimes with the aid of magic spells.

A highly developed magic system existed in ancient **Egypt,** as in Babylonian (see **Semites**) and other early cultures. From these cultures the medieval European system of magic is believed to have evolved. **Greece** and **Rome** also possessed distinct magic systems that were integrated into their religious practice and thus, like the Egyptian and Babylonian rituals, were preserves of the priesthood.

Magic in early Europe was integral to the various religious systems that prevailed throughout that continent and survived into the Middle Ages as **witchcraft.** Christians regarded the practice of magic, at least the popular forms practiced in the Pagan culture competing with their religion, as foreign to the spirit of their faith. Thus the Thirty-Sixth Canon of the Ecumenical Council held at Laodicea in 364 C.E. forbade clerks and priests to become magicians, enchanters, mathematicians, or astrologers. It ordered, moreover, that the church should expel those who employed ligatures or phylacteries, because, it said, phylacteries were the prisons of the soul. The Fourth Canon of the Council of Oxia in 525 C.E. prohibited the consultation of sorcerers, augurs, and diviners, and condemned divinations made with wood or bread, while the Sixteenth Canon of the Council of Constantinople in 692 C.E. excommunicated for a period of six years diviners and those who had recourse to them. The prohibition was repeated by the Council of Rome in 721. The Forty-Second Canon of the Council of Tours in 613 said priests should teach people the inefficacy of magic to restore the health of men or animals, and later councils endorsed the church's earlier views.

Medieval Magic

It does not appear that what may be called "medieval magic" took final and definite shape until about the twelfth century. Modeled after the systems in vogue among the Byzantines and Moors of **Spain,** which evolved from the Alexandrian system (see **Neoplatonism**), what might be called "Oriental" magic gained footing in Europe and superseded the earlier magic based on paganistic practice and ritual. There is evidence that Eastern magic was imported into Europe by persons returning from the Crusades, and magic was disseminated from Constantinople throughout Europe, along with other sciences.

Witches and wizards and professors of lesser magic clung to paganism, whereas among the disciples of Oriental magic were the magicians, necromancers (fortune-tellers), and sorcerers (practitioners of malevolent magic).

The tenets of the higher branches of magic changed little from the eighth to the thirteenth century. There also appears to have been little persecution of the professors of magic. After that period, however, the opinions of the church underwent a radical change, and the life of the magus was fraught with considerable danger. **Paracelsus,** for instance, was not victimized in the same manner as the sorcerers and wizards, but he was consistently baited by the medical profession of his day. **Agrippa** was also continually persecuted, and even mystics like **Jakob Boehme** were imprisoned and mistreated. (Magicians were subject to persecution both for possible acts of sorcery and for allegiance to a heretical religious system.)

It is difficult to estimate the enormous popularity that magic experienced, whether for good or evil, during the Middle Ages. Although severely punished if discovered—or if its professors became notorious enough to court persecution—the power it seems to have conferred upon the practitioner was coveted by scores of people.

Two great names in the history of European magic are those of Paracelsus and Agrippa, who outlined the science of medieval magic. They were also the greatest practical magicians of the Middle Ages—apart from pure mystics, alchemists, and others—and their thaumaturgic and necromantic experiences were probably never surpassed.

Theories Regarding the Nature of Magic

According to Sir James George Frazer, author of *The Golden Bough* (1890), magic and religion are one and the same thing, or at least are so closely allied as to be almost identical.

Frazer's anthropologist successors in the early twentieth century, most notably Malinowski and Marcel Mauss, regarded magic as entirely distinct from religion. Magic possessed certain well-marked attributes that could be traced to mental processes differing from those from which the religious idea springs, they said. The two had become fused by the superimposition of religious rites upon magic practice.

It has also been said that religion consists of an *appeal* to the gods, whereas magic is the attempt to *force* their compliance. Henri Hubert and Marcel Mauss, in *Greatness and Decline of the Celts* (1934), argue that magic is essentially traditional. Holding that the primitive mind is markedly unoriginal, they explain magic as an art that did not exhibit frequent changes among primitive peoples, and was fixed by its own laws. Religion, they claim, was official and organized; magic, prohibited and secret.

Frazer believed all magic was based on the law of sympathy—the assumption that things act on one another at a distance because of their being secretly linked by invisible bonds.

He divided sympathetic magic into homeopathic magic and contagious magic. The first is imitative or mimetic and may be practiced by itself, but the second usually necessitates the application of the imitative principle. Well-known instances of mimetic magic are the forming of wax figures in the likeness of an enemy, which are then destroyed in the hope that he will perish. This belief persisted in European witchcraft into relatively modern times. Contagious magic can be seen in the primitive warrior's anointing the weapon that caused a wound instead of the wound itself, believing that the blood on the weapon continues to feel part of the blood on the body. (See also **Powder of Sympathy**)

L. Marillier divided magic into three classes: the magic of the word or act; the magic of the human being independent of rite or formula; and the magic that demands a person of special powers and the use of ritual. A. Lehmann believed magic to be a practice of superstition, founded in illusion.

The Magic Force

Many peoples have spoken of the operation of a magic cosmic force—something that impinged upon the thought of man from outside. Many tribal cultures postulated the existence of a great reservoir of magic power, the exact nature of which they were not prepared to specify.

Certain American Indian tribes believed in a force called *orenda,* or spirit force. Among the ancient Peruvians everything sacred was *huaca* and possessed magic power. In Melanesia a force called *mana,* transmissible and contagious, could be seen in the form of flames or could even be heard. The Malays used the word *kramat* to signify the same thing, and the Malagasy used the term *hasma.* Some tribes around Lake Tanganyika believed in such a force, which they called *ngai,* and Australian tribes had similar terms, such as *churinga* and *boolya.* In Mexico there was a strange creed named *nagualism* that held the same concept—everything *nagual* was magic or possessed an inherent spiritual force of its own.

The Dynamics of Magic

Earlier practitioners of magic believed that it is governed by a few well-defined laws. Chief among these is that of sympathy, which can be subdivided into the laws of similarity, antipathy, and contiguity.

The law of similarity and homeopathy is divisible into two tenets: (1) the assumption that like produces like—an illustration of which is the destruction of a doll in the form of an enemy; and (2) the idea that like cures like—for instance, that the stone called bloodstone can staunch the flow of blood.

The law dealing with antipathy rests on the assumption that the application of a certain object or drug expels its contrary.

The idea of contiguity assumes that whatever has once formed part of an object continues to form part of it. Thus, if a magician can obtain a portion of a person's hair, he can work harm upon that person through the invisible bonds that are believed to extend between the individual and the hair in the magician's possession. It was commonly believed that if the animal **familiar** of a witch is wounded, the wound will manifest on the witch herself (see **werewolf**). This is called "repercussion."

It was also widely assumed that if the magician procures the name of a person he can gain dominion over that person. This arose from the idea that the name of an individual is the same as the person himself. The doctrine of the "incommunicable name," the hidden name of the god or magician, has many examples in Egyptian legend, usually the deity taking extraordinary care to keep his name secret so that no one might gain power over him. The spell or incantation is connected with this concept.

Associated with these, to a lesser degree, is magic gesture, usually introduced for the purpose of accentuating the spoken word. Gesture is often symbolic or sympathetic; it is sometimes the reversal of a religious rite, such as marching against the sun, which is known as walking "widdershins." The method of pronouncing rites is also of great importance. Archaic or foreign expressions are usually found in spells both ancient and modern, and the tone in which the incantation is spoken is no less important than its exactness. Rhythm is often employed to aid memory. (See also **Mantra**)

The Magician

In early society the magic practitioner, a term that includes the **shaman,** medicine man, piagé, and witch doctor, held his or her position by hereditary right; by an accident of birth, like being the **seventh son** of a seventh son; through revelation from the gods; or through his mastery of ritual.

The shaman operated like a medium, for instead of summoning the powers of the air at his bidding, as did the magicians of medieval days, he found it necessary to throw himself into a **trance** and seek them in their own sphere. (The magician is also often regarded as possessed by an animal or supernatural being.)

The duties of the priest and magician were often combined in tribal society. When one religion was superseded, however, the priests of the old cult were considered, in the eyes of the leaders and believers of the new, nothing but evil or misguided magicians.

Medieval Definition of Magic

The definitions of magic given by the great magicians of medieval and modern times naturally differ greatly from those of anthropologists. For example, nineteenth-century magician **Éliphas Lévi** states in his *History of Magic* (1913):

"Magic, therefore, combines in a single science that which is most certain in philosophy which is eternal and infallible in religion. It reconciles perfectly and incontestably those two terms so opposed on the first view—faith and reason, science and belief, authority and liberty. It furnishes the human mind with an instrument of philosophical and religious certainty were as exact as mathematics, and even accounting for the infallibility of mathematics themselves. . . . There is an incontestable truth; there is an infallible method of knowing that truth; while those who attain this knowledge and adopt it as a rule of life, can endow their life with a sovereign power which can make them masters of all inferior things, all wandering spirits, or, in other words, arbiters and kings of the world."

Paracelsus, writing in the sixteenth century, stated:

"The magical is a great hidden wisdom, and reason is a great open folly. No armour shields against magic for it strikes at the inward spirit of life. Of this we may rest assured, that through full and powerful imagination only can we bring the spirit of any man into an image. No conjuration, no rites are needful; circle-making and the scattering of incense are mere humbug and jugglery. The human spirit is so great a thing that no man can express it; eternal and unchangeable as God Himself is the mind of man; and could we rightly comprehend the mind of man, nothing would be impossible to us upon the earth. Through faith the imagination is invigorated and completed, for it really happens that every doubt mars its perfection. Faith must strengthen imagination, for faith establishes the will. Because man did not perfectly believe and imagine, the result is that arts are uncertain when they might be wholly certain."

Agrippa also regarded magic as the true road to communion with God, thus linking it with mysticism.

Later Magic

With the death of Agrippa in 1535, the old school of magicians ended. But the traditions of magic were handed down to others who were equally capable of preserving them, or were later revived by persons interested in the art. There was a great distinction between those practitioners of magic whose minds were illuminated by a high mystical ideal and those persons of doubtful occult position, like the **Comte de Saint Germain** and others.

At the beginning of the seventeenth century there were many great alchemists in practice who were also devoted to research on transcendental magic, which they carefully and successfully concealed under the veil of hermetic investigation. These included **Michael Maier, Robert Fludd,** Cosmopolite, **Jean D'Espagnet,** Samuel Norton (see **Thomas Norton**), Baron de **Beausoleil, J. Van Helmont,** and **Eirenaeus Philalethes** (see also **alchemy**). The eighteenth century was rich in occult personalities, for example, the alchemists **Lascaris Martines de Pasqually** and **Louis Claude de Saint-Martin,** who founded the Martinist school, which was continued by "Papus" (**Gérard Encausse**).

By the end of the eighteenth century, magic practice had reached its lowest ebb as emphasis on the exploration of causative agents centered on the physical world and supernatural explanations were pushed aside. It was not until the nineteenth century that a spreading mesmerist philosophy offered philosophical underpinnings for a scientific worldview. Magic merged for the moment with **mesmerism,** and many of the secret magic societies that abounded in Europe about this period practiced **animal magnetism** experiments as well as **astrology, Kabbalism,** and **ceremonial magic.**

Mesmerism powerfully influenced mystic life in the time of its chief advocates, and the mesmerists of the first era were in direct line with the Martinists and the mystical magicians of the late eighteenth century. Indeed mysticism and magnetism were one and the same thing to some of these occultists (see **Secret Tradition**), the most celebrated of which were Cazotte, Ganneau, Comte, Wronski, **Baron Du Potet de Sennevoy,** Hennequin, Comte d'Ourches, Baron de Guldenstubbé, and Éliphas Lévi.

Modern Revivals of Magic

During the 1890s there was a revival of interest in ritual magic in Europe among both intellectuals and traditional occultists. This "occult underground" permeated much of the intellectual life and progressive movements in Europe, in contrast to the more popular preoccupation with **Spiritualism** and **table turning.**

Symbolic of this magic revival was the founding of the famous Hermetic Order of the **Golden Dawn,** which numbered among its members such individuals as Annie Horniman (sponsor of the Abbey Theatre, Dublin), Florence Farr (mistress of George Bernard Shaw), **S. L. MacGregor Mathers, William Butler Yeats, Arthur Machen,** and **Arthur Edward Waite.** Another famous member was the magician **Aleister Crowley,** who left the order to found his own organization, A∴A∴, and then become head of the German-based Ordo Templi Orientis. Crowley's more psychologically sophisticated presentation of magic came to dominate twentieth-century thought on magic, even among those who rejected various portions of it, such as its emphasis on sex, mind-altering drugs, and egocentricity. A more sinister aspect of magic was the current of occult thought that flowed into and undergirded Adolf Hitler and Nazism.

During the 1930s there was an outbreak of public interest in the occult in Britain and Europe, and a number of significant books on magic were published. Their influence was limited only by the relatively smaller influence of mass media at that time and by the conservatism of intellectual life. Exceptional individuals like Aleister Crowley flourished in the 1920s and 1930s, but were deplored by polite society, which regarded such occultists as scandalous misfits.

A second wave of popular occultism flared up in the 1950s in Britain and North America, fueled largely by reprints of key books published during the 1930s. This modern interest in magic, however, had little in common with the outlook and ideals of medieval magicians and followers of the hermetic art. It stemmed largely from the trendiness of postwar affluence and the desire for sensationalist indulgence. The occult explosion led in the 1960s to Satanism and black magic cults. Much of modern occultism has been influenced by the use of mind-altering drugs.

During this modern period, one long-kept secret of occultism became generally discussed—that of the importance of sexual energy in dynamizing the processes of magic. Although this factor was well known to some occultists in Persia, China, and India, it was rediscovered in the early twentieth century and increasingly and openly discussed in the writings of Aleister Crowley and his disciples.

Throughout this century practitioners of magic have made some extraordinary claims about achieving desired ends. There are still two opinions among occultists as to how such feats are achieved. One is that desired effects in the physical world are produced through the operator's willpower, assisted by various ritual practices. The other opinion, still held by a minority, is that desired effects are achieved by means of spirit entities evoked during rituals. (Among skeptics there are various mundane explanations for the seemingly positive results of magic activity.)

Conjuring Tricks and Stage Magic

Today the term *magic* normally denotes the performance of conjuring, legerdemain, or illusion, although the term *conjuring* was originally used to indicate the evocation of spirits. Conjuring tricks have been used by priests for thousands of years to create the illusion of miracles. The astonishing and skillful illusions of modern stage magicians show that special caution is necessary in evaluating many apparently paranormal feats of magic, and stage magicians have also performed a valuable service in exposing fraudulent "psychic" feats. Because of their history of exposing fraud and their knowledge of the many techniques for creating illusions, stage magicians tend to be skeptical of all claimed paranormal feats.

Sources:

Agrippa, Henry Cornelius. *The Philosophy of Natural Magic.* London, 1651. Reprint, New Hyde Park, N.Y.: University Books, 1974.

Barrett, Francis. *The Magus: A Complete System of Occult Philosophy.* London, 1801. Reprint, New Hyde Park, N.Y.: University Books, 1967.

Bonewits, Philip E. I. *Real Magic.* New York: Coward, McCann & Geoghegan, 1971. Reprint, New York: Berkeley, 1971.

Christian, Paul. *The History and Practice of Magic.* 2 vols. London: Forge Press, 1952.

Christopher, Milbourne. *The Illustrated History of Magic.* New York: Thomas Y. Crowell, 1973. Reprint, London: Robert Hale, 1975.

———. *Panorama of Magic.* New York: Dover, 1962.

Crow, W. B. *A History of Magic, Witchcraft & Occultism.* London: Aquarian Press, 1968. Reprint, London: Abacus, 1972.

[Crowley, Aleister] The Master Therion. *Magick in Theory and Practice.* Paris, 1929. Reprint, New York: Castle Books, n.d. Rev. ed. *Magick.* Edited by John Symonds and Kenneth Grant. London: Routledge & Kegan Paul, 1973. Reprint, New York: Samuel Weiser, 1974.

Ennemoser, Joseph. *The History of Magic.* 2 vols. London, 1854. Reprint, New Hyde Park, N.Y.: University Books, 1970.

Freedland, Nat. *The Occult Explosion.* New York: G. P. Putnam's Sons, 1972. Reprint, London: Michael Joseph, 1972.

King, Francis. *Ritual Magic in England (1887 to the Present Day).* London: Neville Spearman, 1970. Reprint, New York: Macmillan, 1971.

———. *Sexuality, Magic & Perversion.* London: Neville Spearman, 1971. Reprint, New York: Citadel Press, 1972.

Lévi, Éliphas. *The History of Magic.* London: Rider, 1913. Reprint, New York: David McKay, 1914.

———. *The Mysteries of Magic: A Digest of Éliphas Lévi.* Edited by A. E. Waite. London, 1886. Reprint, New Hyde Park, N.Y.: University Books, 1974.

———. *Transcendental Magic.* London, 1896. Rev. ed. London: Rider, 1923.

Melton, J. Gordon, and Isotta Poggi. *Magic, Witchcraft, and Paganism in America: A Bibliography.* New York: Garland, 1992.

O'Keefe, Daniel Lawrence. *Stolen Lightning: The Social Theory of Magic.* New York: Continuum, 1982.

Seligmann, Kurt. *The History of Magic.* New York: Pantheon Books, 1948. Reprinted as *Magic, Supernaturalism, and Religion.* 1971.

Shah, Sayed Idries. *Oriental Magic.* London: Rider, 1956.

———. *The Secret Lore of Magic: The Books of the Sorcerers.* London: Frederick Muller, 1957.

Summers, Montague. *Witchcraft and Black Magic.* London: Rider, 1946. Reprint, New York: Causeway, 1974.

Thomas, Keith. *Religion and the Decline of Magic.* New York: Charles Scribner's Sons, 1971.

Thompson, C. J. S. *The Mysteries and Secrets of Magic.* London, 1927. Reprint, New York: Causeway, 1973.

Waite, Arthur Edward. *The Book of Ceremonial Magic.* London, 1911. Reprint, New Hyde Park, N.Y.: University Books, 1961.

Webb, James. *The Flight from Reason.* London: Macdonald, 1971. Reprinted as *The Occult Underground.* LaSalle, Ill.: Open Court, 1974.

———. *The Occult Establishment.* LaSalle, Ill.: Open Court, 1975.

Magical Blend Magazine

New Age style publication that embarks "on a voyage of discovery . . . that will take us out of the past and carry us into the future. . . . It charts a course of magic, and sets sail on an excursion into infinite possibilities." Its contributors have included many New Age authorities. Subjects covered have included **trance channeling, occult** systems, visionary art, and the possibilities of extraterrestrial communication. Address: Magical Blend, P.O. Box 600, Chico, CA 95927-0600. Website: http://www.magicalblend.com/.

Sources:

Magical Blend Magazine. http://www.magicalblend.com/. March 23, 2000.

Magical Diagrams

These are geometrical designs representing the mysteries of deity and creation, therefore supposed to be of special virtue in rites of evocation and conjuration. Major diagrams are the Triangle; the Double Triangle, forming a six-pointed star and known as the Sign or Seal of Solomon; the Tetragram, a four-pointed star formed by the interlacement of two pillars; and the Pentagram, a five-pointed star. These signs were traced on paper or parchment or engraved on metals and glass and consecrated to their various uses by special rites.

The Triangle evoked a universal trinity found in all things—deity, time, and creation. The triangle was generally traced on the ground with the magic sword or rod, as in circles of evocation where the triangle was drawn within it and, according to the position of the magician at its point or base, so the spirits were "conjured" (summoned up) from heaven or hell.

The Double Triangle, or the Sign of Solomon, is symbolic of the **macrocosm,** and is formed by the interlacement of two triangles: its points thus constitute the perfect number six. Magicians wore it bound on their brows and breasts during ceremonies, and it was engraved on the silver reservoirs of magic lamps.

The Tetragram, symbolic of the four elements, was used in the conjuration of the **elementary spirits**—sylphs of the air, undines of the water, and the fire salamanders and gnomes of the earth. In **alchemy** it represented the magical elements salt, sulphur, mercury, and azoth; in mystic philosophy, the ideas Spirit, Matter, Motion, and Rest; in hieroglyphs, the man, eagle, lion, and bull.

The Pentagram, the sign of the **microcosm,** was held to be the most powerful means of conjuration in any rite. It might represent good as well as evil, for with one point in the ascendant it was the sign of Christ, and with two points in the ascendant it was the sign of Satan. By the use of the pentagram in these positions, the powers of light or darkness were evoked. The pentagram was said to be the star that led the Magi to the manger where the infant Christ was laid.

The preparation and consecration of this sign for use in magical rites was prescribed with great detail. It might be composed of seven metals, the ideal form for its expression, or traced in pure gold upon white marble never before used for any purpose. It might also be drawn with vermilion upon lambskin without a blemish prepared under the auspices of the Sun.

The sign was next consecrated with the four elements, breathed on five times, dried by the smoke of five perfumes (incense, myrrh, aloes, sulfur, and camphor). The names of five genii were breathed above it, and then the sign was placed successively at the north, south, east, west, and center of the astronomical cross, while the letters of the sacred tetragram and various kabalistic names were prounced over it (See **Kabala**). It was believed to be of great efficacy in terrifying phantoms if engraved upon glass, and the magicians traced it on their doorsteps to prevent evil spirits from entering and good spirits from departing.

This symbol was used by many secret and occult societies, by the **Rosicrucians,** the **Illuminati,** down to the Freemasons of modern times. Modern occultists translate the meaning of the pentagram as symbolic of the human soul and its relation to God.

The Pentagram is placed with one point in the ascendant. That point represents the Great Spirit, God. A line drawn from there to the left-hand angle at the base is the descent of spirit into matter in its lowest form; where it ascends to the right-hand angle, it typifies matter in its highest form: the brain of man. From here, a line is drawn across the figure to left angle, representing man's development in intellect; while progress in material civilization, the point of danger from which all nations have fallen into moral corruption, is signified by the descent of the line to right angle at the base. The soul of man being derived from God cannot remain at this point but must struggle upward, as is symbolized by the line reaching again to the apex, God, from which it issued. (See also **ceremonial magic; magic; magical instruments and accessories; magical vestments and appurtenances**)

Sources:

Barrett, Francis. *The Magus: A Complete System of Occult Philosophy.* London, 1801. Reprint, New Hyde Park, N.Y.: University Books, 1967.

Thompson, C. J. S. *The Mysteries and Secrets of Magic.* London, 1927. Reprint, New York: Causeway Books, 1974.

Waite, Arthur Edward. *The Book of Ceremonial Magic.* London: William Rider & Son, 1911. Reprint, New Hyde Park, N.Y.: University Books, 1961.

Woodroffe, Sir John. *Sakti and Sakta.* Madras, India: Ganesh, 1918.

Magical Numbers

Certain numbers and their combinations were traditionally held to be of magical power, by virtue of their representation of divine and creative mysteries. The doctrines of Pythagoras (see **Greece**) furnished the basis for much of this belief. According to his theory, numbers contained the elements of all things, of the natural and spiritual worlds and of the sciences. The real numerals of the universe were the primaries one to ten, and in their combination the reason of all else might be found.

To the Pythagoreans, one represented unity, therefore God; two was duality, the Devil; four was sacred and holy, the number on which they swore their most solemn oaths; five was their symbol of marriage. They also attributed certain numbers to the gods, planets and elements; one represented the Sun, two the Moon; while five was fire, six the Earth, eight the air, and twelve water. (See also **magic square**)

Cornelius Agrippa, in his work *Occult Philosophy* first published in Latin (1531–33), discourses upon numbers as those characters by whose proportion all things are formed. He enumerates the virtues of numerals as displayed in nature, instancing the herb cinquefoil, which by the power of the number five exorcises devils, reduces fever, and forms an antidote to poisons. He also points to the virtue of seven, as in the power of the **seventh son** to cure the **king's evil.**

One was the origin and common measure of all things. It is indivisible, not to be multiplied. In the universe there is one God; one supreme intelligence in the intellectual world, man; in the sidereal world, one Sun; one potent instrument and agency in the elementary world, the **philosophers' stone;** one chief member in the human world, the heart; and one sovereign prince in the nether world, Lucifer.

Two was the number of marriage, charity, and social communion. It was also regarded sometimes as an unclean number; in the Bible, beasts of the field went into Noah's Ark by twos.

Three had a mysterious value as shown in time's trinity—past, present and future; in that of space—length, breadth, and thickness; in the three heavenly virtues—faith, hope, and charity; in the three worlds of man—brain (the intellectual), heart (the celestial), and body (elemental).

Four signifies solidity and foundation. There are four seasons, four elements, four cardinal points, four evangelists.

Five, as it divides ten, the sum of all numbers, is also the number of justice. There are five senses; the **stigmata,** the wounds of Christ, were five; the name of the Deity, the Pentagram, is composed of five letters; it also is a protection against beasts of prey.

Six is the sign of creation, because the world was completed in six days. It is the perfect number, because it alone by addition of its half, its third and its sixth reforms itself. It also represents servitude by reason of the Divine injunction, "Six days shalt thou labour."

Seven is a miraculous number, consisting of one, unity, and six, the sign of perfection. It represents life because it contains body, consisting of four elements, spirit, flesh, bone, and humor (the ancient concept of bodily fluids affecting the mind); and soul, made up of three elements, passion, desire, and reason. The seventh day was that on which God rested from his work of creation.

Eight represents justice and fullness. Divided, its halves are equal; twice divided, it is still even. In the Beatitudes, eight is the number of those mentioned—peacemakers, those who strive after righteousness, the meek, the persecuted, the pure, the merciful, the poor in spirit, and those that mourn.

Nine is the number of the muses and of the moving spheres.

Ten is completeness, because one cannot count beyond it except by combinations formed with other numbers. In the ancient mysteries, ten days of initiation were prescribed. In ten is found evident signs of a divine principle.

Eleven is the number of the commandments, while twelve is the number of signs in the Zodiac, of the apostles, of the tribes of Israel, of the gates of Jerusalem.

This theory of numbers Agrippa applied to the casting of horoscopes. **Divination** by numbers was one of the favorite methods employed in the Middle Ages.

In magical rites, numbers played a great part. The power of the number three is found in the magic triangle, in the three prongs of the trident and fork, and in the three-fold repetition of names in conjurations. Seven was also of great influence, the seven days of the week each representing the period most suitable for certain evocations, and these corresponding to the seven magical works: (1) works of light and riches; (2) works of divination and mystery; (3) works of skill, science, and eloquence; (4) works of wrath and chastisement; (5) works of love; (6) works of ambition and intrigue; and (7) works of malediction and death. (See also **numerology**)

Sources:

Agrippa, Henry Cornelius. *The Philosophy of Natural Magic.* London, 1651. Reprint, New Hyde Park, N.Y.: University Books, 1974.

Bosman, Leonard. *The Meaning and Philosophy of Numbers.* London: Rider, 1932.

Butler, Christopher. *Number Symbolism.* London: Routledge and Kegan Paul, 1970.

Redgrove, H. Stanley. *A Mathematical Theory of Spirit.* London: Rider, 1912.

Waite, Arthur Edward. *The Holy Kabbalah.* London: Williams & Norgate, 1929. Reprint, New Hyde Park, N.Y.: University Books, 1960.

Westcott, W. Wynn. *Numbers: Their Occult Power and Mystic Virtues.* London: Theosophical Publishing Society, 1890.

Magical Union of Cologne

A society stated in a manuscript of the **Rosicrucians** (under the pseudonym "Omnis Moriar") at Cologne, Germany, to have been founded in that city in the year 1115. In the *Rosenkreutzer in seiner Blosse* (1786) of F. G. E. Weise, it was stated that the initiates wore a triangle, symbolizing power, wisdom, and love. The more exalted orders among them were called Mage or Wise Masters, and these held the greater mysteries of the fraternity. They were masters of secret sciences and achieved feats that seemed supernatural.

Magical Vestments and Appurtenances

The practice of magic generally prescribes various items of clothing and accessories as needful adjuncts to magical rites, in part to assist the magician in imagining himself/herself to be in an otherworldly setting. Their color, name, form, and substance, which were symbolic of certain powers and elements, supposedly added greater efficacy to the evocations.

Abraham the Jew, a magician of the Middle Ages, prescribed a tunic of white linen, with an upper robe of scarlet and a girdle of white silk. A crown or fillet of silk and gold was to be worn on the head, and the perfumes cast on the fire might be incense, aloes, storax, cedar, citron, or rose. According to other authorities on the subject, it was advisable to vary the robe's color and employ certain jewels and other accessories, according to the symbolism of the end desired.

Éliphas Lévi, whose writings stand at the fountainhead of the twentieth-century magical revival, offers instructions for rituals, from which the following details are taken:

If the rites were those of White Magic and performed on a Sunday, then the vestment should be of purple and the tiara, bracelets, and ring of gold, the latter set with chrysolith or ruby. Laurel, heliotrope, and sunflowers are the symbolic flowers, while other details include a carpet of lionskins and fans of sparrow-hawk feathers. The appropriate perfumes were incense, saffron, cinnamon, and red sandal.

If, however, the ceremonial took place on a Monday, the Day of the **Moon,** then the robe must be of white embroidered with silver and the tiara of yellow silk emblazoned with silver characters, while the wreaths were to be woven of moonwort and yellow ranunculi. The jewels appropriate to the occasion were pearls, crystals, and selenite; the perfumes, camphor, amber, aloes, white sandalwood, and seed of cucumber.

In evocations concerning transcendent knowledge, green was the color chosen for the vestment, or it might be green shot with various colors. The chief ornament was a necklace of pearls and hollow glass beads enclosing mercury. Agate was the symbolic jewel; narcissus, lily, herb mercury, fumitory, and marjoram the flowers; while the perfumes must be benzoin, mace, and storax.

For operations connected with religious and political matters, the magician must don a robe of scarlet and bind on his brow a brass tablet inscribed with various characters. His ring must be studded with an emerald or sapphire, and he must burn for incense balm, ambergris, grain of paradise, and saffron. For garlands and wreaths, oak, poplar, fig, and pomegranate leaves should be entwined.

If the ceremonial dealt with amatory affairs, the vestment must be of sky blue, the ornaments of copper, and the crown of violets. The magic ring must be set with a turquoise, while the tiara and clasps were wrought of lapis lazuli and beryl. Roses, myrtle, and olive were the symbolic flowers, and fans must be made of swan feathers.

If vengeance was desired on anyone, then robes must be worn whose color was that of blood, flame, or rust, belted with steel, with bracelets and ring of the same metal. The tiara must be bound with gold and the wreaths woven of absinthe and rue.

To bring misfortune and death on a person, the vestment must be black and the neck encircled with lead. The ring must be set with an onyx and the garlands twined of cypress, ash, and hellebore; the perfumes to be used were sulfur, scammony, alum, and assafoetida.

For purposes of **black magic,** a seamless and sleeveless robe of black was donned, while on the head was worn a leaden cap inscribed with the signs of the Moon, Venus, and Saturn. The wreaths were of vervain and cypress, and the perfumes burned were aloes, camphor, and storax. (See also **ceremonial magic; magic; magical diagrams; magical instruments and accessories**)

Sources:

Knight, Gareth. *The Practice of Ritual Magic.* Toddington, England: Helios Book Service, 1969. Reprint, New York: Samuel Weiser, 1976.

Lévi, Éliphas. *Transcendental Magic.* London: G. Redway, 1896. Reprint, New York: Samuel Weiser, 1970.

Waite, Arthur Edward. *The Book of Ceremonial Magic.* London: Rider, 1911. Reprint, New York: Bell, 1969.

Magic Circle

An important part of **ceremonial magic** was the drawing of a magic circle around the magician to protect him from the malice of evil spirits that he might invoke to perform his will. The circle was symbolic of a sphere that was believed to surround the magician. It both isolated him from the chaos outside and held in the magical power that he raised.

Magic circles were used for thousands of years and often took elaborate forms, requiring the inscribing of magical symbols, such as the Seal of Solomon (a double pentacle). In ancient Hindu folk customs, the bed of a woman in childbirth was encircled by red lead or black pebbles to ward off evil influences.

In medieval magic practice, the circle was usually marked or drawn around the magician with a magic sword or knife. It might be some nine feet in diameter to allow the movements of the magician in his evocations. Portable forms of magic circles were sometimes drawn on parchment and used as **talismans.** (See also **magic square; necromancy**)

The Magic Circle (Organization)

British organization of professional and amateur conjuring **magicians.** It was founded in July 1905 at the famous Pinoli's restaurant in Wardour Street, London (long since vanished), and was originally intended to honor a young professional magician, Martin Charpender, who had just died. Some members preferred an impersonal name to "The Martin Charpender Club," and when it was pointed out that the initials "M. C." might also stand for "Magic Circle," the latter name was agreed upon.

In its early period the Magic Circle convened at St. George's Hall in Portland Place, where the famous stage magicians Maskelyne and Devant performed their feats. In 1910 the Magic Circle moved to Anderton's Hotel, Fleet Street, where it held meetings and monthly concerts (named "séances"). Individual magicians showed off their latest tricks.

The organization still publishes the magazine, *The Magic Circular* ten times a year and maintains two reference libraries. Membership numbers around 1,400 and includes doctors of medicine, philosophy, and divinity, as well as those of more humble occupations. However, full membership is limited to those who have knowledge of and practice magic. Address: 12 Stephenson Way, Euston, London, NW1 2HD England. Website: http://www.themagiccircle.co.uk/Info/mcinfo.html.

Sources:

The Magic Circle. http://www.themagiccircle.co.uk/Info/mcinfo.html. March 8, 2000.

Magic Darts

The Laplanders, at one time said to be great **magicians,** were supposed to launch lead darts, about a finger-length, against their absent enemies, believing that with such **magic** darts they were sending grievous pains and maladies.

Magicians (Illusionists)

The term *magician* can refer to two distinct areas of practice. The first refers to those who claim to practice the art of change by the use of unknown (either natural or supernatural) forces. Such practice is covered in this encyclopedia under the headings **Ceremonial Magic** and **Magic.** The second connotation refers to stage illusionists. These represent those who have perfected acts presenting the same phenomena as those presented by **mediums** and **psychics.** It conjures up many different images in people, some that extend into the far reaches of one's imagination and experience. Since the days of ancient **Egypt** and the Pharoahs, magicians have practiced the art of magic. From the prehistoric caves of Europe and North America, to ancient **Greece** and **Rome,** to the Middle Ages, long before the days of **Vaudeville,** and television, archaeological evidence and historical records show that audiences were held captive by the masters of trickery and illusion. In America, from the 19th century success of the American-born illusionist Harry Kellar to the modern-day magicians, such as Doug Henning and David Copperfield, have captured the attention of the public.

Since the nineteenth century, when Spiritualism took root and gained popularity among the general public, magicians have been skeptical of Spiritualist and psychic claims. Due to their expertise in the area of illusion, they have been at the forefront of exposing **fraud** within the Spiritualist community. The impetus to the birth of the Spiritualism movement in America was linked to two sisters, **Margaret and Kate Fox,** who claimed to be receiving messages "from beyond" in their isolated farmhouse in 1848. It was the Fox sisters, too, who encouraged the beginning of what would become a long history of debate between spiritualists and magic advocates.

The first important challenge to **Spiritualism** by a magician occurred right as the movement was just beginning. In 1853 J. H. Anderson of New York offered a thousand dollars to any "poverty-stricken medium" who would come to his hall and attempt to produce **raps.** Spiritualists were already becoming notorious for calling up the spirits of the dead, often in seances where the deceased would manifest themselves through a knocking on the table where the participants were seated. The Fox sisters accepted Anderson's invitation immediately, and were accompanied by Judge **J. W. Edmonds** and a Dr. Grey. However convinced Anderson might have been, he backed out as they were about to appear. Amid the hisses of the audience, he refused them admission to the stage.

Magicians Confounded

A few of the most famous magicians acknowledged having witnessed genuine phenomena. Spiritualists took such acknowledgement as their blanket approval, and seized upon it. The clairvoyant powers of **Alexis Didier** stupefied the famous conjurer Robert-Houdin. His signed declaration, as published by Edwin Lee in his book *Animal Magnetism* (1866), reads: "I cannot help stating that the facts above related are scrupulously exact and the more I reflect upon them the more impossible do I find it to class them among the tricks which are the objects of my art."

In a letter to M. de Mirville, who introduced him to Didier, Robert-Houdin writes: "I, therefore, came away from this séance as astonished as anyone can be, and fully convinced that it would be quite impossible for anyone to produce such surprising effects by mere skill."

The stage magician Leon Bosco used to laugh at those who thought the phenomena of the famous medium **D. D. Home** could be imitated with the resources of his art. The magician Canti similarly declared to Prince Napoleon that he could "in no way account for the phenomena he saw on the principles of his profession." In the *Outlines of Investigation Into Spiritualism,* (1862) by T. Barkas, he also published a letter expressing the same opinion. Robert-Houdin stated: "I have come away from that **séance** as astounded as I could be, and persuaded that it is perfectly impossible by chance or adroitness to produce such marvelous effects."

The stage magician Hamilton (Pierre Etienne Chocat), successor of Robert-Houdin, in a letter to the **Davenport brothers** published in the *Gazette des Etrangers,* September 27, 1865, declared:

"Yesterday I had the pleasure of being present at the séance you gave, and came away from it convinced that jealousy alone was the cause of the outcry raised against you. The phenomena produced surpassed my expectations; and your experiments were full of interest for me. I consider it my duty to add that those phenomena are inexplicable, and the more so by such persons as have thought themselves able to guess your supposed secret, and who are, in fact, far indeed from having discovered the truth."

This letter was accompanied by a similar statement from M. Rhys, a manufacturer of conjuring implements, who examined the **cabinet** and instruments of the Davenports. He declared that the insinuations about them were false and malevolent. Since the cabinet was completely isolated, all participation in the manifestations by strangers was absolutely impossible, he said.

A Professor Jacobs wrote on April 10, 1881, to the editor of *Licht, Mehr Licht* about the phenomena that occurred through the Davenport brothers in Paris: "As a prestidigitator of repute and a sincere spiritualist, I affirm that the mediumimic facts, demonstrated by the two brothers were absolutely true, and belonged to the spiritualistic order of things in every respect. Messrs. Robin and Robert-Houdin, when attempting to imitate these said facts, never presented to the public anything beyond an infantile and almost grotesque parody of the said phenomena, and it would be only ignorant and obstinate persons who could regard the question seriously as set forth by these gentlemen."

Samuel Bellachini, court conjurer at Berlin, stated in an authenticated statement given to the medium **Henry Slade** (later exposed on several occasions as a fraud) the following:

"I must, for the sake of truth, hereby certify that the phenomenal occurrences with Mr. Slade have been thoroughly examined by me with the minutest observation and investigation of his surroundings, including the table, and that I have not in the smallest degree found anything produced by means of prestidigitative manifestations, or by mechanical apparatus; and that any explanation of the experiments which took place under the circumstances and conditions then obtaining by any reference to prestidigitation is absolutely impossible. It must rest with such men of science as Crookes and Wallace in London, Perty in Berne, Butleroff in St. Petersburg to search for the explanation of this phenomenal power, and to prove its reality."

In January 1882, the great illusionist Harry Kellar witnessed a levitation of the medium **William Eglinton,** in Calcutta, India. Kellar's account of this appeared in the *Proceedings* of the Society for Psychical Research (SPR) (vol. 9, p. 359):

"A circle having been formed, I was placed on Mr. Eglinton's left and seized his left hand firmly in my right. Immediately on the extinction of the lights I felt him rise slowly in the air and as I retained firm hold of his hand, I was pulled to my feet, and subsequently compelled to jump on a chair and then on the table, in order to retain my hold of him. That his body did ascend into the air on that occasion with an apparently utter disregard to the law of gravity, there can be no doubt. What most excited my wonder was the fact, for I may speak of it as a fact without qualification, that Mr. Eglinton rose from my side, and, by the hold he had on my right hand, pulled me up after him, my own body appeared for the time being to have been rendered nonsusceptible to gravity."

In contrast, the case of S. J. Davey is especially noteworthy. He was a magician who attended **slate-writing** séances with Eglinton and was impressed. He studied the problem thoroughly. In agreement with Dr. **Richard Hodgson,** he presented himself as a medium and produced all the characteristic phenomena of the séance room to the complete satisfaction of his sitters. An account of his demonstration was published in the *Proceedings* of the SPR (vol. 4). He revealed that he did everything by trickery; but many committed believers did not believe it. Even **Alfred Russel Wallace** suggested that Davey was also a good physical medium and had produced phenomena supernormally since he exhibited the characteristic physiological symptoms of **trance** convulsions.

The two most tenacious magician opponents of Spiritualism, **J. N. Maskelyne** and **Harry Houdini,** focused public attention on themselves for many years. Both led crusades against mediums. Houdini had sought solace in spiritualism following the death of his beloved mother in 1913. He quickly saw through the deception that ran through many of the claims, and was even more adamant in his denunciation, perhaps, since he felt personally battered from his own experiences. In the preface to his book, *Miracle Mongers and Their Methods,* Houdini said that,

"Much has been written about the feats of miracle-mongers, and not a little in the way of explaining them. Chaucer was by no means the first to turn shrewd eyes upon wonder-workers and show the clay feet of these popular idols. And since his time innumerable marvels, held to be supernatural, have been exposed for the tricks they were. Yet to-day, if a mystifier lack the ingenuity to invent a new and startling stunt, he can safely fall back upon a trick that has been the favorite of press agents the world over in all ages."

Maskelyne, nevertheless, did not absolutely discredit the paranormal, as revealed by a letter he wrote to the *Daily Telegraph* in 1881: "It may surprise some of your readers to learn that I am a believer in apparitions. Several similar occurrences to those described by many of your correspondents have taken place in my own family, and in the families of near friends and relations."

In the *Pall Mall Gazette* of April 20, 1885, Maskelyne acknowledges the phenomenon of **table turning** as genuine. He declared that Faraday's explanation was insufficient and some psychic or nerve force was responsible for the result. At the same time he asserted that he could imitate any Spiritualistic phenomenon provided his own apparatus, which weighed more than a ton, was at his disposal.

Many later psychical researchers were amateur conjurers (notably **Hereward Carrington, Harry Price,** and **W. W. Baggally**) who were well acquainted with the tricks of the trade.

A conjurer's performance may in fact afford evidence that the phenomena produced by the medium are genuine. Admiral Usborne Moore (*Glimpses of the Next State,* 1911) saw a conjurer reproduce the phenomena of the **Bangs sisters** on the stage. The effect was crude at first, although very satisfactory afterward. But the point, Moore remarked, was that the conjurer's conditions were as different from the conditions of the Bangs sisters' séances as a locomotive boiler is different from a teapot. Moore's efforts finally convinced him that he had witnessed genuine spirit manifestations with the Bangs sisters.

After the Reverend **F. W. Monck** was accused of fraud in 1876, Archdeacon **Thomas Colley** offered a thousand pounds to J. N. Maskelyne if he could duplicate Monck's materialization performance. Maskelyne accepted the challenge. His performance was declared unsatisfactory. He sued for the money and lost his reputation when Colley won. Sir Hiram Maxim, the great inventor, later challenged Maskelyne to produce a psychic effect he had seen in the United States under the same conditions, but Maskelyne refused. The challenge and its result were described by the inventor in a pamphlet, *Maxim versus Maskelyne* (1910).

The descendants of J. N. Maskelyne followed in his footsteps. Capt. Clive Maskelyne issued a challenge in February 1925, when the visit of the medium "Margery" (**Mina Crandon**) to England was reported, that he could produce any of the phenomena she had produced in America. Spiritualist author **H. Dennis Bradley,** in an interview for the *Daily Sketch,* promised a hundred guineas to Maskelyne if he could duplicate the **Valiantine** phenomena. Maskelyne at first accepted, but withdrew when he heard what was expected from him.

In 1930 psychical researcher Harry Price offered one thousand pounds to any conjurer who could repeat **Rudi Schneider**'s phenomena under the same conditions. Nobody came forward. A skit, under the title *Olga,* was produced instead, in imitation of Schneider's phenomena at the Coliseum Theatre ("Olga" was Schneider's claimed spirit **control**). Harry Price publicly challenged Noel Maskelyne from the stage of that theater on December 10, 1929, to simulate by trickery, for £250, one single phenomenon of Rudi Schneider's under the identical conditions imposed by the **National Laboratory of Psychical Research.** Maskelyne refused.

Will Goldston, one of the greatest professional magicians in Europe, author of 40 works on legerdemain, founder and former president of the Magicians' Club of London, declared in the *Sunday Graphic,* December 2, 1929, concerning Schneider's phenomena: "I am convinced that what I saw at the séance was not trickery. No group of my fellow-magicians could have produced those effects under such conditions."

Goldston tells the story of his conversion to Spiritualism in *Secrets of Famous Illusionists* (London, 1933). Two of his great fellow magicians—Ottokar Fischer of Vienna, and Harry Rigoletto—were quite accepting of psychic phenomena.

In the *Sunday Dispatch* (August 1931), Goldston testifies about **Hazel Ridley** and her **direct voice** phenomena as follows:

"Miss Ridley sat at a table in our midst, and without the use of trumpets or any of the usual paraphernalia spoke in three different voices. No ventriloquist could possibly produce the effect this girl produced, and I say that after a long experience of ventriloquists. First there was a powerful, clear, man's voice, ringing through the room in tones one would have thought no woman's throat could have produced. The next voice, a very quiet one, like that of a child of six or seven years of age, added to my surprise. The third guide also spoke in a woman's or a child's voice, but quite unlike the normal voice of the medium. The séance lasted an hour and three quarters."

A year later he also spoke up in favor of **Helen Duncan** and declared that he was not aware of any system of trickery that could achieve the astounding results he witnessed. Still, others testified that Duncan's phenomena were fraudulent on some occasions.

Goldston also believed, as did many others, that Houdini was a great psychic. Sir **Arthur Conan Doyle** devoted about sixty pages in *The Edge of the Unknown* (1930) to the claim that Houdini was really a medium masquerading as a conjurer. Whatever the true nature of Houdini's inner belief, his demonstrations during the *Scientific American* investigation of the mediumship of "Margery" (Mina Crandon) did not greatly add to his prestige. The exposures that he publicized throughout the United States were not supported by substantial proof, and privately he backed away from some of his public absolutist admissions.

For example, on January 5, 1925, he wrote to Harry Price: "Another strange thing happened: with the aid of the spirit slates I produced a photograph of Mrs. Crandon's brother, Walter, who was killed, and of all the miracles in the world, I ran across the photograph of the boy as he was crushed between the engine and the tender of the train, and which was taken one minute before he died. . .I doubt very much if there are any duplicates about" (*Light,* August 12, 1932).

Houdini was a clever magician, but considered narrow-minded. According to Doyle, he died disbelieving that the phenomena of **hypnotism** were genuine. *Houdini and Conan Doyle* (1933), by Bernard M. L. Ernst and Hereward Carrington, contains many interesting letters about Houdini's strange adventures in psychic realms.

Modern Debates

With the death of Houdini in 1926 and the decline of physical phenomena in the 1930s, the warfare between Spiritualism and the world of stage conjuring faded, although it by no means died out. It entered the next era during the occult revival of the 1960s, with renewed claims of physical phenomena. As public attention to the paranormal again emerged, **Milbourne Christopher,** a modern illusionist skeptic and member of the Occult Committee of the Society of American Magicians, wrote several books attacking some of the more obvious problems with psychics and the occult.

The continuing issues between magicians and psychics became a public controversy, however, with the advent of **Uri Geller,** an Israeli psychic who claimed extraordinary powers of **psychokinesis** (starting old watches, bending metal spoons) and **telepathy.** He impressed several psychical researchers, and **Andrija Puharich** extolled his abilities in a 1974 book. Christopher was possibly the first to publicly suggest that sleight-of-hand and mentalist tricks accounted for Geller's success.

The Geller controversy brought to the fore Canadian-born magician **James Randi** (stage name "The Amazing Randi"), who had helped organize the **Committee for the Scientific Investigation of Claims of the Paranormal** and subsequently assumed the mantle of Houdini as the archenemy of psychic phenomena and psychics. Randi claimed to be able to duplicate Geller's feats of telepathy and metal bending by trickery. He accused Geller of deception. Their battle was in the forefront of television talk and variety shows throughout the 1970s. Every well-known television host from Merv Griffin to Phil Donahue presented the issue to the American public. When Randi wrote his book, *The Magic of Uri Geller* (1975), both men continued through the 1980s and 1990s with legal battles resulting from the accusations the two exchanged about each other. Randi went on to challenge other psychic claims, explaining to audiences the techniques used by fake occultists.

Master illusionist Doug Henning (d. 2000) was considered by many to be the one responsible for the revival of magic because of his live stage and television performances in the 1970s.

Henning, dressed in the uniform of his generation—blue jeans and a tie-dyed shirt—began to transform magic into a prime-time spectacle. With regular network television specials, and three Broadway shows, he rekindled the public's interest in the glamour of magic. As Randi told *Time* in a 1974 article the new-found interest in magic was, "a sign that our society is still healthy. When people stop being enthralled by a magician who can make a lady vanish, it will mean that the world has lost its most precious possession: its sense of wonder."

With other famous magicians and illusionists such as, Harry Blackstone, Jr. (d. 1997), Penn and Teller, and David Copperfield, magic moved to the grandeur of Las Vegas, and television screens across the world by the end of the twentieth century. Furor entered the public once again in the late-1990s when the Fox television network presented a series of specials which set out to reveal the secrets behind the magician's trade. Although many famous magicians protested the airing of these specials, they proceeded nonetheless. Regardless of whether they revealed any secrets, the specials did not succeed in quieting the public's fascination with magic. In 1999, magician David Blaine stirred up extreme media and public attention by burying himself alive for a week. The media kept close guard to make certain no tricks were used, and Blaine became a cult-hero by lasting out the week and conducting exclusive interviews with television and newspapers.

As the battle rages between those who have come to accept the existence of psychic phenomena and those skeptical of all such claims, both sides have attempted to make use of the work of the magicians. Skeptics have pointed to the exposures of fraud as a good reason to dismiss all claims of paranormal occurrences. Believers, on the other hand, have pointed out that magicians have done a good job in helping them to uncover fraud and drive fakes from the arena of the genuine. The work of magicians and others within the Spiritualist and psychic community in exposing fraud helps define the boundary of real psychic occurrences. It does not speak to the body of parapsychological research or to the experiences of hundreds of thousands of believers.

Sources:

Christopher, Milbourne. *ESP, Seers and Psychics.* New York: Thomas Y. Crowell, 1970.

———. *Houdini: The Untold Story.* New York: Thomas Y. Crowell, 1969.

———. *The Illustrated History of Magic.* New York: Thomas Y. Crowell, 1973. Reprint, London: Robert Hale, 1975.

Dingwall, E. J. and Harry Price, eds. *Revelations of a Spirit Medium.* London: Kegan Paul, 1925.

Doerflinger, William. *The Magic Catalogue, A Guide to The Wonderful World of Magic.* New York: E. P. Dutton, 1977.

Doug Henning's World of Magic 2000. http://doughenning.com/. April 24, 2000.

Duprel, Carl. *Experimental psychologie und Experimental metaphysik.* N.p., 1891.

Dunninger, Joseph. *Inside the Medium's Cabinet.* New York: David Kemp, 1924.

Ernst, Bernard M. L., and Hereward Carrington. *Houdini and Conan Doyle: The Story of a Strange Friendship.* London: Hutchinson, 1933.

Fast, Francis R. *The Houdini Messages: The Facts Concerning the Messages Received Through the Mediumship of Arthur Ford.* New York: The Author, 1929.

Goldston, Will. *Secrets of Famous Illusionists.* London: Long, 1933.

Houdini, Harry. *A Magician Among the Spirits.* New York: Harper & Brothers, 1924.

———. *Miracle Mongers and Their Methods.* Buffalo, N.Y.: Prometheus Books, 1981. Reprint, 1993.

Kanfer, Steven; and Patricia Gordon. "The Magic Boom: New Sorcery." *Time,* 22 July 1974.

Mysteries of the Unknown, Spirit Summonings. Alexandria, Va.: Time-Life Books, 1996.

Proskauer, Julien J. *Spook Crooks.* New York: A. L. Burt, 1946. Reprint, Ann Arbor, Mich.: Gryphon Books, 1971.

Randi, James. *Flim-Flam! Psychics, ESP, Unicorns & Other Delusions.* Buffalo, N.Y.: Prometheus Books, 1982.

———. *The Magic of Uri Geller.* New York: Random House, 1975. Rev. ed. *The Truth About Uri Geller.* Buffalo, N.Y.: Prometheus Books, 1982.

Sexton, George. *Spirit Mediums and Conjurers.* London: 1873.

Truesdell, J. W. *The Bottom Facts Concerning the Science of Spiritualism.* New York: G. W. Carleton, 1883.

Magic Square

An arithmetical curiosity formerly believed to have **occult** significance. A square is divided into smaller squares, each containing a number so arranged that the sum of each row, vertical, horizontal, or diagonal, is the same.

In a variant form, letters are used instead of numbers, the most popular arrangement being the rows:

SATOR
AREPO
TENET
OPERA
ROTAS

A variant form:

SALOM
AREPO
LEMEL
OPERA
MOLAS

The variant form is specified in *The Book of the Sacred Magic of Abra-Melin the Mage* as a charm to obtain the love of a maiden.

Other magic squares were composed of numbers or letters in irregular arrangements that were believed to have magical power. Such squares were inscribed on parchment or other materials and worn as **talismans.**

Other talismans were made in circular format, in wax or in metal, and used to invoke **spirits.** These were sometimes termed "seals." The term **magic circle** more properly indicates the protective circle traced upon the ground by the magician when invoking spirits.

Talismans in the form of magic squares have long been used by Hindus and Moslems for magical purposes and in religious rituals.

Maginot, Adèle (ca. 1848)

Noted early French medium. She was psychic from childhood and was treated by the magnetist **Louis-Alphonse Cahagnet** because of the disturbances in her life caused by lively psychic occurrences. He soon found her an excellent clairvoyant, especially for medical purposes. From this she progressed to serve as a channel for **spirit communications.**

From the summer of 1848, many sittings were held in which visitors were put in touch with their departed relatives. Cahagnet made them sign a statement after the sitting indicating which of the particulars were true and which false, which he later published in the second volume of his book *Magnétisme arcanes de la vie future dévoilé* (1848–60). When Maginot was put into **trance,** she saw the spirits of the departed, described them, and gave an intimate description of their family circumstances.

Baron du Potet, a well-known writer on **animal magnetism** and the editor of the *Journal du Magnetisme,* witnessed a striking **séance** in the company of Prince de Kourakine, who was secretary to the Russian ambassador. Nevertheless, he was inclined to attribute the result to **thought-transference.**

Maginot's most extraordinary phenomena, however, did not consist in communications from the dead but in communications from the living, combined with traveling **clairvoyance.** A. M. Lucas came to inquire after his brother-in-law, who had disappeared after a quarrel 12 years before. Maginot, in trance, found the man and said that he was alive in a foreign country, busy gathering seeds from small shrubs about three feet high. She asked to be awakened since she was afraid of wild beasts. A. M. Lucas returned a few days afterward with the mother of the vanished man. Maginot correctly described the man's appearance and the history of his disappearance. She was asked to speak to the man, and a conversation ensued.

"Get him to tell you the name of the country where you see him," says the record. "He will not answer." "Tell him that his good mother, for whom he had a great affection, is with you, and asks for news of him." "Oh, at the mention of his mother he turned around and said to me 'My mother, I shall not die without seeing her again. Comfort her, and tell her that I always think of her. I am not dead.'" "Why doesn't he write to her?" "He has written to her, but the vessel has no doubt been wrecked—at least he supposes this to be so, since he has received no answer. He tells me that he is in Mexico. He has followed the Emperor, Don Pedro; he has been imprisoned for five years; he has suffered a great deal, and will use every effort to return to France; they will see him again." "Can he name the place in which he is living?" "No, it is very far inland. These countries have no names."

A similar experience was recorded by M. Mirande, the head of the printing office in which the first volume of the *Arcanes* had been printed. His missing brother, whom he believed to be dead, was found by Maginot to be living and a plausible account of his long silence and whereabouts was given. Unfortunately, in neither case was corroboration forthcoming. But there was one instance (quoted in Cahagnet's third volume) in which, a few weeks after the sitting, a mother received a confirmatory letter from her absent son.

Frank Podmore challenged Adèle Maginot's work:

"If Adèle, or any other of Cahagnet's clairvoyants really had possessed the power of conversing with the living at a distance, I cannot doubt that Cahagnet, in the course of his many years' experiments, would have been able to present us with some evidence of such power that was not purely hypothetical. Nothing would be more easy to prove. The fact that no such evidence is forthcoming affords a strong presumption that Adèle did not possess the power, and that the conversations here detailed were purely imaginary, the authentic or plausible details which they contained being filched, it may be, telepathically from the minds of those present."

However, in spite of a lack of convincing evidence from Maginot, Podmore also stated of Cahagnet's investigations: "In the whole literature of Spiritualism I know of no records of the kind which reach a higher evidential standard, nor any in which the writer's good faith or intelligence are alike so conspicuous."

Magnetic Phenomena

Some readily observable phenomena have suggested a connection between psychic abilities and magnetism. The medium **Henry Slade** could influence the movements of a magnetic needle. **Johann Zöllner** made convincing experiments with a glass-covered compass. Slade could also magnetize steel knitting needles, and Zöllner lifted iron filings and sewing needles with their ends. **Stanislawa Tomczyk** could exert a similar influence over the compass.

The British psychic researcher and author **Stanley de Brath** also reported a case in which a young man deflected the magnetic needle. He was searched for a concealed iron or a magnet but nothing was found.

More recently, the controversial psychic **Uri Geller** has also demonstrated deflection of a compass needle, while his skeptical critics also claim that he must have a concealed iron or magnet.

Magnetometer

A device invented by the Abbé Fortin (ca. 1864) consisting of a piece of paper cut to the shape of a compass needle and considered to indicate some kind of electromagnetic force. It was suspended in a glass cylinder by a silk fiber. If the cylinder was approached by a hand, the paper (over a dial of 360 degrees) would either turn toward the hand or away from it.

Carried out in a more substantial form with a "metallic multiplicator," a condenser, and a needle, the magnetometer was used for the study of terrestrial magnetism to solve meteorological problems. Since the beginning of the twentieth century, it has been used for **dowsing.** (See also **Biometer of Baraduc; De Tromelin Cylinder; water witching**)

Magonia (Journal)

Quarterly journal concerned with anomalies, such as **visions, portents,** prodigies, and **UFOs.** The name "Magonia" was given in medieval **France** to a mysterious land beyond the sky, the origin of all kinds of signs and wonders but inextricably bound up with the destinies of human beings. Inhabitants of Magonia traveled in aerial ships and were believed to destroy crops and kidnap human beings. The emperor Charlemagne issued edicts to prohibit the Magonians from troubling the air and provoking storms.

Issues of *Magonia* have covered such subjects as **glossolalia, ouija boards,** pagan **occultism, coincidences, Spiricom,** earth lights, **psychic research, Bigfoot,** and other Fortean topics. Address: John Rimmer, John Dee Cottage, 5 James Terrace, Mortlake Churchyard, London, SW14 8HB England. Website: http://www.magonia.demon.co.uk/.

Sources:

Magonia. http://www.magonia.demon.co.uk/. March 8,2000.

Magpie

The chattering of a magpie was formerly considered a sure **omen** of evil. Another folk belief was that the croaking of a single magpie around a house signified that one of the inhabitants would soon die. In parts of Britain and **Ireland** it was believed that evil could be averted by being respectful to a magpie—bowing or doffing one's hat. Irish folk would sometimes say "Good morning, your reverence" on seeing a magpie first thing in the morning. The magpie also figured in the folklore of the American Indians and was a clan animal among the Hopis.

Maguire, Father Joseph (ca. 1931–)

Catholic priest popularly known as "The Miracle Man," who specializes in spiritual **healing.** He was born in Lowell, Massachusetts; his mother was Irish, from Castlegregory in county Kerry. Maguire was a successful businessman, owning an electronics sales company that sold missile parts to Cape Kennedy, and also operating a chain of hotels, motels, and restaurants. Then, at the age of 38, he left his profitable businesses and became a Catholic priest.

His gift of healing developed slowly over a period of years, commencing the year before his ordination. He has since figured in a large number of medically unexplained cures that followed his touching people who were terminally ill.

In 1984 Father Maguire visited **Ireland,** where he had an enthusiastic reception. More than 2,500 people crowded into the Church of Our Lady Queen of Peace in Merrion Road, Dublin (built to accommodate 1,800 persons). Parents held out babies for Father Maguire to touch. After celebrating mass with eight concelebrants, Father Maguire blessed the congregation and went to pray with the sick. Subsequently a 46-year-old mother, paralyzed for several months with a cancerous tumor, claimed that she regained the use of her left arm and was able to walk again after being virtually immobile. (See also **healing by touch**)

Magus

A master magician or adept. The *Magi,* or **magicians** (plural form of *Magus*), were the "wise men" of the ancient Persian priesthood. It is noted in the Christian New Testament that three magi brought gifts to the infant Jesus. In the later tradition they were given names—Kaspar, Melchior, and Balthasar—and their bones are said to rest in Cologne Cathedral, **Germany.**

The term Magus is also used in magical societies like the **Golden Dawn** to indicate one of its highest grades, between the master of the temple and the ipsissimus.

Sources:

King, Francis. *The Rites of Modern Occult Magic.* New York: Macmillan, 1970.

"Magus"

A spirit **control** of **William Stainton Moses,** supposed to be a member of the Mystic Band that delivered **occult** teaching in Moses's scripts. "Magus" did not disclose his name on Earth, but he said that he lived 4,000 years ago and belonged to an ancient African wonder-working brotherhood. In the nineteenth book of the Moses scripts, a topaz is mentioned as the material counterpart of a spiritual jewel worn by "Magus," which was to be given to Stainton Moses to help him to see visions. The stone, set in a ring, was reportedly dropped from the air in Stainton Moses's bedroom.

Sources:

Moses, Stainton. *Spirit Identity.* London: London Spiritualist Alliance, Ltd., 1908.

———. *Spirit Teachings.* 1883. Reprint, New York: Arno Press, 1976.

Maharaj Ji, Guru (1957–)

Teacher in the Sant Mat tradition and head of Elan Vital (formerly known as the Divine Light Mission). Guru Maharaj Ji, a title rather than a name, was born Prem Pal Singh on December 10, 1957. He moved to the United States as a spiritual teacher in 1971, at the age of 14. He was the son of Sri Hans Maharaj Ji, a spiritual teacher in the Sant Mat Radha Soami tradition and the founder of the Divine Light Mission in India. When Sri Hans died in 1966, his youngest son, only eight but recognized as something of a spiritual prodigy, assumed control of the movement as Guru Maharaj Ji.

On a visit to the United States he was met by a public skeptical of one so young assuming any role in religious leadership, but was welcomed by many young adults as a contemporary spiritual leader. Ten of thousands of "premies," as his followers were called, were initiated, and within a few years hundreds of centers were established in the West.

Through the mid-1970s the rapidly developing movement ran into trouble, beginning with its inability to fill the Houston Astrodome in a highly publicized event, Millennium 73. Then in 1974, Maharaj married his 24-year-old secretary, whom he described as an incarnation of the Hindu goddess Durga. The marriage further disrupted his relationship with his mother and older brothers. A lawsuit in India gave control of the Indian branch of the Divine Light Mission to Maharaj's mother and led to a complete break with her son, who maintained the complete support of the Western disciples.

In the late 1970s the Divine Light Mission had also become the target of the anticult movement, and members were subjected to deprogramming in an attempt to break their allegiance to Maharaj and the group. In the early 1980s Maharaj responded to the problem by disbanding the mission, closing all of the ashrams, and reorganizing his following as merely informal students of his teachings. He has assumed a low profile and largely dropped out of public sight. He spends most of his time traveling the world speaking to his followers.

Sources:

Cameron, Charles. *Who Is Guru Maharaj Ji?* New York: Bantam Books, 1973.

Mahararj Ji, Guru. *The Living Master.* Denver, Colo.: Divine Light Mission, 1978.

Maharishi Mahesh Yogi (ca. 1911–)

A modern Hindu **guru** who began a worldwide Spiritual Regeneration Movement in the late 1950s. The movement, now led by the World Plan Executive Council, is best known for promoting the technique of **Transcendental Meditation** (TM).

Maharishi was born Mahesh Brasad Warma, around the year 1911. Originally a physics graduate of Allahabad University, India, he worked for a time in a factory, then studied spiritual science for some years under Swami Brahmananda Saraswati Shankaracharya of Jyotir Math, a teacher of traditional Hindu transcendentalism. After the death of his teacher in 1953, the Maharishi spent some time trying to develop his own simplified version of traditional Hindu **meditation.**

In 1958 he designed the Science of Creative Intelligence for "the regeneration of the whole world through meditation," known widely as Transcendental Meditation. In a simple initiation ceremony, the guru bestowed a *mantra* (or word of power), which the pupil repeated during a meditation period each day. In this easy technique, the pupil could, it has been claimed, bypass normal intellectual activity and tap a limitless reservoir of energy and creative intelligence.

The system spread around the world through the 1960s but was given a boost in 1967, when the rock music group the Beatles showed interest in the movement. Publicity concerning their relation to the Maharishi made TM seem a viable alternative to psychedelic **drugs.** The Beatles defected some months later, but by then other celebrities were traveling to the Maharishi's ashram at Rishikesh, in the foothills of the Himalayas. The Students' International Meditation Society, which was founded in Los Angeles, California, in 1966, received many of the young adults attracted to TM by its celebrity followers. Since the 1970s, the movement has been boosted by the well-publicized scientific findings that TM produces beneficial results. Various studies, most flawed by the lack of investigation of similar mediative techniques, suggest that TM aids individuals in various manners. The sociological studies, suggesting that a representative number of TM meditators in an area can change its social climate (lower the crime rate, promote peace, etc.), are less conclusive.

The movement adopted a "world plan" to develop the full potential of the individual, to improve governmental achievements, to realize the highest ideal of education, to solve the problems of crime and all behavior that brings unhappiness to the human family, to maximize the intelligent use of the environment, to bring fulfillment to the economic aspirations of individuals and society, and to achieve the spiritual goals of the human race in this generation. The World Plan Executive Council has founded in many countries its own political party, the Natural Law Party, and it runs candidates for public office in order to achieve the goals of the world plan.

In the 1970s, as the number of new people coming into TM dropped, the movement unveiled a "Siddhi" program (*siddhis* are special paranormal powers) based on the claims of the ancient **yoga** treatise *The Yoga Sutras of Patanjali.* The program claimed that students of this special course have successfully achieved the paranormal feat of **levitation.** Photographs of students show them hovering a few feet in the air, but critics (and former students) have stated that the "levitators" merely bounce in the air cross-legged and do not float. To date, no irrefutable evidence of levitation by the Maharishi's students has yet been produced, and several ex-students of the Siddhi program have successfully sued the organization.

In 1968, the council moved its headquarters to Seelisberg, **Switzerland,** and in 1979 established Maharishi International University in Fairfield, Iowa, where they mix courses in TM and academic curriculum. They plan to open an eastern campus in Antrim, New Hampshire. The Maharish was worth $3.5 billion in 1998 and oversaw nearly 1,000 TM centers around the world.

Sources:

Bainbridge, William Sims, and Daniel H. Jackson. "The Rise and Fall of Transcendental Meditation." In *The Future of Religion.* Edited by Rodney Stark and William Sims Bainbridge. Berkeley: University of California Press, 1985.

Jefferson, William. *The Story of Maharishi.* New York: Pocket Books, 1976.

Mahesh Yogi, Maharishi. *The Science of Being and Art of Living.* London: International SRM Publications, 1966.

Mason, Paul. *The Maharishi: The Biography of the Man Who Gave Transendental Meditation to the West.* Shaftesbury, Dorset, UK: Element Books, 1994.

Orme-Johnson, David W., and John T. Farrows, eds. *Scientific Research on the Transcendental Meditation Program: Collected Papers, I.* Seelisberg, Switzerland: Maharishi European Research University Press, 1977.

White, John. *Everything You Want to Know about TM, Including How to Do It.* New York: Pocket Books, 1976.

Mahatma Letters

Communications allegedly from the Mahatmas (Masters or Adepts) of the **Theosophical Society** to **Helena Petrovna Blavatsky** and other leading theosophists during the nineteenth century. These Mahatmas were said to be eastern teachers belonging to the Great White Brotherhood, a group providing overall guidance to human destiny. The brotherhood was said to be living in the Himalayas of Tibet. It included Koot Humi Lal Singh (K. H.) and Morya (M.), the primary masters with whom Blavatsky claimed contact.

Notes signed with the initials of these Masters would be mysteriously precipitated out of the air or discovered in unexpected places. Recipients of such letters included **Henry S. Olcott,** the society's president, and **A. P. Sinnett,** editor of the Anglo-Indian newspaper the *Pioneer.* Sinnett was favorably impressed by such letters as well as other **occult** phenomena demonstrated by Blavatsky, and played a prominent part in the affairs of the **Theosophical Society.** The material received by Blavatsky from the Mahatmas, both in the letters and in other communications, formed the basis of the particular teachings of the society and constituted a new form of Gnosticism.

The reception of communications from the Masters in some unusual and unlikely circumstances became one claim of the society to special revelatory knowledge. Those claims, which had initially impressed some of the leaders of the **Society for Psychical Research,** led it to delegate **Richard Hodgson** to investigate the phenomena in Adyar, the Madras headquarters. He found extensive evidence of **fraud** on Blavatsky's part in producing and delivering the letters and in the arrival of various artifacts, reportedly gifts of the Masters. His discoveries included a shrine with a false back in which letters would mysteriously appear overnight to be found the next morning. He was assisted by Emma Coulomb, a former employee of the society, who claimed to have been a cohort of Blavatsky, but who had subsequently turned on her.

The publication of the Hodgson report created a public controversy and a crisis of major import within the society. While many members left, others preferred to believe that the confession by Coulomb was part of a plot to discredit Blavatsky. After Blavatsky's death, Theosophist co-founder **William Q. Judge** produced furthur Mahatma letters supporting his effort to take charge of the Esoteric Section of the Theosophical Society (in opposition to the leadership of **Annie Besant**). Olcott eventually declared these letters to be fraudulent.

Theosophists have had to live for a century with the Hodgson report and the charge that the society is built upon a fraud. During this time various members have attempted to refute Hodgson's (and additional supporting) claims. For example, all now agree that the original Mahatma letters to Blavatsky were strongly influenced by her personality, since the handwriting and language were typical of her. While skeptics would claim that such influence is an additional sign of conscious fraud, Theosophists would claim that this resulted from the Masters using her as a medium of communication, in much the same way that a psychic delivers **automatic writing.**

More recently (1980), Charles Marshall attempted to prove by computer analysis that there is a strong dissimilarity between Blavatsky's language and that of the Masters. However, the computer program, although extensive, was somewhat arbitrary, being confined to certain prepositions and conjunctions. Moreover the comparison between the Mahatma letters and Blavatsky's writings in such works as *The Secret Doctrine* ignored the extensive editorial work by others on behalf of Blavatsky's writings, and her own extensive and unacknowledged plagiarism from other writers, thus making her claimed style unrepresentative. Other recent defenses of Blavatsky have been made by Vernon Harrison and Walter A. Carrithers.

Some of the original Mahatma letters may be viewed in the Manuscripts Department of the British Library, London.

Sources:

Barker, A. T. *The Mahatma Letters to A. P. Sinnett from the Mahatmas M. and K. H.* London: T. Fisher Unwin, 1924.

Gomes, Michael. *Theosophy in the Nineteenth Century: An Annotated Bibliography.* New York: Garland Publishing, 1994.

Hare, William L., and H. E. Hare. *Who Wrote the Mahatma Letters?* London: William & Norgate, 1936.

Harrison, Vernon. "'J'Accuse': An Examination of the Hodgson Report of 1885." *Journal* of the Society for Psychical Research (April 1986).

Jinarajadasa, C., ed. *The K. H. Letters to C. W. Leadbeater.* Adyar, Madras, India: Theosophical Publishing House, 1941.

———. *Letters from the Masters of Wisdom.* 2 vols. Adyar, Madras India: Theosophical Publishing House, 1919.

———. *The Story of the Mahatma Letters.* Adyar, Madras, India: Theosophical Publishing House, 1946.

Marshall, Charles. "The Mahatma Letters: A Syntactic Investigation into the Possibility of 'Forgery' by Helena Petrovna Blavatsky, a 19th Century Russian Occultist." *Viewpoint Aquarius* 96 (October 1980).

Waterman, Adlai E. [Walter A. Carrithers]. *Obituary: The "Hodgson Report" on Madame Blavatsky.* Adyar, Madras, India: Theosophical Publishing House, 1963.

Mahavira (540 B.C.E.–468 B.C.E.)

Mahavira, Indian guru of the Jain tradition, was born into the *kshatriya* or warrior caste and originally named Vardhamana. His birthdate is traditionally given as 599 B.C.E., but modern dating has suggested a more likely date of 540. He married at a young age, but at the age of 30 left his home on a spiritual quest. After 12 years of wonders and accomplishments in the spiritual life he was given the name Mahavira or Great Hero. He eventually reached a state thought of as complete isolation from harmful karma, called *kevela.* He was acknowledged as the 24th Great Teacher of his tradition, and his new title, *Jaina* or Victor, gave the name to the Jaina community. Mahavira concluded early in his spiritual quest that the key to spiritual advancement was the avoidance of injury to any life form, a difficult process as life was everywhere.

After attaining *kevala,* Mahavira took a student, Makkhali Gosala, who had attained some magical powers. Mahavira questioned the equation of his powers with spiritual enlightenment, and the two went their separate ways. Before their parting, Makkhali Gosala tried to use his powers on Mahavira. Though he lost his first disciple, Mahavira soon gained others, including 11 brahman priests. According to tradition, he had half a million followers by the time of his death. As with his birth, there is a discrepancy between the traditionally accepted date (527 B.C.E.) and the estimates of contemporary scholars (468 B.C.E.).

Since Mahavira's time Jains have followed a path of liberation that has 14 stages. The basics of the life include the successive taking of vows of nonviolence (*ahimsa*), truthfulness, nonstealing, sexual abstinence, and nonpossessiveness. Each vow leads to a releasing of karma. In Jainism, karma is pictured as a sticky substance that adheres to one's life force and prevents liberation. This substance is attracted by violence and the most violent are said to be covered in black karma.

Jainism forms an important element of the Eastern teachings that came into the West, especially England, beginning late in the nineteenth century. These teachings influenced the development of various nonviolent perspectives, some of which became identified with **Spiritualism** and the metaphysical community including the antivivisection movement and vegetarianism.

Sources:

Chalpple, Christopher Key. *Nonviolence to Animals, Earth and Self in Asian Traditions.* Albany: State University of New York Press, 1993.

Jaini, Padmanabh S. *The Jaina Path of Purification.* Berkeley: University of California Press, 1979.

Tatia, Nathmal. *Studies in Jaina Philosophy.* Benares, India: Jaina Cultural Research Society, 1951.

Maier, Michael (ca. 1568–1622)

German alchemist, born at Rensburg in Holstein. He was one of the principal figures in the seventeenth-century **Rosicrucian** controversy in **Germany** and the greatest **adept** of his time. He diligently pursued the study of medicine in his youth, then practiced at Rostock with such success that Emperor Rudolph II appointed him as his physician.

Some adepts eventually succeeded in luring him from the practical work he followed into the complex and tortuous paths of **alchemy.** In order to confer with those who he believed possessed the transcendent mysteries, he traveled all over Germany. The *Biographie Universelle* states that in pursuit of these "ruinous absurdities" he sacrificed his health, fortune, and time. On a visit to England he became acquainted with **Robert Fludd,** the Kentish mystic.

In the controversy that convulsed Germany on the appearance of his Rosicrucian manifestos in the early 1600s, he took a vigorous and enthusiastic share and wrote several works in defense of the mysterious society. He is alleged to have traveled in order to seek members of the "College of Teutonic Philosophers R.C.," and, failing to find them, formed a brotherhood of his own, based on the form of the *Fama Fraternibus.* There is no adequate authority to support the opinion held by some that toward the end of his life he was initiated into the genuine order (there being serious doubt that any such genuine order ever existed).

A posthumous pamphlet of Maier's called *Ulysses* was published by one of his personal friends in 1624. There was added to the same volume the substance of two pamphlets already published in German but which, in view of their importance, were translated into Latin for the benefit of the European literati.

The first pamphlet was entitled *Colloquium Rhodostauroticum trium personarium per Famem et Confessionem quodamodo revelatam de Fraternitate Rosoe Crucis.* The second was an *Echo Colloquii* by Hilarion on behalf of the Rosicrucian Fraternity. From these pamphlets it appears that Maier considered himself a member of the mystical order.

He became the most profuse writer on alchemy of his time. Most of his works, many of which are adorned with curious plates, are obscure with the exception of his Rosicrucian *Apologies.*

Maimonides, Rabbi Moses (1135–1204)

A great Spanish-Hebrew philosopher, theologian, and author of the *Guide for the Perplexed.* His theories were Aristotelian and rational, but there remained in his viewpoint a touch of **mysticism.**

He was born April 6, 1135, in Cordova, southern **Spain,** and was educated by Arabic teachers. After the Moorish conquest of Cordova in 1148, Jews left the province, and Maimonides settled in Fez, Morroco. After five years he moved to Cairo, **Egypt,** where he became physician to Saladin and married the sister of Ibn Mali, a royal secretary.

In his famous treatise, the *Guide for the Perplexed,* he sought to harmonize rabbinical and philosophical teachings but maintained that reason must be supplemented by revelation. His treatise profoundly influenced his Arabic, Jewish, and Christian successors. It has been suggested that Maimonides was sympathetic to the teachings of **Kabala** in his late period. He died December 13, 1204.

Maison des Spirites

Spiritist center founded by **Jean Meyer,** who also assisted the foundation of the **Institut Métapsychique International** (concerned with **psychical research**). The Maison des Spirites was located at 8 Rue Copernic, Paris, and was intended to propagate knowledge of **Spiritism.** It became the secretariat of the Fédération Spirite Internationale (International Spiritualists' Federation) and hosted the Second **International Spiritualist Congress** in Paris in 1925. (See also **France**)

Maithuna

Sanskrit term for sexual intercourse, one practice espoused in **tantric yoga. Tantra** differs from more ascetic forms of Hinduism in eschewing the way of denial. Instead of refraining from such things as alcohol and sex in order to attain spiritual realization, tantra suggests using items commonly denied as a tool to enlightenment. Sexuality is by far the most controversial of such tools. Within tantric systems, the practice of maithuna may be either symbolic (the right-hand path) or actual (the left hand path). Tantra seeks union with the goddess Shakti and speaks of the male's union with the goddess. In left-hand rites, the woman is seen as the goddess present in flesh.

Tantra also developed the understanding of **occult** anatomy in Hinduism focused in the seven **chakras,** or psychic centers, located horizontally in the body from the base of the spine to the top of the head, and **kundalini,** the mystical energy that is usually pictured as lying latent, like a coiled serpent, at the base of the spine. In tantric practice, kundalini is released to travel up the spine, opening the chakras, and eventually bringing enlightenment. In right-hand tantra, this awakening is done with **meditation** and concentration. In the left-hand path, the kundalini is awakened in part by sexual intercourse ending in *coitus interruptus,* with a cooperating female.

There has also existed in the West since the late nineteenth century an occult system that includes sexual practices, its major exponent having been **Aleister Crowley.** This system is often seen as a derivative of tantra, but in fact has quite different origins. Since the 1970s, Western sex magick and tantra have been the subject of many books and articles, and sycretistic forms of sexually oriented practices have begun to emerge.

Maitland, Edward (1824–1897)

Co-founder with **Anna Bonus Kingsford** of Esoteric Christianity and the **Hermetic Society.**

Born October 27, 1824, at Ipswich, England, Maitland graduated from Caius College, Cambridge, 1847. He intended to become a clergyman, but had many reservations about the church, and instead spent some years traveling in California and Australia, studying life firsthand.

Upon returning to England, he devoted himself "to developing the intuitional faculty as to find the solution of all problems having their basis in man's spiritual nature." Through his close friendship with Anna Kingsford, he became an ardent vegetarian and the interpreter of her highly individual mystical Christianity. He collaborated with her on the writing of *The Perfect Way; or, The Finding of Christ* (London, 1882) and related books.

After Kingsford's death in 1888, Maitland published her biography, *Anna Kingsford: Her Life, Letters, Diary* (1896). He died in the following year on October 2, 1897.

Sources:

Kingsford, Anna. *Clothed with the Sun.* London: John M. Watkins, 1889.

Kingsford, Anna, and Edward Maitland. *The Perfect Way; or, The Finding of Christ.* London, 1882. Rev. ed. London, 1887. Reprint, Mokelumne Hill, Calif.: Health Research, 1972. Reprint, Boston: Esoteric Book, 1988.

———. *The Virgin of the World.* 1885. Reprint, Minneapolis: Wizard's Bookshelf, 1977.

Maitland, Edward. *Anna Kingsford: Her Life, Letters, Diary.* London, 1896.

———. *The Story of Anna Kingsford and Edward Maitland and of the New Gospel of Interpretation.* Birmingham, England: Ruskin Press, 1905.

Mak, A(rie) (1914–)

Dutch school director and experimenter in the field of **parapsychology.** He was born November 23, 1914, at Alkmaar, Netherlands. He was an instructor and director at Sneek Technical School, Sneek, Netherlands (1939–56), and later director (1959–60). Mak was a member of the Amsterdam Parapsychologische Kring and served as research officer of the **Studievereniging voor Psychical Research** (Dutch Society for Psychical Research). Contributor of articles to astronomy journals, he won the Van de Bilt gold medal for the best amateur astronomical observations in 1950.

He studied **telepathy, clairvoyance,** and **psychokinesis** and took part in experiments (with **Jan Kappers,** A. H. de Jong, and F. v. d. Berg) to test clairvoyance quantitatively. He also studied the question of evidence for **reincarnation.**

Sources:

Pleasants, Helene, ed. *Biographical Dictionary of Parapsychology.* New York: Helix Press, 1964.

Malachite

A precious stone (a variety of topaz) of basic copper carbonate. Folklore held that it preserved the cradle of an infant from spells.

Malachy Prophecies

St. Malachy O'More was a medieval bishop who is said to have foretold the succession of 112 popes, from Celestinus II (1143) until the final pope in the future yet to come. These predictions were in the form of a long series of Latin character mottos instead of actual names, and there is still scholarly doubt as to whether the prophecies really emanated from St. Malachy. However, other prophecies attributed to him are claimed to have been fulfilled.

He was born Maelmhaedhoc Ua Morgair in Armagh, **Ireland,** in 1095. His biography was written by a famous contemporary, St. Bernard of Clairvaux. Malachy was the son of a well-known scholar; his mother came from a wealthy family in Bangor, county Down. His father died when Malachy was eight years old, and he was subsequently educated by a monk who later became abbot of Armagh.

Malachy was ordained by St. Celsus, an Irish Benedictine of **Glastonbury,** then archbishop of Armagh. He became vicar-general to Celsus, then abbot of Bangor, and later bishop of Connor, succeeding to the archbishopric in 1132. He had a reputation as a firm disciplinarian.

After six years, he resigned in order to make a pilgrimage to Rome. But during the course of his journey, he met St. Bernard at the French abbey of Clairvaux and was so impressed by him that he requested to be allowed to remain at Clairvaux as an ordinary monk. However, Pope Innocent II refused permission, since he had plans for Malachy to be primate of the combined see of Armagh and Tuam, although in the end this did not come to pass.

Malachy traveled through **England, Scotland,** and Ireland, even making a second pilgrimage to **Rome.** On the return journey to Ireland, he died at Clairvaux, which had made such an impression on him.

Malachy had a great reputation as a prophet during his own lifetime. When the son of King David of Scotland was critically ill, Malachy sprinkled him with holy water and predicted that the boy would survive. He did. When one individual tried to prevent the building of an oratory, Malachy correctly foretold his early death. According to St. Bernard, Malachy even predicted the date, place, and circumstances of his own death.

The papal prophecies seem to be extraordinarily apt, beginning with Celestine II (1143) and continuing through to modern times. The first pope was indicated by the motto "Ex Castro Tiberis" (from a castle on the Tiber); Celestine II came from Tuscany, where the Tiber rises, and his family name was Catello. The next pope was indicated by the motto "Inimicus Expulsus" (the enemy driven out); it transpired that his family name was Caccianemici, which combines "cacciare" (to drive out) and "nemici" (enemies). The next pope had the motto "Ex Magnitudine Montis" (from the great mountain); he was born in Montemagno (the great mountain).

Some scholars believe the prophecies to be sixteenth-century forgeries. Nevertheless, some of the mottos predicted for later popes have still been surprisingly apt, e.g., "Flos Florum" (flower of flowers) for Pope Paul VI (1963) seems validated by the fact that the pope had three fleur-de-lys on his armorial bearings.

According to the Malachy prophecies, the line of popes will end after the successor to Pope John Paul II. The last pope will be "Petrus Romanus" (Peter the Roman), and after that Rome will be destroyed and the world will be purified by fire. Some believe that these will be the final days of the Last Judgment, others that there will be a cleansing of the world and the commencement of a new cycle of life.

Sources:

Bander, Peter. *The Prophecies of St. Malachy.* Gerrards Cross, England: Colin Smythe, 1969.

Dorato, M. *Gli ultimi papi e la fine del mondo nelle grandi profezie.* Rome: n.p., 1950.

MALAYSIA

Malaysia now includes the mainland of West Malaysia, sharing a land border with Thailand in the north, and East Malaysia, consisting of the states of Sarawak and Sabah (formerly North Borneo). The ethnic grouping of Malaysia includes Chinese and Indian races, but the largest population is of Malays, predominantly Muslim in faith and speaking their own Malay language.

Much of the folklore and magical tradition of the Malays concerns "sympathetic magic" (see **magic**). The traveler Hugh Clifford, writing in the nineteenth century, stated:

"The accredited intermediary between men and spirits is the *Pawang;* the *Pawang* is a functionary of great and traditional importance in a *Malay* village, though in places near towns the office is falling into abeyance. In the inland districts, however, the *Pawang* is still a power, and is regarded as part of the constituted order of Society, without whom no village community would be complete. It must be clearly understood that he had nothing whatever to do with the official Muhammadan religion of the mosque; the village has its regular staff of elders—the *Imam, Khatio,* and *Bilal*—for the mosque service. But the *Pawang* is quite outside this system and belongs to a different and much older order of ideas; he may be regarded as the legitimate representative of the primitive 'medicine-man,' or 'village-sorcerer,' and his very existence in these days is an anomaly, though it does not strike *Malays* as such. . . .

"The *Pawang* is a person of very real significance. In all agricultural operations, such as sowing, reaping, irrigation works, and the clearing of jungle for planting, in fishing at sea, in prospecting for minerals, and in cases of sickness, his assistance is invoked. He is entitled by custom to certain small fees; thus, after a good harvest he is allowed in some villages five *gantangs* of padi, one *gantang* of rice (*beras*), and two *chupaks of emping* (a preparation of rice and cocoa-nut made into a sort of sweetmeat) from each householder."

The *Pawang* used to regulate taboos, and employ a familiar spirit known as *hantu pusaka*—a hereditary demon. He also acted as a **medium** and divined through **trance.** To become a magician,

"You must meet the ghost of a murdered man. Take the midrib of a leaf of the 'ivory' cocoa-nut palm *(pelepah niyor gading),* which is to be laid on the grave, and two midribs, which are intended to represent canoe-paddles, and carry them with the help of a companion to the grave of the murdered man at the time of the full moon (the 15th day of the lunar month) when it falls upon a Tuesday. Then take a cent's worth of incense, with glowing embers in a censer, and carry them to the head-post of the grave of the deceased. Fumigate the grave, going three times round it, and call upon the murdered man by name: 'Hearken, So-and-so, and assist me; I am taking (this boat) to the saints of God, and I desire to ask for a little magic.'

"Here take the first midrib, fumigate it, and lay it upon the head of the grave, repeating *'Kur Allah'* ('Cluck, Cluck, God!') seven times. You and your companion must now take up a sitting posture, one at the head and the other at the foot of the grave, facing the grave post, and use the canoe-paddles which you have brought. In a little while the surrounding scenery will change and take upon itself the appearance of the sea, and finally an aged man will appear, to whom you must address the same request as before."

Malay magic may be subdivided into preparatory rites, sacrifice, lustration, **divination,** and **possession.** Sacrifice took the form of a simple gift, or act of homage to the spirit or deity. Lustration was magico-religious and purificatory, principally taking place after childbirth. It might be performed by fire or water. Divination consisted for the most part of the reading of **dreams,** and was, as elsewhere, drawn from the acts of men or nature. **Omens** were strongly believed in.

"When a star is seen in apparent proximity to the moon, old people say there will be a wedding shortly. . . .

"The entrance into a house of an animal which does not generally seek to share the abode of man is regarded by the Malays as ominous of misfortune. If a wild bird flies into a house it must be carefully caught and smeared with oil, and must then be released in the open air, a formula being recited in which it is bidden to fly away with all the ill-luck and misfortunes (*sial jambalang*) of the occupier. An iguana, a tortoise, and a snake, are perhaps the most dreaded of these unnatural visitors. They are sprinkled with ashes, if possible to counteract their evil influence.

"A swarm of bees settling near a house is an unlucky omen, and prognosticates misfortune."

So, too, omens were taken either from the flight or cries of certain birds, such as the night-owl, the crow, some kinds of wild doves, and the bird called the "Rice's Husband" (*laki padi*).

Astrology

Divination by **astrology** was, however, the most common method of forecasting the future. The native practitioners possessed long tables of lucky and unlucky periods and reasons. These were mostly translations from Indian and Arabic sources.

The oldest known of these systems of propitious and unpropitious seasons was known as *Katika Lima,* or the Five Times. Under it the day was divided into five parts, and five days formed a cycle. To each division was given a name as follows: Maswara, Kala, S'ri, Brahma, Bisnu (Vishnu), names of Hindu deities, the last name in the series for the first day being the first in that of the second day, and so on until the five days are exhausted. Each of these had a color, and according to the color first seen or noticed on such and such a day would it be fortunate to ask a boon of a certain god.

A variation of this system, known as the "Five Moments," was similar in origin, but possessed a Muslim nomenclature. Still another scheme, *Katika Tujoh,* was based on the seven heavenly bodies, dividing each day into seven parts, each of which was distinguished by the Arabic name for the sun, moon, and principal planets.

The astrology proper of the Malays is purely Arabic in origin, but a system of Hindu invocation was in vogue by which the lunar month was divided into parts called *Rejang,* which resembles the *Nacshatras* or lunar houses of the Hindus. Each division had its symbol, usually an animal. Each day was propitious for something, and the whole system was committed to verse for mnemonic purposes.

Demonology

The demonic form common to Malaysia was that of the **jinn,** 190 in number. These were sometimes subdivided into "faithful" and "infidel," and further into the jinns of the royal musical instruments, of the state, and of the royal weapons. The *afrit* was also known. **Angels** also abounded and were purely of Arabic origin. Besides these, the principal supernatural beings were as follows: the *polong,* or familiar; the *hantu pemburu,* or specter huntsman; the *jadi-jadian,* or wer-tiger; the *hantu,* or ghost of the murdered; and the *jemalang,* or earth-spirit. The *pontianak,* the Malaysian vampire, has become the most famous of the supernatural beings of folklore and the subject of many popular movies.

Minor Sorcery

The rites of minor sorcery and **witchcraft,** as well as those of the **shaman,** were widely practiced among the Malays and were practically identical in character with those in use among other peoples with similar cultures.

Sources:

Clifford, Hugh. *In Court and Kampong.* London: Grant Richards, 1897.

———. *Studies in Brown Humanity.* London: Grant Richards, 1898.

Skeat, W. W. *Malay Magic: Being an Introduction to the Folklore and Popular Religion of the Malay Peninsula.* London: Macmillan, 1900.

Swettenham, Sir Frank A. *Malay Sketches.* London: John Lane, 1895.

Winstedt, R. *The Malays: A Cultural History.* London: Routledge, 1950.

Mallebranche (ca. 1618)

Seventeenth-century Frenchman haunted by his dead wife. Mallebranche was a marker of the game of tennis, living in the Rue Sainte-Geneviève, Paris, who in 1618 was visited by an **apparition** of his wife, who had died five years before. She came to advise him to repent and live a better life and to pray for her also. Both Mallebranche and his wife (for he had married a second time) heard the voice, but the apparition did not become visible.

Sources:

Histoire nouvelle et remarquable de l'esprit d'une femme qui c'est apparue au Faubourg Saint-Marcel après qu'elle a demeué cinq ans entiers ensevelie; elle a parlé a son mari, lui a commandé de faire prier pour elle, ayant commencé de parler le mardi II Decembre, 1618. Paris, 1618.

Malleus Maleficarum

The most authoritative and influential sourcebook for inquisitors, judges, and magistrates in the great **witchcraft** persecutions from the fifteenth through the eighteenth centuries. It was written by **Heinrich Kramer,** leading inquisitors of the Dominican Order; **Jacob Sprenger** merely attached his name to the sourcebook.

The book brought folklore and speculation about witchcraft and **magic** together with the new view identifying witchcraft with devil-worship. That identification turned witchcraft into heresy (rather than a pagan faith) and thus the proper concern of the Inquisition. That change of perspective led to the fierce and relentless persecution that resulted in the deaths of hundreds of individuals accused of practicing the religion of witchcraft, as opposed to merely practicing malevolent magic (i.e., sorcery), which had long been illegal.

This work is in three parts. Part I fulminates against the evil of witchcraft, which is characterized as renunciation of the Catholic faith, homage to the Devil, and carnal intercourse with demons. Even disbelief in the existence of witches and witchcraft was declared a grave heresy. Part II details the specific practices of witches. Part III sets forth rules for legal action and conviction of witches.

The antiquary Thomas Wright, in his book *Narratives of Sorcery and Magic* (2 vols., 1851), stated:

"In this celebrated work, the doctrine of witchcraft was first reduced to a regular system, and it was the model and groundwork of all that was written on the subject long after the date which saw its first appearance. Its writers enter largely into the much-disputed question of the nature of demons; set forth the causes which lead them to seduce men in this manner; and show why women are most prone to listen to their proposals, by reasons which prove that the inquisitors had but a mean estimate of the softer sex.

"The inquisitors show the most extraordinary skill in explaining all the difficulties which seemed to beset the subject; they even prove to their entire satisfaction that persons who have become witches may easily change themselves into beasts, particularly into wolves and cats; and after the exhibition of such a mass of learning, few would venture any longer to entertain a doubt. They investigate not only the methods employed to effect various kinds of mischief, but also the counter-charms and exorcisms that may be used against them. They likewise tell, from their own experience, the dangers to which the inquisitors were exposed, and exult in the fact that they were a class of men against whom sorcery had no power.

"These writers actually tell us, that the demon had tried to frighten them by day and by night in the forms of apes, dogs, goats, etc.; and that they frequently found large pins stuck in their night-caps, which they doubted not came there by witchcraft. When we hear these inquisitors asserting that the crime of which the witches were accused, deserved a more extreme punishment than all the vilest actions of which humanity is capable, we can understand in some degree the complacency with which they relate how, by their means, forty persons had been burnt in one place, and fifty in another, and a still greater number in a third. From the time of the publication of the *Malleus Maleficarum,* the continental press during two or three generations teemed with publications on the all-absorbing subject of sorcery.

"One of the points on which opinion had differed most was, whether the sorcerers were carried bodily through the air to the place of meeting, or whether it was an imaginary journey, suggested to their minds by the agency of the evil one. The authors of the *Malleus* decide at once in favour of the bodily transmission. One of them was personally acquainted with a priest of the diocese of Frisingen, who declared that he had in his younger days been carried through the air by a demon to a place at a very great distance from the spot whence he had been taken. Another priest, his friend, declared that he had seen him carried away, and that he appeared to him to be borne up on a kind of cloud.

"At Baldshut, on the Rhine, in the diocese of Constance, a witch confessed, that offended at not having been invited to the wedding of an acquaintance, she had caused herself to be carried through the air in open daylight to the top of a neighbouring mountain, and there, having made a hole with her hands and filled it with water, she had, by stirring the water with certain incantations caused a heavy storm to burst forth on the heads of the wedding-party; and there were witnesses at the trial who swore they had seen her carried through the air.

"The inquisitors, however, confess that the witches were sometimes carried away, as they term it, in the spirit; and they give the instance of one woman who was watched by her husband; she appeared as if asleep, and was insensible, but he perceived a kind of cloudy vapour arise out of her mouth, and vanish from the room in which she lay—this after a time returned, and she then awoke, and gave an account of her adventures, as though she had been carried bodily to the assembly. . . .

"The witches of the *Malleus Maleficarum* appear to have been more injurious to horses and cattle than to mankind. A witch at Ravenspurg confessed that she had killed twenty-three horses by sorcery. We are led to wonder most at the ease with which people are brought to bear witness to things utterly beyond the limits of belief. A man of the name of Stauff in the territory of Berne, declared that when pursued by the agents of justice, he escaped by taking the form of a mouse; and persons were found to testify that they had seen him perform this transmutation.

"The latter part of the work of the two inquisitors gives minute directions for the mode in which the prisoners are to be treated, the means to be used to force them to a confession, the degree of evidence required for conviction of those who would not confess, and the whole process of the trials. These show sufficiently that the unfortunate wretch who was once brought before the inquisitors of the holy see on the suspicion of sorcery, however slight might be the grounds of the charge, had very small chance of escaping out of their claws.

"The *Malleus* contains no distinct allusion to the proceedings at the Sabbath. The witches of this period differ little from those who had fallen into the hands of the earlier inquisitors at the Council of Constance. We see plainly how, in most countries, the mysteriously indefinite crime of sorcery had first been seized on to ruin the cause of great political offenders, until the fictitious importance thus given to it brought forward into a prominent position, which they would, perhaps, never otherwise have held, the miserable class who were supposed to be more especially engaged in it.

"It was the judicial prosecutions and the sanguinary executions which followed, that stamped the character of reality on charges of which it required two or three centuries to convince mankind of the emptiness and vanity.

"One of the chief instruments in fixing the belief in sorcery, and in giving it that terrible hold on society which it exhibited in the following century, was the compilation of Jacob Sprenger and his fellow inquisitor. In this book sorcery was reduced to a system but it was not yet perfect; and we must look forward, some half a century before we find it clothed with all the horrors which cast so much terror into every class of society."

The work went into some 30 editions between 1486 and 1669 and was accepted as authoritative by both Protestant and Catholic witch-hunters. Its narrow-minded superstition and dogmatic legalism undoubtedly resulted in hundreds of cases of cruel tortures and judicial murders.

An English translation was published in London (1928; 1948; 1974) by the controversial British scholar **Montague Summers,** who embodied in his writings a truly medieval attitude toward witchcraft. He declared (in his learned introduction to the work) that the *Malleus Maleficarum* "is among the most important, wisest, and weightiest books of the world."

Sources:

Robbins, Rossell Hope. *The Encyclopedia of Witchcraft and Demonology.* New York: Crown Publishers, 1959.

Sprenger, Jakob, and Heinrich Kramer. *Malleus Maleficarum.* Edited by Montague Summers. London, 1928.

Malphas

According to demonologist **Johan Weyer,** Malphas was grand president of the infernal regions, where he appeared in the shape of a crow. When he appeared in human form, he had a very raucous voice. He built impregnable citadels and towers, overthrew the ramparts of his enemies, found good workmen, gave familiar spirits, received sacrifices, and deceived the sacrificers. Forty infernal legions were under his command.

Sources:

Weyer, Johannes. *Witches, Devils, and Doctors in the Renaissance: Johann Weyer, De Praestigiis.* Edited by George Mora. Binghamton, N.Y.: Medieval and Renaissance Texts and Studies, 1991.

Mamaloi

An **Obeah** priestess. (See **West Indian Islands**)

Mana

A term indicating vital or magical force used widely throughout Polynesia. From his work in the South Pacific, R. H. Codrington observed:

"The word is common, I believe, to the whole Pacific. . . . It is a power or influence, not physical, and in a way supernatural, but it shows itself in physical force, or in any kind of power or excellence which a man possesses. This *Mana* is not fixed in anything, and can be conveyed in almost anything; but spirits, whether disembodied souls or supernatural beings, have it and can impart it. . . . All Melanesian religion consists in getting this *Mana* for oneself, or getting it used for one's benefit."

The techniques of arousing and acquiring *mana* were extensively explored by **Max Freedom Long** (1890–1971) in his study of the *kahuna* **magic** in Hawaii and described in his books, notably *The Secret Science Behind Miracles* (1948). Long established the **Huna Research Organization** to conduct research and spread knowledge of *mana* and its basis in *kahuna* magic.

The concept of *mana* has been expressed in many cultures under different names. Among the Iroquois and Huron Indians, it is known as *orenda.* In his book *Primitive Man* (vol. 1 of *A History of Experimental Spiritualism,* 2 vols., 1931), Caesar de Vesme wrote:

"We are in a fair way to recognize that we find (approximately) Mana in the *Brahman* and *Akasha* of the Hindus, the *Living Fire* of Zoroaster, the *Generative Fire* of Heraclitus, the *Ruach* of the Jews, the *Telesma* of Hermest Trismegistus, the *Ignis subtilissimus* of Hippocrates, the *Pneuma* of Gallien, the *Soul of the World* of Plato and Giordano Bruno, the *Mens agitat molem* which Vergil drew from the Pythagorean philosophy, the *Astral light* of the Kabbalists, the *Azoth* of the alchemists, the *Magnale* of **Paracelsus,** the *Alcahest* of Van Helmont, the pantheistic *Substance* of Apinoza, the *Subtle Matter* of Descartes, the *Animal magnetism* of **Mesmer,** the *Will* of Schopenhauer, the **Od** of Reichenbach and Du Prel, the *Unconscious* of **Hartmann,** the *Entelechy* of **Driesch,** the *Plastic Mediator* of **Éliphas Lévi,** the *Psychode* and *Ectenic Force* of Thury, the *Force X* and the *Cryptesthesia* of **Richet,** the *Metether* of **F. W. H. Myers,** the *Spiritus* of **Robert Fludd,** the *Spiritus subtilissimus* of Newton, the *Spiritus Vitae* of St. Thomas Aquinas, and many more *Spiritus* besides, if it were permissible to touch upon the different theologies."

Sources:

Codrington, R. H. *The Melanesians: Studies in Their Anthropology and Folk-lore.* Oxford: Clarendon Press, 1891.

Long, Max Freedom. *The Secret Science Behind Miracles.* Vista, Calif.: Huna Research Publications, 1954.

Mananan

Son of the Irish sea-god Lir, magician with strange possessions. His magical boat *Ocean-sweeper,* steered by the wishes of its occupant; his horse Aonban, able to travel on sea or land; and his sword **Fragarach,** a match for any mail, all were brought by **Lugh** from "The Land of the Living" (i.e., fairyland).

As lord of the sea he was the Irish Charon, and his color-changing cloak would flap as he marched around the camp of hostile force invading Ireland. He is comparable with the Cymric Manawiddan and resembles the Hellenic Proteus.

Mandala

A mystical diagram used in **India** and **Tibet** to attract spiritual power or for meditation purposes. The term derives from the Sanskrit word for "circle," although a mandala may embody various geometrical shapes.

The Swiss psychologist **Carl G. Jung,** who regarded the mandala as an archetypal image from the deep unconscious mind, investigated mandalas created spontaneously by psychological patients. (See also **yantra**)

Sources:

Tucci, Giuseppe. *The Theory and Practice of the Mandala.* London: n.p., 1961.

Wilhelm, Richard, and C. G. Jung. *The Secret of the Golden Flower: A Chinese Book of Life.* Rev. ed. New York: Harcourt, Brace, 1962. Reprint, New York: Causeway Books, 1975.

Mandragoras

Familiar demons who appear in the figures of little men without beards. The name is also applied to the plant popularly known as mandrake, whose roots resemble human forms and were believed to be inhabited by demons.

The sixteenth-century **witchcraft** scholar Martin Del Rio stated that one day a *mandragora,* entering a court at the request of a sorcerer who was being tried for wizardry, was caught by a judge (who did not believe in the existence of the spirit), and thrown into the fire, from which it escaped unharmed.

Mandragoras were thought to be little dolls or figures given to sorcerers by the devil for the purpose of consultation and it would seem as if this conception sprung directly from that of the fetish, which is really a dwelling-place made by a **shaman,** or medicine man, to receive any wandering spirit who chooses it.

The anonymous author of the popular magic manual *Secrets merveilleux de la magie et cabalistique de Petit Albert* (1772) stated that once, while traveling in Flanders and passing through the town of Lille, he was invited by one of his friends to accompany him to the house of an old woman who posed as being a great prophetess. This aged person conducted the two friends into a dark cabinet lit only by a single lamp, where they could see upon a table covered with a cloth a kind of little statue, or *mandragoras,* seated upon a tripod, its left hand extended and holding a hank of silk very delicately fashioned, from which was suspended a small piece of highly polished iron.

Placing under this a crystal glass, so that the piece of iron was suspended inside the goblet, the old woman commanded the figure to strike the iron against the glass: "I command you, *Mandragoras,* in the name of those to whom you are bound to give obedience, to know if the gentleman present will be happy in the journey which he is about to make. If so, strike three times with the iron upon the goblet."

The iron struck three times as demanded without the old woman having touched any of the apparatus, much to the surprise of the two spectators. The sorceress put several other questions to the *mandragora,* who struck the glass once or thrice as seemed good to him. But the author claimed that this procedure was an artifice, for the piece of iron suspended in the goblet was extremely light and when the old woman wished it to strike against the glass, she held in one of her hands a ring set with a large piece of magnetic stone, which drew the iron toward the glass. This sounds very much like the folklore practice of putting a ring on a thread and holding it so that it dangles inside a glass and responds to questions put to it (see **pendulums**).

The ancients attributed great virtues to the plant *mandragoras,* or mandrake, the root of which was often uncannily like a human form, and when plucked from the earth was believed to emit a species of human cry. It was also worn to ward off various diseases.

Because of the supposed danger from the resident demon when plucking the plant, an elaborate procedure was prescribed. The mandrake-gatherer was supposed to starve a dog of food for several days, then tie him with a strong cord to the lower part of the plant. The dog was then thrown pieces of meat, and when he leapt forward to seize them, he pulled up the mandrake. Other folklore beliefs included the need for an elaborate prayer ritual before pulling the plant, which should only be gathered at dead of night. (See also **alrunes; exorcism; ginseng**)

Sources:

Thompson, C. J. S. *The Mystic Mandrake.* 1934. Reprint, New Hyde Park, N.Y.: University Books, 1968.

Mandrake

Plant whose roots often bear an uncanny resemblance to a human form. (See **mandragoras**)

Manen

The priest of the **Katean Secret Society** of the Moluccas.

Mangan, Gordon Lavelle (1924–)

University lecturer in psychology who made a special study of **parapsychology.** He was born on December 5, 1924, in Wellington, New Zealand. He studied at the University of New Zealand (M.A., 1945), the University of Melbourne, Australia (Ed.B., 1950), and the University of London, England (Ph.D., 1954).

After working as a high school teacher, he became a fellow of the **Parapsychology Foundation** and a research associate at Duke University (1954–56). After short periods teaching in the department of psychology at Queen's University, Kingston, Ontario, Canada (1956–58) and Victoria University (1958–61) in Canada, he returned to Australia as a senior lecturer in the psychology department at the University of Queensland in 1961.

Mangan published a number of articles on parapsychology and one important monograph, *A Review of the Published Research on the Relationship of Some Personality Variables to ESP Scoring Level* (1958).

Sources:

Mangan, Gordon Lavelle. "An ESP Experiment with Dual-Aspect Targets Involving One Trial Day." *Journal of Parapsychology* (December 1957).

———. "Evidence of Displacement in a Precognitive Test." *Journal of Parapsychology* (March 1955).

———. "How Legitimate Are the Claims for ESP?" *Australian Journal of Psychology* (September 1959).

———. "Parapsychology: A Science for Psychical Research?" *Queen's Quarterly* (spring 1958).

———. "A PK Experiment with Thirty Dice Released for High and Low Face Targets." *Journal of Parapsychology* (December 1954).

———. *A Review of Published Research on the Relationship of Some Personality Variables to ESP Scoring Level.* New York: Parapsychology Foundation, 1958.

Mangan, Gordon Lavelle, and L. C. Wilbur. "The Relation of PK Object and Throwing Surface in Placement Tests." *Journal of Parapsychology* 20 (1956); 21, (1957).

Mankind Research Foundation

A **New Age** organization that aims: "to combine the efforts of leading researchers and experimenters in the multi-disciplinary and interacting fields of human development and humanistic psychology which include research involving the body, mind and those forces and phenomena acting upon the health, education and welfare of mankind. Areas of study include biocommunication, biocybernetics, biophysics, psychophysiology, educational development, cancer research and mind-body developments."

It is located at 1315 Apple Ave., Silver Spring, MD 20910.

Manning, Matthew (1955–)

British psychic, whose phenomena include **poltergeist, apports, automatic writing, telepathy, precognition,** and psychic art. Manning was born August 17, 1955; and at the age of 11, he was the center of a poltergeist disturbance at the family home in Shelford, Cambridge, **England,** which involved repeated knocking and the movement of scores of small articles. After several weeks, the phenomena subsided but returned about a year later, accompanied by childish scribblings on walls and even high ceilings. Chairs and tables were disturbed and dozens of objects moved around.

According to the account in Manning's several books, the phenomena followed him to boarding school, where heavy beds were moved, and knives, nails, electric light bulbs, and other objects were sent flying through the air. Showers of pebbles and pools of water manifested, and strange lights appeared on walls. One day, while writing an essay in his study, Manning found himself involved in automatic writing, at which time the poltergeist phenomena ceased. Since then he has regularly received hundreds of communications apparently from deceased individuals, some in languages unknown to him, including Italian, German, Greek, Latin, Russian, and Arabic.

Following upon the automatic writing, he produced psychic art in the manner of Thomas Bewick, Thomas Rowlandson, Aubrey Beardsley, Paul Keel, Henri Matisse, Picasso, and other great names with remarkable fidelity to the artists' styles. He also discovered an ability to bend spoons in a manner similar to that manifested by **Uri Geller** and to record startling demonstrations of some unknown force in himself by means of **kirlian aura** photography. Matthew duplicated the Geller effect of starting inactive clocks and watches, as well as radios, tape recorders, music boxes, and even electric lights. He had a premonition of the June 1975 plane crash near Kennedy Airport that killed 121 people, as well as the 1975 subway train disaster at Moorgate Station, England, in which 43 people died.

While touring Japan, he appeared on television, and 1,200 callers jammed the studio switchboard with reports of bottles, glasses, and other objects exploding in their homes. Faucets turned on automatically, burglar alarms went off, and auto engines switched themselves on. Lost articles reappeared, small objects materialized in homes, other objects disappeared, and watches and clocks went haywire. Manning has also predicted that his own death will occur at an early date.

On August 7, 1977, he took part in an **ESP** test organized by the British newspaper *Sunday Mirror.* Manning was stationed in London's Post Office Tower (580 ft. high). Between 6 and 6:15 P.M. he mentally transmitted three images: the color green, the number 123, and the shape of a house. Readers of the *Sunday Mirror* were asked to "tune in" to these images and send their results on a postcard. Of the 2,500 readers who responded, 575 scored the right color, 1 in 44 got the three-figure number right, and about 1 in 30 identified a house-like shape. There were some 30 interesting "near-misses" in which readers reported the color green, the figure 123, and a shape of a triangle on top of a square, or the color green, the number 132, and a house. Michael Haslam, deputy honorary secretary of the Institute of Statisticians in London, confirmed that the results were significantly higher than chance expectation.

Manning was also the subject of a Canadian documentary movie, *A Study of a Psychic,* made by the Bruce A. Raymond Company between 1974 and 1977. President Bruce A. Raymond was formerly controller of programs at the Canadian Broadcasting Corporation and one of its chief executives. An objective record of Manning's career, the movie includes interviews with members of his family, his headmaster, and school friends. Extracts were shown on British television on the Brian Inglis *Nationwide* program produced by Granada TV.

In December 1977 Manning announced that henceforth he preferred to be described as a "mentalist" instead of a "psychic." This statement came after three years of worldwide publicity as the Western world's most gifted psychic, on the same day that Manning appeared on the Russell Harty Independent Television talk show in London. The show included filmed accounts from three first-hand witnesses of the poltergeist phenomena that surrounded Manning as a schoolboy. During the program he demonstrated automatic drawing and attempted telepathy tests. He also stated:

"I believe also that a lot of people who are doing debunking in the name of science are merely forming a religion of their own, which I call humanism. . . . They believe there is no more to life than everything they can perceive physically, there is nothing beyond the five senses and that when one dies that is the end. They turn that into a religion. Obviously, what I am doing is to them threatening. That is why they will attack me."

During his 1977 American tour, Manning was vigorously criticized by magician **James Randi,** a well-known and hostile opponent of paranormal phenomena. Randi is a member of the **Committee for the Scientific Investigation of Claims of the Paranormal** and the author of *The Magic of Uri Geller* (1975), in which he accused Geller of "massive fraud."

In September 1977 Randi attacked the British *Sunday Mirror* ESP test in the Post Office Tower, suggesting that Manning could have sent in "an important fraction of the postcards" himself. Manning countered, "The man who talks of 'falsehoods' makes statements himself which can be seen to be totally false by anyone who reads my book." A report on this controversy was carried in the British newspaper *Psychic News* (September 10, 1977).

Manning's preference for the label "mentalist" over "psychic" may be a response to aggressive campaigns such as Randi's. Manning delivered a statement to **Peter Bander,** his former publisher and agent, which became a front-page story in Britain's *Cambridge Evening News* (December 3, 1977) and was also reported in *Psychic News* (December 10, 1977). Manning wrote:

"Dear Peter,—Without any disrespect to anything which may have been said or done in the past, I would prefer from now on to be known as a mentalist and not as a psychic, a description I have always resented and never liked.

"As I have no intention of giving interviews during my short stay in England, I would like you to be the first person to know. Perhaps you might also be so good as to pass this on to any pressman or future inquirers.

"Certain events in America, for example, have made me reconsider my position. I feel this is probably the best description to explain them.

"I reiterate that I do not wish to withdraw anything I have said or done in the past, and that I wish to be judged by what I'm doing now rather than by what I have been doing in the last four years.

"I have no intention of explaining this any further at present."

In his first book, *The Link* (1974), which went into 19 editions and was translated into many languages, Manning accepts the description "teenage psychic" and describes the first occasion that he "entered into direct communication with spirit entities." It may be that like other sensitive individuals in the history of psychic science and **parapsychology,** he felt that a hostile debunking attitude was going beyond criticism and speculation into the realms of psychic persecution.

In recent years Manning has specialized in forms of psychic **healing, healing by touch,** and sympathetic contact between individuals by guided imagery and mental disciplines. He also founded the Matthew Manning Centre at 34 Abbeygate Street, Bury St. Edmonds, Suffolk IP33 ILW, England. He has lectured widely on healing and has issued audiotapes on the subject.

Sources:

Berger, Arthur S., and Joyce Berger. *The Encyclopedia of Parapsychology and Psychical Research.* New York: Paragon House, 1991.

Gregory, Anita. "London Experiments with Matthew Manning." *Proceedings* of the Society for Psychical Research 58 (1982).

Manning, Matthew. *In the Mind of Millions.* London: W. H. Allen, 1977.

———. *The Link.* London: Colin Smythe; New York: Holt Rinehart, 1974.

———. *The Strangers.* London: W. H. Allen, 1978.

Mansfield, J. V. (ca. 1870)

Nineteenth-century American medium who advertised as the "spirit postmaster" in the *Banner of Light.* He obtained thousands of letters in sealed envelopes addressed to spirit-friends, read them clairvoyantly, and wrote out replies automatically in various languages. German, Spanish, Greek, Arabic, Sanskrit, and even Chinese answers were sometimes given.

Many witnesses testified to his powers. His scripts were preserved in evidence. His mediumship is described in N. B. Wolfe's *Startling Facts in Modern Spiritualism* (1875).

However, in the report of the **Seybert Commission,** Dr. H. H. Furness, the acting chairman, discredited Mansfield's powers on the basis of a clairvoyant sitting and a sealed letter test. For a detailed account of Mansfield's handling of an ingeniously sealed letter, see the *Spiritual Magazine* (1868, p. 425).

Sources:

Wolfe, N. B. *Startling Facts in Modern Spiritualism.* Chicago: Religio-Philosophical Publishing House, 1875.

Manson, Charles M. (1934–)

Habitual criminal who was born on November 12, 1934, and achieved notoriety as charismatic leader of the infamous "Family" that indulged in sex orgies and brutal murders. Manson demonstrated that drugs, sex, **occultism,** and crime can be an incredibly dangerous mixture.

As a young man, he was frequently arrested on such charges as car theft, parole violation, and stealing checks and credit cards. He spent most of the 1960s in jail, where he learned to play the guitar and studied hypnotism and various **occult** and metaphysical teachings. He was an avid reader on contemporary culture, including the Vietnam War, peace rallies, rock and roll, and the music of the Beatles. He was greatly impressed by Robert Heinlein's science-fiction story *Stranger in a Strange Land,* which related how an alien intelligence formed a power base of sex and religion on the Earth.

In 1967 Manson was released from jail and wandered around Berkeley, California, as a guitar-toting minstrel, picking up girls and spending time in the Haight-Ashbury section, experiencing the drug scene, occult boom, and communal living. Eventually he collected a kind of tribal family, mostly young adults, and established a hippie-style commune at various locales in the California desert, ranging over Death Valley in stolen dune buggies in an atmosphere of drugs and sex.

In time, Manson developed paranoid fantasies of a forthcoming doomsday situation, supposedly revealed to him by songs on a Beatles album, particularly "Helter-Skelter" and "Piggies." Manson and his followers shared a delusion that "Helter-Skelter" symbolized an uprising of blacks that could be exploited by the Family.

In 1969, under Manson's influence, some members of his Family accepted him as a savior figure and followed his orders to commit a number of sadistic murders. Manson, Patricia Krenwinkle, Susan Atkins, and Leslie Van Houten were found guilty of murdering actress Sharon Tate and four other people at her Bel-Air home in Los Angeles—Voyteck Frykowski, Abigail Folger, Jay Sebring, and Steven Parent, as well as Leno La Bianca and his wife Rosemary, also in Los Angeles. Nine weeks after the verdict, the jury voted death sentences for all the accused. The trial, which opened July 21, 1970, took 32 weeks. During 1976, a movie reconstructing the trial, titled *Helter-Skelter,* was shown on television in the United States.

On February 18, 1972, the California State Supreme Court abolished the death penalty in California, converting the sentences of condemned persons to life imprisonment. Manson and his accomplices now regularly appear at parole hearings, but the state has shown no hint of favor toward his requests for parole.

Manson has become an antihero who still commands attention in the media and in countercultural elements in North American society. Books continue to retell his story, especially amid the wave of true crime books that became popular in the late 1980s.

The violence associated with Manson did not cease with his imprisonment. In September 1984 in Vacaville prison, California, Manson was drenched with paint thinner and set on fire by another convicted killer, who claimed that Manson had threatened him for being a member of a Hare Krishna sect. His head scorched and most of his hair and beard were burned, but Manson survived. A group of Manson's songs, performed by him and recorded prior to the Tate–La Bianca murders, has been issued by Awareness Records (LP disc 0893-0156). The mediocre quality of these songs only enhances their sinister provenance.

Sources:

Atkins, Susan, with Bob Slosser. *Child of Satan, Child of God.* Plainfield, N.J.: Logos International, 1977. Reprint, London: Hodder & Stoughton, 1978.

Bugliosi, Vincent, with Curt Gentry. *Helter Skelter.* New York: W. W. Norton, 1972. Reprint, New York: Bantam, 1975.

Emmons, Nuel. *Manson in His Own Words.* New York: Grove Press, 1986.

George, Edward. *Charles Manson's Life Behind Bars.* Griffin Trade Paperback, 1999.

Livsey, Clara. *The Manson Women: A Family Portrait.* New York: Richard Merek Publishers, 1980.

Sanders, Ed. *The Family.* New York: E. P. Dutton, 1971. Reprint, New York: Avon, 1972.

Mantra (or Mantram)

In Hindu **mysticism,** a mantra is a form of psychoactive speech having a direct effect on the physical body and a claimed effect on the emotions, the mind, and even on physical processes in nature. The term is derived from the root *man* (to think), and *tra* from *trai,* (to protect or to free from bondage). Thus, a mantra is an instrument of thought.

According to Hindu tradition, the material universe is said to be formed from divine **vibration,** a concept echoed in the Judeo-Christian concepts of divine utterance preceding creation—"And God said, let there be light" (Gen. 1:3) and "In the beginning was the Word, and the Word was with God, and the Word was God" (John 1:1). The use of mantras can also be found in Buddhist tantrism, known as *Vairayana.*

The verses of the Hindu sacred scriptures, the Vedas (*veda* means knowledge), are regarded as mantras, because they have been transmitted from a divine source, rather like the Christian concept of the Bible as having power as the Word of God. Hindus, however, also believe that words and phrases have special powers as expressions of the hidden forces of nature. The vibrations of molecules which create the particular sounds of the mantras are thought to resonate with *Shabda* or *Vach* (primal essence of creation.)

Divine creation becomes manifest in form throughout nature, and the latent reality behind form may be affected by correctly uttering the sounds that represent the ideal reality. These mantras were discovered by ancient sages skilled in the knowledge of the Mantra Shastra scripture and taught to initiates.

The universe is called *Jagat* (that which moves), because everything exists by a combination of forces and movement, and every movement generates vibration and has its own sound. These subtle sounds have correspondences in the baser sounds of speech and music, and so everything in the universe has an exact relationship. Everything has its natural name, the sound produced by the action of the moving forces from which it is constructed. Thus, anyone who is able to utter the natural name of anything with creative force can bring into being the thing which has that name.

The most well-known mantra is the trisyllable A-U-M, which precedes and concludes reading from the Vedas and is chanted as an individual mantra or magical prayer. Hindu tradition says it is the origin of all sound, and initially came to those sages who reached the highest state of spiritual development. The three syllables are associated with the processes of creation, preservation, and dissolution and with the three states of consciousness (dreaming, deep sleep, and waking).

The scripture Mandukya Upanishad describes how **AUM,** or "OM," is the basis of all the other letters in the Sanskrit language and is associated with the universe and the human **microcosm** (analgous concepts exist in such kabalistic works as the Sepher Yesirah). A mantra may also be associated with a *yantra,* or mystical diagram.

Mantras are frequently uttered in rhythmic repetition known as *japa,* often with the aid of a *mala,* a set of beads resembling the Catholic rosary. In japa **yoga,** the power of a mantra is enhanced by the accumulation of repetitions. Although mantras have an automatic action, that action is enhanced by proper concentration and attitude of mind. The spoken mantra is also an aid to the mental mantra, which contains the inner meaning and power.

Special mantras called *bija* (seed) mantras are linked with the basic states of matter in connection with the **chakras,** or subtle energy centers, of the human body. These seeds are said to hold the potential to release the powers of the chakras.

Most yogic traditions use some form of mantra initiation, which transmits a particular mantra from guru to student. Spiritual mantras common in India include variants of the "Hari Rama, Hari Krishna" formula, made popular in the West by members of the **International Society for Krishna Consciousness,** and the **Gayatri Mantra,** normally recited by Brahmins during meditation on the sun. Transcendental meditators also reportedly use mantras in their practices. *"Hari Om"* is a common healing mantra performed regularly by the Sivananda Ashram in Rishikesh, India, which invokes Vishnu (Hindu God) to take away illnesses and offenses. *Shiva Hara Shankara,* as chanted by Indira Devi's Ashram in Poona, India, asks the Lord Shiva to free us from the bondage of life. The Shiva Mantra implores "Homage, homage, all homage and glory to you, O Lord Shiva." Similarly, the Lakshmi Mantra calls upon the Goddess Lakshmi, "We pray to you in benign solemnity to bestow your blessings and shower your wealth upon us."

The development of compact discs and digital recordings has made mantra recordings more available in music stores and New Age shops. As this technology has fueled western acceptance of yoga, mantras will gain popularity and perhaps take on a new meaning as more and more westerners practice them.

Sources:

Das, Krishna. *Pilgrim Heart.* New York: Triloka Records, 1998

Easwaran, Eknath. *The Mantram Handbook.* London: Routledge & Kegan Paul, 1978.

Godwin, Joscelyn. *Music and the Occult.* Rochester, N.Y.: University of Rochester Press, 1995.

Gopalacharlu, S. E. *An Introduction to the Mantra Sastra.* Adyar, Madras, India: Theosophical Publishing House, 1934.

Kalisch, Isidor, trans. *Sepher Yezirah: A Book on Creation.* New York, 1877.

Lakshmi Montra. "Mantra on Net." http//:www.mantraonnet.com/. February 26, 2000.

Narayana, Har, trans. *The Vedic Philosophy; or, An Exposition of the Sacred and Mysterious Monosyllable AUM; The Mandukya Upanishad.* Bombay, 1895.

Radha, Swami Sivananda. *Mantras: Words of Power.* Spokane, Wash.: Timeless Books, 1994.

Shiva Montra from Mantra on Net. http//:www.mantraonnet.com. February 26, 2000.

Woodroffe, Sir John. *The Garland of Letters (Varnamala): Studies in the Mantra-Shastra.* Madras, India: Ganesh, 1951.

Manu

According to **Theosophy,** a grade in the theosophical hierarchy below the Planetary Logoi, or Rulers of the Seven Chains. The charge given to *Manus* is that of forming the different races of humanity and guiding humanity's evolution. Each race has its own *Manu,* who represents the racial type. This theosophical concept derives from Hindu mythology of *Manu* (man; thinker), a series of fourteen progenitors of the human race, each creation being destroyed in a Mahayuga (vast cycle of time) involving a deluge.

The *Manu* of the present creation is *Manu Vaivasvata,* who built an ark during a cosmic deluge and afterward renewed the human race. He is the reputed author of the *Manava Dharma Shastra,* or *Laws of Manu,* an ancient Hindu treatise that prescribes human religious and social duties.

Sources:

Das, Ghagavan. *The Science of Social Organisation; or, The Laws of Manu in the Light of Atma-Vidya.* 2 vols. Rev. ed. Adyar, Madras, India: Theosophical Publishing House, 1932.

Mapes, James Jay (1806–1866)

Professor of agricultural chemistry, member of various learned societies, and one of the early American converts to **Spiritualism.** Mapes was born on May 29, 1806, in New York City. After leaving school he worked as a chemist's clerk before entering business for himself. He invented a system of sugar refining in 1831, a machine for manufacturing sugar from cane, and a process for making sugar from West Indian molasses. He also invented a method of tanning hides, as well as improvements in distilling, dyeing, color making, and other industrial innovations. For his contributions, he received an honorary A.M. degree from Williams University in 1840. He was also a colonel in the New York state militia.

His conversion to Spiritualism was the result of an investigation he initiated in order to save his friends from "running to imbecility." **Cora L. V. Richmond** produced for him phenomena he could not explain. Then his wife, a woman of advanced age with no talent for art, developed an **automatic drawing and painting** mediumship. She executed in a marvelously rapid manner several thousand watercolor drawings, which met with praise. His daughter became a writing **medium.**

One of the early messages that came through his daughter purported to emanate from Mapes's father. It asked Mapes to look up an encyclopedia, stored in a packing case 27 years before, and there on page 120 he would find his father's name written. This was found true. With increasing interest Mapes investigated Katie Fox (of the **Fox sisters**) and the **Davenport brothers,** with whom he heard the first **direct voice** phenomena, and the manifestations of **"John King."** He followed every new psychic discovery with keen interest. He died January, 10, 1866.

Maple, Eric (William) (1915–)

British author on **witchcraft, demonology,** the **supernatural,** and folklore. In addition to his books on such subjects, he also lectured widely and in the late 1960s was a consultant on the publication *Man, Myth, and Magic* (1967–70). He gave special attention to the role of the so-called "white witch" in the history of witchcraft persecutions and also showed the interrelationship of witchcraft with ghost lore, **Spiritism,** and the cult of the dead. Maple wrote "Magic is a common bond uniting all races and creeds and therefore, possibly, the most democratic principle in the world."

Sources:

Maple, Eric. *The Dark World of Witches.* London: R. Hale, 1962.

———. *Deadly Magic.* Wellingborough, England: Thursons, 1976.

———. *The Domain of Devils.* London: R. Hale, 1966.

———. *Incantations and Words of Power.* Wellingborough, England: Aquarian Press, 1974.

———. *Magic, Medicine, and Quakery.* London: R. Hale, 1968.
———. *The Realm of Ghosts.* New York: A.S. Barnes, 1964.
———. *Superstition and the Superstitious.* London and New York: W.H. Allen, 1971.
———. *Witchcraft: The Story of Man's Quest for Psychic Power.* London: Octopus Books, 1973.

Marabini, Enrico (1923–)

Italian gynecologist and obstetrician who was also active in the field of **parapsychology.** Marabini was born on November 12, 1923, at Casinalbo, Italy, and studied at Bologna University (M.D., cum laude, 1949). He was a member of the Bologna Center of Parapsychological Studies, and in 1948 he became one of the founders of the **Centro Studi Parapsicologici** (Center for Parapsychological Studies).

Marabini took special interest in **clairvoyance, telepathy, psychokinesis,** and mediumship. He worked with mental and physical **mediums** for several years in controlled experiments concerned with psychosomatic aspects of paranormal behavior. However, he was unable to validate the authenticity of physical mediumship. He afterward studied quantitative testing methods.

Sources:

Marabini, Enrico. "Il Comportamento paranormale in rapporto a stati neuro-endocrini" (Paranormal Behavior in Connection with Neuro-Endocrinological Conditions). *Parapsicologia di Minerva Medica* (November 1957).
———. "Esperienze di Telepatia collectiva eseguite nella Citta' di Bologna" (Experiments in Mass Telepathy in Bologna). *Metapsichica* 1 (1954).
———. "Esperienze triennel di lettura della mano con una sensitiva Bolognese: Maria Guardini" (Three Years of Experiments in Hand-reading with the Sensitive Maria Guardini of Bologna). *Parapsicologia di Minerva Medica* (June 1957).
———. "Il Metodo scientifico in parapsicologia" (Scientific Method in Parapsychology). *Bulletin of the Italian Society for Parapsychology* (July–December 1957).
———. "Problemi parapsicologici e psicosomatica" (Parapsychological Problems and Psychosomatics). *Medicina psicosomatics* 1, no. 2 (1957).
———. "Proposta di una modifica al test di Stuart per la Chiaroveggenza" (Proposal of a Modification of the Stuart Test for Clairvoyance). *Metapsichica* 3 (1954).
———. "La Psi e' stata dimonstrata sperimentalmente?" (Has Psi Been Experimentally Demonstrated?). *Bulletin of the Italian Society for Parapsychology* (July–December 1959).
———. "Sogno paragnosico" (Paragnostic Dreams). *Parapsicologia di Minerva Medica* (June 1957).
———. "La Telapatia" (Telepathy). *Metapsichica* 1–4 (1953).
———. "Una Nuova ESP?" *Bulletin of the Italian Society for Parapsychology* (January–June 1959).

Maranos

A term that generally referred to the "secret" Jews of Portugal and Spain in the fifteenth century, who converted to Christianity when their religion was outlawed, but who continued to practice their religion in the privacy of their families. The existence of such Jews was amply demonstrated by Jews who migrated and soon afterward reemerged to practice publicly the Jewish faith. The term was also applied to a Jewish secret fraternity that arose in Spain in the fourteenth and fifteenth centuries. Its members met in the greatest secrecy at inns, and used grips, signs, and passwords (see *Freemasons' Magazine* 3 [1860]: 416).

The term "marranos" (hogs) was used contemptuously at the time to denote Moors and Jews.

Marcellus Empiricus (ca. 395 C.E.)

A Gallic-Roman writer born at Bordeaux in the fourth century. He was *magister officiorum* under Theodosius (379–395 C.E.). He wrote a work called *De medicamentis conspiricis physicis ac rationalibus,* a collection of medical recipes, for the most part having more in common with popular superstition than with medical science.

March, Marion (1923–)

Marion March, an outstanding American **astrology** teacher, was born on February 10, 1923, in Nürnberg, Germany, though she was raised in Switzerland, the daughter of a banker. She moved to the United States during World War II (1939–45) to pursue an acting career, but after six years joined the American Foreign Service. Stationed in her homeland, she met her husband, a graduate student and future executive with Merrill Lynch. They settled in Los Angeles, California, and she became the mother of two children.

March did not begin the study of **astrology** until 1965 and did not become a professional until 1970. However, she was quickly recognized as an accomplished astrologer and a talented instructor. She developed a large clientele, and as she could speak five languages, she was called upon to lecture across North America and Europe. She was asked to join the faculty of the **American Federation of Astrologers,** the International Society for Astrological Research, and the Southwest Astrology Council. She has been active in both the European International Congress and United Astrology Congress. She was one of the founders of the **Association for Astrological Networking.**

In 1975, March joined forces with Joan McEvers to found Aquarius Workshops, the vehicle for their teaching activity. Their magazine, *Aspects,* soon became one of the most popular in the field, and their multivolume textbook series, *The Only Way to. . .Learn Astrology,* one of the most used textbooks for teaching astrology to newcomers to the field. In addition, she has written numerous articles for the many journals serving astrologers.

March has received a variety of honors for her contributions to the field, including the highly prized Regulus Award in 1972 for service to the astrological community. She received the award again in 1989 (along with McEvers) for her educational activities.

Sources:

March, Marion, and Joan McEvers. *The Only Way to. . . Learn about Horary and Electional Astrology.* San Diego: Astro Computing Services, 1995.
———. *The Only Way to. . . Learn about Relationships.* San Diego: Astro Computing Services, 1992.
———. *The Only Way to. . . Learn about Tomorrow.* San Diego: Astro Computing Services, 1988.
———. *The Only Way to. . . Learn Astrology.* 3 vols. San Diego: Astro Computing Services, 1976–82.

Marciniak, Barbara (fl. ca. 1988)

Barbara Marciniak is a contemporary trance channel best known for her reception of material from entities said to originate in the **Pleiades** star cluster. She was raised in a Polish-American family and in the 1970s became a student of the Seth Material channeled by Jane Roberts. Marciniak emerged out of obscurity on May 18, 1988, when what is described as a collective from the Pleiades began to speak through her. She was on a trip with a New Age group at the time, visiting ancient sites in Egypt and Greece. She felt she was led to reexperience these sites as part of her present life and was in Greece when the channeling emerged.

The Pleiades had been suggested as a source for extraterrestrial contact in the 1980s by **Eduard Albert "Billy" Meier,** a

Swiss flying saucer **contactee.** Two picture books, several volumes recounting his contact claims, and some videos purporting to show saucers from the Pleiades freely circulated through the North American New Age community beginning in 1979. Marciniak's contact with the Pleiadians was among the first contacts independent of references directly to Meier's work. The first significant publication of post-Meier Pleiadian channeled material had been produced by **Barbara Hand Clow,** and it was to the publishing concern at which Clow was employed that Marciniak turned to publish her first book, *Bringers of the Dawn: Teachings from the Pleiadians.* Released in 1992, it became one of the most important volumes of the post-New Age era. Two subsequent books with the same publisher have followed.

Through Marciniak, the Pleiadians suggested that they had come to the Pleiades from another universe that had "attained completion." Earthlings are working on reaching completion, and the Pleiadians are here to assist that process. Their presence heralds the transition from the third dimension to higher dimensions. Also, according to the Pleiadians, humanity was planned as an experiment of the Prime Creator, who sent out extensions of itself into the unknown with the command to create. These extensions, creator gods, began to create new hierarchies, further extensions. Eventually a plan evolved to create Earth. Geneticists took DNA from many species to produce the human race. From these primal observations, the Pleiadians have offered an alternative view of the meaning and purpose of human life.

An organization, Bold Connections (P.O. Box 6521, Raleigh, NC 27628), has been created to distribute Marciniak's tapes and books and to coordinate her teaching activity. She does not have a webpage, but information about the continuing messages from the Pleiadians can be found at http://www.spiritweb.org/Spirit/pleiadians-book.html.

Sources:

Marciniak, Barbara. *Bringers of the Dawn: Teachings from the Pleiadians.* Santa Fe, N.Mex.: Bear & Co., 1992.

———. *Earth: Pleiadian Keys to the Living Library.* Santa Fe, N.Mex.: Bear & Co., 1994.

———. *Family of Light: Pleiadian Tales and Lessons in Living.* Santa Fe, N.Mex.: Bear & Co., 1998.

Margaritomancy

Divination by means of pearls. A pearl was covered with a vase and placed near a fire, and the names of suspected persons were pronounced. When the name of the guilty one was uttered, the pearl was supposed to bound up and pierce the bottom of the vase.

"Margery"

Pseudonym of famous medium **Mina Stinson Crandon** (1888–1941).

Margiotta, Domenico (ca. 1896)

Presumed author of *Souvenirs d'un trente-troisième: Adriano Lemmi, chef suprème des francs-maçons* (1896) and *Le Palladisme: Culte de Satan-Lucifer dans les triangles maçonniques* (1895), which violently impeached the masonic Grand Master Lemmi of the crimes of **devil worship** and **sorcery.** These statements were amply proved to be without foundation. It transpired that these books were part of the **Diana Vaughan** conspiracy of **Gabriel Jogand-Pagés** ("Leo Taxil"), designed to embarrass the Roman Catholic Church and **Freemasonry.**

Sources:

Stein, Gordon. *Encyclopedia of Hoaxes.* Detroit: Gale Research, 1993.

Mariapovch

Povch was a village in northeastern Hungary and the place of origin of one of the more notable weeping icons of the Virgin Mary revered among Eastern Rite Roman Catholic Christians. The icon was prepared by Stefan Papp, the brother of the pastor of the local parish church. Originally, the icon was intended for display in the local parish church. The picture of the Virgin was shown holding the infant Jesus, who in turn held a three-petaled lotus in His hand.

The icon was seen to weep for the first time on November 14, 1696. It again was seen to weep on December 8, and on this second occasion the tears continued to flow for eleven days. The event had such impact that the town became known as Mariapovch. Word of the weeping icon reached the royal court of the Austro-Hungarian Empire in Vienna. The emperor ordered the icon to be brought to Vienna. By the time that the emperor's representatives arrived to pick up the icon for transport back to Vienna, it had become famous and large crowds gathered at every village on the way back to the capital, and they arrived only after many days' delay. On December 1, 1698, the icon was finally placed in St. Steven's Basilica.

The emperor was so impressed by the devotion shown the icon that he hired another artist to make a duplicate of the original icon, which was then given to the village of Mariapovch. It was carried there in a formal procession. On August 1–3, 1715, this second icon also began to weep, and as a result the parish church became a place of pilgrimage. It again shed tears two centuries later, in December 1905.

The original icon remained in the basilica until World War II (1939–45). As the fighting started, it was hidden away until after the war, when it was returned to a new prominent place in the basilica near its entrance. Carpatho-Rusyn immigrants to the United States have continued the veneration that had developed around the icon, and several churches have constructed shrines to house copies of it.

Eastern Roman Catholics are similar to Eastern Orthodox churches and have icons instead of statues. Weeping icons serve the same function in those churches that **weeping statues** serve in Western or Latin Rite churches.

Sources:

Weeping Icon of Mariapovch. http://www.carpatho-rusyn.org/. April 14, 2000.

Marie of Agreda (or Maria de Jesus) (1602–1665)

A Spanish nun, Maria Fernandez Coronel, who founded and was abbess of the Franciscan Recollects at Agreda. She published a work entitled *La mystica ciudad de Dios* (The Mystic City of God, a Miracle of the All-powerful, the Abyss of Grace: Divine History of the Life of the Most Holy Virgin Mary, Mother of God, our Queen and Mistress, manifested in these last times by the Holy Virgin to the Sister Marie of Jesus, Abbess of the Convent of the Immaculate Conception of the town of Agreda, and written by that same Sister by order of her Superiors and Confessors). This work, which was condemned by the Sorbonne, described many strange and miraculous happenings said to have befallen the Virgin Mary from her birth on, including a visit to Heaven in her early years, when she was given a guard of 900 angels. These revelations appear to have come out of her own spiritual raptures, but were full of inaccuracies. She was said to have lived a pious life in spite of the condemnation of her writings.

Marion, Frederick (1892– ?)

Stage name of Josef Kraus, famous European performer of stage **telepathy** and **clairvoyance** during the 1930s, who also claimed paranormal powers. Born in Prague, Czechoslovakia, October 15, 1892, he was the son of a businessman and grew up in a practical atmosphere. When he manifested psychometric and clairvoyant talents, his family was annoyed rather than impressed, and prescribed castor oil for an oversensitivity. At school, however, the boy became adept at games of locating hidden objects and sometimes enlarged this talent by giving detailed descriptions and information relating to the owners of the objects. Towards the end of his school days, he found it expedient to present his psychic abilities in the form of so-called "tricks" at school concerts and other entertainments. He passed his final examination in mathematics, not because he understood the principles involved, but because he had the unusual talent of being able to memorize the test volume of problems and formulae from beginning to end.

After enrolling for university studies, he saw a newspaper report about a Viennese performer named Rubini who claimed special powers of finding concealed objects. Stimulated by his student friends, Marion issued a challenge that he could rival Rubini's feats. The story was taken up by a local newspaper, and a committee was appointed from among the Prague police and personalities of the city. Marion undertook to find, in a stipulated time, several objects hidden by the committee in different parts of Prague and described in a sealed envelope deposited at police headquarters. Marion later stated that his spectacular success was due to the fact that he established telepathic communication with the chairman of the committee, and indeed, there seems no other way in which he could have obtained access to the sealed information.

He became an overnight celebrity, and at the age of 19 was invited to perform at music halls throughout Europe. He was billed as "The Telepathic Phenomenon" or "The Man with Six Senses." In 1913 he appeared in Moscow on the same bill as Fred Karno's "Mumming Birds," a show that included Stan Laurel and a little clown who later became world famous as Charlie Chaplin. In England Marion was sometimes billed as "The Human Bloodhound," since he helped the police in various European countries to unravel crimes through his telepathic powers.

During World War I, Marion served in the Austrian Army, and while stationed in Albania, he tried his hand at water **dowsing.** He rapidly became so well known for his successes that the military authorities commissioned him as an officer and sent him to different areas to find water for the troops. He found traveling around the country somewhat arduous and experimented with what has since become known as "teleradiesthesia," holding his divining twig over a large-scale map instead of visiting the area (see **radiesthesia**). He was remarkably successful, and this gave him more time to spare, which he spent in giving shows to entertain the troops. After a bullet wound and a bout of malaria, he was sent back to base at Innsbruck in the Tyrol.

After the war, he returned to his music hall demonstrations, and in 1920 met the remarkable stage clairvoyant **Erik Jan Hanussen,** who combined extraordinary talents with blatant trickery. Marion warned Hanussen that his growing preoccupation with **black magic** would have disastrous consequences, but the warning was not heeded. According to Marion, it was Hanussen who instructed the inner circle of the young Nazi Party in the power of signs and words and first proposed the **swastika** as the party symbol. Hanussen was murdered by Nazi thugs in 1933, for disclosures that were embarrassing to the party.

In his later years Marion appeared less frequently at music halls and confined his talents chiefly to lecture demonstrations and private consultations. In 1934 he visited England and gave impressive demonstrations of his psychic talents. During a lecture at the Aeolian Hall, New Bond Street, London, he was challenged by Lady Oxford, who stated that his reconstructions of past incidents in the lives of members of his audience were too precise to be genuine and must have involved confederates. Thereupon Marion correctly reconstructed an incident in the life of Lady Oxford's husband, Lord Asquith, in August 1914, which no other person could have possibly known. Lady Oxford was tremendously impressed and made a public apology, acknowledging that Marion's talent was genuine.

In 1934 Marion submitted to a long series of scientific experiments directed by **S. G. Soal** at the **National Laboratory of Psychical Research,** London. Soal was skeptical of Marion's **ESP** but concluded that Marion had unusual **hyperaesthesia,** or unusual acuity of the senses. Soal stated: "My laboratory experiments show that Marion performs his amazing feats by the aid of remarkable powers which are probably possessed by not one man in a million. There can be no question of either collusion or trickery in his public performances, judging from what I have seen him do single-handed in the laboratory. . . ."

However, this hardly did justice to Marion's amazing feats outside the laboratory, including **precognition,** clairvoyance, and telepathy.

Marion was also tested by noted psychic researcher **Harry Price,** chiefly in locating hidden objects. Price, like Soal, concluded that Marion somehow gathered imperceptible indications from the other individuals present who had seen the objects hidden. But he could not say how minute indications were possible, since Marion had no physical contact with the audience (as in the famous **"muscle reading"** technique by which some stage performers make contact with a spectator and can interpret imperceptible movements of their muscles towards or away from objects). Price even attempted to limit Marion's view to only one member of the audience, the others being screened by curtains. Then the single agent's body was further screened off progressively by a box with adjustable panels, so that at times only a fifth of his body was visible to Marion, and eventually only his feet. Even under such extraordinary conditions, Marion had a high rate of success.

After two years of laboratory experiments, **R. H. Thouless** and Dr. B. P. Wiesner stated: "We can say definitely that we are satisfied that Marion shows paranormal capacities of an unusually high order under strictly controlled experimental conditions."

During World War II, Marion joined ENSA (the British troop entertainment service) and traveled around army camps, demonstrating his ESP talents at troop concerts. On May 23, 1946, he took part in a BBC radio program investigating his psychic abilities, one of the first British radio presentations of a subject that was not deemed respectable.

Sources:

Marion, Frederick. *In My Mind's Eye.* London: Rider, 1949.

Preliminary Studies of a Vaudeville Telepathist. Bulletin III. London: London Council for Psychical Investigation, 1937.

Price, Harry. *Confessions of a Ghost Hunter.* 1936. Reprint, Causeway Books, 1974.

Mark Probert Memorial Foundation

Former foundation that preserved tape recordings of sessions with Mark Probert, a **trance medium** of the 1950s.

Marriott, William S. (ca. 1910)

British professional magician and illusionist who investigated and exposed fake mediumship. His stage name was "Dr. Wilmar." One of his noted illusions was the production of apparently paranormal paintings, duplicating the claimed psychic phenomena of the Chicago **mediums,** the **Bangs sisters.** The illusion was presented as "Dr. Wilmar's Spirit Painting" and so impressed fellow magician P. T. Selbit that he agreed to pay Marriott a weekly royalty for the use of the illusion. However, Marriott himself was not entirely straightforward in claiming rights on the illusion, since he had obtained the secret from David P. Abbott, an amateur magician. When Selbit presented the illusion at the Orpheum Theatre in Omaha in 1911, Abbott saw the show and visited Selbit backstage, when he learned that Selbit had already paid Marriott some $10,000 in royalties.

Marriott performed a valuable role in locating and publicizing a rare catalog of fake medium equipment titled *Gambols with the Ghosts: Mind Reading, Spiritualistic Effects, Mental and Psychical Phenomena, and Horoscopy,* issued in 1901 by Ralph E. Sylvestre of Chicago. This catalog was designed for private circulation among fake mediums, on the understanding that it would be returned to Sylvestre when tricks had been selected from it.

The catalog had an introductory note that stated:

"Our experience during the past thirty years in supplying mediums and others with the peculiar effects in this line enable us to place before you only those which are practical and of use, nothing that you have to experiment with. . . . We wish you to thoroughly appreciate that, while we do not, for obvious reasons, mention the names of our clients and their work (they being kept in strict confidence, the same as a physician treats his patients), we can furnish you with the explanation and, where necessary, the material for the production of any known public 'tests' or 'phenomena' not mentioned in this, our latest list. You are aware that our effects are being used by nearly all prominent mediums . . . of the entire world."

This infamous catalog included equipment for fake **slatewriting,** self-playing guitars, self-rapping tables, **materializations,** and a "Complete Spiritualistic Séance." Marriott obtained a number of these illusions and had himself photographed posing with them. Marriott also successfully exposed fake "spirit photographs," obliging that champion of **Spiritualism, Sir Arthur Conan Doyle,** to state ruefully: "Mr. Marriott has clearly proved one point, which is that a trained conjurer can, under the close inspection of three pairs of critical eyes, put a false image upon a plate. We must unreservedly admit it."

A copy of *Gambols with the Ghosts* was obtained by psychic researcher **Harry Price** and is now in the Harry Price Library of Magical Literature at the University of London, England.

Sources:

Sylvestre, Ralph E. *Gambols with the Ghosts: Mind Reading, Spiritualistic Effects, Mental and Psychical Phenomena, and Horoscopy.* Chicago: privately printed, 1901.

Marryat, Florence (1837–1899)

British author, daughter of novelist Frederick Marryat, born July 9, 1837. She later became Mrs. Ross-Church, then Mrs. Francis Lean. Marryat published some 90 novels, about 100 short stories, and numerous essays, poems, and recitations; she lectured, wrote plays, toured as an actress with her own company, and edited a popular magazine. Many of her novels were translated into German, French, Swedish, Flemish, and Russian and were also popular in America.

Marryat is best remembered today, however, as a dedicated Spiritualist who was acquainted with most of the celebrated **mediums** of the 1870s and 1880s both in England and America. She was, for example, a witness to the famous farewell of **"Katie King"** to **Florence Cook** at the **séance** held by **Sir William Crookes.** Florence Marryat recorded her experiences in two books: *There Is No Death* (1891) and *The Spirit World* (1894), and both, especially the first, were frequently reprinted, being immensely popular. The two books are credited with securing hundreds of converts to **Spiritualism.** Later she also claimed mediumistic gifts herself, among them the strange power of summoning the spirits of the living.

She died in London on October 27, 1899. In the 1930s, Sir Oliver Lodge cast doubts upon the accuracy of the phenomena reported by Marryat.

Sources:

Lodge, Sir Oliver. *Letters from Sir Oliver Lodge.* Edited by J. A. Hill. London: Cassell, 1932.

Marryat, Florence. *The Spirit World.* New York: C.B. Reed, 1894.

———. *There Is No Death.* 1891. Reprint, New York: Causeway Books, 1973.

Mars, Face on

In 1977, electrical engineer Vincent DiPietro discovered a photograph released the previous year by the National Aeronautics and Space Administration (NASA) of what appeared to be a stone structure in the shape of a human face on the surface of Mars. The picture had been taken by the Viking spacecraft. Working with a colleague, Gregory Molenaar, DiPietro had the picture computer-enhanced and in 1982 they published a book, *Unusual Martian Surface Features,* displaying their results. Other nearby structures included a pyramid and a grid-like pattern that some saw as the remnants of a city.

The DiPietro/Molenaar book attracted the attention of former museum curator and journalist Richard Hoagland. A self-educated scientist, the widely read Hoagland had placed himself in the midst of several space-related controversies. In the early 1980s he added his voice to several speculative scientists in suggesting the possibility of life on Jupiter's frozen moon Europa. In the mid-1980s he emerged as an enthusiastic supporter of the idea of artificial structures on Mars. In 1987 he published a book, *The Monuments of Mars: A City on the Edge of Forever,* which remains the most cogent statement of the argument. Hoagland's claims found significant support in 1997 in *The Martian Enigmas: A Closer Look,* by Mark Carlotto. Carlotto, a processing engineer, worked with the images and demonstrated their three-dimensional nature. His work provided evidence that, whether natural or artificial, the structures were not a simple simulacra, natural objects that looked like something recognizably human (e.g., a pane of glass which appears to have a face in it). Most simulacra disappear when the object is viewed from a different angle or the lighting direction is changed.

The existence of such structures on Mars, should they prove to be artificial, would have far-reaching implications concerning the place of humans in the solar system and the order of things. There is no place for the construction of such objects in human history as it is currently constructed. Those who accept the possibility that the face, the pyramid, and related structures are artificial, have been integrated into the alternative histories theories that advocate humanity's ancient contacts with extraterrestials. Such alternative histories have been constructed by researchers like **Zecharia Sitchin** and **Alan F. Alford.**

Through the 1990s, scientists at NASA and the Jet Propulsion Laboratory have held to the position adopted when the pictures were initially examined in 1976. They are natural objects that just happen to resemble what some have suggested they are. They have noted that similar objects, such as naturally formed pyramids, may be found on Earth. In the meantime, Hoagland has pressed the case for the Face on Mars and has appeared a number of times on the popular late-night radio talkshow hosted by Art Bell.

The controversy continues, primarily on the fringe of the UFO community, and its ultimate resolution would be possible only with the landing of scientists on Mars and an immediate examination of the artifacts. Hoagland organized a team to study the huge files of photos released by NASA for other possible intelligently constructed artifacts and on several occasions has presented the findings to NASA and to Congressional committees. Those interested in the artifacts, all located in a region of Mars known as Cydonia, forced NASA to include it in their 1999 fly-by of Mars, but the new pictures were no more conclusive than were the earlier ones.

Through the 1990s, Hoagland has developed a conspiracy-theory approach to NASA and the Jet Propulsion Laboratory, and has suggested that they are withholding vital data that would support and further explain his belief concerning the possible ruins on Mars. His ideas may be found at his expansive Internet site, http://www.enterprisemission.com. The Enterprise Mission, Hoagland's research project, may be contacted at P.O. Box 1130, Placitas, NM 87043.

Sources:

Carlotto, Mark J. *The Martian Enigmas: A Closer Look.* Berkeley, Calif.: North Atlantic Books, 1997.

Gardner, Martin. "The Great Stone Face." In *The New Age: Notes of a Fringe Watcher.* Buffalo, N.Y.: Prometheus Books, 1988, 72–78.

Hoagland, Richard. *The Monuments of Mars: A City on the Edge of Forever.* 1987. 4th ed. Frog Ltd., 1996.

Molenaar, Gregory, and Vincent DiPietro. *Unusual Martian Surface Features.* Glen Dale, Md.: Mars Research, 1982.

Mars, Louis (1906–)

Professor of psychiatry and former Haitian ambassador to the United States who was also interested in **parapsychology.** He was born on September 5, 1906, at Grande-Rivière du Nord, Haiti. He studied at the University of Haiti Medical School, Port-au-Prince (M.D., 1927), and took postgraduate training in psychiatry at the Faculté de Médecine in Paris (1935) and at Columbia University in New York City (1939–41).

He became a professor of psychiatry at the Medical School, University of Haiti (1937) and at the Institute of Ethnology, University of Haiti (1946–49). He subsequently served as dean of the Medical School (1947–51) and rector of University of Haiti (1957). Mars joined the Haitian government in 1958 as the minister of foreign affairs. He was subsequently named ambassador to France in 1960 and ambassador to the United States in 1962. After his government service, he became director of Psychiatric Institute of Port-au-Prince (1962).

As a psychiatrist, Mars became interested in the phenomena associated with **voudou** about which he wrote one book and several articles. He contributed to an article, "Phenomena of Possession," published in *Tomorrow* (autumn 1954).

Sources:

Mars, Louis. *The Crisis of Possession in Voudou.* Port-au-Prince, Haiti: State Printing, 1946. Rev. ed. Reed, Cannon and Johnson, 1977.

Mars, Louis, and G. Devereux. "Haitian Voudou and the Revitalization of the Nightmare." *Psychoanlytic Review* 38, no. 4 (1951).

Marsh, Maurice Clement (1922–)

South African university lecturer in psychology who took special interest in **parapsychology.** He was born March 13, 1922, at Bloemfontein, South Africa. He studied at the University of South Africa (B.A., 1942; B.A., hons. psychology, 1946; U.E.D., 1948) and Rhodes University, Grahamstown (Ph.D., 1959). He served as a lecturer in psychology at Rhodes University (1950–61) and in 1962 joined the faculty in psychology at the University of New England, New South Wales, Australia.

Marsh's Ph.D. dissertation dealt with experimental work in **ESP,** and he continued his interest in laboratory investigation of psychic phenomena. He joined the **Society for Psychical Research,** London. He was a guest researcher at the **Parapsychology Laboratory** of Duke University, Durham, North Carolina (1951–52). He has investigated the relationship between subjects and agents in ESP testing and the psychological aspects of conditions favorable to **poltergeists,** using psychological testing techniques.

Sources:

Pleasants, Helene, ed. *Biographical Dictionary of Parapsychology.* New York: Helix Press, 1964.

Marshall, Mary (1842–1884)

The first British professional **medium,** through whom both **Sir William Crookes** and **Alfred Russel Wallace** obtained their introduction to the phenomena of **Spiritualism.** Her manifestations consisted of **raps, movements,** and **levitations** of the table, knotting handkerchiefs under the table-leaf, and writing on glass. This latter appears to have been a rudimentary form of **slate-writing,** with which she later confronted her sitters. The first account of this demonstration was published by Thomas Barkas in *Outlines of Ten Years' Investigations into the Phenomena of Modern Spiritualism* (1862).

On a small scale, Marshall exhibited most of the phenomena of later mediums. From 1867 she held sittings for **direct voice** in which **"John King"** manifested. In her first **séances** she was assisted by her niece and occasionally by her young son. Her husband developed drawing mediumship.

A writer in the journal *All the Year Round* (July 28, 1860) characterized her performance as a "dull and barefaced imposition," but Robert Bell, the celebrated dramatist, writing in the *Cornhill* magazine, was satisfied that the phenomena were genuine **spirit** manifestations.

Sources:

Barkas, Thomas P. *Outlines of Ten Years' Investigations into the Phenomena of Modern Spiritualism.* London, 1862.

The Marsi

According to Pliny, these people of ancient Italy were from the earliest times skilled in magical practices and sorceries.

They were able to charm poisonous serpents by means of songs. St. Augustine also wrote: "One would think that these animals understood the language of the Marsi, so obedient are they to their orders; we see them come out of their caverns as soon as the Marsian has spoken." (See also **Psylli**)

Martel, Linda (1956–1961)

Remarkable child spiritual healer. She was born handicapped, and although she only lived for five years, she became a legend through her ability to heal a wide variety of illnesses through touch or contact with material she had touched. One of the most extraordinary aspects of her healing was that it persisted long after her death.

Born August 21, 1956, at St. Peter Port, Guernsey, Channel Islands, she suffered from hydrocephalus and spina bifida, and her legs were paralyzed. When 11 days old, she was taken to St. Peter Port Hospital, Guernsey, to await death. Over the next few weeks her head grew disproportionately large. During this period, her father experienced a strange phenomenon in which his room was filled with a glowing light and he heard a sound like wind blowing. Linda did not die, and soon afterward the fluid was drained away from her head by means of a new American treatment for hydrocephalus. The operation was successful and the size of the head reduced.

At the age of three, Linda frequently spoke about "my Lady" and about Jesus. The Lady had a blue dress and gold chain and lived in heaven with Jesus and also looked after her. At the age of five, Linda foretold her own death, saying, "My Jesus Christ is not coming to see me many more times, but I shall soon be going to see Him." She died October 20, 1961.

During her brief life, Linda manifested healing gifts as early as the age of three. Sometimes she would simply put her finger on a painful point and a cure would take place. At other times she healed through handkerchiefs she had handled. After her death, a sufferer from asthma asked Linda's father whether he could have a piece of her clothing. Her father gave him a piece of a dress, and the sufferer was healed after contact with the material. After that, there were constant demands for pieces of Linda's clothing, and claimed cures through contact with them included warts, eczema, spinal injury, bone disease, and throat cancer.

Because so many pieces of material associated with Linda were used up, her father presented one of her dresses to the Guernsey Museum, in the hope that it might be effective in healing through people simply looking at it, since the material itself was only the intermediary of some unknown force.

Sources:

Martel, Roy. *The Mysterious Power of Linda Martel.* Guernsey, Channel Islands: Toucan Press, 1973.

Martello, Leo Louis (1931–2000)

Contemporary Wiccan priest. Martello was born on September 26, 1931, in Dudley, Massachusetts. He attended Assumption College and Hunter College and went on to become a Spiritualist minister. In the early 1960s he founded the Temple of Spiritual Guidance and the Spiritual Independents Movement. Through the 1960s he concentrated on his skills as a psychic reader and wrote a series of short booklets: *Your Pen Personality* (1961), *Its in the Cards* (1964), and *How to Prevent Psychic Blackmail* (1966).

By the end of the 1960s, however, he had begun to identify with the slowly emerging neopagan witchcraft movement. In 1970 he founded the Witches Liberation Movement and the Witches Anti-Defamation League as instruments to demand religious rights and reparation payments for the Wiccan community. That same year he organized a Halloween "witch-in" in New York City's Central Park.

Martello was quickly recognized as a leader in the Wiccan community and soon turned out a string of books that were widely read in the community, which had at the time produced only a few texts of its own. His 1973 book *Witchcraft: The Old Religions* was standard reading for young Wiccans through the rest of the decade and was frequently cited as an authoritative presentation of the beliefs and practices of modern witches. He also began to publish a periodical that flourished through the early 1970s, the *WICA Newsletter,* and the *Witchcraft Digest.*

Martello identifies himself as a traditionalist Wiccan with Sicilian roots. His coven operates under the name Witches International Craft Associates. He also founded and heads Hero Press, a small publishing operation. Martello died in June 2000.

Sources:

Martello, Leo Louis. *Curses in Verses.* New York: Hero Press, 1971.

———. *Weird Ways of Witchcraft.* New York: HC Publishers, 1969.

Melton, J. Gordon. *Religious Leaders of America.* 2nd edition. Detroit: Gale Research, 1999.

Martial Arts

A group of Asian skills combining mental, physical, and spiritual energies for self-defense in weaponless fighting, or the achievement of apparently paranormal feats of strength and control. The martial arts derive from the samurai or warrior caste fighting systems of ancient Japan, which were conditioned by **Zen** Buddhism; hence they have a spiritual basis. They are closely related to similar systems in ancient China. Japanese and Chinese martial arts are widely diffused throughout Asia.

These arts have become more widely known and taught in the West since World War II, when many servicemen encountered them in Asian campaigns, and there are now many schools for specific training of the different martial art forms. Symbolic of the growing interest in martial arts has been the popularity of the late Chinese film star Bruce Lee, who popularized the art of *kung-fu* in such films as *Fist of Fury* and *Enter the Dragon.* That particular martial art was further popularized in the television movie series *Kung Fu* starring David Carradine, first shown in the 1970s and revived in the 1990s.

The main martial arts are: *aikido* (a kind of *judo* of graceful movement in which an opponent's force is used against him), *bando* (Burmese boxing and wrestling), *judo* (wrestling with special emphasis on balance and leverage), *jiu-jitsu* (a more comprehensive and aggressive forerunner of *judo*), *karate* (kicking, striking, and blocking with arms or legs), *kung-fu* (a group of various styles of fighting and defense), *shaolin* (Chinese shadow boxing), *tae kwon do* (Korean system of kick-punching), and *t'ai chi chuan* (originally a self-defense art, now a system of physical exercises to harmonize body and mind).

The various forms of martial arts have, as their basis, the attainment of spiritual enlightenment and peace, from which point remarkable feats of skill and strength in self-defense or attack can be generated. In the process of training, practitioners claim to become aware of a subtle vital energy named **ch'i** or *ki. Ch'i* is accumulated, amplified, and directed by willpower to specific parts of the body, which develop strength and resilience. This process is sometimes preceded by a sudden exhalation of breath, often accompanied by a shout or yell. The intake of breath that follows appears to result in hyperventilation of the system, generating vitality that can be directed to hands, feet, or other parts of the body.

This process has been widely demonstrated by practitioners of *karate* in apparently paranormal feats such as breaking bricks, tiles, and planks of wood with a bare hand. It has been suggested that these feats are related to such psychic phenomena as **psychokinesis,** the ability to move objects at a distance by mental action.

Sources:

Barclay, Glen. *Mind over Matter: Beyond the Bounds of Nature.* London: Arthur Barker, 1973. Reprint, London: Pan, 1975.

Ching-nan, Lee, and R. Figueroa. *Techniques of Self-Defense.* New York: A. S. Barnes, 1963.

Feldenkrais, Moshe. *Higher Judo.* New York: Warner, 1952.

Freudenberg, Karl. *Natural Weapons: A Manual of Karate, Judo, and Jujitsu Techniques.* New York: A. S. Barnes, 1962.

Huard, Pierre, and Ming Wong. *Oriental Methods of Mental and Physical Fitness: The Complete Book of Meditation, Kinesitherapy, and Martial Arts in China, India, and Japan.* New York: Funk & Wagnalls, 1971.

Masters, Robert V. *Complete Book of Karate and Self-Defense.* New York: Sterling, 1974.

Medeiros, Earl C. *The Complete History and Philosophy of Kung Fu.* Rutland, Vt.: Charles Tuttle, 1975.

Nakayama, M. *Dynamic Karate.* Cedar Knolls, N.J.: Wehman, 1966.

Tohei, Koichi. *This is Aikido.* Tokyo: Japan Publications, 1975.

Westbrook, A. and O. Ratti. *Aikido and the Dynamic Sphere.* Rutland, Vt.: Charles Tuttle, 1970.

Martian Language

A language purporting to be that of the inhabitants of the planet Mars, written and spoken by the **medium** known as **Hélène Smith** (pseudonym of Catherine Elise Muller). Smith was studied by the celebrated investigator **Theodore Flournoy,** professor of psychology at Geneva. In 1892 Smith joined a Spiritualist circle, where she developed marvelous mediumistic powers.

In 1896, after Flournoy had begun his investigations, Smith claimed to have been spirited during a trance to the planet

Mars, and thereafter described to the circle the manners, customs, and appearance of the Martians. She learned their language, which she wrote and spoke with ease and consistency. Unlike most of the "unknown tongues" automatically produced, the Martian language was intelligible, its words were used consistently, and on the whole it had every appearance of a genuine language.

That it was in any way connected with Mars was, of course, out of the question. The descriptions of that planet and its inhabitants were quite impossible. And the language itself bore remarkable resemblance to French, the native tongue of the medium. The grammar and construction of both languages were the same, and even the vowel sounds were identical, so that the source of the Martian language was clearly an extraordinary construction from the medium's unconscious. As such it greatly resembled the form of religious speech known as **glossolalia,** or speaking in **tongues,** which is a new language that is a cutdown version of the language the speaker uses normally everyday.

Sources:

Flournoy, Theodore. *From India to the Planet Mars.* Reprint, New Hyde Park, N.Y.: University Books, 1963.

Martin, Dorothy R(andolph) (1912–)

Associate professor of psychology with special interest in **parapsychology.** She was born on April 19, 1912, in Denver, Colorado. She studied at the University of Colorado, Boulder, from which she received three degrees (B.A., 1934; M.A., 1936; Ph.D., 1947). She joined the faculty in psychology at the university even prior to completing her doctorate and stayed there through her career.

She was a charter associate of the **Parapsychological Association** and the author of a variety of articles on parapsychology.

Sources:

Martin, Dorothy R. "An Analysis of a Second Series of 25,000 Trials." *Journal of Parapsychology* 2 (1938).

———. "Chance and Extra-Chance Results in Card Matching." *Journal of Parapsychology* 1 (1937).

———. "A Review of All University of Colorado Experiments." *Journal of Parapsychology* 4 (1940).

Martin, Dorothy R., and F. P. Stribic. "Studies in Extrasensory Perception: An Analysis of 25,000 Trials." *Journal of Parapsychology* 2 (1938).

Martin, Stuart (d. 1947)

British Spiritualist and journalist, formerly employed on the *Daily Mirror* newspaper. He was editor of the newspaper *Psychic News* from March 16, 1946, until his death on January 17, 1947.

Martin (of Tours), Saint (ca. 316–400)

One of the most venerated Christian saints in Europe during the Middle Ages. Most of the Christian luminaries were credited with working miracles, and indeed the great majority of them maintained that if the people were to be won for Christ, the one sure way was to show them extraordinary marvels. Even Columba, most engaging of saints, was not averse to practicing deception with a view to making converts, and it has often been suggested, not without considerable reason, that some of these early thaumaturgists brought science to their aid. Perhaps St. Martin was among those who tried this practice, and certainly the list of miracles attributed to him is formidable, for he is traditionally credited with more than 200.

Martin was born about the year 316 at Sabaria, in Pannonia. His parents were heathen, yet he very soon came into contact with Christians, and their teaching impressed him greatly. As a young man he entered the army, and it was soon after this step that, while stationed with his regiment at Amiens, he performed his famous act of charity, dividing his cloak with a beggar who was shivering with cold. The night after this act he had a **vision** of Christ appearing to him and giving him his blessing. Thereupon Martin espoused the Christian faith formally, was baptized, and renounced soldiering.

Going to Poitiers, he then made the acquaintance of Hilary, who wished to make him a deacon, but at his own request ordained him to the humbler office of an exorcist. A little later, during a visit to his home, Martin experienced the joy of winning his mother to the new faith. However, his open zeal in opposing the Arians (heterodox Christians) raised persecution against him, and for some time he found it advisable to live at the island of Gallinaria, near Genoa, where he engaged in scientific research and theological studies.

By the year 365 he was back with Hilary at Poitiers, when he founded the Monasterium Locociagense. In 371 the people of Tours chose him as their bishop, and for some time he was active trying to extirpate idolatry in his diocese and extending the monastic system.

Nevertheless, he was no fierce proseletyzer. At Trèves in 385, he entreated that the lives of the Priscillianist heretics should be spared, and afterward he refused to have anything to do with those bishops who had sanctioned their execution.

Meanwhile, being anxious for a period of quiet study, Martin established the monastery of Marmontier les Tours on the banks of the Loire, and here much of his remaining life was spent, although it was at Candes that his death occurred about the year 400.

Martin left no writings behind him, the *Confessio* with which he is sometimes credited being undoubtedly spurious. His life was written by his ardent disciple, Sulpicius Severus, and it is more a hagiography than a biography, filled with accounts of the miracles and marvels worked by the quondam bishop. Martin was canonized a saint by the church. He is commemorated on November 11, but the feast of Martinmas, which occurs on that date, and which of course derives its name from him, is, nevertheless, a survival of an old pagan festival. It inherited certain pagan usages, which accounts for the fact that Martin is regarded as the patron saint of drinking, joviality, and reformed drunkards.

Certain miracles and other incidents in his life were depicted by noted painters. Perhaps the finest picture of him is one by the Flemish master Hugo van der Goes, which is now in the Municipal Museum at Glasgow.

It should be said that the term "martinet," signifying a severe and punctilious person, is not derived from the saint's name, but from one Jean Martinet, a French soldier who, during the reign of Louis XIV, won fame by his ardor in promoting discipline in his regiment.

Martinez, Louis

Prominent Mexican physical medium, supposed to have demonstrated **levitation** and **materialization** phenomena. In 1964 he was investigated by parapsychologist **W. G. Roll,** who found evidence of **fraud** on the part of one of the sitters.

Martinus Institute of Spiritual Science

The Martinus Institute of Spiritual Science is a **New Age** organization founded in Copenhagen, Denmark, in the 1930s by a teacher known publicly as Martinus (1890–1981). Reportedly, Martinus had undergone an intense experience, after which he could divine spiritual principles and laws of the universe through colored diagrams and symbols. He subsequently claimed to have analyzed the universe, which he understood in a set of logical chains of thought readily accessible to the intelligence. Among the principles he discovered, for example, was that life is eternal and manifests in alternate periods of physical and spiritual existence (that is, **reincarnation**). Martinus's teachings are summarized in his two books, *Livets Bog (The Book of Life)* and *The Eternal World Picture.*

In 1935 he opened what has become the organization's primary center at the seaside resort town of Klint. The work was slowed somewhat by World War II, but by the 1960s affiliated centers had opened in Germany, Holland, Sweden, and Great Britain. *KOSMOS,* the institute's magazine, appears in Danish, German, French, English, Swedish, Esperanto, Spanish, and Dutch editions. The institute may be contacted c/o Mariendalsvej 94–96, 2000 Frederiksberg, Denmark. Website: http://www.martinus.dk/.

Sources:

Martinus. *The Immortality of Living Beings.* Copenhagen, Denmark: Martinus Institute, 1970.

———. *The Principle of Reincarnation.* Copenhagen, Denmark: Martinus Institute, 1938.

———. *The Road to Initiation.* Copenhagen, Denmark: Martinus Institute, 1957.

Martiny, M(arcel) (1897– ?)

Physician with special interests in **parapsychology.** He was born on November 11, 1897, in Nice, France, and studied at the Faculté de Médecine, Université de Paris (M.D. with honors, 1925). He worked for the Rockefeller Institute Mission during World War I and was employed at Beaujon Hospital (1925–32), Léopold Bellan Hospital, Paris (1933–45), and Hospital Foch in the years after the war. From 1949 on he was director of the Anthropotechnical Laboratory, Prophylactic Institute, Paris.

Other appointments include secretary-general, Medico-Surgical Society of the Free Hospitals of France (1932); president of National Union of Physicians, Surgeons, and Specialists of the Free Hospitals of France (1948); president of Physiopsychology Society (1958); and member of Paris Medical Society.

Martiny wrote various medical works and co-authored, with **Alexis Carrel,** *Médecine officielle et médecine hérétique* (Orthodox and Unorthodox Medicine). He also spent many years investigating human bio-types in relation to parapsychological phenomena; parapsychology in relation to psychoanalysis; hypnosis and Pavlov's nervous typology in relation to parapsychology; relationships between neurology, cerebral function, and parapsychology; and space-time concepts in parapsychology. His articles on such subjects have been published in *Revue Métapsychique.* He also contributed papers to international conferences on parapsychology (Utrecht, 1953; St. Paul de Vence, 1954). He was selected president of Institute Métapsychique in 1962.

Sources:

Pleasants, Helene, ed. *Biographical Dictionary of Parapsychology.* New York: Helix Press, 1964.

Mary Celeste

The name of a ship found abandoned at sea December 5, 1872, and one of the most famous unsolved sea mysteries. Her sails were set, she was sound and seaworthy, with plenty of food and water, but not a soul on board. Some garments were hanging out to dry on a line. In the cabin was a slate with notes for the ship's log, with November 25 as the last date. The crew had left pipes, clothing, and even oilskin boots. For some unknown reason the ship had been hurriedly abandoned. The *Mary Celeste* was brought to Gibraltar by the crew of the British brig *Dei Gratia* who claimed salvage. On March 25, 1873, the chief justice awarded £1,700 (about one-fifth of the total value) to the master and crew of the *Dei Gratia.*

Since then, the mystery of the *Mary Celeste* (sometimes inaccurately called "Marie Celeste") has been widely discussed and many theories advanced. There have also been various literary hoaxes, notably "The Marie Celeste: The True Story of the Mystery" (*Strand Magazine,* November 1913) and the book *The Great Mary Celeste Hoax* by Laurence J. Keating (London, 1929).

Several years before the creation of Sherlock Holmes, author Sir Arthur Conan Doyle published "J. Habakuk Jephson's Statement" in *Cornhill* magazine (January 1884), a romantic fictional yarn with an air of verisimilitude. The story was republished in Doyle's volume of short stories *The Captain of the Polestar* (London, 1890).

Sources:

Fay, Charles Eden. *Mary Celeste: The Odyssey of an Abandoned Ship.* Salem, Mass.: Peabody Museum, 1942.

Gould, Rupert T. *The Stargazer Talks.* London, 1944. Reprinted as *More Oddities and Enigmas.* New Hyde Park, N.Y.: University Books, 1973.

Keating, Laurence J. *The Great Mary Celeste Hoax: A Famous Sea Mystery Exposed.* London: Heath-Cranton, 1929.

Stein, Gordon. *Encyclopedia of Hoaxes.* Detroit: Gale Research, 1993.

Maryland Center for Investigation of Unconventional Phenomena

Former Fortean (anomalous) center founded by Willard F. McIntyre and Arthur F. Rosen for the purpose of gathering and disseminating information about such phenomena as **UFOs,** Bigfoot, and **monsters.** The center issued a publication *Believe It.*

Marylebone Spiritualist Association, Ltd. See Spiritualist Association of Great Britain

Maskelyne, John Nevil (1839–1917)

Famous British stage magician who was a strong opponent of fraudulent **Spiritualism.** Born at Cheltenham, Gloucestershire, December 22, 1839, he was the son of a saddlemaker. As a boy he was fascinated by an entertainer who demonstrated spinning plates and practiced this feat himself. He was apprenticed to a clockmaker and at the age of 19 made his first piece of conjuring apparatus, a box with a secret panel. By 1865 he was giving demonstrations of amateur conjuring. After seeing the performance of the famous **Davenport brothers,** he believed that he had observed trickery, and to prove his case he went into partnership with George Alfred Cooke to build a cabinet similar to that of the Davenports and rival their phenomena.

Maskelyne and Cooke were launched on a career of stage magic and leased the Egyptian Hall in London for their entertainments. By 1905 Maskelyne was in partnership with fellow illusionist David Devant (born David Wighton) at St. George's Hall, Langham Place, in West London, where they based many of their presentations of the claimed phenomena of Spiritualism.

In 1906 he was involved in a controversy with Spiritualist sympathizer Archdeacon **Thomas Colley,** who had challenged him to reproduce the phenomena of medium **F. W. Monck** (incidentally exposed in **fraud**). Maskelyne staged a remarkable illusion, but Colley claimed it fell short of the requirements of his challenge. After a court case, Colley's claim was upheld, perhaps surprisingly in view of opposition to Spiritualism at that time.

He died on May 18, 1917, in London.

Sources:

Maskelyne, John N. *The Fraud of Modern "Theosophy" Exposed.* London: G. Routledge, 1913.

———. *Modern Spiritualism: A Short Account of Its Rise and Progress, with Some Exposures of So-Called Spirit Media.* London: F. Warne, 1876.

Masleh

The angel who the Jews believed ruled the zodiac. According to a rabbinical legend, Masleh was the medium through which the power and influence of the Messiah was transmitted to the sphere of the zodiac.

Masse, François (1891– ?)

Commissaire général of the French Navy, with interests in **parapsychology.** He was born on May 10, 1891, at Vendome, France. He entered the French Navy and served in World Wars I and II, finally retiring as commissaire général in 1946.

During his retirement years he became a member of the **Institut Métapsychique International** and for a period served as general secretary and secretary-treasurer. He collaborated with **Rene Warcollier** in **telepathy** experiments and contributed articles on parapsychological topics to *Revue Métapsychique.*

Sources:

Pleasants, Helene, ed. *Biographical Dictionary of Parapsychology.* New York: Helix Press, 1964.

Massey, Gerald (1828–1907)

British poet born May 29, 1828, in Hertfordshire, England. He grew up in poverty, earned a living by working in a factory from the age of eight, and learned to read at a penny school. Massey became a socialist and edited a radical journal, and he also wrote poems, which were favorably noticed by established poets such as Browning and Tennyson. His first wife, Rosina Knowles, was a Spiritualist **medium.**

Massey based one volume of his poetry, *A Tale of Eternity* (1870), on personal experience of a **haunted house.** He soon lost some of his early popularity, however, when he was said to have gone over to the Spiritualists. In response he confessed:

"For the truth's sake I ought to explain that the spiritualism to be found in my poetry is no delusive idealism, derived from hereditary belief in a resurrection of the dead. My faith in the future life is founded upon facts in nature and realities of my own personal experience. These facts have been more or less known to me personally during forty years of familiar face-to-face acquaintanceship, therefore my certitude is not premature; they have given me proof palpable that our very own human identity and intelligence do persist after the blind of darkness has been drawn down in death."

In 1872 Massey presided at the meeting in London marking the departure of **Emma Hardinge Britten** to Australia. His address with some additions was later printed under the title *Concerning Spiritualism.*

In his later years he published four large volumes in which he tried to trace the origin of language, symbols, myths, and religions. The work was reminiscent of **Godfrey Higgins** (1772–1833). His final product was not well received during his lifetime, the idea of Africa as the birthplace of mankind being quite unacceptable in Victorian England. Thus *A Book of the Beginnings* (1881) and his other texts were largely ignored or ridiculed until later archaeological discoveries provided more solid evidence in support of Massey's themes.

He died on October 12, 1907.

Sources:

Massey, Gerald. *Ancient Egypt.* 2 vols. London, 1907. Reprint, New York: Samuel Weiser, 1970.

———. *A Book of the Beginnings.* 2 vols. London, 1881. Reprint, New Hyde Park, N.Y.: University Books, 1974.

———. *The Natural Genesis.* 2 vols. London: n.p., 1883.

Mass of St. Secaire

A form of **black mass** originating in the Basque countryside, possibly in medieval times. It was a travesty of a Christian mass and was celebrated in a ruined church. The intention was not to worship the devil but to direct currents of malevolent spite against a victim. It may have had its origin in ancient folklore practices.

Sources:

Rhodes, H. T. F. *The Satanic Mass.* London, 1954. Reprint, London: Arrow, 1964.

Masters

Occult **adepts** who are supposed to have reached a superhuman stage but have elected to remain on Earth and guide seekers after wisdom. The founding and guidance of the **Theosophical Society** was supposed to be due to the activity of hidden Masters or Mahatmas living in remote Tibet. Since the idea of the Masters and their **Great White Brotherhood** has been popularized, numerous groups such as the several **Alice Bailey** groups, the **I Am Movement,** and the **Church Universal and Triumphant,** now advocate a relationship to the Masters.

Much of Western **occultism** derives from romantic concepts of **adepts** with magical powers, but in Hinduism, mystical awareness of God-realization is considered superior to paranormal feats, and to the Hindu pupil, the Master is his **guru,** or spiritual teacher. The term **Mahatma** is used to indicate a special guru or "great soul," and *Maharishi* or *Maharshi* denotes a great sage of transcendental wisdom. Another Sanskrit term *Paramahansa* (literally "greatest swan") is given to a very exalted mystic.

The primary Masters claimed by **Helena Petrovna Blavatsky,** one of the founders of Theosophy, were: **Koot Hoomi Lal Singh** (usually signing letters "K.H."), the Master **Morya** (known as "Master M."), Master Ilarion or Hilarion (a Greek), Djual Khul (or "D.K."), and the Maha Chohan.

Sources:

Jinarajadasa, C. *The Early Teachings of the Masters.* Chicago: Theosophical Press, 1925.

Johnson, Paul. *In Search of the Masters: Behind the Occult Myth.* South Boston, Va.: The Author, 1990.

Leadbeater, Charles W. *The Masters and the Path.* Adyar, India: Theosophical Publishing House, 1925.

Masters, Robert E. L. (1927–)

Co-founder with wife, **Jean Houston,** of the **Foundation for Mind Research,** Manhattan, New York, conducting experiments in the borderline between mental and physical experience. Masters has a background of poetry and sexology and was formerly director of the Visual Imagery Research Project and the Library of Sex Research. Both Houston and Masters have experimented with psychedelic **drugs** and hypnosis, and in their foundation they have investigated induction of mystical experience and altered states of consciousness.

Sources:

Houston, Jean, and Robert E. L. Masters. *Listening to the Body.* New York: Delacorte Press, 1978.

———. *Mind Games: The Guide to Inner Space.* New York: Viking, 1972.

———. *The Varieties of Psychedelic Experience.* New York: Holt, Rinehart and Winston, 1966.

Masters, Robert E. L. *Eros and Evil: The Sexual Psychopathology of Witchcraft.* New York: Julian Press, 1962.

———. *Forbidden Sexual Behavior and Morality.* New York: Julian Press, 1962.

———. *The Homosexual Revolution: A Challenging Exposé of the Social and Political Directions of a Minority Group.* New York: Julian Press, 1962.

Mastiphal

The name given to the prince of demons in an apocryphal book entitled *Little Genesis,* which was quoted by the Greek monk and historian Cedrenus (eleventh century).

Material for Thought

Journal concerned with Eastern and Western teachings regarding the inner search for self. Address: Far West Editions, P.O. Box 27901-113, San Francisco, CA 94127. Online orders are available at http://www.material4thought.com/.

Sources:

Material For Thought. http://www.material4thought.com/. March 8, 2000.

Materialization

The claimed manifestation of temporary, more or less organized, apparitions in varying degrees of form, often possessing human physical characteristics and said to be shaped for a temporary existence from a substance called "**ectoplasm.**" Materializations were attributed by Spiritualists and some psychical researchers to spirit agency, although a few postulated that they might arise from some unknown natural force independent of departed spirits, but emanating from gifted psychics. Most modern parapsychologists believe that materializations were simply performances staged by mediums and their accomplices to deceive the people sitting with them, who had hoped to come into contact with the supernatural.

For a century psychical researchers investigated claims of materialization and from time to time researchers came forward to declare their belief in the genuineness of the phenomena they had witnessed. Materialization was also closely associated with other physical phenomena such as **apports** and **spirit photography.** As researchers became more sophisticated in detecting **fraud,** the number of people willing to risk announcing themselves as materialization mediums steadily declined. Materialization was pushed to the edge of the Spiritualist movement.

As recently as 1960, there was a major expose of a group of materialization mediums at Camp Chesterfield, an independent Spiritualist camp near Anderson, Indiana. The mediums, including the camp's leading medium Mabel Riffle, were caught on infrared film impersonating spirits and moving in and out of a trap door. Then in the mid-1970s, Lamar Keene, a medium from Florida, resigned from his church and confessed to playing tricks on his congregation and on other clients who came to him for readings.

The manner in which materialization phenomena is finally evaluated will radically affect any account of the era of materialization mediums. It is a unanimous conclusion, however, that fraud occurred and that trade catalogs selling products to help accomplish materializations circulated through the Spiritualist community. It is also true that all of the notable materialization mediums, with the exception of **D. D. Home,** were at one time or another caught in fraud, and that no clear case of even a partial materialization exists. The belief in materialization rests upon evidence of the most questionable kind.

The Origin of Materialization Phenomena

In its early stages, materialization was confined to the appearance of heads and hands, or vague luminous streaks of light. Figures were materialized later. Like much of the physical phenomena of Spiritualism, it had its origin in the United States, where it was reported at a comparatively early period in the history of the movement.

As early as 1860, séances were held with the **Fox sisters** by **Robert Dale Owen** and others, at which veiled and luminous figures were seen. One sitter, a Mr. Livermore, claimed to recognize the spirit of his dead wife during séances with Kate Fox extending over some six years. However, there were no other sitters and the séances were held in the dark. In England the mediums **Frank Herne** and **Charles Williams** succeeded a few months later in "materializing" shadowy forms and faces in a dark séance room.

However, it was **Florence Cook,** whose phenomena was championed by physicist **William Crookes,** who produced the most sensational materializations. At the begining of her Spiritualistic career, she was a pretty young girl of 16 or 17. She was at that time a private medium, though at the outset she held some materialization séances with Herne. From her childhood, it was said, Cook was attended by a spirit girl who said her name on Earth had been Annie Morgan, but that her name in the spirit world was **"Katie King."** Under the latter name, Cook's **control** was destined to become famous in Spiritualist circles.

During a séance the medium was usually put into a sort of cupboard or **cabinet,** tied to her chair, and the cords sealed. After a short interval a form clad in flowing white draperies would emerge from the cabinet.

On one occasion, a séance was held at the Cooks' house, at which several distinguished Spiritualists were present. Among the invited guests was William Volckman, who decided to test for the good faith of the medium and "Katie's" genuineness. After some 40 minutes of close observance of the materialized spirit, Volckman concluded that Cook and Katie were the same, and just as the white-robed figure (probably not Cook, but an accomplice) was about to return to the cabinet he rushed forward and seized her. His indignant fellow sitters released the "spirit," the light was extinguished, and in the confusion that followed the spirit disappeared. Cook was found a few minutes later bound as when she was placed in the cabinet, the cords unbroken, the seal intact. She wore a black dress, and there was no trace of white drapery in the cabinet.

Crookes, whose investigation into the phenomena of this medium extended over a period of years, had better opportunity to examine "Katie's" claims than Volckman. He wrote that the spirit form was taller than the medium, had a larger face and longer fingers, and whereas Cook had black hair and a dark complexion, Katie's complexion was fair, and her hair a light auburn (all observations consistent with the theory that a friend of Cook's portrayed the materialized spirit). Moreover, Crookes, enjoying "Katie's" complete confidence, often had the privilege of seeing her and Cook at the same time.

Strong doubts have been expressed about the genuineness of the spirit form "Katie King." Crucial to the argument is the integrity of William Crookes. In his detailed study of the situation in 1962, **Trevor Hall** concluded that Cook and Crookes were having an affair. Two years later the **Society for Psychical Research** released a report of an interview with a person who claimed to have known Cook and to whom she confessed her fraud.

But Cook was not the only medium who was controlled by "Katie King." With her father, "John King," she became a popular spirit with materialization mediums. From that time on, materialization was extensively practiced both by private and professional mediums. Among them were **Mary Showers** and her daughter, **Lottie Fowler; William Eglinton;** and D. D. Home; in later years materializations were noted to have occurred in the presence of **Eusapia Palladino.**

Many sitters claimed to see in such draped figures and veiled faces the form and features of deceased relatives and friends, although frequently there was little reason for such a claim—parents recognized their daughter by her hair, a man recognized his mother by the sort of cap she wore, and so on.

There is no doubt that fraud entered into materialization séances. Lay figures, muslin draperies, false hair, and similar properties have been found in the possession of mediums; accomplices have been smuggled into the séance room; lights are frequently turned low or extinguished altogether. Add to this the fact that the "spirits" upon being grasped frequently turned into the medium and it will be clear that skepticism was justified.

Psychical Researchers and Materialization

Toward the end of the nineteenth century psychical researchers began to turn their attention toward materialization phenomena and were impressed with what they observed. French researcher **Camille Flammarion** attributed the materializations he had witnessed in the presence of Eusapia Palladino to fluidic emanations from the medium's body, while judging the recognition given them the result of illusion. Other researchers said the physical organization formed by the spirit was composed of fine particles of matter drawn from the material world.

Gustav Geley, in his book *Clairvoyance and Materialisation* (1927), says, "this is no longer the marvelous and quasi-miraculous affair described and commented on in early spiritualistic works." **Charles Richet,** in *Thirty Years of Psychical Research* (1923), was possibly the strongest witness of all. He writes: "I shall not waste time in stating the absurdities, almost the impossibilities, from a psychophysiological point of view, of this phenomenon. A living being, or living matter, formed under our eyes, which has its proper warmth, apparently a circulation of blood, and a physiological respiration which has also a kind of psychic personality having a will distinct from the will of the medium, in a word, a new human being! This is surely the climax of marvels! Nevertheless, it is a fact."

He adds:

"Materialisation is a mechanical projection; we already know the projection of light, of heat and of electricity; it is not a very long step to think that a projection of mechanical energy may be possible. The remarkable demonstrations of Einstein show how close mechanical or luminous energy are to one another.

"I have also, like Geley, Schrenck Notzing, and Mme. Bisson, been able to see the first lineaments of materialisations as they were formed. A kind of liquid or pasty jelly emerges from the mouth or the breast of Marthe which organises itself by degrees, acquiring the shape of a face or a limb. Under very good conditions of visibility, I have seen this paste spread on my knees, and slowly take form so as to show the rudiment of the radius, the cuvitus, or metacarpal bone whose increasing pressure I could feel on my knee."

Richet's Marthe was the medium Marthe Béraud, also known as "**Eva C.**" Geley relates his experiences with her in his 1920 book *From the Unconscious to the Conscious*:

"I have very frequently seen complete representations of an organ, such as a face, a hand, or a finger. In the more complete cases the materialised organ has all the appearance and biologic functions of a living organ. I have seen admirably modelled fingers, with their nails; I have seen compete hands with bones and joints; I have seen a living head, whose bones I could feel under a thick mass of hair. I have seen well-formed living and human faces! On many occasions these representations have been formed from beginning to end under my own eyes. . . . The forms have, it will be observed, a certain independence, and this independence is both physiological and anatomical. The materialised organs are not inert, but biologically alive. A well-formed hand, for instance, has the functional capacities of a normal hand. I have several times been intentionally touched by a hand or grasped by its fingers. . . . Well-constituted organic forms having all the appearance of life, are often replaced by incomplete formations. The relief is often wanting and the forms are flat. There are some that are partly flat and partly in relief, I have seen in certain cases, a hand or a face appear flat, and then, under my eyes assume the three dimensions, entirely or partially. The incomplete forms are sometimes smaller than natural size, being occasionally miniatures."

From Thoughtforms to Full-Grown Phantoms

Many of the photographs taken of Eva C.'s materializations suggest the evolution of **thoughtforms.** A Professor Daumer contended that ectoplasmic forms were neither bodies nor souls. He offered the term *eidolon* (shape). A number of Eva C.'s phantom forms resembled pictures she had seen, caricatures of presidents Wilson and Pioncaré, and they often had folds as if a paper had been uncreased to be photographed.

Richet remarked that the supposition of fraud would presume extreme stupidity on Eva's part because she knew that photographs would be taken; moreover, there was no reason to suppose that a materialization had to be analogous to a human body and three dimensional. "The materialisation of a plaster bust is not easier to understand than that of a lithographic drawing; and the formation of an image is not less extraordinary than that of a living human head," he said.

Daumer's speculation is strangely contrasted by **Glen Hamilton**'s report (in *Psychic Science*) on the building and photographing of a three-dimensional ectoplasmic ship in the Winnipeg circle. The entities "John King" and "Walter" claimed responsibility for the experiment. Coming through the mediums Mary M. and X, they carried on a dialogue feigning that they were aboard "King's" pirate ship among a crew of ruffians. It was hinted that this playacting had a psychological purpose: the recovery of past memories and the creation of the thought image of a sailing ship. Eventually the ship was built, but because of some indecision in giving the signal to take a flash photograph, it "came into port badly damaged." Hamilton remarks:

"No matter how great we may conceive the unknown powers of the human organism to be, we cannot conceive of it giving rise to an objective mass showing purposive mechanistic construction such as that disclosed in the ship teleplasm of June 4th [1903]. We are forced to conclude that the supernormal personalities in this case (by some means as yet unknown to us) so manipulated or otherwise influenced the primary materialising substance after it had left the body of the medium, or was otherwise brought into its objective state, as to cause it to represent the idea which they, the unseen directors, had in view, namely the idea of a sailing ship" (*Psychic Science,* vol. 11, no. 4, Jan. 1933).

The appearance of images instead of forms was said to have something to do with the available power. Geley often observed strange, incomplete forms, imitations or simulacra of organs.

His theory was as follows:

"The formations materialised in mediumistic séances arise from the same biological process as normal birth. They are neither more nor less miraculous or supernormal; they are equally so. The same ideoplastic miracle makes the hands, the face, the viscera, the tissues, and the entire organism of the foetus at the expense of the maternal body, or the hands, the face, or the entire organs of a materialisation. This singular analogy between normal and so-called supernormal physiology extends even to details; the ectoplasm is linked to the medium by a channel of nourishment, a true umbilical cord, comparable to that which joins the embryo to the maternal body. In certain cases the materialised forms appear in an ovoid of the substance. . . . I have also seen on several occasions, a hand presented wrapped in a membrane closely resembling the placental membrane. The impression produced, both as to sight and touch, was precisely that of a hand presentation in childbirth, when the amnion is unbroken. Another analogy with childbirth is that of pain.

The moans and movements of the entranced medium remind one strangely of a woman in travail."

To the legitimate objection that one biological process was natural and the other anomalous, Geley answered: "Normal physiology is the product of organic activity such as evolution has made it. The creative and directive idea normally works in a given sense, that of the evolution of the species, and conforms to the manner of that evolution. Supernormal physiology, on the other hand, is the product of ideoplastic activity directed in a divergent manner by an abnormal effort of the directive idea."

It was also soon noted that the "ectoplasmic" shapes tended to conform to the bodily pattern of the medium. After observing the **Davenport brothers,** Rev. **J. B. Ferguson** said:

"I have seen, with my natural vision the arms, bust and, on two occasions, the entire person of Ira E. Davenport duplicated at a distance of from two to five feet where he was seated fast bound to his seat. I have seen, also, a full-formed figure of a person, which was not that of any of the company present. In certain conditions, not yet clearly understood, the hands, arms and clothing of the Brothers Davenport and Mr. Fay are duplicated alike to the sight and the touch. In other cases, hands which are visible and tangible, and which have all the characteristics of living human hands, as well as arms, and entire bodies, are presented, which are not theirs or those of anyone present."

Crookes was satisfied that "Katie King" was independent from the medium Florence Cook. Yet on certain occasions he noted a striking resemblance between phantom and medium. There is an unusual account in the history of the medium **Elizabeth d'Esperance** that seems to suggest that a total exchange is within the bounds of possibility. During a series of sittings with d'Esperance in Sweden a crucial test was requested and the medium bravely stated to "Walter," her spirit control, that she would take the responsibility. D'Esperance writes:

"A very uncomfortable feeling pervaded the circle but it afterwards gave place to one of curiosity. My senses became keenly alert, the cobwebby sensation, before described, grew horribly intense, and a peculiar feeling of emptiness, which I had previously had, became so strong that my heart seemed as though swinging loosely in an empty space, and resounding like a bell with each stroke. The air seemed to be full of singing, buzzing sounds that pressed on my ears, but through it I could hear the breathing of the sitters outside the curtains. The movements made in the air seemed to sway me backwards and forwards. A fly alighting on my hand caused a pain like that of a toothache to shoot up my arm. I felt faint, almost dying.

"At last the arranged-for signal was given, that all was ready. The curtains were thrown open, and a materialised form stood fully revealed beside me. The lens of the camera was uncovered, the plate exposed, the magnesium light flashed. Then the curtains fell together. I remember the feeling of relief and thinking: Now I can give way. It is possible that I did faint. I do not know. But I was aroused by the sound of a voice saying in my ear: She is not here, she is gone. It was one of the family who spoke and the terror in the boy's voice roused me effectually. I wanted to reassure him, and asked for water, and wondered at the same time whose voice was it that made the request. It was like my own but seemed to come from the air or from another person. The water was brought and drunk, but though I felt refreshed the act seemed to be performed by that other person who had spoken. Then I was left alone . . .

"Now comes the strangest part of this strange experiment. The photographic plate was carefully developed and a print made, which revealed a most astonishing fact. The materialised form, well in focus, was clad in white, flowing garments. The hair was hanging loosely over the shoulder, which, like the arms, were without covering. The figure might have been that of a stranger, but the features were unmistakably mine. Never has a photograph shown a better likeness. On a chair beside it and a little behind, was a figure clad in my dress, the black bands on the wrist, and the tape round the waist showing themselves clearly and intact, but the face was that of a stranger, who seemed to be regarding the proceedings with great complacency and satisfaction. Needless to say, we looked at this extraordinary photograph with something like petrifaction. We were utterly at a loss to understand its meaning, and no explanation was forthcoming, except a rueful remark from Walter, who when questioned replied that 'Things did get considerably mixed up.' "

In *Light* (December 19, 1903), L. Gilbertson remarks:

"My own theory of the strange head is that the manifesting spirit was driven out of the materialised form by Madame's subself, which had gained an abnormal excess of power through the weak condition of her normal organism. Finding itself ousted, the visitor took refuge with Madame's other part, and proceeded to operate on it in the way generally known as transfiguration. Succeeding in this operation, it is not difficult to believe, as Madame says, that it seemed to be regarding the proceedings with great complacency and satisfaction."

To account for the variant phenomena from one séance to the next, Spiritualists hypothesized that if the health of the medium was weak or the power, for any other reason, low, materialization usually did not progress beyond the stage of resemblance to the medium. In line with this hypothesis **Enrico Morselli** proposed a psychodynamic theory (*Psycologia e Spiritismo,* 1907) according to which the ectoplasmic substance resulted from a kind of human radioactivity and the directive idea had its origin in the medium's subconscious mind. But Morselli also added that the medium's subconscious mind may establish telepathic communication with the sitters' subconscious minds and may shape the ectoplasmic forms according to their thoughts and desires. While the second part of the hypothesis seemed far-fetched, the first was supported by many reports. The influence of the human mind, however, was evident to a certain stage only. The phantom shapes did not keep the medium's physiognomy, gestures, and voice for long and displayed, after the transitory period, an apparent independence. Their bodies were said to have temperature and blood circulation and to breathe and behave in every way as an unrelated entity.

Epes Sargent writes in *Proof Palpable of Immortality* (1875) that a feminine spirit who manifested herself at Moravia in the séances of **Mary Andrews** on one occasion produced, in rapid succession, facsimiles of her personal appearance at six different periods of her corporeal life, ranging from childhood to old age. The phantoms of **Etta Roberts** were often said to transform themselves into the forms of other persons in view of the sitters.

From his experiences, E. A. Brackett (another author of books on Spiritualism) concluded that the sitter's will has an influence over the phantom shapes as well. In his séances with **Annie Eva Fay,** he found that by the exercise of his will he could cause the materialized forms to recede.

Interdependence of Phantom and Medium

A **community of sensation** between the medium and the materialized phantom was described as part of the drama of the séance. The interaction between the two bodies was reportedly constant, a fact that is today seen as a rationalization to explain away what is now viewed as further evidence of the fraud in the séance room. Florence Cook once had a dark stain on a covered part of her body after an ink mark had been made on "Katie's" face while the medium was locked in the cabinet. Annie Fairlamb ("Mrs. Mellon") reported: "I feel as though I were that form, and yet I know I am not and that I am still seated on my chair. It is a kind of double consciousness—a faraway feeling, hard to define. At one moment I am hot, and the next moment cold. I sometimes have a choking, fainting, sinking sensation when the form is out."

Describing an early materialization séance of Rosina Thompson, F. W. Thurstan stated: "All this while Mrs. T. was in full consciousness, but she kept exclaiming that she felt 'all hollow' and another thing she noticed was that whenever 'Clare's' fingers touched anyone she distinctly felt a pricking sensation in her body, very similar to her experiences when she had been placed once on an insulating stool and charged with electricity and persons had touched her to make sparks come from her."

D'Esperance, who never touched tobacco, suffered from nicotine poisoning if her sitters smoked during the ectoplasmic process. W. Reichel, author of *Occult Experiences* (1906), observed that the phantoms of the medium **C. V. Miller** smelled of tobacco and even of food and wine if the medium had liberally partaken of them before the séance. When the materilized child of **Florence Marryat** filled her mouth with sugar-plums, she nearly choked the medium. "Mahedi," the Egyptian phantom of medium **F. W. Monck,** discovered a dish of baked apples in the room. "I got him to eat some," wrote Archdeacon **Thomas Colley.** "Our medium was at this time six or seven feet away from the materialised form and had not chosen to take any of the fruit, averring that he could taste the apple the Egyptian was eating. Wondering how this could be, I, with my right hand, gave our abnormal friend another baked apple to eat, holding this very bit of paper in my left hand outstretched towards the medium, when from his lips fell the chewed skin and core of the apple eaten by 'The Mahedi'—and here it is before me now after all these years in this screwed up bit of paper for any scientist to analyse."

Ectoplasm was seen as a sensitive substance. It was to be handled with caution and protected from the light. Gustav Geley observed that the shock of sudden light was proportional to the duration of the light and not to its intensity. A magnesium flash would hurt the medium less than the rays of a pocket lamp. If the ectoplasm had solidified, the danger of injuring the medium was less, but a danger nevertheless. Reportedly, the medium could suffer if the phantom was hurt, but the injury did not necessarily appear on the corresponding part of the medium's body. A phantom hand could be pierced through with a knife and the medium might shriek with pain, yet his hands would bear no trace of the wound. F. L. Willis had an experience of this kind in his mediumship. However, séance-room atrocities seldom went beyond spirit grabbing.

When Florence Marryat was conducted into the cabinet by the materialized spirit of Mary Showers, she was told:

"You see that Rosie is half her usual size and weight. *I* have borrowed the other half from her, which, combined with contributions from the sitters, goes to make up the body in which I show myself to you. If you increase the action of the vital half to such a degree, that, if the two halves did not reunite, you would kill her. You see that I can detach certain particles from her organism for my own use, and when I dematerialise, I restore these particles to her, and she becomes once more her normal size. You only hurry the re-union by violently detaining me, so as to injure her."

In an earlier account given to a Mr. Luxmoore by "Katie King," the danger was graphically but less scientifically pictured. To the question "When you disappear, where is it to?" she answered, "Into the medium, giving her back all the vitality which I took from her. When I have got very much from her, if anyone of you were to take her suddenly round the waist and try to carry her you might kill her on the spot; she might suffocate. I can go in and out of her readily, but understand, I am not her—not her double; they talk a deal of rubbish about doubles; I am myself all the time."

Colley's experience with "Mahedi" appeared to conform to the above theories. This phantom was a giant. His physical strength was so great that he could lift the archdeacon from his chair to the level of his shoulders apparently without effort. He reminded the archdeacon of a mummy of gigantic proportions he once saw in a museum.

Colley described the "Mahedi's" first visit through the medium F. W. Monck:

"He wore a kind of metal skull cap, with an emblem in front which trembled and quivered and glistened, overhanging the brow. I was allowed to feel it, but there was little resistance to my fingers, and it seemed to melt away like a snowflake under my touch, and to grow apparently solid again the moment after. For once (February 18, 1878) by daylight, it was arranged, as a most dangerous experiment, that I should grasp the white-attired Egyptian and try to keep him from getting back to invisibility through the body of the medium. I was, by an invisible force, levitated, as it seemed instantly some eighteen or twenty feet from my drawing room door right up to where the medium stood, whom, strangely and suddenly, wearing white muslin over his black coat, I found in my arms just as I had held The Mahedi. The materialised form had gone, and the psychic clothing that he evolved with him from the left side of my friend must also have gone the same way with the speed of thought back to invisibility through the medium."

It is difficult to find a corroboration of this experience in the literature of Spiritualism. Far more often it was said that the spirit dissolved in the grabber's hand. William Volckman had that experience with "Katie King." Most of the time, however, when the light was switched on the spirit was found to be identical to the medium. Cases of transfiguration in a state of deep trance may offer an excuse, but generally it is a safe assumption that a successful grabbing of the medium in the spirit's guise establishes a *prima facie* case for fraud. The question that usually complicates the case is of the drapery that is visible in the dark and may serve for purposes of transfiguration. The drapery often disappeared when the light was switched on, but often it was found and turned out to be very material and enduring.

Some Early Explanations

According to the explanation of the controls, the phenomena of materialization were not produced by a single spirit. "John King," in a séance with **Cecil Husk,** disclosed to Florence Marryat:

"When the controls have collected the matter with which I work—some from everybody in the circle, mostly from the medium's brain—I mould with it a plastic mask, somewhat like warm wax in feel, but transparent as gelatine, into the rough likeness of a face. . . . I therefore place this plastic substance over the spirit features and mould it to them. If the spirits will have the patience to stand still I can generally make an excellent likeness of what they were in earth life, but most of them are in such haste to manifest that they render my task very difficult. That is why very often a spirit appears to his friends and they cannot recognise any likeness."

The solidity of the materialized form varied. Some mediums only produced vaporous phantoms called "etherealizations." The exertion of force apparently had no relationship to the spirit entity's solidity. For example, an early illustrative account appears in *Spiritualism* by **John Worth Edmonds** and G. T. Dexter (2 vols., 1853–55):

"I felt on one of my arms what seemed to be the grip of an iron hand. I felt distinctly the thumb and fingers, the palm of the hand, and the ball of the thumb, and it held me fast by a power which I struggled to escape from in vain. With my other hand I felt all round where the pressure was, and satisfied myself that it was no earthly hand that was thus holding me fast, nor indeed could it be, for I was as powerless in that grip as a fly would be in the grasp of my hand."

The word *materialization* was first used in 1873 in the United States in place of "spirit forms." Hands and arms were seen in the séances of the Davenport brothers in the earliest days of modern Spiritualism. According to Epes Sargent's *The Scientific Basis of Spiritualism* (1881), "as far back as 1850, a full spirit form would not infrequently appear." Chemist **James J. Mapes** became the first scientist to speculate on a means by which such temporary organisms might be produced in accordance with the kinetic theory of gases, with a minimum of actual material particles, if enough energy of motion were imparted to them.

Phantom Eyes and Hands

A record published in the *Report on Spiritualism* of the **London Dialectical Society** (1871) narrates the metamorphosis of a psychic light into an eye: "Mr W. Lindsay said there was a large bright eye in the centre of the table, from whence other eyes appeared to emanate and approach and retreat." Eyes winking humorously were frequently reported in the Boston séances of "Margery" (the name used in the literature for **Mina Crandon**).

F. W. Pawlowski, professor of aeronautical engineering at the University of Michigan, writes about his experiences with **Franek Kluski** in the *Journal* of the American Society for Psychical Research (1925, pp. 481–504):

"Bright bluish stars appear and begin to move high above the table, near the ceiling. When they approached me at a distance of about 16 inches I recognised to my great astonishment that they were human eyes looking at me. Within a few seconds such a pair of eyes develops into a complete human head, and with a hand moving a luminous palm illuminating it clearly. The hand will move around the head as if to show itself more clearly to the onlooker, the eyes looking at one intensely and the face smiling most pleasantly. I have seen a number of such heads, sometimes two at a time, moving through the air like drifting toy balloons from one sitter to another. On several occasions the apparitions appeared just behind my back, and I was aware of them from the sound of their breathing, which I could hear distinctly before they were noticed by the sitters opposite to me. When I turned around I found their faces just about a foot from me, either smiling or looking intently at me. Some of these were breathing violently as if after a strenuous run, and in these cases I felt their breath on my face. Once I listened to the heartbeat of an apparition. They conducted themselves as callers at a party. The expression of curiosity in their eyes is most appealing. I have seen a similar look only in the eyes of children at the age of the awakening of their intelligence. On one occasion I saw two of them flying high above our heads in the higher room, illuminating each other with the plaques and performing fancy evolutions. It was really a beautiful sight, something like an aerial ballet."

William Crookes testified that the phantom hand ". . . is not always a mere form, but sometimes appears perfectly life-like and graceful, the fingers moving and the flesh apparently as human as that of any in the room. At the wrist, or arm, it becomes hazy and fades off into a luminous cloud."

To the touch the hand was sometimes icy cold and dead, at other times warm and lifelike. Crookes said he saw a luminous cloud hover over a heliotrope, break a sprig off and carry it to a lady; he also claimed to have seen a finger and thumb pick petals from a flower in Home's buttonhole and lay them in front of several persons sitting near him. Phantom hands playing the keys of an accordion floating in the air were frequently seen.

Once in the full light of day in Hall's drawing room, with D. D. Home's feet and hands in full view the entire time, **William Howitt,** S. Carter Hall, and **Emma Hardinge Britten** claimed they saw 20 pairs of hands form and remain visible and active for about an hour. "One evening," wrote John Ashburner of his experiences with the medium **Charles Foster,** "I witnessed the presence of nine hands floating over the dining table" (*Notes and Studies on Animal Magnetism and Spiritualism,* 1867).

Signor G. Damiani testified before the London Dialectical Society as having seen, at a séance of the Davenport brothers in London in 1868, ". . . five pink transparent hands ranged perpendicularly behind the door. Subsequently," he said, "I placed my hand in the small window of the cabinet, when I felt each of my five digits tightly grasped by a distinct hand; while my own was thus held down, five or six other hands protruded from the hole above my wrist. On withdrawing my hand from the aperture, an arm came out therefrom—an arm of such enormous proportions that had it been composed of flesh and bone, it would, I verily believe, have turned the scale (being weighted) against the whole corporeal substance of the small Davenport."

A silver, luminous hand that began at the elbow and was seen in the process of formation is described in the report of a séance with D. D. Home in the *Hartford Times,* March 18, 1853: "In a moment there appeared a rather dull looking, grey hand, somewhat shadowy, and not quite so clearly defined as the first, but it was unmistakably there, and its grey hue could be clearly seen."

Eusapia Palladino was famous for her "third arm," which issued from her shoulders and receded into them. This arm was often seen independently and well materialized. The "counterpartal arms" of **William Stainton Moses,** extending from his shoulders straight out, and above his true arms, presented a similar phenomenon. They simply retracted into the medium, or vanished if an attempt was made to grasp them.

Describing "John King's" materialized hand, Charles Richet stated:

"I held it firmly and counted 29 seconds, during all which time I had leisure to observe both of Eusapia's hands on the table, to ask Mme. Curie if she was sure of her control, to call Courtier's attention, and also to feel, press and identify a real hand through the curtain. After 29 seconds I said: 'I want something more, I want uno anello (a ring) on this hand.' At once the hand made me feel a ring: I said 'adesso uno braceletto' and on the wrist I felt the two ends as of a woman's bracelet that closes by a hinge. I then asked that this hand should melt in mine, but the hand disengaged itself by a strong effort, and I felt nothing further."

Sitting with Eusapia Palladino, **Filippo Bottazzi** "four times saw an enormous black fist come out from behind the left curtain, which remained motionless, and advance toward the head of Mme. B." Eugene Crowell states in *The Identity of Primitive Christianity with Modern Spiritualism* (1874), "At Moravia, at one time, I saw an arm projected from the aperture of the cabinet, which with the hand, was fully three and a half feet in length. It remained in view, in free motion, for a time sufficient for all to observe and remark upon it. Its enormous length and size startled all present."

Despite such startling testimonies, the inference that telekinetic effects are produced by materialized hands should not be drawn hastily. **Julien Ochorowicz** noticed an alternative character about these manifestations: a well-materialized hand, when clearly visible, was mechanically inactive. Mechanical effects were generally produced by invisible hands. The same held true for chemical, luminous, and acoustic effects.

Phantoms of Fame and Name

The best records of full form materializations have been furnished by "familiar" spirits: "Katie King," who attended Florence Cook for three years; "Yolande," who appeared in Elizabeth d'Esperance's séances for a similar period; "Estella," who manifested in the Livermore sittings for five years; and "Bertha," a niece of E. A. Brackett who appeared to him through different mediums for two years. "Yolande's" case was unique in one respect—she was sexually assaulted by a man who took her for a real woman. This resulted in a profound injury and serious illness to the medium.

Materialized spirits seldom came in numbers and their range of activity was limited. The marvelous stories of C. V. Miller's mediumship, which was powerful enough to make 12 materialized figures appear at once, rest mostly on the testimony of W. Reichel. Corroboration by a repetition of the occurrence is also wanting in the case of the peripatetic ghosts of **George Spriggs,** which were said to walk about the house and in the garden, and in the case of the open-air materializations of William Eglinton, in which the spirits walked 66 feet away from the medium.

Crookes was the first modern scientist who studied materializations under laboratory conditions. "Katie King" offered him every opportunity for investigation. She even allowed Crookes to enter the cabinet where, armed with a phosphorus lamp, he saw both the medium and "Katie" at the same time. In studying D. D. Home's mediumship, Crookes did not see many fully materialized figures. He observed: "In the dusk of the evening during a séance with Mr. Home at my house, the curtains of a window about eight feet from Mr. Home were seen to move. A dark, shadowy, semi-transparent form, like that of a man, was then seen by all present standing near the window, waving the curtain with his hand. As we looked, the form faded away and the curtains ceased to move."

Mrs. Crookes described a semitransparent phantom form playing an accordian, which she said was also seen by her husband, the Reverend Stainton Moses, and Sergeant Cox in a Home séance: "As the figure approached I felt an intense cold, getting stronger as it got nearer, and as it was giving me the accordion I could not help screaming. The figure seemed to sink into the floor, to the waist, leaving only the head and shoulders visible, still playing the accordion, which was then about a foot off the floor."

A description of a more solid case was given by **Lord Adare** who also sat in Home's séances:

"Her form gradually became apparent to us; she moved close to Home and kissed him. She stood beside him against the window intercepting the light as a solid body, and appeared fully as material as Home himself; no one could have told which was the mortal body and which was the spirit. It was too dark, however to distinguish features. I could see that she had her full face turned towards us, and that either her hair was parted in the middle, and flowed down over her shoulders or that she had on what appeared to be a veil."

The next systematic investigation was made by Charles Richet, who confides to his readers:

"At the Villa Carmen I saw a fully organised form rise from the floor. At first it was only a white, opaque spot like a handkerchief lying on the ground before the curtain, then this handkerchief quickly assumed the form of a human head level with the floor, and a few moments later it rose up in a straight line and became a small man enveloped in a kind of white burnous, who took two or three halting steps in front of the curtain and then sank to the floor and disappeared as if through a trapdoor. But there was no trap-door."

The phantom "Bien Boa" possessed all the attributes of life. Richet writes: "It walks, speaks, moves and breathes like a human being. Its body is resistant, and has a certain muscular strength. It is neither a lay figure nor a doll, nor an image reflected by a mirror; it is as a living being; it is as a living man; and there are reasons for resolutely setting aside every other supposition than one or other of these two hypotheses: either that of a phantom having the attributes of life; or that of a living person playing the part of a phantom."

At another time he notes, "At certain moments it was obliged to lean and bend, because of the great height which it had assumed. Then suddenly, his head sank, sank right down to the ground, and disappeared. He did this three times in succession. In trying to compare this phenomenon to something, I can find nothing better than the figure in a jack-in-the-box, which comes out all of a sudden."

Hands That Melted Like Snow

The appearance of human organs or of complete bodies was followed by their dissolution. This phenomenon was observed under dramatic circumstances. Testimonies of this phenomenon were numerous: Frank L. Burr, editor of the *Hartford Times,* in a letter to Home's wife, gave his account of one of Home's last séances, held March 14, 1855, before his departure to England:

"Turning this strange hand palm towards me, I pushed my right forefinger entirely through the palm, till it came out an inch or more, visibly, from the back of the hand. In other words, I pushed my finger clean through that mysterious hand. When I withdrew it, the place closed up, much as a piece of putty would close under such circumstances, leaving a visible mark or scar, where the wound was, but not a hole. While I was still looking at it the hand vanished, quick as a lightning flash."

Crookes also wrote of Home: "I have retained one of these hands in my own, firmly resolved not to let it escape. There was no struggle or effort to get loose, but it gradually seemed to resolve itself into vapour, and faded in that manner from my grasp."

Crookes observed that the hands and fingers did not always appear to be solid and lifelike. Sometimes they looked like a cloud partly condensed into the form of a hand.

H. D. Jencken said before the London Dialectical Society, "I have once been enabled to submit a spirit hand to pressure. The temperature was, as far as I could judge, the same as that of the room, and the spirit hand felt soft, velvety; dissolving slowly under the greatest amount of pressure to which I could submit it."

"Katie's" wrist was once seized in anger by G. H. Tapp of Dalston, whom "Katie" had struck on the chest for a joke she resented. As Tapp described it, the hand "crumpled up in my grasp like a piece of paper, or thin cardboard, my fingers meeting through it."

"John King" was seen by Florence Marryat to "hold a slate so that both hands were visible, and then let one hand dematerialise till it was no larger than a doll's, whilst the other remained the normal size."

Filippo Bottazzi of the University of Naples wrote, "I saw and felt at one and the same time a human hand natural in colour, I felt with mine the fingers and the back of a strong, warm, rough hand. I gripped it and it vanished from my grasp, not becoming smaller, but melting, dematerialising, dissolving."

Eugene Rochas wrote in the *Annales des Sciences Psychiques* (vol. 18, 1908, p. 280) of a séance in which M. Montorguiel seized a materialized hand and called for a light. The hand melted and "all of us thought we saw a luminous trail from his hand to F.'s body," Rochas recalls. **Hereward Carrington,** one of the keenest fraudhunters among psychical researchers, wrote:

"I myself have observed materializations under perfect conditions of control, and have had the temporary hand melt within my own, as I held it firmly clasped. This 'hand' was a perfectly formed, physiological structure, warm, life-like and having all the attributes of a human hand—yet both the medium's hands were securely held by two controllers, and *visible* in the red light. Let me repeat, this hand was *not* pulled away, but somehow melted in my grasp as I held it" (*The Story of Psychic Science,* 1930).

Dramatic Exit of Spirit Visitants

The dissolution of a full phantom was one of the most dramatic moments in a materialization séance. "Katie King" agreed to demonstrate it and Florence Marryat captures the moment in her book *There is no Death* (1892):

"She [Katie King] took up her station against the drawing room wall, with her arms extended as if she were crucified. Then three gas-burners were turned on to their full extent in a room about 16 feet square. The effect upon 'Katie King' was marvelous. She looked like herself for the space of a second only, then she began gradually to melt away. I can compare the dematerialisation of her form to nothing but a wax doll melting before a hot fire. First the features became blurred and indistinct; they seemed to run into each other. The eyes sunk in the sockets, the nose disappeared, the frontal bone fell in. Next the limbs appeared to give way under her, and she sank lower and lower on the carpet, like a *crumbling* edifice. At last there was *nothing but her head* left above the ground—then a heap of white drapery only, which disappeared with a whisk, as if a hand had pulled it after her—and we were left staring by the light of three gas burners at the spot on which 'Katie King' had stood."

Sometimes the dissolution is unexpected, the medium later reporting that the power waned and the form could not be held together. In a séance with Annie Eva Fay, a deceased sister appeared to Marryat, who recalled: "Suddenly she appeared to faint. Her eyes closed, her head fell back on my shoulder, and before I had time to realise what was going to happen, she had passed *through* the arm that supported her, and sunk down *through* the floor. The sensation of her weight was still making my arm tingle, but 'Emily' was gone, *clean gone.*"

"Honto," the Indian spirit control of the **Eddy brothers,** smoked a pipe. The light from the burning tobacco enabled Olcott to see her copper-colored cheek, the bridge of her nose, and the white of her eye. She remained out too long. Darting back, she collapsed into a shapeless heap before the curtains, only one hand being distinguishable. In half a minute she appeared again.

The process of dissolution varied. Robert Dale Owen stated that he had seen a form fade from the head downward. William Oxley (author of *Modern Messiahs and Wonder Workers,* 1889) said he saw "Yolande" melting away from the feet upward until only the head appeared above the floor; this grew less and less until only a white spot remained. Then it too disappeared. Her materialization, as a rule, took ten to fifteen minutes. Her disappearance took place in two to five minutes, while the disappearance of the drapery lasted from one-half to two minutes.

At one of Annie Fairlamb's séances in Sydney, Australia, a form lay down on the platform, stretched out its limbs and each member of the body separately dematerialized.

Most often the figures collapsed and disappeared through the floor. The phantoms of Virginia Roberts, however, (as Marryat testified) if they were strong enough to leave the cabinet, invariably disappeared by floating upward through the ceiling. "Their mode of doing this was most graceful," Marryat wrote. "They would first clasp their hands behind their heads, and lean backwards; then their feet were lifted off the ground, and they were borne upward in a recumbent position." The phantoms of **Carlos Mirabelli,** the South American medium, similarly raised themselves and floated in the air before full dissolution, which began with the feet.

When matter apparently passes through matter or when apports are brought into the séance room, the process of dematerialization may be identical. This was suggested by d'Esperance (*Shadow Land,* 1897):

"A lady once brought a brilliantly colored Persian silk scarf, which Yolande regarded with great delight, and immediately draped about her shoulders and waist. This scarf she could not be induced to part with. When she had disappeared and the séance closed a careful search was made, but it was not to be found. The next time she came, the lady asked her what she had done with it. Yolande seemed a little nonplussed at the question, but in an instant she made a few movements with her hands in the air and over her shoulders, and the scarf was there, draped as she had arranged it on the previous evening. . . . She never trusted this scarf out of her hands. When sometimes she herself gradually dissolved into mist under the scrutiny of twenty pairs of eyes, the shawl was left lying on the floor, we would say, 'At last she has forgotten it'; but no, the shawl would itself gradually vanish in the same manner as its wearer and no search which we might afterwards make ever discovered its whereabouts. Yet Yolande assured us gleefully that we failed to see it only because we were blind, for the shawl never left the room. This seemed to amuse her, and she was never tired of mystifying us by making things invisible to our eyes or by introducing into the room flowers which had not been brought by human hands."

Marvels of Materialization

On May 25, 1921, **Juliette Bisson** reported seeing the materialization on the hand of "Eva C." of a naked woman eight inches high, with a beautiful body, long fair hair, and brilliantly white skin. It vanished and returned several times and either her hair was differently arranged or she appeared smaller. The little figure performed various gymnastic exercises and finally stood on Bisson's extended hand. (Bisson was Eva C.'s accomplice in producing materializations.) The materialization of small heads the size of walnuts in a glass of water was the peculiar feature of **Lujza Ignath**'s mediumship. "Nona," the control, said the heads were plastic thoughtforms.

Describing a visit to an unnamed materialization medium, Gladys Osborne Leonard states in her book *My Life in Two Worlds* (1931):

"My husband was sitting with his feet and knees rather wide apart. His gaze suddenly was diverted from the materialised spirit to a kind of glow near his feet. Looking down he saw a tiny man and woman, between 12 and 18 inches high, standing between his knees. They were holding hands and looking up into my husband's face, as if they were thinking 'What on earth is that?' They seemed to be interested, if not more so, in him, and the details of his appearance, as he was in theirs. He was too astonished to call anybody's attention to the tiny people, who were dressed in bright green, like the pictures of elves and fairies, and who wore little pointed caps. A slight glow surrounded them, or emanated from them, he wasn't sure which, but it was strong enough for him to see their little faces and forms clearly. After a moment or two they disappeared, apparently melting into the floor."

In a sitting with Countess Castelwitch in Lisbon, a communicator who called himself "M. Furtado" rapped out through the table that he would not allow himself to be photographed because he had forgotten what his face was like. At the next séance he said: "I have no face, but I will make one." The photographic plate revealed a tall phantom clothed in white, having a death's-head instead of a face. A similar but more gruesome instance was described in the reports of the **Academia de Estudo Psychicos "Cesar Lombroso"** of São Paolo, on the mediumship of Carlo Mirabelli:

"The third sitting followed immediately while the medium was still in a state of exhaustion. A skull inside the closet began to beat against the doors. They opened it and the skull floated into the air. Soon the bones of a skeleton appeared one after another from neck to feet. The medium is in a delirium, beats himself and emits a bad smell like that of a cadaver. The skeleton begins to walk, stumble and walk again. It walks round the room while Dr. de Souza touches it. He feels hard, wet, bones. The others touch it. Then the skeleton disappears slowly until the skull alone remains which finally falls on a table. The medium was bound throughout the performance. It lasted 22 counted minutes in bright sunlight."

Alfred Vout Peters claimed to have seen in a séance with Cecil Husk the materialization of a living friend who was at the time asleep in his home. **Horace Leaf** reported (*Light,* January 29, 1932) on the materialization of the head, shoulders, and arm of a relative living 400 miles away. A conversation was carried on for several minutes on matters thoroughly appropriate, before the head bid him goodbye and vanished.

Colley noticed some unique feature of the mysterious spirit entity "Mahedi." The phantom could not speak English, so Colley had to use signs to make him understand that he wanted him to write. He looked puzzled at the lead pencil. When he was shown how to use it, he held it as he would hold a stylus and began to write quickly from the right to the left in unknown oriental characters, being "in a most peculiar way under the control of 'Samuel' "—one spirit controlling another spirit—the medium having nothing to do with it, since he was fully awake some 17 feet away and talking to a lady. Colley had samples of "Samuel's" handwriting and he understood "Samuel" to be in control. He later argued:

"It was something like what I had before seen and publicly reported relating to the evolution of a spirit form from another spirit form, which first form, as usual, extruded from the medium, so that (December 7, 1877) there stood in line our normal friend (entranced) and next to him the Egyptian thence derived, and from the Egyptian, in turn, the extruded personality of 'Lily,' all at the same time—the three in a row ranked together yet separate and distinct entities."

After all these marvels, Colley's description of the reabsorption of a phantom into the medium's side in plain view appears to lose its wild improbability. Of a séance held on September 25, 1877, Colley stated:

"As I brought my sweet companion close up to him, the gossamer filament again came into view; its attenuated and vanishing point being, as before, towards the heart. Greatly wondering, yet keen to observe, did I notice how, by means of this vapoury cord, the psychic figure was sucked back into the body of the medium. For like a waterspout at sea—funnel-shaped or sand column such as I have seen in Egypt—horizontal instead of vertical, the vital power of our medium appeared to absorb and draw in the spirit-form, but at my desire, so gradually that I was enabled quite leisurely thus closely to watch the process. For leaning against, and holding my friend with my left arm at his back and my left ear and cheek at his breast, his heart beating in an alarming way, I saw him receive back the lovely birth of the invisible spheres into his robust corporeal person. And as I gazed on the sweet face of the disintegrating spirit, within three or four inches of its features, I again marked the fair lineaments, eyes, hair and delicate complexion, and kissed the dainty hand as in process of absorption it dissolved and was drawn through the texture and substance of his black coat into our friend's bosom."

The archdeacon once spoke to a materialized phantom before her extrusion was accomplished and he saw recognition in her eyes and heard her whisper, during the psychic parturition, "so glad to see you."

On one occasion a minister friend of Francis Monck materialized; by common consent the medium was carefully awakened. Colley recalled: "Dazed for a moment, and then most astonished, our aroused friend looked enquiringly at the materialised spirit form, and jumping up from the sofa on which we had placed him he excitedly rushed forward to his one-time fellow-student, shouting 'Why, it is Sam' and then there was handshaking and brotherly greetings between the two. When both friends were about to speak at once there was a momentary impasse and neither seemed able to articulate; the medium's breath appearing to be needed by Samuel when he essayed to speak, while the materialised form was also checked in his utterance when the medium began to speak."

C. V. Miller, the San Francisco materialization medium, as a rule did not pass into trance and took the phantoms that issued from the cabinet by the hand and introduced them to his sitters. His amazing séances were duplicated by R. H. Moore, of San Diego, California. According to N. Meade Layne, in *Psychic Research* (June 1931), Moore was a well-known gentleman past 70 years of age, who did not go into trance and accompanied the forms that issued from behind a curtain within a few steps into the circle. The forms were never fully materialized; as a rule they were invisible below the bust, although the ectoplasmic drapery sometimes trailed nearly to the floor. Layne writes, "At a recent séance one of the forms, while conversing with the person at my side, advanced to within about 18 inches of my face. Dr. Moore then, after telling us what he was about to do, struck the head of the form lightly with his open hand to show the degree of materialization. The movement and the sound were plainly perceived. He then passed his arm through the form at the solar plexus" (*Psychic Research,* July 1930).

Besides the materialization of spirit entities, many other objects came forth in the séance room. Such phenomena, which blend into that of apports, often served to confuse researchers and distract them from the central issues of spirit contact. However, in the end, the other objects served to confirm the fraudulent nature of materializations.

Spirits were often observed enveloped in drapery. This was always considered one of the greatest puzzles of ghost lore, though if one considers materialization as basically fraudulent, the drapery was merely a prop to confuse the issue. The communications received through mediums did little to elucidate the subject, though it was taken up in the discussions of the clothing of spirits in the afterlife. "Spirit drapery" seems to have been constructed of a light material such as cheesecloth and was occasionally coated with a luminous substance such as phosphorus. However, the discussion of the phenomena as part of the larger inquiry into spirit existence is of some interest.

"Julia," in her communications to **W. T. Stead** (*Letters from Julia,* 1897), notes that the spirit "is at the first moment quite unclothed, as at birth. When the thought of nakedness crosses the spirit's mind, there comes the clothing which you need. The idea with us is creative. We think and the thing is. I do not remember putting on any garments." Her observation was confirmed by Caroline D. Larsen in *My Travels in the Spirit World* (1927): "From every spirit emanates a strong aura, a pseudophosphoric light. This aura is completely controlled by the mind. Out of this substance is moulded the vesture of the body."

About a conscious projection of his **astral body, Sylvan J. Muldoon** observed:

"On one occasion I noticed the clothing forming itself out of the emanation surrounding my astral body, when only a few feet out of coincidence, and the clothing was exactly like that covering my physical body. On another occasion I awakened and found myself moving along at the intermediate speed. A very dense aura surrounded me—so dense, in fact, that I could scarcely see my own body. It remained so until the phantom came to a stop, when I was dressed in the typical ghost like garb."

The idea of a power to form spirit clothing seems to have emerged slowly in materialization séances, where the formation of spirit drapery came to be viewed as preliminary to the building up of the body. It served, some speculated, the purpose of covering up imperfections or vacant spots in the temporary organism, protected the ectoplasmic substance from the effects of light, and satisfied the requirements of modesty (very important in both British and American societies). Once while "Yolande," (who was often seen together with medium Elizabeth d'Esperance outside the cabinet) was talking to a sitter, "the top part of her white drapery fell off and revealed her form," writes Oxley. "I noticed that the form was imperfect, as the bust was undeveloped and the waist uncontracted which was a test that the form was not a lay figure."

The drapery observed usually appeared to be white, sometimes of a dazzling whiteness, but could also be greyish in appearance; it was often luminous and so material that it was always the last to disappear when the séance concluded. The reason apparently was that the substance of the drapery, though its texture was finer, withdrawn from the medium's clothes to be molded by the invisible operators, like ectoplasm, into all kinds of patterns.

The medium Franek Kluski noticed that the curtains and carpets of his apartment, where his materialization phenomena were produced, were badly worn in an inexplicable manner. The observation was also made at the **British College of Psychic Science** that the lining of the underarms of a medium's jacket used exclusively for séance purposes and apparently subjected to no rough wear had to be renewed frequently. The wife of medium John Lewis of Wales, who had to repair the garment, said that the wear on the jacket was greater than on garments worn in his work as a coal miner. The color of the garment was apparently of no consequence because the spirit drapery remained white, even if the original dress was black.

In a séance with William Eglinton on September 9, 1877, a Dr. Nichols saw the materialized form "Joey" make, in the presence of three other persons, "20 yards of white drapery which certainly never saw a Manchester loom. The matter of which it was formed was visibly gathered from the atmosphere and later melted into invisible air. I have seen at least a hundred yards so manufactured," he said.

Katherine Bates writes in *Seen and Unseen* (1907), "I stood close over her [the phantom] holding out my own dress, and as she rubbed her hands to and fro a sort of white lace or net came from them, like a foam, and lay upon my gown which I was holding up towards her. I touched this material and held it in my hands. It had substance but was light as gossamer, and quite unlike any stuff I ever saw in a shop."

F. W. Thurstan said that when medium **Rosina Thompson** produced physical phenomena, "a soft, gauzy, scented white drapery was flung over my head and seen by the others on my side of the room." A spirit in séances with Annie Eva Fay supposedly made yards and yards of spirit drapery by rubbing her hands together with bare arms. Once she made a seamless robe and apparently dematerialized it instantaneously. William Harrison, editor of *The Spiritualist,* states in an account of a séance with Florence Cook,

"She ['Katie King'] threw out about a yard of white fabric, but kept hold of it by the other end, saying: 'Look, this is spirit drapery.' I said 'Drop it into the passage Katie, and let us see it melt away; or let us cut a piece off.' She replied: 'I can't; but look here.' She then drew back her hand, which was above the top of the curtain, and as the spirit drapery touched the curtain, it passed right through, just as if there were no resistance whatever. I think at first there was friction between the two fabrics and they rustled against each other, but that when she said 'Look here' some quality which made the drapery common matter was withdrawn from it, and at once it passed through the common matter of the curtain, without experiencing any resistance."

"Katie King" often allowed her sitters to touch her drapery. Sometimes she cut as many as a dozen pieces from the lower part of her skirt and made presents of them to different observers. The holes were immediately sealed. Crookes examined the skirt inch by inch and found no hole, no marks, or seam of any kind.

These pieces of drapery mostly melted into thin air, however carefully they were guarded, but sometimes they could be preserved. If they were, the medium's dress was damaged. "Katie King" said in her attempt to cover up the trickery that nothing material about her could be made to last without taking away some of the medium's vitality and weakening her.

A specimen of "Katie's" drapery was taken by a Miss Douglas to Messrs. Howell and James's cloth and dry goods store, London, with the request to match it. They said that they could not, and that they believed it to be of Chinese manufacture.

At a séance with Elizabeth d'Esperance, a sitter removed a piece of drapery that clothed one of the spirit forms. Later d'Esperance discovered that a large square piece of material was missing from her skirt, partly cut, partly torn. The stolen piece of drapery was found to be of the same shape as the missing part of the skirt, but several times larger, and white, the texture fine and thin as gossamer. After this experience d'Esperance seemed to understand a similar happening in England. "Ninia," a child spirit control, was asked for a piece of her abundant clothing. She complied, but unwillingly. After the séance d'Esperance found a hole in her new dress.

"Katie Brink," the spirit of the medium **Elizabeth J. Compton,** cut a piece of her dress for Richard Cross of Montreal, but on the condition that he would buy a new dress for the medium, for a corresponding hole would appear on her skirt. The cut piece was fine, gossamer-like material. The medium's dress was black alpaca, and much coarser. The cut piece fit the hole in the medium's dress.

William Stainton Moses was once given a piece of spirit drapery sweetened by "spirit musk." He sent it to the wife of his friend Stanhope Speer. The scent on the letter was fresh and pungent 17 years afterward.

Mediums explained that part of the power available to them for the materialization was consumed by the creation of spirit drapery. They added that, in some instances, for purely economical reasons, the operators accepted ready-made cloth brought in for them to wear. **"John King"** was supposedly photographed in such borrowed garments. There were stories that for similar reasons wearing apparel could be "apported."

This speculation made it easy for fraud to flourish. Florence Cook's mother was said to have once caught "Katie King" wearing her daughter's dress. Katie confessed that she borrowed it because the medium's power was weak. She said she would never do it again because the medium might be compromised. In other cases, it was claimed, yards of muslin and grenadine were apported expressly for draping purposes and left in the séance room. Further, traces of spirit cloth appeared in mediumistic **plastics** used to make impressions of spirit faces.

Souvenir Locks of Hair, Materialized Jewels, and Flowers

Materialized phantoms often gave locks of hair to sitters for souvenirs. "Katie King" did it very often. Once in the cabinet, she cut off a lock of her own hair and a lock of the medium's and gave them both to Florence Marryat. One was almost black, soft and silky, the other a coarse, golden red. On another occasion she asked Marryat to cut her hair with a pair of scissors as fast as she could. "So I cut off curl after curl, and as fast as they fell to the ground the hair grew again upon her head," Marryat said.

Severed hair usually vanished, but not always. Crookes, in a later communication, spoke of a lock of "Katie's" hair he still possessed. Similarly a lock that Charles Richet cut from the head of an Egyptian beauty during the mediumship of Marthe Béraud remained intact. Richet stated: "I have kept this lock, it is very fine, silky and undyed. Microscopical examination shows it to be real hair; and I am informed that a wig of the same would cost a thousand francs. Marthe's hair is very dark and she wears her hair rather short."

Materialized phantoms apparently often wore ornaments. Admiral Usborne Moore, in his séances with the medium **J. B. Jonson** of Detroit, found these ornaments yielding to the touch. In other instances they were solid. "Abd-u-lah," the one-armed spirit of William Eglinton, appeared bedecked with diamonds, emeralds, and rubies. The materialization of precious stones is described by a Mrs. Nichols in the *Spiritualist* (October 26, 1877):

"For some time he moved his hands as if gathering something from the atmosphere, just as when he makes muslin. After some minutes he dropped on the table a massive diamond ring. He said: 'Now you may all take the ring, and you may put it on, and hold it while you count twelve.' Miss M. took it and held it under the gaslight. It was a heavy gold ring with a diamond that appeared much like one worn by a friend of mine worth £1000. Joey said the value of this was 900 guineas. Mr. W. examined it as we had done. He now made, as it seemed, and as he said, from the atmosphere two diamonds, very clear and beautiful, about the size of half a large pea. He gave them into our hands on a piece of paper. We examined them as we had the others. He laid the ring and the diamonds on the table before him, and there next appeared a wonderful cluster of rubies, set with a large ruby about half an inch in diameter in the centre. These we all handled as we had the others. Last there came a cross, about four inches in length, having 20 magnificent diamonds set in it; this we held in our hands, and examined as closely as we liked. He told us that the market value of the gems was £25,000. He remarked: 'I could make Willie the richest man in the world, but it would not be the best thing, and might be the worst.' He now took the jewels in front of him and seemed to dissipate them, as one might melt hailstones in heat until they entirely disappeared."

Stainton Moses was told by "Magus," one of his controls, that he would deliver him a topaz, the material counterpart of his spiritual jewel, which would enable him to see scenes in the spheres on looking into it. The jewel was found in his bedroom. Moses was excited. He believed it to be an apport, taken without the consent of the owner. He never received any definite information as to its origin. It cannot be traced how long the stone, which was set in a ring, remained in his possession.

Gems and pearls were frequently brought to Moses' circle. His theory was that they were made by spirits because he could see them falling before they reached the table, while others could not see them until they had fallen. Further, an emerald had flaws in it, and therefore it could not have been cut or have been an imitation.

Flower materializations were more frequent. There was a remarkable instance in d'Esperance's mediumship. On June 28, 1890, at a séance in St. Petersburg, in the presence of **Alexander Aksakof** and one Professor Boutlerof, a golden lily, seven feet high, appeared in the séance room. It was kept for a week and was photographed six times. After the week it dissolved and disappeared.

A record of the Livermore séances with Kate Fox on February 22, 1862, notes:

"Appearance of flowers. Cloudy. Atmosphere damp. Conditions unfavourable. At the expiration of half an hour a bright light rose to the surface of the table, of the usual cylindrical form, covered with gossamer. Held directly over this was a sprig of roses about six inches in length, containing two half-blown white roses, and a bud with leaves. The flowers, leaves and stem were perfect. They were placed at my nose and smelled as though freshly gathered; but the perfume in this instance was weak and delicate. We took them in our fingers and I carefully examined the stem and flowers. The request was made as before to 'be very careful.' I noticed an adhesive, viscous feeling which was explained as being the result of a damp, impure atmosphere. These flowers were held near and over the light, which seemed to feed and give them substance in the same manner as the hand. By raps we were told to 'Notice and see them dissolve.' The sprig was placed over the light, the flowers dropped, and in less than one minute, melted as though made of wax, their substance seeming to spread as they disappeared. By raps 'See them come again.' A faint light immediately shot across the cylinder, grew into a stem; and in about the same time required for its dissolution, the stem, and the roses had grown into created perfection. This was several times repeated, and was truly wonderful."

F. W. Thurstan observed in sittings with Rosina Thompson (*Light*, March 15, 1901) that when a pineapple was to be materialized the smell and notion of it was "in her head" all day. He believed that ideas of forms, actions, and words that would manifest at a séance were placed in the medium's mind days beforehand.

Animal Materializations

One place where animals have made a noticeable impact upon the world of paranormal research has been in claims of their manifestation in the séances of materialization mediums. There are abundant accounts of such apparitions, the strangest reports being attributed to three Polish mediums: Franek Kluski, **Jan Guzyk** and one Burgik.

It was claimed that Guzyk materialized dogs and other animals, and Kluski, a large bird of prey, small beasts, a lion, and an apeman. The year 1919 abounded with apparent animal materializations in the Kluski séances. An account in *Psychic Science* (April 1926) reads in part:

"The bird was photographed, and before the exposure a whirring, like the stretching of a huge bird's wings, could be heard, accompanied by slight blasts of wind, as if a large fan were being used. . . . Hirkill (an Afghan) materialised. . . . Accompanying him always was a rapacious beast, the size of a very big dog, of a tawny colour, with slender neck, mouth full of large teeth, eyes which glowed in the darkness like a cat's, and which reminded the company of a maneless lion. It was occasionally wild in its behaviour, especially if persons were afraid of it, and neither the human nor the animal apparition was much welcomed by the sitters. . . . The lion, as we may call him, liked to lick the sitters with a moist and prickly tongue, and gave forth the odour of a great feline, and even after the séance the sitters, and especially the medium, were impregnated with this acrid scent as if they had made a long stay in a menagerie among wild beasts."

According to one Professor Pawlowski's account in the *Journal* of the American Society for Psychical Research (September 1925), the bird was a hawk or a buzzard. It "flew round, beating his wings against the walls and ceiling, and when he finally settled on the shoulder of the medium he was photographed with a magnesium flash, as the camera was accidently focussed on the medium before, and was ready."

An anthropoidal ape showed itself first in July 1919. Gustav Geley reports in his book *Clairvoyance and Materialisation* (1927):

"This being which we have termed Pithecanthropus has shown itself several times at our séances. One of us, at the séance of November 20, 1920, felt its large shaggy head press hard on his right shoulder and against his cheek. The head was covered with thick, coarse hair. A smell came from it like that of a deer or a wet dog. When one of the sitters put out his hand the pithecanthrope seized it and licked it slowly three times. Its tongue was large and soft. At other times we all felt our legs touched by what seemed to be frolicsome dogs."

Col. Norbert Ocholowicz, in his book on Kluski, quotes an article by Mrs. Hewat McKenzie:

"This ape was of such great strength that it could easily move a heavy bookcase filled with books through the room, carry a sofa over the heads of the sitters, or lift the heaviest persons with their chairs into the air to the height of a tall person. Though the ape's behaviour sometimes caused fear, and indicated a low level of intelligence, it was never malignant. Indeed it often expressed goodwill, gentleness and readiness to obey. . . . After a long stay a strong animal smell was noticed. It was seen for the last time at the séance of December 26, 1922, in the same form as in 1919 and making the same sounds of smacking and scratching."

McKenzie also writes of a small animal reminding the sitters of the "weasel" so often sensed at Guzyk's séances: "It used to run quickly over the table on to the sitters' shoulders, stopping every moment and smelling their hands and faces with a small, cold nose; sometimes, as if frightened, it jumped from the table and rambled through the whole room, turning over small objects, and shuffling papers lying on the table and writing desk. It appeared at six or seven séances, and was last seen in June, 1923."

Charles Richet writes of Burgik in *Thirty Years of Psychical Research* (1923): "In the last séance that I had with him the phenomena were very marked. I held his left hand and M. de Gielski his right. He was quite motionless, and none of the experimenters moved at all. My trouser leg was strongly pulled and a strange, ill-defined form that seemed to have paws like those of a dog or small monkey climbed on my knee. I could feel its weight very light and something like the muzzle of an animal (?) touched my cheek. It was moist and made a grunting noise like a thirsty dog."

Col. E. R. Johnson reported in *Light* (November 11, 1922) of a séance with **Etta Wriedt,**

"It was quite common to meet one's departed dogs. I had one of these, a very small terrier, placed on my knees. It remained there for about a minute, and both its weight and form were all recognised. It was not taken away but seemed gradually to evaporate or melt. Two others, a large retriever and a medium-sized terrier, came very often, and all three barked with their direct voices in tones suitable to their sizes and breeds. Other sitters saw, heard and were touched by them. Those three had died in India some 30 years previously."

The flight of birds was often heard in séances with D. D. Home and later with the Marquis **Scotto Centurione.** A tame flying squirrel was materialized by "Honto," an Indian woman control, in the séances of the Eddy brothers.

Two triangular areas of light, with curved angles like butterfly wings, audibly flitting and flapping, were noticed in the February 24, 1924, séance of "Margery" (Mina Crandon). The flying creature, said to be Susie, a tame bat of the control "Walter," performed strange antics. The wings would hover over roses on the table, pick one up, approach a sitter and hit him over the head with it. Susie pulled the hair of the sitters, pecked at their faces, and flapped her wings in their eyes. Another large, beetlelike area of light that scrambled about the table with a great deal of flapping was called by "Walter" his Nincompoop. Peculiar motions were also performed by a patch of light said to be a tame bear, over a curtain pole. Clicking and whizzing it toboganed down the pole and climbed back again. Nothing definite could be established about these curious animated patches of light.

"Materialisation of both beasts and birds sometimes appeared," writes Gambier Bolton in his book *Ghosts in Solid Form* (1914), "during our experiments, the largest and most startling being that of a seal which appeared on one occasion when Field-Marshal Lord Wolseley was present. We suddenly heard a remarkable voice calling out some absurd remarks in loud tones, finishing off with a shrill whistle. 'Why, that must be our old parrot,' said the lady of the house. 'He lived in this room for many years, and would constantly repeat those very words.'

"A small wild animal from India which had been dead for three years or more, and had never been seen or heard of by the Sensitive, and was known to only one sitter, suddenly ran out from the spot where the Sensitive was sitting, breathing heavily and in a state of deep trance, the little creature uttering exactly the same cry which it had always used as a sign of pleasure during its Earth life. It has shown itself altogether on about ten different occasions, staying in the room for more than two minutes at a time, and then disappearing as suddenly as it had arrived upon the scene.

"But on this occasion the lady who had owned it during its life called it to her by its pet name, and then it proceeded to climb slowly up on her lap. Resting there quietly for about half a minute it then attempted to return, but in doing so caught one of its legs in the lace with which the lady's skirt was covered. It struggled violently, and at last got itself free, but not until it had torn the lace for nearly three inches. At the conclusion of the experiment a medical man reported that there were five green-coloured hairs hanging in the torn lace, which had evidently become detached from the little animal's legs during its struggles. The lady at once identified the colour and the texture of the hairs, and this was confirmed by the other sitter—himself a naturalist—who had frequently seen and handled the animal during its Earth life. The five hairs were carefully collected, placed in tissue paper, and then shut up in a light-tight and damp-proof box. After a few days they commenced to dwindle in size, and finally disappeared entirely."

The story of a materialized seal is told in detail in *Light* (April 22, 1900), on the basis of Gambier Bolton's account before the **London Spiritualist Alliance.** The story goes as follows:

Being well known as a zoologist, Bolton received a note from an auctioneer asking if he would come to see a large seal that had been sent from abroad. "The poor thing is suffering; come round and see what you can do," wrote the seal's temporary owner, and being deeply interested in the welfare of animals of all kinds, Bolton at once obeyed. The poor creature had been harpooned, and was languishing in a large basket. He saw at once that it could not live, but wishing to do what he could to prolong its life, he dispatched it to the Zoological Gardens. Later in the day he called to see how it was faring, and found that it had been put into the seal tank. When Bolton visited the tank the seal rose from the water and gave him a long look, which, as he humorously suggested, seemed to indicate that the animal recognized him and was grateful for its treatment.

The seal died that night, and ten days later Bolton was at a séance at which **Frederick Craddock** was the medium. A number of people of social and scientific repute were present. Suddenly someone called out from the cabinet: "Take this great brute away, it is suffocating me." It was the seal! It came slowly from the cabinet, flopping and dragging itself as do seals, which (unlike sea-lions) cannot walk. It stayed close to Bolton for some moments and then returned to the cabinet and disappeared. "There is no doubt in my mind," said Bolton, "that it was the identical seal."

Asking about the *modus vivendi* of animal materializations, Bolton obtained the following answer from the spirit controls:

"Their actions are altogether independent of us. Whilst we are busily engaged in conducting our experiments with human entities who wish to materialise in your midst, the animals get into the room in some way which we do not understand, and which we cannot prevent; obtain, from somewhere, sufficient matter with which to build up temporary bodies; coming just when they choose; roaming about the room just as they please; and disappearing just when it suits them, and not before; and we have no power to prevent this so long as the affection existing between them and their late owners is so strong as it was in the instances which have come under our notice."

In contradiction to this information, Ocholowicz made it a point that at the Kluski séances the animal apparitions were seen to be in the charge of human apparitions. The only animal that seemed to be able to act independently of a keeper was the "pithecanthropus," he said. Generally the animal and human apparitions were not active at the same time. When the animal was fully materialized and active, the keeper was passive and kept in the background, and vice versa. The testimony of clairvoyants also suggested that when animal apparitions were seen the necessary link was furnished by a friend of the sitter.

Materializations and Apports

In experiments with medium **Thomas Lynn** at the British College of Psychic Science, objects were photographed while supposedly in the process of materialization. They showed flecks and masses of a luminous material, possessing stringlike roots. These light masses floated over a harp lying upon the table and were visible to all present. A fingerlike projection extended from a mass of this luminosity, and extended toward the harp as if to play it. As the photo plates were developed, a bone ring was seen to hang from the medium's nose, and an object similar to the top of an infant's nursing bottle appeared to dangle from his lips by a cord. The medium's features also seemed somewhat altered. At a second sitting, a two-pronged fishhook and a small ring materialized. The photo plates of this materialization showed that some round object proceeded from the region of the medium's solar plexus. It had often appeared in the photographs; from it a root or string seemed to extend to the object materializing. In this case the root was strangely twisted.

Similar observations of what seem in retrospect simple conjuring were reported by Karl Blacher of Riga University, with the apport medium "BX." (*Zeitschrift für Parapsychologie,* June 1933). In trance and under control, nails, screws, or pieces of iron would be visibly drawn out of his chest, armpits, or arms, as could be clearly observed by means of luminous screens. On one occasion wire more than a yard long was drawn from the man's bared chest; at another time Blacher himself caught hold of an end that was protruding from the same spot and drew out a long, leather strap. At another sitting the medium produced a heavy slab of metal from his chest and from his left arm a piece of wrought steel weighing more than three pounds.

In a day when there was serious speculation over the reality of apports and materialization, the problem of explaining the various phenomena was becoming more and more complex. Consider the case of **Lajos Pap,** the Budapest apport medium (*Light,* July 14, 1933). Before his first apport of a frog, for two days he reported that he heard continual croaking. It seemed to him to come from his stomach, and he kept asking people if they heard it. He claimed he heard the chirping of apported grasshoppers long before their arrival; and, before the apport of a large packet of needles, he said he felt pricking sensations over the back of his hand. Pap was discovered in fraud by researcher **Nandor Fodor.**

Modern Views of Materialization

All of the accounts of the marvels of materialization belong to the past; such astonishing phenomena are seldom reported in modern times. There is widespread acceptance of the fraudulence of materializations and related phenomena. The more blatant cases of fraud punctuate any discussions. One of the most impudent was that of **Charles Eldred,** who always took his "highly magnetized" armchair to séances. In 1906 the chair was examined and it was found that the back was really a box with a concealed lock and key. Inside was found a collapsible dummy, yards of cheesecloth for "ectoplasm," reaching rods, wigs, false beards, a music box (for "spirit music"), and even scent (for "spirit perfumes").

Almost all of the materialization mediums who produced results to the point of having their marvels recorded were later caught in fraud.

By World War II the only question remaining for a few who were still interested was whether mediums who had been caught impersonating spirits might also at times have produced genuine materialization phenomena. While it would be untenable to suppose that spirits influenced mediums to purchase wigs, masks, cheesecloth and other properties used fraudulently at séances, it is arguable that genuine mediums might have sometimes cheated to fulfill the expectation of sitters for consistently remarkable phenomena.

A notable example often held up as illustrative of this possibility was the famous Italian medium Eusapia Palladino, who seemed to have produced materialization phenomena under fairly strict conditions with a variety of more-or-less skilled observers, but was also known to take shortcuts and cheat if the opportunity arose. Another controversial medium was **Helen Duncan,** convicted in Edinburgh, Scotland, in 1933 for fraudulent mediumship in which an undervest was used as a materialized spirit. A few reputable observers believed she also produced genuine phenomena, although psychical researchers like **Harry Price** insisted that his photographs of "ectoplasm" clearly showed cheesecloth, rubber gloves, and pictures of heads clipped from magazine covers. Price did not discover how the mediums hid these objects but theorized that the cheesecloth was swallowed and regurgitated, other props perhaps being manipulated by accomplices.

However, the days of materialization mediums are clearly over. No modern medium has come forward with comparable phenomena to be tested in the more rigorous atmosphere of present times. Until they do, materialization must be consigned to the dustbin of rejected phenomena. No evidence of fraud was ever discovered on the part of one medium, D. D. Home, whose séances produced some of the most extraordinary phenomena, but his career now stands as an anomaly.

In his book *The Spiritualists: The Story of Florence Cook and William Crookes* (1962), Trevor H. Hall seeks to show that not only was the mediumship of Florence Cook fraudulent, but that William Crookes became her accomplice because he was infatuated with her. Crookes's psychical research occurred at the beginning of his career, before the unquestioned scientific accomplishments for which he was justly honored. Hall is a noted critic (even debunker) of psychical phenomena, and his book is well documented. The evidence is somewhat speculative and anecdotal, but does demonstrate how Crookes could have been hoodwinked by Cook. Some of Hall's colleagues, including K. M. Goldney and R. G. Medhurst, have attempted to salvage Crookes's reputation in light of Hall's charges.

Sources:

Abbot, David P. *Behind the Scenes with Mediums.* Chicago: Open Court, 1907. Rev. ed. 1926.

Aksakof, Alexander. *A Case of Partial Dematerialization of the Body of a Medium.* Boston, 1898.

Berger, Arthur S., and Joyce Berger. *The Encyclopedia of Parapsychology and Psychical Research.* New York: Paragon House, 1991.

Bisson, Juliette A. *Les Phénomènes dits de Matérialisations.* Paris, 1914.

Bolton, Gambier. *Ghosts in Solid Form.* London, 1914.

Brackett, E. A. *Materialized Apparitions.* Boston, 1886. London: William Rider, n.d.

Carrington, Hereward. *The American Séances with Eusapia Palladino.* New York: Helix, 1954.

———. *The Physical Phenomena of Spiritualism.* New York: Dodd, Mead, 1920. Reprint, London: T. Werner Laurie, n.d.

Colley, Thomas. *Confessions of a Medium.* London, 1882.

———. *Sermons of Spiritualism.* London, 1907.

Crookes, William. *Researches in the Phenomena of Spiritualism.* London: J. Burns, 1874.

Crossley, Alan Ernest. *The Story of Helen Duncan, Materialization Medium.* UK: Stockwell, 1975.

Delanne, Gabriel. *Les Apparitions Materialisées des Vivants et des Morts.* Paris, 1911.

Geley, Gustav. *Clairvoyance and Materialisation.* New York: George Doran, 1927. Reprint, New York: Arno Press, 1975.

———. *From the Unconscious to the Conscious.* London: William Collins, 1920.

Gray, Isa. *From Materialisation to Healing.* London: Regency Press, 1973.

Hall, Trevor H. *The Spiritualist: The Story of Florence Cook and William Crookes.* London: Duckworth, 1962. Reprinted as *The Medium and the Scientist: The Story of Florence Cook and William Crookes.* Buffalo, N.Y.: Prometheus Books, 1984.

Henry, T. Shekleton. *Spookland: A Record of Research and Experiment in the Much Talked of Realm of Mystery.* Chicago, 1902.

Marryat, Florence. *There Is No Death.* 1891. Reprint, New York: Causeway Books, 1973.

Medhurst, R. G., ed. *Crookes and the Spirit World: A Collection of Writings by or Concerning the Work of Sir William Crookes, O.M., F.R.S. in the Field of Psychical Research.* New York: Taplinger; London: Souvenir Press, 1972.

Medium, A. [A. Lunt]. *Mysteries of the Séance.* Boston, 1905.

Olcott, Henry S. *People from the Other World.* Hartford, Conn.: American Publishing, 1875. Reprint, Rutland, Vt.: Charles Tuttle, 1972.

Price, Harry, and Eric J. Dingwall, eds. *Revelations of a Spirit Medium.* London: Kegan Paul, 1922.

Putnam, Allen. *Flashes of Light from the Spirit-Land.* Boston, 1872.

Richet, Charles. *Thirty Years of Psychical Research.* New York: Macmillan, 1923. Reprint, New York: Arno Press, 1975.

Sargent, Epes. *Proof Palpable of Immortality.* Boston: n.p., 1876.

Schrenck-Notzing, Baron von. *Phenomena of Materialisation.* London: Kegan Paul, 1920. Reprint, New York: Arno Press, 1975.

Stein, Gordon. *Encyclopedia of Hoaxes.* Detroit: Gale Research, 1993.

Viereborne, A. *Life of James Riley.* Akron, Ohio: Werner, 1911.

Wolfe, N. B. *Startling Facts in Modern Spiritualism.* Cincinnati, Ohio: The Author, 1874.

Mather, Increase (1639–1723) and **Cotton** (1662–1728)

Father and son, two eminent divines of Boston, Massachusetts. The Mathers were among the first to respond to the wave of skepticism that assaulted Christianity at the end of the seventeenth century and emerged in the next century as Deism. Deism denied the possibility of human contact with what had traditionally been thought of as the supernatural. Both of the Mathers wrote books offering evidence of contact with the spiritual world as an apologetic for Christian faith.

Part of their understanding of the supernatural was supernatural evil. **Witchcraft,** which they equated with Satanism, was one major form taken by supernatural evil, and they saw evidence of witchcraft both among the Native Americans and members of the Boston urban community. This caused them to be seen as believers in the existence of widespread witchcraft throughout New England. Though counseling some degree of caution, especially in responding to the unsupported accounts of people claiming to be afflicted by a witch, they were early supporters of the inquiries at Salem Village (now Danvers), Massachusetts, in 1692. In fact, Increase Mather had chosen the governor, Sir William Phips, who was partly responsible for the Salem Witchcraft trials. However, as the trials proceeded, Cotton Mather especially became one of the strong forces arguing against the litigation. His personal visit with the governor was of great effect in this endeavor.

In the years immediately after the trials, as the people of Massachusetts came to see the error of what had occurred, the Mathers were accused by some of the more skeptical voices in the community, such as Robert Calef, as the real cause of the colony's disgrace. Only in the twentieth century, with the massive reevaluation of the whole of the witchcraft phenomenon in New England, has the Mathers' reputation been somewhat put into a more balanced perspective.

Sources:

Calef, Robert. *More Wonders of the Invisible World; or, The Wonders of the Invisible World Display'd in Five Parts.* London, 1700.

Mather, Cotton. *Memorable Provinces, Relating to Witchcraft and Possessions.* Boston, 1689.

———. *The Wonders of the Invisible World. Observations as Well Historical as Theological, upon the Nature, the Number, and the Operations of the Devil.* Boston: Benjamin Harris, 1693.

Mather, Increase. *Essay for the Recording of Illustrious Provinces.* Boston, 1684.

Mathers, Moina (1865–1928)

Moina Mathers, a leading member of the **Hermetic Order of the Golden Dawn** (HOGD), was largely responsible for the rituals of this ground-breaking magical organization. Born on Feburary 28, 1865, as Mina Bergson, she was the daughter of Jewish parents and the sister of noted philosopher Henri Bergson. Her brother was a professor at the University of Paris, the winner of a Nobel Prize (1927), and president of the Society of Psychical Research. He authored the noted volume *Creative Evolution,* in which he articulated his theory of elan vital, or life urge, an idea integral to magical thought. The elan vital was analogous to the subtle energy that allowed magic to work.

Mina was born and grew up in London, though the family lived briefly in Paris (1868–73). She had an artistic bent and in 1880 enrolled at the Slade School of Art, an affiliated school of the University of London. She had a stellar career and was awarded several certificates of merit. Upon receiving a certificate of completion in 1886 she opened a studio in London. The following year, at the British Museum, she met **Samuel L. MacGregor Mathers.** He was, at the time, doing the initial research that would lead to the founding of the HOGD. The Isis-Urania Temple, the first center of the HOGD, was opened in 1888 and Mina became the first initiate, taking the magical name *Vestigia Nulla Retrorsum.*

The couple was married in 1890, at which time Mina changed her name to Moina. Shortly after their marriage, at a gathering of people interested in psychic matters, Moina's ability as a clairvoyant was discovered. She subsequently played a key role in the development of the order. In 1891, Mathers claimed that he had made contact with the Secret Chiefs, from whom he would be receiving the material to construct the higher grades of the order. As Mathers increased his magical activity, Moina served as his priestess. More importantly, she perfected her abilities to contact the inner magical planes through the process known as scrying. It was she as a scryer who contacted magical sources of information and channeled material that supplied both the rituals and teaching material for the order.

In 1892, the Matherses settled in Paris, where Samuel had access to the large number of manuscripts in the Parisian libraries. They lived a financially restricted life and apparently a celibate one, as Mathers had been instructed to remain sexually pure as he pursued his important magical work. Moina also aided her husband in high political work centered both on his belief that the world was soon to enter a period of massive war and his hope for the independence of Scotland from England. She remained loyal to him through the organizational disruptions that plagued the order in the late 1890s, and was rewarded by losing some of her closest friends who broke with Mathers. Both were expelled from the HOGD when the largely British membership rebelled in 1900. Those members loyal to Mathers reorganized. Meanwhile in Paris, the Matherses formed the Isis Temple.

At the time of revolt of the British members, Mathers had selected a youthful **Aleister Crowley** as his agent. This alliance proved short-lived as Crowley broke with the Matherses in 1904. He would later publish HOGD material in his magazine, *Equinox,* leading Mathers to sue him. Following Mathers' death in 1918, Moina moved back to London where she founded and led the Alpha et Omega Lodge, though the days of its glory were already in the past. Never possessing a large membership, the HOGD ended its days in the 1920s splintered into various factions. Among Moina's notable actions as the leader of one faction was the expulsion of one of the order's American members, **Paul Foster Case,** who would later found a Golden Dawn-like organization, the **Builders of the Adytum.**

Moina Mathers passed away in London on July 25, 1928.

Sources:

Colquhoun, Ithell. *Sword of Wisdom: MacGregor Mathers and the Golden Dawn.* New York: Putnam, 1975.

Greer, Mary K. *The Women of the Golden Dawn: Rebels and Priestesses.* Rochester, Vt.: Park Street Press, 1995.

Howe, Ellic. *The Magicians of the Golden Dawn: A Documentary History of a Magical Order, 1887–1923.* York Beach, Maine: Samuel Weiser, 1972, 1985.

King, Francis. *Ritual Magic in England.* London: Neville Spearman, 1970.

Mathers, S(amuel) L(iddell) MacGregor (1854–1918)

Leading British occultist who was one of the founders of the Hermetic Order of the **Golden Dawn.** Born in Hackney, London, January 8, 1854, he lived with his mother at Bournemouth after the early death of his father. As a boy he was intensely interested in **symbolism** and **mysticism.** He claimed a romantic descent from Ian MacGregor of Glenstrae, an ardent Jacobite who was given the title of Comte de Glenstrae by Louis XIV.

Mathers became a Freemason on October 4, 1877, and a Master Mason on January 30, 1878, soon after his 24th birthday. His mystical interests led him to become a member of the **Societas Rosicruciana in Anglia** (Rosicrucian Society of England), where he was an associate of **William Wynn Westcott, William Robert Woodman,** and **Kenneth Mackenzie.** Together with Westcott and Woodman, Mathers founded the Golden Dawn in 1888. Meanwhile he lived in poverty after the death of his mother in 1885 and spent much time researching **occultism** at the British Museum Library, London.

Anna Kingsford introduced him to **Helena Petrovna Blavatsky.** Blavatsky invited him to collaborate in the building of the **Theosophical Society,** but he declined. In 1890 he married Moina Bergson, sister of the French philosopher **Henri Bergson.** Soon afterward he moved to Paris with his wife.

Mathers and his wife received a small allowance from Annie Horniman (daughter of the founder of the Horniman Museum, London, and a member of the Golden Dawn), so that he might continue his studies on behalf of the order. However, disputes developed between them on financial issues, and in December 1896 Mathers peremptorily expelled Horniman from the organization.

Mathers was also deceived by the charlatans **Theodore and Laura Horos,** who acquired Golden Dawn rituals from him for their own misuse. Other disagreements developed in the order, and during a dispute between Mathers and British officials, a youthful **Aleister Crowley** sided with Mathers and attempted to take over the London premises and documents. The poet **W. B. Yeats,** a noted member, played a prominent part in rejecting Crowley. Eventually Mathers himself was expelled from the Golden Dawn.

Mathers died November 20, 1918. The MacGregor Mathers Society was founded in Britain as a dining club for men only, membership by invitation. The society can be contacted at BM#Spirotos (M.M.S.), London W.C.1, England. Mathers's most lasting contributions to the magical revival of the twentieth century were his many translations of key magical texts, which he rescued from the obscurity into which they had fallen.

Sources:

Colquhoun, Ithell. *The Sword of Wisdom: MacGregor Mathers and The Golden Dawn.* New York: G. P. Putnam's Sons, 1975.

Mathers, S. L. MacGregor. *Astral Projection, Ritual Magic, and Alchemy.* Rochester, Vt.: Destiny Books, 1987.

———. *The Kabbalah Unveiled.* 1907. Reprint, London: Routledge and Kegan Paul, 1926.

———. *The Key of Solomon the King.* 1889. Reprinted as: *The Greater Key of Solomon.* Chicago: De Laurence, 1914.

Mathers, S. L. MacGregor, trans. *The Book of the Sacred Magic of Abra-Melin the Mage.* 1898. Reprint, Chicago: De Laurence, 1932. Reprint, New York: Causeway Books, 1974.

Mathur, Raghuvansh B(ahadur) (1918–)

Indian educator who has investigated parapsychological subjects. He was born September 17, 1918, at Lucknow, India. He studied at the University of Lucknow (B.A., 1937), London University (B.A. with honors, 1940; DPA, 1942; Ph.D., 1947), and Cambridge University (certificate in education, 1942). In 1953 he became the chair of the Department of Education, University of Lucknow. He was interested in **clairvoyance, telepathy,** and **psychokinesis,** and investigated **ESP** in school children.

Sources:

Pleasants, Helene, ed. *Biographical Dictionary of Parapsychology.* New York: Helix Press, 1964.

"Matikon"

A mystical work printed at Frankfurt in 1784, whose theories resemble the doctrines of the Brahmins. It speculated about the biblical creation story that before the Fall, Adam was a pure spirit, a celestial being, surrounded by a mystic covering that rendered him invulnerable to any poison or any power of the elements. The physical body, therefore, is but a coarse husk in which, having lost his primitive invulnerability, a human is sheltered from the elements. In his condition of perfect glory and perfect happiness, Adam was a natural king, ruling all things visible and invisible, and showing forth the power of the Almighty. He also bore "a fiery, two-edged, all-piercing lance"—a living word, which united all powers within itself, and by means of which he could perform all things.

Matter Passing through Matter

Matter interpenetrating matter has been claimed frequently as a **séance**-room phenomenon. It is involved in the marvel of **apports** and **teleportation** of the human body, and its validation under test conditions, which has never occurred, would help toward these greater phenomena becoming recognized. **Robert Hare**'s report of the passing of two small balls of platinum into two hermetically sealed glass tubes was not witnessed by others, and no repetition of the feat has ever been noted.

The possibility of such interpenetration is not generally admitted. The outstanding **medium D. D. Home** denied its possibility, and his **controls** declared that fissures or cracks are necessary to permit the passage of a solid body through another.

Sir William Crookes stated in "Notes of an Enquiry into the Phenomena called Spiritual" (*Quarterly Journal of Science,* January 1894):

"After several phenomena had occurred, the conversation turned upon some circumstances which seemed only explicable on the assumption that matter had actually passed through a solid substance. Thereupon a message was given by means of the alphabet: 'It [is] impossible for matter to pass through matter, but we will show you what we can do.' We waited in silence.

"Presently a luminous appearance was seen hovering over the bouquet of flowers, and then, in full view of all present, a piece of china-grass 15 inches long, which formed the centre ornament of the bouquet, slowly rose from the other flowers, and then descended to the table in front of the vase between it and Mr. Home. It did not stop on reaching the table, but went straight through it and we all watched it till it had entirely passed through. Immediately on the disappearance of the grass, my wife, who was sitting near Mr. Home, saw a hand come up from under the table between them, holding the piece of grass. It tapped her on the shoulder two or three times with a sound audible to all, then laid the grass on the floor and disappeared. Only two persons saw the hand, but all in the room saw the piece of grass moving about as I have described.

"During the time this was taking place Mr. Home's hands were seen by all to be quietly resting on the table in front of him. The place where the grass disappeared was 18 inches from his hands. The table was a telescope dining table, opening with a screw; there was no leaf in it, and the junction of the two sides formed a narrow crack down the middle. The grass had passed through this chink, which I measured and found to be barely one eighth of an inch wide. The stem of the piece of grass was far too thick to enable me to force it through this crack without injuring it, yet we had all seen it pass through quietly and smoothly; and on examination it did not show the slightest signs of pressure or abrasion."

However, some have argued for the reality of such a phenomenon. For example, the psychic researcher **Camille Flammarion** described the passing of a book through a curtain in a séance with **Eusapia Palladino** on November 21, 1898. A book was held up by Jules Bois before the curtain at about the height of a man, 24 inches from each side of the edge. It was seized by an invisible hand, and Flammarion, who observed the rear of the curtain, suddenly saw it coming through, upheld in the air, without hands or arms, for a space of one or two seconds. Then she saw it fall down.

There is some similarity between this observation of Flammarion and an account of Mrs. Speer (friend of **William Stainton Moses**) dated October 17, 1874: "Before the meeting Mr. Stainton Moses had taken three rings from his hands and threaded them on to his watch chain; his watch was on one end of the chain and a small pocket barometer on the other; both of these articles he placed in side pockets of his waistcoat, the rings hanging midway on his chain in full sight of the circle. We suddenly saw a pillar of light advance from a corner of the room, stand between me and Dr. S. then pass through the table to Mr. S. M. In a moment the figure flashed back again between us and threw something hard down upon the table. We passed our hands over the table, and found the rings had been removed from the medium's chain without his knowledge."

Mr. F. Fusedale, testifying to the **London Dialectical Society** in 1869, submitted an account of spirit manifestations in his own house: "The children and my wife would see the things they [the spirits] took (in particular a brooch of my wife's) appear to pass through solid substances, such as the wall or the doors, when they were taken from them; and they would take things out of the children's hands, as if in play, and hide them, and then after a little time return them again."

In a séance with the Italian medium **Francesco Carancini,** a dinner plate, covered with soot and out of the medium's reach, was placed in a padlocked wooden box held by one of the sitters.

In experiments with **Mary Baker Thayer,** Robert Cooper found a Japanese silk handkerchief belonging to one of the sitters and flowers that came from nowhere in the locked box he brought to the séance, and the key of which he retained (*Light,* March 15, 1902).

Gambier Bolton (author *Psychic Force,* 1904) noted:

"During my sixteen years of experiments, investigation into the question of the existence of this psychic force the apparent penetration of matter by matter had been such a common occurrence at our experimental meetings, that unless this happens to take place in connection with some unusually large and ponderous object that is suddenly brought into our midst, or removed from the place in which we are holding our meetings, I take but very little notice of it."

One of the occasions he took notice of came in a séance with the medium **Cecil Husk.** A light table was placed in the middle of the circle and was securely fastened by heavy baize curtains around the four sides, pinning the bottom of the curtain to the floor boards with drawing pins. The table was first heard rocking and tapping the floor boards, and in less than three minutes it had apparently passed through the curtain and was found in its old place, 21 feet away from the curtain.

After having been accused of **fraud,** the American medium **Etta Roberts,** in a test séance on September 3, 1891, was enclosed in a wire cage out of which many phantom forms issued. Finally Roberts herself stepped out through the padlocked and sealed door without breaking the fastenings. The same feat was witnessed by Dr. Paul Gibier, director of the Bacteriological Institute of New York, with Carrie M. Sawyer (Mrs. Salmon) in his own laboratory on three occasions. The trellis of the cage was found to be burning hot by several sitters.

Paranormal Knot-tying

Knots tied in an endless cord was the first phenomenon **Johann Zöllner** witnessed in his experiments with the medium **Henry Slade.** Zöllner made a loop of strong cord by tying the ends together. The ends projected beyond the knot and were sealed down to a piece of paper. In the séance room he hung the loop around his neck until the moment of experiment arrived. Then he took it off, placed the sealed knots on the table, placed his thumbs on each side of the knot, and dropped the loop over the edge of the table on his knees. Slade kept his hands in sight and touched Zöllner's hands above the table. A few minutes later four symmetrical single knots were found on the cord.

Zöllner's knot-tying experiment was repeated by Dr. Nichols with the medium **William Eglinton** in the presence of six observers. Nichols cut four yards of common brown twine from a fresh ball, tied the two ends together with a single knot, then passed each end through a hole in one of his visiting cards, tied another square knot, and firmly sealed this knot to the card. In daylight, the sealed card upon the center of the table, the loop hanging down upon the floor, a minute later five single knots were found tied in the string about a foot apart. (Both Slade and Eglinton were frequently caught in fraudulent mediumship.)

Paranormal Release and Movement of Clothing

The release of the medium from strong bonds without disturbing the knots or seals was claimed by the **Davenport brothers,** although justifiable skepticism surrounds their stage performances. The psychic feat was also claimed by Sir William Crookes in his experiments with **Florence Cook.**

A kindred demonstration, of which the Davenport brothers were the greatest exponents, was the taking on and off of coats while the medium's hands were held. In a letter to the London *Daily News,* Dion Boucicault, the famous English actor and author, spoke of a séance at his house on October 11, 1864, in which, by striking a light, the participants actually witnessed the coat of Mr. Fay, the fellow-medium of the Davenport brothers, flying off. "It was seen quitting him, plucked off him upwards. It flew up to the chandelier, where it hung for a moment and then fell to the ground. Mr. Fay was seen meanwhile bound hand and foot as before."

Robert Cooper wrote in his book *Spiritual Experiences* (1867):

"The coat of Mr. Fay has, scores of times, been taken from his back in my presence, and Mr. Fay at the time might be seen sitting like a statue with his hands securely tied behind him and the knots sealed. I have seen coats of various descriptions, from a large overcoat to a light paletot, put on in the place of his own in a moment of time, his hands remaining securely tied and the seal unbroken. I have known the coat that has been placed on Mr. Fay so small that it could only with difficulty be got off him. I have known a coat that was first placed on Mr. Fay transferred in a moment to the back of Ira Davenport, whose hands, like Mr. Fay's, were tied behind him, and the most curious part of the proceedings was that it was put on inside out. I have also known the waistcoat of Ira Davenport taken from under his coat, all buttoned up, with his watch and guard just as he wore it."

The same feat was witnessed in 1886 in Washington by **Alfred Russel Wallace** in a séance with **Pierre L. O. A. Keeler.**

Italian researcher **Cesare Lombroso** recorded a similar instance with Eusapia Palladino. An overcoat was placed on a chair beyond the reach of the medium whose hands and feet had been continuously controlled. Several objects from an inside pocket of the overcoat had been brought and laid on a phosphorescent cardboard on the table. All at once the medium began to complain of something about her neck and binding her tight. On light being produced it was found that she had the overcoat on.

Accounts of release from bonds and flying clothing must be treated with caution as they are stock feats of stage conjurers.

Ring Experiments and Chair Threading

Ring experiments and chair threading were claimed on many occasions. In October 1872 the *Religio-Philosophical Journal* of Chicago claimed to have witnessed this demonstration. The editor wrote: "We had the pleasure of attending a séance at which Capt. Winslow was the medium. The manifestations were very fine. One remarkable feat is the union of two solid iron rings, leaving them thus interlinked, and yet the metal perfectly sound."

In the majority of cases, however, this plain test was always shirked for the far less convincing demonstration of placing an iron ring on the sitter's arm after the clasping of the hands or of placing a ring too small to pass over the hand on the medium's wrist.

The medium Cecil Husk wore such a ring until his death. The **Society for Psychical Research,** London, investigated it and claimed that the ring could be forced off if the medium were chloroformed. George Wyld, a physician of Edinburgh, said the ring was specially made to Husk's order and secretly marked by him, and that he [Wyld] held the medium's hand tight while the ring was taken from him in the dark.

A similar wrought-iron ring was passed on to the ankle of the medium **F. F. Craddock.** It was very tight and caused him great discomfort and actual pain until it was filed off by a friendly blacksmith. Hearing of this occurrence, Gambier Bolton procured two welded iron rings, and visiting Craddock, he fastened his hands behind his back with strong tape, then led him to a chair and fastened both arms, above the elbows, to the back of the chair with strong tapes and double knots.

Bolton stated:

"Placing the two rings at his feet, I turned to the gas pendant hanging over our heads and lowered it somewhat, and before I had time to turn round again I heard the well-known ring of two pieces of iron being brought into sharp contact with each other, and walking up to him I found both rings on his wrist. To make sure that my eyes were not deceiving me. I pulled them strongly, struck one with the other, and found that they really were on his wrists; and I then carefully examined the tapes and found them not only secure, but so tight that his hands were swollen as a result of the tightness with which I had tied them. I stepped backwards, keeping my eyes on him, when suddenly with a crash both rings fell at my feet. To have withdrawn his hands and arms and replaced them in that time was a physical impossibility. On attempting to untie the tapes I found that I had pulled the knots so tightly that it was only after cutting them with a finely pointed pair of scissors, that I was able to release his hands once more, his wrists being marked for some time with a deep red line as the result."

In his pamphlet *Les Preuves scientifique de la survivance de l'âme* (1905), Dr. L. Th. Chazarain wrote of his experience in meetings organized in Paris by Dr. Puel, director of the *Revue des Sciences Psychiques*: "I took the ring which had been laid on the table and passed it round her right wrist. Immediately afterwards I took hold of the corresponding hand, and waited, holding it firmly between my own. At the end of eight or ten minutes she uttered a cry, like a cry of pain or fright, and at the same instant she woke and the ring was seen on the ground." August Reveillac, observing the same effect, found the fallen ring, when picked up, almost burning hot.

Col. W. A. Danskin described a séance in Baltimore in *How and Why I Became a Spiritualist* (1869), in which a secretly marked iron ring, seven inches smaller than the circumference of the medium's head, was repeatedly placed around the medium's neck. From the *Banner of Light* (January 11, 1868), he reproduced the following testimony, signed by thirty-two names: "We, the undersigned, hereby testify that we have attended the social meetings referred to; and that a solid iron ring, seven inches less in size than the young man's head was actually and unmistakably placed around his neck. There was as the advertisement claims, no possibility of fraud or deception, because the ring was freely submitted to the examination of the audience, both before and while on the neck of the young man."

The medium was a 19-year-old boy. Danskin further wrote:

"Once, when only three persons were present—the medium, a friend and myself—we sat together in the dark room. I held the left hand of the medium, my friend held his right hand, our other hands being joined; and while thus sitting, the ring, which I had thrown some distance from us on the floor, suddenly came round my arm. I had never loosened my hold upon the medium, yet that solid iron ring, by an invisible power, was made to clasp my arm."

The medium **Charles Williams** often demonstrated the ring test. In *Some Reminiscences: An Account of Startling Spiritual Manifestations* (1890), A. Smedley described several instances during which he used a ring that he secretly marked. On one occasion, for example, Col. Lean (husband of **Florence Marryat**) mentally asked the control **"John King"** to fetch the half-hoop diamond ring from his wife's finger and place it on his. The ring, wrote Florence Marryat, "was worn between my wedding ring and a heavy gold snake ring and I was holding the hand of my neighbor all the time and yet the ring was abstracted from between the other two and transferred to Colonel Lean's finger without my being aware of the circumstance."

In experiments with **Maria Vollhardt** in Berlin, two highly skeptical members of the Medical Society for Psychic Research, holding the hands of the medium at either side, found two unbroken wooden rings about their arms.

Robert Cooper, in a séance with the **Eddy brothers,** experienced an electric shock at his elbow and found two iron rings on his arm, which was held by the medium (reported in *Light,* March 15, 1902).

Count Perovsky-Petrovo-Solovovo took a marked ring to a séance with the Russian medium **S. F. Sambor** on November 15, 1894. The ring was placed on M. Vassilief's arm when he was holding the medium's hands (*Rebus,* No. 47, 1894). In séances with the same medium at the Spiritist Club, St. Petersburg, a Dr. Pogorelski suddenly felt a blow on his right arm (close to the shoulder) and felt a chair passed onto his right arm. He held Sambor's hands by interlacing the fingers so that "it was impossible for our hands to become separated, even for a hundredth part of a second, without my feeling it." The experiment was repeated with another sitter whose hand was tied to Sambor's by means of a nearly ten yards long linen ribbon on the ends of which seals were placed.

John S. Farmer, William Eglinton's biographer, wrote in his *Twixt Two Worlds* (1886) that in June 1879 at Mrs. Gregory's house, "in the presence of Mr. Eglinton and a non-professional medium, two chairs were threaded at the same moment of time upon the arms of two sitters, each of whom was then holding the hand of the medium. Mr. Sergeant Cox was holding the hand of Mr. Eglinton and the back of the chair passed through his arm, giving him the sensation of a blow against the elbow when it did so. When a light was struck the chair was seen hanging on Mr. Sergeant Cox's arm and his hand was still grasping that of Mr. Eglinton. An immediate examination of the chair showed that the back of it was in good condition, with none of the woodwork loose or broken."

In *Planchette; or, The Despair of Science* (1880), **Epes Sargent** quoted many testimonies of similar occurrences with Charles Read of Buffalo and other mediums. **Gambier Bolton** wrote of his experience with Cecil Husk as follows:

"With Mrs. Cecil Husk, on half a dozen occasions, in my own room and using my own chairs, I have held both hands of another experimenter with my two hands, about fifteen inches from the top of the back of one of the chairs, when with a sudden snap the back of the chair has passed over our wrists and has been seen by twelve to sixteen other observers hanging from our arms, in gas light, my hands never for an instant releasing those of my fellow-experimenters."

Well-documented experiments in the claimed demonstration of the passage of matter through matter were carried out in June and July 1932, in the **"Margery"** circle in Boston (see also **Mina Crandon**). The phenomena, as reported by William H. Button in the *Journal* of the American Society for Psychical Research (August–September 1932) consisted of the removal of a variety of objects from locked or sealed boxes and the introduction of various objects into such boxes. They were undertaken to confirm some of the results of the Zöllner experiments.

The most astonishing phenomenon of the "Margery" mediumship was the interlocking rings. **Sir Oliver Lodge** had suggested the paranormal linking of two rings made of different woods might provide an irrefutable evidence of psychic force. The rings were duly provided, one of white wood and the other of red mahogany. At a séance with "Margery" in 1932, the rings were interlocked. According to Thomas R. Teitze in his book *Margery* (1973), the Irish poet **W. B. Yeats** was present at this séance. The feat of linking two rings made from different woods was apparently repeated. One set was sent to Sir Oliver Lodge for independent verification, but unfortunately arrived cracked and broken, presumably damaged in the post.

Another set of interlocked rings of different woods was shown to the British Spiritualist journalist **Hannen Swaffer** when he visited the Crandons in 1934. The rings were photographed and show one of white wood and the other of red mahogany. They passed into the care of William Button, then president of the **American Society for Psychical Research,** and were kept in a sealed, glass-covered box. On a return visit to Boston in 1936, Swaffer asked to see the rings again, but when they were taken out of the box it was found that one of the rings was broken.

In 1979 the **SORRAT** group formed by **John G. Neilhardt** attempted to validate such paranormal linkages in an unassailable experiment. Since it could be argued that wooden rings might be cleverly separated along the grain and glued together again, parapsychologist **W. E. Cox** proposed seamless rings made from a single layer of ordinary leather. It would not be possible to cut and rejoin leather without trace of manipulation. In the event, the experiment was successful and film records show the paranormal materializing and dematerializing process. The linkages, however, were not permanent, as the leather rings separated again after a few seconds, a curious echo of the "Margery" experiments.

Sources:

Richards, John Thomas. *SORRAT: A History of the Neilhardt Psychokinesis Experiments, 1961–1981.* Metuchen, N.J.: Scarecrow Press, 1982.

Teitze, Thomas. *Margery.* New York: Harper & Row, 1973.

Transcendental Physics: An Account of Experimental Investigations from the Scientific Treatises of Johann Carl Friedrich Zöllner. Translated by Charles C. Massey. London: W. H. Harrison, 1882. Reprint, New York: Arno Press, 1976.

Maxwell, Joseph (ca. 1933)

Attorney-general at the Court of Appeal at Bordeaux and prominent French psychic investigator. The chance reading of a book on **Theosophy** gave him the first impulse to study **occult** mysteries. He then found a remarkable medium in Limoges. The result, however, was unconvincing. But he realized that certain manifestations could only be studied with the knowledge of nervous and mental pathology, and for six years he studied at the University of Bordeaux for a medical degree.

As a trained investigator he had the rare fortune to find a **medium** in a friend, a Mr. Meurice, who could produce telekinetic phenomena in good light. He obtained further good results with a Miss Agullana of Bordeaux, two young mediums of Agen, and others. In 1895 in l'Agnelas, he and **Eugene Rochas,** Dariex, Sabatier, Count de Gramont, and Watteville attended experiments with **Eusapia Palladino.**

After an extensive study of the phenomena of **raps,** he wrote in *Les Phénoménes psychiques* (Paris, 1903) about the reality of **telekinesis:** "I am certain that we are in the presence of an unknown force; its manifestations do not seem to obey the same laws as those governing other forces more familiar to us; but I have no doubt they obey some law." He admitted that the force is intelligent but wondered if that intelligence did not come from the experimenters. His theory was that a kind of collective consciousness produced the intellectual results. The book, the result of ten years of research, is a valuable contribution to psychical literature.

Sources:

Maxwell, Joseph. *La Divination.* Paris: E. Flammarion, 1927.

———. *La Magie.* Paris: E. Flammarion, 1922.

———. *Les Phénomènes psychiques* (Metapsychical Phenomena). London: Duckworth, 1905.

Maya

A term used in Hinduism to denote the illusory nature of the world or empirical reality. It is to be distinguished from delusion, since it implies that there is something present, although not what it seems to be. According to the Vedas, the ancient scriptures of India, the divine infinity of Brahman (impersonal absolute) or Brahma (creative God) is real and is present in empirical reality but is veiled by the illusory power of *maya.*

Mayavi-rupa

According to **Theosophy** and drawing on Hindu religious insights, the *mayavi-rupa* is the invisible part of the physical body. Its appearance is exactly similar to that of the physical body.

Maynard, Henrietta Sturdevant (1841–1892)

American inspirational speaker known as Nettie Colburn before her marriage. She was born in Bolton, Connecticut, in 1841. **Abraham Lincoln** had a high opinion of her gift and was, to an appreciable extent, influenced by her **trance** exhortations in the issue of the antislavery proclamation. Maynard described her meetings with the president in her book *Was Abraham Lincoln a Spiritualist?* (1891).

She visited Washington in spring 1862 in order to see her brother, then in the Federal Army hospital. Lincoln's wife had a sitting with Maynard and was enormously impressed. The next day she sent a carriage to bring the **medium** to see the president.

In a state of trance, the medium delivered a powerful address relating to the forthcoming Emancipation Proclamation, forcefully urging Lincoln "not to abort the terms of its issue and not to delay its enforcement as a law beyond the opening of the year; and he was assured that it was to be the crowning event of his administration and his life," even though he was being strongly counseled by certain individuals to defer the matter. According to reports, President Lincoln acknowledged the pressures upon him and was deeply impressed by the medium's message.

Maynard died at White Plains, New York, June 27, 1892.

Sources:

Maynard, Henrietta S. *Was Abraham Lincoln a Spiritualist?* Philadelphia, Pa.: R. C. Hartranft, 1891. Reprint, London: Psychic Book Club, 1917.

Mayne, Alan James (1927–)

British researcher and consultant. He was born November 29, 1927, at Cambridge, England, and studied at Oxford University (B.A., 1949; B.S., 1951; M.A., 1953). He held a variety of positions in industry, including work as scientific officer, United Kingdom Atomic Energy Authority (1951–56); research statistician and consultant with A. C. Nielsen Co., Oxford (1956–59); and research fellow with Electronic Computing Laboratory, University of Leeds (1960–61). He edited *The Scientist Speculates,* an anthology, and wrote articles on mathematical statistics and operational research.

Mayne also studied parapsychological phenomena and published contributions in the *Journal of the British Society of Dowsers.* He acted as director of research for the **Society of Metaphysicians** (Archer's Court, Hastings, Sussex, England) and was president of the **Institute of Parascience** (Spryton, Lifton, Devon, England) on its foundation in 1971.

Sources:

Berger, Arthur S., and Joyce Berger. *The Encyclopedia of Parapsychology and Psychical Research.* New York: Paragon House, 1991.

Mayne, Alan James. "The Promotion of Research." *Journal* of the Society for Psychical Research 42 (1963).

Pleasants, Helene, ed. *Biographical Dictionary of Parapsychology.* New York: Helix Press, 1964.

Ma Yoga Shakti International Mission

A Hindu organization founded in 1979 by Maha Mandaleshwar Ma Yoga Shakti Saraswati, an Indian female guru who immigrated to the United States in 1977. She established ashrams in Ozone Park, New York, and Palm Bay and Deerfield Beach, Florida, and alternates her time between them. She has also organized four ashrams in India: Bombay, Calcutta, Delhi, and Gondia.

She teaches a balanced approach to all forms of **yoga**—hatha, rajah, bhakti, and karma. Devotional services, classes and retreats are held at all centers.

Ma Yoga Shakti has published several books or commentaries, including: *Yoga Syzygy, Techniques of Meditation, Shri Satya Narayan Katha, Adhyaatma Sandesh—Spiritual Message,* and *Invisible Psychic Lotuses,* which the mission distributes. It also publishes the *Yogashakti Mission Newsletter.* The address of the New York center is 114-41 Lefferts Blvd., South Ozone Park, NY 11420.

Sources:

Yoga Shakti, Ma. *Adyaatma Sandesh—A Spiritual Message.* Melbourne, Fla.: Yogashakti Mission, 1991.

———. *Invisible Psychic Lotuses.* Bombay: Yogashakti Mission, n.d.

———. *Shri Satya Narayan Katha.* Melbourne, Fla.: Yogashakti Mission, 1979.

———. *Techniques of Meditation.* New York: Ma Yoga Shakti Mission, 1994.

———. *Yoga Para La Salud Fisica Mental.* New York: Yogashakti Publications, 1997.

———. *Yoga Syzygy.* Gherand Samhita Hatha Yoga, New York: Ma Yoga Shakti International Mission, 1984.

Mazdaznan Temple Association

A Zoroastrian group founded in 1890 by Ottoman Zar-Adhusht Hanish (1854–1936). The name Mazdaznan is derived from the Persian *Mazda* and *Znan* which Hanish translated as "master thought," although this interpretation might be questioned by Persian scholars. As a Zoroastrian group, members affirm the monotheistic faith in the Lord God Mazda, the creator of humanity. God finds expression in the Holy Family of Father (the male creative principle), Mother (the procreative female principle), and Child (destiny/salvation).

Hanish was born in Leipzig, Germany. When only a boy, he was supposed to have been taken to a Persian monastery at Math-El-Kharman and taught every major art and science, including occultism. Early in this century, Hanish settled in Chicago, where he founded Mazdaznan. In 1916 he moved to Los Angeles. A European headquarters was established as a colony called Aryana (admitting only white-skinned Aryans) at Herliberg, Lake Zurich.

The Mazdaznans believe that their task is to reclaim the earth and turn it into a paradise, a place suitable for even God to dwell. The process of reclaimation begins with the human body. Hanish taught a series of spiritual exercises centering on breathing and regular prayers and chants. A vegetarian diet is recommended and daily exercise prescribed.

In the 1980s the group moved its headquarters to California. Members are scattered across North America and a number of foreign countries. Hanish wrote several books that embody the group's beliefs and practices. A new magazine is currently being worked on called, *All Is Well.* Address: 4364 Bonita Rd., #617 Bonita, CA 91902. Website: http://www.mazdaznan.org/.

Sources:

Ecroyd, H. R. "A Strange Adventure in Switzerland." *The Quest* 21, 1 (October 1939).

Hanish, O. Z. A. *Health and Breath Culture.* Chicago: Sun Worshipper Publishing, 1902.

———. *Inner Studies.* Mokelumne Hill, Calif.: Health Research, 1963.

———. *Mazdaznan: What It Teaches.* Los Angeles: Mazdaznan Press, 1969.

———. *The Philosophy of Mazdaznan.* Los Angeles: Mazdaznan Press, 1960.

Mazdaznan. http://www.mazdaznan.org/. March 8, 2000.

McConnell, Robert A. (1914–)

Biophysicist and parapsychologist who was president of the **Parapsychological Association** in 1958. McConnell was born in Pennsylvania in 1914, and studied at Carnegie Institute of Technology (B.S., physics, 1935) and the University of Pittsburgh (Ph.D., physics, 1947). He worked as a physicist with Gulf Research and Development, at a U.S. Naval aircraft factory (1937–41), and at the Massachusetts Institute of Technology Radiation Laboratory, where he was a group leader (1944–46). While at MIT he read of **J. B. Rhine**'s work in **parapsychology** and, intrigued, delved into the literature of **psychical research.**

After graduation McConnell joined the faculty at the University of Pittsburgh where he remained until his retirement in 1984, when he was named research professor emeritus. In addition to his work in parapsychology, he also specialized in radar moving target indication, theory of the iconoscope, and ultrasonic microwaves. He was unusual for a parapsychologist in an academic appointment in that he was able to spend the majority of his research time in parapsychological work throughout his active career. He was a founding member of the Parapsychological Association and was the organization's first president (1957–58). He later served a second term in that office (1977–78).

In addition to his articles in technical journals, McConnell has written widely on parapsychology. He contributed chapters to a Ciba Foundation symposium on *Extrasensory Perception* (1956) and a symposium edited by Eileen J. Garrett, *Does Man Survive Death?* During his retirement he wrote *Parapsychology in Retrospect: My Search for the Unicorn* (1987).

Sources:

Berger, Arthur S., and Joyce Berger. *The Encyclopedia of Parapsychology and Psychical Research.* New York: Paragon House, 1991.

McConnell, Robert A. *Encounters with Parapsychology.* Pittsburgh, Pa.: The Author, 1982.

———. *ESP Curriculum Guide.* New York: Simon & Schuster, 1971.

———. *An Introduction to Parapsychology in the Context of Science.* Pittsburgh, Pa.: The Author, 1983.

———. *Parapsychology and Self-Deception in Science.* Pittsburgh, Pa.: The Author, 1982.

———. *Parapsychology in Retrospect: My Search for the Unicorn.* Pittsburgh, Pa.: The Author, 1987.

McConnell, Robert A., and Gertrude Schmeidler. *ESP and Personality Patterns.* New Haven, Conn.: Yale University Press, 1958.

Pleasants, Helene, ed. *Biographical Dictionary of Parapsychology.* New York: Helix Press, 1964.

McDonnell Laboratory for Psychic Research

Parapsychology laboratory at Washington University in St. Louis, Missouri, funded from 1979 to 1986 by a grant from the McDonnell Foundation. The director of the laboratory was Peter R. Phillips, who has worked on high energy physics, cosmology, and **parapsychology.** Address: Washington University, Parapsychology laboratory, One Brookings Dr., St. Louis, MO 63130.

McDougall, William (1871–1938)

Professor of psychology successively at Oxford University, Harvard University, and Duke University who made important contributions to **parapsychology.** He was born June 22, 1871, in Lancashire, England, and was educated at Owens College, Manchester, St. Thomas Hospital, London, and Cambridge, Oxford, and Göttingen universities. He was a fellow of St. John's College, Cambridge (1898; hon. fellow, 1938), a reader at University College London, and a reader in mental philosophy and fellow at Corpus Christi College, Oxford, before becoming a professor at Harvard.

In 1920 he became president of the **Society for Psychical Research,** and the following year became president of the **American Society for Psychical Research** (ASPR). He sat on the Scientific American Committee for the investigation of the mediumship of **"Margery"** (**Mina S. Crandon**) and was a keen but reserved investigator who took great care initially not to commit himself to affirming the genuine occurrence of the supernormal. McDougall later came to believe that Margery's phenomena were created fraudulently and joined with other members of the ASPR to protest the organization's public identification with her. In 1925 he joined with others in the founding of the **Boston Society for Psychical Research.**

McDougall was one of the leading psychologists of his time and the author of numerous books. He contributed an article on hypnotism to the eleventh edition of the *Encyclopaedia Britannica* (1910), as well as articles on **hallucination, suggestion,** and **trance** (11th–14th editions).

His continuing interest in **psychical research** was a dominant influence in the development of modern parapsychology. He is most remembered for the period he spent as head of the Psychology Department at Duke University (1927–38), and he encouraged **J. B. Rhine** in the founding of the **Parapsychology Laboratory,** from which modern research in laboratory controlled experiments developed. He also authored a variety of articles on parapsychology, defended the place of parapsychology as an academic discipline, and co-edited the *Journal of Parapsychology* (1937–38). He died November 28, 1938.

Sources:

Berger, Arthur S., and Joyce Berger. *The Encyclopedia of Parapsychology and Psychical Research.* New York: Paragon House, 1991.

McDougall, William. *Body and Mind: A History and Defense of Animism.* London: Methuen, 1911.

———. "The Case of Sally Beauchamp." *Proceedings* of the Society of Psychical Research 19–20 (1905–07).

———. "Further Observations on the 'Margery' Case." *Journal* of the American Society for Psychical Research 19 (1925).

———. "The Margery Mediumship." *Psyche* 26 (1926).

———. *Modern Materialism and Emergent Evolution.* New York: D. Van Nostrand, 1929.

———. "The Need for Psychical Research." *Harvard Graduate Magazine.* Reprinted in *ASPR Journal* 17 (1923).

———. *The Riddle of Life.* London: Methuen, 1938.

Pleasants, Helene, ed. *Biographical Dictionary of Parapsychology.* New York: Helix Press, 1964.

McKenzie, James Hewat (1869–1929)

Founder of the **British College of Psychic Science.** McKenzie was born in Edinburgh, Scotland, November 11, 1869. He began the study of the paranormal in 1900 as a result of his dissatisfaction with the failure of science or theology to throw any light on human destiny. Years of private study and investigation followed. The fruit of this period of research was a series of lectures in London, Edinburgh, and Glasgow (1915), a book, *Spirit Intercourse: Its Theory and Practice* (1916), and a pamphlet *If a Soldier Die* (1916), which had a wide circulation. In 1917 he toured the eastern United States and the Midwest as far as Chicago in search of **mediums.** After spending a good deal of time in California, he returned home in 1920.

McKenzie raised money to found the British College of Psychic Science in 1920. He started *Psychic Science,* the college's quarterly journal, two years later. In the same year he and his wife, Barbara, who collaborated in all his investigations, visited Germany, Austria, and Poland and had sittings with many of the best psychics on the Continent. In Warsaw they sat with the materializing medium **Franek Kluski** and secured plaster casts of materialized hands, which they brought to London. These casts were the only ones in England at the time. They also brought **Maria Silbert** of Graz, Austria, and a **poltergeist** medium to the college for experimental work. A devoted Spiritualist, McKenzie had no scientific training. Characterized by a strong, assertive personality, he was known to cover up evidence of **fraud** when he discovered it.

McKenzie had a deep interest in physical mediumship in all its aspects and a profound knowledge of the conditions necessary for good results. On many occasions he was asked to investigate cases of **hauntings** and disturbances and was able to clear up annoying conditions. He also made an intensive study of **trance** mediumship with **Gladys Osborne Leonard** and **Eileen Garrett** and assisted in the development of the psychic talents of several other trance mediums. He was convinced that only through psychic "facts" was there any proved knowledge of **survival,** a belief he affirmed continuously in his writings and lectures. During the years in which he acted as honorary president of the college, it was the first substantial organization in London to become a center for psychic demonstration and instruction.

McKenzie died August 29, 1929, in London. Barbara McKenzie, who also brought a fine intellect and understanding to the study of psychic phenomena, was honorary secretary of the college until 1929, and then became honorary president for one year, being succeeded by **Rose Champion de Crespigny.**

Sources:

Berger, Arthur S., and Joyce Berger. *The Encyclopedia of Parapsychology and Psychical Research.* New York: Paragon House, 1991.

Hankey, Muriel. *J. Hewat McKenzie: Pioneer of Psychical Research.* London: Aquarian Press, 1963.

McMahan, Elizabeth Anne (1924–)

Assistant professor of zoology, also active in the field of **parapsychology.** She was born May 5, 1924, at Mocksville, North Carolina, and studied at Duke University (M.A., 1948) and the University of Hawaii (Ph.D., 1960). She was a research fellow at the **Parapsychology Laboratory** at Duke University (1948–54); in 1960 she joined the faculty of the department of zoology at the University of North Carolina. In addition to her many articles on entomology, she published a number of papers on parapsychology, based on her own investigations in **telepathy, psychokinesis,** and **precognition.** She was a charter member of the **Parapsychological Association.**

Sources:

Berger, Arthur S., and Joyce Berger. *The Encyclopedia of Parapsychology and Psychical Research.* New York: Paragon House, 1991.

McMahan, Elizabeth Anne. "An Experiment in Pure Telepathy." *Journal of Parapsychology* 10 (1946).

———. "PK Experiments with Two-Sided Objects." *Journal of Parapsychology* 9 (1945).

McMahan, Elizabeth Anne, and E. K. Bates. "Report of Further Marchesi Experiments." *Journal of Parapsychology* 18 (1954).

McMahan, Elizabeth Anne, and J. B. Rhine. "Extrasensory Perception of Cards in an Unknown Location." *Journal of Parapsychology* 12 (1948).

———. "A Review of the Evidence for Dowsing." *Journal of Parapsychology* 11 (1947).

———. "A Second Zagreb-Durham ESP Experiment." *Journal of Parapsychology* 11 (1947).

Pleasants, Helene, ed. *Biographical Dictionary of Parapsychology.* New York: Helix Press, 1964.

McMoneagle, Joseph (1946–)

Joseph McMoneagle, a psychic known for his **remote viewing** abilities and participation in the **government-sponsored research on parapsychology,** was born in Miami, Florida on January 10, 1946. After high school he enter the army and soon was assigned to the Army Security Agency. After 13 years of service overseas, in 1977 he returned to the United States to work with the Intelligence and Security Command where he became a warrant officer.

In 1978 he was recruited into the secret psychic spy unit of the government program, later known as the STAR GATE Project, designed to develop an operative intelligence operation using remote viewing. He worked with the unit until his retirement in 1984. He moved to rural Virginia where he met and eventually married Nancy Lea Honeycutt, the step-daughter of **Robert A. Monroe,** known for his out-of-body experiences. She was the director of the **Monroe Institute for Applied Sciences.**

Following his retirement, McMoneagle was also hired by the Cognitive Sciences Laboratory, responsible for the research and development side of the STAR GATE Project. He worked both as a remote viewer and as a research assistant. He continues as an employee of the laboratory. McMoneagle has written two nonfiction books about remote viewing, *Mind Trek* (1993) and *The Ultimate Time Machine* (1998). In the wake of the declassification of data on the government's paranormal research in 1995, McMoneagle has made numerous media appearances discussing the subject matter.

McMoneagle and his wife Nancy have founded Intuitive Intelligence Applications, Inc., through which offers astrological consultant and remote viewing services and programs in paranormal research.

Sources:

McMoneagle, Joseph. *Mind Trek.* Charlottesville, Va.: Hampton Roads Publishing Co., 1993. Rev. ed., 1997.

———. *The Ultimate Time Machine: A Remote Viewer's Perception of Time, and Predictions for the New Millennium.* Charlottesville, Va. : Hampton Roads Publishing Co., 1998.

McNallen, Stephen A. (1948–)

Stephen A. McNallen, the pioneer advocate of modern Norse Neo-Paganism in North America, was born in Breckenridge, Texas, on October 15, 1948. He attended Midwestern University in Wichita Falls, Texas, and during his college days discovered the deities of the ancient Norsemen and began to identify with the Viking element in his own ancestry. He eventually dedicated himself to Odin and the whole of the Norse pantheon, though he kept this commitment to himself and a few friends. However, in the winter of 1971–72, as his college career was coming to an end, he released the first issue of *The Runestone.* Previously he had placed an ad in **Fate** magazine, and compiled a list of potential subscribers from it. From those who responded he founded the Viking Brotherhood.

McNallen completed his degree in political science and was commissioned as a second lieutenant in the army. He did his basic training at Fort Benning (Georgia) and was assigned to a unit in Germany, where he served for the remainder of his term. The Viking Brotherhood continued at a minimal level until he returned to the States in 1976. He settled in California and began to meet with Norse Neo-Pagans in the San Francisco Area.

McNallen actively developed his understanding of the **Asatru** (or loyalty to the Germanic deities) and shortly after his assuming active leadership in the brotherhood, he reformed it as Asatru Free Assembly. His efforts received a significant boost when the first edition of Margot Adler's survey of the contemporary community, *Drawing Down the Moon,* appeared in 1979. He even appeared on the radio show of Christian evangelist Bob Larson, which provided further national exposure. He continued to edit *The Runestone* and compiled a book of Norse rituals. Feeling burned out, he dissolved the assembly in 1987, though he did not abandon his faith. Others continued the work of the assembly in various alternative organizations and McNallen moved to northern California. He obtained his teaching credentials and got a job teaching science and math in a junior high school. In his spare time, he traveled to northern India and Burma and turned his observations on the political and military conflicts into articles for national magazines.

In 1992, McNallen felt ready to resume his leadership in what had become an expansive international Asatru community. He revived *The Runestone* and founded a new fellowship group, the **Asatru Folk Assembly,** modelled on the previous Asatru Free Assembly. He has also continued his global travels, beginning with Africa and Bosnia in 1993. He maintains the Internet page for the new assembly at http://www.runestone.org.

Sources:

McNallen, Stephen A. *Rituals of Asatru.* 3 vols. Breckenridge, Tex.: Asatru Free Assembly, 1985.

———. *What Is the Norse Religion?* Turlock, Calif.: The Author, n.d.

Mead, G(eorge) R(obert) S(tow) (1863–1933)

Theosophist, scholar, and writer on **Gnosticism** and early Christianity. Born March 22, 1863, he was educated at St. John's College, Cambridge (M.A., 1885). In 1884 Mead joined the **Theosophical Society,** and in 1889 he gave up his work as a teacher to be closely concerned with the Theosophical Society and its cofounder **Helena Petrovna Blavatsky.** Mead became her private secretary for the last three years of her life and subedited her monthly magazine *Lucifer,* which he renamed the *Theosophical Review* on becoming editor. Mead was one of the few of Blavatsky's associates to have a realistic view of her complex character. He believed her to be a racy personality as well as a powerful **medium,** and not simply a charlatan, as alleged by her critics.

In 1890 Mead was appointed general secretary of the Theosophical Society, a position he held for eight years. Among his first tasks, he helped to edit the second edition of Blavatsky's massive text, *The Secret Doctrine* (1890).

In 1908 he resigned from the society (with some 700 other members) in protest against the sexual scandals concerning **C. W. Leadbeater.** In March of the next year, Mead founded the **Quest Society,** which he saw as a group of sincere seekers after spiritual wisdom without taint of charlatanism. He edited the *Quest,* a quarterly review, for over 20 years (1909–30). After the death of his wife, Mead became actively interested in psychic science and sat with several mediums. He died September 28, 1933, and is remembered for the many books he wrote and edited.

Sources:

Mead, George R. S. *Apollonius of Tyana.* 1901. Reprint, New Hyde Park, N.Y.: University Books, 1966.

———. *Did Jesus Live 100 B.C.?* 1903. Reprint, New Hyde Park, N.Y.: University Books, 1968.

———. *The Doctrine of the Subtle Body.* 1919. Reprint, London: Stuart & Watkins, 1967.

———. *Echoes from the Gnosis.* 1907. Reprint, Hastings, E. Sussex, England: Chthonius Books, 1987.

———. *Fragments of a Faith Forgotten.* 1900. Reprint, New Hyde Park, N.Y.: University Books, 1960.

———. *Pistis Sophia.* London: Theosophical Publishing Society, 1921.

———. *Simon Magus.* London: Theosophical Publishing Society, 1892.

———. *Thrice Greatest Hermes.* London: Theosophical Society, 1906.

Meddelande Fran Sallskapet fur Parapsykologis

Publication in Swedish of the Swedish Society for Psychical Research. Last known address: P.O. Box 7045, Stockholm 10386, Sweden.

Medea

In Greek mythology, an enchantress and daughter of the king of Colchis who fell in love with Jason when he came to that country. Medea enabled him to slay the sleepless dragon that guarded the golden fleece. She fled from Colchis with Jason, who made her his wife, and from whom she exacted a pledge never to love another woman. They were pursued by her father, but she delayed the pursuit by the cruel expedient of cutting her brother Absyrtus to pieces and strewing his limbs in the sea.

Medea accompanied Jason to **Greece,** where she was regarded as a barbarian. Having conciliated King Peleus, who was now a very old man, she induced him to try to regain youth by bathing in a magic cauldron she had prepared. So great was his faith in her powers that the old man unhesitatingly plunged into her cauldron and was boiled alive. Her reason for this act of cruelty was to hasten Jason's succession to the throne. In due course, Jason would have succeeded Peleus, but now the Greeks would have none of either him or Medea, and he was forced to leave Iolcos.

Growing tired of the formidable enchantress to whom he had bound himself, Jason sought to contract an alliance with Glauce, a young princess. Concealing her real intentions, Medea pretended friendship with the bride-elect and sent her as a wedding present a garment, which as soon as Glauce put it on, caused her to die in the greatest agony.

Eventually Medea parted from Jason. Having murdered her two children by him, she fled from Corinth in a car drawn by dragons to Athens, where she married Argeus, by whom she had a son, Medus. But the discovery of an attempt on the life of Theseus forced her to leave Athens. Accompanied by her son, she returned to Colchis and restored her father to the throne, of which he had been deprived by his own brother Perses.

Much literature has been written about the character of Medea. Euripides, Ennius, Aeschylus, and later Pierre Corneille made her the theme of tragedies.

Sources:

Kingsley, Charles. *The Heroes.* 1856. Reprint, New York: Dutton, 1963.

Medhurst, R. G. (1920–1971)

British writer on **parapsychology** and a leading member of the **Society for Psychical Research** (SPR), London. He was attracted to **psychical research** after hearing some of **S. G. Soal**'s lectures on the subject. Medhurst's degree in mathematics and his outstanding work in mathematical engineering were of special value in evaluating the mathematical aspects of **ESP.** His paper "On the Origin of the Prepared Random Numbers Used in the Shackleton Experiments" (1971) was undertaken to defend Soal's reputation, but instead Medhurst discovered flaws in his mentor's work, and he concluded that the common method of constructing quasi-random series in parapsychology was incorrect. Medhurst's work led eventually to Soal's illegitimate manipulation of data being discovered.

Medhurst also contributed work on such subjects as the investigation of Dutch psychic **Gerard Croiset** and Duke University's ESP cards. He discussed one project to discover ESP agents and percipients and wrote a number of book reviews. He headed the SPR's library committee.

Sources:

Berger, Arthur S., and Joyce Berger. *The Encyclopedia of Parapsychology and Psychical Research.* New York: Paragon House, 1991.

Medhurst, R. G. *Crookes and the Spirit World: A Collection of Writings by or Concerning the Work of Sir William Crookes.* Edited by K. M. Goldney and M. R. Barrington. London: Taplinger, 1972.

———. "On the Origin of the Prepared Random Numbers Used in the Shackleton Experiments." *Journal* of the Society for Psychical Research 46 (1971).

Medhurst, R. G., and K. M. Goldney. "William Crookes and the Physical Phenomena of Mediumship." *Proceedings* of the Society for Psychical Research 54, no. 195 (March 1964).

Medicine, Occult

Nineteenth-century magus **Éliphas Lévi** observed:

"The whole power of the **occult** physician is in the conscience of his will, while his whole art consists in exciting the faith of his patient. 'If you have faith,' says the Master, 'all things are possible to him who believes.' The subject must be dominated by expression, tone, gesture; confidence must be inspired by a fatherly manner, and cheerfulness stimulated by seasonable and sprightly talk. Rabelais, who was a greater magician than he seemed, made pantagruelism his special panacea. He compelled his patients to laugh, and all the remedies he administered subsequently succeeded better in consequence. . . . He established a magnetic sympathy between himself and them, by means of which he imparted his own confidence and good humour; he flattered them in his refaces, termed them his precious, most illustrious patients, and dedicated his books to them. So are we convinced that Gargantua and Pantagruel cured more black humours, more tendencies to madness, more atrabilious whims, at that epoch of religious animosities and civil wars, than the whole Faculty of medicine could boast.

"Occult medicine is essentially sympathetic. Reciprocal affection, or at least real good will, must exist between doctor and patient. Syrups and juleps have very little inherent virtue; they are what they become through the mutual opinion of operator and subject; hence homeopathic medicine dispenses with them and no serious inconvenience follows. Oil and wine, combined with salt or camphor, are sufficient for the healing of all wounds, and for all external frictions or soothing applications. Oil and wine are the chief medicaments of the Gospel tradition. They formed the balm of the Good Samaritan, and in the Apocalypse, when describing the last plagues, the prophet prays the avenging powers to spare these substances, that is, to leave a hope and a remedy for so many wounds. What we term Extreme Unction was the pure and simple practice of the Master's traditional medicine, both for the early Christians and in the mind of the apostle Saint James, who has included the precept in his epistle to the faithful of the whole world. 'Is any man sick among you,' he writes, 'let him call in the priests of the church, and let them pray over him, anointing him with oil in the name of the Lord.'

"This divine therapeutic science was lost gradually, and Extreme Unction came to be regarded as a religious formality, as necessary preparation for death. At the same time, the thaumaturgic virtue of consecrated oil could not be effaced altogether from remembrance by the traditional doctrine, and it is perpetuated in the passage of the catechism which refers to Extreme Unction. Faith and charity were the most signal healing powers among the early Christians. The source of most diseases is in moral disorders; we must begin by healing the soul, and then the cure of the body will follow quickly."

Some of these concepts have been revived in the modern New Age concept of holistic medicine.

Sources:

Hartmann, Franz. *The Life and Teachings of Paracelsus.* London: George Redway, 1887. Reprinted with *The Prophecies of Paracelsus.* Blauvely, N.Y.: Rudolf Steiner, 1973.

Lévi, Éliphas. *Transcendental Magic.* London: George Redway, 1896. Rev. ed. London: William Rider, 1923.

Paracelsus. *The Archidoxes of Magic.* Translated by Robert Turner. London, 1656. Reprint, New York: Samuel Weiser, 1975.

Medieval Magic

In the belief of the medieval professors, the science of **magic** conferred upon the adept power over **angels,** demons (see **demonology**), **elementary spirits,** and the souls of the dead, the possession of esoteric wisdom, and actual knowledge of the discovery and use of the latent forces and undeveloped energies resident in man. This was supposed to be accomplished by a combination of will and aspiration, which by sheer force germinated an intellectual faculty of psychological perception, enabling the adept to view the wonders of a new world and communicate with its inhabitants.

To accomplish this magic, the ordinary faculties were almost invariably heightened by artificial means. The grandeur of the magical ritual overwhelmed the neophyte and quickened his senses. **Ceremonial magic** was a spur to the latent faculties of human psychic nature, just as were the rich concomitants of religious **mysticism.**

In the medieval mind, as in other periods of human history, it was thought that magic could be employed both for good and evil purposes, its branches being designated "white" and "black," according to whether it was used for benevolent or wicked ends. The term "red" magic was also occasionally employed, as indicating a more exalted type of the art, but the designation is fanciful.

White magic to a great extent concerned itself with the evocation of angelic forces and the spirits of the elements. The angelology of the Catholic Church was undoubtedly derived from the ancient faith of Israel, which in turn was indebted to **Egypt** and Babylon. The Alexandrian system of successive emanations from the eternal substance evolved a complex hierarchy of angels, all of whom appear to have been at the bidding of the magician who was in possession of the Incommunicable Name, a concept deriving from that of the "Name of Power" so greatly used in Egyptian magic.

The letters that composed this name were thought to possess a great measure of **occult** significance, and a power which in turn appears to have been reflected upon the entire Hebrew alphabet (see **Kabala**). The alphabet was endowed with mystical meaning, each of the letters representing a vital and creative number. Just as a language is formed from the letters of its alphabet, so from the secret powers that resided in the Hebrew alphabet were magical variations evolved. [Comparable concepts existed in esoteric Hinduism (see **AUM**).]

There are many species of angels and powers. More exalted intelligences were conjured by rites to be found in the ancient book known as the **"Key of Solomon the King,"** and perhaps the most satisfactory collection of formulae for the invocation of the higher angels is that included in the anonymous *Theosophia Pneumatica,* published at Frankfurt in 1686, which bears a strong family resemblance to the *Treatise on Magic* by Arbatel. The names in this work do not tally with those that have been already given, but as it is admitted by occult students that the names of all unseen beings are really unknown to humanity, this does not seem of such importance as it might at first sight.

It would seem that such spiritual knowledge as the medieval magus was capable of attaining was insufficient to raise him above the intellectual limitations of his time, so that the work in question possesses all the faults of its age and type. But that is not to say that it possessed no practical value, and it well illustrates the white magic of medieval times. It classifies the names of the angels under the title of "Olympic or Celestial Spirits," who abide in the firmament and constellations: they administer inferior destinies and accomplish and teach whatever is portended by the several stars in which they are insphered. They are powerless to act without a special command from the Almighty.

The stewards of Heaven are seven in number—Arathron, Bethor, Phaleg, Och, Hagith, Ophiel, and Phul. Each of them has a numerous host at his command, and the regions in which they dwell are 196 in all. Arathron appears on Saturday at the first hour and answers for his territory and its inhabitants, as do the others, each at his own day and hour, and each presides for a period of 490 years. The functions of Bethor began in the fiftieth year before the birth of Christ until 430. Phagle reigned till 920 C.E.; Och till the year 1410; Hagith governed until 1900. The others follow in succession.

These intelligences are the stewards of all the elements, energizing the firmament and, with their armies, depending from each other in a regular hierarchy. The names of the minor Olympian spirits are interpreted in diverse ways. Generically, they are called "Astra," and their power is seldom prolonged beyond 140 years. The heavens and their inhabitants come voluntarily to man and often serve even against the will of man, but come much more if we implore their ministry.

Evil and troublesome spirits also approach men through the cunning of the devil, at times by conjuration or attraction, and frequently as a penalty for sins. Therefore he who would abide in familiarity with celestial intelligences should take pains to avoid every serious sin. He should diligently pray for the protection of God to vanquish the impediments and schemes of Diabolus, and God will ordain that the devil himself shall work to the direct profit of the worker in magic.

Subject to divine providence, some spirits have power over pestilence and famine; some are destroyers of cities, like those of Sodom and Gomorrah; some are rulers over kingdoms, some guardians of provinces, some of a single person. The spirits are the ministers of the word of God and of the church and its members, or they serve creatures in material things, sometimes to the salvation of soul and body, or, again, to the ruin of both. But nothing, good or bad, is done without knowledge, order, and administration.

It is unnecessary to follow the angelical host further here, as it has been outlined elsewhere. Many preparations, however, are described by the author of the *Theosophia Pneumatica* for the successful evocation of these exalted beings. The magus must ponder during his period of initiation on the method of attaining the true knowledge of God, both by night and day. He must know the laws of the cosmos, and the practical secrets that may be gleaned from the study of the visible and invisible creatures of God. He must further know himself, and be able to distinguish between his mortal and immortal parts, and the several spheres to which they belong.

Both in his mortal and immortal natures, he must strive to love God, to adore and to fear him in spirit and in truth. He must sedulously attempt to find out whether he is truly fitted for the practice of magic, and if so, to which branch he should turn his talents, experimenting in all to discover in which he is most naturally gifted. He must hold inviolate such secrets as are communicated to him by spirits, and he must accustom himself to their evocation. He must keep himself, however, from the least suspicion of diabolical magic, which has to do with Satan, and which is the perversion of the theurgic power concealed in the word of God.

When he has fulfilled these conditions, and before he proceeds to the practice of his art, he should devote a prefatory period to deep contemplation on the high business he has voluntarily taken in hand, and must present himself before God with a pure heart, undefiled mouth, and innocent hands. He must bathe frequently and wear clean garments, confess his sins, and abstain from wine for the space of three days.

On the eve of operation, he must dine sparely at noon and consume only bread and water for the evening meal (remembering that prior to modern refining techniques that bread was a very substantial food). On the day he has chosen for the invocation, he must seek a retired and uncontaminated spot, entirely free from observation. After offering up prayer, he compels the spirit he has chosen to appear. By this time he should have reached a state of awareness in which it is impossible that the spirit should remain invisible to him.

On the arrival of the angel, the desire of the magus is briefly communicated to him, and his answer is written down. No more than three questions should be asked, and the magician then dismisses the angel to his special sphere. Besides having converse with angels, the magus also has power over the spirits of the elements and may choose to evoke one or more of them.

To obtain power over the salamanders, for example, the **"Comte de Gabalis"** of the **Abbé de Villars** was largely concerned with the elementals and prescribed the following procedure:

"If you would recover empire over the salamanders, purify and exalt the natural fire that is within you. Nothing is required for this purpose but the concentration of the Fire of the World by means of concave mirrors in a globe of glass. In that globe is formed the 'solary' powder, which being of itself purified from the mixture of other elements, and being prepared according to Art becomes in a very short time a sovereign process for the exaltation of the fire that is within you, and transmutes you into an igneous nature."

There is very little information extant to show in what manner the evocation of elementary spirits was undertaken, and no ritual has survived that will acquaint us with the method of communicating with them. In older writers, it is difficult to distinguish between angels and elementary spirits; the lower hierarchies of the elementary spirits were also frequently invoked by the black magician. It is probable that the lesser angels of the older magicians were the sylphs of **Paracelsus,** and the more modern professors of the art.

The nineteenth-century magus **Éliphas Lévi** provided a method for the interrogation and government of elementary spirits, but he did not specify its source, and it was merely fragmentary. It is necessary, he claimed, in order to dominate these intelligences, to undergo the four trials of ancient initiation, and as these are unknown, their room must be supplied by similar tests. To approach the salamanders, therefore, one must expose himself in a burning house. To draw near the sylphs he must cross a precipice on a plank, or ascend a lofty mountain in a storm; and he who would win to the abode of the undines must plunge into a cascade or whirlpool.

The air is exorcised by the sufflation of the four cardinal points, the recitation of the prayer of the sylphs, and by the following formula:

"The Spirit of God moved upon the water, and breathed into the nostrils of man the breath of life. Be Michael my leader, and be Sabtabiel my servant, in the name and by the virtue of light. Be the power of the word in my breath, and I will govern the spirits of this creature of Air, and by the will of my soul, I will restrain the steeds of the sun, and by the thought of my mind, and by the apple of my right eye. I exorcise thee O creature of Air, by the Petagrammaton, and in the name Tetragrammaton, wherein are steadfast will and well-directed faith. Amen. Sela. So be it."

Water is exorcised by the laying on of hands, by breathing and by speech, and by mixing sacred salt with a little of the ash left in an incense pan. The aspergillus is made of branches of vervain, periwinkle, sage, mint, ash, and basil, tied by a thread taken from a virgin's distaff, with a handle of hazelwood which has never borne fruit, and on which the characters of the seven spirits must be carved with a magic awl. The salt and ashes of the incense must be separately consecrated. The prayer of the undines should follow.

Fire is exorcised by casting salt, incense, white resin, camphor, and sulphur therein, and by thrice pronouncing the three names of the genii of fire: Michael, Samael, and Anael, and then by reciting the prayer of the salamanders.

The Earth is exorcised by the sprinkling of water, by breathing, by fire, and by the prayer of the gnomes. Their signs are the hieroglyphs of the bull for the gnomes who are commanded with the magic sword; of the lion for the salamanders, who are commanded with the forked rod, or *magic* trident; of the eagle for the sylphs, who are ruled by the holy pentacles; and finally, of aquarius for the undines, who are evoked by the cup of libations. Their respective sovereigns are Gob for the gnomes, Djin for the salamanders, Paralda for the sylphs, and Necksa for the undines. These names, it will be noticed, are borrowed from folklore.

The "laying" of an elementary spirit is accomplished by its adjuration by air, water, fire, and earth, by breathing, sprinkling, the burning of perfumes, by tracing on the ground the star of Solomon and the sacred pentagram, which should be drawn either with ash of consecrated fire or with a reed soaked in various colors, mixed with pure loadstone.

The conjuration of the four should then be repeated, the magus holding the pentacle of Solomon in his hand and taking up by turns the sword, rod, and cup, this operation being preceded and terminated by the kabalistic sign of the cross.

In order to subjugate an elementary spirit, the magus must be himself free of their besetting sins, thus a changeful person cannot rule the sylphs, nor a fickle one the undines, an angry man the salamanders, or a covetous one the gnomes. (The formula for the evocation of spirits is given under **necromancy.**)

The white magician did not concern himself as a rule with such matters as the raising of demons, animal transformations, and the like, his whole desire being the exaltation of his spiritual nature, and the questions put by him to the spirits he evoked were all directed to that end. However, the dividing line between white and black magic is extremely ambiguous, and it seems likely that the entities evoked might be deceptive as to their nature.

Sources:

De Villars, L'Abbé de Montfaucon. *Comte de Gabalis.* Paris, 1670. Reprint, London: Old Bourne Press, 1913.

The Greater Key of Solomon. Translated by S. L. MacGregor Mathers. London: George Redway, 1888.

Lévi, Éliphas. *The History of Magic.* London: William Rider, 1913. Reprint, New York: Samuel Weiser, 1971.

———. *Transcendental Magic.* London: George Redway, 1896. Reprint, New York: Samuel Weiser, 1970.

Shah, Sayed Idries. *Oriental Magic.* London: Rider, 1956.

———. *The Secret Lore of Magic.* London: Frederick Muller, 1956.

Waite, Arthur E. *The Book of Ceremonial Magic.* London: William Rider, 1911. Reprint, New York: Bell, 1969.

———. *The Holy Kabbalah.* London: Williams & Norgate, 1929. Reprint, New Hyde Park, N.Y.: University Books, 1960.

Walker, D. P. *Spiritual and Demonic Magic: From Ficino to Camperella.* South Bend, Ind.: University of Notre Dame Press, 1975.

Meditation

A traditional spiritual exercise in both Eastern and Western mystical systems, usually involving a static sitting position, a blocking of the mind from normal sensory stimuli, and a concentration upon divine thoughts or mystical centers in the human body.

In Christian and some Eastern traditions, meditation was often enhanced by asceticism—prolonged fasts and other physical mortification practiced in order to assert the supremacy of the soul over all physical and sensory demands. Certain well-defined stages of spiritual growth are recorded by saints and mystics, notably the awakening of the soul, contemplation, the dark night of the soul, illumination, and spiritual ecstasy.

Several basic types of meditation can be distinguished by the particular nature of the alteration of consciousness sought. For example, **Zen** meditation tends to produce a focused concentration in the present. The person who meditates in this way is perfectly alert but takes no notice of surrounding noises or other phenomena. Instead of blocking outside distractions, the meditator allows them to come and go as quickly as they arise, always retaining perfect concentration.

In Hindu-based meditation forms, an attempt is made to distance oneself from the "illusionary" outside world of noise and distractions and retreat completely into the "real" world of the inner self, which causes a trancelike state. In such a condition one can easily step into a state of ecstacy and lose consciousness of the outside world.

Meditation in the West is frequently identified with contemplation of a religious symbol or pious story. That is, the consciousness remains awake and alert as in Zen, but also shut off from the outside world in total concentration upon a predetermined thought. Roman Catholics, for example, have a number of meditative practices built around contemplation of particular episodes in the life of Jesus, the Virgin Mary, or the saints, while Protestants have extolled the value of contemplating verses of Scripture.

Eastern meditation traditions are numerous and complex. In Hinduism, for example, meditation was usually taught by a guru only to a properly qualified pupil who had already followed a pathway of *sadhana,* or spiritual discipline that ensured purification at all levels. The various **yoga** systems describe such spiritual disciplines in detail, with special emphasis on moral restraints and ethical observances. Meditation without such preliminary training was considered premature and dangerous.

The most generally known system has been that of the sage Patanjali (ca. 200 B.C.E.), who taught that in order to experience true reality one must transcend the body and mind. In his *Yoga Sutras,* Patanjali outlines a program of physical exercises (to strengthen a meditation posture), breathing techniques (to purify the body), withdrawal of the senses, concentration, and meditation, culminating in mystical experience.

In this process supernormal powers might be manifested, but were to be ignored. The ultimate goal of meditation was spiritual illumination transcending individuality and extending the consciousness beyond time, space, and causality, but also interfusing it with the everyday duties and responsibilities of the individual. Thus it was not necessary for an illuminated individual to renounce the world, and there are stories in Hindu scriptures of kings and princes who did not forsake their mundane tasks after transcendental experience.

It is clear from consideration of the practices of many religions that meditation may be active or passive, depending upon the techniques employed and the degree of purification of the meditator. Fixed concentration upon one mental image, sound, or center in the body is a passive mechanical technique that may bring relaxation, a sense of well-being, and other benefits, but is not in itself spiritual or transcendental in the traditional sense of those terms. The popular so-called **transcendental meditation** technique of **Maharishi Mahesh Yogi** appears to be of this order, hence criticism from practitioners of other systems.

In active meditation systems, there must be purification at all levels—physical, mental, emotional, and spiritual—and the mind is exercised creatively before it can transcend its own activity. Meditators who have attained stages of higher consciousness or mystical illumination testify that there is a gradual process of refinement arising from the activity of a mysterious energy that Hindu mystics call **kundalini** that modifies the entire organism.

Today the variety of meditation techniques practiced throughout the world all have their advocates and practitioners in the West. Both teachers and texts are available to the aspiring student, and psychologists have dedicated research time to exploring the variant effects of the differing systems, from **Zen** meditation to Sufi dancing to drug-enhanced states of consciousness to Christian contemplative practices. Each of the meditation practices has particular benefits, though the majority of those benefits are only received as the practice is placed within a larger system of spiritual activity, with which it is normally integrated.

Sources:

Augustine of Hippo. *Confessions of St. Augustine.* Edited by Francis J. Sheed. New York: Sheed, 1943.

John of Ruysbroeck. *Adornment of the Spiritual Marriage.* Translated by P. Synschenk. London, 1916.

Gopi Krishna. *Kundalini, the Evolutionary Energy in Man.* Boulder, Colo.: Shambhala, 1970.

———. *Kundalini for the New Age: Selected Writings.* Edited by Gene Kieffer. New York: Bantam, 1988.

Luk, Charles. *The Secrets of Chinese Meditation.* London: n.p., 1964.

Melton, J. Gordon. *The Ways of Meditation.* Evanston, Ill.: Stellium Press, 1974.

Patanjali *The Yoga-Sutras of Patanjali.* Translated by M. N. Dvidedi. Adyar, India: Theosophical Publishing House, 1890.

Underhill, Evelyn. *Mysticism: A Study in the Nature and Development of Man's Spiritual Consciousness.* London: n.p., 1911.

Van Over, Raymond. *Total Meditation.* New York: Collier Books, 1978.

Medium

Throughout the history of **Spiritualism,** a special place has been occupied by the medium as an individual qualified in some special manner to form a link between the living and the dead. Most Spiritualists would agree with the definition adopted by the **National Spiritualist Association of Churches**: "A Medium is one whose organism is sensitive to vibrations from the spirit world and through whose instrumentality intelligences in that world are able to convey messages and produce the phenomena of Spiritualism."

Through the medium, Spiritualism asserts, the spirits of the departed may communicate with their friends or relatives still on earth, either by making use of the material organism of the medium (i.e., through automatic phenomena) or by producing in the physical world certain manifestations that cannot be explained by known physical laws (i.e., physical phenomena).

The essential qualification of a medium is a unique sensitiveness that enables the medium to be readily "controlled" by spirits. Mediums thus stand in contrast to *sensitives* or *psychics,* terms applicable to psychically gifted individuals who are not controlled by spirits of the dead.

If one accepts the possibility of mediumship, the next question is whether mediumship is an inherent faculty or whether it may be acquired. Some Spiritualists hold that all individuals are mediums to some degree, and consequently that everyone is in communication with spirits, from whom proceeds what is called inspiration. Those who are ordinarily designated mediums, say the Spiritualists, are gifted with this common ability to a higher degree than their fellows.

What came to be known as mediumship in nineteenth-century Spiritualism is an ability that was found in the ancient world. Early written records of demonic **possession** afford an excellent example of mediumship, as does the ancient practice of **witchcraft.** The *somnambule* of the eighteenth-century mesmerists provides a more recent example.

In its usual application, the term *medium* is used to describe sensitives associated with the modern Spiritualist movement, which had its origin in the United States in 1848. Spiritualism was distinct as a post-Enlightenment movement in which mediumship was used as a means of demonstrating to the public and proving scientifically the reality of spirit contact and therefore life after death. This peculiar context set it apart from all similar behavior that had preceded it.

In this sense, then, Mrs. Fox and the **Fox sisters,** the subject of the **Rochester rappings,** were the earliest mediums. The phenomena of their séances consisted mainly of knockings, by means of which messages were supposedly conveyed from the spirits to the sitters.

Other mediums rapidly appeared, first in America and later in Britain and throughout Europe. Their mediumship was of both varieties—physical and automatic. One of these phases was exhibited exclusively by some mediums, but others demonstrated both, as in the case of **William Stainton Moses.** Indeed, by the end of the nineteenth century it was practically impossible to find a **trance** speaker who did not at one time or another practice the physical manifestations. **Leonora Piper,** who became well known early in this century, was unusual because the phenomena she demonstrated was purely subjective.

The early rappings of the Fox sisters speedily developed into more elaborate manifestations. For a few years an epidemic of **table turning** caused widespread excitement, and the motions of the table became a favorite means of communicating with the spirits. The playing of musical instruments without visible agency was a form of manifestation that received the attention of mediums from an early date, as was the seemingly paranormal materialization in the séance room of "**apports**": fruit, flowers, perfume, and all manner of portable objects. Darkness was said to facilitate the spirit manifestations, and since there are certain physical processes (such as those in photography) to which darkness is essential, no logical objection could be offered to a dim séance room. The arrival of physical phenomena coincided with the introduction of many amateur conjurers into the movement, who saw a means of making a living bilking sitters hungry for information about their deceased relatives.

Attendees at a Spiritualist séance were generally seated around a table, holding each other's hands, and were often enjoined to sing or talk pending the manifestation of a spirit. All this, although offering grounds of suspicion to the incredulous, was plausible to the Spiritualists.

As the demand for physical manifestations increased through the decades of the nineteenth century, they became more daring and more varied. The moving of objects without contact, the **levitation** of heavy furniture and of medium or sitters, the **elongation** of the human body, and the **fire ordeal** were all practiced by the medium **Daniel Dunglas Home** for a quarter of a century until his death in 1886. At public performances of the **Davenport brothers,** while the brothers were bound hand and foot in a small **cabinet,** musical instruments were played and moved about the room and objects moved without being touched. (The Davenport brothers did not claim to be mediums nor did they identify themselves with Spiritualism, but the Spiritualists certainly welcomed their performances.)

The **slate writing** of "Dr." **Henry Slade** and **William Eglinton** enjoyed considerable attention. The tying of knots in endless cords and the passing of **matter through matter** were typical physical phenomena of the mediumistic circle.

The crowning achievement of mediumship, however, was the **materialization** of the spirit form. Quite early in the history of Spiritualism, hands were materialized, then faces, and finally the complete form of the spirit "**control.**" Thereafter materialized spirits allowed themselves to be touched, and even held conversations with the sitters. Further "proof" of the actuality of the spirits was offered by **spirit photography.**

Physical phenomena were the highlight of Spiritualism through the 1920s. By the beginning of World War II, however, continual exposure of **fraud** within the movement largely drove the physical mediums to the fringe.

To those for whom Spiritualism was a religion, however, the most important part of the mediumistic performances was the trance utterances, which came under the heading of automatic or psychological phenomena, commonly in the form of **automatic speaking** and **automatic writing**. These dealt largely with the conditions of life on the other side of the grave, although in style they often tended to be verbose and vague. Spirit drawings were sometimes amazingly impressive, at other times nondescript (see **Automatic Drawing and Painting**).

Clairvoyance and **crystal vision** were included in the psychological phenomena, and so were the prophetic utterances of mediums and speaking in unknown **tongues.**

According to the Spiritualist hypothesis that all individuals are mediums, it would be necessary to class inspiration—not only the inspiration of genius, but all good or evil impulses—as spiritual phenomena. That idea in turn suggested to the Spiritualist that the everyday life of the normal individual is to some extent directed by spirit controls. Therein lay the responsibility of mediumship, for the medium who desired to be controlled by pure spirits from the higher spheres had to live a well-conducted and principled life. Misuse of the divine gift of mediumship carried with it its own punishment, for the medium became the sport of base human spirits and **elementals,** his or her will was sapped, and the whole being degraded. Likewise the medium had to be wary of giving up individual personality to the first spirit who came by, for the low, earthbound spirits had the least difficulty in communicating with the living.

Great Mediums of the Past

Of the physical mediums, the most noteworthy was Daniel Dunglas Home (1833–86), who claimed to be of Scottish birth. He arrived in the United States at an early age. He is worthy of note in that he was never detected in **fraud** (unlike most physical mediums) although his demonstrations were spectacular. All who came into contact with him were impressed by his simple manners and frank and affectionate disposition, so he possessed the most valuable asset of a medium—the ability to inspire confidence in his sitters.

The production of physical phenomena was promoted at an early date by the Davenport brothers. Although widely popular in their time, they were quite different from Home. Their performance consisted of allowing themselves to be securely bound in a cabinet by the sitters, and while thus handicapped producing the usual mediumistic phenomena. The Davenports were said to be mere conjurers however, and when the stage magicians **John Nevil Maskelyne** and Cooke successfully imitated their feats, the Davenports lost credibility.

Slate writing, which proved one of the most widely accepted forms of psychic phenomena, had as its principal exponents Henry Slade and William Eglinton. The best argument that can be advanced against their feats is to be found in the pseudo-séances of **S. T. Davey,** given in the interests of the **Society for Psychical Research,** London. Davey's slate-writing exhibitions, exposing the methods of producing spirit messages by simple conjuring, were so much like those of the professional mediums that some Spiritualists refused to believe that he was conjuring and hailed him as a renegade medium.

Automatic drawing was principally represented by **David Duguid,** a Scottish medium who attained considerable success in that line. Prominent trance speakers and writers were Duguid, **J. J. Morse, Emma Hardinge Britten,** and **Cora L. V. (Tappan) Richmond.**

One of the best-known and most respected private mediums was Stainton Moses (1839–92), a clergyman and schoolmaster whose normal life was beyond reproach. He produced both automatic and physical manifestations, the former including the writing of a work, *Spirit Teachings* (1894), dictated from time to time by his spirit controls, while the latter consisted of levitations, lights, and apports. His position, character, and education gave to his support of Spiritualism a credibility of considerable value.

It is to later mediums, however, that we must look for proof worthy of scientific consideration, and of these the most important were **Eusapia Palladino** and Leonora Piper. Palladino, an Italian medium, was born in 1854, and for a good many years acted as a medium for scientific investigators. In 1892 séances were held at Milan at which were present Professors Schiaparelli, **Angelo Brofferio, Cesare Lombroso, Charles Richet,** and others. In 1894 Richet conducted some experiments with Palladino at his house in the Ile Roubaud, to which he invited **Sir Oliver Lodge, F. W. H. Myers,** and **Julien Ochorowicz.**

The phenomena occurring in Palladino's presence were the ordinary manifestations of the mediumistic séance, but were of interest because all the distinguished investigators professed themselves satisfied that the medium, with her hands, head, and feet controlled by the sitters, could not herself produce the phenomena. Credible witnesses asserted that she possessed the ability to project psychic limbs from her person. Lodge and Myers were so impressed as to posit the existence of a new force, which they termed **ectenic force,** emanating from the medium.

In 1895, however, some séances with Palladino were held at Myers's home in Cambridge, where it became apparent that she habitually freed a hand or a foot—in short, habitually resorted to fraud if not properly controlled. Yet even these exposures were not conclusive, for in 1898, after a further series of experiments, Myers, Lodge, and Richet once more declared their belief in the genuineness of this medium's phenomena.

Leonora Piper, the Boston medium whose trance utterances and writings contain some of the best evidence forthcoming for the truth of Spiritualism, first fell into a spontaneous trance in 1884, and in the following year she was observed by Professor **William James** of Harvard. Thereafter her case was carefully studied by the American branch of the **Society for Psychical Research,** London.

Her first important **control** was a French physician, "Dr. Phinuit," but in 1892 a new control appeared, "George Pelham," who claimed to be the spirit of a young author who had died in February of that year. So complete was her impersonation of Pelham, and so well was his identity established by the mention of many private matters known only to himself and a few of his friends, that more than thirty of his friends claimed to recognize him.

In 1896 "George Pelham" gave place to "Imperator," "Rector," and other spirits who had formerly controlled Stainton Moses. From that time, and especially after 1900, the interest of the sittings declined, and they offered less material for the investigator.

Another automatic medium, **Hélène Smith,** came under the observation of **Theodore Flournoy.** Smith's trance utterances were spoken in what was claimed to be the **"Martian language,"** and she believed herself to be the reincarnation of Marie Antoinette and a Hindu princess. In his discovery of a more mundane explanation of Smith's phenomena, Flournoy made her one of the most notable mediums in the history of psychical research, if not Spiritualism.

Healing Mediums

The diagnosis and cure of disease were extensively practiced by Spiritualist mediums, following in the path of the older somnambulist and magnetic healers, who not only traced the progress of diseases but also diagnosed and prescribed modes of treatment.

The prescribing aspect of the healing mediums' work has largely been discarded since it frequently falls into the legal category of nonphysicians practicing medicine.

In the beginning it was not considered proper for healing mediums, most of whom practiced part time, to accept any remuneration for their services. As the movement developed and healers became full-time professionals, they either expected a fee or accepted freewill offerings.

Although it may be true that healing mediums, like Christian Science and New Thought practitioners, mesmerists, and others, effected a considerable proportion of bona fide cures, whether the cures were caused by spirit influence, the release of some psychic power, **psychic healing,** or mere suggestion is a point on which controversy continues. Spiritualists, like almost every religious community that practices some form of spiritual healing, can point to people who have been cured of a wide variety of diseases.

Spiritualist Views of Mediumship

Various theories have been advanced to explain mediumistic manifestations. Spiritualists, of course, claim that the phenomena are produced by the spirits of the dead acting on the sensitive organism of the medium. Today, evidence for such a theory is considered to be, at best, inconclusive. In fact, the change from **psychical research** to **parapsychology** was in large part a shift away from **survival** studies to laboratory experiments on basic psychic phenomena.

Observation of Spiritualism by psychical researchers and its claims to demonstrate life after death have been dominated by the question of fraud. The exposure of two generations of physical mediums has largely driven such phenomena from the mainstream of even the Spiritualist movement, although it can still be found in various churches and camps. Fraud was mostly discovered in physical phenomena, but it was also active where mediums practiced mentalist tricks. Information about sitters was collected ahead of time, or, in the case of **pellet reading,** during the session itself. Spiritualists explain these lapses into fraud as being instigated by the spirits themselves, a hypothesis that is clearly untenable in the majority of cases of mediums who practice fraud as a matter of course.

Automatism covers a wider field. The possibility that automatic utterances, writing, drawing, and so on may be involuntary and outside the sphere of the medium's consciousness can no longer be dismissed. The psychological phenomena are sometimes found in small children and in private mediums whose good faith is beyond question. The state is recognized as being allied to **hypnotism** and hysteria. Besides automatism and fraud, there are some other factors to be considered.

Some deception may be practiced by sitters as well as by the medium. It has been said that the ability to inspire confidence in sitters is essential to a successful medium. If the sitters are predisposed to believe in the paranormal, it is easy to imagine a lessening of the attention and observation so necessary to the psychic investigator.

The impossibility of continued observation for even a short period is a fact that can be proved by experiment. Memory defects and proneness to exaggeration are also accountable for many of the claimed marvels of the séance room, and possible **hallucination** must be considered. When the medium is in a trance, with its accompanying hyperesthesia, unconscious suggestion on the part of the sitters might offer a rational explanation for so-called clairvoyance.

Psychical Researchers and Mediumship

Joseph Maxwell defined a medium as "a person in the presence of whom psychical phenomena can be observed." **Gustav Geley**'s definition was "one whose constituent elements—mental, dynamic, and material—are capable of being momentarily decentralised," in other words, an intermediary for communication between the material and spirit worlds. Myers called the word *medium* "a barbarous and question-begging term" since many mediumistic communications were nothing but subconscious revelations; he suggested the use of the word *automatist.* The word *psychic* was proposed by others.

Cesare Lombroso maintained that there was a close relationship between the phenomena of mediumship and hysteria.

Charles Richet believed that "mediums are more or less neuropaths, liable to headaches, insomnia, and dyspepsia. The facility with which their consciousness suffers dissociation indicates a certain mental instability and their responsibility while in a state of trance is diminished."

The same opinion was expressed slightly more circumstantially by psychical researcher **Frank Podmore:** "Physiologically speaking, the medium is a person of unstable nervous equilibrium, in whom the control normally exercised by the higher brain centres is liable, on slight provocation, to be abrogated, leaving the organism, as in dream or somnambulism to the guidance of impulses which in a state of unimpaired consciousness would have been suppressed before they could have resulted in action."

Joseph Maxwell advised caution. He admitted that a certain impressionability—or nervous instability—was a favorable condition for the effervescence of mediumship. But he stressed that the term *nervous instability* was not meant in a negative sense. His best experiments were made with people who were not in any way hysterical; neurasthenics generally gave no result whatever. Nor did instability mean want of equilibrium. Many mediums he had known had extremely well-balanced minds from the mental and nervous point of view. Their nervous systems were even superior to the average person's, he said. The trance was a state such as appears in nervous hypertension.

"There are four chief types of temperament," wrote Dr. **Charles Lancelin,** "nervous, bilious, lymphatic and sanguine. Of these, the nervous temperament is the best suited for psychic experiments of all kinds; the bilious is the most receptive; the sanguine is liable to hallucinations, both subjective and objective; while the lymphatic is the least suitable of all, from every point of view. Of course, one's temperament is usually a compound of all of these, which are rarely found in their ideal state; but the predominantly nervous temperament is the one best suited for this test."

What Mediumship Is and What It Is Not

As mediumship emerged, some understood it to be a pathological state. Psychical researchers considered the question of pathology, but generally were able to draw sharp lines of distinction between dysfunctional mental disorders and unusual states of consciousness such as those displayed by mediums and others demonstrating psychic abilities.

In the late nineteenth century W. F. H. Myers remarked that the confusion on the point was the result of the observation that supernormal phenomena use the same channels for manifestation as the abnormal phenomena. The phenomena of mediumship are developmental, however; they show the promise of powers as yet unknown, whereas abnormal phenomena (like hysteria or epilepsy) show the degeneration of powers already acquired.

Flournoy, after his exhaustive study of the mediumship of Hélène Smith came to the same conclusion:

"It is far from being demonstrated that mediumship is a pathological phenomenon. It is abnormal, no doubt, in the sense of being rare, exceptional; but rarity is not morbidity. The few years during which these phenomena have been seriously and scientifically studied have not been enough to allow us to pronounce on their true nature. It is interesting to note that in the countries where these studies have been pushed the furthest, in England and America, the dominant view among the savants who have gone deepest into the matter is not at all unfavourable to mediumship; and that, far from regarding it as a special case of hysteria, they see in it a faculty superior, advantageous and healthy, but that hysteria is a form of degeneracy, a pathological parody, a morbid caricature."

Dr. Guiseppe Venzano, an Italian psychical researcher, was similarly emphatic: "Mediumship only represents a temporary deviation from the normal psychic state, and absolutely excludes the idea of morbidity; it is even proved that the slightest alteration of a pathological nature is sufficient to diminish or arrest the mediumistic powers."

As Flournoy discovered, the conditions for the successful exercise of mediumistic powers are the same as for the voluntary exercise of any other power—a state of good health, nervous equilibrium, calm, absence of care, good humor, and facilitative surroundings.

Physical defects, significant injury, or serious illness have been suggested as potential causes of mediumistic development. Spiritualist believer **Arthur Conan Doyle** suggested that a bodily weakness causes what may be described as a dislocation of the soul, so that it is more detached and capable of independent action. Eusapia Palladino had a peculiar depression of her parietal bone caused by an accident in childhood. Leonora Piper's mediumship developed after two operations, and her control, "Imperator," in an automatic script by Stainton Moses, said, "The tempering effect of a bodily illness has been in all your life an engine of great power with us." In the case of **Mary Jobson, Mollie Fancher,** Lurrency Vennum (**"the Watseka Wonder"**) and **Vincent Turvey,** prolonged physical agony accompanied the period of their psychic activity.

Spiritualists, however, consider mediumship to be a gift and its development to require great care and understanding. According to Barbara McKenzie (*Light,* March 18, 1932), who worked for many years at the **British College of Psychic Science,** the production and ripening of psychical gifts involves "a lengthy period of homely, warm, appreciative incubation . . . which is found at its best in a family or in a very intimate home circle, in which a continuity of conditions and a warm personal and even reverent interest is assured."

Sir Oliver Lodge believed that the medium should be treated as "a delicate piece of apparatus wherewith we are making an investigation. The medium is an instrument whose ways and idiosyncrasies must be learnt, and to a certain extent humoured, just as one studies and humours the ways of some much less delicate piece of physical apparatus turned out by a skilled instrument maker."

Age, Sex, and Psychical Phenomena

Mediumship may appear spontaneously and early in life, somewhat like artistic gifts. The five-month-old son of **Kate Fox** wrote automatically. **Raps** occurred on his pillow and on the iron railing of his bedstead almost every day. The seven-month-old infant of Margaretta Cooper, the daughter of **LaRoy Sunderland,** gave communications through raps. **Alexander Aksakof,** in his book *Animisme et Spiritism* (1906), records many instances of infantile mediumship. The child Alward moved tables that were too heavy for her normal strength. Another wrote automatically when nine days old.

In Eugène Bonnemère's *Histoire des Camisara* (1869) and in Louis Figuier's *Histoire du Merveilleux* (4 vols., 1886–89), many cases are quoted of mediumistic Camisard babies of 14 to 15 months of age and of infants who preached in French with the purest diction. During the persecution of the Huguenots, these babies were confined to prison in great numbers. The psychic contagion spread to Catholic children as well.

Nationality has no known influence on the development of mediumship, though the peculiar form the mediumship may take and the ideas mediums espouse may show differences across national boundaries. These differences seem more related to social training than to any inherent aspect of mediumship.

Puberty seems to have a peculiar significance. In old chronicles, prepubescent children were mentioned as the best subjects for **crystal reading. Poltergeist** cases mostly occur in the presence of young girls and boys between the ages of 12 and 16. **Hereward Carrington,** in a paper on the sexual aspect of mediumship presented at the First International Congress for Psychical Research in Copenhagen in 1921, speculated that the sexual energies that are blossoming into maturity within the body may, instead of taking their normal course, be somehow turned into another channel and externalized beyond the limits of the body, producing paranormal manifestations:

"There may be a definite connection between sex and psychical phenomena; and this seems to be borne out by three or four analogies. First, recent physiological researches as to the activities of the ductless glands and particularly the sex glands which have shown the enormous influence which these glands have upon the physical and even upon the psychic life. Second, the observation made in the cases of Kathleen Goligher and Eva C. which show that the plasma which is materialised, frequently issues from the genitals. [Given the questionable nature of the mediumship of these two women, however, the observations may have no relevance.] Third, the clinical observations of Lombroso, Morselli and others upon Eusapia Palladino, which brought to light many recognised sexual stigmata. Fourth, the teachings and practices of the Yogis of India, who have written at great length upon the connection between sexual energies and the higher, ecstatic states. Many suggest and explain the way to convert the former into the latter, just as we find instances of 'sublimation' in modern Freudian psychoanalysis, and connection between sex and religion, here in the West."

In his book, *The Story of Psychic Science* (1930), Carrington adds: "These speculations have, I believe, been amply verified by certain recent investigations, wherein it has been shown that (in the case of a celebrated European medium) the production of a physical phenomenon of exceptional violence has been coincidental with a true orgasm. From many accounts it seems probable that the same was frequently true in the case of Eusapia Palladino, and was doubtless the case with other mediums also."

Finally, Carrington pointed out that there was said to be a very close connection between the sexual energies and the **kundalini** energies that may be aroused and brought into activity by various **yoga** exercises.

Health and Mediumship

The practice of mediumship appears to have no adverse affects on health. Recovery from the trance state is usually very quick and, unless too many sittings produce an excessive drain on the vitality of the medium, the results may prove more beneficial than harmful. Many spirit guides have been known to supply regular medical advice, to take care of the medium's health to a greater extent than he or she could, and even to prescribe treatment in case of illness.

The withdrawal of mediumship powers is often evidence of care for the health of the medium. Of course, the lapse may come for entirely different reasons. But recuperative rest was given as an explanation when the "Imperator" group announced on May 24, 1911, that Leonora Piper's trance mediumship would be temporarily withdrawn. The withdrawal lasted until August 8, 1915.

In the case of the Marquis **Centurione Scotto,** it was similarly announced on November 9, 1927, that "he will fall ill if he continues thus. His nerves are shattered. By superior will his mediumistic faculty will be taken from him for a time." On another occasion, his mediumship was suspended, supposedly to allow him to read, study, and acquire more understanding of Spiritualistic belief. Similar experiences befell Stainton Moses, who revolted against his spirit guides when they tried to convince him, as a minister of the Anglican church, that "religion is eternal, whereas religious dogmas are but fleeting." His mediumship was temporarily removed. The powerful mediumship of D. D. Home also lapsed from time to time, probably because he suffered from a tubercular diathesis.

Mediums who are conscious during the production of phenomena appear to suffer more than those in trance. The extrication of power from their organism seems a veritable trial for nerve and flesh. Producing the phenomena is often equivalent to putting the body on the rack.

The Neoplatonist philosopher Iamblichus says in *Divination:*

"Often at the moment of inspiration, or when the afflatus has subsided, a fiery appearance is seen—the entering or departing power. Those who are skilled in this wisdom, can tell by the character of this glory the rank of the divinity who has seized for the time the reins of the mystic's soul, and guides it as he will. Sometimes the body of the man is violently agitated, sometimes it is rigid and motionless. In some instances sweet music is heard, in others discordant and fearful sounds. The person of the subject has been known to dilate and tower to a superhuman height, in other cases it has been lifted into the air. Frequently not merely the ordinary exercise of reason, but sensation and animal life would appear to have been suspended; and the subject of the afflatus has not felt the application of fire, has been pierced with spits, cut with knives and has not been sensible of pain."

However, the disagreeable result of physical phenomena soon vanishes. A quarter of an hour's rest may be enough to dispel the effect.

Curiously enough, the suppression of mediumship may manifest in symptoms of disease. Dr. C. D. Isenberg of Hamburg wrote of a case in *Light* (April 11, 1931) in which a patient of his suffered from sleeplessness and peculiar spasmodic attacks that generally occurred at night. The spasms seized the whole body; even the tongue was affected, blocking the throat and nearly suffocating her. When the patient mentioned that in her youth she tried table tilting, the doctor thought it possible that the mediumistic energy might be blocking his patient's body. A sitting was tried. The lady fell into trance and afterward slept well for a few days. When the sleeplessness recurred the sitting was repeated and the results proved to be so beneficial that treatment with medication was discontinued.

Regarding a deleterious influence on the mind, Gladys Osborne Leonard writes in her book *My Life in Two Worlds* (1931): "I myself have not found that the development of psychic awareness detracts in any way from other so-called normal studies. I am a more successful gardener than I used to be, I am a much better cook; in many quite ordinary but extremely useful directions, I know I have improved; my health and nerves are under better control, therefore they are more to be relied upon than they ever were before I developed what many people think of as an abnormal or extraordinary power."

Dangers of Mediumship

Dangers, nevertheless, do exist in mediumship, but of another kind. Hereward Carrington warned that there is a true "terror of the dark" as well as "principalities and powers" with which, in our ignorance we can toy, without knowing or realizing the frightful consequence that may result from tampering with the unseen world. For that reason, he argued that a few men of well-balanced minds should be designated lifelong investigators in this field; they should be looked upon as recognized authorities, "and their work accepted upon these problems just as any other physicist is accepted on a problem in physics."

Moses agreed, saying, "I do not think it would be reasonable to say that it is wise and well for everyone to become acquainted with mediumship in his own proper person. It would not be honest in me to disguise the fact that he who meddles with this subject does so at his peril. I do not say that peril is anything that should always be avoided. In some cases it is not, but I do say that the development of mediumship is sometimes a very questionable benefit, as in others it is a very decided blessing."

The peril alluded to is the possibility of intrusion and control of undesirable spirits. Moses further stated, "In developing mediumship one has to consider a question involving three serious points. Can you get into relation with a spirit who is wise enough and strong enough to protect and good enough for you to trust? If you do not, you are exposed to that recurrent danger which the old occultists used to describe as the struggle with the dweller on the threshold. It is true that everybody who crosses the threshold of this occult knowledge does unquestionably come into a new and strange land in which, if he has no guide, he is apt to lose his way."

The nervous equilibrium of the medium during the séance may be easily disturbed. **Hudson Tuttle** observed of his own work, "During the physical manifestations I was in semi-trance, intensely sensitive and impressible. The least word, a jarring question, even when the intention was commendable, grated and rasped. Words convey an imperfect idea of this condition. It can only be compared with that physical state when a nerve is exposed."

Yet regarding the moral responsibility of the medium, Tuttle was emphatic: "A medium cannot be controlled to do anything against his determined will, and the plea that he is compelled by spirits is no excuse for wrong-doing. The medium, like anyone else, knows right from wrong, and if the controlling spirit urges towards the wrong, yielding is as reprehensible as it would be to the promptings of passion or the appetite."

Intelligence and Mediumship

The question of the medium's intelligence seems to have nothing to do with psychic powers, but it may greatly influence the power of the communicators to convey clear ideas. The most stolid mediums may exhibit an extraordinary intelligence in trance. If they are educated the manifestation becomes more marvelous. The question naturally arises whether in the long run spirit influence imparts knowledge to rustic minds. The Reverend **J. B. Ferguson** answered the question in the affirmative:

"Supramundane influence in the unfolding and education of mind has been a common and most interesting experience since my own attention was called to this subject. In the case of Mr. H. B. Champion we have a very remarkable instance. This gentleman, now distinguished for his comprehensiveness of thought on all subjects connected with mental and moral philosophy, and for unrivalled force and beauty of expression, was, to my personal knowledge, educated entirely under these influences. He was not educated even in ordinary branches, such as the orthography of his native tongue; was never at school but a few months in life. That which was at first the gift of a supramundane power is now his own; and unless his history were known he would be considered, as he often is, as a man of the highest accomplishments."

Ferguson testified similarly regarding George W. Harrison, another medium he believed to be educated by psychic power. He concluded: "These gentlemen are today highly educated men. They speak and write our language with great precision and accuracy. They converse with men of the first attainments on all questions that engage cultivated thought. They are sought by men distinguished as professors in various departments of science; and where their history is not known, as it is to myself and to others, they are recognised at once as men of very high order of culture."

Physical and Mental Mediums

The classification of mediums is diverse, but in general they fall into two main groups: physical and mental mediums. Physical mediumship as a rule means that there is no intellectual content behind the phenomena. The distinction is useful, as the coexistence of highly developed intellectual and physical phenomena is somewhat rare. These gifts either alternate or develop along lines of specification.

Leonora Piper produced no physical phenomena, and Gladys Osborne Leonard but very few. Franek Kluski was a universal medium. D. D. Home was mostly famous for his telekinetic manifestations. His trance phenomena were not studied in detail. Moses' powerful physical manifestations occurred in a small circle of friends. He was not subject to scientific experiments on these phenomena, but they were recorded. A more valuable record, affording unusual opportunity for study, was left behind in the automatic scripts of his trance phenomena.

The Medium's Source of Power

As a rule, most mediums require assistance for the production of their phenomena. The sitters of the circle often feel drained of power. According to Joseph Maxwell, Eusapia Palladino could quickly discern people from whom she could easily draw the force she needed: "In the course of my first experiments with this medium, I found out this vampirism to my cost. One evening, at the close of a sitting at l'Agnelas, she was raised from the floor and carried on to the table with her chair. I was not seated beside her, but, without releasing her neighbors' hands she caught hold of mine while the phenomena was happening. I had a cramp in the stomach—I cannot better define my sensation—and was almost overcome by exhaustion."

Justinus Kerner stated that the Seeress of Prevorst (**Frederica Hauffe**) ate little and said that she was nourished by the substance of her visitors, especially of those related to her by the ties of blood, their constitution being more sympathetic with her own. Visitors who passed some minutes near her often noticed upon leaving that they were weakened.

Some mediums seemingly draw more of the sitters' vitality than others. These mediums become less exhausted and consequently can sit more often. **Etta Wriedt,** the direct voice medium, always left her sitters weak. Vice-Admiral Usborne Moore complained that he could hardly use his legs after a sitting.

In one instance in **Elizabeth d'Esperance**'s mediumship the draw on the sitter was seen as the cause of death. The materialized phantom was grabbed, and an older woman (the mother of the assailant), who those in attendance suggested had contributed most of the **ectoplasm** for the materialization, was seriously injured. Reportedly, after much suffering, she died. (*Light,* November 21, 1903).

If the sitters of the circle are mediumistic themselves, the phenomena tend to increase in strength. Perhaps the strongest mediumistic circle ever recorded was the family of **Jonathan Koons,** of Ohio. From the seven-month-old infant to the 18-year-old Nahum, the eldest of the family, all the children were mediumistic, making, with the parents, a total of ten mediums. The same curious power was manifest in the family of John Tippie, who had a similar spirit house at a distance of two or three miles from that of the Koons. Ten children formed his "spirit battery."

From 1859 to 1860, D. D. Home often gave joint séances with the American medium and editor, **J. R. M. Squire.** Later he sometimes sat with Kate Jencken, one of the Fox sisters, and with Stainton Moses. **Frank Herne** and **Charles Williams** joined partnership in 1871; Miss C. E. Wood sat with **Annie Fairlamb.** The spirit photographer **William Hope** usually sat with Mrs. Buxton, a member of the Crewe Circle founded by Archdeacon **Thomas Colley.**

Catherine Berry was known as a "developing" medium. According to a note signed by the editor of *Human Nature,* and published in Berry's *Experiences in Spiritualism* (1876), ". . . after sitting with Mrs. Berry a medium has more power to cause the phenomena at any other circle he may have to attend. Messrs. Herne and Williams have been known to visit this lady for the purpose of getting a supply of power when they had a special séance to give. Mrs. Berry is, therefore, successful in developing mediums, and has conferred the spirit voice manifestation, as well as other gifts, upon several mediums. In a public meeting, a speaker or trance medium is benefitted by having Mrs. Berry sitting near him. These facts have not been arrived at hastily, but after years of patient investigation."

Automatic writers have often joined forces. **Frederick Bligh Bond** and the automatists with whom he received the **Glastonbury scripts** presented a case of dual mediumship. Similarly the "Oscar Wilde" scripts were produced through the mediumship of **Hester Dowden** and Mr. V. On the other hand, mediums may antagonize each other and nullify the power. **Florence Cook** always objected on this ground to sitting with her sister Katie.

Machine Mediumship

An early idea in the history of mediumship was the possibility of mechanical communication. The first confused thought of communicating with the spirit world through instruments occurred to **John Murray Spear,** who constructed something called the "**new motor.**" He arranged copper and zinc batteries in the form of an armor around the medium and expected a phenomenal increase of mediumistic powers through the combination of "mineral" and "vital" electricity. The **dynamistograph,** the **Vandermeulen spirit indicator,** the **reflectograph** and the **communigraph** were later developments. The most recent developments concern **electronic voice phenomenon,** also known as **Raudive voices,** and the **SPIRICOM.**

Mediumistic Induction

Incidents with mediums have led some to conclude that, similar to electricity, mediumistic power can be generated by induction. D. D. Home was the most famous medium for imparting his powers to others. Cases are on record in which he levitated others. Once he imparted the power of **elongation** to a Miss Bertolacci, and he bestowed **fire immunity** in a number of cases on his sitters.

The phenomenon of mediumistic induction was observed as modern Spiritualism spread. Those who sat with the Fox sisters sometimes discovered mediumistic abilities in themselves. **Mrs. Benedict** and **Sarah Tamlin,** the two best early mediums, were developed through the gift of Kate Fox. A writer in the *New Haven Journal* in October 1850, refers to knockings and other phenomena in seven different families in Bridgeport; 40 different families in Rochester, Auburn, and Syracuse; some two hundred in Ohio, New Jersey, and places more distant; as well as in Hartford, Springfield, Charlestown, and other cities.

Several famous early investigators went on to become mediums. Judge **John W. Edmonds,** Prof. **Robert Hare,** and **William Howitt,** all confessed to having received the gift. In his last years the psychical researcher **Richard Hodgson** was said to be in direct contact with the "Imperator" group. Sir Arthur Conan Doyle developed automatic writing and direct voice in his family. **H. Dennis Bradley** received the power of direct voice after his sittings with **George Valiantine.** Marquis Centurione Scotto also developed his powers through Valiantine.

Sources:

Bayless, Raymond. *Voices From Beyond.* New Hyde Park, N.Y.: University Books, 1975.

Bouissou, Michaël. *The Life of a Sensitive.* London: Sidgwick & Jackson, 1955.

Britten, Emma Hardinge. *Modern American Spiritualism.* London, 1870. Reprint, New Hyde Park, N.Y.: University Books, 1970.

———. *Nineteenth-Century Miracles.* London & Manchester, 1883.

Carrington, Hereward. *Higher Psychical Development.* London: Kegan Paul, 1920. Reprint, New York: Dodd, Mead, 1924.

———. *Your Psychic Powers and How to Develop Them.* New York: American Universities Publishing, 1920. Reprint, New York: Causeway, 1973.

Chaney, Robert Galen. *Mediums and the Development of Mediumship.* Michigan: Psychic Books, 1946. Reprint, Freeport, N.Y.: Books for Libraries, 1972.

Christopher, Milbourne. *Mediums, Mystics and the Occult.* New York: Thomas Y. Crowell, 1975.

Ellis, D. J. *The Mediumship of the Tape Recorder.* Pulborough, England: The Author, 1978.

Flint, Leslie. *Voices in the Dark: My Life As a Medium.* New York: Macmillan, 1971.

Fodor, Nandor. *The Haunted Mind: A Psychoanalyst Looks at the Supernatural.* New York: Helix/Garrett, 1959.

Garrett, Eileen J. *Adventures in the Supernormal: A Personal Memoir.* New York: Garrett/Helix, 1949. Reprint, New York: Paperback Library, 1968.

———. *My Life As a Search for the Meaning of Mediumship.* London: Rider, 1939. Reprint, New York: Arno Press, 1975.

Home, D. D. *Incidents in My Life.* London, 1863. Reprint, New Hyde Park, N.Y.: University Books, 1973.

Leaf, Horace. *Psychology and the Development of Mediumship.* London, 1926.

Leonard, Gladys Osborne. *My Life in Two Worlds.* London: Cassell, 1931.

Leonard, Maurice. *Battling Bertha; The Biography of Bertha Harris.* London: Regency Press, 1975.

———. *Medium: The Biography of Jessie Nason.* London: Regency Press, 1974.

MacGregor, Helen, and Margaret V. Underhill. *The Psychic Faculties and Their Unfoldment.* London: L.S.A. Publications, 1930.

Manning, Matthew. *The Link: Matthew Manning's Own Story of His Extraordinary Psychic Gifts.* London: Corgi, 1975. Reprint, New York: Holt, Rinehart & Winston, 1975.

Northage, Ivy. *The Mechanics of Mediumship.* London: Spiritualist Association of Great Britain, 1973.

Patanjali. *The Yoga-Sutras of Patanjali.* Translated by M. N. Dvivedi. Adyar, Madras, India: Theosophical Publishing House, 1890.

Piper, Alta. *The Life and Work of Mrs. Piper.* London: Kegan Paul, 1929.

Podmore, Frank. *Modern Spiritualism.* 2 vols. London, 1902. Reprinted as *Mediums of the Nineteenth Century.* 2 vols. New Hyde Park, N.Y.: University Books, 1963.

Price, Harry, and E. J. Dingwall, eds. *Revelations of a Spirit Medium.* London: Kegan Paul, 1922.

Roberts, Estelle. *Fifty Years a Medium.* London: Corgi; New York: Avon Books, 1975.

Salter, W. H. *Trance Mediumship: An Introductory Study of Mrs. Piper and Mrs. Leonard.* Rev. ed. London: Society for Psychical Research, 1962.

Smith, Susy. *Confessions of a Psychic.* New York: Macmillan; London: Collier-Macmillan, 1971.

Spraggett, Allen, and William V. Rauscher. *Arthur Ford: The Man Who Talked with the Dead.* New York: New American Library, 1973.

Stemman, Roy. *Medium Rare: The Psychic Life of Ena Twigg.* London: Spiritualist Association of Great Britain, 1971.

Stokes, Doris, with Linda Dearsley. *Voices in My Ear: The Autobiography of a Medium.* London: Futura, 1980.

Tietze, Thomas R. *Margery.* New York: Harper & Row, 1973.

Tubby, Gertrude Ogden. *Psychics and Mediums.* Boston: Marshall Jones, 1935.

Turvey, Vincent N. *The Beginnings of Seership.* London: Stead Publishing House, 1911. Reprint, New Hyde Park, N.Y.: University Books, 1969.

Wallis, E. W., and M. H. Wallis. *A Guide to Mediumship and Spiritual Unfoldment.* 3 vols. London, 1903.

Zymonidas, A. *The Problems of Mediumship.* London: Kegan Paul, 1920.

The Medium and Daybreak (Journal)

Spiritualist weekly, started in 1869 by **James Burns,** originally published under the title, *Medium,* later absorbing the *Daybreak,* a provincial paper, founded in 1867.

For years it had the largest circulation of any weekly on **Spiritualism.** It was published until Burns died in 1895.

Medjugorje

Name of a village in Yugoslavia that has been the site of claimed **apparitions** of the Virgin Mary. The case follows a pattern seen also at **Lourdes,** La Salette, and **Fatima,** in which teenage visionaries state that the Virgin has given them "secrets" concerning civilization and religion. It is the latest of a series of prominent cases of the apparition of the Virgin that began in the early nineteenth century.

The visionaries have attracted some attention due to their location. They began to report apparitions in 1981 in Yugoslavia, at that time an atheist Marxist country. Although Yugoslavia was independent of the Soviet Union, the state tolerated religion but hardly encouraged it. The reported apparitions brought many tourists, especially from Italy, into the country. Medjugorje is located at some distance from the Serbian-Bosnian war as it progresses into the 1990s, but the number of visitors from outside of the country has definitely dropped. Additional complications concerning the apparitions occurred not only over confrontations between church and state, but also between different branches of Christianity (Roman Catholic and Eastern Orthodox).

The intricate story of the apparitions has been presented in a stream of books and several documentaries such as *The Madonna of Medjugorje,* produced by Angela Tilby, which appeared in the British Broadcasting Company's *Everyman* series in 1986.

Background History of Medjugorje

Medjugorje is a small village of some 3,500 people in Bosnia-Herzegovina, about 200 kilometers inland from the Adriatic coast. The area is a meeting place between Serbs and Croats, between Moslem traditions, the Eastern Orthodox Church, the established Catholic Church, and the Franciscans. The region has a complex and troubled history, involving military and religious conflicts.

For four centuries, the region was under Turkish rule, and many Christians were converted to Islam. The Franciscans kept the Catholic faith alive and became identified with the concept of Croatian identity. When the Turks lost power in 1878, Pope Leo XIII appointed non-Franciscans to work in the parish. This was resisted by the laity, and by the Franciscans themselves, who did not wish to lose their status. Conflict of interest between the established Church and the Franciscans on the issues of lay priests has remained latent into the twentieth century.

Another historical problem dates from World War II, when in 1941 a Croatian fascist group was formed with strong Roman Catholic ties. It lasted only a few years, but during that period these Croats were responsible for terrible atrocities against their Serbian neighbors of the Eastern Orthodox faith. Only a short distance from the site of the modern apparitions, hundreds of Serbian women, children, and babies were thrown to their deaths from the top of a high cliff.

The First Apparitions

The first apparition was reported in 1981. There were six visionaries, all teenagers or younger children: four girls, Marija Pavlovic (16), Vicka Ivankovic (16), Mirjana Dragicevic (16), and Ivanka Ivankovic (15), and two boys, Ivan Dragicevic (16) and Jakov Colo (10).

On the feast of St. John, June 24, 1981, Ivanka, Marija, and Mirjana went for a walk to the hill of Crnica. Ivanka suddenly exclaimed "There's Our Lady!" Mirjana felt unable to look, but Ivanka was convinced that she had seen an apparition of the Virgin Mary. The girls returned home, and a few hours later set out again to help a farmer with his sheep. They left a message for their friends to follow them. The apparition again appeared, and was also seen by some of the other children, who had met up with Ivanka and Mirjana. The apparition was a beautiful smiling mother with child, wearing a starry crown and floating above the ground.

The following day, four of the teenagers returned to the same place, followed by friends, and this time, Jakov Colo and Marija Pavlovic saw the apparition. Similar encounters took place on succeeding days, when the Virgin spoke to the children in excellent Croatian. She said that she was the Blessed Virgin Mary, sent from God with a gospel message. Asked why the message should come through such ordinary children, she replied that it was precisely because they were ordinary and average, neither the best nor worst, that they had been chosen. Thereafter, the children assembled on the hill each day to witness the apparition.

When news of the apparition reached the church, the parish priest was temporarily absent. The assistant priest was not impressed and thought that maybe the children were on drugs and hallucinating. But after a few days, as the news spread, thousands of devout followers flocked to the hill, many in tears as they witnessed the children in a state of ecstasy.

When Father Jozo Zovko, the parish priest, returned from a retreat, he was astonished to find a chaotic situation, with crowds gathering around the hill. His reaction was one of incredulity that people should seek divine revelation on a hillside when the church itself, with its sacraments, was the proper center for worship.

However, Zovko gave the children some prayer books and rosaries, and tried to instruct them about the church in more detail. He also gave Mirjana a book about the apparitions of Lourdes, from which the children concluded that the current apparitions would cease after July 3rd, as they did at Lourdes. In fact, they did not. On the following day, the children did not visit the hill, but each one had a vision wherever he or she happened to be at the time.

By now, there were serious difficulties involving both church and state authorities. According to state laws, gatherings for worship had to be regulated, and the daily assembly on the hill was not authorized by state or church. News of the apparitions had reached Sarajevo, capital of the republic of Bosnia-Herzegovina, where there was alarm that all this might be a right-wing plot in religious disguise. It was thought that this might indicate a return of Croatian nationalism, with a revival of the old Nazi sympathy. Official observers merged with the crowds to report back on this dangerous situation. The children were interrogated by police and examined by doctors. The gatherings on the hillside were forbidden.

The Second Stage

On July 1, the eighth day of the apparitions, the parish priest was troubled by both religious and state problems. In the church, he prayed for divine guidance, while the police went to the hill to arrest the young visionaries. The children fled through the fields and vineyards, followed by the police. There was only one place of sanctuary—the church.

In an answer to prayer, the priest heard a voice saying "Go and protect the children, then I will tell you what to do." He went to the door of the church and found the children pleading to be hidden. He concealed them in a room in the presbytery. That evening, the apparition came to the children again, but this time in the church itself. Now each evening the congregation gathered to pray in the church and the apparitions appeared as usual to the children. Often in tears, the apparition urged the faithful to confess sins, do penance, and fast once a week on bread and water.

The parish priest now supported the apparitions, and indeed also shared the vision in church. The local bishop, Pavao Zanic, visited the parish on several occasions, but was constrained by his theological and political responsibilities. Government observers attending a church congregation reported back that a sermon about the need for personal change was really a disguised criticism of socialism. Father Jozo was arrested by the police and accused of slandering the state system. In October, he was tried and sentenced to three years' imprisonment. He saw the apparition in prison.

The Aftermath of the Apparitions

Meanwhile, in March 1983, Bishop Zanic appointed a theological commission to investigate and form a judgment on the apparitions. The visionaries reported that the Virgin recommended special prayers for the bishop and his heavy responsibility.

The religious authorities in Rome sent representatives to make their own on-the-spot investigations. The children were given extensive medical and psychological tests. Electroencephalographs probed the ecstatic state of the children during the apparitions, and scientists concluded that they were healthy and sane, and not telling lies. The visionaries focused intently on the same spot during the appearance of the apparition. The ecstatic state was genuine and elevating and certainly not a pathological condition. During this state, the children seemed transported into a higher condition of fulfillment.

Thousands of pilgrims continued to flock to Medjugorje, many seeking inspiration and guidance from the young visionaries. Some typical informal question-and-answer sessions in the open air were recorded by the BBC television team. Because of the large number of pilgrims, priests often took confessions in the open air. The main focal point for these gatherings was a cross, which had been erected many years earlier in 1933 and stood opposite the site of the apparitions. People claimed that the cross sometimes changed into a column of light or into the form of the Virgin, and some photographs taken of the cross certainly show "extras" of this nature.

A somewhat disturbing claim was that people believed that they were able to look into the sun and see it dancing, a phenomenon that had been reported earlier in conjunction with the apparitions at Fatima. Naturally gazing at the sun with the naked eye can produce a number of strange visual effects, but it is a highly dangerous practice.

There were also reports of miraculous healings. The BBC television team recorded an interview with a German woman who was previously unable to walk, but now had no difficulty.

These large-scale demonstrations of a revival of faith were alarming both to state and ecclesiastical authorities. Bishop Pavao Zanic found himself in an increasingly delicate position. He had earlier defended the integrity of the children, and was fully aware that their experience might be as valid as those at Lourdes and Fatima, but was reluctant to sanction organized pilgrimages to the site of the apparitions.

While his commission worked slowly in its investigations, an old controversy was now inflamed. The Franciscans had been the parish clergy in Medjugorje for many years. In 1980, during a reorganization instigated by the authorities in Rome, the bishop had attempted to replace two of the Franciscans with secular clergy. The two friars now consulted the visionaries, seeking the opinion of the Virgin, and it was reported that the Virgin told the children that the bishop should not have suspended the friars. The bishop now became critical of the claimed apparitions as hallucinations inflamed by disaffected Franciscans, and refused to endorse the phenomena or to facilitate pilgrimages.

On the other hand, he did not discourage the pilgrims. Consequently a vast pilgrim and tourist trade grew up at Medjugorje without state or religious sponsorship. In spite of primitive conditions in the area and the nearby war, pilgrims have continued to come from all over Europe in the thousands.

Ironically, the Virgin's message had been one of peace and reconciliation. The report of the bishop's commission was secret, but it was believed to have concluded that the claims of the visionaries were false. The bishop himself stated that the apparitions were collective hallucinations, exploited by the Franciscans, and strongly criticized the chaplain at Medjugorje, Father Tomislav Vlasic, as "a mystifier and charismatic wizard."

There was a theological deadlock. The visionaries were banned from seeing apparitions in the church, but continued to do so in a study bedroom in the presbytery. Meanwhile, the international fame of Medjugorje won a grudging tolerance from the government, which saw the influx of pilgrims as a vindication of Yugoslavia as an open country.

Part of the price of the spiritual revival at Medjugorje has been the inevitable commercialization of the religious tourist trade. The simple village life has been totally uprooted by thousands of tourists, ice cream and soft drink stands, stalls for the sale of religious souvenirs, and other worldly activities. But villagers still meet in small groups, sometimes at night. Two younger girls claim to have seen visions and received messages.

The original group of six young visionaries claimed that the Virgin confided ten secrets, including warnings of future world chastisements if people did not return to spiritual life. People were recommended to give up watching television, and return instead to a life of prayer, fasting, and penance. The world had advanced civilization but had lost God. It was prophesied that Russia would come to glorify the name of God. As with apparitions elsewhere, it was said that there would be a visible sign left on the hill. The visions have now ceased so far as the six children are concerned.

Ivanka received her last "secret" from the Virgin in May 1985, and in early 1987 married. Mirjana took up the study of agriculture at the University of Sarajevo. Ivan's apparitions ceased when he was enlisted for a year of military service. Vicka became ill with an inoperable brain tumor. Jakov was still at school in 1986. Marija planned to become a nun. The fascinating film records of the children in states of ecstasy, as well as the EEG tests, remain a permanent record, as do other of the numerous medical and scientific studies.

Psychiatrists, doctors, and scientists concluded that the visionaries were psychologically healthy, without neurosis or hysteria, and that their ecstasies were not a pathological phenomenon. The fasts on bread and water recommended once or twice weekly could merely counteract the excesses of normal diet without risk of starvation. The cures at Medjugorje were reported upon favorably by doctors from the University of Milan.

The apparitions at Medjugorje present many intriguing problems, both for skeptics and believers. Such apparitions now follow a regular pattern within the framework of Catholic theology, just as claims of **UFO** contacts are often consistent with a different pattern of belief.

It could be argued that once such conventions are established, knowledge of them influences other visionaries. In the case of Medjugorje, the parish priest had shown one of the visionaries a book about Lourdes, although it must be remembered that the apparitions had established a regular pattern before this.

The ecstatic state of the young visionaries was undoubtedly very real, and in the audio-visual records they appear to be modest, honest, and touchingly sincere, too simple to be able to fabricate intellectually advanced theological discussions. The occasional contradictory elements in the claimed communications from the Virgin (as in the instance of apparent criticism of the bishop), may be due to the intense pressures from lay and ecclesiastical authorities to which the children were subjected; they may also have been misquoted from time to time. The messages about the need for renewal of religious faith and practice are a relevant comment on the secularism of our time, although with a sophistication normally beyond the awareness of village children.

But, as with Lourdes, Fatima, Garabandal, and other apparitions, the messages are only within the framework of the Roman Catholic faith, and there is no insightful communication for Hindus, Buddhists, or people of other religions.

In the West, the apparitions have produced a wave of enthusiastic acceptance of the visions and organizations have sprung up in every significant Roman Catholic community to spread the message of the Virgin and to facilitate tours to the site. However, there has been some opposition among those elements of the Roman Catholic Church who have not only failed to accept the visions, but who feel that they are false. Among the leading critics is Yugoslavian priest Ivo Sivric. He had compiled and published a host of records, many of which he claimed were suppressed, which cast grave doubts upon the apparitions and the continued attention given to the site. He has argued that the apparitions emanated from the children who first saw them. He was joined by E. Michael Jones, who also found numerous contradictions in the events surrounding the apparitions.

Sources:

Jones, E. Michael. *Medjugorje: The Untold Story.* South Bend, Ind.: Fidelity Press, 1988.

Kraljevic, Svetozar. *Apparitions of Our Lady of Medjugorje (1981–1983).* Chicago: Franciscan Herald Press, 1984.

Laurentin, René, and Henri Joyeux. *Scientific & Medical Studies on the Apparitions at Medjugorje.* Dublin: Veritas, 1987.

Laurentin, René, and L. Rupcic. *Is the Virgin Mary Appearing at Medjugorje?* Washington, D.C.: Word Among Us Press, 1984.

Laurentin, René, L. Rupcic, and René Lejeune. *Messages and Teachings of Mary at Medjugorje.* Milford, Ohio: The Riehle Foundation, 1988.

O'Carroll, Michael. *Medjugorje: Facts, Documents, Theology.* Dublin: Veritas, 1986.

Pelletier, Joseph A. *The Queen of Peace Visits Medjugorje.* Worchester, Mass.: Assumption, 1985.

Sevric, Ivo. *The Hidden Side of Medjugorje.* Saint Francois du Lac, Canada: Psilog, 1989.

Meehl, Paul E(verett) (1920–)

Professor of psychology who has written on **parapsychology.** He was born January 3, 1920, at Minneapolis, Minnesota, and was educated at the University of Minnesota (B.A. summa cum laude, 1941; Ph.D., 1945). Meehl joined the faculty of the psychology department at the University of Minnesota and served as its chair (1951–57); he was also a professor of clinical psychology with the University of Minnesota Medical School department of psychiatry beginning in 1951. He had his own private practice as a psychotherapist and was elected president of the American Psychological Association (1961–62).

Meehl had a continuing interest in parapsychology and belonged to the **American Society for Psychical Research.** He wrote various books and many articles on psychological subjects, as well as articles on the paranormal, which he attempted to integrate into his mainstream psychological insights.

Sources:

Meehl, Paul E., and M. J. Scriven. "Compatibility of Science and ESP." *Science* 123 (1956).

Meehl, Paul E., H. R. Klann, and K. H. Breimeter. *What, Then, Is Man?* N.p., 1958.

Pleasants, Helene, ed. *Biographical Dictionary of Parapsychology.* New York: Helix Press, 1964.

Meerloo, Joost A(braham) M(aurits) (1903–1976)

Psychiatrist, psychoanalyst, and writer on **parapsychology.** He was born on March 14, 1903, at The Hague, Netherlands. He was educated at Leyden University (M.D., 1927) and Utrecht University (Ph.D., 1932). His appointments included psychiatric-neurologic consultant, Municipal Hospital, Voorburg and The Hague (1934–42); chief of the pychological department, Netherlands Army (1943–45); and high commissioner for welfare in the Netherlands (1945–46). He moved to the United States after World War II as an associate in psychiatry at Columbia University (1948–57). In 1958 he became a professor of political science at the New School for Social Research in New York City, then an associate professor of psychiatry at the New York School of Psychiatry in 1962.

He was a member of Royal Society of Medicine, American Psychiatric Association, American Academy of Psychoanalysis, Schilder Society (secretary), Tokyo Institute for Psychoanalysis (honorary member), and Albany Society for Psychosomatic Medicine.

During the 1960s Meerloo was considered an influential thinker in America. Besides his many books, he published over 300 articles on psychology, politics, and literature. Less known was his interest and writings in parapsychology and his membership in the **American Society for Psychical Research.** He was also a corresponding member of the **Studievereniging voor Psychical Research** (Dutch Society for Psychical Research). He delivered a paper at the First International Conference on Parapsychology in the Netherlands. His activity on behalf of the paranormal came in the 1950s and 1960s. He died November 17, 1976.

Sources:

Meerloo, Joost A. M. "The Biology of Time." *Tomorrow* (winter 1954).

———. *Hidden Communion.* New York: Garrett Publications, 1964.

———. "Man's Ecstatic Healing." *Tijdschrift voor Parapsychologie* 27 (1959).

———. *The Rape of the Mind: The Psychology of Thought Control, Menticide, and Brainwashing.* N.p., 1956.

———. "Telepathy and Foreknowledge." In *Proceedings of the First International Conference on Parapsychology.* Utrecht, 1953.

———. "Telepathy as a Form of Archaic Communication." *Psychiatric Quarterly* 23 (1949).

———. *Unobtrusive Communication.* Assen, The Netherlands: Van Gorcum, 1964.

Meher Baba (1894–1969)

Indian spiritual teacher and mystic, born Merwin S. Irani on February 25, 1894 in Poona, India. His parents were Parsees, but he was strongly influenced by both Hinduism and Sufi mysticism and was educated at a Christian high school. At the age of 19, he contacted Hazrat Babajan, an elderly Moslem female saint, who kissed his forehead and, as he later related, induced divine consciousness and a state of ecstatic bliss. After that, he devoted his life to religious teaching, usually expressed in a rather erratic fashion, involving journeys with disciples that apparently led nowhere, or in searching out the eccentric and sometimes deranged wandering monks of India. In 1921 he established an ashram devoted largely to philanthropic work. He had contact with **Sai Baba,** of whom **Satya Sai Baba** is claimed to be a **reincarnation.**

In 1925 Meher Baba entered upon a period of silence, conversing or giving lectures with an alphabet board. He often prophesied in this way that he would one day speak the One Word that would bring spiritualization and love to the world, but he died January 31, 1969, without utterance. Many believe that his prophecy may have been symbolic, like his mysterious life itself, and devotees continue to share the intense affection, of a Sufi kind, that characterized his mission during his lifetime. He came to be regarded by many disciples as an *avatar,* or descent of divine power.

One early American disciple of Meher Baba was Rabia Martin. She led a Sufi group originally established by Pir Inayat Khan (1881–1927). She had a falling out with Pir Khan's successors and looked for a new teacher, began to correspond with Meher Baba, and eventually accepted him as the *Qutb,* a Sufi term for hub of the universe. Martin's successor, Ivy Duce, visited Meher Baba in India, and in 1952 he visited her in Myrtle Beach, South Carolina, and gave her and the Sufis a plan of organization known as Sufism Reoriented.

Since then, however, the followers of Meher Baba have grown quite apart from Sufism Reoriented. They have a very loose, decentralized organization built around independent centers where meetings are held and literature distributed. Because Meher Baba's primary message was one of Divine Love, his followers are generally termed "Lovers of Meher Baba." To make contact with the followers of Meher Baba, write the Meher Spiritual Center, 10200 Hwy. 17 N., Myrtle Beach, SC 29577.

Sources:

Baba, Meher. *Discourses.* Myrtle Beach, S.C.: Sheriar Press, 1987.

———. *God Speaks.* New York: Dodd, Mead, 1973.

Davy, Kitty. *Love Alone Prevails.* Myrtle Beach, S.C.: Sheriar Press, 1981.

Duce, Ivy Oneida. *How a Master Works.* Walnut Creek, Calif.: Sufism Reoriented, 1971.

Hopkinson, Tom, and Dorothy Hopkinson. *Much Silence.* New York: Dodd, Mead, 1975.

Meier, C(arl) A(lfred) (1905–)

Swiss Jungian psychotherapist who wrote on **parapsychology.** He was born on April 19, 1905, at Schaffhausen, Switzerland. He was educated at University of Paris Medical School, the University of Venice, and the University of Zurich Medical School (M.D.).

Besides his private practice as a psychotherapist, he was an assistant, then director, of laboratory research at the Burghölzli Psychiatric Clinic of Zurich University (1930–36) and became a professor of psychology at Swiss Federal Institute of Technology, Zurich, in 1949. Meier served as president of the C. G. Jung Institute, Zurich (1948–57) and was editor of *Studien aus dem C. G. Jung Institute* (1949–57). In 1957 he founded the International Association for Analytical Psychology.

Meier wrote *Jung and Analytical Psychology* (1959) and many articles on psychotherapy, Jungian analysis, and other psychological topics. He had a special interest in relationships between the unconscious and **extrasensory perception.** Meier edited *Studien zu C. G. Jung's Psychologie* written by Toni Wolff (1959).

Sources:

Meier, Carl A. *Ancient Incubation and Modern Psychotherapy.* Evanston, Ill.: Northwestern University Press, 1968.

———. "C. G. Jung's Concept of Synchronicity." In *Proceedings of the First International Conference of Parapsychological Studies* (1955).

———. "Jung's 'Meaningful Coincidence.'&43" *Tomorrow* (spring 1954).

———. "Projection, Transference, and Subject-Object Relation." In *Proceedings of the International Symposium on Psychology and Parapsychology* (1957).

———. "Psychological Background of So-Called Spontaneous Phenomena." In *Proceedings of the Conference on Spontaneous Phenomena* (1957).

Meier, Eduard Albert "Billy" (1937–)

One of the most famous of modern flying saucer **contactees,** Billy Meier emerged out of obscurity in 1975 when he claimed to have encountered people from the Pleiadian star system. To verify his claims he presented some dramatic photos of the spaceship and eventually made some videos of the ship flying near his home in rural Switzerland.

Meier was born on February 3, 1937, in Bulach, Switzerland. According to his story, he had seen a UFO as a child and subsequently heard a voice and saw mental pictures. These communications occurred daily and he learned to respond to them telepathically. In 1944, he met a humanoid named Sfath and took his first ride in a saucer. Sfath told him that he had been chosen and would come to understand his special status at a later date. His telepathic contacts with Sfath continued for some years but he was replaced after Meier's 16th birthday by Asket, a youthful female. These contacts existed side-by-side with outward signs of an unsettled life. As a youth Meier ran away from home several times, eventually landing in the French Foreign Legion. In 1958 he began a period of wandering through the Middle East and southern Asia. Following an accident in 1965, he lost his left arm just above his elbow. He finally returned to Switzerland in 1970 and settled on a farm.

In 1974, he advertised for people who would like to be part of a metaphysical study group, and soon had a small gathering joining him for discussions of occult matters. The next year he announced that he had not only seen a flying saucer, but that it had landed and a beautiful woman disembarked. He talked with her for an hour and a half. The woman, Semjase, hailed from the planet Erra in the **Pleiades.** Of all the people with whom the Pleiadians had made contact, only Meier had passed all the tests. Semjase set the stage for Meier to take a host of pictures of what were termed "beamships," Meier's primary evidence to an unbelieving world. He claimed to have taken a number of rides in the beamships, including a visit to the Pleiades.

European media began to give Meier coverage and controversy grew through 1976. His following also grew and with money they raised, he moved to property purchased near Hinterschmidruti that has been his headquarters ever since. The study group evolved into the **Freie Interessengemeinschaft für Grenz-und Geisteswissenschaften und Ufologie-Studien.** Among the people who learned of the Meier claims were Lou Zinstagg and Timothy Good, who were working on a biography of **George Adamski,** the original 1950s contactee. They brought copies of the Meier pictures to the United States and gave them to contactee enthusiast Wendelle Stevens. Stevens visited Meier in October of 1977, and after investigating his claims, created a company, Genesis III Productions Limited, to market the photos and related stories. In 1979, a coffee-table book, *UFO. . . Contact from the Pleiades, Volume One,* made the world aware of his claims. Additional books and several videos subsequently appeared.

As controversy swelled around Meier, with most ufologists rejecting his contactee claims, in 1981 Kal K. Kroff published the results of his investigation, *The Meier Incident: The Most Infamous Hoax in Ufology.* He demonstrated that Meier's photos were of small models held by string. He followed with a second book, *Spaceships from the Pleiades,* in 1990. Among the most damaging discoveries concerned some pictures supposedly taken from space by Meier that turned out to be NASA photos. More people, however, read writer Gary Kinder's generally favorable book, *Light Years.*

Stevens and his associates have remained staunch supporters of Meier and have continued to distribute the many Genesis III publications through the 1990s. Stevens has edited a multivolume series of Meier's contact notes. The Semjase Silver Star Center was opened as an American counterpart to the Meier organization in Europe. The Meier material freely circulated through the New Age Movement, with New Age bookstores being a major means of distributing it. The impact of this material is visibly demonstrated in the prominence given the Pleiades in channeling material. Beginning in the late 1980s, a host of **New Age** channelers have regularly received messages from entities identifying themselves as Pleiadians.

Sources:

Elders, Lee J., Brit Nilsson-Elders, and Thomas K. Welch. *UFO. . . Contact from the Pleiades, Volume One.* Phoenix, Ariz.: Genesis III Productions, 1979.

———. *UFO. . .Contact from the Pleiades, Volume Two.* Phoenix, Ariz.: Genesis III Productions, 1983.

Kinder, Gary. *Light Years: An Investigation into the Extraterrestrial Experiences of Eduard Meier.* New York: Atlantic Monthly, 1987.

Kroff, Kal K. *Spaceships of the Pleiades: The Billy Meier Story.* Amherst, N.Y.: Prometheus Press, 1995.

———, and William Moore. *The Meier Incident—The Most Infamous Hoax in Ufology.* Fremont, Calif.: The Authors, 1981.

Meier, Eduard "Billy." *Decalogue or the Ten Bids.* Alamogordo, N. Mex.: Semjase Silver Star Center, 1987.

———. *The Psyche.* Alamogordo, N. Mex.: Semjase Silver Star Center, [1986].

Meisner (or **Mesna Lorentz**) (ca. 1608)

Early alchemist whose work is recorded in his tract *Gemma Gemmarum Alchimistarum; oder, Erleuterung der Parabolischen und Philosophischen Schrifften Fratris Basilij, der zwölff Schlüssel, von dem Stein der vharalten Weisen, und desselben aufsdrücklichen und warhaften praeparation; Sampt etlichen seinen Particularen,* published in Leipzig in 1608. This edition also includes a tract on the **philosophers' stone** by Conrad Schülern. (See also **alchemy**)

Mellon, Annie Fairlamb (**Mrs. J. B. Mellon**) (ca. 1850–ca. 1938)

British **materialization medium.** Her first supernormal experience was at the age of nine, when she saw her brother at sea in danger of drowning. Later physical powers manifested in a violent trembling of hand and arm. This was followed, in the family circle, by **automatic writing** with lightning-like speed, by **clairvoyance,** and by **clairaudience.** With bandaged eyes she would fall into a **trance** and describe events happening at the time many miles away, events which were subsequently verified.

In 1873 she and **C. E. Wood** were employed as official mediums of the Newcastle Spiritual Evidence Society. In 1875 they sat for **Henry Sidgwick** and **F. W. H. Myers** of the **Society for Psychical Research** at Cambridge, England. The **séances,** which were held under the strictest test conditions, produced excellent results, but neither Sidgwick nor Myers chose to announce their observations in public.

In 1877 Alderman T. P. Barkas of Newcastle made successful experiments to obtain spirit molds (see **plastics**). Unknown to Fairlamb, he mixed magenta dye with the paraffin. The molds were found to be tinted with magenta, which proved that they were not smuggled in ready-made.

After touring the Continent, during which German investigators found that she lost almost half of her bodily weight during materializations, Fairlamb went to Australia. There she married J. B. Mellon of Sydney but continued to give sittings at her own home. Charles W. MacCarthy, at whose residence Mellon often sat, became convinced of the reality of the phenomena.

On October 12, 1894, a disastrous exposure of her **fraud** took place in Mellon's house. T. Shekleton Henry, another medium and pretended friend, grabbed "Cissie," the materialized spirit, and found it to be the medium half undressed. The missing pieces of garment were found in the cabinet. Mellon defended herself by saying that she seemed to shoot into the grabbed form and became absorbed. She was said to have suffered serious injury in consequence of the spirit grabbing, and after her recovery she resolved never to sit in the cabinet again but always before the curtain in full view of the sitters.

The story of the exposure is told by T. Shekleton Henry in *Spookland* (1902), to which a rebuttal was published by someone under the pseudonym "Psyche" in *A Counterblast to Spookland; or, Glimpses of the Marvellous* (1895).

As late as 1931 Mellon was still active as a medium. H. L. Williams, a retired magistrate from the Punjab, wrote to Harry Price (*Psychic Research,* June 1931): "As regards her (Mrs. Mellon), Dr. Haworth, a well-known doctor of Port Darwin, has testified before me that at Melbourne, in the presence of leading and professional men, he saw many times a spot of mist on the carpet which rose into a column out of which stepped a completely embodied human being who was recognised. . . ." Sir William Windeyer, chief judge, and Alfred Deaking, prime minister of Australia, were, according to the letter, convinced that Mellon was genuine. Of course none of these men, however eminent, were trained observers.

Melton, J(ohn) Gordon (1942–)

Religious studies scholar and director of the **Institute for the Study of American Religion,** Santa Barbara, California. Born September 19, 1942, in Birmingham, Alabama, he attended Birmingham Southern College (A.B. in geology, 1964), Garrett Theological Seminary (M.Div. with distinction, 1968), and Northwestern University (Ph.D. in history and literature of religion, 1975).

Melton was ordained a United Methodist minister in 1968. In 1969, while in graduate school, he founded the Institute for the Study of American Religion to focus research on the many new and small religious groups that were emerging in late twentieth-century America. Melton served as the national field director of the **Spiritual Frontiers Fellowship** (1971–74), and was one of the founders of the **Academy of Religion and Psychical Research.** In 1975 he transferred from the North Alabama Conference to the Northern Illinois Conference of the United Methodist Church and was appointed pastor of the Emmanuel United Methodist Church in Evanston, Illinois. In 1980 he left the pastorate and was appointed director of the Institute for the Study of American Religion, a post he has retained to the present. In 1985 the institute relocated to Santa Barbara, California. Melton is also a research specialist with the department of religious studies at the University of California–Santa Barbara. In 1990 he co-founded the Society for the Study of Metaphysical Religion and sits on its board.

Melton achieved prominence after publishing his *Encyclopedia of American Religions* (1979; 6th ed., 1999), tracking the many different religions as well as the small religious and psychic/occult organizations in the United States and Canada. The encyclopedia documents their origins, interrelationships, and beliefs. He has taken a special interest in the problems of religious pluralism and the growth of many divergent religions in the Christian West. Melton ardently supports religious freedom and actively opposes the efforts of the anticult movement to stigmatize new religions as "destructive cults."

The Institute for the Study of American Religion maintains a unique and comprehensive collection of research materials on religious groups and organizations in North America. The collection is located at the Davidson Library of the University of California–Santa Barbara. For information, address correspondence to the American Religions Collection, c/o Special Collections Department, Davidson Library, University of California–Santa Barbara, Santa Barbara, CA 93106.

Melton has authored or co-authored more than 25 books since his first in 1967, *The History of the Bowling Green Yoked Charge* (1967). He was an associate editor and contributor to the *Encyclopedia of World Methodism* (1968) and senior editor of several book series, including "The Garland Bibliographies on Sects and Cults" (1982–present); "The Churches Speak" (1989–90); "Cults and New Religions" (1990–91); "Cults and Noncoventional Religious Groups: A Collection of Outstanding Dissertations and Monographs" (1992–94); and "Religious Information Systems" (1992–94). He also works on the editorial board of *Theosophical History.* In 1996 he became the senior editor of the multi-volume *International Directory of the World's Religions.*

Melton's avocational study of vampires manifested in 1983 when he served as editor for *Vampires Unearthed* by Martin Riccardo, the first comprehensive bibliography of English-language vampire literature. In 1994 he authored *The Vampire Book: An Encyclopedia of the Undead* (2nd edition, 1999), *Video Hound's Vampires on Video* (1996), and *The Vampire Gallery* (1998).

Sources:

Melton, J. Gordon. *A Directory of Religious Bodies in the United States.* New York: Garland Publishing, 1977.

———. *Directory of Religious Organizations.* Detroit: Gale Research, 1992.

———. *Encyclopedic Handbook of Cults in America.* New York: Garland Publishing, 1986. Rev. ed. 1992.

———. "A History of the New Age Movement." In *Not Necessarily the New Age.* Edited by Robert Basil. Buffalo, N.Y.: Prometheus Press, 1988.

———. *Paganism, Magic, and Witchcraft.* New York: Garland Publishing, 1982.

———. "Paschal Beverly Randolph: America's Pioneer Occultist." In *Le Défi Magique.* Edited by Jean-Baptiste Martin and Franciose LaPlantine. Lyon, France: Presses Universitaires de Lyon, 1994.

———. "The Revival of Astrology in the United States." In *Religious Movements: Genesis, Exodus, and Numbers.* Edited by Rodney Stark. New York: Paragon House Publishers, 1985.

———. "Toward a History of Magical Religion in the United States." *Listening* 9, no. 3 (autumn 1974): 112–33.

Melton, J. Gordon, Jerome Clark, and Aidan Kelly. *New Age Encyclopedia.* Detroit: Gale Research, 1990.

Melton, J. Gordon, and James R. Lewis, eds. *Perspectives on the New Age.* Albany, N.Y.: State Unversity of New York Press, 1992.

Murphy, Larry, J. Gordon Melton, and Gary L. Ward, eds. *Encyclopedia of African American Religion.* New York: Garland Publishing, 1993.

Melusina

The most famous of the fays, or **fairies,** of medieval French legend. Being condemned to turn into a serpent from the waist downward every Saturday, she made her husband, Count Raymond of Lusignan, promise never to come near her on a Saturday. This prohibition finally excited his curiosity and suspicion, and he hid himself and witnessed his wife's transformation.

Melusina was now compelled to quit her mortal husband and was destined to wander about as a specter until the day of doom. She became the **Banshee** of Lusignan. It is said also that the count immured her in the dungeon of his castle.

Sources:

Briggs, Katherine A. *A Dictionary of Fairies.* London: Penguin Books, 1976. Reprinted as *An Encyclopedia of Fairies, Hobgoblins, Brownies, Bogies, and Other Supernatural Creatures.* New York: Pantheon Books, 1976.

Melzer, Heinrich (1873– ?)

German **apport medium** of Dresden, the successor of Anna Rothe. His early **séances** were reported in *Die Übersinnliche Welt* in November 1905. These were held in darkness, but the medium allowed himself to be fastened into a sack. Quanties of flowers and stones were apported to sitters.

The operators were said to be Oriental entities: "Curadiasamy," a Hindu, who spoke with a foreign accent; "Lissipan," a young Indian Buddhist; and "Amakai," a man from China. "Quirinus," who claimed to be a Roman Christian of the time of Diocletian, and "Abraham Hirschkron," a Jewish merchant from Mahren, were other picturesque **controls.** By occupation Melzer was a small tobacconist. It is said that at one time he was an actor, which may account for his powers of declamation under control.

He visited the **British College of Psychic Science** in 1923 and in 1926. Owing to a significant development in his mediumship, he was able to sit in good white or red light. In 1923 he was examined before each séance and dressed in a one-piece linen suit, secured at wrist and ankles. The flowers arrived when the medium was in deep **trance.** He seemed to be able to observe them clairvoyantly before they appeared to the physical sight. Occasionally sitters, who knew nothing of this, spoke of seeing shadows of flowers in the air before they arrived.

Sometimes the medium seized upon the flowers and ate them voraciously, together with stalks and soil, often wounding his mouth by thorns on rose stalks. Returning to normal consciousness, he blamed a particular control for the occurrence. The flowers seemed to arrive toward the medium and were not thrown out from him.

These phenomena were very impressive. The same could not be said of the stone apports. They were invariably very small, and led to his detection in *fraud.* In the sittings of 1926, the doctor in charge slipped his hands at the back of the ears of the medium and discovered two small light colored stones affixed by flesh-colored sticking plaster. The medium's only attempt at excuse was that by that stage his power had gone and that he had been tempted by an undesirable control.

Spiritualist leader **James Hewat McKenzie** defended Melzer in his report in *Psychic Science* (April 1927):

"But there is a difference between stones of a quarter to half an inch in size, and flowers of 18 inches stalk length, with leaves and thorns. Twenty-five anemones—or a dozen roots of lilies of the valley, with soil attached, pure bells and delicate leaves—or violets appearing fresh and fragrant, after two and a half hours sitting—have all been received, when the medium's hands have been seen empty a second before, when no friends of his were in the sittings, and when no opportunity could have presented itself to conceal them that would not have resulted in broken stems and blossoms."

However, the damage had been done to the medium's credibility.

Menger, Howard (1922–)

One of the original flying saucer **contactees** of the 1950s, Howard Menger emerged in 1956 when he told his story to late-night radio talk show host Long John Nebel. Three years later, his book *From Outer Space to You* appeared. Menger told of contacts that began when he was only ten years old. The original contact was with a beautiful blonde woman whom he met in person but who communicated via telepathy. Other contacts followed with other humanoid beings. Then in 1946, the woman disembarked from a spaceship and announced that a wave of contacts was in humanity's immediate future as many space people were coming to Earth to assist in solving its problems.

In 1956, in the wake of the publicity given contactee **George Adamski,** Menger took some photos of flying saucers, and claimed he took a ride in a Venusian ship. Following his appearance on Nebel's show, he was a guest on a national television shows hosted by Steve Allen and Jack Paar. The television exposure led to attacks by critics. An examination of his pictures led to denouncements that they were a hoax, and they caught Menger lying about his having read (and drawing material from) Adamski's books. Amid the controversy, a young blonde woman came to a gathering at the Menger home. He recognized her as the sister of the space person who had originally contacted him as a child. They began an affair and were eventually married. The woman, Connie Weber, wrote her story, which was published in a book under the pseudonym Karla Baxter. It actually appeared in 1958, a year prior to Menger's first book. The title, *My Saturnian Lover,* continued Menger's claim that he was actually an extraterrestrial who had reincarnated on Earth.

Through the 1960s, Menger seemed to back away from some of his claims, but added assertions of government agents involving him in an elaborate hoax. Through the 1970s and 1980s, the Mengers withdrew from the flying saucer scene, but in the 1990s they returned to reassert their contactee claims. They authored a new book in 1991, and subsequently appeared on a 1992 Discovery Channel one-hour special, "Farewell, Good Brothers," that explored the experiences of several contactees. The Mengers were interviewed before the large saucer model that dominates one room of their Florida home.

Sources:

Baxter, Karla [Connie Weber Menger]. *My Saturnian Lover.* New York: Vantage Press, 1958.

Menger, Connie. *Song of Saturn.* Clarksburg, W.Va.: Saucerian Books, 1968.

Menger, Howard. *From Outer Space to You.* Clarksburg, W.Va.: Saucerian Books, 1959.

———, and Connie Menger. *The High Bridge Incident: The Story Behind the Story.* Vero Beach, Fla.: Howard Menger Studio, 1991.

Meng-Koehler, Heinrich Otto (1887– ?)

Physician, psychoanalyst, and author. He was born on July 9, 1887, at Hohnhurst, Baden, Germany, and studied at the University of Heidelberg (M.D., 1912), the University of Leipzig, and the University of Würzburg. He became director of the Institute of Psychoanalysis, Frankfurt (1928–33), and after the fall of Nazism, he emerged as professor of mental hygiene at the University of Basel, Switzerland (1945–55). Following his retirement he was named professor emeritus.

Meng-Koehler edited and contributed to a number of works on mental health and wrote one book, *Psychohygiene* (Mental Hygiene, 1960). In the field of **parapsychology,** he took special interest in connections with psychoanalysis. He attended the International Conference on Parapsychological Studies held in Utrecht, Netherlands, in 1953, and the Conference on Unorthodox Healing at St. Paul de Vence, 1954.

Sources:

Meng-Koehler, Heinrich O. "Parapsychologie, Psychohygiene, and Aerztliche Fortbildung" (Parapsychology, Mental Hygiene and Medical Training). *Hippokrates* (1954).

———. "Wunderheilungen" (Miracles of Healing). *Hippokrates* (1954).

Men in Black

The mysterious and sinister visitors who are supposed to have silenced **flying saucer** investigator **Albert K. Bender,** as described in the book *They Knew Too Much about Flying Saucers* by Gray Barker (1956). They have since become part of flying saucer mythology, with claimed visitations to other UFO investigators and contactees. Some investigators preferred to believe that they were government officials, possibly from the Central Intelligence Agency (CIA), determined to suppress information on the reality of **UFOs.** For most, the Men in Black myth became but a form in which paranoid fears could be expressed within the ufological community.

Sources:

Clark, Jerome. *The Emergence of a Phenomenon: UFOs from the Beginning through 1959.* Vol. 2 of *The UFO Encyclopedia.* Detroit: Omnigraphics, 1992.

Rojcewicz, Peter M. "The 'Men in Black' Experience and Tradition: Analogues with the Traditional Devil Hypothesis." *Journal of American Folklore* 100 (April/June 1987): 148–60.

Mentalphysics

The system developed by **Edwin John Dingle** (1881–1972) as a synthesis of all he had learned as a young man in his travels in the Orient, especially Tibet. Dingle began teaching informally in 1927 in New York City. His early classes grew into the Institute of Mentalphysics in 1934.

Mentalphysics is seen as a super **yoga.** Dingle taught his students a set of what are believed to be universal truths and a system of practice built around pranayama (breathing), diet (vegetarian), exercises, meditation, and a system of working with one's own particular body chemistry. Breathing is especially important as a means of making use of prana, the subtle energy that permeates the universe, which is both the key to good health and contacting the universal realms. The exact details of the teaching are given to students in a set of 26 basic lessons, 124 advanced lessons, and additional "preceptor" lessons.

Current active membership is approximately 5,000 though more than 200,000 different students have at one time studied Mentalphysics. Students come from North America and various foreign countries.

Address: Institute of Mentalphysics, 59700 Twenty-nine Palms Hwy., Joshua Tree, CA 92252.

Sources:

Dingle, Edwin John. *Borderlands of Eternity.* Los Angeles: Institute of Mentalphysics, 1939.

———. *Breathing Your Way to Youth.* Los Angeles: Institute of Mentalphysics, [1931].

———. *The Voice of the Logos.* Los Angeles: Institute of Mentalphysics, 1950.

Mental World (in Theosophy)

Formerly known as the Manas Plane. In the theosophic scheme of things, this is the third lowest of the seven worlds. It is the world of thought into which man passes on the death of the **astral body,** and it is composed of the seven divisions of matter in common with the other worlds. It is observed that the mental world is the world of thought, but it is necessary to realize that it is the world of good thoughts only, for the base thoughts have all been purged away during the soul's stay in the **astral world.**

Depending on these thoughts is the power to perceive the mental world. The perfected individual would be free of the whole of it, but the ordinary individual in past imperfect experience has gathered only a comparatively small amount of thought and is, therefore, unable to perceive more than a small part of the surroundings. It follows from this that although the individual's bliss is inconceivably great, the sphere of action is very limited. This limitation, however, becomes less and less with the individual's abode there after each fresh incarnation.

In the Heaven world-division into which we awake after dying in the astral world, we find vast, unthought-of means of pursuing what has seemed to us good—art, science, philosophy and so forth. Here, all these come to a glorious fruition of which we can have no conception, and at last the time arrives when one casts aside the mental body and awakens in the causal body to the still greater bliss of the higher division of the mental world.

At this stage, one has done with the bodies which form mortal personality, and which form one's home in successive incarnations, and one is now truly whole, a spirit, immortal and unchangeable except for increasing development and evolution. Into this causal body is worked all that one has experienced in the physical, astral, and mental bodies, and when one still finds that experience insufficient for one's needs, one descends again into grosser matter in order to learn yet more and more.

These concepts derive from the Hindu religious classification of three bodies or states of being: gross (or physical), subtle, and causal (known as *sthula, sukshma,* and *karana shariras*). The causal body is pictured as surrounded by five sheaths (or *koshas*): *annamayakosha* (food or physical sheath); *pranamayakosha* (subtle energy sheath); *manamayakosha* (mental sheath); *vijnanamayakosha* (wisdom sheath); and *anandamayakosha* (bliss sheath of spiritual unity).

Sources:

Jinarajadasa, C. *The Early Teachings of the Masters, 1881–83.* Chicago: Theosophical Press, 1923.

Powell, Arthur E. *The Astral Body and Other Astral Phenomena.* London: Theosophical Publishing House, 1927.

"Mentor"

One of the **controls** of **William Stainton Moses,** said to be Al-gazzali or Ghazali, professor of theology at Baghdad in the eleventh century, the greatest representative of the Arabian Philosophical School. "Mentor' "s main duty was to manage the phenomena at the **séances.** He was very successful with lights and scents and brought many **apports.**

In Book 16 of the spirit communications of Stainton Moses there is a story of "Mentor" carving heads on two shells in the dining room while dinner was going on; the sound of the process was heard.

Mephis (or Memphitis)

A fabled precious stone that, when ground to powder and drunk in water, was said to cause insensibility to torture.

Mercurii, Society of the

The Society of the Mecurii was an occult magical organization that operated in London, England, in the 1830s and was one of the primary groups that launched the occult and astrological revival that has led to the spectacular growth of the occult world in the twentieth century. The first public mention of the society seems to have been an announcement in the August 14, 1824, issue of *The Struggling Astrologer,* a magazine that had been launched by astrologer **Robert Cross Smith** (1795–1832), later to become famous under his pen name **Raphael.** According to the brief statement, the society consisted of some "scientific gentlemen" interested in promoting occult science. In a later issue it was noted that the number of the society were few and select and that their meeting place was secret. It was noted, however, that they wished to publish occult books, and could be contacted through Smith.

Beyond Smith, the exact membership of the society is unknown, but some speculation can be made from knowledge of those who were associated with him. One possible early member was artist Richard Cosway (d. 1821). Above and beyond his art, he gathered a large occult library, lectured on occult topics, and practiced spirit contact via clairvoyance. When he died, Smith came into possession of his library.

The Struggling Astrologer was succeeded by a new periodical in 1825, *Urania; or, The Astrologer's Chronicle, and Mystic Magazine,* which listed Smith as the editor under the pseudonym "Mecurius Angelicus, Jur." assisted by members of the Mercurii. Like *The Struggling Astrologer, Urania* lasted only a few issues. However, after it folded Smith published a collection of articles from the two periodicals as a book, *The Astrologer of the Nineteenth Century,* described as a compendium of occult materials by members of the Society of the Mercurii.

From the Smith publications, membership of the Mercurii appears to have included: George W. Graham, an alchemist who assisted Smith in setting up his business; John Varley (1778–1842), a noted artist and friend of the artist/poet William Blake and student of astrology; and John Palmer (1807–1837), a young alchemist who wrote for Smith.

During this period of time, the only other significant occult group in England was the circle that had formed around magician **Francis Barrett,** author of *The Magus,* a seminal text of magical wisdom that stands at the fountainhead of modern magical practice. The Mercurii apparently dissolved following the death of so many of its members in the 1830s, though given its secretive nature it could easily have survived much longer.

Sources:

Godwin, Joscelyn. *The Theosophical Enlightenment.* Albany: State University of New York Press, 1995.

Mercury

Also popularly known as quicksilver. Known for many centuries, the metal has played an important part in the history of **alchemy.** In its refined state it forms a coherent, very mobile liquid that at ordinary room temparature was a well-known unique substance. The early alchemists believed that nature formed all metals from mercury, and that it was a living and feminine principle. It went through many processes, and the metal that evolved was pure or impure according to the locality of its production.

The mercury of the **philosophers' stone** needed to be a purified and revivified form of the ordinary metal; as the Arabian alchemist **Geber** stated in his *Summa perfectionis:* "Mercury, taken as Nature produces it, is not our material or our physic, but it must be added to."

Mercury seems to have been an entirely different substance than any ordinary metal or chemical element. Depending upon one's interprepation of alchemy as a system of spiritual growth, mercury could be one of several substances or states of consciousness.

Merlin

A legendary British enchanter who lived at the court of **King Arthur.** He emerged as a character in Geoffrey of Manmouth's *Historia Regum Britanniae* (completed around 1135 C.E.). Geoffrey later wrote a complete book on Merlin, *Vita Merlini* (ca. 1150). According to Geoffrey, Merlin's mother was a nun, and he was borne of his mother's intercourse with an **incubus.** He lived in the sixth century in north Britain. By the end of the century, he was the subject of poems in Wales, where Geoffrey's character was merged with the folklore image of a Wildman in the Wood.

Merlin seems to have been associated with King Arthur in the poem "Merlin" by Robert de Boron. In Boron's account, Merlin is the product of a demon's mating with a young girl. She confesses the incident to her confessor, who puts the sign of the cross on her. The son, Merlin, is born without the demon's evil nature, but with supernatural abilities. He assists Pendragon, the British king who was slain in a battle with the Saxons. Merlin then assists the king's brother, Uterpendragon. He directs the new king's construction of a roundtable, a replica of the one believed to have been used by Jesus at the Last Supper.

Uterpendragon (with Merlin's magical help) seduces the wife of one of the noblemen. From that union, Arthur is born. Though the king married the woman, who was widowed soon after conceiving Arthur, Merlin advises that Arthur be given to foster parents for his own protection. That action set up Arthur's later claiming the throne based upon his pulling a sword from the stone.

From Boron's basic story, Merlin's story grew and developed. By the nineteenth century, he had become the quinessential magician, and in the twentieth century the number of appearances in fantasy novels soared.

Sources:

Lacy, Norris J., ed. *The Arthurian Encyclopedia.* New York: Garland Publishing, 1986.

Loomis, Roger Sherman, ed. *Arthurian Literature in the Middle Ages.* Oxford: Clarendon Press, 1959.

Mermaids and Mermen

Legendary supernatural sea people, human from the head to the waist but with a fish tail instead of legs. In German folklore, a mermaid was known as "meerfrau," in Danish "maremind," Irish "murduac" (or "merrow"). In Brittany, the "morgans" were beautiful sirenlike women, dangerous to men, while in British maritime lore, seeing a mermaid might precede a storm or other disaster. A traditional ballad, "The Mermaid," tells how a ship's crew sees a mermaid sitting on a rock, combing her hair and holding a mirror. Soon afterward the ship is wrecked in a raging sea. In legend, one can gain power over a mermaid by seizing her cap or belt.

There are many folk tales of marriages between a mermaid and a man, and in Machaire, Ireland, there are individuals who claim descent from such a union. The medieval romance of the fair **Melusina** of the house of Lusignan in France concerns the daughter of a union between a human and a fairy who cursed the daughter Melusine so that she became a serpent from the waist down every Saturday.

Hans Christian Andersen's sad story "The Little Mermaid" echoes folk tales in its theme of a mermaid who falls in love with a prince in a passing ship; the mermaid takes on human form in order to gain a human soul and be close to the prince, but although constantly near him, she cannot speak. When the prince marries a human princess, the mermaid's heart is broken. There is a similar haunting pathos in Matthew Arnold's poem "The Forsaken Merman."

In *Curious Myths of the Middle Ages* (1884) folklorist S. Baring-Gould suggests that mermaid and merman stories originated from the half-fish half-human gods and goddesses of early religions. The Chaldean Oannes and the Philistine Dagon are typical deities of this kind, and a representation of Oannes with a human body down to the waist and a fish tail has been found on sculpture at Khorsabad. Such goddesses as Derceto (Atergatis) and Semiramis have been represented in mermaid form. The classic Venus, goddess of love, was born out of the sea foam, it is told, and was propitiated by barren couples who desired children. The Mexican Coxcox or Teocipactli was a fish god, as were some Peruvian deities. North American Indians have a legend that they were led from Asia by a man-fish. In classical mythology the Tritons and Sirens are represented as half-fish, half-human.

In addition to legends of mythology and folklore, however, there are many claimed accounts of sightings and contact with actual mermaids and mermen throughout history. The twelfth-century *Speculum Regale* of Iceland describes a mermaid called the Margygr found near Greenland: "This creature appears like a woman as far down as her waist, with breast and bosom like a woman, long hands, and soft hair, the neck and head in all respects like those of a human being. From the waist downwards, this monster resembles a fish, with scales, tail, and fins. This prodigy is believed to show itself especially before heavy storms."

In 1187 a merman was caught off the coast of Suffolk in England; it closely resembled a man but was not able to speak, so the story goes. The *Landnama* or Icelandic doomsday book tells of a merman caught off the island of Grimsey, and the annals of the country describe such creatures as appearing off the coast in 1305 and 1329.

In 1430 in Holland violent storms broke the dykes near Edam, West Friesland. Some girls from Edam had to take a boat to milk their cows, and saw a mermaid floundering in shallow muddy water. They brought her home, dressed her in women's clothing and taught her to weave and spin and show reverence for a crucifix, but she could never learn to speak, says the tale.

In 1492 Christopher Columbus claimed to have seen three such creatures leaping out of the sea.

In 1560 some fishermen near the island of Mandar off the west coast of Ceylon caught seven mermen and mermaids, an incident claimed to have been witnessed by several Jesuit fathers and M. Bosquez, physician to the viceroy of Goa. The physician made a careful examination of the "mer-people," dissected them, and pronounced that their internal and external structure resembled that of human beings. There is a well-authenticated case of a merman seen near a rock off the coast of Martinique. Several individuals affirmed that they saw it wipe its hands over its face and even blow its nose; their accounts were attested before a notary.

A merman captured in the Baltic Sea in 1531 was sent as a present to Sigismund, king of Poland, and seen by all his court; the creature lived for three days. In 1608 the British navigator Henry Hudson (discoverer of Hudson Bay) reported the discovery of a mermaid:

"This morning, one of our company looking overboard saw a mermaid; and calling up some of the company to see her, one more came up, and by that time she was come close to the ship's side, looking earnestly at the men. A little after, a sea came and overturned her. From the navel upward, her back and breasts were like a woman's, as they say that saw her; her body as big as one of us, her skin very white and long hair hanging down behind, of colour black. In her going down they saw her tail, which was like the tail of a porpoise, speckled like a mackerel. Their names that saw her were Thomas Hilles and Robert Rayner."

In 1755 Erik Pontoppidan, bishop of Bergen, published his *New Natural History of Norway* (2 vols.), in which there is an account of a merman observed by three sailors on a ship off the coast of Denmark, near Landscrona; the witnesses made a deposition on oath. In another book, *Poissons, écrevisses et crabes de diverses couleurs et figures extraordinaires, que l'on trouve autour des Isles Moluques* (published in 1717 by Louis Renard, Amsterdam), there is an illustration of a mermaid with the following description:

"See-wyf. A monster resembling a Siren, caught near the island of Borné, or Boeren, in the Department of Amboine. It was 59 inches long, and in proportion as an eel. It lived on land, in a vat full of water, during four days seven hours. From time to time it uttered little cries like those of a mouse. It would not eat, though it was offered small fish, shells, crabs, lobsters, etc. After its death, some excrement was discovered in the vat, like the secretion of a cat."

In 1857 two fishermen from Scotland, where numerous reports of mermaids have surfaced, made the following declaration, recorded in the *Shipping Gazette:*

"We, the undersigned, do declare, that on Thursday last, the 4th June 1857, when on our way to the fishing station, Lochindale, in a boat, and when about four miles S.W. from the village of Port Charlotte, being then about 6 p.m., we distinctly saw an object about six yards distant from us in the shape of a woman, with full breast, dark complexion, comely face, and fine hair hanging in ringlets over the neck and shoulders. It was about the surface of the water to about the middle, gazing at us and shaking its head. The weather being fine, we had a full view of it and that for three or four minutes. —John Williamson, John Cameron."

Several more mundane and conventional explanations of reports of mermaids and mermen exist. It is known, for example, that some were the result of hoaxes. As early as the 1820s, for example, Robert S. Hawker, before to his years as a minister, had been known to put on a merman costume and sit on the rocks and sing in the evening to the awe of the local villagers. Japanese fishermen used to manufacture mermaids to supplement their income and P. T. Barnum exhibited similar creatures in his museum. Many reports have been attributed to misidentifications or romantic viewings of a marine mammal called a dugong (*Halicore*), of the order *Sirenia,* which also includes the manatee or sea cow. Such creatures suckle their young at the breast and have a vaguely human appearance. They used to be hunted for their oil, used as a substitute for cod-liver oil, and are now rare.

It is possible that the dugong known as *Rhytina gigas,* or Steller's sea cow, long believed extinct, may survive in the Bering Sea, near the Aleutian Islands. Vitus Bering, after whom the sea is named, was a Danish navigator who was shipwrecked on the desert island of Avacha (now known as Bering Island) in 1741. His party included naturalist George W. Steller, who made copious notes while the party was dying of starvation. Steller observed large herds of *Sirenia* a short distance from the shore.

The creatures were mammals about 25 to 35 feet long and grazed off the kelp like cows on a pasture. They were unafraid of humans, and it was easy to harpoon them, drag them ashore and eat the flesh, which sustained the party. The top half of the creature resembled a seal, and the bottom half a dolphin. It had small flippers, and the females had mammary glands like a woman, suckling their young at the breast. Even courtship habits seemed human, as well as other behavior. When one creature was harpooned, the others would gather around it and try to comfort it, and even swim across the rope and try to dislodge the hook, Steller observed.

Sirenia bear only a very vague resemblance to historic accounts of mermaids, however, especially those brought ashore and kept in captivity before they died. These also have no connection with the stuffed "mermaids" displayed in showmen's booths in the nineteenth and early twentieth centuries, which were invariably clever fakes assembled by Japanese craftsmen.

Contemporary cryptozoologists have included mermen in their area of concern. Gwen Benwell, Arthur Waugh, and Bernard Heuvelmans, who studied the accounts extensively, have suggested that only some type of yet-unrecognized species of dugong or sea cow, or even an undesignated variety of marine primate could account for all of the excellent and detailed reports of mer-hominoids in recent centuries. However, since the habitat of such a creature is in relatively shallow water near shorelines, it is unlikely that some would not at some point have been washed ashore and discovered. Others, primarily folklorists, consider mermaids the products of hallucinatory or visionary experiences. Unfortunately, no extensive scientific expeditions have been launched to either confirm or discover the cause of the widespread reports of mermaid sightings. (See also **Lorelei; Sirens**)

Sources:

Bassett, F. S. *Legends and Traditions of the Sea and of Sailors.* Chicago: Belford, Clarke, 1885.

Benwell, Gwen, and Arthur Waugh. *Sea Enchantress: The Tale of the Mermaid and Her Kin.* London: Hutchinson, 1961.

Clark, Jerome. *Encyclopedia of Strange and Unexplained Phenomena.* Detroit: Gale Research, 1993.

Hutchins, Jane. *Discovering Mermaids and Monsters.* Shire Publications, 1968.

Rappoport, Angelo S. *Superstitions of Sailors.* London: Stanley Paul, 1928. Reprint, Ann Arbor, Mich.: Gryphon Books, 1971.

Merrell-Wolff, Franklin (ca. 1887)

American teacher of a system of higher consciousness deriving from Hindu **yoga** and related philosophies. Born in the late 1880s, Merrell-Wolff was the son of a Christian clergyman but felt himself drawn beyond religious orthodoxy. He graduated Phi Beta Kappa from Stanford University in 1911 with a major in mathematics and minors in both philosophy and psychology. He did graduate work at Stanford and Harvard.

Merrell-Wolff joined the faculty as a lecturer in mathematics at Stanford but soon withdrew from academic life to seek metaphysical knowledge beyond sense perception and conception. After 24 years he claimed to have attained a state of higher consciousness, described in his several books.

Although then in his late eighties, Merrell-Wolff continued teaching students at a community in California, originally designated The Assembly of Man and now known as Friends of the Wisdom Religion, located at the Wolff residence, near Lone Pine, California, U.S. Highway 395, about halfway between Reno and Los Angeles. Meetings, at which Merrell-Wolff's tape-recorded lectures are played, take place at the home of Mrs. James A. Briggs, 4648 East Lafayette Blvd., Phoenix, AZ 85018.

Sources:

Merrell-Wolff, Franklin. *Experience and Philosophy: A Personal Record of Transformation and a Discussion of Transcendental Consciousness.* New York: State University of New York Press, 1994.

———. *Pathways through to Space: A Personal Record of Transformation in Consciousness.* New York: Warner Books, 1976.

———. *The Philosophy of Consciousness without an Object.* New York: Julian Press, 1973.

Mesmer, Franz Anton (1733–1815)

Famous Austrian doctor and originator of the technique that bore his name, **Mesmerism,** forerunner of **hypnotism.** He was born at Weil, near Constance, May 23, 1733. In 1766 he took a degree in medicine at Vienna, the subject of his inaugural thesis being *De planetarum Influxu* (De l'influence des Planettes sur le corps humain). Mesmer identified the influence of the planets with magnetism and developed the idea that stroking diseased bodies with magnets would be curative. On seeing the remarkable cures of J. J. Gassner in Switzerland, he concluded that magnetic force must also reside in the human body, and thereupon Mesmer dispensed with magnets.

In 1778 he went to Paris where he was very favorably received—by the public, that is; the medical authorities there, as elsewhere, refused to countenance him. His curative technique was to seat his patients around a large circular vat, or *baquet,* in which various substances were mixed. Each patient held one end of an iron rod, the other end of which was in the baquet. In due time the crisis ensued. Violent convulsions, cries, laughter, and various physical symptoms followed, these being in turn superseded by lethargy. Many claimed to have been healed by this method.

In 1784 the government appointed a commission of members of the Faculty of Medicine, the Societé Royale de Médecine, and the Academy of Sciences, the commissioners from the latter body including **Benjamin Franklin,** astronomer Jean Sylvain Bailly, and chemist Antoine Lavoisier. The committee reported that there was no such thing as **animal magnetism,** and referred the facts of the crisis to the imagination of the patient. This had the effect of quenching public interest in mesmerism, as animal magnetism was called at the time. Mesmer's ideas were kept alive by a few of his students and reemerged in force during the next century. Mesmer lived quietly for the rest of his life and died at Meersburg, Switzerland, March 5, 1815.

Sources:

Eden, Jerome, trans. *Memoir of F. A. Mesmer, Doctor of Medicine, on His Discoveries, 1799.* Mount Vernon, N.Y.: Eden Press, 1957.

Goldsmith, Margaret L. *Franz Anton Mesmer: The History of an Idea.* Garden City, N.Y.: Doubleday, 1934. Reprint, London: Arthur Barker, 1934.

Wyckoff, James. *Franz Anton Mesmer.* Englewood Cliffs, N.J.: Prentice-Hall, 1975.

Wydenbruck, Nora. *Doctor Mesmer.* London: John Westhouse, 1947.

Mesmerism

A system of **healing,** founded by **Franz Anton Mesmer** (1733–1815), an Austrian doctor who received his degree at Vienna in 1766 and expounded the main principles of his discovery of **animal magnetism** in *De Planetarum Influxu,* his inaugural thesis in which he summarized his position in a series of statements:

"There is a mutual influence between the celestial bodies, the earth and animated bodies.

"The means of this influence is a fluid which is universal and so continuous that it cannot suffer void, subtle beyond comparison and susceptible to receive, propagate and communicate every impression of movement.

"This reciprocal action is subject to as yet unknown mechanical laws.

"The result of this action consists of alternating effects which may be considered fluxes and refluxes.

"It is by this operation (the most universal in nature) that the active relations are exercised between the heavenly bodies, the earth and its constituent particles.

"It particularly manifests itself in the human body with properties analogous to the magnet; there are poles, diverse and opposed, which can be communicated, changed, destroyed and reinforced; the phenomenon of inclination is also observable.

"This property of the animal body which renders it susceptible to the influence of celestial bodies and to the reciprocal action of the environing ones I felt prompted to name, from its analogy to the magnet, animal magnetism.

"It acts from a distance without the intermediary of other bodies.

"Similarly to light it is augmented and reflected by the mirror.

"It is communicated, propagated and augmented by the voice."

By applying magnetic plates to the patient's limbs, Mesmer effected his first cures in 1773. The arousal of public attention was due to a bitter controversy between Mesmer and a Jesuit priest Maximilian Hell, professor of astronomy at the University of Vienna, who claimed priority of discovery. Mesmer won.

In 1778, after a bitter public controversy over the cure of a blind girl, Mesmer went to Paris. In a short time he became famous. His first convert was Charles d'Eslon, medical adviser to Count d'Artois. In September 1780 d'Eslon asked the Faculty of Medicine to investigate Mesmer's ideas and practices. The proposal was rejected, and d'Eslon was told that his name would be struck off the rolls at the end of the year if he did not recant.

In the meantime public enthusiasm grew to such a high pitch that in March 1781 Minister de Maurepas offered Mesmer, on behalf of the king, 20,000 livres (francs) and a further annuity of 10,000 livres if he established a school and divulged the secret of his treatment.

Mesmer refused, but two years later accepted a subscription of 340,000 livres for lectures to pupils. In 1784 the French government charged the Faculty of Medicine and the Societé Royale de Médicine to examine animal magnetism. Nine commissioners convened under the presidency of Benjamin Franklin, including Jean Sylvain Bailly and J. K. Lavater; four more commissioners were added from the Royal Society of Medicine. The delegates restricted their activity to the search for evidence of a new physical force that was claimed as the agent of the cure.

As part of their investigation, they observed Mesmer's use of the famous *baquet*. This baquet was a large circular tub filled with bottles that dipped into the water. The baquet was covered, and iron rods projected from the lid through holes therein. The rods were bent and could be applied to any part of the body by the patients who sat in rows. The patients were tied together by a cord that passed around the circle. Sometimes they held hands in a chain. There was music. The operator, with an iron rod in his hands, walked around and touched the patients; they fell into convulsions, sweated, vomited, cried—and were supposedly cured.

The committees, in their verdict, stated that they found no evidence of a magnetic fluid, and the cures might be due to vivid imagination. De Jussieu was the only member who dissented. He claimed to have discovered something—animal heat—that radiated from the human body and could be directed and intensified by willpower. Later magnetists adopted the theory. It marked the discovery of the human element in animal magnetism.

The next important development is attached to the name of Marquis de Puységur. He began his cures at Busancy in the same year that animal magnetism was officially turned down. He did not employ the baquet. He "magnetized" a tree, which he fastened cords around and invited the sufferers to tie themselves to it. One of his invalid patients, a 23-year-old peasant named Victor, fell asleep in the operator's arms. He began to talk, and on waking he remembered nothing. De Puységur's observation of Victor led to his discovery of the somnambulic stage.

Puységur and the earlier magnetizers attributed many curious phenomena to the state of *rapport,* and they insisted on the theory of a magnetic effluence. Their patients claimed they could see it radiating as a brilliant shaft of light from the operator, from trees, and from other substances. Some substances could conduct it, others not. Water and milk could retain it and work cures.

Tardy de Montravel discovered the **transposition of the senses.** His somnambule not only walked in the town with her eyes fast closed but could see with the pit of her stomach (see also **eyeless sight**). J. H. Desire Pétetin, a doctor at Lyons, enlarged upon these observations. He changed the theory of Mesmer to "animal electricity" and cited many experiments to prove that the phenomena were of an electrical nature.

J. P. F. Deleuze objected, insisted on the magnetic fluid theory, and pointed out its analogies with nerve-force. He explained the phenomena of the transposition of the senses by the idea that it was the magnetic fluid that conveyed the impressions from without. He offered a similar theory to explain medical diagnoses that the patients gave of others and themselves. Every phenomenon was, however, attributed to physiological causes. **Thought-reading** and **clairvoyance** as transcendental faculties were rejected. The phenomena of traveling clairvoyance were yet very rare. Tardy de Montravel was alone in his supposition of a sixth sense as an explanatory theory.

A new approach to Mesmerism was inaugurated by a non-medical man, Abbé Faria. In 1813 he ascribed the magnetic phenomena to the power of imagination. General Noizet and Alexandre Bertrand adopted his view. Bertrand's *Traité du somnambulisme* was published in 1823. It definitely established a new departure. Bertrand denied the existence of the magnetic fluid and pointed out the preternormal sensitivity of the subject to the least suggestion, whether by word, look, gesture, or thought. Yet he admitted the supernormal phenomena of trance.

Marvelous stories were agitating the country. Professional clairvoyants arose. They gave medical diagnosis and treatment. Billot discovered most of the phenomena of **Spiritualism.** From Germany and Russia came rumors of a wide recognition of magnetic treatment. The Royal Academy of Medicine could not long ignore the stir.

On December 13, 1825, the proposal of P. Foissac that another investigation should be ordered was, after a bitter struggle, carried. The report of the committee was not submitted until five and a half years later. It stated that the alleged phenomena were genuine and that the existence of **somnambulism** was well authenticated. They found evidence of clairvoyance and successful medical diagnosis in the state of *rapport.* They also established that the will of the operator could produce the magnetic state without the subject's knowledge, even from another room.

In the meantime, developments in Germany proceeded. Animal magnetism ceased to be a science of healing. Under the influence of Jung-Stilling (see **Johann Heinrich Jung**), it soon developed into a "spiritual" science. While Gmelin, Wienholt, Fischer, Kluge, Kieser, and Weserman observed all the reported properties of the magnetic fluid and insisted on its essential importance, the practice of holding intercourse with the spirits through entranced somnambules soon gained popularity and increasing trust.

In the United States the students of Mesmerism believed they had discovered a new science—**phreno-mesmerism. J. Rhodes Buchanan,** R. H. Collyer, and Rev. **La Roy Sunderland** contended for the honor of the first discovery. Buchanan mapped out an entirely new distribution of the phrenological organs in 1843 and developed the theory of "nerve-aura" as a connecting link between will and consciousness.

The title page of Collyer's *Psychography; or, The Embodiment of Thought* (Philadelphia, 1843) represented two persons looking into a bowl, illustrating, in Collyer's words, that "when the angle of incidence from my brain was equal to the angle of reflection from her brain she distinctly saw the image of my thought at the point of coincidence." Sunderland discovered no less than 150 new phrenologic organs by means of mesmeric experiments. Professor J. S. Grime substituted the magnetic fluid with "etherium," Rev. J. Bovee Dods with "vital electricity."

Andrew Jackson Davis was started on his career of seership by mesmeric experiments for medical purposes. He became the herald of **Spiritualism,** and from the believers of phreno-mesmerism and Mesmerism, Davis gained many believers of the new faith.

In England the beginnings were slow. Not until **John Elliotson** was converted by **Baron Du Potet**'s visit in 1837 did Mesmerism assume the proportions of a widespread movement. For propaganda it relied on the journal the *Zoist* and the short-lived *Phreno-Magnet.* Three main classes of phenomena were thus distinguished: the physical effluence; phreno-mesmerism; and **community of sensation,** including clairvoyance.

From Animal Magnetism to Hypnotism

The controversy between official medical science and Mesmerism raged bitterly. The evolution of animal magnetism into **hypnotism** was due to **James Braid.** But **James Esdaile**'s name also occupies an important place. While Elliotson practically introduced curative magnetism into England, Esdaile proved the reality of mesmeric trance by performing operations under mesmeric anaesthesia.

As early as 1841, Braid read an address before the British Association in which he expounded his discovery of hypnotism. He described it as a special condition of the nervous system, characterized by an abnormal exaltation of suggestibility, which can be brought about automatically by the mere fixation of the eyes on bright objects with an inward and upward squint.

His address was published in 1843 under the title *Neurypnology.* This work was followed three years later by his *Power of the Mind over the Body,* in which he pointed out that the Mesmerists were not on their guard against suggestion and hyperaesthesia. He produced all the characteristic results of Mesmerism without a magnet and claimed that the sensitives could not see flames at the poles of the most powerful magnets until warned to look at them. If warned, they saw flames issuing from any object.

The influence of Braid's discoveries on the Mesmerists themselves was very slight, and strangely enough, official science took little notice. The main attraction of Mesmerism was its therapeutic value. It was the discovery in 1846–47 of the anaesthetic properties of ether and chloroform that deprived mesmeric trance of its most obvious utility. The conquest by Spiritualism soon began, and the leading Mesmerists were absorbed into the ranks of the Spiritualists.

No further advance was registered in England until 1883, when **Edmund Gurney** made his first experiments in hypnotism. He pointed out that in the hypnotic stage, the formerly numerous cases of *rapport* became extremely rare. He and **F. W. H. Myers** reverted to the earlier theory and declared that hypnotism and Mesmerism appeared to be two different states.

Official recognition was first granted to hypnotism in 1893 by a committee of the British Medical Association, which reported to have found the hypnotic state genuine and of value in relieving pain and alleviating functional ailments. Mesmerism remained a controversial subject.

In **France** a great revival began in 1875. A. A. Liébeault published his work on hypnotism in 1866. He sided with Bertrand. In 1875 **Charles Richet** came to the fore. In 1879 **Jean Martin Charcot** began his work in the Salpetrière. Paris, Bordeaux, Nancy, and Toulon became centers of hypnotic activity. The school of Paris, of which Charcot was the chief, adopted and completed the explanation of Braid. Charcot contended that the hypnotic conditions could only be provoked with neuropaths or with hysterical subjects.

The school of Nancy accepted hypnotic sleep but considered suggestion its potent cause. In 1886 in Professor Bernheim's famous work *Suggestion and Its Application to Therapeutics,* he went so far as to declare: "Suggestion is the key of all hypnotic phenomena. There is no such thing as hypnotism, there is only suggestion." The views of Liébeault and Bernheim prevailed almost everywhere over those of Charcot. But animal magnetism was difficult to kill. Boirac was right in saying that "Animal magnetism is a new America which has been alternately lost and found every twenty or thirty years."

In 1887 Dr. Barèty published *Le Magnetisme animal etudié sous le nom de force neurique,* in which he boldly set out to prove the reality of animal magnetism. **Pierre Janet,** reviewing Barèty's work, admitted that certain phenomena of attraction, anaesthesia, etc., produced on subjects apart from all apparent suggestion, by contact alone or the mere presence of the operators, had often struck him as particularly suggestive of the so-called magnetic chain.

Emil Boirac supported this position. He pointed out that although hypnotism and suggestion exist, it does not follow that animal magnetism has no existence. It may be that the effects attributed to hypnotism and suggestion are caused by a third factor. Experiments with several subjects convinced him of the truth of his theory. "We are not prevented from hoping," he wrote in *Psychic Science* (1918),

"that we shall one day succeed in discovering the natural unity of these three orders of phenomena [Mesmerism or animal magnetism, suggestion, and Braidic hypnotism] as we begin to discover the natural unity of heat, light and electricity. They too much resemble each other's path not to betray a secret relationship. They are perhaps the effects of one and the same cause, but these effects are assuredly produced under different conditions and according to different laws."

The claim was further supported in 1921 by Dr. Sydney Alrutz, lecturer on psychology at the University of Upsala. He claimed to have proved experimentally the existence of a nervous effluence. Professor Farny of the Zurich Polytechnicum showed by electrical tests an emission from the fingers and called it "anthropoflux." His results verified the previous investigations of E. K. Muller, an engineer in Zurich and director of the Salus Institute.

Eventually the phenomena of animal magnetism merged with the developing Spiritualist movement, while hypnotism became established as a valid medical technique.

In 1838 **Phineas P. Quimby** began to practice Mesmerism and later developed from it his own concepts of mental healing. One of Quimby's students, **Mary Baker Eddy,** developed her own idealistic approach to healing in the 1870s, embodied in **Christian Science.** Then in the 1880s some of Eddy's students—much to her consternation—began to develop variations on her teachings. One by one they broke away and founded independent movements, which gradually aligned into what became known as **Mind Cure** and then in the 1890s as **New Thought.**

Sources:

Bernheim, H. *Hypnosis and Suggestion in Psychotherapy.* Reprint, New Hyde Park, N.Y.: University Books, 1964.

Bertrand, Alexandre. *Traité du somnambulisme.* Paris, 1824.

Binet, Alfred, and Charles Féré. *Animal Magnetism.* London: Kegan Paul, 1887.

Braid, James. *Magic, Witchcraft, Animal Magnetism, Hypnotism, and Electro-Biology.* London: John Churchill, 1852.

Bramwell, J. Milne. *Hypnotism and Treatment by Suggestion.* London: Cassell, 1909.

Deleuze, J. P. F. *Practical Instruction in Animal Magnetism.* New York: Samuel R. Wells, 1879.

Franklin, Benjamin, and others. *Animal Magnetism: Report of Dr. Franklin and Other Commissioners.* Philadelphia: H. Perkins, 1837.

Goldsmith, Margaret. *Franz Anton Mesmer: The History of an Idea.* London: Arthur Barker, 1934.

Gregory, William. *Animal Magnetism; or, Mesmerism and Its Phenomena.* London: Nichols, 1884.

Ince, R. B. *Franz Anton Mesmer.* London: William Rider, 1920.

Liébeault, A. A. *Du sommeil et des etats analogues.* Paris, 1886.

Mesmer, F. A. *Mesmerism by Doctor Mesmer (1779), Being the First Translation of Mesmer's Historic "Memoire sur la découverte du Magnétism Animal" to Appear in English.* London: Macdonald, 1948.

Podmore, Frank. *Mesmerism and Christian Science.* London: Methuen, 1909.

Sunderland, La Roy. *Pathetism: Man Considered in Relation to His Form, Life, Sensation; An Essay Towards a Correct Theory of Mind.* Boston, 1847.

The Messenger

The Messenger, subtitled "A Guide to Life's Adventures. . .," is a post-**New Age** tabloid that serves Southern California, with a particular focus on those counties immediately east of Los Angeles, popularly referred to as the Inland Empire, and on **Sedona,** Arizona, a small community looked upon by many as the center of the New Age community in North America. Each issue of the monthly newspaper is distributed freely throughout its target area since the initial appearance of *The Messenger* in July of 1997.

The Messenger is built around a set of short feature articles, the great majority of which are written by New Age leaders and practitioners who operate in Southern California. They cover the spectrum of New Age spiritual and **New Thought** metaphysical topics, from metaphysical approaches to business to neurolinguistic programming and various forms of spiritual healing. In addition, there are a large number of monthly columns covering such topics as **astrology, numerology,** and **palmistry.** *The Messenger* also carries the monthly column by popular New Thought writer Louise Hay, and a special section focusing upon events in Sedona.

As with most New Age periodicals, advertising is an important part of each issue's content. There is a relatively brief one-page resource guide, with most of the ads that inform readers of the range of services available to them concentrated in display ads. A monthly book review column carries notices of recent publications, with text drawn primarily from covers and dust jackets of the reviewed items.

The Messenger may be contacted at P.O. Box 1971, Glendora, CA 91740. It has an Internet presence at http://www.themessenger.cc/.

Sources:

The Messenger. Glendora, Calif., n.d.

The Messenger. http://www.themessenger.cc/. May 5, 2000.

Metagnome

Term used by French psychic researchers for a gifted percipient of paranormal knowledge or extrasensory perception. The term avoids the Spiritualist associations of "**medium**" but is now generally superseded by the term "**psychic,**" indicating an individual with **extrasensory perception.** (See also **metagnomy**)

Metagnomy

Term used by French psychic researchers to indicate knowledge acquired through **cryptesthesia,** i.e., without the use of our five senses. Although this term was used by French psychic researcher **Eugèn Osty,** it appears to have been originally coined by researcher **Emile Boirac** (1851–1917) in his book *L'Avenir des sciences psychiques* (Paris, 1917) and was so ascribed in Osty's book *Supernormal Faculties in Man* (London, 1923).

The term derives from the Greek words *meta* (after) and *gnomon* (knower) and designates the phenomenon of supernormal cognition, now generally called **extrasensory perception** by parapsychologists.

Metagraphology

Term indicating psychometric power on the basis of scripts. It has nothing to do with **graphology** (interpretation of personality traits indicated in handwriting), as the reading of the present, past, and future of the subject is not effected by the study of the writing. The script simply serves as an influence, as does any given object in **psychometry.**

The sole justification of the term "metagraphology" is the fact that some graphologists developed their remarkably sensitive powers from the study of scripts. **Raphael Schermann** was the most notable among the metagraphologists. Similar powers were discovered in Otto Reimann of Prague, a bank clerk born in 1903 who, by simply touching a script, would offer a psychometric reading and also imitate the writing. He was studied by Professor Fischer of Prague.

Metal Bending

One of the very few new directions in claimed psychic phenomena in modern times. It was first publicized in the mid-1970s by **Uri Geller,** an Israeli psychic, when he apparently demonstrated paranormal deformation of metal keys and spoons. When these objects were gently stroked or subjected to passes of his hand without actual contact, they tended to bend and often actually break, allegedly by some unknown force directed by the psychic's mind. The phenomenon became known as "the **Geller effect,**" but is now generally classified by parapsychologists as "Psychokinetic Metal Bending" or "PKMB."

In spite of many demonstrations by Geller and hundreds of laboratory experiments with him and other subjects by parapsychologists, the phenomenon remains highly controversial. However, some of the evidence is impressive. Metal samples sealed inside glass tubes appear to have been bent. Some samples have been bent when held by someone other than the **psychic,** while bends have been shown in alloys that normally break rather than bend when stressed. Videotape records appear to show paranormal bending of samples not held by the psychic concerned, but it must be said that other videotapes taken secretly have revealed **fraud** by some metal-benders, notably children, who have become known as "mini-Gellers." Parapsychologists believed for a time that they had found a new Geller in the person of a young Japanese psychic, **Masuaki Kiyota.** However, in 1984 he admitted to having accomplished his feats of metal bending by fraud.

The British scientist **John Taylor** spent three years studying the phenomenon, which he endorsed in his book *Superminds* (1975). Then three years later he retracted his endorsement and announced a position of complete skepticism. However, **John Hasted,** another British scientist who tested Geller and other claimed metal-benders, continues to support the reality of PKMB. For a detailed study of his experiments and conclusions, see his book *The Metal Benders* (1981).

The stage magician **James Randi** has demonstrated various methods of apparent metal bending and also has caused much confusion by planting fake metal benders in parapsychology laboratory tests, to show that scientists may be deceived. One of the most common methods of faking metal bending in tests with spoons is for the operator to surreptitiously weaken the spoon by prior bending, which can be achieved easily with the aid of a strong belt buckle.

Metal bending is a particulalrly spectacular form of **psychokinesis.** In spite of the revelation of fraud in some cases, defense of the ability by some continues among parapsychologists. (See also **movement; psychic force**)

Sources:

Berger, Arthur S., and Joyce Berger. *The Encyclopedia of Parapsychology and Psychical Research.* New York: Paragon House, 1991.

Hasted, John. *The Metal-Benders.* London: Routledge and Kegan Paul, 1981.

Panati, Charles, ed. *The Geller Papers: Scientific Observations on the Paranormal Powers of Uri Geller.* Boston: Houghton Mifflin, 1976.

Randi, James. *The Truth about Uri Geller.* Buffalo, N.Y.: Prometheus Books, 1982.

Taylor, John. *Science and the Supernatural.* London: Temple Smith, 1980.

———. *Superminds: A Scientist Looks at the Paranormal.* New York: Viking Press, 1975.

Metals (in Animal Magnetism)

It was claimed by the practitioners of **animal magnetism** that various metals exercised a characteristic influence on their patients. Physical sensations of heat and cold, numbness, drowsiness, and so on were experienced by the somnambules on contact with metals, or even when metals were secretly introduced into the room. **John Elliotson,** especially, gave much prominence to the alleged power of metal to transmit the hypothesized magnetic fluid.

Gold, silver, platinum, and nickel were said to be good conductors, although the magnetism conveyed by the latter was of a highly dangerous character. Copper, tin, pewter, and zinc were poor conductors. Elliotson found that a magnetized sovereign (British gold coin) would throw into trance his **sensitives,** the **O'Key sisters,** and that although iron would neutralize the magnetic properties of the sovereign, no other metal would do so.

When **Baron Karl von Reichenbach** propounded his theory of **odic force,** his sensitives claimed to see a luminous emanation proceed from metals—silver and gold shone white; lead, blue; and nickel, red. Opponents of Reichenbach's theories ascribed such phenomena to **suggestion.**

Sources:

Elliotson, John. *Human Physiology.* London, 1840.

Reichenbach, Karl von. *Letters on Od and Magnetism.* London: Hutchinson, 1926. Reprinted as *The Odic Force.* New Hyde Park, N.Y.: University Books, 1968.

Metaphysical Digest (Journal) See **Neometaphysical Digest** (Journal)

Metapsichica (Journal)

Semiannual Italian-language publication of the *Associazoine Italiana Scientifica di Metapsichica* (Italian Metaphysical Association). Address: Via S. Vittore 19, 20123 Milano, Italy.

Metapsychics

The term proposed by **Charles Richet** in 1905 (when he was elected president of the **Society for Psychical Research,** London) for phenomena and experiments in **psychical research.** In his inaugural address he defined metapsychics as "a science dealing with mechanical or psychological phenomena due to forces which seem to be intelligent, or to unknown powers, latent in human intelligence." He divided it into objective and subjective metapsychics, the first dealing with material, external facts; the second with psychic, internal, nonmaterial facts.

The term was not generally accepted on the Continent. In Germany, the word "parapsychic" was suggested instead, proposed by **Emile Boirac.** Richet's colleague **Theodore Flournoy** preferred "parapsychics," suggesting that Richet's term should be limited to phenomena definitely proved to be supernormal in character. All three terms have been supplanted by **"parapsychology."**

MetaScience Foundation

A nonprofit organization that pursued scientific information in the field of **parapsychology** and related areas. Originally called the Occult Studies Foundation, the new name reflected reservations about the contemporary connotations of the word "**occult.**" The foundation followed an interdisciplinary approach to paranormal phenomena and endeavored to maintain a high standard of academic and professional responsibility in their investigations. It published *MetaScience Annual* and *Journal of Occult Studies* from its headquarters in Kingston, Rhode Island. It was active for a short period in the 1970s. Website: http://www.metascience.com/.

Metempiric

Term proposed in the 1970s to denote unexplained phenomena such as **UFOs, ghosts,** alien creatures, mysterious fires, and unusual falls from the sky, usually classified as **Fortean phenomena** after the writer **Charles Hoy Fort,** who pioneered the study of such things. The term never became popular and largely passed out of use in favor of "anomalistics." (See also **Occidental Society of Metempiric Analysis**)

Metempsychosis (or **Transmigration of Souls**)

From the Greek *meta,* "after," and *empsychos,* "to animate," the belief that after death, the soul passes into another body, either human or animal. In ancient Greece it was roughly equivalent to the idea of **reincarnation.**

The idea seems to have originated in Egypt but to have first been advocated by Pythagoras around 455 B.C.E. Diogenes Laertius noted that Pythagoras once recognized the soul of a departed friend in a dog that was being beaten. Plato picked up on the idea and expounded it in several of his *Dialogues,* most notably the *Phaedo* and *Republic.* According to the vision of truth that one attains, one will be born in the next life in a body suitable to that attainment, Plato said. The most enlightened will be reborn as a philosopher, musician, artist, or lover. At the lowest level, he placed tyrants. Once a soul has beheld true being, it will pass from animal into human form, he said. Plato also put forth the idea that a person chooses his next life, the very choice being a sign of his character.

The idea of metempsychosis was also held by some of the Gnostics, and it became a source of disagreement between them and the leaders of the Christian church. Irenaeus, the second century bishop of Lyons, wrote at length against the Gnostics in his pacesetting *Contra Heresies* and singled out metempsychosis as an idea that was incompatible with Christianity. The church has essentially followed Irenaeus's lead in its consideration of metempsychosis and reincarnation. Origen, a Christian theologian of the third century with a platonic background, tried to defend some aspects of the metempsychosis doctrine, primarily the prior existence of the soul, but soon gave up, having found the idea contrary to the New Testament teachings.

Metempsychosis found its last great philosophical defender in Plotinus (205–270 C.E.), the Neoplatonic philosopher. He saw repeated births of the soul as a means for its education. By being in the body, the soul learns how desirable is the nonphysical existence, Plotinus taught.

The idea of reincarnation lingered in the West, passing through a succession of Gnostic groups, but experienced a rebirth in the twentieth century. It's current spread, however, has a basis in Indian and Oriental ideas of reincarnation, usually attached to the additional notion of **karma.**

Sources:

Crombie, I. M. *Plato: The Midwife's Apprentice.* London: Routledge & Kegan Paul, 1964.

Ducasse, C. J. *A Critical Examination of the Belief in a Life after Death.* Springfield, Ill.: Charles C. Thomas, 1961.

Meteormancy

A branch of **aeromancy** (**divination** through aerial phenomena such as thunder and lightning), concerned with divination from the appearance and movements of meteors and shooting stars.

Methetherial

A term coined by **F. W. H. Myers** meaning beyond the ether, the transcendental world in which **spirits** exist.

Metopomancy

Metopomancy is a form of **divination** character analysis based upon the reading of the wrinkle lines of an individual's forehead. The use of the forehead wrinkles would appear to be but another one of the many items assigned some divinatory significance in the ancient world, and in fact it was one aspect of the ancient art of face reading or **physiognomy** in China. However, early in the sixteenth century, renowned mathematician, physician, and astrologer Gerolomo Cardano (1501–1576) proposed metopomancy as a new art. In his book, *Metoposcopia,* he covered some 800 wrinkle configurations and related each wrinkle on the forehead to a particular astrological sign. By this method, he claimed to be able, for example, to identify adulterous women and thieves.

Cardano divided the area of the forehead into seven positions, each assigned to one of the then-known heavenly bodies. Beginning at the top, the areas were assigned in order to Saturn, Jupiter, Mars, the Sun, Venus, Mercury, and the **Moon.** The assignment allows the forehead reading to be aligned with the horoscope.

Reading the forehead began with an assessment of the length, depth, and prominence of the lines. Long unbroken lines indicate an honest person while x-shaped lines indicate a deceptive personality. A slight curve in the lines indicate a balanced personality, while wavy lines suggest that the person likes to travel (physically and/or mentally). A diagonal line that reaches downward to the eyebrow indicates that obstacles, possibly misfortune, lie in the person's future.

Cardano's book was republished on several occasions, but his ideas never caught on and he is basically remembered as an odd figure in occult history, seemingly the victim of suicide. He starved himself to death so as to confirm his horoscope reading.

Sources:

Shaw, Eva. *Divining the Future: Prognostication from Astrology to Zoomancy.* New York: Facts on File, 1995.

Metoposcopy

The art of interpreting character and destiny through the lines in the human forehead (Greek *metopon*). It was developed by the celebrated physician, mathematician, and astrologer **Jerome Cardan** (1501–1576). His work, including some 800 illustrations of faces, was published in an edition edited by C. M. Laurenderio, titled *Metoposcopia, libris tredecim, et octingentis Faciei humanae Eiconibus complexa: Cui accessis Melampodia de Navis Corporis Tractatus Graece et Latine nunc primum editus* (Lutetiae Parisorum, 1658). Although his interpretations were confined to lines in the forehead (coupled with **astrology**), his ideas were a forerunner of the physiognomy of J. K. Lavater (1741–1801).

Metratton

According to Jewish rabbinical legend, the angel Metratton is one of the agents by whom God the Father works. He receives the pure and simple essence of the divinity and bestows the gift of life upon all. He dwells in one of the angelic hierarchies.

Metropolitan Spiritual Churches of Christ

The Metropolitan Spiritual Churches of Christ was a Spiritualist church operating in the African American community in the United States. Spiritualism moved into the black community in strength early in the twentieth century, but black people were not welcomed in many Spiritualist congregations. As independent movements began to form around talented individual mediums, they tended to adopt the forms dominant in the pentecostal and holiness churches and retain a central emphasis upon the Bible. They also took the name "spiritual," a reference to the teachings concerning spiritual gifts mentioned in several places in the epistles of St. Paul.

The Metropolitan Spiritual Churches of Christ were founded in Kansas City in 1925 by Bishop William Frank Taylor (formerly a minister in the Christian Methodist Episcopal Church) and Elder Leviticus Boswell (of the Church of God in Christ). It grew quickly and soon had congregations across the Midwest and one in California. In 1942, shortly before Taylor's death, the Metropolitan Churches merged with the Spiritual Churches of the Southwest to create the United Spiritual Churches of Christ. However, soon after Taylor died, a split occurred between Bishop Clarence Cobbs of Chicago, who believed himself Taylor's rightful successor, and Bishop Thomas Watson, who had headed the former Spiritual Churches of the Southwest. Two factions developed, the largest one accepting the leadership of Cobbs, pastor of the First Church of Deliverance.

Under Cobbs's leadership, a revived Metropolitan Spiritual Churches of Christ expanded to encompass close to 100 congregations in the 1960s. It also expanded to West Africa, making it the largest spiritual association operating in the United States. Last known address: 4329 Park Heights Ave., Baltimore, MD 21215.

Sources:

Murphy, Larry G., J. Gordon Melton, and Gary L. Ward. *Encyclopedia of African American Religions.* New York: Garland Publishing, 1993.

Metzger, Herman Joseph (1919–1990)

Herman Joseph Metzger, the outer head of the **Ordo Templi Orientis** (OTO) in Switzerland, was born in Zezikon, Switzerland, on June 20, 1919. Little is known of his youth. He considered the priesthood at one time but eventually became a Marxist. He emerged out of obscurity in 1939 when he moved from Lugano (in Italian-speaking Switzerland) to Zürich. During World War II (1939–45), under the stage name Peter Mano, he worked as a stage magician. He also was an astrologer. In 1947, he inherited a small publishing firm, Psychosophische Gesellschaft, whose owner, F. L. Pinkus, had died. Over the next decades, Metzger's activities would be underwritten by a wealthy friend, Annemarie Aeschbach.

After the war, Metzger founded a lodge of the Ordo Templi Orientis, the initiatory magical group then led internationally by **Karl Johannes Germer** (1885–1962). He also joined the **World League of the Illuminati,** an organization that had attempted to revive the eighteenth-century German **Illuminati.** In 1955, the leader of the Swiss chapter of the World League died and left the small organization to Metzger. In 1957 he was consecrated as a bishop in the Gnostic Catholic Church, one of several small ecclesiastical bodies that traced its apostolic succession to the mystical consecration of French bishop **Jules-Benoit Doniel** (1842–1894). Then in 1960 Metzger became the new patriarch of the church. In 1963, after hearing of the death of Germer, he called the German-speaking leadership of the OTO together and had himself elected the new international outer head of the order (though those in the Spanish- and English-speaking countries did not recognize him).

By this time Metzger was already putting together a new organization that would unite the teachings and practices of the several organizations he had inherited. His headquarters was established in Appenzell in northeast Switzerland. A variety of cottage industries emerged, from a bakery to a movie theater. There was also a chapel for the gatherings of the Gnostic Catholic Church. Metzger led the group until he fell ill toward the end of the 1980s. He died on July 14, 1990. His ashes are kept enshrined at the chapel at Appenzell.

Sources:

Koenig, Peter R. "Herman Joseph Metzger—OHO of the O.T.O. and Patriarch of the Gnostic Catholic Church." http://www.cyberlink.ch/~koenig/bishops.htm. April 23, 2000.

MEXICO AND CENTRAL AMERICA

Sorcerers and Astrologers

Occult science among the ancient Mexicans could be represented as a middle ground derived between the tribal medicine men and the magical practices of the medieval sorcerer. The sources of information are limited, chiefly gleaned either from the works of the early missionaries to the country, or from the legends and myths of the people themselves.

Writing about the sorcerers of Mexico, Bernardino de Sahagun, an early Spanish priest, stated that the *naualli* or magician was one who enchanted men and sucked the blood of infants during the night, a reference to the **vampire**-like characteristics of Central American magical practitioners. He observed that the magician was ignorant of nothing that appertained to sorcery, and possessed great craft. Magicians hired themselves out to people to work evil upon their enemies, and to cause madness and maladies. He added:

"The necromancer is a person who has made pact with a demon, and who is capable of transforming himself into various animal shapes. Such people appear to be tired of life and await death with complaisance. The astrologer practices among the people as a diviner, and has a thorough knowledge of the various signs of the calendar, from which he is able to prognosticate the fortunes of those who employ him. This he accomplishes by weighing the power of one planet against that of another, and thus discovering the resultant applies it to the case in point. These men were called into consultation at births and deaths, as well as upon public occasions, and would dispute with much nicety on their art."

Astrology among the Mexicans was, like their calendar, intricate and advanced. (The reader is referred to **Lewis Spence**'s *The Civilization of Ancient Mexico* (1911), Bernardino de Sahagun's *Historia de la Conquista de Mexico* (1829), and Bulletin 28 of the United States *Bureau of Ethnology.*) In connection with the astrological science of the Aztecs, it is noteworthy that the seventh calendric sign was the one under which necromancers, sorcerers, and evil-doers were usually born. Bernardino de Sahagun noted that:

"These work their enchantments in obscurity for four nights running, when they choose a certain evil sign. They then betake themselves in the night to the houses where they desire to work their evil deeds and sorceries. . .For the rest these sorcerers never know contentment, for all their days they live evilly and know no peace."

The myths of the Mexicans give a good working idea of the status of the enchanter or sorcerer in Aztec society. For example, the Toltec god Quetzalcoatl who, in early times was regarded as a culture-hero, was bewitched by the god of the incoming and rival race, Tezcatlipoca, who disguised himself as a physician and prescribed for an illness of his enemy's an enchanted draught that made him long for the country of his origin—that is, the home of the rains. This would indicate that potions or philters were in vogue among Mexican sorcerers.

In their efforts to rid themselves of the entire Toltec race, the traditional aborigines of Mexico, the incoming race's god Tezcatlipoca was pictured as performing upon a magical drum in such a manner as to cause frenzy among the Toltecs, who leaped by thousands into a deep ravine by their city.

Wonderful stories were told of the feats of the Huaxteca, a people of Maya race dwelling on the Gulf of Mexico. Sahagun related that they could produce from space a spring with fishes, burn and restore a hut, and dismember and resurrect themselves. The Ocuiltec of the Toluca Valley also possessed a widespread reputation as enchanters and magicians.

Divination and Augury

Although **divination** was practiced among the Aztecs by means of astrology, there were other less intricate methods in use. A College of Augurs existed, corresponding in purpose to the Auspices of Ancient **Rome,** the members of which occupied themselves with observing the flight and listening to the songs of birds, from which they drew their conclusions.

The *calmecac,* or training college of the priests, had a department where divination was taught in all its branches. A typical example of augury from birds may be found in the account of the manner in which the Mexicans fixed upon the spot for the foundation of their city.

Halting after years of wandering in the vicinity of the Lake of Tezcuco, they observed a great eagle with wings outspread perched on the stump of a cactus, and holding in its talons a live serpent. Their augurs interpreted this as a good omen, since it had been previously announced by an oracle, and upon the spot where the bird had alighted they drove the first piles upon which they built the city of Mexico—the legend of the foundation of which is still commemorated in the heraldic arms of modern Mexico.

Dreams and visions also played a great part in Mexican divination, and a special caste of augurs called *Teopixqui,* or *Teotecuhtli* (masters or guardians of divine things) were set apart for the purpose of interpreting dreams and of divining through dreams and visions, which was regarded as the chief route between man and the supernatural.

The senses were quickened and sharpened by the use of drugs, and the ecstatic condition was induced by lack of sleep, fixing of the mind upon one subject, swallowing or inhaling cerebral intoxicants such as tobacco, the maguey, coca, the snake-plant or *ololiuhqui,* and similar substances.

Some tribes of Native Americans believed that visions came to the prophet or seer pictorially, or that acts were performed before them as in a play. They also believed that the soul traveled through space and was able to visit those places of which it desired to have knowledge. It was likely that the seers hypnotized themselves by gazing at certain small, highly-polished pieces of sandstone, or that they employed these in a manner similar to the **crystal-gazing** practices found around the globe. The goddess Tozi was the patron of those who used grains of maize or red beans in divination.

On such native group, the Cuna people indigenous to Panama, believed that the Avisua, sang songs of magic that have curative powers—whether it was the healing of the sick, change atmospheric conditions, or inspire a person to act in some oppositive way. The witch doctors, or Neles, claimed powers of extrasensory perception using them to heal, or see into the past, present or future. The main source of those powers was dreams, as well. From 1968 until 1972, Robert Van De Castle conducted ESP tests among Cuna children, both boys and girls. The results were inconclusive, with the girls scoring higher than the boys. Whether or not any of these children were Neles, was also not determined. If that is so, the powers of the witch doctors, remain untested.

Charms and Amulets

The **amulet** was regarded in Mexico as a personal **fetish.** The Tepitoton, or diminutive household deities of the Mexicans, were also fetishistic. It is probable that most of the Mexican amulets were modeled on the various ornaments of the gods. Thus the traveler's staff, carved in the shape of a serpent like that of Quetzalcoatl, was undoubtedly of this nature, and to it occasionally sacrifices would be made. The frog was a favorite model for an amulet. As elsewhere, the thunderbolts thrown by the gods were supposed to be flint stones, and were cherished as amulets and as symbols of the life-giving rains.

Vampirism

Vampirism was an important part of Mexican folk belief and there are various vampire deities. The notion of the vampire that most permeated the life of average people is found in connection with the *ciupipiltin,* or ghosts of women who have died in childbirth. These haunted the crossroads, crying and wailing for the little ones they have left behind them. But as in many other countries, notably in Burma, they are malevolent—their evil tendencies probably being caused by jealousy of the happiness of the living.

In order that they do not enter their houses and injure their children, the Mexicans at certain times of the year stopped up every possible hole and crevice. The appearance of these ghosts (Sahagun described them as "goddesses") at crossroads is highly significant, for we know that the burial of criminals at such junctions was merely a survival of a similar disposal of the corpse of the vampire, whose head was cut off and laid at his side, and entombed at a crossroads for the purpose of confusing him as to his whereabouts.

The Cult of Nagualism

Both in Mexico and Central America a religio-magical system called nagualism existed, the purpose of which was to bring occult influence against the European conquerors for their destruction. The rites of this practice usually took place in caverns and other deserted localities, and were naturally derived to a large extent from those of the suppressed native religion. Each worshiper possessed a magical or animal spirit-guide, with which he or she was endowed early in life. This system flourished as lately as the last quarter of the nineteenth century.

Central America

Information on magic and sorcery amongst the Maya, Kiche, and other Central American peoples is even rarer than that relating to Mexico, and there is little but local legend to guide research in these areas. The great storehouse of Central American legend is the *Popol Vuh,* an early study published by Lewis Spence (1908), with some having appeared in more recent years. This fascinating work of mythological history states that some of the elder gods were regarded as magicians, and the hero-twins, Xblanque and Hun-ahpu, whom they sent to earth to rid it of the Titan Vukubcakix, were undoubtedly possessed of magical powers.

As boys, the twins were equipped with magical tools that enabled them to get through an enormous amount of work in a single day. When they descended into Xibalba (the Kiché Hades) for the purpose of avenging their father and uncle, they took full advantage of their magical propensities in combating the inhabitants of that drear abode. Xibalba itself possessed sorcerers, for within its borders were Xulu and Pacaw, who assisted the hero-gods in many of their necromantic practices.

Regarding divination, the Maya possessed a caste of augurs, called *Cocomes,* or the listeners, while prophecy appears to have been periodically practiced by their priests.

In the books of *Chilan Balam,* which are native compilations of events occurring in Central America previous to the Spanish Conquest, certain prophecies appear that seem to foretell many events, including the coming of the Spaniards. These appear to have been given forth by a priest who bore the title (not the name) of "Chilan Balam," whose offices were those of divination and astrology. These pronouncements were apparently colored at a later date by Christian thought, and not of a genuine aboriginal character. For example, certain astrological formulas in the books exist that are simply borrowed from European almanacs of the century between 1550 and 1650.

Amulets were in great vogue among the Maya, and they had the same fear of the last five days of the year as had the Mexicans, who regarded them as *nemontemi* or unlucky, and did no work of any description upon them. These days the Maya called *uyayayab,* and they believed that a demon entered their towns and villages at the beginning of this period. To avert evil influence they carried an image of him through the village in the hopes that he might afterwards avoid it.

In his book *Atlantis in America* (1925), Lewis Spence, who published several books on the folklore of Mexico and Central America, believed that there was some evidence for the influence of the civilization of an **Atlantis** in what he found.

Death Day

Beginning in the days of the Spanish conquests, the original Indian culture, religion, and superstitions have become inextricably interwoven with Christian beliefs and customs, creating a complex synthesis. With the modern history of war, revolts, and revolution extending into the twentieth century, it is not surprising that death has a special place in the symbolism and folklore of the Mexican people. This is vividly illustrated in the traditional celebration of All Soul's Day on November 2nd, when toys, cakes, and candies in the form of skulls are on sale in the streets, with carnival style costumes and plays depicting skeletons.

Although All Soul's Day is an imported Christian feast, it has blended with the Mexican Indian beliefs in which skulls and death goddesses are typical of pre-Columbian art, with the death orientation of the Spanish monastic orders, and the Christian *memento mori* tradition, as well as the memory of wars and revolutions.

The extraordinary profusion of death images is well illustrated by the work of the Mexican printmaker José Guadalupe Posada (1852–1913), famous for his *calaveras* (skeletons) that ate, drank, made merry, rode bicycles and horses, brandished swords and daggers, or were humble workers and revolutionaries.

Something of the extraordinarily complex history and beliefs of Mexico is captured on film by the great Soviet director S. M. Eisenstein in his uncompleted epic *Que Viva Mexico* of 1932. His vast footage remained in limbo, or was carved into short films by other hands during Eisenstein's lifetime. Political and ideological complications of the time prevented Eisenstein from completing the film as planned; but a 60-minute version titled *Time in the Sun* was completed by Marie Seton in 1940, and a longer reconstruction by G. Alexandrov (Eisenstein's assistant) and N. Orlov titled *Que Viva Mexico* was completed in the U.S.S.R. in 1979. Both are available on videocassette, but the former was released in Britain on the PAL system. The Alexandrov and Orlov film is available on NTSC video from Ifex Films, 201 W. 52nd St., New York, NY 10019. Both versions illustrate the Death Day feast, as well as the history and folklore of Mexico. An earlier short, "Death Day," made from Eisenstein's material was released in cinemas in 1934.

Until his death in 1950, Enrique O. Aragon, a Mexian physician, and dean of the Universidad Nacional Autonoma de Mexico, set out to investigate claims of paranormal activities, including those of poltergeists. He worked not only to clarify the phenomena, but also to expose fraud.

Organizations dedicated to the study of parapsychology and the paranormal are limited throughout Mexico and Central America. Those in Mexico are: Sociedad Mexicana de Parapsicologia, at Apartado 12-699, 03000 Mexico, D.F., Mexico; the Instituto Latinoamericano de Psicologia Paranormal, at Apartado Postal 156, San Juan del Rio, 768000 Queratario; and the Fundacion Interncional Subdud (International Subdud Foundation), located at Plutarco Elias Calles No. 702, Col. Club de Golf, Cuernavaca, Morelos 62030, Mexico. The latter is a branch of the international organization, and was established in 1982 as a charitable organization. The foundation works with the University of Zacatecas and the Instituto Politecnico Nacional to help physically and mentally challenged adults and children in Mexico's rural areas. As therapy, the staff works with the patients using energized gems, acupuncture, and Kirlian photography as a diagnostic tool to determine the psychological health of the children while they are in treatment. Panama's Instituto de Estudios Parapsicologicos, located at Apartado 8000, Panama 7, Panama, and the Sociedad Hispano-Americano para la Investigaticion Filosofica y Metafisica, operating from the same location, also publishes, *Boletin Informativo.* Courses in parapsychology were present from 1982–85, but were suspended at the National University during the time of political unrest. A Spanish-language website for the Parapsychology Institute in Mexico is available through http://www.aliensonearth.com.

Sources:

Berdecio, R., and S. Appelbaum, eds. *Posada's Popular Mexican Prints.* New York: Dover, 1972.

Berger, Arthur S., and Joyce Berger. *The Encyclopedia of Parapsychology and Psychical Research.* New York: Paragon House, 1991.

Recinos, Adriàn, Delia Goetz, and Sylvanus G. Morley, trans. and eds. *Popul Vuh: The Sacred Book of the Ancient Quiché Maya.* London: William Hodge, 1951.

Sahagun, Bernardino de. *Historia de la Conquista de Mexico.* Mexico, 1829.

Spence, Lewis. *Atlantis in America.* London: Ernest Benn, 1925. Reprint, Detroit: Singing Tree Press, 1972.

———. *The Civilization of Ancient Mexico.* London, 1911.

———. *The Gods of Mexico.* London: Fisher, Unwin, 1913.

———. *The Magic and Mysteries of Mexico.* London: Rider, 1930.

———. *The Myths of Mexico and Peru.* London: Harrap, 1913.

———. *The Popul Vuh: The Mythic & Heroic Sagas of the Kichés of Central America.* London: David Nutt, 1908.

Meyer, Gustav (1868–1932)

Famous German occultist and novelist who wrote under the name **Gustav Meyrink.**

Meyer, Jean (d. 1931)

French industrialist, a fervent adherent of the Spiritist doctrines of **Allan Kardec,** founder of the **Maison des Spirites** (8 Rue Copernic, Paris), which aimed, under his personal supervision, at the diffusion of this knowledge. He was also a founder of the **Institut Métapsychique International,** which pursued **psychical research** and was recognized as of public utility by the French government in 1919. He endowed the institution with a portion of his fortune, took a personal interest in its work, and presented it, shortly before his death, with an infrared installation at a cost of 200,000 francs.

The following story indicates the fair-mindedness of Jean Meyer in sponsoring both **Spiritualism** and scientific research. After the death of **Gustav Geley,** director of the Institut Métapsychique, Meyer desired to appoint **Eugèn Osty** as his successor. Osty pointed out that the institute would require complete scientific liberty, and asked, "What would you say, if from the laboratory of the Institut there were to issue some day studies of fact which would suggest that the teaching of the Maison des Spirites is in whole or in part illusory interpretation of facts produced exclusively by the innate powers of man as yet unknown?"

With courageous confidence in both Spiritualism and science, Meyer replied: "Yes, I accept the risk. I know you for a sincere researcher. That is enough for me."

Meyrink, Gustav (1868–1932)

Pseudonym of German novelist Gustav Meyer, famous for his occult fiction. He was also actively concerned with occult and theosophical groups in Europe before and during World War I. Meyrink was born June 19, 1868 in Vienna but was later taken by his family to Prague, Czechoslovakia, where his mother's family owned a bank. As a young man Meyrink worked in the bank, but he was attracted to occult teachings. By 1891 he joined the Theosophical Lodge of the Blue Star, whose members practiced various occult disciplines. Meyrink translated *Nature's Finer Forces* by Rama Prasad, one of the first works to introduce tantra to a popular audience in the West. In 1903 he published his first collection of short stories. Many of his writings have themes of fantasy or occultism, with echoes of E. T. A. Hoffmann, Edgar Allan Poe, and Franz Kafka.

His best-known novel was *Der Golem* (1915; translated by M. Pemberton as *The Golem,* 1928). This is a brilliant and strangely disturbing book concerned with the **Kabala** and the occult, based on Prague legends of the **Golem,** a mysterious man-monster said to have been created from clay by Rabbi Judah Loew of Prague in the seventeenth century. The book had added power in relating to the real-life background of Golem legends, which remained popular in the Prague ghetto, the site of Rabbi Loew's grave. A German silent film *The Golem,* directed and scripted by Paul Wegener, was produced in 1920, adapted very loosely from Meyrink's novel.

Meyrink converted from Protestantism to Buddhism and spent many years in occult investigations, including experiments in **alchemy.** He was present at some of the séances of **Baron Albert von Schrenck-Notzing** in Munich with the medium **"Eva C."** Meyrink also practiced **yoga** and claimed to have achieved telepathic contact with the famous South Indian holy man **Sri Ramana Maharshi,** guru of **Paul Brunton.** After a rich and varied life, Meyrink died in December 1932 in Starnberg, Germany.

Sources:

Frank, Eduard. *Gustav Meyrink.* Budingen-Gettenbach, Germany: Avalun Verlag, 1957.

The Mezazoth

A traditional Jewish schedule that, when fastened on the doorpost, possessed talismanic qualities. It is said in the Talmud that whoever has the mezazoth fixed on his door, and is provided with certain personal charms, is protected from sin.

Mhorag (or Morag)

A Loch Ness-type monster observed and photographed in Loch Morar, West Inverness, Scotland. Accounts of sightings go back to the late nineteenth century, but attracted attention only in the wake of the better-known **Loch Ness monster.** In 1970 members of the Loch Ness Investigation Bureau formed a Loch Morar Survey to begin study of the possible creature in the lake, which is 12 miles long, up to 2 miles wide, and 1,017 feet deep. Investigators Elizabeth Montgomery Campbell and R. Macdonald Robertson collected and published stories of Mhorag over the next several years. Their work was stimulated by a 1969 sighting by two fishermen, Duncan McDonell and William Simpson, which was one of the few sightings reported worldwide.

The magazine *Fortean Times* (no. 22, summer 1977) reproduced a photograph taken by Hazel Jackson (of Wakefield, England), who stayed at Morar with her husband on a touring holiday. The Jacksons, who are skeptical about monsters, took two photographs of their sheepdog by the side of the loch, and both pictures showed what appeared to be the head of a monster in the loch. Two other photographs reproduced in the same issue of *Fortean Times* were taken by an M. Lindsay of Musselburgh, and these were also somewhat ambiguous.

A Loch Morar Expedition headed by Adrian Shine tested underwater surveillance equipment, including a spherical submersible designed by Shine. There are hopes that such equipment may identify the Mhorag monster, since the waters of the loch are crystal clear. But as of the mid-1990s, no clear evidence of Mhorag has been produced.

Sources:

Campbell, Elizabeth Montgomery, and David Solomon. *The Search for Morag.* London: Tom Stacey, 1972.

Clark, Jerome. *Encyclopedia of Strange and Unexplained Phenomena.* Detroit: Gale Research, 1993.

Robertson, R. Macdonald. *Selected Highland Folktales.* North Pomfret, Vt.: David and Charles, 1977.

Michael

An archangel whose Hebrew name means "He who is equal to God." He is mentioned in the book of Daniel as a character in Daniel's visions who is a prince of Persia contending for the Hebrew people. After the Hebrews returned to Palestine from their exile, they began to develop their doctrine of **angels.** Seven archangels, including Michael and Gabriel, emerged into prominence. In one of the uncanonical Jewish writings, the Assumption of Moses, Michael disputes with Satan for the body of Moses, a belief picked up and mentioned in the Christian New Testament (Jude 9).

The most important quote concerning Michael is found in Revelation 12:7: "There was war in heaven. Michael and his angels fought against the dragon." From this it is deduced that Michael is the leader of the celestial hierarchy against Lucifer, the head of the disobedient angels.

His design, according to genealogist Randle Holme, is a banner hanging on a cross, and he is represented as victory with a dart in one hand and a cross on his forehead. Bishop Horsley and others considered Michael as only another name for the Son of God.

In one of the Jewish rabbinical legends, he is the ruler of Mercury, to which sphere he "imparts benignity, motion and intelligence, with elegance and consonance of speech."

Michael Teachings

Michael, a spirit entity, supposedly first manifest during a dinner party in the home of Walter and Jessica Lessing, a couple living in the San Francisco Bay area. The couple were playing with a Ouija board when reportedly a simple message appeared: "We are here with you tonight." When asked who "we" were, an entity replied, "The last name a fragment of this entity used was Michael" and added, "Each soul is a part of a larger body, an entity. Each entity is made up of about one thousand souls, each of which enters the physical plane as many times as necessary is to experience all aspects of Life and achieve human understanding. At the end of the cycles on the physical plane, the fragments once again reunite as we have reunited."

"Michael" indicated that the fragments comprised an ancient entity that comes to those who ask and teaches some understanding of human evolution. They hope to redirect people to their personal life plans and show them that which is wrong so they can come to a personal acceptance of truth. Understanding is achieved when the student can go on to *agape,* a nonsexual and selfless love, the goal toward which all should aspire.

The Lessings and their guests, Craig and Emily Wright, stayed at the board for the next five hours. In the days ahead they were joined by Lucy North (who became the group's typist) and Leah and Arnold Harris. After about six months of intensive reception of material, the small group began to grow until it numbered about thirty. Then in 1978 writer Chelsea Quinn Yarbro was introduced to the teachings and given access to the messages that had accumulated over the eight years since Michael first appeared. Her book *Messages from Michael* (1979) brought attention to the Michael teachings, expanded his audience, especially in the San Francisco area, and has led to the publication of much of the material.

The teachings are set within a familiar Gnostic/theosophical universe that divides existence into seven planes, which Michael calls the physical, astral, causal, akashic, mental, messianic, and buddhaic. Michael resides on the causal.

Sources:

Baumbach, Emily. *Michael's Cast of Characters.* Orinda, Calif.: Affinity Press, 1989.

Pope, Joya. *The World According to Michael.* San Mateo, Calif.: Sage Publications, 1987.

Stevens, Jose, and Simon Warwick-Smith. *Essence and Personality: The Michael Handbook.* Orinda, Calif.: Warwick Press, 1987.

Yarbro, Chelsea Quinn. *Messages from Michael.* Chicago: Playboy Press, 1979.

———. *Michael's People.* New York: Berkeley Books, 1988.

———. *More Messages from Michael.* New York: Berkeley Books, 1986.

Michelsen, Neil Franklin (1931–1990)

Neil Franklin Michelsen, an astrologer and founder of **Astro Communications Services,** was born on May 11, 1931, in Chicago, Illinois. He attended the University of Miami (from which he graduated magnum cum laude in mathematics) and in 1959 went to work for IBM as a systems engineer. Through the 1960s he developed an interest in **astrology** and in 1971, with a primitive computer set up in his home, he began to create the databases of information from which horoscopes could be constructed. In 1973 he incorporated Astro Computing Services, then headquartered in his home in White Plains, New York.

Michelsen resigned from IBM in 1976 to devote full time to his emerging business. That same year the first of what were to become essential reference books for professional astrologers appeared, a computer-generated ephemeris (charts of the daily position of planets) and table of houses (charts showing the locations of the **astrological houses**). As these were expanded through the 1980s and revised by others in the 1990s, they remain popular items in the astrologer's library.

In 1979 Michelsen moved to San Diego and three years later reorganized the company as a California corporation, Astro Communications Services, with ACS Publications as its publication arm. As his work became known, he became the chairman of the **National Council for Geocosmic Research** and gained international recognition for his service to the astrological community, including his generosity with the profits of ACS to the development of the astrological community as a whole. Following his death on May 15, 1990, the National Council created the Neil Michelsen Memorial Fund to continue a set of projects he had previously funded.

Sources:

Astro Communications Services. http://www.astrocom.com/. May 23, 2000.

Michelsen, Neil F. *American Ephemeris for the 20th Century: 1900 to 2000 at Midnight.* Rev. ed., San Diego: ASC Publications, 1990.

———. *American Ephemeris for the 21st Century.* Revised by Rique Pottenger. San Diego: ASC Publications, 1997.

Michigan Canadian Bigfoot Information Center

Founded in 1970, covering the northern and midwestern United States and eastern Canada, to assist persons having a sincere desire for knowledge about the "Sasquatch" or "Bigfoot" (large, hairy, homonoid creature reputedly inhabiting various regions of North America), and to obtain a Sasquatch specimen. The center conducts all-night vigils in classified areas and receives cooperative assistance from anthropologists, wildlife pathologists, and Department of Natural Resources affiliates. It maintains transcript and tape collections as well as a file and indexing system, compiles statistics, and maintains a research program and database. Address: 152 West Sherman, Caro, MI 48723. (See also **Bigfoot Information Center; Monsters; Sasquatch Investigations of Mid-America**)

The Microcosm

From the Greek *Micros,* small; and *Kosmos,* a world. The "little world" of the human being, as distinct from the **macrocosm,** or great world, of the universe. The relationship between microcosm and macrocosm has preoccupied philosophers for many centuries, with the macrocosm believed to be symbolized in the microcosm. According to some occultists, the microcosm was itself symbolized by the pentagram, or **pentacle,**—a five-pointed star believed to represent humanity and the summation of the occult forces. **Paracelsus** held that this sign had a marvelous magical power over spirits and that all magic figures and kabalistic signs could be reduced to two—the microcosm and the macrocosm. (See also **magical diagrams**)

Micro-PK

Term used to denote **psychokinetic** (paranormal movement) effects that are weak or minute, thus requiring statistical analysis or special methods of detection. In contrast, macro-PK effects are paranormal movements sufficiently large or impressive to be observed by the naked eye.

The Microprosopus

One of the four magical elements in the **Kabala,** probably representing one of the four simple elements—air, water, earth, or fire. The word means "creator of the little world."

Mictlan

The Mexican Hades. (See also **Hell; Mexico and Central America**)

Midday Demons

It was the belief of ancient peoples that certain demons became visible especially toward midday to those with whom they had a pact. They appeared in the form of men or of beasts, and would allow themselves be enclosed in a symbolic character, a figure, a vial, or in the interior of a hollow ring. (See also **demonology**)

The Midiwiwin

A secret society or exclusive association of the Ojibway Indians of North America. The myth of the foundation of this society is as follows: "Michabo, the Creator, looking down to earth saw that the forefathers of the Ojibway were very helpless. . . . Espying a black object floating on the surface of a lake he drew near to it and saw that it was an otter [now one of the sacred animals of the *Midiwiwin*]. He instructed it in the mysteries of that caste, and provided it with a sacred rattle, a sacred drum, and tobacco. He built a *Midiwigan,* or Sacred House of Midi, to which he took the otter and confided to it the mysteries of the *Midiwiwin.*"

The society was one of the "medicine" or magical associations so common among the North American Indians (see **America, United States of**). When a candidate was admitted to a grade and prepared to pass on to the next, he gave three feasts and sang three prayers to the Bear Spirit in order to be permitted to enter that grade.

His progress through the various grades was assisted by several snake-spirits. At a later stage, by the power of certain prayers or invocations, a larger snake appeared and raised its body, thus forming an arch under which the candidate made his way to the higher grade.

When the Indian achieved the second grade, he was supposed to receive supernatural power to be able to see into the future, to hear what came from far off, to touch friends and foes no matter how far away, and so on. In higher grades he could assume the form of any animal. The third grade conferred the ability to perform extraordinary exploits and have power over the entire invisible world. The fourth was still more exalted.

When an Indian was ready to undergo initiation, he erected a wigwam in which he took steambaths for four days, one on each day. On the evening of the day before initiation he visited his teachers in order to obtain from them instructions for the following day. Next morning the priests approached with the candidate at their head, entered the *Midiwigan,* and the proceedings commenced.

The publications of the Bureau of American Ethnology contain several good accounts of the ritual of this society.

Midwest Psychic News

Former monthly publication covering psychic events in Illinois and other states. It flourished for several years in the 1970s.

Milk-Drinking Statues

On the morning of September 21 (the fall **equinox**), 1995, a priest of a Hindu temple in New Delhi awakened from a dream in which the deity Genesha asked for a drink of milk. He soon left for a nearby temple dedicated to Genesha and offered the statue a spoonful of milk. To his surprise, the statue drank (absorbed?) the milk. News of the occurrence spread through the neighborhood and across New Delhi within hours. Devotees flocked to the temple to offer Genesha milk and as lines formed, people soon discovered that statues at other temples (almost all of which have a Genesha statue, in the shape of an elephant and located near the door) were also drinking up the milk. By evening, accounts of the event (and the accompanying milk shortage in the Indian capital) were on the news. Phone and e-mail messages went to Indian expatriate communities. By the next day, reports of statues at temples around India drinking milk began to appear, and on the 23rd they were joined by reports from North America, England, and Southeast Asia. Television coverage of the statues showed some of the offerings in which the milk actually disappeared. On the 22nd in Toronto, more than 100 people lined up to feed the statue. The leaders at the temple indicated that the massive feeding frenzy was the sign that a great soul was being born somewhere in the world. They also indicated that the phenomena would cease in some 48 hours.

The Indian government became concerned about the event and sent scientists from its Department of Science and Technology to investigate the situation. They suggested that the small amounts being offered to the statutes were being absorbed by the porous material out of which they were constructed and were coating the surface with a thin film. Other scientists reported similar findings at other locations. Puddles of milk soon appeared around all of the drinking statues. By the end of the day on the 22nd, most of the frenzy had died down, and reports of further drinking by the statues dropped perceptively, and disappeared altogether soon afterwards. Many Hindus consider the events of September 21–22 to have been a miracle. Skeptics have dismissed it as a hysteric reaction to a very mundane occurrence. Many government officials saw it as a move by political conservatives to spread Hindu nationalism.

An archive of e-mail messages and wire service reports has been preserved by the Australian government's Distributed Services Technology Centre in Bribane on an Internet file, "Genesha Is Drinking Milk!!!" at http://archive.dstc.edu.au/TU/staff/timbomb/buddha/ganesha.html.

Sources:

Genesha Is Drinking Milk!!!. http://archive.dstc.edu.au/TU/staff/timbomb/buddha/ganesha.html. March 4, 2000.

Miller, Charles Victor (d. 1943)

Materialization medium of San Francisco, born in Nancy, France. By profession he was a dealer in old pictures and Japanese art. Author Willie Reichel claimed to have witnessed many of Miller's performances. For example, Miller did not go into trance as a séance started. He stood outside the cabinet from which a procession of phantoms issued. Miller took them by the hand, asked their names, and introduced them to the sitters. Later he went into the cabinet, where he was seen with as many as six white robed figures. They came out one by one, spoke to the sitters, and usually dematerialized in front of the cabinet, sinking through the floor.

Although the materialization of figures suggests **fraud** and accomplices rather than genuine psychic phenomena, the variety of Miller's phenomena, the certainty of the witnesses, and the lack of a competent observer leaves the question somewhat open. On one occasion Reichel's nephew disappeared by floating upward through the ceiling. Miller was normally under the **control** of the spirits "Betsy" and "Dr. Benton."

The highest number of materialized spirits Reichel claimed to have seen in a séance was 12. The medium was conscious and kept talking. The phantoms spoke in various languages and many were recognized by the sitters. Once, in Reichel's own house, a materialized spirit walked out into the hall, a distance of 35 feet from the medium.

In the journal *Psychische Studien* (February 1904), Reichel described a séance at which a deceased friend of his materialized eight times, very near to him, at a distance of over three yards from the medium. Reichel stated: "He drew near me like a floating flame, which lowered itself, and in the space of about a minute and a half developed and stood before me quite formed. He held long conversations with me; then, retiring to the curtain, where I followed him, he dematerialised, speaking up to the moment when his head disappeared."

Reichel also witnessed rotating white and blue flames from which voices spoke to him, giving their complete names. In one séance the medium was completely dematerialized and transported to the first floor.

Miller made two visits to Europe. When he first arrived in 1906, much criticism was directed against him because he mostly sat with Spiritists (see **Spiritism**) and avoided researchers such as **Eugene Rochas,** with whom he had corresponded, and a circle of scientists who had arranged to test him scientifically.

However, psychic researcher **Gabriel Delanne** concluded that the apparitions were genuine. Gaston Méry, chief editor of the *Libre Parole* and director of the *Echo du Merveilleux* (which was not a Spiritist journal) admitted that it was highly probable that the phenomena he witnessed were genuine but "until there is fuller information we must be satisfied with not comprehending." The séance took place in Méry's house in a room Miller did not enter before the proceedings. Moreover, he was completely undressed in the presence of three doctors and donned Méry's own garments.

Gérard Encausse ("Papus") also attended a séance and stated in *L'Initiation* that his expectation was fully satisfied and that Miller displayed "mediumistic faculties more extraordinary than he had hitherto encountered."

From Paris, Miller went on to Germany and gave many test séances in Munich at private residences. The accounts appear to corroborate Reichel's observations. The materialized form was often seen to develop from luminous globes and clouds that first appeared near the ceiling. If several forms were materialized at the same time, they were transparent. It often happened that at the end of the séance Miller was violently thrown out of the cabinet, yet he suffered no injury.

On his way back to the United States, Miller again visited Paris and gave a few more séances. According to **Charles Richet,** he would not accept the conditions imposed. Four of his séances were reported in the *Annals of Psychic Science* (vol. 4, 1906). Psychic researcher **Count Cesar de Vesme,** who attended the last séance, objected to not having been given an adequate opportunity to form a well-founded judgment and noted: "A white ball, as of gas, about a quarter of a yard in diameter appeared in the air at the upper extremity of the curtains. Finally it came down, rested on the floor, and in less than a minute, changing into a long shape, was transformed into a draped human form, which subsequently spoke" (*Annals of Psychic Science,* vol. 4, no. 21, 1906). The séance, however, was not sufficient to enable de Vesme to arrive at a definite opinion as to the genuineness of the manifestations.

In 1908 Miller paid another visit to Paris. On June 25, in the presence of 40 persons, a very successful séance was held at the house of a Mrs. Noeggerath under test conditions. The control committee consisted of one Mr. Benezech, Gaston Méry, Cesar de Vesme, and Charles Blech, secretary of the Theosophical Society. The medium was disrobed, medically examined, and put into black garments that were furnished by the committee and had neither lining nor pockets. Numerous phantom shapes evolved and disappeared.

Cesar de Vesme, however, remained unconvinced. In the *Annals of Psychic Science* (vol. 7, 1908), he complained that in the series of séances he attended in almost complete darkness, Miller never allowed the control of his right hand. Sitting on the left side of the cabinet, he could have used his right hand to introduce a white drapery, which he could have manipulated as a small phantom in the course of materialization. He had only been searched in a single séance when 40 people were present. There was no telling whether the drapery might not have been passed to him by one of the sitters. Leon Denis, Baron de Watteville, Charles Blech, de Fremery (director of the *Het Toekomstig Leven,* The Hague), Paul Leymarie (director of the *Reuve Spirite*), M. W. Bormann (director of *Die Übersinnliche Welt*), and **Joseph Maxwell** shared de Vesme's opinion. Of Miller's public séances no more was heard after this Paris series.

Miller died on November 1, 1943 in New York.

Sources:

Reichel, Willie. *Occult Experiences.* N.p., 1906.

Miller, Ellora Fogle (Mrs. R. DeWitt Miller) (1913–1982)

Writer in the fields of publicity and psychical research. She was born June 8, 1913, in Philadelphia, Pennsylvania, and studied at the University of Southern California (M.A., 1945). She was a staff member of the publicity department of Young & Rubicam, Hollywood, California, and national editor of the *Baton* (the publication of Phi Beta Fraternity) (1953–56), and afterward director of honors for the Phi Beta Fraternity. In 1937 she married **R. DeWitt Miller** (1910–1958), with whom she collaborated on two books and several articles concerned with psychical research.

Ellora Miller died in October 1982.

Sources:

Miller, R. DeWitt, and Ellora F. Miller. *Forgotten Mysteries.* Chicago: Cloud Inc., 1947.

———. *You Do Take It with You.* New York: Citadel Press, 1955.

Miller, R(ichard) DeWitt (1910–1958)

Writer on psychical research and parapsychology. Born January 22, 1910, in Los Angeles, California, he was educated at the University of Southern California (B.A., 1933). In 1937 he married **Ellora Fogle Miller.** A freelance writer, Miller contributed many articles to *Coronet, Esquire, Pageant, Popular Mechanics, Popular Science, Tomorrow,* and *Life.*

Many of his writings were concerned with paranormal topics, and he contributed the regular features "Your Other Life," "Forgotten Mysteries," and "Not of Our Species" to *Coronet* magazine. He contributed to the anthology *Beyond the Five Senses,* edited by **Eileen J. Garrett** (1957). He wrote two books and several articles with his wife. He died June 3, 1958.

Sources:

Miller, R. Dewitt. *The Man Who Lived Forever.* N.p., 1956.

———. *Reincarnation.* N.p., 1956.

Miller, R. Dewitt, and Ellora F. Miller. *Forgotten Mysteries.* N.p., 1947.

———. *You Do Take It with You.* New York: Citadel Press, 1955.

Miller, Robin (1950–)

Robin Miller is a poet, songwriter, and musician residing in **Sedona,** Arizona, who during the 1980s found the answer to much of his searching in **New Age** metaphysics. Then in 1987, he began to channel music. The term **channeling** has frequently been applied to the inspiration to which gifted musicians have attributed as the source of their musical innovations. The product of these channelings was released as a series of albums including Paradise View, Magical Spheres, Celestial Bridge, and From the Heart, each of which reached a popular audience in the post-New Age community. Then on January 23, 1991, shortly before Miller and his family moved to Sedona, an unembodied entity named Jonathon manifested early in the morning immediately after an intense dream in which Miller felt he was being taught about the future direction of his life. As he awoke he found himself repeating some thoughts aloud. He sat down to remember and put the thoughts to paper. At that point he found himself tapping into thoughts that did not appear to be his own. He began to record these thoughts by **automatic writing.**

Miller found that he was frequently called upon to write, and he allowed his bonding with the entity who was communicating through him to become stronger. Accompanying the process of communicating, Miller also found that he was transforming into a more loving being.

Jonathon described himself as a seventh ray being and speaker for the Council of the Brotherhood of Light, described as a group of seven beings amid the many organizations and entities in the spiritual realm who are working to reawaken humanity to its true God-self connection. The brotherhood thus works beside the many groups spoken of by other channelers such as the **Great White Brotherhood,** the Celestial Hierarchy of Light, and the **Ashtar Command,** groups of evolved beings who guide humanity in its overall evolution and spiritual life. Jonathon described himself as someone who had been incarnated on various occasions, on the most recent occasion as a Christian monk in the thirteenth century in eastern France. He was also known as Jonathon in that incarnation. He had led a contemplative life and had an awakening in his 46th year. He died three years later.

In returning to speak through Miller, Jonathon explained he is taking part in a coordinated effort from the spiritual realm to push humanity toward enlightenment. As a result, Earth will be transformed into a paradise. The awakening of humanity at this time is the fulfillment of the promise of the Second Coming of Christ. In 1993 Miller published the initial messages from Jonathon as *Talks with Jonathon,* the first of five proposed volumes.

Sources:

Miller, Robin. *Talks with Jonathon, Book I: A Guide to Transformation.* Needham, Mass.: Channel One Communications, 1993.

Millesimo Castle

Located in Italy in the province of Savona. It was the property of the **Marquis Carlo Centurione Scotto** and the scene of important psychic investigations (1927–28) and later on the phenomena of **direct voice, apports, levitation,** and **materialization.**

Mind-Body-Spirit Festival

International festival coordinating and presenting occult, mystical, psychic, astrological, New Age, human potential, and holistic organizations and individuals. Founded in April 1977 in England by new consciousness entrepreneur **Graham Wilson,** the festival has since been presented annually in London and Australia and occasionally in the United States.

The festival provides an annual stage for contemporary alternative lifestyles in a wide spectrum of mystical, holistic, and ecological areas, where traditional philosophies and activities rub shoulders with newer cults. It offers lectures, demonstrations, and workshops as well as exhibits and stands promoting individuals, organizations, and publications concerned with psychic phenomena, healing, **yoga, astrology,** health, physical fitness, dance, **UFOs, meditation,** organic gardening, mystical arts and crafts, and alternative technologies. Address: UK New Life Promotions Ltd., Arnica House, 170 Campden Hill Rd., London W8 7AS, England. Australia Mind Body Spirit Sydney Festival Party ltd., Locked Bag 19, Pyrmont, NSW 2009.

Mind Cure

The name loosely applied to various systems of alternative healing in the late nineteenth century. The name was first applied to the healing system developed by **Phineas Parkhurst Quimby** (1802–66) out of his reflections on **mesmerism** and **hypnotism.** Quimby, a clockmaker who became a professional mesmerist, observed the power of suggestion on his subjects.

Quimby turned his attention from mesmerist power to focus on the idea of mind. He posited that illness comes from holding delusions or false opinions in the mind (such as those put out by the church or the average physician) and the mind will reproduce in the body the false idea. His healing work consisted of presenting wisdom or truth to the patient, who accepted it and then became well. He operated informally out of Portland, Maine, through the years of the Civil War. He died in 1866 having never published any of his writings. His work was carried on by his various pupils.

The most famous of Quimby's students was **Mary Baker Eddy,** who in the months after Quimby's death pushed his system in an idealistic direction. She concluded that God was the only reality and that healing was to be found in accepting that reality. From that insight, which differed radically from that of Quimby, she built the **Church of Christ, Scientist,** the organizational center of the Christian Science movement. Christian Science has four fundamental propositions: (1) God is all in all; (2) God is Good. Good is Mind; (3) God, Spirit, being all, nothing is matter; and (4) Life, God, omnipotent good, deny death, evil, sin, disease. The new church was a phenomenal success and controversy swarmed around it and its founder. Two of Quimby's students, Julius and Annette Dresser, seemingly unaware of how Eddy's system was uniquely her own, challenged Eddy for not giving Quimby the proper credit for originating Christian Science.

Meanwhile, another Quimby student, former Methodist minister turned Swedenborgian, Warren Felt Evans, established a healing practice in Salisbury, Massachusetts, and developed his own healing system as an integral part of his Swedenborgian thought. Ultimately a pantheist, he wrote a number of books.

As the movement developed, a number of students separated from Eddy and began to operate as independent Christian Science healers. One of them, Joseph Addams, began the *Mind Cure Journal* in Chicago in the mid 1880s. Other healers with no connection to Eddy, other than possibly having read her books, also appeared on the scene. Those students most attached to Eddy's thought founded what has been a continuing independent Christian Science movement, while the more autonomous thinkers became the founders of what would in the 1890s become known as **New Thought.** New Thought has been perpetuated through such organizations as the Unity School of Christianity, the Divine Science Association, the Church of Religious Science, and the International New Thought Association. It produced a number of best-selling authors, such as Ralph Waldo Trine, Prentice Mulford, Elizabeth Towne, and Orison Swett Marden.

The term *mind cure* had largely passed from the scene by the beginning of the twentieth century, but the basic movements, Christian Science, independent Christian Science, and New Thought, have continued. New Thought entered into mainline Christian thought through the efforts of Norman Vincent Peale and more recently Robert Schuler, both ministers in the Reformed Church in America.

Sources:

Braden, Charles S. *Spirits in Rebellion.* Dallas, Tex.: Southern Methodist University Press, 1963.

Judah, J. Stillson. *The History and Philosophy of the Metaphysical Movements in America.* Philadelphia: Westminster Press, 1967.

Melton, J. Gordon. *New Thought: A Reader.* Santa Barbara, Calif.: Institute for the Study of American Religion, 1990.

Mind Development and Control Association

Organization founded to develop and promote interest in various facets of paranormal and psychic research and to foster awareness and understanding of the forces that influence and shape human existence. The association sponsored research in the fields of healing and bioenergy and provided monthly correspondence lessons in psychic arts and sciences and classes in psychic development and **ESP** skills. It maintained a haunted-house investigation group, energy and healing group, and other associated groups. It sponsored the U.S. Psi Squad as a nonprofit project that offers assistance to police and law enforcement departments when consulted in cases such as homicide and missing persons. It published *Doorways to the Mind,* a monthly magazine. Last known address: P.O. Box 29396, Sappington, MO 63126.

M'Indoe, John B. (ca. 1936)

A prominent Scottish Spiritualist. He served a tenure as president of the **Spiritualists' National Union** in Britain and was a trustee and advisory committee member of the **Edinburgh Psychic College and Library.** He made a long-term study of **spirit photography** and also reported on the controversial mediumship of **Helen Duncan.**

Mind Science Network

Organization concerned with nontraditional religions, holistic healing, psychic development, and related subjects. Published the quarterly magazine *Mind Science Journal,* which included a calendar of holy days, events, and contacts. Last known address: P.O. Box 1302, Mill Valley, CA 94941.

Mines, Haunted

The belief that mines are haunted is an ancient and universal one, probably arising from the many eerie sounds and echoes that are heard in them and the perpetual gloom, which stimulates belief in apparitions. Sometimes the haunting specters are gigantic creatures with frightful fiery eyes. Such was the German "Bergmönch, a terrible figure in the garb of a monk, who could, however, appear in ordinary human shape to those towards whom he was well-disposed."

Frequently weird knockings were heard in mines. In Germany these were attributed to the **Kobolds,** small black beings of a malicious disposition. White hares or rabbits were also seen at times. The continual dangers attending work underground have been productive of many supernatural "warnings," which generally take the form of mysterious voices.

In the midland counties of England, the "Seven Whistlers" were well known, and miners paid solemn attention to their warnings. A light blue flame settling on a full coaltub was called "Bluecap," and his work was to move the coaltub toward the trolleyway. Bluecap did not give his services for nothing. Every two weeks his wages were left in a corner of the mine and were duly appropriated. A more mischievous elf was "Cutty Soames," who would cut the "soams" or traces yoking an assistant putter to the tub.

Basilisks, fearsome monsters whose terrible eyes would strike the miner dead, were another source of dread to the worker underground. These, as well as other mysterious foes who dealt fatal blows, may be traced to the dreaded, but by no means ghostly, fire-damp or perhaps to underground lizards.

Mines of precious metals were believed to be even more jealously guarded by supernatural beings. Gnomes, the creatures of the earth element, were the special guardians of subterranean treasure, and they were anxious to defend their province. Mines containing precious stones were equally well looked after. The Indians of Peru declared that evil spirits haunted the emerald mines, while a mine in the neighborhood of Los Esmeraldos was said to be guarded by a frightful dragon. It has also been believed that the poisonous fumes and gases that often destroy the lives of miners were baleful influences radiated by evil spirits.

Other stories of haunted mines are linked to legends of secret underground temples of occultists. (See **subterranean crypts and temples**)

Minnesota Zen Meditation Center

This center stemmed from the 1960s, when a group of individuals in Minneapolis met together to practice *zazen* (**Zen** meditation). One of the students was Sekijun Karen Sunna, the center's current head priest. They soon developed an association with the San Francisco Zen Center, and its assistant priest Dainin Katagiri Roshi visited them on several occasions. In 1972, the group invited Katagiri Roshi to become leader of their new Zen Center. He accepted, and the Minnesota Zen Center was formed in January 1973.

Dainin Katagiri Roshi was born in Japan in 1928 and became a Zen monk in 1946. He trained at Eiheji Monastery, the original center of the Soto Shu sect. He came to the United States in 1963 to work with the North American Zen Buddhist Church, the Japanese-American Soto group, and was assigned to their Los Angeles temple. Five months later he was sent to San Francisco to assist Shunryu Suzuki Roshi at both the San Francisco temple (Sokoji) and the independent San Francisco Zen Center. While there he assisted in the opening of the Tassajara Zen Mountain Center.

Since coming to Minneapolis, Katagiri Roshi has attracted students from across the Midwest and has visited various groups interested in Zen. Groups affiliated with the Minnesota Center have been established in Manhattan, Kansas; Iowa City, Iowa; Milwaukee, Wisconsin; and Omaha, Nebraska.

In 1978 the center purchased 280 acres near Houston, Minnesota, which offers meditation, classes and lectures as well as retreats. Since Katagiri Roshi's death in 1990, Sekijun Karen Sunna has acted as head priest. Address: 3343 E. Calhoun Pkwy., Minneapolis, MN 55408. Website: http://www.mnzenctr.com/.

Sources:

Minnesota Zen Center. http://www.mnzenctr.com/. March 8, 2000.

Miñoza, Aurora (1923–)

Psychologist who has written on parapsychology. She was born January 4, 1923, in Cebu City, Philippines, and studied at the University of Michigan (B.S. English, 1947; M.A. psychology, 1953) and the University of the Philippines (Ph.D. educational psychology, 1957). An abstract of her master's thesis, *A Study of Extrasensory Perception,* was published in the *Educational Quarterly,* University of the Philippines (vol. 1, no. 1, September 1953). After graduation she joined the faculty of the Graduate College of Education, University of the Philippines.

She attended the first Parapsychology Workshop at Duke University in June 1957. She has special interests in telepathy, clairvoyance, and psychokinesis, and has experimented with the effect of thought on plant growth. She began a long tenure as president of the Parapsychological Research Society, Philippines, in 1959. She was also a member of the **Parapsychological Association.**

Sources:

Pleasants, Helene, ed. *Biographical Dictionary of Parapsychology.* New York: Helix Press, 1964.

Mirabelli, (Carmine) Carlos (1889–1951)

South American physical medium born on January 2, 1889, in Botucatu, São Paulo, Brazil, of Italian immigrant parents. Mirabelli was a **Spiritist** of the school of **Allan Kardec,** which had become popular in Brazil after its importation from Europe.

Such extraordinary accounts of his phenomena spread through psychical research circles in England and the United States that, if they could have been proved to the satisfaction of psychical researchers, he would have had to be ranked as the greatest medium of all time. Such phenomena included **automatic writing** in more than thirty different languages, **materialization** of persons and objects, **levitation,** impressions of spirit hands, and paranormal musical performances. He also normally produced phenomena in the light of day.

The first description of Mirabelli's feats was published in a booklet, *O Medium Mirabelli,* written anonymously by R. H. Mikilasch, general secretary of the **Academia de Estudos Psychicos de Cesar Lombroso.** Mirabelli had applied to the academy for experiments in **trance** speaking, automatic writing, and physical phenomena. The booklet was published in 1926. It reported 392 sittings in broad daylight or in a room illuminated by electric light. In 349 cases the sittings were held in the rooms of the academy and were attended by a total of 555 people. The summary was as follows:

"The committee carried out with the first group (trance speaking) 189 positive experiments; with the second group (automatic writing) 85 positive and 8 negative; with the third group (physical phenomena) 63 positive and 47 negative experiments. The medium spoke 26 languages including 7 dialects, wrote in 28 languages, among them 3 dead languages, namely Latin, Chaldaic and Hieroglyphics. Of the 63 physical experiments 40 were made in daylight, 23 in bright artificial light."

A second report, based on the first, appeared in a publication of the Academia de Germany, the *Zeitschrift für Parapsychologie,* in August 1929. Fearing a hoax, the German periodical made inquiries first from the Brazilian consul at Munich as to the standing and reputation of Mirabelli's witnesses and supporters. The information was verified, and the consul added that 14 persons on the submitted list were his personal acquaintances, to whose veracity he would testify. He said he had no reason to question the statements of other people on the list, known to him not only as scientists but also as men of character. Thereupon the *Zeitschrift für Parapsychologie* published a summary of the case. (It was later discovered that the Academia de Estudios Psychicos de Cesar Lombroso, named for the famed Italian psychical researcher, was founded and headed by Mirabelli, and hence the objectivity of its report is very much in question.)

The newspapers picked up the story. They wrote of telekinetic **movement,** of **apports,** of a miraculous **teleportation** of the medium from the railroad station of Da Luz to São Vicenti—90 kilometers distance in two minutes; of his **levitation** in the street two meters high for three minutes; of how he caused a skull to float toward an apothecary; of making an invisible hand turn the leaves of a book in the home of Dr. Alberto Seabra in the presence of many scientists; of making glasses and bottles at a banquet play a military march without human touch; of causing the hat of Antonio Canterello to fly off and float ten meters along a public square; of making and quelling fire by will in the home of Alves Lima; of making a cue play billiards without touching it; and finally of having the picture of Christ impressed on plaster in the presence of Dr. Caluby, director of police.

A conjuring magician imitated some of Mirabelli's phenomena, but this did not lessen his reputation as a wonder-worker. Owing to the heated controversy that grew up around him, an arbitration board was instituted for the investigation of the medium. Among the members were Dr. Ganymed de Souza, president of the Republic; a Dr. Brant of the Institute of Technology; and 18 other men of high position and learning.

After the investigation and the testimony of witnesses, the board established that the majority of the manifestations occurred in daylight, that they occurred spontaneously and in public places, that the manifold intellectual phenomena could not easily be based on trickery, and that the statements of persons whose integrity was reputed could not easily be doubted.

Mirabelli's automatic writing was reportedly inspired by the spirits of historical figures. Fifteenth-century reformer John Huss influenced Mirabelli to write a treatise of nine pages on the independence of Czechoslovakia in 20 minutes; French psychical researcher **Camille Flammarion** inspired him to write about inhabited planets—14 pages in 19 minutes in French. "Muri Ka Ksi" delivered 5 pages in 12 minutes on the Russo-Japanese War in Japanese. "Moses" wrote in Hebrew on slandering; "Harun el Raschid" made Mirabelli write 15 pages in Syrian, and an untranslatable writing of three pages came in hieroglyphics in 32 minutes.

The phenomena of **materialization** were astounding, if real. The figures were not only complete, and photographed, but medical men made minute examinations that lasted for sometimes as long as 15 minutes and stated that the newly constituted human beings had perfect anatomical structure. After the examination was completed, one figure began to dissolve from the feet up, the bust and arms floating in the air. One of the doctors exclaimed, "But this is too much!" He rushed forward and seized the remaining half of the body. The next moment he uttered a shrill cry and sank unconscious to the ground. On returning to consciousness, he only remembered that when he had seized the phantom it had felt as if his fingers were pressing a spongy, flaccid mass. Then, he said, he received a shock and lost consciousness.

Reportedly, for 36 minutes in broad daylight the materialization of the young daughter of Dr. Souza, who died of influenza, was visible to all the sitters. She appeared in her burial clothes. Her pulse was tested. Father and child were photographed. Then the phantom raised itself and floated in the air. At the third sitting, supposedly a skull inside the closet began to beat the doors, came out, and slowly grew to a full skeleton.

In another sitting Mirabelli announced that he saw the body of Bishop Dr. Jose de Carmago Barros, who had lost his life in a shipwreck:

"A sweet smell as of roses filled the room. The medium went into trance. A fine mist was seen in the circle. The mist, glowing as if of gold, parted and the bishop materialized, with all the robes and insignia of office. He called his own name. Dr. de Souza stepped to him. He palpated the body, touched his teeth, tested the saliva, listened to the heart-beat, investigated the working of the intestines, nails and eyes, without finding anything amiss. Then the other attending persons convinced themselves of the reality of the apparition. The Bishop smilingly bent over Mirabelli and looked at him silently. Then he slowly dematerialized."

At the sixth sitting, Mirabelli, tied and sealed, disappeared from the room and was found in another room still in trance. All seals on doors and windows were found in order, as well as the seals on Mirabelli himself. Once, among 14 investigators, his arms dematerialized. On the photograph only a slight shadow is visible.

In 1930 the British psychical researcher **Eric J. Dingwall** reviewed and summarized the original Portuguese documents, and stated, "I must confess that, on a lengthy examination of the documents concerning Mirabelli, I find myself totally at a loss to come to any decision whatever on the case."

However, as early as the November 1930 issue of *Psychic Research*, **Hans Driesch** threw cold water on all such marvels on the basis of a personal investigation in São Paulo in 1928. He saw no materializations, no transportation, and heard only Italian and Esthonian, which Mirabelli may have normally known. But he admitted seeing some remarkable telekinetic phenomena that he could not explain, involving the movement of a small vase and the folding of doors in daylight without any visible cause.

In 1934 **Theodore Besterman,** a researcher with the **Society for Psychical Research** in London attended some of Mirabelli's séances in Brazil. Upon his return he wrote a brief, private report claiming that Mirabelli was a fraud, but that report was never published. In his published report, he stated only that he had seen nothing extraordinary. More recent examination of a picture of Mirabelli levitating that the medium gave to Besterman has been shown to be a **fraud.**

Reports of mediumistic phenomena continued throughout Mirabelli's life. Given the general opinion today that apports and materializations do not occur except as magic tricks, it is difficult to believe that Mirabelli can escape broad charges of practicing legerdemain, however extraordinary some of his mental feats may have seemed. Unfortunately, all of the positive reports came from people closely associated with him. Possibly because of the negative nature of the early reports, especially that of Besterman, no conclusive study was ever made.

Mirabelli died April 30, 1951, in an auto accident. For a modern discussion of Mirabelli see Gordon Stein's insightful article from *Fate* and the chapter "Mirabelli!!" in **Guy Playfair**'s study. The former had the opportunity to examine the Mirabelli records in England, and the latter met and interviewed individuals who had known Mirabelli, including living relatives.

Sources:

Playfair, Guy Leon. *The Unknown Power.* Reprinted as *The Flying Cow.* New York: Pocket Books, 1975.

Stein, Gordon. "The Amazing Medium Mirabelli." *Fate* 44, 3 (March 1991): 86–95.

"Mirabilis Liber"

A collection of predictions concerning the saints and the sibyls, attributed to Saint Césaire (470–542 C.E.). The work has appeared in various editions. In the edition of 1522 there is found a prophecy of the French Revolution, including the expulsion and abolition of the nobility, the violent death of the king and queen, the persecution of the clergy, and the suppression of convents. It was followed by a further prophecy that the eagle coming from distant lands would reestablish order in France.

Miracles

Miracles, in the biblical sense are signs and wonders, the extraordinary events that inspire awe and open the world of the divine. By the Middle Ages the differentiation between the natural and supernatural had been made and miracles were redefined as the invasion of the supernatural into the world of the natural. As the concept of natural law and an orderly universe developed, the word *miracle* gradually took on the meaning it has had for the last three centuries—an event that occurs outside the laws of nature as we know them. Christian theologians tended to view a miracle as an event caused by God laying aside one of his own laws out of his concern for humanity.

David Hume (1711–76), the great Scottish philosopher, defined a miracle as "a violation of the laws of nature." The idea that nature follows certain laws and the consideration of whether or not those laws can be violated set the issues of a modern debate. **Alfred Russel Wallace,** prominent nineteenth-century scientist, in his book *On Miracles and Modern Spiritualism* (1881), assumes the existence of natural law and objects to Hume's skepticism by arguing that since we do not know all the laws of nature we cannot rule out the possibility of an unknown law overcoming a known one. He suggests that a miracle is "any act or event necessarily implying the existence and agency of superhuman intelligences."

Contemporary observers of the progress of science have developed a different approach to the question of miracles. They note that the idea of natural law is a concept imposed upon nature by scientists, who have observed its regularities. A miracle, they say, is a religious affirmation in the face of an extraordinary event that affects the individual positively. Calling an event a miracle is but one evaluation among several (e.g., coincidence, trickery) that can be made about the occurrence.

According to Hume, no amount of human testimony can prove a miracle. Hume's philosophy created a scientific environment in which the evaluation of an anomalous extraordinary event could only be explained as a phenomenon already understood. It is on this basis that, in spite of a popular belief in the paranormal, many scientists generally refuse to investigate the nature and evidence of so-called miracles. This resistance is odd since the history of human progress demonstrates that, as **Charles Richet** stated, "the improbabilities of today are the elementary truths of to-morrow." The truth of his statement was amply demonstrated in the lives of great scientists, many of whom had to fight an entrenched scientific community for recognition of their discoveries in an era in which the process of accepting new facts was very slow. Galileo (1564–1642) was persecuted and declared "ignorant of his ignorance;" the evidence of his telescope was rejected without examination; Sir Isaac Newton (1642–1727), born the year Galileo died, had to fight for so long for recognition of his theory of gravitation that he nearly resolved to publish nothing more and said; "I see that a man must either resolve to put out nothing new, or become a slave to defend it." Modern science is replete with stories of people who were ridiculed by their contemporaries for their extraordinary ideas and discoveries and otherwise outstanding scientists who thought the ideas of their younger colleagues to be mere ridiculous flights of fancy.

Belief in the reality of miracles has always been a cornerstone of religion. In former times it was sufficient to have faith that the divine power that created the universe of matter could also transcend its laws either directly or through the agency of particular humans. However, the religious skepticism of the eighteenth and nineteenth centuries—built in large part by the emergence of science and later sustained by its obvious success in changing the world through technology—threw doubt on the reality of all miracles, sacred or secular.

Part of the present-day opposition to claims of the paranormal is based on the brilliant achievements arising from applied scientific laws, reinforcing confidence in the logic of the material world. From this viewpoint, many agnostics and atheists deny the possibility of either religious miracles or secular paranormal happenings, claiming that both are the result of malobservation, superstition, or fraud. Meanwhile many religious authorities have upheld the validity of biblical miracles as indicating God's omnipotence and intervention in human affairs. For example, Vatican Council I (1870–71) denied that miracles are impossible. However, many theologians, responding positively to the world of natural science, have taken the view that miracles are no longer necessary in modern times as evidence for religious faith. Even the Roman Catholic church, informed by its own experience as much as by modern scientific worldviews, champions the idea of caution in evaluating apparent miracles in modern times, since it would be foolish to ignore the possibility of misunderstanding or deception. Ever since the claimed miraculous healings associated with pilgrim centers like **Lourdes,** the church has been careful to insist on satisfactory scientific and medical evidence over a prolonged period of time before placing official confirmation on any claimed miracle.

Through the twentieth century a spectrum of approaches to the question of miracles have been put forth. Older supernatural worldviews have survived and are still championed by conservative Christians. Paranormal events are judged to be either godly miracles (within the context of the Christian community) or devilish deceptions (occurring elsewhere). More liberal Christian leaders have suggested that while miracles are possible, they are rare, and tend to occur spontaneously.

A growing body of believers, members of metaphysical, Spiritualist, ancient wisdom, and other occult religious groups—as well as many parapsychologists—tend to accept the existence of genuine paranormal events, but define them as purely natural events that science is slow in defining. Some would accept basic **ESP,** but not take the additional step and offer a positive evaluation of evidence for spirit communication or human **survival.** Of course, a small but vocal group deny the existence of all paranormal or supernatural events.

The problem of the distinction between religious and secular "miracles" remains a matter of polemics between conservative Christians and other religionists. Parapsychologists, Spiritualists and liberal Christians may point to the many reported miraculous events in the Bible as descriptions of paranormal events that also occur in modern times. Conservative believers accept as miraculous only those events with a clearly established religious purpose and reject all other claimed paranormal happenings. Some conservative Christians claim that all psychic phenomena are mere simulacrum of the miraculous—the work of devils or deceptive spirits counterfeiting real miracles. Of course, non-Christians resent such accusations.

Extraordinary events—miracles to the believer—are the common property of all religious traditions and the nonreligious alike. Every religious community can produce accounts of extraordinary occurrences to strenthen the faith of their believers. Most religious traditions also de-emphazize miracles as secondary to the development of a mature relationship to the transcendent and the performance of spiritual, moral, and social duties within the human community. In such a context, miraculous events may be helpful signposts or motivators at some point, but they do not take the place of spiritual development. In fact, too much attention to the miraculous (or long-term focus on psychic events) may actually be a hindrance to spiritual progress.

Sources:

Ebon, Martin, ed. *Miracles.* New York: New American Library, 1981.

Gopi Krishna. *The Secret of Yoga.* New York: Harper & Row, 1972.

Hill, J. Arthur. *Spiritualism: Its History, Phenomena, and Doctrine.* London: Cassell, 1918.

LeShan, Lawrence. *The Medium, the Mystic, and the Physicist.* New York: Viking Press, 1974.

Nickell, Joe. *Looking for a Miracle: Weeping Icons, Relics, Stigmata, Visions & Healing Cures.* Amherst, N.Y.: Prometheus Press, 1998.

Réginald-Omez, Fr. O. P. *Psychical Phenomena.* London: Burns & Oates, 1959.

Rogo, D. Scott. *Miracles: A Parascientific Inquiry Into Wondrous Phenomena.* New York: Dial Press, 1982.

Stemman, Roy. *One Hundred Years of Spiritualism.* London: Spiritualist Association of Great Britain, 1972.

Thurston, Herbert, S. J. *The Physical Phenomena of Mysticism.* London: Burns & Oates, 1952. Reprint, Chicago: Henry Regnery, 1953.

West, Donald J. *Eleven Lourdes Miracles.* London: Duckworth, 1957.

Miraculous Medal

At the beginning of the nineteenth century, a young nun was privy to several **apparitions of the Virgin Mary.** In the second one she was told to create a medal, the use of which has since become one of the most popular among the many approved practices available to members of the Roman Catholic Church. The story of the Miraculous Medal begins with the arrival of **Catherine Labouré** (1806–1876) at the Convent of the Sisters of Charity of St. Vincent de Paul in Paris, France, in 1830. Just four days after her arrival, she had the first of a series of **visions,** though not of Mary.

On the evening of July 18, she went to bed praying for a vision of the Virgin. She was awakened around 11 P.M. and instructed by a child dressed in white to go to the chapel. There Sister Catherine had her first encounter with the Virgin, in which she was told that she was being given a mission that would entail much suffering on her part. She was also instructed to tell no one but her confessor. The Virgin had predicted some hard times in the immediate future for the Parisian clergy, but noted that the convent would not be disturbed. In fact, within a few days revolution broke out in Paris. The archbishop was forced into hiding. She also predicted that in some 40 years, the ruler would be forced off the throne and the then-Archbishop of Paris killed. These events occurred during the Franco-Prussian War.

On November 27, the second vision of the Virgin occurred, also in the sanctuary. Mary appeared dressed in white and standing on a globe. A smaller globe held in her hands was raised and then disappeared. Mary then dropped her hands to her side and extended them forward with the palms forward as if offering a blessing to the world. Rays of light flowed from her hands and she told the young visionary that they represented the graces she would bestow on all who but asked. Then, an oval of golden letters appeared around the Virgin spelling out a brief prayer. Then the vision changed and she saw a large M surmounted by a cross. Below were the Sacred Hearts of Mary and Jesus. She was given the instruction to have a medal struck after the fashion of what she had just seen. Graces would come to those who wear the medal. This vision was repeated in December, and in the following March, but Sister Catherine's confessor was somewhat cold to the idea. Finally, after the vision reappeared in September, he conferred with the archbishop of Paris, who ordered the medal struck.

The first of the Miraculous Medals, as they came to be known, appeared in 1832, and the first "miracle" attached to them concerned the former archbishop of Malines, who had fallen from his faith and was dying. The archbishop of Paris presented him with one of the new medals, and shortly thereafter the archbishop recanted his errors and died reconciled to the church. As stories of other miracles arrived at his office, the archbishop became its enthusiastic backer. Meanwhile, Sister Catherine was sent to a hospice outside of Paris where she worked with the poor for the next 46 years. No one but her confessor ever heard the story of her visitations from Mary. She was not called to testify at the formal inquiry made in 1936. She did write her account of what occurred in 1856 and added to it shortly before her death. In 1875, she also made known the events to her very surprised Mother Superior and added that Mary had requested a statue of her with the globe in hand be placed in the convent chapel.

Sister Catherine became Saint Catherine in 1947. The church instituted recognition of the apparition in which the Miraculous Medal first appeared for November 27. Millions of the Miraculous Medal have been distributed, and many copies of the statue at the convent in Paris can now be found in Catholic churches around the world.

Sources:

Dirvin, Joseph I. *St. Catherine Labouré of the Miraculous Medal.* Garden City, N.Y.: Doubleday Echo Book, 1965.

Englebert, Omer. *Catherine Labouré and the Modern Apparitions of Our Lady.* New York: P. J. Kennedy & Sons, 1958.

Sharkey, Don. *The Woman Shall Conquer.* Kenosha, Wis.: Franciscan Marytown Press, 1976.

The Mishna

A compilation of Jewish oral traditions containing the religious legal decisions relating to Old Testament laws, gathered together at about the end of the second century by Rabbi Judah, grandson of Gamaliel II. Its doctrines are said to be of great antiquity. It forms the framework of the Talmud.

The Miss Lucy Westenra Society of the Undead

Vampire interest organization named for one of the characters in the novel *Dracula,* the first person Dracula turned into a vampire upon his arrival in England. The society published a newsletter and assisted penpals in locating each other. Last known address: 125 Taylor St., Jackson, IN 38302.

"Miss X"

Pseudonym of psychic researcher **Ada Goodrich-Freer,** used for her early writings on psychic subjects.

Mitchell, Edgar D. (1930–)

American astronaut with an active interest in parapsychology. Born September 17, 1930, at Hereford, Texas, he was educated at the Carnegie Institute of Technology. He entered the U.S. Navy in 1952 and was commissioned a year later. After flight training, he was assigned to Patrol Squadron 29 in Okinawa and flew aircraft on carrier duty and with a heavy attack squadron.

He studied for his doctorate in aeronautics and astronautics at Massachusetts Institute of Technology and became chief of the project management division of the Navy Field Office for Manned Orbiting Laboratory (1964). He later attended Air Force Aerospace Research Pilot School. He was selected by NASA as an astronaut in April 1966 and was lunar module pilot of Apollo 14, which landed on the moon February 5, 1971.

His interest in parapsychology dated from 1967, soon after his arrival at the NASA Manned Spacecraft Center in Houston. He was dissatisfied with orthodox theology and began to investigate areas of psychic phenomena and mysticism. In December 1969 Mitchell became friendly with medium **Arthur Ford,** who suggested an interesting **ESP** test from a man in a rocket to a contact on earth.

Mitchell planned a rocket-to-earth ESP test for the Apollo 14 mission, although Ford died January 4, 1971, 27 days before the mission launch (to which he had been invited as Mitchell's guest). NASA had rejected a telepathy experiment planned by the **American Society for Psychical Research** in 1970, so Mitchell's test was a private affair in his own rest periods. The tests involved the transmission of symbols associated with a range of chosen numbers. Eminent parapsychologists **J. B. Rhine** of the **Foundation for Research on the Nature of Man** and **Karlis Osis** of the ASPR offered cooperation in evaluating the test. The results of the test were ambiguous.

After being the sixth man to walk on the moon, Mitchell was a member of the backup crew of further lunar probes. He retired from NASA and the navy in 1972. His second wife, Anita, whom Mitchell married in 1973 after a divorce, shared his interest in parapsychology. In the same year Mitchell founded the **Institute of Noetic Sciences** for the study of human consciousness and mind/body relationships. He has headed the institute ever since.

Among the projects supported by the institute were the efforts of **Andrija Puharich** to test **Uri Geller,** and supervised experiments with Geller at Stanford Research Institute.

Sources:

Berger, Arthur S., and Joyce Berger. *The Encyclopedia of Parapsychology and Psychical Research.* New York: Paragon House, 1991.

Mitchell, E. D., ed. *Psychic Exploration: A Challenge for Science.* New York: G. P. Putnam's Sons, 1974.

Mitchell, T(homas) W(alker) (1869–1944)

British physician, psychologist, and psychic researcher. He was born January 18, 1869, in Avock, Ross-shire, Scotland, and attended the University of Edinburgh (M.B., C.M., 1890; M.D., 1906). He wrote several books and was the editor of the *British Journal of Medical Psychology* (1920–35).

His favorite topics in psychic research related to hypnosis and multiple personality. He played a prominent part in the **Society for Psychical Research** (SPR), London, and was its president in 1921, the first physician so selected. He was a long-term member of its council (1909–44) and was secretary of the medical section (1911–18). His paper "Phenomena of Mediumistic Trance" was read to the British Association for the Advancement of Science, 1927.

Sources:

Berger, Arthur S., and Joyce Berger. *The Encyclopedia of Parapsychology and Psychical Research.* New York: Paragon House, 1991.

Mitchell, T. W. "The Appreciation of Time by Somnambules." *Proceedings* of the Society for Psychical Research (1908–09).

———. *The Psychology of Medicine.* New York: R. M. McBride, 1922.

———. *Psychology and the Sciences.* Edited by William Brown. London: A & C Black Ltd., 1924.

———. "Psychotherapy and Psychoanalysis." *Proceedings* of the Society for Psychial Research (1912–13).

———. "A Study in Hysteria and Multiple Personality." *Proceedings* of the Society for Psychial Research (1912–13).

Pleasants, Helene, ed. *Biographical Dictionary of Parapsychology.* New York: Helix Press, 1964.

Modern Times, The Socialist Community of

A community founded in 1851 on Long Island that numbered among its members a good many Spiritualists. It was founded by Josiah Warren, formerly associated with the New Harmony community of **Robert Dale Owen.** The versatile Warren was an orchestral leader, an inventor, and a master of printing processes. As distinct from other utopian socialistic communities of nineteenth-century America, Modern Times was nearer to an anarchist society, with principles of complete toleration and without a central government. It suffered hardship in the general slump of 1857, and ceased to be practicable in the turmoil of the Civil War. Warren died in 1874. (See also **Hopedale Community**)

Sources:

Lawson, Donna. *Brothers and Sisters All Over This Land: America's First Communes.* New York: Praeger Publishers, 1972.

Oved, Yaacov. *Two Hundred Years of American Communes.* New Brunswick, N.J.: Transaction Publishers, 1993.

Moghrebi

Arab sorcerer. (See **Semites**)

Mohanes

Shamans, or medicine men, of the Indians of the Peruvian Andes. Joseph Skinner described them at the beginning of the nineteenth century: "These admit an evil being, the inhabitant of the centre of the earth, whom they consider as the author of their misfortunes, and at the mention of whose name they tremble. The most shrewd among them take advantage of this belief, to obtain respect; and represent themselves as his delegates. Under the denomination of *Mohanes,* or *Agoreros,* they are consulted even on the most trivial occasions. They preside over the intrigues of love, the health of the community, and the taking of the field. Whatever repeatedly occurs to defeat their prognostics, falls on themselves; and they are wont to pay their deceptions very dearly. They chew a species of vegetable called *puripiri,* and throw it into the air, accompanying this act by certain recitals and incantations, to injure some, to benefit others, to procure rain, and the inundation of the rivers, or, on the other hand, to occasion settled weather, and a plentiful store of agricultural productions. Any such result having been casually verified on a single occasion, suffices to confirm the Indians in their faith, although they may have been cheated a thousand times. Fully persuaded that they cannot resist the influence of the *puripiri,* as soon as they know that they have been solicited by its means, they fix their eyes on the impassioned object, and discover a thousand amiable traits, either real or fanciful, which indifference had before concealed from their view.

"But the principal power, efficacy, and, it may be said misfortune, of the *Mohanes,* consist in the cure of the sick. Every malady is ascribed to their enchantments, and means are instantly taken to ascertain by whom the mischief may have been wrought. For this purpose the nearest relative takes a quantity of the juice of *floripondium,* and suddenly falls, intoxicated by the violence of the plant. He is placed in a fit posture to prevent suffocation, and on his coming to himself, at the end of three days, the *Mohan* who has the greatest resemblance to the sorcerer he saw in his visions, is to undertake the cure, or if, in the interim, the sick man has perished, it is customary to subject him to the same fate. When not any sorcerer occurs in the visions, the first *Mohan* they encounter has the misfortune to represent his image."

It seems that by practice and tradition, the *Mohanes* acquired a profound knowledge of many plants and poisons, with which they effected surprising cures on the one hand, and did some harm on the other. They also made use of charms and superstitions.

One method of cure was to place two hammocks close to each other, either in the dwelling, or in the open air. In one of them the patient laid extended, and in the other laid the *Mohan,* or *Agorero.* The latter, in contact with the sick man, began by rocking himself, and then proceeded in falsetto voice to call on the birds, quadrupeds, and fishes to give health to the patient. From time to time he rose on his seat, and made extravagant gestures over the sick man, to whom he applied his powders and herbs, or sucked the wounded or diseased parts. Having been joined by many of the people, the *Agoreros* chanted a short hymn, addressed to the soul of the patient, with this refrain: "Thou must not go, thou must not go." In repeating this he was joined by the people and augmented as the sick man became fainter so that it might reach his ears.

Sources:

Skinner, Joseph. *State of Peru.* London, 1805.

Moleoscopy

A system of interpretation of **moles** or **birthmarks** on various parts of the body (usually classed medically as a benign form of *nevus,* and not normally requiring surgery). Moles were considered to have special occult significance in ancient times, and their systematic interpretation as indicative of character and destiny was popularized during the sixteenth and seventeenth centuries. The positions of the moles were linked with astrological signs.

Moles (Animal)

Many superstitions grew up around moles. It was a common error to believe that moles were blind, whereas in fact their eyes are small and often hidden in the hair. As late as Shakepeare's time, moles were popularly believed to be blind, as indicated in the dramatist's play *The Tempest:* "Pray you tread softly, that the blind mole may not hear a footfall."

Other popular beliefs were that if moles came into a meadow it was a sign of fair weather, that if a mole dug his hole very deep, you could expect a very severe winter, and that if a mole threw up earth during a frost, the frost would disappear in two days.

Some Gypsies believed that moles never touched earth that had been stained with blood. In Britain, farm laborers used to wear the forelegs and a hind leg of a mole in a bag around the neck to protect against toothache. It was also believed that if you pulled molehills up on St. Sylvester's Day (December 31), the moles would not throw up earth again.

Moles (Birthmarks)

Birthmarks on the human face or body, usually classed medically as a benign form of *nevus.* Many superstitions exist about moles, and **moleoscopy** arose as a system of **divination** based on the position, character, and astrological connections of these markings. In folk belief, a mole on the throat was said to be a sign of good luck, but unlucky if located on the left side of the forehead near the hair. A mole on the chin, ear, or neck was said to indicate riches, but on the breast to signify poverty.

The position of moles on the various parts of the body had various meanings: On the feet and hands of a woman—many children; on the right arm and shoulder of a man or woman—great lechery; on the ankles or feet—modesty in men and courage in women; on or about the knees—riches and virtue; on a woman's left knee—many children; on the thighs—great poverty and unhappiness. An old folk rhyme from Nottinghamshire, England, indicated the belief that the position of a mole could affect rank in later life:

"I have a mole above my right eye,
And shall be a lady before I die."

Another belief was that hairs growing out of moles portended good luck.

During the great witchcraft manias of the sixteenth and seventeenth centuries, such birthmarks as moles, as well as **warts,** were considered "devil's marks" if they did not bleed when pricked. Professional witch finders like the infamous **Matthew Hopkins** (died 1647) used pricking on suspected witches. Moles, warts, scars, or other birthmarks were pricked with a long pin; if there was no pain or bleeding, the suspect was claimed to be a witch. Special pricking tools like thin daggers were developed, and some enthusiastic witch prickers (who claimed a substantial fee for each convicted witch) even used trick pricking tools with a hollow shaft and retractable blade, to make sure that the suspect would feel no pain and there would be no bleeding.

Molybdomancy

A system of **divination** based on the shapes produced by dropping melted lead or tin into water. Interpretations depended upon the psychic ability of the diviner, much as in tasseography (divination by **tea leaves**). A related system of divination was **ceroscopy** (or ceromancy), in which molten wax was dripped into water and interpreted in a similar way.

Mompesson, John (ca. 1662)

Magistrate at Tedworth, Wiltshire, England, in 1661 whose home was disturbed by **poltergeist** phenomena. (See **Drummer of Tedworth**)

The Monaciello

The *Monaciello,* or "Little Monk," was a spirit who seems to have lived exclusively in and around Naples in southern Italy. Although the precise place is not known, it is supposed to have been in the remains of abbeys and monasteries. When the *Monaciello* appeared to mortals, it was always at the dead of night, and then only to the most desperate—those who had done all that mortals could do to prevent or alleviate their distress, and after all human aid had failed. At such times the Monk occasionally appeared, mutely beckoned them to follow, and led them to a secret treasure. He stipulated no conditions for its expenditure, demanded no promise of repayment, and exacted no duty or service in return. It is not clear whether it was actual treasure that he gave, or whether it merely appeared so to the external senses, to be changed into leaves or stones when the day and the occasion of its requirement had passed.

In Germany, the wood-spirit "Rubezahl" performed similar acts of kindness to poor and deserving persons; it is said that the money he gave always passed for the current coin of the realm.

In Ireland, the O'Donoghue, who lived beneath the waters of an inland lake and rode over its surface on a steed white as the foam of its waves, was said to distribute treasures that proved genuine to the good but were spurious to the undeserving.

Monad (in Theosophy)

Theosophical term that literally means a unit (Greek *monas*). The Monad is frequently described as a "divine spark," which is an appropriate expression, for it is a part of the **logos,** the divine fire. The Logos has three aspects—will, wisdom, and activity, and since the Monad is part of the logos, it also has these three aspects. It abides continually in its appropriate world, the monadic, but in order that the divine evolutionary purposes may be carried out, its ray is borne downward through the various spheres of matter when the outpouring of the third of the three **life waves** takes place.

It first passes into the spiritual **sphere** by clothing itself with an atom of spiritual matter and thus manifests itself in an atomic body, as a **spirit** possessing three aspects. When it passes into the next sphere, the intuitional, it leaves its aspect of will behind, and in the intuitional sphere appears in an intuitional body as a spirit possessing the aspects of wisdom and activity. On passing in turn from this sphere to the next, the higher mental, it leaves the aspect of wisdom behind and appears in a casual body as a spirit possessing the aspect of activity.

To put this somewhat abstruse doctrine in another form, the monad has, at this stage, manifested itself in three spheres. In the spiritual it has transfused spirit with will; in the intuitional it has transfused spirit with wisdom; and in the higher mental it has transfused spirit with activity or intellect; and it is now a human ego, corresponding approximately to the common term "soul," an ego which, despite all changes, remains the same until eventually the evolutionary purpose is fulfilled and it is received back again into the logos.

From the higher mental sphere, the monad descends to the lower mental sphere and appears in a mental body as possessing mind; then betakes itself to the astral sphere and appears in the astral body as possessing emotions; and finally to the physical sphere and appears in a physical body as possessing vitality. These three lower bodies—the mental, the astral, and the physical— constitute the human personality, which dies at death and is renewed when the monad in fulfillment of the process of reincarnation, again manifests itself in these bodies.

Monck, Rev. Francis Ward (ca. 1878– ?)

British clergyman who started his career as minister of the Baptist Chapel at Earls Barton, England, and gave up his ecclesiastical vocation for professional mediumship. His adhesion to **Spiritualism** was first announced in 1873. He claimed great mediumistic powers, toured the British Isles, and healed the sick in Ireland. As a result he was called "Dr." Monck by many people, although he was not a physician.

In London he convinced **Alfred Russel Wallace, William Stainton Moses,** and Hensleigh Wedgwood (brother-in-law of Charles Darwin) of his genuine psychic gifts by giving a remarkable **materialization** séance in bright daylight. He also excelled in **slatewriting.** An account by Wallace of a puzzling slate-writing demonstration was certified by Edward T. Bennett, then assistant secretary to the **Society for Psychical Research,** London. He convinced Judge Dailey, an American, that the dead returned through his body. Monck's reputation was high.

Disaster struck Monck in 1876 shortly after the trial of fellow medium **Henry Slade.** At a Huddersfield séance on November 3, a conjurer named H. B. Lodge suddenly demanded a search of the medium. Monck ran for safety, locked himself into his room upstairs, and escaped through the window. As a further evidence of his guilt, a pair of stuffed gloves was found in his room. In the medium's luggage were found "spirit lamps," a "spirit bird," cheesecloth, and reaching rods, as well as some obscene correspondence from women.

There were other cases in which Monck was caught in flagrant **fraud. Sir William Barrett** wrote of "a piece of white muslin on a wire frame with a black thread attached being used by the medium to simulate a partially materialised spirit." The trial that followed the Huddersfield exposure was a great sensation. Wallace appeared as a witness for the defense and deposed that "he had seen Dr. Monck in the trance state, when there appeared a faint white patch on the left side of his coat, which increased in density and spread till it reached his shoulder; then there was a space gradually widening to six feet between it and his body, it became very distinct and had the outline of a woman in flowing white drapery. I was absolutely certain that it could not be produced by any possible trick."

In spite of the eminent scientist's vote of confidence, the court found Monck guilty and sentenced him to three months' imprisonment. The blow was a stunning one, but some friends never lost their faith in Monck. There was no greater believer in his powers than Archdeacon **Thomas Colley,** who reported the most inexplicable and astounding experiences with Monck. Colley was in India at the time of the Huddersfield incident. After his return, he stoutly maintained that a dreadful miscarriage of justice must have taken place, and he published this account of a séance held on September 25, 1877: "Dr. Monck, under control of Samuel, was by the light of the lamp—the writer not being a yard away from him—seen by all to be the living gate for the extrusion of spirit forms from the realm of mind into this world of matter; for standing forth thus plainly before us, the psychic or spirit form was seen to grow out of his left side. First, several faces one after another, of great beauty appeared, and in amazement we saw—and as I was standing close up to the medium, even touching him, I saw most plainly—several times, a perfect face and form of exquisite womanhood partially issue from Dr. Monck, about the region of the heart. Then after several attempts a full formed figure, in a nebulous condition at first, but growing more solid as it issued from the medium, left Dr. Monck, and stood a separate individuality, two or three feet off, bound to him by a slender attachment as of gossamer, which at my request Samuel, the control, severed with the medium's left hand, and there stood embodied a spirit form of unutterable loveliness."

Colley was so sure of his own powers of observation that he challenged stage magician **John Nevil Maskelyne** and offered him 1,000 pounds if he could duplicate Monck's materialization performance. Maskelyne attempted the feat, and when Colley declared his performance to be a travesty of what had really taken place in Monck's presence, Maskelyne sued for the money. Mainly on the evidence of Wallace on behalf of Monck, judgment was entered against Maskelyne.

In his materialization séances, Monck rarely used a cabinet. He stood in full view of the sitters. Sometimes he was quite conscious. He had two chief controls: "Samuel" and "Mahedi." For a year their individual characters were deeply studied by Stainton Moses and Hensleigh Wedgwood who, with two other men interested in psychic research, secured exclusive rights to Monck's services for a modest salary.

Enduring evidence of Monck's phantasmal appearances was obtained by William Oxley in 1876 in Manchester in the form of excellent paraffin molds of hands and feet of the materialized forms (see **plastics**). Oxley described his psychic experiences in *Modern Messiahs and Wonder Workers* (1889). Oxley's experiences tend to put aside the hallucination theory that psychic researcher **Frank Podmore** proposed in view of Colley's astounding experiences.

In his lecture before the Church Congress at Weymouth in 1903, Colley said: "Often when I have been sleeping in the same bedroom with him, for the near observation of casual phenomena during the night and, specially, that came through the dark I, on such occasions, would hold my hand over his mouth, and he would now and again be startled into wakefulness not unmixed with fear. For he could see the phantoms which I could not, when I had quietly put out the night-light—for he would not sleep in the dark, which made him apprehensive of phenomena, physically powerful to an extraordinary degree."

Colley claimed to have witnessed astonishing marvels with Monck. He said he saw the birth and dissolution of numbers of full-sized solid forms. He saw a child appear, move about, be kissed by those present and then return to the medium and gradually melt into his body. He seized a materialized form and was flung with great force toward the medium and suddenly found himself clasping him. In 1905, when he published his experiences, he wrote: "I publish these things for the first time, having meditated over them in silence for twenty-eight years, giving my word as clergyman for things which imperil my ecclesiastical position and my future advancement."

One of the most astonishing psychic feats ascribed to Monck was his teleportation from Bristol to Swindon, a distance of 42 miles. This claimed miraculous feat in 1871 was described in the *Spiritualist* (1875, p. 55). In his later years, Monck concentrated on healing. The closing period of his life was spent in New York.

Sources:

Oxley, William. *Modern Messiahs and Wonder Workers.* London: Trubner, 1889.

Monen

A term from the **Kabala,** referring to that branch of magic that deals with the reading of the future by the computation of time and observance of the heavenly bodies. It thus includes **astrology.**

Money (in Occult Tradition)

Money that comes from a pact with the devil is of poor quality, and such wealth, like the fairy-money, generally turns to earth, or to lead, toads, or anything else worthless or repulsive. St. Gregory of Tours (d. 594 C.E.) told a illustrative story: "A youth received a piece of folded paper from a stranger, who told him that he could get from it as much money as he wished, so long as he did not unfold it. The youth drew many gold pieces from the papers, but at length curiosity overcame him, he unfolded it and discovered within the claws of a cat and a bear, the feet of a toad and other repulsive fragments, while at the same moment his wealth disappeared."

It is said that an Irishman outsmarted the devil. In his book *Irish Witchcraft and Demonology* (1913; 1973), St. John D. Seymour told the amusing story of Joseph Damer of Tipperary County, who made a bargain with the devil to sell his soul for a top-boot full of gold. On the appointed day, the devil was ushered into the living room, where a top-boot stood in the center of the floor. The devil poured gold into it, but to his surprise, it remained empty. He hastened away for more gold, but the top-boot would not fill, even after repeated efforts. At length, in sheer disgust, the devil departed. Afterward it was claimed that the shrewd Irishman had taken the sole off the boot and fastened it over a hole in the floor. Underneath was a series of large cellars, where men waited with shovels to remove each shower of gold as it came down.

In popular superstition it is supposed that if a person hears the cuckoo for the first time with money in his pocket, he will have some all the year, while if he greets the new moon for the first time in the same fortunate condition, he will not lack money throughout the month.

Monition

Supernormal warning. In the wider sense of the definition of psychic researcher **Charles Richet,** it is the revelation of some past or present event by other than the normal senses. The *Proceedings* of the American Society for Psychical Research (1907, p. 487) published the instance of Mr. McCready, editor of the *Daily Telegraph,* who was in church on a Sunday morning when he heard a voice calling "Go back to the office." He ran and found a petroleum lamp blazing in his room. It threw out such clouds of smoke that everything was covered with soot.

Monitions may range from trifling events to warnings of death. They occur accidentally and are verifiable as true. All the monitive phenomena lie within the field of nonexperimental **telepathy** and **clairvoyance** and include **apparitions** of the dead and of the living, provided that they are message-bearing. It is characteristic of monitions that they deeply impress the mind of the percipients and permit an accurate remembrance even after the lapse of many years.

They may come in the waking state or in dreams, which sometimes repeat themselves. The borderland between waking and sleeping is usually the most favorable for their reception. They may be visual or auditory—seeing apparitions, or hearing voices, and they often take a symbolical form, for instance, the idea of death being presented by a coffin, as seen by Lord Beresford in his cabin while steaming between Gibraltar and Marseilles. The coffin contained the body of his father. On arriving at Marseilles he found that his father had died six days before and was buried on the day he saw the vision (see *Proceedings* of the Society for Psychical Research, vol. 5, p. 461).

As regards perception, monitions may be collective yet non-simultaneous and non-identical, or simultaneous and collective. The former is well illustrated by Mrs. Hunter's case, cited by **Ernesto Bozzano** in the *Annals of Psychical Science* (vol. 6, no. 34, 1907, p. 248). Mrs. Hunter saw, in the waking state and in daytime, a large coffin on the bed and a tall, stout woman at the foot of the bed looking at it. That evening the governess saw a phantom woman in the same dress in the sitting room where there was nothing visible and cried: "Go away, go away, naughty ugly old woman."

To quote another instance: "During the winter of 1899, Richet was at home while his wife and daughter were at the opera. The professor imagined that the Opera House was on fire. The conviction was so powerful that he wrote on a piece of paper "Feu! Feu!" About midnight, on the return of his family, he immediately asked them if there had been a fire. They were surprised and said that there was no fire, only a false alarm, and they were very much afraid. At the very time Richet made his note, his sister fancied that the professor's room was on fire."

In simultaneous and collective monitions, the phantom or symbol is perceived at the same time by several people. (See also **monitions of approach; premonition**)

Monitions of Approach

Unaccountable ideas of an impending meeting with someone. A person seen in the street, for example, is believed to be an old friend, and the next second the mistake is seen. Soon afterward, the real friend appears. Such occurrences are fairly common, but may happen in a somewhat complicated way. A voice may be heard announcing the person's arrival while the percipient is in a dreaming or waking state. The voice may be accompanied by a phantom of the approaching individual. Spiritualists said monitions of approach came from the projection of the human **double** of the person soon to arrive.

Monroe, Robert Allen (1915–1995)

American businessman and an exponent of **out-of-the body travel.** Monroe was born October 30, 1915, and grew up in his native Lexington, Kentucky. Following his graduation from Ohio State University, he went to work in radio and television in New York and then built a successful career in advertising.

His numerous journeys out of his body reportedly began in 1958 following a brief illness. After several somewhat frightening experiences in which his body cramped and vibrated, one day he found himself floating near the ceiling and looking down on his sleeping physical body, a common experience of people who spontaneously leave their body. He became fearful that he was either dying or going insane when subsequent experiences occurred, but his fears were allayed when he learned of **parapsychology** and the frequency of out-of-the-body experiences.

Over the next decade he claimed to have experienced precognitive dreams and visited various "dream worlds" that were largely unknown to anyone else. He came to think of them as extra dimensional. He also participated in tests at both the University of Virginia and the Topeka (Kansas) Veterans Administration Hospital in which he tried to produce his out-of-the-body experience under controlled observation.

His primary concern throughout these years was to verify the new realms he had been exploring and to develop techniques by which others could join him in that endeavor. In 1971 he founded **The Monroe Institute** That same year, an autobiographical volume, *Journeys Out of the Body,* was published. Scientists were impressed by his ability to objectively report on his experiences and to consider alternative explanations.

Monroe went to work developing and improving the methods employed by the institute. By 1975 he claimed to have developed a system to control brain wave emissions and help synchronize the emissions from the right and left hemispheres of the brain.

Although Monroe has critics who have complained about the romanticized and exaggerated accounts included in his autobiography, he also has his enthusiastic supporters, including **Elizabeth Kübler-Ross,** who had an out-of-the-body experience at the institute.

Monroe died March 17, 1995.

Sources:

Monroe, Robert A. *Journeys Out of the Body.* Garden City, N.Y.: Doubleday, 1971.

———. *Ultimate Journey.* New York: Doubleday, 1994.

Rogo, D. Scott. *Leaving the Body: A Complete Guide to Astral Projection.* Englewood Cliffs, N.J.: Prentice-Hall, 1983.

Stockton, Bayard. *Catapult: The Biography of Robert A. Monroe.* Norfolk, Va.: Donning, 1989.

The Monroe Institute

Consciousness research facility specializing in non-physical states of consciousness. The institute was founded in 1971 by businessman **Robert A. Monroe.** For more than a decade Monroe claimed to have had out-of-the-body experiences and was tested on several occasions by psychologists attempting to understand the nature of his inner life. He also began to experiment with the use of sound patterns to affect brain wave production. He developed an audio-technology called Hemi-Sync (Hemispheric Synchronization) that facilitates self-directed exploration of focused states of consciousness.

The institute offers programs that teach individuals the art of switching perceptual modes from the outer to the inner world of their own consciousness and to fields outside the realm of physical matter (i.e., other dimensions). The Gateway program introduces participants, in a step-by-step manner, to inner exploration, allowing time for adjustment to each new experience and the emotions it might create. In 1981 the institute announced the Discovery program, which offers some of the Gateway techniques for use in-home. After Robert Monroe's death in 1998, he was succeeded by his daughter Laurie A. Monroe.

The institute publishes periodicals that report on its research program. It also distributes numerous tapes and CDs. Address: 62 Roberts Mountain Road, Faber, VA 22938. Website: http://www.monroeinstitute.org/.

Sources:

Rogo, D. Scott. *Leaving the Body: A Complete Guide to Astral Projection.* Englewood Cliffs, N.J.: Prentice-Hall, 1983.

Monsters

On the borderland between superstition, **occultism,** and science are the many monsters, human or animal, reported from many parts of the world throughout human history. The word "monster," from the Latin *monstrum,* implies a warning or portent. The term is used derogatorily in reference to malformed or misshapen animals and humans, as well as creatures of great size. Because of the awe and horror excited by monstrous births, they were traditionally regarded as an **omen** or a sign of God's wrath with a wicked world. Many street ballads of the sixteenth century moralized about monstrous animals or malformed human beings. Today, persons born with bodies outside the social norms—giants, dwarfs, and Siamese twins—are studied under the scientific label of "teratology." Deformed and limbless children are now known to be caused by rare genetic factors or by the use of such drugs as thalidomide in pregnancy.

In modern times, much of the superstitious awe surrounding legendary monsters has passed into the world of fiction, and talented novelists have created images of scientific or technological doom like Godzilla and **Frankenstein,** the evil from the subconscious like the vampire **Dracula,** or the product of unrestrained animal-like urges, Dr. Jekyll's Mr. Hyde. Such literary monsters have been powerfully represented in horror movies, which have presented increasingly terrifying creatures from the edge of civilization and human experience—swamps, ocean depths, and outer space. Such fictional monsters undoubtedly owe their power to the eternal fascination of the clash between good and evil in human affairs and the old theological themes of judgment and damnation.

Few stories achieved this metaphysical terror so powerfully as Robert Louis Stevenson's *Dr. Jekyll and Mr. Hyde,* in which the possibilities of evil inherent in all human beings are released from the kindly Dr. Jekyll in the shape of the demonic Mr. Hyde. Stevenson also varied this theme in his short story *Markheim,* where a debauched murderer is confronted by an angelic alter ego.

Mysterious creatures reported from isolated places, having an existence somewhere between myth and natural history, continue to fascinate and attract while playing on subconscious anxieties. The discovery by Western scientists of the gorilla and the colocynth have given substantive hope to the idea that some of the legends of monsters may refer to actual survivors of ancient species. This has generated a new field of research, **cryptozoology.**

Loch Ness Monster

A large, aquatic, dinosaur-like creature is said to inhabit the large area of Loch Ness in Scotland, a lake about 24 miles long and a mile wide with a depth of from 433 to 754 feet. Since a monster was reported in ancient Gaelic legends and in a biography of St. Columba circa 565 C.E., it is supposed that there may be a colony of monsters.

Modern interest dates from the 1930s, when a number of witnesses reported sightings. The creature has been photographed repeatedly and even filmed, though some of the more frequently reproduced films have been shown to be frauds. It appears to be about 45 feet long, of which 10 feet is head and neck, 20 feet the body, and 15 feet the tail. The head is small and sometimes lifted out of the water on the neck, high above the body. The skin is rough and dark brown in color, and in movement the creature sometimes appears to contort its body into a series of humps. It can move at speeds of around 13 knots, and in general appearance resembles a prehistoric plesiosaurus.

On April 8, 1976, the monster made the front page of the *New York Times,* which featured records of an underwater camera using a sonar echo technique. Known in Britain affectionately as "Nessie," in the mid 1970s the creature was given the formal name of *Nessiteras rhombopteryx* by naturalist Sir Peter Scott in an attempt to secure official protection. A British Act of Parliament requires that any rare species of animal qualifying for conservation must have a scientific name.

The Loch Ness Monster is the most famous of a number of reported lake monsters, such as the similar creature reported at Lough Muck in Donegal. In other parts of England and Scotland, reported creatures include **Morgawr** in the area of Falmouth, Cornwall, and **Mhorag** (or Morag) in Loch Morar, West Inverness, Scotland. There are numerous reports of sightings, and some photographs. In 1910, a plesiosaurus-type creature was reported in Nahuel Huapi, Patagonia.

Interest in the Loch Ness monster was stimulated by reports of the decomposing body of a sea creature caught by the Japanese trawler "Zuiyo Maru" about 30 miles east of Christchurch, New Zealand, on April 25, 1977. The carcass was about 30 feet long, weighed two tons, and was raised from a depth of approximately 900 feet. For a time, it was suspended above the trawler deck by a crane, but the captain feared that the evil-smelling fluid dripping from the carcass would pollute his catch of whiptail fish and ordered the creature to be dumped overboard. Before this was done, Michihiko Yano, an official of the Taiyo Fishery Company aboard the vessel, took four color photographs and made a sketch of the carcass, after taking measurements. He described the creature as like a snake with a turtle's body and with front and rear flippers and a tail six feet in length. This suggests a creature resembling the plesiosaurus, which flourished from 200 to 100 million years ago.

When Taiyo Fisheries executives heard about the unusual catch, they radioed their trawlers around New Zealand, ordering them to try to recover the carcass, but without success. Japanese journalists named the creature "The New Nessie" after Scotland's famous Loch Ness Monster, and a large Tokyo department store planned to market stuffed dolls of the creature. Fujior Yasuda of the faculty of fisheries at Tokyo University has examined Yano's photographs and concluded that the creature was definitely not a species of fish, and Toshio Shikama, a Yokohama University paleontologist, was convinced that the creature was not a fish or a mammoth seal. For reports of this incident see the London *Daily Telegraph* (July 21, 1977), London *Times* (July 21, 1977), and *Fortean Times* (no. 22, summer 1977).

Yeti (or Abominable Snowman)

The Yeti is a giant humanoid creature that has long been part of the folklore of the high Himalayan region in Asia. The popular name "Abominable Snowman" derives from the Tibetan term *Metoh-Kangmi* or "Wild Man of the Snows." Other names in the Himalayan regions of Kashmir and Nepal are *Jungli-admi* or *Sogpa*—"Wild Men of the Woods." There are many stories told by Sherpas of the giant Yeti that carried away human children or even adults. In 1951, such stories suddenly attracted scientific interest when a photograph of a large Yeti footprint taken by mountaineer Eric Shipton on an Everest Reconnaissance Expedition appeared.

The Abominable Snowman had been reported by westerners as early as 1832 in an article by B. H. Hodgson for the initial volume of the *Journal of the Asiatic Society of Bengal.* The first European to see Yeti footprints was Major L. A. Waddell, who found them in the snows of northeastern Sikkim at 17,000 feet in 1889, but believed them to be tracks of the great yellow snow bear (*Ursus isabellinus*). Additional reports filtered back to the west through the twentieth century.

In 1925, N. A. Tombazi, a fellow of the Royal Geographical Society, saw a large humanoid creature walking upright at a distance of 300 yards in Sikkim, and afterward examined footprints in the snow. In February 1942, Slavomir Rawicz escaped from a Siberian prisoner-of-war camp with six companions and crossed the Himalayas to India. In his book *The Long Walk* (1956), Rawicz claimed that he saw two Yeti-type creatures, eight feet tall, in an area between Bhutan and Sikkim.

In the 1950s, various expeditions to track down the Yeti failed to produce any tangible evidence of its existence, but in 1972 a Sherpa named Da Temba saw a 4'6" creature, possibly a small Yeti, in Nepal. The cumulative effect of the large number of reports of Yeti sightings from Sherpas reinforces the possibility that there is a large humanoid creature in the Himalayas, but the area is a vast one and the creature could be even more elusive than the Loch Ness monster.

Bigfoot

Other creatures of a Yeti type have been reported frequently from different areas of the world, notably isolated regions of the Pacific Northwest. The popular term "Bigfoot" seems to have been a newspaper invention for the creature named "Sasquatch" by the Salish Indians of southwest British Columbia. The Huppa tribe in the Klamath mountains of Northern California use the name *Oh-mah-'ah,* sometimes shortened to *Omah,* while the name *Seeahtiks* is used in Vancouver Island.

It is interesting to note that reports of Yeti-type creatures cover a fairly consistent trail through the remote mountainous regions of Asia across to similar regions in Alaska, Canada, and North America, suggesting a rare and elusive species distributed over similar isolated areas. In the Russian areas of Asia, such creatures have been named *Almast, Alma* or *Shezhnyy Chelovek.* Bigfoot has been frequently reported in Canadian and North American territories from the early nineteenth century on. In modern times, construction workers in Northern California claimed to have seen a large ape-like creature, eight to ten feet tall, in Bluff Creek in October 1958. It walked upright and left large footprints, which indicated a creature weighing 800 pounds. Investigations were stimulated after the widespread showing of a 16mm color film supposedly of the creature taken by Roger Patterson, a rancher in Bluff Creek, California, on October 7, 1967. This film shows what appears to be an erect ape-like figure at a distance of some 30 feet.

Such creatures were systematically investigated by Irish explorer and big-game hunter Peter Byrne, who organized a three-year search in 1971. He traveled many thousands of miles between Nepal, Canada, and the United States, interviewing hundreds of individuals and evaluating claimed sightings of Bigfoot. Byrne visited Patterson before his death in 1972 and found his story and the film convincing. Byrne, like fellow researchers, was repeatedly distracted by the likes of the 1968 prankster in Colville, Washington, who tied 16 inch foot-shaped plywood boards to his feet and made tracks in the woods. He sent a photograph to Peter Byrne, who dismissed it as an obvious fake. Meanwhile an ordinance in Skamania County, Washington, prohibits wanton slaying of ape-creatures, with substantial penalties.

Further interest in Bigfoot was generated in 1982 by the sighting reported by Paul Freeman, an employee of the U.S. Forest Service. He came face to face with the creature at a distance of no more than 200 feet. Both fled in fear of the other. Interest in Bigfoot continues and over the last generation several research centers such as the **Bigfoot Information Center** and the now defunct **Sasquatch Investigations of Mid-America** were established. While Forteans have kept interest in Bigfoot alive, the dearth of definitive encounters with the creature have caused many to doubt the authenticity of the legends.

Sources:

Baumann, Elwood David. *Bigfoot: America's Abominable Snowman.* New York: Franklin Watts, 1976. Reprint, New York: Dell, 1976.

Bord, Janet, and Colin Bord. *Alien Animals.* Harrisburg, Pa.: Stackpole Books, 1981.

———. *The Bigfoot Casebook.* Harrisburg, Pa.: Stackpole Books, 1982.

Byrne, Peter. *The Search for Big Foot: Monster, Myth or Man.* Washington, DC: Acropolis Books, 1975. Reprint, New York: Pocket Books, 1976.

Campbell, Elizabeth M., and David Solomon. *The Search for Morag.* London: Tom Stacey, 1972.

Clark, Jerome. *Encyclopedia of Strange and Unexplained Phenomena.* Detroit: Gale Research, 1993.

Costello, Peter. *In Search of Lake Monsters.* London: Garnsteon Press; New York: Coward, 1974. Reprint, London: Panther, 1975.

Dinsdale, Tim. *Loch Ness Monster.* London: Routledge & Kegan Paul, 1961.

Farson, Daniel, and Angus Hall. *Mysterious Monsters.* London: Aldus Books, 1978.

Florescu, Radu. *In Search of Frankenstein.* New York: New York Graphic Society, 1975.

Gould, Rupert T. *The Case for the Sea-Serpent.* London: Philip Allan, 1930. Reprint, Detroit: Singing Tree Press, 1969.

———. *The Loch Ness Monster and Others.* London: Geoffrey Bles; New York: Citadel Press, 1976.

Halpin, Marjorie, and Michael M. Ames, eds. *Manlike Monsters on Trial: Early Records and Modern Evidence.* Vancouver, BC: University of British Columbia Press, 1980.

Heuvlmans, Bernard. *In the Wake of the Sea-Serpents.* New York: Hill and Wang, 1868. Reprint, London: Rupert Hart-Davis, 1968.

———. *On the Track of Unknown Animals.* New York: Hill and Wang, 1958. Rev. ed. 1965. Reprint, London: Paladin Books, 1970.

Hodgson, B. H. "On the Mammalia of Nepal." *Journal of the Asiatic Society of Bengal* 1 (1832).

Mackal, Roy Paul. *The Monster of Loch Ness.* Chicago: Swallow Press, 1976.

McNally, Raymont T., and Radu Florescu. *In Search of Dracula: A True History of Dracula and Vampire Legends.* New York: New York Graphic Society, 1972. Rev. ed. Boston: Houghton Mifflin, 1994.

Meredith, Dennis L. *Search at Loch Ness: The Expedition of the New York Times and The Academy of Applied Science.* New York: Quadrangle/New York Times Book Co., 1977.

Meurger, Michel, with Claude Gagnon. *Lake Monster Traditions: A Cross Cultural Analysis.* London: Fortean Tomes, 1988.

Moon, Mary. *Ogopogo: The Okanagan Mystery.* London: David & Charles, 1977.

Napier, John. *Bigfoot: The Sasquatch and Yeti in Myth and Reality.* London: Jonathan Cape, 1972. Reprint, New York: E. P. Dutton, 1973. Reprint, London: Abacus, 1976.

Price, Vincent, and V. B. Price. *Monsters.* New York: Grosset & Dunlap, 1981.

Sanderson, Ivan T. *Abominable Snowman: Legend Comes to Life.* New York: Chilton, 1961.

Scott, Peter. "Naming the Loch Ness Monster." *Nature* (December 11, 1975).

Shackley, Myra. *Wildmen: Yeti, Sasquatch and the Neanderthal Enigma.* London: Thames & Hudson, 1983.

Thompson, C. J. S. *The Mystery and Lore of Monsters.* London, 1930. Reprint, New Hyde Park, N.Y.: University Books, 1968. New York: Citadel Press, 1970.

Witchell, Nicholas. *The Loch Ness Story.* London, 1974. Rev. ed. London: Penguin Books, 1975.

Montgomery, Ruth (Schick)

Award-winning journalist with special interest in psychic **healing, channeling,** and **extrasensory perception.** She was born in Sumner, Illinois, educated at Baylor University (1930–35) and Purdue University (1934). She married Robert H. Montgomery on December 26, 1935. She began a career in journalism as women's editor for the *Louisville Herald-Post,* Kentucky. She later worked as a feature writer for the *St. Louis Post-Dispatch* and the *Indianapolis Star* and as a reporter with the *Detroit News, Detroit Times, Waco News-Tribune, Chicago Tribune,* and the *New York Daily News.* She moved to Washington, D.C., in 1944 and served as a correspondent for the International News Service through the 1950s, frequently traveling around the world as a foreign correspondent. She won the Pall Mall Journalism Award (1947), the Front Page Award from the Indianapolis Press Club (1957), and the George R. Holmes Journalism Award (1958).

In 1958, she became interested in psychic phenomena after writing a series of articles on the **occult.** Although at first skeptical, she continued her research. She met **medium Arthur Ford,** who told her that she had the ability to do **automatic writing,** and has since been influenced by what she calls "my guides," discarnate spirits that have assisted her writings on such subjects as psychic healing, **reincarnation,** and psychic faculties. She broke into the spotlight with her biographical presentation of Washington psychic **Jeane Dixon** in *A Gift of Prophecy* (1965), which the following year won the Best Non-Fiction Book of the Year Award from Indiana University.

Following the death of Arthur Ford in 1971, Montgomery came forward with a volume of communications, *A World Beyond,* which she claimed originated in her contact with his spirit. She built a following in the emerging **New Age** movement and in her 1979 volume *Strangers Among Us* presented the idea of **walk-ins,** people who had died but whose bodies had been immediately taken over and life continued by returning spirits. People claiming to be such walk-ins have now emerged as leaders of various New Age groups. In the 1980s she became a popular spokesperson within the New Age movement and an advocate of a more apocalyptic understanding of society's moving into the New Age through a cataclysmic event, accompanying a pole shift, at the end of the 1990s. In 1986 she released her autobiography, *Ruth Montgomery: Herald of the New Age.*

Sources:

Melton, J. Gordon, Jerome Clark, and Aidan Kelly. *New Age Encyclopedia.* Detroit: Gale Research, 1990.

Montgomery, Ruth. *Born to Heal.* New York: Coward, McCann & Geochegan, 1973.

———. *Companions Along the Way.* New York: Coward, McCann & Geochegan, 1974.

———. *A Gift of Prophecy: The Phenomenal Jeane Dixon.* New York: William Morrow, 1965.

———. *Here and Hereafter.* New York: Coward, McCann & Geochegan, 1966.

———. *A Search for the Truth.* New York: William Morrow, 1967.

———. *Strangers Among Us.* New York: Coward, McCann & Geochegan, 1979.

———. *The World Before.* New York: Coward, McCann & Geochegan, 1976.

———. *A World Beyond.* New York: Coward, McCann & Geochegan, 1971.

———. *The World to Come: The Guide Long-Awaited Predictions for a Dawning Age.* New York: Harmony Books, 1999.

Móo, Queen

According to the anthropological fancies of Augustus le Plongeon, the Queen of Yucatan. Le Plongeon's account of Queen Móo became a major building block in the contemporary myth of the lost continent of **Lemuria.**

Sources:

Le Plongeon, Augustus. *Queen Móo and the Egyptian Sphinx.* London, 1896.

Moody, Raymond Avery, Jr. (1944–)

Raymond A. Moody, whose 1975 book *Life After Life* helped launch a new generation of research on life after death, was born on June 30, 1944 in Porterdale, Georgia. He attended the University of Virginia where he successively earned his B.A. (1966), M.A. (1967), and Ph.D. (1969) in philosophy. While pursuing his education, in 1966 he married Louise Lambach. He joined the faculty at East Carolina University in 1969. He left his university post in 1972 to pursue a degree in medicine (his father was a physician), which he completed at Medical College of Georgia in 1976. He completed his residency in psychiatry at the University of Virginia Medical Center.

While completing his medical degree, Moody began to collect accounts of people who had either died and come back to life or come close to dying, what he termed **near-death experiences.** These accounts became the basis of a best-selling book, *Life after Life* (1975), and along with the work of **Elizabeth Kübler-Ross,** provided the foundation for a generation of research on survival of death and a new starting point for people engaged in counseling the dying. While accounts of the near-death experience had been collected for centuries and had become the subject of attention by psychical research, they were virtually unknown to parapsychologists who had largely abandoned research of life-after-death in favor of laboratory research on basic ESP experiences.

The success of Moody's first book freed him to continue his research on near-death experiences and he wrote a best-selling sequel, *Reflections on Life after Life,* released in 1977. He traveled widely through the 1980s, teaching and lecturing on his work. During the 1990s, his research has taken on a new focus toward those who have lost a loved one. In this regard, he has explored the idea of evoking apparitions of the deceased as a means of resolving unfinished issues in a relationship otherwise ended by the death of one party. To this end he constructed what is known as a **psychomanteum,** a room especially designed to produce a favorable alteration of consciousness and facilitate the production of **apparitions.** This work became the subject of his latest book, *Reunions: Visionary Encounters with Departed Loved Ones* (1994).

The psychomanteum was constructed at Moody's private research center, the **John Dee** Memorial Theater of the Mind, named for the Elizabethan magician. Here he not only counsels people on concerns about death, but carries on a program of research and education, including periodical conferences for professionals. Both his philosophical training and his research have provided Moody with material for his mature reflections on the afterlife which have appeared in his two books, *Coming Back: A Psychiatrist Explores Past Life Journeys* (1991) and *The Last Laugh* (1998).

The Theater of the Mind is located in rural Alabama and may be contacted at P. O. Box 1882, Anniston, AL 36202. Moody has a website at http://www.lifeafterlife.com.

Sources:

Moody, Raymond. *Coming Back: A Psychiatrist Explores Past Life Journeys.* World Publications, 1991.

———. *The Last Laugh.* Charlottesville, Va.: Hampton Road Publishing, 1998.

———. *Life after Life.* New York: Bantam Books, 1975.

———. *Reflections on Life After Life.* Harrisburg, Pa.: Stackpole Books, 1977.

———. *Reunions: Visionary Encounters With Departed Loved Ones.* New York: Ballantine, 1994.

Raymond Moody. http://www.lifeafterlife.com. May 20, 2000. June 20, 2000.

Moon

The Moon was the subject of widespread folklore in ancient times. While the brightest object in the night sky, it is not so bright that its surface texture is obscured. The patterns on the lunar surface have, like clouds, taken on anthropomorphic characteristics. Some saw the face of a man; others, various animals. The changing phases of the Moon and its seeming disappearance for a day or two each month also led to additional speculations. Modern werewolf lore has the wolf-like side of the person showing itself only during the evenings of the full Moon.

The Moon was associated with various gods and goddesses, though primarily the latter. In Hindu astrology, the Moon was associated with the god Nanna, though the more common associations are with the Greek Artemis, the Roman Luna, or the Moonlight-Giving Mother of the Zuni. It was especially associated with females as they identified the lunar cycle with the menstrual cycle. In the contemporary world, the Moon has assumed a central role in the mythology developed by Neo-Paganism, especially its feminist element.

The most comprehensive system for gathering the many observations about the Moon, attempting to understand its significance and drawing implications for behavior from it, was **astrology.** The 28-day cycle of the Moon became a convenient way of dividing the solar year into more manageable units we have come to know as months. (Actually the Moon takes only 27.32 days to orbit the earth, but because of the movement around the Sun it takes 29.53 days for it to complete a cycle from full Moon to full Moon.

In astrology the Moon represents the inner emotional side of the self, the subconscious mind and psyche. The Moon's placement in the chart reveals the creative side of the person, where he/she might give birth to new ideas, how his/her nurturing side is expressed, or where great passion is resting. The Moon is paired off with the Sun, related to the overall aspects of one's outer visible life.

Over the years, from folklore and astrology, the Moon was identified with a variety of behavior patterns, most notably mental disorders, or lunacy. The moon has been seen as effecting crime, suicides, accidents, and births, their occurrences believed to rise and fall with the phases of the Moon. It is believed by many still that, for example, the Moon will stimulate pregnant women to give birth, an observation bolstered by the alternating full and empty birth wards nurses have reported at hospitals. These observations have become the subject of research through the twentieth century, though many of these studies have been somewhat buried in various psychological journals.

In the 1980s and 1990s psychologists I. W. Kelly and R. Martens were the focus of several studies testing lunar assumptions beginning with a sweep of the literature in 1986 attempting to discover any evidence for a correlation between lunar phases and birthrates. They discovered that studies had been done in various settings in different countries with large samples, but that no data tied a higher rate of spontaneous births to a particular phase of the Moon. A similar negative correlation has been found between the Moon and an upsurge of behavior associated with mental illness or suicide (including number of suicides, attempts at suicides, or threats of suicide).

Early in 2000, news reports appeared of a German study that showed a statistical correlation between the Moon phases and alcohol consumption. However, on checking, the report appeared to have garbled the original report written by Hans-Joachim Mittmeyer of the University of Türbingen and Norbert Filipp of the Health Institute in Reutlingen. The pair of researchers had done a study of arrests for alcohol in Germany over a lunar cycle without finding any statistically significant variations from day to day.

While much interesting and suggestive data on astrological relationships have been produced over the twentieth century, especially that associated with **Michel Gauquelin,** the data on the immediate effects of the Moon on behavior as expressed in popular folklore appears to be negative. While there remain areas that have gone unresearched, enough has been done so that the burden of proof has shifted onto the shoulders of those who now make such claims.

Sources:

Carrol, Robert Todd. "Full Moon and Lunar Effects." *Skeptic's Dictionary.* http://www.skepdic.com/fullmoon.html. June 11, 2000.

Chudler, Eric. "Moonstruck! Does the Full Moon Influence Behavior." http://faculty.washington.edu/chudler/moon.html. June 11, 2000.

Kelly, I. W., and R. Martens. "Lunar Phases and Birthrate: An Update." *Psychological Reports* 75 (1996): 507–11.

———, James Rotton, and Roger Culver. "The Moon Was Full and Nothing Happened: A Review of Studies on the Moon and Human Behavior and Human Belief." In J. Nickell, B. Karr, and T. Genoni, eds. *The Outer Edge.* Amherst, N.Y.: CSICOP, 1996.

Moon, Sun Myung (1920–)

Founder of the Holy Spirit Association for the Unification of World Christianity, more popularly referred to as the **Unification Church.** Moon was born in Korea on January 6, 1920, the son of Presbyterian parents. He later noted that on Easter Day in 1936 he was visited by Jesus and told that God had chosen him to establish the kingdom of heaven on earth.

He attended Watseka University. During his early adult years he received revelations on a regular basis, and after World War II he became a full-time independent preacher in North Korea. His activities were curtailed by his arrest by the North Korean government. Released in 1950, he spent three years preaching in Pusan and then moved to Seoul and founded the Unification Church in 1953. Some of his revelations, containing the basic ideas that had been revealed to him, were published in 1957 as *The Divine Principle.*

Moon is seen by his followers as the lord of the second advent, who has come to complete Christ's unfinished work. His teachings strive to create God-centered families in order to make the world a better place for Christ's second coming. In 1960 he married his present wife, Hak Ja Han, who has, in bearing 12 children, helped Moon complete his messianic task. Moon hand-selects marriages between his followers which fulfills his vision of God-centered families. For example, a mass wedding was held in New York's Madison Square Garden to attain this purpose.

In 1959 Moon sent his first church leader to the United States. Moon himself came for the first time in 1965. During that visit he had a sitting with Spiritualist medium **Arthur A. Ford** who spoke glowingly of his work and had his picture taken with President Dwight Eisenhower. He made subsequent visits in 1969, 1971, and 1972, after which he settled in the United States. From that point the church began to grow, but also became an object of controversy as many parents were angered when their sons and daughters dropped out of college and careers to become workers in Moon's organization. The organization also reached out to speak to the influential in a variety of fields, including science, the media, and religion. As the anticult movement formed in the mid-1970s, the Unification Church was singled out as its main target. Moon was criticized from every angle. He was pictured as a power-hungry dictator who turned his followers into mindless zombies.

Finally in the early 1980s, in spite of the widespread support of the religious community, Moon was convicted on a tax violation charge and eventually served 13 months in jail (1984–85), but upon his release he immediately resumed leadership of the church.

Over the years Moon delivered lectures regularly, which have been gathered into a collected work called *The Master Speaks.* In prison he wrote a two-volume book, *God's Warning to the World* (1985). As the anticult controversy receded in the 1990s, Moon and his small church became a more stable part of a wider religious landscape.

Sources:

Barker, Eileen. *The Making of a Moonie.* Oxford, England: Basil Blackwell, 1984.

Mickler, Michael L. *The Unification Church in America: A Bibliography and Research Guide.* New York: Garland, 1987.

Moon, Sun Myung. *Christianity in Crisis: New Hope.* New York: HSA-UWC, 1974.

———. *A Prophet Speaks Today.* New York: HSA-UWC, 1975.

Moonsign Book

Popular publication concerned with influence of the moon on plants and health that has become a key annual publication of Llewellyn Publications, P.O. Box 64383, St. Paul, MN 55164.

Moore, Marcia (1928–1979)

Marcia Moore, an astrologer and metaphysical teacher, was born on May 22, 1928, in Cambridge, Massachusetts, the daughter of Robert L. Moore, the founder of the chain of Sheraton Hotels. She attended Radcliffe, where she chose astrology as the subject of her senior thesis. The heart of the work reported on the results of a questionnaire she had sent to the subscribers of a popular astrological periodical. The finished work would later be published under the title *Astrology Today—A Socio-Psychological Survey* (1960).

Following graduation in 1960, Moore settled into a career as a teacher and writer. After a brief first marriage, in 1966 she married writer Mark Douglas. That same year, they coauthored the first of several books, *Diet, Sex, and Yoga.* It was followed by additional titles on **yoga, reincarnation,** and **astrology.** Increasingly, through the 1970s, Moore became a well-known leader in the astrological world and she was a leading force in integrating it with a reincarnation perspective. Reincarnation was the subject of her work on the faculty for the 1974 convention of the American Federation of Astrologers. She developed a technique called hypersentience that enabled people to recall their previous incarnations, and through the 1970s edited the *Hypersentience Bulletin.*

Moore and Douglas separated in 1972, and she later married Howard Alltourian, Jr. She was at the height of her career in 1979 when she disappeared. On January 15, Alltourian returned home to find his wife missing. Nothing was heard from her. Two years later a portion of a skull was found that was eventually identified as Moore's, though the exact circumstances of her death are unknown. It was known that during her final years she had been experimenting with a mind-altering drug to expand her consciousness (the subject of her last book) and had also become involved with an obscure occult group, but the role of either in her death is unknown.

Sources:

Moore, Marcia. *Astrology Today—A Socio-Psychological Survey.* New York: Lucis Publishing, 1960.

———. *The History of Astrology.* York Harbor, Maine: Arcane Publications, 1974.

———, and Mark Douglas. *Astrology in Action.* York Harbor, Maine: Arcane Publications, 1970.

———, and Mark Douglas. *Diet, Sex and Yoga.* York Harbor, Maine: Arcane Publications, 1966.

———, with Howard S. Alltourian. *Journeys into the Bright World. A Personal Account of the Ketamite Experience.* Rockport, Maine: ParaResearch, 1978.

Mopses, Order of the

A secret association founded in Germany in the eighteenth century, spreading through **Holland,** Belgium, and **France.** It was popularly believed to be a **black magic** order, replacing the Satanic **goat** with a dog as an object of worship. However, it seems clear that it was really a somewhat whimsical crypto-Masonic order, founded partially in reaction to the papal bull of Pope Clement XII on April 24, 1738, which condemned Freemasonry. Immediately after their establishment, they departed from Masonic tradition by admitting females to membership and to all the offices, except that of Grand Master, which was for life. They did, however, create a new office of Grand Mistress, elected every six months.

The ceremonies were a unique variation on Masonic ritual, which probably gave rise to rumors of its worshipping a dog. The candidate for admission did not knock, but had to scratch at the door, and, being purposely kept waiting, was obliged to bark like a dog. On being admitted into the lodge, he had a collar placed round his neck, to which a chain was attached. He was blindfolded and led nine times round the room, while the Mopses present made as great a din as possible with sticks, swords, chains, shovels, and dismal howlings. The candidate was then questioned as to his intentions, and having replied that he desired to become a "Mops," was asked by the master whether he was prepared to kiss the most ignoble part of that animal. Of course this raised the candidate's anger, but in spite of his resistance, the model of a dog, made of wax, wood, or some other material, was pushed against his face. Having taken the oath, he had his eyes unbandaged, and was then taught the secret signs.

Morag See Mhorag

Morgan le Fay

Sister of **King Arthur** and wife of King Urien of Gore. Arthur gave into her keeping the scabbard of his sword Excalibur, but she gave it to Sir Accolon whom she loved and had a forged scabbard made. Arthur, however, recovered the real sheath, but was again deceived by her.

Morgan le Fay seems to have derived from the Celtic deities Morrigan, Macha, and Modron (a divine mother). She figured as a queen of the Land of Faerie and as such appears in French and Italian romance. She first appeared in the Arthurian legends in Geiffrey of Manmouth's twelfth-century volume, *Vita Merlini.* It was she who, on one occasion, threw Excalibur into a lake. She usually presented her favorites with a ring and retained them by her side as did Venus in *Tannhäuser.* Her myth is a parallel of that of Eos and Tithonus and is possibly derived from a sun and dawn myth.

Sources:

Lacy, J. Lacy, ed. *The Arturian Encyclopedia.* New York: Garland Publishing, 1986.

Morgawr

A Loch Ness type monster observed and photographed in the area of Falmouth, Cornwall, England. On November 17, 1976, Morgawr was sighted by Tony "Doc" Shiels and David Clarke (editor of *Cornish Life* magazine) in the Helford estuary near Falmouth. A photograph taken by Clarke was reproduced in *Fortean Times* (no. 22, summer 1977). Although the camera had unfortunately jammed, resulting in a superimposition of pictures, the general impression is of the head of a creature similar to that photographed by Shiels (*Fortean Times* 19) and some photographs taken by Shiels of the **Loch Ness Monster** May 21, 1977 (best one reproduced in both *Cornish Life* and the London *Daily Mirror* for June 9, 1977).

Serious charges of **fraud** have been expressed concerning Shiels's pictures on the grounds that he is well known in conjuring circles as an exponent of magic simulations of psychic effects. However, he claims to be an avid monster-hunter, and has collected other reports of sightings of Morgawr, as well as publishing his own photographs of the Loch Ness monster.

Two photographs of Morgawr taken by Gerry Bennett of Seworgan, Cornwall, from Mawnan beach on January 31, 1977, were also reproduced in *Fortean Times* 22, together with photographs and reports of **Mhorag,** another Scottish monster of a Loch Ness type.

Sources:

Clark, Jerome. *Encyclopedia of Strange and Unexplained Phenomena.* Detroit: Gale Research, 1993.

Morien (or Morienus) (fl. 12th century C.E.)

Twelfth-century alchemist. It is commonly supposed that Morien, or Morienus, as he is sometimes styled, was born at Rome, and it is also reported that, like **Raymond Lully** and several other early practitioners of **alchemy,** he combined evangelical ardor with his scientific tastes. While still a mere boy, and resident in his native city, Morien became acquainted with the writings of Adfar, the Arabian philosopher, and gradually the youth's acquaintance with these developed into tense admiration, the result being that he became filled with the desire to make the personal acquaintance of the author in question.

Accordingly he left Rome and set out for Alexandria, this being the home of Adfar, and, on reaching his destination, did not have to wait long before gaining his desired end. The learned Arabian accorded him a hearty welcome, and a little while afterward the two were living together on very friendly terms, the elder man daily imparting knowledge to the younger, who showed himself a remarkably apt pupil. For some years this state of affairs continued, but at length Adfar died, and thereupon Morien left Alexandria and went to Palestine, found a retreat in the vicinity of Jerusalem, and began to lead a hermit's life there.

Meanwhile the erudition of the deceased Arabian acquired a wide celebrity, and some of his manuscripts chanced to fall into the hands of Kalid, sultan of Egypt. He was a person of active and enquiring mind, and observing that on the cover of the manuscripts it was stated that the secret of the **philosophers' stone** was written within, he naturally grew doubly inquisitive. He found, however, that he himself could not elucidate the precious documents, and therefore he summoned *illuminati* from far and near to his court at Cairo, offering a large reward to the man who should solve the mystery. Many people presented themselves in consequence, but the majority of them were mere charlatans, and thus the sultan was duped mercilessly.

Presently news of these doings reached the ears of Morien. It incensed him to think that his old preceptor's wisdom and writings were being made a laughingstock, so he decided that he must go to Cairo himself, and not only see justice done to Adfar's memory, but also seize what might prove a favorable opportunity of converting Kalid to Christianity.

The sultan was inclined to be cynical when the hermit arrived, nor would he listen to attacks on the Muslim faith, yet he was sufficiently impressed to grant Morien a house wherein to conduct research, and here the alchemist worked for a long time, ultimately perfecting the elixir. However, he did not make any attempt to gain the proper reward, and instead took his leave without the sultan's awareness, simply leaving the precious fluid in a vase on which he inscribed the suggestive words: "He who possesses all has no need of others."

But Kalid was at a loss to know how to proceed further, and for a long time he made great efforts to find Morien and bring him again to his court. Years went by, and all search for the vanished alchemist proved vain, but once, when the Sultan was hunting in the neighborhood of Jerusalem, one of his servants chanced to hear of a hermit who was able to create gold.

Convinced that this must be none other than Morien, Kalid straightway sought him out. Once more the two met, and again the alchemist made strenuous efforts to win the other from Islam. Many discussions took place between the pair, both speaking on behalf of their respective religions, yet Kalid showed no inclination to desert the faith of his fathers. As a result Morien relinquished the quest in despair, but it is said that, on parting with the sultan, he duly instructed him in the mysteries of the transcendent science.

Nothing is known about Morien's subsequent history, and the likelihood is that the rest of his days were spent quietly at his hermitage. He was credited with sundry alchemistic writings, said to have been translated from Arabic, but the ascription rests on the slenderest evidence. One of these works was entitled *Liber de Distinctione Mercurii Aquarum,* and it is interesting to recall that a manuscript copy of this work belonged to the great chemist Robert Boyle (1627–1691), one of the founders of the Royal Society in London, while another is entitled *Liber de Compositione Alchemiae,* and this is printed in the first volume of *Bibliotheca Chemica Curiosa.*

Better known than either of these, and more likely to be really from Morien's pen, is a third treatise styled *De Re Metallica, Metallorum Transmutatione, et occulta summague Antiquorum Medicine Libellus,* which was repeatedly published, the first edition appearing at Paris 1559.

Morin, Jean-Baptiste (1583–1656)

Jean-Baptiste Morin, French physician, mathematician and the leading astrologer of the seventeenth century, was born in Villefranche on February 23, 1583. Morin studied at Avignon, where he received his medical degree and began a career as a physician. However, **astrology** fascinated him, and he secured a position as astrologer to the duke of Luxembourg and later the duke d'Effiat. Then in 1830 the king of France offered him the chair in mathematics at the College of France, and Morin moved to Paris, where he remained for the rest of his life.

While formally a professor of mathematics, he also functioned as court astrologer. As such he was present in the group witnessing the birth of Louis XIV in 1638. He served Cardinal Richelieu (who is noted to have disliked Morin personally but was respectful of his knowledge) and Cardinal Mazarin.

He would be the last of the outstanding French astrologers prior to the modern era, as astrology was on the wane under the attack of the new science. However, he was able to make a number of contributions to the modernizing of astrology, a necessity to prevent its being completely stamped out. Morin developed a system of division of the astrological houses, now called the Morinean system, based upon the equal division of the equator, which is then projected onto an ecliptic as means of handling the elliptical orbit of the earth.

During his life Morin published little. His major work, the *Astrologia Gallica,* was published in Latin in 1661, five years after his death. It was largely unread except by a few intellectuals until 1897, when a French translation was finally published. Thus the work informed the pioneers of the French phase of the modern astrological revival. Morin died in Paris on November 6, 1656.

Sources:

Brau, Jean-Louis, Helen Weaver, and Allan Edmands. *Larousse Encyclopedia of Astrology.* New York: New American Library, 1977.

Morin, Jean-Baptiste. *Astrologia Gallica.* The Hague, Netherlands, 1661.

Mormons See **Church of Jesus Christ of Latter-day Saints**

Morphogenetic Fields

Term normally used somewhat loosely to indicate the mysterious factors that influence the development of form and characteristics in nature. A special theory of the action of morphogenetic fields, relevant to **occult** and **New Age** considerations, was proposed in 1981 by **Rupert Sheldrake** in his theory concerning what he termed **formative causation.** This theory also has relevance to such parapsychological phenomena as **clairvoyance, telepathy,** and **reincarnation.**

Sources:

Sheldrake, Rupert. *A New Science of Life: The Hypothesis of Formative Causation.* London: Blond & Briggs, 1981.

Morris, L(ouis) A(nne) Meurig (1899– ?)

Early twentieth-century British inspirational **medium** through whom an entity who chose the name "Power" delivered religious and philosophical teachings from the platform in a manner analogous to modern **channeling.** Some signs of Morris's psychic gifts were noticeable at an early age, but they were stifled by an orthodox education. However, she began to develop rapidly after a first **séance** with a **direct voice** medium in Newton Abbot in 1922. Within six weeks she went under **control.** "Sunshine," the spirit of a child, spoke through her, and "Sister Magdalene," the spirit of a French nun, assumed charge as principal **trance** control. The prediction came through that Morris would be trained for the delivery of teaching by a spirit called "Power."

Under the control of "Power," the medium's soprano voice changed to a ringing baritone, her mannerisms became masculine and priestly, and the teachings disclosed an erudition and sophisticated philosophy that was far above the intellectual capacities of the medium.

In 1929, Laurence Cowen, well-known author and playwright, came in contact with Morris. "Power" convinced him of the truth of **survival** and filled him with a missionary spirit. Hitherto an agnostic, Cowen became a convert to **Spiritualism,** associated himself with Morris, and arranged a long series of Sunday meetings in the Fortune Theatre in London for the general public. Wide publicity accompanied the sermons for some time in the press. Public attention was further aroused by the provincial tours Cowen arranged at great personal sacrifice.

Morris's rise into the forefront of inspired orators was punctuated with two publicly attested supernormal occurrences. First, an attempt was made by the Columbia Gramophone Company to make a phonograph record of "Power's" voice. According to the publicly rendered account of company spokesperson C. W. Nixon, at the very commencement of the experiment an incident occurred that by all the rules should have spoiled the first side of the record.

Ernest Oaten, president of the International Federation of Spiritualists, was in the chair, and, being unaware that the start was to be made without the appearance of the usual red light, he whispered loudly to Morris as she stood up: "Wait for the signal." These words were picked up by the microphone and heard by the engineers in the recording room after the apparatus had been started, and it was believed they must be on the record. Later, when the second side of the record was to be made, there was confusion in starting, and towards the end, as if to make technical failure a certainty, Morris turned and walked several paces away from the microphone.

A week before the record was ready for reproduction, Cowen telephoned Nixon and told him that "Power" had asserted that notwithstanding the technical mistakes the record would be a success, that Oaten's whispered words would not be reproduced, and that the timing and volume of the voice would not be spoiled by the later accidents.

This statement was so extraordinary and appeared to be so preposterous in view of technical expectations, that Nixon had it taken down word by word, and sent it in a sealed envelope to Oaten in Manchester with the request that he would keep it unopened until the record was ready, and the truth or otherwise of the prediction could be tested. The record was played in the Fortune Theatre on April 25, 1931. It was found perfect. The letter was opened and read. The prediction was true in every detail.

The second strange incident occurred in the studios of the British Movietone Company where a talking film was made of "Power's" oratory. Seventy people saw the microphones high in the air, held up by new half-inch ropes. The rope suddenly snapped (it was found cut as with a sharp knife) and a terrific crash startled all present. Within half an inch of Morris's face, the microphone swept across the space and went swaying to and fro. A foreman rushed up and dragged the rope aside to keep it out of sight of the camera. The cameraman never stopped filming. Nor did Morris falter. In spite of the obvious danger to her life she never stirred and went on undisturbed with her trance speech.

According to expert opinion the voice registering must have been a failure. Yet it was found that the accident had not the least influence. The record was perfect. According to "Power's" later revelation, everything was planned. The ropes were supernormally severed so as to prove, by the medium's demeanor, that she was indeed in trance (which a newspaper questioned) as no human being could have consciously exhibited such self-possession as she did when the accident occurred.

Sir Oliver Lodge, in his book *Past Years* (1931), refers to Morris:

"When the medium's own vocal organs are obviously being used—as in most cases of trance utterances—the proof of supernormality rests mainly on the substance of what is being said; but, occasionally the manner is surprising. I have spoken above of a characteristically cultured mode of expression, when a scholar is speaking, not easily imitated by an uncultured person; but, in addition to that a loud male voice may emanate from a female larynx and may occasionally attain oratorical proportions. Moreover, the orator may deal with great themes in a style which we cannot associate with the fragile little woman who has gone into trance and is now under control. This is a phenomenon which undoubtedly calls attention to the existence of something supernormal, and can be appealed to as testifying to the reality and activity of a spiritual world. It is, indeed, being used for purposes of such demonstration, and seems well calculated to attract more and more attention from serious and religious people; who would be discouraged and offended by the trivial and barely intelligible abnormalities associated with what are called physical (or physiological) phenomena and would not be encouraged by what is called clairvoyance."

In April 1932, Morris sued the *Daily Mail* for a poster reading "Trance Medium Found Out," and also for statements made in the article to which the poster referred. The action lasted for 11 days. The summary of Justice McCardie was dramatically interrupted by the sudden entrancement of Morris and an address of "Power" to the judge. The jury found for the newspaper on the plea of fair comment but added that no allegations of **fraud** or dishonesty against Morris had been proved. Morris's appeal, after a hearing of four days before Lord Justices Scrutton, Lawrence, and Greer, was dismissed. The House of Lords, to which the case was afterward carried, agreed with the Court of Appeal.

Morris, Robert Lyle (1942–)

Parapsychologist at the University of Edinburgh, Scotland. He was born July 9, 1942, in Canonsburg, Pennsylvania, and studied at the University of Pittsburgh (B.S., 1963) and Duke University, North Carolina (from which he received a doctorate in biological psychology). After two years of postdoctoral work at the Duke Medical Center and with **J. B. Rhine,** he became the research coordinator for the **Psychical Research Foundation,** Durham, North Carolina. Over the years he taught **parapsychology** and psychology courses as a visiting lecturer at the University of California—Santa Barbara; the University of California—Irvine; the University of Southern California; John F. Kennedy University (Orinda, California); and Syracuse University (New York). He was named Koestler Professor of Parapsychology at the University of Edinburgh, Scotland, in 1985.

He served on the Council of the American Society for the Advancement of Science (1971–73), the board of the **American Society for Psychical Research** (1979–83; secretary, 1980–82), the board of the Gardner Murphy Research Institute (1971–83; secretary, 1971–74), and the board of the **Society for Scientific Exploration** (1985–86; vice president, 1985). He was on the board of the **Parapsychological Association** for many years, serving additionally as its AAAS representative (1971–77), president (1974 and 1985), vice president (1976 and 1984), secretary (1977), and treasurer (1975). He joined the **Society for Psychical Research,** London, in 1985, and joined its council in 1986. He has written over a hundred professional conference presentations and publications in the area of parapsychology, and he edited the Arno Press reprint program "Perspectives in Psychical Research." His main research interests have included biological aspects of **psi** and **anpsi,** anomalous interactions between people and equipment, psychic development techniques, the psychology of conjuring, mentalism, and deception.

Sources:

Berger, Arthur S., and Joyce Berger. *The Encyclopedia of Parapsychology and Psychical Research.* New York: Paragon House, 1991.

Morris, Robert L. "Biology and Psychical Research." Edited by Gertrude R. Schmeidler. In *Parapsychology: Its Relation to Physics, Biology Psychology, and Psychiatry.* N.p., 1976.

———. "Obtaining Non-Random Entry Points: A Complex Psi Process." In *Parapsychology Today.* Edited by J. B. Rhine and R. Brier. New York: Citadel Press, 1968.

———. "PK on a Bio-Electrical System." In *Parapsychology Today.* Edited by J. B. Rhine and R. Brier. New York: Citadel Press, 1968.

———. "The Psychobiology of Psi." In *Psychic Exploration.* Edited by E. D. Mitchell. New York: G. P. Putnam's Sons, 1974.

———. "Some New Techniques in Animal Psi Research." *Journal of Parapsychology* 31 (December 1967).

Roll, W. G., R. L. Morris, and J. D. Morris, eds. *Research in Parapsychology 1972.* Metuchen, N.J.: Scarecrow Press, 1973.

———. *Research in Parapsychology 1973.* Metuchen, N.J.: Scarecrow Press, 1974.

———. *Research in Parapsychology 1974.* Metuchen, N.J.: Scarecrow Press, 1975.

———. *Research in Parapsychology 1975.* Metuchen, N.J.: Scarecrow Press, 1976.

Pleasants, Helene, ed. *Biographical Dictionary of Parapsychology.* New York: Helix Press, 1964.

Wiseman, Richard and Robert L. Morris. *Guidelines for Testing Psychic Claimants.* Amherst, N.Y.: Prometheus Books, 1995.

Morris Pratt Institute

The Morris Pratt Institute is the primary educational facility serving the **National Spiritualist Association of Churches.** It dates to the 1890s when popular Spiritualist minister/lecturer **Moses Hull** envisioned a training school to pass along the teachings of **Spiritualism** to a new generation, many of the first generation of Spiritualist leaders having already passed from the scene. He opened such a school in Ohio soon after the founding of the National Spiritualist Association (NSA) in 1893, but it survived only a few years. In 1901, Morris Pratt offered the mansion he had constructed at Whitewater, Wisconsin, to the NSA as a place to house a training school like the one Hull had begun. The large mansion seemed ideal; it had one room that could seat 400 people. However, the still-youthful NSA declined the offer, unable to see itself clear financially to manage the property. Pratt went ahead and incorporated the Morris Pratt Institute but died the following year before a school could be organized. Moses Hull picked up the vision in 1903 and organized the new school with himself, his wife and his daughter as the faculty. A few years later, the NSA organized a Bureau of Education. Through the person of Thomas Grimshaw, who succeeded Hull as president of the institute, the two organizations cooperated in the preparation of a course of study consisting of two parts: a general course on the "History, Philosophy, and Religion of Modern Spiritualism," and an advanced course on "Spiritualism, Philosophy, Mediumship, and comparative Religion," the latter completed by Victoria Barnes following Grimshaw's death.

The institute had a shaky history through much of the twentieth century. It closed during the Great Depression, reopened in 1935 but soon closed again. In 1946 the Whitewater property was closed and a new building to house the institute constructed in Wauwatosa, a Milwaukee suburb. In 1977 the building went through a complete renovation and rededication. The institute eventually merged into the NSA and is now its Educational Bureau. The institute is currently located at 111811 Waterplank Rd, Milwaukee, WI 53226-3340. Its website is at http://www.morrispratt.org/.

Morrison, Richard James (1795–1874)

The contemporary revival of interest in **astrology** reversed a trend that saw astrology almost disappear from Western culture by the end of the eighteenth century. Astrology began its slow return in a format capable of existing in the scientifically-oriented world due in large part to the efforts of a series of nineteenth century British astrologers, most of whom wrote under pseudonyms. Richard James Morrison was one of the important writers and publishers who kept astrological knowledge alive.

Morrison was born on June 15, 1795, in London. He joined the navy at the age of 11 and rose to the rank of lieutenant in 1815 during the Napoleonic wars. He retired in 1817, still a young man. He became interested in astrology through R. C. Smith, better known under his pen name, Raphael. Morrison adopted the pen name Zadkiel and began an astrological almanac, *The Herald of Astrology* (later *Zadkiel's Almanac*), modeled upon Raphel's *The Prophetic Messenger.* In 1835 Morrison completed his major literary contribution to the astrological revival, an abridged edition of **William Lilly**'s *Christian Astrology.*

Zadkiel's career was punctuated by a series of incidents that began in 1861 when his almanac predicted a bad year for Prince Albert, the popular consort of Queen Victoria. When Albert died unexpectedly at the end of the year, many gave Zadkiel credit for an accurate prediction, but Edward Belcher, a writer for the *London Daily Telegraph,* attacked Morrison for spreading superstition to the gullible. Morrison countered with a libel suit and won, but was awarded only 20 shillings. His real reward was the publicity the case attracted, which substantially increased his sales. Morrison continued to publish his almanac until his death on April 5, 1874, after which it was continued by his students for many years.

Sources:

Morrison, R. J. *An Introduction to Astrology by William Lilly, being the whole of that Celebrated Author's Rules for the Practice of Horory Astology* . . . London, 1835. Reprint, Hollywood, Calif.: Newcastle Publishing, 1972.

Morrow, Felix (1906–1988)

American publisher who contributed significantly to the **occult** boom in the United States in the 1960s through his publishing house **University Books** and associated Mystic Arts Book Society. Morrow was born on June 3, 1906, in New York City in a Hasidic Jewish family. He grew up in a non-religious atmosphere and became drawn to both Marxism and Freudian teaching. He became a graduate student in philosophy at Columbia University (1929–31), where he researched the history of religions. As editor of the theoretical monthly magazine *Fourth International,* he wrote a thoughtful article on Marxism and religion. For over a decade (1931–46), he devoted himself to the revolutionary socialist movement and was author of an important study: *Revolution and Counter-revolution in Spain* (1938; rev. ed. 1974).

In 1946, he moved from socialism to capitalism in publishing as executive vice president of Schocken Books, a Jewish publishing house in New York City, and became attracted to the writings of Franz Kafka, Martin Buber, and Gershom Scholen, and through them rediscovered his Hasidic roots. However, from 1948 to 1970, he became immersed in Freudian psychoanalytic training and publishing, though at the same time, his association with Mel Arnold at Beacon Press, and later with University of Notre Dame Press, made him responsive to **mysticism.** Throughout this period he remained a socialist at heart, this dichotomy creating many personal conflicts for him while broadening his humanist outlook.

As executive vice president of British Book Center, he took on American rights of *Flying Saucers Have Landed* by **Desmond Leslie** and **George Adamski** (originally published in England in 1953), and this project launched his research into earlier literature in psychic and occult subjects. In 1954, he incorporated University Books, Inc. in New York, and began publishing important out-of-print books on occultism, mysticism, **psychical research,** and comparative religion. These included key works such as A. E. Waite's books on the **tarot** and **ceremonial magic;** Lewis Spence's *Encyclopedia of Occultism;* Montague Summers' books on **witchcraft** and **vampires;** William James's *Varieties of Religious Experience;* R. M. Bucke's *Cosmic Consciousness;* F. W. H. Myers's *Human Personality and its Survival of Bodily Death;* scholarly works by Charles Guignebert on the origins of Christianity; D. T. Suzuki's books on **Zen; Nandor Fodor**'s *Encyclopedia of Psychical Research;* **G. R. S. Mead**'s books on Gnosticism; Alexandra David-Neel's *Magic and Mystery in Tibet;* and scores of similar books that opened large segments of the tradition to a new generation of modern occultists.

Each book carried a new introduction, evaluating the work in a modern context and often supplying original biographical research on the author. Some of these introductions were written by Morrow under the pseudonym 'John C. Wilson;' others were written by such authorities as **E. J. Dingwall,** Kenneth Rexroth, and Leslie Shepard.

University Books also published original works as the occult revival threw up names like **Timothy Leary** and new causes like the psychedelic revolution. In addition to publishing, the company marketed chosen titles each month through the Mystic Arts Book Society. A major event of that period was Morrow's association with William Nyland in distributing the books of **Georgei I. Gurdjieff** through the society. Morrow eventually became a disciple of Nyland and developed a great respect for the Gurdjieff work.

After 15 years of creative and stimulating publishing in the fields of occultism and mysticism, Morrow relinquished the business to Lyle Stuart, who continued the University Books imprint side by side with its own Citadel Press imprint, and moved the operation from New York to Secaucus, New Jersey. In 1973, Morrow launched a second occult series for Causeway Books, an imprint of A. & W. Publishers, Inc., New York. Morrow wrote some of the new introductions for this series under the pseudonym "Charles Sen."

The significant influence of Morrow's publishing work was recognized by the National Endowment for the Humanities and the Rockefeller Foundation, which initiated an oral history recording project on the advanced literary-intellectual life of New York City between 1925 and 1975. Tape recordings have been made of Morrow and other individuals for deposit in the Oral History division of the Columbia libraries.

Morrow extended his psychological studies from Freudianism to Maslow's humanist psychology and the holistic depth psychology of **Ira Progoff.** He was in charge of publishing projects in these areas for Dialogue House Library (80 E. 11th St., New York, NY 10003) prior to resuming independent publishing again with the books of Mantok and Maneewan Chia under the imprint Healing Tao Books, in New York. In his later years he was a regular visitor to the library of the **Parapsychology Foundation** in New York, where he found excellent facilities for research. He died suddenly on May 28, 1988, in New York.

Morse, J. J. (1848–1919)

One of the most prominent trance speakers of the nineteenth century, designated the "Bishop of Spiritualism" by Spiritualist journalist **W. T. Stead.** Morse had been left an orphan at the age of 10, had very little education, and served as pot-boy in a public house before his mediumship was discovered. The difference between the uneducated waking Morse and the erudite entranced Morse is noted by **E. W. Cox** in his book *What Am I?* (1873–74):

"I have heard an uneducated barman, when in a state of trance, maintain a dialogue with a party of philosophers on Reason and Foreknowledge, Will and Fate, and hold his own against them. I have put him the most difficult questions in psychology, and received answers always thoughtful, often full of wisdom, and invariably conveyed in choice and eloquent language. Nevertheless, in a quarter of an hour afterwards, when released from the trance, he was unable to answer the simplest query on a philosophical subject, and was at a loss for sufficient language in which to express a commonplace idea."

James Burns, the well-known Spiritualistic editor and publisher, took an interest in Morse and employed him as an assistant in his printing and publishing office. The spirit entity, "Tien Sien Tie," the Chinese philosopher, who said that he lived on Earth in the reign of the Emperor Kea-Tsing, gave his first addresses through Morse in Burns's offices in 1869. Of the other spirits associated with Morse's mediumship the best known was "The Strolling Player," who supplied the humor and lighter elements in the discourses, which were models of literary grace. Many proofs of spirit identity came through, some of which were years after tabulated and republished by Edward T. Bennett.

Morse's physical mediumship was a powerful one. He could demonstrate the fire test and the phenomenon of **elongation of the human body.** He visited Australia and New Zealand, edited *The Banner of Light* in Boston and *The Two Worlds* of Manchester. *The Spiritual Review* (1901–1902) was his own foundation. His mediumship and general propaganda activity was an important factor in the spread and growth of British **Spiritualism.**

His daughter, Florence, who was clairvoyant from childhood, also developed her abilities as an inspirational speaker. She travelled extensively, visiting the English-speaking world. Unlike her father, however, she was almost fully conscious in the course of her inspirational addresses.

Sources:

Morse, J. J. *Leaves From My Life: A Narrative of Personal Experiences in the Career of a Servant of the Spirits.* N.p., 1877.

Morse Fellowship

The Morse Fellowship was a **channeling** group founded in 1959 by Louise Morse, who channeled an entity she termed the "Holy Spirit." The organization was named for her husband, Elwood Morse, who had died in 1958. She saw her work as a fulfillment of biblical prophecies of the last days. Through the 1970s the group was headquartered in Richardson, Texas, but nothing has been heard from it in recent years and it is presumed defunct.

Sources:

Morse, Louise. *The Living Water.* Richardson, Tex.: Morse Fellowship, 1970.

Morselli, Enrico (1852–1929)

Born July 17, 1852, Enrico Morselli was a professor of psychiatry at the University of Turin and after 1889 at Genoa University. He had been a bitter skeptic of psychic phenomena and had published several books including *Il magnetismo animale; La fascinazione e gli stati ipnotici* (1886) and *I fenomei telepatici e le allucinazioni veridiche* (1897). However, his encounter with the **medium Eusapia Palladino** (later revealed to have been falsified) completely convinced him of the reality of Spiritualist phenomena. He held some 30 sittings with Palladino in 1901–2 and 1906–7. He announced his change of thinking in 1907 in the *Annals of Psychic Science* (vol. 5, 1907, p. 322):

"The question of Spiritism has been discussed for over 50 years; and although no one can at present foresee when it will be settled, all are now agreed in assigning to it great importance among the problems left as a legacy by the nineteenth century to the twentieth.

"If for many years academic science has depreciated the whole category of facts that Spiritism has, for good or ill, rightly or wrongly, absorbed and assimilated, to form the elements of its doctrinal system, so much the worse for science! And worse still for the scientists who have remained deaf and blind before all the affirmations, not of credulous sectarians, but of serious and worthy observers such as Crookes, Lodge and Richet. I am not ashamed to say that I myself, as far as my modest power went, have contributed to this obstinate skepticism, up to the day on which I was enabled to break the chains in which my absolutist preconceptions had bound my judgment."

The next year he published an account of his sightings in the book *Psicologia e Spiritismo.* Here he presented his psychodynamic theory of **materialization** phenomena as a compromise between psychological orthodoxy and the spirit theory.

Morselli died February 18, 1929, in Genoa, Italy.

Sources:

Berger, Arthur S., and Joyce Berger. *The Encyclopedia of Parapsychology and Psychical Research.* New York: Paragon House, 1991.

Morselli, Enrico. *I fenomei telepatici e le allucinazioni veridiche.* N.p., 1897.

Pleasants, Helene, ed. *Biographical Dictionary of Parapsychology.* New York: Helix Press, 1964.

Morya, Master

One of the masters originally contacted by **Helena Petrovna Blavatsky,** cofounder of the **Theosophical Society.** According to theosophical teachings there exists a spiritual hierarchy composed of individuals who have finished their round of earthly reincarnations and have evolved to the spiritual planes, from which they guide the affairs of humanity. Those members of the hierarchy closest to humanity are the "lords of the seven rays" (of the light spectrum). Each ray represents a particular virtue, which the lord of that ray exemplifies.

Master Morya, frequently referred to as simply Master M., is the lord of the first ray and exemplifies will or power. He is one of the two hierarchical founders of the Theosophical Society. Blavatsky claimed a majority of her communications with the masters came from him. He takes as students some members who have been prepared by their past lives and also becomes their guide. He is said to have been a royal personage and appears in the body of an Asian Indian. He reportedly lived in Tibet but was known to travel widely, and many members of the society reported seeing him. Master M. was one of the three main communicators (the others being **Djual Khul** and **Koot Hoomi**) of what were compiled as *The Mahatma Letters,* the ultimate source for many theosophical ideas.

As the Theosophical Society fragmented, leaders of many groups whose organization and beliefs derive in large part from Theosophy have claimed contact with him, including **Helena Roerich** of the **Agni Yoga Society, Mark Prophet** and **Elizabeth Clare Prophet,** and Geraldine Innocente (pen name Thomas Printz) of the **Bridge to Spiritual Freedom.**

Sources:

Barker, A. Trevor, ed. *The Mahatma Letters to A. P. Sennett from the Mahatams M. and K.H.* London: T. Fisher Unwin, 1923. 3d rev. ed. Adyar, Madras, India: Theosophical Publishing House, 1962.

El Morya [through Mark L. Prophet]. *Light From Heavenly Lanterns.* Colorado Springs, Colo.: Summit Lighthouse, 1973.

———. [through Mark L. Prophet and Elizabeth Clare Prophet]. *Morya the Darjeeling Masters Speaks to His Chelas on the Quest for the Holy Grail.* Los Angeles: Summit University, 1973.

Papish, Mary, and Daniel Papish. *We Are Servants of Master M.* Ojai, Calif.: Hanuman Publications, 1973.

Ransom, Josephine. *A Short History of the Theosophical Society.* Adyar, Madras, India: Theosophical Publishing House, 1938.

[Roerich, Helena]. *Leaves of Morya's Garden.* Reprint, New York: Agni Yoga Press, 1952–53.

Moses, William Stainton (1839–1892)

Medium and religious teacher who became one of the most prominent late nineteenth-century British Spiritualists. He was born November 5, 1839, at Donnington, Lincolnshire. His father was headmaster of the Grammar School of Donnington. In 1852, the family moved to Bedford to give young William the advantage of an education at Bedford College. In his school days he occasionally walked in his sleep, and on one occasion in this state he went down to the sitting room, wrote an essay on a subject that had worried him on the previous evening, and then returned to bed without waking. It was the best essay of the class. No other incidents of a psychic nature of his early years were recorded.

He won a scholarship to Exeter College, Oxford. Owing to a breakdown in his health he interrupted his studies, traveled for some time, and spent six months in a monastery on Mount Athos. When he recovered his health he returned to Oxford, took his M.A., and was ordained as a minister of the Church of England by the renowned Bishop Wilberforce. He began his ministry at Kirk Maughold, near Ramsey, in the Isle of Man, at age 24. There he gained the esteem and love of his parishioners. He was remembered for his activity during an outbreak of smallpox, when he helped to nurse and bury a man whose malady was so violent that it was very difficult to find anybody who would approach him.

His literary activity for *Punch* and the *Saturday Review* began at this time. After four years, he exchanged his curacy with that of St. George's, Douglas, Isle of Man. In 1869 he fell seriously ill. He called in for medical aid Stanhope Templeman Speer. As a convalescent he spent some time in Speer's house. This was the beginning of a lifelong friendship.

In 1870, he took a curacy in Dorsetshire. Illness again interfered with his parish work and he was obliged to abandon it, and for the next seven years he was the tutor of Speer's son. In 1871, he was offered a mastership in University College School, London. This office he filled until 1889, when failing health made him resign. He lived for three more years, suffering greatly from gout, influenza, and nervous prostration. He died September 5, 1892.

Moses as a Spiritualist

The period of his life between 1872 and 1881 was marked by an inflow of transcendental powers and a consequent religious revolution that led him away from the Church of England and his former distrust of **Spiritualism.** He had considered all its phenomena spurious and had dismissed **Lord Adare**'s book on **D. D. Home** as the dreariest twaddle he ever came across. **Robert Dale Owen**'s *Debatable Land* (1870) made a deeper impression.

On Mrs. Speer's persuasion, he agreed to have a closer look into the matter and attended his first **séance,** with **Lottie Fowler** operating as the medium, on April 2, 1872. After much nonsense he received a striking description of the spirit presence of a friend who had died in the north of England. **Charles Williams** was the next medium he went to see. A séance with D. D. Home and sittings in many private circles followed. Within about six months, Moses became convinced of the existence of discarnate spirits and of their power to communicate. Soon he himself showed signs of great psychic powers. In 1872, five months after his introduction to Spiritualism, he reported his first experience of **levitation.**

The physical phenomena continued with gradually lessening frequency until 1881. They were of extremely varied nature. The power was often so enormous that it kept the room in constant vibration. **E. W. Cox** describes in his book *What am I?* (2 vols., 1873–74) the swaying and rocking in daylight of an old-fashioned, six-foot-wide and nine-foot-long mahogany table that required the strength of two strong men to be moved an inch. The presence of Moses seemed to be responsible for the table's extraordinary behavior. When Cox and Moses held their hands over the table, it lifted first on one then on the other side. When Moses was levitated for the third time, he was thrown on to the table, and from that position on to an adjacent sofa. In spite of the considerable distance and the magnitude of the force, he was in no way hurt.

Objects left in Moses' bedroom were often found arranged in the shape of a cross. **Apports** were frequent phenomena. They were usually objects from a different part of the house, invariably small, coming mysteriously through closed doors or walls and thrown upon the table from a direction mostly over Moses' head. Sometimes their origin was unknown. Ivory crosses, corals, pearls, precious stones, the latter expressly for Moses, were also brought from unknown sources.

Psychic lights of greatly varying shapes and intensity were frequently observed. They were most striking when the medium was in trance. They were not always equally seen by all the sitters, never lit up their surroundings, and could pass through solid objects, for instance, rising from the floor through a table. Scents were produced in abundance, the most common being musk, verbena, new mown hay, and one unfamiliar odor, which was said to be spirit scent. Sometimes breezes heavy with perfumes swept around the circle.

Without any musical instruments in the room, a great variety of musical sounds contributed to the entertainment of the sitters. There were many instances of **direct writing,** demonstrations of **matter passing through matter** and **direct voice,** and **materializations,** which, however, did not progress beyond luminous hands or columns of light vaguely suggesting human forms.

Moses' continuing circle was very small. Dr. and Mrs. Speer and F. W. Percival were generally the only witnesses of the phenomena. Sergeant Cox, W. H. Harrison, a Dr. Thompson, a Mrs. Garratt, a Miss Birkett, and **Sir William Crookes** were occasional sitters. As a rule, the invisible communicators strongly resented the introduction of strangers. The physical phenomena in themselves were of secondary importance. They were produced in evidence of the supernormal power of the communicators to convince Moses and the sitters of the spirits' claims.

Writing in the *Proceedings* of the Society for Psychical Research (vol. 9, pt. 25), **F. W. H. Myers** asserts that:

". . . they were not produced fraudulently by Dr. Speer or other sitters. . . . I regard as proved both by moral considerations and by the fact that they were constantly reported as occurring when Mr. Moses was alone. That Mr. Moses should have himself fraudulently produced them I regard as both morally and physically incredible. That he should have prepared and produced them in a state of trance I regard both as physically incredible and also as entirely inconsistent with the tenor both of his own reports and those of his friends. I therefore regard the reported phenomena as having actually occurred in a genuinely supernormal manner."

Moses' character and integrity were so well attested that **Andrew Lang** was forced to warn the advocates of **fraud** that "the choice is between a moral and physical miracle." **Frank Podmore** was almost the only critic to charge Moses with trickery. He suggested that the psychic lights at the séances could have been produced by bottles of phosphorized oil and quoted a report by Moses himself in the *Proceedings* of the SPR (vol. 11, p. 45) stating: "Suddenly there arose from below me, apparently under the table, or near the floor, right under my nose, a cloud of luminous smoke, just like phosphorous. . ." It seems most improbable that the medium would write such a report if guilty of fraud, and even Podmore himself concluded: "That Stainton Moses, being apparently of sane mind, should deliberately have entered upon a course of systematic and cunningly concerted trickery, for the mere pleasure of mystifying a small circle of friends, or in the hope of any petty personal advantage, such, for instance, as might be found in the enhanced social importance attaching to a position midway between prestidigator and prophet—this is scarcely credible."

Moses' famous automatic scripts are known from his books *Spirit Teachings* (1883) and *Spirit Identity* (1879) and from the full séance accounts he commenced to publish in *Light* in 1892. The scripts began in 1872 and lasted until 1883, gradually dying out in 1877. They filled 24 notebooks. Except for the third, which was lost, they were preserved by the **London Spiritualist Alliance,** where both the originals and typed copies were accessible to students. They have been complemented by four books of records of physical phenomena and three books of retrospect and summary. In his will Moses entrusted the manuscripts to two friends—C. C. Massey and Alaric A. Watts. They handed them to F. W. H. Myers, who published an exhaustive analysis in the *Proceedings* of the SPR (vols. 9 and 11).

The automatic messages were almost wholly written by Moses's own hand while he was in a normal waking state. They are interspersed with a few words of direct writing. The tone of the spirits towards him is habitually courteous and respectful. But occasionally they have some criticism that pierces to the quick. This explains why he was unwilling to allow the inspection of his books during his lifetime. Indeed, there are indications that there may have been a still more private book into which very intimate messages were entered, but if so it did not survive.

Moses' Controls

The scripts are in the form of a dialogue. The identity of the communicators was not revealed by Moses in his lifetime. Neither did Myers disclose it. They were made public in a later book *The "Controls" of Stainton Moses* by A. W. Trethewy. Considering the illustrious biblical and historical names the communicators bore, Stainton Moses's reluctance was wise. He would have met with scorn. Moreover, for a long time, he himself was skeptical, indeed, at first shocked, and was often reproved for suspicion and want of faith in the scripts.

Moses emerged as the medium for an organized band of 49 spirits. Their leader called himself "Imperator." For some time he manifested through an amanuensis only, and later wrote himself, signing his name with a cross. He spoke directly for the first time on December 19, 1892, but appeared to Moses's clairvoyant vision at an early stage. He claimed to have influenced the medium's career during the whole of his lifetime and said that in turn he was directed by "Preceptor" in the background. "Preceptor" himself communed with "Jesus."

The identity of the communicators was only gradually disclosed and Moses was much exercised as to whether the personalities of the band were symbolical or real. They asserted that a missionary effort to uplift the human race was being made in the spirit realms and, as Moses had the rarest mediumistic gifts and his personality furnished extraordinary opportunities, he was selected as the channel of these communications. Like "Imperator" and "Preceptor" every member of the band had an assumed name at first. The biblical characters included the following names, as revealed later: "Malachias" (Imperator), "Elijah" (Preceptor), "Haggai" (The Prophet), "Daniel" (Vates), "Ezekiel," "St. John the Baptist" (Theologus). The ancient philosophers and sages numbered 14. They were: "Solon," "Plato," "Aristotle," "Seneca," "Athenodorus" (Doctor), "Hippolytus" (Rector), "Plotinus" (Prudens), "Alexander Achillini" (Philosophus), "Algazzali or Ghazali" (Mentor), "Kabbila," "Chom," "Said," "Roophal," "Magus."

It was not until Book XIV of the communications was written that Moses became satisfied of the identity of his controls. In his introduction to *Spirit Teachings* he writes:

"The name of God was always written in capitals, and slowly and, as it seemed, reverentially. The subject matter was always of a pure and elevated character, much of it being of personal application, intended for my own guidance and direction. I may say that throughout the whole of these written communications, extending in unbroken continuity to the year 1880, there is no flippant message, no attempt at jest, no vulgarity or incongruity, no false or misleading statement, so far as I know or could discover; nothing incompatible with the avowed object, again and again repeated, of instruction, enlightenment and guidance by spirits fitted for the task. Judged as I should wish to be judged myself, they were what they pretended to be. Their words were words of sincerity and of sober, serious purpose."

Later, when the phenomena lost strength he was again assailed by doubts and showed hesitation. It is obviously impossible to prove the identity of ancient spirits. "Imperator's" answer to this objection was that statements incapable of proof should be accepted as true on the ground that others that could be tested had been verified. For such evidential purposes many modern spirits were admitted for communication. In several cases satisfactory proofs of identity were obtained. "Imperator's" statement was therefore logical. It should also be noted that each of the communicators had his distinctive way of announcing his presence.

Moses was also well aware of the possible role his own mind might play in the communications, and observed:

"It is an interesting subject for speculation whether my own thoughts entered into the subject matter of the communications. I took extraordinary pains to prevent any such admixture. At first the writing was slow, and it was necessary for me to follow it with my eye, but even then the thoughts were not my thoughts. Very soon the messages assumed a character of which I had no doubt whatever that the thought was opposed to my own. But I cultivated the power of occupying my mind with other things during the time that the writing was going on, and was able to read an abstruse book and follow out a line of close reasoning while the message was written with unbroken regularity. Messages so written extended over many pages, and in their course there is no correction, no fault in composition and often a sustained vigour and beauty of style."

These precautions do not exclude the possibility of the action of the subconscious mind.

Moses' life and activity left a deep impression on Spiritualism. He took a leading part in several organizations. From 1884 until his death he was president of the London Spiritualist Alliance. The phenomena reported in his mediumship served as a partial inducement for the founding of the **Society for Psychical Research.** He was on its foundation council. Later, owing to the treatment the medium **William Eglinton** received (he was accused of fraud), Moses resigned his membership and censured the society for what he considered its unduly critical attitude.

He edited *Light,* contributed many articles on Spiritualism to *Human Nature* and other periodicals, and published a number of books, primarily developed from his automatic writings, under the pen name of "M. A. Oxon," a reference to his degree from Oxford.

Sources:

Berger, Arthur S., and Joyce Berger. *The Encyclopedia of Parapsychology and Psychical Research.* New York: Paragon House, 1991.

Gauld, Alan. *The Founder of Psychical Research.* New York: Schrocken Books, 1968.

Oxon, M. A. [Stainton Moses]. *Higher Aspects of Spiritualism.* N.p., 1880.

———. *Psychography; or, A Treatise on the Objective Forms of Psychic or Spiritual Phenomena.* N.p., 1878. Reprinted as *Direct Spirit Writing.* N.p., 1952.

Moss, Thelma (1918–1997)

Contemporary parapsychologist and medical psychologist at the Neuropsychiatric Institute of the University of California in Los Angeles. Her special interests have included **telepathy,** radiation, Kirlian photography, energy fields, and skin vision, which is akin to **eyeless sight.**

Moss was a professional actress who left the stage after her husband's death. An experience with psychedelic **drugs** in the 1960s led her into psychology, and after receiving her doctorate she joined the staff at UCLA. The psychedelic experience also opened her to parapsychological insights and she began to experiment. In one early experiment in the relationship of creativity and psychic ability, she found artists were scoring higher in **ESP** ability than her control group.

She visited the USSR to investigate Kirlian photography and experimented in the field with a modified high-energy photography system, until it proved a dead end as controls were tightened. She also investigated a **haunted house** in Los Angeles with Gertrude Schmeidler. Moss died February 1, 1997.

Sources:

Berger, Arthur S., and Joyce Berger. *The Encyclopedia of Parapsychology and Psychical Research.* New York: Paragon House, 1991.

"Interview: Thelma S. Moss." *Psychic* 1, no. 1 (1970).

Moss, Thelma. *The Body Electric.* New York: Jeremy P. Tarcher Inc., 1979.

———. "ESP Effects in 'Artists' Contrasted with Non-Artists." *Journal of Parapsychology* 33 (1969).

———. *The Probability of the Impossible.* New York: Dutton/Plume, 1975.

The Moss-Woman

According to German folklore, one of the moss or wood folk who dwelled in the forests of Bavaria, in southern **Germany.** Their stature was small and their form strange and uncouth, bearing a strong resemblance to certain trees. They were a simple, timid, and inoffensive race, and had little intercourse with humankind, approaching only at rare intervals the lonely cabin of the woodsman or forester to borrow some article of domestic use or to beg a little of the food being prepared for the family meal. They would also, for similar purposes, appear to laborers in the fields that lay on the outskirts of the forests. A loan or gift to the moss-people was always repaid manifold.

But the most highly-prized and eagerly-coveted of all mortal gifts was a draught from the maternal breast for their own little ones; for this the moss-people held to be a sovereign remedy for all the ills to which their natures were subject. Yet it was only in the extremity of danger that they could so overcome their natural diffidence and timidity as to ask this boon—for they knew that mortal mothers turned from such nurslings with disgust and fear.

It would appear that the moss or wood folk also lived in some parts of **Scandinavia.** Thus it was believed that in the churchyard of Store Hedding, in Zealand, there were remains of oaks that were trees by day and warriors by night.

Sources:

Arrowsmith, Nancy, and George Moorse. *A Field Guide to the Little People.* New York: Wallaby, 1977.

Mothman

Winged humanoid creature reported in West Virginia from November 1966 to December 1967, along with strange lights, apparitions of **men in black,** and other **occult** phenomena supposedly connected with **UFOs.** These phenomena culminated on December 15, 1967, with the collapse of the Silver Bridge across the Ohio River at Point Pleasant. The name "Mothman" was the inspiration of a newspaper editor, who derived it from the Batman comic book hero, then the subject of a popular television series.

In his book *The Mothman Prophecies: An Investigation Into the Mysterious American Visits of the Infamous Feathery Garuda* (1975), author **John A. Keel** suggests that these and other occult appearances might be the work of evil entities. The term "garuda" derives from ancient Hindu mythology, where Garuda is king of the birds, half-man, half-bird, the vehicle of the god Vishnu. In the religious epic the *Ramayana,* Jatayu is the son of Vishnu's Garuda, and dies fighting against the demon Ravana in an attempt to prevent the abduction of the princess Sita.

In February 1976, three schoolteachers in Texas reported sightings of a "Big Bird," discussed in *Grey Barker's Newsletter* (no. 7, March 1977). An earlier issue of the newsletter (no. 5, March 1976) had reported a more bizarre claimed abductee experience with "Vegetable Man," pictured as a triffid-style animated tree.

UFO authority **Jacques Vallee** compared Mothman and similar apparitions to **Springheeled Jack,** the legendary creature of early nineteenth-century Britain, who attacked travelers and terrified women with his giant leaps and diabolical appearance. Mothman was said to chase motorists and to frighten women. Witnesses stated that he was large, gray in color, without feathers, and with eyes that glowed red. It has been suggested that Mothman is a UFO phenomenon.

Sources:

Clark, Jerome. *Encyclopedia of Strange and Unexplained Phenomena.* Detroit: Gale Research, 1993.

Haining, Peter. *The Legend and Bizarre Crimes of Springheeled Jack.* London: Frederick Muller, 1977.

Keel, John A. *The Mothman Prophecies: An Investigation Into the Mysterious American Visits of the Infamous Feathery Garuda.* New York: Saturday Review Press/Dutton, 1975. Reprint, New York: New American Library, 1976. Reprinted as *Visitors From Space: The Astonishing True Story of the Mothman Prophecies.* St. Albans, England: Panther, 1976.

Mott, George Edward (1935–)

Naval officer who has also experimented in the field of **parapsychology.** He was born on December 3, 1935, at Virginia Beach, Virginia. He studied at Duke University (B.S., electrical engineering, 1958) and joined the U.S. Navy as a lieutenant following his graduation. While at Duke University he assisted **W. C. Stewart** and J. E. Jenkins in developing and testing devices to investigate **extrasensory perception.** He is an associate member of the **Parapsychological Association.**

Sources:

Pleasants, Helene, ed. *Biographical Dictionary of Parapsychology.* New York: Helix Press, 1964.

Stewart, W. C. "Three New ESP Test Machines and Some Preliminary Results." *Journal of Parapsychology* (March 1959).

Mount Shasta See Shasta, Mount

The Mountain Cove Community

A Spiritualist community founded in Mountain Cove, Fayette County, Virginia, in the autumn of 1851 under the leadership of the Rev. James Scott and Rev. **Thomas Lake Harris.** Both were **mediums** who had settled in Auburn the previous year and had obtained a considerable following. While Harris was absent in New York the command to form a community at Mountain Cove was given through the mediumship of Scott, and about a hundred persons accompanied him to Virginia.

Again at the command of the spirits, the members were obliged to deliver up all their possessions. Dissensions soon arose as pecuniary difficulties were experienced, and only Harris's return in the summer of 1852 saved the community from immediate dissolution. However, the dissensions and difficulties remained, and early in 1853 the community finally broke up. (See also **Apostolic Circle**)

Sources:

Noyes, John Humphrey. *Strange Cults and Utopias of 19th-century America.* New York: Dover Publications, 1966.

The Mountain Path (Journal)

Quarterly journal founded in January 1964 dealing with the life and teachings of **Sri Ramana Maharshi** (1879–1950), celebrated Hindu saint credited with many miracles. Address: The Bookstore, Sri Ramanasramam, Tiruvannamalai 606-603, Tamil Nadu, India. Selected articles are available online at http://www.ramana-maharshi.org/.

Sources:

Sri Ramanasramam. http://www.ramana-maharshi.org/. March 8, 2000.

Mourning Star

Mourning Star is an independent Satanist magazine that first appeared in 1997 and superseded *A Taste from the Cauldron,* the magazine of the First Occult Church. *Mourning Star,* like its predecessor, is edited by **William "Starets" Gidney**

(1972–). In the early 1990s Gidney and his wife, Lady Ygraine, operated the First Occult Church, which included in its membership a range of occult perspectives from **Wicca** to **voudou** that were in fellowship with the Satanism of the leaders. In the mid-1970s, the First Occult Church was closed and both Gidney and Lady Ygraine affiliated with the **Church of Satan.** Lady Ygraine, who had previously operated two occult shops, The Cauldron and The Dragon's Lair, also founded a new store dedicated to the left-hand path, Pandora's Box, in Port St. Lucie, Florida. In 1999, in the wake of the Church of Satan's reestablishment of grottos as local church centers, Gidney led in the founding of the Nepotism Grotto and now serves as the grotto master.

Mourning Star is designed as the expression of a maturing Satanic philosophy in the tradition of **Anton Sandor LaVey,** the founder of the Church of Satan. Each issue contains articles, poems, reviews, and additional varied material. All articles must at the least show the author's familiarity with the principles and idea of *The Satanic Bible,* the basic text of the Church of Satan.

While representative of opinions within the Church of Satan, *Mourning Star* is not an official church publication. It is issued irregularly and while each issue is numbered, it is undated. *Mourning Star* is published at Pandora's Box, 321 SE Port Saint Lucie Blvd., Port Saint Lucie, FL 34984.

Sources:

Mourning Star. Port Lucie, Fla., n.d.

Movement (Paranormal)

Paranormal movement has been given various names, among them, *parakinesis,* which refers to movement with some contact but not enough to explain the motion. Movement without perceptible contact is called **telekinesis.** It was a frequently reported séance-room phenomenon during the first century of **Spiritualism.** Telekinesis, in its apparent simplicity, is the most important, and Spiritualists have hypothesized that an invisible intelligence performs complicated operations and exercises a directive influence over mysteriously generated and frequently tremendous forces. Popularly called "mind over matter," the generally accepted modern term for paranormal movement is **psychokinesis** or "PK." This term includes the claimed phenomenon of paranormal **metal bending.**

In the heyday of psychical research, through the 1930s, physical phenomena in the **séance** was a major focus. It was among the most controversial of phenomena, the object of severe debate, resolved only after numerous mediums were caught in **fraud** and the mechanics of that fraud delineated in detail. Such fraud centered upon the production of **materializations** but included **apports** and various extraordinary movements. PK continues as an element of parapsychology and the reported production of such has periodically excited researchers. However, the continued discovery of fraudulent activity by individuals claiming psychic abilities requires constant vigilance, as the 1984 confession of prominent Japanese metal bender **Masuaki Kiyota** to trickery amply demonstrated. The presence of fraud (widespread in Spiritualism) by no means explains physical phenomena, but, it raises the standards any phenomena must pass before it moves from the status of séance-room folklore to established fact.

Shaking of the House

In its initial stage in the séance room, physical movement phenomena commonly begin with the vibration of objects by the sitters; the séance table, upon which sitters have placed their hands, begins to tremble, shake, or jerk. This motion is not always restricted to the table; it may spread over the entire room.

P. P. Alexander, in *Spiritualism: A Narrative with a Discussion* (1871), writes of a séance with the medium **D. D. Home** in Edinburgh: "The first hint or foreshine we had of the phenomena came in the form of certain tremors which began to pervade the apartment. These were of a somewhat peculiar kind; and they gradually increased till they became of considerable violence. Not only did the floor tremble, but the chair of each person, as distinct from it, was felt to rock and—as we Scots say—dirl under him."

Rev. Maurice Davies in the *Daily Telegraph* and a Dr. Gully in the *Morning Star* describe the trembling of the floor during Home's levitation as reminding them of an earthquake. In a similar record, Lord Adare, author of *Experiences in Spiritualism with D. D. Home* (1870), states: "We soon felt violent vibration of the floor, chairs and table—so violent that the glass pendants of the chandelier struck together, and the windows and doors shook and rattled in their frames not only in our room but also in the next."

Such phenomena, not limited to Spiritualism, can, for example, be found scattered through religious literature, such as the incident reported in the journal of George Fox, the Quaker founder: "At Mansfield, where was a great meeting, I was moved to pray, and the Lord's power was so great that the house seemed to be shaken. When I had done, some of the professors said, it was now as in the days of the Apostles, when the house was shaken where they were."

The **levitation** of John Lacy, as described in *Warnings of the Eternal Spirit* (part 2, 1707), made the chamber shake. The Wesley family, during physical manifestations known collectively as the **Epworth phenomena,** heard vast rumblings and clattering of doors and shutters.

Felicia Scatcherd writes of a séance with **Etta Wriedt** in *Light* (August 3, 1912): "We all felt the floor, walls and windows vibrating. I have twice experienced earthquake shocks in the Ionian Islands. The sensation was similar." In the case of **Mary Jobson,** "a rumbling noise was heard like thunder, the tenants downstairs thought that the house was coming down." An excess of power held the room in which **William Stainton Moses** sat in séance in constant vibration. Gambier Bolton writes in *Psychic Force* (1904):

"On several occasions when sitting in my own room with Mr. Cecil Husk, the whole place, floor, walls, and ceiling, have commenced to tremble and vibrate strongly, table and chairs all responding, and glass, china and pictures swaying to and fro, some of the lighter articles eventually falling over; the motion being similar to that experienced when the screw of a steamer, during a gale of wind, and owing to the pitching of the vessel, comes nearly or quite to the surface of the water, and 'races'; or like the tremble of the earthquake which, as I know by experience, when once felt is never forgotten again. So decided was this tremble and vibration that several of the experimenters present not only stated that it made them feel very ill, but their appearance proved to anyone used to ocean travel, that this was not an exaggeration."

Movement of Objects

The telekinetic phenomenon reported from the séance room is varied: a séance curtain sways and bulges out; a table moves, slides or rotates; weights are lifted; small objects stir, jump into the air, and drop slowly or heavily. According to reports, such objects do not follow straight lines but move in curves, as if under the influence of an intelligent mechanical force. Their speed is sometimes alarming. They may come within an inch of some one's face, then suddenly stop. There is no fumbling, no exploration, no accidental collision. If one puts out his hand in the dark for the reception of an object it neatly drops into his palm. The sitters may change seats or posture, yet the objects will seek them out perfectly. The invisible manipulator behind the phenomena seems to have cat's eyes. A table may incline at a considerable angle, yet the objects may remain unmoved on the leaf or they may glide up the slope. A switch may be thrown, gas or electricity turned off, the flame of a candle depressed, cords and handkerchiefs knotted, bonds untied.

Much of the reported phenomena occurred in a darkened séance room. Sitters also reported evidence of the operation of "invisible" hands, whose presence was often felt through touches; frequently the disembodied hands were said to have been seen in operation. The very nature of the reports suggest that much of the phenomena was produced by the mediums and their accomplices.

Lord Adare saw, in a séance with D. D. Home, a hand stretch over the jet of gas. At the same moment eight jets of gas went out in the house. Psychical researcher **Hereward Carrington** wrote of the Naples séances with **Eusapia Palladino:**

"In one of our séances, a white hand appeared, remained visible to all, and untied both Eusapia's hands and one of her feet.

"Once a gentleman seated to the left of Eusapia had his cigar case extracted from his pocket, placed on the table in full view of all of us, opened, a cigar extracted, and placed between his teeth."

Sir William Crookes in his *Researches in the Phenomena of Spiritualism* (1874), gives a good description of the average type of telekinetic phenomena:

"The instances in which heavy bodies, such as tables, chairs, sofas, etc., have been moved, when the medium was not touching them are very numerous. I will briefly mention a few of the most striking. My own chair has been twisted partly around, whilst my feet were off the floor. A chair was seen by all present to move slowly up to the table from a far corner, when all were watching it; on another occasion an armchair moved to where we were sitting, and then moved slowly back again (a distance of about three feet) at my request. On three successive evenings, a small table moved slowly across the room, under conditions which I had specially pre-arranged, so as to answer any objection which might be raised to the evidence. I have had several repetitions of the experiment considered by the Committee of the Dialectical Society to be conclusive, viz., the movement of a heavy table in full light, the chairs turned with their backs to the table, about a foot off, and each person kneeling on his chair, with hands resting over the backs of the chairs, but not touching the table. On one occasion this took place when I was moving about so as to see how everyone was placed."

Julien Ochorowitz recorded some very curious telekinetic phenomena in his experiments with **Stanislawa Tomczyk.** In good light, before a commission composed of physicians, physiologists, and engineers, the medium placed her hands at a small distance on either side of an object. Between her extended fingers, the object rose into the air and floated without apparent support. In fact, the support appeared to be a threadlike, nonmaterial line of force of which Ochorowitz stated,

"I have felt this thread in my hand, on my face, on my hair. When the medium separates her hands the thread gets thinner and disappears; it gives the same sensation as a spider's web. If it is cut with scissors its continuity is immediately restored. It seems to be formed of points; it can be photographed and it is then seen to be much thinner than an ordinary thread. It starts from the fingers. Needless to remark that the hands of the medium were very carefully examined before every experiment."

When these photographs were projected enlarged upon a screen, the psychic structure became visible. There were swellings and nodes along it, like the waves in a vibrating cord. A whole number of filaments surrounded, like a net, a ball that Tomczyk lifted.

With Eusapia Palladino, a marked synchronism was noticed between her movements and that of the objects. She could attract and remove pieces of furniture, cause them to rise into the air or drop to the floor by a corresponding motion of her hands. However, this was an exceptional phenomenon at her séances. Usually mediums profess an inability to account for the movement of objects because they do not know in advance what is going to happen.

In the cases of both **poltergeists** and **apparitions,** spontaneous telekinetic phenomena have been witnessed. **Joseph Maxwell** obtained good phenomena with nonprofessional mediums in public restaurants in daylight. A Miss Cleio made pictures swing out on the wall in the rooms of the Hellenic Society for Psychical Research in full light before dozens of invited guests.

Difficult Operations

The effect of these telekinetic manifestations is often a very complicated one. Pistols were fired in the dark séances of the **Davenport brothers** against a minute mark which was always hit with marvelous precision. The same phenomenon was witnessed earlier in the house of **Jonathan Koons,** under the control of "John King."

In the presence of the Davenport brothers, a billiard room at Milwaukee was darkened. After a few moments the balls were heard to roll and click against each other as if propelled by expert players. The cues moved, the game appeared to be regularly played, and it was marked and counted. The Davenports did not claim to be Spiritualist mediums, however, and are now generally regarded, as is Koons, as clever stage performers.

In the séances of the **Bangs sisters,** the typewriter was held in the hands of the sitters above the table and was heard operating in rapid motion. The operators also inserted paper, addressed the envelopes, and sealed them. The *Posthumous Memoirs* of **Helena Petrovna Blavatsky** (1896) is claimed to have been produced by this technical means. The machine, according to J. M. Wade's introduction, typed nine paper sheets per hour.

Of a sitting with **Franek Kluski** on November 23, 1919, the Polish Society for Psychical Research recorded: "The typewriter on the table, fully illuminated by the red light, began to write. The sitters remarked that it wrote very quickly, the keys being depressed as if by a skilful typist. There was no one near the machine. The persons holding Mr. Kluski's hands noticed that they twitched during the writing."

In Tullio Castellani's record of a sitting on July 6, 1927, in **Millesimo Castle,** there is a description of an artistic exhibition:

"After a little while we heard in perfect rhythm with the music, a dance of two drumsticks upon the floor. Then the rhythm of the drumsticks was heard in the air. On being questioned Cristo d'Angelo described it as the dance of a celebrated American negro upon the ground and in the air. The same phenomena occurred later in the presence of Bozzano, and has been described by him. I think, however, it is useful to emphasize so that the reader may form some idea of how these phenomena took place, and the effect which this dance produced on me also, habituated though I am to spiritistic phenomenology. The dance took place upon the rug but the resonance was like that of wooden drumsticks which were dancing in the void. There was observable all the weight of a normal man dancing with vigour. Thus in the dark, by only the slight spectral light of the phosphorescence from the trumpet, one is reminded of a *dance macabre.*"

Many are the mediums in whose presence musical instruments were played by invisible hands (see **Music**). Other forms of artistic expression through telekinetic movements are on record in independent **direct drawing and painting.**

In volume 14 of the automatic scripts of Stainton Moses there is a description of the carving of two cameo heads by the spirit entities "Mentor" and "Magus." Magus produced his own likeness. Mentor's artistic efforts are thus narrated under the date August 27, 1875:

"A long message was rapped out by Catherine. She said they had brought a shell and were going to cut a cameo. A light was struck, then Dr. and Mrs. S. saw a shell in the middle of the table. Then Mentor came and Imperator. After he left light was called for and in the centre of the table was a cameo and a quantity of debris of shell. Noises had been heard as of picking, and I saw a hand. The shell is more clearly cut than the first, and shows a head laurel-crowned. It is polished inside and shows plain marks of the graving tool."

According to a letter from Moses' unpublished correspondence (*Light,* May, 1902), "Owasso," one of **Henry Slade**'s controls, extracted, without actual pain, a bad tooth of his suffering medium. A reader of *Light* related in the following issue a similar incident, in the presence of several witnesses, in the history of the medium **Miss C. E. Wood.**

The Question of Scientific Verification

Levitation of a table in the full blaze of sunshine was witnessed by **Charles Richet** in front of his Chateau de Carqueiranne with the medium Eusapia Palladino. Again, Ochorowitz, working with Tomczyk, saw a garden chair raised in full light.

An ancient instance of table levitation is described in Samuel Brent's *Judischer agestreifter Schlangen Balg* (1610), and in Zalman Zebi's reply, *Judischer Theriak* 1615). Zebi admits the levitation but argues that it was not caused by magic since "beautiful hymns are sung during the production of the phenomena and no devil is able to approach us when we think of the Lord."

Count Gasparin, **Baron Guldenstubbe, Marc Thury, Robert Hare,** and **James J. Mapes** were the first investigators of table turning. Hare devised special scientific instruments. William Crookes repeated his experiments and improved upon them.

Experiments with an electric bell in a locked and sealed box were successfully carried out with the mediumship of **William Eglinton** by the research committee of the **British National Association of Spiritualists** in January 1878. The bell sounded twice and the armature was depressed with so much force that a spring was strained and an electromagnet disarranged.

Professor **Johann Zöllner**'s famous knot-tying experiments on an **endless cord** were successfully repeated with Eglinton by a Dr. Nichols in his own house. **Mina Crandon** ("Margery") also rivaled Zöllner's experiments by demonstrating the paranormal linking of two rings made of different woods (see **Matter Passing through Matter**).

The "fraudproof" trick table of **Harry Price** was lifted by "Margery" in sittings in London. The telekinetoscope and the shadow apparatus of the same researcher provided some extraordinary phenomena in the presence of **"Stella C."** in the **National Laboratory of Psychical Research.**

The first demand that a **Scientific American** Committee submitted to "Walter," Margery's control, at the time of this well-known investigation was to produce movements inside a closed and sealed space. For this purpose a sealed glass jar with a brass hook projecting down into the bottle was used. Walter was set the task of opening the snap of the hook and hanging upon it the wooden, brass, or cord rings also enclosed in the jar. Two days later the cord ring was found on the hook. A day after its examination by Prof. Daniel F. Comstock, the ring was found removed.

Another experiment with sensitive scales under a celluloid cover produced satisfactory results. With one of the pans weighted and the other empty, Walter held the scales in balance and sent up the weighted pan. This dynamic feat was achieved in good visibility. Similar results were achieved with a bell box, physically operated first by the depression of a key or by throwing a switch, and later (with the instrument revised) by the depression of contact boards. Held in the lap of **Walter Franklin Prince,** Research Officer of the **American Society for Psychical Research** (ASPR), the instrument was operated in daylight.

The voice-cutout machine of Dr. Richardson apparently established the independence of Walter's voice (see *Journal of the American Society for Psychical Research,* vol. 19, no. 12, 1925). Modern psychical research laboratories may boast of a number of other instruments that detect or prevent the slightest movement in the séance room and afford opportunities for observation under strict scientific conditions.

Display of Strength

Occasionally the power that accumulates for telekinetic phenomena is so great that astounding feats of strength are exhibited. At Warsaw, in Ochorowitz's experiments, a dynamometer marked a force three times as great as Eusapia Palladino's and in excess of that of the strongest man present.

The medium of **Elizabeth d'Esperance** recorded that during a séance in Breslau the strongest man in Silesia, a veritable Hercules, vainly tried to prevent the movements of the table.

Zöllner recorded this incident from a séance with Henry Slade:

"A violent crack was suddenly heard as in the discharging of a large battery of Leyden jars. On turning, with some alarm, in the direction of the sound, the before-mentioned screen fell apart in two pieces. The wooden screws, half an inch thick, were torn from above and below, without any visible contact of Slade with the screen. The parts broken were at least five feet removed from Slade, who had his back to the screen; but even if he had intended to tear it down by a cleverly devised sideward motion, it would have been necessary to fasten it on the opposite side."

Zöllner estimated that the strength of two horses would be necessary to achieve this effect. He mentioned that one of his colleagues seriously suggested that Slade carried dynamite about him, concealed it in the furniture, and exploded it with a match.

In a sitting with **Countess Castelvitch** in Lisbon, a small table, strengthened with sheetiron, was rent into 200 pieces. The fragments were found piled in a corner of the room.

This incident is found in the record of a séance with Eusapia Palladino, in which she was supervised by several Italian researchers:

"Dr. Arullani asked that the hand behind the curtain should grasp his. The medium replied in her own voice: 'First I am going to break the table, then I will give you a grasp of the hand.' This declaration was followed by three fresh, complete levitations of the table, which fell back heavily on the floor. All those who were on the left of the medium could observe, by a very good red light, the various movements of the table. The table bent down and passed behind the curtain, followed by one of us (Dr. C. Foà) who saw it turn over and rest on one of its two short sides, whilst one of the legs came off violently as if under the action of some force pressing upon it. At this moment the table came violently out of the cabinet, and continued to break up under the eyes of everyone present. At first its different parts were torn off, then the boards themselves went to pieces. Two legs, which still remained united by a thin slip of wood, floated above us and placed themselves on the séance table."

The astronomer Porro reported from his séance with Palladino in 1891: "Next a formidable blow, like the stroke of the fist of an athlete is struck in the middle of the table. The blows are now redoubled and are so terrific that it seems as if they would split the table. A single one of these fist blows, planted in the back, would suffice to break the vertebral column."

Moses recorded sledgehammer blows in one instance and stated, "The noise was distinctly audible in the room below and gave one the idea that the table would be broken to pieces. In vain we withdrew from the table, hoping to diminish the power. The heavy blows increased in intensity, and the whole room shook with their force."

From the Livermore séance with **Kate Fox,** February 15, 1862, came these notes: "I asked for a manifestation of power; and we at once received the following message: 'Listen, and hear it come through the air; hands off the table.' Immediately a terrific metallic shock was produced, as though a heavy chain in a bag swung by a strong man had been struck with his whole power upon the table, jarring the whole house. This was repeated three times, with decreasing force."

In slate-writing experiments with Henry Slade, the slates were often pulverized. Paul Gibier reports in *Le Spiritisme* (1887): "At ten different trials the slate held by Slade under the table was broken into several pieces. These slates were framed in very hard wood. We endeavoured to break them in the same way by striking them against the table, but never succeeded even in cracking them."

Writing of a visit to a Shaker village with the mediums Miss King and H. B. Champion, the Reverend **J. B. Ferguson** said of the latter: "Although a man of most delicate physical organisation, he was, to my knowledge, without food for ten days, and during that time seemed to possess the strength of three men, when under direct spiritual influence; but when not he was as feeble as an infant, and needed all the care I had promised."

Lifting of Heavy Tables and Pianos

There was a frequent display of great force in the paranormal lifting of heavy tables or pianos. Sir William Crookes saw on five separate occasions a heavy dining table rise from a few inches and one to a half foot off the floor under special circumstances that rendered trickery impossible (R. G. Medhurst, K. M. Goldney, M. R. Barrington, *Crookes and The Spirit World* [1972], 115).

D. D. Home testified before the committee of the **London Dialectical Society:** "I have seen a table lifted into the air with eight men standing on it, when there were only two or three other persons in the room. I have seen the window open and shut at a distance of seven or eight feet, and curtains drawn aside and, in some cases, objects carried over our heads. In the house of Mr. and Mrs. S. C. Hall a table went up so high in the air that we could not touch it."

At a supper party attended by 30 persons, including **Florence Cook,** the heavy dining table, with everything on it, rose in full light into the air, until the feet of the table were level with the knees of those sitting around it; the dishes, plates, and glasses swayed perilously but came to no harm. (Gambier Bolton, *Psychic Force* 1904) **Florence Marryat** also writes of this incident in her book *There Is No Death* (1891). **Robert Dale Owen** claimed to have seen in Paris, in broad daylight in the dining room of a French nobleman, the dinner table seating seven persons, with fruit and wine on it, rise and settle down, while all the guests stood around without touching it.

In another séance, with **Katie Cook,** a piano was carried over the heads of the sitters. One of the ladies became nervous and broke the chain of hands; the piano dropped to the floor the two carved legs were broken and the sounding board smashed.

The levitation of two pianos in the presence of an 11-year-old child was described as early as 1855 in Marc Thury's *Des Tables Tournantes.* The phenomenon of a levitated piano was witnessed by President **Abraham Lincoln** in 1862.

Mr. Jencken, the husband of Kate Fox, said in a paper read before the London Dialectical Society, "As regards the lifting of heavy bodies, I can myself testify I have seen the semigrand at my house raised horizontally eighteen inches off the ground and kept suspended in space two or three minutes."

The Master of Lindsay, before the same body, said, "I was next to him [D. D. Home]. I had one hand on his chair and the other on the piano, and while he played both his chair and the piano rose about three inches and then settled down again."

Dr. John Ashburner, author of *Notes and Studies in the Philosophy of Animal Magnetism and Spiritualism* (1867), recorded the following personal experience: "Mr. Foster, who is possessed of a fine voice, was accompanying himself while he sang. Both feet were on the pedals, when the pianoforte rose into the air and was gracefully swung in the air from side to side for at least five or six minutes. During this time the castors were about at the height of a foot from the carpet."

Sergeant **E. W. Cox,** in *What am I?* (2 vols., 1873–74), writes: "As Mr. Home and myself were entering the drawing room lighted with gas, a very heavy armchair that was standing by the fire, thirteen feet from us, was flung from its place through the whole length of the room and fell at our feet. No other person was in the room and we were crossing the threshold of the door."

Arthur Lévy writes in his report on Eusapia Palladino, November 16, 1898: "Just as if she was defying some monster, she turns, with inflamed looks, toward an enormous divan, which thereupon marches up to us. She looks at it with a Satanic smile. Finally she blows upon the divan, which goes immediately back to its place" (Camille Flammarion, *Mysterious Psychic Forces,* 1907).

Vanishing Objects

In the reported incidents of apports and human **teleportation,** and frequently in the phenomenon of **matter passing through matter**—still among the most controversial of phenomena—there is often reported an intermediate stage in which the objects in question or the human body apparently disappear. Sometimes nothing further than disappearance and subsequent reappearance is accomplished. How it occurs—if it occurs—is the object of speculation. Some have suggested it is accomplished by a great increase in the vibratory rate of the objects or by **dematerialization.** Instances to demonstrate the claimed phenomenon are abundant.

A small table disappeared from underneath a larger one in Zöllner's séance with Slade. They searched the room without result. Five minutes later it was discovered floating in the air, upside down. It dropped and struck Zöllner on the head. The vanishing and reappearance of a book was similarly observed. It struck Zöllner on the ear in its descent (J. C. F. Zöllner, *Transcendental Physics,* 1882).

The records of Stainton Moses dated November 27, 1892, read:

"As Dr. S. and I were pacing up and down the room a whole shower of Grimauve lozenges (the remainder of the packet out of which the cross had been made on Friday last) was violently thrown on to my head, whence they spread over the floor round about where we were standing. There were thirteen or fourteen of them, and that number, together with the nine used in making the cross, would just about make up the two ounce packet which I had. I had looked in every conceivable place for these lozenges (which were missing after the cross was made) but could find them nowhere."

"Lily," the guide of Katie Cook, asked Florence Marryat whether she could take the fur coat that the authoress had put on her shoulders. She was given permission under the stipulation that she return it when Marryat had to go home. Lily asked that the gas be turned up. The fur coat disappeared. During the course of the séance, the coat was flung, apparently from the ceiling, and fell right over the owner's head. The coat had gone through an ordeal for, although it was quite new, all the fur was coming out and an army of moths could not have damaged it more than "Lily's" trick.

Gladys Osborne Leonard, in her book *My Life in Two Worlds* (1931), tells of a **control** named "Joey," a famous clown in mortal life, who as proof of his power made things belonging to her husband disappear in daylight in the house and reappear days later in exactly the same place. "Yolande," d'Esperance's control, often performed similar feats.

In the presence of **Eleonore Zügun,** objects vanished for an indeterminate period. Her patron the Countess Wassilko-Serecki coined the vivid phrase "holes in the world" to describe the effect (Harry Price, "Some Accounts of the Poltergeist Phenomena of Eleonore Zügun" *Journal of the American Society of Psychical Research,* August 1926).

The disappearance usually involves no injury. In experiments with the medium **Thomas Lynn** at the **British College of Psychic Science,** watches frequently vanished from sight without showing harm or stoppage on their reappearance (*Psychic Science,* vol. 8, no. 2, July 1929). With the Austrian medium **Maria Silbert** it was noticed that she seemed to know intuitively a few minutes beforehand what articles would appear, as if the "cloud of invisibility" that surrounded the objects had been of ectoplasmic nature.

The objects that vanish are not necessarily solids. The invisible operators seem to have the same power over liquids. Lord Adare recorded that brandy was invisibly withdrawn from a glass that the medium D. D. Home held above his head. When Lord Adare held his hands above the glass the liquor fell over and through his fingers into the glass, dropping from the air above him. Home explained that the spirit making the experiment was obliged to form a material substance to retain the fluid.

Dr. Eugene Crowell, author of *The Identity of Primitive Christianity with Modern Spiritualism* (2 vols., 1875–79), took a small vial filled with pure water to a séance with the medium Henry Slade to have it "magnetized." He writes:

"We were seated in a well-lighted room, the rays of the sun falling upon the floor, and no one present but us. Twice the medium said he saw a spirit hand grasping the vial, and I supposed the spirits were magnetising it and kept my eyes directing towards it, but I saw nothing, when suddenly at the same instance we both saw a flash of light apparently proceeding from the vial and the latter disappeared. I immediately arose and inspected every part of the room which from the beginning had been closed, under the table, chairs and sofa, but the vial was not found. Then resuming my seat and questions, in about fifteen minutes, while the two hands of the medium were clasping mine upon the table, I felt something fall into my lap, and looking down I observed the vial rolling off my knees on to the floor. Upon my taking it up we both remarked that the water had acquired a slightly purple tinge, but otherwise its appearance was unchanged."

Max George Albert Bruckner describes in the July 1, 1931, issue of the *Zeitschrift für Metapsychische Forschung,* a sitting with Maria Silbert in which a bottle filled with water and sealed was transferred from the top of the table to the undersides of it. On examination it was found that the water had completely disappeared. The seal and the cord remained intact. Not a drop of water was visible on the floor.

Vice-Admiral Usborne Moore noticed that the ink in his bottle disappeared in a séance with the Bangs sisters (*Glimpses of the Next State,* 1911).

Theories of Explanation

Since the first days of modern Spiritualism, speculation has been rife as to the mechanical agency by which movement without contact takes place. **Animal magnetism** was first thought to furnish a clue. Many theories were formulated. All of them (deriving somewhat from the "**od**" of Baron **Karl von Reichenbach**) were more or less similar to the "odylo-mesomeric" theory of E. C. Rogers. Rogers defined a medium as "a person in whom the conscious and personal control of the higher brain centres was for the moment in abeyance leaving the organism open to be acted upon by the universal cosmic forces."

J. Bovee Dods (*Spirit Manifestations,* 1854) posited an electromagnetic cause. He suggested rapping was caused by "an electro-magnetic discharge from the fingers and toes of the medium." About table tilting he stated that "the millions of pores in the table are filled with electro-magnetism from human brains, which is inconceivably lighter than the gas that inflates the balloon." However, the agency of human magnetism or electricity was quickly disproved when no instrument could detect the slightest trace of electromagnetism and neither the smallest iron filing nor the tiniest pith ball was attracted by the charged table.

More mundane explanations—chance, fraud, **hallucination,** or a composite of these suppositions—fail to account for all reported data. The other extreme—that spirits were responsible for the movement—also explains little. It was a comparatively early claim that the contribution of the spirits was at most a directive influence and that in some mysterious way the bodily organism of the medium played a dominant role.

The spirits themselves reportedly described people who act as physical mediums to **Allan Kardec** in the following words: "These persons draw from themselves the fluid necessary to the production of the phenomena and can act without the help of foreign spirits. Thus they are not mediums in the sense attached to this word; but a spirit can assist them and profit by their natural disposition."

The "fluid" mentioned to Kardec at this early period was later replaced by the "**ectoplasm**" of psychical research. The claimed existence of this substance facilitated the idea of a bridge between **telekinesis** and ordinary mechanics. **W. J. Crawford**'s cantilever theory represented a sophisticated attempt in this direction. It essentially claimed that out of ectoplasmic emanations psychic rods so strong as to become semimetallic are formed; that this extrusion acts as a cantilever; and that the phenomena are produced by an intelligent manipulation on the part of unseen operators of these rods.

In his early observations of the Goligher Circle, Crawford found that if the object to be levitated was heavy, the psychic structure beside the medium's body found support on the floor. He made many exact measurements claiming to discover that the objects were usually gripped in a manner resembling suction. He supposedly proved the presence of the psychic rods by their pressure on a spring balance and measured their reaction on the medium's body with scales. Crawford said he photographed psychic structures. He claimed he noticed that if an object was lifted or glued to the floor, the medium's body showed a nearly equivalent increase or decrease in weight. The difference was distributed among the sitters (W. J. Crawford, *Psychic Structures in The Goligher Circle,* 1921).

Crawford's observations were paralleled by others. German zoologist **Karl Gruber** reported experiments with the medium **Willi Schneider** in 1922:

"A rigid body seemed to emanate from the right hip of the medium. At about three quarters of a yard from the floor it traversed the gauze partition, enlarging some of its interstices, and moved objects 80 to 100 centimetres distant from the medium. It seems that the medium has to make a certain effort to cause this fluidic member to traverse the screen. By using luminous bracelets we have verified that during the levitation of a small table a dark stump like that of a member could be distinguished, that it rose up under the table, raised it, and replaced it on the floor and showed itself afresh underneath it."

The advantage of the cantilever theory is its simplicity. For that very reason it only explained an initial stage of telekinetic phenomena. But the theory has many weaknesses, chiefly the later discovery of the fraudulent production of the phenomena in the circle in which he made all of his initial observations. Also, Crawford's theory does not explain movement without contact in haunted houses or in poltergeist cases, and the levitation of the human body, all of which apparently demand a different theory.

Charles Richet suggested that telekinetic phenomena constitute the first stage of materialization which may be called mechanization. When phantom hands or whole bodies are formed, the presence of a separate dynamic organism is suggested. Such a body would be created at the expense of the medium and the sitters. By calculation Julien Ochorowitz announced the finding that the dynamometric energy which a circle lost corresponded to the average energy of a man.

If the theory of a separate dynamic organism were accepted, it could account for experiences like that reported by Lord Adare:

"[D. D.] Home . . . told me to go into the next room and place outside the window a certain vase of flowers. I did so, putting the vase outside the ledge and shutting the window. Home opened the window of the room in which we were sitting. The flowers were carried through the air from the window of the next room in at our open window. We could all hear the rustling, and see the curtains moved by the spirit standing there, who was bringing in the flowers; Lindsay saw the spirit distinctly."

Many psychical researchers refused to accept Ochorowitz's ideas. They did not like to diminish the medium's physical participation in the occurrences. **Theodore Flournoy** suggested an alternative theory,

"It may be conceived that, as the atom and the molecule are the centre of a more or less radiating influence of extension, so the organised individual, isolated cell, or colony of cells, is originally in possession of a sphere of action, where it concentrates at times its efforts more especially on one point, and again on another, *ad libitum.* Through repetition, habit, selection, heredity and other principles loved by biologists, certain more constant lines of force would be differentiated in this homogeneous, primordial sphere, and little by little could give birth to motor organs. For example: our four members of flesh and blood, sweeping the space around us, would be but a more economic expedient invented by nature, a machine wrought in the course of better adapted evolution, to obtain at the least expense the same use full effects as this vague, primitive spherical power. Thus supplanted or transformed, these powers would thereafter manifest themselves, only very exceptionally, in certain states, or with abnormal individuals, as an atavic reapparition of a mode of acting long ago fallen into disuse, because it is really very imperfect and necessitates, without any advantage, an expenditure of vital energy far greater than the ordinary use of arms and limbs. Unless it is the Cosmic power itself, the amoral and stupid 'demiurge,' the Unconsciousness of M. Hartman, which comes directly into play upon contact with a deranged nervous system and realises its disordered dreams without passing through the regular channels of muscular movements."

Edmund E. Fournier d'Albe, author of several books on psychical phenomena, wondered if living principle of the cells that die could in some way still be attached to us. If so, we would be actually living half in this world and half in the next, he theorized. Could not then telekinesis be explained by a resumed embodiment or materialized activity of the disembodied epidermal cell principles? he asked.

Cesare Lombroso suggested:

"I see nothing inadmissible in the fact that, with hysterical and hypnotic subjects the excitation of certain centres which become active in proportion as all other centres become paralysed, may cause a transposition of psychical forces, and thus also bring about a transformation into luminous force or into motor force. It is thus conceivable how the force of a medium, which I may nominate as cortical or cerebral, might, for instance, raise a table or pull someone's beard, or strike or caress him, phenomena which frequently occur under these circumstances."

Joseph Maxwell verified a correlation between the intensity of the muscular effort and the abnormal movement. The movement could sometimes be provoked by shaking the hand at a certain distance above the table. Rubbing the feet on the floor, rubbing the hands, the back, the arms—any quick or slightly violent movement—appeared to liberate this force. The breath appeared to exercise a great influence, as though in blowing on the object the sitters emitted a quantity of energy.

Maxwell had the impression that, within certain limits, the quantity of force liberated varied in direct proportion with the number of experimenters:

"There is a close and positive connection between the movements effectuated by the medium and the sitters, and the displacement of articles of experimentation; there is a relation between these displacements and the muscular contractions of the experimenters; a probable relation, whose precise nature he is unable to state, exists between the will of the experimenters and paranormal movements" (Joseph Maxwell, *Metapsychical Phenomena,* 1905).

Exteriorization of motricity was postulated in the case of Eusapia Palladino by **Enrico Morselli,** Theodor Flournoy, Gustav Geley, and Hereward Carrington. Essentially the same theory was advanced earlier, in 1875, by Francis Gerry Fairfield in *Ten Years With Spiritual Mediums,* suggesting a nerve aura that surrounds every organic structure, capable of receiving sensory impressions, acting as a force and assuming any desired shape. The nerve aura, however, suggests something different from ectoplasm. It suggests the presence of a third factor, a nervous force to which both the medium and the sitters contribute.

During the levitation of a table in the "Margery" séances on June 23, 1923, the sitters felt cold, tingling sensations in their forearms. Dr. Crandon at the same time observed faint, aurora-like emanations from the region of Margery's fingers.

F. W. H. Myers suggested, as a correlative to telepathic effect, a "telergic action," by which he meant the excitation of the motor and sensory centers of the medium by an external mind. He said that in the case of **possession** the external intelligence may directly act upon the body and liberate unknown energies. This theory goes far, as the external mind appears to dwell in the spiritual world, although it is of frequent observation that the sitters' thoughts exercise a certain influence upon the phenomena.

M. Barzini, journalist for *Corriere della Sera,* wrote about his séances with Palladino in Genoa, 1906–07: "It was obvious that our conversations were listened to, so as to yield a suggestion in the execution of the strange performance. If we spoke of levitation the table would rise up. If we began to discuss luminous phenomena instantly a light would appear upon the medium's knees."

If one considers the world of spirits in the search for the agency in psychokinesis, Baron **Lazar de Baczolay Hellenbach**'s suggestion, from his *Birth and Death as a Change of Form of Perception* (1886) might provide a starting point: "I am convinced that the unseen world has first to learn how to act, so as to make themselves accessible to our senses somewhat in the same way that we have to learn how to swim in water, or communicate with the deaf and dumb."

In the weighing-scale experiments of the *Scientific American* Committee with "Margery," the photograph of a curious, semi-transparent cylinder was obtained (with flashlight and a quartz lens). The cylinder looked as if it was made of glass or celluloid. Seven of twelve exposed plates showed the cylinder. It was five or six inches long and three inches or a little less in diameter and stood on a base. When it was photographed on the scale, the pan that carried it was up; when it was photographed on the platform of the scale, the pans balanced. The deduction was that the cylinder acted as a sort of suction pump to keep the lighter pan up. The control "Walter" said that if the cylinders had been taken under long exposure they would have looked as though filled with cotton wool.

There were also observations to suggest that threads finer than a strand of spider's web, may connect the medium with objects in the room. Elizabeth d'Esperance often complained of a feeling of cobwebs on her face. "Margery" and many of her sitters had the same experience.

With Stanislawa Tomczyk, Ochorowitz photographed a balance that was supernormally depressed by fine, hairlike threads. The method must have been similar when Palladino performed the same feat. In fact the thread was seen as it made a glass of water dance. Slowly and cautiously, a sitter drew the thick, white thread to himself. It resisted, then snapped and disappeared with a nervous shock to the medium.

Ernesto Bozzano observed such threads 20 times in the same year. **Juliette Bisson** detected them with the medium **"Eva C."** Dr. Jorgen Bull, of Oslo, found them instrumental in an invisible state in producing direct writing on wax tablets in the presence of **Lujza Linczegh Ignath.**

In some of the excellent photographs obtained by Dr. **T. Glen Hamilton** with "Mary M." of Winnipeg, slight threads can be seen reaching up to a bell fixed high above the curtain. A similar attachment of threads to "apported" objects was observed in photographs taken by Major Mowbray with the medium Thomas Lynn.

The spirit guide of a Frau Ideler explicitly stated, in the experiments conducted by a Professor Blacher of the University of Riga (*Zeitschrift für Parapsychologie,* October 1931), that she spun threads to accomplish telekinetic movement. In red light and later in blue light these attachments were observed and the medium seemed to pull the threads from the inner side of her hand with her fingertips. The threads seemed to be of a doughy, elastic substance, then pulled fine, and felt soft and dry. Even while being handled they diminished perceptibly. A piece was secured and subjected at once to microscopic examination in an adjoining room. An enlargement of the microscopic photo showed that it was composed not of one strand but of many fine but not organized threads. In its chemical composition the structure was not that of the known textile fabrics. Curiously, fire had no power over these threads. They made the flame withdraw. But they were conductors of electricity. The alleged unusual nature and action of such "psychic threads" makes it necessary to be cautious in hastily assuming fraud with ordinary threads.

If the thread connection with the medium is accepted, it would be easy to understand what the medium subconsciously may feel and could indicate in advance what objects are going to be moved. Such an approach proved useful in Eugen Osty's work with the medium **Rudi Schneider** at the Institut Métapsychique. The experience was also well known to sitters with Maria Silbert.

Modern Experiments in Psychokinesis

The bulk of past observation and theory relating to paranormal movement belongs to a period when physical mediums dominated both Spiritualism and the attention of psychical research. Consideration of such phenomena is influenced by the fact that much of the evidence is purely anecdotal or belongs to a period of psychical research less sophisticated than in modern times. Much of the phenomena upon which researchers speculated is now, like that of the Golicher Circle, considered to have been produced deceptively.

In the modern era of **parapsychology,** movement of objects without contact is now studied experimentally under the general term *psychokinesis* or "PK." Parapsychology has attempted to construct more simple laboratory experiments that to demonstrate psychokinetic effects without the complicating and often questionable environment of the séance room. The first important experimental studies of this kind were initiated by **J. B. Rhine** in 1934 after he had encountered a gambler who claimed that he could influence the fall of dice by willpower.

Rhine, who had been involved in investigation of the controversial "Margery" mediumship, was anxious to find some type of phenomenon that could be studied under the exacting conditions in a laboratory, thus avoiding the endless arguments about fraud and faulty observation involved with spontaneous phenomena. Dice-fall experiments could be controlled, and they were also repeatable and subject to statistical assessment. Rhine and his associates duly set up classic experiments at Duke University in North Carolina in which subjects attempted to influence the fall of dice by willpower.

Over the years other parapsychologists verified the successful scores of Rhine and others. Eventually one of Rhine's associates, W. E. Cox, introduced interesting variations, such as "Placement PK," in which subjects attempted to influence movement of various objects in a target direction.

Another interesting direction in scientific PK tests was the introduction of the Minilab, a glass tank containing various small objects as targets for PK. The Minilab can be sealed and locked, and is monitored by a video camera that is activated by a switching apparatus connected to the objects; thus, object movement is automatically recorded.

The Minilab has been used by parapsychologist J. D. Isaacs, who has investigated the phenomenon of paranormal metal bending, introduced by the Israeli psychic **Uri Geller,** whose feats in bending spoons and keys became world-famous, both stimulating imitators and new experiments, and providing accusations of fraud.

Geller produced phenomena for scientists under laboratory conditions that led many of them to back his claims of being psychic with psychokinetic powers. Some later withdrew their enthusiastic endorsements. In the meantime, critics, like stage magician **James Randi,** denied the possibility of paranormal metal bending. Randi questioned the validity of the laboratory tests partly because of the inability of the scientists to detect stage tricks. He backed up his observations by carrying out an experiment in which he sent two amateur magicians into a parapsychological laboratory. They were able to fool the members of the staff of the McDonnell Laboratory for Psychical Research in St. Louis.

Project Alpha, as Randi termed his experiment, was embarrassing to researchers in parapsychology and called attention to the ongoing need to double-check methodological controls, but it did not speak to the large body of data on psychokinesis accumulated during the last half century.

Sources:

Adare, Viscount. *Experiences in Spiritualism with Mr. D. D. Home.* Privately printed, 1870. Reprint, London: Society for Psychical Research, 1924.

Bird, J. Malcolm. *"Margery" the Medium.* Boston: Small, Maynard, London: John Hamilton, 1925.

Bolton, Gambier. *Psychic Force: An Experimental Investigation.* London, 1904.

Carrington, Hereward. *Eusapia Palladino and Her Phenomena.* New York: B. E. Dodge, London: T. Werner Laurie, 1909.

Crawford, W. J. *Experiments in Psychical Science.* London: John M. Watkins, 1919.

———. *The Psychic Structures at the Goligher Circle.* London: John M. Watkins, 1921.

———. *The Reality of Psychic Phenomena.* London: John M. Watkins, 1916.

Crowell, Eugene. *The Identity of Primitive Christianity and Modern Spiritualism.* New York, 1874.

D'Esperance, Elizabeth. *Shadow Land or Light From the Other Side.* London: George Redway, 1897.

Flammarion, Camille. *Mysterious Psychic Forces.* Boston: Small, Maynard, London: T. Fisher Unwin, 1907.

Forwald, Haakon. *Mind, Matter, and Gravitation: A Theoretical and Experimental Study.* New York: Parapsychology Foundation, 1970.

Hasted, John. *The Metal-Benders.* London: Routledge & Kegan Paul, 1981.

Holms, A. Campbell. *The Facts of Psychic Science and Philosophy Collated and Discussed.* London: Kegan Paul, 1925. New Hyde Park, N.Y.: University Books, 1969.

Leonard, Gladys Osborne. *My Life in Two Worlds.* London: Cassell, 1931.

London Dialectical Society. *Report on Spiritualism of the Committee of the London Dialectical Society.* London: Longmans, Green, 1871.

Marryat, Florence. *There Is No Death.* London, 1891. Reprint, New York: Causeway Books, 1973.

Maxwell, Joseph. *Metapsychical Phenomena.* London: Duckworth, 1905.

Medhurst, R. G., and K. M. Goldney, eds. *Crookes and the Spirit World: A Collection of Writings by or Concerning the Work of Sir William Crookes, O.M., F.R.S., in the Field of Psychical Research.* New York: Taplinger, 1972. Reprint, London: Souvenir Press, 1972.

Panati, Charles, ed. *The Geller Papers: Scientific Observations on the Paranormal Powers of Uri Geller.* Boston: Houghton Mifflin, 1976.

"Psychokinetic Metal-bending." *Psi News,* Bulletin of the Parapsychological Association 4, 1.

Rhine, Louisa E. *Mind Over Matter: Psychokinesis.* New York: Macmillan, 1970.

Rogers, E. C. *Philosophy of Mysterious Agents, Human and Mundane.* Boston, 1853.

Zöllner, J. C. F. *Transcendental Physics: An Account of Experimental Investigations.* London: W. H. Harrison, 1882.

Moyes, Winifred (d. 1957)

The **medium** of the spirit **guide** "Zodiac" for the spreading of whose teachings *The Greater World* paper and the **Greater World Christian Spiritualist League** were founded in 1931. "Zodiac" first manifested at Moyes's home circle in 1921. He claimed to have been a teacher at the Temple in the time of Jesus. His earth name was not disclosed but he said he was the scribe who asked Jesus which was the first commandment and to whom Jesus said: "Thou art not far from the Kingdom of God" (Mark 12:28–34). Although Moyes died in 1957, the work of the League continues in spreading the teachings of "Zodiac."

MUFOB (Metempirical UFO Bulletin) See Magonia

MUFON See Mutual UFO Network

Muktananda, Swami (1908–1982)

A Hindu spiritual teacher who was an exponent of what he termed siddha **yoga,** a variation of **kundalini** characterized by the demand that followers give over the guidance in their spiritual development to their teacher. Muktananda was born May 16, 1908, at Dharmasthala, South India. In 1964 he received his master's degree from Jabalpur University and became a lecturer in Hindi at W. M. Ruia College, India.

In February 1966, he first met Swami Nityananda of Ganeshpuri, who became his guru. Swami Nityananda had the power of *shaktipat,* the imparting of spiritual force through touch, thus arousing the kundalini energy believed to be latent in the human organism at the base of the spine. Through initiation by his guru, Muktananda experienced kundalini and its manifestation in various chakras or psychic centers of the body, accompanied by strange visions and enhanced consciousness. He described his remarkable experiences in his book *Guru* (1971), which were similar to those reported by **Pandit Gopi Krishna.**

Muktananda became spiritual head of Shree Gurudev Ashram at Ganeshpuri, near Bombay, and attracted followers from all over India. He taught a traditional Hindu mystical doctrine of *sadhana* or spiritual discipline, enhanced by his ability to awaken spiritual force in others through *shaktipat.*

He first visited the United States in 1970, and four years later made a triumphal tour in California, where he gave an address to a convention of 500 psychologists and psychotherapists in San Diego. Charles Garfield, clinical psychologist at the University of California, described Muktananda as "a highly developed being."

American ashrams were established across the country and additional followers emerged in Europe after Muktananda's successful visits to Britain. Known affectionately as "Baba" to his devotees, he was also given the honorific title "Paramahansa," indicating the highest type of Hindu holy man.

After his death on October 2, 1982, Muktananda was succeeded by a brother/sister team, Swami Nityananda and Swami Chidvilasananda; however, they had a break and Swami Chidvilasananda emerged as Muktananda's primary successor as head of the Siddha Yoga Dham Associates. After a period of inactivity, Swami Nityananda founded a rival organization, the Shanti Mandir Seminars. After Muktananda's death there were also serious charges leveled by a number of former disciples that in spite of his claim to be celibate Muktananda had engaged in sexual activity with, and at times sexually coerced female disciples. More positively Mukatananda is revered for his influence on many American spiritual leaders.

Sources:

Muktananda, Swami. *Guru.* New York: Harper & Row, 1971.

———. *In the Company of a Siddha: Interviews and Conversations with Swami Muktananda.* Ganeshpuri, India: Gurudev Siddha Peth, 1981.

———. *Kundalini: The Secret of Life.* South Fallsburg, N.Y.: SYDA Foundation, 1979.

———. *The Perfect Relationship: The Guru and the Disciple.* South Fallsburg, N.Y.: SYDA Foundation, 1980.

———. *Play of Consciousness.* New York: Harper & Row, 1974.

———. *Satsang with Baba.* Oakland, Calif.: S.T.D.A., 1975.

Mulchuyse, S.

Dr. Mulchuyse is co-author with F. A. Heyne of the book *Vorderingen en Problemen van de Parapsychologie* (Progress and Problems in Parapsychology) (1950).

Muldoon, Sylvan J(oseph) (ca. 1903–1971)

Pioneer American investigator of **astral projection,** also known as **out-of-the-body travel.** His first experience was at the age of twelve, stimulated by a visit with his mother to a Spiritualist Camp at Clinton, Iowa. After going to sleep, he apparently awoke to discover himself outside his physical body, looking down at it, and connected by a kind of elastic cord or cable. He thought at first that he had died, and prowled through the house trying to awaken members of his family, but was eventually drawn back into his physical body. This was the first of hundreds of other projections.

In 1927, Muldoon read some books on the **occult** and psychical science by the famous researcher **Hereward Carrington,** in which Carrington had stated that the book *Le Fantâme des Vivants* by Charles Lancelin covered practically all that was known on the subject of astral projection. Muldoon wrote to Carrington, challenging this statement and saying that he could write a whole book on things that Lancelin did not know.

As a result, Carrington invited Muldoon to collaborate on the book *The Projection of the Astral Body* (1929). The successful collaboration led to two further volumes, *The Case for Astral Projection* (1936) and *The Phenomena of Astral Projection* (1951). These books have become classic works of their kind. Meanwhile Muldoon wrote two additional books on his own: *Sensational Psychical Experiences* (1941) and *Famous Psychic Stories* (1942).

During much of his life, Muldoon suffered from ill health, which may have been facilitated by his frequent separation from the physical body in astral projections. In the latter part of his life, his general health improved, but his ability in astral projection correspondingly decreased and he devoted less time to the subject.

Sources:

Muldoon, Sylvan, and Hereward Carrington. *The Case for Astral Projection.* 1936. Reprint, Chicago: Aries Press, 1946.

———. *The Phenomena of Astral Projection.* London: Rider, 1951.

———. *The Projection of the Astral Body.* London: Rider, 1929.

Mulford, Prentice (1834–1891)

American journalist and philosopher, and popular independent **New Thought** writer and mystic. He was born at Sag Harbour, Long Island, on April 5, 1834, and followed a rambling life. He served as a seaman, ship's cook, and whalerman before becoming a gold prospector. He attempted to run a mining, prospecting and teaching school, then turned to journalism.

From 1863 to 1866 he wrote for the *Democrat,* San Francisco, then *The Golden Era* (a leading literary paper), and the *Dramatic Chronicle.* In 1868 he spent a few months as editor of *The Stockton Gazette,* a Democratic journal.

In 1872 he persuaded a group of San Francisco businessmen to sponsor him for a lecture tour, promoting California in England, a project that lasted for two years. Afterward he worked on the New York *Graphic,* conducting a news column "History of a Day" and in 1878 acted as Paris correspondent for the *San Francisco Bulletin.*

After six years, he retired to the wilderness of New Jersey, where he built a small shanty and commenced writing his famous White Cross Library series of philosophical and occult essays. These covered a wide range of metaphysical, mystical, and practical topics, involving a science of thought, and the nature and application of individual powers.

The titles of some of these essays give a good idea of the range of subjects: "God in the Trees," "The God in Yourself," "The Doctor Within," "Mental Medicine," "Faith: or, Being Led of the Spirit," "The Material Mind versus the Spiritual Mind," "Healthy and Unhealthy Spirit Communion," "You Travel When You Sleep," "The Law of Success," and "Some Laws of Health and Beauty." The first of these essays appeared in May 1886, published in Boston, Massachusetts. One of these White Cross Library series of special interest is "Prentice Mulford's Story," a vigorous autobiographical study to about 1872.

On May 27, 1891, Mulford set out in a small boat, apparently for a vacation cruise, but that same evening died on board during his sleep, while anchored off Long Island.

Sources:

Mulford, Prentice. *Life by Land and Sea.* New York: F. J. Needham, 1889.

———. *Thought Forces.* London: G. Bell & Sons, 1913.

———. *Your Forces and How to Use Them.* 6 vols. White Cross Library. New York: F. J. Needham, 1887–92.

Müller, Auguste (ca. 1817)

German somnambulist of Carlsruhe, the first sensitive in the age of **animal magnetism** who claimed contact with **spirits.** Her **trance** history was carefully recorded by Dr. Meier in his *Höchst Merkwürdige Geschichte der Magnetisch Hellsehenden Auguste Müller* (Stuttgart, 1818). She was controlled by the spirit of her dead mother and gave frequent exhibitions of a remarkable traveling clairvoyant faculty. She gave correct medical diagnoses of herself and others and claimed to discern in trance both the thoughts and the character of others. She could also project herself using **out-of-the-body travel** and appeared one night in the bedroom of her friend Catherine, as she promised her.

Müller, Karl E(ugen) (1893–1969)

Electrical engineer who took a great interest in **parapsychology.** He was born on July 14, 1893, at New Orleans, Louisiana. He studied at the Technical University of Switzerland (B.E.E., D.Sc.Tech.), and after graduation worked for various firms as an engineer and consultant, a major length of time spent with the Oerlikon Engineering Co., Zürich (1930 until retirement in 1958). During his adult life he became a Spiritualist and after his retirement became president of the **International Spiritualist Federation.** He was also a member of the **Society for Psychical Research** (London), the **American Society for Psychical Research,** and the Swiss Society for Parapsychology.

In addition to his many articles in technical journals, Müller published contributions on parapsychology, and also experimented with infrared photography in the investigation of physical mediumship. He also published articles in *Yours Fraternally, Chimes* and other magazines, some of which were translated into Swedish, Danish, and German.

Sources:

Berger, Arthur S., and Joyce Berger. *The Encyclopedia of Parapsychology and Psychical Research.* New York: Paragon House, 1991.

Müller, Karl E. "Aspects of Astral Projection." Introduction for F. C. Sculthorp. *Excursions to the Spirit World.* London: n.p., 1962.

———. "Proofs for Reincarnation." *Psychic News* (October/November 1960).

———. *Reincarnation Based on Facts.* London: Psychic Press, 1970.

———. "Spiritualist Doctrine." *Tomorrow.* (Autumn 1960).

Pleasants, Helene, ed. *Biographical Dictionary of Parapsychology.* New York: Helix Press, 1964.

Mullin, Albert Alkins (1933–)

Mathematician who studied the relationship between **parapsychology** and cybernetics. He was born on August 25, 1933, at Lynn, Massachusetts. He studied at Syracuse University (B.E.E., 1955) and Massachusetts Institute of Technology (M.S., electrical engineering, 1957). After graduation he became a research assistant at the University of Illinois. He was a charter associate of the **Parapsychological Association.**

Sources:

Mullin, Albert A. "Some Apologies by a Cyberneticist." *Journal of Parapsychology* 23, no. 4 (1959).

Mullins, John (1838–1894)

One of the most famous British water diviners. He was born at Colerne, near Chippenham, Wiltshire, on November 12, 1838, into a family of 11 children. His father was a stone mason and Mullins followed the same trade. At the age of 21, while employed by Sir John Ould to build a house in Gloucestershire, a dowser (water diviner) was employed to locate a water supply. Various people present tried their hand with the **divining-rod,** including Ould's daughter, who was frightened when the rod suddenly turned over violently. An abundant water supply was found at the spot.

Ould was most impressed and later asked all the workmen on his estate, about 150 men, to try divining with a rod. When Mullins tried, the rod moved so violently it snapped in two. Thereafter Mullins was considered a dowser, although he continued in his trade as mason. When he first attempted to locate a water source for Ould, he located a spring yielding 200 gallons per hour. After that, Mullins was much in demand as a water diviner.

He married in 1859 and continued his trade as a mason, however he devoted the last twelve years of his life to **dowsing** and well-sinking. Such was his confidence in his talent that he made no charge for the expensive work of well-sinking if a good supply of water was not found. In fact, he was immensely successful, locating over five thousand sources of water.

After his death in May 1894, his business was carried on by his sons, one of whom was a dowser, although not so successful as his father. The firm of John Mullins & Sons was one of the most famous businesses of its kind, claiming royal patronage.

Sources:

Mullins, John. *The Divining Rod and Its Results in Discovery of Springs.* N.p., 1880.

Mumbo-Jumbo

A term used to denote an object of senseless veneration, or a meaningless ceremony designed to overpower impressionable people. It has often been used by individuals as a pejorative label to express their strong personal belief about the **occult.**

Mumbo-Jumbo dates back to the early eighteenth century, when it was reported as an image used by the Mundingo tribe in Gambia, Africa, to keep women in subjection. If the men had a dispute with the women, the "Mumbo-Jumbo" image was brought to adjudicate. This image was eight or nine feet high, made from the bark of trees, with straw on the head, and dressed in a long frock coat. A man of the tribe would be hidden under the coat, and would always give a judgment in favor of the men. The women would usually run away when he was brought to them, although he had power to make them come forward or sing and dance for his pleasure.

A secret society amongst the men maintained the tradition of the Mumbo-Jumbo, and its members were sworn to secrecy. No boy under sixteen was allowed to join.

Mumler, William H. (d. 1884)

The first practitioner of **spirit photography.** He lived in Boston, Massachusetts, where he was employed as the head engraver of the jewelry firm Bigelow, Kennard & Co. According to his account, one day, in a friend's studio, he tried to take a photograph of himself by focusing the camera on an empty chair and springing into position on the chair after uncapping the lens. Upon developing the plate he discovered an extraneous figure, a young, transparent girl sitting in the chair, fading away into a dim mist in the lower parts. He identified the girl as his cousin who had died twelve years before. The experiment was repeated and he became satisfied that the extra faces appearing on his plates were of supernatural origin. The news of Mumler's discovery spread and he was besieged with so many requests for sittings that he gave up his position and became a professional spirit photographer.

Among the first to investigate Mumler's powers was **Andrew Jackson Davis,** then editor of the *Herald of Progress* in New York. He first sent a professional photographer to test Mumler and on his favorable report conducted an investigation himself. He was satisfied that the new psychic manifestation was genuine.

Mumler's reputation was established and, as his fame grew, he did tremendous business. His most famous picture was a photograph of Mary Todd Lincoln on which appeared a spirit portrait of the deceased president.

The first scandal, however, was not long in coming. It was discovered that he obtained from time to time the spirit portraits of men who were very much alive. Apologists claimed that the pictures must be genuine since they had been recognized by relatives and that the processes of production had been properly supervised to obviate **fraud.** It was thought that the living individuals might be doubles of the "spirits." Mumler himself could not explain the result, but eventually even local Spiritualists accused him of trickery. Such a hue and cry was raised that in 1868 he was forced to transfer his headquarters to New York.

He prospered for a while until he was arrested by the order of the mayor of New York on an accusation of fraud raised by a newspaperman. The journalist, P. V. Hickey, of the New York *World,* approached Mumler for a spirit photograph, giving a false name, hoping to get a good story for his newspaper. However, at the trial professional photographers and independent citizens testified for Mumler and he was acquitted.

His further career was filled with ups and downs; Mumler died on May 16, 1884, in poverty.

Sources:

Aksakof, A. N. *Animisme et Spiritisme.* Reprint, Paris, 1985. English ed. as: *Animism and Spiritism.* Leipzig: Oswald Meats, 1890.

Berger, Arthur S., and Joyce Berger. *The Encyclopedia of Parapsychology and Psychical Research.* New York: Paragon House, 1991.

Mumler, William H. *Personal Experiences of William H. Mumler in Spirit Photography.* N.p., 1875.

Sidgwick, Eleanor. "On Spirit Photography: A Reply to Mr. A. R. Wallace." *Proceedings* of the Society for Psychical Research 7 (1891).

Mundle, Clement Williams Kennedy (1916–1989)

Professor of philosophy who was actively involved in the study of **parapsychology.** He was born on August 10, 1916, in Fife, Scotland, and studied at the University of St. Andrews. After time out to serve in the Royal Air Force, Technical Branch (1940–45), Mundle attended Oxford University.

He became head of the Philosophy Department, University College of St. Andrews, Dundee, Scotland (1947–55), during which time he was a holder of a Shaw Philosophical fellowship at Edinburgh University (1948–50). In 1955 he began his long tenure as head of the Philosophy Department at the University College of North Wales, Bangor.

Mundle attended the International Conference of Parapsychological Studies, Utrecht, Netherlands (1953) and the International Conference on Philosophy and Parapsychology, St. Paul de Vence, France (1954). He was a charter member of the **Parapsychological Association** and was president of the **Society for Psychical Research,** London (1971–74). He assisted in the ESP investigations reported by **S. G. Soal** and H. T. Bowden in their book *The Mind Readers* (1959). Mundle died July 27, 1989.

Sources:

Berger, Arthur S., and Joyce Berger. *The Encyclopedia of Parapsychology and Psychical Research.* New York: Paragon House, 1991.

Mundle, C. W. K. "The Experimental Evidence for Precognition and Psychokinesis." *Proceedings* of the Society for Psychical Research 49 (July 1950).

———. "Is Psychical Research Relevant to Philosophy?" *Proceedings, Aristotelian Society* Supplemental Vol. 24 (1950).

———. "Philosophical Implications of ESP Phenomena." In *Encyclopedia of Philosophy.* Edited by P. Edwards. N.p. 1967.

———. "Professor Rhine's Views on Psychokinesis." *Mind* (July 1950).

———. "Selectivity in Extrasensory Perception." *Journal* of the Society for Psychical Research (March 1951).

———. "Some Philosophical Perspectives for Parapsychology." *Journal of Parapsychology* (December 1952).

Pleasants, Helene, ed. *Biographical Dictionary of Parapsychology.* New York: Helix Press, 1964.

Munnings, Frederick T(ansley) (ca. 1928)

British fake **trumpet medium** and former bugler. Writer **H. Dennis Bradley,** who held several experimental sittings with Munnings in his home, dismissed his claims to **direct voice** mediumship. Bradley stated that the sittings were entirely valueless and, in February 1926 a public warning against Munnings was issued in the press by **Sir Arthur Conan Doyle,** Abraham Wallace, R. H. Saunders, and H. D. Bradley.

For publication of the warning, Munnings brought an action for libel against the *Daily Sketch* and the *Sunday Herald* in 1928.

However, he did not face the issue before the court and judgment was entered for the defendants. Thereupon Munnings sold his "Confessions" to *The People* newspaper. It appeared in installments for several weeks, written by journalist Sydney A. Moseley, branding Munnings's whole psychic career as an incident of **fraud.** The understanding between Moseley and Munnings, however, was not perfect and in an interview to the *International Psychic Gazette,* Munnings entered a mild protest against his own sensational disclosures.

Psychical researcher **Harry Price** was instrumental in the exposure of Munnings, who claimed to produce the independent voices of "Julius Caesar," "Dan Leno" (famous nineteenth-century comedian), "Dr. Crippen" (a murderer), and "King Henry VIII." Price had invented a voice control recorder and ultimately proved that all the voices were those of Munnings.

Sources:

Berger, Arthur S., and Joyce Berger. *The Encyclopedia of Parapsychology and Psychical Research.* New York: Paragon House, 1991.

"The Cases of Mr. Moss and Mr. Munnings." *Journal* of the Society for Psychical Research 23 (1926).

Murphy, Gardner (1895–1979)

Distinguished psychologist and pioneer figure in parapsychology. Murphy was born on July 8, 1895, at Chillicothe, Ohio. He studied at Yale University (B.A., 1916), Harvard University (M.A., 1917), and Columbia University (Ph.D., 1923). At Harvard he was the Richard Hodgson Fellow concerned with **psychical research.** While completing his doctorate he became a lecturer at Columbia where he remained through the 1920s. He later served on the faculty of the Department of Psychology at City College of New York (1940–52). In 1952 he became the director of research at the Menninger Foundation, Topeka, Kansas, where he stayed for the remainder of his professional career. He defended parapsychology in the face of a strong vocal attack at the 1938 meeting of the American Psychological Association and went on in 1944 to be elected president of that organization. He also received numerous honors for his psychological studies.

Murphy joined the **Society for Psychical Research,** London, in 1917, while in England during World War I as a soldier in the United States Army. Murphy became involved in the controversy over **Mina Crandon** that divided the **American Society for Psychical Research** in the mid 1920s. Believing Crandon a fraud, he joined with others in the formation of the **Boston Society for Psychic Research** as a rival organization. Once that issue had lost its importance, he led in the reuniting of the two groups. He served as vice president of the ASPR (1940–62), and had a notable tenure as president. Throughout his many years in administering the most prominent parapsychological research institute in the United States, Murphy found time to author over one hundred papers and a number of books, many that are still influential in the field of parapsychology.

Murphy died in George Washington University Hospital, Washington, D.C., March 19, 1979.

Sources:

Berger, Arthur S., and Joyce Berger. *The Encyclopedia of Parapsychology and Psychical Research.* New York: Paragon House, 1991.

Murphy, Gardner. "Difficulties Confronting the Survival Hypothesis." *Journal* of the American Society for Psychical Research 39 (April 1945).

———. *Historical Introduction to Modern Psychology.* New York: Harcourt, Brace and World, 1925.

———. *Human Potentialities.* New York: Basic Books, 1958.

———. *In the Minds of Men.* New York: Basic Books, 1953.

———. *Personality.* New York: Harper & Row, 1947.

———. "Psychical Research and Personality." *Journal* of the American Society for Psychical Research (January 1950).

———. *There Is More Beyond: Selected Papers of Gardner Murphy.* Jefferson, N.C.: McFarland, 1989.

———. "Triumphs and Defeats in the Study of Mediumship." *Journal* of the American Society for Psychical Research 52 (October 1957).

Murphy, Gardner, and Morton Leeds. *Outgrowing Self-Perception.* New York: Basic Books, Inc., 1975.

———. *The Paranormal and the Normal.* Lanham, Md.: Scarecrow Press, Inc., 1980.

Murphy, Gardner, and Robert Ballou. *William James and Psychical Research.* New York: Viking Press, 1960.

Murphy, Gardner, and L. A. Dale. *The Challenge of Psychical Research.* New York: Harper and Row, 1961.

Peatman, John G., and Eugene L. Hartley, eds. *Festschrift for Gardner Murphy.* N.p., 1960.

Pleasants, Helene, ed. *Biographical Dictionary of Parapsychology.* New York: Helix Press, 1964.

Schmeidler, Gertrude. "Some Lines About Gardner Murphy, the Psychologist's Parapsychologist." *Parapsychology Review* (July–August, 1976).

Murphy-Lydy, Mary (ca. 1870– ?)

American **materialization** and **trumpet medium,** who practiced for many years in Chesterfield Camp, Indiana. She was engaged for a year by the Indiana Psychic Research Society at Indianapolis, toured the United States, and attained prominence in 1931 in England by platform demonstration of **direct voice.** Her chief controls were "Dr. Green" and "Sunflower."

Impressive accounts of her phenomena were published in the press, but British writer on psychic phenomena **H. Dennis Bradley** considered her performances highly suspicious. In his book, . . . *And After* (1931) he described sittings with the medium whom he roundly condemned as "deliberately fraudulent." He also stigmatized her public appearances, stating, "There was no semblance whatever of spirituality during the medium's proceedings. The effect produced was merely the boredom of a material and dreary exhibition." The main charge was that in a private sitting the author actually heard the medium speak into the trumpet.

Murray, (George) Gilbert (Aime) (1866–1957)

Born on January 2, 1866, Murray was a Regius Professor of Greek at Oxford University who was a leader in the **psychical research** community in early twentieth-century England. He believed he had the capacity for **thought-transference** and declared in an interview for the *Sunday Express* in the summer of 1929, that he discovered his thought-reading faculty by accident while playing guessing games with his children. At the insistence of his wife, Murray commenced experimenting with grown-ups.

Ultimately he became a famous figure in psychical research for his experiments in thought-transference with investigator **Eleanor Sidgwick,** the results of which were published in the 1924 *Proceedings* of the **Society for Psychical Research.** Sidgwick considered these findings "perhaps the most important ever brought to the notice of the society."

Murray was president of the Society for Psychical Research, London, 1915–16. He did not believe in **communication** with the dead, but he had reached an agreement with psychologist **William James** that there exists a "stream of consciousness, with a vivid centre and dim edges." In moments of inattentiveness, subconscious impressions register themselves and afterward form a sort of dim memory, which may account for certain phases of **clairvoyance.** Murray suspected that around our perceptions is a fringe of still more delicate sensing apparatus. The "feelers" of this apparatus are constantly registering contacts with their surroundings, but the impressions are too weak to enter the field of normal consciousness. This fringe of consciousness is the key to **telepathy.**

In addition, Murray published a number of books concerned with Greek traditions in literature and poetry. He died at Oxford, England, May 20, 1957.

Sources:

Essays in Honor of Gilbert Murray. Freeport, N.Y.: Books for Libraries Press, 1972.

Murray, Gilbert. *Gilbert Murray: An Unfinished Autobiography.* London: Allen and Unwin, 1960.

Sidgwick, Eleanor. "Report on Further Experiments in Thought-Transference Carried Out by Professor Gilbert Murray, LL.D, Litt.D." *Proceedings* of the Society for Psychical Research 34 (1924).

Murray, Margaret A(lice) (1863–1963)

British archaeologist whose writings on **witchcraft** played a prominent part in the modern witchcraft revival. She was born in Calcutta, India, July 13, 1863. She later moved to England and entered University College, London (1894) where she was subsequently a Fellow of University College (D.Lit., F.S.A. (Scot.), F.R.A.I.), and by 1899 became a junior lecturer on Egyptology. She retired in 1935. She participated in excavations in Egypt (1902–4), Malta (1921–24), Hertfordshire, England (1925), Minorca (1930–31), Petra (1937), and Tell Ajjul, South Palestine (1938). During her long career, which included a tenure as president of the Folklore Society, London (1953–55), she published a number of valuable works on archaeology, but is better remembered for her controversial books on witchcraft.

In *The Witch Cult in Western Europe* (1921), Murray proposed the idea that witchcraft was a pre-Christian religion in its own right, rather than a heretical deviation from established Christianity. The book had a great influence on **Gerald B. Gardner** (1884–1964), pioneer of the modern witchcraft revival. Murray in turn contributed an introduction to Gardner's book *Witchcraft Today* (1954). She also wrote two other books on witchcraft: *The God of the Witches* (1931) and *The Divine King in England* (1954). She died November 13, 1963, soon after her hundredth birthday.

Sources:

Murray, Margaret A. *My First Hundred Years.* London: William Kimber, 1963.

Rose, Elliot. *A Razor for a Goat.* Toronto: University of Toronto Press, 1964.

Valiente, Doreen. *An ABC of Witchcraft Past and Present.* New York: St. Martin's Press, 1973.

Muscle Reading

According to psychic researcher **James H. Hyslop,** "the interpretation by the operator of unconscious muscular movements in the subject experimented on." As no paranormal perception is involved in the interpretation, **psychical research** is not specifically concerned in muscle reading, although the special sensitivities involved may have some relevance to the mechanisms of paranormal cognition. Some have suggested that what has been interpreted as **telepathy** may in fact be conscious or unconscious muscle reading.

Sources:

Beard, George Miller. *The Study of Trance, Muscle Reading and Allied Nervous Phenomena.* New York, 1882.

Dessoir, Max. "Experiments in Muscle Reading and Thought-Transference." *Proceedings* of the Society for Psychical Research 4, 10 (1886–87).

Sugden, E. H. "Note on Muscle Reading." *Proceedings* of the Society for Psychical Research 1, 4 (1882–83).

Musès, C(harles) A(rthur) (1919–)

Mathematician, physicist, cyberneticist, and philosopher who worked as a theoretician in the field of **parapsychology.** Born on April 28, 1919, in New Jersey, Musès studied at City College, New York (B.Sc.) and Columbia University (A.M., Ph.D. philosophy). He worked as a chemist and consultant for Gar-Baker Laboratories Inc. (1941–54), was editor in chief of Falcon's Wing Press, Colorado (concerned with philosophical and occult books) (1954–59), and from the beginning of the 1960s held various positions as a writer, editor, and consultant, including a stint as editor of the *Journal for the Study of Consciousness.*

Musès has made myriad contributions in a variety of fields. He worked with the late Norbert Wiener, pioneer of cybernetics, whose posthumously published lectures he edited. In the field of mathematics, Musès discovered root and logarithm operations for hyper-numbers following the square root of minus one. In the field of anthropology he studied the Mayans, the Lacadones of Chiapas, Mexico, and symbolic systems in India. He edited the *Journal of Psychoenergetic Systems,* the *Proceedings of the First International Symposium on Biosimulation* (Locarno, 1960), and the *Aspects of the Theory of Artificial Intelligence* (New York, 1962). For a time he served as director of research for the Center for Research on Mathematics and Morphology, Santa Barbara, California.

In the field of parapsychology, Musès made important contributions to the study of the nature, alterations, and potentials of consciousness, to which he gave the name **noetics.**

Sources:

Musès, Charles A. "Aspects of Some Crucial Problems in Biological and Medical Cybernetics." In Norbert Wiener and J. P. Schade, eds. *Progress in Bio-Cybernetics.* Vol. 2. 1975.

———. *Consciousness and Reality.* New York: Morrow/Avon, 1983.

———. *Destiny and Control in Human Systems.* Dordrecht, Netherlands: Kluwer Academic Publishers Group, 1984.

———. *East-West Fire; Schopenhauer's Optimism and the Lankavatara Sutra: An Excursion toward the Common Ground between Oriental and Western Religion.* London: J. M. Watkins, 1955.

———. *Esoteric Teachings of the Tibetan Tantra.* Falcon's Wing Press, 1961.

———. *An Evaluation of Relativity Theory after a Half-Century.* 1953.

———. *Illumination of Jacob Boehme: The Work of Dionysius Andreas Freher.* 1951.

———. "The Limits of Consciousness." *Journal for the Study of Consciousness* 1 (1968).

———. "The Politics of Psi; Acculturation & Hypnosis." In Joseph K. Long, ed. *Extrasensory Ecology: Parapsychology and Anthropology.* 1977.

———. *Prismatic Voices; An International Anthology of Distinctive New Poets.* 1958.

———. "Psychotronic Quantum Theory; A Proposal for Understanding Mass/Space/Time/Consciousness Transductions in Terms of a Radically Extended Quantum Theory." *Proceedings of International Association for Psychotronic Research,* 1975.

Musès, Charles A., and A. M. Young, eds. *Consciousness and Reality; the Human Pivot Point.* New York: Outerbridge & Lazard, 1972.

Museum of Magic and Witchcraft

Founded in 1951 by **Cecil H. Williamson** as the Folklore Center of Superstition and Witchcraft at the Witches Mill, Castletown, Isle of Man, Great Britain. It contained **witchcraft** relics, as well as reconstructed scenes of **occult** rituals and instruments. **Gerald B. Gardner** (1884–1964), who developed modern Wicca, the neo-Pagan form of witchcraft, presided at the opening ceremony. In 1952 Gardner purchased the museum from Williamson. In the late 1950s as Gardner's health failed, Scottish witch Monique Wilson (witch name "Lady Olwyn") and her husband Campbell Wilson, both Gardner initiates, began to administer the Museum's affairs. They inherited the museum and Gardner's papers after Gardner's death in 1964.

In 1971 Ripley's International purchased the museum and brought its contents to the United States. The company created a Museum of Witchcraft and Magic at Fisherman's Wharf, San Francisco, California, and another at Gatlinburg, Tennessee. Some of the collection was sold and various items distributed to the several Ripley's museums now located in various cities.

Sources:

Kelly, Aidan A. *Crafting the Art of Magic: A History of Modern Witchcraft, 1939–1964.* St. Paul: Llewellyn Publications, 1991.

Mushrooms

The narcotic and hallucinogenic properties of certain mushrooms have been known since ancient times. Some mushrooms were even regarded as sacred, and in some cultures their use was prohibited to ordinary people. In what is now Mexico and the southwestern United States a primary psychedelic source was peyote, a small, spineless, carrot-shaped cactus. Dried, the peyote button was consumed in various ceremonial settings. In the late nineteenth century, the use of peyote began to spread among various tribes, and early in the twentieth century strong opposition developed both among Native Americans who rejected it and whites who sought to control Native American behavior and religion.

The Native American Church was founded in 1906 at the Union Church by peyote users in Oklahoma and Nebraska. It adopted its present name in 1918 in response to a campaign by the Bureau of Indian Affairs to outlaw peyote. The fight to legalize the practices of the church has continued into the 1990s, though major rulings in the 1960s largely established the place of the church and its major sacrament.

Serious medical and scientific interest in hallucinogenic mushrooms dates from the pioneer work *Phantastica: Narcotic and Stimulating Drugs* by Louis Lewin (London, 1931). In this important book, Lewin discusses the use of fly agaric and identifies the peyote plant (which he named *anhalonium Lewinii*) and the active substance, mescaline, obtained from it.

More than two decades later New York banker R. Gordon Wasson and his wife Valentina Wasson published their classic study *Mushrooms, Russia, and History* (Pantheon, 1957). This important work launched a new science of ethnomycology (i.e., the study of the role played by wild mushrooms in various human cultures throughout history). The Wassons took field trips to Mexico during 1955 to study firsthand the sacred mushroom ceremonies of the Indian people. Their record album *Mushroom Ceremony of the Mazatec Indians of Mexico* (Folkways Records, New York, 1957) was the first documented recording of its kind. The studies of the Wassons—along with the popular volume by Aldous Huxley, *The Doors of Perception* (1954)—spread interest in psychedelic drugs and their hallucinogenic properties and stand at the fountainhead of the psychedelic revolution of the 1960s.

The Wassons also gave special attention to fly agaric (*A. muscaria*) in history. In his book *Soma, Divine Mushroom of Immortality* (1968, 1971) Wasson speculates that it was the source of the nectar named **soma** in the ancient Vedic literature of India. Although a few modern writers on psychedelics support the Wassons, this particular suggestion has not found support in the scholarly community.

In 1960 **Timothy Leary,** then an instructor at Harvard University, was introduced to the psychedelic mushroom *trianactyle* by a Mexican anthropologist. The experience totally disturbed his rather settled view of the universe and led directly to his launching research on psychedelic **drugs** at Harvard. In the process, he was introduced to LSD and very soon he left Harvard to become the advocate of a new worldview based on the mind-altering properties of **hallucinogens.**

Emerging as a major prophet of the mushroom was **Carlos Castaneda,** a South American anthropologist who seems to have worked one of the great hoaxes in history with his claims to have been taught by a mushroom-using Yaqui Indian whom he called Don Juan. His writings, using his research in the University of California library, not only influenced hundreds of thousands of readers already seeking justification for their use of psychedelics, but deceived the teachers at UCLA and many in the anthropological community who saw him as the advocate of a new methodology for the study of tribal cultures. In spite of the revelations of his deceit, Castaneda retains a loyal following.

What began as an intellectual exercise to understand tribal cultures led in the 1960s to the development of a new subculture based on the consumption of drugs, and the emergence of prophets like **Richard Alpert,** who found a new vision in Hinduism.

Sources:

Castaneda, Carlos. *The Teachings of Don Juan.* New York: Ballentine Books, 1969.

De Mille, Richard. *Castaneda's Journey: The Power and the Allegory.* Santa Barbara, Calif.: Capra Press, 1976.

———. *The Don Juan Papers.* Santa Barbara, Calif.: Ross-Erikson, 1980.

La Barre, Weston. *The Peyote Cult.* New York: Schocken Books, 1969.

Leary, Timothy. *Flashbacks.* Los Angeles: Jeremy Tarcher, 1983.

Masters, R. E. L., and Jean Houston. *The Varieties of Psychedelic Experience.* New York: Delta, 1967.

Roseman, Bernard. *The Peyote Story.* North Hollywood, Calif.: Wilshire Book, 1963.

Music (Paranormal)

Paranormal music ranges from inspired performances by mediums, to compositions dictated by "spirit musicians," to music that is heard without any apparent earthly source. This latter form of paranormal music is perhaps the most impressive.

During the seventeenth-century persecution of the Huguenots in France, music from invisible sources became a widespread phenomenon. The *Pastoral Letter* of Pierre Jurieu (1689) refers to dozens of instances. The sound of trumpets as if an army were going to battle, the singing of psalms, a choir of many voices, and an ensemble of musical instruments were heard day and night in many places.

After the church in Orthez was razed, there was hardly a house in the city in which people did not hear the music, ordinarily between eight and nine o'clock night. The Parliament of Pau and the Intendant of Bearn forbade citizens to go and hear these psalms under a penalty of 2,000–5,000 crowns. The scale of the phenomenon was too vast to be attributed to **hallucination.** It was experienced throughout the Cevennes. It was largely under the effect of this supernormal phenomenon that Cavalier, Roland, and Marion rose against Louis XIV.

According to Beriah G. Evans, in his account of the Welsh religious revival in the *Daily News* (February 9, 1905), "From all parts of the country come reports of mysterious music descending from above, and always in districts where the Revival fire burns brightly."

Several interesting cases in which music was heard around the deathbed are cited by **Edmund Gurney, F. W. H. Myers** and **Frank Podmore** in their classic study *Phantasms of the Living* (1886). For example, after the death of a Mr. L. (p. 446), three persons in the death chamber heard for several seconds three feminine voices singing softly, like the sounds of an Eolian harp. Eliza W. could distinguish the words: "The strife is o'er, the battle done." Mrs. L., who was also present, heard nothing.

Before a Mrs. Sewell's little girl died (vol. 2, p. 221) "sounds like the music of an Eolian harp" were heard from a cupboard in the room. "The sounds increased until the room was full of melody," the researchers narrate, "when it seemed slowly to pass down the stairs and ceased. The servant in the kitchen, two stories below, heard the sounds." The sounds were similarly heard for the next two days by several people, except the child, who was passionately fond of music. She died when the music was heard for the third time. Following the death of her 21-year-old daughter, a Mrs. Yates heard the sweetest spiritual music, "such as mortals never sang" (vol. 2, p. 223).

As reported in the *Journal of the Society for Psychical Research* (vol. 4, p. 181), music was heard around the sickbed of John Britton, a deafmute who was dangerously ill with rheumatic fever. His face was lit up, and when he had recovered sufficiently to use his hands he explained in sign language that he had heard "beautiful music."

Puritan divine John Bunyan related his observations of an elderly believer, saying that "when his soul departed from him the music seemed to withdraw, and to go further and further off from the house, and so it went until the sound was quite gone out of hearing."

The British *Daily Chronicle* reported on May 4, 1905, the case of a dying woman of the Salvation Army: "For three or four nights mysterious and sweet music was heard in her room at frequent intervals by relatives and friends, lasting on each occasion about a quarter of an hour. At times the music appeared to proceed from a distance, and then would gradually grow in strength while the young woman lay unconscious."

Of course, in some cases the experience appears to have been purely subjective. According to a story told by Count de la Resie in the *Gazette de France* of 1855, Urham's *Chef d'oeuvre Audition* was supernormally produced. In a narrow glade in the Bois de Boulogne, he heard a sound in the air. Urham saw a light without form and precision and heard an air with the accompaniment of an Eolian harp. He fell into a kind of ecstasy and distinctly heard a voice that said to him, "Dear Urham, write down what I have sung." He hurried home and wrote down the air with the greatest ease.

In the famous **Versailles adventure** of C. A. E. Moberley and E. J. Jourdain, two English women walking in the gardens of Versailles were apparently transported to the Trianon (a villa) of 1789, where they heard period music, which has since been transcribed.

Music through Mediums without Instruments

Whereas mediumistic manifestation of the production of music without instruments was rare, the apparent telekinetic playing of instruments was heard fairly frequently. The sitters of **D. D. Home** and **William Stainton Moses** were often delighted by music from an invisible source. Home relates, in *Incidents In My Life* (1863), the following story:

"On going to Boston my power returned, and with it the most impressive manifestation of music without any earthly instrument. At night, when I was asleep my room would be filled as it were with sounds of harmony, and these gradually grew louder till persons in other parts of the house could hear them distinctly; if by any chance I was awakened, the music would instantly cease."

In the second volume of his biography, Home recounts the following well-attested experience that occurred on Easter Eve 1866 in the home of S. C. Hall: "First we had simple, sweet, soft music for some minutes; then it became intensely sad; then the tramp, tramp as of a body of men marching mingled with the music, and I exclaimed 'The March to Calvary.' Then three times the tap-tapping sound of a hammer on a nail (like two metals meeting). A crash, and a burst of wailing which seemed to fill the room, followed; then there came a burst of glorious triumphal music, more grand than any of us had ever listened to, and we exclaimed 'The Resurrection.' It thrilled all our hearts."

Lord Adare, who published *Experiences in Spiritualism with Mr. D. D. Home* (1870), recorded many interesting accounts of the same phenomenon. "We had not been in bed more than three minutes," he writes of an experience in Norwood, London, "when both Home and myself simultaneously heard the music: it sounded like a harmonium; sometimes, as if played loudly at a great distance, at other times as if very gently, close by."

On another occasion, says Adare, "the music became louder and louder, until I distinctly heard the words: 'Hallelujah! Praise the Lord God Almighty!' It was no imagination on my part." The music was the same as at Norwood. The aerial musical sounds sometimes resembled drops of water, and according to Home they were produced by the same method as **raps.** Dr. James H. Gully, in whose house Home was a guest, writes: "Ears never listened to anything more sweet and solemn than these voices and instruments; we heard organ, harp and trumpet, also two voices" (*Spiritualist,* vol. 3, p. 124).

In the presence of Moses, "drum, harp, fairy bells, trumpet, lyre, tambourine, and flapping of wings" were heard (*Proceedings* of the Society for Psychical Research, vol. 11, p. 54). No such instruments were in the room. They were also heard in the open. A Mrs. Speer reflects on the event (*Light,* January 28, 1893):

"September 19, before meeting this evening we heard the fairy bells playing in different parts of the garden, where we were walking; at times they sounded far off seemingly playing at the top of some high elm trees, music and stars mingling together, then they would approach nearer to us, evidently following us into the séance room which opened on to the lawn. After we were seated the music still lingered with us, playing in the corner of the room and over the table, round which we were seated. They played scales and chords by request, with the greatest rapidity and copied notes Dr. Speer made with his voice. After Moses was in trance the music became louder and sounded like brilliant playing on the piano! There was no instrument in the room."

There were similar observations before Home and Moses; in the case of **Mary Jobson** a psychic invasion took place during a spell of mysterious illness.

Taps "as on a bell so pure as to bear no vibration, in the most exquisite tones, quite beyond description" were produced by "Walter" in the "Margery" séances (see **Mina Crandon**) without any visible instrument. Notes were struck on a "psychic piano"; the English call to arms was rendered on a "psychic bugle," sounding at a distance and in an open space; the British reveille was played; an invisible mouth organ and the striking of a "celestial clock," different from any clock known to be in the house or in the neighborhood, were heard (J. Malcolm Bird, *"Margery" the Medium,* 1925).

Music Telekinetically Produced

According to E. W. Capron in *Modern Spiritualism: Its Facts and Fanaticisms* (1885): "Mrs. **[Sarah] Tamlin** was, so far as I have been able to learn, the first medium through whom the guitar or other musical instrument was played, without visible contact, so as to give recognisable tunes. In her presence it was played with all the exactness of an experienced musician, although she is not acquainted with music, or herself able to play on any instrument. The tones varied from loud and vigorous to the most refined touches of the strings that could be imagined."

The playing of a locked piano in a séance with James Sangster is reported in the *Age of Progress* (March 1857).

In the presence of **Annie Lord** and **Jennie Lord** of Maine—both unable to play any instrument—a double bass violincello, guitar, drums, accordion, tambourine, bells, and various small instruments were played "with the most astonishing skill and power," writes Emma Hardinge Britten in *Modern American Spiritualism* (1870). The instruments were played "sometimes singly, at others all together, and not infrequently the strange concert would conclude by placing the young medium, seated in her invalid chair, silently and in a single instant in the centre of the table, piling up all the instruments around her." Britten writes.

In D. D. Home's mediumship, musical feats of **telekinesis** were particularly well attested. **Sir William Crookes** witnessed it under fraud-proof conditions. The quality of the music was mostly fine. **William Howitt** had an experience to the contrary. He is quoted in a letter in D. D. Home's *Incidents In My Life* (1863): "A few evenings afterwards, a lady desiring that the 'Last Rose of Summer' might be played by a spirit on the accordion, the wish was complied with, but in so wretched a style that the company begged that it might be discontinued. This was done, but soon after, evidently by another spirit, the accordion was carried and suspended over the lady's head, and there, without any visible support or action on the instrument, the air was played through most admirably, in the view and hearing of all."

Lord Adare noted a peculiarity:

"The last few notes were drawn out so fine as to be scarcely audible—the last note dying away so gradually that I could not tell when it ceased. I do not think it possible for any human hand to produce a note in that way."

Robert Bell gives the following account in the *Cornhill Magazine* (August 1860), under the title "Stranger than Fiction":

"The air was wild and full of strange transitions, with a wail of the most pathetic sweetness running through it. The execution was no less remarkable, for its delicacy than its powers. When the notes swelled in some of the bold passages, the sound rolled through the room with an astounding reverberation; then gently subsiding, sank into a strain of divine tenderness."

The experience was the same when Bell held the accordion in his own hand, with full light upon it; during the loud and vehement passages it became so difficult to hold that he had to grasp the top with both hands, he said.

In a letter to the *Morning Star* (October 1860), a Dr. Gully stated, "I have heard Blagrove repeated; but it is no libel on that master of the instrument to say that he never did produce such exquisite distant and echo notes as those which delighted our ears."

Alfred Russel Wallace writes in his book *My Life* (1902) of his first séance in the company of Crookes and Home:

"As I was the only one of the company who had not witnessed any of the remarkable phenomena that occurred in his presence, I was invited to go under the table while an accordion was playing, held in Home's hand, his other hand being on the table. The room was well lighted and I distinctly saw Home's hand holding the instrument which moved up and down and played a tune without any visible cause. He then said 'Now I will take away my hand,' which he did; but the instrument went on playing, and I saw a detached hand holding it while Home's two hands were seen above the table by all present."

There were other mediums who apparently performed similar feats of telekinetic music, **Henry Slade** and the Reverend **F. W. Monck** among them. Of **Eusapia Palladino Hereward Carrington** gives the following account, in *The Story of Psychic Science* (1930):

"One of the most remarkable manifestations, however, was the playing of the mandolin, on at least two occasions. The instrument sounded in the cabinet first of all—distinct twangings of the strings being heard, in response to pickings of Eusapia's fingers on the hand of one of her controllers. The mandolin then floated out of the cabinet, on to the séance table, *where, in full view of all, nothing touching it, it continued to play for nearly a minute*—first one string and then another being played upon. Eusapia was at the time in deep trance, and was found to be cataleptic a few moments later. Her hands were gripping the hands of her controllers so tightly that each finger had to be opened in turn, by the aid of passes and suggestion."

H. Dennis Bradley writes in . . . *And After* (1931):

"I have had instruments of an orchestra placed in the centre of my own study, with luminous paint covering them so that every movement could be seen instantly, and these instruments have been played by unseen forces in perfect harmony. Whilst operatic selections were being played upon the gramophone, they have been supernormally conducted with a luminous baton in a majestic manner."

Musicians Who Were Mediums

There were also musical mediums who achieved fame, even though they were often without musical training or were unable to play in a conscious state. Among these, **Jesse F. G. Shepard** was the most astonishing.

Well-known classical composers were said to play through **George Aubert,** a nonprofessional medium who was investigated at the Institut Genéral Psychologique in Paris.

At the International Psychical Congress in 1900, **Charles Richet** introduced Pepito Ariola, a three-and-a-half-year-old Spanish child who played classical pieces.

Blind Tom, a child living in south Georgia described as otherwise intellectually deficient, played the piano impressively with both hands, using the black and the white keys, when four years old. At age five he composed his "Rainstorm" and said it was what the rain, wind, and thunder had said to him. He could play two tunes on the piano at the same time, one with each hand, while he sang a song in a different tempo. Each tune was set to a different key as dictated by the audience.

In 1903 the famous palmist "Cheiro" (Count **Louis Hamon**) introduced to London a M. de Boyon, a French musical medium to whose extraordinary gift **Victorien Sardou,** actress Sarah Bernhardt and other musicians of the day testified. M. de Boyon had no memory of what he played. He employed a unique fingering, and he could not play the same piece twice.

The most remarkable musical medium of the late twentieth century has been **Rosemary Brown,** a British housewife who performs musical compositions on the piano, claimed to originate from such great composers as Beethoven, Mozart, Liszt, and Chopin. Brown has no musical training, but these psychic compositions have been endorsed by established musicians.

Paranormal Aspects of Music

Because of its powerful influence directly on emotions, music often achieves remarkable effects on humans and even on animals. Music therapy is now a recognized treatment for mentally handicapped children.

Ancient legends tell of the paranormal effects of music. Orpheus of ancient Greece charmed wild animals and even trees by his music, and the modal system of the Greeks was said to influence the social and emotional attitudes of listeners. Naik Gopal, a musician of ancient India, was said to have caused flames to burst forth by his performance of Dipak Raga (associated with heat), even when the musician stood in water.

The musical system of India has always emphasized the powerful effects of musical vibration. Different *ragas* (scale patterns) are regarded as specific for certain times of the day or seasons of the year, and their microtonal intervals and grace notes involve vibrations that are unknown to the well-tempered scale of Western nations. Ragas, properly performed, are said to evoke beautiful forms or have paranormal effects.

In Hinduism, the first manifestation of creation was said to be that of subtle sound vibration, giving rise to the forms of the material world. Each sound produced a form, and combinations of sound created complicated shapes. This is also the basis of mantra yoga. The creative power of sound is also echoed in the Christian Scripture: "In the beginning was the Word, and the Word was with God, and the Word was God" (John 1:1).

Through this century attempts have been made to explore the legendary traditions from scientific perspectives. The great Indian scientist Sir **Jagadis Chunder Bose** devised sensitive apparatus to demonstrate subtle plant reactions, many of which resembled nervous responses in animal or human life. Prof. T. C. N. Singh and Stells Ponniah of Annamalai University in India carried out experiments to measure the growth in plants as a result of musical sounds (see **Plants, Psychic Aspects of**). Western scientists have demonstrated that ultrasonic sounds can destroy bacteria, guide ships in the dark, and weld together materials.

In recent years, the Hindu musician Swami **Nadabrahmananda Saraswati** has demonstrated an ancient **yoga** of music, involving the arousal of **kundalini** energy through the psychic power of musical vibrations. In a Western context, psychic effects from music were claimed by the singing teacher **Alfred Wolfsohn.**

In contrast, some have suggested that the aggressiveness and violence of much of modern popular rock music seems to have had a negative and sinister influence on a younger generation, recalling the fears of the ancient Greeks that certain musical modes would have a harmful social effect.

Sources:

Brown, Rosemary. *Immortals at My Elbow.* London: Bachman & Turner, 1974. Reprinted as *Immortals by My Side.* Chicago: Henry Regnery, 1975.

Crookes, William. *Researches in the Phenomena of Spiritualism.* London: J. Burns, 1974.

Danielou, Alain. *The Ragas of Northern Indian Music.* London: Barrie & Rockliff, 1968.

Gurney, Edmund. *The Power of Sound.* London: Smith, Elder, 1880. Reprint, New York: Basic Books, 1966.

Parrott, Ian. *The Music of "An Adventure."* London: Regency Press, 1966.

Podolsky, Edward. *Music Therapy.* New York: Philosophical Library, 1954.

Rogo, D. Scott. *Nad: A Study of Some Unusual "Other-World" Experiences.* 2 vols. New Hyde Park, N.Y.: University Books, 1970–72.

Scott, Cyril. *Music: Its Secret Influence Throughout the Ages.* 6th ed. London: Rider, 1956.

Sivananda, Swami. *Music as Yoga.* Sivananda Nagar, India: Yoga-Vedanta Forest University, 1956.

Musso, J(uan) Ricardo (1917–1989)

Business consultant, author, editor, and professor of parapsychology whose research centered on the testing of **ESP** by statistical methods. Musso was born on June 9, 1917, in Buenos Aires, Argentina, and studied at the School of Economic Sciences, Buenos Aires University (Doctor of Economic Sciences, 1944). He became a lecturer on parapsychology at the Argentine Institute of Parapsychology, Buenos Aires (1956–58) and at the National University of the South, Bahia Blanca, Argentina (1957). Beginning in 1959 he was a professor of parapsychology and psychostatistics at the School of Philosophy, Letters and Educational Sciences, National Littoral University, Rosario Argentina.

In 1953 he helped found the Argentine Institute of Parapsychology. He was also a consultant to the **Parapsychology Foundation,** director of Biblioteca de Parapsicología (Parapsychology Publications), and director and editor of *Revista de Parapsicología* (Parapsychology Review). In 1971, he attended the Twentieth International Conference of the Parapsychology Foundation, held at Le Piol, St. Paul de Vence, France. He died October 28, 1989.

Sources:

Musso, J. Ricardo. *En los Límites de la Psicología: Desde el Espiritismo hasta la Parapsicología* (On the Frontiers of Psychology: From Spiritualism to Parapsychology). N.p., 1954.

———. "Il Movimiento Parapsicologico in Argentina" (The Parapsychology Movement in Argentina). *International Review of Parapsychology* (1956).

Musso, J. Ricardo, and M. Granero. "An ESP Drawing Experiment with a High-Scoring Subject." *Journal of Parapsychology* 37 (1973).

Mutual UFO Network, Inc. (MUFON)

One of the largest and most influential UFO investigation organizations. MUFON was founded as the Midwest UFO Network in 1969 at Quincey, Illinois, by Walter H. Andrus, Jr., formerly a member of the **Aerial Phenomena Research Organization.** In 1975 Andrus moved the headquarters to Texas, where it is currently headquartered.

Conceived as a grassroots organization, MUFON currently has over one thousand members and investigators spread over various parts of the world. The organization holds an annual symposium, the papers of which are published in an annual *MUFON Proceedings,* and publishes the *MUFON UFO Journal* (formerly *Skylook*), a monthly publication. Working with Andrus is a board of directors and a director for investigations. MUFON may be contacted at 103 Oldtown Rd., Seguin, TX 78155-4099. Website: http://mufon.com/.

Sources:

Clark, Jerry. *UFOs in the 1980s.* Vol. 1 of *The UFO Encyclopedia.* Detroit: Apogee Books, 1990.

Fowler, Raymond. *MUFON Field Investigator's Manual.* 3d ed. Seguin, Tex.: Mutual UFO Network, 1983.

———. *UFOs, Interplanetary Visitors.* New York: Exposition, 1974.

MUFON: The Mutual UFO Network. http://mufon.com/. March 8, 2000.

MYANMAR

An independent republic of Southeast Asia, known until 1989 as Burma, located east of India and south of China, and formerly a province of British India, inhabited by an indigenous stock of Indo-Chinese people who originally migrated from Western China at different periods, represented by three principal groups, the Talaings, the Shans, and the Bama, although groups of several other allied races are also found.

The largest religious community is the Theravada Buddhist, though there are significant minority communities of Hindus, Muslims, Christians, and those who follow forms of indigenous tribal religions. Many beliefs were affected by the Japanese occupation during World War II and by the internal power struggles following independence in 1948, culminating in the creation of the present socialist republic in 1974.

Some traditional beliefs still linger on. In general, the Burmese believed the soul is immaterial and independent of the body, to which it is only bound by a special attraction. It can quit and return to the body at will, but can also be captured and kept from returning to it. After death the soul hovers near the corpse as an invisible butterfly, known as *leippya.* A witch or demon may capture the leippya while it wanders during the hours of sleep, and sickness is sure to result. Offerings are made to the magician or devil to induce him to release the soul. The Kachins of the northern hills of Burma believed that persons having the **evil eye** possessed two souls, the secondary soul being the cause of the malign influence.

Belief in Spirits

Beliefs in spirits, mostly malign, took a prominent place in the religious beliefs of the people of Myanmar. The spirits of rain, wind, and the heavenly bodies were in that condition of evolution that usually results in their becoming full-fledged deities, with whom placation gives way to worship. But the spirits of the forest are true demons with well-marked animistic characteristics. Thus the *nat* or *seiktha* dwells in trees or groves. His nature is usually malign, but occasionally we find him as the guardian of a village. In any case, he possesses a shrine where he may be propitiated by gifts of food and drink. Several of these demonic figures have almost achieved godhead, so widespread did their particular veneration become, and Hmin Nat, Chiton, and Wannein Nat may be named as fiends of power, the dread of which spread across extensive districts.

The nats were probably of Indian origin, and the now thoroughly indigenous creatures may at one time have been members of the Hindu pantheon. Many spirit families such as the *Seikkaso, Akathaso,* and *Bommaso,* who inhabit various parts of the jungle trees, are of Indian origin. The fulfillment of every wish depends upon the nats or spirits, who are all-powerful as far as humans are concerned. They are innumerable. Any house might have its complement, who swarmed in its several rooms and took up their abode in its hearth, doorposts, verandas, and corners. The nats also inhabited or inspired wild beasts, and all misfortune was supposed to emanate from them.

The Burmese used to believe that the more materialistic dead haunted the living with a malign purpose. The people had a great dread of their newly-deceased relatives, whom they imagined to haunt the vicinity of their dwellings for the purpose of ambushing them.

No dead body would be carried to a cemetery except by the shortest route, even should this necessitate cutting a hole in the wall of a house. The spirits of those who died a violent death haunted the scene of their fatality. Like the ancient Mexicans (see **Ciupipiltin**), the Burmese had a great dread of the ghosts of women who died in childbirth. The Kachins believed such women to turn into **vampires** (*swawmx*) who were accompanied by their children when these died with them. The spirits of children were often supposed to inhabit the bodies of cats and dogs.

The Burmans were extremely circumspect as to how they spoke and acted towards the inhabitants of the spirit world, as they believed that disrespect or mockery would at once bring down upon them misfortune or disease. An infinite number of guardian spirits were included in the Burmese demonological system, and these were chiefly supposed to be Brahmanic importations. These dwelt in the houses like the evil nats and were the tutelars of village communities, and even of clans. They were duly propitiated, at which ceremonies rice, beer, and tea-salad were offered to them. Women were employed as exorcists to drive out the evil nats, but at the festivals connected with the guardian nats, women were not permitted to officiate.

Necromancy and Occult Medicine

Necromancy used to be common among the Burmese. The *weza* or wizards were of two kinds, good and evil, and these were each subdivided into four classes, according to the materials they employed, such as, for example, magic squares, mercury, or iron. The native doctors professed to cure the diseases caused by **witchcraft,** and often specialized in various ailments. Besides being necromantic, medicine was largely astrological. There was said to be in Lower Burma a town of wizards at Kale Thaungtot on the Chindwin River, and many journeyed there to have the effects of bewitchment neutralized by its chief. Sympathetic magic was employed to render an enemy sick. Indian and native **alchemy** and **cheiromancy** were widespread. Noise is the universal method of exorcism, and in cases of illness the patient was often severely beaten, the idea being that the fiend that possessed him was the sufferer.

Mediums and Exorcists

The *tumsa* or *natsaw* were magicians, diviners, or wise men and women who practiced their arts in a private and in a non-hierophantic capacity among the rural Burmese. The wise man physician who worked in iron (*than weza*) was at the head of his profession, and sold **amulets** that guarded their purchasers from injury. Female mediums professed to be the spouses of certain nats, and could only retain their supernatural connection with a certain spirit so long as they were wedded to him.

With the exorcists, training was voluntary and even perfunctory. But with the mediums it was severe and prolonged. Among the civilized Burmanese a much more exhaustive apprenticeship was demanded. Indeed a thorough and intricate knowledge of some departments of magical and astrological practice was necessary for recognition by the brotherhood, the entire art of which was medico-magical, consisting of the **exorcism** of evil spirits from human beings and animals.

The methods employed were such as usually accompanied exorcism among tribal cultures, that is, dancing, flagellation of the afflicted person, induction of ecstasy, oblation to the fiend in possession, and noise.

Prophecy and Divination

Prophecy and **divination** have been quite popular in Myanmar, and were in some measure controlled by the use of the *Deitton,* an astrological book of Indian origin. Observation of the direction in which the blood of a sacrificed animal flowed, the knots in torn leaves, the length of a split bamboo pole, and the whiteness or otherwise of a hardboiled egg were utilized as methods of augury. But by far the most important mode of divination in use in the country was the bones of fowls. It was indeed an almost universal way of deciding all the difficulties of Burmese existence. Those wing or thigh bones in which the holes exhibit regularity were chosen. Pieces of bamboo were inserted into these holes, and the resulting slant of the stick defined the augury. If the stick slanted outwards it decided in favor of the measure under test. If it slanted inwards, the omen was unfavorable. Other materials of divination were the entrails of animals and the contents of blown eggs.

Astrology

Burmese **astrology** derived both from Indian and Chinese sources, and powerfully affected the entire people, most of whom had a private astrologer who would be consulted for knowledge of the trend of the horoscope regarding the near future. Burmese would be active and enterprising on lucky days, but nothing would induce them to undertake any form of work should the day be *pyatthadane* or ominous.

The *bedinsaya,* or astrologers proper, practiced a fully developed Hindu astrology, but being few in number, they were not as influential as the rural soothsayers, who followed the Chinese system known as *Hpewan,* almost identical to the Taoist astrological tables of Chinese diviners. From this system were derived horoscopes, fortunes, happy marriages, and prognostications regarding business affairs. But in practice the system was often confounded with the Buddhist calendar and much confusion resulted. The Buddhist calendar was in popular use, while the *Hpewan* was purely astrological. Therefore the Burmese ignorant of the latter was obliged to consult an astrologer who was able to collate the two regarding his lucky and unlucky days. The chief horoscopic influences were day of birth, day of the week, represented by the symbol of a certain animal, and the position of the dragon's mouth to the terminal syllables of the day-names.

Magic

Burmese **magic** consisted in the making of charms and the manufacture of occult medicine to cause hallucination, second sight, the prophetic state, invisibility, or invulnerability. It was frequently sympathetic and overlapped with necromancy and astrology. It did not appear to be at all ceremonial, and was to a great extent unsophisticated, save where it had been influenced by Indian and Buddhist monks, who also drew on native sources to enlarge their own knowledge.

Sources:

Fielding, H. *The Soul of a People.* London: n.p., 1902.

Fytche, A. *Burma, Past & Present.* 2 vols. London: n.p., 1878.

Spiro, Melford E. *Burmese Supernaturalism.* Englewood Cliffs, N.J.: Prentice-Hall, 1967.

Temple, Sir Richard C. *The Thirtyseven Nats (Burmese Animism).* London: n.p., 1906.

Myers, A(rthur) T(homas) (1851–1894)

Brother of **F. W. H. Myers** and a founding member of the **Society for Psychical Research** (SPR), London, serving on the society's council from 1888 to 1894. He used his medical knowledge to investigate cases of alleged paranormal healing and also made a special study of **hypnotism.** He was largely responsible for forming the Edmund Gurney Library of books and pamphlets on hypnotism and related subjects. Myers also participated in the experiments of the French neurologist **Pierre Janet** in telepathic hypnotism, as well as some of the SPR sittings with the American medium **Leonora Piper.** He died in London, England, January 10, 1894.

Sources:

Myers, Arthur Thomas. "Report on a Alleged Physical Phenomenon." *Proceedings* of the Society for Psychical Research 3, no. 9 (1885).

Myers, Arthur Thomas, and F. W. H. Myers. "Mind-Cure, Faith-Cure, and the Miracles of Lourdes." *Proceedings* of the Society for Psychical Research 9, no. 24 (1893).

Myers, Frederic William Henry (1843–1901)

A leading theoretician during the first generation of psychical research. He was born February 6, 1843, at Keswick, Cumberland, England, and educated at Trinity College, Cambridge. For 30 years Myers filled the post of an inspector of schools at Cambridge. Here his resolve to pursue psychical investigation was born in 1869 after a starlight walk and talk with **Henry Sidgwick.**

His theory was that if a spiritual world ever manifested to humans, a serious investigation must be made to discover unmistakable signs of it. For "if all attempts to verify scientifically the intervention of another world should be definitely proved futile, this would be a terrible blow, a mortal blow, to all our hopes of another life, as well as of traditional religion" for "it would thenceforth be very difficult for men to be persuaded, in our age of clear thinking, that what is now found to be illusion and trickery was in the past thought to be truth and revelation."

Myers had in mind an empiric method of deliberate, dispassionate, and exact inquiry. It was in this spirit that, in 1882, the **Society for Psychical Research** (SPR), London, of which he was a cofounder, came to be established. He devoted all his energies to its work and concentrated with a deep grasp of science on the psychological side. Of the 16 volumes of the society's *Proceedings* published while he lived, there are few without an important contribution from his pen.

In *Phantasms of the Living,* a collaboration with **Edmund Gurney** and **Frank Podmore** (and one of the society's first major studies of the paranormal), the system of classification of paranormal phenomena was entirely his idea. The words "telepathy," "supernormal," "veridical," and many others less in use today were coined by Myers.

In the SPR he filled the post of honorary secretary. In 1900, Myers was elected to the presidential chair, a post that only distinguished scientists had previously filled.

To periodicals such as the *Fortnightly Review* he contributed many articles. They were collected and published in 1893 under the titles *Science and a Future Life* and *Other Essays.*

His chief work, *Human Personality and its Survival of Bodily Death,* was posthumously published in 1903. It is an exposition of the potential powers of the subliminal self, which Myers pictured as the real ego, a vast psychic organism of which the ordinary consciousness is but an accidental fraction, the life of the soul, not bound up with the life of the body, of which the so-called supernormal faculties are the ordinary channels of perception.

Myers challenged the Spiritualist position that all, or most of, supernormal phenomena were due to the spirits of the dead, contending to the contrary that by far the largest proportion was due to the action of the still embodied spirit of the agent or of the percipient himself. The theory brought order into a chaotic mass of psychical phenomena. On the other hand, it greatly enhanced the probability of **survival** after death. As the powers of the subliminal self did not degenerate during the course of evolution and served no purpose in this life they were obviously destined for a future existence. Why, for instance, should the subconscious so carefully preserve all thoughts and memories if there would be no use for them?

William James suggested that the problems of the subliminal mind should be called "the problem of Myers." And he added, "Whatever the judgment of the future may be on Mr. Myers' speculation, the credit will always remain to them of being the first attempt in any language to consider the phenomena of hallucination, automatism, double personality, and mediumship as connected parts of one whole subject."

Theodore Flournoy, a profound psychologist himself, considered Myers "one of the most remarkable personalities of our time in the realm of mental science." Further, he observed, "If future discoveries confirm his thesis of the intervention of the discarnate, in the web and the woof of our mental and physical world then his name will be inscribed in the golden book of the initiated, and, joined to those of Copernicus and Darwin, he will complete the triad of geniuses who have the most profoundly revolutionised scientific thought, in the order, Cosmological, Biological and Psychological."

Walter Leaf compared Myer to Ruskin and considered him in some respects his peer. According to **Charles Richet** "if Myers were not a mystic, he had all the faith of a mystic and the ardour of an apostle, in conjunction with the sagacity and precision of a *savant.*"

"I never knew a man so hopeful concerning his ultimate destiny," wrote **Sir Oliver Lodge** in memoriam. "He once asked me whether I would barter—if it were possible—my unknown destiny, whatever it might be, for as many aeons of unmitigated and wise terrestrial happiness as might last till the secular fading of the sun, and then an end. He would not."

Myers was working not only in the first generation of parapsychology, but at a time when psychology was struggling to separate itself from the dominance of physiology. The kind words of Myers's contemporaries about his psychological theories reflect his general high standing in the intellectual community and the larger consideration that was being given to Myers's theories concerning the human personality. His psychological theories, which could possibly have made a significant place for the paranormal in the consideration of the psychological community, were, however, displaced by the competing thought of his contemporary, **Sigmund Freud,** and the emergence of psychotherapy. In the success of Freudian thought, Myers's ideas were pushed to the fringe.

Myers on Spiritualist Phenomena

In *Human Personality and Its Survival of Bodily Death,* physical phenomena received but little consideration. Myers believed in **telekinesis,** but in spite of his own experiments and those of **Sir William Crookes,** its genuine occurrence did not appear to him sufficiently believable to justify discussion in his book. Nevertheless, in dealing with **possession** he suggested an ingenious explanation, i.e., that the possessing spirit may use the organism more skillfully than its owner and may emit some energy that can visibly move ponderable objects not actually in contact with the flesh. Of his own investigations between 1872 and 1876 he said that they were "tiresome and distasteful enough."

On May 9, 1874, in the company of Edmund Gurney, he made the acquaintance of medium **William Stainton Moses.** The two became such close friends that when Moses died on September 5, 1982, his notebooks were handed to Myers for study.

Myers's articles in the *Proceedings* of the Society for Psychical Research (vols. 9 and 11) contain the best accounts of this remarkable mediumship, although his conclusions were not solely based on personal experiences with Moses. He also participated in some startling sessions involving **C. E. Wood** and **Annie Fairlamb Mellon.**

In 1894, on the Ile Roubaud, Myers was the guest of Charles Richet and participated with Sir Oliver Lodge and **Julien Ochorowicz** in the experiments conducted with **Eusapia Palladino.** The Cambridge exposure of Palladino's **fraud** shook his belief and he then wrote: "I had no doubt that systematic trickery had been used from the first to last, and that there was no adequate ground for attributing any of the phenomena occurring at these sittings to a supernormal cause." Later, however, he participated in another series of sittings with Palladino in Paris and at the solemn adjuration of Richet he declared himself convinced that both telekinesis and **ectoplasm** were genuine phenomena. He also sat with **Mrs. Thomas Everitt, Elizabeth d'Esperance,** and **David Duguid.**

Further, Myers experienced **crystal gazing** and he investigated the haunted Ballechin House in Perthshire, Scotland. As a result, he published two papers in the *Proceedings* of the Society for Psychical Research: "On Alleged Movements of Objects without Contact, occurring not in the Presence of a Paid Medium" (vol. 7, pts. 19 and 20, 1891–92).

Myers Speaks from the Grave?

Myers died January 17, 1901, in Rome, Italy. After his death, a flood of claimed communications from his spirit came from many mediums. The most important ones were those received through **Leonora Piper, Margaret Verrall,** and **Alice K. Fleming** (known publicly as Mrs. Holland). As regards the latter, Frank Podmore and **Alice Johnson** agreed that the "Myers" **control** was a subconscious creation of the medium. The views there expressed were alien to the mentality of the living Myers.

Verrall apparently obtained the contents of a sealed letter that Myers had written in 1891 and left in the care of Sir Oliver Lodge for such a test. However, when the letter was opened in 1904 the contents were found to be entirely different.

In 1907, **Eleanor Sidgwick** obtained good identity proofs through Leonora Piper. On her behalf, Verrall asked some questions to which she did not know that answer and received correct replies as regards the contents of the last conversation that had taken place between Mrs. Sidgwick and Myers.

Many other impressive indications of his surviving self were found in **cross-correspondences,** especially during Piper's second visit to England in 1906–07. The whole system of cross-correspondences appears to have been elaborated by him, and the wealth of classical knowledge displayed in the connected fragments given by several mediums raises a strong presumption that they emanated from Myers' mind.

The most striking evidence of this nature was obtained after Piper's return to the United States by G. B. Dorr in 1908. Frank Podmore considered it "perhaps the strongest evidence yet obtained for the identity of any communicator."

In *The Road to Immortality* (1932), a book supposedly written by Myers through **Geraldine Cummins,** a stupendous vista was opened up, apparently by Myers, of the soul's progression through the after-death states. As regards the authorship of the book, Sir Oliver Lodge received independent testimony through **Gladys Osborne Leonard** from "Myers" of his communications through Cummins. Lodge saw no reason to dissent from the view that the remarkable accounts of the fourth, fifth, sixth, and seventh states "are the kind of ideas which F. W. H. Myers may by this time [1932] have been able to form."

Sources:

Berger, Arthur S., and Joyce Berger. *The Encyclopedia of Parapsychology and Psychical Research.* New York: Paragon House, 1991.

Gauld, Alan. *The Founders of Psychical Research.* New York: Schocken Books, 1968.

Haynes, Renée. *The Society for Psychical Research, 1882–1982: A History.* London: Mcdonald, 1982.

Myers, F. W. H. *Human Personality and the Survival of Bodily Death.* London: Longmans, Green, 1903.

———. *Science and a Future Life: With Other Essays.* London: Macmillan, 1901.

Myers, F. W. H., Edmund Gurney, and Frank Podmore. *Phantasms of the Living.* London: Trubner, 1886.

Pleasants, Helene, ed. *Biographical Dictionary of Parapsychology.* New York: Helix Press, 1964.

Salter, W. H. "F. W. H. Myers' Posthumous Message." *Proceedings* of the Society for Psychical Research 52 (1958).

Myers, John (d. 1972)

Prominent British medium who demonstrated psychic healing and **spirit photography.** Originally a London dentist, he visited a psychical research society in 1931 where a medium warned him of a possible defect in his automobile. His interest in psychic phenomena so piqued, Myers visited the Stead Bureau (see **Julia's Bureau**), founded by **W. T. Stead.** He met the medium **Ada Emma Deane,** who practiced **psychic photography** and tried the phenomena for himself, with successful results. He also discovered a mediumistic talent.

In his séances, Myers would enter into semi-trance while standing and was controlled by "Blackfoot," an American Indian. From clairvoyant impressions, he would describe the presence of spirit forms and, quite frequently, the extra that would appear on a photographic plate.

He was challenged by the Marquess of Donegall. In the presence of the art editor of the *Sunday Dispatch,* journalist **Hannen Swaffer,** and stage magician Will Goldston, Donegall filled Myers's camera (which he examined) with his own marked plates, took six pictures in bright light while Myers simply stood by, and developed them himself.

Two of the plates showed extras that neither Donegall nor the art editor could explain (*Sunday Dispatch,* October 9, 1932). The following week, however, after another sitting, Donegall accused Myers of substituting plates.

In the 1930s, Myers was consulted by Laurence Parish, a New York businessman, who was greatly impressed by his psychic photography. Myers was also instrumental in the psychic healing of Parish's sciatica and restoring normal eyesight after years of defective vision. After these miraculous cures, Parish invited Myers to join his company in New York. Myers accepted and eventually became vice president of the company.

Sources:

Barbanell, Maurice. *He Walks in Two Worlds: The Story of John Myers, Psychic Photographer, Healer and Philanthropist.* London: n.p., 1964.

Myomancy

A method of divination by rats or mice, supposedly alluded to in the biblical book of Isaiah (62:17). Their peculiar cries, or some marked devastation committed by them, was taken for a prognostic of evil. Aeilan related that Fabius Maximus resigned the dictatorship in consequence of a warning from these creatures, and Cassius Flaminius retired from the command of the cavalry for no greater reason.

Herodotus stated that when the army of Sennacherib invaded Egypt, mice invaded their camp by night and gnawed their quivers and bows to pieces. In the morning, therefore, without arms, they fled in confusion; many were slain.

Horapollo, in his work on the hieroglyphics of Egypt, described the rat as a symbol of destruction and said that the Hebrew name of this animal is from a root that means to separate, divide, or judge. It has been remarked by one of the commentators on Horapollo that the mouse has a finely discriminating taste.

An Egyptian manuscript in the Bibliothèque Royale in Paris contains the representation of a soul going to judgment, in which one of the figures is depicted with the head of a rat. It is understood that the Libian rats and the mouse of Scripture are the same as the Arabian *jerboa,* which is characterized by a long tail, bushy at the end, and short forelegs.

Sources:

Waite, Arthur Edward. *The Occult Sciences.* 1891. Reprint, Secaucus, N.J.: University Books, 1974.

Mysteria Mystica Aeterna

A lodge of the occult society **OTO** (Ordo Templi Orientis) licensed to **Rudolf Steiner** (1861–1925) in 1906, some years before Steiner fully developed his own interpretations of **Theosophy,** which culminated in his concept of Anthroposophy (man-wisdom).

Mysteria Mystica Maxima

Name given to the British lodge of the occult society **OTO** (Ordo Templi Orientis) when **Theodor Reuss,** head of the German order, proposed that **Aleister Crowley** start a British section.

Mysteries

From the Greek word *muein,* to shut the mouth, and *mustes,* an initiate: a term for what is secret or concealed in a religious context. Although certain mysteries were probably part of the initiatory ceremony of the priests of ancient Egypt, we are ignorant of their exact nature, and the term is usually used in connection with certain semi-religious ceremonies held by various cults in ancient Greece.

The mysteries were secret cults, to which only certain initiated people were admitted after a period of preliminary preparation. After this initial period of purification came the mystic communication or exhortation, then the revelation to the neophyte of certain holy things, the crowning with the garlands, and lastly the communion with the deity. The mysteries appear to have revolved around the semi-dramatic representation of the life of a deity.

It is believed that these mystic cults were of pre-Hellenic origin, and that the Pelasgic aboriginal people of Greece strove to conceal their religions from the eyes of their conquerors. However, it is interesting to note that for the most part the higher offices of these cults were in the hands of aristocrats, who, it may be reasonably inferred, had little to do with the strata of the population that represented the Pelasgic peoples.

Again, the divinities worshiped in the mysteries possess for the most part Greek names and many of them are certainly gods evolved in Greece at a comparatively late period. We find a number of them associated with the realm of the dead. The Earth-god or goddess is in most countries often allied with the powers of darkness. It is from the underworld that grain arises, and therefore it is not surprising to find that Demeter, Ge, and Aglauros are identified with the underworld. But there were also the mysteries of Artemis, of Hecate, and the Cherites—some of which may be regarded as forms of the great Earth mother.

The worship of Dionysus, Trophonious, and Zagreus was also of a mysterious nature; however it is the Eleusinian and Orphic mysteries that undoubtedly are the most important to the occult student, and though archaeological findings (such as vase-painting) it has been possible to glean some general idea of these. That is not to say that the heart of the mystery is revealed by any such illustrations, but that these, supplemented by what the Christian fathers were able to glean regarding these mystic cults, give useful hints for further investigations.

Eleusis

The mysteries of Eleusis had for their primal adoration Demeter and Persephone (the mother and the daughter).

Other "nameless" divinities appear to have been associated with Eleusinian mysteries, usually signified by terms such as "the gods" or "the goddesses." Mythological science suggests that such nameless gods are merely those whose higher names are hidden and unspoken. In Egypt, for example, the concept of the concealed name was extremely common. The name of the power of a god, if discovered, bestowed on the discoverer control over that deity.

Dionysus is also a figure of some importance in the Eleusinian mystery. It has been thought that Orphic influence was responsible for his presence in the cult, but traces of Orphic doctrine have not been discovered in what is known of the mysteries.

A more baffling personality in the great ritual drama is that of Iacchus, who appears to be none other than Dionysus under another name. In either case Dionysus (or Iacchus) does not appear to be a primary figure of the mystery.

In early Greek legends there are allusions to the sacred character of the Eleusinian mysteries. From the fifth century their organization was in the hands of the Athenian city, the royal ruler of which, along with a committee of supervision, undertook the general management. The rites took place at the city of Eleusis and were celebrated by a hereditary priesthood, the Eumolpedie. They alone (or rather their high priest) could penetrate into the innermost holy of holies, but there were also priestesses and female attendants of the goddesses.

The celebration of the mysteries was somewhat as follows: in the month of September the Eleusinian Holy Things were taken from the sacred city to Athens and placed in the Eleusinion. These probably consisted to some extent of small statues of the goddesses. Three days afterward, the catechumens assembled to hearken to the exhortation of one of the priests, during which those who were for any reason unworthy of initiation were solemnly warned to depart. All Greeks or Romans above a certain age were admitted, including women and even slaves, but foreigners and criminals could not partake.

The candidates were questioned about their purification, especially regarding the food they had eaten. After this assembly, they went to the seashore, bathed, and were sprinkled with the blood of pigs. A sacrifice was offered up, and several days later the Eleusinian procession commenced its journey along the sacred way, its central figure being a statue of Iacchus. Many shrines were visited on the way to Eleusis, where, upon arrival, the supplicants celebrated with a midnight orgy.

It is difficult to know what occurred in the inner circle, but there appear to have been two grades in the celebration, and we know that a year elapsed before a person who had achieved one grade became fit for election to the higher. Regarding the actual ritual in the hall of mystery, a great deal of controversy has taken place, but it is certain that a dramatic representation was the central point of interest, the chief characters in which were probably Demeter and Persephone, and that the myth of the lost daughter and the sorrowing mother was enacted before an audience. Of scenic display there was probably little or none, as excavation has proved that there was not room for it, and we find nothing regarding scenery in the accounts presented in many inscriptions; but the apparel of the actors was probably most magnificent, heightened by the effect of gloom and torch-light.

Certain sacred symbols were also displayed before the eyes of the elect. These appear to have been small idols of the goddesses, of great antiquity and sanctity. We know that the original symbols of deity are jealously guarded by many priesthoods. For example, the Uapes of Brazil kept careful watch over the symbols of Jurupari, their god, and they were shown only to the initiated. Any woman who cast eyes on them was instantly poisoned.

It was also stated by Hippolytus that the ancients were shown a cut corn stalk, the symbol of Demeter and Persephone. This, however, is debatable, as is the theory that the Eleusinians worshiped the actual corn as a clan totem. Corn as a totem is not unknown elsewhere, as for example in Peru, where the *cconopa* or godlings of the maize fields were probably originally totemic.

But if the Eleusinian corn was a totem, it was certainly the only corn totem known to Greece, and corn totems are rare. The totem was usually initiated with the hunting condition of peoples. When they arrived at the agricultural stage a fresh pantheon usually slowly evolved, in which full-fledged gods took the place of the old totemic deities. The corn appears as a living thing. It is growth, and within it resides a spirit. Therefore the deity that evolves from this concept is more likely to be of animistic than of totemistic origin.

The neophyte was then made one with the deity by partaking of holy food or drink. This recalls the story of Persephone, who, upon reaching the dark shores of Hades, partook of the food of the dead—thus rendering it impossible for her to return. Once the human soul eats or drinks in Hades, it may not return to Earth. This belief is universal, and it is highly probable that it was symbolized in the Eleusinian mysteries.

M. Foucart ingeniously put forward the theory that the object of the Eleusinian mysteries was much the same as that of the Egyptian *Book of the Dead,* i.e., to provide the initiates with elaborate rules for avoiding the dangers of the underworld, and to instruct them in the necessary magical formula. Thus, friendship with the Holy Mother and Daughter (Demeter and Persephone), to the Eleusinian votary, was the chief assurance of immortality.

Dionysiac

A great many offshoots of the Eleusinian cult were established in several parts of Greece. The most important cult next to the Eleusinian was the Orphic, which probably arose in Phrygia, and which came to be associated with Dionysus, originally a god of vegetation, who was also a divinity of the nether world. By entering into communion with Dionysus it was believed that immortality might be assured. His celebrations were marked by orgies of a bacchic description, in which it was thought that the neophyte partook for the moment of the character and the power of the deity himself.

The rites of the cult of Dionysus were of a much more barbaric nature than those of Eleusis. For instance, the devouring of an animal victim was supposed to symbolize the incarnation, death, and resurrection of the divinity. Later the Dionysiac mysteries were somewhat tempered, but always retained something of their earlier character. The cult does not appear to have been highly regarded by the sages of its time.

The golden tablets relating to the Orphic mystery found in tombs in Greece, Crete, and Italy contain fragments of a sacred hymn. As early as the third century C.E., it was buried with the dead as an **amulet** to protect the deceased from the dangers of the underworld.

Attis and Cybele

The Phrygian mysteries of Attis and Cybele focused on the rebirth of the god Attis, who was also of an agrarian character. Communion with the deity was usually attained by bathing in blood in the *taurobolium* or by the letting of blood.

Mithraic Mysteries

The Mithraic cult was of Persian origin, having at its center Mithra, a personification of light worshiped in that country some five hundred years before the Christian era. Carried into Asia Minor by small colonies of **magi,** it was largely influenced by the religions with which it was brought into contact.

For instance, Chaldean **astrology** inspired much of the occult traditions surrounding the creed of the sun-god; the art of Greece influenced the representation of Mithra Tauroctonous that graced the temples of the cult; and the Romans gave it a wide geographical area and immense influence.

According to Plutarch, the rites originally reached Rome through the agency of Cilician privates conquered and taken there by Pompey. Another source, doubtless, was the large number of Asiatic slaves employed in Roman households. Again the Roman soldiery must have carried the Mithraic cult as far north as the mountains of Scotland, and south to the borders of the Sahara Desert.

Mithraism may be said to have been the only living religion Christianity found a need to combat. It was strong enough to exert a formative influence on certain Christian doctrines, such as those relative to the end of the world and the powers of hell.

Mithra was essentially the divinity of beneficence. He was the genius of celestial light, endowing the Earth with all its benefits. As the sun he put darkness to flight, so by a natural transition he came to represent truth and integrity, the sun of goodness that conquers the night of evil. To him was ascribed the role of mediator between God and humanity. His creed promised a resurrection to a future life of happiness and felicity.

Briefly the story of Mithra is as follows. Mithra sprang to being in the gloom of a cavern from the heart of a rock, seen by none but humble shepherds. He grew in strength and courage, excelling all, and used his powers to rid the world of evil.

Of all his deeds of prowess, however, the one upon which the cult centered was the slaying of a bull, itself possessed of divine potentialities. From the spinal cord of the bull sprang the wheat of the human race's daily bread, from its blood the vine, source of the sacred drink of the mysteries, and from its seed all the different species of useful animals. After this beneficent deed, Mithra ruled in the heavens, yet still kept watch over human beings, granting the petitions asked in his name. Those who followed him, who were initiated into his mysteries, passed under his divine protection, especially after death, when he would rescue their souls from the powers of darkness. In addition, when the Earth failed in her life-sustaining powers, Mithra would slay a divine bull and give to all abundant life and happiness.

Among Mithra's worshipers were slaves and soldiers, high officials and dignitaries, who worshipped in temples, mithraeums as they were called, built underground or in caves and grottoes in the depths of dark forests, symbolizing the birthplace of their god.

The rites in which they participated were of magical significance and an oath of silence was taken by all.

In order to bring their lives into closer communion with the divinity of Mithra, the neophytes had to pass through seven degrees of initiation, successively assuming the names of Raven, Occult, Soldier, Lion, Persian, Runner of the Sun, and Father. Each of these grades carried with it symbolic garments and masks, donned by the celebrants. The masks represented birds and animals and seem to indicate belief in the doctrine of metempsychosis, or perhaps they point to a remnant of totemic belief. An almost ascetic habit of life was demanded, including prolonged fasting and purification.

Before the supplicants entered the higher grades, a ceremony called the Sacrament was held where they partook of consecrated bread and wine. Believers were also expected to undergo dramatic trials of strength, faith, and endurance, a stoical attitude and unflinching moral courage demanded as sign of fitness in the participant. The drinking of the sacred wine and the baptism of blood were supposed to bring to the initiate not only material benefit but wisdom. They gave the power to combat evil and the power to attain the immortality of their god.

An order of priests was connected with this cult, which faithfully carried on the occult tradition and usages, such as that of initiation, the rites of which were arduous; the tending of a perpetual fire on the altars; and prayers to the sun at dawn, noon, and evening. There were sacrifices, libations, and musical rites including long psalmodies and mystic chants.

The days of the week were each sacred to a planet, the day of the sun being held especially holy. There were seasonal festivals: the birth of the sun was solemnized on the 25th of December, and the equinoxes were days of rejoicing, while the initiations were held preferably in the spring, in March or April.

It is believed that in the earliest days of the cult, some of the rites were of a savage and barbaric character, especially the sacrificial element, but these, as indicated, were changed and ennobled as the beneficence of Mithra took precedence over his warlike prowess.

The Mithraic brotherhoods were involved with secular interests as well as spiritual ones and were in fact highly organized communities, composed of trustees, councils, senates, attorneys, patrons, and people of high status and wealth. Belonging to such a body gave the initiate a sense of brotherhood and comradeship that was doubtless a powerful reason for the popularity the Mithraic cult gained in the Roman army, whose members, dispersed to the ends of the Earth, relied on such fraternal comfort and solace.

Sources:

Angus, Samuel. *The Mystery Religions and Christianity.* London: John Murray, 1928. Reprint, New York: Dover, 1975.

Burkert, Walter. *Ancient Mystery Cults.* Cambridge, Mass.: Harvard University Press, 1987.

Cumont, F. V. M. *Mysteries of Mithra.* London: Kegan Paul; Chicago: Open Court, 1910.

Harrison, Jane E. *Prolegmena to the Study of Greek Religion.* Cambridge University Press, 1922.

Masks of Dionysus. Ithaca, N.Y.: Cornell University Press, 1993.

Mylonas, George E. *Eleusis and the Eleusian Mysteries.* Princeton, N.J.: Princeton University Press, 1961.

Nilsson, Martin P. *The Dionysian Mysteries of the Hellenistic and Roman Age.* Lund, Sweden: C. W. K. Gleerup, 1957.

Ouvaroff, M. *Essay on the Mysteries of Eleusis.* London: Rodwell & Martin, 1817.

Mystic Order of Veiled Prophets of the Enchanted Realm

In spite of its name, the Mystic Order of Veiled Prophets of the Enchanted Realm is not an occult or mystical organization, but entirely a fellowship association for Master Masons. The order was created in 1889 by LeRoy Fairchild and members of a Masonic lodge in Hamilton, New York. It grew out of an expressed desire of lodge members for diversions from the mundane concerns. Meeting for the first time in September of 1889, the order was originally known as the Fairchild Deviltry Committee. The idea proved a popular one, and the next year, members of the growing organization formally instituted the Supreme Council of the Mystic Order of Veiled Prophets of the Enchanted Realm. From the beginning, membership was limited to Master Masons in good standing.

In spite of its major membership requirement, the order is not formally connected to any particular Masonic organization and does not engage in Masonic rituals. It does encourage the members' participation in their lodge, but the rituals and activities of the order are strictly for fun. The unique ritual of the order is an elaborately staged production that amid its humor offers lessons in optimism, brotherhood, and the benefits of fellowship.

Order chapters are known as grottoes, a number of which are found across North America. New members receive a fez, a distinctive pin, and a membership card, which will admit a member to any grotto in North America. Members of the order can be recognized by their wearing of the pin in their everyday life. The order's supreme council may be contacted at 1696 Brice Rd., Reynoldsburg, OH 43068. Its Internet page is found at http://members.tripod.com/%7Ebelagrotto/GrottoH.htm.

Sources:Mystic Order of Veiled Prophets of the Enchanted Realm. http://members.tripod.com/%7Ebelagrotto/GrottoH.htm. February 20, 2000.

Mystical Night (of the Sufis)

It was believed by the **Sufis** that to attain the coveted state of mystical contemplation, it was necessary to close the gateway of the physical senses, so that the inner or spiritual senses might operate more freely.

This injunction was sometimes taken literally, as by the Brahmin Yogis, who carefully closed eyes, ears, nose, and mouth in order to attain visionary ecstasy.

The Mystical Night was thus a shutting out of all external sense impressions—of hope, fear, consciousness of self, and every human emotion—so that the interior light might be more clearly perceived. (See also **meditation; yoga**)

Mysticism

The attempt of man to attain the ultimate reality of things and experience direct communion with the highest. Mysticism maintains the possibility of a relationship with God, not by means of revelation or the ordinary religious channels, but by introspection and **meditation** in conjunction with a purified life, culminating in the awareness that the individual partakes of the divine nature. Mysticism has been identified with pantheism by some authorities, and many pantheists have been mystics. However, mysticism is not tied to any particular philosophical or theological perspective.

Mysticism tends to differ from public religion, which emphasizes a worshipful submission to the deity and the ethical dimension of life, while mysticism strains after the realization of a personal union with the divine source itself. The mystic desires to be as close to God as possible, part of the divine essence itself, whereas the ordinary devotee of most religious systems merely desires to walk in God's way and obey his will.

Historical Survey

Mysticism has emerged as a strain in all of the major religious systems, both East and West. It tends to have a particular affinity, however, with some systems. While there is, for example, a perceptible mystical stain in Christianity, Judaism (Hassidism), and Islam (Sufism), Western systems that emphasize the transcendence of a personal all-powerful deity have made mysticism a secondary concern. In the East, where the unreality of material things is emphasized, mysticism is a more dominant form of spiritual life. The **Sufis** of Persia may be said to be a link between the more austere Indian mystics and those of Europe.

With the rise of Alexandrian **Neoplatonism,** mysticism attained a new level of presence in Europe. Neoplatonism made a definite mark upon early Christianity, and we find it mirrored in many of the patristic writings of the sixteenth century.

It was Erigena who, in the ninth century, transmitted to Europe the so-called writings of Dionysius the Areopagite, the sixth century Syrian thinker who synthesized Christian theology and Neoplatonism and thus greatly influenced the mysticism of the Middle Ages. Erigena based his own system upon that of Dionysius. This was the so-called "negative theology," which placed God above all categories and designated him as nothing, or the incomprehensible essence from which the world of primordial causes is eternally created. This creation is the work of the Son of God, in whom all substantial things exist; but God is the beginning and end of everything. On this system Christian mysticism may be said to have been founded with little variation.

With Erigena, reason and authority are identical, and in this he agrees with all speculative mystics. Scholasticism, however, is characterized by the acceptance by reason of a given matter that is presupposed even when it cannot be understood. It seemed to Erigena that in the scholastic system, religious truth was external to the mind, while the opposite view was fundamental to mysticism.

That is not to say that mysticism according to Erigena is a mere subordination of reason to faith. Mysticism indeed places every confidence in human reason, and it is essential that it should have the unity of the human mind with the divine as its main tenet, but it accepts nothing from without, and it posits the higher faculty of reason over the realization of absolute truth.

Medieval mysticism may be said to have originated from a reaction of practical religion against the dialectics in which the true spirit of Christianity was then enshrined. Thus St. Bernard opposed the dry scholasticism of Abelard. His mysticism was profoundly practical, and dealt chiefly with the means by which human beings may attain the knowledge of God. This is to be accomplished through contemplation and withdrawal from the world.

Asceticism is the soul of medieval mysticism, but St. Bernard averred regarding self-love that it is proper to love ourselves for God's sake, or because God loved us, thus merging self-love in love for God. We must, so to speak, love ourselves in God, in whom we ultimately lose ourselves. In this, St. Bernard is almost Buddhistic, and indeed his mysticism is of the universal type.

Perhaps Hugh of St. Victor, a contemporary of St. Bernard's, did more to develop the tenets of mysticism, and his monastery of Augustinians near Paris became a great center of mysticism. One of his apologists, Richard of St. Victor, declared that the objects of mystic contemplation are partly above reason, and partly, as regards intuition, contrary to reason. The protagonists of this theory, all of whom issued from the same monastery, were known as the Victorines and put up a stout fight against the dialecticians and schoolmen. Bonaventura, who died in 1274, was a disciple of this school and a believer in the faculty of mystic intuition.

In the twelfth and thirteenth centuries, the worldliness of the church aroused much opposition among laymen, and the church's cold formalism created a reaction towards a more spiritual regime. Many sects arose, such as the **Waldenses,** the Cathari (see **Gnosticism**), and the Beguines, all of which strove to infuse into their teachings a warmer spirituality than that which burned in the heart of the church of their time.

In Germany, mysticism made great strides, and Machthild of Magdeburg and Elizabeth of Thuringia were, if not the originators of mysticism in Germany, certainly among its earliest supporters. Joachim of Flores and Amalric of Bena wrote strongly in favor of a reformed church, and their writings are drenched with mystical terms, derived for the most part from Erigena. Joachim mapped out the duration of the world into three ages, that of the Father, that of the Son, and that of the Spirit—the last of which was to commence with the year 1260, and to be inaugurated by the general adoption of monastic and contemplative life.

A sect called the New Spirit, or the Free Spirit, became widespread through northern France, Switzerland, and Germany; and these did much to infuse the spirit of mysticism throughout Germany.

It is with Meister Eckhart, who died in 1327, that we get the juncture of mysticism with scholastic theology. Of his doctrine it has been said:

"The ground of your being lies in God. Reduce yourself to that simplicity, that root, and you are in God. There is no longer any distinction between your spirit and the divine—you have escaped personality and finite limitation. Your particular, creature self, as a something separate and dependent on God is gone. So also, obviously, your creaturely will. Henceforth, therefore, what seems an inclination of yours is in fact the divine good pleasure. You are free from law. You are above means. The very will to do the will of God is resolved into that will itself. This is the Apathy, the Negation, the Poverty, he commends."

With Eckhart personally this self-reduction and deification is connected with a rigorous asceticism and exemplary moral excellence. Yet it is easy to see that it may be a merely intellectual process, consisting in a man's thinking that he is thinking himself away from his personality. He declares the appearance of the Son necessary to enable us to realize our sonship; and yet his language implies that this realization is the perpetual incarnation of that Son—does, as it were, constitute him. Christians are accordingly not less the sons of God by grace than is Christ by nature. Believe yourself divine, and the Son is brought forth in you. The Saviour and the saved are dissolved together in the blank absolute substance."

With the advent of the Black Death, a great spirit of remorse swept over Europe in the fourteenth century, and a vast revival of piety took place. This resulted in the foundation in Germany of a society of Friends of God, whose chief object was to strengthen each other in intercourse with the creator. Perhaps the most distinguished of these were John Tauler and Nicolas of Basle, and the society numbered many inmates of the cloister, as well as wealthy men of commerce and others. **Ruysbroek,** the great Flemish mystic, was connected with them, but his mysticism is perhaps more intensely practical than that of any other visionary. The machinery by which the union with God is to be effected is the most attractive. In Ruysbroek's lifetime, a mystical society arose in Holland called the Brethren of Common Lot, who founded an establishment at which Groot dispensed the principles of mysticism to Radewyn and Thomas Kempis.

The attitude of mysticism at the period of the Reformation is peculiar. We find a mystical propaganda sent forth by a body of **Rosicrucians** denouncing Roman Catholicism in the fiercest terms, and we also observe the spirit of mysticism strongly within those bodies that resisted the coldness and formalism of the Roman Catholic Church of that time.

On the other hand, however, we find the principles of Luther strongly opposed by some of the most notable mystics of his time. But the Reformation passed, and mysticism went on its way, divided, it is true, so far as the outward theological principles of its votaries were concerned, but strongly united in its general principles.

It is with Nicolas of Kusa, who died in 1464, that mysticism triumphs over scholasticism. Nicolas was the protagonist of super-knowledge, or that higher ignorance which is the knowledge of the intellect in contra-distinction to the mere knowledge of the understanding. His doctrines colored those of Giordano Bruno (1550–1600) and his theosophy certainly preceded that of **Paracelsus** (1493–1541). The next great name in mysticism is that of **Jakob Boehme** (1575–1624), a German Rosicrucian mystical teacher.

The Roman Catholic Church produced many mystics of note in the sixteenth and seventeenth centuries, including Francis of Sales, Madame Guyon, and Molinos—the last two of which were the protagonists of Quietism, which set forth the theory that there should be no pleasure in the practice of mysticism, and that God did not exist for the enjoyment of man. Perhaps the greatest students of Boehme were **William Law** (1686–1761) and **Saint-Martin** (1743–1803).

The Universality of Mystical Experience

It is clear from the statements of mystics that they are not limited to any given religion or theology. Given the elevation of the mystical experience over any theological reflection upon that experience, it has been relatively easy for mystics of different traditions to relate to each other, often finding a more natural affinity that with the non-mystic members of their own religious tradition. It is obvious that they are dealing with an element in human experience common to all of humankind. When Meister Eckhart stated, "If I am to know God directly, I must become completely He, and He I: so that this He and this I become and are one I," he comes to the same point as the Advaita Vedanta doctrine of Hinduism, where the *jiva* (individual soul) merges with Brahma the creator before absorption in Brahman, the non-personal divine ground.

Sufism, Islamic mysticism, first arose in the ninth century among the Persian Moslems, probably as a protest against the severe monotheism of their religion, but in all likelihood more ancient springs contributed to its revival. In the Persia of Hafiz and Saadi, pantheism abounded, and their magnificent poetry is read by Moslems as having a deep mystical significance, although for the most part it deals with the intoxication of love. It is certain that many of them exhibit the fervor of souls searching for communion with the highest.

The apparent differences between Hindu mysticism and Christian mysticism are nominal. Although Christian theology postulates the divine in the form of God as Father, Son, and Holy Spirit, such distinctions become largely unimportant in the actual mystical experience. Similarly, popular Hinduism postulates hundreds of different gods and goddesses, but these are merely legal fictions to the Indian mystic, melting away in the totality of higher consciousness.

Because mind and emotion are transcended in the higher reaches of mysticism, they are seen by mystics as merely ways of reaching a reality that lies beyond them, a totality of consciousness without object, beyond the normal human limitations of individual body, ego, personality, hopes, and fears.

Like Christianity, Hindu Vedanta (inquiry into ultimate reality), has different schools of theology, ranging from *Advaita* (monism or non-dualism, claiming that all is one and only the divine ultimate has actual existence, all else being illusory) to degrees of *Dvaita* or dualism (claiming that there is one ultimate divine principle of God but that the soul is a separate principle with independent existence). Such schools are not really contradictory to the mystic, but rather different degrees of interpretation of one reality on the way to an actual mystical experience in which intellectual distinctions vanish.

The Way of the Mystic

In both Eastern and Western mysticism, withdrawal from the everyday life of a householder is recognized as an aid to mystical progress, thus both have monastic establishments at which one follows a life of prayer and meditation. In the initial stages, self-purification is facilitated by dedicated service to others, prior to the more secluded life of the contemplative.

Mystics have sometimes been accused of escapism, of retreating from the responsibilities of everyday life into a private world, and indeed, the descriptions of the ecstasies of spiritual awareness often sound rather like a selfish indulgence, oblivious to the problems of the outside world.

It is clear that the ideal mystic partakes fully of the duties and social responsibility of life after spiritual enlightenment, since mystical experience should give deeper meaning to the reality behind the everyday mundane world. For most individuals, however, a period of retreat from everyday life is helpful in disengaging oneself from the fears, desires, and egoism of mundane existence.

Hinduism places great stress on *dharma,* the duties and responsibilities of the individual, which take priority over any desire for transcendentalism. During this period one would observe the everyday religious rites and rituals related to the gods and goddesses of an individual's life. Later, however, when one had fulfilled one's responsibilities, married, begat a family, and provided for them, the realization that everything connected with the material world and physical life was transient would grow steadily, culminating in a hunger for knowledge of what is eternal.

At such a time, one might seek a qualified **guru** or spiritual preceptor and follow an ascetic life, discarding all material possessions, egoism, hopes, and fears in the quest for a higher spiritual awareness not subject to birth and death, or change and decay. Various pathways of **yoga** facilitated that quest, involving self-purification, service to others, and refinement of perception based upon physical health and its spiritual counterpart.

The Hindu emphasis on the duties and responsibilities of a householder taking priority over the quest for mystical enlightenment have something in common with Judaism, which does not seek to separate mystical experience from everyday life. Judaism is essentially pragmatic in its approach to the spiritual life and requires that mystical experience be interfused with daily life and religious observance.

The Jewish mystic typified in the period of eighteenth- to nineteenth-century **Hasidism,** was a pious rabbi, living a life of prayer, study, and meditation within his community and sharing everyday social life and responsibility. In this respect he resembled the Eastern teacher around whom a group of pupils would gather for spiritual teaching and experience.

The Mechanisms of Mysticism

It is clear that the concept of self-purification in mystical progress involves psycho-physical mechanisms. Fasting, asceticism, mortification, and intense meditation have profound effects on the individual nervous system and other aspects of the body and mind. Very little discussion on this important area appeared in Western literature until Aldous Huxley published *The Doors of Perception* (1954) and *Heaven & Hell* (1956). The starting point for Huxley's speculations about the psychophysical mechanisms of mystical experience was his own experiment in taking mescaline, a psychedelic drug, and unfortunately this particular stimulus has overshadowed the wider implications of his discussion.

A more simplistic interpretation of Huxley's speculations leads directly to the psychedelic revolution of the 1960s, spearheaded by **Timothy Leary** and **Richard Alpert,** based on the conviction that by merely taking certain chemical substances one could have a spiritual experience comparable with that of the great mystics of history. This was a concept that Huxley himself deplored in his later years.It is now obvious that the chemical ecstasy and visions produced by psychedelic drugs are qualitatively different from the transcendental union experienced by the mystic who has devoted years to self-purification of mind, inner exploration, and spiritual perception, and that unless there is such a purification of the individual, the consumption of drugs can produce an intense but ultimately shallow experience. The search for chemical ecstasy was soon abandoned by its major early exponents, such as **Walter Houston Clark.**

It is now clear that the gradual transformation of the personality on all levels—physical, mental, emotional and spiritual—involves specific psycho-physical concomitants. Some of these may be accessible to scientific inspection. It may also be possible to evaluate various degrees of transcendental experience, ranging from emotional euphoria to progressively more profound areas of higher consciousness.

The modern Hindu mystic **Pandit Gopi Krishna,** who experienced a dramatic development of higher consciousness following a period of intense yoga discipline and meditation, has published his experiences and the perceptions accompanying them in a series of books, which during the last years of his life attracted the attention of scientists in investigating the phenomenon.

Paranormal Side Effects

Most religions have reported miraculous phenomena associated with the path of mysticism, including visions, disembodied voices, **levitation,** and gifts of healing. Christian saints have their miracles and the yogis have their occult powers. It would seem that with the transcendence of normal mental and emotional life, there is an area of transcendence of normal physical law. However, the mystic is warned not to be snared by such phenomena, since it will activate egoism and pride, common faults of the beginner on the spiritual path.

A Turning Point in Western Mysticism

Recent studies of Christian mysticism recognize 1200–1350 C.E. as a crucial period in Western mysticism history. The era witnessed new styles and forms of religion, including reformed attitudes toward the relation of the world and the church. No longer was withdrawal from the worldly considered necessary to experience the mystical. Language styles changed in mystical poetry, sermons, and hagiography. Most significantly, there was a growth in the number of mystics, both male and female, as women began to take on a more influential role in mysticism during this time. Among these women visionaries was the ecstatic mystic Angela of Foligno and several great spiritual leaders of the Beguine movement: Mary of Oignies, Hadewijch of Antwerp, Mechthild of Magdeburg, and Marguerite Porete.

Sources:

"AE" [George W. Russell]. *The Candle of Vision.* London: Macmillan, 1919. Reprint, New Hyde Park, N.Y.: University Books, 1965.

Augustine, St. *Confessions.* N.p., n.d.Blakney, Raymond B. *Meister Eckhart: A Modern Translation.* New York: Harper, 1941.

Brinton, Howard H. *The Mystic Will: Based on a Study of the Philosophy of Jacob Boehme.* New York: Macmillan, 1930.

Buber, Martin. *Tales of the Hasidim: The Early Masters.* London: Thames & Hudson, 1956. Reprint, New York: Schocken, 1961.

Bucke, Richard M. *Cosmic Consciousness: A Study in the Evolution of the Human Mind.* 1901. Reprint, New Hyde Park, N.Y.: University Books, 1961.

Cheney, Sheldon. *Men Who Have Walked with God.* New York: Alfred A. Knopf, 1968. Reprint, New York: Dell, 1974.

Clement, Olivier and Theodore Berkeley. *The Roots of Christian Mysticism : Text and Commentary.* New York: New City Press, 1995.

Ferguson, John. *An Illustrated Encyclopaedia of Mysticism and The Mystery Religions.* London: Thames & Hudson, 1976.

Gall, Edward. *Mysticism Throughout the Ages.* London: Rider, 1934.

Gopi Krishna, Pandit. *The Biological Basis of Religion and Genius.* New York: Harper & Row, 1972.

Hartmann, Thom. *The Last Hours of Ancient Sunlight: Waking Up to Personal and Global Transformation.* Northfeld, Vt.: Mystical Books, 1998.

Huxley, Aldous. *The Doors of Perception.* London: Chatto & Windus, 1954.

———. *Heaven & Hell.* London: Chatto & Windus, 1956.

James, William. *The Varieties of Religious Experience.* London, 1902.

Johnston, William. *Christian Mysticism Today.* San Francisco: Harper & Row, 1984.

Jones, Richard H. *Mysticism Examined: Philosophical Inquiries into Mysticism.* Albany: State University of New York Press, 1993.

Lawrence, Brother. *The Practice of the Presence of God.* London, 1691. *Light from Light: An Anthology of Christian Mysticism.* Edited by Louis Dupre and James A. Wiseman. New York: Paulist Press, 1988.

Maeterlinck, Maurice. *Ruysbroeck and the Mystics.* London, 1908.

McGinn, Bernard. *The Flowering of Mysticism: Men and Women in the New Mysticism (1200-1350).* New York: Crossroad, 1998.

McGinn, Bernard. *The Foundations of Mysticism (Presence of God : A History of Western Christian Mysticism, Vol 1).* New York: Crossroad, 1994.

O'Brien, Elmer. *Varieties of Mystical Experience.* New York: Holt, Rinehart, and Winston, 1964.

Pandit, Madhav Pundalik. *Traditions in Mysticism.* New Delhi, India: Sterling, 1987.

Patanjali. *The Yoga-Sutras of Patanjali.* N.p., n.d.Roth, Ron and Peter Occhiogrosso. *The Healing Path of Prayer: The Modern Mystic's Guide to Spiritual Power.* New York: Harmony Books, 1997.

Swedenborg, Emanuel. *Divine Love and Wisdom.* New York: Swedenborg Foundation, n.d.

Underhill, Evelyn. *The Mystic Way: A Psychological Study in Christian Origins.* London and New York, 1913.

———. *Mysticism: A Study in the Nature & Development of Man's Spiritual Consciousness.* London: Methuen; New York: E. P. Dutton, 1911.

Waite, Arthur E. *Lamps of Western Mysticism.* London: Kegan Paul; New York: Alfred A. Knopf, 1923. Reprint, Blauvelt, N.Y.: Multimedia, 1973.

———. *Studies in Mysticism.* London: Hodder & Stoughton, 1906.

Younghusband, Francis. *Modern Mystic.* London: John Murray, 1935. Reprint, New Hyde Park, N.Y.: University Books, 1970.

Zaehner, R. C. *Mysticism: Sacred, and Profane.* London: Oxford, 1957.

N

NAA See National Astrological Association

Nacht, Sacha (1901–)

Physician and psychoanalyst concerned with relationships between psychology and parapsychology. He was born on September 23, 1901, in Bacau, Romania, but later moved to **France,** where he studied at the Faculté de Médecine de Paris, and was director of the Institut de Psychanalyse de Paris from 1952. Author of *La Psychanalyse d'aujourd'hui* (1956, American ed. 1959).

Sources:

Pleasants, Helene, ed. *Biographical Dictionary of Parapsychology.* New York: Helix Press, 1964.

Nada

A Sanskrit term used in Hindu musical theory to denote subtle aspects of musical sound. There are two kinds of nada: *anahata* is the mystical essence of sound; *ahata* is the conscious realization of musical sound by human beings. Anahata is heard by yogis in **meditation** and is related to different *chakras* (psychic centers) in the human body. *Nada upasana* is the **yoga** of **music,** which brings God-realization through pure forms of music and meditation. (See also **Swami Nadabrahmananda Saraswati; vibrations; Alfred Wolfsohn**)

Sources:

Rogo, D. Scott. *Nada: A Study of Some Unusual "Other World" Experiences.* 2 vols. New Hyde Park, N.Y.: University Books, 1970, 1972.

Sivananda, Swami. *Music as Yoga.* Rishikesh, India, 1956.

Nadabrahmananda Saraswati, Swami (1896– ?)

A Hindu musician who developed a **yoga** of **music,** involving the arousal of **kundalini** energy through the psychic power of sound vibrations. Born May 5, 1896, in Mysore, India, he studied music under Shri Sadasiva Bua, and Ustad Alladiya Khan of Dolahpur, eventually becoming a disciple of Tata Bua of Benares. He spent 15 years in perfecting his skills and was a devotee of the late **Swami Sivananda.** Saraswati taught music to students at the Sivananda Ashram (Divine Life Society), Rishikesh, Himalayas, North India.

He not only played various instruments like *swara mandala* (Indian zither) and *tabla* (Indian drums), but was also a master of the intricate graces of Thaan or vocal exercises. During his vocal performances he directed the sound vibration to various parts of his body, and sent out **vibrations** through his ears and the top of his head when his mouth was covered. In his performances on the tabla, he suspended respiration for nearly half an hour in a state of **trance,** playing the most intricate and complex rhythms without movement of his eyes or head. He also used sound vibrations for psychic **healing.** (See also **nada**)

Naddeo, Alighiero (1930–)

Italian professor of statistics who has conducted investigations in parapsychology. He was born on August 18, 1930, in Rome, Italy. He studied at the University of Rome (LL.B., 1952; B.S. statistics, 1953). He joined the faculty at the university (1954–61) and eventually in 1961 was named a professor of statistics at the University of Trieste. He is the author (with M. Boldrini) of *Le statistiche empirische e la teoria dei campioni* (Empirical Statistical Studies on the Sample Theory, 1950). In his investigation of **ESP** ability with 500 students he concluded that the correct results were higher than random expectation.

Sources:

Pleasants, Helene, ed. *Biographical Dictionary of Parapsychology.* New York: Helix Press, 1964.

Nakaidokilini (d. 1881)

Nakaidokilini or Nochaydel-klinne was an Apache visionary who emerged in 1881 during the time that the U.S. government's attempts at pacification of the Native American population was being hampered by Geronimo. During a lull in the ongoing hostilities, Nakaidokilini emerged claiming that he possessed power to raise the dead and that he regularly communed with spirit entities. He also brought the welcome message that the whites would soon be driven from the land. From his spirit contacts he had learned a dance that he taught his followers. With Nakaidokilini assuming a position in the center, dancers would be arranged in lines outward, much as spokes on a wagon wheel. They faced inward and as they moved in a circular pattern around him, he sprinkled them with *hoddentin,* a sacred yellow powder made from the pollen of the tule-rush, a plant widely used by the Apache.

In June of 1881, he asserted his position by offering to raise two prominent Apache chiefs who had been recently killed, if a sufficient number of blankets and horses were brought to him. The excited Apache accumulated the horses and blankets with the understanding that they would seek the return of their property if the chiefs did not reappear. Nakaidokilini began his spiritual work and the dancers kept up the new dance they had been taught. After a few days, the prophet announced that the chiefs would not return until the whites were out of the land, and that they would be gone before the corn was ripe (it was already July).

The antiwhite statements called the government's attention to the prophet and his followers, and white officials decided to arrest him. They had learned that at the end of August he was to make an appearance at the area designated for the dancing. Eighty-six soldiers and 26 Native scouts arrived at the spot and placed Nakaidokilini under arrest. On their way back to their post, the soldiers were attacked, with their scouts joining the attackers. They fought off their attackers, but in the process Nakaidokilini was killed. His movement soon fell apart.

Sources:

Debo, Angie. *A History of the Indians of the United States.* Norman: University of Oklahoma Press, 1970.

Mooney, James. "The Ghost-Dance Religion and the Sioux Outbreak of 1890." In the *Fourteenth Annual Report of the Bureau of Ethnology.* Compiled by J. W. Powell. Washington: Government Printing Office, 1896.

Napellus

A plant with narcotic properties, with which J. B. Van Helmont (1577–1644) experimented. He stated that, having on one occasion roughly prepared the root, he tasted it with his tongue, and in a very short time found that his center of thought and intellect was situated in the pit of his stomach. An unusual clarity and distinctness of thought rendered the experience a pleasant one, and he sought on future occasions to repeat it by the same means, but without success. After about two hours he felt a slight dizziness and thereupon thought in the normal fashion with his brain. But throughout the strange experience he claimed that he was conscious that his soul still remained in the brain as a governing power.

The plant with which Van Helmont experimented was *Aconitum napellus,* or monkshood, a species of poisonous aconite. (See also **drugs;** seeing with the **stomach**)

Naphology

Term coined by ufologists to denote a field of study that examines a wide range of reported phenomena and events for which there appears no acceptable scientific explanation, such as **astrology,** ufology, and **occultism.** A more popular term for such apparently inexplicable events is "**Fortean phenomena,**" deriving from the research and books of **Charles Fort** (1874–1932), who first classified reports of unexplained phenomena.

Napper (or Napier), Richard (1559–1634)

British astrologer and doctor of medicine of Great Linford, Buckinghamshire. He attended Oxford University, but never got a degree, and in 1589 was ordained and admitted to the rectory of Great Linford, a position he held for 44 years. He was a pupil of astrologer Simon Forman (1552–1611) and, according to **William Lilly** (1602–1681), "outwent Forman in physic and holiness of life, cured the falling-sickness perfectly by constellated rings, and some diseases by amulets."

Sources:

The Dictionary of National Biography. London: Oxford University Press, 1953.

Nash, Carroll B(lue) (1914–1998)

Professor emeritus of biology and former director of the parapsychology laboratory at St. Joseph's College, Philadelphia, Pennsylvania. He was born on January 29, 1914, in Louisville, Kentucky. He studied at George Washington University, Washington, D.C. (B.S., 1934) and the University of Maryland (M.S., 1937; Ph.D, 1939). Following graduation, he became an instructor in zoology at the University of Arizona (1939–41) and subsequently served as an associate professor of biology at Pennsylvania Military College, Chester (1941–44), assistant professor of biology at American University, Washington, D.C. (1944–45), and chairman of the biology department at Washington College, Chestertown, Maryland (1945–48). He moved to the faculty at St. Joseph's College in 1948 where he remained during the next four decades.

Nash was a founding member of the **Parapsychological Association** and was selected as its president in 1963. He received the William McDougall Award for Distinguished Work in Parapsychology in 1960, the first American so honored. He had, as early as 1940, developed dice tests for psychokinesis and soon afterward began to pursue interests in precognition and personality variables in psi. He authored a number of articles and one important book, *Parapsychology: The Science of Psiology* (1986). Nash was consultant and adviser for the television production "ESP" in 1958, and taught college-level courses in parapsychology at St. Joseph's College. He died May 30, 1998.

Sources:

Berger, Arthur S., and Joyce Berger. *The Encyclopedia of Parapsychology and Psychical Research.* New York: Paragon House, 1991.

Nash, Carroll B. "Can Precognition Occur Diametrically?" *Journal of Parapsychology* 27 (1963).

———. *Parapsychology: The Science of Psiology.* Springfield, Ill.: Charles C. Thomas, 1986.

———. "Psi and Probability Theory." *Science* 120 (1954).

———. "Psychokinesis Reconsidered." *Journal of Parapsychology* 45 (1951).

———. *Science of Psi: ESP and PK.* Springfield, Ill.: Charles C. Thomas, 1978.

———. "The Unorthodox Science of Parapsychology." *International Journal of Parapsychology* 1 (1959).

Nash, Caroll B., and M. G. Durkin. "Correlation Between ESP and Religious Value." *Journal of Parapsychology* 22 (1958).

Pleasants, Helene, ed. *Biographical Dictionary of Parapsychology.* New York: Helix Press, 1964.

Nash, Catherine S(tifler) (Mrs. Carroll B. Nash) (1919–)

Professor emeritus of biology and charter associate of the **Parapsychological Association.** She was born on August 31, 1919, in Woodbrook, Maryland. She studied at Goucher College, Baltimore, Maryland (B.A., 1939) and Ohio State University (M.S., 1950). In 1941 she married **Carroll B. Nash.** At the time she finished her graduate work, she was a lecturer on biology at Washington College, Chestertown, Maryland, where she remained until taking a position in 1958 as an assistant professor of biology at St. Joseph's College, Philadelphia, where her husband also taught and had founded a parapsychology laboratory.

She conducted research in parapsychology, including some joint experiments with her husband. She has taken particular interest in telepathy and clairvoyance and published a number of articles in the field.

Sources:

Berger, Arthur S., and Joyce Berger. *The Encyclopedia of Parapsychology and Psychical Research.* New York: Paragon House, 1991.

Nash, Carroll B., and C. S. Nash. "An Exploratory Analysis for Displacement in PK." *Journal* of the American Society for Psychical Research 50 (1956).

———. "Relation Between ESP Scoring and Minnesota Multiphasic Personality Inventory." *Journal* of the American Society for Psychical Research 60 (1960).

Nash, C. S. "Checking Success and the Relationship of Personality Traits to ESP." *Journal of the American Society for Psychical Research* 52 (1958).

———. "Experiments in Plant Growth." *International Journal of Parapsychology* (autumn 1959).

———. "Report on the Second Annual Convention of the Parapsychological Association." *Newsletter, Parapsychology Foundation* (September–October 1959).

———. "A Test of Adding Extrasensorially Perceived Digits." *Journal of Parapsychology* 23 (1959).

Pleasants, Helene, ed. *Biographical Dictionary of Parapsychology.* New York: Helix Press, 1964.

NASO See National Astrological Society

NASO International Astrological Directory

A former publication (1970s and 1980s) compiled by Henry Weingarten that listed local, national, and international astrology societies, organizations, periodicals and practitioners, published by the now defunct **National Astrological Society.**

Sources:

Weingarten, Henry, comp. *The NASO International Astrological Directory.* New York: National Astrological Society, 1977–78. Rev. ed. 1980–81.

Nastrond

The "Strand of the Dead"—the Scandinavian and Icelandic **hell,** said to be of an icy temperature. It lies in the lowest depths of **Niflheim,** is a "dark abode far from the sun," and its gates face "the cutting north." Its "walls are formed of wreathed snakes, and their venom is ever falling like rain." It is surrounded by dark and poisonous streams, and Nidhog, the great dragon that dwells beneath the central root of Ygdrassil, torments and gnaws the dead. Here Loki is chained to a splintered rock, where the venom of the snake Skada falls on him unceasingly, and it was believed that his shuddering was the cause of earthquakes.

Nastrond is featured in the *Voluspa,* a poem in the Icelandic *Poetic Edda.*

Sources:

The Poetic Edda. Oxford: Clarendon Press, 1969.

Nat

An evil spirit. (See also **MYANMAR**)

National Astrological Association (NAA)

At various intervals throughout the twentieth century, the growing astrological community has been engaged in the arduous process of organizing. The NAA, founded by **Llewellyn George,** was one important step toward a national federation of astrologers. It was organized in Hollywood, California, at a convention held July 19–23, 1927. George was elected the first president. In spite of the organizational name, membership was drawn mainly from the West Coast. Original cooperating members included most of the leading astrologers and astrological organizations in California, the Torch Center of Vancouver, British Columbia, and the Astrological Research Bureau and School of Boston, Massachusetts. The NAA's plans for a campus-based astrological college were never brought to fruition. It was eventually superseded by the **American Federation of Astrologers,** organized in 1938.

Sources:

Hartman, William C. *Who's Who in Occultism, New Thought, Psychicism, and Spiritualism.* Jamaica, N.Y.: Occult Press, 1927.

Weschcke, Carl Llewellyn, and Stan Baker. *The Truth About Astrology.* St. Paul: Llewellyn Publications, 1989.

National Astrological Society (NASO)

Non-profit organization founded in 1968 to promote high standards of practice and instruction in astrology, to facilitate communications among astrologers through meetings and publications, and to foster cooperation among persons and organizations concerned with astrology. During the years of its existence, NASO held annual conferences in cities throughout North America, acted as an educational institution, maintained an astrological library, and facilitated access to IBM computing for members with high level projects.

Voting membership was open to professional or qualified astrologers, non-voting membership for associates. The society published the *NASO Journal* and the *NASO International Astrological Directory* from it headquarters in New York City.

National Colored Spiritualist Association of Churches

African Americans were among people attracted to the Spiritualist movement, especially in the years following the formation of the National Spiritualist Association (NSA) (now the **National Spiritualist Association of Churches**) in 1893. A few emerged as talented **mediums.** Because American society was segregated at that time, African American members were organized in "colored" auxiliary societies attached to the association. In the period of heightened racial tension following World War I, the leadership of the NSA decided to create a separate all-black Spiritualist organization for their African American members and appointed president Joseph P. Whitwell to lead a meeting held in Cleveland, Ohio, on April 21, 1925.

Twenty delegates attended the meeting but six withdrew in protest of the establishment of yet another segregated organization. The remaining 14 formed themselves into what became the first convention of the National Colored Spiritualist Association of Churches (NCSAC). It elected Rev. John R. White president; Sarah Harrington, vice-president; Mrs. C. W. Dennison, secretary; and a Mr. Smith as treasurer.

The second national meeting of the NCSAC, held in 1926, adopted a new constitution modeled on that of the NSA and established a loose association of churches, mediums, and healers. It followed the NSA "Declaration of Principles," which affirmed God as "Infinite Intelligence" and the possibility of communication with the so-called dead through mediumship. Happiness in this life came from obedience to the natural and spiritual laws of the universe, according to the declaration.

Churches emerged from the auxiliary societies previously established and the group served the African American community into the 1970s. The NCSAC had strong competition from the **Spiritual churches,** independent spiritualist churches that also emerged in the 1920s and grew strong over the years. The NCSAC continued into the 1970s but has not been heard from in recent years and its present status is unknown.

Sources:

Murphy, Larry, J. Gordon Melton, and Gary L. Ward. *Encyclopedia of African American Religion.* New York: Garland, 1993.

The National Spiritualist Association of United States of America. *One Hundredth Anniversary of Modern Spiritualism.* The Author, 1948.

National Council for Geocosmic Research (NCGR)

Organization devoted to medical **astrology** in North America. The NCGR was founded in Massachusetts in 1971 by a group of astrologers and physicians interested in exploring areas of mutual concern and possible research. The organization traces its beginning to an informal study group that originally met in 1957 in New York City.

The NCGR has developed an interdisciplinary program that includes scientists from many fields. Members seek to discover new means of correlating earthly events with celestial phenomena, especially as such discoveries might lead to new insights into human nature. They conduct research on a variety of topics, including astrological characteristics of gifted and mentally challenged persons, timing of earthquakes, the astrological correlates of SIDS (sudden infant death syndrome), and other issues in astrology and psychotherapy. The NCGR has also established the *DAV Database* which is available on CD Rom.

The NCGR has developed a curriculum for young astrologers leading to national certification. The curriculum was developed with the idea that it might eventually become the basis of a college major in astrology.

The NCGR sponsors an annual conference and publishes two periodicals, *Geocosmic Magazine* and **NCGR Journal** as well as a series of monographs. The organization has over 3,000 members that can be found in 26 countries on 6 continents. Address: P.O. Box 38866, Los Angeles, CA 90038. Website: http://www.geocosmic.org/.

Sources:

National Council for Geocosmic Research. http://www.geocosmic.org/. March 8, 2000.

National Council for Geocosmic Research Journal

Journal of the National Council for Geocosmic Research, concerned with correlations between astrological observations and human behavior. Once a year, as a part of the journal, the council publishes *Geocosmic Magazine.* Address: NCGR, Inc., P.O. Box 38866, Los Angeles, CA 90038.

National Directory of Psychic Counselors

Former comprehensive directory which listed astrologers, healers, card and palm readers, hypnotherapists, graphologists, trance mediums, and other psychics in the United States. The directory offered addresses and telephone numbers and also listed metaphysical organizations, publishers, resources, and psychic products (tapes, books, courses). It was published by Carma Press, Box 12633, St. Paul, MN 55112.

National Enquirer (Newspaper)

A nationally distributed weekly newspaper that gives special attention to psychical phenomena and the paranormal, including the publication of regular forecasts of future events by different psychics. It is noted for its sensationalistic approach to the subject, but is not noted for its validity or the quality of its sources of information on the paranormal or related issues such as **UFOs.** Address: PO Box 420235, Palm Coast, FL 32142-0235. Website: http://www.nationalenquirer.com/.

Sources:

National Enquirer Online. http://www.nationalenquirer.com/. March 8, 2000.

National Federation of Spiritual Healers (NFSH)

British organization founded in 1955 "to establish a national body which would coordinate, protect, and advance the work of spiritual healing." Its fourfold purpose is "To speak for the concept of spiritual healing in the councils of this country [Britain] and internationally; to participate in developments promoted by the federation or elsewhere related to increasing knowledge and understanding of the healing gift; to provide opportunities for its members to develop their full healing potential; to ensure that the public who seek healing receive a proper service and correct advice."

The federation registers as "healer members" those for whom authenticated evidence of spiritual healing has been obtained and accepted by the membership panel of the NFSH. "Spiritual healing" is understood to be the healing of the sick in body, mind, and spirit by means of the laying-on of hands, prayer, or meditation, whether or not in the actual presence of the patient.

It operates a national healer referral service to put members of the public seeking spiritual healing in touch with approved "healer members" of the federation. Since 1965 (under an agreement with more than 1,500 National Health Service Hospitals), NFSH healer members may attend to those hospitalized patients who request the services of a healer. An important development took place in 1977, when the General Medical Council in England agreed to allow doctors to recommend spiritual healing to their patients.

The federation has approximately 6,500 members and may be contacted at Old Manor Farm Studio, Church St., Sunbury-on-Thames, Middlesex, TW16 6RG, England. Website: http://www.nfsh.org.uk/. (See also **healing by touch**)

Sources:

National Federation of Spiritual Healers. http://www.nfsh.org.uk/. March 8, 2000.

National Investigations Committee on Aerial Phenomena (NICAP)

Early **UFO** organization. By the mid-1950s speculation about flying saucers, begun in 1947, had developed into a massive controversy. The possibility of extraterrestrial visitors and the scientific advances that a culture with interplanetary or even interstellar travel could bring captured the interest of a number of scientists. Among those in the midst of the controversy was Donald E. Keyhoe, journalist and retired marine officer. Beginning in 1950 Keyhoe wrote three books—*The Flying Saucers Are Real* (1950), *Flying Saucers from Outer Space* (1953), and *The Flying Saucer Conspiracy* (1955)—in which he argues that flying saucers were extraterrestrial in origin, that the United States Air Force knew what they were, but that the government, fearful of public reaction, was covering up the evidence.

By 1956, Keyhoe, popular radio host Frank Edwards, physicist T. Townsend Brown, and several retired officers from the armed forces said they felt that an organization was needed to address the issues created by the "space visitors" controversy. After some initial organizational struggles, Keyhoe emerged as the group's director. The organization's periodical, *The U.F.O. Investigator,* promoted discussion of the extraterrestrial hypothesis and openly criticized both the air force for hoarding needed data and the contactees for their unsupported claims of contact with extraterrestrials.

Although continually on the verge of collapse, NICAP became the symbol of conservative scientific ufology and found some stability with the assistance of Richard Hall, who became secretary of the organization in 1958 and wrote *The UFO Evidence* (1964). That document was part of an effort by NICAP members to attract the attention of Congress to the UFO question. NICAP hoped the legislators would override the air force's reticence to share what it allegedly knew.

NICAP initially supported the efforts of the **Condon Committee,** headed by physicist Edward U. Condon as an independent and well-funded effort to study the question. However, it quickly withdrew cooperation when it was learned that Condon believed that UFOs were nonexistent and had no intention of conducting any "real" investigation. NICAP announced it would expand its activity to do what Condon was supposed to do, but NICAP's resolve came too late. When the Condon report was published it declared that further study of UFOs was unlikely to produce results, and NICAP was unable to respond to the massive drop in public interest in the UFO question.

NICAP continued to exist into the early 1980s, when it was disbanded. Its files were eventually turned over to the J. Allen

Hynek Center for UFO Studies. Keyhoe, who had resigned as chairman of NICAP, retired to his home in Virginia and wrote his last book, *Aliens from Space* (1973), in which he targets the CIA rather than the air force as the source of the government's UFO coverup. He also endorses a plan to entice alien craft to land at an isolated air strip decorated with unusual and novel displays.

Sources:

Clark, Jerome. *The Emergence of a Phenomenon: UFOs from the Beginning through 1959.* Vol. 2 of *The UFO Encyclopedia.* Detroit: Omnigraphics, 1992.

Hall, Richard H. *The UFO Evidence.* Washington, DC: National Investigations Committee on Aerial Phenomena, 1964.

Jacobs, David M. *The UFO Controversy in America.* Bloomington: Indiana University Press, 1975.

Keyhoe, Donald E. *Aliens from Space: The Real Story of Unidentified Flying Objects.* Garden City, N.Y.: Doubleday, 1973.

———. *The Flying Saucer Conspiracy.* New York: Henry Holt, 1955.

———. *The Flying Saucers Are Real.* New York: Fawcett Publications, 1950.

———. *Flying Saucers from Outer Space.* New York: Henry Holt, 1953.

National Investigations Committee on UFOs (NICUFO)

Non-profit organization founded in 1967 to investigate "the truth surrounding UFOs and associated phenomena." It probes unidentified flying object (**UFO**) reports and relates its findings to governmental agencies and the general public via press, radio, television, and newsletters. It organizes conventions, lectures, seminars, and various activities related to UFOs, with special interest in claimed contracts with UFO occupants. It publishes the *Confidential Space-Link* newsletter at 14617 Victory Blvd., Ste. 4, Van Nuys, CA 91411. Website: http://www.nicufo.org.

National Laboratory of Psychical Research (NLPR)

Research facility established by psychical researcher **Harry Price** in 1925 at 13 Roland Gardens, London, S.W.7, "to investigate in a dispassionate manner and by purely scientific means every phase of psychic or alleged psychic phenomena." The honorary president was The Lord Sands, K.C., LL.D., and acting president H. G. Bois. Price served as the laboratory's honorary director. The laboratory continued into the 1930s and its major product was the set of publications it published. It issued two periodicals: the *British Journal of Psychical Research* (bimonthly, discontinued in 1929) and the *Proceedings of the National Laboratory of Psychical Research* (discontinued in 1929).

The laboratory also issued occasional *Bulletins of the National Laboratory of Psychical Research,* which include: (I) *Regurgitation and the Duncan Mediumship,* by Harry Price (1932); (II) *Fraudulent Mediums,* an essay by D. S. Fraser-Harris, formerly published from *Science Progress* (January 1932); (III) *The Identification of the "Walter" Prints,* by E. E. Dudley (1933); (IV) *An Account of Some Further Experiments with Rudi Schneider,* by Harry Price (1933); and (V) *Rudi Schneider: The Vienna Experiments of Prof. Meyer and Przibram* (1933).

One of the most valuable issues of the NLPR *Proceedings* was vol. 1, pt. 2 (April 1929), comprising the *Short-Title Catalogue of Works on Psychical Research, Spiritualism, Magic, Psychology, Legerdemain and Other Methods of Deception, Charlatanism, Witchcraft and Technical Works for the Scientific Investigation of Alleged Abnormal Phenomena from circa 1450 A.D. to 1929 A.D.* compiled by Harry Price. This catalog (supplemented by Bulletin I, (1935) listed the splendid collection assembled by Price himself. Since Price's death (1948), the collection has existed as the Harry Price Collection, at the Senate House, University of London.

Sources:

Tabori, Paul. *Harry Price: The Biography of a Ghost-Hunter.* London: Atheneum Press, 1930.

National New Age Yellow Pages

Directory listing holistic practitioners, astrologers, psychics, social justice organizations, and mail-order businesses, intended as a national networking tool. Two editions were issued in the late 1980s from the Light Connection, Fullerton, CA 92635.

Sources:

Ingenito, Marcia Gervase, ed. *National New Age Yellow Pages.* Fullerton, Calif.: National New Age Yellow Pages, 1987. Rev. ed. Fullerton, Calif.: Highgate House, 1988.

National Psychic Science Association

A group of lecturers, healers, preachers, and ministers, founded in 1929 "to promote the religion of Spiritualism, psychic science and morality and demonstrate the phenomena of the continuity of life through spirit communication and psychic healing through prayer." Last known address: c/o Rev. Marion Odom, 17 Baird Pl., Whippany, NJ 07981.

National Psychological Institute, Inc.

Founded for scientific research in normal and abnormal psychology, spirit **obsession,** and the complex problem "What becomes of the dead?" by **Carl A. Wickland,** who was active in Spiritualist circles in California in the 1920s. It was headquartered in Los Angeles, California.

National Spiritual Aid Association

The National Spiritual Aid Association was a Spiritualist church founded in 1937. It operated among the independent-minded Spiritualists as a corporation to hold church charters and ministerial credentials for churches and ministers who otherwise operated as autonomous Spiritualist centers and independent mediums. The association held that **Spiritualism** was the true religion sent by God to Earth. However, it did not specify a set of teachings to which its member churches and ministers had to conform. Last known address: 5239 40th St. N., St. Petersburg, FL 33714.

National Spiritual Alliance of the United States of America

A Spiritualist organization founded in 1913 by Rev. (and medium) G. Tabor Thompson, formerly of the **National Spiritualist Association of Churches** and other individuals who believed that "intercommunication between the denizens of different worlds is scientifically established." The alliance promoted studies of **Spiritualism** and prescribed qualifications of ministers, including the method of examination and ceremony by which they were set apart. It also set the qualifications of associated ministers, licentiates, healers, mediums, missionaries, and other official workers, and issues certificates. Last known address: RFD 1, Lake Pleasant, MA 01347.

National Spiritualist Association of Churches (NSAC)

The National Spiritualist Association (later renamed the National Spiritualist Association of Churches) was founded in 1893 to bring some order out of the chaotic and decentralized Spiritualist movement and to respond to the charges and revelations of **fraud** that had hindered the movement through the last half of the nineteenth century. Leading in the formation of the association were former Unitarian clergymen Harrison D. Barrett and James M. Peebles and the medium Cora L. V. Richmond. An initial six-article "Declaration of Principles" was adopted. As later amended by additions, NSAC's statement affirms the following:

"1. We believe in Infinite Intelligence [i.e., God].

"2. We believe that the Phenomena of Nature, both physical and spiritual, are the expression of Infinite Intelligence.

"3. We affirm that a correct understanding of such expression and living in accordance therewith constitute true religion.

"4. We affirm that the existence and personal identity of the individual continue after the change called death.

"5. We affirm that communication with the so-called dead is a fact, scientifically proven by the phenomena of Spiritualism.

"6. We believe that the highest morality is contained in the Golden Rule: 'What so ever ye would have that other do unto you, do ye also unto them.'

"7. We affirm the moral responsibility of the individual, and that he makes his own happiness or unhappiness as he obeys Nature's physical and spiritual laws.

"8. We affirm the doorway to reformation is never closed against any human soul here or hereafter.

"9. We affirm that the receipt of Prophecy and Healing contained in the Bible is a divine attribute proven through Mediumship."

These beliefs are largely shared by all Spiritualist groups, although the NSAC has continually been the target of controversy as pockets of members and leaders have professed a belief in reincarnation. Traditionally, Spiritualism in America and England has opposed the idea of reincarnation in favor of the idea of continuing mediumistic contact. As belief in reincarnation spread among Americans in general, however, different groups withdrew from the NSAC to found new denominations. To a lesser degree the association also argued against the distinctly Christian nature of Spiritualism and found itself competing with the Christian Spiritualist movement. In the 1920s African American members were set apart in the **National Colored Spiritualist Association of Churches.**

The NSAC has been the most stable of the several Spiritualist organizations. It is affiliated fraternally with the National Spiritualist Churches of Canada, which has congregations in Ontario and Quebec. It issues a periodical, the *National Spiritualist Summit.* Affiliated youth work is organized through the association's Lyceum movement. Address: NSAC, 3521 W. Topeka Dr., Glendale, AZ 85308-2325. Website: http://www.nsac.org/.

Sources:

Holms, A. Campbell. *The Fundamental Facts of Spiritualism.* Indianapolis: Stow Memorial Foundation, n.d.

Melton, J. Gordon. *Encyclopedia of American Religions.* 6th edition. Detroit: Gale Research, 1999.

The National Spiritualist Association of Churches. http://www.nsac.org/. March 8, 2000.

The National Spiritualist Association of United States of America. *One Hundredth Anniversary of Modern Spiritualism.* Chicago: The Author, 1948.

National Spiritual Science Center

The National Spiritual Science Center was established in Washington, D.C., by Rev. Alice Welstood Tindell, who had been trained by Mother Julia O. Forrest, a medium and the founder of the Spiritual Science Mother Church. For many years after its opening in 1941, the Washington center was an integral part of the mother church. In 1969, while attending a meeting of the Federation of Spiritual Churches and Associations, Tindell had a disabling accident. This occasioned her retirement and she turned the center over to two of her students, Revs. Henry J. Nagorka and Diane S. Nagorka. During the 1970s the Nagorkas reorganized the center independently of the mother church.

The Nagorkas developed a vigorous program at the church. They moved into new enlarged facilities and founded ESPress, Inc., a publishing concern headed by Henry Nagorka. Diane Nagorka founded a School of Spiritual Science and, with her assistant Margaret Moum, developed its curriculum. The school includes classes for training mediums and pastors for Spiritual Science congregations. Henry Nagorka died in 1986, and ESPress ceased operation. Diane Nagorka headed the center and school until her retirement in 1989. She was succeeded by a board of directors, who presently manage the center and its associated congregations.

The center's beliefs were similar to that of the parent body, though many of the specifically Christian elements have been deleted. A nine-point statement affirmed these beliefs: God as the universal Creative Energy; the dynamic growing nature of the universe; the drive of every entity to unite with God; the immortality of the soul; individual free will; wisdom as the latent power of God within; the reality of communication with spirit; soul unfoldment and service as one's purpose in life; and God as a just, accepting, and impersonal force, drawing all to perfection.

Last known address: 409 Butternut St., Ste. 1, Washington, DC 20012.

Sources:

Moum, Margaret R. *Guidebook to the Aquarian Gospel of Jesus the Christ.* Washington, DC: ESPress, 1974.

Nagorka, Diane S. *Spirit as Life Force.* Washington, DC: ESPress, 1983.

Natsaw

Burmese wizards. (See also **MYANMAR**)

Natural Health

One of the early periodicals of the **New Age** movement. *East West Journal* was published monthly and featured articles on personal transformation, spiritual life, holistic health, and diet. It gave special focus to macrobiotics. It began publication in 1971 and continued through 1991, when its name was changed to *East West Natural Health.* The magazine was informally associated with the East West Foundation headed by Michio Kushi, a teacher of macrobiotics. Last known address: 17 Station St., Brookline, MA 02147.

Nature Spirits (or Elementals)

According to **Theosophy,** nature spirits have bodies composed of the finer kinds of matter. There are countless hosts of them, divided into seven classes, which, allowing for two unmanifested forms, belong to the ether, air, fire, water, and earth—the last four being called by followers of the **Kabala,** sylphs, salamanders, undines, and gnomes respectively. At the head of each class is a *deva* or inferior god.

Nature spirits are said to work in unsuspected ways, sometimes lending their aid to human beings in the form of certain faculties, while those in the **astral world** are engaged in the creation of form out of the matter that the outpouring of the **Logos** has quickened, hence they form minerals, flowers, and other aspects of nature.

These nature spirits of the astral worlds of course have bodies of astral matter, and they frequently form mischievous or other impulses and change the appearance of these bodies. They are just beyond the limits of normal human vision, but many sensitives of more acute vision can see them, while the action of drugs is also believed to make them visible. (See also **elementary spirits; fairies**)

Nayler, James (ca. 1617–1660)

An English religious leader of the seventeenth century. He was born around 1617 in the diocese of York and served for a time in the army before joining the Quakers where his discourses gained for him a reputation for sanctity. Eventually, his followers hailed him as a Messiah and accompanied him in a dramatic entrance in Bristol in 1656. Nayler, mounted on a horse led by a man and a woman, was followed by others who chanted "Holy, holy, holy, is the god of Sabaoth."

Authorities did not appreciate Nayler's messianic pretensions and had him arrested, charging him with blasphemy and punishing him by having his tongue pierced with a hot iron and his forehead marked with the letter "B" (blasphemer). This done, prior to his imprisonment, he was forced to ride into Bristol in disgrace, his face turned towards the horse's tail. After two years in prison Nayler was released sobered and penitent. His return to Quaker preaching was sanctioned by Quaker founder George Fox and Nayler preached with George Whitehead. After a period of ill health, Nayler died in October 1660.

Sources:

Bittle, William G. *James Nayler, 1618–1660: The Quaker Indicted by Parliament.* Richmond, Ind.: Friends United Press, 1986.

Brailsford, Mabel Richmond. *A Quaker from Cromwell's Army: James Nayler.* London: Swathmore Press, 1927.

Nazca "Spaceport"

A mysterious area of desert markings on the plains of Nazca, Peru, about 250 miles southeast of Lima between the towns of Nazca and Palpa.

This barren plateau covering 200 square miles has over 13,000 lines, 100 spirals, trapezoids, and triangles, and about 800 large animal drawings, etched in the desert through removal of surface stones with lighter colored soil underneath. Many of the lines extend for miles, radiating from centers like star shapes. It is estimated that the markings were made between 400 B.C.E. and 900 C.E. and their construction may have occupied several centuries.

During the 1970s, as part of a larger theory of ancient astronauts having visited Earth, **Erich von Däniken** suggested that these markings were the work of ancient spacemen who landed on the plain and marked out an airfield for their spacecraft. Actually, as early as 1955 James W. Moseley had proposed such a hypotheses in an article in **Fate** magazine. In one of his later books, *Gods From Outer Space* (1973), von Däniken states:

"At some time in the past, unknown intelligences landed on the uninhabited plain near the present-day town of Nazca and built an improvized airfield for their spacecraft which were to operate in the vicinity of the earth."

The hypothesis has little to commend it. For example, Ronald D. Story pointed out a number of weaknesses in von Däniken's reasoning in an article in the *The Zetetic* in 1977. First of all, there should be no need for a runway several miles long for a space vehicle capable of vertical landing (only modern air liners need a long runway). Secondly, many of the lines run right into hills, ridges, and the sides of mountains. Thirdly, the markings are on soft, sandy soil, unsuitable for any heavy vehicle to land on. Maria Reiche, an expert on Nazca, has commented: "I'm afraid the spacemen would have gotten stuck."

Story cited Professor Kosok of Long Island University, who first mapped and photographed the mysterious markings from the air in June 1941 and discovered apparent alignment with solstices and equinoxes. Perhaps the markings were "the largest astronomy book in the world." Similar astronomical ground markings have been discovered in what is termed the **Glastonbury Zodiac** in England.

While the ideal viewing position for such markings as Nazca is from a point about 600 feet above the plain, it does not necessarily follow that they were actually designed for viewing from the air. They could be interpreted as a giant image of astronomical mysteries, in which the construction and traversal of competed markings might be in the nature of a religious ritual. Many magical ceremonies involve physical traversing of geometrical forms inscribed on the ground.

An ingenious theory cited by Story is that of the International Explorers Society (IES) of Florida, who suggested that the "chariots of the gods" sailing over Nazca might have been ancient smoke balloons piloted by early Peruvians. This theory was presented in some detail by IES member Jim Woodman in his book *NAZCA: Journey to the Sun* (1977). Woodman has discovered that the thousands of ancient gravesites around Nazca contain finely woven textiles (suitable for balloon fabric), braided rope, and ceramic pottery. One clay pot has a picture suggesting a hot-air balloon with tie ropes.

It is not generally known that manned balloon flights were recorded in Brazil as early as 1709, when Bartolomeu de Gusmao made his first flight on August 8.

Jim Woodman has actually tested his theory in collaboration with balloonist Julian Nott. They constructed a balloon using the same materials as those available to the ancient Nazcans. The envelope used cotton fabric similar to that in the gravesites; the basket for pilot and co-pilot was woven from native fibers. On November 28, 1975, Woodman and Nott actually flew their balloon (named *Condor I*) over the Nazca plains.

However, this impressive demonstration hardly settles the mystery of Nazca, since it is not plausible that the Nazcans would have spent centuries constructing these markings for the benefit of occasional balloonists to view from the air. Validation of the theory would require evidence of a religious and cultural milieu in which such balloonists had maintained an elite status for hundreds of years, and it is hardly likely that such balloons would have vanished without a trace.

Sources:

Charroux, Robert. *The Mysteries of the Andes.* New York: Avon, 1977.

Clark, Jerome. *Encyclopedia of Strange and Unexplained Phenomena.* Detroit: Gale Research, 1993.

Morrison, Tony. *Pathways to the Gods: The Mystery of the Andes Lines.* London: Granada Publishing, 1980.

Moseley, James W. "Peruvian Desert Map for Saucers?" *Fate* 8, no. 10 (October 1055): 28–33.

Story, Ronald D. "Von Däniken's Golden Gods." *The Zetetic* 2, no. 1 (1977).

Von Däniken, Erich. *Chariots of the Gods?: Unsolved Mysteries of the Past.* New York: G. P. Putnam's Sons, 1970.

NCGR See National Council for Geocosmic Research

Ndembo (or Kita)

A former African secret society that had widespread influence in the lower Congo, and especially in the districts lying to the south of that river. Initiation was made through the *ganga* or chief, who instructed the neophyte at a given signal suddenly to lie down as if dead. A shroud was spread over him, and he was carried off to an enclosure outside the village called *vela* and pronounced to have died a *ndembo.*

Perhaps 20, 30, or even 50 candidates "died" at one time. It was then assumed that persons "dying" in this manner decayed until only a single bone remained, and this the ganga took charge of. The process varied from three months to as many years, and the ganga was supposed by art magic to bring every one of the dead back to life within that period.

On a festival day of the ndembo, the members marched through the village in a grand procession amidst universal joy, carrying with them the persons who were supposed to have died. The neophytes who were supposed to have perished comported themselves as if in reality they had come from another world. They took new names, pretended that everything in the terrestrial sphere was new to them, turned a deaf ear to their parents and relatives, and even affected not to know how to eat. They further desired to have everything they set eyes on, and if it was not granted to them immediately, they might fall upon the unhappy owner and beat and even kill him without any consequence to themselves. It was assumed that they were mere children in the affairs of the terrestrial sphere, and therefore knew no better.

Those who went through this rite were called *nganga,* or the "knowing ones," while the neophytes were designated *vanga.* During their occupation of the vela they learned an esoteric language, which they constantly employed. Perhaps the best record of the group was made by ethnologist Adolf Bastian (1826–1905), who stated:

"The Great Nkissi (who here replaces the fetish) lives in the interior of the woodlands where nobody can see him. When he dies the Nganga carefully collect his bones in order to bring them back to life, and nourish them that they may again put on flesh and blood. But it is not well to speak about it. In the Ambamba country everybody must have died once, and when the Nganga (replacing the fetish-priest) shakes his calabash against a village, those men and youths whose hour is come fall into a state of lifeless torpor, from which they generally rise up in three days.

"But the man whom the Nkissi loves he carries off to the bush and often buries him for a series of years. When he again awakens to life, he begins to eat and drink as before, but his mind is gone, and the Nganga must himself educate him and instruct him in every movement, like the smallest child. At first that can only be done with the rod, but the senses gradually return, so that you can speak with him, and when his education is finished the Nganga takes him back to his parents. These would seldom recognize him but for the positive assurance of the Nganga, who at the same time reminds them of earlier occurrences. Whoever has not yet undergone the experience in Ambamba is universally despised, and is not allowed to join in the dances."

This account in curiously reminiscent of the Haitian tradition of **zombies.**

Near-Death Experience Project

This now-defunct project was devoted to collecting written, audio, and video interviews with individuals who have had **near-death experiences** or related mystical experience. It provided public education and workshops connected with such experiences. The project was originally run by Professor Howard Mickel at Wichita State University, Wichita, Kansas.

Near-Death Experiences

Individuals who have shown many of the characteristics of death (stopped heart, flat brain scan, etc.) but have survived and been brought back to consciousness often report experiences that seem to have a bearing on the questions of individual **survival** of death and the possible existence of a human soul or surviving individual consciousness. Such experiences have been studied in modern times under the category of "near-death experiences."

Common to many such experiences is the powerful sensation of rushing through a long dark tunnel with a bright light at the end. This light brings an ecstatic feeling of joy, peace, and freedom from the body. Often the tunnel experience is preceded by a detached awareness in which some higher reality is interfused with perception of the physical environment surrounding the body, which may be perceived from a detached viewpoint, in which the self can look down on its own body, as in **out-of-the-body travel.** [Crucial to understanding the accounts of such experiences is separating the elements of the experience from the interpretation placed upon it by the person who has had the experience.]

Psychologists and doctors who have studied near-death experiences have also examined reports of out-of-the-body experiences, and have found enough commonalities to suggest that they are varieties of the same experience, the near-death experience often being distinguished by its intensity, its vividness, and its impact upon the person having the experience. For example, tunnel experiences are common to both, and as is the experience of viewing the physical body from a perspective outside of it. Many individuals find that such experiences are a powerful vindication of religious beliefs such as the existence of a soul as a separate entity from the body and the possibility of the continuation of the soul beyond the experience of bodily death. Clergy who undergo the experience are likely to change their views and teachings.

Various mundane theories have been offered to account for near-death and out-of-the-body experiences in terms of hallucination. For example, the tunnel sensations might be a reliving of the powerful experience of passing through the birth canal, since the baby usually emerges head first. Another psychological explanation centers upon the behavior of cells in the visual cortex when the brain is hyperactive through lack of oxygen. For a thoughtful examination of psychological theories, see the 1989 article, "Down the Tunnel" by Susan Blackmore. Blackmore has studied out-of-body experiences as a psychological phenomenon, but unlike most psychologists who theorize about such experiences, she has actually had such an experience herself. She rightly draws attention to the fact that skeptical explanations ignore the intense insightful and spiritual aspects of such experiences.

Investigators from different disciplines will emphasize their own bias. Allan Kellehear, who comes from a sociological perspective, compares the experience to crisis situations that happen to those lost at sea or trapped in a mine. Melvin Morse is a pioneer working with children who have NDEs and he finds that experiencers in this group to be contaminated by the life experiences that adults have accumulated.

Since 1981, research on the near-death experience has been focused by the **International Association for Near-Death Studies** founded in 1981 and headed by Kenneth Ring. It published a monumental study of the phenomenon in 1980 and has an active presence on the web. Whether the phenomenon is completely understood or not it has become increasingly important because half the recipients of medical procedures are likely to have a near-death experience.

Sources:

Atwater, P. M. H. *Coming Back to Life: The After Effects of the Near-death Experience.* New York: Dodd, Mead, 1988.

Blackmore, Susan J. *Beyond the Body.* London: Heinemann, 1982.

———. "Down the Tunnel." *British and Irish Skeptic* 3, no. 3 (May/June 1989).

———. *Dying to live: Near-death experiences.* Buffalo, N.Y.: Prometheus Books, 1993.

Crookall, Robert. *Out-of-the-Body Experiences: A Fourth Analysis.* New Hyde Park, N.Y.: University Books, 1970.

———. *The Techniques of Astral Projection: Denouement After Fifty Years.* London: Aquarian Press, 1964.

Gallup, George, Jr., with William Proctor. *Adventures in Immortality.* New York: McGraw-Hill, 1982. London: Souvenir Press, 1983.

Greyson, Bruce. "The Near-Death Experience as a Focus of Clinical Attention." *Journal of Nervous and Mental Disease* 185, no. 5 (May 1997).

Groth-Marnat, G. and J. Schumaker. "The Near-Death Experience: A Review and Critique." *Journal of Humanistic Psychology* 29, no. 1 (January 1989).

International Association for Near-Death Studies. http://www.iands.org. April 10, 2000.

Kellehear, Allan. *Experiences Near Death: Beyond Medicine and Religion.* New York: Oxford Univ Press, 1996.

Kübler-Ross, Elisabeth. *On Death and Dying.* New York: MacMillan, 1969.

Moody, Raymond. *Life After Life.* New York: Bantam Books, 1975.

Morse, Melvin. *Closer to the Light.* New York: Villard, 1990.

Near-Death Experiences and the Afterlife. http://www.near-death.com. April 10, 2000.

Ring, Kenneth. *Life at Death: A Scientific Investigation of the Near-Death Experience.* New York: William Morrow, 1980.

———, and Evelyn E. Valarino. *Lessons from the Light: What We Can Learn from the Near-Death Experience.* New York: Insight Books/Plenum Press, 1998.

SpiritWeb: NDE, Near Death Experiences. http://www.spiritweb.org/Spirit/nde.html. April 10, 2000.

Wilson, Ian. *The After Death Experience.* London: Sidgwick & Jackson, 1987.

Zaleski, Carol G. *Otherworld Journeys: Accounts of Near-Death Experiences in Medieval and Modern Times.* New York: Oxford University Press, 1987.

Necedah

Necedah, Wisconsin, was the site for almost 30 years of regular **apparitions of the Virgin Mary** to **Mary Anne Van Hoof** (1909–1984). The apparitions began on April 7, 1950, and attracted thousands to the small town in central Wisconsin for what became one of the most controversial incidents in Marian devotional history. Van Hoof initially saw the Virgin on November 12, 1949, the one-year anniversary of the last of a set of apparitions that had taken place in Lipa, Philippines. Then some months later, on April 7, 1950, the Virgin appeared again and for the first time spoke to Van Hoof, and told her to pray for the peoples of the world. Then on May 28, she appeared in what became a pattern, as a blue mist that would then turn into the figure of the Virgin. Over the next several days she came daily and then continued to appear quite frequently. She left lengthy messages relating her appearances to the previous apparitions in **Fatima** and Lipa. Van Hoof was asked to mark the spot of the apparitions and then to construct a shrine.

News of the apparition soon reached the parish priest and a report was sent to the bishop in La Crosse. By the time of the fifth appearance of the Virgin on June 16, Necedah was front-page news in Chicago, and large crowds, in the tens of thousands, began to gather at the stand of ash trees near Van Hoof's home on the edge of town. During the apparitions, Van Hoof would generally kneel, receive the message, and then step to a microphone and repeat what she had seen and heard. The next apparitions were promised for August 15 and October 7. Over the summer, Catholic periodicals and some bishops began to warn their people to stay away following the announcement by the bishop of La Crosse that there were some questionable aspects to the apparitions, but the crowds continued to arrive. On October 7, many in the crowd reported seeing a miracle of the sun, such as had occurred at Fatima, though others saw nothing.

In 1955, the bishop of La Crosse took a more definitive step and declared the apparitions false and prohibited Roman Catholics from participating in any worship that might occur at the apparition site. In the face of the pronouncements, the crowds dwindled but did not disappear. The faithful at the shrine continued and Van Hoof still received apparitions. An organization arose to manage the shrine that had been built, and efforts were begun to have the bishop reconsider his judgment. Eventually in 1975, those associated with the shrine were placed under interdict, an action one step short of excommunication. This action barred them from all the sacraments except confession. By this time, a number of shrines had been constructed in the general area of the central shrine at the spot of the apparitions. In 1977 the group commenced building its own church. An order of nuns was created, the Sisters of the Seven Dolors of the Sorrowful Mother, and the Seven Dolors of Our Sorrowful Mother Infants Home opened.

Two years later the Sisters of the Seven Delors organizations formally severed any remaining ties to the Roman Catholic Church, and realigned with a small independent Catholic jurisdiction, the American National Catholic Church, though that relationship ended in scandal in 1981. Since that time the shrine has operated under a separate corporation, For My God and My Country, Inc. Van Hoof died in 1984. The group that grew out of her apparitions continues as does its charity work. They have transcribed all of the messages that she received over the years and now circulate them in a several-volume work. Followers around the country are kept in touch with a monthly periodical.

Sources:

Revelations and Messages as Given to Mary Ann Van Hoof. 2 vols. Necedah, Wis.: For My God and My Country, Inc., 1971, 1978.

Swan, Henry. *My Work at Necedah.* 4 vols. Necedah, Wis.: For My God and My Country, Inc., 1959.

Necromancy

Divination by means of the spirits of the dead, from the Greek *nekrosh* (dead), and *manteia* (divination). It is through its Italian form *nigromancia* that it came to be known as the "black art." With the Greeks it originally signified the descent into **Hades** in order to consult the dead rather than summoning the dead into the mortal sphere again.

The art is of almost universal usage. Considerable difference of opinion exists among modern **adepts** as to the exact methods to be properly pursued in the necromantic art, and it must be borne in mind that necromancy, which in the Middle Ages was included in the practice of sorcery (malevolent **magic,** usually traditionally accomplished through the assistance of a demonic spirit), shades into modern spirit contact in **Spiritualism.** Necromancy has long been regarded as the touchstone of occultism, for if, after careful preparation, the adept can successfully raise a soul from the other world, he has proved the success of his art. The occult sages of the past have left full details as to how the process should be attempted.

In the case of a compact existing between the sorcerer and the devil, of course, no ceremony is necessary, as the **familiar** is ever at hand to do the bidding of his masters. This, however, is never the case with the true sorcerer, who preserves his independence and trusts to his profound knowledge of the art and his powers of command. His object therefore is to "constrain" some spirit to appear before him, and to guard himself from the danger of provoking such beings.

The magician normally has an assistant, and every article and procedure must conform to rules well known in the black art. In the first place, the magician and his assistant must locate a suitable venue for their procedures, which may be either a subterranean vault, hung with black and lighted by a magical torch, or else the center of some thick wood or desert, or some extensive unfrequented plain where several roads meet, or amid the ruins of ancient castles, abbeys, and monasteries, or among the rocks on the seashore, or some private detached churchyard, or any other solemn, melancholy place between the hours of twelve and one at night, either when the moon shines bright, or else when the elements are disturbed with storms of thunder, lightning, wind, and rain, for in these places, times, and seasons, it is contended that spirits can manifest themselves to mortal eyes with less difficulty and continue to be visible with the least pain in this elemental external world.

When the proper time and place is fixed on, a magic circle is to be formed, within which the master and his associate are carefully to retire. The dimensions of the circle are as follows: a piece of ground is usually chosen, nine feet square, at the full extent of which parallel lines are drawn one within the other, having sundry crosses and triangles described between them, close to which is formed the first or outer circle, then, about half-a-foot within the same, a second circle is described, and within that another square correspondent to the first, the center of which is where the master and associate are to be placed.

According to one authority:

"The vacancies formed by the various lines and angles of the figure are filled up with the holy names of God, having crosses and triangles described between them. The reason assigned by magicians and others for the institution and use of circles, is, that so much ground being blessed and consecrated by such holy words and ceremonies as they make use of in forming it, hath a secret force to expel all evil spirits from the bounds thereof, and, being sprinkled with pure sanctified water, the ground is purified from all uncleanness; besides, the holy names of God being written over every part of it, its force becomes so powerful that no evil spirit hath ability to break through it, or to get at the magician or his companion, by reason of the antipathy in nature they bear to these sacred names. And the reason given for the triangles is, that if the spirit be not easily brought to speak the truth, they may by the exorcist be conjured to enter the same, where, by virtue of the names of the essence and divinity of God, they can speak nothing but what is true and right. The circle, therefore, according to this account of it, is the principal fort and shield of the magician, from which he is not, at the peril of his life, to depart, till he has completely dismissed the spirit, particularly if he be of a fiery or infernal nature. Instances are recorded of many who perished by this means; particularly 'Chiancungi,' the famous Egyptian fortune-teller, who was so famous in England in the 17th century. He undertook for a wager, to raise up the spirit 'Bokim,' and having described the circle, he seated his sister Napula by him as his associate. After frequently repeating the forms of exorcism, and calling upon the spirit to appear, and nothing as yet answering his demand, they grew impatient of the business, and quitted the circle, but it cost them their lives; for they were instantaneously seized and crushed to death by that infernal spirit, who happened not to be sufficiently constrained till that moment, to manifest himself to human eyes."

The magic circle is consecrated by special rituals. The proper attire, or "pontificalibus," of a magician is an ephod made of fine white linen, over that a priestly robe of black bombazine reaching to the ground, with the two seals of the Earth drawn correctly upon virgin parchment, and affixed to the breast of his outer vestment. Around his waist is tied a broad consecrated girdle, with the names "Ya, Ya,—Aie, Aaie,—Elibra,—Elchim,—Sadai,—Pah Adonai,—tuo robore,—Cinctus sum." Upon the magician's shoes must be written "Tetragrammaton," with crosses around it; upon his head a high-crowned cap of sable silk, and in his hand a Holy Bible, printed or written in pure Hebrew.

Thus attired, and standing within the charmed circle, the magician repeats the awful form of exorcism, and presently the infernal spirits make strange and frightful noises, howlings, tremblings, flashes, and most dreadful shrieks and yells before they become visible. Their first appearance is generally in the form of fierce and terrible lions or tigers, vomiting forth fire, and roaring hideously about the circle, during which time the exorcist must not suffer any tremor of dismay, for, in the event the spirits gain the ascendancy, the consequences may endanger his life. On the contrary, he must summon up firm resolution and continue repeating all the forms of constriction and confinement until the spirits are drawn nearer to the influence of the triangle, when their forms will change to appearances less ferocious and frightful, and become more submissive and tractable.

When the forms of conjuration have in this manner been sufficiently repeated, the spirits forsake their bestial shapes and enter into human form, appearing like naked men of gentle countenance and behavior, yet the magician must remain warily on his guard so that they do not deceive him by such mild gestures, for they are exceedingly fraudulent and deceitful in their dealings with those who constrain them to appear without compact, having nothing in view but to accomplish his destruction.

The spirit must be discharged with great care after the ceremony is finished and he has answered all the demands made upon him. The magician must wait patiently until he has passed through all the terrible forms that announced his coming, and only when the last shriek has died away and every trace of fire and brimstone has disappeared may he leave the circle and depart home safety.

If the ghost of a deceased person is to be raised, the grave must be resorted to at midnight, and a different form of conjuration is necessary. Still another is the infernal sacrament for "any corpse that hath hanged, drowned, or otherwise made away with itself," and in this will at last arise, and standing upright, answer with a faint and hollow voice the questions that are put to it.

Lévi's Instructions

The occultist **Éliphas Lévi** stated in his book *Transcendental Magic* (1896) that "evocations should always have a motive and a becoming end, otherwise they are works of darkness and folly, dangerous of health and reason." The permissible motive of an evocation may be either love or intelligence. Evocations of love require less apparatus and are in every respect easier.

Lévi describes the procedure as follows:

"We must collect in the first place, carefully the memorials of him (or her) whom we desire to behold, the articles he used, and on which his impression remains; we must also prepare an apartment in which the person lived, or otherwise one of a similar kind, and place his portrait veiled in white therein, surrounded with his favourite flowers, which must be renewed daily. A fixed date must then be chosen, being that of the person's birth or one was that especially fortunate for his and our own affection, one of which we may believe that his soul, however blessed elsewhere, cannot lose the remembrance. This must be the day of the evocation, and we must prepare for it during the space of two weeks.

"Throughout the period we must refrain from extending to anyone the same proofs of affection which we have the right to expect from the dead; we must observe strict chastity, live in retreat, and take only one modest and light collation daily. Every evening at the same hour we must shut ourselves in the chamber consecrated to the memory of the lamented person, using only one small light, such as that of a funeral lamp or taper. This light should be placed behind us, the portrait should be uncovered and we should remain before it for an hour, in silence; finally, we should fumigate the apartment with a little good incense, and go out backwards.

"On the morning of the day fixed for the evocation, we should adorn ourselves as if for a festival, not salute anyone first, make but a single repast of bread, wine, and roots, or fruits. The cloth should be white, two covers should be laid, and one portion of the broken bread should be set aside; a little wine should also be placed in the glass of the person we design to invoke. The meal must be eaten alone in the chamber of evocations, and in presence of the veiled portrait; it must be all cleared away at the end, except the glass belonging to the dead person, and his portion of bread, which must be placed before the portrait. In the evening, at the hour for the regular visit, we must repair in silence to the chamber, light a clear fire of cypress-wood, and cast incense seven times thereon, pronouncing the name of the person whom we desire to behold. The lamp must then be extinguished, and the fire permitted to die out.

"On this day the portrait must not be unveiled. When the flame dies down, put more incense on the ashes, and invoke God according to the forms of the religion to which the dead person belonged, and according to the ideas which he himself possessed of God.

"While making this prayer we must identify ourselves with the evoked person, speak as he spoke, believe in sense as he believed. Then, after a silence of fifteen minutes, we must speak to him as if he were present, with affection and with faith, praying him to appear before us. Renew this prayer mentally, covering the face with both hands; then call him thrice with a loud voice; remain kneeling, the eyes closed or covered, for some minutes; then call again thrice upon him in a sweet and affectionate tone, and slowly open the eyes. Should nothing result, the same experiment must be renewed in the following year, and if necessary a third time, when it is certain that the desired apparition will be obtained, and the longer it has been delayed the more realistic and striking it will be.

"Evocations of knowledge and intelligence are performed with more solemn ceremonies. If concerned with a celebrated personage, we must meditate for twenty-one days upon his life and writings, form an idea of his appearance, converse with him mentally, and imagine his answers. We must carry his portrait, or at least his name, about us; follow a vegetable diet for twenty-one days, and a severe fast during the last seven.

"We must next construct the magical oratory . . . [This oratory must be invariably darkened]. If, however, the proposed operation is to take place during the daytime, we may leave a narrow aperture on the side where the sun will shine at the hour of the evocation, place a triangular prism facing the opening, and a crystal globe, filled with water, before the prism. If the experiment has been arranged for the night, the magic lamp must be so situated that its single ray shall upon the altar smoke. The purpose of the preparations is to furnish the Magic Agent with elements of corporeal appearance, and to ease as much as possible the tension of imagination, which could not be exalted without danger into the absolute illusion of dream. For the rest, it will be easily understood that a beam of sunlight, or the ray of a lamp, coloured variously, and falling upon curling and irregular smoke, can in no way create a perfect image. The chafing-dish containing the sacred fire should be in the centre of the oratory, and the altar of perfumes hard by. The operator must turn towards the East to pray, and the West to invoke; he must be either alone or assisted by two persons preserving the strictest silence; he must wear the magical vestments, which we have described in the seventh chapter, and must be crowned with vervain and gold. He should bathe before the operation, and all his under garments must be of the most intact and scrupulous cleanliness.

"The ceremony should begin with a prayer suited to the genius of the spirit about to be invoked and one which would be approved by himself if he still lived. For example, it would be impossible to evoke Voltaire by reciting prayers in the style of St. Bridget. For the great men of antiquity, we may see the hymns of Cleanthes or Orpheus, with the adjuration terminating the Golden Verses of Pythagoras. In our own evocation of Apollonius, we used the Magical Philosophy of Patricius for the Ritual, containing the doctrines of Zoroaster and the writings of Hermes Trismegistus. We recited the Nuctemeron of Apollonius in Greek with a loud voice and added the following conjuration: 'Vouchsafe to be present, O Father of All, and thou Thrice Mighty Hermes, Conductor of the Dead. Asclepius son of Hephaistus, Patron of the Healing Art; and thou Osiris, Lord of strength and vigour, do thou thyself be present too. Arnebascenis, Patron of Philosophy, and yet again Asclepius, son of Imuthe, who presidest over poetry. Apollonius, Apollonius, Apollonius, Thou teachest the Magic of Zoroaster, son of Oromasdes; and this is the worship of the Gods.'

"For the evocation of spirits belonging to religions issued from Judaism, the following Kabalistic invocation of Solomon should be used, either in Hebrew, or in any other tongue with which the spirit in question is known to have been familiar: 'Powers of the Kingdom, be ye under my left foot and in my right hand! Glory and Eternity, take me by the two shoulders, and direct me in the paths of victory! Mercy and Justice, be ye the equilibrium and splendour of my life! Intelligence and Wisdom, crown me! Spirits of *Malchuth,* lead me betwixt the two pillars upon which rests the whole edifice of the temple! Angels of *Netsah* and *Hod,* strengthen me upon the cubic stone of *Jesod! O Gedulael! O Geburael! O Tiphereth! Binael,* be thou my love! *Ruach Hochmael,* be thou my light! Be that which thou art and thou shalt be, *O Ketheriel!* Tschim, assist me in the name of *Saddai!* Cherubim, be my strength in the name of *Adonai!* Beni-Elohim, be my brethren in the name of the Son, and by the power of *Zebaoth!* Eloim, do battle for me in the name of *Tetragrammation!* Melachim, protect me in the name of *Jod He Vau He!* Seraphim, cleanse my love in the name of *Eloi* and Schechinah! Aralim, act! Ophanim, revolve and shine! Hajoth a Kadosh, cry, speak, roar, bellow! Kadosh, Kadosh, Kadosh, *Saddai, Adonai, Jotchavah, Eieazereie:* Hallelu-Jah, Hallelu-jah, Hallelu-jah. Amen.'

"It should be remembered above all, in conjurations, that the names of Satan, Beelzebub, Adramelek, and others do not designate spiritual unities, but legions of impure spirits. 'Our name is legion, for we are many,' says the spirit of darkness in the Gospel. Number constitutes the law, and progress takes place inversely in hell as the domain of anarchy. That is to say, the most advanced in Satanic development, and consequently the most degraded, are the least intelligent and feeblest.

"Thus, a fatal law drives demons downward when they wish and believe themselves to be ascending. So also those who term themselves chiefs are the most impotent and despised of all. As to the horde of perverse spirits, they tremble before an unknown, invisible, incomprehensible, capricious, implacable chief, who never explains his laws, whose arm is ever stretched out to strike those who fail to understand him. They give this phantom the names of Baal, Jupiter, and even others more venerable, which cannot, without profanation, be pronounced in hell. But this Phantom is only the shadow and remnant of God disfigured by their wilful perversity, and persisting in imagination like a visitation of justice and a remorse of truth.

"When the evoked spirit of light manifests with dejected or irritated countenance, we must offer him a moral sacrifice, that is, be inwardly disposed to renounce whatever offends him; and before leaving the oratory, we must dismiss him, saying: 'May peace be with thee! I have not wished to trouble thee; do thou torment me not. I shall labour to improve myself as to anything that vexes thee. I pray, and will still pray, with thee and for thee. Pray thou also both with and for me, and return to thy great slumber, expecting that day when we shall wake together. Silence and adieu!'"

Necromancy Around the World

The last example is, of course, of modern European necromancy, from France, the center of the modern magical revival. The evocation procedure followed by various peoples elsewhere is totally different. Among certain Australian tribes, for example, the necromants were called "Birraark." It is said that a Birraark was supposed to be initiated by the "mrarts" (ghosts) when they met him wandering in the bush. It was from the ghosts that he obtained replies to questions concerning events passing at a distance, or yet to happen, that might be of interest or moment to his tribe.

An account of a spiritual séance in the bush is given in a discussion of the Kamilaroi and Kurnai peoples: "The fires were let down; the Birraark uttered the cry 'Coo-ee' at intervals. At length a distant reply was heard, and shortly afterwards the sound as of persons jumping on the ground in succession. A voice was then heard in the gloom asking in a strange intonation 'What is wanted?' At the termination of the séance, the spirit voice said, 'We are going.' Finally, the Birraark was found in the top of an almost inaccessible tree, apparently asleep."

In **Japan,** ghosts were traditionally raised in various ways. One mode was to "put into an andon (a paper lantern in a frame) a hundred rushlights, and repeat an incantation of a hundred lines. One of these rushlights is taken out at the end of each line, and the would-be-ghost-seer then goes out in the dark with one light still burning, and blows it out, when the ghost ought to appear. Girls who have lost their lovers by death often try that sorcery."

The mode of procedure as practiced in **Scotland** was thus. The haunted room was made ready. He, "who was to do the daring deed, about nightfall entered the room, bearing with him a table, a chair, a candle, a compass, a crucifix if one could be got, and a Bible. With the compass he cast a circle on the middle of the floor, large enough to hold the chair and the table. He placed within the circle the chair and the table, and on the table he laid the Bible and the crucifix beside the lighted candle. If he had not a crucifix, then he drew the figure of a cross on the floor within the circle. When all this was done, he rested himself on the chair, opened the Bible, and waited for the coming of the spirit. Exactly at midnight the spirit came. Sometimes the door opened slowly, and there glided in noiselessly a lady sheeted in white, with a face of woe and told her story to the man on his asking her in the name of God what she wanted. What she wanted was done in the morning, and the spirit rested ever after. Sometimes the spirit rose from the floor, and sometimes came forth from the wall. One there was who burst into the room with a strong bound, danced wildly round the circle, and flourished a long whip round the man's head, but never dared to step within the circle. During a pause in his frantic dance he was asked, in God's name, what he wanted. He ceased his dance and told his wishes. His wishes were carried out, and the spirit was in peace."

In Sir N. W. Wraxall's *Memoirs of the Courts of Berlin, Dresden, Warsaw, and Vienna* (2 vols., 1799), there is an account of the raising of the ghost of the Chevalier de Saxe. Reports had been circulated that at his palace at Dresden there was a large sum of money hidden, and it was said that if his spirit could be compelled to appear, interesting secrets might be extorted from him. Curiosity, combined with avarice, accordingly prompted his principal heir Prince Charles to try the experiment. On the appointed night, one Schrepfer was the operator in raising the apparition. He commenced his proceedings by retiring into the corner of the gallery, where, kneeling down with many mysterious ceremonies, he invoked the spirit to appear. At length a loud clatter was heard at all the windows on the outside, resembling more the effect produced by a number of wet fingers drawn over the edge of glasses than anything else to which it could well be compared. This sound announced the arrival of the good spirits, and was shortly followed by a yell of a frightful and unusual nature, which indicated the presence of malignant spirits. Schrepfer continued his invocations, when "the door suddenly opened with violence, and something that resembled a black ball or globe rolled into the room. It was enveloped in smoke or cloud, in the midst of which appeared a human face, like the countenance of the Chevalier de Saxe, from which issued a loud and angry voice, exclaiming in German, 'Carl, was wollte du mit mir?'" (Charles, what would thou do with me?) By reiterated exorcisms Schrepfer finally dismissed the apparition, and the terrified spectators dispersed fully convinced of his magical powers.

Since the rituals of magical evocation date back to the ancient East, it is not surprising to find that European rituals have parallels in Arabia, Persia, India, China, Tibet and Japan. In the modern occult revival, such rituals have been popularized side by side with European traditions; various hybrid forms have also evolved. (See also **ceremonial magic; magical diagrams; magical instruments and accessories; New Zealand**)

Sources:

Lévi, Éliphas. *The History of Magic.* London: William Rider, 1913.

Shah, Sayed Idries Shah. *Oriental Magic.* London: Rider, 1956.

———. *The Secret Lore of Magic: Books of the Sorcerers.* London: Frederick Muller, 1957.

Smedley, Edward, W. C. Taylor, Henry Thompson, and Elihu Rich. *The Occult Sciences.* London and Glasgow: Richard Griffin, 1855.

Waite, Arthur E. *The Book of Ceremonial Magic.* London: William Rider & Son, 1911. Reprint, New Hyde Park, N.Y.: University Books, 1961. Reprinted as *The Book of Black Magic and Ceremonial Magic.* New York: Causeway Books, 1973.

———. *The Occult Sciences.* 1891. Reprint, Secaucus, N.J.: University Books, 1974.

Necronomicon

A **grimoire,** or textbook of black magic for evoking demons, supposedly compiled by the "mad Arab Abdul Alhazred," but in fact an invention of **H. P. Lovecraft,** early twentieth-century writer of supernatural and fantasy fiction. The name Abdul Alhazred was adopted playfully by Lovecraft around the age of five, after he read an edition of *The Arabian Nights.* He later used it in his fiction. It may also refer to an old Rhode Island family name, Hazard.

In 1936 Lovecraft wrote a pseudoscholarly essay titled *A History of the Necronomicon,* which claimed that its original title was *Al Azif,* derived from the word used by Arabs to designate the nocturnal sound of insects resembling the howling of demons. There followed an account of various editions of the *Necronomicon,* beginning in 730 C.E. Lovecraft claimed that there was a copy of the work in the equally fictional library of Miskatonic University, in Arkham (a city he invented in his fiction). Lovecraft's essay was published in leaflet form by Wilson H. Shepherd in 1938 and has since been reprinted. The *Necronomicon* was cited in various stories by Lovecraft and gradually acquired a spurious life of its own.

For example, someone inserted an index card for the book in the files of the Yale University Library. A New York bookseller could not resist inserting an entry for a Latin edition in one of his sale catalogs. Eventually a group of writers and researchers headed by occult scholar **Colin Wilson** solemnly presented *The Necronomicon: The Book of Dead Names* as a newly discovered lost masterpiece of occult literature.

In an introduction to this publication, Wilson suggested that Lovecraft's invention may have had some substance in fact, perhaps revealed through Lovecraft's subconscious mind. Wilson told a story as fabulous as that of the origin of the **Golden Dawn** cipher manuscript. Wilson's story concerned a Dr. Stanislaus Hinterstoisser, president of the Salzburg Institute for the Study of Magic and Occult Phenomena, who was said to have claimed that Lovecraft's father was an Egyptian Freemason. Lovecraft Sr. saw a copy of *The Necronomicon* in Boston (where he worked), which was a section of a book by Alkindi (d. 850 C.E.) known as *The Book of the Essence of the Soul*—so the story went.

Science fiction writer L. Sprague de Camp (who published a biography of Lovecraft in 1975) is said to have acquired an Arabic manuscript from Baghdad titled *Al Azif.* The British occultist Robert Turner, after researching in the British Museum

Library, claimed that the Alkindi work was known to the magician **John Dee** (1527–1608), who had a copy in cipher manuscript. This book, known as *Liber Logaeth,* was recently examined by computer analysis, and so *The Necronomicon: The Book of Dead Names* has now been researched, edited, and published (Neville Spearman, U.K., 1978).

No doubt other recensions of *The Necronomicon* will be discovered in the course of time. It might seem inevitable that once *The Necronomicon* appeared, a group accepting it as a valid magic text would soon follow. In the 1980s there surfaced on campuses across the United States flyers from what was termed "the Campus Crusade for Cthulhu," drawing upon Lovecraft in a parody of the Evangelical Christian organization, Campus Crusade for Christ. While the organization appears to be based in satire, it nevertheless demonstrates the comprehensive nature of the mythology created by Lovecraft and the seriousness with which some of his readers have taken the idea of the old gods enunciated therein.

Sources:

De Camp, L. Sprague, ed. *Al Azif (The Necronomicon).* Philadelphia: Owlswoch, 1973.

Hay, George, ed. *The Necronomicon: The Book of Dead Names.* UK: Neville Spearman, 1978. Reprint, London: Corgi, 1980.

Simon, ed. *The Necronomicon.* New York: Schlangekraft, Inc.; Barnes Graphics, 1977. Reprint, New York: Avon Books, 1977.

———. *Necronomicon Spellbook.* New York: Magickal Childe, 1986.

Nederlandse Vereniging voor Parapsychologie

The Nederlandse Vereniging voor Parapsychologie (Dutch Society of Parapsychology) was founded in 1960 by George A. M. Zorab and other Dutch parapsychologists who rejected what they considered the authoritarian leadership of the Studievereniging voor Psychical Research's **Wilhelm H. C. Tenhaeff.** They considered Tenhaeff overly ambitious, an observation which later proved to have a degree of truth when it was discovered that Tenhaeff had been altering data from his research to make his claims more impressive.

The society conducts some research but has made public education its major focus. It sponsors public lectures and publishes a journal, *Spiegel der Parapsychologie.* It may be contacted at Postbus 271, 3720 AG Bilthoven, The Netherlands.

Neihardt, John G(neisenau) (1881–1973)

Eminent American poet and author who also founded an organization for parapsychological research known as **SORRAT** (the Society for Research on Rapport and Telekinesis). Neihardt was born on January 8, 1881, near Sharpsburg, Illinois, the son of a farmer. He was educated at Nebraska Normal College (now Nebraska State Teachers College at Wayne), obtaining a diploma in science 1897.

From a period he lived among Native Americans, first with the Omaha (1901–07) and later among the Lakota (Sioux). Out of his relationship with the Lakota would come his single most famous book, *Black Elk Speaks* (1932). He then became the literary editor of the *Minneapolis Journal* (1911–20). In 1923, he was appointed professor of poetry at the University of Nebraska, Lincoln, and later held jobs as literary editor of the *St. Louis Post-Dispatch* (1926–38), director and field representative for the Bureau of Indian Affairs, U.S. Department of the Interior (1943–48) and lecturer in English and poet-in-residence at the University of Missouri–Columbia (1949–65).

Through his life Neihardt was repeatedly honored. He received the Poetry Society of America Prize for best volume of verse in 1919 and was named poet laureate of Nebraska by an act of the legislature, 1921. He was awarded the Gold Scroll Medal of Honor of National Poetry Center (1936) and the Writers Foundation award for poetry (1964). He was elected to the Nebraska State Hall of Fame in 1974. A bronze bust of Neihardt had already been placed in the rotunda of the Nebraska capital by an act of the state legislature in 1961. The Garden Club of Bancroft, Nebraska, acquired the cottage in which he lived and where he did much of his writing as a museum of Neihardt memorabilia, and there is a special Neihardt Memorial Collection at the University of Missouri.

Neihardt was friendly with **Joseph B. Rhine,** famous parapsychologist and director of the **Foundation for Research on the Nature of Man.** Neihardt's experience with the Omaha and Lakota probably influenced his philosophical views expressed in what has been called "pragmatic mysticism," involving the heightened awareness of prayer and meditation being applied to everyday life. In 1908, he married Mona Martensen, who had earlier spent some time as companion to a Spiritualist and who was convinced that psychic experience could not be dismissed. Apparently she had considerable mediumistic talents herself.

From the 1920s on, Neihardt spent some time investigating psychic phenomena at first hand, and he was also well aware of paranormal experiences among the Lakota. In 1926, he met Caspar Yost, a journalist who had investigated the famous phenomena of **Pearl Curran,** through whom the **"Patience Worth"** scripts were produced. Neihardt himself made an in-depth study of Curran.

In 1960, with John T. Richards and other associates, Neihardt formed the Society for Research on Rapport and Telekinesis in order to develop the investigation of psi faculties under favorable conditions. Some remarkable effects of **psychokinesis** were obtained. The story of the group has been recorded by Richards in his 1982 book. Neihardt died November 3, 1973.

Sources:

Aly, Lucile Folse. *John G. Neihardt: A Critical Biography.* Amsterdam: Radopi, 1977.

Berger, Arthur S., and Joyce Berger. *The Encyclopedia of Parapsychology and Psychical Research.* New York: Paragon House, 1991.

Neihardt, John G. *All Is But a Beginning.* New York: Harcourt, Brace, Jovanovich, 1972.

———. *Patterns and Coincidents: A Sequel to All Is but a Beginning.* Columbia: University of Missouri Press, 1978.

———. *The Sixth Grandfather: Black Elk's Teachings given to John G. Neihardt.* Lincoln: University of Nebraska Press, 1984.

———. *When the Tree Flowered: The Fictional Biography of Eagle Voice, a Sioux Indian.* Lincoln: University of Nebraska Press, 1970.

Richards, John Thomas. *SORRAT: A History of the Neihardt Psychokinesis Experiments, 1961–1981.* Metuchen, N.J.: Scarecrow Press, 1982.

A Sender of Words: Essays in Honor of John G. Neihardt. Salt Lake City, Utah: Howe Brothers, 1984.

Neil-Smith, Christopher (1920–)

Vicar of a Church of England parish church in London, and a leading British exorcist. He was born November 11, 1920, ordained in 1944 and soon after became aware of a healing power, which he has since used for dealing with possessed individuals. He performed his first exorcism in 1949, and has since performed as many as 500 exorcisms in a single year. By 1974, he had performed some 2,200 exorcisms, one of which was filmed for television.

He became well known in the public debates about exorcism in the mid-1970s following the popular response to Peter Blatty's *The Exorcist.* He has appeared on radio and television programs in North America, continental Europe, and Africa as well as in the United Kingdom. He describes his experiences and beliefs in his 1974 book, *The Exorcist and the Possessed.*

Sources:

Deutsch, Richard. *Exorcism: Possession or Obsession?* Foreword by Christopher Neil-Smith. London: Bachman & Turner, 1975.

Neil-Smith, Christopher. *The Exorcist and the Possessed: The Truth about Exorcism.* Cornwall, England: James Pike, 1974. Reprint, New York: Pinnacle Books, 1974.

Nelson, John

John Nelson, a radio engineer specializing in the study of shortwave radio propagation, made discoveries that have had a profound effect upon the study of contemporary **astrology.** As an employee of the Radio Corporation of America, he had the task of exploring the fluctuations in the Earth's magnetic field that affected communications systems. If those fluctuations could be understood and predicted, then steps could be taken to diminish their effects.

Disturbances in the magnetic field were directly tied to the magnetic storms on the Sun. The one factor that correlated with magnetic disturbances on the Sun was the position of the planets relative to the Sun. When two planets were either lined up with the Sun (what in astrology is termed an opposition) or at a 90-degree angle (a square), there would be disturbances. However, when the planets were at 120 degrees (trine) or 60 degrees (sextile), disturbances were noticeably quiet. Nelson eventually found that he could predict the disturbances on the sun with better than 90 percent accuracy. His results were published in several scientific articles at the beginning of the 1950s.

Nelson's work, while not directly related to astrology, was soon recognized as supportive of some significant conclusions of astrology. Traditionally, astrologers had suggested that oppositions and squares in a horoscope represented more negative aspects while trines and sextiles were more favorable. Nelson's research became a major element in the current scientific argument for astrology, but more recent attempts to replicate it have proven unsuccessful. Although many of his specific findings have been discarded, his work provided the foundation upon which additional research has been conducted concerning the relationship between planetary configuration and sunspot activity.

Nelson's work (and the work that followed from it) concerned the relationship of planets to the Sun, not to the Earth, as in the average horoscope, which is drawn with the Earth in the center. Such work provided additional impetus to the creation of a heliocentric (or Sun-centered) astrology. With the development of the computer in the last generation, such a heliocentric horoscope has become as simple to draw as has the traditional horoscope, and several astrologers have begun creating such a system of planetary interpretation.

Sources:

Nelson, John H. "Planetary Position Effect on Short Wave Signal Quality." *Electrical Engineering* 71, no. 5 ((May 1952): 421–24.

———. "Shortwave Radio Propagation Correlation with Planetary Positions." *RCA Review* 12 (March 1951): 26–34.

Seymour, Percy. *The Scientific Basis of Astrology.* New York: St. Martin's Press, 1992.

West, John Anthony, and Jan Gerhard Toonder. *The Case for Astrology.* New York: Coward-McCann, 1970.

Nengraphy

Japanese term for the **psychic photography** (or **thoughtography**) of the young Japanese psychic **Masuaki Kiyota,** who emerged in 1977 claiming and demonstrating a number of unusual psychokinetic abilities. He later admitted that he had accomplished everything through **fraud.** The Japan Nengraphy Association, headed by Tsutomu Miyauchi, was formed to investigate such phenomena, which appears to have some genuine practitioners. The association is headquartered at Awiji-cho 2-25, Kannda, Chioda, Tokyo. (See also **T. Fukurai; Ted Serios; thoughtforms**)

Sources:

Berger, Arthur S., and Joyce Berger. *The Encyclopedia of Parapsychology and Psychical Research.* New York: Paragon House, 1991.

Neometaphysical Digest

Publication of the **Society of Metaphysicians,** Inc., Archers' Court, Stonestile Lane, The Ridge, Hastings, East Sussex, England.

Neoplatonism

A mystical philosophical system initiated by Plotinus of Alexandria in 233 C.E. that combined the Platonic philosophy of ancient **Greece** with later Gnostic spiritual cravings. Although to some extent founded on the teachings of Plato, it was undoubtedly sophisticated by a deep mysticism, which in all probability emanated from Greece. To a great extent, Neoplatonism colored the thought of medieval mysticism and magic. Plotinus, its founder, commenced the study of philosophy in Alexandria at the age of 28. He early experienced an earnest desire to reach the truth concerning existence, and to that end made a deep study of the dialogues of Plato and the metaphysics of Aristotle. He practiced severe austerities and attempted to live what he called the "angelic" life, or the life of the disembodied in the body.

He was greatly drawn to **Apollonius of Tyana** by reading his *Life* by Philostratus. The union of philosopher and priest in the character of Apollonius fired the imagination of Plotinus, and in his Pythagorean teachings the young student discovered the elements of both Orientalism and Platonism, for both Pythagoras and Plato strove to escape the sensuous and to realize in contemplative abstraction the tranquility, superior to desire and passion, that made men approach the gods. However, in the hands of the later Pythagoreans and Platonists, the principles of the Hellenic masters were carried off into popular magical speculations. Many of the Pythagoreans joined the various Orphic (mystery religion) associations, becoming little more than itinerant vendors of charms.

It is probable that even before he left Alexandria Plotinus began to absorb some of the gnostic mysticism circulating throughout the Mediterranean Basin. But everywhere he also found a growing indifference to religion as known to the more ancient Greeks and Egyptians. By this time, the pantheons of Greece, Rome, and Egypt had become fused in the worship of Serapis, and this fusion had been forwarded by the works of Plutarch, Apuleius, and Lucian. The position of metaphysical philosophy at this time was by no means a strong one. In fact, metaphysical emphases had given place to ethical teachings, and philosophy was regarded as a branch of literature, or an elegant recreation. Plotinus persuaded himself that philosophy and religion should be one, and that speculation should be a search after God. It was at this time that he first heard of Ammonius Saccas, who shortly before had been a porter in the streets of Alexandria, and who lectured upon the possibilities of reconciling Plato and Aristotle.

"Skepticism," stated Ammonius, "was death." He recommended men to travel back across the past, and out of the whole bygone world of thought to construct a system greater than any of its parts. This teaching formed an epoch in the life of Plotinus, who was convinced that Platonism, exalted into a species of illuminism and drawing to itself like a magnet all the scattered truths of the bygone ages, could alone preserve mankind from skepticism. He occupied himself only with the most abstract questions concerning knowledge and being.

"Truth," according to Plotinus, "is not the agreement of our comprehension of an external object with the object itself, but rather, the agreement of the mind with itself. For the philosopher the objects we contemplate, and that which contemplates are identical; both are thought." All truth is then easy. Reduce the soul to its most perfect simplicity, and we find it is capable of exploration into the infinite; indeed it becomes one with the infinite. This is the condition of ecstasy, and to accomplish it, a stoical austerity and asceticism was necessary.

The Neoplatonists were thus, like the Gnostics, ascetics and enthusiasts. Plato was neither. According to Plotinus, the mystic contemplates the divine perfection in himself; all worldly things and logical distinctions vanish during the period of ecstasy. This approach has some similarity with the stages of **yoga meditation.**

Plotinus regarded the individual existence as phenomenal and transitory, and subordinated reason to ecstasy where the Absolute was in question. It is only at the end of his chain of reasoning that he introduces the supernatural. He is first a rationalist, afterwards a mystic, and only a mystic when he finds that he cannot employ the machinery of reason. The following letter of Plotinus, written about 260 C.E., embodies his conclusions:

"*Plotinus to Flaccus.*—I applaud your devotion to philosophy; I rejoice to hear that your soul has set sail, like the returning Ulysses, for its native land— that glorious, that only real country—the world of unseen truth. To follow philosophy, the senator Rogatianus, one of the noblest of my disciples, gave up the other day all but the whole of his patrimony, set free his slaves, and surrendered all the honours of his station.

"Tidings have reached us that Valerian has been defeated and is now in the hands of Sapor. The threats of Franks and Allemanni, of Goths and Persians, are alike terrible by turns to our degenerate Rome. In days like these, crowded with incessant calamities, the inducements to a life of contemplation are more than ever strong. Even my quiet existence seems now to grow somewhat sensible of the advance of years. Age alone I am unable to debar from my retirement. I am weary already of this prisonhouse, the body, and calmly await the day when the divine nature within me shall be set free from matter.

"The Egyptian priests used to tell me that a single touch with the wing of their holy bird could charm the crocodile into torpor; it is not thus speedily, my dear friend, that the pinions of your soul will have power to still the untamed body. The creature will yield only to watchful, strenuous constancy of habit. Purify your soul from all undue hope and fear about earthly things, mortify the body, deny self—affections as well as appetites, and the inner eye will begin to exercise its clear and solemn vision.

"You ask me to tell you how we know, and what is our criterion of certainty. To write is always irksome to me. But for the continual solicitations of Porphyry, I should not have left a line to survive me. For your own sake, and for your father's, my reluctance shall be overcome.

"External objects present us only with appearances. Concerning them, therefore, we may be said to possess opinion rather than knowledge. The distinctions in the actual world of appearance are of import only to ordinary and practical men. Our question lies within the ideal reality which exists behind appearance. How does the mind perceive these ideas? Are they without us, and is the reason, like sensation, occupied with objects external to itself? What certainty could we then have, what assurance that our perception was infallible? The object perceived would be a something different from the mind perceiving it. We should have then an image instead of reality. It would be monstrous to believe for a moment that the mind was unable to perceive ideal truth exactly as it is, and that we had not certainty and real knowledge concerning the world of intelligence. It follows, therefore, that this religion of truth is not to be investigated as a thing external to us, and so only imperfectly known. It is *within* us. Here the objects we contemplate and that which contemplates are identical—both are thought. The subject cannot surely *know* an object different from itself. The world of ideas lies within our intelligence. Truth, therefore, is not the agreement of our apprehension of an external object with the object itself. It is the agreement of the mind with itself. Consciousness, therefore, is the sole basis of certainty. The mind is its own witness. Reason sees in itself that which is above itself as its source; and again, that which is below itself as still itself once more.

"Knowledge has three degrees—Opinion, Science, Illumination. The means or instrument of the first is sense; of the second, dialectic; of the third, intuition. To the last I subordinate reason. It is absolute knowledge founded on the identity of the mind knowing with the object known.

"There is a raying out of all orders of existence, an external emanation from the ineffable One [*prudos*]. There is again a returning impulse, drawing all upwards and inwards towards the centre from whence all came [epistrophe]. Love, as Plato in the *Banquet* beautifully says, is the child of Poverty and Plenty. In the amorous quest of the soul after the Good, lies the painful sense of gall and deprivation. But that Love is blessing, is salvation, is our guardian genius; without it the centrifugal law would overpower us, and sweep our souls out far from their source toward the cold extremities of the Material and the Manifold. The wise man recognises the idea of the Good within him. This he develops by withdrawal into the Holy Place of his own soul. He who does not understand how the soul contains the Beautiful within itself, seeks to realize beauty without, by laborious production. His aim should rather be to concentrate and simplify, and so to expand his being; instead of going out into the Manifold, to forsake it for the One, and so to float upwards towards the divine fount of being whose stream flows within him.

"You ask, how can we know the Infinite? I answer, not by reason. It is the office of reason to distinguish and define. The Infinite, therefore, cannot be ranked among its objects. You can only apprehend the Infinite by a faculty superior to reason, by entering into a state in which you are your finite self no longer, in which the Divine Essence is communicated to you. This is Ecstasy. It is the liberation of your mind from its infinite consciousness. Like only can apprehend like; when you thus cease to be finite, you become one with the Infinite. In the reduction of your soul to its simplest self (aplosis), its divine essence, you realize this Union, this Identity [enosin].

"But this sublime condition is not of permanent duration. It is only now and then that we can enjoy this elevation (mercifully made possible for us) above the limits of the body and the world. I myself have realized it but three times as yet, and Porphyry hitherto not once. All that tends to purify and elevate the mind will assist you in this attainment, and facilitate the approach and the recurrence of these happy intervals. There are, then, different roads by which this end may be reached. The love of beauty which exalts the poet; that devotion to the One and that ascent of science which makes the ambition of the philosopher; and that love and those prayers by which some devout and ardent soul tends in its moral purity towards perfection. These are the great highways conducting to that height above the actual and the particular where we stand in the immediate presence of the Infinite, who shines out as from the deeps of the soul."

Plotinus appears to have been greatly indebted to Numenius for some of the ideas peculiar to his system. Numenius attempted to harmonize Pythagoras and Plato, to elucidate and confirm the opinions of both by the religious dogmas of the Egyptians, the **Magi,** and the Brahmans, and he believed that Plato was indebted to the Hebrew as well as to the Egyptian theology for much of his wisdom. Like Plotinus he was puzzled that the immutable One could find it possible to create the manifold without self-degradation, and he therefore (from Plato) posited a being whom he calls the Demi-urge, or Artificer, who merely carried out the will of God in constructing the universe.

Expressed in summary, the mysticism of Plotinus is as follows: One cannot know God in any partial or finite manner. To know him truly we must escape from the finite, from all that is earthly, from the very gifts of God to God himself, and know him in the infinite way by receiving, or being received into him directly. To accomplish this, and to attain this identity, we must withdraw into our inmost selves, into our own essence, which alone is susceptible of blending with the Divine Essence. Hence the inmost is the highest, and as with all systems of mysticism introversion is ascension, and God is found within.

Porphyry entered the school of Plotinus when it had become an institution of some standing. At first he strongly opposed the teachings of his master, but soon became his most devoted scholar. He directed a fierce assault on Christianity, and at the same time launched strictures at paganism, but both forces were too strong for him.

Porphyry modified the doctrine of Plotinus regarding ecstasy by stating that in that condition the mind does not lose its consciousness of personality. He called it a dream in which the soul, dead to the world, rises to a species of divine activity, to an elevation above reason, action and liberty. He believed in a certain order of evil genii, who took pleasure in hunting wild beasts, and others of whom hunted souls that had escaped from the fetters of the body, so that to escape them, the soul must once more take refuge in the flesh. Porphyry's theosophical conceptions, based on those of Plotinus, were strongly and ably traversed by the theurgic mysteries of Iamblichus, to whom the priest was a prophet full of deity. Criticizing Porphyry, Iamblichus stated:

"Often, at the moment of inspiration, or when the afflatus has subsided, a fiery Appearance is seen—the entering or departing Power. Those who are skilled in this wisdom can tell by the character of this glory the rank of divinity who has seized for the time the reins of the mystic's soul, and guides it as he will. Sometimes the body of the man subject to this influence is violently agitated, sometimes it is rigid and motionless. In some instances sweet music is heard, in others, discordant and fearful sounds. The person of the subject has been known to dilate and tower to a superhuman height; in other cases, it has been lifted up into the air. Frequently, not merely the ordinary exercise of reason, but sensation and animal life would appear to have been suspended, and the subject of the afflatus has not felt the application of fire, has been pierced with spits, cut with knives, and been sensible of no pain. Yea, often, the more the body and the mind have been alike enfeebled by vigil and by fasts, the more ignorant or mentally imbecile a youth may be who is brought under this influence, the more freely and unmixedly will the divine power be made manifest. So clearly are these wonders the work, not of human skill or wisdom, but of supernatural agency! Characteristics such as these I have mentioned, are the marks of the true inspiration.

"Now, there are, O Agathocles, four great orders of spiritual existence—Gods, Demons, Heroes or Demi-gods, and Souls. You will naturally be desirous to learn how the apparition of a God or a Demon is distinguished from those of Angels, Principalities, or Souls. Know, then, that their appearance to man corresponds to their nature, and that they always manifest themselves to those who invoke them in a manner consonant with their rank in the hierarchy of spiritual natures. The appearances of Gods are uniform, those of Demons various. The Gods shine with a benign aspect. When a God manifests himself, he frequently appears to hide sun or moon, and seems as he descends too vast for earth to contain. Archangels are at once awful and mild; Angels yet more gracious; Demons terrible. Below the four leading classes I have mentioned are placed the malignant Daemons, the Anti-gods.

"Each spiritual order has gifts of its own to bestow on the initiated who evoke them. The Gods confer health of body, power and purity of mind, and, in short, elevate and restore our natures to their proper principles. Angels and archangels have at their command only subordinate bestowments. Demons, however, are hostile to the aspirant, afflict both body and mind, and hinder our escape from the sensuous. Principalities, who govern the sublunary elements, confer temporal advantages. Those of a lower rank, who preside over matter, often display their bounty in material gifts. Souls that are pure are, like Angels, salutary in their influence. Their appearance encourages the soul in its upward efforts. Heroes stimulate to great actions. All those powers depend, in a descending chain, each species on that immediately above it. Good Demons are seen surrounded by the emblems of blessing, Demons who execute judgment appear with the instruments of punishment."

We thus see how in the process of time the principles on which the system of Plotinus rested were surrendered little by little, while **divination** and evocation were practiced with increasing frequency. Plotinus had declared the possibility of the absolute identification of the divine with human nature—the broadest possible basis for mysticism. Porphyry took up narrower ground and contended that in the union which takes place in ecstasy, we still retain consciousness of personality. Iamblichus diminished the real principle of mysticism still farther in theory, and denied that man has a faculty, eternally active and in accessible, to passion; the intellectual ambition so lofty in Plotinus subsided among the followers of Iamblichus into magical practice.

Proclus was the last of the Greek Neoplatonists. He elaborated the Trinity of Plotinus into a succession of impalpable triads, and surpassed Iamblichus in his devotion to the practice of theurgy. With Proclus, theurgy was the art that gave human beings the magical passwords that carried them through barrier after barrier, dividing species from species.

Above all being is God, the Non-Being, who is apprehended only by negation. When we are raised out of our weakness and on a level with God, it seems as though reason were silenced for we are above reason. In short we become intoxicated with God.

Proclus was an adept in the invocation rituals of every people in the world, and a great magical figure. With the advance of Byzantinism, he represented the old world of Greek thought, and even those who wrote against him as a heathen show the influence he exercised on their doctrines. Thus Dionysius attempted to accommodate the philosophy of Proclus to Christianity, and greatly admired his asceticism. The theology of the Neoplatonists was always in the first instance a mere matter of logic. They associated universals with causes. The highest became with them merely the most comprehensive.

As has been said, Neoplatonism exercised great power among the scholiasts and magicians of the Middle Ages. In fact most of what medievalism knew of Plato was through the medium of the Neoplatonists. In Germany in the fourteenth century it became a vivifying principle, for although its doctrine of emanation was abandoned, its allegorical explanation and its exaltation of the spirit above the letter was retained, and Platonism and mysticism together created a party within the church—the sworn foes of scholasticism and mere lifeless orthodoxy.

Sources:

Brehier, Emile. *The Philosophy of Plotinus.* Chicago: University of Chicago Press, 1958.

Gerson, Lloyd P. *Plotinus.* London: Routledge, 1994.

Hadot, Pierre. *Plotinus; or, The Simplicity of Vision.* Chicago: University of Chicago Press, 1993.

Mead, G. R. S. *Essay Written as a Preface to a New Edition of T. Taylor's "Select Works of Plotinus."* London: Theosophical Publishing Society, 1895.

Neoplatonism and Gnosticism. Albany, N.Y.: State University of New York Press, 1992.

Plotinus Amid Gnostics and Christians: Papers Presented at a Plotinus Symposium held at the Free University, Amsterdam, on January 25, 1984. Amsterdam: Free University Press, 1984.

Rist, J. M. *Plotinus: The Road to Reality.* Cambridge: Cambridge University Press, 1967.

Turnbull, Grace, ed. *The Essence of Plotinus.* New York: Greenwood Press, 1934.

Neppe, Vernon M.

Vernon M. Neppe, founder of the **Pacific Neuropsychiatric Institute** in Seattle, Washington, is a prominent neuropsychiatrist who has also engaged in significant parapsychological research. He attended the University of Witwatersrand in Johannesburg, South Africa, where he completed his medical degree in 1973. He later served as a specialist for post-graduate training and as a senior consultant at the school. In 1982 he was named the Witwatersrand University Overseas Traveling Fellow for 1982–83. He developed a specialization in psychopharmacology, forensic psychiatry, and geriatric psychiatry.

In 1986, Neppe established and was named director of the first division of neuropsychiatry in a department of psychiatry in the United States, at the University of Washington. In 1992 he founded the Pacific Neuropsychiatric Institute, a facility that conducts both clinical and forensic consultations for patients suffering from neuropsychiatric disorders and conducts research in a variety of related fields.

Over the years, one area that attracted Neppe's interest was paranormal experience, the subject of his master's thesis in 1979. He later came to refer to such experiences as anomalous experiences, those events humans perceive as paranormal, psychic, or bizarre and not easily explained by the conventional laws of science. Such events would include ESP and **psychokinesis.** He has advocated the use of a new set of terms in describing such experiences that are less prejudicial than many commonly employed in discussions of psychic phenomena. For example, ESP seems to carry with it the idea of contradicting well-known laws of physics. Neppe has argued that if, in fact, such events occur they should link with natural laws. Through the institute he conducts research in anomalous experiences in the attempt to understand them, especially in relation to his own fields of specialization.

Sources:

Neppe, V. M. "Anomalous Experience and Psychopathology." In Betty Shapin and Lisette Cody, eds. *Spontaneous Psi, Depth Psychology and Parapsychology.* New York: Parapsychology Foundation, 1992.

———. "Extrasensory Perception—an Anachronism and Anathema." *Journal of the American Society for Psychical Research* 52, no. 789 (October 1984): 365–70.

———. *An Investigation of the Relationship Between Temporal Lobe Symptomatology and Subjective Paranormal Experience.* Johannesburg, South Africa: University of Witwatersrand, Med Psych thesis, 1979.

———. "The Relevance of the Temporal Lobe to Anomalous Subjective Experience." In Rhea A. White and R. S. Broughton, eds. *Research in Parapsychology 1983.* Methuchen, N.J.: Scarecrow Press, 1984.

"Nessie"

Popular affectionate name for the **Loch Ness monster,** who is said to reside in a lake in northern Scotland. In an article in *Nature* titled "Naming the Loch Ness Monster," naturalist Sir Peter Scott and Robert Rines bestowed the scientific name *Nessiteras rhombopteryx.* They felt obliged to do this following modern photographic evidence suggesting the reality of the monster, since a British Act of Parliament (1975) requires a scientific name for any rare species of animal qualifying for conservation. Some newspapers gleefully pointed out that this scientific name may be converted to the anagram "Monster Hoax by Sir Peter."

Nessletter (Newsletter)

Newsletter concerned with reports and news of **monsters,** especially the **Loch Ness monster.** It is published by the Ness Information Service, 7 Huntshieldford, St. Johns Chapel, Bishop Aukland, Co. Durham DL13 1RQ, England.

Nester, Marian L(ow) (1910–)

A researcher in parapsychology, she was born on June 8, 1910, in Jamaica Plain, Massachusetts. She studied at Smith College (B.A., 1932) and Boston University (M.Ed., 1940). She was a school teacher (1933–44), a staff member of the United Service Organization, Travelers Aid Society (1944–46), a staff member of a publishing firm (1946–51), and a freelance editor and researcher (beginning in 1951). She was an associate member of the **Parapsychological Association** and a research assistant at the Parapsychology Foundation (1958–62) where she worked on experiments connected with survival and mediumship and assisted in a survey of death-bed hallucinations.

Sources:

Nester, Marian L. "New Methods of Parapsychology." *Tomorrow* 9, no. 4 (1961).

Pleasants, Helene, ed. *Biographical Dictionary of Parapsychology.* New York: Helix Press, 1964.

Nettles, Bonnie Lu Truesdale (1924–1985)

Bonnie Lu Truesdale Nettles, cofounder of the **Heaven's Gate** group, known for having ended its existence with the suicide of 39 members in 1997, was born in Houston, Texas. She grew up in a Baptist home, married, and became the mother of four children. She graduated from the Herman Hospital School of Professional Nursing in 1948 and subsequently worked as a registered nurse. In midlife, she developed an interest in things occult and in February 1966 joined the Houston Lodge of the **Theosophical Society in America,** which she remained affiliated with until she allowed her dues to lapse in 1973. She also attended a group centered upon **channeling** various noncorporeal entities.

In 1972 she met **Marshall Applewhite.** At the time Nettles was heading toward a divorce, while Applewhite had already been divorced and subsequently lost his teaching job because of an extramarital affair. The two developed a friendship and then a partnership in what was called the Christian Art Center where they offered classes in religion, art, and music. It was superseded by the Know Place, a metaphysical center, a reflection of the theosophical and occult teachings that Nettles introduced to Applewhite.

In 1973 the pair left Houston for the West Coast. They slowly began to see themselves as the Two Witnesses mentioned in the Bible (Revelation 11) who spread a message of judgment, are martyred, and then are resurrected and taken to heaven in a cloud. They identified the cloud as a flying saucer. They developed a perspective that interpreted biblical passages in light of contemporary thought about extraterrestrial contact. They believed that Jesus had ascended to heaven (the Level above Human, or T.E.L.A.H.) in a spacecraft and that Applewhite had arrived on Earth from that same T.E.L.A.H. realm and brought with him the Heavenly Father in the person of Nettles.

They began gathering followers in Los Angeles, California, and then set out on a tour that took them north to Oregon and eastward to Chicago, Illinois. Now known as Bo (Applewhite) and Peep (Nettles), they offered prospective members deliverance from Earth in a spaceship in the immediate future. Amid news coverage that ranged from hostility to ridicule, the group continued to gather members, but in 1976, Nettles announced the doors to the next level were now closed. The group did no further proselytizing and began to concentrate on teaching their followers. In 1977, they received a windfall in the form of a large inheritance received by one of the members. They began to rent houses in which to live, but moved frequently to avoid attachments to any location or home. They also withdrew contact from family and friends.

In the early 1980s, Nettles became ill from cancer. In 1983 she had one eye removed, but the cancer continued to spread. It eventually affected her liver and in June of 1985, she died in Dallas, Texas. Her **death** seemed to contradict the group's teachings, but Applewhite was later able to explain and justify her moving on ahead of the group. The group stayed together for another decade until the surviving members, including Applewhite, committed suicide at the spring equinox 1997.

Sources:

Perkins, Rodney, and Forrest Jackson. *Cosmic Suicide: The Tragedy and Transcendence of Heaven's Gate.* Dallas: Pentaradial Press, 1997.

Wessinger, Catherine. *How the Millennium Comes Violently.* New York: Seven Bridges Press, 2000.

Networking

A system of communication praised by many in the **New Age** movement as the best means of organizing people horizontally around common concerns (rather than veritically around leadership structures) and of data sharing. Networking of one kind or another has been practiced for many decades by means of directories, yearbooks, encyclopedias, specialized magazines, and groups, but with the development of modern computer resources, the facilities for accumulating, storing, and disseminating data on a wide scale have been greatly enhanced and accelerated. R. Buckminster Fuller observed,

"The new human *networks* emergence represents the natural evolutionary expansion into the just completed, thirty-years-in-its-building, world-embracing, physical communications network. The new reorienting of human 'networking' constitutes the heart and mind pumped flow of life and intellect into the world arteries."

The concept of rapid access to topical information has special value in relation to New Age beliefs and practices, since so many groups and centers flourish for a while, then change name or address or disappear, sometimes giving rise to splinter movements. Many networking guides are presented in magazine format for distribution at occult and holistic health shops. Some have related publications in different countries through international networking. Many such publications have diaries of forthcoming events, exhibitions, and lectures. Other networking publications appear in a more traditional directory format, regularly updated.

Networking makes it possible to accumulate and disseminate New Age information in a variety of formats and at local, state, or city levels. Typical networking publications in magazine and/or tabloid newspaper format include *Common Ground* (San Francisco), *PhenomeNews* (Detroit), *Whole Life* (New York), and *Whole Life Times* (Los Angeles). Such publications tend to have a relatively short life, though these mentioned have lasted for more than a decade.

The Whole Life World Fair Expo, organized annually by the *Whole Life Times,* publishes a catalog that includes networking information on related events, individuals, and publications. The comparable British annual Festival for **Mind-Body-Spirit** has a special networking feature, inviting the public to "play the Networking Game," i.e., join a network to exchange information with other people, to keep track of meetings and contacts, and to benefit from the use of computers for exchange of information.

The Networking Game charges a small fee and provides guidance notes, a personal networking diary, a networking badge, personal address labels, and information on contacts in one's local area, as well as information on such facilities as Net Workshops, Playshops, a Networking Market for goods and services, and a computer conferencing network for "screen-to-screen" meetings. The Networking Game may be contacted c/o Sabine Kurjo, 21A Goldhurst Terrace, London, NW6 3HD, England.

Sources:

Lipnack, Jessica, and Jeffrey Stamps. *The Networking Book: People Connecting with People.* New York: Methuen; London: Routledge & Kegan Paul, 1986.

Network News

Bimonthly publication of the Stewards of the Findhorn Foundation, Scotland, a **New Age** spiritual center. Address: Stewards of the Findhorn Foundation, The Park, Findhorn Bay, Forres, Moray, Scotland IV36 OTZ. Website: http://www.findhorn.org/.

Neuburg, Victor (Benjamin) (1883–1940)

Poet, editor, and associate of occultist **Aleister Crowley.** Neuburg was born on May 6, 1883, in London, England. He was educated at the City of London School, southwest London, and at Trinity College, Cambridge. An early Freethinker, his first poems were published in the *Agnostic Journal* and *Freethinker.*

Around 1906 at Cambridge, Neuburg came in contact with Crowley, also a poet, who had read some of Neuburg's pieces in the *Agnostic Journal.* Crowley initiated Neuburg into his secret society, the **A∴A∴,** giving him the name "Frater Omnia Vincam." He also initiated a homosexual relationship with Neuburg. In 1909 Crowley took Neuburg to Algiers, and they set off into the North African desert, where they performed a series of occult rituals. In the midst of these, Crowley put the ideas of sex and "magick" together and performed his first "sex magick" ritual.

In 1913 Crowley and Neuburg again joined forces in a homosexual ritual magic operation known as "the Paris Working." Neuburg appears to have broken with Crowley some time in 1914, before Crowley left for the United States on a magick tour. Supposedly, Neuburg was ritually cursed by Crowley and suffered a nervous breakdown.

From 1916 to 1919 Neuburg served in the army in World War I. Thereafter, he avoided Crowley and spent most of his time at Vine Cottage, Steyning, Sussex, where he operated a hand printing press. Many of his poems were issued under the imprint "Vine Press." In addition to works published under his own name, he used a number of pseudonyms: Alfricobas, Benjie, M. Broyle, Richard Byrde, Christopher Crayne, Lawrence Edwardes, Arthur French, Paul Pentreath, Nicholas Pyne, Harold Stevens, Shirley Tarn, and Rold White. His books include *The Green Garland* (1908), *The Triumph of Pan* (1910), *Lillygay, an Anthology of Anonymous Poems* (1920), *Swift Wings, Songs in Sussex* (1921), *Songs of the Groves* (1921), and *Larkspur, a Lyric Garland* (1922).

In 1933 Neuburg edited a section called "The Poet's Corner" in the British newspaper the *Sunday Referee.* This encouraged new talent by awarding weekly prizes. A group of talented young writers and poets grew up around Neuburg. He gave an award to a then-unknown poet named Dylan Thomas. As a result of Neuburg's enthusiasm, the publisher of the *Sunday Referee* sponsored the first book of poems by Dylan Thomas, titled *18 Poems.* The first publication is now a prized collector's item.

Although a minor poet, Neuburg's work has a magical lyric quality. Known affectionately as "Vickybird," he was a generous and warmhearted friend of other writers. Neuburg died May 30, 1940.

Sources:

Calder-Marshall, Arthur. *The Magic of My Youth.* N.p., 1951.

Crowley, Aleister. "The Book of the High Magick that as Worked by Frater O.S.V. 6-5 and Frater L. T. 2-9: The Paris Working." *The Equinox* (Nashville, Tenn.) 5, 4 (1981): 171–228.

———. *The Confessions.* New York: Hill & Wang, 1969.

Fuller, Jean Overton. *The Magical Dilemma of Victor Neuburg.* London: W. H. Allen, 1965.

Neuburg, Victor E. *Vickybird: A Memoir by His Son.* London: The Polytechnic of North London, 1983.

Neumann, Thérèse (1898–1962)

Bavarian peasant girl of Konnersreuth, whose **stigmata,** visions of the Passion of Christ, and other supernormal phenomena aroused worldwide attention. Neumann was born on April 8, 1898. As a young girl she was educated to have a religious mentality and aspired to become a missionary sister. Constitutionally she appeared robust.

In March 1918, while she aided in putting out a fire that had broken out in a neighboring house, she was stricken by a violent pain in the lumbar regions and collapsed. In the hospital of Waldsassen she was seized with terrible cramps, became blind, from time to time deaf, and paralyzed, first in both legs, then in the right and left cheeks. She spent miserable years at the home of her parents in constant suffering and religious meditation.

On April 29, 1923, the beatification day of St. Thérèse de Lisieux, she suddenly recovered her sight. On May 3, 1923, an ulcer between the toes of her left foot that might have caused the foot to be amputated was unaccountably healed after she put three rose leaves from the tomb of St. Thérèse in the bandage. On May 17, 1925, the canonization day of St. Thérèse, she saw a light and heard a voice that comforted her and assured her that she would be able to sit up and walk. She sat up immediately and afterward could walk about the room with the help of a stick and a supporting arm. On September 30 she dispensed with this support and went to church alone.

In December she was seized with violent intestinal pains. An urgent operation for appendicitis was recommended. She had a vision of St. Thérèse and heard a voice that told her to go to church and thank God. During the night the pus found a natural outlet and she was cured.

The stigmata appeared during Lent in 1926. An abscess developed in her ear, causing violent headaches. She saw in a vision Jesus in the Garden of Olives and felt a sudden stinging pain in the left side. A wound formed and bled abundantly. It was followed by stigmatic wounds in the hands and legs. There was no pus and no inflammation, but there was a fresh flow of blood every Friday. She also shed tears of blood and became, by Friday, almost blind.

With an awe-inspiring dramatic vividness she lived through the whole tragedy of the crucifixion; and in ancient Aramaic (which famous linguists established as such) she reproduced what were claimed to be the words of Christ and the vile swearing of the crowd as she clairaudiently heard them in that archaic language. Her pronunciation was always phonetic and many believed that she was in communication with someone who was a spectator of the events.

At Christmas in 1922, an abscess developed in Neumann's throat and neck. From this date until Christmas 1926 she abstained from solid food. She took a little liquid—three or four spoonfuls of coffee, tea, or fruit juice. After Christmas 1926, she only took a drop of water every morning to swallow the sacred host. From September 1927 until November 1928 she abstained even from this drop of water. Nevertheless she retained her normal weight. But four Roman Catholic sisters declared on oath that during the Friday ecstasies Neumann lost four pounds of weight, which she regained by the following Thursday without taking nourishment in any form. On August 15, 1927, Neumann had a vision of the death, burial, and ascension of Mary. She visualized Mary's tomb at Jerusalem and not at Ephesus, as usually assumed.

In the socialist and communist presses of Germany, Russia, and Austria, many libellous statements and quasiexposures were published about Neumann. Whenever they were followed by suits for libel the editors were found guilty and sentenced to imprisonment and fine. Neumann was something of an embarrassment to the Nazis during World War II, and the authorities made difficulties for visitors to Konnersreuth, but immediately after the war, hundreds of thousands of American and other servicemen lined up to visit her. She often gave accurate information on distant events through **out-of-the-body travel,** and appears to have traveled astrally to the death chamber of Pope Pius XII.

Although pilgrims presented many gifts to her, she would not use these for her own comfort and, before her death September 18, 1962, she had contributed to the church a training seminary for priests, as well as a convent. During her lifetime over 133 books or papers were written about her. (See also **Catherine Emmerich; Padre Pio**)

Sources:

Danemarie, J. *The Mystery of Stigmata from Catherine Emmerich to Theresa Neumann.* N.p., 1934.

Fahsel, K. *Konnersreuth: Le mystère des stigmatisés.* N.p., 1933.

Graef, Hilda. *The Case of Thérèse Neumann.* Westminister, Md.: Newman Press, 1951.

Hynek, R. W. *Konnersreuth: A Medical and Psychological Study of the Case of Teresa Neumann.* N.p., 1932.

Messmer, Joseph, and Sigismund Waitz. *A Visit to the Stimatized Seer: Therese Neumann.* Chicago: John P. Dalriden, 1929.

Pater, Thomas. *Miraculus Abstinence: A Study of the Extraordinary Mystical Phenomena.* Washington, DC: Catholic University of Medica, 1946.

Siwek, Paul. *The Riddle of Konnersreuth.* Milwaukee: Bruce Publishing, 1953.

Steiner, Johannes. *Thérèse Neumann: A Portrait Based on Authentic Accounts, Journals, and Documents.* Staten Island, N.Y.: Alba House, 1967.

Theodorowicz, Jose. *Mystical Phenomena in the Life of Therese Neumann.* St. Louis: B. Herder, 1940.

Von Lama, Frederick. *Thérèsa Neumann, une stigmatisée de nos jours.* N.p., 1928.

Neurypnology

James Braid's first term for **hypnotism.**

New Age

The New Age movement was a revivalist movement that swept through metaphysical New Thought churches and Spiritualist and occult organizations in the 1970s and 1980s. As a result, many people accepted either a metaphysical or Spiritualist perspective and both communities grew significantly. The New Age idea of replacing the present society with a coming of the golden age of peace and love for the next generation transformed both communities. By the mid-1990s, the idea of a New Age had largely died out but had left the psychic community permanently changed.

Roots of the New Age Movement

A noticeable New Age vision, the triumph of the hopes and ideals to which occultists gave their allegiance, was given a certain limited expression throughout the twentieth century. Often that hope was seen in the arrival of what was termed the Aquarian Age. In **astrology,** an "age" is defined by the location of the sun at the moment of the spring equinox each year. Because of the tilt of the Earth's axis, that sign changes approximately every 2,160 years. Depending upon the astrological system one uses, the sun is making the transition from the sign of Pisces to that of Aquarius sometime in this century.

Pisces, the fish sign, is often associated with Christianity, in which the fish is frequently used as a symbol of Jesus; in Greek the word for fish, *ichthus,* was a acronym for the phrase "Jesus Christ, God's son and Saviour." The passing of the Earth to a new astrological age would bring a new religion or spiritual perspective to dominance. However, during the last half of the twentieth century, as a new millennium loomed on the horizon, a variety of occult groups predicted the coming new age at the same time as the new millennium.

Among the early groups predicting the New Age was the London-based **Universal Link,** which originated in the contact of Richard Grave of Worthing, England, with a spirit entity who came to be known only as "Limitless Love." This entity first appeared in 1961 and gave Grave a variety of messages on the impending return of Christ in the midst of the seemingly destructive course of action being followed by the human race. Publicity given Grave's messages in a Spiritualist newspaper and his subsequent meeting with Spiritualist artist Libby Pugh led to the development of a network of interested individuals.

Crucial to the message was a prediction that by Christmas morning of 1967 Christ would reveal himself through the medium of nuclear evolution. That prediction brought many into the network, including Sir Anthony Brooke, the former ruler of the Indonesian island of Sarawak, who spent his retirement years traveling the world spreading the message.

When no visible event occurred to coincide with the predicted nuclear event, the most dedicated of the Universal Link members concluded that the event was an invisible one. Nellie Cane, founder of the **Spiritual Research Society,** and a key American figure spreading the Universal Link message, suggested that the event was the completion of the international linking of groups and individuals who need to join in a common effort to radiate God's light to the world.

Among the groups linked in the 1960s was the Findhorn Foundation, a communal association in northern Scotland in large part held together by **channeling.** Channeling is similar to mediumships in **Spiritualism**— the ability to contact spirit entities. However, in Spiritualism, a mediumship had concentrated upon the communication with a large number of spirit entities bringing greetings or messages to their still-living relatives with the aim of proving their continued existence after the transition of bodily death. Channeling, in contrast, assumed the existence of a spiritual world with which contact could be made for the purpose of learning about the nature of the world and receiving guidance on how to live. Mediumship was seen as the special prerogative of a few special individuals, while channeling was seen as possible for almost anyone.

A **medium** usually had a control, one or a few individual spirit entities who facilitated contact with the deceased relatives of the sitter(s). The channel usually contacted one or a few master teachers who regularly delivered philosophical discourses. The entities channeled, while usually the spirits of long-deceased individuals, could also be creatures from other planets, angelic beings, nature spirits, the channels' own higher self, or even Christ or God. The theosophical tradition had been built from the initial channelings of **Helena Petrovna Blavatsky** from the Masters or Mahatmas. While little channeling activity took place in the post-Blavatsky **Theosophical Society,** numerous splinter groups emerged around a new channel, sometimes referred to as a Messenger. Most prominent of these subsequent channels were **Alice A. Bailey** of the **Arcane School** and **Guy W. Ballard,** founder of the **I Am Movement.** The practice of channeling was given a tremendous boost in the 1970s by the publication of the material channeled by **Jane Roberts** from an entity known as "Seth."

Findhorn had been sustained through the 1960s, its developing years, by the channeling activity of Eileen Caddy. In the early 1970s, it was joined by a young student of the Alice Bailey teachings, David Spangler, who channeled material from an entity called "John." Spangler would, during his three years at Findhorn, construct a vision of the New Age as a time when important new energies from the cosmos were available to the human race. If these energies were accepted and worked with over the next generation, a New Age could be brought to pass. According to Spangler, the coming of the New Age was dependent upon the dedicated spiritual work of the people. He published his views first in a small book published by Findhorn, *The New Age Vision* (1973), upon which he expanded in his widely circulated volumes *Revelation: The Birth of a New Age* (1976) and *Towards a Planetary Vision* (1977).

Through the 1970s the New Age vision as articulated by Spangler spread through the groups and individuals that had constituted the network created by the Universal Link and spread far beyond it. The basic ideas were quite simple: There is a New Age coming and this present generation is the transition generation, though most will live to see and enjoy the imminent new society of peace and love. As society goes through the birth pangs of the new society and the turmoil and displacement it will bring, individuals can experience a foretaste of the social transformation in an immediate and personal transformation occasioned by a healing, a new personal insight, or the realization of a spiritual truth. Facilitating the personal transformation were a number of New Age transformative tools: channeling, crystals, divinatory techniques (**tarot** cards, astrology, etc.) and a whole range of **holistic** health practices. Responsibility for bringing in the New Age is in the hands of individuals who must take responsibility for their lives and the direction of society.

As the New Age movement emerged through the 1970s, it had a social vision that saw the merging of New Age vision to older movements centered upon world peace, environmentalism, and multiethnic cooperation. Healing became an important metaphor of the New Age and the holistic health perspective provided an alternative program to the common scientific medicine built upon drugs and surgery. It suggested an emphasis upon preventive medicine and the eradication of disease through a natural (and frequently vegetarian) diet, healthful practices (exercise, **hatha yoga,** living in a nonpolluted environment), and attention to clearing problems by developing spiritually and cleansing the emotions. The various forms of body work (chiropractic, massage, and related practices) have been immensely popular in New Age circles.

Rise and Fall of the New Age

The New Age movement grew through the 1970s and by 1980s had become a recognizable social phenomena. In that year Marilyn Ferguson would describe it as The Aquarian Conspiracy, a decentralized network of people who have forsaken the past for a coming new world. They are bonded by their experience of inner transformation and their common work for the coming transformed society. Through the next decade channeling became a well-known phenomenon, the use of crystals (the effect of which was described in great detail by channeler **Frank Alper**) spread, the publication of metaphysical and occult books burgeoned, and hundreds of thousands of people in Europe, North America, and urban centers around the world were swept up into the movement. An estimated four million adherents could be found in the United States alone.

The movement seemed to peak in the late 1980s following the airing in 1987 of *Out on a Limb,* a television movie based upon the New Age awakening of actress **Shirley MacLaine.** MacLaine had written a series of popular New Age books and publicly identified with the movement, in which she developed an avocation as a teacher. In 1989 she released a video, *Shirley MacLaine's Inner Workout.*

However, through the 1980s, the New Age movement received a significant amount of criticism, the most telling accusing it of being a shallow spiritual vision built upon the questionable practices of channeling and crystals and a naive (and false) hope of a significant systemic change in society. Internally, New Age leaders began to reexamine the movement. The first of an important set of redefining articles by David Spangler began to appear in 1988. Over the next few years, prominent leaders of the movement announced their abandonment of the New Age vision of a transformed society and publicly distanced themselves from channeling and crystals. They suggested that the heart of the movement had always been the personal transformations experienced by individuals and the spiritual perspective on life it gave to people. The social vision was abandoned and the people left in the movement reoriented entirely around personal development and improvement.

By the early 1990s, it was obvious that the New Age movement was dying. The passing of the New Age movement did not leave the metaphysical, Spiritualist, and occult communities unchanged. The hundreds of thousands of individuals brought into the communities by the New Age did not leave. Hundreds of New Age bookstores still dot the landscape, and New Age publishing remains a healthy concern. Most importantly, the concept of "New Age," which largely replaced "occult" in popular parlance, gave occultism a positive image in popular culture, the lack of which was a major barrier to its growth. The New Age movement left the occult community in a most robust state.

During the nineties the New Age has shifted from its premillennialist stance where an "overnight" scenario was expected to occur to a more postmillennial outlook where each person is expected to create their own heaven on earth by personal spiritual transformation over time. This evolution can be seen in the progression of books by James Redfield starting with *The Celestine Prophecy* and continuing with many sequels. The new emphasis has been on the issue of ascension, but with no crystallized consensus from the many authors that promote it. Such authors grace the pages of *Sedona Journal of Emergence* with an eclectic mix of views. Another huge archive of New Age information is the SpiritWeb Internet site.

Sources:

Anderson, Walter Truett. *The Upstart Spring: Esalen & the American Awakening.* Reading, Mass.: Addison-Wesley, 1983.

Basil, Robert, ed. *Not Necessarily the New Age.* Buffalo, N.Y.: Prometheus Books, 1988.

Celestine Vision. http://www.celestinevision.com/main.html. April 10, 2000.

Ferguson, Marilyn. *The Aquarian Conspiracy: Personal and Social Transformation in Our Time.* New York: St. Martin's Press, 1980.

Lewis, James R., and J. Gordon Melton, eds. *Perspectives on the New Age.* Albany, N.Y.: State University Press of New York, 1992.

MacLaine, Shirley. *Out on a Limb.* New York: Bantam Books, 1983.

Melton, J. Gordon, Jerome Clark, and Aidan Kelly, eds. *New Age Encyclopedia.* Detroit: Gale Research, 1990.

Mystic Planet and New Age Directory of Planet Earth. http://www.mysticplanet.com/. April 10, 2000.

New Age Reading Room. http://www.wholeagain.com/news.html. April 10, 2000.

New Age Web Works. http://www.newageinfo.com. April 10, 2000.

New Age On-line Australia. http://www.newage.com.au. April 10, 2000.

Schultz, Ted. *The Fringes of Reason: A Whole Earth Catalog.* New York: Harmony Books, 1989.

Sedona Journal of Emergence. http://www.sedonajo.com/sje. April 10, 2000.

Spangler, David. *Revelation: The Birth of a New Age.* San Francisco: Rainbow Bridge, 1976.

Spangler, David, and William Irwin Thompson. *Reimagination of the World: A Critique of the New Age, Science, and Popular Culture.* Sante Fe, N.Mex.: Bear and Company Publishing, 1991.

Spiritual Consciousness on WWW. http://www.spiritweb.org. April 10, 2000.

Wilson, Robert Anton. *The New Inquisition: Irrational Rationalism and the Citadel of Science.* Las Vegas: Falcon Press, 1986.

New Age Bible and Philosophy Center

The New Age Bible and Philosophy Center is a Rosicrucian study center in Santa Monica, California, founded in 1931 by Mary Elizabeth Shaw. Though Shaw led the center, it was also for many years a vehicle for the teaching activity of Corinne Heline and her husband, Theodore Heline. Corinne Heline was a prominent student of Max Heindel, founder of the **Rosicrucian Fellowship,** and she remained a member of the fellowship through the 1920s. During this period she began work on metaphysical Bible interpretation, a project that eventually resulted in a seven-volume series. In 1930 she married Theodore Heline, and they founded the New Age Press and affiliated with the center in Santa Monica. Many of the Helines' writings remain in print and may be obtained from the center.

Shaw was succeeded by Rev. Gene Sande, who after many years was succeeded by the present leader, Rev. Patricia Tallis. The center is located at 1139 Lincoln Blvd., Santa Monica, CA 90403.

Sources:

Heline, Corinne. *Color and Music in the New Age.* La Canada, Calif.: New Age Press, 1964.

———. *New Age Bible Interpretation.* 7 vols. Los Angeles: New Age Press, 1938–54.

Heline, Theodore. *America's Destiny: A New Order of the Ages.* Oceanside, Calif.: New Age Press, 1941.

New Age Church of Truth

The New Age Church of Truth was founded in the mid-1960s by Gilbert N. Holloway (b. 1915), who emerged in the 1930s as a metaphysical teacher. He was widely read in the available Rosicrucian and theosophical literature and conscious of his own psychic powers, and by the 1960s he worked as a psychic with a national following. In 1967 a Pentecostal experience (which included speaking in **tongues**) converted him to Christianity, though Holloway cast his faith in a metaphysical thought world. He then changed his organization's name to New Age Church of Truth, the Christ Light Community. From the headquarters of his church in Deming, New Mexico, he traveled widely as a lecturer, healer, and psychic reader into the 1980s. Current address unavailable.

Sources:

Holloway, Gilbert N. *Let the Heart Speak.* Los Angeles: DeVorss, 1951.

———. *New Ways of Unfoldment.* Deming, N.Mex.: New Age Truth Publications, n.d.

———. *The Way Up.* Deming, N.Mex.: New Age Church of Truth, 1975.

New Age Journal

Journal of **New Age** and holistic topics published by New Age Publishing and concerned mainly with achievement, commitment, health, creative living, and holistic nutrition. It includes a calendar of a wide range of New Age seminars, lectures, training courses, and symposia. Since the late 1980s the

Journal has also published annual networking books from their editorial offices at 42 Pleasant St., Watertown, MA 02472. Website: http://www.newage.com/.

Sources:

Holistic Health Directory and Resource Guide, 1994–1995. Watertown, Mass.: New Age Journal, 1994.

New Age: The Journal for Holistic Living. http://www.newage.com/. March 8, 2000.

Sourcebook 1994. Watertown, Mass.: New Age Journal, 1994.

New Age Media Resource Directory

Quarterly networking publication concerned with **New Age** information, listing books, publishers, audiotapes, periodicals, film and video productions, and therapeutic and spiritual centers. It is concerned with psychic studies, Eastern religion and yoga, macrobiotics, holistic health, and related topics. Address: Box 419, New York, NY 10002.

New Age Retailer

New Age Retailer is the major trade journal serving the chain of metaphysical bookstores that emerged in the 1980s as the **New Age** Movement came into existence. From its beginning in the mid-1980s, the magazine has grown into a large bimonthly report on new publications in the post-New Age spirituality, including books, music, and various related products from jewelry to greeting cards. For example, **crystals,** which lost the central place that they had in the New Age community of the 1980s, have remained popular as art objects. Each issue of *New Age Retailer* is built around a listing of several hundred new books, many of which come from small independent publishers. A picture of the book cover is accompanied by basic ordering information and a brief description of the content supplied by the publishers (usually the same material found on the book's cover or dust jacket). A similar treatment is offered for new cds and products. While *New Age Retailer* is built around providing basic information on new products, it also provides additional guidance to assist retail outlets improve their sales, the major factor affecting the health of the metaphysical wholesale community. On a regular basis, the magazine offers information on contacting sales representatives and wholesale jobbers, attending trade shows, and expanding inventory. Each issue also features a set of articles on a particular topic of interest to store owners on such diverse topics as building a store website and doing effective but inoffensive advertising. *New Age Retailer* generally circulates only within the psychic/occult business community, but may be ordered from Continuity Publishing, Inc., 1300 N. State St., Ste. 105, Bellingham, WA 98225-4730. Its webpage can be found at http://www.newageretailer.com/. It provides clear insight into the business world that undergirds the current metaphysical/spiritual community and offers a means of contacting small publishers issuing metaphysical products.

Sources:

New Age Retailer. Bellingham, Wash., n.d.

New Age Retailer. http://www.newageretailer.com/. February 28, 2000.

New Age Teachings

New Age Teachings, one of the original **New Age** organizations in the United States, was founded by New Age channel Anita Afton (b. 1922). Better known as Illiana, she regularly channeled messages for more than 25 years. As a young seeker, Illiana, a Unitarian, became interested in the teachings of **Paramahansa Yogananda.** She affiliated with the **Self-Realization Fellowship** and began the practice of kriya **yoga.** She learned to meditate and became aware of her past lives in India. In 1965 she received her first channeled messages. Her early messages came from entities identifying themselves as residents of the planet Jamel. Within a few years she experienced what she described as a lifting of her own consciousness and since then the "I AM THAT I AM" has been the only voice speaking through her. After she founded New Age Teachings, she began publishing a regular bulletin containing transcripts of the messages. Illiana also became part of the original international network established in the 1960s by the Universal Link.

New Age Teachings emphasized that New Age vibrations were causing increasing light to come to Earth. The work expanded in 1976 with the addition of a Spanish edition of the bulletin, published from Houston, Texas. A music ministry began in the 1980s. Last known address: P.O. Box 346, Brookfield, MA 01506.

New Age World Religious and Scientific Research Foundation

Formerly Inner Sense Scientist Association, this organization was founded in 1976 with a membership of persons interested in **New Age** religious and scientific culture, including inventors, authors, lecturers, students, and scientists.

The purpose of the foundation is to bring forth the highest and best of religious and scientific understanding to humankind and to serve as a balance between religion and science. It maintains a 4,000-volume library and sponsors a correspondence course in New Age World Religious Millennium Teachings. Address: 62091 Valley View Cir. No. 2, Joshua Tree, CA 92252. Website: http://www.joshuatreevillage.com.

Sources:

Vandertuin, Victoria. *My God: The Power and Wisdom of the Universe.* Calif.: New Age Press, 1978.

New Atlantean Research Society

Former nonprofit organization that investigated all relevant aspects of the unknown, unexplained, and unexplored, especially Atlantis, UFO sightings, and Earth changes. The society, which was headquartered in St. Petersburg, Florida, published a quarterly, the *New Atlantean Journal.*

Newbold, William Romaine (1865–1926)

Philosopher with a special interest in psychical research. He was born November 20, 1865, at Wilmington, Delaware. He studied at the University of Pennsylvania (B.A., 1887; Ph.D., 1891) and did post-graduate study at the University of Berlin (1891–92). He was a member of the faculty of the University of Pennsylvania for 37 years, of which the last two decades were spent as the Adam Seybert Professor of Intellectual and Moral Philosophy (1907–26). He was an authority on Oriental languages and Greek philosophy. He became famous for his achievement in deciphering a medieval manuscript, which he showed to be the work of Roger Bacon, and for his translation of Semitic scrawls on the walls of the Roman catacombs.

He was a member of both the **Society for Psychical Research** (SPR), London, and the **American Society for Psychical Research** (ASPR). He was deeply interested in psychical research and contributed a number of important articles on the subject to the *Journal* and *Proceedings* of the ASPR and the SPR. He died September 26, 1926, in Philadelphia, Pennsylvania.

Sources:

Berger, Arthur S., and Joyce Berger. *The Encyclopedia of Parapsychology and Psychical Research.* New York: Paragon House, 1991.

Newbold, William R. *The Cipher of Roger Bacon.* Philadelphia: University of Pennsylvania Press, 1928.

———. "Subconscious Reasoning." *Proceedings* of the Society for Psychical Research 12 (1896).

Pleasants, Helene, ed. *Biographical Dictionary of Parapsychology.* New York: Helix Press, 1964.

Newbrough, John Ballou (1828–1891)

A New York dentist who was clairvoyant and clairaudient from childhood and who, through **automatic writing** (on a typewriter), produced **"Oahspe"** (1881), a channeled volume published as a new bible. He was born on June 5, 1828, near Springfield, Ohio, the son of a schoolteacher. He was educated in the local schoolhouse, and from the age of 16 continued to educate himself. He attended the Cincinnati Medical College and practiced both medicine and dentistry.

He migrated to California in 1849 and was fortunate in becoming a gold miner. Several years later, he married Rachel Turnbull, the sister of his partner John Turnbull. They moved to New York, where Newbrough resumed his dental and medical practice. He associated himself with the emerging Spiritualist movement, and became a trustee of the New York Spiritualist Association. Eventually his Spiritualist interests led to disagreements with his wife, and some years later they divorced.

His own psychic gifts were remarkable. He could paint in total darkness with both hands at once. It was claimed that, by closing his eyes, he could read printed pages of any book in any library, that he could bring back recollections of astral travels (or **astral projections**), and that under control he could lift enormous weight, even a ton, without apparent effort. However, bored with the commonplace messages that dominated Spiritualist spirit contact, he was anxious to utilize the spirits' time for more metaphysical information.

Thus he initiated the events that culminated in his production of *Oahspe: A Kosmon Bible in the Words of Jehovah and his Angel Ambassadors.* He described these events in a letter dated January 21, 1883, to the editor of the *Banner of Light:*

"I was crying for the light of Heaven. I did not desire communication for friends or relatives or information about earthly things; I wished to learn something about the spirit world; what the angels did, how they travelled, and the general plan of the universe. . . . I was directed to get a typewriter which writes by keys, like a piano. This I did and I applied myself industriously to learn it, but with only indifferent success. For two years more the angels propounded to me questions relative to heaven and earth, which no mortal could answer very intelligently. . . .

"One morning the light struck both hands on the back, and they went for the typewriter for some fifteen minutes very vigorously. I was told not to read what was printed, and I have worked myself into such a religious fear of losing this new power that I obeyed reverently. The next morning, also before sunrise the same power came and wrote (or printed rather) again. Again I laid the matter away very religiously, saying little about it to anybody. One morning I accidentally (seemed accidental to me) looked out of the window and beheld the line of light that rested on my hands extending heavenward like a telegraph wire towards the sky. Over my head were three pairs of hands, fully materialised; behind me stood another angel with her hands on my shoulders. My looking did not disturb the scene, my hands kept right on printing . . . printing. For 50 weeks this continued, every morning, half an hour or so before sunrise, and then it ceased, and I was told to read and publish the book 'Oahspe.' The peculiar drawings in Oahspe were made with pencil in the same way."

He claimed that "Oahspe" came from the higher heavens, and was "directed and looked over by God, the creator's chief representative in the heavens of this earth."

A group formed around Newbrough's revelations, and in 1883 they gave themselves the name "Faithists of the Seed of Abraham" (a term used in "Oahspe"). They moved to Las Cruces, New Mexico, and established Sholam, a community to implement the "Oahspe" injunction to care for foundlings and orphans.

Newbrough married again, choosing a companion from the community. By 1891, a residential home had been completed, housing some 50 children, but in the following year an outbreak of influenza devastated the area, and Newbrough himself was struck down, dying that year. For a time, his associate Andrew M. Howland continued the community, but it soon disintegrated. However, Newbrough's very dispersed and decentralized followers continued under such names as the "Essenes of Kosmon" or "Universal Faithists" and are still active today. "Oahspe" is kept in print through the Universal Faithists of Kosmon (Box 664, Salt Lake City, UT 84110), and a journal, *The Faithist Journal,* is published at 2324 Suffock Ave., Kingman, AZ 86401.

Sources:

Denton, Jim. *Dr. Newbrough and Oahspe.* Kingman, Ariz.: Faithist Journal, 1975.

———. *The Oahspe Story.* Kingman, Ariz.: Faithist Journal, 1975.

Miller, Timothy. *American Communes, 1860–1960: A Bibliography.* New York: Garland Publishing, 1990.

Stowes, K. D. *The Land of Shalam: Children's Land.* Evansville, Ind.: Frank Molinet Print Shop, n.d.

The New Celtic Review (Journal)

Former quarterly publication of the British based GSO Society for the Preservation of Celtic Lore, Monuments and Antiquities. The journal included details of festivals, mail order books, cards (of the ancient Celtic Ogham Tree Alphabet), and publications, as well as events throughout Celtic regions and countries.

New Christian Church of Full Endeavor

During the 1980s, **A Course in Miracles** emerged as a text around which thousands of people found guidance for their spiritual life. While many simply read the text and integrated it into a previously existing metaphysical worldview already in large agreement with the teachings, many found in the text a new profound spiritual direction. Many found their participation primarily in weekly study groups and noted how helpful the *Course* insights were for their life. Others found in the *Course* the catalyst to completely reorient their life and perception. Among the latter are the members of the New Christian Church of Full Endeavor.

Catalyst for the coming together of the church in the 1980s is Chuck Anderson, today known as simply Master Teacher. He and the members found in the *Course* a restatement of the perennial philosophy, a mystical visionary worldview that has appeared in other times and places as, for example, advaita vedanta, **Zen,** or **Taoism.** The perennial philosophy recognizes a Divine Reality behind the visible world of sense experience (described by Vedantists as maya or illusion). In discovering that reality behind the illusion, humans discover their essence as equal to the Divine Reality and perceive that their highest purpose is in knowledge of that Ground of Being. They see in Master Teacher a person who facilitates the **enlightenment** of those around him.

The church teaches that *A Course in Miracles* is a contemporary restatement by Christ of the teachings of Jesus of Nazareth. Church members have come into an experience of the Divine Reality and are attempting to learn always with that reality and out of that reality. In the real world, fear and evil do not exist. In that reality love is perfected and joy established. They also believe that a process of transformation is going on in their lives and in the world. The keynote of that transformation is healing and forgiveness. That process will continue through their full endeavor.

The church is headquartered in Lake Delton, Wisconsin. Also established there is the Endeavor Academy, the church's educational arm, which offers a variety of courses drawing upon *A Course in Miracles* and the vast literature representative of the perennial philosophy. Located in a former resort hotel, it provides residential space for students who may come to the classes that are offered on a quarterly basis. The church and academy may be contacted at P.O. Box 206, Lake Delton, WI 53940. It has an Internet site at http://www.endeavoracademy.com/. Besides the center in Wisconsin, there are groups related to the church across North America and in Europe.

The church emerged in the very diverse environment of the movement built around *A Course in Miracles.* That movement has been seen as somewhat centered in the Foundation for Inner Peace, a corporation that owned the copyright of the *Course* and has been primarily responsible for its printing and distribution. The New Christian Church of Full Endeavor is one of several groups that have come into conflict with the foundation for reprinting sections of the *Course* as part of their effort to spread the message. They are currently in litigation with the foundation over their right to reprint the material. Part of the case hinges upon the claimed authorship of the *Course,* namely Christ, and whether a work by a Divine Being can be copyrighted under United States law.

Sources:

Endeavor Academy. http://www.endeavoracademy.com/. April 7, 2000.

"New Christian Church of Full Endeavor." *Out of Time: A Journal of Endeavor Academy* 1 (1993): 14.

The New Church See Church of the New Jerusalem

New Civilization Network

During the 1990s, by far the best-selling metaphysical text was **The Celestine Prophecy** by **James Redfield.** It offered the idea that an increasing number of people were gaining new insights into their own nature and the inner structure of the universe. In fact, as a critical mass of such people who shared these insights became aware of each other, they would realize a common world vision. Working together, awakened people could produce a new spiritualized world culture.

As the readership of *The Celestine Prophecy* and its sequels, *The Tenth Insight* (1996) and *The Celestine Vision* (1997), grew, study groups began to form. Redfield also produced several study guides and a newsletter for people who took the content of the books most seriously. At the same time he has resisted becoming the leader of a new movement.

However, in 1995, Flemming Funch, the head of a computer web development and networking company (Synchronicity Network in Van Nuys, California), sent out an e-mail letter calling for people who were interested in working toward a new spiritual culture. He received an unexpected amount of feedback and organized the New Civilization Network and a loose association of people conversing on the Internet. Since that time, the network has grown into what is described as a "self-organizing international grass-roots association" of people interested in building a better world. The members of the network share a positive vision of the future and seek appropriate means for working with each other. As the network has increased in size, in those geographical areas where members are concentrated, network members have organized salons, gatherings at which they meet and discuss their new ideas. The largest number of these are in southern California.

Members come to the network from a wide range of backgrounds and have appropriated the Redfield material in quite diverse manners. Respect for the diversity and the very different ideas being expressed is a hallmark of the network, holding it together even as commonalities are being sought. Members may join simply by submitting their name to the network, where they are placed on a membership list and begin receiving the messages posted by other members. They may also participate in Internet chat rooms and bulletin boards. In some places they may attend meetings and work with others on mutually agreed upon projects. Funch has also put together a reading list of complementary material.

As of the beginning of 2000, the network is not incorporated, its major emphasis being on providing a space in which the spontaneous cooperation of its members may occur. Contact with the network is through its webpage, http://www.newciv.org/.

Sources:

New Civilization Network. http://www.newciv.org/. February 25, 2000.

Redfield, James. *The Celestine Prophecy.* New York: Warner Books, 1994.

———. *The Celestine Vision: Living the New Spiritual Awareness.* New York: Warner Books, 1997.

———. *The Secret of Shambhala: Search for the Eleventh Insight.* New York: Warner Books, 1999.

———. *The Tenth Insight.* New York: Warner Books, 1996.

Newcomb, Simon (1835–1909)

Astronomer, mathematician, and first president (1885–86) of the **American Society for Psychical Research.** He was born on March 12, 1835, at Wallace, Nova Scotia. He studied at Lawrence Scientific School (B.S., 1858), and Harvard University. He joined the U.S. Navy during the Civil War as a professor of mathematics (1861), and was later assigned to the U.S. Naval Observatory (1867). He subsequently became the director of the American Nautical Almanac (1877–97) and a professor of mathematics and astronomy at Johns Hopkins University (1884–94). A world-famous astronomer and mathematician, Newcomb's research made possible the construction of accurate lunar tables. In spite of his interest in psychical research, he remained an outspoken skeptic, a position he explained in his autobiography. He died July 11, 1909.

Sources:

Berger, Arthur S., and Joyce Berger. *The Encyclopedia of Parapsychology and Psychical Research.* New York: Paragon House, 1991.

Hyslop, James H. "Professor Newcomb and Occultism." *Journal* of the American Society for Psychical Research 5 (1909).

Newcomb, Simon. *Reminiscences of an Astronomer.* Boston: Houghton, Mifflin, 1903.

Pleasants, Helene, ed. *Biographical Dictionary of Parapsychology.* New York: Helix Press, 1964.

New Consciousness Sourcebook

Important **New Age** guide issued by the followers of Yogi Bhajan (founder of the Sikh Dharmma) in the San Francisco Bay area. The original edition was issued in 1972 as the *Spiritual Community Guide for North America.* New editions were released periodically through the 1970s. The new name was adopted for the fifth edition in 1982. The last edition, the sixth, appeared in 1985.

The directory covered organizations concerned with spiritual growth as well as such New Age subjects as nutrition, holistic health, healing, therapies, kundalini, bodywork, lifestyles, and meditation. It listed New Age bookstores, publications, occult supply houses, records, and tapes. It was published by Spiritual Community Publications in Berkeley, California. The group also published *A Pilgrim's Guide to Planet Earth,* an international directory covering the same areas of concern as the *Sourcebook.*

Sources:

The New Consciousness Sourcebook, #5. Berkeley, Calif.: Spiritual Community Publications, 1982. Rev. ed. Pomona, Calif.: Arcline, 1985.

A Pilgrim's Guide to Planet Earth. San Rafael, Calif.: Spiritual Community Publications, 1981.

New Dimensions (England)

Briefly published British quarterly publication dealing with the **Kabala** and magical teachings in the tradition of the Hermetic Order of the **Golden Dawn** and **Dion Fortune.**

New Dimensions (Florida)

Occasional newsletter of the Florida Society for Psychical Research, Inc., dealing with society activities and psychic topics. Last known address: 2837 1st Ave. N., St. Petersburg, FL 33713.

New Dimensions Broadcasting Network

New Dimensions Broadcasting Network is the producer and distributor of post-**New Age** radio and short wave programs. New Dimensions was created in 1973, as an expression of the human potentials movement. Founders Michael and Justine Toms were, at that time, inspired by the work of parapsychologist **Charles T. Tart,** one of the founders of the discipline of transpersonal psychology, who had observed that a new revolution in consciousness was beginning. New Dimensions was incorporated as a nonprofit educational foundation to address the issues raised by the approaching change in culture and value systems.

New Dimensions began modestly as a program for a single station in Northern California. In 1980 the program reached a national audience with a weekly program over a satellite network. Through the 1990s more than a hundred different stations across the United States have aired the ongoing series of programs and it has been picked up by the Armed Forces Radio Network and the Radio for Peace International shortwave network. Beginning in May 2000, New Dimensions was aired by the Merlin shortwave system. It is also available on the Internet. As the twenty-fist century begins, *New Dimensions* is the most widely heard New Age broadcast in the world.

New Dimensions programs are commonly built around an interview with one or more persons representative of what is perceived as the new consciousness. Guests have included spiritual leaders from a variety of Eastern and alternative traditions, environmental spokespersons, and exponents of various forms of esoteric wisdom and **New Thought** metaphysics.

The New Dimensions Broadcast is currently supported by the New Dimensions Foundation, P. O. Box 569, Ukiah, CA 95482. The Foundation issues a bi-monthly periodical, *New Dimensions: The Journal of New Dimensions Radio,* that provides a guide to upcoming programs. It also supports a website at http://www.newdimensions.org/, and makes available tape recordings of past programs. The work of the foundation is supported by a cadre of listeners known as the Friends of New Dimensions.

Sources:

New Dimensions: The Journal of new Dimensions Radio. Ukiah, Calif., n.d.

New Dimensions. http://www.newdimensions.org/. January 15, 2000.

New England Journal of Parapsychology

Quarterly journal that publishes papers from undergraduates of a college course in parapsychology at Franklin Pierce College, Rindge, New Hampshire.

New Existence of Man upon the Earth (Journal)

Short-lived British journal founded in 1854 by socialist reformer **Robert Owen** (1771–1858), the only European journal of the period concerned with **Spiritualism.** The issues included an early report on automatic writing by a four-year-old child who wrote in Latin. The journal ceased publication after the death of Owen.

New Frontiers Center Newsletter

Now-defunct publication that contained news and views from parapsychologist **Walter Uphoff** and his associates.

NewHeavenNewEarth

NewHeavenNewEarth (NHNE) is an online newsletter operating out of a post-**New Age** vision of planetary transformation. It was founded in 1994 by David Sunfellow out of his realization of the power of the Internet as a tool for communication and cooperation among humans on a global scale. NHNE operates through an online mailing list to which news stories are regularly sent and an extensive webpage that carries news and reports of interest to the "planetary transformation movement," the name given by Sunfellow to the post-New Age.

NHNE has set as its mission the tracking of planetary transformation and using the Internet to bring together a group of people in cyberspace to focus upon the basic age-old religious/philosophical questions of "Who are we? "Where did we come from?" and "Why are we here?" Having rejected the use of traditional (and authoritarian) sources of religious teachings, NHNE opts instead for a new methodology for arriving at Truth. It attempts to bring together contemporary spiritual seekers, both professional and lay, to pool their wisdom in a process of encouraging enlightenment. The understanding that the planet is undergoing a period of significant change underlies the discussions pursued through NHNE.

Besides simply passing along news items on topics such as environmental concerns, the paranormal, relevant developments in science, etc., NHNE has focused on selected topics for concentrated research and reporting. NHNE has also posted its findings from investigations of **A Course in Miracles** court cases, crop circles, and the claims of visionary musician James F. Twyman, leader of the **Community of the Beloved Disciple.**

NHNE can be contacted at P.O. Box 10627, Sedona, AZ 86339-8627. Its large Internet site is at http://www.nhne.com/.

Sources:

NewHeavenNewEarth. http://www.nhne.com/. June 11, 2000.

New Horizons (Journal)

Former semi-annual journal of New Horizons Research Foundation, Toronto. It contained articles on the research of the Toronto Psychical Society and other parapsychological work. It was edited by **A. R. G. Owen,** a mathematician at the University of Toronto, who was one of the group of experimenters who created the experimental ghost **"Philip."** Last known address: P.O. Box 427, Station F, Toronto, ON, Canada M4Y 2L8.

New Horizons Newsletter

Monthly publication devoted to spiritual movements, alternate energies, and related New Age subjects. Last known address: 1 Palomar Arcade, #124, Santa Cruz, CA 95060.

Newhouse, Flower (1909–1994)

Metaphysical teacher Flower Newhouse was born Mildred Arlene Sechler on May 10, 1909, in Allentown, Pennsylvania. From her childhood days, she told her parents that her real name was Flower, but they did not choose to follow her lead. Her father died when she was six, and two years later her mother remarried. They then moved out of Allentown and eventually settled in Scranton. Shortly after that, the still-prepubescent Mildred claimed that she was confronted by her guardian angel, who told her that he was now taking charge of her development. At the age of 13, Mildred again announced that she wanted to be called Flower, and her mother and sister finally gave in.

Through the next years, Mildred developed her own independent ways, and her family learned to trust her inner promptings. Thus, in 1924, they took very seriously the story of her encounter of a new entity in her life whom she described as John the Beloved. The spirit had come to her and called for an immediate move to California. Within weeks they were in Los Angeles. Flower found work as a salesperson in a retail store, but twice a week began to teach what she had learned from her spiritual contacts. Within a short time she was able to become a full-time teacher. In 1933, while in San Bernardino, California, to speak, she met Lawrence Newhouse, whom she would marry later that year. He would become her confidant and helpmate for the rest of his life. That same year she issued the first of many booklets, *The School of Life.*

By this time Newhouse had come to see herself as the product of a set of previous incarnations. She had returned this time to be a teacher and to found a teachings center. She was in contact with the broad range of spiritual entities from nature spirits to the theosophical hierarchy, but saw her special emphasis to be the enlightening of people concerning the ministry of **angels.**

Soon after their marriage, she and her husband began traveling throughout North America and she built a large following. She launched a periodical, the *Inspiration Newsletter,* in 1934, as a means to stay in contact. Finally in 1940, she found a suitable and affordable tract of land upon which to build Quest Haven, the spiritual center she had envisioned. When dedicated, it became the headquarters of the Christward Ministry, the name she gave to her far-flung work. People began to move to land close by Quest Haven so they would be able to attend the regular weekly events at the center.

The rest of her life, Newhouse concentrated her efforts on building Quest Haven, writing a series of books, and composing a set of lessons summarizing her teachings. Lawrence died in 1963, but Flower lived for another 30 years, passing away in 1994.

Sources:

The Christward Ministry. Vista, Calif.: Christward Ministry, n.d.

Isaac, Stephen. *The Way of Discipleship to Christ.* Escondido, Calif.: Christward Ministry, 1976.

Newhouse, Flower. *The Christward Ministry.* 4 vols. (lessons 1–208). Vista, Calif.: Christward Publications, n.d.

———. *The Meaning and Value of the Sacraments.* Escondido, Calif.: Christward Ministry, 1971.

New Humanity (Journal)

British newsstand magazine founded in February 1975 as "the world's first politico-spiritual journal." Its purpose is "to create Peace on Earth, the alleviation of suffering, and the promotion of well-being among mankind. We are neither Left nor Right but Uplifted Forward. We work for Peace, Non-Confrontation, Unity in Diversity, Mental Liberation and Harmony with the God-head." Articles cover a wide range of **New Age** topics relating to the improvement of humanity through new consciousness awareness. It is issued six times annually from editorial offices at 51A York Mansions, Prince of Wales Dr., London, SW11 4BP, UK.

New Isis Lodge

An original lodge of the British **OTO** (Ordo Templi Orientis) organization. The New Isis Lodge was established by **Kenneth Grant** in 1955, during the period of turmoil that hit the organization following the death of the outer head of the order, **Aleister Crowley,** in 1947. During Crowley's last years, aided by the chaos of World War II, the order virtually ceased to exist in Europe. Crowley passed his job to **Karl Germer,** then living in the United States. Germer operated as a caretaker for the order, but was more interested in seeing to the publication of Crowley's manuscripts than in aiding the revival of the organization after its decimation by the Nazis. Germer had himself spent several years in a concentration camp prior to escaping to England and then the United States.

In 1951 Germer granted a charter to Kenneth Grant, a young magician who had known Crowley during the last years of his life. Originally Grant was limited to performing only the first three of the order's eleven degrees, but he had access to copies of all of the secret material. In 1955, Grant formally organized the New Isis Lodge of the OTO. The "New" was a pun on "Nu," or "Nuit," a term borrowed from Egyptian mythology that symbolized absolute consciousness. It was associated with the Crowley concept of the Scarlet Woman, whose formula was "love under will." "New-Isis" or "Nu-Isis" therefore symbolized the heavenly and earthly goddess. Grant also began to work all eleven degrees of the order.

Accompanying the organization of the lodge, Grant issued a manifesto announcing the discovery of a new planet in this solar system beyond Pluto, a planet unknown to astronomy, which he named Isis. Quickly after receiving the manifesto and news of Grant's actions, Germer expelled Grant from the OTO. Grant ignored the expulsion and continued to build his organization. He had no competition in the United Kingdom until the 1970s.

Grant had access to Crowley's library, which was eventually deposited at an academic library in London, and as his organization grew he began to write books both on the Crowley legacy and on his own peculiar revisions of it. He gained considerable status in the larger magical community in 1969 as the co-editor of Crowley's autobiographical *Confessions.*

Grant, while working the OTO rituals, offered a new variation that had grown out of his own magical experiments with what was termed the shadowside or backside of the Kabalistic system, work which resembled **Satanism** to many magicians. Since Grant's death, the work of the British OTO has continued independently of the larger OTO movement, one branch of which is headquartered in Germany and one in the United States.

Sources:

Grant, Kenneth. *Cults of the Shadow.* London: Frederick Muller, 1975.

———. *Nightside of Eden.* London: Frederick Muller, 1977.

———. *Outside the Circles of Time.* London: Frederick Muller, 1980.

King, Francis. *The Rites of Modern Occult Magic.* New York: Macmillan, 1970.

The New Motor

A strange machine constructed in 1854 by Spiritualist medium **John Murray Spear** in association with another medium, Charles Hammond, at the instigation of the "Association of Electricizers," one of the bands of spirits by whom he was controlled. The motor was to derive its motive power from the magnetic store of nature and was therefore to be independent of artificial sources of energy, like the human body. The machine was hailed as the "physical saviour of the race," and the "new messiah." Mrs. Alonzo Newton, wife of one of Spear's collaborators, obeyed a vision by going to High Rock, Lynn, Massachusetts, where the new motor was located, and for two hours suffering "birth-pangs," whereby she judged that the essence of her spiritual being was imparted to the machine.

At the end of that time it was claimed that pulsations were apparent in the motor. Newton continued to act as nurse to the contraption for several weeks, but the only observed movements seemed to be a slight oscillation of some of the metal balls that adorned it. One disappointed Spiritualist complained that the new motor could not even turn a coffee mill. **Andrew Jackson Davis** visited the new motor at High Rock and expressed the belief that the design was the work of spirits of a mechanical turn of mind, but that the machine was of no practical value.

The new motor was finally smashed by a mob at Randolph, New York, where it had been taken. In all it cost its builder some two thousand dollars. In common fairness to the Spiritualists it must be said that Spear was widely recognized as a kind and honest man who had championed many liberal reforms. His earlier experience of spirit messages was remarkable, resulting in a healing ministry. It seems that he was deceived by misleading communications from "the Association of Electricizers" (which supposedly included the spirit of Benjamin Franklin).

It is possible that the new motor may have suggested a line of research to **John Worrell Keely** (1837–1898), who claimed the discovery of a new motive force in his invention of the Keely motor. This force was said to be a "vibratory etheric force" or cosmic energy. After the death of Keely, evidence of **fraud** was revealed.

From time to time since the new motor fiasco, Spiritualists have constructed various apparatus to facilitate **communication** with the spirit world, sometimes basing their constructions on spirit messages. Among modern inventors who were more successful than Spear were those comprising the group known as the **Ashkir-Jobson Trianion,** ca. 1930, who built various apparatus that seemed to work. The psychotherapist **Wilhelm Reich** also claimed the discovery of a cosmic motor force in what was termed **orgone** energy. (See also **Communigraph**)

New Perspectives

New Perspectives is one of a host of periodicals established during the late 1980s as the **New Age** Movement peaked and one of the few to survive into the post-New Age era. In its broad statement of purpose, it focuses attention on the emergence of a new consciousness and information considered by many to be esoteric. It is also tracing the movement of the movements of the last generation, from human potentials to **New Thought** metaphysics, into the self-conscious and self-critical mainstream culture.

Each issue of *New Perspectives* is built around a set of feature articles, often grouped around a single theme, that highlight issues within the larger community of people who accept an esoteric and holistic perspective on the world. Articles treat psychic reality, various forms of spiritual and alternative healing, and varieties of esoteric practice. A strong concern for healthy living is projected with articles that advocate practices (from dietary changes to spiritual exercises) that promote a healthful lifestyle in general. Each issue also contains a set of columns that include book reviews, movie and video reviews, and evaluation of New Age/holistic health spas, hotels, and retreats. Unlike most New Age periodicals, formed with an emphasis on networking between New Age organizations, practitioners, and devotees, *New Perspectives* has followed a more traditional magazine format centered upon providing its readers information and a perspective on what is seen as a forward-looking emerging culture. That perspective includes the attempt to highlight the similarities between people in spite of their apparent differences.

New Perspectives has been published quarterly since its founding in 1987. Editor/publisher Allan Hartley may be contacted at P.O. Box 3208, Hemet, CA 92546. In 1999 it added an Internet presence at http://www.newperspectivesjournal.com/.

Sources:

New Perspectives. Hemet, Calif., n.d.

New Perspectives. http://www.newperspectivesjournal.com/. (March 12, 2000).

New Realities

New Age magazine issued through the 1980s that presented a wide range of new age topics. It was initially issued in 1969 under the name *Psychic,* and quickly gained the respect of the psychic-oriented community for its coverage of parapsychology and psychic phenomena and its in-depth interviews with leading personalities in the field. It had a high standard of popular presentation without the sensationalism or vulgarity of so many of the competing periodicals dealing with the occult.

In 1977, after Vol. 7, No. 6, *Psychic* changed its title to *New Realities,* indicating its new direction as an organ serving the New Age community by its stated desire to focus upon "developments in the emergent areas of human possibilities that affect our everyday lives" in addition to psychic phenomena and new psychic research. This wider view embraces "holistic health" (total approach to human well-being on all levels), aspects of consciousness, Eastern and Western mysticism, new lifestyles and parapsychology.

In 1986 editor/publisher James Bolen transferred control of *New Realities,* which had been published in San Francisco, to Heldref Publications in Washington, D.C. The magazine was discontinued several years later.

New Reformed Orthodox Order of the Golden Dawn (NROOGD)

The NROOGD is an American Witchcraft tradition which was founded by a group of San Franciscans interested in the occult; they banded together to perform an archetypal Witches' Sabbath for a class at a San Francisco university in 1968. Using published sources from Robert Graves, **Margaret Murray,** and **Gerald Gardner,** a ritual was composed which serves as the basis of the NROOGD practice. After repeat performances, the group created an identity for themselves and trained others in its performance. The name they chose, New Reformed Orthodox Order of the Golden Dawn, is a play on the attitudes they had toward what they were doing and upon their spiritual antecedents. NROOGD is a wholly new tradition stemming from the magical order known as the **Hermetic Order of the Golden Dawn;** they consider themselves their spiritual and magical successors.

The mother circle of NROOGD "hived off" (branched off into) daughter and granddaughter covens. In 1976, the governing body of the order, called the Red Cord Council, was dissolved and the NROOGD became known as a tradition. Those groups tracing their lines of initiation back to a member of the original group and that share certain forms of liturgy consider themselves part of the NROOGD tradition. Covens are autonomous and recognize one another's initiates. The identities of initiates are held in strictest confidence.

Coven esbats are usually held skyclad; they work on ethical magic and the celebration of the divinity of each participant. The covens recognize and greet the force of a Goddess and God.

Initially, the ritual performance required three priestesses and one priest, but now this form is usually reserved for large public rituals; the smaller coven meetings require only one of each. Although magical workings vary in form and content, they often include charms and simple poetry. Mythic enactments corresponding to a needed transformation may also be performed.

During the late 1980s and 1990s, younger members expanded inherited liturgy by writing new poetry and songs for new rituals. The NROOGD encourages creative expression, and these new writings serve to keep the tradition alive.

The core NROOGD ritual, written by Aidan Kelly and others, begins with a line dance in the form of an inward and then outward spiral, representing death and rebirth, with coveners singing a chant—"Tout, tout, tout, throughout and about!" Afterward, conjurations of elements, which go into a central "Charging Bowl," begin with "I conjure salt for savor. . . ." Gods, demigods, or other spirits at each of the cardinal directions serve as Guardians of the Circle and of the Elements. Each coven has their own guardians that are unique from other covens. Names of the Gods are idiosyncratic to each group and the names are kept secret.

The sharing of food and drink (called a Love Feast) concludes the ritual, as members prepare themselves to reenter their daily lives.

Three initiations distinguish the practice of NROOGD. The first initiation, called the White Cord, marks the entrance either into the NROOGD community, or into a particular coven's instruction. The second initiation, called the Red Cord, is a full initiation into the Mysteries of Witchcraft. Red Cord initiates are elders of the tradition, and are empowered to lead their own covens and train and initiate. The third initiation is not bestowed by human hand but rather by the Gods themselves, and is called a Black Cord, or Taking the Garter. This last is the most intensely personal of the three.

The order holds large public ritual celebrations at each of the eight Sabbats for the benefit of the greater Pagan community. The most unique of these celebrations is the re-enactment of the Eleusinian Mysteries in the fall. Area covens also meet periodically to decide responsibilities for the coming year.

NROOGD member covens are primarily in the San Francisco Bay Area, yet elders are found all over California, the Pacific Northwest, Michigan, and on the East Coast. There is no central authority nor spokesperson for the tradition.

The order publishes a quarterly magazine called *The Witches Trine,* consisting of news, articles, poetry and reviews relating to the NROOGD tradition and Witchcraft in general.

Sources:

About the NROOGD. http://www.conjure.com/TRINE/nroogd.html. May 1, 2000.

The News (Journal) See **Fortean Times**

New Sense (Bulletin)

A newsletter, formerly known as the *Brain/Mind Bulletin,* published on first and third Mondays of the month, dealing with frontiers of research, theory, and practice in such fields as **parapsychology,** physics of consciousness, perception, **dreams, biofeedback, acupuncture, hypnosis,** psychiatry, creativity, memory, and humanistic medicine. Included news of conferences and workshops, significant trends, books, and journals. Edited by **Marilyn Ferguson,** author of *The Brain Revolution: The Frontiers of Mind Research* (1973) and *The Aquarian Conspiracy* (1980). Last known address: Interface Press, P.O. Box 42211, Los Angeles, CA 90042.

Newsletter of the Parapsychology Foundation

Former publication of the **Parapsychology Foundation,** which appeared as a bimonthly giving news in the field of parapsychology and psychical research with world coverage, from vol. 1 (1956) through vol. 16 (1969), when it was merged into the **Parapsychology Review.** For back issues of the newsletter, contact the Parapsychology Foundation, 288 E. 71st St., New York, NY 10021.

Newspaper Tests

Ingenious experiments devised by séance-room communicators to exclude **telepathy** as an explanation of hypothesized spirit communication. Rev. **C. Drayton Thomas** in *Some Recent Evidence for Survival* (1922) published many remarkable instances as recorded in sittings with the medium **Gladys Osborne Leonard.**

The method of the communicators was to give in the afternoon names and dates that were to be published the next day in certain columns of *The Times,* or, if so requested, in coming issues of magazines. The information so obtained was immediately posted to the **Society for Psychical Research** (SPR), London. The results when verified were so much more striking since neither the editor nor the compositor in the offices of *The Times* could tell at the hour when the communication was made what text would occupy the column mentioned in the next edition.

The following tests were given on February 13, 1920:

"The first page of the paper, in column two and near the top the name of a minister with whom your father was friendly at Leek. (Perks was found, a name which verified from an old diary.)

"Lower in this column, say one quarter down, appears his name, your own, your mother's and that of an aunt; all four within the space of two inches. (John and Charles were correctly found, then came the name Emile Souret which presumably suggested Emily and Sarah, his aunt and mother.)

"Near these the word 'Grange.' (It was not found.)

"In column one, not quite half-way down, is a name which is your mother's maiden name or one very like it. (The maiden name was 'Dore,' the name found 'Dorothea.')

"Somewhat above that is named a place where your mother passed some years of her girlhood. (Hants. Correct. Shirley, where she spent her girlhood, being in Hampshire, for which 'Hants.' is the recognized abbreviation.)

"Close to the foregoing is a name, which suggests an action one might make with the body in jumping. (Cummock, a bad pun: come knock.)

"Towards the bottom of the column is named a place where you went to school. (Lincolnshire. Correct.)

"There is a word close by which looks to your father like Cheadle. (Not found.)

"Higher in column one, say two-thirds down, is a name suggesting ammunition. (Found the ecclesiastical title Canon.) Between that and the teacher's name is a place-name, French, looking like three words hyphened into one. (Braine-le-Chateau.)

"About the middle of this page, the middle both down and across, is a mistake in print; it cannot be right. Some wrong letters inserted or something left out, some kind of mistake just there. (The word 'page' printed imperfectly: 'Paae.')"

Out of the items in this test, two entirely failed, the others forecast at 3 P.M. the day previous to the publication of the paper were correct. At 6 P.M. a copy of this test was posted to the SPR. Inquiries at *The Times* revealed the fact that in some cases the particular notices referred to might have already been set up in type at the time of the sitting, in other cases they were probably not set up and in any case their ultimate position on the page could not be normally known until late in the afternoon.

By the spirit of his father the following explanation was furnished to Thomas:

"These tests have been devised by others in a more advanced sphere than mine, and I have caught their ideas. I am not yet aware exactly how one obtains these tests, and have wondered whether the higher guides exert some influence whereby a suitable advertisement comes into position on the convenient date. I am able to sense what appears to me to be sheets and slips of paper with names and various information upon them. I notice suitable items and, afterwards, visualise a duplicate of the page with these items falling into their places. At first I was unable to do this. It seems to me that it is an ability which throws some light upon foretelling, a visualising of what is to be, but based upon that which already is. Sometimes I see further detail upon visualising which I had not sensed from the letters. I think there is an etheric foreshadowing of things about to be done. It would probably be impossible to get anything very far ahead, but only within a certain number of hours, and I cannot say how many. I scarcely think it would be possible to get a test for the day after the morrow, or, even if possible, that it could result in more than a jumble of the morrow's with a few of the day following. I think they should impress people more than book tests. It becomes clear that telepathy cannot explain; you find in the paper that for which you seek, but given in a form which you did not expect and about which you could, in the nature of the case, have known nothing. Two sets of memory are combined to produce them, my memories of long ago, and my memory of what I found this morning about preparations for the Press." (See also **Book Tests; Chair Test; Prediction; Prevision**)

Sources:

Thomas, C. Drayton. *Some Recent Evidence for Human Survival.* London: William Collins, 1922.

New Thought

A late-nineteenth-century religious movement that wedded the spiritual idealism of philosopher Ralph Waldo Emerson with the pursuit of healing alternatives through various mental and psychological processes. The origin of New Thought is generally traced to **Phineas Parkhurst Quimby** (1802–1866), a mesmerist from the state of Maine. Quimby had become fascinated with the phenomena associated with **mesmerism** (or **hypnotism**) but began to notice that its healing potential really came from the transfer of healing thoughts. He concluded that mind was the major factor in healing. The mind of the patient had come to accept thoughts that caused disease, and healing was accomplished when the mind came to believe the truth. For Quimby, the mind's operation upon the body brought health.

Quimby lived in Portland, Maine, far from the centers of culture. He wrote down his ideas but never published them, and only a few students found their way to his door. When he died as a relatively unknown and unheralded healer in 1866 there was nothing like a movement built around either him or his ideas. One of his students, Warren Felt Evans, a Swedenborgian minister, settled in Salisbury, Massachusetts, and in 1869 wrote the first of a series of books on mental healing, acknowledging in passing his debt to Quimby. However, his developing ideas left Quimby behind for a form of pantheism.

The most notable of Quimby's students was **Mary Baker Eddy.** She found significant relief from her chronic medical problems under Quimby's tutelage, but had questioned the fact that her symptoms returned when she left Maine and tried to resume her normal life. She also was offended by Quimby's disparagement of ministers, churches, and religion in general. She went to the Bible as a means of answering her questions.

Eddy reached a crisis in 1866 a few weeks after Quimby's death. She slipped on some ice and injured herself to the extent that she was bedridden. Some thought she was going to die. However, during her recovery, all of her study came together in a new revelation that God was all, the sum of reality. Since God is all, and in his presence there can be no illness, she concluded that illness must be an error in the individual's mind. The realization of this new insight led to her immediate healing. She would embody this new idealistic understanding of the universe in a booklet, *The Science of Man* (1870), and then more completely in her textbook, *Science and Health* (1875). She taught informally for several years but in 1876 encouraged the formation of the Christian Science Association, an organization of her students and the root of the Church of Christ, Scientist, which she would found three years later.

The Christian Science movement placed a new healing emphasis before the American public. Eddy regularly offered classes at which she trained people to become practitioners. Her students in turn moved out to establish offices and offer their services to their suffering neighbors. Led by the distribution of *Science and Health* (soon expanded with a biblical key to become *Science and Health with Key to the Scriptures*), the Christian Science movement spread across North America and into Europe during the 1880s.

The Emergence of New Thought

Eddy built this large movement, with which Quimby was never involved. It was built around her own particular healing vision, the core of which had been revealed to her in 1866 and which she developed throughout the rest of her life. She had little patience with students who wished to take her ideas and make personal elaborations upon them. Students who deviated from Eddy's own presentation of Christian Science were soon separated from the organization. By the mid 1880s there were a number of independent Christian Science practitioners, including some who moved away due to Eddy's insistence upon the centrality of Christian faith and symbols. Collectively they became known as the **mind cure** movement.

In 1885, one of Eddy's most talented students, to whom she had entrusted the *Christian Science Journal,* broke with Eddy and moved from Boston to Chicago to establish an independent private practice. After a year as merely a practitioner, **Emma Curtis Hopkins** was talked into opening a school at which she could teach Christian Science and train practitioners. The school opened in 1886 as the Hopkins Metaphysical Association. By the end of 1887, affiliated associations managed by her students could be found from Maine to California. Hopkins' efforts pulled together the independents into a coherent competing movement that grew and diversified over the next decade. Among Hopkins's students were a number of capable leaders who, with her encouragement, founded their own independent movements. Over the years she taught Melinda Cramer (founder of Divine Science), Myrtle and **Charles Fillmore** (cofounders of Unity), Annie Rix Militz (founder of the Homes of Truth), and **Ernest Holmes** (founder of Religious Science).

Hopkins thus mobilized the followers and trained the leaders of what would in the 1890s become known as the New Thought movement and is rightly remembered as the movement's founder. Hopkins would largely resign from any leadership role in 1895 after launching the movement, which consisted of several large associations of churches and centers (Unity, Divine Science, Homes of Truth, and later the Church of Truth and Religious Science) and many independent churches and centers. Various attempts to organize the movement were made through the early years of the twentieth century, culminating in the formation of the International New Thought Alliance in 1915. Several years later the alliance adopted a "Declaration of Principles" which guided it for forty years until the present "Declaration," which was adopted in 1957, appeared.

The 1957 Declaration affirmed the oneness of God and humanity, a major implication being that humans can reproduce divine perfection in the body. God is defined as universal wisdom, love, life, truth, power, peace, joy, and beauty, and the universe is seen as the body of God. Mental states manifest in human life to good or ill. God manifests as the divine virtues in humans. Humans are basically an invisible spiritual dweller in the body.

Today the International New Thought Alliance is headquartered at 5003 E. Broadway Rd., Mesa, AZ 85206.

Sources:

Beebe, Tom. *Who's Who in New Thought.* Lakemount, Ga.: CSA Press, 1977.

Braden, Charles S. *Spirits in Rebellion.* Dallas, Tex.: Southern Methodist University Press, 1963.

Dresser, Horatio W. *History of the New Thought Movement.* New York: Thomas Y. Crowell, 1919.

———. *The Spirit of New Thought.* New York: Thomas Y. Crowell, 1917.

Fuller, Robert C. *Mesmerism and the American Cure of Souls.* Philadelphia: University of Pennsylvania Press, 1982.

Judah, J. Stillson. *The History and Philosophy of the Metaphysical Movements in America.* Philadelphia: Westminster Press, 1967.

Melton, J. Gordon. *New Thought: A Reader.* Santa Barbara, Calif.: Institute for the Study of American Religion, 1990.

Meyer, Donald. *The Positive Thinkers.* New York: Doubleday, 1965.

Parker, Gail. *Mind Cure in New England.* Hanover, N.H.: University Press of New England, 1973.

Podmore, Frank. *Mesmerism and Christian Science.* London: Metheun, 1909.

Quimby, Phineas P. *The Complete Writings.* Edited by Ervin Seale. 3 vols. Marina del Rey, Calif.: DeVorss, 1987.

———. *The Quimby Manuscripts.* Edited by Horatio Dresser. New York: Thomas Y. Crowell, 1919. Reprint, New York: Julian Press, 1961.

Trine, Ralph Waldo. *In Tune With the Infinite.* New York: Thomas Y. Crowell, 1897.

Troward, Thomas. *The Edinburgh Lectures on Mental Science.* London, 1904.

———. *The Hidden Power and Other Papers on Mental Science.* New York: Dodd, Mead, 1917.

New Thought (Organ)

Quarterly organ of the International New Thought Alliance (INTA), the major ecumenical organization bringing together the congregations of the large **New Thought** groups (Divine Science, Religious Science, and the Unity School of Christianity) with the many small and independent congregations that follow New Thought metaphysics. It includes a directory of the affiliated congregations. Founded in 1914, it was published in Los Angeles for many years; however, its editorial offices were moved in the 1980s to the new permanent headquarters of INTA, 5003 E. Broadway Rd., Mesa, AZ 85206.

The New Times

The New Times is a post-**New Age** networking monthly that serves the Northwest United States, primarily Washington and Oregon. It has adopted a tabloid newspaper format and is distributed free through a variety of metaphysical and health food establishments in the Seattle metropolitan area and beyond.

Each issue of *The New Times* includes a host of original feature articles, most written by local authors, that cover the wide range of typical concerns that had been brought together by the New Age Movement of the 1980s with spirituality philosophies and practices heading the list. **Holistic** health is a close second. There is additional concern for such topics as ecology and psychic phenomena. Monthly columns cover **astrology,** reviews of books, music and transformational tools, and herbalism.

The heart of each issue is the "Resource Directory," the pages of advertisements that effectively delineate the range of metaphysical and health services and activities available for seekers throughout the Northwest. As is common in similar publications, the ads are classified into six major divisions: classes, workshops, and trainings; health services; intuitive arts and sciences; professional services; spiritual organizations and practices; and tools for your journey.

The New Times began publication in the mid-1970s, and continues under the leadership of publisher Deverick Martin and editor David Young. Its publishing headquarters may be contacted at P.O. Box 51186, Seattle, WA 98115-1186 and through its website at http://www.newtimes.org/.

Sources:

The New Times. Seattle, Wash., n.d.

The New Times. http://www.newtimes.org/. April 27, 2000.

New Times Network (Directory)

One of several **New Age** directories compiled in the early 1980s. It included sections on health and healing, growth and human potential, holistic education, spiritual traditions, New Age communities, networks, associations, and information centers. Unfortunately, like so many of the New Age directories that appeared in the 1980s, new editions were never issued and the volume quickly became outdated.

Sources:

Adams, Rovert. *New Times Network: Groups Centers for Personal Growth.* London: Routledge & Kegan Paul, 1982.

New Ways of Consciousness Foundation See Intuition Network

New Wiccan Church

The New Wiccan Church, originally the New Celtic Church, was founded in the early 1970s to practice **Witchcraft** in the British tradition. Membership is restricted to adult witches who have been initiated in the Gardnerian tradition or one of the several variations of the Gardnerian practice, the most well known being the Alexanderian. **Gerald B. Gardner,** generally considered the father of modern Wicca, established a new form of Witchcraft in England in the 1950s. He instituted three degrees of accomplishment, the third being admittance into the priesthood.

In the statement of belief, called the "Dedication," the New Wiccans identify themselves with a form of traditional monotheism by affirming belief in Dyghtyn, the name they give to the ultimate godhead. They follow modern Wicca, however, by noting that the godhead, who is all knowing and all pervasive, differentiates itself into male and female as the "Lady of the moon" and the "Lord of Death and Resurrection." The Lord and Lady further differentiate themselves into a myriad of lesser deities that have been recognized throughout human history in the various world mythologies. Members are free to acknowledge these lesser deities in their rites as they see fit, save only that such practice does not lead to harm to people or animals. In addition to the "Dedication," the church circulates the statement issued in 1974 by the now-defunct Council of American Witches whose "Principles of Wiccan Belief" has become a popular statement defining the community.

The actual rites used in the church are secret, but the published Gardnerian rituals provide a close approximation of typical practice. There is a degree of variation from coven (small worshipping group) to coven. Traditionally, Gardnerians worship in the nude, but many New Wiccan coven dress for rituals.

There are annual dues for members and each coven may ask for an additional fee to cover the small costs involved in running the coven. However, no fees may be charged for initiating anyone into the craft or for the performance of an act of magic. Church members are very active in the larger Wiccan community, especially with the covens of the **Covenant of the Goddess.** Most New Wiccan covens are found in the Western United States. Headquarters are at Box 162046, Sacramento, CA 95816. Information about the group can be found in its periodical, *Red Garters,* and on its website, http://www.angelfire.com/ca/redgarters.

Sources:

Adler, Margot. *Drawing Down the Moon.* Boston: Beacon Press, 1997.

Newton, J. R. (1810–1883)

American healing medium. He began his healing career in 1855 and is said to have cured thousands of sufferers from a variety of ailments. He claimed to be aided by Christ and other spirits. He usually healed in large halls or other areas with space to move about in and used to handle patients, often giving a sufferer a push and telling him he was cured, which he usually was.

Newton gave most of his healing free. Many of his cures were reliably recorded both in the United States and in England, which he visited the first time in 1870. The publication *The Spiritualist* (June 15, 1870) listed 105 cases of persons cured or benefitted by Newton on that visit, while the *Spiritual Magazine* (July 1870) cited full particulars of many cures.

New York Circle

The first experimental Spiritualist organization in the United States. It was an exclusive body in the initial stages, later broadening its membership. The principal medium was **Edward P. Fowler,** who had sat with **Kate and Margaretta Fox.** Fowler provided the location. Early members included the judge **John W. Edmonds.** At one sitting of the circle, the medium Henry Gordon demonstrated the feat of floating in the air, i.e., **levitation,** in the presence of many unimpeachable witnesses.

At the initiative of the circle, the New York Conference was established in November 1851, providing a focal point for the growing interest in **Spiritualism.**

NEW ZEALAND

The Maori

Among the Maori, the indigenous inhabitants of New Zealand, (known by the Maori as "Aotearoa") the spirits of the dead played a prominent role, with the priests (or *tohungas*) functioning in a manner quite similar to Spiritualist mediums. Some were born with their gift. Others were devoted to the priestly office by their parents and acquired their power after the fashion of Eastern ecstatics, by prayer, fasting, and contemplation.

Prophets emerged among the Maoris during the early colonization phase of the islands. As Great Britain established hegemony in the land, her officials frequently wrote home that the Maori would never be conquered wholly. Information of the parties sent out to attack them, the color of the boats and the hour when they would arrive, the number of the enemy, and all particulars essential to Maori safety were invariably communicated to the tribes beforehand by their tohungas.

The best prophets and seers among the Maori were female. Christian missionaries tried to account for the extraordinary powers they exhibited. For example, these women listened for the sound of the spirit voice, a common designation that occurred in their communion with the dead. Skeptical observers suggested that the women who practiced such "arts of **sorcery,**" were really ventriloquists; yet this attempted explanation rarely accounted for the intelligence received.

In his book *Old New Zealand* (1863), F. E. Maning cites an interesting case of tohungaism. A certain young chief had been appointed registrar of births and deaths, when he suddenly came to a violent end. The book of registries was lost, and much inconvenience ensued. The man's relatives notified their intention of invoking his spirit and invited General Cummings to be present at the ceremony, an invitation he accepted. Cummings's story continues as follows:

"The appointed time came. Fires were lit. The Tohunga repaired to the darkest corner of the room. All was silent, save the sobbing of the sisters of the deceased warrior-chief. There were 30 of us, sitting on the rush-strewn floor, the door shut and the fire now burning down to embers. Suddenly there came a voice out from the partial darkness, 'Salutation, salutation to my family, to my tribe, to you, pakeha, my friend!' Our feelings were taken by storm. The oldest sister screamed, and rushed with extended arms in the direction from whence the voice came. Her brother, seizing, restrained her by main force. Others exclaimed, 'Is it you? Is it you? Truly it is you! aue! aue!' and fell quite insensible upon the floor. The older women and some of the aged men were not moved in the slightest degree, though believing it to be the spirit of the chief.

"Whilst reflecting upon the novelty of the scene, the 'darkness visible' and the deep interest manifest, the spirit spoke again, 'Speak to me my family; speak to me, my tribe: speak to me, the pakeha!' At last the silence gave way, and the brother spoke: 'How is it with you? Is it well with you in that country?' The answer came, though not in the voice of the Tohunga-medium, but in strange sepulchral sounds: 'It is well with me; my place is a good place. I have seen our friends; they are all with me!' A woman from another part of the room now anxiously cried out, 'Have you seen my sister?' 'Yes, I have seen her; she is happy in our beautiful country.' 'Tell her my love so great for her will never cease.' 'Yes, I will bear the message.' Here the native woman burst into tears, and my own bosom swelled in sympathy.

"The spirit speaking again, giving directions about property and keepsakes, I thought I would more thoroughly test the genuineness of all this: and I said, 'We cannot find your book with the registered names; where have you concealed it?' The answer came instantly, 'I concealed it between the tahuhu of my house, and the thatch; straight over you, as you go in at the door.' The brother rushed out to see. All was silence. In five minutes he came hurriedly back, with the book in his hand! It astonished me.

"It was now late, and the spirit suddenly said, 'Farewell my family, farewell, my tribe; I go.' Those present breathed an impressive farewell, when the spirit cried out again, from high in the air, 'Farewell!'

"This, though seemingly tragical, is in every respect literally true. But what is that? ventriloquism, the devil, or what!"

Emma Hardinge Britten, in her book *Nineteenth Century Miracles* (1883), notes:

"The author has herself had several proofs of the Mediumistic power possessed by these 'savages' but as her experiences may be deemed of too personal a character, we shall select our examples from other sources. One of these is furnished by a Mr. Marsden, a person who was well-known in the early days of New Zealand's colonial history, as a miner, who grew rich 'through spiritual communications.' Mr. Marsden was a gentleman who had spent much time amongst the Maoris, and who still keeps a residence in 'the King country,' that is—the district of which they hold control.

"Mr. Marsden informed the author, that his success as a gold miner, was entirely due to a communication he had received through a native woman who claimed to have the power of bringing *down* spirits—the Maoris, be it remembered, always insisting that the spirits *descend* through the air to earth to visit mortals.

"Mr. Marsden had long been prospecting unsuccessfully in the gold regions. He had a friend in partnership with him, to whom he was much attached, but who had been accidentally killed by a fall from a cliff.

"The Spirit of this man came unsolicited, on an occasion when Mr. Marsden was consulting a native seeress, for the purpose of endeavouring to trace out what had become of a valuable watch which he had lost.

"The voice of the Spirit was the first heard in the air, apparently above the roof of the hut in which they sat, calling Mr. Marsden by his familiar name of 'Mars.' Greatly startled by these sounds, several times repeated, at the Medium's command, he remained perfectly still until the voice of his friend speaking in his well-remembered Scotch accent sounded close to his ear, whilst a column of grey misty substance reared itself by his side. This apparition was plainly visible in the subdued light of the hut, to which there was only one open entrance, but no window. Though he was much startled by what he saw and heard, Mr. Marsden had presence of mind enough to gently *put his hand through the misty column* which remained intact, as if its substance offered no resistance to the touch. Being admonished by an earnest whisper from the Maori woman, who had fallen on her knees before the apparition, to keep still, he obeyed, when a voice—seemingly from an immense distance off—yet speaking unmistakably in his friend's Scotch accents, advised him to let the watch alone—for it was irreparably gone—but to go to the stream on the banks of which they had last had a meal together; trace it up for six miles and a half, and then, by following its course amidst the forest, he would come to a *pile* which would make him rich, if he chose to remain so.

"Whilst he was waiting and listening breathlessly to hear more, Mr. Marsden was startled by a slight detonation at his side. Turning his head he observed that the column of mist was gone, and in its place, a quick flash, like the reflection of a candle, was all that he beheld. Here the séance ended, and the astonished miner left the hut, convinced that he had heard the Spirit of his friend talking with him. He added, that he followed the directions given implicitly, and came to a mass of surface gold lying on the stones at the bottom of the brook in the depth of the forest. This he gathered up, and though he prospected for several days in and about that spot, he never found another particle of this precious metal. That which he had secured he added, with a deep sigh, was indeed enough to have made him independent for life, had it not soon been squandered in fruitless speculations.

"Many degrees of superstition exist among the Maoris," states a writer in the *Pall Mall Gazette.* "In the recesses of the Urewera country for example, diablerie has lost little of its early potency; the *tohunga* there remains a power in the land. Among the more enlightened natives a precautionary policy is generally followed; it is always wiser and safer, they say, to avoid conflict with the two mysterious powers *tapu* and *makuta.* Tapu is the less dangerous of the two; a house, an individual, or an article may be rendered tapu, or sacred, and if the tapu be disregarded harm will befall someone. But makuta is a powerful evil spell cast for the deliberate purpose of accomplishing harm, generally to bring about death. The *tohunga* is understood to be in alliance with the spirits of the dead. The Maori dreads death, and he fears the dead. Places of burial are seldom approached during the day, never at night. The spirits of the dead are believed to linger sometimes near places of burial. Without going to experts in Maori lore, who have many and varied theories to set forth, a preferable course is to discover what the average Maori of to-day thinks and believes respecting the strange powers and influences he deems are at work in the world around him.

"A Maori of this type—who can read and write, is under 40 years of age, and fairly intelligent—was drawn into a lengthy conversation with the writer. He believed, magistrates notwithstanding, that *tohungas,* somehow, had far more power than ordinary men. He did not think they got that power from the 'tiapo' (the devil?); they just were able to make themselves masters of men and many things in the world. There are many degrees of Tohungaism. An ordinary man or woman was powerless against a *tohunga,* but one *tohunga* could overcome another. The speaker knew of an instance of one *tohunga* driving the tohunga power entirely out of a weaker rival. It was a fairly recent east coast occurrence. Three Maoris had accidentally permitted their pigs to trespass into the *tohunga's* potato paddock, and much damage and loss was the result. The *tohunga* was one of the dangerous type, and being very wroth, he *makutued* the three men, all of whom promptly died. Nobody was brave enough to charge the *tohunga* with causing the death of the men; they were all afraid of this terrible *makuta.* At length another *tohunga* was heard of, one of very great power. This oracle was consulted, and he agreed to deal effectively with *tohunga* number one, and punish him for killing the owner of the pigs. So, following his instructions, the first-mentioned individual was seized, and much against his will, was conveyed to the home of the greater magician. Many Maoris, it should be known, stand in awe of hot water, they will not handle it, even for purposes connected with cooking or cleaning. Into a large tub of hot water the minor *tohunga* struggling frantically, was placed, then he was given a page torn from a Bible, which he was ordered to chew and swallow. The hot water treatment, combined with the small portion of the white man's sacred volume, did the expected work; the man was no longer a *tohunga,* and fretting over his lost powers, he soon afterwards died."

Spiritualism in New Zealand

Among the earliest adherents to **Spiritualism** in New Zealand was John Logan of Dunedin. Before he had become publicly identified with the cause of Spiritualism, an association had been formed, the members of which steadily pursued their investigations in private circles and semi-private gatherings. Logan became well known when he became the subject of a church trial. Although holding a high position in the first Presbyterian church of the city, he had been attracted to Spiritualist circles and witnessed Spiritualistic phenomena. Rumors spread around the small community that one of his own near relatives was a very remarkable medium. On March 19, 1873, Logan was summoned to appear before a church convocation, to be held for the purpose of trying his case, and if necessary, dealing with his "delinquency." That was when he was deprived of his church membership.

In many of the principal towns besides Dunedin, circles, held at first in mere idle curiosity, produced their usual fruit of mediumistic power. This again was extended into associative action, and organization into local societies. For over a year, the Spiritualists and Liberalists of Dunedin secured the services of Charles Bright as their lecturer. Bright had once been a member of the editorial staff of the Australian *Melbourne Argus,* and he had obtained a good reputation as a capable writer and liberal thinker. Bright's lectures in Dunedin were highly appreciated. By their scholarly style and attractive manner they served to band together those citizens who were not attracted to orthodox Christianity, both the liberal dissenting element and those attracted to Spiritualism.

In Auckland, the principal town of the North Island, the same good service was rendered to the cause of religious thought by the addresses of a Rev. Edgar, a clergyman whose absorption of Spiritualist doctrines had tended to sever him from more traditional churches and drew around him the Spiritualists of the town.

Besides the work effected by these men, the occasional visits of well-known personalities like Rev. J. M. Peebles and J. Tyerman and the effect of the many private circles held in every portion of the islands tended to promote a general, although quiet, diffusion of Spiritualist belief and practice throughout New Zealand. In 1879, a lecture tour by Emma Hardinge Britten gave added impetus to public interest and discussion concerning Spiritualism.

By 1930, the Spiritualist Church of New Zealand, headquartered in Wellington, had branches throughout New Zealand. One of the most prominent mediums was **Pearl Judd,** who demonstrated **direct voice** phenomena in full light.

Psychical Research

Interest in New Zealand in psychical research flared briefly on the heels of the development of psychical research in Australia in the 1870s; but as in the neighboring land, soon died away. Only after World War II did interest revive. In the 1990s, there was an Auckland Psychical Research Society and a branch of the **Churches' Fellowship for Psychical and Spiritual Studies,** as well as the Federation of Spiritual Healers. There is also a New Zealand UFO Studies in New Plymouth.

Sources:

Britten, Emma Hardinge. *Nineteenth Century Miracles.* New York: William Britten, 1884.

Maning, F. E. *Old New Zealand.* London: R. Bentley, 1884. Reprint, Auckland: Whitcombe & Tombs, 1922.

Nexus

Nexus is among the more distinctive newsstand magazines reporting on paranormal realities. This Australian-based publication takes a decidedly countercultural and antigovernment perspective and is especially attuned to what it sees as possible conspiracies operating against the public's welfare. It was born out of the **New Age** belief in humanity's current transition in consciousness, but believes that sinister forces are at work to block human progress. Thus *Nexus* has assigned itself the task of reporting on what it believes to be the news behind the news, hard-to-gather facts and suppressed information that are needed by people making the consciousness transformation.

Each issue of *Nexus* begins with approximately ten feature stories that cover such topics as natural health cures, UFO **abductions,** natural disasters and Earth changes, government wrong-doing, and possible future scientific catastrophes. Particular attention has been paid to alternative cancer therapies and government efforts to suppress their use. This overall perspective is carried over to the many short news items reprinted from around the world. *Nexus* is especially helpful for its extensive book review column that highlights many books on alternative science, UFOs, psychic phenomena, ancient mysteries, and conspiracy theories not generally reviewed in the mainstream UFO and New Age periodicals.

Nexus sponsors an annual conference (in Australia) that includes speakers on **psychical research, holistic** health, ancient mysteries, UFOs, and related topics.

Nexus was first issued as a quarterly in 1987. The present editors, Duncan M. Roads and Catherine Simons, purchased it in 1990. They adopted the present bimonthly schedule, removed articles on subjects like the environment of primary New Age interest, and gave it its present distinctive editorial perspective. Through the 1990s it gained an international audience. *Nexus* is published in **Australia,** but has developed an American and a British edition and a number of foreign-language editions (Polish, Italian, Swedish, Japanese, French, Korean, and Greek). Its editorial offices are located at P.O. Box 30, Mapleton, Queensland 4560, Australia. It has a webpage at http://www.nexusmagazine.com/.

Sources:

Nexus. Mapleton, Queensland, Australia. N.p.

Nexus. http://www.nexusmagazine.com/. June 10, 2000.

NFSH See National Federation of Spiritual Healers

Nganga

Members of the **Ndembo** secret society of the Lower Congo. *Nganga*—literally "the knowing ones"—was a term applied to those who had passed certain rites to distinguish them from the *vanga,* or uninitiated.

NICAP See National Investigations Committee on Aerial Phenomena

Nichusch

A Kabalistic term for prophetic indication, in accordance with the view that all events and natural happenings have a secret connection and interact upon one another. It was believed that practically everything could become an object of soothsaying—the flight of birds, movement of clouds, cries of animals, events happening to man, and so on. A person might become *nichusch* by saying that if such and such a thing took place it would be a good or a bad omen. (See also **divination; Kabala**)

"Nick" (or "Old Nick")

A well-known British nickname for the devil, comparable with the American "Mr. **Splitfoot**" or **"Old Scratch."** It seems probable that this name is derived from the Dutch *nikken,* the devil, which again comes from the Anglo-Saxon *noec-an,* to slay, deriving from the theological view that the devil was "a murderer from the beginning."

In northern countries there is a river spirit named "Neck," "Nikke," or "Nokke," of the same nature as the water **kelpie** and the **merman** or triton.

Nicol, Betty (Elizabeth) Humphrey (1917–1993)

Psychologist and parapsychologist. She was born Elizabeth Humphrey on June 7, 1917, in Indianapolis, Indiana. She studied at Earlham College, Richmond, Indiana (B.A. philosophy, 1940), and Duke University (Ph.D. psychology, 1946). While at Earlham she became interested in psychical research and pursued her doctoral degree at Duke in order to work with **J. B. Rhine.** In the early 1950s she collaborated with her future husband on attempts to discern the personality correlates of psychic ability. In 1955 she married parapsychologist **J. Fraser Nicol.** She undertook a detailed analysis of published precognition cases in order to ascertain optimal psychological and physical conditions for spontaneous precognition, a project sponsored by a grant from the **Parapsychology Foundation.** She also wrote a number of articles.

Nicol died in January 1993.

Sources:

Berger, Arthur S., and Joyce Berger. *The Encyclopedia of Parapsychology and Psychical Research.* New York: Paragon House, 1991.

Humphrey, Elizabeth. *Handbook of Tests in Parapsychology.* Durham, N.C.: Parapsychology Laboratory, 1948.

———. "Simultaneous High and Low Aim in PK Tests." *Journal of Parapsychology* 11 (1947).

Pleasants, Helene, ed. *Biographical Dictionary of Parapsychology*. New York: Helix Press, 1964.

Nicol, J(ohn) Fraser (d. 1989)

Parapsychologist born in Edinburgh, Scotland. He was educated at Heriot's School, Edinburgh, and Heriot-Watt College, Edinburgh University. Quite early in his life he became a research member of the **Society for Psychical Research,** London (1934–51); he also became a member of its council (1948–1957). Then in 1951 he moved to the United States to spend a year as a research associate at the **Parapsychology Laboratory,** Duke University, where he met his future wife (known after her marriage as **Betty Nicol**). They worked together for many years, funded in part by grants from the Rockefellar Foundation, the **American Society for Psychical Research,** and the **Parapsychology Foundation.**

Among Nicol's early research projects carried out with his future wife—they were married in 1955—was on the personality components of psyhically aware people. Besides his numerous articles, many written with his wife, Nicol is also remembered as a historian of psychical research, about which he authored several important articles.

Sources:

Berger, Arthur S., and Joyce Berger. *The Encyclopedia of Parapsychology and Psychical Research*. New York: Paragon House, 1991.

Gilbert, Mostyn. "J. Fraser Nicol: An Appreciation of His Dedication to Psychical Research." *Journal* of the Society for Psychical Research 56, no. 818 (January 1990).

Nicol, J. Fraser. "The Founders of the Society for Psychical Research." *Proceedings* of the Society for Psychical Research 55 (1972).

———. "The Fox Sisters and the Development of Spiritualism." *Journal* of the Society for Psychical Research 34 (1948).

———. "The Silences of Mr. Trevor Hall." *International Journal of Parapsychology* 1, no. 1 (1966).

Pleasants, Helene, ed. *Biographical Dictionary of Parapsychology*. New York: Helix Press, 1964.

Nicolai, Christoph Friedrich (1733–1811)

German critic, novelist, and bookseller of Berlin, who is of special interest from the occult point of view because of his peculiar experiences, described in a presentation read before the Royal Society of Berlin. The case is one of the most celebrated in the annals of psychology. Nicolai reported:

"In the first two months of the year 1791, I was much affected in my mind by several incidents of a very disagreeable nature; and on the 24th of February a circumstance occurred which irritated me extremely. At ten o'clock in the forenoon my wife and another person came to console me; I was in a violent perturbation of mind, owing to a series of incidents which had altogether wounded my moral feelings, and from which I saw no possibility of relief, when suddenly I observed at the distance of ten paces from me a figure—the figure of a deceased person. I pointed at it, and asked my wife whether she did not see it. She saw nothing, but being much alarmed, endeavoured to compose me, and sent for the physician. The figure remained some seven or eight minutes, and at length I became a little more calm, and as I was extremely exhausted, I soon afterwards fell into a troubled kind of slumber, which lasted for half an hour. The vision was ascribed to the great agitation of mind in which I had been, and it was supposed I should have nothing more to apprehend from that cause, but the violent affection had put my nerves into some unnatural state. From this arose further consequences, which require a more detailed description.

"In the afternoon, a little after four o'clock, the figure which I had seen in the morning again appeared. I was alone when this happened, a circumstance which, as may be easily conceived, could not be very agreeable. I went therefore to the apartment of my wife, to whom I related it. But thither also the figure pursued me. Sometimes it was present, sometimes it vanished, but it was always the same standing figure. A little after six o'clock several stalking figures also appeared, but they had no connection with the standing figure. I can assign no other cause for this apparition than that, though much more composed in my mind, I had not been able so soon entirely to forget the cause of such deep and distressing vexation, and had reflected on the consequences of it, in order, if possible, to avoid them; and that this happened three hours after dinner, at the time when digestion just begins.

"At length I became more composed with respect to the disagreeable incident which had given rise to the first apparition, but though I had used very excellent medicines and found myself in other respects perfectly well, yet the apparitions did not diminish, but on the contrary rather increased in number, and were transformed in the most extraordinary manner.

"The figure of the deceased person never appeared to me after the first dreadful day, but several other figures showed themselves afterwards very distinctly, sometimes such as I knew, mostly, however, of persons I did not know, and amongst those known to me, were the semblance of both living and deceased persons, but mostly the former, and I made the observation, that acquaintance with whom I daily conversed never appeared to me as phantasms; it was always such as were at a distance.

"It is also to be noted, that these figures appeared to me at all times, and under the most different circumstances, equally distinct and clear. Whether I was alone, or in company, by broad daylight equally as in the night-time, in my own as well as in my neighbour's house; yet when I was at another person's house, they were less frequent, and when I walked the public street they very seldom appeared. When I shut my eyes, sometimes the figures disappeared, sometimes they remained even after I had closed them. If they vanished in the former case, on opening my eyes again, nearly the same figures appeared which I had seen before.

"I sometimes conversed with my physician and my wife concerning the phantasms which at the time hovered around me; for in general the forms appeared oftener in motion than at rest. They did not always continue present—they frequently left me altogether, and again appeared for a short or longer space of time, singly or more at once; but, in general, several appeared together. For the most part I saw human figures of both sexes. They commonly passed to and fro as if they had no connection with each other, like people at a fair where all is bustle. Sometimes they appeared to have business with one another. Once or twice I saw amongst them persons on horseback, and dogs and birds; these figures all appeared to me in their natural size, as distinctly as if they had existed in real life, with the several tints on the uncovered parts of the body, and with all the different kinds and colours of clothes. But I think, however, that the colours were somewhat *paler* than they are in nature.

"None of the figures had any distinguishing characteristic, they were neither terrible, ludicrous, nor repulsive; most of them were ordinary in their appearance—some were even agreeable.

"On the whole, the longer I continued in this state, the more did the number of the phantasms increase, and the apparitions became more frequent. About four weeks afterwards I began to hear them speak. Sometimes the phantasms spoke with one another, but for the most part they addressed themselves to me, these speeches were in general short, and never contained anything disagreeable. Intelligent and respected friends often appeared to me, who endeavoured to console me in my grief, which still left deep traces on my mind. This speaking I heard most frequently when I was alone; though I sometimes heard it in company, intermixed with the conversation of real persons; frequently in single phrases only, but sometimes even in connected discourse.

"Though at this time I enjoyed rather a good state of health both in body and mind, and had become so very familiar with these phantasms, that at last they did not excite the least disagreeable emotion, but on the contrary afforded me frequent subjects for amusement and mirth, yet as the disorder sensibly increase, and the figures appeared to me for whole days together, and even during the night, if I happened to awake, I had recourse to several medicines."

Nicolai then recounted how the apparitions vanished upon blood being let.

"This was performed on the 20th of April, at eleven o'clock in the forenoon. I was alone with the surgeon, but during the operation the room swarmed with human forms of every description, which crowded fast one on another. This continued till half-past four o'clock, exactly the time when the digestion commences. I then observed that the figures began to move more slowly; soon afterwards the colours became gradually paler; every seven minutes they lost more and more of their intensity, without any alteration in the distinct figure of the apparitions. At about half-past six o'clock, all the figures were entirely white, and moved very little, yet the forms appeared perfectly distinct. By degrees they became visibly less plain, without decreasing in number, as had often formerly been the case. The figures did not move off, neither did they vanish, which also had usually happened on other occasions. In this instance they dissolved immediately into air; of some even whole pieces remained for a length of time, which also by degrees were lost to the eye. At about eight o'clock there did not remain a vestige of any of them, and I have never since experienced any appearance of the same kind. Twice or thrice since that time I have felt a propensity, if I may be allowed to express myself, or a sensation as if I saw something which in a moment again was gone. I was even surprised by this sensation whilst writing the present account, having, in order to render it more accurate, perused the papers of 1791, and recalled to my memory all the circumstances of that time. So little are we sometimes, even in the greatest composure of mind, masters of our imagination."

Nicolai was a greatly respected writer who became an organizer and leader of the Enlightenment in northern Germany, together with G. E. Lessing and Moses Mendelssohn. He died January 1, 1811.

Sources:

Nicolai, Christoph Friedrich. "An Account of the Apparition of Several Phantoms." *The German Museum* (1800).

Nicoll, (Henry) Maurice (Dunlap) (1884–1953)

Prominent British physician and psychologist who became a leading exponent of the teachings of **G. I. Gurdjieff** and his most prominent pupil, **P. D. Ouspensky.** Nicoll was born in 1884. He was educated at Aldenham School and Caius College, Cambridge University, going on to study medicine at St. Bartholomew's Hospital, London, and in Vienna, Berlin, Paris, and Zürich (B.A., M.B., B.C., Cambridge; M.R.C.S., London). He was medical officer to Empire Hospital for injuries to the nervous system, a lecturer in medical psychology at Birmingham University, England, and a member of the British Psycho Medical Society. He became a member of the editorial staff of *Journal of Neurology and Psychopathy.* During World War I he served in Gallipoli in 1915 and Mesopotamia in 1916.

After his study in Zürich, Nicoll emerged as an early Jungian psychotherapist. In 1923 he spent a year with Gurdjieff and later spent several years with Ouspensky. In his mature life he founded his own groups based upon his understanding of his teachers' ideas, and ultimately became known as one of the most perceptive of their interpreters. The problems of traveling and meeting with his groups during World War II spurred his putting his insights on paper, a practice he continued until his death on August 30, 1953.

Sources:

Driscoll, J. Walter. *Gurdjieff: An Annotated Bibliography.* New York: Garland Publishing, 1985.

Nicoll, Maurice. *Dream Psychology.* Oxford: Henry Frowde, 1917.

———. *Living Time and the Integration of Life.* London: Vincent Stuart, 1952.

———. *The Mark (On the Symbolism of Various Passages from the Bible).* London: Watkins, 1954.

———. *The New Man: An Interpretation of Some Parables and Miracles of Christ.* London: Start & Richard, 1950.

———. *Psychological Commentaries on the Teaching of G. I. Gurdjieff and P. D. Ouspensky.* 5 vols. London: Vincent Stuart, 1954, 1964, 1966.

Nictalopes

Name given to human beings who can see in the dark. They are extremely rare. For example, a Dr. Tentin of Paris reported in 1874 the case of Marie Verdun, a girl of 18:

"Although her eyes do not present any special morbid character she is forced to keep her eyelids closed during the day, and to cover her head with a thick veil. On the other hand, when the shutters of the room are hermetically fastened, she reads and writes perfectly in the deepest darkness." Auguste Müller, the Stuttgart somnambulist, saw perfectly well and recognized all persons and objects in the greatest darkness.

In view of the remarkable precision with which objects move in the darkness of the séance room, it was suggested that some mediums might be nictalopes. As, however, the same precision has been observed when the medium goes into trance, the theory as a normal explanation seems untenable. (See also **eyeless sight**)

NICUFO See National Investigations Committee on UFOs

Nielsen, Einer (d. 1965)

Danish materialization medium whose phenomena were first publicized by the report on experiments recorded by **Baron Schrenck-Notzing** in his book *Physikalische Phaenomene des Mediumismus* (1920). In 1922 in Christiania, Oslo, Nielsen was pronounced a **fraud** but seemed to have completely reinstated himself in 1924 in Reykjavik, in sittings for the Psychical Research Society of Iceland. The report of the novelist Einar H. Kvaran, endorsed by scientists and other people of high standing, recorded the materialization of forms, sometimes two appearing simultaneously near the medium while he himself was within view. **Levitation** and other telekinetic phenomena were also seen in abundance.

After his exposure in 1922, Nielsen refused to sit with researchers. However, that did not prevent further exposure. Several years later in Copenhagen, he was accused of fraud by Johs. Carstensen, the leader of his own circle, and a convinced Spiritualist. After his exposure in a pamphlet, the medium went to court but lost his case in April 1932. He continued to work but was never considered credible again by people outside of his small circle of influence. He died February 26, 1965.

Sources:

Berger, Arthur S., and Joyce Berger. *The Encyclopedia of Parapsychology and Psychical Research.* New York: Paragon House, 1991.

Nielsen, Einer. *Solid Proofs of Survival.* Translated by Helmi Krohn. London: Psychic Book Club, 1950.

Nielsen, Winnifred Moon (1917–)

Assistant professor of psychology who experimented in the field of parapsychology. She was born on August 16, 1917, in Key West, Florida, and later studied at the University of Florida (B.A., 1958; Ph.D., 1962). Even before completing her first college degree, she worked for two years as a research fellow at the **Parapsychology Laboratory,** Duke University (1954–56). She later joined the faculty in psychology at Mary Washington College, University of Virginia. She was a charter associate of the **Parapsychological Association.** She investigated relationships between psi and personality.

Sources:

Nielsen, Winnifred M. "An Exploratory Study in Precognition." *Journal of Parapsychology* (March 1956).

———. "Mental States Associated with Precognition." *Journal of Parapsychology* (June 1956).

Pleasants, Helene, ed. *Biographical Dictionary of Parapsychology.* New York: Helix Press, 1964.

Nielsson, Haraldur (d. 1928)

Professor of theology at the University of Iceland who became convinced by experiences with the medium **Indridi Indridason** that modern **Spiritualism** was identical with primitive Christianity. Three lectures in which he affirmed this faith were published in a small book: *Mes Expériences en Spiritualisme Experimentale.* Nielsson died in 1928.

Nif

An Egyptian symbol in the form of a ship's sail widely spread, symbolizing breath. (See also **Egypt**)

Niflheim

The region of everlasting cold, mist, and darkness in Teutonic mythology. It is situated north of Midgard (middle earth—the present human abode), across the river Gjol. It was into this region that the god Odin banished the goddess Hel to rule over the worlds of the dead. The lowest depths are named **Nastrond**—"Strand of the Dead."

Nightmare

Possibly deriving from the Old English *night* and *mara,* a specter, indicating a terrifying dream. It is said to be caused by a disorder of the digestive functions during sleep, inducing the temporary belief that some animal or demon is sitting on the chest. Among primitive people it was thought that the affliction proceeded from the attentions of an evil spirit.

Johann Georg Keysler, in his work *Antiquitates selectae Septentrionales et Celticae* (1720), collected interesting particulars concerning the nightmare. *Nactmar,* he stated, is from *Mair,* an old woman, because the specter which appears to press upon the breast and impede the action of the lungs is generally in that form. The English and Dutch words coincide with the German. The French *cochemar* is *Mulier incumbens* or *incubus.* The Swedes use *Mara* alone, according to the *Historia de omnibus Gothorum Sueonumque Regibus* of J. Magnus (1554), where he stated that Valender, the son of Suercher, succeeded to the throne of his father, who was suffocated by a demon in his sleep, of that kind which by the scribes is called *Mara.*

Others "we suppose Germans," continued Keysler, "call it *Hanon Tramp.*" The French peasantry called it *Dianus* which is a corruption either of Diana or of *Daezmonium Meridianum* for it seems there is a belief which Keysler thought might not improbably be derived from a false interpretation of an expression in the 91st Psalm ("the destruction that wasteth at noonday") that persons are most exposed to such attacks at that time and therefore women in childbed are then never left alone.

But though the *Daezmonium Meridianum* is often used for the Ephialtes, nevertheless it is more correctly any sudden and violent attack which is deprives the patient of his senses.

In some parts of **Germany,** the name given to this disorder is *das Alpdructen,* either from the "mass" which appears to press on the sufferer or from *Alp* or *Alf* (elf). In Franconia it is *die Drud* or *das Druddructern,* from the Druid or Weird Women, and there is a belief that it may not only be chased away, but be made to appear on the morrow in a human shape, and lend something required of it by the following charm: "Druid tomorrow / So will I borrow."

These Druids, it seems were not only in the habit of riding men, but also horses, and in order to keep them out of the stables, the salutary *pentalpha* (which bears the name of *Drudenfuss* (Druids foot) should be written on the stable doors, in consecrated chalk on the night of St. Walburgh. It should also be mentioned that the English familiar appellation "Trot" as traced to "Druid," "a decrepit old woman such as the Sagas might be," and the same might perhaps be said of a Scottish Saint, Triduana or Tredwin.

In the *Glossarium Suiogothicum of Johann Ihre* (1769), a somewhat different account of the *Mara* is given. Here again, we find the "witch-riding" of horses, against which a stone **amulet** was suggested by the antiquarian John Aubrey, similar to one described below.

Among the incantations by which the nightmare may be chased away, Reginald Scot recorded the following in his *Discovery of Witchcraft* (1584):

St. George, St. George, or lady's knight,
He walked by day so did he by night:
Until such times as he her found,
He her beat and he her bound,
Until her troth to him plight,
He would not come to her that night.

"Item," continued this author, "hand a stone over the afflicted person's bed, which stone hath naturally such a hole in it, as wherein a string may be put through it, and so be hanged over the diseased or bewitched party, be it man, woman, or horse."

Readers of these lines may be reminded of the similar charm which Shakespeare put into the mouth of Edgar as Mad Tom in *King Lear:*

Saint Withold footed thrice the wold:
He met the night-mare and her ninefold
Bid her alight,
And her troth plight
And aroint thee, witch, aroint thee.

Another charm of earlier date occurs in Chaucer's *Miller's Tale.* When the simple Carpenter discovers the crafty Nicholas in his feigned abstraction, he thinks he may perhaps be hagridden, and address him thus:

I crouch from the Elves and fro wikid wightes
And there with the night-spell he seide arightes,
On four halvis of the house about,
And on the dreshfold of the dore without,
'Jesus Christ, and seint Benedight,
Blesse this house from evrey wikid wight,
Fro the night's mare, the wite paternoster,
Where wennist thou Seint Peter's sister.

A later author has pointed to some other formularies, and has noticed the Asmodeus was the fiend of most evil repute on these occasions. In the *Otia Imperiala* of Gervase of Tilbury, some other protecting charms are said to exist.

To turn the medical history of the **incubus, Pliny** recommended two remedies for this complaint, one of which was the herbal remedy wild peony seed. Another, which it would not be easy to discover in any modern pharmacopoeia, was a decoction in wine and oil of the tongue, eyes, liver, and bowels of a dragon, wherewith, after it has been left to cool all night in the open air, the patient should be anointed every morning and evening.

Dr. Bond, a physician, who stated that he himself was much afflicted with the nightmare, published an *Essay on the Incubus* in 1753. At the time at which he wrote, medical attention appears to have been very little called to the disease, and some of the opinions hazarded were sufficiently wild and inconclusive. Thus, a certain Dr. Willis said it was owing to some incongruous matter which is mixed with the nervous fluid in the cerebellum (*de Anima Brutorum*), while Bellini thought it imaginary and to be attributed to the idea of some demon which existed in the mind the day before.

Both of these writers might have known better if they would have turned to Fuchsius (with whom Dr. Bond appeared to be equally acquainted), who in his work *de Curandi Ratione*, published as early as 1548, had an excellent chapter (I, 31) on the causes, symptoms, and cure of nightmare, in which he attributed it to repletion and indigestion, and recommends the customary discipline.

Much of Gothic literature has been ascribed to dreams and nightmares. Horace Walpole's famous story *The Castle of Otranto* (1764) derived from a dream in which Walpole saw upon the uppermost banister of a great staircase a vision of a gigantic hand in armor.

In 1816, Mary Shelley had a gruesome and vivid nightmare which was the basis for her story *Frankenstein.*

Nearly seventy years later, novelist Robert Louis Stevenson had a nightmare that inspired his famous story *The Strange Case of Dr. Jekyll and Mr. Hyde,* which he completed in only three days.

Bram Stoker's immortal creation of *Dracula* (1897) was claimed to be the result of a nightmare after a supper of dressed crab, although clearly many of the elements in the story had been germinating in the author's mind much earlier. Many horror stories have also been inspired nightmares. (See also **fiction; Succubus**)

Nirmala Devi Srivastava (1923–)

Modern Hindu teacher, and wife of a United Nations diplomat. She was born on March 21, 1923, in Chindawara, a small hill station near Nagpur, India. Although born into a Christian family, she has embraced the concept of the basic truth of all religions in a universal teaching, based on ancient Hindu concepts of **kundalini,** the latent power believed to reside in the human organism and to be an evolutionary force in nature. Kundalini operates as a psycho-physical force in human beings, as the dynamic of sexual activity and also, when properly aroused, as the mechanism of higher consciousness and God-realization.

Kundalini **yoga** is concerned with the opening of *chakras* or psychic centers in the body, culminating in an energy flow to the highest center in the head. The arrival of kundalini energy in the top of the head is believed to result in an expansion of consciousness and mystical awareness.

On May 5, 1970, Nirmala Devi experienced the awakening of the *sahasrara* chakra (the highest center) through kundalini arousal and perceived a vision of her ability to communicate this arousal to other individuals (an ability generally termed *shaktipat*). She began teaching other people a technique called Sahaja Yoga (inborn technique) in order to transform their lives.

A center was established in New Delhi, India, and through the decade centers came into being in Great Britain, Australia, France, Switzerland, Hong Kong, Canada, and more recently in the United States. Known to her followers as "Mataji," Nirmala Devi travels to centers abroad, keeping contact in different countries. A bimonthly magazine, *Nirmala Yoga,* is published from the international headquarters at 43, Banglow Road, Delhi 110007, India. In the west the movement may be contacted at Nirmala Palace, 99 Nightingale Ln., Clapham South, Balham, London, SW12, United Kingdom or at 12416 Reva St., Cerritos, CA 90701.

Sources:

Barker, Eileen. *New Religious Movements: A Practical Introduction.* London: HMSO, 1989.

Coney, Judith. *Sahaja Yoga.* Richmond, Surrey, UK: Curzon Press, 2000.

Pullar, Philippa. *The Shortest Journey.* London: Hamish Hamilton, 1981.

Nixon, Queenie (ca. 1918–1989)

British transfiguration medium. Her psychic gifts manifested in childhood, when she grew up in the care of two aunts, both Spiritualist mediums. She spent 35 years as a medium, traveling widely in Europe, North America, and Australia. In addition to trance communications through her spirit guide "Paul," she manifested the rare phenomenon of **transfiguration,** when her features reportedly took on the appearance of deceased persons speaking through her.

These transfiguration demonstrations would sometimes last as long as three hours, with various personalities manifesting. In 1967, infrared photographs captured a record of such appearances, including what appeared to be clouds of **ectoplasm** around her face. Two newspapers accused her of **fraud,** but the reporters in each incident had neither interviewed her nor attended her séances. She died at the age of 71, following several heart attacks.

NLPR See National Laboratory of Psychical Research

Noah's Ark Society for Physical Mediumship

Noah's Ark Society for Physical Mediumship originated on April 25, 1990, in a Spiritualist home circle in Ilkeston, Derbyshire, England. The people sitting in attempt to communicate heard an independent voice message (heard apart from any of their member's speaking), that urged those present to form an organization specifically devoted to the promotion of physical mediumship and the development of mediums in whose present physical **mediumship** occurs. The voice identified himself as Noah Zerdin, a Spiritualist known for his having founded **The Link**, a network of Spiritualists groups built around small groups that sat for spirit contact in their homes. Zerdin had been the mentor of Leslie Flint, who died in 1994.

Physical mediumship includes those paranormal phenomena that has an effect upon the medium, others present, or an object in the immediate space where spirit contact is being attempted. It would include the **materialization** of spirit entities, **apports, transfiguration** (when a spirit's face is superimposed on that of the medium), **psychic photography, direct voice** through a **trumpet,** independent voices, and **electronic voice phenomena** (imposition of voices on an electronic tape). Such physical mediumship has all but disappeared in the wake of discoveries of numerous fraudulent mediums. Most of these phenomena have never been known to occur apart from stage magic.

Soon after its founding, the society began promoting what it termed the safe practice of physical mediumship and encouraged the development of home circles for the development of its practice. The society also holds weekend seminars, limited to society members, which incorporate experimental seances. The society now claims some functioning physical mediums among its members. The Society is not affiliated with any religious body, though it recognizes its primary members appear to be Spiritualists.

Noah's Ark Society operates primarily in England, thou it claims affiliates in other countries. It began publishing the *Noah's Ark Society Newsletter* soon after its formation. The *Newsletter* became *The Ark Review* in 1988, which includes speculative articles on physical mediumship as well as accounts of the experiences of affiliated home circles with physical mediumship. The society supports an Internet site at http://home.clara.net/noahsark/ind1.htm.

Sources:

Noah's Ark Society for Physical Mediumship. http://home.clara.net/noahsark/ind1.htm. May 23, 2000.

Noetics

Term used by scientific writer **Charles A. Musès** and others to denote the science of consciousness and its alterations. He noted in 1977, "Noetics is concerned with the nature, alterations and potentials of consciousness, and especially human consciousness." (This parapsychological use of "noetic" is, of course, distinct from its prior use as a synonym for "noachian," meaning pertaining to Noah and his period.)

An earlier use of the word noetic in relation to states of consciousness was in the article "Psychic and Noetic Action" by Theosophist **Helena Petrovna Blavatsky** (1831–1891), originally published in the journal *Lucifer* (October–December 1890) during the last years of her life. In this article, Blavatsky equated noetic with *manasic* (deriving from *manas,* a Sanskrit term for mind) and compared materialistic psychological views of her time with ancient Hindu religious teachings and occultism. She concluded that there is a higher noetic character of the mind principle than individual ego, a "spiritual-dynamical" force relating to divine consciousness, as distinct from mechanistic psychological dogmas or passive psychicism. This interesting article was reprinted in volume 3 of *Studies in Occultism,* a series of reprinted articles by Blavatsky.

Musès's use of noetics has been picked up by **Edgar D. Mitchell** for his psychical research organization, the **Institute of Noetic Sciences.**

Sources:

Blavatsky, Helena P. "Psychic and Noetic Action." In *Studies in Occultism.* Boston: New England Theosophical Corporation, 1895.

Musès, Charles A. "The Politics of Psi: Acculturation and Hypnosis." In *Extrasensory Ecology,* edited by Joseph K. Long. Metuchen, N.J.: Scarecrow Press, 1977.

Nolan, Finbarr (1952–)

Contemporary Irish healer who is the **seventh son** of a seventh son, and was thus, according to folk tradition, destined to begin **healing by touch.** He was born October 2, 1952, at Loch Gowna, county Cavan, Republic of Ireland. His mother stated "I knew . . . God would give him the power to heal." There were requests for healing when Nolan was only three months old, but his mother insisted that healing wait until the boy was at least two years old. At that time, a man brought his five-year-old child, who was suffering from ringworm. Nolan's mother circled the spots with holy water, making the sign of the cross in the middle, then placed the two-year-old Nolan's hand on each spot in turn, while she prayed for healing and asked her son to repeat the prayers after her. She claims that the ringworm was cured after two visits.

However, Nolan did not immediately undertake regular **healing,** although at the age of nine he touched the paralyzed hand of a local hotel proprietor and the hand became normal in three days' time. The father of this man was confined to a wheelchair with severe arthritis, but the day after Nolan touched him he was able to use his hands, and a month later he had recovered sufficiently to resume his job as a butcher.

At the age of sixteen, while still attending school, Nolan was asked to go to Donegal to cure an aunt. She notified the local newspaper, with the result that the young Nolan arrived to find a crowd of three hundred people and a television film crew. For several weeks afterward, some five thousand people a day came to his home for healing, and he touched them in groups of 14 or 15 at a time in the kitchen of the house. After that Nolan decided to leave school and devote himself full time to healing.

His reputation as a healer spread rapidly, and visitors came from around the world for treatment. Since county Cavan is located near the border of Northern Ireland, the political unrest and disorders began to discourage visitors, so Nolan moved with his parents and brothers to a house in the suburbs of Dublin. Here the large number of visitors seeking healing soon made it difficult for the family to live a normal life in an average-sized house, so Nolan hired halls and hotel rooms for regular clinics.

In the early period, Nolan had been influenced by his mother's religious outlook and used holy water, making the sign of the cross when touching each patient, but eventually he discarded such specifically Catholic tradition. As he said: "It deterred a lot of Protestants and I have nearly as many Protestant patients at my clinic as I do Catholic." Moreover he came to believe that his healing power had nothing to do with religion, and rejected the term "faith healer." He stated: "People should understand my healing has nothing to do with faith; I believe my power is a gift . . . I've proved that faith is not needed by curing animals and babies." Indeed, he became well known for treating injured race horses, and one horse he treated won nine races afterward.

His healing power appears to be in his right hand, and he therefore places it on each part of a patient's body that is afflicted. He lays his hand on the patient for several seconds and does not himself feel anything unusual happening, although patients often state that they feel a sensation of heat. His healing technique was monitored at a Belfast hospital, and it was found that during healing sessions there were changes in his respiration, pulse rate, and the electrical potential of his skin.

Like other seventh son healers, he has found that three visits are usually necessary. Patients sometimes feel worse after the first healing session, usually a sign that some changes have commenced. Healing is usually consolidated at the second and third visits.

Most patients pay a small voluntary contribution for healing, but some wealthier individuals have been very generous. An elderly lady in New York suffering from rheumatoid arthritis paid for Nolan's 6,000-mile journey and gave him an additional check for several thousand dollars. Nolan has also flown to Washington to treat a young Vietnamese war soldier. Nolan has held clinics in London as well as the United States and is credited with some remarkable cures.

An interesting experiment with Nolan was carried out by Robert E. Willner, diplomate of the Board of Family Practice, in his office in Florida. Willner selected ten patients on the basis of severity of their disease and failure to respond to multiple attempts at medical therapy. Nolan was introduced to them as "Dr. Finn, a medical student from the medical school in Dublin, Ireland." His function was ostensibly to confirm Willner's observations and provide an independent evaluation of each patient's disease process. The ten patients were involved with the experiment for three visits a week over a period of two weeks. Under these conditions, Nolan's touching appeared part of normal medical examination, so suggestion or placebo effect was eliminated, as no therapy was indicated.

Willner reported as follows:

"Four of the ten patients were completely unaffected by the examinations; five patients showed definite response of a positive nature and the improvement was thought to be of significant nature, in some cases 60% to 100% improvement. Two of these cases were extremely difficult and showed dramatic results. . . . It is also extremely important to note that all of these patients have been under the care of extremely fine specialists in the fields to which their diseases were related. Except for the increased attention that the patients were getting, I am not aware of any other positive influencing factor on the progress of the disease in any of them. One would expect that a patient in this setting would continue with their symptomatology in the hope that they would be chosen for the continuation of the experiment because their symptoms persisted. . . . The patients were not charged for their visits. Therefore, monetary incentive was absent."

Nolan is an amiable and, apart from his healing activity, eminently normal individual, with none of the mystique of many professionals in the paranormal. He does not think about anything in particular during the laying on of hands and exudes a friendly matter-of-fact atmosphere. His relaxations include Gaelic football, golf, and water skiing. His may be contacted at 11 Foxfield Rd., Raheny, Dublin 5, Republic of Ireland. (See also **Danny Gallagher; King's Evil**)

North American UFO Federation

A short-lived organization, founded in 1983 with the object of uniting other **UFO** organizations in an effort (1) to study and resolve the UFO phenomenon, (2) to develop a standard manual, reporting form, and vocabulary for investigation and reporting UFO sightings, (3) to inform the general public through educational materials and speakers, and (4) to provide a forum for discussion. The federation compiled a library and planned to develop and maintain a computer file of UFO reports and to establish a speakers bureau. The federation was headquartered in Los Altos, California.

North Door

In a possible remnant of pagan beliefs, some old Christian churches in Europe have a bricked-up doorway on the north side. There is an old tradition that witches used to enter on the north, which is connected with superstitions concerning the devil.

Northern UFO News

British publication concerned with UFOs and related topics, such as **crop circles.** It is edited by **Jenny Randles.** Address: Halsteads Close, Dove Holes, Buxton, High Peak, Derbyshire SK17 8BS, England.

Norton, Rosalind (1917–1979)

Rosalind Norton, an Australian occultist and avant-garde artist whose life anticipated the modern Wiccan movement, was born in Dunedin, **New Zealand.** As a child she had a vision of a shining dragon beside her bed, one of several events that convinced her of the existence of a spirit world. When she was seven, her family moved to Sydney, **Australia.** As she grew into her teen years, she felt increasingly alienated from mainstream life and by her 14th birthday decided to make her own way and express her unique vision in her art. During her years at East Sydney Technical College, she developed a deep interest in **witchcraft** and magic and began reading **Éliphas Lévi, Dion Fortune,** and **Aleister Crowley.**

After college Norton supported herself with a variety of menial jobs in King's Cross, where she had moved, but increasingly lived for her art and occult life. She experimented with self-hypnosis as a means of inducing a trance state during which she would produce her art. Meanwhile she continued her reading in the occult and Eastern religion. Her paintings became increasingly demonic complete with **ghoul**s, werewolves, and even **vampire**s, She also increasingly focused her subconscious on Pan, the ancient Greek deity, whose spirit she felt pervaded the Earth. She decorated her apartment with a Pan mural, did rituals invoking his presence, and felt him when she entered her trance states.

In 1949 she moved with her husband, Gavin Greenlees, to Melbourne. The next year, she had her first major encounter with the law. An exhibit of her art at the University of Melbourne was raided by the police, and Norton was charged with obscenity; the court ruled in her favor. In 1952, a limited edition book of her art was judged to contain two obscene pictures; the publisher was fined, and future copies were produced with the two pages blacked out.

Then in 1955, a woman who was being questioned by police on other matters began to make statements claiming that Norton was leading black masses as part of a Satanic cult. She described her as the "black witch of King's Cross," a label that would be frequently repeated by the press. While the woman later recanted some of her statements, they had already made their way to the newspapers, and Norton was forced to defend her attachment to Pan. No sooner had the issue died, than a film of her and her husband performing a ritual to Pan, which had been stolen from their apartment, found its way to the police. The film included some sex scenes, and the pair were arrested again. The trials of both the men who had stolen the film and of Norton entertained the public for almost two years. In the midst of the publicity, a café where Norton's paintings were hanging was raided and the owner fined. Norton and Greenlees were eventually found guilty of making obscene pictures.

After the lengthy court proceeding, Norton became reclusive and stayed out of the public eye for the remaining 20 years of her life. She died in King's Cross on December 5, 1979. In the years since, her work has been reevaluated and her artistic accomplishments praised by a new generation of art critics. Her magical career has found appreciation by the expanding Australian Wiccan movement who now see her as a herald of their community.

Sources:

Drury, Nevill, and Gregory Tillett. *Other Temples/Other Gods: The Occult in Australia.* Sydney: Methuen, 1982.

Norton, Rosalind. *The Art of Rosalind Norton.* Sydney: Wally Glover, 1952.

Norton, Thomas (d. ca. 1477)

The exact date of this alchemist's birth is wrapped in mystery, and little is recorded about his life in general. But at least it is known that he was born in Bristol, England, towards the end of the fourteenth century, and that in the year 1436 he was elected to represent that town in Parliament. This suggests that he was an upright and highly-esteemed person, and the conjecture is strengthened by the fact that Edward IV made him a member of his privy council and employed him repeatedly as an ambassador.

At an early age Norton showed curiosity concerning **alchemy,** demonstrating his predilection by attempting to make the personal acquaintance of **George Ripley,** sometime canon of Bridlington, who was reputedly a man of extraordinary learning, author of numerous alchemical works. For many months Norton sought Ripley in vain, but at length the canon, yielding to the other's importunity, wrote to him in the following manner: "I shall not longer delay; the time is come; you shall receive this grace. Your honest desire and approved virtue, your love of truth, wisdom and long perseverance, shall accomplish your sorrowful desires. It is necessary that, as soon as convenient, we speak together face to face, lest I should by writing betray my trust. I will make you my heir and brother in this art, as I am setting out to travel in foreign countries. Give thanks to God, Who next to His spiritual servants, honours the sons of this sacred science."

After receiving this very friendly and encouraging letter, Norton hurried straightway to Ripley's presence, and thereafter for more than a month the two were constantly together. The elder man taught the novice many things, and he even promised that, if Norton showed himself an apt and worthy pupil, he would impart to him the secret of the **philosophers' stone.** In due course this promise was fulfilled, though it is reported that Norton's own alchemical research met with various disappointments.

On one occasion, for instance, when he had almost perfected a certain tincture, his servant absconded with the crucible containing the precious fluid; while at a later time, when the alchemist was at work on the same experiment and thought he was just about to reach the goal, his entire paraphernalia was stolen by a mayoress of Bristol. This defeat must have been doubly galling to the unfortunate philosopher, for soon afterwards the mayoress became very wealthy, presumably as a result of her theft.

Norton himself does not appear to have reaped pecuniary benefit at any time from his erudition, but to have been a comparatively poor man throughout the whole of his life. This is a little surprising, for his *Ordinall of Alchemy* was a popular work in the Middle Ages and was repeatedly published. The original edition was anonymous, but the writer's identity has been determined because the initial syllables in the first six lines of the seventh chapter compose the following couplet:

> Tomas Norton of Briseto A parfet master ye maie him trowe.

Norton died circa 1477, and his predilections descended to one of his great grandsons, Samuel Norton. The younger Norton was born in 1548, studied science at St. John's College, Cambridge, and afterward became a justice of the peace and sheriff of Somersetshire. He died about 1604, and in 1630 a collection of his alchemistic tracts was published at Frankfort.

The Nostradamian

Monthly journal that analyzed the predictions of **Nostradamus** (1503–1566), discussing prophecies fulfilled and interpreting those that have not yet come to pass. Last known address: Nostradamus Research, P.O. Box 6463, Lincoln, NE 68506.

Nostradamus (1503–1566)

Medieval French physician and prophet. Nostradamus was born Michel de Nostredame on December 24, 1503, in St. Remey de Provence. A short time before his birth his Jewish family had changed its name from Gassonet to Nostredame as a reaction to a "convert or go into exile" order of the government in Provence. He received his medical training at Montpellier. He sometimes voiced dissension with the teachings of the Catholic priests, who dismissed the study of astrology and the assertions of Copernicus that the Earth and other planets revolved around the sun—contrary to the Christian appraisal of the heavens. Nostradamus's family warned him to hold his tongue, since he could be easily persecuted because of his Jewish background. Earlier, from his grandfathers he had secretly learned mystical areas of Jewish wisdom, including the Kabbalah and alchemy. He graduated in 1525 and was licensed as a physician. Four years later he received his full medical degree. He established his reputation by treating the ill during the plague in southern France. For a while he lived in Agen to work with Julius Caeser Scaliger, a prominent physician of the day, but moved on to Aix-en-Provence and Lyons during the 1530s. He eventually settled in Salon.

Over the years Nostradamus (the Latin version of his name) became a practitioner of astrology and related occult arts. He published his first book, an astrological almanac (issued annually for several years), in 1550. Five years later he issued a popular book of recipes for cosmetics and various medical remedies. That same year he also published the first edition of the book from which his current fame is largely derived, *The Centuries.*

In reference to Nostradamus's writings, a "century" referred to a grouping of one hundred verses, each verse being a four-line poem called a quatrain. It was this work that brought Nostradamus his fame. The 1555 edition contained the first three centuries and 53 quatrains of "Century Four." A second edition two years later had 640 quatrains and Centuries Eight through Ten were published as a separate volume in 1558. The first English edition, published in 1672, also had eight additional quatrains from the "Century Seven" not in the French editions. As a result of the success of the first edition, in 1556 Nostradamus was invited to Paris as a guest of the French queen Catherine de Médicis. With the financial support she gave him, he was able to complete his writings of the prophetic verses.

The quatrains were written in a cryptic and symbolic fashion requiring some interpretation and thus offering room for a wide variety of understandings of exactly to which events and persons Nostradamus was making reference. Among the most famous of quatrains is one often seen as referring to the London Fire of 1666 (though more critical interpreters see a reference to the burning of Protestants by Queen Mary I of England, a contemporary of Nostradamus):

> The blood of the just shall be wanting in London, Burnt by thunderbolts of twenty three the Six(es), The ancient dame shall fall from [her] high place, Of the same sect many shall be killed.

Nostradamus died in June 1566 of congestive heart failure. He was succeeded by a colleague, Jean-Aimé de Chavigny, also a physician, who immediately began work on a biography. De Chavigny also published his interpretations of 126 of the quatrains. Over the centuries a number of additional interpreters have arisen (including Theophilus de Garencieres, who translated the quatrains into English (1672)), all of whom have championed the reputed accomplishments of Nostradamus as a seer of future events and emphasized those quatrains presaging events soon to occur. Garancieres's effort was marred by his acceptance of two fake quatrains written to attack French Roman Catholic Cardinal Jules Mazarin, who also served as the French prime minister.

Modern interest in Nostradamus, which has spawned a massive popular literature during the last generation, began with Charles Ward's work, *Oracles of Nostradamus* (1891). One prominent student of the quatrains, Edgar Leoni, submitted his lengthy treatise as a master's thesis at Harvard University (1961). Interpreters claim Nostradamus predicted Hitler's rise to power as well as the explosion of the U.S. space shuttle *Challenger* in 1986.The popular interest in Nostradamus has been countered by the observations of a variety of historians who have offered other explanations of his prophetic verse (often to the detriment of his reputation), and by some modern psychic debunkers, such as stage magician James Randi.

Sources:

[Note: There is a large literature on Nostradamus, of which only a selected list is given here. For a bibliography of the 25 oldest editions of Nostradamus, published up to 1689, compiled by Carl Graf von Klinckowstroem, see *Zeitschrift für Bücherfreude,* March 1913.]

Cheetham, Erika. *The Prophecies of Nostradamus.* New York: G. P. Putnam's Sons, 1972. Reprint, London: Neville Spearman, 1973. Reprint, London: Corgi, 1975.

Du Vignois, Elisée. *Notre histoire racontée à l'avance par Nostradamus.* Paris, 1910.

Hogue, John. *Nostradamus and the Millennium.* Garden City, N.Y.: Doubleday, 1987.

Howe, Ellic. *Urania's Children: The Strange World of the Astrologers.* London: William Kimber, 1967. Rev. ed. as *Astrology and Psychological Warfare During World War II.* London, 1972. Reprinted as *Astrology: A Recent History Including the Untold Story of Its Role in World War II.* New York: Walker, 1968.

Laver, James. *Nostradamus, or the Future Foretold.* London: Collins, 1942. Reprint, UK: Penguin Books, 1952. Reprint, London: George Mann, 1973.

Leoni, Edgar. *Nostradamus and His Prophecies.* New York: 1961.

Le Pelletier, Anatole. *Les Oracles de Michel de Nostredame.* 2 vols. Paris, 1867.

Le Vert, Liberte E., ed. *The Prophecies and Enigmas of Nostradamus.* Glen Rock, N.J.: Firebell Books, 1979.

Prieditis, Arthur A. *Fate of the Nations.* London: Neville Spearman; St. Paul: Llewellyn Publications, 1973.

Randi, James. *The Mask of Nostradamus.* Buffalo, N.Y.: Prometheus Books, 1993.

Roberts, Henry C. *The Complete Prophecies of Nostradamus.* New York, 1947.

Torné-Chiavigny, H. *L'Histoire prédite et jugée par Nostradamus.* 3 vols. Bordeaux, 1860–62.

Voldben, A. *After Nostradamus.* London: Neville Spearman, 1973. Reprint, New York: Citadel, 1974.

Ward, Charles A. *Oracles of Nostradamus.* London, 1891. Reprint, New York: Modern Library, 1942.

Noualli

Aztec magicians. (See **MEXICO AND CENTRAL AMERICA**)

Nous Letter (Journal)

Semi-annual journal of **noetics,** the science of states of consciousness. The *Nous Letter* also absorbed *Astrologica,* formerly a separate journal. Last known address: 1817 De La Vina St., Santa Barbara, CA 93101.

NROOGD See New Reformed Orthodox Order of the Golden Dawn

NSAC See National Spiritualist Association of Churches

Nuan

In ancient Irish romance, the last of the sorceress-daughters of Conaran. Having put **Finn Mac Cummal** under taboo to send his men in single combat against her as long as she wished, she was slain by Goll Mac Morna, her sister's slayer.

Numerology

A popular interpretive and prediction system deriving from the mystic values ascribed to numbers. In Jewish mysticism, for example, **gematria** refers to the traditional association of numbers with Hebrew letters, and the practice of seeking hidden meanings in words by systematically converting them into numbers.

Modern numerology was popularized by the palmist and fortune-teller **"Cheiro"** (Count Louis Hamon), who developed a system of what he called "fadic" numbers. These were arrived at by adding together all the digits in the subject's birth date to produce a number of destiny to which special planetary and other significance was then attached.

In general, numerology systems assign numerical values to the letters of one's name and/or birthplace. These are added together to ascertain a basic number, which has a special symbolic interpretation, much as astrological types are traditionally assigned particular characteristics of helpful and harmful influences. Sometimes lucky or unlucky numbers are also related to the 22 symbols of the major arcana of the **Tarot** pack.

Sources:

Bosman, Leonard. *The Meaning and Philosophy of Numbers.* 1932. Reprint, London: Rider, 1974.

Buess, Lynn M. *Numerology for the New Age.* Marina del Rey, Calif.: DeVorss, 1978.

Bunker, Dusty. *Numerology and Your Future.* Rockport, Mass.: Para Research, 1980.

Cheiro [Count Louis Hamon]. *The Book of Numbers.* London, 1926. Revised as *Cheiro's Book of Numbers.* London: Barrie & Jenkins, 1978.

Coates, Austin. *Numerology.* London: Frederick Muller, 1974. Reprint, London: Mayflower, 1978.

Konraad, Sandor. *Numerology: Key to the Tarot.* Rockport, Mass.: Para Research, 1983.

Kozminsky, Isidore. *Numbers, Their Meaning and Magic.* New York: G. P. Putnam's Sons, 1927.

Misegades, Charles. *Know Your Number.* Marina Del Rey, Calif.: DeVorss, 1980.

Moore, Gerun. *Numbers Will Tell.* London: Barker; New York: Grossett & Dunlap, 1973.

Sepharial [W. G. Old]. *The Kabala of Numbers.* 2 vols. London, 1913. New York: MacKay, 1928. Reprint, San Bernadino, Calif.: Borgo Press, 1980.

Stein, Sandra Kovacs. *Instant Numerology: Charting Your Road Map to the Future.* New York: Harper & Row, 1979.

Westcott, W. W. *Numbers: Their Occult Power and Mystic Virtue.* London: Theosophical Publishing House, 1890. Reprint, 1974.

Numeromancy

Alternative term for **numerology,** or **divination** by the letter and word values ascribed to numbers. Other synonyms are arithmancy and arithomancy.

Nurse, Rebecca (1621–1692)

Alleged witch executed at Salem Village (now Danvers), Massachusetts, in 1692. Rebecca Nurse was born Rebecca Towne in Yarmouth, England, and baptized on February 21, 1621. She was still a youth when her family moved to Massachusetts and settled at Topsfield. At some point she married Francis Nurse, and they settled at Salem. In 1678 they purchased a farm near Salem Village. They had fours sons and four daughters. Until 1692 Rebecca Nurse was well-respected by her neighbors.

After several young girls in the community began to complain of being attacked by the spectres of several women who were accused of **witchcraft,** accounts of such affliction grew. One of the girls interrupted a church service with her accusations, and afterward the Nurses stopped going to church.

Eventually the young girls singled out Rebecca Nurse, and on March 23, 1692, she was arrested and, although sick at the time, confined to jail. During her initial hearing a number of her acquaintances spoke highly of her. The primary evidence against her were the spectral allegations, the girls' claim she afflicted them through her spirit. Possibly her deafness, a condition she developed in later years, and her subsequent inability to respond adequately to questions put to her tilted the jury against her in the end. She was finally excommunicated from her church and was hung on July 19, 1692, the same day as **Goodwife Good** and three other convicted witches were hung.

Sources:

Hansen, Chadwick. *Witchcraft at Salem.* New York: George Braziller, 1969.

Tapley, Charles Sutherland. *Rebecca Nurse.* Boston: Marshall Jones, 1930.

O

"Oahspe"

A "New Bible" revealed to **John Ballou Newbrough** (1828–1891), a New York **medium,** and received through **automatic writing** on the newly invented typewriter in 1881. Newbrough spent ten years in self-purification so that he could become inspired by a higher power. The result was *Oahspe, The Kosmon Bible in the words of Jehovah and his angel ambassador.* It took fifty weeks to complete, with Newbrough working half an hour each morning. A movement grew out of people who responded to the teachings of *Oahspe,* which survives as a set of loosely organized groups that can be contacted through the Universal Faithists of Kosmon, Box 154, Riverton, UT 84065.

Sources:

Denton, Jim. *Dr. Newbrough and Oahspe.* Kingman, Ariz: Faithist Journal, 1975.

———. *The Oahspe Story.* Kingman, Ariz.: Faithist Journal, 1975.

Newbrough, John Balllou. *Oahspe.* New York; London: Oahspe Publishing Association, 1882. Reprint, Los Angeles: Essenes of Kosmon, 1950.

Oak-Apples

An oak-apple is a spongy, brightly colored gall found on the leaf bud of oak trees; it is globular in shape. In folklore, oak-apples could be used in **divination.** To discover whether a child was bewitched, three oak-apples were dropped into a basin of water under the child's cradle, at the same time preserving the strictest silence. If the oak-apples floated, the child was not fascinated, but if they sank, the child was believed to be bewitched.

Oak Tree

Much folklore belief surrounds the oak tree. From ancient times it has been regarded as sacred tree. The Druids venerated the oak and performed many of their rites under the shadow of its branches. When St. Augustine (the sixth-century archbishop of Canterbury) preached Christianity to the ancient Britons, he stood under an oak tree.

The ancient Hebrews also evidently held the oak as a sacred tree. It is believed that Abraham received his heavenly visitors under an oak. Rebekah's nurse was buried under an oak, called afterward the oak of weeping. Jacob buried the idols of Shechem under an oak. It was under the oak of Ophra that Gideon saw the angel sitting who gave him instructions as to what he was to do to free Israel.

When Joshua and Israel made a covenant to serve God, a great stone was set up in evidence under an oak that was by the sanctuary of the Lord. The prophet sent to prophesy against Jeroboam was found at Bethel sitting under an oak. Saul and his sons were buried under an oak, and, according to Isaiah, idols were made of oak wood. Abimelech was made king beneath an oak located in Shechem.

As late as the eighteenth century the oak was used in curing diseases. It was believed that a toothache could be cured by boring the tooth or gum with a nail to draw blood, and then driving the nail into an oak tree. Another folk belief was that a child with rupture could be cured by splitting an oak branch, and passing the child through the opening backwards three times; if the splits grew together the child would be cured.

It was widely believed that carrying acorns brought long life and good luck, since the oak tree itself is used as a symbol of strength and endurance.

Oaten, Ernest W(alter) (ca. 1937)

Prominent British Spiritualist, and former president of the International Federation of Spiritualists. He was president of the **Spiritualists' National Union** from 1915 and edited the journal *Two Worlds* (1919–36). He was also a **medium** and believed that his leading articles were inspired by the spirit of **Emma Hardinge Britten,** whose work had inspired the formation of the Union in 1890. As chairman of the Parliamentary Committee of the Spiritualists National Union he pressed for reform of the Fortune Telling Act, the British law relating to mediumship.

OBE (or OOBE or OOB) See Out-of-the-Body Travel

Obeah

West Indian **witchcraft.** The term is believed to derive from an Ashanti word, *obayifo,* a wizard or witch, although there are claims that it refers to Obi, a West African snake god. Author M. G. Lewis (1775–1818) spent some time in Jamaica, where his father owned large estates, and reported cases of obeah. In his posthumously published *Journal of a West India Proprietor* (1834), he wrote an entry on January 12, 1816, describing how ten months earlier a black man "of very suspicious manners and appearance" was arrested,

". . . and on examination there was found upon him a bag containing a great variety of strange materials for incantations; such as thunder-stones, cat's ears, the feet of various animals, human hair, fish bones, the teeth of alligators, etc.: he was conveyed to Montego Bay; and no sooner was it understood that this old African was in prison, than depositions were poured in from all quarters from negroes who deposed to having seen him exercise his magical arts, and, in particular, to his having sold such and such slaves medicines and charms to deliver them from their enemies; being, in plain English, nothing else than rank poisons. He was convicted of Obeah upon the most indubitable evidence. The good old practice of burning had fallen into disrepute; so he was sentenced to be transported, and was shipped off the island, to the great satisfaction of persons of all colours—white, black, and yellow."

Jamaican legislation of 1760 enacted that "any Negro or other Slave who shall pretend to any Supernatural Power and be detected in making use of any materials relating to the practice of Obeah or Witchcraft in order to delude or impose upon the Minds of others shall upon Conviction thereof before two Magistrates and three Freeholders suffer Death or Transportation." (See also **Voudou; West Indian Islands**)

Sources:

Bell, Hesketh J. *Obeah: Witchcraft in the West Indies.* London: Sampson, Low & Co., 1889.

Emerick, Abraham J. *Obeah and Duppyism in Jamaica.* Woodstock, N.Y.: privately printed, 1915.

Lewis, Matthew Gregory. *Journal of a West Indian Proprietor.* London: J. Murray, 1861. Reprint, New York: Negro University Press, 1961.

Williams, Joseph J. *Voodoos and Obeahs; Phases of West Indian Witchcraft.* New York: Dial Press, 1933.

Obercit, Jacques Hermann (1725–1798)

Swiss mystic and alchemist. He was born December 2, 1725, in Arbon, **Switzerland,** the son of a scientist keenly interested in Hermetic philosophy. Early in his life he decided to search for the **philosophers' stone,** hoping to resuscitate the fortunes of his family, which were at a low ebb. The young man worked strenuously, maintaining that whoever would triumph in this endeavor must not depend on scientific skill alone but rather on constant communion with God.

Notwithstanding this theory, he soon found himself under the ban of the civic authorities, who came to his laboratory and forced him to forego further experiments, declaring that these constituted a danger to public health and safety. Obercit was incensed and appears to have left and gone to live for some time thereafter with a brother of the noted physiognomist Johann Lavater. At a later date, Obercit renounced the civilized world altogether and took up residence in the Alps.

However, he did not live the solitary life of a hermit, since according to his own account, he took as bride a shepherdess named Theantis. Obercit's writings include *Disquisitio de Universali Methodo Medendi* (1767) and *Défense du Mysticisme et de la Vie Solitaire* (1775). He died at Weimar, Germany, February 2, 1798.

Oberion

One of three spirits (the others were "Andrea Malchus" and "Inchubus") said to have been raised up by the parson of Lesingham and Sir John of Leiston in Norfolk, **England,** ca. 1528.

Objective Phenomena

Term used in **psychical research,** together with "subjective phenomena" as an alternative classification to "physical" and "mental" phenomena, terms which emerged out of the study of **Spiritualism.**

Object Reading

A term for **psychometry,** in which the operator may form impressions of events relating to an object associated with those events, usually by holding the object in his or her hand.

Obsession and Possession

Obsession, from Latin *obsidere* (to besiege), is a form of insanity caused, according to traditional belief, by the persistent attack of an invading spirit from outside the individual. Obsession is the opposite of possession, control by an invading spirit from within. Both, however, involve the usurpation of the person's individuality and control of the body by a foreign and discarnate entity.

In the Western Christian context, both obsession and possession, but especially possession, have been viewed as completely negative, a perspective somewhat enforced by the modern concern for the autonomous individual, possession implying a giving over of one's freedom. In most cultures, however, there is a distinction between dysfunctional possession and possession that occurs voluntarily, usually in a religious context. Numerous religions, like Spiritualism, are possession-oriented religions, in which a central feature is the voluntary possession of members by what is believed to be a deity, a spirit, or a deceased person. These religious functionaries may periodically become possessed, usually in a ritual context, during their entire active lives, but without the otherwise dysfunctional consequences so evident in pathological possessed states.

During the 1960s anthropologist Erika Bourguignon conducted a study of possession in 488 societies about which data was available. Seventy-four percent of them maintained some belief in spirit possession, of which more than half had some form of positive institutionalized structure in which possession occurred and was appropriated by believers.

Historical Background

This belief may be found in the earliest records of human history—in the ancient magic rites and in the pronouncements often used as charms against and for the **exorcism** of these invading influences. The oldest literary remains from **India, Greece,** and Rome are filled with references to possession. While there are passing references to demons and demon obsession or possession in sacred Jewish writings—such as the case of Saul, who was "troubled with an evil spirit from God" only to be relieved by the music of David's harp (1 Sam. 16:14–16)—it is with the Christian movement that a major emphasis on spirit possession emerges. Jesus regularly healed by casting possessing spirits out of the mentally ill. Crucial to later understanding of possessing spirits in the Western tradition are incidents such as Jesus' driving the legion of demons into the swine (thus demonstrating their existence apart from the psychology of the possessed individual) and Paul's driving out of the divining spirit who possessed a young woman of Thyatira (thus associating spirit possession with fortune-telling).

Plato, in the *Republic,* not only speaks of demons of various grades, but mentions a method of treating and providing for those obsessed by them. Sophocles and Euripides described the possessed, and mention of the subject is also found in Herodotus, Plutarch, Horace, and many other classical writers.

Appalling episodes in the Middle Ages can be traced to the unquestioned belief in possession and obsession by the Devil and his demonic legions. Many believed that all madness was caused by possession, the visible manifestation of the Evil One. Such madness had to be exorcised by charms and averted by the observance of sacred rites. In extreme cases the possessed body was to be burned and destroyed for the good of the tortured soul within. The rites of **black magic,** in all ages and places, deliberately evoked this possession by the Devil and his demons to obtain the benefit of the extensive knowledge it was believed they conferred and the consequent power and control over man and his destinies.

In the Middle Ages, when an intense belief in angels, saints, and devils flourished, the imagination of the individual was dominated by such beings.

A variation on the belief in obsession and possession can be found in the condition known as **lycanthropy** (the delusion that one has become a wolf), which afflicted large numbers of people in **France** and **Germany** in the fourteenth and sixteenth centuries.

The mania of **flagellation** took its rise in Perouse in the thirteenth century, caused by the panic accompanying an outbreak of the plague. Flagellants preached that there was no remission of sins (and dissipation of accompanying disasters such as epidemics) without their self-inflicted punishment offered as penance. Bands of them, gathering adherents everywhere, roamed through city and country, clad in scanty clothing on which were depicted skeletons, and with frenzied movements publicly lashed themselves. It was to these exhibitions the name "Dance of Death" was first applied.

The dancing mania, accompanied by aberration of mind and maniacal distortions of the body, was prevalent in Germany in the fourteenth century, and in the sixteenth century in Italy, where it was termed *tarantism* and was ascribed to the bite of the tarantula spider. The music and songs employed for the cure are still preserved. Edmund Parish, in his book *Hallucinations and Illusions* (1897), summarizes the activity of the dancers:

"If not reckoned as true chorea, the epidemic of dancing which raged in Germany and the Netherlands in the Middle Ages comes under this head. Appearing in Aix it spread in a few months to Liège, Utrecht and the neighbouring towns, visited Metz, Cologne and Strasburg (1418) and after lingering into the sixteenth century gradually died out. This malady consisted in convulsions, contortions accompanying the dancing, hallucinations and so forth. The attack could be checked by bandaging the abdomen as well as by kicks and blows on that part of the body. Music had a great influence on the dancers, and for this reason it was played in the streets in order that the attacks might by this means reach a crisis and disappear the sooner. Quite trifling circumstances could bring on these seizures, the sight of pointed shoes for instance, and of the colour red which the dancers held in horror. In order to prevent such outbreaks the wearing of pointed shoes was forbidden by the authorities. During their dance many of the afflicted thought they waded in blood, or saw heavenly visions."

Tying the dancing to possession, Parish continues,

"To this category also belongs the history of demoniacal possession. The belief of being possessed by spirits, frequently met with in isolated cases, appeared at certain periods in epidemic form. Such an epidemic broke out in Brandenburg, and in Holland and Italy in the sixteenth century, especially in the convents. In 1350–60 it attacked the convent of St. Brigitta, in Xanthen, a convent near Cologne, and others. The nuns declared that they were visited by the Devil, and had carnal conversation with him. These and other 'possessed' wretches were sometimes thrown into dungeons, sometimes burnt. The convent of the Ursulines at Aix was the scene of such a drama (1609–11) where two possessed nuns, tormented by all kinds of apparitions, accused a priest of witchcraft on which charge he was burnt to death [see **Urbain Grandier**]. The famous case of the nuns of **Loudun** (1632–39) led to a like tragic conclusion, as well as the Louvier case (1642) in which the two chief victims found their end in life-long imprisonment and the stake."

Religious Possession

The widespread belief in and fear of magic and **witchcraft** produced some hallucinations. Certain levels of religious ecstasy partake of the same character, the difference being that they involve possession by and contact with so-called angelic or good (i.e., socially approved) spirits. The sacred books of all nations teem with instances of this and history can also furnish examples. The many familiar cases of ecstatic visions and revelations in the Torah may be cited, as well as those found in the legends of saints and martyrs, where they either appear as revelations from heaven or temptations of the Devil.

In the latter case, the sexologist Richard von Krafft-Ebing pointed out the close connection of religious ecstasy with sexual disturbances, especially in situations where the sexual drive was suppressed and diverted into religious activity. The religious ecstatic condition was frequently sought and induced. Von Kraftt-Ebing noted as follows:

"Among Eastern and primitive peoples such as Hindoos, American Indians, natives of Greenland, Kamtschatka and Yucatan, fetish-worshipping Negroes, and Polynesians, the ecstatic state accompanied with hallucinations is frequently observed, sometimes arising spontaneously, but more often artificially induced. It was known also among the nations of antiquity. The means most often employed to induce this state are beating of magic drums and blowing of trumpets, howlings and hour-long prayers, dancing, flagellation, convulsive movements and contortions, asceticism, fasting and sexual abstinence. Recourse is also had to narcotics to bring about the desired result. Thus the flyagaric is used in Western Siberia, in San Domingo the herb coca, tobacco by some tribes of American Indians, and in the East opium and hashish. The ancient Egyptians had their intoxicating drinks, and receipts for witch's salves and philtres have come down to us from medieval times."

In many countries this condition of possession was induced for a spectrum of purposes from the higher mystical and prophetic to mere fortune-telling. Anthropologist Edward Tylor, in his *Primitive Culture* (1871), testifies to the extent to which this belief in obsession and possession persisted into the nineteenth century: "It is not too much to assert that the doctrine of demoniacal possession is kept up, substantially the same theory to account for substantially the same facts, by half the human race, who thus stand as consistent representatives of their forefathers back in primitive antiquity."

Such beliefs persisted in the development of **Spiritualism.** Pioneer Spiritualist seer **Andrew Jackson Davis** developed a theory of obsession to account for forms of insanity and crime. The following passage taken from his book *Diakka and Their Victims* (1873) indicates this belief:

"The country of the diakka is where the morally deficient and the affectionately unclean enter upon a strange probation. . . . They are continually victimizing sensitive persons still in the flesh making sport of them and having a jolly laugh at the expense of really honest and sincere people. They [these demonlike spirits] teach that they would be elevated and made happy if only they could partake of whiskey and tobacco, or gratify their burning free-love propensities. . . . Being unprincipled intellectualities their play is nothing but pastime amusement at the expense of those beneath their influence."

Davis saw some of these creatures as having such a malignant and bloodthirsty nature as to incite the beings they possessed to murder.

Recorded Instances of Possession

The sixteenth-century writer Jean Boulaese told how 26 devils came out of the body of the possessed Nicoli of Laon:

"At two o'clock in the afternoon, the said Nicoli, being possessed of the Devil, was brought to the said church, where the said de Motta proceeded as before with the exorcism. In spite of all entreaty the said Beelzebub told them in a loud voice that he would not come out. Returning to their entreaties after dinner, the said de Motta asked him how many had come out, and he answered, 'twenty-six.' 'You and your followers,' then said de Motta, 'must now come out like the others.' 'No,' he replied, 'I will not come out here, but if you like to take me to Saint Restitute, we will come out there. It is sufficient for you that twenty-six are out.' Then the said de Motta asked for a convincing sign of how they had come out. For witness he told them to look in the garden of the treasury over the front gate, for they had taken and carried away three tufts (i.e., branches) from a green maypole (a small fir) and three slates from above the church of Liesse, made into a cross, as others in France commonly, all of which was found true as shown by the Abbot of Saint-Vincent, M. de Velles, Master Robert de May, canon of the Church Notre-Dame of Laon, and others."

The same author gave an account of the contortions of the possessed woman:

"As often as the reverend father swung the sacred host before her eyes, saying, 'Begone, enemy of God,' so did she toss from side to side, twisting her face towards her feet, and making horrible noises. Her feet were reversed, with the toes in the position of the heel, and despite the restraining power of eight of the men, she stiffened herself and threw herself into the air a height of six feet, the stature of a man, so that the attendants, sometimes even carried with her into the air, perspired at their work. And although they bore down with all their might, still could they not restrain her, and torn away from the restraining hands, she freed herself without any appearance of being at all ruffle.

"The people, seeing and hearing such a horrible sight, one so monstrous, hideous and terrifying cried out, 'Jesus, have mercy on us!' Some hid themselves, not daring to look; others, recognising the wild cruelty of such excessive and incredible torment, wept bitterly, reiterating piteously, 'Jesus, have mercy on us!' The reverend father then gave permission to those who wished to touch and handle the patient, disfigured, bent, and deformed, and with the rigidity of death. Chief among these were the would-be reformers, such men as Francois Santerre, Christofle, Pasquot, Gratian de la Roche, Masquette, Jean du Glas, and others well-known for their tendencies towards reform, all vigorous men. They all endeavored, but in vain, to straighten her limbs, and bring them to a normal position, and to open her eyes and mouth—it was futile. Further, so stiff and rigid was she, that the limbs would have broken rather than give, as also the nose and ears. And then, as she said afterwards, she was possessed, declaring that she was enduring incredible pain. That is, by the soul torment, the devil makes the body become stone or marble."

A Dr. Ese exponded on the case of Sister Mary, one of Louviers' nuns:

"The last was Sister Mary of St. Esprit, supposedly possessed by Dagon, a large woman, slender-waisted, and of good complexion, with no evidence of illness. She came into the refectory. . . head erect and eyes wandering from side to side, singing, dancing and skipping. Still moving about and touching lightly those around her, she spoke with an elegance of language expressive of the good feeling and good nature which were his (using the person of the devil). All this was done with movements and carriage alike haughty, following it up with a violence of blasphemy, then a reference to his dear little friend Magdalen, his darling and his favourite mistress. And then, without springing or using effort of any kind, she projected herself into a pane of glass and hanging on to a central bar of iron passed bodily through it, but on making an exit from the other side the command was given in Latin, 'est in nomine Jesu rediret non per aliam sed per eadem viam.' After some discussion and a definite refusal to return she, however, returned by the same route, whereupon the doctors examined her pulse and tongue, all of which she endured while laughing and discussing other things. They found no disturbance such as they had expected, nor any sign of the violence of her actions and words, her coming to being accompanied with some trivial remarks. The company then retired."

As at Louviers, nuns at Auxonne also experienced a problem with possession, an account of which is in the *Relation des Ursulines possedées d'Auxonne* (ca. 1660):

". . . the bishop of Chalons, with the intention of exorcising Denise Lamy, sent for her and when she was not found, he inwardly commanded her to come to him in the chapel of St. Anne where he was. It was striking to see the prompt obedience of the demon to this command, formulated merely in the mind, for in about a quarter of an hour a violent knocking was heard at the door of the chapel, as if by one hard pressed. On opening the door this girl entered the chapel abruptly, leaping and bounding, her face changed greatly and with high colour and sparkling eyes. So bold and violent was she that it was difficult to restrain her, nor would she allow the putting on of the stole which she seized and threw violently into the air despite the efforts of four or five clerics who did their best to stop her, so that finally it was proposed to bind her, but this was deemed too difficult in the condition in which she was.

"On another occasion, at the height of her frenzy. . . the demon was ordered to stop the pulse in one of her arms, and it was immediately done, with less resistance and pain than before. Immediate response was also made to the further order to make it return. The command being given to make the girl insensible to pain, she avowed that she was so, boldly offering her arm to be pierced and burnt as wished. The exorcist, fortified by his earlier experience, took a sufficiently long needle and drove it, full length, into the nail and flesh, at which she laughed aloud, saying that she felt nothing at all. Accordingly as he was ordered, blood was allowed to flow or not, and she herself took the needle and stuck it into different parts of her arm and hand. Further, one of the company took a pin and, having drawn out the skin a little above the wrist, passed it through and through so that the two ends were only visible, the rest of the pin being buried in the arm. Unless the order was given for some no blood issued, nor was there the least sign of feeling or pain."

As proof of the possession of the Auxonne nuns, the same account continues:

"Violent agitation of the body only conceivable to those who have seen it. Beating of the head with all their might against the pavement or walls, done so often and so hard that it causes one to shudder on seeing it and yet they show no sign of pain, nor is there any blood, wound or contusion.

"The condition of the body in a position of extreme violence, where they support themselves on their knees with the head turned round and inclined towards the ground for a foot or so, which makes it appear as if broken. Their power of bearing, for hours together without moving, the head being lowered behind below the level of the waist; their power of breathing in this condition; the unruffled expression of the face which never alters during these disturbances; the evenness of the pulse; their coolness during these movements; the tranquil state they are in when they suddenly return and the lack of any quickening in the respirations; the turning back of the head, even to the ground, with marvelous rapidity. Sometimes the movement to and fro is done thirty or forty times running, the girl on her knees and with her arms crossed in front; at other times, in the same position with the head turned about, the body is wound around into a sort of semicircle, with results apparently incompatible with nature.

"Fearful convulsions, affecting all the limbs and accompanied with shouts and cries. Sometimes fear at the sight of certain phantoms and spectres by which they say they are menaced, causes such a change in their facial expression that those present are terrified; at other times there is a flood of tears beyond control and accompanied by groans and piercing cries. Again, the widely-opened mouth, eyes wild and showing nothing but the white, the pupil being turned up under cover of the lids—the whole returning to the normal at the mere command of the exorcist in conjunction with the sign of the cross.

"They have often been seen creeping and crawling on the ground without any help from the hands or feet; the back of the head or the forehead may be touching the soles of the feet. Some lie on the ground, touching it with the pit of the stomach only, the rest of the body, head, feet and arms, being in the air for some length of time. Sometimes, bent back so that the top of the head and the soles of the feet touch the ground, the rest of the body being supported in the air like a table, they walk in this position without help from the hands. It is quite common for them, while on their knees to kiss the ground, with the face twisted to the back so that the top of the head touches the soles of the feet. In this position and with the arms crossed on the chest they make the sign of the cross on the pavement with their tongues.

"A marked difference is to be noticed between their condition when free and uncontrolled and that which they show when controlled and in the heat of their frenzy. By reason of their sex and delicate constitutions as much as from illness they may be weak, but when the demon enters them and the authority of the church compels them to appear they may become at times so violent that all the power of four or five men may be unable to stop them. Even their faces become so distorted and changed that they are no longer recognisable. What is more astonishing is that after these violent transports, lasting sometimes three or four hours; after efforts which would make the strongest feel like resting for several days; after continuous shrieking and heart-breaking cries; when they become normal again—a momentary proceeding—they are unwearied and quiet, and the mind is as tranquil, the face as composed, the breathing as easy and the pulse as little changed as if they had not stirred out of a chair.

"It may be said, however, that among all the signs of possession which these girls have shown, one of the most surprising, and at the same time the most common, is the understanding of the thought and inward commands which are used every day by exorcists and priests, without there being any outward manifestation either by word or other sign. To be appreciated by them it is merely necessary to address them inwardly or mentally, a fact which has been verified by so many of the experiences during the stay of the bishop of Chalons and by any of the clergy, who wished to investigate, that one cannot reasonably doubt such particulars and many others, the details of which cannot be given here."

Simon Goulart, in *Histoires admirables et mémorables de nostre temps* (2 vols., 1610), culled many stories of demonic possession from demonologist **Johan Weyer,** including the following:

"Antoine Benivenius in the eighth chapter of the *Livre des causes cachées des maladies* tells of having seen a girl of sixteen years whose hands contracted curiously whenever she was taken with a pain in the abdomen. With a cry of terror her abdomen would swell up so much that she had the appearance of being eight months pregnant—later the swelling went down and, not being able to lie still, she tossed about all over the bed, sometimes putting her feet above her head as if trying a somersault. This she kept up throughout the throes of her illness and until it had gone down by degrees. When asked what had happened to her, she denied any remembrance of it. But on seeking the causes of this affection we were of opinion that it arose from a choking of the womb and from the rising of malignant vapours affecting adversely the heart and brain. We were at length forced to relieve her with drugs but these were of no avail and becoming more violent and congested she at last began to throw up long iron nails all bent, brass needles stuck into wax, and bound up with hair and a part of her breakfast—a mass so large that a man would have had difficulty in swallowing it all. I was afraid, after seeing several of these vomitings, that she was possessed by an evil spirit, who deluded those present while he removed these things and afterwards we heard predictions and other things given which were entirely beyond human comprehension.

"Meiner Clath, a nobleman living in the castle of Boutenbrouch in the duchy of Juliers, had a valet named William who for fourteen years had the torments of a possession by the devil, and when, at the instigation of the devil, he began to get ill, he asked for the curé of St. Gerard as confessor. . . who came to carry out his little part . . . but failed entirely. Seeing him with a swollen throat and discoloured face and with the fear of his suffocating, Judith, wife of Clath and an upright woman, with all in the house, began to pray to God. Immediately there issued from William's mouth, among other odds and ends, the whole of the front part of the trousers of a shepherd, stones, some whole and other broken, small bundles of thread, a peruke such as women are accustomed to use, needles, a piece of the serge jacket of a little boy, and a peacock's feather which William had pulled from the bird's tail eight days before he became ill. Being asked the cause of his trouble he said that he had met a woman near Camphuse who had blown in his face and that his illness was the result of that and nothing else. Some time after he had recovered he contradicted what he had said and confessed that he had been instructed by the devil to say what he had. He added that all those curious things had not been in his stomach but had been put into his throat by the devil despite the fact that he was seen to vomit them.

"On the 18th March, 1566, there occurred a memorable case in Amsterdam, Holland, on which the Chancellor of Gueldres, M. Adrian Nicolas, made a public speech, from which is the following: 'Two months or so ago thirty children of this town began to be strangely disturbed, as if frenzied or mad. At intervals they threw themselves on the ground and for half an hour or an hour at the most this torment lasted. Recovering, they remembered nothing, but thought they had a sleep and the doctors, sorcerers, and exorcists were all equally unable to do any good. During the exorcism the children vomited a number of pins and needles, finger-stalls for sewing, bits of cloth, and of broken jugs and glass, hair and other things. The children didn't always recover from this but had recurrent attacks of it—the unusualness of such a condition causing great astonishment."

Dr. Jean Languis gives the following example in the first book of his *Epitres,* saying they happened in 1539 in Fugenstall, a village in the bishopric of Eysteten, and were sworn to by a large number of witnesses:

"Ulric Neusesser, a ploughman in this village, was greatly troubled by a pain in the side. On an incision being made into the skin by a surgeon an iron nail was removed, but this did not relieve the pain, rather did it increase so that, becoming desperate, the poor man finally committed suicide. Before burying him two surgeons opened his stomach, in front of a number of persons, and in it found some long round pieces of wood, four steel knives, some sharp and pointed, other notched like a saw, two iron rods each nine inches long and a large tuft of hair. One wondered how and by what means this mass of old iron could be collected together into the space of his stomach. There is no doubt that it was the work of the devil who is capable of anything which will maintain a dread of him."

Views of Obsession from Psychical Research

As Nandor Fodor pointed out, obsession in psychiatry means that the mind of the patient is dominated by fixed ideas to which an abnormal mental condition corresponds. In psychical research, obsession is an invasion of the living by a discarnate entity, tending to a complete displacement of normal personality for purposes of selfish gratification that is more or less permanent. The difference between mediumship and obsession is not in principle but in purpose, duration, and (most important) effect. Mediumship, or trance possession, does not interfere with the ordinary course of life, does not bring about a demoralizing dissociation or disintegration; it shows consideration for the medium and its length is limited. After a certain time it ceases automatically and the medium's normal self resumes its sway.

Obsession is always abnormal; it is an accompaniment of a shock, organic lesion, or, as has been observed among psychics, of low morale and weakening will power, induced by an unstable character and debility of health. Once the existence of spirits is admitted, the possibility of obsession cannot be disregarded.

Psychical researcher **James H. Hyslop** in *Contact with the Other World* (1919), observes:

"If we believe in telepathy we believe in a process which makes possible the invasion of a personality by someone at a distance. . . . It is not at all likely that sane and intelligent spirits are the only ones to exert influence from a transcendental world. If they can act on the living there is no reason why others cannot do so as well. The process in either case would be the same; we should have to possess adequate proof that nature puts more restrictions upon ignorance and evil in the next life than in this in order to establish the certainty that mischievous personalities do not or cannot perform nefarious deeds. The objection that such a doctrine makes the world seem evil applies equally to this situation in the present life."

How are we to distinguish obsession from multiple **personality?** It was explained to Hyslop by the "**Imperator**" group of controls of medium **William Stainton Moses** that even for the spirits it is sometimes difficult to state how far the subconscious self of the patient is acting under influence and suggestion from spirits or as a secondary personality. Nevertheless Hyslop claimed to have found a satisfactory method to find out the truth in **cross-reference:**

"I take the patient to a psychic under conditions that exclude from the psychic all normal knowledge of the situation and see what happens. If the same phenomena that occur in the patient are repeated through the medium; if I am able to establish the identity of the personalities affecting the patient; or if I can obtain indubitably supernormal information connecting the patient with the statements made through the psychic, I have reason to regard the mental phenomena observed in the patient as of external origin. In a number of cases, persons whose condition would ordinarily be described as due to hysteria, dual, or multiple personality dementia precox, paranoia, or some other form of mental disturbance, showed unmistakable indications of invasion by foreign and discarnate agencies."

Hyslop tells the readers of his *Life After Death* (1918), "Before accepting such a doctrine, I fought against it for ten years after I was convinced that survival after death was proved. But several cases forced upon me the consideration of the question. The chief interest in such cases is their revolutionary effect in the field of medicine. . . . It is high time for the medical world to wake up and learn something."

William James, shortly before his death, surrendered to the same belief. He wrote:

"The refusal of modern enlightenment to treat obsession as a hypothesis to be spoken of as even possible, in spite of the massive human tradition based on concrete experience in its favor, has always seemed to me a curious example of the power of fashion in things scientific. That the demon theory (not necessarily a devil theory) will have its innings again is to my mind absolutely certain. One has to be 'scientific' indeed to be blind and ignorant enough not to suspect any such possibility."

James was affected by the account of the Thompson-Gifford case published in the *Proceedings* of the American Society for Psychical Research (vol. 3, part 8, 1909). According to the report, F. L. Thompson, a Brooklyn goldsmith, was seized in 1905 with an irresistible impulse to sketch and paint. The style was that of Robert Swain Gifford. The American artist had died six months previously but this fact was unknown to Thompson, who hardly knew of him and, except for a slight taste for sketching in his early years, had never shown artistic talent.

Supposedly, Thompson had visions of scenes of the neighborhood of Gifford's country house and often had the hallucination that he was Gifford himself. He saw a notice of an exhibition of Gifford's paintings. He went in and heard a voice whisper, "You see what I have done. Can you take up and finish my work?" The desire to paint became stronger. Soon it was so overpowering that he was unable to follow his former occupation.

Thompson grew afraid that he was losing his sanity. Two physicians diagnosed the case as paranoia. One of them, without offering to cure it, expressed a desire to watch the progress of the malady. Thompson went to Hyslop for advice, who took him to three different mediums. They all claimed to sense the influence of Gifford, described his character and life and confirmed the vague possibility, which Hyslop wished to investigate, that the case was not the result of mental disorder. As soon as the case was determined to be spirit obsession, a course of treatment was decided upon. Reportedly, Gifford, the spirit entity, was reasoned with and persuaded to desist.

Spirit Obsession and Personality Displacement

If one assumes the possibility of obsession being actually caused by a spirit entity, the importance of such treatment as Hyslop gave Thompson and Gifford seems appropriate. The obsessing spirit entity, if driven out either by strengthened willpower of the victim or by psychotherapeutic means, would logically seek and find another subject, but if it is convinced of the error of its ways, the danger is eliminated. Work of this kind was done in the Temple of Light in Kansas City in 1910. Hyslop was impressed with the importance of this cure and established the James J. Hyslop Foundation for the Treatment of Obsession in New York. Physician **Titus Bull** served as its director.

The systematic practice of curing obsession through such means was soon taken up by Dr. and Mrs. **Carl Wickland** in their Psychopathic Institute of Chicago. The patient was brought to Mrs. Wickland, who operated as a medium. She went into trance. Her controls influenced the obsessing spirit to step into Mrs. Wickland's body. If the obsessor was unwilling it was forced to do so by means known to the controls. Dr. Wickland then began to parley with the spirit, usually ending in convincing the invader that it did a great wrong to its spiritual evolution by strengthening ties to the Earth. The invader usually promised to depart and the patient became normal. Later Wickland moved to California and founded the National Psychological Institute for the Treatment of Obsession. His experiences are chronicled in his book *Thirty Years Among the Dead* (1924).

The Wicklands considered the obsessing entities to be mostly earthbound spirits—spirits of the recently deceased. They do not necessarily mean harm, the Wicklands said, but only wish to enjoy earthly existence again. Some may commit acts of revenge or do other harm, however, and if an occasional evil personality takes control, the obsessed individual could be driven to criminal, insane acts.

Just as the trance control will become perfect by practice, the obsessor will feel more at home in the victim's organism after repeated possession and will settle as permanently as possible, said the Wicklands.

Certain historic records suggest that obsession may attain an epidemic character. The case of the Ursuline Nuns of Loudon in 1632–34 has already been cited. Several of the nuns of the convent, including the mother superior, were seized with violent convulsions, symptoms of catalepsy and demonic possession. Blasphemies and obscenities poured from their mouths, confessed to come from the devil. The priest **Urbain Grandier** was accused of immoralities preceding the outbreak. The devils indicated him as the cause of their troubles. He was burned alive in April 1634.

In February 1874 Franklin B. Evans was executed in Concord, New Hampshire, for the murder of a 12-year-old child. In his confession made just before his execution he said that "for some days before the murder I seemed to be attended continually by one who seemed to bear a human form, urging me on to the deed. At length it became fixed in my mind to take her life."

Hudson Tuttle, in his book *The Arcana of Spiritualism* (1871), describes a suicidal obsession:

"While sitting in a circle at the home of the venerable Dr. Underhill, I was for the time in an almost unconscious state, and recognised the presence of several Indian spirits. The roar of the Cayahoga River over the rapids could be heard in the still evening air, and to my sensitive ear was very distinct. Suddenly I was seized with a desire to rush away to the rapids, and throw myself into the river. . . someone caught hold of me, and aroused me out of the impressible state I was in, so that I gained control of myself. Had the state been more profound, and had I once started, the end might have been different. The desire remained all the evening."

On occasion the obsession might serve a beneficial end. An example is the case of **Lurancy Vennum, Watseka Wonder.** Her obsessors, it was said, were forced out by the spirit of Mary Roff, who had died 18 years earlier in the same city. "Mary Roff" supposedly lived in Lurancy Vennum's body, but haunted the house of her own parents for 16 weeks and convinced everyone of her identity. Her long inhabitation somehow made Vennum's body safe from malicious invasions, and when she finally yielded its control to the returning ego of Lurancy Vennum, the girl's health was mentally and physically reestablished.

As a result of his twenty years' study of obsession as head of the James Hyslop Institute, Titus Bull published in 1932 some conclusions, as follows:

"An obsessing personality is not composed of the soul, mind and will of one disembodied being, but is, in reality, a composite personality made up of many beings. The pivot obsessor, or the one who first impinges upon the sensorium of the mortal, is generally one with little resistance to the suggestions of others. He or she, therefore, becomes an easy prey to those who desire to approach a mortal in this way.

"Some people, moreover, may be born with tendencies which make it easier for them to become victims of mental alterations later in life. . . . There is an influence which can be exerted upon the minds of mortals by ideas embodied in thoughts from their departed ancestors. In other words, some departed ancestors, whenever possible, attempt to mould the lives of those incarnated who are akin. . . . There is a type of mortal whose mind is easily influenced by the stronger minds of the family group. . . . The more clannish the family group, the more likely is this to be true on both sides of the veil. It is, however, not to be considered as spirit obsession in the true sense. . . . The intervention of shock, however, or anything that could upset the nerve balance of a member of such family group, would place him in actual danger of becoming a victim of true spirit obsession. . . . The primary obsessor, in this case, would likely be one who claimed the right by ties of blood, who had no desire to do anything but to keep the mortal in line with family ideals."

According to Bull, obsessors ". . .have three major points of impingement; namely, the base of the brain, the region of the solar plexus and at the center governing the reproductive organs. As there are three major points of impingement, it may be assumed that there can be three composite groups, each starting with a pivot entity. What satisfaction is to be gained this way includes the whole gamut of human emotions."

Objections to the Concept of Spirit Obsession

Much of the evidence for spirit obsession is subjective, based on the observations, feelings, and prejudices of investigators, many of whom have been reputable individuals. However, so far no conclusive evidence has been found that will resolve this question definitively.

The subconscious mind has the ability to weave convincing fantasies of personality, just as novelists create imaginary characters who seem to have lives of their own. Some cases of apparent secondary or multiple personality seem to be a dramatization of the subject's unconscious emotional desires and fears. Children often pretend to be different personalities, while even the effect of a powerful movie portrayal often awakens both conscious and unconscious imitation of personality traits in impressionable viewers.

For a time it was thought that the technique of hypnotic regression, in which a subject's memory is progressively explored into the past and then into apparent former lives, might offer reliable evidence of the continuity of personality from one life to another. However, although there are case histories, the evidence so far is not conclusive.

It may well be discovered that there is no one simple explanation for or against the concept of spirit obsessions, that certain cases may be genuinely spirit obsession, others only subconscious impersonation. The concept of spirit obsession/possession has suffered from the same doubts that have discouraged continued research on spirit communication. Such experiments as the conjuring of **"Philip"** by members of the Toronto Society for Psychical Research have done much to call into question the possibility of investigating spirit **survival** and working with a spirit hypothesis.

Exorcism

Pagan and Christian beliefs in demonic obsession and possession brought about complex rituals of exorcism, designed to drive out the diabolical entities. Although such rituals had virtually fallen into disuse in Christian countries with the more pragmatic materialist philosophy of the twentieth century, they were revived on a startling scale with the occult boom of the 1960s. The theme permeated popular books and movies through the early 1970s and led to a revival of forgotten rituals of exorcism.

Active belief in demonic possession seems to be a causative force in generating apparent cases. Among Pentecostal Christians, who discuss demons and possession regularly from the pulpit and hold periodic exorcism services, cases of possession appear to be in response to the group's belief. Among liberal Christians and conservative groups who do not believe in demon possession, members manifest no symptoms of possible possession.

Sources:

Ebon, Martin, ed. *Exorcism: Fact Not Fiction.* New York: New American Library, 1974.

Huxley, Aldous. *The Devils of Loudon.* London: Chatto & Windus, 1952. Reprint, New York: Harper & Row, 1971.

Hyslop, James H. *Contact with the Other World; The Latest Evidence as to Communication with the Dead.* New York: Century, 1919.

Nicola, John T. *Diabolical Possession and Exorcism.* Rockford, Ill.: TAN Books, 1974.

Oesterreich, T. K. *Possession, Demoniacal and Other.* London: Kegan Paul; New York: R. R. Smith, 1930. Reprint, New Hyde Park, N.Y.: University Books, 1966. Reprinted as *Possession and Exorcism.* New York: Causeway Books, 1974.

Pettiward, Cynthia. *The Case for Possession.* UK: Colin Smythe, 1975.

Sargant, William. *The Mind Possessed: A Physiology of Possession, Mysticism & Faith Healing.* London: Heinemann, 1973. Reprint, Philadelphia: J. B. Lippincott, 1974.

Shepard, Leslie. *How to Protect Yourself Against Black Magic & Witchcraft.* New York: Citadel, 1978.

Walker, Sheila S. *Ceremonial Spirit Possession in Africa and Afro-Americana.* Leiden, Netherlands: E. J. Brill; New York: Humanities Press, 1972. Wickland, Carl A., et al. *Thirty Years among the Dead.* Los Angeles: National Psychological Institute, 1924.

Occidental Society of Metempiric Analysis

Founded in 1977, to investigate all types of anomalistic or "metempiric" phenomena (unexplained occurrences ignored or discounted by scientists) such as sightings of **UFOs,** space aliens, **ghosts,** and "Bigfoot." The society maintains a speakers bureau, museum, and charitable program, and compiles statistics. It maintains a library of 1,500 volumes on metempirical, **occult,** and UFO topics and issues a periodical, *Beacon,* semiannually. The society can be contacted at its headquarters, 32055 Hwy. 24E, Simla, CO 80835.

Occult

General term (derived from Latin *occultus, occulere,* to hide; the opposite of *apocalypse,* that which is revealed). The word has come to denote that which is hidden from the uninitiated, which is imperceptible by normal senses, and thus refers to various magical and divinatory beliefs and practices, beginning with **astrology, tarot, palmistry, numerology** and other divinatory arts and especially including various forms of spirit contact—**Spiritualism** (and the various forms of mediumship), **magic,** and **witchcraft.** It also applies to specific practices such as the **prediction** of the future, exploring past lives (**reincarnation**), casting spells, and psychokinesis (mind over matter).

The word exists as a derogatory label tending to denigrate and marginalize those against whom it is used. Those interested in the paranormal have often taken pains to isolate selected areas of paranormal activity and separate them from other areas, which are left to the "occult." Modern practitioners have also taken the opportunity offered by the relatively open context of contemporary society to attempt the recovery of classically occult terms such as witchcraft and astrology. The New Age movement, a contemporary phase of the life of the occult community, has allowed a significant revamping of the occult. Divinatory practices such as astrology and the tarot have been redefined as counseling methodologies, and Wiccans have joined together to denounce anti-witchcraft activities as religious bigotry.

In ancient times, it was believed that apparent deviations from natural law involved mysterious and miraculous "supernatural" or occult (i.e., hidden) laws, deriving from gods, invisible entities, or the souls of the dead. The rituals of magic were designed to evoke entities and spirits, to ward off misfortune, or to perform actions in defiance of natural law, such as obtaining knowledge of distant or future events, causing injury or death to one's enemies, or securing sudden wealth (usually in the form of gold). In most tribal cultures, shamans or similar practitioners claimed the specialized ability to work magic, especially as relating to healing the sick or obtaining useful information.

Modern Spiritualism was an attempt to substantiate the ancient belief in the continued existence of personality after death and the evolution of the individual soul to perfection, a belief challenged by modern worldviews. The **Spiritism** inaugurated by **Allan Kardec** is a form of Spiritualism with an emphasis on reincarnation. Both Spiritualism and Spiritism are essentially religious movements, endorsing the miracles cited in the Bible and citing continuing paranormal phenomena as evidence of survival.

In pre-modern cultures occultism was an integral part of a religious worldview deriving from the mystery, wonder, and fearfulness of the environment in which human beings found themselves. By the Middle Ages, the occult had been separated from its religious base and competed with the dominant religious belief and practice. The magic spells and rituals of the Middle Ages contain popular practices of pre-Christian religions in the Mediterranean Basin.

One's opinion of the validity of the occult and the meaning of claimed paranormal phenomena depends in large part upon one's philosophical or religious viewpoint. From the early nineteenth century on, the successes of science and technology in achieving apparent miracles led to the widespread adoption of a materialist view of life and natural law, and to some extent encouraged the growth of agnosticism and atheism. Both the irreligious and those with a religion informed by the findings of the new sciences often ridiculed simplistic and literal belief in biblical teachings, the creation story in the book of Genesis being a particular target. They disparaged the accounts of scientifically impossible events in sacred texts and publicized the many instances of the abuse of power by religious authorities, vividly illustrated by the often violent suppression of heresies and blood-thirsty religious wars.

In the twentieth century, liberal Christianity has tended to play down the question of miraculous phenomena, although conservative voices still cite persuasive evidence that such miracles still occur. At the same time worldviews not so dependent on either a personal deity and/or a law-abiding universe have emerged. Many scientists have argued that what were formerly thought of as "natural laws" were imposed upon nature as observers made note of regularities. Such a worldview leaves room for spontaneous, supernatural, or miraculous occurrences.

Belief has always appeared to be a powerful creative factor in occult practice, and it is not impossible that even initial fraud could sometimes be a stimulating factor in producing paranormal phenomena by "priming the pump," so to speak. Ancient religions sometimes used mechanical contrivances to simulate divine power, rather like religious conjuring tricks.

Many have argued that the reputed power of prayer may be more closely connected with the creative power of the praying individual rather than derived from the action of God (or the gods). Prayers to Eastern or Western deities appear equally to produce results. The mental state appears to be a relevant factor. Closely related is the willpower of the magical practitioner, which again has some relevance to the mystical concept of concentration and **meditation** being preliminaries to the manifestations of paranormal phenomena.

At a secular level, psychical researchers and parapsychologists have attempted to bring scientific method into the investigation of claims of the paranormal, attempting to extract the paranormal subject from any religious context. Such scientific endeavors may in many ways be an essential step in the learning process, but sometimes tend to bypass the possible religious dimension and ignore the broader aspects of the meaning and purpose of life and the interpretation of natural phenomena. The clinical atmosphere of a parapsychology laboratory, with its scientific controls, specialized jargon, and mathematical evaluation, as has been repeatedly noted, tends to remove the paranormal from a natural setting.

Sources:

Crow, W. B. *A History of Magic, Witchcraft, and Occultism.* London: Aquarian Press, 1968. Reprint, London: Abacus, 1972.

Freedland, Nat. *The Occult Explosion.* New York: George Putnam's Sons; London: Michael Joseph, 1972.

Godwin, John. *Occult America.* Garden City, N.Y.: Doubleday, 1972.

Gratton-Guinness, Ivor. *Psychical Research: A Guide to Its History, Principles & Practices.* London: Aquarian Press, 1982.

James, William. *The Varieties of Religious Experience.* London, 1902.

Rhine, J. B., and Associates. *Parapsychology From Duke to FRNM.* Durham, N.C.: Parapsychological Press, 1965.

Thomas, Keith. *Religion and the Decline of Magic.* New York: Charles Scribner's Sons, 1971.

Underhill, Evelyn. *Mysticism: A Study in the Nature and Development of Man's Spiritual Consciousness.* London: Metheun, 1911.

Waite, Arthur E. *The Book of Ceremonial Magic.* London: William Rider & Son, 1911. Reprint, New Hyde Park, N.Y.: University Books, 1961. Reprint, New York: Causeway Books, 1973.

Wilson, Colin. *The Occult.* London: Hodder & Stoughton; New York: Random House, 1971. Reprint, New York: Vintage Books, 1973. Reprint, London: Mayflower, 1973.

Occult Americana (Magazine)

Bimonthly magazine published during the 1970s that included articles, interviews, and other material relating to **occultism** and **psi** phenomena. It was issued from Painesville, Ohio.

Occultism

A collective term for the various doctrines, theories, ideas, and principles believed to underlie and hold together the practices of **magic,** and related topics such as **alchemy, demonology, ghosts, poltergeists, prediction,** psychic powers, **spells,** and **Spiritualism.** The term "the **occult"** is often used synonymously with "occultism." The term is most frequently used by those who oppose the existence of magic or the work of its practitioners. It is sometimes viewed as a derogatory label, and many involved in occultism have preferred other labels such as **New Age.**

Occult Observer (Magazine)

British journal first published May 1949 by **Michael Houghton.** Houghton was a well-known occultist and proprietor of the

Atlantis Book Shop. The journal failed to find its audience and ceased publication after completion of one volume.

The Occult Review

A journal dedicated to psychic and **occult** topics. *The Occult Review* was a British monthly journal published in London beginning in 1877 and edited by **Ralph Shirley.** In September 1933, its title was changed briefly to *The London Forum.* From January 1936 to Christmas 1948, it resumed the title *Occult Review,* but in 1949 it changed again to *Rider's Review,* after which it soon ceased publication.

Occult Studies Foundation See MetaScience Foundation

Ochorowicz, Julien (1850–1917)

Lecturer in psychology at the University of Lemberg, co-director from 1907 of the Institut Général Psychologique of Paris, and distinguished psychical researcher. He was born in Radzyn, Poland, on February 23, 1850, and educated at the University of Warsaw.

The **medium Eusapia Palladino** was his guest from November 1893 until January 1894 in Warsaw. Ochorowicz's conclusions did not favor the spirit hypothesis and he expressed his conviction that the phenomena were due to a "fluidic action" and were performed at the expense of the medium's own powers and those of the persons present.

The mediumship of **Stanislawa Tomczyk** was discovered by Ochorowicz. In his experiments with her, he achieved conspicuous success in **psychic photography,** having photographed what he believed was an etheric hand on the film, rolled together and enclosed in a bottle. Tomczyk was also successful in raising and suspending small objects in the air without contact with her hands. In 1911, Ochorowicz was awarded a prize of 1,000 francs by the Comité d'Etude de Photographie Transcendental for his experiments. A similar prize was awarded to him by the Academie des Sciences de Paris.

Ochorowicz was an honorary member of the **Society for Psychical Research,** London, the **American Society for Psychical Research,** and other societies in Hungary and **Germany.** He was author of over one hundred books, papers, and articles on psychology, philosophy, and **psychical research.** He died in Warsaw, **Poland,** on May 1, 1917.

Sources:

Ochorowicz, Julien. *Mediumistic Phenomena.* N.p., 1913.

———. *Mental Suggestion.* New York: The Humbolt Publishing, 1891.

———. *Psychology and Medicine.* N.p., 1916.

———. *Psychology, Pedagogics, and Ethics.* N.p., 1917.

Oculomancy

An obscure system of identifying thieves by the turning of their eyes when associated with certain ceremonies.

Od (Odic Force) (or Odyle)

The term first used by **Baron Karl von Reichenbach** to denote the subtle effluence that he claimed emanated from every substance in the universe, particularly from the stars and planets, and from **crystals,** magnets, and the human body. The term "od" was derived from Odin, the Norse deity, indicating a power that permeated the whole of nature. The name "od" was retained by Dr. John Ashburner (1816–1878) in his translation of Reichenbach's writings, but another translator, William Gregory (1803–1858), substituted "odyle," probably hoping it would sound more scientific than "od."

Od or odyle was perceptible to **sensitives,** in whom it produced vague feelings of heat or cold, according to the substance from which it radiated. A sufficiently sensitive person might perceive the odic light, a clear flame of definite color, issuing from the human fingertips, the poles of the magnet, various metals, crystals and chemicals, and seen over new graves. The colors varied with each substance; thus silver and gold had a white flame; cobalt, a blue; copper and iron, a red.

The English mesmerists speedily applied Reichenbach's methods to their own sensitives, with results that surpassed their expectations. These observations were confirmed by experiments with persons in perfect health. Prof. D. Endlicher of Vienna saw on the poles of an electromagnet unsteady flames forty inches high, exhibiting numerous colors, and ending in a luminous smoke, which rose to the ceiling and illuminated it. The experiments were controlled by Ashburner and Gregory.

According to the sources from which the energy proceeded, Reichenbach, a chemist, employed the following nomenclature: crystallod, electrod, photod, thermod, and so on. He claimed that this peculiar force also existed in the rays of the sun and the moon, in animal and human bodies. The force could be conducted to distances yet unascertained by all solid and liquid bodies, bodies may be charged with od, or od may be transferred from one body to another. Reichenbach believed this transference was apparently affected by contact. But mere proximity, without contact, was sufficient to produce the charge, although to a lesser degree. The mouth, the hands, the forehead, and the skull were the main parts of the body in which the od force manifested.

Reichenbach claimed that the odic tension varied during the day; it diminished with hunger, increased after a meal, and also diminished at sunset. He insisted that the odic flame was a material something, that it could be affected by breath or a current of air.

The thoroughness of Reichenbach's many experiments made an impression on the public mind, though his colleagues saw significant methodological flaws in his work. The objections of James Braid, a British surgeon, who at this time advanced his theory of suggestion, were ignored by the protagonists of od. Years later when **Spiritualism** had established itself in America, there remained a group of "rational" defenders of the movement, who attributed the phenomena of Spiritualism as well as those of **poltergeist** to the action of odylic force.

Others, such as Samuel Guppy, regarded the so-called "spirit" intelligences producing the manifestations as compounded of odic vapors emanating from the **medium,** and probably connected with an all-pervading thought-atmosphere—an idea sufficiently like the "cosmic fluid" of the early magnetists.

Reichenbach's odic force clearly had possible relevance to **psychical research,** and in 1883 the **Society for Psychical Research** in London formed a committee to report on "Reichenbach Phenomena." The committee's first report was published in the society's *Proceedings* and contributions on the subject also appeared from time to time in the *Proceedings* and the *Journal* of the Society for Psychical Research.

Reichenbach's experiments with od made an interesting comparison with the phenomenon of the human **aura** reported by **Walter J. Kilner, Oscar Bagnall** and others, and also with the research of **Wilhelm Reich** and his concept of **orgone** energy.

Sources:

Bagnall, Oscar. *The Origin and Properties of the Human Aura.* New Hyde Park, N.Y.: University Books, 1970.

Kilner, Walter J. *The Human Aura.* New Hyde Park, N.Y.: University Books, 1965.

Reich, Wilhelm. *The Discovery of the Orgone.* 2 vols. New York, 1948.

Reichenbach, Karl von. *Letters on Od and Magnetism.* Translated by F. D. O'Byrne. 1926. Reprinted as *The Odic Force: Let-*

ters on Od and Magnetism. New Hyde Park, N.Y.: University Books, 1968.

———. *Physico-Physiological Researches on the Dynamics of Magnetism, Heat, Light, Crystallization, and Chemism, in their relations to Vital Force.* Translated by John Ashburner. London, 1851.

———. *Researches on Magnetism, Electricity, Heat, Light, Crystallization and Chemical Attraction, in their relations to the Vital Force.* Translated by William Gregory. 1850. Reprint, New Hyde Park, N.Y.: University Books, 1974.

O'Donnell, Elliott (1872–1965)

Author of popular books on **occult** subjects. Born February 27, 1872, in England, he claimed descent from Irish chieftains of ancient times, including Niall of the Nine Hostages (the King Arthur of Irish folklore) and Red Hugh, who fought the English in the sixteenth century. O'Donnell was educated at Clifton College, Bristol, England, and Queen's Service Academy, Dublin, Ireland. He had a psychic experience at the age of five, in a house where he saw a nude elemental figure covered with spots. As a young man, he claimed he was half strangled by a mysterious phantom in Dublin.

In later life he became a **ghost** hunter, but first he traveled in America, working on a range in Oregon and becoming a policeman during the Chicago Railway Strike of 1894. Returning to England, he worked as a schoolmaster and trained for the theater. He served in the British army in World War I, and later acted on stage and in movies.

His first book, written in his spare time, was a psychic thriller titled *For Satan's Sake* (1904). From this point onward, he became a writer. He wrote several popular novels but specialized in what were claimed as true stories of ghosts and **hauntings.** These were immensely popular, but his flamboyant style and amazing stories suggest that he embroidered fact with a romantic flair for fiction.

As he became known as an authority on the supernatural, he was called upon as a ghost hunter. He also lectured and broadcast (radio and television) on the paranormal in Britain and the United States. In addition to his more than 50 books, he wrote scores of articles and stories for national newspapers and magazines. He claimed "I have investigated, sometimes alone, and sometimes with other people and the press, many cases of reputed hauntings. I believe in ghosts but am not a spiritualist."

The O'Donnells were reputed to have a **banshee**—the wailing ghost that heralds a death, and O'Donnell wrote the first book devoted entirely to the subject. It is not known whether his own passing evoked this phantom, but he lived to the age of ninety-three years. He died on May 8, 1965. His entry in the British publication *Who's Who,* listed his hobbies as "investigating queer cases, inventing queer games, and frightening crooks with the Law." His books include: *The Banshee* (1926), *Ghosts with a Purpose* (1952), *Spiritualism Explained* (1917), *Strange Cults & Secret Societies of Modern London* (1934), *Werewolves* (1912), *For Satan's Sake* (1904), *Unknown Depths* (1905), *Some Haunted Houses* (1908), *Haunted Houses of London* (1909), *Reminiscences of Mrs. E. M. Ward* (1910), *The Meaning of Dreams* (1911), *Byways of Ghostland* (1911), *Scottish Ghost Stories* (1912), *The Sorcery Club* (1912), *Animal Ghosts* (1913), *Ghostly Phenomena* (1913), *Haunted Highways and Byways* (1914), *The Irish Abroad* (1915), *Twenty Years' Experience as a Ghost Hunter* (1916), *The Haunted Man* (1917), *Fortunes* (1918), *Haunted Places in England* (1919), *Menace of Spiritualism* (1920), *More Haunted Houses of London* (1920), *Ghosts, Helpful and Harmful* (1926), *Strange Disappearances* (1927), *Strange Sea Mysteries* (1927), *Confessions of a Ghost Hunter* (1928), *Fatal Kisses* (1929), *Famous Curses* (1929), *Great Thames Mysteries* (1929), *Rooms of Mystery* (1931), *Ghosts of London* (1932), *The Devil in the Pulpit* (1932), *Family Ghosts* (1934), *Spookerisms; Twenty-five Weird Happenings* (1936) *Haunted Churches* (1939), *Dead Riders* (1953), *Phantoms of the Night* (1956), *Haunted Waters,* and *Trees of Ghostly Dread* (1958).

Odor of Sanctity

Perfume said to be exhaled by Christian saints, even after death. The idea that sin has a disagreeable odor and holiness a sweet perfume occurs in Romance literature and reflects folk beliefs of medieval times. Over the centuries, the idea of the sweet smell has been tied to that of the incorruption of the body of some saints.

In Sir Thomas Malory's *Morte d'Arthur* (translated as *History of Prince Arthur*), the death of the wicked Sir Corsabrin is described as follows: "Then they smote off the head of sir Corsabrin, and therewithal came a stench out of the body, when the soul departed." And in contrast, the death of the noble Sir Launcelot is described: "When sir Bors and his fellows came to sir Launcelot's bed, they found him stark dead, and the sweetest savour about him that ever they did smell."

St. Benedicta (ca. 1643) claimed that angels had perfumes as various as those of flowers; Benedicta herself was supposed to exhale the sweet perfume of the love of God. The body of St. Clare (660 C.E.), abbot of Ferriol, exhaled a sweet odor after death, which pervaded St. Blandina's church. When St. Hubert of Britanny (714 C.E.) died, the whole province was said to be filled with sweet perfume. St. Casimir, Patron of Poland, died in 1483, and when his body was exhumed one hundred and twenty years later, it exhaled a sweet smell.

Odyssey

Odyssey, the leading New Age periodical in South Africa, was founded in 1977 by Jill Iggulden as a networking organ for the emerging New Age scene in the country. Iggulden continued as editor until June 1984 when the magazine was turned over to Rose de la Hunt, then the part-time leader of a small New Age center in the Cape Town area. In August 1986 the editorial offices moved into a new building in suburban Wynberg called The Wellstead. Within a short time, The Wellstead emerged as the center of the New Age Movement in the Cape region and offered a full range of programs. It is generally the first stopping place of spiritual teachers visiting the Cape. At first, the magazine was published informally with a staff consisting only of de la Hunt and one other. In addition, for several years the pair headed the annual "Health for Africa" holistic health conferences, though these were discontinued in the early 1990s. Then in 1994, de la Hunt was asked to take over the Cape Town Mind Body Spirit Festival, the largest New Age gathering in South Africa. She revamped the festival as the Art of Living Festival, now presented biannually in Cape Town. *Odyssey* has emerged as a 60-page periodical featuring articles of general interest to the post-New Age community, ranging from **channelling** and **crystals** to the wide variety of holistic health practices. South African metaphysical groups are regularly highlighted and their leaders and teachers profiled. In addition, a running list of up-coming events are included. *Odyssey* is published bimonthly. On alternate months, a second periodical, *Link-Up,* is issued as a newsletter carrying announcements of upcoming events and ongoing services offered by various esoteric/metaphysical and holistic health organizations. *Link-Up* is issued in six regional editions specific to the different areas of the country. The Wellstead and the editorial offices of *Odyssey* and *Link-Up* are at 1 Wellington Ave., Wynberg 7800, South Africa. Its website can be found at http://www.odyssey.org.za/.

Sources:

de la Hunt, Rose. "Odyssey Comes of Age." *Odyssey* 22, no.4 (August/September 1998): 2.

Oenomancy

An ancient system of **divination** based on interpretations of the patterns made by wine that had been poured out as an offering to the gods.

Oesterreich, Traugott Konstantin (1880–1949)

German professor of philosophy, an authority on religious philosophy, and one of the first modern scientists in Germany to declare publicly his belief in psychic phenomena. He taught philosophy at Tübingen University in 1910 and was appointed professor in 1922. He somehow survived in Nazi Germany, in spite of his Jewish wife and his anti-militarist views, although he was dismissed from his post in 1933, reinstated in 1945 and again forced into retirement on reduced pension soon afterward.

He was originally skeptical of psychic phenomena, and in the fourth volume of Friedrich Ueberweg's *Geschichte der Philosophie* he referred to **Baron Schrenck-Notzing,** pioneer of investigations into **materialization** phenomena, as the dupe of tricksters. In private correspondence with Oesterreich, Schrenck-Notzing protested at this sweeping charge and submitted his entire literary and photographic material on **Eva C.,** the **medium.** Oesterreich became interested, investigated the mediumships of **Maria Silbert** and **Willi Schneider,** and finally became convinced of the reality of such phenomena.

In 1921 he published two books: *Grundbegriffe der Parapsychologie* and *Der Okkultismus im modernen Weltbild;* and in the latter title testified to materializations and **telekinesis** as facts. He also presented his revised conclusions in Ueberweg's *Geschichte der Philosophie* published in 1923. His book *Weltbilder der Gegenwart* contained further contributions to psychic science. As an active and thorough psychical researcher, Oesterreich also published a number of scientific papers and monographs supporting psychic science.

His classic work, however, was a study of psychic **obsession and possession,** *Possession: Demoniacal and other among Primitive Races, in Antiquity, the Middle Ages, and Modern Times,* translated into English by D. Ibberson from the German publication of 1921. This is a detailed study of possession and multiple **personality** from earliest times onward. For many years it failed to secure other than a highly specialized readership, but following the 1966 reprint by University Books, it attracted the attention of William Peter Blatty, who derived much of the background material for his book, *The Exorcist* (1971), from it. After the movie of the book, there was a new wave of interest in demonic possession and **exorcism,** and Oesterreich's book was again reprinted by various publishers, sometimes under variant titles such as *Possession and Exorcism* and *Possession and Obsession.*

He died in 1949. His wife Maria wrote a biography of him that was published in 1954.

Sources:

Oesterreich, Maria. *Traugott Konstantin Oesterreich—Lebenswerk und Lebensschicksal.* N.p., 1954.

Oesterreich, T. K. *Die Bessessenheit.* English ed. as *Possession: Demoniacal and Other among Primitive Races, in Antiquity, the Middle Ages, and Modern Times.* Translated by D. Ibberson. New Hyde Park, N.Y.: University Books, 1966.

———. *Occultism and Modern Science.* New York: McBride, 1923.

———. *Occultism of the Present Day.* London, 1922.

Office of Paranormal Investigations

The Office of Paranormal Investigations (OPI) is an organization focused upon scientific research on spontaneous occurrences of psi phenomena, an area abandoned by most contemporary parapsychologists who concentrate on repeatable laboratory results. Of primary concern are sightings of ghosts, hauntings, and poltergeists, for which the office provides consulting services, especially to people who have been disturbed by such phenomena occurring in their homes or place of business. Though aware of the problems of proving scientifically the phenomena with which it is primarily concerned, OPI personnel attempt to assist people in understanding what is happening and if possible take steps to remove it. Most on-site investigations occur in the San Francisco Bay area, but OPI associates are located across the United States.

Founder and head of OPI is Lloyd Auerbach, best known for his writings, including three books, *ESP, Hauntings and Poltergeists*(1986), *Psychic Dreaming* (1991), and *Mind Over Matter* (1996), and his regular column in **FATE** magazine. Auerbach is a graduate of Northwestern University (B.A., 1978) and JFK University (M.S. in parapsychology, 1981). Since 1983 he has been an adjunct professor at JFK University. He served as the president of the California Society for Psychical Research for four years (1988–1992), and in 1989 he became the president of the Assembly of American Magicians (the first person to serve as the head of both a professional magicians' association and a parapsychological research organization). He founded the Office of Paranormal Investigations in 1989.

OPI publishes a monthly newsletter, *Invisible Signals.* It maintains an Internet site at http://www.mindreader.com/. The office has no physical facilities but may be contacted through its website or telephone hotline.

Sources:

Auerbach, Lloyd. *ESP, Hauntings and Poltergeists.* New York: Warner Books, 1986.

———. *Mind Over Matter.* New York: Kennsington Books, 1996.

———. *Psychic Dreaming.* New York: Warner Books, 1991.

Office of Paranormal Investigations. http://www.mindreader.com/. May 20, 2000.

Official UFO (Magazine)

Newsstand magazine, published nine times per year during the 1980s, that included articles, photographs, charts, and other information relating to extraterrestrial phenomena.

Ohio Sky Watcher

Former quarterly publication of Ohio UFO Investigators League, Inc. It included news and discussion of **UFO** sightings and other mysteries such as **monsters** and the **Bermuda Triangle.**

Ointment, Witches'

It was believed in medieval times that the wonders performed by witches such as changing themselves into animals or being transported through the air (i.e., **transvection**) were accomplished by anointing themselves with a potent salve. As ointments had been used in the ancient world as a means of inducing visions, many believe that a similar ointment may account for the hallucinations the witches may have experienced.

At the beginning of the fifteenth century, a trial was held near Bern, Switzerland, where the accused were said to have drained the juices of stolen children to make an ointment for flying. *The Witches Hammer* stated that the flying ointment was made "at the devil's instruction" from "the limbs of children, particularly of those whom they have killed before baptism." Francis Bacon stated: "The *ointment,* that witches use, is reported to be made of the *fat* of *children,* digged out of their *graves;* of the *juices* of *smallage, wolfebane,* and *cinque foil,* mingled with the *meal* of fine *wheat:* but I suppose that the soporiferous medicines are likest to do it, which are *hen-bane, hemlock, mandrake, moonshade, tobacco, opium, saffron, poplar leaves,* etc."

Other recipes that have been handed down as flying ointments for witches include the following: 1) Parsley, water of aconite, poplar leaves and soot 2) Water parsnip, sweet flag, cinquefoil, bat's blood, deadly nightshade and oil 3) Baby's fat, juice of water parsnip, aconite, cinquefoil, deadly nightshade and soot.

It should be noted that such poisonous **drugs** as aconite, hemlock, and belladonna, absorbed through the skin, would probably cause mental confusion, dizziness, irregular heart action, and shortness of breath. These effects might give the sensation of flying through the air, although **witchcraft** authorities during the great witch hunts have claimed that witches did actually travel in the air.

Sources:

Krammer, Heinrich, and James Sprenger. *The Malleus Maleficarum (Witches Hammer)*. Translated by Montague Summers, 1928. Reprint, New York: Dover Publications, 1971.

Robbins, Rossell Hope. *The Encyclopedia of Witchcraft and Demonology*. New York: Crown Publishers, 1959.

Russell, Jeffrey Burton. *Witchcraft in the Middle Ages*. Ithaca, N.Y.: Cornell University Press, 1972.

Ojai Foundation

A **New Age** foundation founded by Dr. Joan Halifax in Ojai, California. It was situated on 40 acres of former semi-wilderness land in the Upper Ojai Valley, some 80 miles from Los Angeles. Through the 1980s, the foundation offered retreats with well-known healers, scientists, artists, and others from various religious traditions and spiritual disciplines. At the end of the 1980s the foundation ran into a zoning quarrel with the community that eventually led to its demise.

O'Key Sisters, Jane and Elizabeth (ca. 1838)

Two somnambules or hypnotized subjects of **John Elliotson,** an early British experimenter in **animal magnetism.** The two girls were supposedly put into a **trance** by passes on the part of Elliotson and two different states induced: a condition of coma with insensibility and lack of consciousness, and ecstatic delirium in which they spoke, sometimes making clairvoyant predictions and also being subject to the operator's suggestions. In the ecstatic condition, which occasionally lasted for days, one of the girls claimed to be able to see with the back of her hand.

After many "successful" demonstrations, Elliotson one day met with a complete failure, which excited his opponents to accusations of imposture on the part of the girls. Elliotson was stigmatized as a weak and credulous man. Eventually he was obliged to resign his position as physician at University College Hospital, London. However, Elliotson persisted with his experiments and published his conclusions in an appendix to his textbook *Human Physiology* (1840) in which he detailed his further experiments with the O'Key sisters.

Oki, Masahiro (1921–)

Idiosyncratic teacher-healer-philosopher, originator of a very individual system of **yoga.** Oki was born in Korea in 1921, and brought up in a strictly religious environment. His early education familiarized him with **martial arts** and **Zen.** He was influenced by the politician Ottama Daisojo, who played an important part in the history of Burma (now Myanmar). Oki asked him about such great individuals as Buddha, Christ, and Muhammed, and their spiritual eminence. Daisojo explained that all three practiced something called yoga, which he would understand through later experience. At the time Oki was only eight years old.

As a young man, he studied at a military academy and also took a brief course in medicine before becoming a soldier. He became a spy for the Korean government in 1939, after **Japan** had seized areas on the China coast. Oki's task was to enter parts of southern Asia and cooperate with Islamic independence movements. As a cover for this, he went to Tibet to train as a lama. At that time, this was a purely utilitarian move without religious significance.

His religious experience was later stimulated when he was arrested on an assignment in Iran and thrown in jail, with a leg chain and an iron ball. He shared a cell with an older man who, although facing a death sentence, was always serene and peaceful. Oki himself was scared that he would be executed, so he became a pupil of the older man, learning from his chanting, **meditation,** and religious observances that gave him serenity. Later, both men were freed when a raiding party liberated the jail. Oki's first teacher turned out to be Hoseini-shi, father of the Ayatollah Khomeini, the former spiritual leader of Islam in Iran.

After the war was over, Oki concentrated on earning a living. He ran a medical clinic and also operated a profitable smuggling business between Japan, Korea, and Taiwan. Becoming dissatisfied with material success, he joined a Japanese peace movement, but was soon disillusioned. He decided to become a Zen monk. He divorced his wife, built six orphanages, gave away the remainder of his money, and joined a monastery. After some time he grew restless in the monastery and concluded that he should do something more practical than simply purifying himself.

United Nations Educational, Scientific, and Cultural Organization (UNESCO) officials employed him to work for peace in India and Pakistan, where he lectured, practiced medicine, and taught practical skills in housing and food production. He stayed at the ashram of Mahatma Gandhi in India, where the concept of yoga in relation to practical life matured in Oki's experience.

During 1960 he worked as a researcher for a Japanese newspaper, traveling Europe and North America and lecturing on Zen to religious groups. In 1962 the Buddhist Society of America invited him to teach yoga. Oki also taught in Brazil before returning to Japan, where he founded the International Oki Yoga Institute in Mishima in 1967. He has since authored a number of books on **healing,** mastered thirty-two martial arts and taught them to students from all walks of life, and has given private lectures on the **Oki yoga** system to the Japanese royal family.

Oki has been criticized for violence in his teaching sessions by people who are unaware of the traditional use of a training stick in the old Zen tradition. However, his success with students and his uncompromisingly individualistic attitude to teaching and living rank him as a kind of Japanese Gurdjieff.

Sources:

"Behind the Scenes of Oki Yoga." *East West Journal* 15, 9 (September 1985).

Oki Yoga

The highly individual system of Japanese teacher-healer-philosopher **Masahiro Oki.** Oki Yoga is a unique blend of traditional Indian **hatha yoga** with **Zen meditation,** dancing, physical games, **martial arts,** and chanting. The training method emphasizes balance between opposites: tension and relaxation, heat and cold, stillness and movement. Oki's system of *shusei taiso* or corrective exercise through yoga postures stemmed from his detailed observations of the sleeping postures of students. He claims that during sleep people take postures that attempt to correct their physical imbalance.

The headquarters of the Oki system is The International Oki Yoga Institute in Mishima, Japan; there is another full-time center in Shimoda, on the Izu peninsula. There are over 250 centers throughout Japan, and others scattered around the world in North and South America, Europe, and Australia.

Olcott, Henry Steel (1832–1907)

Joint founder with **Helena Petrovna Blavatsky** and **William Q. Judge** of the **Theosophical Society.** Olcott was born August 2, 1832, in Orange, New Jersey, where his father had a farm. At the age of twenty-six, Olcott was associate agricultural editor of the *New York Tribune* and traveled abroad to study European farming methods. Olcott served in the Civil War and afterward became a special commissioner with the rank of colonel. In 1868, he was admitted to the New York bar. In 1878, he was commissioned by the president to report on trade relations between the U.S. and **India.**

His first contact with psychic phenomena was in 1874. The *New York Daily Graphic* had assigned him to investigate the phenomena of the **Eddy brothers** in Vermont. He spent ten weeks at the Chittenden farm and came away convinced of the genuineness of the phenomena he witnessed. The fifteen articles in which he summarized his experiences began his career as a leader in the psychic community.

His next opportunity was the Holmes scandal, when the **materialization mediums Mr. and Mrs. Nelson Holmes** were accused of **fraud.** Olcott sifted through all the records, collected new affidavits, and concluded that as the evidence of fraudulent mediumship was very conflicting, the mediums should be tested. After conducting tests, as with the Eddy brothers, he affirmed his belief in their powers.

Olcott related accounts of his investigations to the spiritualist community in his book, *People from the Other World.* Included was an account of his experiences with the medium **Elizabeth Compton,** who allegedly was able to accomplish an entire **dematerialization.** While some praised his work, as a whole, the book was heavily criticized. Among his harshest critics was **D. D. Home,** who denounced Olcott's account in his *Lights and Shadows of Spiritualism* as "the most worthless and dishonest" book.

As a result of his writing on the the Eddy brothers and the Holmeses, Olcott soon became known as a person aware of the spiritualist scene. When the professors of the Imperial University of St. Petersburg decided to make a scientific investigation of **Spiritualism,** they asked Olcott and his associate Helena Petrovna Blavatsky, who had worked with the Eddys, to select the best American medium they could recommend. Their choice fell on **Henry Slade,** later to become known as one of the most notorious of frauds.

Enter Madame Blavatsky

The association between Olcott and Blavatsky began at their meeting at the Chittenden farm. Blavatsky had identified with the Spiritualists but she broke with the Spiritualist movement soon after the Theosophical Society was founded in December 1875. Olcott was elected president; he worked at founding and organizing the society worldwide. The society was firmly established in New York by the time of the Blavatsky exposure by the **Society for Psychical Research.**

Nobody witnessed more apparent Theosophic episodes through Blavatsky than Olcott. In those early days, she professed to have been controlled by the spirit **"John King."** She first specialized in precipitated writing, independent drawing, and supernormal duplication of letters and other things (among them a $1,000 banknote in the presence of Olcott and the Hon. J. L. Sullivan). Reportedly, the duplicate mysteriously dissolved in a drawer.

Olcott was convinced that Blavatsky could produce such illusions by hypnotic suggestion. Blavatsky once disappeared from his presence in a closed room and appeared again a short time afterward from nowhere. This admission called into question Olcott's observations and records and his testifying in "good faith" to the appearance of Mahatmas and to the souvenirs they left behind.

In 1878, Olcott and Blavatsky sailed for Bombay with a brief stop in London. **A. P. Sinnett** in his book *The Early Days of Theosophy in Europe* suggested that the manners of Blavatsky and Olcott caused offense in polite society and the beginning of the unfriendly attitude of the Society for Psychical Research was to be traced to a society meeting at which Olcott made a speech in his worst style.

The Blavatsky exposure in 1895 left Olcott's reputation damaged. According to Dr. **Richard Hodgson,** who compiled the Society for Psychical Research report, Olcott's statements were unreliable either owing to peculiar lapses of memory or to extreme deficiency in the faculty of observation. Hodgson could not place the slightest value upon Olcott's evidence. But he stated definitely also: "Some readers may be inclined to think that Col. Olcott must himself have taken an active and deliberate part in the fraud, and been a partner with Blavatsky in the conspiracy. Such, I must emphatically state, is not my own opinion." On the other hand Vsevolod Solovyoff in *A Modern Priestess of Isis* called Olcott a "liar and a knave in spite of his stupidity."

For his critics, a problematic instance of psychic phenomena is the story of the **William Eglinton** letter. From the boat *Vega,* the letter was claimed to be "astrally" conveyed first to Bombay, then with the superimposed script of Blavatsky carried to Calcutta, where it fell from the ceiling in Mrs. Gordon's home while Olcott pointed to the apparition of two brothers outside the window. According to Mrs. Gordon's testimony, Olcott told her that the night before he had an intimation from his chohan (teacher) that K. H. (a Mahatma) had been to the *Vega* and had seen Eglinton.

If the delivery of this letter was fraudulent (and it has been convincingly argued by experts that the K. H. letters were written by Blavatsky), the only excuse for Olcott is that he acted unconsciously from suggestions fed him by Blavatsky.

It is believed Olcott will be remembered in the future not so much for his leadership of the Theosophical Society as for his public espousal of Buddhism in 1880 in Sri Lanka (then known as Ceylon). His action on behalf of Buddhism began with the writing and publication of his *Buddhist Catechism,* which introduced the religion to many people and remains in print. He also promoted and helped pay for the presence of Buddhists at the 1893 World's Parliament of Religions which led to the founding of the first Buddhist organizations to formally receive Americans into the faith.

Olcott remained president of the society until his death on February 17, 1907, at Adyar, India. During the last years of his life he worked with **Annie Besant,** who succeeded Blavatsky as head of the Esoteric section and then succeeded Olcott as president.

Sources:

Gomes, Michael. *The Dawning of the Theosophical Movement.* Wheaton, Ill.: Theosophical Publishing House, 1987.

Karunaratne, K. P. *Olcott Commemoration Volume.* Ceylon: Olcott Commemoration Society, 1967.

———. *Olcott's Contribution to the Buddhist Renaissance.* Colombo, Sri Lanka: Publication Division, Ministry of Cultural Affairs, 1980.

Murphet, Howard. *Hammer on the Mountain: Life of Henry Steel Olcott, 1832–1907.* Wheaton, Ill.: Theosophical Publishing House, 1972.

Olcott, Henry Steel. *Old Diary Leaves.* 6 vols. Adyar, Madras, India: Theosophical Publishing House, 1895–1910. Reprinted as *Inside the Occult: The True Story of Madame H. P. Blavatsky.* Philadelphia: Tunning Press, 1975.

———. *People From the Other World.* Hartford, Conn., 1875. Reprint, Rutland, Vt.: Charles E. Tuttle, 1971.

Prothero, Stephen. *The White Buddhist: The Asian Odyssey of Henry Steel Olcott.* Bloomington: Indiana University, 1996.

Old, Walter G(orn) (1864–1929)

British author on **astrology** who became famous under his pseudonym, "Sepharial." Originally named Walter Richard Old, he also wrote under the name Walter Gorn Old. He was born on March 20, 1864, at Harndsworth, Birmingham, England, and educated at King Edward's School, Birmingham.

At an early age he studied books on **Kabala** and astrology, and became friendly with astrologer **Alan Leo** (1860–1917). He went on to study a variety of subjects, including medical dispensing, Orientalism, and ancient languages.

He moved to London in 1889 and joined the **Theosophical Society,** where he became a member of the inner group, known as the Esoteric Section, around **Helena Petrovna Blavatsky.** He was very interested in **astral projection.** Old left the Society after Blavatsky's death.

Beginning in the 1890s, Old wrote extensively on astrology and his books remained popular through the twentieth century. In addition to his basic astrological texts, he developed a system of astrological prediction for the stock market and successfully predicted futures in basic commodities. His most profitable income came from his astrological horseracing systems. He died December 23, 1929, a year before newspaper astrology columns became popular in England. Old also wrote a number of books on general **occult** themes.

Sources:

Old, Walter [Sepahrial]. *The Book of Charms and Talismans.* N.p., 1974.

———. *Book of the Crystal and the Seer.* N.p., 1897.

———. *Book of the Simple Way of Laotze.* N.p., 1904.

———. *The Kabala of Numbers.* 2 vols. N.p., 1913. Revised ed., 1928.

———. *A Manual of Occultism.* N.p., 1910.

———. *Prognostic Astronomy.* N.p., 1901.

———. *Second Sight.* N.p., 1911.

———. *What Is Theosophy?* N.p., 1891.

Old Hat Used for Raising the Devil

One mode of "summoning" the **devil** was to make a circle, place an old hat in the center, and recite the Lord's Prayer backwards.

"Old Moore" (1657–ca. 1714)

Pseudonym assumed by a succession of British astrologers for more than three centuries. The original Dr. Francis Moore, a physician, was born in 1657 and published *Vox Stellarum,* an almanac with predictions based on **astrology,** in 1701. Henry Andrews was a later "Old Moore" whose editions of *Vox Stellarum* had a circulation of five hundred thousand. *Vox Stellarum* had become *Old Moore's Almanack* by the twentieth century and in the 1960s, "Old Moore" was Edward W. Whitman, secretary of the Federation of British Astrologers.

There is a "Genuine Old Moore" ("Beware of Spurious Editions") credited to John Arigho featuring a portrait of Theophilus Moore, said to have lived ca. 1764. The Irish Old Moores contained word games, by "Lady Di." There were four rival Old Moores in Britain, all claiming "Original Editions." Foulsham states their own original Old Moore ("Beware of Imitations") dates back to a copyright of 1697. Their predictions are now calculated by a team of four astrologers.

A comparable American publication is the *Old Farmer's Almanac,* by Robert B. Thomas and rivals Old Moore in claiming centuries of continuous publication. It maintains the tradition established by Benjamin Franklin's *Poor Richard's Almanac,* started in 1732.

Sources:

Capp, Bernard. *Astrology and the Popular Press: English Almanacs 1500–1800.* London: Faber & Faber, 1979.

Howe, Ellic. *Urania's Children; The Strange World of the Astrologers.* London: William Kimber, 1967.

The Old Religion

Folklore term popularized in the 1960s for **witchcraft** as an older paganism displaced by Christianity.

"Old Scratch"

One of the appellations given to the Devil. It is supposed to have been derived from *Skrati,* an old Teutonic faun or Satyr, a horned half-man and half-goat. (See also **"Nick"; Splitfoot**)

Oliveto Citra

Oliveto Citra, a town in Italy south of Naples, was the site in the 1980s of a series of **apparitions of the Virgin Mary,** unusual for the number of people who reported sightings. They began on May 24, 1985, the feast day of Saint Macarius, the patron saint of Oliveto Citra. In the evening, as the townspeople gathered for the celebration, some dozen boys ages eight to ten were playing at a small square just off the piazza Garibaldi, where the main celebration took place. Suddenly, behind the iron gate that led to the castle ruins that dominate the town, the boys heard a baby crying. It startled them, and they did not know what to do. Then, they saw what was variously reported as a light, or a light in the shape of a person. A few saw a young woman; several reported seeing an infant in her arms. Excited, they ran to the piazza to report that they had seen the Virgin. Two women returned to the spot, and one of them, Anita Rio, saw the young woman and the infant with a rosary in his hands. The woman spoke to Rio and said that she would see the woman in the evenings. Rio entered a state of shock and was taken to the town's small hospital. One of the boys who had seen the woman asked her who she was, and she replied, "I am Our Lady of Graces." The next evening, Gino Acquaviva and his twin brother, Carmine, saw the Virgin again, and asked her name. This time she replied, "I am Our Lady of Consolation." The Lady appeared frequently over the next months. Rio saw her regularly and was told that she wished a small chapel built at the castle gate. That chapel was dedicated in 1987. As word spread of the sightings, the castle gate became a place of pilgrimage and by the end of the 1980s, a site of nightly worship services built around the recitation of the rosary and the mysteries of Mary. One resident wrote a hymn to the Virgin, and one evening as it was being sung, she supplied a new melody heard by some as coming from a heavenly choir. One man in the village, crippled since birth, was healed. A number of subsequent healings have been reported. Some 20 people saw the Virgin with some degree of regularity and by the end of the decade over 100 had signed statements recording at least one sighting. While many are children or youth, a number of adults have become a part of the group who regularly sees and/or speaks to the Virgin. Many also report a sweet-smelling perfume as indicative of her presence. Of those who have heard her speak, the Lady has spoken words of personal admonition as well as general admonitions supportive of Catholic piety. Several of the visionaries have been told secrets by the Virgin that they have not revealed to anyone. The parish priest at Oliveto Citra, Don Peppino, took a pastoral interest in the visionaries and soon took it upon himself to record all that has happened. He became convinced of the reality of the apparitions and believes the number of people who have seen the Virgin makes the sightings unique among the many reported sightings worldwide. Though the local archdiocese has made an initial investigation of the events, the archbishop has yet to make a definitive statement. The sightings continued through the 1990s, though they have remained spontaneous and sporadic. Regular services continue at the site of the chapel, and several books have been written about the sightings. Like Medjugore, in Herzegovina, it appears that Oliveto Citra will remain a site of pilgrimage well into the twenty-first century.

Sources:

Faricy, Robert, and Luciano Pecoraio. *Mary Among Us: The Apparitions at Oliveto Citra.* Stubenville, Ohio: Franciscan University Press, 1989.

OM (or AUM)

A Sanskrit word of special sanctity in the Hindu religion, generally interchangable with **AUM.** It is pronounced at the beginning and end of every lesson in the *Vedas* (ancient scriptures) and is also the introductory word of the *Puranas* (religious works embodying legends and mythology). The *Katha-Upanishad* states: "Whoever knows this syllable obtains whatever he wishes."

There are various accounts of its origin; one that it is the term of assent used by the gods and possibly an old contracted form of the Sanskrit word *evam* meaning "thus." The *Manu-Sangita* (Laws of Manu), a religious work of social laws, states the word was formed by Brahma himself, who extracted the letters *a-u-m* from the *Vedas.*

Om is also the name given by the Hindus to the spiritual sun, as opposed to *Surya,* the natural sun.

Omarr, Sydney (1926–)

U.S. astrologer born on August 5, 1926. He served with the Air Force in the Pacific during World War II. After predicting the death of President Roosevelt, the Armed Forces Radio assigned him to a horoscope show; he thus became the first official astrologer in U.S. Army history.

After the war, he wrote articles on astrology and appeared in radio shows. He was also a CBS radio news editor in Los Angeles. His astrology columns appeared in some 225 newspapers, and at the height of his success he moved to Hollywood. His books on astrology include: *Astrology: Its Role in Your Life* (1963); *My World of Astrology* (1965); *Dream-Scope* (1973); *The Thought Dial Way to a Healthy & Successful Life* (1973); *Sydney Omarr's Astrological Guide* (1974); *Sydney Omarr's Astrological Guide to Sex and Love* (1974).

Omega Directory

Monthly publication of psychic and **New Age** resources in the Southwest United States that includes articles and information on regional groups. Address: New Age Community Church, 6418 S. 39th Ave., Phoenix, Ariz. 85041.

Omen

Believed to be a sign or portent of some future event, occurring either as a result of some form of **divination,** or as an unusual or supernatural event prior to some great development or catastrophe. (See Paranormal **Signs**)

Omez, Réginald, O.P. (Order of Dominicans) (1895– ?)

Dominican priest who studied parapsychological subjects. He was born October 12, 1895, at Tourcoing (Nord), France. He studied at Le Saulchoir, Université Francaise des Dominicains (D. Theol., 1922), and the Dominican University, Rome, Italy (Ph.D., 1924). Omez joined the faculty of Dominacan University in 1922 and taught while completing his doctorate. He remained there until the beginning of World War II. In 1942, he became the French and international chaplain of Catholic Writers and Journalists. He was a member of the French Association for Metapsychical Studies and the Society of Friends of the Institut Métapsychique International.

Omez authored a number of books and articles on religious subjects and has also published in the paranormal field. His books include: *Le Subconscient* (The Subconscious Mind) (5 vols., 1949–1953), *Etudes sur le subconscient* (Studies of the Subconscious) (1954), *Peut-on communiquer avec les morts?* (Can We Communicate with the Dead?) (1955), *Supranormal ou surnaturel?* (Supernormal or Supernatural?) (1956), *Religione E. Scienze Metapsichiche* (Religion and the Metaphysical Sciences) (1957), *Médecine et Merveilleux* (Medicine and the Supernatural) (1956), *Le Gouvernement Divin: Coopération des hommes et des esprits* (God's Rule: Cooperation of Men and Spirits) (1959), *Le monde des ressuscités* (The World After Resurrection) (1961), *Jeunesse eternelle* (Everlasting Youth) (1962), and *L'Occultisme devant la science* (Occultism and Science) (1963).

Omphalomancy

A system of **divination** using the navel of the first newborn child to ascertain future conceptions by the mother. Indications were obtained from the number of markings or bands on the navel.

Onec, Omnec

Omnec Onec is the name of a woman who claims to be an extraterrestrial from Venus and is the subject of a book, *From Venus I Came,* published by **Wendelle Stevens,** best known for his promotion of the claims of Swiss contactee Billy Meiers in North America. According to Onec's account, she had lived for 210 years (Earth time) on Venus prior to taking on the form of a seven-year-old Earth girl and came to Earth in 1955 in a spaceship accompanied by her uncle.

Onec claims that she was born and raised in the Venusian city of Teutonia (a city whose name reflects earlier Venus-Earth contacts that included a trip to Venus by a German scientist). From the Temple of History she learned of the long-term monitoring of Earth by scientists from many planets and of the nature of life on all of these planets. Earth, the youngest of the planets in this solar system, is plagued by the imbalance caused by its singular Moon, which works an alternating influence on people as it moves through the heavens. The other planets are organized into a Brotherhood of Planets and their monitoring of Earth includes the era of Atlantis and Lemuria. The different races of earth have ties to the inhabitants of the various planets.

According to Onec, a set of teachings called Om-Notia Zedia, the laws of the Supreme Deity, exists on Venus. These teachings start with the utterly transcendent Supreme Deity from whom there issues an audible life stream of Spirit. This life stream sustains the existence of all worlds and universes. Human beings are Soul existing in the ocean of Spirit. Souls have been placed in physical embodiment to awaken to their true nature. The Soul may learn to exist apart from its physical body and to travel in the planes of existence between the physical world and God, beginning with the astral, causal, and mental planes. Wendelle Stevens has noted the similarity of these teachings with **ECKANKAR.**

Onec believed in **reincarnation** and **karma** and accepted the idea of coming to Earth to balance her personal karma. After landing, she said she was substituted for a seven-year-old girl who had just been killed in an accident. She was raised in Chattanooga, Tennessee, by the grandmother of Sheila, the girl whom she had replaced. She grew up in what was to all outward appearances a normal life, never speaking of Venus, and endured the struggles that allowed her to deal with her own karmic past. As a young adult, however, she began to manifest her second mission, to offer humanity an increased awareness of their relation to spirit. As an initial step, she wrote a book published by Stevens in 1986. The account included a variety of problems, including claims of significant habitation of all of the planets of the solar system and assertions of conditions existing on these planets that contradict the repeated observations of various space probes. To defend the account, it had to be assumed that the inhabitants resided on something other than the physical plane of existence.

Sources:

Onec, Omnec. *From Venus I Came.* Tucson, Ariz.: W. C. Stevens, 1986.

Oneiromancy

Term for **divination** by **dreams,** possibly the oldest of the divinatory systems. Written records exist of dream interpretation in a papyrus ca. 1250 B.C.E. Prophetic dreams involving the interpretation of symbolic images and information are also in biblical history (See Gen. 41:1–36; Matt. 2:12, 22).

Psychologists and psychoanalysts claim that dreams include symbolic hopes and fears, sexual anxieties, and recollections of past events, as well as possible precognitive images. An attempt to isolate claimed precognitive factors in dreams was made by **J. W. Dunne** (1875–1949) in his book *An Experiment With Time* (1927).

Onimancy (or Onycomancy)

An elaborate ritual of **divination,** possibly based on the observation of the angel Uriel. Olive oil or walnut oil mixed with tallow is put on the nails of the right hand or in the palm of a young boy or girl. To recover money or hidden objects, the face of the child must be turned toward the east; for inquiry into a crime or romance toward the south; for robbery toward the west; and for murder toward the south.

Then the child must repeat the seventy-two verses of the Psalms, which the Hebrew Kabalists (see **Kabala**) collected for the Urim and Thummim. In each verse the venerable name of four letters and the three lettered name of the seventy-two angels occurs. Believers claim that at the end of this process would be the answer.

Other authorities give the name **onychomancy** to the interpretation of the spots on the human nails.

Onion

The onion was regarded as a symbol of the universe by the ancient Egyptians, and many beliefs were associated with it. It was believed that it attracted and absorbed infectious matters and was usually hung in rooms to prevent illness. This belief in the absorptive power of the onion is still prevalent.

British folklorist James Napier noted:

"When a youth, I remember the following story being told, and implicitly believed by all. There was once a certain king or nobleman who was in want of a physician, and two celebrated doctors applied. As both could not obtain the situation, they agreed among themselves that the one was to try to poison the other, and he who succeeded in overcoming the poison would thus be left free to fill the situation. They drew lots as to who should first take the poison. The first dose given was a stewed toad, but the party who took it immediately applied a poultice of peeled onions over his stomach, and thus abstracted all the poison of the toad. Two days after, the other doctor was given the onions to eat. He ate them, and died. It was generally believed that the poultice of peeled onions laid on the stomach, or underneath the armpits, would cure anyone who had taken poison."

Onomancy (or Onomamancy)

Divination using a person's name, satirically said to be nearer to divination by a donkey, and more properly termed onomamancy or onomatomancy. The notion that an analogy existed between men's names and their fortunes is supposed to have originated with the Pythagoreans.

Onomancy had two rules: first, that an even number of vowels in a man's name signifies something amiss in his left side; an uneven number, a similar affection on the right. Second, of two competitors, success was based on the competitor with the longest name; thus Achilles triumphed over Hector.

According to Caelius Rhodiginus, the Gothic King Theodotus practiced an unusual version of onomancy recommended by a Jew. The diviner advised the prince, on the eve of a war with Rome, to enclose 30 hogs in three different sties, having previously given some Roman and others Gothic names. On an appointed day, when the sties were opened, all the Romans were found alive, but with half their bristles fallen off; all the Goths were dead. From this, the onomantist predicted that the Gothic army would be destroyed by the Romans, who would lose half their own force.

The system uses the rationale of Jewish **gematria** to assign numerical values to the letters of names.

Sources:

Waite, Arthur Edward. *The Occult Sciences.* N.p., 1891. Reprint, Secaucus, N.J.: University Books, 1974.

Onychomancy

Divination by fingernails. It was practiced by watching the reflection of the sun in the nails of a boy, and judging the future by the shape of the figures displayed on their surface. (See also **onimancy**)

Sources:

Waite, Arthur Edward. *The Occult Sciences.* N.p., 1891. Reprint, Secaucus, N.J.: University Books, 1974.

Onyx

A precious stone whose properties were believed to resemble those of jasper; it was also supposed to increase saliva in boys and cause bad dreams. If applied to the eye, it was believed to remove anything noxious.

The onyx was also believed to create strife, cause melancholy, and cure epilepsy. According to the Bible, an onyx was the eleventh stone in the breastplate of the High Priest (Exod. 28:20), but it is possible that this stone (in Hebrew, *shoham*) is known today as **beryl.**

Oomancy

A system of **divination** using the outer and inner forms of eggs. One method was to break an egg into a glass of water and interpret the shapes assumed by the white. (See also **ooscopy**)

Sources:

Waite, Arthur Edward. *The Occult Sciences.* N.p., 1891. Reprint, Secaucus, N.J.: University Books, 1974.

Oom the Omnipotent

Title given to **Pierre Bernard,** pioneer of **hatha yoga** study in the United States and founder of the New York Sanskrit College in 1909.

Ooscopy and Oomantia

Two methods of **divination** using eggs, similar to **oomamcy.** An example of ooscopy was related by the Roman historian Suetonius (ca. 98–138 C.E.), who stated that Livia, when anxious to know whether she should be the mother of a boy or girl, kept an egg in her bosom at the proper temperature, until a chick was born.

The name oomantia denoted a method of divining the signs or characters appearing in eggs. John Brand, an English clergyman, described the custom of giving away pasche or paste eggs at Easter. These are eggs stained with various colors. The custom was religiously observed in Russia, where it was derived from the Greek Church. Gilded or colored eggs were mutually exchanged by men and women, who kissed one another and, if any coolness existed previously, became good friends again on these occasions.

The egg is one of the most ancient symbols of new birth and has been applied to natural philosophy as well as the spiritual creation of man.

Sources:

Brand, John. *Observations on Popular Antiquities.* 2 vols. London, 1813.

Waite, Arthur Edward. *The Occult Sciences.* N.p., 1891. Reprint, Secaucus, N.J.: University Books, 1974.

Opal

Gemstone of quartz or silica, praised by **Pliny the Elder** (ca. 23–79 C.E.), who wrote: "For in them you shall see the living fire of the ruby, the glorious purple of the amethyst, the green sea of the emerald, all glittering together in an incredible mixture of light." In ancient times many legends existed around its claimed virtues. It was believed to recreate the heart, ward off airborne contagions, and dispel sadness. It was also good for weak eyes. The name *poederos,* applied to the opal, refers to the complexion of youth.

The superstition that opals were unlucky seems to have been popularized by Sir Walter Scott's novel *Anne of Geirstein* (1829). The story claims the opal worn by Baroness Hermione of Arnheim lost its luster after a drop of water touched it.

Open Deck

Term used by parapsychologists in card guessing tests, where each symbol in the pack is chosen at random, versus a Closed Deck, where each symbol occurs a set number of times.

Open Letter (Newsletter) See Network News

The Open Mind (Newsletter)

Former bimonthly newsletter edited by parapsychologist **Charles T. Tart** devoted to increasing self-knowledge. Many of the articles featured in the newsletter were put together in a book, *Open Mind, Discriminating Mind: Reflections on Human Possibilities.* Copies of the now out-of-print book can be obtained from Tart's own website: http://www.paradigm-sys.com/cttart/.

Sources:

Home Page and Virtual Library: Charles T. Tart. http://www.paradigm-sys.com/cttart/. March 24, 2000.

Open Mind Magazine

Publication by a group of Australian experimenters in the **Christos Experience,** a technique of traveling by mind to other places, identities, and time periods. The Open Mind group can be contacted at Open Mind Publications, c/o Post Office, Mahogany Creek, Western Australia 6072.

Sources:

Glaskin, G. M. *Worlds Within: Probing the Christos Experience.* London: Wildwood House, 1976.

"Ophiel"

Pseudonym of Edward C. Peach, a writer on **occultism.** In 1961, after receiving a claims settlement of $1,000 for an accident, he spent the money publishing his own manuscript *The Art and Practice of Astral Projection,* using a Hong Kong printer. Over the next decade, Peach published several **occult** books and continued to write through the 1970s.

Sources:

Ophiel [Edward C. Peach]. *Art and Practice of Talismanic Magic.* West Hollywood, CA: Peach Publishing, 1973.

———. *The Oracle of Fortuna.* St. Paul: Llewellyn Publications, 1971.

Ophiomancy

A system of **divination** based on the color and movements of serpents.

Ophites

This sect of **Gnostics** appears to date from the second century. A system of initiation was popular among the members and they possessed symbols to represent purity, life, spirit, and fire. Beliefs were based on mysteries of the Egyptian goddess Isis, concepts of Oriental mythology, and Christian doctrine.

According to the theologian Origen (ca. 185–ca. 254 C.E.), the sect was founded by a man named Euphrates. The sect was believed to have given special prominence to serpents in their rituals.

Sources:

Legge, Francis. *Forerunners and Rivals of Christianity from 330 B.C. to 333 A.D.* Reprint, New Hyde Park, N.Y.: University Books, 1964.

Oracle Bones

Oracle bones were popular tools for **divination** in ancient China, during that period of the Shang Dynasty, 1776–1122 B.C.E. Two primary objects were utilized, the bones of a now-extinct species of tortoise (*Pseudocardia anyangensis*) and the shoulder bones of oxen. The tortoise was a sacred animal in China and appears as a symbol in various divinatory systems including **astrology.** It was symbolic of long life and was considered a guardian of graves. The ox also acquired an array of symbolic meanings.

Pseudocardia anyangensis was bred in ancient China. The part utilized for divination was the relatively soft and flat underlayer called the plastron. It was cleaned, and a number of cavities were cut into the surface. Questions would then be put to the plastron. To discover an answer, a heated rod would be pressed on one of the cavities and in a short time, a crack would appear on the reverse side of the surface. The crack would then be analyzed for its suggested portents. The majority of the surviving examples appear to have been used on behalf of the ruler by court diviners. Many exist only as fragments, as the process of divination often caused the plastron to break in two. In the case of shoulder bones, one end of which is flat, a similar process to that used on the tortoise plastrons was used. Half of the socket would be removed along with the longitudinal ridge, leaving a flat piece of bone with a handle. The first burns would be made on the end of the blade away from the handle. It also appears that the questions put to the bones would have been asked multiple times in order to determine the drift of the answers rather than simply relying on one response.

Archeologists have uncovered extensive collections of oracle bones of both varieties, in many cases bearing a number indicating the use of a filing system. At some point, however, after the fall of the Shang Dynasty, the use of oracle bones gave way to other popular systems of divination, especially the **I Ching.**

Sources:

Chang, Kwang-Chih. *Shang Civilization.* New Haven, Conn.: Yale University Press, 1980.

Keightley, David N. *Sources of Shang History: The Oracle-Bone Descriptions of Bronze Age China.* Berkley, Calif.: University of California Press, 1985.

Temple, Robert K. G. *Conversations with Eternity: Ancient Man's Attempt to Know the Future.* London: Rider, 1984.

Oracles

Shrines where a god was believed to speak to human beings through the mouths of priests or priestesses. The concept of the god becoming vocal was not confined to ancient **Greece** or **Egypt.** The Eskimos used to consult spirits for hunting and fishing expeditions. It is believed their wizards were as familiar with the art of giving ambiguous replies to their clients as were the Oracle keepers of Greece. The direction of the gods was also sought in all affairs of private and public life.

The Oracle of Delphi at Greece

In Greek mythology, when Jupiter wished to learn where the central point of the earth was, he dispatched two eagles, or two crows, named by Strabo. The birds took flight in opposite directions from sunrise and sunset, and they met at Delphi. The site was given the title "the navel of the earth" and the central point has white marble.

Delphi became a place of distinction. It was designated as oracular when the fumes coming from a neighboring cave were first discovered by a shepherd named Coretas. His attention was attracted to the spot by his goats gambolling and bleating more than usual.

It is not known whether these fumes arose due to an earthquake or whether they were generated by human act. According to the story, Coretas, on approaching the spot, was seized and uttered words deemed to be inspired. Later as the danger of inhaling the fumes without proper caution was known, the fissure was covered by a table, with a hole in the center and called a tripod, so that those who wished to try the experiment could safely.

Eventually, a young girl became the **medium** for responses, now deemed oracular and called "Pythian," as proceeding from Apollo, the slayer of Python, to whom Delphi was consecrated. A wooden structure of laurel branches was erected over the spot and the Pythoness sat on throne to receive Apollo's dictation.

As the oracle became better known, the structure was constructed of more costly materials. The tripod was made of gold but the lid continued to be made of brass. The Pythoness began by drinking from a "sacred" fountain (Castalia) adjoining the crypt (the waters were reserved for her only), chewing a laurel leaf, and placing a laurel crown on her head.

The person making an inquiry from the oracle first offered a victim and then, having written his question in a notebook, handed it to the Pythoness before she ascended the tripod. The inquisitor and the priestess wore laurel crowns. Originally the oracle spoke only on the seventh day of the month "Byssus." This was regarded as the birthday of Apollo and was called "Polypthonus."

According to Diodorus, virginity was originally a prerequisite in the Pythoness, due to the purity of that state and its relation to Diana; moreover, virgins were thought better adapted than other women to keep oracular mysteries secret and inviolate. But after an accident had occurred to one of the Pythonesses, the guardians of the temple permitted no one to fulfil the duties of the office until she had attained the age of 50.

The Oracle of Dodona

Another celebrated oracle, that of Jupiter, was at Dodona in Epirus, Greece (from which Jupiter derived the name of Dodonus). It was situated at the foot of Mount Tomarus, in a grove of oaks, and there answers were given by a woman named Pelias. "Pelias" means dove in the Attic dialect. The fable arose that the doves prophesied in the groves of Dodona.

The historian Herodotus (ca. 484–425 B.C.E.) cites a legendary tale concerning the origin of the oracle. Supposedly two priestesses from Thebes, Egypt, were carried away by Phoenician merchants; one went to Libya, where she founded the oracle of Jupiter Ammon, the other to Greece. There she had a temple built at the foot of an oak in honor of Jupiter, whose priestess she had been in Thebes. Herodotus added that this priestess was called a dove, because her language could not be understood.

The Dodonic and African oracles were probably connected. Herodotus stated that the manner of prophecy in Dodona was the same as that in Thebes, Egypt. Diana was worshiped in Dodona in conjunction with Zeus, and a female figure was associated with Amun in the Libyan Ammonium. According to some authors, there was an intoxicating spring at Dodona and later other materials were employed to produce the prophetic spirit.

Several copper bowls and bells were placed on a column beside the statute of a boy. When the wind blew a chain attached to a rod or scourge with three bones struck the metallic bowls and bells, and the sound was heard by the applicants. These Dodonian tones stated the proverb: *Oes Dodonoekum*—an unceasing babbler.

The tree, the "incredible wonder," as Aeschylus calls it, was an oak, with evergreen leaves and edible acorns that the Greeks and Romans believed to be the first sustenance of mankind. The Pelasgi regarded this tree as the tree of life. In this tree the god was supposed to reside and the rustling of its leaves and the voices of birds showed his presence. When the questioners entered, the oak rustled and the Peliades said, "Thus speaks Zeus." Incense was burned beneath it. According to the legend, sacred doves continually inhabited the tree, like the Marsoor oracle at Tiora Mattiene, where a sacred hawk predicted the future from the top of a wooden pillar.

At the foot of the oak, a cold spring gushed and supposedly the inspired priestesses prophesied from this murmur. According to legend, when lighted torches were thrust into this fountain they would be extinguished and would rekindle without assistance. Ernst von Lasaulx in *Das pelasgische Orakel d. Zeus zu Dodona* speculated:

"That extinction and rekindling has, perhaps, the mystical signification that the usual sober life of the senses must be extinguished, that the prophetic spirit dormant in the soul may be aroused. The torch of human existence must expire, that a divine one may be lighted; the human must die that the divine may be born; the destruction of individuality is the awakening of God in the soul, or, as the mystics say, the setting of sense is the rising of truth."

It appears predictions were drawn from the tones of the Dodonian brass bowls, the rustling of the oak, and the murmuring of the well. The Dodonian columns appear to express the following: The medium-sized brazen bowl was a hemisphere, and symbolized heaven; the boy-like male statue was a figure of the Demiurgos, or constructor of the universe; the bell-like notes were a symbol of the harmony of the universe and music of the spheres. That the Demiurgos was represented as a boy is in the spirit of Egypto-Pelasgian theology as it reigned in Samothrace (Greek Island). It is believed the bell told all who came to Dodona to question the god that they were on holy ground, must inquire with pure hearts, and be silent when the god replied. Those who questioned the god were also obliged to take a purificatory bath in the temple, similar to that of the Delphian Pythia when preparing herself for prophecy.

Besides soothsaying from signs, divination by the prophetic movements of the mind was practiced. Sophocles called the Dodonean priestesses divinely inspired. Plato (Phaedrus) stated the prophetess at Delphi and the priestesses at Dodona had done much good while in a state he termed "sacred madness," but while in their senses accomplished little or nothing.

We may infer from this that the Delphian Pythia as well as the Dodonian priestesses did not give their oracles in the state of waking consciousness but with the assistance of incense and drink. Aristides stated the priestesses at Dodona neither knew (before being seized upon by the spirit) what would be said, nor remembered afterward when their natural consciousness returned, what they had uttered, so that all others, rather than they, knew it.

The Oracle of Jupiter Trophonius

According to Pausanias (ca. 470 B.C.E.), Trophonius was the most skillful architect of his day. There are various opinions regarding the origin of his oracle. Some say he was swallowed up by an earthquake in the cave and became prophetic; others, that after having completed the Adytum of Apollo at Delphi, he declined asking any specific pay, but requested the god to grant him whatever was the greatest benefit a man could receive—and three days later he was found dead.

This oracle was discovered after two years, when the Pythoness ordered the starving population who applied to her to consult Trophonius in Lebadaea. The deputies sent for that purpose could not find any trace of such an oracle until Saon, the oldest among them, followed the flight of a swarm of bees.

The responses were given by Trophonius to the inquirer, who descend into a cave. The inquirer resided for a certain number of days in a sanctuary, performed ceremonial purification, and abstained from hot baths, but dipped in the river Hercyna and was supplied with meat from the victims he sacrificed.

From an inspection of the entrails, a soothsayer decided if Trophonius could be consulted. The night of the decent a ram was sacrificed to Agamedes at the mouth of the cave. When the signal had been given, the priests led the inquirer to the river Hercyna, where he was anointed and washed by two Lebadaean youths, thirteen years of age, named "Hermai."

He was then carried to the two spring-heads of the stream, and there he drank first of Lethe to forget all past events and present his mind to the oracle as a "tabula rasa" (cleaned tablet); and secondly of Mnemosyne, to remember every occurrence about to happen within the cave. An image, reputed to be the workmanship of Daedalus, was then shown to him. Because of its sanctity, no other eyes but those of a person about to undertake the adventure of the cave were ever permitted to see it.

Next he was clad in a linen robe, tied with ribbons, and shod with sandals peculiar to the country. The entrance to the oracle was a very narrow aperture in a grove on the summit of a mountain, protected by a marble wall about two cubits in height with brass spikes above it. The upper part of the cave was artificial, like an oven. No steps were cut in the rock; to descend a ladder was brought to the spot on each occasion.

On approaching the mouth of the temple, the adventurer lay flat, first inserting his feet into the aperture, then drawing up his knees and the remainder of his body, until caught by a hidden force and carried downward like a whirlpool.

The responses were given sometimes by a vision, sometimes by words, and a forcible exit was then made through the original entrance, feet first. Supposedly there was only one instance on record of any person who had descended failing to return.

Immediately upon returning from the cavern, the inquirer was placed on a seat called that of Mnemosyne, not far from the entrance. The priests demanded an account of everything he had seen and heard; he was then carried once again to the sanctuary of good fortune, where he remained for some time.

The antiquary Dr. Edward D. Clarke (1769–1822) during his visit to Lebadaea found everything belonging to the hieron of Trophonius in its original state, except the narrow entrance to the temple was filled with rubbish. The Turkish governor was afraid of civil unrest if he gave permission to clean the aperture. In modern times, the waters of Lethe and Mnemosyne are used for the wash of Lebadaea.

The Oracles of Delos and Branchus

The oracle of "Delos" was derived from the nativity of Apollo and Diana in that island. At Dindyma, or Didyma, near Miletus, Apollo presided over the oracle of the "Branchidae," so called from either one of his sons or of his favorites Branchus of Thessaly, whom he instructed in soothsaying while alive and canonized after death.

The responses were given by a priestess who bathed and fasted for three days before consultation, then sat upon an axle or bar, with a charming-rod in her hand, and inhaled the steam from a hot spring. Offerings and ceremonies were necessary, including baths, fasting, and solitude.

The Oracle at Colophon

Of the oracle of Apollo at Colophon, Iamblichus (ca. 330 C.E.) left an account relating that it prophesied by drinking water:

"It is known that a subterranean spring exists there, from which the prophet drinks; after he has done so, and has performed many consecrations and sacred customs on certain nights, he predicts the future; but he is invisible to all who are present. That this water can induce prophecy is clear, but how it happens, no one knows, says the proverb.

"It is believed, God is in all things, and is reflected in this spring, thereby giving it prophetic power. Supposedly the inspiration of the water prepares and purifies the light of the soul, to receive the divine spirit. The soothsayer uses this spirit like a work-tool over which he has no control. After the moment of prediction he does not always remember what has happened. Before drinking the water, the soothsayer must fast for day and night and observe religious customs in order to receive the god."

The Oracle of Amphiaraus

Another celebrated oracle was Amphiaraus, who distinguished himself in the Theban war. He was venerated at Oropus, in Boeotia, as a seer. This oracle was consulted more in sickness than on any other occasion. The applicants had to lie upon the skin of a sacrificed ram and during sleep had the remedies of their diseases revealed to them. Not only were sacrifices and ceremonial purifications performed here, but the priests also prescribed other preparations for the minds of the sleepers to be enlightened. They had to fast one day and refrain from wine for three.

Amphilochus, the son of Amphiaraus, had a similar oracle at Mallos, in Cilicia, which Pausanias called the most trustworthy and credible of the age. Lucian mentioned that all those who wished to question the oracle had to lay down two oboles (small silver coins).

Egyptian Oracles

The oracles of ancient Egypt were as numerous as those of Greece. Herodotus claimed that at least seven gods in Egypt spoke by oracles. Supposedly, the most reliable were considered to give an intimation of their intentions by means of "remarkable events." These were carefully observed by the Egyptians, who recorded these events.

The Egyptians also considered the fate of a person was determined by the day of his birth—every day belonged to a special god. The oracle of Jupiter Ammon and the same deity at Thebes existed from the twentieth to the twenty-second Dynasty. He was consulted not only concerning the fate of empires but also for the identification of a thief. In all serious matters, however, it was sought to ascertain his views. Those about to make their wills sought his oracle and judgments were ratified by "his" word. For example, surviving inscriptions described what occurred when a king consulted a god:

"The King presented himself before the god and preferred a direct question, so framed as to admit of an answer by simple yes or no; in reply the god nodded an affirmative, or shook his head in negation.

"This has suggested the idea that the oracles were manipulated statues of divinities mechanically set in motion by the priests. But as yet no such statues have been found in the Valley of the Nile. It was customary for the king to visit the god alone and in secret. It is believed the king presented himself on such occasions before the sacred animal the god was incarnate, believing the divine will would be manifested by its movements." (See also moving **statues**)

The Apis bull also possessed oracles, as did Bes, the god of pleasure or of the senses, whose oracle was located at Abydos.

American Oracles

Among the peoples of the Americas many of the principal deities acted as oracles. For example, the ancient inhabitants of Peru, the *huillcas,* believed the noises made by serpents, trees, and rivers to be of the quality of articulate speech. Both the Huillcamayu and the Apurimac rivers at Cuzco were *huillca oracles* of this kind, as their names, "Huillcariver" and "Great Speaker," denote. These oracles often set the mandate of the Inca himself, occasionally supporting popular opinion against his policy.

As late as the nineteenth century, the Peruvian Indians of the Andes mountain range continued to believe in oracles they had inherited from their fathers. One account of this says they:

". . . admit an evil being, the inhabitant of the centre of the earth, whom they consider as the author of their misfortunes, and at the mention of whose name they tremble. The most shrewd among them take advantage of this belief to obtain respect, and represent themselves as his delegates. Under the denomination of *mohanes,* or *agoreros,* they are consulted even on the most trivial occasions. They preside over the intrigues of love, the health of the community, and the taking of the field. Whatever repeatedly occurs to defeat their prognostics, falls on themselves; and they are wont to pay for their deceptions very dearly. They chew a species of vegetable called *piripiri,* and throw it into the air, accompanying this act by certain recitals and incantations, to injure some, to benefit others, to procure rain and the inundation of rivers, or, on the other hand, to occasion settled weather, and a plentiful store of agricultural productions. Any such result, having been casually verified on a single occasion, suffices to confirm the Indians in their faith, although they may have been cheated a thousand times."

Supposedly there is an instance on record of how the *huillca* could refuse on occasion to recognize even royalty itself. Manco, the Inca who had been given the kingly power by Spanish conqueror Francisco Pizarro, offered a sacrifice to one of these oracular shrines. The oracle refused to recognize him; through the medium of its guardian priest, the oracle stated Manco was not the rightful Inca. According to legend Manco had the rock shaped oracle thrown down, whereupon its guardian spirit emerged in the form of a parrot and flew away. But upon Manco commanding the parrot be pursued, the spirit sought another rock to receive it, and the spirit of the *huillca* was transferred.

Similar to the idols of Mexico, most of the principal *huacas* of Peru seem to also have been oracles. It is believed the guardians of the speaking *huacas* were not influenced by the Apu-Ccapac-Inca himself. There was a tradition that the Huillacumu, a venerable *huillac* whom the rest acknowledged as their head, at one time possessed jurisdiction over the supreme war chiefs.

Sources:

Bouché-Leclercq, A. *Histoire de la divination dans l'antiquité.* Paris, 1879. Reprint, New York: Arno Press, 1975.

Dempsey, T. *The Delphic Oracles.* Oxford: B. H. Blackwell, 1918.

Halliday, W. R. *Greek Divination.* London: Macmillan, 1913. Reprint, Chicago: Argonaut, 1967.

Parke, Herbert W. *Greek Oracles.* London: Hutchinson, 1967.

———. *Oracles of Zeus.* Oxford: Blackwell, 1967.

Parke, Herbert W., and Donals Ernest Wilson Wormell. *The Delphic Oracles.* Oxford: Blackwell, 1956.

Oram, Arthur T(albot) (1916–   )

British accountant and statistician who conducted research on card guessing. He was born June 27, 1916, at Devizes, Wiltshire, England, and worked both for the Civil Service and industry. His interest in parapsychology led to his joining and eventually serving on the council of the **Society for Psychical Research,** London. His work on the "displacement effect" in card guessing was reported in *Nature* (vol. 157, 1946).

Sources:

Oram, Arthur T. "An Experiment with Random Numbers." *Journal* of the Society for Psychical Research (1954) 37; (1955) 38.

Pleasants, Helene, ed. *Biographical Dictionary of Parapsychology.* New York: Helix Press, 1964.

Orbas

The name given by the French to a species of metallic electrum. According to the Roman historian **Pliny,** a vessel of this substance has a magical property—when added to liquor it reveals poison by displaying colored semicircles: the fluid also sparkles and hisses as if on the fire.

Orchis, Root of

In ancient times, the root of the *Satyrios Orchis* from the orchid family was believed to be a sure remedy against enchantment.

Order of Bards, Ovates & Druids

A British Druid Order that claims to continue the traditions of the ancient Bardic and Druid Order. One order is concerned with the arts, history, and archaeology and performs outdoor ceremonies. The initiatory order undertakes mystical studies. Public ceremonies are arranged at ancient sites based on the summer and winter solstices and the equinoxes of March and September. After the distance program was initiated in 1988 over 7,000 people have joined the order. Address: PO Box 1333, Lewes, E. Sussex, BN7 1DX England. Website: http://www.druidry.org/.

Sources:

Order of Bards, Ovates & Druids. http://www.druidry.org/. March 8, 2000.

Order of Elect Cohens

An occult Masonic group founded by **Martinees de Pasqually** (ca.1710–1774) in Bordeaux, France, in 1760. The French title *Rite des Élus Cohens* refers to cohens, the Hebrew word for "priests." The rituals for the order's magical invocation of spirits, with the ultimate purpose of communication with the "Active and Intelligent Cause" (i.e., God), were written by Pasqually. He drew upon Roman Catholic, astrological, and various occult texts, especially the **Kabbalah.**

The group appears to have had a Sovereign Tribunal at Paris in 1767 with Pasqually at its head. After the death of Pasqually in Port-au-Prince, Haiti, on September 20, 1774, the order was headed by J. B. Willermoz, then residing in Lyons. The order died out at Lyons following Willermoz's death in 1815, but survived in Italy and Germany. It was later reestablished in Lyons and subsequently spread to Haiti and other islands of the Caribbean and to North America, where it survives today. The archives of the order passed to G. M. Profe Willermoz's nephew, and then to a M. Cavernier, who finally returned them to the reestablished lodge at Lyons.

In 1887 a period of reorganization and diffusion of the order began that led in 1891 to the creation of a council of 21 members who supervised the work in France, across Europe, and in the Americas.

One of Pasqually's students, Louis Claude de Saint-Martin, emerged as a mystic who gained much respect in Europe and is highly revered among Martinists today. Also connected with the order in the nineteenth century was Papus (**Gérard Encausse**).

Sources:

Le Forestier, René. *La Franc-maconnerie occultiste au XVIII siecle et l'ordre des Elus Coens.* Paris: Dorbon, 1928.

McIntosh, Christopher. *Éliphas Lévi and the French Occult Revival.* New York: Samuel Weiser, 1974.

Waite, Arthur Edward. *The Unknown Philosopher: Louis Claude de St. Martin.* Blauvelt, N.Y.: Rudolf Steiner Publications, 1970.

Order of Napunsakäs in the West

The Order of Napunsakäs in the West (ON) was founded in 1996 as a special interest group (SIG) associated with the thelemic magical order the **Servants of the Star and the Snake** (SSS). It was inspired by the writings of the late scholar of Hinduism, Alain Daniélou (author of such books as *The Gods of India: Hindu Polytheism; Shiva and Dionysus* and *While the Gods Play*). The Hindu word "napunsakä" designates some 16 categories of non-heterosexual, gender variant types mentioned in the Sanskrit dictionary of V. S. Apete. Members of the order seek to reestablish the natural, divine order found in pre-Aryan Shaivism, but with an emphasis on gay, lesbian, bisexual, and transgendered **Tantra.** The outer order is open to all napunsakäs (people who define themselves as other than heterosexual); affiliates are considered associate members. An inner order, the Cultus Skanda-Karttikeya (CS-K), is open to gay males only, and only upon formal, in-person *diksha,* or initiation. The focus of the CS-K is on gay Tantra with special emphasis on the *sadhana* (or worship or more properly, adoration) of the Hindu deity Skanda as patron of gays, in His many forms (Kumara, Marugan, etc.). The current head of the Order of Napunsakäs in the West and the Cultus Skanda-Karttikeya is known by his religious name, Sahajananda Skanda-Das. The order is headquartered at P.O. Box 1219, Corpus Christi, TX 78403-1219. It publishes a periodical, *Zibaq.* Information on the order can be found on the Internet through the site of the Servants of the Star and the Snake at http://www.wild.au/sss/index.html.

Order of New Templars

German occult sect organized between 1894 and 1907 by Austrian occultist **Jörg Lanz von Liebenfels** (1874–1954) at Burg Werfenstein near the river Danube. The Order used the swastika symbol, advocated master-race ideals, and developed rituals from appropriation of the Holy "Grail" traditions and Parsifal. Von Liebenfels published a journal, *Ostara.* The Order of New Templars survived for a generation but went underground after the German invasion of Austria in 1938.

Sources:

Webb, James. *The Occult Establishment.* LaSalle, Ill.: Open Court Publishing, 1976.

Order of the Black Ram

The Order of the Black Ram, founded and headed by its grand magister, Rev. Seth-Klippoth, was a Satanic organization that appeared in Detroit during the 1980s. Mixing elements of Nazism and racism with the teachings of the **Church of Satan** and neo-paganism, the order was closely associated with the neo-Nazi National Renaissance party. It published an irregular periodical, *Liber Venifica.*

Order of the Cross

The Order of the Cross is a Christian theosophical group founded in 1904 by former Congregational minister J. Todd Ferrier (1855–1943). Born and raised in Scotland, Ferrier began to read theosophical and other esoteric materials that led him to a very different understanding of the purpose and mission of Jesus. He resigned from the monastery in 1903 and the following year began what was to become his life's work. The first sign of his new ministry was the initial issue of a new periodical, *The Herald of the Cross,* which continues in publication to the present. He also began work on what were to become his two most important books, *The Master: His Life and Teachings* (1913) and *The Logia, or Sayings of the Master.* He moved to London, where he established the order's headquarters. Important in Ferrier's development was participation in the animal rights movement. He became a vegetarian, which he described as a "bloodless" diet, and campaigned against vivisection. It led him to adopt what he termed the Christ-life, a path of self-denial, self-sacrifice, and self-abandonment to the Divine Will. Ferrier believed that Jesus had come into the world to prevent its further disintegration. Over the centuries, the Earth had gradually experienced an increasing disorder in both nature and society caused by the fading of the divine light in human beings. Jesus' work was beginning to show signs of success in the twentieth century. Ferrier saw the changes occurring as the century progressed as signs of the increase of light. Those who actively align themselves with the effort to restore the light to human life will be endowed with a sense of purpose and an ability to communicate with the unseen (i.e., psychic abilities). According to Ferrier, the message of Jesus had been missed by the mainstream of Christianity. He intended not to create the vast earthly institution, but to restore spirituality to individuals. Thus the Order of the Cross has adopted a somewhat anti-institutional bias and devoted itself to introducing people to Jesushood, a state of spiritual realization. Jesushood leads to Christhood, a state of mystical illumination. The order is focused in a number of small groups, most in the British Isles, but some in North America and other English-speaking communities worldwide. International leadership is vested in a self-perpetuating executive council that seeks assistance from an advisory committee of representatives of the groups. International headquarters is located at 10 De Vere Gardens, London W8 5AE, United Kingdom and American headquarters at P.O. Box 2477, LaGrange, IL 60525. The order has a website at http://www.ourworld.compuserve.com/homepages/GabrielBuist/OrdCross.htm. The order has published more than 50 books and booklets of Ferrier's writings and transcribed talks.

Sources:

Ferrier, J. Todd. *The Logia, or Sayings of the Master.* London: Percy, Lund, Bradford and Co., 1916, 1926.

———. *The Master: His Life and Teachings.* London: Order of the Cross, 1913.

Kemmis, E. Mary Gordon. *Shepherd of Souls: Some Impressions of the Life and Ministry of John Todd Ferrier.* Santa Barbara, Calif.: J. F. Rowney Press, 1947.

Order of the Cubic Stone

A group in the Hermetic Order of the **Golden Dawn** tradition, founded in Britain in the 1930s by Theodore Howard and two technicians, David Edwards and Robert Turner. The Order believes in a system of Enochian magic and trains students in **ceremonial magic.**

In the early 1990s, Robert Turner was severely injured in a criminal assault, which has resulted in disruption of the order and its magazine, *The Monolith.* The order is currently attempting a comeback, more information can be found at http://guildnavigator.demon.co.uk/the_monolith.htm.

Sources:

Edwards, David. *Dare to Make Magic.* London: Regal Press, 1971.

The Order of the Cubic Stone. http://guildnavigator.demon.co.uk/the_monolith.htm. March 8, 2000.

Turner, Robert, and David Edwards. *The Outer Court.* Woverhampton, UK: Order of the Cubic Stone, 1968.

Order of the Sacred Word

A breakaway order of the society Aurum Solis, founded in 1897. The Order developed separately in 1957 but was reunited with the main Society in 1971. (See also **Aurum Solis**)

Order of the Silver Star

The **A∴A∴** (Argenteum Astrum), a secret order founded by occultist **Aleister Crowley.**

Order of the Star

Revival of the earlier **Order of the Star in the East,** formed to promote **Jiddu Krishnamurti** as the Great World Teacher. At its peak, the old order had over 45,000 members, but was suddenly suspended in 1929 after Krishnamurti had publicly rejected the role of Great World Teacher. He maintained that people should seek the truth within themselves rather than rely upon the authority of external teachers.

The present Order of the Star was founded by a group claiming a Spiritual Hierarchy had decided to reactivate the order in preparation for the second coming of Christ. The order worked "to establish a peripheral group on the outskirts of the major ashram under the sponsorship of the Master K. H., to initiate an active unit of service in the world, to raise the banner laid down temporarily by the old Order of the Star and to hold it aloft once again and to offer groups and individuals shelter under it." The order published *Star Bulletin* and the *Embers from the Fire.* Last known address: 57 Warescot Road, Brentwood, Essex, CM15 9HH, England.

Order of the Star in the East

Organization promoting the teachings of **Jiddu Krishnamurti** as a World Teacher. The Order was developed by Theosophical president **Annie Besant** in July 1911, as an international movement, extending the scope of the Order of the Rising Sun (founded seven months earlier). The Star in the East had been founded

"...out of the rapidly growing expectation of the near coming of a great spiritual Teacher, which is visible in many parts of the world today. In all the great faiths at the present time, and in practically every race, there are people who are looking for such a Teacher; and this hope is being expressed quite naturally, in each case, in the terms appropriate to the religion and the locality in which it has sprung up. It is the object of the Order of the Star in the East, so far as is possible, to gather up and unify this common expectation, wherever and in whatever form it may exist, and to link it into a single great movement of preparation for the Great One whom the age awaits."

The Order expanded with the assistance of active branches of the **Theosophical Society.** A junior Order of the Servants of the Star was established for members under twenty-one years of age. Membership in the Theosophical movement peaked in the late 1920s.

Order Under Attack

Attacks by the Indian newspaper *The Hindu,* revived the Hodgson Report scandal of the **Society for Psychical Research.** The report alleged fraud by **Helena Petrovna Blavatsky** and sex scandals involving **Charles W. Leadbeater** and young boys in 1906. However, in spite of the attacks, the OSE survived. In 1911, Krishnamurti was claimed to be "the chosen Vehicle of the Lord Maitreya-Bodhisattva-Christ."

In October 1912, J. Narayniah, the father of Krishnamurti, and his brother, started legal proceedings against Besant for the guardianship of the two boys. Narayniah claimed that because of Leadbeater's influence, Besant was unfit to have custody. The case was heard two years later in Madras, the judge concluded that charges of sexual immorality against Leadbeater in relation to Krishnamurti were unfounded. However, he also ruled that Leadbeater was not a suitable person to associate with children, Besant should no longer have custody, and the boys were to become wards of the court. After an appeal court upheld this decision, Besant appealed to the Privy Council in England, and in May 1914, the original judgment was reversed.

Meanwhile, **Katherine Tingley,** head of the American branch of the Theosophical Society also attacked Leadbeater, Besant, and the OSE, declaring that "Krishnamurti is a fine chap who has been hypnotized by Mrs. Annie Besant, and is really an unwilling follower."

In 1912, American members of the Esoteric Section of the Theosophical Society (Adyar) formed a school and community named "Krotona" ("the place of promise") in the Hollywood Hills. Krotona was similar to the community Tingley had developed at Point Loma (San Diego). The complex included a temple, vegetarian cafeteria, metaphysical library, and experimental center. Disciples invented "stereometry," a three-dimensional geometric alphabet, involving a structure weighing three tons and using redwood. After an internal conflict concerning money, the property was sold and the group relocated to the Ojai Valley, a desert in California. Krishnamurti moved Besant to Ojai in hopes of reviving the health of his brother who was suffering from tuberculosis. His brother did not recover but Krishnamurti made Ojai his American headquarters.

On January 23, 1927, Besant announced the arrival of the World Master and that a new utopian colony would be set up in Ojai. Subscriptions were requested to establish a $200,000 Happy Valley Foundation, covering 465 acres and comprising temples, an art center, places for worship and meditation, and a playground for Greek games.

During his world lecture tours, Krishnamurti was favorably received by his followers. However, in June 1927, he gave a speech that disturbed believers in the Vehicle of the Great Teacher. Krishnamurti suggested that **Masters** and other gurus were superfluous and there was a more direct route to the truth within every individual. Meanwhile, the objectives of OSE were revised as follows: "1. To draw together all those who believe in the presence in the world of the World Teacher. "2. To work for Him in all ways for His realization of His ideal for humanity. "The Order has no dogmas, no creeds or systems of belief. Its inspiration is the Teacher, its purpose to embody His universal life."

On June 28, 1927, the name of the Order was changed to the Order of the Star, implying the World Teacher had "arrived," but on August 1, Krishnamurti gave an address on "Who brings the truth?" In this speech, he claimed the Masters had no objective existence—they were mental images shaped by belief and imagination. Krishnamurti stated: "What you are troubling about is whether there is such a person as the World Teacher who has manifested Himself in the body of a certain person, Krishnamurti." He believed the truth must be sought inside each individual rather than relying on an external authority such as himself. In effect, he renounced the role of World Teacher as defined by Besant and Leadbeater. The following day, at the Star Camp at Ommen, The Netherlands, Krishnamurti reiterated this message.

The Order of the Star was formally suspended in 1929. However, Krishnamurti continued to teach as an independent teacher and drew followers throughout his life. Many of his speeches were transcribed and published as books.

From time to time, the messianic concept of a coming World Teacher was similar to that of the Lord Maitreya/Jesus. The concept continued to find support from various theosophical teachers such as **Alice A. Bailey** and was revived as one theme within the **New Age** movement by Bailey student **Benjamin Creme.** In 1982, the Order of the Star was revived similar to its earlier form by a group in Britain.

Sources:

Jayakar, Pupul. *Krishnamurti: A Biography.* San Francisco: Harper & Row, 1986.

Lutyens, Mary. *Krishnamurti: The Years of Awakening.* New York: Farrar, Straus, and Giroux, 1975.

Mills, Joy. *100 Years of Theosophy: A History of the Theosophical Society in America.* Wheaton, Ill.: Theosophical Publishing House, 1987.

Order of the Thelemic Golden Dawn

The Order of the Thelemic Golden Dawn (OTGD) is an initiatory magical group that adheres to the teachings of **Aleister Crowley.** Originally known as The Thelemic Temple and Order of the Golden Dawn, it was founded in Los Angeles in 1990 by David Cherubim who now serves as its Frater Superior Chief. It exists to assist people in their initiation as thelemic magicians and to spread the Law of Thelema worldwide. Thelema (from the Greek word for will) is an approach to magic which attempts to assist the magician in the location of his/her particular destiny or True Will. The thelemic magician, having discovered his/her True Will is bound to identify with and follow it.

Members enter the order as a neophyte. Work is then pursued in seven successive grades beginning with Zelator. These grades or levels closely resemble the grades of the **Ordo Templi Orientis,** the order that Crowley headed during his lifetime. The seven grades are seen as corresponding to the seven chakras of the subtle body in the Indian tantric system, the seven planets found in traditional **astrology,** and the seven metals included in **alchemy.**

Members consider themselves a body of Free Warriors whose task is to extend the Law of Thelema as contained in *The Book of the Law,* the text of which Crowley claimed to have received from a preternatural entity named Aiwass in 1904. To this end members engage in occult research, practical mysticism, **ceremonial magic,** and tantric alchemy. Members are also expected to be thoroughly grounded in Crowley's thought as found in his many books.

The OTGD is headquartered in Los Angeles. Its website can be found at http://www.tgd.org/.

Sources:

Crowley, Aleister. *Magick: Book Four, Parts I-IV.* York Beach, ME: Samuel Weiser, 1994. [Includes *The Book of the Law,* a brief text that has been reprinted numerous times.]

———. *Magick in Theory and Practice.* New York: Dover Publications, 1976.

Order of the White Rose

The order of the White Rose was an esoteric Spiritualist organization that included elements of Rosicrucianism and mysticism not generally associated with **Spiritualism.** Its founder was Jesse Charles Fremont Grumbine (1861–1938), who created the order in the 1890s in Chicago. Around 1900 he moved to Boston, where he lived for many years. Then in 1921 he moved first to Cleveland, Ohio, and two years later to Portland, Oregon.

For Grumbine, there was a distinction between Universal Spirit and personal individual spirits. Universal Spirit does not exist as a deity outside of the universe, but as the radiant center from which spirits draw their life. Matter is the substance of form. Form defines and limits spirits, which are temporal, relative, and finite. Spiritualism reveals the spirit of God within each human spirit. By bringing evidence of **survival** of death and of disencarnate spirits, Spiritualism demonstrates the divinity of each spirit. Psychic abilities (clairvoyance, telepathy, healing, and prevision) are innate divine powers. Grumbine believed that the proper use and control of those powers could produce a divine manhood and womanhood.

The order was organized into two branches, the order of the Red Rose, an outer branch, and the order of the White Rose, its esoteric branch. Both branches were believed to lead members to the inner celestial branch of the order. Members were organized into chapters, though no information on the size of the order has survived. It published a number of books by Grumbine, an indication of at least some degree of success. There is no record of the order surviving Grumbine.

Sources:

Grumbine, J. C. F. *Clairaudience.* Boston: Order of the White Rose, 1911.

———. *Clairvoyance.* Boston: Order of the White Rose, 1911.

———. *Melchizedek; or, The Secret Doctrine of the Bible.* Boston: Order of the White Rose, 1919.

Ordo Rosae Rubeae et Aureae Crucis (Order of Rose of Ruby and Cross of Gold)

The second order or level of the Hermetic Order of the **Golden Dawn,** usually known by the initials R. R. et A. C. It included the grades of zelator adeptus minor, theoricus adeptus minor, adeptus major, and adeptus exemtis. The group was formed in 1892 by **S. L. M. Macgregor Mathers,** with **William W. Westcott** as Chief Adept.

It was kept secret from some members of the Golden Dawn and accessible only to those who had passed through the basic four grades. The R. R. et A. C. gave instructions in ritual **magic.** The poet, **W. B. Yeats** was initiated into the 5°=6° grade January 20–21, 1893. During later controversies in 1901, Yeats privately published a pamphlet titled *Is the R. R. et A. C. to Remain a Magical Order?*

Sources:

Harper, George Mills. *Yeat's Golden Dawn.* Wellingsborough, Northamptonshire, UK: Aquarian Press, 1974.

King, Francis. *The Rites of Modern Occult Magic.* New York: Macmillan Co., 1970.

Yeats, William Butler. *Is the R. R. et A. C. to Remain a Magical Order?* Privately printed, 1901.

Ordo Stellae et Serpente

The Ordo Stellae et Serpente (Order of the Star and the Serpent) is a magical order in the thelemic tradition founded on June 21 (the summer solstice), 1999, in Sacramento, California. It is headed by several advanced teachers, Adepti of the "Inner Continuum," who serve as personal mentors of the order's newer members.

Neophytes begin their work with basic studies in occult wisdom, including instruction in **gemantria, numerology, astrology,** and **tarot.** They are introduced to the understanding of the universe symbolized in the cabalistic Tree of Life diagram, the body's subtle energy system centered in the **chakras** and the **kundalini** energy, and the basics of **ceremonial magic.** Neophytes are expected to develop a daily practice in meditation and ritual and to broaden their knowledge with reading in the literature of Western magic. During this training period, the Adepti provide personal guidance and offer discourses that may be experienced in person (for those who live in northern California) or online. Regular rituals are held in the temple of the order. Members at a geographical distance participate in their own personal temple at an astrologically coordinated time. The goal of the basic training is the initiate's becoming an independent practitioner of ceremonial magic while at the same time learning to work in concert with others. It is the belief that both solitary and group work is necessary in the present age.

It is also the belief of the order that magical work will lead to an awareness of the meta-dimensional harmonious Unity. Encounter with the Unity does not lead to absorption, but to a more clearly defined individual who also feels at One with the totality of the universe. It is the teaching of the order that magical activity does not make us more than human, but grants knowledge of what it means to be fully human.

Advanced students are free to explore the variety of distinct magical systems, from Enochian to Egyptian to Tantric and Thelemic. In the process, the initiate remembers him/herself as a Divine Being of his/her own creation. This realization provides the entrance into the mysteries of the Inner Order that guides the Ordo Stellae et Serpente, known as the Elect Order of **Melchizedek.**

The order may be contacted through its Internet site at http://members.aol.com/Yechidah37/ossintro.html. It does not ask for set dues, but is supported by the tithing and gifts of its members.

Sources:

Ordo Stellae et Serpente. http://members.aol.com/Yechidah37/ossintro.html. May 20, 2000.

Ordo Templi Orientis (Grant)

Aleister Crowley served as outer head of the Order of the Ordo Templi Orientis (OTO), until his death in 1947, when he was succeeded by Karl Germer. Germer died in 1962 without naming a clear successor, and among the people who emerged to succeed him was Kenneth Grant. Germer had given Grant a charter to begin a lodge in London to work the first three of the nine degrees of the OTO system, and in 1955 he founded New Isis Lodge. However, when Grant began working the higher degrees using his own material, Germer expelled him from the order. After Germer died in 1962, there was no one in England to challenge Grant's authority, and for a decade he operated unchallenged. In 1969 Grant co-edited *The Confessions of Aleister Crowley,* and in 1973 he published *Aleister Crowley and the Hidden God,* the first of a series of books on the thelemic magical tradition. As these books appeared, they described his work with the **Kabala** (the Hebrew system of magic that became very popular in western magic in the twentieth century). He described his experiences exploring the Qliphoth, the negative side of the kabalistic work. While some accused Grant of flirting with **black magic,** other magical students were drawn to his work. Grant also brought out new editions of the work of the eccentric artist and magician Austin O. Spare.

Grant's OTO practiced a program similar to other OTO groups. Its goal was the establishment of the Law of Thelema (Will) in the world. New members had to have been practicing magic for at least nine months prior to being accepted in the order and had to agree to disseminate Liber LXXVII, the brief statement of thelemic principles written by Crowley. Grant also dropped the masonic initiatory degree system found in most magical groups, including the American OTO. Members are expected to seek their own true will (destiny) by their magical work.

Under Grant, the OTO dominated the British ritual magic scene into the 1970s. Over the last two decades a number of other thelemic magical groups have arisen in Great Britain and Grant's OTO has come to the United States, though it has remained small.

Ordo Templi Orientis (OTO)

A ritual magic organization founded in **Germany** around 1904. The order found its inspiration in the medieval Knights Templar, who were suppressed through most of Europe in the fourteenth century. Among the charges made against the order were that they practiced various forms of illicit sex, specifically sodomy and bestiality. Through the nineteenth century a number of groups had emerged in both **France** and Germany claiming to carry on the Templar tradition. However, this order seems to have originated out of a Masonic group founded by Karl Keller and **Theodor Reuss** and chartered in 1902 by English Mason John Yarker. They began publishing a magazine, *Oriflamme,* in which the first mention of the OTO occurred. There was mention that the order possessed the key of all hermetic and Masonic secrets (i.e., sex magic).

Keller claimed to have learned his secrets from three adepts, two Hindu and one Arab. His adepts seem to have been the sex manuals from India, the *Kama Sutra* and *Ananda Ranga,* and the Arab manual the *Perfumed Garden.* Keller died in 1905 and Reuss succeeded him as outer head of the order.

Meanwhile, in England, magician **Aleister Crowley** had emerged as head of his own magic order, the Astrum Argentinum. In 1909, with one of his initates, Victor Neuberg, Crowley conducted a series of magic spells modeled after the invocations in the Enochian language produced by Edward Kelley, the clairvoyant who worked with Elizabethan magician John Dee. Crowley would pronounce the invocation, hoping to receive a vision, the content of which Neuberg would write down. Halfway through the invocations, Crowley had the idea of the two of them performing a ritual sex act. Several years later he published a volume of free verse, *The Book of Lies.*

Theodor Reuss read the book and perceived that Crowley had discerned the secret of the OTO and confronted him with his discovery. Reportedly, Crowley at that point perceived that the ritual sex in which he had engaged was the key to understanding Rosicrucian, Masonic, and magic symbolism.

Crowley was invited to join the OTO and became the outer head of the order for England. He was also invited to rewrite much of the ritual material. The order was organized in a Masonic manner, with a system of ten degrees, progress upward through the degrees admitting the member to more of the inner teachings. In the first six degrees of the OTO students were taught a general occult system that prepared them for the introduction of the sexual magic presented in the seventh, eighth, and ninth degrees. The tenth degree was purely administrative. Crowley later introduced an eleventh degree based upon his homoerotic predilections.

During the 1970s the secret materials of the OTO were published. They revealed a system of sexual magic based on the use of sex to accomplish goals in magic. Crowley's system is very different from the mystical sexual practices of tantric yoga, with which it has often been compared.

Reuss resigned his position in 1922 and Crowley became the outer head of the order. The order became his major means of spreading his particular magical philosophy based on the revelatory *The Book of the Law,* which he claimed he had received from a disembodied intelligence in 1904. This book was translated into German in the mid-1920s, and many of the German members rejected Crowley and his perspective. They withdrew and continued as a pre-Crowleyite OTO, although enough German members accepted Crowley that he could count one German lodge in his branch of the order. Both of the German groups were destroyed by the Nazi regime. A group continuing the anti-Crowley lineage reemerged in Switzerland after the war.

During the time he headed the OTO Crowley experimented with a variety of magic practices, wrote widely, and compiled a curriculum consisting of his own books and some additional valuable works on magic for the order members. He died in 1947 and left the leadership of the order to **Karl Germer,** a German who had moved to the United States after a nasty encounter with the Nazis. Germer was a loyal member but the order languished under him. He did charter a lodge in England under the leadership of **Kenneth Grant,** but then withdrew the charter when Grant began to operate outside its dictates.

Germer died in 1962. He had initiated no new members nor arranged for a successor. He was so out of touch with the members that for many years some did not even know that he had died. The order languished and could easily have dissolved. However, in 1969 Grady McMurtry, a member residing in the San Francisco Bay area, began to reorganize the OTO. McMurtry had been given a document by Crowley containing broad emergency measures. Through the 1970s and until his death in 1985, McMurtry rebuilt the order (assisted by the publication of many of Crowley's books), and by the time of his death there were lodges across the United States and in a number of foreign countries. By 1992 the order had approximately 2,100 members in 135 lodges and local groups in some twenty countries.

Several months after McMurtry's death, the ninth-degree members met and elected a new caliph (the title assumed by McMurtry because of the way he came to head the order). The new caliph has chosen to keep his identity a secret from all except the higher-degree members and has never published his real name. He goes by his title, Hymenaeus Beta, acting outer head of the order.

One part of the organization of the OTO is an ecclesiatical structure, the Ecclesia Gnostica Catholica (or Gnostic Catholic Church). The church offers a Gnostic-like mass written by Crowley that embodies the order's perspective in a public, ritualized, and celebratory setting. Crowley was consecrated a bishop in the French Gnostic tradition of Charles J. Doinel, and he in turn passed that episcopal authority to the OTO leadership.

The order values and uses all of Aleister Crowley's writings on magic. In the 1980s it published two collections of the most important writings, one concerning the OTO and its organizational structure, and a second consisting of the "holy books" (the revelatory material received, i.e., channeled, by Crowley, as opposed to the books he consciously wrote). The first was issued as Volume 3, number 10 of *The Equinox,* one of the order's periodicals.

Address: JAF Box 7666, New York, NY 10116.

Sources:

Crowley, Aleister. *Magick in Theory and Practice.* 4 vols. Paris, 1929.

Heidrick, Bill. *Magick and Qaballah.* Berkeley, Calif.: Ordo Templi Orientis, 1980.

Hymenaeus Beta, comp. *The Equinox* 3, no. 10. New York: Thelema Publications, 1986.

King, Francis. *The Holy Books of Thelema.* York Beach, Maine: Samuel Weiser, 1988.

———. *O.T.O. System Outline.* San Francisco, Calif.: Stellar Vision, 1981.

———. *The Rites of Modern Occult Magic.* New York: Macmillan, 1970.

———. *Sexuality, Magic and Perversion.* New York: Citadel Press, 1972.

Symonds, John. *The King of the Shadow Realm.* London: Duckworth, 1989.

Ordo Templi Orientis (Roanoke, Virginia)

The Ordo Templi Orientis (Roanoke, Virginia) was one of several ritual magic groups to emerge in the 1970s. **Karl Germer** had served as outer head of the order for 15 years (1947–62), but after his death, the order endured a period of leaderlessness and corporate chaos. While several leaders stepped forward with papers and claims from either **Aleister Crowley** or Germer, Robert E. L. Snell put forward other credentials. He suggested that the mission of the OTO was to facilitate the movement of humanity into the new age of the Aeon of Horus, which had been announced by Crowley in 1904. Snell suggested that leaders must validate their role by their allegiance to the Law of Thelema (Will), the primary principle guiding the order. He also claimed direct contact with the secret chiefs, those preternatural beings (similar to the Theosophical Society's **Great White Brotherhood**) believed to be ultimately guiding the order.

Ordre Kabbalistique de la Rosecroix

A French Rosicrucian order founded by Joséphin Péladan (1858–1918) and the Marquis Stanislas de Guaita (1860–1898). The occultist **Gérard Encausse** (known as "Papus") was a member on the Supreme Council.

Orenda

A magical force. (See **America, United States of**)

Oresme, Nicole (ca. 1320–1382)

Bishop of Lisieux, France, in 1378, who published works on theology, politics, economics, mathematics, and physical science. His book *Livre de Divinacions* expresses orthodox theological thought on various aspects of medieval occultism. The book is titled after the *De Divinatione* of Cicero and defines the arguments for and against belief in the occult, lists frauds and deceptions in divination, and distinguishes between **astrology** and astronomy. Oresme accepted **alchemy** and ascribed occult success to demons.

Oresme was born ca. 1320, probably in Normandy, and entered the College of Navarre in Paris in 1348. As Archdeacon of Bayeux, he accepted the Deanship of Rouen but retained his university office until obliged to relinquish it due to a decision by the Parliament of Paris. In 1378, after his translation of the works of Aristotle into French, he was given the bishopric of Lisieux. He died in 1382.

His *Livre de Divinacions* was originally written in Latin, subsequently in French. In the absence of an English translation, there was little scholarly discussion of the work until the 1900s. In 1934, Lynn Thorndike devoted three chapters in Volume 3 of *History of Magic and Experimental Science* to a detailed study of Oresme's work.

Sources:

Coopland, G. W. *Nicole Oresme and the Astrologers; A Study of His "Livre de Divinacions."* Liverpool, UK: University Press of Liverpool, 1952.

Thorndike, Lynn. *History of Magic and Experimental Science.* Vol. 3. New York: Columbia University Press, 1923–58.

Organisation pour la Recherche en Psychotronique

The Organisation pour la Recherche en Paychotronique was founded in 1987 in Toulouse, France, by the leadership of the **Laboratorie Universitaire de Parapsychologie et d'Hygiene Mental** to promote research in parapsychology in France and other French-speaking countries and throughout Europe. Its major contribution to the field was the formation of l'Oeil (the Eye), a library and data bank of parapsychological publications, through which it attempted to keep people in the field aware of research that had been conducted in order to avoid needless repetition of work in what has become a vast field. L'Oeil provided a mail order service for members who request articles from the library and data files.

The organization published two periodicals, including a journal, *Revue Francaise de Parapsychologie,* and a bulletin. Last known address: c/o Yves Lignon-OEIL, Laboratorie de Parapsychologie, UER Mathématiques, Université Toulouse-Le-Mirail 31058, Toulouse CEDEX, France.

Organization of Awareness (Canada)

The Organization of Awareness (now **Cosmic Awareness Communications**) underwent a splintering following the death in 1967 of its channel, William Ralph Duby. One group, headquartered in Calgary, Alberta, Canada, under the leadership of Nick Chwelos, attempted to carry on the original effort, but it lasted only a few years.

Organization of Awareness (Federal Way)

Channel William Ralph Duby, whose messages had tied together the Organization of Awareness (now **Cosmic Awareness Communications,**) died in 1967. At that time the original group, which included adherents from around North America, splintered into a number of factions. One independent branch was established in Federal Way, Washington, by Frances Marcx. As with most of the splinter groups, it survived only a few years.

Organization of Awareness (Olympia)

The Organization of Awareness (now **Cosmic Awareness Communications**) was originally founded in the early 1960 and was built around the channeled material of William Ralph Duby. In 1967 Duby died, and the organization broke into a number of independent factions. One such faction, the Organization of Awareness of Olympia, Washington, was headed by David DeMoulin. It lasted only a few years.

Orgone

Primordial cosmic energy, claimed to have been discovered by **Wilhelm Reich** between 1936 and 1940. It is believed to be universally present and demonstrable visually (a blueness in the atmosphere), thermically, electrosopically, and by means of a Geiger-Müller counter. It manifest in living organisms as biological energy.

Reich invented what he termed an "orgone energy accumulator," a device to concentrate orgone energy in a box constructed from metallic material and covered by organic material. Reich found a temperature difference between the inside and outside of the accumulator and believed that the accumulated energy had a therapeutic effect on individuals. He performed experiments using the accumulator on cancer patients and reported substantial improvement in the health of patients. He authorized use of the accumulator for "therapeutic" purposes provided it was used in conjunction with "reputable" medical advice. As a result, he was the subject of court action instituted by the Food and Drug Administration in the United States. The FDA argued the accumulator had no demonstrable scientific effect on the human body.

As physician and psychotherapist, Reich rejected the charges against him and the accumulator and denied the right of federal inspectors to arbitrate in matters of natural science, an argument not accepted by the court. His attack upon the court's authority caused his imprisonment for contempt of court. The court also ordered the destruction of his apparatus and the burning of his books. He died in prison. Many of his writings have been republished.

Currently, the idea of a static device accumulating some form of energy is being investigated; it has yet to be demonstrated scientifically. In the 1970s and 1980s, some people experimented with pyramid forms in an effort to claim this effect and sharpen old razor blades. Reich also claimed discovery of a motor force in orgone energy comparable with similar claims by **John Ernst Worrell Keely** and **John Murray Spear.**

Compared to Other Occult Concepts

Some have noticed the similarity of orgone energy to earlier ideas of **"Od"** and the occult concepts of vital force. The biological manifestation of orgone energy in humans as described by Reich is comparable to the **kundalini** energy of Hindu **yoga** science, but more closely resembles the idea of **prana.**

An account of the construction of an orgone accumulator was given in Vol. 2 of *The Discovery of the Orgone* by Wilhelm Reich or the booklet *The Orgone Energy Accumulator.* Observations on orgone energy were published in the journal *Orgonomic Functionalism* edited by Paul and Jean Ritter, published between 1954 and 1963 from Nottingham, England, and in *Energy and Character; the Journal of Bioenergetic Research* published from 1970 onwards by David Boadella (an associate of Paul Ritter) from Abbotsbury, Dorset, England. In June 1955, the official American Association for Medical Orgonomy began publishing *Orgonomic Medicine* (c/o Orgonomic Publications Inc., 515 E. 88 St., New York, N.Y. 10028).

Sources:

Boadella, David. *Wilhelm Reich: the Evolution of His Work.* Chicago: Henry Regnery, 1973.

Mann, William Edward. *Orgone, Reich and Eros.* New York: Simon and Schuster, 1973.

Raknes, Ola. *Wilhelm Reich and Orgonomy.* New York: St. Martin's Press, 1970.

Reich, Wilhelm. *The Discovery of the Orgone.* 2 vols. New York: Orgone Institute Press, n.d.

———. *The Orgone Energy Accumulator.* New York: Orgone Institute Press, n.d.

———. *Selected Writings: An Introduction to Orgonomy.* New York: Farrar, Straus, and Giroux, 1973.

Schul, Bill, and Ed Pettit. *The Secret Power of Pyramids.* Greenwich, Conn.: Fawcett, 1975.

Sharaf, Myron. *Fury on Earth: A Biography of Wilhelm Reich.* New York: St. Martin's Press, 1983.

The Origin

The "Origin" is the name given the source of the channelled material received by Canadian businessman Amyn Dahya. Dahya was born to an Indian family of Muslim background living in Arusha, Tanzania, in West Africa, but as a child moved to Mombasa, Kenya, where he grew up. He was sent to England for college, and after receiving his degree in chemical engineering, he moved to Canada. Shortly thereafter he married his wife Karina, and subsequently fathered four children. In 1987 he founded the Casmyn Corporation, a company whose business took Dahya around the world. During his travels he visited his family's homeland in India and discovered firsthand the poverty in which many children were born. He developed a vision of spending his life improving the lives of others, especially children. To that end, in 1992 he founded the Bismallah Children's Fund. In 1993, Dahya began to receive messages from the Origin via automatic writing. The first messages were received when he was awakened in the middle of the night. At a later date he began to hear the messages, which he transcribed. The messages asked him to deliver the content, summarized in a "Statement of Universal Truth," to the world. The Origin is described as the Creator of All Things. Origin is believed to have given human beings all that was necessary for their service to the world, including freedom to act and flexibility to think. The Origin guides humanity and has offered a fundamental guiding principle: "Each of Us is a part of the Creator. Therefore, I am You and You are Me. Together We are Everything." The continued reception of information, at first considered merely a personal event, soon took on more expansive dimensions as Dahya understood that the messages were meant to be broadly shared. He received messages of general significance along with messages for specific groups. The most important of the latter was a set of messages on the nature of the scientific task and the problems currently faced by scientists who do not understand the consequences of their actions for the environment. The first collection of messages from the Origin was released in 1997. Further messages are expected to be released in the future.

Sources:

Dahya, Amyn. *Reflections from the Origin.* Vancouver, BC: Reflections Publishing, 1997.

The Orion Mystery

A book proposing that the **pyramids** of Giza, Egypt, are a terrestrial map of the constellation Orion, traditional home of the soul of the reborn kings of **Egypt.**

Sources:

Bauval, Robert, and Adrian Gilbert. *The Orion Mystery.* London: Heinemann, 1994.

Oris (1954–)

Oris is the spiritual name of Tsvelev Sergei Vassillievich, a psychic channel who emerged in Russia in the 1990s following the demise of the Soviet Union. Oris was born on January 25, 1954, in Mariinka, a town in the Donetsk. In 1978 he entered the Crimean Agricultural Institute, but his work in farming merely concealed his real interests. He became a student of martial arts and mastered kung-fu, karate, and judo, along with dim-mak, the art of deferred death. From his accomplishments, he wrote three books, which he were published in 1992 as *A Way of Karate: From the Pupil Up to the Master* (in Russian).

More importantly, Oris had become a channel, regularly receiving messages from a group of entities he came to know as the Universal Teachers. Many of these teachers come from the **Pleiades** and the Sirius star systems. Through the 1980s he spoke little about his channeling work for fear of being diagnosed as mentally deranged and placed in an asylum. Only in the 1990s did he begin sharing the information he had received. In 1990 he began to channel regularly and received the material for a book that he called *Life After Life, or the Revelation of Aquarius.* In the late 1990s, an English translation of that book, on the destiny of the human soul, was made available to a Western audience through the Internet. The book describes the movement of the soul after death into various spheres of the fiery world, its meeting with spiritual hierarchies in space, and its preparation for reincarnation.

While Oris' understanding of the destiny of the soul contradicts that of traditional Russian Christianity, he insists that his message is Christian in its emphasis on the essential truth of love and its attempt to highlight Jesus' words that his followers would surpass his deeds. The channeled messages attempt to free people from the bondage of dogmatism and conservatism. It is his belief that the One Truth had been split by various churches into competing truths. This competition will have disastrous results.

Oris believes the Earth is about to make a leap into the next dimension when many will experience **ascension** (known as the day of judgment in traditional religion). Those with love in their hearts and the truth of what is occurring will be able to overcome space and time and unite with the Higher Cosmic Consciousness. The continued bickering of religious groups is counterproductive to that end. While some accept ascension, others will be killed as ecological disasters and a world war wipe out a large percentage of humanity.

Oris currently resides in Yalta. His work can be accessed on the Internet at http:/members.xoom.com_XMCM/orisde/English/.

Sources:

The Channel Oris. http://members.xoom.com_XMCM/orisde/English/. March 1, 2000.

Ornithomancy

The ancient Greek term for augury, the method of **divination** by the flight or song of **birds.** For the Romans, it became a part of their national religion and had a distinct priesthood. The practice was also popular among the Spanish people, the Amoganenses.

Orton

A spirit alluded to by the historian, Jean Froissart (1338–ca. 1410) as the **familiar** of the Lord of Corasse. According to legend a clerk whom his lordship had wronged had the spirit torment his superior, but through conversation the Lord of Corasse won the spirit over and Orton became his familiar. Nightly Orton would shake his pillow and waken him to tell him the news of the world. Froissart wrote:

"So Orton continued to serve the Lord of Corasse for a long time. I do not know whether he had more than one master, but, every week, at night, twice or thrice, he visited his master, and related to him the events which had happened in the different countries he had traversed, and the lord of Corasse wrote of them to the Count of Foix, who took a great pleasure in them, for he was the man in all the world who most willingly heard news of strange countries.

"Now it happened that the Lord of Corasse, as on other nights, was lying in his bed in his chamber by the side of his wife, who had become accustomed to listen to Orton without any alarm. Orton came, and drew away the lord's pillow, for he was fast asleep, and his lord awoke, and cried, 'Who is this?' He answered, 'It is I, Orton.' 'And whence comest thou?' 'I come from Prague, in Bohemia.' 'And how far from hence is this Prague, in Bohemia?' 'Why,' said he, 'about sixty days' journey.' 'And thou hast come so quickly?' 'Faith, I go as quickly as the wind, or even swifter.' 'And thou hast wings?' 'Faith, none.' 'How then canst thou fly so quickly?' Orton replied—'It does not concern thee to know.' 'Nay,' said he, 'I shall be very glad to know what fashion and form thou art of,' Orton answered, 'It does not concern thee to know; it is sufficient that I come hither, and bring thee sure and certain news.' 'By G—, Orton,' exclaimed the lord of Corasse, 'I should love thee better if I had seen thee.' 'Since you have so keen a desire to see me,' said Orton 'the first thing thou shalt see and encounter tomorrow morning, when you rise from your bed, shall be—I.' 'That is enough,' said the Lord of Corasse. 'Go, therefore; I give thee leave for the night.'

"When the morrow came, the Lord of Corasse began to rise, but the lady was so affrighted that she fell sick and could not get up that morning, and she said to her lord, who did not wish her to keep her bed, 'See if thou seest Orton. By my faith, I neither wish, if it please God, to see nor encounter him.' 'But I do,' said the Lord of Corasse. He leapt all nimbly from his bed, and seated himself upon the edge, and waited there to see Orton, but saw nothing. Then he went to the windows and threw them upon that he might see more clearly about the room, but he saw nothing, so that he could say, 'This is Orton.' The day passed, the night returned.

"When the Lord of Corasse was in his bed asleep, Orton came, and began speaking in his wonted manner. 'Go, go,' said his master, 'thou art a fibber: thou didst promise to show me to-day who thou wert, and thou hast not done so.' 'Nay,' said he, 'but I did.' 'Thou didst not.' 'And didst thou not see anything,' inquired Orton, 'when thou didst leap out of bed?' The Lord of Corasse thought a little while, and said—'Yes, while sitting on my bed, and thinking of thee, I saw two long straws upon the pavement, which turned towards each other and played about.' 'And that was I,' cried Orton, 'I had assumed that form.' Said the Lord of Corasse: 'It does not content me: I pray thee change thyself into some other form, so that I may see and know thee.' Orton replied: 'You will act so that you will lose me.' 'Not so,' said the Lord of Corasse: 'When I have once seen you, I shall not want to see you ever again.' 'Then,' said Orton, 'you shall see me tomorrow; and remember that the first thing you shall see upon leaving your chamber, will be I.' 'Be it so,' replied the Lord of Corasse. 'Begone with you, therefore, now. I give thee leave, for I wish to sleep.'

"Orton departed. When the morrow came, and at the third hour, the Lord of Corasse was up and attired in his usual fashion, he went forth from his chamber into a gallery that looked upon the castle-court. He cast therein his glances, and the first thing he saw was the largest sow he had ever seen; but she was so thin she seemed nothing but skin and bones, and she had great and long teats, pendant and quite attenuated, and a long and inflamed snout.

"The Sire de Corasse marvelled very much at this sow, and looked at her in anger, and exclaimed to his people, 'Go quickly, bring the dogs hither, and see that this Sow be well hunted.' The varlets ran nimbly, threw open the place where the dogs lay, and set them at the sow. The sow heaved a loud cry, and looked up at the Lord of Corasse, who supported himself upon a pillar buttress in front of his chamber. She was seen no more afterwards, for she vanished, nor did any one note what became of her. The Sire de Corasse returned into his chamber pensively, and bethought himself of Orton, and said, 'I think that I have seen my familiar; I repent me that I set my dogs upon him, for I doubt if I shall ever behold him again, since he has several times told me that as soon as I should provoke him I should lose him, and he would return no more.' He spoke truly; never again did Orton return to the Lord of Corasse, and the knight died in the following year."

Ortt, Felix (1866–1959)

Dutch engineer who developed a philosophy of "pneumatic-energetic monism," proposing that a spirit revealed itself under energy and entelechy. Ortt wrote on parapsychological subjects, including a theory of temperature drop in relation to psychical phenomena and "Philosophy of Occultism and Spiritualism," on concepts of substantiality and causality.

Osborn, Arthur W(alter) (1891– ?)

British author of books on the paranormal, higher consciousness, and mysticism. He was born March 10, 1891, in London, England, and privately educated. He became a businessman in the Dutch East Indies (1913–14) and later in Australia (1920–54). His career was interrupted by service in the British Army, Royal Field Artillery, during World War I. He received the Military Cross. Though he lived in Australia, Isborn was a member of the **Society for Psychical Research,** London.

Sources:

Berger, Arthur S., and Joyce Berger. *The Encyclopedia of Parapsychology and Psychical Research.* New York: Paragon House, 1991.

Osborn, Arthur W. *The Axis and the Rim: The Quest for Reality in a Modern Setting.* London: V. Stuart, 1963.

———. *The Cosmic Womb: An Interpretation of Man's Relationship to the Infinite.* Wheaton, Ill.: Theosophical Publishing House, 1969.

———. *The Expansion of Awareness: One Man's Search for Meaning in Living.* Wheaton, Ill.: Theosophical Publishing House, 1967.

———. *The Future Is Now: The Significance of Precognition.* New Hyde Park, N.Y.: University Books, 1961.

———. *The Meaning of Personal Existence in the Light of Paranormal Phenomena: The Doctrine of Reincarnation & Mystical States of Consciousness.* London: Sidgwick and Jackson, 1966.

———. *Occultism, Christian Science and Healing.* 1926.

———. *The Superphysical; A Review of the Evidence for Continued Existence, Reincarnation, and Mystical States of Consciousness.* 1937.

———. *What Am I Living For?* 1974.

Pleasants, Helene, ed. *Biographical Dictionary of Parapsychology.* New York: Helix Press, 1964.

Osborn, Edward Collet (1909–1957)

British publicist and parapsychologist. He was born on November 4, 1909, at Irvingdean, Sussex, England and later studied at Giggleswick School, Yorkshire. Osborn was active in the **Society for Psychical Research** for the last decade of his life (1947–57). During this time he served on the council and edited the *Journal.* He also edited the society's *Proceedings* (1951–57). Osborn worked with the publishing company of Benn, and from 1932, with the Royal Institute of International Affairs. He died March 27, 1957, in London.

Sources:

Osborn, Edward Collet. "The Woman in Brown, an Investigation of an Apparition." *Journal* of the Society for Psychical Research (1939).

Osborn, Edward Collet, and C. C. Evans. "An Experiment in the Electro-Encephalography of Mediumistic Trance." *Journal* of the Society for Psychical Research (1952).

Oscilloclast

An apparatus invented by "healer" Dr. **Albert Abrams** (1863–1924), pioneer of **radionics.** It is better known by its popular name, the **black box.**

Sources:

Scott, G. Laughton. *The Abrams Treatment in Practice; an Investigation.* London: n.p., 1925.

Osis, Karlis (1917–1997)

Parapsychologist who investigated extrasensory perception, spontaneous psi phenomena, and mediumship. He was born on December 26, 1917, at Riga, Latvia. After World War II he completed his graduate training in Germany at the University of Munich (Ph.D., 1950). His doctoral thesis concerned interpretations of Extrasensory Perception (ESP). He moved to the United States in 1950 on the displaced persons program after graduation and became a United States citizen in 1959.

His professional career in parapsychology began as a research associate at the **Parapsychology Laboratory** at Duke University (1951–57). Osis subsequently became director of research at the **Parapsychology Foundation** in New York City (1957–62), and in 1962 became director of research at **American Society for Psychical Research.** He was a council member of the **Parapsychological Association** and served as its president for one term (1961–62).

At Duke University from 1951–1957, he worked with **J. B. Rhine** and explored the relationship between ESP and psychokinesis, precognition, and psi between men and animals. In 1958, Osis investigated the poltergeist phenomena at Seaford, Long Island, N.Y., and concluded the facts did not support a paranormal explanation. His report was published in the March-April 1958 *Newsletter* of the Parapsychology Foundation. Among his studies were those concerning the effect of distance on ESP and the relationship between meditation and ESP. Before moving to the American Society for Psychical Research he began work on deathbed experiences indicative of survival.

Osis died December 26, 1997.

Sources:

Berger, Arthur S., and Joyce Berger. *The Encyclopedia of Parapsychology and Psychical Research.* New York: Paragon House, 1991.

Osis, Karlis. *Deathbed Observations by Physicians and Nurses.* New York: Parapsychology Foundation, 1961.

———. "ESP Tests at Long and Short Distances." *Journal of Parapsychology* 20, 2 (1956).

———. "Out-of-the-Body Research at the ASPR." *ASPR Newsletter* 22 (1974),

———. "A Test of the Relationship Between ESP and PK." *Journal of Parapsychology* 17, 4 (1953).

———. "What Did The Dying See?" *ASPR Newsletter* 24 (1975).

Osis, Karlis, and Erlendur Haraldsson. *At the Hour of Death.* New York: Avon Books, 1977. Rev. ed.: New York: Hasting House, 1986.

Pleasants, Helene, ed. *Biographical Dictionary of Parapsychology.* New York: Helix Press, 1964.

Osmond, Humphrey (Fortescue) (1917–)

Psychiatrist who studied psychedelics and parapsychology. He was born July 1, 1917, at Milford, Surrey, England. He studied at the Royal College of Physicians and Surgeons, Canada, receiving a certificate in psychiatry in 1952; Guy's Hospital, London, England, receiving a M.R.C.S. and L.R.C.P. in 1942; and St. George's Hospital, London receiving a diploma in psychological medicine in 1949. During World War II, Osmond served as a surgeon lieutenant in the Royal Navy (1942–47), and afterward served in various positions in hospitals in London. In 1953, he moved to Canada as a physician superintendent and director of research (1953–61) at Saskatchewan Hospital, Weyburn, Canada. In 1961, he became the director of the Bureau of Research in Neurology and Psychiatry for the State of New Jersey.

In the 1950s, Osmond became interested in psychedelics, the study of mental activities and states of consciousness in relation to drugs and other pharmacological substances. His research then veered into parapsychology and the study of imagery in mediumship. He authored papers and books from his two decades of research. He was co-chairman with **Emilio Servadio** at the Conference on Parapsychology and Pharmacology held in 1959 at St. Paul de Vence, France.

Sources:

Osmond, Humphrey. "A Call for Imaginative Theory." *International Journal of Parapsychology* (Autumn 1959).

Osmond, Humphrey, and Abram Hoffer. *The Chemical Basis of Clinical Psychiatry.* Springfield, Ill.: Thomas, 1960.

Osmond, Humphrey, and Abram Hoffer. *The Hallucinogens.* New York: Academic Press, 1967.

Osmond, Humphrey, and Bernard Aaronson, eds. *Psychedelics: The Uses and Implications of Hallucinogenic Drugs.* Cambridge, Mass.: Schenkman, 1971.

Osmond, Humphrey, H. Yaker, and F. Cheek. *The Future of Time: Man's Temporal Environment.* Garden City, N.Y.: Doubleday, 1971.

Pleasants, Helene, ed. *Biographical Dictionary of Parapsychology.* New York: Helix Press, 1964.

Osmont, Anne (1872–1953)

Clairvoyant, author, and lecturer. Born August 2, 1872, at Toulouse, France. Osmont published articles on psychic subjects in *Initiation et Science* and *Psychic* magazine (a French journal). She died in Paris May 13, 1953.

Sources:

Osmont, Anne. *Envoutements et exorcisms à travers le ages* (Sorcery and Exorcism Through the Ages) N.p., 1954.

———. *Le Mouvement Symboliste* (The Symbolist Movement). Paris: Maison du livre, 1917.

———. *Le Rythme Créateur de forces et de formes* (The Creative Rhythm of Forces and Forms). Paris: Les Editions de Champselysees, 1942.

Ossowiecki, Stephan (1877–1944)

Polish engineer and clairvoyant. Reportedly, he read thoughts from early childhood. At the Engineering Institute at Petrograd, where Ossowiecki studied, he reportedly answered questions enclosed in sealed envelopes. Supposedly he described the colored **auras** of people in his presence, heard raps, and could move objects telekinetically (without physical means). Reportedly when Ossowiecki practiced **telekinesis,** his clairvoyant powers diminished. At the age of thirty-five he "lost" his telekinetic powers and his "gift" of reading sealed papers developed.

With human subjects Ossowiecki claimed to know their most intimate thoughts and read their past, present, and future. Reportedly on several occasions, mostly involuntarily, but once by an effort of will, he projected his likeness over a distance. His friends claimed to have received the impression that he was near in flesh and blood.

Ossowiecki's "powers" were possibly **psychometry** rather than **clairvoyance.** It was claimed he never read the sealed letters word for word but perceived the ideas. He was unable to perceive ideas from typewritten or printed texts. Letters had to be written by a living person. If the writing was in a language he did not know, he could not disclose the contents but supposedly could describe the circumstances connected with the writer and the writing.

He impressed **Charles Richet, Gustave Geley,** and other scientists in reading sealed letters, the contents of which in many cases were unknown to the investigator. To Geley, he read the contents of a letter as follows: "I am in a zoological garden; a fight is going on, a large animal, an elephant. Is he not in the water? I see his trunk as he swims. I see blood."

Geley said: "Good, but that is not all."

Ossowiecki: "Wait, is he not wounded in his trunk?"

Geley: "Very good. There was a fight."

Ossowiecki: "Yes, with a crocodile."

The sentence Geley wrote was "An elephant bathing in the Ganges was attacked by a crocodile who bit off his trunk."

In 1923, at the International Psychical Research Congress in Warsaw, Poland, Ossowiecki "read" the contents of a note sent by the **Society for Psychical Research** and sealed by Dr. **Edwin J. Dingwall** in an envelope. The note had been wrapped in several pieces of colored paper. The note contained the sketch of a flag, a bottle, and the date August 22, 1923. Reportedly Ossowiecki reproduced correctly the flag and the bottle and wrote the numerals of the date, although not in correct order. After the seal was broken, Ossowiecki was accepted by the Congress. The psychical researcher, **Baron Schrenck-Notzing** said: "Thank you, thank you, in the name of science."

Ossowiecki remained in Warsaw during World War II. He was killed in August 1944 during an uprising in which the Nazi occupation forces killed 9500 civilians.

Sources:

Berger, Arthur S., and Joyce Berger. *The Encyclopedia of Parapsychology and Psychical Research.* New York: Paragon House, 1991.

Besterman, Theodore. *Collected Papers on the Paranormal.* New York, Garrett Publications, 1968.

Dingwall, E. J. "An Experiment with Polish Medium Stefan Ossowiecki." *Journal* of the Society for Psychical Research 21 (1924).

Geley, Gustav. *Materialisation and Clairvoyance.* London, 1927.

———. "Une sensationelle expérience de M. Stephan Ossowiecki au Congrès de Varsovie." *Revue Métapsychique* (September-October 1923).

Osty, Eugèn (1874–1938)

French physician and director of the **Institut Métapsychique Internationale.** Osty was born May 16, 1874. He was physician at Jouet sur l'Aubor's from 1901 through 1924.

In 1910, Osty investigated psychical phenomena and summed up his research three years later in *Lucidity and Intuition.* Osty claimed the acquisition of knowledge through paranormal means was possible. His subsequent research was published in *Supernormal Faculties in Man.* He described the source of after-death communication as "crypto-psychism" (lingering after bodily death).

Osty was succeeded by **Gustave Geley** as the head of the Institut Métapsychique. Geley considered Osty "the first living authority on lucidity as applied to a human being, both under its practical and its theoretical aspect. His book *Supernormal Faculties in Man (Une Faculté de Connaissance Supra-Normale)* is truly epochal in the study of subjective metapsychics."

In 1931 and 1932, with the collaboration of his son, Marcel, Osty employed infra-red and ultra-violet rays in the study of physical and physiological phenomena of **Rudi Schneider.** The results were published in *Les Pouvoirs inconnus de l'esprit sur la matiere.* Osty died August 20, 1938.

Sources:

Berger, Arthur S., and Joyce Berger. *The Encyclopedia of Parapsychology and Psychical Research.* New York: Paragon House, 1991.

Osty, Eugene. *Une Faculté de connaissance Supra-Normal.* (Super Normal Faculties in Man). Paris: Felix Alcan, 1926.

Osty, Marcel. "Eugene Osty: Pioneer Researcher." *Tomorrow.* 7, 1 (1959).

Otani, Soji (1924–)

Japanese psychologist who founded the **Japanese Society for Parapsychology.** He was born on December 8, 1924, in Chiba Prefecture, Honshu, Japan. He studied at the University of Tokyo (B.A. 1949), became a research fellow at the National Institute of Education, Tokyo (1951–52), and a lecturer at Chiba University, Chiba-shi (1952–60). In 1960, Otani began his career as a professor at the Defense Academy Yokosuka-shi.

Otani was a charter associate of the Parapsychological Association and councilor at the Japan Psychic Science Association, Tokyo. Otani studied and conducted experiments in Extrasensory Perception (ESP) and Psychokinesis (PK) through the 1970s. In the late 1970s, he headed a team studing the Japanese psychic Masuaki Kiyota in **metal-bending** and nengraphy **(psychic photography);** Kiyota later admitted the results were fraudulent. Otani is generally credited with helping to establish parapsychology in Japan.

Sources:

Otani, Soji. "The Aim of Parapsychology." *Journal of Psychical Research and Spiritualism* (1955).

———. "The Method of ESP Card Testing." *Journal of Psychical Research and Spiritualism* (1951).

———. "Relations of Mental Set and Change of Skin Resistance to ESP Scores." *Journal of Parapsychology* (1955).

———. "Studies on the Influence of Mental and Physiological Conditions Upon ESP Function." *Journal of the Department of Liberal Arts* (Defense Academy) (1959).

———. "A Survey of Public Opinion on Psychical Phenomena" *Journal of Psychical Research and Spiritualism* (1951).

OTO See Ordo Templi Orientis

Ouija Board

Apparatus for psychic **communication.** The name was derived from the French word *oui* and the German word *ja* meaning 'yes.' A medium spells out messages by pointing out letters on a board with the apex of a wooden tripod on rollers. It is an ancient invention; a similar device was used in the days of Pythagoras, about 540 B.C.E. According to a French historical account of the philosopher's life, his sect held séances or circles at "a mystic table, moving on wheels, moved towards signs, which the philosopher and his pupil, Philolaus, interpreted to the audience as being revelations supposedly from the unseen world."

The original ouija board was replaced with a piece of alphabetical cardboard, and a finger-like pointer was added to the narrow end of the wooden tripod. If the pointer and the roll at the apex is replaced by a pencil to form a third leg, the ouija board becomes a **planchette.**

Mrs. Hester Dowden, an English medium stated: "The words come through so quickly that it is almost impossible to read them, and it requires an experienced shorthand writer to take them down when the traveller moves at its maximum speed." She also believed the cooperation of two automatists led to the best results.

It is believed the ouija board, when used as a method of communication, is slow and laborious but frequently works for those unable to receive **automatic writing** with a pencil.

While the ouija board remains popular and is sold commercially as a "game," it has been attacked both by critics of the occult and those within the occult community who consider it unsafe. Some mediums claim to have started with the board and "discovered" their psychic abilities as a result of using it.

Sources:

Gruess, Edmond G. *The Ouija Board: Doorway to the Occult.* Chicago: Moody Press, 1975.

White, Stewart Edward. *The Betty Book.* New York: E. P. Dutton, 1937.

"The Oupnekhat"

According to **Lewis Spence** in *An Encyclopaedia of Occultism,* the *Oupnekhat* or *Oupnekhata* (Book of the Secret) is a work written in Persian providing the following instructions for the production of visions:

"To produce the wise Maschqgui (vision), we must sit on a four-cornered base, namely the heels, and then close the gates of the body. The ears by the thumbs; the eyes by the forefingers; the nose by the middle; the lips by the four other fingers. The lamp within the body will then be preserved from wind and movement, and the whole body will be full of light. Like the tortoise, man must withdraw every sense within himself; the heart must be guarded, and then Brahma will enter into him, like fire and lightning. In the great fire in the cavity of the heart a small flame will be lit up, and in its center is Atma (the soul); and he who destroys all worldly desires and wisdom will be like a hawk which has broken through the meshes of the net, and will have become one with the great being." Thus will he become Brahma-Atma (divine spirit), and will perceive by a light that far exceeds that of the sun. "Who, therefore, enters this path by Brahma must deny the world and its pleasures; must only cover his nakedness, and staff in hand collect enough, but no more, alms to maintain life. The lesser ones only do this; the greater throw aside pitcher and staff, and do not even read the *Oupnekhata.*"

This book is possibly a revision of one of the Hindu *Upanishads. Oupnekhata* is probably from a nineteenth-century German translation titled *Das Oupnekhat; die aus den Veden zusammengefasste Lebre von dem Brahm* (Dresden, 1882), derived from an earlier Latin edition of 1801.

There is no single *Upanishad* "Book of Secrets." All the *Upanishads* contain the esoteric wisdom of Hindu metaphysics (derived from the *Vedas.*) Comparable forms of meditation are also found in various Hindu **yoga** treatises and in the *Bhagavad-Gita,* a Hindu scripture derived from the *Mahabharata,* a religious epic.

Our Lady of Endor Coven

Our Lady of Endor Coven was an early semipublic Satanic group, which grew out of the appearance of "Satanas, the Horned God," to Herbert Arthur Sloane of Toledo, Ohio. Sloane was a child at the time. He later saw the same entity pictured on the dust jacket of a study of **witchcraft,** *The God of the Witches.* When Sloane was 25 years old, Satanas appeared again.

In structuring Our Lady of Endor Coven, Sloane was heavily influenced by his reading of *The Gnostic Religion,* a scholarly treatise on gnosticism by Hans Jonas. In gnosticism, the creator God (of the Christians), is considered a lesser deity than another God. Satan is that God's messenger. Satan brought knowledge of God to Eve in the Garden of Eden. That God takes no direct interest in this world, except for his concern that the sparks of deity trapped in this world return to their origin. This return occurs through gnosis, occult wisdom.

Sloane taught that this gnostic form of **Satanism** was the oldest religion, dating to the worship of the horned god pictured in the ancient cave paintings of Europe. As developed by Sloane, the religion emerged in the context of the neo-pagan revival of the late 1960s. It differed from **Wicca** by refusing to turn the Horned God into a fertility god.

The coven dissolved following Sloane's death in the early 1980s.

Ouroboros (or Uroboros)

Ancient Greek alchemical symbol of a serpent eating his tail. The mystical work *The Chrysopoeia of Kleopatra* has a drawing of the Serpent Ouroboros eating his tail, with the text "One is All." Another emblem illustrates the symbols of gold, silver, and mercury enclosed in two concentric circles with the text "One is the serpent which has its poison according to two compositions" and "One is All and through it is All and by it is All and if you have not All, All is Nothing." The symbol of Ouroboros has also been interpreted as the unity of sacrificer and sacrificed, relating to the symbolism of the mystical life.

The symbol dates back to Mesolithic (Azilian) culture and appeared in the symbolism of many races. The Gnostic text *Pistis Sophia,* describes the disc of the sun as a great dragon with his tail in his mouth. The fourth-century writer Horopollon stated the Egyptians represented the universe as a serpent devouring its own tail, a symbol of eternity and immortality, an image also found on Gnostic gems.

In **alchemy,** the tail-eating dragon represented the guardian of mystical treasure, symbolized by the sun. Alchemy was to destroy or dissolve this guardian as a stage towards knowledge of this treasure.

Possibly the familiar Chinese Yin-Yang symbol is related to the tail-devouring serpent—here the masculine-feminine principles throughout nature are held in balance.

Sources:

Eddison, E. R. *The Worm Ouroboros.* New York: E. P. Dutton, 1952.

Oursler, Will (William Charles) (1913–1985)

Author concerned with certain areas of parapsychology. He was born on July 12, 1913, in Baltimore, Maryland. Oursler attended Harvard College and received a B.A. (cum laude) in 1937. He then launched a career as an editor and writer. Oursler was a police reporter, magazine editor, and war correspondent accredited to the U.S. Army and U.S. Navy in World War II. As a writer he took a particular interest in inspirational subjects and often wrote and lectured on religion and narcotics. He was a member of the Overseas Press Club, Dutch Treat Club, The Players, P.E.N., Harvard Club of New York, Baker Street Irregulars. His books include: (with the late Fulton Oursler) *Father Flanagan of Boys Town* (1949), (with Lawrence Dwight Smith) *Narcotics: America's Peril* (1952), *The Boy Scout Story* (1955), *The Healing Power of Faith* (1957), *The Road to Faith* (1960), *Family Story* (1963), *The Atheist: A Novel* (1965), *Marijuana: The Facts and the Truth* (1968), *Religion: Out or Way Out?* (1968). He has published a number of articles dealing with human problems and religious faith in such magazines as *Collier's, Reader's Digest, True, American Weekly, Photoplay.* Oursler died January 7, 1985, after a long illness.

Ousby, W(illiam) J(oseph) (1904–)

British investigator on hypnosis. Ousby performed field studies of **yoga** and African witchcraft. He was born in Liverpool, England, and worked as a journalist then as an industrial psychological consultant; he also studied hypnosis. Ousby lectured and taught self-hypnosis in Britain, Australia, and New Zealand. He spent several years in Africa, where he studied the methods of witch doctors. In India, he trained in **hatha yoga** and investigated **fire walking** and **trance** conditions. Ousby later practiced as a specialist in hypnosis and self-hypnosis in London.

Sources:

Ousby, W. J. *A Complete Course of Auto-Hypnosis—Self Hypnotism and Auto-Suggestion.* London & Durban, 1950.

———. *Methods of Inducing and Using Hypnosis.* London, 1951.

———. *The Theory and Practice of Hypnotism.* London, 1967.

Ouspensky, P(eter) D(emianovitch) (1878–1947)

Follower of early twentieth-century spiritual teacher **Georgei I. Gurdjieff** (1877–1949) and interpreter of his system. Ouspensky was born in Russia in 1878. He became a student of mathematics at Moscow University, then went on to become a journalist.

In 1907, motivated by the conviction that some higher form of knowledge must exist beyond the tangent fields of science and math, Ouspensky became aware of Theosophical literature and the possible synthesis of religion, mysticism, and science. In 1909, he published *The Fourth Way,* dealing with abstract mathematical concepts. He later published a book on **yoga,** followed by *Tertium Organum; the Third Canon of Thought; a Key to the Enigmas of the World* (English translation London, 1923). It offered his synthesis of time, space, relativity, Theosophy, cosmic consciousness, and Eastern and Western philosophy.

From 1913, Ouspensky traveled on an extended journey to Egypt, India, and Ceylon, searching for the miraculous, and upon his return gave a series of lectures on his experiences. In 1915, he met Sophia Grigorievna Maximenko (who later became his wife) and the mystic G. I. Gurdjieff (who became his guru).

Ouspensky became a disciple and interpreter of Gurdjieff's system (i.e., that there exists real possibilities for individuals to evolve psychologically into a state of consciousness far higher than that in which they spend the whole of their ordinary lives) until 1924, when he decided to follow his own path. He lectured, wrote books, and conducted study groups in England and the United States on the work of Gurdjieff until his death in 1947. Rom Landau attended and wrote an account of an Ouspensky lecture in London.

Sources:

Driscoll, J. Walter. *Gurdjieff: An Annotated Bibliography.* New York: Garland Publishing, 1985.

Landau, Rom. *God Is My Adventure.* London: Ivor Nicholson & Watson, 1935.

Ouspensky, P. D. *The Fourth Way.* New York: Alfred A. Knopf, 1953.

———. *In Search of the Miraculous.* New York: Harcourt, Brace, 1949.

———. *A New Model of the Universe.* New York: Alfred A. Knopf, 1931.

———. *Tertium Organum; the Third Canon of Thought; a Key to the Enigmas of the World.* Rochester, N.Y.: Manas Press, 1920.

Webb, James. *The Harmonious Circle: The Lives and Work of G. I. Gurdjieff, P. D. Ouspensky, and Their Followers.* New York: G. P. Putnam's Sons, 1980.

Wintle, Justin, ed. *Makers of Modern Culture.* New York: Facts on File, 1981.

Out-of-the-Body Travel

A phenomenon based on the belief that individual consciousness can leave the physical body during sleep or trance and travel to distant places or into an ethereal or astral realm. Different religions in the ancient world taught that men and women were essentially spiritual beings (souls) incarnated for a divine purpose, and that they shed the body at death and survived in an afterlife or a new incarnation.

The ancient Hindus believed in the phenomenon of out-of-the-body travel, featured in such Scriptures as the Yoga Vashishta-Maharamayana of Valmiki. Hindu teachings recognize three bodies—physical, subtle, and causal. The causal body builds up the characteristics of one's next reincarnation by the desires and fears in its present life, but the subtle body may sometimes leave the physical body during its lifetime and reenter it after traveling in the physical world. Ancient Egyptian teachings also represented the soul as having the ability to hover outside the physical body in the *ka,* or subtle body.

In the twentieth century, psychical researchers began to study and conduct experiments on the possibility of out-of-the-body travel. Their interest was provoked by its possible contribution to evidence of the **survival** of death. Beginning in 1920 **Hugh G. Callaway,** under the pseudonym Oliver Fox, published a series of articles in *The Occult Review.* His articles would later become the basis of a book, *Astral Projection* (1939). Meanwhile, **Sylvan J. Muldoon,** an American experimenter who professed an ease with **astral projection** (another name for out-of-the-body travel), began to work with psychical researcher **Hereward Carrington,** their work resulting in the first of a series of books, *The Projection of the Astral Body,* in 1929.

Both Callaway and Muldoon gave detailed firsthand accounts of consciously controlled and involuntary journeys outside the body. Sometimes these involved appearances to other individuals or the obtaining of information that could not have been ascertained by other means. Such accounts were thus highly suggestive.

Certain techniques were also described by both Callaway and Muldoon for facilitating the release of the astral or ethereal body from the physical body. These included visualizing such mental images as flying or being in an elevator traveling upward, just before going to sleep. Some involuntary releases occurred as a result of regaining waking consciousness while still in a dream state (i.e., lucid dreaming). This was often stimulated by some apparent incongruity in the dream, such as dreaming of one's own room but noticing that the wallpaper has the wrong pattern. Such awareness sometimes resulted in normal consciousness, but with a feeling of being *outside* the physical body and able to look down at it.

Many individuals who claimed to have experienced astral projection describe themselves as joined to the physical body by an infinitely extensible connection—rather like a psychic umbilical cord—that would snatch the astral body back to the physical body if one were disturbed by fear.

Some cases of astral projection have reportedly occurred as a result of anesthetization (during operations) or even a sudden shock.

In spite of the significance attributed to out-of-the-body experiences (OBEs), both as a parapsychological phenomenon and for their relevance to the question of survival after death, they did not receive the acknowledged attention of the parapsychological community until British scientist **Robert Crookall** began to publish a number of books in which he cataloged and analyzed hundreds of cases of astral projection from individuals in all walks of life. It seems that the phenomenon is much more widespread than generally supposed, but some people are sensitive about discussing such experiences. Moreover, the majority of cases are of involuntary projection; consciously controlled projection under laboratory conditions is rare.

Crookall distinguished between the physical body of everyday life, a "vehicle of vitality," and a "soul body," connected by an extensible cord. Movement from one body to another is reported as often accompanied by strange sounds and sensations—a "click" in the head, a "blackout," or a "journey down a long tunnel." Reportedly, the projector often sees his own physical body lying on the bed and sometimes the semiphysical vehicle of vitality is observed by other people. Crookall also cited instances of the condition of consciousness in which one sees a **double** of oneself (see also **Vardøgr**).

Again, while much astral travel is supposedly in the world of everyday life, one sometimes moves into regions of otherworldly beauty or depression, characterized by Crookall as "Paradise condition" (the finer area of earth) or "Hades condition" (a kind of purgatorial area). Here one sometimes encounters friends and relatives who have died, or even angelic or demonic beings. Return to the physical body is often accompanied by violent loud "repercussion" effects. Sometimes the transition to and from the physical body appears to be assisted by "deliverers" or spirit helpers, or even obstructed by "hinderers."

Projection may be preceded by a cataleptic condition of the body in which there are **hypnogogic** illusions. Because of the close association of dreaming and hallucinatory images, many people have dismissed claimed OBEs as illusory or merely dreams.

One controlled experiment in astral projection was undertaken by the medium **Eileen J. Garrett** in 1934, when a test was set up between observers Dr. Mühl in New York and Dr. D. Svenson in Reykjavik, Iceland. Reportedly, Garrett projected her astral double from New York to Iceland and acquired test information afterward verified as correct. The case is described in her book *My Life as a Search for the Meaning of Mediumship* (1939), although at the time the experimenters were not named, in order to protect their anonymity, and "Newfoundland" was substituted for Reykjavik.

Since World War II, parapsychologists have given special attention to the phenomenon of OBEs. A number of special terms were devised by Celia Green, director of the Institute of Psychophysical Research, Oxford, England, in a scientific study of approximately four hundred individuals claiming OBEs. The general term *ecsomatic* was applied where objects of perception appeared organized in such a way that the observer seemed to observe from a point of view not coincident with the physical body. *Parasomatic* was defined as an ecsomatic experience in which the percipient was associated with a seemingly spatial entity with which he felt himself to be in the same kind of relationship as, in the normal state, with his physical body. *Asomatic* denoted an ecsomatic state in which the subject was temporarily unaware of being associated with any body or spatial entity at all.

Other experiments have been conducted at the **American Society for Psychical Research** (ASPR) in New York and the Psychical Research Foundation, Durham, North Carolina. At the ASPR Dr. **Karlis Osis** used a special target box designed to eliminate ordinary ESP. Subjects were invited to "fly in" astrally and read the target. Over a hundred volunteers participated in the test. Although Osis reported that the overall results were not significant, some of the subjects were tested further under laboratory conditions. Among those who reportedly performed well in such tests was psychic **Ingo Swann.**

At the Psychical Research Foundation, brain wave recordings were taken from OBE subjects, with special attention given to detection of the subject at the target location. There is a suggestion that some subjects may have been able to manifest psychokinetic effects while projecting. PK effects had been reported earlier in the experiments of Sylvan J. Muldoon in the book *The Projection of the Astral Body* (1929).

In 1956 Dr. **Hornell Hart** made a survey of reported apparitions of the dead, which he compared with apparitions of living persons when having OBE experiences. He concluded that "the projected personality carries full memories and purposes."

As with other laboratory experiments in parapsychology, OBE tests lack the intrinsic interest of involuntary experiences, and acceptable evidence is correspondingly reduced. Many laboratory experimenters regard OBEs as a form of traveling clairvoyance and have criticized the methodology employed in many experiments because the methodology fails to distinguish between the two. A person experiencing astral travel may be having an experience somewhat analogous to "virtual reality." It remains to be seen whether scientists can devise techniques that can validate objectively the phenomena of OBEs.

Meanwhile, in the many cases of involuntary projection, it is belived the experience itself often has a profound effect on the outlook of the subject, since it seems to give firsthand subjective evidence for the existence of a soul that survives the death of the physical body. Such experiences have become the subject of study by psychologists such as **Elizabeth Kübler-Ross** and Raymond Moody, who claimed to have been affected by the intensity of the accounts and their long-term, life-changing quality. Critics of such stories have noted that ultimately there is little independent confirmation of the stories, and while there is a high degree of similarity between the experiences, there is enough divergence to call the nature of the experience into question. Others have also noted that the use of OBEs as evidence of survival is somewhat limited in that even if the consciousness could leave a living body and return there is no reason to jump to the conclusion that the consciousness could survive the death of its host body.

Some psychologists are confident that OBEs can be fully explained as hallucinatory mental phenomena. British parapsychologist **Susan J. Blackmore** has given special attention to the phenomenon in attempting to discover a psychological explanation. Her book *Beyond the Body* (1981) proposes that the experience is an altered state of consciousness characterized by vivid imagery, in which the subject's cognitive system is disturbed, losing input control and replacing normal reality with one drawing upon memory. Blackmore's experiments and theories have special interest to parapsychologists because, unlike so many investigators of claimed out-of-the-body phenomena, she has had such experiences herself.

Sources:

Battersby, H. F. Prevost. *Man Outside Himself.* London, 1942. Reprint, New Hyde Park, N.Y.: University Books, 1969.

Black, David. *Ekstasy: Out-of-the-Body Experiences.* Indianapolis: Bobbs-Merrill, 1975.

Blackmore, Susan J. *Beyond the Body: An Investigation of Out-of-the-Body Experiences.* London: Heinemann, 1981.

Crookall, Robert. *Case-Book of Astral Projection. 545–746* New Hyde Park, N.Y.: University Books, 1972.

———. *Ecstasy: The Release of the Soul from the Body.* Moradabad, India: Darshand International, 1975.

———. *Out-of-the-Body Experiences.* New Hyde Park, N.Y.: University Books, 1970.

———. *The Study and Practice of Astral Projection.* London, 1960. Reprint, New Hyde Park, N.Y.: University Books, 1966.

Fox, Oliver. *Astral Projection.* London, 1939. Reprint. New Hyde Park, N.Y.: University Books, 1963.

Green, Celia E. *Out-of-the-Body Experiences.* Oxford, England, 1968.

Greenhouse, Herbert B. *Astral Journey: Evidence for Out-of-the-Body Experiences from Socrates to the ESP Laboratory.* Garden City, N.Y.: Doubleday, 1975.

King, Francis. *Astral Projection, Ritual Magic, and Alchemy: Being Hitherto Unpublished Golden Dawn Material.* London: Neville Spearman, 1971.

Mead, G. R. S. *The Doctrine of the Subtle Body in Western Tradition.* London, 1919.

Monroe, Robert A. *Journeys Out of the Body.* Garden City, N.Y.: Doubleday, 1971.

Muldoon, Sylvan J., and Hereward Carrington. *The Phenomena of Astral Projection.* London, 1951.

———. *The Projection of the Astral Body.* London, 1929.

Shirley, Ralph. *The Mystery of the Human Double.* London, 1938. Reprint, New Hyde Park, N.Y.: University Books, 1965.

Smith, Susy. *The Enigma of Out-of-body-Travel.* New York: Helix, 1968. Reprint, New York: New American Library, 1968.

Turvey, Vincent N. *The Beginnings of Seership.* London, 1911. Reprint, New Hyde Park, N.Y.: University Books, 1969.

Walker, George B. *Beyond the Body: The Human Double and the Astral Planes.* London/Boston: George Benjamin Walker, 1974.

Wilkins, Hubert, and Harold Sherman. *Thoughts Through Space.* London: Frederick Muller, 1971.

Yram [Marcel L. Forham]. *Le Medecin de l'Ame'.* Translated as *Practical Astral Projection.* London, 1935. Reprint, New York: Samuel Weiser, 1966.

Owen, Alan Robert George (1919–)

Mathematician and parapsychologist. He was born July 4, 1919 at Bristol, England. During World War II, he studied at Cambridge University (B.A. 1940, M.A. 1945, Ph.D. 1948). After graduation he became a research fellow at Trinity College, Cambridge (1948–52) and met C. D. Broad, who kindled Owen's interest in parapsychology. Owen also met and, in 1952, married Iris May Pepper. He joined and became president of the Cambridge Society for Psychical Research, and was a council member of the Society for Psychical Research. While at Cambridge, he conducted research on poltergeist. The published results, *Can We Explain the Poltergeist?*, received the 1964 award from the Parapsychology Foundation as the best book of the year. Owen later moved to Canada where he taught genetics and mathematics at the University of Toronto. He cofounded with his wife, **Iris Owen,** the New Horizons Research Foundation in Toronto and the Toronto Society for Psychical Research. Before moving to Canada, he had investigated the British psychic, **Matthew Manning.** He stayed in contact with Manning, and in 1974 invited him (then 18 years old) to Toronto, to be studied at a seminar on psychokinesis. During this visit, Manning successfully tried the metal-bending phenomenon popularized by **Uri Geller.** Electroencephalograph recordings revealed significant movements toward theta and delta frequencies prior to Manning bending metal objects. Owen retired in 1988.

Sources:

Berger, Arthur S., and Joyce Berger. *The Encyclopedia of Parapsychology and Psychical Research.* New York: Paragon House, 1991.

Owen, A. R. G., *Can We Explain the Poltergeist?* New York: Garrett Publications, 1964.

———. *Hysteria, Hypnosis, and Healing.* 1971.

———. *Psychic Mysteries of Canada.* New York: Harper & Row, 1975.

Owen, A. R. G., J. P. Rindge, and W. Cook. "An Investigation of Psychic Photography with the Beilleux Family." *New Horizons* (1972).

Owen, A.R.G. and J. Whitton. "Proceedings of the First Canadian Conference on Psychokinesis." *New Horizons* (1975).

Pleasants, Helene, ed. *Biographical Dictionary of Parapsychology.* New York: Helix Press, 1964.

Owen, George Vale (1869–1931)

British clergyman and convert of Spiritualism. Owen was born on June 26, 1869, in Birmingham, England. He was educated at the Midland Institute and Queen's College in Birmingham and ordained in the Church of England. After curacies at Seaforth, Fairfield and Liverpool, he became vicar of Orford, New Warrington. Here he created a new church and worked for twenty years.

After some psychic experiences Owen developed **automatic writing,** and received, from high spirits, an account of life after death and further philosophical teachings. After Lord Northcliffe published the scripts in his newspaper, the *Weekly Dispatch,* Owen was forced out of ministry by the Church authorities. He resigned his vicarage and went on a lecture tour in America and in England, eventually settling in a pastorate of a Spiritualist congregation in London. Through 1920, he authored a number of books about his new faith, his most notable being the five-volume *Life Beyond the Veil.*

He died March 8, 1931. Messages purported to emanate from the surviving ego of Owen were supposedly published in *A Voice from Heaven* by **Frederick H. Haines.** The clairvoyant Haines claimed the book contained messages he had "received automatically" from the deceased Owen.

Sources:

Owen, George Vale. *Facts and the Future Life.* London: Hutchinson & Co., 1922.

———. *How Spirits Communicate.* N.p., n.d.

———. *Jesus the Christ.* N.p., 1929.

———. *The Life Beyond the Veil.* 5 vols. London: Greater World Association, 1926.

———. *What Happens After Death.* London: Hutchinson & Co., 1924.

Owen, George Vale, and H. A. Dallas. *The Nurseries of Heaven.* (1920).

Owen, Iris M.

Nurse and psychical researcher. As a registered nurse and volunteer in social work, Owen became a member of the governing board of schools and chairperson of governors of an approved school for delinquent boys. In 1962, she married parapsychologist **Alan Robert George Owen.** They shared an interest in poltergeist phenomena. She moved to Canada in the 1960s and became secretary of the Toronto Society for Psychical Research. Owen also assisted her husband's work at the New Horizons Research Foundation, Toronto.

In the early 1970s, she led the **"Philip"** experiment. A group of people sitting as a séance circle created a fictitious figure whom they named Philip and who then began to manifest physical phenomena. The result destroyed the "spirit" hypothesis by demonstrating that spirits were unnecessary in the production of phenomena—it could be produced by the sitters.

Sources:

Berger, Arthur S., and Joyce Berger. *The Encyclopedia of Parapsychology and Psychical Research.* New York: Paragon House, 1991.

Owen, Iris M., and P. Mitchell. "The Alleged Haunting of Borley Rectory." *Journal* of the Society for Psychical Research 50 (1979).

Owen, Iris M., and Margaret Sparrow. *Conjuring Up Philip; An Adventure in Psychokinesis.* New York: Harper and Row, 1976.

Owen, Robert (1771–1858)

British socialist and humanitarian. Owen was born May 14, 1771, at Newtown, Montgomeryshire. He was successful in the cotton mill industry and, in 1800, established a utopian society based on his cotton mills at New Lanark.

Owen established a community at New Lanark. This news induced the settlers of the Harmony Society in Indiana to sell land to Owen, who purchased Harmony with its mills, factories, houses, and land when the Harmonists moved to Pennsylvania. Owen came to the United States in December 1824 and established the community of New Harmony, based on socialist principles; the experiment did not succeed. For an account of New Harmony see *Strange Cults & Utopias of 19th Century America* by J. H. Noyes (Dover, 1966).

On May 14, 1856, at The First Meeting of the Congress of the Reformers of the World, detailed plans, based on spiritually-inspired architectural conceptions, were submitted through Owen's agency for building Homes of Harmony.

At the age of 83, Owen developed an interest in **Spiritualism** after several sittings with **Maria B. Hayden,** the first American medium who visited England. In 1853, in his journal, the *Rational Quarterly Review,* Owen published a formal profession of his new faith. In the same year he issued as a separate pamphlet *The Future of the Human Race; or great, glorious and peaceful Revolution, to be effected through the agency of departed spirits of good and superior men and women.* The periodical installments of his *New Existence of Man Upon Earth* (1854–55) were, for some time, the only British publications dealing with Spiritualism.

Nevertheless, Owen cannot be ranked as a typical Spiritualist. Communication with the Beyond for him was another means for the advancement of mankind. Supposedly Andrew Jackson Davis, who saw him when lecturing in America in 1846, wrote in November 1847, some months before the Rochester knockings, that according to a message he received from the spiritual spheres, Robert Owen was destined to hold "open intercourse" with the higher world. Reportedly some of the prophecy communications were printed in Owen's autobiography *The Life of Robert Owen* (2 vols., London, 1857–58). Owen died at Newtown November 17, 1858, and his Spiritualist interests were carried forward by his son, **Robert Dale Owen.**

Sources:

Freudenberg, Gideon G. *Robert Owen: Educator of the People.* Tel Aviv, Israel: Dvir, 1970.

Harrison, John F. C. *Quest for the New World.* New York: Charles Scribner's Sons, 1969.

Oved, Yaacov. *Two Hundred Years of American Communes.* New Brunswick, N.J.: Transaction Publications, 1993.

Owen, Robert Dale. *The Debatable Land Between this World and the Next.* London: Trubner, 1871.

———. *Footfalls on the Boundaries of Another World.* Philadelphia: J. B. Lippincott, 1860.

———. *The Life of Robert Owen.* 2 vols. Hamden, Conn.: Archon Books, 1966.

Owen, Robert Dale (1801–1877)

Son of the British socialist **Robert Owen.** He was born November 9, 1801 in Glasgow, Scotland, and educated in Switzerland. Owen eventually emigrated to America. He lived for several years in his father's socialistic community, New Harmony, in Indiana. He served in the Indiana legislature and in Congress. He introduced the bill organizing the Smithsonian Institution and in 1846 became one of its regents and chairman of its Building Committee. Owen was a member of the Indiana Constitutional Convention in 1850. In 1853, Owen was appointed Chargé d'Affaires at Naples and Minister in 1855. He remained there until 1858.

Owen was disappointed to learn of his father's attachment to **Spiritualism.** But experiences with the famous medium **D. D. Home** during his stay in Naples started his career of psychic investigation. Owen worked to prove whether **survival** was a certainty or delusion. He published two books, *Footfalls on the Boundaries of Another World* (1860) and *The Debatable Land Between this World and the Next* (1871), in support of the Spiritualist movement. In spite of scandals, such as cheating on the part of the mediums **Mr. and Mrs. Nelson Holmes** in 1874, Owen continued to advocate his new faith until his death. He died June 17, 1877.

Sources:

Harrison, John F. C. *Quest for the New World.* New York: Charles Scribner's Sons, 1969.

Oved, Yaacov. *Two Hundred Years of American Communes.* New Brunswick, N.J.: Transaction Publications, 1993.

Owen, Robert Dale. *The Debatable Land Between this World and the Next.* London: Trubner, 1871.

———. *Footfalls on the Boundaries of Another World.* Philadelphia: Lippencott, 1860.

———. *Threading My Way; Twenty-Seven Years of Autobiography.* 1874. Reprint, New York: A. M. Kelley, 1967.

Owens, Ted (1920–)

Psychic who in the 1960s claimed contact with intelligences from flying saucers. Unlike other contactees, Owens does not claim to have taken a ride on a saucer but uses his brain as a radio set for telepathic messages, to pass on to anyone interested. According to Owens, the ultimate purpose of the **space intelligences** was for him to act as an ambassador for them to world governments.

As a psychic, Owens claimed to control weather, predict events, and heal the sick. He has an IQ of 150, and is a member of Mensa, a well known organization of individuals with high mental test scores.

Sources:

Owens, Ted. *Flying Saucer Intelligences Speak: A Message to the American People from the Flying Saucer Intelligences.* New Brunswick, N.J.: Interplanetary News Service, [1966].

———. *How to Contact Space People.* Clarksburg, W.Va.: Saucerian Books, 1969.

Oxford Golden Dawn Occult Society

The Oxford Golden Dawn Occult Society is a magical order that, as its name implies, is based in Oxford, England. It takes its name (without any claim of organizational continuity) from the **Hermetic Order of the Golden Dawn** and teaches a form of **magic** that it describes as a modern equivalent of the Golden Dawn system, the pioneering system of modern ceremonial magic. The society has a more public program aimed at disseminating authentic information about occultism and magic that includes lectures, workshops, and conferences, and a discussion seminar on the last Friday of each month. These are open to the public and run the gamut from magic to shamanism, to qabala (or **Kabbalah**) and **Witchcraft.**

Members of the society follow different traditions of magical practice including Neo-Pagan/**Wicca** traditions. Many find the society a place to meet others who share their magical interests but operate different magical systems. Often meetings involve the working of various rituals on an experimental basis. The society has served as a catalyst for new groups to form by people who wish to follow up on a particular ritual or idea.

The society also teaches a system of magic that combines insights from the Western Hermetic tradition with Eastern Tantric practice. Training is open to associate members of the society who can present themselves at one of their centers in Oxford and London. There is also a correspondence course in magic. The society considers itself a sister group to **AMOOKOS,** which it recommends to members especially interested in Tantra.

The society meets in various venues for its different activities. The Oxford group has an Internet page at http://www.cix.co.uk/~mandrake/ogdos.htm and the London group maintains a page at http://www.lawbright.com/logdos/. The society may be contacted through either site. The society is a small organization of fewer than 100 members in the United Kingdom.

Sources:

Oxford Golden Dawn Occult Society. http://www.cix.co.uk/~mandrake/ogdos.htm. May 20, 2000.

London Lodge of the Oxford Golden Dawn Occult Society. http://www.lawbright.com/logdos/. May 20, 2000.

Ozanne, Charles E(ugene) (1865–1961)

History and philosophy teacher, who devoted many years to research in parapsychology after retirement from teaching. He was born April 14, 1865, in Cleveland, Ohio. Ozanne studied at Western Reserve University, Cleveland (B.A. 1889), Yale University (B.S.T. 1892), and Harvard University (M.A. 1895). He taught history and civics at Central High School, Cleveland, Ohio, until 1935. During those years he provided financial support for research in parapsychology at Duke University, Durham, North Carolina, and after 1951 moved to Durham because of the research at the **Parapsychology Laboratory.**

In 1961, Ozanne founded the **Psychical Research Foundation, Inc.** at Durham, N.C. The foundation is an independent research organization concerned with mental, spiritual, or personality characteristics associated with survival after death. **William G. Roll** was director of the Foundation. Ozanne died April 5, 1961, at Durham, North Carolina.

Sources:

Ozanne, Charles. "A Layman Looks at Psychical Research." *Journal* of the American Society for Psychical Research (April 1942).

———. "Significance of "Non-Evidential" Material in Psychical Research." *Hibbert Journal* (October 1913).

Oz Factor

The Oz Factor, a term coined by ufologists and author **Jenny Randles** (b. 1951), refers to the experience of being isolated or transported by the real world of everyday life into another environment which is quite similar to the real world but changed enough to be noticeable and disturbing. Such reports have been common in both UFO and paranormal accounts, but had been pushed aside (their evidential value being somewhat limited) until Randles called attention to such experiences as a common element in some types of UFO encounters.

Folklorist Peter M. Rojcewicz recounted such an experience in 1980 while working on his Ph.D. dissertation, which happened to be on UFOs. While working in the library, he had a strange encounter with a man who approached the table at which he worked and engaged him in conversation. As they talked on the subject of his dissertation, the man suddenly shouted accusingly, "Flying saucers are the most important fact of the century, and you are not interested?" Shortly thereafter he left. Rojcewicz was relieved at his departure, thinking the man disturbed. However, as he tried to return to his work, he had a feeling that all was not right. Unable to stay seated, he wandered around the library. He noticed that no librarians were staffing the desks and that no patrons seemed to be in the library. In a mild panic, he returned to his working space and tried to settle his mind. An hour later when he finally left the library, all seemed to have returned to normal.

Such experiences often appear as an aspect of a longer story of paranormal encounters, doing more to describe the atmosphere surrounding more spectacular or definitive experiences. Also, such stories appear closely related to phenomena like **déjà vu,** which make an impact upon the person experiencing them, but only minimally impress one to whom the story is told. Stories abound of people who have felt a presence, sensed some guidance or seen something that led them to sense that they had been unwittingly pulled away from the normal sequence of experiences. It is almost impossible to further investigate the anecdotal accounts, however reality-shattering they might be to the person experiencing them.

Sources:

Randles, Jenny. "In Search of the Oz Factor." *BUFORA Bulletin* 26 (July 1987): 17–18.

Rojcewicz, Peter M. *The Boundaries of Orthodoxy: A Folkloric Look at the UFO Phenomenon.* Bloomington, Ind.: Indiana University, Ph.D. diss., 1984.

P

Pacific Neuropsychiatric Institute

The Pacific Neuropsychiatric Institute, founded in 1992 in Seattle, Washington, by South African psychiatrist **Vernon M. Neppe,** serves primarily as a center treating patients suffering from neuropsychiatric disorders, but also as a center for research on neuropsychiatric-related phenomena, including paranormal phenomena. Prior to establishing the institute, Neppe had an outstanding career as a professor of psychiatry at the University of Witwatersrand in Johannesburg, South Africa, and the University of Washington.

Along with his work on specialized areas from forensic psychiatry to geriatric psychiatry, Neppe has had a long-term interest in paranormal phenomena that manifests as early as his masters thesis in 1979, in which he documented a correlation between the subjective experience of having a paranormal experience with the activity of the brain. Over the years he became convinced that if such experiences are real, then they should have links to more phenomena documented in psychiatric literature.

At the institute, Neppe has made use of a set of what he considers more neutral descriptive terms for phenomena such as ESP, **remote viewing,** or **psychokinesis.** The whole area of anomalous or paranormal phenomena is referred to as "delta." A clairvoyant event, an experience of reception of a delta experience, is termed an "afferent delta," and an event such as psychokinesis, or mind over matter, is termed an "efferent delta," an outgoing element of an anomalous experience. The new language recognizes the problem of researching subjective experiences of persons, which, while very real to the individual, is most difficult to understand in objective terms. Neppe has been especially concerned with correlating anomalous experience with brain activity. The institute may be contacted on the Internet at http://www.pni.org.

Sources:

Neppe, V. M. "Anomalous Experience and Psychopathology." In Betty Shapin and Lisette Cody, eds. *Spontaneous Psi, Depth Psychology and Parapsychology.* New York: Parapsychology Foundation, 1992.

———. "Extrasensory Perception—an Anachronism and Anathema." *Journal of the American Society for Psychical Research* 52, no.789 (October 1984): 365–70.

———. *An Investigation of the Relationship between Temporal Lobe Symptomatology and Subjective Paranormal Experience.* Johannesburg, South Africa: University of Witwatersrand, Med Psych thesis, 1979.

———. "The Relevance of the Temporal Lobe to Anomalous Subjective Experience." In Rhea A. White and R. S. Broughton, eds. *Research in Parapsychology 1983.* Methuchen, N.J.: Scarecrow Press, 1984.

Pack, John L(ee) (1927–)

Research physicist who has experimented in the field of **parapsychology.** He was born on June 7, 1927, in Silver City, New Mexico, and later attended the University of New Mexico (B.S., 1950; M.S., 1952). After graduation he became a research engineer at the Westinghouse Research Laboratories, Pittsburgh, Pennsylvania (1952–85). In addition to his work in physics, Pack tested a number of subjects under hypnosis for enhanced extrasensory ability as compared with a normal state of consciousness. He believes hypnosis may enable subjects to develop **ESP.** Pack was a charter associate of the **Parapsychological Association.**

Sources:

Pleasants, Helene, ed. *Biographical Dictionary of Parapsychology.* New York: Helix Press, 1964.

Pacts with the Devil

Throughout history there have been documentations of individuals making agreements with the Devil. An agreement said to have been entered into between **Louis Gaufridi** and the Devil follows:

"I, Louis, a priest, renounce each and every one of the spiritual and corporal gifts which may accrue to me from God, from the Virgin, and from all the saints, and especially from my patron John the Baptist, and the apostles Peter and Paul and St. Francis. And to you, Lucifer, now before me, I give myself and all the good I may accomplish, except the returns from the sacrament in the cases where I may administer it; all of which I sign and attest."

On his side, Lucifer made the following agreement with Louis Gaufridi: "I, Lucifer, bind myself to give you, Louis Gaufridi, priest, the faculty and power of bewitching by blowing with the mouth, all and any of the women and girls you may desire; in proof of which I sign myself Lucifer."

Accounts of pacts with the devil emerged after Satan became an important figure in Christian theology and an image of the devil began to spread abroad in popular preaching. It was given a biblical basis from a reading of Isaiah 28:15, "We have entered into a league with death; we have made a covenant with hell." Thus Origen (185–254 C.E.) and, more important, St. Augustine (354–430 C.E.) could speak of a pact with demons.

The earliest Christian legend involving a pact with the devil is a story concerning St. Basil (ca. 329–379 C.E.). The most important was that of Theophilus, bursar of the church of Adam in Northern Cilicia (ca. 538 C.E.). After his bishop withdrew his employment, Theophilius sold his soul to the devil to recover the position. This story, translated into Latin in the eighth century by Paul the deacon, became a popular tale and was used as the basis of the drama *Le Miracle de Théophile,* by Ruteboeuf of Arras.

It was not until the medieval period however, that numerous accounts of pacts with the devil appear in literature. From the sixteenth century, the pact included homage and reverence to the devil and was thus considered a form of apostasy and heresy, crimes pursued by the Inquisition.

The first extended description of a pact with the devil seems to have been published in 1435 by Johannes Nider in his book

Formicarius. Then in 1486 the *Malleus Maleficarum* (The Witches' Hammer)—the main text used by the Inquisition and Protestant witch-hunters over the next centuries—tied the worship of Satan to **witchcraft.** Witches were branded as evil for, among other reasons, having made a pact with the devil and then having intercourse with him. The publication of *The Witches' Hammer* launched the great era of witch-hunts that culminated in the incidents at Salem Village, Massachusetts, three centuries later. Overwhelmingly, accounts of pacts with the devil are tied to witchcraft persecution.

In 1587 the first book appeared recounting the story of Johannes Faust, the legendary magician who made the most famous pact with a devil figure, the demon Mephistopheles. In exchange for his soul, Mephistopheles agreed to serve Faust for 24 years. He was granted every wish for that period, only to be killed by the demon when the 24 years ended. Faust has inspired a number of literary reflections upon the individual's relationship with evil.

Signs of the Devil's Presence

F. Pierre Crespet described the mark with which Satan brands his own:

"It may be assumed that it is no fallacy but very evident that Satan's mark on sorcerers is like leprosy, for the spot is insensitive to all punctures, and it is in the possession of such marks that one recognizes them as true sorcerers for they feel the puncture no more than if they were leprous, nor does any blood appear, and never indeed, does any pain that may be inflicted cause them to move the part.

"They receive, with this badge, the power of injuring and of pleasing, and, secretly or openly, their children are made to participate in the oath and connection which the fathers have taken with the devil. Even the mothers with this in view, dedicate and consecrate their children to the demons, not only as soon as born but even when conceived, and so it happens that, through the ministrations of these demons, sorcerers have been seen with two pupils in each eye, while others had the picture of a horse in one eye and two pupils in the other, and such serve as marks and badges of contracts made with them, for these demons can engrave and render in effigy such or similar lines and features on the bodies of the very young embryo."

Jacques Fontaine writes,

"These marks are not engraved on the bodies of sorcerers by the demons for recognition purposes only, as the captains of companies of light-horse know those of their number by the colour of their coats, but to imitate the creator of all things, to show his power and the authority he has gained over those miserable beings who have allowed themselves to be caught by his cunning and trickery, and by the recognition of these marks of their master to keep them in his power. Further, to prevent them, as far as possible, from withdrawing from their promises and oaths of fidelity, because though breaking faith with him the marks still remain with them and serve, in an accusation, as a means of betraying them, with even the smallest amount of evidence that may be brought forward.

"Louis Gaufridi, a prisoner, who had just been condemned to be burnt . . . was marked in more than thirty places over the body and on the loins especially there was a mark of lust so large and deep, considering the site, that a needle could be inserted for the width of three fingers across it without any feeling being shown by the puncture."

The same author claimed that the marks on sorcerers were areas that had mortified from the touch of the devil's finger.

"About 1591, Leonarde Chastenet, an old woman of eighty, was taken up as a sorceress while begging in Poitou. Brought before Mathurin Bonnevault, who deponed to having seen her at the meeting of witches, she confessed that she had been there with her husband, and that the devil, a very disgusting beast, was there in the form of a goat. She denied that she would have carried out any witchcraft, but nineteen witnesses testified to her having caused the death of five labourers and a number of animals.

"Finding her crimes discovered and herself condemned she confessed that she had made a compact with the devil, given him some of her hair, and promised to do all the harm she could. She added that at night in prison the devil had appeared to her, in the form of a cat, to which she expressed the wish to die, whereupon the devil presented her with two pieces of wax telling her to eat them and she would die, but she had been unwilling to do it. She had the pieces of wax with her, but on examination their composition could not be made out. She was then condemned and the pieces of wax burnt with her."

An Exorcism

According to French Catholic Bible scholar **Dom Augustin Calmet** at the Jesuit Chapel of St. Ignatius in Molsheim, a well-known inscription gave the history of a young German nobleman named Michel Louis, of the family of Boubenhoren. He was sent as a youth to the court of the duke of Lorraine to learn French, and there lost all his money at cards. Reduced to despair, he decided to give himself to the devil if that spirit would give him *good* money, for he was afraid that the devil would be able to supply him only with counterfeit.

While Louis was thinking this over, a young man his own age, well built and well clothed, suddenly appeared before him. Asking him the cause of his distress, the young man put out a handful of money and invited him to prove its worth, telling Louis to look him up again the next day. Louis returned to his companions, who were still playing, won back all he had lost, and won all his companions' money as well.

Then he called on his Devil who asked in return three drops of blood, which he collected in an acorn shell. Offering a pen to Louis, the devil told him to write his dictation. This consisted of unknown words, written on two different contracts, one of which the Devil retained. The other was put into Louis's arm, in the place from which the blood had been taken. The Devil then said, "I undertake to serve you for seven years, after which you belong to me without reserve."

The young man agreed, though with some dread, and the Devil appeared to him day and night in various forms, inspiring him to various strange deeds, always with a tendency to evil.

The fatal period of seven years began drawing to an end when Louis was about 20 years old. He went home, where the Devil inspired him to poison his father and mother, burn the castle, and kill himself. He tried to carry out all these crimes, but God prevented their success—the poison failed to act on his parents, and the gun with which he would have killed himself misfired twice.

Becoming more and more uneasy, he revealed his plight to some of his father's servants and begged them to get help. The Devil seized him, twisting his body around and stopping very short of breaking his bones. His mother was forced to put him in the care of monks. He soon left them and escaped to Islade, but was sent back to Molsheim by his brother, canon of Wissbourg, who again put him into the hands of the monks.

It was then that the demon made the most violent efforts against Louis, appearing to him in the form of wild animals. In one attempt the demon, in the form of a wild man covered with hair, threw on the ground a contract different from the original, trying by this false show to get Louis out of the hands of those who were looking after him and to prevent his making a full confession.

Finally, October 20, 1603, was set aside for proof in the Chapel of St. Ignatius, and for reproduction of the true contract containing the deal made with the demon. The young man made profession of the orthodox Catholic faith, renounced the demon, and received the Holy Eucharist. Then with terrible cries he said that he saw two **goats** of immense size standing with their forefeet in the air, each holding between its hoofs one of the contracts.

But when the **exorcism** began and the name of St. Ignatius was invoked, the two goats disappeared and there issued from the arm or left hand of the young man—practically without pain and leaving no scar—a contract, which fell at the feet of the exorcist. There remained the contract that had been retained by the demon. The exorcisms began once more. St. Ignatius was invoked and a mass was promised in his honor. A stork appeared—large, deformed, and ill-shapen—and dropped from its beak the second contract, which was found on the altar.

Of Magic and Medicine

There is frequent mention among ancient writers of certain demons that showed themselves, especially at midday, to those with whom they were on familiar terms. They visited such persons in the form of men or animals or allowed themselves to be enclosed in a letter, account, or vial, or even in a ring, wide and hollow within. "Magicians are known," states **Pierre Le Loyer,** "who make use of them [demons], and to my great regret I am forced to admit that the practice is only too common."

Housdorf in his *Théâtre des exemples du 8e commandement,* quoted by Simon Goulart, states,

"A doctor of medicine forgot himself so far as to form an alliance with the enemy of our salvation whom he called up and enclosed in a glass from which the seducer and familiar spirit answered him. The doctor was fortunate in the cure of ailments, and amassed great wealth in his practice, so much so that he left his children the sum of 78,000 francs. Shortly before his death, when his conscience began to prick him, he fell into such a frenzy that he never spoke but to invoke the devil or blaspheme the Holy Ghost and it was in this unfortunate condition that he passed away."

A Priest's Pact

In the celebrated case of **Urbain Grandier** and the **Nuns of Loudon,** the diabolical pact between Grandier and the devils was produced as evidence in his trial in 1634. It survives today in the Bibliothèque Nationale in **France.** This extraordinary document is handwritten in looking-glass letters in Latin (presumably devils did everything in reverse) and bears the signatures (also reversed) of Satanas Beelzebub, Elimi Leviathan, and Astaroth. Urbain Grandier's pact, in his own handwriting and signed, states his allegiance to Lucifer and his renunciation of the Christian faith. In return, the pact promises Grandier the love of women, wealth, and worldly honor. There are, of course, doubts as to the authenticity of this document, which the prosecution at Grandier's trial claimed had been stolen by the demon Asmodeus from Lucifer's private files.

Charges of a pact with the devil were also entered in the trials of **Jeanne D'Arc** and **Gilles de Laval.**

Modern Satanism

With the revival of **occultism** in the nineteenth century and the emergence of **Satanism** in France, a new set of modern accounts of pacts with the devil began to appear. Such pacts were discussed at length by **Paul Christian** in his monumental *History and Practice of Magic* (1870). Montague Summers, for example, describes an incident reported in 1929 by Maurice Garcon, who claimed to have watched a sorcerer invoke Satan in a secluded location near Fontainebleau. At the peak of the midnight ceremony, the sorcerer offered the devil a pact written in his own blood. He offered his soul and another soul to the devil for every wish he was granted in life. However, the devil did not appear.

Gracon said he believed that the devil refused to become visible because he (Gracon) was spying upon the sorcerer.

Sources:

Christian, Paul. *The History and Practice of Magic.* N.p., 1870. Revised edition, New York: Citadel Press, 1969.

Robbins, Rossell Hope. *The Encyclopedia of Witchcraft and Demonology.* New York: Crown Publishers, 1959.

Russell, Jeffrey Burton. *Witchcraft in the Middle Ages.* Ithaca, N.Y.: Cornell University Press, 1972.

Summers, Montague. *A Popular History of Witchcraft.* New York: Causeway Books, 1973.

Padrick, Sid (fl. 1965)

UFO **contactee** Sid Padrick rose out of obscurity in 1965 when he claimed that on January 30 a spacecraft landed near his home in Watsonville, California. A high school graduate, Padrick worked as a radio/television repairman. He was married and the father of three sons. Frightened at the sight of the ship, he dropped his guard after the being from the ship assured him that they were not hostile. He invited Padrick aboard their ship. Walking into the saucer-shaped ship, he met a humanoid being who spoke English and indicated his name was Xeno. All the entities on the craft were young. The single female among the crew was attractive. The other crew members did not speak, and Padrick concluded that they communicated by **telepathy.** This observation appeared to be confirmed by Xeno's slowness in answering Padrick's questions. He seemed to be receiving his answers through telepathic contact with another source.

Xeno indicated that he came from a planet hidden by another planet that could be seen from Earth. He told Padrick of his hometown on that planet. There was no crime or sickness. People lived long lives and the society practiced strict birth control. Children were trained for the single task they would work at later in life.

Unusual in contact claims, Padrick said he was led into a room on the spaceship that functioned as a chapel and was invited to "pay his respects to the Supreme Deity." He offered prayer in the manner he had been accustomed to do through his life, but for the first time actually felt the presence of God. He concluded that these advanced beings had found the means to unite science and religion.

The contact had been made in the early morning hours while Padrick's family was asleep and he was walking outside. He was returned to his home around 4 a.m. Several days later he reported the incident to nearby Hamilton Air Force Base and announced plans to write a book, though it was never published. He lectured for several years to contactee audiences and claimed further contacts, though he did not elaborate on them. Eventually he moved back into the obscurity from which he had emerged.

Sources:

Clark, Jerome. "Two New Contactee Claims." *Flying Saucer Review* 11, no.3 (May/June 1965): 20–23.

Lorenzen, Coral, and Jon Lorenzen. *Encounters with UFO Occupants.* New York: Berkley Medallion, 1976.

Pagan Alliance

The Pagan Alliance is the major networking organization of Pagans and Witches in Australia. As in the United Kingdom and North America, nature-centered Goddess worship spread through Australia during the 1970s and 1980s. The movement was based in a number of small autonomous covens and groves and in somewhat limited associations of covens that shared the same heritage and approach to **magic** and **witchcraft.** The Pagan Alliance, founded in 1991, emerged to promote communication and cooperation between the very decentralized movement. Members affirm their love for and kinship with nature; an ethic of individual responsibility; and an acceptance of the many-faceted nature of divinity.

The alliance is organized through a set of state councils, each of which seeks to have at least three members and represent three different Pagan/Wiccan traditions. The alliance attempts to network different groups and individuals and to serve as a contact between the Pagan community and outsiders, especially the news media. On a national level, the alliance involves itself as an advocacy group on issues of interest to Pagans including freedom of religion. In this regard, it monitors news coverage and responds to attacks, especially those involving negative stereotypes. It has also compiled a list of Pagans licensed to perform official functions such as marriages and funerals.

The alliance is currently administered by Chel and Jon Bardell, who may be contacted at P.O. Box 823, Bathurst, New South Wales 2795. The alliance's Internet site is found at http://www.geocities.com/Athens/Thebes/4320. It publishes the *Pagan Times* quarterly.

Sources:

Pagan Alliance. http://www.geocities.com/Athens/Thebes/4320. February 20, 2000.

Pagenstecher, Gustav (1855–1942)

Nineteenth-century German physician who conducted important experiments in **psychometry.** He was born in Germany in 1855, and received his medical degree from Leipzig University. Shortly afterward he moved to Mexico where he practiced medicine for some four decades.

One day Pagenstecher treated a patient, **Maria Reyes Zierold,** for insomnia by using hypnosis. During treatment she claimed to see beyond the closed doors of her room and could describe accurately individuals and events outside the range of normal vision. With Zierold's permission Pagenstecher conducted further experiments to test this paranormal perception. He discovered her normal physical senses were blocked by hypnotic sensation; nevertheless, she reported sensations of vision, smell, taste, hearing, or feelings from objects held by her. These sensations enabled her to report information connected with the history or associations of the objects held by her.

In 1919 Pagenstecher reported on these experiments to a medical society in Mexico City, which appointed a committee to study this psychometric ability. The committee gave Zierold pumice stones to hold while in trance, and she accurately reported information concerning the stones, their origin, and other details. The committee reported favorably on Pagenstecher's view that the phenomena appeared genuinely paranormal.

The next year Pagenstecher reported the facts to the **American Society for Psychical Research** via an article in the Society's *Journal.* In 1921 **Walter Franklin Prince** visited Mexico to observe Pagenstecher's experiments and to conduct his own. Prince also endorsed the phenomena in his reports to the society. Pagenstecher died December 26, 1942, in Mexico City.

Sources:

Pagenstecher, Gustav. *Die Geheimnisse der Psychometrie oder Hellsehen in die Vergangenheit* (Secrets of Psychometry or Clairvoyance into the Past). N.p., 1928.

———. "A Notable Psychometrist." *Journal* of the American Society for Psychical Research 14 (1920).

———. "Past Events Seership." *ASPR Proceedings* 16 (January 1922).

Prince, Walter Franklin. "Psychometrical Experiments with Señora Maria Reyes de Z." *ASPR Journal* 16 (January 1922).

———. "Psychometrical Experiments with Señora Maria Reyes de Z." *ASPR Proceedings* 15 (1921).

Page Research Library Newsletter

A 1970s publication giving news on **apparitions, mysteries,** and general **Fortean phenomena.** In 1979, it merged with *Ohio Sky Watcher* to become the *UFO Ohio Newsletter* and continued to be published for several years by the now defunct **UFO Information Network** in Rome, Ohio.

The Paigoels

According to Nathaniel E. Kindersley, these were devils of Hindustan mythology. Some of the Hindus believed that the *paigoels* were originally created devils; other believed they were individuals put out of heaven because of their great sin. Some of these devils had individual names and were the tempters of men to special sins; others entered into the bodies of men and took possession of them. It was also believed that the souls of wicked men joined the *paigoels.*

Sources:

Kindersley, Nathaniel E. *Specimens of Hindoo Literature.* N.p., 1794.

Palingenesy

A term employed by the philosophers of the seventeenth century to denote the "resurrection of plants," and the method of achieving their astral appearance after destruction.

The Roman poet/philosopher Lucretius (ca. 98–55 B.C.E.) attacked the popular notion of ghosts by claiming they were not spirits returned from the mansions of the dead, but nothing more than thin films, pellicles, or membranes, cast off from the surface of all bodies like the exuviae (sloughs of reptiles).

An opinion by no means dissimilar to that of the Epicureans was revived in Europe about the middle of the seventeenth century and the process was performed by the likes of Sir Kenelm Digby, Athanasius Kircher, Abbé de Vallemont, and others. The complicated and exacting procedure began with a selected plant, a rose, for example. The operator then bruised it, burnt it, collected its ashes, and, in the process of calcination, extracted from it a salt. This salt was then put into a glass vial and mixed with some peculiar undisclosed substance.

When the compound was formed, it was pulverulent (crumbly) and blue. The powder was next submitted to a gentle heat. With its particles instantly set into motion, it then gradually arose (it was claimed) from the midst of the ashes—a stem, leaves, and flowers. It appeared as an apparition of the plant, which had been submitted to combustion. But as soon as the heat was removed, the form of the plant that had been sublimed was precipitated to the bottom of the vessel. Heat was then reapplied and the plant form was resuscitated; when it was withdrawn the form once more became latent among the ashes.

This notable experiment was said to have been performed before the Royal Society of England, and to have satisfactorily proved that the presence of heat gave a sort of life to the plant apparition, and that the absence of nourishment caused its death. The poet Abraham Cowley was quite delighted with the story of the experiment of the rose and its ashes, since he believed that he, too, had detected the same phenomenon in letters written with the juice of lemons, which were revived with the application of heat. He celebrated the mystic power of caloric in a poem:

> "Strange power of heat, thou yet dost show,
> Like winter earth, naked, or cloth'd with snow.
> But as the quick'ning sun approaching near,
> The plants arise up by degrees, new line
> A sudden paint adorns the trees,
> And all kind nature's characters appear.
>
> So nothing yet in thee is seen,
> But when a genial heat warms thee within,
> A new-born wood of various lines there grows;
> Here buds an A, and there a B,
> Here sprouts a V, and there a T,
> And all the flourishing letters stand in rows."

The rationale of this famous experiment made on the rose ashes was attempted by Kircher. He supposed the seminal virtue of every known substance and even its substantial form resided in its salt. This salt was concealed in the ashes of the rose, and adding heat put it in motion. The particles of the salt were quickly sublimed and by being moved about in the vial like a vortex, the particles arranged themselves in the same general form they had possessed from nature. Other particles were subject to a similar law, and accordingly, by a disposing affinity, they resumed their proper position, either in the stalk, the leaves, or the flowers.

The next object of these philosophers was to apply their doctrine to explain the popular belief in ghosts. As the experimenters claimed the substantial form of each body resided in a sort of volatile salt, it was believed that superstitious notions must have arisen about ghosts haunting churchyards. When a dead body had been committed to the earth, the salts were exhaled during the heating process of fermentation. Each saline particle then resumed the same relative situation it had held in the living body, and thus a complete human form was induced.

Palingenesy was similar to the early claims of Lucretius involving a chemical explanation of the discovery of filmy substances, which he had observed to arise from all bodies. Yet, in order to prove that apparitions might really be explained on this principle, a crucial experiment was necessary.

Three alchemists obtained a quantity of earth-mould from St. Innocent's Church in Paris, believing that this matter might contain the true **philosophers' stone.** They subjected it to a distillatory process. They saw (it was claimed) the forms of men produced in their vials, which immediately caused them to end the project. This was brought to the attention of the Institute of Paris (under the protection of Louis XIV), which, in turn, took up the business with much seriousness. The result of its own investigations appeared in the *Miscellania Curiosa.* James F. Ferrier, in a volume of the *Manchester Philosophical Transactions,* made an abstract of one of these French documents:

"A malefactor was executed, of whose body a grave physician got possession for the purpose of dissection. After disposing of the other parts of the body, he ordered his assistant to pulverize part of the cranium, which was a remedy at that time admitted in dispensatories. The powder was left in a paper on the table of the museum, where the assistant slept. About midnight he was awakened by a noise in the room, which obliged him to rise immediately. The noise continued about the table, without any visible agent; and at length he traced it to the powder, in the midst of which he now beheld, to his unspeakable dismay, a small head with open eyes staring at him; presently two branches appeared, which formed into arms and hands; then the ribs became visible, which were soon clothed with muscles and integuments; next the lower extremities sprouted out, and when they appeared perfect, the puppet (for his size was small) reared himself on his feet; instantly his clothes came upon him, and he appeared in the very cloak he wore at his execution. The affrighted spectator, who stood hitherto mumbling his prayers with great application, now thought of nothing but making his escape from the revived ruffian; but this was impossible, for the apparition planted himself in the way, and, after divers fierce looks and threatening gestures, opened the door and went out. No doubt the powder was missing next day."

But older analogous results are on record, suggesting that the blood was the chief part of the human frame in which those saline particles resided. These arrangements gave rise to the popular notion of ghosts. John Webster's book *The Displaying of Supposed Witchcraft* (1677) related an experiment, given on the authority of **Robert Fludd,** in which this conclusion was drawn.

"A certain chymical operator, by name La Pierre, near that place in Paris called Le Temple, received blood from the hands of a certain bishop to operate upon. Which he setting to work upon the Saturday, did continue it for a week with divers degrees of fire. But about midnight, the Friday following, this artificer, lying in a chamber next to his laboratory, betwixt sleeping and waking, heard a horrible noise, like unto the lowing of kine, or the roaring of a lion; and continuing quiet, after the ceasing of the sound in the laboratory, the moon being at the full, and, by shining enlightening the chamber suddenly, betwixt himself and the window he saw a thick little cloud, condensed into an oval form, which, after, by little and little, did seem completely to put on the shape of a man, and making another and a sharp clamour, did suddenly vanish. And not only some noble persons in the next chambers, but also the host with his wife, lying in a lower room of the house, and also the neighbours dwelling in the opposite side of the street, did distinctly hear as well the bellowing as the voice; and some of them were awaked with the vehemency thereof.

"But the artificer said, that in this he found solace, because the bishop, of whom he had it, did admonish him, that if any of them from whom the blood was extracted should die, in the time of its putrefaction, his spirit was wont often to appear to the sight of the artificer, with perturbation. Also forthwith, upon Saturday following, he took the retort from the furnace, and broke it with the light stroke of a little key, and there, in the remaining blood, found the perfect representation of an human head, agreeable in face, eyes, nostrils, mouth, and hairs, that were somewhat thin, and of a golden colour."

Regarding this narrative Webster added:

"There were many ocular witnesses, as the noble person, Lord of Bourdalone, the chief secretary to the Duke of Guise; and he [Fludd] had this relation from the Lord of Menanton, living in that house at the same time from a certain doctor of physic, from the owner of the house, and many others."

Apart from such credulous statements, the claimed results of early experiments in palingenesy have long since been abandoned by science, but curious echoes of the subject have appeared in twentieth-century borderland researches. For example, Charles W. Littlefield, a physician of Seattle, Washington, published a book titled *"M. M. M."—Man, Minerals and Masters* (1937) in which he described his experiments as showing by demonstration and illustration that thoughts are things, and that their power may be expressed through certain mineral compounds occurring in organic nature. Littlefield claimed the crystallization of solutions of organic salts could be modified by mental energy, and stated that he had produced microscopic animal or human-like forms in this way.

The work of another experimenter was reminiscent of the seventeenth-century Royal Society claim of the restoration of the form of a destroyed plant. In the 1920s a British biological chemist named Morley-Martin claimed the forms of fishes, plants, and animals continued to exist in miniature in ancient azoic rocks. Morley-Martin experimented by taking fragments of such rock and submitting them to a temperature of 2,000–3,000 degrees Fahrenheit in an electric oven. He isolated what he named "primordial protoplasm" from the ashes, which he transformed into crystalloids with Canada balsam. In the course of time the crystalloids condensed and produced numerous organisms that were creature-like, even having life and movement.

These little-known and bizarre experiments are described by **Maurice Maeterlinck** in his book *La Grande Porte* (Paris, 1939), and the work of both Littlefield and Morley-Martin is described in the booklet *The Morley-Martin Experiments* issued by the Borderland Sciences Research Associates. In these experiments palingenesy merged with the old theory of spontaneous generation, which was considered to have been solved by Louis Pasteur's experiments on micro-organisms, although P. J. A. Béchamp in France and H. Charlton Bastian in Britain claimed Pasteur's work did not cover all the facts.

Of possible relevance to the palingenesy experiments were the "osmotic growths" produced by Dr. Stéhane Leduc of Nantes. These were formed from crystal solutions and not only presented the cellular structure of living matter, but also reproduced such functions as food absorption, metabolism, and the excretion of waste products. These beautiful growths are described in Leduc's book *The Mechanism of Life* (1914).

Sources:

Littlefield, Charles W. *"M. M. M."—Man, Minerals and Masters.* Los Angeles: DeVorss, 1937.

The Morley-Martin Experiments. BSRA booklet No. 1. San Diego: Borderland Sciences Research Associates, 1948.

Palladino, Eusapia (1854–1918)

The public name of Signora Raphael Delgaiz, the first physical **medium** who stood in the crossfire of collective scientific investigation for more than twenty years all over Europe and in America. It was largely due to her career that physical phenomena was given center stage by **psychical research** and the psychological complex of **fraud** was, in the early twentieth century, introduced to an array of brilliant minds.

Palladino was born in Minervo-Murge, Italy, on January 21, 1854. Her birth cost her mother's life; her father was assassinated by brigands in 1866. As a little girl she heard **raps** on the furniture against which she was leaning; she saw eyes glaring at her in the darkness and was frequently frightened in the night when invisible hands stripped off her bedclothes.

When she became orphaned, a family of the upper bourgeoisie received her in Naples as a nursemaid. They soon detected that she was not an ordinary girl, but her real discovery and mediumistic education was due to Signor Damiani, a noted Italian psychic investigator. His wife went to a **séance** in London. **"John King"** manifested and spoke about a powerful medium in Naples who was his reincarnated daughter. He gave her address, street and number. In 1872 Damiani went to the house and found Palladino, of whom he had never heard before. The development of her abilities progressed at a rapid rate. In the first five or six years she devoted herself mainly to phenomena of **movements** without contact. Then came the famous spectral appearances, the phantom limbs so often noticed to issue from her body, and the **materialization** of full but incomplete figures.

Her **control** "John King" communicated through raps and in **trance** spoke in Italian alone. Palladino always knew what phenomenon was going to take place and could warn the sitters. She appeared to suffer extremely during the process and exhibited a synchronism between her gestures and the movement without contact. If she glared defiantly at a table it began to move towards her, if she warned it off it backed away. A forcible motion of her head was accompanied by raps and upward movements of her hand would cause the table to lift in the air. Another peculiarity of her séances was that any particular phenomenon had to be wished for incessantly. Strong desire on the part of the sitters present usually brought about the occurrence.

The first scientist who proclaimed the reality of her phenomena was **Ercole Chiaia.** An opportunity to invite public attention to Palladino was occasioned by **Cesare Lombroso**'s article on "The Influence of Civilisation upon Genius," which concluded:

"Twenty or thirty years are enough to make the whole world admire a discovery which was treated as madness at the moment when it was made. Even at the present day academic bodies laugh at hypnotism and homeopathy. Who knows whether my friends and I, who laugh at Spiritualism, are not in error, just as hypnotised persons are?"

On August 9, 1888, Chiaia addressed an open letter to Lombroso and challenged him to observe Palladino, saying:

"The case I allude to is that of an invalid woman who belongs to the humblest class of society. She is nearly thirty years old and very ignorant; her appearance is neither fascinating nor endowed with the power which modern criminologists call irresistible; but when she wishes, be it by day or by night, she can divert a curious group for an hour or so with the most surprising phenomena. Either bound to a seat, or firmly held by the hands of the curious, she attracts to her the articles of furniture which surround her, lifts them up, holds them suspended in the air like Mahomet's coffin, and makes them come down again with undulatory movements, as if they were obeying her will. She increases their height or lessens it according to her pleasure. She raps or taps upon the walls, the ceiling, the floor, with fine rhythm and cadence. In response to the requests of the spectators something like flashes of electricity shoot forth from her body, and envelop her or enwrap the spectators of these marvellous scenes. She draws upon cards that you hold out, everything that you want—figures, signatures, numbers, sentences—by just stretching out her hand towards the indicated place.

"If you place in the corner of the room a vessel containing a layer of soft clay, you find after some moments the imprint in it of a small or a large hand, the image of a face (front view or profile) from which a plaster cast can be taken. In this way portraits of a face at different angles have been preserved, and those who desire so to do can thus make serious and important studies.

"This woman rises in the air, no matter what bands tie her down. She seems to lie upon the empty air, as on a couch, contrary to all the laws of gravity; she plays on musical instruments—organs, bells, tambourines—as if they had been touched by her hands or moved by the breath of invisible gnomes. This woman at times can increase her stature by more than four inches.

"She is like an India rubber doll, like an automaton of a new kind; she takes strange forms. How many legs and arms has she? We do not know. While her limbs are being held by incredulous spectators, we see other limbs coming into view, without her knowing where they come from. Her shoes are too small to fit these witch-feet of hers, and this particular circumstance gives rise to the suspicion of the intervention of mysterious power."

Two years later Lombroso visited Naples for a sitting. His first report stated:

"Eusapia's feet and hands were held by Professor Tamburini and by Lombroso. A handbell placed on a small table more than a yard distant from Eusapia sounded in the air above the heads of the sitters and then descended on the table, thence going two yards to a bed. While the bell was ringing we struck a match and saw the bell up in the air."

A detailed account of his observations and reflections appeared in the *Annales des Sciences Psychiques* (1892). Lombroso admitted the reality of the phenomena and, on the basis of the analogy of the **transposition of the senses** observed in hypnotic cases, suggested a transformation of the powers of the medium as an explanation. He continued his researches for many years and ended in the acceptance of the spirit theory.

In his book *After Death—What?* (1909) he expanded upon his observation of the medium:

"Her culture is that of a villager of the lower order. She frequently fails in good sense and in common sense, but has a subtlety and intuition of the intellect in sharp contrast with her lack of cultivation, and which make her, in spite of that, judge and appreciate at their true worth the men of genius whom she meets, without being influenced in her judgments by prestige or the false stamp that wealth and authority set upon people.

"She is ingenuous to the extent of allowing herself to be imposed on and mystified by an intriguer, and, on the other hand, sometimes exhibits, both before and during her trance states, a slyness that in some cases goes as far as deception. . . .

"She possesses a most keen visual memory, to the extent of remembering five to ten mental texts presented to her during three seconds. She has the ability to recall very vividly, especially with her eyes shut, the outlines of persons, and with a power of vision so precise as to be able to delineate their characteristic traits.

"But she is not without morbid characteristics, which sometimes extend to hysterical insanity. She passes rapidly from joy to grief, has strange phobias (for example the fear of staining her hands), is extremely impressionable and subject to dreams in spite of her mature age. Not rarely she has hallucinations, frequently sees her own ghost. As a child she believed two eyes glared at her from behind trees and hedges. When she is in anger, especially when her reputation as a medium is insulted, she is so violent and impulsive as actually to fly at her adversaries and beat them.

"These tendencies are offset in her by a singular kindness of heart which leads her to lavish her gains upon the poor and upon infants in order to relieve their misfortunes, and which impels her to feel foundless pity for the old and weak. . . . The same goodness of heart drives her to protect animals that are being maltreated, by sharply rebuking their cruel oppressors."

Arthur Levy also left a description of Palladino in his report on a séance held in the house of **Camille Flammarion** in 1898:

"Two things arrest the attention when you look at her. First, her large eyes, filled with strange fire, sparkle in their orbits, or again, seem filled with swift gleams of phosphorescent fire, sometimes bluish, sometimes golden. If I did not fear that the metaphor was too easy when it concerns a Neapolitan woman, I should say that her eyes appear like the glowing lava fires of Vesuvius, seen from a distance in a dark night. The other peculiarity is a mouth with strange contours. We do not know whether it expresses amusement, suffering or scorn."

Lombroso made a thorough psychological study of Palladino. He wrote:

"Many are the crafty tricks she plays, both in the state of trance (unconsciously) and out of it—for example, freeing one of her two hands, held by the controllers, for the sake of moving objects near her; making touches; slowly lifting the legs of the table by means of one of her knees and one of her feet, and feigning to adjust her hair and then slyly pulling out one hair and putting it over the little balance tray of a letter-weigher in order to lower it. She was seen by Faifofer, before her séances, furtively gathering flowers in a garden, that she might feign them to be 'apports' by availing herself of the shrouding dark of the room."

Similar observations were made by **Enrico Morselli** and later investigators. Her penchant to cheat caused Palladino trouble in her later years and destroyed any contribution her career might have made in the long run.

The sittings in Naples, which started Lombroso on his career as a psychical researcher, were followed by an investigation in Milan in 1892. Professor Schiaparelli, director of the Observatory of Milan, Professor Gerosa, **G. B. Ermacora, Alexander Aksakof, Baron Carl du Prel** and **Charles Richet** were among the members of the Milan Commission. Part of the report, based on a series of seventeen sittings, observed:

"It is impossible to count the number of times that a hand appeared and was touched by one of us. Suffice it to say that doubt was no longer possible. It was indeed a living human hand which we saw and touched, while at the same time the bust and the arms of the medium remained visible, and her hands were held by those on either side of her."

At the end of the report the committee concluded:

"1) That in the circumstances given, none of the phenomena obtained in more or less intense light could have been produced by the aid of any artifice whatever.

"2) That the same opinion may be affirmed in a large measure with regard to the phenomena obtained in complete darkness. For some of them we can well admit, strictly speaking, the possibility of imitating them by means of some adroit artifice on the part of the medium; nevertheless, according to what we have said, it is evident that this hypothesis would be not only improbable, but even useless in the present case, since even admitting it, the assembly of facts clearly proved would not be invalidated by it."

In the following year, a series of séances took place in Naples under the direction of a Professor Wagner of the University of St. Petersburg. The next series was in Rome in 1893–94 under the direction of Mr. de Semiradski, but was interrupted by a visit to Warsaw where **Julien Ochorowicz** conducted additional experiments. He worked out the hypothesis of a "fluidic double" which, under certain conditions, detaches itself and acts independently of the body of the medium. In 1894, at Richet's home on the Ile Roubaud, **Sir Oliver Lodge** and **F. W. H. Myers** had their first opportunity to witness what they believed to be genuine physical phenomena of an unusual order. Lodge reported to the **Society for Psychical Research** that he had no doubts that movement occurred without contact.

Richard Hodgson, of Boston, criticized the report and pointed out that the precautions described did not exclude trickery. He suggested explanations for various phenomena on the theory that the medium could get a hand or foot free. Lodge, Myers, and Richet each replied. Richet pointed out that he attended 15 séances with Palladino in Milan and Rome and held 40 at Carquieranne and in the Ile Roubaud over a period of three months under his own supervision. He concluded: "It appears to me that after three months' practice and meditation one can arrive at the certainty of holding well a human hand."

Palladino at Cambridge (1895)

As an outcome of the critical reception of this report, Palladino was invited to England. In August and September 1895 twenty sittings were held at Myers's house in Cambridge. Hodgson and **J. N. Maskelyne,** the professional conjurer, were also invited. The sitters' attitude was not so much to prevent fraud as to detect it. Hodgson intentionally left Palladino's hand free. She was given every opportunity to cheat and she availed herself of this generosity.

In communicating the findings of the Cambridge investigation to the Society for Psychical Research, Myers, who on the Ile Roubaud was convinced of having witnessed supernormal phenomena, reversed himself in a most decisive fashion:

"I cannot doubt that we observed much conscious and deliberate fraud, of a kind which must have needed long practice to bring it to its present level of skill. Nor can I find any excuse for her fraud (assuming that such excuse would be valid) in the attitude of mind of the persons, several of them distinguished in the world of science, who assisted in this inquiry. Their attitude was a fair and open one; in all cases they showed patience, and in several cases the impression first made on their minds was distinctly favourable. With growing experience, however, and careful observation of the precise conditions permitted or refused to us, the existence of some fraud became clear; and fraud was attempted when the tests were as good as we were allowed to make them, quite as indisputably as on the few occasions when our holding was intentionally left inadequate in order to trace more exactly the *modus operandi.* Moreover, the fraud occurred both in the medium's waking state and during her real or alleged trance. I do not think there is adequate reason to suppose that any of the phenomena at Cambridge were genuine."

The Cambridge report was not well received by some psychical researchers. Lodge only attended two of the sittings but declared that he failed to see any resemblance between the phenomena there produced and those witnessed on the Ile Roubaud. He reaffirmed his belief in what he observed there. **Ada Goodrich-Freer** soon broke with the Society for Psychical Research and defended Palladino in her book *Essays in Psychical Research* (1899): "The Italian medium, Eusapia Palladino, may have been a fraud of the deepest dye for anything I know to the contrary, but she never had a fair chance in England. Even her cheating seems to have been badly done. The atmosphere was inimical; the poor thing was paralysed."

In his book *Metapsychical Phenomena* (1905), **Joseph Maxwell** concluded, "I cannot help thinking that the Cambridge experimenters were either ill-guided, or ill-favoured, for I have obtained raps with Eusapia Palladino in full light, I have obtained them with many other mediums, and it is a minimum phenomenon which they could have and ought to have obtained, had they experimented in a proper manner."

Meanwhile, Ochorowitz argued that Palladino frequently released her hand for no other reason than to touch her head, which was in pain from the manifestations. It was a natural reflex and a fixed habit. Immediately before the mediumistic doubling of her personality, her hand was affected with hyperaesthesia and consequently, the pressure of the hand of another made her ill, especially in the dorsal quarter. The medium acted by autosuggestion and the order to go as far as an indicated point was given by her brain simultaneously to the dynamic hand and the corporeal hand, since in the normal state they form only one. Sometimes the dynamic hand remained in place, while her own hand went in the indicated direction. Ochorowitz concluded that "not only was *conscious* fraud not proved on Palladino at Cambridge, but not the slightest effort was made to do so. *Unconscious* fraud was proved in much larger proportion than in all the preceding experiments. This negative result is vindicated by a blundering method little in accordance with the nature of the phenomena."

It appears from the *Journal* of the Society for Psychical Research that the dynamic hands of which Ochorowitz spoke created a strong presumption against Palladino. The paper said: "It is hardly necessary to remark that the continuity of the spirit limbs with the body of the medium is, *prima facie,* a circumstance strongly suggestive of fraud."

The issue of the "phantom limbs" continued to intrigue researchers, while at the same time it was well recognized that Palladino frequently resorted to fraud whenever allowed. Camille Flammarion tried to defend her:

"She is frequently ill on the following day, sometimes even on the second day following, and is incapable of taking any nourishment without immediately vomiting. One can readily conceive, then, that when she is able to perform certain wonders without any expenditure of force and merely by a more or less skillful piece of deception, she prefers the second procedure to the first. It does not exhaust her at all, and may even amuse her. Let me remark, in the next place, that, during these experiments, she is generally in a half-awake condition which is somewhat similar to the hypnotic or somnambulistic sleep. Her fixed idea is to produce phenomena; and she produces them, no matter how."

In the very month of the exposure a new series of experiments was made at l'Agnelas, in the residence of **Eugene Rochas,** president of the Polytechnic School. Dr. Dariex, editor of the *Annales des Sciences Psychiques,* Count de Gramont, Joseph Maxwell, Professor Sabatier, and Baron de Watteville participated. They all attested that the phenomena produced were genuine. On the result of the observations, Rochas built up his theory of "externalisation of motricity."

On December 1, 1898, a séance was arranged in Richet's library in Paris for the purpose of assisting Palladino to regain her reputation. The séance took place in good light, her wrists and ankles were held by the sitters, and before each experience she warned the sitters what she was going to do in order that they might establish the phenomenon to the best of their faculties and observation. She did not cease to admonish Myers to pay the closest attention and to remember exactly afterwards what had happened. "Under these conditions," wrote **Theodore Flournoy,** "I saw phenomena which I then believed, and still believe, to be certainly inexplicable by any known laws of physics and physiology." When Myers was begged by Richet to state his view, he again reversed himself and avowed his renewed belief in the supernormal character of Palladino's mediumship. Lombroso adopted the spirit hypothesis and Flammarion became firmly convinced of the reality of Palladino's phenomena.

In 1901 Genoa was the scene of important experiments in the presence of Enrico Morselli, professor of psychology at the University of Genoa, and the astronomer Porro, director of the observatories of Genoa, Turin, and later La Plata in Argentina. Much instrumental investigation was carried on by Herdlitzka, Charles Foà, and Aggazotti; assistants of Professor Mosso, the distinguished physiologist in Turin; and by **Filippo Bottazzi,** director of the Physiological Institute at the University of Naples, with the assistance of six other professors.

The Institut Général Psychologique of Paris carried on extensive experiments in 43 sittings from 1905 to 1907. Pierre and Marie Curie were among the investigators. Fraud and genuine phenomena were observed in a strange mixture. Jules Courtier's report states that movements seemed to be produced by simple contact with the medium's hands; even without contact, such movements were registered by automatic recording instruments that ruled out the hypothesis of collective hallucination. The instruments show that molecular vibrations in distant external objects could be positively asserted. They explained the fraud by suggesting that Palladino was growing old and that she was strongly tempted not to disappoint her clients when genuine power failed. On the whole, the phenomena were less striking and abundant as the years passed. On one or two occasions she succeeded in discharging an electroscope without anybody being able to find out how it was done.

In consequence of this report and under the effect of a growing number of testimonies to the genuine powers of Palladino, the council of the Society for Psychical Research reconsidered its attitude and delegated in 1908 a committee of three very capable and skeptical investigators: **W. W. Baggally,** a practical conjurer; **Hereward Carrington,** an amateur conjurer, whose book *The Physical Phenomena of Spiritualism* (1907) is a reliable authority on fraudulent performances; and **Everard Feilding,** who also brought many a fraudulent medium to grief. They held eleven sittings in November and December in a room of a member of the committee at the Hotel Victoria in Naples.

Finally, they admitted that the phenomena were genuine and inexplicable by fraud. Their report was published as Part 59 of the *Proceedings* of the Society for Psychical Research, and even **Frank Podmore,** the most hardened skeptic of the time, felt compelled to say: "Here, for the first time perhaps in the history of modern spiritualism, we seem to find the issue put fairly and squarely before us. It is difficult for any man who reads the Committee's report to dismiss the whole business as mere vulgar cheating."

It is sufficient, however, against any outside criticism to quote the opinion of Everard Feilding as expressed after the sixth séance:

"For the first time I have absolute conviction that our observation is not mistaken. I realise as an appreciable fact in life that, from an empty curtain, I have seen hands and heads come forth, and that behind the empty curtain I have been seized by living fingers, the existence and position of the nails of which were perceptible. I have seen this extraordinary woman, sitting outside the curtain, held hand and foot, visible to myself, by my colleagues, immobile, except for the occasional straining of a limb while some entity within the curtain has over and over again pressed my hand in a position clearly beyond her reach. I refuse to entertain the possibility of a doubt that it could be anything else, and, remembering my own belief of a very short time ago, I shall not be able to complain, though I shall unquestionably be annoyed when I find that to be the case."

By this verdict, Palladino's standing was enormously enhanced, and not without reason. Richet wrote:

"There have perhaps never been so many different, sceptical and scrupulous investigators into the work of any medium or more minute investigations. During twenty years, from 1888 to 1908, she submitted, at the hands of the most skilled European and American experimentalists, to tests of the most rigorous and decisive kind, and during all this time men of science, resolved not to be deceived, have verified that even very large and massive objects were displaced without contact."

In discussing **materializations** he added: "More than thirty very sceptical scientific men were convinced, after long testing, that there proceeded from her body material forms having the appearances of life."

The most extraordinary séance recorded with Palladino was probably the one described in full detail by Morselli in *Psicologia e 'Spiritismo'* (Turin, 1908, Vol. 2, pp. 214–237). The séance was held in Genoa on March 1, 1902. Besides Morselli, **Ernesto Bozzano,** Dr. Venzano, and six other persons were present. The cabinet was examined by Morselli and he himself tied the medium to a camp bed. In fairly good light six phantoms presented themselves in succession in front of the cabinet, the last one a woman with a baby in her arms. Each time after the phantom retired, Morselli rushed into the cabinet and found the medium tied as he left her. No doubt was left in Morselli's mind of the genuineness of the phenomena, yet strangely his materialistic attitude remained unshaken.

Palladino in America (1909–10)

Still one final blow was in store for Palladino. Owing to the success of the Naples sittings, the story of which was ably told in Hereward Carrington's *Eusapia Palladino and Her Phenomena* (1909), she was invited in 1909 to visit America. She landed in New York on November 10, 1909, and left on June 18, 1910.

Her first twenty séances were comparatively good ones. In the later sittings at Columbia University and at the house of Professor Lord she was caught in the use of her old trickery. The press made a tremendous sensation of the exposure. The authenticity of the published account, however, was questioned by Carrington. It said that at a sitting held on December 18, a young man crept under the cover of darkness into the cabinet and, during the movement of a small table, while Professor Hugo Munsterberg was controlling the left foot of Palladino, the young man grabbed a human foot, unshod, by the instep. Palladino's foot was pulled out of the shoe. Later she was watched from a concealed window in the cabinet and from a bureau provided with a secret peephole. She achieved the desired effect by gradual substitution, i.e., making one foot do duty for two as regards the control of her limbs, and acting freely with the loose foot.

It had not been emphasized that Paladino, at this stage, was so apprehensive of her investigators that she did not allow herself to go into trance for fear that an injury might be done to her. The psychological attitude of her sitters was reflected by the following statement of Palladino to a newspaper man: "Some people are at the table who expect tricks—in fact they want them. I am in a trance. Nothing happens. They get impatient. They think of the tricks—nothing but tricks. They put their minds on the tricks and I automatically respond. But it is not often. They merely will me to do them. That is all."

Carrington contended that far from having been exposed in America, as the public imagined, Palladino presented a large number of striking phenomena that have never been explained; only a certain number of her classical and customary tricks were detected, which every investigator of this medium's phenomena had known to exist and had warned other investigators against for the past twenty years. No new form of trickery was discovered and Carrington had warned the sitters against the old and well-known methods in a circular letter in advance.

According to Palladino, when her power was strong, the phenomena began almost at once. When it was weak, long waiting was necessary. It was on such occasions that she was tempted to cheat. She did this so often that, as Carrington stated: "practically every scientific committee detected her in attempted fraud, but every one of these committees emerged from their investigations quite convinced of the reality of these phenomena, except the Cambridge and American investigation which ended in exposure."

This was not the case as stated in a document from April 1910 at Columbia in which she was again exposed by a set of conjurors. Nevertheless, Palladino did not depart from America without her convert Howard Thurston, a magician, who declared: "I witnessed in person the table levitations of Madame Eusapia Palladino . . . and am thoroughly convinced that the phenomena I saw were not due to fraud and were not performed by the aid of her feet, knees, or hands."

He also offered to give a thousand dollars to a charitable institution if it could be proved that Palladino could not levitate a table without trickery.

To the Present

In December 1910 Everard Feilding stated in documents in Naples that Palladino's observed phenomena were produced by fraud. Carrington, who had worked with Feilding earlier but was not with him in Naples, remained a supporter of her phenomena throughout his life and as late as 1930 concluded:

"To sum up the effects of these séances upon my own mind, I may say that, after seeing nearly forty of her séances, there remains not a shadow of doubt in my mind as to the reality of the vast majority of this phenomena occurring in Eusapia Palladino's presence . . . I can but record the fact that further study of this medium has convinced me more than ever that our Naples experiments and deductions were correct, that we were not deceived, but that we did, in very truth, see praeternormal manifestations of a remarkable character. I am as assured of the reality of Eusapia Palladino's phenomena as I am of any other fact in life; and they are, to my mind, just as well established."

Paole Carrara, the daughter of Lombroso, published a biography of Palladino in 1907. A comprehensive bibliography related to her work is in Morselli's *Psicologia e spiritismo* (Turin, 1908).

Sources:

Barzini, Luigi. *Nel mondo dei Misteri con Eusapia Palladino.* Milan, 1907.

Berger, Arthur S., and Joyce Berger. *The Encyclopedia of Parapsychology and Psychical Research.* New York: Paragon House, 1991.

Bottazi, F. *Nelle regioni inesplorate della Biologia Umana.* Rome, 1907.

Carrington, Hereward. *The American Séances with Eusapia Palladino.* New York: Helix Press, 1954.

———. *Eusapia Palladino and Her Phenomena.* New York: B. W. Dodge, 1909. Reprint, London: T. Werner Laurie, 1910.

Dingwall, Eric J. *Very Peculiar People: Portrait Studies in the Queer, the Abnormal and the Uncanny.* London: Rider, 1950. Reprint, New Hyde Park, N.Y.: University Books, 1962.

Feilding, Everard. *Sittings with Eusapia Palladino & Other Studies.* New Hyde Park, N.Y.: University Books, 1963.

Flammarion, Cesar. *After Death—What?* London: T. Fisher Unwin, 1909.

Ochorowicz, Julien. *La Questione della frode negli Experimenti coll' Eusapia Palladino.* Milan, 1896.

Podmore, Frank. *The Newer Spiritualism.* New York: Henry Holt, 1911.

———. *Studies in Psychical Research.* New York: George Putnam's, 1897.

Rochas, Albert de. *L'Extériorisation de la Motricité.* Paris, 1906.

Palladium, Order of

Said to have been a Masonic order, also entitled the Sovereign-Council of Wisdom, founded in Paris on May 20, 1737. It initiated women under the name of "Companions of Penelope." As proof of its existence, Jean Marie Ragon, the Masonic antiquary, published its ritual.

The "Palladium" was also one name used by Leo Taxil (**Gabriel Jogand-Pagés**) to refer to the Masonic order he made a part of his 1880s hoax, which was aimed at showing that the Roman Catholic church secretly sponsored freemasonry.

Palmer, Raymond Alfred (1910–1977)

Entrepreneur publisher of **occult** and science-fiction magazines, who first published the series of stories in *Amazing Stories* known as the **Shaver Mystery.** He was born August 1, 1910, in Milwaukee, Wisconsin. Palmer began writing science fiction as a teenager, sold his first science-fiction story in 1930, and three years later had founded the Jules Verne Prize Club.

At age 28 Palmer became editor of *Amazing Stories,* which had just been bought by the Ziff-Davis Company. He transformed *Amazing Stories* by colorful editing, utilizing old and new science-fiction writers, and even writing much of the magazine himself under various pseudonyms such as G. H. Irwin, Frank Patton, and A. R. Steber. He is said to have boosted circulation from 25,000 to over 185,000. Although there were waves of protests from readers at the Shaver Mystery, Palmer's successor Howard Browne ended the series when he took over *Amazing Stories* in 1949. He later edited *Fantastic Adventures* for Ziff-Davis.

With fellow writer **Curtis Fuller,** Palmer also launched **Fate Magazine** a pocket-size pulp specializing in **occultism.** The first issue in spring 1948 contained an article by Kenneth Arnold, "I *Did* See the Flying Disks," which launched the **flying saucer** craze in North America. Palmer followed up with his own book on saucers, written in collaboration with Arnold.

With his unique flair for popular fantasy, Palmer started his own publication business from a dairy farm in Amherst, Wisconsin. In his magazines *Flying Saucers* and *Search* he generated a new mythology about saucers coming from holes in the polar ice caps. Palmer also promoted the medium Mark Probert and the New Age bible, **"Oahspe."** He died August 15, 1977, after suffering several strokes.

Sources:

Arnold, Kenneth, and Ray Palmer. *The Coming of the Saucers: A Documentary Report on Sky Objects that Have Mystified the World.* Boise, Idaho; Amherst, Wis..: The Authors, 1952.

Clark, Jerome. *The Emergence of a Phenomenon: UFOs from the Beginning through 1959.* Vol. 2, *The UFO Encyclopedia.* Detroit: Omnigraphics, 1992.

"Ray Palmer Dies." *Fate* 30, no. 12 (December 1977): 53.

Palmistry

The art of **divination** by means of lines and marks on the human hand. It is said to have been practiced in very early times by the Brahmins of India and to have been known to Aristotle, who discovered a treatise on the subject written in letters of gold. He presented the treatise to Alexander the Great and was afterward translated into Latin by Hispanus. There are also extant works on the subject by Melampus of Alexandria, Hippocrates, and Galen; several Arabian commentators have also dealt with it.

In the Middle Ages the science was represented by Cocles (ca. 1054) and Hartlieb (ca. 1448). In the early modern period, by which time its practice was identified with the **Gypsies, Robert Fludd** (1574–1637), Indigane, Rothmann, and many others wrote on "cheiromancy," as the subject was then known. D'Arpentigny, Desbarolles, Carus, and others kept the subject alive in the earlier half of the nineteenth century. Since 1860, or thereabouts, palmistry's popularity has grown steadily and has experienced a revival.

Practicing Palmistry

Palmistry is subdivided into three lesser arts—*cheirognomy,* the art of recognizing the type of intelligence from the form of the hands; *cheirosophy,* the study of the comparative value of manual formations; and *cheiromancy,* the art of divination from the form of the hand and fingers, and the lines and markings thereon.

The palmist, first of all, studies the shape and general formation of the hand as a whole; afterward she regards its parts, details, lines, and markings. From cheirognomy and cheirosophy, the general disposition and tendencies are ascertained, and future events are foretold from the reading of the lines and markings.

There are several types of hands: the elementary or large-palmed type; the necessary, with spatulated fingers; the artistic, with conical-shaped fingers; the useful, the fingers of which are square-shaped; the knotted or philosophical; the pointed, or psychic; the mixed, in which the types are blended.

The principal lines are those that separate the hand from the forearm at the wrist, which are known as the rascettes, or the lines of health, wealth, and happiness. The line of life stretches from the center of the palm around the base of the thumb almost to the wrist and is joined for a considerable part of its course by the line of the head. The line of the heart runs across two-thirds of the palm, above the head line; and the line of fate between it and the line of the head runs nearly at right angles extending towards the wrist. The line of fortune runs from the base of the third finger towards the wrist parallel to the line of fate. If the lines are deep, firm, and of narrow width, the significance is good—excepting that a strong line of health shows constitutional weakness.

At the base of the fingers, beginning with the first, lie the mounts of Jupiter, Saturn, Apollo, and Mercury; at the base of the thumb the mount of Venus; opposite to it, that of Luna. If well-proportioned they show certain virtues, but if exaggerated they indicate the vices that correspond to these. The first displays religion, reasonable ambition, or pride and superstition; the second wisdom and prudence, or ignorance and failure; the third when large, makes for success and intelligence, when small for, meanness or love of obscurity; the fourth desire for knowledge and industry, or disinterestedness and laziness. The Lunar mount indicates sensitiveness, imagination, morality or otherwise, and self-will; the mount of Venus, charity and affection, or if exaggerated, viciousness.

The phalanges of the fingers are also indicative of certain faculties. For example, the first and second of the thumb, according to their length, indicate the value of the logical faculty and of the will; those of the index finger in their order—materialism, law, and order; of the middle finger—humanity, system, intelligence; of the third finger—truth, economy, energy; of the little finger—goodness, prudence, and reflectiveness.

There are nearly a hundred other marks and signs, by which certain qualities, influences, or events are believed to be recognized. The length of the line of life indicates the length of existence of its owner. If it is short in both hands, the life will be a short one; if broken in one hand and weak in the other, a serious illness is denoted. If broken in both hands, it means death. If it is much chained it means delicacy. If it has a second or sister line, it shows great vitality. A black spot on the line shows illness at the time marked. A cross indicates some fatality. The line of life coming out far into the palm is a sign of long life.

The line of the head, if long and well-colored, denotes intelligence and power. If descending to the mount of the Moon it shows that the head is much influenced by the imagination. Islands on the line denote mental troubles. The head line forked at the end indicates subtlety and a facility for seeing all sides of the question. A double line of the head is an indication of good fortune. The line of the heart should branch towards the mount of Jupiter. If it should pass over the mount of Jupiter to the edge of the hand and travel round the index finger, it is called "Solomon's ring" and indicates ideality and romance; it is also a sign of occult power. Points or dots in this line may show illness if black, and if white love affairs, while islands on the heart line indicate disease. If the line of fate or Saturn rises from the Lunar mount and ascends towards the line of the heart, it is a sign of a rich marriage. If it extends into the third phalange of Saturn's finger it shows the sinister influence of that planet. A double line of fate is ominous. There are also numerous other lesser lines and marks the hand contains, which are detailed in a number of books on the subject.

Many practitioners of palmistry have their own special interpretations. A few of these works are on scientific lines, but others are merely empirical, and their forecasts of events to come are on a par with newspaper **astrology** columns.

The popularity of palmistry was raised to a new height, especially in the English-speaking world, by **"Cheiro,"** the public name of Count Louis Hamon (1866–1936), who was patronized by royalty and distinguished individuals of his time. He wrote a number of books on palmistry, which were frequently reprinted in both England and the United States and taught and inspired a generation of palmists. Modern palmistry is largely an outgrowth of his efforts.

Sources:

Abayakoon, Cyrus D. F. *Astro-Palmistry: Signs and Seals of the Hand.* New York: ASI Publishers, 1975.

Anderson, Mary. *Palmistry—Your Destiny In Your Hands.* London: Aquarian Press, 1973.

Bashir, Mir. *Your Past, Your Present, and Your Future Through the Art of Hand Analysis.* Garden City, N.Y.: Doubleday, 1974.

Benham, W. G. *Laws of Scientific Hand Reading.* Rev. ed. New York: G. P. Putnam's Sons, 1928. Reprinted as *The Benham Book of Palmistry.* North Hollywood, Calif.: Newcastle, 1988.

Broekman, Marcel. *The Complete Encyclopaedia of Practical Palmistry.* Englewood, N.J.: Prentice-Hall, 1972. Reprint, London: Mayflower, 1975.

Cheiro [Louis Hamon]. *Cheiro's Complete Palmistry.* New Hyde Park, N.Y.: University Books, 1968. Reprint, New York: Dell, 1969.

———. *Cheiro's Guide to the Hand.* London: Nichols, 1900. Reprint, London: Corgi, 1975.

———. *Cheiro's Language of the Hand; A Complete Practical Work on the Science of Cheirognomy and Cheiromancy.* 28th ed. London: H. Jenkins, 1949. Reprint, London: Corgi, 1975.

———. *Cheiro's Memoirs: The Reminiscences of a Society Palmist.* London: William Rider, 1912.

———. *You and Your Hand.* Garden City, N.Y.: Doubleday, Doran, 1935.

Desbarolles, A. *Les Mysteres de la Main.* Paris, 1860.

Hipskind, Judith. *Palmistry: The Whole View.* St. Paul: Llewellyn Publications, 1977.

Jaquin, Noel. *The Hand of Man: A Practical Treatise of the Science of Hand Reading.* London: Faber & Faber, 1933.

———. *Man's Revealing Hand.* London: Routledge, 1934.

Niblo. *The Complete Palmist.* 1900. Reprint, North Hollywood, Calif.: Newcastle, 1982.

Saint-Germain, Comte C. de. *The Practice of Palmistry for Professional Purposes.* 2 vols. 1897–98. Reprint, Hollywood, Calif.: Newcastle, 1973.

Steinbach, Marten. *Medical Palmistry: Health & Character in the Hand.* New Hyde Park, N.Y.: University Books, 1975. Reprint, New York: New American Library, 1976.

Wilson, Joyce. *The Complete Book of Palmistry.* New York: Bantam Books, 1971.

Wolff, Charlotte. *The Human Hand.* London: Methuen, 1942.

Pansini Brothers (ca. 1904)

Italian mediumistic children, chiefly known for the reports of their mysterious bodily **transportations.** In 1901 their father Signor Mauro Pansini, a building contractor, went to live in an old house close to the town hall at Ruvo, in Apulia. A few days later **poltergeist** phenomena broke out in the house, articles were thrown about, and crockery was broken.

One evening Alfredo Pansini, then seven years of age, fell into **trance** and began to speak and recite in French, Latin, and Greek. These manifestations continued until he was sent to a seminary where he was entirely free from them.

When he returned home in 1904 at age ten, a new series of phenomena commenced in which, besides Alfredo, his eight-year-old brother Paolo was also involved. In a few minutes they were, according to reports, bodily transported to places ten to fifteen miles distant (see also **teleportation**). This phenomena created great bewilderment. The parents appealed to the bishop of Bitonto to deliver the children from the obsession of which they were supposed to be the victims. While their mother was talking to the bishop both boys mysteriously disappeared from the room.

Alfredo Pansini could answer mental questions by **automatic writing.** The spirit speaking through him explained that he achieved the transportation by the **dematerialization** of their bodies. No observer could explain the phenomena. Italian scientists who looked into the matter put forward the theory of "ambulatory automatism," moving about in a secondary state and forgetting it when returning to the normal state. This, however, did not explain how the boys ran nine miles in half an hour without anybody seeing them on the road.

Sources:

Lapponi, Joseph. *Hypnotism and Spiritism.* New York: Longmans, Green, and Co., 1907.

Pansophic Institute

A Tibetan Buddhist educational organization founded in Reno, Nevada, in 1973 by Simon Grimes and sponsored by the School of Universal Wisdom. It received its initial corporate status through the Church of Universal Light. The institute is intended to serve as "a voice for the perennial philosophy or ageless wisdom leading to liberation and enlightenment in the New Age. It united Eastern and Western forms of *gnosis* (spiritual wisdom) and *theurgy* (techniques of enlightenment) in the light of modern science." It also provided an educational program consisting of courses in **meditation,** esoteric cosmology, **divinations,** spiritual **healing,** superhealth and longevity, thanatology, and empowerment. It offered courses for ministership in four types of theurgy and theurgic cosmology, and in child education, creativity, and world responsibility. The institute discouraged intellectual learning for one's own sake in favor of learning "that assists one to become enlightened for the sake of all things."

Last known address: P.O. Box 2422, Reno, NE 89505.

Pantomnesia

Term coined by **Charles Richet** to denote "regression of memory, the imagination that a thing experienced has been seen before." Richet also stated: "I propose *pantomnesia* to indicate that no vestige of our intellectual past is entirely effaced. Probably we are all pantomnesic. In weighing metapsychic facts it should be taken for granted that we do not absolutely forget anything that has once impressed our senses."

Pap, Lajos (1883– ?)

Hungarian carpenter and nonprofessional **medium** for **apports** and **telekinesis.** A resident of Budapest, his powers first manifested in 1922 in a casual sitting for table movement and were developed by Major Cornelius Seefehlner, Dr. John Toronyi, and later by Dr. Elmer Chengery Pap (not a relative), a retired chief chemist to the government and president of the Budapest Metapsychical Society. For some years Lajos Pap gave joint sittings with Tibor Molnar, another Hungarian medium. "Rabbi Isaac," his **control,** first communicated through table rapping, then through **trance** speaking.

Chengery Pap gradually developed scientific control, not only searching the medium and dressing him in a special séance robe but also providing special garments for his immediate controls and searching every sitter. The medium wore luminous stripes; the sitters tied luminous straps on their ankles and wrists. Instead of red light, a 100 watt green lamp was used; Pap permitted it to be switched on during the proceedings for repeated examination.

Under such conditions telekinetic movements of luminous baskets, strange white and colored lights, and the arrival of hundreds of living and inanimate objects were observed. The majority of the apports were small animals and insects, including living beetles, butterflies, caterpillars, frogs, lizards, birds, mice, fish, and squirrels, as well as liquids, perfumes, flowers, and other objects.

In an article in the *Proceedings* of the Society for Psychical Research (vol. 38), **Theodore Besterman** described a sitting with Lajos Pap at John Toronyi's flat on November 18, 1928. He witnessed telekinetic phenomena and the apport of three stones. However, Besterman's verdict was **fraud,** and his general attitude was the subject of a strongly worded protest addressed by Pap's advocates to the **Society for Psychical Research.**

For an amusing account of the phenomena of Lajos Pap and probable explanation of the rationale of fraud, see the chapter "Apports of a Carpenter" in Nandor Fodor's *The Haunted Mind* (1959). Fodor also indulged some shrewd speculations about the psychology of fraud.

Sources:

Fodor, Nandor. *The Haunted Mind.* New York: Helix Press, 1959.

Papaloi

An Obeah priest. (See **West Indian Islands**)

Papus

Pseudonym of occultist **Gérald Encausse** (1865–1916).

Parabola (Journal)

Journal of the Society for the Study of Myth & Tradition, concerned with exploring the inner being through myth and its manifestations. Published quarterly. Address: 656 Broadway, New York, NY 10012. Website: http://www.parabola.org/.

Sources:

Parabola Online. http://www.parabola.org/. March 8, 2000.

Parabrahman (or Para Brahm)

Term used in Hindu religious philosophy to denote the supreme absolute transcendental reality. Brahman is the nonpersonal divine beyond manifestation as gods and goddesses, as distinct from Brahma, the form as divine creator of the universe. Comparable concepts exist in most forms of **mysticism** and **Gnosticism.**

Paracelsus (1493–1541)

One of the most striking and picturesque figures in the history of medicine, **alchemy,** and **occultism,** full name Auraelus Philippus Theophrastus Paracelsus Bombast von Hohenheim, this illustrious physician and exponent of the hermetic philosophy was renowned under the name of Paracelsus.

He was born December 26, 1493, in Einsideln, near Zürich, Switzerland. His father, the natural son of a prince, himself a physician, desired that his only son should follow the same profession. The fulfillment of that desire was directed during the early training of Paracelsus. The training fostered his imaginative rather than his practical tendencies, which first cast his mind into the alchemical mould.

He freed himself from the constraining bonds of medicine as practiced by his contemporaries, who chiefly applied bleeding, purging, and emetics, and set about evolving a new system to replace the old. In order to study the book of nature better, he traveled extensively between 1513 and 1524 and visited almost every part of the known world. During his travels he compiled the wisdom present at the time on metallurgy, chemistry, and medicine, and the folk wisdom of the untutored.

Paracelsus met the Cham of Tartary, conversed with the magicians of **Egypt** and Arabia, and is said to have even reached **India.** At length his protracted wanderings came to a close, and in 1524 he settled in Basel, then a favorite resort of scholars and physicians, where he was appointed to fill the chair of medicine at the university.

His inflated language, eccentric behavior, and the splendor of his conceptions attracted, repelled, and gained him friends and enemies. His antipathy to the Galenic school became ever more pronounced, and the crisis came when he publicly burned the works of Galen and Avicenna in a vase into which he had cast nitrate and sulphur. By such a proceeding he incurred the hatred of his more conservative brethren and cut himself off forever from the established school of medicine. He continued his triumphant career, however, until a conflict with the magistrates brought it to an abrupt close. He was forced to flee from Basel, and thereafter wandered from place to place, earning a living as best he could.

An element of mystery surrounds the manner of his death, which took place September 24, 1541. Some say that he was poisoned at the instigation of the medical faculty, others that he was thrown down a steep incline.

But interesting as were the events of his life, it is to his work that most attention is due. Not only was he the founder of the modern science of medicine, but the magnetic theory of **Franz A. Mesmer,** the "astral" theory of modern **Spiritualism,** and the philosophy of Descartes were all foreshadowed in the fantastic, yet not always illogical, teachings of Paracelsus.

He revived the "microcosmic" theory of ancient Greece, and sought to prove the human body analogous to the solar system by establishing a connection between the seven organs of the body and the seven planets. He preached the doctrines of the efficacy of willpower and the imagination (i.e., magic):

"It is possible that my spirit, without the help of my body, and through an ardent will alone, and without a sword, can stab and wound others. It is also possible that I can bring the spirit of my adversary into an image and then fold him up or lame him at my pleasure.

"Resolute imagination is the beginning of all magical operations.

"Because men do not perfectly believe and imagine, the result is, that arts are uncertain when they might be wholly certain."

He was thus a forerunner of **New Thought** teachings. The first principle of his doctrine was the extraction of the quintessence, or philosophic mercury, from every material body. He believed that if the quintessence were drawn from each animal, plant, and mineral, the combined result would equal the universal spirit, or **astral body** in human beings, and that a draught of the extract would renew youth.

He came to the conclusion that "astral bodies" exercised a mutual influence on each other, and declared that he himself had communicated with the dead and with living persons at a considerable distance. He was the first to connect this influence with that of the magnet, and to use the word "magnetism" with its modern application in the **occult.** It was on this idea that much of Franz A. Mesmer's work was built.

While Paracelsus busied himself with such problems, however, he did not neglect the study and practice of medicine, into which both **astrology** and the magnet entered largely. When he was sought by a patient, his first care was to consult the planets, where the disease had its origin, and if the patient were a woman he took it for granted that the cause of her malady lay in the moon.

His anticipation of the philosophy of Descartes consisted in his theory that by bringing the various elements of the human body into harmony with the elements of nature—fire, light, earth—old age, and death might be indefinitely postponed.

His experiment in the extraction of essential spirits from the poppy resulted in the production of laudanum (a popular form of opium through the nineteenth century), which he prescribed freely in the form of "three black pills." The recipes he gives for the **philosophers' stone,** the **elixir of life,** and various universal remedies are exceedingly obscure. He was known as the first physician to use opium and mercury, and to recognize the value of sulphur.

He applied himself also to the solution of a problem that exercised the minds of scientific men in the nineteenth and twentieth centuries—whether it was possible to produce life from inorganic matter. Paracelsus asserted that it was, and left on record a quaint recipe for a **homunculus,** or artificial man. By a peculiar treatment of certain "spagyric substances" (which he unfortunately omitted) he declared that he could produce a perfect human child in miniature.

Medical, alchemical, and philosophical speculations were scattered so profusely throughout his teaching that one concludes that here was a master-mind, a genius, who was a charlatan, by reason of training and temperament. Paracelsus displayed a curious singleness of purpose and a real desire to penetrate the mysteries of science.

He left on record the principal points of the philosophy on which he founded his researches in his *Archidoxa Medicinae.* It contains the leading rules of the art of healing as he practiced and preached them. He stated that he had resolved to give ten books to the *Archidoxa,* but had reserved the tenth in his memory. He believed it was a treasure that men were not worthy to possess and should only be given to the world when it abjured Aristotle, Avicenna, and Galen, and promised a perfect submission to Paracelsus. The world did not recant, but Paracelsus relented and at the entreaty of his disciples published his *Tenth Book of the Arch-Doctrines,* also known as *On the Secret Mysteries of Nature.*

At the beginning Paracelsus hypothesized, and then attempted to substantiate, the existence of a universal spirit infused into the veins, which forms within us a species of invisible body, of which our visible body directs and governs at its will. This universal spirit is not simple—not more simple, for instance, than the number 100, which is a collection of units. The spiritual units are scattered in plants and minerals, but principally in metals. There exists in these inferior productions of the earth a host of sub-spirits that sum themselves up in us, as the universe does in God. So the science of the philosopher has to unite them to the body, disengage them from the grosser matter that clogs and confines them, and separate the pure from the impure. To separate the pure from the impure is to seize upon the soul of the heterogeneous bodies and evolve their "predestined element," "the seminal essence of beings," and "the first being, or quintessence."

To understand this latter word "quintessence," it is necessary to postulate that every body is composed of four elements. The essence compounded of these elements forms a fifth, which is the soul of the mixed bodies, or, in other words, its "mercury." "I have shown," stated Paracelsus, "in my book *Elements,* that the quintessence is the same thing as mercury. There is in mercury (soul) whatever wise men seek." That is, not the mercury of modern chemists, but a philosophical "mercury" of which every body has its own. "There are as many mercuries as there are things. The mercury of a vegetable, a mineral, or an animal of the same kind, although strongly resembling each other, does not precisely resemble another mercury, and it is for this reason that vegetables, minerals, and animals of the same species are not exactly alike. . . ."

Paracelsus sought a plant in the vegetable kingdom that was worthy of holding the same rank as gold in the metallic—a plant whose "predestined element" united in itself the virtues of nearly all the vegetable essences. Although this was not easy to distinguish, he claimed to recognize at a glance the supremacy of excellence in the *melissa,* and first decreed to it the pharmaceutical crown. Then:

"He took some balm-mint in flower, which he had taken care to collect before the rising of the sun. He pounded it in a mortar, reduced it to an impalpable dust, poured it into a long-necked vial which he sealed hermetically, and placed it to digest (or settle) for forty hours in a heap of horse-dung. This time expired, he opened the vial, and found there a matter which he reduced into a fluid by pressing it, separating it from its impurities by exposure to the slow heat of a *bain-marie* (a vessel of hot water in which other vessels are heated). The grosser parts sunk to the bottom, and he drew off the liqueur which floated on the top, filtering it through some cotton. This liqueur having been poured into a bottle he added to it the fixed salt, which he had drawn from the same plant when dried. There remained nothing more but to extract from this liqueur the first life or being of the plant. For this purpose Paracelsus mixed the liqueur with so much 'water of salt' (understand by this the mercurial element or radical humidity of the salt), put it in a matrass, exposed it for six weeks to the sun, and finally, at the expiration of this term, discovered a last residuum which was decidedly, according to him, the first life or supreme essence of the plant. But at all events, it is certain that what he found in his matrass was the genie or spirit he required; and with the surplus, if there were any, we need not concern ourselves."

Those who wished to know what this *genie* was like were informed that it as exactly resembled, as two drops of water, the spirit of aromatic wine known today as *absinthe suisse.* It was a liquid green. Unfortunately, it failed as a specific in the conditions indispensable for an elixir of immortality.

By means and manipulations as subtle and ingenious as those that he employed upon the melissa, Paracelsus learned to extract the "predestined element" of plants that ranked much higher in the vegetable aristocracy—the "first life" of the gilly-flower, the cinnamon, the myrrh, the scammony, and the celandine. All these supreme essences, which, according to the fifth book of *Archidoxa,* united with a mass of "magisteries" as precious as they were rude, were the base of so many specifics, equally reparative and regenerative. This depended upon the relationship that existed between the temperament of a privileged plant and the temperament of the individual who asked of it his rejuvenescence.

However brilliant were the results of his discoveries, those he obtained or those he thought he might obtain, they were for Paracelsus but the beginning of magic. To the eyes of so consummate an alchemist, vegetable life was not important; it was the mineral—the metallic life—that was significant. Paracelsus believed it was in his power to seize the first life-principle of the moon, the sun, Mars, or Saturn; that is, of silver, gold, iron, or lead. It was equally facile for him to grasp the life of the precious stones, the bitumens, the sulphurs, and even that of animals. Paracelsus set forth several methods of obtaining this great arcanum. Here is the shortest and most simple explaination as recorded by Incola Francus:

"Take some mercury, or at least the element of mercury, separating the pure from the impure, and afterwards pounding it to perfect whiteness. Then you shall sublimate it with sal-ammoniac, and this so many times as may be necessary to resolve it into a fluid. Calcine it, coagulate it, and again dissolve it, and let it strain in a pelican [a vessel used for distillation] during a philosophic month, until it thickens and assumes the form of a hard substance. Thereafter this form of stone is incombustible, and nothing can change or alter it; the metallic bodies which it penetrates become fixed and incombustible, for this material is incombustible, and changes the imperfect metals into metal perfect. Although I have given the process in few words, the thing itself demands a long toil, and many difficult circumstances, which I have expressly omitted, not to weary the reader, who ought to be very diligent and intelligent if he wishes to arrive at the accomplishment of this great work."

Paracelsus himself described in *Archidoxa* his own recipe for the completion of it, and profited by the occasion to criticize his fellow-workers.

"I omit what I have said in different places on the theory of the stone; I will say only that this *arcanum* does not consist in the blast [*rouille*] or flowers of antimony. It must be sought in the mercury of antimony, which, when it is carried to perfection, is nothing else than the *heaven* of metals; for even as the heaven gives life to plants and minerals, so does the pure quintessence of antimony vitrify everything. This is why the Deluge was not able to deprive any substance of its virtue or properties, for the heaven being the life of all beings, there is nothing superior to it which can modify or destroy it.

"Take the antimony, purge it of its arsenical impurities in an iron vessel until the coagulated mercury of the antimony appears quite white, and is distinguishable by the star which appears in the superficies of the regulus, or semi-metal. But although this regulus, which is the element of mercury, has in itself a veritable hidden life, nevertheless these things are in virtue, and not actually.

"Therefore, if you wish to reduce the power to action, you must disengage the life which is concealed in it by a living fire like to itself, or with a metallic vinegar. To discover this fire many philosophers have proceeded differently, but agreeing to the foundations of the art, have arrived at the desired end. For some with great labour have drawn forth the quintessence of the thickened mercury of the regulus of antimony, and by this means have reduced to action the mercury of the antimony: others have considered that there was a uniform quintessence in the other minerals, as for example in the fixed sulphur of the vitriol, or the stone of the magnet, and having extracted the quintessence, have afterwards matured and exalted their *heaven* with it, and reduced it to action. Their process is good, and has had its result. Meanwhile this fire—this corporeal life—which they seek with toil, is found much more easily and in much greater perfection in the ordinary mercury, which appears through its perpetual fluidity—a proof that it possesses a very powerful fire and a celestial life similar to that which lies hidden in the regulus of the antimony. Therefore, he who would wish to exalt our *metallic heaven,* starred, to its greatest completeness, and to reduce into action its potential virtues, he must first extract from ordinary mercury its corporeal life, which is a celestial fire; that is to say the quintessence of quicksilver, or, in other words, the metallic vinegar, that has resulted from its dissolution in the water which originally produced it, and which is its own mother; that is to say, he must dissolve it in the arcanum of the salt I have described, and mingle it with the 'stomach of Anthion,' which is the spirit of vinegar, and in this menstruum melt and filter and consistent mercury of the antimony, strain it in the said liquor, and finally reduce it into crystals of a yellowish green, of which we have spoken in our manual."

As regards the **philosophers' stone,** he gave the following formula:

"Take the electric mineral not yet mature [antimony], put it in its sphere, in the fire with the iron, to remove its ordures and other superfluities, and purge it as much as you can, following the rules of chymistry, so that it may not suffer by the aforesaid impurities. Make, in a word, the regulus with the mark. This done, cause it to dissolve in the 'stomach of the ostrich' (vitriol), which springs from the earth and is fortified in its virtue by the 'sharpness of the eagle' (the metallic vinegar or essence of mercury). As soon as the essence is perfected, and when after its dissolution it has taken the colour of the herb called *calendule,* do not forget to reduce it into a spiritual luminous essence, which resembles amber. After this, add to it of the 'spread eagle' one half the weight of the election before its preparation, and frequently distil the 'stomach of the ostrich' into the matter, and thus the election will become much more spiritualized. When the 'stomach of the ostrich' is weakened by the labour of digestion, we must strengthen it and frequently distil it. Finally, when it has lost all its impurity, add as much tartarized quintessence as will rest upon your fingers, until it throws off its impurity and rises with it. Repeat this process until the preparation becomes white, and this will suffice; for you shall see yourself as gradually it rises in the form of the 'exalted eagle,' and with little trouble converts itself in its form (like sublimated mercury); and that is what we are seeking.

"I tell you in truth that there is no greater remedy in medicine than that which lies in this election, and that there is nothing like it in the whole world. But not to digress from my purpose, and not to leave this work imperfect, observe the manner in which you ought to operate.

"The election then being destroyed, as I have said, to arrive at the desired end (which is, to make of it a universal medicine for human as well as metallic bodies), take your election, rendered light and volatile by the method above described.

"Take of it as much as you would wish to reduce it to its perfection, and put it in a philosophical egg of glass, and seal it very tightly, that nothing of it may respire; put it into an athanor until of itself it resolves into a liquid, in such a manner that in the middle of this sea there may appear a small island, which daily diminishes, and finally, all shall be changed to a colour black as ink. This colour is the raven, or bird which flies at night without wings, and which, through the celestial dew, that rising continually falls back by a constant circulation, changes into what is called 'the head of the raven,' and afterwards resolves into 'the tail of the peacock,' then it assumes the hue of the 'tail of a peacock,' and afterwards the colour of the 'feathers of a swan;' finally acquiring an extreme redness, which marks its fiery nature, and in virtue of which it expels all kinds of impurities, and strengthens feeble members. This preparation, according to all philosophers, is made in a single vessel, over a single furnace, with an equal and continual fire, and this medicine, which is more than celestial, cures all kinds of infirmities, as well in human as metallic bodies; wherefore no one can understand or attain such an arcanum without the help of God: for its virtue is ineffable and divine."

Sources:

Hartmann, Franz. *The Life of Philippus Theophrastus Bombast of Hohenheim Known by the Name of Paracelsus and of the Substance of his Teachings.* London: George Redway, 1887; Retd. with: *The Prophecies of Paracelsus; Occult Symbols and Magic Figures.* Blauvelt, N.Y.: Rudolf Steiner Publications, 1973.

The Hermetic and Alchemical Writings of Aureolus Philippus Theophrastus Bombast, of Hohenheim, called Paracelsus the Great. 2 vols. Edited by Arthur E. Waite. London: James Elliott, 1894. Reprint, New Hyde Park, N.Y.: University Books, 1967.

Stillman, John M. *Theophrastus Bombast von Hohenheim called Paracelsus; his Personality and Influence as Physician, Chemist and Reformer.* LaSalle, Ill.: Open Court Publishing, 1920.

Webster, Charles. *From Paracelsus to Newton: Magic and the Making of Modern Science.* Cambridge, Mass.: Cambridge University Press, 1982.

Para Committee

Popular term for the **Committee for the Scientific Investigation of Claims of the Paranormal,** established April 30, 1976, at a meeting of the American Humanist Association in Buffalo, New York.

Paradise

A word derived from the old Persian (Zeud) *pairedaèza,* an enclosure, a walled-in place; old Persian *pairi,* around, *dig,* to mould, form, shape (hence to form a wall of earth). The word moved into Greek (paradeisos), Latin (paradisus), and Hebrew (pardes). It literally denotes an enclosure or park planted with fruit trees and abounding with various animals, i.e., a pleasure garden or park. Josephus referred to Solomon's garden at Etham and to the hanging gardens of Babylon as paradises. Eden is not termed a "paradise" in the Hebrew text of Gen. 2:8, but a place where God planted a garden. The term, however, was inserted in the text in the Greek Septuigant translation, which read that God planted a paradise in Eden.

While the biblical paradise is located in reference to several well-known geographic reference points such as the Euphrates and Hiddekrl (Tigris) rivers, the failure to find such a paradisical place in that area in modern times has suggested the possibility that the paradise of Eden might be found elsewhere.

Paradise has been sought for or located in many regions of the earth: on the banks of the Euphrates and of the Ganges, in Tartary, Armenia, India, China, Mesopotamia, Syria, Persia, Arabia, Palestine, Ethiopia, and near the mountains of Libanus and Anti-libanus. Some place it in Judea, what is now the sea of Galilee; others in Armenia or Syria, near Mount Ararat, toward the sources of the Orontes, the Chrysorrhoas, and the Barrady. In the early nineteenth century the Island of Ceylon (now known as Sri Lanka), which was the "Serendib" of the ancient Persians and the "Taprobane" of the Greek geographers, was cited as a possibility. Robert Percival, in his book *An Account of the Island of Ceylon* (1803), suggested:

"It is from the summit of Hamalleel or Adam's Peak that Adam took his last view of Paradise before he quitted it never to return. The spot on which his feet stood at the moment is still supposed to be found in an impression on the summit of the mountain, resembling the print of a man's foot, but more than double the ordinary size. After taking this farewell view, the father of mankind is said to have gone over to the continent of Judea, which was at that time joined to the island, but no sooner had he passed Adam's Bridge than the sea closed behind him, and cut off all hopes of return. This tradition, from whatever source it was derived, seems to be interwoven with the earliest notions of religion entertained by the Cingalese; and it is difficult to conceive that it could have been engrafted on them without forming an original part. I have frequently had the curiosity to converse with black men of different castes concerning this tradition of Adam. All of them, with every appearance of belief, assured me that it was really true, and in support of it produced a variety of testimonies, old sayings, and prophecies, which have for ages been current among them. The origin of these traditions I do not pretend to trace; but their connection with Scripture history is very evident, and they afford a new instance how universally the opinions with respect to the origin of man coincide."

We are further informed by this writer that a large chair fixed in a rock near the summit of the mountain is said to be the workmanship of Adam. It has the appearance of having been placed there at a very distant period, but who really placed it there, or for what purpose, it is impossible to discover.

However, long before Percival travelled to Sri Lanka, this apparently oversize footprint had been venerated equally by Buddhists and Hindus, who ascribe it respectively to Gautama, Buddha, or the god Siva.

Some believed Eden represented the whole earth, which was of surprising beauty and fertility before the Fall. A curious notion prevailed to a great extent among the various nations that the Old World was under a curse and the earth became very barren. This view is reflected in the Apostle Paul's letter to the Romans (8:22) where he refers to the whole of creation groaning in pain.

Eastern Philosophies of Paradise

Some Eastern philosophies shared the idea that nature had been contaminated, and that the earth labored under some defilement—a sentiment that might have resulted from obscure traditions connected with the first human pair. The Hebrew historian Josephus stated that the Sacred Garden was watered by one river, which ran round the whole earth and was divided into four parts, but he appeared to think Paradise was merely a figurative or allegorical locality. Some of the peoples of Hindustan had traditions of a place resembling Paradise on the banks of the river Ganges; their accounts were completely blended with mythology and legends respecting the Deluge and the second peopling of the world.

One writer who had diligently studied the Indian Puranas (religious and mythological works) placed Eden on the Imaus Mountains of India. He stated:

"It appears from Scripture that Adam and Eve lived in the countries to the eastward of Eden; for at the eastern entrance of it God placed the angel with the flaming sword (Gen. 3:24). This is also confirmed by the Puranics, who place the progenitor of mankind on the mountainous regions between Cabul and the Ganges, on the banks of which, in the hills, they show a place where he resorted occasionally for religious purposes. It is frequented by pilgrims. At the entrance of the passes leading to the place where I suppose was the Garden of Eden, and to the eastward of it, the Hindoos have placed a destroying angel, who appears, and it is generally represented with a cherub; I mean Garudha, or the Eagle, upon whom Vishnu and Jupiter are represented riding. Garudha is represented generally like an eagle, but in his compound character somewhat like a cherub. He is represented like a young man, with the countenance, wings, and talons of the eagle. In Scripture the Deity is represented riding upon a cherub, and flying upon the wings of the wind. Garudha is called Vahan [literally the Vehicle] of Vishnu or Jupiter, and he thus answers to the cherub of Scripture; for many commentators derive this word from the obsolete root c'harab, in the Chaldean language, a word implicitly synonymous with the Sanscrit Vahan."

In the fabled Mount Meru of Hindu mythology there is also a descriptive representation of a Mosaic-like garden of Eden. Meru is a conical mountain; the exact locality of which is not fixed, but Hindu geographers considered the earth as a flat table with the sacred mountain of Meru rising in the middle. It became at length their decided conviction that Meru was the North Pole, from their notion that the North Pole was the highest part of the world. Some Hindu writers admitted that Mount Meru must be situated in the central part of Asia. Rather than relinquish their notion of and predilection for the North Pole as the real locality of Paradise, they actually forced the sun out of the ecliptic and placed the Pole on the elevated plains of Lesser Bokhara. However, the Hindu description of this Paradise seems to be analogous to the Mosaic account.

The traditions of Kashmir represented that country as the original site of Paradise and the abode of the first human pair, while the Buddhists of Tibet held opinions respecting the mountain Meru similar to those of the Hindus. They located the sacred garden, however, at the foot of the mountain near the source of the Ganges.

The Muslims inhabiting adjacent countries adopted the belief that Paradise was situated in Kashmir. They believed the first man was driven from it, he and his wife wandered separately for some time, then meeting at a place called Bahlaka, or Balk. Two gigantic statues, which the Moslems said were yet to be seen between Bahlaka and Bamiyan, represented Adam and Eve. A third statue was that of their son Seish or Seth, whose tomb, or its site, was pointed out near Bahlaka.

Some writers maintained that Paradise was under the North Pole. They argued over the idea of the ancient Babylonians and Egyptians that the ecliptic or solar way was originally at right angles to the Equator, and so passed directly over the North Pole. Some Moslems speculated that it was in one of the seven heavens. One commentator summed up extravagant theories respecting the locality of Paradise. "Some place it as follows: In the third heaven, others in the fourth, some within the orbit of the moon, others in the moon itself, some in the middle regions of the air, or beyond the earth's attraction, some on the earth, others under the earth, and others within the earth."

Before leaving the East, it may be observed that Oriental people generally reckoned four sites of Paradise in Asia: the first Ceylon, already mentioned; the second in Chaldea; the third in a district of Persia, watered by a river called the Nilab; and the fourth in Syria near Damascus, and near the springs of the Jordan. This last supposed site was not peculiar to Oriental writers, as it was maintained by some Europeans, especially Heidegger, Le Clerc, and Hardouin. The following are the traditions once believed by inhabitants of the city of Damascus—a city which the Emperor Julian the Apostate styled "the Eye of all the East," the most sacred and most magnificent Damascus. For example, M. de Lamartine observed:

"I understand that Arabian traditions represent this city and its neighbourhood to form the site of the lost Paradise, and certainly I should think that no place upon earth was better calculated to answer one's ideas of Eden. The vast and fruitful plain, with the seven branches of the blue stream which irrigate it—the majestic framework of the mountains—the glittering lakes which reflect the heaven upon the earth—its geographical situation between the two seas—the perfection of the climate—every thing indicates that Damascus has at least been one of the first towns that were built by the children of men—one of the natural halts of fugitive humanity in primeval times. It is, in fact, one of those sites pointed out by the hand of God for a city—a site predestined to sustain a capital like Constantinople."

According to Muslim beliefs, Damascus stood on the site of the Sacred Garden. Outside this city was a meadow divided by the river Barrady, and is alleged that Adam was formed from its red earth. This field was designated Ager Damascenus by the Latins, and nearly in the center formerly stood a pillar, intended to mark the precise spot where the Creator breathed the breath of life into the first man.

Other Philosophies of Paradise

Other traditions that existed among ancient nations of the Garden of Eden doubtless inspired the magnificent gardens that were designed and planted by Eastern princes, such as the Golden Garden, which was consecrated by Pompey to Jupiter Capitolinus of Aristobulus, King of the Jews. Nor is mythology deficient in similar legends. There are the Gardens of Jupiter, of Alcinous, of the Fortunate Islands, and of the Hesperides. These not only contain descriptions of the primeval Paradise, but also include the traditions of the Tree of Knowledge and of the original promise made to the woman. The Garden of the Hesperides produced golden fruit, guarded by a dangerous serpent—this fierce reptile encircled with its folds a mysterious tree—and Hercules procured the fruit by encountering and killing the serpent.

The story of the constellation, as related by Eratosthenes, is applicable to the Garden of Eden and the primeval history of mankind.

"This serpent," said that ancient writer, alluding to the constellation, "is the same as that which guarded the golden apples, and was slain by Hercules. For, when the gods offered presents to Juno on her nuptials with Jupiter, the Earth also brought golden apples. Juno, admiring their beauty, commanded them to be planted in the garden of the gods; but finding that they were continually plucked by the daughter of Atlas, she appointed a vast serpent to guard them. Hercules overcame and slew the monster. Hence, in this constellation the serpent is depicted rearing its head aloft, while Hercules, placed above it with one knee bent, tramples with his foot upon its head, and brandishes a club in his right hand."

The Greeks placed the Garden of the Hesperides close to Mount Atlas, and then claimed it was far into the regions of western Africa, yet all knowledge of its Asiatic site was not erased from the classical mythologists. Apollodorus states that certain writers situated it not in the Libyan Atlas, but in the Atlas of the Hyperboreans.

Others believed the world was originally a paradise, and its first inhabitants were human, whose dwelling was a magnificent hall glittering with fine gold and where love, joy, and friendship presided. But this happiness was soon overthrown by certain women from the country of the giants, to whose seductions the first mortals yielded, losing their innocence and integrity forever. The transgression of Eve was the obvious prototype of the fatal curiosity of Pandora.

The legends of Hindustan also supply accounts of the happiness of paradise in the Golden Age of classic mythology. Thomas Maurice, author of *Indian Antiquities* (1793–1800), observed at the end of the eighteenth century,

"There can arise little doubt that by the Satya age, or Age of Perfection, the Brahmins obviously allude to the state of perfection and happiness enjoyed by man in Paradise. It is impossible to explain what the Indian writers assert concerning the universal purity of manners, and the luxurious and unbounded plenty prevailing in that primitive era, without this supposition. Justice, truth, philanthrophy, were then practised among all the orders and classes of mankind. There was then no extortion, no circumvention, no fraud, used in the dealings one with another. Perpetual oblations smoked on the altars of the Deity; every tongue uttered praises, and every heart glowed with gratitude to the Supreme Creator. The gods, in token of their approbation of the conduct of mortals, condescended frequently to become incarnate, and to hold personal intercourse with the yet undepraved race, to instruct them in arts and sciences; to unveil their own sublime functions and pure nature; and to make them acquainted with the economy of those celestial regions into which they were to be immediately translated, when the period of their terrestial probation expired."

Sources:

Baring-Gould, S. "The Terrestrial Paradise." In *Curious Myths of the Middle Ages.* 1872. Reprint, New Hyde Park, N.Y.: University Books, 1967.

Doane, T. W. "The Creation and Fall of Man." In *Bible Myths and Their Parallels in Other Religions.* 1884. Reprint, New Hyde Park, N.Y.: University Books, 1971.

Jacoby, Mario. *The Longing for Paradise: Psychological Perspectives on an Archetype.* Boston: Sigo Press, 1985.

Pagel, Walter. *Paracelsus: An Introduction to Philosophical Medicine in the Era of the Renaissance.* New York: Karger, 1982.

Paragnost

Term coined by Dutch parapsychologist **W. H. C. Tenhaeff** in 1932 to indicate an individual gifted with **psi** or psychic faculties. The term derives from the Greek *para* (beyond) and *gnosis* (knowledge), i.e., paranormal knowledge.

Paranormal and Psychic Australian (Magazine)

Former name of a quarterly Australian magazine devoted to psychic phenomena, unexplained mysteries, news, and book reviews. Since the death of its editor in May 1999, the publication has been incorporated into *Masque Noir.* Address: P.O. Box 19, Spit Jct., New South Wales 2088, Australia.

Paraphysical Laboratory

A research unit organized by some members of the **Society for Psychical Research** (London) that specialized in study of the physical aspects of **psi** phenomena. The laboratory published the *International Journal of Paraphysics* Last known address: Summerhayes Hotel, 12 Cambridge Rd., Bournemouth, Dorset BH2 6AQ, England.

Parapsychic Phenomena

A term coined by psychologist **Max Dessoir** (1867–1947) in Germany in 1889 and picked up by psychical researcher **Emile Boirac** (1851–1917) and used to refer to "all phenomena produced in living beings or as a result of their action, which do not seem capable of being entirely explained by already known natural laws and forces." According to Boirac, the term "psychical" is not satisfactory because it is synonymous with "mental." The prefix "para" denotes that it relates to exceptional, abnormal, paradoxical phenomena. The term found some acceptance in Germany during the establishment of **psychical research.**

Sources:

Boirac, Emile. *La Psychologie Inconnue; Introduction et contribution à l'étude expérimentale des sciences psychiques.* Paris, 1908. English edition as *Psychic Science: An Introduction and Contribution to the Experimental Study of Psychical Phenomena.* London, 1918.

Dessoir, Max. "Die Parapsychologie, Eine Entgegnung auf den Artikel 'Der Prophet.' " *Sphinx* (June 1889): 341–44. Reprinted as "Parapsychology, A Response to the Article 'The Prophet.' " *Journal* of the Society for Psychical Research 53, 802 (January 1986).

Parapsychika (Journal)

A German bimonthly journal of the Swiss Parapsychological Society (Parapsychologische Arbeitsgruppe Base l). It included papers on theoretical and experimental aspects of **parapsychology.** Last known address: c/o K. Berber, Leonhardsgraben 2, CH-4057, Basel, Switzerland.

Parapsychological Association, Inc.

Formed in 1957 as the professional society for parapsychologists following an initiative of **J. B. Rhine.** Its purpose has been "to advance parapsychology as a science, to disseminate knowledge of the field, and to integrate the findings with those of other branches of science." It holds an annual convention, which is reported in its *Proceedings,* and the proceedings of which are published annually as *Research in Parapsychology.*

In 1969 the association took a giant step in advancing the field by affiliating with the American Association for the Advancement of Science. The work of the association is reported in *Journal of Parapsychology* and *Journal* of the American Society for Psychical Research. Address: P.O. Box 92209, Durham, NC 27708-2209. Website: http://www.parapsych.org/.

Sources:

The Parapsychological Association, Inc. http://www.parapsych.org/. March 8, 2000.

Parapsychological Journal of South Africa

Bi-annual publication of South African Society for Psychical Research (founded in 1955). It publishes lectures given by the society and can be contacted at P.O. Box 23154, Johannesburg 2044, South Africa.

Parapsychological Research Society (Turkey)

Turkish organization concerned with parapsychological research. Last known address: c/o Mr. Selman Gerceksever, Sakizzülü Sokak, No. 21 Kat: 1 Bahariye, Kadiköy, Istanbul, Turkey.

Parapsychologischen Arbeitsgruppe Basel

The Parapsychologischen Arbeitsgruppe Basel (Parapsychology Work Group of Basel) was a small Swiss organization founded in 1967 at the suggestion of German parapsychologist Hans Bender, a professor at the University of Freiburg, Germany. It established a program of research and public lectures and annually cooperated with the Schweizer Parapsychologische Gesellschaft in sponsoring the *Basel PSI Days,* a congress that brought together an international audience for lectures on a variety of subjects. Last known address: c/o Psi Zentrum Basel, Guterstrasse 144, CH-4053, Basel, Switzerland.

Parapsychology

The name given to the scientific study of psychic or paranormal phenomena. The **Parapsychological Association,** refers to it as, "The scientific and scholarly study of certain unusual events associated with human experience." The association also pointed out in its *Parapsychology FAQs,* on its website in 2000, that:

> In spite of what the media often imply, parapsychology is not the study of 'anything parnormal' or bizarre. Nor is parapsychology concerned with astrology, UFOs, searching for Bigfoot, paganism, vampires, alchemy, or witchcraft.

Parapsychology largely replaced the earlier term "psychical research," the change indicating a significant shift in emphasis and methodology. The term "parapsychology" is an old one. It appears to have been coined in Germany in or before 1889 by psychologist **Max Dessoir** (1867–1947). Dessoir first used the term in an article the June 1889 issue of the German periodical *Sphinx.* Dessoir's use of the term "parapsychology," as also the term "parapsychic," predates the later use of the term by **Emile Boirac** (1851–1917) in a book in 1908.

The term "parapsychology," as used currently was popularized by **J. B. Rhine** (1895–1980) and fellow pioneers **William McDougall** and **Louisa E. Rhine** to distinguish the laboratory based study, including the use of careful experimental methodology, of psychic phenomena in both its mental (telepathy, clairvoyance, and precognition) and physical (psychokinesis) form. In 1927, McDougall and the Rhines began research on mediumship, survival, and telepathy in the Department of Psychology at Duke University, Durham, North Carolina.

Rhine established the now familiar outlines of laboratory method with card-guessing and dice-rolling experiments. Card-guessing had been used already in scientific tests implemented by psychical researchers in Britain. It was Rhine who popularized the use of **Zener cards,** devised by his colleague psychologist **Karl Zener.** This experiement of sorts consisted of holding 25 cards bearing simple symbols in groups of five of a kind: star, circle, square, cross and waves. The pack simplified the mathematical calculations involved in evaluating chance factors in guessing.

In addition to this work, Rhine popularized the terms "parapsychology," "extrasensory perception" and "psi." In the 1930s his attempts to find a statistical validation of ESP transformed parapsychology into a legitimate area for scientific research for many who had eschewed psychical research previously.

Assisted by **J. Gaither Pratt,** who later became a prominent parapsychologist himself, Rhine looked for psychically gifted people to study. One prominent subject was a Duke student, Hubert E. Pearce. In a significant set of 74 runs which Rhine named the Pearce-Pratt Series, the odds against the successful guesses being merely chance were estimated as 1 in 10,000,000,000,000,000,000,000. Many variants in experimental setup were developed in card-guessing, and the results were often significantly above chance expectation.

The idea for the classic psychokinetic (PK) experiments developed after a casual visitor to Duke boasted that he could will dice to fall so that he could get the numbers he needed to win. Experimental techniques were devised in which subjects threw dice for the face of their choice The results were analyzed mathematically. The results over several years indicated strong evidence for the reality of PK. Such findings were later confirmed by experimenters elsewhere, using a variety of experimental techniques. Various methods were developed to ensure that PK tests with dice were not influenced by mechanical factors (weight of dice, etc.) or unconscious skills in throwing. Apparatus was designed which threw dice automatically.

Some special terms that have developed in the study of PK are: PK-MT (psychokinetic effect on moving targets such as dice); PK-LT (influence on living matter, such as growth in plants, healing, influencing animals); PK-ST (influence on static targets). Another initialism that grew up in evaluating PK was "QD," which indicated the division of record sheets into four equal quarters. Study of quarter divisions showed a consistent pattern of fall-off in scoring results as between upper left and lower right quarters of the record sheet, with the other two quarters bridging the gap in success fall-off. It became clear that this fall-off in success during the course of a series of tests was a characteristic feature of PK, suggesting the operation of some unknown mental process which affected the continuity of PK achievement.

In 1934, Rhine published his first book, *Extrasensory Perception,* which caused something of a furor in scientific and academic circles. For a time it was fashionable to attack his preliminary findings favoring ESP. The scientific community especially, and a large portion of the general public, were still much opposed to, and highly suspcious of parapsychology as a study. The identification of Duke University with such controversial and scientifically marginalized research, was also highly criticized; and eventually Rhine was obliged to open a separate **Parapsychology Laboratory,** seeking outside sponsorship for research. The persistent patient work of Rhine, his associates and other parapsychologists over decades eventually established a place for parapsychology as a proper scientific study, however many skeptics stood by with disbelief.

The early years of parapsychology were chronicled in a book by Rhine and others: *Extrasensory Perception after Sixty Years; a Critical Appraisal of the Research in Extrasensory Perception* (1940). In it they detailed the ESP research at Duke University from 1927 through 1940 in the context of the former period of psychical research from 1882 to 1927. Valuable scientific investigation of ESP and related phenomena and some laboratory research had been conducted during this earlier period by both the **Society for Psychical Research,** founded in London in 1882, and the **American Society for Psychical Research,** founded in 1885. For example, from 1921 on, an important series of card tests was conducted by **G. N. M. Tyrrell** in Britain. The British experimenter **W. Whately Carington** did important tests on telepathy and PK and developed a stimulating "association theory" of telepathy. Other British experimenters included: **G. W. Fisk** and **Donald J. West** working on PK scoring, **S. G. Soal,** and **Kathleen M. H. Goldney.**

In the United States, notable ESP pioneers included **Gardner Murphy** and **Gertrude R. Schmeidler.** Murphy joined the Society for Psychical Research, London, as early as 1917. He did graduate work at Harvard University in the field as the Richard Hodgson Fellow from 1922 to 1925, and also served as vice-president and president of the American Society (1940–62).

In 1937, Rhine began publication of the *Journal of Parapsychology,* devoted to original publication of experimental results and other research findings in extra-sensory perception and psychokinesis.

Rhine's early work with **Eileen J. Garrett,** a notable psychic whom he tested in the early days at Duke, bore fruit in 1951 when she established the **Parapsychology Foundation,** in New York City, to promote laboratory parapsychology and fund and sponsor research. From 1953 on, the foundation published a bimonthly newsletter, *Newsletter of the Parapsychology Foundation,* which was superseded in 1970 by the bimonthly journal *Parapsychology Review.* Between 1959 and 1968 the foundation also published a valuable *International Journal of Parapsychology.* The Parapsychology Foundation plays an important role in encouraging parapsychological research in universities and among scholars with established scientific reputations.

The Second Generation

A new day arrived for parapsychology with the founding of the **Parapsychological Association** in 1957 as *the* professional society for parapsychologists. The association projected a threefold effort to advance parapsychology as a scientific discipline, engage in public education, and integrate the results of their research with the findings of other branches of science.

By 1957 parapsychology and psychical research had developed a working partnership and tolerance of the particular contributions both made. Boundaries were blurred as individuals worked both areas. Researchers saw the need to investigate the claims and phenomena which emerged in the noticeable revival of the occult and occult religion in the 1960s. As psychical researchers examined a broad range of phenomena (Spiritualism, evidence for survival after death, hauntings, poltergeist occurrences, out-of-the-body traveling, reincarnation, psychical healing, and magical practices) parapsychologists expanded the range of topics covered by laboratory experimentation.

Popular interest in psychic and occult phenomena in the 1960s helped create a general climate of belief in the paranormal at both critical and uncritical levels. The most significant sign of the changing climate was the acceptance of the Parapsychological Association into membership of the American Association for the Advancement of Science in December 1969, after three previous rejections. This improved scientific status of parapsychology owed much to the patient laboratory work on ESP by Rhine and others since the 1930s.

Parapsychology and Fraud

Parapsychology, as science in general, is a very competitive field. The sense of urgency to produce results is heightened in this field. Undergirded as it is with the belief that positive results would necessitate a significant revision of currently operative scientific models of the universe the pressure is great. With such high stakes, the field has had to pay constant attention to improving its methodology and tightening its controls. Consequently, it has also had to watch out for the occasional production of fraudulent reports, especially the altering of laboratory statistics, in order to give significance to mundane or negative experimental results. With parapsychology being such a controversial field, it is not unexpected that ideological critics of the field have seized such revelations of fraud and widely publicized them. Many of these critics of parapsychology organized and affiliated with the **Committee for the Scientific Investigation of Claims of the Paranormal** (CSICOP).

While parapsychology has some well-publicized cases of fraud, the cases must be understood in the larger context of fraud that afflicts every field of science. Most cases of fraud go undetected as they concern peripheral matters of insignificant technological or philosophical consequence. Yet it only would follow that the temptation to fraud is everywhere. This temptation was vividly illustrated by CSICOP itself in their early investigation of the work of **Michel Gauquelin** in astrology. When

CSICOP results confirmed Guaquelin's results, data was changed to conceal that fact. Even after the fraud was pointed out to the committee, the original papers were republished without any reference to the cheating that had occurred. That refusal to deal with internal fraud has blunted much of the usefulness that the committee might have had as a watchdog in the field.

Two revelations of fraud have had the most effect on parapsychology. The first concerned the experiments in telepathy carried out by S. G. Soal with the percipient Basil Shackleton from 1941–1943. They had been regarded as highly evidential for many years. In 1971, serious doubts were raised about the experiments and Soal's handling of them. An article by R. G. Medhurst in the *Journal* of the S.P.R. in 1971 questioned the method of constructing quasi-random series in the tests. Medhurst implied inaccuracy (or worse) in Soal's methods. As early as 1960, Gretl Albert, an agent at some of the sittings, had alleged that she had seen Soal "altering the figures" several times on the score sheets. Thus the Medhurst article opened a controversy within parapsychology which resulted in a 1978 article by Betty Markwick in the *Proceedings* of the S.P.R. Markwick presented an overwhelming case for conscious or unconscious manipulation of data by Soal, based on computer analysis of his records. (Not all parapsychologists agree that Soal was deliberately fraudulent; but the validity of his telepathy experiments with Basil Shackleton has been shown to be inadmissible.)

In another case, the research of **Walter J. Levi, Jr.,** formerly the director of the Institute for Parapsychology offered a rival for the Soal experiments as an instance of fraud. In 1974 J. B. Rhine reported that Levy had been caught falsifying results in an experiment. Levy was asked to resign and left the field. A re-examination of all his research in the field, including independent replication of his experiments, began. His papers were from that time no longer cited as providing any evidence of psi.

During the 1980s a controversy developed around the **ganzfeld** psi experiments of Carl Sargent at Cambridge University. An article "A Report of a Visit to Carl Sargent's Laboratory" authored by **Susan Blackmore** (*Journal* of the S.P.R., vol. 54, 1987) cast serious doubt on the methods and validity of Sargent's experiments. A defense of Sargent against the implication of fraud, "Cheating, Psi, and the Appliance of Science; A Reply to Blackmore" by Trevor Harley & Gerald Matthews, was published in the same issue of the *Journal.*

Contemporary Parapsychology

The general openness to psychic and occult phenomena that led to the burgeoning of the New Age movement and the acceptance of the Parapsychological Association into the American Association of the Advancement of Science served to create a decade of heightened parapsychological research in the 1970s. The founding of new research organizations such as the **Academy of Parapsychology and Medicine** (1970); the **Institute of Parascience** (1971); the **Academy of Religion and Psychical Research;** the **Institute for Noetic Sciences** (1973); and the **International Kirlian Research Association** (1975) created an optimistic climate. It offered promise that new breakthroughs were imminent. The reports of new work in parapsychology at the **Stanford Research Institute** further inflated the hope.

Parapsychology had become an international affair before World War II. During the last half of the twentieth century it became even more intricately woven into the everyday lives of people the world over. The decade of the 1970s saw further expansion of parapsychology. By the end of the 1980s the Parapsychological Association reported approximately 300 members working in more than 30 countries. In the United States alone by 1990, the organization listed over 150 members, including many professionals and scientists. Additionally, research not affiliated with the association was being carried out in Eastern Europe and the former Soviet Union.

Not surprisingly, both the scope and methods of parapsychology expanded greatly by the end of the twentieth century. Notable new directions included Kirlian photography, remote viewing, the investigation of altered states of consciousness (including alpha-related states and dream experiences) prompted by the influx of spiritual teachers from the East who made extraordinary claims for the abilities produced by **meditation** and related disciplines; experiments in the paranormal healing of animals; and, possibly the most controversial of all, the work of **Ian Stevenson** in the investigation of the evidence for reincarnation. The 1970s and 1980s also saw a significant amount of attention paid to the testing of the claims of paranormal feats by psychic **Uri Geller** followed by the emergence of a number of others, especially in Japan, who claimed similar abilities.

Parapsychologists still found themselves faced with strong opposition from their academic colleagues. Research and teaching positions were difficult to obtain, and unstable at best. No university seemed willing to establish a parapsychological department. Continued opposition both to parapsychological findings and the lack of any formal acknowledgement to the field remained a constant aggravation and threat to the work. The core of the opposition was focused in the Committee for the Investigation of the Claims of the Paranormal, founded in 1976, (CSICOP) and in its periodical, *Skeptical Inquirer.*

New lines of hopeful research soon proved to be dead-ends. The effects of Kirlian photography disappeared as more stringent controls were applied, as did most of the effects produced by Geller and his imitators. Stevenson was unable to pass on the enthusiasm he had for his reincarnation research. The Stanford Research Institute abandoned its parapsychological research. The Academy for Parapsychology and Medicine disbanded and the problem of the nonacceptance of parapsychology by the academic world continued to provoke concern and debate in parapsychological circles.

Charles Thomas Cayce, the grandson of **Edgar Cayce,** and director of the **Edgar Cayce Foundation,** and the **Association for Research and Enlightenment,** (ARE) reported in 1995 that the foundation's **Atlantic University,** was expected offer the first Master's Degree in Transpersonal Studies, much of the program directed to the readings of the elder Cayce and the meaning of his psychic revelations. Much of the research that previously had been conducted at Duke University, was being conducted through Atlantic and the ARE, as well as programs and seminars around the United States, and internationally. ARE's approach to studying paranormal phenomena consisted of understanding the whole person. Through holistic medical clinics, spiritual reflection and meditation the work to develop psychic ability must be a lifelong process. Again, the true believers worked hard to overcome the impression the non-believers had that the entire pursuit of uncovering the complexities of the paranormal world was the domain of the non-thinking person. While the Parapsychological Association wanted to specifically exclude paranormal as a part of their ongoing scientific research, and disassociate from the term, "paranormal," many outside the organization insisted on using both the terms and the phenomena in conjunction with any unexplained occurrence that involved the human mind.

Yet if the experts and scientists were skeptical, in 1991, *American Demographics,* reported that a **Gallup** poll indicated that people in the age group of 30 to 49, a generation more educated than any previous one in America, were more likely than any other to believe in paranormal phenomena. According to that poll, between 1978 and 1991, certain statistics emerged: 1), the proportion of people believing in ghosts increased to 25 percent from 11 percent; 2), belief in devils increased to 55 percent from 39 percent; 3), belief in **deja vu,** the belief that a person holds when a new experience gives the feeling that it has already occured, in this life or another, increased to 55 percent from 30 percent; 4) 18 percent of adults believe in the possibility of communicating with the dead; and, 5), 70 percent believe in an afterlife. That poll also indicated a decline in certain paranormal beliefs, including a drop from 51 percent to 49 percent of the people who claimed to believe in **ESP.** One person who appeared on television sets at the end of the 1990s was **James Van Praagh.** Van Praagh, a world-famous medium, wrote books and produced audio tapes, recounting his communication with the spirits of dead people. He received wide acclaim, particularly regarding his spiritual approach.

Popular television shows and movies at the end of the twentieth century belied, too, that skepticism was as rampant as CSICOP claimed. In any case, Hollywood especially took advantage of the interest the average person seemed to have in the area of parapsychology—from ghosts to satanic possession. One popular network show, "Unsolved Mysteries," featured at least one piece a week on some paranormal occurrence, right along with their true-crime mysteries of kidnapping, murder, and other crime-related stories. The weekly television series, "The X-Files," had its two fictional heros, FBI agents, experiencing the "out of the ordinary" phenomena as they hunted down mysterious criminals and sometimes supernormal forces. A 1999 hit summer movie, "The Sixth Sense," even won an Academy Award nomination for its 11 year-old star. The line that became most infamous was familiar to those who did not see the movie, as well as those who had. "I see dead people." A line that revealed the perplexed youngster's dilemma, was pronounced on movie trailers for the months surrounding the picture's opening. Indeed, the idea fascinated people enough to give the movie some of the highest ratings and biggest box office sales of the year.

Parapsychological phenomena did not abide by the constraints of time or space, according to those involved in its research. It does not distinguish between mind and matter—both are one, inextricably connected to each other. Still, the majority of parapsychologists believed that all of the unexplained experiences that included, ESP, PK, and the body surviving after death, to name only a few, would eventually be explained scientifically as scientific knowledge expanded.

Sources:

Beloff, John, ed. *New Directions in Parapsychology.* London, 1974. Reprint, Metchen, N.J.: Scarecrow Press, 1975.

Blackmore, Susan. *Adventures of a Parapsychologist.* Buffalo, N.Y.: Prometheus Books, 1986.

Boirac, Emile. *Psychic Science; An Introduction and Contribution to the Experimental Study of Psychical Phenomena.* London, 1918.

Brodeur, Nicole. "Reporter has a close encounter with a psychic." *Knight-Ridder/Tribune News Service,* 16 August 1993.

Dessoir, Max. "Die Parapsychologie, Eine Entgegnung auf den Artikel 'Der Prophet.'" *Sphinx* (June 1889): 341–44. Reprinted as "Parapsychology, A Response to the Article 'The Prophet.'" *Journal* of the S.P.R. 53, 802 (January 1986).

Dougherty, Robin. "It's uncanny! Networks are invaded by 'paranoia shows'." *Knight Ridder/Tribune News Sercie,* 18 Sept.1996.

Edge, Hoyt L., Robert L. Morris, John Palmer, Joseph H. Rush. *Foundations of Parapsychology; Exploring the Boundaries of Human Capability.* London: Routledge & Kegan Paul, 1986.

Grattan-Guinness, Ivor. *Psychical Research; A Guide to its History, Principles and Practices, in Celebration of 100 Years of the Society for Psychical Research.* UK: Aquarian Press, 1982.

Hansel, C. E. M. *ESP and Parapsychology: A Critical Re-Evaluation.* Buffalo, N.Y.: Prometheus Books, 1980.

Haynes, Renée. *The Society for Psychical Research 1882–1982, a History.* Macdonald & Co., London, 1982.

Holden, Constance. "Parapsychology Update." *Science,* 2 December 1983.

Lindsey, Charley. "Skeptics attempt to debunk unusual beliefs." *Knight Ridder/Tribune News Service,* 3 August 1998.

McConnell, R. A. *An Introduction to Parapsychology in the Context of Science.* Pittsburgh, Penn.: University of Pittsburgh, Biological Sciences Department, 1983.

Markwick, Betty. "The Soal-Goldney Experiments with Basil Shackleton; New Evidence of Data Manipulation." *Proceedings* of the S.P.R. 56 (1978).

"Max Dessoir and the Origin of the Word 'Parapsychology.'" *Journal* of the S.P.R. 54, 806 (January 1987).

Medhurst, R. G. "The Origin of the Prepared Random Numbers Used in the Shackleton Experiments." *Journal* of the S.P.R. 46 (1971).

Moore, R. Lawrence. *In Search of White Crows: Spiritualism, Parapsychology, and American Culture.* New York: Oxford University Press, 1977.

Murphy, Gardner, and Laura A. Dale. *Challenge of Psychical Research: A Primer of Psychical Research.* New York: Harper & Row, 1961.

Parapsychological Association Web Site. http://www.parapsych.org. July 31, 2000.

Pratt, J. Gaither. *ESP Research Today: a Study of Developments in Parapsychology since 1960.* Metuchen, N.J.: Scarecrow Press, 1963.

Price, Harry. *Fifty Years of Psychical Research: A Critical Survey.* London: Longmans Green, 1939. Reprint, New York: Arno Press, 1975.

Rao, K. Ramakrishna. *Experimental Parapsychology: a Review and Interpretation, with a Comprehensive Bibliography.* Springfield, Ill.: Charles Thomas, 1966.

Rhine, J. B. *Extrasensory Perception.* Boston, Mass.: Boston Society for Psychic Research, 1934. Rev. ed., Boston: Bruce Humphries, 1964.

———. "History of Experimental Studies." In Benjamin B. Wolman, et al. *Handbook of Parapsychology.* New York: Van Norstrand Reinhold, 1986.

———, ed. *Progress in Parapsychology.* Durham, N.C.: Parapsychology Press, 1971.

———. *The Reach of the Mind.* New York: William Sloane, 1947. Reprint, New York: William Morrow, 1971.

Rhine, J. B., et al. *Extrasensory Perception after Sixty Years: a Critical Appraisal of the Research in Extrasensory Perception.* New York: Henry Holt, 1940. Reprint, Boston: Bruce Humphries, 1966.

Rhine, J. B., and R. Brier. *Parapsychology Today.* New York: Citadel, 1968.

Richet, Charles. *Thirty Years of Psychical Research.* London: W. Collins Sons, 1923. Reprint, New York: Arno Press, 1975.

Rush, Joseph H. "What is Parapsychology?" In Hoyt L. Edge, Robert L. Morris, Joseph H. Rush, & John Palmer. *Foundations of Parapsychology.* London: Routledge & Kegan Paul, 1986.

Schmeidler, Gertrude R. *Extrasensory Perception.* New York: Atherton, 1969.

Schwartz, Joe. "The baby boom taks to the dead." *American Demographics,* April 1991.

Science News. "Believe it or not." 9 March 1991.

Soal, S. G., and F. Bateman. *Modern Experiments in Telepathy.* New Haven, Conn.: Yale University Press, 1954.

Sudre, René. *Parapsychology.* New York: Citadel, 1960.

Thalbourne, Michael A. *A Glossary of Terms Used in Parapsychology.* London: Heinemann, 1982.

Thouless, Robert H. *Experimental Psychical Research.* London, 1963. Reprint. Santa Fe, N.M.: Gannon, 1969.

Vasiliev, L. L. *Experiments in Mental Suggestion.* Church Crookham, UK: Institute for the Study of Mental Images, 1963. Reprinted as *Experiments in Distance Influence.* New York: E. P. Dutton/London: Wildwood House, 1976.

———. *Studies in Mental Telepathy.* New York: CCM Information Corp., 1971.

White, Rhea A., and Laura A. Dale. *Parapsychology: Sources of Information.* Metuchen, N.J.: Scarecrow, 1973.

———. *Surveys in Parapsychology.* Metuchen, N.J.: Scarecrow Press, 1976.

Wolman, Benjamin B., ed. *Handbook of Parapsychology.* New York: Van Nostrand Reinhold, 1977. Rev. ed., Jefferson, N.C.: McFarland & Co., 1986.

Parapsychology (Newsletter)

Quarterly journal in Chinese language that was published in Taiwan. Last known address: Society for Parapsychological Studies, 6 Lane 4, Huang Puh Village 7, Genshan, Taiwan.

Parapsychology Abstracts International See Exceptional Human Experience (Abstracts)

Parapsychology Association of Riverside

Organization sponsoring lectures and study groups on parapsychology and acting as a center for information. It issued a monthly newsletter titled **PARINFO.** Last known address: 6370 Magnolia Ave., no. 219, Riverside, CA 92506.

Parapsychology Bulletin

Former publication of Parapsychology Press that brings together parapsychologists through the medium of their scientific publications. The main functions of *Parapsychology Bulletin* have been taken over by a section of news and comments in the *Journal of Parapsychology.* Back issues of *Parapsychology Bulletin* are available from the **Foundation for Research on the Nature of Man** (Box 6847, College Station, Durham, NC 27708) or from UMI, 300 N. Zeeb Rd., Ann Arbor, MI 48106.

Parapsychology Foundation

Founded in 1951 as a nonprofit educational organization to support "impartial scientific inquiry into the psychical aspect of human nature such as telepathy, clairvoyance, precognition, and psychokinesis." The foundation stems from the work of **Eileen J. Garrett,** the first president, and Frances P. Bolton. The foundation provides grants for research in **parapsychology** and maintains an active program of publications, including monographs, books, and journals. It holds both national and international conferences. It periodically issued journals beginning with *Tomorrow* and more recently the **International Journal of Parapsychology** (1959–1968) and *Parapsychology Review* (1970–1990). The *International Journal of Parapsychology* resumed publication in the spring of 2000. The foundation's web site offers answers to frequently-asked-questions, **The Parapsychology F.A.Q.,** and other information regarding the organization's history, research, and membership.

The foundation also maintains the Eileen J. Garrett Library, which provides valuable reference to students and researchers in the field of parapsychology. The main emphasis of the library is to disseminate information on the history of parapsychology, contemporary and experimental parapsychology, and related subjects. It warehouses publications that approach parapsychology from an objective and analytical point of view. The library also has access to various parapsychological databases, as well as, to current journals and periodicals. The foundation may be contacted at 228 E. 71st St., New York, NY 10021. Website: http://www.parapsychology.org.

Sources

The Parapsychological Association Web site. http://www.parapsych.org. April 25, 2000.

Parapsychology Laboratory (Duke University)

In 1927 **J. B. Rhine** and his wife, **Louisa Rhine,** moved to College Station, North Carolina, where they had found the support of **William McDougall,** chairman of the psychology department, in pursuing parapsychology. By the time McDougall died in 1931 they were settled in and working on the experiments that would lead to J. B. Rhine's early important work, *Extra-Sensory Perception* (1934). The next year, with the cooperation of McDougall's successor, a separate division of parapsychology was established in the psychology department and designated the Parapsychology Laboratory. Rhine was placed in charge. For the next 30 years, the Parapsychology Laboratory was the primary scene of major experiments in parapsychology. Among them were those of the well-known medium, **Eileen J. Garrett.** She conducted a series of experiments there, known as the **Zner Card Experiements,** studying the phenomenon of ESP.

The laboratory's controversial work made **ESP** a household word. It also met with mixed reactions from the faculty at the university, mostly critical. In 1950 it was made an autonomous unit, and in 1962, when Rhine formerly retired, the laboratory was discontinued altogether and support of this field by Duke came to an end. That same year Rhine created the **Foundation for Research on the Nature of Man** to continue the work of the laboratory and established the **Institute for Parapsychology** as a new laboratory.

Sources:

Garrett, Eileen J. *Adventures in the Supernormal.* New York: Creative Age Press, Inc., 1949.

———. *Many Voices, The Autobiography of a Medium.* New York: G. P. Putnam's Sons, 1968.

Rhine, J. B. *New World of the Mind.* New York: William Sloane, 1953.

Rhine, Louisa E. *ESP in Life and Lab: Tracing Hidden Channels.* New York: Macmillan, 1967.

Parapsychology Laboratory (Netherlands)

A former Dutch institute founded by **W. H. C. Tenhaeff** in 1933. The institute was supported by state funds, conducted experimental programs, and published books, periodicals, and reports on parapsychological research. It published the *European Journal of Parapsychology,* which is now distributed through the Koestler Chair of Parapsychology at the University of Edinburgh, 7, George Sq., Edinburg EH8 9JZ, Scotland, UK. Website: http://moebius.psy.ed.ac.uk/.

Parapsychology Now (Journal)

Quarterly journal of **parapsychology** that included feature stories, book reviews, and news of parapsychological events in the Midwest. Last known address: 324 Touhy St., Park Ridge, IL 60068.

Parapsychology Research Group, Inc.

Nonprofit organization founded in Palo Alto, California, to conduct investigations into **psychical research** in 1962. The president was **Russell Targ,** with **Stanford Research Institute.** Targ collaborated with **Harold E. Puthoff** on parapsychological research involving psychics **Uri Geller** and **Ingo Swann.**

Current address unavailable.

Parapsychology Review (Journal)

Published bimonthly from 1970 to 1990 by the **Parapsychology Foundation** to give news of individuals and organizations associated with **parapsychology;** information on courses, lectures, and grants; book reviews; and obituaries.

Parapsychology Sources of Information Center See Exceptional Human Experience Network, Inc.

Parapsychology: The Indian Journal of Parapsychological Research

An Indian journal (text in English) published quarterly by the University of Rajasthan. Last known address: University of Rajasthan, Department of Parapsychology, Jaipur (Rajasthan), India.

Parascience Proceedings

Publication of the **Institute of Parascience,** England. It included research papers and reports of conferences on **psi** subjects. Last known address: Institute of Parascience, Spryton, Lifton, Devon PL16 OAY, England.

Parascience Research Journal

Quarterly journal published by the **Institute of Parascience,** England, dealing with theoretical and experimental research into **ESP, PK, out-of-the-body travel**, and related subjects. Last known address: Parascience Centre, Sprytown, Devon PL16 OAY, England.

Paraskeva, Saint

A saint of the Russian calendar, whose feast day is August 3. On that day, pilgrims from all parts of Russia used to congregate in St. Petersburg for the purpose of casting out devils. A newspaper report of the proceedings as they occurred in 1913 is as follows:

"Another St. Paraskeva's day has come and gone. The usual fanatical scenes have been enacted in the suburbs of St. Petersburg, and the ecclesiastical authorities have not protested, nor have the police intervened. Special trains have again been run to enable thousands of the lower classes to witness a spectacle, the toleration of which will only be appreciated by those acquainted with the writings of M. Pobiedonostzeff, the late Procurator of the Holy Synod.

"The Church of St. Paraskeva is situated in a factory district of the city. On the exterior side of one of the walls is an image of the Saint, to whom is attributed the power of driving out devils and curing epileptics, neurotics, and others by miraculous intervention. At the same time, the day is made a popular holiday, with games and amusements of the all sorts, booths, and lotteries, refreshment stalls and drinking bars.

"The newspapers publish detailed accounts of this year's proceedings without comment, and it is perhaps significant that the *Novoe Vremya,* a pillar of orthodoxy, ignores them altogether. Nor is this surprising when one reads of women clad in a single undergarment with bare arms being hoisted up by stalwart peasants to the level of the image in order to kiss it, and then having impure water and unclarified oil forced down their throats.

"The treatment of the first sick woman is typical of the rest. One young peasant lifted her in the air, two others held her arms fully extended, while a fourth seized her loosened hair, and, dragging her head from side to side and up and down, shouted 'Kiss, kiss St. Paraskeva!' The woman's garment was soon in tatters. She began groaning. One of the men exclaimed: 'Get out! Satan! Say where thou art lodged!' The woman's head was pulled back by the hair, her mouth was forced open, and mud-coloured water (said to be holy water) was poured into it. She spat the water out, and was heard to moan, 'Oh, they are drowning me!'

"The young man exultantly exclaimed, 'So we've got you, devil, have we? Leave her at once or we will drown you!' He continued pouring water into the victim's mouth, and after that unclarified oil. Her lips were held closed, so that she was obliged to swallow it. The unfortunate woman was again raised and her face pressed against the image. 'Kiss it! kiss it!' she was commanded, and she obeyed. She was asked who was the cause of her being 'possessed.' 'Anna,' was the whispered reply. Who was Anna? What was her village? In which cottage did she live? A regular inquisition.

"The physical and mental sufferings of the first victim lasted about an hour, at the end of which she was handed over to her relatives, after a cross had been given to her, as it was found that she did not own one. According to accounts published by the papers *Retch* and *Molva,* many other women were treated in the same fashion, the exercises lasting a whole day and night. The men 'pilgrims' would seem to have been less severely handled. It is explained that the idea of unclothing the woman is that there should be no knot, bow, or fastening where the devil and his coadjutors could find a lodgment. And one is left with the picture of scores of women crawling around the church on their knees, invoking the aid of the Almighty for the future of His pardon for sins committed in the past."

The treatment of the "possessed" is analogous to that employed by many peoples for the casting out of devils. Non-Western cultures such as the Chams of **Cambodia** forced the possessed to eat garbage in order to disgust the fiend they harbored and medieval Roman Catholic exorcisms occurred among the nuns of **Loudon.** Even at the end of the twentieth century similar practices that however effective are culturally offensive to most religious people can be found among contemporary Western religions that practice exorcism.

PARINFO

Monthly newsletter of the **Parapsychology Association of Riverside.** Last known address: 6370 Magnolia Ave., no. 219, Riverside, CA 92506.

Parish, W. T. (1873–1946)

Pioneer British spiritual healer, whose profession commenced in 1929 after a surgeon warned that his wife would die from inoperable cancer within six months. A Spiritualist friend suggested psychic **healing,** and during a Spiritualist séance, a spirit guide informed Parish that he was a natural healer and would cure his own wife.

Parish did in fact effect a cure within nine months, after which he began regularly to practice as a healer. Over seventeen years he received more than 500,000 letters of thanks from grateful patients, many of whom had been declared incurable by doctors. He became popularly known as "Parish the Healer." He died in January 1946.

Sources:

Barbanell, Maurice. *Parish the Healer.* London: Psychic Book Club, 1938.

Parkes, F. M. (ca. 1872)

British Spiritualist who practiced **spirit photography.** In association with a Mr. Reeves, the proprietor of a dining room, he obtained recognized spirit extras in 1872 after three months of experiments. That same year **Frederick A. Hudson** also obtained the first such pictures in England. Without the presence of Reeves or his own wife, Parkes could not get a full form and clearly defined pictures, only white patches and cloudy appearances.

In accordance with spirit directions, Parkes set it as a condition to have the plates in his possession in the dark room prior to their being placed in the camera for purposes of magnetization. To avert suspicion he had an inspection hole cut in the dark room through which the sitters could see the plate through its entire process.

Sexton wrote enthusiastically of Parkes's powers in the *Christian Spiritualist.* **William Stainton Moses** gave the following interesting description in *Human Nature:*

"A considerable number of the earlier pictures taken by Messrs. Parkes and Reeves were allegorical. One of the earliest, taken in April, 1872, shows Mr. Reeves' father holding up a cross above his head and displaying an open book on which is written "Holy Bible." Another shows a cloud of light covering two-thirds of the pictures, and made up of the strangest medley of heads and arms, and flashes of light, with a distinct cross in the centre. Another, in which Mr. and Mrs. Everitt were the sitters, taken June 8, 1872, is a symbolical picture of a very curious nature. Mr. Everitt's head is surrounded with a fillet on which 'Truth' is inscribed, while three pencils of light dart up from it. There are at least two figures in the picture which blot out Mrs. Everitt altogether.

"In a later photograph, in which Mr. Burns is the sitter, is a giant hand of which the thumb is half the length of the sitter's body. It is just as if a luminous hand had been projected or flashed on the plate without any regard to focus. Another very startling picture is one which shows on a dark background a huge luminous crucifix. Then we have angels with orthodox wings hovering over some sitters. One is a very striking model: the face of great beauty and of pure classical design. The figure floats with extended arm over the sitter, and below it, almost on the ground, appear nine faces, and, strangest of all, close by the sitter's head, a large eye, with beams of light proceeding from it. The eye is larger than the head of the sitter, and the whole picture presents a most curious appearance. Some show mere faces; some heads; some, again, whole bodies floating in the air; and some partially formed bodies projected on the plate, apparently at haphazard."

Paroptic Vision

Term coined by French author **Jules Romains** (Louis Farigoule) for the ability to see without the use of the eyes. (See **Eyeless Sight**)

Parrish-Harra, Carol W. (1935–)

Carol W. Parrish-Harra—author, **New Age** leader, and founder of the Light of Christ Community Church—emerged in the 1980s after establishing the Sparrow Hawk Spiritual Community in Tahlequah, Oklahoma, and publishing several popular New Age books. She was born on January 21, 1935, and in 1958 had a life-changing experience. A Florida housewife at the time, she was given a pain killer during the birth of her sixth child. In an allergic reaction to the drug, her lung collapsed and she slipped into unconsciousness. She would later claim that her consciousness left her body, and a new consciousness, who retained the memories of her previous earthly years, replaced it. As a result, she emerged as a new person. Formerly passive, she became assertive and outgoing. No longer content at home, she got a job and soon worked her way into an executive position.

In 1969 Parrish-Harra attended a lecture at a Spiritualist church in St. Petersburg, Florida, and began studying there. Two years later she was ordained as a minister in the Christian Metaphysical Church, became an associate minister (medium) at the church, and through the 1970s gave lectures around the United States. In 1976 she founded the Villa Serena Spiritual Community in Sarasota, Florida.

In 1981 she founded a New Age community on 300 acres in Oklahoma with five families from Florida. Parrish-Harra's Light of Christ Community Church ministered to the spiritual welfare of the residents. Planned to be the home of approximately 150 people, the community is organized into clusters (tribes) to allow for both intimacy and community and serves as a prototype for other communities and as a training ground for future leaders.

Many people first heard of Parrish-Harra in 1983 in **Ruth Montgomery**'s *Threshold to Tomorrow.* In the book Montgomery describes people who had had experiences similar to the one Parrish-Harra had in 1958. Montgomery designates such people as "**walk-ins,**" and suggests that such changes represent the actual replacement of the consciousness of one person with the consciousness of another (rather than a new integration of the individual's personality). In any case, Parrish-Harra's experience was noted as a heretofore unrecognized type of personal event.

Sources:

Montgomery, Ruth. *Threshold to Tomorrow.* New York: Putnam, 1983.

Parrish-Harra, Carol W. *Messengers of Hope.* Black Mountain, N.C.: New Age Press, 1983.

———. *A New Age Handbook on Death and Dying.* Marina del Rey, Calif.: DeVorss, 1982.

Parsons, Denys (1914–)

British administrator and documentary film director who for some years was joint honorary secretary of the **Society for Psychical Research,** London. He was born on March 12, 1914, in London, England. He was educated at Eton, the University of London (B.Sc., 1936), and the Imperial College of Science and Technology, London (M.S., A.R.I.C., 1938). He was a research chemist (1939–45); a director of scientific, medical, and industrial films (1945–51); a manager with Applied Physics Group, National Research Development Corporation, London (1952–73); and the head of press and public relations for the British Library, London (1973–80). Parsons published a number of humorous books and guides and edited *The Directory of Tunes and Musical Themes* (1975). Parsons took special interest in research relating to quantitative evaluation of **extrasensory perception,** on which he published a number of articles.

Sources:

Parsons, Denys. "Attempts to Detect Clairvoyance and Telepathy with a Mechanical Device." *Proceedings* of the Society for Psychical Research 48 (1946).

———. "Cloud Busting: A Claim Investigated." *Journal* of the Society for Psychical Research 38 (December 1956).

———. "Experiments on PK with Inclined Plane and Rotating Cage." *Proceedings* of the Society for Psychical Research 47 (1945).

———. "A Nonexistent Building Located." *Journal* of the Society for Psychical Research 41 (July 1962).

———. "On the Need for Caution in Assessing Mediumistic Material." *Proceedings* of the Society for Psychical Research 48 (1949).

Parsons, Jack (1914–1952)

Jack Parsons, an explosives expert, pioneer in rocket propulsion, and follower of the thelemic **magic** of **Aleister Crowley** (1875–1947), was born Marvel Whiteside Parsons, the son of Marvel and Ruth Whiteside Parsons in Los Angeles, California, on October 2, 1914. Shortly after his birth, his parents separated, and his mother raised him as John Parsons. His friends and magical associates would know him as Jack.

During his teen years he developed an interest in rocketry and explosives, and carried out a number of amateur experiments. In 1932, while still in high school, he landed a job with the Hercules Powder Company. He graduated the following year and entered Pasadena Junior College and then spent two years at the University of Southern California, though he never graduated. In 1935 he married Helen Northrup and shortly thereafter left school to take a job at the California Institute of Technology, even though he lacked the formal training that such a job usually required. He took the lead in the development of liquid-fuel propellants, and made a secure place for himself in the history of rocket science.

In 1939 Parsons discovered a book by Crowley and then met Winifred Smith, a resident of Pasadena, who also led what was then the only active chapter of Crowley's organization, the **Ordo Templi Orientis** (OTO), then in existence. Thus began his double life, rocket scientist by day and magical student by night. In 1941 he and his wife both formally joined the OTO. From that time forward he would be the occasional object of surveillance by law enforcement officials who were concerned with his keeping explosive materials at his home. Also, neighbors and some who had attended various events at Parsons' home reported that he was engaged in immoral actions and black magic. As a whole, the police discounted them. In 1943, Parsons and his wife divorced, and he began a relationship with Helen's sister Sara Elizabeth "Betty" Northrup.

In the months immediately after World War II (1939–45), Parsons began a set of independent magical operations that would become known collectively as the Babalon Workings. These workings brought him into contact with a preternatural entity and also coincided with another shift in his personal relations. Betty was attracted to a new friend of Parsons', **L. Ron Hubbard.** Soon after the workings began, Marjorie Cameron came to Pasadena, and Parsons introduced her to magic work. They would eventually marry.

The results of the Babalon Workings were manifold. Parsons channeled a document, "Liber 49," which he came to believe was a fourth chapter to Crowley's basic magic text, *The Book of the Law.* As the workings became more involved, Crowley, then living out his last years in England, became concerned and sent a representative to examine the situation with the Pasadena OTO. Parsons formed a company with Hubbard and Betty to purchase boats on the East Coast and transport them to California. This company failed after Parsons and Hubbard had a disagreement and the assets were divided in a court settlement. Hubbard would later go on to found the **Church of Scientology.**

Parsons went through a period of disillusionment with magic and the OTO and resigned. He became convinced that the organization had proven itself an obstacle to reach its own magical goals. He began to work his magic outside of the OTO system. In 1948 he lost his security clearance at the California Institute of Technology. It was reinstated the following year, but in January of 1952, he lost it again. His involvement in magic was the stated reason for his lost status. Then on June 17, 1952, Parsons died when his home was destroyed in an explosion. The exact nature of what occurred has never been satisfactorily explained. His mother committed suicide after hearing of his death.

Parsons was a minor figure in the magical world at the time of his death. However, in the wake of the revival of interest in Crowley and magic in the 1970s, his work was rediscovered and in the early 1980s published. It has remained in print and been reproduced widely on the Internet. A first biography appeared in 1999.

Sources:

[Carter, John.] *Sex and Rockets: The Occult World of Jack Parsons.* Venice, Calif.: Feral House, 1999.

Parsons, Jack. *The Book of AntiChrist.* Edmonton: Isis Research, 1980.

———. *The Book of B.A.B.A.L.O.N.* Berkeley, Calif.: O.T.O., 1982.

———. *Freedom Is a Two Edged Sword, and Other Essays.* Edited by Marjorie Cameron Parsons Kimmel and Hymanaeus Beta. New York: Ordo Templi Orientis, 1989.

Partridge, John (1643–1715)

John Partridge, an influential member of the large astrological community in late seventeenth-century London, was one of several people known for his production of almanacs. As a youth he was apprenticed to a shoemaker, but in his leisure moments he educated himself and learned the several classic languages. He also mastered **astrology,** and there is evidence that he studied with **John Gadbury.** In 1678 his first book, *Mikropanastron,* was published and became the catalyst for his leaving his shoemaking career for life as an astrologer. Two years later he published his first almanac, *Merlinus Liberatus.*

Political changes in 1685 (the year of the death of King Charles II) led Partridge to leave England and take up residence in Leyden, Holland. He returned four years later, having acquired a medical degree. He married a well-to-do widow and resumed his astrological practice. He is remembered as a prominent British exponent of a new system of division of the astrological house in the horoscope originated by Italian mathematician, Placidus de Tito. In the midst of several systems of house division, Placidus began by measuring the time needed for a point on the ascendent (horizon) to reach the midheaven (directly above the observer). The degree thus obtained is divided by three. The Placidean system, introduced in the late seventeenth century, was shunned by many British astrologers. It found its major exponent in Partridge.

By the end of the century, Partridge had emerged as the most prominent astrologer in England, a role he inherited from the late **William Lilly** (1602–1681). He also continued Lilly's attacks on fellow astrologer John Gadbury. In the early eighteenth century, his colleagues began to take advantage of Partridge's reputation by issuing competing almanacs in Partridge's name. Then in 1708 he became the victim of a vicious hoax. Author Jonathan Swift (1667–1745), writing under the pseudonym Isaac Bickerstaff, published a fake almanac that included a prediction of Partridge's death on March 29, 1708. He followed his almanac on March 30 with a brief tract that regretfully noted that the prediction of Partridge's death had been true and described Partridge's passing. Many almanac readers did not perceive the hoax, and Partridge was presented with the task of proving that he was still alive. He discontinued his almanac for several years and when he resumed, he included an attack on Swift's character.

Partridge died in London on June 24, 1715.

Sources:

Holden, James H., and Robert A. Hughes. *Astrological Pioneers of America.* Tempe, Ariz.: American Federation of Astrologers, 1988.

McCaffery, Ellen. *Astrology: Its History and Influence in the Western World.* New York: Charles Scribner's Sons, 1942.

Partridge, John. *Mikropanastron; or, an Astrological Vade Mecum. . .* London, 1679.

———. *Nebulo Anglicanus; or, the First Part of the Black Life of John Gadbury.* London, 1693.

———. *Opus Reformatum; or, a Treatise of Astrology in which the Common Errors of the Art Are Exposed and Rejected.* London, 1693.

Pascal, Guillermo B. (1906–)

Uruguayan instructor in parapsychology. He was born on June 6, 1906, at Montevideo, Uruguay. He is a member of the Brazilian Academy of Social and Political Sciences, the Argentine College for Psychic Studies, Buenos Aires, and the International Institute for Scientific Research, Paris. Pascal was president of the Parapsychology Society of Montevideo from 1952 onward and is instructor in parapsychology at the Institute of Advanced Studies, Montevideo. He also taught parapsychology at the University of San Salvador, El Salvador. He takes special interest in **telepathy, clairvoyance, precognition,** and mediumship.

Pasqually, Martines de (ca. 1710–1774)

French Kabbalist, Mason, and mystic, and founder of the **Order of Elect Cohens.** The date of his birth is not known definitely, and even his nationality is a matter of uncertainty. It is commonly supposed, however, that he was born about 1710 somewhere in the south of France, most likely Grenoble. Several writers have maintained that his parents were Jewish, but this theory has largely been dismissed.

It is said that from the outset he evinced a predilection for mysticism in its various forms, while it is certain that in 1754, at Montpellier, he founded an organization called the Scottish Judges, most likely a lodge of speculative **Freemasonry.** It failed, but around 1760 at Bordeaux he instituted a ceremonial magic organization that combined elements of the Catholic mass with any material from magic texts that he could gather. The members of his order were styled *cohens,* Hebrew for "priests."

He propagated this *Rite des élus Cohens* (Order of Elect Cohens) in several Masonic lodges of France, notably those of Marseilles, Toulouse, Bordeaux, and Paris. In 1767 he settled in Paris, where he gathered around him many people ready to pursue the magic rituals he proposed. In 1772 he left after he heard that some property had been bequeathed to him on the island of Haiti, and he hastened there with the intention of asserting his rights; but he did not return to France, his death occurring in 1774 at Port-au-Prince, the principal town in Haiti. Pasqually is credited with having written a book, *Traité de la réintegration des etres,* but this was not published until the end of the nineteenth century. A rather extensive summary of the rituals he proposed for the order were gathered and published by René Le Forestier in 1928.

The rituals drew heavily upon the **Kabala,** which Pasqually felt was the essence of true Judaism. The format, however, followed one that would have been familiar to a pious Roman Catholic. The members began the day with a reading of the office of the Holy Spirit. Around ten in the evening, following a time of prayer, the members entered a private ritual space where a ritual diagram would be drawn on the floor. The invocation would begin at midnight. Its purpose was to communicate with what Pasqually termed the "Active and Intelligent Cause" (God).

Members of the order were forbidden to consume blood, fat, or kidneys of any animal, were to refrain from fornication, and not indulge the senses.

Pasqually was succeeded as head of the order by his chief disciple, J. B. Willermoz, but is largely remembered today because of the work of a younger disciple, Louis Claude de Saint-Martin, who carried his work toward a mystical, rather than magical, direction.

Sources:

Le Forestier, René. *La Franc-maconnerie occultiste au XVIII siecle et l'ordre des Elus Coens.* Paris: Dorbon, 1928.

McIntosh, Christopher. *Eliphas Levi and the French Occult Revival.* New York: Samuel Weiser, 1974.

Pasqually, Martines de. *Traité de la réintegration des etres.* Paris: Chacorac, 1899.

Patanjali

Patanjali was an Indian teacher traditionally thought of as the person who gathered and systematized the teachings of **meditation** and **yoga.** He is believed to have lived between 200 B.C.E. and 450 C.E. However, he is credited with composing the small Sanskrit volume of *Yoga Sutras* from which the modern practice of yoga is derived.

The *Sutras* laid out a system of practice by which one can attain a pure state free of illusion. The practice begins with the adoption of a fivefold ethic (call *yama*), very similar to that taught by **Mahavida** and the Jains—nonviolence, truthfulness, non-stealing, sexual restraint, and non-attachment. It is followed by the adoption of five virtues (*niyama*)—purity, contentment, austerity, study, and dedication. These practices inhibit the negative influences of being in the world. After adopting a lifestyle centered on *yama* and *niyama,* one begins the step-by-step adoption of the *asanas* (postures), breath control, control over the sense, concentration, and meditation, each of which should lead to the goal of *samadhi* (variously described as absorption or liberation).

According to Patanjali, the practice of yoga has a number of side effects. For example, the practice of nonviolence will lead to the cessation of violence in one's presence. Some of these side effects involve distinctly paranormal activity. For example, truthfulness in one's life leads to the ability to speak the future. The practice of concentration and meditation grants a number of *siddhas,* unusual powers, such as the ability to remain hidden or to greatly increase one's strength. It also leads to an understanding of the subtle anatomy of the body, including an awareness of the mysterious psychic/spiritual centers generally referred to as **chakras.** The practice of yoga then leads to the valuing of the *siddhas* and those who practice them throughout Indian society.

The practice of yoga (especially that part of Patanjali's system that included the *asanas,*) reached a low point in the nineteenth century, but was reborn early in the twentieth century. Simultaneously, **hatha yoga,** that aspect of the teachings devoted to the postures, was exported to the West as a discipline centered upon the improvement of bodily health. Hatha yoga has actually enjoyed a greater response in non-Indian cultures than in the land of its birth.

Sources:

Majumdar, Sachindra Kumar. *Introduction to Yoga Principles and Practice.* Secaucus, N.J.: Citadel Press, 1976.

Patanjali. *The Yoga Sutras of Patanjali: A New Translation and Commentary.* Edited by Georg Feuerstein. Folkstoone, UK: Dawson, 1979.

Paterson, T(homas) T(homson) (1909–)

Scottish professor of industrial administration who took a special interest in **parapsychology.** He was born on September 29, 1909, at Buckhaven, Fife, Scotland. He studied at the University of Edinburgh (B.S. chemistry, mathematics, 1930; B.S. geology, zoology, anatomy, 1932) and Cambridge University (M.A. anthropology, 1938; Ph.D. anthropology, 1940).

He was a staff member of the Medical Research Council, Scotland (1948–51), senator lecturer in industrial relations, Glasgow University (1951–62), and a professor of industrial administration from 1962 onward at Royal College of Science and Technology, Glasgow. He authored many papers and books on anthropology, geology, psychology, administration, and sociology.

In the field of parapsychology he took a special interest in **telepathy** and **clairvoyance** in relation to psychedelics. He was chairman of the symposium on Methodology of Research at the Conference on Parapsychology and Psychedelics held in November 1958 in New York.

The Path

A popular term to indicate the way an individual leads a religious life, especially if the way is prescribed with stages leading toward a preset goal. With **Theosophy** this term has taken on a special meaning in that it is used to denote not only the path itself but also the probationary path along which an individual must journey before he can enter on the path proper.

In order to begin the journey down a path, the individual first must be wholeheartedly devoted to this service. At the entrance to the probationary path, one becomes the *chela* or disciple of one of the **masters** or perfected beings who have all finished the great journey, and one must devote oneself to acquiring four qualifications, which are (1) knowledge of what only is real; (2) rejection of what is unreal; (3) the six mental attributes of control over thought, control over outward action, tolerance, endurance, faith, and balance; and (4) the desire to be one with God.

During the period of efforts to acquire these qualifications, the *chela* advances in many ways. The master imparts wise counsel and teaches the *chela* through meditation how to attain divine heights unthought of by ordinary human beings. The *chela* constantly works for the betterment of others, usually in the hours of sleep. Striving thus and in similar directions, he or she becomes fitted for the first initiation at the entrance to the path proper. It may be mentioned that the *chela* has the opportunity either during probation or afterward to forego the heavenly life that is due. The *chela* may allow the world to benefit by the powers that he or she has gained, which in ordinary course would have been utilized in the heavenly life. In this case, the *chela* remains in the **astral world,** from whence he or she makes frequent returns to the physical world.

There are four initiations that begin a new stage on the path, and each manifests the knowledge of that stage. On the first stage there are three obstacles or, as they are commonly termed, fetters, that must be cast aside, and these are the illusion of self, which must be realized to be only an illusion; doubt, which must be cleared away by knowledge; and superstition, which must be cleared away by the discovery of what in truth is real.

After this stage is traversed, the second initiation follows, and after this comes the consciousness that earthly life will now be short; only once again will physical death be experienced and the disciple begins more and more to function in the mental body.

After the third initiation, the disciple has two other fetters to unloose—desire and aversion, and now knowledge becomes keen and piercing and the disciple can gaze deep into the heart of things.

After the fourth initiation, the disciple enters on the last stage and is finally freed of what fetters remain—the desire for life whether bodily or not and the sense of individual difference from fellow human beings. The disciple has now reached the end of the journey and is no longer trammelled with sin or with anything that can hinder him or her from entering the state of supreme bliss, where he or she is reunited with the divine consciousness.

This theosophical scheme of spiritual realization has similarities with other mystical paths both East and West, but has a special affinity with Hinduism.

Sources:

Leadbeater, Charles W. *The Masters and the Path.* Chicago: Theosophical Press, 1925.

Pathetism

Term used to denote **mesmerism** or **animal magnetism** by **La Roy Sunderland** (1804–1885), a minister and prominent public advocate of the magnetist movement in America in the middle of the nineteenth century. Sunderland is a contemporary of **James Braid,** who is generally credited with secularizing mesmerist practice as **hypnotism.**

In his book *Pathetism* (1843), Sunderland wrote:

"I use this term to signify, not only the AGENCY, by which one person by manipulation, is enabled to produce *emotion, feeling, passion,* or any physical or mental effects, in the system of another but also that SUSCEPTIBILITY of *emotion* or *feeling,* of any kind, from manipulation, in the subject operated upon, by the use of which these effects are produced; as also the *laws* by which this agency is governed. I mean it as a substitute for the terms heretofore in use, in connection with this subject, and I respectfully submit it to all concerned, whether this be not a far better term for the *thing signified,* than either Magnetism or Mesmerism."

Most magnetists had their own favorite term, such as "etherology" (J. Stanley Grimes), "neurology" (**Joseph Rhodes Buchanan**), "electrobiology" (John Bovee Dods), or "electropsychology" (Dr. Fiske), but eventually the term "hypnotism," devised by Braid, was generally adopted.

Sources:

Sunderland, La Roy. *Book of Human Nature.* New York: Sterns, 1853.

———. *Ideology.* Boston: J. P. Mendum, 1885–87.

———. *Pathetism.* New York: P. P. Good, 1843.

———. *Trance and Correlative Phenomena.* Chicago: J. Walker, 1868.

Path of Gnostic Light

The Path of Gnostic Light is a new form of **Gnosticism** that was originated by a man known only as Master Leo, a resident of Macedonia. In the early 1980s, after a period of working with *The Book of the Law,* the holy book of the thelemic magick tradition, Master Leo claimed to have made contact with the entity Aiwaz, which he described as an energetic current, the same entity who had dictated *The Book of the Law* to **Aleister Crowley** early in the twentieth century. Aiwaz provided insight into the old magical formula Abrahadabra which gave rise to a set of magical techniques that connected the energy centers in the human body, the **chakras,** to the energies of Abrahadabra. The communication from Aiwaz led to the founding of the Path of Gnostic Light in 1985.

The Path of Gnostic Light was created as an outer order on April 16, 1985. Subsequently, Master Leo compiled the teachings of the order into a book, *Knjiga Gnoze* (Book of Gnosis), and published 121 copies, all of which were distributed in the former Yugoslavia. In the meantime, Master Leo had come into contact with Michael Bertiaux, a thelemic magician residing in Chicago, Illinois, who noted that while a new form of magical Gnostic teachings, Master Leo's perspective was very close to his own and that of Kenneth Grant, the head of the **Ordo Templi Orientis** organization based in London, England.

Following the opening of the Path of Gnostic Light, a set of inner orders were created. They include the Order of the Gnostic Black Serpent (for males), the Order of the Gnostic Black Dove (for females), the Order of the Gnostic Black Star (for both males and females) and a fourth order known only by its initials, P.O.K.A. Included in the work of these orders is the practice of left-hand tantra, that is, sex magick.

The teachings of the Path are a path of self-exploration that begins in the direct experience of one's personal nature and the destruction of the illusionary presentation of the mind about oneself. Following the Path leads to the complete identification of the self to the primal It. The teachings of the Path of Gnostic Light use the symbolism of the snake and the associated **kundalini** energy as central to its teachings. That symbol brings together such diverse esoteric teachings as the ancient cult of Orpheus and the modern **Voudou** cult of Damballah. Identification with the snake (and other animals on the astral plane) involves a magical transformation, a form of **lycanthropy.**

The Path of Gnostic Light has an Internet site at http://www.mnsi.net/~miskovic/pglvx.htm through which Master Leo in Macedonia and his representative in Canada may be contacted.

Sources:

The Path of Gnostic Light. http://www.mnsi.net/~miskovic/pglvx.htm. May 14, 2000.

Pathways

The name of a number of esoteric and **New Age** periodicals. Among them are *Pathways,* a British directory which provides a concise listing of New Age and **psi** events, organizations, periodicals, and meetings in England. It is published quarterly at 16 Great Ormond St., London, WC1N 3RB, England.

Pathways Journal is a quarterly publication of "ideas concerning personal and social transformation." Each issue includes a directory of services and events and book reviews. It is issued by the Yes Educational Society, P.O. Box 5719, Takoma Park, MD 20912.

A second *Pathways Journal* is a quarterly publication edited by B. C. Jaegers, head of the State Licensed Psychic Detective Bureau, P.O. Box 24571, Creve Coeur, MO 63141.

"Patience Worth"

A spirit entity, communicating from 1913 on through **Pearl Lenore Curran** (Mrs. John H.), of St. Louis, Missouri, first through the **ouija board,** then through **automatic speaking** and dictating in a late medieval English prose and poetry with extreme rapidity on a wide range of subjects.

The literary merit of the books was quite good and received favorable reviews apart from any notice of their unusual origin. Four novels were published: *The Sorry Tale, Hope Trueblood, Light from Beyond,* and *The Pot upon the Wheel. Telka,* a lengthy play of 60,000–70,000 words was considered by psychical researcher **Walter Franklin Prince** superior to analogous works.

"Patience Worth" claimed to have lived in Dorsetshire, England, in the seventeenth century and to have been killed in America by the Indians. Some of her statements as to her home and environment were verified. Caspar Yost, the editor of the *St. Louis Globe-Democrat,* took a great personal interest in the "Patience Worth" phenomenon and edited the publication of the texts.

Out of his study of the "Patience Worth" texts, Prince concluded, "Either our concept of what we call the subconscious mind must be radically altered so as to include potencies of which we hitherto have had no knowledge, or else some cause operating through, but not originating in, the subconsciousness of Mrs. Curran must be acknowledged." Most psychical researchers today would opt for the former of Prince's two choices.

Prof. Allison of Manitoba University said of the case in a personal study that "it must be regarded as the outstanding phenomenon of the age." Dr. Usher, a professor of history at Washington University, considered *The Sorry Tale,* a composition of 350,000 words, "the greatest story penned of the life and times of Christ since the Gospels were finished." On occasions "Patience Worth" demonstrated before professors. Starting in March 1918, a monthly called *Patience Worth's Magazine* was published for ten months to provide an outlet for her prolific literary activity.

Sources:

Douglas, Alfred. *Extrasensory Powers.* New York: The Overlook Press, 1977.

Hickman, Irene. *I Knew Patience Worth.* Sacramento, Calif., The Author, 1971.

Litvag, Irving. *Singer in the Shadows: The Strange Story of Patience Worth.* Macmillan, 1972; New York: Popular Library, 1973.

Prince, Walter Franklin. *The Case of Patience Worth: A Critical Study of Certain Unusual Phenomena.* Boston: Society for Psychical Research, 1927; New Hyde Park, N.Y.: University Books, 1964.

"Worth, Patience." *Hope Trueblood.* New York: Henry Holt, 1918.

———. *The Pot upon the Wheel.* New York: Patience Worth Publishing, 1916.

———. *The Sorry Tale.* New York: Henry Holt, 1917.

Yost, Casper S. *Patience Worth; A Psychic Mystery.* New York: Henry Holt, 1916. Reprint, London: Skeffington, 1919.

Paton, Mrs.

Nonprofessional **apport** medium of Melbourne, Australia, who flourished in the 1870s. She accepted no fees for her séances.

The objects apported were distinguished by the place where the objects came from. It often happened that things were brought from her own house over a distance of two miles. Occasionally, the objects were very heavy or difficult to handle like a glass of wine. A stone apported from the seashore was found to weigh 14 pounds and came with a mass of seaweed with shrimp-like creatures on it. One of the most notable apported household objects was a soup plate with twenty eggs on it.

Paton was not usually entranced during her apport phenomena, but was often markedly convulsed. She worked under strict test conditions: she was searched before a séance and completely enveloped in a large mosquito net bag, which was tied and sealed. The apports arrived on a table in the dark, but on some occasions, arrived even in bright light.

One of the most astonishing apports occurred at the house of a Miss Finlason, a resident of Castlemaine. During the séance, Paton mentioned to one of the sitters that before leaving her home, two miles away, she had made a cup of tea, but had forgotten to drink it. The cup of tea and saucer appeared as an apport on the table. At another séance on April 6, 1874, an iron wheel weighing sixteen and a half pounds fell with a crash on the table, brought from the yard outside.

Sources:

Denovan, W. C. D. *Evidences of Spiritualism.* Melbourne, 1882.

Patterson, Mrs. S. E.

American **slate-writing** medium, the first subject of the experiments of the **Seybert Commission** in 1884. In two sittings, no results were obtained, and evidence of **fraud** appeared.

A slate given to the medium was returned six months later without any writing inside. Dr. Horace Howard Furness, a member of the commission, gave her a second slate. At the end of a fortnight, the announcement was made that the slate pencil inside had disappeared, as it was not heard rattling. This was taken as a sign of success, as in Patterson's case the completion of the writing was not indicated by **raps,** but by the sudden appearance of the slate fragment on the top of the slates.

When, however, the committee opened the slates, no writing was seen inside. On the other hand, according to the report, the wooden frames bore telltale marks of a knife which was inserted to force an aperture for the slate pencil.

Pauwels, Louis (1920–)

Co-author with **Jacques Bergier** of the sensational bestselling French work, *Le Matin des Magiciens* (1960), later translated into English as *The Dawn of Magic* (London, 1963) and reprinted in America as *The Morning of the Magicians* (1971). The book had a significant influence on the occult revival in Europe and elsewhere, and it contained revelations of the part played by occultism in the career of Adolf Hitler and the establishment of Nazi philosophy.

Pauwels and Bergier have also collaborated on *Der Planet der unmöglichen Möglichkeiten* (1968), translated into English as *Impossible Possibilities* (1971).

Pauwels was born in Paris, August 2, 1920, and worked in journalism and French television. As a student he was fascinated by the romance of alchemy. His collaborator Bergier was born 1912 and qualified as a chemical engineer during World War II. Pauwels was an active member of the French resistance movement. In the 1970s he was employed as the chief editor of *Figaro* magazine.

Sources:

Pauwels, Louis, and Jacques Bergier. *The Eternal Man.* London: Souvenir, 1972.

———. *Le Matin des Magiciens.* Paris: Editions Gallimard, 1960. English edition as: *The Dawn of Magic.* London: Anthony Gibbs and Phillips, 1963. Reprinted as *The Morning of the Magicians.* New York: Stein and Day, 1964.

———. *Der Planet der unmöglichen Möglichkeiten.* Bern: Scherz Verlag, 1968. English edition as *Impossible Possibilities.* New York: Stein and Day, 1971.

PEAR See Princeton Engineering Anomalies Research

Pearls

Various occult properties were ascribed to pearls. Among the early Greeks and Romans, the wearing of the gem as an **amulet** or **talisman** was much in vogue, and pearls were often made into crowns. Smedley, Taylor, Thompson and Rich noted, "Pope Adrian, anxious to secure all the virtues in his favour, wore an amulet composed of a sun baked toad, arsenic, tormentil, pearl, coral, hyacinth, smarag, and tragacanth."

It was popularly believed that to dream of pearls meant many tears. The occult virtues of pearls were said to be brought forth by boiling them in meat. When bruised and taken with milk, they were believed to be good for ulcers and to clear the voice. They were also said to comfort the heart and render their possessor chaste.

The mysterious **Mr. Jacob** ("Jacob of Simla") (ca. 1850–1921) described himself as a "Healer of Pearls," able to restore color to a "sick" pearl.

Sources:

Smedley, E., W. C. Taylor, H. Thompson, and E. Rich. *The Occult Sciences.* N.p., 1855.

Pederson-Krag, Geraldine Huanayra (1901–1995)

Psychoanalytic psychiatrist with interests in parapsychology. She was born on July 23, 1901, in Schenectady, New York. She was a member of the Royal College of Surgeons and a licentiate of the Royal College of Physicians, London. She began her medical career as an assistant surgeon and house physician at Westminster Hospital, London, but moved to New York at the beginning of the 1930s and held various positions through the next three decades. In 1960 she became the director of Huntington Township Mental Health Clinic. Over the years she has authored one book in a specialized area of concern, *Personality Factors in Work and Employment* (1955), and various articles in the *Psychoanalytic Quarterly.* She took a special interest in telepathy and clairvoyance. Pederson-Krag died June 23, 1995.

Sources:

Pederson-Krag, Geraldine H. "Telepathy and Repression." *Psychoanalytic Quarterly* 16 (1947).

Peebles, J(ames) M(artin) (1822–1922)

Prominent American Spiritualist, author, and lecturer. He was born on March 23, 1822, in a log cabin in Whittingham, Vermont. He studied at Oxford Academy, New York, graduating with a Ph.D. and LL.D.; he subsequently practiced as a physician. He was also ordained as a minister and preached in parishes in Kellogsville, Elmira, New York and Baltimore.

After preaching a sermon in Kellogsville, he was invited by one of his parishioners to attend a séance in Auburn, New York, where he first heard spirit rapping. Soon afterwards he heard a trance lecture delivered by an uneducated boy; the subject was chosen by Peebles: "The Philosophical Influence of the Nations of Antiquity Upon the Civilization and Sciences of Modern Europe and America." As Dr. Peebles described the event: "The boy at once stepped forward and commenced, and for one hour and three-quarters one continual stream of history and philosophy fell from his lips." When Peebles preached on "The Spiritual Gifts" in his own church, the deacons and congregation protested; Peebles resigned in disgust to follow a secular career and continue his investigation of **Spiritualism.** He wrote and lectured for more than eighty years, mainly in the cause of Spiritualism. He was also one of the earliest temperance workers and joined the abolition movement together with John Brown and William Lloyd Garrison.

In 1866 Peebles became western editor of the Spiritualist journal *Banner of Light.* His brilliant editorials greatly extended circulation. He became editor-in-chief of *The Spiritual Universe,* a journal devoted to Freethought and Spiritualism, which frequently joined in common causes in the nineteenth century. He subsequently became editor-in-chief of *The American Spiritualist,* published in Cleveland. In addition to his editorial and other newspaper contributions, he also published many books and pamphlets on Spiritualism.

Peebles was an advocate of Spiritualism, and traveled around the world five times in its behalf. He died February 15, 1922, in Los Angeles, California.

Sources:

Barrett, J. O. *The Spiritual Pilgrim: A Biography of James M. Peebles.* Boston: William White, 1872.

Peebles, James M. *Around the World: or, Travels in Polynesia, China, India, Arabia, Egypt, Syria.* Boston: Colby & Rich, 1875.

———. *Celebration of the Fiftieth Anniversary of Modern Spiritualism at Its Birthplace.* Battle Creek, Mich.: The Author, 1898.

———. *The Demonism of the Ages, Spirit Obsessions So Common in Spiritism, Oriental and Occidental Occultism.* Battle Creek, Mich.: Peebles Medical Institute, 1904.

———. *Five Journeys around the World: or, Travels in the Pacific Islands, New Zealand, Australia, Ceylon, India, Egypt and Other Oriental Countries.* Los Angeles: Peebles Publishing, 1910.

———. *Seers of the Ages.* 1869. Reprint, Chicago: Progressive Thinker, 1905.

Peebles, James M., Helen Densmore, and W. J. Colville. *Reincarnation; or the Doctrine of "Soul's" Successive Embodiment.* Battle Creek, Mich.: Peebles Medical Institute, 1904.

Pegomancy

A branch of **hydromancy** (**divination** by water), also associated with crystalomancy (also known as **crystal gazing** or scrying). Interpretations were made by dropping stones in sacred pools or springs and observing their movements. (See also **lecanomancy**)

"Pelham, George"

Pseudonym of "George Pellew," **control** of the famous medium **Leonora E. Piper** (1859–1950). In earthly life, Pellew was a lawyer by education but a writer by preference. He often argued with his friend, researcher **Richard Hodgson,** that the idea of survival after death was not only improbable but inconceivable. Hodgson claimed that if not probable, it was at least conceivable. Pellew promised that if he died first he would return and "make things lively." In February 1892, when he was 32 years old, he was killed in New York by a fall.

On March 22, the spirit entity "George Pellew" made his first appearance in Piper's automatic script and from 1892 to 1898 he talked with some 130 people of whom 30 had previously known him. He addressed each of them in the tone and manner which he used in his lifetime.

From 1892 until 1897 he shared control with **"Phinuit."** With the appearance of the **"Imperator"** group, who assumed the control function in Piper's mediumship, "Phinuit" completely disappeared and "Pellew's" communications became rare. He said that he was "advancing" in the afterlife and thus getting farther away from the physical realm. Finally he disappeared altogether. He was originally referred to in séance reports as "Pelham" or "G.P." to protect anonymity.

Pellet Reading (or Billet Reading)

A popular means of demonstrating psychic ability in **Spiritualism.** Sitters at a séance or other gathering are each requested to write the name of a deceased person or persons whom they wish to contact or know about, and/or questions to which they seek an answer, on a slip of paper. The slips are either folded into billets or tightly screwed up into pellets, which are sometimes sealed in envelopes. The medium would hold each billet or pellet (often to the forehead) and give a message relating to the deceased individual or question on the slip of paper. The American medium **Charles H. Foster** specialized in this type of clairvoyance.

Variants of this performance are common with stage magicians and the very nature of the procedure suggests a conjuring trick. The psychical researcher **Harry Price** described in his book *Confessions of a Ghost Hunter* (1974) how he bought the secret of the trick from a man from Oshkosh, Wisconsin.

As practiced by fake mediums, such billet-readings sessions begin with the medium taking a piece of paper, holding it in his or her hand (or at the forehead for dramatic effect) and giving an initial reading. The first reading is not for the person who wrote the billet but for a person in cahoots who agrees with whatever is said. The medium then reads the billet and places it aside. The process is repeated and the answer is now given to the first billet, pretending it to be a reading for the billet in hand. By this manner the medium is always one billet ahead. After the session, the billets are collected and become part of a file on those persons who are regular attendees at the medium's public events.

Sources:

Keene, Lamar. *Psychic Mafia.* New York: St. Martin's Press, 1976.

Pellevoisen

In 1876, Pellevoisen, a town in central France, became the site of an **apparition of the Virgin Mary** and an accompanying spectacular healing of Constance Estelle Faguette. Faguette had been ill for several years. She was wasting away with tuberculosis (at the time an incurable disease) and related complications and had finally reached a point that she could not retain any food. She was given the last rites and a grave was being prepared. She had been the sole means of support for her aging parents and her death threatened to reduce them to beggars. As her illness had taken its toll, she had composed a letter to the Virgin and placed it under the statue of Mary at the local church.

On the evening of February 14, as friends kept a death watch, Faguette awoke to a strange sight at the foot of her bed. A demon-like figure appeared and then the Virgin. She banished the demon and told the dying young woman not to fear. She would suffer for five more days and then be healed. The Virgin returned each evening to assure her. When she told her friends and neighbors about the apparitions, they assumed that it was the sickness talking, though many showed up on the fifth day to see what would occur. After taking Communion, Faguette announced her cure, got out of bed, put on her street clothes, and asked for food. She would live an additional 63 years.

Over the next year, Faguette had ten additional encounters with the Virgin, in one of which she was shown what is known as the red scapular, a square of red cloth with the picture of a heart pierced with a lance and surrounded by thorns. Over the next century, it would be a new item in the church's depository of pious practices. In the last apparition, Faguette was told to make the spread of the scapular her mission in life.

Following a study of the apparitions, the local bishop reported favorably, but sent the results to the Vatican asking the pope's blessing. Given a positive response, the bishop organized the Confraternity of Our Lady of Pellevoisen. The regular holding of services at Pellevoisen was only a matter of time, and soon a regular stream of pilgrims began to appear. It has also been added to the short list of approved Marian apparitions.

Sources:

Beaumont, Barbara. *Pellvoisen: Our Lady Reveals the Devotion to the Sacred Heart Scapular.* Chulmleugh, Devon, UK: Augustine Publishing House, 1986.

Sharkey, Don. *The Woman Shall Conquer.* Kenosha, Wis.: Franciscan Marytown Press, 1976.

Pencovic, Francis Heindswater (1911–1958)

Founder of the **WFLK Foundation of the World,** a communal religious group with roots in Hinduism. Pencovic operated under his religious name, **Krishna Venta.** Raised a Mormon, Pencovic became a public figure in his new identity in the 1930s and founded the group he led in the 1940s. He was killed by some dissident members in 1958 and the group finally disbanded in the early 1980s.

Sources:

Mathison, Richard. *Faiths, Cults, and Sects of America.* Indianapolis: Bibbs-Merrill, 1960.

Ormont, Arthur. *Love Cults & Faith Healers.* New York: Ballantine Books, 1961.

Pendulums

A divination device. Small pendulums are often used in **dowsing, radiesthesia,** and related divination systems instead of **divining-rods.** Questions can be put, and the clockwise or anticlockwise rotation of the pendulum gives an answer, rather like the **raps** in Spiritualist séances.

In earlier forms of pendulum divination, a wedding ring was suspended on a silk thread. Today, practitioners of radiesthesia obtain a number of subtle indications from the nature of the oscillations of the pendulum, which is used for water divining, discovery of metals, indications of health and medical remedies, and even discovery of missing persons.

Sources:

Bird, Christopher. *The Diving Hand: The 500 Year-Old Mystery of Dowsing.* New York: E. P. Dutton, 1979.

De France, Henry. *The Elements of Dowsing*. London: G. Bell, 1971.
Hitching, Francis. *Pendulum: The Psi Connection*. London: Fontana, 1977.
Letbridge, T. C. *The Power of the Pendulum*. London: Routledge & Kegan Paul, 1976.
Nielsen, Greg, and J. Polansky. *Pendulum Power: A Mystery You Can See, a Power You Can Feel*. New York: Destiny Books, 1977.
Wethered, V. D. *A Radiesthetic Approach to Health and Homeopathy, or Health and the Pendulum*. London: British Society of Dowsers, 1950.

Penelhum, Terence Michael (1929–)

Associate professor of philosophy who also studied in the field of parapsychology. He was born on April 26, 1929, at Bradford-on-Avon, England. He attended the University of Edinburgh (M.A., 1950) and Oxford University (B.Phil., 1952), England. Following graduation he joined the faculty of the Department of Philosophy of the University of Alberta, Edmonton, Canada.

In the field of parapsychology, he studied the question of personal identity with reference to the possibility of a purely psychical entity. He was also interested in theories of survival and discussed questions of identity and survival in his book *Survival and Disembodied Existence* (1970).

Pentacle (or Pantacle or Pentagram)

A five-pointed star formed from five straight lines of equal length, a symbol frequently used in magical rituals. When a single point projects upward, with two points on the base projecting downward, it is used in modern neo-paganism and Wicca (witchcraft) groups as a symbolic invocation of positive influences. When turned upside-down, it is used by post-Christian Satanic groups as symbolic of the invocation of Satan and evil (in the Christian sense of that term). Satanists frequently impose the figure of a goat with two ears pointing upward and its beard pointing downward on the reverse pentagram.

The pentacle has a wide use in religions. It has been used within Christianity in such a way that the five points represent the wounds of the crucified Christ. A more common contemporary use refers back to the star which hovered in the sky when the baby Jesus was born. It is found on the flag of many Muslim countries. In ancient Greece, the pentacle was used by the Pythagoreans to symbolize perfection. In folklore, the sign has been traced on windows and doors in order to repel witches.

In ritual magic, the pentacle has played an important part in evoking or repelling spirits. It was usually associated with holy or unholy names of power and inscribed or engraved with great care and concentration. A six-pointed version or hexagram is often known as "The Seal of Solomon." (See also **magical diagrams**)

Sources:

Valiente, Doreen. *The ABC of Witchcraft Past and Present*. New York: St. Martin's Press, 1973.

Pentecost Miracles (with D. D. Home)

Pentecostalism

A modern revival movement within free church Protestantism characterized by the appearance of the biblical gifts of the spirit as outlined in the Apostle Paul's First Epistle to the Corinthians 12. These gifts include the working of miracles, healing, prophecy, and speaking in tongues. Of the several gifts, the speaking in tongues has been the most controversial.

The Pentecostal movement began in 1901 in a Bible school in Topeka, Kansas. The school's teacher, Charles Parham, assigned his students the project of researching the sign of the baptism of the Holy Spirit in the lives of the first Christian apostles. Upon questioning, the students agreed that the baptism of the spirit was always accompanied by the individual "speaking in tongues." Thus the group began to pray for the baptism, and on January 1, 1901, Agnes Oznam was the first to receive an answer to her prayer and began to speak in tongues. The other students also soon spoke in tongues, and over the next few years news of the experience was spread through Kansas, Missouri, Oklahoma, and Texas. In 1906, a student from Parham's school in Houston carried the experience to Los Angeles. William J. Seymour, an African American led a small black congregation that became the center from which the movement spread to the world. It eventually took organizational form in a number of denominational bodies such as the Assemblies of God and the Church of God (Cleveland, Tennessee).

It is a doctrine of Pentecostals that every person who receives the baptism of the Holy Spirit will initially speak in tongues, and then subsequently manifest one or more of the other gifts of the spirit. Within Pentecostal congregations, members look for manifestations of all of the gifts.

The early Pentcostals believed that they were living in the last days prior to the return of Jesus. Therefore they interpreted the sounds which they heard as people were speaking in tongues as a foreign language, a supernatural tool to assist them in converting the nations of the world. Numerous accounts appear in the early Pentecostal literature of someone recognizing a specific foreign language being spoken despite the ignorance of the person speaking of that language. The speaking of a foreign language while in an altered state of consciousness is termed **xenoglossia.** Documented cases of xenoglossia are quite rare.

However, most people who speak in tongues speak sounds not translatable into any known language. In the Bible, the words spoken are described as the "words of men and of angels," and many have suggested that the unintelligible sounds were really angelic. These unintelligible vocalizations are referred to as glossolalia.

With the popularization of Pentecostalism in the last half of the twentieth century, research on the nature of glossolalia has been done. Among the most useful was the work of linguist William Samarin who studied a number of people who spoke in tongues and discovered that their vocalizations constituted a proto-language. The sounds were related to the language they spoke every day, but had only a limited number of vowels and consonants. Their speech did not have enough different sounds from which to construct a language, but was quite distinct from the gibberish spoken by someone trying to imitate someone speaking in tongues.

Pentecostal Happenings in Spiritualism

Within Spiritualism, the full range of phenomena generally referred to as the gifts of the spirit by Pentecostals also manifest. Among notable examples is the "Martian" language spoken by French medium Helene Smith and reported by Theodore Flournoy. Smith claimed that she had astrally visited Mars and while in trance spoke "Martian." Her claim was thus that she exhibited an instance of xenoglossia. Flournoy demonstrated that the language was related to her everyday French, that is, she was demonstrating glossolalia.

Viscount Adare, in his book *Experiences in Spiritualism with Mr. D. D. Home* (1870), claimed to have witnessed a broad modern duplication of the Pentecostal experience in the mediumship of **D. D. Home:**

"We now had a series of very curious manifestations. Lindsay and Charlie [Charles Wynne] saw tongues or jets of flame proceeding from Home's head. We then all distinctly heard, as it were, a bird flying round the room whistling and chirping, but saw nothing, except Lindsay, who perceived an indistinct form resembling a bird. Then came a sound as of a great wind rushing through the room, we also felt the wind strongly; the moaning rushing sound was the most weird thing I ever heard. Home then got up, being in trance, and spoke something in a language that none of us understood; it may have been nonsense, but it sounded like a sentence in a foreign tongue. Lindsay thought he recognized some words of Russian. He then quoted the text about the different gifts of the spirit, and gave us a translation in English of what he had said in the unknown tongue. He told us that Charlie had that day been discussing the miracles that took place at Pentecost, and that the spirit made the sound of the wind; of the bird descending; of the unknown tongue, and interpretation thereof, and the tongues of fire to show that the same phenomenon could occur again." (See also **Daniel Dunglas Home; Luminous Phenomena; Sounds; Winds; Xenoglossis**)

Sources:

Dunraven, Windham Thomas Wyndham-Quin. *Experiences in Spiritualism with Mr. D. D. Home.* Glasgow: R. Maclehose & Co. Ltd., 1924.

Flournoy, Theodore. *From India to the Planet Mars.* New York: Harper, 1901.

Goodman, Felicitas D. *Speaking in Tongues: A Cross Cultural Study of Glossolalia.* Chicago: University of Chicago Press, 1972.

Kydd, Ronald A. N. *Charismatic Gifts in the Early Church.* Peabody, Mass.: Hendrickson Publishers, 1984.

Samarin, William J. *Tongues of Men and Angels.* New York: Macmillan, 1972.

Synan, Vincent, ed. *Aspects of Pentecostal-Charismatic Origins.* Plainfield, N.J.: Losgos International, 1975.

Peoples Temple

A congregation led by Pastor **Jim Jones.** It fell victim to a massive murder-suicide in November 1978. In the wake of the tragedy, the Peoples Temple has become a symbol of the dangers of cults and Jones the model of the evil, manipulative cult leader. The Peoples Temple was for the last 15 years of its existence a part of the Christian church (Disciples of Christ), a large mainstream Christian denomination. In the 1960s it was hailed by liberal Protestants for its social activism. Within the loose structure of the Christian church, however, it developed a unique internal life.

The Peoples Temple was founded in Indianapolis, Indiana, in 1955 by a youthful Jim Jones as an independent congregation. He eventually brought the congregation into fellowship with the Disciples of Christ and he was ordained as a minister in that church in 1965. The next year he led most of the congregation's members to Ukiah, California, and once settled the group began to take on the elements of its unusual life. Although Jones was white, his efforts at recruiting were focused in the African American community, and the great majority of members were black. Worship services took on the free style of black Holiness churches.

Jones had been deeply influenced by his perception of black religious leader **Father Divine,** both in his ability to build an interracial community and in his godlike status. At one point he even attempted to merge his efforts with those of Divine's Peace Mission. Jones also came to see himself as possessing some of the godlike abilities claimed by Divine. This new self-perception was also influenced by Jones's experience among Brazilian Spiritists, and he was seen by followers as a prophet and miracle worker. Not only could he heal, but there were a number of cases of reported resurrection from the dead. Church services came to feature psychic readings and healings by Jones. Equally strong in Jones were the Marxist leanings underlying his social idealism.

By 1972 the Peoples Temple had grown to include several congregations, with groups in San Francisco and Los Angeles joining the older groups in Indianapolis and Ukiah. That same year Jones leased land in the South American nation of Guyana and the temple initiated an agricultural colony. The colony prospered and in 1977 Jones and a number of the members moved there. Eventually approximately one thousand members resided at Jonestown, as the colony was named. Jones's move to Guyana coincided with a rising criticism of the church by former members (including accusations of violence directed toward some) and the prospect of several very negative media reports on the temple.

By this time a variety of government investigations had been launched into temple activities, including its use of the welfare checks received by many of the members. In the midst of the ongoing controversy, Congressman Leo J. Ryan went to Guyana to see the colony, claiming he was interested because many of its residents had formerly lived in his district. After what had been to all outward appearances a cordial visit, Ryan and his party were murdered as they were about to board an airplane to return to the United States. Within hours most of the temple members were dead; some committed suicide, but many were murdered. Very few survived to tell what had happened.

In the wake of the tragedy, the U.S. Congress conducted an extensive investigation. Unfortunately, though a lengthy report was issued, the mass of materials, including the files of the various government investigations of the temple, have never been made public, and the truth of what actually occurred at Jonestown remains shrouded in mystery. Substantive revelations of what occurred there will likely be made when those files become available. In the meantime, completely distancing herself from the standard anticult rhetoric concerning the temple, Patricia Ryan, Ryan's daughter, filed a lawsuit against the U.S. Central Intelligence Agency, claiming that it was in large part responsible for her father's death.

Sources:

Hall, John R. *Gone from the Promised Land: Jonestown in American Cultural History.* New Brunswick, N.J.: Transaction, 1987.

Klineman, George, and Sherman Butler. *The Cult That Died.* New York: G. P. Putnam's Sons, 1980.

Melton, J. Gordon, ed. *The Peoples Temple and Jim Jones: Broadening Our Perspectives.* New York: Garland, 1990.

Moore, Rebecca, ed. *New Religious Movements, Mass Suicide, and Peoples Temple: Scholarly Perspectives on a Tragedy.* New York: Edwin Mellen Press, 1989.

Reiterman, Tom. *Raven.* New York: E. P. Dutton, 1982.

Pepper, May S. (1868– ?)

Pastor of the First Spiritualist Church of Brooklyn, whose powers of **clairvoyance** were a subject of lively discussion in the American press for a considerable time. She was born in Mansfield, Massachusetts, in May 1868. When only 16 years old, after the death of her mother, she became controlled by the spirit "Bright Eyes." As she demonstrated her mediumistic talent at public meetings, she was ostracized by members of the public and even her father, who claimed that her phenomena were from "the evil one." She became one of the leading American mediums and president of the Rhode Island State Spiritualist Association.

According to contemporary accounts, her congregation wrote letters to deceased friends and put them in a plain envelope on a small table. After a prayer and short sermon, Pepper would take a letter and return a correct answer to the question if it was put in a spirit of serious inquiry, or declare it to be an attempt to mislead her. It also was said that she asked the spirit she clairvoyantly saw to look for the letter addressed to him. Before all eyes, the pile of letters moved and one of them was taken as though by an invisible hand and thrown on the floor.

James H. Hyslop, William James, J. D. Quackenbos and many others expressed their confidence in Pepper's supernormal faculties.

Percipient

General term in parapsychology to denote an individual taking part in a test of **extrasensory perception.** In the case of a subject who is involved in an experiment to receive impressions from an **agent** or sender of information, the term "percipient" is usually used.

Percival, Harold Waldwin (1868–1953)

Harold W. Percival, Theosophist and founder of the Word Foundation, was born April 15, 1868, at his parents' plantation near Bridgetown, Barbados, in the British West Indies. He lived on Barbados until his father's death when Harold was ten; he then moved with his mother to Boston and later New York City. As a youth he rejected the Christianity of his parents, and once in New York he discovered **Theosophy** and in 1892 joined the American **Theosophical Society** under the leadership of **William Q. Judge.** Four years later Judge died, and the society experienced a period of disruption in large part by members who rejected the leadership of **Katherine Tingley,** whom Judge wished to succeed him. Percival was among the members in New York City who left to found the independent Theosophical Society of New York. Percival founded the Theosophical Publishing Company of New York and emerged as a major writer, publisher, and distributor of theosophical literature.

In 1904 Percival launched the *Word,* which became the official journal of the Theosophical Society of New York. He wrote several books, including *The Zodiac* (1906), *Karma: The Law of Life* (1910), and *Hell and Heaven, on Earth and After Death* (1911).

Increasingly during his years with the Theosophical Society of New York, Percival worked on creating his own synthesis of knowledge. The beginning point of his thought was a personal mystical experience that had occurred in 1893. He described what happened to him as becoming "conscious of Consciousness." It was an experience he had a number of times over the years. As early as 1902 he attempted to explain his experience in terms of Theosophy, and by 1912 was outlining a book that would contain his developing synthesis. He dictated the massive volume to a colleague, Benoni B. Gattell. A first edition appeared in 1932 as *The Law of Thought.* A completely rewritten edition appeared in 1946 as *Thinking and Destiny.* He subsequently published three books expanding upon topics in light of his system: *Man and Woman and Child* (1951), *Masonry and Its Symbols* (1952), and *Democracy Is Self-Government* (1952).

Percival believed that the state of being conscious of Consciousness allowed one to know about any subject simply by taking thought of that subject. Thinking, he defined, is the "steady holding of the Conscious Light within on the subject of the thinking. Briefly stated, thinking is of four stages: selecting the subject; holding the Conscious Light on that subject; focusing the Light; and the focus of the Light. When the Light is focused, the subject is known."

In 1946 Percival founded the Word Publishing Company to print and distribute his books. In 1950 he founded the Word Foundation to perpetuate his teachings. The company and foundation have continued in the years since Percival's death on March 6, 1953.

Sources:

Percival, Harold W. *Democracy Is Self-Government.* New York: Word Publishing, 1952.

———. *Man and Woman and Child.* New York: Word Publishing, 1951.

———. *Masonry and Its Symbols.* New York: Word Publishing, 1952.

———. *Thinking of Destiny.* New York: Word Publishing, 1946.

Perelandra

Title of a 1943 science fiction story by British Christian writer C. S. Lewis, denoting Venus, planet of perfection. The book deals with the play between the forces of good and evil, and the need to resolve this conflict with harmonious balance.

The name Perelandra has also been given to a garden established by Machaelle Small Wright and Clarence Wright covering some twenty-two acres near Jeffersonton, Virginia. The garden is the showpiece of the Wrights' Center for Nature Research, which seeks to harmonize the forces of nature in a joint creative process between the Wrights, nature spirits (or **fairies**) and **devas** (divine intelligences). Perelandra has been compared to the experimental **Findhorn Community,** Scotland, U.K., which has also claimed gardening success due to cooperation between human beings and nature spirits. In fact, books on Findhorn stimulated the Wrights to experiment with Perelandra.

Machaelle Wright believes that *devas* are the architects of growth in nature: if they are contacted through **meditation,** they will facilitate harmonious growth, communicating instructions for seed choice and planting, arrangement of intervening space, and other data. Wright distinguishes between *devas* and nature spirits. The latter are "more dense in vibration" and closer to the earth, whereas the *devas* guide the overall development of plant forms.

Perelandra is laid out in eighteen concentric circles, the innermost circle being a herb ring with a large quartz crystal in the center. The garden does not use chemical or organic repellents of any description, but produces unusually attractive flowers and vegetables without pest problems.

In the summer of 1986, writer P. M. H. Atwater visited Perelandra. At that time, this area of Virginia had been officially declared a drought disaster, but the vegetables and roses of Perelandra flourished without added moisture. Various neighbors who did not share the Wrights' belief in nature spirits nevertheless commented that the garden always looked great and produced good food. One remarked, "It's not normal."

Wright has refreshingly original concepts of a harmonious balance between insects, weather, climate, and soil in nature. She is quoted as saying:

"What I am finding that works best is a garden which constantly changes, that is free to breathe and grow on its own without set rules. An organic garden will selectively repel some life but an energy garden repels nothing and includes everything. It took me a long time to learn that . . . once animals and insects realize they don't have to fight for their lives, that they are free to live and grow, their aggression subsides and they regulate themselves! I had a rabbit living in the herb ring for several years. It never did any damage. I've had turtles, skunks, and all manner of animals living in the garden without difficulty. My few Japanese beetles, for instance, stick to the same flower and leave the others alone now that they are no longer threatened with extinction." Wright leaves ten percent of all produce for animal or insect consumption, and certain sections of land are also left unmowed for their benefit."

Perelandra is open for day-long tours and occasionally sponsors workshops. For information on activities and visiting, write Perelandra, Box 136, Jeffersonton, VA 22724. (See also **crystal healing**)

Sources:

Atwater, P. M. H. "The Magic of Perelandra." *East-West* (August 1986).

Wright, Machaelle S. *Behaving As If the God in All Life Mattered.* N.p., 1983.

———. *The Perelandra Garden Workbook.* N.p., 1987.

"Perfect Sermon"

A Hermetic book. (See **Hermes Trismegistus; hermetica**)

Perfumes

Perfumes are substances, generally made by blending plant oils, selected animal secretions, and synthetic chemicals, to produce a pleasant odor. Such substances were highly valued and sought after throughout human history, especially before regular bathing and the widespread use of deodorants altered the significance of human body odors. During earlier centuries, for a body to smell of a pleasant odor was noteworthy. Modern medicine has observed that in certain illnesses the skin gives out a scent of violets, pineapple, and musk, among others.

Whatever the explanation may be, this observation helps one understand the perfumes produced by mediums and makes the phrase "the **odor of sanctity**" appear in a new light. Christian saints are said to exhale a sweet perfume which increases at **death** and may remain for weeks, months, or even years afterwards. When the body of St. Casimir, Patron of Poland, was exhumed in 1603, 120 years after his death, it was found entire and exhaled a sweet smell. St. Cajetan emitted the scent of orange blossoms, St. Francis that of musk. Other saints stated to have given forth fragrance include St. Clare of Ferriol (660 C.E.), St. Hermann of Britanny (714 C.E.) and St. Patrick (461 C.E.).

Some Hindu yogis are credited with the ability to create perfumes by miraculous means. In his famous book *Bengal Lancer* (1930), F. Yeats-Brown described his encounter with a Mahatma named Babu Bisudhanan Dhan at Puri, Calcutta. With nothing more than a magnifying-glass and a piece of cotton-wool, the Mahatma conjured perfumes out of the air by focusing light on the cotton-wool through the glass. Each scent was waved away with the hand, to be succeeded by the next request. He produced in quick succession the scents of violets, musk, sandalwood, opium, heliotrope, flowering bamboo, nicotine plant, jasmine, and even cow-dung. A later book, *Naked Ascetic* by Victor Dane (1933), described a Tantric yogi in Bhawanipore who produced on request the smell of violets on Dane's handkerchief without it leaving Dane's hand; the perfume lasted for twelve hours.

In the records of **William Stainton Moses,** we find highly illustrative experiences recorded. For example, at the closing of a séance, scents were often found to be issuing out of his head. The more they were wiped away, the stronger and more plentiful they became. The most common scents were musk, verbena, new-mown hay and an unfamiliar odor which was assumed to be a "spirit scent." During the séance it usually came down in showers. On Dr. Stanhope Templeman Speer's request a good tablespoonful was once poured into a glass. Moses was fully aware that his body played an important part in the production of scents. He wrote on July 4, 1874:

"While in the garden, before we began to sit, I was conscious of scent all round me, especially on my hair. When I rubbed my hair my hand was scented strongly. I tried the experiment many times. When the peppermint came I was conscious of its presence first near my head, and it seemed, as it were, to be evolved out of the hair. I have before noticed the same thing, but not so markedly on this occasion."

He suspected that the process was remedial, as the scent from his scalp was most marked when he was suffering pain. He believed that scents were employed to harmonize conditions. As he noted,

"If a new sitter is present, he or she is sensed, and so initiated. The chair which the stranger occupies is surrounded by luminous haze, from which issues the perfume; and very frequently wet scent, more or less pungent, according to conditions, is sprinkled from the ceiling at the same time. If a new intelligence is to communicate, or special honour to be paid to a chief, the room is pervaded by perfume which grows stronger as the spirit enters. This scenting of the room in which we are about to meet will sometimes commence many hours before we begin. There is a subtle odour in it which is perpetually being changed. Sometimes the aroma of a flower from the garden is drawn out, intensified, and insinuated throughout the house. Sometimes the odour is like nothing of this earth's production, ethereal, delicate, and infinitely delightful. Sandalwood used to be a favourite, and rose, verbena, and odours of other flowers have been plentifully used.

"I find it difficult to convey any idea of the subtle odours that have been diffused throughout the room, or of the permanence of the scent. It is usually the first manifestation and the last. The perfume is sprinkled in showers from the ceiling, and borne in waves of cool air round the circle, especially when the atmosphere is close and the air oppressive. Its presence in a particular place is shown to me by the luminous haze which accompanies it. I can trace its progress round the circle by the light . . . and can frequently say to a certain sitter: 'You will smell the scent directly. I see the luminous form going to you.' My vision has always been confirmed by the exclamations of delight which follow.

"When we first observed this manifestation, it was attended by a great peculiarity. The odour was circumscribed in space, confined to a belt or band, beyond which it did not penetrate. It surrounded the circle to a few feet, and outside of that belt was not perceptible; or it was drawn across the room as a cordon, so that it was possible to walk into it and out of it again—the presence and absence of the odour and the temperature of the air which accompanied it being most marked. . . . Within it the temperature was cool and the scent strong, outside of it the air was decidedly warmer, and no trace of the perfume was perceptible. It was no question of fancy. The scent was too strong for that.

"I have known the same phenomenon to occur in the open air. I have been walking with a friend, for instance, and we have walked into air laden with scent, and through it again into the natural atmosphere . . . I have even known cases where wet scent has been produced and showered down in the open air. On one special occasion, in the Isle of Wight, my attention was attracted by the patter of some fine spray on a lady's [Mrs. Speer's] silk dress, as we were walking along a road. One side of the dress was plentifully besprinkled with fine spray, which gave forth a delicious odour, very clearly perceptible for some distance round.

"During a séance the scent is either carried, as it seems, round the circle, and is then accompanied by cool air, or it is sprinkled down from the ceiling of the room in liquid form. In the clairvoyant state I am able to see and describe the process before the scent is sprinkled, and can warn a special sitter not to look upwards. For, on certain occasions, when conditions are not favourable, the scent is pungent and most painful if it gets into my eye, and it has caused no more pain than water would. On the contrary, I have seen the effect caused on another [Mrs. Speer] by a similar occurrence. The pain caused was excruciating, the inflammation was most severe, and the effects did not pass off for 24 hours or more. In fact, whatever the liquid was, it caused severe conjunctivitis.

"This variety in the pungency and potency of perfume I attribute to variety in the attendant circumstances. The illness of one of the sitters will cause the scent to become coarse and pungent. Harmonious conditions, physical and mental, are signalised by the presence of delicate subtle odours which are infinitely charming. I have said that sometimes the odour of flowers, either in the house or garden, will be intensified. A vase of fresh flowers put on the table causes the natural perfume in this way. We used frequently to gather fresh flowers, and watch the process. Flowers which had a very slight smell when gathered would, by degrees, throw off such a perfume as to fill the room and strike anyone who came into it most forcibly. In this case the natural odour of the flower was intensified and the bloom received no harm. At other times, however, some liquid was apparently put upon the blossom, and an odour, not its own given to it. In that case it invariably withered and died very rapidly. I have frequently had flowers in my buttonhole scented in this way.

"Great quantities of dry musk have been from time to time thrown about in the house where our circle meets. On a late occasion it fell in very considerable quantities over a writing-desk at which a lady was sitting in the act of writing letters. It was mid-day, and no one was near at the time, yet the particles of musk were so numerous as to pervade the whole contents of the desk. They were placed, for no throwing would have produced such a result, at the very bottom of the desk, and between the papers which it contained. The odour was most pronounced; and the particles, when gathered together, made up a considerable packet. Some time after this when at a séance, I saw something which looked like luminous dust on the table. No odour was perceptible, but in my clairvoyant state I saw a heap of luminous particles which appeared to be extremely brilliant. I described it, and putting out my hand I found that there was really a heap on the table. I inquired what it was and musk was rapped out. We demurred, for no odour was perceptible, but the statement was reiterated. After the séance we gathered up the dust, which looked like musk, but had no smell whatsoever. The next morning, however, the odour was powerful enough; and the powder still exists, and is indubitably a very good powdered musk. By what imaginable process can that phenomenon have been accomplished?"

The scents were not always welcome. In his note of July 4, 1874, Moses referred to a pungent odor of peppermint which was very unpleasant. Stanhope Speer described this happening more outspokenly:

"The other evening a newcomer slipped in, and stank us out of the room by throwing down from the ceiling a large quantity of Sp. Pulegii. Everything that it touched was impregnated for 24 hours. The dining-room cloth and my own nether habiliments had to be exposed to view in the back garden; and on the following morning our dining-room floor and passage had to be freely fumigated with pastilles. That spirit has not been invited to join us again."

The experience suggests that the stench observed in some curious cases of haunting have a similar cause. Dr. **Justinus Kerner** recorded the case of Frau Eslinger who, in 1835, in the prison of Weinberg, was visited and talked to by a ghost that emitted an intolerable stench, felt by many others, as well.

The sickening stench of a charnel house was reported in a house near London (*Daily Chronicle,* April 15, 1908). On examination it was revealed that a body had been left unburied in the house until advanced putrefaction had occurred.

Florence Marryat wrote about the phantom "Lenore" of **Mary Showers:** "On one occasion . . . there was a charnel house smell about her, as if she had been buried a few weeks and dug up again. . . . One evening at Mrs. Gregory's . . . I nearly fainted from the smell. It resembled nothing but that of a putrid corpse, and when she returned to the cabinet, I was compelled to leave the room and retch from the nausea it had caused me."

The medium **Carlos Mirabelli** of São Paolo once produced a skeleton via **materialization.** An odor as that of a cadaver was emitted from his body.

The withdrawal of the scents of flowers of which Moses wrote was the only physical phenomenon known in **Leonora Piper**'s mediumship. "Mrs. Piper's fingers," wrote **Richard Hodgson,** "moved near the flower, as if withdrawing something from it; and in a few hours it had withered."

Lord Adare witnessed the famous medium **D. D. Home** extending his hand towards the flowers on a small table, the fingers pointing towards them. "His hand remained there for few seconds, and was then brought round, and with a motion like sprinkling, cast the perfume of the flowers towards each of us in turn; the perfume was so strong that there could be no mistake about it. This was done twice. Home then made some very curious experiments with flowers; he separated the scent into two portions—one odor smelling exactly like earth; the other being sweet.

Essences were also similarly withdrawn,

"I am going to take the strength from the brandy—and he began to make passes over the glass and flipping his fingers, sending a strong smell of spirit through the room; in about five minutes he had made the brandy as weak as very weak brandy and water, it scarcely tasted at all of spirit; both Lindsay and I tasted it, at the moment, and also some time after the séance was over.

"He withdrew the acid flavour from a half a lemon, freshly cut and tasted. He held it up above his head; a yellowish light came over it, and when offered to taste again the lemon was found most disagreeable, the flavour was like magnesia or washing soda. He then restored the acid. Holding it up, a rose coloured flame came over it. After a little while, he offered it and it was found all right." (See *Experiences in Spiritualism with D. D. Home* by Viscount Adare [1870]).

The psychical researcher Dr. **Joseph Maxwell** found the luminous phenomena of the medium **Eusapia Palladino** at the sittings of Choisy not very convincing because a strong aroma of phosphorus permeated the room. Later, however, he found this odor characteristic and discovered that it was more like the odor of ozone than that of phosphorus. It was like the odor perceptible in the vicinity of frictional electrical machines when in activity.

It is curious to note that this smell often disturbed clairvoyants during their visions. **Emanuel Swedonborg** was one of the first to record his annoyance over it. In the **poltergeist** disturbance of the **Drummer of Tedworth** in 1661, the manifestations were sometimes accompanied by "a bloomy noisome smell" as of sulphur.

There are early records of paranormal scents in the correspondence of Dr. **G. P. Billot** with J. P. F. Deleuze in 1839. Billot stated that superior intelligences presented themselves through his somnambules, presided at séances, and manifested themselves by the delicious odors which they diffused around them.

In the séances of the medium **David Duguid,** perfumes were administered to one sitter at a time, and the recipient felt the cooling odors gently blown over his face. The manifestation was not confined to the séance room; it was sometimes experienced in the open air.

Among later mediums in whose séances the phenomenon was often recorded the Marquis **Centurione Scotto** and **Mina Crandon** ("Margery") stand foremost.

Sources:

Dane, Victor. *Naked Ascetic.* N.p., 1933.

Dunraven, Windham Thomas Wyndham Quin. *Experiences in Spiritualism with D. D. Home.* 1871. Reprint, New York: Arno Press, 1976.

Kennett, Frances. *History of Perfume.* London: Harrap, 1975.

Thompson, C. J. S. *The Mystery and Lure of Perfume.* London: J. Lane; Detroit: Singing Tree Press, 1969.

Yeats-Brown, F. *Bengal Lancer.* London: V. Gollancz Ltd., 1930. Reprinted as *The Life of a Bengal Lancer.* New York: Viking Press: 1931.

Perispirit

The term applied by Spiritist **Allan Kardec** to denote the spirit body.

Pernety, Antoine Joseph (1716–1801)

Author of the *Dictionnaire Mytho-Hermetique* (1787) and *Les Fables Egyptiennes et Grecques* (1758). According to Pernety, the Golden Fleece in the Jason-Medea legend is symbolic. The labors of Jason represent human strivings towards perfection.

Perovsky-Petrovo-Solovovo, Count (1868–1954)

Distinguished Russian-born psychical researcher. He was born Michael Solovioy, succeeded to the title of Count, and was generally known as "Count Solovovo" among members of the **Society for Psychical Research,** London. He joined the society in 1890 at a time when it had commenced the collection of cases for the important **Census of Hallucinations** (published in vol. 10 of the society's *Proceedings*), and he contributed Russian cases to this project.

He investigated the Russian medium **S. F. Sambor** and uncovered his methods of producing phenomena by **fraud,** and in 1910 he cooperated with **Everard Feilding** and W. Marriott in sittings with the famous medium **Eusapia Palladino** in Naples. He reported on these sittings in *Proceedings* of the SPR (vol. 25, pp. 57–69). He took a special interest in the question of whether competent researchers, qualified to detect fraud, might still be influenced by illusions induced by séance room conditions. He also contributed to the SPR *Proceedings* and *Journal* on such topics as **extrasensory perception** and the medium **D. D. Home.** He also reviewed for the *Journal* those continental journals devoted to psychical research. He was honorary secretary for Russia for the society for many years. In view of his eminent services, the society conferred honorary membership upon him.

In 1936, he moved to London and in his later years acquired British citizenship.

Sources:

Berger, Arthur S., and Joyce Berger. *The Encyclopedia of Parapsychology and Psychical Research.* New York: Paragon House, 1991.

Perovsky-Petrovo-Solovovo, Count. "My Experiments with S. F. Sambor." *Journal* of the Society for Psychical Research 30 (1937).

———. "On the Production of Spurious 'Spirit Raps.' " *Journal* of the Society for Psychical Research 6 (1893).

Perriman, Florence (Mrs. A. E. Perriman) (d. 1936)

Voice medium tested by **Nandor Fodor,** who was not favorably impressed at the time. Perriman's séance at Victoria Hall, London, is described in Fodor's book *The Haunted Mind* (1959) and was also reported in the *Psychic News* of May 4, 1936.

Florence Perriman, also known by her married name, Mrs. A. E. Perriman, spent many years of her life as a society clairvoyant, using the professional name Madame Faustina. She was consulted by famous stars of stage and screen, including Esme Percy, Ivor Novello, Viola Tree, Isabel Jeans, and Gladys Cooper. She died in 1936.

Sources:

Fodor, Nandor. *The Haunted Mind.* New York: Garrett Publications, 1959.

Perriman, A. E. *Broadcasting From Beyond.* London, 1952.

Perriman, Florence. *Secrets of a Famous Clairvoyante.* London, 1936.

Perrott-Warrick Research Unit

The Perrott-Warrick Research Unit, a parapsychological research program located within the Psychology Department at the University of Hertfordshire in England, was launched in 1995 following Richard Wiseman's reception of a Perrott-Warrick Fellowship (administered by Trinity College Cambridge). Wiseman, a practicing stage magician, had received his Ph.D. in psychology from Edinburgh University before joining the faculty at Hertfordshire. Since receiving the fellowship, he has launched a multifaceted research program that includes probes into the paranormal, intuition, **false memory syndrome,** and lying and deception. He has also worked on promoting the public understanding of science and has frequently appeared on television discussing his research and related topics. In 1998 he brought together psychologists, historians, magicians, and professional actors to stage "Séance," a show that encouraged the public to think critically about claims of the paranormal, and the following year he was awarded Britain's first Readership in the Public Understanding of Psychology.

To carry out his research, Wiseman has assembled a team of doctoral students, each of which are exploring different topics under his supervision. Emma Greening, while pursuing a Ph.D. in psychology, possesses a scholarship funded by the **Society for Psychical Research** and is conducting a research project on belief in the paranormal and the development of false memories. Before beginning her graduate program, she had been the editor of *The Paranormal Review* (for the Society for Psychical Research), and she serves as secretary of its research activities committee.

Ciaran James O'Keefe completed his master's thesis on the utility of psychic detectives and analyzed the style of their narrative, which he concluded tended to convince the listener that there was a higher degree of accuracy in the psychic words than actually existed. Building on this research, he is currently researching the discourse that occurs in psychic readings, both mediumistic session and phone sessions on psychic hotlines. Paul Rogers is working on people with reputed intuitive powers. He is testing their ability to size up other people's personality relative to the ability of nonintuitive people. In the process, he is trying to discover which factors convince a person of his/her own intuitive abilities.

The Perrott-Warrick Research Unit may be reached c/o Psychology Department, University of Hertfordshire, Hatfield Campus, University of Hertfordshire, College Lane, Hatfield, Herts, AL10 9AB, England. The unit has an Internet site at http://phoenix.herts.ac.uk/PWRU/hmpage.html.

Sources:

The Perrott-Warrick Research Unit. http://phoenix.herts.ac.uk/PWRU/hmpage.html. May 23, 2000.

Perry, Michael C(harles) (1933–)

British clergyman concerned with parapsychology. He was Born June 5, 1933, at Ashby-de-la-Zouch, Leicestershire, England. He studied at Trinity College, Cambridge University, England (first class honors in natural sciences and theology). He obtained his B.A. in 1955, his M.A. in 1959, and was ordained as a priest of the Church of England in 1959.

In 1963, he was appointed chief assistant for publishing at the Society for the Promotion of Christian Knowledge, London. He has written a number of books, edited the series "Mowbray's Library of Theology," and has contributed articles and reviews to various theological journals. He also served as Secretary to the Archbishops, Commission on Christian Doctrine (1967–1971). Perry was made assistant editor of report of the Lambeth Conference of Anglican Bishops in 1968 and became senior editor in 1978. He became student associate (1951) and later a member of the **Society for Psychical Research,** London, and also became a member of the **Churches' Fellowship for Psychical and Spiritual Studies.** He was coeditor of the fellowship's periodical, *Christian Parapsychologist,* for a year (1977–78) prior to becoming editor in 1978. He is particularly interested in the relationship between parapsychology and Christianity, about which he has written a number of articles.

Sources:

Berger, Arthur S., and Joyce Berger. *The Encyclopedia of Parapsychology and Psychical Research.* New York: Paragon

House, 1991. Perry, Michael C. *Crisis for Confirmation.* N.p., 1967.

———. *The Eastern Enigma.* N.p., 1959.

———. *Meet the Prayer Book.* N.p., 1963.

———. "A New View of the Resurrection." *Tomorrow* (Summer 1954).

———. "Parapsychology in Apologetics." *Church Quarterly Review* (January 1959).

———. *The Pattern of Matins & Evensong.* N.p., 1961.

———. *The Resurrection of Man.* N.p., 1975.

———. *Sharing in One Bread.* N.p., 1980.

Personality

Term that has three uses in describing the self: (1) the sum of the characteristics that make up physical and mental being, including appearance, manners, habits, tastes, and moral character; (2) the characteristics that distinguish one person from another (individuality); and (3) the capacity to engage in mental processes, that is, possessing consciousness (according to psychical researcher **James H. Hyslop**).

For psychical researchers, this last definition is of primary importance. The question of **survival** after death cannot be decided until the continuance of personality as a stream of consciousness is proved. A stream of consciousness is proof of the presence of a personality.

The identity of this personality, however, is inseparably bound up with the faculty of remembrance. With a complete loss of memory a new personality will develop. If the former memory returns, the new personality tends to disappear. It may be resuscitated by another attack of amnesia or under hypnosis, in which case it will act as an independent personality.

The case of Anselm Bourne, investigated by **William James** and **Richard Hodgson** in 1890, is illustrative. Bourne suddenly lost his memory in 1887 in Providence, Rhode Island, and eight weeks later awoke in Norristown, Pennsylvania, as a shopkeeper. He knew nothing of Albert John Brown, the name under which he lived, nor of the shop or the business. In hypnosis a secondary personality came forward and Bourne's movements were satisfactorily traced from the moment of his disappearance.

This was a plainly degenerative case. Bourne suffered from a postepileptic condition. He had fits of depression from childhood and in later life presented symptoms suggestive of epilepsy. Such degenerative instances are numerous. In other cases the secondary state is an improvement on the primary one.

F. W. H. Myers gave an account of such a case, that of a Dr. Azam's patient, "Felida X." She was born in Bordeaux, France, in 1843, exhibited symptoms of hysteria around age 13, felt pains in her forehead and fell into a profound sleep, from which she awoke in a secondary condition. Whereas in her original condition she exhibited a melancholy disposition, constantly thought of her maladies, and suffered acute pain in various parts of her body, in the secondary state she appeared to be an entirely different person, happy and free from pain.

Such changes at first occurred every five or six days and were marked by a more complete development of her faculties. Her memory in the secondary state was continuous. This state was her lucid one; the primary state was marked by fits of melancholy. The secondary personality became more frequent and, relapses of short duration disregarded, slowly suppressed the melancholy one.

Multiple Personality

A well-developed secondary personality is often followed by the appearance of other personalities. As many as 11 personalities were recorded in the case of "Mary Barnes" (see *Journal* of the Society for Psychical Research, vol. 11, p. 231; vol. 12, p. 208). They may come and go, like lodgers in a tenement house. Among the better-investigated cases of multiple personality in the literature of psychical research was that of a Miss Beauchamp, discussed by **Morton Prince** in *Dissociation of a Personality* (1906). Under emotional shocks, Beauchamp developed four personalities antithetic to her original one. They not only differed markedly in health, in memories, and in knowledge of their own life, but they were formally at war with one another. The third personality, "Sally," was the most interesting. She had all the appearance of an invading, outside entity. She wrote her autobiography, in which she claimed conscious but suppressed existence as far back as Beauchamp's infancy. She had a will of her own, could hypnotize the other personalities, had no notion of time, and exhibited complete tactile anesthesia. She persistently said that she was a spirit.

Prince attempted with hypnotic suggestion to weld the four personalities into one. Sally was bitterly resistant. After a long struggle and much reasoning, however, she agreed to be "squeezed" out of existence, and Beauchamp was restored to one personality commanding the memories of all her former selves with the exception of Sally.

In the remarkable case of Doris Fischer, Prince had to deal with five personalities. They were called "Real Doris," "Margaret," "Sleeping Margaret," "Sick Doris," and "Sleeping Doris." Real Doris barely had five minutes' conscious existence a day. The alternating personalities were veritably chasing after one another for years. After lengthy efforts, Prince finally effected a cure.

In the October 1931 issue of the British medical journal *The Lancet,* a case of eight distinct personalities is recorded by Robert M. Riggall, clinical psychologist at the West End Hospital of Nervous Diseases, London. The personalities were (1) "Mabel," the patient herself—good, composed, moral, and economical, without many faults, but usually unhappy; (2) "Miss Dignity," who considered it her duty to do all in her power to hurt Mabel. Miss Dignity went so far in her hostility as to write a letter to Mabel, urging her to commit suicide and saying that she had enclosed a packet of poison; (3) "Biddy"—bright, cheerful, laughing, and helpful; (4) "Hope"; (5) "Faith"; and (6) "Dame Trot," who were harmless and seldom appeared; (7) "Miss Take," so named because she did not know when she first appeared or what her name was, and added that she was just a mistake; and (8) another unnamed personality of an evil stripe.

Slight causes such as hunger, fatigue, or fever are sometimes sufficient to produce a transient but violent perturbation of personality. The novelist Robert Louis Stevenson, if ill or feverish, always felt possessed in part of his mind by another personality. According to **Frank Podmore,** overindulgence in daydreams is probably the first indication of a tendency to isolated and unregulated psychic activity, which, in its extreme form, may develop into a fixed idea or an obsession. **Theodore Flournoy** added:

"As a crystal splits under the blow of a hammer when struck according to certain definite lines of cleavage, in the same way the human personality under the shock of excessive emotions is sometimes broken along the lines of least resistance or the great structural lines of his temperament. A cleavage is produced between the opposite selves—whose harmonious equilibrium would constitute the normal condition—seriousness and gaiety; optimistic tendencies and pessimistic; goodness and egoism; instincts of prudery and lasciviousness; the taste for solitude and the love of Nature, and the attractions of civilization, etc. The differences, in which the spiritists see a striking proof of an absolute distinction between the spirits and their so-called instruments, awaken, on the contrary, in the mind of the psychologist the irresistible suspicion that these pretended spirits can be nothing but the products of the subconsciousness of the medium himself."

F. W. H. Myers argued that the first symptom of disintegration of personality is an *idée fixe,* the persistence of an uncontrolled and unmodifiable group of thoughts or emotions, which, from their brooding isolation, from lack of interchange with the general current of thought, become alien and intrusive, so that some special idea or image presses into consciousness with undue and painful infrequency. (Such a fixed idea has also, of course, led to some of the major new contributions by individuals to society.)

In the second stage, Myers maintained, there is a confluence of these obsessive notions overrunning the whole personality, often accompanied by something of a somnambulic change. This is the birth of the secondary personality from emotionally selected elements of the primary personality. It may attain a morbid intensity, and it may lead to so-called demonic possession. In other cases, arbitrary development of a scrap of personality is responsible for the dissociation. Its most common mode of origin, Myers believed, is in sleepwalking that is repeated until the mind acquires a chain of memories related exclusively to the sleepwalking state; this chain then alternates with the primary chain.

Sleepwalkers may display a secondary personality as the acts in repeated spontaneous **somnambulism** form a chain of memory. Considering the wide power and tenacious memory of the subconscious, Myers suggested that the conscious personality should be regarded as a privileged case of personality, a special phase, easiest to study because it is accessible. Its powers of perception he similarly considered a special case of the subliminal faculties.

The question of secondary personalities is unanswered, in spite of continued research over the decades. No single explanation has emerged as dominant. Within the psychic community, interest has centered on cases that seem to provide some evidence of possession or obsession by spirit entities or **reincarnation.** Many cases appear to be a matter of abnormal psychology in which artificial personalities are created from repressed desires, anxieties, or traumas. The question has been the center of a new debate within the psychological community with the emergence of a new set of multiple personality cases claiming origin in childhood trauma from ritual sexual abuse.

Much obscurity surrounds the development of normal personality in individuals, a situation likely to remain the case given the aversion of psychologists to researching personality using models with large groups of people. Character traits often change during the course of time. Many apparently normal individuals sometimes present different personalities in public from those exhibited in private.

The maintenance of a recognizable personality depends heavily on accumulated experiences and memories (the most obvious attribute of an individual personality) and the reassurance of a familiar body and sensory perception. If one grants the possibility of survival after death, the sudden removal of memories, sensory associations, and bodily presence must be a traumatic experience. The confusing or vague messages relating to identity received at many séances could be explained on this basis. Even the triviality of many communications seems explicable, since the departed spirit might place great value on such trivialities as reassurance of a continuation of personality.

How real are our personalities? Fantasy plays a great part in the maintenance of personality, nourished by the myriad fictions of novels, movies, and television shows. Our personalities have been shaped by fashion and role models that have had powerful influence through the modern mass media society. Talented actors and actresses have shown that it is possible to change roles night after night in a physical and psychological masquerade that becomes an intensely shared experience with an audience.

The larger implications of personality involve philosophies and religions, which often differ markedly in their understanding of personality. The imperfections and contradictions of earthly personality constitute unfinished chapters in the fascinating story of life, and it is reasonable to postulate sequels in an afterlife involving progressive evolution of personality.

Sources:

Bernstein, Morey. *The Search for Bridey Murphy.* Garden City, N.Y.: Doubleday, 1956.

Blythe, Henry. *The Three Lives of Naomi Henry.* London: Frederick Muller, 1956.

Congdon, M. H., J. Hain, and Ian Stevenson. "A Case of Multiple Personality Illustrating the Transition from Role-Playing." *Journal of Nervous and Mental Disease* 132 (1961).

Flournoy, Theodore. *From India to the Planet Mars.* New York: Harper & Row, 1900. Reprint, New Hyde Park, N.Y.: University Books, 1963.

Geley, Gustav. *From the Unconscious to the Conscious.* London: William Collins, 1920.

Iverson, Jeffrey. *More Lives Than One?* London: Souvenir Press, 1976. Reprint, London: Pan, 1967.

Mitchell, T. W. *Medical Psychology and Psychical Research.* London: Methuen, 1922.

Myers, F. W. H. *Human Personality and Its Survival of Bodily Death.* 2 vols. London: Longmans, Green, 1903. Reprint, New York: Longmans, 1954.

Oesterreich, T. K. *Possession: Demoniacal and Other, Among Primitive Races, in Antiquity, the Middle Ages, and Modern Times.* London, 1930. Reprint, New Hyde Park, N.Y.: University Books, 1966.

Prince, Morton. *The Dissociation of a Personality.* London: Longmans, 1906.

Solfvin, J., W. G. Roll, and E. F. Kelly. "A Psychophysical Study of Mediumistic Communications." In *Research in Parapsychology, 1976,* edited by J. D. Morris, W. G. Roll, and R. L. Morris. Metuchen, N.J.: Scarecrow Press, 1977.

Stevens, E. W. *The Watseka Wonder.* Chicago: Religion-Philosophical Journal, 1879.

Stevenson, Ian. *Twenty Cases Suggestive of Reincarnation.* New York: American Society for Psychical Research, 1966.

Thigpen, C. H., and H. Cleckley. *The Three Faces of Eve.* New York: McGraw-Hill, 1957.

Personation

The portrayal of alien personalities by a temporary assumption of their bodily and mental characteristics. It is a frequent psychical phenomenon and differs from **trance** possession in that it does not necessarily involve a loss of consciousness or personal identity.

Personation is an impressive indication of the communicator's identity. It is an indication rather than proof, as experiments in **hypnotism** suggest the need for careful consideration in attributing the phenomena of personation to an outside intelligence. Under the effect of suggestion, the subconscious displays surprising histrionic abilities. The hypnotized subject is not only capable of successfully imitating any suggested personality, but may even sometimes take on animal similitudes. **Charles Richet** hypnotized a friend and suggested that he was a parrot. Richet asked him: "Why do you look preoccupied?" The friend answered: "How can I eat the seed in my cage?"

Richet compared the phenomenon of personation to crystallization from a saturated solution. Remembrances and emotions concentrate upon the personality invented like crystals form around a center.

Frank Podmore, in *Modern Spiritualism* (1902), quoted a curious instance of personation verging on possession in which the subject of personation was alive.

A Miss A. B. had a passionate love affair with a young man, C. D., and continued to cherish the belief, even after the young man broke off the relationship that he was still profoundly attached to her. "A few weeks after the breach she felt one evening a curious feeling in the throat, as of choking, the prelude probably, under ordinary circumstances to an attack of hysteria. This feeling was succeeded by involuntary movements of the hands and a fit of long-continued and apparently causeless sobbing. Then, in the presence of a member of her family she became, in her own belief, possessed by the spirit of C. D., personating his words and gestures and speaking in his character. After this date she continually held conversation, as she believes, with C. D.'s spirit; 'he' sometimes speaking aloud through her mouth, sometimes conversing with her in the inner voice. Occasionally 'he' wrote messages through her hand, and I have the testimony of a member of her family that the writing so produced resembled that of C. D. Occasionally also, A. B. had visions in which she claimed to see C. D. and what he was doing at the moment. At other times she professed to hear him speaking or to understand by some inner sympathy his feelings and his thoughts." Podmore believed the phenomena to be a delusion.

An account of personation experiences was rendered by Charles Hill-Tout, principal of Buckland College, Vancouver, Canada, in *Proceedings* of the Society for Psychical Research (vol. 11, pp. 309–16). On one occasion, during a séance, he was oppressed by a feeling of coldness and loneliness, as of a recently disembodied spirit. His misery was terrible, and he was only kept from falling to the floor by some of the other sitters. At this point one of the sitters

". . . made the remark, which I remember to have overheard 'It is father controlling him,' and I then seemed to realise who I was and whom I was seeking. I began to be distressed in my lungs, and should have fallen if they had not held me by the hands and let me back gently upon the floor. As my head sunk back upon the carpet I experienced dreadful distress in my lungs and could not breathe. I made signs to them to put something under my head. They immediately put the sofa cushion under me, but this was not sufficient—I was not raised high enough yet to breathe easily—and they then added a pillow. I have the most distinct recollection of a sigh of relief I now gave as I sank back like a sick, weak person upon the cool pillow. I was in a measure still conscious of my actions, though not of my surroundings, and I have a clear memory of seeing myself in the character of my dying father lying in the bed and in the room in which he died. It was a most curious sensation. I saw his shrunken hands and face and lived again through his dying moments; only now I was both myself—in some distinct sort of way—and my father, with his feelings and appearance."

The flaw, from the viewpoint of the theory of an extraneous influence, is that Hill-Tout personated his own father with whose circumstances of death he must have been familiar. But many mediums reenact the death-bed scenes of people they have never heard of and furnish, in the process, evidential details. This was a feature of the mediumship of a Mrs. Newell of Lancashire, England. As a rule such re-enactments were accompanied by great suffering. The medium seemed to experience the symptoms of illness and the agonies of dying.

The American medium **Mrs. J. H. Conant,** was recorded once to have shown the signs of hydrophobia; she foamed at the mouth and snapped at the sitters. The man whom she personated had died from the bite of a mad dog.

People who practice **pychometry** also exhibit this curious phenomenon. The object which they hold as a clue may establish a community of sensation with both men and beasts. Mrs. Denton, in describing her impressions from a fragment of mastodon tooth felt herself to be in the body of the monster, although she could not very well personate it. Personation of a dying animal, through **telepathy,** was illustrated by the vivid dream of the novelist **H. Rider Haggard** on the night when his dog Bob was struck and killed by a train.

If the assumption of the bodily characteristics of the departed is effected by the adaptation of **ectoplasm,** as in **materialization** séances, the case is known as **transfiguration.** (See also **personality; trance personalities**)

Perty, Maximilian (ca. 1861)

Professor at the University of Berne who suggested that the supernormal manifestations of mediums were caused by communion with planetary spirits through an unconscious exercise of latent occult powers.

Sources:

Perty, Maximilian. *Die Mystischen Erscheinungen der menschlichen Natur.* Leipzig, 1861.

Pessomancy (or Psephomancy)

A system of **divination** using pebbles or beans marked with symbols and colors relating to issues such as health, communications, success, and travel. The stones were either thrown out after shuffling in a bag or drawn out at random. (See also **aleuromancy; astragalomancy; belomancy; sortilege**)

Peter of Abano (Petrus de Abano) (1250–1318)

Famous medieval philosopher, mathematician, and astrologer who also wrote treatises on **magic.** He was born in Abano, near Padua, and became a learned scholar. He traveled widely, visiting France, Sardina, and Constantinople, and he once met the famous traveler Marco Polo, from whom he obtained information on Asia. During his travels he also discovered one of the lost books of Aristotle and translated it into Latin.

He practiced medicine in Paris with success and became rich, but his wealth and attainments were annulled by the accusation of sorcery brought against him. He was said to receive instruction in the seven liberal arts from seven spirits that he kept in crystal vessels. Other rumors claimed that he had the curious and useful ability to make the money he spent to return to his own purse.

An act of revenge, for which he was called to account by the Inquisition, brought about his downfall. A neighbor of his had been possessed of a spring of excellent water in his garden, from which he allowed Peter to drink at will. For some reason, the permission was withdrawn, and it was claimed that with the assistance of the devil, Peter caused the water to leave the garden and flow uselessly in some distant street.

The unfortunate physician died before his trial was finished, but the inquisitors were so bitter that they ordered his bones to be dug up and burned. This public indignity to his memory was averted by some of his friends, who, hearing of the vindictive sentence, secretly removed the remains from the burying-ground where they lay. The inquisitors satisfied their animosity by burning him in effigy.

Peter had a considerable literary output. He translated the astrological work *Nativities* by Abraham Aben Ezra, and wrote books on physiognomy, **geomancy, prophecy,** and the practice of occult **magic.**

Sources:

Seligman, Kurt. *The History of Magic.* New York: Pantheon Books, 1948. Reprined as: *Magic, Supernaturalism and Religion.* New York: Pantheon Books, 1971.

Peters, Alfred Vout (1867– ?)

British clairvoyant and trance **medium.** When still a child he was conscious of the presence of other ghostly children and remarked to his mother, "I suppose they are God's angels who come and play with me after you leave me?" He often had dreams that came true, saw visions, and heard voices. His mediumship began in 1895 when he attended a séance at his sister-in-law's house. Three years later he acted regularly as a medium controlled by a guide named "Moonstone."

Peters's mediumship figured in **Sir Oliver Lodge**'s book *Raymond, or Life & Death* (1916), which largely concerned séances with Peters and **Gladys Osborne Leonard.** In 1899, Peters held a séance in London in which he had the strange experience of being controlled by a living person. There were two ladies at the sitting and a third, a well-known medium, acted as the **control** of Peters from Paris. Evidential messages were reportedly given.

Peters scored some notable success in demonstrating **psychometry** in connection with the box of religious enthusiast **Joanna Southcott** at the **National Laboratory of Psychical Research** in 1927, before the box was officially opened by psychical researcher **Harry Price.**

Phantasmagoria

Term generally used for a shifting series of imaginary or fantastic images as seen in a dream or fevered imagination. The term appears to have been derived from a magic lantern entertainment presented in 1802 by the Frenchman M. Philipstal. Variants of the term have been used to describe the appearance of phantoms, as in the collection of stories by Jean Baptiste Eyries, *Fantasmagoriana, or Collection of the Histories of Apparitions, Spectres, Ghosts, etc.* (1812). This was the volume that Lord Byron read aloud to Percy Shelley, Mary Wollstonecraft (later Mary Shelley), Claire Clairmont, and J. W. Polidori on the night of June 16, 1816, which, along with the consumption of opium, stimulated their imaginations after Byron suggested that each should write a ghost story. The game culminated in Mary Shelley's **Frankenstein,** first published in 1818.

Sources:

Eyries, Jean Baptiste. *Fantasmagoriana, or Collection of the Histories of Apparitions, Spectres, Ghosts, etc.* Paris: F. Schoell, 1812.

Phelps, Eliakim (fl. 1850)

Presbyterian minister and early mesmeric healer of Stratford, Connecticut, whose house was the scene of alarming **poltergeist** disturbances from March 10, 1850, for a period of eight months. The documents on the phenomena consist mostly of letters written to the *New Haven Journal* during the progress of the events. Additional testimony from neighbors was collected and published by C. W. Elliott in his book *Mysteries or Glimpses of the Supernatural* (1852).

The phenomena started with the mysterious displacement of objects when the family was at church. After their return, inanimate things began to fly about and stuffed effigies were discovered in empty rooms.

The following letter in the *New Haven Journal* describes the early activity:

"While the house of Dr. Phelps was undergoing a rigid examination from cellar to attic, one of the chambers were mysteriously fitted up with eleven figures of angelic beauty, gracefully and imposingly arranged, so as to have the appearance of life. They were all female figures but one, and most of them in attitudes of devotion, with Bibles before them, and pointing to different passages with the apparent design of making the Scriptures sanction and confirm the strange things that were going on. . . .

"Some of the figures were kneeling beside the beds, and some bending their faces to the floor in attitudes of deep humility. In the center of the group was a dwarf, most grotesquely arrayed; and above was a figure so suspended as to seem flying through the air. These manifestations occurred sometimes when the room was locked, and sometimes when it was known that no person had been there. Measures were taken to have a special scrutiny in regard to every person who entered the room that day, and it is known with the most perfect certainty that many of these figures were constructed when there were no persons in the room, and no visible power by which they could have been produced. The *tout ensemble* was most beautiful and picturesque, and had a grace and ease and speaking effect that seemed the attributes of a higher creation."

The effigies were constructed from clothing and other materials in the house, stuffed with pillows to represent human figures.

The *New Haven Journal* correspondence reported that on another occasion, Phelps was writing in his room alone. For a moment he turned away, and resuming his seat he found the sheet of paper, which was quite clean before, now covered with strange-looking writing, the ink still wet. Thus began spirit correspondences to him which mostly came in hieroglyphs. Jocular messages on scraps of paper fluttered down from the ceiling. Other communications were scrawled on walls inside and outside the house. In one case, mysterious symbols were inscribed on a large turnip.

Phelps never discovered how the phenomena were produced. "I witnessed them," he said, "hundreds and hundreds of times, and I know that in hundreds of instances they took place when there was no visible power by which the motion could have been produced."

The family had four children: two girls; Harry, a stepson of eleven; and another son of six years of age. The phenomena mostly seemed to attach themselves to Harry. In one case, his bed was set on fire. When he was sent to school in Philadelphia he was pursued there, his books destroyed, and his clothes torn. There was such an uproar in the school that he had to be brought home. One of the girls also had some invisible share in the disturbances. When both Harry and she were away, peace reigned in the house.

Andrew Jackson Davis, the pioneer Spiritualist medium, paid a visit to the house. His explanation was that the raps were produced by discharges of vital electricity from Harry's being. Indeed he attributed an actual share in the phenomena to Harry, in saying: "Young Harry frequently failed to discriminate during certain moments of mental agitation between the sounds and effects which he himself made and those sounds which were produced by spiritual presence." Davis also offered lofty spiritual interpretations of the symbolic communications. (See also **Ashtabula Poltergeist; Cock Lane Ghost; Drummer of Tedworth; Enfield Poltergeist; Epworth Phenomena**)

Sources:

Capron, E W. *Modern Spiritualism, its Facts and Fanaticisms.* 1855. Reprint, Boston: B. Marsh; New York: Partridge and Brittan, 1976.

Elliott, C. W. *Mysteries or Glimpses of the Supernatural.* New York: Harper, 1852.

PhenomeNews (Periodical)

Monthly publication that features news and information of **New Age** events. It includes articles on topics such as **astrology, holistic** health, diet, Eastern religions, and psychic subjects. It also includes a listing of groups and ongoing events and a calendar of lectures, workshops, and meetings.

Previously this publication served only the Michigan area, but with the addition of their online service the *PhenomeNews* reaches over 100,000 readers monthly. Address: 18444 W. 10 Mile Rd., Ste. 105, Southfield, MI 48075. Website: http://www.phenomenews.com/.

Sources:

PhenomeNews On-Line Publication. http://www.phenomenews.com/. March 8, 2000.

The Philadelphia Experiment

Title of a 1979 book by **Charles Berlitz** and William Moore that investigated the rumor that a top secret U.S. Navy experiment in 1943 had succeeded in rendering a destroyer, most likely the *Eldridge,* and its crew temporarily invisible and teleported it from its berth in Philadelphia to Norfolk, Virginia.

(The name "The Philadelphia Experiment" had earlier been used by various writers to denote the classic electrical experiments of Benjamin Franklin.)

The story of the Philadelphia Experiment stems largely from Carlos Allende (born in 1925 as Carl M. Allen). He claimed to have served as a deck hand on the S.S. *Andrew Furuseth* in 1943 and to have witnessed the experiment that rendered the *Eldridge* invisible. In 1956 he initially communicated with Morris K. Jessup (1900–1959), author of *The Case for the UFO* (1955), citing the Philadelphia Experiment as rationale for Jessup to stop researching unified field theory. A short time afterward, a copy of Jessup's book with numerous annotations relative to UFOs and the Philadelphia Experiment arrived in the office of Naval Research.

In 1959, Jessup committed suicide, and the issue seemed to be closed. Then in 1963, Gray Barker published a book about Jessup and his unexpected death. In 1968 Brad Steiger and Joan Whritenour wrote a second book. Allende, angry that he had received nothing as a result of either the Barker or Steiger title, allowed L. J. Lorenzen, director of the **Aerial Phenomena Research Organization** (APRO), to interview him in 1969. He stated that his annotations on Jessup's book were part of the hoax as were his letters to Jessup. Allende subsequently told William Moore that his confession was made in the expectation of financial gain from its publications. However, he later retracted that confession. **Gray Barker** published a facsimile edition of Jessup's book, containing the annotations, in 1973 through his Saucerian Press.

In the face of a series of inquiries concerning the Philadelphia Experiment, on July 23, 1976, the Department of the Navy, Office of Information, Washington, D.C., stated in a letter regarding the Philadelphia Experiment (reproduced in full in Berlitz & Moore's book): "ONR [Office of Naval Research] has never conducted any investigations on invisibility, either in 1943 or at any other time. . . . In view of present scientific knowledge, our scientists do not believe that such an experiment could be possible except in the realm of science fiction. A scientific discovery of such import, if it had in fact occurred, could hardly remain secret for such a long time."

Berlitz and Moore revealed that Albert Einstein was employed as a scientific consultant to the U.S. Navy from May 31, 1943 to June 30, 1944, and made speculations that both Einstein and philosopher Bertrand Russell might have been involved in the Philadelphia Experiment. The Philadelphia Experience has continued to be a matter of entertainment on the fringe of the UFO community. (See also **invisibility; teleportation**)

Sources:

Barker, Gray. *The Strange Case of Dr. M. K. Jessup.* Clarksburg, W.Va.: Saucerian Books, 1962.

Clark, Jerome. *Encyclopedia of Strange and Unexplained Phenomena.* Detroit: Gale Research, 1993.

Moore, William L., and Charles Berlitz. *The Philadelphia Experiment.* New York: Grosset & Dunlap, 1979.

Steiger, Brad, and Joan Whritenour. *New UFO Breakthrough: The Allende Letters.* New York: Award Books, 1968.

Stein, Gordon. *Encyclopedia of Hoaxes.* Detroit: Gale Research, 1993.

Philalethes (or Philaletha), Eirenaeus (ca. 1660)

The life of this alchemist is wrapped in mystery although a considerable mass of writing stands to his credit. The name, a pseudonym, is similar to the one used by **Thomas Vaughan,** who wrote as **Eugenius Philalethes**). Whoever Eirenaeus Philalethes was, however, he was not Vaughan. Others have striven to identify him with George Starkey, the doctor and author of *Liquor Alchahest,* but Starkey died of the plague in London in 1665, and it is known that Eirenaeus was living for some years after that date.

Philalethes appears to have been on intimate terms with Robert Boyle and, although this points to his having spent a considerable time in England, it is certain that he emigrated to America. Starkey was born in the Bermudas, and practiced his medical crafts in the English settlements in America, where, according to his contemporary biographers, he met Eirenaeus Philalethes. This meeting may have given rise to the identification of Starkey as Philalethes, while it is probably Starkey to whom Philalethes referred when, in a preface to one of his books, he told of certain of his writings falling "into the hands of one who, I conceive, will never return them," for in 1654 Starkey issued a volume with the title, *The Marrow of Alchemy by Eirenaeus Philoponus Philalethes.*

It is to prefaces by Philalethes that we must chiefly look for any information about him. In the thirteenth chapter of his *Introitus Apertus ad Occlusum Regis Palatium* (Amsterdam, 1667) he also made a few autobiographical statements which illuminate his character and career.

"For we are like Cain, driven from the pleasant society we formerly had," he wrote, which suggests that he was persecuted. Elsewhere he heaped scorn on most of the hermetic philosophers of his day. Elsewhere, again, he criticized the popular worship of money. "I disdain, loathe, and detest the idolizing of silver and gold, by which the pomps and vanities of the world are celebrated. Ah! filthy, evil, ah! vain nothingness."

In his preface to *Ripley Revived* (London, 1678), he gave some account of those who wrote on **alchemy** to whom he felt himself chiefly indebted. "For my own part, I have cause to honour Bernard Trévisan, who is very ingenious, especially in the letter to Thomas of Boulogne, when I seriously confess I received the main light in the hidden secret. I do not remember that ever I learnt anything from Raymond Lully. . . . I know of none like Ripley, though Flamel be eminent."

Lenglet du Fresnoy, in his *Histoire de la Philosophie Hermétique* (1742), referred to numerous unpublished manuscripts by Eirenaeus Philalethes, but nothing is known about these today.

Sources:

Philalethes, Eirenaeus. *Enarratio methodica trium Gebri medicinarum.* N.p., 1678.

———. *Introitus apertus ad occlusum Regis Palatium.* N.p., 1667.

———. *The Marrow of Alchemy.* N.p., 1654.

———. *Ripley Reviv'd; or an Exposition upon Sir George Ripley's Hermetico-Poetical Works.* 5 vols. London: T. Ratcliff and N. Thompson, 1677–78.

———. *Tractatus tres: (i) Metallorum Metamorphosis; (ii) Brevis Manuductio ad Rubinum Coelestem; (iii) Fons Chymicae Veritatis.* N.p., 1678; 1694.

Philalethes, Eugenius (1622–1666)

Pseudonym of alchemist **Thomas Vaughan,** brother of Henry Vaughan, the "Silurist" poet. Eugenius Philalethes has often been confused with **Eirenaeus Philalethes** (or Philaletha), another alchemist. The scholar **Arthur E. Waite** made this error in his book *The Real History of the Rosicrucians* (1887). He corrected it the following year, both in his new edition of the *Lives of Alchemystical Philosophers* (1888) and his edition of *The Magical Writings of Thomas Vaughan* (1888).

"Philip"

An experimental ghost created by **Iris M. Owen** and members of the Toronto Society for Psychical Research, Canada, who wanted to test the connections between living individuals and paranormal phenomena. In the past, many psychical researchers have hypothesized that the entities manifesting at séances may be artificial personalities created by the unconscious attitudes of the sitters. Many "spirit guides" and "spirits" have been self-evidently synthetic and illusory entities, although acceptance of them as real personalities often favorably influences paranormal phenomena.

In September 1972, the Toronto experimenters began meditating on "Philip," a deliberately created ghost with a personal history, idiosyncratic characteristics, and even an appearance consciously worked out by the group. The eight members of the group other than Owen (a former nurse) were Margaret Sparrow (former chairman of MENSA in Canada, an organization of individuals with high IQs), Andy H. (housewife), Lorne H. (industrial designer, husband of Andy H.), Al P. (heating engineer), Bernice M. (accountant), Dorothy O'D. (housewife and bookkeeper), and Sidney K. (sociology student). At times A. R. G. Owen (mathematician and Iris Owen's husband) or Joel Whitton (a psychologist) attended meetings as an observer.

After nearly a year without significant results, the group changed their method of sitting to conform with that of a traditional nineteenth-century Spiritualist séance, in which participants were seated around a table and sang or talked to enhance the atmosphere. This approach embodied the suggestions of British psychologist **Kenneth Batcheldor,** who claimed that skepticism inhibited paranormal phenomena but that the conventional form of a séance tended to dispel skepticism and provide an atmosphere in which paranormal phenomena seemed natural.

Within only a few weeks, the group elicited raps from the table and communications from "Philip" on conventional yes-no lines. On one occasion this phenomenon was successfully demonstrated before a live audience of fifty individuals for a videotaped TV show. In addition, there have been instances of noises from various parts of the room, a light blinking, and an apparent levitation of the table.

The results attained by the group have provided insight on the nature of spirit **personality,** the phenomena of the **poltergeist, hauntings,** and the claims of **Spiritualism.**

Sources:

Owen, Iris M., and Margaret Sparrow. *Conjuring up Philip.* New York: Harper & Row, 1976.

Philips, James B. (1907–1987)

British businessman who played a prominent part in the practical affairs of the **Society for Psychical Research,** London (SPR). He was born on December 20, 1907. Philips traveled widely throughout his life, and at different periods he was in business in New Zealand, Nigeria, and South Africa.

He did not join the SPR until 1970, but soon became a member to the Council (June 1973) and subsequently accepted the post of deputy treasurer. His wide experience of practical business affairs proved of great value to the society. In May 1975, he became honorary secretary and treasurer. Two years later he resigned as honorary secretary, but continued as treasurer for another year. He retired in 1978, when he was elected an honorary associate. He returned to service on the executive committee for further short periods as needed. He died in London on August 7, 1987.

Phillimore, Mercy (d. 1975)

Pioneer British journalist and organizer in the field of **Spiritualism** and psychical research. She became a member of the staff of the **London Spiritualist Alliance** (since 1955 known as the **College of Psychic Studies**) in 1913, and she stayed with the organization for the next 39 years. She retired in 1952.

As secretary, she came in contact with such leading mediums as **Eileen Garrett,** as well as many well-known personalities in the British psychic scene, such as **Arthur E. Waite, W. B. Yeats, Stanley De Brath, Sir Arthur Conan Doyle, Sir Oliver Lodge,** and **Paul Brunton.**

In 1928, Phillimore and the medium Clare Cantlon were arrested for vagrancy by two police officers who had come to the Alliance headquarters for a reading. Both were found guilty.

Phillimore contributed a number of articles to the British journal *Light* and gave many lectures. She was a tireless worker in the cause of Spiritualism and played a significant but unobtrusive part in the modern history of the movement. She was associated with **Nandor Fodor** in Britain, and after his death she wrote a tribute to him in the journal *Light* (Autumn, 1964).

Sources:

Edmunds, Simeon. *Spiritualism: a Critical Survey.* London: Aquarian Press, 1966.

Philosophers' Stone

A legendary substance which enabled **adepts** in **alchemy** to compass the transmutation of metals. Alchemists believed that one definite substance was essential to the success of the transmutation operation. By the application or admixture of this substance, often called the "Powder of Projection," any metal might be transmuted into gold or silver.

Zosimus, who lived at the beginning of the fifth century, was one of the first to allude to the philosophers' stone. He said that it was a powder or liquor formed of diverse metals, fused under a favorable astrological condition. The stone was supposed to contain the secrets not only of transmutation, but of health and life, for through it the **elixir of life** could be distilled.

The author of a *Treatise on Philosophical and Hermetic Chemistry,* published in Paris in 1725, stated:

"Modern philosophers have extracted from the interior of mercury a fiery spirit, mineral, vegetable and multiplicative, in a humid concavity in which is found the primitive mercury or the universal quintessence. In the midst of this spirit resides the spiritual fluid. . . .

"This is the mercury of the philosophers, which is not solid like a metal, nor soft like quicksilver, but between the two. They have retained for a long time this secret, which is the commencement, the middle, and the end of their work. It is necessary then to proceed first to purge the mercury with salt and with ordinary salad vinegar, to sublime it with vitriol and saltpetre, to dissolve it in aquafortis, to sublime it again, to calcine it and fix it, to put away part of it in salad oil, to distill this liquor for the purpose of separating the spiritual water, air, and fire, to fix the mercurial body in the spiritual water or to distill the spirit of liquid mercury found in it, to putrefy all, and then to raise and exalt the spirit with non-odorous white sulphur—that is to say, sal-ammoniac—to dissolve the sal-ammoniac in the spirit of liquid mercury which when distilled becomes the liquor known as the Vinegar of the Sages, to make it pass from gold to antimony three times and afterwards to reduce it by heat, lastly to steep this warm gold in very harsh vinegar and allow it to putrefy. On the surface of the vinegar it will raise itself in the form of fiery earth of the colour of oriental pearls. This is the first operation in the grand work.

"For the second operation, take in the name of God one part of gold and two parts of the spiritual water, charged with the sal-ammoniac, mix this noble confection in a vase of crystal of the shape of an egg: warm over a soft but continuous fire, and the fiery water will dissolve little by little the gold; this forms a liquor which is called by the sages "chaos" containing the elementary qualities—cold, dryness, heat and humidity. Allow this composition to putrefy until it becomes black; this blackness is known as the "crow's head" and the "darkness of the sages," and makes known to the artist that he is on the right track. It was also known as the "black earth." It must be boiled once more in a vase as white as snow; this stage of the work is called the "swan," and from it arises the white liquor, which is divided into two parts—one white for the manufacture of silver, the other red for the manufacture of gold. Now you have accomplished the work, and you possess the Philosophers' Stone.

"In these diverse operations, one finds many by-products; among these is the "green lion" which is called also "azoph," and which draws gold from the more ignoble elements; the "red lion" which converts the metal into gold; the "head of the crow," called also the "black veil of the ship of Theseus," which appearing forty days before the end of the operation predicts its success; the white powder which transmutes the white metals to fine silver; the red elixir with which gold is made; the white elixir which also makes silver, and which procures long life—it is also called the white daughter of the philosophers."

In the lives of the various alchemists, we find many notices of the philosophers' stone in connection with those adepts who were supposed to have arrived at the solution. Thus in the story of **Alexander Seton,** a Scotsman who came from Port Seton, near Edinburgh, it is stated that on his various travels on the continent he employed in his alchemical experiments a blackish powder, the application of which turned any metal given him into gold.

Numerous instances are on record of Seton's projections, the majority of which were verified by multiple observers. On one occasion, while in Holland, he went with some friends from the house at which he was residing to undertake an alchemical experiment at another house near by. On the way there, a quantity of ordinary zinc was purchased, and reportedly Seton succeeded in projecting the zinc into pure gold by the application of his powder. A similar phenomenon occurred at Cologne, and even the most extreme torture could not wring the secret from him.

Seton's pupil or assistant, Sendivogius, made great efforts to obtain the secret from Seton before he died, but without success. However, out of gratitude Seton bequeathed him what remained of his marvelous powder, which Sendivogius employed with the same results Seton had achieved.

Sendivogius fared badly, however, when the powder came to an end. He had used it chiefly in liquid form, and into this he had dipped silver coins which immediately had become pure gold. When the powder gave out, Sendivogius was driven to the practice of gilding coins, which, it was reported, he had previously transmuted by legitimate means, and this brought upon him the wrath of those who had trusted him.

There are many intriguing accounts of successful alchemical operations with the philosophers' stone, but most students of the field have surmised that the great work accomplished was a personal and spiritual transformation rather than any chemical miracle. The close association of ideas of the philosophers' stone with the elixir of life reinforces this view.

The idea of the philosophers' stone is an ancient one. In Egyptian alchemy, which seems one of the oldest, the idea of a black powder (the detritus or oxide of all metals mingled) is already found.

The ancient Chinese believed that gold was immortal and that when absorbed in the human body could bestow immortality, thus we find here ideas of the mystical value of gold again associated with the concept of the elixir of life.

The art of Chinese alchemists can be traced back to circa 100–150 B.C.E., long before records of alchemy being practiced in the West appear. Gold was regarded as a medicine for long life, and there is a story that the great Wei Po-Yang (ca. 100–150 C.E.) succeeded in manufacturing the gold medicine and he and his pupil Yu, together with the wise man's dog, thereby became immortal.

The idea that the philosophers' stone could grant wishes is found in ancient Indian religious tradition, where this magical stone was named "Chintamani" and cited in scriptures. Similar ideas were carried over into Buddhism.

The antiquarian Sabine Baring-Gould suggested that legends of the philosophers' stone ultimately could be traced to reflections upon the life-giving properties of the sun, which was a prominent symbol in many alchemical works. He reviewed such concepts in a chapter on the philosophers' stone in his book *Curiosities of Olden Times* (1895).

Sources:

Bacon, Roger. *Mirror of Alchemy.* London, 1597. Reprint, Los Angeles: Globe Bookshop, 1975.

Barring-Gould, Sabine. *Curiosities of Olden Times.* London, J. T. Hayes, 1895.

Chkashige, Masumi. *Oriental Alchemy.* New York: Samuel Weiser, 1936.

Eliade, Mircea. *The Forge and the Crucible; The Origins and Structures of Alchemy.* New York: Harper & Row, 1956.

Jung, C. G. *Alchemical Studies.* Vol. 13, *Collected Works.* Princeton: Princeton University Press, 1967.

Redgrove, H. Stanley. *Alchemy: Ancient & Modern.* London: William Rider, 1911. Reprint, New Hyde Park, N.Y.: University Books, 1969.

Regardie, Israel. *The Philosophers' Stone.* St. Paul: Llewellyn Publications, 1958.

Waite, Arthur E. *Alchemists Through the Ages.* Blauvelt, N.Y.: Rudolf Steiner Publications, 1970.

———, ed. *The Hermetic and Alchemical Writings of Paracelsus.* 2 vols. London: James Elliott, 1894. Reprint, New Hyde Park, N.Y.: University Books, 1967.

Philosophical Research Society

Founded in 1934 by **Manly Palmer Hall,** the Philosophical Research Society grew out of Hall's early successful work in **astrology** and occult philosophy and superseded the Hall Publishing Company and the Church of the People, which he had previously headed. The society was created:

". . . to investigate the essential teachings of scientific, spiritual, and cultural leaders and further clarify and integrate man's body of knowledge, to apply this knowledge to the present needs of mankind by means of modern skills and the cooperation of outstanding experts, to make available these vital concepts to the public through lectures, publications and other medium to increase public awareness of the usefulness of these ideas and ideals in solving the personal and collective problems of modern man."

The society maintains a research library of over 50,000 volumes and a collection of art and rare books, conducts a weekly program of lectures, seminars, and special events, and publishes a quarterly *Journal.* The society has also published over 130 books, most by Hall, and produces audiocassettes. The society is located at 3910 Los Feliz Blvd., Los Angeles, CA 90027. Website: http://www.prs.org/.

Sources:

Philosophical Research Society Home Page. http://www.prs.org/. March 8, 2000.

"Philosophus"

One of the spirit **controls** of **William Stainton Moses.** It was said to have been the spirit of Alexander Achillini, who succeeded Francatiano in the chair of philosophy at Padua in 1506.

"Phinuit"

A spirit entity, the earliest permanent **control** of the medium **Leonora E. Piper.** "Phinuit," who succeeded the *soi-disant* spirit of Sebastian Bach, said that he was French and a physician in Metz, but never furnished convincing proof of identity. His statements about himself were hazy and contradictory. As N. S. Shaler wrote in a letter to William James of "Phinuit's" first year of manifestation in 1894, "Whatever the medium is, I am convinced that this influence is a preposterous scoundrel."

Attempts to verify the statements of "Phinuit" resulted in failure. The archives of Metz were searched. No trace was found of him. He could not even speak French. When an explanation was asked, he declared that he had forgotten his maternal tongue. Later, on closer questioning, he disclosed uncertainty over whether he was born at Metz or Marseilles, and finally concluded that his name was not "Phinuit," but "Jean Alaen Scliville."

Richard Hodgson regarded the existence of "Phinuit" as an open question. To **F. W. H. Myers,** it seemed clear that the name "Phinuit" was the result of a suggestion at one of the early séances. Other psychical researchers thought it most probable that "Phinuit" was nothing more than a secondary **personality** of Piper.

According to "Imperator," a later control, "Phinuit" was an earthbound spirit who had become confused and bewildered in his first attempts at **communication** and had lost his consciousness of personal identity. The "Edmund Gurney" control also bore out "Phinuit's" claim to an independent existence. He said to **Sir Oliver Lodge** in 1889: "Dr. Phinuit is a peculiar type of man . . . he is eccentric and quaint, but good-hearted . . . a shrewd doctor, he knows his own business thoroughly."

"Phinuit's" regime was exclusive from 1884 to 1892, but beginning in 1892 he shared control with **George Pelham.** In 1897 the "Imperator" group took over Piper's sessions and "Phinuit" was entirely suppressed.

Sources:

Piper, Alta C. *The Life and Work of Mrs. Piper.* London: K. Paul, Trench, Trubner, & Co. Ltd., 1929.

Sage, M. *Mrs. Piper and the Society for Psychical Research.* New York: Scott-Thaw, 1904.

Phoenix, William

A **direct voice** medium of Glasgow, Scotland, who attempted feats of **xenoglossia.** Spiritualist **Sir Arthur Conan Doyle,** never known as a qualified observer of mediumistic phenomena, had a number of sittings with him and thought highly of his powers. However, Phoenix was later demonstrated to have been a clever **fraud.**

Lord Charles Hope of the **Society for Psychical Research** invited **Neville Whymant,** a professor of oriental literature and philosophy, to join him for a sitting with Phoenix in Glasgow and later in London. In the first Glasgow sitting, the voice of an Indian attempted to speak in a variety of Persian. In the second sitting a conversation of real import was being worked up in Italian but the control's power failed too soon. Modern Greek was also heard. The Persian voice reappeared and was a little more explicit than on the previous occasion. Finally, a Chinese voice, that of a scribe or commentator apparently, also spoke and something was said in Japanese. Hope said of the Glasgow sittings, "Although the Glasgow sittings had not resulted in any communication of the order of importance of Dr. Whymant's experience in New York they had apparently established a strong case for the speaking of languages unknown to the medium."

Thereupon Phoenix was invited to London. In September and October 1927, he gave six sittings. In the first, Chinese and Japanese voices spoke to Gonoské Komai. But Whymant observed,

"I cannot truthfully say that I gathered anything at all from this voice. It was over-anxious to tell me something and probably the keenness of its desire prevented its being understood. Other voices struggled for expression without achieving more than whispering and trumpet taps. Then came a voice speaking a queer idiom; it sounded almost like a jargon of some kind and I called out that it sounded like Indo-Chinese border dialect, later giving the impression that it might have been badly spoken Yunnanese. The voice gave bugle calls of a military nature easily recognized and several people suggested that it might have been a soldier."

Of another voice Whymant surmised, "It seemed to me that the voice was that of a Straits Chinese who had lived in Singapore."

Hope added his own conclusion,

"I had become convinced that at any rate on most occasions the medium left his chair before voices spoke to the sitters. I had sat next to the medium on several occasions and had distinctly heard sounds like a creaking boot. After the sitting at which I had heard these sounds I noticed that one of the medium's boots creaked as he walked. The sounds were similar."

In a late sitting, Hope obtained proof that the medium left his chair. Phoenix protested that he was under control. Hope suggested that he should turn out his pockets to prove that he had no appliance with which to produce the psychic lights which appeared at each sitting. Upon Phoenix's refusal, Hope gave up and concluded, "reluctantly I had come to the conclusion that Phoenix was at least in part a fraud."

Hope published an account of the sittings in the *Proceedings* of the SPR (vol. 40, pp. 419–427).

Phoenix: New Directions in the Study of Man (Journal)

A semi-annual scholarly publication published in the 1970s by Phoenix Associates of Stanford, California. It was concerned with the advancement of the scientific and philosophical study of paranormal phenomena.

Phone-Voyance

A kind of psychic television, named as a special form of **clairvoyance** by British psychic **Vincent N. Turvey** in 1905, when the telephone was still a relatively new device to most people. Phone-voyance implies four things: psychic vision, physical contact, the wires and instruments of a telephone company, and simultaneity of clairvoyance with physical contact. Turvey often described things which the listener at the other end of the telephone wire did not know, for instance, what his daughter was doing in the room above him or what a man behind his back was reading in a book.

Turvey saw things habitually worn by his listener, although they may not have been on the listener at the particular time. He also claimed to see spirits in the room of his listener. Once he described the picture of a young lady known to the listener, but then at a distant location, and told him that she was not dead and yet not actually in the room.

Turvey demonstrated this faculty intermittently from 1905 to 1908, but complained that it was a great strain on the brain and that too frequent use would lead to very serious injury. In most cases, he reported that he saw

". . . through a halo, or aura, of bright heliotrope, or pale violet-coloured fire, the flashes or sparks of which do not appear to cover *all* the window, so to speak, but to leave the centre clear and colourless, and in that centre appears the person or object that is seen. Another extraordinary thing is that occasionally a part of my mentality seems to ooze out of me, and to run along the line for a little distance, say a yard or two; and as "I" (his spirit) go, so little pieces of the copper wire which lay together, A-B, seem to turn over to B-A, i.e., reverse their position as if on a hinge. These pieces appear to be about four inches in length. At other times phone-voyance seems to be very like mental body-traveling, because "I" appears to be in the room at the one end of the line, and by a sort of living cord to communicate with "ME" (his body)] at the other end, and to make "ME" speak about that which "I" see."

The famous spiritualist editor **W. T. Stead,** in his preface to Turvey's *Beginnings of Seership* (1911), quoted the case of Mrs. A. T. Giddings, a professional music hall performer, who trained the faculty of "phone-voyance" to such perfection that it could be exercised at will under the most adverse conditions. Experiments with Giddings were carried out by a committee of investigators between the stage of the Alhambra Theater in London and the office of the *Daily Mirror.* Articles presented at random to Mr. Zomah (professional name of A. T. Giddings) by members of the committee in the Alhambra were immediately seen and described by his wife who was at the other end of the telephone in the newspaper office.

Of course this demonstration may have been simply long-distance telepathy or even clever stage mentalism, but according to Stead (to judge from the reports that were published), Giddings claimed to actually see the article which was held in her husband's hand at the other end of the telephone wire.

Sources:

Turvey, Vincent N. *The Beginnings of Seership.* 1911. Reprint, New Hyde Park, N.Y.: University Books, 1969.

Phouka (or Puca)

The Irish form of a European field spirit, the kornböcke, one of various kinds of animal **fairies.** The phouka would appear as a goat, a pig, or, most frequently, as a horse. It would lure its victims to mount it, then take them for a wild ride and throw them off. It is possible that the word *puca* is related to Puck, another mischievous fairy figure.

Sources:

Arrowsmith, Nancy, and George Moorse. *A Field Guide to the Little People.* New York: Wallaby Books, 1977.

Phrenology

A nineteenth-century proto-science claiming that character and personality could be ascertained by the shape and size of various areas or "bumps" on the skull, resulting from development of the brain centers. It derives from the traditional belief that character traits are reflected in physical appearance, and was associated with physiognomy, the study of outward aspects of the individual.

Phrenology was first systematically developed by Franz Joseph Gall (1758–1828) at the end of the eighteenth century. He made observations on hundreds of heads and skulls, and in 1796 lectured in Vienna on the anatomy of the brain and the elements of phrenology. His pupil J. K. Spurzheim continued his work in England and America, where phrenology vied with **mesmerism** and spiritualist phenomena as a popular subject of study during the nineteenth century. Initially, Gall and Spurzheim encountered opposition from some church leaders because their system appeared to imply that personality characteristics were inborn instead of being subject to modification by leading a good life.

Gall was an accredited physician with a detailed knowledge of the brain and nervous system, and he proposed phrenology to his colleagues for their serious scientific consideration. Phrenology became the province of many original thinkers of the day. However, phrenology also was popularized and practiced by non-medical individuals and even fairground charlatans.

Essentially, phrenology defined more than thirty areas of the skull related to such instincts as amativeness, philogeniture, habitativeness, affection, combativeness, destructiveness, alimentiveness, secretiveness, acquisitiveness, and constructiveness, and to such moral faculties as self-esteem, approbativeness, circumspection, benevolence, veneration, firmness, conscientiousness, hope, admiration, idealism, cheerfulness, and imitativeness.

The size and development of these areas implied strong or weak aspects of these instincts and faculties. The areas were measured by calipers and marked off on a chart, so that a complete character reading could be made.

Early exponents of **animal magnetism** (a precursor of **hypnotism,** but allied with psychic faculties) developed a new approach named "phreno-magnetism" or **"phreno-mesmerism."** Operators claimed that when any phrenological area of the subject was touched during a trance, the subject acted out the particular faculty associated with that area. Thus, when the operator touched the bump of "combativeness," the entranced subject would exhibit belligerent behavior.

Although now discarded as a failed scientific option, phrenology flourished side by side with mesmerism and **Spiritualism** during the nineteenth century. Noted scientists were sympathetic, and additional supporters could be found among the literary elite such as Walt Whitman and Edgar Allan Poe.

Interest in phrenology continued in America well into the twentieth century, and the British Phrenological Society, founded in 1886 by Lorenzo J. Fowler, was still in existence in the 1960s, though it had long ceased to affect the culture that surrounded it.

Sources:

Chambers, Howard V. *Phrenology.* Sherbourne, 1968.

Davies, John D. *Phrenology, Fad and Science: A Nineteenth Century American Crusade.* Archon, 1955. Reprint, Shoe String, 1971.

De Giustino, David. *Conquest of Mind: Phrenology and Victorian Social Thought.* London: Croom Helm; Totowa, N.J.: Rowman & Littlefield, 1975.

Gall, Franz J. *On the Functions of the Brain and of Each of Its Parts: with Observations on the Possibility of Determining the Instincts, Propensities and Talents, or the Moral and Intellectual Dispositions of Men and Animals, by the Configuration of the Brain and Head.* 6 vols. Boston, 1835.

Stern, Madeleine B. *Heads and Headlines: The Phrenological Fowlers.* Norman, Okla.: University of Oklahoma Press, 1971.

Wells, Samuel R. *How to Read Character: A New Illustrated Handbook of Phrenology and Physiognomy.* New York: Samuel R. Wells, 1871. Reprint, Rutland, Conn.: C. E. Tuttle, 1971.

Phreno-Magnet and the Mirror of Nature (Journal)

Nineteenth-century British journal devoted to **phrenology** in relation to **animal magnetism.** It was founded in London in 1843 and edited by S. T. Hall.

Phreno-Mesmerism (or Phreno-Magnetism or Phrenopathy)

An application of the principles of **mesmerism** to **phrenology,** a means of discerning the nature of an individual's personality from examining the skull. Mesmerism (or **animal magnetism**) and phrenology, both proposed as sciences in the mid-nineteenth century, had been regarded by English mesmerists as related topics after it was observed that a sleepwalker whose phrenological "bumps" were touched would respond to the stimulus by exhibiting every symptom of the mental trait corresponding to the bump touched. Thus signs of joy, grief, destructiveness, combativeness, and friendship might be exhibited in rapid succession by the entranced patient.

Among those who claimed to have discovered the new science were Dr. R. H. Collyer, a pupil of Dr. **John Elliotson,** and **La Roy Sunderland,** although the former afterwards repudiated it. As time went on, enterprising phreno-mesmerists discovered many new cerebral organs, as many as a hundred and fifty more than those already mapped out by J. K. Spurzheim and Franz Joseph Gall.

Phreno-mesmerism numbered among its supporters James Braid (credited with demythologizing mesmerism into **hypnotism**), who expressed himself fully satisfied of its reality. He recorded a number of cases in which the patient correctly indicated by his actions the organs touched, although the patient was by all accounts demonstrably ignorant of phrenological principles and inaccessible to outside information.

Concerning this evidence, it would seem advisable to admit the possibility of **suggestion,** (or even **telepathy**), by means of which the expectation of the operator, reproducing itself in the mind of the patient, would give rise to the corresponding reactions.

Phrygian Cap

Hargrave Jennings, in his book *The Rosicrucians: Their Rites and Mysteries* (1870), argued for the common ancestry of the Phrygian Cap, which is the classic cap of the god Mithra; the sacrificial cap; and the miter. The Mithraic or Phrygian Cap is the origin of the priestly miter in all faiths. The Phrygian Cap was worn by the priest in sacrifice. When worn by a male, it had its crest, comb, or point set jutting forward; when worn by a female, the same prominent part of the cap is in reverse, or on the nape of the neck, as in the instance of the Amazon's helmet, displayed in antique sculptures, or that of the goddess Athena.

According to Jennings, the peak of caps or hats (the term "cocked hat" is a case in point) all refer to the same idea. This point had a sanctifying meaning afterward attributed to it, when it was called the christa, crista, or crest, which signifies a triumphal top or tuft. The Grenadier Cap and the loose black Hussar Cap derive remotely from the same sacred Mithraic bonnet, or high pyramidal cap.

The Phrygian Cap comes from the highest antiquity. It is displayed on the head of the figure sacrificing in the celebrated sculpture it *Mithraic Sacrifice* (or the Mythical Sacrifice) in the British Museum, London. This loose cap, with the point protruding, gives the original form from which all helmets or defensive headpieces, whether Greek or not, derive.

When a Phrygian Cap, or Symbolizing Cap, is bloodred, it stands for the cap of liberty, a revolutionary symbol; in another way, it is even a civic or incorporated badge. It marks the needle of the obelisk, the crown or tip of the phallus, whether human or representative. It may have had its origin in the rite of circumcision. The real meaning of the *bonnet rouge* or cap of liberty is obscure, but it has always been regarded as a most important hieroglyph or figure. It signifies the supernatural simultaneous sacrifice and triumph. It has descended from the time of Abraham, and it is supposed to be an emblem of the strange mythic rite of the *circumcision preputii.*

The Phrygian Cap stands as the sign of the Enlightened. The heroic figures in most Gnostic gems have caps of this kind. The sacrificer in the sculptured group of the *Mithraic Sacrifice,* among the marbles in the British Museum, has a Phrygian Cap on his head. He performs the act of striking the bull with a dagger, which is the office of the immolating priest. The *bonnet conique* is the miter of the Doge of Venice. Cinteotl, a Mexican god of sacrifice, wears such a cap made from the thigh-skin of a sacrificed virgin. This headdress is shaped like a cock's comb. The Scotch Glengarry cap also seems, upon examination, to be "cocked."

Besides the "bonnet rouge," the Pope's miter and other miters or conical head-coverings derive their names from the terms "Mithradic," or "Mithraic," and the origin of the whole class of names is Mittra, or Mithra.

Sources:

Cumont, Franz. *The Mysteries of Mithra.* LaSalle, Ill.: Open Court Publishing, 1903. Reprint, New York: Dover Publications, 1956.

Jennings, Hargrave. *The Rosicrucians: Their Rites and Mysteries.* 3rd ed. 2 vols. London: J. Nimmo, 1887.

Vermaseren, M. J. *Mithras, The Secret God.* London: Chatto & Windus, 1963.

Wynne-Tyson, Esmé. *Mithras, the Fellow in the Cap.* London: Rider, 1968.

Phyllorhodomancy

Divination by rose leaves. The ancient Greeks clapped a rose leaf on the hand and judged from the resulting sound the success or failure of their desires.

Physical World

In theosophical thought, the lowest of the seven **worlds,** the world in which ordinary man moves and is conscious under normal conditions (formerly known as the Sthula Plane). It is the limit of the ego's descent into matter, and the matter which composes the appropriate physical body is the densest of any of these worlds. Physical matter has the seven divisions of solid, liquid, gas, ether, super-ether, sub-atom, and atom in common with the matter of the other worlds.

Beside the physical body, familiar to ordinary vision, there is a finer body, the **etheric double,** which plays a very important part in collecting vitality from the sun for the use of the denser physical body through its etheric centers, the **chakras.** At death, the physical body and the etheric double are cast aside and slowly resolved into their components. **Theosophy** adopted these ideas from Hindu teachings.

Physiognomy

Physiognomy, also known today as personology, is an ancient form of **divination** based upon reference of the physical appearance of the individual. It was a widespread practice in the ancient Mediterranean Basin and in China, and also appears in India and the ancient Arab world. During the Renaissance, Gerolamo Cardano and Giovanni Battista della Porta emerged as popular exponents. As did other forms of divination, it came under heavy attack by the eighteenth-century Enlightenment and following the work of J. C. Lavater largely died. Its post-Enlightenment revival was delayed by the emergence of phrenology, which could be seen as a form of physiognomy that concentrated attention on the shape and appearance of the head.

In China, a form of physiognomy, called *Siang Mien,* developed that concentrated on face readings tied to the acupuncture points. Each of the 100 points on the face are numbered and named, assigned to a year in one's life, and carry a range of meanings. The Chinese measure life from conception, hence one must add a year to one's age to find the applicable point. At age 41, for example, one can make reference to point 42, the Delicate Cottage. It represents a place of seclusion and may be interpreted as an appropriate time to shift concentration from outer to inner concerns. A variety of face readers may be found throughout Chinese ethnic communities in the West.

In the mid-twentieth century new attention to physiognomy was proposed by Edward Vincent Jones, a judge with the U.S. Superior Court who did his primary research on defendants brought before him over a number of years. His modern development of physiognomy was called personology. During World War II (1939–45) he founded the Personology Foundation of California, which graduated its first class in 1942. Jones' work is being carried on by Paul Eisner, who founded the Personology Foundation of the Pacific. Its Learning Center is located at P.O. Box 3301, Honokaa, HI 96727. It has a website at http://www.users.totalise.co.uk/~tmd/person.htm.

The measurable growth of interest in physiognomy associated with the **New Age** Movement can be traced both to Personology and to the influx of Chinese into North America since 1965. Pushing the practice of physiognomy ahead is Rose Rosetree, a former **Transcendental Meditation** instructor who now teaches both aura readings and face readings and trains teachers in suburban Washington, D.C. Based on her initial study of both European and Chinese texts, she developed her own new system of physiognomy. She is the author of one of the most popular contemporary texts in the field, *The Power of Face*

Reading. She may be contacted through her webpage at http://www.rose-rosetree.com/.

Sources:

Lin, Henry B. *What Your Face Reveals*. St. Paul, Minn.: Llewellyn Publications, 1999.

Personology Foundation of the Pacific. http://www.users.totalise.co.uk/~tmd/person.htm. April 23, 2000.

Rose Rosetree. http://www.rose-rosetree.com/. April 23, 2000.

Rosetree, Rose. *The Power of Face Reading for Sales, Self-Esteem, and Better Relationships*. Women's Intuition Worldwide, 1998.

Yong, Wu. *Face Reading*. Longmead, Dorset, UK: Element Books, 1998.

Pickering, Edward Charles (1846–1919)

Distinguished astronomer and a founding member of the **American Society for Psychical Research.** He was born on July 19, 1846, in Boston, Massachusetts. He studied at the Lawrence Scientific School of Harvard University (B.S., 1865). After graduation he taught mathematics and physics at Lawrence (1865–67) and then became a professor of physics at the Massachusetts Institute of Technology (1868–77). In 1877 he was appointed director of the Harvard Observatory, a position he held for 42 years. Pickering devised methods of measuring the magnitudes of stars and supervised the cataloguing of some 80,000 stars. He also established the Harvard Observatory auxiliary station at Arequipa, Peru, in 1891.

In the field of parapsychology, Pickering was vice president of the American Society for Psychical Research from 1885 to 1888 and served on the society's Committee on Thought Transference. He participated in the statistical analysis of experiments in **telepathy** using cards, dice, and numbers, a precursor to the methods later championed by **parapsychology.** He died on February 3, 1919, in Cambridge, Massachusetts.

Sources:

Berger, Arthur S., and Joyce Berger. *The Encyclopedia of Parapsychology and Psychical Research*. New York: Paragon House, 1991.

Pickering, Edward Charles. "Possibility of Errors in Scientific Researches, Due to Thought-Transference." *Proceedings* of the American Society for Psychical Research 1 (1885).

Pickering, Edward Charles, and J. M. Peirce. "Discussion of Returns in Response to Circular No. 4." *Proceedings* of the American Society for Psychical Research 1 (July 1885).

Pleasants, Helene, ed. *Biographical Dictionary of Parapsychology*. New York: Helix Press, 1964.

Pico della Mirandola, Giovanni (1463–1494)

Italian astrologer and Kabbalist born February 24, 1463. His family played a prominent part in a number of the civil wars which convulsed medieval Italy; they owned extensive lands in the neighborhood of Modena, the most valuable of their possessions being a castle bearing their own name of Mirandola. It was here that Giovanni was born.

He appears to have been a versatile student. According to tradition, before he was out of his teens he had mastered jurisprudence and mathematics, had studied philosophy and theology, and had dabbled in occultism.

As a young man, Mirandola soon left his brothers in charge of the family estate and proceeded to various universities in Italy and France. While in the latter country, his interest in **astrology** and related subjects deepened, thanks partly to his making a close study of the works of alchemist **Raymond Lully.** In 1486 Giovanni went to Rome, where he delivered a series of lectures on various branches of science.

While thus engaged, his erudition won high praise from some of his hearers, but certain members of the clergy suspected him of heresy, reported his doings to the Inquisition, and even sought to have him excommunicated. The pope, however, was rather averse to quarrelling with a member of so powerful a family as the Mirandolas, and accordingly he waived violent measures, instead appointing a body of church leaders to argue with the scientist.

A lengthy dispute ensued. Mirandola published a defence (under the title *Apologia*) of the ideas and theories promulgated in his lectures and in 1493 the pope, Alexander VI, brought the affair to a conclusion by granting him absolution.

Thereupon Mirandola went to live in Florence, and stayed there until his death in 1494, occasionally experimenting with **alchemy,** but chiefly busy with further study of the **Kabala.** He died November 17, 1494, in Florence.

Apart from the *Apologia Pici Mirandoli* cited above, Giovanni was author of several books of a theological nature, the most important of these being his *Conclusiones Philosophicae, cabalisticae et theologicae,* published in 1486, and his *Disputationes adversus Astrologiam Divinaticum,* issued in 1495. His works appear to have been keenly admired by those of his contemporaries who were not averse to speculative thought, and a collected edition of his writings was printed at Bologna in 1496, and another at Venice two years later.

Piddington, J(ohn) G(eorge) (1869–1952)

Officer of the **Society for Psychical Research,** London. He served successively as a member of council (1899–1932), secretary (1899–1907), treasurer (1917–21) and president (1924–25). He was born J. G. Smith in 1869, but he took his mother's family name in order to avoid confusion with other leading members of the Society for Psychical Research. He joined the SPR in 1890 and subsequently devoted the rest of his life to the cause of psychical research. He helped to create the SPR research endowment fund in 1902, which enabled the Society to have a full-time paid research officer. In 1905 Piddington visited the United States and assisted in the organization of the American branch of the SPR as an independent society.

In the field of psychical research, he worked with **Eleanor Sidgwick, G. W. Balfour, Sir Oliver Lodge,** and **Alice Johnson** in interpreting the scripts of the "SPR group" of automatic writers concerned with **cross correspondence.** The SPR group of mediums consisted of **Margaret Verrall,** Helen Verrall, **Leonora Piper, Winifred Coombe-Tenant** (usually identified in the literature as Mrs. Willett), **Alice Fleming** (Mrs. Holland), **Dame Edith Lyttelton** (Mrs. King), and Mrs. Stuart Wilson. There were over three thousand of these scripts, which became fully meaningful when correctly juxtaposed. These cross correspondences have been cited as among the very best evidence of individual **survival** of death.

Piddington's presidential address in 1924 was directed to the issue then dividing psychical research: the strict standards of investigation and reporting on the observation of mediums. The issue divided the American Society for Psychical Research in 1925 and would lead to the resignation of Spiritualist believer **Sir Arthur Conan Doyle** from the SPR. Piddington died in April 1952.

Sources:

Berger, Arthur S., and Joyce Berger. *The Encyclopedia of Parapsychology and Psychical Research.* New York: Paragon House, 1991.

Gauld, Alan. *The Founders of Psychical Research.* New York: Schrocken Books, 1968.

Piddington, John George. "Cross Correspondences of a Gallic Type." *Proceedings* of the Society for Psychical Research 29, 72 (1916).

———. "Presidential Address." *Proceedings* of the Society for Psychical Research 34, 89 (1924).

———. "A Reply to Sir Oliver Lodge's Note." *Proceedings* of the Society for Psychical Research 30, 77 (1918).

———. "A Series of Concordant Automatisms." *Proceedings* of the Society for Psychical Research 22, 57 (1908).

Piddington, John George, and Eleanor Sidgwick. "Note on Mrs. Piper's Hodgson-Control in England." *Proceedings* of the Society for Psychical Research 23, 58 (1909).

Pleasants, Helene, ed. *Biographical Dictionary of Parapsychology.* New York: Helix Press, 1964.

Salter, W. H. "J. G. Piddington and His Work on the Cross-Correspondence 'Scripts.' " *Journal* of the Society for Psychical Research 36 (1952).

Piddington, Sydney (1918–1991) and Lesley (1925–)

A husband-wife team who gave one of the most famous stage **telepathy** acts of modern times. Sydney Piddington was born in Australia in 1918. During World War II he served in an artillery regiment in Singapore. After the fall of Singapore he was imprisoned for four years in the dreaded Changi Camp, immortalized by fellow prisoners Russell Braddon, author of *The Naked Island* (1952), and artist Ronald Searle, who drew illustrations of his life in the camp.

As a relief from harsh treatment, forced labor, malnutrition, and disease, the camp prisoners staged theatrical entertainments. An article by Dr. **J. B. Rhine** on parapsychology in a stray copy of *Digest* magazine stimulated Piddington and Braddon to experiment with telepathy, and they devised an act which became a notable feature of the prison camp entertainments. After his release from the camp, Piddington returned to Australia where he met and married radio-actress Lesley Pope in 1946. The couple worked up a telepathy act based on Sydney's experience in Changi jail, and the Piddingtons became a successful show on 2UE in Sydney and 3K2 in Melbourne, followed by live stage shows.

In 1949 the couple went to England, where they appeared over eight weeks on BBC radio programs, which were a sensational success. The Piddingtons became a household name almost overnight. In one remarkable program, twenty million listeners waited with bated breath while Lesley Piddington, sequestered in the Tower of London, correctly stated the difficult test sentence "Be abandoned as the electricians said that they would have no current" relayed by Sydney telepathically from a BBC studio in Piccadilly, several miles away. The line had been chosen independently of the Piddingtons, and it was only revealed to Sydney when he was asked to concentrate upon it in the studio.

Throughout the BBC shows, the tests were rigorously controlled, and if there *was* a code (as so many theorists suggested) it would have to have been independent of aural and visual signals and able to operate at a distance. The possibility of concealed electronic devices (in a period long before micro transistor techniques) was also ruled out by searching the Piddingtons. One by one each ingenious "explanation" of trickery was eliminated under conditions that precluded codes and confederates. Everyone had his pet theories about how it might be done, and part of the success of the shows was the challenge issued to the public by the Piddingtons: "You are the judge." Some psychical researchers (including Dr. **S. G. Soal**) objected to the shows, presumably on the ground that telepathy should be restricted to laboratory investigation. However, the Piddingtons made telepathy a topic of conversation throughout Britain, and years later there has been no revelation of trickery. Skeptics have not offered a viable explanation, other than a staged hoax by the BBC that could account for the Piddington's performance.

Russell Brandon later wrote a book about his former campmate and his wife and the *Journal* of the **Society for Psychical Research** provided lengthy discussion of their work (vol. 35, pp. 83–85, 116–19, 187, 244–45, 316–18; vol. 42, p. 250).

Sources:

Braddon, Russell. *The Piddingtons.* London: T. Werner Laurie, 1950.

Pienaar, Domenick Cuthbert (1926–1978)

South African personnel officer who took an active interest in parapsychology. He was born on August 2, 1926, at Krugersdorp, Transvaal, South Africa. He studied at the University of Potchefstroom (B.S., 1950) and the University of South Africa (B.S. hons., psychology 1956). After graduation he worked as an assistant personnel officer at Daggafontein Mines, Springs, Transvaal (1957), a vocational guidance officer at the Department of Labour, Johannesburg (1958–61), and in 1961 he joined the personnel study section of South African Coal, Oil and Gas Corporation.

In 1971, Pienaar received his Ph.D. from the University of South Africa for his thesis "Studies in ESP; an Investigation of Distortion in ESP Phenomena." This study was aided by a grant from the **Parapsychology Foundation** and used clock cards as targets in testing for ESP. He has tested ESP ability in abnormal personalities using Zener Cards. Pienaar has also studied factors in the relationship between percipient and agent. He distinguished two primary factors: the "sheep/goat" effect and "friends/strangers" differences, as well as other agent-centered or percipient-centered factors.

He was associated with the South African Society for Psychical Research and the South African Parapsychology Institute for more than twelve years. He was a council member of the Society, served as secretary, and was president for seven years.

Sources:

Pienaar, Domenick C., and Karlis Osis. "ESP Over Seventy-Five Hundred Miles." *Journal of Parapsychology* 20, no. 4 (1956).

Pleasants, Helene, ed. *Biographical Dictionary of Parapsychology.* New York: Helix Press, 1964.

Piérart, Z. J. (d. 1878)

Founder of the rival branch of **Spiritualism** in France against the **Spiritism** of **Allan Kardec.** As a more traditional Spiritualist than Kardec, Piéare did not accept the doctrine of compulsory **reincarnation.**

At one time, Piérart was a professor at the College of Maubeuge and afterward secretary to **Baron du Potet.** In 1858, he founded the Spiritualist journal *La Revue Spirtualiste* which engaged Kardec's journal *La Revue Spirite* in debate. Eventually Kardec's journal was sufficiently successful to overwhelm *La Revue Spiritualiste,* which was discontinued during the 1860s. It was revived in 1870 under the title *Concile de la Libre Pensée,* but in 1873 it was suppressed under pressure generated by clerical authorities.

Among the ideas Piérart advocated was a form of psychic vampirism. He though **vampires** were the ghostly or astral bodies of deceased persons which vampirized the living to keep their physical bodies (still in graves) vitalized. His idea would explain why some bodies that were later dug up showed signs of life.

Sources:

Rogo, Scott. "In-depth Analysis of the Vampire Legend." *Fate* 21, no. 9 (September 1968): 77.

Pierrakos, Eva (1915–1979)

Eva Pierrakos, a psychic channel who developed a system of spiritual development called Pathwork, was born in Vienna, Austria. Her father, Jakob Wasserman (1873–1934), was a famous Jewish novelist. As a young woman, she began to do **automatic writing** and developed her relationship to an entity known only as The Guide. The Guide never identified itself, and pushed away inquiries of its identity. Out of the material she received, however, she came to feel that she was called to help people with their spiritual development. As World War II (1939–45) approached, she moved to the United States and continued to work as a trance channel and produced a series of lectures that were transcribed and circulated among those who came to hear her.

In 1971 she met and married psychiatrist **John C. Pierrakos,** a Greek expatriate who, like her, had moved to the United States as World War II approached. He had been one of the founders of bioenergetics, a system of bodywork partially inspired by the teachings of **Wilhelm Reich** and based upon an understanding of the way that psychological energy is reflected in body states. She added some of the energy teachings to her own work and developed the Pathwork. In 1972 she opened the first Pathwork Center in the Catskill Mountains near Phonecia, New York.

Pierrakos' teachings are contained in the 258 *Guide Lectures,* and an additional 100 transcripts of question-and-answer sessions. Through her, the *Guide* taught that humans have problems from a distorted picture of reality that separates us from the flow of life energy and our true feelings and prevent insights into the nature of the world. The Pathwork offers techniques for dissolving misconceptions about the world.

Pierrakos died in 1979. Since that time her work has been carried on by her students and expanded from the two centers opened in 1979 to include work across North America and Europe, with newer centers now functioning in Africa, South America, and Australia. The Pathwork Foundation is headquartered at 13013 Collingwood Ter., Silver Spring, MD 20904-1414. It has an Internet site at http://www.pathwork.org/. Pierrakos' husband went on to develop the Institute of Core Energetics.

Sources:

Hanegraaff, Wouter J. *New Age Religion and Western Culture: Esotericism in the Mirror of Secular Thought.* Leiden: E. J. Brill, 1996.

Pathwork Foundation. http://www.pathwork.org/. June 10, 2000.

Pierrakos, Eva. *Guide Lectures for Self-Transformation.* New York: Pathwork Press, 1985.

———. *The Pathwork of Self-Transformation.* New York: Bantam Doubleday, 1990.

Pierrakos, John C. (1921–)

Psychiatrist John Pierrakos, the husband of psychic channel Eva Pierrakos, was a student of controversial psychiatrist **Wilhelm Reich** and the founder of a system of bodywork called core energetics. Pierrakos was born in a small town, Neon Oitylon, in Greece. In 1939, as World War II loomed on the horizon, he left Greece for the United States. He settled in New York and attended Columbia University eventually earning an M.D. with a specialization in psychiatry. He eventually earned a Ph.D. in psychiatry. In the late 1940s, he came to know Reich and studied with him until he ran into trouble with the authorities for his teachings and practices concerning Orgone energy (his version of what was otherwise known as **prana** or psychic energy).

Pierrakos worked on the staff of a hospital for several years and then settled in private practice with another former Reichean, Alexander Lowen. The two created bioenergetics, a new system of bodywork that drew inspiration from Reich and dealt with the manner in which the inner life of people and energetic states were manifest in the body.

Around 1964, he was given a copy of a lecture of a medium, Eva Broch, a trance channel whose lectures were devoted to personal growth. The two were drawn to each other from their initial meeting, and he began to study with her on what she called the Pathwork. The teaching seemed to provide what he had found missing from Reich and from bioenergetics. He also began to share with her what he had learned about the body's energies. They were married in 1971.

As **Eva Pierrakos** (1915–1979), she opened the first Pathwork Center in 1972. He supported her work while continuing to integrate the Pathwork insights into his own practice. He has seen the Pathwork as causing a shift of emphasis toward the development of the spiritual self in his bodywork and counseling practice. According to Pierrakos, "Core Energetics is based on a deep understanding of the ways in which energy and consciousness work together in the transformative process of healing." Following his wife's death in 1979, he founded the Institute of Core Energetics, now the Institute of Core Energetics International.

The institute may be contacted c/o Joan Groom, 47 Moseman Ave., Katonah, NY 10536. It offers an expansive program of professional workshops and symposia at locations across North America, Europe, and **Australia.** It has a webpage at http://www.core-energeticsintl.org/.

Sources:

Institute for Core Energetics. http://www.core-energeticsintl.org/. June 10, 2000.

Pierrakos, John C. *Core Energetics: Developing the Capacity to Love and Heal.* Mendocino, Calif.: Liferhythms, 1990.

———. *Eros, Love, and Sexuality: The Forces that Unify Men and Women.* Mendocino, Calif.: Liferhythm, 1997.

Pike, Albert (1809–1891)

Albert Pike, the leading American Masonic scholar of the nineteenth century, was born on December 20, 1809, in Boston, Massachusetts, the son of an alcoholic father and a mother who tried to push him into the ministry. In 1925 he was sent to live with his uncle, who discovered that Pike had a photographic memory and was able to recall large volumes at will. He soon mastered several languages and passed his entrance exams for Harvard. Unable to afford tuition, he taught school at Gloucester. A free spirit, in 1831 he moved to New Mexico and joined several exploration expeditions. He finally settled in Fort Smith, Arkansas, in 1833 and taught school for a year while he studied law. He opened his practice in 1834.

He enjoyed some degree of prestige and in the 1850s became politically active. He organized the Know-Nothing Party (Order of United Americans), a reactionary political movement opposed to foreigners, and came to see the continuance of slavery as better for the country than farmers importing foreign laborers. At the same time he was pro-Indian, and as the representative of several tribes of Native Americans before the government, won some large settlements. At the beginning of the Civil War (1861–65), Pike, then living in New Orleans, Louisiana, was named commissioner of Indian Affairs for the Confederacy. He eventually was named a brigadier general and he organized several regiments from the Arkansas tribes. Unfortunately, some of his soldiers mutilated Union soldiers in a battle in 1862. In the midst of that controversy, he quarreled with his superiors and accused the Confederacy of neglecting its treaty obligation to the tribes. He was arrested for treason, but released as the war effort collapsed. Now hated by both sides, he retreated to the Ozark Mountains.

It is possible that Pike's sojourn into the occult started during his days in hiding. Rumors emerged that he was conjuring the devil and engaging in sexual orgies (charges discussed by Montague Summers in his *History of Witchcraft and Demonology*). He had joined the Freemasons in 1850 and began working seriously on reforming what he thought of as worthless rituals. He became accomplished in hermetic, Rosicrucian, and continental Masonic traditions and incorporated extensive esoteric content. His monumental textbook, *Morals and Dogma of Freemasonry,* appeared in 1872. Since Pike had dumped so much material acquired from his memory, he refused to claim authorship. He could not determine what was his own contribution.

He was never able to recover his prewar prominence in law, and increasingly he lost himself in **Freemasonry.** In 1873 he moved into the Temple of the Supreme Council of the Scottish Rite in Washington, D.C. The council offered him a stipend and he would remain there the rest of his life. He dominated Scottish Rite Masonry for the next two decades. During this time he wrote several additional books on Masonry (and left behind a number of manuscripts still unpublished), but is still remembered for his early text and reformed rituals. He died in Washington on April 2, 1891.

In 1899 the Scottish Rites erected a statue of Pike in Washington. Ninety years later, civil rights activists brought up the old accusation of Pike having written the rituals of the Ku Klux Klan and demanded that it be removed. Lacking clear evidence of their accusations, they were unsuccessful.

Sources:

Brown, Walter Lee. *Albert Pike, 1809–1891.* Fayetteville: University of Arkansas Press, 1997.

Duncan, Robert Lipscomb. *Reluctant General: The Life and Times of Albert Pike.* N.p., 1961.

[Pike, Albert]. *Morals and Dogma of Freemasonry.* 1871, 1905. Reprint, Kila, Mont.: Kessinger Publishing, 1992.

Pike, James A(lbert) (1913–1969)

Former Episcopalian bishop of California, whose bestselling book *The Other Side* (1968) was a powerful argument for psychic phenomena and communication with the dead. Pike was born on February 14, 1913, in Oklahoma City, Oklahoma. He was educated at the University of Santa Clara (1930–32), the University of California at Los Angeles (1932–33), the University of Southern California (A.B., 1934; LL.B., 1936), and Yale University (J.S.D., 1938). He later studied at Virginia Theological Seminary (1945–46), General Theological Seminary (1936–47), and Union Theological Seminary (B.D. magna cum laude, 1951).

Though raised a Roman Catholic, he converted to the Episcopal Church, in which he was ordained a priest in 1944. He was successively curate of St. John's Church, Washington, D.C. (1944–46), chaplain at Vassar College (1947–49), chaplain and head of the department of religion at Columbia University (1949–52), adjunct professor of religion and law (1952–58), and dean of the Cathedral of St. John the Divine, New York City (1952–58). He was elected the bishop coadjutor (i.e., with right of succession) of the diocese of California, San Francisco in 1958 and became bishop a few months later.

During his pastoral career, Pike wrote a number of popular books, but his popularity jumped significantly in 1964 with the publication of *A Time for Christian Candor* (1964). That volume became one of several volumes published during the 1960s that offered somewhat radical reinterpretations of traditional Christian doctrines, ideas freely discussed in a seminary context, but rarely openly discussed between pastors and church members. This volume, two subsequent titles, *If This Be Heresy* (1967) and *You and the New Morality* (1967), the admission of some failures in his personal life, and some happenings at the cathedral in San Francisco, combined to create significant enemies in the church. Pike was forced out of office. He resigned as bishop in 1966 to become theologian in residence at the Center for Study of Democratic Institutions in Santa Barbara, California.

Among the personal problems with which Pike was confronted was the death of his son Jim, who had committed suicide at the age of twenty after experimenting with LSD. In a 1967 Canadian television program, American medium **Arthur A. Ford** communicated a message to Pike apparently from his son Jim. The message, in the full glare of the television lights, was highly evidential and was augmented by strongly suggestive messages purportedly from several of Pike's deceased colleagues, including theologian Paul Tillich. Pike soon publicly affirmed his belief in the reality of the phenomena he had experienced, and this affirmation made up the substance of his book *The Other Side* (1968). More quietly he also received messages through mediums **Ena Twigg** in London and George Daisley in Santa Barbara.

In 1969 he founded, with his wife Diane, the Foundation of Religious Transition to focus upon people who, like himself, had problems because of their demythologizing approach to Christian belief and practice. Soon afterward, Pike died when he wandered off and became lost in the Israeli desert in 1969. (Three days before the discovery of his body a communication claiming to be from him came through medium Ena Twigg stating what had occurred and where the body would be found.)

Diane Pike changed the name of the foundation to the Bishop Pike Foundation, and it eventually (1972) merged into the Love Project (now the Teleos Foundation) led by Arleen Lorrance. Diane and Lorrance have worked together ever since.

In the early 1970s, following the medium Arthur Ford's death, author Alan Spraggett (who had hosted the television show during which Ford spoke to Pike) discovered material in Ford's papers which conclusively proved that Ford had faked the séance. Ford's **fraud** was discovered in his papers, which had been left in the care of William Rauscher, an Episcopal minister in New Jersey, in a file of material that contained all of the "evidential" facts stated by the supposedly entranced Ford. Prior to the television séance Ford had thoroughly researched Pike's career.

Sources:

Berger, Arthur S., and Joyce Berger. *The Encyclopedia of Parapsychology and Psychical Research.* New York: Paragon House, 1991.

Spraggett, Alan, with William Rauscher. *Arthur Ford: The Man Who Talked with the Dead.* New York: New American Library, 1973.

Pilgrim's Guide to Planet Earth: A New Age Traveler's Handbook & Spiritual Directory

A directory published in 1981 of shrines, temples, churches, monasteries, holy places, spiritual and New Age teachings. It covers some 50 countries. It also cites schools, publications, communes, food stores, and vegetarian and macrobiotic restaurants and offers useful advice to international travelers (pilgrims) on the customs and facilities of unfamiliar countries and cultures. The guide was published by Spiritual Community Publications, formerly of San Rafael, California. Several years after the guide appeared Spiritual Community Publications went out of business, and no one has attempted an update of the original directory.

Sources:

A Pilgrim's Guide to Planet Earth: A Traveler's Handbook and New Age Directory. San Rafael, Calif.: Spiritual Community Publications, 1981.

Pincott, Hugh (1941–)

British chemist and psychical researcher. He was born on October 11, 1941, in Swansea, Wales. He was educated at Pontardawe Grammar School and the Universities of St. Andrews and Dundee. He obtained the first Ph.D. from Dundee University on its foundation in 1967, and he later became a chartered chemist. He was employed for nearly a quarter of a century by the British Petroleum group of companies and occupied several commercial positions of increasing seniority, eventually becoming assistant coordinator of BP's chemicals operation in the Western Hemisphere. Following a rationalization of company interest in 1984, Pincott left BP and established his own organization, **Specialist Knowledge Services** (SKS), which does marketing consultancy and specialist bookselling.

Pincott joined the **Society for Psychical Research** in 1971, was appointed a member of its Council in 1974, and became its honorary secretary and treasurer in 1976. He was one of the founding members of the **Association for the Scientific Study of Anomalous Phenomena** (ASSAP) in 1981 and acted as the external affairs officer for two years. Since 1983 he has been the association's honorary general secretary. Among his wide research activities have been mental mediumship, paranormal metal bending, and, more particularly, regressive hypnosis to alleged previous lives.

Pinto

The grand master of Malta, who was assisted in alchemical experiments by **Cagliostro.**

Pio, Padre (da Pietralcini) (1887–1968)

Italian friar of the Capuchin monastery of San Rotundo, near Foggia, with reputed powers of **clairvoyance** and **precognition,** who also demonstrated the **stigmata** (wounds of Christ) from 1915 onward. Born Francesco Forgione, he lived a simple life and was a sympathetic personality who did not seek public notice. Among the phenomena he demonstrated that have excited some parapsychologists are instances of apparent bilocation. The most notable example occurred in 1941 when his friend Monsignor Damiani died in far-off Urugary. On the evening of Damiani's death, the Cardinal Archbishop or Montevideo admitted a hooded Capuchin monk who Damiani testified before his death was Pio.

The phenomena surrounding Pio have been neither endorsed nor condemned by the official office of the church charged with the evaluation of such occurrences, but they have been widely accepted by the public. Pio has been the subject, especially since his death in 1968, of a large body of literature. (See also **Therese Neuman**)

Sources:

Berger, Arthur S., and Joyce Berger. *The Encyclopedia of Parapsychology and Psychical Research.* New York: Paragon House, 1991.

Grosso, Michael. "Padre Pio and the Paranormal." *Christian Parapsychologist* 4, no. 7 (1982).

Schug, J. A. *Padre Pio.* Huntington, Ind.: Our Sunday Visitor, 1976.

The Pioneer of Progress (Newspaper)

British Spiritualist weekly, published in London from January 1874 until November of the same year.

Piper, Leonora E(velina Simonds) (1859–1950)

Trance medium of Boston, among the most renowned in the history of psychical research. Her work is credited with convincing **Sir Oliver Lodge, Richard Hodgson, James H. Hyslop,** and many others to believe in **survival and communication** with the dead.

Early Life

Piper was born Leonora Simmonds on June 27, 1859, in Nashua, New Hampshire. There has been some discussion of the correct spelling of her first name, though it is now largely agreed to have been "Leonora," rather than "Leonore," as is often found in the literature. This issue became the subject of a paper in the *Journal* of the American Society for Psychical Research.

When eight years old, playing in the garden, she suddenly felt a sharp blow on her right ear, accompanied by a prolonged sibilant sound. This gradually resolved itself into the letter *s*, which was then followed by the words "Aunt Sara, not dead, but with you still." The child was terrified.

Her mother made a note of the day and the time. Several days later it was found that Piper's aunt Sara had died at that very hour on that very day. A few weeks later the child cried out that she could not sleep because of "the bright light in the room and all the faces in it," and because the bed "won't stop rocking." However, discounting occasional experiences of this kind, her childhood was relatively normal.

At age 22 she married William Piper of Boston. Soon after this she consulted Dr. J. R. Cocke, a blind professional clairvoyant who was attracting considerable attention by his medical diagnoses and cures. She fell into a short trance.

At the second visit to the clairvoyant's circle, which was held for effecting cures and developing latent mediumship, when Cocke put his hand on her head, Piper again saw in front of her "a flood of light in which many strange faces appeared." In a trance, she rose from her chair, walked to a table in the center of the room, picked up a pencil and paper, and wrote rapidly for a few minutes before handing the written paper to a member of the circle and returning to her seat. The member was Judge Frost of Cambridge, a noted jurist; the message, the most remarkable he ever received, came from his dead son.

The report of Frost's experience spread and Piper was soon besieged for sittings. She was not at all pleased by this sudden notoriety, and apart from members of her family and intimate friends she refused to see anyone. However, when the mother-in-law of **William James** applied for a sitting (after hearing strange stories through servant gossip), for some inexplicable reason her request was granted. Her own experience, the subsequent experience of her daughter (i.e., James's wife), and the marvelous stories they told finally induced James to visit Piper in order to explain away her reputed psychic talents. But his impression of her supernormal powers was so strong that he not only continued sittings, but for the next eighteen months monitored Piper and controlled virtually all of her séance arrangements.

Referring mainly to this first period of his experiences, he wrote in 1890 in *Proceedings* of the Society for Psychical Research (vol. 6, pt. 17): "And I repeat again what I said before, that, taking everything that I know of Mrs. Piper into account, the result is to make me feel as absolutely certain as I am of any personal fact in the world that she knows things in her trances which she cannot possibly have heard in her waking state, and that the definite philosophy of her trances is yet to be found."

James also made the famous statement: "If you wish to upset the law that all crows are black . . . it is enough if you prove that one crow is white. My white crow is Mrs. Piper."

Piper's Controls

When James began his experiments, a claimed French doctor, **"Phinuit,"** was in exclusive **control** of the sittings. He appeared to have been inherited from Cocke. He was known there as "Finne" or "Finnett." His manifestation was not immediate. The first of Piper's controls was an Indian girl of the strange name "Chlorine." "Commodore Vanderbilt," "Longfellow," "Lorette Penchini," "J. Sebastian Bach" and "Mrs. Siddons," the actress, were the next communicators encountered.

"Phinuit" had a deep gruff voice, in striking contrast with the voice of the medium. His exclusive regime lasted from 1884 to 1892 when **"George Pelham,"** who had died in an accident, appeared and manifested in **automatic writing.** Still, the trance speaking was left for "Phinuit" and the control, speaking and writing, was often simultaneous.

In 1897 the **"Imperator"** group took charge of the séance proceedings. "Phinuit" disappeared and "Pelham" became relegated to the role of a minor communicator. While "Phinuit" had much difficulty in keeping back other would-be communicators, the advent of the "Imperator" group of controls made the communications freer from interruptions and from the admixture of apparently foreign elements. They excluded "inferior" intelligences (whom they spoke of as "earth-bound" spirits) from the use of the light.

Under the new regime, the communications assumed a dignity and loftiness of expression, as well as a quasi-religious character, which they had heretofore entirely lacked. Moreover, the passing in and out of the trance state, which in the earlier stages had been accomplished with a certain amount of difficulty, now, under the new conditions, became quiet and peaceful.

James called special attention to the fact that the "Imperator" group of controls not only exhibited characteristic personalities, but they could also divine the most secret thoughts of the sitters. As a lasting influence of this regime in later years, Piper showed remarkable development as spiritual adviser in her waking state. "It is almost," wrote Alta L. Piper in 1929, "as if, since the trance state has been less and less resorted to, the cloak of 'Rector' has fallen upon Mrs. Piper herself, and the good that she has been able to do along these lines, during the past nine or ten years, is almost unbelievable."

Piper did not exhibit physical phenomena, except for one single strange manifestation: she could withdraw the scent from flowers and make them wither in a short time. To establish rapport with her spirit communicators, she utilized psychometric influences (see **psychometry**), usually asking for an object belonging to the departed. James succeeded in hypnotizing her and found the conditions of the hypnotic and medium trances entirely different. He found no signs of thought transference either in the hypnotic condition or immediately after it.

Of the earliest trances there is no contemporary record. When, owing to other duties, James relinquished direct control of the Piper séances he wrote to various members of the **Society for Psychical Research** of the puzzling and remarkable facts of the mediumship. It was as a result of these letters that Richard Hodgson arrived in the United States for the express purpose of continuing the investigation on behalf of the SPR.

With his arrival began the most famous period of Piper's mediumship. Hodgson was a keen **fraud**-hunter, having previously caught **Eusapia Palladino** and **Helena Petrovna Blavatsky** in trickery. He took every precaution to bar the possibility of deception including hiring a detective to follow Piper and watch for possible attempts to obtain information by normal means. On the first three days of the week, when sittings were given, Hodgson forbade her to see a morning newspaper. He arranged the sittings without communicating the name of the sitters and the sitters were in most cases unknown to her. They were introduced under the pseudonym "Smith." The sittings were often improvised for the benefit of chance callers.

She was usually weakest precisely where the pseudo-medium is most successful. She was vague about dates, preferred to give Christian names to surnames, and mostly concentrated on the sitters diseases, personal idiosyncrasies, and characters. On the other hand, she often failed to answer test questions. For example, the spirit of "Hannah Wild" manifesting through her could not describe the contents of the sealed letter she wrote before her death.

The possibility of fraud was discussed at length by Hodgson, James, **William R. Newbold** (of Pennsylvania University), **Walter Leaf,** and Sir Oliver Lodge. In 1898 James wrote in the *Psychological Review:*

"Dr. Hodgson considers that the hypothesis of fraud cannot be seriously maintained. I agree with him absolutely. The medium has been under observation, much of the time under close observation, as to most of the conditions of her life, by a large number of persons, eager, many of them to pounce upon any suspicious circumstance for (nearly) fifteen years. During that time not only has there not been one single suspicious circumstance remarked, but not one suggestion has ever been made from any quarter which might tend positively to explain how the medium, living the apparent life she leads, could possibly collect information about so many sitters by natural means. The scientist who is confident of 'fraud' here must remember that in science as much as in common life a hypothesis must receive some positive specification and determination before it can be profitably discussed, and a fraud which is no assigned kind of fraud, but simply 'fraud' at large, fraud in *abstracto,* can hardly be regarded as a specially scientific explanation of concrete facts."

He added, at a later period:

"Practically I should be willing now to stake as much money on Mrs. Piper's honesty as on that of anyone I know, and I am quite satisfied to leave my reputation for wisdom or folly, so far as human nature is concerned, to stand or fall by this declaration."

In 1888–89, Hyslop joined the investigation. On the first two or three occasions he took the extraordinary precaution of putting on a mask before he got out of the cab, removing it only after Piper was entranced, and resuming it before she awoke. Twelve sittings were sufficient to convince him of the untenability of the secondary **personality** hypothesis. He declared, without hesitation, that "I prefer to believe that I have been talking to my dead relatives in person; it is simpler." His first report was published in *Proceedings* of the Society for Psychical Research (vol. 16, pt. 41) and concluded: "I give my adhesion to the theory that there is a future life and persistence of personal identity."

Piper in England

With unabated zeal, Hodgson sought still more stringent precautions and conceived the idea of removing Piper from her normal surroundings and placing her in a foreign country among strangers. As a result Piper made her first visit to England in November 1889. She was met at the station by Lodge and escorted the next day to Cambridge by **F. W. H. Myers,** at whose house she stayed. Myers later stated,

"I am convinced, that she brought with her a very slender knowledge of English affairs and English people. The servant who attended on her and on her two children was chosen by myself, and was a young woman from a country village, whom I had full reason to believe to be trustworthy and also quite ignorant of my own or my friend's affairs. For the most part I had myself not determined upon the persons whom I would invite to sit with her. I chose these sitters in great measure by chance; several of them were not residents of Cambridge; and except in one or two cases where anonymity would have been hard to preserve, I brought them to her under false names—sometimes introducing them only when the trance had already begun."

Piper gave, under the supervision of Myers, Lodge, and Leaf, 88 sittings between November 1889 and February 1890. Wherever she stayed in England, her movements were planned for her, and even when shopping she was accompanied by a member of the SPR Lodge, which even exceeded Myers in caution. Prior to Piper's stay in Liverpool, Lodge's wife engaged an entirely new staff of servants. Lodge safely locked away the family Bible, and throughout the duration of her stay, all of Piper's correspondence passed through the hands of Lodge, who had permission to read it.

In Lodge's first sitting, his father, his Uncle William, his Aunt Ann, and a child of his who died very young were described. There were some flaws in the descriptions that were later rectified. Many personal and intimate details of their lives were given. In subsequent sittings the names of the dead relatives were communicated in full, and supernormal knowledge of the history of the whole family was exhibited. Sir Oliver Lodge's report, published in 1890, concluded:

"1. That many of the facts given could not have been learnt even by a skilled detective.

"2. That to learn others of them, although possible, would have needed an expenditure of money as well as of time which it seems impossible to suppose that Mrs. Piper could have met.

"3. That her conduct has never given any ground whatever for supposing her capable of fraud or trickery. Few persons have been so long and so carefully observed, and she has left on all observers the impression of thorough uprightness, candor and honesty."

Lodge enumerated 38 cases in which information not within the conscious knowledge of the sitter was given. In only five instances did the sitter acknowledge that the facts were at one time known to him. Considering the extraordinary familiarity of "Phinuit" with the boyhood days of two of his uncles, Lodge was curious how much of this knowledge might be obtained by normal means. He sent a professional inquiry agent to the scene for the purpose of making full and exhaustive inquiries. "Mrs. Piper," reported the agent, "has certainly beat me. My inquiries in modern Barking yield less information than she gave. Yet the most skilful agent could have done no more than secure the assistance of the local record keepers and the oldest inhabitants living."

In his summary, Lodge added,

"By introducing anonymous strangers and by catechising her myself in various ways, I have satisfied myself that much of the information she possesses in the trance state is not acquired by ordinary common-place methods, but that she has some unusual means of acquiring information. The facts on which she discourses are usually within the knowledge of some person present, though they are often entirely out of his conscious thought at the time. Occasionally facts have been narrated which have only been verified afterwards, and which are in good faith asserted never to have been known; meaning thereby that they have left no trace on the conscious memory of any person present or in the neighborhood and that it is highly improbable that they were ever known to such persons. She is also in the trance state able to diagnose diseases and to specify the owners or late owners of portable property, under circumstances which preclude the application of ordinary methods."

Further he stated:

"That there is more than can be explained by any amount of either conscious or unconscious fraud—that the phenomenon is a genuine one, however it is to be explained—I now regard as absolutely certain; and I make the following two statements with the utmost confidence:

"1.That Mrs. Piper's attitude is not one of deception.

"2. No conceivable deception on the part of Mrs. Piper can explain the facts."

Further Work with Hodgson

After Piper's return to the United States, Hodgson took charge again. His first report was published in 1892 in the *Proceedings* of the Society Psychical Research. He refused to consider spirit hypothesis acceptable. In 1892 the Piper phenomena underwent a notable evolution in the quality of trance communications. Automatic writing developed and "Pelham" a became the primary control.

Hodgson's second report, which appeared in the *Proceedings* of the SPR in 1897, ended with the adoption of the spirit hypothesis. His statement was quite firm:

"I cannot profess to have any doubt but that the 'chief communicators . . . are veritably the personalities that they claim to be; that they have survived the change we call death, and that they have directly communicated with us whom we call living through Mrs. Piper's entranced organism. Having tried the hypothesis of telepathy from the living for several years, and the "spirit" hypothesis also for several years, I have no hesitation in affirming with the most absolute assurance that the "spirit" hypothesis is justified by its fruits and the other hypothesis is not."

It is interesting to quote here the following note from Alta L. Piper's biography of her mother: "During the latter years of his investigation I more than once heard Dr. Hodgson say, ruefully, that his *amour propre* had never quite recovered from the shock it received when he found himself forced to accept unreservedly the genuineness of the so-called Piper phenomena."

Hodgson's intended third report was cut short by his unexpected death in 1905. **J. G. Piddington** came over from England to go through his papers and a committee was formed to dispose of the material on hand. The reports were filled with intimate and personal data concerning the sitters, who trusted Hodgson but would not trust anybody else. Finally, despite Hyslop's efforts, all these reports were returned to the original sitters and the valuable material was lost. Piper remained under the jurisdiction of the SPR, and the sittings were continued under Hyslop's charge.

The Hyslop Era

In 1906, Piper made a second visit to England. It was mainly devoted to elucidating the mystery of **cross-correspondences.** Several famous investigators (such as Myers, **Edmund Gurney,** and Hodgson) had died and communications of an intricate nature were purported to emanate from their surviving spirits. Piper held 74 sittings. Many others were held with **Margaret Verrall** and **Alice K. Fleming** (usually cited as Mrs. Holland in the literature to protect her privacy). The results were summed up and analyzed by Piddington and others. According to their findings, the coincidences of thought and expression in the various messages were too numerous and too detailed to be accounted for by chance.

In 1909, James published his report on the Hodgson communications jointly in the *Proceedings* of the SPR and the ASPR. He judged the findings to be inconclusive. Writing on the Myers, Gurney, and Isaac Thompson communications in the same number of the *Proceedings,* Lodge showed none of James's reserve,

"On the whole they [the messages] tend to render certain the existence of some outside intelligence or control, distinct from the consciousness, and, so far as I can judge, from the subconsciousness also, of Mrs. Piper or other mediums. And they tend to render probable the working hypothesis, on which I choose to proceed, that the version of the nature of the intelligences which they themselves present and favour is something like the truth. In other words, I feel that we are in the secondary or tertiary touch—at least occasionally—with some stratum of the surviving personality of the individuals who are represented as sending messages."

In only one instance were aspersions cast, in public, on Piper's character and phenomena, and this happened simply as an advertising stunt. On October 20, 1901, the *New York Herald* published a statement by Piper, advertised as a "confession," in which she was quoted to say that she intended to give up the work she had been doing for the SPR, as fourteen years' work was not enough to clear up the subject and summed up her own views as follows: "The theory of telepathy strongly appeals to me as the most plausible and genuinely scientific solution of the problem . . . I do not believe that spirits of the dead have spoken through me when I have been in the trance state. . . . It may be that they have, but I do not affirm it."

According to the inquiries made by the editor of *Light,* Piper forbade the publication of the article as soon as she learned that they had advertised it with the word "confession" above it. She received a telegram from the *New York Herald* assuring her that the word was used for advertising only and would not appear in the article. On October 25, 1901, Mrs. Piper stated in *The Boston Advertiser:*

"I did not make any such statement as that published in the *New York Herald* to the effect that spirits of the departed do not control me. . . . My opinion is today as it was eighteen years ago. Spirits of the departed may have controlled me and they may not. I confess that I do not know. I have not changed. . . . I make no change in my relations."

As Lodge pointed out, her honesty was not in question and the *New York Herald* spoke of her throughout in laudatory terms, "since little value would be attached to her opinion in favour of the spiritistic hypothesis, it cannot fairly be urged that her opinion on the other side would weigh with us. Mrs. Piper in fact . . . is not in a more favourable, but even in a less favourable position for forming an opinion than those who sit with her, since she does not afterwards remember what passes while she is in trance."

The Closing of a Career

In October 1909, Piper made her third visit to England. Prostrated by a heavy cold, she was not able to give her first sittings until the late spring and early summer of 1910. Lodge supervised these sittings, during which Piper's return from the trance state was very difficult. Both the sitters and the controls were disturbed by these conditions and at a sitting on May 24, 1911, a coming suspension of Piper's mediumship was announced. The last sitting was held on July 3. After the appearance of a new control, "Mme. Guyon," the sitting was closed by "Imperator." In the years that followed, communications by automatic writing remained intermittent but the trance state did not make its appearance until 1915 when the famous "Faunus" message, relating to the forthcoming death of Sir Oliver Lodge's son Raymond, was given.

Between 1914 and 1924 Piper did no regular work. Her mother's failing health made increasing demands upon her time and strength. Further, no suitable supervisor for her work was found. In October 1924, Dr. **Gardner Murphy** conducted a series of sittings, at the end of which the SPR agreed that Piper should sit with the newly formed Boston Society for Psychical Research during the season of 1926–27. She complied.

Piper's work in the cause of psychical research was of tremendous importance. For several decades her powers were tested to a degree that no other medium had approximated. Psychical research owes an enormous debt to her generous and sustained cooperation, often under difficult circumstances. The literature covering her work is vast and is spread out over several decades of the publication of both the SPR and the ASPR. Piper died in 1950.

Sources:

Berger, Arthur S., and Joyce Berger. *The Encyclopedia of Parapsychology and Psychical Research.* New York: Paragon House, 1991.

Bull, K. T. "Mrs. Piper—A Study." *Harper's Bazaar* 33 (1900).

Matlock, James G. "Leonor*a* or Leonor*e*? A Note on Mrs. Piper's First Name." *Journal* of the American Society for Psychical Research 82, no. 3 (July 1988).

Piper, Alta L. *The Life and Work of Mrs. Piper.* London: Kegan Paul, 1929.

Pleasants, Helene, ed. *Biographical Dictionary of Parapsychology.* New York: Helix Press, 1964.

Robbins, Anne Manning. *Both Sides of the Veil: A Personal Experience.* Boston: Sherman & French, 1909.

Sage, M. *Mrs. Piper and the Society for Psychical Research.* London, 1903.

Salter, W. H. *Trance Mediumship: An Introductory Study of Mrs. Piper and Mrs. Leonard.* London: Society for Psychical Research, 1950.

PK

Initialism for **psychokinesis,** the ability to move objects at a distance by mental power. (See also **movement**)

PKMB

Initialism for psychokinetic **metal-bending,** the claimed paranormal bending or deformation of metal objects such as spoons and keys by psi action. (See **psychokinesis**)

Plaat, Lotte (Mme. von Strahl) (1895– ?)

Dutch psychometrist whom, for some time, the German police regularly employed to trace criminals. She was born December 30, 1895. Plaat was under the observation of Drs. Paul Sünner, Gustave Pagenstechner, Harms, Ludwig Jahn, Kasnacich, and other scientists, who recorded significant results with her. In 1930, important experiments in psychometry took place at the **National Laboratory of Psychical Research** in London at the conclusion of which Plaat left for the United States where further experimental work was performed.

Sources:

Sünner, Paul. *Die psychometrische Bebabung der Frau Lotte Plaat.* Leipzig, 1929.

Placement Test

Term used by parapsychologists to indicate a test for **psychokinesis** in which the subject attempts to make objects land in a given area.

Placidus de Titis (or Titus) (1603–1668)

Italian astrologer, mathematician, and Roman Catholic monk, born at Perugia, Italy, into a prominent noble family. Little is known of his early life prior to his joining the Olivetian order around 1624 at age 21. He later became a reader of mathematics and physics at the University of Padua and then in 1657 was appointed professor of mathematics at the Milanese University in Pavia. He remained at Pavia for the rest of his life.

In Placidus's lifetime, **astrology** was still the proper concern of scholars and churchmen, and Placidus served as astrologer to a number of prominent political leaders, including Leopold William (1614–62), the archduke of Austria. In his studies he focused upon **Claudius Ptolemy**'s ancient astrological work the *Tetrabiblos,* and in it he believed he had discerned Ptolemy's lost method of "dividing houses." (In reading an astrology chart, one must not only divide the chart into the 12 astrological signs but also rotate the chart to account for the rotation of the earth during a 24-hour period. **Astrological houses** serve as a second division system that (among other functions) facilitates that rotation. Placidus published his findings in two volumes in 1650 and 1657.

The work of Placidus had little immediate impact on astrology, which was entering a period of decline even as he was writing. At the end of the eighteenth century, however, as the revival of astrology began in England, Manoah Sibley translated some writings of Placidus into English, and a second translation, by John Cooper, was published in 1814. R. C. Smith, better known under his pen name, Raphael, used Sibley's translation in his annual *Raphael's Ephemeris,* the most popular ephemeris for the next century. (An ephemeris provides the daily charts of the planets and is used by astrologers to quickly prepare a horoscope chart.) *Raphael's Ephemeris* is still published and is used by many astrologers in Great Britain. Through Raphael the Placidian system became the dominant system in astrolgy today.

Sources:

Baugnet, Michael. Introduction to *Primum Mobile. . . .* by Placidus de Titis. Translated by John Cooper. London: Davis and Dickson, 1814.

Brau, Jean-Louis, Helen Weaver, and Allan Edwards, eds. *Larousse Encyclopedia of Astrology.* New York: New American Library, 1982.

Holden, James H., and Robert A. Hughes. *Astrological Pioneers of America.* Tempe, Ariz.: American Federation of Astrologers, 1988.

Lewis, James L. *The Astrology Encyclopedia.* Detroit: Gale Research, 1994.

Placidus de Titus. *Astronomy and Elementary Philosophy.* Translated by Manoah Sibley. London: W. Justins, 1789.

———. *A Collection of Thirty Remarkable Nativities.* Translated by Manoah Sibley. London: W. Justins, 1789.

Planchette

A simple instrument designed for the purpose of communication with spirits. It consists of a thin heart-shaped piece of wood mounted on two small wheels that carries a pencil, point downward, for the third support. The hand is placed on the wood and the pencil writes automatically, or presumably by spirit control operating through the psychic force of the medium.

In 1853, a Mr. Planchette, a well-known French Spiritualist, invented this instrument, to which he gave his name. For some fifteen years it was utilized exclusively by French Spiritualists, but then in the year 1868, a firm of American toy makers took up the idea and flooded the shops of booksellers with great numbers of planchettes. They became a popular item and the instrument sold in the thousands in the United States and Great Britain. It was used largely as a toy and any results obtained that were arresting or seemingly inexplicable were explained by **animal magnetism** or ascribed to the power of subconscious thought.

Amongst Spiritualists the planchette has been used for spirit communication, and **automatic writing** has often resulted from its use. Some mediums published books that, they claimed, were written wholly by their spirit-controls through the use of planchettes.

An early attempt to explain the phenomenon was put forward by **Samuel Guppy** in his book *Mary Jane: or Spiritualism Chemically Explained* published under the modest pseudonym "A Child at School" in 1863. He stated that the human body is a condensation of gases, which constantly exude from the skin in an invisible electrical vapor and that the fingers coming in contact with the planchette transmit to it an "odic force," and thus set it in motion. He went on to say that some people have excess phosphorous in their systems and the vapor "thus exuded forms a positively living, thinking, acting body, capable of directing a pencil."

There are variations on the planchette form, such as the dial-planchette, which consists of a foundation of thick cardboard nine inches square on the face of which the alphabet and the numerals one to ten are printed. Also printed are the words "Yes," "No," "Goodbye" and "Don't know." These letters, words, and numerals are printed on the outer edge of a circle, the diameter of which is about seven inches. In the center of this circle, firmly affixed to the cardboard, is a block of wood three inches square.

The upper surface of this block has a circular channel in which balls run. Over the balls a circular piece of hard wood, five inches in diameter, is placed and attached to the outer edge of this a pointer. The upper piece of wood is attached to the lower by an ordinary screw, upon which the upper plate revolves when used for communication.

Another form is the **ouija** board, on which, in a convenient order, the letters of the alphabet are printed and over which a pointer easily moves under the direction of the hand of the person or persons acting as medium. It is stated that a form of this "mystic toy" was in use in the days of Pythagoras, about 540 B.C.E. One French author described his celebrated school of philosophy, asserted that the brotherhood held frequent séances or circles at which a mystic table, moving on wheels, moved towards signs inscribed on the surface of a stone slab. The author stated that probably Pythagoras, in his travels among the Eastern nations, observed some such apparatus in use amongst them and adapted his idea from them.

Another trace of some such communicating mechanism is found in the legend told by the Scandinavian Blomsturvalla of how the people of Jomsvikingia in the twelfth century had a high priest, one Völsunga, whose predictions were renowned for their accuracy throughout the land. He had in his possession a little ivory doll that drew with "a pointed instrument" on parchment or "other substance," certain signs to which the priest had the key. The communications were prophetic utterances, and it is said in every case they came true.

The writer who recounted this legend thought it probable that the priest had procured the doll in China. In the National Museum at Stockholm there is a doll of this description that is worked by mechanism, and when wound up it walks around in circles and occasionally uses its right arm to make curious signs with a pointed instrument like a pen that is held in the hand. Its origin and use have been connected with the legend recounted above.

The planchette and ouija board are devices to assist automatic writing. Such instruments allow use by more than one individual during a sitting, as distinct from other forms of automatic writing when only the operator handles the pen or pencil.

How It Works

The content of such messages may suggest either communications from spirit entities or unconscious mental processes on the part of the individuals concerned. Sometimes artificial entities appear to be created from the combined energies and the messages, although often startling and apparently authentic, may be deceptive. It is generally assumed that the actual movement of the planchette is due to unconscious muscular effort on the part of the operator or operators using the instrument, but as in **table-turning** and the **divining-rods** used in **dowsing,** it is by no means certain that this explanation covers all the facts.

Clearly the actual contact between fingers and instrument can communicate subtle muscular exertion, but the conversion of this exertion to the complex movements involved in writing intelligible messages is difficult to explain. Even granting the operation of unconscious muscular effort, it is not clear how this is adapted to constructing messages which are often not visible to the operator. Again, the planchette may sometimes move at remarkable speeds, far in advance of the normal intellectual mode or reflex muscular actions of the operator. The same phenomenon also occurs in automatic writing.

There are also some cases reported of **direct writing,** in which there was no contact between the operator and the writing.

It should be noted that the results of the use of the planchette and similar devices often reflect the intellectual and emotional status of the operator or operators involved, and most knowledgeable people advise against use of the planchette or ouija board in the frivolous atmosphere of party games. Suggestible individuals may become obsessive about the messages obtained.

Sources:

A Child at School [Samuel Guppy]. *Mary Jane: or Spiritualism Chemically Explained.* London: John King, 1863.

Ellis, Ida. *Planchette and Automatic Writing.* Blackpool, UK, 1904.

Hyslop, James H. *Contact With the Other World.* New York: Century, 1919.

Mühl, Anita M. *Automatic Writing: An Approach to the Unconscious.* Steinkopff, 1930. Reprint, New York: Helix Press, 1964.

Sargent, Epes. *Planchette, or the Despair of Science.* Boston, 1869.

Truthseeker, A. *The Planchette Mystery: Being a Candid Inquiry Into the Nature, Origin, Import, and Tendencies of Modern Signs and Wonders.* New York: Samuel R. Wells, 1870.

Planetary Light Association

The Planetary Light Association was founded in 1983 by Jane Weiss, a channel. She claimed that the messages she channels come from "Anoah." Described as a member of the Melchizedek Order of the White Brotherhood, the groups of advanced beings believed to be guiding the course of human history, "Anoah" spoke at Golden Circle sessions to assist the transition into the **New Age,** which many hoped would arrive during the next generation. These channeled messages were distributed worldwide through a newsletter and tapes. Weiss also gave psychic development workshops. Last known address: P.O. Box 180786, Austin, TX 78718.

Sources:

Weiss, Jane. *Reflections by Anoah.* Austin, Tex.: Planetary Light Association, 1986.

Planetary Logos

According to the **Theosophy** scheme of creation, the Planetary Logos or Ruler of Seven Chains is one of the grades in the hierarchy assisting in the creation and guidance. It is the supreme Logos who initiates this work, but he is helped by the "seven." The seven receive from the Logos the inspiration and each carries on the work in his own Planetary Chain. (See also **Logos; planetary spirits**)

Sources:

Jinarajadasa, C. *The Early Teachings of the Masters, 1881–1883.* Chicago: Theosophical Press, 1923.

Planetary Spirits

In **Theosophy,** the number of these spirits is seven. They are emanations from the Absolute and are the agents used by the Absolute to effect all changes in the Universe. (See also **Logos; Planetary Logos**)

Planetary Travels

Mediums in a trance state claim to travel to other planets. Descriptions of astral travel, inner vision, or spirit enlightenment and life on the planets were first given by **Emanuel Swedenborg** in the seventeenth to eighteenth century.

Swedenborg claimed the people of Mars were the best in the whole planetary system. Physiognomy, with them, was an expression of thought. They judged each other by it. They were God-fearing, and the Lord sometimes appeared among them. Of the inhabitants of Venus and the moon, Swedenborg said:

"They are of two kinds; some are gentle and benevolent others wild, cruel and of gigantic stature. The latter rob and plunder, and live by this means; the former have so great a degree of gentleness and kindness that they are always beloved by the good; thus they often see the Lord appear in their own form on their earth.

"The inhabitants of the Moon are small, like children of six or seven years old; at the same time they have the strength of men like ourselves. Their voices roll like thunder, and the sound proceeds from the belly, because the moon is in quite a different atmosphere from the other planets."

Swedenborg's accounts of planetary travel was limited to those planets known to exist in the eighteenth century.

Planetary exploration in the form of what appeared to be traveling **clairvoyance** was first recorded with Fraulein Romer, a German somnambule who in November 1813, at the age of 15, was seized with convulsive attacks and developed mediumship.

In 1921, C. Romer described how the spirits of dead relatives but more often the spirit of a living companion, Louise, led the medium to the moon. She described its flora, fauna and inhabitant and the spirits of the dead who spend there their first stage of existence in their progress to higher spheres. Romer claimed the descriptions were in accord with those offered by the subjects of **Joseph Ennemoser**'s experiments.

Andrew Jackson Davis followed in the footsteps of Swedenborg. **Victorien Sardou** reportedly drew automatic sketches of houses and scenes on the planet Jupiter. **Auguste Henri Jacob** executed drawings of fruits and flowers he claimed grew on the planet Venus. **Thomas Lake Harris,** in *Celestial Arcana,* described the inhabitants on other planets of the solar system and also some of remote fixed stars. Harris claimed to have had conversations with them.

Statements and disclosures were also exemplified by a revelation of Hélène Smith. **Theodore Flournoy** in *From India to the Planet Mars* (1900), traced the origin of Smith's Martian Cycle to chance remarks and the desire expressed by Georges-Henri Lemaitre a Belgian astro physicist, to know more about the planet. On November 25, 1884, Flournoy noted:

"From the beginning . . . Mlle. Smith perceived, in the distance and at a great height, a bright light. Then she felt a tremor which almost caused her heart to cease beating, after which it seemed to her as though her head were empty and as if she were no longer in the body. She found herself in a dense fog, which changed successively from blue to a vivid rose color, to gray, and then to black. She is floating, she says, and the table, supporting itself on one leg, seemed to express a very curious floating movement. Then she sees a star growing larger, always larger, and becomes finally 'as large as our house.'

"Hélène feels that she is ascending; then the table gives, by raps: 'Lemaitre, that which you have so long desired!' Mlle. Smith, who had been ill at ease, finds herself feeling better, she distinguishes three enormous globes, one of them very beautiful. 'On what am I walking?' she asks. And the table replies: 'On a world—Mars.' Hélène then began a description of all strange things which presented themselves to her view, and caused her as much surprise as amusement. Carriages without horses or wheels, emitting sparks as they glided by; houses with fountains on the roof; a cradle having for curtains an angel made of iron with outstretched wings, etc. What seemed less strange were people exactly like the inhabitants of our earth, save that both sexes wore the same costume, formed of trousers, very ample, and a long blouse, drawn tight about the waist and decorated with various designs. The child in the cradle was exactly like our children, according to the sketch which Hélène made from memory after the séance. . . .

"We are struck by two points, the complete identity of the Martian world, taken in its chief points, with the world in which we live, and its puerile originality in a host of minor details. . . . One would say that it was the work of a young scholar to whom had been given the task of trying to invent a world as different as possible from ours, but real and who had conscientiously applied himself to it loosening the reins of his childish fancy in regard to a multitude of minor points in the limits of what appeared admissible according to his short and narrow experience. All the traits that I discover in the author of the Martian romance can be summed up in a single phrase, its profoundly infantile character."

New Languages Appear

Flournoy claimed the Martian language, was not only revealed but also translated into French and bore the stamp of a "natural" language. "I will add that in speaking fluently and somewhat quickly, as Hélène sometimes does in somnambulism, it has an acoustic quality altogether its own due to the predominance of certain sounds, and has a peculiar intonation difficult to describe."

Seventeen days later a medium attempted to depict life in an undetermined planet farther away than Mars. Reportedly, medium saw a world, with a different language than the Martian, the tallest people were three feet high, with heads twice as broad as high, living in low, long cabins without windows or doors but with a tunnel about ten feet long running from it into the earth.

Flournoy believed there was an earthly origin of both the Ultra-Martian and the Uranian language and writing.

In August 1895, Hélène Smith found a rival in America. The medium, Mrs. Willis M. Cleveland (generally known as **Mrs. Smead**), made several revelations about the planets Mars and Jupiter. After a period of five years, the detailed descriptions according to Flournoy, presented "the same character of puerility and naive imagination as those of Mlle. Smith."

Planetary Visitor

Isaac K. Funk, in his book *The Widow's Mite* (1904), wrote of a medium who impersonated "a lady eight feet tall from the planet Mars" by the use of a wire bust with rubber over it, and a false face. The wire bust fitted snugly on the shoulders of the medium and was inflated with air when in use. When not in use it could be made into a small package and concealed.

Numerous mediums have given descriptions of Martian life. Eva Harrison's *Wireless Messages from Other Worlds* (London, 1916) introduced planetary visitors from the constellation Orion. The medium **George Valiantine,** through "Dr. Barnett" predicted Martians would communicate with us before we communicated with them.

The Martian fascination of Mansfield Robinson should also be mentioned. Through a Mrs. James, the author claimed to have obtained a Martian alphabet, a Martian trance control "Oumaruru," and gave a number of Martian revelations based on trance excursions to the red planet.

Many of the claimed spiritual revelations of life on other planets betray their terrestrial origins by everything being bigger and better than on earth. This is demonstrated in the pamphlet *A Description of the Planet Neptune; or, A Message From the Spirit World* by Japssa Seniel, Spiritual, from the Planet Naculo or Neptune (London, ca. 1872), from which the following quotations are typical:

"We have horses, which we call nemilis, but they stand nearly as high again as yours, and are very far superior to any that I have seen on this globe. We have a great variety of peculiar animals called denfan; they resemble your dogs; they are quite harmless, but very useful. . . . In the city of Zinting, which is distant from Vanatha about 80,000 miles, is a carnil or match factory, which employs 30,000 hands. These matches are made of wax, and can only be lighted by dipping them in water. . . .

"Now, we will return to Vanatha, and I will describe a grand piece of workmanship—namely a bridge of metal, which is in length about 59 miles. It passes over two rivers, each seven miles in width, also over corn fields, grazing pastures, and railways; it supporters are black marble pillars. The metal is composed of iron, steel, copper, gold, and silver; but we have another kind of metal we call accelity verua, which far exceeds all the rest in strength and durability. The cross supporters of this magnificent bridge are made of this durable material; they are nine feet in diameter.

"The immense bridge is only for foot passengers; its width is about 2000 feet; it has 2000 lamps of large dimensions—namely, nine feet in diameter; they are circular in form, and are lighted with gas. This bridge took 300 years to construct it, at a cost of £300,000,000 sterling; it employed about 40,000,000 workmen. It was laid out by a seraph; it is paved with pantine pardia, which is more durable than any other material we have. It is neither stone nor iron, yet it is harder than the diamond or sapphire. The pavement is all cut in stars; the balustrade is about twelve feet high, and all this stupendous bridge is covered with lemena or glass. There is on this bridge 500 drinking fountains, and about 200 filestres or water closets; these are placed over the rivers. There is about 300 approaches to this bridge, which are ascended by 300 steps, with landings and windings, and seats to recline on. In the ascent to the top, there are small houses built in the centre of this bridge, where the inhabitants can take tea or coffee, or what you call luncheon or meals. . . ."

Similar contacts with extraterrestrials and descriptions of their planets appeared throughout the first half of the twentieth century. However, a new era began in 1952 with the public attention being given to flying saucers. Claims of contacts with extraterrestrials and accompanying descriptions of their home planets, almost totally received by psychic means, began to appear with the publication of **George Adamski**'s first book. Through the 1950s people such as Truman Bethrum, Ernest Norman, and Howard Menger described life on other planets. However, in the 1950s, a new element was added. Space aliens traveled to Earth on space ships . . . thus supplemented their telepathic and related communications with actual physical contact.

These claims of contact with aliens from other planets were concurrent with the exploration of space by improved telescopes and space probes. Such data gave a better picture than previously possible of the different planets in this solar system and disproved the history of contact literature concerning life on the moon, Venus, Mars, and the other planets. By the end of the 1960s, almost no one continued to claim such contact, but claims of contact with planets beyond the reach of contemporary science in other solar system continued. Among the few claims for life on Mars was made by Ruth Norman in her 1977 *Martian Underground Cities Discovered!*

Sources:

Clark, Jerome. *The UFO Encyclopedia.* Vol. 2. Detroit: Omnigraphics, 1992.

Flournoy, Theodore. *From India to the Planet Mars.* 1900. Reprinted, New Hyde Park, N.Y.: University Books, 1963.

Harris, Thomas Lake. *Arcana of Christianity: Celestial Sense of the Divine Word.* 2 vols. New York, 1858.

Leslie, Desmond, and George Adamski. *Flying Saucers Have Landed.* London: T. Werner Laurie, 1953.

Lunan, Duncan. *Man and the Stars.* London: Souvenir Press, 1974. Reprinted as *Interstellar Contact; Communication with Other Intelligences in the Universe.* Chicago: Henry Regnery, 1975.

Melton, J. Gordon. "The Contactees: a Survey." In *The Spectrum of UFO Research: Proceedings of the Second UFO Conference.* Chicago: Center for UFO Studies, 1975.

Melton, J. Gordon, and George M. Eberhart. *The Flying Saucer Contactee Movement: 1950–1990.* Santa Barbara, Calif.: Santa Barbara Centre for Humanistic Studies, 1990.

Romer, C. *Ausführliche historische Darstellung einer höchst merkwürdigen Somnambule.* Stuttgart, 1821.

Swedenborg, Emanuel. *Earths in Our Solar System Which Are Called Planets, and Earths in the Starry Heaven, Their Inhabitants, and the Spirits and Angels There.* London: Swedenborg Society, 1860. Frequently reprinted.

Plants, Psychic Aspects of

Plant life has always been of interest to mankind. Plants have provided food, medicine, and hallucinogenic substances. However, beginning in the 1970s, there was more, public interest in the behavior and psychic aspects of plant life. Evidence was presented suggesting plants may diagnose disease, react to music and human emotions, and act as lie detectors.

Legends told of the power of sound to influence plants. In Hindu mythology, the flute music of Shri Krishna made flowers bloom. Reportedly the musician Tansen, during the era of Moghul Emperor Akbar could cause the flowers to blossom by singing a particular musical *raga* or mode. Tamil literature described how sugarcane grew in response to the musical sounds of beetles, wasps, and bees.

Scientific interest in the sensitivities of plants dates from the experiments of Charles Darwin, who attempted to stimulate *Mimosa pudica* by playing a bassoon in close proximity, hoping to bring about movements of the pinnae. There was no measurable response and twenty years later in 1877 the German plant physiologist Wilhelm Pfeffer reported in his book *Physiology of Plants* (translated into English 1900) another unsuccessful experiment he hoped would stimulate the stamens of *Cynararae* by sound.

In 1903, the Indian scientist, **Jagadis Chunder Bose,** reported in *Philosophical Transactions* of the Royal Society, Britain, his results from experiments with plants. He concluded "all characteristics of the responses exhibited by the animal tissues, were also found in those of the plant." Bose devised an apparatus to demonstrate plant reactions, many of which resembled nervous responses in animal or human life. He also measured the electrical forces released in the "death-spasms" of vegetables. The American scientist George Crile also conducted experiments to measure the vital response of plant life.

Following Bose, T. C. N. Singh at Annamalai University, India, continued experiments on plants from 1950 and reported plants respond measurably to music, dance, and prayer. After publication of his papers, similar experiments were also conducted in Canada and the United States.

From 1966 onward, **Cleve Backster,** an American polygraph specialist, conducted experiments in plant extrasensory perception, using polygraph techniques. His experiments, as reported in the *International Journal of Parapsychology,* (vol. 10, 1968), supported the thesis that plants were sensitive to human thoughts. Backster's conclusions have been independently confirmed by other experimenters, including research chemist Marcel Vogel, who claimed plants and human beings shared a common energy field and may affect each other in a manner he could record with instruments. Vogel recorded the ability of Debbie Sapp, who claimed to "enter the consciousness of a plant."

Other experimenters have shown plants may be used to trigger electric relays and open doors, stimulated by emotional suggestions from human operators. Many owners of garden plots and window boxes take it for granted their plant life may be favorably affected by human feelings and talk regularly to their plants.

Sources:

Bolton, Brett L. *The Secret Powers of Plants.* New York: Berkley, 1974. Reprint, London: Abacus, 1974.

Bose, J. C. *Plant Autographs and Their Revelations.* London: Longmans Green, 1927.

Crile, George. *The Phenomena of Life: A Radio-Electric Interpretation.* London, 1936.

Loehr, Franklin. *The Power of Prayer on Plants.* New York: New American Library, 1969.

Tompkins, Peter, and Christopher Bird. *The Secret Life of Plants.* New York: Harper & Row, 1973. Reprint, New York: Avon, 1974.

Whitman, John. *The Psychic Power of Plants.* New York: New American Library, 1974. Reprint, London: W. H. Allen, 1974.

Plastics (Spirit Markings)

Paranormally obtained plastics may be divided into two groups: imprints and molds. The first may be produced in any soft, yielding substance or on smoked or chemically treated surfaces; for the second, melted paraffin wax is employed.

Paranormal Imprints

Johann C. F. Zöllner, in his experiments with the medium **Henry Slade,** placed a dish filled to the brim with flour under the table hoping the spirit hand that took hold of him might leave an impression in the flour. **Baron Lazar Hellenbach** testified to having seen an impression of a hand larger than Slade's or any other individual present. None of their hands had any trace of flour. Zöllner also obtained the imprint of a foot on two sheets of paper covered with lamp black between two closed slates.

The imprint of a hand with four fingers, the imprint of a bird, two feet, and a materialized butterfly were supposedly obtained during the **George Valiantine**–Bradley sittings in 1925, in England. Charles Sykes, the British sculptor, was unable to give an explanation, as was Noel Jaquin, a fingerprint expert. In 1931, however, the same experts claimed to have caught Valiantine in a **fraud.** They smeared printing ink in secret on the modeling wax, stripped Valiantine after the séance and found a large stain on his left elbow corresponding with the lines of the imprint. Other imprints were found identical to those of his toes.

Palladino's Mediumship

Eusapia Palladino produced hand and face imprints in putty and clay. Reportedly they bore her characteristics, although she was held at a distance from the tray while the impression was made. Numerous imprints were obtained by the psychical researchers **Cesare Lombroso, Enrico Morselli, Ercole Chiaia,** and **Guillaume de Fontenay.**

Camille Flammarion claimed to be a witness of the process at Monfort-l'Amaury in 1897. Supposedly the resemblance of the spirit head to the medium was undeniable, yet seemingly she could not have imprinted her face in the putty. Besides having been physically controlled, Ms. Z. Blech kissed Palladian on the cheeks, searching for the odor of putty on her face.

Julien Ochorowitz wrote of Palladino's mediumship at Rome:

"The imprint of this face was obtained in darkness, yet at a moment when I held two hands of Eusapia, while my arms were entirely around her. Or, rather, it was she who clung to me in such a way that I had accurate knowledge of the position of all her limbs. Her head rested against mine even with violence. At the moment of the production of the phenomena a convulsive trembling shook her whole body, and the pressure of her head on my temples was so intense that it hurt me."

Paranormal Molds

In normal wax molding, the technical process of the production of paraffin wax casts begins with the placement of buckets of hot and cold water placed side by side. The hot water will melt the paraffin. If one dips a hand in and withdraws it, a thin shell of the liquid will settle and congeal. If a hand is dipped alternately into the hot paraffin and into the cold water the shell will thicken. When the hand is freed, a wax glove is left behind. These gloves are fragile. They must be filled with plaster of Paris to preserve. Then if the paraffin wax is melted off, the texture of the skin appears in the plaster. The hand freed from the paraffin shell must be washed in soap and water before another experiment, or the second shell will stick to the fingernails. Altogether, it takes about twenty minutes to deliver a finished shell. The fingers of the hand must be held fairly straight, otherwise they will break the shell when withdrawn. For the same reason no full cast, up to the wrist, can be obtained.

Supposedly molds obtained by psychical researchers in séances with mediums have bent fingers, joined hands, and wrists. These molds are fine and delicate, whereas those obtained from living hands are thick and solid.

The first paraffin wax casts were obtained by **William Denton** in 1875, in Boston with the medium **Mary M. Hardy.** Hardy produced the paraffin wax gloves in public halls. To test Hardy's ability, the dish of paraffin was weighed before the mold appeared and after. In later years, another test was devised, locking up the liquid paraffin wax and cold water in a wire cage. After Denton, **Epes Sargent** investigated Hardy.

In England, **William Oxley** produced the first psychic molds in 1876 with **Elizabeth d'Esperance** and later with **Mrs. A. H. Firman** and the Rev. **Francis W. Monck.** Similar success was claimed with the **Davenport Brothers, William Eglinton,** and **Annie Fairlamb** around the same time. T. P. Barkas of Newcastle, England, mixed magenta dye in the paraffin wax during experiments with Fairlamb in 1876. The gloves had traces of the dye.

The psychical researcher **Alexander Aksakof** hypothesized that the plaster casts showed similar characteristics between the medium and the **materialization.** He noted that Oxley made similar observations and quoted his letter:

"It is a curious fact that one always recognises in the casts the distinctive token of youth or age. This shows that the materialised limbs, whilst they preserve their juvenile form, evince peculiarities which betray the age of the medium. If you examine the veins of the hand you will find in them characteristic indications which indisputably are associated with the organism of the medium."

It had been suggested the wax gloves may have been prepared from inflated rubber gloves. **Gustav Geley** produced some casts using rubber gloves for comparison. They were also put on display. The charge that the gloves may have been made previous to the séance could not be sustained.

One variety of plastics is the working of linen into the semblance of human features by psychic means. Reportedly Dr. **Eliakim Phelps** left a well-detailed description of an instance, including the appearance of 11 figures of "angelic beauty." Occasionally similar phenomena have been reported as a manifestation in haunted houses, with cushions assuming the shape of human forms.

There are also artistic efforts under the heading of **direct paintings**—the paint appears to give three-dimensional effects. Many such pictures were produced during the late nineteenth and early twentieth centuries.

There are various methods to produce imprints. Mrs. Albert Blanchard, an American medium, produced imprints by depositing sediment under water in a dish. **F. Bligh Bond** discussed her work in *Psychic Research* (October 1930) using data collected from Horace Newhart. Blanchard put clay and water in a shallow dish, stirred the sediment with her fingers, and let it settle. When the water evaporated, supposedly the clay had assumed the outlines of a human face or head in low relief.

Playfair, Guy Lyon (1935–)

Writer and investigator concerned with anomalous and paranormal phenomena. He was born on April 5, 1935, in Quetta, India and educated at Pembroke College, Cambridge University (B.A., 1959). After graduation he moved to Brazil and from 1961 through 1975 was a freelance writer and photographer. From 1967 through 1974, he also worked for the Information Office of the United States Agency for International Development in Rio de Janeiro as a writer. Playfair is a member of the the Society for Psychical Research, the Society of Authors, and the College of Psychic Studies.

Although considered by many as a writer on occultism, he has stressed that his interest actually lies in the "border areas of human experience and in anomalous phenomena of all kinds." As he stated, "I am not concerned with the 'supernatural' but with unexplored areas of nature that are by definition natural." Playfair is the author of a number of books on the psychic and related subjects and was also a contributor to the series *The Unexplained.*

Sources:

Berger, Arthur S., and Joyce Berger. *The Encyclopedia of Parapsychology and Psychical Research.* New York: Paragon House, 1991.

Playfair, Guy Lyon. *The Indefinite Boundary.* London: Souvenir Press, 1976.

———. *The Unknown Power.* 1975. Reprinted as *The Flying Cow.* London: Souvenir Press, 1975.

This House is Haunted: The True Story of a Poltergeist. London: Souvenir Press, 1980.

Pleiades

The Pleiades is a star cluster an approximately 400 light-year distance from Earth and near the constellations of Orion and Taurus in the night sky. The cluster includes seven bright stars that are easily seen with the naked eyes. In more recent years, astronomers equipped with telescopes have found the cluster to contain some 400 stars and to be surrounded by a nebula. As with many of the heavenly bodies, the Pleiades has attracted the speculation of people who have imposed a mythological significance on the objects seen in the night sky. And such speculations have not been limited to prescientific cultures. Early in the twentieth century, the leader of the group later known as the Jehovah's Witnesses suggested that one of the stars of the Pleiades was actually the throne of the Lord God Jehovah.

In ancient **Greece,** the seven prominent stars were named after the seven daughters of Atlas and Pleione. Atlas, a titan who warred against the gods, was condemned by Zeus to hold up the heavens on his shoulders. His daughters were named Alcyone, Asterope, Celaeno, Electra, Maia, Merope, and Taygete. Each has her own story from the mythological cycles.

Pleiades, largely a concern for the astronomical community in recent centuries, broke into the news in 1975 when **Eduard Albert "Billy" Meier,** the leader of a small metaphysical study group in his native **Switzerland,** announced that he had seen a saucer-shaped craft land and had communicated with its pilot, a woman named Semjase. Semjase claimed to reside on a planet in the Pleiades. Having discovered Earth in the distant past, some Pleiadians settled here and intermarried. The peace-loving Semjase was part of a group who were attempting to assist humanity out of its warlike tendencies. Meier claimed that Semjase allowed him to take pictures of the Pleiadian spacecraft, called beam ships, and that he even took a trip to the Pleiades himself. While the photographs were the most important aspect of the Meier contact claims, he also asserted that he had telepathic contacts with Semjase.

A first volume of photographs and an outline of the Meier story was published in English in 1979, and a number of additional books appeared over the next few years as ufologists debated the pros and cons of the Meier pictures. American inventor **Fred Bell** also claimed to have been in touch and received a variety of technological information from Semjase. But, although Meier received much support, mainstream ufologists denounced him. Kal K. Kroff authored two books condemning him as a hoaxer. Kroff's attacks on Meier were countered by Meier's supporters with more than a dozen books, illustrated with his many photos of the spaceships, and several video tapes. Together they made the Pleiades a well-known item within the lay community of people interested in flying saucers.

Beginning in the late 1980s, channelers (mediums), people who receive information from various extrasensory sources, appeared within the larger New Age community and claimed that they were **channeling** material from Pleiadians. The results of these contacts began to appear in 1991 with **Jani King**'s book, *The P'taah Tapes: Transmissions from the Pleiades.* It was followed the next year by possibly the most influential volume, **Barbara Marciniak**'s *Bringers of the Dawn: Teachings from the Pleiadians.* Additional Pleiadian **contactees** include **Amorah Quan Yin,** Nina Jenice, Susan Drew, **Barbara Hand Clow,** and Lyssa Royal, whose channeled material appears regularly in the monthly magazine of channeled material, *Sedona: A Journal of Emergence.* In 1996 Preston Nichols, the man who made some extraordinary claims concerning his secret work on a U.S. government project with mind control, materialization, and weather control known as the **Montauk Project,** revealed that he had also taken a trip to the Pleiades on a spaceship.

Together these New Age Channelers have led in the development of that segment of the New Age community who look to extraterrestrials as the source of the teaching material they are releasing.

Sources:

Amorah Quan Yin. *Pleiadian Perspectives on Human Evolution.* Santa Fe, N.Mex.: Bear & Co., 1996.

———. *The Pleiadian Workbook.* Santa Fe, N.Mex.: Bear & Co., 1996.

Bell, Fred. *Rays of Truth-Crystals of Light.* Blue Hill, Maine: Medicine Bear Publishing, 1999.

Clark, Jerome. *UFO Encyclopedia.* 2 vols. 2nd ed. Detroit: Omnigraphics, 1998.

Klimo, Jon. *Channeling: Investigations on Receiving Information from Paranormal Sources.* Rev. ed. Berkeley, Calif.: North Atlantic Books, 1998.

Nichols, Preston B., and Peter Moon. *Encounter in the Pleiades: An Inside Look at UFOs.* New York: Sky Books, 1996.

Rutherford, J. F. *Reconciliation.* Brooklyn, N.Y.: Watchtower Bible and Tract Society, 1917.

Winters, Randolph. *The Pleiadian Mission: A Time of Awareness.* Atwood, Calif.: The Pleiades Project, 1994.

Pliny the Elder (Galius Plinius Secundus) (ca. 23–79 C.E.)

Roman historian who studied firsthand, and died during, the eruption of Vesuvius on August 24, 79 C.E., and was one of the earliest writers to record that animals behaved in an unusual way prior to earthquakes. Many of his writings no longer exist, but one surviving work is *Naturalis Historia.* It consists of 37 books, with a mathematical and physical description of the world, and covering geography, ethnography, anthropology, human physiology, zoology, botany, agriculture, horticulture, materia medica, mineralogy, painting, modelling, and sculpture. Although Pliny was skeptical about magic and **astrology,** he described many of the occult beliefs of his time. (See also **earthquake prediction**)

Plummer, George Winslow (1876–1944)

George Winslow Plummer, cofounder of the **Societas Rosicruciana in America,** was born August 25, 1876, in Boston, Massachusetts. He graduated from Brown University and moved to New York City as an artist. Along the way he joined the Masons. At this time there was within the Masonic movement a Rosicrucian society, but its membership was limited to Masons. In 1907 Sylvester C. Gould decided to found a Rosicrucian group that would be open to all. Plummer worked with Gould in the formation of the group, the Societas Rosicruciana in America, and the founding of a periodical, *The Rosicrucian Brotherhood.* Gould died in 1909, and Plummer emerged as the sole leader of the society, a position he held for the rest of his life. He also founded the First Rosicrucian Church in America. He was ordained and later consecrated as a bishop (1918) by Manuel Ferrando of the Reformed Episcopal Church.

In 1916 Plummer founded the Mercury Publishing Company and launched *Mercury,* a quarterly, as the official periodical of the Societas Rosicruciana in America. By 1920 he was able to quit his secular job and become the full-time executive of the society. He led in the founding of six colleges (Rosicrucian groups) in the United States and one overseas in Sierre Leone.

Plummer expanded his interest in an esoteric Christian mysticism in early 1902 with the founding of the Seminary of Biblical Research, a correspondence school, for which he wrote a series of lessons called *Christian Mysticism.* In 1924, with Episcopal priest Arthur Wolfort Brooks, he founded the Anglican Universal Church of Christ in the U.S.A. He and Brooks went their separate ways in 1927, and Plummer emerged as archbishop. In 1934 he was reconsecrated by William Albert Nichols of the Holy Orthodox Church in America. The Anglican Universal Church and Holy Orthodox Church in America merged and took the name of the latter body.

Plummer developed congregations of the Holy Orthodox Church in all of the cities where Rosicrucian lodges had previously been developed. He also consecrated four men to assist him, one of whom, Stanislaus Wotowski, eventually succeeded Plummer as head of the church.

Plummer wrote a number of books, including the *Rosicrucian Fundamentals* (1920), *Principles and Practice for Rosicrucians* (1947), *The Art of Rosicrucian Healing* (1947), and *The Science of Death* (1978). He also wrote the lessons for the Rosicrucian society. Plummer died January 26, 1944, and was succeeded by Witowski and his wife, Gladys Plummer. His widow eventually married Witowski and succeeded him. She was known during the last years of her life as Mother Serena.

Sources:

Plummer, George Winslow. *The Art of Rosicrucian Healing.* New York: Society of Rosicrucians, 1947.

———. *Consciously Creating Circumstances.* New York: Society of Rosicrucians, 1939.

———. *Principles and Practices for Rosicrucians.* New York: Society of Rosicrucians, 1947.

———. *The Science of Death.* New York: Society of Rosicrucians, 1978.

Voohris, Harold V. B. *Masonic Rosicrucian Societies.* New York: Press of Henry Emmerson, 1958.

Ward, Gary L. *Independent Bishops: An International Directory.* Detroit: Apogee Books, 1990.

PMIR

Initialism for **Psi-Mediated Instrumental Response,** an experimental concept developed by parapsychologist **Rex. G. Stanford.**

Pneumatographers

Term used to denote **direct writing** mediums.

Podmore, Frank (1856–1910)

British opponent of **Spiritualism,** well-known psychical investigator, and author. He was born February 5, 1856, at Elstree, Hertfordshire. In 1874, he received a classical scholarship to Pembroke College, Oxford University, England. In 1879, he became a higher division clerk in the secretary's department of the post office.

His personal experiences in paranormal matters date from his academic studies at Oxford University. He believed in the survival and communication with the dead. In 1875, he became a contributor to *Human Nature* on Spiritualist subjects. His early belief in Spiritualism arose from his experiences with the medium **Henry Slade** (later discovered to be a **fraud**) in 1876. By 1880, in his address to the **British National Association of Spiritualists,** his belief was wavering.

He gradually developed into a skeptical critic and acted as a brake in the early years of the **Society for Psychical Research,** London. He was elected to the council of the Society for Psychical Research in 1882 and served for 27 years. **F. W. H. Myers** jointly held the office of honorary secretary for eighty years. He collaborated with Myers and **Edmund Gurney** in the producing *Phantasms of the Living.*

He admitted he was profoundly impressed by Slade and puzzled by **David Duguid** until, many years later, he considered the possibility of fraud. He did not believe the materialization demonstration of **Miss C. E. Wood** and proved he had reason to reject manifestations in the **Morell Theobald** case.

Podmore's Beliefs Challenged

Podmore believed all physical phenomena were due to fraud. **Ernesto Bozzano** in the *Annals of Psychical Science* (February 1905) claimed Podmore selected as proof those single incidents or episodes fitting his proposed theories and ignoring any contradictions to his theories. Nevertheless, Bozzano held that "we cannot refuse Mr. Podmore the extenuating circumstances of comparative good faith."

Podmore concluded: "Whether the belief in the intercourse with spirits is well-founded or not, it is certain that no critic has yet succeeded in demonstrating the inadequacy of the evidence upon which the spiritualists rely." In his book *The Newer Spiritualism,* published posthumously in 1910, Podmore stated his research had left him of the opinion:

"So far as the evidence at present goes, clairvoyance and precognition are mere chimeras, and telepathy may be no more than a vestigial faculty, to remind us, like the prehensile powers of the newly-born infant, of a time when man was in the making."

Although, in regard to trances, he stated:

"I should, perhaps, state at the outset, as emphatically as possible that it seems to me incredible that fraud should be the sole explanation of the revelations made in trance and automatic writing. No one . . . will believe that any imaginable exercise of fraudulent ingenuity, supplemented by whatever opportuneness of coincidence and laxness on the part of the investigators, could conceivably explain the whole of these communications."

Podmore resigned his position as a post office civil servant in 1906 after 25 years to devote himself fully to literary activities. His death on August 14, 1910, was an accidental drowning in the Malvern Hills.

Sources:

Berger, Arthur S., F. E. Gurney, and F. W. H. Myers. *Phantasms of the Living.* 2 vols. London: Trubner, 1986.

Berger, Arthur S., and Joyce Berger. *The Encyclopedia of Parapsychology and Psychical Research.* New York: Paragon House, 1991.

Pleasants, Helene, ed. *Biographical Dictionary of Parapsychology.* New York: Helix Press, 1964.

Podmore, Frank. *Apparitions and Thought Transference: an Examination of the Evidence for Telepathy.* London: Walter Scott Publishing, 1896.

———. *Biography of Robert Owen.* London: Hutchinson, 1906.

———. *Mesmerism and Christian Science.* Philadelphia: G. W. Jacobs, 1909.

———. *Modern Spiritualism.* 2 vols. London: Methuen, 1902. Reprinted as *Mediums of the Nineteen Century.* New Hyde Park, N.Y.: University Books, 1963.

———. *The Naturalisation of the Supernatural.* New York; London: G. P. Putnam's Sons, 1908.

———. *The Newer Spiritualism.* New York: Arno Press, 1975.

———. *Studies in Psychical Research.* London: Kegan Paul, Trench, Tubner, 1897.

———. *Telepathic Hallucination; the New View of Ghosts.* Halifax, Milner, & Co., 1909.

Pohl, Hans Ludwig (1929–)

Patent engineer who also investigated parapsychology. He was born on April 16, 1929, at Krefeld, Germany and was educated at Bad Godesberg and Staatliche Ingeniurschule, Essen. He was an engineer at the Institute of Research, Deutsche Edelstahlwerke, Krefeld (1952–57) and a patent engineer at Deutsche Edelstahlwerke beginning in 1957. He is interested in the phenomena of **psychokinesis.**

Sources:

Pleasants, Helene, ed. *Biographical Dictionary of Parapsychology.* New York: Helix Press, 1964.

Pohl, Hans Ludwig. "Investigation of the PK-Effect." *Journal of Parapsychology* 24, no. 3 (September 1960).

"Poimandres" (or "Poemander")

Texts of the **Hermetica,** ascribed to **Hermes Trismegistus.**

POLAND

Poland's history of staunch Roman Catholic beliefs has offered an interesting perspective on that country's interest in parapsychology and the paranormal. For observers, the belief in miracles and other spiritual phenomena alone might have qualified as testimony to belief in the supernatural. In 2000 the country's Roman Catholic population was estimated at 80 percent of all Poles. Eastern Orthodoxy shares the majority of the remaining population but remaines isolated to the eastern frontier, representing approximately one percent-still making it second to Roman Catholicism. Other communities of Protestants and Buddhists exist on a small scale. Prior to World War II, psychical phenomena not necessarily related to religion could be found throughout Poland. In the nineteenth century, Poland was the home of psychical researcher **Julien Ochorowicz** (1850–1917). He investigated the medium **Eusapia Palladino** who visited Warsaw from 1892 through 1894. Ochorowicz testified to the **levitation** of Palladino. He also experimented with the medium **Stanislawa Tomczyk.** His 1887 book, *Mental Dominance-Classics of Personal Magnetism and Hypnotism* was considered by experts to be the most comprehensive work on mental suggestion to appear in the nineteenth century.

After World War I, in the 1920s, a Metapsychical Society was founded in Crakow with approximately one hundred members, including authors and lecturers. The medium **Stefan Ossowiecki,** born in Moscow to Polish parents, served as the honorary chairman of the society. He also "demonstrated" telepathy, clairvoyance, psychokinesis, and the projection of the astral body (also known as **out-of-the-body** travel).

Ossowiecki was investigated by researchers such as **Charles Richet, Gustave Geley,** and **Baron Schrenck-Notzing.** His psychic abilities were also investigated by the Polish Society for Psychical Research. Ossowiecki was murdered by the Nazis in the final days of World War II.

Also active in the 1930s, was the Psycho-Physical Society in Warsaw. Its president, P. de Szmulro, edited the journal *Zagadnienia Metapsychiczne.*

As Poland began to recover from World War II, psychical research reappeared with an informal parapsychological network in Western Europe and North America. Psychical research in Poland has developed its own terminology.

Research on **radiesthesia,** hypnosis, and **clairvoyance** was conducted by the Bio-Electronic Section of the Copernicus Society of Naturalists, whose president was Dr. Franciszek Chmielewski. The section's activities included investigations of electric phenomena in living organisms, higher nerve activity in connection with parapsychological phenomena and hypnosis, and the influence on living organisms of cosmic and earth radiation.

Psychotronika embodies the papers of the proceedings presented at the biennial symposium of the Society of Radiesthesists held annually in Poland. Address: Towarzystwo Psychotroniczne w Warszawie, ul Noakowskiego 10 m 54, 00-666 Warszawa. The Polish monthly journal *Trzecie Oko* (Third Eye) is published by Stowarzyszenie Radiestetow, ul Noakowskiego 10 m 54, Warzawa.

In a country that can boast of a cultural life especially in literature and music that has crossed several centuries, and with education a top priority, Poland is shaping its future in the twenty-first century with the political freedom for which its people have fought. An economy and lifestyle that will open to more Western and American influences could broaden the landscape in a way yet to be determined.

Sources:

Berger, Arthur S., and Joyce Berger. *The Encyclopedia of Parapsychology and Psychical Research.* New York: Paragon House, 1991.

Dydyriski, Krzysztof. *Krakow.* Melbourne: Lonely Planet Publications, 2000.

Materialy z Konfernecji Parapsychologów '94. Warsaw: Polskie Towarzystwo Psychotroniczne, 1994.

Ochorowica, Julien. *Mental Dominance-Classics of Personal Magnetism and Hypnotism (1887).* http://www.tranceworks.com/history.htm. 2000.

Swick, Thomas. *Unquiet Days.* New York: Ticknor & Fields, 1991.

Politi, Auguste (1855– ?)

Italian watchmaker and physical medium. His mediumship was developed by the psychical researcher Captain Enrico de Albertis. In 1902, a series of experiments were conducted on Politi in Paris by de Albertis, Col. **Eugene Rochas,** Taton, Lemerle, Baclé, **Guillaume de Fontenay,** and Dariex. Photographs were taken of table **levitations.** In 1904, he was studied by a group in Rome under the direction of Professor Milesi.

In the Paris séances, a piano was supposedly raised several times and noisly dropped. A table of 39 pounds was lifted over the sitters' head, went through the opening of the curtain, and dropped upside down upon the floor. Supposedly luminous phenomena were also obtained. In the fifth séance, two luminous crosses, about four inches in high, appeared. The sitters were touched by a hairy hand and phantoms were seen. The medium sat in a sack fastened at the neck, wrists, and feet.

In 1908, Politi gave more than 70 séances in Milan at the Societe d'Etudes Psychiques.

Polong

A Malay **familiar** spirit. (See also **MALAYSIA**)

Poltergeist

The name of unexplained rappings, noises, and similar disturbances. The term poltergeist (*Polter Geist,* or rattling ghost) is indicative of the character of these "beings." It is believed poltergeists rarely cause serious physical injury, but can cause much damage by breaking fragile objects and occasionally setting fire to pieces of furniture or clothing. Supposedly a person may be pulled out of bed or levitated.

Most psychic manifestations require darkness, but poltergeists act in daylight. However, the movement of objects usually happens when no one is looking. One frequently reported claim is that objects rose or fell through the air *slowly.* Otherwise objects are often seen in flight but seldom beginning to move.

In the late nineteenth century, to explain the crashing noises that occurred such as the sounds of breaking crockery later found intact, Adolphe d'Assier advanced a theory in his book *Posthumous Humanity* (1887). He suggested inanimate objects also possess a double, a phantasmal image and it is the duplicate that is flung by the poltergeist. D'Assier stated the sum of motion a moving body possesses is found by multiplying the mass of the moving body by its velocity and its live force at the moment of fall is equal to half the bulk by the square of velocity. D'Assier's theory was discarded.

Reportedly, Italian psychical researcher **Ernesto Bozzano** collected statistics on hauntings and claimed that out of 532 cases, 374 were ghostly manifestations and 158 were poltergeists.

Historical Poltergeists

Supposedly the poltergeist is not indigenous to any one country or any particular period. Author **Andrew Lang** claimed several cases belonging to the Middle Ages and at least one dates back to 856 B.C.E. In different cultures around the world, the reported phenomena are similar regardless of the country of origin.

Believers claim the disturbances are particularly active in the neighborhood of one person, generally a child, a young woman, an epileptic, or a hysterical subject. According to the theory advanced by Spiritualists, the center of the disturbances is a natural medium, through whom the spirits desire to communicate with the world of living beings. In earlier times, such a person might be regarded as a witch, the victim of a sorcerer, or even an evil spirit. Some believe the poltergeist developed out of witchcraft and is a direct forerunner of modern Spiritualism, possibly a link between the two.

Amongst the earliest poltergeist cases recorded were those of the **Drummer of Tedworth** (1661) and the **Epworth Phenomena** (1716). Supposedly the case of the Drummer of Tedworth began in 1661. A vagrant drummer was taken before a justice of the peace and deprived of his drum. The instrument was found in the house of Mr. Mompesson. Later, disturbances broke out in the house. Loud knockings and thumpings and the beating of an invisible drum were heard. Articles flew around the rooms and the beds (particularly those of the children) were shaken. After the drummer was sentenced to leave the manifestations ceased, but reoccurred when he returned.

Contemporary opinion classified the case as witchcraft by the drummer. Modern psychical researchers such as **Frank Podmore** believe the "two little modest girls in the bed" were responsible for the knockings and scratchings of the poltergeist rather than the drummer.

In the Epworth case, the family of the Reverend Samuel Wesley (father of Methodist founder John Wesley) reportedly described **levitations,** loud noises, and rappings, together with apparitions such as rabbits and badgers. Podmore was of the opinion that Hetty, one of John's sisters, was in some way responsible for the disturbances. Hetty did not give an individual account of the manifestations.

Poltergeists Around the World

Supposedly in Germany, **Justinus Kerner** recorded a poltergeist case in his book *The Seeress of Prevorst* (1845) that occurred in 1806–07 in the Castle of **Slawensik,** Silesia.

In Italy, the newspaper *La Stampa* of Turin claimed on November 19, 1900, poltergeist occurrences in a wine and spirit shop. **Cesare Lombroso** investigated the case and wrote:

"I went into the cellar, at first in complete darkness, and heard a noise of broken glasses and bottles rolled at my feet. The bottles were ranged in six compartments one above another. In the middle was a rough table on which I had six lighted candles placed, supposing that the spirit phenomena would cease in the bright light. But, on the contrary, I saw three empty bottles, standing on the ground, roll as though pushed by a finger, and break near the table. To obviate any possible trick, I felt and carefully examined by the light of a candle all the full bottles which were on the racks, and assured myself that there was no cord or string which could explain their movements. After a few minutes first two, then four, then two other bottles on the second and third racks detached themselves and fell to the ground, not suddenly but as though carried by someone; and after their descent, rather than fall, six of them broke on the wet floor, already soaked with wine; only two remained whole. Then at the moment of leaving the cellar, just as I was going out, I heard another bottle break."

In America, reportedly in 1850, disturbances occurred in the house of the Reverend **Eliakim Phelps** at Stratford, Connecticut. Twelve-year-old Harry Phelps was put in a water cistern and suspended from a tree. Mrs. Phelps was often pinched and pricked, and once, from a vacant room, a bottle of ink was thrown at her white dress.

The story known as "The Great Amherst Mystery" (after the 1888 book by Walter Hubbell) occurred between 1878–79 at Amherst, Nova Scotia, in the Teed family. The phenomena centered around Esther Cox, a sister of Mrs. Teed. A cardboard box, moving beneath the bed of its own accord, was the first manifestation. The next night Cox's body began to swell to an abnormal size. Soon after, a noise, "like a peal of thunder" woke everyone in the house.

Supposedly the bedclothes flew off Cox's bed, night after night; an invisible hand wrote in the plaster: "Esther Cox, you are mine to kill." Cold water on the kitchen table bubbled and hissed like boiling water, yet its temperature remained unaffected; and a voice announced the house would be set on fire and for many days lighted matches were seen falling from the ceiling on the bed.

The spirit communicated by raps, and said he was an evil spirit bent on mischief and would torment Esther until she died. Things became so bad that Esther left. In the house of a friend, Mr. White, for a month everything was quiet. One day, while Esther was scrubbing the hall floor, the brush suddenly disappeared from under her hand. A few moments later, it fell from the ceiling. The spirit was heard to walk about the house, banged the doors, attempted to set the house on fire, stabbed Esther in the back with a knife, and piled up seven chairs in the parlor and pulled one out near the bottom allowing them to fall with a crash. This lasted for nearly a year.

Walter Hubbell, the actor, was supposedly a witness. In 1907, the psychical researcher **Hereward Carrington** interviewed some of the surviving witnesses at Amherst. The testimonies he gathered confirmed Hubbell's narrative.

The Staus Poltergeist

One case occurred in the home of the Joller family in Switzerland. In 1860-62, disturbances broke out in Staus, in the home of Mr. Joller, a lawyer. Knocks were first heard by a maid, who also claimed she was haunted by grey shapes and the sound of sobbing. In the autumn of 1861, she was dismissed and another maid hired.

In the summer of 1862 the disturbances began again. Joller's wife and his seven children claimed to have heard and seen many sights and sounds, though Joller remained skeptical. After a while he was convinced that neither trickery nor imagination would suffice as an explanation of the phenomena. Meanwhile the manifestations appeared before thousands who were attracted by stories of the phenomena circulating around town. The Land-Captain Zelger, the Director of Police Jaun, the President of the Court of Justice, and other people arrived to investigate the disturbances and some suggested a commission be appointed to examine the house.

Three of the police were to conduct a formal inquiry. They demanded the withdrawal of Joller and his family, and remained in the house for six days without witnessing anything abnormal. They drew up a report to this effect. However, after the Joller family returned to their home, the interruptions were renewed. Joller became the butt of ridicule and jokes and finally left his ancestral home.

Poltergeist Fires

Alexander Aksakof described several instances of poltergeist fires in his book *Animisme et Spiritisme* (1906). One occurred in 1870, at the country house of a Mr. Shcnapoff, near Orenburg, Russia and was investigated by various locals. It seems that Mrs. Shcnapoff was the medium in this case. When she was sent away from the house, the phenomena ceased. On one occasion a bluish phosphorescent spark was seen flying through the air, bursting a cotton dress into flames in her bedroom. Another time the dress she was wearing caught fire. In extinguishing it her husband was severely burned, yet she suffered no injury.

Sporadically, events were claimed to have occurred to justify the Russian belief in the "domovoy," the Slavic house elf who performs various domestic duties during the night and watches over the sleeping household. The Shcnapoff case is similar to the **Morell Theobald** case where the poltergeist obligingly lit the kitchen fires. An even more domesticated poltergeist was recorded by J. A. Gridley in his book *Astounding Facts from the Spirit World* (1854). He wrote that on one occasion the breakfast table was laid by spirit agency.

Stone Throwing

The medieval *Annales Fuldenses* includes a chronicle of stone throwing approximately 858 C.E. in the town of Bingen on the Rhine. It was believed stones were thrown by a malignant spirit, and they struck dwelling walls.

Joseph Glanvill in his study *Sadducismus Triumphatus* (1681), recorded the witch trial of Mary London. She was a servant girl who, in addition to vomiting pins, had stones flung at her. The stones vanished after falling on the ground.

Poltergeists in the 1900s

In the early period of the **Society for Psychical Research,** London, opinions about poltergeist phenomena were dominated by the skeptical theories of Frank Podmore, but an alternative view was presented by Sir William Barrett in 1911. Amongst reported cases, Barrett investigated one at Derrygonnelly, in Ireland, where he claimed the phenomena had intelligence. Four times he got answers to numbers that he mentally asked.

In 1926, **Eleonore Zügun,** a Romanian peasant girl, was brought to London by psychical researcher **Harry Price** to London, and studied at the **National Laboratory of Psychical Research** for more than three weeks. The girl exhibited **stigmata.** Poltergeists stuck pins and needles into her body. Objects wandered around the room when she was in it. Reportedly no **fraud** was detected.

Hereward Carrington investigated the Windsor Poltergeist case involving a haunted town. Many of the Windsor residents conspired to play a prank on an old judge to mock his belief in Spiritualism. Carrington's account of the hoax was published in his book *Personal Experiences in Spiritualism* (1918, pp. 112–24). As is the case with many believers confronted with evidence of having been defrauded the judge refused to accept Carrington's explanation and insisted the manifestations were genuine.

One of the most interesting things about poltergeist phenomena is that in modern times, when there has been a marked decline in the physical phenomena of mediumship (most of which was fraudulently produced by tricks that will no longer work), poltergeists (not the product of fraud) continue to be reported, and many have been accessible to parapsychologists with modern monitoring equipment.

In Germany, the Institut für Grenzgebiete der Psychologie (Institute for Border Areas of Psychology) under the direction of Dr. **Hans Bender** has studied 35 cases of poltergeists since World War II. Of these, the Rosenheim Case, 1967–68, attracted the most attention. In a lawyer's office in Rosenheim, Bavaria electric lamp bulbs exploded, neon tubes continually went out, fuses blew, photostatic copying machines did not work, telephones rang or conversations were cut off unaccountably, and sharp bangs were reported. The focus of these events seemed to be Annemarie Sch., a nineteen-year-old employee. The disturbances ceased when she left the office, although witnesses claimed further events took place in her new office.

In Britain in 1977, the **Enfield Poltergeist** attracted wide attention. The poltergeist effects reportedly appeared in-house in the North London suburb of Enfield and focused its activity around the Hodgson family, Peggy Hodgson and her four children. Events recorded included inexplicable movements of objects, often flying through the air, levitation and transportation of one of the children, and noisy knockings. The case was investigated by members of the Society for Psychical Research, and author **Guy Lyon Playfair** who published a book on the phenomena.

In the United States, parapsychologist **William G. Roll** of the **Foundation for Research on the Nature of Man,** made poltergeists one of his specializations following his initial investigation of the Seaford Poltergeist of Long Island in 1958, when disturbances took place in the family of Mr. and Mrs. James Herrmann and their two children. Bottles were uncapped and the contents spilled, and toys were broken, in addition to the usual noises and movement of objects. Roll's monograph, *The Poltergeist* (1976), summarized the parapsychological aspects of the subject.

Sources:

Barrett, Sir William. "Poltergeists, Old and New." *Proceedings* of the Society for Psychical Research 25, no. 64 (August 1911).

Bell, Charles Bailey. *A Mysterious Spirit.* N.p., 1934.

Bell, Charles Bailey, and Harriet Parks Miller. *Bell Witch of Tennessee.* Reprint, Nashville, Tenn.: C. Elder, 1972.

Beloff, John, ed. *New Directions in Parapsychology.* London: Paul Elek (Scientific Books), 1974. Reprint, Metuchen, N.J.: Scarecrow Press, 1975.

Bender, Hans. "Modern Poltergeist Research—A Plea for an Unprejudiced Approach." In *New Directions in Parapsychology,* edited by John Beloff. London: Paul Elek (Scientific Books), 1974. Reprint, Metuchen, N.J.: Scarecrow Press, 1975.

Britten, Emma Hardinge. *Nineteenth Century Miracles.* N.p., 1883.

Carrington, Hereward, and Nandor Fodor. *Haunted People; Story of the Poltergeist Down the Centuries.* New York: E. P. Dutton, 1951. Reprinted as *The Story of the Poltergeist Down the Centuries.* London: Rider, 1953.

Dingwall, E. J., K. M. Goldney, and Trevor H. Hall. *The Haunting of Borley Rectory.* London: Duckworth, 1955.

Fodor, Nandor. *On the Trail of the Poltergeist.* New York: Citadel, 1958. Reprint, London: Arco Publications, 1959.

Gauld, Alan, and A. D. Cornell. *Poltergeists.* London: Routledge & Kegan Paul, 1979.

Lang, Andrew. *Cock Lane and Common-Sense.* London: Longmans Green, 1896.

Owen, A. R. G. *Can We Explain the Poltergeist?* New York: Helix Press, 1964.

Playfair, Guy Lyon. *This House is Haunted; An Investigation of the Enfield Poltergeist* London: Souvenir Press, 1980.

Price, Harry. "Same Account of the Poltergeist Phenomena of Eleonore Zügun." *Journal* of the American Society for Psychical Research (August 1926).

Richat, Charles. *Thirty Years of Psychical Research.* New York: Macmillan, 1923. Reprint, New York: Arno Press, 1975.

Roll, William G. *The Poltergeist.* Metuchen, N.J.: Scarecrow Press, 1976.

Sitwell, Sacheverell. *Poltergeist.* London: Faber & Faber, 1940.

Thurston, Herbert. *Ghosts and Poltergeists.* Chicago: Henry Regnery, 1954.

POLYNESIA

The name Polynesia means "region of many islands," and Polynesia comprises a group of central Pacific islands, including the Hawaiian, Rotuma, Uved, Tokelau, Samoan, Cook, and Easter Islands as well as Tuvalu, Tonga, Niue, and **New Zealand.** Many traditions were also shared with Melanesians of the central and western Pacific islands. Under the impact of their discovery by the Europeans in the nineteenth century and their subsequently being drawn into affairs of the larger world, including World War II, customs, beliefs, and lifestyles have undergone radical change.

Traditional Magic and Sorcery

Magic in Polynesia used to be the preserve of the priestly and upper classes, although lesser sorcery was practiced by individuals not of these castes. There was a prevailing belief in what was known as *mana,* or supernatural power in certain individuals. The method of using this power was twofold. One of these was practiced by a society known as the Iniat, where certain rites were carried out that were supposed to bring calamity upon the enemies of the tribe.

The ability to exercise magic was known as *agagara,* and the magician or wizard was termed *tena agagura.* If the wizard desired to cast magic upon another man, he usually tried to secure something that the person had touched with his mouth, and to guard against this, the natives were careful to destroy all food that they did not consume. They carefully gathered up even a single drop of blood when they received a cut or scratch, and burned it or threw it into the sea, so that the wizard might not obtain it.

The wizard, having obtained something belonging to the person whom he wished to injure, buried it in a deep hole with leaves of poisonous plants and sharp-pointed pieces of bamboo, accompanying the action by suitable incantations. If he chanced to be a member of the Iniat society, he would place on the top of this package one of the sacred stones. The Iniat believed that as long as the stone was pressing down on the article that had been buried in the hole, the man to whom it belonged would remain sick.

Because of this, as soon as a man fell sick he sent to find out who had bewitched him, and there was usually someone who did not deny it. If the victim did not succeed in having the spell removed he would almost certainly die, but if he succeeded in having it taken away, he began to recover almost immediately. The strange thing was that he showed no enmity toward the person or persons who bewitched him—indeed it was taken as a matter of course, and he quietly waited until the time when he could return the "compliment."

These practices applied mostly to New Britain, now Papua New Guinea, but its system of magic was practically the same as that known in Fiji as *vakadraunikau,* about which very little is known. In his book *Melanesians and Polynesians* (1910) the Reverend Dr. George Brown, pioneer missionary and explorer, gives an interesting account of the magic systems of these people, in which he incorporated several informative letters from brother missionaries. For example, the Rev. W. E. Bromilow gives the following account of the magic system at Dobu, in southeastern New Guinea:

"*Werabana* (evil spirits) are those which inhabit dark places, and wander in the night, and gave witches their power to smite all round. *Barau* is the wizardry of men, who look with angry eyes out of dark places, and throw small stones, first spitting on them, at men, women, and even children, thus causing death. A tree falls, it is a witch who caused it to do so, though the tree may be quite rotten, or a gust of wind may break it off. A man meets with an accident, it is the *werabana.* He is getting better through the influence of the medicine-man, but has a relapse; this is the *barau* at work, as we have ascertained from the terrified shouts of our workmen, as some sleeper has called out in a horrid dream. These medicine-men, too, have great power, and no wonder, when one of our girls gets a little dust in her eye, and the doctor takes a big stone out of it; and when a chief has a pain in the chest, and *to obaoba* takes therefrom a two-inch nail.

"The people here will have it that all evil spirits are female. *Werabana* is the great word, but the term is applied to witches as well, who are called the *vesses* of the *werabana,* but more often the single word is used. I have the names of spirits inhabiting the glens and forests, but they are all women or enter into women, giving them terrible powers. Whenever any one is sick, it is the *werabana* who has caused the illness, and any old woman who happened to be at enmity with the sick person is set down as the cause. A child died the other day, and the friends were quite angry because the witches had not heeded the words of the *lotu,* i.e., the Christian religion *Taparoro,* and given up smiting the little ones. 'These are times of peace,' said they, 'why should the child die then?' We, of course, took the opportunity and tried to teach them that sickness caused death without the influence of poor old women.

"Sorcerers are *barau,* men whose powers are more terrible than those of all the witches. I was talking to a *to obaoba*—medicine-man—the other day, and I asked him why his taking a stone out of a man's chest did not cure him. 'Oh,' said he, 'he must have been smitten by a *barau.*' A very logical statement this. Cases the *to obaoba* cannot cure are under the fell stroke of the *barau,* from which there is no escape, except by the sorcerer's own incantations.

"The Fijian sorcery of *drau-ni-kau* appears here in another form called *sumana* or rubbish. The sorcerer obtains possession of a small portion of his victim's hair, or skin, or food left after a meal, and carefully wraps it up in a parcel, which he sends off to as great a distance as is possible. In the meantime he very cunningly causes a report of the *sumana* to be made known to the man whom he wishes to kill, and the poor fellow is put into a great fright and dies."

The Rev. S. B. Fellows gives the following account of the beliefs of the people of Kiriwina (Trobiand Islands group):

"The sorcerers, who are very numerous, are credited with the power of creating the wind and rain, of making the gardens to be either fruitful or barren, and of causing sickness which leads to death. Their methods of operation are legion. The great chief, who is also the principal sorcerer, claims the sole right to secure a bountiful harvest every year. This function is considered of transcendent importance by the people.

"Our big chief, Bulitara, was asking me one day if I had these occult powers. When I told him that I made no such claim, he said, 'Who makes the wind and the rain and the harvest in your land?' I answered, 'God.' 'Ah,' said he, 'that's it. God does this work for your people, and I do it for our people. God and I are equal.' He delivered this dictum very quietly, and with the air of a man who had given a most satisfactory explanation.

"But the one great dread that darkens the life of every native is the fear of the *bogau,* the sorcerer who has the power to cause sickness and death, who, in the darkness of the night, steals to the house of his unsuspecting victim, and places near the doorstep a few leaves from a certain tree, containing the mystic power which he, by his evil arts, has imparted to them. The doomed man, on going out of his house next morning, unwittingly steps over the fatal leaves and is at once stricken down by a mortal sickness. Internal disease of every kind is set down to this agency. Bulitara told me the mode of his witchcraft. He boils his decoctions, containing numerous ingredients, in a special cooking-pot on a small fire, in the secret recesses of his own house, at the dead of night; and while the pot is boiling he speaks into it an incantation known only to a few persons. The bunch of leaves dipped in this is at once ready for use. Passing through the villages the other day, I came across a woman, apparently middle-aged, who was evidently suffering from a wasting disease, she was so thin and worn. I asked if she had any pain, and her friends said 'No.' Then they explained that some *bogau* was sucking her blood. I said, 'How does he do it?' 'Oh,' they said, 'that is known only to herself. He manages to get her blood which makes him strong, while she gets weaker every day, and if he goes on much longer she will die.'

"Deformities at birth, and being born dumb or blind, are attributed to the evil influence of disembodied spirits, who inhabit a lower region called *Tuma.* Once a year the spirits of the ancestors visit their native village in a body after the harvest is gathered. At this time the men perform special dances, the people openly display their valuables, spread out on platforms, and great feasts are made for the spirits. On a certain night, when the moon named *Namarama* is at the full, all the people—men, women and children—join in raising a great shout, and so drive the spirits back to *Tuma.*

"A peculiar custom prevails of wearing, as charms, various parts of the body of a deceased relative. On her breast, suspended by a piece of string round her neck, a widow wears her late husband's lower jaw, the full set of teeth looking ghastly and grim. The small bones of the arms and legs are taken out soon after death, and formed into spoons, which are used to put lime into the mouth when eating betel-nut. Only this week a chief died in a village three miles from us, and a leg and an arm, for the above purpose, were brought to our village by some relatives as their portion of their dead friend."

Some of the unusual magic traditions of Polynesia were also noticed by the ethnologists working in the area. In New Guinea and Fiji the custom prevailed of cutting off a finger joint in mourning a dead relative, as did the bushmen of South Africa. They firmly believed in **mermaids,** tailed men, and dwarfs. One group of natives in fact declared to a missionary that they had caught a mermaid, who had married a certain native, and that the pair had several children. "But unfortunately," stated the storyteller, "I could never get to see them." Another tradition connected to the Polynesian belief in magic, noted by the Europeans, was the practice of tattooing. The practice is represented widely in bodies of mythology, as being connected to the people's process of migration.

Like many other races, the Polynesians used to work themselves into a great state of terror whenever an eclipse took place, and during the phenomenon they beat drums, shouted, and invoked their gods.

In Samoa, magic was not practiced to such an extent as in other Melanesian groups, the magician being much more sophisticated. Instead of asking for any trifling object connected with the person he desired to bewitch, he demanded property, such as valuable mats and other things of use to him.

His method of working magic was to get into communication with his god, through his body, which became violently contorted and convulsed. The assembled residents of the village would then hear a voice speaking from behind a screen (possibly through ventriloquism), which indicated the presence of the god invoked.

Sickness was generally believed to be caused by the anger of some god, who could thus be concealed by the priest or wizard and duly placated. The "god" invariably required some present of substantial value, such as a piece of land, a canoe, or other property, and if the priest happened to know of a particularly valuable object belonging to the person who supposed himself bewitched, he stipulated that the property should be given up to the "god." This caste of priests was known as *taula-aitu,* and they also acted as physicians.

Lost Secrets of Polynesian Magic

In 1917 **Max Freedom Long** went as a teacher to rural Hawaii and subsequently became fascinated by the idea of discovering the lost secrets of the *kahuna* magician priests, whose leadership role in the social order had been disrupted in the nineteenth century. Long obtained valuable information on the fire walk ceremony from Dr. William Tufts Brigham, who had taken part in a fire walk 40 years earlier. Brigham had also investigated the ancient *kahuna* practice of charging wooden sticks with some vital energy, the sticks being used in combat and giving opponents some kind of electric shock that rendered them unconscious.

It was difficult for Long to obtain precise information on *kahuna* magic, since the laws of Hawaii had, many years earlier, outlawed it through strictures against what was termed **sorcery** and **witchcraft,** but Long continued to investigate the subject even after leaving Hawaii in the 1930s. He found his most valuable clues in the Hawaiian language, describing *kahuna* magic and the use of *mana,* or vital force.

Eventually Long believed that he had rediscovered the secrets of Polynesian magic, and the concepts of a high, low, and middle self or *aka* body through which power, *mana,* was generated and applied for magic purposes. He collated his discoveries with the information on psychic phenomena in the literature of psychical research and published his finding initially in a short work, *Recovering the Ancient Magic,* in 1936. In 1945 he founded the Huna Fellowship and soon issued several more substantive summaries of his conclusions, *The Secret Science Behind Miracles* (1948) and *The Secret Science at Work* (1953). The Huna Fellowship grew into **Huna Research Associates** for research and experiment in Polynesian magic, now continued by **Huna Research, Inc.**

Hawaiianists continue their efforts to recover as much of the Hawaiian magical teachings as possible before all traces of them disappear. The sacred sites of the old religion are protected by the state, and still occasionally show signs of private use. Several healing kahunas have survived and pass on the teachings to a select few.

Long's theories of *huna* and *mana* make interesting comparison with the researches of **Baron Karl von Reichenbach** into a vital force that he named "**od,**" and parallels can also be found in the nineteenth-century concepts of **animal magnetism.**

In 1952 George Sandwith, a British exponent of **radiesthesia** (**dowsing** with **pendulums**) who was familiar with Long's work, visited the South Sea islands and made his own investigation of magic practices. In Fiji he investigated fire walking (see **fire immunity**) firsthand and discussed with local priests the concept of *mana* or vital energy involved. He also studied the *atua* or ancient phallic stones of Fiji, regarded as shrines of ancestral spirits, and their activation for magic purposes. Sandwith tested the magical charge of these stones by radiesthesia, using a pendulum. He experienced firsthand the way in which *mana* is used in magic when he was bewitched by a local chief.

In sharp contrast to the European accounts of the Polynesian practices and myths, today, these rich cultural tales are used as a tool to expand children's creativity, especially American children's creativity. The creation tales, specifically, are short and vivid enough to attach in a child's mind and therefore aid in their creativity. Today, the religious make-up of Polynesia is largely Catholic and Protestant, with some traditional beliefs and myths incorporated into the Christian ideology.

Sources:

Black, Sharon. "Using Polynesian Legends and Folktales to Encourage Culture Vision and Creativity." *Childhood Education* 75 (September 1, 1999): 332–35.

Gall, Timothy, ed. "Polynesia." *Worldmark Encyclopedia of Cultures and Daily Life.* Vol. 3. Farmington Hills, Mich.: The Gale Group, 1998.

Guerreiro, Antonio. "The Pacific: The Coming of the Ancestors." *UNESCO Courier* (December 1997): 14.

Long, Max Freedom. *Recovering the Ancient Magic.* London, 1936. Cape Girardeau, Mo.: Huna Press, 1978.

———. *The Secret Science Behind Miracles.* Kosmon Press, 1948. Reprint. Vista, Calif.: Huna Research Publications, 1954.

———. *The Secret Science at Work.* Vista, Calif.: Huna Research Publications, 1953.

Sandwith, George, and Helen Sandwith. *Research in Fiji, Tonga, and Samoa.* Reigate, England: Omega Press, 1954.

Wingo, E. Otha. *The Story of the Huna Work.* Cape Girardeau, Mo.: Huna Research, Inc., 1981.

Polytrix

According to ancient belief, this was a stone causing hair to fall off the head of anyone who had it about his person.

Pontica

According to ancient belief, this was a blue stone with red stars or drops and lines like blood. It compelled the **devil** to answer questions, and also put him to flight.

Pontmain

Pontmain, a town not far from the border of Britanny and Normandy, was, in the year 1871, the scene of one of the more important of the modern **apparitions of the Virgin Mary.** Early on the evening of January 17, members of the Barbadette family were at work in their barn when Eugene (age 12) went to the door and looked at the starry sky. He noticed something unusual, a blank patch of sky over the house opposite theirs. Then within the patch, he saw stars appear in the shape of a triangle. Within the stars appeared a beautiful young woman. An expression of surprise brought his 10-years-old brother Joseph, who saw the Lady immediately, and his father, who saw nothing at all. The two boys began to describe what they were viewing. The Lady wore a blue dress decorated with stars and blue shoes with a gold buckle. She had a black veil on her head and a gold crown. The boys' mother arrived on the scene and saw nothing.

Their mother sent for a nun from the local convent school and she arrived with three children. Two of the three immediately saw the Lady. Soon other villagers arrived. Everyone could see the triangle of stars but not the Lady, seen only by the four children. The woman unrolled a scroll upon which a message calling for prayer was printed. She also showed the children various symbols—a red cross, some candles, and two luminescent crosses. She then assumed the same position she had in the apparition to Catherine Labouré in Paris in 1830, with her arms to her side and hand extended in a blessing.

The local priest who had joined the group witnessing the apparition sent a report to his bishop, who appointed an investigating commission. Its report was positive; the bishop also ruled favorably. The Barbadette barn became a pilgrimage site. The two Barbadette children entered the priesthood and lived to see the completion and consecration of a large church near their family's house that was dedicated in 1900. Then in 1901 they participated in a second study of Pontmain ordered by Pope Leo XIII that also ruled favorably. Benedict's successor, Pius XI, gave permission for a special mass and liturgy for "Our Lady of Pontmain."

The Pontmain apparition took on special significance for many French Catholics as it occurred at the point that the Germans made their deepest penetration of the country. On January 17, 1871, the army stood on the outskirts of Lavel (just 30 miles from Pontmain) and were prepared to take it the next day. Instead, they received orders to withdraw. Many came to believe that the Virgin appeared at Pontmain to stop the German advance.

Sources:

Sharkey, Don. *The Woman Shall Conquer.* Kenosha, Wis.: Franciscan Marytown Press, 1976.

Sullivan, T. S. *Our Lady of Hope: The Story of the Apparition at Pontmain.* St. Meinrad, Ind.: Grail, 1954.

Poortman, J(ohannes) J(acobus) (1896– ?)

Professor of metaphysics who wrote on parapsychology. Poortman was born on April 26, 1896, in Rotterdam, Netherlands and educated at the universities of Gröningen, Hamburg, Paris (Sorbonne), Geneva, and Vienna. He was a research fellow in philosophy at Harvard University (1935–36) and received his Ph.D. from the University of Amsterdam in 1954.

Poortman was coeditor of *Tijdschrift voor Parapsychologie* (1937–38), the year before he began as head of the Library of the Theosophical Society (Netherlands Section), Amsterdam (1938–59). Simultaneously he was secretary of the Division of Philosophy for the *Winkler Prins Encyclopedia* (1944–51), a lecturer in metaphysics at Leyden University (1945–53), and beginning in 1954, secretary of Netherlands Theosophical Research Center. In 1958, he became a special professor for "metaphysics in the spirit of theosophy" at Leyden University.

Poortman was a charter member of the Studievereniging voor Psychical Research (Dutch Society for Psychical Research) and for four years its treasurer (1934–38). He was a charter member of the **Parapsychological Association** and a member of Korrespondierendes Mitglied Österreichische Gesellschaft für Psychische Forschung. He took a special interest in the relationships between philosophy and parapsychology.

Sources:

Poortman, J. J. *De Grondparadox.* N.p., 1961.

———. *Drei Vorträge Über Philosophie und Parapsychologie.* N.p., 1939.

———. "The Feeling of Being Stared At." *Journal* of the Society for Psychical Research (1959).

———. "Henri Bergson and Parapsychology." *Tijdschrift voor Parapsychologie* N.p., 1941.

———. "Mysterious Words." *Tijdschrift voor Parapsychologie.* N.p., 1939, 1940.

———. *Occult Motives in Literature.* N.p., 1937.

———. "Psychophysical Parallelism or Interactionism?" *Journal* of the American Society for Psychical Research (1937).

———. *Variaties op een en meer Themata* (Collected Essays on Philosophy, Parapsychology and Theosophy). N.p., 1947.

Pope, Dorothy Hampson (1905–)

Parapsychologist and editor of the *Journal of Parapsychology* published by the **Foundation for Research on the Nature of Man.** Pope was born on December 28, 1905, in Providence, Rhode Island. She received her B.A. from Brown University, Providence (1927) and later did graduate work at Duke University (1939–41).

Pope was a staff member of the **Parapsychology Laboratory** at Duke University (1938–59) and assumed duties as managing editor of the *Journal of Parapsychology* in 1942. Four years later she also became the managing editor of the *Parapsychology Bulletin* (1942–63), and later coeditor. In 1963 Pope became an editorial consultant for the *Journal of Parapsychology.* She was a charter member of the **Parapsychological Association** and was named its treasurer in 1963.

Sources:

Pope, Dorothy H. "The Search for ESP in Animals." *Tomorrow* (Summer 1953).

Pope, Dorothy H., and J. G. Pratt. "Five Years of the Journal of Parapsychology." *Journal of Parapsychology* (March 1942).

———. "The ESP Controversy." *Journal of Parapsychology* (September 1942).

Poppy Seeds

Divination by smoke was sometimes practiced by **magicians.** A few jasmine or poppy seeds were flung upon burning coals; if the smoke rose lightly and ascended, straight into the heavens, it augured well; but if it hung about it was regarded as a bad omen. In parts of Europe, a pregnant woman would place poppy seeds on a window sill if she wanted a boy; sugar if she wanted a girl.

Popular Astrology (Magazine)

Monthly magazine with astrological forecasts for the year, universal zodiac, and day-to-day guides. Last known address: P.O. Box 3728, Marion, Ohio 43302.

Portent

An event or object seen as an omen to a future event. (See also paranormal **signs**)

Possession

An altered state of consciousness in which the conscious personality of the individual is replaced with that of another personality, commonly thought of as a possessing spirit entity. Possession is a phenomenon common to all religious traditions but some traditions have a greater focus upon it. For example, many of the Afro-Cuban religions (**Voudou,** Santeria, Macumba) can be described as possession religions, and the being possessed by the deity is central to worship in these groups.

In the Christian West, possession, with rare exceptions, has been viewed as a negative phenomena. Taking the lead from New Testament examples in which several people are described as possessed by demons and are healed by Jesus, Christian leaders have largely equated possession with possession by a demonic force, or even the devil himself.

The negative evaluation of possession in the West has been reinforced by the development of secular worldviews that champion the autonomous individual, the maker of choices. Such worldviews emerged in the nineteenth century from European encounters with what were deemed "primitive" cultures with possession-oriented beliefs and practices, and by the spread of the practice of hypnotism, in which people could seemingly be made to do things that they would not or could not do if conscious. More recently, in this century, negative views of possession have been reinforced as a by-product of contemporary psychological exploration of the phenomena of multiple personalities, in which a secondary personality of the individual comes forward, usually as a result of extreme trauma.

Spiritualism

Spiritualism emerged as a possession-oriented religion in the mid-nineteenth century. In Spiritualist mediumship, and its contemporary derivations such as **New Age channeling,** possession is a developed form of motor **automatism** in which the personality of the automatist is substituted by another, usually by as a discarnate spirit. The possessing personality aims to establish **communication** with this world through the organism of the entranced medium, by writing or speech.

The incipient stage of possession is **personation,** during which the medium's own personality is still in the body but is assuming the characteristics of someone departed. The next stage is partial possession, the excitation of the medium's motor or sensory centers by a discarnate agent either through the subconscious self or in some direct way. **F. W. H. Myers** suggested the word "telergic" as a correlative to telepathic for such action.

Full possession postulates the vacation of the organism by the medium to allow the entrance of another spirit. Alternating personalities offer the first suggestion of the possibility of possession. An arbitrary personality may possess the organism of the hypnotic subject at the hypnotizer's suggestion. Secondary personalities are often hostile and antagonistic to the primary one.

Traveling **clairvoyance** in dream states points to the wandering of the spirit while the body is asleep. Cases of religious ecstasy in which an excursion is made into the spiritual world furnish another instance of the temporary separation of body and soul. Once we admit the possibility of the soul leaving the body, we have to admit the possibility of another spirit entering it.

Whether possession actually takes place or whether a secondary personality speaks through the organism is a question of evidence. Such evidence has to be furnished by the nature and content of the communications. The testimony of the medium is usually not available, as she or he often does not remember what happened.

Swedish seer **Emanuel Swedenborg** remembered his excursions into the spiritual world, but in his case there was no possession. The subjects of **Alphonse Cahagnet** described heavenly visions in trance, but there was not enough evidence to rule out the possibility that even when evidential communications from discarnate spirits were produced, they did not come from the subconscious self alone. If no new knowledge is shown in the trance state, there is no reason to ascribe the communication to an external intelligence. The character of the communicator alone does not furnish convincing proof.

The medium **Leonora Piper** never remembered her visions of the spiritual world and, the fragmentary utterances during her passing from **trance** to waking life aside, she was the tool for the writing and utterances of "alien entities".

Paranormal knowledge the medium could not have acquired is an indispensable condition for proving the presence of an external spirit. It is believed incoherence in the communicator does not militate against possession. It is rather in favor of it. If the spirit of the medium vacates the body, his or her brain will be left behind in a dreamlike state. To control such a brain and to make it obey the will of the communicator may not only be an enervating process, but full of pitfalls and possibilities of confusion.

Possession and Psychical Research

Taken as a phenomenon, possession presents one of the central mysteries of human life. It involves a mind using a brain. Possession is always temporary and implies a surrender of the body on the part of the medium. If possession takes place against the will of the medium and endures in the waking state, the phenomenon is called **obsession.**

The possibility of an instrumental test of possession was first suggested by **W. Whateley Carrington.** He advised the use of a galvanometer, which measured the emotional reactions of the medium to a certain set of questions. The different controls, if they are different personalities, should exhibit different emotional reactions to the same questions. It was by such tests that the independence of the controls of the medium **Eileen Garrett** was established at Johns Hopkins University and the New York Psychical Institute in 1933.

Postel, Guillaume (ca. 1510–1581)

A sixteenth-century visionary born around 1510 in the diocese of Avranches, France. At fourteen years of age, Postel was made master of a school. Postel believed he had been called by God to reunite all men under one law, either by reason or the sword. The pope and the king of France were to be the civil and religious heads of his new republic.

Postel was made almoner to a hospital at Venice, where he met Mére Jeanne, a woman who had visions. Because of his heterodox preachings, Postel was denounced as a heretic, but later was regarded as merely mad.

A follower of **Kabbalah** he spoke internationally about his belief in astrology wrote several works on the visions of his coadjutor. Postel retired to the priory of St. Martin-des-Champs at Paris, where he died penitent.

Posthumous Letters

Many investigators of psychic science, members of the **Society for Psychic Research** and others, have left sealed letters, whose contents are known only to the writer. On the death of the writer and before the letter is opened, an attempt is made by a medium to reveal the contents.

Since only the writer knows what the letter contains, it is presumed that on his death this knowledge can only be communicated through his discarnate spirit.

A notable posthumous letter from the escapologist **Harry Houdini,** was a code message apparently confirmed to his widow by the medium **Arthur A. Ford.** However, the genuineness of this story has been alternately confirmed, denied, and confirmed again.

Potawatomi Prophet

By the 1880s, the Native American tribes who had been pushed from their traditional homes in the East to new lands in the former Louisiana Territory had experienced a variety of new movements. Each movement had been led by a prophet/visionary who spoke to their new situation, including the loss of their land to white settlers and their forced removal to new land. Most offered some hope that the whites would be driven from the land. Among the Kickapoo, a prophet named **Kanakuk** had arisen calling for a heightened morality as a condition for the favor of the Great Spirit. From his visions, he had developed a new religion that came to dominate his people and found great favor among the Potawatomis. First introduced before removal to the West, it led to the Kickapoo remaining in the homeland for more than a decade after they should have moved. It continued in their new home in Kansas until Kanakuk's death in 1852, after which it appeared to die out.

At the beginning of the 1880s there appeared among the Potawatomi of Wisconsin a new prophet/visionary known only as the Potawatomi Prophet. He began to spread his message from the Great Spirit among the Winnebago and Ojibwa. In 1883 followers of the prophet introduced the prophet's teachings among the Kickapoo, and Potawatomi people then living in Kansas. The teachings appeared to have been a mixture of Christianity and traditional Native American beliefs but arose as competition to the missionary efforts of various Christian churches that were working among all the Native American people at the time. The movement spread quickly, aided by the memory of Kanakuk's teachings.

The movement called for moral living according to the Ten Commandments and offered special condemnation of some particular evils attendant upon reservation life: drunkenness, horse racing, and gambling. The apocalyptic element, offering the imminent end to white rule, had been abandoned in favor of rewards in the next life. It found a response among those Native Americans who had not joined a Christian church and who remembered Kanakuk. While surviving for some years, it was eventually overwhelmed by Christian missionary efforts.

Sources:

Mooney, James. "The Ghost-Dance Religion and the Sioux Outbreak of 1890." In the *Fourteenth Annual Report of the Bureau of Ethnology.* Compiled by J. W. Powell. Washington: Government Printing Office, 1896.

Pottenger, Maritha (1952–)

Maritha Pottenger, a contemporary astrologer, was born on May 21, 1952, in Tucson, Arizona, the daughter of famed astrologer **Zipporah Dobyns.** Dobyns began the study of **astrology** in 1956, the year she separated from Maritha's father. She moved the family to Los Angeles, California, in 1969 and became active in the Church of Religious Science (a **New Thought** church in which she was eventually ordained). Maritha assumed her mother's maiden name. She attended the University of California–Berkeley, where she earned her degree in psychology (1974) and did graduate work in clinical psychology at the California School of Professional Psychology (M.A., 1976).

Pottenger learned her astrology from her mother and in the 1980s began to work with **Astro Communications Services** (ACS), the original astrological computer company founded in 1973 by **Neil Franklin Michelsen.** Through ACS she began to write computerized interpretive reports profiling various aspects of astrology interpretation, and she offers on-line interpretations of individual charts based on her profiles, the most recent being a comparison of horoscopes with the chart of the new millennium.

Pottenger is a member of the **National Council for Geocosmic Research** (chaired by Michelsen) and the International Society for Astrological Research. She has integrated her psychological training into her approach and encourages her clients to see their horoscope as a map of the psyche that assists them in making optimum choices. Her insights have been gathered in her encyclopedic work, *Complete Horoscope Interpretation* (1986). She has also authored a number of other books including *Encounter Astrology* (1978), *Healing with the Horoscope* (1982), *What Are Astrological Maps: All About Astrology* (1996), *Your Love Life, Venus in Your Chart* (1996), and *Astro-Essentials* (1991).

Pottenger is an editorial director at Astro Communications Services, where her brother Rique Pottenger also is employed.

Sources:

Pottenger, Maritha. *Astro-Essentials.* San Diego: ASC Publications, 1991.

———. *Complete Horoscope Interpretation.* San Diego: ASC Publications, 1986.

———. *Healing with the Horoscope.* San Diego: ASC Publications, 1982.

———. *What Are Astrological Maps: All About Astrology.* San Diego: ASC Publications, 1996.

———. *Your Love Life, Venus in Your Chart.* San Diego: ASC Publications, 1996.

The Poughkeepsie Seer

Title given to **Andrew Jackson Davis** (1826–1910), a pioneer Spiritualist medium from Poughkeepsie, New York.

Powder of Projection

A powder claimed to assist alchemists in the transmutation of base metal into pure gold. (See also **Philosophers' Stone**)

Powder of Sympathy

An occult remedy applied to the weapon that caused a wound, and which supposedly cured the hurt. This method was in vogue during the reigns of James I and Charles I, when its chief exponent was Sir Kenelm Digby. Digby published his theory in a volume entitled *A late Discourse . . . by Sir Kenelm Digby, Kt. & c. Touching the Cure of Wounds by the Powder of Sympathy* (London, 1658). Sir Francis Bacon had also written on the subject a generation earlier in his book *Sylva Sylvarum: or, a Natural History* (1627), in which he quoted a recipe for the powder:

"It is constantly Received, and Avouched, that the Anounting of the Weapon, that maketh the Wound wil heale the Wound it selfe. In this Experiment, upon the Relation of Men of Credit, (though my selfe, as yet, am not fully inclined to beleeve it,) you shal note the Points following; First, the Ointment . . . is made of Divers ingredients; whereof the Strangest and Hardest to come by, are the Mosse upon the Skull of a dead Man, Unburied; And the Fats of a Boare, and a Beare, killed in the Art of Generation. These Two last I could easily suspect to be prescribed as a Starting Hole; That if the Experiment proved not, it mought be pretended, that the Beasts were not killed in due Time . . ."

A summary of Digby's theory was presented at an assembly at Montpellier in France. According to T. J. Pettigrew's book *On Superstitions connected with the History and Practice of Medicine and Surgery* (1844), his instruction for making the powder was simple:

"Take Roman vitriol six or eight ounces, beat it very small in a mortar, sift it through a fine sieve when the sun enters Leo; keep it in the heat of the sun by day, and dry by night."

Sources:

Pettigrew, T. J. *On Superstitions connected with the History and Practice of Medicine and Surgery.* N.p., 1844.

Redgrove, H. Stanley. *Bygone Beliefs: Being a Series of Excursions in the Byways of Thought.* London: Rider, 1920. Reprinted as *Magic & Mysticism: Studies in Bygone Beliefs.* New Hyde Park, N.Y.: University Books, 1971.

Powell, Ellis T(homas) (1869–1922)

British barrister, journalist, and Spiritualist. Powell was born in Ludlow, Shropshire, and educated at Ludlow Grammar School. He served an apprenticeship to a draper in Ludlow, then came to London, where he became a journalist on the *Financial News,* eventually becoming editor. He mastered several languages, including Hebrew, Greek, and Latin. In his spare time, he studied law and became a barrister. Powell was a fellow of the Royal Historical and Royal Economic Societies, the Institute of Journalists, and the Royal Colonial Institute (member of council). He lectured at the London School of Economics and Political Science (University of London).

Powell became a supporter of the Spiritualist movement, traveling throughout Britain and lecturing on psychic subjects. He was a member of the **British College of Psychic Science** and was a council member of the **London Spiritualist Alliance.** He frequently contributed to the Spiritualist journal *Light.*

As a good friend of **Sir Arthur Conan Doyle,** Powell's name figured in the séance conducted by Doyle and his wife for **Harry Houdini.** In 1922, when the Doyles were in Atlantic City, they met Houdini on the sea front. Lady Jean Doyle offered to give Houdini an **automatic writing** séance. This took place at the Ambassador Hotel, where they were staying.

Lady Doyle produced automatic writing purporting to come from Houdini's dead mother. At the end of the message, Houdini took up the pencil and wrote on the pad—the name "Powell." This convinced Doyle that Houdini was a medium, since his friend Ellis Powell had died a few days earlier. Houdini later stated the message claimed to be from his mother was not evidential, since she would have been unable to communicate in fluent English, moreover he had been thinking of Frederick Eugene Powell, a fellow stage magician.

As a barrister, Powell brought his legal training to the problem of what he termed the "barbaric legislation" against mediums, campaigning to amend the Witchcraft Act of George II, still used against mediums during the twentieth century. He died June 1, 1922.

Sources:

Pleasants, Helene, ed. *Biographical Dictionary of Parapsychology.* New York: Helix Press, 1964.

Powell, Ellis T. *The Essentials of Self-Government.* N.p., 1909.

———. *The Mechanism of the City.* London: P. S. King & Son, 1910.

———. *The Practical Affairs of Life.* N.p., 1918.

———. *The Psychic Element of the New Testament.* N.p, n.d.

Powell, Evan (1881– ?)

British physical medium of Paignton, South Devon. Powell was originally a coal miner and later a tradesman in Wales. Powell usually sat tied to a chair before a cabinet with drawn curtains. His chief control was "Black Hawk," a Native American. **Movements** of objects, psychic lights (see **luminous phenomena**), and **direct voice** phenomena were supposedly witnessed at his séances. He gave many sittings at the **British College of Psychic Science.**

"Black Hawk" claimed that a book had been published about him in the United States. A friend of Powell's commissioned a book agent to locate it and present it to the medium. The title was: *Life of Ma-Ka-Tai-Me-She-Kia-Kiak or Black Hawk, dictated by himself* (Boston, 1834). "Black Hawk" also maintained there was a memorial to him in Illinois, a fact subsequently proven wrong. For a discussion of Powell's mediumship, see *Revue Métapsychique* (1924, p. 326) and *Journal* of the Society for Psychical Research (vol. 44, p. 161).

Powell, Kenneth F(rancis) (1923–)

Engineer who investigated parapsychology. Powell was born on March 4, 1923, in Boston, Massachusetts, and later studied at the University of Pittsburgh (B.S., 1949; M.A., 1951). After graduation Powell became an analytical engineer at Babcock & Wilcox (1951–55) and manager at International Business Machines in Pittsburgh. He was a member of the **Parapsychological Association.** He took a special interest in **psychokinesis.**

Sources:

Pleasants, Helene, ed. *Biographical Dictionary of Parapsychology.* New York: Helix Press, 1964.

Powell, Kenneth F., R. A. McConnell, and Ruth J. Snowden. "Wishing With Dice." *Journal of Experimental Psychology* 50 (1955).

Powell, W. H. (ca. 1879)

Slate-writing medium of Philadelphia with whom **Epes Sargent** conducted experiments in Boston on June 21, 1879. Under a chandelier, "without touching the surface of the slate, he made motions over it with his forefinger in the air, as if making a drawing, and then writing something. I reversed the slate, and there on the under surface, was a neat drawing of a flower, and under it in clear, bold letters, the word 'Winona.' " Powell was tested by a committee, including chemists and physicians in 1879 in Philadelphia. The committee reported Powell's slate-writing was "one of those peculiar psychological manifestations that we cannot account for."

Power Spots

Within traditional religious thought as well as occult spirituality, different physical locations are believed to be holy sites because they possess an access to spiritual energy. Common sacred sites include many mountains, caves, springs, and the locations of unusual natural phenomena. This concept of power spots has received special emphasis in the contemporary occult community through the **New Age** movement. Recognized power spots are places that intensify whatever people bring to them, so that spending even short periods of time in them can lead to spiritual transformation.

The modern theory of power spots can be traced to the literature of the 1920s on the old monolithic culture in Great Britain that erected many stone monuments, of which **Stonehenge** is the most notable. In 1925 Alfred Watkins proposed that a system of straight lines, which he called "ley" lines, could be traced across England and from there to other parts of the world, and that these lines were aligned with the sun and various star clusters. This idea was expanded by later writers to suggest that the lines, which tended to cross at the sites of ancient pagan temples, manifested psychic energy. These writers compared the lines with the acupuncture meridians believed to crisscross the human body and hypothesized that ancient peoples intuitively chose the points where ley lines crossed as places to build their holy shrines. Archaeological evidence has proved that some straight paths actually exist, and, apart from any speculations about psychic energy, modern research has shown that magnetic forces surround the Earth relative to its magnetic pole. Published maps show those lines of forces as well as spots of strong deviation from the norm, which has led to the designation of new power points such as **Sedona,** Arizona, which is believed to be home to four power spots.

Power spots tend to be sites of striking natural beauty (such as **Mount Shasta,** in northern California), ancient holy sites (such as the Egyptian pyramids, or the Incan temple in Machu Picchu, Peru), and unexplained human constructions (such as the massive earth drawings on the plains of Nasca in Peru, which many believe were built to guide UFO landings). Such sites have become the object of pilgrimages.

Sources:

Corbett, Cynthia L. *Power Trips.* Santa Fe, N.Mex.: Timewindow Publications, 1988.

Sutphen, Dick. *Sedona: Psychic Energy Vortexes.* Malibu, Calif.: Valley of the Sun Publishing, 1986.

PPCC Bulletin

Organ of the Planetary Professional Citizens Committee, established as an international organization concerned with UFOs and the **orgone** energy concepts of **Wilhelm Reich.** It was edited by **Jerome Eden,** and superseded his personal journal, the *Eden Bulletin.* PPCC operated as a small organization in the 1970s and 1980s and supported the idea UFOs were connected with the development of global deserts. It was published from Eden's home in Careywood, Idaho.

Prana

According to Hindu **yoga** teachings, a subtle vitality contained in the air, modified by the human body to govern essential functions. In **hatha yoga** training, this vitality is enhanced by special yoga exercises known as **pranayama.** A combination of hatha yoga exercises and pranayama techniques created a latent force called **kundalini** in the body. Reportedly Kundalini usually supplies energy for sexual activity, but when fully aroused can be conducted up the human spine to a center in the head, resulting in higher consciousness or transcendental states.

Many writers have noted the similarity of teachings on prana and other teachings concerning subtle energies such as **od** or **orgone.**

Sources:

Kuvalayananda, Swami. *Pranayama.* Bombay, India: Popular Prakashan, 1966.

Prasad, Rama. *The Science of Breath and the Philosophy of the Tattvas.* 3rd ed., rev. London: Theosophical Publishing Society, 1897.

Prasad, Kali (1901–)

Indian professor of psychology who investigated parapsychology. Prasad was born in 1901, in Sitapur, India, and studied at Allahabad University (Ph.D.). He was professor and head of the Department of Philosophy and Psychology of Lucknow University beginning in 1944. He was the Fulbright Visiting Professor at the Massachusetts Institute of Technology (1954–56).

Prasad was author of the book *The Psychology of Meaning* (1949), was responsible for the section on 'Communal Tensions' in the United Nations Educational, Scientific, and Cultural Organization *Report on India* (1952), and was also included in the book, *In the Minds of Men* (1953) by **Gardner Murphy.** Prasad was interested in telepathy and psychokinesis and was involved in various research projects funded by the **Parapsychology Foundation.** These projects concerned experiments in extrasensory perception (ESP) and the influence of interpersonal relations between subject and experimenter on ESP results.

Sources:

Pleasants, Helene, ed. *Biographical Dictionary of Parapsychology.* New York: Helix Press, 1964.

Pratt, J(oseph) G(aither) (1910–1979)

Parapsychologist and chief assistant to **J. B. Rhine** at Duke University. Pratt was born on August 31, 1910, at Winston-Salem, North Carolina. He entered Duke University during the 1920s with the idea of becoming a Methodist minister (Duke is sponsored by the Methodist Church) but was diverted into parapsychology and stayed to complete work with Rhine and eventually earned his Ph.D. (B.A., 1931; M.A., 1933; Ph.D., 1936). After graduation he became a research associate and the assistant director at the **Parapsychology Laboratory,** a position he held (except for service with the United States Navy during World War II) until joining the Department of Psychiatry at the University of Virginia in 1964. He remained at Virginia until his retirement. Pratt was a charter member of the **Parapsychological Association** and elected its president in 1960. He also served for many years on the editorial staff of the *Journal of Parapsychology.*

Pratt took a special interest in quantitative experiments in extrasensory perception. His early investigations at Duke University included the Pearce-Pratt series (with Hubert E. Pearce Jr.) and the Pratt-Woodruff series (with **J. L. Woodruff.**) These ESP tests were critiqued by **C. E. M. Hansel.**

Pratt investigated the card-guesser Pavel Stepanek in Prague, Czechoslovakia. Stepanek was discovered by parapsychologist Milan Ryzl in 1961. Pratt and Ryzl collaborated on experiments with Stepanek in Prague and Charlottesville, Virginia, for several years.

As a parapsychologist, Pratt traveled in Europe, India, South Africa, and the Soviet Union. He had hoped to study the talented Russian PK subject **Nina Kulagina,** but did not obtain permission, although he saw her informally in a hotel. Pratt collaborated with H. J. Keil, Benson Herbert, and **Montague Ullman** on a monograph about Kulagina, published in *Proceedings* of the **Society for Psychical Research,** January 1976. He died November 3, 1979, at his home near Charlottesville, Virginia.

Sources:

Pratt, J. G. "A Decade of Research with a Selected Subject." *Proceedings* of American Society for Psychical Research (1973).

———. *ESP Research Today: A Study of Developments in Parapsychology Since 1960.* Metuchen, N.J.: Scarecrow Press, 1973.

———. *On the Evaluation of Verbal Material in Parapsychology.* New York: Parapsychology Foundation, 1969.

———. *Parapsychology: An Insider's View of ESP.* Metuchen, N.J.: Scarecrow Press, 1977.

———. *The Psychic Realm.* New York: Random House, 1975.

Rhine, J. B., J. G. Pratt, et al. *Extrasensory Perception After Sixty Years.* New York: Henry Holt, 1940.

Pratt, Morris (d. 1901)

Morris Pratt, the founder of the **Morris Pratt Institute,** currently the educational arm of the National Spiritualist Association of Churches, was a successful nineteenth-century businessman and Spiritualist. Little is known of his early life, but in 1851, just three years after **Spiritualism** emerged in the United States, he visited the Lake Mills (New York) Spiritualist Center. The visit launched his interest in psychic phenomena and he soon became a dedicated Spiritualist. Over the years he enjoyed provoking ministers with the phenomena of Spiritualism, and on at least one occasion was arrested and fined for his interruption of a church meeting to argue his position.

In the 1880s, an investment in the Ashland Mine at Ironwood, Michigan, provided him with a large amount of cash. He had made the investment due to information that had come through a medium from an Indian spirit guide. True to a promise made earlier in his life, he dedicated part of that money to Spiritualism. He constructed a large mansion in Whitewater, Wisconsin, specifically designed to house gatherings for seances and lectures. Dedicated in 1889, the "Temple," as it was known, included classrooms, office space, and dormitories. The main lecture hall could comfortably seat 400 people.

The National Spiritualist Association (later the **National Spiritualist Association of Churches**) was founded in 1893, the first national organization representative of Spiritualism's maturing into a religious community. In 1901, the aging Pratt offered the house and property in Whitewater to the association for the purpose of opening an educational institution modeled on the training school that Spiritualist teacher **Moses Hull** had led for several years in the mid-1890s in Ohio. The association felt financially unable to assume the responsibility, and Pratt incorporated the Morris Pratt Institute separately. Unfortunately, he died on December 2, 1902, before the school could open. Hull assumed control of the corporation the next year and operated the institute for the rest of his life. In spite of some shaky years following the Great Depression, the institute has continued to the present and now serves as the educational arm of the National Spiritualist Association of Churches.

Sources:

Morris Pratt Institute. http://www.morrispratt.org. April 25, 2000.

Pratyahara

One of the advanced stages of the Hindu system of **yoga** practice. According to the Indian teacher Patanjali (ca. 200 B.C.E.), the following stages are prescribed: *yama* and *niyama* (ethical restraints and moral observances), **asanas** (the physical positions of **hatha yoga**), *pranayama* (breathing exercises), *pratyahara* (sense withdrawal), *dharana* (concentration), and dhyana (**meditation**), culminating in various degrees of samadhi (superconsciousness).

Pratyahara involves withdrawing sensory perception from external objects to concentrate on single-minded contemplation as a preliminary phase of meditation.

Sources:

Inengar, B. K. S. *Light on Yoga.* New York: Schocken Books, 1966.

Majumdar, Sachindra Kumar. *Introduction to Yoga Principles and Practices.* Secaucus, N.J.: Citadel Press, 1976.

Prayer

Prayer is a name given to the primary means for humans to make contact with the divine. In Western religion, especially, it is the means of contact between God and the individual believer. Prayer generally consists of one or more of the following elements: adoration and praise, thanksgiving, confession of sin, intercession for others, and supplication.

The belief that God intervenes to grant the petitions of fervent prayers, especially in the matter of healing the sick, has long been a central aspect of Christian theology, although in modern times more emphasis has been laid on submission to divine will than on desire for special favors. Such intervention is seen as the cause of most miracles and raises questions of the persistence of supernaturalism. Faith remains an essential component of successful prayer.

Samuel Jackson, in his biographical sketch of Jung-Stilling (**J. Heinrich Jung**), records that he attained the means for his education by a succession of miracles in answer to fervent prayer. J. K. Lavater's life abounded in similar incidents. Augustus Franke of Halle erected a vast orphanage and yearly fed and educated thousands of children by the power of prayer, he said.

Christopher Blumhardt (1805–1880) of Württemberg, Germany, was not only famous for his prayer cures but also for his philanthropy, the means of which were procured by answer to prayer. Hundreds of persons reported to have been compelled by a power they could not resist to send presents of clothes or food to Blumhardt.

The **Curé d'Ars,** Jean Baptiste Vianney (1786–1859), furnishes a similar example of an extraordinary life of faith. He built three chapels and established a home for destitute children and another home for friendless women. Constant prayer, he said, was the source of his beneficence. When food, fuel, or money was wanted, he prayed for it and it came.

George Muller of Bristol, as related in his *Life of Trust, being a Narrative of Some of the Lord's Dealings with George Muller* (2 vols., 1837–41), depended on prayer for half a century for his own maintenance and that of his charitable institutions. He never asked anyone, or allowed anyone to be asked, directly or indirectly, for a penny. No subscriptions or collections were ever made. Hundreds of times there was no food in his house, yet he never took a loaf or any other article on credit even for a day. During the 30 years covered by his narrative, neither he nor the hundreds of children dependent on him for their daily food were ever without a regular meal. Secret prayer was his only resource, he claimed. The donors always described sudden and uncontrollable impulses to send him a definite sum at a certain date, the exact amount he was in want of.

F. W. H. Myers states in *Human Personality and Its Survival of Bodily Death* (2 vols., 1903) that "the recorded appearances, intimations, and messages of the departing and the departed" prove that "between the spiritual and material worlds an avenue of communication does exist—that which we call the despatch and receipt of telepathic messages, or the utterance and the answer of prayer and supplication."

Traditional prayer in Western religions (Judaism, Christianity, and Islam) that imply a direct relationship between the believer and a beneficent deity have always been severely challenged by the existence of significant evil. The idea of a loving and omnipotent God acting on behalf of human life was put to its most intense test by the Holocaust of World War II. If there is any simple efficacy to devout and heartfelt prayers to a deity, why did the inconceivably monstrous horrors of the Nazi persecutions and prison camps fail to be averted? Reflection on this question has provided a watershed in theological thinking. It led in the short term to the emergence of the "death of God" movement in theology and only as some distance and reappraisal of the Holocaust has occurred has a theological reconstruction of faith been possible for many.

Less affected by the Holocaust were those who had adopted the alternative perspective on prayer offered by the metaphysical movements of the nineteenth century. **Christian Science** and **New Thought** metaphysics jettisoned a personal deity in favor of an underlying divine principle or law undergirding the visible structures of the universe. Prayer is seen much more as atuning oneself with the underlying universal spirit, in which condition anything is believed possible, especially on a personal scale. Numerous reports indicate that prayer with faith and confidence in this metaphysical context has produced the desired results in both a religious and secular setting. One wing of New Thought has retained a religious prayerful context, while a secular wing has simply emphasized the creative powers of the mind in achieving fulfillment of desire.

It seems possible that there are factors in prayer that are applicable to both religious and secular frames of thought, that faith and confidence enhance psychic factors at present not clearly identified. Even such mundane attempts to influence events as the willing of the fall of dice in parapsychological research may hold clues to the mechanisms of prayer.

Again, it is interesting to note that in such ancient religions as Hinduism, the gods are said to be unable to avoid granting requests when the petitioner has practiced intense austerities. This idea suggests that spiritual disciplines may bring about psychophysical changes in the petitioner that influence events. Secondary aspects of traditional prayer that may also have relevance are the ritualistic forms of prayers and the need for constant repetition, which, like **autosuggestion,** may enhance subconscious powers. The concept of faithful prayer often gradually drifts into various attempts not just to petition the divine but to assist or coerce the deity's action.

Ultimately, however, divine will takes priority over the mundane desires of petitioners, and even in mystical Hinduism the highest wisdom is said to be transcendental awareness, which is beyond desires and fears in the mundane world and which accepts favorable or unfavorable destiny with equanimity, much as the petitioner in the Christian tradition concludes, "Thy will be done."

Sources:

Bounds, E. M. *Power Through Prayer.* London, 1912. Reprint, Chicago: Moody Press, 1979.

Brown, William A. *The Life of Prayer in a World of Science.* London: Hodder & Stoughton, 1927.

Carrol, F. *The Prayer of the Early Christians.* London: Burns & Oates, 1930.

Fillmore, Charles, and Cora Fillmore. *Teach Us to Pray.* New York: Seabury Press, 1976.

Greene, Barbara, and W. Gollancz. *God of a Hundred Names.* London: Gollancz, 1962.

Humbard, Rex. *Prayer With Power.* Grand Rapids, Mich.: Baker Books, n.d.

James, William. *The Varieties of Religious Experience.* London, 1902. Reprint, New Hyde Park, N.Y.: University Books, 1963.

Loehr, Franklin. *The Power of Prayer on Plants.* Garden City, N.Y.: Doubleday, 1959.

Patton, William P. *Prayer and Its Answers.* New York, 1885.

Petuchowski, Jacob J., ed. *Understanding Jewish Prayer.* New York: Ktav Publications, 1972.

Sherman, Harold. *How to Use the Power of Prayer.* New York: C. & R. Anthony, 1959.

Stanton, Horace. *Telepathy of the Celestial World.* New York, 1913.

Steiner, Rudolf. *The Lord's Prayer.* London: Anthroposophic Press, n.d.

Theresa, St. *The Interior Castle.* London: Baker, 1921.

Yatiswarananda, Swami. *Universal Prayers.* 6th ed. Hollywood, Calif.: Vedanta Press, 1963.

"Preceptor"

Pseudonym of one of the spirit **controls** of **William Stainton Moses,** who later claimed to be the biblical Elijah. "Imperator" (another control) frequently referred to "Preceptor" as his "Great Master" and director of the movement to uplift humanity through the teachings they delivered to Moses under the leadership of Jesus. Reportedly "Preceptor's" first signed communication was May 27, 1876. He was seen clairvoyantly by Moses as a communications link between himself and Malachi in the chain of spirit influence from Melchizedek to Jesus.

Precession of the Equinox

Astrology as it is known today was developed between the fourth and first centuries B.C.E. in the Mediterranean Basin. At the beginning of the year, marked by the spring **equinox,** the sun rose in the constellation Aries. After several centuries of observations, around 125 B.C.E., a Greek astrologer named Hipparchus discovered that very gradually the sun was moving in relation to the zodiac; that is, the precession of the equinoxes. There is some evidence that the phenomenon had been discovered earlier, but since Hipparchus, Western astrologers in general were aware of it.

The precession is caused in part by the slant of the Earth. It spins on an axis slanted at 23 degrees relative to its orbit around the Sun. That slant immediately accounts for the seasons. As the Earth moves around the Sun, where the axis is pointed toward the Sun, summer occurs, and where it is inclined away from the Sun, there is winter. However, as the Earth spins on its axis, because it is not a perfect sphere, it also wobbles slightly. It is this wobble that causes it to move slightly backward each year. That movement is hardly noticeable, being only one degree every 71 years.

Most Western astrologers use what is termed the tropical **zodiac.** The beginning of the year is marked by positioning 0° Aries at the point where the sun is located on the spring equinox. However, that point changes slightly every year, hence the zodiac moves slightly every year. Some astrologers use what is termed a sidereal equinox, in which the sun's true alignment with the constellations is retained. In the sidereal zodiac, the traditional relationship of the zodiac with the seasons of the year is lost.

This movement is slight from year to year but over the centuries makes a real difference. It takes approximately 2,150 years for the spring equinox to move from one sign to another and approximately 27,000 years for the wobble to make that point to return to its previously held position. The movement of the Sun's position at 0° Aries within one sign over a 2,100-year period defines an astrological age. Astrologers believe that different historical periods are ruled by different signs. In our own day we are believed to be experiencing the transition of the sun from the sign Pisces to Aquarius. The sign of Pisces the fish is often associated with Christianity, of which the fish has been a popular symbol. The contemporary revival of astrology has seen the twentieth century as the beginning of the **Aquarian Age** and has projected a hope that it will bring broad characteristic changes.

Sources:

Bach, Eleanor. *Astrology from A to Z: An Illustrated Source Book.* New York: Philosophical Library, 1990.

Campion, Nicolas. "The Age of Aquarius: A Modern Myth." In *The Astrology of the Macrocosm.* Edited by Joan Evbers. St. Paul, Minn.: Llewellyn Publications, 1990.

Filbey, John, and Peter Filbey. *The Astrologer's Companion.* Wellingsborough, Northampton, UK: Aquarian Press, 1986.

Precipitation of Matter

One of the phenomena of Spiritualism known as the "passing of solids through solids." The theory suggests before one solid body passes through another it is resolved into its component atoms, to be precipitated in its original form when the passage is completed. **Camille Flammarion** suggested a parallel: the passage of a piece of ice (a solid) through a napkin. The ice passes through the napkin in the form of water, and may afterwards be re-frozen.

Sources:

Zöllner, J. C. F. *Transcendental Physics.* London: W. H. Harrison, 1882.

Precognition

Paranormal knowledge of impending events, also referred to as **prediction, premonition,** and **prophecy.** See also **retrocognition.**

Prediction (Magazine)

British magazine founded in 1936 dealing with astrology and the occult. Brief features articles in each issue cover such topics as the tarot, palmistry, graphology, yoga, and magic. Astrological forecasts are featured. *Prediction* is published from Link House, Dingwall Ave., Croydon, CR9 2TA, England.

Pre-Existence

The question of pre-existence has come to the fore throughout Western history. Some people adhere to the Hebraic and Christian notions that the individual is created during the period between conception and birth and other people believe the human soul is somehow immortal, neither created nor destined for destruction. For example, according to Christianity, God creates the person for life in this world and prepares a person for a life extended beyond death. A variety of positions arrayed themselves against Christianity.

The question of pre-existence is often tied to the religious issue of **reincarnation,** a belief that individuals now living on earth have had a series of previous human lives as they have moved from body to body, a position found in the Hindu text, the *Bhagavad-Gita.* Traditional Spiritualism believes a new soul is created at birth and goes on to other levels of existence. However, French **Spiritism** and Theosophy argue for reincarnation.

It is rare to believe in pre-existence without reincarnation. One person who articulated such a belief was **Sir Oliver Lodge.** In *Phantom Walls* (1929), he wrote:

"When the question of pre-existence arises I should say that the individual as we know him is a fresh apparition, a new individualisation of something preexisting. . . . We can imagine that, every now and then, an opportunity arises for spirit to enter into relation with matter, and to become gradually an individual, and develop a character and personality which will persist; so that there is almost a kind of 'choice' whether we enter into life or what sort of life we enter into. In that sense we may be said—with apparent absurdity, but possibly with some kind of truth—to select our parentage; and thus may some facts of heredity be accounted for."

Premonition

A paranormal impression warning of a future event. Premonitions may range from vague feelings of disquiet, suggestive of impending disaster, to actual **hallucinations,** visual or auditory. **Dreams** are frequent vehicles of premonitions, either direct or symbolical, as well as veridical dreams. Spiritualists do not know if the warning comes from an external intelligent source such as a knowledgeable spirit being, from claivoyance (precognition), the intuitive projection of the outcome of presently existing trends, or coincidence or self-fulfilling prophecy, a form of **autosuggestion.**

A premonition differs from **prediction.** Reportedly the latter has a degree of precision and tends to detail the basic who, what, when, where, and how questions. When the event foreseen is not precisely outlined or is too insubstantial to prompt a prophetic utterance, "premonition" is the more appropriate term. For vague future events of a personal nature, "presentiment" is employed.

Richet's Conditions

According to psychical researcher **Charles Richet,** premonitions should have two fundamental conditions:

"1. The fact announced must be absolutely independent of the person to whom the premonition has come."

"2. The announcement must be such that it cannot be ascribed to chance or sagacity."

Richet did not employ the term "presentiment." He also ruled out personal premonitions. It was believed subconscious perception or suggestion is possible if sickness or death were announced. Richet claimed a photograph taken of a person suffering from a slight attack of fever may show signs of a rash or eruption on the face invisible to ordinary sight. The photograph "foresees" the sickness. However, Richet accepted personal premonitions ("auto-premonitions," to use his term) in cases when accidental death figured in the paranormal perception.

According to legend, the Earl of Hartington's dream illustrates pseudo-premonitions. In good health, he dreamt of a skeleton that looked like him; it raised the coverlet bedclothes and slipped in bed between him and his wife. He died fifteen days later.

Premonitions where the subconscious is ruled out may be received under hypnosis, in trance, or accidentally in the dream or waking state. The Seeress of Prevorst (**Frederica Hauffe**), claimed while in hypnotic sleep she saw a spirit anxious to speak of misfortune threatening her daughter. Reportedly a few weeks later, the girl was almost killed by a tile falling on her head.

If the percipient is positive the event in question is about to happen, the term "precognition" is used. If it takes visual form, "prevision" is the appropriate label. When predictions involving the fate of larger units, countries, or nations are made, "prophecy" is the appropriate term. Premonition may be conceived of as the lowest degree of prophecy. Whether the premonition comes in the waking state or during sleep, it is believed the impression is usually deep and lasting. The recipient may write it down or narrate it for later verification.

In the 1880s, the **Society for Psychical Research** collected 668 cases of death premonitions; 252 more were added in 1922. **Camille Flammarion** collected 1,824 cases. From time to time, cases were registered in English, German, French, and Italian psychical periodicals. **Ernesto Bozzano** collected 260 cases in his *Des Phénomènes Premonitoires.* **Count Cesar Baudi de Vesme** analyzed premonition in games of chance (*Le Merveilleux dans les jeux de hasard,* Paris, 1930). An earlier work of William MacKenzie (*Metapsichica moderna,* Rome, 1923) related experiments in the same field with mediumistic intervention.

In *L'Avenir et la Premonition* (1931), Richet referenced **Julien Ochorowicz**'s experiment (*Annales des Sciences Psychiques,* 1909–10), stating a telekinetic explanation in stopping the roulette ball at the announced number should be considered.

Incidents of Premonitions

Many prominent people have left records illustrative of the general nature of premonitions:

Charles Dickens dreamed of a lady in a red shawl, who said: "I am Miss Napier." He did not know who this woman was. Some hours later, he was visited by two ladies, and a girl in a red shawl was introduced as Miss Napier. (*Proceedings* of the American Society for Psychical Research, vol. 14, 1920).

Sir Oliver Lodge quoted the account of an English minister who dreamed of a terrible storm and lightning that entered the dining room and destroyed the chimneys of the roof opposite. Under the impression of the dream, although it was bright sunshine, he directed his wife to prepare lunch at an early hour. Events happened just as in the dream. Soon a storm broke out, and lightening struck through the dining room and demolished the chimneys of the neighboring roof.

Field-Marshal Earl Roberts (1832–1914), in his autobiography *Forty-one Years in India* (1897), related his experiences when commanding: "My intention, when I left Kabul, was to ride as far as the Kyber Pass, but suddenly a presentiment which I have never been able to explain to myself, made me retrace my steps and hurry back to Kabul, a presentiment of coming trouble which I can only characterise as instinctive. The feeling was justified when, about half way between Butkhak and Kabul I was met by Sir Donald Stewart and my Chief of Staff, who brought me the astounding news of the total defeat by Ayub Khan of Brigadier General Burrow's brigade at Maiwand and of Lieutenant-General Primrose, with the remainder of his force, being besieged at Kandahar."

President **Abraham Lincoln** had strange presentiments of his coming end. John Forster, in his *Life of Dickens* (3 vols., 1872), quoted a letter written to him by Dickens, dated February 4, 1868. Charles Summer had told Dickens that on the day of Lincoln's assassination an extraordinary change was noticeable in him. Lincoln said: "Gentlemen, something extraordinary will happen, and that very soon." Later he spoke of a dream that came to him for the third time and said: "I am on a deep, broad, rolling river; I am in a boat, and I am falling in! I am falling in!" Six weeks before his assassination he saw a great concourse of mourners in the White House in a dream. The mourners surrounded a coffin in which he saw his own body. Presidents Garfield and McKinley also had premonitions of their violent ends.

William T. Stead, the Spiritualist journalist, had a presentiment that he would not die normally. He thought he would be kicked to death by a mob. Instead, he went down in the "Titanic" in 1912. In 1892 Stead had written a fictional story about a ship called the "Majestic," that received a psychic message from a survivor of another ship that had struck an iceberg in the Atlantic. The novelist Emile Zola always dreaded asphyxiation by gas. It was the cause of his death.

A method of experimental premonitions was described by Richet in *L'Avenir et la Premonition* (1931) and *La Grande ésperance* (1933). To quote from the latter (p. 198):

"Thirty six pieces of paper, each containing a number written in pencil. They are carefully folded, all alike. Armand, a painter of my friends, the brother of Brigitta, indicates the number which Brigitta is going to draw. There are errors, certainly. Armand is not always correct, but the result is far superior to the probability. There are periods of error and periods of astonishing lucidity. At my formal recommendation Armand only makes one experiment per day which gives the probability of 1/36. Well, during a certain week, in six draws, his predictions was five times correct. This is about 1/30,000,000."

We have no satisfactory explanation for premonitions. Possibly Richet was right when he stated: "If we knew the totality of things in the present we should know the totality of things to come. Our ignorance of the future is the result of our ignorance of the present."

According to novelist **Maurice Maeterlinck,** the phenomenon of premonitions is far less exceptional than generally thought. He believed in "human foreknowledge" and observed that the great catastrophes usually claim fewer victims than the probabilities of each case would allow. He found that generally some strange chance keeps a number of people away who otherwise would be there and perish. They are warned by a mysterious, unfailing instinct.

Richet concluded, from his belief in the reality of premonitions, that the future is determined. His conclusion is a possible logical surmise from his line of reasoning, but it is not the only or right one. The basis of premonitions need not be the supposition of either a closed future or an eternal present. The consideration of the presence of presupposition leads directly to questions of freedom and the nature of the future. Do premonitions announce an unalterable future or suggest a future that can with attention be altered?

More recently an extended study of precognitive dreaming was done by Mary Stowell with a group of five women tabulating 32 characteristics of such dreams. Syntheses of the narratives of interviews indicated common patterns across the dream descriptions and the responses to the experiences. Both traumatic and nontraumatic situations arose, some of which would benefit by professional counseling to assuage guilt and a sense of helplessness. In some cases intervention was possible to prevent the dreams from coming true.

Premonitions registries founded in recent decades included (with their last known address) the **Central Premonitions Registry** (Box 482, Times Square Station, New York, NY 10023);

the Southern California SPR (via Carolyn Jones, 4325 E. Broadway, Long Beach, CA 90803); and the Toronto Society for Psychical Research (10 North Sherbourne St., Toronto 5, ON, Canada).

Sources:

Barker, J. C. *Scared to Death; An Examination of Fear, Its Causes and Effects.* London: Muller, 1958. Reprint, New York: Dell, 1969.

Brier, Robert. *Precognition and the Philosophy of Science; An Essay on Backward Causation.* New York: Humanities Press, 1973.

Central Premonitions Registry. http://clever.net/yaron/precog/precog.htm. April 10, 2000.

Dunne, J. W. *An Experiment With Time.* London: Macmillan, London, 1927. Reprint, New York: Hillary, 1958.

Greenhouse, Herbert B. *Premonitions: A Leap Into the Future.* London: Turnstone Press, 1972. Reprint, London: Pan, 1975.

Jaffé, Aniela. *Apparitions and Precognition: A Study From the Point of View of C. G. Jung's Analytical Psychology.* New Hyde Park, N.Y.: University Books, 1963.

MacKenzie, Andrew. *The Riddle of the Future: A Modern Study of Precognition.* London: Barker, 1974. Reprint, New York: Taplinger, 1975.

Osborn, Arthur W. *The Future Is Now: The Significance of Precognition.* New Hyde Park, N.Y.: University Books, 1962.

Saltmarsh, H. F. *Foreknowledge.* London: G. Bell, 1938.

Stowell, Mary S. "Precognitive dreams: A phenomenological study. Part I. methodology and sample cases." *Journal of the American Society for Psychical Research* 91 no. 3 (July 1997).

———. "Precognitive dreams: A phenomenological study. Part II. Discussion." *Journal of the American Society for Psychical Research* 91 no. 3 (July 1997).

———. "Researching precognitive dreams: A review of past methods, emerging scientific paradigms, and future approaches." *Journal of the American Society for Psychical Research* 89 no. 2 (April 1995).

UK Psychics—Premonitions Registry. http://www.ukpsychics.com/premonitions.html. April 10, 2000.

The Prenestine Lots

Also known as *Sortes Prenestinae.* A method of **divination** by lots, in vogue in Italy in early times. The letters of the alphabet were placed in an urn, shaken, and dropped on the floor; the words thus formed were received as omens. In the East, a similar method of divination was also common.

Presentiment

Personal **premonition** of vague events in the future.

Preta

Hindu term for the soul of a departed. After death the soul was said to inhabit a subtle body the size of a man's thumb and remain in the keeping of Yama, judge of the dead. Punishment or reward arises for the *preta* depending upon the actions of the individual's life and may involve many rebirths.

Eventually through faith and enlightenment, the soul is translated to the heaven of the *Pitris* (the Manes or progenitors of the human race).

Prevision

Foreknowledge of the future acquired in a visual form. Reportedly, such visions are mostly spontaneous, but there are means of experimentally inducing them through **crystal gazing** and other forms of **divination.**

In the experiments of Col. **Eugene Rochas,** he supposedly took his hypnotic subjects on longitudinal passes into past phases of their lives and brought them back to transversal passes. Reportedly, if these passes were continued beyond the present age the subject went into the future. These experiments are also known as "hypnotic regression."

Florence Marryat, in her book *There is No Death* (1892), claims her spirit was summoned by friends, sitting in a circle, while she was fast asleep in her home. Her spirit begged to be sent back with the words: "There is a great danger hanging over my children, I must go back to my children." The day after the séance, her brother-in-law accidentally discharged a rifle in the midst of her seven children and a bullet passed through the wall close to her eldest daughter's head.

The mechanism of prevision was described in Vincent Turvey's *The Beginnings of Seership* (1911):

"At certain times I see a sort of film or ribbon continually moving as does an endless belt in a cinematograph film. This film is in colour of a very, very pale pinky-heliotrope, and it seems to vibrate with very great velocity. Upon it are numerous little pictures, some of which appear to be engraved on the film itself, whilst others are like pale blue photographs stuck on the film. The former I have found to refer to past events, the latter to those about to happen. The locality of the event is judged by the scenery and the climatic heat. I have to estimate dates by the clearness of the pictures. I foresee more unpleasant than pleasant things. I believe the reason to be that evil, being nearer to matter than to spirit, is more ponderous in the ether than its opposite, and is therefore sensed more easily by a Seer. I not only see, but feel, the density of evil."

(See also **Arnall Bloxham**)

Sources:

Besterman, Theodore. *Crystal Gazing: A Study in the History, Distribution, Theory and Practice of Scrying.* London: William Rider, 1924. Reprint, New Hyde Park, N.Y.: University Books, 1965.

Grey, E. Howard. *Visions, Previsions and Miracles in Modern Times.* London: L. N. Fowler, 1915.

Turvey, Vincent N. *The Beginnings of Seership.* London: Stead's Publishing House, 1911. Reprint, New Hyde Park, N.Y.: University Books, 1969.

Price, E(lias) Alan (1918–)

Physician and radiologist concerned with parapsychology. Price was born on April 15, 1918, in Dolhinow, Poland. He moved to South Africa and studied at the University of Witwatersrand, South Africa (M.B., Ch.B).

Price served in the Israeli Army from 1948 to 1949, during the formation of the state of Israel. He then returned to South Africa as a resident house physician from 1949 to 1951 and then went to England to study at London University College Hospital (D.M.R.D. diagnostic radiology, 1953). Price became a consulting radiologist (1954–58) at Johannesburg General Hospital, South Africa. He reentered private practice in Johannesburg in 1958.

Price was a member of the **Society for Psychical Research,** London and a founder and leader in 1955 of the South African Society for Psychical Research (vice president, 1956–57; president, 1958; and executive member from 1959).

Sources:

Price, E. Alan, Marius Valkhoff, and J. H. Van Der Merwe. *Parapsychology and Modern Science.* South African Society for Psychical Research, 1958.

Price, George R(obert) (1922–1975)

Chemist and science writer, who published articles critical of parapsychology findings. Price was born on October 16, 1922, in Scarsdale, New York. He studied at Harvard University and at the University of Chicago (B.S., 1943; Ph.D. chemistry, 1946). He worked on the Manhattan Project during the last days of World War II and then from 1946 to 1957 worked at various teaching and industrial positions. In 1957, he became a full-time writer of material on science, primarily chemistry and biology.

In August 1955, Price started a controversy by publishing an article in *Science* magazine (the periodical of the American Association for the Advancement of Science). He dismissed parapsychologists (then attempting to gain admittance to the circles of the AAAS) with the observation that their positive results were "dependent on clerical and statistical errors and unintentional use of sensory clues" and claimed that "all extrachance results not so explicable are dependent on deliberate fraud or mildly abnormal mental conditions."

This article was quoted by newspapers and journals. It suggested various fraudulent methods used to show such results as those claimed by parapsychologists like **J. B. Rhine** and **S. B. Soal,** and stated their claims were not acceptable as proof of extrasensory perception. Rhine and Soal responded to these criticisms in the *Newsletter of the Parapsychology Foundation* (October 1955), which also published a further communication from Price.

It is believed the skeptical attitude of Price represented a backlash against parapsychology by orthodox scientists of the time, particularly by members of the American Association for the Advancement of Science, a body having refused to permit affiliation to the **Parapsychological Association.** Reportedly the skeptical and hostile criticisms stimulated parapsychologists to develop methods of testing extrasensory perception that could not be faulted by their colleagues in other fields on simple methodological grounds. An indication of the acceptability of parapsychology as a recognized scientific discipline was the acceptance of the Parapsychological Society into membership of the AAAS in December 1969.

In 1972, Price changed his mind about what he had written in the 1950s. In an article in *Science,* he apologized to Soal and Rhine for treating them unfairly. Shortly afterward, it was discovered that Price had been right about Soal, who had faked the data he had presented.

Sources:

Berger, Arthur S., and Joyce Berger. *The Encyclopedia of Parapsychology and Psychical Research.* New York: Paragon House, 1991.

Markwick, Betty. "The Soal-Goldney Experiments with Basil Shackleton: New Evidence of Data Manipulation." *Proceedings* of the Society for Psychical Research 56 (1978).

Pleasants, Helene, ed. *Biographical Dictionary of Parapsychology.* New York: Helix Press, 1964.

Price, George R. "Apology to Rhine and Soal." *Science* 175 (1972).

———. "Science and the Supernatural." *Science* 122 (August 26, 1955).

———. "Where Is the Definitive Experiment?" *Science* (January 6, 1956).

Price, Harry (1881–1948)

Prominent British psychical researcher. Price was born January 17, 1881, and was educated at London and Shropshire. His interest in conjuring dated from his boyhood, when he watched the medicine show of "The Great Sequah" at a fairground, a performance with quack remedies, tooth drawing, and magical tricks. At the age of fifteen, he conducted his first scientific investigation of poltergeist phenomena, staying until midnight in a reputed haunted house with photographic equipment.

Price was involved in archaeological excavations in Greenwich Park and discovered a prehistoric cave in Shropshire. He assisted the early flying experiments of José Weiss, a year before the Wright Brothers at Kitty Hawk. Price was an amateur conjurer, a member of the Magic Circle, elected to the Society of American Magicians, and from 1921 onward was honorary librarian of the exclusive Magician's Club.

As a psychical researcher, Price investigated **Stella C.** (Stella Cranshaw Deacon), **Eleonore Zügun,** and **Rudi Schneider.** He was a publicist for the cause of psychical research. Price went on an expedition to the Hartz Mountains, Germany, during the Goethe centenary of 1932, to test a fifteenth-century white magic ritual said to change a goat into a "fair youth of surpassing beauty." The goat was not metamorphosed. Price was also founder of Britain's National Laboratory of Psychical Research (which became the University of London Council for Psychical Research).

Price also attracted attention for his investigation of Borley Rectory, Essex, "The Most Haunted House in England," and his connection with **R. S. Lambert** and the story of the **Talking Mongoose** of the Isle of Man. Price published many books and pamphlets concerning his research and other experiences in the Spiritualist and occult community. He also made an early talking picture, *Psychical Research,* in 1935, contributed an article on "Faith and Fire-Walking" to the *Encyclopedia Britannica* (1936), and collaborated on a film script of the Borley hauntings with novelist Upton Sinclair. Price died March 29, 1948. His collection of some 20,000 volumes of works on psychical research, magic, and related subjects, was donated to the University of London as the Harry Price Library of Magical Literature.

After his death, Price was accused by fellow psychical researchers of helping out or faking some of the Borley Rectory phenomena. One of those, Trevor Hall, went on to write a biography of Price critical of every aspect of his activities. Hall presented him as a pretender, fraud, and dishonest investigator.

Sources:

Berger, Arthur S., and Joyce Berger. *The Encyclopedia of Parapsychology and Psychical Research.* New York: Paragon House, 1991.

Dingwall, E. J., K. M. Goldney, and Trevor H. Hall. "The Haunting of Borley Rectory; A Critical Survey of the Evidence." *Proceedings* of the Society for Psychical Research 51 (1956).

Hall, Trevor H. *Search for Harry Price.* London; Duckworth, Tex.: Southwest Book Services, 1978.

Pleasants, Helene, ed. *Biographical Dictionary of Parapsychology.* New York: Helix Press, 1964.

Price, Harry. *Confessions of a Ghost-Hunter.* London: Putnam, 1936. Reprint, New York: Causeway Books, 1974.

———. *The End of Borley Rectory.* London: Harrap, 1946.

———. *Fifty Years of Psychical Research: A Critical Survey.* London: Longmans, 1939. Reprint, New York: Arno Press, 1975.

———. *Leaves From a Psychist's Case-Book.* London: Gollancz, 1933.

———. *The Most Haunted House in England.* London: Longmans, Green, 1940.

———. *Poltergeist Over England.* London: Country Life, 1945.

———. *Search for Truth: My Life for Psychical Research.* London: Collins, 1942.

Price, Harry, and E. J. Dingwall, eds. *Revelations of a Spirit Medium.* London: Kegan Paul, 1922.

Tabori, Paul. *Harry Price: The Biography of a Ghost-Hunter.* London: Athenaenum Press, 1930.

Price, Henry Habberley (1899–1984)

Emeritus professor of logic who also became a prominent figure in the field of parapsychology. Price was born on May 17, 1899, at Neath, South Wales, Britain. He was educated at Winchester College and New College, Oxford (B.S., M.A.). He was a fellow of Magdalen College, Oxford (1922–24) and a fellow of Trinity College, Oxford (1924–35) prior to beginning his long tenure as Wykeham Professor of Logic, University of Oxford and fellow of New College, Oxford (1935–59). He was named emeritus fellow of New College at the time of his retirement. Price was honored as the Gifford Lecturer at Aberdeen University for the 1959–60 school year.

Price was president of the **Society for Psychical Research,** London (1939–41) and subsequently a council member. He was a charter member of the Parapsychology Association. An outstanding philosopher, he lectured and wrote articles and books on the philosophical problems raised by parapsychology. He lectured on "Some Philosophical Implications of Paranormal Cognition" at the International Conference on Philosophy and Parapsychology, St. Paul de Vence, France, in 1954. He died in Oxford, England, November 26, 1984, at the age of 85.

Sources:

Price, Henry H. *Belief.* Gifford Lectures, 1969.

———. *Essays in the Philosophy of Religion.* Oxford: Claredon Press, 1972.

———. "Haunting and the 'Psychic Ether' Hypothesis" *Proceedings* of the Society for Psychical Research (vol. 45, 1939).

———. *Hume's Theory of the External World.* Oxford: Claredon Press, 1940. Reprint, Greenwood Press, 1981.

———. *Perception* (1932; 1973).

———. "Psychical Research and Human Personality." *Hibbert Journal* (January 1949).

———. "Some Philosophical Questions About Telepathy and Clairvoyance." *Philosophy* (October 1940). Reprint in: J. M. O. Wheatley and H. L. Edge, eds. *Philosophical Dimensions of Parapsychology.* Springfield, Ill.: Charles C. Thomas, 1976.

———. "Survival and the Idea of Another World." *Proceedings* of the Society for Psychical Research 50 (January 1953).

———. *Thinking and Experience.* Cambridge: Harvard University Press; London; New York: Hutchinsons University Library, 1953.

Price-Mars, Jean (1875–1969)

Haitian educator and diplomat who also studied parapsychology. He was born on October 15, 1875, at Grande-Rivière du Nord, Haiti. Price-Mars was a professor and rector at the University of Haiti and a member of the Haitian Senate. Beginning in 1900 he served in the Haitian diplomatic service in Germany, the United States, France, the Dominican Republic, and the United Nations and served as Haiti's Minister of Foreign Affairs. He was the founder of the Institute of Ethnology, Haiti, and president of the African Society of Culture. He published various books on the folklore, history, culture and ethnology of Haiti and took a special interest in parapsychology in relation to **voudou.**

He died March 2, 1969.

Sources:

Price-Mars, Jean. "Africa in the Americas." *Tomorrow* (Autumn 1954).

Prince, Morton (1854–1929)

Physician, neurologist, and psychologist whose career peaked as psychical research was maturing. He was born on December 21, 1854, at Boston, Massachusetts. He studied at Boston Latin School, Harvard (B.A., 1875), and Harvard Medical School (M.D., 1879). He was particularly interested in the work of Jean Charcot and Pierre Janet in hysteria and hypnosis. He was a physician for diseases of the nervous system at Boston Dispensary (1882–86) and Boston City Hospital (1885–1913), an instructor in neurology at Harvard Medical School (1895–98), a professor of neurology at Tufts Medical School (1902–12), and subsequently professor emeritus. He was an associate professor in abnormal and dynamic psychology at Harvard University for two years at the end of his life (1926–28).

Prince was an outstanding neurologist. He founded and, for almost a quarter of a century, edited the *Journal of Abnormal Psychology* (1906–29), and in 1911 he was elected president of the American Psychological Association. His book on *The Dissociation of a Personality* (1906) dealt with the famous case of "Sally Beauchamp" and is considered a basic work in the field of abnormal psychology, with an important bearing on the parapsychological phenomenon of secondary and multiple personality.

Prince was a member of the **American Society for Psychical Research** and contributed articles to the Society's *Proceedings.* He authored a number of books including *The Nature of Mind and Human Automatism* (1885), the title most directly related to parapsychological concerns. He died August 31, 1929.

Sources:

Prince, Morton. "A Contribution to the Study of Hysteria." *Proceedings* of the Society for Psychical Research 14 (1899).

———. "The Development and Genealogy of the Misses Beauchamp." *Proceedings* of the Society for Psychical Research 15 (1900–01).

———. *The Nature of Mind and Human Automatism.* Philadelphia: J. B. Lippincott, 1885.

Taylor, W. S. *Morton Prince and Abnormal Psychology.* New York; London: D. Appleton & Co., 1928.

Prince, Walter Franklin (1863–1934)

Prominent American psychical researcher, research officer of the **American Society for Psychical Research** (1920–25) and cofounder and research officer of the **Boston Society for Psychical Research** (1925–32). He was born in Detroit, Maine, April 22, 1863. After graduating from the Maine Wesleyan Seminary in 1881, he attended Yale University (B.A., 1896; Ph.D, 1899), and Drew Theological Seminary (B.D., 1896). He became the pastor of Methodist Episcopal congregations in Maine and Connecticut and then joined the Protestant Episcopal Church and served parishes in Brooklyn, Pittsburgh, and San Bernardino, California.

From church social work, he was led to study abnormal psychology and became the director of psychotherapeutics at St. Mark's Episcopal Church in New York City (1916–17). While there, he met and became the assistant to **James Hervey Hyslop,** who had reestablished the American Society for Psychical Research. In 1925 he became the Society's research officer, a post he held until the controversy over Mina Crandon ("Margery") flared in the mid-1920s. The controversy split the society. Prince believed Margery a fraud and resigned from his position with the Society over his differences with the board on how to handle the data that it had assembled.

Along with Elwood Worcester and Gardner Murphy, Prince led in the founding of the rival Boston Society for Psychical Research in 1925 and became its research officer. While operating out of Boston, he was responsible for a remarkable cure in the multiple personality case of Doris Fischer and conducted important investigations of the cases of **"Patience Worth"** and the Antigonish poltergeist. His excellent work led to his twice being elected president of the Society for Psychical Research, London, in 1930 and 1931. He died on August 7, 1934.

In eighteen years of research with the American Society for Psychical Research and the Society for Psychical Research, London, Prince investigated many different kinds of paranormal phenomena in hundreds of cases, but in spite of his doubts about certain phenomena, he eventually concluded that a case for the reality of telepathy and clairvoyance has been "absolutely and scientifically proved." In addition, he was inclined to belief in survival of personality after death and considered the evidence "very promising."

Sources:

Berger, Arthur S., and Joyce Berger. *The Encyclopedia of Parapsychology and Psychical Research.* New York: Paragon House, 1991.

Pleasants, Helene, ed. *Biographical Dictionary of Parapsychology.* New York: Helix Press, 1964.

Prince, Walter Franklin. *The Enchanted Boundary: A Survey to Negative Reactions to Claims of Psychical Phenomena.* Boston: Boston Society for Psychic Research, 1930.

———. *Leonard and Soule Experiments.* Boston: Boston Society for Psychical Research, 1929.

———. *Noted Witnesses for Psychic Occurrences.* Boston: Boston Society for Psychical Research, 1928. Reprint, New Hyde Park, N.Y.: University Books, 1963.

———. *The Psychic in the House.* Boston: Boston Society for Psychical Research, 1926.

Prince, Walter Franklin, and Lydia W. Allison. *The Case of Patience Worth.* Boston: Boston Society for Psychical Research, 1927. Reprint, New Hyde Park, N.Y.: University Books, 1964.

Smith, Anson J. "Walter Franklin Prince." *Tomorrow* (Summer 1955).

Walter Franklin Prince: A Tribute to His Memory. Boston: Boston Society for Psychical Research, 1935."

Princeton Engineering Anomalies Research (PEAR)

The Princeton Engineering Anomalies Research (PEAR) program was founded in 1979 by Robert G. Jahn, a physicist, engineer, and former dean of the School of Engineering and Applied Science, to pursue the study of the interaction of human consciousness with various mechanical devices and to measure the effects of such interaction. The ultimate goal was better understanding of the role of consciousness in establishing physical reality.

PEAR has emphasized research on attempts by humans to affect the behavior of various mechanical, electrical, and other devices apart from mundane physical forces. Utilizing various sophisticated machines that generally give random outputs, researchers found that various subjects had been able to produce outputs that varied considerably from expected random results. Among the more interesting experiments were those involving people located at some distance from the machine being affected, pairs of people with emotional bonds, and experiments in which the results were produced either prior to or after the actual attempt to make changes occurred.

PEAR also has become involved in the popular remote viewing experimentation that has dominated much parapsychological research through the 1980s and 1990s. PEAR experiments tended to be based on telepathy (rather than clairvoyance), as the experiments were set up between a recipient at one location attempting to reproduce the images perceived by a second participant who was at another location. Researchers also ran a lengthy remote viewing experiment using Urquardt Castle at Loch Ness in Scotland as a target. Repeated positive effects have been reported from these experiments.

The results of two decades of work, demonstrating the correlation of human intention and physical effects, has led Jahn and his associates to the conclusion that a larger model of reality exists, one that provides for an active role of consciousness in controlling the physical world. Jahn has called for his colleagues to alter their methodology based upon the phenomena he has explored.

The Princeton Engineering Anomalies Research program is headquartered at C-131, Engineering Quadrangle, Princeton University, Princeton, NJ 08544. It maintains an Internet site at http://www.princeton.edu/~pear/index.html.

Sources:

Dunn, Brenda J., and R. G. Jahn. "Experiments in Remote Human/Machine Interactions." *Journal for Scientific Exploration* 6, no. 4 (1993): 311–32.

Jahn, R. G., and B. J. Dunne. *Margins of Reality: The Role of Consciousness in the Physical World.* San Diego: Harcourt Brace Jovanovich, 1987.

Jahn, R. G., B. J. Dunne, and R. D. Nelson. "Engineering Anomalies Research." *Journal for Scientific Exploration* 1, no. 1 (1987): 15–26.

Princeton Engineering Anomalies Research. http://www.princeton.edu/~pear/index.html. May 20, 2000.

Private UFO Investigations (Group)

Organization of the 1970s concerned with UFO reports and international sightings which issued a quarterly publication *The UFO Examiner.* It was headquartered in Hazelton, Iowa.

Probe (Woonsocket) (Magazine)

Quarterly newsstand magazine concerned with controversial phenomena which was edited by Joseph L. Ferriere and published in Woonsocket, Rhode Island, in the 1970s.

Probe—The Unknown (Magazine)

Bimonthly newsstand publication published in Burbank, California in the 1970s that included articles on psychic phenomena, astrology, tarot and ESP generally.

Probing the Unexplained (Newsletter)

Former newsletter of the International Association for Investigation of the Unexplained. It included articles and news concerning **UFOs** and other mysteries and scientific anomalies. It was published in Edmond, Oklahoma.

Proceedings (of Psychical Research Societies)

Official publications of the societies for psychical research. The first in the field was the *Proceedings* of the **Society for Psychical Research,** London, the second the *Proceedings* of the old **American Society for Psychical Research** (1885–89), the third the *Proceedings* of the independent American Society for Psychical Research (1907–27) and the fourth the *Proceedings* of the **National Laboratory of Psychical Research.** The **Boston Society for Psychical Research** issued books and *Bulletins,* but nothing titled *Proceedings.*

Proceedings of the first four psychical research societies cited above and the reconstituted American Society for Psychical Research from 1907 onward are the subject of separate entries.

Proceedings of the College of Universal Wisdom

Official publication of the College of Universal Wisdom, the educational branch of the ministry of Universal Wisdom, founded by **George W. Van Tassell** (1910–1978). Van Tassell was the author of *I Rode in a Flying Saucer* (1952) and other books and the organizer of **Giant Rock Space Convention,** held annually at Giant Rock Airport, near Yucca Valley, California. The ministry was founded to perpetuate the teaching received from **UFO** visitors. The messages from outer space were published in the *Proceedings.* Toward the end of Van Tassel's life the *Proceeding* became irregular and then ceased to exist altogether.

Proceedings of the Institute of Psychophysical Research

Irregular publication in book form of research undertaken by the Institute during the 1960s into paranormal phenomena. The first volume was titled *Lucid Dreams* and the second, *Out-of-the-Body Experiences.* Both were by **Celia E. Green** and issued in 1968. The Institute of Psychophysical Research was headquartered in Oxford, England.

Proceedings of the National Laboratory of Psychical Research

The **National Laboratory of Psychical Research** was founded by psychical researcher **Harry Price** for scientific investigation of phenomena. The *Proceedings* published from 1927–29 contain research reports. Part 2, issued in April 1929, was the still valuable *Short-Title Catalogue of Works on Psychical Research, Spiritualism, Magic, Psychology, Legerdemain and Other Methods of Deception, Charlatanism, Witchcraft and Technical Works for the Scientific Investigation of Alleged Abnormal Phenomena from circa 1450 A.D. to 1919 A.D.*.

In 1934, the National Laboratory of Psychical Research was taken over by the University of London Council for Psychical Research, London, and published various issues of a *Bulletin* concerned with psychical research. *Bulletin I,* issued in 1935, was a *Supplement* to the *Short-Title Catalogue.* The National Laboratory of Psychical Research also issued a *Bulletin* of psychical investigations.

Proceedings of the Old American Society for Psychical Research

The American Society for Psychical Research was originally formed in 1885 and existed as an independent organization until 1889, when it became a branch of the British Society for Psychical Research, under the leadership of **Richard Hodgson.** When Hodgson died in 1905, the branch was dissolved, and after a year of preparation, the present American Society for Psychical Research was formed under the leadership of **James H. Hyslop.** The main *Proceedings* of the original Amerian Society for Psychical Research from 1885–89 continued reports of research by the Society and its members on such areas as thought-transference, the Supernatural Among the Omaha Tribe, hypnotic phenomena, telepathy, and automatic writing. The American Society for Psychical Research was reconstituted in 1907.

Proceedings of the Parapsychological Association

Annual publication from 1966 onward "to provide a published record of the annual convention of the Parapsychological Association." This scholarly journal was edited by **W. G. Roll,** R. L. Morris and J. D. Morris. Numbers 1–7 were published by the Parapsychological Association, and subsequent issues have been published by Scarecrow Press as an annual volume of abstracts and papers under the running title *Research in Parapsychology.* The current address of the Parapsychological Association is: P.O. Box 3695, Charlottesville, VA 22903-3695. The association's home page organizes these issues from current to past issues at http://www.parapsych.org/.

Sources:

Parapsychological Association. http://www.parapsych.org/. March 8, 2000.

Proceedings of the Psychological Society of Great Britain

A volume, published in London in 1880, with reports of the papers and discussions in **Sergeant Cox**'s Society for 1875–79. The society dissolved in 1880, and no further papers were published. The papers offered reflection on the common concerns of psychology and parapsychology. There is a copy of this volume in the library of the Society for Psychical Research, London.

Proceedings of the Society for Psychical Research

The society was founded in 1882 and has published *Proceedings* since then. The *Journal* was first published from 1883 onward and until 1949 was available only to members of the Society. The *Proceedings* for the first half century of the Society's existence offer a comprehensive view of psychical research over that period. A *Combined Index* to the *Journal* and the *Proceedings* is issued by the society.

Procter & Gamble Logo

The familiar logo of Procter & Gamble for decades was a design of thirteen stars enclosed in a circle, with a man-in-the-moon. In the wake of the rise of a popular interest in Satanism and anti-Satanism in the late 1960s, the logo gave rise to persistent rumors that the company was run by Satan sympathizers and that the logo expressed allegiance to the devil. The rumor was spread by many conservative Christians and others who had come to believe in an international underground Satanic conspiracy, such as that described in the black magic novels of popular occult writer Dennis Wheatly. The company took a number of public relations countermeasures through the 1970s, but unable to stamp out the rumor, in 1982 it was obliged to take legal measures to defend itself. Procter & Gamble filed two libel suits in July 1982, one against a WXIA television weatherman, another against a Tennessee couple, for spreading such rumors. On April 24, 1985, Procter & Gamble dropped the suits when all three individuals publicly apologized. The logo was, nonetheless, removed from its products.

Professional Psychics United

Organization founded in 1977 by professional psychics with the object of helping police in crime solving. It provided a psychic rescue team to assist in locating missing persons, offered educational programs on the nature of extrasensory perception, and conducted teaching seminars. It maintained biographical archives and a library of 203 volumes and sponsored psychic fairs. It bestowed awards, maintained a speakers bureau, offered placement service, and conducted research programs. The organization, which survived only a few years, was headquartered in Berwyn, Illinois.

Progoff, Ira (1921–1998)

Jungian psychologist who has investigated areas of parapsychology. Progoff was born on August 2, 1921, in New York City. He studied at the New School for Social Research in the city from which he received his Ph.D. in 1951. He was a Bollingen fellow from 1952–58, during which time he spent a year in Zürich as a lecturer at the Jung Institute (1953). In 1959 he became the director of Institute for Research in Depth Psychology at Drew University, Madison, New Jersey. He was a member of the **Parapsychology Association,** a member of the advisory board of the Institute for Religion in an Age of Science, and a member of the board of editors of *Journal of Humanistic Psychol-*

ogy. Progoff took a special interest in mediumship, psychedelics, religious and creative experience, personality growth and psychic sensitivity, and image-making at depth-psychological levels. He also developed a system of Process Meditation, characterized by the individuals' use of an "Intensive Journal" to record their progress. He organized Life Context Workshops and published the *National Intensive Journal* at Dialogue House, 80 E. 11th St., New York, N.Y. 10003. His meditation system was the subject of his book *The Practice of Process Meditation* (1980). Progoff died December 28, 1998.

Sources:

Pleasants, Helene, ed. *Biographical Dictionary of Parapsychology*. New York: Helix Press, 1964.

Progroff, Ira, ed. *The Cloud of Unknowing*. N.p., 1957.

———. *Death and Rebirth of Psychology*. N.p., 1956.

———. *Depth Psychology and Modern Man*. N.p., 1959.

———. *Jung's Psychology and Its Social Meaning*. N.p., 1953.

———. "Parapsychology in Modern Thinking." *International Journal of Parapsychology* 1, 1 (Summer 1959).

———. *The Practice of Process Meditation*. N.p., 1980.

———. *The Symbolic and the Real*. N.p., 1963.

———. "Transformation of Jewish Mysticism." *International Journal of Parapsychology* 2, 2 (Autumn 1960).

Progressive Library & Spiritual Institution

Established by pioneer British Spiritualist **James Burns** in 1863. The organization included a lending library of several thousand volumes on Spiritualism and related subjects, with a reading room and rooms for séances or experiments relating to Spiritualism.

In addition, the Institution included a publishing department to assist and promote literature connected with Spiritualism. These included an edition of the writings of prominent American Spiritualist Judge Edmonds and the important *Report on Spiritualism of the London Dialectical Society* (1872). The Institution was an influential meeting place for nineteenth-century Spiritualists in London.

The Progressive Thinker (Newspaper)

American Spiritualist weekly, founded by J. R. Francis in 1899 and edited and published for many years by M. E. Cadwallader. The Progressive Thinking Company, headquartered in Chicago, also published a variety of Spiritualists books.

Project Starlight International

Founded in 1964, to gather and disseminate a broad range of instrumented **UFO** data to the scientific community. During its existence, the project has utilized magnetometers, a gravimeter, spectrometer, radar, laser-telescope-video system, and other electronic and optical systems for recording the physical effects, optical images, and location of UFOs. The project conducts in-depth analyses of motion-picture films of UFOs obtained by PSI staff members, along with magnetometric, spectrographic, and other data recorded during UFO events. Address: P.O. Box 845, College Park, MD 20740.

Project VISIT—Vehicle Internal Systems Investigative Team

Founded in 1976 with a membership of researchers, including engineers, scientists, analysts, and investigators, interested in **UFOs.** The project exists to conduct research in order to determine whether or not there is a correlation of engineering systems among UFO cases, to identify and evaluate such systems and determine the mode of operation of UFOs, and to share research findings with government agencies, public corporations, and the general public. The project maintains an archives containing 10,000 clippings, reports, and reviews on current UFO cases and also compiles statistics. It sponsored the 1980 **Mutual UFO Network** Conference. It has also published study and monographs. Project VISIT may be reached at P.O. Box 890327, Houston, TX 77289.

Prophecy

In premodern society, prophets appeared both informally as gifted individuals with a sudden prophetic insight or as functionaries identical with what Western scholars in the nineteenth and twentieth century called witchdoctors, priests or **shaman.** For an example of the prophet/seer/judge functionary, see the biblical book of I Samuel which traces the history of the last judge to rule the Hebrew tribe. Samuel was, as a child, dedicated to God and placed in the care of Eli, the corrupt judge/seer of Israel. His career includes a number of clairvoyant and prophetic (precognitive) utterances, but the most illustrative of his daily functions is pictured in I Sam. 9 in which Samuel helps locate the lost donkeys of the future king Saul.

In many instances prophetic utterances were made in what appeared to be a normal state (see the references to prophecy in the biblical book of Acts) but often occurred in an altered or ecstatic state of consciousness (see the opening verse of the book of Ezekiel, or the sixth chapter of Isaiah). In general the Hebrew prophets went through a period in which "the word of the Lord" spoke to them and then they in turn went among the populace and spoke what they had been told. We know that the pythonesses attached to the oracles of ancient **Greece** uttered prophetic words under the influences of natural gases or drugs, and when the magical practitioners in tribal cultures attempt to peer into the future they often attain a condition of ecstasy by taking some drug, the action of which is well known to them. But this was not always the case; the shaman often summoned a spirit to his aid to discover what portents and truths lie in the future.

Most often **divination** is not prophecy in the true sense of the term, as artificial aids are employed. Those aids can stimulate the psychic attunement, but most of the time appear merely as a pretended **prediction** of future events by the chance appearance of certain objects that the augur supposedly understands. We often find prophecy disassociated from the ecstatic condition, as among the priests of the Maya Indians of Central America, known as *Chilan Balam,* who, at stated intervals in the year, made certain statements regarding the period which lay immediately before them.

Prophecy may be regarded as a direct utterance of the deity, taking a human being as mouthpiece, or the statement of one who seeks inspiration from the fountain of wisdom. In the biblical writings, Yahweh desired to communicate with human beings and chose certain persons as mouthpieces. Again individuals (often the same as those chosen by God) applied to the deity for inspiration in critical moments. Prophecy then may be the utterances of the deity(ies) through the instrument of an entranced shaman or seer, or the inspired utterance of a seer who later repeats what has been learned while in an altered state (hearing the word of the Lord).

In ancient Assyria the prophetic class were called *nabu,* meaning "to call" or "announce"—a name probably adopted from that of the god Na-bi-u, the speaker or proclaimer of destiny, the tablets of which he inscribed.

Among the ancient Hebrews the prophet was called *nabhia,* a borrowed title probably adopted from the Canaanites. They differed little in function from similar functionaries in the surroundings cultures, but differed greatly in the particular deity to which they were attached. Prophets were important functionaries in the ancient Near East. Four hundred prophets of Baal reportedly sat at Queen Jezebel's table (I Kings 18:19). The fact that they were prophets of this deity would almost go to prove that they were also priests. We find that the most celebrated prophets of Israel belonged to the northern portion of that country, which was more subject to the influence of the Canaanites.

Association of prophets appeared in Israel quite early (see I Sam. 10:5) and records of such appear periodically through Israel's history. In the era after the death of Ahab and Jezebel they appear to have had some formal organization (see II Kings 2) with chapters in various towns (II Kings 2–5). They served to consolidate Elijah's victories over the prophets of the hated deity Baal. They seem to have died out by the time of the exile.

The general idea in Hebrew Palestine was that Yahweh, or God, was in the closest possible touch with the prophets, and that he would do nothing without revealing it to them. While often ignored or persecuted during their lifetime, their preserved written words were later given greatest veneration and still later canonized.

In ancient Greece, the prophetic class were generally found attached to the oracles and in Rome were represented by the augurs. In **Egypt,** the priests of Ra at Memphis acted as prophets as, perhaps, did those of Hekt. Among the ancient Celts and Teutons prophecy was frequent, the prophetic agent usually placing him or herself in the ecstatic condition. The Druids were famous practitioners of the prophetic art, and some hint of their utterances may be still extant in the so-called "Prophecies of Merlin."

In **America,** as has been stated, prophetic utterance took practically the same forms as in Europe and Asia. Captain Jonathan Carver, an early traveler in North America, cited a peculiar instance where the seers of a certain tribe stated that a famine would be ended by assistance being sent from another tribe at a certain hour on the following day. At the very moment mentioned by them, a canoe rounded a headland, bringing news of relief.

A story was told in the *Atlantic Monthly* many years ago by a traveler among the Plains tribes, who stated that an Indian medicine-man had prophesied the coming of himself and his companions to his tribe two days before their arrival among them.

In recent years, **channeling** and **contactees** contributed more to American prophecy than any other sources. Hundreds of channeling books have been published in the past few decades, but the majority contain unspecified prophetic content. More often than not, the predictions are about millennial earth changes and a new era of spiritual transformation and peace. Prophetic channeling by **Edgar Cayce,** Kryon and Elizabeth Clare Prophet are considered the most prominent. More traditional psychic seers such as **Jeanne Dixon, Ruth Montgomery,** Gordon Scallion, Dannion Brinkley and Lori Toye are in the forefront due to the lack of more particulars from channeled sources. Today, mass market prophecy paperbacks are just a number of hodge-podge collections of bits and pieces from Cayce, **Nostradamus,** Native American lore, etc. Much analysis on prophecy is rare, but works by John White and Tom Kay are considered noteworthy in their field.

Sources:

Alschuler, Alfred S. "When prophecy succeeds: Planetary visions near death and collective psychokinesis." *Journal of the American Society for Psychical Research* 90 no. 4 (October 1996).

Ascension, Soul Ways and Its Meaning. http://www.spiritweb.org/Spirit/ascension.html. April 10, 2000.

Cannon, Dolores. *Conversations with Nostradamus, vol 1.* Huntsville: Ozark Mountain Publishing, 1997.

Cayce, Hugh Lynn. *Earth Changes Update.* Virginia Beach: ARE Press, 1980.

Center for Millennial Studies. http://www.mille.org. April 10, 2000.

Ellis, Keith. *Prediction and Prophecy.* London: Wayland, 1973.

Garrison, Omar V. *Encyclopedia of Prophecy.* New York: Citadel, 1979.

Geertz, Armin W. *The Invention of Prophecy : Continuity and meaning in Hopi Indian religion.* Berkeley: University of California Press, 1994.

Kirkwood, Annie. *Mary's Message to the World.* Nevada City: Blue Dolphin Publishing, 1994.

Kay, Tom. *When The Comet Runs.* Norfolk, Va.: Hampton Roads Publishing, 1997.

Millennial Prophecy Links. http://www.wholeagain.com/millennial.html. April 10, 2000.

The Millennium Matters. http://www.mm2000.nu. April 10, 2000.

Morgana's Observatory. http://www.dreamscape.com/morgana. April 10, 2000.

Montgomery, Ruth. *The World To Come.* New York: Random House, Harmony Books, 1999.

Prophet, Elizabeth Clare. *Saint Germain on Prophecy II.* Livingston: Summit University Press, 1986.

Rowley, Harold H. *Prophecy and Religion in Ancient China and Israel.* New York: Harper, 1956.

Shellhorn, G. Cope. *Surviving Catastrophic Earth Changes.* Madison: Horus House, 1994.

Stanford, Ray. *Fatima Prophecy,* New York: Random House, Ballantine Books, 1990.

Timms, Moira. *Prophecies and Predictions: Everyone's Guide to the Coming Changes.* Santa Cruz, Calif.: Unity Press, 1981.

Vaughan, Alan. *Patterns of Prophecy.* New York: Hawthorn Books, 1973. Reprint, London: Turnstone, 1974.

White, John. *Pole Shift.* Virginia Beach: ARE Press, 1980.

"The Prophet"

A **control** of the medium **William Stainton Moses,** said to have been the biblical Haggai, a contemporary of Malachi, brought in by "Imperator" as an assistant with Vates (Daniel), another contemporary. He signed communications several times jointly with "Imperator" but never gave independent teaching.

Prosperity Paths (Newsletter)

Newsletter published six times a year, which presents the teachings of Eastern mystic Yogi Bhajan and news of the activities of the **3HO Organization.** Address: P.O. Box 2337, Espanola, NM 87532. The newsletter is also available on the organization's website: http://www.3ho.org/.

Sources:

Healthy Happy Holy Organization. http://www.3ho.org/. March 8, 2000.

The Prosperos

A group stemming from the "Fourth Way" philosophy of **Georgei Ivanovitch Gurdjieff** founded in 1956 by **Thane Walker,** a charismatic student of Gurdjieff, and Phez Kahlil. The Prosperos were chartered in Florida, but moved around the country, and they reported a some 3,000 members in California.

The Prosperos believed in One Mind and claimed that reality can be experienced only from its perspective by removing the distortions of the senses and memory that hide the true self. This was generally in accord with traditional mystical teaching, but whereas the way of the fakir is through willpower, the yogi through intellect and the monk through emotions, the "Fourth Way" was available to individuals within world experience. The Prosperos believed that God is pure consciousness and use five processes to achieve identification of the individual with the One Consciousness: 1) Statement of Being (the facts of reality); 2) Uncovering the Lie or Error (the claims of the senses); 3) Argument (resting of claims); 4) Summing up the Results; and 5) Establishing the Absolute.

Lectures and classes were conducted on such topics as "Translation," and "Releasing the Hidden Splendor," and there was also an inner circle named High Watch, for those who complete three classes of development.

The name "Prosperos" derived from the magician Prospero in Shakespeare's play *The Tempest.* Through his magical powers, Prospero could interpret, project, rationalize and imagine life as he wishes, but on his island he was interconnected with Caliban the monster (who parallels the unconscious mind) and Ariel (the intuitive agent who aids Prospero when called upon).

Current address unavailable.

Sources:

Ritley, Mary. *Invitation to a Hungry Feast.* Santa Monica, Calif.: The Prosperos Inner Space Center, 1970.

Proxy Sitting

A consultation with a medium in which the individual uses a substitute or "proxy," in order to avoid possible telepathic communication or other indications from the sitter.

Pruden, Laura A. (d. 1939)

Slate-writing medium of Cincinnati, widow of a judge, who practiced mediumship for well over half a century. She did not go into trance. **Hereward Carrington** sat with her on October 27, 1925, and in his book, *The Story of Psychic Science* (1930), he included an account of his experiences. After describing the result of his preliminary examination of the table and the slates, he stated that, at the medium's request, he wrote two questions on slips of paper, one addressed to **Richard Hodgson,** and the other to his own father. He folded them up and placed one upon the floor under the séance table, the other on a small table to his right where it remained visible throughout the sitting, until used.

Pruden, sitting on a very low rocking chair, thrust the pair of slates, a small piece of slate pencil between them, through the slit on the tablecloth, with her right hand under the table. Her left hand rested in her lap and remained visible throughout the séance.

Carrington continued:

"The first pair of slates remained under the table for about half an hour, when they were removed and a brief message was found written upon one of the inner surfaces, signed "R. Hodgson," and answering my question, written upon the first slip. These slates were then put to one side. I was then requested to remove the first slip from under the séance table and place the second one there. This I did. The second pair of slates was then examined and held under the table in the same manner as the first pair. At the end of about half an hour these were removed and a general message from my 'father' was found upon them, answering the question written upon the second slip. The slips and slates I took with me, and now have them in my possession."

Carrington further stated:

"It is my opinion that, on any theory whatever, Pruden's slate-writing is a very remarkable performance. The table and slates were certainly free from any previous preparation. She certainly could not have seen the written questions before they were placed on the floor under the séance table. She certainly keeps up an animated conversation with her sitter throughout the sitting. Her left hand is always visible and her body appears to be practically stationary throughout. At no time does she stoop to pick up anything from the floor."

Carrington advanced a theory as a hypothetical explanation of the feat, but he himself admitted that his observations tended to support the genuine character of the manifestation.

A series of articles which gave a favorable impression of Pruden's powers was published in the *Journal* of the American Society for Psychical Research (1926–27). The British psychical researcher **Harry Price,** in his report of séances held with Pruden in London in 1925, withheld favorable pronouncement, as he found fault with Pruden's conditions. See also *Journal* of the Society for Psychical Research (vol. 23, pp. 76, 97, 139; vol. 24, p. 128). Pruden died March 10, 1939, at age 86.

Sources:

Carrington, Hereward. *The Story of Psychic Science.* New York: Ives Washburn, 1931.

"Prudens"

One of the spirit **controls** of **William Stainton Moses,** said to be Plotinus. He contributed a Greek philosophical tone of thought to the spirit teachings. At an early stage he was appointed one of Moses's guardians and was left in charge of him during the absence of the controls "Imperator" and "Doctor."

Pryse, James Morgan, Jr. (1859–1942)

James Morgan Pryse, Jr., founder of the Gnostic Society, was born on November 14, 1859, in New London, Ohio, the son of a Welsh Presbyterian minister. His father, who belonged to the Welsh Order of Druid Bards, filled Pryse with the legends of the Druids along with the Presbyterian faith. As a young man Pryse pursued a law career but gave it up for journalism. He moved around frequently during his early adulthood, joined in the effort to create a colony at Topolobampo, Mexico, and from his New Jersey residence edited the Topolobampo periodical.

After moving to Los Angeles, Pryse joined the **Theosophical Society** in 1886. Within a few years he was one of its most active members and moved to New York to work for the society's Aryan Press. Late in 1889 he moved on to London at the request of **Helena Petrovna Blavatsky,** cofounder of the society, to work with her in the founding of HPB Press.

In 1894, following Blavatsky's death, Pryse moved to Ireland to work with the *Irish Theosophist.* While there he wrote the book *The Sermon on the Mount* (1896), the first of a series of theosophical treatments of the Bible and Christian theology. In 1895 Pryse returned to the United States to work with **William Quan Judge,** then the head of the American Theosophical Society, which had broken with the international theosophical movement. Following Judge's death in 1896, Pryse remained in New York and affiliated with the independent Theosophical Society of New York, which had broken with Judge's successor, **Katherine Tingley.** Pryse's next books were published by the society's Theosophical Publishing Co.

After 15 years in New York, Pryse returned to Los Angeles, where he wrote his most important text, *The Restored New Testament,* a theosophical translation of the New Testament. It was completed and published in 1914. While continuing to flirt with the larger Theosophical Society and writing articles for its periodicals, he remained aloof and led independent gatherings in Los Angeles. In 1925 he founded the Gnostic Society with six people who met in his home to discuss his metaphysical interpretation of Christianity. The small group is important as possibly the first modern group to describe itself as Gnostic. The society disbanded soon after Pryse's death on April 22, 1942, but has been revived by Stephan A. Hoeller.

Sources:

Pryse, James Morgan. *The Apocalypse Unsealed.* Los Angeles: The Author, 1931.

———. *Reincarnation in the New Testament.* New York: Theosophical Publishing Co. of New York, 1900.

———. *The Restored New Testament.* Los Angeles: The Author, 1914.

———. *The Sermon on the Mount.* New York: Theosophical Society, 1904.

Psi

Greek letter used in **parapsychology** to indicate psychic or paranormal phenomena such as **extrasensory perception** (ESP) or **psychokinesis** (PK).

PSI Center See Exceptional Human Experience Network, Inc.

Psi-Conducive

Term used by parapsychologists to indicate environmental or personal factors in the test situation that are favorable for the occurrence of **psi.** It is the opposite of **Psi-inhibiting.**

Psi-Forum (Journal)

Former Dutch-language journal published in the 1980s in Belgium by De Werkgroep Parapsychologie. It ceased publication after the third volume in 1986.

Psi-Hitting

Term used by parapsychologists to indicate a situation in a test of **extrasensory perception** when the subject's rate of scoring is above chance. It is the opposite to **Psi-missing.**

Psi-Inhibiting

Term used by parapsychologists to indicate environmental or personal facts in the test situation which inhibit the occurrence of **psi.** It is the opposite of **Psi-conducive.**

Psi-line Database System

Computer service providing online reference materials on parapsychology, covering dissertations, chapters from books, and psi-related publications. It is a service provided by the Exceptional Human Experience Network, Inc.; the service was established by parapsychologist **Rhea A. White** in 1983.

Psiline can be contacted at 414 Rockledge Rd., New Bern, NC 28562.

Psi Magazine

Former bimonthly periodical published by the Bartonian Metaphysical Society of Ottawa, Ontario, Canada. It was originally titled *Metaphysical Society Newsletter.*

Psi-Mediated Instrumental Response

An experimental concept developed by parapsychologist **Rex G. Stanford,** who proposed a model for spontaneous psi events where individuals may unconsciously obtain extrasensory knowledge of events relevant to their personal needs and use this knowledge to modify their behavior in a way which will be instrumental in satisfying those needs. Stanford and other parapsychologists have published a series of papers on experimental research relating to the PMIR model.

Sources:

Stanford, Rex G., and Angelo Castello. "Cognitive Mode and Extrasensory Function in a Timing-Based PMIR Task." In J. D. Morris, W. G. Roll, and R. L. Morris, eds. *Research in Parapsychology 1976* Metuchen, N.J.: Scarecrow Press, 1977.

Stanford, Rex G., and Peter Rust. "Psi-mediated Helping Behavior: Experimental Paradigm and Initial Results." In J. D. Morris, W. G. Roll, and R. L. Morris, eds. *Research in Parapsychology 1976* Metuchen, N.J.: Scarecrow Press, 1977.

Stanford, Rex G., and Angela Stio. "Associative Mediation in Psi-mediated Instrumental Response (PMIR)." In J. D. Morris, W. G. Roll & R. L. Morris, ed. *Research in Parapsychology 1975.* Metuchen, N.J.: Scarecrow Press, 1976.

Stanford, Rex G., and Gary Thompson. "Unconscious Psi-mediated Instrumental Response and its Relation to Conscious ESP Performance." In W. G. Roll, R. L. Morris, and J. D. Morris, eds. *Research in Parapsychology 1973* Metuchen, N.J.: Scarecrow Press, 1974.

Stanford, Rex G., R. Zennhausern, A. Taylor, and M. Dwyer. "Psychokinesis as a Psi-mediated Instrumental Response." *Journal* of the American Society for Psychical Research 69 (1975).

Psi-Missing

Term used by parapsychologists to indicate a situation in a test of **extrasensory perception** when the subject's rate of scoring is below chance. This is the opposite of **Psi-hitting.**

Psi Network

Organization formed "to promote a broader understanding and acceptance of psychic phenomena through lectures, discussions and experiments." Psi Network shared information with members and also with the general field of parapsychology research. Last known address: Psi Network, P.O. Box 998, Carpinteria, CA 93013.

Psi News

Quarterly bulletin of the **Parapsychological Association,** an international society for professional parapsychologists and psychical researchers. It featured news on scientific and educational activities in the field of parapsychology and included reviews of new books and correspondence from readers. Address: PO Box 92209, Durham, NC 27708-2209.

Psionics

A term coined by science-fiction editor John W. Campbell, Jr. to denote a combination of **radionics** and **psi** phenomena. His editorial "The Science of Psionics," published in the February 1956 issue of his magazine *Astounding Science Fiction,* discussed "psychic electronic machines." One such machine was invented by Thomas G. Hieronymus (U.S. Patent No. 2,482,773) and resembles the **black box** of radionics. Campbell described the machine in an article later that year. Campbell is also remembered as the publisher of **L. Ron Hubbard**'s initial article introducing **Dianetics** to the public.

Sources:

Campbell, John W., Jr. "Psionic Machine-Type One." *Astounding Science Fiction* (June 1956).

Psi Patterns (Journal)

Monthly publication of Midwestern Institute of Parapsychology which included articles on parapsychology and information on local psi events. Last known address: P.O. Box 262, Mason City, IA 50401.

Psi Research (Journal)

International publication that dealt with psi research. *Psi Research* was ceased in 1986.

Psi Science Institute of Japan

Organization concerned with parapsychological research in **Japan.** Its *Journal,* first published in 1977, is now an annual. It is in Japanese, but includes English abstracts. The institute is headquartered at Nishi-cho 786-3, Soka City, Saitama Prefect., 340-0035 Japan.

Psi-Trailing

A term used to indicate a form of **anpsi** or the **psi** faculty in **animals,** in which a pet may trace its owner in a distant location it has not previously visited.

Psyche

Anglicization of the Greek term for soul which has been adopted in a number of ways by various parapsychological and occult authors and organizations. Among them are:

(1) A German spiritualist monthly founded in 1894 and later, following the union in 1900 of the three largest Spiritualist societies of Berlin, superseded by a joint organ, the *Spiritistische Rundschau,* of which Karl Obertimpfler became the editor.

(2) An English monthly magazine devoted to the philosophy and phenomena of life, beginning in 1899.

(3) An English quarterly journal which succeeded **W. Whateley Carington**'s *Psychic Research Quarterly* in 1921 as a journal of general and applied psychology. It was edited by C. K. Ogden out of London.

Psychenautics

Term coined by **Robert E. L. Masters** and **Jean Houston** to denote the combination of mechanical and hypnotic techniques by means of which they have probed the **psi** faculty in their **Foundation for Mind Research** in Manhattan, New York.

Psychic

A term denoting (1) as an adjective, the paranormal character of certain phenomena and (2) as a noun, a sensitive individual, one susceptible to psychic influences. A psychic is usually not a medium and tends to attribute his/her ability to clairvoyance or ESP rather than spirit contact. The term psychic, however, is used very loosely in an inclusive manner to include the medium, the somnambule, and the magnetic or mesmeric subject, i.e., anyone who is in any degree sensitive. **Camille Flammarion** seems to have been the first to use the word as a French term while **Edward William Cox** seems to have introduced it into England.

Psychic (Magazine) See **New Realities**

Psychical Research

Scientific inquiry into the facts surrounding and causes underlying reports of paranormal and mediumistic phenomena. Psychical research's first concern has been to establish the occurrence of the claimed events. If such events are not due to obvious mundane causes, including **fraud,** observational error, or the laws of chance, the next stage of the inquiry is to establish a reason for their occurrence—whether known natural laws are sufficient to explain them or whether there is reason to assume action by an unknown force.

Determining the nature of such an unknown force and the mode of its manifestation forms a third level of investigation. If it is not a blind force but operated by intelligence, it must be determined whether this intelligence is earthly. Not until every other explanation and test fails can the claim of a paranormal source be accepted.

The Historical Background

The term *psychical research* covers all scientific investigation into the obscure phenomena traditionally connected with the so-called supernatural, undertaken with a view to their elucidation. Certain of these phenomena are known all over the world and have remained practically unaltered almost since prehistoric times. Such are the phenomena of **levitation, fire ordeal, crystal gazing, thought reading,** and **apparitions.** Even though the formal discipline of psychical research rests on the scientific method of the nineteenth century, these phenomena have been investigated throughout the ages.

John Gaule, in his *Select Cases of Conscience Touching Witches and Witchcraft* (1646), observes:

"But the more prodigious or stupendous [of the feats mentioned in the witches' confessions] are effected meerly by the devil; the witch all the while either in a rapt ecstasie, a charmed sleepe, or a melancholy dreame; and the witches' imagination, phantasie, common sense, only deluded with what is now done, or pretended."

A few other writers of the same period arrived at similar conclusions. The result of many of these medieval records was to confirm the genuineness of some of the phenomena witnessed, but here and there, even in those days, there were skeptics who refused to give them any supernatural significance.

Poltergeist disturbances received a large share of attention and investigation. The case of the **Drummer of Tedworth** was examined by Joseph Glanvill and the results set forth in his *Saducisimus Triumphatus,* published in 1668. The **Epworth phenomena,** which occurred in the house of John Wesley's father, elicited many comments, as did the **Cock Lane ghost,** the Stockwell poltergeist, and many others.

Those who investigated **animal magnetism** and **mesmerism** may be considered psychical researchers, since these forerunners of **hypnotism** were the fruits of prolonged investigation into the phenomena connected with the **trance** state.

The writings of **Paracelsus** and **Franz A. Mesmer** show that they had glimpses of perspectives that were ahead of their time, foreshadowing the work of psychical researchers. Paracelsus, for example, stated in his writings,

"By the magic power of the will, a person on this side of the ocean may make a person on the other side hear what is said on this side. . . . The ethereal body of a man may know what another man thinks at a distance of 100 miles and more."

This reads like an anticipation of **telepathy,** which has since attained remarkable prominence, although it is by no means attributed to "the ethereal body of a man." Such writings would seem to entitle many of the mesmerists and the older mystics to the designation of protopsychical researchers. As knowledge increased and systematized methods came into use, such inquiries became more focused and fruitful.

The introduction of modern **Spiritualism** in 1848 undoubtedly set the stage for psychical research. The movement was so widespread and the reports of its effects so numerous and impressive that it was inevitable that scientists (especially those facing the spiritual questions to which the movement spoke) would be attracted to the movement and then drawn into an examination of the alleged phenomena.

Thus we find engaged in the investigation of Spiritualism such individuals as William Carpenter, **Michael Faraday** and **Augustus De Morgan,** and on the Continent, **Count de Gasparin, Marc Thury** and **Johann C. F. Zöllner.** One of the most important investigators was undoubtedly **Sir William Crookes,** who worked independently for some time before the founding of the **Society for Psychical Research.**

However, although much good work was done by independent students of psychic science, as it came to be called, more systematic investigation was inevitable. The **London Dialectical Society** was established in 1867, and a resolution was carried out two years later to "investigate the phenomena alleged to be Spiritual Manifestations, and to report thereon." The committee included many distinguished individuals. An initial report was published in 1871.

In 1875 **Edward William Cox,** also connected with the London Dialectical Society, founded the **Psychological Society** of Great Britain for similar investigation. Cox included C. C. Massey, Walter H. Coffin, and Spiritualist medium **W. Stainton Moses** among the members. A single volume of *Proceedings* of the society's work was published in 1878. The society came to an end the next year, following Cox's death.

From 1878 on, the **British National Association of Spiritualists,** London (founded in 1873), appointed a research council that carried on significant research work with well-known mediums of the day under test conditions. Their work bore fruit early in 1882 when **William F. Barrett** presided over several conferences held by the association that resulted in the formation of the Society for Psychical Research.

The Establishment of Psychical Research

The Society for Psychical Research (SPR) was founded largely by a group of scientists and philosophers connected with Trinity College, Cambridge. The society was formed to "examine without prejudice or prepossession and in a scientific spirit those faculties of man, real or supposed, which appear to be inexplicable in terms of any generally recognized hypothesis."

The society's prospectus indicates its proposed aim and methods:

"It has been widely felt that the present is an opportune time for making an organised and systematic attempt to investigate that large group of debatable phenomena designated by such terms as mesmeric, psychical, and spiritualistic.

"From the recorded testimony of many competent witnesses, past and present, including observations recently made by scientific men of eminence in various countries, there appears to be, amid much delusion and deception, an important body of remarkable phenomena, which are *prima facie* inexplicable on any generally recognised hypothesis, and which, if incontestably established, would be of the highest possible value.

"The task of examining such residual phenomena has often been undertaken by individual effort, but never hitherto by a scientific society organised on a sufficiently broad basis."

The first president of the society was **Henry Sidgwick,** and among later presidents were **Balfour Stewart,** Sir William Crookes, **Arthur James Balfour,** and **Sir Oliver Lodge. William James** and **Charles Richet** were the first American and French researchers to serve as presidents, respectively. Prominent among the original members were **Frank Podmore, F. W. H. Myers, Edmund Gurney,** William F. Barrett, W. Stainton Moses, and **Eleanor Sidgwick** (later the first female to become president), **Lord Rayleigh,** and **Andrew Lang.** Many of these would eventually be honored with a term in the president's chair.

James initiated work in America that was later carried on by **Richard Hodgson** and **James H. Hyslop.**

On the Continent the Italian **Cesare Lombroso,** and French researchers **Joseph Maxwell, Camille Flammarion,** and Richet—all men of the highest standing in their respective branches of science—conducted exhaustive research into the phenomena of mediumship, chiefly with the Italian medium **Eusapia Palladino** as a subject.

At first the members of the Society for Psychical Research found it convenient to work in concert, but as they became more conversant with the broad outlines of the subject, it was necessary to specialize in various branches. The original plan, roughly sketched in 1882, grouped the phenomena to be researched under five different heads, each of which was placed under the direction of a separate committee. The five goals and their committee chairs were as follows:

"1. An examination of the nature and extent of any influence which may be exerted by one mind upon another, apart from any generally recognized mode of perception. (Hon. Secretary of Committee, Professor W. F. Barrett.)

"2. The study of hypnotism, and the forms of so-called mesmeric trance, with its alleged insensibility to pain; clairvoyance, and other allied phenomena. (Hon. Secretary of Committee, Dr. G. Wyld.)

"3. A critical revision of Reichenbach's researches with certain organisations called 'sensitive,' and an inquiry whether such organisations possess any power of perception beyond a highly-exalted sensibility of the recognised sensory organs. (Hon. Secretary of Committee, Walter H. Coffin.)

"4. A careful investigation of any reports, resting on strong testimony, regarding apparitions at the moment of death, or otherwise, or regarding disturbances in houses reputed to be haunted. (Hon. Secretary of Committee, Hensleigh Wedgwood.)

"5. An inquiry into the various physical phenomena commonly called Spiritualistic; with an attempt to discover their causes and general laws. (Hon. Secretary, Dr. C. Lockhart Robertson.)"

A committee was also appointed to consider the literature of the subject; honorary secretaries were Edmund Gurney and Frederic W. H. Myers, who, with Frank Podmore, collected a number of historic examples.

Of the various goals of the SPR, however, the first is now generally considered the most important, and is certainly the one that has yielded the best results to investigators. In the case of hypnotism, the work of psychical researchers contributed to its admission to the sphere of legitimate physiology. It was formerly classed among doubtful phenomena, even at the time the society was founded.

The examination of Baron von Reichenbach's claims of having discovered a new psychic fluid or force, the "**od**" (or odyle), which issued like flame from the points of a magnet or the human fingertips, was at length abandoned since nothing was found to verify his conclusions.

The investigations in connection with apparitions, **haunted houses,** and Spiritualist phenomena continued for many years, although on the whole no definite conclusions were arrived at.

The members of the society attempted to carry out their investigations in an entirely unbiased spirit. Some members who had joined the society originally as avowed Spiritualists soon dropped out. After prolonged and exhaustive research the opinions of the various investigators often changed. Far from being pledged to accept the spirit hypothesis—or any other specific hypothesis—the SPR expressly stated that "membership of this Society does not imply the acceptance of any particular explanation of the phenomena investigated, nor any belief as to the operation, in the physical world, of forces other than those recognised by Physical Science."

Nevertheless, two prominent researchers, F. W. H. Myers and Sir Oliver Lodge, found evidence sufficient to convince them of the operation in the physical world of disembodied intelligences who manifest themselves through the organisms of special people generally referred to as mediums or sensitives.

Frank Podmore, on the other hand, was the exponent of a telepathic theory. Any phase of the manifestations that could not be explained by means of such known physiological facts as suggestion and hyperesthesia (the so-called subconscious whispering), exaltation of memory and automatism, or the unfamiliar but presumably natural telepathy, according to him, fell under the grave suspicion of fraud. His theory of poltergeists, for example, which he regarded as the work of naughty children, did not admit the intervention of a mischievous disembodied spirit. He considered telepathy a suitable explanation for "coincident hallucination" (hallucinatory apparitions that coincide with the death of the person represented or with some other crisis in that person's life), as well as for all cases of "personation" by the medium. His view—one shared by Andrew Lang, several of his contemporaries, and many present-day parapsychologists—was that if telepathy were established the spirit hypothesis would not only be unnecessary, but impossible to prove.

The most important of telepathic experiments were those conducted by Henry and Eleanor Sidgwick (1889–91). The percipients were hypnotized by G. A. Smith, who also acted as agent, and the matter to be transmitted consisted at first of numbers and later of mental pictures. The agent and percipient were generally separated by a screen, or were sometimes in different rooms, although the results in the latter case were perceptibly less satisfactory. On the whole, however, the percentage of correct guesses was far above what could be attributed to chance, and the experiments did much to encourage a belief that some hitherto unknown mode of communication existed.

At a later date, the trance communication of **Leonora Piper** seemed to point to some such theory, although Myers, Hodgson, and Hyslop, who conducted a thorough investigation into those communications, were inclined to believe that the spirits of the dead were the agencies in this case.

Telepathy was never established in the early experiments of psychical research, yet something similar to telepathy (various names have been suggested) must be working to explain the results attained by the ESP experiments carried out over the last half century by parapsychologists. During the first generations of psychical research, many worked with the idea that the machinery of telepathy existed in the form of ethereal vibrations, or brain waves, acting in accordance with natural laws (although Gerald Balfour and others argued that the action did not conform to the law of inverse squares). The remnants of such material notions of telepathy were quickly disposed of by parapsychology.

The subject of **hallucinations** has also been investigated over the years, and has been found to be closely connected with the question of telepathy. Apparitions were in former times regarded as the **double** or ethereal body of the persons they represented, but they are now mainly considered to be subjective phenomena.

Nevertheless, the study of coincidental hallucinations, now termed **near-death experiences,** raises the question as to whether the agent can produce such a hallucination in the mind of the percipient by the exercise of telepathic influence, which may be judged to be more powerful during an emotional crisis.

Hallucinations have been shown to be fairly common among otherwise sane and normal people, about one person in ten having experienced one or more, but the odds that a hallucination will coincide with the death of the person it represents are about one in 19,000.

The SPR undertook a **Census of Hallucinations** in 1889. Henry Sidgwick and a committee of members of the society conducted the investigations, with Eleanor Sidgwick collating the results and writing the final report. Printed forms were distributed among 410 accredited agents of the society, including many medical men and others belonging to the professional classes, all of whom gave their services without fees in the interest of science.

In all, some 17,000 persons were questioned, and negative as well as affirmative answers were sent in just as they were received, the agents being instructed to make no discrimination between the various replies. Out of 8,372 men, 655 claimed to have had a hallucination, as did 1,029 out of 8,628 women—9.9 percent of the total. When ample allowance had been made for defects of memory with regard to early hallucinations by multiplying the 322 recognized and definite cases by 4, it was found that 62 coincided with a death; again making allowances, this number was reduced to 30.

Thus the survey results showed one coincidental hallucination in 43 instead of the expected one in 19,000. Clearly, then, if these figures are accepted, there must be some causal connection between the death and the apparition, whether it be a Spiritualist, telepathic, or other cause.

Apart from telepathy, perhaps the most interesting field of psychical research is **automatism.** Trance writings and utterances have been known since the earliest times, when they were attributed to demonic possession, or, sometimes, to angelic possession. By means of the **planchette,** the **Ouija board,** and other contrivances people were able to write automatically and divulge information they were unaware of possessing.

The phenomena are purely subjective, however, and are the result of cerebral dissociation such as may be induced in hypnosis. In this state, exaltation of the memory may occur, accounting for such phenomena as **xenoglossis** (speaking in foreign **tongues** with which the medium is not acquainted). Cerebral dissociation may also produce a sensitiveness to telepathic influences, as would seem apparent in the case of the medium Leonora Piper, whose automatic productions in writing and speaking supplied investigators with plentiful material and did more in the early twentieth century, perhaps, than anything else to stimulate an interest in so-called Spiritualist phenomena.

In connection with the "physical" phenomema—probably no less the result of automatism than the "subjective"—the Italian medium Eusapia Palladino was carefully studied by many eminent investigators, both in Great Britain and on the Continent. Camille Flammarion, Charles Richet, and Sir Oliver Lodge (to mention only a few) satisfied themselves with regard to the genuineness of some of her phenomena (although other equally eminent researchers dissented).

On the whole, even if psychical research has not succeeded in scientifically validating such matters as **survival** of death or the possibility of communication between the living and the dead, it can be credited with having widened the field of psychology and therapeutics and gaining support from the medical profession for the concept of suggestion.

In the United States, the **American Society for Psychical Research,** founded in 1885, and the **Boston Society for Psychic Research,** founded in 1925, were similar to the SPR of London. The American Society for Psychical Research (ASPR) was founded on the initial suggestion of William F. Barrett with the active cooperation of Richard Hodgson. A number of distinguished scientists were involved, many at the request of William James, and the general attitude was at first somewhat skeptical toward psychical phenomena.

The first period of the old ASPR lasted for four years (1885–89), after which it was absorbed by the Society for Psychical Research, London. It was briefly dissolved following Hodgson's death in 1905, but was reconstituted in 1906 as Section B of the American Institute for Scientific Research, an organization that James H. Hyslop founded at Columbia University, where he taught. Section A was devoted to abnormal psychology. The name American Society for Psychical Research was not readopted until 1922.

After Hyslop's death in 1920, the work of the society was carried on by his assistant **Walter Franklin Prince,** who became director of research and edited the society's publications. In 1921 **William McDougall,** a noted psychologist, became president. He was succeeded the following year by Frederick Edwards, a clergyman.

During the 1920s there were strong policy dissensions within the society, sparked by the American tour of Spiritualist **Sir Arthur Conan Doyle** but substantively related to the controversial investigations of the mediumship of **Mina S. Crandon,** popularly known as **"Margery."** In 1925, complaining of shoddy work and a lack of professionalism, Prince, McDougall, **Elwood Worcester,** and **Gardner Murphy** led a group that split off from the ASPR and formed the Boston Society for Psychical Research, which existed through the 1930s. During this period the most substantive psychical research was carried on by the Boston Society; the ASPR continued to be preoccupied with the problem of the "Margery" mediumship.

From Psychical Research to Parapsychology

Meanwhile, beginning in the 1930s, a new phase in American psychical research was beginning, spearheaded by **J. B.**

Rhine, whose experimental work at Duke University was encouraged by McDougall. This work involved using college students as subjects instead of mediums, with emphasis on statistical and scientific methods in evaluating experiments. Rhine's initial report, *Extra-sensory Perception,* published by the Boston Society in 1934, described 85,724 card-guessing trials. Rhine's work aroused a storm of controversy, and was attacked from every angle, most severely on methodological grounds. The sting of the controversy was removed in 1938 when the American Psychological Association (APA) upheld Rhine's testing procedures and his statistical method (if not his results). The APA report was confirmed by the American Institute of Mathematical Statistics, which issued this statement: "If the Rhine investigation is to be fairly attacked, it must be on other than mathematical grounds."

It was through the work of Rhine that the terms **parapsychology, extrasensory perception,** and **psychokinesis** became widespread. The *Journal of Parapsychology* was first published in 1937, and the Parapsychological Association was founded in 1957.

The work of Rhine and his associates established parapsychology—laboratory-based research on the paranormal—as a reputable field for scientific study. As another generation of researchers appeared, the boundary between parapsychology and the older concerns of psychical research became blurred. In the decades since World War II a new movement, in addition to the purely statistical studies, has embraced all the phenomena formerly associated with Spiritualist mediums, and the spontaneous phenomena of poltergeists and **out-of-the-body travel** has been reconsidered. In the 1970s and 1980s, a new wave of interest in psychokinesis was stimulated by widely heralded claims of psychic **Uri Geller.**

(Note: Developments in psychical research and parapsychology and their precursors in Continental Europe are dealt with under the headings of the various countries—**France, Holland, Switzerland, Germany,** and **Italy.**)

Sources:

Carrington, Hereward. *The Story of Psychic Science.* London: Rider, 1930.

Coover, J. E. *Experiments in Psychical Research at Leland Stanford Junior University.* Palo Alto, Calif.: Stanford University, 1917. Reprint, New York: Arno Press, 1975.

Crookes, William. *Researches in the Phenomena of Spiritualism.* London: J. Burns, 1874.

Douglas, Alfred. *Extra-sensory Powers: A Century of Psychical Research.* Woodstock, N.Y.: Overlook Press, 1977.

Driesch, Hans. *Psychical Research: The Science of the Supernormal.* London: G. Bell, 1933. Reprint, New York: Arno Press, 1975.

Edge, Hoyt L., Robert L. Morris, John Palmer, and Joseph H. Rush. *Foundations of Parapsychology: Exploring the Boundaries of Human Capability.* London: Routledge & Kegan Paul, 1986.

Gauld, Alan. *The Founders of Psychical Research.* London: Routledge & Kegan Paul, 1968.

Grattan-Guinness, Ivor, ed. *Psychical Research: A Guide to Its History, Principles and Practices, in Celebration of 100 Years of the Society for Psychical Research.* London: Aquarian Press, 1982.

Haynes, Renée. *The Society for Psychical Research 1882–1982: A History.* London: Macdonald, 1982.

Hyslop, James H. *Enigmas of Psychical Research.* New York: G. P. Putnam's Sons, 1906.

London Dialectical Society. *Report on Spiritualism of the Committee of the London Dialectical Society.* London: Longmans, Green, Reader & Dyer, 1971.

Maxwell, Joseph. *Metapsychical Phenomena.* London: Duckworth, 1905.

Podmore, Frank. *Studies in Psychical Research.* New York: G. P. Putnam's Sons, 1897. Reprint, New York: Arno Press, 1975.

Price, Harry. *Fifty Years of Psychical Research: A Critical Study.* London: Longmans, Green, 1939. Reprint, New York: Arno Press, 1975.

Richet, Charles. *Thirty Years of Psychical Research.* London: Collins; New York: Macmillan, 1923.

Rhine, J. B. *Extra-sensory Perception.* Boston: Boston Society for Psychical Research, 1934. Rev. ed. Boston: Branden, 1964.

Rhine, J. B., et al. *Extrasensory Perception After Sixty Years.* New York: Holt, 1940. Reprint, Boston: Branden, 1966.

Rhine, J. B., ed. *Progress in Parapsychology.* Durham, N.C.: Parapsychology Press, 1971.

Rhine, J. B., and Robert Briwer, eds. *Parapsychology Today.* New York: Citadel, 1968.

Thouless, Robert H. *From Anecdote to Experiment in Psychical Research.* London: Routledge & Kegan Paul, 1972.

Tyrrell, G. N. M. *Science and Psychical Phenomena.* New York: Harper, 1938. Reprint, New York: Arno Press, 1975.

White, Rhea A., and Laura A. Dale. *Parapsychology: Sources of Information.* Metuchen, N.J.: Scarecrow Press, 1973.

Psychical Research Foundation

A parapsychological research facility established in 1960 with funds from **Charles E. Ozanne,** a high school and college teacher interested in the question of survival of death. The foundation was created to investigate phenomena relating to the survival of human personality after death. The foundation serves as a scientific and educational research center to investigate the possibilities of continuation of consciousness after death of the physical body. Its research program includes study of sensitives, haunting and poltergeist phenomena, as well as **out-of-the-body travel.**

In 1960, William G. Roll became project director and is now president. Under Roll's leadership the foundation has established an outstanding record of parapsychological research on meditation, haunts, poltergeists, out-of-the-body experiences, and mediumship. Roll can be reached at Isleway House, Fairfield Plantation, Villa Rica, GA 30180.

The foundation conducts lectures, workshops and seminars on topics related to the question of survival after death. It sponsers volunteer field investigators to assist in its research. The foundation has a research division that is directed by Dr. Andrew Nichols, City College, Gainesville, Florida 32608. News of its activities are published in its quarterly bulletin *Theta.*

Psychic Body

A Spiritualist term loosely applied to an impalpable body which clothes the soul on the "great dissolution of death" or to the soul itself. **Edward William Cox** in his book *Mechanism of Man* (2 vols., 1876) declared that the soul (quite distinct from mind, or intelligence, which is only a function of the brain) is composed of attenuated matter and has the same form as the physical body that it permeates in every part. From the soul radiates the psychic force, by means of which all the wonders of **Spiritualism** are performed. Through its agency, human beings become endowed with telekinetic and clairvoyant powers, and with its aid they can affect such natural forces as gravitation. When free of the body, the soul can travel at a lightning speed, nor is it hindered by such material objects as stone walls or closed doors.

The psychic body is also regarded as an intermediary between the physical body and the soul, a sort of shell or envelope, more material than the soul itself, which encloses it at death. It is this envelope, the psychic body or *nervengeist,* that, some believed, became visible during **materialization** by attracting to itself other and still more material particles.

According to traditional Spiritualist teachings, in time the psychic body decays just as did the physical and leaves the soul free. During trance, the soul leaves the body, but the vital functions are continued by the psychic body. (See also **astral body; etheric double**)

Psychic Detective Bureau

State licensed organization, also known as the U.S. Psi Squad, headed by psychic **Beverly Jaegers,** who also edited a quarterly publication *Pathways,* containing articles, reports on activities, reviews and comments. The organization brought together "persons interested in utilizing mind skills such as psi to combat crime as a public service, to work with and for law enforcement officials in solving mysteries, to learn mind development to a higher, more useful stage."

Last known address: P.O. Box 29396, Sappington, MO 63126.

The Psychic Directory

A directory published once in 1984, as a comprehensive guide to practicing psychics in Britain, with additional listing of Spiritualist churches, associations, societies, festivals and bookshops.

Sources:

Rodway, Howard. *The Psychic Directory: A Comprehensive Guide to Practicing Psychics in the U.K.* London: Futura/ Macdonald, 1984.

Psychic Esperanto League (Palka Esperantista Ligo)

Founded in Britain by Alexander W. Thomson, F.B.E.A. in August 1934, with members in eleven countries. The work of the League was carried on mainly by correspondence, and its aim was to educate individuals concerning psychic awareness in various parts of the world untouched by other means because of the language barrier. Esparanto is an artificial language created in the 1880s by L. L. Zamehhof of Poland to assist communication between people with incompatible languages. It was developed from root words taken from all of the European languages. It is the most successful of all of the artificial languages, and an estimated eight million people speak it (a relatively small number but far larger than the communities which speak most of the world's hundreds of languages). The league appears to have ceased operation after World War II.

The Psychic Evidence Society

An organization for inquiry into the actuality and meaning of psychical phenomena for clergymen throughout Great Britain. It was founded in London, England, in 1931 by John Engledow, who also served as its general secretary. It existed only briefly, but its work has been assumed by the **Churches' Fellowship for Psychical and Spiritual Studies.**

The Psychic Eye Directory

Annual listing of psychics, healers, dowsers, and lecturers published in the 1970s by the now defunct Parapsychology League of Toledo (Ohio).

Psychic Force

Nineteenth-century psychical researchers posited the existence of a psychic force, the existence of which had a direct inspiration from the force described by Franz A. Mesmer in the previous century and which was investigated by different researchers and occultists under different names. The primary reference to such a force was as a healing power and a hypnotizing influence. It was soon discarded as having any relation to hypnotism and now survives as a psychokinetic force. In addition it was claimed by inquirers into **Spiritualism** that the human organism, i.e., the sitters, is in some mysterious way bound up with séance room phenomena. They posited the existence of a psychic force which operated beyond the periphery of the body, apart from any physical contact.

The researches of **Baron von Reichenbach** suggested the term "Odic force" to Dr. E. C. Rogers of Boston in 1852, Asa Mahan, also in America, and **Count Agenor de Gasparin** in France, and they accepted it as such. **Marc Thury** called it "ectenic force." Mayo at the Royal College of Surgeons, London, postulated on "exo-neural action of the brain." **Edward William Cox** recommended the term "psychic force" and this rather vague inclusive term came into general use by psychical research through the era of concentrated research on physical mediums.

In a letter to **Sir William Crookes,** Cox wrote in 1871:

"I noticed that the force was exhibited in tremulous pulsations, and not in the form of steady, continuous pressure, the indicator rising and falling incessantly throughout the experiment. The fact seems to me of great significance as tending to confirm the opinion that assigns its source to the nerve organisation, and it goes far to establish Dr. Richardson's important discovery of a nerve atmosphere of various intensity enveloping the human structure. . . . To avoid the appearance of any foregone conclusion, I would recommend the adoption for it of some appropriate name, and I venture to suggest that the force be termed Psychic Force; the persons to whom it is manifested in extraordinary power Psychics; and the science relating to it Psychism as being a branch of psychology."

Later he added:

"The theory of Psychic Force is in itself merely the recognition of the fact that under certain conditions, as yet but imperfectly ascertained, and within limited, but as yet undefined, distance from the bodies of certain persons having a special nerve organisation, a Force operates by which, without muscular contact or connection, action at a distance is caused, and visible motions and audible sounds are produced in solid substances."

The speculation of the existence of a nervous atmosphere to which Cox alluded was expounded by Dr. Benjamin W. Richardson in the *Medical Times,* on May 6, 1871. As it came from a medical source, Crookes welcomed it, and noted in the *Quarterly Journal of Science,*

"I think I perceive what it is that this psychic force uses up for its development. In employing the terms *vital force,* or *nervous energy,* I am aware that I am employing words which convey very different significations to many investigators; but after witnessing the painful state of nervous and bodily prostration in which some of these experiments have left Mr. Home [The medium **D. D. Home**]—after seeing him lying in an almost fainting condition on the floor, pale and speechless—I could scarcely doubt that the evolution of psychic force is accompanied by a corresponding drain on vital force."

Joseph Maxwell observed,

"Certain peculiar sensations accompany the emission of this nervous force, and with custom the passage of the energy expanded in a séance can be felt, just as the interruption of the flow can be discerned."

Maxwell was inclined to discern four principal sensations in connection with the generation of the force:

"1) The sensation of cool breezes, generally over the hands.

"2) The sensation of a slight tingling in the palm of the hand, and at the tips of the fingers, near the mounts.

"3) The sensation of a sort of current through the body.

"4) The sensation of a spider's web in contact with the hands and face, and other parts of the body—notably the back and the loins. "If the sensation of the 'passage of the current' may be feeble, it is not so with its abrupt interruption. . . . It may even cause a sensation of sudden indisposition, if the interruption coincide with the phenomenon in course of production. . . .

The sensation of the breaking of the current is distinctly felt; and it is this which makes me think, that the feeble impression of the passage of the current is not altogether imaginary."

The medium **Gladys Osborne Leonard** in her book *My Life in Two Worlds* (1931) wrote of a visit to a materializing medium:

"He [the **control**] instructed the sitter who sat at the extreme end of the left side of the horse-shoe, to release her left hand and throw it out towards him. She did so, and we could all see a stream of pale grey matter, like fog or steam from a kettle, oozing from her fingers. It was shaped like rods, about a foot long and an inch thick. The medium reached out his hands carefully towards the end of the rods, and seemed to try and coax the grey material to come farther away from the sitter, towards himself. The rods thinned slightly, as he induced them to extend, and after a couple of minutes the French control said, speaking through the medium again "No, not strong enough, link hands up, and close in the power again."

Harry Price wrote in 1930:

"I cannot help wondering whether there is really anything in the curious stroking movements which Rudi (or Olga) [Schneider] makes during the height of the trance and when she is leaving us. She 'gathers power' she says, by drawing his hands down my body and legs, or those of the second controller's. She 'releases' it at the end of the séance by similar movements, but in a reverse direction."

On the basis of his observations in the **Goligher Circle, W. J. Crawford** elaborated a more precise theory of psychic force:

"Operators are acting on the brains of the sitters and thence on their nervous systems. Small particles, it may even be molecules, are driven off the nervous system, out through the bodies of the sitters at wrists, hands, fingers, or elsewhere. These small particles, now free, have a considerable amount of latent energy inherent in them, an energy which can react on any human nervous system with which they come into contact. This stream of energized particles flows round the circle, probably partly on the periphery of their bodies. The stream, by gradual augmentation from the sitters, reaches the medium at a high degree of 'tension,' energises her, receives increment from her, traverses the circle again, and so on. Finally, when the 'tension' is sufficiently great, the circulating process ceases, and the energized particles collect on or are attached to the nervous system of the medium, who has henceforth a reservoir from which to draw. The operators having now a good supply of the right kind of energy at their disposal, viz., nerve energy can act upon the body of the medium, who is so constituted that gross matter from her body can, by means of the nervous tension applied to it, be actually temporarily detached from its usual position and projected into the séance room."

Crawford put both his sitters and his **medium** on the scale and found that the loss of weight of the sitters was, at the end of the séance, greater than that of the medium. The sitters lost, on an average, 5–10 ounces and were more exhausted than the medium. His speculations were favorably received by many when published in his 1916 volume *The Reality of Psychic Phenomena* as it seemed to accord with other observations.

For example, the control "Walter," in the "Margery" sittings, (see **Mina S. Crandon**) always stated that he used the brain of the sitters. His assertion was no novelty. The control of the great medium Home indicated the same source of power at an early period.

Neurologist Charles Féré noticed that excitation of almost any kind tended to increase "dynamometrical" power. The average squeezing power exhibited by educated students was greater than that of robust laboring men. Maxwell observed in his 1895 sittings with the medium **Eusapia Palladino** that there was a marked loss in dynamometric force not only on the part of the medium, but also on the part of the sitters at the end of the séance. Sometimes the loss amounted to six kilos on the right side and fourteen on the left.

Admiral Usborne Moore complained of a drain on his vitality after his direct voice séances with medium **Etta Wriedt.** One of the reasons why **Lord Adare** retired from his researches with D. D. Home was that the séances physically exhausted him. **Cromwell Varley,** who assisted Crookes in his experiments with the medium **Florence Cook,** always felt depleted, while Crookes himself remained unaffected. **James H. Hyslop** had to go to bed for two days after his first sitting with the medium **Leonora Piper. Richard Hodgson** was also markedly affected.

Eugene Rochas said, in describing the case of levitation with Eusapia Palladino in his home: "We ought to add that one of the persons who was quite close to the table [Dr. Maxwell]; see Mediums almost completely fainted away, not from emotion, but through weakness, saying that he felt drained of his strength as the result of Eusapia's efforts."

The Nature of the Force

The method of the liberation of this vital force, the circumstances regulating the quantity of the supply, its use by the invisible operators of the séance room, and its relation to **ectoplasm** remained elusive. Reportedly, the force was subject to an ebb and flow. In some cases fasting or seclusion increased it, in some others a hearty meal. Psychological factors also enter to a great extent. In a calm, harmonious atmosphere it is more liberally generated. The operators spoke of lines of force and of a vibratory synchronization. They often asked the sitters to change places, the resulting combination frequently being surprising. Dr. Féré stated that "all our sensations are accompanied by a development of potential energy which passes into a kinetic state and externalises itself in motor manifestations."

The observations on psychic force and its generation offered a rationale for the disappearance of the reported phenomena of the séance room when a skeptical observer was present—the cold and suspicious observer destroys the harmonious atmosphere, disrupts the psychic forces, and hence cannot witness strong manifestations. In the absence of sensations, he may not contribute to the psychic power in the same proportion as other sitters do. He may even have an effect of negative force.

It was also claimed that certain bodies and materials such as tables, linen, wood, and dresses appear to conduct the force. Perhaps this is why women's dresses so frequently bulge out and approach the table during a séance. It also appears that some of the nervous force or fluid settles in the séance room or in the objects in use. According to the statements of controls, once the séance "room" has become charged the manifestations are easier to produce in that space at the next sitting. Controls often protested against the use of the séance room for other purposes. Again, in other instances, for reasons of their own, they had no concern for the preservation of the remains of the force.

Mrs. Stanhope Speer, in an account given to **F. H. Myers,** described nocturnal disturbances in her house after a séance with **William Stainton Moses.**

"The servants heard so much pounding in the séance room that they felt frightened and went to bed as quickly as possible. We were told afterwards that so much power had been generated that the spirits had to make the noise to get rid of it."

She also described a similar circumstance which occurred to her and her husband. Their bedroom door was violently shaken after they went to bed and they were afterward told that a spirit had been attracted by the spiritual light over the house and had used up power that had been left by shaking the doors.

P. P. Alexander, in his book *Spiritualism; A Narrative with a Discussion* (1871), gave evidence of a physical phenomena that transpired after D. D. Home had left the house of a scientific friend and his wife. Chairs moved slowly across the carpet and set themselves beside his own.

In the early mediumship of **Agnes Guppy-Volckman** (then Agnes Nichols), powerful phenomena were witnessed in the empty séance room afterward. Displacement of furniture was recorded in the adjoining rooms. And Robert Cooper stated in his book *Spiritual Experiences, Including Seven Months with The Brothers Davenport* (1867):

"I have occasionally heard the furniture in the room where we had been holding a séance, in motion after retiring to bed . . . On leaving a room in which I had been with Ira Davenport for the purpose of talking with the spirits in a chair followed me into the passage, myself being the last to leave."

When a medium-visitor of Eugene Rochas was shown into the room where the séance-suit of medium **Auguste Politi** was lying folded up and where, unknown to her, the investigations with Politi were going on, she became almost immediately controlled by an adverse and highly disagreeable influence. Rochas took up part of the suit and gave it to the medium. The effect was instantaneous; the controlling influence became violent and furious and was thought to be the spirit of a deceased monk who sometimes got hold of Politi and damaged the conditions as much as he could.

In one of W. J. Crawford's photographs, a vaporous substance seems to connect the medium Kathleen Goligher with the various sitters. Whether it was ectoplasmic emanation or a nervous fluid he did not attempt to answer.

The problem with the hypothesized psychic force, quite apart from the fraud committed by the mediums whose séances were the source of speculation about it, was the inability of researchers to find a way to have the force manifest in a way which would register on an instrument for measurement. The disconnection between the hypothesized source (cause) and the observed occurrence (effect) left too many explanations, quite apart from either fraud or psychic force, possible. Pierre Curie was occupied with the idea of devising an instrument which could register and direct the liberated psychic power. His death cut short his experiments. Before such an instrument could be devised, the era of the study of physical mediums ended. (See also **Od**)

Sources:

Crawford, William J. *The Reality of Psychic Phenomena, Raps, Levitations, etc.* London: J. M. Watkins, 1919.

Crookes William. "Some Further Experiments on Psychic Force." *Quarterly Journal of Science* (October 1, 1871).

Leonard, Gladys Osborne. *My Life in Two Worlds.* London: Cassell, 1931.

Maxwell, Joseph. *Metaphysical Phenomena.* New York: G. P. Putnam's Sons; London: Duckworth, 1905.

Price, Harry. *Rudi Schneider; A Scientific Examination of his Mediumship.* London: Methuen, 1930.

Psychic Museums

A museum was founded in 1925 by veteran Spiritualist **Sir Arthur Conan Doyle,** (1859–1930) and located at 2 Victoria Street, London, S.W. The museum housed an interesting collection of apports, automatic scripts, automatic and direct sketches and paintings, paraffin molds, photographs and other psychic objects. Unfortunately, at a later date, the museum was closed and its collection was dispersed. A number of the items have been lost or destroyed.

Some archives of the **British College of Psychic Science** were also dispersed, but items from the Institute for Psychic Research (of which **Nandor Fodor** was Research Officer) were absorbed by the **Society for Psychical Research,** London. The **Harry Price** archives are still kept at University of London, Senate House, Malet Street, London, W.C.I., England.

There are probably many psychic collections in existence in various corners of the world. T. W. Stanford, a Melbourne millionaire, collected all the **apports** of the controversial medium **Charles Bailey** and donated them to the Psychical Research Department of Stanford University, Palo Alto, California. In Budapest (I. Mészáros u.2.) Dr. Chengery Pap established a museum of the objects apported through the mediumship of **Lajos Pap.** There was an *Other World Museum* in Rome, Lungo-Tevere Prati 12, founded by Father V. Jouet, containing many rare objects and documents bearing upon different manifestations of the departed.

In Virginia, the **Association for Research and Enlightenment** has preserved for study 15,000 transcripts of the psychic readings of **Edgar Cayce.**

The most recent psychic museum is the **Britten Memorial Museum** on the grounds of the **Arthur Findlay College** (of the **Spiritualists National Union**) in Essex, England.

Psychic News (Newspaper)

The oldest Spiritualist weekly newspaper in Britain. It was founded in 1932 and for many years it was edited by **Maurice Barbanell** (1902–1981). After Barbanell's passing, Tony Ortzen became the new editor. *Psychic News* has always been the preeminent source for news, discussion, and controversy on Spiritualism in Britain, and, in the absence of a comparable organ in North America, exerted influence in the United States and Canada.

For many years the *Psychic News* maintained a bookshop for books and magazines connected with Spiritualism and psychical research. In November 1989, the proprietors, Psychic Press Ltd., acquired the long established **Atlantis Book Shop,** 49a Museum Street, London, WC1A 1LY, and moved their own book shop to these premises, with an augmented stock of new and secondhand books on the paranormal, Spiritualism, occult studies, and New Age topics.

The office of the *Psychic News* can be contacted at Clock Cottage, Stansted Hall, Stansted, Essex CM24 8UD, England.

Psychic Observer and Chimes (Magazine)

Prominent American Spiritualist magazine founded in 1974 by the merger of *Chimes* and the *Psychic Observer.* The Psychic Observer Corporation was founded in 1937 in Jamestown, New York, by Ralph and Juliette Pressing. The first issue of the *Psychic Observer* appeared in August 1938. In 1957 the Pressings retired and Agnes F. Reuther became editor. Two years later Tom O'Neill acquired the periodical, then issued as a tabloid. In 1960 he was informed by **Andrija Puharich,** then a young researcher, that he had discovered several of the more prominent mediums at Camp Chesterfield engaged in a conspiracy to conduct fake **materialization** séances. Puharich presented the photographic proof, pictures taken with an infrared camera. O'Neill published the pictures and announced the findings as a dark day for **Spiritualism.**

As a result of the exposé, O'Neill almost went bankrupt, as advertisers loyal to the camp pulled their support from the periodical. He relocated his publishing enterprise to North Carolina and for a brief period published under another title.

O'Neill died in 1965 and the *Psychic Observer* ceased publication. In 1968 it was purchased by Alice Tindell and moved to Washington, D.C. It was issued as an open forum magazine, but in effect it was the periodical of the **National Spiritual Science Center,** the church headed by Tindell. It was published by the ESPress, the church's publishing concern. Henry Nagoka edited the new publication.

Chimes began in 1942 under the editorship of Bert Welch and his wife. It was later purchased by June and Leighton Denton. Chimes, Inc., the publishing company, also had a book distribution service and facilitated the Dentons' healing ministry. *Chimes* faithfully served the American Spiritualist community for a generation until it was discontinued as an independent publication in 1974.

Psychic Observer and Chimes was discontinued after the July/October 1981 issue.

Psychic Register International

An annual directory listing psychics in Great Britain, Canada and the United States published in 1977, 1978, and 1979 in Erie, Pennsylvania.

Sources:

The International Psychic Register. Edited by Donald McQuaid. 3 vols. Erie, Pa.: Ornion Press, 1977, 1978, and 1979.

Psychic Research (Journal)

The *Journal* of the **American Society for Psychical Research** was published under this title for four years (1928–1932), during which time it was edited by **Frederick Bligh Bond.** After 1932 it returned to its former title.

Psychic Research Quarterly

British journal issued in 1920, edited by **W. Whately Carington.** The title was changed to *Psyche* in 1921, and the scope was enlarged to deal with psychology.

Psychics and Mystics Fayre

An offshoot of the **Mind-Body-Spirit Festival** in Britain started by **Graham Wilson,** comprising smaller exhibitions held regularly at different London and provincial centers, featuring practitioners and groups concerned with **yoga, tarot, astrology, clairvoyance,** health and healing, arts and crafts, ufology, and related topics. Wilson sold the Fayres in 1986 and similar shows are now commonplace in most major UK cities. For information write: New Life Promotions Ltd., Arnica House, 170 Campden Hill Rd., London, W8 7AS, England.

Psychic Science

A compilation and examination of data with the aim of demonstrating the possible existence of spirits independent of the human body and to validate their ability to communicate with humanity. According to **J. Hewat McKenzie**'s summary in his book *Spirit Intercourse,* (1916), the following claims fall within the proper research perimeters of psychic science:

1) That at the death of the body, a human being continues to function as a conscious being.

2) That he or she functions after death in a refined spirit-body or soul, which has substance and weight, and which can be seen and photographed.

3) That this soul existed within the physical body during life, and is organic, having brain, nerves, blood-vessels, heart, etc.

4) That the soul can communicate in various ways with persons on earth both before and after death.

5) That the world in which the soul dwells after the death of the body lies immediately around the physical earth.

6) That a man or woman while alive may leave the physical body, and by use of the soul, may explore spheres of refined physical states, commonly called the spirit world.

Abstractly, psychic science might seem to be but a focus within psychical research or parapsychology, however, in practice, it has functioned as a synonym of **Spiritualism.** The foundation of various British societies and colleges of "psychic science" and the dropping of the term "Spiritualist" in favor of "psychic science," without any appreciable redirection of program stems from the Spiritualist's claims that their religion can be scientifically demonstrated. (See also **British College of Psychic Science; College of Psychic Studies**)

Psychic Science (Journal)

Quarterly journal of the **British College of Psychic Science,** founded in 1920 in London by **James Hewat McKenzie.** The first issue of the journal, April 1922, bore the title *Quarterly Transactions of the British College of Psychic Science,* but beginning with the April 1923 issue was shortened to *Psychic Science.* In 1945 *Psychic Science* was absorbed into **Light,** the journal of the **College of Psychic Studies.** Last known address: 16 Queensberry Pl., South Kensington, London, SW7 2EB England.

Sources:

Edmonds, Simeon. *Spiritualism: a Critical Survey.* London: Aquarian Press, 1966.

Psychic Science International Special Interest Group

A now-defunct group founded in 1976 from among members and associates of Mensa (persons who have established by score in a standard intelligence test that their intelligence is higher than that of 98 percent of the population). PSISIG was concerned with interest in and conducting of scientific research in the psychic sciences and arts, such as theories of existence and reality, states of mind, human **auras, clairvoyance,** mental and thought projection, **telepathy, dowsing, psychometry, healing** and defense, multiple personalities and possession, psychokinesis, survival after death, discarnate entities, and extraterrestrial life. It disseminated research findings and applied research and education for the benefit of humanity in mental health, reduction of superstition and **fraud,** safety, and enhancement of human relations.

PSISIG provided educational programs to promote awareness and capabilities in the psychic sciences and arts and offers grants, scholarships, and other aids to persons or organizations studying psychic sciences. It also operated a speakers bureau, provided members for surveys by responsible, noncommercial organizations, and compiled statistics. The group published the *PSI-M* Newsletter/Journal and a *Yearbook.*

Psychic Surgery

A term which is applied to two very distinct branches of psychic **healing.** It sometimes denotes psychic healers who believe that they are making "surgical" changes in the astral double that upon completion of the "operation" are reflected in the physical body. Such psychic surgeons believe that the spirit of a dead doctor influences them, and observers see them enter a trance state from which they mime an operation over the body of the person seeking healing.

Typical of the first type is British healer George Chapman, who claimed to be controlled by the dead surgeon "Dr. Lang." Chapman diagnosed while in trance and simply laid his hands on the patient or made movements indicative of a phantom operation.

More interesting to psychic researchers, because of their extraordinary claims, have been the psychic surgeons in the Spiritualist communities of the Philippines and Brazil. They appear to perform real operations making an incision with bare hands, removing pathological matter, and causing an instantaneous healing of the incision. Such healers in the Philippines have been the subject of numerous popular books, including vivid pictures of apparent operations, and several volumes by observers who have dismissed the phenomena as a complete hoax. The two most famous psychic surgeons of this second type have been **Tony Agpaoa** in the Philippines and **José Arigó** in Brazil.

Accounts of Tony Agpaoa began to emerge in the 1960s. He used no anesthetic or scalpel, yet appeared to make an incision in which there was a liberal flow of blood. He appeared to insert his hands into the body and either remove pathological tissue with his hands or cut it away with unsterilized scissors. He then moved his hand over the incision, which seemed to close instantaneously, leaving no scar.

Operations conducted by Agpaoa and similar psychic surgeons in the Philippines have been photographed and even filmed and are impressive, especially to the untrained eye. However, there is every reason to believe that these "operations" have been faked. There is to date no clear incident of either Agapoa or any of the Philipine healers having ever opened the body and closed it again without leaving any evidence of their having operated. To the contrary, a spectrum of practicing magicians from a skeptic such as the **Amazing Randi** and **Milbourne Christopher** to a professional psychic such as David Hoy have agreed that the operations are done with slight of hand and have easily been able to duplicate every effect. It is suggested that if a small quantity of dried blood and a piece of animal tissue is palmed, the flesh "operated" on can be pinched and made to appear as if an incision has been made. The cure that follows would then be a matter of strong suggestion rather than actual surgery.

The issue is not so simple among the Brazilian healers. **Andrija Puharich,** himself a physician, visited Argió in Brazil and was the subject of a psychic operation for a small lipoma on the elbow. Arigó, who claimed to be controlled by the spirit "Dr. Fritz," made an incision with a pocket knife without anesthetic or sterilization and removed the tumor. A small incision scar was left (thus there was no paranormal opening or closing of the body), and the elbow healed over the next four days (there was no instantaneous healing). The operation was filmed, and it was clear that the tumor had been removed by rather mundane, if crude, means, and that the extraordinary character of the event was the lack of infection. Arigó was killed in an automobile accident before he could be more completely tested.

Thousands of invalids and the merely curious travelers have visited the Philippines, especially through the 1970s and 1980s, with an interest in psychic healing. While some have been healed, many have returned disillusioned after an expensive and tiresome trip. There they have also encountered what became a highly competitive business between the various healers and those who provide transportation to the various locations (mostly outside of Manila) where the healers operate. Over the years, the number of reported healings is no higher than that reported by more domestic healers be they psychic or religious.

Australian journalist Gert Chesi investigated the Philippine healers and warned readers about the situation they will encounter should they choose to go to the Philippine Islands. In his *Geistheiler auf den Philippinen* (English edition as *Faith Healers in the Philippines,* 1981), he draws upon his prior observation of tribal magical practices in Africa.

Chesi discovered what he believed were genuine as well as fake healers, and concluded that the dividing line is often a confusing one, since although the blood and the objects apparently removed from a patient's body may be unrelated to genuine surgery, they may still be part of a mysterious shamanistic healing process. He also discovered that some healers appeared to remove objects from a diseased body which are clearly unrelated to any genuine illness, such as coins, leaves, nails, plastic objects, or even garbage. Chesi suggests that such objects, as well as the blood, may be the products of the healer's imagination, becoming solidified as **materializations** or **apports.** Journalist Tom Valentine found that some of the psychic surgeons in the Philippines have "removed" not only tissue from the body of their patients, but also such things as eggshells, coffee grounds and even a crayfish. Like Chesi, Valentine concluded that such phenomena might be related to **apports** and that healers like Agpaoa materialize and dematerialize matter. This observation offers little help as it merely introduces one equally dubious phenomenon to explain another. The tissue from the operations that has been tested has been non-human in origin, instead generally that of chickens.

Some healers have argued that patients will not believe in the healer's power unless they see an apparent incision with plenty of blood, and a tangible object removed from the body. Other Philippine healers eschew such practices and regard such bloody operations as unnecessary. They practice a more traditional form of psychic or "magnetic healing."

Sources:

Chesi, Gert. *Faith Healers in the Philippines.* Perlinger Verlag, 1981.

Christopher, Milbourne. *Mediums, Mystics & the Occult.* New York: Thomas Y. Crowell, 1975.

Fuller, John G. *Arigó. Surgeon of the Rusty Knife.* New York: Thomas Y. Crowell, 1974.

Randi, James. *Flim-Flam: Psychics, ESP, Unicorns, and Other Delusions.* Buffalo, N.Y.: Prometheus Books, 1987.

Sherman, Harold. *Wonder Healers of the Philippines.* Los Angeles: DeVorss & Co., 1967.

Valentine, Tom. *Psychic Surgery.* Chicago: Henry Regnery, 1973.

Psychic Telephone

An instrument invented by F. R. Melton of Nottingham, England, consisting of a box inside of which was a rubber bag connected with a pair of earphones from a radio set. The idea was that if a medium inflated the bag with his or her breath and then sealed it, the bag would take the place of the medium and direct voices would be heard through the earphones in his absence. The psychical researcher **Harry Price** subjected the instrument to a thorough test in the **National Laboratory for Psychical Research,** London. It did not work.

The Psychic Yellow Pages

A 1977 listing of psi practitioners and organizations in Northern California. It includes psychics, astrologers, holistic centers, palmists, and tarot readers. It was issued from Saratoga, California.

Psychische Studien (Journal)

Journal of psychical studies, founded by **Alexander Aksakof** in 1874. It was published for many years in Leipzig, Germany. It changed its name to *Zeitschrift für Parapsychologie* in 1925 and ceased publication in 1934.

Psychode

Term proposed by psychical researcher **Marc Thury** to designate what others called **ectoplasm.**

Psychoenergetic (Journal)

Quarterly British publication edited by American parapsychologist **Stanley C. Krippner,** included discussions on psi phenomena by distinguished writers and parapsychologists. Last known address: Gordon & Breach, 41 William IV St., London, WC2, England.

Psychograph

Paranormal script obtained through **spirit photography** on a sensitive plate. (See also **psychic photography; skotograph**)

Psychography

Term used by British medium **William Stainton Moses** (1839–1892) to denote all forms of **direct writing** by spirit entities.

Psychokinesis

The ability to move objects at a distance by mental power. The term has now largely displaced "telekinesis," formerly used by psychical researchers and Spiritualists. The term "psychokinesis" or "PK" was proposed by psychologist **J. B. Rhine** and his associates at the Psychology Department, Duke University, Durham, North Carolina, in 1934 in relation to experiments with influencing the fall of dice by mental concentration.

Special terms have developed as the study of PK has expanded, such as: "PK-MT" (psychokinetic effect on moving targets, such as dice), "PK-LT" (influence on living target, such as plants, healing, influencing of animals), and "PK-ST" (influence on static targets). A "PK Placement Test" denotes a PK-MT experiment in which the subject attempts to influence falling objects to land in a designated area. (See also **movement**)

The Psychological Society

The Psychological Society, a precursor to the **Society for Psychical Research,** was founded in England in April 1875 by **Edward William Cox.** Cox counted among his associates **William Stainton Moses,** Walter H. Coffin, and C. C. Massey. Cox articulated the aim of the society was the study and elucidation of those Spiritualist and related problems now grouped under the term **psychical research,** to which he somewhat loosely attached the designation of "psychology."

To this end Cox proposed to collect and consider the available material bearing on psychic phenomena. In reality the members accomplished little of any practical value, as may be seen from their published *Proceedings* (1875–79), published in London in 1880. Cox did not possess the necessary scientific background for investigation of such phenomena. In November 1879, on his death, the society came to an end.

Although the Psychological Society regarded psychic phenomena from a more or less popular standpoint, and conducted its investigations in a somewhat superficial manner, it nevertheless contained the germ of scientific inquiry into the domain of psychic science that, a few years later with the founding of the **Society of Psychical Research,** was to raise the study to a level where it became worthy of the attention of the academy. Up to that time, those intrigued by Spiritualist phenomena had to content themselves with the explanation of spirit intervention. The Psychological Society was the crystallization of a small body of "rationalist" opinions which had existed since the days of **Mesmer.**

Sergeant Cox, in his book *The Mechanism of Man* (2 vols., 1876–79) stated that "spirit" was refined matter, or molecular matter split into its constituent atoms, which thus become imperceptible to our physical organism; this view may have been shared by some members of the Psychological Society. (See also **London Dialectical Society**)

Psychology

Originally the name given to the branch of philosophy dealing with the soul (from the Greek *psyche,* or soul), then to the science of the mind, and now generally understood to be the science of behavior, both human and animal, and of human thought processes. Early **psychical research,** in contrast, concerned itself with the demonstration and investigation of paranormal faculties and the concept of the soul, with the question of **survival** after bodily death as a legitimate inference.

According to the criterion of **Charles Richet,** everything that the human intelligence can do, even when it is most profound and penetrating, is psychological. Everything of which such intelligence is incapable belongs to metapsychics.

The crux of the matter is that the greatest difficulty is experienced in drawing the line between what the human intelligence can and cannot do, because many paranormal faculties appear to originate in the subconscious mind and manifest along the same channels as the phenomena of abnormal psychology. Their difference from abnormal phenomena seems to be primarily their social functionality.

Abnormal Psychology and the Paranormal

Some would contend that an abnormal bodily condition may facilitate the function of a paranormal faculty without being the reason and cause of it. **Hereward Carrington,** in *The Story of Psychic Science* (1930), relates the story of a female acquaintance who fell into Lake Minnetonka, sank three times, and was rescued unconscious. A severe illness complicated with pneumonia followed her misadventure. During her convalescence she became clairvoyant and could tell what letters were in the mailbox in the morning and often their approximate contents. When she was completely restored her clairvoyant faculty disappeared.

Neither pneumonia nor near-drowning can be supposed the cause of such **clairvoyance.** Similarly it is reasonable to infer that in the clairvoyance of hysteric subjects, the abnormal bodily condition is simply a coincidental phenomenon but not the cause and explanation of the clairvoyance. An abnormal condition may open up a channel of function for paranormal faculties. If the abnormal condition becomes permanent, mediumship may develop in organisms that constitutionally were not adapted for paranormal manifestations.

The study of abnormal psychology may also have relevance to the emotional and temperamental problems of some mediums, particularly those who are disposed to fraudulent tricks, even if gifted with some genuine psychic faculties.

Parapsychology adopted much from modern behavioral studies and does not assume any particular psychological structure, as did psychical research. Its name implies that it is a branch of psychology that specializes in the study of paranormal behavior. Parapsychologists seek to use appropriate psychological methodologies and integrate their findings into the larger body of psychological knowledge.

Sources:

Beloff, John. *The Existence of Mind.* London: MacGibbon, 1962. Reprint, New York: Citadel, 1965.

Brown, William. *Science and Personality.* New Haven, Conn.: Yale University Press, 1929. Reprint, College Park, Md.: McGrath, 1972.

Burt, Cyril. *Psychology and Psychical Research.* London: Society for Psychical Research, 1968.

Ehrenwald, Jan. *Telepathy and Medical Psychology.* New York: W. W. Norton, 1948.

Eysenck, H. J. *Sense and Nonsense in Psychology.* London: Penguin, 1957.

Hudson, Thomas J. *The Law of Psychic Phenomena: A Working Hypothesis for the Systematic Study of the Vast Potential of Man's Mind.* New York: G. P. Putnam's Sons, 1894. Reprint, Chicago: Hudson-Cohan, 1970. Reprint, New York: Weiser, 1972.

LeShan, Lawrence. *The Medium, the Mystic, and the Physicist: Towards a General Theory of the Paranormal.* New York: Viking Press; London: Turnstone Books, 1974.

McCreery, Charles. *Science, Philosophy, and ESP.* London: Faber & Faber, 1967. Reprint, Hamden, Conn.: Archon Books, 1968.

Mitchell, T. W. *Medical Psychology and Psychical Research.* London: Methuen, 1922.

Myers, F. W. H. *Human Personality and Its Survival of Bodily Death.* 2 vols. London: Longmans, Green, 1903. Reprint, New York: Longmans, Green, 1954. Abr. ed. New Hyde Park, N.Y.: University Books, 1961.

Osty, Eugene. *Supernormal Faculties in Man.* London: Methuen, 1923.

Rhine, J. B., and Robert Brier. *Parapsychology Today.* New York: Citadel, 1968.

Rosenthal, Robert. *Experimenter Effects in Behavioral Research.* New York: Appleton-Century-Crofts, 1966.

Schmeidler, Gertrude R. *ESP in Relation to Rorschach Test Evaluation.* New York: Parapsychology Foundation, 1960.

Wolman, Benjamin B., ed. *Handbook of Parapsychology.* New York: Van Nostrand Reinhold, 1977. Reprint, Jefferson, N.C.: McFarland, 1986.

Psychomancy

Divination by spirits or the art of evoking the dead. (See also **ceremonial magic; necromancy**)

Psychomanteum

A psychomanteum is a room set aside for communication with those who have died and are believed to have passed to the world beyond. It is specially designed to promote an altered state of consciousness that facilitates such contact. Essential to the décor is a mirror into which the person wishing to communicate with a deceased loved one gazes. The use of the psychomanteum is traced to the ancient Mediterranean Basin, where its use is described in various writings and to the sleep temples of the followers of Asklepios.

The modern use of the psychomanteum had been advocated by **Raymond Moody,** a physician most known for his study of the near-death experience. Moody had noted that having an apparition of a loved one who had recently died had a healing effect on many people. They were given a sense of peace by knowing that their loved ones were alive and in a better place. They were also, on occasion, to complete their grieving process by resolving a broken relationship that had been present at the time of the death of the other party.

Following the publication of his highly successful books, *Life After Life* and *Reflections on Life After Life,* Moody constructed a psychomanteum and developed a simple process of inducing apparitions that including sitting inside the mirrored room and sending telepathic messages to the person with whom contact was desired. He discovered that the great majority of the people who went through a process of preparation for the psychomanteum actually saw an apparition within the room or later in their bedroom. Moody reported on his research in his 1993 book, *Visionary Encounters with Departed Loved Ones.*

The successes of the initial attempts at encounter have led Moody to train facilitators to spread the psychomanteum work. In his book, he offers instructions on constructing a psychomanteum. He has also initiated a research program to quantify the results of contacts made within the psychomanteum. Moody believes that it will provide further evidence of communication between the living and the dead.

Sources:

Moody, Raymond, with Paul Perry. *Visionary Encounters with Departed Loved Ones.* New York: Ballantine Books, 1993.

Psychometry

A faculty, claimed by many psychics and mediums, of becoming aware of the characters, surroundings, or events connected with an individual by holding or touching an object, such as a watch or ring, that the individual possessed or that was strongly identified with the person. Medium **Hester Dowden** described psychometry as "a psychic power possessed by certain individuals which enables them to divine the history of, or events connected with, a material object with which they come in close contact."

No doubt such an ability has been manifest from ancient times, but it was first named and discussed in modern history by the American scientist **Joseph Rhodes Buchanan** in 1842. The term derives from the Greek *psyche* (soul) and *metron* (measure) and signifies "soul-measuring," or measurement by the human soul. Buchanan's theory was based on the belief that everything that has ever existed—every object, scene, or event that has occurred since the beginning of the world—has left on the ether, or astral light, a trace of its being. This trace is indelible while the world endures and is impressed not only on the ether but on more palpable objects, such as trees and stones. Sounds and perfumes also leave impressions on their surroundings, said Buchanan. Just as a photograph may be taken on film or plate and remain invisible until it has been developed, so may those psychometric "photographs" remain impalpable until the developing process has been applied. That which can bring them to light is the psychic faculty and mind of the medium, he said.

Buchanan claimed that this faculty operated in conjunction with what he termed a **community of sensation** of varying intensity. The psychometric effect of medicines in Buchanan's experiments as a physician was similar to their ordinary action. When an emetic was handed to a subject, the subject could only avoid vomiting by suspending the experiment. Buchanan's earliest experiments, with his own students, showed that some of them were able to distinguish different metals merely by holding them in their hands. Later he found that some among them could diagnose a patient's disease simply by holding his hand. Many of his acquaintances, on pressing a letter against their foreheads, could tell the character and surroundings of the writer, the circumstances under which the letter was written, and other details.

Many mediums who have practiced psychometry have since become famous in this line. As has been said, their method is to hold in the hand or place against the forehead some small object, such as a fragment of clothing, a letter, or a watch; appropriate visions are then seen or sensations experienced.

While on rare occasions a psychometrist may be entranced, normally he or she is in a condition scarcely varying from the normal. The psychometric pictures, presumably somehow imprinted on the objects, have been likened to pictures carried in the memory, seemingly faded, yet ready to start into vividness when the right spring is touched. Some have suggested, for example, that the rehearsal of bygone tragedies so frequently witnessed in haunted houses is really a psychometric picture that, during the original occurrence, impressed itself on the room. The same may be said of the sounds and smells that haunt certain houses.

The psychological effect of the experimental objects appears to be very strong. When a Mrs. Cridge, William Denton's subject, examined a piece of lava from the Kilauea volcano she was seized with terror and the feeling did not pass for more than an hour.

On examining a fragment of a mastodon tooth, Elizabeth Denton said,

"My impression is that it is a part of some monstrous animal, probably part of a tooth. I feel like a perfect monster, with heavy legs, unwieldy head, and very large body. I go down to a shallow stream to drink. I can hardly speak, my jaws are so heavy. I feel like getting down on all fours. What a noise comes through the wood! I have an impulse to answer it. My ears are very large and leathery, and I can almost fancy they flap my face as I move my head. There are some older ones than I. It seems, too, so out of keeping to be talking with these heavy jaws. They are dark brown, as if they had been completely tanned. There is one old fellow, with large tusks, that looks very tough. I see several young ones; in fact, there is a whole herd."

She derived further impressions from a fragment of a meteorite: "It carries my eyes right up. I see an appearance of misty light. I seem to go miles and miles very quickly, up and up. Streams of light come from the right, a great way off. . . . Light shining at a vast distance."

Some negative impressions can prostrate the psychic and cause illness. On occasion, if the impressions are too antagonistic, the psychic will refuse to handle the object. Some psychometrists have been known, when given an object belonging to a deceased person, to take on the personal appearance and mannerisms of the owner and even to suffer from his or her ailments.

Eugene Crowell, in *The Identity of Primitive Christianity and Modern Spiritualism* (2 vols., 1875–79), writes of a sentry box in Paris in which the sentry on duty committed suicide by hanging. Another soldier was assigned to the same duty, and within three weeks took his life by similar means. Still another succeeded to the post, and in a short time met a similar fate. When these events were reported to Emperor Louis Napoleon, he ordered the sentry box removed and destroyed.

There are many instances on record in which corpses have been traced through psychometric influence. Attempts have also been made to employ it in criminology with varying results. In his book *Thirty Years of Psychical Research* (1923), **Charles Richet** narrates the experience of a Dr. Dufay with a nonprofessional somnambulist called Marie. He handed her something in several folds of paper. She said that the paper contained something that had killed a man. A rope? No. A necktie, she continued. The necktie had belonged to a prisoner who hanged himself because he had committed a murder, killing his victim with a gouet (a woodman's hatchet). Marie indicated the spot where the gouet was thrown on the ground. The gouet was found in the place indicated.

While most psychometrists give their readings in a normal state, a few are hypnotized. Maria Reyes de Z. of Mexico, with whom **Gustav Pagenstecher** conducted a series of successful experiments, belongs to the latter class. From a shell picked up on the beach of Vera Cruz she gave the following reading: "I am under water and feel a great weight pressing upon my body. I am surrounded by fishes of all kinds, colors, shapes, and sizes. I see white and pink coral. I also see different kinds of plants, some of them with large leaves. The water has a dark green, transparent colour. I am among the creatures but they do not seem to notice my presence, as they are not afraid of me in spite of touching me as they pass by."

Many psychometrists in the Spiritualist community have asserted that they are simply instruments and that spirits do the reading. Trance mediums often ask for objects belonging to the dead to establish contact. It was a habit with **Leonora Piper.** But other psychics, like **Pascal Forthuny,** repudiated the theory of spirit intervention and considered psychometry a personal gift, a sensitivity to the influence of the objects possessed. This influence, or emanation, was likened by Waldemar Wasielawski to the "rhabdic force" that he believed bends the rod of the water-witcher while **dowsing.**

William T. Stead suggested that very slight contact would suffice to impart such personal influence. On one occasion he cut pieces of blank paper from the bottom pages of letters of eminent people, just below the signature of each, and sent them to a Miss Ross marked "No. 1. Lady," "No. 2. Gentleman." The readings were very successful (see Stead's journal, *Borderland,* October 1895).

The psychometric vision sometimes comes in quickly flashed images and requires an effort of will to slow down, say mediums. Acccording to D'Aute Hooper in *Spirit Psychometry,* "It would be impossible to follow up and write the impressions as they pass through my consciousness. It is far too rapid. They are like cinematographic pictures. I seem to fly, and at other times I seem to be the piece of stone, without thinking power but seeing things and happenings around me."

The scope of the visions has been described as small or encompassing the whole room. There is no definite order in their emergence. The picture is kaleidoscopic, there is an oscillation in periods of time, but the images of more important events seem to have better sway, say mediums.

The exercise of the faculty requires a relaxed, receptive mind. After the object is touched, some psychometrists feel they are immediately at the location; others mentally travel there first. Some may tear off a piece of paper from an envelope and put it into their mouths. Others are satisfied to handle an object, or hold it wrapped up in their hands.

As a rule, a clue containing an "influence" is indispensable for psychometric readings. But experiments with exceptional psychics led Joseph Buchanan to the conclusion that the clue may be supplanted by an index, for instance, by a name written on a piece of paper. Such cases appear to be rare.

It is usually said that a medium cannot get a reading for himself or herself by psychometry. An incident told some years ago in the journal *Light* is therefore very interesting. E. A. Cannock was handed, without her knowing the origin, a broad piece of elastic that was actually her own. She not only gave a character reading of herself, but also made a prediction that proved to be correct.

It is said that the image of engravings is retained by the glass and that by some processes, such as the use of mercury vapor, this image can be developed. There is a suggestion of some similar effect in an incident related by Elizabeth Denton. She had entered a car from which the passengers had gone to dinner and was surprised to see all the seats occupied. She later recalled:

"Many of them were sitting perfectly composed, as if, for them, little interest was attached to this station, while others were already in motion (a kind of compressed motion), as if preparing to leave. I thought this was somewhat strange, and was about turning to find a vacant seat in another car, when a second glance around showed me that the passengers who had appeared so indifferent were really losing their identity, and, in a moment more, were invisible to me. I had sufficient time to note the personal appearance of several; and taking a seat, I awaited the return of the passengers, thinking it more than probable I might find them the prototypes of the faces and forms I had a moment before so singularly beheld. Nor was I disappointed. A number of those who returned to the cars I recognized as being, in every particular, the counterparts of their late, but transient representatives."

Psychometric impressions may come so spontaneously as to seriously distract the medium in the daily course of life. The British medium **Bessie Williams** complained of this troubie. The Dutch psychometrist **Lotte Plaat** said she could not go into the British Museum in London because she felt that the exhibits were literally shouting their history. By a strong effort of will, however, such impressions can usually be dispelled.

Buchanan made a suggestion to test **direct writing** by spirits by submitting it to psychometric reading. He thought that if the writing was purely the product of the medium, the reading would give the medium's character; if not, the character of the spirit author would be described. The experiments were unsuccessful, however, because he had seemingly overlooked the complications of the **ectoplasm** from which the "spirit" hand was said to be formed. If the writing was done by a materialized hand built out of the bodily substance of the medium, it might bear as little impression of the spirit as a dictated text bears of the dictator, he reasoned.

As already mentioned, psychometry has been utilized to gain information about hauntings. "That the victim of some century old villainy," writes **Sir Arthur Conan Doyle** in his book *The Edge of the Unknown* (1930), "should still in her ancient garments frequent in person the scene of her former martyrdom, is indeed, hard to believe. It is more credible, little as we understand the details, that some thought-form is used and remains visible at the spot where great mental agony has been endured." But he was not unmindful of the difficulties of such speculation, adding, "Why such a thought-form should only come at certain hours, I am compelled to answer that I do not know." The psychometric impression should always be there and should always be perceived, if the theory is correct. The ghost apparently is not; its ways are strange.

Searching for Explanations

Psychometry was identified by Buchanan and entered into the terminology of Spiritualism at a time when a somewhat elaborate and detailed understanding of the spirit world was being conceived in order to explain the many varied phenomena emerging in the séance room. Many of these ideas were offered in an attempt to explain one mystery, such as psychometry, by another, such as ectoplasm. Much of that speculation disappeared along with the mass of physical phenomena. **Stephan Ossowiecki,** a prominent modern psychometrist, has noted correctly that should the psychometric speculation be even partially true, it would explain nothing. Psychometry is just a word and not an explanation, he said. Its essential nature, its exercise, is a mystery. He writes:

"I begin by stopping all reasoning, and I throw all my inner power into perception of spiritual sensation. I affirm that this condition is brought about by my unshakable faith in the spiritual unity of all humanity. I then find myself in a new and special state in which I see and hear outside time and space. . . . Whether I am reading a sealed letter, or finding a lost object, or psychometrising, the sensations are nearly the same. I seem to lose some energy; my temperature becomes febrile, and the heartbeats unequal. I am confirmed in this supposition because, as soon as I cease from reasoning, something like electricity flows through my extremities for a few seconds. This lasts a moment only, and then lucidity takes possession of me, pictures arise, usually of the past. I see the man who wrote the letter, and I know what he wrote. I see the object at the moment of its loss, with the details of the event; or again, I perceive or feel the history of the thing I am holding in my hands. The vision is misty and needs great tension. Considerable effort is required to perceive some details and conditions of the scenes presented. The lucid state sometimes arises in a few minutes, and sometimes it takes hours of waiting. This largely depends on the surroundings; skepticism, incredulity, or even attention too much concentrated on my person, paralyses quick success in reading or sensation."

Illuminating as this subjective account is, it conveys little about the specific nature of psychometric influence. Gustav Pagenstecher conjectured as follows:

"The associated object which practically witnessed certain events of the past, acting in the way of a tuning fork, automatically starts in our brain the specific vibrations corresponding to the said events; furthermore, the vibrations of our brain once being set in tune with certain parts of the Cosmic Brain already stricken by the same events, call forth sympathetic vibrations between the human brain and the Cosmic Brain, giving birth to thought pictures which reproduce the events in question."

Spiritualist Sir Arthur Conan Doyle, in plainer language, compared psychometric impressions to shadows on a screen. The screen is the ether, "the whole material universe being embedded in and interpenetrated by this subtle material which would not necessarily change its position since it is too fine for wind or any coarser material to influence it." Doyle himself, although by no means psychic, would always be conscious of a strange effect—almost a darkening of the landscape with a marked sense of heaviness—when he was on an old battlefield. A more familiar example of the same faculty may be suspected in the gloom that gathers over the mind of even an average person upon entering certain houses. Such sensitivity may find expression in more subtle and varied forms. "Is not the emotion felt on looking at an old master [painting] a kind of thought transference from the departed?" asked **Sir Oliver Lodge.** The query cannot be answered conclusively, since the labels attached to psychic phenomena are purely arbitrary.

Akashic Records

Attempts at such a synthesis have been made by Theosophists. In his introduction to W. Scott-Elliot's *The Story of Atlantis and the Lost Lemuria* (1904), the first book drawn from the so-called **akashic records, A. P. Sinnett** explains that the pictures of memory are imprinted on some nonphysical medium; they are photographed by nature on some imperishable page of superphysical matter. They are accessible, but the interior spiritual capacities of ordinary humanity are as yet too imperfectly developed to establish touch, he says. He further notes:

"But in a flickering fashion, we have experience in ordinary life of efforts that are a little more effectual. Thought-transference is a humble example. In that case, 'impressions on the mind' of one person, Nature's memory pictures with which he is in normal relationship, are caught up by someone else who is just able, however unconscious of the method he uses, to range Nature's memory under favourable conditions a little beyond the area with which he himself is in normal relationship. Such a person has begun, however slightly, to exercise the faculty of astral clairvoyance."

Such highly speculative ideas are beyond the scope of psychical research, but the concept of the akashic records in its philosophical depths can be partly supported by an astronomical analogy. Because of the vastness of interstellar distances it takes hundreds of thousands of years for light, traveling at the enormous speed of 186,000 miles per second, to reach us from distant stars. Anyone who could look at the Earth from such a distant star would witness, at the present moment, the primeval past. From various distances the creation of our world could be seen as a present reality. Theoretically, therefore, astronomy admits the existence of a scenic record of the world's history. The concept of this **cosmic picture gallery** and that of the akashic records is similar.

There is no generally validated method of access to such records in sublimated psychometry. However, Theosophist G. R. S. Mead, in his book *Did Jesus Live 100 B.C.?* (1903), asserted the following regarding akashic research:

"It would be as well to have it understood that the method of investigation to which I am referring does not bring into consideration any question of trance, either self-induced, or mesmerically or hypnotically effected. As far as I can judge, my colleagues are to all outward seeming in quite their normal state. They go through no outward ceremonies, or internal ones for that matter, nor even any outward preparation but that of assuming a comfortable position; moreover, they not only describe, as each normally has the power of description, what is passing before their inner vision in precisely the same fashion as one would describe some objective scene, but they are frequently as surprised as their auditors that the scenes or events they are attempting to explain are not at all as they expected to see them, and remark on them as critically, and frequently as sceptically, as those who cannot 'see' for themselves but whose knowledge of the subject from objective study may be greater than theirs."

Simultaneous Perception of "Memory Records"

One need not go to occultists for psychic experiences in which there is a clear suggestion of memory records existing independently of individual powers of cognition. Something of that nature has been perceived by several people simultaneously, thus suggesting some sort of objectivity.

The Battle of Edge Hill (on the borders of Warwickshire and Oxfordshire, England) was fought on October 22, 1624. Two months later a number of shepherds and village people witnessed an aerial reenactment of the battle with all the noises of the guns, the neighing of the horses and the groans of the wounded. The vision lasted for hours and was witnessed by people of reputation for several consecutive days. When rumors of it reached the ears of Charles I, a commission was sent out to investigate. The commission not only reported having seen the vision on two occasions, but actually recognized fallen friends of theirs among the fighters; one was Sir Edmund Varney.

A similar instance was recorded by Pausanias (second century B.C.E.), according to whom on the plains of Marathon, four hundred years after the great battle, the neighing of horses, the shouts of the victors, the cries of the vanquished, and all the noise of a well-contested conflict, were frequently to be heard.

Patrick Walker, the Scottish Presbyterian covenanter, is quoted in *Biographia Presbyteriana* (1827) as stating that in 1686, about two miles below Lanark, on the water of Clyde, "many people gathered together for several afternoons, where there were showers of bonnets, hats, guns and swords, which covered the trees and ground, companies of men in arms marching in order, upon the waterside, companies meeting companies . . . and then all falling to the ground and disappearing, and other companies immediately appearing in the same way." But Patrick Walker himself saw nothing unusual occur. About two-thirds of the crowd saw the phenomena; the others saw nothing strange. "Patrick Walker's account," states Andrew Lang in his book *Cock Lane and Common Sense* (1896), "is triumphantly honest and is, perhaps, as odd a piece of psychology as any on record, thanks to his escape from the prevalent illusion, which, no doubt, he would gladly have shared."

Under the pseudonyms Miss Morrison and Miss Lamont, Anne Moberly, daughter of the bishop of Salisbury, and Eleanor Jourdain published in 1911 a remarkable book entitled *An Adventure,* in which they claim that in 1901 and 1902 they had a simultaneous vision, on the grounds of Versailles, of the place as it was in 1789. Some time after the first publication of their account of their **Versailles adventure,** testimony was given by people who lived in the neighborhood of Versailles that they also had seen the mysterious appearances, the strange phenomena being witnessed only on the anniversary of the attack on Versailles during the French Revolution. The most inexplicable feature of the story is that the people of the eighteenth century saw, heard, and spoke to the people of the twentieth century, who never doubted at the time that they were in communication with real individuals.

Psychometric Premonitions

Another class of phenomena could be classified as psychometric foreshadowings of the future. The report on the **Census of Hallucinations** made by the Society for Psychical Research in Great Britain in 1889 recorded one incident concerning a solitary excursion to a lake. The individual noted:

"My attention was quite taken up with the extreme beauty of the scene before me. There was not a sound or movement, except the soft ripple of the water on the sand at my feet. Presently I felt a cold chill creep through me, and a curious stiffness of my limbs, as if I could not move, though wishing to do so. I felt frightened, yet chained to the spot, and as if impelled to stare at the water straight in front of me. Gradually a black cloud seemed to rise, and in the midst of it I saw a tall man, in a suit of tweed, jump into the water and sink. In a moment the darkness was gone, and I again became sensible of the heat and sunshine, but I was awed and felt eery. . . . A week afterwards Mr. Espie, a bank clerk (unknown to me) committed suicide by drowning in that very spot. He left a letter for his wife, indicating that he had for some time contemplated death."

Princess Karadja narrates in the *Zeitschrift für Metapsychische Forschung* (March 15, 1931) a story of a personal experience of the late Count Buerger Moerner that contains this incident:

"Passing through the little garden and glancing in at the window as he approached the house (looking for public refreshment) the Count was horrified to see the body of an old woman hanging from a ceiling beam. He burst into the room with a cry of horror, but once across the threshold was stunned with amazement to find the old woman rising startled from her chair, demanding the reason of his surprising intrusion. No hanging body was to be seen and the old lady herself was not only very much alive, but indignant as well. . . . Some days later, being again in that locality, he decided to visit the hut once more, curious to see if by some peculiarity of the window pane he might not have been observing an optical illusion. Nearing the hut through the garden as before, the same terrible sight met his eye. This time, however, the Count stood for some minutes studying the picture, then after some hesitation knocked at the door. No answer, even to repeated knocks, until at length Count Moerner opened the door and entered to find what he saw this time was no vision. The old woman's body was indeed hanging from the beam. She had committed suicide."

Psychometry remains a popular practice in both psychic and Spiritualist circles. There has been little work done on it in parapsychology since it is difficult to quantify results and many consider it but a variation on clairvoyance. It may also be seen as merely a helpful tool to assist the psychic into the proper state for receiving clairvoyant impressions.

Sources:

Buchanan, J. Rhodes. *Manual of Psychometry: The Dawn of a New Civilization.* Boston: Dudley M. Holman, 1885.

Butler, W. E. *How to Develop Psychometry.* London: Aquarian Press; New York: Samuel Weiser, 1971.

Denton, William, and Elizabeth Denton. *Nature's Secrets, or Psychometric Researches.* London: Houston & Wright, 1863.

Ellis, Ida. *Thoughts on Psychometry.* Blackpool, England, 1899.

[Hooper, T. D'Aute]. *Spirit Psychometry and Trance Communications by Unseen Agencies.* London: Rider, 1914.

Pagenstecher, Gustav. "Past Events Seership." *Proceedings* of the American Society for Psychical Research 16 (January 1922).

Prince, Walter Franklin. "Psychometrical Experiments with Senora Maria Reyes de Z." *Proceedings* of the American Society for Psychical Research 15 (1921).

Richet, Charles. *Thirty Years of Psychical Research.* N.p., 1923.

Verner, A. *Practical Psychometry* (pamphlet). Blackpool, England, 1903.

Psychophone

Term suggested by **James Coates** for **direct voice** communications at séances.

Psychophysical Research Laboratories

An organization founded in 1979 by James S. McDonnell at the Forrestal Research Center, Princeton, New Jersey. It was devoted to laboratory investigation of **psi** phenomena, **extrasensory perception,** and **psychokinesis.** Under its director, **Charles Honorton,** it became known as the location of experiments using the **Ganzfeld** procedures, the subject of major controversy within parapsychology in the 1980s. The center closed in the late 1980s due to a lack of financial resources.

Sources:

Honorton, Charles. "Meta-Analysis of Psi Ganzfeld Research: A Response to Hyman." *Journal of Parapsychology* 49 (1985): 59.

Hyman, Ray. "The Ganzfeld Psi Experiment: A Critical Appraisal." *Journal of Parapsychology* 49 (1985): 3.

Psychoplasm

Alternative term for **ectoplasm.**

Psychorrhagic Diathesis

Formidable term used by psychical researcher **F. W. H. Myers** for his theory of phantasmal appearances, a psychic faculty of detaching elements of personality and transforming by them a certain part of space into a phantasmogenetic center. In this center, in a manner not material or optical, the phantasm of the psychorrhagist appears and may become collectively visible. (See also **apparitions**)

Psychosynthesis Institute

A facility founded to promote the psychotherapeutic approach of **Roberto Assagiolo,** a psychiatrist who attempted to integrate theosophical ideas, especially those of **Alice A. Bailey,** into his psychotherapeutic work. Basic concepts in psychosynthesis include the supraconscious (a higher unconscious, source of meaning and purpose in life), the Self and the will.

Essentially psychosynthesis is a psychological and educational method of harmonizing one's relationship to environment through inner integration and synthesis. This involves a continuing process of expanding self-awareness and higher consciousness, leading from the personal to the transpersonal or universal. The approach varies according to the needs of the individual and the most suitable way of releasing inner guidance, combining the methods of psychology and spiritual disciplines.

The institute offered theoretical and practical training for professionals and concerned individuals, as well as supporting research on psychosynthesis. Last known addresses: High Point Foundation, 647 N. Madison Ave., Pasadena, CA 91101, and Nan Clark Ln., Mill Hill, London, NW7, England.

Sources:

Assagioli, Roberto. *The Act of Will.* New York: Viking Penguin, 1973.

———. *Psychosynthesis: A Manual of Principles and Techniques.* New York: Viking Penguin, 1971.

The Psycho-Therapeutic Society

Founded in London, England, on April 1, 1901, for the advocacy of health reform, medical hypnotism, suggestive therapeutics, curative human radiations, and general drugless healing. The first president was **George Spriggs,** whose services as healing medium were at the disposal of patients for a generation. It is no longer active.

Psychotronics

A modern term favored in Eastern Europe for what in the West is termed parapsychology. It attempts to extend parapsychology by indicating the relationship of man to the universe, interaction with other physical bodies and matter, and fields of energy, known or unknown.

The First International Conference on psychotronics was held in Prague, Czechoslovakia, in 1974. Delegates included professors of physics and psychology, doctors of medicine and psychiatry, and parapsychologists. Subjects discussed included **dowsing** (water-witching and location of hidden objects), **radionics, telepathy, Kirlian aura, out-of-the body travel,** and bioelectric energy fields. Psychotronics organizations now exist in Poland, the Czech Republic and several other Eastern European countries.

Sources:

Wilczewski, Janusz, Zbigniew Szczerba, and Barbara Szbicka, eds. *Materialy z Konferencji Parapsychologow '94.* Warsaw: Polskie Towarzystwo Psychotroniczne, 1994.

The Psychotronics and Folk Medicine Center

A research center dedicated to collecting and disseminating information on **psi** and alternative (especially folk) medicine. Since the fall of the Soviet Union, Russian study of parapsychology (or **psychotronics**) and contact with the West has increased measurably. The Psychotronics and Folk Medicine Center, established in the 1990s, initiated communication with Western scientists and businesses concerning psi knowledge. It developed and published relevant literature and films on these subjects, working with such prominent healers as Nickolay Kasyan and psychic **Nina S. Kulagina.**

Edward Naumov, president of the center, was a corresponding member of the **Parapsychological Association.** He was known in the West for his work on "bioinformation" and healing. He dispensed information on what he called "the mystery of Psy-weapon," and the center's literature outlined examples of former Soviet government interest in "radioson," which allegedly was capable of causing "acoustic modulations in the brain." Naumov claimed that the representatives of the KGB and the CIA reported the creation of "a generator [that can] transmit information regardless of distance."

Last known address: House 1, Block B, Apt. 60, Pl. Poebody, 12193 Moscow, Russia, Commonwealth of Independent States.

Psylli

A class of persons in ancient Italy who had the power of charming serpents. This name was also given by various writers to the snake charmers of Africa, and it is claimed that the serpents twisted round the bodies of these *Psylli* without doing them any injury, although the reptiles did not have their fangs extracted or broken.

In Kahira, when a viper entered a house, the charmer was sent for, and he enticed it out by the use of certain words. At other times, music was used, and it is believed that the serpents understood what was said to them by the snake charmers, and they acted with complete obedience.

Since vipers do not have ears, thus eliminating the effect of words or music, they may instead respond to movements and body heat.

Ptolemy, Claudius (100–178 C.E.)

Greek scholar and the father of Western **astrology.** Ptolemy lived in the Greek community of Alexandria, Egypt, then one of the major centers of learning in the Mediterranean basin. He is most remembered as the author of *Mathematikê Syntaxis.*

In *Mathematikê Syntaxis* (also known as the *Almegest,*) Ptolemy synthesized current knowledge of the solar system. His earth-centered astronomy was accepted for centuries until finally overthrown by the solar-centered view of Copernicus (1473–1543).

From his earth-centered astronomy Ptolemy derived his perspective on astrology (the two disciplines not then so rigidly separated as they are today). In the *Tetrabiblos,* he organized the astrological knowledge then available into a unified system and tied it to a set of ethical principles that stress the proper function of astrology and the ways in which it can be properly used. Although his system has been modified in a number of ways in modern astrology, its basic structure remains.

Sources:

Brau, Jean-Louis, Helen Weaver, and Allan Edwards, eds. *Larousse Encyclopedia of Astrology.* New York: New American Library, 1982.

Holden, James H., and Robert A. Hughes. *Astrological Pioneers of America.* Tempe, Ariz.: American Federation of Astrologers, 1988.

Lewis, James R. *The Astrology Encyclopedia.* Detroit: Gale Research, 1994.

Puharich, Andrija (Henry Karl) (1918–1995)

Physician and parapsychologist. He was born on February 9, 1918, in Chicago, Illinois, of Yugoslavian ancestry. He studied at Northwestern University (B.A., 1942) and Northwestern University Medical School (M.B. and M.D., 1946). He developed an interest in psychic phenomena in 1947 and the following year set up the Round Table Foundation, Glen Cove, Maine, to study the physico-chemical basis for paranormal phenomena. However, it was after his period of service in the army (1953–59) that his true interests emerged.

Through the 1960s, Puharich was an independent scientist and inventor operating with the funds and patronage of various funding sources including the Mind Science Foundation, San Antonio, Texas; the Belk Research Foundation, New York City; the Consciousness Research Foundation; and various industrial and scientific organizations. He holds some 50 patents. He did both psychological and non-parapsychological work; his several books reflect his exploration of hallucinogens and ESP.

In April 1971 he decided to change directions and devote himself fully to his first love, parapsychological investigation. This decision was stimulated by his brief contact in 1962 with the Brazilian psychic surgeon **José Arigó,** who died suddenly in an auto accident in 1971. Shortly thereafter he went to Tel Aviv, Israel, to meet **metal bending** psychic **Uri Geller** and commenced a series of tests of Geller's talents.

During these tests Geller apparently manifested psychokinetic ability and dematerialization of objects which reappeared elsewhere. Under hypnosis, a mysterious voice was heard in the same room as Geller, claiming to be a superior intelligence of an extraterrestrial nature. Similar messages had been conveyed to Puharich by a Hindu scholar and psychic Dr. D. G. Vinod in 1953, and also by Dr. Charles Laughead of Whipple, Arizona, three years later. These messages are described in detail in Puharich's biography of Geller, *Uri: A Journal of the Mystery of Uri Geller* (1974). It must be emphasized that these astonishing communications, claiming to originate from superior intelligences in spaceships, manifested in the Puharich's presence and seemed to follow him around from one psychic to another, and the reports of these voices led many of Puharich's colleagues to question his work otherwise.

Puharich continued to work quietly through the 1970s, and little has been published since concerning his direction or results. He died January 3, 1995.

Sources:

Puharich, Andrija. *Beyond Telepathy.* Garden City, N.Y.: Doubleday, 1962.

———. *The Sacred Mushroom: Key to the Door of Eternity.* Garden City, N.Y., Doubleday, 1959.

———. *Time No Longer.* N.p., 1980.

———. *Uri: A Journal of the Mystery of Uri Geller.* Garden City, N.Y.: Doubleday, 1974.

Puharich, Andrija, and Harold E. Puthoff. *The Iceland Papers.* Amherst, Wis.: Essentia Research Associates, 1979.

Purce, Jill (1947–)

British biophysicist, author, editor, and lecturer on mystical aspects of sound vibration and the human voice. Purce was born October 10, 1947, in Newcastle, Staffordshire. She attended Headington School, Oxford, Reading University (B.A. Hons., 1970), the Chelsea College of Art, London (1970–71), and Kings College, London (1971–72). Her special interest in the mystical aspects of life began when she studied the fine arts at Reading University and became fascinated with relationships between form and pattern in nature, and patterns in the development of human consciousness. She was awarded a research fellowship in the biophysics departments at Kings College and studied the spiral form in science, religion, and art. This became the basis for her book *The Mystic Spiral: Journey of the Soul* (1974), concerned with the evolution of consciousness in spiritual traditions and in psychology.

She also investigated the effect of sound vibrations on particles and on water, a subject that had been much neglected since the early experiments of E. F. F. Chladni in 1785 and Margaret Watts Hughes between 1885–1904.

Purce first introduction to the effect of sound in matter came from seeing photographs concerning the work of Hans Jenny, a Swiss engineer and doctor who had been influenced by the teachings of **Rudolph Steiner.** Jenny used liquids, pastes, and fine powders to demonstrate that formless matter could be organized into exquisite and precise patterns through sound vibration. In 1885, Hughes had studied the patterns formed by lycopodium seeds, sand, and also semi-liquid pastes when vibrated by the human voice. To assist her research, she invented the eidophone, an instrument to facilitate control of and the direction of the voice vibrations on any given medium.

Purce spent a period studying **music** with the eminent composer Karlheinz Stockhausen in Germany. It was at this time that Stockhausen composed his *Alphabet for Lieges,* illustrating relationships between sound vibration and matter. Afterwards she extended her studies with special reference to vibrations of the human voice. She studied Mongolian and Tibetan overtone chanting (producing chords of simultaneous notes octaves apart, with harmonics) in the Indian Himalayas, her teacher being the chantmaster of the Gyutö Tibetan Monastery and Tantric College. She subsequently developed her studies with American Indians and shamans from various traditions.

Purce has offered her research for the light it might shed on the mystic power of sound vibrations as they have operated in ancient traditions and practices. She has also tried to show that the human voice can act as a creative link between body and mind. In her lectures and workshops in various countries, Purce demonstrates to students the manner in which understanding and liberation of the voice can transform the personality, in both a psychotherapeutic and a spiritual way. She has also used her voice techniques as a tool of positive value for women in childbirth. She has conducted workshops on the healing and meditative effects of sound and voice across Europe and North America.

In addition to this specialized work, Purce is also general editor of the Thames & Hudson series of books on sacred traditions, art, and imagination. She is married to the biologist **Rupert Sheldrake** who has offered some new theoretical approaches to biologists about the origin and growth of form in nature. (See also **Mantra; Nada; Alfred Wolfsohn**)

Purna Yoga (Journal)

Annual publication of **Atmaniketan Ashram,** devoted to the teachings of **Sri Aurobindo** as interpreted by Sadhu Loncontirth the ashram's founder. The journal included news of **Auroville,** the new religious city in India. Current address unavailable.

Purohit, Swami Shri (1882–ca. 1936)

Hindu monk, poet and spiritual teacher, who greatly influenced the poet **W. B. Yeats** and (through him) actress Margot Ruddock, a close friend of Yeats in his later years. Swami Purohit was born on October 12, 1882, at Badnera, near Amraoti in Berar, India (Central Provinces), of a religious and wealthy Brahmin family. His father had renounced a large fortune out of respect for the memory of his own father. As a boy, Purohit grew up in a devout religious atmosphere and had several encounters with wonder-working Mahatmas.

After attending a local Anglo-vernacular school, he studied at University of Bombay, enrolling in 1898. He went on to the Morris College at Nagpur, where he entered the Arts course. After passing his examination in 1901 he joined the B.A. class and studied philosophy. After failing this examination, he took a position as teacher at Amraoti, eventually receiving his B.A. from Calcutta University in 1903. He went on to Poona and studied at Deccan College, where he obtained his LL.B. degree.

However, he was more interested in obtaining spiritual experience from yogis and mahatmas than in practicing law. He made several religious pilgrimages. At the request of his parents, he married a sixteen-year-old girl Godu Bai, but after the birth of two daughters and a son, he obtained his wife's permission to renounce the life of householder. He studied under his guru Bhagwan Shri Hamsa and in about 1923 became a renunciate and traveling monk. He practiced severe austerities and made religious pilgrimages throughout India. At the request of his guru, he traveled to Europe in 1930.

In London, he became a close friend of W. B. Yeats, then in his sixties, and strongly influenced his outlook on Hindu philosophy and mysticism. Yeats wrote introductions to the Swami's autobiography *An Indian Monk* (1932) and his translation of his guru's book *The Holy Mountain* (Faber, London, 1934).

In 1935, the Swami published a translation of *Bhagavad-Gita* under the title *The Geeta; The Gospel of the Lord Shri Krishna* (1935) which he dedicated "To my friend William Butler Yeats" on his seventieth birthday. In the same year, the Swami published a translation of the *Mandukya Upanishad,* for which Yeats provided an introduction. Yeats had planned to travel to India to assist the Swami in translating the ten principal Upanishads, but eventually the work was completed by the two friends at Majorca in 1936.

From 1934 onward, Yeats developed a romantic friendship with the young actress Margot Ruddock, then twenty-seven years old. He introduced her to the Swami, who thereafter became her spiritual adviser and influenced the poems which she wrote. The Swami also composed many religious poems, some of which Margot Ruddock translated into English.

The Swami featured frequently in the correspondence between Yeats and Margot Ruddock, published as *Ah, Sweet Dancer; W. B. Yeats and Margot Ruddock* edited by Roger McHugh (1970). Yeats corresponded with the Swami for some years before his own death. The Swami returned to India in 1936 after receiving news of the illness of his guru, who died the same year. The Swami died soon afterward.

Yeats's letters to the Swami were bought privately by Claude Driver, director of the Rosenbach Foundation, Philadelphia. Extracts from some letters were quoted in *The Later Phase of the Development of W. B. Yeats* by S. Mokashi-Punekar (1966).

Sources:

Patanjali, Bhagwan Shree. *Aphorisms of Yoga.* London: Faber, 1938.

The Purrah

A former secret society of the Tulka-Susus, a tribe whose members dwelled between the Sierra Leone river and Cape Mount in West **Africa.** The *Tulka* consisted of five small communities which together formed a kind of republic. Each group had its own chiefs and council, but all were under a controlling power that was called the *purrah.* Each of the five communities also had its own *purrah,* from which was formed the great or general *purrah,* which held supreme sway over the five bodies.

Before an African could join a district *purrah,* he had to be thirty years of age, and before being received into membership of the great *purrah,* he had to have reached the age of fifty. Thus the oldest members of each district *purrah* were members of the head *purrah.* On desiring admittance to the examination for the district *purrah,* the relations of the candidate had to swear to kill him if he did not stand the test, or if he revealed the mysteries and the secrets of the society. The explorer Leo Frobenius stated:

"In each district belonging to a *purrah* there is a sacred grove to which the candidate is conducted, and where he must stay in a place assigned to him, living for several months quite alone in a hut, whither masked persons bring him food. He must neither speak nor leave his appointed place of residence.

"Should he venture into the surrounding forest, he is as good as dead.

"After several months the candidate is admitted to stand his trial, which is said to be terrible. Recourse is had to all the elements in order to gain satisfaction as to his firmness and courage. We are even assured that at these mysteries use is made of fettered lions and leopards, that during the time of the tests and enrolment the sacred groves echo with fearful shrieks, that here great fires are seen at night, that formerly the fire flared up in these mysterious woods in all directions, that every outsider who through curiosity was tempted to stray into the woods was mercilessly sacrificed, that foolish people who would have penetrated into them disappeared and were never heard of again.

"If the candidate stands all the tests, he is admitted to the initiation. But he must first swear to keep all the secrets and without hesitation carry out the decisions of the *purrah* of his community and all the decrees of the great head *purrah.* If a member of the society betrays it or revolts against it, he is condemned to death, and the sentence is often carried out in the bosom of his family. When the criminal least expects it, a disguised, masked and armed warrior appears and says to him:—

" 'The great *purrah* sends thee death!'

"At these words everybody stands back, no one dares to offer the least resistance, and the victim is murdered.

"The Court of each district *purrah* consists of twenty-five members, and from each of these separate courts five persons are chosen, who constitute the great *purrah,* or the High Court of the general association. Hence this also consists of twenty five persons, who elect the head chief from their own body.

"The special *purrah* of each community investigates the offenses committed in its district, sits in judgment on them, and sees that its sentences are carried out. It makes peace between the powerful families, and stops their wranglings.

"The great *purrah* meets only on special occasions, and pronounces judgment on those who betray the mysteries and secrets of the order, or on those who show themselves disobedient to its mandates. But usually it puts an end to the feuds that often break out between two communities belonging to the confederacy. When these begin to fight, after a few months of mutual hostilities, one or other of the parties, when they have inflicted sufficient injury on each other, usually wants peace. The commune repairs secretly to the great *purrah,* and invites it to become the mediator and put an end to the strife.

"Thereupon the great *purrah* meets in a neutral district, and when all are assembled announces to the communes at war that it cannot allow men who should live together as brothers, friends and good neighbors, to wage war, to waste each others' lands, to plunder and burn; that it is time to put an end to these disorders; that the great *purrah* will inquire into the cause of the strife; that it requires that this should cease and decrees that all hostilities be forthwith arrested.

"A main feature of this arrangement is that, as soon as the great *purrah* assembles to put a stop to the feud, and until its decision is given, all the belligerents of the two districts at war are forbidden to shed a drop of blood; this always carries with it the penalty of death. Hence everybody is careful not to infringe this decree, and abstains from all hostilities.

"The session of the High Court lasts one month, during which it collects all necessary information to ascertain which commune caused the provocation and the rupture. At the same time it summons as many of the society's fighting-men as may be required to carry out the decision. When all the necessary particulars are brought in, and everything is duly weighed, it settles the question by condemning the guilty commune to a four days' sack.

"The warriors who have to give effect to this decision are all chosen from the neutral districts; they set out by night from the place where the great *purrah* is assembled. All are disguised, the face being covered with an ugly mask, and armed with lighted torches and daggers. They divide into bands of forty, fifty, or sixty, and all meet unexpectedly before dawn in the district that they have to pillage, proclaiming with fearful shouts the decision of the High Court. On their approach men, women, children and old people, all take to flight, that is, take refuge in their houses, and should anyone be found in the fields, on the highway, or in any other place, he is either killed or carried off and no more is ever heard of him.

"The booty obtained by such plundering is divided into two parts, one of which is given to the injured commune, the other to the great *purrah,* which shares it with the warriors that have executed its decree. This is the reward for their zeal, their obedience and loyalty.

"If one of the families in a commune subject to the *purrah* becomes too powerful and too formidable, the great *purrah* meets, and nearly always condemns it to unexpected sack, which is carried out by night and, as usual, by masked and disguised men. Should the heads of such a dangerous family offer any resistance, they are killed, or carried off, and conveyed to the depths of a sacred and lonely grove where they are tried by the *purrah* for their insubordination; they are seldom heard of again.

"Such, in part, is the constitution of this extraordinary institution. Its existence is known; the display of its power is felt; it is dreaded; yet the veil covering its intentions, decisions and decrees is impenetrable, and not till he is about to be executed does the outlaw know that he has been condemned. The power and reputation of the *purrah* is immense, not only in the homeland, but also in the surrounding districts. It is reported to be in league with the spirits (instead of the devil).

"According to the general belief the number of armed men who are members and at the disposal of the *purrah* exceeds 6,000. Moreover, the rules, the secrets and the mysteries of this society are strictly obeyed and observed by its numerous associated members, who understand and recognise each other by words and signs."

Pursuit (Journal)

Quarterly publication of the **Society for the Investigation of the Unexplained.** The Society for the Investigation of the Unexplained was founded in 1966 by explorer-author **Ivan T. Sanderson** (1911–1973), an enthusiastic student of the research of **Charles H. Fort** into strange and anomalous phenomena and events. *Pursuit* included reports on the wide range of Fortean phenomena, i.e., bizarre events, strange anomalies, synchronicities and scientific ambiguities often ignored or explained away, such as unusual falls from the skies, mysterious **disappearances** and reappearances, **stigmata,** earthquake and tornado anomalies, invisible assassins, **teleportation, UFOs**, **levitation, monsters,** inexplicable fires and explosions. The society died soon after Sanderson's death in 1973 and with it went *Pursuit.*

Purucker, Hobart Lorentz Gottfried de (1874–1942)

Hobart Lorentz Gottfried de Purucker, a prominent American theosophical author and leader, was the son of a pastor of the German Reformed church. He was born January 15, 1874, in Suffern, New York. He grew up in parsonages in several states and also as a youth lived in Geneva, Switzerland, where his father moved to become chaplain of the American church. He attended the Collège de Genève for a short time but returned to the United States during his eighteenth year. After a period of wandering, he settled in San Diego, California, where he discovered the **Theosophical Society.** He met the leader of the American Theosophists, **William Q. Judge,** and became an assistant to Judge's successor, **Katherine Tingley.** In 1903 Purucker moved to Point Loma, California, where Tingley had established a theosophical community.

Purucker served as Tingley's personal secretary, and in 1911 he assumed additional duties as editor of the *Theosophical Path,* the group's periodical. His years of work were acknowledged in 1929 when he succeeded Tingley as head of the society. He soon began a second periodical, the *Theosophical Forum.* He also took over Tingley's role as spokesperson of the society and began to give public lectures, which were later collected into some of his more popular books. The early 1930s were his most productive literary period. He completed *Questions We All Ask* (1930–31); *Theosophy and Modern Science* (1930); *Golden Precepts of Esotericism* (1931); *Fundamentals of Esoteric Philosophy* (1932); and *The Esoteric Tradition* (1935).

World War II presented a significant challenge to the community at Point Loma, which was located on Pacific coastal property adjacent to a major U.S. naval facility. The location was a vulnerable position should Japanese forces reach the West Coast, which many felt to be a real possibility at the time. That threat and the financial problems being experienced by the group led Purucker to close the community and sell the site. He died September 27, 1942, just a few weeks after new headquarters were established in Covina, California.

Following his death, the society published a variety of Purucker's writings, including *Studies in Occult Philosophy* (1945) and *Dialogues with G. de Purucker* (1948). Purucker's work is not very well known, because the branch of the society over which he presided has dwindled in size through the last half of the twentieth century.

Sources:

Purucker, Gottfried de. *Dialogues with G. de Purucker.* 3 vols. Covina, Calif.: Theosophical University Press, 1948.

———. *The Esoteric Tradition.* 2 vols. Point Loma, Calif.: Theosophical University Press, 1935.

———. *Fundamentals of Esoteric Philosophy.* London: Rider, 1932.

———. *Questions We All Ask.* 4 vols. Covina, Calif.: Theosophical University Press, 1930–31.

Puthoff, Harold E. (1936–)

Physicist and parapsychologist born June 20, 1936, in Chicago, Illinois. He earned his Ph.D. from Stanford University where he worked from 1972 onward in the field of lasers. He was responsible for developing a tunable Raman laser that produced high-power radiation throughout the infrared section of the spectrum. He has supervised research for Ph.D. candidates in electrical engineering and applied physics at Stanford.

His interest in parapsychology was first manifest in his initiating research in **biofeedback** and biofield measurements. However, he has become most known for his research with his colleague **Russell Targ** at **Stanford Research Institute** on remote viewing, a type of test for ESP in which one person goes to a specified location and another person attempts to describe what the first person is seeing. They reported remarkable success and following the publication of their book, *Mind Reach* (1977), others replicated the process with equally remarkable success. Critics, however, found a methodological flaw in the giving of cues to the percipient. The critics stimulated new research which prevented the cueing and researcher Robert Jahn has also reported (in Beloff, 1988) positive results with the new format. Puthoff and Targ have also done research on **Uri Geller.** (See also **Ingo Swann**)

Sources:

Beloff, John. *The Importance of Psychical Research.* London: Society for Psychical Research, 1988.

Puharich, Andrija, and Harold E. Puthoff. *The Iceland Papers.* 1979.

Puthoff, Harold E., and Russell Targ. "ESP Experiments with Uri Geller" In J. D. Morris, W. G. Roll, and R. L. Morris, eds. *Research in Parapsychology 1973.* Metuchen, N.J.: Scarecrow Press, 1974.

———. "Information Transmission under Conditions of Sensory Shielding." *Nature* (October 1974).

———. "A Perceptual Channel for Information Transfer over Kilometer Distances: Historical Perspective and Recent Research." *Proceedings, Institute of Electrical and Electronics Engineers* 64 (1975).

———. "PK Experiments with Uri Geller and Ingo Swann." In J. D. Morris, W. G. Roll, and R. L. Morris, eds. *Research in Parapsychology 1973.* Metuchen, N.J.: Scarecrow Press, 1974.

———. "Remote Viewing of Natural Targets." In J. D. Morris, W. G. Roll, and R. L. Morris, eds. *Research in Parapsychology 1974.* Metuchen, N.J.: Scarecrow Press, 1975.

———. "Replication Study on the Remote Viewing of Natural Targets." In J. D. Morris, W. G. Roll, and R. L. Morris, eds. *Research in Parapsychology 1975.* Metuchen, N.J.: Scarecrow Press, 1976.

Pyramid Church of Truth and Light

The Pyramid Church of Truth and Light is a Spiritualist church founded in 1941 in Ventura, California, by Revs. John Kingham and Emma Kingham. They led the church through its first generation after which, in 1962, Rev. Steele Goodman became the new head. Under the Kinghams, four congregations were chartered, but none have survived. Under Goodman two centers have been noted, one in Sacramento, California, and one in Phoenix, Arizona. The Phoenix church is pastored by Isaiah Jenkins, an African American who has emerged as a popular medium in the Spiritualist community. The church has a minimal set of beliefs and emphasizes personal development. It lives by the basic principle of love, upon which laws should be based.

Pyramid Guide (Newsletter)

Former bimonthly newsletter of the Life Understanding Foundation, concerned with **pyramids** and pyramid energy and related subjects, in the early 1990s superseded by **Univercolian** magazine. Back issues (1-55) are available from PO Box 30305, Santa Barbara, CA 93130.

Pyramids and Pyramidology

The large pyramid structures built by the ancient peoples of Egypt, Peru, and Central America have fascinated scholars and lay people through the centuries. In the wake of the emergence of modern Egyptology, they have been the subject of religious and millennial speculation, and more recently occult speculation. In spite of the efforts of Egyptologists, who have done much to discover and describe the building, the structure, and the purposes of the pyramids, a number of unanswered questions, such as the unit of measurement used by the pyramid architects, remain, and provide a basis for broad speculation. The discovery and spread of public knowledge concerning the pyramids in the Americas only added fuel to the fires of imagination. Although the Egyptian pyramids served as tombs for royalty and the wealthy of society, some pyramids had no clearly discernible purpose and others had structures that seemed to have no relation to the primary burial function.

There were some eighty pyramids in Egypt, built under the reign of the Pharaohs from 3,100 to 332 B.C.E. Egyptian tombs reflect the early religious ideas about the afterlife. In predynastic times, the dead were buried in sand pits of an oval or square shape; in the dynastic era a structure called a *mastaba* was erected over the burial place of kings and nobles. This was made of dried mud bricks and reproduced the house or palace of the deceased, so that his soul could have a replica of earthly existence.

Eventually stone was used instead of mud bricks, and the process of development culminated in the Step Pyramid of the Third Dynasty (ca. 2686–2181 B.C.E.) The familiar square-based, triangular-sided pyramid is seen at its best in the Great Pyramid of Giza, built in the reign of Cheops (or Khufu) of the Fourth Dynasty, regarded as one of the Seven Wonders of the World. It measures 756 feet square, with a height of 480 feet. It is made of some 2,300,000 blocks of stone that average 2 1/2 tons each. The core is of local stone and the outer facing of limestone, while the granite and limestone blocks are hewn with a high level of precision.

The pyramid is entered through a shaft on the north side, where a descending corridor leads to an unfinished chamber with a blind passage; an ascending corridor leads to what is called "the Queen's Chamber," containing two-dead end shafts, and eventually to the "Grand Gallery," 100 feet long and 30 feet high, and the "King's Chamber," containing an empty sarcophagus. It is thought that it originally contained a mummy, rifled by tomb robbers who surmounted the granite plugs, false passages and other precautions of the pyramid builders.

Occult speculations regarding the Great Pyramid have arisen mainly around its construction, dimensions, and possible use. It is certainly a remarkable engineering feat, and it has been suggested that it could have been achieved only by supernormal techniques, such as levitating the great blocks of stone by mysterious occult force. However, tomb paintings, tool marks on stone, and quarry workings suggest more conventional technology.

Ruins found near the pyramid are thought to have been the barracks for about 4,000 skilled workmen. The heavy work could have been done by conscripted labor, as depicted on other tomb paintings. One such painting depicts about 172 men shifting a sixty-ton statue. The stones were probably moved on sleds and by barges and rafts. Earthen mounds may have surrounded the pyramid in the course of construction, with ramps for elevating the stones.

Pyramidology, the attempt to impose metaphysical and cosmological meaning upon the Great Pyramid, dates back to the 1830s, after Colonel Howard Vyse blasted a way inside and took measurements. The British mathematician John Taylor and Scottish astronomer Charles Piazza Smyth claimed that the pyramid embodied divine revelations and prophecy, calculated from its measurements, assuming a unit of a "pyramid inch" which was later the Anglo-Saxon inch. After Smyth pyramidology became the domain of British Israelites (who tried to prove that contemporary Anglo-Saxons were the descendants of the fables ten lost tribes of Israel) and various conservative Christians who looked to the pyramid to verify biblical speculations concerning the end of the world.

For example, by considering the inch a symbol for a year, the internal structures of the pyramid are calculated to indicate the important dates of the world's past and present history. This involves identifying the pyramid itself with biblical versions of history, such as the traditional view that the world was created about 4,004 B.C.E., duly verified by pyramid measurements, that also showed that the Second Coming of Christ was due in 1881. When this prophecy was not fulfilled, pyramidologists revised their calculations to produce a score of other dates.

It was from Smyth's calculations that Charles Taze Russell, founder of International Bible Students Association, the precursor of what today is known as the **Jehovah's Witnesses,** based his own prophecy of the Second Coming of Christ. The Edgar brothers, Scottish Bible students produced a massive two volume work on pyramidology beginning with Russell's early writings.

However, the majority of pyramidology texts were put to use by the British Israelites, and the decline of British Israelism that had followed the dismantling of the British Empire had manifested in a marked reduction of interest in pyramidology in the last half of the twentieth century. Among the last noteworthy attempts at selling pyramidology was one made by the

Institute of Pyramidology. Adam Rutherford founded the institute in London, England, in 1940, and it became an international body a year later with the launching of *Pyramidology Magazine*, with special emphasis on "Divine Revelation" and prophecies. The Institute for Pyramidology is located at 108 Broad St., Chesham, Bucks. HP5 3ED, England.

Occult speculations on the Great Pyramid have been varied and somewhat disjuncted. For example, in the 1880s, **Ignatius Donnelly** had suggested that the Great Pyramid had been built by the descendants of the Atlanteans. That idea was picked up in the 1920s by **Manly Palmer Hall** who went one to suggest that they were the focus of the ancient Egyptian wisdom schools. **Edgar Cayce** built upon Hall's speculations.

Through this century, other writers have suggested that the plan of the Great Pyramid and its internal structures may have embodied a mystical symbolism of the journey of the soul, as described in the Egyptian *Book of the Dead* (Papyrus of Ani). It is also not unlikely that the north-south orientation of the pyramid and the nature of its dimensions reveal astronomical and geometrical knowledge of a high order. It seems clear that the Egyptians were aware of the mathematical radio of *pi*.

During the last generation, widespread publicity has been given to two interesting speculations about pyramids. The first was proposed by Erich von Däniken who, drawing upon popular ignorance about the broad findings of Egyptology, suggested that the pyramids had been built by extraterrestrials. Through the asking of rhetorical questions, he proposed a system by which the space visitors used anti-gravity devices to lift the very heavy block from which the structures were built. He failed to account for numerous other observations as to why the pyramids did not embody any modern technology or advanced architectural discoveries, not even the Roman arch. His speculations where soon put to rest and remain the property of a small circle of followers.

Pyramid Energy

The second set of speculations concerning pyramids have centered upon the possible existence of an unknown energy concentrated in pyramidical structures. Pyramid energy was rediscovered in the early 1970s after it was introduced in the popular best-selling *Psychic Discoveries behind the Iron Curtain* by journalists Sheila Ostrander and Lynn Schroeder. They described their experience with a Czech radio engineer, Karl Drbal, who had taken out a patent on a pyramid razor blade sharpener. The idea was picked up by **New Age** writer Lyll Wat and then a host of others including Peter Toth, Greg Nielsen, and Pat Flanagan. Through the 1970s, it was a common theme at psychic and New Age gatherings.

The idea of pyramid energy goes back to the 1920s. As early as 1928, at Lyons, a 33-year old Frenchman named Georges Gaillard demonstrated the ability to mummify two mutton chops by holding them in his hands for a minute. The French radiesthetist Antoine Bovis reported that meat, eggs and other organic substances could be mummified by placing them in a cardboard model of the Great Pyramid, which he claimed accumulated the same radiations as the King's chamber of the pyramid. It was Bovis's claims which were later picked up by Karl Drbal.

In 1950, at the Scientific and Technical Congress of Radionics and Radiesthesia, held in London, England, Noel Macbeth claimed that a cardboard model pyramid could mummify organic substances such as an egg and that this energy was connected with that radiated by the hands of gifted human healers. Such claims had also been made in Britain during World War II, when there was a shortage of razor blades.

Through the 1970s into the 1980s, experimentation with pyramids was one of the prominent New Age fads. For the most serious, pyramid tents and energy generators are marketed by Pyramid Products of Glendale, California. Interest in pyramids faded through the 1970s and exists in the mid 1990s as a mere shadow of its peak in the 70s.

In spite of all of the claims made for pyramids, from sharpening razors to the beneficial effects on the health of the persons sitting in one of the larger models, to date no scientific study has validated the reality of pyramid energy and the evidence of its effectiveness remains entirely anecdotal.

Sources:

Clark, Jerome. "Life in a Pyramid." *Fate* 36, no. 6 (June 1983): 38–44.

Davidson, David. *The Great Pyramid: Its Divine Message.* London, 1924.

De Camp, L. Sprague. *The Ancient Engineers.* Garden City, N.Y.: Doubleday, 1960. Reprint, New York: Ballantine Books, 1974.

Ostrander, Sheila, and Lynn Shroeder. *Psychic Discoveries Behind the Iron Curtain.* Englewood Cliffs, N.J.: Prentice Hall, Inc., 1970.

Smyth, Charles Piazzi. *Our Inheritance in the Great Pyramid.* London, 1864.

Stewart, Basil. *The Mystery of the Great Pyramid: Traditions Concerning It and Its Connection with the Egyptian Book of the Dead.* London, 1929.

Tompkins, Peter. *Mysteries of the Mexican Pyramids.* New York: Harper & Row, 1976.

———. *Secrets of the Great Pyramid.* New York: Harper & Row, 1971.

Toth, Max, and Greg Nielsen. *Pyramid Power.* London: Freeway, 1974. Reprint, New York: Warner Books, 1976.

Watson, Lyall. *Supernature.* Garden City, N.Y.: Anchor Press, 1973.

Pyromancy

Divination by fire, already alluded to in **extispicy.** The presage was good when the flame was vigorous and quickly consumed the sacrifice; when it was clear of all smoke, transparent, neither red nor dark in color; and when it did not crackle, but burnt silently in a pyramidal form. On the contrary, if it was difficult to kindle, if the wind disturbed it, or if it was slow to consume the victim, the presage was evil.

Besides the sacrificial fire, the ancients divined by observing the flames of torches and even by throwing powdered pitch into a fire; if it caught quickly, the omen was good. The flame of a torch was good if it formed one point, bad if it divided into two; but three was a better omen than one. Sickness for the healthy, and death for the sick, was foreshadowed by the bending of the flame and some frightful disaster by its sudden extinction.

The vestal virgins in the Temple of Minerva at Athens were charged to make particular observations on the light perpetually burning there.

Pyroscopy

A branch of **pyromancy** (**divination** by fire), based on the burn stains left on a light surface after burning a sheet of paper on it.

Q

The Q Directory

British directory published in London of **occult,** pagan, and **New Age** groups, services, and publications that appeared periodically from 1977 through the early 1980s. It was superseded by the **Quest List of Esoteric Sources.**

Sources:

The Q Directory. London: Aquariana, 1978–79. Rev. ed. London: Pallas Aquariana, 1980–81.

Qi

Qi is the Chinese name for the vital energy that undergirds the universe, analogous to the Indian **prana.** Its literal translation is "gas" and hence is similar to the Hebrew concept of spirit which is associated with breath. In **China,** qi is usually thought of as *yaunqi,* the original vital energy. Qi is the energy that flows through the body and is the subject of treatment in **acupuncture** and acupressure. Blockage of the flow of qi is the source of disease and the free natural flow of qi is the underpinning basis of health. The flow of qi, it is believed, can be stimulated by the practice of a series of exercises called **qigong.** Teaching about qi reaches into ancient China and much of the traditional Chinese understanding of the universe is based upon a belief in its existence. It is integral to Chinese medicine, including the understanding of the power of herbs, and basic to a vital sexual life.

Common throughout China were a wide range of practices designed to raise qi and hence invigorate the body and serve as a system of preventive medicine. These wide-ranging techniques are generally grouped under the name qigong, and include practices known elsewhere as **meditation** and exercise. Some form of qigong was integrated into Chinese religious practices, especially Buddhism and **Taoism.**

Working with qi was greatly affected by the Chinese Revolution in the mid-twentieth century, and especially during the brief period known as the Cultural Revolution. Religious institutions and practices were heavily suppressed and the secret books that held the teachings on qi were either destroyed or placed in government archives. Following the Cultural Revolution, Deng Xiao Peng went about rebuilding China's past, but in the light of the Communist present. Most importantly, he promoted traditional Chinese medicinal practice and the revival of qigong. In the meantime, people knowledgeable of qi migrated to the West and began to talk openly about traditional Chinese practices, thus creating a demand from the West for more information. The flow of material on qi began with President Nixon's trip to China in 1972 and the American government's support for a new scientific look at acupuncture. Acupuncture has subsequently become a popular alternative medical practice, though its use by Western physicians remains limited.

In China in the 1980s and 1990s, extensive experimentation has proceeded aimed at gathering scientific data on the existence and beneficent effects of qi. These experiments parallel Western attempts to measure the effects of spiritual/psychic healing. Using the EEG and related instruments, Chinese scientists believe that they have documented the existence of qi and in a wide range of experiments have documented the power of qi in the treatment of different diseases. It has, for example, appeared helpful in curing cancer in experiments involving the progress of carcinoma cells and leukemia in mice. These experiments are now being offered to Western scientists for duplication and verification.

Meanwhile, the promotion of qigong among the population has proved a two-edged sword for the Chinese. In the late 1990s, it was discovered that qigong had become the basis of the creation of new unofficial religious groups built around the mental and spiritual effects of the experience of qi. The most successful, a Buddhist movement named **Falun Gong,** now has followers in the millions and has become very popular in many countries with Chinese expatriate communities. In 1998, the Chinese government began an effort to suppress the movement in China.

Sources:

He, Hong-Zhen, et al. "A 'Stress Meter' Asesssment of the Degree of Relaxation in Qigong vs. Non-Qigong Meditation." *Frontier Perspectives* 8, no.1 (Spring 1999): 37–42.

Lee, Richard E. *Scientific Investigations in Chinese Qigong.* San Clemente, Calif.: China Healthways Institute, 1999.

Peisheng, Wang, and Chen Guanhua. *Relax and Calming Qigong.* Hong Kong: Peace Book Co., 1986.

Qigong

Qigong is an ancient Chinese practice believed to invigorate the body and bring health and well-being. It is based upon the belief in the existence of **qi,** also called ki or ch'i, the universal energy that undergirds the cosmos. The practice of qigong is related to **acupuncture,** the ancient form of medicine also based upon the flow of energy through the body. Acupuncture has mapped a series of channels or meridians that exist as part of the subtle anatomy of the body. If these meridians are blocked, the qi cannot flow freely, and ill health results.

Qigong has been practiced for millenia in China and has been exported to surrounding countries. It is intimately associated with Taoism, though it also freely mixes with Buddhism. Through the centuries, the practice was kept from the general public and its secrets passed orally from teacher to master, and through various families. Very few books were written prior to the 1950s and those were closely guarded in private monastic libraries. The changes accompanying the Chinese Revolution of 1948 forced qigong into the open.

Maoist leaders moved against the monasteries and forebade many traditional practices. Within China, the secret qigong texts were largely destroyed or confiscated and buried in government libraries. However, a few qigong masters left China and some texts were smuggled out of the country. Over the next decades, these masters resurfaced and began to teach qigong openly. Also, the first Western books on the practice were published. In the meantime, China went through a generation of intensive change, culminating in the Cultural Revolution, that attempted to cut the people's ties with a large part of their religious and cultural heritage, and to eradicate what were seen as non-Chinese and particularly Western intrusions. In the wake of the Cultural Revolution, under Deng Xiao Peng, a reevaluation of the tradition began and limited reemergence of various practices was encouraged and allowed.

The recovery of Chinese medicine in general led to the encouragement of qigong practice and hundreds of qigong groups appeared. The government also encouraged the formation of a national association of qigong groups which most joined, and as the benefits were documented, further encouragement of the practice came forth. Qigong was included, for example, in the training of fighter pilots, as it appeared to improve their reflexes. In the 1980s, a number of studies attempting to provide modern scientific underpinnings to the practices of qigong, especially documenting the existence of qi, were initiated. Qigong practitioners became guinea pigs for such research, which was similar to research done on spiritual healing in the West.

Qigong and Religion

Qigong practice had primarily been the special property of Taoist and Buddhist monasteries prior to the Chinese Revolution. When it resurfaced, inevitably the religious connections were present, in spite of efforts to keep the practice in a secular context. The existence of such a mysterious invisible force as qi is in itself encouragement to many to assume a spiritual explanation. At the same time, the Chinese government has given some limited space for the revival of religion, as long as it is kept within the confines of the several national religious organizations; there is one national Buddhist federation and one national Taoist federation.

In the mid-1990s, various popular qigong groups emerged apart from the national gigong federation. One, the Fakun Gong, operated in a Buddhist context and offered the peculiar form of qigong as taught by its Master Hongzi Lee as the superior form of qigong and as leading to a Buddhist-like enlightenment. Thus it existed as both unofficial religion and unofficial qigong. In 1999, in the midst of a nationwide crackdown on unoffical religion, the Chinese government began a systematic suppression of **Falun Gong** that has brought the country under the scrutiny of human rights groups around the world. By the end of 1999, a second group, **Zhong Gong,** was also under attack. Both groups were charged with practicing medicine without proper training and causing the death of people who used qigong in the place of modern medicine. There is little evidence to support these charges.

Sources:

Lee, Richard E. *Scientific Investigations in Chinese Qigong*. San Clemente, Calif.: China Healthways Institute, 1999.

Peisheng, Wang, and Chen Guanhua. *Relax and Calming Qigong*. Hong Kong: Peace Book Co., 1986.

Qi Magazine

Qi Magazine is a newsstand periodical launched in the mid-1990s to cover the world of **qigong** and inform the English-speaking world of the spectrum of practice and thought being offered by various master practitioners in the West. Qigong is the collective name of a number of exercise systems that emerged through the centuries in China. On one end of the spectrum, hard qigong, designed to build the body, grades into Tai Chi and the martial arts. On the other end, soft qigong, designed to relax the body and improve health, fades into **acupuncture** and the practice of Chinese medicine.

Each issue of *Qi Magazine* is built around a number of short feature articles that provide insight from the wisdom of one of the more notable qigong masters, introduce an element of basic practice, or discuss the value of a form of Chinese medicine. Many of these are illustrated with detailed diagrams of the body or of the movements being discussed. There is a large letters-to-the-editor column in which readers are invited into a lively dialog with the editorial staff. In addition, the e-mail address of most writers for the magazine is given so that readers may respond to their articles immediately and directly. A selection of both Eastern and Western authors also write regular columns.

Qi Magazine is published by the Tse Qigong Centre in suburban Seattle, Washington. Its editor, Michael Tse, authors much of the content of each issue as well as translating material from the Chinese for inclusion. The Tse Qigong Centre offers a full range of student training, extension classes in New York and London, and teacher training and certification. *Qi Magazine* appears bimonthly. Address: P.O. Box 2697, Kirkland, WA 98083. Website: http://www.qimagazine.com/.

Sources:

Qi Magazine. Kirkland, Wash., n.d.

Quaesitor (Organization)

A British human potentials center, modeled on the **Esalen Institute.** It was concerned with such subjects as **meditation** and body-mind relationships. The word *quaesitor* means seeker, and the organization's workshops, courses, and sessions "are to explore this longing, to give us insight into how our lives can become more rich and more fulfilling." Last known address: Quaesitor II, Top Flat, 17 Hornsey Lane Gardens, London, N6 5NX, England.

Quest List of Esoteric Sources (Directory)

Comprehensive directory of British groups, societies, and courses, and publications and suppliers in the occult, neopagan, and mystical fields that appeared in 1984. It was compiled and edited by Marian Green, one of the leading neopagans in Great Britain and named after her neo-pagan organization and periodical. It superseded the **Q Directory,** which had appeared in several editions beginning in 1977. Quest still exists but no recent editions of the directory have appeared.

Sources:

Green, Marian, ed. *Quest List of Esoteric Sources*. London: Quest, 1984.

The Quest Society

An offshoot of the **Theosophical Society,** founded by scholar **G. R. S. Mead** (1863–1933), who had been secretary to **Helena Petrovna Blavatsky** and general secretary of the Theosophical Society. He resigned (in company with some 700 other members) in protest over the scandals concerning **C. W. Leadbeater**'s love of young boys.

In March 1909, Mead founded the Quest Society as a group of sincere seekers after spiritual wisdom without any taint of charlatanism. The objects were "to promote investigation and comparative study of religion, philosophy and science on the basis of experience; to encourage the expression of the ideal in beautiful form." For 21 years (1909–30), the society published a quarterly journal, *The Quest,* edited by Mead and with an extremely high standard of contributions. The society faded away after the death of Mead in 1933.

Quigley, Joan (1927–)

San Francisco astrologer who claims that her astrological advice had "absolute control" over the movements, and influenced the decisions, of former United States president Ronald Reagan. She was born April 10, 1927. Her secret role as an astrological influence at the White House was referred to by Donald Regan, former chief of staff to Ronald Reagan, who was quite critical of Nancy Reagan's influence on decisions made by the president. Regan's remarks caused a major controversy that eventually led to the complete revelation of the name and role of Nancy Reagan's astrologer.

In her book, *What Does Joan Say? My Seven Years as White House Astrologer to Nancy and Ronald Reagan* (1990), Quigley made far-reaching claims. She advised Nancy Reagan from 1981 through 1989 and is sure that her astrological advice decided the timing of key political events, including speeches, televised campaign debates, the signing of arms control treaties, and even the dates for Ronald Reagan's cancer surgery and the announcement that he would run for a second term. Quigley claims that Air Force One would only take off if she reported a favorable alignment of the planets and that she sometimes also gave the president and his wife political advice.

Quigley states, "I was responsible for timing all press conferences, most speeches, the State of the Union addresses, the take-offs and landing of Air Force One. . . . I picked the time of Ronald Reagan's debate with Carter and the two debates with Walter Mondale, all extended trips abroad, as well as the shorter trips and one-day excursions, the announcement that Reagan would run for a second term, and briefings for all the summits except Moscow." Quigley also claims credit for influencing the president's favorable view of the Soviet leader Gorbachev, whose astrological chart indicated a genuine reformer.

The title of Quigley's book derives from the period in late 1986 when the Iran-Contra scandal broke. She claims that the president asked "What does Joan say?" and that her advice was to stay in the White House and say nothing, because his stars were bad and she feared another assassination attempt.

Although the revelations of astrological influence on a modern leader's actions and decisions may seem bizarre to Western people, it is my no means unusual in Eastern countries. **Astrology** plays a significant part in the life of people in India, and marriages, dates of important meetings, dedication of temples, and other decisions normally involve the services of an astrologer for millions of Indians in all walks of life, including politics.

Sources:

Quigley, Joan. *What Does Joan Say? My Seven Years as White House Astrologer to Nancy and Ronald Reagan.* New York: Birch Lane Press, 1990.

Reagan, Nancy. *My Turn: The Memoirs of Nancy Reagan.* New York: Random House, 1989.

Regan, Donald. *For the Record.* San Diego: Harcourt Brace Jovanovich, 1988.

Quimby, Phineas P(arkhurst) (1802–1866)

An early influential exponent of **Mind Cure,** later known as **New Thought.** Born February 16, 1802 in Lebanon, New Hampshire, he became a clockmaker before becoming interested in **Mesmerism** in 1838. He had great success in treating patients but eventually developed his own system based on mental influence. He practiced in Portland, Maine, from 1859 on, treating some 12,000 individuals during seven years.

Several of Quimby students, such as Warren Felt Evans (1817–1899), went on to pursue careers that built on Quimby's insights. Another student, **Marry Baker Eddy** (1821–1910), dropped Quimby's approach and developed her own system of spiritual healing which she termed **Christian Science.** One of Eddy's students, **Emma Curtis Hopkins** (1849–1925), brought a number of Eddy's former students together and created the New Thought Movement.

Quimby died January 16, 1866.

Sources:

Quimby, Phineas P. *The Complete Writings.* Edited by Ervin Seale. 3 vols. Marina del Rey, Calif.: DeVorss & Co., 1987.

———. *The Quimby Manuscripts.* Edited by Horatio Dresser. New York: Thomas Y. Crowell, 1919. Reprint, New York: Julian Press. 1961.

The Quincey P. Morris Dracula Society

Defunct **vampire** interest group in the United States. It was named for the most obscure of the major characters in the novel *Dracula,* the one most often written out of the story in Dracula plays and movies. The society issued a quarterly newsletter called *Transfusion.*

Quincunx

An **astrology** term denoting planets at a distance of five signs of 150 degrees from each other. The term was once generally used to denote a disposition of five objects (especially plants or trees) placed so that there is one in each corner of a square or rectangle with the fifth in the center. The use of the quincunx in various aspects throughout history was exhaustively discussed by the English physician and author **Sir Thomas Browne** (1605–1682) in his book *The Garden of Cyrus* (1658).

Quirinus (or Quirus)

A fabled precious stone, described as "a juggling stone, found in the nest of the hoopoo" (hoopoe bird). If laid on the chest of a sleeping person, it "forces him to discover his rogueries." The word quirinus is also used to describe the third of the ancient gods (after Jupiter and Mars).

Qvarnstrom, S(ven) Birger (1897– ?)

Swedish teacher and journalist active in the field of parapsychology. He was born on June 22, 1897, at Vissefjärda, Kalmer län, Sweden. He studied at University of Lund and later held positions as an instructor in languages and political economics at colleges in the Swedish cities of Hälsingborg, Eskilstuna, Malmö, Orebro, and Norrköping.

He contributed to a number of Swedish newspapers as a columnist and literary critic, and as a member of the Swedish Society for Psychical Research he spent some years investigating psychic phenomena such as clairvoyance, telekinesis, and precognition.

Sources:

Qvarnstrom, S. Birger. *Parapskologi Resultat och Perspecktiv* (Parapsychology—Results and Perspectives). N.p., 1959.

R

Radcliffe, Maud Elizabeth Furse (Lady Gorell) (d. 1954)

In December 1980, an auction sale at Sotheby's, London, included a batch of over thirty letters to Bessie (Elizabeth) Radcliffe from poet **William Butler Yeats,** revealing that Radcliffe had acted as a Spiritualist medium for **automatic writing** during the occult researches of Yeats.

Radcliffe had been introduced to Yeats in the summer of 1913, possibly through Eva Fowler, friend of Olivia and Dorothy Shakespear and of Ezra Pound. The mediumship continued for some four years until Yeats married Georgie Hyde-Lees in 1917, after which his wife acted as his medium. Before his marriage, Yeats had initiated Georgie into the Stella Matutina temple of the Hermetic Order of the **Golden Dawn** occult society.

Radcliffe's mediumistic activities remained through her lifetime. In 1922, she married Ronald Gorell Barnes, 3rd Baron Gorell (1884–1963); they had two sons and a daughter. Baron Gorell, C.B.E., O.B.E., had a distinguished military career, was deputy director of staff duties (Education) at the War Office (1918–20), and later served as Under-Secretary of State for Air (July 1921–October 1922). He was also the president of various societies, editor of *Cornhill Magazine* (1933–39), and the author of multiple volumes of poetry, fact, fiction, and religion.

The correspondence from Yeats sold at a Sotheby sale revealed that Radcliffe's mediumship had a profound influence on the poet, and in one letter he stated that her script "contained the most important evidence of the most important problem of the world" and in others: "I can never make known to you my profound gratitude. You have changed most things for me and I know not how far that change will go. A year ago your spirits saved me from serious error in a crisis of life."

Radha, Swami Sivananda (1911–1995)

Founder and spiritual leader of **Yasodhara Ashram,** Kootenay Bay, British Columbia, Canada. Swami Radha (born Ursula Sylvia Hellman) was born March 20, 1911, in Germany and demonstrated psychic ability when only a child. She was widowed twice during World War II and emigrated to Canada, in an effort to forget the horrors of the Nazi regime.

Hellman felt a strong urge for spiritual fulfillment, and during meditation she had a vision of a Hindu sage. A few days later, while looking at books in a Montreal store, she saw a photograph of the Hindu sage she had seen in meditation. His name was **Swami Sivananda Saraswati,** a famous yogi with an ashram at Rishikesh, India, in the foothills of the Himalayas.

Hellman wrote to Swami Sivananda and received a reply asking her to "come home" to India. With some considerable sacrifices, she finished up her job and traveled to Rishikesh, where she received intensive training in Hinduism and the integral yoga system taught by Sivananda. In January 1956, she was initiated as a renunciate (sannyasi) by Swami Sivananda and instructed to carry his spiritual message to the West. At that period, women swamis, particularly Westerners, were rare, and the prospect of returning to Canada without income was a daunting one, but with faith in her guru, Swami Radha returned to Canada. Slowly a society grew around her to spread **yoga** teachings of the spiritual life.

The Sivananda Ashram was originally founded at South Burnaby, Vancouver, British Columbia, but later moved to Kootenay Bay, British Columbia. While searching for a possible site in this area, Swami Radha found an ideal setting by the side of a lake, officially listed since 1897 as "Yasodhara." It was a good omen, since in Hinduism Yasoda is the foster-mother of Shree Krishna, an incarnation of God.

Under the name Yasodhara Ashram, the society occupied an 83-acre site with a lake, forests, and mountains, reminiscent of the foothills of India. Several acres have been cleared, and the ashram premises include residential buildings, a guest lodge, prayer room, print shop, bookstore, office, recording studio, and a Temple of All Faiths. Various workshop programs and courses are given in yoga and the spiritual teachings of East and West. There are no religious limitations, as the aim of the ashram is to integrate the spiritual ideals and practices of all major religions.

As spiritual director, Radha took steps to avoid a personality cult growing up around her and allowed no pictures of herself or of Sivananda in the prayer rooms. Instead, the basic spiritual light of different religions was emphasized by their traditional symbols. Besides her many books, Radha was responsible for issuing various recordings, including her teachings, which were available on *Divine Light Invocation* and *Mantras: Songs of Yoga,* published by Ashram Records.

Radha died November 30, 1995.

Sources:

Radha, Swami Sivananda. *Gods Who Walk the Rainbow.* Porthill, Idaho: Timeless Books, 1981.

———. *Hatha Yoga, Hidden Language.* Porthill, Idaho: Timeless Books, 1987.

———. *Kundalini Yoga for the West.* Spokane, Wash.: Timeless Books, 1978.

———. *Mantras, Words of Power.* Porthill, Idaho: Timeless Books, 1980.

———. *Radha, Diary of a Woman's Search.* Porthill, Idaho: Timeless Books, 1981.

Radhasoami Satsang

An Indian spiritual movement, also known as *Sat May* (the way of the Saints), that emerged in the nineteenth century in northern India. It is one of the most important but least known of Indian religious movements, its teachers often being cited as either Hindus or Sikhs. The movement was founded in 1861 by Shiv Dayal Singh (1818–1878) of Agra, but had its base in the earlier teachings of Tulsi Singh who taught through the first four decades of the century. Known as "Soamiji Maharaj" by his disciples, he taught three basic principles of religious life: 1) *Satguru,* a term embracing the Absolute Lord and living human Master; 2) *Shabd* or sound current (spoken or written expression, and also inner spiritual sound); and 3) *Satsang,* association of devotees seeking spiritual truth.

Although drawing on Sikhism, Radhasoami had discarded the Sikh bible, the *Adi Granth,* in favor of a living Master Teacher (the Satguru). It has also elevated the yoga of the sound current to a preeminent position. The Satguru (or his appointed representative) initiates people into the practice. Members also gather in community, satsang, much as do Christians.

After Soamiji Maharaj passed away, he was succeeded by Rai Salig Ram, and in turn by Pandit Brahma Shankar Misra in 1907. After the passing of Brahma Shankar Misra, questions over the succession led to a division of the movement under two competing gurus: Sri Kamta Prasad Sinha (known as "Param Guru Sarkar Sahib") and Buaji Maharaj, sister of Brahma Shankar Misra. Further divisions occurred throughout the twentieth century as different rival leaders emerged claiming a succession. Among the different Stagurus who have appeared in America seeking followers are Kirpal Singh, Guru Maharaj Ji, and Ajaib Singh. **ECKANKAR** and the several groups that have developed from it are Westernized groups based on Radhasommi teachings but without the Punjabi appearance of its leaders.

The two groups within the larger movement became known as the Radhasoami Satsang, Beas, and the **Ruhani Satsang,** both descended from the founder Shiv Dayal Singh through Baba Jaimal Singh, whose satsang was based at Beas, Punjab.

Baba Jaimal Singh passed away in 1903 and was succeeded by his disciple Sawan Singh (1858–1948). Sawan Singh had a profound influence in the spread of teachings relating to *Shabd-Yoga,* the pathway of sacred sound current. On the passing of Sawan Singh, he was succeeded by his grandson Charan Singh (b. 1916). Some disciples challenged Charan Singh's leadership and began alternative movements. Amongst these was Kirpal Singh, who established the Ruhani Satsang in Delhi. Charan Singh initiated many thousands of people and the Beas groups expanded remarkably under his leadership. Kirpal Singh began the Ruhani Stasang in 1951 and in 1955 made the first of several trips to the west. An energetic leader, his movement spread around India, and because of his periodic present, his movement grew in North America. Paul Twitchell (founder of ECKANKAR) was disciple of Kirpal Singh and left to found a movement which kept all of the substance of the tradition but had a new terminology and a Western facade. From ECKANKAR came the Movement of Spiritual Inner Awareness (MSIA) founded by John-Roger Hinkins; MasterPath founded by Gary Olsen; and the Ancient Teachings of the masters founded by Darwin Gross. The Divine Light Mission (now known as Elan Vital), brought to the West by Guru Maharaj Ji in the early 1970s, represents a new infusion of an Indian-based Radhasoami lineage.

The teaching that a mystical sound current heard in meditation may bring about higher consciousness is central to Radhasoami beliefs and also had been an important part of the **meditation** techniques of traditional yoga practice, though it was a rare practice by the time of the career of Tulsi Singh. It was cited in such yoga manuals as the *Hatha-Yoga-Pradipika* of Svatmarama Svamin and the *Siva Samhita.* It is also loosely related to the special significance attached to the sacred trisyllable AUM in the Hindu Vedanta.

The main address of Radhasoami Satsang is: P.O. Dera Baba Jaimal Singh, Via Beas, Dist. Amritsar, India.

Sources:

Cameron, David. *Who Is Guru Maharaj Ji?* New York: Ballantine Books, 1973.

Fripp, Peter. *The Mystic Philosophy of Sant Mat.* London: Neville Spearman, 1964.

Lane, David Christopher. *The Making of a Spiritual Movement.* Del Mar, Calif.: Del Mar Press, 1983.

———. *The Radhasoami Tradition: A Critical History of Guru Successorship.* New York: Garland Publishing, 1992.

Radhasoami Satsang Beas and its Teachings. Beas, India: Radha Soami Satsang, n.d.

Singh, Charan. *Light on San Mat.* Beas, India: Radha Soami Satsang, Beas, 1958.

Radiant School of Seekers and Servers

The Radiant School of Seekers and Servers was one of a number of occult groups drawn to **Mount Shasta,** the prominent mountain in northern California. Founded by Kenneth Wheeler in 1963, the original small group moved some years later to the village of Mount Shasta, at the base of the mountain. The school was a **channeling** group through whom "Phylos the Tibetan" spoke. "Phylos" is a disembodied entity who is claimed to have first spoken in the 1890s through Frederick Spencer Oliver. These channelings were collected and published in a book, *A Dweller on Two Planets* (1899). A second volume reported to be by "Phylos" appeared in 1940 as *An Earth Dweller Returns* and was channeled through one of the founders of the **Lemurian Fellowship.** In the 1960s "Phylos" began to speak again, and the material became the basis of the regular mailings sent to the supporters of the Radiant School.

The school taught a message of personal development in line with humanity's ultimate life pattern, which in turn is in line with God's universal plan. All people are expected to unfold their patterns in full. During our various lives on Earth, we are allowed to meet again all those we have previously interfered with and thus created karma (consequences). The divine plan assumes the right to health, happiness, and prosperity.

The school existed for several decades but disbanded in the early 1980s.

Sources:

Van Valer, Nola. *My Meeting with the Masters of Mount Shasta.* Mount Shasta, Calif.: Radiant School, 1982.

Radiesthesia

A development of the art of **dowsing** (water witching) which extends the specific use of indicators such as rod and pendulum form water finding, to various additional uses such as the tracing of missing persons, treasure hunting, and/or the diagnosis and treatment of disease. The term *radiesthésie* was coined in 1930 by the Abbé Bouly, in France, where the use of a pendulum has largely replaced the divining rod. L'Association des Amis de la Radiesthésie was founded in 1930 and the **British Society of Dowsers** in 1933. International Congresses of Radiesthesia are held regularly in Europe. The terms "dowsing" and "radiesthesia" have become virtually synonymous, and in France "radiesthésie" is used to include all forms of dowsing.

The dowser or radiesthetist is an individual who is sensitive (and often unconsciously so) to hidden objects or other information and uses a simple indicator, primarily a **dowsing rod** or **pendulum,** to amplify this sensitivity. It is still not entirely clear if, or just what kind of, radiation might be involved, and many investigators believe the individual to be rather like a psychic medium, and certainly some of the special applications of radiesthesia seem nearer to **ESP** than conventional physics.

The pendulum is usually a small ball attached to a thread on the end of a short stick. It is best to use a nonspun thread or thin nylon since the twist in a thread may communicate extraneous movement to the pendulum bob. The stick is held just above its connection with the thread and the pendulum bob tends to gyrate or oscillate. The length of the thread can be adjusted by winding it round the stick, so that the pendulum movement is clearly visible. There are characteristic pendulum movements relating to various substances, indicated by the number of gyrations and whether their movement is clockwise or counterclockwise. Like the dowsing rod, the pendulum also seems to be drawn toward hidden objects.

The pendulum is often used to diagnose disease conditions in the body or indicate remedies. The pendulum is first adjusted over a healthy part of the body. When moved to an unhealthy area its movement changes.

Another use of the pendulum is simply to answer questions put to it, rather in the manner of a **ouija board;** "Yes" is usually indicated by a clockwise gyration and "No" by counterclockwise movement. An even more psychic use of the pendulum is known as "teleradiesthesia" or "superpendulism." Instead of using a pendulum over an actual area in which underground water or minerals are sought, the operator holds the pendulum over a map of the district. Some claim that a subtle link exists between a locality and its symbolic representation on a map. Some teleradiesthetists have also used a map to trace the movements of a missing person.

Some operators use a hollow pendulum that accommodates a sample of the material sought. Others hold something connected with the object of their inquiries in one hand while using the pendulum in the other. Since the indications of a pendulum are subtle and may also be deflected by conscious or unconscious muscular movements, some preliminary study is recommended before practice. There is considerable literature on the subject and various reports of its use.

In the United States, the **American Society of Dowsers,** which encourages the practice of various forms of dowsing and gives guidance and information on the subject, may be contacted at P.O. Box 24, Brainerd St., Danville, VT 05828. In Great Britain, the British Society of Dowsers is concerned with all aspects of dowsing and radiesthesia and publishes a journal. It is located at Sycamore Cottage, Tamley Lane, Hastingleigh, Ashford, Kent, TN25 5HW, England.

Sources:

Beasse, Pierre. *A New and Rational Treatise of Dowsing according to the methods of Physical Radiesthesia.* France, 1941.

Cameron, Verne. *Map Dowsing.* El Carismo, 1971.

Cooper, Irving S., and Willi Kowa. *The Pendulum: Operational Practice and Theory.* Haywards Heath, UK: Academic Publications, 1978.

De France, Henry. *The Elements of Dowsing.* London, 1971.

Franklin, T. Bedford. *Radiations.* London, 1949.

Hitching, Francis. *Pendulum: The Psi Connection.* London: Fontana, 1977.

Nielsen, Greg, and Joseph Polansky. *Pendulum Power: A Mystery You Can See, A Power you Can Feel.* New York: Destiny Books, 1977; Wellingborough, UK: Excalibur, 1981.

Wethered, V. D. *A Radiesthetic Approach to Health and Homeopathy, or Health and the Pendulum.* London, 1950.

Radiesthésie

Radiation-perception, the French word usually transliterated **radiesthesia,** the divining with pendulum or rod.

Radionic Association

Organization formed to promote knowledge and understanding of **radionics** as a method of healing at a distance using a specially designed instrument (the **black box,** originally developed by American physician **Albert Abrams**). The association also encourages use of the faculty of **ESP.**

The association includes a school of radionics, provides professional training, houses a library of relevant literature, and sponsors annual conventions. Publications include *Radionics Quarterly,* pamphlets, and monographs. Address: Baerlein House, Goose Green, Deddington, Banbury, Oxon OX15 0SZ, England.

Radionics

The instrumental detection of hypothesized vital energy patterns as a means of diagnosis and therapy of disease. In radionic theory, all living things radiate an electro-magnetic field which has different characteristics in health and disease conditions. Energy patterns are given a numerical value or "rate" usually calibrated on the dials of a diagnostic apparatus called a **black box.** The original black box, sometimes called the E.R.A. or **Oscilloclast,** was the invention of Dr. **Albert Abrams,** a San Francisco physician.

The black box consisted of several variable rheostats and a thin sheet of rubber mounted over a metal plate. A blood sample from the patient was put into the machine, which was connected with a metal plate placed on the forehead of a healthy person. By tapping on the abdomen of this person, the doctor determined the disease of the patient according to "areas of dullness" in relation to dial readings on the apparatus. This strange procedure brought together the special sensitivities of **radiesthesia** or **dowsing** and medical auscultation.

After the death of Abrams in 1924, his procedures were developed by **Ruth Drown** of the United States in the 1930s and **George De la Warr** in Britain. De la Warr devised black boxes that dispensed with the auscultation techniques of Abrams and even an apparatus which produced photographs relating to the condition of the patient whose sample was placed in the machine. De la Warr claimed that they registered a radiation pattern showing the shape and chemical structure of the radiating body, and given a suitable sample the camera plate would register not only regional tissue but also its pathology.

It should be noted that Abrams was attacked by the American Medical Association, but in England a committee of the British Medical Association gave him some initial approval in 1924. Then in 1950 Drown was given a test under the auspices of the American Medical Association. It was completely negative and had the effect of driving radionics out of the United States. Defenders of radionics have argued that the worth of the diagnostic techniques is based upon the consciousness of the operator, a fact which in itself takes the practice out of the realm of medical science and into the field of parapsychology and spiritual healing.

In England, the De la Warr Laboratories designs and manufactures radionic instruments and offers diagnosis and treatment for patients. It may be contacted at Raleigh Park, Oxford, UK. There is also a Radionic Association in Britain, which trains and represents radionic practitioners, located at Field House, Peaslake, Guildford, Surrey.

In the late 1960s, William A. Tiller, then chairman of the Department of Material Medicine at Stanford University, reported favorably on his experience in 1971. In 1975 an important development in American radionics studies was the U.S. Radionic Congress held in Indianapolis, Indiana, April 19–20, 1975, at which papers on research in the field were presented and discussed. Amongst those present was Thomas G. Hieronymus, regarded as the dean of American radionics researchers, whose patented invention of a machine to analyze a new type of radiation in 1949 led to American interest in radionics under the name **psionics.** Psionic was a term coined by John Campbell, Jr., editor of *Astounding Science Fiction,* to denote a combination of radionics and **psi** phenomena. He gave instructions for building a Hieronymus machine in the June 1956 issue of *ASF.*

Sources:

Abrams, Albert. *New Concepts in Diagnosis and Treatment.* Physico-Clinical, 1924.

Day, Langston & G. De la Warr. *New Worlds Beyond the Atom.* London, 1956.

Inglis, Brian. *The Case for Unorthodox Medicine.* New York: Berkeley Publishing, 1969.

Proceedings of the Scientific and Technical Congress of Radionics and Radiesthesia London May 16–18, 1950, London, n.d.

Tiller, William A. "Radionics, Radiesthesia and Physics." In *The Varieties of Healing Experience.* Palo Alto, Calif.: Academy of Paraspsychology & Medicine, 1971.

Young, James Harvey. *The Medical Messiahs.* Princeton N.J.: Princeton University Press, 1967.

Raelian Movement

A flying saucer religious movement that originated in France in 1973 from the claims of contact with extraterrestrials by former motor-racing journalist Claude Vorilhon. Vorilhon claimed that on December 1, 1973, he encountered a small humanoid being who arrived on Earth in a spacecraft. The entity, addressing him in French, told Vorilhon that he had been chosen to spread a message of love, peace, and fraternity to all people. The substance of their continued contacts was published in 1974 in *The Message Given to Me by Extra-Terrestrials* (originally published in French). Vorilhon was given a new name, Rael, by the extraterrestrials.

According to the space beings, humankind is the product of experiments by an extraterrestrial race, the Elohim (a hebrew term generally translated in the Bible as "God"). In their scientific experiments, the Elohim succeeded in creating life and eventually produced a humanlike creature. Their governmental authorities ordered them to continue their work elsewhere, and Earth was the chosen site.

The Elohim eventually left Earth, but returned in 1973 because of the threats of atomic war. The Elohim, according to Vorilhon, now wish to assist humanity in controlling aggressive urges that threaten the race with total annihilation. They have requested that an embassy be constructed where they can meet with world leaders. The construction of such a meeting place is high on the Raelians' agenda.

Rael organized those who read his book and adhered to his message into a Raelian movement. It is structured hierarchically. Leaders are termed guides, with Rael designated a sixth-level guide. He is assisted by 12 fifth-level guides scattered around the world overseeing the spreading movement. The growth of the movement has been assisted by the translation of Rael's work into some 25 languages. The movement moved into North America through French-speaking Canada in 1976.

American headquarters: P.O. Box 611793, North Miami Beach, FL 33261. Canadian headquarters: P.O. Box 86, Youville Sta., Montreal, PQ, Canada H2P 2V2. International headquarters: CP 225, CH-1411 Geneva 8, Switzerland.

Sources:

Rael [Claude Vorilhon]. *Sensual Meditation.* Tokyo: AOM Corp., 1986.

———. *Space Aliens Took Me to Their Planet.* Liechtenstein: Foundation pour l'Accueil des Elohim, 1978.

———. *Welcome Our Fathers from Space: They Created Humanity in Their Laboratories.* Tokyo: AOM Corp., 1986.

Raffé, W(alter) G(eorge) (1888–ca. 1950)

British writer, lecturer, and designer, who took a special interest in the occult in relation to art and color. He was educated at Halifax Technical College, Leeds College of Art, and the Royal College of Art, South Kensington, England. He was art director of the Northern Polytechnic, London (1919–21); principal, Lucknow School of Art, India (1921–23); and lecturer to the London County Council (1925), before a lengthy career as an independent writer and designer. He contributed to many periodicals dealing with arts, crafts, color, psychology of art, and occultism.

Sources:

Raffé, W. G. *Art and Labour.* N.p., 1927.

———. *The Control of the Mind.* N.p., 1934.

———. *Graphic Design.* London: Chapman and Hall, Ltd., 1927.

———. *Poems in Black & White.* N.p., 1922.

Ragnarok

A term meaning "rain of dust," derived from an ancient Scandinavian legend of a titanic conflict between gods and giants. It was also the title of a book by the Minnesota congressman and senator **Ignatius Donnelly** (1831–1901). More than a century before **Immanuel Velikovsky**'s bestselling *Worlds in Collision,* Donnelly's book speculates that a comet passed close to or struck the earth in ancient times, causing cataclysmic changes dimly remembered in mythologies and scripture history.

Donnelly was an original thinker, and although some of his ideas may not stand up to modern scientific scrutiny, the theme of catatrophism has remained a persistent if minority opinion in contemporary science.

Sources:

Donnelly, Ignatius. *Ragnarok: the Age of Fire and Gravel.* 1883. Reprint, New Hyde Park, N.Y.: University Books, 1970.

Rahu

According to Hindu mythology, Rahu is a demon who swallows the sun and moon. He is the cause of eclipses, and Rahu and Ketu are the ascending and descending nodes in Hindu astronomy.

Rajneesh (Journal)

A publication formerly issued by the Shree Rajneesh Ashram located in Poona, India. It contained lectures by **Bhagwan Shree Rajneesh,** a controversial Spiritual teacher (guru) who expounded an eclectic teaching which combined elements of Sufism, Hinduism, and modern human potentials perspective. Translated into a variety of languages, it tied together the growing international movement through the 1970s.

During the last years of his life, Rajneesh took the name Osho and the Center in Poona became known as Osho Commune International. The worldwide Osho movement is now served by the *Osho International Times.*

Rajneesh, Bhagwan Shree (1931–1990)

Controversial Indian spiritual teacher, known since 1988 within the movement he established as "Osho." From modest beginnings in India, he built up a worldwide following, which experienced a major crisis in 1985 when the community he was building in Oregon fell apart after four years of conflict with residents of the town of Antelope, Oregon, and their allies throughout the state. The disintegration of the center occurred in the midst of scandal surrounding various criminal exploits planned and committed by community leaders, several of whom were later tried and convicted.

Rajneesh was born Mohan Chandra Rajneesh, on December 11, 1931, in Kutchwara, India, with a Jain religious background. At age seven he attended the Gunj School at Gadwara, where he showed great intelligence. He went on to study at Jabalpur University (B.A., 1955) and the University of Saugar (M.A., 1957).

According to those who knew him, he was a fearless child, given to playing pranks and fascinated by the **occult** and **hypnosis.** He was also said to have been obsessed with death and sex. An astrologer had predicted that he might die at age 21. In surviving that year, he was said to have achieved total enlightenment.

He read widely, was an independent thinker, and displayed an original approach to traditional Indian concepts, often at odds with authority. In 1968 he became a traveling lecturer on the theme of the importance and sacredness of sex as a step on the path to higher consciousness. He was greatly impressed with the personality and teachings of **Georgei Gurdjieff,** whose concepts he knew through reading the books of his disciple **Peter D. Ouspensky.** His absorption of Gurdjieff's philosophy affected his style of leadership as a **guru** (teacher). He began to write books as Acharya [Professor] Rajneesh.

Basic to his teachings was a spiritual practice called "dynamic (or chaotic) meditation," said to be especially suitable for Western consciousness and physique. This involved fast intensive breathing, intended to break through tensions and related emotional blocks, followed by a cathartic release of emotional energy (rather like the **latihan** in **Subud**). The Sufi mantra "Hoo" was then shouted intensely, to further raise the energy level, with special effects on the sexual centers of the body. This was followed by a period of absolute stillness and silence, during which a form of meditation ensued.

The concept of emotional tensions rooted in different segments of the body recalls the "muscular armoring" postulated by **Wilhelm Reich,** whose therapeutic techniques also involved intensive breathing to achieve catharsis. The relationship between sexual energy and higher consciousness had been charted in ancient Hindu texts on **kundalini,** but the idea of achieving higher consciousness through unrestrained sexual expression differs somewhat from Hindu **tantric yoga** teachings, which involve disciplined sexual activity under exacting conditions. Rajneesh's teachings, which seemed to offer sanction for unrestrained sexual activity, had a great appeal to Western seekers of Eastern wisdom who were experiencing the freedoms of the modern sexual revolution.

In 1970 Rajneesh established a following in Bombay, where he assumed the title "Bhagwan" (Lord) and was seen by his followers as a spiritually enlightened master. In 1974 he acquired land for an ashram in Poona (southeast of Bombay), which became his headquarters for the rest of the decade. Here Western devotees flocked for a period before returning to their homes to spread the movement worldwide. Rajneesh himself is author of more than a hundred books in Hindu, and almost as many in English (almost all transcripts of the talks he gave over the years). Many have been translated into German, Japanese, Dutch, Italian, French, Spanish, and Portuguese.

Rajneesh retained some aspects of the traditional Hindu *guru-chela* (teacher-pupil) relationship. He termed his devotees *neosannyasins.* Devotees initiated into his movement were required to don the traditional robe of a renunciate (though it was red rather than ocher) and wear a *mala* (rosary necklace). They assumed new spiritual names. Seeing Rajneesh's followers adopt the trappings of the renounced life (sannyas) was greatly offensive to many Hindus, since a renunciate normally renounced sex, wealth, and family ties. The neosannyasins did not renounce ties to the world; rather, they saw themselves entering into a more conscious life. The spectacle of devotees advocating wildly permissive sexual activity while clad in the robes of renunciation, however, seemed a travesty of Hindu religion.

Through the late 1970s there were many complaints from local residents about the activities of the Rajneesh Foundation. A few of the female devotees turned to prostitution in order to make enough money to stay at the ashram. Drugs were forbidden at the ashram, but some devotees succumbed to the temptation of lucrative rewards as drug runners, and several were caught and prosecuted. There were also problems of sexually transmitted diseases, especially herpes, among the promiscuous followers. At one point, a British devotee allegedly made advances to an Indian lady outside the ashram, and enraged local residents attacked the devotees. The Indian authorities questioned the charitable status of the ashram, which had reputedly acquired some $80 million in donations in only a few years, and the ashram accountants were accused of not keeping proper receipts and documentation. The state charity commissioners in Bombay ruled against the ashram, which was pursued for some $4 million in unpaid taxes.

In 1981 Rajneesh astonished and bewildered many of his followers by suddenly leaving the ashram with a handful of key workers who were involved in his secret plans and moving to the United States. Shortly thereafter the ashram was closed and many of the items accumulated there were sold. The Rajneesh Foundation was disbanded, and a new corporation, Rajneesh International, was founded in the United States.

The American Years

A prominent figure in handling Rajneesh's practical affairs was his disciple Ma Anand Sheela (Sheela Ambalal Patel), who had been a key figure in ashram activities since first joining the guru in 1972. She had found the mansion in Montclair, New Jersey, where the guru and his staff first became established in the United States, and she next set about locating a larger site for a more ambitious American ashram community.

In July 1981 she oversaw the purchase of the 64,000-acre Big Muddy Ranch and lands in eastern Oregon, near the village of Antelope, for $5.75 million. Over the next two months, some two hundred devotees settled in, building 50 new houses. Rajneesh himself had arrived in August, ostensibly "on a visit," in order to avoid immigration rules. Plans were made to construct an ashram city on 2,000 acres of the site, to be named Rajneeshpuram. Large sums of money amounting to some $120 million flowed into the project from sympathizers and Indian assets.

Local residents fiercely opposed the creation of an ashram city, and environmentalists organized against the movement. In the face of an increasingly hostile situation, with those opposed to the ashram taking every legal means to slow its development and harass its members, Sheela and her associates became increasingly paranoid and moved to solidify their position. Their plans began to take on a conspiratorial nature, and efforts were made both to subvert Oregon's liberal voting laws (which allowed new residents to vote immediately), and to organize criminal acts to stop their local detractors (including plans to spread salmonella bacteria). The commune eventually collapsed when some of the criminal plans became known to authorities and a federal court ruled against the union of religion and government implied in the Rajneeshpuram charter.

During the period of disintegration, internal conflict at the highest level broke out. It was discovered that Sheela had installed listening devices at houses in the commune and even bugged Rajneesh's own bedroom. The two severed their relationship. In September 1985 Sheela and some other officials fled from Oregon to Europe, and Rajneesh called news conferences to state that the commune was now "free from a fascist regime," accusing Sheela of maintaining a secret "poison lab" and trying to kill his personal doctor, dentist, and housekeeper. He claimed that she poisoned Jefferson County District Attorney Michael Sullivan, who had suffered a serious undiagnosed illness during a 1983 dispute with Sheela. In response, in an interview with a German magazine, Sheela denied these charges and also the accusation that she had created a $55 million debt at the commune in a fraud scheme, diverting some of the funds to a Swiss bank account. She countercharged that the commune debts arose from the guru's opulent tastes.

Meanwhile back at the Rajneesh ranch, the guru ordered the burning of 5,000 copies of *The Book of Rajneeshism,* along with many pendants and the red robes formerly worn by Sheela, thus symbolizing a repudiation of the ideas and projects that he attributed to Sheela rather than to himself.

In October 1985, as authorities were building a strong case against him on a variety of charges, Rajneesh suddenly left Rajneeshpuram. A Lear jet took him and a few officials of his movement to an undisclosed destination, but when the jet landed at Charlotte, North Carolina, for refueling, police had already been alerted. On October 28 he was arrested, together with six followers. Coincidentally, on the same day, Sheela and two associates were arrested in Germany. Rajneesh was handcuffed and taken back to Oregon to stand trial, but his progress in and out of jail and across several states was marked by a manner of simple dignity and became more like a triumphant procession.

The authorities were never able to connect him with crimes on the ranch, but he was found guilty of immigration violation and conspiracy to evade visa regulations (charges his followers claimed were entirely bogus). He was fined $400,000, given a suspended prison sentence of ten years, and ordered to leave the United States for a minimum of five years. Sheela was returned from Germany on charges of attempted murder, poisoning, and wiretapping. She was jailed for four and a half years. After his sentence, Rajneesh left the country on what became a world tour. He became persona non grata all over the world. Countries that refused him entry or expelled him after entry include Antigua, Australia, Bermuda, Canada, Costa Rica, England, Fiji, France, Greece, Holland, Ireland, Italy, Jamaica, Mauritius, Seychelles, Spain, Sweden, Switzerland, Uruguay, Venezuela, and West Germany. Legal proceedings growing out of the fall of Rajneeshpuram continued into the mid-1990s.

Eventually Rajneesh returned to Poona and reestablished the ashram there. Eventually the ranch and its assets were sold and the movement in the United States returned to the decentralized state it was in before the founding of the Rajneeshpuram. In the wake of the fall, a number of books, including several by former members in the leadership of Rajneeshpuram, appeared. At Poona, Rajneesh continued to teach, and his disciples published an equal number of volumes aimed at his vindication. In 1988 the first national gathering of American followers since the fall of Rajneeshpuram was held. The movement reorganized and has continued to the present.

In 1988 Rajneesh changed his name to Osho (i.e., one upon whom the heavens shower flowers). He had begun to develop some new meditation techniques that were barely shared with the followers in India when on January 19, 1990, he suddenly died amid charges that the American government had poisoned him. The international movement continued under the leadership of senior disciples in Poona, there being no guru arising to take Rajneesh's place. Osho Commune International is headquartered at 17 Koregeon Park, Poona 411 001, MS, India. The American headquarters can be reached at Osho Viha Meditation Center, P.O. Box 352, Mill Valley, CA 94942.

Sources:

Belfage, Sally. *Flowers of Emptiness.* New York: Dial Press, 1981.

Braun, Kirk. *The Unwelcome Society.* West Linn, Ore.: Scout Creek Press, 1984.

Gordon, James S. *The Golden Guru.* Lexington, Mass.: Stephen Greene Press, 1986.

Milne, Hugh. *Bhagwan: The God That Failed.* New York: St. Martin's Press, 1986. Reprint, London: Sphere Books, 1987.

Rajneesh, Bhagwan Shree. *The Great Challenge: A Rajneesh Reader.* New York: Grove Press, 1982.

———. *I Am the Gate.* New York: Harper & Row, 1977.

———. *The Orange Book.* Rajneeshpuram, Ore.: Rajneesh Foundation, 1983.

———. *Tantra, Spirituality, and Sex.* San Francisco, Calif.: Rainbow Bridge, 1977.

Rajneesh: The Most Dangerous Man Since Jesus Christ. Zürich, Switzerland: Rebel Publishing House, 1983.

Strelley, Kate. *The Ultimate Gate.* San Francisco: Harper & Row, 1987.

Raj-Yoga Math and Retreat

A monastic community founded in 1974 by Yogi Father Satchakrananda Bodhisattvaguru on an ecumenical basis, combing both Hindu and Christian traditions and practices. Satchakrananda started **yoga** practice in 1967 and is said to have experienced the raising of **kundalini** energy after only two months. He went on to spend a period at a Trappist monastery, attended Kenyon College, and became coordinator of the Northwest Free University, where he taught hatha yoga. In 1973, he was mystically initiated by the late **Swami Sivananda** (1887–1963), founder of the **Divine Life Society,** Rishikesh, India, and went on to found his own monastic community the following year. In 1977, he was ordained a priest by independent Archbishop H. Adrian Spruit of the Church of Antioch and has since combined teaching of traditional yoga practices with regular celebration of the Mass.

The small community is located in the foothills of Mt. Baker overlooking the Nooksuck River near Deming, Washington. The Math offers classes for residents and may be contacted at P.O. Box 547, Deming, WA 98244.

Sources:

Satchakrananda, Yogi. *Coming and Going: The Mother's Drama.* Deming, N.Mex.: Raj-Yoga Math & Retreat, 1975.

———. *Thomas Merton's Dharma.* Deming, N.Mex.: Raj-Yoga Math & Retreat, 1986.

Rakoczi, The Master the Prince

One of the masters originally contacted by **Helena Petrovna Blavatsky,** cofounder of the **Theosophical Society.** According to theosophical teachings there exists a spiritual hierarchy composed of individuals who have finished their round of earthly reincarnations and have evolved to the spiritual planes, from which they guide the affairs of humanity. Those members of the hierarchy closest to humanity are the "lords of the seven rays" (of the light spectrum). Each ray represents a particular virtue, which the lord of that ray exemplifies.

The prince Rakoczi is the master of the seventh ray, concerned with ordered service or **ceremonial magic.** He is involved with the ceremonial aspect of religion and magic, especially the ancient mysteries. He is also occupied with the volatile political situation in Europe and North America and speaks many languages.

Reportedlty, Rakoczi has had numerous incarnations. He was, successively, Saint Alban (third century C.E.), Proclus (a Neoplatonic philosopher, 410–85 C.E.), Roger Bacon (1220–92), Christian Rosencrutz (1378–1484), Hunyadi Janos (1387–1456), Robertus the monk (sixteenth century), and Francis Bacon (1561–1626). In his last incarnation he was a Hungarian prince, the last surviving member of the Hungarian Rokoczi family, and known throughout Europe as the **Comte de Saint Germain.** He still inhabits that body.

As Prince Rakoczi, this master was not as prominent in theosophical literature as some others, even though he became the subject of a popular book by **Isabel Cooper-Oakley.** He was lifted out of obscurity, however, after Guy W. Ballard claimed to have encountered him in 1929 on the slopes of Mt. Shasta. Saint Germain became the patron of the "I Am Religious Activity," and all of the groups that have emerged from it, such as the **Bridge to Spiritual Freedom** and the **Church Universal and Triumphant,** have given him a prominent place in their teachings.

Sources:

Cooper-Oakley, Isabel. *The Comte de Saint Germain.* Milan, Italy: Libreria Editrice del Dr. G. Sulli-Roa, 1912.

King, Godfre Ray [Guy W. Ballard]. *Unveiled Mysteries.* 4th ed. Chicago: Saint Germain Press, 1934.

Ransom, Josephine. *A Short History of the Theosophical Society.* Adyar, Madras, India: Theosophical Publishing House, 1938.

Saint Germain. *Violet Fire: The Torch of Freedom's Holy Light.* Portland, Ore.: Universariun Foundation, 1983.

Rakshasa

An Indian demon. In one of the Indian folktales he appears black as soot, with hair yellow as the lightning, looking like a thunder-cloud. He made himself a wreath of entrails and wore a sacrificial cord of hair; he gnawed the flesh of a man's head and drank blood out of a skull, thus adding him to the list of the world's **vampires.** In other stories, these *rakshasas* have formidable tusks, flaming hair, and insatiable hunger. They wander about the forests catching animals and eating them.

Rakshasas feature in the Hindu religious epic of the *Ramayana.* When the monkey god Hanuman goes to the city of Lanka in search of Sita, he sees *rakshasas* of many varied kinds, some disgusting in appearance, others quite beautiful.

"Some had long arms and fearful shapes; some were fat, others very lean, some were dwarfs, others exceedingly tall. Some had only one eye and others one ear. Some had monstrous bellies, hanging breasts, projecting teeth and crooked thighs; others were exceedingly beautiful in appearance and clothed in splendor. Some had two legs, some three legs and some four legs. Some had the heads of donkeys, some the heads of horses and some the heads of elephants."

Sources:

Sutherland, Gail Hinich. *The Disguises of the Demon: The Development of the Yaksa in Hinduism and Buddhism.* Albany: State University of New York Press, 1991.

Rama, Swami (1925–1996)

Well-known Indian teacher of **yoga, meditation,** and holistic health. At an early age he was ordained as a monk by a great sage of the Himalayas and later journeyed to numerous monasteries and caves, studying with many spiritual masters. Notable teachers he encountered included Mahatma Gandhi, Rabindranath Tagore, **Sri Aurobindo,** and **Sri Ramana Maharshi.** He studied psychology and philosophy in Varanasi and Prayas, India, and received a medical degree from Darbhanga Medical School in 1945. At a later date, he pursued a formal education at Oxford University, continuing his studies of Western psychology and philosophy in Germany and Holland for three years before coming to the United States in 1969. In the following year, he served as a consultant to the Voluntary Controls Project of the Research Department of the Menninger Foundation at Topeka, Kansas. Under scientific controls, he demonstrated such feats as manipulating his heartbeat at will to 300 beats per minute (effectively stopping the flow of blood) for seventeen seconds.

The publication of the results of such tests generated a new medical interest in body-mind relationships and spurred public interest in yoga techniques among young adults already involved in reacting to the steady arrival of new Indian spiritual teachers.

Swami Rama consistently sought to establish a clear scientific basis for the practice of yoga and meditation. He published books and audiotapes for the **Himalayan International Institute of Yoga Science and Philosophy,** first located in a Chicago suburb, which he founded in 1971. The institute later moved to Honesdale, Pennsylvania, and has a 422-acre campus in the Pocono Mountains of northeastern Pennsylvania. Branch centers have also been established throughout the United States. The Swami also continued to teach and write from his centers in India. He is widely respected in the East, where he held, and later renounced, the office of Shankaracharya, Indian's highest spiritual position. His lifetime of contributing to a reconciliation of scientific and spiritual knowledge brought him the Martin Buber Award for Service to Humanity in 1977. As the scientific interest in yoga declined through the 1980s, Swami Rama lead the Himalayan Institute until his death in 1996. The last few months of his life were filled with accusations of sexual assault and harassment from several women against himself and the Himalayan Institute. In 1997, after the Swami had died, one of the women pressing charges was awarded almost two million dollars in damages posthumously.

Sources:

Boyd, Doug. *Swami.* New York: Random House, 1976.

Rama, Swami. *Lectures on Yoga.* Arlington Heights, Ill.: Himalayan International Institute of Yoga Science and Philosophy, 1978.

———. *Living with the Himalayan Masters: Spiritual Experiences of Swami Rama.* Edited by Swami Ajaya [Allan Weinstein]. Honesdale, Pa.: Himalayan Institute, 1978.

———. *A Practical Guide to Holistic Health.* Honesdale, Pa.: Himalayan International Institute of Yoga Science and Philosophy, 1978.

Rama, Swami, Rudolph, and Swami Ajaya. *Yoga and Psychotherapy.* Glenview, Ill.: Himalayan Institute, 1976.

Tigunait, Pandir Rajmani. *Swami Rama of the Himalayas: His Life and Mission.* Honesdale, Pa.: Himalayan Institute Press, 1999.

Ramacharaka, Yogi (1862–1932)

Religious name of American writer/editor William Walker Atkinson. He was born on December 5, 1862, in Baltimore, Maryland. He went into business as a young man and was admitted to the Pennsylvania bar in 1894 and the Illinois bar 1903. He underwent a profound change after experiencing a nervous breakdown. He found healing through New Thought metaphysics and moved to Chicago where he emerged as a major advocate of the new faith. In that cause he became associate editor of the magazine *Suggestion* (1900–05), co-editor with his colleague Sydney Flowers of *New Thought* (1901–5), and later edited *Advanced Thought* (Chicago, 1916–19). He founded the Atkinson School of Mental Science and authored a large number of popular books on New Thought, Self-Healing, Mind-Power, and psychic phenomena.

During this time he was also introduced to yoga exercises, and the whole of the yogi philosophy. In 1903 he began to write books on yoga using the pseudonym Yogi Ramacharaka. Through the next several decades thirteen titles appeared and Atkinson thus became one the earliest propagandists of and an important figure in the development of Hinduism in North America. His books on yoga and occultism were issued by the Yogi Publication Society, now located in Jacksonville, Florida, and continue to be reprinted. Atkinson died in California on November 22, 1932.

Sources:

Melton, J. Gordon. *Religious Leaders of America.* Detroit: Gale Research, 1991.

Ramacharacka, Swami [William Walker Atkinson]. *Advanced Course in Yogi Philosophy and Oriental Occultism.* Chicago: Yogi Publication Society, 1904.

———. *Hatha Yoga.* Chicago: Yogi Publication Society, 1932.

———. *The Hindu-Yogi System of Breath.* Chicago: Yogi Publication Society, 1904.

———. *Raja Yoga, or Mental Development.* Chicago: Yogi Publication, 1905.

———. *The Spirit of the Upanishads; or, The Aphorisms of the Wise.* Chicago: Yogi Publication Society, 1936.

Ramakrishna, Sri (1836–1886)

An important Indian spiritual teacher on **Vedanta** and mystic of the nineteenth-century Hindu Renaissance. He was born February 18, 1836, in a village in Bengal, after the divine hero Sri Rama had appeared in a vision to an old Brahmin named Khudiram, saying that he would be reborn as his son. In due course, the boy was born and named Gadadhar. He grew up to worship the goddess Kali, the great mother, and even when he was obliged to marry, he directed his veneration toward his bride, identifying her with Kali. At the age of eighteen, Gadadhar was taken to Calcutta by his brother Ramkumar, whom he assisted as a teacher.

He settled in a temple at Dakshineswar, where he became known as "Ramakrishna," and after a period of intense spiritual discipline had ecstatic visions and trances. He was virtually intoxicated with the bliss of *samadhi* or divine **trance,** and a number of miracles were credited to him. A group of young spiritual seekers informally gathered around him. One of these, **Swami Vivekananda,** went to the United States in 1893 to speak to the World's Parliament of Religions. Given the strong public response to his presentation, he stayed on and in 1894 founded the Vedanta Society of New York, the first of a number of similar centers now present in the west. Upon his return to India he organized the followers of Ramakrishna into the Ramakrishna Order, which continues to spread the teachings of Ramakrishna and Vivekananda worldwide.

Sri Ramakrishna passed into the *mahasamadhi* (great sleep) of death August 16, 1886. The Ramakrishna Order is today the largest and most widely known monastic order in India, with colleges, schools, hospitals, relief projects, and publishing houses. Publications and information are available from Sri Ramakrishna Math, Mylapore, Madras 4, India, or from the American branches: Vedanta Press & Book Shop, 1946 Vedanta Pl., Hollywood, CA 90028; Vedanta Society, 2323 Vallejo St., San Francisco, CA 94123; Vedanta Society, 34 W. 71 St., New York, NY 10023.

Sources:

Gambhrananda, Swami. *History of the Ramakrishna Math and Mission.* Calcutta, India: Advaita Ashraam, 1957.

Isherwood, Christopher. *Ramakrishna and His Disciples,* New York: Simon & Schuster, 1965.

Melton, J. Gordon. *Religious Leaders of America.* Detroit: Gale Research, 1991.

Ramakrishna, Sri. *The Gospel of Ramakrishna.* Boston: Beacon Press, 1947.

Raman, Bangalore Venkata (1912–1998)

Prominent Indian astrologer, born in Madras, India, on August 12, 1912. His grandfather **B. Suryanarain Rao** was also a prominent astrologer. In 1930 Raman became coeditor with his grandfather of *The Astrological Magazine,* founded by Rao in 1895, and gradually assumed complete control of it and of Raman Publications, an astrological publishing house in Bangalore. He published his first book, *A Manual of Hindu Astrology,* in 1935.

Raman spent his life writing on **astrology,** challenging the Western scientific view of the field as a pseudoscience or under the umbrella of occultism. After World War II his works began to circulate in England and the United States, introducing Vedic astrology to Europe and North America. Raman died in December 1998.

Sources:

Holden, James H., and Robert A. Hughes. *Astrological Pioneers of America.* Tempe, Ariz.: American Federation of Astrologers, 1988.

Raman, B. V. *Astrology and Modern Thought.* 5th ed. Bangalore, India: Raman Publications, 1965.

———. *Hindu Predictive Astrology.* Bangalore: Raman Publications, 1938.

———. *A Manual of Hindu Astrology.* Bangalore: Raman Publications, 1935.

———. *Notable Horoscopes.* Bangalore: Raman Publications, 1956.

Ramana Maharshi, Sri (1879–1950)

An important twentieth-century Indian spiritual teacher, whose life and teachings have been cited as an example of the classic God-realized sage. Born December 30, 1879, in the village of Tiruchuzhi, near Madura, South India, he was the second son of a pleader or solicitor. The boy attended elementary school at Tiruchuzhi and Dindigul, and went on to Scott's Middle School, Madura, and the American Mission High School.

As a boy, he was impressed by a casual remark from a visitor that he had come from Arunachalam, a holy place in Tiruvannamalai, and his mind was directed to study of the lives of Tamil saints. At the age of seventeen, he had a strange mystical experience following a period in a **trance**-like condition. He felt that he was going to die, but perceived that only the body could die, the true self being independent. He lost interest in his studies and felt an intense desire to go to Arunachalam.

On August 29, 1896, he renounced his everyday life and set out for Arunachalam, where he spent the rest of his life in a condition of mystical meditation which transformed his understanding. Impervious to physical or mental discomforts, he remained in ecstatic spiritual meditation, at first in complete silence, living under a tree, or in temples, accepting minimum food which he ate mechanically.

In the course of time, the young renunciate attracted the attention of devotees, who found that he was able to answer the most abstruse metaphysical questions with wit and incisive wisdom. Eventually a religious settlement grew up around him, and he was visited by devotees from all over India and even from western countries.

He gave no formal teaching as such, but merely answered questions put to him in such a way that traditional Hindu metaphysical teachings had personal relevance to the questioner. His constant theme was the discovery of the essential Self present in all beings, summarized in the formulation "Who Am I?"

His statements combined metaphysical subtlety and simplicity, while his gentle and perceptive presence was inspiring to his devotees. Even the local creatures (monkeys, cows, peacocks, birds) were attracted to him as if to a latter-day St. Francis of Assisi. He was also visited by leading Western scholars and seekers, including **Paul Brunton** and **W. Y. Evans-Wentz.**

In his later years, he developed various illnesses and a cancerous tumor on his left elbow, but remained indifferent to intense physical pain. He passed into the *mahasamadhi* (great sleep) of death on April 14, 1950, after assuring devotees of continued presence. He stated "I am not going away. Where could I go? I am here." This implied the omnipresence of the Universal Self. At the precise moment of death a large star was seen to trail slowly across the sky. It was witnessed by the famous French photographer Henri Cartier-Bresson, who was visiting the ashram at the time.

The ashram is still in existence and has published a number of books dealing with the teachings of Sri Ramana Maharshi. A biography by Arthur Osborne was published in London, 1957, and reissued by Jaico paperbacks, Bombay, 1958. The ashram is located at: Sri Ramananasramam, Tiruvannamalai, South India.

A North American branch, the Arunchala Ashrama, with centers in Canada and the United States, has been founded with headquarters at 72–63 Yellowstone Blvd., Forest Hills, NY 11375.

Sources:

Brunton, Paul. *A Message from Arunchala.* 1936. Reprint, New York: Samuel Weiser, 1971.

Melton, J. Gordon. *Religious Leaders of America.* Detroit: Gale Research, 1991.

Osborne, Arthur. *Ramana Maharshi and the Path of Self-Knowledge.* New York: Samuel Weiser, 1970.

———, ed. *The Teachings of Ramana Maharshi.* 1963. Reprint, New York: Samuel Weiser, 1978.

Ramana Maharshi. *The Collected Works of Ramana Maharshi.* 20 vols. London: Rider, 1970.

Ram Dass, Baba

Name assumed by **Richard Alpert,** associate of Dr. **Timothy Leary,** after giving up the psychedelic revolution of the 1960s and embracing traditional Hindu mysticism.

Ramer, Andrew (1951–)

Andrew Ramer, a contemporary channeler and angelologist, was born into a Jewish family. He attended the University of California–Berkeley, from which he graduated in 1973 with a B.A. in religious studies. He held a variety of jobs through the next decade, but also began to teach **meditation** and gay spirituality in the San Francisco Bay area and emerged as a channeler of various spirit entities. In his workshops, he began to relate traditional heterosexual occult techniques such as tantra to homoeroticism. In his first book, *Two Flutes Playing: Spiritual Love/Sacred Sex: Priests of Father Earth and Mother Sky* (1990), his spirit guides spoke to the situation of gay men seeking a spiritual way of being. They asserted that gay men are tuned differently, a fact that allows them to be drawn to each other. The same year his book appeared, Ramer joined with three like-minded associates, including Atlanta spiritual writer **John R. Stowe,** to found Gay Spirit Visions, a national association of men exploring alternative spiritualities, and remains an active leader.

Through the 1990s, Ramer has become best known for his writing about and channeling of angels. He believed that angels, who neither marry nor are given in marriage, appear to be genderless or of the same gender, and that they can be considered homosexual, and thus fitting spiritual resources for gay men. He argues that there are gay guides, gay angels, and gay heavens. His speculation resulted in two bestselling books, *Ask Your Angels: A Practical Guide to Working with Angels to Enrich Your Life* (1992) and *Angel Answers: A Joyful Guide to Creating Heaven on Earth* (1995). His most recent book, *Revelations for a New Millennium,* appeared in 1997.

Sources:

Ramer, Andrew. *Angel Answers: A Joyful Guide to Creating Heaven on Earth.* New York: Pocket Books, 1995.

———. *Ask Your Angels: A Practical Guide to Working with Angels to Enrich Your Life.* San Antonio, Tex.: Alamo Square Press, 1992.

———. *Revelations for a New Millennium.* San Francisco: Harper San Francisco, 1997.

Ramer, Andrew, and Mark Thompson. *Two Flutes Playing: Spiritual Love/Sacred Sex: Priests of Father Earth and Mother Sky.* N.p., 1990.

Thompson, Mark. *Gay Soul.* San Francisco: Harper San Francisco, 1995.

Ramirez, Richard (1960–)

Richard Ramirez, Satanist and serial killer, was born on February 29, 1960, in El Paso, Texas, the son of Julian and Mercedes Ramirez, Mexican immigrants. In his childhood, it was discovered that he was epileptic and subject to sporadic seizures. He also came under the influence of his Green Beret cousin who introduced him to marijuana and who taught him to fight and kill. He took to a life of crime, stealing money to pay for his drugs. Still in his teens, he began to imagine himself a child of Satan. At age 16 he was arrested for breaking into a room at the hotel where he worked part time, and raping a woman. He was released when the judge believed his story that the woman had lured him to the room for sex. In 1978, after turning 18, he moved to Los Angeles, California. By this time he was an accomplished burglar.

In Los Angeles, Ramirez's drug habit deepened as did the intensity of his crimes. He briefly flirted with the **Church of Satan** but quickly reverted to his loner ways. He did, however, have a deep belief that Lucifer would both protect and empower him. He was seemingly proved correct, as for several years he existed freely as a criminal. In June of 1984, however, he began the new phase of his life that was to bring him both notoriety and a lifetime in jail. For more than a year he operated in the Los Angeles suburbs burglarizing homes and savagely killing the residents, leaving **occult** symbols, usually an inverted pentagram (five-pointed star), behind.

In June of 1985, the police announced that a serial killer was loose in Los Angeles. The press called him the "Night Stalker." The following month, Ramirez finally left a clue to his identity behind, a fingerprint in a getaway car. Identified, Ramirez soon found his picture everywhere in the media, and people in the Mexican-American community where he lived recognized him and almost killed him before the police arrived to arrest him.

Ramirez was convicted on multiple counts of murder and rape and sentenced to death. Defiant, he scrawled a pentagram on the palm of his hand to show reporters. After the trial he still believed that Lucifer would avenge him. Though there was an overtone of occultism to his crimes, Ramirez proved in the end to be more like other serial killers than those involved in the occult, even the great majority of those who consider themselves Satanists.

As this edition goes to press, Ramirez remains alive and in prison while appeals to his death sentence are proceeding through the courts. In 1996 he married Doreen Lloyd, one of a handful of Ramirez female groupies who emerged over the years since his trial.

Sources:

Carlo, Philip. *The Night Stalker: The Life and Crimes of Richard Ramirez.* New York: Pinnacle Books, 1996.

Lane, Brian. *The Encyclopedia of Occult and Supernatural Murder.* London: Brockhampton Press, 1995.

Rampa, T(uesday) Lopsang (ca. 1911–1981)

Pseudonym of British author Cyril Henry Hoskins, whose first book, *The Third Eye* (1956), became a sensational bestseller. It purported to be written by a Tibetan lama and described a kind of occult leucotomy in which his "third eye," in the center of his forehead, was opened surgically, resulting in his psychic powers. It was soon followed by a sequel, *Doctor From Lhasa* (1959).

The books were well-written, but people knowledgeable of Tibet soon began to find numerous errors and inconsistencies. There is no tradition of surgical opening of the third eye, which is considered a structure in the subtle body, a concept underlying the practice of **meditation** techniques in various **yoga** systems.

An initial perceptive review appeared in the journal *Tomorrow* in 1958, in which the Tibetan scholar **Chen Chi Chang** declared the book literary entertainment, stating: "we have here a work of interesting and highly imaginative fiction—but certainly not . . . a source of authentic information on Buddhist teachings or training."

While this review was being published, an independent inquiry was undertaken by Clifford Burgess, a Liverpool (England) detective, on behalf of a group of Tibetan scholars. Burgess tracked down Hoskins to a village overlooking Dublin Bay in the Irish Republic and revealed that Hoskins had never been in Tibet or had an operation on his forehead.

Hoskins was the son of Joseph Henry Hoskins, a plumber. After leaving school he assisted his father for a time, and when his father died in 1937 he lived with his mother in Nottinghamshire. He worked for a surgical instrument company, then became a clerk with a correspondence school, teaching time and motion studies. About this time he shaved his head, grew a beard and adopted the name of "Dr. Kuan-suo." Later, with his wife, Sanya, he moved to Ireland. After exposure of his hoax, Hoskins attempted to recover by arguing that his own body had been taken over by the spirit of a Tibetan lama. He went on to write a number of other successful books that built on the original story and rehashed standard occult and psychic themes.

He died of heart trouble January 25, 1981, in Calgary, Alberta, Canada. His books have remained in print and continue to sell to an audience unaware of the **fraud.**

Sources:

Chan, Chen Chi. "Tibetan Phantasies." *Tomorrow* 6, 2 (spring 1958).

Rampa, T. Lopsang [Cyril Henry Hoskins]. *As It Was!* N.p., 1976.

———. *Beyond the Tenth.* N.p., 1969.

———. *Candlelight.* N.p., 1974.

———. *Cave of the Ancients.* N.p., 1963.

———. *The Hermit.* N.p., 1971.

———. *Living With the Lama.* N.p., 1964.

———. *My Visit to Venus.* N.p., 1966.

———. *The Rampa Story.* London: Souvenir Press, 1960.

———. *The Saffron Robe.* N.p., 1964.

———. *The Thirteenth Candle.* N.p., 1972.

———. *Wisdom of the Ancients.* N.p., 1965.

———. *You—Forever.* N.p., 1965.

Stein, Gordon. *Encyclopedia of Hoaxes.* Detroit: Gale Research, 1993.

"The Tibetan Lama Hoax." *Tomorrow* 9, 2 (spring 1958).

"Ramtha"

Spirit guide channeled through **J. Z. Knight.** According to Knight, "Ramtha" first made himself known in 1977 when he appeared to her one Sunday afternoon in 1977 in her home in Tacoma, Washington. Over a period of months, she became used to his presence and to his use of her body, through which he began to speak. In the 1980s he became the center of a movement that emerged in the context of the larger **New Age** movement. Knight became the most successful of the plethora of channels who became so definitive of the New Age.

Ramtha described himself as having lived on Earth some thirty-five thousand years previously. He was born in Lemuria, described as a section of the ancient continent of Atlatia (or Atlantis). When Ramtha was still a youth, the Atlatians misused their vast technology and created a disaster—the northern half of the continent, including Lemuria, was destroyed. The Lemurians had to seek a new home in the south; Ramtha's family relocated to Onai, the great port city of Atlatia.

After the disaster the Atlatian social system fell apart and was replaced with a feudal-like structure with the Lemurians at the bottom. After his mother's death, Ramtha fled to the mountains to nurture his anger. It became focused on the Atlatians, and he soon returned to Onai at the head of an army. He conquered the city and found a new life as a warrior. He became a conqueror who was stopped only by an assassin's sword.

He survived, but had to endure a lengthy healing process. He used the time for contemplation of the Unknown God to be found in the life force. The death wish that had dominated his life to that point and led him to become a warrior was replaced with a desire to embrace life. His search for the Unknown God led him to contemplate the wind. The wind was powerful, free-moving, without boundaries, limits, or form. The image of the wind beckoned to Ramtha to exist unbounded by the common human limitations, including death. His contemplation over a number of years led first to an out-of-the-body experience. But as his concentration continued, his very bodily vibration changed and he rose as a body of light. He had conquered life, and, leaving his earthly existence, he ascended.

Now, thirty-five thousand years later, he returned to teach what he had learned, through the instrument of a young woman. The essence of his teachings was that each person is a god, a master, who has forgotten his or her origin. In remembering and coming to understand one's true nature, the individual can become a creator who can have whatever he or she desires.

Ramtha's teachings came forth in the mid 1980s through a series of "dialogues," usually weekend gatherings at which Knight would channel Ramtha. These came to an end in 1987 and were replaced by Ramtha's School of Enlightenment (RSE), a more structured course that included a program developed for students. While the dialogue sessions had been held around the country, and even overseas, RSE is centered entirely on Knight's ranch in rural Washington, where students gather several times a year for intensive sessions of philosophical instruction and spiritual practice.

RSE allows more systematic instruction in Ramtha's Gnostic theology. The universe emanated in stages from God, described as absolute potentiality, says Ramtha. Each stage of creation was marked by a slowing of the frequency of the energy out of which the universe has been created. Individual entities, gods, have been embodied in each stage of creation and now have come into physical embodiment to grow and experience life, he says.

The primary problem of humans is having accepted the limitation of physical existence, Ramtha teaches, when in fact, they are gods with vast powers. The spiritual practice of the school, based in concentration and **pranayama**-like breathing, is designed to teach students to remember and use their godly powers.

Ramtha's School of Enlightenment may be contacted at Box 1210, Yelm, WA 98597

Sources:

Kerins, Deborah, ed. *The Spinner of Tales: A Collection of Stories as Told by Ramtha.* Yelm, Wash.: New Horizon Publishing, 1991.

Knight, JZ. *A State of Mind: My Story.* New York: Warner Books, 1987.

Ramtha (as channeled by JZ Knight). *The Ancient Schools of Wisdom.* Transcribed by Diane Munoz. Yelm, Wash.: Diane Munoz, 1992.

———. *I Am Ramtha.* Edited by Cindy Black, Richard Cohn, Greg Simmons, and Wes Walt. Portland, Ore.: Beyond Words Publishing, 1986.

Ramtha (The White Book). Edited by Steven Lee Weinberg, with Randall Weischedel, Sue Ann Fazio, and Carol Wright. Eastsound, Wash.: Sovereignty, 1986.

Ramtha's School of Enlightenment: The American Gnostic School. Yelm, Wash.: JZK, 1994.

Rand, William

William Rand, prominent teacher of the **Reiki** system of healing and founder of the Center for Reiki Training in suburban Detroit, Michigan, was a professional astrologer and hypnotherapist living in Hawaii in the 1970s at the time that the existence of the Reiki healing system became known. Reiki, a Japanese healing system, had been developed early in the twentieth century by **Mikao Usui,** a Buddhist layman. He passed his teachings to several students, among whom was Dr. Chujiro Hayashi. In the 1930s Hayashi passed his succession to a Ms. **Hawayo Takata** (1900–1980), a Japanese-American who resided in Hawaii. Takata practiced Reiki quietly in the Japanese-American community until the 1970s, when she began to teach non-Japanese for the first time and made the Anglo world aware of its existence.

Rand took his initial Reiki class from Bethal Phaigh in Hawaii in 1981, the year after Takata's death. Phaigh was one of the first Reiki Masters, who had the knowledge to pass on the teachings initiated by Takata. He took the second intermediate degree from Phaigh in 1982 and subsequently studied with other Reiki teachers. He received his own Reiki Master training from Diane McCumber and Marlene Schilke in 1989, and repeated the course with Cherie Prasuhn (1990) and Leah Smith (1992). Meanwhile, he met and studied with Phyllis Furumoto, Takata's daughter and one of the two people she named a Grand Master.

In the mid-1980s, Rand moved to Michigan and in 1988 opened the Center for Reiki Training (now the International Center for Reiki Training). Shortly after receiving his Reiki Master attunement, Rand created a virtual revolution in the larger community when he challenged a practice followed by Takata and both Grand Masters she initiated, of charging $10,000 to become a Reiki Master as a means of emphasizing the value of what the students were learning. At the center, Rand dropped the fee to a mere $600.00. He also authored *Reiki: The Healing Touch: First and Second Degree Manual,* a textbook that included most of Reiki's heretofore confidential teachings, though he refrained from revealing the unique Reiki symbols, a key esoteric element in the technique that the Reiki practitioner acquired to gain the initial attunement to the chi energy. In setting up the inexpensive training courses, Rand challenged the assumption that a Reiki practitioner Master should turn to one of the Grand Masters for Master training. His action would, in fact, stimulate the spread of the movement in the manner he envisioned.

Among the early students to take Rand's Master class was Kathleen Milner. Milner in turn became an associate of a channeler through whom she began to develop an expanded version of Reiki. Milner soon became a channel for some spirit entities known only as "Higher Beings," and under their guidance developed what became known as the Tera-Mai Reiki System. Rand began to work with Milner's system and then began to further alter it. He eventually experienced a new shift in energy and developed a further variation of the traditional Reiki system which he termed Karuna Reiki. He claimed that in his system the energy seemed "much more definite and focused" and helps release **karma** and deeply seated issues that are often stored at the cellular level. This difference seemed sufficient to demand he trademark the name Karuna Reiki to insure the quality of its transmission to students.

Rand heads the International Center for Reiki Training, now located at 21421 Hilltop, No. 28, Southfield, MI 48034. He has also founded Vision Publications, which issues books and the quarterly *Reiki News.* His second book, *Reiki for a New Millennium,* appeared in 1998. The website is: http://www.reiki.org/.

Sources:

Rand, William. *Reiki for a New Millennium.* Southfield, Mich.: Vision Publications, 1998.

———. *Reiki: The Healing Touch: First and Second Degree Manual.* Southfield, Mich.: Vision Publications, 1991.

Randall, Edward Caleb (1860–1935)

American lawyer, author, Spiritualist, and psychical researcher. He was born at Ripley, New York, on July 19, 1860. He was educated at Allegheny College and practiced as a lawyer in Buffalo, New York, from 1884 onward. He became president of the Niagara Terminal Corporation, the American Super-Power Corporation and the South Buffalo Gas Corporation.

He experimented with the **direct voice** medium **Emily S. French** for 20 years, during which period she refused to accept fees or compensation. Randall also carried on Spiritualist work with **rescue circles** and contributed articles to Spiritualist journals. He died in Buffalo on July 3, 1935.

Sources:

Randall, Edward Caleb. *The Dead Have Never Died.* New York: A. A. Knopf, 1917.

———. *Frontiers of the After Life.* New York: A. A. Knopf, 1922.

———. *Future of Man.* Buffalo, N.Y.: O. Ulbrich, 1908.

———. *Life's Progression.* Buffalo, N.Y.: H. B. Brown, 1906.

———. *The Living Dead.* N.p., 1927.

———. *Told In The After Life.* N.p., 1925.

Randall, John L(eslie) (1933–)

British school teacher and parapsychologist. Randall was born on November 27, 1933, in Warwick, England. He studied at Leicester University (graduate certificate in education), Leicester College of Technology (honors degree in chemistry; minor in biology), and the University of London (B.Sc., honors). He taught at secondary schools for four years prior to his position as biology master at Leamington College, a grammar school for boys (1962–79). In 1979 he became a biology teacher at the King Henry VIII School, Coventry.

He was a member of the **Society for Psychical Research,** London, and served on the council from 1978 onward. He introduced **psi** experiments and the study of **parapsychology** into a General Studies course for sixth form students. He has a special interest in the philosophical implications of psi and biological theories relating to psi and is a supporter of **Rupert Sheldrake**'s theories concerning **formative causation.** He has written a number of papers and books on parapsychology.

Sources:

Pleasants, Helene, ed. *Biographical Dictionary of Parapsychology.* New York: Helix Press, 1964.

Randall, John L. "Biological Aspects of Psi." In John Beloff, ed. *New Directions in Parapsychology.* London, 1974; Metuchen, N.J.: Scarecrow Press, 1975.

———. *Childhood and Sexuality: A Radical Christian Approach.* Pittsburgh, Pa.: Dorrance Publishing Company, Inc., 1992.

———. "A New Science of Life: The Hypothesis of Formative Causation." *Journal* of the Society for Psychical Research 51, 1981.

———. *Parapsychology and the Nature of Life.* New York: Harper & Row, 1975.

———. "Psi Phenomena and Biological Theory." *Journal* of the Society for Psychical Research 46, 1971. Reprint in Rhea A. White's *Surveys in Parapsychology.* N.p., 1976.

———. *Psychokinesis: A Study of Paranormal Forces Through the Ages.* N.p., 1982.

———. *Tests for Extrasensory Perception & Psychokinesis.* N.p., 1980.

Randi, James (1928–)

Pseudonym of stage magician James Randall Zwinge who has developed what amounts to a second vocation as a cofounder and leading spokesperson of the **Committee for the Scientific Investigation of Claims of the Paranormal** (CSICOP) and debunker of both psychics and their paranormal claims and religious claims of supernatural occurrences. Born August 7, 1928, in Toronto, Canada, he was exceptionally talented as a child, although he did not have the advantage of a college education. He was passionately interested in conjuring **magic,** and in adult life he achieved worldwide fame for his skill in legerdemain. He performed before royalty in Europe and Asia and appeared on national television programs and at college campuses under the stage name of "The Amazing Randi." In the lineage of many stage **magicians** over the last two centuries, Randi has assumed a watchdog role over people who would perform conjuring tricks while trying to pass them off as either supernatural or paranormal events. He has also been somewhat incensed at "experts" who have been fooled by hoaxing through their naive trust of the hoaxer, their own will to believe ideas which the paranormal event seems to confirm, or a simple lack of attention in seeing a trick being worked on them. Randi's own skepticism concerning the paranormal has a strong foundation in the significant element of **fraud** which permeated Spiritualism in past generations and is still present in the world of fortunetellers and psychics. In this work, Randi performs an unquestioned public service.

According to journalist Richard Pyatt in *USA Today* (August 29, 1986), Randi's interest in investigating psychic phenomena started at the age of fifteen. Randi is quoted as stating:

"When I was 15 years of age, I had already started out on my career as an amateur magician. When I attended a spiritualist church in Toronto, I saw they were using the same gimmicks that I had been reading about in the catalog and had been learning to do myself. Ministers were apparently speaking with the dead. I saw people in that congregation who really believed that the minister was able to read the contents of sealed envelopes and bring them messages from beyond the grave. I resented that highly, and I tried to expose that. I was arrested for my troubles. So at 15, I ended up in a police station, sitting there for four hours waiting for my father to come and get me out. I guess that was the worst four hours the psychic world ever spent, though they didn't know it until recently." Like the late **Harry Houdini** (1874–1926), also a brilliant stage magician, he has made his concern for psychic tricks a public issue. He has made himself available to the media to attack specific psychics and has given public demonstrations imitating their feats and explaining the means by which some of the tricks were accomplished. He has also issued challenges to psychics to perform paranormal feats under his own exacting conditions and to his satisfaction for a prize of ten thousand dollars. One of his major targets has been **Uri Geller,** and he has published a book claiming that Geller's **metal-bending** feats are not paranormal: *The Magic of Uri Geller* (1975).

Among his most successful exposes were of several Christian healers, the primary one being Peter Popoff in San Francisco in 1986. In his healing crusades, Popoff actually called sufferers by name and described their ailments, claiming to receive such information directly from God. Actually he had developed a rather elaborate and involved system which Randi began to uncover when he noticed that Popoff had a "hearing aid" inside his ear. That ear piece suggested that someone might be broadcasting information to Popoff; the problem was how to obtain definite evidence that the identification of sufferers was fraudulent. Randi enlisted the aid of trusted individuals from the Bay Area Skeptics group and the Society of American Magicians. Some members of the group took up strategic places in the Civic Auditorium in San Francisco, where the crusade was held. Robert Steiner and Alexander Jason (an electronics expert) established themselves behind the balcony of the auditorium with hidden tape recorders and electronic listening equipment.

Just before the healing service started, Jason succeeded in tuning into and recording a backstage broadcast from Elizabeth Popoff to her husband, the minister. The message began: "Hello Petey. I love you. I'm talking to you. Can you hear me? If you can't, you're in trouble." Here was firm evidence that the claimed messages from God were in fact information relayed to Popoff by his wife, and received through Popoff's hearing aid. The broadcast continued: "I'm looking up the names right now." This appeared to be a reference to the "prayer cards" which those attending the healing service were asked to fill out, giving names, description of ailments, and other information.

The tape recordings of a claimed healing from a service of the Popoff Crusade a few weeks later in Anaheim, California, on March 16, 1986, provided evidence of a backstage prompting broadcast by Elizabeth Popoff to her husband. She gave the name "Virgil Jorgenson. Virgil. . . . Way back in the back somewhere. Arthritis in knees. He's got a cane . . . He's got arthritis. He's praying for his sister in Sweden, too."

In the auditorium, the Rev. Popoff called out: "Virgil. Is it Jorgenson? Who is Virgil?" A man, apparently in his sixties and limping with a cane, came forward, and Popoff continued: "Are you ready for God to overhaul those knees?" Jorgenson then appeared to walk more easily, and Popoff continued: "Oh, glory to God. I'll tell you, God's going to touch that sister of yours all the way over in Sweden." Popoff then broke Jorgenson's cane, while the sufferer, apparently cured of his arthritis, walked about the auditorium, praising God and the minister Popoff.

This healing was so impressive that Peter Popoff used the film clip for three consecutive weeks on his television show. Unfortunately for the Popoff Crusade, "Virgil Jorgenson" was Don Henvick, program coordinator for Bay Area Skeptics and president of Assembly #70 of the Society of American Magicians, and he does not suffer from arthritis. His disguise as "Virgil Jorgenson" was only one of several appearances that challenged the claimed divine source of Peter Popoff's information and healing. Under the name "Tom Hendrys," Henvick was "healed" of nonexistent alcoholism at the San Francisco Civic Auditorium. In a Detroit healing crusade, Popoff "healed" Henvick of uterine cancer when this master of disguise appeared dressed in woman's garb under the name "Bernice Manicoff," seated in a wheelchair.

The decisive exposure of the electronic source of Popoff's claimed divine messages from God was made by Randi nationwide on a Johnny Carson "Tonight" show on April 22, 1986, when scenes of a claimed healing were shown with a soundtrack of the secret information broadcast identifying the sufferer.

This brilliantly organized and presented exposure of Popoff showed Randi at his best, identifying the techniques of an intricate hoax set within the trusting environment of a church service. At the same time it provided a platform for him at his worst, making broad generalizations branding all faith healers by associating them with the guilt of the few. His attempts to push his conclusions far beyond what the data would suggest has tended to sever Randi from the larger audience who would be open to his actual uncovering of hoaxing.

Randi went beyond the uncovering of hoaxes to perpetuating one himself in what was termed Project Alpha. He sent two magicians to the McDonnell Laboratory for Psychical Research at Washington University in St. Louis. Their ability to fool the researchers into believing that they were genuine psychics became a matter of great embarrassment to the parapsychological community and the university and the laboratory was closed a short time afterward. This project was based upon the idea that most people in parapsychology are ill-equipped to do psychical research and need the help of a trained magician.

Randi served as a founding member of the Committee for Scientific Investigation of Claims of the Paranormal (CSICOP) and a member of the editorial board of their journal *The Skeptical Inquirer: The Zetetic.* When he is not traveling the world performing and exposing the paranormal as fraud and conjuring, Randi lives in New Jersey in a house full of unusual and remarkable illusions, with doors that open unexpectedly on the side opposite the door knob and clocks that run backward.

On July 14, 1986, Randi was the recipient of a $272,000 award by the MacArthur Foundation of Chicago through his efforts in "alerting the unsuspecting public to hoaxers who, for example, claim to perform miracle cures of cancer, and also to support his exposure of shoddy, pseudo-science through his investigations and public lectures." The MacArthur Fellow Awards are tax-free, no-strings grants to individuals to permit them to continue their work without economic hindrance.

In 1992, the *Skeptical Inquirer* noted that Randi is no longer associated with CSICOP due to two libel suits; he resigned in order to protect the committee from further suits because of legal issues. But in 1999 Randi was still in the public eye when he addressed the U.S. Congress on medical and scientific quackery.

Sources:

Berger, Arthur S., and Joyce Berger. *The Encyclopedia of Parapsychology and Psychical Research.* New York: Paragon House, 1991.

Randi, James. *The Faith Healers.* Buffalo, N.Y.: Prometheus Books, 1987.

———. *Flim-Flam! Psychics, ESP, Unicorns and Other Delusions.* Buffalo, N.Y.: Prometheus Books, 1980.

———. *The Magic of Uri Geller.* New York: Ballantine Books, 1975. Reprinted as *The Truth About Uri Geller.* Buffalo, N.Y.: Prometheus Books, 1982.

———. "Project Alpha Experiment." In Kenneth Frazier, ed. *Science Confronts the Paranormal.* Buffalo, N.Y.: Prometheus Books, 1986.

Steiner, Robert A. "Exposing the Faith-Healers." *The Skeptical Inquirer* 11, 1 (fall 1986).

Randles, Jenny (Jennifer Christine) (1951–)

British ufologist. She was born on October 30, 1951, in Bacup, England, and studied chemistry, mathematics, and physics, receiving advanced level General Certificates of Education in these subjects. She went on to post advanced level studies in geography and geology, receiving City and Guilds Certificates with distinctions in audio-visual technology and education. She was a teacher at a Cheshire Middle School (1972–74), a Research Coordinator on the council of the **British UFO Research Association** (BUFORA) (1975–77), and an audio-visual technician in a college of education, servicing teachers (1977–78). Through the 1970s she became increasingly involved in **UFO** research. She has held a variety of positions and has done a variety of tasks simultaneously.

In 1973 she helped form the Northern UFO Network and became the editor of the **Northern UFO News** in 1974. In 1977 she became a columnist for *Flying Saucer Review.* After 1978 she became secretary of the Northern UFO Network (NUFON) and the UFO Investigators' Network (UFOIN), concerned with procuring reports on UFO sightings in Britain. Her first book, co-authored with Peter Warrington, *UFOs; A British Viewpoint,* appeared in 1979.

In the 1980s Randles also allowed her interest in psychic phenomena and the paranormal to emerge. In 1983, she wrote and presented a thirty-week series of features on mysterious phenomena for the independent British radio station Radio City. She has also appeared in, researched, and helped to produce numerous other radio and television programs on British and foreign channels. During these media appearances, she met many celebrities who provided the inspiration and material of her book *Beyond Explanation?* (1985). This deals with the paranormal experiences of past and present public figures such as John Lennon, Edgar Allan Poe, Susannah York, Kevin Keegan, Donald Sutherland, Arthur Koestler, Winston Churchill, Anthony Hopkins, Lindsay Wagner, **Sir Arthur Conan Doyle,** and many others. It was followed by *Sixth Sense* (1986).

As a result of many years of study and investigation of the UFO phenomenon and the paranormal, she advised caution in reaching firm conclusions about UFOs and stated that she had found no objective evidence to support the belief that we are visited by extraterrestrials. She suggested that there may be several different answers to the unexplained cases, some of them possibly relating to new types of natural, physical phenomena. She has now explored the UFO question from almost every angle and continues to produce a new book based on her recent research every few years.

Sources:

Clark, Jerome. *UFOs in the 1980s. The UFO Encyclopedia. Volume 1.* Detroit: Apogee Books, 1990.

Randles, Jenny. *Abduction: Over 200 Documented UFO Kidnappings Investigated.* London: Robert Hale, 1988.

———. *The UFO Conspiracy: The First Forty Years.* Poole, England: Blandford Press, 1987.

———. *UFO Reality: A Critical Look at the Physical Evidence.* London: Robert Hale, 1983.

Randles, Jenny, and Peter Warrington, *UFOs; A British Viewpoint.* N.p., 1979.

Randolph, Paschal Beverly (1825–1875)

Paschal Beverly Randolph, an early leader of American Rosicrucianism, was born on October 8, 1825, in New York City, the son of William Beverly Randolph and Flora Beverly, a black woman who claimed descent from Madagascan royalty. At age 16 he went to sea, but this career ended five years later, when he was injured in an accident. He settled in Philadelphia and worked as a barber, while he trained as an eclectic (natural) physician and avidly studied magnetism and spiritualism. He later claimed to have been named the supreme hierarch of the Rosicrucian Fraternity in 1846.

Randolph, who traveled to Europe in 1854, claimed that he met occult magician **Éliphas Lévi** and began a relationship with the European **Rosicrucians** (a claim which can neither be proven nor contradicted). In 1858, on a trip to England, he was made the Supreme Grand Master of the Western World and Knight of L'Ordre du Lis. Following this trip he founded the first modern Rosicrucian group in the United States. In the 1850s he wrote his first articles for Spiritualist publications and in 1860 published his first independently published work, a pamphlet, *The Unveiling; or, What I Think of Spiritualism.* His own Rosicrucian system developed from his reading of occult texts and his dialogue with **Spiritualism.** Randolph, though, described the afterlife in terms quite different from the familiar Summerland of the Spiritualists. The concept of "will" and the exercising of volition dominated Randolph's mature thought. While he acknowledged the success of mediums, he suggested that they vacated their will and thus became subject to every wind of influence around them and thus reached contradictory results. He advocated a method of active mediumship called blending. Rather than operating in a trance, the medium identified with the soul of the deceased and thus developed a knowing without giving up will.

Randolph became best known for his teachings on sexuality, a largely taboo subject in public, but one about which as a physician he had some freedom to counsel and to write. At that time almost anyone who gave advice on sexual issues would be branded as an advocate of "free love." However, Randolph believed that he had discovered a great secret about the mysterious fluid produced by people when they became sexually aroused. This fluid was the secret of marital success and happiness, he contended, while its block was a bane to humankind. As a herbal physician and mesmerist, Randolph developed ways to cure the blockages to the production of this fluid. His final words on this topic were published in 1874 in his last book, *Eulis! The History of Love* (later reprinted under the title *Affectional Alchemy*). Two years earlier he had been brought to trial in Boston, charged with advocating free love, but he was found not guilty. In 1874 he reorganized the fraternity for the last time. That same year Randolph married, and his wife bore a son, Osiris Budha Randolph, for whom Randolph had great hopes. However, on July 29, 1875, despair overcame him, and for reasons not altogether understood, he killed himself. He was succeeded as head of the fraternity by Freeman B. Dowd and later Edward H. Brown and **R. Swinburne Clymer.** Under Clymer's leadership, the largely moribund fraternity was brought back to life and has since enjoyed a successful existence, though because of a rule against advertising itself, it has remained less known than some other groups.

Randolph is one of the lesser known but more important occult leaders of the nineteenth century. His many books were widely read. Randolph's teachings on occult sexuality were carried to Europe and fed the development of **sex magic.** Both his ethnicity and his manner of death, which is something of an embarrassment to occultists, have contributed to his being forgotten.

A French-language book on occult sexuality was published in Paris in 1931 under Randolph's name, claiming to be the product of his secret teachings among European students. In fact, the book, which appeared in English in 1988, was taken from several of Randolph's published works mixed with other writings. It was denounced by the Fraternitas Rosae Crucis as a fraudulent work.

Sources:

Deveney, John Patrick. *Paschal Beverly Randolph: A Nineteenth-Century Black American Spiritualist, Rosicrucian, and Sex Magician.* Albany: State University of New York Press, 1996.

Melton, J. Gordon. "Pascal Beverly Randolph: America's Pioneer Occultist." In *Le Défi Magique,* edited by Jean Baptiste Martin and Francois Laplantine. Lyon, France: Presses Universitaires de Lyon, 1994.

Randolph, Paschal Beverly. *After Death: The Disembodiment of Man.* 4th ed. Toledo, Ohio: Randolph Publishing, 1886.

———. *Dealings with the Dead.* 1861. Reprinted as *Soul! The Soul World: The Homes of the Dead.* Quakertown, Pa.: Confederation of Initiates, 1932.

———. *Eulis! The History of Love.* Toledo, Ohio: Randolph Publishing, 1874.

———. *Magia Sexualis.* Paris: R. Telin, 1931. Published in English as *Sexual Magic.* Translated by Robert North. New York: Magickal Childe Publishing, 1988.

———. *Pre-Adamic Man.* Reprint, Toledo, Ohio: Randolph Publishing, 1888.

———. *Ravalette, Rosicrucian's Story.* 1863. Reprint, Quakertown, Pa.: Philosophical Publishing, 1939.

———. *The Unveiling; or, What I Think of Spiritualism.* Newburyport, Mass.: The Author, 1860.

Random Event Generator (REG)

Electronic apparatus which generates random numbers, used as targets in a **psi** test. A basic form of REG is an electronic coin-tossing machine, generating a series of "heads and tails" outputs. Other REGs have more complex outputs. Tests with REGs are often conducted in conjunction with computers, so that the timing and running of the experiment can be mechanically controlled and analyzed, thus obviating fraud on the part of the subject, and facilitating evaluation of a long series of runs.

Sources:

Schmidt, Helmut. "A PK Test with Electronic Equipment." *Journal of Parapsychology* 34 (1970).

Ransom, Champe (1936–)

Editor in a law book publishing company and writer on parapsychology. He was born in San Diego, California, and became a seaman in the Merchant Marines after leaving high school. He obtained a B.A. degree from Lawrence University with a major in history (1961) and a J.D. degree from St. Mary's University School of Law (1966). He then served as legislative counsel to the state legislature in Juneau, Alaska (1966–70). During his final year in law school he had taken an interest in parapsychology and in 1970 was finally able to become a research assistant at the **Division of Parapsychology,** University of Virginia (1970–72). He then became an editor with Michie Company, law book publishers, Charlottesville, Virginia, and later owned a chimney sweeping business.

While at the University of Virginia he worked off of a grant for the **Parapsychology Foundation,** which supported his research on parapsychology's critics. He also assisted J. G. Pratt with experiments in **PK** and **ESP.**

Sources:

Pleasants, Helene, ed. *Biographical Dictionary of Parapsychology.* New York: Helix Press, 1964.

Pratt, J. G., with Champe Ransom. "Exploratory Observations of the Movement of Static Objects Without the Apparent Use of Known Physical Energies by Nina S. Kulagina." *Proceedings of the Parapsychological Association* 8 (1971).

———. "Extrasensory Perception or Extraordinary Sensory Perception?" *Journal* of American Society for Psychical Research 66 (1972).

Ransom, Champe. "Recent Criticisms of Parapsychology: A Review." *Journal* of American Society for Psychical Research 65 (1971).

Rao, Bangalore Suryanarain (1856–1937)

Indian astrologer, born in Srikakulam, India, on February 12, 1856. Rao graduated from Central College in Bangalore and practiced law at Bellary, India, for a decade. He also became interested in **astrology** and pioneered the introduction of Vedic astrology from the several Indian languages into the dominant English-speaking culture then existing in India. He published his first book in 1882 and his *Astrological Self-Instructor* in 1892. In 1895 he began an English-language periodical, *The Astrological Magazine.* The magazine continued until 1923, when it was suspended for seven years because of Rao's ill health. It was revived with Rao and his grandson **B. V. Raman** serving as coeditors. Over the next few years Raman gradually assumed control of the family business.

Rao wrote some of the first English-language books on Indian astrology, and his books introduced the topic to the West. Through his grandson's books, Vedic astrology has found a large following.

Rao died in March 1937.

Sources:

Holden, James H., and Robert A. Hughes. *Astrological Pioneers of America.* Tempe, Ariz.: American Federation of Astrologers, 1988.

Rao, B. Suryanarain. *Compendium of Astrology.* Bagalore: Raman Publications, n.d.

———. *Strijataka, or Female Horoscopy.* Bangalore: Raman Publications, 1933.

Rao, K(oneru) Ramakrishna (1932–)

Lecturer in philosophy and parapsychologist. Rao was born on October 4, 1932, in India. He did his college and graduate work at Andhra University, Waltair, India (B.A. hons., philosophy 1953; M.A. hons., psychology 1955; Ph.D., 1962). He was a lecturer in the Departments of Philosophy and Psychology at Andhra University from 1953–58. He left in 1958 to come to the United States as a Fulbright scholar. His stay at the University of Chicago was extended a year with a Rockefeller Fellowship. He returned to India in 1960 as chief librarian at Andhra University (1960–61), but then moved on to North Carolina to work with J. B. Rhine at the Parapsychology Laboratory at Duke University, Durham, North Carolina.

He returned to Andhra University in the mid-1960s and in 1967 established the Department of Parapsychology, the only such university department of its kind in the world. In the meantime he had become a charter member of the **Parapsychology Association** and was elected as its secretary in 1963 and its president in 1965. (He was again elected president in 1978). In 1977 he became the director of the Institute for Parapsychology, but again in 1984 went back to Andhra to become the university's vice-chancellor. The following year he established the Institute for Yoga and Consciousness at Andhra and became its director. In 1987 he again became head of the Institute for Parapsychology, where he has remained to the present.

Rao has authored a number of papers and books on parapsychology and related fields. More than any other person, he embodies the internationalization of parapsychology and the involvement of a growing edge of the field among scholars with non-Western backgrounds in the last half of the twentieth century.

Sources:

Rao, K. Ramakrishna. *The Basic Experiments in Parapsychology.* Jefferson, N.C.: McFarland, 1984.

———. "A Consideration of Some Theories in Parapsychology." *Journal of Parapsychology* (March 1961).

———. *Experimental Parapsychology.* Springfield, Ill.: Charles C. Thomas, 1966.

———. *Gandhi and Pragmatism.* Calcutta & Oxford, N.p., 1968.

———. *J. B. Rhine: On the Frontiers of Science.* Jefferson, N.C.: McFarland, 1982.

———. *Mystic Awareness.* Mysore, India, 1972.

———. *Psi Cognition.* India: Tagore Publishing House, 1957.

———. "Vedanta and the Modus Operandi of Paranormal Cognition." *Philosophical Quarterly* 1955.

Rao, K. Ramakrishna, and K. S. Murty. *Current Trends in Indian Thought.* New Delhi, 1972.

Rao, K. Ramakrishna, and P. Sailaja. *Experimental Studies of the Differential Effect in Life Setting.* N.p., 1972.

Raphael

An angel whose name means "God has healed." He first appeared in the *Apocrypha,* those honored but uncanonical books of the Hebrew people that were considered but not included in their Bible (i.e., the Christian Old Testament). The book of Tobit, written in the second century B.C.E., concerns a man who was blind. Raphael was the angel sent to heal him. In the pseudepigraphical (falsely ascribed) book of *Enoch* it was said that: "Raphael presides over the spirits of men." In Jewish rabbinical legend of the angelic hierarchies, Raphael was the medium through which the power of Tsebaoth, or the Lord of Hosts, passed into the sphere of the sun, giving motion, heat, and brightness to it.

As one of the angels named in the ancient writings, Raphael reappears in the Kabalistic literatures of the Middle Ages. As an archangel, Raphael was identified with Hod, one of the ten sephiroth iminated by the Ein Soph (God) who implements God's creative purposes, in this case healing. He then reappears in a variety of magical operations of ceremonial magic and is one of the four angels called upon in, for example, the basic "Ritual of the Pentagram" which was taught to neophytes in the Hermetic Order of the **Golden Dawn.**

The name "Raphael" was also adopted by pioneer British astrologer Robert Cross Smith (1795–1832) whose career really marks the beginning of the modern astrological revival from the low point of astrological interest in the eighteenth century. Smith founded a successful astrological publishing house and compiled *Raphael's Astronomical Ephemeris,* the book of sun, moon, and planet position for each day of the year, a necessary tool for the preparation of an accurate horoscope. Since his death, the publishing house continues to publish his ephemeris which remains one of the most popular used today.

Through the nineteenth century, individual astrologers also assumed the name and operated as "Raphael." Raphael II was John Palmer (1807–1837), editor of *Raphael's Sanctuary of the Astral Art* (1834), Raphael III was a Mr. Medhurst, who edited the *Prophetic Messenger* almanac (1837–ca. 1847), Raphael IV was Mr. Wakeley (d. 1853) who wrote under the name "Edwin Raphael," and Raphael V was a Mr. Sparkes (1820–1875) who edited *The Oracle* (May–June 1861). Raphael VI was Robert C. Cross (1850–1923) who acquired the Raphael copyrights, including the ephemeris. Since Cross's death, a company has continued the Raphael publications.

Sources:

Christian, Paul. *The History and Practice of Magic.* New York: Citadel Press, 1969.

Halevi, Z'ev ben Shimon. *A Kabbalistic Universe.* New York: Samuel Weiser, 1977.

Lewis, James R. *Astrology Encyclopedia.* Detroit: Gale Research, 1994.

Regardie, Israel. *The Golden Dawn.* 4 vols. Chicago: Aries Press, 1937–40. Revised ed., St. Paul: Llewellyn Publications, 1969.

Rapping

Phenomena of knockings or rappings have usually accompanied **poltergeist** disturbances, even before the commencement of the modern Spiritualist movement. Thus they were observed in the case of the **Drummer of Tedworth,** the **"Cock Lane Ghost,"** and other disturbances of the kind, and also in the presence of various somnambules, such as **Frau Frederica Hauffe,** known as the Seeress of Prevorst.

With the **"Rochester Rappings"**—the famous outbreak at Hydesville in 1848—to which may be directly traced the beginning of modern **Spiritualism**—the phenomenon took on a new importance, rapidly increasing to an epidemic, remaining throughout the earlier stages of the movement the chief mode of communication with spirits.

Although it was afterward supplanted to some extent by more elaborate and complicated phenomena, it continued to occupy a place of some importance among the manifestations of the séance-room into the early twentieth century. It is apparent from descriptions furnished by witnesses that raps varied considerably both in quality and intensity, being sometimes characterized as dull thuds, sometimes as clear sounds like an electric spark, and again as deep, vibrating tones.

It has been shown that raps may be produced by the movement of various body parts (ankle-joints, knee-joints, shoulders, and other joints), and one man, Rev. Eli Noyes, claimed to have discovered seventeen different methods.

There are also instances on record where specially constructed "medium" tables were responsible for the manifestations. Besides the Spiritualist explanation and the frankly skeptical one of **fraud,** there have been other scientific (and pseudoscientific) theories advanced which ascribe the raps to various forces such as **od** (or odyle), **ectenic force,** or **animal magnetism.** (See also **Raps**)

Sources:

Brown, Slater. *The Heyday of Spiritualism.* New York: Hawthorne Books, 1970.

Pearsall, Ronald. *The Table-Rappers.* New York: St. Martin's Press, 1972.

Pond, Mariam Buckner. *Time Is Kind.* New York: Centennial Press, 1947.

Rapport

A mystical sympathetic or antipathetic connection between two persons. It was formerly believed that for a witch to harm her victims, the latter must first have become in *rapport* with her, either by contact with her person or by contact with some garment she has worn. A certain Irish witch, Florence Newton (tried in 1661), was accused of establishing *rapport* between herself and those she sought to bewitch by kissing them, whereby she was able to compass their destruction.

In the practice of **animal magnetism,** it was considered that the only invariable and characteristic symptom of the genuine trance was the *rapport* between patient and operator. It consisted of a **community of sensations**—the subject perceiving the sensations of the magnetizer and also divining his thought. In modern **hypnotism,** *rapport* denotes the community of sensation between the hypnotizer and his subject.

According to the psychical researcher **Julien Ochorowicz,** *rapport* was solely a "magnetic" condition. He observed that under hypnosis his subject was indifferent to anybody with whom he came in contact but in animal magnetism he had an incontestable preference for the magnetizer. In general, the touch of the magnetizer was agreeable while that of others was painful. This condition is not found in hypnosis.

The term *rapport* is also used in **Spiritualism,** signifying sympathy between the spirit **control** and the **medium** or any of the sitters. The control (through the medium) may be placed in *rapport* with anyone who is absent or dead, merely by handling something which has belonged to him or her. It is for a similar reason that in **crystal gazing** the crystal is sometimes held for a few moments prior to the inspection by the person on whose behalf the crystal-gazer is about to examine it.

The term *rapport* has also been employed by spiritual healers to describe the necessary relationship between the healer and the patient as a prerequisite for the successful flow of the healing power. *Rapport* is thus seen as an alternative to the patient's faith, sometimes suggested in religious healing circles as the necessary precondition for healing. (See also **psychometry**)

Raps

Percussive sounds of varying intensity without visible, known or normal agency, a common phenomenon of nineteenth-century **Spiritualism. Typtology** was the name given to the "science" of communicating with spirits by means of raps. While a simple phenomenon, raps were considered to be of tremendous importance by nineteenth-century psychical researchers. **Charles Richet,** for example, wrote in *Thirty Years of Psychical Research* (1923):

"The reality of these raps is of primary importance, and this phenomenon carries the implication of the whole of metapsychics. If it is established that mechanical vibrations can be produced in matter, at a distance, and without contact, and that these vibrations are intelligent, we have the truly far-reaching fact that there are in the universe human or non-human intelligences that can act directly on matter."

Modern Spiritualism began with **rappings** at Hydesville, New York, in 1848 in connection with the **Fox Sisters.** But the history of this paranormal manifestation reaches back into antiquity and the belief that it was in the house of the Fox family that intelligent contact with the unseen world through such agency was established for the first time is shortsighted.

Historical Background

Rudolf of Fulda, a chronicle dating from 858 C.E. spoke of communications with a rapping intelligence. The sixteenth-century physician **Paracelsus** called it "pulsatio mortuorum"—an omen of approaching death. The early church knew of *spiritus percutiens* (rapping spirits). They were conjured away by old Catholic formulae at the benediction of churches.

Raps were recorded by the theologian Philipp Melancthon in 1520 at Oppenheim, Germany. Montalambert, chaplain to François I, described raps which he heard in Lyon about 1521. According to a manuscript from 1610 at the University of Glasgow, Scotland, Mr. Welsh, a clergyman in Ayr, conversed with spirits by raps and observed movements of objects without contact.

The first detailed account of the phenomenon is in **Joseph Glanvill**'s *Saducismus Triumphatus* (1681). It described the disturbances of the so-called **Drummer of Tedworth** in the home of Magistrate Mompesson in 1661. It was discovered that an invisible entity would answer in drumming anything that was beaten or called for. But no further progress was made.

The phenomenon was a part of the **Epworth Phenomena** noticed at the home of Rev. Samuel Wesley, the father of John Wesley, in 1716. In the first quarter of the nineteenth century, **Justinus Kerner** detected in raps a means of conversation with the spirit visitants of **Frederica Hauffe,** better known as the Seeress of Prevorst. Then came the historic outbreak at Hydesville, followed two years later by the Stratford disturbances chronicled by Rev. **Eliakim Phelps.** Amid much public acrimony a literature grew up around the reality of the strange knocks.

The theories which have been advanced to explain the phenomenon are of historic interest. The cracking of knee joints and toe joints, the snapping of fingers, and the contraction of the respiratory muscles were variously called the scientific solution to the mystery. S. L. Loomis (1822–1896) offered one of the more creative theories. He discovered the effect of the vibrations of a dam over which water plunged. These sounds, transmitted to a distance by the earth, would produce sudden alarming knocking sounds in dwellings.

Raps were very likely often the product of **fraud.** British surgeon William Faulkner testified before the committee of the **London Dialectical Society** in 1869 that he was in the habit of selling trick magnets to produce rapping sounds at Spiritualist séances. The magnets could be concealed about the person or attached to furniture. By pressing a small brass button, raps could be produced whenever desired. Methods of fraud were described in various books by **Hereward Carrington,** Ed Lunt, and **David P. Abbott.**

Underneath the scientific theories there was a physiological foundation that suggested the use of a bodily mechanism of the medium that is responsible for the raps. Still it is one of the aberrations of scientific orthodoxy that when the **Seybert Commission** investigated the raps of Margaret Fox, one of the Fox Sisters, in 1884, the evidence for the genuine nature of the phenomenon was ruled out because one of the members of the committee, when placing his hand on her feet, distinctly felt an unusual pulsation although there was not a particle of motion in it.

Early Explanations of the Raps

But why should spirits knock and rap? According to **Andrew Lang**: "Were we inventing a form for a spirit's manifestation to take, we never should invent that." He frankly admitted that medieval and later tales of rapping have never been satisfactorily accounted for on any theory. He advanced a theory of "spectral aphasia," suggesting that raps may be the easiest signs which a spirit wishing to affect the physical plane may produce, though he may aim at a different effect.

In the March 1888 issue of *Psyche,* a Dr. Purdon reported on the curious connection he had discovered between raps and chorea. He noted the case of two soldiers in Guernsey, both of them of neurotic temperament, in whose presence rappings of an unnatural character were heard. Under the administration of iodide of potassium, salicylate of soda, and arsenic in full doses, the men improved wonderfully, and the rappings became less frequent.

E. Howard Grey, in his book *Visions, Previsions and Miracles in Modern Times* (1915), quoted a similar experience with a member of his own family. The attack commenced during the cutting of a child's permanent teeth, sometimes convulsions occurred in the night, and these generally seized upon the little girl about the same hour. He stated:

"We were usually well prepared for these nocturnal troubles by explosive and other auditory sounds, either on the wall or by Drs. Drury and Purdon, indeterminate or derial. Sometimes a tinkling sound as of dropping water would be heard, but none was visible, they occurred when the child was asleep, also in her absence . . .

"When she was in bed upstairs, they heard them in a room below; sometimes her mother heard them sounding like little taps on a newspaper she was reading. They did not exhibit intelligence. The last, or departing rap was especially loud. The cure was effected in a few months by the administration of bromide of potassium."

In speaking of the curious "thrilling" of the table in the presence of the great medium **D. D. Home,** Mrs. Augustus de Morgan wrote in *From Matter to Spirit* (1863):

"The last time I witnessed this phenomenon, an acute surgeon present said that this *thrilling,* the genuineness of which was unmistakable, was exactly like what takes place in that affection of the muscles called *subsultus tendinum.* When it ceased the table rose more than two feet from the floor."

In the closing years of the medium **Henry Slade,** loud raps were heard on the bedstead, walls, and furniture while he was asleep. Chairs and other furniture moved about. The phenomena occurred even after he sank into senile dementia. The same phenomenon was observed around the deathbed of Margaret Fox. The mysterious illness of **Mary Jobson** started with loud rapping sounds. When D. D. Home was ill the same manifestation was continually witnessed. Many observed a connection between abnormal conditions and paranormal phenomena, but the larger percentage of such manifestations involves no bodily affliction.

The Varieties of Rapping Experience

Simple as the phenomenon appears to be, various important accounts reflect an astounding variety of manifestation. **John Worth Edmonds** heard raps on his own person. The Rev. Samuel Watson, a nineteenth-century British Methodist preacher, had similar experiences. "The noise made on my shirt bosom," he wrote, "resembled more the telegraph machine than anything else." **Abby Warner,** of Massillon, Ohio, was prosecuted in 1851 for disturbing the Christmas service in St. Timothy's Church by raps which sounded in her presence.

Considerable excitement was caused in New York in 1871 in the prominent Brooklyn, New York, congregation of Henry Ward Beecher. In front of the rostrum at the reporter's table, raps were heard for a succession of Sabbaths, and slow and deliberate motion of the table was witnessed. Eugene Crowell reported that it kept time with the preacher's words and assented to Beecher's demands for reform with great pushes and movement to the opposite side of the sanctuary as if to say: "That's so, that is the truth."

Leah Underhill, the eldest of the Fox Sisters, wrote in her book *The Missing Link in Modern Spiritualism* (1885) that during the funeral of Calvin Brown, her second husband, raps were heard all over the room while S. B. Brittan delivered the funeral sermon and Edmonds the eulogy.

Robert Dale Owen recorded some very curious experiments in raps with Underhill in 1861. He heard raps on the seaside in a ledge of rock. "Placing my hands on the same ledge, a few steps from Mrs. Underhill and asking for raps, when this came audibly I felt, simultaneously with each rap, a slight but unmistakably distinct vibration or concussion of the rock." Owen heard raps onboard an excursion boat and later in a sailing boat sounding from underneath. He also obtained them in the open air on the ground; "a dull sound, as of blows struck on the earth; then I asked Mrs. Underhill to touch one of the trees with the tips of her fingers and applying my ear to the tree I heard the raps from beneath the bark." In an account of a séance on February 22, 1860, in which psychic lights were seen, Owen wrote:

"While I was looking intently at such a light, about as large as a small fist, it rose and fell, as a hammer would, with which one was striking against the floor. At each stroke a loud rap was heard in connection. It was exactly as if an invisible hand held an illuminated hammer and pounded with it."

As to the objectivity of the raps produced by Kate Fox, **Sir William Crookes** argued,

". . . it seems only necessary for her to place her hand on any substance for loud thuds to be heard in it, like a triple pulsation, sometimes loud enough to be heard several rooms off. In this manner I have heard them in a living tree—on a sheet of glass—on a stretched iron wire—on a stretched membrane—a tambourine—on the roof of a cab—and on the floor of a theatre. Moreover, actual contact is not always necessary. I have had these sounds proceeding from the floor, walls, &c. when the medium's hands and feet were held—when she was standing on a chair—when she was suspended in a swing from the ceiling—when she was enclosed in a wire cage—and when she had fallen fainting on a sofa. I have heard them on a glass harmonium—I have felt them on my own shoulder and under my own hands. I have heard them on a sheet of paper, held between the fingers by a piece of thread passed through one corner."

The membrane of which Crookes spoke was part of a complicated apparatus. A small piece of graphite was placed on it so as to be thrown upward by the slightest jar. The point of a lever registered in curves the amount of mechanical energy employed in the effect.

As to the sounds, Crookes observed:

". . . delicate ticks, as with the point of a pin; a cascade of sharp sounds as from an induction coil in full work; detonations in the air; sharp, metallic taps; a cracking like that heard when a frictional machine is at work; sounds like scratching; the twittering as of a bird, &c."

"We have been present with Kate Fox," wrote **J. J. Morse** in *The Two Worlds* newspaper (vol. 19) "when the raps were heard on a sheet of paper, held between the thumb and forefinger of another person standing beside the medium, the paper visibly shaking from the violence of the raps produced upon its surface."

Lord Adare's father, in experiments with D. D. Home, heard raps upon the medium's hand when he placed it upon his head. Raps came on a sheet of paper which they held by the corners. Adare heard raps under his feet and distinctly felt the jar while the raps were taking place. He saw a table leg rap. The spirits by raps joined into their conversation and signified approval in a most emphatic way. Adare was told to understand that by remaining in the earth's atmosphere, spirits get so charged that it is a positive relief to make sounds. Sometimes they cannot help rapping, and cannot control them. They discharge their electricity by a whole volley of taps.

The sounds may be single or combined knockings. "It was the most singular noise," wrote **William Stainton Moses** on December 5, 1873, "that the combined knockings made. The room seemed to be full of intelligences manifesting their presence." The sounds had distinct individuality. They had characteristics as permanent as the voice, and the communicator could often be recognized by his rapping style.

Dr. J. Garth Wilkinson wrote of an inward thrill going through the table and chairs and found the sensation best conveyed by the exclamation of his daughter: "Oh, papa, there is a heart in my chair."

"The departure of the spirits," wrote J. H. Powell in *Spiritualism; Its Facts and Phases* (1864), "was preceded by an indistinguishable number of raps, loud at first, then gradually faint and fainter until, like echoes on a hill, they faded away in the echoing distance."

In volume, the sounds may grow from a tiny tick to a loud crash. But the crashing blows leave no mark, although normally such force would be expected to smash the table. The tonality of the raps differs according to the object upon which they resound. They may resemble the slight noises made by a mouse, a fretsaw, or the scratching of a fingernail on wood or cloth, and their rhythm is as varied as their tonality.

They often sound like detonations. There are instances in which the impression is borne out by effect. Archdeacon **Thomas Colley,** in a **slate-writing** experiment with the medium **Francis W. Monck,** placed his foot on the slate and felt a sensation of throbbing in the enclosed space—a heaving as when the confined steam lifts the lid of a kettle—and in a moment, an explosion took place that scattered the slate in fragments over the carpet, like spray from a fountain. Such explosions and shatterings of the slate were frequently reported in séances with the medium Henry Slade.

Helena Petrovna Blavatsky, the co-founder of the **Theosophical Society,** was a powerful rapping medium in her teens. While later accused of reproducing Spiritualist tricks, she was said to have caused raps inside the spectacles of a skeptical professor with such force that they were sent flying from his nose. In reply to a somewhat frivolous woman who asked what was the best conductor for raps, the table spelt out "gold," and the next moment the lady in question rushed out of the room with her hand clapped on her mouth, as she had felt the raps on the gold in her artificial teeth.

Joseph Maxwell obtained raps in restaurants and railway refreshment rooms which were loud enough to attract public attention. In his book *Metapsychical Phenomena* (1905), he described experiences of "Doctor X." with the medium Meurice:

"The raps on the open umbrella are extremely curious. We have heard raps on the woodwork and on the silk at one and the same time; it is easy to perceive that the shock actually occurs in the wood—that the molecules of the latter are set in motion. The same thing occurs with the silk, and here observation is even more interesting still; and each rap *looks* like a drop of some invisible liquid falling on the silk from a respectable height. The stretched silk of the umbrella is quickly and slightly but surely dented in; sometimes the force with which the raps are given is such as to shake the umbrella. Nothing is more absorbing than the observation of an apparent conversation—by means of the umbrella—between the medium's personifications. Raps, imitating a burst of laughter in response to the observer's remarks, resound on the silk, like the rapid play of strong but tiny fingers. When raps on the umbrella are forthcoming, M. Meurice either holds the handle of the umbrella, or someone else does, whilst he simply touches the handle very lightly with his open palm. He never touches the silk."

Maxwell concluded,

"(1) Every muscular movement, even a feeble one, is generally followed by a rap. (2) The intensity of the raps does not strike me as being in proportion with the movement made. (3) The intensity of the raps did not seem to me to vary proportionately according to their distance from the medium."

He questioned mediums about their sensations when raps were being produced. They acknowledged a feeling of fatigue, of depletion, after a good séance, a feeling perceptible to observers. One of the mediums reported a cramp-like feeling in the epigastric region when the raps were particularly loud.

In *From Matter to Spirit* (1863), the wife of **Augustus de Morgan** wrote that once, through typtological communication (i.e., through raps), she was informed that raps would come through herself that day.

"This was not expected but it was worth trying, and I therefore went into an uncarpeted room barely furnished, and sat down by the table, on which I laid my arm. Very soon loud raps, which I called some of the family to hear, resounded on the table. There seemed to be power enough to rap the number of times desired, but not to indicate letters so as to spell anything. The sounds soon ceased and never returned. As each rap seemed to be shot through my arm it was accompanied by a feeling like a slight blow or shock of electricity and an aching pain extending from the shoulder to the hand, which remained for more than an hour after they had entirely ceased. This experiment seemed to prove that the nerves of the human body were necessary, if not for the production, at least for the propagation of the sounds.

In the experiments of **W. J. Crawford,** the loudness of the raps varied with weight and massiveness of the psychic "rods." Crawford put the medium, later discovered to be producing phenomena by trickery, on a weighing machine and measured the exact amount of ectoplasm necessary for the increase of rapping strength. He also found that the raps reacted upon the medium's body but that she was not conscious of any stress. The reaction, however, was not always the case, as he noted:

"As soon as the séance begins, we hear noises, raps, rap, rap on the floor near the medium. They become louder and louder, on the table, on the chairs of the sitters. Sometimes they are like hammerblows, so loud that they can be heard outside, and they shake the floor and the chairs. They can imitate any different sounds, the step of a man, the trot of a horse, the rubbing of a match, or the bouncing of a ball."

Sir William F. Barrett, who like Crawford also sat in the **Goligher circle,** wrote in *On the Threshold of the Unseen* (1917): "Very soon knocks came and messages were spelt out as one of us repeated the alphabet aloud. Suddenly the knocks increased in violence, and being encouraged, a tremendous bang came which shook the room and resembled the blow of a sledge hammer on an anvil.

In *Proceedings* of the Society for Psychical Research (vol. 17, p. 726), a case of rapping was described by a Mrs. Davis who had received a letter from India with the request to forward it to a Mrs. W. She placed the letter on the mantelpiece. Some time after, raps were heard. They seemed to emanate from the neighborhood of the letter. She placed it on another spot. The raps followed the letter. It was discovered afterward that the letter had some urgency attached to it as it announced the death of Mrs. W.'s husband.

James H. Hyslop, in a sitting with a young non-professional female medium, heard loud raps in a closed piano. He wrote, in *Contact with the Other World* (1919):

"After getting raps under her feet I had her stand on a very thick cushion. When she was standing on the cushion, which was at least six or eight inches thick, the raps occurred exactly as before, with the same quality of sound. If made by the joints, the raps would have been muffled when the feet were on the cushion. I then had her stand with a foot on each of my hands, which rested on the cushion, and the raps occurred apparently on the floor with the same quality of sound as when her feet were on the floor. I then tried the steam radiator some distance away, and the rap had a metallic ring, as if on iron. I then tried the piano experiment again. . . . The raps were very loud, and made the string ring so that the sound could be heard perhaps a hundred feet away."

Again Barrett, in his *On the Threshold of the Unseen,* observed: "On one occasion I asked for the raps to come on a small table near me, which Florrie [the medium] was not touching, they did so; I then placed one of my hands on the upper and the other on the under surface of the table, and in this position I felt the slight jarring made by the raps on the part of the table enclosed between my hands. It made no difference whether Florrie and I were alone in the room, as was often the case, or other observers were called in."

The distance to which the sound of raps carry may be considerable. In Southend, England, metallic raps produced on the rail in the presence of Moses and Dr. Stanhope T. Speer were audible to both of them when they were seventy yards apart. The raps were apparently made in the space between them.

An interesting non-psychic method of procuring raps was described in *Psychic Research* (February 1930) by John E. Springer, a attorney from Palo Alto, California:

"In one face of a small cardboard box I cut an aperture the size and shape of my ear. When fitted to the ear the box sticks on securely and becomes a sort of sounding board. Upon retiring I affix the box to the ear which is not to rest on the pillow, and I will as strongly as possible that as I fall asleep I shall be awakened by a given series of raps upon the cardboard. It frequently—but not always—happens that when I reach the stage of drowsiness where unconsciousness is about to supervene, loud and clear raps upon the box in the predetermined series bring me back to wakefulness with a start. The raps may be subjective, but it is difficult for one who experiences them to escape from the conviction that they are objective psychic raps."

The medium **Eusapia Palladino** frequently rapped a certain number of times on the table with her fingers. Holding her hands about eighteen inches above the table the faint echoes of the raps were heard in the wood about two seconds later. She produced the same phenomenon with scratching sounds.

In the séances with **Mina A. Crandon** ("Margery"), the first raps were faint but definite, sounding like something soft inside a wooden box. Dr. Crandon listened to them through a stethoscope applied to the table. They were so magnified as to be unlike anything in his experience. Later they developed to such a degree that the **control** "Walter" could render tunes or rhythmical phrases with a marked syncopation upon the cabinet, the table, the arm of "Margery," the hands of the sitters, and even on the limited surface of a ring. Once he rapped out a popular tune unknown in his day and answered in explanation that they (the spirits) go everywhere, to our theaters and other places.

There are some rare cases on record in which raps were produced in the distance. The Seeress of Prevorst (Frederica Hauffe) could cause raps in the houses of others. There were similar testimonies in the mediumship of D. D. Home. **Cromwell Fleetwood Varley** stated before the London Dialectical Society that he heard raps in his home after his arrival from a séance with D. D. Home. The next morning he received a letter from Home which disclosed that the medium knew of the occurrence.

Countess Panaigai wrote in a letter to *Human Nature* (vol. 11) that in a sitting with Home the name of her deceased child was rapped out and that Home predicted the hearing of raps in her own house. The prediction not only came true, but when a friend called her attention to it she found the little boot of her child (kept in a locked box in a bureau) from which the raps appeared to proceed, imprinted by a perfect star with a letter at each of the six points forming the name "Stella," as the deceased was called. Not even the family of the Countess knew anything of the box and Home, to whom she was an utter stranger, was never in her house.

Interconnection of Psychic Phenomena

According to the hypothesis of spirit communication, raps represent the most primitive form of such communication. They may be manifest independently or through the faculties of a psychic individual. They may be obtained collectively through table-tipping or **table-turning,** in which a group sits round a table with their hands resting on it, and the raps indicate a letter of the alphabet, or a simple "yes" or "no" by one rap or two. This is a slow and tedious procedure.

Much more rapid communication is established through such simple devices as the **ouija board** or the **planchette.** Much swifter and more direct is **automatic writing,** in which the communicating entity operates the hand of the psychic.

In the presence of specially gifted mediums, **direct writing** by spirit hands has been reported. More direct still are the messages received vocally through a medium and, in rare instances, **direct voice** independent of the vocal apparatus of the medium.

It is not always clear if claimed spirit messages are the product of the subconscious mentation of the medium or the sitters, since fictitious entities can be created in séances (see **"Philip"**). Evaluation depends upon the detail and overall paranormal quality of the evidence in individual cases.

Sources:

Abbott, David P. *Behind the Scenes With the Mediums.* LaSalle, Ill.: Open Court, 1907.

Brownson, Orestes Augustus. *The Spirit-Rapper.* Boston: Little, Brown, 1854.

Carrington, Hereward. *The Physical Phenomena of Spiritualism.* Boston: Small; London: T. Werner Laurie, 1907.

Crowell, Eugene. *Identity of Primitive Christianity and Modern Spiritualism.* 2 vols. 1875–79.

Doyle, Arthur Conan. *The History of Spiritualism.* 2 vols. London: Cassell New York: Geo. H. Doran, 1926. One volume. Reprint, New York: Arno Press, 1975.

Jackson, Herbert G., Jr. *The Spirit Rappers.* Garden City, N.Y.: Doubleday, 1972.

Lang, Andrew. *Cock Lane and Common-Sense.* London: Longmans, Green, 1896. Reprint, New York: AMS Press, 1970.

A Medium [Ed Lunt]. *Mysteries of the Séance.* Boston: Lunt Brothers, 1905.

Pearsall, Ronald. *Table-Rappers.* London: Joseph, 1972. Reprint, New York: St. Martin's Press, 1973.

Rochester Knockings! Discovery and Explanation of the Source of the Phenomena Generally Known as the Rochester Knockings. Buffalo, N.Y., 1851.

"A Searcher After Truth." *The Rappers; or, the Mysteries, Fallacies, and Absurdities of Spirit Rapping, Table-Tipping and Entrancement.* Long, N.Y. 1854.

Rasmussen, Anna (Melloni) (1898– ?)

Danish medium for physical and intellectual phenomena. Her mediumship was first manifested at the age of twelve, when a table moved both with and without contact. **Poltergeist** phenomena developed, then died out to give place to a range of phenomena: **telekinesis, raps, slate-writing,** automatic writing, **luminous phenomena** and **trance** speech under the control of an entity "Dr. Lasaruz."

In October and November 1921, the mediumship was examined at Fritz Grünewald's laboratory at Berlin. The results were placed before the second International Congress for Psychical Research at Warsaw, Poland, in 1923. The electrical condition of the séance room was a particularly noticeable phenomenon.

In September 1922, Christian Winther, of the Polytechnic Academy of Copenhagen, commenced a series of scientific experiments in which a Professor Bondorff, of the Danish Agricultural High School, the Laboratory Director R. Dons, and Dr. A. Marner, a practicing physician also participated. According to Winther's detailed account in *Psychic Research* (1928) among 116 séances which he had with the medium not a single one was completely negative.

There appeared a steady outpouring of psychical energy and if a séance was not organized the medium became restless and felt ill. In many cases she gave two, three, or even four sittings in a single day. All the sittings took place in actual daylight or in very strong artificial light. The medium sat quietly in the circle at the table, took her share of the conversation, took refreshments, read a newspaper and had apparently no connection with what was going on. Trance, however, was always a great fatigue, and it was only employed when this was the special subject of study.

Some of the automatic scripts came in English. A unique feature of her mediumship was that raps emanated from her left shoulder and answered questions. The British psychical researcher **Harry Price** placed his ear against the medium's shoulder and distinctly heard decided thumps from her body (*Psychic Research,* 1928, p. 377).

Rasputin, Gregory Efimovitch (1869–1916)

Charismatic Russian monk, who became a powerful figure in the court of Czar Nicholas II, before the Romanov dynasty was swept aside by the Russian Revolution of 1917. The son of a peasant, Rasputin joined a monastery as a novice at the age of sixteen. As the Orthodox Church established hegemony in Russia, various dissenting sect groups emerged, among them the Khlysty. The Khlysty were supposedly founded in the seventeenth century by Daniel Filippov. They deviated from Orthodoxy in numerous ways. Several different splinter groups developed through the nineteenth century and by the beginning of the twentieth century the Khlysty numbered approximately 65,000 people.

Rasputin came into early contact with the Khlysty, though it is unclear just how dedicated a member he had been. Rasputin married around 1890, but his first son died when only six months old. The tragedy sent Rasputin to a strange hermit named Makary, and subsequently Rasputin became absorbed in scriptures, prayer, and meditation. One day he saw an image of the Virgin in the sky, and Makary told him, "God has chosen you for a great achievement. In Order to strengthen your spiritual power, you should go and pray to the Virgin in the convent of Afon."

The convent was at Mount Athos, in Greece, two thousand miles away, but in 1891, Rasputin made the pilgrimage on foot. Later he made a pilgrimage to the Holy Land, traveling across Turkey. For the next few years he became a wandering *staretz* (lay priest). He was widely believed to possess occult power, which made him both loved and feared. He manifested gifts of healing and prophecy. In 1903, he traveled to St. Petersburg, where he met influential churchmen, including the monk Illiodor, who later became a hateful rival. Rasputin's reputation as a prophet and miracle worker spread widely, and he was sought by rich and poor.

In those days, Russian court life and high society were still strongly attracted to the marvels of Spiritualism which had been introduced in the 1860s by Alexander N. Aksakof, and any wonder worker was in great demand. Soon Rasputin came to the attention of the czar of Russia to whom he became an indispensable adviser and healer to the royal family.

Surrounded by the madhouse of tyranny, secret police, bomb plots, crippling wars, and the ruthless suppression of liberty of the Romanov empire, Rasputin, self-absorbed in his own sense of destiny, towered above the sycophants, bureaucrats, and plotters. He treated the czar and czarina with complete familiarity, and they welcomed Rasputin because of the healing powers he supposedly possessed; he seemed to be able to treat the couple's only son, Alexis, who was a hemophiliac. In 1911, tiring of court life, he undertook another pilgrimage to the Holy Land, and during his absence his enemies intrigued against him. In the fall of 1915, when the czar left to take command of the Russian army, Rasputin took on more power as the czarina's chief aide. Rasputin forced many of the cabinet ministers to resign, and he replaced them with his cronies. His enemies, headed by Prince Yussupov, felt he had taken on too much political power and planned his murder.

The day before Rasputin was killed, Czar Nicholas requested his blessing and with curious presence, Rasputin said, "This time it is for you to bless me." Yussupov invited Rasputin to his palace and persuaded him to eat poisoned food and drink poisoned wine. The poison was ineffectual. Thereupon the treacherous Yussupov sang gypsy songs and played the guitar before leaving the room and returning with a loaded revolver, shooting his victim in the back. Other conspirators rushed in clumsily, accidentally switching off the room light. When the light was switched on again, Rasputin appeared dead, but was still alive. Another conspirator shot Rasputin again; the body was dragged from the house and battered with a steel press. But Rasputin was still alive when he was pushed through a hole in the ice on the River Neva. And although his wrists had been bound, he had still managed to free his right hand and make the sign of the cross before drowning. He died December 31, 1916.

Sources:

Bolshakoff, Serge. *Russian Nonconformity.* Philadelphia: Westminster Press, 1950. Reprint, New York: AMS Press, 1973.

Fülop-Miller, René. *Rasputin; The Holy Devil.* New York: Viking Press, 1928.

Klibanv. A. I. *History of Religious Sectarianism in Russia (1860s–1917).* Oxford: Pergamon Press, 1982.

Rasputina, Maria. *My Father.* London: McClelland/Cassell, 1934. Reprint, New Hyde Park, N.Y.: University Books, 1970.

Vogel-Jorgensen, T. *Rasputin: Prophet, Libertine, Plotter.* London: T. Fisher Unwin, 1917. Reprint, New Hyde Park, N.Y.: University Books, 1970.

Wilson, Colin. *Rasputin and the Fall of the Romanovs.* London: Arthur Barker, 1964.

Ratte, Rena J(osephine) (1928–)

Instructor in philosophy who has experimented in the field of parapsychology. She was born on September 7, 1928, at Waterville, Maine. She studied at the University of Maine (B.A., 1951) and Duke University, (M.A., 1958; Ph.D., 1959). After receiving her doctorate, Ratte was a research fellow at the **Parapsychology Laboratory,** (1959–60), and joined the faculty in philosophy at Lewis and Clark College, Portland, Oregon, from 1960 onward.

She joined the **Parapsychology Association.** In her parapsychological work she focused on **psychokinesis** and experimented in the use of game techniques in PK to ascertain whether the PK effect would be enhanced by a game atmosphere.

Sources:

Pleasants, Helene, ed. *Biographical Dictionary of Parapsychology.* New York: Helix Press, 1964.

Ratte, Rena J. "Three Exploratory Studies of ESP in a Game Situation." *Journal of Parapsychology* 25 (1961).

Ratte, Rena J., and Frances M. Greene. "An Exploratory Investigation of PK in a Game Situation." *Journal of Parapsychology* (1960).

Raudive, Konstantin (1909–1974)

Latvian psychologist and parapsychologist who spent many years investigating **electronic voice phenomenon,** involving electronic tape recordings of voices allegedly belonging to dead individuals, which has been popularly known as **Raudive voices.** His surname is pronounced "Row-dee-vay." Born in Uppsala, Sweden, on April 30, 1909, he studied psychology in Switzerland, Germany, and England. For some time he was a teacher at the University of Riga and also edited a Latvian newspaper. In Switzerland he had studied psychology under **Carl Jung** and was also a pupil of the Spanish philosopher Ortega y Gasset. He left Latvia when the Soviet Army invaded the Baltic and absorbed Latvia in 1945. With his wife, Dr. Zenta Maurina, he lived for a time in Sweden, later moving to Bad Kroningen, Germany, near the border with Switzerland.

It was during his period in Sweden in 1965 that Raudive met **Friedrich Jürgenson** who had pioneered the study of paranormal voice recordings. In 1959, Jürgenson tape-recorded a Swedish finch, and on playback he heard what appeared to be a human voice in addition to the bird. He thought there must be some fault in the apparatus, but subsequent recordings contained a message which seemed to be recognizably from his dead mother. Jürgenson described his experiments in his book *Rösterna från Rymden* (Voices From Space), published in Sweden in 1964. Prior to Jürgenson, **Raymond Bayless** had reported such phenomena. Raudive published an account of his research in 1968.

Starting in 1965, Raudive and his wife devoted themselves to investigating this phenomenon of paranormal voices manifesting on tape recordings, later assisted by Swiss physicist Alex Schneider and various engineers. Other scientists and parapsychologists who investigated the electronic voice phenomenon included Professor **Hans Bender** of the University of Freiburg, Germany, and Dr. Friedebert Karger of the Max Planck Institute in Munich. After 1969, differences of opinion arose between Jürgenson and Raudive, and thereafter they conducted their research independently.

Essentially the electronic voice phenomenon consists of paranormal voice communications (apparently from dead individuals) manifesting on recordings made on a standard tape recorder (sometimes enhanced by a simple diode circuit). The voices are also apparent on the "white noise" of certain radio bands.

The communications are usually fragmentary and ambiguous, rather like those produced by a **ouija board,** and need considerable amplification. The voices are sometimes in a mixture of different languages, rather like scrambled radio bands, but in many cases they appear to be recognizably from persons known to the experimenters during their lifetimes. They comment on the experimenters or convey cryptic messages in a kind of terse, disjointed telegram style. So far no communications appear to indicate high intelligence and seem relatively trivial.

Various explanations of the voices have been suggested. They may be sounds relayed back to earth from other planets by some unknown natural phenomenon or a potpourri of ordinary radio communications. Some skeptics think the voices may be imaginary, since listening to amplified electronics static and hum may suggest voices that do not really exist. Another theory is that the voices come from the subconscious of the experimenters, impressed on the tapes like the thought-forms of **psychic photography.**

Against such theories and criticisms, a number of highly qualified researchers have conducted and analyzed thousands of careful experiments which lead them to suggest that some of these recordings are of paranormal voices, and voice prints of communications purporting to be from the same source show matching patterns.

In June 1970, David Ellis, a Cambridge graduate, had been elected to the Perrott-Warrick Studentship which grants aid to conduct psychic research. He studied a selection of Raudive tapes in 1970. In his 1978 book, his findings were largely skeptical, and he believed that on occasion Raudive may have mistaken fragments of foreign language broadcasts for paranormal voice communications. However, Ellis was inclined to believe some of the voices might be paranormal, but their faintness and the background noise prevented positive identification.

Raudive died September 2, 1974, and his widow Dr. Zenta Maurina-Raudive published a tribute to his work. After his death, controversy arose on the question of archive storage and availability for study of the Raudive Collection, which the **Society for Psychical Research** expressed willingness to house.

Sources:

Bander, Peter. *Carry On Talking: How Dead are the Voices?* London: Colin Smythe, 1972. Reprinted as *Voices from the Tapes.* New York: Drake Publishers, 1973.

Berger, Arthur S., and Joyce Berger. *The Encyclopedia of Parapsychology and Psychical Research.* New York: Paragon House, 1991.

Ellis, David J. *The Mediumship of the Tape Recorded.* West Essex, UK: The Author, 1978.

Maurina-Raudive, Zenta, ed. *Konstantin Raudive zum Gedaechtnis.* München: Maximilian Dietrich Verlag, 1975.

Ostrander, Sheila, and Lynn Schroeder. *Handbook of Psi Discoveries.* New York: G. P. Putnam's Sons, 1974. Reprint, New York: Berkeley Publishing, 1975. Reprint, London: Abacus, 1977.

Raudive, Konstantin. *Unhörbares Wird Hörbar* (The Inaudible Made Audible). N.p., 1968. English edition as *Breakthrough: An Amazing Experiment in Electronic Communication with the Dead.* Translated by Peter Bander. New York: Taplinger, 1971.

Raudive Voices

Popular term for the electronic voice phenomenon first reported by Raymond Bayless, but rediscovered by **Friedrich Jürgenson** in 1959. Voices, apparently from deceased individuals, are found to be electronically impressed on tape recordings made on standard apparatus (sometimes enhanced by a simple diode circuit). The voices are also apparent on the "white noise" of certain radio bands. The suggestion that they are communications from the dead is based on many thousands of experimental recordings made by Jürgenson and later **Konstantin Raudive,** and later replicated by various parapsychologists, including **Hans Bender.**

Konstantin Raudive (1909–1974), a Latvian psychologist, conducted joint experiments with Jürgenson between 1964 and 1969 after reading a reference to the paranormal voice phenomenon in Jürgenson's book. Subsequently the two men had some differences of opinion and conducted their further researches independently.

Raudive's researches were very extensive and included collection and study of over 100,000 recordings. After the publicity given to his book *Unhörbares Wird Hörbar,* translated into English in an enlarged edition as *Breakthrough: An Amazing Experiment in Electronic Communication* (1971), the phenomenon became generally known and discussed as "Raudive voices." The book was translated by **Peter Bander,** a British psychologist who subsequently appeared on a number of television and radio programs to discuss the subject. His own book reviewed replication experiments in Britain and the Irish Republic, the attitudes of religious authorities, the experiments carried out by the electronic experts, and the alternative theories to explain the phenomenon.

Bender, working at Freiburg University in Germany, suggested that electronic impulses might be transmitted by the subconscious mind and impressed on tapes, rather like **psychic photographs.** However, there is some evidence tending to suggest that the communications are mainly from dead individuals.

A later development of Raudive's researches into paranormal voices were his investigation of a budgerigar (a bird) named Putzi, owned by Editha von Damaros in Germany. In March 1972, von Damaros wrote to Raudive stating that a few weeks after the death of her daughter Barbara at the age of fourteen, her pet budgerigar started giving extraordinary messages suggestive of spirit communications; one of these advised contacting "the Latvian doctor." Raudive made a careful investigation of the budgerigar and took a number of recordings. It concluded that possibly the bird was being used as an energy field for the direct transmission of paranormal voices.

This investigation has led to some confusion, since Jürgenson's original researches into paranormal voices on tape recordings were stimulated by attempts to record bird song. "Bird voices," however, remain a quite separate phenomenon from "Raudive Voices."

Sources:

Bander, Peter. *Carry On Talking: How Dead are the Voices?* London: Colin Smythe, 1972. Reprinted as *Voices from the Tapes.* New York: Drake Publishers, 1973.

Berger, Arthur S., and Joyce Berger. *The Encyclopedia of Parapsychology and Psychical Research.* New York: Paragon House, 1991.

Jürgenson, Friedrich. *Rösterna från Rymden* (Voices From Space). Sweden, 1964. German edition as *Sprechfunk mit Verstorbenen.* Freiburg i. Br.: Herman Bauer, 1967.

Ray, P(ramode) C(handra) (1916–)

Psychologist who carried out research in the field of parapsychology. He was born on January 1, 1916, in East Bengal, India. He studied at the University of Calcutta (M.Sc. psychology, 1940) and did graduate work in clinical psychology at the Institute of Psychiatry, Maudsley Hospital, London, England. After graduation he joined the staff of the Anthropological Survey of India of the Government of India and rose from lab assistant to psychologist and officer in charge of the Department of Psychology. In addition to his studies and papers on psychological subjects, he carried out a research project on possession amongst the Lodha tribe of Bengal.

Rayleigh, Lord (1842–1919)

World-famous as experimental physicist, the discoverer of argon, and president of the **Society for Psychical Research** (SPR), London (1919). He was born John William Strutt on November 12, 1842. He inherited the title as the 3rd Baron Rayleigh from his father. He attended Trinity College, Cambridge (Senior Wrangler and Smith's Prizeman 1865, Fellow 1866). He was the Cavendish professor of experimental physics at Cambridge (1879–84) and a professor of natural philosophy at the Royal Institution (1887–1905). He was secretary of the Royal Society (1884–1896) and was awarded the Nobel Prize for physics in 1904 for his discovery of argon. He published many scientific papers and one important book *Theory of Sound* (2 vols., 1894–96).

One of several members of royalty interested in psychical research, Lord Rayleigh married Evelyn Balfour, the sister of **Arthur James Balfour,** one of the presidents of the SPR in the 1890s. Evelyn Balfour's other sibling was Eleanor Sidgwick, wife of SPR founder **Henry Sidgwick.** In 1876 in the discussion of **William F. Barrett**'s paper on **Spiritualism** before the British Association for the Advancement of Science, he declared that his own interest in the subject dated from 1874. He was first attracted to it by the investigations of **Sir William Crookes.** "Although," he stated, "my opportunities have not been so good as those enjoyed by Professor Barrett, I have seen enough to convince me that those are wrong who wish to prevent investigation by casting ridicule on those who may feel inclined to engage in it."

Physical phenomena impressed him more than mental phenomena. He had many sittings with Kate Fox-Jencken, one of the **Fox sisters,** and with **Eusapia Palladino.** He was nonplussed by the result. Yet he never felt sufficiently convinced to declare himself in public. He paid little attention to **automatic writing** and **trance** phenomena. He did not think the evidence for **telepathy** conclusive, but he declared that, given irrefragable evidence for telepathy between living persons, he would have no difficulty in extending it to telepathy from the dead.

Speaking of Kate Fox-Jencken and the famous medium **D. D. Home** in his presidential address before the Society for Psychical Research, London, in 1919 (see pp. 275–290) he said: "I repudiate altogether the idea of hallucination as an explanation. The incidents were almost always unexpected, and our impressions of them agreed" (Rayleigh, pp. 275–90). He died June 30, 1919.

Sources:

Berger, Arthur S., and Joyce Berger. *The Encyclopedia of Parapsychology and Psychical Research.* New York: Paragon House, 1991.

Pleasants, Helene, ed. *Biographical Dictionary of Parapsychology.* New York: Helix Press, 1964.

Rayleigh, Lord. "Presidential Address." *Proceedings* of the Society for Psychical Research 30, 70 (1918–1919).

Rays from the Rose Cross (Magazine)

Monthly publication of the **Rosicrucian Fellowship** founded by **Max Heindel** (1865–1919). It may be ordered from the fellowship's headquarters at 2222 Mission Ave., Oceanside, CA 92054-2399. The magazine is also available on the society's homepage at http://www.rosicrucian.com/rays.htm.

Sources:

Rays from the Rose Cross Magazine. http://www.rosicrucian.com/rays.htm. March 8, 2000.

Reality Change (Magazine)

Quarterly magazine "for people who want to change their lives," discussed the Seth Material channeled through medium **Jane Roberts** (1929–1984). The magazine contained news of **Seth** conferences and local groups, as well as contributions reporting personal experiences in relation to the Seth teachings. Last known address: **Austin Seth Center,** P.O. Box 7786, Austin, TX 78713-7786.

"Rebazar Tarzs"

Claimed to be the Tibetan lama guide of **Paul Twitchell,** founder of the religious organization **ECKANKAR** promoting "the ancient science of soul travel," a kind of **out-of-the-body travel** or **astral projection** to other planes. Researcher David Christopher Lane raised serious questions about the existence of "Rebazar Tarzs."

Sources:

Lane, David Christopher. *The Making of a Spiritual Movement.* Del Mar, Calif.: Del Mar Press, 1983.

Rebus (Newspaper)

The first Spiritualist periodical in Russia, founded in 1881, that, owing to the antagonism of the authorities to **Spiritualism,** was professedly devoted to rebuses and charades. It was commenced by Captain (later Admiral) Victor Ivanovitch Pribytkoff, and it was largely financed by **Alexander Aksakof.**

Reclaiming

The Reclaiming tradition of contemporary American **witchcraft** developed from a working collective in San Francisco in the summer of 1980 when Diane Baker and **Starhawk** decided to co-teach a basic class in Witchcraft. The initial class became so popular that a series of three classes were created which became known as the original Core Classes—The Elements of Magic, the Pentacle of Iron, and Rites of Passage. Classes were team-taught within a sacred space. This group of teachers and their students shared what they learned and eventually coalesced into a Reclaiming Collective. Soon classes were offered in groups consisting of all women, all men, or mixed genders; many of these classes evolved into future covens.

During the 1980s, many Collective members and people from the larger Reclaiming community were active in antinuclear civil disobedience. The Collective's activities, from designing classes to dealing with domestic concerns to public political protests, stemmed from the Religious Society of Friends (Quakers). These concepts and method of decision-making fostered close bonds among participants.

Concurrently, Reclaiming Collective began four public sabbat rituals at the Cross-Quarters and four issues of a small newsletter at the Solstices and Equinoxes. The Collective wrote a statement which appeared in each issue of the *Reclaiming Newsletter:*

"Reclaiming is a community of San Francisco Bay Area women and men working to unify spirit and politics. Our vision is rooted in the religion and magic of the Goddess—the Immanent Life Force. We see our work as teaching and making magic—the art of empowering ourselves and each other. In our classes, workshops, and public rituals, we train our voices, bodies, energy, intuition, and minds. We use the skills we learn to deepen our strength, both as individuals and as community, to voice our concerns about the world in which we live, and bring to birth a vision of a new culture."

So unlike most other Craft traditions, Reclaiming espouses a connection between spirituality and political action.

The Core Classes of the Reclaiming Tradition

The development of the core classes derived from Starhawk's and Diane Baker's basic classes in Witchcraft. The first class, known as the Elements of Magic, teaches basic ritual, concepts and correspondences, energy sensing and projecting, shifting consciousness, spellwork, and theology.

The second, or Iron Pentacle class, based upon a Faery Witchcraft concept, focuses on trance work and the discovery of the healing powers of the human body through meditations on the five-pointed star. The points represent sex, self, passion, pride, and power. Its opposite is the Pentacle of Pearl whose points represent love, law, wisdom, knowledge, and power. Both pentacles have correspondences with the head, hands and feet, going round and transversing the human body touching the points of a five-pointed star.

The third, or Rites of Passage, is the most adaptable class; it is usually redesigned, or created anew, by different teachers.

Besides the three classes, Reclaiming developed a concept in the 1990s known as the Three Souls—a concept sharing Faery Tradition Witchcraft, Hawaiian, Jewish, and Celtic cultures. Starhawk's own adaptation of this concept is called the Three Selves: The Spiral Dance, which represents the Younger Self; the Talking Self, or unconscious mind, which gives verbal and conscious expression; and Deep Self or God Self, which deals with the Divine within oneself.

Rituals Roles of Reclaiming

The leading of public rituals teach new ways of doing magic in large groups with participants of all degrees of magical expertise and inspire the creation of methods and roles to meet these changing circumstances.

Among those roles are "Crows," who oversee everything from an individual ritual to teaching plans to overall Collective activities. Snakes view things from the ground, the "little, down-to-Earth things." "Dragons" guard the perimeters of circles in public outdoor spaces such as beaches so that participants can work undistracted by curious passersby; they do not directly participate in the work of a ritual because they are providing a buffer between the public and the inner circle. In this role, Dragons are similar to what are called in other traditions Guardians, the Summoner or the Man in Black. "Graces" act as assistant priest or priestesses; they welcome people, guide them, keep aisles clear, get people standing, sitting, chanting, dancing, assembled for a spiral dance, all in different and appropriate parts of the ritual. Graces could be compared, in some sense, to Maidens in other Craft traditions.

In recent years Reclaiming employed "Anchors" in large public rituals. Anchors are individuals who help focus and contain the energy of the circle in settings where it might be prone to fragmentation and dissolution. They act to contain the energy until it's time to release and direct it. It's important that the anchor not try to control the energy of the ritual or to ground it through their body.

Currently, some Reclaiming Witches are trained in *aspecting*—a technique which closely corresponds to what in traditional British Craft traditions more commonly known as *Drawing Down the Moon.* Not all Reclaiming Witches practice all these techniques. Many full-fledged and respected Reclaiming Witches were trained and proceeded in their personal and coven practices before some of these techniques were commonly used.

Distinguishing Features of Reclaiming

In *The Pagan Book of Living and Dying,* Starhawk describes Reclaiming's style of ritual as *EIEIO*—Ecstatic, Improvisational, Ensemble, Inspired, and Organic. Practices are constantly growing, being "extended, refined, renewed and changed as the spirit moves us and need arises, rather than . . . learned and repeated in a formulaic manner."

Distinguishing features of Reclaiming Tradition Witchcraft are:

(1) non-hierarchal covens and group priest- or priestess-hoods;
(2) no specific pantheon;
(3) no requirement of initiation, and when initiations are undertaken, customized ones;
(4) strong emphasis on political involvement and social and ecological responsibility/consciousness;
(5) no set liturgy (except in certain large, rehearsed or semi-rehearsed public sabbat rituals) but rather training in principles of magic and the structure of ritual, and how to "speak as the spirit moves you" within that structure;
(6) cultivation of ecstatic states (customarily without the use of entheogens or psychotropics) and divine colloquy—more shamanic than ceremonial;
(7) cultivation of self-empowerment, self-discovery, and creativity;
(8) extensive use of chanting and breathwork in magical rites;
(9) intense "energy-raising," often using our trademark spiral dance (or even double helix/DNA molecule dance);
(10) magical use of the Pentacle of Iron construct and its obverse, the Pentacle of Pearl;
(11) concept of Three Souls;
(13) encouragement of the creation of new ritual forms by anyone.

Reclaiming rituals are typically loose in structure, high in energy, and ecstatic in nature.

Deities

Reclaiming has no specific pantheon, rather, invokes Goddess into circles and often, but not always, God. Collective classes, covens, and community usually have had more women than men. Eventually, two particular deities seemed to have adopted the Bay Area Reclaiming community—Brigit and Lugh.

Initiation, or Not

Initiation—though not required to perform rituals—is performed by "committees" of teachers selected by the candidate who must ask for initiation; it is not offered, or even suggested. Just asking for an initiation does not guarantee that the request is granted; one or more teachers may refuse. It may take some years before all on the "committee" agree that the candidate is ready. If the candidate works in a coven, they usually are simultaneously initiated into the Craft and that coven, and any initiates within the coven are invited to be part of the initiation whether they were the candidate's teachers or not.

Reclaiming initiations are customized to the individual seeker. First, the initiators give challenges to the candidate. The candidate must accept the challenges from each initiators and fulfill them to everyone's satisfaction before the actual ceremony takes place. Each initiator creates these challenges according to what that priest or priestess feels the candidate needs to improve upon. The initiator's challenge is a task, which they have already done, or would and could do. They can also require the candidate to complete a challenge if they determine it would foster the candidate's development. It must be a task the person is actually capable of completing. A challenge is never given if it poses a danger to the candidate's health or welfare.

Reclaiming Collective Today

Over the years, Reclaiming Collective expanded from teaching Craft and providing public sabbat rituals to recording chants, publishing books, and maintaining an internet presence with website and listserves. The Reclaiming Newsletter developed into *Reclaiming Quarterly,*—a magazine of articles, poetry, and photos.

After years of discussion, the Collective (which varied in size from about 10 to 20 or more at its largest) dissolved itself as a collective in 1999 and turned over its authority to the Wheel—a representative body comprised of spokespersons from all the many different witchcraft groups. About 52 people had, over the years, been members of Reclaiming Collective, for greater or lesser periods of time.

With the dissolution of Reclaiming Collective and its evolution into a more inclusive complex, the Collective wrote Principles of Unity.

Reclaiming Principles of Unity

The values of the Reclaiming tradition stem from the understanding that the Earth is alive and all life is sacred and interconnected. The Goddess is seen as immanent in the Earth's cycles of birth, growth, death, decay, and regeneration. This practice comes from a deep, spiritual commitment to the Earth, to healing and to the linking of magic with political action.

Each of the members embodies the Divine. The ultimate spiritual authority is within oneself, and no other person is needed to explain its interpretation. A member's questions are welcomed, as well as, intellectual, spiritual, and creative freedoms.

Reclaiming is an evolving tradition honoring both Goddess and God. Members work with female and male images of divinity, but remember their essence is a mystery which goes beyond form. The community rituals celebrate the cycles of the seasons and their lives, and raise energy for personal, collective and earth healing.

It is known that everyone can do the life-changing, world-renewing work of magic and change one's consciousness at will. Reclaiming strives to teach and practice in ways that foster personal and collective empowerment, to model shared power and to open leadership roles to everyone. It makes decisions by consensus, and balance individual autonomy with social responsibility.

The tradition of Reclaiming honors the Wild, and calls for service to the Earth and the community. Its members value peace and practice non-violence, in keeping with the Rede, "Harm none, and do what you will." They also work for all forms of justice: environmental, social, political, racial, gender, and economic. Their feminist views include a radical analysis of power, seeing all systems of oppression as interrelated, rooted in structures of domination and control.

The organization welcomed all genders, races, ages, and sexual orientations before its disbandment. It strived to make public rituals and events accessible and safe. Members tried to balance the need for compensated labor with a commitment to make their work available to people of all economic levels.

The Reclaiming Tradition believed all living beings are worthy of respect and that the sacred Elements of Air, Fire, Water, and Earth support everything. The group worked to create and sustain communities and cultures that embody their values, that can help to heal the wounds of the earth and her peoples, and that can sustain and nurture future generations.

In the San Francisco Bay Area today Reclaiming, the entity, is the Wheel and many specialized cells or smaller groups. Several "daughter" collectives are spread over a widespread geographic area. Reclaiming Tradition Witch Camps, which began in 1985, are still conducted in the United States, Canada, and Europe. The camps are a series of intensive lessons held in a retreat-like setting. The people trained in these camps, in turn, train others in their communities. They are connected to Reclaiming's representative body called the Wheel through their Witch Camp spokescouncil called the Web.

Sources

NightMare, M. Macha. "Reclaiming Tradition Witchcraft." http://www.reclaiming.org/about/history-mmnm.html. May 11, 2000.

Reclaiming Principles of Unity. http://www.cog.org/wicca/trads/reclaiming.html. May 11, 2000.

The Reclaiming Tradition. http://www.spiralheart.org/orgtradfiles/rectrad.html. May 11, 2000.

Reclaiming Tradition Witchcraft. http://www.aracnet.com/~ravnglas/tradition.html. May 8, 2000.

Records and Cassettes: A Selected Guide (Catalog)

Comprehensive mail order catalog issued by the **Yes! Bookshop** founded by Cris Popenoe. It lists records and cassette tapes of New Age music, non-Western music, choral music, instrumental music, and spoken tapes on health, healing and meditation, past lives, relaxation, sleep, dreams, visualization, weight control, yoga, and related subjects. It forms a useful companion to the Yes! Bookshop Guide *Inner Development.* The Yes! Bookshop is located at 1035 31st St. NW, Washington, D.C. 20007.

ReCreation

ReCreation is an organization founded out of the response to the three-volume set of the metaphysical best-seller *Conversations with God,* received over a three-year period (1992–1995) by **Neal Donald Walsch.** Walsch was a radio talk show host in Ashland, Oregon, who in 1992 vented his frustration over his lot in life in a letter to God. To his surprise God answered back, and thus began his three-year dialogue. The messages from God were received by a process generally termed **automatic writing.** The three volumes of *Conversations with God* appeared in 1995, 1997, and 1998 respectively. They each became best-sellers, and Walsch was faced with a massive response by people who were positively affected by his writing. He founded ReCreation to channel that response into action.

ReCreation is based upon the notion that deep within our memory, each human carries the awareness that there once existed a race of beings who had a deep acceptance of love as the only reality and thus lived without anger, fear, struggle, and war. Bonded by love, these people lived by three rules: Love is all there is; Do harm to no one; and We are all One. They had a code of ethics based on three imperatives: Awareness, honesty, and responsibility. Having once existed, a society of such people of love can be rebuilt, and that is the goal of ReCreation.

To that end, ReCreation now sponsors a full schedule of programs (seminars, workshops, and lectures) at various locations across North America and overseas. A *Conversations with God* in Action program seeks to mobilize people to create centers to actualize the ideals of *Conversations with God* in their own community. These centers will be able to offer many of the same programs heretofore only available in Oregon. CWG in Action also has a "Little Masters" program for children. Walsch leads an annual Empowerment Week at which interested people may learn to be CWG leaders, both those who wish to work at the local level and those who wish to train other leaders. ReCreation certifies those who complete the training as Message senders.

ReCreation publishes a newsletter and study materials for people reading *Conversations with God.* It is headquartered at PMB #1150, 1257 Siskiyou Blvd., Ashland, OR 97520. Its Internet site is at http://www.conversationswithgod.org/.

Sources:

Varble, Bill. "Former Rogue Valley Radio Host Finds Success in Conversations with God." *Mail Tribune* (Ashland, Ore.) (September 14, 1997).

Walsch, Neal Donald. *Conversations with God I, II, III.* Charlottesville, Va.: Hampton Roads Publishing, 1995, 1997, 1998.

"Rector"

One of the spirit controls of **William Stainton Moses,** said to have been Hippolytus, pupil of Irenaeus, who was Bishop of

Portus, the harbor of Rome opposite to Ostia. He was banished in 235 C.E., when Maximin succeeded Alexander Severus. "Rector" first manifested on January 4, 1873. His distinctive sign was his heavy tread, which shook the room. His main duty was to act as amanuensis for "Imperator" and the other spirits. After the earlier books, almost all the writing was done by him.

He had the power of reading books paranormally. The experiments which were conducted to test this ability proved highly successful. When the "Imperator" group took control of the séances of the medium **Leonore E. Piper,** "Rector" manifested in his old role as amanuensis and spiritual adviser again.

Recurrent Spontaneous Psychokinesis (RSP)

A term suggested by parapsychologist **W. G. Roll** to denote **poltergeist** phenomena.

Red Cap (of Witches)

The witches of Ireland used to put on a magical red cap before flying through the air to their meeting-place. It has been suggested that witches in various countries may have experienced the illusion of traveling through the air after ingesting the "red cap" hallucinatory mushroom *amanita muscaria* (fly-agaric).

In Scotland the red caps were bloodthirsty elves who were said to live in the castles in the Lowlands. They dyed their caps red with human blood.

Redfield, James (1950–)

James Redfield, the author of the post-**New Age** spiritual classic **The Celestine Prophecy,** was born on March 19, 1950, in rural Alabama. He grew up near Birmingham, Alabama, and attended Auburn University, where he majored in sociology. After receiving his bachelor's degree, he continued at Auburn and received a master's degree in counseling. In 1974 he began work as a therapist for abused adolescents. During his college years and subsequent period as a counselor, he became a student of Eastern religions and the human potentials movement. He increasingly turned to theories of psychic phenomena and intuition as resources to assist his clients.

In 1989, Redfield quit his job to write and to synthesize his interests. The results of his initial effort, which included a trip to the New Age sacred sites in **Sedona,** Arizona, were completed in 1991 as his first book, *The Celestine Prophecy.* He self-published the book in 1992 and within a year over 100,000 copies had been printed. Eventually Warner Books bought the rights to the title and in 1994 brought out the first hardback edition. The book soon became number one on the *New York Times* nonfiction best-seller list. It remained on the list for three years, was translated into several languages, and was soon joined by its sequel, *The Tenth Insight* (1996).

The Celestine Prophecy appeared as it became evident that the vision of a New Age that had so transformed the metaphysical community through the 1980s had died. Many who had identified themselves with the New Age sought new understanding of what had been occurring. Redfield's book appeared to provide that new direction. *The Celestine Prophecy* described nine insights that Redfield felt were emerging in prominence among those who chose to be aware of them. The insights suggested that since the 1960s people had become more attuned to their intuitive self and the coincidences that filled their life. As a result of the attunement to these insights, a new vision of the transformation of human consciousness would emerge in the next century. *The Tenth Insight* explored the results of working with these insights.

People not only read *The Celestine Prophecy,* but study groups formed to work with the insights. For these people, Redfield authored "experiential guides" for both *The Celestine Prophecy* and *The Tenth Insight.* He began a newsletter, *The Celestine Journal,* in 1994 that in 1998 became a monthly Internet newsletter on his website at http://www.celestinevision.com. More recently he continued to develop his perspectives in additional books, *The Celestine Vision* (1997) and *The Secret of Shambhala* (1999). He has been aided in his endeavors by his wife, Salle Merrill Redfield, who has authored several related books and who lectures with Redfield on their speaking tours around the world. Beyond supplying material for study of the nine insights, Redfield has done little toward organizing any movement out of the response to his writings. However, some readers of his works have formed the **New Civilization Network,** a loose association operating primarily through the Internet.

Sources:

Redfield, James. *The Celestine Prophecy.* New York: Warner Books, 1994.

———. *The Celestine Vision: Living the New Spiritual Awareness.* New York: Warner Books, 1997.

———. *The Secret of Shambhala: Search for the Eleventh Insight.* New York: Warner Books, 1999.

———. *The Tenth Insight.* New York: Warner Books, 1996.

Red Man

The demon of the tempests. He was supposed to be furious when the rash voyager intruded on his solitude and would show his anger in the winds and storms. The French peasants believed that a mysterious little red man appeared to Napoleon to announce coming military reverses.

Red Pigs

It was formerly believed that Irish witches could turn wisps of straw or hay into red pigs, which they sold at the market. But when the pigs were driven homeward by the buyers, they resumed their original shape on crossing running water.

Reese, Bert (1851–1926)

American-Polish medium with whom remarkable experiments in clairvoyance were conducted by **Baron von Schrenck-Notzing,** Thomas A. Edison, **Hereward Carrington,** and Felix Hollaender. Reese was said to have manifested extraordinary psychic faculties at the age of six. According to Felix Hollaender, writing in the *Annals of Psychic Science* (September 1913), these abilities so terrified the people of the little town where he was born that they deserted the shop where his father sold miscellaneous goods, and to avoid ruin he had to send his son away to Posen. The people of the country town were filled with horror. They considered the child a wizard and possessed by the devil.

In America, Reese was arrested and condemned for disorderly conduct. Appealing against his sentence he appeared before Judge Rosalsky and proved his powers to him. He asked the Judge to write something on three different pieces of paper, to fold them up and place them in three different pockets, mixing them in such a way that they could not be recognized.

Then Judge Rosalsky took one of the pellets and pressed it against Reese's forehead. He immediately answered: "You have fifteen dollars in the bank mentioned in your question." He continued by reading the second paper, which contained the name of a Miss O'Connor, a former governess to Judge Rosalsky's children. He also read the third paper, whereupon Judge Rosalsky acquitted him.

Schrenck-Notzing considered him one of the most extraordinary men of the time. Thought reading could not sufficiently account for his performances as the experimenters mostly took care that they themselves should not know which piece of paper contained which question. In certain performances, "X-ray clairvoyance" also fell short as an explanation; his success must have been due to **psychometry.** According to the account of Felix Hollaender, he indicated to a commercial firm the pages on which there was a fraudulent entry. He was given five percent of the amount of the fraud.

However, **Harry Houdini** claimed Reese was a **fraud,** and that he knew his methods. In a letter to **Sir Arthur Conan Doyle,** Houdini wrote: "I have no hesitancy in telling you that I set a snare at the séance I had with Reese, and caught him cold-blooded. He was startled when it was over, as he knew that I had bowled him over. So much so that he claimed I was the only one that had ever detected him."

Reese was at one time an assistant to Thomas A. Edison, who held séances with him. In his later years, Edison worked on apparatus to communicate with the dead. Reese also had a reputation for **dowsing** and was said to have discovered valuable oil deposits for the Rockefeller company.

Sources:

Ernst, B. M. L., and Hereward Carrington. *Houdini and Conan Doyle.* New York: A & C Boni, 1932.

Reeves, M.

London restaurant proprietor who, in association with **F. M. Parkes,** gained renown in 1877 as one of the earliest practitioners of **spirit photography** in England. He was said to have contributed a considerable part of the team's power, as without him Parkes could not obtain recognizable spirit "extras" on his photographic plates. The association was dissolved when Reeves emigrated to Canada. Many of the psychic pictures that appeared on their plates were symbolic. (See also **psychic photography**)

Reflectograph

An instrument for mechanical communication with spirits, invented by George Jobson and B. K. Kirkby. It consisted of a large typewriter, the key-contacts of which were so sensitive that by merely blowing upon them they could be depressed, closing an electric circuit and making an illuminated letter appear. The machine, however, was by no means independent of human action. The presence of the medium L. E. Singleton was necessary. When she was entranced, a hand (suggestive of **fraud**) appeared out of the cabinet, tapped the keys, and spelled out messages which were then flashed in luminous letters on a six-foot indicator. (See also **Ashkir-Jobson Trianion; communigraph**)

Re-formed Congregation of the Goddess-International

The Re-formed Congregation of the Goddess-International is one expression of feminist **Wicca** that has emerged in stages through the 1980s and 1990s. Wicca emerged as a religion built around the worship of the Goddess. It elevated the role of the priestess as a means of balancing the more traditional all-male leadership role in Western religion. Many women found Wicca and **magic** to be a means of empowerment. In the early 1970s Dianic Wicca took the notion of the feminine role in the religion one step further and began to speak of Wicca as "wimmen's" religion. Feminist leaders began to organize all-female covens with a range of opinion from all-lesbian separatist groups to those groups that merely supplied women with a place for religious self-expression without male interference.

Feminist consciousness emerged within the strongest of the Wisconsin-based Wiccan groups, Circle, but generally manifested as all-female events during gatherings in which males otherwise participated. A more separatist format of feminist Wicca emerged in 1983 with the first issue of *Of a Like Mind,* a periodical that became the focus of a network of goddess-worshipping women. *Of a Like Mind* covered such areas as women's spirituality, Goddess religions around the world, nature-centered spirituality, and feminism. Each issue centered upon a particular Goddess and a singular theme, the subjects of feature articles, and included a number of columns that facilitated networking.

Over the years the Re-formed Congregation emerged as a network of groups (called **circles**) and then in the 1990s as a formal corporate structure that chartered member organizations and trained and ordained leaders. The congregation organized its own publishing house, Triple Crescent Press, and a school, the Women's Theological Institute. The Grove is a retreat center near Madison, Wisconsin. It sponsors a number of celebrative and training events through the year.

The Re-formed Congregation is headquartered at Box 6677, Madison, WI 53726. *Of a Like Mind* is issued quarterly. It has an Internet presence at http://www.cae.wisc.edu:80/~cashd/pathways/rcg.html.

Sources:

Of a Like Mind. Madison, Wisconsin, n.d.

Re-formed Congregation of the Goddess-International. http://www.cae.wisc.edu:80/~cashd/pathways/rcg.html. January 12, 2000.

REG See Random Event Generator

Regang

Malay system of astrology. (See **MALAYSIA**)

Regardie, (Francis) Israel (1907–1985)

Ritual magician, student of **Aleister Crowley,** and later a chiropractor who utilized the thought of **Wilhelm Reich** in his work. He was born in England on November 17, 1907, but emigrated to the United States with his family at age 13. He discovered the theosophical writings of **Helena Petrovna Blavatsky,** which provided him an entrée into the occult. Then through the writings of **Charles Stansfeld Jones,** he became more aware of the occult tradition and fascinated by Crowley's outlook and exploits.

Beginning in 1928 he traveled through Europe as Crowley's secretary and student. Although he later parted company with Crowley, he defended him from those who disliked his exploits in magic and sexual liberties, and spoke of his "real genius and grandeur." Regardie was well aware of Crowley's more controversial exploits, but was willing to overlook much that might be objectionable because of what he recognized as Crowley's true magical genius.

Regardie began to write in the early 1930s, his first books being *The Tree of Life* (1932) and *The Garden of Pomegranates* (1932). In 1934, after parting with Crowley, he joined the **Stella Matutina,** an offshoot of the former Hermetic Order of the **Golden Dawn.** He despaired of the corrupt nature of the order's leadership and saw no hope of reform. Enthused with the rituals, he broke his oath of secrecy and revealed all he had learned in a book, *My Rosicrucian Adventure* (1935). Several years later he published the complete rituals in a four-volume set, *The Golden Dawn: An Encyclopedia of Practical Occultism* (1937–40). (While angering his fellow magicians, these published rituals interested only a few until the renewal of the occult revival in the 1960s, when Regardie's compendium was reprinted in a revised and enlarged edition in 1969.)

Regardie later became a chiropractor and, following the outbreak of hostilities with Japan, served in the U.S. Army. After the war he settled in southern California, where he practiced chiropractic and psychoanalysis. He had studied with

Nandor Fodor in the mid-1930s in New York City and later became an enthusiastic supporter of Wilhelm Reich and his theories of **orgone** energy.

In his highly individual linking of the Golden Dawn teachings with Reich's psychophysical therapy, Regardie created a unique synthesis of mysticism, occultism, and psychotherapy. In his introduction to the second edition of *The Golden Dawn* (1969), Regardie notes that, "Reich has succeeded in building a bridge between the modern psychologies and occultism. What he had to say, and the therapeutic method he developed and called vegetotherapy, have been found of inestimable value in my life, and the two hundred hours of therapy I had years ago comprise an experience that today, in retrospect, I would not be without."

Regardie retained his respect for the Golden Dawn teachings, and during the last years of his life he accepted a few magic students and nurtured the birth of several new organizations that drew inspiration from both the Golden Dawn and Crowley. In 1983 he visited New Zealand, where a Stella Matutina lodge had been founded by R. W. Felkin in 1912 and continued to function.

Regardie died March 10, 1985, at age 77, in Sedona, Arizona, where he lived for several years after he retired from some 30 years in practice as a Reichian therapist in Los Angeles. The forename "Francis" was adopted by Regardie in the 1930s at the suggestion of Winifred Burke (wife of the famous novelist Thomas Burke), who thought that his spiritual direction was reminiscent of St. Francis of Assisi, noted for his faith, humility, and love.

Sources:

Regardie, Israel. *The Art and Meaning of Magic.* Dallas, Tex.: Sangreal Foundation, 1964.

———. *The Eye in the Triangle.* St. Paul: Llewellyn Publications, 1970.

———. *The Garden of Pomegranates.* London: Rider, 1932. Reprint, St. Paul: Llewellyn Publications, 1970.

———. *The Golden Dawn: An Encyclopedia of Practical Occultism.* 4 vols. Chicago: Aries Press, 1937–40.

———. *Middle Pillar.* Chicago: Aries Press, 1938. Rev. ed. St. Paul: Llewellyn Publications, 1971.

———. *My Rosicrucian Adventure.* Chicago: Aries Press, 1936. Reprint, St. Paul: Llewellyn Publications, 1971.

———. *What You Should Know about the Golden Dawn.* Phoenix, Ariz.: Falcon Press, 1983.

Regurgitation

An explanatory theory of **materialization** phenomena that suggests that the white substance issuing from a medium's body, which is taken for **ectoplasm,** is something that the medium swallowed before the sitting and brought up at the appropriate moment. The theory was put forward by the **Society for Psychical Research,** London, in the case of **Eva C.,** accused of **fraud** in 1922. Wide public attention was also aroused by the case of the British medium **Helen Duncan,** in which the theory was considered a satisfactory explanation.

Sources:

Price, Harry. *Regurgitation and the Duncan Mediumship.* Council at the Rooms of the National Laboratory of Psychical Research, London, 1931.

Reich, Wilhelm (1897–1957)

Austrian psychoanalyst, whose later ideas on life energy had analogies with occult and mystical concepts. Reich was born on March 24, 1897, in Dobrzcynica, Galicia. The son of a farmer, he was tutored at home for entrance to the German Gymnasium at Czernowitz (Cernauti) at the age of 14. He boarded with a family in Czernowitz and helped out on his father's farm during vacations. Reich passed his Abiturium in 1915 just as World War I was heating up. He joined the Austrian army and served on the Italian front.

In 1918, he returned to study in Vienna. He matriculated in law at the University of Vienna, then went on to study medicine. He obtained his M.D. in 1922 and after graduate studies in neurology and psychiatry became the first clinical assistant at **Sigmund Freud**'s Psychoanalytic Polyclinic in 1922 and vice-director in 1928. He joined the Austrian Socialist Party in 1924 with the hope of reconciling Freudian and Marxist theories. He had become convinced that much neurosis was caused by poverty, bad housing conditions, and various social ills. His actions alienated him from orthodox psychoanalysts and doctrinaire Marxists.

He joined the Communist Party in 1928 and became a pioneer in advocating health centers, but after a visit to Russia in 1929 he was disappointed with Russian bureaucracy and bourgeois moralistic attitudes toward sexuality. He was expelled from the Communist party in 1933 because of his advocacy of sexual politics. Later, the International Psychoanalytic Association excluded him because of his Communist associations.

He moved to Berlin in 1930 and the following year helped establish Verlag für Sexualpolitik (Sexpol-Verlag) for the sexual education of young people. He followed the logic inherent in the original Freudian concept of the overriding importance of the sexual urge in human affairs. A vicious newspaper smear campaign centered in Scandinavia hounded him through the mid-1930s (1933–39). He left Germany to escape the Nazis in 1939, after exposing what he considered the sham Socialism and perverse character of the Hitler regime.

He escaped to the United States and settled in Forest Hills, Long Island, but moved to Oregon, Maine, in the 1940s, where he established the Orgone Institute Research Laboratories. He was once again the subject of attacks from journalists and was persecuted by the Food and Drug Administration (FDA) on charges arising from a tragi-comic misunderstanding of Reich's theories of cosmic **"orgone"** energy in relation to a cure for cancer.

He developed what he called an "orgone accumulator," a large box-like arrangement of materials that, he claimed, trapped orgone energy, which entered the device more rapidly than it exited. Reich believed that this energy had a tonic effect on individuals sitting in the accumulator, and that it was particularly beneficial for cancer sufferers.

He supplied this device only to individuals who would use it experimentally under the guidance of a qualified physician. But the FDA proceeded against Reich as if he were a common charlatan peddling a worthless cancer cure. Reich refused to comply with a court injunction banning the use of his "orgone accumulator" and insisting on the removal of the word "orgone" from all his books, and he was eventually sentenced to two years imprisonment for contempt of court. Most of his books (some of which had been burned in Nazi Germany) were seized by the American authorities and burned at the Gansevoort Incinerator, New York, August 23, 1956.

Reich was a brilliant if eccentric thinker who continually ran up against intense social and government forces. Many of his ideas, especially those concerning sexuality, would be quite acceptable today. His championing of the importance of sexual expression in Freudianism was rejected by most psychoanalysts, although they used many of his therapeutic insights. His reconciliation of psychic and somatic aspects of psychoanalysis, long desired by Freud, was regarded with suspicion and mistrust by Freud himself. Reich's teachings on "sexual revolution," as opposed to authoritarian repression, were grossly misinterpreted after his death by cranks, pornographers, and hippies on one hand, and by a humorless orthodoxy of authoritarian Reichian physicians on the other.

Reich died in the federal penitentiary in Lewisburg, Pennsylvania, November 3, 1957.

Sources:

Berger, Arthur S., and Joyce Berger. *The Encyclopedia of Parapsychology and Psychical Research.* New York: Paragon House, 1991.

Constable, T. J. "Orgone Energy Engineering through the Cloudbuster." In John White and Stanley Krippner, eds. *Future Science.* Garden City, N.Y.: Doubleday, 1977.

Reich, Ilse Ollendorff. *Wilhelm Reich: a Personal Biography.* New York: St. Martin's Press, 1969.

Reich, Peter. *A Book of Dreams.* New York: Harper & Row, 1973.

Reich, Wilhelm. *Character Analysis.* New York: Orgone Institute Press, 1949. Reprint, New York: Farrar, Straus & Giroux, 1961.

———. *The Discovery of the Orgone.* Vol. 1, *The Function of the Orgasm; Sex-economic Problems of Biological Energy.* New York: Orgone Institute Press, 1942.

———. *The Discovery of the Orgone.* Vol. 2, *The Cancer Biopathy.* New York: Orgone Institute Press, 1948.

———. *The Mass Psychology of Fascism.* New York: Orgone Institute Press, 1946.

Sharaf, Myron. *Fury on Earth: A Biography of Wilhelm Reich.* New York: St. Martin's Press, 1983.

Reichenbach, Baron Karl von (1788–1869)

Nineteenth-century German chemist, expert on meteorites, and discoverer of kerosene, parrafin, and creosote. He also spent over two decades experimenting with the mysterious force which he named **"od"** (also known as odic force or odyle in various translations). This claimed force, which has its intellectual roots in mesmerism, had particular relevance to concepts of the human **aura.**

Reichenbach was born on February 12, 1788, at Württemberg and died at Leipzig on January 22, 1869. He was educated at the gymnasium (high school) in Württemberg and afterward at the State University of Tübingen, where he studied natural science, political economy, and law. During Reichenbach's student days, Germany was under the military control of Napoleon's France, and at the age of sixteen Reichenbach founded a secret society to set up a German state in the South Sea Islands. However, he was arrested by the Napoleonic police and detained for some months as a political prisoner. After his release he continued his studies and obtained his Ph.D.

He later traveled in France and Germany investigating the construction and operation of ironworks, and in 1815 he set up his own plant at Villigen in Baden. He later built a large charcoal furnace at Hausach in Baden. He established a beet-sugar factory, steelworks, and blast furnaces and devoted much time to experimental research. He discovered paraffin in 1830 and other coal-tar products such as eupion, creosote, and pittacal (pitch) in the following years. Between 1835 and 1860, he also published a long series of scientific papers on meteorites. His many contributions earned him a well-deserved reputation as a brilliant scientist and industrialist.

Meanwhile his experiments in human sensitivity from 1839 onward were not as well received by his colleagues; in fact, he was harshly criticized. These experiments involved attempts to demonstrate a mysterious vital force which he named "od," for the Norse deity Odin, indicating a power, like the **animal magnetism** conceived by **Franz A. Mesmer,** which permeates the whole of nature.

Detection and demonstration of this force depended upon sensitives—specially gifted individuals rather like psychics, although Reichenbach's sensitives were ordinary people from all walks of life. These individuals experienced specific reactions to the proximity of other people—feelings of pleasant coolness and drowsiness or, on the other hand, disagreeable, numbing, or exciting feelings. They also manifested a special right-hand/left-hand polarity, which affected their reactions to other people standing or sitting near to their right or left sides, and particularly to sleeping positions with partners. They were also sympathetic to the color blue, and antipathetic to yellow; they had particular food fetishes; were sensitive to certain metals; and unpleasantly affected by mirrors.

In a long series of experiments with some two hundred individuals, Reichenbach documented the reports of sensitives to seeing **emanations** from crystals and magnets in total darkness and detecting alternations of electric current. They could also perceive an aura surrounding the human body.

Reichenbach studied the various manifestations of this vital force in its relationship to electricity, magnetism, and chemistry. He experimented with its connection to water-witching (or **dowsing**), **mesmerism,** and similar psychic subjects. He tried to show that the force could move objects without conscious effort, as in the **table-turning** of the Spiritualists.

However, Reichenbach was neither a Spiritualist nor a mesmerist. His interest was purely scientific, his hundreds of experiments were conducted with empirid precision. Unfortunately, his experiments ran both against the dominant mechanistic view of the universe held by most mid-nineteenth-century scientists and had a significant methodological flaw. While he could and did produce a wide range of positive results, he was never able to demonstrate his major causative agent, the od. He was never able to eliminate a variety of possible causes, both paranormal and mundane, for the effects.

Reichenbach's researches were published in Germany in 1850. There were two English translations, one by William Gregory in 1850 and another by John Ashburner the following year. Both translations are good, but Gregory's was the official translation and is generally regarded as the best. Gregory translated Reichenbach's "od" as "odyle," perhaps feeling that this term would sound more acceptable to scientists. Gregory also translated Reichenbach's essays *Letters on Od and Magnetism* (1926), which are a simpler general introduction to Reichenbach's experiments and concepts than his main work.

Reichenbach died on January 22, 1869, at the age of eighty, and as Gustav Fechner, another scientist, commented: "Up to the last days of his life, he grieved at the thought of having to die without obtaining recognition for his system, and such was the tragic fate that actually befell him."

Some years after Reichenbach's death, there was a belated revival of interest in his work by the **Society for Psychical Research** in Britain, which formed a Reichenbach Committee that included **William F. Barrett, Edmund Gurney,** and **F. W. H. Myers.** In this case, it was precisely the possible connection with psychic phenomena that inspired this renewal of interest in a subject pointedly ignored by orthodox science. The committee made careful investigations, but was less fortunate than Reichenbach in obtaining suitable sensitives. Only three out of the forty-five individuals tested possessed the sensitivity postulated by Reichenbach, but these three provided interesting confirmation of Reichenbach's observations.

In 1908, **Walter J. Kilner,** who was familiar with the work of Reichenbach, developed a technique for making the human **aura** visible. In this century, **Wilhelm Reich**'s theories of "orgone energy" seem to be about the same energy Reichenbach explored under the label "od."

Sources:

Bagnall, Oscar. *The Origin and Properties of The Human Aura.* London, 1937. Rev. ed. New Hyde Park, N.Y.: University Books, 1970.

Gopi Krishna. *Kundalini: The Evolutionary Energy in Man.* New Delhi, 1967. Reprint, Boulder, Colo.: Shambhala, 1970.

Kilner, Walter J. *The Human Atmosphere.* London, 1911. Reprinted as *The Human Aura.* New Hyde Park, N.Y.: University Books, 1965.

Reich, Wilhelm. *The Function of the Orgasm.* New York: Orgone Institute Press, 1948. Reprint, New York: Farrar, Straus & Giroux, 1973.

Reichenbach, Karl von. *Letters on Od and Magnetism.* London, 1926. Reprinted as *The Odic Force; Letters on Od and Magnetism.* New Hyde Park, N.Y.: University Books, 1968.

———. *Physico-Physiological Researches on the Dynamics of Magnetism, Electricity, Heat, Light, Crystallization, and Chemism, in their Relations to Vital Force.* Translated by H. John Ashburner. London: H. Baillière, 1851.

———. *Researches on Magnetism, Electricity, Heat, Light, Crystallization and Chemical Attraction in relation to the Vital Force.* Translated by William Gregory. 1850. Reprint, New Hyde Park, N.Y.: University Books, 1974.

Reiki

A Japanese healing system built around the use of *ki,* the universal life energy, analogous to the Hindu **prana** and the **od** force described in the research of **Baron von Reichenbach.** Reiki can be traced to the discoveries of Mikao Usui, a Christian minister working in Kyoto in the 1880s. Challenged by his contemporaries concerning the Christian claims of biblical miracles, he began a search that led him to the United States to study at the University of Chicago, where he worked toward a Ph.D. However, he did not find answers to his questing until he investigated Buddhism.

Unable to find any Buddhists practicing healing, he learned Chinese and Sanskrit in order to read the early Buddhist sutras in their original languages. There he found a discussion of the healing power, and during a 21- day retreat he welcomed the power into himself. Soon afterward he was able to be the facilitator for several spectacular healings and he settled down in Kyoto to learn about this new power he had discovered and to perfect the techniques for using it. He eventually passed his knowledge to Chijuro Hayashi.

An event of great importance to the spread of reiki occurred in the 1930s when a young Japanese American, Hawayo Takata, ill and believing herself soon to die, returned to her native land. There she met several reiki healers and they facilitated her complete recovery. As a result she became the first woman, and first American, reiki master. She returned to Hawaii and taught quietly for many years. Then in the late 1970s she moved to the Midwest, where she began to share reiki healing with a larger audience of metaphysically-oriented Americans. Virginia Samdall of Chicago became the first of a new generation of reiki masters. In 1978 Takata initiated Barbara Ray of Atlanta, Georgia, and went on to teach her the secrets of initiating other reiki masters. She had previously taught the secrets to her granddaughter, Phillis Lei Furomoto.

Takata died in 1980. Both Ray and Furomoto, as reiki grand masters, assumed leadership for the development of the movement built around what Takata had taught them. Ray founded the American Reiki Association (later renamed the Radiance Technique Association International) and Furomoto founded the Reiki Alliance. Both have initiated further masters who formed different lineages of reiki practice.

Reiki is taught in three degrees. Students having mastered the first degree are equipped to use the reiki technique to heal others. The second degree provides a deeper knowledge of the reiki work. The third degree must be taught by a reiki grand master and allows one to become a reiki master and a teacher of reiki at the first and second levels. Today, an individual may learn reiki through classes or workshops at any number of special institutes or centers designed to teach reiki healing energy and educate the public. Each institute may teach its own unique system or interpretation of reiki based on traditional teachings. Completion of a reiki class usually leads to a certificate.

Legal requirements to practice reiki usually depend on the place where it is practiced. Regulation varies from state to state and any licenses are issued primarily by governmental bodies.

There are certain procedures and guidelines that are recommended with reiki treatments and therapy, although some reiki masters claim that reiki cannot cause harm or be performed incorrectly (it is possible to perform reiki illegally if there is inappropriate touching). Some masters also claim that it makes no difference if the person receiving treatment has Eastern or Western beliefs. Several styles of reiki are practiced around the world. Different reiki styles apply different methods to conduct the flow of energy during a treatment or therapy session. Methods or tools may include meditation, prayer, use of colors or sounds, chants, mantras, applying hot and cold sensations, elements or healing rays (fire, air, water, earth), use of crystals, **astrology,** tantric healing, karmic body education, chakras, breathing exercises, and attunement openings.

Sources:

Arnold, Larry, and Sandy Nevius. *The Reiki Handbook.* Harrisburg, Pa.: PSI Press, 1982.

Barnett, Libby. *Reiki Energy Medicine: Bringing Healing Touch into Home, Hospital, and Hospice.* Rochester, Vt.: Healing Arts Press, 1996.

Henderson, Jaclyn Stein. "Insights to Reiki: Existing in a state of balance." *Massage & Bodywork.* June/July 1999. pp.96–99.

Ray, Barbara Weber. *The Reiki Factor.* St. Petersburg, Fla.: Radiance Associates, 1983.

Ray, Barbara Weber, and Nonnie Green, eds. *The Official Reiki Handbook.* Atlanta: The American-International Reiki Association, 1982.

Reiki Plus Institute of Natural Healing and Energetic Healing. http://www.reikiplus.com. June 15, 2000.

Stein, Diane. *Essential Reiki: A Complete Guide to an Ancient Healing Art.* Freedom, Calif.: Crossing Press, 1995.

Reincarnation

The return to a new corporeal life of a soul (the incorporeal true self) that had previously been embodied and passed through bodily death. The idea of reincarnation—that the soul passes through a series of embodiments—stands in contrast to the dominant Western Christian idea of a single corporeal embodiment followed by resurrection (reunion of the soul with a spiritual body) and life with God in heaven. Reincarnation is often associated with, but is not necessarily connected with, transmigration, the idea that at death the soul might pass into the body of an animal, a plant, or even an inanimate object such as a stone. The belief in reincarnation was tied to moral categories in ancient religions, especially the Eastern concept of **karma,** which viewed the present life as the working out of consequences from previous lives. Future embodiments will also be determined by the consequences of this present life. One must remove oneself from the realm of consequences through spiritual activity or be stuck in the endless cycle of reincarnation forever. The belief in a form of reincarnation is fundamental to both Hinduism and Buddhism and had some popularity in the ancient Mediterranean basin. Pythagoras, for example, claimed that he was Euphorbus in a previous existence. In modern times, reincarnation has spread in the West through the efforts of French **Spiritism** and **Theosophy.**

Reincarnation in the East

The idea of reincarnation is usually associated with India. It is found in most of the forms of Hinduism; there are hundreds, with some variation in the different theologies and schools of thought. Basically, the soul is an immortal entity that has continuity through eternity, but falls into material existence and is trapped in the illusion that this physical world is ultimately real. Through multiple lives the soul becomes subject to karma, or consequences. Good karma leads to noble birth; bad karma to a lower birth, even to rebirth as an animal. The idea of karma and reincarnation was integral to social organization in the caste system and thus had practical application in everyday life. The caste system in turn dictated proper action that was sanctioned by the rewards and punishments of karma.

In the mainstream of Hindu thought—which found truth in the timeless eternal world beyond this world of illusion—while a favorable reincarnation was desirable, the ultimate goal was to escape the wheel of reincarnation totally. The means of such escape was spiritual discipline encased within a renunciation of the world. By withdrawing and concentrating on the spiritual realm, one ceased to create karma and dissolved old karma. Eventually, one could rid oneself of karma entirely and escape.

The essential soul is said to be pure and impersonal, part of a universal soul, but overlaid by illusions of individual egoism relating to desires and fears of the body and senses. The classic statements relating to reincarnation are to be found in the Hindu scripture Bhagavad-Gita, which stresses: "The soul is never born nor dies, nor does it exist on coming into being. For it is unborn, eternal, and primeval. Even although the body is slain, the soul is not" (2:20).

Buddhism emerged as a reform movement in Hinduism. It challenged the traditional Hindu system at a number of points, including its understanding of human life. In particular, Buddhism challenged the idea of a substantial soul that existed in and of itself apart from the body. The rather sophisticated understanding of the self in Buddhism is often likened to a candle flame. Obviously, as the candle burns down the flame will eventually die out. It has no existence apart from its burning. Buddhists suggest that reincarnation is as if, just as the flame is about to go out, it finds a new candle wick—a new body within which to burn.

In the nineteenth century, during the height of British rule in India, Christianity challenged Hinduism, especially as it existed in village temple worship. Christian leaders denounced animal sacrifice and the sexual promiscuity of some tantric groups, while slowly discovering the sophistication of Hindu philosophy. One of the responses to Christianity's invasion of the country, with the backing of colonial authorities, however, was a revival of philosophical Hinduism in light of new nineteenth century Western notions of progress, evolution, and moral striving.

In this new Hinduism of the nineteenth century, the succession of lives of the soul in different bodies is regarded as one indivisible life. The soul uses the experience of each incarnation as an opportunity for expiating sins in former lives, of balancing bad karma with good, and perfecting the soul through a process of evolution so that further incarnations will not be necessary and the individual soul can be absorbed in the divine plan. Until then, the body of the next life (whether human or animal) is shaped by actions in the present life. Moral striving is the means of gaining good karma. Ultimately, all lives may be seen as illusions of consciousness. This form of reincarnationist thought—which called for the good life, rather than the more traditional form calling for withdrawal from life—influenced Western visitors to India and was ultimately imported to the West through Theosophy and the various Indian teachers who successfully established themselves in the United States (notably Swamis **Vivekananda** and **Yogananda**).

Some religions, like Hinduism, teach that reincarnation is not always immediate, but that some souls may enjoy a period in a transitional state, either heavenly or purgatorial, before rebirth.

An idea of reincarnation, though not karma, is also found in some early Greek philosophy, including that of both Pythagoras and Plato. It actually emerges in the Mediterranean basin simultaneously with its emergence in India, around 600 B.C.E. In the fourth century, Plato's Phaedrus presents a reincarnation myth that seems to have been derived from the ophite religion. A preexistent soul falls from the realm of the gods into earthly existence, where it migrates from one body to the next for some ten thousand years before it returns upward to a place of judgment. Plato also introduced into Greek thought the possibility of a transmigration of the soul into an animal.

In Roman literature, the idea of reincarnation is found in the writings of Ennius, probably deriving from Greek thought. There is no trace of it in Jewish literature, although it later entered into some Kabalistic teaching. From Greek philosophy, it came into the Gnostic tradition, and from second- and third-century Gnosticism it passed to the Manichaeans and **Cathari.**

The theory underlying the concept of reincarnation differs from the eschatology of rewards and punishments in Christianity. Each individual soul will eventually attain perfection, although some will take more reincarnations than others, learning by painful experience, in one life after another, the inexorable laws of karma—of cause and effect. All actions involve consequences, some immediate, others delayed, others in future lives. We punish ourselves by our actions, and the very defects and difficulties under which we suffer offer scope for expiation and perfection.

The Jewish and Christian traditions were (and largely remain) inimical to reincarnation. All of the Christian theologians who spoke of reincarnation denounced it in no uncertain terms. The only break in the antireincarnationist view appears in the early writings of Origen, the third-century theologian who as a young man had converted to Christianity. Before his conversion he was an accomplished Platonist, and he attempted to integrate Platonic philosophy and Christian thinking in his earliest writings, which, if not affirming reincarnation, do speak of the preexistence of the soul and its possible transmigration. Origen later dropped his beliefs and in his biblical commentaries emerged as hostile to reincarnationist thought.

A major controversy involving Origen's early thought emerged in the sixth century surrounding a group of people who adopted Origen's early writings as part of their larger challenge to the Roman Empire. Thus it was that several councils reaffirmed the church's opinion on reincarnationist ideas and, in the style of the times, pronounced them anathema. In the early twentieth century, several proponents of reincarnation, primarily Theosophists working against the opposition of Christian leaders, countered with the story of a sixth-century plot. According to the idea, Christianity had taught reincarnation until the Roman empress Theodosia forced the church to edit the Bible and remove any reference to it. This theory shows a great ignorance of the history of the period and has no foundation in fact. In recent decades the primary presentation of this idea appeared in a book by Noel Langley, *Edgar Cayce and Reincarnation,* and has passed into **New Age** literature.

Theosophical Teachings on Reincarnation

The major conduit of reincarnationist teachings in the West during the twentieth century has been the **Theosophical Society.** According to Theosophy, the various manifestations in the flesh are merely small portions of one whole. The **monad,** the divine spark, or individuality, remains the same throughout the whole course of reincarnation and is truly a denizen of the three higher worlds—the spiritual, the intuitional, and the higher mental. In order to further its growth and the widening of its experience and knowledge, however, it is necessary for the monad to descend into the worlds of denser matter—the lower mental, the astral, and the physical—and take back with it to the higher worlds what it learns there. Since it is impossible to progress far during one manifestation, the monad must return again and again to the lower worlds.

The laws of progress, the laws that govern reincarnation, are those of evolution and of karma. The scheme of the **evolution of life** decrees that all shall sooner or later attain perfection by developing to the utmost their latent powers and qualities, and each manifestation in the lower worlds is but one short journey nearer to the goal. Those who realize this law shorten the journey by their own efforts while those who do not realize it, of course, lengthen the journey.

Karma decrees that both good and bad effects follow whoever caused them. Hence, what an individual has done in one manifestation he will benefit by or suffer for in another. It may be impossible that actions should be immediately effective, but each is stored up and sooner or later will bear fruit.

It may be asked why one long life in the lower worlds should not suffice in place of a multitude of manifestations, but this is explained by the fact that the dense matter that is the vehicle of these bodies becomes, after a time of progress, incapable of further alteration to suit the developing monad's needs and must accordingly be laid aside for a new body.

After physical death, the individual passes first to the **astral world,** then to the heavenly portion of the **mental world.** Most time is spent in the latter, except when descending into the denser worlds to garner fresh experience and knowledge for further development in preparation for passage into a higher sphere.

In the heaven world these experiences and this knowledge are woven together into the texture of the individual's nature. In those who have not progressed far on the journey of evolution, the manifestations in the lower worlds are comparatively frequent, but with passage of time and development, these manifestations become rarer and more time is spent in the heaven world, until at last, the great process of reincarnation draws to an end, and the pilgrims enter the **path** that leads to perfection.

Reincarnation and Spiritism

In France reincarnation was advocated before the time of **Allan Kardec** by several philosophers and mystics, such as Henri de St. Simon, Prosper Enfantin, Charles Fourier, Pierre Leroux, and Jean Reynaud. From an article by **Alexander Aksakof** in the *London Spiritualist* during 1875, it appears that Kardec adopted the doctrine of reincarnation from spirit communications that were received by the medium Celina Japhet. Japhet's mediumship was developed by one M. Roustan, a mesmerist who believed in reincarnation.

If the medium disclosed the doctrine under the effect of the mesmerist's belief, it is easy to understand how Kardec and his school could receive ample confirmation through automatists of his tenet that spiritual progress is achieved through a series of incarnations, always in the human race, that successive corporeal existences are the necessary steps to perfection and that the soul retains its individuality and memory after separation from the body.

The influence of the Kardec school was powerful and, by the appeal of its reconciliation with the apparent injustices of life, it bacame more popular than the teachings of the Spiritualist **Z. J. Piérart** and his followers, who denied reincarnation and relied on the same kind of evidence as that which the Kardecists produced. Indeed, **Alphonse Cahagnet,** who kept the earliest careful trance records in France, was the first to whom the communicators emphatically denied reincarnation, but admitted the existence of the soul anterior to its appearance on Earth.

Outside France, the doctrine of Allan Kardec was denounced by many Spiritualists. In the United States, **Andrew Jackson Davis** declared it to be "a magnificent mansion built on sand." But he also believed in preexistence and taught that "all souls existed from the beginning in the divine soul; all individuality which is, has been, or will be, had its pre-existence, has its present existence in creative being."

In England, **William Howitt** was the chief antagonist. He said that the doctrine was pitiable and repellent, and argued that if it were true there must have been millions of spirits who, on entering the other world, have sought in vain their kindred, children, and friends.

A very pertinent remark may be quoted from a published letter of the great medium **D. D. Home:** "I have had the pleasure of meeting at least twelve Marie Antoinettes, six or seven Marys of Scotland, a whole host of Louis and other kings, about twenty Great Alexanders, but never a plain John Smith. I, indeed, would like to cage the latter curiosity."

For its psychological import, it is also interesting to note that at the exact time of Kardec's death, Home claimed to have received the following communication: "I regret having taught the Spiritist doctrine. Allan Kardec." (See Home's book *Lights and Shadows of Spiritualism,* 1877.)

Among Spiritualists, those who favored reincarnation countered Home. His argument was no argument; reincarnation, if true, may not necessarily be a universal fact. It may not take place at once. In *The Road to Immortality,* by Geraldine Cummins (1932), the spirit of **F. W. H. Myers,** communicating from "the other side," admits reincarnation as an optional choice and as a necessity for "animal men," but not through a series of existences, and counters Theosophical notions of karma by a fascinating theory of **group souls.**

Regarding Howitt's objection it may be claimed that the **double,** in sleep, may establish meetings without recollecting them on awakening. **Sir Arthur Conan Doyle** pointed out that since reincarnation for the spirits is a question of their own future, they may not be more enlightened on it than we are on our own fate.

Reincarnation could be optional; it could be punitive. It could be imposed for the purposes of retribution or it could be undertaken for the fulfillment of a mission. The teachings of the spirit **control "Imperator"** through medium **W. Stainton Moses** admitted the possibility of reincarnation as another chance for souls that had sunk so low as practically to lose identity, and in the case of high spirits who descend with a mission.

The opposition to Kardec's philosophy in England was not universal; he had some followers. Theosophist **Anna Kingsford** translated many of his books. She believed herself to be the reincarnation of the Virgin Mary, while her follower **Edward Maitland** believed that he had been St. John the Divine.

Reincarnation and Spiritualism

Outside France, Spiritualist experience offered little to support the theory of reincarnation. "John King," the famous control of the medium **Eusapia Palladino,** claimed to have been Palladino's father in a previous existence. "John King" claimed manifestation through many different mediums at different times, however.

The experiences of **Carl A. Wickland** and his wife in **obsession** cases did not bear out the theory. They were told by earthbound spirits, brought into their **rescue circles,** that on passing over they had entered the auras of young children and obsessed them. The children, however, never ceased to struggle against these invaders. In those cases in which the Wickland rescue circle enlightened the obsessors of their error, the sanity of the patient quickly returned as the obsessing influence was relieved.

In the nineteenth century, however, hints of support for reincarnation began to emerge. **Charles Richet** gives one illustrative case from *Les Miracles de la Volonté,* by E. Duchatel and R. Warcollier:

"A distinguished physician of Palermo, M. Carmelo Samona, well acquainted with metapsychic science, lost his little daughter, Alexandrina, aged five, in 1910. Mme. Samona was wild with grief. Three days after she saw the child in a dream who said to her: 'I have not left you; I have become tiny like that,' designating some very small object. A fresh pregnancy was the more unlikely in that Mme. Samona had undergone a serious ovarian operation a year previously. On April 10, however, she became aware that she was pregnant. On May 4th it was predicted by Alexandrina, communicating by means of the table, that Mme. Samona would be delivered of twin girls, one of whom would entirely resemble Alexandrina. This came to pass. One of the twins had a mark on the left eye and another mark on the right ear with a symmetry of the face, precisely like the deceased child."

Among various **automatic writing** scripts, **Frederick Bligh Bond,** whose famous discovery of Edgar Chapel, Glastonbury Abbey, is described in his book *The Gate of Remembrance* (1918), noticed reincarnation claims in the communications he received through "Miss X." The old monks who communicated asserted that Miss X was one of the early Glastonbury monks and addressed her as "Brother Simon." Neither Miss X nor Bond believed in reincarnation when the script came through. The incident is referred to in Bond's book *The Company of Avalon* (1924).

Spiritualist J. Arthur Hill presented his reflections on scripts received by a Mrs. Cary (pseudonym), a British working woman of about 50. The scripts detailed episodes involving reincarnation. The impact of "Some Reincarnationist Automatic Scripts," in the *Proceedings* of the Society for Psychical Research (vol. 38), was weak, however, since no attempt had been made to verify the historic accuracy of the names. It was also noted that Cary was a Theosophist.

The Strange Experiments of Eugene Rochas

The feeling of **déjà vu** has often been cited as an argument for reincarnation. However, this phenomenon yields to a variety of explanations. More interesting than the rather vague feelings of déjà vu are claimed memories of past incarnations. **Eugene Rochas** was among the first to explore such memories. Rochas claimed that certain subjects, if put into hypnotic sleep by means of longitudinal passes, could be made to retrace the previous phases of their existence down to their birth and beyond "into the grey" and then into an even earlier state of incarnation. By means of transversal passes the subject was brought back to his normal state by going through the same phases in order of their time. If the transversal passes were continued, the subject was led into the future.

Marie Mayo, the daughter of a French engineer, was one of Rochas's subjects. She passed through various stages of hypnotic sleep into the first stage of lethargy, in which she was suggestible for brief moment, into the first state of **somnambulism,** in which she was not at all suggestible and retained the memory of what happened in her preceding state and in her waking life. She then passed into the state of **rapport,** in which she heard no one but the hypnotizer.

In this state she began to exteriorize herself, a half phantom formed at the left and a half at the right, the colors red and blue. In a successive state, the phantom halves united; the exteriorization of the **astral body** became complete but was attached to the body by a fluidic cord. In this state of exteriorization, the astral body assumed shapes in accord with the age in which the subject saw herself going through the stages of her life.

At age eight, she wrote her name in Arabic. At that age she had attended a school in Beirut. Beyond that birth she called herself Lina, the daughter of a fisherman in Brittany. She married at age 20. Her husband was also a fisherman; his name was Yvon, but she did not remember his family name. She had one child who died at the age of two; her husband perished in a shipwreck. In a fit of despair she had thrown herself into the sea from the top of a precipice. Her body was eaten by fish.

All this information was successively elicited. She first passed through the convulsions of drowning and then went back to her life as Lina, through the childbirth to girlhood, infancy, the state of "grey" and then spoke in a previous incarnation as a man, named Charles Mauville, who lived in the time of Louis XVIII. He was a clerk in a ministerial office in Paris, a bad man, a murderer who died at age 50.

Still further back, she was a lady whose husband was a gentleman attached to the court. Her name was Madeleine de Saint-Marc. Being brought back to the present by transversal passes Mayo successively reached her real age of 18 and then was pushed, by a continuation of the passes, two years into the future. Beyond this she could not go. She saw herself in a strange country with Africans, in a house far away from a railway station, the name of which she could not read. She could not give any precise information that could be used for identification.

Rochas was also possibly the first to explore the fact that similar visions occur if a hypnotized subject is moved into the future instead of into the past. He pushed Juliette Durand, a girl of 16, ahead nine years up to age 25, when she reported dying at Nice. After a time, she reportedly was reincarnated in the future as Emile Chaumette in a family of easy circumstances, studied for the ministry, and was appointed vicaire at Havre in 1940.

Rochas's research soon reached the same dead end as did most of those to follow. It could never be proved that the past personalities enacted by the subjects had really lived, even though they were often very plausible. In some cases, the places and the families spoken of existed, but the individuals could never be traced in parish registers or family documents and the incarnations swarmed with improbabilities.

Rochas rejected the idea that the accounts were the result of suggestion:

"They certainly do not come from me, for I have not only avoided everything that could lead the subject into any determined path, but I have often tried in vain to lead her astray by different suggestions; and the same has been the case with the experimenters who have devoted themselves to this study. . . . Are we to assimilate these phenomena to mere dreams? Certainly not. There is in them a constancy, a regularity, which we do not find in ordinary dreams. . . . And besides, how are we to explain why physical causes, such as longitudinal and transversal passes should have absolutely certain effects on the memory of the subjects between the moments of their birth and that of their present life, and they produce phenomena which do not rest on any basis of fact. I believe that we must compare these manifestations with those which have been studied in the case of Mlle. Hélène Smith, and generally with all those which are provisionally attributed to spirits, and in which we see the true and the false intermingled in a way calculated to drive to despair those who do not reflect upon the darkness in which all observers have to struggle at the beginning of every new science."

Psychical Researchers and Reincarnation

When Allan Kardec died, **Leon Denis** and **Gabriel Delanne** became the main pillars of the reincarnationist school in France. The general evidence they relied on was fourfold: (1) infant prodigies, (2) spontaneous recollection of past lives, (3) exploration of memory under hypnosis, and (4) the claims announced of coming reincarnation.

They found a powerful supporter in psychical researcher **Gustav Geley.** His book *From the Unconscious to the Conscious* (1920) was described as a veritable Bible for reincarnation by Innocinzo Calderone, founder and director of the Italian review *Filosofia della Scienza,* which made a widespread international inquiry on reincarnation in 1913. Geley asserted, "I am a reincarnationist for three reasons: (1) because the doctrine seems to me from the moral point of view fully satisfactory, (2) from the philosophic point of view absolutely rational, and (3) from the scientific point of view likely, or—better still—probably true."

Reminding all that French thought was by no means unanimous on the subject, another distinguished representative of French psychical thinking, **René Sudre,** ranked himself definitely in the opposite camp, declaring in an article in *Psychic Research* (May 1930), "Even as I can admit the faith in survival from the religious point of view, I should in like measure reject as absurd the doctrine of reincarnation and I well understand how it is that the common-sense of the Anglo-Saxon refuses to bow to this teaching."

Modern Experiments in Hypnotic Regression

Through the twentieth century, reincarnation garnered its supporters with little fanfare. Then in 1954 the subject of reincarnation became the subject of a public controversy following the serialization of the story of Bridey Murphy in the *Denver Post* and the subsequent publication of **Morey Bernstein**'s best-selling book *The Search for Bridey Murphy* in 1956.

Bernstein was a businessman in Pueblo, Colorado, who had hypnotized a housewife, Ruth Simmons (the pseudonym of Virginia Tighe). In those sessions Bernstein probed Tighe's memories back to childhood and then, as it seemed, to an earlier life as Bridey Murphy, an Irish girl. The book stimulated "come as you were" social parties, pop songs, and a spate of amateur hypnotic sessions. More important, it launched attempts to find remaining traces of Bridey Murphy. As the controversy seemed to be reaching a dead end, the *Chicago American* published a series of articles that effectively disproved the claim that Tighe was really Bridey Murphy in a former existence. Not only had the evidence for a Bridey Murphy been lacking, but an Irish woman turned up from Tighe's early life who proved the likely model from which the past life could have been constructed. Today most people consider Bridey Murphy to have been a case of **cryptonesia.**

A few other experimenters in hypnotic regression techniques produced more convincing results. Among these is the British hypnotherapist **Arnall Bloxham,** who spent more than 20 years tape recording hypnotic subjects. These sessions convinced many that they presented actual memories of former incarnations.

Reincarnation and Parapsychology

Renewed popular interest in reincarnation also led to serious research by parapsychologists, most notably that of **Ian Stevenson,** of the Department of Neurology and Psychiatry, School of Medicine, University of Virginia. Stevenson collected cases from around the world of people, primarily children, who remembered an immediately previous life, and was able to provide some convincing evidence when confronted with the actual locations and people in those former lives. His book *Twenty Cases Suggestive of Reincarnation* was initially published by the American Society for Psychical Research as the society's *Proceedings* for September 1966. It presented similar cases, each investigated personally by Stevenson on field trips to Alaska, Brazil, Ceylon, India, and Lebanon. Additional cases were documented in subsequent volumes.

Stevenson's research received mixed reactions. Many of his parapsychologist colleagues, having given up on the possibility of doing **survival** research, had moved away from that whole area of research. A few actively attacked his cases as representative of biased sources and the imposition of Stevenson's own well-known prior commitment to a belief in reincarnation. However, they remain the best contemporary attempt of psychical research to compile evidence on so complex a subject. (See also **Glastonbury Scripts**)

Sources:

Banerjee, H. N., and W. C. Oursler. *Lives Unlimited: Reincarnation East and West.* Garden City, N.Y.: Doubleday, 1974.

Bernstein, Morey. *The Search for Bridey Murphy.* Garden City, N.Y.: Doubleday, 1956.

Duncasse, C. J. *A Critical Examination of the Belief in a Life after Death.* Springfield, Ill.: Charles Thomas, 1961.

Ellwood, Gracia Fay. *Psychic Visits to the Past: An Exploration of Retrocognition.* New York: New American Library, 1971.

Fisher, Joe. *The Case for Reincarnation.* New York: Bantam, 1985.

Guirdham, Arthur. *The Cathars and Reincarnation.* London: Neville Spearman, 1960.

Head, Joseph, ed. *Reincarnation in World Thought: A Living Study of Reincarnation in All Ages.* New York: Julian Press, 1967.

Head, Joseph, and S. L. Cranston, eds. *Reincarnation: An East-West Anthology.* New York: Julian Press, 1961. Reprint, Wheaton, Ill.: Theosophical Publishing House, 1968. Rev. ed. *Reincarnation: The Phoenix Fire Mystery, an East-West Dialogue on Death and Rebirth.* New York: Julian Press/Crown Publishers, 1977.

Holzer, Hans. *Born Again: The Truth about Reincarnation.* Garden City, N.Y.: Doubleday, 1970. Reprint, London: Bailey Bros. & Swinfen, 1975.

Leek, Sybil. *Reincarnation: The Second Chance.* New York: Stein & Day, 1974. Reprint, New York: Bantam, 1975.

Osborn, Arthur. *Superphysical: A Review of the Evidence for Continued Existence, Reincarnation, and Mystical States of Consciousness.* Rev. ed. New York: Barnes & Noble; London: Frederick Muller, 1974.

Pierce, Henry W. *Science Looks at ESP.* New York: New American Library, 1970.

Rochas, Eugene. *Les Vies Successives.* N.p., 1911.

Stevenson, Ian. *Cases of the Reincarnation Type.* 3 vols. Charlottesville: University Press of Virginia, 1975–80.

———. *Twenty Cases Suggestive of Reincarnation.* Rev. ed. Charlottesville: University Press of Virginia, 1974.

Story, Francis, and Nyanaponika Thera. *Rebirth as Doctrine and Experience.* Kandy, Sri Lanka: Buddhist Publication Society, 1975.

Underwood, Peter, and Leonard Wilder. *Lives to Remember: A Case Book on Reincarnation.* London: Robert Hale, 1975.

Wilson, Ian. *Mind out of Time? Reincarnation Claims Investigated.* London: Gollancz, 1981. Revised as *Reincarnation?* Baltimore: Penguin Books, 1982.

The Religio-Philosophical Journal

Prominent American Spiritualistic weekly founded in 1865 in Chicago. Its founder and publisher, Stevens J. Jones, was murdered in 1877. His son-in-law, Col. J. C. Bundy, assumed charge. Successive editors were M. E. Bundy, B. F. Underwood, and T. G. Newan. In the 1890s the *Journal* moved to San Francisco and a new series (vols. 34–42) began. The publication of this long-running periodical ceased on April 22, 1905. It was superseded briefly by *The Mountain Pine* (1906–1908).

Religious Experience Research Centre

Originally founded in 1969 as the **Religious Experience Research Unit** at Manchester College, Oxford, England, by Professor Sir **Alister Hardy** after his retirement from the chair of zoology at Oxford University. In 1985, shortly before he died, Sir Alister was named before a group of eminent churchmen and scientists at the Church Centre of the United Nations as the winner of the Templeton Prize, awarded annually for progress in religion. Following Hardy's death in 1985, the name of the unit was briefly changed to the **Alister Hardy Research Centre.** In 1991 the name of the organization was renamed the **Religious Experience Research Centre** when it moved to Westminster College.

The purpose of the Religious Experience Research Centre is "to make a disciplined study of the frequency of report of first hand religious or transcendent experience in contemporary members of human species and to investigate the nature and function of such experiences." The centre explores such questions as: How many people in the modern world report religious or transcendent experiences? What do people mean when they say they have had one of these experiences? What sort of things do they describe? How do they interpret them? What effects do they have on their lives? Are the sorts of people who report them more likely to be: Well or poorly educated; impoverished or well provided for; happy or unhappy; mentally unbalanced or stable; socially responsible or self-preoccupied; members of religious institutions or not?

Since its foundation, the centre has built up a unique body of research data consisting of more than 5,000 case histories of individuals who have had some form of such experience. Although these case histories have come mainly from Britain, and, to a lesser degree, from other English-speaking countries, many other cultural and religious traditions are represented.

The centre has also conducted a number of large scale and in-depth surveys of reports of religious experiences in Britain and the United States.

Repeated national polls indicate that between a third and a half of the adult populations in Britain and the United States claim to have been "aware of or influenced by a presence or a power, whether they call it God or not, which is different from their everyday selves." Parallel studies in the United States and Australia (e.g., by the National Opinion Research Center at the University of Chicago, the Survey Research Center of the University of California at Berkeley, and Gallup International) have produced similarly high figures. The centre has now completed a number of in-depth studies in Britain, in which random samples of particular social groups (e.g., adult members of the population of an industrial city, a sample of postgraduate students, and a sample of nurses in two large hospitals) have been interviewed personally and at length about their experiences. In all these groups the positive response rate has been over 60 percent.

The centre believes that such research is particularly important "in view of the crisis through which Western culture (and hence the world affected by it) is now passing, in part the result of an intellectually restricted perspective which appeared at the time of the European Enlightenment, especially during the eighteenth century." The centre claims that modern analyses of the alienation, meaninglessness, and violence increasingly endemic to society have been limited by the proscriptions enforced by this dominant (and materially successful) thought pattern, particularly in failing to comprehend or dismissing the religious or transcendent dimension of human experience.

The mailing address of the Religious Experience Research Centre is Westminster College, Oxford, OX2 9AT England.

REM

Initialism for "rapid eye movement," a physical phenomenon during which the most active, visually rich, and bizarre dreaming occurs.

Remy, Nicolas (1530–1612)

Nicolas Remy, a French demonologist, was the author of the frequently reprinted *Demonolatry* (1595), a standard reference for witch-hunters in the next centuries. He was born around 1530 at Charmes, Vosges Department, in Lorraine. His father, Gérard Remy, was provost of Charmes and his uncle held a prominent position in the department. Following their lead, he also became a lawyer. He studied at the University of Toulouse where fellow demonologist **Jean Bodin** (1529–1596) also studied and later taught. He married Anne Marchand with whom he had seven children. In 1563 Remy relocated to Paris where his career blossomed. In 1570 he was appointed lieutenant general of Vosges, succeeding his retiring uncle. Five years later he was also named privy councilor to the Duke Charles III of Lorraine. In 1591 he became attorney general of Lorraine.

Remy traced his interest in **witchcraft** to his childhood, when he first witnessed a trial of an accused witch. Once placed in a position of power in Lorraine, he persecuted them mercilessly, and bragged that he had been responsible for the condemnation of over 900. In 1582 he personally prosecuted one woman on charges of working malevolent magic after his eldest son had died, believing she was responsible for his death. In 1592 the plague hit Nancy, and he retired to the country to write his book, concerned that all should know the power of witches. He wrote in haste, and the volume was unorganized and abruptly changed subjects.

Demonolatry covers two broad subjects, the nature of **Satanism** and the activities of witches, especially their sexual lives. Following the lead of the *Witches Hammer,* the fountainhead of witch-hunting books, Remy assumed that witches are worshipping Satan. He also assumed that a sexual relationship with His Infernal Majesty was essential to the witchcraft rites as were illicit relationships with other members of the secret witchcraft fraternity. The strength of Remy's text was the material he brought from his personal involvement with numerous cases. His own personal reflections gave the volume an air of authority that previous witch-hunting volumes had lacked, which accounts for its widespread acceptance as a standard authority on the subject. Remy argued that the influence of Satan was everywhere, in fact that whatever was out of the normal was probably due to the devil. There are no unexplained facts, hence whatever is unknown is of the realm of demons.

Remy remained at his post until his death in April of 1612. As attorney general he was able to prioritize **witchcraft** cases and alter decisions in instances where local magistrates had, in his opinion, been too lenient on witches. It was noted that he retained his hatred and fear of witches to the very end.

Sources:

Robbins, Russell Hope. *The Encyclopedia of Witchcraft and Demonology.* New York: Crown Publishers, 1970.

Shumaker, Wayne. *The Occult Sciences in the Renaissance: A Study in Intellectual Patterns.* Berkeley: University of California Press, 1972.

Renier, Noreen

Contemporary professional psychic with ten years' experience as a teacher, investigator, and lecturer. Originally from Massachusetts, Noreen lived in Florida for eighteen years, working in advertising and public relations. In 1976, she was introduced to **meditation** and discovered a psychic ability. She submitted her gift to scientific testing and research, working with the **Psychical Research Foundation** in Durham, North Carolina, and the **Department of Personality Studies** at the University of Virginia in Charlottesville. Her experiments in archaeology and anthropology with Dr. David Jones at the University of Central Florida were reported in his book *Visions of Time* (1979).

Noreen became a consultant to law enforcement agencies, and she claims to have worked on more than a hundred cases. She briefly had a weekly call-in radio program "In Touch with Noreen" (1980–82). In 1984, she began work on a book about her experiences, returning to Orlando in 1985 to continue teaching, consultation, and lecturing.

During 1985, John D. Merrell of Beaverton, Oregon, published an article in the *Newsletter* of the Northwest Skeptics (a group of which Merrell was co-founder) questioning Noreen's background credentials and what he claimed were "fraudulent claims" of psychic ability. Northwest Skeptics is a group dedicated to combating pseudoscience and uncovering false claims of paranormal phenomena, with loose ties to the **Committee for the Scientific Investigation of Claims of the Paranormal.** The *Newsletter* was mailed to newspapers, broadcast media, and police departments.

Noreen filed a defamation suit against Merrell, claiming that the *Newsletter* had damaged her reputation as a practicing psychic. The case was heard in September 1986, when Noreen testified that she lost at least one lecturing job with Oregon State Police trainees because of Merrell's article. The suit claimed that Merrell's statements "held the plaintiff up to public ridicule, humiliation, embarrassment, and loss of reputation causing her to suffer loss of self-esteem, mental anguish, humiliation, and loss of reputation regarding her occupation." The jury's verdict was that Merrell knew that at least some of his story was false or written with a reckless disregard for the truth. Noreen was awarded $25,000 damages.

The case was something of a landmark in the present battle between skeptics and psychics. Militant skeptics claim that belief in paranormal phenomena is unscientific and socially irresponsible and must be exposed as pseudoscience or fraud.

Some skeptics have performed a useful service in joining with psychical researchers in exposing a variety of fraudulent claims; others have been irresponsible in attempting to use guilt by association to brand all psychics and all claims of the paranormal as **frauds.**

Sources:

Jones, David. *Visions of Time.* Wheaton, Ill.: Theosophical Publishing House (Quest), 1979.

Res Bureaux Bulletin

A Canadian bulletin about Fortean type phenomena (scientific anomalies), published in the 1970s by a person known only as Mr. X of Kingston, Ontario, Canada. It circulated among serious students of unusual and obscure events in exchange for reciprocity on cuttings and articles.

Reschith Hajalalim

The name of the ministering spirit of the angelic hierarchies in Jewish rabbinical legend. To this angel, the pure and simple essence of the divinity flows through Hajoth Hakakos; he guides the *primum mobile,* and bestows the gift of life on all.

Rescue Circles

Groups formed by Spiritualists for the purpose of "waking up" the dead and freeing them from their earthbound state. These spirits exist closer to the material plane than to the spiritual world and in many cases they do not realize that they are dead at all, and live in a state of bewilderment. If they are enlightened as to their true condition and if prayers are offered for them, they will progress to a higher existence. The origin of rescue circles may be traced to the **Shaker** communities of America.

The first such circles were held by the wife of a Col. Danskin of Baltimore and her other female acquaintances. The most renowned work was performed by a circle in Buffalo between 1875 and 1900 and by **Carl Wickland** and his wife.

The mediums in the Buffalo circle were Marcia M. Swain and Leander Fischer (a professor of music). The circle consisted of Daniel E. Bailey and his wife, Fischer's mother, and Aline M. Eggleston, the stenographer. The identity of the spirit brought to be "woken" was often verified but as the search for such proof entailed considerable labor and time it was, after a while, given up. The circle's work was described by D. E. Bailey in his book *Thoughts from the Inner Life* (1886). Twelve impressive records of these rescue séances were published in an appendix in Admiral Usborne Moore's *Glimpses of the Next State* (1911). Similar mission work was carried on by **E. C. Randall,** also in Buffalo. The medium was **Emily S. French.**

Carl Wickland and his wife worked on literally hundreds of cases and kept detailed records which were published in his 1924 book *Thirty Years Among The Dead.* The work of the Tozer rescue circle in Melbourne is described by **Sir Arthur Conan Doyle** in *Wanderings of a Spiritualist* (1921).

Sources:

Bailey, D. E. *Thoughts from the Inner Life.* Boston: Colby & Rich, 1886.

Doyle, Sir Arthur Conan. *Wanderings of a Spiritualist.* New York: G. H. Doran;London: Hodder & Stoughton, 1921. Reprint, Berkeley, Calif.: Ronin Publishing, 1988.

Moore, Usborne. *Glimpses of the Next State.* London: Watts & Co., 1911.

Randall, E. C. *Frontiers of the After Life.* New York, A. A. Knopf, 1922.

Research Institute for Psi and Psychics

The Research Institute for Psi and Psychics was founded in 1980 by Dutch parapsychologist Dick Bierman and others as a research organization to conduct theoretical speculation and laboratory experiments highlighting the relationship of psychic phenomena to biology, psychology, and physics. Last known address: Alexanderkade 1, NL-1018 Amsterdam, Netherlands.

Research Institute for Supersensonic Healing Energies (RISHE)

Branch of **University of the Trees,** founded by **Christopher Hills** in 1973 at Boulder Creek, California. RISHE is devoted to practical, applied research in subtle energy therapeutics. This includes such subject areas as **radiesthesia, radionics,** homeopathy, Bach flower remedies, negative ionization, and healing with **crystals** and gemstones. Last known address: P.O. Box 644, 13151 Pine St., Boulder Creek, CA 95006.

Resurrection

The central claim of Christianity, that the pre-existent Son of God was incarnated in the man Jesus, that Jesus was the Christ (or Anointed One), and that Jesus died an agonizing death and three days later came back to life in the flesh. Underlying Christianity is a belief in the goodness of material creation and the necessity of a body for a human individual to be a complete person. Future existence will be in a "spiritual body," though there is some disagreement as to what the Apostle Paul means by that term (I Cor. 15:44). Jesus in his resurrected body, as recorded in the gospel accounts and the books of Acts, had what appeared to be a physical body. He ate food and invited Thomas to touch his body. Again, he did extraordinary things such as suddenly appear in a closed room.

Many Spiritualists' and Christians' acceptance of Spiritualist claims have argued for "resurrection" in what might be termed an astral or light body, a non-corporeal body suitable for life in an existence analogous to earthly life but quite distinct from the material world.

As the theory of reincarnation has become the dominant belief within the **New Age** community, there has been an attempt to confuse the two terms both out of ignorance of Christian belief and in an attempt to lessen the tension in a society in which the majority believe in "resurrection" in a Christian sense.

Retrocognition

Term used in psychical research and parapsychology to indicate a form of extrasensory perception in which the subject obtains knowledge of some event in the past by paranormal cognition. This amounts to a kind of backward **precognition. F. W. H. Myers** combined retrocognition with his theory of **"psychorrhagic diathesis"** to explain the phenomena of haunting. It was also suggested that apparitions of the dead and visions of the future, owing to a curious inversion of time, may be amenable to retrocognition.

Retropsychokinesis

Retropsychokinesis (RPK) refers to the possibility of someone in the present affecting an event that occurred in the past. The study of possible RPK events grew out of the studies on **psychokinesis** (mind over matter) conducted by **J. B. Rhine** at Duke University. Rhine explored the possibility that human subjects could affect the roll of dice or the toss of coins. Rhine's experiments raised a variety of methodological issues involving assumptions about, for example, the behavior of a pair of dice tossed numerous times under "normal" conditions and what might constitute paranormal alteration of those conditions. They also raised questions about the nature of probability. More recently, **Helmut Schmidt** conducted similar experiments using an electronic random number generator, which ensured the randomness of the events being altered. The use of the random number generator greatly increased the sophistication of the experiments, and while laying to rest some of the questions concerning the Rhine experiments, it raised others, especially about the nature of time.

In the case of the random number generator, a series of numbers were generated and recorded, and the experiment was actually run at a later time. Subjects were then asked to force the choice which the random generation had already selected. After a series of experiments, and a variety of philosophical discussions about the nature of reality, causation, and the contemporary state of quantum theory, Schmidt concluded that his subjects seemed to be able to influence selected events in the past.

In the later 1990s, Matthew R. Watkins and Peter Moore of Cambridge University launched the RetroPsychoKinesis Project with the idea of continuing the work that Schmidt, now retired, had initiated. It is their understanding that the existence of the Internet has created a new possibility for testing Schmidt's assertions that developed out of his two decades of work. It is Watkins' belief that the use of the Internet can overcome a host of problems previously inherent in laboratory-based research and can eliminate many of the charges brought against parapsychology by the skeptics.

The use of the computer will allow a large number of subjects to be tested and untalented ones to be screened out. By having the computer handle the numbers, the opportunity for fraud will largely disappear. A major problem will, however, be the distinguishing of RPK from precognition, the most obvious alternative explanation for any positive results once fraud is eliminated. It is yet to be seen if the project can produce any positive results and deal satisfactorily with the multitudinous methodological problems. Those wishing to participate in the experiments may contact the project at its Internet site at http://www.fourmilab.c/rpkp/.

Sources:

Schmidt, Helmut. "A PK Test with Electronic Equipment." *Journal of Parapsychology* 34 (1970): 175–81.

———. "PK Tests with a High Speed Random Number Generator." *Journal of Parapsychology* 37 (1973): 105–18.

———. "Precognition of a Quantum Process." *Journal of Parapsychology* 33 (1969): 99–108.

Reuss, Theodor (1855–1023)

German occultist who recruited **Aleister Crowley** to the **OTO** (Ordo Templi Orientis). Reuss was a mysterious and many-sided man. He was born on June 28, 1855 and lived in Britain during the 1880s and earned a living as a music-hall singer under the name Charles Theodore. He sang at fund-raising concerts organized by the British Social League (of which he was an executive member) while acting as an under-cover agent for the German Secret Service, spying on the Karl Marx family. Eleanor Marx considered him a vulgar and dirty man, and he was expelled from the league when his spying was discovered.

In 1902 Reuss was one of the three people named on the charter given by **John Yarker** for the establishment of a German Masonic lodge, which later emerged as the OTO. Reuss, then residing in England, most likely served as liaison between Yarker and Karl Keller, the German founder and leader of the order. Reuss became head of the OTO in 1905 after the death of Karl Keller and was from then on known by his occult name, Frater Merlin.

The most closely guarded secret of the OTO was that of **sex magic,** the use of sexual energy for occult purposes. In 1912 Crowley published *The Book of Lies,* which Reuss read and from one passage inferred that Crowley had discovered and was writing about this secret. Soon thereafter Reuss visited Crowley in London and begged him to conceal the secret, inviting him to enter the OTO as head of a British branch. The British lodge was duly launched under the name **Mysteria Mystica Maxima.**

In 1916 Reuss chartered a North American branch, which was organized as the **Ancient and Mystical Order of the Rosicrucians** (AMORC), headed by **H. Spencer Lewis.** In the legal battles between the several American Rosicrucian groups, the connection with the OTO became a matter of great embarrassment to AMORC, but while denying any connection with Crowley or sex magic, it has continued to publish its charter from Reuss.

After World War II Reuss resided in Switzerland, where he claimed to be a grand master of a Masonic order. He became friendly with Heinrich Tränker, a member of a Rosicrucian society, who had links with other German occult groups such as the **Fraternitas Saturni.** Reuss retired as outer head of the order in 1922, a year before his death, and nominated Crowley as his successor.

Sources:

King, Francis. *Sexuality, Magic, and Perversion.* Secaucus, N.J.: Citadel Press, 1972.

Reuter, Florizel von (1893– ?)

Professor and director of the Master School for Violin at the Vienna State Academy of Music. His mother developed **automatic writing,** receiving messages in seventeen languages, many of them being evidential in character and often coming in mirror writing. In *The Psychic Experiences of a Musician* (1928), von Reuter gave a full analytical account of these phenomena.

His second book *The Consoling Angel* (1930), narrated the receipt of automatic-writing messages from a school friend of his mother's, including over three hundred proofs of identity, all dealing with matters totally unknown to von Reuter and his mother. **Ernesto Bozzano** considered the book to be one of the most evidential publications of the time.

A third book, *A Musician's Talks with Unseen Friends* (1931), is a record of automatic scripts received by von Reuter alone, dealing with ethical and philosophical matters, and given (as in the case of **William Stainton Moses**) by a band of communicators.

Later von Reuter and his mother also developed **direct voice** and received **apport** phenomena in their own circle. Von Reuter lectured on psychic matters all over Germany and the British Isles. He was associated with **Baron von Schrenck-Notzing** in a series of experiments with the **Schneider** brothers.

Sources:

Reuter, Florizel von. *A Musician's Talks with Unseen Friends.* London: Rider, 1931.

Review of Indian Spiritualism

Indian monthly publication issued from 39 S.R. das Road, Calcutta 700026, India.

ReVision: A Journal of Consciousness and Transformation

Quarterly journal devoted to scholarly articles on consciousness and change in modern society. Typical subjects include interdisciplinary studies on Eastern and Western **meditation** and philosophy, **mysticism,** religion in contemporary transpersonal experiences, and research on higher consciousness. The journal is published by Heldref Publications (division of the

Helen Dwight Reid Educational Foundation) in cooperation with the International Transpersonal Association. The editorial staff has included such distinguished individuals as Stanislav Grof, **Stanley Krippner,** Ralph Metzner, and Dr. Karan Singh. Heldref Publications is located at 1319 18th St. NW, Washington, DC 20036-1802. Online subscriptions to the magazine are available at http://www.heldref.org/.

Sources:

Heldref Publications. http://www.heldref.org/. March 8, 2000.

Revista de Parapsicologia (Brazil)

Bimonthly Brazilian publication (in Spanish or Portuguese) of Centro Latino Americano de Parapsicologia. Illustrated articles covered parapsychological phenomena and research. Last known address: Caixa Postal 11.587, 05.000, São Paulo, Brazil.

Revista de Parapsicologia (Chile)

Annual publication of Laboratorio de Investigaciones Parapsicologicas in Chile. It gave national and internal news in the field of parapsychology; reviews of experiments, books and journals; and critical and bibliographical surveys. Last known address: Centro de Investigationes Parapsicologia J. B. Rhine, Constitution 187, Santiago, Chile.

Revivals

Outbreaks of religious mass enthusiasm, often inspired by a new wave of spiritual fervor and/or in reaction to persecution. They have often been accompanied by a variety of paranormal manifestations, such as **luminous phenomena,** aerial music, miraculous **healing,** speaking in **tongues,** and **prophecy.**

From June 1688 to February 19, 1689, five to six hundred prophets emerged in France (in Dauphiny and in the Vivarez) as a result of the revocation of the Edict of Nantes by Louis XIV and the consequent persecution of Protestants. Under its effect, eight thousand seers were counted in Languedoc in the first year.

There hardly was a house that did not have its inspired orators. Even children prophesied in tongues unknown to them. Heavenly music was heard day and night in the air, tongues of fire were observed and, in at least one case, the ordeal of the pyre was harmlessly undergone by the entranced leader Claris. Cavalier, Roland, and Marion, the organizers of the insurgency, were all inspired orators. The army which they assembled chose its own chief by their gifts of the spirit.

The great Irish revival in 1859 and the Welsh revival in 1904 were accompanied by similar phenomena, especially the sound of unearthly music and the sight of inexplicable lights.

The Reverend John Crapsey of Brookfield, Tioga County, was quoting the words of Jesus on the cross when:

"a mighty invisible power seemed suddenly to possess him, and a luminous appearance scintillated upon and around his hand, shining with brilliant effulgence in the eyes of all beholders. Under an impulse which I could not resist, I sprang from the desk out upon the middle of the floor into the midst of the congregation. Fire and pillars of smoke and luminous light rose up bodily in our midst; men, women and even stammering children were seized, speaking with new tongues, and uttering prophecies. Prayers and exhortations were poured forth in abundance, and many of the congregation broke out into the most marvelous and heavenly singing."

McLoughlin, in *Modern Revivalism* (1959) cites three great revival periods in the United States history, each lasting about a generation, each spurred on by national periods of intellectual and cultural conflict and change. The First Great Awakening (1725–1750) followed a period of colonial growth prior to the Revolution, featuring the immigration of the religiously persecuted. The Second Great Awakening (1797–1835), emerged as the new United States sought to establish its identity, expanding its political boundaries through western expansion.

The Second Great Awakening, in particular, emerged out of the rural camp meetings of Tennessee and Kentucky, on the western borders of the burgeoning United States. One of the most famous of these camps took place over five successive days in August of 1801. As many as 10,000 to 30,000 traveled to east of Paris, Kentucky from parts throughout the East and Midwest, to listen to ministers from the Presbyterian, Methodist, and Baptist churches preach adherence to fundamental Christian ideals.

". . .from rotting stumps, fallen tree trunks, horse-drawn wagons, and makeshift platforms, they sermonized and admonished, cajoled and exulted, often all at the very same time. . .As many as 3000 to 5000 made their confessions of faith right there, many displaying involuntary physical convulsions as evidence of their heart-felt conversions: they jerked and twitched, barked and bayed, sang and chanted, cried like babies, and fainted dead away, often remaining unconscious for hours on end."

The Third Great Awakening (1875–1915) followed the Reconstruction Period after the Civil War, as the country attempted to redefine itself as it moved toward the Industrial Revolution. Each of these Awakening periods swept through the growing nation, creating new sects, reviving old ones, and inspiring an infectious spiritual fervor. Among the most famous evangelists of the Great Awakenings included Charles Finney, Dwight Moody, and Billy Sunday, each paving the way for revivalists of future generations.

A peculiar form of revivalism is said to have arisen by the late twentieth century, culminating with the explosion of television evangelists in the politically conservative 1980s. Televangelists such as Oral Roberts, Billy Graham, Jimmy Swaggert, Jerry Falwell, and Jim and Tammy Bakker reached huge audiences through broadcast and cable television, virtually recreating the Great Awakenings' revivalist meetings in the American living room. These televangelists reflected much of the same fervor, fundamentalism, and showmanship of 19th century preachers. Scandals erupted among some of them in 1987, but by then the phenomenon of the televised revival had affixed itself to the modern cultural landscape. (See also **Convulsionaries of St. Médard; Pentecostalism; snake-handling; Tremblers of the Cevennes**)

Sources:

Buchanan, Paul D. *Historic Places of Worship.* Jefferson, N.C.: McFarland and Co., Inc., 1999.

Grey, E. Howard. *Visions, Previsions and Miracles in Modern Times.* London: L. N. Fowler, 1915.

Hadden, Jeffrey K. and Shupe, Answen. *Televangelism.* New York: Henry Holt and Co., 1988.

Kelsey, Morton T. *Tongue Speaking.* Garden City, N.Y.: Doubleday, 1964.

Lewis, Mrs. J. *The Awakening in Wales.* London: Marshall; New York: Revell, 1905.

McLoughlin, William G. *Modern Revivalism: Charles Grandison Finney to Billy Graham.* New York: The Ronald Press Co., 1959.

Simson, Eve. *The Faith Healer: Deliverance Evangelism in North America.* Concordia/Pyramid, 1977.

Revue des Études Psychiques

French edition of the *Rivista di Studi Psichici,* founded by **Count Cesar Baudi de Vesme** in 1898, after the death of **G. B. Ermacora** whom he succeeded in the editorial chair of the *Rivista di S.P.* In 1905 it was amalgamated with the *Annales des Sciences Psychiques,* which ceased publication in 1924.

Revue Métapsychique

Official organ of the Institut Métapsychique Internationale (IMI). It was founded in 1920, with the IMI president **Eugèn Osty** as editor. The review, which published parapsychological research in France and elsewhere, was discontinued in 1981. Back issues from the 1930s onwards are available from the Institut Metapsychique, 1 Place Wagram, Paris 75017, France.

Revue Scientifique et Morale du Spiritisme

Periodical founded by Spiritist **Gabriel Delanne,** running from 1894–1923.

Revue Spirite

Monthly journal founded by **Allan Kardec** in 1858, and for many years the official journal of French **Spiritism,** published in Paris. After Allan Kardec's death, P. G. Ley-marie succeeded to the editorial chair. In the 1920s, it was directed by **Jean Meyer** and edited by **Pascal Forthuny.**

Revue Spiritualiste

Journal representing French **Spiritualism** (as distinct from the more popular school of **Spiritism**) founded by **Z. J. Pierart.** It was published from 1858 until 1870.

Rhabdic Force

Name given to the force which causes muscular contortions in the hands of sensitives while **dowsing.** The force can violently bend a hazel switch being used as a **divining-rod,** or oscillate a **pendulum.** Sometimes called "telluric force."

Rhabdomancy

Term for **divination** by **divining-rods.** Deriving from Greek words meaning "a rod" and "divination," it was thus alluded to by Sir Thomas Browne (1605–82): "As for the divination or decision from the staff, it is an augurial relic, and the practice thereof is accused by God himself: 'My people ask counsel of their stocks, and their staff declareth unto them.' Of this kind was that practised by Nabuchadonosor in that Caldean miscellany delivered by Ezekiel."

John Brand's *Observations on Popular Antiquities* (1777) cited a manuscript, John Bell's *Discourse on Witchcraft* (1705):

"They set up two staffs, and having whispered some verses and incantations, the staffs fell by the operation of demons. Then they considered which way each of them fell, forward or backward, to the right or left hand, and agreeably gave responses, having made use of the fall of their staffs for their signs."

The practice is said to have passed from the Chaldeans and Scythians to the German tribes, who used pieces from the branch of a fruit tree, which they marked with certain characters and threw at hazard upon a white cloth. Something like this, according to one of the rabbis, was the practice of the Hebrews, only instead of characters, they peeled their rods on one side and drew the presage from their manner of falling. The Scythians and the Alani used rods of the myrtle and sallow, and as the latter chose "fine straight wands" according to Herodotus, it may be inferred that their method was that of the Hebrews, or some modification of it. (See also **Aaron's rod**)

Rhapsodomancy

Divination by means of opening the works of a poet at hazard and reading the verse which first presents itself. This is similar to **bibliomancy,** the well-known divination technique of opening a Bible at random and reading the verse on which the finger or other indicator lights as an oracular statement relative to the inquirer's problem.

Rhasis (or Rhazes) (ca. 825–925)

Name given to the famous Arabian physician, chemist, and alchemist Abu Bekr Muhammed Ben Zakeriyah er-Rasi. His popular name "Al-Rhasis" (Man of Ray) derives from his birthplace of Ray, near Teheran, on the frontiers of Khorassan. He first studied philosophy, logic, metaphysics, poetry, and music, and became a skilled player on the lute. At the age of thirty, he began to study medicine and soon became one of the most famous physicians of his time. He was director of the famous hospital of Bhagdad, and a great many books on medicine, chemistry, and philosophy are ascribed to him.

He also wrote treatises on **alchemy** and the transmutation of metals. Some commentators have compared his intellectual attainments with those of Galileo and Robert Boyle. He had a great reputation for his insistence upon the importance of practical experiment over theory. He was one of the first experimenters to mention borax, orpiment, realgar, and other chemical compounds.

There is a probably apocryphal story that he dedicated an alchemical work to the Emir El Mansur, prince of Khorassan, who rewarded him with a thousand pieces of gold, but desired to witness a transmutation. Rhasis was by now an elderly man and his experiment was unfortunately unsuccessful.

El Mansur was enraged, and struck him with a whip, saying "I have rewarded you richly for your trouble, and now I must punish you for your affirmation of lies!" As a result, Rhasis was blinded. However, other explanations have been offered for his failing eyesight, including the claim that it resulted from an inordinate appetite for eating beans.

In his studies in chemistry he left some results of real value, notwithstanding the time and trouble he spent in the pursuit of the **philosophers' stone.** Another theory which he held in common with **Geber** and others was that the planets influenced metallic formation under the earth's surface.

Sources:

Barrett, Francis. *The Lives of the Alchemystical Philosophers.* 1815. Rev. ed. as *Alchemists Through the Ages.* Blauvelt, N.Y.: Rudolf Steiner Publications, 1970.

Rhine, J(oseph) B(anks) (1895–1980)

One of the pioneers of **parapsychology** and co-founder with **William McDougall** of the **Parapsychology Laboratory** at Duke University, Durham, North Carolina. He was born on September 29, 1895, in Juniata County, Pennsylvania. He studied at the University of Chicago (B.S., 1922; M.S., 1923; Ph.D., 1925) where he majored in botany. In 1920 he married Louisa Ella Weckesser, who as **Louisa Rhine,** also became a noted parapsychologist. After graduation Rhine became an instructor in plant physiology at West Virginia University (1924–26) before moving to Duke University where he would remain for the rest of his active career with the department of psychology. Rhine's interest in parapsychology grew out of his investigations of mediumship with Dr. **Walter Franklin Prince** at Harvard University in 1926. Rhine went on to Duke University the following year and studied psychic phenomena with William McDougall, head of the psychology department. It was Rhine's training in plant physiology which gave him the idea that psychic faculties might be tested with scientific disciplines.

With the encouragement of McDougall, Rhine commenced a program for statistical validation of **ESP** (extrasensory perception), a term he invented, working in collaboration with colleagues on the psychology faculty, with students as subjects.

The emphasis was first on **clairvoyance** and **telepathy,** transmitting images from sender to receiver, and the now familiar **Zener cards,** the simple symbols of cross, star, circle, square and waves assisting statistical evaluation of tests. Later work included experiments in **psychokinesis** using dice to test the ability of the human mind to affect movement of objects at a distance. Psychokinesis or "PK" has since largely displaced the term "telekinesis" formerly used in psychical research. The publication of Rhine's monograph *Extrasensory Perception* by the **Boston Society for Psychic Research** in 1934 was a key point in the development of parapsychology as a scientific study, and opinion sharply divided on the validity of the work. Duke, like the rest of the academic world, was home to strong opposition to parapsychology. Thus Rhine amd MacDougal were obliged to open a separate Parapsychology Laboratory in 1935 and seek outside financial sponsorship for research.

From 1937, Rhine launched the *Journal of Parapsychology* at Duke and settled down to create the basic foundational methodology and to generate the body of knowledge upon which laboratory parapsychology would build. In 1957 he led in the foundation of the **Parapsychology Association.** He retired from Duke in 1965 and lost the power base that allowed him to operate the Parapsychology Laboratory. Three years before, in anticipation of the lack of support for parapsychology, he began the reorganization of the endeavor he had managed for the last three decades. He founded the **Foundation for Research on the Nature of Man,** an organization to continue his parapsychological work. The foundation established a new research facility, the **Institute for Parapsychology.**

Through the years Rhine authored a set of basic texts in parapsychology, still necessary reading for any one interested in the field. Though he published many impressive reports, he was repeatedly dogged by criticism that he ignored much of the negative data he had gathered and reported only the positive. Because of these flaws, Rhine's work was not often taken seriously. He died February 20, 1980, at the age of 84. Shortly before his death he had been elected president of the Society for Psychical Research, a recognition of his monumental contributions to the field.

Financial support for the work at the Parapsychology Laboratory at Duke University owed much to the generosity of **Charles E. Ozanne** who made regular financial gifts to support research. In 1960 he helped establish the **Psychical Research Foundation** at Duke Station, Durham, N.C., as an independent research center to investigate phenomena relating to survival of human personality after death as well as other aspects of parapsychology. Another generous donor in the field of parapsychology was the late Chester F. Carlson, inventor of xerography, whose financial support assisted the establishment of the Foundation for Research on the Nature of Man. Situated at Durham, N.C., this foundation made possible the transition from the Parapsychology Laboratory at Duke University to an independent world center for the study of parapsychology and related fields.

Sources:

Berger, Arthur S., and Joyce Berger. *The Encyclopedia of Parapsychology and Psychical Research.* New York: Paragon House, 1991.

Pleasants, Helene, ed. *Biographical Dictionary of Parapsychology.* New York: Helix Press, 1964.

Rhine, J. B. *New Frontiers of the Mind.* New York: Farrar and Rinehart, 1939.

———. *New World of the Mind.* New York: William Sloane Associates, 1953.

———. *The Reach of the Mind.* New York: William Sloane Associates, 1947.

———, ed. *Progress in Parapsychology.* N.p., 1971.

Rhine, J. B. et al. *Parapsychology from Duke to FRNM.* Durham, N.C.: Parapsychology Press, 1965.

Rhine, J. B., and R. Brier. *Parapsychology Today.* New York: Citadel Press, 1968.

Rhine, J. B., and J. G. Pratt. *Parapsychology, Frontier Science of the Mind.* N.p., 1957.

Rhine, J. B., and J. G. Pratt, Charles E. Stuart, Burke M. Smith, and Joseph A. Greenwood. *Extrasensory Perception After Sixty Years; a Critical Evaluation.* New York: Henry Holt, 1940. Reprint, Boston: Bruce Humphries, 1960.

Rhine, Louisa Ella Weckesser (1891–1983)

Pioneer worker in the field of parapsychology. She was born on November 9, 1891, at Sanborn, New York. She studied at the University of Chicago (B.S., 1919; M.S., 1921; Ph.D., biology, 1923). In 1920 she married **Joseph Banks Rhine.** Like her husband, she found parapsychology a much more intriguing field than biology, and began to work in the area from the 1930s. She became a staff member of the Parapsychology Laboratory at Duke University (1948–62) and then research director of the **Institute for Parapsychology** which superseded it as the research branch of the **Foundation for Research on the Nature of Man.** She was a charter member of the Parapsychology Association and co-edited the *Journal of Parapsychology.*

She is known for her work on spontaneous psi cases, reports of which flooded into Duke University as the work of the Parapsychology Laboratory became known across the country. She studied the reports using categories and data coming out of the laboratory's work. In this endeavor she in effect provided the laboratory's transition from the older psychical research and the newer parapsychology that J. B. Rhine was developing. She authored a number of articles and books. She died March 17, 1983, at the age of 91.

In addition to substantial joint contributions to parapsychology, she and her husband also raised four children. Although committed to scientific disciplines in their parapsychology work, both the Rhines shared a humane and religious view of the implications of the subject.

Sources:

Berger, Arthur S., and Joyce Berger. *The Encyclopedia of Parapsychology and Psychical Research.* New York: Paragon House, 1991.

Pleasants, Helene, ed. *Biographical Dictionary of Parapsychology.* New York: Helix Press, 1964.

Rhine, Louisa E. *ESP in Life and Lab: Tracing Hidden Channels.* New York: Macmillan, 1967.

———. *Hidden Channels of the Mind.* New York: William Sloane, 1961.

———. *The Invisible Picture.* Jefferson, N.C.: McFarland, 1981.

———. *Mind Over Matter.* New York: Macmillan, 1970.

———. *Psi: What Is It?* New York: Harper & Row, 1975.

———. *Something Hidden.* Jefferson, N.C.: McFarland, 1983.

Rhine Research Center

The Rhine Research Center is a nonprofit organization devoted to parapsychological research and education. Established as the Foundation for Research on the Nature of Man in 1962 by **J. B. Rhine** and renamed in 1995, the RRC comprises two subsidiaries: The Institute for Parapsychology and Parapsychology Press. The institute is the research arm of the RRC, and its staff conducts experimental research into the apparently psychic **(psi)** functions of **extrasensory perception** (ESP) and **psychokenisis** (PK). As the designated successor to Rhine's famous Duke University Parapsychology Laboratory, the institute maintains access to all records and other properties acquired by that laboratory during its three decades at Duke. The Parapsychology Press publishes the **Journal of Parapsychology,** a professional quarterly. Recognized worldwide as a cornerstone of the professional parapsychological community, the RRC serves the lay public as a reliable resource of authoritative information on psi research. The center is supported through private funding and is sustained in part by memberships. It is currently directed by Richard S. Broughton, 402 N. Buchanan Blvd., Durham, NC 27701-1728. Website: http://www.rhine.org.

Ricerca Psichica (Journal)

The title which **Luce e Ombra,** the oldest Italian Spiritualist monthly, assumed in 1932.

Richet, Charles (1850–1935)

Pioneer psychical researcher, honored professor of physiology at the Faculty of Medicine in Paris, and winner of the 1913 Nobel Prize in Physiology and Medicine. He was also the honorary president of La Societé Universelle d'études Psychiques, president of the **Institut Métapsychique Internationale,** and president of the **Society for Psychical Research,** London (1905).

Richet was born on August 26, 1850, and educated at the University of Paris. He had an initial personal experience in **lucidity** (paranormal knowledge) in 1872. He confessed that although it had tremendous effect on him, he lacked the requisite intellectual courage to draw conclusions. In 1875, while yet a student, he demonstrated that the hypnotic state was a purely physiological phenomenon which had nothing to do with "magnetic fluids." "Following my article," he wrote of the result, "many experiments were widely made, and **animal magnetism** ceased to be an occult science."

A few years later, he published his studies in multiple **personality.** He sat with various mediums, including **William Eglinton** and **Elizabeth d'Esperance,** and in 1886–87 conducted many experiments in **cryptesthesia** with four subjects—Alice, Claire, Eugenie, and Leontine. Some were in a hypnotic, some in a waking state. They reproduced drawings enclosed in sealed envelopes. As a result of these experiments Richet formulated the theory of cryptesthesia in these words: "In certain persons, at certain times, there exists a faculty of cognition which has no relation to our normal means of knowledge."

He founded with Dr. Dariex the *Annales des Sciences Psychiques* in 1890, and two years later he took part in the investigation conducted by the Milan Commission with the medium **Eusapia Palladino.** The report admitted the reality of puzzling phenomena, expressing also the conviction that the results obtained in light, and many of those obtained in darkness, could not have been produced by trickery of any kind.

Richet did not sign the report and in his notes on it in the *Annales des Sciences Psychiques* carefully stated his conclusions as follows:

"Absurd and unsatisfactory though they were, it seems to me very difficult to attribute the phenomena produced to deception, conscious or unconscious, or to a series of deceptions. Nevertheless, conclusive and indisputable proof that there was no fraud on Eusapia's part, or illusion on our part, is wanting: we must therefore renew our efforts to obtain such proof."

He became convinced of the reality of **materialization** phenomena by his experiments with the medium Marthe Béraud (better known as **Eva C.**) at the Villa Carmen, Algiers, in General Noel's house. His report, published in the *Annales des Sciences Psychiques* (April 1906) aroused wide attention. He confirmed his experiments in later sittings at the house of Juliette Bisson and at the Institut Métapsychique of which, after the resignation of Professor Santoliquido, he was elected president. He was unable to detect Eva C.'s fraud which was conclusively revealed only in the 1950s.

He conducted experiments with a number of different mediums including **Franek Kluski, Jan Guzyk,** and **Stephen Ossowiecki,** both in Paris and Warsaw.

His book *Traité de Métapsychique* (1922; translated as *Thirty Years of Psychical Research,* 1923) summed up the experiences of a lifetime. The book was dedicated to **Sir William Crookes** and **F. W. H. Myers.** It became a sign of repentance for his earlier skepticism. He stated in his work:

"The idolatry of current ideas was so dominant at that time that no pains were taken either to verify or to refute Crookes' statements. Men were content to ridicule them, and I avow with shame that I was among the wilfully blind. Instead of admiring the heroism of a recognized man of science who dared then, in 1872, to say that there really are phantoms that can be photographed and whose heart beats can be heard, I laughed."

He accepted **cryptesthesia, telekinesis, ectoplasm,** materializations, and **premonitions** as abundantly proved. On the other hand, he considered doubtful **apports, levitations,** and the phenomena of the **double,** which he had no opportunity to examine thoroughly. He was most emphatic in stating: "The fact that intelligent forces are projected from an organism that can act mechanically, can move objects and make sounds, is a phenomenon as certainly established as any fact in physics." As if to leave a loophole for more definite proofs on **psychic photography, direct writing,** apports, psychic **music,** and **luminous phenomena** he added, somewhat naively: "No one would have thought of simulating them if they had never really occurred. I do not hesitate to think them fairly probable, but they are not proven."

His struggle with the problem of **survival** was very interesting. He stated: "I admit that there are some very puzzling cases that tend to make one admit the survival of human personality—the cases of **Leonora E. Piper**'s George Pelham, of Raymond Lodge and some others."

His basis for disbelief in survival was twofold: first, the human mind has mysterious faculties of cognition; second these mysterious cognitions have an invincible tendency to group themselves around a new personality. He explained:

"The doctrine of survival seems to me to involve so many impossibilities, while that of an intensive cryptesthesia is (relatively) so easy to admit that I do not hesitate at all. I go so far as to claim—at the risk of being confounded by some new and unforeseen discovery—that subjective metapsychics will always be radically incapable of proving survival. Even if a new case even more astounding than that of George Pelham were to appear, I should prefer to suppose an extreme perfection of transcendental cognitions giving a great multiplicity of notions grouping themselves round the imaginary centre of a factitious personality, than to suppose that this centre is a real personality—the surviving soul, the will and consciousness of a self that has disappeared, a self which depended on a brain now reduced to dust. . . .

"But except in a few rare cases, the inconsistency between the past and the present mentality is so great that in the immense majority of spiritist experiences it is impossible to admit survival, even as a very tentative hypothesis. I could more easily admit a non-human intelligence, distinct from both medium and discarnate, than the mental survival of the latter." Treating of the so-called **death** bed meeting cases he stated: "Among all the facts adduced to prove survival, these even seem to me to be the most disquieting."

He did not accept the facts of materialization as proof of survival.

"The case of George Pelham, though there was no materialization, is vastly more evidential for survival than all the materializations yet known. I do not even see how decisive proof could be given. Even if (which is not the case) a form identical with that of a deceased person could be photographed I should not understand how an individual two hundred years dead, whose body has become a skeleton, could live again with this vanished body any more than with any other material form."

He called the phenomena of materialization absurd, yet true, and explained:

"Spiritualists have blamed me for using this word 'absurd'; and have not been able to understand that to admit the reality of these phenomena was to me an actual pain; but to ask a physiologist, a physicist, or a chemist to admit that a form that has a circulation of blood, warmth, and muscles, that exhales carbonic acid, has weight, speaks, and thinks, can issue from a human body is to ask of him an intellectual effort that is really painful."

In concluding his weighty *Thirty Years of Psychical Research,* he was assailed by doubts:

"Truth to tell—and one must be as cautious in denial as in assertion—some facts tend to make us believe strongly in the survival of vanished personalities. Why should mediums, even when they have read no spiritualist books, and are unacquainted with spiritualist doctrines, proceed at once to personify some deceased person or other? Why does the new personality affirm itself so persistently, so energetically, and sometimes with so much verisimilitude? Why does it separate itself so sharply from the personality of the medium? All the words of powerful mediums are pregnant, so to say, with the theory of survival? These are semblances, perhaps, but why should the semblances be there?" Then, again, as if repenting his doubts, he explained:

"Mysterious beings, angels or demons, existences devoid of form, or spirits, which now and then seek to intervene in our lives, who can by means, entirely unknown, mould matter at will, who direct some of our thoughts and participate in some of our destinies, and who, to make themselves known (which they could not otherwise do) assume the bodily and psychological aspect of vanished human personalities—all this is a simple manner of expressing and understanding the greater part of the metapsychic phenomena."

His next book, *Notre Sixième Sens* (1927; translated as *Our Sixth Sense,* 1929), was a courageous attempt to grapple with the problem of cryptesthesia. He conceived it physiologically as a new **sixth sense** which is sensitive to what he called the vibrations of reality. It is a sweeping theory that, in its implications, is nearly as far-reaching as the spirit theory.

In *La Grande Espérance* (1933), following an important monograph, *L'Avenir et la Premonition* (1931), he himself admitted that this vibratory theory is far from being sufficient for "there are cases in which *á la rigeur* one could suppose the intervention of a foreign intelligence."

These were the cases of veridical **hallucinations.** Even there he would have preferred to fall back on the vibratory explanation but for the puzzle of collective veridical hallucinations in which "one is almost compelled to admit the objective reality of the phantom." That admission did not allow him to doubt that "in cases of simple veridical hallucinations there is an objective reality as well." Pursuing this line of reasoning, he stated: "It appears that in certain cases phantoms are also inhabiting a house. I hesitate to write this down. It is so extraordinary that my pen almost refuses to write but just the same it is true."

Still, after having analyzed the purely psychological phenomena, if the choice was between the spirit hypothesis and a prodigious lucidity he would lean towards the second. For that explained all cases, whereas the former, although it is the better one in a small number of cases, was inadmissible in many others.

The grand hope of humanity lay in psychical research, in that immense incertitude which we feel in face of its extraordinary, truly absurd phenomena.

"The more I reflect and weigh in my mind these materializations, hauntings, marvelous lucidity, apports, xenoglossie, apparitions and, above all, premonitions, the more I am persuaded that we know absolutely nothing of the universe which surrounds us. We live in a sort of dream and have not yet understood anything of the agitations and tumults of this dream.

"Everything came down to this:

"Either the human intelligence is capable of working miracles. I call miracles the phantoms, ectoplasm, lucidity, premonitions. Or assisting in our doings, controlling our thoughts, writing by our hand, or speaking by our voice there are, interblending with our life, mysterious, invisible entities, angels or demons, perhaps the souls of the dead, as the spiritualists are convinced. Death would not be death but the entrance into a new life. In each case we hurl ourselves against monstrous improbabilities (*invraisemblances*), we float in the inhabitual, the miraculous, the prodigious."

Richet died December 3, 1935.

Sources:

Berger, Arthur S., and Joyce Berger. *The Encyclopedia of Parapsychology and Psychical Research.* New York: Paragon House, 1991.

Gauld, Alan. *The Founders of Psychical Research.* New York: Schrocken Books, 1968.

Jules-Bois, A. H. "Charles Richet: Father of Metaphysics." *Journal* of the American Society for Psychical Research 30 (1936).

Richet, Charles. *Notre Sixième Sens.* N.p., 1927. English ed. as *Our Sixth Sense.* N.p., 1929.

———. *Traité de Métapsychique.* N.p., 1922. English ed. as *Thirty Years of Psychical Research.* New York: Macmillan, 1923.

Richmond, Cora L(inn) V(ictoria) (1840–1923)

The most famous American Spiritualist inspirational speaker and healer, variously known under her married names as Cora Scott, Cora Hatch, Cora L. V. Tappan, and Cora L. V. Tappan-Richmond. She was born April 21, 1840, a noteworthy event in that she had a veil (membrane) covering her face, an event often seen as portending a psychically aware life. She was named Cora, a seeress. Her family was attracted to Spiritualism and in 1851, as a child of eleven, she resided some months in the Spiritualist community headed by **Adin Ballou** at **Hopedale** and at the ranch community at Waterloo, Wisconsin. Passing into a **trance** while at Waterloo, she was controlled by the spirit of young Ballou. Two years later, she was appearing as a public speaker. At the age of sixteen she was famous, had traveled throughout the United States, often lecturing with great elocution before scientists on randomly-selected subjects.

She married while still a teen, but soon got a divorce because of spousal abuse. She worked out of Baltimore for many years prior to moving to England in 1873. While in England, she delivered some three thousand lectures. **Frank Podmore** wrote of her in his book *Modern Spiritualism* (2 vols., 1902),

"That the flow of verbiage never fails is a small matter; Mrs. Tappan's trance-utterances surpass those of almost every other automatist in that there is a fairly coherent argument throughout. Two at least of the subjects sent to her in 1874 'The Origin of Man' and 'The Comparative Influence of Science and Morality on the Rise and Progress of Nations,' may be presumed to have been little familiar. But the speaker is never at a loss . . . Again, we find none of the literary artifices by which ordinary speakers are wont to give relief—there is no antithesis, no climax, no irony or humour in any form. And the dead level of style reflects a dead level of sentiment; there is no scorn or indignation, no recognition of human effort and pain, no sense of the mystery of things. The style is clear, as jelly is clear; it is the proto-plasm of human speech; and it is flavoured throughout with mild, cosmic emotions.

"Frequently at the close of an address Mrs. Tappan would recite an impromptu poem, again on a subject chosen at the moment by the audience. Some of these poems are strikingly melodious, and it is interesting to note how the melody continually overpowers the sense."

After her return to America, Richmond married William Richmond and settled in Chicago. She pastored the First Society of Spiritualists and he operated as her publisher and book agent. From her platform in Chicago she became one of the movement's most famous leaders. In 1892, she officiated at the funeral of Nettie Colburn Maynard (also known as **Henrietta S. Maynard**), the medium who had worked with **Abraham Lincoln.** The next year she assisted in the founding of the **National Spiritualist Association of Churches** and became its first vice president and a national lecturer through the first decades of the new century.

She was equally renowned for her healing power and for her trance utterances. Of her excursions into the spirit world in trance she brought back recollections of an absorbing interest. She died January 2, 1923.

Sources:

Barrett, Harrison D. *The Life and Work of Cora L. V. Richmond.* Chicago: Hack & Anderson Printers, 1895.

Melton, J. Gordon. *Religious Leaders of America.* Detroit: Gale Research, 1991.

Podmore, Frank. *Modern Spiritualism.* London: Methuen, 1902. Reprinted as *Mediums of the Nineteenth Century.* New Hyde Park, N.Y.: University Books, 1963.

Richmond, Cora L. V. *Discourses Through the Mediumship of Mrs. Cora L. V. Tappan.* Boston: Colby & Rich, 1876. Reprint, London, N.p., 1878.

———. *My Experiments While out of the Body and My Return after Many Days.* Boston: Christopher Press, 1915.

———. *Psychosophy.* Chicago: The Author, 1888. Reprint, Chicago: Regan Printing House, 1915.

———. *The Soul in Human Embodiment.* Chicago: Spiritualist Publishing, 1887.

Richmond, Kenneth Forbes (1882–1945)

Scottish writer and educational psychologist who assisted the **Society for Psychical Research** (SPR), London, during the crucial years of World War II. He edited the *Journal* of the SPR (1939–45) and served as the Society's part-time secretary (1944–45). Richmond was born on August 8, 1882, at Glenarmond, Scotland, and was educated at Glenarmond School. His wife, **Zoe Richmond,** was a sensitive who was tested by the SPR.

His interest in psychical research was stimulated by the book *Raymond: Or Life After Death* by **Sir Oliver Lodge** (1916), which Richmond reviewed. He became a member of the SPR and investigated the phenomena of mediumship, especially the medium **Gladys Osborne Leonard** and her **control,** "Feda." He wrote a number of popular articles which appeared in newspapers and magazines, one book, *Evidence of Identity* (1939), and several articles in the *Proceedings* of the SPR. He died November 30, 1945.

Sources:

Berger, Arthur S., and Joyce Berger. *The Encyclopedia of Parapsychology and Psychical Research.* New York: Paragon House, 1991.

Richmond, Kenneth F. *Evidence of Identity.* London: G. Bell, 1939.

———. "Preliminary Studies of the Recorded Leonard Material." *Proceedings* of the Society for Psychical Research (1936).

Richmond, Thomas (1796– ?)

United States Senator, a leading man of Chicago, and also a medium. He was author of the book *God Dealing with Slavery* (1870), which told the story of his psychic influence which, along with that of **Henrietta S. Maynard,** prevailed upon **Abraham Lincoln** to abolish slavery.

Richmond, Zoe Blanche Russell (1888–1986)

Honorary associate of the **Society for Psychical Research** (SPR), London. Born June 14, 1888, in London, England. In 1914 she married **Kenneth Forbes Richmond,** whom she assisted in investigations of mediumship, in particular the phenomena of **Gladys Osborne Leonard.**

She joined the Society for Psychical Research in 1922. Subsequently she developed the faculty of **automatic writing** and was herself the subject of SPR experiments. She contributed a number of articles to *Light* (published by the London Spiritualist Alliance), and published *Evidence of Purpose* (1938), in which she reviewed purposive messages through mediums from deceased individuals.

Sources:

Berger, Arthur S., and Joyce Berger. *The Encyclopedia of Parapsychology and Psychical Research.* New York: Paragon House, 1991.

Richmond, Zoe. *Evidence of Purpose.* N.p., 1938.

Ridley, Hazel (Hurd) (ca. 1900–)

American **direct voice** medium of Buffalo, New York. Her psychic development began at the age of 18. "Grey Wolf," an American Indian **control,** manifested in trance and declared that the medium would develop voices. She did. The voices were of a curious, whispering quality, coming from her larynx alone with no function of her mouth, lips, or tongue.

Wilson G. Bailey, a physician of Camden, New Jersey, wrote in his book *No, Not Dead; They Live* (1923): "I filled her mouth with water and then with salt, and still the voice came through without interruption or impediment and I also punctured her arm when in trance, and though I drew blood she did not feel any pain."

Ridley toured the American continent and paid three visits to England, the first in 1926, the second in 1931, and the third in 1932. While hailed by some, she also encountered strong opposition to her performances. Spiritualistist author **H. Dennis Bradley,** not known for his critical appraisals, caustically condemned her performance as fraudulent rubbish in his book... *And After* (1931). Against Bradley's comments stands the testimony of Will Goldston, one of the renowned professional magicians in Europe, that she had genuine powers. In *Death Unveiled,* Mrs. D. U. Fletcher, wife of a senator from Florida, described how through Ridley's mediumship a violin was restored to its owner after thirty-seven years.

Sources:

Bailey, Wilson G. *No, Not Dead; They Live.* N.p., 1923.

Bradley, H. Dennis. . . . *And After.* London: T. W. Laurie Ltd., 1931.

Rinaldo des Trois-Echelles du Mayne (d. ca. 1571)

A much-dreaded French sorcerer of the reign of Charles IX, who, at his execution, boasted before the king that he had in France three hundred thousand confederates, whom they could not burn—meaning, perhaps, the demons of the witches **sabbat.** Trois-Echelles is cited in **Jean Bodin**'s *De la démonomanie des Sorciers.*

Sources:

Bodin, Jean. *De la Démonomanie des Sorciers.* Paris, 1580.

Ringger, Peter (1923–)

Swiss author who has written on parapsychological subjects. He was born on February 1, 1923, in Zürich, Switzerland, and he studied at Zürich University (Ph.D., 1948). In 1950 he became editor of the journal *Neue Wissenschaft,* in which he published a number of his own articles. In 1951 he founded and became the director of the Swiss Society for Parapsychology (Schweizer Parapsychologische Gesellschaft). Ringer is cited for having contributed his financial resources to the building of Swiss **parapsychology.**

Sources:

Berger, Arthur S., and Joyce Berger. *The Encyclopedia of Parapsychology and Psychical Research.* New York: Paragon House, 1991.

Pleasants, Helene, ed. *Biographical Dictionary of Parapsychology.* New York: Helix Press, 1964.

Ringger, Peter. *Parapsychologie: Die Wissenschaft des Okkulten* (Parapsychology: The Science of the Occult). N.p., 1957. Reprint, Zürich; Stuttgart: Werner Classen, 1972.

———. *Das Problem der Besessenheit* (The Problem of Possession). N.p., 1953.

———. *Das Weltbild der Parapsychologie* (The World View of Parapsychology). N.p., 1959.

Ring of Thoth

The Ring of Thoth is a contemporary Norse Pagan association founded shortly after the disbanding of the **Asatru Free Assembly** in 1987. The Asatru Free Assembly had been the first and most prominent organization attempting to revive the acknowledgment of the pre-Christian deities once generally worshiped throughout Germany and the Scandinavian countries. The Ring of Thoth was founded by Edred Thorsson (Stephen Edred Flowers) and James Chisholm as an explicitly non-racist organization dedicated to the promotion of the religion of the Germanic peoples. (During the 1980s racism was a persistent charge leveled against groups promoting Norse Paganism.) It sees itself as taking a more liberal and scholarly approach than that taken by the other major group formed somewhat simultaneously, the **Asatru Alliance.** In other respects it continues the beliefs and practices of the former Asatru Free Assembly.

The Ring allows considerable variation in belief and practice but is united by a common loyalty to, or "Troth" with, the Norse gods and goddesses; a respect for the religious, cultural, and historical heritage of the Northern Europeans; and a commitment to the virtues of Courage, Truth, Honor, Loyalty, Discipline, Hospitality, Industriousness, Self-reliance, and Steadfastness. Membership is open to all regardless of racial or ethnic background or sexual orientation, and the Ring is opposed to racialist definitions of the Germanic Heathen people. The Asatru religion emerged from the experiences of the pre-Christian Germanic peoples of pre-Christian Northern Europe. While universalist in orientation, it would be impossible to understand without an appreciation of the cultural context that gave it birth.

The Ring of Thoth may be contacted at P.O. Box 25637, Tempe, AZ 85285. Its webpage can be found at http://asatru.knotwork.com/troth/index.html. Thorsson has authored several books on the Asatru traditions, especially on the magical practices associated with **runes.**

Sources:

Gundarsson, KveldulfR Hagan, ed. *Our Thoth.* N.p.: Ring of Thoth, 1992.

Thorsson, Edred. *A Book of Thoth.* St. Paul, Minn.: Llewellyn Publications, 1989.

———. *Futhark: A Handbook of Rune Magic.* York Beach, Maine: Samuel Weiser, 1984.

———. *The Nine Doors of Midgard: A Complete Curriculum of Rune Magic.* St. Paul, Maine: Llewellyn Publications, 1991.

———. *The Truth about Teutonic Magick.* St. Paul, Maine: Llewellyn Publications, 1989.

Rinpoche

An honorific used in Tibetan Buddhism meaning "precious master," now commonly encountered among Tibetan groups operating in the West.

Ripley, George (ca. 1415–1490)

British alchemist born in Ripley, Yorkshire, England, where his kinsfolk appear to have been powerful and numerous. He entered the Roman Catholic Church, became an Augustinian monk, and was subsequently appointed Canon of Bridlington in his native Yorkshire, a priory which had been founded in the time of Henry I by Walter de Ghent.

Ripley's priestly office did not prevent him from traveling, and he studied physical science and **alchemy** in France, Germany, and Italy, even voyaging as far as the island of Rhodes, where he is said to have made a large quantity of gold for the knights of St. John of Jerusalem.

Afterward he went to Rome, where he was dignified by the Pope, the result being that when he returned to Bridlington, he found his friends there intensely jealous of him. It was reported that he even resigned his position and retired to a priory at Boston, in Lincolnshire, but this story is probably unfounded, the likelihood being that Ripley the alchemist was confused with George Ripley, a Carmelite friar, who lived at Boston in the thirteenth century and wrote a biography of St. Botolph.

Ripley died in England in 1490, but his fame did not die with him; his name continued to be familiar for many years after his death. He was among the first to popularize the alchemical writings attributed to **Raymond Lully,** which first became known in England about 1445. An interest in alchemy was increasing steadily among English scholars at this time—the more so because the law against multiplying gold had lately been repealed.

Ripley wrote a number of learned treatises himself, notably *Medulla Alchimioe, The Treatise of Mercury* and *The Compound of Alchemie* (first printed 1591), the latter work dedicated to King Edward IV. A collected edition of his writings was issued at Kassel Germany in 1649.

Sources:

Ripley, George. *The Compound of Alchemie.* N.p., 1591.

———. *Medulla Alchimioe.* N.p., n.d.

———. *The Treatise of Mercury.* N.p., n.d.

Ripley Revived, or an Exposition upon George Ripley's Hermetico-Poetical Works. London, 1978.

RISHE See Research Institute for Supersensonic Healing Energies

"Rita"

Pseudonym of British novelist and Spiritualist **Eliza M. Y. Humphreys,** who died in 1938.

Rita, A.

British private medium, who only sat with friends, in darkness, without passing into **trance,** and kept up a running conversation throughout with **apparitions** who apparently brought their own light. In 1878, in a séance in Amsterdam, Holland, he impersonated the spirit entity **"John King"** and was exposed as a **fraud** and accomplice of the medium **Charles Williams.** Masks, false beard, and white muslin were found secreted on him.

Sources:

Berger, Arthur S., and Joyce Berger. *The Encyclopedia of Parapsychology and Psychical Research.* New York: Paragon House, 1991.

Rivers, Olivia Burnett (Mrs. Doris Wilmer Rivers) (1919–)

Assistant professor of psychology and a parapsychologist. She was born on June 16, 1919, at Booneville, Mississippi. She studied at Blue Mountain College, Mississippi (B.A., 1941) and Peabody College, Nashville, Tennessee (M.A., 1942). After graduation she taught at Southwestern Louisiana Institute, Lafayette (1942–44), the Woman's College, University of North Carolina, Greensboro, (1944–47), and Mississippi State University (1947–49). In 1950 she joined the staff of the **Parapsychology Laboratory,** at Duke University.

Sources:

Pleasants, Helene, ed. *Biographical Dictionary of Parapsychology.* New York: Helix Press, 1964.

Rivista Di Studi Psichici (Journal)

The first Italian psychical research periodical, founded by Dr. **G. B. Ermacora** with Georgio Finzi in January 1895. The journal was carefully and critically conducted on principles analogous to those of the *Proceedings* of the Society of Psychical Research. After the death of Ermacora in 1898, **Count Cesar Baudi de Vesme** became its editor, publishing a simultaneous French edition (*Revue des Etudes Psychiques*) until 1905, when the journal was amalgamated with the *Annales des Sciences Psychiques.*

Robbins, Shawn (1945–)

Shawn Robbins, a popular psychic best known for her many prophecies, was born and raised in the Queens section of New York City, the daughter of a businessman. As a child, her clairvoyant and precognitive powers began to manifest. She recalls that on her 16th birthday her mother tested her abilities by hiding all of her presents around the house. She found them quickly by simply walking around the room and pointing to where they were. As a teenager she read widely in the available literature trying to understand her gift.

She did not complete high school, and after dropping out she joined a band. For the next five years she attempted to establish herself as a musician in an all-female band. She grew bored with the grind, however, and in the early 1970s settled in New York as a professional psychic. Her first job was as a consultant to a large cosmetics company, but eventually she opened an office and began to offer psychic readings to the general public. Her career took an upward swing after she began doing call-in talk shows answering questions and giving brief readings to the audience. Her appearances led to her being featured in the pages of the popular tabloid, *The National Enquirer,* which regularly ran features on psychic predictions. While largely dismissed by many in the psychic community, the coverage in the *Enquirer* made her a national celebrity. That celebrity status was confirmed by several outstanding successes. Then, while in Boston to do a talk show, she was contacted by the local police who used her in the pursuit of some money that had been hidden by several robbers. Her success in assisting with the find created another area in which she could apply her skills.

Many of the stories of her early adventures, including her prediction of Patty Heart's arrest in 1975, were recounted in her autobiographical volume, *Ahead of Myself,* in 1980. During the 1990s, Robbins expanded her occasional prophecies and focused her attention on the new millennium. The effort resulted in two books filled with prophecies for the twenty-first century. It is yet to be determined how accurate she is, but by the end of her life the record she has produced will provide a wealth of material for evaluation.

Sources:

Robbins, Shawn, and Edward Susman. *More Prophecies for the Coming Millennium.* New York: Avon, 1996.

———. *Prophecies for the End of Time.* New York: Avon, 1995.

Robbins, Shawn, with Milton Pierce. *Ahead of Myself: Confessions of a Professional Psychic.* Englewood Cliffs, N.J.: Prentice-Hall, 1980.

Roberts, Estelle (1889–1970)

One of the more famous British Spiritualist mediums of the mid-twentieth century. Born May 10, 1889, she claimed to have first seen a spirit at the age of ten. At school, she constantly heard voices and saw apparitions. Her parents scolded her for having a too-vivid imagination. At the age of fifteen, she was employed as a nursemaid, but the visions and voices followed her wherever she went. She married at the age of seventeen and later foretold her husband's untimely death. After that she had a hard struggle to support her three children, and she took a job as a waitress, working from 7 a.m. until late at night.

One day a neighbor persuaded her to attend a Spiritualist service, where the clairvoyant said: "You are a born medium. You have great work to do in the world." In due course, she became a medium, controlled by the spirit guide "Red Cloud." She operated in complete darkness and manifested **clairvoyance, clairaudience, direct voice, materialization, psychometry,** psychic **healing, trance** oratory, **automatic writing,** and production of **apports.**

While hailed by Spiritualists, she would never allow trained observers to examine her work. She even gave a demonstration of **Spiritualism** in the august surroundings of the House of Commons in Britain, but she turned down a formal offer from the **Society for Psychical Research** to investigate her physical mediumship.

Estelle Roberts died in 1970.

Sources:

Berger, Arthur S., and Joyce Berger. *The Encyclopedia of Parapsychology and Psychical Research.* New York: Paragon House, 1991.

Roberts, Estelle. *Fifty Years a Medium.* London, 1969. Reprint, New York: Avon, 1972.

Roberts, Etta

American **materialization** medium. After being accused of fraud she held a remarkable test séance at Onset Grove, Onset Bay, Massachusetts, on September 3, 1891, before sixty people. She was enclosed in a wire cage. Phantoms not only appeared, but the medium herself was mysteriously brought out of the cage without disturbing the seals.

Many of the phantoms were seen to build up before the cage and also to transform into other shapes. The full account of the séance, signed by twelve people present, was published in the *Banner of Light* (September 1891). Paul Joire wrote a brief description of this test séance in *Psychical and Supernormal Phenomena* (1916).

Roberts, Jane (1929–1984)

Public name of Jane Butts, an American psychic who became the medium for communications from an entity named **"Seth"** who claimed to be a minor pope of the fourth century.

In 1963, Roberts and her husband, Robert Butts, experimented with a **ouija board** and received the first "Seth" messages. Later, she started going into trance, and when "Seth" spoke through her, Roberts's voice and features changed character. In her autobiographical work *Adventures in Consciousness: An Introduction to Aspect Psychology* (1975), Roberts gives the background and development of the "Seth" communications and discusses what she calls "aspect psychology," based on the concept that human consciousness is mobile.

The "Seth" communications developed in various levels of awareness (Seth I, II, and III). They were tape recorded, and have been transcribed and published in a series of books, notably *Seth Speaks; The Eternal Validity of the Soul* (1972) and *The Nature of Personal Reality: A Seth Book* (1974). The popularity of the volumes led to the production of a series of texts through the 1970s and have been credited with generating the renewed interest in **channeling** so evident in the **New Age** movement of the 1980s. These communications cover a whole range of topics of concern to religious and metaphysical belief, from personal belief and development to mental and physical health, illumination, good and evil, sexuality, art, creativity, spiritual grace, and modern problems.

An early book by Roberts titled *How to Develop Your ESP Power* (1966) was reissued under the title *The Coming of Seth* (1976). It describes the day-to-day emergence of the personality of "Seth" and the experiments involved, with suggestions for experiments that readers can attempt. Roberts subsequently regarded this early book as occasionally naive, reflecting her own inexperience at the time. It was supplemented by *The God of Jane; A Psychic Manifesto* (1981), discussing her early life, psychic experiences, and outlook. Other "Seth" books include: *The "Unknown" Reality* (1977), *The Nature of the Psyche; Its Human Expression* (1979), and *The Individual and the Nature of Mass Events* (1981). Some of the "Seth" titles have been reprinted by Bantam in paperback.

Roberts lived a quiet life in spite of the demands of a growing readership. She rarely spoke in public and refused all suggestions that she head a "Seth" organization. She died September 5, 1984, in her home town, Elmira, New York. The **Austin Seth Center** was formed to spread the ideas of the "Seth" Material; it also publishes the quarterly magazine *Reality Change.*

In Roberts's posthumously published book *Seth, Dreams and Projection of Consciousness* (1986), her husband Robert Butts stated: "I think that I've had a number of waking and dreaming experiences in which Jane and I have communicated with each other since her physical death. So have others."

Sources:

Berger, Arthur S., and Joyce Berger. *The Encyclopedia of Parapsychology and Psychical Research.* New York: Paragon House, 1991.

Melton, J. Gordon. *Religious Leaders of America.* Detroit: Gale Research, 1991.

Roberts, Jane. *Adventures in Consciousness: An Introduction to Aspect Psychology.* Englewood Cliffs, N.J.: Prentice-Hall, 1975.

———. *Dreams, "Evolution," and Value Fulfillment; A Seth Book.* 2 vols. Englewood Cliffs, N.J.: Prentice-Hall, 1986.

———. *The God of Jane: A Psychic Manifesto.* Englewood Cliffs, N.J.: Prentice-Hall, 1981.

———. *How to Develop Your ESP Power.* New York: Frederick Fell, 1966. Reprinted as: *The Coming of Seth.* New York: Pocket Books, 1976.

———. *The Nature of Personal Reality: A Seth Book.* Englewood Cliffs, N.J.: Prentice-Hall, 1974.

———. *Seth, Dreams and Projection of Consciousness.* Stillpoint Publishing, 1986.

———. *The Seth Material.* Englewood Cliffs, N.J.: Prentice-Hall, 1970.

———. *Seth Speaks: The Eternal Validity of the Soul.* Englewood Cliffs, N.J.: Prentice-Hall, 1972.

Watkins, Susan. *Conversations with Seth. The Story of Jane Roberts's ESP Class.* 2 vols. Englewood Cliffs, N.J.: Prentice-Hall, 1980–81.

Robertson, Olivia (1917–)

Irish neo-pagan writer and painter who founded the **Fellowship of Isis** to revive worship and communication with the feminine principle in deity. She was born in London on April 13, 1917, and later worked as a play leader in Dublin Corporation playgrounds, Eire (1941–45). Her book *St. Malachy's Court* (1946) is based on these experiences. Other publications include *Field of the Stranger* (1948, a Book Society choice and also published in a Braille edition); *The Golden Eye* (1949); *Miranda Speaks* (1950); *It's an Old Irish Custom* (1954); and *Dublin Phoenix* (1957). She has exhibited her paintings in Dublin.

Robertson founded the Fellowship of Isis at Clonegal Castle, Enniscorthy, Eire, in 1976, and subsequently has used her literary skills in service to the Fellowship.

Sources:

Robertson, Olivia. *The Call of Isis.* Enniscorthy, Eire: Cesara Publications, 1975.

———. *Dea: Rites and Mysteries of the Goddess.* Enniscorthy, Eire: Cesara Publications, 1975.

———. *The Isis Wedding Rite.* Enniscorthy, Eire: Cesara Publications, 1975.

———. *Ordination of a Priestess.* Enniscorthy, Eire: Cesara Publications, n.d.

———. *Rite of Rebirth.* Enniscorthy, Eire: Cesara Publications, 1977.

"Robert the Devil"

A popular thirteenth-century romance legend, known in France in both prose and verse forms as *Robert le Diable.* The story was printed in England ca. 1502 by Wynkyn de Worde (Caxton's assistant) as *Lyfe of Robert the Devyll.*

According to the story, Robert was the son of a duke and duchess of Normandy. He was endowed with marvelous physical strength, which he used only for evil. Explaining to him the cause of his wicked impulses, his mother told him that he had been born in answer to prayers addressed to the devil. He sought religious advice and was directed by the Pope to a hermit, who ordered him to maintain complete silence, to take his food from the mouths of dogs, to feign madness, and to provoke abuse from common people without attempting to retaliate.

He became court fool to the Roman emperor, and three times delivered the city from Saracen invasions, having, in each case, been prompted to fight by a heavenly message. The emperor's dumb daughter was given speech in order to identify the savior of the city with the court fool, but he refused his due reward, as well as her hand in marriage, and went back to the hermit, his former confessor.

Rocail

According to ancient Oriental legend, Rocail was the younger brother of Seth, the son of the biblical Adam. The circumstances of his history were picturesque and unique. A dive, or giant, of Mount Caucasus, finding himself in difficulties, applied for aid to the human race. Rocail offered his services to the giant, and these proved so acceptable that the dive made his benefactor his grand vizier.

For a long period Rocail successfully governed the giant's realm and reached a position of dignity and honor. However, when he felt himself growing old, he desired to leave behind him a more lasting monument than public respect, so he built a magnificent palace and sepulcher. The palace he peopled with statues, which, by the power of magic, he made to walk and talk.

Sources:

Herbelot, Barthélemy d'. *Bibliotheque Oriental.* Paris, 1697.

Rochas d'Aiglun, Lt.-Col. Eugene Auguste-Albert de (1837–1914)

Prominent French psychical investigator, famous for his researches in human **emanations, hypnotism, reincarnation,** and physical phenomena. He served as attaché to the French General Staff during the Franco-Prussian War and was administrator of the École Polytechnique of Paris, but owing to his interest in occult investigations was forced to resign.

Rochas was the first writer to acquaint the French public with the claims concerning the **od** made by **Baron von Reichenbach.** His own experiments in the **exteriorization of sensitivity** were preceded by those of **Paul Joire,** but he had unique observations to his credit.

He contributed new perspectives on the theoretical elucidation of the mystery of physical phenomena—the **exteriorization of motricity.** Rochas's book of the same title, in which his theory is expounded, summed up his experiments with the medium **Eusapia Palladino,** who was his guest in his country house at l'Agnelas, near Voiron, and sat in the presence of a large committee of scientists. Much of this work, of course, has been discarded as psychical research discounted physical phenomena as largely the product of fraud.

The interest of Rochas extended to every branch of psychical research. As an investigator he was keen and competent. **Charles Victor Miller,** the San Francisco materialization medium, came to Europe at his request, although he did not sit for Rochas. Nor did Rochas succeed in witnessing full materializations with other mediums. The second visit of **Charles Bailey,** the Australian **apport** medium, was arranged by him. Bailey came to Grenoble in 1910 and, as it turned out, was exposed as a fraud amid much excitement.

Sources:

Berger, Arthur S., and Joyce Berger. *The Encyclopedia of Parapsychology and Psychical Research.* New York: Paragon House, 1991.

Reichenbach, Karl von. *Aphorismen Über Sensitivität und Od.* French ed. as *Le Fluide des Magnétiseurs.* Edited by Albert De Rochas. N.p., 1891.

———. *Les effleuves odique; L'envoutement; Les frontières de la science.* N.p., 1902.

———. *Les états profonds de l'hypnose.* N.p., 1892.

———. *Les états Superficiels de l'hypnose.* N.p., 1898.

———. *L'Exteriorisation de la motricité.* N.p., 1896.

———. *L'Exteriorisation de la Sensibilité.* N.p., 1895.

Rochas, Eugene Albert de. *Les Forces non définies.* Paris: Masson, 1887.

———. *Receuil de documents relatifs à la levitation du corps humain.* N.p., 1897.

———. *La Science des Philosophes et l'Art des Thaumaturges dans l'Antiquité.* N.p., 1882.

———. *Les Sentiments, la Musique et le Geste; Les Vies Successives.* N.p., 1911.

———. *La Suspension de la Vie.* N.p., 1913.

Rochester Rappings

The outbreak of **rappings** that occurred in Hydesville, near Rochester, New York, in 1848, and which became popularly known as the "Rochester Rappings," was of peculiar importance, not because of its intrinsic superiority to any other **poltergeist** disturbance, but because it inaugurated the movement of modern **Spiritualism.**

Hydesville is a small village in Arcadia, Wayne County, New York, and there, in 1848, lived John D. Fox with his wife and two young daughters, Margaretta, aged fifteen, and Kate, aged twelve. Their house was a small wooden structure previously tenanted by Michael Weekman, who afterward claimed that he had frequently been disturbed by knockings and other strange sounds in the Hydesville house.

Toward the end of March 1848, the Fox family was disturbed by mysterious rappings, and on the evening of the 31st, they went to bed early, hoping to get some undisturbed sleep. But the rappings broke out even more vigorously than they had on previous occasions, and Mrs. Fox, much alarmed and excited when the raps manifested signs of intelligence, decided to call in her neighbors to witness the phenomenon.

The neighbors heard the raps distinctly and it was decided to try to communicate with the unseen forces. Questions were asked by the "sitters" of this informal séance—if the answer was in the affirmative, raps were heard, if in the negative, there was silence. By this means the knocker indicated that he was a ghost, the spirit of a peddler who had been murdered for his money by a former resident of the house.

The raps also answered correctly other questions relating to the ages of those present and other particulars concerning persons who lived in the neighborhood. In the few days immediately following, hundreds of people made their way to Hydesville to witness the marvel.

Fox's married son, David, who lived about two miles from his father's house, recorded a statement to the effect that the Fox family, following the directions of the raps, which indicated that the peddler was buried in the cellar, had begun to dig early in April, but were stopped by water.

Later, however, hair, bones, and teeth were found in the cellar. Vague rumors were afloat that a peddler had visited the village one winter, had been seen in the kitchen of the house afterward inhabited by the Foxes, and had mysteriously disappeared without fulfilling his promise to the villagers to return the next day. There was not a scrap of real evidence, whether for the murder or for the existence of the peddler, particulars of whose life were furnished by the raps.

Soon after these happenings, Kate Fox went to Auburn, and Margaretta to Rochester, New York, where her married sister Leah lived, and at both places outbreaks of rappings subsequently occurred. New mediums sprang up, circles were formed, and soon Spiritualism started.

Sources:

Brown, Slater. *The Heyday of Spiritualism.* New York: Hawthorne Books, 1970.

Rock Music

Soon after rock music began making an impact on youth during the 1950s it was denounced by parents, clergymen, educators, and others in positions of authority. The new music was antitraditional, antiauthoritarian, and disparaging of adult influence over teenagers. Pastors denounced it as evil—the product of Satan.

Rock music of the 1950s, however, did not prepare people for the upheaval of the 1960s and the open defiance against societal mores. In particular, the Rolling Stones' image as a "bad boy" band continued the identification of rock music with antiestablishment values in contrast to the "tamer" persona exemplified by the Beatles. In 1967 the Rolling Stones released *Their Satanic Majesties Request.* This was a harbinger of future events—two years later on December 6, 1969, some 300,000 young people gathered for a free pop music festival at Altamont Raceway, California, featuring the band. The crowd heard Mick Jagger singing "Sympathy for the Devil" while

Hell's Angels, who had been engaged as bodyguards, beat up spectators and clubbed and kicked a man to death. After the event, no one was willing to take responsibility for the debacle.

Some rock bands turned up the power on their electric instruments and created the sound known as heavy metal, a name that seems to have been derived from a line in the 1968 Steppenwolf song, "Born to Be Wild." One performer, Alice Cooper, moved into shock entertainment by integrating the occult, sadomasochism, and animal abuse in his act. The shock element developed from an unplanned event in 1969. During a concert in Detroit, Michigan, Cooper released some chickens into the audience at the close of his act. The audience killed them and tore them to pieces, a fact subsequently noted in the press.

A new connection between rock music and the occult was made in the late 1960s by another British band, Led Zeppelin. Formed in 1968, their first album went gold the next year. Guitarist Jimmy Page had a strong interest in magic and the occult and upon attaining fame and fortune purchased the house on Loch Ness once owned by **Aleister Crowley.** Crowley's advocacy of drugs and **sex magic** had already earned him a reputation as a supporter of **black magic** and **Satanism** (though he was into neither), and that image began to follow Page, Led Zeppelin, and the bands that followed their lead.

In 1970 Black Sabbath followed on the heels of the Rolling Stones and Led Zeppelin. In spite of lack of interest from radio stations and the music press, their first album hit the charts and remained for 13 weeks. Other albums followed that kept the band popular for the next two decades. While its predecessors had some ties to the occult, Black Sabbath actively cultivated an image of evil and darkness—its name suggestive of a satanic mass and its use of black in their stage clothing and album covers. Lyrics explored mystical fantasy themes. Among the early members of the band was Ozzy Osbourne who would leave in 1979 and cultivate a more graphic satanic image.

Through the 1970s and 1980s, heavy metal was on the edge of the larger rock community as music expressing teenage rebellion in both England and the United States. As such, it was music enjoyed for a relatively few years before its followers reached adulthood. The music survived because there was always a new crop of teenagers entering the market each year. However, due to the rapidly changing audiences it was difficult for many bands to survive on top for more than five to seven years. In order to capture the attention of an audience with an increasingly short attention span, some bands moved into the most graphic portrayals of sex, sadism, and Satanism, themes that played predominantly to male teenagers.

Satanist themes dominated heavy metal lyrics and images, horrifying pastors and parents (even those raised on Elvis Presley and the Rolling Stones). These people saw heavy metal music as both a direct attack upon the mind and morals of their children and a new low in cultural degeneracy.

Performers such as Ozzy Osbourne were singled out for particular criticism. After leaving Black Sabbath, Osbourne formed a new band that later released the albums *Talk of the Devil* (1982), *Bark at the Moon* (1983) with Osbourne as a **werwolf** on the cover, and *Ultimate Sin* (1984). Incidents in which teen delinquency was tied to listening to heavy metal rock received wide publicity and Osbourne was accused of instigating crimes and suicides.

Another band drawn into the Satanism/antiSatanism controversy was Judas Priest. They were accused of releasing albums that contained subliminal messages encoded into the songs via a process known as **backward masking.** A Reno, Nevada, couple charged that their son attempted suicide after listening to their *Stained Glass* (1978) album, which they argued contained subliminal messages ordering the suicide. The courts dismissed the case but not before rock music received a significant amount of negative publicity.

More contemporary groups that actively cultivated the satanic image include Slayer, a relatively unknown band on the rock scene whose albums covers include an inverted satanic pentagram as their logo and other satanic symbols (such as an inverted cross) and whose lyrics cultivate satanic and black magic themes. Slayer was considered extreme, but other bands such as the obscure Possessed to the more widely recognized Motley Crüe (*Shout at the Devil,* 1983) also drew on satanic symbolism.

Contemporary rock has been criticized especially for the values it incorporates. However, to date, no valid evidence has been produced to link even the more objectionable form of heavy metal music as a causal agent to specific patterns of antisocial behavior or to long-term negative effects among devoted fans.

Sources:

Aranza, Jacob. *Backward Masking Unmasked: Backward Satanic Messages of Rock and Roll Exposed.* Shreveport, La.: Huntington House, 1983.

Clifford, Mike, ed. *The Harmony Illustrated Encyclopedia of Rock.* New York: Harmony Book, 1992.

Godwin, Jeff. *The Devil's Disciples: The Truth About Rock.* Chino, Calif.: Chick Publications, 1985.

Rascke, Carl A. *Painted Black.* San Francisco: Harper & Row, 1990.

Scott, Cyril. *Music: Its Secret Influence Throughout the Ages.* Reprint, London: Rider, 1950.

Stuessy, Joe. *Rock and Roll: Its History and Stylistic Development.* Englewood Cliffs, N.J.: Prentice-Hall, 1994.

Tane, David. *The Secret Power of Music: The Transformation of Self and Society Through Musical Energy.* New York: Destiny Books, 1984.

Wedge, Thomas W. *The Satan Hunter.* Canton, Ohio: Daring Books, 1988.

Rodhe, Gosta (1912–)

Swedish physician with special interest in psychical research. Born on May 11, 1912, at Kristanstad, Sweden, he later studied at Caroline Medical School, Stockholm (M.D., 1939). Before becoming the chief medical officer of the (Swedish) National Board of Education in 1959, he had been a practicing pediatrician (1948–53), a child psychiatrist, and school psychiatrist (1948–59). He was president of the Swedish Society for Psychical Research for many years.

Sources:

Pleasants, Helene, ed. *Biographical Dictionary of Parapsychology.* New York: Helix Press, 1964.

Roerich, Helena (1879–1949)

Author and channeler, born in Russia on February 13, 1879. Roerich was not formally educated but early developed a love of reading that included serious works in philosophy. She married artist **Nicholas Roerich** in 1901. Both she and her husband had a leaning toward Theosophy, and soon after their marriage she came into contact with **Master Morya,** the teacher whom **Helena Petrovna Blavatsky,** the co-founder of the **Theosophical Society,** had heralded as the primary source of theosophical teachings.

In 1915 the Roerichs left Russia for England, but moved on to New York in 1920. Through the early 1920s Helena Roerich received the messages that would constitute her first book, *Leaves of Morya's Garden* (a second volume appeared in 1925). Over the rest of her life she operated quietly as a channel and produced a host of books from Morya, including *New Era Community* (1926); *Infinity* (2 vols., 1930); *Hierarchy* (1931), and *The Fiery World* (2 vols., 1933–34). During these years her own work, which constituted the teachings of the **Agni Yoga Society,** founded in the mid-1920s, was overshadowed by that of her husband and his very public activities as an artist and peace advocate.

In 1929 she and her husband moved to the Punjab and lived near the Urusvati, the Himalayan Research Institute of the Roerich Museum. Through the 1930s she wrote letters on theosophical themes, which were assembled and published as *Letters of Helena Roerich.*

Sources:

Balyoz, Harold. *Three Remarkable Women.* Flagstaff, Ariz.: Altai Publishers, 1986.

Roerich, Helena. *Fiery World.* 2 vols. New York: Agni Yoga Press, 1943.

———. *Hierarchy.* 3d ed. New York: Agni Yoga Press, 1947.

———. *Infinity.* 2 vols. New York: Agni Yoga Press, 1956, 1957.

———. *Leaves of Morya's Garden.* 2 vols. New York: Agni Yoga Press, 1952, 1953.

———. *Letters of Helena Roerich.* New York: Agni Yoga Press, 1954, 1967.

Roerich, Nicholas K(onstantin) (1874–1947)

Versatile Russian-born painter, poet, writer, and mystic, and founder of the **Agni Yoga Society.** He was born in St. Petersburg on September 27, 1874, and educated at the University of St. Petersburg, becoming a graduate of the law school. He studied drawing and painting at the Academy of Fine Arts, St. Petersburg, and in Paris, France. In 1901, he married Helena Ivanov Shaposhnikov; they had two children. Both Nicholas and Helena Roerich were initially influenced by the theosophical writings of **Helena Petrovna Blavatsky,** the co-founder of Theosophy, and later by **Rudolf Steiner,** founder of Anthroposophy, and **Alice A. Bailey.**

Between 1901 and 1904, Roerich made a pilgrimage through Russia during which he produced some 75 paintings, exhibited at La Purchase Exposition, St. Louis. From 1906 to 1910, he was director of the School for Encouragement of Fine Arts, Russia, president of the Museum of Russian Arts, first president of *Mir Iskusstva,* and a leader in Moscow Art Theatre Diagilev Ballet.

The Roerichs escaped Russia at the time of the revolution and in 1920 migrated to the United States under the auspices of the Art Institute of Chicago. Roerich established a number of institutions with the aim of bringing humanity together through education, art, and culture. He traveled extensively and spent much time in Eastern countries, which strongly influenced his philosophy.

He exhibited his paintings in New York in December 1920. In 1921, he showed his work at the Institute of United Arts in New York. He took an active part in the foundation of Cor Ardeus (Flaming Heart) by a group of artists in Chicago, and in September 1922, he associated himself with an international cultural center named Corona Mundi (Crown of the World), promoting cooperation among scientists and cultural workers in different countries.

In 1923, the Roerich Museum was inaugurated in New York, an occasion marked by President Calvin Coolidge with a greeting to the founders. Roerich was also concerned with the American-Russian Cultural Association. Although the Roerichs had left Russia after the revolution, they devoted much time to attempting to bring about friendly cultural relations between the newly-established Soviet Union and the United States. Their efforts were appreciated by the Soviet authorities. Georgi Chickerin, a People's Commissar for Foreign Affairs, once described Roerich as "a half-Communist and a half-Buddhist."

Roerich spent five years in Central Asia as head of an expedition, making 500 paintings. He took a great interest in United States agriculture at a time when soil erosion threatened the holdings of American farmers during the thirties. Roerich had established an institute at Uruswathi, in Kulu, India, and sent specimens of drought-resistant plants collected in Central Asia to botanical research agencies in the United States. At the suggestion of the U.S. Department of Agriculture he headed an expedition to collect seeds of plants that prevented the destruction of fertile layers of soil. He also headed a further expedition to Japan in May 1934 and later continued these studies in Manchuria.

Roerich was internationally accepted at a time when his mysticism and artistic talents ranked equally with his efforts to improve agriculture and to bring about world peace. He was honored by many counties, and awards included: Commander, lst class, Royal Swedish Order of North Star; Grand Cross, Legion of Honor (France); Order of Saint Sava, lst class (Yugoslavia); Commander of Order of Imperial Russians of St. Stanislas, St. Anne and St. Vladimir; medal of city of Bruges, Belgium (for plan of Roerich Pact and Banner of Peace). His Roerich Pact and Banner of Peace was signed by twenty-two Pan-American countries at the White House, Washington, D.C., in 1935.

Among his many artistic activities, he was responsible for a number of works for the Chicago Opera Company, for the Russian Ballet (scenery in *Prince Igor*), and for Konstantin Stanislavsky (setting of *Peer Gynt*). He wrote libretto, and designed scenery and costumes for *Sacre du Printempts,* for which Stravinsky composed music. Ten Roerich Halls were established, in Paris, Belgrade, Riga, Benares, Bruges, Allahabad, Zagreb, Buenos Aires, Kyoto, and Praha. Roerich authored books on all of the artistic and social activities which he sponsored.

In all these activities, he was assisted by his wife Helena, who had in the meantime become a channel for Master Morya, one of the masters first brought forth by Blavatsky. Her channelled materials became the basis of what became known as Agni Yoga, a variation on theosophical teachings very much like those of Alice Bailey.

Roerich died December 12, 1947. The books of the Roerichs are kept in print by the Agni Yoga Society and the Roerich Museum, 319 W. 107 St., New York, NY 10025.

Sources:

Conlan, Barnett D. *Nicholas Roerich: A Master of the Mountains.* Liberty, Ind.: Flamma, Association for Advancement of Culture, 1938.

Fosdick, Sara. *Nicholas Roerich.* New York: Nicholas Roerich Museum, 1964.

Melton, J. Gordon. *Religious Leaders of America.* 2nd edition. Detroit: Gale Research, 1999.

Nicholas Roerich, 1874–1947. New York: Nicholas Roerich Museum, 1974.

Pealian, Gerhard. *Nicholas Roerich.* Agoura, Calif.: Aquarian Education Group, 1974.

Roerich, Nicholas. *Adamant.* New York: Corona Mundi, 1922.

———. *Flame in Chalice.* New York: Nicholas Roerich Museum, 1929.

———. *Heart of Asia.* New York: Atlas Publishing, 1929.

———. *Realm of Light.* New York: Nicholas Roerich Museum, 1931.

Roessling, Bernhardt Emil (1892–1961)

Teacher who wrote on parapsychology. He was born on November 27, 1892, in Brussels, Belgium. He completed his doctorate at Louvain University, Belgium (1914), moved to the United States and became a language teacher at St. Joseph's College, Philadelphia (1919–23), and was later an assistant to an agronomy professor at the University of Florida (1924–27) and a high school teacher in the Florida and Georgia public school systems (1929–52).

While in Florida he was executive secretary of the Florida Society for Psychical Research. During his retirement years, beginning in 1955, Roessling investigated mental and physical mediumship and contributed articles on psychical research to the Spiritualist periodical, **Psychic Observer and Chimes.**

Sources:

Pleasants, Helene, ed. *Biographical Dictionary of Parapsychology.* New York: Helix Press, 1964.

Rofé, (Fevzi) Husein (1922–)

Author, teacher, orientalist, and advocate of **Subud,** an Indonesian mystical movement closely associated with the work of **George I. Gurdjieff.** He was born May 3, 1922, in Manchester, England and studied at the University of London. He traveled widely as a lecturer and teacher, particularly in Eastern countries, and became a fellow of the Royal Asiatic Society, London.

During World War II Rofé served in the Royal Air Force (1940–45) and afterward became a teacher at the London School of Languages (1945–46). He moved to Morrocco in 1947 as an interpreter for the British Consulate (1947–49) and was successively a teacher in government secondary schools, Djokjakarta, Indonesia (1950–54); a Turkish lycée, Nicosia, Cyprus (1955–56); a language tutor, University of Hong Kong (1959–65); and head of the translation service for the Asian Development Bank, Manila, Philippines, through the 1970s.

He took special interest in spiritual **healing** and during his stay in Indonesia associated with the Subud movement, on which he published two books: *Path of Subud* (1959) and *Reflections on Subud* (1961). He also authored several other books out of his Asian wanderings and frequently contributed articles on psychical research and related topics to popular journals around the world.

Sources:

Pleasants, Helene, ed. *Biographical Dictionary of Parapsychology.* New York: Helix Press, 1964.

Rofé, Husein. *Path of Subud.* London: Rider & Co., 1959.

Rogo, David Scott (1950–1990)

Parapsychologist and writer on psychological, scientific, and psychic subjects. Rogo was born February 1, 1950, in Los Angeles and studied at the University of Cincinnati for a year before finishing his degree at San Fernando Valley State College (B.A., 1971). Originally a musician, he became a student of parapsychology and in 1968–69 coordinated an experimental course in parapsychology at the University of California, Los Angeles. He joined the **American Society for Psychical Research** and the **Society for Psychical Research,** London. Over the years he educated himself in parapsychology and became one of the important interpreters of its findings to the public.

As a professional writer, he regularly contributed to various psychic and New Age periodicals such as *Fate* and *Psychic* (renamed *New Realities*), for whom he became a review editor. He authored several papers for parapsychology journals, but is most remembered for his many thoughtful books. He was tragically killed during a break-in at his apartment in Northridge, California on August 14, 1990. The Parapsychology Foundation has established the "D. Scott Rogo Award for Parapsychology Literature" in his memory.

Sources:

Berger, Arthur S., and Joyce Berger. *The Encyclopedia of Parapsychology and Psychical Research.* New York: Paragon House, 1991.

Rogo, Scott. *An Experience of Phantoms.* New York: Taplinger, 1974.

———. *The Haunted Universe.* New York: New American Library, 1977.

———. *Methods and Models for Education in Parapsychology.* N.p., 1973.

———. *Minds and Motion.* New York: Taplinger, 1978.

———. *Miracles: A Parascientific Study into Wondrous Phenomena.* New York: Dial Press, 1982.

———. *NAD: A Study of Some Unusual Other-World Experiences.* N.p., 1970.

———. *NAD Vol. 2: A Psychic Study of "The Music of the Spheres."* N.p., 1972.

———. *The Welcoming Silence.* New Hyde Park, N.Y.: University Books, 1973.

Rogo, Scott, and Raymond Bayless. *Phone Calls from the Dead.* Englewood Cliffs, N.J.: Prentice-Hall, 1979.

"Rohmer, Sax"

Pseudonym of British author **Arthur Henry (Sarsfield) Ward,** creator of the celebrated fictional character Dr. Fu-Manchu, and a student of the occult.

Roll, William George, Jr. (1926–)

Roll, a prominent parapsychologist, was born on July 3, 1926, in Bremen, Germany. He grew up in Denmark and studied at the University of California, Berkeley (B.A., 1949) and with **Henry Habberley Price** at Oxford University, England (B.Litt, 1960; M.Litt., 1961). While in England, he was president of the Oxford University Society for Psychical Research (1952–57). His Oxford researches covered the effects of hypnosis and the correlation of ESP with personality traits. With the help of the **Parapsychology Foundation** he was able to establish a laboratory and reading room for psi experiments at the university.

In 1957 he became Louis K. Anspacher Visiting Research Fellow at Duke University, Durham, North Carolina, and stayed on as a research associate at the **Parapsychology Laboratory** (1958–60). While at Duke he directed a research project on incorporeal personal agency concerned with survival (1960) and was a member of the editorial staff of the *Journal of Parapsychology* (1958–60). In 1958 he first investigated a poltergeist and launched himself upon the area of research with which he has become most identified.

While at Duke he also became a member of the founding council of the **Parapsychology Association** (1957) and was later the association's treasurer (1958), secretary (1959–60), vice president (1963), and president.

In 1960 **Charles Eugene Ozanne** chose Roll to become the new project director of the **Psychical Research Foundation.** In 1986 the foundation moved from Durham, North Carolina, to the campus of West Georgia College, Carrollton, Georgia.

Beginning in 1963 Roll edited *Theta,* a quarterly journal for research on the problem of survival after bodily death; this publication ceased in 1991. He also authored more than 100 scholarly papers on parapsychological topics, edited eleven volumes of research in parapsychology for the Parapsychology Association, and authored thirteen books.

Sources:

Berger, Arthur S., and Joyce Berger. *The Encyclopedia of Parapsychology and Psychical Research.* New York: Paragon House, 1991.

Pleasants, Helene, ed. *Biographical Dictionary of Parapsychology.* New York: Helix Press, 1964.

Roll, William G. "ESP and Memory." In *Philosophical Dimensions of Parapsychology,* edited by J. M. O. Wheatley and H. L. Edge. Springfield, Ill.: Charles C. Thomas, 1976.

———. *The Poltergeist.* New York: New American Library, 1972. Reprint: Methuchen, N.J.: Scarecrow Press, 1976.

———. *Theory and Experiment in Psychical Research.* n.p.: Arno Press, 1975.

Romains, Jules (1885–1972)

Famous French author who first studied the phenomenon of **eyeless sight.** Born Louis Farigoule on August 26, 1885, at Saint-Julien, Chapteuil in Velay, in the Haute-Loire district of France, he grew up in Paris. He was a talented scholar and received his bachelor's degree by 1903. In that year Romains also had a sudden mystical experience of universalism, which he embodied in a philosophy he called "Unanism" and expressed in his book of poems *La Vie Unanime* (1908).

In 1909, he received his degree in philosophy and science, and become a professor of philosophy at the Lycée of Brest. He published more poems, a play, and a novel before World War I shattered his universalist hopes of human society. After the war he devoted much time to travel and writing.

His book on eyeless sight is his only scientific work. First published in France in the early 1920s, it deals with his research in developing vision in blind people through a little-known faculty of perception usually associated with psychics. The book was ridiculed by his colleagues and he was refused access to subjects for experiments. He abandoned his scientific research, and under the name "Jules Romains" became a universally acclaimed poet, dramatist, and novelist. He is best known for his vast series of novels surveying the world scene from the beginning of the twentieth century on, published in English as *Men of Good Will* in 27 volumes (1932–48). Romains died August 14, 1972.

The subject of eyeless sight was revived in the 1960s with the Soviet experiments in "fingertip vision" with **Rosa Kuleshova,** and Romains lived to see his own research taken up again by Dr. Yvonne Duplessis in France.

Sources:

Romains, Jules. *La vision extra-rétinienne.* English edition as: *Eyeless Sight.* London, 1924. Reprint, New York: Citadel Press, 1978.

Rome (Ancient Religion & Magic)

Magical practice was widespread among the ancient Romans. Magic was integral to their worship and operated as an organized system of magical rites for communal ends. Magic formed a foundation for thought and outlook upon the world, entered daily life, and directly affected many laws and customs. This ingrained tendency eventually developed into a broad polytheistic system, which led during bad times, especially in the later years of the Empire, to a frenzied search for new gods, borrowed from various countries Rome had conquered. In times of misfortune and disaster, the Romans were always ready to utilize a non-Roman deity if his or her favors promised more than those of their own deities.

Although there was a strong conservative element in the populous, and the "custom of the elders" was strongly upheld by the priestly fraternity, this usually gave way before the momentary impulses of the people. Thus, as a rock shows its geological history by its differing strata, so the theogony of the Roman gods tells its tale of the race that conceived it. There are prehistoric nature deities, borrowed from indigenous tribes; gods of the Sabines, from whom the young colony stole its wives; gods of the Etruscans, and of the Egyptians, Greeks, and Persians. The temple of Jupiter on the capitol contained the altar of an ancient deity, a stone-god, Terminus, the spirit of boundaries. In the temple of Diana of the Grove, a fountain nymph was worshiped. Additional instances of this kind abound.

Belief in Spirits

In addition to the gods, the spirits needed to be propitiated. Indeed the objects offered to the Roman for veneration were seemingly numberless. Apuleius gave a description of popular supernaturalism when he told of a country road where one might meet an altar wreathed with flowers, a cave hung with garlands, an oak tree laden with horns of cattle, a hill marked by fences as sacred, a log rough-hewn into shape, an altar of turf smoking with libations, or a stone anointed with oil.

Every single action of man's daily life had a presiding spirit, as did commerce and husbandry. Ednea was concerned with eating and Potina with drinking. Other spirits oversaw departures, travel, approaching, and homecoming. In commerce Mercurius reigned as the spirit of gain and Pecunia of money. Farmers had to pay attention to the spirits of cutting, grinding, sowing, and bee-keeping. A deity presided over streets and highways; Cloacina served as goddess of the sewers, while the lowly Mephitis was the spirit of bad smells. Spirits of evil, such as Robigo, the spirit of mildew, also had to be propitiated by pacificatory rites. In Rome there was an altar to fever and bad fortune.

From the country came Silvanus, god of farms and woods, and his fauns and nymphs with Picus, the woodpecker god who fed the twins Romulus and Remus with berries. Each deity or spirit possessed some influence, and had to be approached with proper rites. The names of these spirits were inscribed on tablets, *indigitamenta,* which were in the charge of the pontiffs (priests), who thus knew which spirit to evoke according to need. Most of these spirits were animistic in origin.

Rites and Worship

Worship in ancient Rome consisted largely of magical rites destined to propitiate the powers controlling human beings, to bring people into touch with those powers, to renew life and the land that supported it, and to stop that process of degeneration constantly set in motion by evil influences. Everything connected with worship typified this restoration. The priests, who represented the life of the community, were therefore bound by strict observances from endangering it in any way. Rules as to attire, eating, and touch were numerous. Sacrifices were systematized according to the end desired and the deity invoked.

Worship instructions designated the age and gender of all animal sacrifices; oxen were to be offered to Jupiter and Mars, and swine to Juno, Ceres the corn-goddess, and Silvanus. At one shrine, a pregnant cow was sacrificed and the ashes of the unborn young were considered to be of special magical efficacy. Even human sacrifice existed within historical times. After the battle of Cannæ, the Romans sought to divert misfortune by burying two Greeks alive in the cattle-market, while in the time of Julius Cæsar, two men were put to death with sacrificial solemnities by the pontiff and flamen of Mars. Again, in the time of Cicero and Horace, boys were killed for magical purposes.

Fire possessed great virtue and was held sacred in the worship of Vesta, in early belief Vesta being the fire itself; it presided over the family hearth; it restored purity and conferred protection.

Blood had the same quality and, smeared on the face of the god, symbolized and brought about the oneness of the deity with the community. On great occasions the statue of Jupiter was treated thus: the priests of Bellona made incisions in their shoulders and sprinkled the blood upon the image. The face of a triumphant general was painted with vermilion to represent blood.

Kneeling and prostration brought one into direct contact with the earth of the sacred place.

Music was also used as a species of incantation, probably deriving its origin in sounds made to drive away evil spirits. Dancing too was of magical efficacy. In Rome there were colleges of dancers for the purposes of religion, youths who danced in solemn measure about the altars, who, in the sacred month of Mars, took part in the festivals and were sent throughout the city dancing and singing. One authority stated that there were four kinds of "holy solemnity"—sacrifice, sacred banquets, public festivals, and games. Theatrical performances also belonged to this category, in one instance being used as a means of diverting a pestilence.

Sacred banquets were often decreed by the Senate as thanksgiving to the gods. Tables were spread with a sumptuous repast in the public places and were first offered to the statues of the deities seated around.

The festivals were numerous, all of a magical and symbolic nature. In the spring there was the *Parilia,* when fires of straw were lighted, through which persons passed to be purified, and the *Cerealia,* celebrated with sacrifice and offerings to Ceres, the corn-goddess, and followed by banquets. The *Lupercalia,* the festival of Faunus, was held in February and symbolized the wakening of spring and growth. Goats were slain as sacrifice and with their blood the *Luperci,* youths clad in skins, smeared their faces. They took thongs made of the goatskin and, laughing wildly, rushed through the city striking the crowd, Roman matrons believing that the blows thus received rendered them prolific.

Juno, the goddess of marriage and childbirth, also had her festival, the *Matronalia,* celebrated by the women of Rome. During festivals of the dead, the door leading to the other world was opened, the stone removed from its entrance in the Comitium, and the dark spirits who came forth were appeased with offerings. On these days, three times in the year, when the gods of gloom were abroad, complete cessation from all work was decreed. No battle could be fought nor ship set sail, neither could a man and woman marry.

To the sacred games were taken the statues of the gods in gorgeous procession, chariots of silver, companies of priests, and youths singing and dancing. The gods viewed the games reclining on couches.

The chariot races also partook of the nature of rites. After the races, in the Field of Mars, came one of the most important Roman rites, the sacrifice of the October Horse. The right-hand horse of the victorious team was sacrificed to Mars, and the tail of the animal, running with blood, carried to the Altar of the Regia. The blood was stored in the temple of Vesta until the following spring and used in the sacrifice of the festival of Parilia. The sacrifice was essentially magical, all citizens present being purified by the blood-sprinkling and bonfire.

The Roman outlook upon life was largely colored by magic. Bodily foes had their counterpart in the unseen world—wandering spirits of the dead, spirits of evil, the anger of innocently offended deities, and the menace of the evil eye. Portents and prodigies were everywhere. In the heavens, strange things might be seen. The sun had been known to double, even treble itself, its light turn to blood, or a magical halo to appear round the orb. Thunder and lightning were always fraught with presage. Jove was angered when he opened the heavens and hurled his bolts to earth.

Phantoms, too, hovered amid the clouds. Upon the Campagna, the gods were observed in conflict, and afterward tracks of the combatants were visible across the plain. Unearthly voices were heard amid the mountains and groves and cries of portent sounded within the temples.

Blood haunted the Roman imagination. Sometimes it was said to have covered the land as a mantle, the standing corn dyed with blood, the rivers and fountains flowing with it, while walls and statues were covered with a bloody sweat.

The flight and song of birds might foretell the decrees of Fate; unappeased spirits of the dead were known to lurk near and steal away the souls of men, who then died. All these happenings were attributable to the gods and spirits, who, if the portent was one of menace, must be propitiated, if one of good fortune, thanked with offerings.

Down to later times, this deep belief in the occurrence of prodigies persisted. When Otho set out for Italy in 69 C.E., Rome rang with reports of a gigantic phantom rushing forth from the Temple of Juno and of the statue of Julius turning from east to west.

Divination and Augury

Divination was connected with Roman worship. There was a spot on the Capitol from which the augur, with veiled head, read the auspices in the flight of birds. Augurs also accompanied armies and fleets and read the omens before an engagement was entered upon. Divination was also practiced by reading the intestines of animals, by dreams, by divine possession, as in the case of the Oracles, when prophecies were uttered. These had been gathered together in the **Sibylline Books** and were consulted as oracles by the state. With the worship of fortune were connected the *Lots of Praœneste.* The questions put to the goddess were answered by means of oaken lots a boy drew from a case made of sacred wood. The fortune-tellers also used a narrow-necked urn that, filled with water, only allowed one lot at a time to rise. Astrologers from Chaldea were also much sought after and were attached to the kingly and noble houses.

Familiar things of everyday life took on magical import. Words and numbers, especially odd ones, were of special significance. The Kalends, Nones, and Ides were so arranged as to fall upon odd days. Touch was binding, and so recognized in the law of Rome, as the grasp of a thing sold, from a slave to a turf of distant estate. Knotting and twisting of thread was injurious, so that women must never pass by cornfields twisting their spindles.

A strange sympathy existed between the trees and humankind, and great honor was paid to the sacred trees of Rome. On the oak tree of Jupiter, the triumphant general hung the shield and arms of his fallen foe, while the hedges about the Temple of Diana at Nemi were covered with votive offerings. The trees also harbored the spirits of the dead, who came forth as dreams to the souls of men. **Pliny the Elder** stated in this matter:

"Trees have a soul since nothing on earth lives without one. They are the temples of spirits and the simple countryside dedicates still a noble tree to some god. The various kinds of trees are sacred to their protecting spirits: the oak to Jupiter, the laurel to Apollo, olive to Minerva, myrtle to Venus, white poplar to Hercules."

These trees therefore partook of the nature of their presiding spirits and it was desirable to bring about communion with their magical influence, as in the spring, when laurel boughs were hung at the doors of the flamens and pontiffs, and in the temple of Vesta, where they remained hanging until the following year. Trees and their leaves were also possessed of healing and purifying value. Laurel was used for the latter quality after triumphs, when the spears and javelins of legionaries were wreathed with its branches to purify them from the blood of the enemy.

Man himself had a presiding spirit, his genius, each woman her "Juno" and the Saturnalia was really a holiday for this "other self." The Roman kept his birthday in honor of his genius. He would offer frankincense, cakes, and unmixed wine on an altar garlanded with flowers while making solemn prayers for the coming year. Cities and villages had their genii.

Beliefs About Death

Death was believed to be the life and soul enticed away by revengeful ghosts, hence death would never occur save by such agencies. The dead therefore must be appeased with offerings or else they wandered abroad working evil among the living.

One manifestation of this belief appeared in Ovid's lines,

"Once upon a time the great feast of the dead was not observed and the manes failed to receive the customary gifts, the fruit, the salt, the corn steeped in unmixed wine, the violets. The injured spirits revenged themselves on the living and the city was encircled with the funeral fires of their victims. The townsfolk heard their grandsires complaining in the quiet hours of the night, and told each other how the unsubstantial troop of monstrous specters rising from their tombs, shrieked along the city streets and up and down the fields."

Beans were used in the funeral feasts. They were supposed to harbor the souls of the dead, and the bean-blossom to be inscribed with characters of mourning.

Dreams were considered of great importance by the Romans and many historical instances of prophetic dreams may be found. They were thought to be like birds, the "bronze-colored" hawks; they were also thought to be the souls of human beings visiting others in their sleep or the souls of the dead returning to earth. In Virgil much may be found on this subject. Lucretius tried to find a scientific reason for dreams; Cicero, although writing in a slighting manner of the prevalent belief in these manifestations of sleep, recorded dreams of his own.

Sorcery & Witchcraft

Sorcery in all its forms, from love-magic to death-magic, was rife among all classes, as were necromantic practices. There were charms and spells for everything under the sun. The rain-charm of the pontiffs consisted of the throwing of puppets into the Tiber. The charm against thunderbolts was compounded of onions, hair, and sprats. The charm against an epidemic required the matrons of Rome to sweep the temple-floors with their hair. There were many more charms, including the simple love-charm strung around the neck of the country maiden.

Witches were prevalent. The poets often chose these sinister figures for their subjects, as when Horace described the ghastly rites of two witches in the cemetery of the Esquiline. Under the light of the new moon they crawled about looking for poisonous herbs and bones. They called the specters to a banquet consisting of a black lamb torn to pieces with their teeth, and afterward these phantoms had to answer the questions of the sorceresses.

Witches made images of their victims and prayed to the infernal powers for help; hounds and snakes glided over the ground, the moon turned to blood, and as the images were melted so the lives of the victims ebbed away.

Virgil gives a picture of a sorceress performing love-magic by means of a waxen image of the youth whose love she desired. Lucan, in his *Pharsalia,* discusses Thessaly, notorious in all ages for sorcery, and drew a terrific figure of Erichtho, a sorceress of illimitable powers, one whom even the gods obeyed, and to whom the forces of earth and heaven were bond-slaves.

Both Nero and his mother Agrippina were reported to have had recourse to the infamous arts of sorcery, while in the New Testament may be found testimony as to these practices in Rome.

The attitude of the cultured class towards magic is illustrated by an illuminating passage to be found in the writings of Pliny the Elder. He states,

"The art of magic has prevailed in most ages and in most parts of the globe. Let no one wonder that it has wielded very great authority inasmuch as it embraces three other sources of influence. No one doubts that it took its rise in medicine and sought to cloak itself in the garb of a science more profound and holy than the common run. It added to its tempting promises the force of religion, after which the human race is groping, especially at this time. Further it has brought in the arts of astrology and divination. For everyone desires to know what is to come to him and believes that certainty can be gained by consulting the stars. Having in this way taken captive the feelings of man by a triple chain, it has reached such a pitch that it rules over all the world and in the East, governs the King of Kings."

Roosevelt Spiritual Memorial Benevolent Association

The Roosevelt Spiritual Memorial Benevolent Association was founded in 1949 among independent Spiritualists as a corporation to hold church charters and ministerial credentials for otherwise autonomous congregations and mediums. The association promoted **Spiritualism** but held a minimum of beliefs, including the idea that Spiritualist communication with the deceased is taught by the Bible. It provided a study course in Spiritualism. Last known address: P.O. Box 68-313, Miami, FL 33138.

Rose

In ancient Rome, the rose, the flower of Venus, was the badge of the sacred prostitutes. The rose additionally symbolized silence. Eros, in Greek mythology, presents a rose to the god of silence. Things spoken under the rose or *sub rosa* were the secrets of Venus' sexual mysteries, later generalized to refer to keeping any secret. The use of red and white roses symbolized the sexually active and virginal goddess respectively and set the stage for the later Christian sexual symbolism possessed by the rose. That symbolism survives today in the predominate use of roses at weddings and as gifts for Valentine's Day.

In Christian Rome it was the custom to bless the rose on a certain Sunday, called Rose Sunday. The custom of blessing the golden rose came into vogue about the eleventh century. The golden rose thus consecrated was given to princes as a mark of the Roman pontiffs' favor. The Christian use of the older rose symbolism achieved its most artistic expression in the rose windows of the medieval cathedrals.

In the East, it was believed that the first rose was generated by a tear of the prophet Mohammed, and it was further believed that on a certain day in the year the rose had a heart of gold.

In the west of Scotland, if a white rose bloomed in autumn it was a token of an early marriage. The red rose, it was said, would not bloom over a grave. If a young girl had several lovers and wished to know which of them would be her husband, she would take a rose leaf for each of her sweethearts, and, naming each leaf after one of her lovers, she would watch them until one after another they sank, and the last to sink would be her future husband.

Rose leaves thrown upon a fire gave good luck. If a rose bush was pruned on St. John's Eve, it would bloom again in the autumn. Superstitions respecting the rose are more numerous in England than in Scotland.

The rose became a prominent symbol in occultism at the beginning of the modern age. It appeared on the family crest of Martin Luther, seemingly the ultimate source of the **Rosicrucians**' juxtaposition of the rose and cross. Earlier it had been used in the symbolism of **alchemy.** Both pagan and Christian folklore cites the rose as a symbol of regeneration and love.

Sources:

Walker, Barbara. *The Woman's Encyclopedia of Myths and Secrets.* San Francisco: Harper & Row, 1983.

Wilkins, Eithne. *The Rose-Garden Game.* London: Victor Gallancz, 1969.

Rose, Ronald K(riss) H(ume) (1920–)

Australian author who has investigated parapsychology and written extensively on the subject. He was born on March 9, 1920, at Lakemba, New South Wales, **Australia.** After many years of employment in public relations for the New South Wales Railways (1935–49) he returned to school and earned his degree at the University of Queensland (B.A., 1953). In 1957 he became an information officer of the Department of Territories, Commonwealth of Australia.

His special interest involved investigating parapsychology among the original peoples of Australia, New Zealand, and Samoa, about whom he wrote extensively. He and his wife appear to have been the first to conduct **ESP** and **PK** tests with them.

Sources:

Berger, Arthur S., and Joyce Berger. *The Encyclopedia of Parapsychology and Psychical Research.* New York: Paragon House, 1991.

Pleasants, Helene, ed. *Biographical Dictionary of Parapsychology.* New York: Helix Press, 1964.

Rose, Ronald. "Australia's Medicine Men." *Tomorrow* (spring 1954).

———. "Crisis Telepathy in Australia." *Tomorrow* (winter 1957).

———. "Experiments in ESP and PK with Aboriginal Subjects." *Journal of Parapsychology* (September 1952).

———. *Living Magic.* 1956. Reprint as *Primitive Psychic Power; the Realities Underlying the Psychical Practices and Beliefs of Australian Aborigines.* New York: New American Library, 1968.

———. *South Seas Magic.* London: R. Hale, 1959.

"Rosemary's Baby"

The sensational Satanist novel by Ira Levin, first published in 1967. It was issued the year after the public announcement of the founding of the Church of Satan by **Anton La Vey** and the popular interest in Satanism evidenced by several front page stories concerning La Vey's activities (including a military funeral) and his appearance on the Johnny Carson television show.

The Paramount movie version starring Mia Farrow was directed by Roman Polanski. La Vey was hired as a consultant and appeared briefly as the devil. La Vey called the film "the best paid commercial for Satanism since the Inquisition," and saw it as contributing to the growth of his church.

Some interesting coincidental events surrounded the film's release. On June 5, 1968, ten days before *Rosemary's Baby* was released, Polanski and his wife Sharon Tate dined with Robert Kennedy in Malibu; shortly afterward Kennedy left for the Ambassador Hotel, where he was assassinated.

A year later, on August 7, 1969, followers of **Charles Manson** brutally stabbed, mutilated, and murdered Sharon Tate and her unborn baby, together with four other people at the Polanski residence, Los Angeles.

The premises of the **American Society for Psychical Research** were housed immediately behind the famous Dakota Apartments in Manhattan, the large Gothic building that was the setting for *Rosemary's Baby.*

Sources:

Levin, Ira. *Rosemary's Baby.* New York: Random House, 1967.

Rosen, (Samuel) Paul

A sovereign grand inspector-general of the 33rd degree of the French rite of Masonry, who in 1888 decided that Masonry was diabolical in conception and to prove his strictures published a work called *Satan et Cie.* The Satanism credited to Freemasonry by Rosen was social anarchy and the destruction of the Catholic religion.

In 1890, he published a further attack titled *L'ennemie sociale; Histoire documentée des faits et gestes de la Franc-Maçonnerie de 1717 à 1890 en France, en Belgie et en Italie.* He made accusations of a "supreme directory" of Freemasonry in Berlin.

Such conspiracy accusations were common from the eighteenth century onward, reflecting social unrest and the involvement of Freemasons in the various revolutionary causes of the period. Freemasonry was generally pictured as anti-Catholic, pro-Jewish, subversive, and even diabolical. Substance for these acusations was provided by the prominent role of Freemasons, from George Washington to Garibaldi, in the anti-monarchical and secularizing trends of the eighteenth and nineteenth centuries.

Rosen's delusions were soon eclipsed by the infamous and sustained hoaxes of **Gabriel Jogand-Pagès,** who, under the name "Léo Taxil," claimed to have exposed Satanism in Freemasonry. This plot was double-edged, since it was also designed to embarrass and compromise the Catholic Church.

Rosetree, Rose

Rose Rosetree is an innovative teacher of **physiognomy,** the art of face reading, who has named her own system Face Reading Secrets. Following her graduation from Brandeis University, she became initially a student and then a teacher of **transcendental meditation** (TM). Among the highlights of her 15-year career was her pioneering the introduction of the TM program into the high school system of Miami, Florida, in the early 1970s. In 1974–75 she authored a syndicated column on meditation for newspapers in Massachusetts, and in 1981–82 she worked with the Environmental Protection Agency to develop a meditation program for its employees. This later program coincided with the challenge in the courts of TM's role in government agencies and its eventual banishment because of its religious nature. In 1986, Rosetree left the TM movement and began teaching independently.

During this time she began the study of physiognomy. She published her first book on the subject, *I Can Read Your Face,* in 1989. She continued to read widely in both the Chinese *Siang Mien* and Western texts, only a handful of which had been written over the nineteenth and twentieth centuries. Based upon her study and her own experiments in reading people's faces, she created her new system. This was also developed along with her abilities in reading the human aura, and greatly expanded the average person's ability to utilize aura reading skills.

Although teaching both physiognomy and aura reading, Rosetree, who resides in suburban Washington, D.C., has focused on teacher training, a key to spreading the practice of face reading, and upon application in the business world. The first book based upon her new system, *The Power of Face Reading for Sales, Self-Esteem, and Better Relationships,* appeared in 1998.

Sources:

Rose Rosetree. http://www.rose-rosetree.com/. April 23, 2000.

Rosetree, Rose. *Aura Reading Through All Your Senses: Celestial Perception Made Practical.* Sterling, Va.: Women's Intuition Worldwide, 1996.

———. *The Power of Face Reading for Sales, Self-Esteem, and Better Relationships.* Sterling, Va.: Women's Intuition Worldwide, 1998.

Rosher, Grace (d. 1980)

Noted British exponent of **automatic writing.** She was an artist who exhibited miniature paintings in the Royal Academy, London. Her psychic talent became manifest after the loss of her fiancé Gordon E. Burdick, whom she had known for many years. In June 1956, he was serving in the Canadian Navy, stationed at Vancouver, and intended to come to London to marry Rosher. A week before sailing, he died.

Fifteen months later, Grace Rosher had written a letter concerning an aunt and was wondering if she had time to write another letter before tea-time when she had a strong urge to keep her hand on the writing pad. The pen began to move without her conscious volition, and she discovered to her astonishment that it had written a letter in the handwriting of her dead fiancé. In the course of time, many other such automatic letters followed, stating that this phenomenon would be the means of bringing other people to realize that life continues after death.

Rosher was not a Spiritualist, and sought guidance from the Rev. **G. Maurice Elliot,** then secretary of the **Churches' Fel-**

lowship of Psychic and Spiritual Studies. Elliot enlisted the aid of handwriting expert F. T. Hilliger who studied the automatic scripts and compared them to the handwriting of Burdick when alive. Although initially skeptical, Hilliger reported that the automatic scripts bore a close resemblance to the genuine writing of Burdick in a large number of different ways, and were so consistent that "the writing reproduced by Grace Rosher was, if it were humanly possible, genuinely inspired by the personality of Gordon E. Burdick."

Rosher subsequently produced many other scripts, including messages from her mother, father, and three sisters, and a relative who had died in 1752. On one occasion, she produced a communication claimed to be from the famous scientist **Sir William Crookes,** in handwriting remarkably similar to that of Crookes in his lifetime.

A special characteristic of these automatic scripts was the way in which they were written with a pen lying loosely across the joint of Rosher's index finger, the nib resting on a writing pad. Although she did not hold the pen, it wrote swiftly and intelligently. Skeptical stage magicians have pointed out that it is possible to guide a pen under these circumstances, but it is not clear whether they are suggesting a conscious or even subconscious deception on her part. The circumstances of the production of Rosher's automatic scripts are in no way comparable with the deliberate mystification of a professional magician. Grace Rosher died in July 1980.

Sources:

Rosher, Grace. *Beyond the Horizon.* London, 1961.

Rosicrucian Anthroposophical League

The Rosicrucian Anthroposophical League was founded in 1932 by Samuel Richard Parchment (b. 1881), an astrologer and occultist who trained with **Max Heindel.** During the 1920s, Parchment became a leader in the **Rosicrucian Fellowship,** founded by Heindel, which published his early writings. However, he broke away from the fellowship after Heindel's death and formed an independent organization out of the former fellowship center in San Francisco. Parchment is best remembered as the author of a classic textbook, *Astrology, Mundane and Spiritual,* which was used by many astrologers not affiliated with the league and later reprinted by the American Federation of Astrologers. He also wrote a number of booklets that became league texts: *The Just Law of Compensation; The Middle Path, the Safest; Ancient Operative Masonry;* and *Steps to Self-Mastery.*

The league strove to investigate occult laws, to practice the brotherhood of man, to disseminate spiritual truth, and to facilitate the attainment of self-conscious immortality by its members. During Parchment's lifetime, league centers developed on both coasts, but in recent years little has been heard of it. Its present status is unknown. In the 1970s the New York League became the independent **Ausar Auset Society.**

Sources:

Parchment, S. R. *Ancient Operative Masonry.* San Francisco: San Francisco Center—Rosicrucian Fellowship, 1930.

———. *Astrology, Mundane and Spiritual.* San Francisco: Anthroposophical Rosicrucian League, 1933.

———. *The Just Law of Compensation.* San Francisco: San Francisco Center—Rosicrucian Fellowship, 1932.

———. *Steps to Self-Mastery.* Oceanside, Calif.: Fellowship Press, 1927.

Rosicrucian Digest

The *Rosicrucian Digest,* the outer organ of the **Ancient and Mystical Order Rosae Crucis** (AMORC), is one of the oldest occult magazines being published in the Western world, having been established in the early 1920s. The *Digest* continues *The American Rosae Crucis,* the original periodical established by **H. Spencer Lewis** (1883–1939) in 1915 when he opened the AMORC. The organization passed through an unstable initial decade before settling in San Jose, California, where its headquarters has remained and from which it has grown into a worldwide **occult** fellowship, possibly the largest in the contemporary world.

The *Rosicrucian Digest* is built around a set of feature articles expounding upon various Rosicrucian themes. The order traces its origins to ancient Egypt, and has founded an Egyptian museum that remains a popular tourist stop in San Jose. Articles discuss the museum's artifacts, its staff's archeological work, and ancient Egypt in general. The emphasis upon Egypt provides a foundation for regular treatments of the Hermetic tradition, also traced to Egyptian roots. Generally each issue begins with an article by the leader of the order, and recently each issue has reprinted an article from the many written by Lewis, the founding imperator.

Through the years, the *Digest* was issued as a monthly magazine. However, in the 1990s the order went through a major upheaval when it came into conflict with its imperator, Gary Stewart. Stewart was forced out of office after being accused of attempting to steal substantial funds. For several years the order faced severe financial problems. Eventually a new imperator, Christian Bernard, was named. Through the unrest, the *Digest* became a quarterly periodical. It currently circulates approximately 15,000 copies per issue (with parallel issues serving the order in other countries). Once a year, the *Digest* publishes a list of Rosicrucian lodges and centers around the world.

The *Rosicrucian Digest* may be ordered from the Grand Lodge of the English Language Jurisdiction, AMORC, Inc., 1342 Naglee Ave., San Jose, CA 95191.

Sources:

Rosicrucian Digest. San Jose, Calif., n.d.

Rosicrucian Fellowship

An occult organization founded in 1907 by Carl Louis van Grashoff who used the pseudonym **Max Heindel.** Born in **Germany** in 1865, he came to America in 1895 and in 1904 was vice president of a **Theosophical Society** lodge in Los Angeles.

He claimed that during a visit to Europe in 1907 he met a mysterious occult Rosicrucian who took him to a Rose Cross temple on the borders of Germany and Bohemia, where he was initiated. Heindel expounded his version of Rosicrucian teachings, with obvious roots in Theosophy, in his book *The Rosicrucian Cosmo-Conception* (1909) and established various Fellowship Centers. He also founded the fellowship's magazine **Rays from the Rose Cross.**

In 1911, the fellowship was established at Mt. Ecclesia, a plot of land in Oceanside, California, to disseminate Rosicrucian philosophy through books, magazines, lectures, and correspondence courses. The Oceanside headquarters now cover a vast estate with stucco temples, a healing department, and a vegetarian restaurant at nearby El Toro Marine base.

Much of Heindel's teachings seem to derive from the lectures he attended of Anthroposophist **Rudolf Steiner** (1861–1925) in Germany during the 1900s, and Steiner, who saw himself standing in the Rosicrucian tradition, may have been Heindel's mysterious Rosicrucian.

Heindel died in 1919, and his widow Augusta Foss Heindel became leader and director of the Fellowship until her own death in 1938. Another prominent official of the Fellowship during this later period was **Manly Palmer Hall.**

In 1995 the fellowship reported 8,000 members worldwide with 700 in the United States. Address: 2222 Mission Ave., Oceanside, CA 92054-0713. Website: http://www.rosicrucian.com/.

Sources:

Heindel, Max. *Rosicrucian Cosmo-Conception.* Oceanside, Calif.: Rosicrucian Fellowship, 1937.

Heindel, Mrs. Max [Augusta Foss]. *The Birth of the Rosicrucian Fellowship.* Oceanside, Calif.: Rosicrucian Fellowship, n.d.

The Rosicrucian Fellowship. http://www.rosicrucian.com/. April 14, 2000.

Rosicrucians

The idea of a Rosicrucian brotherhood arose in the early seventeenth century and through the succeeding decades aroused considerable interest among those with occult leanings. In the absence of an organization to coincide with the early documents that presented the basic Rosicrucian myth, numerous occultists filled the vacuum and invented a new mystical life. Over the next centuries, books appeared to present the true Rosicrucian teachings; Rosicrucian degrees appeared in speculative masonry; and different Rosicrucian orders emerged. During the nineteenth century, fiction writers found the idea of Rosicrucianism a suitable topic for romantic novels, such as **Bulwar Lytton**'s *Zanoi,* Percy Shelley's *St. Irvyne the Rosicrucian,* and Harrison Ainworth's *Auriol.*

The name Rosicrucian is derived from *rosa* (a rose) and *crux* (a cross); the general symbol of the supposed order was a rose placed on the center of a cross. In a Rosicrucian book of the nineteenth century, there is a symbol of a red cross-marked heart in the center of an open rose, which the writer **Arthur E. Waite** believed to be a development of the monogram of Martin Luther, which was a cross-crowned heart rising from the center of an open rose.

History of the Brotherhood

Little was known concerning the Rosicrucians before the publication of Waite's work *The Real History of the Rosicrucians* in 1887 (later revised and enlarged as *The Brotherhood of the Rosy Cross,* 1924). Waite's writing on the Rosicrucians laid the groundwork for serious study of the subject. Prior to that, a great deal had been written concerning Rosicrucianism by people claiming to be Rosicrucians or representatives of the brotherhood, including the most questionable volume by Hargrave Jennings, *The Rosicrucians: Their Rites and Mysteries* (1870). It was typical of many writings regarding the fraternity of the Rosy Cross, and as the *Westminster Review* wittily commented in its notice of the volume, it dealt with practically everything under the sun except the Rosicrucians. In contrast, working as a critical historian, Waite gathered all that could be known regarding Rosicrucians at that time. Assembling all the relevant manuscripts, some of which he discovered, he was the first to put together a believable account of the origins of this branch of the occult world.

The name Rosicrucian appears to have been unknown before the year 1598. The movement originated in Germany, where, in the town of Cassel in the year 1614, the public was surprised by the publication of a pamphlet bearing the title *The Fama of the Fraternity of the Meritorious Order of the Rosy Cross Addressed to the Learned in General and the Governors of Europe.*

It purported to be a message from certain anonymous **adepts** who were deeply concerned for the condition of humankind and who greatly desired its moral renewal and perfection. It proposed that all men of learning throughout the world should join forces for the establishment of a synthesis of science, through which would be discovered the perfect method for all the arts. The squabblings and quarrelings of the literati of the period were to be ignored, and the antiquated authorities of the old world to be discredited. It pointed out that a reformation had taken place in religion, that the church had been cleansed, and that a similar new career was now open to science. All this was to be brought about by the assistance of the illuminated Brotherhood, the children of light who had been initiated in the mysteries of the Grand Orient and would lead the age of perfection.

The fraternity supplied what purported to be an account of its history. The head and front of the movement was one C. R. C., a magic hierophant of the highest rank, who at age five had been placed in a convent where he studied the humanities. At age 15, he had accompanied one Frater (brother) P. A. L. on his travels to the Holy Land. To the great grief of C. R. C., Frater P. A. L. died at Cyprus, but C. R. C. resolved to continue the arduous journey himself.

Arriving at Damascus, he obtained knowledge of a secret circle of mystics, experts in all magic arts, who lived in an unknown city of Arabia called Damcar. Turning aside from his quest for the Holy Sepulcher, the lad made up his mind to trace these illuminati and sought out certain Arabians, who took him to the city of Damcar. He arrived there at age 16 and was graciously welcomed by the magi, who told him they had long been expecting him, and related to him several occurrences from his past.

They proceeded to initiate him into the mysteries of occult science, and he quickly became acquainted with Arabic, from which he translated the divine book *M* into Latin. After three years of mystic instruction, he departed from the mysterious city for Egypt, then sailed to Fez, as the wise men of Damcar had instructed him to do. There he fell in with other masters who taught him how to evoke the elemental spirits.

After a further two years' sojourn at Fez, his period of initiation was over, and he proceeded to Spain to confer with the wisdom of that country and convince its professors of the errors of their ways. The scholars of Spain, however, turned their backs upon him with loud laughter and intimated to him that they had learned the principles and practice of **magic** from a much higher authority, namely, Satan himself, who had unveiled to them the secrets of **necromancy** within the walls of the University of Salamanca.

With noble indignation, the young man shook the dust of Spain from his feet and turned his face to other countries, only to find the same treatment within their boundaries. At last he sought his native land of Germany, where he pored over the great truths he had learned in solitude and seclusion and reduced his universal philosophy to writing. Five years of a hermit's life, however, only served to strengthen him in his opinions and he continued to feel that one who had mastered the arts of **alchemy,** had achieved the transmutation of metals, and had manufactured the **elixir of life** was designed for a nobler purpose than rumination in solitude.

Slowly and carefully he began to gather assistants, who became the nucleus of the Rosicrucian fraternity. When he had gathered four of these into the brotherhood, they invented among them a magic language, a cipher writing of equal magic potency, and a large dictionary replete with occult wisdom. They erected a House of the Holy Ghost, healed the sick, and initiated further members, then, calling themselves missionaries, went to the various countries of Europe to disseminate their wisdom.

In course of time, C. R. C. died, and for 120 years the secret of his burial place was concealed. The original members also died one by one, and it was not until the third generation of adepts had arisen that the tomb of their illustrious founder was unearthed during the rebuilding of one of their secret dwellings. The vault in which this tomb was found was illuminated by the sun of the magi, and inscribed with magic characters. The body of the illustrious founder was discovered in perfect preservation, and a number of marvels were discovered buried beside him, which convinced the existing members of the fraternity that it was their duty to make these known to the world.

It was this discovery that immediately inspired the brotherhood to make its existence public in the aforementioned circular, and they invited all worthy persons to apply to them for initiation into their order. They refused, however, to supply their names and addresses, and asked those who wished for initiation to signify their intention by the publication of printed letters, which they would be certain to notice. In conclusion they assured the public that they were believers in the reformed Church of Christ (i.e., Lutheranism) and denounced in the most solemn manner all pseudo-occultists and alchemists.

The *Fama* created tremendous excitement among the occultists of Europe, and a large number of pamphlets were published criticizing or defending the society and its manifesto, in which it was pointed out there were a number of discrepancies. To begin with, no such city as Damcar existed in Arabia. Where, it was asked, was the House of the Holy Ghost, which the Rosicrucians stated had been seen by 100,000 persons but was concealed from the world? C. R. C., the founder, as a boy of 15 must have achieved great occult skill to have astonished the magi of Damcar, skeptics said.

Despite these objections, however, considerable credit was given to the Rosicrucian publication. The *Confession of the Rosicrucian Fraternity,* addressed to the learned in Europe, appeared one year later. This offered initiation by gradual stages to selected applicants, and revealed its ultra-Protestant character by what an old Scottish minister used to call "a dig at the Pope," whom it publicly execrated, expressing the hope that his "asinine braying" would finally be put a stop to by tearing him to pieces with nails! This impious comment did little to enhance the reputation of Rosicrucians among Roman Catholics.

A year later, in 1616, *The Chemical Nuptials of Christian Rosencreutz* was published, purporting to recount incidents in the life of the mysterious founder of the Brotherhood of the Rosy Cross. But the "chemical marriage" makes Christian Rosencreutz an old man when he achieves initiation, and this hardly squared with the original account of his life as given in the *Fama.* By that time a number of persons had applied for initiation but had received no answer to their applications. Since many believed themselves to be alchemical and magical adepts, great irritation arose with the brotherhood, and it was generally considered that the whole business was a hoax. By 1620 the Rosicrucians and their publication had lapsed into obscurity.

Numerous theories were advanced as to the probable authorship of these manifestos, and it is now known that these documents were written by Johann Valentin Andrae (1586–1654), a Lutheran pastor who had absorbed both occult and magical teachings as well as a desire for social change in Germany. His aim in producing the books seems to have derived from a plan to attempt the formation of a secret society that could encourage the reformation of values among the public, but it is not impossible that the documents were simply a hoax. It is most unlikely that they describe an actual organization existing in Germany in the early seventeenth century or that C. R. C. ever existed.

Rosicrucian Groups

So far as can be gleaned from their publications, the Rosicrucians (or the person in whose imagination they existed) were believers in the doctrines of **Paracelsus.** They believed in alchemy, astrology, and occult forces in nature, and their belief in these is identical to the doctrines of that great master of occult philosophy and medicine. They were thus essentially modern in their occult beliefs, just as they were modern in their religious ideas.

Waite thought it possible that in Nuremburg, in the year 1598, a Rosicrucian society was founded by a mystic and alchemist named Simon Studion, under the name Militia Crucifera Evangelica, which held periodical meetings in that city. Its proceedings were reported in an unprinted work of Studion's, and in opinions and objects it was identical with the supposed Rosicrucian Society. "Evidently," stated Waite, "the Rosicrucian Society of 1614 was a transfiguration or development of the sect established by Simon Studion." But Waite's idea remains unsupported speculation.

In 1618 Henrichus Neuhuseus published a Latin pamphlet that stated that the Rosicrucian adepts had migrated to India. This pamphlet received little response until the nineteenth century, when some Theosophists proposed the notion that Rosicrucians still existed in the tablelands of Tibet. It was even alleged that the Rosicrucians developed into a Tibetan brotherhood, and exchanged their Protestant Christianity for esoteric Buddhism.

On a more serious level, in England the Rosicrucian idea was taken up by **Robert Fludd** (1574–1637), who wrote a spirited defense of the brotherhood; by the alchemist **Thomas Vaughan** (1622–1666), who wrote as **Eugenius Philalethes** and translated the *Fama* and the *Confession;* and by **John Heydon** (ca. 1629–1668), who furnished a peculiarly quaint and interesting account of the Rosicrucians in *The Wise Man's Crown; or, The Glory of the Rosie-Cross* (1664). Heydon also wrote a variety of other treatises regarding alchemical skill and medical ability in *El Havareuna; or, The English Physician's Tutor* (1665), and *A New Method of Rosie Crucian Physick* (1658). In France, Rosicrucianism was also widely discussed. It has been stated that there was a strong connection between Rosicrucians and Freemasons.

In Germany, Rosicrucianism became identified with various Pietist movements, movements that attempted to revive spiritual life above and beyond that to be found in the many parish churches. One Pietist leader was Johann Jacob Zimmerman, a theologian and occultist who emerged in the 1680s. Zimmerman also believed that Christ would return at some point in the 1690s. He found an apt pupil in Johannes Kelpius, whom he brought into the Pietist movement and with whom he organized a small disciplined brotherhood ready to accept William Penn's offer of a home in the American colonies. Zimmerman died before this small group of Rosicrucians could migrate, which they finally did in 1694. They arrived in Philadelphia on June 23, just in time to celebrate St. John's Eve.

The group settled on Wissahickon Creek in what is today the Germantown section of Philadelphia and there erected a cubic house with 40 foot sides and America's first astrological observatory on its roof. They believed that by observation of the heavens, they would be able to discern the first signs of Christ's anticipated arrival. Kelpius died in 1708, and soon thereafter, Christ having not returned, the group disintegrated. It became the basis of the continuing magic (or powwow) tradition in southeastern Pennsylvania.

Early in the eighteenth century another Rosicrucian impulse appeared in Germany. In 1710 a certain Sincerus Racatus, or Sigmund Richter, published *A Perfect and True Preparation of the Philosophical Stone according to the Secret Methods of the Brotherhood of the Golden and Rosy Cross,* and annexed to this treatise were the rules of the Rosicrucian Society for the initiation of new members.

Waite considered these rules additional indication of the society's existence at the period, and he believed that Richter's group continued the Nuremburg group originally established by Studion. In 1785 the publication of *The Secret Symbols of the Rosicrucians of the Sixteenth and Seventeenth Centuries* took place at Altona, showing, in Waite's opinion, that the mysterious brotherhood still existed, but this was their last manifesto. These bits of evidence are so scanty that any reasonable and workable hypothesis that such a society ever existed can scarcely be founded upon them.

Waite humorously stated that he was not able to trace the eastern progress of the brotherhood further than the Isle of Mauritius, where it is related in an odd manuscript that a certain Comte De Chazal initiated **Sigismond Bacstrom** into the mysteries of the Rose Cross Order in 1794, but nothing is known about the Comte De Chazal or his character, and it is possible that Bacstrom might have been one of those persons who, in all times and countries, have been willing to purchase problematical honors. Bacstrom's manuscripts attained a new importance later, when they passed into the hands of **Frederick Hockley,** an important figure in the revival of magic in the nineteenth century in England and who was later concerned with a revival of the Rosicrucian society.

Rosicrucian Theories

Rosicrucianism fit into the stream of Gnosticism that emerged in the Mediterranean basin in the second century and coexisted with Christianity through the centuries. At times, as Manicheanism or as the **Cathari,** it attained a significant popular following, and in the late middle ages undergirded alchemy. From the *Fama* and *Confession,* it is possible to glean some definite ideas of the occult concept of the Rosicrucians. In these documents is included the doctrine of the **microcosm,** which teaches that man contains the potential of the universe. This is a distinctly Paracelsian belief. There is also the belief of the doctrine of **elementary spirits,** which many people wrongly think originated with the Rosicrucians, but which was probably reintroduced by Paracelsus.

The manifestos contain the doctrine of the *Signatura Rerum,* which is also of Paracelsian origin. This is the magic writing referred to in the *Fama* and the mystical characters of a book of nature, which, according to the *Confession,* stands open for all eyes but can be read or understood by only a very few. These characters, it is written, are the seal of God imprinted on the wonderful work of creation, on the heavens and Earth, and on all beasts.

It would appear, too, that some form of practical magic was known to the brotherhood. They were also, they said, alchemists, and claimed to have achieved the transmutation of metals and the manufacture of the elixir of life.

Modern Rosicrucianism

The flurry of interest in Rosicrucianism in the century following the initial announcement of the existence of a Rosicrucian Brotherhood was followed in the eighteenth and nineteenth centuries by the development of speculative masonry, especially in Scotland, and the inclusion of Rosicrucian degrees amid the mass of others. Such Rosicrucian degrees survive to the present in the eighteenth degree, "the Rose-Croix," of the Ancient and Accepted Rite and the RSYCS degree of the Royal Order of Scotland. However, the first of the modern Rosicrucian organizations was founded around 1861 by **Paschal Beverly Randolph** (1825–1875). Randolph claimed that in the 1850s he traveled to France, made contact with the **Rosicrucian Fraternity,** and was named grand master for the Americas of the organization. Unfortunately, no independent record of the Rosicrucians with whom he met was available, and some doubt exists as to from whom he received his commission. What is less in doubt is his founding the First Supreme Grand Lodge of the Rosicrucian Fraternity in San Francisco on November 5, 1861, just as the Civil War was beginning. Shortly thereafter, however, he left on a trip around the world, and then settled in Boston.

Randolph's travel required at least two reorganizations of the fraternity during his lifetime, the second in 1874 in Toledo, Ohio. Following Randolph's death in 1875, he was succeeded by Freeman B. Dowd (1875–1907) and Edward H. Brown (1907–1922). In 1922 Reuben Swinburne Clymer, under whose leadership the order found a stabilized existence, established the present headquarters in rural Pennsylvania near Quakertown. Clymer was eventually succeeded by his son Emerson Clymer. The Rosicrucian Fraternity differs from other Rosicrucian groups in its refusal to advertise or engage in self-promotional activities.

In England the idea of Rosicrucianism was passed through the masonic orders and thereby came to Frederick Hockley. In 1865 a small group of masons founded the Societas Rosicruciana in Anglia (RSIA; the Rosicrucian Society of England). (There is some hint of a "Rosicrucian" society having been founded in the 1830s, but its existence is somewhat shadowy.) The RSIA published a small quarterly magazine, beginning in 1868 and continuing through the end of the 1870s, which in an early number stated that the society was "calculated to meet the requirements of those worthy masons who wished to study the science and antiquities of the craft, and trace it through its successive developments to the present time; also to cull information from all the records extant from those mysterious societies which had their existence in the dark ages of the world, when might meant right."

To join, it was necessary to be a mason. The officers of the society consisted of three magi, a master-general for the first and second orders, a deputy master-general, a treasurer, a secretary, and seven ancients. The assisting officers numbered a precentor, organists, torchbearer, herald, and so forth. The society was composed of nine grades or classes. These objects were, however, fulfilled in a very perfunctory manner, if the magazine of the association is any criterion of its work, for this publication was filled with occult serial stories, reports of masonic meetings, and verse. Waite observed (though he seemed to be speaking in heightened hyperbole) that the most notable circumstance connected with this society was the complete ignorance that seemed to have prevailed among its members concerning everything connected with Rosicrucianism.

The prime movers of the association were Robert Wentworth Little, (1840–1878); its first supreme magus, Frederick Hockley; **Kenneth Mackenzie,** author of *The Royal Masonic Cyclopaedia* (1877); and Hargrave Jennings, author of the infamous text, *The Rosicrucians: Their Rites and Mysteries* (1870). A Metropolitan College was founded in London in 1866, and the Soc. Ros. in Scotia about the same time. Other colleges were later formed in the provinces. W. R. Woodman succeeded Little as grand magus in 1878. Mackenzie was named honorary magus and gave many lectures to the society.

In 1891 **William Wynn Westcott** succeeded Woodman as supreme magus. Three years earlier, Westcott had become one of the founders of the Hermetic Order of the **Golden Dawn** occult society, whose grade system and rituals drew heavily on Rosicrucian concepts. **S. L. MacGregor Mathers,** another of the Golden Dawn chiefs, formed a second order known as R.R. et A.C. (Rose of Ruby and Cross of Gold), supposed to be a British branch of a German occult order known as Ordo Roseae Rubeae et Aureae Crucis. The Golden Dawn was regarded as the probationary order of the R.R. et A.C. and the initiation rite dramatized the Rosicrucian legend of Christian Rosenkreutz in his tomb. When executive dissension arose in the Golden Dawn in 1901, member W. B. Yeats privately published a pamphlet titled *Is the Order of R.R. & A.C. to Remain a Magical Order?*

Meanwhile, in the United States, a set of Rosicrucian orders began to emerge. The first was the Societas Rosicruciana Republicae Americae (now known as the Societas Rosicruciana in Civitatibus Foederatis), established by a set of masons who received their authorization in 1878 from the Societas Rosicruciana in Anglica, through the college in York. Like its British counterpart, one had to be a mason to join. Out of it grew the Societas Rosicruciana in America, founded in 1907, which opened its doors to non-masons. Founder Sylvester Gould was succeeded by George Winslow Plummer (1876–1944), under whose leadership the society flourished up to World War II. Plummer was succeeded by Stanislaus Witowski (or de Witow). He was succeeded by Gladys Plummer de Witow and more recently, Lucia L. Grosch.

Also based in the Western occult tradition is the **Ancient and Mystic Order of the Rosicrucians,** popularly known by its acronym, AMORC. AMORC was founded in 1915 by **H. Spencer Lewis,** and after locating the headquarters in San Jose, California, in the mid-1920s, Lewis built the order into the largest Rosicrucian organization in the world with an aggressive program of advertising and recruitment and a popular correspondence course for members.

Several Rosicrucian groups grew out of the Theosophical Society and the teachings of **Helena Petrovna Blavatsky** and **Rudolf Steiner,** an early theosophical leader in German-speaking Europe. Steiner was the leading champion of a Christ-centered approach to Theosophy and promoted Rosicrucian ideals. In 1907 Louis van Grashof, known under his public name, **Max Heindel,** founded the **Rosicrucian Fellow-**

ship. Heindel had attended Steiner's lectures, and he incorporated Steiner's ideas in his many books. The Rosicrucian Fellowship became an important force in reestablishing **astrology** in the West in this century. The Rosicrucian Fellowship became the source of several other Rosicrucian groups, including the **Lectorium Rosicrucianum,** the **Rosicrucian Anthroposophical League,** and the **Ausar Auset Society,** unique for its adaptation of Rosicrucian teachings to the needs of the African American community.

Sources:

Allen, Paul M. *Christian Rosenkreutz Anthology.* Blauvelt, N.Y.: Steiner Books, 1974.

Arnold, Paul. *Histoire des Rose-Crois.* Paris, 1934.

Dickson, Donald R. *The Tesserea of Antilia: Utopian Brotherhoods and Secret Societies in the Early Seventeenth Century.* Leiden: Brill, 1998.

Gardener, F. Leigh. *A Catalogue Raisonne of Works on the Occult Sciences.* Vol. 1 of the *Rosicrucian Books.* Privately printed, 1923.

Howe, Ellic. *The Magicians of the Golden Dawn.* London: Routledge & Kegan Paul, 1972.

McIntosh, Christopher. *The Rosy Cross Unveiled: The History, Mythology, and Rituals of an Occult Order.* Wellingborough, England: Aquarian Press, 1980.

Pryse, F. N., ed. *The Fame and Confession of the Fraternity of R:C: Commonly of the Rosie Cross . . . by Eugenius Philalethes . . . now reprinted in facsimile together with an Introduction, Notes and a Translation of the letter of Adam Haselmeyer.* Societas Rosicruciana in Anglia, 1923.

Silberer, Herbert. *The Hidden Symbolism of Alchemy and the Occult Arts.* New York: Dover, 1971.

Waite, A. E. *The Real History of the Rosicrucians.* London: George Redway, 1887. Reprint, Blauvelt, N.Y.: Steiner Books, 1977. Revised as *The Brotherhood of the Rosy Cross.* London: William Rider & Son, 1924. Reprint, New Hyde Park, N.Y.: University Books, 1961.

Yates, Frances. *The Rosicrucian Enlightenment.* London: Routledge & Kegan Paul, 1972.

Rosma, Charles B.

Claimed as the murdered peddler of Hydesville, New York, in 1848, when spirit rappings were heard in the Fox household. The supposed source of the **Rochester Rappings** produced by the **Fox sisters.**

Rossetti, Dante Gabriel (1828–1882)

English author and painter Gabriel Charles Dante Rossetti, commonly known as Dante Gabriel Rossetti, was born in London, May 12, 1828. His father was an Italian who had settled in England.

While yet a boy, Rossetti manifested artistic talent, and accordingly was sent to study drawing under John Sell Cotman, Shortly afterward he entered the Royal Academy Schools. In 1848, he commenced working in the studio of Ford Madox Brown, during which time he began to show himself a painter of distinct individuality, while simultaneously he made his first essays in translating Italian literature into English and became known among his friends as a poet of rare promise.

Meanwhile, however, Rossetti was really more interested in painting rather than writing, and soon after leaving Brown's studio he brought about a memorable event in the history of English painting by founding the Pre-Raphaelite Brotherhood, a body consisting of seven members, whose central aim was to render precisely and literally every separate object figured in their pictures. Leaving his father's house in 1849, Rossetti went to live at Chatham Place, Blackfriars Bridge, London, and during the next ten years his activity as a painter was enormous.

The year 1860 was a notable one in his career, as it marked his marriage to Eleanor Siddal. The love between the pair was of an exceptionally passionate order, and from it sprang Rossetti's later sonnet sequence called *The House of Life,* published in 1881. However, Eleanor died in 1862. The loss of his wife preyed upon him persistently; he was tortured by insomnia and, in consequence, began to take occasional doses of the drug chloral. Gradually this practice developed into a habit, and it soon became evident that his death was imminent unless he gave up his addiction to the drug. He died April 9, 1882, at Birchington, near Margate, and his remains were interred in the cemetery there.

Rossetti had a marked bias for mysticism in various forms. William Bell Scott, in his *Autobiographical Notes* (2 vols., 1892), told how the poet became at one time much enamored of **table-turning.** His temperament was undoubtedly a very religious one, and once toward the close of his life he declared that he had "seen and heard those that died long ago."

A belief in the possibility of communicating with the dead may have induced him on his wife's death to have some of his love poems enclosed in her coffin. Whatever the truth of his poems, it is by his painting rather than by his poetry that Rossetti holds a place as a great mystic, for despite his fondness for precise handling, most of his pictures are essentially of a mystical nature. They embody the scenes and incidents beheld in dreams in a manner similar to the work of **William Blake.**

Rothe, Frau Anna (1850–1907)

German working woman who, after the death of her daughter's fiancé in about 1892, developed mediumship. She constantly saw the deceased seated on the sofa in his accustomed attitude. She saw visions as a child, too, but soon physical phenomena also developed and Rothe soon specialized in **apports** of flowers and fruits in quantity. Her mediumistic career, however, was a stormy one and finally her fraud led to a sensational trial and a prison sentence.

Camille Flammarion held a séance with Rothe in May 1901, at his own apartment. He wrote:

"During its continuance, bouquets of flowers of all sizes did, in truth, make their appearance, but always from a quarter in the room opposite to that to which our attention was drawn by Frau Rothe and her manager, Max Jentsch.

"Being well-nigh convinced that all was fraud, but not having the time to devote to such sittings, I begged M. Cail to be present, as often as he could, at the meetings which were to be held in different Parisian salons. He gladly consented, and got invited to a séance at the Clément Marot house. Having taken his station a little in the rear of the flower-scattering medium, he saw her adroitly slip one hand beneath her skirt and draw out branches which she tossed into the air."

He also saw her take oranges from her corsage, and ascertained that they were warm.

"The imposture was a glaring one, and he immediately unmasked her, to the great scandal of the assistants, who heaped insults upon him. A final séance had been planned, to be held in my salon on the following Tuesday. But Frau Rothe and her two accomplices took the train at the Eastern Railway station that very morning and we saw them no more."

Charles Richet stated in his book *Thirty Years of Psychical Research* (1923):

"The first time that I saw the surprising performances of Anna Roth, The 'Blumen-medium,' I was dazzled; at a second sitting I was perplexed; at the third I was convinced that the thing was a fraud. I asked Anna Roth to allow a more complete control which would have settled the question. She refused."

The fact on which Richet based his belief in the imposture of Rothe was that he weighed her before the séance and after. The difference was two pounds, exactly the weight of the "apported" flowers. Therefore, he concludes, they must have been secreted about her person.

A serious exposure took place in Germany in 1902, as a result of which Rothe was kept in prison for over a year before the trial and was afterward sentenced to eighteen months imprisonment and a fine of 500 marks. Detectives posing as inquirers found 150 flowers and several oranges and apples in a series of bag-like folds in her petticoat.

At the trial, Judge Georges Sulzer, President of the Zurich High Court of Appeal, stated on oath that Rothe put him in communication with the spirits of his wife and father, who gave information unknown to any mortal. He also declared that the medium produced flowers in quantity in a room flooded with light. They came down slowly from above, and he saw four nebulous points on the hand of the medium condense into bonbons. Altogether forty witnesses, mostly doctors and professors, gave evidence on behalf of the medium. But the presiding judge stated in the sentence:

"The Court cannot allow itself to criticize the spiritistic theory, for it must be acknowledged that science, with the generality of men of culture, declares supernatural manifestations to be impossible."

In *Die Zukunft* (April 4, 1903), journalist Maxmilian Harden criticized the sentence,

"Before the conclusion of the testimony one could not but ask: Does this Rothe case, taken as a whole, show the proofmarks of fraud? This question was answered by us in the negative; but the court answered it affirmatively after a short deliberation. The flower medium was condemned to imprisonment for a year and half—a strange transaction, an incomprehensible sentence. The court summons witnesses for the defence—dozens—although the proof-notes show that almost all testify to the same effect. They come, are sworn, and declare almost without exception 'we feel ourselves in no way injured.' The most say 'we are convinced that no false representations were worked off on us by the Rothe woman.' . . . But the sentence has been pronounced on Frau Rothe in the name of justice."

Sources:

Bohn, Erich. *Der Fall Rothe.* Breslau, 1901.

Roy, William (1911–1977)

Pseudonym of William George Holroyd Plowright, a notorious mediumistic fraud in British Spiritualist history. He boasted that he had earned £50,000 by cheating the bereaved and others who attended his fraudulent séances. He even made money out of publishing his own confessions. It is to the credit of the British Spiritualist movement that its members took the lead in first exposing Roy.

Born in Cobham, Surrey, England, Roy was boastful and deceptive even at an early age. He was seventeen years old when he married Mary Castle, who owned a nightclub in the Soho area of London's West End. Mary was the first of many women who were deceived by Roy's glamorous tall tales.

During the 1930s, his wife died and Roy married again. He set up in business as a professional psychic medium. Roy used ingenious technical devices for fraudulent mediumship and also employed confederates. He concealed a microphone in the séance room and recorded the conversations of sitters before commencement of a séance.

When people wrote to ask if they could attend his séances, Roy researched at the registry of births, deaths, and marriages in order to obtain detailed information about their relatives. When they visited his house for a sitting, they would be asked to leave their bags and coats outside the séance room. These were searched by a confederate for letters, tickets, bills, or other scraps of personal information. All the facts concerning sitters were recorded in a detailed card index system, and cleverly worked into Roy's "psychic" messages during séances.

Roy also produced "spirit voices" and **"materialization"** phenomena through use of amplifiers, butter muslin, masks, and tape recorders and microphones in the hands of confederates. One of Roy's most shameless con tricks was the exploitation of a widow who attended his séances. Through a female accomplice, Roy obtained detailed information about the widow's dead husband and son, duly relayed to the widow at séances as messages from her loved ones. At the same time, Roy made advances to the widow and claimed that he wanted to marry her as soon as he could obtain a divorce.

During a séance, the widow was given "spirit messages" advising her to offer Roy's wife £15,000 in return for an arranged divorce. In due course, Roy produced a letter apparently from his wife through a firm of solicitors, giving consent for this arrangement. The letter and the firm of solicitors were both bogus, but the widow paid Roy £15,000, which went into his own pocket, and the pair went away on a "honeymoon."

Meanwhile Roy's second wife Dorothy committed suicide. Three weeks after her death, Roy married Mary Rose Halligan. Roy had rich clients and lived in style, with expensive motorcars. He separated from his third wife in 1956.

Meanwhile in August 1955, after almost 20 years of mediumistic trickery, his activity was first exposed by veteran Spiritualist **Maurice Barbanell** (editor of *Psychic News*) in an article in the journal *Two Worlds.* The exposure did not occur until Roy quarreled with his accomplice, who left him and supplied evidence and explained Roy's methods and apparatus. Roy instituted libel proceedings, but withdrew the action in 1958.

In 1958, Roy unblushingly published his own confessions in the *Sunday Pictorial* newspaper. But he continued operating as a fake medium, using a new name "Bill Silver." At the age of 58, Roy bigamously married Ann Clements. He finally died at Hastings, Sussex, suffering from cancer, leaving three children from his various alliances.

Roy's ingenious apparatus for fake mediumship is now in the care of Scotland Yard, in a museum at the Metropolitan Police Detective Training School. After Roy's death and twenty years after his original exposure, Barbanell devoted a whole front page of *Psychic News* (August 13, 1977) to the story of Roy's frauds, illustrated by photographs of the apparatus and techniques used for fake mediumship.

Royal Priest Research

Royal Priest Research is an Arizona-based company that facilitates the channeling work of Lyssa Royal, one of the more prominent **New Age** channels to arise in the 1980s. During her college years in the later 1970s, Royal studied self-hypnosis and learned to enter altered states of consciousness for purposes of stress management. In the early 1980s, having completed her degree in psychology, she had a dream in which she was told that she would become a channel. She developed her skills over the next few years and began channeling professionally in 1985. She was one of the first and most successful of the New Age channels to rely primarily on information claimed to be from extraterrestrial sources.

Priest's early work focused on the **contactee** and abductee phenomena and resulted in three books, *The Prism of Lyra* (1989), *Visitors from Within?* (1992), and *Preparing for Contact: A Metamorphosis of Consciousness* (1993), all written with Keith Priest, a musician, alternative health therapist, and independent researcher who works with Royal. These books explored the possibilities of human contact with space visitors through telepathic means and were among the first to suggest that the **abduction** experience was not necessarily negative, but could be used for personal and planetary evolution. Through the 1990s, Royal has become identified with the post-New Age channels operating out of **Sedona,** Arizona, and her work has frequently appeared in **Sedona Journal of Emergence.** Also working with Royal Priest Research is Ron Holt, Lyssa's husband, who has been a leader in the **Flower of Life** organization headed by Drunvalo Melchizedek.

During the 1990s, Royal and Priest have continued to produce books based upon her channeling work. In 1997 Royal released a book, *Millennium,* in preparation for the changes she saw coming as the new century began. She offered a more mundane view of the changing times, noting that the millennium was a manmade marker that designates the collective recognition of a milestone in human life. However, she also believes in the post-New Age vision of coming human transformation. She views this as a movement from the third density state to the fourth density state. In the new state, humans will have a higher vibratory rate, will radiate more light, and the illusion of separation from the Divine will come to an end.

Royal Priest Research can be reached at P.O. Box 30973, Phoenix, AZ 85046. It has a website at http://www.royalpriest.com. Royal's books have now been translated into a number of languages.

Sources:

Royal, Lyssa. *Millennium.* Phoenix: Royal Priest Research, 1997.

Royal, Lyssa, and Keith Priest. *Preparing for Contact: A Metamorphosis of Consciousness.* Phoenix: Royal Priest Research, 1993.

———. *The Prism of Lyra: An Exploration of Human Galactic Heritage.* Phoenix: Royal Priest Research, 1989.

———. *Visitors from Within?* Phoenix: Royal Priest Research, 1992.

Royal Priest Research. http://www.royalpriest.com. June 10, 2000.

Royce, Josiah (1855–1916)

Philosopher and a founding member of the **American Society for Psychical Research.** He was born on November 20, 1855, at Grass Valley, California. He studied at University of California (B.A., 1875) and later did graduate work at Johns Hopkins University (Ph.D., 1878) and in Germany at the universities of Leipzig and Göttingen. In 1880 he married Katharine Head.

After his return from Germany he became an instructor in English literature and logic at the University of California. Then in 1882 he joined the Harvard faculty where in 1914 he was named Alford Professor of Religion, Moral Philosophy, and Civil Polity. He authored a number of books and professional papers.

As a prominent modern American philosopher, Royce investigated the problem of the individual self as part of the world mind. In part due to his friendship with William James, he became a founding member of the ASPR in 1884 and served as chairman and vice president of the Committee on Apparitions and Haunting Houses. The committee's name was changed later to Committee on Phantasms and Presentiments; it classified cases sent in from individuals all over the United States and published his report in the first volume of the *Proceedings* of the ASPR. Royce died September 14, 1916, at Cambridge, Massachusetts.

Sources:

Royce, Josiah. "Report of the Committee on Phantasm and Presentiments." *Proceedings* of the American Society for Psychical Research 1, 3 (December 1877); 1, 4 (March 1889).

———. *William James and Other Essays on the Philosophy of Life.* N.p., 1911. Reprint, Freeport, N.Y.: Books for Libraries Press, 1969.

RSP See **Recurrent Spontaneous Psychokinesis**

Rudhyar, Dane (1895–1985)

Musician, painter, poet, novelist, and one of the most important voices redirecting **astrology** in the twentieth century. Rudhyar was born in Paris, on March 23, 1895. At age 12 a severe illness and surgery disabled him and he turned to music and intellectual development to compensate for his lack of physical agility. He studied at the Sorbonne, University of Paris (graduating at age 16) and at the Paris Conservatoire. His early ventures into philosophy and association with the artistic community in Paris led to his conviction that all existence is cyclical in character.

His music led him to New York in 1916, where he composed some of the first polytonal music performed in the United States. He also met Sasaki Roshi, one of the early Japanese **Zen** teachers in America, who led him in the study of Oriental philosophy and occultism. His interest was further stimulated by his association with Theosophy, which began when he was asked to compose music for a production at the society's headquarters in Los Angeles in 1920. Rudhyar became a naturalized citizen of the United States in 1926. He stayed in California (often commuting to New York) through the 1920s and in 1930 married Marla Contento, secretary to independent Theosophist Will Levington Comfort. Comfort introduced Rudhyar to **Marc Edmund Jones,** who in turn introduced him to astrology.

Rudhyar learned astrology during a period when he was also studying the psychological writings of **Carl G. Jung,** and he began to think in terms of bringing astrology and Jungian psychology together. The marriage overcame some basic problems of astrology, including its deterministic approach to life and the trouble of designating an agreeable agent to produce the astrological effects. Rudhyar postulated that the stars did not cause the effects seen in human life but were pictures synchronistically aligned to human beings. They detailed psychological forces working in individuals, but did not override human freedom in responding to those forces, he said. At first he called his new interpretation "harmonic astrology" and as the ideas matured renamed it "humanistic astrology," the subject of his monumental volume, *The Astrology of Personality,* published in 1936. A friend, **Alice A. Bailey,** encouraged the development of his thought and published his book.

Over the next two decades Rudhyar continued to write and lecture on astrology, but while he was honored within the astrological community he was little known outside of it. It was not until the 1970s, as the **New Age** movement emerged, that major publishing houses discovered him and began to publish his writings: among the first was *The Practice of Astrology,* published in 1970 by Penguin Books.

In 1969 Rudhyar founded the International Committee for Humanistic Astrology, a small professional society that would work on the development of his perspective. He began one of the most fruitful periods of his life, turning out several books a year for the next decade. He began to absorb the insights of transpersonal astrology, which concentrated on exploring altered and exalted states of perception, and by the mid-1970s had moved beyond humanistic astrology to what he termed "transpersonal astrology." He also began to reflect upon the New Age movement and wrote several of the more sophisticated volumes on planetary consciousness and New Age philosophy.

He died September 15, 1985, in California.

Sources:

Melton, J. Gordon, Jerome Clark, and Aidan A. Kelly. *New Age Encyclopedia.* Detroit: Gale Research, 1990.

Rudhyar, Dane. *The Astrology of Personality: A Reformulation of Astrological Concepts and Ideals, in Terms of Contemporary Psychology and Philosophy.* New York: Lucis Publishing, 1936.

———. *The Astrology of Transformation: A Multilevel Approach.* Wheaton, Ill.: Theosophical Publishing House, 1980.

———. *From Humanistic to Transpersonal Astrology.* Palo Alto, Calif.: Seed Center, 1975.

———. *Occult Preparations for the New Age.* Wheaton, Ill.: Theosophical Publishing House, 1975.

———. *Person-centered Astrology.* Lakemont, Ga.: CSA Press, 1972.

———. *The Planetarization of Consciousness.* New York: Harper, 1972.

———. *Rhythm of Wholeness: A Total Affirmation of Being.* Wheaton, Ill.: Theosophical Publishing House, 1983.

Ruggles, A. D. (ca. 1853)

Early American Spiritualist medium, the subject of experiments by Prof. **Robert Hare.** According to testimonies in contemporary periodicals, Ruggles's abilities included **xenoglossia,** the skill of writing and speaking in foreign languages that one does not understand.

Ruhani Satsang

A major branch of the **Radhasoami Satsang** spiritual movement of India, stemming from the guru Sawan Singh (1858–1948), a disciple of Baba Jaimal Singh. Central to the teaching is the concept of an inner light and inner sound experienced in meditation. After Kirpal Singh's death in 1974, his son Darshan Singh succeeded him. The Satsang currently operates in the West as the Sawan Kirpal Ruhani Mission.

There is an international headquarters at: Kirpal Ashram, 2 Canal Road, Vijay Nagar, Delhi 11009. In the United States, the mission may be contacted at 8605 Village Way, No. C, Alexandria, VA 22309-1605.

Ruh Ve Madde (Journal)

Monthly journal (in Turkish language) of the Metaphysic Research Society of Turkey that covered **Spiritualism,** healing, **astrology, UFOs,** and **parapsychology.** Last known address: P.O. Box 1157, Istanbul, Turkey.

Rumi, Jalal al-Din (1207–1273)

A Sufi poet born in 1207 in Balkh (now Afganistan). He taught the Sufi doctrine that the chief end of life is to emancipate oneself from human thoughts and wishes, human needs, and the outward impressions of the senses, so that one may become a mere mirror for the Deity. So refined an essence does one's mind become that it is as nearly as possible nothing, yet while in this state it can, by a union with the Divine Essence, mysteriously become the All.

In his teachings, Rumi declared that names and words must not be taken for the things they represent:

"Names thou mayest know; go, seek the truth they name
Search not the brook, but heaven, for the moon."

Nature figured largely in the imagery of Rumi's poems. He also used the image of the reed-pipe, which figures largely in the symbolism of the Mevlevi order **Sufism,** popularly known as the whirling **dervishes,** which his followers founded after his death in 1273.

Sources:

Classical and Medieval Literature Criticism. Vol. 20, Detroit: Gale Research, 1997.

Jackson, Guida M. *Encyclopedia of Literary Epics.* Santa Barbara: ABC-CLIO, 1996.

Runes

An ancient alphabet found in inscriptions on stone in Scandinavian countries. The runic alphabet belongs to the Germanic group of languages, but is related to Greek and Latin alphabets. The earliest inscriptions were pictured in the hands of the goddess Idun, the keeper of the gods' magic apples of immortality. Dating from the 3rd century C.E., runic inscriptions have been found in areas between the Black Sea and the Baltic (territories occupied by Goths) as well as throughout Scandinavia.

At one point, Odin dies to acquire the runes for humankind, and, as men were expected to imitate his sacrifice, high praise was given to one who died in battle. In place of dying in battle, a Norse warrior might carve the runes on his body and bleed to death, that day thus being marked as a "red-letter day."

Runes were inscribed on stone monuments to commemorate events and individuals as well as for magical purposes. They were also used on objects like brooches. Typical of runic inscriptions is the writing on an ancient Danish monument which reads: "Rolf raised this stone, priest and chieftain of the Helnaes dwellers, in memory of his brother's son, Gudmund. The men were drowned at sea. Aveir wrote (the runes)." A Norwegian monument indicates that runes were believed to give magical protection: "This is the secret meaning of the runes; I hid here power-runes, undisturbed by evil witchcraft. In exile shall he die by means of magic art who destroys this monument."

The use of runic inscriptions has been revived in both the modern magical and New Age ideas and activities, and crated a vast contemporary literature. Among the most popular, Ralph Blum has adapted runes for **divination** purposes. His publications *The Book of Runes* (1984) and *Rune Play* (1985) are issued in conjunction with a package of twenty-five runic letters on ceramic counters. These counters are "cast," rather in the manner of a simplified **I Ching** system, to give oracular guidance on personal questions and decisions.

The concept of "casting the runes" also occurs in Western magical practice, where spells are inscribed on a slip of paper in runic letters, to be unobtrusively delivered to and accepted by the victim of the spell. This is brilliantly described in the short story *Casting the Runes* by M. R. James (included in *More Ghost Stories of an Antiquary,* 1911) in which one character takes a ticket-case belonging to the victim and places the slip of paper with the runic spell on it inside the case. He then hands it to the victim, implying casually that he must have dropped it. The victim recognizes the ticket-case as his own, and gratefully accepts it, so the runes are cast.

Sources:

Blum, Ralph. *The Book of Runes.* New York: St. Martin's Press, 1984.

———. *Rune Play.* New York: St. Martin's Press, 1985.

Branston, Brian. *Gods of the North.* London: Thames & Hudson, 1955.

Elliott, R. W. V. *Runes.* Rev. ed. UK: Manchester University Press, 1963.

Flowers, Stephen E. *Runes and Magic: Magical Formulaic Elements in the Older Runic Tradition.* New York: Kang, 1986.

Hermannsson, H. *Catalogue of Runic Literature Forming Part of the Icelandic Collection at Cornell University.* Ithaca, N.Y.: Cornell University Press, 1918.

Howard, Michael. *The Magic of Runes.* New York: Samuel Weiser, 1980.

Peschel, Lisa. *The Runes.* St. Paul: Llewellyn Publications, 1989.

Thorsson, Edred. *Futjhark: A Handbook of Rune Magic.* York Beach, Maine: Samuel Weiser, 1984.

Tyson, Donald. *Rune Magic.* St. Paul: Llewellyn Publications, 1989.

Willis, Tony. *The Runic Workbook.* New York: Sterling Publishers, 1986.

Rupa

In theosophical teachings, *rupa* denotes form, appearance, or the physical body, the most gross of the **seven principles** of which personality consists. It is a term originating in Hindu philosophy denoting the subtle essence of form. (See also **Mayavi-rupa.**)

Rusalki

The lovely river nymph of southern Russian legend endowed with human beauty and the gentle characteristics of the **Mermaids** of northern European nations. Shy and benevolent, she lived on the small alluvial islands that stud the rivers or in the detached coppices of their banks. Her pastime and occupation was to aid in secret the poor fishermen in their laborious and precarious calling.

The rusalki (also spelled "rusalky" or "rusalka") were believed to have originated with young women who met an untimely death either by suicide, drowning, or murder by strangling or were not buried in holy ground. At times the rusalki would turn on people and kill them, especially young men who would go bathing in the streams without wearing a cross around their necks.

Little is known of these beautiful creatures. Thomas Keightley, a knowledgeable source in the lore of **fairies,** says little of *rusalki* in his book *The Fairy Mythology* (1850) and gives only this brief notice:

"They are of a beautiful form, with long green hair; they swim and balance themselves on the branches of trees, bathe in the lakes and rivers, play on the surface of the water, and wring their locks on the green meads at the water's edge. It is chiefly at Whitsuntide that they appear; and the people then, singing and dancing, weave garlands for them, which they cast into the stream."

Sources:

Arrowsmith, Nancy, and George Moorse. *A Field Guide to the Little People.* New York: Wallaby, 1977.

Cherryh, C. J. *Rusalka.* New York: Ballantine Books, 1989.

Rush, J(oseph) H(arold) (1911–)

Physicist and science writer who also studied aspects of parapsychology. He was born on April 17, 1911, at Mount Calm, Texas. He studied at the University of Texas (B.A., 1940; M.A., 1941) and Duke University (Ph.D., 1950). He worked as a physicist and teacher of physics through the 1940s, including work on the development of the atomic bomb during World War II, prior to becoming a physicist at the National Center for Atmospheric Research in Boulder, Colorado, in 1962. He has published a number of papers on astronomy and physics and is author of *The Dawn of Life* (1958). He was in Boulder at the end of the 1960s when the **Condon** Committee on **UFOs** was established and he was invited to participate on it.

Rush's interest in parapsychology dates to the mid-1930s when he discovered some of the early texts on the subject by **J. B. Rhine.** His acceptance of parapsychology came in part because of his early experiences of clairvoyance and precognition. He became a charter member of the **Parapsychology Association.** In the field of parapsychology, he has studied and written about the associative aspects of psi phenomena and the functioning of psi with ordinary sensorimotor activities. He has emerged as a sympathetic critic of the field and claimed that much of parapsychology had been wasted by scientists using inadequate methodologies.

Sources:

Berger, Arthur S., and Joyce Berger. *The Encyclopedia of Parapsychology and Psychical Research.* New York: Paragon House, 1991.

Edge, H. L., J. Morris, J. Palmer, and J. H. Rush. *Foundations of Parapsychology: Exploring the Boundaries of Human Capabilities.* London: Routledge & Kegan Paul, 1986.

Pleasants, Helene, ed. *Biographical Dictionary of Parapsychology.* New York: Helix Press, 1964.

Rush, J. H. *The Dawn of Life.* New York: Doubleday, 1958.

———. "Parapsychology: Some Personal Observations." In *Men and Women of Parapsychology.* Edited by R. Pilkington. Jefferson, N.C.: McFarland, 1987.

———. "A Reciprocal Distance GESP Test with Drawings." *Journal of Parapsychology* (1949).

———. "Some Considerations as to a Physical Basis of Extrasensory Perception." *Journal of Parapsychology* (1943).

Rushton, W(illiam A(lbert) H(ugh) (1901–1980)

Distinguished British physiologist who also took an active interest in parapsychology, becoming president of the **Society for Psychical Research,** London, (1969–71). Rushton was born on December 8, 1901. He was educated at Gresham's, Bolt; Emmanuel College, Cambridge and University College Hospital, London. He joined the faculty at Cambridge University in physiology and taught until 1968 when he moved to Florida State University as the Distinguished Resident Professor in Psychobiology. Following his retirement in 1977 he was named emeritus professor of physiology.

He contributed to the *Journal of Physiology* and took a special interest in nerve excitation and vision. In the field of psychical research, his expert physiological knowledge stimulated inquiry into the possible mechanisms of ESP. He was critical about false assumptions or unscientific thinking in study of the paranormal, but maintained a keen interest in the subject and believed in the reality of some phenomena. He died June 21, 1980.

Ruskin, John (1819–1900)

Famous British author and critic born in London on February 8, 1819, who owed his belief in survival to **Spiritualism.** In *Pre-Raphaelitism and the Pre-Raphaelite Brotherhood* by W. Holman Hunt (2 vols., 1913) there occurs the following conversation:

"When we last met," said Holman Hunt to Ruskin, "you declared you had given up all belief in immortality." "I remember well," Ruskin replied, "but what has mainly caused the change in my views is the unanswerable evidence of spiritualism. I know there is much vulgar fraud and stupidity connected with it, but underneath there is, I am sure, enough to convince us that there is personal life independent of the body, but with this once proved, I have no further interest in spiritualism."

Also during one summer in Switzerland Ruskin had a startling experience with a child who saw a ghost that had long been known to haunt a particular spot in the valley of Chamonix. He described the female spirit as having no eyes, but only holes where they were supposed to be.

Ruskin died January 20, 1900.

Sources:

Berger, Arthur S., and Joyce Berger. *The Encyclopedia of Parapsychology and Psychical Research.* New York: Paragon House, 1991.

Prince, Walter F. *Noted Witnesses for Psychic Occurrences.* Boston: Boston Society for Psychical Research, 1928. Reprint, New Hyde Park, N.Y.: University Books, 1963.

Russell, Eric Frank (1905–1978)

Prolific science-fiction writer, who based some of his stories on the ideas and data of **Charles Fort**; British representative of the **Fortean Society.** Russell was born on January 6, 1905, at Sandhurst, Surrey, England. He spent his early years at military bases abroad before returning to England, where he had a scientific and technical education. In the 1930s he published science-fiction stories, later serving in the Royal Air Force during World War II. He was active in promoting Fortean ideas at a time when Fort's books were little known in Britain and difficult to obtain.

His first major novel *Sinister Barrier* (1943), published serially in 1939, was built around the Fortean theme "I think we're property," suggesting that the inhabitants of Earth may be controlled by alien entities. His story *Three to Conquer* (1956) is a science-fiction treatment of the theme of psi powers.

Other Russell books include: *Dreadful Sanctuary* (1953), *Sentinels From Space* (1954), *Deep Space* (1956), *Men, Martians & Machines* (1956), *Wasp* (1958), *The Space Willies* (U.K. title *Next of Kin*) (1959), *Far Stars* (1961), *The Great Explosion* (1962), *With a Strange Device* (1964), and *Somewhere a Voice* (1965).

With the decline of the Fortean Society, his enthusiasm waned and during the 1960s he also stopped writing.

Although never officially dissolved, the work of the Fortean Society was later taken over by the **International Fortean Organization** in North America and the **Fortean Times** in Great Britain. Russell died February 28, 1978.

Sources:

Russell, Rick Frank. *The Best of Eric Frank Russell.* Edited by Alan Dean Foster. New York: Del Rey, 1978.

———. *Sinister Barrier.* Reading, Pa.: Fantasy Press, 1948.

Russell, George W(illiam) (1867–1935)

Irish poet, essayist, and mystic, who wrote under the pseudonym "AE." Born April 10, 1867, at Lurgan, County Armagh, Northern Ireland, his family moved to Dublin when he was ten, where he was able to attend Rathmines School. He had a natural talent for painting and attended the Metropolitan School of Art in Dublin, where he met **William Butler Yeats,** who introduced him to **Theosophy.** At that time, Russell earned his living by working as a clerk and soon began contributing poems and articles to *The Irish Theosophist.*

Theosophical teachings and the literature of Hindu philosophy opened his mind to heightened consciousness of Celtic myth and nature spirits. He painted visionary pictures of the Irish landscape.

He felt a strange impulse to call one of his paintings "The Birth of Aeon," a Gnostic concept, and signed one of his articles "AEON." A proof reader rendered this as "AE-?" and thereafter Russell used the initials for his poems. In 1894 he allowed some of his poems to be published as a book, *Homeward: Songs of the Way,* and the response thrust him to the fore of Ireland's literary community. In 1913 the first edition of his collected poems was published.

He also wrote many political articles and became organizer for the Irish Agriculture Organization, successfully combining his mystical visions with everyday practical tasks, in the spirit of the ancient Hindu scripture, the *Bhagavad Gita,* a work which greatly impressed him. He edited the Irish Homestead for the Organization from 1906 to 1923. In 1923 he became the editor of the *Irish Statesman* in which he tried to steer a moderate course for the newly founded Irish Free States. He gave expression to his political idealism in two novels, *The Interpreters* (1922) and *The Avatars* (1932).

His major mystical book was *The Candle of Vision* (1918). His book *Song and Its Fountains* (1932) developed the mystical meditations of *Candle of Vision* and spoke of poetry as "oracles breathed from inner to outer being." *The Avatars: A Futurist Fantasy* (1933) indicated his debt to Hindu philosophy. Russell died July 17, 1935.

Sources:

AE [George Russell]. *The Candle of Vision.* 1918. Reprint, New Hyde Park, N.Y.: University Books, 1965.

———. *Homeward: Songs of the Way.* Portland, Maine: T. B. Mosher, 1895.

———. *The Interpreters.* New York: Macmillian, 1922.

———. *Song and Its Foundations.* New York; London, Macmillian, 1932.

de Zirkoff, Boris, comp. "General Bibliography with Selected Biographical Notes." In *Collected Writings.* Vol XII. by H. P. Blavatsky. Wheaton, Ill.: Theosophical Publishing House, 1980.

Denson, Alan. *Printed writings of George W. Russell (AE): A Bibliography.* London: Northwestern University Press, 1961.

Eglinton, John. *A Memoir of AE: George William Russell.* London: Macmillian, 1937.

Merchant, Francis. *A.E.: An Irish Promethean.* Columbia, S.C.: Benedict College Press, 1954.

RUSSIA

Spiritualism was first introduced in Russia by people who had been introduced to the subject abroad, witnessing manifestations of psychic phenomena and acquaintance with the works of **Allan Kardec,** the French exponent of **Spiritism.**

The new doctrine found its followers chiefly among the members of the professions and the aristocracy, finally including the reigning monarch of that time, Alexander II. Members of his family and entourage also became devoted adherents. Because of the immense influence of such converts, the progress of Spiritualism in Russia was made smoother.

Much of the spiritualist propaganda, manifestations, and publications were conducted under various ruses and deceptions such as the circulation of a paper entitled "The Rebus," professedly devoted to innocent rebuses and charades and only incidentally mentioning Spiritualism, the real object of its being.

Among the distinguished devotees of the subject was Prince Wittgenstein, aide-de-camp and trusted friend of Alexander II, who not only avowed his beliefs openly but arranged for various mediums, including **D. D. Home,** to give séances before the emperor. The Czar was impressed, and, from that time onward he consulted mediums and their prophetic powers as to the advisability of any contemplated change or step in his life.

Another Russian of high position socially and officially was **Alexander N. Aksakof,** who interested himself in Spiritualism, arranging séances to which he invited the scientific men of the University, editing a paper *Psychische Studien,* translating into Russian the works of **Emanuel Swedenborg** and various French, American, and English writers of the same subject, thus becoming a leader in the movement.

Later, with his friends Boutlerof and Wagner, professors respectively of chemistry and zoology at the University of St. Petersburg, he specially commenced a series of séances for the investigation of the phenomena in an experimental manner and a scientific committee was formed under the leadership of Professor Mendeleyef, who afterward issued an adverse report on the matter. This accused the mediums of trickery and their followers of easy credulity and the usual warfare proceeded between the scientific investigators and spiritual enthusiasts.

At the other extreme of the social scale, among the peasantry and uneducated classes generally, the grossest superstition existed, a profound belief in supernatural agencies and cases were often reported in the columns of Russian papers. Stories abounded of wonder-working, obsession and various miraculous happenings, all ascribed to demoniac or angelic influence, or in districts where the inhabitants were still pagan to local deities and witchcraft.

The final years of the Romanov dynasty were dominated by the strange charismatic figure of the monk **Rasputin,** murdered shortly before the outbreak of the Russian Revolution of 1917. **Grigory Yefimovich,** was a Siberian peasant who had entered a monastery at 18, but left, married and had 4 children. He became absorbed in a peculiar sect that promoted licentious behavior—"Rasputin" was the nickname he was given because it means, "debauched one." Rasputin entered the royal circle in 1903 in the height of the popularity of the occult among the socially elite. He did not meet the royal family until 1905, but quickly gained favor particularly with the Czarina because he was able to help control the young Alexander's bleeding due to his hemophilia. Evidence suggests that Rasputin engaged his hypnotic prowess to calm the child which resulted in easing the bleeding.

During the same period, Russian philosopher and mystic, **Peter Demianovitch Ouspensky,** (1878–1947) who was a disciple of **Georgei Ivanovitch Gurdijeff** in connection with the Theosophy movement of **Helena Petrovna Blavatsky** began to rise to prominence in small elite circles of Europe. According to Peter Washington in his 1993 book, *Madame Blavatsky's Baboon,* "The self-taught Ouspensky was tempted more by Luciferean visions of self-transcendance, dreaming of a humanity remade in the image of gods by its own strenuous efforts." Ouspensky was never officially a member of the **Theosophical Society,** which was banned in Russia until 1908. By 1914 when World War I began and the revolution in Russia became imminent, Ouspensky moved away from Theosophy. He was in an ongoing search to raise consciousness—his own and others—in order to understand why, as was his belief, humans continued to relive past lives, and past mistakes.

In the modern era, especially during the 1960s, there was widespread modern interest in parapsychology in the USSR. Its popularity emerged again after the ultraconservative science of the Stalin era. One of the pioneers in this psychic renaissance was **Leonid L. Vasiliev** (1891–1966), who helped to establish the first parapsychology laboratory in the Soviet Union, at Leningrad. His book *Mysterious Manifestations of the Human Psyche* (1959) was published in the United States under the title *Mysterious Phenomena of the Human Psyche* (University Books, 1965).

One possible stimulus for Soviet interest in **extrasensory perception** (ESP) was the belief that ESP might have military significance. In 1959, a story was leaked in the French press that the United States Navy had experimented with telepathic communication between the atomic submarine *Nautilus* and a shore base.

Another surprising Soviet interest was disclosed in the readiness of the authorities to permit lectures and demonstrations by Hindu hatha yogis. This had nothing to do with prerevolutionary bourgeois cults of mysticism, but rather indicated willingness to learn about the alleged paranormal physical feats claimed for **yoga.** Russians have always placed great importance on physical training and sport. In addition, any system of physical culture that promised unusual feats of endurance or control of automatic nervous functions might also have relevance to the physical stresses involved in space travel.

By 1966 the Soviet Union was financing more than twenty centers for the scientific study of the paranormal, involving an annual budget of around 12 to 20 million rubles ($13 to $21 million). Soviet parapsychologists studied reports of such American psychics as **Edgar Cayce, Jeane Dixon,** and **Ted Serios,** as well as the parapsychological research of **J. B. Rhine** and his colleagues.

Throughout the 1960s, Soviet parapsychologists investigated the phenomena of their own sensitives in such fields as **dowsings, psychokinesis, telepathy,** psychic **healing,** and **eyeless sight.** Soviet individuals such as **Nina Kulagina** in psychokinesis and **Rosa Kuleshova** who claimed abilities such as fingertip vision (eyeless sight) became widely known and discussed even outside the Soviet Union.

Perhaps because of such international publicity, Soviet authorities sporadically suppressed information on parapsychological research, while a backlash of dogmatic conservatism impeded parapsychology studies. The essentially practical investigations into paranormal faculties by Soviet scientists did hold out hope through the 1970s that they might achieve a real breakthrough in such fields of study.

In his book *Psychic Warfare: Threat or Illusion?* (1983), Martin Ebon claims that in the early 1970s the KGB took over extensive parapsychological research to attempt to identify **psi** particles in order to discover unknown communication channels in living cells for the transfer of information and to conduct follow-up studies on such subjects as **hypnosis** at a distance. On a popular level, interest has grown in such areas as **thoughtography** and **UFOs.**

In the book *Psychic Discoveries Behind the Iron Curtain* (1970), Sheila Ostrander and Lynn Schroeder revealed the wide range of Soviet research in parapsychology. Much of their book was based on firsthand interviews and observations during visits to the Soviet Union and other Eastern European countries. The book is useful as a record of information on individuals and organizations at the peak of Communist psychic research.

Eyeless Sight and Psychokinesis

Rosa Kuleshova, exponent of fingertip vision or eyeless sight, reportedly suffered from overexposure of her talent and for a time was accused of cheating before her strange abilities were reasserted. Meanwhile, Abram Novemeisky at the Nizhnig Tagil Pedagogical Institute in the Urals experimented with graphic arts students; he claimed that one in six individuals could distinguish between two colors by fingertip vision.

Yakov Fishelev of the Sverdlovsk Pedagogical Institute confirmed such findings and also experimented with subjects at the Pyshma school for the blind, starting with fingertip color recognition and then developing the ability to distinguish shapes of letters. S. N. Dobronravov of Sverdlovsk reported that he had found "skin sight" potential in 72 percent of children, mostly between the ages of 7 and 12.

At the Filatov Institute Laboratory of the Physiology of Vision, in Odessa, an experiment was conducted by Dr. Andrei Shevalev. His subject was Vania Dubrovich, an eight-year-old boy blind from early childhood, whose eyes and optical nerves had been removed. Shevalev attached a lens to Vania's forehead, and the boy learned to distinguish degrees of light through the lens. This experiment claimed to open up new possibilities of "skin glasses."

In the field of psychokinesis (PK), the unusual ability of Nina Kulagina to move small objects at a distance without contact was first discovered by L. L. Vasiliev, after Kulagina had demonstrated a talent for "skin vision." Vasiliev found that she could influence a compass needle by holding her hands over it. In further PK tests it was discovered that she could disturb or move objects at a distance. Film records were made demonstrating her PK ability. Among other feats Kulagina apparently changed the flow of sand in an hourglass and made letters appear on photographic paper by mental force. In early reports, her identity was at first hidden under the pseudonym Nelya Mikhailovna.

In March 1988 Kulagina won a libel action against the magazine *Man and Law,* published by the Soviet Justice Ministry. Two articles by Vyacheslav Strelkov published in the magazine described her as "a swindler and a crook." The Moscow court ruled that Strelkov had no firm evidence on which to base his allegations, and the magazine was ordered to publish an apology. In a subsequent appeal to the Moscow city court, the district court's ruling was upheld: "the articles published by *Man and Law* besmirch the honor and dignity of Nina Kulagina and. . .it must publish an apology."

Recent Developments

In the freer atmosphere of public debate and expression of opinion arising from the Mikhail Gorbachev policy of *glasnost,* public support and discussion of psychic matters increased. Psychic healing received much attention, and the healer Barbara Ivanova treated many prominent officials. She has also undertaken distant healing through the telephone.

In the field of dowsing and **radiesthesia,** Soviet scientists like G. Bogomolov and Nikolai Sochevanov have collected data to support the reality of such phenomena. With recently developed techniques and apparatus, dowsers have been used to locate damaged cables, water pipes, and electrical lines, as well as underground minerals and water. One series of dowsing tests suggested that women dowsers have a higher ability than men. Dowsing and radiesthetic work is now reported as the "biophysical effect."

Soviet experiments in telepathy are well advanced. Vasiliev studied spontaneous telepathy for nearly 40 years and collected hundreds of circumstantial accounts. In 1967 Yuri Kamensky in Moscow claimed to successfully relayed a telepathic message to Karl Nikolaiev in Leningrad; the message was in a form of Morse code. Other telepathy experiments involved the transmission of emotions, monitored by EEG records. A number of experiments were conducted to ascertain optimum conditions for telepathic transmission, involving a complex of touch, visualization, and thought.

Sometimes a biological sympathy between sender and receiver (heartbeat, brain wave, and similar synchronism) was found to facilitate transmission. Even the influence of high-frequency electromagnetic waves on telepathy was studied, while the neurologist Vladimir Bekhterev experimented with telepathy between human beings and animals.

One development in Soviet parapsychology claiming a significant amount of attention in the 1970s was **Kirlian photography,** developed by Semyon D. Kirlian and Valentina C. Kirlian, as a method of photographing a corona discharge in human beings and other objects both living and inanimate. It was hoped that an auralike phenomena had been discovered, but the effects reported early in experimentation were later shown to be an effect of differential pressure placed on the film by objects being photographed.

In 1960 the Soviet Academy of Sciences declared that the search for UFOs was "unscientific." However it seems that reports of UFOs were closely studied, a matter of control of Soviet air space, and some Soviet researchers were prepared to consider the possibility of extraterrestrial intelligences.

Over the past two or three decades, there have been many reports of UFO phenomena from the USSR. On October 9, 1989, the Soviet news agency, TASS, astonished the world by reporting claims that a UFO had landed on the evening of September 27, 1989, in a park at Voronezh, a city of 900,000 inhabitants some three hundred miles southeast of Moscow, and that the UFO occupants had walked about and been seen by many people (cf. *Flying Saucer Review,* vol. 34, no. 4, 1898).

The practical and scientific investigations of Soviet scientists into every major aspect of the paranormal was in sharp contrast to the more romantic interest of Western countries, where psychics demonstrate for entertainment. The down-to-earth Soviet approach into the how and why of the paranormal appeared to be yielding results with clearly practical applications.

The strong, and long-held folk traditions of the Russian people are expected to emerge as the country re-shapes its identity. In his book, *The Russian Challenge and the Year 2000,* Russian ex-patriate Alexander Yanov, living in the United States since 1975, discussed the issues facing the country since the fall of the Soviet Empire. He noted that, "Orthodox marxisim has been exhausted as an ideological resource for the system, just as the ideology of tsarism was exhausted at the beginning of the twentieth century. Alternative ideological resources are needed to enable the empire to survive a 'systemic' crisis." Published two years before the fall of the Berlin Wall, Yanov's book offered an interesting perspective while reform was anticipated. As Russians continue to pursue a free, elective government as a commonwealth, political reform will begin to shape other apsects of Russian life, as well. The curiosity that they have demonstrated for centuries regarding the inner workings of their consciousness—throughout artistic, cultural and religious pursuit especially—could evolve dramatically in the area of parapsychology, as well. While continuing in the economically stressed atmosphere of the demise of the USSR and the emergence of the Commonwealth of Independent States, parapsychology has suffered and its future is as yet not discernible. (See also **Slavs**)

Sources:

[Note: For an authoritative survey of Soviet research in parapsychology and psychotronics, see the journal *Psi Research,* edited by Larissa Vilenskaya, published quarterly by Washington Research Institute and Parapsychology Research Group, San Francisco, California.]

Berger, Arthur S., and Joyce Berger. *The Encyclopedia of Parapsychology and Psychical Research.* New York: Paragon House, 1991.

Ebon, Martin. *Psychic Discoveries by the Russians.* New York: Parapsychology Foundation, 1963. Reprint, New York: New American Library, 1971.

———. *Psychic Warfare: Threat or Illusion?* New York: McGraw-Hill, 1983.

Hobana, Ion, and J. Weverbergh. *Unidentified Flying Objects from Behind the Iron Curtain.* London: Souvenir Press, 1974. Reprint, London: Corgi, 1975.

Ostrander, Sheila, and Lynn Schroeder. *Psychic Discoveries Behind the Iron Curtain.* Englewood Cliffs, N.J.: Prentice-Hall, 1970. Reprint, New York: Bantam, 1971.

Washington, Peter. *Madame Blavatsky's Baboon.* New York: Schocken Books, 1993.

Yanov, Alexander. *The Russian Challenge and the Year 2000.* Oxford: Basil Blackwell, 1987.

Rutot's Spirit Indicator See **Vandermeulen Spirit Indicator**

Ruysbroek (or **Ruysbrock**), **Jan van** (1293–1381)

Flemish mystic, whose name probably derived from the village of Ruysbroek, near Brussels, where he was born in 1293. As a child he showed distinct religious inclinations and spent his adolescence exploring a wealth of mystical literature. He decided to follow the clerical profession, and in 1317 he was duly ordained. A little later he became vicar of St. Gudule, a parish in Brussels.

During his long term in this capacity he became widely esteemed for his erudition and for his personal piety, while his sermons and even his letters were passed from hand to hand and perused with great admiration by many of his fellow clerics.

He did not court fame nor publicity of any kind, and at the age of sixty he retired to Groenendale, not far from the battlefield of Waterloo, where he founded a monastery. There he lived until his death, devoting himself chiefly to the study and practice of mysticism, and maintaining those charitable actions befitting a monk. Ruysbroek was known to his disciples as "the ecstatic teacher." As a thinker he was speculative and broad-minded, and indeed was one of those who prefigured the Reformation, the result being that although he won the encomiums of many famous theologians in the age immediately succeeding his, an attempt to beatify him was sternly suppressed.

Ruysbroek wrote a great deal, and at Cologne, in 1552, one of his manuscripts found its way into print with the title, *De Naptu svel de Ornatu Nuptiarum Spiritualium,* while subsequently a number of his other works were published, notably *De Vera Contemplatione* and *De Septem Gradivus Amoris* (Hanover, 1848).

The central tenet of his teaching was that "the soul finds God in its own depths." But in contradistinction to many other mystics, he did not teach the fusion of the self in God, holding that at the summit of the ascent toward righteousness the soul still preserves its identity. Ruysbroek and his teaching gave rise to many voluminous commentaries throughout the Middle Ages, and he has attracted a number of great writers.

Ruysbroek died in 1381.

Sources:

Jones, Rufus Matthew. *Studies in Mystical Religion.* N.p., 1909. Reprint, New York: Russell & Russell, 1970.

Maeterlinck, Maurice *L'Ornemant des Noces Spirituelles, de Ruysbroeck l'admirable.* English ed. as: *Ruysbroeck and the Mystics with Selections fron Ruysbroeck.* N.p., 1894.

Ryerson, Kevin (1953–)

Kevin Ryerson is a contemporary channel who became nationally known due to his association with actress **Shirley MacLaine,** who wrote about her interaction with him in her international best-seller *Out on a Limb* (1983). Born in 1953, Ryerson's childhood consisted of a number of psychic experiences, which he came to understand during his teen years in light of his study of occult literature. He joined a study group sponsored by the **Association of Research and Enlightenment (ARE),** through which he studied the **Edgar Cayce** materials and learned to meditate. One evening, during a meeting of his ARE study group, Ryerson slipped into a trance, and a voice claiming to be a spirit guide, "John," began to speak through him.

The study group members became fascinated with "John" and with Ryerson's **channeling** and began to tape the sessions. "John" identified himself as the biblical apostle John and said that he had returned to assist people in the transformational process and make them aware of the Christ within. Ryerson later sought out Richard Ireland, a Spiritualist medium from Phoenix, Arizona, and was eventually licensed as a minister by Ireland's University of Life Church. In 1976 Ryerson became a full-time professional channel.

Ryerson's career has encompassed several projects. In 1979 he met Gurudas, an herbalist and natural healing practitioner. Gurudas taped a number of channeling sessions at which "John" spoke of natural healing processes and substances, which became the basis of a series of books. Early in the 1980s Ryerson met Shirley MacLaine and conducted several channeling sessions with her. The convincing nature of these sessions was quite important to her development, and Ryerson subsequently recreated their meetings for the film version of *Out on a Limb* (book, 1983; movie, 1987). He has also made several other media appearances, in *Poltergeist II, The Magic Boat,* and *Palooka.* Ryerson's character is also featured in MacLaine's books *Dancing in the Light* (1985) and *It's All in the Playing* (1987). He allowed himself to be studied by Dr. Jeffrey Mishlove and William Krautz at the Center for Applied Intuition.

Ryerson has his own website at http://www.kevinryerson.com/.

Sources:

Gurudas. *Flower Essences.* Albuquerque, N.Mex.: Brotherhood of Life, 1983.

Kevin Ryerson Home Page. http://www.kevinryerson.com/. May 30, 2000.

———. *Gem Elixirs and Vibrational Healing.* 2 vols. Boulder, Colo.: Cassandra Press, 1985–86.

MacLaine, Shirley. *Dancing in the Light.* New York: Bantam Books, 1985.

———. *Out on a Limb.* New York: Bantam Books, 1983.

Raskin, Paula B. "Kevin Ryerson." *Pychic Guide* 4, no. 4 (March–April 1986): 16–21.

Ryerson, Kevin. *Spirit Communication of the Souls.* New York: Bantam Books, 1991.

Ryzl, Milan (1928–)

Czech biochemist who experimented in the field of parapsychology. Born May 22, 1928, at Prague, Czechoslovakia, he studied at Charles University, Prague (D.Sc., 1952). He became a biochemist at the Institute of Biology of the Czechoslovak Academy of Science, was a charter associate of the **Parapsychology Association,** and the winner of the 1962 McDougall Award for parapsychology research. He is considered one of the leading authorities on parapsychology in the West.

Ryzl took a special interest in paranormal cognition of subjects under hypnosis, and developed a method by which the **ESP** of such subjects may be brought under voluntary control. He organized a parapsychology study group in Prague, but later defected from Czechoslovakia and obtained a position as a biochemist at San José College, California. He worked for a time at the Parapsychology Laboratory at Duke University and in 1963 wrote a series of papers with **J. G. Pratt.** He is credited as being the first person to write on parapsychology in Communist Europe.

Sources:

Ryzl, Milan. "How Not to Test a Psychic." *Journal of Parapsychology* 54 (September 1990).

———. "Training the Psi Faculty by Hypnosis." *Journal* of the Society for Psychical Research 41 (1962).

Ryzl, Milan, and J. T. Barendregt, P. R. Barkema, and Jan Kappers. "An ESP Experiment in Prague." *Journal of Parapsychology* 29 (1965).

Ryzl, Milan, and J. Bekoff. "Loss of Stability of ESP Performance in a High-Scoring Subject." *Journal of Parapsychology* 29 (1965).

Ryzl, Milan, and J. G. Pratt. "The Focusing of ESP Upon Particular Targets." *Journal of Parapsychology* 27 (1963).

———. "A Further Confirmation of Stabilized ESP Performance in a Selected Subject." *Journal of Parapsychology* 27 (1963).

———. "A Repeated-Calling ESP Test with Sealed Cards." *Journal of Parapsychology* 27 (1963).

S

S.I.

Initialism for **Space Intelligence.**

Saba

In ancient Irish legend, the wife of **Finn Mac Cummal** and mother of Oisin. Finn captured her in the form of a fawn while hunting, but noticing that his hounds would not hurt her, he gave her shelter. The next morning he found her transformed into a beautiful woman. She told him than an enchanter had compelled her to take the shape of a fawn, but that her original form would be restored when she reached Dun Allen, where she had just spent the night. Finn made her his wife and ceased for a while from battle and hunting.

Hearing one day that the Northmen's warships were in the Bay of Dublin, he mustered his men and went to fight them. He returned victorious, but found Saba gone. The enchanter, taking advantage of Finn's absence, had appeared to her in the likeness of Finn with his hounds and lured her from the dun. Away from the dun, she became a fawn again.

Sabbats

In modern Neo-Paganism, the sabbats are the eight great festivals of the sacred year. The sabbats follow the ancient festival days that were common throughout Europe, though different cultures poured variant meanings into their celebrations. Over the centuries, as Christianity became the dominant form in the West, ancient pagan worship sites were replaced with churches and the festival days integrated into the Christian liturgical calendar. Many of these older pagan festivals survived in secularized form and many of the practices were reinterpreted by Christians, especially the Yule (winter solstice) practices that became part of the celebration of Christmas.

The eight sabbats are defined by the principal points in the changing relationship of the Sun and the Earth over the year. These points are measured by the easily observable point of the sun's daily emergence on the eastern horizon. Through the spring, as the days grow longer, the sun appears to rise at a point slightly further north each day and then as the days reach their longest, it appears to pause and then start moving south. As the shortest day of the year is reached, it again pauses and starts north. The points of the pauses (the solstices), and half way between them, when the length of the day and night are equal (the equinoxes, formed four easily marked points in the years. They, and the four additional points halfway between them that mark points in the planting and harvest process, became the eight evenly spaced holidays of the ancient world.

During the Middle Ages, the ancient Pagan practices were invoked to supply content with the new understanding of **Witchcraft** as **Satanism** advocated by the Inquisition. The sabbats were identified as a time for Witches to gather to worship His Infernal Majesty. That mythology survived in the secularized celebration of Halloween.

In the 1950s, **Gerald B. Gardner** introduced his modern reconstruction of Witchcraft which drew on ancient Pagan practices mixed with elements of Asian beliefs and practices. It was a nature oriented religion in which the worship of the Goddess was central. Integral to the new Witchcraft were the ancient eight festivals that became times of gathering for the emerging Pagan community. In the Wiccan faith, the years begin on the evening of October 31, Samhein. This day culminated the harvest season, and heralds the coming of winter, a period of waiting until the planting can begin a new food production cycle. It is also a night in which the veil between the living and the dead is thin and communication with spirits is facilitated. It is a time to remember the dead and complete relationships with them.

Seven other sabbats follow:

Yule (December 21)
Imbolc or Candlemas (Feb 1)
Spring equinox
Beltane (May 1)
Summer solstice
Lamas (August 1)
Fall Equinox

These festivals marked important events in agricultural communities, though most modern Pagans are urban dwellers. In the rituals, while some recognition of their past significance is still noted, the sabbats have been reinterpreted as occasions for personal magic and reformation and the veneration of the deities.

As distinct from the eight major Sabbats, witchcraft covens also hold a bi-monthly **esbat** at each new and full moon. These are the coven's regular meetings for its ongoing magical work and group worship. (See also **litanies** of the sabbat)

Sources:

Ravenwolf, Silver. *To Ride a Silver Broomstick: New Generation Witchcraft.* St. Paul, Minn.: Llewellyn Publications, 1995.

Valiente, Doreen. *The ABC of Witchcraft Past and Present.* New York: St. Martin's Press, 1973.

Sabbathi

This angel, in the Jewish rabbinical legend of the celestial hierarchies, is assigned the sphere of Saturn. He receives the divine light of the Holy Spirit and communicates it to the dwellers in his kingdom.

Sabellicus, Georgius (ca. 1490)

A magician who lived about the same time as the legendary necromancer **Faust,** at the end of the fifteenth century. Sabellicus's chief claim to fame as a sorcerer rests on his own wide and arrogant advertisement of his skill in **necromancy.** He styled himself: "The most accomplished Georgius Sabellicus, a second Faustus, the spring and centre of necromantic art, an astrologer, a magician, consummate in chiromancy, and in agromancy, pyromancy and hydromancy inferior to none that ever lived." However, no proof is forthcoming that he ever substantiated these claims.

Sabian Assembly

Founded in Los Angeles, California, in 1923 by **Marc Edmund Jones,** the Sabian Assembly is dedicated to the "mastery of self and the world." The object of the assembly was the restoration of the Solar Mysteries.

Jones was a writer and exponent of astrology, and for many years students of the assembly requested him to give spontaneous interpretations of charts without study or prior knowledge of them. Five hundred of these horoscope sessions were tape-recorded and transcribed, and the first volume of *The Marc Edmund Jones 500* was published in 1977 by ASI Publishers, Inc. Address: P.O. Box 417, 1 Faurie Rd., Lakehills, TX 78063. Website: http://www.sabian.org.

Sabine, William H(enry) W(aldo) (1903–1994)

Author, historian and writer on parapsychological subjects. He was born on April 2, 1903, in Birkenhead, England. He was educated in private schools and emigrated to the United States in 1947. Before leaving England, Sabine taught at schools in Middlesex and London. In the United States he worked as an author, editor, and book dealer from 1947 onward, and he completed a number of books on American and European history. He had a number of spontaneous psi experiences, mainly of a precognitive kind, some of which he recorded in his book *Second Sight in Daily Life* (1949).

He died on July 13, 1994.

Sources:

Pleasants, Helene, ed. *Biographical Dictionary of Parapsychology.* New York: Helix Press, 1964.

Sabine, William Henry Waldo. "Is There a Case for Retrocognition?" *Journal of the American Society for Psychical Research* 44 (April 1950): 43–64. Reprint as *Surveys in Parapsychology.* Edited by Rhea A. White. 1976.

———. *A Prophecy Concerning the Swedish Monarchy.* N.p., 1968.

Strommenburg, Aaders Gabriel. *A Prophecy Concerning the Swedish Monarchy As It was Related in 1809.* New York: Colburn & Tegg, 1968.

———. *Second Sight in Daily Life.* New York: Coward-McCann, 1949.

SAC See Society for the Anthropology of Consciousness

SAC See Spiritual Advisory Council

Sacha Runa

Sacha Runa is the name of a section of the Amazonian Rain Forest at the upper reaches of the Madeira River in northern Bolivia. It is an area where **shamans** still function as religious functionaries for the residents. The Sacha Runa people describe themselves as the people who know how to live on the Earth and who are descended from ancestors in ancient times.

Stepping into this ancient culture is Bolivian spiritual seeker/guide Miguel A. Kavlin. Kavlin grew up in Bolivia but moved to the United States when he was 17, where he resided for a time amid the ancient Anazazi site in the Southwest. At a gathering of Sun Dance followers he met Beautiful Painted Arrow, a Ute painter and visionary with whom he began to study. He moved on to complete his graduate studies in anthropology and philosophy. He also studied martial arts and traditional Chinese medicine.

In 1987, Kavlin went to Peru, where in the rain forest near Iquitios, he met and became a student of Don Agustin Rivas Vazques. He eventually was authorized by Don Agustin to conduct rituals outside of Peru, and in 1989, Kavlin began to take people to Peru to meet with Don Agustin. In the early 1990s, he returned to his homeland where he met two Bolivian shamans, Don Hector Aguanari and Don Jose Coral, and began studying with them. In 1996, Kavlin built what he termed a Peace Chamber, an underground ceremonial space for people to use and dedicated to instilling in all who come to it a heart of peace.

All of the people and events in Kavlin's life have subsequently come together in Sacha Runa Productions, the organization through which he brings people to Peru and Bolivia to meet with his teachers and to experience the shamanistic culture. Integral to that culture is the production and use of **ayahuasca,** a brew made from locally grown plants that have a psychedelic effect upon those who consume them.

Kavlin sees the meeting of modern Westerners with indigenous leaders as a tool in assisting them in reconnecting with the life-giving forces of the universe. It empowers them to become their own teacher as they realize their own self-knowledge and reach a point of self-realization. Self-realized people will, Kavlin believes, become pillars of the next generation and real caretakers within the culture.

Sacha Runa Productions may be reached through its website at http://www.sacharuna.com/.

Sources

Sacha Runa. http://www.sacharuna.com/. February 12, 2000.

SAFE Newsletter

Quarterly publication of the Society for the Application of Free Energy (associated with the **Mankind Research Foundation**), dealing with **dowsing, radiesthesia** and **pyramid** energies. Last known address: 1640 Kalmia Rd., Washington, DC 20012.

Saga UFO Report

A magazine, now out of print, edited by Martin M. Singer and published in the 1980s ten times a year by Gambi Publications in Brooklyn, New York. It was a spin-off of *Saga Magazine,* a long-running men's magazine that carried UFO articles during the 1970s, a time when many periodicals discontinued these articles following the skeptical **Condon Report.**

SAGB See Spiritualist Association of Great Britian

Sahu

The Egyptian name for the spiritual or incorruptible body. It is symbolized in the *Book of the Dead* by a lily springing from the Khat, or corruptible body.

Sai Baba (ca. 1856–1918)

Indian spiritual teacher and mystic who, like the celebrated spiritual poet **Kabir,** was accepted equally by both Hindus and Moslems. Little is known of his early life. It is believed that he was born into a Brahmin family in Hyderabad State, left home at an early age to follow a Moslem fakir, and on the death of his teacher became attached to a Hindu guru whom he called

"Venkusa." Even these details are uncertain, however, since there was a profound symbolism attached to all the utterances of Sai Baba.

It is known that in 1872 he appeared as a lad of 16 in the village of Shirdi, in the Ahmadnagar district of Bombay. He first attempted to settle at a small Hindu temple but was asked to go to a half-ruined mosque nearby.

He made his home at the mud-walled mosque, where he kept an oil lamp burning and occasionally smoked a clay pipe. He muttered to himself and performed such strange secret rites as emptying and refilling water pots, regarded by devotees as symbolic gestures relating to divine grace. His actions and instructions were unconventional and erratic but often culminated in a great many extraordinary miracles and an outpouring of divine grace. His following grew among both Hindus and Moslems.

In 1886, almost as a rehearsal for death, he told a devotee that he was going to Allah and that his body should be preserved carefully for three days against a possible return. His heart stopped beating, his breathing ceased, and local authorities pronounced him dead. On the third day he opened his eyes and started breathing again.

Sai Baba died October 15, 1918, and was buried in a Hindu shrine. Since his death, the miracle-working guru **Satya Sai Baba** has been regarded by many devotees as a reincarnation of Sai Baba.

Sources:

Osborne, Arthur. *The Incredible Sai Baba.* New Delhi: Orient Longmans, 1957.

Pradhan, Rao Bahadur M. W. *Shri Sai Baba of Shirdi: A Glimpse of Indian Spirituality.* Bandra, India: R. A. Turkhud, n.d.

Saintes Maries de la Mer

A small village in the Camargue, France, on the shores of the Mediterranean, where every year, about the 24th and 25th of May, **gypsies** congregate to celebrate the feast day of their patron saint Sara. Sara, seemingly a survival of the Indian deity Kali, has been tied to Christian folklore in a story of the three Marys of the Christian New Testament traveling to France. Upon their arrival they were met and assisted by Sara. Like Kali, Sara is pictured with black skin. The Gypsies gather to keep a vigil before the statue that has been set up in the basement of the church.

Sources:

Clébert, Jean-Paul. *The Gypsies.* Hammondsworth, UK: Penguin Books, 1967.

Saint Germain, Comte de (ca. 1710–ca. 1780)

One of the most celebrated mystic adventurers in history. Like **Cagliostro** and others of his kind, little is known concerning Saint Germain's origin, but there is reason to believe that he was a Portuguese Jew. There were claims that he was of royal birth, but these have never been substantiated.

It is fairly certain that he was an accomplished spy, for he resided at many European courts, spoke and wrote various languages, including Greek, Latin, Sanskrit, Arabic, Chinese, French, German, English, Italian, Portuguese, and Spanish, and was even sent upon diplomatic missions by Louis XV. Horace Walpole mentioned him being in London about 1743 and being arrested as a Jacobite spy, but later being released.

Walpole wrote: "He is called an Italian, a Spaniard, a Pole, a somebody who married a great fortune in Mexico and ran away with her jewels to Constantinople, a priest, a fiddler, a vast nobleman. The Prince of Wales has had unsatiated curiosity about him, but in vain. However, nothing has been made out against him; he is released, and, what convinces me he is not a gentleman, stays here, and talks of his being taken up as a spy."

Saint Germain claimed to have lived for centuries and to have known Solomon, the Queen of Sheba, and many other persons of antiquity. Although regarded as a charlatan, the accomplishments upon which he based his reputation were in many ways real and considerable. He was alluded to by Baron Friedrich Melchior Grimm as the most capable and able man he had ever known. He was a composer of music and a capable performer on the violin.

This was especially the case regarding chemistry (or **alchemy**), a science in which he was certainly adept. He claimed to have a secret for removing the flaws from diamonds, to be able to transmute metals, and to possess the secret of the **elixir of life.**

Five years after this London experience, Saint Germain attached himself to the court of Louis XV, where he exercised considerable influence over the monarch and was employed on several secret missions. He was much sought after and discussed, since at this time Europe was fascinated by the occult, and Saint Germain combined mystical conversation with a pleasing, flippant character, he was extremely popular. But he ruined his chances at the French court by interfering in a dispute between Austria and France, and he was forced to leave for England.

He resided in London for one or two years, but in 1762 was in St. Petersburg, where he is said to have assisted in the conspiracy that placed Catherine II on the Russian throne. After this he traveled in Germany, where he was reported in the *Memoirs of Cagliostro* to have become the founder of **Freemasonry,** and to have initiated Cagliostro into that rite. If Cagliostro's account can be credited, Saint Germain set about the business with remarkable splendor and bombast, posing as a "deity" and behaving in a manner calculated to delight pseudo-mystics of the age.

Saint Germain died at Schleswig, Germany, somewhere between the years 1780 and 1785, but the exact date of his death and its circumstances are unknown.

Assessing Saint Germain's Career

It would be difficult to say whether Saint Germain really possessed genuine occult power. A great many people of his own time thoroughly believed in him, but we must also remember the credulous nature of the age in which he flourished. It has been said that eighteenth-century Europe was skeptical regarding everything except occultism and its professors.

Saint Germain possessed a magnificent collection of precious stones, which some considered to be artificial, but others believed to be genuine. He presented Louis XV with a diamond worth 10,000 livres (a livre is an old French monetary unit).

All sorts of stories were in circulation concerning Saint Germain. One old lady professed to have encountered him at Venice fifty years before, posing as a man of sixty, and even his valet was supposed to have discovered the secret of immortality. On one occasion a visitor teased this man, asking if he had been present at the marriage of Cana in Galilee. "You forget, sir," was the reply, "I have only been in the Comte's service a century."

Legend has it that Saint Germain made various appearances after his death. He is said to have appeared to Marie Antoinette and to other individuals during the French Revolution. He was also believed to have been one of the **Rosicrucians,** from whom he obtained his occult knowledge.

The deathless count was also resurrected in modern times by **Helena Petrovna Blavatsky** as one of the masters of the Great White Brotherhood, and he thus became an important figure in all of the more than a hundred theosophical splinter groups now active. **Guy W. Ballard** claimed that Saint Germain had appeared to him at Mt. Shasta, California, and from Saint Germain's teachings, Ballard built the **I Am Movement.** The centrality of Saint Germain has been common to all "I Am"-

related groups such as the Bridge to Spiritual Freedom and the **Church Universal and Triumphant.** Within the New Age movement, a number of psychics have emerged **channeling** an entity called Saint Germain. In the 1970s, author Chelsea Quinn Yarbro drew on the Saint Germain story to begin production of a series of novels and short stories that describe the mysterious count as a **vampire.** The novels helped begin the current popular interest in the vampire as hero.

Sources:

Cooper-Oakley, Isabel. *The Comte de Saint-Germain.* New York: S. Weiser, 1970.

King, Godfre Ray [Guy Ballard]. *Unveiled Mysteries.* Chicago: Saint Germain Press, 1934.

Lang, Andrew. *Historical Mysteries.* London: Smith, Elder, 1904.

Prophet, Elizabeth Clare. *Saint Germain on Prophecy.* Livingston, Mont.: Summit University Press, 1986.

Prophet, Mark L., and Elizabeth Clare Prophet. *Saint Germain on Alchemy.* Livingston, N.Y.: Summit University Press, 1962.

Seligmann, Kurt. *Magic, Supernaturalism, and Religion.* New York: Pantheon Press, 1971.

Wraxall, Lascelles. *Remarkable Adventurers and Unrevealed Mysteries.* 2 vols. London, 1863.

Yarbro, Chelsea Quinn. *The Vampire Stories of Chelsea Quinn Yarbro.* White Rock, BC: Transylvania Press, 1994.

Saint-Jacques, R. P. de

A monk of the seventeenth century, who published a book entitled *Lumiere aux vivants par l'expérience des morts, ou diverses apparitions des âmes du Purgatoire* (Light to the living by the experiences of the dead, or divers apparitions of souls from purgatory) in Lyons in 1675.

Saint-Martin, Louis Claude de (1743–1803)

French mystic and philosopher, commonly known as "le philosophe inconnu" (the unknown philosopher), the pseudonym under which his books were published. The name of Louis de Saint-Martin is a familiar one, which is partly due to his having been a voluminous author, and partly due to his being virtually the founder of a sect, the Martinistes. Literary critic Augustin Sainte-Beuve wrote about him in his *Causeries du Lundi.* Saint-Martin was born on January 18, 1743, at Amboise. He came from a family of some wealth, but his mother died while he was a child. Fortunately his stepmother, besides lavishing a wealth of affection on him, early discerned his rare intellectual gifts and made every effort to nurture them.

The boy was educated at the Collège de Pontlevoy, where he read with interest numerous books of a mystical order. One that impressed him particularly was Jacques Abbadie's *Art de se connaître soi-même* (1692). At first he intended to make law his profession, but he soon decided on a military career instead and accordingly entered the army. A little before taking this step, he affiliated himself with the Freemasons, and when his regiment was sent to the garrison at Bordeaux, he became intimate with certain mystical rites that **Martines de Pasqually** had introduced into the masonic lodge there. His immersion in the philosophy of Pasqually, who became his teacher, and the writings of **Emanuel Swedenborg** alienated him from regimental life, and thus, in 1771, he resigned his commission, determined to devote the rest of his life to philosophical speculations.

He then began writing a book *Des Erreurs et de la Vérite, ou les Hommes rappelés au Principe de la Science,* which was published in 1775 at Edinburgh, Scotland, at this time a center of literary activity. This initial work by Saint-Martin was brought to the notice of Voltaire, the old cynic observing shrewdly that half a dozen folio volumes might well be devoted to the topic of *erreurs,* but that a page would suffice for the treatment of *vérité!*

The next years were spent in travel to England, Italy, and Germany (where an interest in the teachings of the mystic **Jakob Boehme** would eventually lead to his translating a number of the German mystic's writings into French). He never married, but he appears to have exercised a most extraordinary fascination over women, and in fact various scandalous stories were told, some of them implicating various courtly women of the French nobility.

Upon returning to France, he found his outlook suddenly changed. The revolution had broken out in 1789, and a reign of terror had set in. No one was safe. Saint-Martin was arrested in Paris simply because he was a gentleman by birth, but he was saved by his affiliation with the Freemasons. He resumed writing, and in 1792 he issued a new book, *Le Nouvel Homme.* Two years later he was commissioned to go to his native Amboise, inspect the archives and libraries of the monasteries in that region, and draw up occasional reports on the subject.

Shortly afterward, he was appointed an *élève professeur* at the *École Normale* in Paris, in consequence of which he now made his home in that city. He became acquainted there with Chateaubriand, of whose writing Saint-Martin was an enthusiastic devotee, but who appears to have received the mystic with his usual haughty coldness.

Saint-Martin had a large circle of admirers, and he continued to work hard, publishing in 1795 one of his most important books, *Lèttres à un Ami, ou Considérations politiques, philosophiques et réligieuses sur la Révolution,* which was succeeded in 1800 by two speculative treatises: *Ecce Homo* and *L'Esprit des Choses.* What proved to be his final volume appeared in 1802 as *Ministère de l'Homme Esprit.* In the following year his labors were brought to an abrupt close, for while staying at Annay, not far from Paris, with a friend, he succumbed to an apoplectic seizure, and died October 23, 1803. After his death it was found that he had left a considerable mass of manuscripts, and some of these were issued by his executors in 1807. In 1862 a collection of his letters appeared.

Martinism

As a philosopher, Saint-Martin found a host of disciples among his contemporaries, who gradually formed themselves into a cult and took the name of their teacher. His teachings are best summarized in his latter volumes *L'Homme du Désir* (1790) and *Tableau natural des Rapports qui existent entre Dieu, et l'Homme et l'Univers* (1782).

He suggests that human beings are divine, despite the fall recounted in the Hebrew/Christian scriptures. Dormant within lies a lofty quality of which we are too often scarcely conscious, and it is incumbent on us to develop this quality, striving without ceasing and avoiding the snares of materialism. This lifestyle is exemplified by a life of occult striving. This basic perspective is common to the Gnostic writings of the Rosicrucians, past and contemporary theosophists, and ritual magicians. In writing in this vein, Saint-Martin owed a good deal to Freemasonry, Swedenborg, and Boehme. Saint-Martin also developed a system of numerical correspondences that are easily adapted to **gematria.**

Saint-Martin's teaching found their greatest response, as might be expected, in French-speaking areas and the lack of English translations of his works limited his influence in a large part of the world. Martinist themes, however, permeated the occult revival of the nineteenth century and can be seen in both the writings of **Éliphas Lévi** and the teachings of the Gnostic churches that began to appear toward the end of the century. Gérard Encausse, who authored numerous occult texts, emerged as the primary Martinist interpreter to the next generation. In England, **Arthur E. Waite** developed a great appreciation for Saint-Martin and tried to make his work known to his contemporaries in the Hermetic Order of the Golden Dawn. Waite wrote three separate titles about Saint-Martin, and for the first he received an honorary doctorate from the École Hermetique, an indication of esteem from Encausse and the French Martinists. Saint-Martin's ideas spread to Haiti and from there entered the United States, where a new Martinist thrust emerged in the late twentieth century in the person of Michael Bertieaux, a thelemic magician residing in Chicago.

Sources:

Matter, A. J. *Saint-Martin, le philosophe inconnu.* Paris, 1862.

Waite, A. E. *The Life of Louis Claude de Saint-Martin, The Unknown Philosopher.* London: Philip Welby, 1901.

———. *Saint-Martin.* Monroe, N.C.: The Sunnside Press, 1935.

———. *Saint-Martin, The French Mystic, and the Story of Modern Martinism.* London: William Rider & Son, 1922.

Salagrama

A stone credited with possessing magical properties and worn in parts of India as an amulet. This stone is black in color, about the size of a billiard ball, and pierced with holes. It is actually a fossilized ammonite, and it is valued according to the number of its spirals and holes. It is said that it is found in the Gandaki, a river in Nepal, which some, depending upon their theological perspective, believe rises at either the foot of Vishnu or the head of Siva. The stone is kept in a clean cloth and often washed and perfumed by its fortunate owner.

The water in which it has been dipped is supposed to gain the power to expel evil and is therefore drunk and greatly valued. This water possesses other occult powers, and it is a necessary ingredient of the preparations for those about to die. The departing Hindu holds it in his hand and, believing in its powers, has hope for the future and dies peacefully.

Salamander's Feather

Another name for **asbestos.** It is an incombustible mineral that resembles flax, being of fine fibrous texture. It was used by pagans in their temples.

Saleh, Wadih (1910–)

Attorney and parapsychologist born on October 31, 1910, at Mansura, Egypt. He was educated in Egypt, Lebanon, and at the University of Lyon in France. He served for two years as a research associate of the **Parapsychology Laboratory** at Duke University (1958–60). He became a charter associate of the **Parapsychological Association** and has taken special interest in the question of the psychological conditions favoring psi phenomena.

Sources:

Pleasants, Helene, ed. *Biographical Dictionary of Parapsychology.* New York: Helix Press, 1964.

Saller, K(arl) F(elix) (1902–1969)

German professor of anthropology and genetics who has also studied parapsychology. He was born on September 3, 1902, at Kempten, Germany and did his college work at the University of Münich (Ph.D., 1924; M.D., 1926). He was a lecturer in anthropology and anatomy at the Universities of Kiel and Göttingen but was dismissed in 1935 for opposing Nazi racial doctrines. He entered private medical practice and became the sanatorium physician at Badenweiler (1936–39) and served in the German Army during World War II. After the war he became director of the Robert Bosch Hospital, Stuttgart (1945–48), but was able to return to teaching as a professor of anthropology and genetics at the University of Münich in 1948. In 1949 he became the director of the Institute of Anthropology and Human Genetics at Münich.

He published his paper "Die Parapsychologie vom Standpunkt des Anthropologen" in the journal *Die Heilkunst,* in 1955. He took an interest in the question of parapsychology as related to racial and age differences. He attended the First International Conference of Parapsychological Studies, Utrecht, Netherlands, in 1953 and the International Study Group on Unorthodox Healing at St. Paul de Vence, France, in 1954.

Saller died on October 15, 1969.

Sources:

Pleasants, Helene, ed. *Biographical Dictionary of Parapsychology.* New York: Helix Press, 1964.

Saller, K. F. "Die Parapsychologie vom Standpunkt des Anthropologen" (Parapsychology from the anthropologist's point of view). *Die Heilkunst* 68, no. 7 (1955).

Sallow

A willow tree or shrub. Rods made from this particular wood were much in use among the ancient Scythians and the Alani for purposes of augurial **divination.** The magician chose fine straight wands, wrote certain characters on them, and threw them on a white cloth. From the way in which they fell the magician gained the desired information.

Salter, Helen Woollgar de Gaudrion Verrall (1883–1959)

Daughter of medium **Margaret Verrall.** Salter developed the faculty of **automatic writing** and was a prominent member of the **Society for Psychical Research,** London. She was an assistant research officer (1910–16), research officer (1916–21), a member of the council (1921–57), vice president (1953–57), editor of the *Journal* of the SPR (1921–29), and for many years editor of the *Proceedings* (1921–46, 1948–54). She was born July 4, 1883, in Cambridge, England, and was educated at Newnham College, Cambridge University (M.A., 1906). In 1915 she married **William Henry Salter,** president of the SPR.

Some of her automatic writing scripts form part of the important **"cross-correspondence"** project, which involved piecing together a number of scripts from different communicators that were meaningful only as a whole. Salter also participated in various telepathy experiments. She wrote a number of articles for the SPR's publications and interpreted the SPR for American colleagues. She died April 22, 1959.

Sources:

Berger, Arthur S., and Joyce Berger. *The Encyclopedia of Parapsychology and Psychical Research.* New York: Paragon House, 1991.

Pleasants, Helene, ed. *Biographical Dictionary of Parapsychology.* New York: Helix Press, 1964.

Salter, Helen. "Evidence for Telepathy." *Journal* of the American Society for Psychical Research (1951).

———. "The History of George Valiantine." *Proceedings* of the Society for Psychical Research (1931).

———. "Some Experiments with a New Automatist." *Proceedings* of the Society for Psychical Research (1918).

———. "Some Observations on Scripts of the SPR Group of Automatists." *Journal* of the American Society for Psychical Research (1951).

Salter, W(illiam) H(enry) (1880–1970)

British lawyer who was president of the **Society for Psychical Research,** London. He was born on March 19, 1880, in London, England. He was educated at St. Paul's School, London and Trinity College, Cambridge University (M.A., LL.B.). In 1915 he married Helen Woollgar de Gaudrion Verrall, the daughter of medium **Margaret Verrall. Helen Salter,** who actually introduced her husband to psychical research, became an important officer at the SPR and even served a term as vice president.

Salter served with the Ministry of Munitions during World War II (1916–21) and was awarded the Member of the British Empire in 1918. He joined the SPR in 1916, and was honorary treasurer (1920–31), honorary secretary (1924–48), and president (1967–68). Salter participated in a number of experiments and became an authority on the subject of **automatic writing.** He was also interested in **telepathy, apparitions,** mediumship, and the evidence for **survival.** Helen Salter, above and beyond her work for the society, was well-known for her automatic writing and took part in the famous **"cross-correspondence"** tests. After his death in 1970, William Salter left a series of papers concerned with these correspondences and his reminiscences of life at the SPR at Trinity College, Cambridge, with instructions that they were not to be opened until 1995 and 1996 respectively.

Sources:

Berger, Arthur S., and Joyce Berger. *The Encyclopedia of Parapsychology and Psychical Research.* New York: Paragon House, 1991.

Pleasants, Helene, ed. *Biographical Dictionary of Parapsychology.* New York: Helix Press, 1964.

Salter, William H. "An Experiment in Pseudo-Scripts." *Proceedings* of the Society for Psychical Research 36, no. 103 (1927).

———. *Ghosts and Apparitions.* London: G. Bell & Sons, 1938.

———. *The Society for Psychical Research; An Outline of Its History.* London: Society for Psychical Research, 1948.

———. "Some Automatic Scripts Purported to be Inspired by Margaret Veley." *Proceedings* of the Society for Psychical Research 38, no. 110 (1928–29).

———. *Trance Mediumship: An Introductory Study of Mrs. Piper and Mrs. Leonard.* London: Society for Psychical Research, 1950.

———. *Zoar: The Evidence of Psychical Research Concerning Survival.* New York: Arno Press, 1961.

Saltmarsh, H. F. (1881–1943)

Shipping agent who became a prominent member of the **Society for Psychical Research,** London. He was born in London on July 16, 1881. His business career was interrupted by ill health, and in his early retirement he became interested in theosophical literature and philosophy, which eventually led him to psychical research. He joined the SPR in 1921 and served on the council for more than a decade (1931–43). Saltmarsh organized sittings with the medium Mrs. Warren Elliot, which were reported in the *Proceedings* of the SPR (vol. 39; parts 112, 114; 1930) and made a special study of **"cross-correspondence"** tests. He also classified evidence for precognition and survival. He died February 24, 1943.

Sources:

Saltmarsh, Herbert Francis. "Ambiguity in the Question of Survival." *Proceedings* on the Society for Psychical Research 46, no. 165 (1941).

———. *Evidence of Personal Survival from Cross Correspondences.* New York: Arno Press, 1975.

———. *Foreknowledge.* London: G. Bell & Sons, 1938. Reprint, New York: Arno Press, 1975.

———. "Is Proof of Survival Possible?" *Proceedings* of the Society for Psychical Research 40, no. 122 (1931–32).

———. "Report on the Investigation of Some Sittings with Mrs. Warren Elliott." *Proceedings* on the Society for Psychical Research 39, no. 112 (1930).

Saltmarsh, H. F., and S. G. Soal. "A Method of Estimating the Supernormal Content of Mediumistic Communications." *Proceedings* of the Society for Psychical Research 39, no. 114 (1930).

Sambor, S. F. (d. 1902)

A Russian telegraph operator who was discovered and promoted as a powerful **materialization** and **telekinesis** medium. A series of his sittings between 1896 and 1902 was recorded in the Russian Spiritualist journal *Rebus.* Phantoms materialized from luminous vapor before the sitters and were seen together with the medium. Telekinetic phenomena were produced in abundance. Many of the experiments were conducted by **Count Perovsky-Petrovo-Solovovo.** However, the count's belief in Sambor's phenomena was considerably shaken when he discovered that one of the sitters, an accomplice, intentionally released Sambor's hand when he was supposed to be holding it.

This discovery of **fraud** offered a convenient general explanation for the movement of objects although not for the action of a white mandolin (as reported by Mme. Youdenitch in the *Annales des Sciences Psychiques,* vol. 14, 1904, p. 193), which began to play in the adjoining room and, visible in the faint light, was seen to come in and settle on the table in the séance room.

Neither Perovsky-Petrovo-Solovovo nor Youdenitch (who were far from trained observers) could explain the phenomena of a white column rising from the floor and turning into a human form in good light. Some other phenomena, for instance, the threading of a chair on the medium's or on a sitter's arm while all hands were held in a chain, were also difficult to explain. Such events were observed on several occasions, in conditions which caused Perovsky-Petrovo-Solovovo to observe in the *Annales des Sciences Psychique* ". . . if they do not absolutely eliminate all possibility of error, render it improbable to a degree which almost amounts to absolute certainty." Perovsky-Petrovo-Solovovo also heard sounds from a piano after the lid had been locked with a key that remained on the table in the midst of the experimenters. Sambor died a few months after the séances in 1902.

Sanders, Alex(ander) (1926–1988)

Known as "the King of the Witches," a title he gave himself during the early years of the Gardnerian Neo-Pagan Revival in the 1960s, Alexander Sanders became the originating point for a number of witchcraft covens that in acknowledgment of his leadership called themselves Alexandrian. In light of the revelations concerning the origins of modern Wicca, few Alexandrian covens now remain.

Sanders was born in Manchester, England, the son of a music hall entertainer. According to a story he told in the 1970s, when he was seven years old he discovered his grandmother in the kitchen performing a magic ritual. She was completely naked. She confided in him that she was a witch, and she initiated the young Alex then and there. She subsequently gave him a **Book of Shadows,** which he copied and from which he learned his magic rites. He held a number of jobs over his young adult years and became involved in ritual magic and even Satanism. In the 1960s he formed his first coven and began to initiate people into witchcraft.

In fact, Sanders encountered one of the covens of **Gerald B. Gardner** in the 1960s. From it he attained an initiation into the craft and a copy of Gardner's rituals. He eventually left that coven and began his own group independently. His version of witchcraft differed little from that of Gardner and included all of his distinctives.

About this same time he met Maxine Morris, a young woman some twenty years his junior. He married her and made her his high priestess. They were discovered by the media in 1969, the same year June Johns's fictionalized biography of Sanders appeared. Over the next decade he, Maxine, and their coven were the subject of numerous magazine and newspaper articles, most frequently appearing in the nude and occasionally while engaged in symbolic sexual acts.

In 1971 Sanders and Maxine separated, and he largely retired. Interestingly, that same year, a book, *What Witches Do,* by Stewart Farrar, a close associate of Sanders, appeared and gave Sanders his most lasting fame as a Wiccan leader. Farrar and his wife Janet moved to Ireland where they became Wiccan leaders in their own right and together wrote a number of authoritative books on Wicca.

Sanders died April 30, 1988, from lung cancer. His movement spread around the English-speaking world during the 1970s, but following the revelations of his unacknowledged use of Gardner's rituals and his plagiarizing of material from **Éliphas Lévi** and **Franz Bardon,** most of the covens that had identified themselves as Alexandrian dropped any relationship with him.

Sources:

Farrar, Stewart. *What Witches Do.* New York: Coward, McCann & Geoghegan, 1971.

Guiley, Rosemary Ellen. *The Encyclopedia of Witches and Witchcraft.* New York: Facts on File, 1989.

Johns, June. *King of the Witches: The World of Alex Sanders.* London, 1969. Reprint, London: Pan, 1971.

[Sanders, Alexander]. *The Alex Sanders Lectures.* New York: Magickal Childe Publishing, 1980. Rev. ed. 1982.

Sanders, C. B. (1831– ?)

A Presbyterian minister of Alabama, a **sleeping preacher,** who became subject to attacks over a 22 year period (1854–1876), during which a secondary **personality,** assuming the title of "X + Y = Z," developed and exhibited startling powers of **telepathy** and **clairvoyance.** His story is told in the book *X + Y = Z; or the Sleeping Preacher of North Alabama* (1876). It appears that the secondary personality had command over the memories of the normal self whereas the primary consciousness remained ignorant of the doings of "X + Y = Z." There are twelve cases on record in which this mysterious secondary personality found lost objects, money, or jewelry; he could shoot ducks at night that were invisible to his companions; and he could write letters and sermons with his hand completely concealed under the bedcloth. A review of the case was published by **Walter Franklin Prince** in the *Bulletin* of the Boston Society for Psychical Research.

Sources:

Mitchell, G. W. *X + Y = Z; or the Sleeping Preacher of North Alabama.* New York, 1876. Reprint, Owens Cross Roads, AL: Drake Publications, 1981.

Prince, Walter F. *Two Old Cases Reviewed.* Boston: Boston Society for Psychical Research, n.d.

Sanders, Celestine G.

Noted American **trance** medium. Reports on her trance phenomena were published by **James H. Hyslop** in *Proceedings* of the American Society for Psychical Research (vol. 15, 1921) and by **Walter Franklin Prince** in *Proceedings* of American Society for Psychical Research (vol. 18, 1924).

Sanderson, Ivan T(erence) (1911–1973)

Scottish-born naturalist, traveler, collector and exhibitor of rare animals, radio and television commentator, and author. In addition to his many books on nature, travel, and zoology, Sanderson also had special interest in such anomalous mysteries as the **Abominable Snowman,** the **Loch Ness Monster,** and **UFOs.** In 1965 he founded the **Society for the Investigation of the Unexplained.**

Sanderson was born on January 30, 1911, in Edinburgh, Scotland, the son of Arthur Buchanan, a famous whisky manufacturer who also founded the first game reserve in Kenya, East Africa. He was educated at Eton College (1924–27), Trinity College, Cambridge (1930–32), and the University of London (1933–34). He started collecting animals in 1924 and traveled around the world collecting for the British Museum (1927–29). He also led the Percy Sladen Expedition to Cameron, West Africa for the British Museum, the Royal Society of London, and other institutions (1932–33). Through the 1930s he traveled widely, exploring and collecting animals, a career cut short by World War II. He served in British Naval Intelligence (1940–45) and finished the war with the rank of commander. He continued in intelligence work with the British government through 1957.

He moved to the United States in the 1950s and became a regular on television shows as a naturalist spreading knowledge about the world's animals. He also edited books and wrote widely on animals and his favorite hobby, Forteana (the study of bizarre phenomena, named for **Charles Fort.**) Through the last two decades of his life he averaged more than a book a year. His books were commonly illustrated with photographs he had taken on his world tours. His Fortean interests become widely known after the publication of his memorable book on the Abominable Snowman in 1961. It was followed by a series of volumes on Fortean topics.

Sanderson died on February 19, 1973. His Society for the Investigation of the Unexplained continued his work into the 1980s, collecting data and maintaining the library he had assembled.

Sources:

Clark, Jerome. *Encyclopedia of Strange and Unexplained Phenomena.* Detroit: Gale Research, 1993.

Sanderson, Ivan T. *Abominable Snowmen: Legend Comes to Life.* New York: Chilton, 1961. Abridged ed., New York: Pyramid Publications, 1968.

———. *Investigating the Unexplained.* Englewood Cliffs, N.J.: Prentice-Hall, 1972.

———. *Invisible Residents: A Disquisition Upon Certain Matters Maritime, and the Possibility of Intelligent Life Under the Waters of This Earth.* New York: World Publishing, 1970.

———. *More "Things."* New York: Pyramid Books, 1969.

———. *"Things."* New York: Pyramid Books, 1967.

———. *Uninvited Visitors; A Biologist Looks at UFO's.* New York: Cowles, 1967.

Sandwich, The Earl of (Edward George Henry Montague) (1839–1916)

British baron who, in the later years of a life spent in diplomatic service, was prominent before the public because he claimed to be able to cure both organic diseases and functional derangement by prayer and the laying on of hands. In June 1912 he testified before the clerical and medical committee of inquiry into spiritual, faith, and mental healing, over which the Dean of Westminster presided, that his power was a divine gift that he was unable to explain. He never accepted money for his services.

Accounts of many of his cases, with letters of gratitude, are published in his autobiography.

Sources:

Erskine, Steuart *Memoirs of Edward, Eighth Earl of Sandwich, 1839–1916.* London, N.p., 1919.

Sandwich, The Earl of [Edward George Henry Montague]. *My Experiences in Spiritual Healing.* London, N.p., 1915.

Sangha Newsletter

Former quarterly publication devoted to the mysticism of various Tibetan Buddhist teachers, primarily **Chogyam Trungpa.** It was issued by Trungpa's organization, Vajradhatu, headquartered in Boulder, Colorado.

Santa Maria

Santa Maria, California, is the site of a set of **apparitions of the Virgin Mary** to Barbara Matthias that began on March 24, 1990. Santa Maria, a town on California's central coast, had been the site since 1970 of several active charismatic prayer groups. Within the groups, charismatic gifts, especially spiritual healing and prophecy, had been common. Several members of the groups periodically received **locutions,** direct communications via **telepathy,** from Jesus. In the 1980s these groups had become a center of Marian piety and many had received with enthusiasm the news of the apparitions that were occurring at **Medjugorje,** in Yugoslavia (Bosnia). Eventually, a prayer group centered on the Medjugorje events would arise.

In 1987, a young couple, Charlie and Carol Nole, attended a Holy Spirit seminar, a class to introduce the idea of the range of charismatic spiritual gifts (as mentioned in the Bible in 1 Corinthians 12) to new members of the charismatic prayer groups. The following year, on March 24, 1988, Carol began receiving locutions from the Virgin Mary. She was subsequently told to place a cross on a hill north of Santa Maria and given instructions as to its size and exact location. The project to place a cross on the hill was tied to the message of peace from the visionaries in Medjugorje and Santa Maria was designated a "City of Peace." In September the prayer group that the Noles attended was finally informed of the messages that Carol had been receiving and plans were made to publish them. A booklet, "A Cross Will Be Built. . .," was released in March of 1989. A movement grew up around the crusade to place a cross on the designated hill, but was blocked as the site was on private land and the owner had indicated his unwillingness to cooperate with the project. Groups began to gather on the highway right away near the hill, and their daily prayer meetings became a matter of media interest. Media coverage attracted visitors from across California, among them Barbara Matthias.

Matthias reported that the Virgin had appeared to her as Our Lady of the Immaculate Conception, a popular image in Roman Catholic circles since the apparitions at Lourdes. After the first few apparitions, Mary began to appear daily, usually in the later afternoon. Matthias would enter a trance-like state and stay in that state for several hours, on occasion approaching six hours. Crowds gathered in the afternoon and often stayed late into the evening. Many reported various unusual phenomena, including a dancing sun, the well-known miracle that so many had seen the day of the last apparitions at **Fatima.** However, no general miracles such as those that occurred at Fatima were reported. The attention to the apparitions completely overwhelmed the movement to erect the cross on the still-inaccessible hill.

On March 29, 1990, Mgr. John H. Rohde, Matthias' spiritual director, expressed some doubts about the apparitions. As a result, the public apparitions ceased in May of 1990, but Matthias continued to receive daily apparitions privately. In 1991, a request was made for an investigation of Matthias by the Diocese of Monterey. An agreement to proceed was reached in June of 1991. In October of 1991 she went to Berkeley, California, and underwent the first of a series of tests that would be conducted over the period of a year. These ruled out a number of alternative explanations for her apparitions, and Mgr. Rohde announced that all of his questions had been favorably resolved.

While the diocese has yet to rule on the apparitions to Matthias, in 1993 a book was published that recounted the history of the apparitions, summarized the testings, and offered the opinions of various people, including Fr. René Laurentin, the famous French Mariologist. While public apparitions have not resumed, a group of people in Santa Maria now circulate the messages received and are attempting to implement the admonitions contained therein, much of which is directed to the Catholic community of the region.

Sources:

Castro, J. Ridley. *Mary's Plan: The Madonna Comes to Santa Maria.* Santa Barbara, Calif.: Queenship Publishing, 1993.

Santo Daime

Santo Daime is a new religion founded in Brazil at the beginning of the twentieth century when Raimundo Irineu Serra was introduced to the use of a powerful hallucinogenic brew called **ayahuasca** while in the upper Amazon. The drug is made from boiling the vine Banisteriopsis Caapi in water along with various other plants. The resultant mixture contains several psychedelic substances that produce a unique ecstatic experience that has been compared to that produced by peyote. In the case of Maestre Irineu, as he is called by those affiliated with the movement, his use of ayahuasca was accompanied by an **apparition of the Virgin Mary** in which she began to expound the doctrine of what would become the Santo Daime religion. Mary appeared as Our Lady of Conceição and opened the way for viewing Christian teachings through the new experience.

Soon after his initial experience Maestre Irineu received the text of new songs that now comprise a hymnal for the movement. He also received the movements to three dances, each with very simple steps, that are used to accentuate the flow of divine energy. Additional hymns have been received through the years and as the group has spread to other countries, new hymns in languages other than Portuguese have begun to be received and accepted for use in the rituals.

Santo Daime rituals begin with the separation of the men and women into two groups in the meeting hall. Two lines are formed and the ayahuasca is received. Then the hymns are sung and dancing begins. Different songs have different purposes (healing, communicating with spirits, celebration). Additional sips of the sacramental substance are handed out every few hours. The ceremony may last as long as eight to twelve hours.

Maestre Irineu was succeeded by Padrinho Sabastiao de Melo, who was in turn succeeded by his son, Padrinho Alfredo Gregório de Melo, the present international leader. A second smaller group is headed by Padrinho Alfredo's brother, Paulo Roberto de Melo. The larger group was incorporated in Brazil in 1974 as the Eclectic Center of the Universal Flowing Light, the term "Eclectic" referring to the mixing of Christian and traditional beliefs within the church. It is headed by a spiritual council, and headquartered at Céu do Mapiá, a community created by Padrinho Sabastiao de Melo. Céu de Mapiá is located in the jungle on the Purus River, a tributary of the Amazon River. The branch of the movement led by Paulo Roberto has established centers in Hawaii, California, and the Netherlands.

The Eclectic Center of the Universal Flowing Light may be contacted through its website at http://www.santodaime.org/.

Sources:

The Eclectic Center of the Universal Flowing Light. http://www.santodaime.org/. June 12, 2000.

Santoliquido, Rocco (1854–ca. 1930)

Italian scientist and Italy's director general of Public Health who became the first president of the **Institut Métapsychique International,** which was founded in 1919 in Paris by **Jean Meyer** on the initiative of Santoliquido and **Gustav Geley.**

Santoliquido's first experience in psychical research took place in 1906 in his own home. The table rapped out messages in the presence of his niece, "Louise." He soon became convinced that the information furnished could not have been acquired normally. Among the messages was one directed to him: "Instead of criticising my experiments you ought to be working on your report which is not yet finished." Santoliquido believed that the report had been posted, but found out that owing to the negligence of an employee, it was still in his office. He published a pamphlet on these experiments under the title *Observation d'un cas de mediumnité intellectuel.*

During World War I his international hygienic activities obliged him to reside in Paris. He became acquainted with Gustav Geley and took him on as a secretary. They often discussed the problems of psychical research. Santoliquido found the rich and generous Jean Meyer to endow a research facility, and in 1918 Meyer founded the **Institut Métapsychique International** in Paris, following up on Santoliquido's and Geley's initiative. Santoliquido remained its president for ten years and was then elected honorary president.

To provide permanent headquarters for international psychical congresses and research, he founded another center in Geneva with a provisional committee consisting of Hans Driesch, Dr. Young, Professor Grandjean and Eugen Osty. This *Centre International de Conferences et de Congres de Recherches Psychiques de Geneve* dissolved after his death.

Sanyojanas

According to **Theosophy,** these are obstacles that the traveler along the **Path** must surmount. There are ten of them:

(1) Belief in the Ego as unchangeable.
(2) Lack of faith in higher effort.
(3) Reliance on ritual.
(4) Lust.
(5) Ill-will.
(6) Love of the world.
(7) Egotistic longing for a future life.
(8) Pride.
(9) Self-righteousness.
(10) Nescience.

Sources:

Leadbeater, Charles W. *The Master and the Path.* Adyar, Madras, India: Theosophical Publishing House, 1925.

Saphy (or Grigris)

Perhaps deriving from the Arabic *safi* ("pure, select, excellent"), saphy were charms or **amulets** worn by Africans as protection against thunderbolts and diseases, to procure wives, and to avert disasters of all kinds. They are composed of strips of paper on which sentences from the Koran are inscribed, sometimes intermixed with Kabbalistic signs. These strips are enclosed in silver tubes or silk bags, which are worn near the skin, often fastened in the dress. This is by no means a practice limited to Muslims; Africans of both sexes and many faiths have been believers in the occult properties of such talismans. The Scottish explorer Mungo Park (1771–ca. 1806) is said to have depended on the making of saphy or grisgris, as they are sometimes called.

Sapphire

Many legends of occult properties surround this precious stone, whose name derives from the Sanskrit *sanipriya,* i.e., dear to the planet Saturn. Next to the diamond, it is the hardest mineral; its true color is blue, but it may also be red, yellow, violet, green, or brown. It was also known in ancient times as lapis lazuli. According to folklore, the vision seen by Moses and the Law given to him were inscribed on sapphire. The sapphire was one of the twelve stones on the Jewish high priest's breastplate, located on the second row in the middle. It attained an eschatological significance as a foundation stone for the New Jerusalem (Isaiah 54:11 and Rev. 21:19).

When Roman Catholics select a new pope, a gold ring set with a sapphire is traditionally placed on his ring finger, symbolizing marriage to the church. Buddhists ascribed sacred magical power to the sapphire and believed that it reconciled mankind to God.

It was said to be a good **amulet** against fear, to promote the flow of good spirits, to prevent ague and gout, and to prevent the eyes being affected by smallpox. The sixteenth-century writer Camillo Leonardo claimed: "The sapphire heals sores, and is found to discharge a carbuncle with a single touch." The occult writer Francis Barrett stated in his book *The Magus* (1801): "A Sapphire, or a stone that is of a deep blue colour, if it be rubbed on a tumour wherein the plague discovers itself, (before the party is too far gone) and if, by and by it be removed from the sick, the absent jewel attracts all the poison, or contagion therefrom."

Sara, St.

A patron saint of Gypsies, especially in France and Western Europe. According to Gypsy lore, she was a maid to Marie Jacobé and Marie Salomé, two sisters of the Holy Virgin. The three Maries (the biblical Marys) are thought to have come to France after the resurrection of Jesus, where Sara met and served them. In fact, she seems to be an adaptation to Christian folklore of the goddess Kali, brought by the Gypsies from India. St. Sara is a local saint at les **Saintes Maries de la Mer** in the Camargue, France.

Sources:

Clébert, Jean-Paul. *The Gypsies.* Hammondsworth, UK: Penguin Books, 1967.

Sarcognomy

A term coined by **J. Rhodes Buchanan,** pioneer writer on **psychometry,** to denote a therapeutic science of the relationship between body and brain. He advanced the ideas that the whole body is expressive; that the entire form is an embodiment of character; that each part of the evolving surface not only possesses a physiological characteristic but also psychological powers; and that each portion of this cutaneous surface exercises, through the nervous system, a direct action upon some particular part of the brain. Buchanan believed that understanding these relationships could have great value in the treatment of disease.

Sardius (or Sard)

A precious stone that is a variety of cornelian, varying in color from pale yellow to reddish orange. According to ancient tradition, it is an antidote to the onyx. It was believed to prevent unpleasant dreams, to make its possessor wealthy, and to sharpen the wit. It was one of the twelve stones in the breastplate of the Jewish high priest and a foundation stone of the New Jerusalem yet to appear (Revelation 21:20).

Sardou, Victorien (1831–1908)

Famous French dramatist and member of the Académie Francuise who attracted considerable attention in Spiritistic circles in the 1860s with curious automatic drawings, signed "Bernard Palissy, of Jupiter." He was born on September 5, 1831, in Paris. For a short period, he studied medicine, but gave it up in order to devote himself to writing. He was not successful at first, and was seriously ill and in great poverty when rescued by a Mlle. de Brécourt (whom he later married). She introduced him to a Mlle Déjazet, for whom he wrote successful plays.

In due course, many outstanding actors and actresses acted in a long line of successful plays by Sardou. His plays enjoyed long runs in France, England, and America, and his drama *La Tosca* became the basis of Puccini's opera *Tosca.* He wrote plays for the great actress Sarah Bernhardt. One controversial play by Sardou in which Bernhardt appeared was titled *Spiritisme.* It had a plot that involved mediumship, and it included a discussion between believers in occultism and skeptics.

Sardou himself was a remarkable medium and produced many intricate automatic drawings. Some of these were supposed to delineate the dwellings of people in Jupiter. He sketched the houses of Mozart, Zoroaster, and Bernard Palissy, who were country neighbors on the immense planet that, at the time, was commonly believed to be inhabited by a superior race of beings.

He made his own opinions clear in a letter published in *Le Temps* at the time when he was putting on his drama *Spiritisme.* He spoke of himself as an observer, incredulous by nature, who had been obliged to admit that **Spiritism** concerns itself with facts that defy any present scientific explanation. Further:

"Respecting the dwellings of the planet Jupiter, I must ask the good folks who suppose that I am convinced of the real existence of these things whether they are well persuaded that Gulliver (Swift) believed in Lilliput, Campanella in the City of the Sun, and Sir Thomas More in his Utopia."

In another letter, written to Charles Frohman on the same occasion, he spoke with much greater freedom:

"Everybody knows that for forty years I have been a wonderful medium myself, and I have had in my own house wonderful manifestations. My piano has played by itself. Flowers have fallen from my ceiling upon a table; and it is I who have brought this about, and they dare not lay at my door calumnies such as true mediums are exposed to, and say of me, as they had the impudence to say of Home, that I am a charlatan."

Sardou was elected to the French Academy in 1878. He died in Paris November 8, 1908.

Sargent, Epes (1813–1880)

Well-known American author, editor, and psychical investigator. He was born on September 27, 1813, in Gloucester, Massachusetts. He graduated from Boston Latin School in 1829 and joined the editorial staff of the *Boston Daily Advertiser.* He subsequently worked for the *Daily Atlas* as its Washington correspondent. He wrote two plays, *The Bride of Genoa* and *Velasco,* which led to a move to New York City, where he worked as a journalist, founding the short-lived *Sargent's New Monthly Magazine* (January–June 1843). He also published a biography of Henry Clay (1842) and a popular novel *Fleetwood, or the Stain of Birth* (1845).

Returning to Boston, he edited the *Boston Transcript* (1847–1853) and published his own works, including two volumes of verse, the song "A Life on the Ocean Wave," *The Woman Who Dared* (1870), and a number of widely used textbooks for schools.

His attention was drawn to **mesmerism** as it emerged in New England around 1837. He studied the subject and soon became convinced clairvoyance and thought-reading were actually occurring. When the phenomena at Hydesville broke out, he was editing the *Boston Transcript* and did much to direct public attention to the problem.

This life-long interest resulted in a set of books during his mature years beginning with *Planchette; or, The Despair of Science* (1869). He wrote extensively on the subject of Spiritualism. He died in Boston on December 30, 1880.

Sources:

Sargent, Epes. *Planchette; or, The Despair of Science.* Boston: Roberts Brothers, 1869.

———. *The Proof Palpable of Immortality.* Boston: Colby & Rich, 1881. Reprint, Boston: Banner of Light Publishing, 1901.

———. *The Scientific Basis of Spiritualism.* Rev. ed. Boston: Banner of Light Publishing, 1891.

Sarkar, Probhat Ranjan (1923–1990)

Known primarily under his religious name, Shrii Anandamurti, the founder of the Hindu religious community, the **Ananda Marga Yoga Society.** Sarkar was born in 1923 in Jamalpur, India. His father died when he was still a youth, and he went to work for the railroad in order to provide for his family. In 1955, however, he announced to his fellow employees that he had attained enlightenment and was leaving his secular occupation to found a spiritual movement that he termed the path (*marga*) of bliss (*ananda*). The movement expanded rapidly.

Ananda Marga was envisioned as a fully integrated social-spiritual movement and members were expected to practice yoga (a form of tantric yoga) and to engage in social work. The group founded over 400 schools and 250 children's homes.

In 1958, under his given name, Sarkar launched Renaissance Universal, an organization designed to propagate his social ideals, which he presented as the Progressive Utilization Theory (Prout). Prout was offered as a political alternative to both the communists and the philosophy of the then Indian government. The Indian government became a particular target because of its perceived corruption, and in 1967 and 1969, Anandamurti's followers ran candidates. Indira Ghandi retaliated by issuing orders against any government employee joining Ananda Marga. Then in 1971 Anandamurti was arrested, ostensibly for giving orders to members to kill some former members. He was still in jail when Ghandi issued the Emergency Rule in 1975, and he was sentenced to life imprisonment in November 1976. Ananda Marga was banned, many of its members arrested, and its assets seized.

Finally, in August 1978, after the fall of the Ghandi government, Anandamurti's case was reviewed, the fictitious nature of the charges against him ascertained, and he was released. In the meantime his movement had spread around the world. He died in October 1990.

Sources:

Anandamurti, Shrii [P.R. Sarkar]. *The Spiritual Philosophy of Shrii Anandamurti.* Denver, Colo.: Ananda Marga Publications, 1981.

Sarkar, P. R. *Idea and Ideology.* Calcutta, India: Ananda Marga Pracaraka Research, 1967.

Tadblavananda, Avadhuta Archrya. *Glimpses of Prout Philosophy.* Copenhagen, Denmark: Central Proutish Publications, 1981.

Sasportas, Howard (1948–1992)

Howard Sasportas, an important voice in contemporary **astrology** supportive of the psychological interpretation of astrological theory, was born in Hartford, Connecticut, on April 12, 1948. He studied at Antioch University in New York, and received his master's degree in humanistic psychology. Shortly afterward, in 1973, he moved to England, where he pursued his psychological studies at the Psychosynthesis and Education Trust. (**Psychosynthesis,** developed by Italian psychotherapist **Roberto Assagioli,** is a form of psychotherapy that has been found compatible with occult perspectives.) He also developed an interest in **astrology.** As his interest grew, he became an associate of the **Faculty of Astrological Studies,** a prominent British astrological organization founded by a group of leading astrologers including Margaret Hone and **Charles E. O. Carter.** He became a stellar student and in 1979 was awarded the school's gold medal. That same year he also joined the school's staff as a tutor.

Sasportas' astrological career led him to make the acquaintance of **Liz Greene,** another exponent of the psychological approach to astrological interpretation. Together, in 1983, they founded the **Centre for Psychological Astrology** in London. The school offered a spectrum of seminars and a broad course of study in psychology and mythology, in addition to a standard curriculum in astrology.

Beginning in 1985, Sasportas authored a set of books, including the three volumes of the "Seminars in Psychological Astrology" series with Liz Greene, that quickly became popular texts for his colleagues. Then in 1987 he became the series editor for the Arkana Astrology series published by Viking-Penguin. He not only assembled volumes from some of the most important voices in contemporary astrology for the series, but contributed what most consider to be his finest volume, *The Gods of Change.* Unfortunately, at the height of his career, he passed away in London on May 12, 1992.

Sources:

Sasportas, Howard. *The Gods of Change: Pain, Crisis, and the Transits of Uranus, Neptune, and Pluto.* New York: Arkana, 1989.

———. *The Twelve Houses.* Wellingborough, Northamptonshire, UK: Aquarian Press, 1985.

Sasportas, Howard, and Liz Greene. *The Development of Personality.* Vol. 1. Seminar in Psychology Astrology. York Beach, Maine: Samuel Weiser, 1987.

———. *The Dynamic of the Unconscious.* Vol. 2. Seminar in Psychology Astrology. York Beach, Maine: Samuel Weiser, 1989.

———. *The Luminaries: Sun and Moon.* Vol. 3. Seminar in Psychology Astrology. York Beach, Maine: Samuel Weiser, 1992.

Sasquatch

Another name for Bigfoot, the mysterious humanoid creature reported to inhabit remote areas of North America. (See **monsters**)

Sasquatch Investigations of Mid-America

An organization founded in 1976, one of several which functioned in the 1970s and 1980s whose membership was interested in the scientific study of the Sasquatch, also known as Bigfoot, a large hairy nocturnal creature allegedly sighted in thickly-wooded, mountainous regions throughout the world. Sasquatches are reportedly about eight feet tall, walk upright, and appear to be intelligent and peaceful.

About 1,000 Sasquatch sightings were documented through the 1970s in the United States, primarily in the northwestern states. SIA collected and evaluated data on Bigfoot and released findings to the general public through lectures, publications, and radio and television programs. It maintained a library of books and magazines and published *Bigfoot News,* in which members reported their investigations and sightings. SIA was headquartered in Edmond, Oklahoma. (See also **Bigfoot Information Center; Michigan Canadian Bigfoot Information Center; Monsters**)

Satanic Bible

The basic text of the **Church of Satan** (founded April 1966), written and compiled by the church's founder, **Anton Szandor LaVey.** The book includes the basic principles, the texts of the rituals, and basic invocations and conjurations.

Sources:

LaVey, Anton S. *The Satanic Bible.* New York: Avon, 1969.

Satanic Ritual Abuse

Satanic ritual abuse is narrowly defined as an assault (either psychological, physical, or sexual) that takes place on an individual as part of a liturgy or ordered pattern incorporated into a ceremony of worship aimed at Satan, the Christian **devil.** As such, ritual abuse is one type of occult-related crime but different from other types of occult crimes such as the adoption of Satanic symbols and language by a serial killer or Satanic ceremonies that include only legal and voluntary activities.

The idea of Satanic ritual abuse was brought to the fore in the 1980s with the publication of a book, *Michelle Remembers,* which recounted the reputed memories/experiences of Michelle Smith (the pseudonym of Michelle Pazder, the wife of Lawrence Pazder, a psychiatrist and author of the book). The book recounted the story of Michelle's teen years in which she was forced into a Satanic cult, abused, and forced to forget her traumatic experiences. Her memory of the experience only reemerged 20 years later when she underwent psychiatric treatment. It would be followed later in the decade by a growing number of reports of Satanic abuse following the pattern of and expanding upon Michelle's story. These reports were accompanied by additional accounts of contemporary abuse of children by parents in Satanic cults. Graphic accounts of Satanic ritual abuse were supplied in books such as Lauren Stafford's *Satan's Underground* (1988) and Rebecca Brown's *He Came to Set the Captives Free* (1993). By the end of the decade, it was apparent that a major wave of concern focused upon the belief in widespread Satanic abuse had emerged. Several cities established agencies to handle the problem.

The belief in Satanic abuse was greatly aided by the McMartin case, in which the teachers and employees of a preschool in Manhattan Beach, California, were accused of sexually and otherwise abusing the children left in their care. The case began with a letter by the Manhattan Beach police chief to the parents of children who had attended or were currently attending the preschool seeking confirmation that Ray Buckley, who worked at the school, had molested some children. When the letter became public, panic followed. Literally hundreds of children were interviewed at the Children's Institute International, a research facility that specialized in problems of child abuse, and by 1984 the doctors in charge had concluded that some 360 children had been abused over the years. Their report built upon a 1978 paper by Dr. Roland Summit who had argued that children's reports of sexual abuse were almost always factual. The accounts derived from the interviews included incidents of Satanic rituals complete with animal sacrifice and the drinking of blood.

The McMartin case lasted for six years. It was placed in the hands of prosecutor Marcia Clark (later to lose the equally high-profile O. J. Simpson case). The McMartin case fell apart when the videos of the interviews of the children revealed the manner in which interviewers planted the story of abuse in the minds of the children and in some of the factually unsubstantiated statements made by the children. Most important of the unsubstantiated claims from the interviews were the descriptions of an extensive set of tunnels under the school building. No such tunnels were ever found, in spite of the building being dismantled and the lot dug up in several different searches.

The multiplying accounts of ritual abuse began to coalesce into a very new picture of Satanism. They described an extensive Satanic network that had been in place for many decades. This picture contradicted all of the previous work that had basically described Satanism at best as a very small phenomenon on the cultural fringe. This network was seen to be responsible for thousands of kidnappings of infants and children who were then abused or killed. Adult members of these groups would give up infants for sacrifice in a black mass or allow their older children to become the object of rape by the cult. These children would otherwise seemingly lead a normal life, their trauma undetected by their friends and schoolmates, and later assume a normal role in society as an adult. They would only remember the childhood trauma years later under hypnosis or similar techniques used during psychotherapy. As the veracity of the accounts of Satanic ritual abuse was called into question, stories adopted more extreme elements to account for an increasing number of inconsistencies.

In the early 1990s, the expansive hysteria over Satanism was called into question in books by FBI agent Robert Hicks and several sociologists such as James V. Richardson and David Bromley, who specialized in the study of new religious movements. Many psychologists who reviewed these reports along with other similar cases accusing parents of sexual abuse but without the Satanic element concluded that they had been falsely diagnosed. According to the psychologists, the memories were not recovered memories, but imposed memories. These patients were not suffering from their prior abuse; they were victims of a memory disorder called the **false memory syndrome.** In 1992 many of these psychologists banded together to form the **False Memory Syndrome Foundation.** Also, beginning in 1991, a series of government reports (including reports from England and other areas where abuse reports had surfaced) reached the conclusion that no evidence of the Satanic conspiracy or of widespread Satanic abuse could be found. Controversy peaked through the early 1990s with support for the idea coming mainly from individuals identified as "survivors" of ritual abuse, therapists who were specializing in counseling such survivors, and policemen who were conducting seminars on occult-related crimes. It was noted that much of the support was from therapists and police who were affiliated with conservative Christian churches.

A significant aspect of Satanic ritual abuse was the large number of court cases that arose (as opposed to the UFO **abductee** cases) in which parents were tried for abusing their children. Convictions were handed down in early cases, but through the 1990s those convictions tended to be reversed and not only were accused parents found not guilty, but civil cases were launched against therapists who testified to the truth of recovered memories of ritual child abuse.

In the midst of the controversy, a series of exposés occurred demonstrating that many prominent exponents of Satanic ritual abuse were in fact lying to an extent that called their entire story into question. These hoaxes included the books by Michelle Smith, Lauren Stafford, Rebecca Brown, and self-confessed Satanic priest Mike Warnke. While these fictionalized stories did not discredit the large number of reports by survivors who have come to be seen as victims of the false memory syndrome, they did much to quiet the support of the Christian community in the widespread panic over Satanism.

The scholarly attack upon the idea of ritual abuse, the government reports on the lack of evidence for such occurrences, and the court cases directed against exponents of Satanic ritual abuse combined in the late 1990s to destroy the popular wave of interest in Satanic ritual abuse, though for many reasons, religious and otherwise, many believers remain.

Sources:

Hicks, Robert. *In Pursuit of Satan: The Police and the Occult.* Buffalo, N.Y.: Prometheus Books, 1991.

Nathan, Debbie, and Michael Snedeker. *Satan's Silence: Ritual Abuse and the Making of a Modern American Witch Hunt.* New York: Basic Books, 1995.

Richardson, James V., et al, eds. *The Satanism Scare.* New York: Alsdine de Gruyter, 1991.

Ross, Colin. *Satanic Ritual Abuse: Principles of Treatment.* Toronto: University of Toronto Press, 1995.

Victor, Jeffrey. *Satanic Panic: The Creation of a Contemporary Legend.* Chicago: Open Court, 1993.

Satanic Society

The Satanic Society is a small Satanic organization in the tradition of **Anton LaVey** and one of a number of groups that emerged out of the **Church of Satan** that he founded. The Satanic Society was founded in the early 1990s by its High Priestess Jessica as the Society of Sin, and took its present name toward the end of the decade. Jessica was raised in a Christian home from which she rebelled and was led to Satanism through reading the writing of LaVey and others and through guidance from several older Satanists who served as her mentors. Since the death of LaVey, she considers herself no longer a supporter of the Church of Satan, but recommends both the **First Church of Satan** and the **First Satanic Church.**

Membership in the Satanic Society follows application and screening. Members must demonstrate their possession of a set of traits and abilities, including a sense of personal responsibility, a goal-centered approach to the future, the ability to organize and manage their life, the ability to listen and work with a team, and the ability to reform and revive the self. Prospective members must complete a lengthy membership application. The Satanic Society accepts the Nine Satanic Statements originally articulated by LaVey and promotes both **magic** and self-aggrandizement. It is opposed to illegal acts and abusive behavior.

The Satanic Society may be contacted at P.O. Box 109, 2025 Guelph Line, Burlington, ON, Canada L7P 4X4. It has an Internet site at http://www.thesatanicsociety.net/ which includes an extensive collection of documents on **Satanism** and related topics for the use of its members.

Sources:

The Satanic Society. http://www.thesatanicsociety.net/. May 20, 2000.

Satanism

The worship of Satan, the Christian devil. The idea that such a parody of Christian worship could and did exist emerged in several stages. Central to Satanism was the idea of **magic** and that extraordinary miracles, if not performed by God in answer to the prayer of one of his servants (i.e., a Christian), had to be accomplished by the devil in cooperation with someone who had made a pact with the devil. Once the idea of the pact became commonplace, it was but a short step to the notion of an organized community of devil-worshippers. Some substance was provided by the small pockets of paganism that had not succumbed to the church's evangelical efforts.

Before the fifteenth century, the magic practices (i.e, **witchcraft)** associated with paganism had been defined as unreal and pagan belief as disbelief. However, for several centuries the Roman Catholic Church had been engaged in a struggle to eliminate heresy, especially in southern France. That successful effort had left it with a large and efficient organization, the Inquisition, essentially bereft of a job. Thus the redefinition of witchcraft as Satanism served the purpose of providing work for those conducting the Inquisition. It transferred witchcraft from the realm of doubt to that of heresy and apostasy, and thus the concern of the Inquisition. Satanism implies the acceptance of Christianity and the subsequent transfer of allegiance to the Christian anti-God.

Immediately after the papal bull *Summis desiderantes affectibus,* issued in 1484, which unleashed the Inquisition, two German Dominicans, **Jakob Sprenger** and **Heinrich Kramer,** wrote a massive text, *Malleus Maleficarum* (The Witches Hammer), which became the textbook for witch-hunters in understanding the evil of witchcraft and in locating and identifying witches. Witches were accused of sacrificing infants and of having sexual intercourse with the devil (most witches were women). Since the Bible affirmed the existence of witchcraft, to believe it did not exist was to be considered in itself a heresy, according to the inquisitors.

Thus was initiated the era of the great witch-hunts. In spite of the Reformation, which split the church and commanded so much attention in the sixteenth century, the crusade against witches continued and was pursued by Protestants and Catholics alike. Confessions were obtained by torture and tended to conform to the image expected by the inquisitors after having read the *Malleus Maleficarum.*

There is no real evidence that a devil cult existed. Its description in the *Malleus Maleficarum* was the result of the imaginings of a group of people who had never seen what they described. The confessions were extracted from people informed as to the nature and content of what the inquisitor sought. Such has remained the case to the present. Even though some groups of Satanists emerged, they were always adult converts and created the organization *de novo* each generation. There was no Satanic organization to carry the tradition from generation to generation. Thus the imagination of Christian clergymen was necessary to inform each new group of Satanists as to the beliefs and activities of Satanism. Without the writings of Christian anti-Satanists, Satanism could not exist.

The anti-Satanist literature defined the practices proper to any self-respecting Satanist, including the Black Mass (a parody of the Roman Catholic Mass), the saying of the Lord's Prayer backwards, the destruction/profanation of sacred objects, the sacrifice of an infant, and the invocation of Satan for the purpose of working malevolent magic (**sorcery**). It was not until the late seventeenth century that something similar to the Satanism described in the *Malleus Maleficarum* came into being.

The Affair La Voisin

In the year 1679, King Louis XIV set up a secret court to deal with several cases of poisoning of the French nobility. The investigations and findings of the court centered around the activities of Catherine Deshayes, better known as La Voisin. La Voisin operated as an adviser and fortune-teller to ladies at the court. She supplied them with love potions, charms, and occasionally, poison. However, things turned in a more sinister direction in 1667.

In that year La Voisin was consulted by the Marquise de Montespan, Françoise-Athenais, who was ambitious in the extreme. She wanted to become the queen of France. Her goal was, through magic, to alienate Louis from both the queen and his current mistress. Reportedly, following a mass during which two doves were killed, she became Louis's mistress. Further masses were said to secure her position. Then in 1673, with the Abbé Guibourg officiating, a mass was said over Montespan's nude body, during which an infant was sacrificed and the blood used to create a host that was then added to the king's food.

These later masses seemed to have no effect, and Louis was perceived to be changing his affections to another. Finally, in 1879, she had a mass for the dead said for Louis, followed by an attempt to poison him. The plot was discovered. La Voisin was arrested and Montespan distanced from the king (though for the sake of appearances she was never publicly accused). The affair, as the extent of La Voisin's activities became known, threatened to bring down the monarchy if made public. It was handled with the utmost discretion. La Voisin was executed, but most of the people involved were merely banished.

Since the era of the affair, sporadic incidents of Satanism and ephemeral Satanic magic groups have appeared. Among the more renowned were those described in a fictionalized account in J. K. Huysman's novel *La Bas* in 1891. The groups that appeared were largely made of young people using Satanism as an expression of their youthful rebellion. They came and went with little sign of their existence except a desecrated graveyard or church. A few were discovered during a ceremony or soon afterward. The number of such groups seemed to rise in the years after World War II, though that may have been a result of better reporting and the correlation of the scattered accounts facilitated by improved communications. However, a new thrust developed in the 1960s.

The Church of Satan

A new era began on Walpurgis Night (May Eve), 1966. **Anton LaVey** announced the first day of the year of Satan (anno Satanas) marked by the founding of the **Church of Satan.** The very affront of such an organization in an ostensibly Christian nation was newsworthy, but LaVey, an old carnival performer, was able to make good use of publicity events—the first Satanic wedding and the first funeral—to have his picture on the front page of newspapers across the United States.

To some, the very appearance of the Church of Satan was all they needed to project it as a symbol of all that was wrong with contemporary society and to associate the new organization with every occult-related crime that was uncovered. The reality was more mundane. The Church of Satan was, in fact, a fairly small group (never more than a few thousand members), which affirmed some of the values that LaVey saw as dominant in secular society but counter to traditional values. People were trapped in a value system that affirmed mutually contradictory goals. He advocated indulgence of the senses, individual responsibility, selfishness, life in the present, and ego strength and assertion. He specifically denounced love for ingrates, turning the other cheek, and obscurantism.

The main holiday in the church was an individual's birthday. The primary ritual was the Black Mass, which served as a psychodrama for people, allowing them to overcome inhibitions and move ahead with their lives. He specifically eschewed any illegal activities and told members to pursue their goals, but to do so without harming others.

The Church of Satan gave Satanism a new respectability. Its scripture, *The Satanic Bible,* became a steady seller at newsstands, and LaVey attracted some celebrities to his organization. During the early 1970s, however, the church went through a period of turmoil and a number of splinter groups emerged. The most substantive of these (and the only one to survive the decade) was the Temple of Set. Founded by Michael Aquino and Lilith Sinclair, two prominent leaders in the Church of Satan, the temple became the home of a sophisticated Satanic theology developed from Egyptian thought.

Satanism in the 1980s

Satanism had plainly declined by the end of the 1970s; however, in the mid 1980s reports that it had merely gone underground began to surface. Claims of the existence of a massive Satanic underground emerged around a set of reports concerning ritual child abuse. Amid the heightened concern for child abuse generated during the era, children began to tell horrendous stories of having been abused as part of forced participation in Satanic rituals, both in homes and in day care centers. These stories were soon joined by an increasing number of stories of women, and a few men, mostly in their thirties, who told stories of having been abused as children and youth, and then having suppressed the memories until they were recalled twenty years later in sessions with counselors.

These two types of reports generated much attention in the press, a heated debate among psychological professionals, and a variety of court cases. In the end, little substance concerning Satanic activity emerged, though a core of childhood trauma was discovered at the heart of many of the reports. Some cases were discovered to be lies told to reclaim custody of children lost in a divorce settlement, and many were generated by psychological counselors using unprofessional techniques and practices. As the cases were investigated and no supporting evidence was discovered, the stories became increasingly conspiracy oriented. By the 1990s little support remained for the veracity of the accounts of widespread Satanism.

Sources:

Kelly, Henry Ansgar. *The Devil, Demonology, and Witchcraft.* Garden City, N.Y.: Doubleday, 1974.

LaVey, Anton. *The Satanic Bible.* New York: Avon, 1969.

Lyons, Arthur. *Satan Wants You.* London: Rupert Hart-Davies, 1970.

Richardson, James T., Joel Best, and David G. Bromley. *The Satanism Scare.* New York: Aldine de Gruyter, 1991.

Robbins, Rossell Hope. *The Encyclopedia of Witchcraft and Demonology.* New York: Crown Publishers, 1959.

Sat B'Hai

A Masonic type of society supposed to be of Anglo-Indian origin. The name signifies "Seven Feathers," and it alludes to the bird *Malacocersis Grisis,* which flies in groups of seven. The society was introduced into England about the year 1872 by J. H. Lawrence Archer. It had seven descending degrees, each of seven disciples, and seven ascending degrees of perfection, Ekata or Unity. Occult historian **Arthur E. Waite** believed that the rituals were compiled by Masonic writer **John Yarker.** Waite also believed that occultist **Kenneth MacKenzie** may have been involved and may have incorporated some of these rites into the Order of Light, another Masonic society.

Satchidananda, Swami (1914–)

Disciple of the late Swami **Sivananda** and founder of **Integral Yoga International.** He was born December 22, 1914, into a wealthy family. He married, but his wife died only five years later. Following World War II he began a wandering life that led him for a brief period to the monastery of the Ramakrishna order at Timpurraiturai, and then to Sivananda's forest academy at Rishikesh. He was initiated as a renunciate in 1949 and emerged as Swami Satchidananda. He served as a professor of raja and hatha **yoga** at the academy, the educational arm of the **Divine Life Society.**

Toward the end of his life, Sivananda assigned different parts of the world to his leading disciples and gave them a commission to spread his yoga teaching around the globe. In 1953 Satchidananda settled in Sri Lanka, where he founded a branch of the Divine Life Society and led in the spread of its work of social service, so integral to Sivananda's life and work.

Then in 1966 he undertook a global tour sponsored by artist Peter Max, during which he visited the United States and gained popularity in the counter culture. He became widely recognized as a result of his making the opening address for Woodstock. While in America, not part of his assigned territory, he established the Integral Yoga Institute (now Integral Yoga International) in New York. Shortly thereafter he broke with the Divine Life Society and settled permanently in the United States. As a master of hatha yoga, in 1970 he wrote what has become one of the most popular yoga texts in the English language. To his students he taught the integral yoga system of Sivananda, which attempted to integrate the various branches of yoga into a unified practice.

In the 1980s Satchidananda established a new headquarters complex near Buckingham, Virginia, which included the Light of Truth Universal Shrine (LOTUS), a temple embodying the universalist religious perspective taught by Satchidananda and honoring all religious traditions. In his later years Satchidananda was known for his busy schedule of writing and lecturing, which he has since cut back.

Sources:

Satchidananda, Swami. *Beyond Words.* New York: Holt, Rinehart and Winston, 1977.

———. *The Glory of Sannyasa.* Pomfret Center, Conn.: Integral Yoga Institute, 1975.

———. *Integral Hatha Yoga.* New York: Holt, Rinehart and Winston, 1970.

Satchidananda, Swami, et al. *Living Yoga: The Value of Yoga in Today's Life.* New York: Gordon and Beach Science Publishers, 1977.

———. *Sri Satchtheidananda: A Decade of Service.* Pomfret Center, Conn.: Satchidananda Ashram–Yogaville, 1976.

Saturn-Gnosis

The teachings of the **Fraternitas Saturni,** or Brotherhood of Saturn, a German occult group dating from about 1930 and continuing after World War II. One essential feature of the Gnosis was the sex-magic adjustment of coital positions to match planetary movements.

Sources:

Flowers, Elred. *Fire and Ice: Magical Teachings of Germany's Greatest Secret Occult Order.* St. Paul: Llewellyn Publications, 1990.

Satya Sai Baba (1926–)

Modern Hindu guru, regarded by his devotees as a **reincarnation** of an early twentieth century holy man, **Sai Baba** (d. 1918). He was born Sathyanarayana Ratnakaru Raju, November 23, 1926, in the village of Puttaparthi, South India. As a thirteen year old, in 1940, he was bitten by a scorpion and remained unconscious for some time. He emerged from the experience, however, a changed person. He stated to those around him, "I am Sai Baba," a name hardly known to anyone in his obscure village. He then became a religious teacher and healer, manifesting extraordinary miracles.

He quite frequently "materializes" small objects out of the air—pictures, statuettes, prayer beads, or rings—which he gives to his devotees. A widespread religious movement has grown up around him, and he has directed devotees into social work, resulting in the building of a number of schools and medical centers. His fame has spread far beyond India into both African and Western countries due to the distribution of his writings and the books about him written by **Indra Devi,** Howard Murphet, and other Western writers. A charismatic figure, he is regarded by many devotees as a divine *avatar.*

Sai Baba remains something of an enigma. He has refused many parapsychologists the opportunity to study him. Many have, however, joined his audiences and reported seeing the extraordinary feats his followers have reported. C. T. K. Chari raised the question of trickery, but gathered no substantial proof of it.

Sources:

Berger, Arthur S., and Joyce Berger. *The Encyclopedia of Parapsychology and Psychical Research.* New York: Paragon House, 1991.

Chari, C. T. K. "Regurgitation, Mediumship, and Yoga." *Journal* of the Society for Psychical Research 47 (1973).

Haraldsson, Erlendur. *Modern Miracles.* New York: Fawcett Columbine, 1988.

Murphet, Howard. *Sai Baba Avatar.* London, Frederick Muller, 1979.

———. *Sai Baba, Man of Miracles.* Levittown, N.Y.: Transatlantic Arts, 1972.

Schulman, Arnold. *Baba.* New York: Viking Press, 1971.

Saucer and Unexplained Celestial Events Research Society

A flying saucer organization founded on paper in 1954 by James W. Moseley as the sponsoring organization for his periodical, *Saucer News.* SAUCERS was never established as a group. It still exists, one of the oldest in ufology. *Saucer News* made its most lasting contribution in the 1950s with its exposés of contactee **George Adamski.** *Saucer News* was sold to **Gray Barker** in 1968, and it continued to appear until 1972. In 1976 Moseley began a new periodical entitled *Nexus* and eventually changed the name to *Saucer Smear.* It was sent gratis to several hundred of Moseley's acquaintances. Address: P.O. Box 1709, Key West, FL 33041. Website: http://www.martiansgohome.com/smear/.

Savage, Minot Judson (1841–1918)

Unitarian clergyman, author, and an early member of the **American Society for Psychical Research.** He was born on June 10, 1841, at Norridgewock, Maine. He studied at Bangor Theological Seminary, graduated in 1864, and was ordained as a Congregational minister a short time afterward. He served churches in California, Massachusetts, and Missouri. In 1873 he left Congregationalism and joined the Unitarian Church. He subsequently pastored the Third Unitarian Church, Chicago (1873–74), the Church of the Unity, Boston (1874–96), and the Church of the Messiah (now the Community Church), New York City (1896–1906).

Savage frequently advocated the examination of Darwin's evolutionary theories and their acceptance by the church. Evolution, he believed, tended to strengthen rather than weaken religious faith. His views were expressed in his books: *Christianity, the Science of Mankind* (1873), *The Religion of Evolution* (1876), and *The Morals of Evolution* (1880).

As were many liberal thinkers of the day, he became interested not only in the scientific approach to origins supplied by biology, but the light shed on the end of earthy life by psychical research. He wrote several books dealing with issues of religion and survival. He died May 22, 1918, in Boston, Massachusetts.

Sources:

Savage, Minot J. *Can Telepathy Explain?* New York; London: G. P. Putnam's & Sons, 1902; 1903.

———. *Immortality.* N.p., 1906.

———. *Life Beyond Death.* New York; London: G. P. Putnam's & Sons, 1899; 1902; 1903.

Sawyer, Carrie M.

American **materialization** medium with whom **Paul Gibier,** director of the Bacteriological Institute of New York, conducted experiments in his own laboratory for ten years. According to Gibler's report, published in 1901 in the *Annales des Sciences Psychiques,* he enclosed the medium in a large wire cage, the meshes of which were so small that they only admitted his little finger. The cage was darkened. After the appearance of several spirit forms, Gibier was asked to tend to the medium, who required his care.

Stepping before the door of the cage, he was astounded to see the medium fall into his arms through the door, which was locked with intact paper slip fastenings and a stamp over the keyhole. The phenomenon was repeated on three occasions. According to sitters, the wire cage felt burning hot when the medium exited it, though Gibier could not confirm this observation.

Gibier intended to take Sawyer on a three-years tour of England, France, and Egypt, but he died in an accident before the project could be realized.

E. A. Brackett, a Boston sculptor, attended a séance in the mid-1880s during which he was led into the cabinet by a spirit. Sawyer was not entranced. Arm in arm, the three of them walked out of the cabinet in full view of 25 sitters. In his account of Sawyer, Brackett also wrote of evil influences that were sometimes noticeable in her séances.

Sources:

Brackett, E. A. *Materialized Apparitions.* Boston: Colby & Rich, 1886.

Scallion, Gordon Michael

Gordon-Michael Scallion, a contemporary prophet known for his predictions of vast changes, began his current career in 1979. As an electronic consultant, he had been meeting with a client when unexpectedly, he lost his voice. He checked into a hospital, and during his stay had an **apparition** of a woman who came into his room and hovered several feet above him. She began to tell him about his life, what was in store for the next month and then events that would occur over the next decades. Most importantly, she predicted major changes to the Earth that would begin at the end of the 1980s and increase annually through the 1990s. Immediately after the woman departed, Scallion's voice returned. It also appeared that he had experienced a psychic awakening. He began to see auras around people and emerged as a healer.

He continued to receive visions of future events and through the 1980s had a series of successful predictions, including the 1984 Mexico City earthquake and George Bush's election as president in 1988. In 1984, inner guidance told him to move to a location within ten miles of the New Hampshire border at an elevation 300 feet above sea level. He settled in Chesterfield, New Hampshire. Then in 1991 he had a set of disturbing dreams that took place over 29 evenings. He wrote down the contents of the dreams and sent the transcript to a number of his friends. This report is now seen as the origin of what would become his periodical, *The Earth Changes Report.* The subject of his **dreams** was worldwide changes, many of a catastrophic nature.

In the 1990s, Scallion unveiled maps of North America and the world that indicated a series of significant geographical changes that he predicted would occur between 1998 and 2012. They bear some resemblance to the **I AM America** map published in 1989. Scallion's map shows the American West Coast, the Mississippi River Valley, and Florida now covered by water. It also shows the emergence of new land masses east of Australia, south of the southern tip of South America, and in the midst of the South Pacific Ocean. Concurrent with the map, Scallion predicted that a great spiritual awakening would occur worldwide during the 1990s. He saw that by the year 2002 humanity would be reborn and living in harmony with each other, and that a new utopian society would arise. Many of Scallion's predicted changes are based upon his appropriation of a form of what is termed the Gaia hypothesis, the idea that the Earth is itself a living organism that reacts to human disturbance of the natural order of things.

Scallion and his wife, Cynthia Keyes, now head the Matrix Institute and send out *The Earth Changes Newsletter* bimonthly. The institute may be reached at P.O. Box 336, Chesterfield, NH 03443. It has a website at http://www.matrixinstitute.com/. A complete evaluation of Scallion's career rests on the dramatic predictions he has made for the first decade of the new millennium. Objective looks at his predictions to date note both significant hits and misses among those predictions that were falsifiable.

Sources:

Matrix Institute. http://www.matrixinstitute.com/. June 10, 2000.

Scallion, Gordon-Michael. *Notes from the Cosmos: A Futurist's Insights into the World of Dream Prophecy and Intuition.* Chesterfield, N.H.: Matrix Institute, 1997.

Sunfellow, David. "Gordon-Michael Scallion: A Summary of His Most Important Predictions." Sedona, Ariz.: NewHeaven-NewEarth Special Report, 1995. http://www.v-j-enterprises.com/scalpred.html. June 10, 2000

Virato, Swami Nostradamus. "An Interview with Gordon-Michael Scallion." *New Frontier Magazine* (May 1995). http://www.v-j-enterprises.com/scallion.html. June 10, 2000.

SCANDINAVIA

[For the early history of occultism in Scandinavia, see the entry on the **Teutons.**]

Witchcraft

In medieval times, Scandinavian examples of the **witchcraft** persecutions that arose in much of Europe were rare, but in 1669–70 a great outbreak against witchcraft commenced in Sweden, in the villages of Mohra and Elfdale in the district of Elfdale. In 1669 a strange report was circulated that the children of the neighborhood were carried away nightly to a place they called **Blockula,** where they were received by Satan in person. The children themselves, who were responsible for the report, pointed out numerous women, who, they said, were witches and carried them there.

The alarm and terror in the district became so great that a report was at last made to King Charles XI, who nominated commissioners, partly clergy and partly laymen, to inquire into the extraordinary circumstances that had been brought to his notice. These commissioners arrived in Mohra and announced their intention of opening proceedings on August 13, 1670.

One day preceding, the commissioners met at the parsonage-house and heard the complaints of the minister and several people of the upper class, who told them of the miserable condition they were in. They gravely told the commissioners that by the help of witches, hundreds of their children had been drawn to Satan, who had been seen to go in a visible shape through the country and to appear daily to the people. They said that the poorer people had been seduced by him feasting them with meat and drink.

The commissioners entered upon their duties the next day with the utmost diligence, and the result of their misguided zeal formed one of the most remarkable examples of cruel and remorseless persecution that stains the annals of sorcery. No fewer than 70 inhabitants of the village and district of Mohra, 23 of whom made confessions, were condemned and executed. One woman pleaded that she was with child, and many denied their guilt, but they were sent to Fahluna, where most of them were put to death.

Among those who suffered death were 15 children, and 36 more, of different ages between nine and sixteen, were forced to run a gauntlet and be scourged on the hands at the church door every Sunday for one year. Twenty more, who had been drawn into these practices more unwillingly, and were very young, were condemned to be scourged with rods upon their hands for three successive Sundays at the church door. Some 300 children were accused in all.

It appears that the commissioners began by taking the confessions of the children, and then they confronted them with the witches, whom the children accused as their seducers. Most of the latter, to use the words of the authorized report, had ". . . children with them, which they had either seduced or attempted to seduce, some seven years of age, nay, from four to sixteen years."

"Some of the children complained lamentably of the misery and mischief they were forced sometimes to suffer of the devil and the witches." Being asked, if they were sure that they were at any time carried away by the devil, they all replied in the affirmative. "Hereupon the witches themselves were asked, whether the confessions of those children were true, and admonished to confess the truth, that they might turn away from the devil unto the living God." One account noted,

"At first, most of them did very stiffly, and without shedding the least tear, deny it, though much against their will and inclination. After this the children were examined every one by themselves, to see whether their confessions did agree or no, and the commissioners found that all of them, except some very little ones, which could not tell all the circumstances, did punctually agree in their confessions of particulars.

"In the meanwhile, the commissioners that were of the clergy examined the witches, but could not bring them to any confession, all continuing steadfast in their denials, till at last some of them burst into tears, and their confession agreed with what the children said; and these expressed their abhorrence of the fact, and begged pardon. Adding that the devil, whom they called Locyta, had stopped the mouths of some of them, so loath was he to part with his prey, and had stopped the ears of others. And being now gone from them, they could no longer conceal it; for they had now perceived his treachery."

The witches asserted that the journey to "Blockula" was not always made with the same kind of conveyance. They commonly used humans, animals, and even spits and posts, according to opportunity. They preferred, however, riding upon goats, and if they had more children with them than the animal could conveniently carry, they elongated its back by means of a spit annointed with their magical ointment.

It was further stated that if the children did at any time name the names of those, either man or woman, that had been with them and had carried them away, they were again carried by force, either to "Blockula" or the crossway, and there beaten, insomuch that some of them died of it, "and this some of the witches confessed, and added, that now they were exceedingly troubled and tortured in their minds for it."

One thing was lacking to confirm these confessions: the marks of the whip could not be found on the bodies of the victims, except on one boy, who had some wounds and holes in his back that were given him with thorns; but the witches said they would quickly vanish.

As described in the court records, the mysterious "Blockula" was situated in a large meadow, like a plain sea, "wherein you can see no end." The house they met at had a great gate painted with many different colors. Through this gate they went into a little meadow distinct from the other, and here they turned their animals to graze. When they had used men for their beasts of burden, they set them up against the wall in a state of helpless slumber, and there they remained until needed for the homeward flight. In a very large room of this house stood a long table, at which the witches sat down, and adjoining this room was another chamber, where there were "lovely and delicate beds."

As soon as they arrived at the ritual site, the visitors were required to deny their baptism and devote themselves body and soul to Satan, whom they promised to serve faithfully. Hereupon the devil cut their fingers, and they wrote their names with blood in his book. He then caused them to be baptized anew, by priests appointed for that purpose.

Upon this the devil gave them a purse, wherein there were filings of clocks, with a big stone tied to it, which they threw into the water, and said, "As these filings of the clock do never return to the clock, from which they were taken, so may my soul never return to heaven!"

Since few of the children had any marks on their fingers to show where they had been cut, another difficulty arose in verifying their statement. But here again the story was helped by a girl who had hurt her finger, and who declared that because she would not stretch out her finger, the devil in anger had wounded it.

When the ceremonies were completed, the witches sat down at the table, those whom the devil esteemed most being placed nearest to him, but the children were made to stand at the door, where he himself gave them meat and drink. The food with which the visitors to "Blockula" were regaled consisted of "broth, with coleworts and bacon in it, oatmeal bread spread with butter, milk and cheese." They said that the food sometimes tasted very good, and sometimes very bad.

After meals, they danced, and it was one peculiarity of these northern witches' sabbaths that the dance was usually followed by fighting. Those of Elfdale confessed that the devil used to play upon a harp before them. Another peculiarity of these northern witches was, it was said, that children resulted from their intercourse with Satan, and these children, having married together, became the parents of toads and serpents.

The witches of Sweden appear to have been less noxious than those of most other countries, for, whatever they confessed, there seems to have been no real evidence of mischief done by them. They confessed that they were obliged to promise Satan that they would do all kinds of mischief and that the devil taught them to "milk" in the following manner. They used to stick a knife in the wall and hang a kind of label on it, which they drew and stroked, and as long as this lasted, the persons they had power over were miserably plagued. The beasts that were milked like this sometimes died.

One woman confessed that the devil gave her a wooden knife, with which, going into houses, she had the power to kill anything she touched. However, there were few that could confess that they had hurt any man or woman. Being asked if they had murdered any children, they confessed that they had indeed tormented many, but did not know whether any of them died of these plagues. They also said that the devil had showed them several places where he had power to do mischief.

The minister of Elfdale declared that one night these witches were, to his thinking, on the crown of his head, and that from this he had a long-continued headache. One of the witches confessed that the devil had sent her to torment the minister, and that she was ordered to strike a nail into his head, but his skull was so hard that the nail would not penetrate it and merely produced that headache. The minister said further that one night he felt a pain as if he were torn with an instrument used for combing flax, and when he awoke, he heard somebody scratching and scraping at the window, but could see nobody. One of the witches confessed that she was the person who had disturbed him.

The minister of Mohra also claimed that one night one of these witches came into his house and so violently took him by the throat that he thought he would choke. Upon awaking, he saw the person that did it, but did not recognize her, and for some weeks he was not able to speak or perform divine service. An old woman of Elfdale confessed that the devil had helped her make a nail, which she stuck into a boy's knee, of which stroke the boy remained lame a long time. She added that before she was burned or executed by the hand of justice, the boy would recover.

Another circumstance confessed by these witches was that the devil gave them a beast, about the shape and size of a cat, which they called a "carrier," and a bird as big as a raven, but white, and these they could send anywhere, and wherever they went, they took away all sorts of victuals, such as butter, cheese, milk, bacon, and all sorts of seeds, and carried them to the witches.

What the bird brought, they kept for themselves, but what the carrier brought they took to "Blockula," where the arch-fiend gave them as much of it as he thought good. The carriers, they said, often filled themselves so full that they were forced to disgorge by the way, and what they thus rendered fell to the ground, and was found in several gardens where coleworts grew, and far from the houses of the witches. It was of a yellow color like gold and was called witches' butter.

Such were the details, as far as they can now be obtained, of this extraordinary occurrence, the only one known to have occurred in the northern part of Europe during the age of the witchcraft trials. In other countries, we can generally trace some particular cause that gave rise to great persecutions of this kind, but here, as the story is told, we see none, for it is hardly likely that such a strange series of accusations should have been the mere involuntary creation of a party of little children.

Suspicion is excited by the peculiar part the two clergymen of Elfdale and Mohra played in this affair, and perhaps they were not altogether innocent of fabrication. They seem to have been weak, superstitious men, and perhaps they had been reading the witchcraft books of the south until they imagined the country around them to be overrun with witches. Perhaps the two clergymen themselves became alarmed, but one thing seems certain, that the moment the commission was revoked and the persecution ceased, no more witches were heard of.

The proceedings at Mohra caused so much alarm throughout Sweden that prayers were ordered in all the churches for delivery from the snares of Satan, who was believed to have been let loose in that kingdom. A new edict of the king suddenly put a stop to the whole process, and the matter was brought to a close rather mysteriously. It is said that the witch prosecution was increasing so much in intensity that accusations began to be made against people of a higher class in society, and then a complaint was made to the king, and the mania brought to a close.

Spiritualism

In 1843, an epidemic of "preaching" occurred in southern Sweden, which provided Joseph Ennemoser with material for an interesting passage in his *History of Magic* (1854). The manifestation of this was similar in character to outbreaks described elsewhere. A writer in the London *Medium and Daybreak* of 1878 states,

"It is about a year and a half since I changed my abode from Stockholm to this place, and during that period it is wonderful how Spiritualism has gained ground in Sweden. The leading papers, that used in my time to refuse to publish any article on Spiritualism excepting such as ridiculed the doctrine, have of late thrown their columns wide open to the serious discussion of the matter. Many a Spiritualist in secret, has thus been encouraged to give publicity to his opinions without standing any longer in awe of that demon, public ridicule, which intimidates so many of our brethren.

"Several of Allan Kardec's works have been translated into Swedish, among which I may mention his *Evangile selon le Spiritisme* as particularly well-rendered in Swedish by Walter Jochnick. A spiritual Library was opened in Stockholm on the 1st of April last, which will no doubt greatly contribute to the spreading of the blessed doctrine. The visit of Mr. Eglinton to Stockholm was of the greatest benefit to the cause. Let us hope that the stay of Mrs. Esperance in the south of Sweden may have an equally beneficial effect.

"Notwithstanding all this progress of the cause in the neighbouring country, Spiritualism is looked upon here as something akin to madness, but even here there are thin, very thin rays, and very wide apart, struggling to pierce the darkness."

In Norway, **Spiritualism** as known to modern Europe, did not seem to have become existent until about 1880. A writer in a number of the *Dawn of Light* published in that year states,

"Spiritualism is just commencing to give a sign of its existence here in Norway. The newspapers have begun to attack it as a delusion and the 'expose' of Mrs. C., which recently took place at 38 Great Russell St., London, has made the round through all the papers in *Scandinavia*. After all, it must sooner or later take root as in all other parts of the world. Mr. Eglinton, the English medium, has done a good work in Stockholm, showing some of the great savants a new world; and a couple of years ago Mr. Slade visited Copenhagen. The works of Mr. Zollner, the great astronomer of Leipzig, have been mentioned in the papers and caused a good deal of sensation.

"Of mediums there are several here, but all, as yet, afraid to speak out. One writes with both hands; a gentleman is developing as a drawing medium. A peasant, who died about five years ago, and lived not far from here, was an excellent healing medium; his name was Knud, and the people had given him the nickname of Vise Knud (the wise Knud); directly when he touched a patient he knew if the same could be cured or not, and often, in severe cases, the pains of the sick person went through his own body. He was also an auditive medium, startling the people many times by telling them what was going to happen in the future; but the poor fellow suffered much from the ignorance and fanaticism around him, and was several times put in prison. I am doing all I can to make people acquainted with our grand cause."

A second and more hopeful letter of 1881, addressed to the editor of the *Revue Spirite,* was as follows:

"My dear Brothers, Here our science advances without noise. An excellent writing medium has been developed among us, one who writes simultaneously with both hands; while we have music in a room where there are no musical instruments; and where there is a piano it plays itself. At Bergen, where I have recently been, I found mediums, who in the dark, made sketches—were dessinateurs—using also both hands. I have seen, also, with pleasure that several men of letters and of science have begun to investigate our science spirite. The pastor Eckhoff, of Bergen, has for the second time preached against Spiritualism, 'this instrument of the devil, this psychographie'; and to give more of eclat to his sermon he has had the goodness to have it printed; so we see that the spirits are working. The suit against the medium, Mme. F., in London, is going the rounds of the papers of Christiania; these journals opening their columns, when occasion offers, to ridicule Spiritualism. We are, however, friends of the truth, but there are scabby sheep among us of a different temperament. From Stockholm they write me that a library of spiritual works has been opened there, and that they are to have a medium from Newcastle, with whom séances are to be held."

In the *London Spiritual Magazine* of May 1885, is a long and interesting paper on Swedish Spiritualism by **William Howitt,** in which he gives quite a notable collection of narratives concerning the "Phenomenal Spiritual Manifestations in Sweden," most of which were furnished by an eminent and learned Swedish gentleman—Count Piper. Howitt stated that the public had become so thoroughly sated with tales of hauntings, apparitions, previsions, etc., that Piper's narrations would present few, if any, features of interest, save in justification of one assertion, that Spiritualism was rife in human experience everywhere, although it might not take the form of a public movement, as it had in America and England.

As early as 1864, the *Afton Blad,* one of the most popular journals circulated in Sweden, published a number of excellent leading articles commending the belief in spiritual ministry, and the study of such phenomena that would promote communion between the "two worlds."

Psychical Research and Parapsychology

Scandinavia has produced some notable psychical researchers, including Sydney Alrutz (1868–1925) of Uppsala University; Chr. Winther of Copenhagen, who was president of the Danish Society for Psychical Research (Selskapet for Psykisk Forsking) and experimented with the medium **Anna Rasmussen;** and **Aage Slomann** (died 1970), a full-time parapsychologist and president of the Danish Society. Professor Jaeger and **Thornstein Wereide** (who edited the Oslo *Psykisk Tidsschrift*) led the effort in Norway, and in Iceland could be found **Harald Nielsson** (died 1928), who wrote books on theological and psychic subjects; Gudmundur Hannesson of the University of Reykjavik; and Einar Hjorleifsson Kvaran (1859–1938), who founded the Icelandic Society for Psychical Research in 1918.

In 1942, the Swedish Sällskapet för Parapsykologisk Forskning (Society for Parapsychological Research) was founded in Stockholm. Well-known members included **Gosta Rodhe,** Rolf Evjegärd, Eric Uggla, and **Eva Hellström** (who was also clairvoyant). The engineer **Haakon Forwald** (1897–1978) carried out valuable studies in psychokinesis. Other Swedish parapsychologists include Martin Johnson and Nils Olof Jacobson.

In Norway, there is the Norsk Parapsykologist Selskap, under Kirsten Pauss (Dahlsgt. 33, Oslo 3). The dramatist **Wiers Jensen** (1866–1925) made notable contributions to the study of the "vardøgr" or "projected double" phenomenon, and also edited the journal *Norsk Tiddesskrift for Psykisk Forskning* from 1922 to 1925.

In Finland there has also been much activity in parapsychological research, which has received favorable notice from such scientists as Sven Segerstråle, professor of biology; **Sven Krohn,** professor of philosophy and former president of Parapsykologinen Tutkimusseura; Väinö Auer, famous geologist; and Uuno Saarnio, philosopher and mathematician. The Finnish Society for Psychical Research was established as early as 1907 under the name Sällskapet för Forsking i Finland-Suomen Psyykkinen Tutkimusseura. The psychical researcher **Jarl Fahler** was president for a number of years, and also experimented with ESP and psychokinesis; a later president was Stefan Talqvist. In 1938, the Parapsykologinen Tutkimusseura was established and has been active ever since. In 1965, an Institute of Parapsychology was established in Helsingfors, directed by Jarl Fahler, who is also president of the Society for Hypnosis in Finland. Another parapsychological organization is Tampereen Parapsykologinen Tutkimusseura, in Tammersfors, under the presidency of Gunnar Strömmer.

Scandinavian UFO Information (Organization)

Founded in 1957 to research and disseminate information relating to UFO phenomena. It publishes the quarterly *UFO-Nyt* (Danish language), UFO-VISION (Yearbook of UFO Literature, Danish language), and an occasional *Newsletter* in English. Address: P.O. Box 6, DK 2820 Gentofte, Denmark. Website: http://www.ufo.dk.

Scapulomancy

An ancient branch of **pyromancy** (**divination** through fire) based on the interpretation of the cracks in the shoulder blade of an animal burned in sacrifice.

Schaefer, Hans (1906–)

Physiologist, director of the Department of Physiology, College of Medicine, University of Heidelberg, Germany, who has also written on parapsychology. He was born on August 13, 1906, in Düsseldorf, Germany, and studied at the University of Bonn (M.D., 1931). He held teaching positions beginning in 1935 at the University of Bonn (1935–40), the Kerckhoff Foundation, Bad Nauheim (1940-41), Giessen University (1941–50), and at Heidelberg University after 1950. He was an editor of *Medizin, Theorie and Klinik,* a winner of the Adolf Fick Prize in Physiology (1944), and an honorary life member of New York Academy of Sciences.

Sources:

Pleasants, Helene, ed. *Biographical Dictionary of Parapsychology.* New York: Helix Press, 1964.

Schaefer, Hans. "Ist die Existenz Parapsychologischer Phènomene Bewiesen?" (Have Parapsychological Phenomena Been Proved?) *Münchner Medizinische Wochenschrift* 99 (1957).

———. "Parapsychologie." *Arztliche Praxis* 3, no. 48 (1951).

———. "Telepathie und Hellshehen" (Telepathy and Clairvoyance). *Die Umschau* 52 (1952).

Schepis, Giovanni (1894–1963)

Italian official who experimented in the field of parapsychology. He was born on June 3, 1894, at Catania, Italy, and studied at the University of Rome. He was a lecturer in statistics at the University of Rome for many years (1936–63). In 1963 he became the director of the mechanographic center of Italy's Department of Elections, of the Ministry of the Interior. In 1937 he co-founded and became the first general secretary of the **Società Italiana de Metapsichica.** He went on to become its president (1959–63). Schepis conducted mass experiments in telepathy using radio and television. He also studied the personality of sensitives, but made his major contribution with his work on the statistical approach to parapsychological experiments. He published a number of papers in various Italian journals. He died December 1, 1963.

Sources:

Schepis, Giovanni. "La Esplorazione delle Percezioni Extra-Sensoriali col Metodo Statistico" (Exploring extrasensory perception by statistical methods). *Notiziario di Metapsichica* (March 1949).

———. "I 'Poteri magici' e l'Uomo Normale" ("Magical powers" and the normal man). *Ulisse* (October 1948).

———. "La Parapsicologia in Italia e la scienza ufficiale: Anno Zero" (Parapsychology in Italy and official science: The year zero). *Studies and Problems of Parapsychology* (1961).

———. "Questioni di Metodo in Parapsicologia" (Questions of method in parapsychology). *Revista de Parapsicologia* (April–June 1955).

———. "Un Nuovo Campo di Applicazione del Metodo Statistico: Lo Studio dell' effetto detto di ESP" (A new field for the application of statistical methods: The study of so-called extrasensory perception). *Proceedings,* Società Italiana di Demografia e Statistica (1947).

Scherer, Wallace B(rown) (1913–)

Director of Psychological Instrument Company and experimenter in parapsychology. He was born on January 27, 1913, in Bristol, Tennessee. He studied at Davidson College in North Carolina (B.S., 1940) and Duke University (M.A., 1948). He taught at Atlantic Christian College, Wilson, North Carolina and Richmond Professional Institute at the College of William and Mary prior to becoming the director and owner of Psychological Instruments in 1953.

Scherer took special interest in the spectrum of ESP: telepathy, clairvoyance, precognition, and psychokinesis. He conducted experiments to ascertain whether spontaneous responses enhanced ESP results, and he reported on this in the *Journal of Parapsychology.*

Sources:

Pleasants, Helene, ed. *Biographical Dictionary of Parapsychology.* New York: Helix Press, 1964.

Scherer, Wallace B. "Spontaneity as a Factor in ESP." *Journal of Parapsychology* (June 1948).

Schermann, Raphael (1879– ?)

Austrian clairvoyant mostly known as a graphologist but with powers far transcending reading character from handwriting samples. He was credited with telling the past and future with an uncanny precision. From the writing Schermann could visualize the writer, from a face he could visualize and reproduce the script. "Psycho-graphology," the term employed by E. S. Bagger as the title of his book on Schermann, was coined to refer to this strange gift of combining the science of graphology with psychic talents.

Schermann was born in Cracow, then part of Austrian Galicia, in 1879. He was self-educated, and by the age of 12 he had developed a serious study of the characteristics of handwriting. He visited the United States early in the twentieth century, but soon returned to Europe and settled down in Vienna, where he earned a living as a claims inspector for an insurance company. His privately exhibited talents as a psycho-graphologist soon earned him a considerable reputation, and he was consulted by the police to assist their work, eventually being appointed an official handwriting expert at the Vienna Central Law Court.

During World War I, Schermann served in the Austrian army. In 1923, he again visited the United States, where he delivered lectures and cooperated with the New York police in solving a murder mystery. Back in Vienna, he acted in two silent movies based on some of his most interesting cases. After this, he continued to work as a consultant for a group of insurance companies, but spent his spare time on psychographology. He charged nothing for his talents and took part in many experiments conducted by psychical researchers. Oskar Fischer, of the University of Prague, conducted between 1916 and 1918 a series of experiments in character reading from writing with Raphael Schermann.

During World War II, Schermann returned to his birthplace in Cracow and became a victim of the Nazi occupation of Poland.

Sources:

Bagger, E. S. *Psycho-Graphology.* London; New York: G. P. Putnam's & Sons, 1924.

Fischer, Oskar. *Experimente mit Raffael Schermann. Ein Beitrag zum Problem der Graphologie, Telepathie und des Hellsehens.* N.p., 1924.

Hayek, Max. *Der Schriftdeuter Raffael Schermann.* N.p., 1921.

Tabori, Paul. *Pioneers of the Unseen.* London: Souvenir Press, 1972.

Schierling, Charlotte Anna (1911–)

German archivist and evangelical Christian who conducted research in parapsychology. She was born on January 10, 1911, at Tiegenhof, West Prussia. She received her doctorate at the University of Berlin. After World War II, she joined the staff of the Danzig Library (1946) and then became the archivist of the Federal Board for Employment Service, Frankfurt am Main, West Germany. Schierling published a number of books and pamphlets for children and on religious subjects. She also studied shamanism in Asia and the United States and took special interest in telepathy and the study of poltergeist phenomena. She published an article "Red Indian Studies," in *Dakota Scout* (1960) and subsequently undertook research in shamanistic practices among Native Americans.

Schiller, F(erdinand) C(anning) S(cott) (1864–1937)

Author, philosopher, and president of the **Society for Psychical Research,** London (1914). He was born on August 16, 1864, at Ottensen, near Altona, Germany. He was educated at Rugby School, and Balliol College, Oxford University (M.A., D.Sc., LL.D.). He moved to the United States, taught philosophy at Cornell University for four years and then spent many years as a private tutor. He joined the SPR in 1884.

He became an active member of the SPR and served terms as president and vice president (1920–28). His earliest contribution to the society's *Proceedings* was on **automatic writing** experiments (vol. 4, pt. 11, 1887). He later contributed frequent reviews and articles on psychological and philosophical aspects to both the *Proceedings* and the *Journal* of the SPR and other psychic and non-psychic periodicals.

He was author of the articles on psychical research in the *Encyclopedia Britannica* (11th edition, 1920) and of articles on **Spiritism** and **telepathy** in Hasting's *Encyclopedia of Religion and Ethics.* He also authored a number of books on various philosophical questions. He died August 6, 1937.

Sources:

Berger, Arthur S., and Joyce Berger. *The Encyclopedia of Parapsychology and Psychical Research.* New York: Paragon House, 1991.

Pleasants, Helene, ed. *Biographical Dictionary of Parapsychology.* New York: Helix Press, 1964.

Schiller, F. C. S. *Humanism.* N.p., 1903. Reprint, Freeport, N.Y.: Books for Libraries Press, 1969. Reprint, Westport, Conn.: Greenwood Press, 1970.

———. "On Some Philosophical Assumptions in the Investigation of the Problem of a Future Life." *Proceedings* of the Society for Psychical Research 15 (1900).

———. "Philosophy, Science, and Psychical Research. A Presidential Address." *Proceedings* of the Society for Psychical Research 27 (1914).

———. *Problems of Belief.* London: Hodder & Stoughton; New York: George H. Doran, 1924. Reprint, New York: AMS Press, 1980.

———. *Psychology and Logic in Psychology and the Sciences.* N.p., 1924.

———. "The Progress of Psychical Research." *Fortnightly Review* 77 (1905).

———. *The Riddle of the Sphinx.* N.p., 1891. Reprint, New York: Greenwood Press, 1968. Reprint, Freeport, N.Y.: Books for Libraries Press, 1970.

———. *Studies in Humanism.* N.p., 1907. Reprint, Freeport, N.Y.: Books for Libraries Press, 1969. Reprint;, Westport, Conn.: Greenwood Press, 1970.

———. *Tantalus, or the Future of Man.* N.p., 1924. London: K. Paul, Trnch, Trubner & Co.; New York: E. P. Dutton, 1924.

Schlatter, Francis (1855–1895)

Mystic and miracle worker of the nineteenth century. Born in Alsace in 1855, he emigrated to the United States and traveled the country with head and feet bare, preaching the love of God and peace amongst men. When imprisoned as a vagrant, he continued to preach in jail. He had a gift of healing and cured many sick individuals merely by placing his hand on their heads. He appeared in San Francisco, California, in 1894, traveled through Mexico, and crossed the Mohave Desert. He spent several weeks at Flagstaff, then wandered among the Indian tribes, staying with the chief of the Navajos five days and performing many miracles.

Thousands came to see him in Denver, Colorado, where he once identified a secret murderer. He reputedly healed blindness, deafness, diphtheria, cancer, and other diseases with a touch of the hand, and also cured a number of handicapped people. He claimed that faith was the cause of his cures, and that even touching was unnecessary. He would sometimes sensitize a piece of material or a handkerchief with healing force. He treated from three to five thousand people a day by standing with outstretched hands blessing them.

Eventually he undertook a forty-day fast, during which he continued to heal the sick. In November 1895 he disappeared from Denver without warning. He left a note at the house of Alderman Fox, where he was a guest, stating "Mr. Fox—my mission is ended, and the Father calls me. I salute you. Francis Schlatter, November 13th." He was never heard from again.

Schmeidler, Gertrude Raffel (1912–)

Professor of psychology and parapsychologist, she was born Gertrude Raffel on July 15, 1912, in Long Branch, New Jersey. She studied at Smith College, Northampton, Massachusetts (B.A. magna cum laude, 1932), Clark University, Worcester, Massachusetts (M.A., 1933), and Radcliffe College/Harvard University, Cambridge, Massachusetts (Ph.D., 1935). She first encountered parapsychology by reading a just-published copy of **J. B. Rhine**'s first book, *Extra-Sensory Perception,* in 1934. Before she completed her Ph.D. she took a course in psychical research with **Gardner Murphy.**

After graduation she taught at Monmouth College, Long Branch, New Jersey (1935–37), was a research associate at Harvard University (1942–44) and a research officer at the **American Society for Psychical Research** (1945–46) before beginning her long tenure at the City College of New York in 1945. She was a charter member of the **Parapsychological Association** and was elected vice president (1958, 1960) and president (1959). She also received a grant for research from the **Parapsychology Foundation** (1955–59).

Schmeidler has conducted quantitative experiments in telepathy and clairvoyance with hundreds of students and other subjects in an attempt to evaluate connections between objective interpersonal and personality factors and success or failure in **ESP** experiments. She has also taken an interest in the question of theories of survival after death. She attained fame in the 1940s for her "sheep-goat" experiments based upon the hypothesis that subjects who believed in ESP scored better as subjects in ESP tests than those who did not. Also among her many noteworthy experiments were PK tests with psychic **Ingo Swann.** She has contributed to over 150 articles for professional journals.

Sources:

Berger, Arthur S., and Joyce Berger. *The Encyclopedia of Parapsychology and Psychical Research.* New York: Paragon House, 1991.

Pleasants, Helene, ed. *Biographical Dictionary of Parapsychology.* New York: Helix Press, 1964.

Schmeidler, Gertrude. *ESP in Relation to Rorschach Test Evaluation.* New York: Parapsychology Foundation, 1960.

———. *Extrasensory Perception.* New York: Atherton Press, 1969.

———. *Parapsychology; Its Relation to Physics, Biology, Psychology, and Psychiatry.* Metuchen, N.J.: Scarecrow Press, 1976.

———. *Parapsychology and Psychology; Matches and Mismatches.* Jefferson, N.C.: McFarland, 1988.

———. "Separating the Sheep from the Goats." *Journal* of the American Society for Psychical Research (1945).

Schmeidler, Gertrude, and R. A. McConnell. *ESP and Personality Patterns.* New Haven, Conn.: Yale University Press, 1958.

Schmidt, Helmut (1928–)

Physicist who has specialized in parapsychology. He was born in Danzig, Germany, February 21, 1928. He was educated at the University of Göttingen (M.A., 1953) and the University of Cologne (Ph.D. Physics, 1958). He moved to North America in 1964 as a visiting lecturer at the University of British Columbia and stayed to become senior research physicist at Boeing Science Research Laboratory (1966–69) and a resident associate at the **Institute of Parapsychology** (1969–70). In 1970 he was named director of the institute, a position he held until 1973. More recently he became associated with The Mind Science Foundation in San Antonio, Texas.

Schmidt has been praised by critics of parapsychology as the person with the most sophisticated approach to the methodological design of parapsychological experiments. He has conducted research with electronic random generators (with which he is most identified), and with E. H. Walker he proposed a "psi enhancement" paradigm in which it is suggested that psi faculty is triggered at the instant of positive feedback. He also worked with **Walter J. Levy, Jr.** on possible PK in chickens, cockroaches, and rats, though the studies with Levy were called into question after it was discovered that he had been manipulating data.

Sources:

Berger, Arthur S., and Joyce Berger. *The Encyclopedia of Parapsychology and Psychical Research.* New York: Paragon House, 1991.

Pleasants, Helene, ed. *Biographical Dictionary of Parapsychology.* New York: Helix Press, 1964.

Schmidt, Helmut. "Clairvoyance Tests with a Machine." *Journal of Parapsychology* 33 (1969).

———. "PK Experiments with Animals as Subjects." *Journal of Parapsychology* 34 (1970).

———. "A PK Test with Electronic Equipment." *Journal of Parapsychology* 34 (1970).

———. "PK Tests with a High Speed Random Number Generator." *Journal of Parapsychology* 37 (1973).

———. "Precognition of a Quantum Process." *Journal of Parapsychology* 33 (1969).

Schneider Brothers, Willi (1903–1971) and Rudi (1908–1957)

Physical mediums of Braunau, Austria, initially discovered by **Baron Schrenck-Notzing** and tested by him under stringent conditions in the presence of a number of scientists. The father of the Schneider brothers was a linotype compositor. Of his six sons, four—Willi, Rudi, Hans and Karl—had psychic power, though the latter two only in a slight degree.

The trance personality of Willi was a woman, "Olga," who said that her full name was Olga Lintner, and that she was the notorious Lola Montez, the mistress of Ludwig I, the king of Bavaria, who died in New York in 1861. Willi's mediumistic development was taken up by Schrenck-Notzing.

Between December 3, 1921, and July 1, 1922, a hundred scientists witnessed Willi's **telekinesis** and **ectoplasm** phenomena under very strict test conditions and declared themselves completely convinced of their reality. The room was searched, the medium was examined by specialists, and glowing pins were affixed to his clothing so that his slightest movements could be seen by witnesses even in the dark. Willi sat outside the cabinet. Two witnesses held his wrists and a third sat in front of him, holding his hands and keeping his legs between his own. Both medium and experimenters were shut off from the objects to be telekinetically moved by a gauze screen in the form of a cage. The severity of the control did not prevent the phenomena. The result of these sittings was published in Schrenck-Notzing's *Experimente der Fernbewegung* in 1924.

In English-speaking countries, the mediumship of the Schneider brothers began to be known after British psychical researcher **Harry Price,** accompanied by **Eric J. Dingwall,** attended some sittings in 1922 in Munich. Both Price and Dingwall signed statements that they witnessed genuine phenomena.

Meanwhile Willi aspired to be a dentist. When he concentrated on his studies, his mediumship showed signs of weakening. Having left Schrenck-Notzing he went to Vienna where he lived with E. Holub, the head of a large asylum at Steinhof. He gave a series of sittings. When Holub died in 1924 Willi continued sitting with university professors.

Late in 1924, at the invitation of the **Society for Psychical Research,** Willi Schneider, accompanied by Mrs. Holub, came to London, and from November 12 to December 13 he gave twelve sittings on the society's premises. According to E. J. Dingwall's report in *Proceedings* of the SPR (vol. 36): "The only phenomena clearly observed were telekinetic, and even these were only striking upon a few occasions."

Making every effort to find a normal explanation Dingwall stated:

"In order to raise an object 2–3 feet distant from him, the medium must have had concealed in his mouth an extensible apparatus workable by the mouth alone and by this means have supported a flat object lying on the table and raise it into the air from below. This feat must have been accomplished without any obvious interference with his breathing or speech; and when completed the rod must have been in some inexplicable manner withdrawn and again concealed in his mouth. We frankly do not believe such a device exists, and therefore are driven to the conclusion that the only reasonable hypothesis which covers the facts is that some supernormal agency produced the results."

The development of Rudi Schneider's powers was also under Schrenck-Notzing's supervision. One night in a séance with Willi, "Olga" said that the power was not strong enough and that she wanted Rudi to assist. As Rudi was only eleven years of age then and was asleep in bed, the parents objected. "Olga" did not answer.

A few minutes later, however, the door opened and Rudi, in deep trance, entered and joined the circle. After that night, "Olga" permanently attached herself to Rudi and never spoke through Willi again. Her place was taken by "Mina," another female personality.

Rudi's first independent séance was held in November 1919, at Braunau. The **materialization** of a tiny hand was witnessed. One peculiarity of his sittings was the frequent intermissions that "Olga" demanded.

In 1923–24, Stefan Meyer and Karl Przibram, of the Institut für Radiumforschung der Academie der Wissenschaffen, Vienna, detected Rudi evading control. After that they had no reason to believe that any of the phenomena they witnessed were of supernormal character. Actually, however, **fraud** was more assumed than proved. Rudi went on with his sittings and several reports of his mediumship appeared through the 1920s in the *Journal* of the ASPR. Then in April 1927, the journal *Psyche* published an article by Warren Jay Vinton that made a detailed and categorical charge of fraud through confederacy. Vinton was introduced at Braunau by Dingwall, attended a total of ten séances and concluded that the phenomena were caused by someone who secretly invaded the séance room.

The article made a stir and provoked strong comment both for and against these claims. **J. Malcolm Bird,** the research officer of the **American Society for Psychical Research,** decided to see the evidence for himself. He arrived at Braunau in October 1927, but owing to pressure of business could only stay for a single séance. His conclusion was that all the essentials of the Dingwall-Vinton theory were verified and all the conditions requisite to its operation were reproduced.

Harry Price and the VX

Some time after, **Walter F. Prince** attended a series of ten sittings with Rudi in Braunau and in Rudolf Lambert's house at Stuttgart. Phenomena were scarce. In his notes in *Bulletin VII* of the Boston Society for Psychical Research, published under the title *Experiments with Physical Mediums in Europe* (1928), Prince came to the conclusion that the phenomena could not be considered genuine. He observed,

"Throughout the thirteen sittings, despite my studied and unremitting complaisance, no phenomena have occurred when I had any part in the control, save curtain movements which were capable of the simplest explanation."

These events somewhat dimmed the luster of Rudi's reputation. Schrenck-Notzing desired to settle the matter definitely and arranged an elaborate program of experiments for 1929. They were to be conducted in Herr Krall's laboratory under a completed system of partly electrical, partly tactual control. Early in 1929, before the test could be conducted, both Schrench-Notzing and Krall died. Later that year, psychical research **Harry Price** paid a visit to Münich. On this occasion he made arrangements with Rudi to visit the **National Laboratory for Psychical Research** in London. Karl Amereller, an electrician who employed Rudi, accompanied him to London and installed his electric indicator in the laboratory. This indicator was developed from Price's electric chair idea. As developed at the beginning of 1923, it consisted of a number of electric contact-makers, normally kept apart by light springs which corresponded to various parts of the medium's anatomy. The contacts were connected up with a row of colored indicator lights, so that should a person under test move or rise from the chair, the corresponding light immediately failed.

The plan of this indicator had been submitted to Baron Schrenck-Notzing and perfected by him and Amereller. In its latest phase, it controlled the four limbs of the medium by four separate electric circuits. In the experiments at the National Laboratory, however, Harry Price decided to control the hands and feet of the sitters in the same way, making six separate circuits and corresponding lights for all.

The first series of séances took place between April 12 and April 22, 1929. The second series lasted from November 14, 1929, to January 20, 1930. Both were eminently successful. As Harry Price stated in the conclusion to his book *Rudi Schneider: A Scientific Investigation of his Mediumship* (1930):

"But the fact remains that Rudi has been subjected to the most merciless triple control ever imposed upon a medium in this or any other country and has come through the ordeal with flying colours. The genuineness of the phenomena produced at his London séances has impressed nearly one hundred persons, including scientists, doctors, business men, professional magicians, journalists, etc. The triple control involved: The holding of Rudi's hands and feet by one controller, a second person always having one hand upon the four locked hands of the medium and the controller; the electric indicator; the dressing of the medium in a pajama jacket to which metallic gloves were sewn, he being invariably searched besides."

The phenomena witnessed were summed up by Harry Price as follows:

". . . cold breezes felt by everyone; an occasional fall in the temperature of the cabinet . . . violent movements of the pair of curtains . . . movements and levitations of the luminous waste paper basket . . . and the coffee table . . . the ringing of the bells and the twanging of the toy zither, even in mid-air; the emergence from, and withdrawal into, the cabinet of a handkerchief, afterwards found in a far corner, tied into a *tight* knot, the 'touchings' and 'brushings' of the sitters at the wonderful thirteenth, fifteenth, twenty-first and other séances; the intelligent knocking of the table . . . when it was resting against a sitter's leg near the end of the circle farthest from the medium; the tugs-of-war with Olga, and finally the emergence from, and withdrawal into, the cabinet of 'hands,' 'arms,' and 'tubes,' some perfectly formed. . . .

". . . the following scientists have been present at the Rudi experiments: **Lord Rayleigh,** Prof. A. O. Rankine, **F. C. S. Schiller,** Dr. William Brown, Prof. Nils von Hofsten, Prof. A. F. C. Pollard, Mr. C. E. M. Joad, Mr. A. Egerton, Prof. A. M. Low, Dr. Braun, Dr. David Efron, Dr. **Eugen Osty** and Dr. Jeans."

After the end of the séance on April 15, Price casually remarked to journalist **Hannen Swaffer** that he would give a thousand pounds to any person who could produce the same effects under identical conditions, provided that if the person failed he would pay a like sum to the laboratory. This was published as a challenge in the *Daily Express* and other papers. "No one appeared," wrote Harry Price, "to want a thousand pounds, and the magical fraternity showed a sudden and strange lack of interest in psychic things. . . . What baffled magicians was the fact that the phenomena occurred inside the cabinet while Rudi was outside, nearly five feet away."

Will Goldston, the famous stage magician, attended some séances and declared that under the same conditions a whole group of prestidigitators could not produce the phenomena which he witnessed.

As regards the personality, "Olga": "After many séances and 'confidential talks' with her," wrote Harry Price, "I am completely at a loss to know whether she is really a figment of Rudi's subconscious mind or actually a discarnate entity." After the experiments were over, Harry Price handed a certificate to Rudi Schneider on behalf of the Council of the National Laboratory of Psychical Research, stating that absolutely genuine phenomena have been produced through his mediumship. He added:

"If the Laboratory issued a 'gold medal,' or 'diploma' for genuine mediumship under our own scientific conditions, we should have no hesitation in awarding it to Rudi. I know of no other physical medium who could claim it—except perhaps Miss Stella C. . . . If Rudi were to be 'exposed' a hundred times in the future it would not invalidate or affect to the slightest degree our considered judgment that the boy has produced genuine abnormal phenomena while he has been at the National Laboratory of Psychical Research."

The Schneider brothers did not accept payment for their services. In London, Rudi was only paid as much as he would have earned at his trade as a motor engineer, from which he was taken. In 1932, however, he raised his maintenance fees considerably.

In October and November 1930, Rudi sat at the **Institut Métapsychique** in Paris. According to Eugen Osty's report, in the fourteenth séance infra-red photography revealed, at a distance from the medium, the existence of an invisible substance, localized in space but rigorously commanded by the psychical organism of the medium. Sound registering and recording instruments signaled the movements of this invisible substance. No screens and meshes of various materials, nor electrically charged plates, could intercept it. An increase in red light, a change in the conditions of the room, or a change in the medium's position however, always sensibly diminished the action of the substance.

Under the conditions laid down by Osty, no fraud seemed possible. He was satisfied as to the reality of telekinetic movements. At the end of ninety sittings, Rudi was presented with a gift of 5,000 francs from the institute in recognition of the willing manner in which he had submitted to experimentations. For details of the experiments see Osty's book *Les Pouvoirs inconnus de l'esprit sur la matière* (1932).

In the spring of 1932, Rudi again sat at the National Laboratory of Psychical Research. Out of twenty-seven séances, eighteen were negative. His powers appeared to be on the wane. Nevertheless Osty's infra-red experiments were successfully duplicated and a number of distinguished scientists were convinced of the reality of the phenomena.

As, however, an automatic photograph taken in the twenty-fifth sitting apparently revealed (as disclosed a year later in Price's report *An Account of Some Further Experiments with Rudi Schneider*), there was an arm free behind Rudi when both his hands were supposed to be controlled by the sitter in front. Price concluded that "it will be necessary for previous investigators to revise their findings."

Both this conclusion and its basis were subjected to vigorous attack by Professor Fraser-Harris (*Light,* March 17, 1933). He gave his unqualified testimony to the genuineness of the medium. Several members of the laboratory's council resigned to protest the report.

Strong exception to Price's methods was also taken by Osty in an offprint from the *Revue Metapsychique,* April 1933, *L'Etrange Conduit de M. Harry Price.* It has also been suggested that Price misinterpreted or deliberately falsified this photograph.

In October–December 1932, Rudi gave 27 sittings in London to Lord Charles Hope's research group. According to the report in *Proceedings* of the SPR (vol. 41, p. 131): "On the whole, the phenomena noted were weaker and less frequent than those reported as having taken place with the same medium elsewhere, but the results obtained go far to support the claims put forward by Dr. Osty in his report." Replying to Price's allegation of trickery, Lord Charles Hope stated in a special section of the report:

"I submit that neither the evidence Mr. Price adduces nor his method of presentation is such as to make his charges count for anything against a medium with Rudi's record. What does emerge damaged from Mr. Price's report is his own reputation as controller, conductor of investigations and critic."

In an addendum, **Theodore Besterman** stated: "Quite apart from other and important considertions, Mr. Price's report appears to me to be in itself quite worthless as an exposure. It can have no effect on Rudi Schneider's standing."

The next development was *Bulletin V* of the National Laboratory of Psychical Research (*Rudi Schneider, the Vienna Experi-*

ments of Professors Meyer and Przibram). This referred to sittings in 1924. The theories of fraud there advanced, however, had been dealt with earlier in Schrenck-Notzing's posthumous *Die Phenomene des Mediums Rudi Schneider* (December 1932) and by Osty in his book. The rest of the *Bulletin* was devoted to answering the criticism that Osty and others levelled against Price.

Meanwhile, Willi Schneider had retired from mediumship much earlier, after the sittings with Schrenck-Notzing. His psychic talents had waned, and he transferred his attention to studying dentistry. He died in 1971. Rudi gave up mediumship, married, and became an automobile mechanic, eventually owning a garage. He died April 28, 1957, at Weyer, Austria.

Sources:

Berger, Arthur S., and Joyce Berger. *The Encyclopedia of Parapsychology and Psychical Research.* New York: Paragon House, 1991.

Gregory, Anita. *The Strange Case of Rudi Schneider.* Metuchen, N.J.: Scarecrow Press, 1985.

Hall, Trevor H. *Search for Harry Price.* London: Duckworth, 1978.

School of Economic Science

British-based organization that helped to promote the **Transcendental Meditation** technique of **Maharishi Mahesh Yogi** in Britain in the 1960s. The school's roots actually stem from the land reform economic theories of Henry George (author of *Progess and Poverty,* 1879) and the mystical theories of **Georgei I. Gurdjieff** and his disciple **P. D. Ouspensky.** It commenced primarily as a political and economic group, founded by Andrew MacLaren in Glasgow. It was developed by his son Leon (Leonardo da Vinci), who added the esoteric philosophy of Gurdjieff and later the meditation popularized by Maharishi Mahesh Yogi in the belief that the practical problems of the world could best be solved by transforming the nature of human beings.

Leon MacLaren was strongly attracted to the teachings of the Mahareshi at the latter's first visit to London in 1960, and in the following year MacLaren organized the Maharishi's first world assembly in the prestigious Albert Hall, London. In that year a school of meditation was established by members of the SES. Leon MacLaren made a pilgrimage to India and became convinced of the importance of Hindu-based meditation and philosophy. The connection with Maharishi appears to have been short lived and was eventually discarded as the school's own technique was put in place.

Leon MacLaren began to devote more time to the SES, giving up his professional work as a lawyer. The SES acquired a number of valuable properties throughout the United Kingdom and, with the success of its teachings, soon expanded abroad, with branches in Europe, Cyprus, Malta, Australia, New Zealand, South Africa, North America, Trinidad, and Fiji. The organization was variously styled the "School of Philosophy," and/or the "School of Economics and Philosophy." The enormous successful expansion appears to owe much to MacLaren's systematic method and his firm control over the organization's branches.

As with the esoteric tradition in general and the Gurdjieff tradition in particular, some degree of secrecy veils much of the SES program from the uninitiated public. It appears to have an eclectic program for personal development drawing on the Sufism so central to Gurdjieff and various more or less familiar Hindu and yogic techniques.

The organization has encountered some criticism. Several people who had a bad experience with the group have branded it with the "cult" and "brainwashing" labels of the anti-cult movement, which the leadership of SES has chosen to ignore. Address: 90 Queen's Gate, London, SW7 5AB England. Website: http://www.schooleconomicscience.org/.

Sources:

Hounam, Peter, and Andrew Hogg. *Secret Cult.* London: Lion, 1984.

School of Economic Science. http://www.schooleconomicscience.org/. April 6, 2000.

School of Natural Science See The Great School of Natural Science

School of Universal Philosophy and Healing

British Spiritualist organization founded in 1946 by the medium Grace Spearman-Cook, based on the teachings of her spirit guide "Ra-Men-Ra." The purpose of Universal Philosophy was to awaken the soul to its spiritual destiny so that it may participate actively in the working and unfolding of the cosmos. The school also published the monthly *The Occult Gazette,* Last known address: 6 Phillimore Place, Kensington, London, W8, England.

Schrenck-Notzing, Baron Albert von (1862–1929)

German pioneer of psychical research, a physician of Münich who specialized in psychiatry, which eventually led him into psychical research. He was born May 18, 1862, at Oldenburg, Germany, and educated at the University of Münich. He investigated the mysteries of somnambulism while a student, when, in hypnotic experiments, he succeeded in obtaining duplications of **personality.** He soon realized that there was a new realm of science awaiting discovery.

With a young woman of Münich, Lina M., he made experiments in **thought-transference.** They were described by **Baron Carl du Prel** in his books. Lina M. also presented the curious phenomenon of the **transposition of the senses,** when senses blocked from normal activity reappear and operate from another place on the body.

Magdeleine C., a musical medium, gave Schrenck-Notzing opportunity to study hypnotic alterations of personality. She was a dancer who, in trance, interpreted the feelings and reproduced the actions of various personalities and played any piece of music suggested mentally by a committee on the stage.

These cases, the study of which was described in Schrenck-Notzing's monograph *Die Traumtanzerin Magdeleine C.* (1904) marked the transition between his research on hypnosis and metapsychics. He resigned from the Gesellschaft für Wiessenschaftliche Psychologie, a Spiritualist society which Carl du Prel founded, established himself as an authority in sexual anomalies and criminal psychopathy, published essays upon the importance of **suggestion** in medico-legal practice, and wrote many other remarkable books.

By his marriage to Gabrielle Siegle in 1892, he suddenly became financially independent, and he surrendered his medical practice and devoted himself exclusively to research. With the awakening of his interest in metapsychics he founded the Gesellschaft für Metapsychische Forshung and began the study of **telekinesis** and teleplastics (or **ectoplasm**) that rendered him famous. Up to the time of his death, there was no important medium in Europe with whom he did not conduct personal experiments.

He commenced with **Eusapia Palladino,** at whose séances in Rome he was present as early as 1894. He followed her all over Europe and invited her twice to Münich as his guest. But he did not declare his belief in the reality of her phenomena until 1914 and only published his Rome and Münich séance records in *Physikalische Phenomena des Mediumismus* in 1920.

For many years he studied the phenomena of **materialization** of **Eva C.** (Marthe Béraud), in Munich and at Juliette Bisson's house in Paris. His book, *Materialisations-Phenomene,* published in Germany in 1914, at the same time as Bisson's work in France, is amply illustrated with photographs. He discussed the phenomena, concluding, "I am of the opinion that the hypothesis of spirits not only fails to explain the least detail of these processes, but in every way it obstructs and shackles serious scientific research." However, he put forward the equally vague theory of teleplasmic (ectoplasmic) phenomena. (In recent years Eva C. has been shown to have been a clever fraud who seems, with Bisson's help, to have completely fooled Schrenck-Notzing.) The book evoked much public criticism. The pros and cons were summed up by Schrenck-Notzing in a later book, *Der Kampf um die Materialisations Phenomene* (Battle for the Phenomena of Materialization). The two main works appeared in English translation under the title *Phenomena of Materialisation* (London, 1920, 1923; New York, 1975).

A supplementary volume to the original book was published in 1922. In it the cases of **Willi Schneider, Stanislava P., Maria Silbert** and **Einer Nielsen** were presented. Schrenck-Notzing also sat with **Stanislawa Tomczyk, Franek Kluski, Linda Gazzera, Lucia Sordi,** and many other mediums. Their cases were reviewed in his book *Physikalische Phenomene des Mediumismus* (1920). He expressed his conclusions as follows:

"The telekinetic and teleplasmic phenomena are not only different degrees of the same animistic process, they depend in the end upon physical manifestations in the subconscious sphere of the medium. The *soi-disant* occult intelligences which manifest and materialize themselves in the séance, never display any higher spiritual faculty than is owned by the medium and the sitters; they are wholly of oneiric type, dream personifications that correspond to detached memories, to beliefs, to all the miscellaneous things that lie dormant in the minds of the participants. It is not on a foundation of extra-corporeal beings that one will find the secret of the psycho-dynamical phenomena of these subjects, but rather through consideration of hitherto unknown transformations of the biopsychical forces of the medium's organism."

When he discovered the mediumistic gifts of the Schneider children, he trained Willi Schneider so that the same phenomenon could be repeated under similar conditions at specified times and before varying observers. The conditions of these experiments were very strict and the records considered unimpeachable. An electrical system of control made the phenomena apparently fraud-proof. Schrenk-Notzing's work was criticized by **Harry Price,** but supported by a group of scientists who witnessed the phenomena in 1922 and declared themselves completely convinced of the reality of telekinesis and ectoplasm. The book, *Experimente der Fernbewegung,* Stugggart, 1924, in which he summed up the story of these researches, is one of the most important works on telekinesis.

In *Der Betrug des Mediums Ladislaus László,* published in the same year in Leipzig, he described his experiences in Budapest with a pseudo-medium, László. At the conclusion of a series of four sittings he advised the sponsor of the medium, a Mr. Torday, of his uncertainties. Soon after László confessed to gross **fraud.** When Willi Schneider "lost" much of his power, the Baron trained his brother, Rudi. He discovered another subject, Karl Weber (Karl Kraus), a young man who produced **levitations** at will and while awake. He reported on him at the Paris Congress.

However, **Malcolm Bird** in *Psychic Research* (July 1930) accused Schrenk-Notzing of "extraordinary improprieties in the way of suppressing unfavorable evidence," and cited as one instance that Schrenk-Notzing had completely concealed at the Paris Congress that "Karl Weber" was identical to the notorious Karl Kraus.

In his last years, Schrenck-Notzing devoted much attention to the phenomena of haunting. He left behind a posthumous book, *Gefälschte Wunder: Kraus-László-Schlag,* in manuscript. In 1929, his widow published his collected articles; *Gesammelte Aufsätze zur Parapsichologie* devoted 47 pages to intellectual and more than 300 to experimental physical phenomena.

Another posthumous volume (*Die Phenomene des Mediums Rudi Schneider*) was published in December 1932. As **René Sudre** pointed out in his memorial article in *Psychic Research* (May 1929), Schrenck-Notzing never made any attempt at an inner interpretation of the phenomena he observed. "He lacked the spirit of the philosopher. With him there existed no urgent need for construction; he felt only the urge of accumulating material."

He died February 12, 1929, at Münich, Germany.

Sources:

Berger, Arthur S., and Joyce Berger. *The Encyclopedia of Parapsychology and Psychical Research.* New York: Paragon House, 1991.

Pleasants, Helene, ed. *Biographical Dictionary of Parapsychology.* New York: Helix Press, 1964.

Schrenck-Notzing, Albert von. *Materialisations-Phenomene.* Munich: Ernst Reinhardt, 1914.

———. *Phenomena of Materialisation.* London, 1920. Reprint, New Hyde Park, N.Y.: University Press, 1975.

———. *Die Traumtanzerin Magdeleine C.* Stuttgart, 1904.

Sudre, Rene. "The Life and Works of Schrenck-Notzing." *Psychic Research* 23 (1929).

Tabori, Paul. *Pioneers of the Unseen.* London: Souvenir Press, 1972.

Schucman, Helen (1910–1981)

Helen Schucman, the psychologist and channel who received the material later incorporated into *A Course in Miracles* (ACIM), the most successful channelled work of the late twentieth century, was born Helen Cohn, the daughter of Sigmund Cohn, a chemist. Her mother had dabbled both in **Theosophy** and Christian Science, but Helen had not been interested in either. She was influenced by a Roman Catholic governess and throughout her life she periodically attended mass and possessed a number of rosaries she had collected over the years. During her teens, she was attended by an African-American maid who saw to her baptism as a Baptist. However, through most of her life, she was a professing atheist who was quite aware of the dominant secularism of her professional colleagues.

She attended New York University, aiming for a career as a writer or possibly an English teacher, but following her graduation suffered a traumatic experience from complications following a gall bladder operation. In 1933 she married Louis Schucman, the owner of an antiquarian bookstore, and settled down to life as a housewife and sometime assistant to her husband. In 1952, however, she decided to return to school and entered the psychology program at her alma mater. She specialized in clinical psychology and concentrated upon the problems of mental retardation in children.

Following her graduation with a Ph.D., in 1958 she accepted a position at Colombia-Presbyterian Medical Center. Here she met **William N. Tetford,** the new head of the hospital's Psychology Department. The pair was temperamentally very different, and the next seven years they had an often stormy relationship. Then in 1965, Tetford, who had been dabbling in metaphysical literature, suggested that they attempt to change their relationship and shortly thereafter, at Tetford's suggestion, they began to practice meditation. Schucman began to have vivid visual experiences. Tetford suggested that she record her experiences, but and on October 21, 1965, she heard an inner voice that told her, "This is a course in miracles. Please take notes." Again Tetford suggested that she do what the voice told her.

Schucman recorded what she was told in shorthand and over the next seven years read her notes to Tetford, who transcribed them. Eventually some 1,200 pages were received. She then worked with Kenneth Wapnick to edit the materials that would later be published as the three-volume *A Course in Mira-*

cles. The material, whose teachings are very close to those found in New Thought metaphysics, claims to have been dictated by Jesus Christ. It offers a means to a more meaningful life as an awakened child of god who learns the self-recrimination that manifests as guilt and hostility can be overcome through forgiveness and learning to forgive.

Schucman was ambivalent about the material and the method of its reception, both of which contradicted her self-professed atheism. However, she slowly became more comfortable with the material and finally allowed its publication in 1975. She assigned the copyrights to the Foundation for Inner Peace, a corporation set up to publish the books and disseminate the teachings. The *Course* took off and quickly spread through the New Thought and New Age communities. However, Schucman continued to be in the background and, while identified as the channel, was known only to a small circle of early leaders in the New York area.

In 1980, she developed pancreatic cancer and withdrew even more and lived largely cut off from the growing ACIM community until her death in 1981. Only in the years after her death was the story of her life made known.

Sources:

A Course in Miracles. 3 vols. New York: Foundation for Inner Peace, 1975.

Koggend, John. "The Gospel According to Helen." *Psychology Today* 14 (September 1980): 74–78.

Miller, D. Patrick. *The Complete Story of the Course: The History, The People and the Controversies Behind A Course in Miracles.* Berkeley, Calif.: Fearless Books, 1997.

Skutch, Judith. "A Course in Miracles, the Untold Story." Parts 1 &2. *New Realities* 4, no. 1, 2 (August, September/October 1984): 17–27; 8–15, 78.

Wapnick, Kenneth. *Absence of Felicity: The Story of Helen Schucman and Her Scribing of A Course in Miracles.* Roscoe, N.Y.: Foundation for "A Course in Miracles," 1991.

Schuetzinger, C(aroline) E(va) (1909–)

Psychologist and linguist who also explored parapsychological subjects. She was born on February 14, 1909, in Münich, Germany. She attended the Pädagogisches Institut, Münich (M.Ed., 1945), Incarnate Word College, San Antonio, Texas (B.A., 1951), and St. Louis University, St. Louis, Missouri (M.A., 1955). She taught at the Pädagogisches Institut (1947–60) before moving to Detroit, Michigan and assuming a position at Mercy College. She was a member of the **Parapsychological Association,** the author of the *German Controversy on St. Augustine's Illumination Theory* (1960), and has studied such parapsychological subjects as telepathy, clairvoyance, psychokinesis and theories of survival.

Schwartz, Emanual K(ing) (1912–1973)

Psychologist who wrote on parapsychology. He was born on June 11, 1912, in New York City. He studied at College of the City of New York (B.S., 1932; M.S., 1933) and New York University (Ph.D., 1937). He was a practicing psychoanalyst for the United States Army during World War II (1942–46). After the war he worked as dean and director of the Postgraduate Center for Psychotherapy, New York (1947–73), and as a teacher at Long Island University (1951–57), New York University (1960–73), and Adelphi University, Garden City, New York (1960–73). His studies in the field of parapsychology concerned personality determinants in psychical experiences, and he conducted research to ascertain whether hypnosis can facilitate such experiences. He died January 22, 1973.

Sources:

Pleasants, Helene, ed. *Biographical Dictionary of Parapsychology.* New York: Helix Press, 1964.

Schwartz, Emanual K. "The Psychodynamics of Spontaneous Psi Experiences." *Journal* of the American Society for Psychical Research 46 (1952).

———. "The Study of Spontaneous Psi Experiences." *Journal* of the American Society for Psychical Research 43 (1949).

Schweighöfer, Jurgen (1921–)

German psychologist who has written on parapsychology. He was born on June 22, 1921, at Allenstein, Germany. He served in the German Army during World War II (1940–46). He studied at the University of Mainz (Diplom-psychologe 1951; Ph.D. 1956). His psychology degree thesis in 1950 was entitled *Probleme der Aussersinnlichen Wahrnehmung und Telekinese im Lichte der Amerikanischen Forschung* (Problems of Extrasensory Perception and Psychokinesis in the Light of American Researches). After the war and the completion of his doctoral program, he worked as a vocational guidance officer. He was a charter associate of the **Parapsychological Association.** He translated **Betty Humphrey Nicol**'s book, *Handbook of Tests in Parapsychology,* into German.

Schweizerische Vereinigung für Parapsychologie

Semi-annual German-language publication containing information on parapsychological research in Switzerland and elsewhere and reports on conferences and details of courses at Berne University. It is published from Brückfeldstrasse 19, 3012 Bern, Switzerland.

Scientific American (Journal)

In the summer of 1922, this New York journal, known for its outstanding presentation of scientific findings to the American lay public, decided to investigate the subject of psychical research. Contributions were invited, but as these proved to be rather contradictory, a plan was worked out for first-hand investigation, and the sum of $2,500 was promised for the demonstration of an objective psychic phenomenon before a committee of five.

The offer was to remain open from January 1923, when it was published in the *Scientific American,* until December 31, 1924. The committee consisted of **William McDougall,** a professor of psychology at Harvard; Daniel Frost Comstock, formerly of the Massachusetts Institute of Technology and then a retired inventor; **Walter Franklin Prince,** principal research officer of the **American Society of Psychical Research; Hereward Carrington,** the well-known psychical investigator and author; and **Harry Houdini,** the stage magician and escapologist. **J. Malcolm Bird,** associate editor of the *Scientific American,* was assigned to the committee as a non-voting member to perform secretarial duties.

Psychics and mediums proved reluctant to appear before the committee, some objecting to its composition. In fourteen months, the committee had only three applicants. The verdict in each case was **fraud,** conscious or otherwise.

The offer of the *Scientific American* was enlarged in April 1924. It comprised the payment of the expenses of any high-class medium who would come forward, regardless of the verdict. No response came, but Bird succeeded in making arrangements with **Mina Crandon,** soon to become famous as "Margery," the wife of L. R. Crandon of Boston, to sit for investigation in Boston. In return for the change of scene, necessitated by L. R. Crandon's professional engagements, the doctor waived the *Scientific American*'s offer to pay expenses and himself undertook to pay the committee's expenses in Boston.

The "Margery" Sittings

The first séance was held on April 12. The committee witnessed gradual development of interesting phenomena and made good headway into the investigation by using scientific instruments. Final judgment might have been reached; however, friction, dissension, and distrust arose between the members.

One focus of tension was Houdini. He had established, at that time, a reputation in the unmasking of fraudulent mediums. In the end, possibly not without justification, he openly accused Bird with confederacy in producing the mediumistic phenomena. Other members of the committee had come to believe that Bird was at best highly incompetent.

Houdini obtained no direct proof against "Margery," yet after two sittings in July, he published a document attacking both the Crandons and Malcolm Bird. He began to give lectures in which he claimed to have infallibly demonstrated that the rest of the committee was duped.

Orson D. Munn, the publisher of the *Scientific American,* now stepped in and, noting that the finality of the exposure was in no way acknowledged by the committee itself, prevailed upon Houdini to go back for further sittings in August and to make an attempt to reach a final verdict. At that stage, since Carrington had pronounced the mediumship genuine, he withdrew from further sittings. McDougall was otherwise engaged, so Comstock, Houdini, and Prince remained on the scene.

Houdini constructed a supposedly "fraud-proof" wooden cage for the critical séance, but refused to sit with it in red light, demanded total darkness, and categorically denied the request of his colleagues for its examination. The committee yielded to Houdini but some suspicion was present. In any case, after a few minutes of the séance the entire top of the cage was found open and Houdini at once stated that anybody sitting in it could throw it open with her shoulders. It appeared, therefore, that the problem at this point was Houdini's design. This incident was followed with confrontations between Houdini and "Margery's" spirit **control** "Walter," who demanded to know how much Houdini was getting for stopping phenomena. "Walter" advised Comstock to take the bell box out into white light and examine it. Sure enough, a rubber eraser, off the end of a pencil, was found tucked down into the angle between the contact boards, necessitating four times the usual pressure to ring the bell.

At the next séance, when the top of the cage was properly secured, Houdini, on some pretext, put his arm in through the porthole at the last minute. "Walter" thereupon denounced Houdini and accused him of putting a ruler in the cage under the cushion on which "Margery's" feet rested. The accusation was proved. A two-foot jointed ruler, of the sort used by carpenters, folded into four sections, was found at the designated spot. After this, Houdini was delivered an ultimatum for handing over the cage to the committee. Houdini refused to comply, packed the cage up, and carted it away.

The attitude of the rest of the committee towards the mediumship of "Margery" was also open to criticism. Prince sat ten times, Comstock 56 times, McDougall 22 times; none of them uncovered any fraud, yet they came increasingly to agree that the phenomena were not genuine.

Malcolm Bird's Role

The next crisis came with Malcolm Bird's unofficial (and very favorable) account of the investigation in the *Scientific American.* In the press reproductions, the distinction between the *Scientific American* and the committee was lost; headlines shrieked across the country that "Margery" was about to win the prize. Prince insisted that the *Scientific American* articles be stopped until the committee was through with the case and threatened resignation. Houdini sided with him. The articles were discontinued, and Bird was pressured to resign from further association with the committee.

When the August séances were over and still no verdict had been reached, the *Scientific American* insisted on its rights and demanded a statement from the committee or from its individual members. These statements were published in November 1924. Carrington pronounced the mediumship genuine and so proved, Houdini pronounced it fraudulent and so proved. Comstock said he found it interesting and wanted to see more of it. Prince disclaimed to have seen enough. McDougall could not be reached, but later sided with Comstock. After this, Prince and McDougall attended some more séances. Prince witnessed bell ringing in perfect daylight with the bell box in his lap; McDougall saw it ringing while being carried about the room, yet they still refused to commit themselves. Thus ended the investigation of the committee of the *Scientific American.*

In April 1925, O. D. Munn announced: "The famous Margery case is over so far as the *Scientific American* investigation is concerned." The question of the "Margery" mediumship was now transferred from the *Scientific American* fiasco to the ASPR. Bird left the editorial board of the *Scientific American* and became a staff member of the ASPR. As a result the "Margery" question became central to the organization. Prince, who considered Bird incompetent, resigned, and, with others who had come to doubt Crandon's abilities, he founded the Boston Society for Psychical Research. He was joined by William MacDougall, **Gardner Murphy** and **Elwood Worcester.** Bird's book on "Margery" appeared in 1925.

The affair seemed to have reached a stalemate: the ASPR basically backed "Margery," and the Boston SPR opposed her. Then Bird submitted a confidential report to the ASPR board in which he revealed that, contrary to his own book, he was aware that at least some of the phenomena produced by Margery were produced in a mundane manner and that he had been approached to become the Crandons' accomplice. Bird soon resigned and dropped out of sight.

Sources:

Berger, Arthur S., and Joyce Berger. *The Encyclopedia of Parapsychology and Psychical Research.* New York: Paragon House, 1991.

Bird, Malcolm. *Margery the Medium.* New York: Maynard, 1925.

Tietze, Thomas R. *Margery.* New York: Harper and Row, 1973.

Scientology, Church of

In 1950 writer L. Ron Hubbard announced the discovery of **Dianetics** as a new system of mental health. Several years later he announced the further development of Dianetics into a comprehensive system of spiritual philosophy and religion, which he termed Scientology. Both Dianetics and Scientology now form the teachings and practice of the Church of Scientology.

Dianetics

Developed in part in reaction to the dominance of behavioral approaches to psychology and then-current psychotherapeutic practices such as electric shock therapy, Dianetics is based upon the idea that the human is identified with the soul (termed the Thetan), and Dianetics identifies what the soul does to the body through the mind. It was first exposed to the public in the article "Dianetics . . . An Introduction to a New Science" in the pages of *Astounding Science Fiction* (May 1950), a magazine published by one of Hubbard's friends who had become enthusiastic about the possibilities of the new approach. Several weeks later Hubbard's book *Dianetics: The Modern Science of Mental Health* was published, on May 9, 1950, and became an overnight best-seller.

Hubbard suggested that the goal of life was what he termed "infinite survival." Pain, disappointment, and failure are the results of actions that do not promote survival, he said. The mind operates to solve the problems relating to survival. From the information it receives, stored in mental pictures, it directs the individual in actions geared toward surviving. Such mental images are three dimensional—they have energy and mass, they exist in space, and they tend to appear when someone thinks of them, Hubbard said. They are strung together in a consecutive record accumulated over a lifetime Hubbard called a "time track."

The theory of Dianetics is a variation on preexisting concepts of conscious and unconscious mind, using the terms *analytic* and *reactive* mind. The analytic mind, according to Hubbard, records the mental image pictures derived from our experiences. However, pictures of experience which contain pain or painful emotions are recorded in the reactive mind. Also, experiences that occur when a person is unconscious (on the operating table, for example) or partially conscious (when inebriated) are recorded by the reactive mind and are not available to the analytic mind, he said.

The problem with the reactive mind is that it stores particular types of mental images called "engrams" (a term borrowed from psychologist Richard Semon to denote a memory trace), creating a complete record of unpleasant or unconscious experiences. It also thinks in identities, equating the various elements of a painful experiences. In the future, when one experiences several elements in the engram, all of the pain and emotion of past experiences will flood back into the present. Over a lifetime, the cumulative effect of engrams can be a set of unwanted and little-understood negative conditions, including, but not limited to, pains, emotional blocks, and even physical illnesses, according to Hubbard. Armed with Hubbard's book, any ordinary individual was considered competent to practice a simple system of psychotherapy superior to those involving specialized training.

Having discovered the nature of the human psyche, Hubbard set out to discover the means of addressing psychological disorders. His techniques are supposed to erase the contents of the reactive mind, rendering them useless in further affecting the person without his/her conscious knowledge.

The aim of the techniques is the production of a "clear," a person whose reactive mind has been cleared, who has no engrams. The primary technique is called "auditing," a one-on-one counseling process that uses an instrument called an "E-meter," a modified whetstone bridge that measures the level of electrical resistance in the human body. It is the belief that such resistance is directly related to the focus upon an engram. The process of becoming a clear occurs in a series of classes and personal counseling sessions. Participants record the state of clear in degrees.

Hubbard founded the Hubbard Dianetic Research Foundation in June 1950. He spent the rest of the year traveling and lecturing and the following year opened the Hubbard College in Wichita, Kansas. By this time Hubbard had speculated that human beings are basically spiritual, and that once cleared, have great potential. These insights led to what would be termed "Scientology." The Hubbard Association Scientology International was founded in 1952, and the first Church of Scientology opened two years later. Dianetics became the method of entering the church and discovering its teachings.

Scientology

Hubbard proposed the existence of engrams—painful impressions from past experiences, extending back into innumerable previous incarnations. According to his book *The History of Man* (1952), the human body houses two entities—a genetic entity (for carrying on the evolutionary line), and a *Thetan,* or consciousness, like an individual soul, that has the capacity to separate from body and mind. In man's long evolutionary development the Thetan has been trapped by the engrams formed at various stages of embodiment, Hubbard says.

As soon became obvious in Dianetics, clears were not the fully liberated individuals it had been hoped they would be. The idea of engrams from past lives explained the problem, thus a new concept appeared in Scientology—the "MEST-Clear" (MEST = Matter-Energy-Space-Time). Much of Hubbard's thinking resonates with the concepts of **reincarnation** and **transmigration** of souls found in Eastern religions. The goal of Scientology training thus became the final clearing of the individual of all engrams and the creation of what is termed an "Operating Thetan." Among the abilities of the operating Thetan is the soul's capacity to leave and operate apart from the body.

The exact content of the teachings of the Church of Scientology are imparted in the classes attended by church members and are not revealed to the public. Such is especially true of the highest classes (OT-4–7 levels), though jumbled accounts have been presented in books by former members, several of whom left the church with the confidential materials used in the classes and who tried to hurt the church by making these materials available to the general public. As in Dianetics, one progresses through the OT levels on a degree basis, the mastering of one level being a prerequisite to the next.

Scientology's Controversy

Almost from its beginning, Scientology has been a controversial religion. Soon after his announcement of the discovery of Dianetics, Hubbard encountered opposition by the American Medical Association, and in 1958 a two-decade battle with the Food and Drug Administration began. The initiation of these continuing battles had immense consequences, and critics of the church used the actions in one country as a basis for initiating actions elsewhere. Also, government files, not checked for accuracy, were passed to other government agencies and to other countries. Suddenly, in the 1960s, Scientology found itself under attack from a variety of quarters and has spent 30 years in the courts in the attempt to vindicate its existence and program.

Through the 1970s and 1980s, the church fought battles with the Internal Revenue Service in the United States (finally resolved in the early 1990s) and with several former members and anticult organizations who accused it of brainwashing church members. The church itself initiated legal action against publications that it believed libeled the organization and its founder. Important international cases were fought and won in **Australia,** Canada, and Great Britain, and ongoing cases are pending in **Germany,** among the most conservative of Western countries concerning religious freedom issues.

In the midst of its fight with the U.S. government, and continually blocked in its attempt to gather documentation of covert government actions against the church, in the mid-1970s several high officials conspired to infiltrate targeted agencies and obtain copies of files on the church. The FBI, CIA, and IRS were especially high on their list. When the plan was discovered, it resulted in a massive raid on the church's headquarters. Several church officials were arrested and convicted of theft of government property.

As of the 1990s, with the solving of its problems with the U.S. government, the church has moved to gain its rights as a viable religion in Germany and to oppose the actions of the Cult Awareness Network—which it believes is simply an antireligious organization—and similar groups internationally.

The Church of Scientology reports members in 129 countries and the words of L. Ron Hubbard have been translated into over 30 languages. They also maintain social reform and community activities among services such as the World Institute of Scientology Enterprises (WISE), that provide professional groups with strategies to find harmony in the workplace.

For an authoritative account of Dianetics and Scientology, see current editions of L. Ron Hubbard's books *Dianetics: The Modern Science of Mental Health* and *History of Man,* both published by the Church of Scientology, Los Angeles, and available at local Scientology organizations. Address: US IAS Members Trust, 1311 N. New Hampshire Ave., Los Angeles, CA 90027. Website: http://www.scientology.com/.

Sources:

Atack, Jon. *A Piece of Blue Sky: Scientology, Dianetics, and L. Ron Hubbard Exposed.* New York: Lyle Stuart, 1990.

Church of Scientology. http://www.scientology.com/. April 14, 2000.

Corydon, Bent, and L. Ron Hubbard, Jr. *L. Ron Hubbard: Messiah or Madman?* New York: Lyle Stuart, 1987.

Evans, Christopher. *Cults of Unreason.* New York: Farrar, Straus & Giroux, 1973. Reprint. New York: Dell, 1975.

Hubbard, L. Ron. *Dianetics 55!* Los Angeles: Publications Organization, 1954.

———. *Dianetics: The Modern Science of Mental Health.* New York: Hermitage House, 1950.

———. *Handbook for Preclears.* Los Angeles: Publications Organization, 1951.

———. *Science of Survival.* Los Angeles: Publications Organization, 1951.

———. *Scientology: The Fundamentals of Thought.* Los Angeles: Publications Organization, 1956.

———. *Self-Analysis.* Los Angeles: Publications Organization, 1951.

———. *You Have Lived Before This life?* Los Angeles: Publications Organization, 1977.

Miller, Russell. *Bare-Faced Messiah: The True Story of L. Ron Hubbard* New York: Henry Holt; London: Michael Joseph, 1987.

Wallis, Roy. *The Road to Total Freedom.* New York: Columbia University Press, 1976.

What Is Scientology? Los Angeles: Bridge Publications, 1992.

Sciomancy

A somewhat obscure branch of **divination** concerned with the evocation of astral reflections to ascertain future events.

Scoresby, William (1789–1857)

British Arctic explorer, whaler, physicist, author, and clergyman who was also a pioneer in the study of **animal magnetism.** He was born on October 5, 1789, at Cropton, near Whitby, England. At the age of eleven, he accompanied his father (a master mariner) on a whaling expedition, afterward resuming his education at a simple country school. Three years later, he was apprenticed to his father on a whaler. He made annual voyages to Greenland, and became a ship's chief officer in 1806. Later in the same year, he resumed his studies, entering Edinburgh University, Scotland, and studying chemistry and natural philosophy.

In 1807, he undertook a voyage to survey and chart the Balta Sound in the Shetland Islands. Afterward he served with the fleet at Copenhagen. He left the navy a year later and became acquainted with Joseph Banks, who introduced him to other scientists of the day. Scoresby made studies of natural phenomena and resumed attendance at Edinburgh University. From 1813 to 1817, he was at sea again, in charge of whaling vessels. In January 1819, he was elected a fellow of the Royal Society of Edinburgh, and in the following month he contributed a paper on variations of the magnetic needle to the Royal Society of London. The next year he published his first book, *An Account of the Arctic Regions, with a History and Description of the Northern Whale-Fishery* (2 vols., 1820), for many years the standard work on the subject. This was the first of a number of books that grew out of his worldwide travels.

In 1819, Scoresby moved with his family to Liverpool, where he superintended the building of the *Baffin,* a vessel fitted for the Greenland trade. He made three successful voyages in this vessel, but on returning to Liverpool in 1822, he found that his wife had died. Her death stimulated his strong religious convictions. Following his next voyage in 1823, he entered Queen's College, Cambridge, England, to prepare for the ministry. He was ordained in 1825, and for two years he was curé of Bessingby, near Bridlington Quay, in the north of England.

He became successively chaplain of Mariners Church, Liverpool (1827–32), incumbent of Bedford Chapel, Exeter (1932–39), and vicar of Bradford (1839–47). He resigned because of ill health, having spent six months leave on a voyage to the United States in search of a replacement. He lived his last years at the English seaside resort of Torquay when he was not traveling in search of some relief from his illness. He died at Torquay on March 21, 1857.

It was during his years at Exeter that Scoresby's interest in animal magnetism (**mesmerism**), arising from his observations on terrestrial magnetism during his polar voyages, emerged. During his last years at Torquay, he conducted a number of experiments, having found that he could mesmerize subjects easily. He gave the name "zoistic magnetism" to this hypnotic faculty. His third wife was one of his hypnotic subjects.

Scoresby's careful research into the possibility of clairvoyance resulted in persuasive evidence for **thought transference** or **community of sensation** between operator and subject. One entranced subject was able to describe accurately food that Scoresby tasted and also identified physical sensations in Scoresby's body. Another subject was immobilized as she sat on a sofa that had been "magnetized" by Scoresby and was unable to move outside an imaginary circle that Scoresby had traced on the floor. The power of purely imaginary diagrams to imprison hypnotized subjects was often explored by early mesmerists and suggests affinities with the magic circles of occult magicians.

Scoresby's work in the field of animal magnetism is of special importance. His book *Zoistic Magnetism* influenced **James Esdaile,** who read it while he was in India. Esdaile claimed to have successfully repeated Scoresby's experiment in "magnetizing" a sofa, using an armchair with knobs that Esdaile "magnetized." The subject was unable to remove his hands from the chair knobs until Esdaile had made mesmeric passes over him.

Sources:

Scoresby, William. *Journal of a Voyage to Australia for Magnetical Research.* London: Longman, Green, Longman, & Roberts, 1859.

———. *Magnetical Investigations.* 2 vols. London: Longman, Brown, Green, and Longmans, 1844–52.

———. *Zoistic Magnetism.* London: Longman, Brown, Green, and Longmans, 1849.

Stamp, Tom, and Cordelia Stamp. *William Scoresby, Arctic Scientist.* Whitby, U.K.: Whitby Press, 1975.

Scoriton Affair

As he later told the story, on April 24, 1965, at about 5:30 in the late afternoon, Ernest Arthur Bryant, a resident of Scoriton, Devonshire, England, saw a flying saucer approach. It stopped near to him, and a door opened. Three beings appeared and beckoned to him. He approached the saucer. Two of the three beings appeared to be nonhuman, but the third seemed to be a youth in his teens. The youth spoke with an accent that Bryant thought might be Russian and called himself Yamski. He said that he was from Venus, and then remarked that he wished Des was there, as he would understand what was happening. At the close of their conversation, he said that in a month he would return and bring proof of Mantell.

Ufologists who would eventually hear the story immediately associated Yamski with **George Adamski,** the controversial flying saucer contactee who had died on April 23, 1965. Adamski was of Polish background and had a noticeable accent. If this were Adamski, he would have immediately lost the signs of his aging. Adamski had a friend Desmond Leslie with whom he had written his first book. Captain Thomas F. Mantell, piloting an F-51, had been killed when he began chasing what he thought was a flying saucer. According to Bryant, the saucer returned in June and left some items, including several pieces of metal that could have possibly come from an F-51.

He reported the story to the **British UFO Research Association** (BUFORA), and an investigation was launched. The various items Bryant turned over to the two investigators proved to be mundane and of no relation to the F-51. In spite of problems with the story, one of the investigators, Eileen Buckle, rushed into print with a book. Shortly thereafter, Bryant unexpectedly took ill and died from a brain tumor. The other investigator, Norman Oliver, visited his widow. She reported that she was familiar with the story in the book as her husband has presented it to her first as the script for a science fiction novel. It was only after the investigation was well along that she realized her husband was trying to sell the story as a real event. She indicated that the supposed items related to Mantell had been purchased at a naval surplus store.

Alice Wells, head of the Adamski Foundation, dismissed the Scoriton story from the beginning, as did Desmond Leslie. Between their rejection and Oliver's uncovering of the hoax, few remained to support Bryant except Buckle. It is remembered amid the many UFO hoax attempts primarily because it extends, however briefly, the entertaining story of George Adamski.

Sources:

Buckle, Eileen. *The Scoriton Mystery.* London: Neville Spearman, 1967.

Oliver, Norman. *Sequel to Scoriton.* London: The Author, 1968.

Zinstagg, Lou, and Timothy Good. *George Adamski—The Untold Story.* Beckenham, Kent, UK: Ceto Publications, 1983.

SCOTLAND

[For early historical material on Scotland, see the entry on the **Celts**].

Witchcraft

Witchcraft and, more commonly, **sorcery,** malevolent magic, appear to have been practiced in the earliest historical and traditional times in Scotland. It is related that during the reign of Natholocus in the second century there lived in Iona a witch of great renown, so celebrated for her marvelous power that the king sent one of his captains to consult her regarding the issue of a rebellion then troubling his kingdom. The witch declared that within a short period the king would be murdered, not by his open enemies but by one of his most favored friends, in whom he had most special trust. The messenger inquired the assassin's name. "Even by thine own hands as shall be well known within these few days," replied the witch.

So troubled was the captain on hearing these words that he abused her bitterly, vowing that he would see her burned before he would commit such a crime. But after reviewing the matter carefully in his mind, the captain arrived at the conclusion that if he informed the king of the witch's prophecy, the king might, for the sake of his personal safety, have him put to death, so thereupon he decoyed Natholocus into his private chamber and killed him with a dagger.

In about the year 388, the **devil** was said to be so enraged at the piety of St. Patrick that he assailed the saint with a whole band of witches in Scotland. The story goes that St. Patrick fled to the river Clyde, embarking in a small boat for Ireland. As witches cannot pursue their victims over running water, they flung a huge rock after the escaping saint, which fell harmlessly to the ground, and which tradition says now forms Dumbarton Rock.

Catholic and Protestant church leaders alike pursued the crusade against witchcraft with equal vigor, drawing their support from biblical passages such as Exodus 22:18, which commands, "Thou shalt not suffer a witch to live." Witches were believed to have sold themselves, body and soul, to the devil. Their ceremony was said to consist of kneeling before the devil, who placed one hand on the individual's head and the other under her feet, while she dedicated all between to the service of the devil and renounced baptism. The witch (usually thought of as a female) was thereafter deemed to be incapable of reformation. No minister of any denomination whatever would intercede or pray for her. On sealing the compact, the devil then proceeded to put his mark upon her.

Writing on the "Witches' Mark," the Reverend Bell, minister of Gladsmuir, in 1705 states,

"The witches' mark is sometimes like a blew spot, or a little tale, or reid spots, like fleabiting, sometimes the flesh is sunk in and hollow and this is put in secret places, as among the hair of the head, or eyebrows, within the lips, under the armpits, and even in the most secret parts of the body."

The Reverend Robert Kirk of Aberfoyle in his *Secret Commonwealth of Elves, Fauns and Fairies* (written in 1691) notes,

"A spot that I have seen, as a small mole, horny, and brown colored, throw which mark when a large brass pin was thrust (both in buttock, nose, and roof of the mouth) till it bowed [bent] and became crooked, the witches, both men and women, nather felt a pain nor did bleed, nor knew the precise time when this was doing to them (their eyes only being covered)."

In many cases the mark was invisible, and according to popular lore, no pain accompanied the pricking of it. Thus, there arose a group of experts who pretended great wisdom and skill concerning the marks. They referred to themselves as "witch prickers" and it became their business to discover and label witches.

The method employed was barbarous. First, having stripped and bound his victim, the witch pricker proceeded to thrust his needles into every part of the body. When at last the victim, worn out with exhaustion and agony, remained silent, the witch pricker declared that he had discovered the mark.

The witch pricker could also resort to trial by water. The suspects were tied, wrapped in a sheet, and flung into a deep pool. In cases where the body floated, the water of baptism was supposed to be giving the accused, while those who sank to the bottom were absolved, but no attempt was made at rescue.

If a confession was demanded, tortures was resorted to, burning with irons being generally the last torture applied. In some cases a diabolic contrivance called the "witches' bridle" was used. The "bridle" encircled the victim's head while a pronged iron bit was thrust into the mouth, piercing the tongue, palate, and cheeks. In cases of execution, the victim was usually strangled and her body later burned at the stake.

Witches were accused of a great variety of sorceries. Common offenses were bewitching milk cattle by turning their milk sour or curtailing the supply, raising storms, stealing children from their graves, and promoting various illnesses. A popular device was to make a waxen image of the victim, thrust pins into it, and sear it with hot irons, all of which the victim was supposed to feel. Upon domestic animals witches cast an **evil eye,** causing emaciation and refusal to take food until at length death ensued. On the other hand, to those who believed in them and acknowledged their power, witches were supposed to use their powers for good by curing disease and causing prosperity.

Witches were believed to meet weekly, at which time the devil presided. Saturday was commonly called "the witches' sabbat," as their meetings were generally believed to be held on that day in a desolate place or possibly a ruined church building (a number of which had been left by the invading Vikings). They rode to the gatherings through the air on broomsticks (see **transvection**). If the devil was not present on their arrival, they evoked him by beating the earth with a fir stick and saying "Rise up foul thief."

The witches appeared to see the devil in different guises; to some he appeared as a boy clothed in green, others saw him dressed in white, while to others he appeared mounted on a black horse. After delivering a mock sermon, he held a court at which the witches had to make a full statement of their doings during the week. Those who had not accomplished sufficient "evil" were beaten with their own broomsticks, while those who had been more successful were rewarded with enchanted bones. The proceedings finished with a dance, the music to which the fiend played on his bagpipes.

The poet Robert Burns in his *Tale of Tam o'Shanter* gave a graphic description of a witches' gathering. There were great annual gatherings at Candlemas (February 2), Beltane (April 30), and Hallow-eve (October 31). These were of an international character and the witch sisterhood of all nations assembled, those who had to cross the sea performing the journey in barges of eggshell, while their aerial journeys were on goblin horses with enchanted bridles.

Laws Against Witchcraft

Through the confessions extracted from accused witches, guided by the fantasies about witchcraft in the several manuals that circulated through Europe beginning late in the fifteenth century, a picture of witchcraft was constructed and then promulgated into a society that still strongly believed in the powers of supernatural magic. In response to the fear of sorcerers and witches, the government passed laws outlawing their reported activities. In Scotland, less than a century after the redefinition of witchcraft as apostasy by the Roman Catholic Church in the 1480s, the first witchcraft law was enacted in the form of statute passed in 1563 in the Parliament of Queen Mary. It read (in the now archaic English of the time),

"That na maner of person nor persons of quhatsumever estaite, degree or condition they be of, take upon hand in onie times hereafter to use onie maner of witchcraft, sorcerie, or necromancie, under the paine of death, alsweil to be execute against the user, abuser, as the seeker of the response of consultation."

Scottish Catholics then accused Protestant reformer John Knox of being a renowned wizard and having by sorcery raised up saints in the churchyard of St. Andrews, when Satan himself was said to have appeared and so terrified Knox's secretary that he became insane and died. Knox was also charged with using his magical arts in his old age to persuade the beautiful young daughter of Lord Ochiltree to marry him.

There were numerous trials for witchcraft in the Justiciary Court in Edinburgh and at the circuit courts, while session records preserved from churches all over Scotland also show that numerous cases were dealt with by local authorities and church officials.

C. Rodgers, in his book *Social Life in Scotland,* (3 vols., 1884–86) states:

"From the year 1479 when the first capital sentence was carried out thirty thousand persons had on the charge of using enchantment been in Great Britain cruelly immolated; of these one fourth belonged to Scotland. No inconsiderable number of those who suffered on the charge of sorcery laid claim to necromantic acts with intents felonious or unworthy."

When James VI of Scotland in the year 1603 was called upon to ascend the throne of Great Britain and **Ireland** (as James I), his own native kingdom was in a rather curious condition. James himself was a man of considerable learning, intimate with Latin and theology, while his book, *Daemonologie* marks him as a person completely absorbed in the supernatural. Moreover while education and even scholarship were comparatively common at this date in Scotland (more common in fact than they were in contemporary **England**), the great mass of Scottish people shared abundantly their sovereign's dread of witches and sorcery. The efforts of Knox and his associates had brought about momentous changes in Scottish life, but if the Reformation rejected certain popular beliefs, Presbyterianism (the particular form of Protestant Christianity that came to power in Scotland) undoubtedly tended to introduce others. For that stern Calvinistic faith that now began to take root in Scotland nourished the idea that sickness and accident were a mark of divine anger. This theory did not cease to be common in the north till long after King James' day.

King James mentioned few precise facts concerning the practitioners of magic who were said to flourish in Scotland during his reign. But other sources of information claimed that these people were very numerous, and whereas in Elizabethan England it was customary to put a witch to death by hanging, in Jacobean Scotland magistrates employed harsher measures. In fact, the victim was burned at the stake, and it is interesting to note that on North Berwick Law, in the county of East Lothian, there is a tall stone that, according to local tradition, was formerly used as a site for such burnings.

Yet it would be wrong to suppose that witches and sorcerers, although handled roughly, were regarded with universal hatred, for in seventeenth- century Scotland medicine and magic went hand in hand, and the man suffering from a physical malady (particularly one whose cause he could not understand) very seldom entrusted himself to a professional leech (a physician whose medical technique was the placement of bloodsucking leeches on the patient's body) and much preferred to consult one who claimed healing capacities derived from intercourse with the unseen world.

Sorcerers, however, were generally also experts in the art of poisoning, and while a good many cures are credited to them, their triumphs in the opposite direction would seem to have been much more numerous. Thus we find that in July 1702, a certain James Reid of Musselburgh was brought to trial, being charged not merely with achieving miraculous cures, but with contriving the murder of one David Libbertoun, a baker in Edinburgh. This Libbertoun and his family, it transpired, were sworn enemies of a neighboring household, by the name of Christie, and eventually their feud grew as fierce as that between the Montagues and Capulets. The Christies swore they would bring things to a conclusion, and going to Reid they petitioned his nefarious aid.

His first act was to bewitch nine stones, these to be cast on the fields of the offending baker with a view to destroying his crops. Reid then proceeded to enchant a piece of raw flesh and also to make a statuette of wax. The nature of the design is not recorded, but presumably Libbertoun himself was represented. Mrs. Christie was instructed to thrust the meat under her enemy's door, and then to go home and melt the waxwork before her own fire. These instructions she duly obeyed, and a little later the victim breathed his last. Reid did not escape justice and after his trial suffered the usual fate of being burned alive.

Isobel Griersone, a Prestonpans woman who was burned to death on the Castle Rock, Edinburgh, in March 1607, had a record of poisonings rivalling that of Cellini himself, and it is even recorded that she contrived to put an end to several people simply by cursing them.

Equally sinister were the exploits of another sorceress, Belgis Todd of Longniddry, who was reported to have brought about the death of a man she hated just by enchanting his cat. This picturesque method was scorned by notorious Perthshire witch Janet Irwing, who in about the year 1610 poisoned various members of the family of Erskine of Dun, in the county of Angus. The criminal was eventually detected and suffered the usual fate.

The wife of John Dein, a burgess of Irvine, conceived a violent aversion for her brother-in-law, Archibald, and on one occasion, when the latter was setting out for France, Margaret hurled imprecations at his ship, vowing none of its crew or passengers would ever return to their native Scotland. Months went by, and no word of Archibald's arrival reached Irvine, until one day a peddler named Stewart came to John Dein's house and declared that the baneful prophecy had been duly fulfilled.

Learning of the affair, municipal authorities arrested Stewart, whom they had long suspected of practicing magic. At first he confessed innocence, but under torture he confessed how, along with Margaret Dein, he had made a clay model of the ill-starred ship, and thrown this into the sea on a particularly stormy night. His audience was horrified at the news, but they hastened to lay hands on the sorceress, whereupon they dealt with her as noted above.

No doubt the witches of Jacobean Scotland were credited with triumphs far greater than what they really achieved. At the same time, a number of the accused sorcerers firmly maintained, when confronted by a terrible death, that they had been initiated in their craft by the devil himself, or perhaps by a band of **fairies.** It is not surprising that they were dreaded by the simple, illiterate folk of their day, and, musing on these facts, we may feel less amazed at the credulity displayed by King James, who declared that all sorcerers "ought to be put to death according to the law of God, the civill and imperiale Law, and municipall Law of all Christian nations."

The last execution of a witch in Scotland took place in Sutherland in 1722. An old woman residing at Loth was charged, among other crimes, with having transformed her daughter into a pony, shod by the devil, which caused the girl to turn lame both in hands and feet. Sentence of death was pronounced by Captain David Ross, the Sheriff-substitute. C. Rodgers relates: "The poor creature when led to the stake was unconscious of the stir made on her account, and warming her wrinkled hands at the fire kindled to consume her, said she was thankful for so good a blaze. For his rashness in pronouncing the sentence of death, the Sheriff was emphatically reproved."

In more recent centuries witchcraft has been dealt with under laws pertaining to rogues, vagabonds, gamesters, and practitioners of **fortune- telling.**

Magic and Demonology

Magic appears to have been common in Scotland until a late period. In the pages of Adamnan, Abbot of Iona (ca. 625–704 C.E.), St. Columba and his priest regarded the Druids as magicians, and he countered their sorcery with what was believed to be a superior celestial magic of his own. Thus does the religion of one race become magic in the eyes of another.

Notices of sorcery in Scotland before the thirteenth century are scanty, if we except the tradition that Macbeth encountered three witches who prophesied his fate to him. There is no reason to believe that **Thomas the Rhymer** (who was endowed by later superstition with adventures similar to those of Tannhauser) was really other than a minstrel and maker of epigrams, or that Sir **Michael Scott** was other than a scholar and man of letters.

The rhymed fragment known as "The Cursing of Sir John Rowil," by a priest of Corstorphine, near Edinburgh, which dates perhaps from the last quarter of the fifteenth century, provides a glimpse of medieval Scottish **demonology.** The poem is an invective against certain persons who rifled his poultry-yard, upon whom the priest called down divine vengeance. The demons who were to torment the evildoers were Garog, Harog, Sym Skynar, Devetinus "the devill that maid the dyce," Firemouth, Cokadame, Tutivillus, Browny, and Syr Garnega, who may be the same as Girnigo, to whom cross children are often likened by angry mothers of the Scottish working classes. The Scottish verb, "to girn" (to pull grotesque faces or grin), may find its origin in the name of a medieval fiend, the last shadow of some Teutonic or Celtic deity of unlovable attributes.

In Sym Skynar, we may have Skyrnir, a Norse giant in whose glove Thor found shelter from an earthquake, and who sadly fooled him and his companions. Skyrnir was one of the Jotunn or Norse Titans, and probably one of the powers of winter, and he may have received the popular surname of "Sym" in the same manner as we speak of "Jack" Frost.

A great deal has still to be done in unearthing the minor figures of Scottish mythology and demonology, and even the greater ones have not received the attention due to them. For example, in Newhaven, a fishing district near Edinburgh, we find the belief in a fiend called Brounger, who is described as an old man who levies a toll of fish and oysters upon the local fishermen. If he is not placated with these, he wreaks vengeance on the persons who fail to supply him. He is also described as "a Flint and the son of a Flint," which strongly suggests that, like Thor and many other gods of Asia and America, he was a thunder or weather deity. In fact his name is probably a mere corruption of an ancient Scandinavian word meaning "to strike," which still survives in the Scottish expression "make a breenge."

With regard to practical magic, a terrifying and picturesque legend tells how Sir Lewis Bellenden, a lord of session and superior of the Barony of Broughton, near Edinburgh, succeeded by the aid of a sorcerer in raising the devil in the backyard of his own house in the Canongate, somewhere around the end of the sixteenth century. Bellenden was a notorious trafficker with witches, with whom his barony of Broughton was reportedly overrun. Wanting to see the devil in person, he secured the services of one Richard Graham. The results of the evocation were disastrous to the inquisitive judge, whose nerves were so shattered at the devil's appearance that he fell ill and soon expired.

The case of Major Thomas Weir in 1670 is one of the most interesting in the annals of Scottish sorcery. Master storyteller Sir Walter Scott recounts the major aspects of the curious occurrence:

"It is certain that no story of witchcraft or necromancy, so many of which occurred near and in Edinburgh, made such a lasting impression on the public mind as that of Major Weir. The remains of the house in which he and his sister lived are still shown at the head of the West Bow, which has a gloomy aspect, well suited for a necromancer. It was, at different times, a brazier's shop and a magazine for lint, and in my younger days was employed for the latter use; but no family would inhabit the haunted walls as a residence; and bold was the urchin from the High School who dared approach the gloomy ruin at the risk of seeing the Major's enchanted staff parading through the old apartments, or hearing the hum of the necromantic wheel, which procured for his sister such a character as a spinner.

"The case of this notorious wizard was remarkable chiefly from his being a man of some condition (the son of a gentleman, and his mother a lady of family in Clydesdale), which was seldom the case with those that fell under similar accusations. It was also remarkable in his case that he had been a Covenanter, and peculiarly attached to that cause. In the years of the Commonwealth this man was trusted and employed by those who were then at the head of affairs, and was in 1649 commander of the City-Guard of Edinburgh, which procured him his title of Major. In this capacity he was understood, as was indeed implied in the duties of that officer at the period, to be very strict in executing severity upon such Royalists as fell under his military charge. It appears that the Major, with a maiden sister who had kept his house, was subject to fits of melancholic lunacy, an infirmity easily reconcilable with the formal pretences which he made to a high show of religious zeal. He was peculiar in his gift of prayer, and, as was the custom of the period, was often called to exercise his talent by the bedside of sick persons, until it came to be observed that, by some association, which it is more easy to conceive than to explain, he could not pray with the same warmth and fluency of expression unless when he had in his hand a stick of peculiar shape and appearance, which he generally walked with. It was noticed, in short, that when this stick was taken from him, his wit and talent appeared to forsake him.

"This Major Weir was seized by the magistrates on a strange whisper that became current respecting vile practices, which he seems to have admitted without either shame or contrition. The disgusting profligacies which he confessed were of such a character that it may be charitably hoped most of them were the fruits of a depraved imagination, though he appears to have been in many respects a wicked and criminal hypocrite. When he had completed his confession, he avowed solemnly that he had not confessed the hundredth part of the crimes which he had committed.

"From this time he would answer no interrogatory, nor would he have recourse to prayer, arguing that, as he had no hope whatever of escaping Satan, there was no need of incensing him by vain efforts at repentance. His witchcraft seems to have been taken for granted on his own confession, as his indictment was chiefly founded on the same document, in which he alleged he had never seen the devil, but any feeling he had of him was in the dark.

"He received sentence of death, which he suffered 12th April, 1670, at the Gallow-hill, between Leith and Edinburgh. He died so stupidly sullen and impenitent as to justify the opinion that he was oppressed with a kind of melancholy frenzy, the consequence perhaps of remorse, but such as urged him not to repent, but to despair. It seems probable that he was burnt alive.

"His sister, with whom he was supposed to have had an incestuous connection, was condemned also to death, leaving a stronger and more explicit testimony of their mutual sins than could be extracted from the Major. She gave, as usual, some account of her connection with the queen of the fairies, and acknowledged the assistance she received from that sovereign in spinning an unusual quantity of yarn. Of her brother she said that one day a friend called upon them at noonday with a fiery chariot, and invited them to visit a friend at Dalkeith, and that while there her brother received information of the event of the battle of Worcester. No one saw the style of their equipage except themselves.

"On the scaffold this woman, determining, as she said, to die with the greatest shame possible was with difficulty prevented from throwing off her clothing before the people, and with scarce less trouble was she flung from the ladder by the executioner. Her last words were in the tone of the sect to which her brother had so long affected to belong: 'Many,' she said, 'weep and lament for a poor old wretch like me; but alas, few are weeping for a broken covenant.' "

Alchemy

While fearful of sorcery and witchcraft, James IV was attracted to the science of **alchemy.** The poet William Dunbar described the patronage the king bestowed upon certain adventurers who had studied the mysteries of alchemy and were ingenious in making "quintiscence," which should convert other metals into pure gold. In the *Treasurer's Accounts* there are numerous payments for the "quinta essentia," including wages to the persons employed, utensils of various kinds, coals and wood for the furnaces, and for a variety of other materials such as quicksilver, aqua vitae, litharge, auri, fine tin, burnt silver, alum, salt and eggs, and saltpeter.

The Scottish monarch appears to have collected around him a multitude of quacks of all sorts for mention is made of "the leech with the curland hair," of "the lang Dutch doctor," of one Fullertone, who was believed to possess the secret of making precious stones, of a Dr. Ogilvy who labored hard at the transmutation of metals, and many other empirics, whom James not only supported in their experiments, but himself assisted in their laboratory. The most noted of these adventurers was Master **John Damian,** the French Leich. He probably held an appointment as a physician in the royal household.

John soon ingratiated himself with the king, who had a strong passion for alchemy. He remained in James's favor throughout the rest of his life, the last notice given to him being on March 27, 1513, when the sum of £20 was paid to him to travel to the mine in Crawford Moor, where the king had artisans at work searching for gold.

From the reign of James IV to that of Mary Stuart, no magician or alchemical practitioner of note appears to have existed in Scotland, and in the reign of James VI, too great a severity was exhibited against such to permit them to avow themselves publicly. In the reign of James VI, however, lived the celebrated **Alexander Seton** of Port Seton near Edinburgh, known abroad as "The Cosmopolite," who is said to have succeeded in achieving the transmutation of metals.

Magic and Religion in the Scottish Highlands

Pagan Scotland appears to have been lacking in benevolent deities. Those representatives of the spirit world who were on friendly terms with mankind were either held captive by magic spells or had some sinister object in view which caused them to act with the most plausible duplicity. The chief demon or deity (one hesitates which to call her) was a one-eyed hag who had tusks like a wild boar. She was referred to in folk tales as "the old wife" (Cailleach), "Grey Eyebrows," or "the Yellow Muitearteach," and reputed to be a great worker of spells. Apparently she figured in a lost creation myth, for fragmentary accounts survive of how she fashioned the hills, brought lochs into existence, and caused whirlpools. Echoes of this boar-like hag survive in folk ballads of "Old Bangum" and "Sir Lionel" (Child No. 18), prefigured in ancient Hindu legends of the god Vishnu as the giant boar Vahara.

The hag was a lover of darkness, desolations, and winter. With her hammer she alternately splintered mountains, prevented the growth of grass, and raised storms. Numerous wild animals followed her, including deer, goats, and wild boars. When one of her sons was thwarted in his love affairs by her, he transformed her into a mountain boulder "looking over the sea," a form she retained during the summer. She was liberated again on the approach of winter. During the spring months, the hag drowned fishermen and preyed on the food supply; she also stole children and roasted them in her cave.

Her progeny included a brood of monstrous giants, each with several heads and arms. These were continually operating against mankind, throwing down houses, abducting women, and destroying growing crops. Heroes who fought against them required the assistance of a witch who was called the "Wise Woman," from whom they obtained magic wands.

The witch of Scottish folk tales is the "friend of man" and her profession was evidently regarded in ancient times as a highly honorable one. Wizards also enjoyed high repute; they were the witch-doctors, priests, and magicians of the Scottish Pagans, and it was not until the sixteenth century that legal steps were taken to suppress them in the Highland districts.

There seems to have been no sun-worship or moon-worship in Scotland, for neither sun nor moon was individualized in the Gaelic language; these bodies, however, were reputed to exercise a magical influence. The moon especially was a "Magic Tank," from which supplies of power were drawn by those capable of performing requisite ceremonies. This practice has been revived by modern neo-pagan witches in the ritual referred to as "drawing down the moon."

But although there appear to have been no lunar or solar spirits, there were numerous earth and water spirits. The "water wife," like the English "mer wife," (see **mermaids**), was a greatly dreaded being who greedily devoured victims. She must not be confused with the **banshee,** that Fate whose chief business it was to foretell disasters, either by washing blood-stained garments or knocking on a certain boulder beside the river.

The water wife usually confronted a late traveler at a ford. She claimed him as her own, and if he disputed her claim she asked what weapons he had to use against her. The unwary one named each in turn, and when he did so, the power to harm her passed away. One story of this character is as follows:

"The wife rose up against the smith who rode his horse, and she said, 'I have you: what have you against me?' 'My sword,' the man answered. 'I have that,' she said, 'what else?' 'My shield,' the man said. 'I have that and you are mine.' 'But,' protested the man, 'I have something else.' 'What is that?' the water wife demanded. To this question the cautious smith answered, 'I have the long, grey, sharp thing at my thigh.' This was his dirk, and not having named it, he was able to make use of it. As he spoke he flung his plaid round the water wife and lifted her up on his horse behind him. Enclosed in the magic circle she was powerless to harm him, and he rode home with her, deaf to her entreaties and promises.

"He took her to his smithy and tied her to the anvil. That night, her brood came to release her. They raised a tempest and tore the roof off the smithy, but the smith defied them. When day dawned they had to retreat. Then he bargained with the water wife, and she consented that if he would release her, neither he nor any of his descendants should ever be drowned in any three rivers he might name. He named three and received her promise, but as she made her escape she reminded him of a fourth river. 'It is mine still,' she added. In that particular river the smith himself ultimately perished."

Ever since, fishermen have not liked to name either the fish they desire to procure or those that prey on their catches. Haddocks are "white bellies," salmon "red ones," and the dog-fish "the big black fellow." It is also regarded as unlucky to name a minister, or refer to Sunday, in a fishing boat—a fact that suggests that in early Christian times fishermen might be pious churchmen on land but continued to practice paganism when they went to sea, like the Icelandic Norsemen who believed that Christ ruled their island, and Thor the ocean. Fairies must not be named on Fridays, at Halloween, or on Beltane (May Day) when charm fires were lit.

Earth worship, or rather the propitiation of earth spirits, was a prominent feature of Scottish paganism. There too magic played a leading role. Compacts were confirmed by swearing over a piece of turf, certain moors or mounds were set apart for ceremonial practices, and these were visited for the performance of child-procuring and other ceremonies, which were performed at a standing stone.

In cases of sickness, a **divination** cake was baked and left at a sacred place: If it disappeared during the night, the patient was supposed to recover, if it remained untouched until the following morning it was believed that the patient would die.

Offerings were constantly made to the earth spirits. In a witch trial recorded in *Humbie Kirk Session Register* (September 23, 1649) one Agnes Gourlay was accused of having made offerings of milk, saying, "God preserve us too; they are under the earth that have as much need of it as they that are above the earth."

The milk poured out upon the earth at magical ceremonies was supposed to go to the fairies. "Gruagach" stones survived into relatively modern times in the Highlands. These were flat stones with deep "cup" marks. After a cow was milked, the milker poured into a hole the portion of milk required by the Gruagach, a long-haired spirit who is usually "dressed like a gentleman." If no offering was given to him, the cream would not rise on the milk, or even if it did, the churning would be a failure. There are interesting records in the Presbytery records of Dingwall, Ross-shire, regarding the prevalence of milk pouring and other ceremonies during the seventeenth century.

The seer was usually wrapped in the skin of a sacrificed bull and left lying all night beside the river. He was visited by supernatural beings in the darkness and obtained answers regarding future events. Another and horrifying way to perform this divination ceremony was to roast a live cat. The cat was turned on a spit until the "Big Cat" (the devil) appeared and either granted the wish of the performer of the ceremony, or foretold what was to take place in answer to a query. In the twentieth century, there are still memories of traditional beliefs regarding witchcraft, fairies, the evil eye, second sight, and magical charms to cure or injure.

Individuals, domesticated animals, and dwellings were charmed against witchcraft by iron and certain herbs or berries. The evil eye influence was dispelled by drinking "water of silver" from a wooden bowl or ladle. The water was taken from a river or well of high repute, silver placed in it, then a charm repeated. When it had been passed over a fire, the victim was given it to drink and what remained was sprinkled around the hearth-stone with a ceremony that varied according to district.

Curative charms were handed down in families from a male to a female and a female to a male. Blood-stopping charms were regarded with great sanctity and the most persistent folklore collectors were unable to obtain them from those who were reported to be able to use these with effect.

Accounts were given of "blood-stopping" from a distance. Although the possessor of the power usually had a traditional charm, he or she rarely used it without also praying. Some Highland doctors testified in private to the wonderful effects of "blood-stopping" operations. In relatively recent times, a medical officer of Inverness-shire stated in his official report to the county council that he was watching with interest the operations of "King's Evil Curers," who still enjoyed great repute in the Western Isles. These were usually **seventh sons.**

Second sight, like the power to cure and stop blood, runs in families. There is scarcely a parish in the Scottish Highlands without a family in which one or more individuals are reputed to have occult powers. Some had visions, either while awake or asleep. Others heard ominous sounds on occasions and were able to understand what they signified. Certain individuals confessed, but with no appreciation of the faculty, that they were sometimes able to foretell that a person was likely to die soon.

Two instances of this kind may be cited. A younger brother caught a chill. When an elder brother visited him, he knew at once that the young man would die soon, and communicated a statement to that effect to a mutual friend. According to medical opinion, the patient, who was not confined to bed, was in no danger, but three months afterward, he developed serious symptoms and died suddenly. When news of the death was communicated to the elder brother, he had a temporary illness.

The same individual met a gentleman in a friend's house and had a similar experience; he "felt," he could not explain how, that this man was near death. On two occasions within the following week he questioned the gentleman's daughter regarding her father's health and was informed that he was "as usual." The daughter was surprised at the inquiries. Two days after this meeting, the gentleman in question expired suddenly while sitting in his chair.

Again the individual, on hearing of the death, had a brief but distressing illness, with symptoms usually associated with shock. The mother of this man had a similar faculty. On several occasions she saw lights. One day during the Boer War, an officer passing her door bade her goodbye, since he had been ordered to South Africa. She said, "He will either be slain or come back deformed," and turned ill immediately. A few months later the officer was wounded in the lower jaw with a bullet and returned home with his face much deformed.

The faculty of second sight manifests itself in various ways, as these instances show, and evidence that it is possessed by individuals may occur only once or twice in a lifetime. There are cases, however, in which it is constantly active. Those reputed to have the faculty are most reticent regarding it and appear to dread it.

At the close of the nineteenth century, "tow-charms" to cure sprains and bruises were sold in a well-known Highland town by a woman who muttered a metrical spell over each magic knot she tied as the afflicted part was treated by her. She had numerous patients among all classes. Bone-setters (the precursors of modern chiropractors) enjoyed high repute in some localities. In modern memory a public presentation was made to a Ross-shire bone-setter in recognition of his life-long services to the community. His faculty was inherited from his forbears.

Numerous instances may be gleaned in the Highlands of the appearance of the spirits of the living and the dead. The appearance of the spirit of a living person is said to be a sure indication of the approaching death of that individual. It is never seen by a member of the family, but appears to intimate friends. Sometimes it speaks and gives indication of the fate of some other mutual acquaintance.

The Supernatural in Scottish Fiction

While Sir Walter Scott frequently introduced supernatural traditions into his novels and poems, and writers like Robert Louis Stevenson published powerful stories on occult subjects (see **fiction, English occult**), the magical and supernatural stories of the land go back to the ancient balladry of Scotland. Many of the 305 ballads collected and classified by Francis James Child (regarded as definitive in its time) echo ancient stories and beliefs from a magical past. Some of these themes seem to have descended from Scandinavian balladry.

From Folklore to Psychical Research

The study of Scottish **occultism** was begun by the collectors of folklore. Among the earliest was the Reverend Robert Kirk, whose *The Secret Commonwealth of Elves, Fauns and Fairies,* (written in 1691, but not published until 1815) reads like an anthropologist's report on a foreign country. The work is precise in its descriptions of fairy life and customs, and some believed that Kirk himself became a prisoner of the fairies.

Among Scottish folklorists whose research preserved ancient legends and magical traditions, the most prominent was John Francis Campbell of Islay (1822–1885). His great collection, *Popular Tales of the West Highlands, Orally Collected* (4 vols., 1860–62), achieved for Scotland what Jacob Grimm had done for the *Household Tales* of Europe. Alexander Carmichael (1832–1912) collaborated with Campbell and preserved the ancient Gaelic culture in his collection *Carmina Gadelica, Hymns and Incantations, With Illustrated Notes in Words, Rites, and Customs, Dying and Obsolete, Orally Collected in the Highlands and Islands of Scotland* (2 vols., 1900).

The versatile genius Andrew Lang (1844–1912) published over fifty major works concerned with poetry, book collecting, classical studies, Scottish history, English literature, anthropology, folklore, and fairy tales. Lang was a founder-member and later president of both the **Society for Psychical Research,** and the **Folk-Lore Society.** Lang was one of the earliest writers on psychical research to collate modern phenomena with the traditions and beliefs of ancient peoples, and his knowledge in this wide field was encyclopedic. He noted, for example, in regard to reports of **crystal gazing** that he found it difficult to understand why as long as such things rested only on tradition, they were a matter of respectable folklore, but whenever contemporary evidence was produced, folklorists dropped the subject hastily.

In 1897, he published *The Book of Dreams and Ghosts,* in which he collated stories from all ages dealing with the whole field of the supernatural, including uncanny dreams, hauntings, bilocation, crystal gazing, animal ghosts, and poltergeists. His classic study, *Cock Lane and Common-Sense* (1894), reviewed ancient spirit contact, haunted houses, the famous Cock Lane poltergeist of London in 1762, apparitions, ghosts, hallucinations, second sight, table-turning, and comparative psychical research.

Modern-day Scotland

In Scotland, the study of parapsychology has become a degree-bestowing science. Noted writer and critic **Arthur Koestler** provided in his will the establishment of an endowed Chair of Parapsychology at a British University. His intention was to further objective scientific research into ". . .the capacity attributed to some individuals to interact with their environment by means other than the recognised sensory and motor channels." Following Koestler's death in 1982, his trustees advertised the post and in 1984 awarded the Chair to the University of Edinburgh. Today, The University of Edinburgh's **Koestler Parapsychology Unit,** a part of the Department of Psychology, offers a doctorate program in parapsychology and publishes the **European Journal of Parapsychology.** Similarly, St. Andrews University has also offered courses in parapsychology.

Scotland remains famous for its ghost tales and haunted dwellings, with the natives proud to quip that "ghostly spirits are second only to the drinkable kind in the hearts of Highlanders." Cities such as Edinburgh offer organized ghost walks and haunted tours through selected castles and ancient hotels. Ghostly notoriety is shared among spectors of famous as well as common folk, male and female, young and old. It is the spirit of Mary Queen of Scots that seems to be the most prevalent among Highland haunters. The queen's spiritual presence has reportedly appeared in nearly every castle she visited during her life. In addition to ghost tours for mortal visitors to Scotland, interested parties can learn more about Scottish hauntings at web sites devoted to the subject, as well as the bimonthly magazine, *Haunted Scotland.*

Sources:

Black, George F. *A Calendar of Cases of Witchcraft in Scotland 1510–1727.* New York: New York Public Library, 1938.

Bliss, Douglas Percy, ed. *The Devil in Scotland.* London: Alexander MacLehose, 1937.

Bronson, Bertrand Harris. *The Traditional Tunes of the Child Ballads.* 4 vols. Princeton, N.J.: Princeton University Press, 1959–72.

Campbell, John F. *Popular Tales of the West Highlands, Orally Collected.* 4 vols. Edinburgh, 1860–62. Rev. ed. London and Paisley: Alexander Gardner, 1890–93. Reprint, Detroit: Singing Tree Press, 1969.

Campbell, John L., and Trevor H. Hall. *Strange Things: The Story of Fr. Allan McDonald, Ada Goodrich Freer, and the Society for Psychical Research's Enquiry into Highland Second Sight.* London: Routledge & Kegan Paul, 1968.

Carmichael, Alexander. *Carmina Gadelica, Hymns and Incantations.* 2 vols. 1900. 2nd ed. 5 vols. Edinburgh & London, 1928–54.

Chambers, Robert. *Traditions of Edinburgh.* N.p., 1825.

Child, Francis J. *The English and Scottish Popular Ballads.* 5 vols. Boston, 1882–98. Reprint, Folklore Press; Pageant Book, 1957.

Davidson, Thomas. *Rowan Tree and Red Thread.* Edinburgh: Oliver and Boyd, 1949.

Ferguson, John. *Witchcraft Literature of Scotland.* Edinburgh: Edinburgh Bibliographical Society Papers, 1899.

Ghosts of Scotland. http://www.tartans.com/articles/ghostwomen.html. June 19, 2000.

James I. *Daemonologie.* Edinburgh, 1597. Reprint, London, 1603. Reprint, London: John Lane/New York: E. P. Dutton, 1924.

Kirk, Robert. *The Secret Commonwealth of Elves, Fauns and Fairies.* Edinburgh, 1815. Reprint, Stirling, Scotland: Eaneas Mackay, 1933.

Koestler Parapsychology Unit at the Department of Psychology, University of Edinburgh, Scotland, U.K. http://moebius.psy.ed.ac.uk/. June 19, 2000.

Lang, Andrew. *The Book of Dreams and Ghosts.* London, 1897. Reprint, New York: Causeway Books, 1974. Lowry, Betty. "Scotland's Lady Ghost Scream in Shades of Gray and Green." *The Denver Post.* October 31, 1999. Pp. T03.

———. *Cock Lane and Common-Sense.* London: Longmans, Green, 1894. Reprint, New York: AMS Press, 1970.

Macgregor, Alexander. *Highland Superstitions Connected with the Druids, Fairies, Witchcraft, Second-Sight, Hallowe'en, Sacred Wells and Lochs.* Stirling, Scotland: Eaneas Mackay, 1922.

———. *The Prophecies of the Brahan Seer.* Stirling, Scotland: Eaneas Mackay, 1935.

Maclagan, Robert Craig. *The Evil Eye in the Western Highlands.* London: David Nutt, 1902. Reprint, U.K.: E. P. Publishing, 1972. Reprint, Norwood, Pa.: Norwood Editions, 1973.

MacLeod, Nicholas A. *Scottish Witchcraft.* St. Ives, England: James Pike, 1975.

Macrae, Norman, ed. *Highland Second-Sight: With Prophecies of Conneach Odhar of Petty.* Dingwall, Scotland: G. Souter, 1908. Reprint, Norwood, Pa., 1972.

McNeill. F. Marian. *Scottish Folklore and Folk-Belief.* Glasgow: William Maclellan, 1957.

Scott, Sir Walter. *Letters on Demonology and Witchcraft.* London, 1830. Reprint, New York, 1831.

Sharpe, Charles Kirkpatrick. *Historical Account of the Belief in Witchcraft in Scotland.* N.p., 1819.

Sinclair, George. *Satan's Invisible World Discovered.* Edinburgh, 1685. Reprint, Edinburgh: Thomas G. Stevenson, 1865.

Sutherland, Elizabeth. *Ravens and Black Rain: The Story of Highland Second Sight.* London: Constable, 1986.

Thompson, Francis. *The Supernatural Highlands.* London: Robert Hale, 1976.

Scott, Christopher S(avile) O'D(onoghue) (1927–)

British sociologist who has experimented in the field of parapsychology. He was born on August 12, 1927, at Cuckfield, Sussex, England, and he studied at Cambridge University (B.A., 1948; M.A., 1952). Following his graduation, he became a statistician at UNESCO, Paris (1952–55), and a research officer of The Social Survey at the British Central Office of Information, London (1955–61), prior to returning to work with the United Nations in Africa.

He joined the **Society of Psychical Research,** London, and was an SPR council member during the years he lived in London (1957–60). He conducted experiments in an attempt to find a repeatable technique for the demonstration of extrasensory perception. He has also done theoretical work on models for psi and examined the work of **Gertrude R. Schmeidler** on the so-called "sheep-goat" effect on scoring in quantitative psi experiments.

Scott was among the first researchers to call into question the experiments of **S. G. Soal** based upon his statistical analysis. Based upon Scott's initial critique, much of Soal's work was reexamined and found to have been faulty and his spectacular results probably a matter of conscious **fraud.** Scott's conclusions were initially attacked, but later independently confirmed.

Sources:

Berger, Arthur S., and Joyce Berger. *The Encyclopedia of Parapsychology and Psychical Research.* New York: Paragon House, 1991.

Pleasants, Helene, ed. *Biographical Dictionary of Parapsychology.* New York: Helix Press, 1964.

Scott, Christopher S. O. "Experimental Object-Reading: A Critical Review of the Work of Dr. J. Hettinger." *Proceedings* of the Society for Psychical Research (November 1959).

———. "Fresh Light on the Shackleton Experiments." *Proceedings* of the Society for Psychical Research 56 (1974).

———. "G. Spencer Brown and Probability: A Critique." *Journal* of the Society for Psychical Research (June 1958).

———. "Models for Psi." *Proceedings* of the Society for Psychical Research (October 1961).

Scott, Cyril (Meir) (1879–1970)

Eminent British composer, librettist, poet, author, and Theosophist. He was born on September 27, 1879, at Oxton, Birkenhead, England. He studied music at Frankfort-on-Main, Germany. He was only 21 when his *Heroic Suite* was first performed at Darmstadt, Germany, and launched him on a successful music career. He wrote for the piano, on which he also performed capably, as well as composing orchestral pieces, chamber and choral works, and violin studies. He composed an opera, *The Alchemist,* a ballet and a cantata, and songs and ballads. In addition he published several volumes of his poetry: *The Celestial Aftermath, The Vales of Unity,* and *The Voice of the Ancient.*

Scott was an outspoken Theosophist, and he gave much thought to the occult meanings of music, a topic to which only a few, for example, Corinne Helene, had given any consideration. He published his conclusions in the book *Music; Its Secret Influence Throughout the Ages* (1933; enlarged ed. 1950), a volume dedicated to "Master Koot Hoomi Lal Singh and his pupil Nelsa Chaplin." It dealt with occult aspects of musical inspiration and the effects on the morals and aesthetics of different periods in history.

He also authored a series of books on the occult: *The Initiate* (1920), *The Initiate in the New World* (1927), and *The Initiate in the Dark Cycle* (1932). His autobiography, *Memoirs, Entitled My Years of Indiscretion,* appeared in 1924. He died December 31, 1970.

Sources:

Scott, Cyril. *The Adept of Galilee.* N.p., 1920.

———. *Bone of Contention* N.p., 1969.

———. *The Christian Paradox.* N.p., 1942.

———. *The Initiate.* London: Routledge & K. Paul, 1920; York Beach, Maine: St. Weiser, 1977.

———. *The Initiate in the Dark Cycle.* N.p., 1932; 1977. Reprint, York Beach, Maine: Samuel Weiser, 1991.

———. *The Initiate in the New World.* N.p., 1927; 1977. Reprint, York Beach, Maine: Samuel Weiser, 1991.

———. *Memoirs, Entitled My Years of Indiscretion.* N.p., 1924.

———. *An Outline of Modern Occultism.* New York: E. P. Dutton, 1935. Reprint, New York: Dutton, 1950.

———. *The Vision of the Nazarene.* N.p., 1933.

Scott, David (1806–1849) and William Bell (1811–1890)

These two brothers displayed unusual talent in the treatment of supernatural themes in art. David Scott was born October 10 (or 12), 1806, in Edinburgh, Scotland, and lived a comparatively uneventful life, his remarkable gifts being largely unrecognized by his contemporaries. He died on March 5, 1849.

In modern times, however, connoisseurs have appreciated his paintings, perceiving in his work great technical merits. In addition, people who care for art dealing with the supernatural have noted that Scott's *Paracelsus* and *Vasco de Gama* are in the forefront of work of this kind. His beautiful drawings for *The Ancient Mariner* express the very spirit of Coleridge, the arch-mystic, rendering it with a skill unsurpassed in any previous or subsequent illustrations to this poem.

David's brother, William Bell Scott, was also born in Edinburgh, his birth date being September 12, 1811. His career was very different from David's, for he won worldly success from the outset, and before his death on November 22, 1890, he had received much acclaim.

Etching some of his brother's works, and painting a host of pictures, he was also a voluminous writer, and his *Autobiographical Notes of the Life of William Bell Scott* (2 vols., published posthumously, 1892) contains insights concerning the mystic symbolism permeating the painting of the Middle Ages. It also contains a shrewd and interesting account of D. G. Rossetti's essays on **table-turning** and other Spiritualist practices.

William Bell's poems are almost all of a metaphysical order, and although it is extravagant to call him "the Scottish Blake," as many people have done, his mystical verse undoubtedly reflects a certain "meditative beauty," as "Fiona Macleod" (**William Sharp**) once wrote on the subject.

Scott, Michael (ca. 1175–ca. 1234)

Scottish mathematician, physician, astrologer, and reputed magician. Although Michael Scott's life is shrouded in obscurity, his name is familiar for various reason. First, the poet Dante referred to him in his *Inferno,* speaking of him as one singularly skilled in magical arts, while Scott was also mentioned by Boccaccio, who hailed him as among the greatest masters of **necromancy.** Moreover, Samuel Taylor Coleridge planned a drama dealing with Scott, who Scott asserted was a much more interesting personality than **Faust.** There is a novel about him by Allan Cunningham, but above all, he figures in Sir Walter Scott's *The Lay of the Last Minstrel.*

Sir Walter Scott, not a very careful antiquarian, identified the astrologer with one Sir Michael Scott of Balwearie, who, along with Sir David Wemyss of Wemyss, went to bring the Maid of Norway to Scotland in 1290. However, this identification is manifestly wrong, for in a poem by Vincent de Beauvais published as early as 1235, Michael Scott was mentioned as lately deceased.

This does not altogether dispose the idea that he emanated from the family of Balwearie, whose estates were situated near Kirkcaldy, in Fife, and it is almost certain that Scott was a man of high birth, since he studied at Oxford University.

When his Oxford days were over, Scott proceeded to the Sorbonne in Paris, where he acquired the title of *mathematics,* and from the French capital he wandered on to Bologna, in those days famous as a seat of learning. He did not stay for long, however, but went on to Palermo. He subsequently settled for a while at Toledo to study Arabic.

He appears to have been successful with these studies, thoroughly mastering the intricacies of the Arabic language. He next went to Sicily, where he became attached to the court of Ferdinand II, probably in the capacity of state astrologer. At least, he is so designated in an early manuscript copy (now in the Bodleian Library, Oxford, England) of his book on astronomy.

Scott had also at some time taken holy orders. In 1223, Pope Honorius III wrote to the Archbishop of Canterbury, urging him to procure an English benefice for Scott. It appears that in the following year, Scott was offered the Archbishopric of Cashel in Ireland, but he declined it on account of his total ignorance of the Irish language.

Scott was clearly highly esteemed at the Vatican, for in 1227 Gregory IX, successor to Honorius, made further overtures to the English primate on behalf of Scott. Whether these proved fruitful or not, according to **Roger Bacon,** Scott came to England in 1230, bringing with him the works of Aristotle—at that date virtually unknown in that country—and giving them a certain popularity among scholars.

Although no documentary evidence is forthcoming to support this theory, local tradition at Melrose, Scotland, contends that the astrologer came to that town in his old age, and that he died there and was buried somewhere in the neighborhood. Various other places in the Borders area of Scotland likewise claimed this distinction, and Sir Walter Scott stated that throughout the south of Scotland, "any great work of great labour or antiquity is ascribed either to Auld Michael, Sir William Wallace, or the Devil."

One popular story about Scott maintains that he used to ride through the air on a demon horse, and another claims that he used to sail the seas on the back of some fabulous animal. Yet a further legend recounts that Scott went as Scottish envoy to the king of France, and that the first stamp of his black steed's hoof rang the bells of Notre Dame, whereupon his most Christian majesty granted the messenger all he desired.

As regards the writings of Scott, he is credited with a translation of Aristotle's *De Animalibus,* but the ascription is not very well founded. However, it is almost certain that he wrote *Quvœsto Curiosa de Natura Solis et Lunae,* which is included in the *Theatrum Chemicum.* He was undoubtedly the author of *Mensa Philosophica,* published at Frankfurt in 1602, and also of *Liber Physiognomiœ Magistri Michaelis Scot,* a book that was reprinted nearly twenty times and translated into various languages.

Reference has already been made to a manuscript attributed to Scott in the Bodleian Library, and it should be noted that at Corpus Christi College, Oxford, the Vatican, and at the Sorbonne, there are further documents purporting to have been written by the astrologer himself, at his dictation, or copied out by scribes soon after the actual author's death.

Scottish Society for Psychical Research

Organization concerned with the study of parapsychology in Scotland. It sponsors meetings and lectures and issues a regular newsletter. It may be contacted c/o Archie Lawrie, 5 Church Wynd, Kingskettle, By Cupar, Fife, KY15 7PS Scotland, U.K.

Screech Owl

A variety of owl (*Megascops asio*) commonly found in the United States. The cry of the screech owl at midnight is said to portend evil. In Italy, the screech owl became the basis of the stories of a night demon, which further developed into the *strega,* the witch/vampire who under slightly different names appears in the folklore of various southern European countries.

Scriven, Michael John (1928–)

Professor of the logic of science who has written widely on parapsychology. He was born on March 28, 1928, at Beaulieu, Hampshire, England. He studied at University of Melbourne, Australia (B.A., 1948; M.A., 1950) and returned to Oxford for his doctorate in 1956. Following his graduation he taught at Swarthmore College (1956–60) and Indiana University (1960–66) prior to joining the philosophy department at the University of California in 1966.

While in Australia, Sciven founded and served as secretary of the Melbourne University Society for Psychical Research and then presided over the Oxford University Society for Psychical Research. Scriven's interests included, research in psychokinesis and spontaneous phenomena and the theoretical and philosophical implications of parapsychology. He has contributed a variety of articles on the philosophical implications of psychical research.

Sources:

Scriven, Michael John. "Modern Experiments in Telepathy." *Philosophical Review* (April 1956).

———. "New Experimental Designs for Psi Research." *Journal* of the Society for Psychical Research (June 1956).

———. "Randomness and the Causal Order." *Analysis* (October 1956).

———. "Some Theoretical Possibilities in Psi Research." *Journal* of the Society for Psychical Research (June 1957).

Scrying

Divination by gazing into crystals or at shining surfaces. Scrying is commonly simple **crystal-gazing** but also includes the use of a magical mirror in ceremonial magic.

Seabrook, William (Buehler) (1886–1945)

American traveler and author who explored paranormal phenomena and occultism many years before the occult revival of the 1960s and 1970s. From the 1920s onward, he lived with a Bedouin tribe in Arabia, witnessed whirling **dervish** dancing at a monastery in Tripoli, saw Yezidee devil worshipers in Kurdistan, studied **voudou** in Haiti for a year, and also investigated **black magic** in West Africa. Born February 22, 1886, in Westminster, Maryland, he was educated at Mercersburg Academy; Roanoke College, Salem, Virginia (Ph.B.); Newberry College, South Carolina (M.A.); and the University of Geneva.

In 1908 he worked as a reporter on the *Augusta (Ga.) Chronicle* and became city editor at the age of 22. He went on to become a partner in an advertising agency in Augusta, then enlisted in the French Army in 1915. He was discharged after a gas attack at Verdun and awarded a Croix de Guerre. After a period as a farmer in Georgia, he went to New York, where he worked as a reporter for the *New York Times,* then as a writer for King Features Syndicate.

In 1924, he visited Arabia, where he lived with a Bedouin tribe, and thereafter he devoted himself to traveling and writing. In 1933, he committed himself to a New York hospital where he was treated for alcoholism; his seven-month treatment became the basis of his book *Asylum* (1935). He died on September 20, 1945, at Rhinebeck, New York, by committing suicide.

Sources:

Seabrook, William Buehler. *Adventures in Arabia Among the Bedouins.* New York, Blue Ribbon Books, 1930.

———. *Jungle Ways.* N.p., 1931.

———. *The Magic Island.* 1929. Reprint. New York: Paragon House, 1989.

———. *No Hiding Place.* Philadelphia; New York: J. B. Lippencott, 1942.

———. *These Foreigners.* New York: Harcourt, Brace & Co., 1938.

———. *The White Monk of Timbuctoo.* New York: Harcourt, Brace & Co., 1934.

———. *Witchcraft: Its Power in the World Today.* New York: Harcourt, Brace & Co., 1940.

Séance

A major structure of **Spiritualism,** the séance is a gathering of a small group of individuals who sit together to obtain paranormal manifestations or establish communication with the dead. At least one member of the group is usually a **medium** or at least possessed of some mediumistic powers.

In 1848 the **Fox** family at Hydesville, New York, called in their neighbors to listen to mysterious rapping sounds, which later became famous as the "**Rochester rappings**" and were responsible for inaugurating the modern Spiritualist movement. The gathering was too informal to be called a séance, although all the necessary elements were present, but within the following two or three years, the concept of spirit communication spread throughout a large part of the eastern states and many Spiritualist séance **circles** were formed.

In the early stages of the movement these séances were conducted by private mediums who took no fee for their performances; later, professional mediums arose whose séances were open to the public for a fee. Both public and private séances continue to be an indispensable feature of Spiritualism. Unfortunately, much of the common wisdom concerning séances was derived from sittings that later proved to be fraudulent, including the great majority of séances involving physical phenomena, and many of the conditions for a successful séance touted by Spiritualists have little relationship to the manifestation of psychic phenomena or spirit contact. Also, over the years many mediums developed personal peculiarities that they passed on to the mediums they trained. Such mannerisms have no bearing on the success or failure of a séance beyond the medium's belief in them.

The Sitters

The sitters need not have psychic powers, although the phenomena reported are generally more impressive if they do. As a rule séances are held with a single medium, because, according to Spiritualists, a second powerful medium introduces another spirit **control** and the ensuing conflict between the controls can lead to confusion.

The optimum number of sitters is generally believed to be eight or nine, but many mediums sit in larger circles. The great medium **D. D. Home,** even at the risk of offending the empress of France, refused to sit with more than eight individuals. However, the number of sitters in **Indridi Indridason**'s séances sometimes approached seventy. **Lujza Ignath** demonstrated **direct writing** before a hundred people.

In isolated instances mediums have been known to demonstrate psychic phenomena onstage, although doubts surround the genuineness of such displays. The **Davenport brothers** demonstrated before as many as a thousand people, but there is no firm evidence that their phenomena were genuinely psychic. Others who held séances in public halls include the **Bangs sisters,** for spirit paintings; a Mrs. Suydam, for immunity to fire; **Annie Eva Fay,** Lulu Hurst, Annie Abbot, and a Miss Richardson, for feats of strength; **Etta Roberts** and a Mrs. Bliss, for **materializations;** Mary M. Hardy, for paraffin wax molds (see **Plastics**); **William Eglinton,** for **slate writing;** and **Mary Murphy-Lydy,** for **direct voice.**

Composition and Conditions of the Séance

Ideally, according to Spiritualists, males and females should be about equally represented at séances. The majority of the sitters should not be too old. Young sitters provide favorable conditions if their attitude is serious and not flippant. Persons of questionable moral character should not be admitted into the circle. Those in ill health, preoccupied, or nervous should withdraw. Skepticism does not prevent success, but the effect of a hostile or suspicious mind is not helpful and may be a hindrance.

Strangers should not be introduced frequently into the circle. A series of at least six sittings should be held without modifying the group. New sitters should be admitted one by one at intervals of three or four sittings. No more than two or three sittings should be held a week.

A favorable environment is an essential condition for a séance. Excitement or fatigue before the sitting should be avoided. The medium should not take any stimulants. He or she should be comfortable and maintain a genial frame of mind.

Both the medium and the experimenters have an equal share in success or failure. As the psychical researcher **Gustav Geley** aptly remarked, "Mediumistic investigations belong to the class of 'collective experiments,' for the phenomena are the result of subconscious psycho-physiological collaboration between the medium and the experimenters." **Augustus De Morgan** wrote to **Alfred Russel Wallace** at an early period: "There is much reason to think that the state of mind of the inquirer has something—be it external or internal—to do with the power of the phenomena to manifest themselves. This I take to be one of the phenomena—to be associated with the rest in inquiry into cause. It may be a consequence of action of incredulous feeling on the nervous system of the recipient; or it may be that the volition—say the spirit if you like—finds difficulty in communicating with a repellent organization; or, may be, is offended."

A dark or semi-dark séance room is believed to be favorable for phenomena, according to Spiritualists, because light often interferes with spirit manifestation. Critical observers have often noted that it favors **fraud,** and the demand for darkness was an early hindrance to discovering the manipulations of fake mediums. However, darkness is by no means essential for the production of psychic phenomena, and many remarkable effects have been produced in good light.

The placement of the sitters appears to be a matter of consequence. The controls often make changes to produce a better combination of "psychic currents." After sitters form a chain by holding hands or placing them on the table with fingertips touching, they are requested to engage in general conversation or to sing. It is said that talking or singing creates **vibrations** that help produce the phenomena. For the same purpose, phonographs and audio tape players have been used in recent years.

Spiritualist medium **W. Stainton Moses** believed that the chief merit of music in the séance room was its soothing effect, that it harmonized conditions. In his own circle, music was very seldom asked for by the communicators. Harmony was effected by means of perfume and breezes of cool scented air.

The utility of general conversation, free and easy chatter, is that it prevents the sitters from concentrating too much. Tension, solemnity, eagerness, depression are obstructive. Even with the great medium D. D. Home intense attention often prevented manifestations. When everybody stopped talking and looked at him, he awoke from **trance.** (Mediums often enter into a trance condition during a séance, although they sometimes retain normal consciousness throughout.)

A natural, easy, relaxed attitude on the part of the sitters is most conducive to phenomena. Fear or terror usually breaks a manifestation. A table, partly levitated, may drop or a phantom may disappear at a scream. During his **levitations,** Home always asked the sitters not to get excited and to talk of something else because, until he had risen above their heads, any movement or excitement could thwart the force at work. Once in Nice in 1874, Home, in trance, reportedly buried his face and hands in the flames of the open fireplace. On seeing his head encircled by flames, Count de Komar started from his chair, crying, "Daniel! Daniel!" Home recoiled brusquely, and after some moments he said, "You might have caused great harm to Daniel by your want of faith; and now we can do nothing more."

In 1867, Frederick L. H. Willis, professor of the New York Medical College, described his experience with a musical medium in *The Spiritual Magazine:*

"Scarcely had the medium struck the first note upon the piano when the tambourine and the bells seemed to leap from the floor and join in unison. Carefully and noiselessly I stole into the room, and for several seconds it was my privilege to witness a rare and wonderful sight. I saw the bells and tambourine in motion. I saw the bells lifted as by invisible hands and chimed, each in its turn, accurately and beautifully with the piano. I saw the tambourine dexterously and scientifically manipulated with no mortal hand near it. But suddenly . . . the medium became aware of my presence . . . instantly everything ceased. . . . A wave of mental emotion passed over her mind, which was in itself sufficient to stop the phenomena at once."

Emma Hardinge Britten, testifying before the **London Dialectical Society,** narrated the case of the medium **J. B. Conklin,** who was invited to hold a number of séances in Washington:

"The manifestations were very marked and decisive until Mr. Conklin discovered that one of the gentlemen present was no other than President Lincoln, when his anxiety and surprise became so great as entirely to stop the manifestations which were not again renewed till a mutual explanation had restored him to his normal state of mind."

According to Spiritualists, the medium should not be pressured to produce phenomena. Psychical researcher **Sir William Crookes** wrote of Home:

"I used to say [to Home], let us sit round the fire and have a quiet chat and see if our friends are here and will do anything for us; we won't have any tests or precautions. On these occasions, when only my own family were present, some of the most convincing phenomena took place."

Atmospheric conditions also can have an important bearing on séances. Dry climates are seemingly more favorable than wet ones, and a thunderstorm is believed inimical. **Joseph Maxwell** observed that dry cold is helpful and rain and wind often cause failure.

The medium William Eglinton kept a careful record of the atmospheric conditions during his séances. He found that during the 170 failures in 1884–85 the weather was either very wet, damp, or dreary in the majority of instances.

Some Spiritualists believe that the location and furnishing of the séance room are also of considerable consequence. A place saturated with historic atmosphere facilitates manifestations, as does one with powerful emotional associations. With the marquis **Carlo Centurione Scotto** much better results were obtained in the medieval **Millesimo Castle** than in Genoa. The psychical researcher **Harry Price** reputedly had striking clairvoyant descriptions of the life of St. Agnes in a séance held in the Roman catacombs (*Psychic Research,* 1928, p. 665).

The séance room, according to most practitioners, should be plainly furnished. Spiritualists have argued that the table should be entirely of wood and the chairs plain and wooden. Carpets, cushions, and heavy drapes should be dispensed with because they appear to absorb the **psychic force,** whereas a wooden table apparently stores it up. If possible the same room should be used on subsequent occasions and should not be disturbed in the interval.

The Phenomena of Séances

Sitters have frequently reported that the advent of different manifestations, especially physical ones, is usually preceded by a current of cold air passing through the hands of the sitters or by a chilling of the atmosphere. Sometimes there are rapping sounds or moving furniture. In some cases there are moving lights.

If there is a medium in the circle, he or she may breathe heavily or groan before becoming entranced. The medium may then speak and deliver messages in the character of a spirit entity, often with a marked change of voice. In some sittings an alleged spirit control takes charge of the proceedings and indicates how the séance may best be conducted or reveals what departed spirit is conveying a message. With certain powerful mediums, messages may be given in direct voice, supposedly without use of the medium's vocal apparatus.

In one simple form of séance, communication is accomplished through **raps** or audible movements of a table. Questions are asked, and the answers are given by a single rap for "yes" or a double rap for "no," or by some other code of communication agreed upon by the circle. The **Ouija board** and **planchette** are more sophisticated forms of such communication, suitable for one to three individuals rather than a full séance sitting. Another mode of communication for a single sitter or a small group is slate-writing, although considerable doubt surrounds the genuineness of communications received via this method because it is most amenable to fraud.

It is convenient to classify parapsychological phenomena such as **automatic writing** or speaking by a medium as "psychical," as distinct from the "mental" phenomena of, say, **telepathy.** Such manifestations as raps, **table turning,** and slate writing are also largely psychical, but also partly "physical." Physical manifestations properly involve more remarkable phenomena, such as the paranormal **movement** of objects (**telekinesis**), the levitation of objects or human beings, the summoning of small objects such as flowers, fruit, or jewels from a distance through closed doors (**apports**), the transformation of heavy objects or people into very light ones, or the manifestation of spirits (materialization).

Mediums who regularly manifested materialization phenomena (few have attempted such feats in the last several decades) usually sat inside a small **cabinet** with a heavy curtain in front. Materialized forms issued from the cabinet. The cabinet was believed to conserve and condense psychic force in the production of spirit forms. Not all materializations were of full-length spirit forms. Some were only faces or other partial human shapes, in some instances even grotesque forms. Materialization mediums were sometimes securely tied inside the cabinet as a check against fraud, but of course they frequently merely demonstrated their abilities as escape artists.

A few of the more renowned physical mediums of the nineteenth and early twentieth centuries demonstrated astonishing phenomena, such as the ability to handle live coals without injury and the manifestation of spirit hands that wrote messages in clear daylight instead of the darkness or subdued light of a séance room. The most talented medium was undoubtedly D. D. Home, who was never detected in fraud. An account of one of his most remarkable séances is given by H. D. Jencken in the journal *Human Nature* (February 1867):

"Mr. Home had passed into the trance still so often witnessed, rising from his seat, he laid hold of an armchair, which he held at arms' length, and was then lifted about three feet clear of the ground; travelling thus suspended in space, he placed the chair next Lord Adare, and made a circuit round those in the room, being lowered and raised as he passed each of us. One of those present measured the elevation, and passed his leg and arm under Mr. Home's feet. The elevation lasted from four to five minutes. On resuming his seat, Mr. Home addressed Captain Wynne, communicating news to him of which the departed alone could have been cognizant.

"The spirit form that had been seen reclining on the sofa, now stepped up to Mr. Home and mesmerised him; a hand was then seen luminously visible over his head, about 18 inches in a vertical line from his head. The trance state of Mr. Home now assumed a different character; gently rising he spoke a few words to those present, and then opening the door proceeded into the corridor; a voice then said: 'He will go out of this window and come in at that window.'

"The only one who heard the voice was the Master of Lindsay, and a cold shudder seized upon him as he contemplated the possibility of this occurring, a feat which the great height of the third floor windows in Ashley Place rendered more than ordinarily perilous. The others present, however, having closely questioned him as to what he had heard, he at first replied, 'I dare not tell you,' when, to the amazement of all, a voice said, 'You must tell; tell directly.'

"The Master then said, 'Yes; yes, terrible to say, he will go out at that window and come in at this; do not be frightened, be quiet.' Mr. Home now re-entered the room, and opening the drawing-room window, was pushed out semi-horizontally into space, and carried from one window of the drawing-room to the farthermost window of the adjoining room. This feat being performed at a height of about 60 feet from the ground, naturally caused a shudder in all present. The body of Mr. Home, when it appeared at the window of the adjoining room, was shunted into the room feet foremost—the window being only 18 inches open. As soon as he had recovered his footing he laughed and said, 'I wonder what a policeman would have said had he seen me go round and round like a teetotum!'

"The scene was, however, too terrible—too strange, to elicit a smile; cold beads of perspiration stood on every brow, while a feeling pervaded all as if some great danger had passed; the nerves of those present had been kept in a state of tension that refused to respond to a joke. A change now passed over Mr. Home, one often observable during the trance states, indicative, no doubt, of some other power operating on his system.

"Lord Adare had in the meantime stepped up to the open window in the adjoining room to close it—the cold air, as it came pouring in, chilling the room; when, to his surprise, he only found the window 18 to 24 inches open! This puzzled him, for how could Mr. Home have passed outside through a window only 18 to 24 inches open. Mr. Home, however soon set his doubts at rest; stepping up to Lord Adare he said, 'No, no; I did not close the window; I passed thus into the air outside.' An invisible power then supported Mr. Home all but horizontally in space, and thrust his body into space through the open window, head-foremost, bringing him back again feet foremost into the room, shunted not unlike a shutter into a basement below.

"The circle round the table having re-formed, a cold current of air passed over those present, like the rushing of winds. This repeated itself several times. The cold blast of air, or electric fluid, or call it what you may, was accompanied by a loud whistle like a gust of wind on the mountain top, or through the leaves of the forest in late autumn; the sound was deep, sonorous, and powerful in the extreme, and a shudder kept passing over those present, who all heard and felt it. This rushing sound lasted quite ten minutes, in broken intervals of one or two minutes. All present were much surprised; and the interest became intensified by the unknown tongue in which Mr. Home now conversed. Passing from one language to another in rapid succession, he spoke for ten minutes in unknown languages.

"A spirit form now became distinctly visible; it stood next to the Master of Lindsay, clad, as seen on former occasions, in a long robe with a girdle, the feet scarcely touching the ground, the outline of the face only clear, and the tones of the voice, though sufficiently distinct to be understood, whispered rather than spoken. Other voices were now heard, and large globes of phosphorescent lights passed slowly through the room."

The following extract is taken from an account of a séance held by **Cesare Lombroso** with the famous Italian medium **Eusapia Palladino:**

"After a rather long wait the table began to move, slowly at first—a matter explained by the skepticism, not to say the positively hostile spirit, of those who were this night in a séance circle for the first time. Then little by little, the movements increased in intensity. M. Lombroso proved the levitation of the table, and estimated at 12 or 15 pounds the resistance to the pressure which he had to make with his hands in order to overcome that levitation.

"This phenomenon of a heavy body sustained in the air, off its centre of gravity and resisting a pressure of 12 or 15 pounds, very much surprised and astonished the learned gentleman, who attributed it to the action of an unknown magnetic force.

"At my request, taps and scratchings were heard in the table. This was a new cause for astonishment, and led the gentlemen to themselves call for the putting out of the candles in order to ascertain whether the intensity of the noises would be increased, as had been stated. All remained seated and in contact.

"In a dim light which did not hinder the most careful surveillance, violent blows were first heard at the middle point of the table. Then a bell placed upon a round table, at a distance of a yard to the left of the medium (in such a way that she was placed behind and to the right of M. Lombroso), rose into the air, and went tinkling over the heads of the company, describing a circle around our table where it finally came to rest."

At this séance the sitters also felt themselves pinched and their clothes plucked and felt invisible hands on their face and fingers. The accuracy of the account was testified to by Lombroso himself.

The Problem of Verification

It may seem surprising that a group of people sitting together can induce extraordinary phenomena that appear to defy normal physical laws. It has been argued that suggestion may play a part, and it is difficult to rule out the possibility of conscious or even subconscious suggestion as a factor. The important thing is that the paranormal character of phenomena be established, that fraud, chance, unconscious muscular action, and so on should be excluded. In the case of mental phenomena, the possibility of subconscious suggestion should also be examined. It is helpful to use visual and aural recording apparatus to register the objectivity of the manifestations. Experiments have shown that the senses may be deceived in the séance-room atmosphere and that individuals do not always remember accurately things seen or heard.

The availability of modern cameras and film, tape recorders, camcorders, and other highly sensitive electronic surveillance devices greatly simplifies accurate documentation of séances.

The Wider Implications of the Séance

As mentioned earlier, the purposes and aims of a group of people sitting together may influence the result, although little research has been done on the mechanics of séance phenomena. It is clear that the medium and the sitters frequently have reported a drain on their energies, manifested in fatigue and weakness afterward; loss of weight has also been reported.

We do not at present know how nervous energy is related to any psychic forces. There are analogies to be drawn from the séance room to the claimed currents of energy in the human body that may be modified by **acupuncture** techniques and result in improvements in health. There are also comparable concepts in **yoga** and in the psychophysical energy popularly termed **kundalini,** expressed alternatively in either sexual activity or transformations of higher consciousness, sometimes with paranormal side effects. Large groups of people in an atmosphere of emotional fervor may contribute to the spiritual or psychic **healing** of revival meetings. Analogies can also be drawn to the changed atmosphere that often exist between entertainer and audience at concerts and theaters and even the atmosphere at traditional religious services in churches.

In each case, there is a single individual (or small group of individuals) acting as a focal point for the mass vital energies of the group. Entertainer, actor, minister, or medium: all are involved in vital energy exchanges and transformations. Although the nature of such energy transformations is clearly affected by the established conventions of the group occasion, it is not clear how a street demonstration accumulates and releases the lowest common impulse of the mob, resulting in stone throwing, window smashing, or other antisocial behavior while a revival meeting may result in paranormal healing, or a séance in levitation or telekinetic phenomena.

Sources:

Abbott, David P. *Behind the Scenes With the Mediums.* La Sale, Ill.: Open Court, 1907.

Bayless, Raymond. *Voices From Beyond.* New Hyde Park, N.Y.: University Books, 1975.

Britten, Emma Hardinge. *Modern American Spiritualism: A Twenty Years' Record of the Communion Between Earth and the World of Spirits.* London, 1869. Reprint, New Hyde Park, N.Y.: University Books, 1970.

Carrington, Hereward. *The Physical Phenomena of Spiritualism: Fraudulent and Genuine.* New York: Dodd, Mead, 1920.

———. *The Story of Psychic Science.* London: Rider, 1930.

Flammarion, Camille. *Mysterious Psychic Forces.* London: T. Fisher Unwin, 1907.

Hints on Sitting With Mediums. London: Society for Psychical Research, 1965.

Holms, A. Campbell. *The Facts of Psychic Science.* London: Kegan Paul, 1925. Reprint, New Hyde Park, N.Y.: University Books, 1969.

Hyslop, James H. *Contact With the Other World.* New York: Century, 1919.

Le Bon, Gustave. *The Crowd: A Study of the Popular Mind.* London: T. Fisher Unwin, 1896.

Leonard, Gladys Osborne. *My Life in Two Worlds.* London: Cassell, 1931.

MacGregor, Helen, and Margaret V. Underhill. *The Psychic Faculties and Their Development.* London: LSA Publications, 1930.

Maxwell, Joseph. *Metapsychical Phenomena.* London: Duckworth, 1905.

Myers, F. W. H. *Human Personality and Its Survival of Bodily Death.* 2 vols. London: Longmans, 1903. Reprint, New Hyde Park, N.Y.: University Books, 1961.

Owen, Iris M., and Margaret Sparrow. *Conjuring Up Philip.* New York: Harper & Row, 1976.

Richards, John Thomas. *SORRAT: A History of the Neihardt Psychokinesis Experiments, 1961–1981.* Metuchen, N.J.: Scarecrow Press, 1982.

Richmond, Kenneth. *Evidence of Identity.* London: G. Bell, 1939.

Stemman, Roy. *Spirits and Spirit Worlds.* London: Aldus Books, 1975. Reprint, Garden City, N.Y.: Doubleday, 1976.

Sea Phantoms and Superstitions

Sailors in general are often superstitious, as are fishermen and others who live by deep bodies of water. The old songs of the outer Hebrides off the coast of Scotland are full of wizardry, with figures in some of the old sea shanties as well. The novelist Captain Frederick Marryat (1792–1848), who understood sailors as few others have, testified repeatedly to their firm belief in the supernatural.

He is the not only author who has dealt with this subject: Coleridge also touched on the matter in his *Rime of the Ancient Mariner.* Turning from literature to painting, Scottish master **David Scott,** in a memorable canvas now in the seaport town of Leith, Scotland, showed Vasco de Gama and his henchmen gazing thunderstruck at an apparition rising from the waves.

It is scarcely surprising that the supernatural should be a preoccupation of sailors, as they have lived until this century with the constant possibility of sudden death.

In Cornwall, England, so rich in romantic associations of all sorts, quite a number of stories concerning marine specters have been handed down from generation to generation and are still remembered.

One of these stories relates how, on a winter's evening when a fierce gale was raging around the Cornish headlands, a fisherman chanced to see a ship in distress. The man called on some of his friends to aid him in the rescue. In a few minutes, a row boat had been manned, for Cornish fisherfolk are accustomed to being on the water in all weather despite the danger of drowning. Very soon the rescuers were almost within earshot of the distressed vessel and could see her name clearly on the stern. They planned to jump on board, their idea being that if the ship had a skillful pilot acquainted with the coast's dangers, the ship might be steered safely into Falmouth harbour. However, just as one of the fishermen stood up in the prow of the boat intending to throw a rope, the great vessel looming before him disappeared from sight.

The ship could not have sunk, for some relics would certainly have survived. Fearing that the devil had conjured up a phantom to induce them to put out to sea, the rowers put retreated speedily, and pulled for home. One and all, they were more afraid of the devil's machinations than of the more genuine perils they were encountering.

Another Cornish fishing tradition is associated with the village of Sennen Cove. This place is situated at the head of a bay flanked by two capes. Sometimes a band of misty vapor stretches across the bay, obscuring the villagers' outlook on the sea. Whenever this occurs, the fisherfolk believe that it warns them not to put out in their boats. At one time, Sennen Cove numbered among its inhabitants a group of skeptical fishermen who laughed at this superstition. Accordingly, when the warning band of vapor next made its appearance, they sailed off singing gaily. But their boat never returned, their fate remained a mystery, and they strengthened rather than weakened the belief they had ridiculed.

Scotland has stories of phantom ships. Near Ballachulish, on the west coast of Argyllshire, there is a rocky island on which the Macdonalds of Glencoe used to bury their honored dead. The tradition of the district tells that once, some hundreds of years ago, a skiff bearing a beloved chieftain's corpse to this place foundered before reaching its destination. For the Macdonalds, it was a horrible catastrophe that a leader of their clan should be denied a resting place beside his ancestors. Soon the accident came to seem supernatural, for invariably, just before any misfortune overtook the Macdonald tribe, the wrecked skiff was seen drifting about the sea, its dead oarsman clinging to it, and a coffin floating in its wake. This weird vision appeared only too often, and it was said that on the eve of the massacre of Glencoe, the specter boat bore a crew of ghostly female mourners who sang a loud coronach.

Another Scottish Highland story claims that a large ship, wrecked off the coast of Ross at the time of the first Celts voyages to Canada, still rises occasionally from the waves and, after sailing for a few minutes, suddenly lurches and sinks beneath the ocean. Dwellers by the shores of the Solway tell how a certain craft, which went down there while conveying a happy bridal party towards Stranraer, is frequently seen sailing at full speed before the gale, the bride and bridegroom clinging to the rigging as though in terror of immediate death by drowning.

Nor is this the only Solway phantom, for that treacherous seaway once witnessed the foundering of two Scandinavian pirate vessels, which are said to rise periodically from the water, the crew of each calling for mercy.

Religion has played a prominent part in some stories of specter ships. At Boulogne, France, for example, there is a tradition to the effect that on one occasion in the Middle Ages, the townspeople wanted to build a church, for they were without any public place of worship. They were anxious to choose a site God would approve, but found it difficult to come to a decision, as everyone concerned suggested a different place.

Finally, a group assembled on the beach, intending to offer up a prayer for a solution to the problem. While they were thus engaged, they happened to look out to sea, where to their astonishment a vessel was seen sailing toward them, the sacred Virgin herself on board. Standing in the bow, she pointed in a certain direction, and the devout people concluded that their petition had been answered. The mysterious phantom vanished as quickly as it had come.

Another French specter ship, however, used to remain in sight for longer periods. The vessel was manned by a crew of demons and great dogs—the perjured souls of men who had been guilty of fearful crimes. Yet the pious knew that they had little to fear, the priests having told them that the repetition of a *paternoster* would guard against the hideous vision.

Somewhat similar to this story is one associated with Venice, where one stormy evening about the middle of the fourteenth century, a fisherman was requested to row three saints to a neighboring village on the Adriatic. After rowing for a while, he suddenly stopped as though petrified, a galley filled with Saracens having risen beside his boat. The oarsman wanted to start back, but his godly passengers calmed him, and while they sang an *Ave Maria* the ominous galley was submerged by the waves. The fisherman rowed on and reached his haven. The three saints rewarded him with a present of a gold ring. That ring figures in the old coat-of-arms of the Venetian Republic.

There are legends of the sea in most countries. In Japan, there are tales of phantom junks, distinctive Chinese ships. The Chinese used to paint a pair of great eyes on the prow of each craft to detect any monsters prowling afloat. On the coasts of the United States, there are traditions of spectral vessels. Kindred stories are known in the Ionian Islands, and the folklore of the Shetlands has a wealth of such tales. Around the coast of Denmark and the fiords of Norway, many a phantom vessel was supposed to hover as well.

It was on the North Sea that the most famous of all supernatural ships was said to sail, the ship known as *The Flying Dutchman.*

The story goes that a sailor who had loved a woman but wronged her, left her to languish, and put forth on the high seas, where he committed many flagrant acts of piracy. But the fates condemned him to sail wearily and everlastingly from shore to shore. He was to endure this punishment until he could win the staunch affection of a virtuous woman and prove faithful to her.

The guilty man longed to walk solid ground once more, but whenever he dared to put in to port to try to win the woman who might be able to save him, the devil drove him on board ship again, and his interminable voyage commenced again.

Century after century passed in this way, the ill-fated vessel gradually becoming familiar to all who sailed the North Sea or lived by its shores. The legend did not disappear with a more skeptical age, for Richard Wagner evolved a drama from the legend, and his powerful music—charged so abundantly with the weirdness, mystery, and glamour of the surging ocean—vividly evokes the Dutchman's ship driving before a gale, the criminal sitting terrified and hopeless at his useless helm.

Sea Monsters

Among persistent legends of the sea is the belief in great monsters of the deep. The sea serpent has been reported since earliest times. The Roman historian Pliny the Elder (ca. 23–79 C.E.) described in his *Naturalis Historia* how a Greek squadron on a voyage for Alexander the Great saw a shoal of sea serpents, each thirty feet long, in the Persian Gulf.

Much more terrifying is the great sea serpent two hundred feet long and twenty feet broad cited by Olaus Magnus in his *History of Northern People* in 1555. It would be a mistake to assume that all reports of great sea serpents belong to the fabulous past or represent confused accounts of known sea creatures, like whales or giant squids. Sea serpents continued to be reported into modern times, although some accounts would indicate creatures nearer to a plesiosaurus than a serpent. This is understandable, as the prehistoric plesiosaurus had a long neck which might appear to look like a serpent. One of the most celebrated of such creatures is the famed **Loch Ness Monster** of Scotland.

More legendary are the ancient accounts of a gigantic sea creature named the Kraken. Bishop Eric Pontoppidan discussed the Kraken in his *Natural History of Norway* (1751) and concluded that it was an enormous polyp (octopus) or starfish. It is probable that it was one of the cephalopods popularly known as cuttlefish.

Less ominous are the stories of **mermaids,** around whom many strange myths have grown. It is generally supposed that mermaid stories grew up around the dugong or sea-cow, which superficially resembles a human form. However, there are early accounts of mermaids that do not seem to fit this description. In an old history of the Netherlands, there is the following account of a sea-woman of Harlem in the fifteenth century:

"At that time there was a great tempest at sea, with exceeding high tides, the which did drowne many villages in Friseland and Holland; by which tempest there came a sea-woman swimming in the Zuyderzee betwixt the towns of Campen and Edam, the which passing by the Purmeric, entered into the straight of a broken dyke in the Purmermer, where she remained a long time, and could not find the hole by which she entered, for that the breach had been stopped after that the tempest had ceased.

"Some country women and their servants, who did dayly pass the Pourmery, to milk their kine in the next pastures, did often see this woman swimming on the water, thereof at the first they were much afraid; but in the end being accustomed to see it very often, they viewed it neerer, and at last they resolved to take it if they could. Having discovered it they rowed towards it, and drew it out of the water by force, carrying it in one of their barkes unto the towne of Edam.

"When she had been well washed and cleansed from the sea-moss which was grown about her, she was like unto another woman; she was appareled, and began to accustome herself to ordinary meats like unto any other, yet she sought still means to escape, and to get into the water, but she was straightly guarded.

"They came from farrre to see her. Those of Harlem made great sute to them of Edam to have this woman by reason of the strangenesse thereof. In the end they obtained her, where she did learn to spin, and lived many years (some say fifteen), and for the reverance which she bare unto the signe of the crosse whereunto she had beene accustomed, she was buried in the church-yarde. Many persons worthy of credit have justified in their writings that they had seene her in the said towne of Harlem."

A strange superstition of seafaring life related to the **caul,** a thin membrane found around the head of some new-born babies. A caul was considered a good omen for the child, and also for anyone who acquired it. Many seamen considered a caul to be a powerful lucky charm against shipwrecks or death from drowning. There are many allusions to the occult power of the caul by early writers, and in Ben Jonson's play *The Alchemists* (act I, section 2), the character Face says to Dapper: "Ye were born with a Cawl o' your head."

Belief in the power of the caul persisted even into the late nineteenth century, when advertisements relating to the sale of a caul frequently appeared in British newspapers. As much as fifteen, twenty, or even thirty guineas were asked by sellers. In the *Western Daily News* of Plymouth (February 9, 1867) a notice offered mariners a child's caul for five guineas. The *Times* (May 8, 1848) offered a caul for six guineas and described it as "having been afloat with its last owner forty years, through all the perils of a seaman's life, and the owner died at last in his bed, at the place of his birth."

Great stress was laid on the soundness of the article, thus in the *Times* (February 17, 1813) an advertisement stated, "A child's caul in a *perfect state* for sale."

The notion that a child's caul could prevent drowning prevailed in France as well as in England. It was alluded to in a *rondeau* by Claude de Malleville (born 1597).

The superstition concerning the caul is from remote antiquity and was prevalent in the days of the Roman empire. Ælius Lampridius in his life of Antonine (surnamed Diadumeninus) stated that paidumeninus was so called from having been brought into the world with a band of membrane around his forehead in the shape of a diadem, and that he enjoyed perpetual happiness from this circumstance. Pagan midwives had no scruples about selling cauls, and their best market was the Forum, where they got high prices from lawyers. Many of the councils of the early Christian Church denounced the superstition. St. John Chrysostom frequently inveighed against it in his homilies.

"Il est né coiffé," is a well-known French expression describing a lucky man, and indicating that he was born with a caul.

It was believed that so long as the child from whom the caul had been taken enjoyed good health, the caul experienced the same and was dry, flexible, and healthy, but when the caul-born person suffered from any sickness, the membrane also underwent a change, either becoming totally crisp or regaining its former flexibility, according to whether the person died or recovered. Often these cauls became heirlooms, handed down from father to son (especially if it had been born in the family), and were regarded by their owners with as much superstition as if the caul-born person were still living. (Of course, the caul, a relatively unusual birth event, meant different things in different cultures. In Poland, for example, a child born with a caul was a potential **vampire** and the caul had to be treated precisely to prevent that fate.) (See **monsters**)

Sources:

Bassett, F. S. *Legends and Traditions of the Sea and Sailors.* Chicago & New York: Belford, Clarke, 1886.

Benwell, G., and A. Waugh. *The Sea Enchantress: The Tale of the Mermaid and Her Kin.* London: Hutchinson, 1961.

Clark, Jerome. *Encyclopedia of Strange and Unexplained Phenomena.* Detroit: Gale Research, 1993.

Gibson, John. *Monsters of the Sea: Legendary and Authentic.* London: T. Nelson & Sons, 1887.

Gould, Rupert T. *The Case for the Sea-Serpent.* London: Philip Allan, 1930. Reprint, Detroit: Singing Tree Press, 1969.

Heuvelmans, Bernard. *In the Wake of the Sea-Serpents.* London: Rupert Hart-Davis, 1968.

Jones, William. *Credulities Past and Present.* London: Chatto & Windus, 1880. Reprint, Detroit: Singing Tree Press, 1967.

Rappoport, Angelo. *Superstitions of Sailors.* London: Stanley Paul, 1928. Reprint, Ann Arbor, Mich.: Gryphon Books, 1971.

The Searcher

A bi-monthly publication for followers of the teachings of the New Age bible *Oahspe.* Address: Kosmon Publications, P.O. Box 4670, Hualapai, AZ 86412-4670.

Search Magazine

Former quarterly publication dealing with UFOs and other mysteries, founded as *Mystic* in the early 1950s by entrepreneur occult publisher **Raymond A. Palmer.** In the 1970s *Search* magazine absorbed *Flying Saucers* magazine, formerly a separate publication issued by Palmer. *Search* continued into the 1980s.

Sebottendorf, Rudolf Freiherr von (1875–1945)

Name assumed by Adam Glauer, founder of the occult political **Thule Society** in pre-war Germany, and the Germanen Order.

Second Sight

Paranormal perception at a distance in time and space, today classified by parapsychology under such labels as ESP, **clairvoyance, precognition** and **remote viewing.** Second sight, as a faculty of foreseeing future events or occurrences happening at the moment at a distance, is traditionally attributed to certain individuals in the Highlands of **Scotland.**

The medium **Daniel Dunglas Home,** who claimed descent from a Highland family, was supposed to have second sight and described it in the following way: "A deadly tremor comes over me, and there is a film on my eyes, and I not only see persons, but hear conversations taking place at a distance." While in Paris Home saw his brother, who was then in the North Sea. He saw his fingers and toes fall off. Six months afterward tidings came of the brother having been found dead on the ice, his fingers and toes having fallen off from scurvy.

The chief peculiarity of second sight is that the visions are often of a symbolic character. For example, in March 1927, in a lecture before the Societé Internationale de Philologie, Sciences et Beaux Arts, F. G. Fraser noted: "The vision of coming events which some of the Highlanders possess, used to be accompanied, in some cases, by a nerve storm and by a subsequent prostration. It must not be confused with the sight of apparitions, nor does it depend upon artificial aids, such as accompanied by the invocation of the oracles in classic times."

Samuel Johnson took note of the phenomenon in his 1775 account of *A Journey to the Western Islands of Scotland:* "The foresight of the seers is not always prescience. They are impressed with images, of which the event only shows them the meaning." He denied that "to the second sight nothing is presented but phantoms of evil. Good seems to have the same proportion in those visionary scenes as it obtains in real life." According to some old books (Ranulf Higden's *Polychronicon,* 1482 and Robert Kirk's *Secret Commonwealth of Elves, Fauns and Fairies,* 1691) second sight is communicated by touch. Napier's *Folklore or Superstitious Beliefs in the West of Scotland* (1879) mentions the practice as surviving in the nineteenth century.

The belief in second sight dates back to a very early period in the history of these regions, and has not been altogether eradicated by the encroachments of the twentieth century. And, of course, apart from the name, which is used primarily in Scotland, second sight itself is not exclusive to the Celts of Scotland, for it is allied to the clairvoyance, prophetic vision, soothsaying, and so on, that have been reported from time immemorial in practically every part of the world. Yet the second sight has certain distinctive features of its own.

It may, for instance, be either congenital or acquired. In the former case, it generally falls to the **seventh son** of a seventh son, by reason of the potency of the mystic number seven. In the days of large families and no birth control, such a person appeared far more frequently than in modern society. Yet again, sometimes Highlanders would find themselves suddenly endowed with the mysterious faculty. A person gifted with second sight is said to be "fey." Generally there is no apparent departure from the normal consciousness during the vision, although sometimes a seer may complain of a feeling of disquiet or uneasiness. A vision may be communicated from one person to another, usually by contact, but the secondary vision is dimmer than that of the original seer.

A frequent vision is that of a funeral, a **premonition** of a death shortly to occur in the community. This is an instance of the second sight taking a symbolical turn. Occasionally the apparition of the doomed person will be seen—his wraith, or **double**—while he himself is far distant.

Another form second-sight visions often take is that of "seeing lights." The lights, too, may indicate death, but they may likewise predict lesser happenings. In one instance, a light was seen by two persons to hover above the mansion of an estate, then to travel swiftly in the direction of the gamekeeper's cottage, where it remained stationary for a while. The next day the gamekeeper was found dead.

Animals also are said to possess second sight, especially dogs and horses. Two men were travelling in Scotland from Easdale to Oban on a stormy night. In making a short cut through a wood, one of them died from fatigue and exposure. That night more than one horse had to be carefully led past the spot by his driver, who as yet knew nothing of the tragedy. Many Highlanders used to believe that the faculty was common to all the lower **animals,** since they whine and bristle when there is nothing visible to human eyes or audible to human ears.

The march of civilization has eroded the occult beliefs of the Highlanders, but they still believe in second sight, even those who claim that they are not in the least "superstitious."

Sources:

Campbell, John L., and Trevor H. Hall. *Strange Things: The Story of Fr. Allan McDonald, Ada Goodrich Freer, and the Society for Psychical Research's Enquiry into Highland Second Sight.* London: Routledge & Kegan Paul; Philadelphia: Folklore Associates, 1968.

Mackenzie, Alexander. *The Prophecies of the Brahan Seer.* Stirling, Scotland: Eneas Mackay, 1935. Reprint, London: Constable, 1977.

Macrae, Norman, ed. *Highland Second-Sight: With Prophecies of Conneach Odhar of Petty.* Dingwall, Scotland: G. Souter, 1908.

Napier, James. *Folklore, or Superstitious Beliefs in the West of Scotland, within this Century.* Paisley, Scotland, 1879.

Spence, Lewis. *Second Sight: Its History and Origins.* London: Rider, 1951.

Sutherland, Elizabeth. *Ravens and Black Rain: The Story of Highland Second Sight.* London: Constable, 1986.

Thompson, Francis. *The Supernatural Highlands.* London: Robert Hale, 1976.

Secret Chiefs

A term which emerged in the nineteenth century to designate the superhuman **adepts** who were attributed with the founding of several secret magical orders. They were the real founders of the Hermetic Order of the **Golden Dawn,** for example, analogous to the Mahatmas or Masters who supposedly led the **Theosophical Society** (founded in 1875). Together they formed the **Great White Brotherhood** who from their lofty perspective secretly guided and influenced human history. They also had a model in the *Superiores Incogniti,* or hidden superiors, introduced by Baron Hund (1722–76) for his *Strikt Observanz* Masonic system.

The Secret Chiefs of the Golden Dawn were said to be unknown magi who were "Concealed Rulers of the Wisdom of the True Rosicrucian Magic of Light." Human founders **W. Wynn Westcott, S. L. MacGregor Mathers** and **W. R. Woodman** are supposed to be in contact with them.

Sources:

King, Francis. *The Rites of Modern Occult Magic.* New York: Macmillan, 1970.

Secret Fire

Described by Philostratus (ca. 170–245 C.E.) in his *Life of Apollonius* as issuing from a basin in a well on the hill **Athanor.** A blue vapor was said to rise from the well and change into all the colors of the rainbow. The bottom was strewn with red arsenic; on it was the basin full of fire, and from it rose flame without smell or smoke. Two stone reservoirs were beside it, one containing rain, the other wind. This description is probably a symbolic one.

Secrets of Fatima

During 1917, three children in the town of **Fatima,** Portugal, claimed to have witnessed an **apparition of the Virgin Mary** some six times between May 13 an October 13. The attention of the public and the Roman Catholic Church was captured by the phenomenon in the sky over Fatima on the day of the last apparition, but as devotion to Mary as advocated at Fatima spread, a second element of the apparitions emerged to also claim widespread attention. During the July 13 apparition, the Virgin shared information with the children that they were to keep secret. This occurrence repeated the course of the apparition at **La Salette** several decades previously.

For a time, all that was known of the secret message was that while receiving it, the children were heard to groan aloud. Two of the children, Jacinta and Francisco Marto, died in 1919 and 1920 respectively, but did not speak of the message that they had been given. Subsequently, some years later Lucia Dos Santos, who had been the third child, made two parts of the secret message known. The first part consisted of a vision of hell, with an accompanying admonition that the children should sacrifice themselves for sinners in reparation for the many offenses against the Immaculate Heart of Mary. The second part was an admonition to spread the devotion to the Immaculate Heart of Mary, which has become a popular form of devotion in the Roman Catholic Church. Added to this admonition was a prediction that World War I (1914–18) would soon end, but another one would soon begin if people did not cease their offending behavior. The war would occur during the reign of Pope Pius XII. She added that five scourges would come upon the world and that as a sign they were about to appear, the night would be illuminated by an unknown light. Speaking to the three children, she asked that **Russia,** in particular, be consecrated to the Immaculate Heart, and that a communion of reparation be received on the first Saturday of each month. If that happened, Russia would be converted. If it did not, Russia would spread its errors throughout the world.

In 1925, Mary again appeared, this time privately to Lucia, and asked that she initiate the devotion to the Immaculate Heart of Mary through the Communion of Reparations on the first Saturdays. Lucia began to advocate the Communions but did not tie them to the original apparitions until 1927, when she received a further message from Christ to reveal that part of the secret. She would spend the next decade promoting the devotion.

When Lucia saw the extraordinary aurora borealis on January 25, 1938, she believed it to be the sign that the punishment of the world was about to begin. Most believers equate the Spanish Civil War (1936–39) and the succeeding Second World War (1939–45) as confirmation of the **prophecy.** In 1940 she wrote to Pope Pius XII, asking for the consecration of Russia to the Immaculate Heart of Mary and tied the request to the secret received in 1917. Pius XII did consecrate Russia to the Immaculate Heart in 1942 and again in 1952.

In 1941, she wrote the last of several documents recording her memories of the 1917 apparitions, apart from the third secret. But two years later, when Lucia fell ill, her bishop finally ordered her to write down the rest of the secret. The brief message was sealed in an envelope and passed to the bishop of Leiria. On several occasions through the 1940s and 1950s, the bishop indicated that the letter would be opened in 1960 and/or after Lucia's death (she is still alive as of 2000). There was great expectation that the rest of the secret would be revealed in 1960. The sealed letter was transferred to Rome in 1957 and in 1960 was presented to Pope John XXIII, who did read it. He also shared its contents with several of his close advisors. Afterwards, he placed the message in another envelope, sealed it, and returned it to the archives.

The non-publication of the final secret came as a disappointment to many who had been swept up into the international community of Fatima devotees. Speculation as to the nature of the secret ranged from the bizarre to the mundane. Some suggested that it contained prophecies of imminent world disaster. Others suggested that it was quite unspectacular, anticlimactic. The idea of the secret was integrated into many conspiracy theories already present about the papal role in secret world government intrigues.

In what became one of the most widespread of reports, the German newspaper *Neues Europa* claimed that the third secret spoke of important treaties to be concluded in the years 1963–65 between the Anglo-Saxon nations and the Soviet Union. Following the test ban treaty of 1963, the newspaper went on to publish what it claimed was the exact text of the third secret document. The lengthy document referred to the previous secret at La Salette, internal church conflict, and the endtimes for humanity. It suggested that this text was being circulated to the rulers of Europe and helped bring about the 1963 treaty. The article was republished in French by *Le Monde de la Vie* in Paris and in English in a book printed and widely circulated by a conservative Catholic businessman, Emmett Culligan. Culligan tied his own understanding of the document to the assassination of U.S. president John F. Kennedy in 1963 and the predictions of seeress **Jeanne Dixon** that the antichrist was born in Egypt in 1962. Many Fatima experts have pointed out that this 1963 document is far too long to be the final secret which was written in longhand on a small piece of paper.

In 1971, **Ray Stanford,** a psychic channel and head of the Association for the Understanding of Man in Austin, Texas, did a set of readings in which the source that spoke through him discussed Fatima. It suggested that the children had been in contact with beings from the angelic realm. It also suggested that the third secret spoke of the assassination of a pope and the end of the papacy. Many Fatima enthusiasts believe that there will be only five popes installed after 1960 (Pope John Paul II being the third). The idea that the papacy would end, also suggested by some of the interpreters of **Nostradamus,** has become a popular theme in speculation on Fatima.

Still others, relying primarily on statements made by people such as Lucia or those from the Vatican known to have been privy to the secret, agree that the document speaks of the last days but suggest that it refers to a falling away of the faithful and a great apostasy among church teachers. In May of 2000, Pope John Paul II revealed the third secret of Fatima. The third secret dealt with an assassination attempt on a "bishop in white" by an atheist system against the Catholic Church and Christians in the twentieth century. This was considered to be the assassination attempt of Pope John Paul II in 1981.

Apart from speculation over the content of the Fatima secret, the idea of Mary sharing a secret with the persons to whom she appears has become a common element in more recent apparitions. It was integral to the apparitions at **Beauraing** (1932), **Lipa** (1948), and **Bayside** (1968), among others. By its association with Fatima, the granting of a secret has come to be viewed as an element contributing to the authenticity of any given apparition.

In 2000, Pope John Paul II finally released the text of the third secret. The brief description of the vision seen by the three children in 1917 included an angel with a flaming sword. This angel spoke the words "Penance! Penance! Penance!;" a bishop dressed in white who while in prayer for the souls of the martyrs around him was killed; and an angel who gathered the blood of the martyrs to sprinkle on the faithful. At the time of the release of the third secret, the pope was quoted as identifying the image of the martyred bishop in white as a reference to himself and to the attempted assassination of him on May 13, 1981, which occurred on the anniversary of the first vision at Fatima.

It was hoped by many that the release of the third vision would end the many speculations concerning its content.

Sources:

Alonso, Joaquin Maria. *The Secret of Fatima: Fact and Legend.* Cambridge, Mass.: Ravengate Press, 1979.

Culligan, Emmet. *The 1960 Fatima Secret.* Rockford, Ill.: Tan Books and Publishers, 1967.

Francois de Marie de Anges, Frere. *Tragedy and Triumph.* Buffalo, N.Y.: Immaculate Heart Publications, 1994.

Martin, Malachi. *The Keys of This Blood.* New York: Simon and Schuster, 1990.

"The Message of Fatima." http://www.cesnur.org. June 28, 2000.

Simpson, Victor L. "Vatican reveals third secret told at Fatima." *Detroit News* (May 14, 2000): 11A.

Stanford, Ray. *Fatima Prophecy: Days of Darkness/Promise of Light.* Austin, Tex.: Association for the Understanding of Man, 1974.

Secret Tradition

Since the medieval period, students of occultism (that which is hidden) have professed a belief that the ancient wisdom and secret tenets of the various psychic sciences have been preserved to modern times by a series of **adepts,** who have handed these secrets down from generation to generation in their entirety. Leaders have gained authority by claiming to be in contact with such secret adepts, for proficiency in any one of the occult sciences requires instruction from a master of that branch.

It is possible that in neolithic times, societies existed among our ancestors similar in character to the **Midiwiwin** of the North American Indians, the snake-dancers of the Hopi of New Mexico, or the numerous secret societies of aboriginal Australians. This is inferred from the probability that **totemism** existed amongst neolithic peoples. Hierophantic castes would hand down secret traditions from one generation to another.

The early **mysteries** of Egypt, Eleusis, Samothrace, and Cabiri were probably the elaboration of such primitive mysteries. There would appear to be what might be called a fusion of occult beliefs throughout the ages. It has been said that when the ancient mysteries are spoken about, it should be understood that the same sacred ceremonies, initiatory processes, and revelations are intended, and that what is true of one applies with equal certainty to all the others.

Thus the Greek geographer Strabo recorded that the strange orgies in honor of the mystic birth of Jupiter resembled those of Bacchus, Ceres, and Cybele, and the Orphic poems identified the orgies of Bacchus with those of Ceres, Rhea, Venus, and Isis. Euripides also mentioned that the rites of Cybele were celebrated in Asia Minor in a manner identical with the Grecian mysteries of Dionysius and the Cretan rites of the Cabiri.

The Rev. Geo. Oliver, in his book *The History of Initiation* (1829), asserted that the rites of **Freemasonry** were exercised in the antediluvian world, were received by Noah after the Flood, and were practiced by people at the building of Babel. These rites spread and were molded into a form, the great outlines of which can be traced in the mysteries of every heathen nation. These mysteries are the shattered remains of the one true system, from which they were derived.

Although there may have been likenesses between the rites of certain societies, the idea that all sprang from one common source has never been proved. One thing, however, is fairly certain. Anthropology permits us to believe that human concepts, religious and mystical, are practically identical whereever people exist, and there is every possibility that this brought about a strong resemblance between the mystical systems of the older world.

The principles of magic are universal, and these were probably handed on throughout the centuries by hereditary castes of priests, **shamans,** medicine-men, magicians, sorcerers, and witches. But the same evidence does not exist with regard to the higher magic. Was this handed on by means of secret societies, occult schools or universities, or from adept to adept?

This magic is that spiritual magic that, taken in its best sense, shades into **mysticism.** The schools of Salamanca and the mystic colleges of Alexandria could not impart the great truths of this science to their disciples. Its nature is such that communication by lecture would be worse than useless. It is necessary to suppose then that it was imparted by one adept to another. But it is not likely that this magic arose at a very early period in human history, probably not before some three or four thousand years B.C.E. The undisturbed nature of Egyptian and Babylonian civilization leads to the belief that these countries brought forth a long series of adepts in the higher magic.

We know that Alexandria was heir to the works of these adepts, but it is unlikely that their teachings were publicly disseminated in her public schools. Individuals of high magical standing would, however, be in possession of the occult knowledge of ancient Egypt, and it seems likely that they imparted this to the Greeks of Alexandria. Later Hellenic and Byzantine magical theory is distinctly Egyptian in character, and we know that its esoteric forms were disseminated in Europe at a comparatively early date, placing all other systems in the background.

Regarding **alchemy,** the evidence is much more sure, and the same may be said regarding **astrology.** These are occult studies in which it is peculiarly necessary to obtain the assistance of an adept if any excellence is to be gained in their practice, and it is known that the first originated in Egypt, and the second in ancient Babylon.

The names of those early adepts who carried the sciences forward until the days of Alexandria are not known, but subsequent to that period the identity of practically every alchemical and astrological practitioner of any note is known. In the history of no other occult study is the sequence of its professors so clear as is the case in alchemy, and the same might almost be said of astrology.

In the case of mystical brotherhoods, a long line of these have probably existed from early times, sharing the traditions. Many persons would be members of several and would import the conceptions of one society into another, as we know **Rosicrucian** ideas were imported into Masonry.

In the mystic societies of the Middle Ages there seem to be reflections of the older Egyptian and classical mysteries, and some support the theory that the spirit and, in some instances, even the letter of these may have descended to medieval and perhaps to present times.

Such organizations die much harder than any credit is given them for doing. We know, for example, that Freemasonry was transformed at one part of its career, about the middle of the seventeenth century, by an influx of alchemists and astrologers who crowded out the operative members and strengthened the mystical position of the brotherhood.

It is therefore possible to suppose that on the fall or disuse of the ancient mysteries, their disciples, looking eagerly for some method of saving their cults from entire extinction, would join the ranks of some similar society, or would keep the flame alive in secret.

The occult idea has been preserved through the ages, the same in essence among the believers in all religions. To a great extent, the occult's trend was in one direction, so that the fusion of the older mystical societies and their rebirth as a new brotherhood is a plausible hypothesis.

The entry on the **Templars,** for example, suggests the possibility of that brotherhood having received its tenets from the East. It seems very likely that its rites were oriental in origin, and certainly the occult systems of Europe owed much to the Templars, who, probably, after the fall of their own order, secretly formed others or joined existing societies.

Masons have a hypothesis that they inherited traditions from the Dionysian artificers, the artisans of Byzantium, and the building brotherhoods of Western Europe. This is not a proven theory; however, it is much more feasible than the romantic legend concerning the rise of Freemasonry at the time of the building of the Temple of Solomon.

One of the chief reasons that we know so little concerning these brotherhoods in medieval times is that the charge of dabbling in the occult arts was a serious one in the eyes of the law and the church; therefore, occultists found it necessary to carry on their practices in secret.

But after the Reformation, a modern spirit took possession of Europe, and protagonists of the occult sciences came out of their secrecy and practiced in the open light of day. In England, for example, numerous persons avowed themselves alchemists; in Germany the "Rosicrucians" sent out a manifesto; in Scotland, **Alexander Seton,** a great master of the hermetic art, flourished.

But it was nearly a century later when further secret societies were formed, such as the Academy of the Ancients and of the Mysteries in 1767; the Knights of the True Light, founded in Austria about 1780; the Knights and Brethren of Asia, which appeared in Germany in the same year; the Order of Jerusalem, which originated in America in 1791; and the Society of the Universal Aurora, established in Paris in 1783.

Besides being masonic, these societies practiced **animal magnetism,** astrology, **Kabala,** and even **ceremonial magic.** Others were political, such as the **Illuminati.** But the individual tradition was kept up by an illustrious line of adepts, who were more instrumental in keeping the flame of mysticism alive than even such societies as those mentioned.

Anton Mesmer, Emanuel Swedenborg Louis Claude de Saint-Martin and **Martines de Pasqually** all labored to that end. We may regard all these as belonging to the school of Christian magicians, distinct from those who practiced the rites of the **grimoires** or Jewish Kabalism. The line may be carried back through Lavater, **Karl von Eckartshausen,** and so on to the seventeenth century. These men were mystics besides being practitioners of theurgic magic, and they combined in themselves the knowledge of practically all the occult sciences.

With Anton Mesmer began the revival of a science that cannot be altogether regarded as occult when consideration is given to its modern developments, but that powerfully influenced the mystic life of his time and even later. The Mesmerists of the first era were in a direct line from the Martinists and the mystical magicians of France in the late eighteenth century. Indeed, for some English mystics, such as **Valentine Greatrakes,** mysticism and "magnetism" are one and the same thing. But when **hypnotism,** to give it its modern name, became numbered with the more practical sciences, persons of a mystical cast of mind appear to have deserted it.

Hypnotism does not bear the same relation to mesmerism and animal magnetism that modern chemistry does to alchemy, but those who practice it are as dissimilar to the older professors of mesmirism as the modern practitioner of chemistry is to the medieval alchemist. It is symptomatic of the occult studies that its students despise knowledge that is "exact" in the common sense of the term, that is to say, pertaining to materialistic science. Students of the occult do not delight laboring upon a science whose basic laws are already known.

The occultists of the twentieth century, however, draw upon an ancient inspiration. They recognize that their forerunners of the seventeenth and eighteenth centuries were influenced by older traditions and may have had access to records and traditions that are now obscure. The recovery of these is, perhaps, the great question of modern occultism. But apart from this, modern occultism strains towards mysticism. It ignores ceremony and exalts the spiritual. (See also **Gnosticism; Neoplatonism**)

Sources:

Hall, Manly P. *An Encyclopedic Outline of Masonic, Hermetic, Qabbalistic and Rosicrucian Symbolical Philosophy.* Los Angeles: Philosophical Research Society, 1928.

Hartmann, Franz. *Magic White and Black; or, The Science of Finite and Infinite Life.* London: George Redway, 1886. Reprint, New York: University Books, 1970.

Maeterlinck, Maurice. *The Great Secret.* London: Methuen, 1922. Reprint, New York: University Books, 1969.

Shirley, Ralph. *Occultists & Mystics of All Ages.* London: William Rider, 1920; Reprint, New York: University Books, 1972.

Waite, Arthur E. *The Brotherhood of the Rosy Cross.* London: William Rider, 1924; Reprint, New York: University Books, 1961.

———. *The Life of Louis Claude de Saint-Martin: The Unknown Philosopher.* London: Philip Wellby, 1901. Reprinted as *The Unknown Philosopher: The Life of Louis Claude de Saint-Martin.* Blauvelt, N.Y.: Rudolf Steiner, 1970.

———. *The Secret Tradition in Alchemy.* Kegan Paul, London, Alfred A. Knopf, 1926. Reprint, New York: S. Weiser, 1969.

———. *The Secret Tradition in Freemasonry.* London, Rider, 1937. Reprint, New York: S. Weiser, 1969.

Yarker, John. *The Arcane Schools: A Review of Their Origin and Antiquity; With a General History of Freemasonry.* Belfast: William Tait, 1909.

Secret Words

According to Christian folklore, Christ communicated certain words relating to the Eucharist to Joseph of Arimathea, who was described as a secret disciple in John 19:38, and these words were committed orally from keeper to keeper of the **Holy Grail.** In Robert de Borron's (ca. 1170–1212) metrical romance, *Joseph of Arimathea,* material power is added to the spiritual efficacy of these words, and whoever could acquire and retain them had a mysterious power over all around him, could not suffer by evil judgments, could not be deprivated of his rights, and need not fear the result of battle, provided his cause was good.

The words were the secret of the Grail and were either incommunicable in writing or were written only in the Book of the Grail, which, de Borron implied, was itself written by Joseph of Arimathea. These words are the chief mystery of the *Lesser Holy Grail,* as the prose version of de Borron's poem is called. They were most probably a form of eucharistic consecration, and there is evidence that the Celtic church, following the example of the Eastern Church, used them in addition to the usual consecration as practiced in the Latin Church, which is merely a repetition of the New Testament account of the Lord's Supper. The separate clause they are supposed to have formed was called Epiclesis and consisted of an invocation of the Holy Ghost.

De Borron's account also ties the Grail to **Glastonbury,** a borough in England that had also been identified with King Arthur by the reported discovery of his body and that of his queen, Guenevere. According to de Borron, the Grail was to be conveyed to the Far West, to the veils of "Avaron" (i.e., "Avalon," i.e., Somerset).

Sources:

Furnivall, F. J., ed. *The History of the Holy Grail . . . from the French prose of Sires R. de Borron.* London: Early English Text Society, 1874.

Lacy, Norris J. *The Arthurian Encyclopedia.* New York: Farland, 1986.

Loomis, Roger Sherman. *The Grail: From Celtic Myth to Christian Symbol.* Cardiff: University of Wales, 1963.

Waite, Arthur E. *The Holy Grail; The Galahad Quest in the Arthurian Literature.* London: Rider, 1933. Reprint, New York: University Books, 1961.

Weston, Jessie L. *The Quest of the Holy Grail.* London: G. Bell, 1913. Reprint, London: Frank Cass, 1964.

Sedona

During the last quarter of the twentieth century, Sedona, Arizona, a small city south of Flagstaff, emerged as a center of the New Age Movement, and in the 1990s, as the **New Age** waned, it has become a major center of the successive focus upon ascension and human transformation. Sedona has been touted as a remnant of the ancient mythical continent of **Lemuria,** and contemporary psychics have claimed that it is the center of various energy vortexes that make it a place especially accommodating to psychic/spiritual awakening and **channeling** work.

Sedona's present role as a metaphysical center can be traced to the late 1950s when Mary Lou Keller moved to the area and opened the Sedona Church of Light. The church became a center for disseminating metaphysical teachings both by Weller and the many outside speakers who came to Sedona. She was joined in the early 1960s by Evangeline and Carmen Van Pollen, two teachers who led the Ruby Focus of Magnificent Consummation, an independent "I AM" group. The Van Pollens operated as messengers of the **ascended masters,** much as had **Guy W. Ballard** in the 1930s, and their work continues under the name Rainbow Focus.

As the New Age Movement began to identify different significant locations as power spots, places where the Earth's configuration creates a spiritual energy vortex, Sedona was touted as such a location. As the image of Sedona developed, New Age writer/publisher **Dick Sutphen** joined the chorus of Sedona supporters and in 1986 published a new book, *Sedona Psychic Energy Vortexes.* He built his discussion both upon the ancient designation of sacred spaces by Native Americans and the more modern mapping of the lines of magnetic forces on the earth's surface. The area around Flagstaff has been noted as an area of deviation from the expected pattern of the Earth's magnetic field. Sutphen argued that Sedona is a sight at which several vortexes, peculiar places where energy is emitted on the Earth's surface, are located. He identified these particular locations (while offering practical advice on visiting the more remote spots that require hiking through the snake-infested countryside). He also explained the power vortexes on the Earth as similar to acupuncture points on the human body. Others tied Sedona to UFO activity.

During the 1990s, many holistic healers and channelers settled in Sedona, while others visit regularly. Around 1989, *Emergence—a Journal for the Golden Age* began to feature the people, organizations, and events in the larger New Age community of Sedona. In the mid-1990s, renamed *Sedona: Journal of Emer-*

gence, it became the voice of the new generation of channelers across North America and around the world, and has established Sedona as the vocal center of the post-New Age vision of the ascended life. Light Technology Publishing also publishes and distributes a wide range of channeled material both from the Sedona channels and other like-minded channels around the world.

Sources:

Dannelley, Richard. *Sedona Power Spot, Vortex, and Medicine Wheel Guide.* Sedona, Ariz.: R. Dannelley with the Cooperation of the Vortex Society, 1991.

———. *The Sedona Guide Book of Channeled Wisdom.* Sedona, Ariz.: Light Technology Publishing, 1991.

Dongo, Tom. *The Alien Tide: The Mysteries of Sedona II.* Sedona, Ariz.: Hummingbird Press, 1990.

———. *The Mysteries of Sedona.* Sedona, Ariz.: Color Pro Graphics, 1988.

Sutphen, Dick. *Sedona: Psychic Energy Vortexes.* Malibi, Calif.: Valley of the Sun Publishing, 1986.

Sedona Journal of Emergence

Sedona Journal of Emergence is one of the most important expressions of the post-New Age spirituality as it has become focused in the **channeling** activity of a group of channelers who have emerged to prominence in the 1990s. The monthly publication began as a local networking magazine serving the **Sedona,** Arizona, community which became known in the 1980s as a peculiar spot favoring psychic and spiritual activity. Over the decade it transformed into a large monthly magazine circulated nationally and throughout the English/speaking world.

Each issue of *Sedona* is built around excerpts of channeled material produced by a spectrum of individuals, a number of whom reside in the Sedona area, though increasingly channelers from around the world contribute material. Occasionally, this material is grouped around particular themes to which a variety of channeled entities have spoken. While these entities have their differences, they tend to speak out of the common worldview supplied by the Western Esoteric tradition as exemplified in **Theosophy.** In the post-New Age environment, the two strains of channeling work, that based primarily on conversations with **ascended masters** and that with extraterrestrials, has merged and many channelers have both members of the spiritual hierarchy and space beings speaking through them. Particularly prominent is Robert Shapiro, who channels Zoosh, Isis, and other entities. These entities are listed along with the magazine staff as the magazine's "Interdimensional Board of Directors."

Along with the channeled material, *Sedona* also carries a monthly **astrology** column and a column by **New Thought** metaphysician Louise Hay. There is relatively little space devoted to advertising, most of which advertises the counseling sessions and books by the channels. In the late 1990s *Sedona* nurtured the development of an **Australia/New Zealand** edition, which after a year-and-a-half, in 1999, became **Elohim.** *Elohim* continues as a sister publication following the format of *Sedona.*

Sedona Journal of Emergence is published at 2020 Contractors Rd., #4, Sedona, AZ 86336. Its Internet presence is found at http://www.sedonajo.com/.

Sources:

Sedona Journal of Emergence. Sedona, Ariz., n.d.

Sedona Journal of Emergence. http://www.sedonajo.com/. March 10, 2000.

The Seekers

A spiritual healing organization founded in London in 1926 by C. A. Simpson, formerly a New Zealand electrical engineer, who gave up his profession to establish this center under the direction of the spirit guide "Dr. Lascelles." The center was originally named The Guild of Spiritual Healing. Many cures were reported in cases generally classed as incurable. Associated Harmony Prayer Circles throughout Britain provided absent healing treatment. In 1933, the Seekers center moved to larger premises at West Malling, Kent, where over 5,000 members were linked in prayer circles. Last known address: Seekers' Trust, The Close, Addington Park, West Malling, Kent, England.

The Seer (Journal)

Early twentieth-century monthly review of occult and psychic sciences, founded 1928, published in Nice, France, and later in Carthage, Tunisia. It was edited by Francis Rolt Wheeler. Contributors included **Ernesto Bozzano, Lewis Spence,** and Jollivet Castelot.

Seer (or Seeress)

A traditional term for a person who manifests **clairvoyance** or **precognition.** In ancient Israel the term was replaced by "judge." The judges used their psychic abilities to guide the twelve tribes from the time of the settlement in Palestine until the establishment of the monarchy under Saul (I Samuel 9:9). In Scotland it is equated with the possession of **second sight.**

"Seer" (Software)

An **astrology** software program that purportedly indicates from their star signs how well business partners will perform with each other. From the proposed partners' date and place of birth, the program calculates the planetary conjunction believed to determine personal characteristics and behavior patterns. An index of business compatibility is then generated using a scale from 0 to 30. "Seer" was marketed by British-born Peter Mackenzie through the Triangle Group in California, and customers are said to have included Pizza Hut and Motorola. The package was also tested on a KOBA Television program.

Seik Kasso

Burmese evil spirits inhabiting trees. (See **MYANMAR**)

Seiktha

A Burmese evil spirit. (See **MYANMAR**)

Self-Realization Fellowship

An early American Hindu organization founded in 1920 as the Yogoda Satsang Society by Swami **Paramahansa Yogananda.** Yogananda was the inheritor of a tradition of kriya yoga, which had been revived in the 1860s by Mahavatar Babaji, a guru who lived in the foothills of the Himalayas and was believed to be an incarnation of Shiva, the Hindu deity. The lineage was passed to Swami Sri Yukteswar, who passed it to Yogananda.

Yogananda traveled to Boston in 1920 for the tricentennial anniversary of the Pilgrims' landing, sponsored by the International Congress of Religious Liberals, and decided to stay in the United States, one of the few Hindu teachers to settle in the country before immigration from India was stopped in 1924. He moved the headquarters to California in 1925. He wrote several books and began a magazine, *East-West* (later *Self-Realization*). He also developed a set of correspondence lessons, which facilitated the spread of the movement to all parts of the country.

The Self-Realization Fellowship was incorporated in 1935. As its name implies, it emphasizes the attainment of *ananda,* through self-realization, which it teaches is accomplished "through definite techniques for attaining a personal experience of God." Central to Yogananda's teachings is the practice of kriya yoga, which reinforces and revitalizes subtle currents of life energy in the body, enabling the normal activities of the heart and lungs to slow down naturally. It is based on a form of **meditation,** the details of which are taught only to students of the Self-Realization Fellowship Lessons.

The fellowship also emphasizes what it sees as the essential unity of Eastern and Western spiritual teachings. To that end, its teachers often provide interpretations of parallel passages in the Christian New Testament and the Hindu Bhagavad Gita.

Following Yogananda's death in 1952, Swami Rajasi Janakananda (James J. Lynn) led the organization for three years but died in 1955. He was succeeded by Sri Daya Mata, who has led the organization since. SRF has more than 500 meditation centers in 56 countries, including twelve temples and ashram centers: nine in California and one each in Arizona, Virginia, and Nuremburg, Germany.

Yogananda's *Autobiography of a Yogi,* first issued in 1946, has proved to be a widely popular text and has influenced people far beyond the Self-Realization Fellowship. Among the more famous members of the fellowship is **W. Y. Evans-Wentz,** scholar of Eastern mysticism and author of various books dealing with Tibetan and yogic texts. Website: http://www.yogananda-srf.org/.

Sources:

Mata, Sri Daya. *Only Love.* Los Angeles: Self-Realization Fellowship, 1976.

New Pilgrims of the Spirit. Boston: Beacon Press, 1921.

Self-Realization Fellowship Highlights. Los Angeles: Self-Realization Fellowship, 1980.

Self-Realization Fellowship Manual of Services. Los Angeles: Self-Realization Fellowship, 1965.

Yogananda, Swami Paramahansa. *Autobiography of a Yogi.* New York: Philosophical Library, 1946. Reprint, Los Angeles: Self-Realization Fellowship, 1971.

———. *Descriptive Outlines of Yogoda.* Los Angeles: Yogoda Satsang Society, 1928.

The Semites

This entry on the Semites applies to the more ancient divisions of the race, such as the Babylonians and Assyrians, and the Hebrews in Biblical times. For later Semitic occultism, see **Arabs** and **Kabala.**

In ancient **Babylonia** and Chaldea, magic was a department of priestly activity. In Mesopotamia a sect of priests named the *Asipu* were set apart for the practice of magic, which in their case probably consisted of hypnotism, the casting out of demons, the banning of troublesome spirits and so forth.

The caste of priests called the *Baru* consulted the oracles on the future by inspecting the entrails of animals, the flight of birds, "the observation of oil in water, the secret of Anu, Bel, and Ea, the tablet of the gods, the sachet of leather of the oracles of the heavens and earth, the wand of cedar dear to the great gods."

These priests of *Baru* and *Asipu* wore clothing peculiar to their rank, which they changed frequently during the ceremonies in which they took part. In ancient tablets we find kings making frequent inquiries about the future through these priestly castes: in a tablet of Sippar, we find treated the royal Sennachrib seeking through the *Baru* the causes of his father's violent death. The *Asipu* were exorcists, who removed taboos and laid ghosts. An *Asipu*'s functions are set forth in the following incantatory poem:

[The man] of Ea am I,
[The man] of Damkina am I,
The messenger of Marduk am I,
My spell is the spell of Ea,
My incantation is the incantation of Marduk,
The circle of Ea is in my hand,
The tamarisk, the powerful weapon of Anu,
In my hand I hold,
The date-spathe, mighty in decision,
In my hand I hold.
He that stilleth all to rest, that pacifieth all,
By whose incantation everything is at peace,
He is the great Lord Ea,
Stilling all to rest, and pacifying all,
By whose incantation everything is at peace.
When I draw nigh unto the sick man
All shall be assuaged.
I am the magician born of Eridu,
Begotten in Eridu and Subari.
When I draw nigh unto the sick man
May Ea, King of the Deep, safeguard me!
O Ea, King of the Deep, to see. . . .
I, the magician, am thy slave.
March thou on my right hand,
Assist [me] on my left;
Add thy pure spell to mine,
Add thy pure voice to mine,
Vouchsafe (to me) pure words,
Make fortunate the utterances of my mouth,
Ordain that my decisions be happy,
Let me be blessed where'er I tread,
Let the man whom I [now] touch be blessed.
Before me may lucky thoughts be spoken.
After me may a lucky finger be pointed.
Oh that thou wert my guardian genius,
And my guardian spirit!
O God that blesseth, Marduk,
Let me be blessed, where'er my path may be!
Thy power shall god and man proclaim;
This man shall do thy service,
And I too, the magician thy slave.
Unto the house on entering. . . .
Samas is before me,
Sin [is] behind [me],
Nergal [is] at (my) right hand,
Ninib [is] at my left hand;
When I draw near unto the sick man,
When I lay my hand on the head of the sick man,
May a kindly Spirit, a kindly Guardian, stand at my side.

The third caste was the *Zammaru,* and its members sang or chanted certain ceremonials.

The lower ranks of sorcery were represented by the *Kassapu* and *Kassaptu,* the wizard and witch, who, as elsewhere, practiced black magic and were fiercely combated by the priest-magician caste. In the code of Hammurabi there was a stringent law against the professors of black magic:

If a man has charged a man with sorcery and has not justified himself, he who is charged with sorcery shall go to the river, he shall plunge into the river, and if the river overcome him, he who accused him shall take to himself his house. If the river makes that man to be innocent, and he be saved, he who accused him shall be put to death. He who plunged into the river shall take to himself the house of him who accused him.

This recalls the water test for a witch in the seventeenth century: if she sank when thrown in a pond, she was innocent, but if she floated, she was a witch.

Another series of tablets dealt with the black magician and the witch, who were represented as roaming the streets, entering houses, and prowling through towns, stealing the love of men, and withering the beauty of women. The exorcist made an image of the witch and he called upon the fire-god to burn it. He seized the witch's mouth, tongue, eyes, feet, and other members and prayed that sin would cast her into an abyss of water and fire, and that her face would grow yellow and green. He feared that the witch was directing a similar sorcery against himself, but sent the *haltappan* plant and sesame to undo her spells and force the words back into her mouth. The exorcist trusted that the images she had fashioned against him would assume her own character, and her spells would be turned back on her.

Another tablet expressed the desire that the god of night would strike the witch's magic, that her mouth become fat and her tongue salt, that the words of evil she had spoken be poured out like tallow, and that the magic she was working be crumbled like salt.

The tablets abound in magical matter, and in them we have a record of the actual wizardry in vogue at the time they were written, which runs at least from the seventh century until the time when cuneiform inscription ceased to be used.

Chaldean magic was renowned throughout the world, especially for its astrology. The book of Isaiah states: "Let now the astrologers, star-gazers, monthly prognosticators, stand up and save thee from the things that shall come upon thee." In the book of Daniel, magicians are called Chaldeans, and even in modern times occultists have praised Chaldean **magi.** The Greek geographer Strabo and the Roman rhetorician Ælian alluded to Chaldean knowledge of astrology, and it is supposed to have been the Chaldean magician Œthanes who introduced his science into Greece, which he entered with Xerxes.

The great library of Assurbanipal, king of Assyria, who died in 626 B.C.E., affords first-hand knowledge of Assyrian magic. Assurbanipal gathered together numerous volumes from the cities of Babylonia, stored them in his great library at Nineveh, and had them copied and translated. In fact, letters have been discovered from Assurbanipal to some of his officials, giving instructions for the copying of certain incantations. Many **grimoires** also come from Babylonia, written during the later empire, the best known of which are the series entitled *Maklu* (burning), *Utukki limnuti* (evil spirits), *Labartu* (hag-demon), and *Nis kati* (raising of the hand).

There are also many ceremonial texts available that throw considerable light on magical practice. The *Maklu,* for example, contains eight tablets of incantations and spells against wizards and witches—the general idea running through it being to instruct the bewitched person how to manufacture figures of his enemies and thus destroy them.

The series dealing with the **exorcism** of evil spirits enumerates demons, goblins, and ghosts, and consists of at least sixteen tablets. They were for the exorcist's use in driving devils out from possessed people. This was to be accomplished by invoking the aid of the gods, so that the demons might be placed under a divine taboo. The demon who possessed the unfortunate victim had to be described in the most minute manner.

The series dealing with the *Labartu* or hag-demon, a kind of female devil who delighted in attacking children, gave directions for making a figure of the *Labartu* and the incantations to be repeated over it. The magician and philosopher appear to have worked together in Assyria, for medical men constantly used incantations to drive out demons, and incantations were often associated with prescriptions. Medical magic indeed appears to have been of much the same sort as we find among the Native American.

The doctrine of the "Incommunicable Name" was established among the early Semites, as among the Egyptians. It related to the secret name of a god that, when discovered, gave the speaker complete power over him by its mere utterance. Knowing the name or description of the person or demon against whom the magician directed his charm was also essential to success. Drugs were originally ascribed the power vouchsafed by the gods for the welfare of mankind and were supposed to aid greatly in exorcism.

In Assyrian sorcery, Ea and Marduk were the most powerful gods, Marduk being an intermediary between human beings and their father, Ea; indeed the legend of Marduk going to his father for advice was commonly repeated in incantations. When working magic against an individual it was necessary to have something belonging to him or her—clippings of hair, or fingernails if possible. The possessed person was usually washed, the principle of cleansing probably underlying this ceremony. An incantation called the Incantation of Eridu was often prescribed, and this must have related to some such cleansing, for Eridu was the Home of Ea, the Sea-god.

A formula for exorcising or washing away a demon named Rabesu stated that the patient was to be sprinkled with clean water seven times. Of all water none was so sacred as that from the Euphrates river, and its water was frequently used for charms and exorcisms.

Fumigation with a censor was also employed by the Assyrians for exorcism, but the possessed person was often guarded from the attack of fiends by being placed in the middle of an enchanted circle of flour, through which it was thought no spirit could break. Wearing the glands from the mouth of a fish was also a charm against possession. In making a magic circle, the sorcerer usually formed seven little winged figures to set before the god Nergal, blessing them with a long spell that stated he had completed the *usurtu* or magic circle with a sprinkling of lime. The wizard further prayed that the incantation might be performed for his patient by the god. This would seem to be a prototype of the use of the circle among magicians of medieval times.

R. Campbell Thompson, in his book *Semitic Magic* (1908), stated:

"Armed with all these things—the word of power, the acquisition of some part of the enemy, the use of the magic circle and holy water, and the knowledge of the magical properties of substances—the ancient warlock was well fitted for his trade. He was then capable of defying hostile demons or summoning friendly spirits, of driving out disease or casting spells, of making amulets to guard the credulous who came to him. Furthermore, he had a certain stock-in-trade of tricks which were a steady source of revenues. Lovesick youths and maidens always hoped for some result from his philtres or love-charms; at the demand of jealousy, he was ever ready to put hatred between husband and wife; and for such as had not the pluck or skill even to use a dagger on a dark night, his little effigies, pierced with pins, would bring death to a rival. He was at once a physician and wonder-worker for such as would pay him fee.

"Among the more modern Semites magic is greatly in vogue in many forms, some of them quite familiar to Europeans: indeed we find the *Arabian Nights* edited by Lane, a story of old women riding on a broom-stick. Among Mahommedans the wizard is thought to deserve death by reason of the fact that he is an unbeliever. Witches are fairly common in Arabic lore, and we usually find them figuring as sellers of potions and philtres. . . . In Arab folk tales the *moghrebi* is the sorcerer who has converse with demons, and we find many such in the Old and New Testaments, as well as diviners and other practitioners of the occult arts. In the *Sanhedrin,* Rabbi Akiba defines an enchanter as one who calculates the times and hours, and other rabbis state that 'an enchanter is he who grows ill when his bread drops from his mouth, or if he drops the stick that supports him from his hand, or if his son calls after him, or a crow caws in his hearing, or a deer crosses his path, or he sees a serpent at his right hand, or a fox on his left.' "

The Arabs used to believe that magic would not work while he that employs it was asleep. In this belief system it is possible to overreach Satan himself, and many Arabic tales exist in which men of wisdom and cunning have succeeded in accomplishing this. The Devil Iblis once sent his son to an assembly of honorable people with a flint stone, and told him to have the stone woven. He came in and said, "My father sends his peace, and wishes to have this flint stone woven." A man with a goatbeard said, "Tell your father to have it spun, and then we will weave it."

The son went back, and Iblis was very angry and told his son never to make any suggestion when a goat-bearded man was present, "for he is more devilish than we."

Curiously enough, the rabbi Joshua ben Hananiah made a similar request in a contest against the wise men of Athens, who required him to sew together the fragments of a broken millstone. He asked in reply for a few threads made of the fiber of the stone. The good folk of Mosul, too, always prided themselves on a ready wit against the Devil. Once upon a time, the devil Iblis came to Mosul and found a man planting onions. They fell to talking, and in their fellowship agreed to divide the produce of the garden. On the day when the onions were ready, the partners went to their vegetable patch and the man said, "Master, wilt thou take as thy half that which is above ground or that which is below?"

The Devil saw the green shoots of the onions sprouting high and carried these off as his share, leaving the gardener chuckling over his bargain. But when wheat time came round, the Devil looked over the land and complained that he had made nothing out of their previous compact. "This time," he said, "we will divide differently, and thou shalt take the tops," and so the bargain fell to the gardner's advantage again.

When they visited the land together when the corn was ripe, the man reaped the field and took away the ears, leaving the Devil stubbing up the roots. After he had been digging for a month, he began to realize his error and went to the man, who was cheerily threshing his portion.

"This is a paltry quibble," said Iblis, "thou hast cozened me this twice." "Nay," said the former, "I gave thee thy desire, and furthermore, thou didst not thresh out thine onion-tops, as I am doing this." So it was a hopeful Devil that went away to beat the dry onion-stalks in vain. Iblis left Mosul sullenly, stalking away in frustrated anger, stopping once in a while to shake his hand against so crafty a town. "Cursed be he, ye tricksters! who can outmatch devilry like yours?"

"In modern times in the East," stated R. C. Thompson, "from Morocco to Mesopotamia, books of magic are by no means rare, and manuscripts in Arabic, Hebrew, Gershuni, and Syriac can frequently be bought, all dealing with some form of magic or popular medicine. In Suakin in the Soudan I was offered a printed book of astrology in Arabic illustrated by the most grotesque and bizarre woodcuts of the signs of the Zodiac, the blocks for which seem to have done duty in other places. Such books existed in manuscript in ancient days, as is vouched for by the story of the Sibylline books or the passage in Acts XIX, 19; 'Not a few of them that practised curious arts brought their books together, and burned them in the sight of all.' "

It is curious to find the charm for raising hatred was practically the same among the Semites and the peoples of Hungary and the Balkan States—that is, through the agency of the egg of a black hen.

We find, too, many minor sorceries the same among the Semites as among European races. To be invisible was on attainment much sought after, and it was thought that if one wore a ring of copper and iron engraved with certain magic signs this result would be secured. The heart of a black cat, dried and steeped in honey, was also believed to be effective.

(For various instances of potent enchantments, see **Solomon.**)

Sympathetic magic was often resorted to by the Arabic witch and wizard, just as it was among the ancient Hebrews and Assyrians. The great repertory of Semitic occultism is the Kabala, but here the occult has been transmuted into Hebrew **mysticism.**

Sources:

Thompson, C. J. S. *The Mysteries and Secrets of Magic.* London: Allen Lane, 1927. Reprint, Causeway, 1973.

Thompson, R. C. *Devils & Evil Spirits of Babylonia* 2 vols. London: Luzac, 1903–04/

———. *Semitic Magic.* London: Luzac, 1908.

Sensitive

The term "sensitive," often interchangeable with **"psychic,"** refers to a person with psychic powers, but eschews communication with the dead. A sensitive is thus distinguished from the **"medium,"** or "channel." A medium is usually also a sensitive. According to Spiritualism, a medium is not necessarily a sensitive but may be simply an instrument for spirit communication. (It must be remembered that such a distinction was made in the days in which may "mediums" accepted by the movement were frauds. This distinction explained why they made no pretense of being "psychic" except in the séance room.)

Sensitives ordinarily believe that their psychic abilities are a natural ability that they possess to a greater degree than most, either through natural endowment or a process of psychic development. Many believe in reincarnation, a belief that is often incompatible with Spiritualist contact with the dead, and they may explain many events (such as seeing an apparition) that Spiritualists ascribe to spirit agency to memories from previous lives. Sensitives may specialize in one form of psychic ability, be it **psychometry, precognition, telepathy,** or **clairvoyance.** Many emerge as healers with some ability in **psychokinesis.**

During the nineteenth century, prior to the rise of Spiritualism, German scientist **Baron Karl von Reichenbach** conducted numerous experiments with "sensitives" in order to validate his concept of a mysterious vital force in nature which he termed **"od"** or "odyle." These individuals, drawn from all walks of life, were selected on the basis of specific sensitive reactions—feelings of pleasant coolness or alternatively disagreeable feelings in relation to other people or to metals, as well as reactions to colors and foods.

Sources:

Reichenbach, Karl von. *Der sensitive Mensch und sein Verhalten zum Ode* (The sensitive man and his relation to od). 2 vols. Stuttgart and Tübingen, 1854–55.

Sensory Deprivation

The process of psychic development generally entails learning to refocus attention from the outer world of sensory input and directing attention inward in some form. One popular form is meditation, in which the person consciously withdraws attention from sensory data. Various attempts to readjust the environment to reduce sensory input have been made. Lights can be dimmed, a quiet location selected, a comfortable posture assumed, and breathing regulated.

The heightened blocking of normal sensory input has been found to result in **hallucinations** and vivid fantasies. Such a heightened blockage can be attained by placing a person in a sensory neutral environment. In the **Ganzfeld setting,** the eyes and ears are covered, and a sensory neutral environment is created with blue light and white noise.

An even more intense experience is provided by the isolation tank, in which an individual can float in water at a controlled temperature in a soundproof, lightproof chamber. While such experiments may be exhausting and affect mental process in an unstable individual, they can throw light on personality disorders and apparent paranormal experiences. An apparatus called the **Witches' Cradle,** devised by **Robert E. L. Masters** and **Jean Houston** of the **Foundation for Mind Research,** has been developed to study heightened sensory deprivation.

Sources:

Hooper, Judith, and Dick Teresi. *Would a Buddha Wear a Walkman?* New York: Simon & Schuster, 1990.

Solomon, P., and others eds. *Sensory Deprivation.* Cambridge, Mass.: Harvard University, 1961.

Zubeck, John P., ed. *Sensory Deprivation: Fifteen Years of Research.* Appleton-Century-Crofts, 1969.

"Sepharial"

Pseudonym of British astrologer and occult author **Walter Gorn Old** (1864–1929).

Serios, Ted (1918–)

A former Chicago bellhop, born November 27, 1918, with a claimed ability to project photographic images onto camera film by staring into the lens of a Polaroid camera. He sometimes used a piece of rolled cardboard to look into the camera lens at the moment the picture was taken. This "gismo," as he called it, tended to arouse suspicions of **fraud,** although there was no evidence that it was a device for trickery. Serios also produced images using a camera without a lens.

A report of Serios's strange talent by Pauline Oehler of the Illinois Society for Psychic Research was published in *Fate* magazine. **Curtis Fuller,** proprietor of *Fate,* sent a copy of the article to parapsychologist **Jule Eisenbud,** and as a result Eisenbud conducted an extensive investigation of Serios's phenomena in 1964, the results of which were published in *The World of Ted Serios: "Thoughtographic" Studies of an Extraordinary Mind* (1966). Eisenbud found the phenomena as erratic as Serios himself, but probably genuine.

Critics charged fraud and James Randi claimed to have been able to reproduce pictures like Serios's by use of a "gizmo-like" device. While Randi had suggested a means by which the pictures could be reproduced, at least those in which Serios held the camera in his hand and used the cardboard device, he did not explain how the pictures were produced when the camera was at some distance. Among some of the extraordinary images produced by Serios with a Polaroid camera were pictures of Mariner IV and Russian Vostok rockets. Many pictures produced by Serios are ambiguous, in soft focus, or too vague to identify. Some contained mistakes which would have been absent from a picture of an object that had merely been reproduced via the "gizmo."

At one point, a rumor circulated that Serios had confessed to fraud, a fact that both Eisenbud and Serios staunchly denied. His work has fallen into the shadow created by the confession of Masuki Kiyota to having faked similar effects after he had passed a number of tests by both Japanese researchers and Eisenbud.

Sources:

Berger, Arthur S., and Joyce Berger. *The Encyclopedia of Parapsychology and Psychical Research.* New York: Paragon House, 1991.

Eisenbud, Jule. "On Ted Serios' Alleged 'Confession.'&43" *Journal* of the American Society for Psychical Research 69 (1975).

———. *The World of Ted Serios: "Thoughtographic" Studies of an Extraordinary Mind* New York: William Morrow, 1966.

Serling, Rod (1924–1975)

Writer, dramatist, television producer, and creator of the classic science fiction/horror series, *Twilight Zone.* He was born in Syracuse, New York, on December 25, 1924. During World War II, he served with the paratroopers, and after the war he studied at Antioch College (B.A., 1950), but even before completing his degree he had become a writer for radio (beginning in 1946) and television (beginning in 1948). His plays were produced on a variety of popular drama shows such as the Kraft Theatre, Studio One, U.S. Steel Hour, Playhouse 90, Suspense, and Danger. He later became writer-producer for *The Twilight Zone,* and *Rod Serling's Night Gallery,* and the narrator for *In Search of Ancient Astronauts.* He received Emmy awards for best teleplay writing in 1955–57, 1959–61, and 1963–64 and numerous additional awards for his teleplay writing. He also authored a number of books. He died on June 28, 1975.

Sources:

Serling, Rod. *More Stories From the Twilight Zone.* New York: Bantam Books, 1961.

———. *Night Gallery.* New York: Dember Books, 1987. Distributed by W. W. Norton.

———. *Night Gallery Two.* Toronto; New York: Bantam Books, 1972.

———. *Patterns.* New York: Simon & Schuster, 1957.

———. *Stories from the Twilight Zone.* N.p., 1960. Reprint, New York; Toronto: Bantam Books, 1986.

Servadio, Emilio (1904–1995)

Italian psychoanalyst, author, and co-founder in 1937 of the **Societa Italiana Di Parapsychologia** (the Italian Society for Psychic Research, now Italian Society for Parapsychology). He was born on August 14, 1904, in Genoa, Italy. He studied at Genoa University (LL.D., 1926). In private practice for much of his life, he took special interest in the psychodynamic and psychoanalytic aspects of ESP. In 1932 he investigated the phenomena of the medium **Pasquale Erto,** and in 1957 he investigated the miraculous healers in Lucania, South Italy.

Highlighting his outstanding career, he was named president of the Psychoanalytic Center of Rome in 1962, and he was elected to terms as vice president of the Italian Society for Parapsychology (1955–56) and vice president of Italian Psychoanalytic Society (1953–55, 1958–60). He was a charter member of the **Parapsychological Association** and in 1982 was elected president of the Parapsychological Association of Italy. He was chairman of the International Committee for the Study of Methods in Parapsychology and a subeditor and contributor to the *Enciclopedia Italiana* and various scholarly and scientific journals. He is author of *La Ricerca Psichica* (Psychical Research, 1930, 1946), and contributed to *Proceedings of an International Conference on Methodology in Psi Research: Psi Favorable States of Consciousness* edited by Roberto Cavanna (Parapsychology Foundation, 1970) and *Proceedings of an International Conference: Psi Factors in Creativity* edited by Allan Angoff and Betty Shapin (Parapsychology Foundation, 1970).

Servadio died January 18, 1995.

Sources:

Berger, Arthur S., and Joyce Berger. *The Encyclopedia of Parapsychology and Psychical Research.* New York: Paragon House, 1991.

Pleasants, Helene, ed. *Biographical Dictionary of Parapsychology.* New York: Helix Press, 1964.

Servadio, Emilio. "Le conditionnement transferentiel et contre-transférentiel des événements 'psi' au cours de l'analyse" (Transference and counter-transference conditioning of 'psi' events during analysis). *Acta Psychotherapeutica* (1955).

———. "Freud et la Parapsychologie." *Revue Francaise de Psychoanalyse* 3 (1956).

———. "The 'Normal' and the 'Paranormal' Dream." *International Journal of Parapsychology* (1962).

———. "A Presumptively Telepathic-Precognitive Dream During Analysis." *International Journal of Psycho-Analysis* 1 (1955).

———. "Psychoanalyse and Telepathie" (Psychoanalysis and telepathy). *Imago* 4 (1935). Reprinted in *Psychoanalysis and the Occult,* edited by 1953 George Devereux.

———. "Transference and Thought-Transference." *International Journal of Psycho-Analysis* 4, no. 5 (1956).

Servants of Awareness

The Servants of Awareness was one of a several organizations that formed in response to the turbulence in the **Organization of Awareness** (now **Cosmic Awareness Communications**) that arose after the death of William Ralph Duby in 1967. Since the Organization of Awareness's founding, Duby had served as the channel for messages from "Cosmic Awareness," upon which the group's teachings were based. Servants of Awareness was formed by David E. Worcester in Seattle, Washington. It gained some support through the 1970s but has since disappeared.

Servants of the Light (SOL)

The Servants of the Light is a contemporary ritual **magic** group founded by **William E. Butler** (1898–1978) in early 1965. Butler had studied with **Dion Fortune** and the **Society of the Inner Light,** which he founded and had gone on to establish his own direct contact with the higher magical planes. In the years following Dion Fortune's death, Butler wrote several basic magical textbooks, several of which became quite popular in occult circles for their clarity and readability: *Magic: Its Ritual, Power, and Work* (1952), *The Magician: His Training and Work* (1959), and *Apprenticed to Magic* (1962).

In 1965, along with fellow society member **Gareth Knight,** he left the society and founded the Helios Book Service and a new correspondence course of study in magic, the Helios Course, similar to that taught by Dion Fortune. In 1972, Knight departed and the following year founded a new magical group. Butler continued to offer the Helios Course, which evolved into the curriculum of the Servants of the Light School of Occult Science. He was joined in this endeavor by Michael and **Delores Ashcroft-Nowicki.** Together they built the school into an international training instrument with students in more than 20 countries.

Delores Ashcroft-Nowicki eventually came into direct contact with the same inner plane teacher that Butler had contacted. She decided to dedicate her life to the service of this inner plane adept. She was appointed to succeed Butler as the director of studies for the school and Michael was named the school's guardian. In the decades since assuming leadership of the school, as the school has expanded, Delores Ashcroft-Nowicki has emerged as a teacher in her own right and has authored a number of books, both beginning and advanced.

The Servants of the Light offers a 50-lesson correspondence course in magic (with each lesson taking approximately one month). The content of the course is drawn from the **Kabbalah,** the **tarot,** and the Arthurian myths. It supplies a basic understanding of the esoteric tradition and the fundamentals of magical practice. Students study in their own home but are assigned a personal teacher to whom they may direct questions and from whom they can receive guidance. The school is not sectarian and teaches a system of magic that is compatible with a variety of religious backgrounds.

As of the beginning of the new millennium, the school reports some 2,600 students in 23 countries. Contact may be made through the international headquarters at P.O. Box 215, St Helier, Jersey, Channel Islands, Great Britain JE4 9SD. An Internet site is found at http://www.servantsofthelight.org/.

Sources:

Ashcroft-Nowicki, Delores. *First Steps in Ritual.* Wellingsborough, Northamptonshire, UK: Aquarian Press, 1982.

———. *The Tree of Ecstasy.* Wellingsborough, Northamptonshire, UK: Aquarian Press, 1991.

Butler, William E. *Apprenticed to Magic.* London: Aquarian Press, 1962.

———. *The Magician: His Training and Work.* London: Aquarian Press, 1959.

Servants of the Light. http://www.servantsofthelight.org/. May 16, 2000.

Servants of the Star and the Snake

The Servants of the Star and the Snake (SSS), founded in 1995, grew out of the remnants of the Ordo Templi Baphemetis (OTB), a thelemic magical order which had functioned earlier in the decade, and it retains the thelemic character of the OTB. SSS exists as a free association of magical practitioners, members variously defining themselves as ceremonial magicians, shamans, witches, neopagans, sorcerers, or tantrikas. Having jettisoned the hierarchical structures and degree systems of what is considered the Old Aeon, the magicians of the SSS come together for mutual sharing, learning, and networking. There are no leaders, no holy books, and no formal initiations; however, the group does have a special respect for the teachings of the late Sri Gurudeva Mahendrabath Paramahamsa, known to his followers as Dadaji, the cofounder of AMOOKOS (the Arcane, Magikal Order of the Knights of Shambhala) and the late Alain Daniélou.

The association is overseen by an administrator-general, a revolving office; the current administrator-general of the SSS is known by his magical name, Frater Eeyore. SSS may be contacted at P.O. Box 642, Weslaco, TX 78599-0642. It publishes a periodical, *Lila.* Closely associated is the American Gnostic Church, founded in 1985, headed by the Rev. James M. Martin. The church serves as an umbrella organization for several closely related spiritual movements, each claiming some form of illumination by stellar-gnosis. Through it, the SSS is closely related to the **Order of Napunsakas in the West** (ON), a tantrick Order for non-heterosexuals. The ON exists through an outer order for both males and females, though its inner order, the Cultus Skanda-Karttikeya (CS-K), is open only to males. The Tantra (from Hinduism) and Thelema (the magical system developed by **Aleister Crowley**) systems have a common interest in sex magick, though traditionally they approach sexuality from different perspectives.

The SSS has a webpage at http://www.wild.au/sss/index.html.

Sources:

Servants of the Star and the Snake. http://www.wild.au//sss/index.html.

Servier, Jean H(enri) (1918–)

Professor of ethnology who has written on parapsychology. He was born on November 2, 1918, in Constantine, Algeria. He moved to France and studied at the Sorbonne. After graduation he became a professor of sociology and ethnology at the University of Montpellier, France. He was a member of Société des Africanistes. In addition to his studies in ethnology and anthropology, Servier has taken special interest in clairvoyance, mediumship, and the ethnological aspects of the history of magic.

Sources:

Pleasants, Helene, ed. *Biographical Dictionary of Parapsychology.* New York: Helix Press, 1964.

Servier, Jean H. "Geomancy, Clairvoyance and Initiation." *La Tour Saint-Jacques* (September–December 1956). Reprinted in the *Proceedings of Four Conferences of Parapsychology* (1957).

———. *L'Homme et l'Invisible.* Paris: R. Laffonto, 1964.

———. *Les Partes de l'Année.* Paris: R. Laffonto, 1962.

"Seth"

Entity channeled through the medium **Jane Roberts,** the public name of Jane Butts (1929–1984). The communications from Seth began in 1963, when Jane and her husband Robert

Butts first experimented with an **ouija board.** Later, Jane went into a trance, and when "Seth" spoke through her, Jane's voice and features changed character.

The "Seth" material comprises a mass of teachings in manuscript and on tape recordings, much of which has been edited and issued in a series of books. The philosophy presented is coherent and continuous, covering teachings on dreams, health, **reincarnation, astral projection,** and the relationship of human beings to their creator. The teachings are comprehensive, dealing with "aspect psychology" (different levels of awareness and grades of reality in relation to mobile consciousness), the nature of the soul, death, and after-death experiences.

In a communication titled "The Unknown Reality," "Seth" stated:

"The individual self must become aware of far more reality, it must allow its identity to expand to include previously unconscious knowledge. Your species is in a time of change—you are now poised on the threshold from which the race can go many ways. Potentials within the body's mechanisms, not as yet used, can immeasurably enrich the race and bring it to levels of spiritual, psychic, and physical fulfillment. But if some changes are not made, the race will not endure. . . . I am suggesting ways in which the unknown reality can become a known one."

Sources:

Roberts, Jane. *The God of Jane: A Psychic Manifesto.* Englewood Cliffs, N.J.: Prentice-Hall, 1981.

———. *How to Develop Your ESP Power.* New York: Frederick Fell, 1966. Reprinted as *The Coming of Seth.* New York: Pocket Books, 1976.

———. *The Nature of Personal Reality: A Seth Book.* Englewood Cliffs, N.J.: Prentice-Hall, 1974.

———. *Seth, Dreams and Projection of Consciousness.* Walpole, N. H., Stillpoint Publishing, 1986.

———. *The Seth Material.* Englewood Cliffs, N.J.: Prentice-Hall, 1970.

———. *Seth Speaks: The Eternal Validity of the Soul.* Englewood Cliffs, N.J.: Prentice-Hall, 1972.

Sethos (ca. 12th century C.E.)

According to M. A. Del Rio (1561–1608), Sethos was a diviner, who was deprived of his sight by the Emperor Manuel because of his addiction to magic. It is said that the emperor Andronicus Comnenus, cousin of Manuel, had Sethos divine by **hydromancy** an answer to the question of who was to succeed him. The spirit gave the letters "S I" in reply; and on being asked when, said before the feast of the exaltation of the Cross. This prediction was fulfilled, for before the date mentioned, Isaac Angelus had thrown Andronicus to the mob to be torn to pieces. It is said that when the devil spells, he spells backwards, so that "S I" may be taken to represent Isaac.

Setna, Papyrus of

An ancient papyrus said to have been discovered by Prince Setna Kha-em-ust, son of Rameses II of Egypt, under the head of a mummy in the Necropolis at Memphis. The Egyptologist Alfred Wiedemann stated in his book *Popular Literature in Ancient Egypt* (1902):

"The first text, which has been known to us since 1867, tells that this prince, being skilled and zealous in the practice of necromancy, was one day exhibiting his acquirements to the learned men of the court, when an old man told him of a magic book containing two spells written by the hand of Thoth himself, the god of wisdom.

"He who repeated the first spell bewitched thereby heaven and earth and the realm of night, the mountains and the depth of the sea; he knew the fowls of the air and every creeping thing; he saw the fishes, for a divine power brought them up out of the depth. He who read the second spell should have power to resume his earthly shape, even though he dwelt in the grave; to see the sun rising in the sky with all the gods and the moon in the form wherein she displays herself.

"Setna inquired where this book was to be found, and learned that it was lying in the tomb of Nefer-ka-Ptah, a son of King Mer-neb-ptah (who is nowhere else named), and that any attempt to take away the book would certainly meet with obstinate resistance. These difficulties did not withhold Setna from the adventure. He entered the tomb of Nefer-ka-Ptah, where he found not only the dead man, but the Ka of his wife Ahuri and their son, though these latter had been buried in Koptos.

"Ahuri told all the trouble that the possession of the book had brought upon her husband and herself, but her tale of woe produced no effect upon the intruder. Setna persisted in his undertaking, and at length, by the help of magic, he gained his end.

"But as in many other tales among many other peoples, success brought no blessing to the man who had disturbed the repose of the dead. Setna fell in love with the daughter of a priest at Memphis, who turned out to be a witch, and took advantage of his intimate connection with her to bring him to ignominy and wretchedness.

"At length the prince recognized and repented of the sacrilege he had committed in carrying off the book, and brought it back to Nefer-ka-Ptah. In the hope of atoning to some extent for his sin he journeyed to Koptos, and finding the graves of the wife and child of Nefer-ka-Ptah, he solemnly restored their mummies to the tomb of the father and husband, carefully closing the tomb he had so sacrilegiously disturbed.

"The second text, edited two years ago by Griffith from a London papyrus, is also genuinely Egyptian in its details. Three magic tales, interwoven one with another, are brought into connection with Saosiri, the supernaturally born son of Setna.

"In the first, Saosiri, who was greatly Setna's superior in the arts of magic, led his father down into the underworld. They penetrated into the judgment-hall of Osiris, where the sights they saw convinced Setna that a glorious future awaited the poor man who should cleave to righteousness, while he who led an evil life on earth, though rich and powerful, must expect a terrible doom. Saosiri next succeeded in saving his father, and with him all Egypt, from great difficulty by reading without breaking the seal a closed letter brought by an Ethiopian magician, whom he thus forced to recognize the superior power of Egypt.

"The last part of the text tells of a powerful magician once dwelling in Ethiopia who modelled in wax a litter with four bearers to whom he gave his life. He sent them to Egypt, and at his command they sought out Pharaoh in his palace, carried him off to Ethiopia, and, after giving him five hundred blows with a cudgel, conveyed him during the same night back to Memphis. Next morning the king displayed the weals on his back to his courtiers, one of whom, Horus by name, was sufficiently skilled in the use of amulets to ward off by their means any immediate repetition of the outrage.

"Horus then set forth to bring from Hermopolis, the all powerful magic book of the god Thoth, and by its aid he succeeded in treating the Ethiopian king as the Ethiopian sorcerer had treated Pharaoh. The foreign magician then hastened to Egypt to engage in a contest with Horus in magic tricks. His skill was shown to be inferior, and in the end he and his mother received permission to return to Ethiopia under a solemn promise not to set foot on Egyptian territory for a space of fifteen hundred years."

Seton (or **Sethon**) **Alexander** (d. ca. 1604)

One of the very few alchemists, reportedly, who succeeded in the great experiment of the transmutation of metals. He was said to have taken his name from the village of Seton, in the vicinity of Edinburgh, Scotland.

In the year 1601, the crew of a Dutch vessel was wrecked on the coast near Seton's dwelling, and he personally rescued several of them, lodged them in his house, and treated them with great kindness, ultimately sending them back to Holland at his own expense. In the following year, he visited Holland and renewed his acquaintance with at least one of the shipwrecked crew, James Haussen, the pilot, who lived at Arksun.

Haussen, determined to repay Seton for the hospitality he had received in Scotland, entertained him for some time in Haussen house, and to him Seton disclosed the information that he was a master of the art of **alchemy** and proved his words by performing several transmutations. Haussen could not keep this information to himself and confided it to Venderlinden, a physician of Enkhuysen, and showed him a piece of gold that had been transmuted from lead. Venderlinden's grandson, in turn, showed it to the celebrated author D. G. Morhoff, who wrote a letter concerning it to Langlet du Fresnoy, author of the *Histoire de la Philosophie Hermétique* (3 vols., 1742).

Seton visited Amsterdam and Rotterdam, traveled by sea to Italy, then went through Switzerland to Germany, accompanied by Wolfgang Dienheim, a professed skeptic of alchemy, whom Seton convinced of the error of his views at Basel, before the eyes of several of its principal inhabitants. Dienheim described Seton, and the pen picture he made resembles a typical Scot of the seventeenth century. "Seton," Dienheim said "was short but stout, and high coloured, with a pointed beard, but despite his corpulence, his expression was spiritual and exalted." "He was," added Dienheim, "a native of Molier, in an island of the ocean."

Seton demonstrated several experiments of importance. In one of these the celebrated physician Zwinger himself brought the lead that was to be transmuted. A common crucible was obtained at a goldsmith's, and ordinary sulphur was bought on the road to the house where the experiment was to take place. Seton handled none of these materials and took no part in the operation except to give those who followed his directions a small packet of powder that transformed the lead into the purest gold of exactly the same weight. Zwinger appears to have been absolutely convinced of the genuine nature of the experiment, for he wrote an account of it to his friend Dr. Schobinger, which appears in Lonig's *Ephemerides.*

Shortly after this Seton left Basel and, changing his name, went to Strasbourg before traveling to Cologne, where he lodged with Anton Bordemann, who was something of an alchemist himself. In this city, Seton was sufficiently imprudent to exhibit his alchemical skill openly, on one occasion producing six ounces of gold through the application of one grain of his magical powder. The incident seems to have made an impression on at least one of the savants of Cologne, for Theobald de Hoghelande in his *Historiæ Aliquot Transmutationis Mettalicæ,* which was published in Cologne in 1604, alluded to it.

Seton then went to Hamburg and traveled south to Munich, where something more important than alchemy engaged his attention: he eloped with the daughter of a citizen of that city. Christian II, the young elector of Saxony, had heard of Seton's brilliant alchemical successes and invited him to his court, but Seton, reluctant to leave his young wife, sent his friend William Hamilton (probably a brother-Scot) instead, with a supply of the transmuting agent.

In the presence of the whole court, Hamilton undertook and carried through an experiment with complete success, and the gold manufactured resisted every known test. This excited the elector's desire to see and converse with Seton himself, and a pressing invitation, which amounted to a command, was dispatched to Seton, who, unable to refuse, came to the electoral court.

He was received there with every mark of honor, but it soon became evident to him that Christian II had only invited him for the purpose of learning his secret, but Seton, as an adept in the mysteries of alchemy, remained true to his calling and flatly refused to gratify the elector's greed.

In the end the elector ordered him to be imprisoned in a tower, where he was guarded by forty soldiers. There he was subjected to every conceivable species of torture, but it failed to extort from him his methods. The elector at last ceased the torture.

At this point, Michael Sendivogius, a Moravian chemist who happened to be in Dresden, heard of Seton's terrible experiences and possessed sufficient influence to obtain permission to visit him. Himself a searcher after the **philosophers' stone,** he sympathized with the adept, and proposed to him that he should attempt a rescue. Seton agreed to this and promised that if he were fortunate enough to escape, he would reward Sendivogius with his secret.

The Moravian traveled back to Cracow, where he resided, sold his property, and returned to Dresden. He lodged near Seton's place of confinement, entertaining the soldiers who guarded the alchemist and judiciously bribing those who were directly concerned in his imprisonment.

At last he judged that the time was ripe to attempt Seton's rescue. He feasted the guards and they were soon in a condition of drunken carelessness. Sendivogius hurried to the tower in which Seton was imprisoned, but found him unable to walk through the severity of his tortures. He therefore supported Seton to a carriage, which they reached without being observed. They halted at Seton's house to pick up his wife, who had in her possession some of the all-important powder, and sped to Cracow, which they reached in safety.

When quietly settled in that city, Sendivogius reminded Seton of his promise to assist him in his alchemical projects, but was met with a stern refusal. Seton explained to him that it was impossible for him as an adept to reveal to his rescuer the terms of such a great mystery. The health of the alchemist, however, had been shattered by the torture he had suffered, and upon his death he presented the remains of his magical powder to his preserver.

The possession of this powder made Sendivogius more eager than ever to discover the mysteries of alchemy. He married Seton's widow, perhaps with the idea that she was in possession of her late husband's occult knowledge, but she was absolutely ignorant of the matter.

Seton left behind him a treatise entitled *The New Light of Alchymy,* which Sendivogius published as his own. In its pages he thought he saw a method of increasing the powder, but he only succeeded in lessening it.

With what remained he posed as a successful alchemist. In his own country of Moravia, he was imprisoned, but escaped. His powder was rapidly diminishing, but he still continued his experiments. Pierce Borel, in his work *Tresor de Recherches et Antiquites Galoises et Françoises* (1655), mentioned that he saw a crown piece that had been partially dipped into a mixture of the powder dissolved in wine, and that the part steeped in the elixir was gold, porous, and was not soldered or otherwise tampered with.

The powder expended, Sendivogius degenerated into a charlatan, pretending that he could manufacture gold, and receiving large sums on the strength of being able to do so. He survived until the year 1646 when he died at Parma at the age of eighty-four. Seton's book *The New Light of Alchymy* would appear to deny that the philosophers' stone was to be achieved by the successful transmutation of metals. It stated:

"The extraction of the soul out of gold or silver, by what vulgar way of alchymy soever, is but a mere fancy. On the contrary, he which, in a philosophical way, can without any fraud, and colourable deceit, make it that it shall really tinge the basest metal, whether with gain or without gain, with the colour of gold or silver (abiding all requisite tryals whatever), hath the gates of Nature opened to him for the enquiring into further and higher secrets, and with the blessing of God to obtain them."

Seven Principles (in Theosophy)

According to the teachings of **Theosophy** (derived from Hinduism), there are seven principles or parts of the human being that reflect cosmic principles. These concern the **evolution of life** from the unmanifest principles through creation. The seven principles of the human being are: *Atman* (the universal self), *Buddhi* (the intellectual principle), *Manas* (the mental principle), *Kama* (desire), *Prana* (subtle vitality), *Linga-sarira* (astral body), and *Sthula-sarira* (gross physical matter).

For convenience, these are sometimes simplified into three principles of the human being: spirit, soul, and body, as in Christianity. These three parts are first and highest, the Divine Spirit or the Divine Monad, rooted in the universe, whose spirit is linked with the All, being in a mystical sense a ray of the All; second, the intermediate part of Spiritual **Monad,** which in its higher and lower aspects is the spiritual and human soul; third, the lowest part of the human constitution, the vital-astralphysical part, composed of material or quasi-material life atoms. (See also **Logos; Planetary Logos; Rupa**)

Sources:

Besant, Annie. *The Seven Principles of Man.* 1892. Reprint, New York: London & Bernes; Theosophical Publishing Society, 1904.

Seven Stewards of Heaven

According to the sixteenth-century magical ritual system **Arbatel,** these are the spirits through whom God governs the world. They are known as the Olympian spirits, and they govern the Olympian spheres, which are composed of 196 regions. Their names in the Olympian language are: Aratron, the celestial spirit of Saturn, whose day is Saturday; Bethor, the angel of Jupiter, whose day is Monday; Phaleg, the prince of Mars, whose day is Tuesday; Och, the master of the Sun, whose day is Sunday; Hagith, the sovereign of Venus, whose day is Friday; Ophiel, the spirit of Mercury, who must be invoked on Wednesday; Phul, the administrator of affairs in the Moon, whose day is Monday. Each of these Seven Celestial Spirits may be invoked by magicians with the aid of ceremonies and preparations.

Seventh-Day Adventism

Heterodox Christian cult stemming from the teachings of William Miller (1782–1849), formerly a Baptist convert, whose simplistic interpretation of scripture led him to asssert that Christ would return to earth March 21, 1843. He built up a considerable following, but lost support when the return did not take place, even for a revised calculation of October 22, 1844.

His teachings were later modified by the Millerite Hiram Edson in New York State, who claimed that he had a vision which confirmed that Miller was right about the time of redemption but wrong about the *place,* which should have been the "heavenly sanctuary" and not the earth. Edson's doctrine was further developed by "Father Bates" (former sea captain), Elder James White of the S.D.A. church which had been organized in 1860 and his wife Ellen G. White.

Since then, S.D.A. has built up a membership claimed at over two million in the United States and abroad. Two of its doctrinal points influenced Charles Taze Russell (1870–1916) in the formation of his evangelical cult of 'Russellites' which became known as **Jehovah's Witnesses** under Joseph Rutherford (1916–1942). These doctrines were those of a "soul-sleep" after death, and of annihilation of the wicked. Other specifically S.D.A. doctrines include the concept of a completion of Christ's atonement which had remained unfinished and the need to observe the Sabbath on Saturday.

Sources:

Land, Gary, ed. *Adventism in America.* Grand Rapids, Mich.: William B. Eerdmans Publishing Co., 1986.

Nichol, Francis D. *The Midnight Cry.* Tacoma Park, Md.: Review and Herald Publishing Association, 1944.

Seventh Son

It has long been believed in Europe and the United States that a seventh son is especially lucky or gifted with occult powers, and that the seventh son of a seventh son has healing powers. In Scotland, the seventh daughter of a seventh daughter was said to have the gift of **second sight** (prophetic vision). In Ireland, the saliva of a seventh son was said to have healing properties. However, in Romanian folklore, a seventh child was believed to be fated to become a **vampire.**

As early as the beginning of the seventeenth century, the *Diary of Walter Yonge 1604–1628* (published by the Camden Society, 1847, edited by G. Roberts) had a negative reference to the healing powers of a seventh son:

"In January, 1606–7, it is reported from London by credible letters, that a child being the seventh son of his mother, and no woman child born between, healeth deaf, blind, and lame; but the parents of the child are popish, as so many say as are healed by it. The Bishop of London, Doctor Vaughan, caused divers [various people] to be brought to the child as aforesaid, who said a short prayer as [he] imposed his hands upon, as 'tis said he did unto others; but no miracle followeth any, so that it appeareth to be a plain lie invented to win grace to the popish faction."

Thomas Lupton, in the second edition of his book *A Thousand Notable Things* (1660), noted, "It is manifest, by experience, that the seventh male child, by just order (never a girl or wench being born between) doth heal only with touching (through a natural gift) the king's evil [scrofula], which is a special gift of God, given to kings and queens, as daily experience doth witnesse."

In France, there was also a tradition that a seventh son had the power to cure the **king's evil.** He was called a "Marcou" and branded with a fleur-de-lis. The Marcou breathed on the part affected, or else the patient touched the Marcou's fleur-de-lis.

Robert Chambers, in his *Domestic Annals of Scotland from the Reformation to the Revolution* (1858), stated that in February 1682, a certain Hugh McGie, ". . . gave in a bill to the Privy Council, representing that, by the practice of other nations, any tradesman having seven sons together, without the intervention of a daughter, is declared free of all public burdens and taxes, and has other encouragements bestowed on him, to enable him to bring up the said children for the use and benefit of the commonwealth; and claiming a similar privilege on the strength of his having that qualification. The Council recommended the magistrates [of Edinburgh] to take Hugh's seven sons into consideration when they laid their 'stents' (trade taxes) upon him."

A tradition in Donegal, Ireland, claimed that the healing powers of a seventh son required a special ceremony at the moment of the infant's birth. The woman who received the child in her arms should place in its hand whatever substance she decided that he should use to heal in later life. This substance could be metal (e.g., a silver coin) or a common substance like salt, or even hair; when the child was old enough, it would rub the substance and the patient would apply it to an afflicted part for healing purposes. There was also an Irish tradition similar to the Scottish belief that a seventh son of a seventh son possessed prophetic as well as healing powers.

There was a general belief in Britain that the seventh son of a seventh son was destined to be a physician and would have an intuitive knowledge of the art of healing, often curing a patient simply by touching an afflicted part. This belief also extended to the seventh daughter of a seventh daughter. A contributor to *Notes & Queries* (June 12, 1852) observed: "In

Saltash Street, Plymouth [England], my friend copied, on the 10th December, 1851, the following inscription on a board, indicating the profession and claims of the inhabitant: 'A. Shepherd, the third seventh daughter, Doctress.'"

The belief in the healing powers of a seventh son of a seventh son has persisted into the twentieth century, and there are two Irish healers of this kind: **Danny Gallagher** and **Finbarr Nolan.** Both are "touch healers," although Gallagher additionally "blesses" soil that is to be mixed with water and applied to the afflicted area of the patient; both healers recommend a sequence of two or three visits for maximum healing. They are credited with remarkable cures. Gallagher is reported to have restored the sight of a woman blind for twenty-two years, and Nolan claims to have successfully healed injured race horses as well as human beings.

Sources:

Chambers, Robert. *Domestic Annals of Scotland from the Reformation to the Revolution.* 2 vols. Edinburgh, 1858.

Lupton, Thomas. *A Thousand Notable Things.* London, 1660.

Sex Magic

The sexualization of spirituality has a long tradition in most non-Western religious traditions and is especially prominent in Hindu **tantric yoga,** which strongly influenced Tibetan Buddhism. Sex was utilized as a means to unite with the goddess, in one of her several guises. It also emerged in Chinese Taoist traditions, where it was integrated into speculations of longevity and immortality.

In the West, sexual activity was to a large extent denigrated and identified with original sin. Thus the idea of positively integrating sexuality and religion was considered somewhat scandalous. With the emergence of alternative forms of spirituality, however, new attention was given to sexuality.

Within **Spiritualism** a new attention to sexuality began quite early as the basis of the concept that would become known as "soul mates." Early speculation would be passed on to **Pascal Beverly Randolph,** an eclectic physician who specialized in marital problems. Randolph developed a teaching of occult sexuality centered upon a hypothesized energy transfer between couples during intercourse. His ideas led directly to a full-blown "sex magick" as embodied in the **OTO** (Ordo Templi Orientis), a German magic order founded in the 1890s.

Through the nineteenth century the basic problem in **ceremonial magic** was the building of energy for the accomplishment both of mundane goals and the great work of union with the ultimate. A variety of different methods, from chanting to using mind-altering drugs, was used. The Ordo Templi Orientis proposed that sex was the best means of raising such energy. The order developed a degree system that taught basic magic practice and then introduced sexual techniques at the eighth (autoerotic) and ninth (heterosexual intercourse) degree levels. Through the early decades of the twentieth century, sex magic was the great secret of the OTO.

Independently of the OTO, **Aleister Crowley** (1875–1947), a former member of the Hermetic Order of the **Golden Dawn** who had formed his own small group, pursued his development of magic through attempts to repeat some of the operations described in older texts. In 1909 he was in Egypt attempting to understand works of magic originally described by Elizabethan magicians **John Dee** and Edward Kelly. Assisting Crowley was **Victor Neuburg.** In the midst of these studies Crowley was inspired to conduct his first act of sex magic, with Neuburg as his partner. Crowley's work led to the publication *The Book of Lies,* which contains, in allegorical phrasing, some of the insights on sex and magic he had acquired.

Following the publication of *The Book of Lies,* **Theodor Reuss,** the outer head of the order of the OTO, contacted Crowley and complained that he had published the secret of the OTO. The result of their encounter was Crowley's induction into the OTO and his quick rise to a position of power as head of the British section. He then succeeded Reuss as outer head of the order. Crowley rewrote the ritual material for the order and added an eleventh, homoerotic, degree. Crowley also experimented with sex magic at an intense level over the next decade and kept detailed journals of his endeavors.

Through the decades after World War I several other sex magic groups were born, most founded by former members of the OTO. They included the Fraternal Saturni (Germany) and the Choronzon Club, also known as the Great Brotherhood of God (United States).

The OTO itself was never a large organization and few knew about and practiced its sex magic techniques. Crowley was succeeded by Carl Germer, whose administrative leadership was almost nonexistent. Through the 1950s the secret materials were dispensed to a variety of people internationally. Germer died in the early 1960s without designating a successor, and the order fell into chaos. In the meantime a set of Crowley's papers were deposited at the Warburg Institute in London and became known to various British magicians (especially **Kenneth Grant**).

Then in 1969 Louis Culling, a former member of the OTO who had left to join an American offshoot, published the *Complete Magick Curriculum of the Secret Order of the G.B.G.,* and shortly thereafter a commentary on it, *A Manual of Sex Magick.* Beginning with the publication in 1972 of an edited edition of Crowley's *Magical Diaries,* which contained the account of some of his sexual experiments, within a decade all of Crowley's writings on sex magic and all of the secret materials of the OTO were published. These books provided the basis for the spread of sex magic throughout the Western world. At the same time, through the Bihar School of Yoga in Bengal, the sexual teachings of Indian tantra were for the first time spread to the West in such detail that tantric practice could be institutionalized.

From the 1980s to the present a host of different sex magic groups drawing upon the Crowley/OTO tradition have arisen. At the same time a number of tantric groups (and a few Taoist groups) have also appeared. While each tradition seems to be aware of the other and has some superficial similarity in its use of sexual intercourse for religious and magical ends, they have remained separate. The Western and Eastern teachings on sexuality are quite different. While the same basic practices are present in both Eastern and Western forms of occult sexuality, the ideas under which they were organized do not easily mix.

Sources:

Crowley, Aleister. *De Arte Magica.* San Francisco: Level Press, [1974].

———. *Magical Diaries of Aleister Crowley.* Edited by John Symonds and Kenneth Grant. Montreal: Next Step Publications, 1972.

———. *The Magical Record of the Beast 666.* Edited by John Symonds and Kenneth Grant. Montreal: Next Step Publications, 1972.

Culling, Louis, ed. *A Manual of Sex Magick.* St. Paul: Llewellyn Publications, 1971.

King, Francis, ed. *The Secret Rituals of the O.T.O.* New York: Samuel Weiser, 1973.

———. *Sexuality, Magic, and Perversion.* Secaucus, N.J.: Citadel Press, 1972.

Sexton, George

British secularist teacher of the nineteenth century. **Robert Owen** invited his attention to the phenomena of **Spiritualism.** After a crusade against its doctrines, personal experiences with the **Davenport Brothers** convinced Sexton of their genuine validity. Continuing his experiments, he finally ended by accepting Spiritualism and proclaimed its truth in lectures with the same outspokenness with which he formerly fought against it. He denounced the pretensions of conjurers who claimed to have exposed Spiritualism and, pointing out the difference in condition and effect, he actually performed sham spiritual manifestations before his audience.

Sexton authored one pamphlet, a transcript of a lecture: *Scientific Materialism Calmly Considered; A Reply to Prof. Tyndall's Belfast Address* (1874). He also served as editor of the *Spiritual Magazine* and became a member of the **British National Association of Spiritualists.**

Sextus V. Pope (1521–1590)

One of the popes accused of sorcery. J. A. de Thou said of him in his *Histoire Universelle* (1734, Vol. II):

"The Spaniards continued their vengeance against this Pontiff even after his death, and they forgot nothing in their anxiety to blacken his memory by the libels which they flung against him. Sextus, said they, who, by means of the magical art, was for a long time in confederacy with a demon, had made a compact with this enemy of humanity to give himself up to him, on condition he was made Pope, and allowed to reign six years.

"Sextus was raised to the chair of St. Peter, and during the five years he held sway in Rome he distinguished his pontificate by actions surpassing the feeble reach of the human intellect. Finally, at the end of this term, the Pope fell sick, and the devil arriving to keep him to his pact, Sextus inveighed strongly against his bad faith, reproaching him with the fact that the term they had agreed upon was not fulfilled, and that there still remained to him more than a twelve-month.

"But the devil reminded him that at the beginning of his pontificate he had condemned a man who, according to the laws, was too young by a year to suffer death, and that he had nevertheless caused him to be executed, saying that he would give him a year out of his own life; that this year, added to the other five, completed the six years which had been promised to him, and that in consequence he did very wrong to complain.

"Sextus, confused and unable to make any answer, remained mute, and turning himself towards the *ruelle* of his bed, prepared for death in the midst of the terrible mental agitation caused by the remorse of his conscience." De Thou added, "For the rest, I only mention this trait as a rumor spread by the Spaniards, and I should be very sorry to guarantee its truth."

During his papacy, Sextus authorized very large sums to be expended on public works, including completion of the dome of St. Peter's, the loggia of Sextus in the Lateran, and the chapel of the Praesepe in Sta. Maria Maggiore. In spite of the controversy, today Sextus is ranked among the greatest popes.

Seybert Commission

A commission for the investigation of **Spiritualism,** appointed by the wish of Henry Seybert, a Philadelphia Spiritualist who, in his will, left $60,000 to the University of Pennsylvania to be devoted "to the maintenance of a chair in the said University to be known as the 'Adam Seybert Chair of Moral and Intellectual Philosophy,' upon the condition that the incumbent of the said chair, either individually or in conjunction with a commission of the university faculty will make a thorough and impartial investigation of all systems of morals, religion, or philosophy which assume to represent the truth, and particularly of Modern Spiritualism."

The commission, which began its investigations in March 1884, was composed as follows: William Pepper, Joseph Leidy, George A. Koenig, Robert Ellis Thompson, George S. Fullerton, and Horace Howard Furness; added afterward were Coleman Sellers, James W. White, Calvin B. Knerr, and S. Weir Mitchell. Pepper, as provost of the university, was ex-officio chairman. Furness acted as chairman and Fullerton was secretary to the committee.

Seybert was represented in the committee by Thomas R. Hazard, a personal friend. Hazard was charged by Seybert to prescribe the methods to be used in the investigation, designate the mediums to be consulted, and reject the attendance of those whose presence might be in conflict with the harmony or good order of the spirit circles. In May 1887, the committee published a preliminary report with negative conclusions in the whole field of Spiritualist phenomena. No final report was ever published, nor was the investigation continued.

The committee first turned its attention to **slate-writing.** Two séances with **Mrs. S. E. Patterson** led to no result. The committee then sent to New York for **Henry Slade** and promptly caught him in **fraud.** As no other slate-writing medium was available for testing, a mock séance was arranged for the committee by Harry Kellar, one of the more capable magicians of the day, and he proceeded to deliver messages in French, Spanish, Dutch, Chinese, Japanese, Gujerati, and German, without the committee being able to discover the trick.

The committee then turned to the issue of spirit **rappings.** Margaret Kane-Fox (of the **Fox Sisters**), the medium of these experiments, stood on four glass tumblers, the heels of her shoes resting upon the rear tumblers and the soles upon the first tumblers. After many attempts, raps were heard and Furness remarked to the medium, "This is the most wonderful thing of all, Mrs. Kane, I distinctly feel them in your feet. There is not a particle of motion in your foot, but there is an unusual pulsation." After two séances the experiments were abandoned as the medium expressed doubt that in her state of health a third meeting would bring more striking results. According to the committee, this investigation was not sufficiently extensive to warrant any positive conclusions. The report, however, points out that "sounds of varying intensity may be produced in almost any portion of the human body by voluntary muscular action. To determine the exact location of this muscular activity is at times a matter of delicacy."

An attempt was made to study **spirit photography.** This was frustrated as the committee felt disinclined to accept the high fees of **William M. Keeler.** He asked three hundred dollars for three séances and the right to demand, if conditions made it necessary, the exclusive use of the dark room and his own instruments. The committee refused and concluded "that in these days of composite photography it is worse than childish to claim a spiritual source for results which can be obtained at any time by any tyro in the art."

The investigations into **materialization** with **Pierre L. O. A. Keeler,** into **telekinesis** phenomena with Dr. Rothermel, and into **direct voice** with **Maud E. Lord** were declared to have been negative.

In 1886 Fullerton visited to Germany to reexamine psychic researcher **Johann C. F. Zöllner**'s experiments with Henry Slade. He interviewed William Wundt, philosopher of the University of Leipzig; Gustave Theodore Fechner, emeritus physicist at the University of Leipzig; W. Schneibner, mathematician of the University of Leipzig; and Wilhelm Weber, emeritus physicist at the University of Göttingen. With the exception of Weber, the learned professors declared that Zöllner's mental condition was not normal. The results of Fullerton's investigation in Europe appeared as an appendix to the Seybert Report.

The report of the Seybert Commission was received with indignation by Spiritualists. Thomas R. Hazard, the only Spiritualist on the committee, declared that he repeatedly protested against the committee's methods, but his protests were disregarded. In the *Philadelphia North American,* Hazard publicly argued for the removal of Fullerton, Thompson, and Koenig as prejudiced researchers. For, he continued, ". . . had the object in view been to belittle and bring into discredit, hatred and general contempt the cause . . . the Trustees could scarcely have selected more suitable instruments for the object intended from all the denizens of Philadelphia than are the gentlemen who constitute a majority of the Seybert Commission."

This protest was considered and rejected. The report subsequently appeared, and A. B. Richmond, a Philadelphia lawyer, replied in two books. Frank Podemore observed, "Spiritualists contend, and not apparently without justification, that the intentions of Mr. Seybert were never fairly carried out, and that the prepossessions of the committee against the subject under investigation are demonstrated by their willingness to leave the inquiry unfinished and to divert the funds entrusted to them to an object which was regarded by the testator as at most of secondary importance."

The negative results attained by the Seybert Commission, and its implicit condemnation of the movement for harboring fraudulent mediums, which has been substantiated by later research, did much to set the intellectual community in the United States against Spiritualism and marginalize it in the religious community.

Sources:

Berger, Arthur S., and Joyce Berger. *The Encyclopedia of Parapsychology and Psychical Research.* New York: Paragon House, 1991.

Podmore, Frank. *Modern Spiritualism.* London: Methuen, 1902. Reprinted as *Mediums of the Nineteenth Century.* New Hyde Park, N.Y.: University Books, 1963.

Preliminary Report of the Commission Appointed by the University of Pennsylvania to Investigate Modern Spiritualism. Philadelphia: J. B. Lippincott, 1887.

Richmond, A. B. *What I Saw at Cassadaga Lake; A Review of the Seybert Commissioners' Report.* N.p., 1888.

Shaddai

According to the mysticism of **Kabbalah,** this was one of ten divine names in the angelic hierarchy. The *Zohar* speaks of three supernal degrees or divine hypostases (that which stands under), the first being Kether. When the world of manifest things was in the condition of Tohu, God revealed himself in the hypostasis Shaddai; when it had proceeded to the condition called Bohu, he manifested as the hypostasis Tsabaoth, but when the darkness had disappeared from the face of things he appeared as Elohim.

Shah, (Sayed) Idries (1924–1996)

Author and translator of important works on occultism and Eastern mysticism. He was born on June 16, 1924, in Simla, India. He came from an Afghan family of Arabian origin that claims descent through the prophet Mohammed to the Sasanian emperors of Persia. He was educated privately, and became a British citizen. He became the proprietor of the International Press Agency in 1953, and from 1966 until his death he was the director of studies of the Institute for Cultural Research in London. He was also the literary and film director of Mulla Nasrudin Enterprises.

Shah wrote over 30 books and translated others, and through them he became a major force in the movement of Islamic, especially Sufic, thought into the West. He also had a broad knowledge of the occult and reportedly ghostwrote the early biography of **Gerald B. Gardner,** the founder of the neopagan revival in the 1940s.

He was awarded the Dictionary of International Biography Certificate of Merit for Distinguished Service to Human Thought, and in 1972 he was appointed Visiting Professor in Intercultural Studies at the University of Geneva, Switzerland. He was the Professor Honoris Causa, National University of La Plata, Argentina, from 1974 to his death on November 23, 1996, in London.

Sources:

Shah, Idries. *The Exploits of the Incomparable Mulla Nasrudin.* London: Cape, 1966. Reprint, New York: Simon & Schuster, 1967.

———. *Learning How to Learn; Psychology and Spirituality in the Sufi Way.* London: Octagon Press, 1978. San Francisco: Harper & Row, 1981.

———. *Oriental Magic.* London; New York: Rider, 1956. Reprint, New York: Penguin Arkana, 1993.

———. *Reflections.* London: Zenith Books; Octagon Press, 1968. Reprint, Baltimore: Penguin Books, 1972.

———. *The Secret Lore of Magic.* New York: Citadel Press, 1957.

———. *Special Problems in the Study of Sufi Ideas.* London: London Society for Understanding Fundamental Ideas, 1966. Reprint, London: Octagon Press, 1974.

———. *The Sufis.* New York: Anchor Books, 1940. Reprint, London: Cape, 1969.

———. *Tales of the Dervishes.* London: Cape, 1967. Reprint, New York, Dutton, 1969.

———. *Way of the Sufi.* London: Cape, 1968. Reprint, New York: Dutton, 1969.

———. trans. *The Subtleties of the inimitable Mulla Nasrudin.* New York: Dutton; London: Cape, 1973.

Shakers

A spiritual community established in New Lebanon, New York, near the Massachusetts line, formally known as the United Society of Believers in Christ's Second Appearing. It had its origin in England in 1747, when Jane and James Wardley became the first leaders of a Lancashire revivalist sect. They were Quaker tailors influenced by the French prophets, an enthusiastic movement that had spread through southern France earlier in the century. Ann Lee, 22-year-old daughter of a Manchester blacksmith, joined this group of "shaking Quakers" in 1758 and through her strange visionary gifts became their leader. She was imprisoned in 1772 for disturbing the Sabbath and preaching a doctrine of celibacy, an idea stemming from her own experience of losing four children at or soon after their birth.

In 1774, after visions and inspired revelations, she moved to America with a handful of followers. By 1780 the Shaker colony had grown, attracting many settlers. Men and women lived together in celibacy with common ownership of property.

Between 1781 and 1783 Lee and her elders visited 36 towns in Massachusetts and Connecticut on a missionary campaign, but the Shakers were ridiculed. They had become especially unpopular for their pacifist ideas during the Revolution.

Lee died in 1784. The community eventually prospered, especially under Lee's successor, Joseph Meacham, and established an enviable reputation for hard work, excellent furniture making, and community spirit. The most characteristic behavior of the Shakers, from which their popular name derived, was an ecstatic dance. It seems clear that much of the very genuine joy and creativeness of the Shaker community arose from the intense energy of sexual sublimation.

Starting in 1837, the Watervliet community near Albany, New York, was visited by Spiritualist-type manifestations of shaking and jerking, and some Shakers were possessed by Indian spirits and spoke in tongues (see **Xenoglossis**). Some of them became Spiritualists.

The Shaker community grew throughout the nineteenth century. The Shakers were able to gather many converts on the frontier and found other members among the many orphans to whom they provided a home. They originally had functioned informally as an orphanage in many areas, but the creation of a system of government and church-sponsored orphanages had a significant impact on the movement's development. The eventual decline of Shakerism owed partly to materialistic influences from outside and partly to the inevitable dwindling of a community that outlawed sexual activity.

Sources:

Andrews, Edward Deming. *The People Called Shakers: A Search for the Perfect Society.* New York: Oxford University Press, 1953.

Desroche, Henri. *The American Shakers.* Amherst, Mass.: University of Massachusetts Press, 1971.

[Evans, Frederick W.]. *Autobiography of a Shaker.* Mount Lebanon, N.Y., 1869.

Evans, Frederick W. *Shakers and Shakerism.* New York, 1859.

Flinn, H. C. *Spiritualism Among the Shakers.* East Canterbury, N.H., 1899.

Garrett, Clarke. *Spirit Possession and Popular Religion: From the Camisards to the Shakers.* Baltimore, Md.: Johns Hopkins University Press, 1987.

Holloway, Emory. "Walt Whitman's Visit to the Shakers; With Whitman's Notebook Containing his Description and Observations of the Shaker Group at Mt. Lebanon." *The Colophon* 1 (spring 1930).

MacLean, John P. *Bibliography of Shaker Literature.* 1905. Reprint, Burt Franklin, 1971.

Taylor, Michael Brooks. "&43'Try the Spirits': Shaker Responses to Supernaturalism." *Journal of Religious Studies* 7 (fall 1979): 30–38.

Shaman

The magician or "medicine man" of primitive tribes, with powers of healing, prophecy, or paranormal phenomena. The term is thought to derive from Tungus *shaman* and Sanskrit *sramana* (ascetic). As distinct from priests, shamans have no ritualistic knowledge, but operate rather as occult adepts. Their primary ability, at least in their Siberian setting, was the power of astral travel. The gift of shamanism is often a hereditary function, and its nature is communicated orally from one shaman to another.

Shamanism has been studied among the Eskimos and in Scandinavia, Tibet, China, Japan, Korea, Siberia, Manchuria, Mexico, Yutacan, Guatemala, and the North Pacific coast. A shamanistic performance often includes dancing, a mediumistic trance, and spirit possession. The role of the shaman (and shamaness) became the subject of a new movement in the West that began in the 1980s primarily through the work of Michael Harder and a number of popular teachers (many with Matove American backgrounds) who have developed a neo-Shamanism that draws on many themes emphasized in the **New Age** movement. Neo-Shamanist leaders have varied: some, such as Sun-Bear, have attempted to translate traditional Native American themes into useful practice for those outside of the Native American community. Other have developed new systems claiming Native American esoteric traditions as a base (Lynn Andrews) and still others have simply taken traditional occult teachings upon which they have placed a Native American overlay.

Sources:

Andrews, Lynn V. *Star Woman.* New York: Warner Books, 1986.

Eliade, Mircea. *Shamanism: Archaic Techniques of Ecstasy.* Princeton, N.J.: Princeton University Press, 1964.

Harder, Michael. *Way of the Shaman: A Guide to Power and Healing.* New York: Bantam Books, 1982.

Sun Bear. *Path of Power.* Spokane, Wash.: Bear Tribe Publishing, 1983.

Shaman's Drum

Shaman's Drum: A Journal of Experiential Shamanism & Spiritual Healing is a newsstand magazine that has through the 1990s emerged as the major voice of neoshamanism, the new appropriation of shamanism by modern Westerners. **Shamans** are the major bearers of the spiritual wisdom of pre-modern, preliterate societies (once termed primitive) that underwent a significant reappraisal in the last half of the twentieth century. Anthropologists who had led in the study of such societies discovered a level of sophistication in the thought of pre-modern peoples and others found in their holistic worldviews a wisdom they believed had much to teach contemporary society. Not a small part of the attractiveness of pre-modern cultures was their use of various psychedelic substances as an integral element in their psychic and spiritual activity. The appropriation of wisdom came from around the world, but special attention was paid to the peoples of the Amazon, Tibetan cultures, and Native Americans.

Shaman's Drum emerged in the late 1980s to provide education, information, and networking in the growing neoshamanistic community. It is published quarterly by Cross-Cultural Shamanism Network, a small nonprofit corporation whose major program is the sustaining of the magazine. *Shaman's Drum* is a subsidized publication, with a minimum of advertising, all directly related to the subject matter.

The majority of the space in each issue of the magazine includes a set of feature articles on such topics as traditional shamanism, environmentalism, and contemporary spiritual healing. The magazine functions in the space between the scholarly study of shamanism and its popular appropriation. *Shaman's Drum* has given significant space to airing the controversy of non-Indians claiming status as teachers of Native American wisdom and the business of selling Native sacred artifacts for use in secular and other non-Native contexts. Each issue also contains a news column, a book review column, and a directory of individuals and organizations that offer resources for studying shamanism.

Shaman's Drum may be contacted at P.O. Box 97, Ashland, OR 97520.

Sources:

Shaman's Drum. Ashland, Ore., n.d.

Shamballah

Fabulous mystical city of ancient legend, believed to be the site of the Garden of Eden.

Shanti Nilaya

A healing and growth center founded in Escondido, California, in 1978. The name means "final home of peace" and the organization is concerned with the work of physician **Elisabeth Kübler-Ross,** author of the book *On Death and Dying* (New York, 1970). An extension of Kübler-Ross's earlier well-known "Life-Death and Transition" workshops, Shanti Nilaya offers short- and long-term therapeutic sessions connected with the experience of death and the question of life after death. The *Shanti Nilaya Newsletter,* giving news of the work of Kübler-Ross and Shanti Nilaya centers, is published from the center, now located in Virginia: General Delivery, Headwaters, VA 24442.

Sharp, William (1856–1905)

Scottish poet, biographer, and editor, who also achieved fame under the name of "Fiona Mac-Leod"—not so much a literary pseudonym as virtually a psychic secondary personality. Sharp was born in Paisley, Scotland, on September 12, 1856, and spent his childhood in the Scottish Highlands. He ran away from home three times, on one occasion spending a whole summer in a gypsy encampment. He studied for two years as a student at Glasgow University before becoming an attorney's clerk.

He suffered from ill health and his family sent him on a Pacific cruise. Afterward he settled in London as a bank clerk, eventually becoming acquainted with literary circles that included B. G. Rossetti and Walter Pater.

Pater encouraged his literary work, which first appeared in the *Pall Mall Gazette.* Then in 1885 Sharp became the art critic for the *Glasgow Herald.* In the same year he married his first cousin Elizabeth Amelia Sharp, who became companion and co-worker as well as wife. They worked jointly on the anthology *Lyra Celtica* (1896). Sharp abandoned banking for a journalistic career, becoming editor of *The Pagan Review* in 1892. He traveled throughout Europe and even visited the United States, where he met Walt Whitman.

Sharp's enthusiasm for the Celtic literary revival brought him into contact with **William Butler Yeats** and the Isis Urania Temple of the famous Hermetic Order of the **Golden Dawn** magical society. Here he was initiated into the Neophyte grade. This occult connection may have been a stimulus to the development of his *anima* personality of "Fiona MacLeod." Sharp and "Fiona" remained distinctly different identities in literary style and outlook, even corresponding with friends as separate personalities for many years.

Sharp himself kept up a correspondence with Yeats and **George W. Russell** on occult and mystical experiments, while also writing to them on literary, poetical, and Celtic matters as "Fiona Mac-Leod."

The identical nature of the two personalities remained a closely guarded secret among Sharp, his wife, and one or two personal friends until after Sharp's death. The "Fiona" letters were in the handwriting of Sharp's sister, but their style and personality were those of a distinct individual. "Fiona's" letters, poems, and books were quite feminine in outlook, quite unlike the masculine lifestyle and writings of the bearded Sharp.

The "Fiona" works played a leading part in the Scottish Celtic literary revival and were the product of automatic writing by Sharp, who virtually acknowledged "Fiona" as a separate personality. She was said to be a distant cousin and even had a biography in the prestigious British biographical annual *Who's Who.*

Sharp died December 12, 1905, after catching a cold during a visit to a friend in Sicily. His widow died a few years later, leaving two large packets of materials "to be destroyed unexamined." It is believed that these may have contained Golden Dawn documents.

Sources:

MacLeod, Fiona. *The Divine Adventure.* Portland, Maine: T. B. Mosher, 1903.

———. *The Dominion of Dreams.* New York: F. A. Stokes, 1900.

———. *Green Fire.* N.p., 1896.

———. *The Immortal Hour.* Portland, Maine: T. B. Mosher, 1907.

———. *The Mountain Lovers.* N.p., 1895.

———. *Pharais.* Chicago: Stone & KImball, 1895.

———. *The Sin-Eater.* New York: Duffield, 1910.

———. *The Washer of the Ford.* New York: Stone & Kimball, 1896.

———. *Winged Destiny.* New York: Dufdfield, 1910.

Sharp, William. *Earth's Voices.* N.p., 1884.

———. *Flower o' the Vine.* N.p., 1894.

———. *Human Inheritance.* N.p., 1882.

———. *Life of D. G. Rossetts.* N.p., 1882.

Shasta, Mount

Mount Shasta is an awe-inspiring volcanic cone in northern California. Long a sacred site for Native American tribes, it became a magnet for many occult speculations in the twentieth century. As early as 1899 Mount Shasta was an element in the Spiritualist world created in a channeled book, *An Earth Dweller Returns,* by Phylos (the pseudonym of Frederick William Oliver), an early text discussing the lost Pacific continent of **Lemuria.** After the publication of this book, California and Mount Shasta began to be seen as a remnant of Lemuria. The Lemurian hypothesis was developed by **H. Spencer Lewis,** who, under the penname Wishar Spenie Cerve, wrote a text for the Ancient and Mystical Order of the Rosae Crucis, *Lemuria, the Lost Continent of the Pacific* (1931).

Two years before the publication of Lewis's work, **Guy W. Ballard,** walking the slopes of Mount Shasta, had an encounter with a mysterious person whom he later identified as Saint Germain, an ascended master of the **Great White Brotherhood** (the spiritual hierarchy believed by many occultists to be guiding the destiny of humankind). Out of this encounter, Ballard later led in the founding of the **I Am Movement.** The story of his encounter appears in Ballard's 1934 book *Unveiled Mysteries,* published under the penname Godfre Ray King. In recent years, the "I Am" has presented an annual pageant centered upon their unique interpretation of the life of Jesus.

Over the years since the Rosicrucian and "I Am" publications on Mount Shasta, numerous authors have described mystical experiences associated with the mountain and offered their speculations about its significance. The resort community of Mount Shasta, California, became a unique gathering place for metaphysical people, a trend further spurred by the beginning of the **flying saucer** era.

Sources:

Andrews, Richard. *The Truth behind the Legends of Mount Shasta.* New York: Carlton Press, 1976.

Cerve, W. S. [H. Spencer Lewis]. *Lemuria, the Lost Continent of the Pacific.* San Jose, Calif.: Supreme Lodge of the AMORC, 1931.

Chaney, Earlyne. *Secrets from Mount Shasta.* Anaheim, Calif.: Stockton Trade Press, 1953.

King, Godfre Ray [Guy W. Ballard]. *Unveiled Mysteries.* Chicago: Saint Germain Press, 1934.

Walton, Bruce. *Mount Shasta, Home of the Ancients.* Mokelumna Hill, Calif.: Health Research, 1985.

Shaver, Richard S(harpe) (1907–1975)

Pennsylvania welder and author born on October 8, 1907, responsible for the series of revelations known as the "Shaver Mystery," originally published by **Raymond A. Palmer** in *Amazing Stories* from 1945 to 1949. Drawing upon "racial memories," Shaver described a race of "deros" or vicious dwarfs living in underground caverns, indulging in sexual orgies and harassing human beings by means of secret rays and telepathy.

Shaver's somewhat crude original manuscript, titled *A Warning to Future Man,* was extensively worked over by Palmer and emerged in the March 1945 issue of *Amazing Stories* as "I Remember Lemuria." At first the series boosted the magazine's circulation to a record 185,000. Many earnest readers described their own knowledge of secret influences from deros who were also apparently responsible for the disaster of Pearl Harbor. More traditional science fiction readers were indignant at such stories being presented as factual, and after thousands of protests, Howard Browne, who took over from Palmer, ended the series. Browne described the Shaver material as "the sickest crap I'd run into."

However, Palmer kept the the Shaver legend alive and revived it from time to time in *Search* and *Flying Saucers* magazines and *The Hidden World,* a series of periodicals in trade paperback format. For a while there was also a fanzine, the *Shaver Mystery Magazine,* and *I Remember Lemuria* and *The Return of Sathanas* were reissued in book format in 1948.

Shaver died on November 5, 1975.

Sources:

Clark, Jerome. *Encyclopedia of Strange and Unexplained Phenomena.* Detroit: Gale Research, 1993.

Shavick, Nancy (1957–)

Nancy Shavick, a contemporary author and **tarot** counselor, was born in Englewood, New Jersey, in 1957. Following high school graduation she entered Hampshire College (Massachusetts), from which she graduated in 1979 with a degree in creative writing. Through the 1980s she taught creative writing, worked as an editor, and became an accomplished student of the tarot cards. In 1984 she founded Prima Materia Books, a publishing house, through which she published her first book, *The Tarot: A Guide to Reading Your Own Cards.* In the process of mastering the tarot, she became a gifted reader with a growing clientele. In 1991 she closed Prima Materia and moved to San Francisco.

Shavick felt that the tarot should be demystified and was most useful as a tool for self-transformation and personal development. These themes dominated the four best-selling books she wrote for Berkley Books between 1988 and 1993: *The Tarot* (1988), *The Tarot Reader* (1991), *Traveling the Royal Road: Mastering the Tarot* (1992), and *The Tarot Guide to Love and Relationships* (1993). Along the way she also acquired a working knowledge of astrology and in 1994 authored her first volume on it, *Reach for the Stars.* Her most recent work, *Nancy Shavick's Tarot Universe* (2000), is a comprehensive text summarizing her previous five books.

Sources:

Shavick, Nancy. *Nancy Shavick's Tarot Universe.* Santa Monica, Calif.: Santa Monica Press, 2000.

———. *The Tarot.* New York: Berkley Books, 1988.

———. *The Tarot Guide to Love and Relationships.* New York: Berkley Books, 1993.

———. *The Tarot Reader.* New York: Berkley Books, 1991.

———. *Traveling the Royal Road: Mastering the Tarot.* New York: Berkley Books, 1992.

Sheargold, Richard K(empsell) (1911–1988)

British parapsychologist. He was born on December 20, 1911, at Caterham, Surrey, England. He was departmental manager at McMichael Radio, Slough, England. He joined the **Society for Psychical Research** and took a special interest in scientific experiments relating to the question of human survival. In 1963 he became the first chairman of the Survival Joint Research Committee Trust.

Under the sponsorship of the SPR, he completed a series of card-guessing tests with mediums as percipients, in order to investigate the possibility of a relationship between telepathic faculty and the ESP demonstrated by mental mediums. These experiments were reported in the *Journal* of the SPR (June 1961). From 1971 on, Sheargold experimented with the **electronic voice** phenomenon, also known as **Raudive Voices,** that had just been publicized in the West by Friedrick Jürgenson and **Konstantin Raudive.** In September 1973, he gave a talk on "Experiments on the Jürgenson Voice Phenomena" at a symposium organized by The Institute of Parascience. He died January 25, 1988.

Sources:

Berger, Arthur S., and Joyce Berger. *The Encyclopedia of Parapsychology and Psychical Research.* New York: Paragon House, 1991.

Ellis, David J. *The Mediumship of the Tape Recorder.* Pulborough: The Author, 1978.

Pleasants, Helene, ed. *Biographical Dictionary of Parapsychology.* New York: Helix Press, 1964.

Sheargold, Richard K. "The Ghost of Twenty-Nine Megacycles." *Journal* of the Society for Psychical Research 53 (1986).

———. *Hints on Receiving the Voice Phenomenon.* N.p., 1973.

———. "The Occultism of Occultism." *Journal* of the Society for Psychical Research 45 (1970).

Sheep-Goat Hypothesis

A concept in parapsychology relating to the effect of belief and attitude to success in **ESP** scoring. The term derives from the pioneer researches of parapsychologist **Gertrude R. Schmeidler** in 1958. She conducted experiments in which her subjects were divided into two groups—"sheep" and "goats." The sheep had belief in the possibility of **psi,** while the goats rejected the possibility.

It was observed that, in individual and group tests, the sheep scored higher in ESP trials than the goats, suggesting that belief strongly influenced successful ESP. The differences in scoring were relatively small, although statistically significant. Many later experiments have been conducted by other parapsychologists to test the hypothesis, and the term "sheep-goat" has now become commonplace in parapsychological discussions.

Sources:

McConnell, R. A., and Gertrude Schmeidler. *ESP and Personality Patterns.* New Haven, Conn.: Yale University Press, 1958.

She-Goat

One of the branches of divination in ancient Rome dealt especially with the signs that might be derived from animals, and it was believed that if a she-goat crossed the path of a man who was stepping out of his house, it was a good omen.

Sheldrake, Rupert (1942–)

British biochemist with specialized experience in plant research who has proposed a bold new theory of **formative causation,** concerned with the origin and growth of form and characteristics in nature. While not denying the inheritance of characteristics through the gene complex, he has suggested a literal view of what has been termed for convenience "morphogenetic fields" as actual structures independent of time and space. Although Sheldrake's field theory applies primarily to organisms, plants, and animals, it also has important relevance to concepts of parapsychological phenomena, such as **telepathy, clairvoyance** and **reincarnation.**

Robert Sheldrake was born June 28, 1942, in Newark Notts, England. He was educated at Clare College, Cambridge University, England, becoming a fellow and director of studies in biochemistry and cell biology. In 1973, he was awarded a Rosenheim Research Fellowship of the Royal Society. Instead of taking a professorship at a university, he decided to study growing plants first hand, and he became a member of the staff of the International Crops Research Institute for the Semi-Arid Tropics in Hyderabad, India. He became a consultant to the institute in 1978.

In 1966, Sheldrake was associated with the Epiphany Philosophers, a group of scientists and philosophers at Cambridge University concerned with exploring interconnections between science, philosophy, and mysticism. This contact stimulated his early ideas on formative causation. Other influences were the theories of **Henri Bergson** and **Hans Driesch.**

Sources:

Berger, Arthur S., and Joyce Berger. *The Encyclopedia of Parapsychology and Psychical Research.* New York: Paragon House, 1991.

Sheldrake, Rupert. *A New Science of Life: the Hypothesis of Formative Causation.* London: Blond & Briggs; Los Angeles: J. P. Tarcher, 1981.

———. *The Presence of the Past.* New York: New York Times Books, 1988.

———. *The Rebirth of Nature: The Greening of Science and God.* New York: Bantam, 1990.

———. *Seven Experiments That Could Change the World: A Do-It-Yourself Guide to Revolutionary Science.* n.p.: Riverhead Books, 1995.

Sheldrake, Rupert and Matthew Fox. *Natural Grace.* Garden City, N.Y.: Doubleday, 1996.

Shelta Thari

An esoteric language spoken by the tinkers (a **Gypsy**-type people) of Britain and Ireland and possibly a descendant of an "inner" language employed by the ancient Celtic Druids or bards. It was in 1876 that the first hint of the existence of Shelta Thari reached the ears of **Charles Godfrey Leland.** It seems strange that George Borrow, the first authority on Romany and Gypsy lore, had never stumbled upon the language, and that fact may be taken as evidence of the jealousy with which the nomadic classes guarded it.

Leland related how he and E. H. Palmer were wandering on the beach at Aberystwyth in Wales when they met a wanderer who heard them conversing in Romany. Leland questioned the man as to how he made a living, and he replied, "Shelkin gallopas." The words were foreign even to Leland, and he asked what they meant. "Why," said the man, "it means selling ferns. That is tinker's language or minklers' thari. I thought as you knew Romany, you might understand it. The right name for the tinkers' language is Shelta."

"It was," said Leland, "with the feelings of Columbus the night before he discovered America that I heard the word Shelta, and I asked the fern-dealer if he could talk it." The man replied "A little," and on the spot the philologist collected a number of words and phrases from the fern-seller that gave him sufficient insight into the language to prove that it was absolutely different from Romany.

The Celtic origin of the dialect soon began to suggest itself to Leland, and he attempted to obtain from the man some verse or jingle in it, for the purpose of observing its syntactical arrangement. But all he was able to learn from his informant were some rhymes of no philological value, and he found he had soon exhausted the fern-seller's knowledge.

It was later on in the United States that Leland terrified a tinker by speaking to him in the lost dialect. The man, questioned as to whether he could speak Shelta, admitted that he could. He proved to be an Irishman, Owen Macdonald by name, and he furnished Leland with an invaluable list of several hundred words. But Leland could not be sure upon which of the Celtic languages the dialect was based. Owen Macdonald declared to him that it was a fourth language that had nothing in common with old Irish, Welsh, or Gaelic and hazarded the information that it was the idiom of the "Ould Picts," inhabitants of Scotland, but this did not convince the philologist.

Shelta is not a jargon, for it can be spoken grammatically without using English, as in the British form of Romany. Pictish in all probability was not a Celtic language, nor even an Aryan one, however intimately it may have been affected by Celtic speech in the later stages of its existence.

Leland's discovery was greeted in some quarters with laughter. The *Saturday Review* jocosely suggested that he had been conned and that old Irish had been palmed off on him for a mysterious lingo. Leland put this view of the matter before his tinker friend, who replied with grave solemnity, "And what'd I be after makin' two languages av thim for, if there was but wan av thim?"

Since Leland's time, much has been done to reclaim this mysterious tongue, chiefly through the investigations of John Sampson and professor Kuno Meyer. The basis of these investigations rested on the fact that the tinker caste of Great Britain and Ireland was a separate class—so separate indeed as almost to form a "race" by itself. For hundreds of years, possibly, this caste existed with nearly all its ancient characteristics, and on the general disuse of Celtic speech had conserved its language as a secret dialect.

The peculiar thing concerning Shelta is the extent of territory over which it is spoken. That it was known rather extensively in London itself was discovered by Leland, who heard it spoken by two small boys in the Euston Road. They were not Gypsies, but Leland found out that one of them spoke the language with great fluency. Since Leland's discoveries Shelta has been to some extent mapped out into dialects, one of the most important of which is Ulster. The Ulster dialect of this strange and ancient tongue differed from that in use in other parts of Britain and Ireland.

John Sampson, the successor to Borrow and Leland, and a linguist of repute, published in the *Journal* of the Gypsy Lore Society (new series, vol. 1, 1908), a number of sayings and proverbs that he had collected in Liverpool from two old Irish tinkers—John Barlow and Phil Murray. Sampson stated that these were in the Ulster dialect of Shelta.

Some of these may be quoted to provide the reader with specimens of the language: "Krish gyukera have muni Sheldru" (Old beggars have good Shelta). "Stimera dhi-ilsha, stimera aga dhi-ilsha" (If you're a piper, have your own pipe). "Mislo granhes thaber" (The traveler knows the road). "Thom Blorne mjesh Nip gloch" (Every Protestant isn't an Orangeman). "Nus a dhabjon dhuilsha" (The blessing of God on you). "Misli, gami gra dhi-il" (Be off, and bad luck to you).

There seems to be considerable reason to believe that the tinker (or more properly "tinkler") class of Britain and Ireland sprang from the remnants of its ancient Celtic inhabitants and differed as completely from the Gypsy or Romany as one people can well differ from another. This is strongly suggested by the criterion of speech, for it is now generally believed that Shelta is a Celtic tongue and that Romany is a dialect of Northern Hindustan. Those who now speak Romany habitually almost invariably make use of Shelta as well, but that only proves that the two nomadic groups, having occupied the same territory for hundreds of years, gained a knowledge of each other's languages. Who, then, were the original progenitors of the tinkers? Whoever they were, they were a Celtic-speaking people and probably a nomadic one. Shelta has been referred to as the language of the ancient bards of Ireland and the esoteric tongue of an Irish priesthood.

Leland put forward the hypothesis that the Shelta-speaking tinker is a descendant of a prehistoric guild of bronze-workers. This, he thought, accounted in part for the secretiveness as regards this language. In Italy, to this very day, the tinker class is identified with the itinerant bronze workers. The tinker fraternity of Britain and Ireland existed with perhaps nearly all its ancient characteristics until the advent of railroads. But long before this, it had probably amalgamated to a great extent with the Gypsy population, and the two languages had become common to the two peoples.

It seems to be highly probable that Shelkta originated in Ireland, for in no other part of these islands during the later Celtic period was technology sufficiently advanced to permit of the existence of a close corporation of metalworkers possessing a secret language. Moreover, the affinities of Shelta appear to be with old Irish more than with any other Celtic dialect. One other theory that presents itself in connection with the origin of Shelta that it is the modern descendant of the language of the "Ould Picts" mentioned by Owen Macdonald, Leland's tinker friend. But there are great difficulties in accepting the hypothesis of the Pictish origin of Shelta, the chief among them being its obvious Irish origin. There were, it is known, Picts in the north of Ireland, but they were almost certainly a small and primitive colony and a very unlikely community to form a metalworking fraternity that possessed the luxury of a private dialect.

It still remains for the Celtic student to classify Shelta in a definitive way. It may prove to be "Pictish," strongly influenced by the Gaelic of Ireland and Scotland. A comparison with Basque and the dialect of the Iberian tribes of Morocco might bring affinities to light and thus establish the theory of its non-Aryan origin, but its strong kinship with Gaelic seems likely.

Sources:

Leland, Charles Godfrey. *The Gypsies.* Boston: Houghton, Mifflin, 1882.

MacRithie, David. *Shelta: The Cairds' Language. Transactions* of Gaelic Society of Inverness 24 (1904).

Shemhamphorash

In the Talmud, the external term representing the hidden word of power, by whose virtues a new world might be. This word is lost to the human race, although even sounds approximating it have a magic power and can give to whomever pronounces them dominion in the spirit world.

Some of the old rabbis believed that the word of power contains 12 letters, others, 42, and yet others 72, but these are the letters of the divine alphabet, which God created from certain luminous points made by the concentration of the primal universal light. *Shemhamphorash* is, in fact, the name of this word.

In the **Kabala,** the *Shemhamphorash,* or 72 syllabled name of God, is related to three verses of the Hebrew Bible, Exodus 14, 119–21. Each of these verses, in Hebrew, contains 72 letters. If one writes the 72 letters or verse 19 in correct order, and under them write the letters of verse 20 in a similar manner in reverse order, and then the letters in verse 21 in correct order below the first two, one creates 72 three-letter names. By adding either AL or IH to these names the names of the 72 angels of Jacob's ladder were created.

This ancient Jewish mystical concept is somewhat paralleled by the ancient Hindu teachings of the creation of the world through the mystical trisyllable **"AUM,"** said to contain the origin of the alphabet and all sounds. related to such concepts are the use of certain letters and sounds known as **mantras** for magical purposes. (See also **Nada; Yoga**)

Sources:

Poncé, Charles. *Kabblah: An Introduction and Illumination for the World Today.* San Francisco: Straight Arrow Books, 1973.

Shepard, Jesse Francis Grierson (1848–1927)

Mystic, seer, author, and musical medium who performed before famous musicians and royal personages. His musical séances were held both in light and darkness. In darkness his renderings were marvelous. He did not always actually play the piano: the music sometimes came through the shut keyboard. He rendered duets and sang simultaneously in bass and soprano. He also played the organ and sang in cathedrals. He could give trance addresses in English, French, German, Latin, Greek, Chaldean, and Arabic on any subject.

His full name was Benjamin Henry Jesse Francis Grierson Shepard. He was born on September 18, 1848 and was of Scottish-Irish descent but moved to the United States with his family in his first year. He spent his boyhood on the Illinois prairie. At the age of 13 he became a pageboy to General John C. Frémont and made the acquaintance of both Generals Grant and Sherman.

When in his twenty-first year, he set out for Paris without any funds. Within a short time he became one of the most famous mediums in Europe, demonstrating **psychometry, clairvoyance, prediction,** and diagnosis of disease. He also displayed uncanny musical gifts. Without extensive formal training in music, he gave performances at the piano and claimed to be possessed by the spirits of Mozart, Beethoven, Meyerbeer, Rossini, Sontag, Persiani, Malibran, Lablache, Liszt, Berlioz, and Chopin. He performed to the rich, the famous, and the royal in Europe. The audience at one concert in Holland in 1894 included the duchess of Cumberland, the queen of Hanover, the reigning duke of Saxe-Altenburg, and the queen of Denmark.

In addition to his piano performances, Shepard sometimes sang, in every range of voice from bass to soprano. Henry Kiddle, superintendent of schools in New York, was imprudent enough to state that he heard Shepard playing a splendid piano symphony under the control of Mozart, while at the same time delivering a learned philosophical discourse under the influence of Aristotle. Kiddle was forced to resign his position.

In Catherine Berry's *Experiences in Spiritualism* (1876), historical fragments relating to Assyrian queen Semirami were published as recorded after Shepard's trance statements under the control of an Egyptian spirit. In 1889 he published two volumes of which **Maurice Maeterlinck** declared that he knew nothing in literature more admirable or profound.

Prince Adam Wisniewski wrote in an account quoted by *Light* in 1894:

"After having secured the most complete obscurity we placed ourselves in a circle around the medium, seated before the piano. Hardly were the first chords struck when we saw lights appearing at every corner of the room . . . The first piece played through Shepard was a fantasie of Thalberg's on the air from "Semiramide." This is unpublished, as is all the music which is played by the spirits through Shepard. The second was a rhapsody for four hands, played by Liszt and Thalberg with astounding fire, a sonority truly grand, and a masterly interpretation. Notwithstanding this extra ordinarily complex technique, the harmony was admirable, and such as no one present had ever know paralleled, even by Liszt himself, whom I personally knew, and in whom passion and delicacy were united. In the circle were musicians who, like me, had heard the greatest pianists of Europe; but we can say that we never heard such truly supernatural execution."

Shepard was also occasionally a **direct voice** medium. During a séance at The Hague, Holland, in 1907, direct voices were heard speaking in Dutch. High officials of the Dutch government who were present also heard voices speaking in Sundanese and Mandarin Chinese.

In 1907, after his fabulous success in Europe and return visits to America, Shepard broke with his psychic connections and mediumship and settled in London, where he ceased his musical exhibitions and devoted himself to writing. He changed his name to Francis Grierson and made a reputation through his essays in both English and French. At the age of fifty, he published his book *Modern Mysticism and Other Essays* (1899), followed by *The Celtic Temperament and Other Essays* (1901). The latter work was adopted as a textbook by Japanese universities. Other publications included *The Valley of Shadows: Recollections of the Lincoln Country, 1858–63* (1909), *Portraits* (1910), *La Vie* and *Les Hommes* (1911), *The Humour of the Underman* (1911), *The Invisible Alliance* (1913), *Illusions and Realities of the War* (1918), and *Abraham Lincoln: The Practical Mystic* (1918).

The quality of his literary work secured him a place in the prestigious Kunitz and Haycraft *Twentieth Century Authors* (1942). Many of Shepard's readers were unaware of his earlier psychic activities until he published a Spiritualist pamphlet, *Psycho-Phone Messages,* in 1921.

In spite of Shepard's mystical and artistic talents or perhaps because of his dedication to mystic insight rather than material things, he died in utter poverty. As an old man of 78, he died from hunger May 29, 1927, while a case worker from the Los Angeles Assistance League was knocking on his door. She was unaware of his glittering past as a musician or his fame as a writer. He had earlier pawned his last valuable—a watch given to him by the king of England.

Sources:

Endore, Guy. *King of Paris.* New York: Pocket Books, 1958.

Grierson, Francis [Jesse Shepard]. *Abraham Lincoln: The Practical Mystic.* New York: John Lane, 1918.

———. *The Celtic Temperament and Other Essays.* London: John Lane, 1913.

———. *Modern Mysticism and Other Essays.* London: G. Allen, 1899.

Shepard, Jess F. G. "How I Became a Musical Medium." *Medium* (May 6, 1970).

Tonner, W. "The Genius of Francis Grierson." *Trend* (March 1914).

Sherman, Harold (Morrow) (1898–1987)

Author, broadcaster, and lecturer in the field of parapsychology. Born July 13, 1898 in Traverse City, Michigan, he was educated at Traverse City High School and the University of Michigan. In 1920 he married Martha Frances Bain. Memberships include Authors League of America and the Dramatists Guild. After working as a freelance writer, he was employed at CBS-Radio in New York from 1935–36. He was founder and president of E.S.P. Research Associates Foundation, Little Rock, Arkansas from 1964 onward.

He conducted experiments in **clairvoyance, telepathy, psychokinesis, precognition,** mediumship, and survival; he lectured on ESP. With psychologist **Leslie LeCron** and scientists affiliated with the University of California, L.A., he investigated the question and the method of operation of ESP faculty. Sherman contributred articles to *Mind Digest, Journal of Living, Success Unlimited,* and *Tomorrow.*

By the age of twenty-two, Sherman authored approximately sixty books on such subjects as sports, adventure, and short stories, as well as books on **extrasensory perception** and mental power. He was also interested in the theater and produced plays and a Hollywood movie "The Adventures of Mark Twain." His book *Your Key to Happiness* (1935) was presented on radio and he conducted a radio series on philosopy three times a week under the title "The Man Who Helped You to Help Yourself."

Sherman died August 19, 1987, at Mountain View, Arkansas. One of his final messages to his many friends was, "I expect it will be a great moment when I greet you in the next dimension."

Sources:

Sherman, Harold. *Adventures in Thinking.* Master Publications, 1956.

———. *How to Foresee and Control Your Future.* New York: Information, Inc., 1970.

———. *How to Know What to Believe.* New York: Fawcett, 1976.

———. *How to Make ESP Work for You.* Greenwich, Conn.: Fawcett, 1964.

———. *How to Picture What You Want.* New York: Fawcett, 1978.

———. *How to Turn Failure into Success.* Englewood Cliffs, N.J.: Prentice-Hall, 1958.

———. *How to Use the Power of Prayer.* Unity Village, Mo.: Unity Books, 1985.

———. *Know Your Own Mind.* New York: G. & R. Anthony, 1953.

———. *TNT—The Power Within You.* Englewood Cliffs, N.J.: Prentice-Hall, 1959.

———. *Wonder Healers of the Philippines.* Los Angeles: DeVross, 1967.

———. *You Can Communicate with the Unseen World.* New York: Fawcett, 1974.

———. *You Live After Death.* New York: Creative Age Press, 1949.

———. *Your Key to Happiness.* 1935. Reprint, New Canaan, Conn.: Mulvey Books, 1990.

———. *Your Power to Heal.* New York: Harper & Row, 1972.

Shermer, Michael (1954–)

Michael Shermer, cofounder of the **Skeptics Society,** one of the major organizations debunking what it considers pseudoscientific claims, especially of a psychic or occult nature, was born on September 8, 1954, in Glendale, California. He attended Pepperdine University, where he majored in psychology. He later received an M.A. in experimental psychology from California State University–Fullerton and a Ph.D. in the history of science from the Claremont Graduate School (1991).

During the 1980s Shermer launched a ten-year career as a professional cyclist, the high point of which was his participation in a 30,000-mile transcontinental Race Across America. His racing activity, which led to his first media appearances on various sports broadcasts, led to his first books, including *Sport Cycling* (1985), *Cycling for Endurance and Speed* (1987), *The Woman Cyclist* (with Elaine Mariolle, 1989), and *Race Across America: The Agonies and Glories of the World's Toughest Bicycle Race* (1994).

Shermer's racing career coincided with a growing interest in the movement started by the **Committee for the Scientific Claims of the Paranormal** (CSICOP), based in Buffalo, New York. Though he was a member, he also felt that more could be done, and in January of 1992, with Pat Linse and Kim Ziel Shermer, he founded the Skeptics Society, with its base in the Greater Los Angeles area. Several months later the first issue of *Skeptic,* a new periodical, joined the newsstand shelves next to CSICOP's *Skeptical Inquirer.* Shermer envisioned the Skeptics Society as treating traditional pseudoscience issues concerning psychic and occult claims, but also was concerned with other boundary issues in science where no such paranormal element was present (cold fusion, cryonics, nanotechnology, etc.) as well as controversial issues in social science and history, such as Holocaust denial.

Shermer has supplied much of the energy that has seen the Skeptics Society, which he directs, grow into a significant organization challenging occult claims, and the *Skeptic* magazine, which he edits, gain national circulation. He has authored several related books, including *Why People Believe Weird Things* (1997), *How We Believe: The Search for God in an Age of Science* (2000), and *Denying History* (2000). He created the Skeptics Lecture Series at the California Institute of Technology and is an adjunct professor at Occidental College in Los Angeles. Shermer also put the media attention he gained in his cycling era to good use and has been a popular guest on talk shows. Most recently he has hosted a weekly radio show, "Science Talk," on the NPR affiliate in Southern California and a national television show on the Fox Family Channel.

Sources:

Shermer, Michael. *Denying History.* Berkeley: University of California Press, 2000.

———. *How We Believe: The Search for God in an Age of Science.* New York: W. H. Freeman and Co., 2000.

———. *Why People Believe Weird Things.* New York: W. H. Freeman and Co., 1997.

Sherwood, Carlton M(ontgomery) (1895–1970)

Financial counselor also active in the field of parapsychology. He was born on April 12, 1895, in Buffalo, New York. After serving in the Army during World War I, he worked for various agencies, mostly Christian organizations, through the next two decades. They included the New York State Christian Endeavor Union (1919–27), the Citizens Committee of 100 (1926–36), and the International Society of Christian Endeavor (1926–34). He edited *Christian Endeavour World* (1930–34). After two years as the executive director of Associated Boards for Christian Colleges in China (1934–36) he began a long tenure as president of Pierce, Hedrick & Sherwood, counselors in institutional financing.

Over the years he became interested in psychical research. He joined and served on the boards of both the **Parapsychology Foundation** and the **American Society for Psychical Research.** He was also a member of the **Society for Psychical Research,** London, and chaired the Conference on Parapsychology and Psychedelics, New York, November 1958. He died on September 14, 1970.

Sources:

Pleasants, Helene, ed. *Biographical Dictionary of Parapsychology.* New York: Helix Press, 1964.

Shiatsu (or Shiatzu)

A Japanese term from the root words *shi* (fingers) and *atsu* (pressure). Shiatsu is an applied system of massage which, like **acupuncture,** seeks to release and facilitate the flow of vital life energy, known as *Qi* (*chi* in Chinese, *ki* in Japanese), within the body. Shiatsu incorporates a number of massage techniques, such as pressing, sweeping, rotating, and patting. More than techniques, however, shiatsu has been described as a dance of two, a touch communication between practitioner and client, grounded in the traditional Chinese medicine concept of balance.

In the 10th century, a contingent of Japanese monks reportedly traveled to China to study Buddhism. While there, they observed the tenets of traditional Chinese medicine. They learned of the Qi (analogous to **kundalini** in Hindu tradition), the balancing life concepts of **yin and yang,** plus the body's energy pathways called meridians. They also gleaned the connections between the meridians, the five basic elements (earth, metal, water, fire, and wood) and corresponding organs of the body. The monks combined this acquired knowledge with the ancient medicinal practices of Japanese massage, which over time has become known as Shiatsu.

Shiatsu was introduced to the United States by individuals such as Wataruu Ohashi, founder of Ohashiatsu. Ohashi was a protégé of Japanese psychologist and Zen student Shizuto Masunaga. Instrumental in the repeal of governmental restrictions on massage, Masunaga reincorporated psychological and spiritual dimensions to shiatsu. Another instrumental pioneer of shiatsu was Tokujiro Namikoshi. Working as a masseur, he developed a chart comparable to the acupuncture chart, showing where the appropriate pressure could be applied to relieve pain in specific parts of the body, as well as affect underlying conditions.

In the United States a variation on shiatsu, *jin shin jyutsu,* has been developed by Jiro Murai. Also closely related are the Chinese system of *do-in* and reflexology.

Sources:

The Burton Goldberg Group *Alternative Medicine: The Definitive Guide.* Tiburon, Calif.: Future Medicine Publishing, Inc., 1997.

Chung, Hazel. "Shiatsu: Therapeutic Art of Japan." http://www.doubleclickd.com/shiatsu.html. March 31, 2000.

Namikoshi, Tokujiro. *Shiatsu.* Tokyo: Japan Publications, 1969.

Ohashi, Wataru. *Do It Yourself Shiatsu.* New York: ASI Publishing, 1976.

Tappan, Frances M. *Healing Massage Techniques: A Study of Eastern and Western Methods.* Reston, Va.: Reston Publishing Co., Inc., 1980.

Shiatsu: Japanese Massage. http://www.rianvisser.nl/shiatsu/e_index.htm. March 31, 2000.

Shiels, Tony ("Doc")

Well-known contemporary magician who presents **conjuring** and mentalism in a setting of "psychic power." In his publicity to fellow stage magicians, Shiels gives instructions on how "to bend metal in the Geller style . . . to teleport and levitate . . . to become a successful witch . . . to raise ghosts and poltergeists, etc." However, Shiels also acknowledges the reality of **PK** and **ESP** as well as the effects produced by conjuring and mentalism.

Shiels claims to have taken several photographs of the **Loch Ness monster** but most researchers have dismissed them as a hoax attempt. He has also been accused as the hoaxer behind some photos of fairies and Morgawr the Cornish sea serpent.

Sources:

Chorvinsky, Mark. "The Mary F. Morgawr Photographs Investigation." *Strange Magazine* 8 (Fall 1991): 8–9, 11, 46–48.

———. "The Shiels-Related Fairy Photos." *Strange Magazine* 9 (spring/summer 1992): 24–25, 60.

Clark, Jerome. *Encyclopedia of Strange and Unexplained Phenomena.* Detroit: Gale Research, 1993.

Shiels, Tony. *Entertaining With "ESP."* UK: David & Charles, 1974.

Ship of the Dead

Similar to the idea of the death-coach is the belief that at times a phantom ship carries away the souls of men. In the form of a cloud-ship, or wrapped in a driving mist, it sails over mountains and moors, and at sea it sails without hindrance.

A story is told of a certain pirate, at whose death a spectral ship approached in a cloud. As it sailed over the roof, the house was filled with a sound as of a stormy sea, and when the ship had passed by, the soul of the pirate accompanied it. (See also **Flying Dutchman**)

Shipton, Mother

Legendary British prophetess, supposed to have been born in the reign of King Henry VII and to have predicted the deaths of Cardinal Wolsey and Lord Percy, as well as other events. Her prophecies had a clarity quite unlike the cryptic verses of **Nostradamus.** Shipton was also credited with even more remarkable prescience in the following rhymed couplets:

"Carriages without horses shall go,
And accidents fill the world with woe.
Around the world thoughts shall fly
In the twinkling of an eye.
The world upside down shall be
And gold be found at the root of a tree.
Through hills man shall ride,
And no horse be at his side.
Under water men shall walk,
Shall ride, shall sleep, shall talk.
In the air men shall be seen,
In white, in black, in green;
Iron in the water shall float,
As easily as a wooden boat.
Gold shall be found and shown
In a land that's now not known.
Fire and water shall wonders do,
England shall at last admit a foe.
The world to an end shall come,
In eighteen hundred and eighty one.

These alleged prophecies occurred in a chapbook pamphlet published in 1862 by the bookseller Charles Hindley, who claimed that they were reprinted from an earlier chapbook by Richard Head titled *The Life and Death of Mother Shipton,* first published in 1684.

The final couplet about the end of the world caused a great deal of panic in country districts of Britain during 1881, with people leaving their houses and spending the night in the open fields or praying in churches and chapels.

Meanwhile Hindley had already confessed that these lines were a fabrication in 1873, but by then they had passed into folk tradition, and ordinary country folk did not read learned antiquarian journals. Even in modern times, these spurious prophecies of Hindley, which seem to predict automobiles, steamships, submarines, the telegraph, radio, and aircraft, are still often quoted as Shipton's. (For details of Charles Hindley's confession of having invented Shipton prophecies, see *Notes and Queries*, 4th series, vol. 9.)

Richard Head's chapbook of 1684 contains an undoubtedly imaginary account of the birth of Shipton from a union between her mother Agatha and the Devil in Yorkshire, England. That account appears to be an embellished version of an earlier pamphlet of 1641 titled *The Prophesie of Mother Shipton, In the Raigne of King Henry the Eighth. Fortelling the death of Cardinall Wolsey, the Lord Percy and others, as also what should happen in ensuing times.*

Four years later, the famous astrologer **William Lilly** published *A Collection of Ancient and Moderne Prophesies* that included what he called "Shipton's Prophecy, after the most exact Copy." This gave 20 prophecies attributed to Shipton, most of which were said to have been fulfilled.

There is no validation that these prophecies were actually made or that Shipton was even a real person, but she rapidly became a folk heroine and even the subject of stage comedies. In *The Life of Mother Shipton: A New Comedy* (1660), the heroine and prophetess is named Agatha Shipton, daughter of Solomon Shipton. In a later work titled *Mother Shipton and Nixon's Prophecies* (1797), she is stated to have been born in July 1488 and to have been baptized Ursula Sonthiel. This account added: "Her stature was larger than common, her body crooked, her face frightful; but her understanding extraordinary."

Early chapbook portraits of Shipton represent her as an ugly woman with the characteristic hooked nose, chin, and humped back associated with Punch in the traditional Punch and Judy puppet show. Shipton is probably wholly legendary, and many prophecies attributed to her are spurious inventions.

Sources:

Harrison, William H. *Mother Shipton Investigated.* Reprint, London: The Author, 1881.

Hindley, Charles. *Curiosities of Street Literature.* 1871. London: The Broadsheet King, 1966.

Shirley, Ralph (1865–1946)

Leading British pioneer in the publication of occult and mystical literature. Ralph Shirley was born at Oxford, England, December 30, 1865, of aristocratic stock, brother of the eleventh Earl Ferrers and a direct descendant of Robert Devereux, Earl of Essex. He was educated at Winchester and New College, Oxford University.

For more than three decades (1892–1925) he was director of William Rider & Son, the foremost British publishers of literature dealing with **occultism, mysticism, New Thought, astrology, psychical research,** and related subjects. Rider's authors included **Éliphas Lévi, Arthur Edward Waite, Hereward Carrington,** and **Franz Hartmann** in addition to many others who became legendary in the field.

In 1905, Shirley founded the *Occult Review,* which he edited for 21 years. It included contributions from the leading occultists of the time and set a high standard of both popular and scholarly occultism. Shirley also became vice president of the **International Institute for Psychic Investigation,** for whom he edited **Ernesto Bozzano**'s important study *Discarnate Influence in Human Life* (1938).

It was in the pages of the *Occult Review* that Shirley published the important firsthand experiences of Oliver Fox (pseudonym of **Hugh G. Callaway**) on **astral projection** and **out-of-the-body travel** from April to May 1920. Shirley also published other pioneer writings on the subject, including his own book *The Mystery of the Human Double: The Case for Astral Projection* (1938; reprinted University Books, 1965).

Shirley had a special interest in astrology and had edited *The Horoscope* (under the pseudonym Rollo Ireton). From 1943 to 1944 he was chairman of the Spiritualist journal *Light,* but suffered from failing health and was obliged to retire. He also published a pamphlet *The Angel Warriors at Mons* (1915) reviewing the legends that accumulated around **Arthur Machen**'s famous short story *The Bowmen.* He died December 29, 1946.

Sources:

Shirley, Ralph. *The Mystery of the Human Double: The Case for Astral Projection.* 1938. Reprint, New Hyde Park, N.Y.: University Books, 1965.

———. *The New God, and Other Essays.* N.p., 1911.

———. *Occultists and Mystics of All Ages.* London: W. Rider & Son, 1920.

———. *The Problem of Rebirth.* N.p., 1936.

———. *A Short Life of Abraham Lincoln.* New York: Funk & Wagnalls; London: W. Rider & Son, 1919.

Shivapuri Baba (Sri Govinananda Bharati) (1826–1963)

Hindu mystic who made a great impression on his biographer **J. G. Bennett,** who met him in 1961 when the sage was already a reported 135 years old. Bennett stated: "He was a true saint who produced an immediate and uplifting effect on everyone who entered his presence." Shivapuri Baba had a profound influence on many individuals during his long life, including Hindus, Buddhists, Moslems, and Christians.

When he was born, Britain was under the reign of George IV, and the future Queen Victoria was only a child of seven. Later in life, Shivapuri Baba visited England and made no fewer than 18 visits to Queen Victoria; he was possibly the first Indian holy man invited to meet the queen.

Shivapuri Baba was born in a Brahmin family in Kerala. His grandfather, a famous astrologer, announced that the boy would become a great *sannyasin* (renunciate or wandering monk) and became his guru until about 1840.

Shivapuri Baba decided to leave a worldly life in 1844, at age 18. After making a will leaving his rights of succession in his father's property to his sister, he joined his grandfather in the forest of the upper Deccan, near the banks of the river Narbada. The grandfather insisted that after his own death, the boy should meditate until he obtained God-realization, then make a pilgrimage on foot not only through India, but also around the world, and he set aside money for this purpose.

After the death of his grandfather, the young man received initiation as a sannyasin and took the name of Govindananda Bharati. He then retreated to the Narbada forest and spent 25 years in absolute seclusion. During this period he was even completely unaware of the Indian Mutiny of 1856. At the age of 50, he achieved the beatific vision and became aware of the divine as absolute, beyond name and form, which in Hinduism is considered the highest and most difficult stage of God-realization. He then undertook his great pilgrimages.

He visited all the holy places of India, meeting **Sri Ramakrishna** and **Sri Aurobindo.** He went on to travel through Afghanistan and Persia, then made a pilgrimage to Mecca. After this experience of the Moslem shrine, he next traveled to Jerusalem, the holy city of Judaism and Christianity. He went on to Turkey, through the Balkans into Greece and then through Italy to Rome, so that he might better understand the Christian religion. After visiting most European countries, he was invited to England by Queen Victoria's Indian Secretariat and had 18 private visits with the queen.

In 1901, after the death of the queen, Shivapuri visited the United States and met President Theodore Roosevelt. He spent two or three years in America before going to Mexico, where he met Porfirio Diaz before going on through the Andes to Colombia and Peru. After a period in South America, he embarked on a ship for the Pacific Islands, moving through New Zealand and Australia and visiting Japan in 1913. He then followed an ancient pilgrim route into Nepal, then back to India, visiting Benares. He traveled more than 25,000 miles, eighty percent on foot.

He then returned to his own home in Kerala as a wandering sannyasin after 70 years. He found no trace of his sister, who had also become a renunciate. He concluded remaining family affairs, then retired to the forests of Nepal. Although he was known as a holy man, equally at ease with the religions of Buddhism, Christianity, and Islam (a task made easier by Hindu ideas about the nature of religion), he insisted on remaining isolated, living in a small wooden hut and seeing only a few genuine seekers. Those who saw him received a sense of inner peace and realization from him, and one visitor suggested that even the wild beasts of the forest were on friendly terms with him.

J. G. Bennett, a disciple of **G. I. Gurdjieff** who later promoted the mission of **Subud,** met the Shivapuri Baba in Easter 1961 and found him, at the age of 135 years, alert, quick, and graceful, with a phenomenal memory and an inspiring spiritual presence. One of the most remarkable features of his teaching was his ability to communicate spiritual wisdom in only a few works in the idiom of his questioners. He explained his teaching in three words to S. Radhakrishnan, famous philosopher and former president of India, and afterward Radhakrishnan expounded for 15 minutes on the theme of these three words.

Shivapuri Baba died on January 28, 1963. His final message was: "Live Right Life, Worship God. That is all. Nothing more." He took a drink of water then said "Gaya" (I'm gone), laid down on his right side and passed away. His teaching of right living involved duty, morality, and worship. The sole purpose of human life was to find the Ultimate Truth, or God, and to this end a certain code of life was required—a spiritual, moral, and intellectual order.

Sources:

Bennett, John G., with Thakur Lal Manandhar. *Long Pilgrimage: The Life and Teaching of Sri Govinananda Bharati known as the Shivapuri Baba.* London: Hodder & Stoughton, 1965.

Showers, Mary (ca. 1857– ?)

British **materialization** medium, daughter of General C. L. Showers of the Bombay Army. As a child she conversed with invisible people, sat for the first time in the circle of her family in the spring of 1872, produced **raps** and **movement** without contact, obtained **poltergeist** manifestations in daylight, performed **direct writing,** and saw spirit forms among which **"John King"** and "Peter" rose to prominence.

In 1874, Showers and her mother came from Teignmouth to London to give séances to representative Spiritualists. The test conditions in these early séances were taken charge of by the spirits. At the beginning of the séance, coils of rope or tape would be placed in the cabinet. At a signal, the curtain of the cabinet was drawn aside and the medium was discovered tightly bound.

The usual materialized spirit form was a girl, "Florence," who was eight inches taller than the medium, could vary her height, and was often seen by **Florence Marryat** together with the medium. Marryat describes these experiences in her book *There is No Death* (1891).

Marryat found herself so much in rapport with Showers that she wrote:

"We could not sit next each other at an ordinary tea or supper table when we had no thought of, or desire to hold a séance, without manifestations occurring in the full light. A hand that did not belong to either of us would make itself apparent under the table-cloth between us—a hand with power to grasp ours—or our feet would be squeezed or kicked beneath the table, or fingers would suddenly appear and whisk the food off our plates."

An attempt at exposure of Showers was made on April 2, 1874, at the house of **Edward William Cox.** When "Florence" appeared between the curtains of the cabinet, Cox's daughter Mrs. Edwards opened the curtains wider. The spirit resisted; in the struggle the headdress fell off and revealed Showers. Cox, however, seemed satisfied that the medium was entranced and had unconsciously impersonated the spirit.

Although Cox may have believed that the medium was entranced, the episode cast strong doubts upon the genuineness of Showers's phenomena. Cox himself reinforced such doubts in a letter dated March 8, 1876, to the medium **D. D. Home** (printed in full in Home's *Light and Shadows of Spiritualism,* London, 1877):

"I am satisfied that a large amount of fraud has been and still is practiced. Some of it is, doubtless, deliberately planned and executed. But some is, I think, done while the medium is in a state of somnambulism, and therefore unconscious. As all familiar with phenomena of somnambulism are aware, the patient acts to perfection any part suggested to his mind, but wholly without self-perception at the time, or memory afterwards. But such an explanation serves only to acquit the medium of deliberate imposture; it does not affect the fact that the apparent manifestation is not genuine.

"The great field for fraud has been offered by the production and presentation of alleged spirit-forms. All the conditions imposed are as if carefully designed to favour fraud if contemplated, and even to tempt to imposture. The curtain is guarded at either end by some friend. The light is so dim that the features cannot be distinctly seen. A white veil thrown over the body from head to foot is put on and off in a moment, and gives the necessary aspect of spirituality. A white band round head and chin at once conceals the hair, and disguises the face. A considerable interval precedes the appearance—just such as would be necessary for the preparations. A like interval succeeds the retirement of the form before the cabinet is permitted to be opened for inspection. This just enables the ordinary dress to be restored. While the preparation is going on behind the curtain the company are always vehemently exhorted to sing. This would conveniently conceal any sounds of motion in the act of preparation. The spectators are made to promise not to peep behind the curtain, and not grasp the form. They are solemnly told that if they were to seize the spirit they would kill the medium. This is an obvious contrivance to deter the onlookers from doing anything that might cause detection. It is not true. Several spirits have been grasped, and no medium has died of it; although in each case the supposed spirit was found to be the medium. That the detected medium was somewhat disturbed in health after such a public detection and exposure is not at all surprising. Every one of the five mediums who have been actually seized in the act of personating a spirit is now alive and well. There need be no fear for the consequences in putting them to the proof.

"But I have learned how the trick is done. I have seen the description of it given by a medium to another medium who desired instruction. The letter was in her own handwriting, and the whole style of it showed it to be genuine.

"She informs her friend that she comes to the *séance* prepared with a dress that is easily taken off with a little practice. She says it may be done in two or three minutes. She wears two shifts (probably for warmth). She brings a muslin veil of thin material (she gives its name, which I forget). It is carried *in her drawers!* It can be compressed into a small space, although when spread it covers the whole person. A pocket-handkerchief pinned around the head keeps back the hair. She states that she takes off all her clothes except the two shifts, and is covered by the veil. The gown is spread carefully upon the sofa over the pillows. In this array she comes out. She makes very merry with the spiritualists whom she thus gulls, and her language about them is anything but complimentary.

"This explains the whole business. The question so often asked before was—where the robe could be carried? It could not be contained in the bosom or in a sleeve. Nobody seems to have thought of the drawers.

"But it will be asked how we can explain the fact that some persons have been permitted to go behind the curtain when the form was before it, and have asserted that they saw or felt the medium. I am sorry to say the confession to which I have referred states without reserve that these persons knew that it was a trick, and lent themselves to it. I am, of course, reluctant to adopt such a formidable conclusion, although the so-called 'confession' was a confidential communication from one medium to another medium who had asked to be instructed how the trick was done. I prefer to adopt the more charitable conclusion that they were imposed upon, and that it is easy to find how this was likely to be. The same suspicious precautions against detection were always adopted. The favoured visitor was an assured friend; one who, if detecting trickery, would shrink from proclaiming the cheat. But one was permitted to enter. A light was not allowed. There was nothing but the 'darkness visible' of the lowered gas rays struggling through the curtain. I have noted that no one of them ever was permitted to see the face of the medium. It was always 'wrapped in a shawl.' The hands felt a dress, and imagination did the rest. The revealer of the secret above referred to says that, when she took off her gown to put on the white veil, she spread it upon the sofa or chair with pillows or something under it, and this is what they felt and took for her body!

"The lesson to be learned from all this is, that no phenomena should be accepted as genuine that are not produced under strict test conditions. Investigators should be satisfied with no evidence short of the very best that the circumstances will permit."

Cox's reference to the means by which "spirit forms" were produced fraudulently in a "communication from one medium to another medium who had asked to be instructed how the trick was done" is thought by **Trevor H. Hall** (in his book *The Spiritualists*, London, 1962) to refer to **Florence Cook** and Mary Showers, who were known to each other and indeed collaborated with each other in a joint performance of fully materialized "spirit forms" at the house of **Sir William Crookes.** It is particularly significant that at the final séance with the phantom **"Katie King"** on May 21, 1874, Crookes himself noted that the face of the medium Florence Cook was covered with a red shawl, ostensibly to protect her from the effects of light, and that this established the separate identity of phantom and medium, seen together.

Although some sitters at the Crookes séances with Florence Cook noted marked similarities between the medium and the phantom "Katie King," Crookes himself was at pains to establish specific differences. If the phenomena of Florence Cook was fraudulent, it is likely that her friend Showers was an accomplice at séances when the differences between medium and "spirit form" were apparent.

Both Trevor H. Hall and **E. J. Dingwall** are satisfied that the circumstantial evidence strongly indicates that Cook's phenomena were fraudulent and that Showers was an accomplice. Their conclusion that such **fraud** was known to Crookes and that he connived at it, using the séances as a cover for an affair with Cook, is much more speculative, although it is undeniable that Crookes was tremendously impressed and captivated by the beauty of the materialized phantom "Katie King."

The story of the connections between Showers, Cook, and the investigations of Crookes and Cox is a complex one. The best sources are the writings of Hall and Dingwall.

Sources:

Dingwall, E. J. *The Critic's Dilemma.* Dewsbury, England: The Author, 1966.

Hall, Trevor H. *Florence Cook and William Crookes: A Footnote to an Enquiry.* London: Tomorrow Publications, 1963.

———. *New Light on Old Ghosts.* London: G. Duckworth, 1965.

———. *The Spiritualists.* New York: Heliz Press, 1963. Reprinted as *The Medium and the Scientist.* Buffalo, N.Y.: Prometheus Books, 1984.

Marryat, Florence. *There is No Death.* 1891. Reprint, New York: Causeway Books, 1973.

Thouless, R. H. "Crookes and Cook." *Journal* of the Society for Psychical Research 42 (1963).

Shrine of Sothis

The Shrine of Sothis was a short-lived occult organization that made its public appearance in 1973 through ads placed in a variety of occult periodicals. It stressed a system of practical theurgy (magick) as the best form of communication between the individual and the inner self. It offered a set of lessons on the occult and magical disciplines, including the pentagram, the deities, initiation, reincarnation, black magick, divination, and the construction of talismans. Progressing through the lessons led the student to a realization of "the great concealed one," i.e., God.

The shrine was headquartered in San Francisco. After several years it dropped out of sight.

Shrine of the Eternal Breath of Tao/ Universal Society of the Integral Way

Organization founded by Master Ni, Hua Ching, who had studied **Taoism** as a child in China. He moved to Taiwan after the Chinese Revolution. He continued his studies and became a teacher of Taoism and related martial and healing arts. During the 1970s, he moved to the United States and began to teach in Los Angeles.

This Toaist teaching concerns a universal law of subtle energy response. According to Master Ni, everything in the universe is a manifestation of energy in either its grosser or more subtle states. An understanding of how to develop the proper response to the energies of one's environment will bring harmony to one's life. The practice of Taoist meditation, **martial arts** (kung fu and **t'ai chi ch'uan**), and medical practices (**acupuncture** and herbs) assist in attaining a balanced relationship to life. The universal law of response is claimed to be the basis of all spiritual practices.

The shrine is located in Los Angeles and sponsors the College of Tao and the Yo San University of Traditional Chinese Medicine. Website: http://www.usiw.org/.

Sources:

Ni, Hua-Ching. *The Subtle Universal Law and the Integral Way of Life.* Malibu, Calif.: Shrine of the Eternal Breath of Tao, 1979.

Shroud of Turin Research Project

Former project founded in 1978, with a membership of professionals, logistics support personnel, and physical scientists whom acted as principal investigators in research work being performed on the **Turin Shroud.**

The purpose of the project was to determine the physics and chemistry of both the cloth and image in order to verify or refute the authenticity of the Shroud. The project conducted nondestructive testing and research and attempted to simulate and analyze various images and stains found on the Shroud through laboratory testings, including chemical analysis, infrared spectroscopy and thermography, optical and ultraviolet reflectance and fluorescent spectroscopy, photography, X-radiography, and X-ray fluorescence.

The project reported findings in the form of technical papers to the scientific press, seeked to coordinate all activities in the field, reviewed research proposals, and distributed funding. It published a quarterly called *Update.* The project was formally dissolved by the Connecticut Secretary of State in 1993.

Siberia

Siberia is a vast territory of northern Asia, part of the Commonwealth of Independent States (formerly the U.S.S.R.). It is bounded by the Urals on the west, by Kazakhstan, China, and North Korea on the south, by the Pacific on the east, and by the Arctic on the north.

In former times, most of the tribal cultures of Siberia practiced the art of sorcery through the expertise of the **shaman.** The definitive characteristic of the shaman, as opposed to other tribal ritual leaders, was the ability to go into trance and travel in the spirit world.

The Samoyeds of Siberia believed in the existence of an order of invisible spirits called *tadebtsois.* These were ever circling through the atmosphere and were a constant menace to the people, who were anxious to propitiate them. This propitiation could only be effected through the intervention of a *tadibe,* or necromancer, who, when his services were requisitioned, attired himself in a magic costume of reindeer leather trimmed with red cloth, a mask of red cloth, and a breastplate of polished metal. He then took a drum of reindeer skin ornamented with brass rings and, attended by an assistant, walked in a circle and invoked the spirits while shaking a large rattle. The practice was very similar to that found among the Lapps in **Lapland.**

As the noise grew louder the spirits were supposed to draw near the sorcerer, who addressed them, beating his drum more gently and pausing in his chant to listen to their answers. Gradually he worked himself into a condition of frenzy, beat the drum with great violence, and appeared to be possessed by the spirit's influence, writhing and foaming at the mouth. All at once he stopped and oracularly pronounced the will of the spirits.

The tadibe's office was a hereditary one, but a member of the tribe exhibiting special qualifications was adopted into the priesthood, and through fasts, vigils, and the use of narcotics and stimulants—in the same manner as employed by some Native Americans—came to believe that he or she was visited by the spirits. The initiate was then adopted as a tadibe in a midnight ceremony and invested with a magic drum.

Many of the tricks of the priesthood were merely those of ordinary conjuring, such as the rope trick, but some of the illusions were exceedingly striking. With their hands and feet tied together, the tadibe sat on a carpet of reindeer skin and, putting out the light, summoned the assistance of the spirits. Peculiar noises heralded the spirits' approach, snakes hissed and bears growled, the lights were rekindled, and the tadibe's hands and feet were untied.

The Samoyeds sacrificed often to the dead and performed various ceremonies in their honor, but they believed that only the souls of the tadibes enjoyed immortality, hovering in the air and demanding frequent sacrifices.

Further to the east, inhabiting the more northerly part of Siberia, lived the Ostiaks, who nominally adopted the rites of the Greek church, but magic was also common among them. Many Ostiaks carried a kind of fetish they called *schaitan.*

Larger images of this kind were part of the furnishings of an Ostiak lodge, but they were attired in seven pearl-embroidered garments and suspended from the neck by a string of silver coins. In a strange sort of dualism they were placed in many of the huts cheek by jowl with the image of the Virgin Mary, and at mealtimes their lips were smeared with the blood of raw game or fish.

The Mongols, who inhabited the more southern parts of the vast expense of Siberia, were also ancient practitioners of magic and relied greatly on **divination.** To prognosticate the weather they employed a stone endowed with magic virtues, called *yadeh-tash,* which was suspended over or laid in a basin of water with sundry ceremonies.

Many of the old beliefs and practices in Siberia died out following the Russian Revolution of 1917 and the subsequent development of the area. (See also **Fetishism**)

Sibley, Ebenezer (1751–1799)

Ebenezer Sibley, British astrologer, **magician,** and practitioner of herbal medicine, was born on January 30, 1751. He had a conservative upbringing in a Calvinist Baptist church and later attended the Aberdeen Medical College. He studied orthodox medicine, but also had an interest to study **animal magnetism** under **Franz Anton Mesmer;** he joined Mesmer's Harmonic Philosophical School. Then Sibley also taught himself the basics of occultism. In 1784 he joined the Freemasons.

Sibley is best remembered for two books. In 1784 the first volume of his four-volume magnum opus, *The Complete Illustration of the Celestial Art of Astrology.* It summarized the work of the previous century of astrological writing and became a steady seller for the rest of Sibley's life in spite of the reviews. *The Conjurer's Magazine,* the only occult periodical in England at the time dismissed it as derivative. The final volume, concerning magic, that appeared in 1792, presented an interesting variation on **Emanuel Swedenborg**'s vision of the spiritual world. According to Sibley, spirits live in another world that is neither heaven nor hell. Magic can summon only the evil spirit. Good spirits watch over humans, but do not respond to any summoning. Sibley went on to highlight seven good spirits that watch over human affairs and noted seven corresponding wicked spirits. He noted that since God had removed his wrath through Christ, these seven spirits made but few appearances.

The same year that his fourth volume was purchased, Sibley also completed *A Key to the Physic and the Occult Sciences,* a systematic statement of his occult philosophy. Like Mesmer, he suggested that the world was animated by a universal spirit, the operative agent in both astrology and healing work. This spirit works on matter and can be used by the magician for his purposes. This understanding would become standard for magical thought through the century and anticipates the more heralded work of **Éliphas Lévi.** Also included in the *Key,* published a supplement to the famous work on herbal medicine by **Nicolas Culpepper.**

Ebenezer's brother **Manoah Sibley** became a prominent Swedenborgian minister.

Ebenezer Sibley styled himself an "astro-philosopher." He claimed to have cast the horoscope of the forger-poet Thomas Chatterton, and to have predicted his fatal end, such as "death by poison." Among various successful prognostications made through **astrology,** Sibley claimed to have foretold the American War of Independence in a symbolic picture in his book. Sibley was sufficiently enterprising to design a small notebook for astrologers, engraved from plates but with blank spaces for recording the positions of various planets and noting horoscopes.

Sources:

Godwin, Joscelyn. *The Theosophical Enlightenment.* Albany, N.Y.: State University of New York Press, 1995.

Sibley, Ebenezer. *Celestial Science of Astrology.* 1776. Revised as *New and Complete Illustration of the Celestial Science of Astrology.* 2 vols. N.p., 1817.

Sibley, Ebenezer. *A Key to Physic and the Occult Sciences.* 1792. 5th ed. London W. Lewis and G. Jones, 1814.

———. *The Medical Mirror; or, A Treatise on the Impregnation of the Human Female.* N.p., 1800.

———. *Uranoscopia; or, The Pure Language of the Stars Unfolded by the Motion of the Seven Erratics.* N.p., 1780.

Sibley, Manoah (1757–1840)

Swedenborgian minister and astrologer, born in Bristol, England, on August 20, 1757, the younger brother of astrologer **Ebenezer Sibley.** Unlike his college-educated brother, Manoah Sibley had to study on his own from age 11, but through his teens he mastered several languages, which, along with shorthand, he taught through the 1760s and 1770s. He married in 1780 and opened a bookshop, which he and his wife managed. Sibley dropped his own work to align with the church that had been established in London by **Robert Hindmarsh.** Swedenborg's teachings were received as the end of his spiritual quest and by Easter of the next year he began preaching. He was ordained in 1790. Hindmarsh, a former Methodist, modeled his church on that which was familiar to him. Sibley found his approach too restrictive and in 1793 he left to found his own Swedenborgian congregation. He preached weekly for the next forty years.

Apart from pioneering the beliefs of **Emanuel Swedenborg** in England, Sibley is most remembered today for his publication of translations of the writings of **Claudius Ptolemy** and **Placidus.** Sibley's translation of the *Tetrabiblos* (four books) of Ptolemy, the major work from which Western **astrology** developed, appeared in 1786, and the writings of Placidus, whose system of arranging the astrological houses would come to dominate astrology in the next century, appeared in several volumes in 1789 and 1790.

Astrologers hail Sibley for making these works available and note their importance in directing the astrological revival in England in the nineteenth century. Critics have charged Sibley with theft, first of Whalley's earlier translation of the *Tetrabiblos,* and then of a manuscript of a translation of the writing of Placidus. All of his books are full of errors that, in spite of his linguistic accomplishments, he could not correct because he did not have copies of the Latin originals.

Whatever the problems with the translations, Sibley went on to an even more prestigious career with the Bank of England, beginning in 1797, and was appointed principal of the Chancery Office in 1815.

Sibley died in December 1840 in London.

Sources:

Astronomy and Elementary Philosophy, Translated from the Latin of Placidus de Titus. London: W. Justins, 1789.

Godwin, Joscelyn. *The Theosophical Enlightenment.* Albany: State University of New York Press, 1995.

Holden, James H., and Robert A. Hughes. *Astrological Pioneers of America.* Tempe, Ariz.: American Federation of Astrologers, 1988.

Ptolemy, Claudius. *The Quadripatite, or Four Books.* Translated by J. Whalley. Edited by Manoah Sibley and J. Browne. London, 1786.

Sibyl

General term for a prophetess. The original Sibyl was believed to have lived in Asia Minor in the seventh century B.C.E., but three centuries later various sibyls were claimed in different parts. Sibylline prophecies in hexameters ascribed to Sibyl were current in classical Greece and were referred to by Aristophanes and Plato.

Sibylline Books

The manuscripts that embodied the secrets of human destiny, the work of the **sibyls** or prophetesses of the ancient world. According to the historian Tacitus (ca. 55–120 C.E.), these books were first preserved in the Roman Capitol. When it burned down, the previous leaves were preserved and removed to the temple of Apollo Palatinus. Their subsequent fate is enshrouded in mystery, but it would seem that the Cumean books existed until 339 C.E., when they were destroyed by the consul Stilikon.

Augustus sent three ambassadors—Paulus Gabinus, Marcus Otacillius, and Lucius Valerius—into Asia, Africa, and Italy to collect whatever could be discovered of the Sibylline Oracles in order to replace those that had been lost or burned.

The books are of two kinds: the books of the elder Sibyls, (that is, of the earlier Greek and Roman times) and those of the later Sibyls, which are falsified and disfigured with numerous interpolations. Of the latter, eight books in Greek and Latin are still said to exist.

Those preserved in Rome had been collected from various places, at various times, and contained predictions of future events couched in the most mysterious of symbolic languages. At first they were permitted to be read only by descendants of Apollo, then later by priests, until their care was entrusted to certain officials.

Siddhas

According to Hindu mythology, the 88,000 semi-divine beings of great holiness dwelling between the Earth and the Sun.

Siddhis

The eight occult powers resulting from the practice of yoga, according to the system of Patanjali (ca. 200 B.C.E.). These powers are *anima* (to become infinitely small at will), *mahima* (large), *laghima* (light), *garima* (heavy), *prapti* (to reach anywhere), *prakamya* (to gratify any wishes), *ishatwa* (to create), and *vashitwa* (to command).

There are many accounts of Hindu yogis possessing and manifesting such powers, even in relatively modern times. However, at the same time the *siddhis* are regarded by many as obstacles to spiritual realization as they might distract the seeker from his or her true goal. In recent years, the **Transcendental Meditation** movement founded by **Maharishi Mahesh Yogi** inaugurated a controversial Siddha Course for advanced students and claimed the ability to teach students the power of levitation.

Sources:

Dvidedi, M. N., ed. *The Yoga-Sutras of Patanjali.* Adyar, Madras, India: Theosophical Publishing House, 1890.

Siderealist (Journal)

Former publication for professional astrologers and students concerned with sidereal aspects of **astrology.** Among astrologers, there are several systems of calculating the divisions of the horoscope chart and devising its relation to the actual stars that constitute the 12 signs of the zodiac. The sidereal zodiac places the division according to the present locations of these signs, which, because of a phenomenon known as the procession of the equinoxes, are constantly changing. In contrast, the tropical zodiac always measures the divisions from the position of the sun at the annual spring equinox. *The Siderealist* included charts of public personalities in relation to star patterns.

Siderite

An old name for a loadstone or magnet. The term has also been variously used to indicate a steel-colored stone (possibly sapphire), a blue-colored quartz, carbonate of iron, and meteorites containing iron.

Sideromancy

A branch of **pyromancy** (**divination** by fire), based on interpretation of the flame, smoke, and pattern of straws placed on a hot piece of iron.

Sidgwick, Eleanor Mildred Balfour (1845–1936)

Psychical researcher and president of the **Society for Psychical Research** (SPR). Sidgwick was born on March 11, 1845, the older sister of **Arthur James Balfour** (later British Prime Minister Premier) and **Gerald William Balfour,** both of whom were also elected president of the SPR. In 1876 she married Henry Sidgwick, who would go on to become a professor of moral philosophy at Cambridge and in 1882 the first president of the SPR. Though without formal training, she was of great intellect and began to participate in research alongside her husband. Her sister Evelyn Balfour married **John William Strutt** (Lord Rayleigh), also an SPR president.

Mathematics was her forte. With her brother-in-law Lord Rayleigh, she conducted several experiments in electricity and with him published three papers in the *Philosophical Transactions of the Royal Society.* Lord Rayleigh later won the Nobel Prize for physics.

She joined the SPR, and in 1888 she assumed the duties formally assigned to her husband as editor of the society's *Journal* and *Proceedings.* In the 1890s, deemed the best at handling large masses of information, she was placed in charge of the **Census of Hallucinations** and was the author of the final report. She was elected president of the SPR for 1908–09. After her term of office was finished, she acted as honorary secretary until 1931. At the society's Jubilee Celebrations in 1932, she was appointed as President d'Honneur. Over a 30 year period she collected and analyzed the many communications that made up the bulk of the **cross-correspondences.**

Over the years she wrote a number of papers for the *Journal* and *Proceedings* of the SPR. She assisted **Edmund Gurney, F. W. H. Myers,** and **Frank Podmore** in the compilation of their key work *Phantasms of the Living* (2 vols., 1886) and edited an abridged edition in 1918. She also contributed the entry on **Spiritualism** to the 9th edition of the *Encyclopedia Britannica* (1875–89). She died February 10, 1936.

Sources:

Berger, Arthur S., and Joyce Berger. *The Encyclopedia of Parapsychology and Psychical Research.* New York: Paragon House, 1991.

Gauld, Alan. *The Founders of Psychical Research.* New York: Schrocken Books, 1968.

Pleasants, Helene, ed. *Biographical Dictionary of Parapsychology.* New York: Helix Press, 1964.

Sidgwick, Eleanor. "Discussion of the Trance Phenomena of Mrs. Piper." *Proceedings* of the Society for Psychical Research (1899).

———. "An Examination of Book-Tests Obtained in Sittings with Mrs. Osborne Leonard." *Proceedings* of the Society for Psychical Research (1921).

———. "Hindrances and Complications in Telepathic Communication." *Proceedings* of the Society for Psychical Research (1923).

———. "History of the SPR." *Proceedings* of the Society for Psychical Research (1932–33).

———. "Phantasms of the Dead." *Proceedings* of the Society for Psychical Research (1885).

———. "The Physical Phenomena of Spiritualism." *Proceedings* of the Society for Psychical Research (1886).

Sidgwick, Henry (1838–1900)

First president of the **Society for Psychical Research** (SPR), London, a professor at Cambridge University who filled the chair of moral philosophy, and who once was described as "the most incorrigibly and exasperatingly critical and sceptical mind in England." **F. W. H. Myers** (who pursued investigations with Sidgwick) and **Edmund Gurney** made their cooperation with the fledgling SPR contingent upon his acceptance of the presidential post.

Sidgwick was born May 31, 1838, at Skipton, Yorkshire, England. He attended Rugby and Trinity College, Cambridge (fellow, 1859–69). In 1876, he married Eleanor Mildred Balfour, the sister of **Arthur James Balfour,** later British Prime Minister.

In his first presidential address to the SPR, on July 17, 1882, Sidgwick used plain words:

"We are all agreed that the present state of things is a scandal to the enlightened age in which we live, that the dispute as to the reality of these marvelous phenomena of which it is quite impossible to exaggerate the scientific importance, if only a tenth part of what has been alleged by generally credible witnesses could be shown to be true—I say it is a scandal that the dispute as to the reality of these phenomena should still be going on, that so many competent witnesses should have declared their belief in them, that so many others should be profoundly interested in having the question determined, and yet the educated world, as a body, should still be simply in an attitude of incredulity."

He declared that he did not expect to produce evidence of a better quality than that of **Sir William Crookes, Alfred Russel Wallace,** and **Augustus de Morgan,** but wanted a great deal more of it. Speaking on scientific incredulity he concluded:

"We have done all that we can when the critic has nothing left to allege except that the investigator is in the trick. But when he has nothing else left he will allege that. . . . We must drive the objector into the position of being forced either to admit the phenomena as inexplicable, at least by him, or to accuse the investigators either of lying or cheating or of a blindness or forgetfulness incompatible with any intellectual condition except absolute idiocy."

For 18 years Sidgwick claimed an active share in the work of the SPR, contributed many important studies to the *Proceedings,* and helped the investigations by his personal means. He edited the society's *Journal* in 1885.

He died without admitting any reality to either **telekinesis** or **ectoplasm.** But as early as 1864 he wrote to a Mr. Dakyns, a friend: "I (fancy I) have actually heard the raps . . ." and added: "However, I have no kind of evidence to come before a jury. So keep it still till I blaze forth." He never blazed forth.

He had sittings with mediums **Frank Herne** and **Henry Slade** and **materialization** séances with **C. E. Wood** and **Annie Fairlamb** in his own home at Cambridge under the most stringent test conditions, as testified by Myers's notes. **Eleanor Sidgwick** published an account of those she attended in the SPR *Proceedings* (vol. 4) and admitted that it was exceedingly difficult "but not perhaps impossible" to impute the results to imposture. In justice, however, it should be added that the most astounding and conclusive phenomena, according to Myers, occurred in the absence of both Sidgwicks.

It is more widely known that Sidgwick was impressed by the phenomena of **Eusapia Palladino,** which he witnessed with his wife on the Ile. Roubaud in 1894, as the guest of **Charles Richet.** During the latter part of Palladino's stay there, her phenomena were less spectacular, and he then took a leading part in the sittings held at Cambridge in 1895 that resulted in her exposure. He had a number of sittings with **Leonora Piper** in 1889–90 and retained the keenest interest in her trance phenomena.

He died August 28, 1900. The first communications purporting to come from Sidgwick after his death were obtained through **Rosina Thompson** on January 11, 1901. According to **J. G. Piddington,** who was present, the diction, manner, and voice were astonishingly lifelike, and he felt that he was indeed speaking with and hearing the voice of the man he had known. The written communications that followed the oral one bear out a striking resemblance to Sidgwick's handwriting. The first such script was received through Thompson in Piddington's presence. Other messages, of varying evidential value, were received through the hand of **Margaret Verrall.**

Sources:

Berger, Arthur S., and Joyce Berger. *The Encyclopedia of Parapsychology and Psychical Research.* New York: Paragon House, 1991.

Gauld, Alan. *The Founders of Psychical Research.* New York: Schrocken Books, 1968.

Pleasants, Helene, ed. *Biographical Dictionary of Parapsychology.* New York: Helix Press, 1964.

Sidgwick, Henry. "Canons of Evidence in Psychical Research." *Proceedings* of the Society for Psychical Research (1888–90).

———. "Disinterested Deception." *Journal* 6 (1894).

Sidgwick, Henry, A. Johnson, F. W. H. Myers, Frank Podmore, and Eleanor Sidgwick. "Report on the Census of Hallucinations." *Proceedings* of the Society for Psychical Research 10 (1894).

Sierra, Ralph U(son) (1904–1982)

Chiropractic doctor who conducted research in parapsychology. Sierra was born December 6, 1904, in San Juan, Puerto Rico, and graduated from Atlantic States Chiropractic Institute of New York. He was a physical therapist at Kings County Hospital, Brooklyn, New York (1935–47), an instructor in neurology at Atlantic States Chiropractic Institute (1947–49), and a lecturer on healing and natural sciences. He wrote the *Handbook of Neurology,* a chiropractic text. Sierra investigated respiratory and diaphragmatic changes in mediums during manifestation of phenomena. He died in November of 1982.

Sources:

Pleasants, Helene, ed. *Biographical Dictionary of Parapsychology.* New York: Helix Press, 1964.

Sigil

A sign or seal for an occult entity. Sigils, especially those that are the marks of angels, deities, or demons, are often used on **amulets** and **talismans.** According to occultists, such signs are like the signatures of gods and other supernatural entities, and the inscribing of such sigils evokes the entities that they symbolize. (See also **Yantra**)

In this century, the art of creating sigils was recreated by artist-magician Austin Osman Spare. He saw in sigils a means of concentrating the magical will. He would write his magic intention or will down in a sentence or word, and then combine the major letters (without repeating any letter) into a patterned shape, the sigil. The symbolic shape thus created could be impressed upon the subconscious for working magic.

Sources:

Drury, Nevill, and Stephen Skinner. *The Search for Abraxas.* London: Neville Spearman, 1972.

Gettings, Fred. *Dictionary of Occult, Hermetic and Alchemical Sigils.* London: Routledge & Kegan Paul, 1981.

Signs (Paranormal)

At various moments in history and in times of great stress, suffering, and persecution, reports of paranormal signs (believed to portend great events) frequently emerged. Under these conditions it was not unusual for ecstatic states to become epidemic, prophecies to be uttered, and unusual physical phenomena to appear. Many of these reports appear to be a mixture of misobservation of mundane if unusual occurrences and hallucinations.

The ancient historians Josephus and Tacitus wrote of fearful sights and great signs from heaven before the judgment on Jerusalem. When, three centuries later, Julian the Apostate attempted to rebuild Jerusalem, fiery balls burst forth upon the workmen and took strange shapes. This was recorded not only by Julian's own historian but by Jewish and non-Roman writers as well. Many accounts testify of the signs and wonders during the persecution of the Huguenots in France.

From the dawn of printing onward, unnatural events and prodigies of nature became the subject of broadside ballad-sheets and chapbook pamphlets, the street literature of poor people. Monstrous births and other signs and wonders were made the occasion for moralizing about the sins of the day and predicted divine judgment. Even in modern times, visions of the Virgin Mary are often considered signs of divine wrath at a sinful world. (See also **Fatima; Garabandal**)

Sources:

Eniatos. *Mirabilis Annus; or, The Year of Prodigies and Wonders; Being a Collection of Several Signs That Have Been Seen in the Heavens, in the Earth, and in the Waters, Together with Many Remarkable Accidents and Judgments . . . Within the Space of One Year Last Past.* London, 1661.

Grey, E. Howard. *Visions, Previsions and Miracles in Modern Times.* London: L. N. Fowler, 1915.

Rollins, Hyder E., ed. *The Pack of Autolycus or Strange and Terrible News of Ghosts, Apparitions, Monstrous Births, Showers of Wheat, Judgments of God, and other Prodigious and Fearful Happenings as told in Broadside Ballads of the Years 1624–1693.* Cambridge, Mass.: Harvard University Press, 1927.

Thompson, C. J. S. *The Mystery and Lore of Monsters.* London: Williams & Norgate, 1930. Reprint, New Hyde Park, N.Y.: University Books, 1968.

Silberhartz, Allen (1947–)

Allen Silberhartz, the host of the national **New Age** television show **Bridging Heaven and Earth,** was born on February 28, 1947, in New York City. He grew up in a Jewish home and had his Bar Mitzvah at age 13. He completed his degree at the University of Pennsylvania (1967), where he majored in accounting, and earned a law degree at George Washington University (1971). He moved to rural Maryland, where he joined a commune residing on an organic farm. While there he learned to practice meditation which has subsequently remained a part of his daily schedule.

Having joined the bar in Maryland, in 1975 Silberhartz began practicing law, but in 1980 moved to Santa Barbara, California, where he became an investment counselor. During his Maryland years, he had had a profound mystical experience of oneness that changed his outlook on life and that he has since sought to manifest in all his various activities. In 1985 he began to teach meditation and spiritual development. He became close friends with another independent spiritual teacher named Wistancia.

In 1995, along with Wistancia and a group of spiritual friends, he launched a television show on the local community access station in Santa Barbara. The show grew out of a conversation reflecting upon the negativity that appeared to dominate many of the daytime talk shows then running on national television. Silberhartz and his colleagues attempted to put together a show that would be positive and uplifting and reflect his own experience of oneness which he had come to feel transcended any particular organizational expression. In the beginning, he and Wistancia served as cohosts, but since 1997 he has been the sole host.

By the end of the decade, *Bridging Heaven and Earth* had become a national show, having been picked up on a number of community access stations. Silberhartz continues his financial counseling work and role as a teacher.

Sources:

Bridging Heaven and Earth. http://www.heavenonearth.com/. March 23, 2000.

Manville, Rhonda Parks. "Local Metaphysical Talk Show Resonates with Viewers." *Santa Barbara News Press* (March 7, 1999).

Silbert, Maria (d. 1936)

Austrian physical medium of Waltendorf, near Graz, mainly known for **telekinesis, stigmata, apport,** and **trance** phenomena. As a child she reportedly could predict future events, but her later physical powers were developed at the expense of her clairvoyant abilities.

Her apports were preceded by remarkable lights resembling lightning strokes. A deceased doctor, calling himself "Franciscus Nell," was her chief control. One of his curious demonstrations was engraving cigarette cases with his name when they were held under the table. However, such a feat is more reminiscent of **conjuring** than paranormal phenomena. Paul Sünner recorded in *Psychic Science* (January 1931) some sittings in which, while the medium's hands were visible above the table, the engraving feat was demonstrated five times in succession, additions being scratched on the same cigarette case on his request.

Silbert's standing on the Continent was high. But except for her three visits to the **British College of Psychic Science** in London, she did not have the good fortune to sit with sympathetic British investigators. **Walter Franklin Prince,** of the **Boston Society for Psychical Research,** published a negative report after two sittings in Graz in 1927. **Theodore Besterman,** in an account of a personal investigation in November 1928 (*Proceedings* of the Society for Psychical Research, vol. 38), admitted some interesting phenomena that he could not explain but nevertheless concluded **fraud.**

During 1925, the British psychical researcher **Harry Price** was in Graz, and on November 3 he attended a sitting with Silbert. Various objects, including Price's gold cigarette lighter, were placed under the table. The lighter suddenly appeared on top of the table with the word "well" engraved on it.

Price obtained permission to look under the table to see the movement of the objects. After 30 minutes he saw Silbert's right foot outside her shoe with her toes visible where the end of a stocking had been cut off. Price was satisfied that the medium used her toes to handle objects. He did not accuse the medium of fraud because he was hoping to make further investigations later, and because he learned that five other individuals who had publicly criticized Silbert had suffered inexplicable misfortunes. (Price believed that Silbert actually possessed some paranormal powers, especially in regard to the **raps** she produced.)

Silbert died in September 1936.

Silva, Edivaldo Oliveira (ca. 1930–1974)

Brazilian Spiritualist healer specializing in **psychic surgery.** Born in Vitoria da Conquista, Bahia, he became a schoolteacher, taxidermist, and entomologist. In his later years he studied medicine and law, hoping thereby to qualify as a doctor so that his spiritual healing would be secured against prosecution for illegal medical practice. Although brought up as a Roman Catholic, he was an unconventional Christian who did not endorse the monopoly of the church authorities and developed his own personal theological approach. He did not claim to be formally aligned to **Spiritism,** the Brazilian form of **Spiritualism,** although his healing work was ascribed to spirit controls.

He first discovered his healing abilities in 1962, when he visited a neighbor who had a fit of temporary insanity. Silva went into a **trance** and was taken over by a spirit personality, becoming very violent. When he recovered normal consciousness, his neighbor had been cured.

Later, Silva visited a Spiritist center where he again went into trance, discovering on his way home that he had performed psychic surgery while in this state. Over the next ten years, he performed psychic **healing** on some 65,000 individuals.

During his healing sessions, Silva went into a trance-like condition while his spirit controls performed the work. He only learned the details of his healing afterward from conversations, photographs, or tape recordings. His spirit controls consisted of an international team that included "Dr. Calazans," "Pierre" (a Frenchman), and "Dr. Fritz" (a German), as well as an Englishman, a Japanese person, an Italian, and a Brazilian.

Silva believed that the psychic surgery operated on two planes—plasmic and ectoplasmic. In the former, red globules were actually separated from the plasma; in the latter, the operation was on a subtle body rather than a physical body. As with other psychic surgeons, he would make instantaneous incisions that were afterward apparently paranormally healed.

Silva was investigated by author **Guy Lyon Playfair,** a member of the Brazilian Institute for Psycho-Biophysical Research, who spent two years studying Brazilian healers firsthand. Two operations were performed on Playfair himself, who also witnessed the making of an incision in another patient and was allowed to place his fingers into the hole before the flesh was reunited.

Silva performed over 10,000 psychic operations during his lifetime. He died in 1974 after being involved in a car accident.

Sources:

Playfair, Guy Lyon. *The Flying Cow.* 1975. Reprinted as *The Unknown Power.* New York: Pocket Books, 1975.

Silvester II, Pope (d. 1003)

Silvester II (Gerbert), a distinguished scholar, statesman, and pope (999–1003 C.E.), was one of a number of popes from the tenth century on who were regarded as sorcerers. It was said that Silvester had evoked a demon who obtained for him the papacy, and who further promised him that he should die only after he had celebrated High Mass in Jerusalem.

One day while he was saying mass in a church in Rome, he felt suddenly ill, and, remembering that he was in a church called the Holy Cross in Jerusalem, suddenly knew that the demon had played him a trick. Before he died, he confessed to his cardinals his compact with the devil. However, as Silvester had been preceptor of two monarchs, and a friend of others, it is more likely that he owed his preference to one of these.

He was one of the most learned men of his day, proficient in mathematics, astronomy, and mechanics. He introduced clocks, and some writers credit him with the invention of arithmetic. It is not at all improbable that his scientific pursuits and the technical language involved might have appeared to the less educated to savor of magic. The brazen head that the chronicler William of Malmesbury stated as belonging to Silvester, which answered questions in an oracular manner, probably had its origin in a similar misinterpretation of scientific apparatus. It also recalls folk stories of the wonderful brazen head of **Roger Bacon.**

There is no lack of picturesque detail in some of the stories told of Silvester. He was said to have discovered buried treasure by the aid of sorcery and to have visited a marvelous underground palace, whose riches and splendor vanished at a touch. His tomb was believed to possess the powers of sorcery and to shed tears when one of the succeeding popes was about to die.

Simmonite, William Joseph (ca. 1800–ca. 1862)

Prominent leader of the nineteenth-century astrology revival in England. Little is known of Simmonite's life prior to his appearance as a schoolteacher in Sheffield, England, in the 1830s. He knew several languages and was a mathematician. It appears he also practiced herbal medicine. His first book, *The Practical Self-teaching Grammar of the English Language,* appeared in 1841.

Simmonite emerged as an astrologer in the mid-1840s with the publication of his first astrological text, *Prognostications on Revolutions, or Solar Figures* (1845). He continued to write through the remainder of his life, greatly expanding the minuscule number of books available to would-be astrologers of the era. His books went through many editions and were republished in the United States at the end of the century as the American phase of the astrology revival commenced. His work was noted for its erudite cast. Simmonite is also credited with simplifying the nature of the calculations required to construct a horoscope chart.

Simmonite lived into the early 1860s, but the date and place of his death are unknown.

Sources:

Holden, James H., and Robert A. Hughes. *Astrological Pioneers of America.* Tempe, Ariz.: American Federation of Astrologers, 1988.

Simmonite, W. J. *The Celestial Philosopher.* 2d ed. London: Simpkin, Marshall, 1847.

———. *Medical Botany, or Herbal Guide to Health.* London: Simpkin, Marshall, [1848].

———. *The Prognostic Astronomer, or Horary Astrology.* London: Simpkin, Marshall, 1851.

———. *Prognostications on Revolutions or Solar Figures.* London: Simpkin, Marshall, 1845.

Simon Magus (ca. 67 C.E.)

Founder of the heterodox sect of Simonites, often identified with the sorcerer mentioned in the New Testament (Acts 8) who was said to have bewitched the people of Samaria and made them believe that he was possessed of divine power.

He was born in Samaria or Cyprus and was among the number of Samaritans who came to Philip for baptism after hearing him preach. Later, when Peter and John laid their hands on the new converts, so that they received the Holy Ghost, Simon offered the disciples money to procure a similar power. But Peter sternly rebuked him for seeking to buy the gift of God with money (a practice afterward called simony) and bade him pray that his evil thought might be forgiven, whereupon the already repentant Simon said, "Pray ye to the Lord for me, that none of these things which ye have spoken come upon me."

Though we are not told in detail the sorceries with which Simon was supposed to have bewitched the people of Samaria, certain early ecclesiastical writers have left a record of his doings. They claimed that he could make himself invisible when he pleased, assume the appearance of another person or of one of the lower animals, pass unharmed through fire, cause statues to come alive, make furniture move without any visible means of imparting motion, and perform many other miracles. In explanation of his desire to possess the apostles' power of working miracles, he is said to have affirmed that his sorceries took a great deal of time and trouble to perform, owing to the necessity for a multitude of magical rites and incantations, while the miracles of the apostles were accomplished easily and successfully by the mere utterance of a few words.

The adept from whom Simon was supposed to have learned the art of magic was Dositheus, who pretended to be the Messiah foretold by the prophets and who was contemporary with Christ. From this person Simon was said to have acquired a great store of occult erudition, and owed his power chiefly to the hysterical conditions into which he was capable of throwing himself. Through these, he was able to make himself look either old or young, returning at will to childhood or old age.

It seems that he had not been initiated into transcendental magic, but was merely consumed by a thirst for power over humanity and the mysteries of nature. Repulsed by the apostles, he is said to have undertaken pilgrimages, like them, in which he permitted himself to be worshiped by the mob. He declared that he himself was the manifestation of the Splendor of God, and that Helena, his Greek slave, was its reflection. Thus he imitated Christianity in the reverse sense, affirmed the eternal reign of evil and revolt, and was, in fact, an antichrist.

After a while, according to popular legend, he went to Rome, where he appeared before the Emperor Nero. He is said to have been decapitated by him; however, his head returned to his shoulders, and he was instituted by the tyrant as court sorcerer. Legend also states that St. Peter, alarmed at the spread of the doctrine of Simon in Rome, hurried there to combat it. When Nero was made aware of Peter's arrival, he imagined Peter to be a rival sorcerer and resolved to bring Simon and Peter together for his amusement.

An account ascribed to St. Clement states that upon the arrival of Peter, Simon flew gracefully through a window into the outside air. The apostle made a vehement prayer, whereupon the magician, with a loud cry, crashed to the earth and broke both his legs. Nero, greatly annoyed, immediately imprisoned the saint, and it is related that Simon died of his fall. He had, however, founded a distinct school, headed by Merrander, that promised immortality of soul and body to its followers.

In the mid-nineteenth century, a sect existed in France and the United States that credited the principles of this magician.

French scholar Jacques Lacarrière viewed Simon Magus as one of the precursors of **Gnosticism.**

Sources:

Lacarrière, Jacques. *The Gnostics.* London: Owen, 1977. Reprint, San Francisco: City Lights, 1989.

SIMS See Student's International Mediation Society

Sinclair, Upton (Beall) (1878–1968)

Famous American novelist, fearless champion of many unpopular causes. He was born on September 20, 1878, in Baltimore, Maryland, and later studied at the City College of New York. He was a Socialist candidate for the U.S. House of Representatives (1906, 1920); for the Senate (1922); and for governorship of California (1926, 1930). In 1934, he was narrowly defeated as the Democratic candidate for governor of California.

He published over 80 books, some of which were translated into more than 50 languages. His most well-known books include *The Jungle* (1906), *King Coal* (1917), *The Brass Check* (1919), *The Goose Step* (1923), *Oil* (1927), *Between Two Worlds* (1941), *Presidential Agent* (1944), *Presidential Mission* (1947), and *O Shepherd Speak* (1947).

In his book *Mental Radio: Does it Work, and How?* (1930), he detailed his investigations into the phenomena of **telepathy** with his wife, Mary Craig Sinclair. The book, to which **William McDougall** wrote the introduction to the English edition and Albert Einstein to the German edition, presents a lively account of the abilities of Mary Sinclair as a **sensitive,** or psychic. She first became aware of her powers after the death of several intimate friends. They were further awakened by her contact with Jan, a Pole, who had studied **yoga** in India and performed some of the feats of the **fakirs.** He was, for some time, a guest in the Sinclair home.

Upton Sinclair himself was, for some time, irritated by his wife's gift. In the waking state and in her dreams she could follow her husband and describe his doings. Finally he decided to experiment. The usual method was to make half a dozen drawings of anything that came into his mind. These were folded. His wife, in a dark room, would take them one by one, place them on her abdomen and then write or draw her impression.

The curious thing was that sometimes the second drawing was registered on her mind before she finished with the first one. When, for instance, a necktie was drawn, she added puffs of smoke at the end of the tie. The next object was a burning match.

Sinclair concluded:

"We have something more than telepathy, for no human mind knows what drawings she has taken from that envelope. No human mind but her own even knows that she is trying an experiment. Either there is some super-human mind or else there is something that comes from the drawings, some way of 'seeing' other than the way we know and use all the time."

Walter Franklin Prince made the Sinclair experiments the subject matter of the sixteenth bulletin of the **Boston Society for Psychic Research,** dealing also with a great deal of unpublished material and giving an account of a series of control tests with ten different persons. Upton Sinclair died November 25, 1968.

Sources:

Berger, Arthur S. and Joyce Berger. *The Encyclopedia of Parapsychology and Psychical Research.* New York: Paragon House, 1991.

Prince, Walter Franklin. *The Sinclair Experiments Demonstrating Telepathy.* Boston: Boston Society for Psychic Research, n.d.

Sinclair, Upton. *The Autobiography of Upton Sinclair.* N.p., 1962.

———. *Mental Radio: Does it Work, and How?* Pasadena, Calif.: The Author, 1930.

Sindonology

Term given to studies relating to the **Turin Shroud,** a burial shroud that some people have promoted as the one in which Jesus was wrapped after his crucifixion. A first Sindonological Congress, held in Turin in 1939, was attended by scholars, primarily Roman Catholic, who supported the claims of the Shroud, though the majority of those who have studied the cloth have pronounced it a product of the Middle Ages.

Sinnett, A(lfred) P(ercy) (1840–1921)

British journalist and occultist who played an important part in the affairs of the **Theosophical Society** during its first generation. He was born on January 18, 1840, in London. His father was a journalist and his mother a writer who had published numerous books. Sinnett became a journalist himself at the age of 19, working on the staff of the London *Globe.* Later he went to Hong Kong, where he became editor of the *Daily Press.* He returned to England in 1868 and became a writer on the *Standard,* then traveled to India to take a position as editor of the *Pioneer* in Allahabad in 1871.

He published some articles on **Spiritualism,** which led to a meeting with **Helena Petrovna Blavatsky** and **Henry S. Olcott,** founders of the Theosophical Society. Sinnett and his wife Patience became members. The subsequent publicity given to **Theosophy** in the *Pioneer* assisted its membership growth, but it cost Sinnett his job. He returned to London in 1883, where he became friendly with **Frederic W. Myers,** who (with **Edmund Gurney** and **Henry Sidgwick**) had founded the **Society for Psychical Research** a year earlier.

For a period, Sinnett was vice president of the Theosophical Society, but his independent views made it difficult for him to cooperate fully with other officials, although Sinnett's book *The Occult World* had attracted many individuals to the society. During his association with the society, Sinnett received a number of **Mahatma letters,** supposedly from the mysterious Masters who had directed the formation of the society. Sinnett's book *Esoteric Buddhism* was said to have derived from communications from the "Master K. H." on human evolution and cosmogony.

By 1887, Sinnett and his wife had formed associations with the Hermetic Order of the **Golden Dawn,** the pioneering **ceremonial magic** society. In 1896 the poet **William Butler Yeats,** a prominent member of the Golden Dawn, wrote that Sinnett was in charge of the order's neophytes. Sinnett was also friendly with the important occult and mystical writer **Arthur Edward Waite,** and with **Mary A. Atwood,** who sent Sinnett her library of alchemical texts.

Sinnett died June 26, 1921, at the age of 81. He had written a number of books, including many that grew out of his theosophical experience.

Sources:

Blavatsky, H. P. *Letters of H. P. Blavatsky to A. P. Sinnett.* Edited by A. T. Barker. London: T. Fisher Unwin, 1925.

Sinnett, A. P. *The Autobiography of Alfred Percy Sinnett.* London: Theosophical History Centre, 1986.

———. *Early Days of Theosophy in Europe.* London: Theosophical Publishing House, 1922.

———. *Esoteric Buddhism.* London: Trubner, 1883.

———. *The Growth of the Soul: A Sequel to "Esoteric Buddhism."* London: Theosophical Publishing Society, 1896.

———. *Incidents in the Life of Madame Blavatsky.* London: George Redway, 1886.

———. *The Mahatma Letters to A. P. Sinnett.* Edited by A. T. Barker. London: T. Fisher Unwin, 1924.

———. *The Occult World.* London: Trubner, 1881.

———. *The "Occult World Phenomena," and the Society for Psychical Research.* London: George Redway, 1886.

———. *The Rationale of Mesmerism.* Boston: Houghton, Mifflin, 1892.

Sirens

The sea nymphs of Greek mythology whose hypnotically sweet song lured mariners to their deaths. The island of the sirens had a meadow strewn with the bones of the victims of these deadly nymphs. In Homer's *Odyssey,* Odysseus has to steer his vessel past the island and takes the precaution of having his men fill their ears with wax to avoid hearing the siren song, while he himself is lashed to the vessel's mast. Jason and his band of heroes also had to sail past that island, but Orpheus sang so sweetly that he drowned out the song of the sirens. After Orpheus's song vanquished them, the sirens sprang into the sea and became rocks.

The sirens, two or three in number, were said to be the offspring of Phorcys or Achelous, and were part women, part birds. Some believed they were unhappy souls of the dead, envious of the living. The modern story of the **Lorelei** has something in common with the myths of the sirens.

The Sirius Mystery

Title of a book by Robert K. G. Temple (1972), discussing his discovery that a primitive African tribe, the Dogon of Mali in former French Sudan, apparently had been aware for centuries that the Dog Star Sirius was orbited by a white dwarf neighbor invisible to the naked eye and only recently discovered by astronomers. Temple claimed that this knowledge of the Dogon tribe was five thousand years old, that the white dwarf was known also to the ancient Egyptians in pre-dynastic times prior to 3200 B.C.E., and that the Dogon people may have partially descended from them. His idea was quickly integrated into the ancient astronaut hypothesis.

Sources:

Temple, Robert K. G. *The Sirius Mystery.* Folkstone, Kent, England: Bailey Brothers and Swinfen, 1972.

Sisters of the Amber

The Sisters of the Amber was an early **New Age** network around Merta Mary Parkinson. Parkinson headed two interlocking networks. The Dena Foundation catered to the general audience. The more committed female members were invited to be part of the Sisters of the Amber. Parkinson was intrigued by the healing power of amber, and she sent a piece of the fossil resin to each of the women who dedicated themselves to be linked to each other in a life of loving service.

Parkinson was among the early supporters of the Universal Link network, which developed in England in the 1960s and was active in the United States into the 1980s. She wrote several books, but her loosely organized network died soon after her death in 1983.

Sitchin, Zecharia

Zecharia Sitchin, an author of books offering an alternative history of the extraterrestrial origins of ancient humanity, was born in the 1920s in Baku, Russia. Soon after his birth his family moved to Palestine, where he grew up. He learned a variety of Near Eastern languages including Hebrew and Sumerian. He moved to England for college and attended both the London School of Economics and the University of London, from which he graduated with a degree in economics. He returned to Palestine, where he became a journalist. During World War II (1939–45) he served in the British Army. He moved to the United States in the mid-1950s.

In the 1970s, Sitchin's lifelong interest in the archeology of the Middle East culminated in a book, *The 12th Planet,* published in 1976. It appeared at the height of the **ancient astronaut** controversy that had been generated by claims of **Erich von Däniken** that he had discovered evidence of the presence of UFOs and extraterrestrials in the artifacts from various ancient cultures. Sitchin, out of his knowledge of ancient languages, proposed a new option concerning ancient history and lifted the debate to a new level. While the debate generated by von Däniken was largely resolved, Sitchin's hypothesis survived and has continued to be the subject of a series of books through the 1990s.

The von Däniken approach centered upon pictures from ancient sites that, taken out of context, could be seen as resembling contemporary astronauts and objects similar to items reported as unidentified flying objects. Sitchin started with a somewhat different hypothesis, that ancient mythology should be read as historical documents, as reports of actual occurrences. His starting point was the biblical book of Genesis, chapter 6, and the cryptic references to the sons of God marrying the daughters of men and the giants or *nephilim* who were on Earth in the era prior to the biblical flood. Using a variety of ancient documents, though primarily the Babylonian epic known as "Enuma Elish," he hypothesized the existence of another planet in our solar system, which he named Nibiru, that travels an eliptical orbit that brings it into the area between the orbits of Jupiter and Mars every 3,600 years. The planet is inhabited by a humanoid race called the Anunnaki, who created homo sapiens.

A war in the heavens, as described in the ancient Sumerian chronicles and the Bible, Sitchin believes, accounts for the ancients' knowledge of information that had only become available to modern science in recent centuries, especially the existence of the outer planets, Neptune, Uranus, and Pluto. He believes that the Anunnaki first arrived on Earth almost half a million years ago, their arrival motivated by the problem of an eroding atmosphere. They established a large gold mining operation in South **Africa,** and gold was shipped to Mesopotamia where the space port was set up to transport it to Nibiru. The Anannaki created humans to work the mines, then later intermarried with their creation. The near approach of Nibiru around 11,000 B.C.E. led to the destructive flood recounted in Genesis. Noah and his family escaped in a submersible ship. After the flood, life began again with the Anunnaki's assistance.

Given the hypothesis of human interaction with the Anunnaki, Sitchcin has been able to present an alternative reading of ancient history that, while ignored by the mainstream of modern archeologists and astronomers, has found a broad popular audience. *The 12th Planet* has been followed by five additional volumes, collectively termed the Earth Chronicles, that expand and undergird the original hypothesis. The most recent volume, *The Cosmic Code,* appeared in 1998.

Sitchin's hypothesis was given additional credibility by a lively debate among astronomers in the 1970s over the possible existence of an additional planet in the solar system, commonly referred to as Planet X. Sitchin identified Nibiru with the hypothesized Planet X. The astronomical debate, however, proceeded without reference to Sitchin, and by the 1990s astronomers had abandoned the search for Planet X. At the end of the 1990s, **Alan F. Alford,** whose 1998 book *Gods of the New Millennium* had been most supportive of Sitchin, attempted independently to verify Sitchin's hypothesis with his own research. In the end, however, he too abandoned Sitchin after encountering astronomical data suggesting the impossibility of some of Sitchin's claims about the way that Nibiru's close approach affected the Earth. He subsequently has produced a significant variant hypothesis that nevertheless retains much of Sitchin's alternative approach to history.

Sitchin resides in New York City. He has an Internet site: http://www.crystalinks.com/sitchen.html. There are a number of additional sites that discuss Sitchin's work.

Sources:

Alford, Alan F. *Gods of the New Millennium.* 1998. Reprint, London: Hodder and Stoughton, 1999.

———. *When the Gods Came Down.* London: Hodder and Stoughton, 2000.

Sitchin, Zecharia. *The Cosmic Code.* New York: Avon, 1998.

———. *The Stairway to Heaven.* Santa Fe, N.Mex.: Bear & Co., 1993.

———. *The 12th Planet.* 1976. Reprint, Santa Fe, N.Mex.: Bear & Co., 1991.

———. *The Wars of Gods and Men.* Santa Fe, N.Mex.: Bear & Co., 1992.

SITU See Society for the Investigation of the Unexplained

Sivananda, Swami (1887–1963)

One of the most influential modern Hindu spiritual teachers, whose most important contribution was the wedding of the traditional concept of *sannyas,* the renounced life, with social service directed toward people in need. Born Kuppuswami Iyer on September 8, 1877, in Pattamadai, near Tirunelveli in southern India, he was a son of Vengu Iyer, a revenue official and devotee of the Hindu deity Siva. Kuppuswami was educated in Ettayapuram, attending the Rajah's High School, where he was a good scholar and proficient in athletics. In 1903 he matriculated and went on to the Society for the Propagation of the Gospel College at Tiruchirappalli.

In 1905 he entered the Tanjore Medical Institute but was obliged to leave when the death of his father made it financially impossible to continue at the institute. He moved back to

Tiruchirappalli, where he started a medical journal, *Ambrosia,* in 1909. Soon afterward, he supplemented his small income from the journal by working at a pharmacy in Madras.

In 1913 Kuppuswami decided to take up medical work in Malaya, where he eventually earned a reputation for combining medical work, spiritual observance, and selfless service to the poor. By 1920 he was working with three European doctors and managing a hospital. He became a member of the Royal Institute of Public Health, London, a member of the Royal Asiatic Society, London, and an associate of the Royal Sanitary Institute, London. In addition he published several books, including *Household Remedies, Fruits and Health, Diseases and their Tamil Terms, Obstetric Ready Reckoner,* and *Fourteen Lectures on Public Health.*

During his spare time, he studied traditional **yoga** and **Vedanta,** spending much time in **meditation.** In 1923 he became increasingly preoccupied with the desire to realize spiritual truth. He gave up his job and returned to India. He became a religious mendicant, making pilgrimages to Varanasi (Benares), Poona, Nasik, Pandharpur, and Hardwar, staying at ashrams. In Rishikesh in northern India, a traditional holy place, he was formally initiated as a *sannyasi,* or renunciate, by Swami Viswananda, an elderly monk, and became Swami Sivananda Saraswati on June 1, 1924.

For some time, he lived at Swargashram by the side of the river Ganges, subjecting himself to intense spiritual discipline and using his medical knowledge to help the sick. He also made pilgrimages to Kedarnath and Badrinath, holy places high in the Himalayan mountains. He excited great enthusiasm by his popular lectures, inspiring chanting and singing of spiritual verses. In 1933 he was invited to attend the birthday celebration of Swami Ram Tirtha in Lucknow, and he subsequently traveled through India inspiring a great spiritual revival.

Returning to Rishikesh, he established an ashram in abandoned cowsheds on the banks of the Ganges in March 1934. With the help of disciples and supporters, the humble premises, named *Ananda Kutir* (hut of bliss), grew into a large self-contained community with a temple, hospitals, a pharmacy, a printing press for literature, and even a post office. As the **Divine Life Society,** the ashram sent its spiritual literature all over the world.

The rapid and successful establishment of the ashram was accelerated by the swami's dynamic personality and an astonishingly simple financial routine involving the spending of all donations on the day of receipt. Hindu swamis traditionally renounce the accumulation of wealth, so all contributions were immediately applied to practical purposes—feeding the sadhus of the district, maintaining hospital and medical treatment for the poor, leper relief, building huts, and developing a printing department for literature.

Integral yoga, Sivananda's unique system, which combined the practices of the various branches of traditional yoga, and Vedanta were propagated in hundreds of books and pamphlets and in the several magazines issued by the swami. They were often printed on poor-quality paper in quaint English as well as in the vernacular, yet they powerfully influenced thousands of devotees all over the world.

The Sivananda Ashram or Divine Life Society became a kind of Shangri-La in the foothills of the Himalayas, a half unreal world poised between past and present, between materialism and religion, between popular and advanced teaching. Part of its strange power lay in its paradoxical contrasts as a world in miniature, where high government officials and maharajahs rubbed shoulders with wandering mendicants, saints, and rogues. Each day, the swami would receive visitors and resident monks, giving instructions with a few succinct words, a gift, or a good-humored joke. In the evening, he would preside over *Satsang* (association of the wise), a kind of religious meeting at which visitors, Indian or Western, were encouraged to lecture, sing, dance, or tell a joke. Many individuals underwent a sudden uprush of spiritual awareness in this highly charged atmosphere.

Sivananda was credited with many miracles, and his teaching was often manifested obliquely in the collective unconscious of the ashram itself. The key to someone's problem might come from a casual remark from a stranger or the events of the day. One of the quaint but practical mottoes of the swami was, "Do it now!" In the same succinct manner, he condensed all religious teachings of various creeds to the simple formula, "Serve—Love—Give—Purify—Meditate—Realise. Be Good—Do Good—Be Kind—Be Compassionate. Inquire 'Who am I?'—Know the Self, and Be Free!"

Many swamis now well known in the Western world were disciples of Swami Sivananda or were influenced by his teachings. These include **Swami Vishnudevananda** (famous teacher of **hatha yoga**), Swami Venkateshananda, Swami Hridayananda (a woman, formerly an eye surgeon), **Swami Satchidananda** (founder of Integral Yoga Institute), Swami Jyotir Maya Nanda, **Swami Nadabrahmananda** (famous for his application of yoga principles to music), and **Swami Sivananda Radha** (Western founder of the **Yasodhara Ashram**).

After the death of Swami Sivananda on July 14, 1963, his successor as president of the ashram was his leading disciple, **Swami Chidananda,** the secretarial work continuing in the hands of Swami Krishananda.

Sivananda wrote a great number of books, and several biographies about him have been published. There are also two recordings of life at the Sivananda Ashram: *The Sounds of Yoga-Vedanta: Documentary of Life in an Indian Ashram* (Folkways Records, 33 1/3 rpm, Album 8970) and *Sounds of Sivananda Ashram,* volumes 1 and 2 (two C60 cassette tapes), issued by Ashram Records, Box 9, Kootenay Bay, BC, Canada VOB 1XO.

Sources:

Ananthanarayan, N. *From Man to God-Man.* New Delhi: The Author, 1970.

Krishnananda, Swami. *Swami Sivananda and the Spiritual Renaissance.* Sivanandanagar, India: Sivananda Literature Research Institute, 1959.

Omkarananda, Swami. *In Sivananda Literature.* Rishikesh, India: Sivananda Literature Research Institute, 1960.

Sivananda, Swami. *Practical Lessons in Yoga.* Sivanandanagar, India: Divine Life Society, 1978.

———. *Practice of Karma Yoga.* Sivanandanagar: Divine Life Society, 1980.

———. *Sadhana.* Sivanandanagar: Divine Life Society, 1967.

———. *Science of Yoga.* 18 vols. Durban, South Africa: Sivananda Press, 1977.

Sivananda Yoga Vedanta Centers See International Sivananda Yoga Vedanta Centers

Sixth Sense

The theory of the existence of a sixth sense as a convenient explanation of paranormal phenomena was first put forward in the era of **animal magnetism** by Tardy de Monravel in his *Essai sur la Théorie du Somnambolisme Magnétique* (1785). Departing from his mesmerist contemporaries, he considered the sixth sense as the source and sum of all our partial senses. (His colleagues attempted to explain **clairvoyance** and **prevision** by positing the existence of a "magnetic fluid.")

More recently the sixth sense has been given prominence as **Charles Richet**'s comprehensive term for the phenomena of **telepathy,** clairvoyance, **psychometry, premonition, prediction, crystal gazing,** and phantasmal appearances. They were, in Richet's view, manifestations of a new unknown sense that perceives the vibrations of reality. The conception is largely an attempt to do away with the spirit hypothesis, making its invocation unnecessary. Richet admitted, however, that the working of this sense is incomprehensible when a choice has to be made between vibrations of reality, for instance in the case of a **book test,** when the **sensitive** is called upon to read a certain line on a certain page in a certain book that nobody has opened.

His main argument in favor of his theory was that the hypothesis of the sixth sense as a new physiological notion contradicted nothing that we learn from physiology, whereas the spirit hypothesis does. A hint of Richet's term survived in the concept of **extrasensory perception** as used by **J. B. Rhine.**

Sources:

Richet, Charles *Notre Sixième Sens.* Paris: Editions Montaigne, 1928.

Sinel, Joseph. *The Sixth Sense.* London: T. W. Laurie, 1927.

The Skeptic (Newsletter)

Newsletter issued by a group associated with CSICOP (the **Committee for Scientific Investigation of Claims of the Paranormal**) and formerly named **The British & Irish Skeptic.** It is published four times a year, and the first issue (January/February 1987) included notes on the **James Randi** exposure of faith healer Peter Popoff, Ireland's claimed phenomena of Marian apparitions at **Knock,** and moving **statues.** The newsletter is edited by Wendy M. Grossman, at The Skeptic, PO Box 475, Manchester M60 2TH, England. Website: http://www.cix.co.uk/~philmck/skeptic/.

Sources:

The Skeptic. http://www.cix.co.uk/~philmck/skeptic/. March 8, 2000.

Skeptics Society

The Skeptics Society, one of the major American groups challenging claims to paranormal and supernatural reality which it considers largely in the realm of pseudoscience, was founded in 1991 by **Michael Shermer,** Pat Linse, and Kim Ziel Shermer. Michael Shermer, formerly a professional cyclist, completed his Ph.D. in the history of science in 1991. A former member of the **Committee for the Scientific Investigation of Claims of the Paranormal** (CSICOP), he felt that much more could be done in public education in this area by an organization that was located in the media nexus of Los Angeles and aggressively used radio and television as educational tools. He also wanted to launch a periodical that would allow for articles presenting more in-depth treatments of subjects and original research articles. Shortly after its founding, the society launched a quarterly newsstand magazine, *Skeptic,* which has a circulation of 40,000.

While focused upon claims of a psychic or occult nature, and the investigation of claims of supernatural miracles, the society has also involved itself in a variety of controversial issues of a scientific, psychological, historical, and religious nature, where no claim of paranormal or miraculous phenomena is present. Thus, while attacking such phenomena as claims to spirit contact or UFOs, the society has also attacked Holocaust denial as pseudo history and joined in the general denigration of minority religions (popularly called cults). Any issues that arise in public debate and include a crucial element of scientific (or social scientific) information in their resolution is considered an area of consideration.

The society currently pursues its expansive program through a monthly lecture series at the California Institute of Technology; an annual conference; a weekly radio show, "Science Talk," on the Southern California NPR affiliate, KPCC; and a national weekly television show on the Fox Family Channel. The society carries out its education through a book service that sells skeptical literature and cassette tapes. The Skeptics Society may be contacted at P.O. Box 338, Altadena, CA 91001. Its website can be found at http://www.skeptic.com/.

Sources:

Shermer, Michael. *Denying History.* Berkeley: University of California Press, 2000.

———. *How We Believe: The Search for God in an Age of Science.* New York: W. H. Freeman and Co., 2000.

———. *Why People Believe Weird Things.* New York: W. H. Freeman and Co., 1997.

Skoob Occult Review

Modern occult periodical reviving the title of the former *Occult Review,* which flourished in Britain from 1877 to 1948. *Skoob Occult Review* commenced publication in the spring of 1990 and has been published irregularly by Scoop Two Books, which has become a significant London-based occult publishing house and bookstore. The substantive periodical focuses on magic, occult, and esoteric subjects. Address: Skoob Two Books, 19 Bury Pl., London, WC1 2JH England.

Skotograph

A term (from the Greek for "dark-writing") proposed by Felicia Scatcherd for psychographs, spirit writing on photographic plates in unopened packets, and similar effects. Scatcherd was a member of the **Society for Psychical Research,** London, and helped **W. T. Stead** found **Julia's Bureau.** She was associated with the study of **psychic photography.** She died in 1927.

Madge Donohoe, widow of Martin H. Donohoe, British war correspondent of the *Daily Chronicle,* was known to produce a bewildering variety of skotographs—landscapes (often peopled), flowers, star constellations, jewels, birds, dogs, hands, eyes, and faces. Her gift was tested by F. W. Warrick, a chemical manufacturer and well-known British psychical researcher.

SKS See Specialist Knowledge Services

Skylook Bulletin See Mutual UFO Network (MUFON)

Skynet (Project)

Founded in 1965 by a team of physicists, engineers, scientists, and other individuals interested in **UFO** research. Project Skynet conducted scientifically-oriented research into UFOs in the Los Angeles and southern California area, investigated sightings worldwide, engaged in statistical studies, operated a tracking system to help identify UFOs, and worked with other UFO networks. Leaders of Skynet held no socioeconomic or philosophical opinions on the sightings, though individuals associated with it had reached various conclusions. Among those associated with Skynet was Ann Druffel, now an investigator for the **Mutual UFO Network.**

Skywatch (Journal)

Former quarterly publication of the Manchester Aerial Phenomena Investigation Team in England. Each issue included reports on local **UFO** sightings, information from other areas, letters from readers, and editorial comment on ufology.

Slade, Henry (d. 1905)

Controversial American medium, best known for his **slate-writing** phenomena. He was familiar to the American public for 15 years when the choice fell on him to demonstrate paranormal phenomena in St. Petersburg, Russia, before the investigators of the university of that city. **Helena Petrovna Blavatsky** and **Henry S. Olcott,** cofounders of the **Theosophical Society,** were asked to find a suitable medium and sit with him for weeks. They testified to "messages inside double slates, sometimes tied and sealed together, while they either lay upon the table in full view of all, or were laid upon the heads of members of the committee, or held flat against the under surface of the table-top, or held in a committee man's hand without the medium touching it."

En route to Russia, Slade arrived in England on July 13, 1876. He gave many sittings in London and was examined by both Spiritualists and non-Spiritualists. Besides slate writing he produced partial **materializations** and strong **telekinesis** phenomena. Observers reported seeing tables being moved, **matter passing through matter, levitation,** and musical instruments played by invisible hands. For six weeks all went well, his fame spread, and J. Enmore Jones, the editor of *The Spiritual Magazine,* declared that he was taking the place vacated by the great medium **D. D. Home.** *The World* wrote in a long article on August 30, 1876:

"Then came more and violent knockings at the table, a chair at the farthest corner from Dr. Slade was lifted rapidly in the air and hurled to the ground without visible agency. My coat and trousers were plucked violently, and I was pinched and patted, all with great rapidity, and in quarters which it seemed absolutely impossible Dr. Slade could reach. A hand appeared and disappeared fitfully, but with unmistakable reality, close to me; and when the slate was produced with a similar crumb of pencil, once on it when it was held under the table, and once under it when it was placed on the table, messages of various kinds were inscribed rapidly and in different handwritings. One, the longest, was of a religious character, and inculcated the usual religious lessons. Others were in reply to questions in which I pressed hard for a communication on some subject which could be only known to myself."

The article on the séance at which the reporter was alone with Slade and, presumably from the context, in daylight, concluded: "I had not, and have not, a glimmering of an idea how the effects described had been produced, and I came away inexpressibly puzzled and perplexed."

Slade was visited by men of science who were unable to explain what they saw. **Lord Rayleigh** stated at a meeting of the British Association for the Advancement of Science in September 1876 that he had attended a séance with Slade in the company of a professional conjurer, who admitted that he was completely puzzled. Slade convinced **Alfred Russel Wallace** of his genuine powers and "finally" solved the doubts of skeptic **Frank Podmore** as to the truth of **Spiritualism.**

Podmore, author of the skeptical work *Modern Spiritualism* (1902), preserved silence in his later writings over this stage of his beliefs, but he frankly admitted that he was profoundly impressed by Slade's performance.

Then, early in September 1876, at the peak of his fame, Slade was entangled in a serious controversy with accusations of **fraud.** Ray Lankester, who was outvoted as a member of the Selecting Committee of the British Association for the Advancement of Science when **William F. Barrett**'s paper on Spiritualism was admitted, intended to strike a deadly blow at this new "superstition" and when **Edward William Cox** told him of the puzzling slate-writing demonstrations of Slade, he went to Slade with his friend Dr. Donkin determined to unmask the medium at whatever cost.

He paid the usual fee of a pound, and in the second sitting he suddenly seized the slate before the writing was supposed to have taken place. He found a message ready, published his exposure on September 16 in *The Times,* and brought an action against the medium for obtaining money under false pretenses.

Over this exposure a fierce controversy ensued. Besides Lankester the skeptics were represented by **Henry Sidgwick,** R. H. Hatton, **Edmund Gurney,** and W. B. Carpenter. According to Podmore,

". . . the Spiritualists were perhaps justified in not accepting the incident as conclusive. Slade defended himself by asserting that, immediately before the slate was snatched from his hand, he heard the spirit writing, and had said so, but that his words were lost in the confusion which followed. If we grant that Slade's testimony was as good as Prof. Lankester's or Dr. Donkin's it was difficult summarily to dismiss this plea."

The case came up for trial at the Bow Street Police Court, London, on October 1, 1876. Evidence in favor of the genuineness of Slade's mediumship was given by Wallace, Cox, and George Wyld. Only four witnesses were allowed. The magistrate overruled their evidence, saying that he must base his decision on "inferences to be drawn from the known course of nature," and, on the ground of the deposition of Lankester and Donkin, he sentenced Slade, under the Vagrancy Act, to three months' imprisonment with hard labor.

In the course of the appeal, the conviction was nullified on technical grounds and Slade quickly left for the Continent before Lankester could obtain a fresh summons. However, Slade wrote from Prague, Czechoslovakia, offering exhaustive private tests to Lankester if he would let him come. To this he received no answer, nor did Slade come to London again until 1878, and later in 1887 under the assumed name of "Dr. Wilson."

Armed with many testimonies of Spiritualists and other people of distinction against the blot of the conviction, Slade spent interesting months on the Continent in the Hague, in Berlin, and in Denmark. In Berlin, Bellachini, the famous conjurer, testified on oath to his powers.

In St. Petersburg the séances were satisfactory, but owing to the disturbed state of Russia the investigation did not assume the character originally intended. A successful sitting was given to the Grand Duke Constantine in the presence of **Alexander Aksakof** and one Professor Boutlerof. According to an account there had been accidentally two bits of pencil on the slate. When he held it under the table the writing of two pencils was heard at the same time and when he drew out the slate it was found that one pencil had written from left to right, the other from right to left.

In December 1877, the experiments of **Johann Zöllner,** well-known in psychical literature, commenced in Leipzig. Zöllner hoped to establish his theory of four-dimensional space. Professors Fechner, Scheibner, and Weber participated in the investigation. Writing on sealed slates was produced under the strictest test conditions, knots were tied on an endless string, there were remarkable displays of force, and the apparent penetration of matter through matter was several times demonstrated.

After this brilliant success, Slade went to Paris and placed himself at the disposal of **Camille Flammarion,** "but I obtained nothing certain," stated Flammarion. He added:

"In the cases that did succeed, there was possible substitution of slates. Tired of so much loss of time, I agreed with Admiral Mouchez, director of the observatory of Paris, to confide to Slade a double slate prepared by ourselves, with the precautions which were necessary in order that we should not be entrapped. The two slates were sealed in such a way with paper of the observatory that if he took them apart he could not conceal the fraud. He accepted the conditions of the experiment. I carried the slates to his apartment. They remained under the influence of the medium, in this apartment, not a quarter of an hour, not a half hour or an hour, but ten consecutive days, and when he sent them back to us there was not the least trace of writing inside."

Charles Richet writes of the same period:

"I saw Slade once with Gibier. Slade handed me a slate and put a small fragment of a slate-pencil on it. I held one end and Slade the other, and we put the slate under the table. In a few moments we heard a noise as of writing. There was some writing and the bit of slate-pencil was worn. But I give this experiment (my only one of the kind) under all reserves: (1) It was long ago; (2) I cannot find the notes I took; (3) Slade's honesty is open to question; and (4) Experiments with slates lend themselves to trickery."

The next stage of Slade's career was his visit to Australia. His activities there were recorded in a book by James Curtis titled *Rustlings in the Golden City* (1894).

In 1885, he appeared before the **Seybert Commission** in Philadelphia. He was caught in glaring fraud. On one occasion, the sitters distinctly saw that his foot, before he had time to get it back into its slipper, was the instrument of claimed telekinetic phenomena. Once a slate, resting against the leg of the table, was upset by a sitter. It was seen that it had a message on it prepared in advance.

The writing obtained was generally of two kinds. The general messages were very legible and clearly punctuated, but when the communication came in answer to questions it was clumsy, scarcely legible, abrupt and vague. It bore traces of hasty work under difficult conditions, as these impromptu messages could not be prepared in advance.

According to the Seybert Committee's report, Slade declared that Zöllner watched him closely only during the first three or four sittings, but afterward let him do as he pleased. This was the starting point of Fullerton's trip to Germany to interview Zöllner's surviving colleagues in an attempt to discredit his favorable findings.

The exposure by the Seybert Commission was preceded by J. W. Truesdell's revelations. In *Bottom Facts of Spiritualism* (1883), he claimed to have caught Slade in cheating and narrates an amusing incident. He had discovered a slate with a prepared message in the séance room. He stealthily added another message of his own: "Henry, look out for this fellow; he is up to snuff—Alcinda." He says that he enjoyed Slade's discomfiture when, at the appropriate moment, the unrehearsed message came to light.

Another highly damaging incident was recorded on February 2, 1886, in the *Boston Herald,* namely an account of the denunciation of Slade as an impostor in Weston, West Virginia. Both Slade and his business manager were arrested but they were afterward released without prosecution.

During the last years of his life Slade fell victim to alcohol addiction; his moral standing was far from high, and he sank lower and lower. He died penniless and in mental decrepitude in a Michigan sanatorium in 1905.

Sources:

Curtis, James. *Rustlings in the Golden City.* Ballard, 1894.

Podmore, Frank. *Modern Spiritualism.* London: Methuen, 1902. Reprinted as *Mediums of the Nineteenth Century.* New Hyde Park, N.Y.: University Books, 1963.

Truesdell, J. W. *Bottom Facts of Spiritualism.* New York, 1883.

Slater, John (1861–1932)

American clairvoyant who, for 50 years, gave remarkable demonstrations of reading sealed letters and giving names, data, and specific information on deceased people from the platform. He traveled all over the United States and attracted big audiences. In 1930, he established his right to function as a medium in Detroit, Michigan. A clergyman had him arrested for making predictions, then a statutory offense, but he won the case with costs and continued his work thereafter undisturbed. He later moved to San Francisco.

Sources:

Slater, John. "Memories." *National Spiritualist* (September 1926).

Slater, Thomas (ca. 1872)

British spirit photographer, the first after the initial success of **Frederick A. Hudson** in England. He was an established optician and amateur photographer in London. After a sitting with Hudson in 1872, he experimented at his own home and, the family being mediumistic, obtained striking success.

By the side of a portrait of his sister two heads appeared on the plate. One of them was unmistakably Lord Brougham, the other, much less distinct, was recognized by Slater as **Robert Dale Owen.** The curious thing about this picture is that in 1856, when Slater was holding a séance with Lord Brougham and Robert Dale Owen, it was predicted by **raps** that the time would come when he would be engaged in **spirit photography.** Owen immediately remarked that if dead at the time he would attempt to appear.

Alfred Russell Wallace believed that the Slater pictures were genuine.

Slate Writing

A form of **direct writing,** or "autography," that has been one of the popular phenomena of séances. The method is the same in the majority of cases. The medium and the sitter take their seats at opposite ends of a small table, each grasping a corner of an ordinary school slate that they thus hold firmly pressed against the underside of the table. A small fragment of slate-pencil is first enclosed between slate and table, for the use of the spirit-writer. Should the séance be successful, a scratching sound, as of someone writing on a slate, is heard at the end of a few moments; three loud raps indicate the conclusion of the message; and on the withdrawal of the slate, it is found to be partly covered with writing—either a general message from the spirit world, or an answer to some question previously written down by the sitter.

Among the mediums who were most successful in obtaining spirit writing in this manner were **Henry Slade** and **William Eglinton.** The former, an American medium, came to England in 1876 and succeeded in mystifying a number of people of education and of scientific attainments. His critics attributed his success, in part at least, to his frank and engaging manner.

Ray Lankester exposed his trickery, and Henry Slade was prosecuted. Although sentenced to three months' hard labor, the omission of certain words in the accusation made the conviction of no effect. But Slade found that England had become too hot for him and speedily left.

Many of the accounts of his séances in different countries are of interest, chiefly because of the discrepancy that exists between the observations of credulous Spiritualists and those of trained investigators. **Richard Hodgson,** however, has pointed out that even in the latter class, instances of flawed observation were the rule rather than the exception, particularly where sleight of hand played a prominent part.

William Eglinton was a worthy successor to Slade as a medium for slate-writing manifestations and attained extraordinary popularity, with more than a hundred people testifying to his mediumistic powers in the Spiritualist journal *Light.* Speaking of Eglinton's performances, C. C. Massey of the Psychological Society said: "Many, of whom I am one, are of the opinion that the case for these phenomena generally, and for autography, in particular, is already complete."

Eglinton's manifestations were produced in full light, and his séances were seldom without results, so it is hardly surprising that many persons, ignorant of the lengths to which conjuring can be carried and overconfident in their own ability to observe correctly, should have seen in slate-writing a phenomenon explicable only by a Spiritualist theory.

But there was definite proof of **fraud** in several cases. Muslin and a false beard, part of the make-up of a "spirit," had been found in Eglinton's portmanteau, and various persons declared that they had seen his messages written on prepared slates previous to séances.

Other well-known exponents of slate-writing were **Fred P. Evans** and **Laura A. Pruden.**

Spiritualists themselves responded to exposures by asserting that fraud might occasionally be practiced by genuine mediums, owing to the uncertainty of the "power" and the constant expectation of phenomena. Particularly was this so in the case of professional mediums, who felt obliged to produce *some* results, and who had to resort to trickery when other means failed them.

S. J. Davey, an associate of the **Society for Psychical Research,** London, having discovered the tricks of slate-writing, practiced them himself and was accordingly claimed by certain Spiritualists as a medium as well as a conjurer, notwithstanding his protestations to the contrary! This was undoubtedly a powerful argument against the good faith of slate-writing. If his sitters could mistake these sleight-of-hand tricks (which Davey practiced with the express purpose of discrediting professional mediums) for genuine spirit manifestations, they might also be misled by the legerdemain of Slade and Eglinton, and other well-known mediums. It has been objected that even a skilled conjurer such as Professor Hoffmann (Angelo J. Lewis) professed himself mystified by slate-writing performances.

The methods adopted by Davey were of a simple nature, requiring little or no apparatus. In the case of a long, general message, he would prepare a slate beforehand and substitute it for the test slate. A shorter message, or a reply to a question, he would write on the reverse side of the slate, with a scrap of pencil fastened in a thimble, and so withdraw the slate that the side written on would be uppermost. There is reason to believe that similar devices were used in other séances for their simplicity and the absence of all apparatus rendered them particularly difficult to detect. But where the sitters were more credulous, intricate furniture and appliances were used and the most elaborate preparations made for the séance.

Slate writing is now a largely discredited phenomenon because it is open to conjuring fraud and it has never required anything in the nature of the reverent atmosphere of a Spiritualist séance. The businesslike way in which vague messages or answers to questions are obtained does not suggest either spirit agency or the operation of a paranormal faculty.

Sources:

Abbott, David P. *Behind the Scenes with the Mediums.* Chicago: Open Court; London: Kegan Paul, 1909.

———. *The Revelations of a Spirit Medium.* St. Paul: Farrington, 1891. Rev. ed., edited by Harry Price and E. J. Dingwall. London: Kegan Paul, 1922.

Farmer, John S. *'Twixt Two Worlds: A Narrative of the Life and Work of William Eglinton.* London: The Psychological Press, 1886.

Owen, J. J. *Psychography: Marvelous Manifestations of Psychic Power Given Through the Mediumship of Fred P. Evans.* San Francisco, 1893.

Slavs

The early Slavonic races passed down an extensive demonology embedded in a polytheistic religious system. It included reference to spirits of nature. According to folklorist F. S. Krauss:

"In the *vile,* also known as *Samovile, Samodivi,* and *Vilivrjaci,* we have near relations to the forest and field spirits or the wood and moss-folk of Middle Germany, France and Bavaria, the 'wild people' of Hesse, Eifel, Salzburg and the Tyrol, the woodwomen and woodmen of Bohemia, the Tyrolese Fanggen, Fanken, Norkel and Happy Ladies, the Roumanish Orken, Euguane, and Dialen, the Danish Ellekoner, the Swedish Skogsnufvaz, and the Russian Ljesje, while in certain respects they have affinity with the Teutonic Valkyries."

The vila were, however, more like divine beings, constantly watching over and controlling the destiny of mortals. They were prayed to or exorcised on all occasions. In short, their origin was shamanistic.

Nineteenth-century American writer and folklorist **Charles Godfrey Leland** remarked of this unseen spirit world, "We can still find the *vila* as set forth in old ballads, the incarnation of beauty and power, the benevolent friend of sufferers, the geniuses of heroes, the dwellers by rock and river and greenwood tree. But they are implacable in their wrath to all who deceive them, or who break a promise. Nay, they inflict terrible punishment even on those who disturb their rings, or the dances which they make by midsummer moonlight. Hence the proverb applied to any man who suddenly fell ill, 'he stepped on a fairy ring.' "

There were three varieties of nature spirits among the southern Slavs: the *Zracne vile,* or aerial spirits, which were evilly disposed to human beings and inflicted serious injuries upon them; will-'o-the-wisps, which led people astray by night; the *pozemne vile,* companionable spirits who gave sage counsel to humankind and dwelled in the earth; and the *podovne vile,* or water spirits, kindly to people on shore but somewhat treacherous in their own element.

Another water spirit was the *likho,* the Slavonic Polyphemus, a dreaded and terrible monster. The *leshy* was a wood demon, *Norka* was the frightful lord of the lower world, and *Koschei* was a kind of ogre whose specialty was the abduction of princesses.

Witchcraft

The witch was frequently mentioned in Slavonic folktales, especially among the southern Slavs. She was called *vjestica* (masculine *viestae*), meaning originally "the knowing one" or "the well-informed one." In Dalmatia and elsewhere among the southern Slavs the witch was called *krstaca,* "the crossed," in allusion to the idea that she was of the horned race of hell. It was said that it enraged the witches so much to be called by this word that when they heard that anyone had used it they went to his house by night and tore him into four pieces, which they cast to the four winds of heaven, and drove away all his cattle and stock. Therefore, the shrewd farmers of the country called the witch *hmana zena,* or "common woman."

There were many forms of Slavonic witches, however, and the *vjestica* differed from the *macionica* and the latter from the *zlokobnica,* or "evil-meeter," whom it was unlucky to encounter in the morning and who possessed the **evil eye.**

One Serbian authority related that he had often heard that "every female Wallach [Slav] as soon as she is forty years old, abandons the 'God be with us,' and becomes a witch (*vjestica*) or at least a *zlokobnica* or *macionica.* A real witch has the mark of a cross under her nose, a *zlokobnica* has some hairs of a beard, and a *macionica* may be known by a forehead full of dark folds with blood-spots in her face."

In southern Slavonian countries on St. George's Day, the peasants adorned the horns of the cattle with garlands to protect them from witches. They attached great importance to a seventh or a twelfth child, believing that children born in that order were the great protectors of the world against witchcraft. But children of that order were thought to be in great danger on St. John's Eve, for then the witches, having the most power, attacked them with stakes or the stumps of saplings, which is why the peasantry carefully removed everything of the kind from the ground in the autumn.

The Slavs believed that on St. George's Day the witches climbed into the steeples of churches to get the grease from the axle of the bell, which, for some reason, they greatly prized.

The *krstnik,* or wizards, notoriously attracted female vila, who in most instances desired to be their mistresses, just as female salamanders desired to mate with men. (See the *Curiosa* of Heinrich Kornmann, 1666.) The man who gained the love of a vila was supposed to be extremely lucky.

Transformation stories were also fairly common in Slavonic folklore, which indicates that this was a form of magic practiced by the witches of those countries. (See also **Seventh Son**)

Slawensik Poltergeist

A curious **poltergeist** case in 1806 in the Castle of Slawensik, Upper Silesia. Councillor Hahn, in the service of the Prince of Hohenlohe, was directed to proceed to Slawensik, where he stayed in the castle with his old friend Charles Kern, attended by John, Hahn's servant.

On the third day of their residence, the disturbances commenced with a shower of lime, apparently from the ceiling. This was repeated the next day, accompanied by the sound of heavy blows. Soon afterward, noises like a beating drum and a sound as if someone was walking around the room with slippers on and striking a stick on the door were heard. Soon various small articles in the room were thrown around, including knives, forks, brushes, caps, slippers, padlocks, funnels, snuffers, and soap, while lights darted from corner to corner. The showers of lime and heavy noises continued. Various witnesses were called and confirmed the phenomena.

One day, Kern saw a figure in the mirror staring at him, apparently interposed between himself and the glass. Another evening, Hahn was about to shave when the soapbox, razor, brush, and soap flew at him and fell at his feet. When he tried to sleep he was awakened by the heavy noises, and once it seemed as if someone had sprinkled water on him while he lay in bed, although he could find no water.

Hahn then made a journey to Breslau, but when he returned he was told that rather than be alone, Kern had asked Hahn's servant John to stay in the room with him.

As Kern lay in his bed, John was talking to him when he saw a jug of beer slowly lift to a height of about three feet and pour into a glass until it was half full. The jug was then gently replaced and the glass lifted and emptied as if by some invisible specter. John exclaimed in terrified surprise, "Lord Jesus! It swallows!" The glass was quietly replaced.

After some time, the disturbances ceased as suddenly as they had begun. Hahn wrote a detailed narrative of the events and signed it November 19, 1808. Many years later the castle was destroyed by lightning, and among the ruins was found the coffinless skeleton of a man, his skull split open and a sword by his side. It was believed by some that Kern may have been a powerful sensitive.

Sources:

Crowe, Catherine. *The Night Side of Nature; or, Ghosts and Ghost Seers.* N.p., 1848. Reprint, Philadelphia: R. West, 1978.

Sleep

A state of unconsciousness or partial consciousness in which, according to psychical belief, the human organism is being perpetually replenished with energy from an unseen world. **Hereward Carrington,** writing in *Your Psychic Powers and How to Develop Them* (1920), notes: "Various theories have been advanced in the past to explain sleep, but no satisfactory theory has even been fully accepted. Thus we have the so-called 'chemical theories,' which endeavor to account for sleep by assuming that certain poisonous substances are formed in the body during waking hours and are eliminated during sleep. Others have suggested that sleep is due to peculiar conditions of the circulations of blood in the brain; still others that the action of certain glands explains sleep; others that muscular relaxation accounts for it, others that the lack of external stimuli is sufficient to induce profound slumber. All these theories have been shown insufficient to explain the facts. We shall never arrive at a satisfactory theory of sleep, doubtless, until we admit the presence of a *vital force* and the existence of an individual *human spirit* which withdraws more or less completely from the body during the hours of sleep, and derives spiritual invigoration and nourishment during its sojourn in the spiritual world."

In the paranormal phenomena observed in dreams and the hypnotic state, **F. W. H. Myers** found indications that "the self of sleep is a spirit freed from ordinary material limitations, and this conclusion conforms to the hypothesis that we live in two worlds; the waking personality is adapted to the needs of terrestrial life, the personality of sleep maintains the fundamental connection between the spiritual world and the organism, so as to provide the latter with energy while developing itself by the exercise of its spiritual powers."

Related to theories of sleep are theories on **astral projection,** also known as OBE (out-of-body experience) or soul traveling, in which the soul is said to leave its body, and travel about the astral plane. People who experience this, claim OBEs eliminate their fears of death, while convincing them of their connection to the spiritual realm. Writer **Sylvan J. Muldoon,** explains the theory through his own experience: "the astral body discoincides during sleep for the purpose of recharging and the depth of sleep and the amount of recuperation depend upon the distance between the astral and physical bodies; i.e., the greater the distance of separation, the freer the inflow of cosmic energy, or prana, into it." Precursors to astral projection are lucid dreaming (an awareness of the self in dream state) and interrupted sleep (in which the physical body arises during the sleep state).

Considerable study is presently being conducted in the area of Rapid Eye Movement (REM) sleep. REM sleep is said to constitute between 20 and 50 percent of sleep activity. During this type of sleep, the brain seems to behave as if the body is awake: brainwave activity is high, heart rate increases, and sexual stimulation occurs. It is during this REM period that most of the night's dream activity—and perhaps paranormal activity—occurs.

While the increased neural activity during REM sleep may facilitate the development and maturation of the nervous system in infants, the role of REM in adults remains unclear. William C. Dement of the Stanford Sleep Disorders Clinic proposes some of the possibilities:

"There is strong evidence that REM sleep plays a role in the regulation of mood and/or drive; that it is related in some way to excitability of the central nervous system; and that its suppression may in some way jeopardize the learning and memory functions. The occurrence of large amounts of REM sleep among newborn infants remains possibly the most provocative puzzle of all; it suggests a very important role for REM in the earliest stages of life."

Another subject currently receiving significant attention is sleep deprivation. Murphy, in an article written for the *Atlantic Monthly* (1996), asserts Americans living a century ago could sleep 20% longer than the average American today. Ten million Americans each year seek medical, alternative medical, or therapeutic help for the treatment of sleeping disorders. Also sleep deprivation is thought to be a greater contributor to traffic fatalities than intoxication. Severe sleep deprivation is known to cause substantial detrimental alterations in both behavior and perception. Since a considerable amount of people who have been deprived of sleep report paranormal experiences, there exists the question of what role sleep deprivation plays in perceived paranormal incidents.

Sources:

Angoff, Allan, ed. *The Psychic Force: Essays in Modern Psychical Research from the International Journal of Parapsychology.* New York: G. P. Putnam's Sons, 1970.

Bigelow, J. *The Mystery of Sleep.* London: Unwin; New York: Harper, 1903.

Braid, James. *Neurypnology; or, The Rationale of Nervous Sleep.* London, 1843. Reprint, AMS Press, 1976.

Cohen, D. *Sleep and Dreaming: Origins, Nature and Functions.* New York: Pergamon Press, 1981.

Crookall, Robert. *During Sleep: The Possibility of "Co-operation" Between the Living and the Dead.* New Hyde Park, N.Y.: University Books, 1974.

Dement, William C. *Sleepwatchers.* Stanford: Stanford Alumni Association, 1992.

———. *Some Must Watch While Some Must Sleep: Exploring the World of Sleep.* San Francisco: San Francisco Book, 1976. Reprint, New York: Norton, 1978.

Green, Celia E. *Lucid Dreams.* London: Hamish Hamilton, 1968.

Hammon, A Christopher. "If You Don't Snooze, You Lose: Getting a Good Night's Sleep is Critical to Productivity and Creativity." *http://www.quantadynamics.com.* September 27, 1997.

Jones, Richard M. *The New Psychology of Dreaming.* New York: Grune & Stratton, 1970.

Jyotir Maya Nanda, Swami. *Waking, Dream, and Sleep.* Miami, Fla.: Yoga Research Foundation, 1974.

Muldoon, Sylvan, and Hereward Carrington. *The Projection of the Astral Body.* London: Rider, 1929.

Murphy, Cullen. "Hello Darkness: Dealing with Yet Another Deficit." *Atlantic Monthly* March 1996. 22–24.

Perl, James. *Sleep Right in Five Nights.* New York: William Morrow and Co., Inc. 1993.

Taylor, Albert. *Soul Traveler.* Covina, Calif.: Verity Press, 1996.

Ullman, Montague, and Stanley Krippner. *Dream Studies and Telepathy: An Experimental Approach.* New York: Parapsychology Foundation, 1970.

The Sleeping Preacher (1794– ?)

Rachel Baker, known as "the Sleeping Preacher," was born at Pelham, Massachusetts, in 1794. When she was nine years old, her parents moved to Marcellus, New York. As a child she had religious training, her parents being devout people, and she manifested a strong conviction about sinfulness. In 1811 she showed symptoms of **somnambulism,** in which she seemed stricken with horror and despondency. But gradually her mind became calmer, and she delivered discourses of singular clarity, marked by a devout and solemn tone. Reportedly, these fits of somnambulism, or trance-speaking, seized her regularly every day.

She began and concluded her devotional exercises with prayer, between which came the discourse. Then a period of apparent physical distress appeared, characterized by shaking, sobs, and groans. At length the paroxysms passed, and she would fall into a natural sleep. Change of scene did not affect these exercises, but the administration of opium would interrupt them.

Such **trance** sermons later became an integral phenomenon of the Spiritualist movement. Among famous later trance speakers were Nettie Colburn (**Henrietta Maynard**), remembered for the trance address before **Abraham Lincoln,** and **Louis Anne Meurig Morris** in Britain. Trance addresses of an inspirational or a spiritually guiding nature became an important part of the modern **New Age** movement under the label **channeling.**

Sources:

Devotional Somnium; or a Collection of Prayers and Exhortations Uttered by Rachel Baker . . . During her Abstracted and Unconscious State. New York, 1815.

Remarkable Sermons of Rachel Baker and Pious Ejaculations Delivered During Sleep Taken Down in Shorthand. London, 1815.

Sloan, John C. (1870–1951)

British physical medium of Glasgow, Scotland. He worked as a packer in a warehouse and later operated a small shop. Unlike many professional mediums, he accepted no remuneration for his séances, and worked without the use of a **cabinet.** He had as a spirit control "White Feather," a Native American, a genial personality who preferred to be called "Whitey." He spoke both through the medium's vocal organs and provided **direct voice** phenomena through a **trumpet.**

To have the medium at the disposal of the **British College of Psychic Science, James Hewat McKenzie** found employment for Sloan in a London garage and made him accessible to various experimenters. After his return to Glasgow, Sloan cooperated in experiments with **J. Arthur Findlay.**

In 1924, Findlay published a small book on his findings: *An Investigation of Psychic Phenomena,* with a preface by **Sir William Barrett.** This was followed by a larger volume: *On the Edge of the Etheric* (1931), in which Findlay graded his evidential cases A1 and A2, according to the quality of the evidence.

Examining three of the 180 A1 communications, he stated: "An eminent mathematician on calculating the chances of correctly guessing all the facts recorded, answers that to have reached such accuracy, represented the equivalent of 1 to 5,000,000,000,000 in other words the odds were 5,000,000,000,000 to 1 against chance being the explanation."

Sources:

Findlay, J. Arthur. *An Investigation of Psychic Phenomena.* N.p., 1924.

———. *On the Edge of the Etheric.* London: Rider, 1931.

Slocum, John (1842–1897)

John Slocum, a Native American prophet and visionary, was a member of the Squaxin people who resided on Puget Sound in the state of Washington. Among his people he was known as Squ-sacht-un. As a young man he had lived on the Skokomish reservation, where he attended a Presbyterian church and also became familiar with the Roman Catholic faith. In October of 1881 he found himself giving strong consideration to the problems that afflicted the Native Americans of Puget Sound and the manner in which they had been ravaged by alcohol, gambling, and general immorality. He was himself among the guilty. As he contemplated his condition, he became ill and apparently died one morning about 4 a.m. He was considered dead by those present and preparation began for his burial. Then in the middle of the afternoon, he awoke and announced to all present that he had been to heaven. He saw the light, so frequently mentioned in accounts of **near-death experiences,** and faced a life review. He also, at one point, looked down upon his own body.

At the gates of heaven, according to Slocum's account, he had been turned back because of his immoral life. He encountered some angelic beings who gave him a choice of going to Hell or returning to Earth to teach his people the way to heaven. He announced that all should be Christians and requested that a church be built. Within a short time, some 50 people associated with the church. The movement subsequently spread among the various Native American groups in the area.

The teachings of the new church combined elements of Presbyterianism, Catholicism, and the traditional religion of his people. Among the traditional practices, members of a secret society were known to go into a **trance** and commune with various spirit entities. Slocum taught a form of Christianity, but downplayed the Bible in favor of his own contacts with heaven that he felt were more immediate and relevant than an old book. He emphasized moral living as a prerequisite to heaven.

A short time after the founding of the church, he fell ill again. His wife, Mary, began to pray for him. In her concern she began to shake and tremble. When Slocum recovered, he attributed his getting better to the shaking. Very soon afterwards, the members began to copy Mary Slocum's movements and soon were demonstrating a range of exuberant body movements that had been a familiar part of revival and camp meetings among Protestant religious groups. Because of this shaking, they became known as the Shaker religion. The members also adopted a form of ritualized prayer for the sick.

The Shaker Church was incorporated in 1892. Slocum led it for the rest of his life but as the end of his earthly life drew near, he withdrew from the public, and the exact place and date of his death is unknown. His church continues to the present.

Sources:

Barnett, H. G. *Indian Shakers: A Messianic Cult of the Pacific Northwest.* Carbondale, Ill.: Southern Illinois University, 1957.

Mooney, James. "The Ghost-Dance Religion and the Sioux Outbreak of 1890." In the *Fourteenth Annual Report of the Bureau of Ethnology.* Compiled by J. W. Powell. Washington: Government Printing Office, 1896.

Slomann, Aage (1891–1970)

Danish chemical engineer who was concerned with parapsychology. He was born on October 25, 1891, at Copenhagen. He graduated as a chemical engineer in 1914 at the Technical University of Denmark. He worked as a chemical engineer in Denmark (1914–18), in Bordeaux, France (1919–20), and in New York (1920–31). He returned to Denmark where he was a factory superintendent for Colgate-Palmolive in Copenhagen until his retirement (1932–56).

Slomann was particularly interested in qualitative research and philosophical aspects of parapsychology, and he lectured on psychical research throughout Scandinavia and broadcast over Danish radio. He was a member of the executive committee of the Danish Society for Psychical Research beginning in 1950, named honorary librarian and research officer in 1956, and elected president in 1961. He was a member of the **Society for Psychical Research** (SPR) and the Swedish Society for Parapsychological Research, and he was a charter associate of the **Parapsychological Association.**

In 1959, he completed a two-year survey of paranormal phenomena in Denmark. He published many articles on parapsychology in the *Journal* of the American Society for Psychical Research, the *Journal* of the SPR, and the Danish parapsychological journals *Psykisk Forum* and *Psykisk Information.*

Sources:

Pleasants, Helene, ed. *Biographical Dictionary of Parapsychology.* New York: Helix Press, 1964.

"Smagorad"

A mysterious book of magic power in the possession of Arnaud Guillaume in 1393, during the reign of Charles VI of France.

Smaragdine Table

Believed to be the earliest statement of the principles of spiritual **alchemy,** ascribed to **Hermes Trismegistus.** It was said to have been inscribed on emerald (smaragdine) in Phoenician letters and was generally referred to as the **Emerald Table of Hermes.**

Smead, Mrs. (ca. 1902)

Pseudonym of Mrs. Willis M. Cleveland, wife of an American preacher to whom **James H. Hyslop**'s attention was invited in December 1901. Smead had occasionally practiced **planchette** writing from her childhood and began systematic experiments in 1895. Records were kept of the communications received and put at Hyslop's disposal. He was impressed with both Willis Cleveland and Mrs. Smead as honest, conscientious people. The communicators claimed to be the deceased children of the couple and a deceased brother of Willis Cleveland's. Their identities were very plausible.

A curious feature of Smead's mediumship began to develop when in August 1895 several references were made to the planets Mars and Jupiter. A short time before, an article by Percival Lowell was published in the *Atlantic Monthly* that referred to the canals of the planet Mars. This article may have had something to do with Smead's new variety of phenomena in which Jupiter played an additional but minor part.

A crude map of Jupiter's surface was given, and the planet was said to be the "babies' heaven." At the next sitting, the map of Mars was drawn, the different zones were named in Martian, and several communications were given about the inhabitants and the canals.

There followed then an incubation period of five years during which no Martian revelations were granted. In September 1900, the communications returned in a developed state. Men, boats, houses, and flowers were drawn, named in Martian, and written in hieroglyphic characters. Some of the sketches, such as one of a self-winding double clock, were very ingenious; others, like a Martian airship, were peculiar but unconvincing. A curious coincidence existed with **Hélène Smith,** the French medium studied by **Theodore Flournoy,** who also produced Martian drawings.

In general, according to Flournoy's review in *Spiritism and Psychology,* "the Martian revelations of Mrs. Smead present the same character of puerility and naive imagination as those of Mlle. Smith." He could only think that the psychological explanation was at basis the same. Flournoy's book was actually in the house, but it was carefully kept from the medium.

The number of Martian scripts continued to increase until a new **personality,** calling himself "Harrison Clark," abruptly came on the scene and shut out all other communicators. He showed great facility in inverted and mirror writing and gave his autobiography. When he was confronted by Hyslop with the findings of his investigation, he began "a battle of intellectual sparring and defiance which perhaps has hardly its equal in the annals of secondary personality."

For a considerable period, Hyslop attributed all the communications to a secondary personality. In this view Hyslop was confirmed by the controls of the medium **Leonora Piper.** They sent a message to Hyslop that he should be wary. "The so-called light as seen by us is not a light given from our world at all, but the conditions are hypocritic and fanciful."

Later, however, the mediumship improved, scraps and bits of paranormal information came through, and, although at first Hyslop only classified the case as an intermediate one between Smith and Piper, he later surrendered his hesitations and admitted the existence of genuinely paranormal phenomena beyond question.

Smells (Psychic)

Smells appearing in the séance room have often been ascribed to a paranormal origin. **Materializations** in sittings with the medium **Franek Kluski** were associated with strong animal odors. Psychic perfumes were reported at séances of **Carlos Mirabelli** and **Daniel Dunglas Home.** (See also **Odor of Sanctity; Perfumes**)

Smith, Alson Jesse (1908–1965)

Writer and lecturer on religion and parapsychology. He was born on August 12, 1908, at Danbury, Connecticut. He studied at Dickinson College, Carlisle, Pennsylvania (B.A., 1930) and Garrett Biblical Institute (now Garrett Theological Seminary), Evanston, Illinois (B.D., 1933). He was ordained as a minister in the Methodist Episcopal Church, and after a year in Montana (1933–34) he served churches in New York and Connecticut for 20 years (1935–54). He retired from the active ministry in 1954 and became a full-time author and lecturer. In the years after World War II he wrote a number of books including several on the psychic. He was a member of Spiritual Frontiers fellowship (now the International Spiritual Frontiers Fellowship) in its initial years. He died May 17, 1965.

Sources:

Pleasants, Helene, ed. *Biographical Dictionary of Parapsychology*. New York: Helix Press, 1964.

Smith, Alson Jesse. *Faith to Live By*. Garden City, N.Y.: Doubleday, 1949.

———. *Immortality: The Scientific Evidence*. N.p., 1954.

———. *Psychic Source Book*. New York: Creative Age Press, 1951.

———. *Religion and the New Psychology*. Garden City, N.Y.: Doubleday, 1951.

Smith, Barbara Gosline (1909–1994)

Newspaper columnist who studied parapsychological subjects. She was born on November 4, 1909, in Dallas, Texas. She studied at the University of California at Los Angeles (B.A., 1929) and the University of Southern California (M.A., 1933). She was successively an elementary school teacher (1930–35), high school teacher (1935–45), and college instructor (1945–50). In 1950 she became a freelance writer. She was a member of Bema Forensic Society. With **Karlis Osis** she investigated possible relationships between religious backgrounds and ESP among elementary school children.

She died on January 7, 1994.

Sources:

Pleasants, Helene, ed. *Biographical Dictionary of Parapsychology*. New York: Helix Press, 1964.

Smith, Hélène (1861–1929)

Pseudonym of Catherine Elise Muller of Geneva, the medium whose case caused much dissension among continental psychologists for many years and was considered as the Dreyfus case of science by some. Had **Theodore Flournoy** not written his brilliant work *Des Indes à la Planète Mars* (English ed. as *From India to the Planet Mars,* 1900), in which he psychoanalyzed and presented the more mundane explanations of some of her more extraordinary phenomena, she might have been acclaimed as the greatest medium of her time, the first human being to whom the glory was due of having established intelligent communication with Mars and of having revealed the language and writing of the red planet. Her work occurred, of course, long before the modern triumphs of interplanetary research and space probes that have revealed the actual nature of the surfaces of Mars and Venus.

Smith's father, a merchant, was a Hungarian who possessed a remarkable facility for languages; her mother had sporadic visions but showed no mediumistic powers. As a young girl, Smith was always fond of indulging in daydreams. She used to see highly colored landscapes, a lion of stone with a mutilated head, and fanciful objects on pedestals. These visions made her discontented. She asked her parents on one occasion whether she was really their child or a changeling. When 14 or 15 years old, she saw a bright light thrown against the wall of her room, which then seemed to be filled with strange and unknown things.

She heard of **Spiritualism** for the first time in the winter of 1891–92. An acquaintance lent her the book *D'Après la Mort* by Leon Denis. It excited her curiosity and led her to a Spiritualist circle. At the second séance that she attended, her hand moved automatically. Soon the table began to move and in April 1892, a spirit communicated through **typtology** and said that he was **Victor Hugo,** her guide and protector. His reign as a **control** lasted undisturbed for about six months. Then another control appeared, "Leopold," who, against the warning of "Victor Hugo," forced the medium into trance and, after a struggle lasting for a year, completely ousted his predecessor.

At this period Smith possessed every attribute of a powerful medium. She produced **telekinesis** phenomena and strange **apports,** found lost objects, predicted future events, saw spirit visitors, clairaudiently heard their names, and received the explanation of visions that unfolded before her eyes by **raps.**

Flournoy was admitted to her circle in the winter of 1894–95. The séances that he attended for five years alternated with a series given to August Lemaitre and one Professor Cuendet, vice president of the Geneva Society for Psychic Studies. In his book *From India to the Planet Mars* (1900), Flournoy notes,

"I found the medium in question to be a beautiful woman about thirty years of age, tall, vigorous, of a fresh, healthy complexion, with hair and eyes almost black, of an open and intelligent countenance, which at once invoked sympathy. She evinced nothing of the emaciated or tragic aspect which one habitually ascribes to the sybils of tradition, but wore an air of health, of physical and mental vigour, very pleasant to behold, and which, by the way, is not often encountered in those who are good mediums."

In describing her triple mediumship (visual, auditive and typtological) he admitted:

"Speaking for myself alone . . . I was greatly surprised to recognize in scenes which passed before my eyes events which had transpired in my own family prior to my birth. Whence could the medium, whom I had never met before, have derived the knowledge of events belonging to a remote past, of a private nature, and utterly unknown to any living person?"

The professor made good friends with the spirit control "Leopold." The secret of his identity, which for a long time he refused to reveal, was already known. He claimed to have been Guiseppe Balsamo, alias **Cagliostro.** With the exception of Flournoy, everybody believed in his existence as a spirit. Even he admitted that "it would be impossible to imagine a being more independent and more different from Smith herself, having a more personal character, and individuality more marked, or a more certain actual existence."

When "Leopold" wrote with Smith's hand she held the pen in a different way and her handwriting differed from her usual calligraphy and showed the style of the last century. The voice of "Leopold" was a deep bass. He had a strong, easily recognizable Italian accent.

But Flournory was firm in his conviction that "there is no reason to suspect the real presence of Joseph Balsamo behind the automatisms of Mlle. Smith." He traced the psychogenesis of "Leopold" to a great fright that she had when ten years old. She was attacked in the street by a big dog. She was terrified but the terror was dispelled by the sudden appearance, as if by a miracle, of a personage clothed in a long brown robe with flowing sleeves and with a white cross on the breast who chased the dog away and disappeared before she had time to thank him.

"Leopold" claimed that this was his first appearance. Whenever some unpleasant sight or a dangerous encounter lay in her way the phantom always rose at a distance of about ten yards, walked or glided in silence at the same rate as she advanced toward him, attracting and fascinating her gaze in such a manner as to prevent her turning her eyes away either to the right or left, until she passed the place of danger.

Flournoy found some curious analogies between what is known to us of Cagliostro and certain characteristics of "Leopold," but he believed that they accorded well with the subliminal medley. "Leopold" did not know Italian and turned a deaf ear if anyone addressed him in that language. His handwriting showed striking dissimilarities to that known of the real Cagliostro. His answers to questions regarding his terrestrial existence were evasive or vague. He did not furnish a single name, date, or precise fact. He was, on the other hand, as archaic in his therapeutics as in his orthography and treated all maladies in an old-fashioned way. He claimed that his sentiments for Smith were only the continuation of those of Cagliostro for Marie Antionette.

Marie Antoinette was the first great romance of Smith's mediumship. Flournoy called it the "Royal Cycle." It was roughly outlined at séances in the house of Cuendet in December 1893. The announcement that Smith was the reincarnation of the late queen was made by the table on January 30, 1894. In the interval she had for some time believed herself to be the reincarnation of Lorenze Feliciani. When, however, she was told that Lorenze Feliciani only existed in the fantasy of novelist Dumas, she quickly dropped this role.

There was less difference between the autograph of Cagliostro and "Leopold" than between the handwriting of the real Marie Antoinette and the somnambulistic one. The role of the queen was acted in a very lifelike manner. Probably Smith's tastes for everything that was noble, distinguished, and elevated made the task easier. In the surroundings of the queen, the king was conspicuous by his absence. Three personages figured most often. "Cagliostro" ("ce cher sorcier"), "Louis Philippe d'Orleans," and the "Marquis de Mirabeau." They were discovered reincarnated in two sitters: M. Eugene Demole and M. August de Morsier. For the spectators, the royal somnambulism was the most interesting on account of the brilliancy and life of the role and the length of time during which it was sustained. But for lovers of the paranormal it was not in the least extraordinary.

The Hindu dream in which Flournoy was cast in the role of Prince Sivrouka Nayaka began on October 16, 1894, eight weeks before his admission to the circle. The Martian romance dated from the same period and was to be attributed, in Flournoy's view, to an involuntary suggestion of one Professor Lemaitre. In the Oriental Cycle, Smith was Simandini, the daughter of an Arab sheik in the sixth century, and was courted and married by Prince Sivrouka, lord of the fortress of Tchandraguiri built in the province of Kanara, Hindustani, in 1401. After many years of married life she was burned alive on her husband's funeral pyre.

In enacting the role of the Oriental princess, Smith spoke Hindustani and wrote a few words in good Arabic. She did not speak it. While recovering in trance the use of Hindustani, which she formerly spoke at the court of Sivrouka, she appeared to have forgotten her mother tongue. Her Hindustani was a mixture of improvised articulations and of veritable Sanskrit words well adapted to the situation. This means that it expressed personal thought and was not merely a series of senseless phrases. Besides Flournoy, Professor Seipel, another investigator, also figured in the Oriental romance. He was an Arab slave.

Historians appeared to be singularly ignorant of Kanara, Sivrouka, and Simandini. One day, however, Flournoy accidentally came across an old history of India by De Marles printed in Paris in 1828 and found in it a confirmation of the main facts. It was objected that De Marles was a very unreliable historian. The fact was, however, that only two copies of the work existed in Geneva, both covered with dust. Only in a combination of absolutely exceptional and almost unimaginable circumstances could the work have found its way into Smith's hands.

Flournoy saw himself forced to admit that the precise historical information given by "Leopold" and the language spoken by "Simandini" defied normal explanation. He said:

"The Hindoo romance, in particular, remains for those who have taken part in it a psychological enigma, not yet solved in a satisfactory manner, because it reveals and implies in regard to Hélène, a knowledge relative to the costumes and languages of the Orient, the actual source of which it has up to the present time not been possible to discover."

The Martian romance, one of the outstanding modern claims of **planetary travels,** was the most striking of all. In November 1894, the spirit of the entranced medium was carried to the planet Mars. She described the human, animal, and floral life of the planet from night to night and supported her story by writing in Martian characters and speaking fluently in that language. Suggestive of **xenoglossis,** the characters were unlike any written characters used on the Earth, and the language had many characteristics of genuineness. From the translation she furnished in French, Flournoy concluded that the Martian language was a subconscious elaboration.

The vowels and consonant sounds were the same as in French, and the grammar, the inflections, and the construction were modeled on French. As a work of art Flournoy considered the subconscious construction of this language infantile, as a feat of prodigious transpose memory. The Martian descriptions he found similarly childish and the landscapes suggested Japanese lacquer and Nankin dishes.

Curiously enough, when the defects were pointed out to the medium by Flournoy, her subconscious mind appeared to be impressed and set a new task before itself. Not long afterwards an Ultra-Martian romance developed and descriptions were given of the life of still another, more distant planet (Uranus), with grotesque inhabitants and a language totally different from the former one and having apparently no relationship with the known languages of the Earth.

The medium and the other investigators of the phenomena did not share Flournoy's view of the earthly origin of the Martian romance. In articles published in the *Annales des Sciences Psychiques* (in March–April and May–June, 1897), Lemaitre argued for the extraterrestrial origin of Smith's Martian language. The medium's defense was also taken up in an anonymous volume (*Autour des Indes à la Planète Mars*) published under the auspices of the Societé d'Etudes Psychiques de Genève (1901). On the other hand, V. Henry, professor of Sanskrit at the Sorbonne, completely vindicated Flournoy's conclusions in his book *La Language Martien* (1901) and showed how the Martian words, with the exception of a residue of two percent, were derived from known terrestrial words.

Flournoy did not stop at the claim that all the controls of the medium were secondary personalities. He proposed that the source of the incarnation dreams was to be found in the influence **Allan Kardec**'s belief in **reincarnation** exercised on the minds of various automatic writers. Flournoy also disputed the paranormal character of the other manifestations. He stated:

"As to the Supernormal, I believe I have actually found a little telekinesis and telepathy. As to lucidity and spiritistic messages, I have only encountered some brilliant reconstructions, which the hypnoid imagination, aided by latent memory, excels in fabricating in the case of mediums."

At a séance in 1899, Smith had a vision of a village and a landscape that she could not recognize. At the same time, an old man whom she also saw possessed her hand and wrote: "Chaumontet Syndic." Later, further information was divulged. The old man was syndic of Chessenaz in 1839. At another séance these words came: "Burnier, Curé de Chessenaz." Flournoy made inquiries and found out there was a little village named Chessenaz in Haute Savoie, that in 1839 the syndic of the village was Jean Chaumontet, and the curé was named Burnier; furthermore the signatures resembled the authentic signatures of these two people. Nevertheless he dismissed the case, as he found out that Smith had relations in a neighboring village and had been to visit them.

To the physical phenomena of the mediumship he devoted little attention. He was inclined to admit that a force may radiate from the medium that may be capable of attracting or repelling objects in the neighborhood. How such a force could be employed to levitate a table, play on distant instruments, or apport branches of trees, leaves of ivy bearing the name of the control, shells filled with sand and still wet from the sea, a China vase full of water containing a rose, or Chinese money, he did not even attempt to explain. The physical phenomena did not last long and ceased at an early period.

In 1901, Flournoy published another extensive study on some further developments in the *Archives de Psychologie (Nouvelles Observations sur un case de Somnambulisme avec Glossolalie).* He related that owing to the sensation that his previous work created, Smith was inundated with letters and requests for sittings. A rich American lady provided her with a life income. Smith resigned her position and gave many sittings to her new friends, but Flournoy and Lemaitre were not among the invited ones. In the summer of 1900 there came a complete break. Flournoy was no more accorded facilities for study. The material that he dealt with in his new book hardly covered the period of a year.

He stated that the Martian romance passed into oblivion, but the Martian personalities "Astané" and "Ramier" were retained as guides and interpreters in the exploration of the Ultra-Martian and Uranian worlds. A Lunarian phase also developed at a later period, with descriptions, language, and writing. But of this Flournoy had no firsthand information. The Ultra-Martian romance was accompanied by several painted scenes. The writing was ideographic. Its curious hieroglyphs did not express letters but words. The ideograms showed no resemblance to the objects that they represented.

In this, Flournoy found another proof of infantile imagination. This essential characteristic was omitted because the medium strove to create something defying all analysis. The Uranian language and writing differed totally from the Ultra-Martian. But, stated Flournoy, the phonetic and alphabetic system was a copy of the Martian, and the Uranian language differed less from French than French from the languages of the neighboring countries. The origin of the strange notion of Lunarian inhabitants presumably sprung from Smith reading an article in *La Paix Universelle* in which, after flattering allusions to Smith, mention was made of the claims of certain yogis of psychic visits to the inhabitants of that side of the moon that is turned away from the Earth.

The duration of the astronomic cycle was not long. It was superseded, after a complete break with the Spiritualists, by a religious cycle in which Christ, the Virgin, the apostles, and the archangels played the dominant roles. In 1903, a luminous vision filled Smith's room. "Christ" appeared and she heard the voice of "Leopold": "You will draw him." Two years later, Smith began with crayon. This was later changed to oil. On large wooden boards, in a state of trance, she executed 12 religious tableaus.

Lemaitre stated in a study that, according to certain mediumistic communications she had received, Smith was a reincarnation of "Raphael," or of "Michaelangelo"; the medium herself, however, did not accept his conclusion.

In May 1913, at the International Congress for Psychical Research at Geneva, eight of her striking pictures were exhibited. In a statement to *Light* (October 11, 1913) she said:

"On the days when I am to paint I am always roused very early—generally between five and six in the morning—by three loud knocks at my bed. I open my eyes and see my bedroom brightly illuminated, and immediately understand that I have to stand up and work. I dress myself by the beautiful iridescent light, and wait a few moments, sitting in my armchair, until the feeling comes that I have to work. It never delays. All at once I stand up and walk to the picture. When about two steps before it I feel a strange sensation, and probably fall asleep at the same moment. I know, later on, that I must have slept because I notice that my fingers are covered with different colours, and I do not remember at all to have used them, though, when a picture is being begun, I am ordered to prepare colours on my palette every evening, and have it near my bed."

A brush was very seldom used in these pictures. She put on the first coating of paint with her three middle fingers. For the second coating, she moved the same fingers very lightly from right to left and back, thus producing a very smooth surface. The outlines were made by the nails and the sky with the palm of her hand.

This last phase of Smith's mediumship was exhaustively dealt with by W. Deonna in his book *De La Planète Mars en Terre Sainte* (1932). As the medium did not again subject herself to scientific investigation, Deonna's psychoanalytic examination was based on the voluminous correspondence that Smith left behind and on the paintings themselves. The religious cycle was arrested in 1915 in its further progress by the shock that the medium received when her dearest Italian friend died. Her later years were dominated by visions and automatic communications of and from this friend.

Deonna attached no particular value to the paintings. He stated that their inspiration did not surpass the usual level of religious imagery. The tableaus did not have an elevating effect, indeed a striking mediocrity was often noticeable. But he also admitted certain qualities and said that the paintings were far above what Smith could produce normally. He looked for an explanation to the regression of infantile memories. He offered no explanation for certain paranormal features.

It was Smith's habit to have photographs taken of the successive stages of the pictures. To her utter despair, some of the negatives of the painting "Judas" were spoiled. Her guardian angel appeared and announced a miracle. Two days later, the portrait began to fade out. The beards, the moustache, the tears of Judas, and other details gradually disappeared until the painting returned to the stage where it was last successfully photographed. Then an inscription appeared: "God's will, November 18, 1913." The photographs were taken again. The inscription vanished and Smith finished the picture as before.

She always painted from visions. The eyes appeared first. But Judas was painted into the landscape from the leg upward. The visions were accompanied by luminous phenomena. They began with a ball of light that expanded and filled the room. This was not a subjective phenomenon. Smith exposed photographic plates that indeed registered strong luminous effects. But to Deonna, they had no scientific value as they were only supported by the good faith of the medium.

The Smith case is, on perspective, one of the more important in parapsychology. It illustrated many of the phenomena encountered by parapsychologists as they dealt with Spiritualist claims. Flournoy proved the equal of the task and was able, through his long-term observation and study, to understand the dynamics operating in Smith's life. He was able to show the mundane sources for her extraordinary material without falling into name calling and charges of fraud and to present the material fully without the need of an exposé format.

Sources:

Flournoy, Theodore. *Des Indes à la Planète Mars.* English ed. as *From India to the Planet Mars: A Study of a Case of Somnambulism with Glossolalia.* New York: Harper, 1900. Reprint, New Hyde Park, N.Y.: University Books, 1963.

Maxwell, J. *Metapsychical Phenomena: Methods and Observations.* London: Duckworth, 1905.

Smith, Helene Veeder Altpeter (1890– ?)

Worker in the field of parapsychology. She was born on July 31, 1890, at Redding, California. She became a school teacher, college instructor, and secretarial worker. From 1957 on Smith was secretary, treasurer, and librarian for the **California Society for Psychical Studies,** meeting in Berkeley. Her own special interests included telepathy, clairvoyance, and spontaneous psi phenomena.

Smith, Robert Cross (1795–1832)

Robert Cross Smith, a pioneering modern astrologer, was the first of a lineage of British astrologers to use the pseudonym **Raphael** with his writings. He was born in Bristol, England, on March 19, 1795. He became a carpenter and in 1820 married Sarah Lucas. Soon after his marriage he moved to London. In the city he became interested in **astrology,** possibly due to his acquaintance with G. W. Graham, the balloonist. The pair authored a book on **geomancy,** *Philosophical Merlin,* in 1822. In 1824, Smith became the editor of a new magazine, *The Struggling Astrologer,* but it failed for lack of subscribers after only a few issues. Then, two years later, he was offered the opportunity to edit an almanac, *The Prophetic Messenger.* The first issue appeared in 1827 under his pen name and carried the ephemeris (chart of daily planetary positions) that was to become so identified with him.

Smith edited *The Prophetic Messenger* annually for the rest of his life. It was widely read and the ephemeris used by an increasing number of astrologers. Following Smith's death on February 26, 1832, in London, his work as Raphael would be continued by a series of astrologers who successively inherited the title. Eventually, *Raphael's Ephemeris* would be issued as a separate volume and become the standard text consulted by both British and American astrologers for the construction of their clients' horoscopes. The *Ephemeris* was unique in introducing in its table of houses the system of house division developed by the Italian monk **Placidus de Titus** (1603–1668). Through the success of *Raphael's Ephemeris,* the Placidian system of house division would come to dominate English-speaking countries.

Smith also wrote several books, the most important being *A Manual of Astrology* (1828), which joined **James Wilson**'s *Dictionary of Astrology* as a basic textbook for astrology. It continued to be reprinted into the twentieth century. Raphael thus joined Wilson, his older contemporary, in creating the astrological revival that, following a century of decline, would initiate two centuries of steady growth.

Sources:

Brau, Jean-Louis, Helean Weaver, and Allan Edwards. *Larousse Encyclopedia of Astrology.* New York: New American Library, 1982.

Raphael [pseudonym of Robert C. Smith]. *The Familiar Astrologer.* London: Knight & Lacey, 1828.

———. *A Manual of Astrology.* London: C. S. Arnold, 1828.

———, and G. W. Graham. *Philosophical Merlin.* London, 1822.

Smith, Susy (1911– ?)

Journalist and author of a number of books on psychical subjects and parapsychology. She was born on June 2, 1911, in Washington, D.C. She attended the University of Texas and the University of Arizona. She was a columnist for the *Salt Lake Tribune* and the *Desert News,* in Salt Lake City, Utah, and also conducted radio programs on shopping information at Daytona Beach, Florida.

Smith has spent most of her life as a freelance writer, and for a period she worked as an editor at Sherbourne Press on the popular ". . . for the Millions" series. Besides her own many books, she edited the one-volume edition of **F. W. H. Myers**'s *Human Personality and Its Survival of Bodily Death* for University Books in 1961. She was a member of the **Society for Psychical Research,** London; the **American Society for Psychical Research;** the International Spiritual Frontiers Fellowship; the **Association for Research and Enlightenment;** and founded the **Survival Research Foundation** in 1971.

In addition to her many popular books on parapsychology she also lectured on the subject and has operated as a psychic and channeled one book from **William James.** She is herself psychic, as related in her book *Confessions of a Psychic* (Macmillan, 1971). Toward the end of her life, she also had a religious awakening and renounced some of her previous psychic activity.

Sources:

Smith, Susy. *The Book of James.* New York: Putnam, 1974.

———. *Confessions of a Psychic.* New York: Macmillan, 1971.

———. *The Conversion of a Psychic.* Garden City, N.Y.: Doubleday, 1978.

———. *The Enigma of Out-of-the-Body Travel.* New York: Helix Press, 1965.

———. *ESP.* New York: Pyramid Books, 1962.

———. *ESP for the Millions.* Los Angeles: Sherbourne Press, 1965.

———. *Haunted Houses for the Millions.* Los Angeles: Sherbourne Press, 1967.

———. *The Mediumship of Mrs. Leonard.* New Hyde Park, N.Y.: University Books, 1964.

———. *More ESP for the Millions.* Los Angeles: Sherbourne Press, 1969.

———. *Reincarnation.* N.p., 1969.

———. *A Supernatural Primer for the Millions.* Los Angeles: Sherbourne Press, 1966.

———. *Today's Witches.* Englewood Cliffs, N.J.: Prentice-Hall, 1970.

Smith, W. W. (1884–1947)

Original name of **Walter Whateley Carington,** British psychical researcher. He changed his name in 1933 for family reasons.

Smohalla (1815?–1907)

Smohalla, a chief of the Wanapum, a small Native American group in the state of Washington, became famous as a visionary and dreamer among the Native Americans of the Northwest in the 1880s. As a youth he attended a Catholic mission operating among the Yakima, where he learned French and absorbed some Christianity. He distinguished himself as a warrior during his early manhood and participated in the Yakima war of 1855–56. He had also become known as a powerful medicine man and possessed great occult power and the knowledge to use it.

In 1860 he had a life-changing experience. A chief of another tribe, believing that Smohalla was engaging in malevolent occultism (making medicine) against him, almost killed him and left him for dead. Smohalla was able to crawl away and after a long period of recovery, he became a wanderer. Finally reaching Mexico, he traveled for several years throughout the West. He finally returned to his people, who, believing him dead, listened in awe as he told them a story of his journeys. He claimed that he had visited the spirit world and had returned as a teacher. His message was that Saghalee Tyee, the Great Chief Above, wanted his people to return to their old ways. His teachings included a mixture of what he knew of traditional Native American beliefs along with Catholicism and Latter-day Saints teachings. Because of their departure from the old ways, whites had been allowed to come into the land, Smohalla told them.

Smohalla's message was emphasized by his falling into **trance** states (during which times he was stuck with sharp objects and he offered no response). During these times he would claim to visit the spirit world, much as a **shaman,** and upon his return relate the latest message. White people who were present at these trance sessions compared him to Spiritualist **mediums.** Others called him the Dreamer and his followers the Dreamers. He was also able to predict eclipses.

Smohalla's movement spread among the Native people of Washington and Oregon and westward into Idaho. It had a teaching based upon the Earth as the Mother of All and articulated a program that opposed the attempts of the U.S. government to force the various groups into reservations and favored individuals integrating into the larger economic system. Church-like buildings were constructed for the gathering of the Dreamer religion. Out of his teachings a new Native American church developed that would prosper for a generation and remnants of which, known as the Feather Religion or Seven Drums religion, can still be found. His ideas influenced the Paiute prophet **Wovoka,** the founder of the Ghost Dance movement. Among his converts was Old Joseph (d. 1871) of the Nez Perce who passed the Dreamer religion on to his son, Chief Joseph, who would later adopt Wovoka's message.

Smohalla lived into his 90s. He died in 1907.

Sources:

Debo, Angie. *A History of the Indians of the United States.* Norman, Okla.: University of Oklahoma Press, 1970.

Dictionary of American Biography. 20 vols. and 7 supps. New York: Charles Scribner's Sons, 1928–36. 1944–81.

Mooney, James. "The Ghost-Dance Religion and the Sioux Outbreak of 1890." In the *Fourteenth Annual Report of the Bureau of Ethnology.* Compiled by J. W. Powell. Washington: Government Printing Office, 1896.

Smythies, J(ohn) R(aymond) (1922–)

University lecturer and psychiatrist who has written widely on parapsychology. He was born on November 30, 1922, at Naini Tal, U.P., India. He studied at Cambridge University and the University of British Columbia. He settled in Edinburgh and for many years was a senior lecturer at the Department of Psychological Medicine, University of Edinburgh, and a consultant psychiatrist at Royal Edinburgh Hospital, Scotland (1961–73). In 1973 he was named C. B. Ireland Professor of Psychiatry at the University of Alabama at Birmingham. In 1957 he began a lengthy tenure as editor of the *International Review of Neurobiology.*

In addition to his many papers on psychological and psychiatric subjects, Smythies has special interest in the theoretical basis of **ESP.** He was a member of the **Society for Psychical Research** (SPR), London, and has published various articles in the *Journal* of the SPR and *Tomorrow.* He also attended the International Conferences on Philosophy and Parapsychology and Unorthodox Healing, St. Paul de Vence, France, 1954, and the Conference on Parapsychology and Psychedelics, New York, 1958.

Sources:

Berger, Arthur S., and Joyce Berger. *The Encyclopedia of Parapsychology and Psychical Research.* New York: Paragon House, 1991.

Pleasants, Helene, ed. *Biographical Dictionary of Parapsychology.* New York: Helix Press, 1964.

Smythies, John Raymond. *Science and the ESP.* London: Routledge & K. Paul: 1922. Reprint, New York: Humanities Publications, 1967.

Smythies, John Raymond, and Arthur Koestler, ed. *Beyond Reductionism: New Perspectives in the Science of Life.* London: Hitchinson, 1969. Reprint, New York: Macmillian, 1970; London: Hutchinson, 1972.

Snake Handling

Snakes played a prominent part in pagan mythologies and religious ceremonies long before the Judeo-Christian story of the Garden of Eden. The snake has often been regarded as a fertility symbol. In the Mayan scripture *Popul Vuh,* the plumed serpent assists in the creation of life, as it does in the beliefs of the Aztec and the Pueblo Indians. The deity Dambollah, an African deity most frequently pictured as a serpent, is central to Haitian **voudou.** Various American Indian tribes have dances in which live snakes are carried, while the Yokut shamans of central California handled rattlesnakes at public ceremonies.

In the early twentieth century, among members of the Church of God (Cleveland, Tennessee), one of the early Pentecostal churches to emerge in the Appalachian Mountains of the American Southeast, the handling of poisonous snakes took on a new life and importance. These practices arose from a quite literal application of the "signs" of Jesus' disciples mentioned in the biblical gospel of Mark (16:17–18): "And these signs shall follow them that believe; In my name shall they cast out devils; they shall speak with new tongues; They shall take up serpents; and if they drink any deadly thing, it shall not hurt them; they shall lay hands on the sick, and they shall recover."

While Pentecostals had practiced **speaking in tongues** and healing—both also mentioned as gifts of the Holy Spirit in the writings of the apostle Paul—no one had paid attention to the signs in the passage in Mark until 1909. That year George W. Hensley of Tennessee captured a rattlesnake and brought it to a church service for snake handling as a test of religious faith. In 1914, Hensley was invited to an annual meeting of the Church of God, whose leader Ambrose Tomlinson gave the practice tacit approval. In 1928, the leadership of the church realized their mistake and distanced themselves from the practice, but by that time it had spread among church members throughout the Appalachian Mountains and as far south as central Florida.

Hensley, Raymond Hays, and Thomas Harden eventually founded the Dolley Pond Church of God with Signs Following, in Pine Mountain, Tennessee; it became the mother church of Southern snake handling. Pushed out of the Church of God, the "signs" people founded similar churches in a loose fellowship that became in effect a new denomination. Snake handling became clandestine after World War II, when Tennessee led other states in passing laws to forbid the practice, following the publicity given to the death of a member of the Dolly Pond church. Less known is the associated practice of drinking poison, usually a solution of strychnine, at church services, also forbidden by law.

The astonishing fact is that scores of sincere devotees of snake handling have survived the bites of deadly snakes and the effects of drinking poisons at church ceremonies. Less than 75 deaths have been recorded as of the mid-1990s. The deaths that occurred were ascribed to lack of faith. Interestingly enough, Hensley, after surviving numerous snake bites, died after being bitten during a church service in Florida in 1965. Snake handling adds a dramatic element to religious faith, and has much in common with the earlier practice of the **fire ordeal** in non-Christian religions.

Present-day members of the Holiness Church of God in Jesus' Name in the Southeast are more concerned about the dangers of persecution through punitive laws against snake handling than from the practice itself. They regard such laws as a breach of their freedom to exercise their religious convictions sincerely in accordance with Holy Scripture.

Estimates place the number of snake-handling church members at about 3000, living chiefly in Ohio, Indiana, and Appalachia.

Sources:

Carden, Karen W., and Robert W. Pelton. *The Persecuted Prophets: The Story of the Frenzied Snake Handlers.* New York: A. S. Barnes; London: Thomas Yoseloff, 1976.

Covington, Dennis. *Salvation on Sand Mountain: Snake Handline and Redemption in Southern Appalachia.* New York: Penguin, 1996.

Kimbrough, David L. *Taking Up Serpents: Snake Handlers of Eastern Kentucky.* Chapel Hill, N.C.: University of North Carolina, 1995.

La Barre, Weston. *They Shall Take up Serpents.* New York: Schocken Books, 1969.

Sewell, Dan. "Snake Handlers Put Bite into Religion." *Santa Barbara News-Press* (May 1,1995).

Stekert, Ellen. "The Snake Handling Sect of Harlan County, Kentucky: Its Influences on Folk Tradition." *Southern Folklore Quarterly* 27 (December 1963).

Sneezing

There are many superstitions concerning sneezing. It is said that the custom of blessing one who sneezes originated in Italy in the time of Pope Gregory the Great (ca. 540–604) during a pestilence that proved fatal to those who sneezed. A still older date is given to this custom by some writers, who traced the idea to the biblical Adam and to his descendent Jacob, who supposedly begged that its fatal effects might be removed. On his request being granted, the people gratefully instituted the custom of saluting the sneezer.

In some diseases, sneezing was a bad omen, while in others it was a good omen. Sneezing to the right was lucky, to the left, unlucky; from noon to midnight good, from night to noon, bad. St. Augustine (d. 430) stated that the ancients would return to bed if they sneezed while putting on a shoe.

Snowdon, Ruth J(ohnson) (1896– ?)

Research associate in biophysics who published articles on parapsychology. She was born in 1896 in Philadelphia, Pennsylvania, and studied at Vassar College. In 1948 she became a research associate in biophysics at the University of Pittsburgh, where **R. A. McConnell** established his center for parapsychological research. She was a charter member of the **Parapsychological Association.**

Sources:

Snowdon, Ruth J., R. A. MacConnell, and K. F. Powell. "Wishing with Dice." *Journal of Experimental Psychology* 50 (October 1955).

Soal, S(amuel) G(eorge) (1889–1975)

Mathematician and important figure in British parapsychology whose credibility has been attacked. He was born on April 29, 1889, at Kirby Moorside, Yorkshire, England. He received his degrees at London University (B.S. first class honors mathematics, 1910; M.A. mathematics, 1914). He was for many years a lecturer in mathematics at Queen Mary College, University of London (1911–54). After his retirement he was a part-time lecturer at Queen Mary College (1954–58) and an examiner at London University (1960–62).

Soal was one of the shining stars of British parapsychology. From 1919 onward he conducted parapsychological studies, in mediumship (1919–24), automatic writing (1923–28), and statistical experiments in telepathy and clairvoyance (1927 on). He collaborated in quantitative research with **Kathleen M. Goldney,** Frederick Bateman, and **J. G. Pratt.** He lectured widely on parapsychology in Britain and the United States.

He was the Myers Memorial lecturer (1947); Perrott Student in Psychical Research, Cambridge (1948–49); Fulbright Research Scholar in Parapsychology (1951); and president of the Nottingham University Society for Psychical Research (1938). In 1950 he was elected president of the **Society for Psychical Research.**

Soal, at first critical of **J. B. Rhine**'s early work, carried out some very successful experiments with Basil Shackleton. The Soal-Goldney experiments became one of the foundation stones of the emerging field. As early as 1949 critics began to complain that the results were too good, that they had to have been produced by error or **fraud.** In 1960, **C. E. M. Hansel** criticized the claimed precognitive findings in the card-guessing experiments and suggested a number of ways in which there might have been conscious or unconscious falsification of the evidence.

A March 1971 article in the *Journal* of the SPR by **R. G. Medhurst** initially pointed out inaccuracies in the method of constructing quasi-random series in the experiments. By 1974, such criticism had become hostile, with papers by other experimenters suggesting that Soal had deliberately falsified or manipulated his data.

It was also suggested that experimenters J. G. Pratt and J. B. Rhine, who had checked Soal's statistical evaluation, had failed to disclose in detail a glaring error in the assessment of probability, using instead the vague term "very significant." There may, of course, have been a number of quite valid reasons for Pratt and Rhine to have failed to be specific. Soal himself ascribed his initial error to an assistant.

Soal died in 1975. Three years later Betty Markwick, a computer expert, published a complex technical paper in which computer analysis indicated that Soal was guilty of fraud. Other researchers have attempted to defend Soal from the charge of conscious deception, but their arguments have been unconvincing. The effect has been to destroy whatever value had been attached to the Shackleton experiments and, more significantly, to call into question Soal's lifetime of contributions to the field.

Sources:

Berger, Arthur S., and Joyce Berger. *The Encyclopedia of Parapsychology and Psychical Research.* New York: Paragon House, 1991.

Markwick, Betty. "The Soal-Goldney Experiments with Basil Shackleton: New Evidence of Data Manipulation." *Proceedings* of the Society for Psychical Research 56 (1978).

Medhurst, R. G. "On the Origin of the 'Prepared Random Numbers' Used in the Shackleton Experiments." *Journal* of the Society for Psychical Research 46 (March 1971).

Pleasants, Helene, ed. *Biographical Dictionary of Parapsychology.* New York: Helix Press, 1964.

Soal, S. G. "Experiments in Supernormal Perception at a Distance." *Proceedings* of the Society for Psychical Research 123 (1932).

———. "Fresh Light on Card Guessing." *Proceedings* of the Society for Psychical Research 46 (1940).

———. "A Report on Some Communications Received Through Mrs. Blanche Cooper." *Proceedings* of the Society for Psychical Research 35 (December 1925).

Soal, S. G., and F. Bateman. *Modern Experiments in Telepathy.* New Haven, Conn.: Yale University Press, 1954.

Soal, S. G., and H. T. Bowden. *The Mind Readers.* London: Faber and Faber, 1959.

Soal, S. G., and K. M. Goldney. "Experiments in Precognitive Telepathy." *Proceedings* of the Society for Psychical Research 47 (1943).

Soal, S. G., and J. G. Pratt. "ESP Performance and Target Sequence." *Journal of Parapsychology* (September 1951).

———. "Some Relations Between Call Sequence and ESP Performance." *Journal of Parapsychology* (September 1952).

Sociedad Espanola de Parapsychologia

The Sociedad Espanola de Parapsychologia (Spanish Parapsychological Society) was founded in 1973 and grew out of the fledgling interest in parapsychology that emerged in Spain in the 1960s. In 1971 Ramos Molina Perera became the first person to offer courses in parapsychology at a Spanish university, the Universidad Autónoma Madrid. Two years later Perera became one of the founders of the Sociedad Espanola de Parapsicologia.

The society was an open membership group with members from many segments of Spanish society, including psychologists, newspaper reporters, and scholars of various backgrounds. Its program had both research and educational components, and it published a journal, *Psi Communicación.* Last known address: Belen 15—1 Derecha, 28004, Madrid, Spain.

Sociedad Mexicana de Parapsicologia

The Sociedad Mexicana de Parapsicologia (Mexican Parapsychological Society) was founded in 1974 by Carlos B. Trevino and Marcela G. de Trevino. Its formation was occasioned by the perception that the general public was being defrauded by people claiming various paranormal abilities, from tea leaf reading to **witchcraft,** and by various self-appointed parapsychologists. The society immediately became controversial, and many who did not believe in the existence of psychic phenomena protested the formation of the organization.

The society found an ally in the Roman Catholic Church. The church has made use of the society's expertise in cases of reported diabolical possession. It occasionally sends people to the parapsychologists for an initial assessment of their condition and psychological health. The primary objectives of the society, however, remain the battle against psychic trickery and public gullibility and the perennial attempt to gain some acceptance for psychical research from the mainstream of the scholarly world. Its major focus is education rather than research, and it sponsors frequent programs to alert the public to the tricks of fake psychics. In 1984, it sponsored its first symposium on parapsychology, at which a number of international speakers were featured. The symposium was held at the Centro Universitario México, Mexico City. Address: CDA Nicolas San Juan No. 16, D. F. Mexico 12 D.F.

Societa Italiana di Parapsicologia

The Societa Italiana di Parapsicologia (Italian Society of Parapsychology) was founded in Milan, Italy, in 1946 as the Associazióne de Metapsíchica. It was an educational association and does not engage in research. It sponsored an annual series of lectures on psychical research and publishes a journal, *Rasségna Italianan di Ricérca Psichica* (*Italian Journal of Psychic Research*). Last known address: Via dei Montecatini 7, Rome, Italy.

Societas Rosicruciana in Anglia

The Rosicrucian Society of England, organized in 1865 by Robert Wentworth Little (who claimed to have found some old Freemasonry rituals) and **Kenneth R. H. Mackenzie** (who claimed to have received Rosicrucian initiation in Austria). The Metropolitan College was founded in London in 1865 with Little as supreme magus, and a Societas Rosicruciana in Scotia was started soon afterward, followed by provincial lodges.

Some famous names associated with the Societas Rosicruciana in Anglia include Sir Francis Burdett (vice president) and author-occultist-politician Lord Edward Bulwer Lytton (grand patron 1871–73). Kenneth Mackenzie became an honorary magus. **William Wynn Westcott** was supreme magus in 1916.

The aims of the society were:

". . . to afford mutual aid and encouragement in working out the great problems of Life, and in discovering the Secrets of Nature; to facilitate the study of the system of Philosophy founded upon the Kabala and the doctrines of Hermes Trismegistus, which was inculcated by the original Fratres Rosae Crucis, of Germany; and to investigate the meaning and symbolism of all that now remains of the wisdom, art and literature of the ancient world."

In spite of these resounding aims, the society confined itself mainly to lectures and Freemasonry rituals.

In 1887, Westcott, Mackenzie, and **W. R. Woodman** were concerned in the formation of the Isis-Urania Temple of the Hermetic Order of the **Golden Dawn,** in which the esoteric Freemasonry of the Societas Rosicruciana in Anglia was expanded into a more complex occult system. The Societas Rosicruciana in America was modeled on the Societas Rosicruciana in Anglia.

Sources:

King, Francia. *The Rites of Modern Occult Magic.* New York: Macmillan, 1970.

Societas Rosicruciana in Civitatibus Foederatis

The Societas Rosicruciana in Civitatibus Foederatis was founded in Boston in 1878 by Charles E. Meyer (1839–1908) with a Mason from Pennsylvania. The Mason had headed the **Societas Rosicruciana in Anglia,** the British branch of the society founded in the 1860s by Robert Wentworth Little. Within a few years the American group had established lodges, called colleges, across the country. With several others, Meyer traveled to England and was initiated at the college in Sheffield. When Sheffield blocked their request for a charter, they turned to the college in Edinburgh, which issued a charter in 1879. The next year a second charter was issued for a college in New York, and the two American colleges jointly founded the Society Rosicruciana Republicae Americae. Almost immediately, colleges were chartered for Baltimore and Boston. As did the English body, the American group limited membership to Masons.

The society remained stable for a generation but experienced a schism shortly after the turn of the century. At that time some of its members, led by Sylvester C. Gould and George Winslow Plummer (1876–1944), formed the **Societas Rosicruciana in America,** with membership not limited to Masons. However, the losses were compensated for by the chartering of new colleges in Duluth, Minnesota (1911), and Texas (1918). The society enjoyed a brief period of growth during the 1930s when new colleges were chartered for New Jersey (1931), North Carolina (1932), Virginia (1933), Illinois (1934), and Colorado and Long Island, New York (both in 1935). The society expanded to Canada with colleges chartered in Nova Scotia in 1936 and Ontario in 1937.

The society issues the periodical *Rosicrucian Fama.* The membership in 1990 was 1400 and as of 1996 there were 32 active colleges. Website: http://www.geocities.com/Athens/2092/.

Sources:

Societas Rosicruciana in Civitatibus Foederatis. http://www.geocities.com/Athens/2092/. April 14, 2000.

Voohis, Harold V. B. *Masonic Rosicrucian Societies.* New York: Press of Henry Emerson, 1958.

Societies of Harmony

Associations formed for the practice of **animal magnetism** by the pupils of **Franz Anton Mesmer.** The first *Société de Harmonie* was formed in Paris, and its members seem to have acted in a manner that was anything but "harmonious." After some quarreling among themselves, they broke their contract with Mesmer, whereby they had promised before being admitted to his lectures that they would not practice on their own account or give away the secret of his methods without his consent. Other Societies of Harmony soon sprang up, the most important being that of Strasbourg, founded in 1785 by the Marquis Chastenet de Puységur.

Society for Astrological Research

British organization that superseded the older **Astrological Society,** which had been formed in 1895 but had been criticized by astrologers around England as being primarily a London operation. In 1903, the older society was disbanded and a new one reorganized with a seven-person leadership committee. The committee consisted of **Walter Gorn Old, Alan Leo,** Bessie Leo, H. S. Green, E. H. Bailey, Robert King, and G. T. Elliot. This body gave way to the Astrological Lodge of the Theosophical Society (now the **Astrological Lodge of London**).

Sources:

Naylor, P. I. H. *Astrology: A Fascinating History.* North Hollywood, Calif.: Wilshire Book Co., 1970.

Society for Interdisciplinary Studies

British organization founded in 1974 to act as a link between specialists in various disciplines who are interested in the theories of **Immanuel Velikovsky.** The aim of the society has been ". . . to bring a rational and objective approach to the study of Velikovsky's theories and encourage the detailed evaluation which is their due in the light of the evidence accumulating in their favour."

Meetings for members are held throughout the United Kingdom and public seminars and conferences are organized at universities. While activities are focused in England, membership comes from around the world. The society maintains an extensive archive of reviews, reports, and other material. The society publishes a journal, *Chronology & Catastrophism Review* and the *SIS Internet Digest.* Address: 10 Witley Green, Darley Heights, Stopsley, Beds, LU2 8TR England. Website: http://www.knowledge.co.uk/sis/.

Sources:

Society for Interdisciplinary Studies. http://www.knowledge.co.uk/sis/. March 8, 2000.

Society for Parapsychological Studies (Taiwan)

Organization for parapsychological investigations. It published a newsletter, *Parapsychology,* in Chinese.

Current address unavailable.

Society for Psychical Research (SPR)

The British organization that became the focus for the emerging field of psychical research in the nineteenth century. Its establishment was proposed on June 6, 1882, at a meeting, by **Sir William F. Barrett,** and on February 20, 1882, the society came into being. **Henry Sidgwick,** professor of moral philosophy at Cambridge, was elected president. The first council included Barrett, **Edmund Gurney, Balfour Stewart, F. W. H. Myers,** Richard Hutton (all non-Spiritualists) and **W. Stainton Moses,** Dawson Rogers, **Morell Theobald, E. N. Bennett,** George Wyld, and others (all Spiritualists). The investigation of Spiritualist phenomena was to be the focus of the society's work. **Eleanor Sidgwick, Frank Podmore,** and **Richard Hodgson** were among the first to join.

The objects of the society consisted of the following points:

1. An examination of the nature and extent of any influence that may be exerted by one mind upon another, apart from any generally recognized mode of perception.

2. The study of hypnotism and the forms of so-called mesmeric trance, with its alleged insensibility to pain; clairvoyance and other allied phenomena.

3. A critical revision of Reichenbach's research with certain organizations called sensitive, and an inquiry whether such organizations possess any power of perception beyond a highly exalted sensibility of the recognized sensory organs.

4. A careful investigation of any reports, resting on strong testimony regarding apparitions at the moment of death, or otherwise, or regarding disturbances in houses reputed to be haunted.

5. An inquiry into the various physical phenomena commonly called spiritualistic; with an attempt to discover their causes and general laws.

6. The collection and collation of existing materials bearing on the history of these subjects.

The early activity of the society was devoted to an experimental investigation of **thought transference.** They established it to their satisfaction as a fact. Equally important to this achievement was the discovery of the authors of *Phantasms of the Living* (Gurney, Myers, and Podmore) that between death and apparitions a connection existed that was not due to chance alone. The report of the committee on the **Census of Hallucinations** came to the same conclusion. It was largely attributable to the SPR's investigation that **hypnotism** was officially received by the British Medical Association.

Hysteria, **haunted houses,** Reichenbach's phenomena, the **divining rod,** multiple personality, **automatic writing,** and trance speaking were other subjects taken up in due course.

Very valuable work was done in the study of **cross-correspondence** and in the investigation of the mediumship of **Leonora Piper.** The specific subject of communication with the dead was not included in the original program of the society, but the presumption for evidence became so strong that much of the SPR's activity was devoted to its consideration.

In 1889, the **American Society for Psychical Research** was affiliated. From 1887 until his death in 1905, Hodgson was in charge and concentrated most of his activity on the mystery of Piper's trance communications. This investigation is one of the most memorable events in the whole existence of the society, for, to the satisfaction of many distinguished psychical researchers, it dealt with the question of **survival** and the possibility of holding intercourse with the departed. Hodgson himself accepted the evidence of survival, to the great jubilation of Spiritualists, for, in the words of E. Dawson Rogers, then president of the **London Spiritualist Alliance,** "he was a very Saul persecuting the Christians." Officially, however, the society reached no conclusions, and in the century of its existence it has made no collective pronouncement on the question of survival, maintaining that the constitution of the society precludes a collective opinion.

At first the cooperation between the SPR and the Spiritualists was friendly. The line of distinction was that psychical researchers only attempted to establish the veracity of the phenomena whereas Spiritualists not only considered them proved but also attributed them to the action of disembodied spirits. Sympathy, however, soon changed to hostility as the society refused to endorse, and then in many ways became antagonistic to, the views of the Spiritualists (in spite of the personal views of many of the society's members).

Spiritualists objected to the extreme suspicion and the frequently voiced charges of **fraud** by psychical researchers and said that their standard of evidence, when they wished to prove fraud, was far more elastic than when the genuine occurrence of phenomena was in question.

Early resentment was shown for the treatment of mediums Kate Fox-Jencken (one of the **Fox Sisters**), **Henry Slade,** and **William Eglinton,** and that this feature of the situation remained constant through a great many years is best evidenced by the statement of **Sir Oliver Lodge** in his book *The Survival of Man,* published in 1909: "It has been called a society for the suppression of facts, for the wholesale imputation of imposture, for the discouragement of the sensitive, and for the repudiation of every revelation of the kind which was said to be pressing itself upon humanity from the regions of light and knowledge."

It cannot be denied that a certain bias against physical phenomena was observable in the society. The exposure by Hodgson of **Helena Petrovna Blavatsky,** cofounder of the Theosophical Society, of performing the same kind of tricks that were present throughout Spiritualism, appears to have prejudiced the society against this side of psychical research.

Eusapia Palladino was branded an impostor in 1895, and it was only after the society's commitment had been reduced to an amusing anachronism by many years of competent investigation all over Europe that the case was reopened in 1908. A committee was delegated to sit with her in Naples; the later verdict was in favor of Palladino.

E. N. Bennett, who was assistant secretary to the society for 20 years, published a book in 1904 under the title *Twenty Years of Psychical Research.* It is a review of the work of the society and states:

". . . the question of the movement of tables without contact is exactly in the state in which it was left by the Dialectical Society in the year 1869. In all the series of the *Proceedings* there is no light whatever thrown on this simple phenomenon. Some investigation was made as regards direct writing and spirit photography, but to a large extent with negative result.'

As far as the official attitude of the society is concerned the question is in about the same state even now. In a century of research, not a single physical phenomenon has been established as an unquestionably genuine fact. This attitude of reserve and the gradual dying out of the first famous group of psychical investigators dimmed the luster of the society for many years. The society could have never been accused of being unduly credulous. Only the most hostile and defensive of debunkers could disagree with **William James** in his widely read volume, *The Will to Believe and Other Essays* (1902), "In fact, were I asked to point to a scientific journal where hard-headedness and never-sleeping suspicion of sources of error might be seen in their full bloom, I think that I should have to fall back on the Proceedings of the Society for Psychical Research."

The reserve shown by the society, so necessary if the findings of psychical research were to be integrated into the larger body of scientific knowledge, led to criticism by those who had too quickly jumped to unwarranted conclusions. Otherwise outstanding scientists such as **Gustav Geley** scathingly criticized the society's report on **Eva C.** The **William Hope** scandal reflected on the good reputation of the society. In public protest against its methods, **Sir Arthur Conan Doyle** resigned his membership in 1930. His example (as pointed out in an indictment by **H. Dennis Bradley**) was followed by some other members supporting his views. This indictment was published in the daily press in March 1931 but elicited no public reply on the part of the society.

In his Jubilee address in June 1932, Sir Oliver Lodge remarked that up to that time, in its corporate capacity, the society had entertained no corporate conviction and reported no progress except to the extent that it might have committed itself to a corporate belief in **telepathy.** He also remarked:

"Many of us are now similarly convinced of the reality of a spiritual world and of its interaction with this world. I wonder whether it would be premature to say so and thus show that we are not merely working towards some unknown and perhaps unprofitable end, but are really in our opinion making progress. . . . I suggest that time has now arrived and that during the next 50 years we might announce this as a verified hypothesis and use it as an explanation of occurrences in which it is evidently an operative factor."

Against criticisms of negative or over-skeptical attitudes, it must be said that the society has maintained a high standard of investigation and discussion. The middle period of elitism and rejection has long passed; the membership has broadened and the scope of investigations is a wide one. In the middle of the twentieth century the society went through a shift from emphasis on psychical research to laboratory experimental **parapsychology.** The society has successfully avoided the uncritical contagion of the "occult explosion" of the 1960s and also the negative backlash of the 1980s, and has thus retained its leadership in the scientific investigation of the paranormal in England.

The style of contributions to the society's *Journal* and *Proceedings* now varies from the simple clarity of a down-to-earth investigation to the highly technical project heavily structured with statistical analysis. Members hold a wide variety of viewpoints and there are lively and stimulating controversies.

The presidential chair of the society has been filled by a veritable who's who of the leading researchers in the field and public personalities who have lent their names to the cause. They include: Henry Sidgwick, 1882–84; Balfour Stewart, 1885–87; Henry Sidgwick, 1888–92; **Arthur James Balfour,** 1893; William James, 1894–95; **Sir William Crookes,** 1896–99; F. W. H. Myers, 1900; Sir Oliver Lodge, 1901–03; Sir William Barrett, 1904; **Charles Richet,** 1905; **Gerald William Balfour,** 1906–07; **Eleanor Sidgwick,** 1908–09; H. Arthur Smith, 1910; **Andrew Lang,** 1911; The Rt. Rev. Bishop W. Boyd Carpenter, 1912; **Henri Bergson,** 1913; **F. C. S. Schiller,** 1914; **Gilbert Murray,** 1915–16; **L. P. Jacks,** 1917–18; **John William Strutt** (Lord Rayleigh), 1919; **William McDougall,** 1920–21; **T. W. Mitchell,** 1922; **Camille Flammarion,** 1923; **J. G. Piddington,** 1924–25; **Hans Driesch,** 1926–27; Sir Lawrence J. Jones, 1928–29; **Walter Franklin Prince,** 1930–31; Eleanor Sidgwick (President of Honour) and Sir Oliver Lodge, 1932; Dame **Edith Lyttelton,** 1933–34; **C. D. Broad,** 1935–36; **R. J. Strutt** (Baron Rayleigh), 1937–38; **Henry Habberley Price,** 1939–41; **Robert H. Thouless,** 1942–44; **G. N. M. Tyrrell,** 1945–46; W. H. Slater, 1947–48; **Gardner Murphy,** 1949–50; **S. G. Soal,** 1950–51; **Gilbert Murray,** 1952; **F. J. M. Stratton,** 1953–55; **G. W. Lambert,** 1955–58; **C. D. Broad,** 1958–60; Henry Habberley Price, 1960–61; **E. R. Dodds,** 1961–63; **D. J. West,** 1963–65; **Sir Alister Hardy,** 1965–69; **W. A. H. Rushton,** 1969–71; **C. W. K. Mundle,** 1971–74; **John Beloff,** 1974–76; A. J. Ellison, 1976–79; **J. B. Rhine,** 1980; **Louisa E. Rhine,** 1980; A. J. Ellison, 1981–83; **D. J. West,** 1983–87; **Ian Stevenson,** 1988–89; **Alan Gauld,** 1989–92; Archie E. Roy, 1992–95; David G. J. Fontana, 1995–98; D. J. West, 1998–2000.

In addition to the *Journal* and *Proceedings,* the society has published a number of books and pamphlets on a wide range of topics concerned with psychical research as well as recordings of important lectures. It also publishes its own quarterly *Paranormal Review.*

The society is headquartered at 49 Marloes Rd., Kensington, London, W8 6LA, England. Website: http://moebius.psy.ed.ac.uk/~spr/.

Sources:

Grattan-Guinness, Ivor, ed. *Psychical Research: A Guide to Its History, Principles and Practices, in Celebration of 100 Years of the Society for Psychical Research.* London: Aquarian Press, 1982.

Haynes, Renee. *The Society for Psychical Research 1882–1982: A History.* London: MacDonald, 1982.

Thouless, R. H. *Psychical Research Past and Present.* London: Society for Psychical Research, 1952.

Society for Psychic Research (Australia)

The Society for Psychic Research was founded in 1933 by Spiritualists who wished to assemble evidence that human personality survives death. **Spiritualism,** as a religion, has as a major objective obtaining proof that humans survive into a spirit existence. While it carried on occasional research, none of the society's work was scientifically valid, and the major effect of the organization was to stimulate the Australian public's interest in psychical research.

The society continued to function into the 1980s; however, during the last years of its existence it gave up all pretense of being a research organization. It moved its headquarters into a personal growth center and operated a referral agency for various mediums and psychic readers.

Society for Psychic Research (California)

Present name of the organization for many years known as the **Southern California Society for Psychical Research.** Not to be confused with the long-established British organization, the California group conducts research into **extrasensory perception,** altered states of consciousness, and related subjects, and it issues a monthly newsletter to members.

Current address unavailable.

Society for Research on Parapsychological Phenomena (Germany)

A parapsychological organization founded in 1976 in Freiburg, Germany. In March 1980, the society organized an International Congress of Parapsychology in Freiburg, attended by eminent parapsychologists from a number of different countries.

Current address unavailable.

Society for Scientific Exploration

Society devoted to advancing the study of anomalous phenomena of the kind **Charles Fort** called attention to. It operates in various areas both inside and outside established science. It publishes a semiannual *Journal of Scientific Exploration.* Address: P.O. Box 5848, Stanford, CA 94309-5848. Website: http://www.scientificexploration.org/.

Sources:

Society of Scientific Exploration. http://www.scientificexploration.org/. March 8, 2000.

Society for the Anthropology of Consciousness (SAC)

An interdisciplinary organization (formerly the Association for the Anthropological Study of Consciousness) interested in states of consciousness; shamanic, spiritual, and magic phenomena; indigenous healing practices; mythological and religious studies; and **psi** phenomena. SAC publishes a quarterly journal, *The Anthropology of Consciousness* (formerly the *AASC Newsletter*). and sponsors an annual spring meeting consisting of monograph readings, panel discussions and workshops. Address: Box 13758, Berkeley, CA 94712.

Society for the Diffusion of Spiritual Knowledge

The first American Spiritualist organization, established in New York on June 10, 1854. It published the *Christian Spiritualist* and engaged mediums to give séances free. New York judge **John Worth Edmonds** and governor **N. P. Tallmadge** were among its members.

Society for the Investigation of the Unexplained (SITU)

An organization founded by naturalist **Ivan T. Sanderson** in 1965, ". . . for the acquisition, investigation and dissemination of information on reports of all tangible items in the fields of chemistry, astronomy, geology, biology and anthropology, that are not readily explained." For a generation it was the leading organization pursuing research on anomalous phenomena of the kind usually associated with **Charles Fort.** It encouraged fieldwork and on-the-spot investigation by offering advice, helping to raise funds, and arranging contacts for members who planned field trips and expeditions. Fieldwork and research were reviewed by a panel of 20 scientists.

The society disseminated information on findings through a quarterly journal, *Pursuit,* and through papers and reports. Investigations by society members included such areas as claims of ancient Egyptian television, ringing rocks, entombed toads, and poltergeist manifestations. The society maintained information files of original material, a map collection, and a specialized library. It was disbanded in the 1980s.

Society for the Study of Physiological Patterns

The Society for the Study of Physiological Patterns is a prominent British **palmistry** organization founded around 1945 by Noel Jaquin (1893–1974) and Beryl Hutchinson to further the science of hand analysis. The society arose amid the vacuum created by the demise of the **Cheirological Society of Great Britain** at the end of the 1930s, and many former members of the Cheirological Society joined the new organization. It differed from the older organizations in that it included a place for related occult interests such as **astrology, graphology,** and **phrenology.**

As a young man, Jaquin had studied with William G. Benham, the prominent palmist and author of *The Laws of Scientific Hand Reading* (1900). He later developed his own approach to palmistry based upon the idea that the shape of the fingers, palms, and nails, and the texture of the skin were the primary elements indicative of the personality traits of the individual. By the 1930s he concentrated his studies on the fingerprint and the five major patterns, the loop, whorl, arch, tented arch, and composite (a subfield of palmistry called **dermatoglyphics**). He published his initial findings in two books, *The Hand of Man* (1933) and *The Signature of Time* (1940). Jaquin, in particular, was an amazingly productive author and reportedly was the only palmist ever invited to work with Scotland Yard on their investigations. In addition, both Jaquin and Hutchinson worked in the field of medical palmistry, their findings being published in Jaquin's book, *Hand and Disease* (1926), and Hutchinson's *Your Life in Your Hands* (1967).

The Society for the Study of Physiological Patterns has grown into an international organization with members throughout the English-speaking world. It is headquartered at 39 Larchwood House, Baywood Sq., Chigwell, Essex 1G7 4AY, United Kingdom.

Sources:

Campbell, Edward D. *The Encyclopedia of Palmistry.* New York: Perigee, 1996.

Hutchinson, Beryl. *Your Life in Your Hands.* London: Sphere, 1967.

Jaquin, Noel. *The Hand of Man.* London: Faber, 1933.

———. *The Hand Speaks: Your Health, Your Sex, Your Life.* New Delhi: Sagar Publications, 1973.

———. *The Human Hand—The Living Symbol.* Bombay: Taraporevala, 1958.

The Society for the Study of Supernormal Pictures

Small psychical research organization established in 1918 in London, England, to promote the scientific study and investigation of supernormal pictures. Its members consisted largely of professional photographers. The first president was Abraham Wallace. He was assisted by first vice presidents W. G. Mitchell, **Sir Arthur Conan Doyle,** and H. Blackwell.

After many hundreds of experiments, the society reported in May 1920:

"The members here present desire to place on record the fact that after many tests and the examination of thousands of pictures, they are unanimously of opinion that results have been obtained supernormally on sensitive photographic plates under reliable test conditions. At present the members do not undertake to explain how the results have been obtained, but they assert that they have undoubtedly been secured under conditions excluding the possibility of fraud."

The society's views were not found acceptable to other psychical researchers and it ceased operation in 1923.

Society of Metaphysicians

British organization devoted to a science of unity between physical and psychical fields, founded by J. J. Williamson, an electronic engineer, in 1948. Williamson experienced such psychic abilities as **astral projection,** also known as **out-of-the-body travel,** and **clairvoyance** at an early age, and in later life attempted to find a basis for integrating such faculties with normal physical science. An early associate of the society was "Oliver Fox" (**Hugh G. Callaway**), pioneer of astral projection, who prepared a mail-order course on the subject for the society.

The society commenced by experimenting in such areas as out-of-the-body travel, **aura** studies, and **dowsing,** and later explored **biofeedback** phenomena. The society concentrates largely on postal courses in conjunction with a mail-order business for books and such psychic appliances as aura goggles for viewing the human aura (as described in the books of **Walter J. Kilner** and **Oscar Bagnall**). It is headquartered at Archers Ct., Stonestile Ln., The Ridge, Hastings, East Sussex, England.

Society of Novus Spiritus

The Society of Novus Spiritus was founded in 1986 by spirit medium **Sylvia Browne** (1936–), who has been **channeling** a spirit, Francine, since the 1960s. The society was created to disseminate the teachings that have been received over the past 25 years. Novus Spiritus strives to uncover all of the "mysteries" regarding the nature of life, death, God, and the role humans play in life's scheme. Members believe that God never withholds information, though individuals may choose to ignore it.

Novus affirms the existence of an all-loving God and is dedicated to eliminating what it considers the false concepts of Satan, hell, sin, guilt, and the fear of God, all of which are contrary to its understanding of a benevolent Creator. The pain of life is not punishment from God; rather it is a learning tool, and a very necessary one in the larger scheme of life.

The society also affirms that after "death," the human soul goes to the Other Side, which is better known as heaven. This place is the true reality, as opposed to the temporal planet Earth. The Other Side is eternal, a place of total harmony, no physical limitations. The individual's identity is intact. Life exists in its most wondrous and joyous form on the Other Side. Even though the Other Side is total beauty and happiness, the soul may not be at peace and will still seek to better itself. This seeking drives an urge again to enter life on Earth to experience God's knowledge, gaining perfection in the process. Each soul decides how much experience it wants. While some may never have a life on Earth, others will choose 50 or more lives.

Based upon the observation that everything in nature exhibits a dual nature, most notably in the pairing of male/female, the society teaches that this pattern extends even to the Most High, to God. Members believe in both Mother God and Father God who reflect the patterns of nature. While God the Father holds creation in a constant state of being, God the Mother actively works with and through human beings for learning and perfection. Each is a distinct entity, not just a nebulous force, and they are addressed as Om (male) and Azna (female).

The society exists to help prepare individuals to receive God's wisdom. It teaches that knowledge provides the key needed to unlock the mind, and considers itself to be a Gnostic organization, by which it means that members are seekers after truth (gnosis). God is the source of all truth, available to all who are ready to receive it. The society promotes a community of people who seek to be guided by the Light and dedicated to living a spiritual life.

The society holds weekly celebration services in Campbell, California, and Seattle, Washington. The work of the society is expanded through study groups which utilize a 16-volume set of books written by Browne, *Journey of the Soul.* Monthly, related study groups receive two cassette tapes by Browne to focus their meetings. Those who complete the *Journey of the Soul* lessons may choose to take more advanced lessons leading to becoming a deacon and ordained minister of the society.

The Society of Novus Spiritus is headquartered at 35 Dillon Ave., Campbell, CA 95008-3001. Its website can be found at http://www.sylvia.org/novusdoc.htm.

Sources:

Browne, Sylvia. *Adventures of a Psychic.* Carlsbad, Calif.: Hay House, 1998.

———. *Journey of the Soul.* 16 vols. Campbell, Calif.: Society of Novus Spiritus, 1991–94.

———. *Meditation Book I.* Campbell, Calif.: Society of Novus Spiritus, 1994.

———. *The Other Side and Back.* New York: E. P. Dutton, 1999.

Dufresne, Chris. *My Life with Sylvia Browne.* Carlsbad, Calif.: Hay House, 1999.

Society of Rosicrucians in America See Societas Rosicruciana in Anglia

Society of the Inner Light

The Society of the Inner Light was founded by the British occultist "Dion Fortune" (**Violet Mary Firth**) in 1924. Originally known as the Community then Fraternity of the Inner Light, it became the Society of the Inner Light when incorporated as a registered charity in 1946.

Firth was a member of the **Stella Matutina,** an outer order of the famous Hermetic Order of the **Golden Dawn,** and the Community of the Inner Light was originally intended by Golden Dawn members as a recruitment body for suitable prospects. Firth came into conflict with Golden Dawn leaders, however, and she split away from the parent body. Firth remained warden of the fraternity until her death in 1946.

The fraternity was headquartered in London and maintained a library of occultism and mysticism, including the various works on occultism by Fortune herself. It also organized public lectures and published a monthly journal, the *Inner Light Magazine,* devoted to esoteric Christianity, occult science, and the psychology of superconsciousness.

The fraternity purchased a site at **Glastonbury,** long considered a holy place in Britain, a power center associated with legends of Joseph of Arimathea. A guest house was established on this site on the side of the Tor, the famous Hill of Vision supposed to overlook the Isle of Avalon. Here, Fortune could retreat from the continued tensions she experienced from her interactions with the older, male-dominated magic community. The guest house became a meeting place and social center for those interested in mysticism.

After the death of Dion Fortune, the fraternity continued her teachings virtually unchanged for a time, but eventually its scope broadened, embracing a wider range of occult practices and dispensing with the initiation oath. The society recommenced the publishing of *The Inner Light* as a quarterly in 1993. Website: http://www.innerlight.org.uk.

Sources:

Chapman, Janine. *Quest for Dion Fortune.* York Beach, Maine: Samuel Weiser, 1993.

Fielding, Charles, and Clark Collins. *The Story of Dion Fortune.* York Beach, Maine: Samuel Weiser, 1985. Reprint, Loughborough, England: Thoth Publications, 1999.

Knight, Gareth. *Dion Fortune and the Inner Light.* Loughborough, England: Thoth Publications, 2000.

Richardson, Alan. *Priestess: The Life and Magic of Dion Fortune.* Wellingborough, England: Aquarian Press, 1987.

Society Ordo Templi Orientis (SOTO)

The Society Ordo Templi Orientis (SOTO) is one of several groups to emerge following the death in 1962 of **Karl Germer,** the outer head of the **OTO** (Ordo Templi Orientis). In the English-speaking world the OTO had been headed by **Aleister Crowley** until his death in 1947. Crowley appointed Karl Germer as his successor. Germer, however, was inactive during much of the 15 years of his administration, which allowed contact with many of the order's members to be broken. When Germer died, several different people emerged to lead the leaderless organization. A Brazilian, **Marcelo Ramos Motta** (1931–1987), claimed that on his deathbed, Germer had appointed him as the new head. Motta was not at the time sufficiently advanced to assume the office, but over the next years he completed his initiate work and assumed control of a reorganized order, which he named the Society Ordo Templi Orientis.

Through the society, Motta issued in 1975 the first of four massive volumes of a revived *Equinox,* modeled on the journal Crowley had published early in the century. Each issue contained writings by Motta and documents that supported his claims, as well as writings by Crowley. Various issues of the *Equinox* also denounced the rival claimants to OTO leadership who came forward. The issue came to a head in the United States when the OTO sued the SOTO on several legal actions. The publication house Samuel Weiser was caught in the middle as the publisher of both organizations. The primary ruling occurred in 1985, when the court declared the OTO, then led by Grady McMurtry, to be the legal entity who owned all Crowley copyrights and trademarks. In effect, the court turned back all Motta's claims to OTO lineage and leadership.

It may be contacted throught the Parzival XI O.T.O. Foundation, P.O. Box 979, Belconnen, ACT 2616 Australia.

Sources:

Motta, Marcelo. *Letter to a Brazilian Mason.* Nashville, Tenn.: Troll Publishing, 1980.

———. *Manifesto.* Nashville, Tenn.: Society Ordo Templi Orientis in America, 1978.

———. *The Political Aims of the O.T.O.* Nashville, Tenn.: Ordo Templi Orientis in America, 1980.

———. *Thelemic Political Morality.* Nashville, Tenn.: Society Ordo Templi Orientis in America, 1978.

Solar Systems (in Theosophy)

Theosophy has presented a unique perspective on the formation of solar systems. It postulates the existence of an all pervading ether (a popular concept of nineteenth-century science, later discarded), known as **koilon,** which is imperceptible to ordinary senses and indeed even to clairvoyants except the most highly-developed. It is considered dense despite its diffusion.

The Deity, intending to create a universe, invests this ether with divine force to become matter in the shape of minute drops or bubbles and the universe with its solar systems is formed. First, a mass is aggregated by the appropriate agitation of these drops and added to this mass is a rotatory motion. The formed mass contains the matter to create all the seven worlds. It may be possible to observe that these worlds are not separate in the manner we usually conceive separate worlds to be, but interpenetrate each other.

The substance in its original form is the texture of the first world and to create the texture of the second–and lower–world, the Deity sets up numerous rotatory agitations to collect 49 atoms arranged in a certain way, sufficient for the first atom to form the first world.

This process continues six times, the atoms of the succeeding lower worlds are formed from the world immediately higher and each time with a multiple of forty-nine atoms. Gradually, and with time, the aggregation containing the atoms of all seven worlds completely intermingled, contracts until it forms a nebula with the flat, circular form familiar to astronomy students.

The center is more dense than the fringes. During the process of flattening and due to the initial revolving motion, rings are formed encircling the center. From these rings the planets are formed and later these planets can support human life.

The various worlds penetrate each other substantially within the same bounds, with the exception being the worlds of finer texture that extend beyond those relatively more dense. The names of the worlds are: first, the **Divine World,** which has not yet been experienced by man; second, the Monadic whence come the impulses that form human beings; third, the Spiritual World, which is the highest world humans have experienced; fourth, the **Intuitional World;** fifth, the **Mental World;** sixth, the Emotional or **Astral World;** and seventh is the world of matter familiar to us.

Some of these worlds are referred to in other entries as: *Adi* or Divine plane; *Anupadaka* plane (see **Monad**); *Atmic, Nirvanic,* or Spiritual plane; and *Buddhic* or Intuitional plane. (See also **Evolution of Life**)

Sources:

Jinarajadasa, C. *The Early Teachings of the Masters.* Chicago: Theosophical Society, 1923.

Leadbeater, C. W. *A Textbook of Theosophy.* Adyar, Madras, India: Theosophical Publishing House, 1956.

SOL See Servants of the Light

Solar Temple

The Solar Temple (officially the Ordre du Temple Solaire or OTS) was an obscure French-speaking initiatory occult order that made front-page headlines following the suicide death of its leaders among 52 people who died in a 72-hour period in three incidents on October 3–5, 1994, in Switzerland and Quebec. Sixteen additional members of the group died on the winter solstice in 1995 and five more on March 22, 1997, in Quebec. It appears that some of those who died committed suicide in hopes of making a transition to a higher world. A few people were murdered, considered traitors by the larger group. The remainder were considered weaker members and were assisted (i.e., murdered) to make the transition.

The Solar Temple was one of a number of groups that emerged in France and neighboring countries in the years since 1804 that traced their authority to a lineage of grand masters of the Order of the Temple, a medieval order of knights that was suppressed at the beginning of the fourteenth century. In 1804, a Parisian physician, Bernard-Raymond Fabré-Palaprat (1773–1838), claimed that he was the successor to a secret line of Templar grand masters who had kept the order alive through the years since its disappearance from public view. Following his death the order began to splinter. Among the modern splinters from this millieu was the Renewed Order of the Temple founded around 1970 by Julian Origas (1920–1983).

The Solar Temple was founded in 1984 as the Ordre International Chevalresque Tradition Solaire by **Luc Jouret** (1947–1994) and **Joseph Di Mambro** (1924–1994). Jouret was born in the Belgian Congo, but as a youth his parents returned to Belgium where he attended the Free University of Brussels and became a physician. After a short time in the army, he took training as a homeopathic physician and established a practice in France. In the early 1980s he became a popular speaker on alternative medicine in French-speaking Europe and Quebec. His travels brought him into contact with Di Mambro. Di Mambro was a French jeweler and watchmaker who as a young man had joined the **Ancient and Mystical Order of the Rosae Crucis** (AMORC). In 1973, he founded the first of several successive organizations, the Center for the Preparation of the New Age, in Annemasse, France. One of the successor groups, the Golden Way Foundation, in Geneva, Switzerland, hosted Luc Jouret for some of his health lectures.

The Solar Temple was founded as a secret order in the 1980s. Its members were drawn from affiliates of the Amenta and Archédia Clubs, esoteric groups founded by Jouret, and the Golden Way Foundation. The Solar Temple members saw themselves as assisting in the arrival of the coming New Age. They practiced various meditative and occult disciplines and participated in elaborate rituals to achieve an enlightened state of consciousness. The rituals invoked the spiritual hierarchy of ascended masters to send light and love to bring in the New Age. The recitation of the popular "Great Invocation" that originated in the Alice Bailey's Arcane school was an integral part of their ritual life. Members also believed that the group would produce a next generation of exceptional children, including nine cosmic children who would initiate the New Age. To this end, group members listened to Di Mambro's identification of them with famous people in previous incarnations, his pairing them in cosmic marriages.

The group prospered through the 1980s, reaching a peak of 442 members in 1989, but in the early 1990s it began to lose members, a number of whom demanded the money they had contributed be returned. The leadership became increasingly pessimistic as members defected, no signs of the coming New Age appeared, and Di Mambro's health suffered.

By 1994, Di Mambro, Jouret, and a few members in their confidence began to think in terms of an alternate plan. Since the world was not responding to their message, they decided to escape the world to a higher reality via suicide. In the process, they also decided to take revenge on some of the former members.

In 1982, Di Mambro had fathered a female child, Emmanuelle, who was assigned a messianic role in the New Age. At a later date, against Di Mambro's orders not to have children, Nicki Dutoit became pregnant, and she and her husband left the order. When their child arrived, he was named Christopher Emmanuel. Di Mambro saw this act as a challenge to Emmanuelle's status and labeled the young boy the Antichrist. When the decision was made to make the transition, the Dutoits and their son were the first victims. They were murdered on October 3, 1994, and their two assailants then committed suicide in the house in Morin Heights, Quebec. On that same day, 22 people were found dead in Cheiry, Switzerland, 18 of whom were found in a room with their bodies arranged in a circular patterns as if they were the spokes of a wheel. On October 25 bodies were found in two chalets in Granges-sur Salvan, Switzerland.

It was later concluded that of the total of 52 dead, only 15 were suicides. Besides the three people murdered in Canada, the majority had been drugged and killed, many by shooting. Di Mambro and Jouret were among those who committed suicide. However, the next year 16 more who had not been invited to the original event in Switzerland died at their own hand near Grenoble, France. A final five died on March 22 (spring equinox), 1997, in Canada. In the meantime, the Solar Temple had been disbanded and its surviving members have melded back into the population.

The Solar Temple deaths were a unique event for the European Templar and occult community, though it has in the popular consciousness been tied to several other violent incidents involving small new spiritual/religious groups such as the murders committed by leaders of the **AUM Shinrikyo** Buddhists in Japan and the suicides of 39 members of **Heaven's Gate,** the American UFO contactee group. In France and Belgium, it led to a backlash against minority religions that continues to the present. The government of Switzerland carried out an extensive investigation of the deaths and concluded that it had been the outcome of the group's theological choices. Religious scholar Jean François Mayer consulted with the police in their investigation.

Sources:

Introvigne, Massimo. "The Magic of Death: The Suicides of the Solar Temple." In Catherine Wessinger, ed. *Millennialism, Persecution, and Violence: Historical Cases.* Syracuse, N.Y.: Syracuse University Press, 2000.

Meyer, Jean François. " 'Our Terrestrial Journey is Coming to an End:' The Late Voyage of the Solar Temple." *Nova Religio* 2, 2 (April 1999): 172-196.

Palmer, Susan. "Purity and Danger in the Solar Temple." *Journal of Contemporary Religion* 11, 3 (October 1996): 303-318.

Wessinger, Catherine *How the Millennium Comes Violently.* New York: Seven Bridges Press, 2000.

Solomon

Legends have connected the biblical King Solomon, son of David, with magical practices. Although it does not possess any biblical authority, there is a considerable body of Middle Eastern folklore concerning Solomon that grows out of his reputation as one of the wisest of men, coupled with the possible identification of Solomon with a still older mythical figure named Suleiman. Arabic and Persian legends speak of a prehistoric race that was ruled by 72 monarchs by the name of Suleiman.

Nineteenth-century occultist John Yarker, author of *The Arcane Schools* (1909), stated: "It does not seem that these Suleimans who are par excellence the rulers of all Djinn, Afreets and other elemental spirits, bear any relationship to the Israelite King." The name, he said, is found in that of a god of the Babylonians. Dr. Kenealy, the translator of Hafiz, said that the earliest Aryan teachers were named Mohn, Bodles, or Solymi, and that Suleiman was an ancient title of royal power, synonymous with "Sultan" or "Pharaoh."

A Persian legend states that in the mountains of **Kaf,** there is a gallery built by the giant Arzeak, where there are statues of a race who were ruled by the Suleiman or wise King of the East. There is a great chair or throne of Solomon hewn out of the solid rock called the Takht-i-Suleiman or throne of Solomon.

It is to these older Suleimans that we must look for a connection with the tradition of occultism. It is not unlikely that the legend relating to Solomon and his temple have been confused with these, and that the protagonists of the antiquity of **Freemasonry,** who trace their organization to the building of Solomon's Temple, have intermingled some still older rite or mystery relating to the ancient dynasty of Suleiman with the circumstances of the Masonic activities of the Hebrew monarch. Hebrew historian Josephus notes,

"God enabled Solomon to learn that skill which expels demons, which is a science useful and sanative to men. He composed such incantations, also, by which distempers are alleviated, and he left behind him the manner of using exorcisms, by which they drive away demons, so that they never return. And this method of cure is of great force unto this day; for I have seen a certain man of my own country, whose name was Eleazar, releasing people that were demoniacal, in the presence of Vespasian and his sons, and his captains, and the whole multitude of his soldiers.

"The manner of the cure was this. He put a ring that had a root of one of these sorts mentioned by Solomon to the nostrils; and when the man fell down immediately, he adjured him to return unto him no more, making still mention of Solomon, and reciting the incantations which he composed. And when Eleazar would persuade and demonstrate to the spectators that he had such a power, he set, a little way off, a cup, or basin full of water, and commanded the demon as he went out of the man, to overturn it, and thereby to let the spectators know that he had left the man."

Some claimed fragments of these magical books of Solomon are mentioned in the Codex Pseudepigraphus of Fabricius, and Josephus himself has described one of the antidemoniacal roots, which appears to refer to legends of the perils involved in gathering the mandrake root, or **mandragoras.**

The Islamic Solomon

The Qur'an alleges that Solomon had power over the winds, and that he rode on his throne throughout the world during the day, and the wind brought it back every night to Jerusalem. This throne was placed on a carpet of green silk, of a prodigious length and breadth, and sufficient to afford standing room to all Solomon's army, the men on his right hand and the **jinn** on his left. An army of the most beautiful birds hovered near the throne, forming a kind of canopy over it and the attendants, to screen the king and his soldiers from the sun.

A certain number of evil spirits were also made subject to Solomon, whose business it was to dive for pearls and perform other work.

It is also stated that the devils, having received permission to tempt Solomon, in which they were not successful, conspired to ruin his character. They wrote several books of magic, and hid them under his throne, and when he died they told the chief men among the Jews that if they wished to ascertain the manner in which Solomon obtained his absolute power over men, Genii, and the winds, they should dig under his throne. They did so and found the books, abounding with the most impious superstitions.

The more learned and enlightened refused to participate in the practices described in those books, but they were willingly adopted by the common people. Muslims asserted that the Jewish priests published this scandalous story concerning Solomon, which was believed until Mahomet, by God's command, declared him to have been no idolater.

It was further maintained by some Muslims that Solomon brought a thousand horses from Damascus and other cities he conquered, although some say they were left to him by his father David, who seized them from the Amalekites; others claimed that they came out of the Red Sea and were provided with wings. The king wished to inspect his horses and ordered them to be paraded before him. Their symmetry and beauty so much occupied his attention that he gazed on them after sunset, and thus neglected evening prayers until it was too late. When aware of his omission, he was so greatly concerned at it that he ordered the horses to be killed as an offering to God, keeping a hundred of the best of them. This, we are informed, procured for him an ample recompense, as he received for the loss of his horses dominion over the winds.

The following tradition was narrated by Muslim commentators relative to the building of the temple of Jerusalem. According to them, David laid the foundations of it, and when he died he left it to be finished by Solomon. That prince employed Jinn, and not men, in the work; and this idea may relate to what is said in Kings 6:7, that the temple was "built of stone, made ready before it was brought thither, so that there was neither hammer, no axe, nor any tool of iron, heard in the house while it was building." The rabbis noticed a worm that they claimed assisted the workmen, the power of which was such as to cause the rocks and stones to separate in chiseled blocks.

While engaged in the erection of the temple, Solomon found his end approaching, and he prayed that his death might be concealed from the Jinn until the building was finished. His request was granted. He died while in the act of praying, leaning on the staff that supported his body in that posture for a whole year. The Jinn, who believed he was still alive, continued their work. At the expiration of the year the edifice was completed. When a worm that had entered the staff ate through it and, to the amazement even of the Jinn, the body fell to the ground, the king was discovered to be dead.

The inhabitants of the valley of Lebanon believed that the celebrated city and temple of Baalbec were erected by the Jinn under Solomon's direction. The object of the erection of Baalbec was variously stated, one tradition affirming that it was intended to be a residence for the Egyptian princess whom Solomon married, and another that it was built for the Queen of Sheba.

The Magical Solomon

From the sixteenth century on, occultists have studied the great grimoire known as *The Key of Solomon* (*Clavicula Salomonis*) to which tradition ascribes an ancient history before it was committed to writing. This book of ceremonial magic has two sections: the *Great Key* and the *Lemegeton or Lesser Key.* The first is concerned with magic spells, rituals, and talismans, the second with the evocation of spirits.

There is also another work known as *The Testament of Solomon* that was translated into German from an ancient Greek manuscript. Manuscripts of the *Testament* have also been reported from Greek monasteries, and the work is extremely rare in any format. The work claims to be Solomon's own story covering the period between the building of the Temple in Jerusalem and his own fall from grace. It tells the story of a vampire-like Jinn and the magic ring of Solomon and details the various spirits and the magical means of controlling them. The ring of Solomon is also the subject of stories in the *Arabian Nights.*

In the seventeenth century, Freemasons began to trace their work backward to Hiram, the architect of Solomon's kingdom. This indirect reference to Solomon has possibly been the single reference that has kept Solomon associated with the occult world.

Sources:

Conybeare, F. C., ed. *The Key of Truth.* London, 1898.

Mathers, F. L. MacGregor, ed. *The Key of Solomon the King.* London: George Redway, 1908. Reprint, London: Routledge and Kegan Paul, 1972.

Shah, Sayed Idires. *The Secret Lore of Magic: Books of the Sorcerers.* London: Frederick Muller, 1957.

Waite, Arthur E. *The Book of Ceremonial Magic.* London: William Rider, 1911. Reprint, New Hyde Park, N.Y.: University Books, 1961. Reprint, New York: Causeway Books, 1973.

Solomon, Mirror of

Popular name given to a "magic mirror" used for **divination.** Various magical signs and devices have been attributed to the biblical **Solomon,** but they were derived from folk legends rather than any statements in the Hebrew Bible. The Mirror of Solomon is constructed from a shining and well-polished plate of fine steel, slightly concave. The blood of a white pigeon is inscribed at the four corners with the names "Jehovah," "Eloym," "Metatron," and "Adonay."

The newly constructed mirror is placed in a clean and white cloth. Its owner, when beholding a new moon during the first hour after sunset, would repeat a prayer that the angel Anaël might command and ordain his companions to act as they are instructed, that is, to assist the operator in divining from the mirror. He or she would then cast a suitable perfume upon burning coals, at the same time uttering a prayer.

After repeating this process three times, the person breathes on the mirror and evokes the angel Anaël. The sign of the cross is then made upon the operator and upon the mirror for 45 days in succession, at the end of which period, if all goes as planned, Anaël appears in the form of a beautiful child to accomplish the operator's wishes. Sometimes he appears on the fourteenth day, according to the devotion and fervor of the operator. The perfume used in evoking him is saffron.

For another method of constructing a magic mirror that does not involve the sacrifice of a white pigeon, see the appendix to *The Philosophy of Natural Magic* by Henry C. Agrippa (University Books, 1974).

Solomon Ibn Gabirol (ca. 1021–ca. 1058)

Spanish-Hebrew poet and mystic philosopher. He was an advocate of **neoplatonism,** but also ascribed to the *via negativa,* the mystical doctrine that holds that the deity can only be understood as a negation of all attributes (which are in themselves limiting and human in our thoughts). He considered this view essential to the preservation of Jewish monotheism.

Solovovo, Count See Perovsky-Petrovo-Solovovo, Count

Solstices

As ancient peoples began systematic observation of heavenly phenomena, they noticed the wandering habits of the Sun, easily measured by its changing location at its daily rising. Over half a year the rising point would be a little further to the north each day and then it would appear to pause and begin moving south. In the Northern Hemisphere, it would reach its northernmost point just as the summer began and its southernmost point as a prelude to the coldest days. The word "solstice" is derived from the apparent pause, from the Latin *sistere,* to stand still. The phenomena of the changing position of the rising sun is due to the 23-degree tilt to the Earth's axis. The axis changes daily as the Earth rotates around the Sun.

The Sun's movements were so obvious, and so equated with changing weather, that some form of acknowledgment of the solstices occurred in cultures around the world. Some of these festivals continue into the present and many were observable in the recent past. Among the oldest records of solstice celebrations are found in the remains of the ancient megalithic cultures, such as the one that led to the building of **Stonehenge.** Such stone monuments were frequently oriented to include an alignment to the point of the rising sun at the summer solstice, presumably an occasion for the community to gather for ritual observances.

In **astrology,** the solstices were important markers. The Sun entered Capricorn at the winter solstice and Cancer at the summer solstice. While important markers in constructing a horoscope, the solstices were little used in its interpretation.

In modern times, as Paganism has been revived, the summer solstice has become a major occasion for ritual gatherings, among the oldest and certainly the most famous being the gatherings of the Druids at Stonehenge. Until quite recently, the summer solstice was celebrated in Germany with a picnic and bonfire. Couples would attempt to jump the bonfire as a sign of the strength of their relationship. Neo-Pagans mark the solstices as two of the major festival occasions (called **sabbats**). The ancient winter solstice, called Yule, has survived in a radically altered form as the Christian's Christmas, but is now being celebrated in its own right.

Sources:

Cunningham, Scott. *Wicca: A Guide for the Solitary Practitioner.* St. Paul, Minn.: Llewellyn Publications, 1988.

Farrar, Stewart. *What Witches Do.* New York: Coward, McCann & Geoghegan, 1971.

Lewis, James R. *Encyclopedia of Astrology.* Detroit: Gale Research, 1994.

Spicer, Dorothy Gladys. *The Book of Festivals.* New York: Womans Press, 1937.

Soma

A term found in the hymns of the *Rig-Veda,* one of the four sacred scriptures of ancient **India** (the others are the *Sama Veda, Yajur Veda,* and *Artharva Veda*). The essential teachings of the *Vedas* were recast in the form of the **Upanishads,** of which there are 108 principal scriptures and a number of minor ones.

The ninth chapter of the *Rig-Veda* comprises 114 verses in praise of *soma,* the ambrosia of the gods and the elixir of immortality. It is clear that soma was also an intoxicating drink (possibly made from the milk-weed *asclepias acida* described in the *Yajur Veda* as a dark, sour creeper without leaves). This drink was offered by the priests as a libation to the gods, much as wine is used sparingly in the sacraments of the Christian religion for symbolic purposes.

In the twentieth century, several writers, most notably R. Gordon Wasson in his book *Soma, Divine Mushroom of Immortality* (1968), have speculated that soma was the *amanita muscaria* (a mushroom with hallucinogenic properties) and that Hindu mysticism arose from intoxication of the priests. This suggestion stemmed from Wasson's research in Mexico, when he discovered a Mazatec Indian religious practice based on the use of a hallucinogenic mushroom.

Wasson's soma theory became attractive during the psychedelic revolution of the 1960s, and it became fashionable to expand upon Wasson's view to assert that transcendental revelation had always been stimulated by the use of psychedelic drugs. Another writer, John M. Allegro, suggested in his book *The Sacred Mushroom and the Cross* (1970) that the crucifixion story of Jesus was a symbolic myth of the ecstasy produced by a psychedelic drug.

Intoxicating (as opposed to psychedelic) beverages have certainly been known since ancient times in **Egypt,** India, **Greece,** and Rome. Warnings about intoxication abound in ancient writings, notably in the Bible, in the Proverbs of Solomon, in Isaiah, Jeremiah, Amos, and Hosea. In the Christian religion, the apostle Paul complained of drunkenness at the *agape,* or love feasts, celebrated in common. Novatian, a Church father of the third century, spoke of Christians who, in the morning after fasting, began the day by drinking, pouring wine into their still "empty veins," and were drunk before eating.

In India, the *Manava Dharma Shastra* (Ordinances of Manu), a code of religious and civil duties, prohibited intoxication on the part of Brahmin priests and made it clear that the soma drink was from a plant, not a mushroom. This plant is sometimes called the "moon plant," and soma was traditionally associated with the moon.

Yoga treatises on meditation suggest that the true soma, or elixir of life, is the union of the twin currents of **kundalini** energy in the human body, culminating in higher consciousness. Some Hindus believe in kundalini as a latent energy situated at the base of the spine that is activated in normal life in sexual activity, but which may also be drawn upward in subtle channels of the spine to a center in the head, illuminating the consciousness with mystical awareness. The goal of some forms of yoga practice is often referred to as the union of the sun and moon, the fiery and cool kundalini currents in the spinal column. At the junction of these currents, the blissful condition is described as "drinking the soma juice," and the energy flow as "*amaravaruni*" (wine drinking).

The elaborate symbolism and metaphor of Hindu mysticism has often misled commentators into literal interpretations. While intoxicants and hallucinatory drugs may produce transcendental experiences, throughout history great prophets and mystics, as well as scientists and geniuses, have been inspired by a higher consciousness that owed nothing to intoxication or hallucinogenic mushrooms. The twentieth-century discovery of psychedelic drugs and their power to transform normal consciousness have misled many people into vastly overstating the role of such substances in the history of mystical experiences. Critics of drug use have also complained that the use of drugs for mystical purposes has yet to "produce a single inspiring statement on the philosophy and meaning of life comparable with the wisdom of the prophets and mystics of history."

In the 1960s, several groups were formed in the United States to promote the idea of the religious use of psychedelics, but most of these dissolved following negative court actions. Outside of these circles, as recently as 1988, a short-lived attempt to defend the psychedelic/soma connection was made in the journal *ReVision* (vol. 10, no. 4, spring 1988). There was little positive response and a strong rebuttal by Gene Kieffer, a follower of Indian teacher **Gopi Krishna.**

Sources:

Allegro, John M. *The Sacred Mushroom and the Cross.* London: Hodder & Stoughton, 1970; Garden City, N.Y.: Doubleday, 1970.

Gopi Krishna. *The Awakening of Kundalini.* New York: E. P. Dutton, 1973.

Iyangar, Yogi Srinivasa. *Hatha-Yoga-Pradipika of Svatmarama Svamin.* Adyar, Madras, India: Theosophical Publishing House, 1933.

Kieffer, Gene. "An Appeal for Common Sense." *SFF Newsletter* [Spiritual Frontiers Fellowship] (October 1988).

———. "It's Not the Soma that the Brahmans Know!" *SFF Newsletter* [Spiritual Frontiers Fellowship] (September 1988).

———. "*ReVision* Revisits the Sacred Mushroom." *SFF Newsletter* [Spiritual Frontiers Fellowship] (August 1988).

Masters, R. E. L., and Jean Houston. *The Varieties of Psychedelic Experience.* New York: Delta, 1967.

Rele, Vasant G. *The Mysterious Kundalini: The Physical Basis of the "Kundalini (Hatha) Yoga" in Terms of Western Anatomy and Physiology.* Rev. ed. Bombay, India: D. B. Taraporevala, 1950.

Wasson, R. Gordon. *Soma, Divine Mushroom of Immortality.* New York: Harcourt Brace Jovanovich, 1971.

Zaehner, R. C. *Mysticism: Sacred and Profane.* London: Clardenon Press, 1957. Reprint, Galaxy Book, 1961.

Somatography

A fringe medical technique deriving from study of the human **aura,** devised by Welsh healer Bryn Jones. The term derives from the Greek and implies "mapping-out of the soul." Jones "massages" the auras of his patients, using a diagnostic device taken over from **radionics** and designed by an American named Mark Gallot. This therapy of healing through the human aura recalls an earlier technique of **Hyppolite Baraduc,** who used to "clip" a short distance around the face and body of his patient with large copper scissors to free the etheric body from the physical part of the aura.

Jones operates a center for healing known as the Company of Somatographers, located in Nottingham Pl., London, W.1., England.

Sommer, Robert (1929–)

Research psychologist with special interest in imagery and its relationship to paranormal experience. He was born April 26, 1929, in New York City. He studied at Hobart College, Geneva, New York (B.A., 1950), the University of Oklahoma (M.S., 1952), and the University of Kansas (Ph.D., 1956). Following his graduation he was a research psychologist at Saskatchewan Hospital, Canada (1957–63) and assistant professor, University of Alberta, Edmonton (1961–63) prior to joining the Department of Psychology at the University of California, Davis, California, in 1963. He contributed a paper on parapsychology to *The Psychic Force: Essays in Modern Psychical Research* edited by Allan Angoff (1970).

Sources:

Angoff, Alan, ed. *The Psychic Force: Essays in Modern Psychical Research.* New York: Putnam, 1970.

Pleasants, Helene, ed. *Biographical Dictionary of Parapsychology.* New York: Helix Press, 1964.

Somnambulism

Term derived from Latin *somnus* (sleep) and *ambulare* (to walk). A state of **sleep,** or half-waking **trance,** spontaneously or artificially induced, in which subconscious faculties take the place of normal consciousness and direct the body in the performance of various actions from the erratic (sleep walking) to the highly intellectual (solving problems). Somnambulism may start as an exaggerated dream and lead to the development of what resembles a secondary personality with a chain of memory of its own. This chain of memory will often be found as part of the hypnotic memory. The personality itself, in some cases, may exhibit wisdom beyond that of the waking subject and perform paranormal feats.

The somnambulist may have his or her eyes closed, and ears deaf to auditory impressions or sense impressions, without awakening any gleam of consciousness. This lack of attention to sensory impressions may have some effect in rousing new trains of association and suggesting a new line of action. It is suggested that the sleepwalker may see only a mental picture of what he or she is doing as in a dream instead of objective reality, and certain experimental tests have suggested that this occurs in some cases.

The somnambulic state was the discovery of the Marquis Chastenet de Puysègur in 1784 in the context of **mesmerism** and **animal magnetism.** He induced it by passes, and finally, by a simple act of will. The Abbé Faria brought it on by shouting; Chevalier de Barbarin by praying; and **James Braid** by staring at a bright object, usually his lancet case.

The nineteenth-century physician Alexandre Bertrand assigned somnambulism to four causes: (1) A particular nervous temperament that predisposes individuals otherwise in good health to paroxysm of somnambulism during their ordinary sleep. (2) It is sometimes produced in the course of certain diseases of which it may be considered a symptom of a crisis. (3) It is often seen in the course of the proceedings necessary to bring on the condition known as animal magnetism. (4) It may result as a consequence of a high degree of mental exaltation. Accordingly, he distinguished four kinds of somnambulism: the natural, the symptomatic, the artificial, and ecstatic. **Hypnotism** would fall under the artificial category, and trance under the ecstatic.

Physiologically, somnambulism differs from sleep in that the muscles retain the ordinary tension of the waking life. The eyeballs are usually in an unnatural position, drawn upward and inward so that the vision is directed to the top of the forehead. There is an insensibility to pain; taste and smell are paralyzed. The external senses are perfectly sealed. No memory is carried into the waking state.

There are various degrees of somnambulism. **Charles Richet** spoke of semi-somnambulism, the state in which the medium retains consciousness while automatic manifestations take place. Catalepsy is a deep stage of somnambulism. The fakirs and yogis of India induced it by an effort of will.

The mildest form of somnambulism is typified in the inarticulate murmurings or vague gestures of a dreaming child, while in the most extreme cases where all the senses are active and the actions apparently as purposive as in the normal waking state, it borders on the condition of spontaneous hypnotism.

Its affinity with hypnosis was recognized early, when the hypnotic subjects of the animal magnetists were designated "somnambules." It is remarkable that somnambulists may walk in dangerous paths with perfect safety, but if they are suddenly awakened they are liable to fall. Spontaneous somnambulism generally indicates some tendency of the nervous system, since as a rule, only in some abnormal state could the dream ideas exercise so exciting an influence on the brain as to rouse to activity centers normally controlling voluntary movements.

Sylvan J. Muldoon (with **Hereward Carrington**) in *The Projection of the Astral Body* (1929) writes of "astral somnambulism," a state of unconscious **astral projection** that, according to Muldoon, was far more common than generally supposed. It mostly occurred in the dream state.

It should be noted that in the wake of contemporary language concerning altered states of consciousness, somnambulism has dropped out of the language of psychology and parapsychology.

Sources:

Belden, L. W. *Somnambulism: The Extraordinary Case of J. C. Rider, the Springfield Somnambulist.* London, 1834.

Bertrand, A. *Traité du Somnambulisme.* Paris, 1824.

Braid, James. *Neurpnology; Or, The Rationale of Nervous Sleep.* London, 1843. Reprint, New York: Arno Press, 1975.

Cahagnet, L. A. *The Celestial Telegraph; Or, Secrets of the Life to Some Revealed Through Magnetism.* London, 1850. Reprint, New York: Arno Press, 1976.

Colquhoun, J. C. *Report of the Experiments on Animal Magnetism; Made By a Committee of the Medical Section of the French Royal Academy of Sciences . . . 1831.* Edinburgh, 1833. Reprint, New York: Arno Press, 1975.

Esdaile, James. *Natural and Mesmerism Clairvoyance.* London, 1852. Reprint, New York: Arno Press, 1975.

Haddock, Joseph W. *Somnolism and Psycheism; Or, The Science of the Soul and the Phenomena of Nervation as Revealed by Vital Magnetism or Mesmerism.* London, 1851. Reprint, New York: Arno Press, 1975.

Fahnestock, W. B. *Statuvolism: Artificial Somnambulism.* Chicago: Religio-Philosophical Publishing House, 1871.

Tuke, W. H. *Sleep-walking and Hypnotism.* Philadelphia: Blakiston; London: Churchill, 1884.

Weinhold, Arnold. *Seven Lectures on Somnambulism.* Edinburgh, Scotland, 1845.

Sons Ahman Israel See Suns Ahman Ishrael—I:A:O:

Sorcery

Term originating in the 14th century. From Middle English *sorcerie,* and Old French *sorcier,* derived from the Vulgar Latin *sortiarius,* traced back to the original Latin, *sors,* meaning lot, or chance, and *sortis,* the genitive case meaning *of,* or *by,* lots. Indicating the practice of **divination** by lots. Its practices date back to prehistoric and pre-Columbian religions, as well as those of the Middle East and ancient Egypt; by the Middle Ages it referred to the practice of malevolent **magic,** or **black magic,** most commonly the use of supposed supernatural power by the agency of evil spirits called forth by spells by any person with a desire for malice, often motivated out of envy or revenge. Contrasted from **witchcraft,** referring to the destructive methods that can be used by anyone, rather than by one with the special innate powers attributed to witches. Also connotes the use of special charms, potions, or rituals to cast a particular spell. Practices abounded in certain regions of Africa and Oceania among the tribal peoples into the 21st century.

Sources:

Encyclopedia Brittanica. http://www.brittanica.com/. April 11, 2000.

Sordi, Signora Lucia (1871– ?)

Italian physical medium, a working-class woman controlled by "Remigio," a spirit who specialized in giving demonstrations, under test conditions, of **matter passing through matter,** producing many-colored psychic lights, **materializations,** and **telekinesis.**

The clothes of the securely-fastened medium were often removed from under a labyrinth of knots while not the slightest ringing was heard from the small bells attached to her garments. Handcuffs and a straitjacket were similarly taken off, and the medium herself was repeatedly placed outside a padlocked wooden fence more than two yards high.

In 1911, the Societa de Studi Psichici de Milano engaged Sordi's services for test sittings during a period of not less than a year. During this investigation, **Baron Schrenck-Notzing** attended two of the sittings. He discovered no trickery but expressed an opinion in *Psychische Studien* that the results might have been obtained by purely mechanical means. This opinion stimulated an animated controversy. In December 1911, and in the following January, the medium sat for scientists in Rome. An interesting account of an attempted exposure is given by Professor V. Tummolo in *Luce e Ombra.* A sitter being touched by a solid materialized limb switched on an electric lamp and produced a dazzling light. Tummolo continues,

"Then to my sight there appeared a sort of transparent shirt, which vanished immediately, instantaneously entering the medium. The latter, who happened to be standing at some distance from the cabinet and not far from the individual responsible for the sudden illumination, fell to the ground like a corpse, and then commenced to wail in an indescribable manner. Every possible attention was hastily rendered her; but she expectorated blood, and felt terrible pains in the region of the heart until the next day—pains which forced her to utter cries which she was unable to repress. . . . In the cabinet, immediately after the event just narrated, the medium's gown was found completely buttoned up, in spite of the fact that she was still bound in the manner previously described—bound, that is to say, in respect to her hands and body, with a network of ribbon."

Tummolo expressed his conviction of the genuineness of Sordi's mediumship.

Sorokin, Pitirim Alexandrovitch (1889–1968)

Professor of sociology with special interest in the supraconscious, manifestations of genius, and creativity. He was born January 21, 1889, at Turya, Vologda Province, Russia. He studied at the University of St. Petersburg (M.A. criminal law, 1916; Ph.D. sociology, 1922). He became a lecturer at the University of St. Petersburg but was eventually banished by the Soviet government in 1922.

He moved to the United States and became a professor of sociology at the University of Minnesota (1924–30). In 1930, he moved to Harvard University, where he founded and headed the department of sociology (1930–43). In 1943, he became the director of the Harvard Research Center in Creative Altruism where he remained until his retirement. Sorokin published 30 books on sociology and history.

He contributed an introduction to *The Psychic Source Book,* edited by **Alson J. Smith,** which includes an appendix in which Sorokin wrote on the importance of parapsychology. He died February 19, 1968.

SORRAT

Acronym for the Society for Research on Rapport and Telekinesis, a group founded by **John G. Neihardt.** Meetings were usually held at Neihardt's home at Skyrim Farm, near Columbia, Missouri.

Neihardt's interest in psychic matters stemmed from his close association with the Indian Rights movement from 1903 on. Neihardt was accepted as a participant in secret healing ceremonies and was actively concerned with the Indian shaman Black Elk, the subject of his book *Black Elk Speaks* (William Morrow, 1932). Neihardt's wife, Mona, had been associated with

Spiritualism and was mediumistic, and Neihardt investigated the phenomena of various mediums.

The SORRAT group was formed during the mid-1960s with a primary focus on the manipulation of matter by conscious mental effort. Neihardt discussed the group methods with veteran parapsychologist **J. B. Rhine,** in order to conduct experiments in a congenial atmosphere that would also be **fraud**-proof.

One technique employed was the "mini-lab"—a sealed transparent box containing target objects for testing psychokinesis. With the assistance of parapsychologist **Edward William Cox,** an automatic filming method was developed in which a fixed movie camera and lights were trained on a mini-lab and activated by an electrical signal. The former **McDonnell Laboratory for Psychic Research** also supported these techniques. From 1965 on, the SORRAT group performed experiments tending to validate **psychokinesis, levitation, apports, apparitions,** and **communication** with entities. However, the methods of recording the phenomena were so poor that most parapsychologists have dismissed the experiments as the unfortunate work of unprepared amateurs and hence of no evidential value.

Sources:

Berger, Arthur S., and Joyce Berger. *The Encyclopedia of Parapsychology and Psychical Research.* New York: Paragon House, 1991.

Richards, John Thomas. *SORRAT: A History of the Neihardt Psychokinesis Experiments, 1961–1981.* Metuchen, N.J.: Scarecrow Press, 1982.

Sorrel Leaf

A sorrel leaf was sometimes used to bewitch people, as in the case of the Irish witch mentioned in George Sinclair's *Satan's Invisible World Displayed* (1685), who gave to a girl a leaf of sorrel that the child put into her mouth. Great torture ensued for the child and increased on the approach of the witch.

Sortilege

Divination by lots, one of the most ancient and common superstitions. It was used among Oriental nations to detect a guilty person, as when Saul by this means discovered that Jonathan had disobeyed his command by taking food, and when the sailors by a similar process found Jonah to be the cause of the tempest by which they were overtaken.

The various methods of using the lot have been very numerous, including **rhabdomancy,** clidomancy, the Sortes Sagittariae or **belomancy,** and the common casting of dice. The following are the more classical methods:

Sortes Thriaecae, or Thriaen lots, were chiefly used in Greece; they were pebbles or counters distinguished by certain characters that were cast into an urn, and the first that came out was supposed to contain the right direction. This form of divination received its name from the Thriaej, three nymphs supposed to have nursed Apollo and to have invented this mode of predicting futurity.

Sortes Viales, or street and road lots, were used both in Greece and Rome. The person that wanted to learn his fortune carried with him a certain number of lots, distinguished by several characters or inscriptions. Walking to and fro in the public ways he asked the first boy whom he met to draw, and the inscription on the lot thus drawn was received as an infallible prophecy. Plutarch declared that this form of divination was derived from the Egyptians, by whom the actions and words of boys were carefully observed as containing in them something prophetical.

Another form of the Sortes Viales was exhibited by a boy, or sometimes by a man, who positioned himself in a public place to give responses to all comers. He was provided with a tablet, on which certain predictive verses were written; when consulted, he cast dice on the tablet, and the verses on which they fell were supposed to contain the proper direction. Sometimes instead of tablets they had urns, in which the verses were thrown, written upon slips of parchment. The verse drawn out was received as a sure guide and direction. Tibullus alluded to this custom as follows: "Thrice in the streets the sacred lots she threw, and thrice the boy a happy omen drew." This form of divining was often practiced with the Sibylline oracles, and hence was named Sortes Sibyllina.

Sortes Prenestinae, or the Prenestine lots, were used in Italy. The letters of the alphabet were placed in an urn and shaken; they were then turned out upon the floor, and the words that they accidentally formed were received as omens.

This divinatory use of letters is still known in Eastern countries. The Muslims had a divining table that they said was invented by the prophet Edris or Enoch. It was divided into a hundred little squares, each of which contained a letter of the Arabic alphabet. The person who consulted it repeated three times the opening chapter of the Qur'an, and the 57th verse of the 6th chapter: "With Him are the keys of the secret things; none knoweth them but Him; He knoweth whatever is on the dry ground, or in the sea: there falleth no leaf but he knoweth it; neither is there a single grain in the dark parts of the earth, nor a green thing, nor a dry thing, but it is written in a perspicuous book."

Having concluded this recitation, he averted his head from the table and placed his finger upon it; he then looked to see upon what letter his finger was placed, wrote that letter; the fifth following it; the fifth following that again; and so on until he came back to the first he had touched. The letters thus collected formed the answer.

Sortes Homericae and Sortes Virgilianae involve divination by opening some poem at hazard and accepting the passage that first turns up as an answer. This practice probably arose from the esteem that poets had among the ancients, by whom they were reputed divine and inspired persons. Homer's works among the Greeks had the most credit, but the tragedies of Euripides and other celebrated poems were occasionally used for the same purpose. The Latins chiefly consulted Virgil, and many curious coincidences were related by grave historians, between the prediction and the event; thus, the elevation of Severus to the Empire is supposed to have been foretold by his opening at this verse, "Remember, Roman, with imperial sway to rule the nations."

It is said that Charles I and Lord Falkland made trial of the Virgilian lots a short time before the commencement of the great Civil War. The former opened at that passage in the fourth book of the Æneid where Dido predicts the violent death of her faithless lover; the latter at the lamentation of Evander over his son in the eleventh book. If the story is true, the coincidences between the responses and events are remarkable.

Sortes Biblicae was divination by the Bible, which the early Christians used instead of the profane poets. Nicephorus Gregoras recommended the Psalter as the fittest book for the purpose, but Cedrenus stated that the New Testament was more commonly used. St. Augustine denounced this practice in temporal affairs, but declared in one of his letters that he had recourse to it in all cases of spiritual difficulty. Another form of the Biblical lots was to go to a place of worship and take as an omen the first passage of Scripture read by the minister or the text from which he preached.

Muslims consulted the Qur'an in a similar manner, but one of their methods was to deduce their answer from the seventh line of the right-hand page. Others counted how often the letters *kha* and *shin* occurred in the page; if *kha* (the first letter of *kheyr,* "good") predominated, the answer was deemed favorable, but if *shin* (the first letter of *shin,* "evil") appeared more frequently, the inference was that the projects of the inquirer were forbidden or dangerous.

It would be easy to multiply examples of these efforts to obtain guidance from blind chance. They were once so frequent that it was deemed necessary to denounce them from the pulpit as being clearly forbidden by the divine precept, "Thou shalt not tempt the Lord thy God."

Soul

The term soul is used in two senses—it indicates the ego and the spirit-body. In ancient writings, an individual was described as a triune being: body, soul, and spirit. According to this concept, the soul is just as much an envelope, animated by the spirit, as the physical body is an envelope for the soul. At death the soul withdraws and continues to function in the spiritual world. **Astral body** and soul are almost equivalent terms.

Some occult and Eastern teachings, however, speak of five bodies of differing degrees of refinement that will be cast away in time just as the physical body is left behind.

In his book *Man and the Universe* (1908), **Sir Oliver Lodge** defined the soul and ego as,

". . . that controlling and guiding principle which is responsible for our personal expression and for the construction of the body, under the restrictions of physical condition and ancestry. In its higher development it includes also feeling and intelligence and will, and is the storehouse of mental experience. The body is its instrument or organ, enabling it to receive and convey physical impressions, and to effect and be effected by matter and energy."

Because such concepts as "soul" and "spirit" (as its animating essence) are not available for scientific scrutiny like the body or the world of matter generally, many scientists have either denied their existence as real entities or as a reality not subject to scientific scrutiny, although retaining as useful the concept of consciousness, with which the ego is associated.

Spiritualists claim that there is evidence for **survival** of consciousness after death, and that there is sufficient individuality in the surviving consciousness to justify the use of the term soul. A good deal of psychical research tends to confirm this position, without necessarily accepting the religious implications of such survival.

Christianity has generally taught the resurrection of the body, although, in light of Paul's mention of a spiritual resurrection body, there has been some disagreement on the exact nature of that revived body. The doctrine of the soul has always vied for attention with the Greek notion of the immortality of the soul.

In Eastern religious philosophy, there are clear distinctions between the gross ego of name and form (with individual experience) and the subtle ego that is claimed as a universal substratum of all individual souls. The gross ego, by reason of its limitations of experience and consciousness, is tied to the world of matter, which is transient. This ego is an obstruction to fuller awareness of reality and must be transcended by selfless service and refinement of consciousness. In this process, the individual soul loses its attachment to the transient desires and fears of material life and is eventually subsumed in a divine consciousness. In this progress, the world of matter becomes like an illusion that ceases to have validity when divine reality supervenes. As long as an attachment to the world of matter and sense experience remains, the soul must go through a process of **reincarnation.**

The concept of the soul remains unverifiable by experimental method that is based on the limitations of material existence itself. But it is a useful concept insofar as it relates to individual subjective experience, which is often more relevant to ethical goals than laboratory experiments.

For many individuals, the conviction that there is a soul that is independent of (although shaped by) the physical body occurs as they experience **out-of-the-body travel** or **astral projection.** Such an experience is an overwhelming one to most who have it and has become a profound religious experience to many individuals.

Sources:

Bernard, Theos. *The Philosophical Foundations of India.* London: Rider, 1945.

Broad, C. D. *The Mind and Its Place in Nature.* London: Kegan Paul, 1925.

Carrington, Hereward. *Psychic Science and Survival.* Manchester, England: Two Worlds Publishing; New York: American Psychical Institute, 1939.

Carus, Paul. *The Soul of Man.* Chicago: Open Court, 1900.

Crookall, Robert. *Out-of-the-Body Experiences and Survival.* UK: World Fellowship Press, 1970.

———. *The Supreme Adventure.* London: James Clarke, 1961.

Ducasse, C. J. *A Critical Examination of the Belief in a Life After Death.* Springfield, Ill.: Charles C. Thomas, 1961.

Head, Joseph, and S. L. Cranston. *Reincarnation: The Phoenix Fire Mystery.* New York: Julian Press; Crown Publishers, 1977.

James, William. *The Varieties of Religious Experience.* London: Longmans, Green, 1903.

Myers, F. W. H. *Human Personality and Its Survival of Bodily Death.* 2 vols. London: Longmans, Green, 1903.

Purohit, Swami Shri. *The Geeta: The Gospel of the Lord Shri Krishna.* London: Faber & Faber, 1935.

Soule, Minnie Meserve (d. 1936)

Trance medium of the **American Society for Psychical Research,** known in early experiments under the pseudonym "Mrs. Chenoweth." For many years **J. H. Hyslop** made interesting tests in cases of **obsession** with her mediumship. She produced excellent trance phenomena, similar to those of **Leonora Piper.** Soule was controlled by "Imperator" and "Sunbeam," the spirit of a child.

In the publications of the **Boston Society for Psychic Research,** an interesting record of séances narrates the experiences of **Lydia W. Allison,** with supplementary material by **Walter Franklin Prince,** under the title *Leonard and Soule Experiments in Psychical Research* (1929). An earlier work, *Spirit Messages* (Rochester, 1914), dedicated to the medium Hiram Corson of Cornell University, recorded unique communications received through Soule, apparently from Robert and Elizabeth Barrett Browning, Alfred Lord Tennyson, Henry Wadsworth Longfellow, and many other eminent minds.

Sources:

Allison, Lydia W. *Leonard and Soule Experiments in Psychical Research.* Boston: Boston Society for Psychic Research, 1929.

Thomas, John F. *Beyond Normal Cognition.* Boston: Boston Society for Psychic Research, 1937.

SoulSongs, Inc., The Center for Sound Healing

SoulSongs, Inc., The Center for Sound Healing is an organization founded and led by a woman known only as Shulamit (from the Hebrew word *Shalam,* meaning whole or complete), described as a gifted healer and a Kabbalistic vocal toner. Her work is based upon the **Kabbalah,** the ancient Jewish system of mystic wisdom. The Kabbalah pictures the universe as having emanated from God through a series of levels, each of which is entered through a gate or *sephiroh* (sephira). These ten gates are often pictured on a diagram called the Tree of Life. The highest of the sephiroh are named Kether and Chochmah.

As a tonal healer, Shulamit uses her voice to produce sacred tones (the sounds of the Hebrew vowels that are identified as the breath of God in the Kabbalistic literature). Her intoning the sounds allows her to access what is thought of as the Chochmah consciousness, a level of wisdom that exists beyond words and concepts, a realm that is boundless and infinite. She then brings that wisdom into a realm of verbal and conceptual understanding (the sephiroh call Binah) and relates it to each person with whom she works.

Shulamit teaches that according to Kabbalah, each person has a higher self (the Neshamah) that in most cases is dormant and must be awakened. Shulamit offers personal sessions to individuals who wish to stimulate their higher self into action or who are in need of healing.

The Center for Sound Healing may be contacted at P.O. Box 465, High Falls, NY 12440. It maintains two webpages, http://www.soulsongs.com/ and http://www.kabbalah.com/.

Sources:

Soul Songs. http://www.soulsongs.com/. May 20, 2000.

Soul Travel

The primary spiritual experience of practitioners of **ECKANKAR,** a religious system developed by Sir **Paul Twitchell.** While connections are denied by the organization, soul travel closely resembles **astral projection** or **out-of-the-body travel.** Travel is seen as taking place on the various planes of existence as originally described in the literature of the Radhasoami Beas.

Sounds (in Psychical Research)

Sounds produced in the séance room fall into two main categories: ordinary and psychic. In the first category belong all the natural sounds emitted by the manipulation of certain objects without any visible agency. In the second are the sounds that apparently do not relate to any visible object; both the source and the production of these sounds are unknown.

The noises that accompany the movement of objects, such as the lifting of a table or the shaking of bells or tambourines, are ordinary noises. **Raps, direct voice,** direct music, sounds of invisible instruments, machines, the rattle of chains, the clashing of swords, and sounds of galloping, without having the noise-producing object in the room, would be considered psychic.

Another differentiation may be made according to the intelligence required for the sound production. No intellectual effort is necessary to bang a table or shake a bell. The phonograph requires certain experience, the playing of an instrument artistic education.

The simplest psychic sounds are the raps. Their tonal scale and expressive power is surprising and their strength may increase to formidable blows. For example, as Lord Adare in *Experiences in Spiritualism with D. D. Home* (1870) notes, "At one time, Miss Wynne, Home and I heard a very singular rumbling and rolling sort of sound in the air behind us, which was repeated three times."

The sounds in the séances of **W. Stainton Moses** showed an extraordinary range. The first sound, as distinct from raps, was heard on March 23, 1873, and resembled the plucking of a string in midair. It soon imitated a musical clock that was in the next room. Two months later, the sound became so loud that the vibration of the table was marked.

"The sound would traverse the room and seem to die away in the distance, and suddenly burst forth into great power over the table, which appeared, in some inexplicable way, to be used as a sounding board. The wood of the table vibrated under our hands exactly as it would have done had a violincello been twanged while resting upon it. . . . The sounds were at times deafening and alternated between those made by the very small strings of a harp and such as would be caused by the violent thrumming of a violincello resting on the top of a drum. . . . With them, as with other phenomena, a great variety was caused by good or bad conditions. Just as illness or atmospheric disturbance made the perfumes and drapery coarse and unrefined, so the lyre sounds became harsh, unmusical and wooden. . . . The table was used until at times the musical twang would shade into a sort of musical knock, and finally become an ordinary dull thud upon the table. . . . When things were not all right, the sound would assume a most melancholy wailing character, which was indescribably weird and saddening. It was not unlike the soughing of the wind through trees in the dead of night; a ghost-like dreary sound that few persons would sit long to listen to. That sound was always accompanied by black darkness in the room. . . . No point, indeed, connected with these strange sounds is more remarkable than the intensity of feeling conveyed by them. . . . Anger, sadness, content and mirth, solemnity and eagerness, are conveyed in a way that is quite inexplicable. . . . The wailing sounds above noticed seem at times almost to sob and shriek as if in a burst of sadness. Sometimes to a question put silence will be maintained for a while, and then little hesitating sounds will be made, very slowly and tremulously, as to convey perfectly the idea of uncertainty and doubt. Then again the reply will come clear, sonorous, and immediate as the 'I do' of a witness in the box who has no doubt as to the answer he should give.

"The sounds used always to commence near the circle, and, so to say, radiate from it as a centre into different parts of the room. Of late they have changed, and are usually audible to me before they strike the ear of any other person. How far this may be attributable to clairaudience, a faculty lately developed in me, I cannot say positively. But at any rate, they seem to me to commence by a distant rumble, not unlike the roll of a drum. This gradually draws nearer until it is audible to all, and the old sounds are in our midst.

"Hitherto I only mentioned the stringed musical sounds. . . . But there are other sounds which professedly emanate from the same source and which resemble the sound of a tambourine played over our heads, or, at times, the flapping of a pair of large wings. . . . Still later other sounds, like those made by a small zither, have presented themselves."

Charlton Speer, in an account given to **F. W. H. Myers,** described four kinds of musical sounds produced without any instrument in the room. The first was called "fairy bells." These resembled the tones produced by striking musical glasses with a small hammer. No definite tune was ever played, but the bells, on request, would always run up and down a scale in perfect tune. It was difficult to judge where the sounds came from, but when Speer applied his ear to the top of the table it seemed to be somehow in the wood. The second was a stringed instrument, akin to a violincello but more powerful and sonorous. It was only heard in single notes and was employed to answer questions. The third sound was an exact imitation of an ordinary handbell. It denoted the presence of a particular spirit. The fourth sound could best be described by imagining the soft tone of a clarinet gradually increasing in intensity, until it rivaled the sound of a trumpet, then by degrees gradually diminished to the original subdued tone of the clarinet, until it eventually died away in a drawn-out, melancholy wail. In no case were more than single notes, or at best isolated passages, produced. The controlling agencies accounted for this with the peculiarly unmusical organization of the medium.

Various sounds were used by some of the spirit **controls** as a special mark of identity. "Grocyn" produced pure sounds like those of a thick harp string; "Chom" made the sound of an old Egyptian harp with four strings; "Said" used a three stringed lyre; "Roophal" a seven-stringed one with a rippling sound; and "Kabbila's" sound was like a drum, very deep, a sort of prolonged roll.

It is said in mediumistic communications that the spirits, in their world, can create for themselves from fluidic material the things they wish. Spirits have claimed that they can produce the sound of anything in this same way.

In Gwendolyn K. Hack's *Modern Psychic Mysteries at Millesimo Castle* (1929), there is the interesting note that the spirit of the young aviator Vittorio Centurione always arrived and departed in his airplane. The coming of the airplane was heard from a distance, then it descended into the séance room with the characteristic noise and flew above as if there was no limit of space and finally stopped. On the first occasion when "Centurione" manifested, the approach of the plane was followed by the sound of falling, hissing, and splashing into the water illustrating the very manner by which this aviator had perished over Lake Varese.

Dancing performances and duels were executed for the sitters' entertainment at the séances at Millesimo Castle. In the notes of the séance August 12, 1928, we find:

"D'Angelo: 'Here, in the midst of you, a little battle between two Romans is going to take place' . . . we heard the sound of two swords hastily withdrawn from their scabbards. They were crossed and glanced off each other in a sinister manner. Then we heard the most formidable blows, given first by one side and then by the other. These blows rained upon metal, echoing upon the shields and helmets of the warriors. We heard rapid footsteps pounding the floor as the combatants fought, now advancing, now retreating. It was quite alarming, and one could not avoid cowering instinctively, when a powerful thrust came too close, for one felt that the next blow might glance off and strike one's head or neck."

Will Goldston wrote an account of a séance with **Rudi Schneider** in the *Sunday Graphic* (December 22, 1929):

"Several heavy thuds followed, as though a giant were striking a block of marble with a mallet. The extraordinary thing was that the thuds did not seem to come from the walls, the ceiling or the floor, but from the table. They were powerful thuds, and yet they did not cause any vibration in the room, as such thuds caused by normal means would create."

Sources:

Adare, Lord. *Experiences in Spiritualism with D. D. Home.* Glasgow: R. Maclehose, 1924.

Hack, Gwendolyn Kelley. *Modern Psychic Mysteries at Millesimo Castle Italy.* London: Rider, 1929.

South African Society for Psychical Research

The first South African Society for Psychical Research was founded in 1910 but existed for only a few years. It was not until 1955 that a second attempt to form such an organization was attempted, this time by Arthur E. H. Bleksley and others at the University of Witwatersrand. The previous year an informal group had gathered to study psychic phenomena, and the interest stimulated by this group led directly to the society's formation.

No sooner had the society formed than it came under a strong ideological attack by a group of psychic debunkers, described as "Marxists, atheists, and communists," and the original program of the group was diverted to answering the challenge. It developed a public program to establish the existence of psi phenomena and the legitimacy of scientific efforts to study it. It was able to survive this crisis successfully and has continued to exist to the present. In 1968, it founded the South African Institute for Parapsychological Research and moved from an exclusive emphasis on education to the development of a research program. The institute survived for several years but eventually ran out of funds.

Over the long haul, the society has suffered from the country's former apartheid policies, which prohibited the participation of black people in the organization. Social customs also prevented research among the native population, which would have provided a unique resource for the society. Also, the relatively small white population has had difficulty keeping the society functioning on a steady basis. Its meetings and publications are sporadic, and it has been unable to establish a headquarters or hire staff. However, the society now publishes the *Parapsychological Journal of South Africa,* and in 1974 a branch of the society opened at the University of Natal in Durbin. It may be contacted at P.O. Box 23154, Joubert Park, Johannesburg 2044, South Africa.

Sources:

"The South African Society for Psychical Research." *Journal of the Psychical Research Society* 40 (1959): 43.

SOUTH AMERICA

[Note: See the related article on Native North Americans in the entry **America.**]

South American Indians

Throughout South America, the magician caste analogous to the medicine men or shamans of North America were known as *piaies* or *piaes.* Of those of British Guiana (now Guyana), W. H. Brett gives the following account in *The Indian Tribes of Guiana* (1868):

"They are each furnished with a large gourd or calabash, which has been emptied of its seeds and spongy contents, and has a round stick run through the middle of it by means of two holes. The ends of this stick project—one forms the handle of the instrument, and the other has a long string to which beautiful feathers are attached, wound round it in spiral circles. Within the calabash are a few small white stones, which rattle when it is shaken or turned round. The calabash itself is usually painted red. It is regarded with great awe by the heathen Indians, who fear to touch it, or even to approach the place where it is kept.

"When attacked by sickness, the Indians cause themselves to be conveyed to some friendly sorcerer, to whom a present of more or less value must be made. Death is sometimes occasioned by those removals, cold being taken from wet or the damp of the river. If the patient cannot be removed, the sorcerer is sent for to visit him. The females are all sent away from the place and the men must keep at a respectful distance, as he does not like his proceedings to be closely inspected. He then commences his exorcisms, turning, and shaking his *marakka,* or rattle, and chanting an address to the *yauhahu.* This is continued for hours, about midnight the spirit is supposed to be present, and a conversation to take place, which is unintelligible to the Indians, who may overhear it. These ceremonies are kept up for successive nights.

"If the patient be strong enough to endure the disease, the excitement, the noise, and the fumes of tobacco in which he is at times enveloped, and the sorcerer observes signs of recovery he will pretend to extract the cause of the complaint by sucking the part affected. After many ceremonies he will produce from his mouth some strange substance, such as a thorn or gravel-stone, a fish-bone or bird's claw, a snake's tooth, or a piece of wire, which some malicious *yauhahu* is supposed to have inserted in the affected part. As soon as the patient fancies himself rid of this cause of his illness his recovery is generally rapid, and the fame of the sorcerer greatly increased. Should death, however, ensue, the blame is laid upon the evil spirit, whose power and malignity have prevailed over the counteracting charms. Some rival sorcerer will at times come in for a share of the blame, whom the sufferer has unhappily made his enemy, and who is supposed to have employed the *yauhahu* in destroying him. The sorcerers being supposed to have the power of causing, as well as of curing diseases, are much dreaded by the common people, who never willfully offend them. So deeply rooted in the Indian's bosom is this belief concerning the origin of diseases, that they have little idea of sickness arising from other causes. Death may arise from a wound or a contusion, or be brought on by want of food, but in other cases it is the work of the *yauhahu.*

"I once came upon a Warau practising his art upon a woman inflicted with a severe internal complaint. He was, when I first saw him, blowing violently into his hands and rubbing them upon the affected part. He very candidly acknowledged his imposture when I taxed him with it, put up his implements, and went away. The fate of the poor woman, as it was related to me some time afterwards, was very sad. Though a Venezuelan half-breed, and of the Church of Rome, she was wedded to the Indian superstitions, and after trying the most noted sorcerers without relief, she inflicted on herself a mortal wound with a razor in the vain attempt to cut out the imaginary cause of her internal pain.

"Some have imagined that those men have faith in the power of their own incantations from their performing them over their own children, and even causing them to be acted over themselves when sick. This practice it is indeed difficult to account for. The juggling part of their business is such a gross imposture as could only succeed with a very ignorant and credulous people; but it is perhaps in their case, as in some others, difficult to tell the precise point where credulity ends and imposture begins. It is certain that they are excited during their incantations in a most extraordinary way, and positively affirm that they hold intercourse with spirits; nor will they allow themselves to be laughed out of the assertion however ridiculous it may appear to us.

"The Waraus, in many points the most degraded of the tribes, are the most renowned as sorcerers. The huts which they set apart for the performance of their superstitious rites are regarded with great veneration.

"Mr. Nowers, on visiting a Warau settlement, entered one of those huts, not being aware of the offense he was committing and found it perfectly empty, with the exception of the gourd, or *mataro,* as it is called by the tribe. There was, in the centre of the hut, a small raised place about eighteen inches high, on which the fire had been made for burning tobacco. The sorcerer being asked to give up the gourd, peremptorily refused, saying that if he did so his two children would die the same night."

Franz Keller, in *Amazon and Madeira Rivers* (1874), observes of the Brazilian tribes as follows:

"As with the shamans of the North Asiatic nations, the influence a Pajé may secure over his tribe depends entirely on the success of his cures and his more or less imposing personal qualities. Woe to him if by some unlucky ministration or fatal advice he forfeits his prestige. The hate of the whole tribe turns against him, as if to indemnify them for the fear and awe felt by them until then; and often he pays for his envied position with his life.

"And an influential and powerful position it is. His advice is first heard in war and peace. He has to mark the boundaries of the hunting-grounds; and, when quarrels arise, he has to decide in concert with the chieftain, sometimes even against the latter's wishes. By a majestically distant demeanour, and by the affectation of severe fasting and of nightly meetings with the spirits of another world, these augurs have succeeded in giving such an appearance of holiness to the whole caste, that their influence is a mighty one to the present day, even with the Indians of the Aldeamentos, where contact with the white race is sure by-and-by to produce a certain degree of scepticism.

"When I was at the Aldeamento of San Ignacio, on the Paranapanema, Cuyaba, chieftain and Pajé of an independent horde of Cayowa Indians made his appearance, and I had the honour of being introduced to this magnificent sample of a conjurer. He was a man of about fifty, with large well-cut features, framed within a dense, streaming mane of long black hair. The long *xerimbita* on his under lip (a long, thin, cylinder of a resin resembling amber), a great number of black and white beads covering his chest in regular rows like a cuirass, and a broad girdle holding his *cherapi* (sort of apron), which was fringed all round with rich, woven ornaments, gave him quite a stately, majestic appearance."

The Chileans called their magicians *gligua* or *dugol,* and they were subdivided into *guenguenu, genpugnu,* and *genpiru,* meaning respectively "masters of the heavens," "of epidemics," and "of insects *or* worms." There was also a sect called *calcu,* or "sorcerers," who lived in caves, and who were served by *ivunches,* or "man-animals," to whom they taught their terrible arts.

The Araucanians believed that these wizards had the power to transform themselves at night into nocturnal birds, to fly through the air, and to shoot invisible arrows at their enemies, besides indulging in the malicious mischief with which folklore credits the wizards of all countries. They believed their priests possessed numerous familiars who were attached to them after death—similar to the beliefs of the magicians of the Middle Ages. These priests or diviners were celibate, and led an existence apart from the tribe, in some communities being dressed as women. Many tales are told of their prowess in magic, that indicate that they were either natural epileptics or ecstatics, or that disturbing mental influences were brought about by the use of drugs. The Araucanians also held that to mention their real personal names gave magic power over them that might be turned to evil ends. Regarding the wizards of the inhabitants of the territory around the River Chaco in Paraguay, Barbrook Grubb records as follows in *An Unknown People in an Unknown Land*:

"The training necessary to qualify an Indian to become a witch-doctor consists, in the first place, in severe fastings, and especially in abstention from fluid. They carry this fasting to such an excess as to affect the nervous system and brain. Certain herbs are eaten to hasten this stage. They pass days in solitude, and, when thoroughly worked up to an hysterical condition, they see spirits and ghosts, and have strange visions. It is necessary, furthermore, that they should eat live toads and some kinds of snakes. Certain little birds are plucked alive and then devoured, their power of whistling being supposed to be thus communicated to the witch-doctor. There are other features in the preliminary training which need not be mentioned, and when the initiatory stage has been satisfactorily passed, they are instructed in the mysteries under pledge of secrecy. After that their future depends upon themselves.

"It is unquestionable that a few of these wizards understand to a slight degree the power of hypnotism. They appear at times to throw themselves into a hypnotic state by sitting in a strained position for hours, fixing their gaze upon some distant object. In this condition they are believed to be able to throw their souls out—that is, in order to make them wander. It seems that occasionally, when in this state, they see visions which are quite the opposite of those they had desired. At other times they content themselves with concentrating their attention for a while upon one of their charms, and I have no doubt that occasionally they are sincere in desiring to solve some perplexing problems.

"One of the chief duties of the wizard is to arrange the weather to suit his clansmen. If they want rain it is to him they apply. His sorceries are of such a kind that they may be extended over a long period. He is never lacking in excuses, and so, while apparently busy in combating the opposing forces which are hindering the rain, he gains time to study weather signs. He will never or rarely venture an opinion as to the expected change until he is nearly certain of a satisfactory result. Any other Indian could foretell rain were he to observe signs as closely as does the wizard. The killing of a certain kind of duck, and the sprinkling of its blood upwards, is his chief charm. When he is able to procure this bird he is sure that rain cannot be far off, because these ducks do not migrate southwards until they know that there is going to be water in the swamps. These swamps are filled by the overflowing of the rivers as much as by the local rainfalls, and the presence of water in the rivers and swamps soon attracts rain-clouds.

"The wizards also observe plants and animals, study the sky and take note of other phenomena, and by these means can arrive at fairly safe conclusions. They are supposed to be able to foretell events, and to a certain extent they succeed so far as these events concern local interest. By judicious questioning and observation, the astute wizard is able to judge with some amount of exactitude how certain matters are likely to turn out.

"After we had introduced bullock-carts into their country, the people were naturally interested in the return of the carts from their periodical journeys to the river. When the wizards had calculated carefully the watering-places, and had taken into consideration the state of the roads, the character of the drivers, and the condition and number of the bullocks, all that they then required to know was the weight of the loads and the day on which it was expected that the carts would leave the river on their return journey. The last two items they had to obtain from us. When they had these data, by a simple calculation they could make a very shrewd guess, not only at the time when they might be expected to arrive at the village, but also at what particular part of the road they might happen to be on any given day. A great impression was made upon the simple people by this exhibition of power, but when we discovered what they were doing, we withheld the information, or only gave them part, with the result that their prophecies either failed ignominiously or proved very erroneous. Their reputation accordingly began to wane.

"The wizards appear to be authorities on agricultural matters, and when application to the garden spirit has failed, the witch-doctor is called in. He examines the crop, and if he thinks it is likely to be a poor one, he says it is being blighted by an evil spirit, but that he will use what sorceries he can to preserve it. If, on the other hand, he has reason to believe that the crop will be a good one, he spits upon it here and there, and then assures the people that now they may expect a good harvest.

"Some of the chief duties of the witch-doctor consist in laying ghosts, driving off spirits, exorcising *kilyikhama* in cases of possession, assisting wandering souls back to their bodies, and generally in the recognising of spirits. When a ghost is supposed to haunt a village, the wizard and his assistants have sometimes an hour's arduous chanting in order to induce the restless one to leave. When he considers that he has accomplished this, he assures the people that it is done, and this quiets their fears. Evil spirits frequenting a neighbourhood have also to be driven off by somewhat similar chanting."

Through the twentieth century, practices first described in the nineteenth century by anthropologists have been integrated into the Spiritualist groups of the countries of South America, especially **Brazil.**

Sources:

Brett, William H. *The Indian Tribes of Guiana.* London, 1868.

Grubb, W. Barbrook. *An Unknown People in an Unknown Land.* London, 1911.

Keller, Franz. *Amazon and Madeira Rivers.* London, 1874.

McGregor, Pedro. *Jesus of the Spirits.* New York: Stein & Day, 1966.

Playfair, Guy Lyon. *The Flying Cow.* London, 1975. Reprinted as *The Unknown Power.* New York: Pocket Books, 1975.

Southcott, Joanna (1750–1814)

British prophetess of the eighteenth and nineteenth centuries who announced that she had a divine pregnancy. She was born on April 25, 1750, one of the daughters of a farmer in the village of Gittisham, East Devon, England. She grew up in a devout religious atmosphere, being obliged to read a chapter of the Bible daily and discuss it with her father. She became a sturdy, vivacious, self-reliant young woman.

When she was 21, her father because ill, obliging her to take charge of the farm, which she managed admirably for a couple of years until her father recovered. Southcott left the farm and went into domestic service for five years at the house of an upholsterer in Exeter, where she also became skilled in the trade. She next went to work as a maid for a couple named Taylor.

For 42 years Joanna had lived a normal life, but in 1792, at the time of her menopause, she began to have strange experiences.

Southcott's Prophetic Career

These were apocalyptic times. In France, revolutionary mobs had stormed the king's palace, and the houses of noblemen were in flames. Radical propagandists sought to foment revolution in Britain. Tom Paine's *The Rights of Man* had just been published. Several extreme religious movements had appeared.

Among the prophetic voices was that of a young naval officer, Richard Brothers. Brothers immersed himself in Bible study and preached powerful sermons on his apocalyptic visions, with warnings of the Day of Doom. He believed that the time had come for the Jews to regain Palestine, that the British were a lost tribe of Israel, and that the Second Coming of the Lord was at hand. Brothers was eventually arrested and charged with "maliciously publishing fantastical prophecies with intent to cause disturbances," certified as insane, and sent to a mental asylum, where he stayed for 11 years.

About this time Southcott also began to have similar apocalyptic dreams and visions. She was visited by a "voice," which told her,"The Lord is awakened out of sleep. He will terribly shake the earth." At first, Southcott thought she was being deluded by Satan, but the voice began to make amazingly accurate prophecies about events, both great and small.

Asked for a sign, the voice knocked three times on the bedstead—an early precursor of the **raps** at nineteenth-century Spiritualist séances. Then she suddenly found her hand writing messages without conscious guidance. She stated, "The writing comes extremely fast, much faster than I could keep up by voluntary effort. I have to turn over the pages and guard the lines of writing from running into each other; but, except for this, I need not look at the paper. I can talk on other subjects while writing. The mass of the writings consists in teachings on Religion. Some messages, however, deal with earthly matters." Many of the writings were in simple verse form.

When her prophecies on domestic affairs began to be vindicated, Southcott became confident that the voice was a true guide, and she attempted to interest religious authorities in her messages. A Methodist preacher listened to her, then pronounced, "This is from Satan to disturb your peace." She approached the Dissenters, but their minister stated that her revelations were unscriptural. She then turned to the established Church and wrote to a preacher named Joseph Pomeroy, vicar of St. Kew in Cornwall, who had himself warned of perilous times to come.

Pomeroy received her kindly and said he saw nothing diabolical in the messages, but he told her mistress, Mrs. Taylor, "She will be out of her mind soon." On a subsequent visit, Southcott spoke to Pomeroy of impending events of an apocalyptical nature, and he said, "You have advanced things that make me shudder. It is bordering on blasphemy." At a loss to refute her sincerity, he suggested that she have her writings examined by a jury of clergymen.

Thereupon Southcott sent Pomeroy a number of prophecies that were fulfilled. She predicted that the bishop of Exeter, then in good health, would not live until Christmas of that year. He died on December 12. In 1796 Lord Malmesbury went on a peace mission to Paris. Southcott foretold that it would fail, and so it did. At that time it would have seemed unreasonable to believe that the French revolutionary armies would conquer Italy, as predicted by Southcott, but young Bonaparte's success brought this to pass. Southcott was sincerely convinced that her messages were from God.

In 1797, Southcott left the service of the Taylors and went to work for several Exeter tradesmen in upholstering. She was a good worker, and her income helped to support her father, who was ill again. She also saved some money for her eventual retirement.

All this time her messages continued. Joanna introduced an early feminist view into her messages, claiming that when the time was right, God would use a woman to fulfill divine purpose. She stated, "Is it a new thing for a woman to deliver her people? Did not Esther do it? And Judith? Was it not a woman that nailed Sisera to the ground?" She became convinced that she herself was the destined "Bride of the Lamb," "woman clothed with the sun" in Revelation (12:1). In 1794, her voice had stated, "Now I'll tell thee who thou art, The true and faithful Bride."

Southcott alarmed Pomeroy with what seemed to him a blasphemous claim, as well as with more prophecies. She demanded that her messages be considered by a panel of clergymen. She wrote to the bishop, the archdeacon, and the chancellor, urging them to visit Pomeroy and test her teaching. On January 5, 1801, she wrote again to five clergymen, asking them to prove within seven days that the messages were not divine revelations. After a week she heard nothing, so she took her messages to an Exeter printer, paying him £100 she had saved for her old age.

In February of that year, *The Strange Effects of Faith* appeared as a 48-page, nine-penny pamphlet describing how the messages had come to Southcott and how she had sought to get clerical recognition of them. The following month she published *Second Part.* By now, her life savings were exhausted, so she borrowed from a moneylender to sponsor publication of further parts.

Rev. T. P. Foley, fellow of Jesus College, Cambridge, an intelligent, educated man and a former follower of the unfortunate fanatic Richard Brothers, saw these modest pamphlets and was immediately impressed with them. He consulted other friends, including the engraver William Sharp (who had also been a follower of Brothers's), and they attempted to interest clergymen in forming a jury to consider Southcott's writings. Afterward, many of the prophecies and other papers were put in a box fastened with cords and sealed with seven seals. Sharp had charge of this. The sealed box was later to become a central point in controversies over the writings.

When some of Southcott's followers printed her letters, Pomeroy was alarmed to find his name frequently quoted, and in a weak moment threw her papers on the fire. Almost immediately he had a letter from Southcott demanding their return, and thereafter his life was made miserable by scores of letters from her and her followers, denouncing him as a second Johoiakim who burned the roll of the prophet and threatening him with divine and diabolical justice.

The Seals

As Southcott's followers increased, she devised a strange sign of her mission, her famous "seal." Years earlier, when working in the shop of Mr. and Mrs. Taylor, she had found a seal with the initials "I. C." and two stars. One day she formed the idea that these were the initials of Jesus Christ ("I" and "J" were then interchangeable as initials) and marked her prophecies with this seal. Now the idea came to her that this also indicated the sealing of believers as well as prophetic writings, as cited in Rev. 7:3: "Hurt not the earth till we have sealed the servants of our God."

She cut paper into squares and marked a circle on each square, writing inside, "The Seal of the Lord, the Elect and Precious, Man's Redemption to Inherit the Tree of Life, to be made Heirs of God and Joint Heirs with Jesus Christ." Her followers received one of these squares after signing it, and it was folded up like an envelope and marked with the "I. C." seal.

Within a year she had issued several thousand of these "seals." Unfortunately she was accused of selling them and making a handsome income, although she claimed the seals were freely issued without any charge. (It is possible that middlemen asked money for them, since many people regarded them as lucky charms or passports to heaven.)

The Ministry Prospers

From time to time, Southcott was genuinely tortured by doubts as to whether her inner voice was a delusion of Satan, and she toyed with the idea of giving up her mission and going back to the upholstery trade. Some of her prophecies had failed. After one period of depression, she published her doubts in a pamphlet titled "A Dispute between the Woman and the Powers of Darkness." It seemed to be an honest work by a sincere woman, caught up in a strange mission that she had never sought.

But after 18 months her mission grew rapidly, with followers in London and the provinces, and she soon enrolled more than eight thousand disciples. She continued to demand that the bishops examine her claims and prophecies and agreed to abide by their decision, but the church dignitaries were unwilling to become involved.

Her mission continued to grow in spite of various unfortunate setbacks. One of these was the case of the infamous Mary Bateman, thief and abortionist, who had obtained a seal from Southcott and claimed that her hens were laying eggs with an inscription announcing the coming of Christ. Mary Bateman was executed for the murder of Rebecca Perigo, whom she had unmercifully fleeced for years by selling her charms against evil. For a time this scandalous episode of one of the "sealed followers" caused much embarrassment to the movement.

But Southcott's writings sold well, and many people who had followed the unfortunate Richard Brothers now came to join her mission. In 1812 a legacy from a disciple gave her financial independence. During 1813 her ecstasies increased and she felt surrounded by angels.

Shiloh

Southcott was 64 years old when her "voice" commanded, "Order twelve gowns for thy wedding." She was greatly disconcerted by this, as she had no desire for matrimony, but in early 1814 the voice added, "This year in the sixty-fifth year of thy age thou shalt bear a son by the power of the Most High." Back in 1794, she had already declared her conviction that she was "the Bride of the Lamb," but now the full significance of this dawned on her. The Virgin Mary had born a divine son. Southcott's child would have a divine destiny.

In Genesis (49:10) Jacob says that the scepter will not depart from Judah "until Shiloh come." This passage has confused and comforted many religious prophets, including Richard Brothers, who had declared at one point, "I am Shiloh." Southcott believed Brothers misunderstood the passage; Shiloh was to arise in the Last Days. In March 1814 she declared her belief that Shiloh was her unborn child. By then she showed every sign of pregnancy, and astonishingly enough this was confirmed by a leading surgeon and no fewer than 20 other medical practitioners.

The followers received the news of the coming divine virgin birth with great joy, and gifts flowed in. A satinwood cradle for the baby was prepared at a cost of £200. A superbly bound Bible was presented, and dozens of christening mugs and pap spoons. Recalling her message to Pomeroy (the Cornwall vicar) that she was the bride mentioned in Scripture, Southcott concluded that she must make an earthly marriage so that Shiloh would have a foster father, as with Joseph and the child Jesus. Accordingly on November 12 she was married in her bedroom to John Smith, steward of the earl of Darnley.

Southcott expected the divine birth in July, but as late as September nothing had happened. During November, painful doubts began to manifest in her mind, and once again she began to wonder if her voice had misled her. She called her close friends to her bedside and confessed despairingly, "Now it all appears delusion." She grew weaker, and by December 16 the symptoms of pregnancy had vanished. She told her doctor she was gradually dying, and requested that after her presumed death her body be kept warm for four days, in case she was only in a trance. She died early in the morning on December 27.

After the four days had elapsed, her doctor and 14 other medical practitioners examined the body and found no organic disease beyond a condition of dropsy, which may have enhanced the false pregnancy. It is probable that Southcott suffered a deep depression and no longer wished to live after her final disillusionment with her divine mission.

Just before her death she had made a will in which she sadly claimed that she had been deceived by the Devil and directed that all the gifts intended for the coming Shiloh be returned to their donors. She was buried in Marylebone Cemetery, London, on January 2, 1815, and her tombstone, evidently supplied by a follower, predicted great wonders yet to come but inaccurately stated her age as 60 instead of 64. The tombstone was shattered in a gunpowder explosion at Regent's Park in 1874.

The Successors of Joanna Southcott

Her death and recantation left her thousands of followers in great confusion. A large number refused to believe that her mission had been a delusion. Others formed splinter groups. Among these was a group led by George Turner, "Herald of Shiloh," who claimed to be Southcott's successor. He explained that Shiloh had been taken from Southcott's womb into Paradise until the appointed time.

Turner's demented "Proclamation of the Final Days" was to be delivered in Palace Yard, London. It denounced "the Treasury, Horse Guards, Carlton House, the Playhouses, Churches and Chapels, the Tower, Somerset House, and other public places. The Angel of the Lord shall sink all by earthquake." His radical manifesto dictated, "The whole United Kingdom is to be divided to the People on the Roll. Those who are not worth a penny now must be lords of the land. No rents must be paid. No postage for letters. No turnpikes. No taxes. Porter a gallon for one half-penny. Ale the same. The dead must be carried in carts three miles from the city and put into deep pits covered with pigs' flesh."

Confined to a Quaker asylum for the insane, Turner continued with fantastic directions for his faithful followers. Shiloh's palace must have walls of pure gold adorned with precious stones. "There must be in attendance 70,000 men that play musical instruments and 70,000 singing women. He must have 500,000 servants, and his carriages must be of pure gold." Turner himself was to have 300,000 servants and accommodations similar to those of Shiloh.

In 1820 Turner was declared cured of insanity, and his followers petitioned the lord chancellor for his release, granted a few months later. After an extravagant "marriage supper," Turner promised that Shiloh would appear in London on October 14, being born as a boy already six years old. When the date passed uneventfully, the faithful took it as merely a divine test of their love. Turner's own "voice" ordered him to marry, so that Shiloh might have a foster mother. Accordingly Turner chose a wife, and a new date of April 10, 1821, was pronounced for the birth of Shiloh. When nothing happened, some followers were disillusioned; others followed rival leaders.

Visions came to a wool comber named John Wroe, another Southcott follower, who came into prominence when he challenged Turner's original prophecy of October 14, 1820, as the date of birth of Shiloh. Wroe now assumed control of Turner's group, and his followers proclaimed themselves Christian Israelites. Wroe dictated new laws for the Final Days. Males were to be circumcised, and everyone was to eat only kosher meat. Men had to wear dark, broad-brimmed hats and special clothing; even the sober dress for women was stipulated in great detail. Men were also to give up shaving and wear beards. Everyone was to give up snuff, tobacco, and alcohol. Those who transgressed these laws were to be severely beaten.

One child died after circumcision and the man performing the operation was charged with manslaughter. He was acquitted after Jewish leaders pressured the government, fearing that their own legitimate rite would be prohibited.

Eventually the movement renounced Wroe after persistent debaucheries on his part, but he emigrated to the United States and then to Australia, where his mission continued to have followers. He died in 1863. The Christian Israelite church continues in Australia, and there was one congregation in the United States as of the mid-1990s.

Meanwhile another large group of Southcott believers had followed John Ward, a pauper Irish shoemaker. He had been a disciple of George Turner's before his faith in Southcott was shaken when he read an attack on the New Testament account of Christ by the freethinker Richard Carlile. Eventually he concluded that the Scriptures were not history but prophecies, foretelling future events, and that the accounts of the birth of Jesus were allegorical. He had visions of Southcott, who told him, "Thou art Shiloh."

Ward eventually decided that he himself was the Jesus foretold in the Gospels, in part because he had been born on Christmas Day and his mother's name was Mary. Even more fantastic was Ward's belief that he was Satan before becoming Christ, and that the Devil was now the Son of God. All the Scriptures implicated him in a multiplicity of roles. He was Adam, Judah, and Elijah. He claimed, "There is no name in Scripture which I may not with propriety apply to myself." Because of the many texts using the name Zion, he chose this designation for himself, becoming known as "Zion Ward."

Ward escaped from the poorhouse where he had been confined and talked followers into supporting his mission by publishing literature and handbills. He roamed the country preaching his unique variety of messianism, which included attacks on landlords, the government, and the established Church. He was a remarkable orator and obtained considerable support for his mission. Eventually his health broke down, and he died of a stroke on March 12, 1837. Faithful followers continued to support him long after his death, and as late as 1921 one supporter published his book *The Shilohites' Bible.* By then there was no public mission, and a handful of the faithful simply read his books and meditated on his message.

In 1875, the Southcott followers were given a new direction by another prophet, a soldier named James White, whose friends called him "The Stranger." Like Southcott, he was inspired by a mysterious voice that ordered him to regroup the faithful. He adopted the name James Jershom Jezreel. "Jershom" was a misspelling of "Gershom," the name of the first child of Moses. "Jezreel" came from Hosea: "Then shall the children of Israel and the children of Judah be gathered together and appoint themselves one Head, for great shall be the day of Jezreel."

White published a book, titled *The Flying Roll* (derived from the book of Zechariah), outlining his new creed. In Rev. 8:2, seven angels are given seven trumpets to sound before the Day of Doom. According to White, these angels were seven prophets. The first five were Richard Brothers, Southcott, George Turner, a man named Shaw (another Southcott successor), and John Wroe. White was the sixth angel. One more prophet would arise, then Shiloh would come.

One of Jezreel's important converts was a girl of 15 named Clarissa Rogers. She too heard a mystical voice, which called on her to preach in the United States. Her beauty and eloquence converted many Americans, some of whom returned with her to Gillingham, Kent, where Jezreel had become established. Jezreel married her, and they both toured America in 1880 with six wagons, a large tent, and a hundred benches.

They collected enough financial support to enable them to buy a 20-acre site in Gillingham, where they built a housing estate for their followers, with shops and bakeries so that they could pursue a trade. They ran a successful delivery service in Gillingham and Chatham with their carts, selling bread, meat, produce, and other provisions. The Jezreel estate also had the International College for boys and girls, with special emphasis on harp playing and study of Jezreel's writings.

In 1884, after a successful tour in Australia, Jezreel returned with ambitious plans for a temple, cubic in shape, 100 feet high, 100 feet wide, and 100 feet long. It was to house printing presses, offices, and an assembly hall seating six thousand people. The walls were to be reinforced with steel girders and cement used instead of mortar, and it was to last for a thousand years. After six months' building, Jezreel died in March 1885.

His wife, who had adopted the name Esther, continued to develop the movement effectively, opening Jezreel chapels in many areas and employing hawkers to carry the movement's literature all over the country. There were Jezreel followers in the United States, Australia, and New Zealand. Esther was accepted as the seventh angel with a trumpet, to be followed by Shiloh. She died in 1888, only three years after her husband. The great temple remained unfinished.

After her death, quarrels and schisms arose in the movement. One branch followed Michael Keyfor Mills, who organized a Jezreel community in Detroit, Michigan, but it soon broke up. In 1903 Benjamin Purnell, who had been expelled from the Detroit community, founded his own colony, the House of David, in Benton Harbor, Michigan. Things went well for several years, and their orchestra and baseball team became famous.

Problems began in 1926, when the community had nine hundred colonists. Four years earlier, Purnell had stopped making public appearances and disappeared from public sight, but in 1926 he was arrested during a police raid on the community. A lengthy investigation and court proceeding followed. In 1927 the colony was declared a public nuisance and moved into receivership. Purnell and his wife, Mary, were excluded from further association with the colony. Purnell died on December 16. Mary Purnell began a lengthy fight for the return of the colony's property, and in 1930 a settlement was reached. Assets were divided between her and H. T. Dewhist, who had assumed control of the House of David following Purnell's arrest.

The House of David continues on its original land. Mary Purnell and her followers established a second community a short distance away. Both continue to the present time. An Australian branch of the House of David also survives.

The Panacea Society

The final phase of the Southcott movement commenced in 1907 and involved four ladies who became skillful propagandists for the movement. They were Alice Seymour, who edited editions of Southcott's books; Rachel Fox, a Quaker; her friend Helen Exeter, who received Spiritualistic messages about Joanna Southcott's sealed box; and Mabel Barltrop, widow of an Anglican curate, who was a godchild of the poet Coventry Patmore.

Mabel Barltrop pestered innumerable clergymen and bishops, demanding that they open Southcott's box. She joined forces with Helen Exeter, whose spirit messages through **automatic writing** informed her that she would be the mother of Shiloh. Exeter, who was to be the eighth prophet, adopted the name Octavia.

Octavia established a settlement at Bedford, and many supporters of the emerging suffragette movement joined her. She continued to badger the bishops to open Southcott's box and study the writings and prophecies it contained. For 20 years she propagandized with handbills, posters, and petitions.

In 1918 the bishop of Lambeth stated that he had the consent of 24 bishops to receive the box and open it on March 7 or 8. But Octavia's followers were not satisfied unless all the bishops were prepared to spend a whole week studying the contents. Not surprisingly, Bishop Carpenter could not agree, and the matter was dropped. It was the nearest the famous box ever came to being officially examined as Southcott had always desired.

By this time Octavia had been declared to be Shiloh by her followers. By 1920 she had a team of 36 residents at Bedford and a large following in Britain, Australia, and America.

In 1923 the movement took a new direction. One night Octavia tried to swallow a pill, but it slipped away and rolled under a cupboard. Accordingly she took the glass of water and prayed that it would serve the purpose of the pill. When it did, her voice proclaimed that she had been given healing powers. Thereafter the community prepared small linen squares "with the breath of prayer." These were to be dipped in water, which was to be drunk or poured onto wounds. The community adopted the name The Panacea Society, convinced that they had a universal remedy for all ills.

Octavia herself died in 1934, notwithstanding the universal remedy, but her movement continues.

The Opening of the Southcott Box

For decades, quaint notices continued to appear in British newspapers stating, "War, disease, crime and banditry will increase until the Bishops open Joanna Southcott's box."

In 1927 an attempt to resolve this persistent controversy was undertaken by the British psychical researcher **Harry Price,** who had a great flair for publicity. On April 28, 1927, he arrived at his **National Laboratory of Psychical Research** to be greeted by his secretary with the news "Joanna Southcott's box has arrived!" According to Price, it had been sent by the employer of two servants who were descendants of Mrs. Rebecca Morgan (née Pengarth), said to have been the sole companion of Southcott between 1798 and 1814. The cover letter stated that the Morgans had become custodians of Southcott's box, which had been earlier entrusted to Rebecca, and that the National Laboratory of Psychical Research should arrange for a formal opening of the box because the writer was moving to the United States.

This account has been challenged by **Trevor H. Hall** in his book *The Search for Harry Price* (1978), which suggests that the letter was a forgery by Price to obtain publicity for the box. It is true that there is no mention of Rebecca Pengarth as a companion to Southcott in histories of the movement, although the box itself appeared to be a genuine Southcott relic, however Price came into possession of it. It was a strongly built casket of walnut, stained with age, with a heavy lid with a mother-of-pearl plate bearing the engraved initials "I. S." (i.e., J. S.). The casket was secured by two rusty steel bands and by strong silk tapes secured in five places with large black seals bearing a profile of George III.

Price invited eight psychics, a psychologist, and a dowser to inspect the box and give their impressions of its contents. Most of the psychometric impressions proved reasonably accurate. When Price later x-rayed the box in his laboratory he identified the following objects: an old horse pistol, a dice box, a fob purse with coins in it, a bone puzzle with rings, some blocks (one with metal clasps), a framed painting or miniature, a pair of earrings, and a cameo or engraved pebble.

Price secured much publicity for the box, and sensational stories were published that it might contain a boobytrap bomb intended to kill the bishops. Price wrote to three archbishops and 80 bishops stating his intention to make a formal opening of the box, and asking if they would consent to be present to honor Southcott's wishes and perhaps to end the persistent superstition surrounding the box.

Some replies were noncommittal. The bishop of Derby hoped that Price could get a quorum for the opening in order to "lay to rest the Joanna Southcott legend." The bishop of Lincoln strongly advised opening the box "with or without the presence of bishops." The bishop of Liverpool wrote: "I join you in hoping that the Southcott myth will be exploded." In contrast, the bishop of Kensington was unsympathetic, saying that he did not wish to be a party to providing amusement for a public that would like nothing better than to see a company of bishops the victims of a hoax, even if it had been arranged one hundred years earlier.

However, the bishop of Chichester wrote that he would be glad if the Southcott myth could be exploded and would be willing to be present, if in London at the time. The bishop of London replied that he would try to be present. The bishop of Carlisle replied that he would be present if the archbishop of Canterbury "should be satisfied as to the propriety of bishops being present at the opening of the box."

The archbishop of Canterbury replied that his correspondence over Southcott's box had been voluminous and extended over many years. He was not sympathetic to the idea, "partly profane and partly comic," that 24 bishops representing the 24 elders in Revelation should sit around the box. He believed the box should be opened speedily, but also thought that as soon as it was opened a rival box would be found. Other bishops expressed interest in being present if in London, or if given permission by the archbishop of Canterbury.

The opening of the box took place before a large audience at the Hoare Memorial Hall, Church House, Westminster, London, on July 11, 1927. For the event, only the bishop of Grantham turned up, but the bishop of Crediton was represented by his son, the Reverend Trefusis.

As already mentioned, the psychometric impressions given by the psychics contained many accurate statements. Not surprisingly, the X-rays of the solid objects were also correct. Among the 56 objects in the box, the pamphlets and books included: *The Surprises of Love, Exemplified in the Romance of a Day . . .* (1765), with annotations; *Rider's British Merlin* (1715); *Calendier de la Cour* (1773); and Ovid's *Metamorphoses* (1794). There was a paper souvenir "printed on the River Thames, Feb. 3rd, 1814," and a lottery ticket for 1796. Among the objects were a fob purse (containing silver and copper coins and tokens), a horse pistol, a miniature case, an ivory dice cup, a bone puzzle, a woman's embroidered nightcap, and a set of brass money weights.

Naturally the loyal Southcottians did not accept that these pathetic souvenirs were the contents of the right box, and the appeals to bishops to attend the opening of the true box continued, although it was by no means clear where this box might be. Certainly one would have expected the real Southcott box to contain voluminous prophecies, correspondence, and religious pamphlets.

The incredible story of Joanna Southcott and her prophecies has continued over nearly two centuries and is still not wholly extinct. The Southcott literature is voluminous. She herself published some 65 books and pamphlets, while her followers in the various groups added a flood of additional communications.

Sources:

Adkin, Clare E. *Brother Benjamin: A History of the Israelite House of David.* Berrien Springs, Mich.: Andrews University Press, 1990.

Balleine, G. R. *Past Finding Out: The Tragic Story of Joanna Southcott and Her Successors.* London: SPCK, 1956.

Lane, C. *Life and Bibliography of Joanna Southcott.* London, 1912.

Matthews, Ronald. *English Messiahs.* London: Methuen, 1936.

Octavia. [Helen Exeter]. *Healing for All: The "Joanna Southcott Healing."* London: Panacea Society, 1925.

Panacea Society. *Transactions of the Panacea Society with the Archbishops and Bishops of the Church of England with Reference to Joanna Southcott.* London: Panacea Society, 1935.

Pullen, Philip. *Index to the Divine and Spiritual Writings of Joanna Southcott.* Ashford, England: Clock House Press, 1921.

Reece, Richard. *A Correct Statement of the Circumstances that Attended the Last Illness and Death of Mrs. Southcott.* London, 1815.

Southcott, J. *The Book of Wonders, Marvelous and True.* 5 parts. London, 1813–14.

———. *The Divine Writings of Joanna Southcott.* 2 vols. Bolton, England, 1931.

———. *Prophecies: A Warning to the Whole World from the Sealed Prophecies of Joanna Southcott.* 2 parts. London, 1803.

———. *The Strange Effects of Faith; with Remarkable Prophecies.* 2 parts. Exeter, England, 1801–2. With three "*Continuations.*" 1802–3.

"Xenes." *Joanna Southcott and Her Box.* London: W. Foulsham, 1927.

Southern California Society for Psychical Research, Inc. See **Society for Psychic Research** (California)

Sovereign and Military Order of the Temple of Jerusalem

The Sovereign and Military Order of the Temple of Jerusalem, incorporated in Belgium in 1932, is the largest group growing out of the Neo-Templar Movement launched by Bernard-Raymond Fabré-Palaprat (1773–1838) in the years following the French Revolution. The Order of the Temple, commonly called the Templars, was a medieval monastic order virtually destroyed by King Philip the Fair of France and formally dissolved by Pope Clement V in 1307. The order survived for another century in Portugal, but by the beginning of the fifteenth century had completely disappeared.

However, as Speculative **Freemasonry** spread through Europe in the eighteenth century, a rumor developed that the order had survived in the person of knights who sought protection in the masonic guilds of Scotland and Ireland. They were the sources of the "Templar" degrees in the Masonic initiatory structure. Then, at the time of the French Revolution, some French masons began to argue that since the **Templars** came before Freemasonry, it was logically independent of it and hence not subordinate to it. Their cause was championed by Fabré-Palaprat, a physician residing in Paris, who claimed to have found documents proving the existence of a lineage of grand masters who continued to operate from the time of the order's official suppression to 1792 when the then-grand master was killed by political opponents. The most important of these documents was the Lamenius charter which specifies the passing of the grand mastership by the last public master, Jacques de Molay, to one John Mark Lamenius who he met in prison while awaiting his execution.

In the freer atmosphere of post-Revolutionary France, in 1804 Fabré-Palaprat organized a new Templar Order and four years later received the approbation of Napoleon. Since the Roman Catholic Church had not changed its official stance against the Templars, he also organized an esoteric Johannite church and consecrated its first bishop. After his death in 1838, the order experienced the first of many schisms. Over the next century, a number of branches and derivative groups would appear, including the German **Ordo Templi Orientis** and the French-based Independent Group of Esoteric Studies founded by **Gérard Encausse.** Among the more than 30 Neo-Templar groups operating in the 1990s was the infamous **Solar Temple** whose leaders committed suicide in 1994.

Fabré-Palaprat's Order of the Temple existed as an informal association until 1932, when it was legally incorporated in Belgium as the Sovereign and Military Order of the Temple of Jerusalem, under the leadership of Theodore Covais. Covais assumed the title of regent rather than grand master. Then, as Belgium was engulfed by World War II (1939–45), the regency was passed to Antonio Campello Pinto de Sousa Fontes, who resided in neutral Portugal. After the war, he continued as the regent, though not without opposition from some of the French-speaking Templars. He issued charters in many countries and the order grew significantly. An American branch was chartered in 1962.

Antonio Campello Pinto de Sousa Fontes died in 1960 and was succeeded by his son, Fernando Campello Pinto de Sousa Fontes. However, not all approved his election and in 1970, a French-speaking group gathered in Paris where Antoine Zdrojewski was elected regent of what became a rival body. This rival body included a number of people with right-wing political affiliations. They soon involved the order in their political intrigues and it was disbanded in France in 1973. Internationally it became the source of a variety of new orders.

The order that remained loyal to Antonio Campello Pinto de Sousa Fontes has grown and prospered while at the same time it has played down its occult roots. Like Freemasonry, the contemporary Templars (especially in North America) have emerged as a fraternal organization dedicated to work for their community and country, to support the poor and the unjustly accused, to stand against oppression, and to encourage the ideal of medieval chivalry. Harking back to the Templar history during the Crusades, the modern Templars see it their duty to assist Christian pilgrims and to maintain a Christian presence in the Holyland. One must be a professed Christian to be a member.

The current grand prior of the order in the United States is Col. Chev. Stewart McCarty. He may be contacted through the order's Internet site at http://www.smotj.org/. Internationally, the order is led by the current Grand Master MG Sir Roy Redgrave, who resides in London, England. He may be contacted through the Internet site at http://www.osmth.org/index.html. Grand priories may be found in Austria, England and Wales, Scotland, Finland, France, and Italy.

Sources:

Introvigne, Massimo. *Il cappello del mago: I nuovi movimenti magici dallo spiritismo al satanismo.* Milan: SugarCo, 1990.

Kovarik, Robert J. "Chronology of the Sovereign Military Order of the Temple of Jerusalem." 1977. http://members.aol.com/TemplarNY/TemplarNY.html. June 11, 2000.

Sovereign and Military Order of the Temple of Jerusalem (International). http://www.osmth.org/index.html. June 11, 2000.

Sovereign and Military Order of the Temple of Jerusalem (United States.). http://www.smotj.org/. June 11, 2000.

Space and Unexplained Celestial Events Research Society

A paper organization created to cover the activities of James W. Moseley, an early flying saucer enthusiast and journalist. It was founded at the time of the preparation of the first issue of his magazine, originally called *Nexus* but quickly changed to *Saucer News.* In 1968 Moseley sold *Saucer News* to Gray Barker of Saucerian Press in Clarksburg, West Virginia. The name **Space and Unexplained Celestial Events Research Society** appeared on the masthead of Barker's issues of *Saucer News* through 1972, but it continued as a paper organization.

In 1976 Moseley started another newsletter. Each issue of this humor- and gossip-oriented periodical had a different title, the first word being saucer and the second word rhyming with "smear." *Saucer Smear* can be ordered from Moseley at Box 1709, Key West, FL 33041.

Sources:

Clark, Jerome. *The Emergence of a Phenomenon: UFOs from the Beginning through 1959.* Vol. 2 of *The UFO Encyclopedia.* Detroit: Omnigraphics, 1992.

Space Intelligence

Alleged extraterrestrial entities. Prior to the 1970s such entities usually claimed to be inhabitants of the Moon, Mars, Venus, or another planet of this solar system. In the last two decades such claimed inhabitants have tended to come from far distant solar systems. Space Intelligences (SIs) allegedly communicate telepathically to chosen individual channels or through Spiritualist mediums. The most consistent Space Intelligences are those that communicate to the several contactee organizations such as the Raelian Movement, Unarius-Science of Life, the **Aetherius Society,** and Mark-Age, Inc.

SPAIN

Witchcraft

Modern Spain emerged in the fifteenth century. The land had previously been occupied by the Romans, Visagoths, and the **Moors,** who remained dominant beginning in the eighth century C.E. From early times, Spain was regarded as a special abode of superstition and **sorcery,** malevolent magic, and, in the Middle Ages, as the home of witchcraft, much of that reputation deriving from the notoriety of the Moorish alchemists. Spain was a major point of dissemination of Arab learning into Christian Europe. As early as 1370, the kingdom of Castile (a major component of what would become Spain) declared **divination** to be heresy. Writing about 1458 C.E., Alfonso de Spina, a Franciscan brother from Castile, created a work especially directed against heretics and nonbelievers, in which he gave a chapter on those articles of popular belief that were derived from ancient pagan beliefs. Among these, witches, called *Xurguine (jurgina)* or *bruxe,* held a prominent place. He stated that in his time offenders abounded in Dauphiny and Gascony, where they assembled in great numbers by night on a wild tableland, carrying candles with them to worship Satan, who appeared in the form of a boar on a certain rock, popularly known by the name Elboch de Biterne, and that many of them had been taken by the Inquisition of Toulouse and burned.

Spain reemerged as a Christian kingdom during the reign of Ferdinand V (1474–1504) and Isabella. They introduced the Inquisition, expelled the Jews, and financed Columbus's voyages to America. Their reign coincided with the redirection of the Inquisition against witchcraft in the 1480s and from that time in Spain, the charge of **witchcraft** and **sorcery** was frequently made under different forms and circumstances. Local inquisitors operated without clear guidelines, especially regarding exactly what constituted sorcery, and had considerable latitude in their prosecution of the accused.

The first *auto-da-fé* (act of faith) against witchcraft appears to have been that of Calahorra in 1507, when 30 women charged before the Inquisition as witches, were burned. In 1527 a great number of women were accused in Navarre of the practice of sorcery through the information of two girls, one 11, the other only nine years old, who confessed before the royal council of Navarre that they had been received into the sect of the jurginas. They promised, on condition of being pardoned, to expose all the women who were involved in these practices.

The prevalence of various magic practices in the Basque provinces became notorious, and Charles V, judging that it was to be attributed more to the ignorance of the population of those districts than to any other cause, directed that preachers should be sent to instruct them.

The first treatise in the Spanish language on the subject of sorcery was by a Franciscan monk named Martin de Castanaga, printed under approbation of the bishop of Calahorra in 1529. About this time, the zeal of the inquisitors of Saragossa was excited by the appearance of many witches who were said to have come from Navarre, and to have been sent by their sect as missionaries to make disciples of the women of Aragon. This sudden witch persecution in Spain appears to have had an influence on the fate of the witches of Italy. Pope Adrian IV, who was raised to the papal chair in 1522, was a Spanish bishop, and had held the office of inquisitor-general in Spain.

In the time of Pope Julius II (1503–13), a large sect of witches and sorcerers had reportedly been discovered in Lombardy who had their Sabbats and all the other activities of the Continental witches. The proceedings against them had been hindered by a dispute between the inquisitors and the ecclesiastical judges who claimed jurisdiction in such cases. Then on July 20, 1523, Pope Adrian issued a bull against the crime of sorcery, equating divination with its practice, and by naming both as heresy, placed sorcery clearly under the sole jurisdiction of the inquisitors. This bull freed the Inquisition to act against witches in Spain.

Of the cases that followed during more than a century, the most remarkable was that of the *auto-da-fé* at Logrono on November 7 and 8, 1610, which arose in some measure from a visit to the French Basque province in the preceding year. The valley of Bastan is situated at the foot of the Pyrenees on the French frontier, near Labourd. It was within the jurisdiction of the Inquisition established at Logrono in Castille. The mass of the population of this valley were said to have been sorcerers, and they held their meetings or Sabbats at a place called Zugarramurdi.

A woman who was condemned implicated a number of other persons. All the persons arrested on this occasion agreed in their description of the Sabbat and of the practices of the witches, who in their general features bore a close resemblance to the witches of Labourd. The usual place of meeting was known here, as in Labourd, by the popular name of Aquelarre, a Gascon word signifying "the meadow of the goat." Their ordinary meetings were held on the nights of Monday, Wednesday, and Friday, every week, but they had grand feasts on the principal holidays of the church, such as Easter, Pentecost, and Christmas. All these feasts appear to have been fixed by the Christian teachers at the period of older pagan festivals. The accounts of their claimed Sabbats were similar to those given of such meetings elsewhere. They supposedly danced, sang, took part in orgies, and came into personal contact with Satan.

The *auto-da-fé* of Logrono, as far as it related to the sect of the sorcerers of Zugarramurdi, caused a sensation, and brought the subject of witchcraft under the consideration of the Spanish theologians. They were far more enlightened than most of their contemporaries in other countries, that they generally held the opinion that witchcraft was a mere delusion and that the details of the confessions of its victims were all creations of the imagination. They were punished because their belief was a heresy, contrary to the doctrines of the church. Llorente gave the abstract of a treatise on this subject by a Spanish ecclesiastic named Pedro de Valentia, addressed to the grand inquisitor in consequence of the trial at Logrono in 1610. It remained in manuscript among the archives of the Inquisition.

Valentia adopted the opinion that the acts confessed by the witches were imaginary; he attributed them partly to the methods in which the examinations were carried out—and to the desire of the people examined to escape by saying what seemed to please their persecutors—and partly to the effects of the ointments and draughts they had been taught to use. These were composed of ingredients that produced sleep and acted upon the imagination and the mental faculties.

Although the heresy-hunting of the Spanish Inquisition resulted in a vast number of victims being burned throughout Europe, in Spain itself witchcraft persecutions were relatively more restrained than elsewhere, and there were relatively fewer burnings. An entrenched skepticism on the part of the Suprema as to the reality of witchcraft discouraged mass persecutions from 1526 onward. During the witchcraft panic of 1610 in Navarre, the secular judges had burned their victims before the Inquisition could act. Subsequently the Suprema restrained punishment for alleged witches and in some cases denounced the charges as a delusion.

Spiritualism

A writer in the *Religio-Philosophical Journal* (flourished 1865–1905) states: "The language that furnishes the largest number of periodicals devoted to the dissemination of the doctrine and philosophy of modern Spiritualism, is the Spanish. This statement will be somewhat surprising to many of our readers, for we have been accustomed to look upon the Spaniards as non-progressive and conservative in the extreme. Spain, until a few years, has always been intolerant of any religions except the Roman Catholic, and was the latest of European nations to yield to the spirit of religious progress. Protestantism has with the greatest difficulty obtained a foothold in that country within the last few years, but it has been attended with annoying restrictions and persecutions, while its progress has been exceedingly slow and discouraging."

Spiritualism in Spain began, as in many other lands, with a series of disturbances, which took place in a family residing in the outskirts of Cadiz. Stone throwing, bell ringing, and other **poltergeist**-style annoyances were the first means of awakening attention to the subject. Because they occurred at the house of a Spanish gentleman who had just returned from the United States, full of the marvels of the **Rochester rappings,** circles were at once formed, intelligent responses by rappings obtained, and a foothold for Spiritualism established. So rapidly did interest in Spiritualism spread, that the first promulgators were soon lost sight of. As early as 1854, a society was formed at Cadiz for the sole purpose of publishing the communications received from the spirits during the two preceding years.

From 1854 to 1860, Spiritualism spread through the principal towns and villages of Spain in the usual fashion, aided in large part by Spiritualism's claim to be a nonreligious, scientific movement. Circles were held in private families, and an endless number of societies were formed and dissolved, according to the exigencies of the time.

One of the first public events of note in connection with Spanish Spiritualism deserves special mention. It was no other than a modern *auto-da-fé,* held on the morning of October 9, 1861, at the Esplanade Barcelona. The difference between this burning and the fiery executions of earlier centuries was that the early victims were humans, while these were all the books, pamphlets, and works of a Spiritualist character that could be procured at that period of the movement. Resting on the "funeral pyre" were the writings of **Allan Kardec** and **Baron Ludwig von Guldenstubbe,** some copies of English and American Spiritualist papers, and a large collection of tracts issued by the Spiritualists of Spain. Some change of attitude soon occurred.

Among the well-known residents of Barcelona was a Señor Navarez, whose daughter Rosa had, for many years, been the subject of spasmodic attacks, called by some of the Roman Catholic clergy "the obsession of demons," and by the medical faculty, "an aggravated condition of epilepsy." Within two years following the Barcelona burning, Rosa was pronounced entirely cured by the magnetic passes of a gentleman who was the medium of the private circle held in the city.

Shortly after this, Barcelona could boast of its well-approved Spiritualist publications, numerous societies for investigation, and several mediums. A journal published by a Señor Alcantara was supported by the Viscount de Torres Solanot and many other leaders of science and literature in Spain. Through this publication the opponents of Spiritualism were amazed to learn of the immense progress the cause was making, and the number of distinguished persons who assembled nightly in circles to promote its investigation.

A circular calling the attention of the Spanish public to the phenomena of Spiritualism was published in 1875 by Viscount Solanot. The authors of this circular met with no little response. However, the energetic viscount again promoted the subject before the Paris Exposition of 1878. In articles written for *El Criterio,* he argued for the development of an international cooperative effort by Spiritualists and named among those societies prepared to promote such a structure as including: La Federation Espirita, of Belgium; The British National Association of Spiritualists, England; La Sociedad Central Espirita, of the Republic of Mexico; and El Central General del Espiritismo. There was also an attempt to form a national association and unite all the discordant elements under the one broad banner of Spiritualism. Instead of further development, however, by the end of the century Spiritualism had ceased to exist as a vital movement in Spain.

Animal Magnetism and Mediums

In Spain, as in Italy, a considerable amount of attention was directed toward exploring mediumistic abilities by means of **animal magnetism.** Magnetic societies abounded in Spain prior to World War I, but internal discord eventually dissolved the bonds that had united flourishing associations.

Among the numerous groups formed in the different parts of Spain in the late nineteenth century to study Spiritualism and its phenomena was one of long standing at Tarragona called The Christian Circle. The president of this circle sent the following communication to the *Revue Spirite* of Paris:

"The convict prison here in Tarragona has 800 inmates sentenced to forced labour. By some means, Spiritualistic books have been introduced among the prisoners. The circulation of these books among them has been the means of bringing seventy or eighty of them to be believers in our doctrine. These converts have ceased to regard their miserable position from their old point of view; they no longer entertain schemes of revolt against the authorities. They endure their lot with resignation under the influence of the teaching that this world is but a preliminary stage to another, where, if repentant of the ill they have done, and seeking the good of others, they will be better off than here.

"Not long since one of these men died; at his death he declined the established offices of the prison priest, on the ground that he was a Spiritualist and did not need them. The priest then discovered that Spiritualism was a subject of discussion with many of the prisoners. He made a representation of the matter to his bishop, who made formal complaint of it to the commandant of the prison, and the commandant made an investigation. In the end a particular prisoner was selected for punishment in the form of an additional weight of fetters. This coming to the knowledge of the Spiritualists of Tarragona, Barcelona, and Lerida, they had a meeting upon the subject and delegated one of their number, a man of position, to interview the commandant. The representations which he made, led the commandant to cancel his order as to the additional fetters. The bishop's censure against Spiritualist books placed them under prohibition, which was maintained. It is known, however, that although never found by gaolers, the books are still there."

In April 1881 the editor of the Madrid *El Criterio* stated that ". . . great progress has been made in the cause of Spiritualism; that the hall of meeting of the Spiritual Society is completely full every Thursday evening, and is not now large enough to hold the public who come to the sessions, that Dr. Merschejewski has called the attention of the University of St. Petersburg to a psychometric phenomena of much importance; to wit: A young man deemed from childhood to be an idiot, who will in some seconds solve any mathematical problem, while if a poem be read to him, even of many hundred verses, he will repeat the whole of it without failing in a single word."

In the same issue of *El Criterio* Señor Manuel Lopez wrote on the progress of a society of Spiritualists in Madrid: "We have received a mediumistic work of extraordinary merit, executed by a medium of the Society of Spiritualists of Zaragoza. It consists of a portrait of Isabel the Catholic, made with a pencil, and is a work truly admirable. It is said by intelligent persons who have examined it to be an exact copy of one preserved in the Royal Museum of Painters of this court. Many thanks are tendered to the Zaragozan Society for this highly appreciated present."

It was about the end of the year 1880 that the Spiritualists of Spain sustained another series of attacks from the church. The first of these was the refusal of the clergy to accord the customary rites of interment to the remains of two women, both of irreproachable character and good standing in society, but both "guilty" of having believed in Spiritualist manifestations.

The second attack by the church about this time was the suppression of a Spiritualist paper published at Lerida, entitled *El Buen Sentido.* The bishop of Lerida had long threatened this step and warned the editor to beware allowing any writings reflecting upon clerical doings to appear in his columns.

One article that seemed to inflame the clergy to such threats was an article that appeared in *El Buen Sentido* protesting the condemnation of a working man to three years' imprisonment, leaving a family of children destitute, and all for daring to speak in public against the intolerance of the church.

In an issue of *El Criterio* dated 1881 was a letter from Don Migueles in which he gave a somewhat discouraging account of the cause of Spiritualism as it existed at that time in Spain. The editor commented, "Don Migueles visited many cities to examine into the state of affairs of a spiritual nature, but found many who were only to be enticed by physical phenomena, caring nothing for the esoteric beauties of our faith; many who were convinced that they knew all there was to be known concerning it, and others who were timid fearing the disapproval of neighbours."

In some places, however, excellent mediums were discovered. In Santiago, in Oviedo, in Corunna, and in Valladolid an exceptional interest was manifest. Near Santiago, there was a young girl said to be possessed of remarkable faculties. Two bars of magnetized iron held over her horizontally, half a meter distant, were reportedly sufficient to suspend her body in the air.

In 1881 the Barcelona *Lux* gave encouraging accounts of séances held at Cordova, Tarragona, Seville, and many other places. The editor, Madame Soler, also referred to an archbishop's prohibiting Catholics from possessing or reading the Spiritualist work of Niram Aliv of the Society of Spiritualists of Tarrasa; that of the circle of Santa Cruz of Tenerif; that of Faith, Hope, and Charity, of Andujar, and that of St. Vincent de Bogota.

Psychical Research

Psychical research emerged in Spain but had an extremely spotty existence. Some research was carried on by the Ferderacion Espirita Española, a Spiritualist group in Sabadel. Periodicals included *Hacia La Iguidad y el Amor* of Barcelona and *Lumen* of Tarrasa. Spain was also represented at the several international congresses of psychical research. By 1930 Don Manuel Otero of Madrid and Signor Tassi of Perugia were active psychical researchers who had investigated the phenomena of the medium **Eusapia Palladino** in Naples in 1899.

The Civil War and World War II disrupted developments from the 1930s on. However, interest in parapsychology reappeared in 1971 when Ramos Molina Perera began to teach courses at the Universidad Autónoma de Madrid. Two years later Perera, several colleagues, and others interested in the field founded the Sociedad Española de Parapsicologia. Perera served as president for many years. The society, which at one time had several thousand members, conducts research, sponsors courses at colleges and universities, and issues *Psi Comunicacíon.*

Sources:

Baroja, Julio Caro. *The World of the Witches.* Chicago: University of Chicago Press, 1961.

Berger, Arthur S., and Joyce Berger. *The Encyclopedia of Parapsychology and Psychical Research.* New York: Paragon House, 1991.

Lea, Henry. *History of the Inquisition in Spain.* New York and London, 1906.

Llorente, J. A. *History of the Inquisition of Spain.* 1826.

Robbins, Rossell Hope. *The Encyclopedia of Witchcraft and Demonology.* New York: Crown, 1959.

The Roots of the New Age Movement. http://www.xs4all.nl/~wichm/newage3.html. June 19, 2000.

Spangler, David (1945–)

David Spangler, prominent architect and theoretician of the **New Age** movement, was born in Columbus, Ohio, on January 7, 1945. He was raised in a family open to the psychic realm, and as a boy of seven he had his first mystical experience. As a teenager he affiliated with several theosophical groups, and through the writings of **Alice A. Bailey,** Spangler first learned of the coming New Age at the end of the twentieth century. In 1964 he settled in Los Angeles, where he and Myrtle Glines opened a counseling service. He began to channel an entity named "John," who would periodically emerge over the next decades, and in 1967 he authored the booklet *The Christ Experience and the New Age.*

In 1970, Glines and Spangler traveled to Great Britain, where Spangler decided to pay a brief visit to the **Findhorn** Community in northern Scotland, an early New Age center. He then canceled his travel plans and joined the 15-member community for three years. Here Spangler began to articulate an idea that the coming New Age would be a cooperative venture between humans and cosmic forces. He disagreed with Findhorn leader Peter Caddy, who believed that the New Age would be brought in by a cataclysmic event.

In 1973 Spangler returned to the United States as an apostle of the New Age movement and founded the Lorian Association in Belmont, California, based on the Findhorn model. He lectured widely and wrote a series of books about the New Age. Major titles include *Revelation: The Birth of a New Age* (1976), *Towards a Planetary Vision* (1977), *Explorations: Emerging Aspects of the New Culture* (1980), and his autobiography *Emergence: The Rebirth of the Sacred* (1980).

By the 1980s, the New Age idea had become a mass movement. Spangler, who had worked so hard on popularizing the idea, now found himself in the role of critic of the more dubious aspects of the New Age. He vilified the interest in crystals, psychic phenomena, and even **channeling,** as taking people away from a focus on self-transformation and upon developing a compassionate and creative life. In 1988, after several years of silence, Spangler published a series of articles in which he professed to have given up on the idea of the New Age as a social event. He now described the New Age as a metaphor for personal transformation and said that its essence would be found in the change and growth of individuals. He called upon such people to work for real change in the social order.

Sources:

Spangler, David. *The Call.* New York: Putnam, 1997.

———. *Emergence: The Rebirth of the Sacred.* New York: Delta, 1980.

———. *Everyday Miracles: The Inner Art of Manifestation.* New York: Bantam/Doubleday/Dell, 1996.

———. *Explorations: Emerging Aspects of the New Culture.* Forres, Scotland: Findhorn Publications, 1980.

———. *Parent as Mystic, Mystic as Parent.* New York: Berkeley Publishing Group, 2000.

———. *Revelation: The Birth of a New Age.* San Francisco: Rainbow Bridge, 1976.

———. *Towards a Planetary Vision.* Forres, Scotland: Findhorn Publications, 1977.

Spare, Austin Osman (1886–1956)

Artist and magician. Spare was born on December 13, 1886, in London. At the age of seven, he met a Mrs. Paterson, a fortune-teller and witch, with whom he kept company for many years. She eventually initiated him into her magical work. At the age of thirteen he dropped out of school and began to work in a stained glass factory while attending school at night. He won a scholarship to the Royal Academy and in 1905 published his first book of drawings, *Earth Inferno.* He emerged as a precursor to the surrealists by calling attention to an inner world. The book also brought him to the attention of magician **Aleister Crowley,** who commissioned drawings by Spare for his magazine, *The Equinox.*

Spare served in the British army in Egypt during World War I and then settled down to life as a poor painter, his pictures being the expression of the inner world he was exploring. Integral to that world was sexuality, and Spare took many partners through his lifelong practice of sexual magic. Spare died on March 15, 1956, in London. Though Spare wrote, illustrated, and circulated two books during his life, *The Focus of Life* and *The Book of Pleasure,* it was only after his death that some appreciation of his system could be found and his work made available to the larger magical community.

Spare's teachings have been referred to as the cult of the Zos and Kia, centered upon the polarized (positive and negative) interplay of sexual energy. The two currents are symbolized by the hand (touch) and the eye (vision). The hand and the eye become the magical instruments of the innate obsession to embody the cosmic in the flesh. Expositions of Spare's system have been offered by Kenneth Grant, head of the British OTO in several books.

Sources:

Ericson, Eric. *The World, The Flesh, and the Devil: A Biographical Dictionary of Witches.* New York: Mayflower Books, 1981.

Grant, Kenneth. *Cults of the Shadow.* New York: Samuel Weiser, 1976.

———. *Images of Austin Osman Spare.* London: Frederick Muller, 1975.

Spare, Austin Osman. *A Book of Automatic Drawing.* London: Catalpa Press, 1972.

———. *The Book of Pleasure (Self-Love): The Psychology of Ecstasy.* London: Co-operative Printing Society Limited, 1913. Reprint, Montreal: 93 Publishing, 1975.

———. *The Focus of Life.* London: The Author, 1921.

Speal Bone (Divination by)

An early form of **divination** used in Scotland. A speal bone, or blade bone of a shoulder of mutton, was used, but full details of the method are lacking. A soldier accompanying Lord Loudon on his retreat to Skye foretold the result of the battle of Culloden at the very moment it was decided, claiming to have seen the event by looking through the bone.

Spear, John Murray (ca. 1804–1887)

Famous American Universalist preacher and an outstanding figure in the history of early American **Spiritualism.** He was baptized by John Murray, the founder of the Universalist Church, whose name he bore. In the early years of his public activity he distinguished himself as an ardent abolitionist. In 1845, with his brother Charles, he published a weekly newspaper, *The Prisoner's Friend,* in Boston, and for many years devoted himself to helping the poor, especially prisoners and their relatives. In one year alone he delivered 80 lectures on criminal reform and against capital punishment, distributing 7,500 books to prisoners and traveling 8,000 miles in the cause.

His attention was first drawn to Spiritualism in 1851. A year later, he developed **automatic writing** and **healing.** Messages came through his hand giving addresses and names of sick people. He visited them and drove the pain out of their bodies by his touch.

Later he began to draw and deliver inspirational discourses. It was asserted that they came from John Murray. Under the title *Messages from the Superior State* they were published in 1852. In the following year he was made the instrument of a spirit band called the "Association of Beneficents" and produced a large work that bore resemblance in scope to the *Divine Revelations* of **Andrew Jackson Davis** (1847).

The first volume of Spear's work was published in 1857 in Boston under the title *The Educator, being Suggestions, theoretical and practical, designed to promote Man-Culture and Integral Reform, with a view of the Ultimate Establishment of a Divine Social State on Earth.* In the spirit world several similar organizations to the Association of Beneficents appear to have existed. One of them, the "Association of Electricizers," involved John Murray Spear in one of the strangest adventures in the history of Spiritualism.

As announced in April 1854, in *The New Era,* they instructed him to construct a "new motor" that would be self-generative, drawing upon the great reservoir of the magnetic life in nature and acting, like the human body, as a living organism. The machine was duly built at High Rock, near Lynn, Massachusetts, of zinc and copper at the cost of $2,000. One of Spear's disciples, Mrs. Alonzo E. Newton (the wife of one of his assistants), was appointed in a vision to be "the Mary of the New Dispensation." At High Rock, near the machine, she fell into trance and went through frightful convulsions for a period of two hours, at the end of which there were said to be indications of life in the machine. The machine was considered a newborn child; the medium nursed it for weeks and the enthusiastic band announced it as "the Art of Arts, the Science of all Sciences, the New Messiah, God's last Best Gift to Man."

Reports of a shocking nature were circulated about the birth of this modern **Frankenstein**-style creation and the practices by which the life principle had been infused. Andrew Jackson Davis explained ". . . that by means of a spiritual overshadowing, à la Virgin Mary, the maternal functions were brought into active operation; a few of the usual physiological symptoms followed; the crisis arrived and being in presence of the mechanism, the first living motion was communicated to it." In an anonymous article Newton's husband proceeded to show that Newton had been the subject of a set of remarkable psychological experiences and prophetic visions at the time Spear was engaged in directing the construction of the machinery at High Rock, that the coincidence between their experiences was later discovered, and that the crisis reached its apex when Newton visited the machine. She communicated, and subsequently maintained through certain mediumistic processes, an actual living principle until the machine was pronounced "a thing of life."

When the machine did not work, Davis concluded that mechanically minded spirits, deficient in practical knowledge, were conducting experiments at Spear's expense. A few months later in Randolph, where the machine was moved to have the advantage of a lofty electrical position, superstitious villagers destroyed the new motor in the night.

The destruction of the new motor had a certain advantage in silencing critics of the machine's failure to work as predicted. Other Spiritualists took the loss philosophically, S. B. Brittan commenting in the *Spiritual Telegraph* that, "If the New Motor is to be the physical savior of the race, it will probably rise again." John Murray Spear also projected plans for the building of a "circular city," or "perfect earthly home." These plans were also inspired by spirits. Emma Hardinge Britten, writing in *Modern American Spiritualism* (1869), observes,

" . . . that Mr. Spear honestly believed in a spiritual origin for the various missions he undertook, and the remarkable part he played, none who ever have come into personal relations with him can question. The unwavering patience with which he endured reproach and odium of their execution, would attest his sincerity, were other evidence wanting."

On April 15, 1869, Spear made a statement about his introduction to Spiritualism at a meeting of the **London Dialectical Society.** Since the time of John Murray Spear, other individuals, such as **John Worrell Keely** and **Wilhelm Reich,** have claimed to have discovered a motor force in nature.

Sources:

Hewit, S. C. *Messages from the Superior State.* Boston: B. Marsh, 1853.

Report on Spiritualism of the Committee of the London Dialectical Society. London: Longmans, Green, Reader, & Dyer, 1871. Reprint, New York: Arno Press, 1976.

Spear of Destiny

A legendary Christian relic, the Spear of Longinus, identified in folklore with the spear that pierced the side of Christ (John 19:34) nearly two thousand years ago. Occult legend states that whoever claims this spear and understands its occult significance holds the destiny of the world in his hands. According to **Houston Stewart Chamberlain,** British-born propagandist for anti-Semitism and the German philosophy of an Aryan master race, this spear was claimed by Constantine the Great, Justinian, Charles Martel, Charlemagne, and various German emperors, all men of destiny.

Before World War II, the Spear of Destiny (more properly known as the Maurice Spear) was exhibited in the Hofburg Museum in Vienna. It attracted the attention of the young Adolf Hitler, who linked it with legends of the Holy Grail and made his own plans to be a man of destiny. The spear held a special fascination for Hitler and his associates in the hothouse atmosphere of occultism and evil philosophies that gave rise to the Nazi plan for world domination. In 1935, Heinrich Himmler had a replica of the spear made and kept it in his private room. Three years later, Hitler led his troops into Austria, the first stage of his plan for world conquest. One of his first acts was to remove the Spear of Destiny from the Hofburg Museum.

The spear was buried beneath the Nuremberg Fortress, where it was discovered on the day that Hitler shot himself in the Berlin bunker on April 30, 1945. It was recovered together with other treasures of the Imperial collection. On January 6, 1946, these treasures were returned to the authorities at Vienna, and the spear was reinstated in the Hofburg Museum.

Trevor Ravenscroft has compiled an exhaustive account of the story of the spear. The manner in which it influenced Hitler was integral to the occult philosophy that permeated the upper echelons of the Nazi movement and effected the actual events of World War II. Ravenscroft drew much of his unique research information from Walter Johannes Stein (1891–1957) who knew Hitler as a young man and saw Hitler's books concerned with occultism and Grail legends, with copious manuscript notes by Hitler himself indicating the beginnings of his Nazi philosophy.

Sources:

Ravenscroft, Trevor. *The Spear of Destiny.* London: Spearman, 1972. Reprint, New York: Putnam, 1973.

Specialist Knowledge Services (SKS)

A now-defunct British organization that conducted research, consultancy, and information in the fields of the paranormal, Fortean and anomalous phenomena, ufology, earth mysteries, and occultism. SKS was founded by **Hugh Pincott,** secretary of the ASSAP (**Association for the Scientific Study of Anomalous Phenomena**).

Spectral Flames

Luminous phenomena seen in cemeteries and around churches, believed by some to be paranormal.

Spectrum—Society for Psychical and Spiritual Studies

Irish society that conducted study of such paranormal phenomena as haunted sites, **ESP, psychokinesis,** and spiritual healing. It provided a healing service for individuals in need and was available to investigate hauntings. It was also associated with the **Irish UFO Organisation,** with which it shares a headquarters. Last known address: 70 Glasmeen Rd., Glasnevin, Dublin 11, Republic of Ireland.

Specularii

The name by which those who engaged in **crystal gazing** were known in the sixteenth century.

Speculum

The crystal ball or any shining, light-refracting surface that a scryer uses for divination, i.e., **crystal gazing.**

Spells

Spells are incantations, written or spoken formulas of words believed to be capable of magical effects. The term "spell" derives from the Anglo-Saxon *spel,* a saying or story, hence a form of words; the Icelandic *spjall,* a saying; and the Gothic *spill,* a fable.

The conception of spells appears to have arisen from the idea that there is some natural and intimate connection between words and the things signified by them. Thus if one repeats the name of a supernatural being the effect will be analogous to that produced by the being itself. It is assumed that all things are in a "sympathetic" connection and act and react upon one another; things that have once been in contact continue to act on each other even after the contact has been removed. People in ancient **Egypt** believed that certain secret names of gods, demi-gods, and demons unknown to human beings might be discovered and used against them by the discoverer.

The power of the spoken word was a ubiquitous belief in nearly all ancient societies and continues among pre-industrial societies to the present. Magical practitioners also developed a special language, known only to them, that became an object of mystery and a source of their power in the society. Thus the magicians of ancient Egypt employed foreign words for their incantations, such as *tharthar, thamara, thatha, mommon, thanabotha, opranu, brokhrex,* and *abranazukhel.* These occurred at the end of a spell with the purpose of bringing dreams. The development of magic was integral to the development of writing, and magical writings reveal the manner in which the simple knowledge of writing, especially of a foreign language, was a magical skill of great import.

The magicians and sorcerers of the Middle Ages likewise employed words of a similar kind that were unknown to most people, as did the medicine men of the North American Indians into relatively modern times. The reason the spell was usually couched in a well-known formula may have been that it was the most efficacious. Thus in ancient Egypt not only were the formulas of spells well fixed, but the exact tone of voice in which they were to be pronounced was specially taught. The power of a spell remained until it was broken by an antidote or exorcism.

Spells belong to what modern magicians call low magic, that which attempts to effect the mundane world, as opposed to high magic, which attempts to change the consciousness of the magician and bring him or her into contact with the transcendent realm. Spells or enchantments can be divided into several classes: (1) Protective spells; (2) The curse or taboo; (3) Spells by which a person, animal, or object is to be injured or transformed; (4) Spells to procure some minor end, love-spells, or the curing of persons and animals.

Protective Spells

The protective spell commonly appeared as an incantation, usually rhymed, imploring the protection of certain gods, saints, or beneficent beings, who in waking or sleeping hours would guard the speaker from maleficent powers. For example: "Matthew, Mark, Luke and John, Bless the bed that I lie on."

Of a deeper significance were those spells thought to be spoken by a dead Egyptian on his journey through Amenti (the kingdom of the dead), by which he warded off the evil beings who would hinder his way. The serpent who would bite the dead was addressed thus: "O serpent come not! Geb and Shu stand against thee. Thou hast eaten mice. That is loathsome to the Gods. Thou hast gnawed the bones of a putrid cat."

E. A. W. Budge stated in his book *Egyptian Magic* (1899), "The Book of the Dead says, 'Whoever readeth the spells daily over himself, he is whole upon earth, he escapes from death, and never doth anything evil meet him.'"

The deceased placed great confidence in his words of power. The gods of Thoth and Isis were the sources from which these words sprang. It will be remembered that Thoth is called the "scribe of the gods," the "lord of writing," the "master of papyrus," the "maker of the palette and the ink-jar," and the "lord of divine words," i.e., the holy writings or scriptures. As he was the lord of books and master of the power of speech, he was considered to be the possessor of all knowledge both human and divine. The priests of Thoth were the learned magicians skilled in the written language for which Thoth had been responsible.

At the creation of the world, it was he who reduced to words the will of the unseen and unknown creative power, who uttered them so wisely that the universe came into being, and who proved himself by the exercise of his knowledge to be the protector and the friend of Osiris and of Isis, and of their son Horus.

From the evidence of the texts we know that it was not by physical might that Thoth helped these three gods, but by giving them words of power and instructing them how to use them. We know that Osiris vanquished his foes, and that he reconstituted his body and became the king of the underworld and god of the dead. It is this belief that made the deceased cry out, "Hail, Thoth, who madest Osiris victorious over his enemies, make thou Ani to be victorious over his enemies in the presence of the great and sovereign princes who are in Tattu, or in any other place."

Without the words of power given to him by Thoth, Osiris would have been powerless under the attacks of his foes, and similarly the dead man, who was always identified with Osiris, would have passed out of existence at his death but for the words of power provided by the writings that were buried with him. In the Judgment Scene it is Thoth who reports to the gods the result of the weighing of the heart in the balance, and who has supplied its owner with the words that he has uttered in his supplications, and whatever can be said in favor of the deceased he says to the gods, and whatever can be done for him he does.

But apart from being the protector and friend of Osiris, Thoth was the refuge to which Isis fled in her trouble. The words of a hymn declare that she knew "how to turn aside evil happening," and that she was "strong of tongue and uttered the words of power which she knew with correct pronunciation, and halted not in her speech, and was perfect both in giving the command, and in saying the word," but this description only proves that she had been instructed by Thoth in the art of uttering words of power with effect, and to him, indeed, she owed more than this. Spells to keep away disease are of this class.

The **amulets** found upon Egyptian mummies and the inscriptions on Gnostic gems are, for the most part, of a protective nature. The protective spell may be said to be an amulet in words and is often found in connection with the amulet on which it is inscribed.

Taboos

The curse or taboo may appear as (a) the word of blighting, the damaging word, or (b) the word of prohibition or restriction.

The curse is of the nature of a spell, even if it is not in the shape of a definite formula. Thus we have the Highland Scottish curses: "A bad meeting to you," "Bad understanding to you," and "A down mouth be yours," which are popular as formulas.

Those who had seen old women, of the type of Madge Wildfire (in Sir Walter Scott's novel *The Heart of Midlothian*), cursing and banning, say their manner is well-calculated to inspire terror. Some years ago, a party of Scottish tinkers quarreled and fought, first among themselves, and then with some Tiree villagers. In the excitement, a tinker wife threw off her cap and allowed her hair to fall over her shoulders in wild disorder. She then bared her knees, and falling on them to the ground in a praying attitude, poured forth a torrent of wishes that struck awe into all who heard her.

She imprecated: "Drowning by sea and conflagration by land; may you never see a son to follow your body to the graveyard, or a daughter to mourn your death. I have made my wish before this, and I will make it now, and there was not yet a day I did not see my wish fulfilled."

Curses employed by witches usually invoked a blight upon the person cursed and their flocks, herds, and crops. Barrenness, too, was frequently called down upon women. A person under a curse or spell was believed in the Scottish Highlands "to become powerless over his own volition . . . alive and awake but moves and acts as if asleep." Curses or spells that invoked death were frequently mentioned in works that deal with Medieval magic (see **summons by the dying**).

The taboo was a word of prohibition or restriction. This is typified in the mystic expression "thou shalt not." Thus a number of the Biblical commandments are taboos, and the book of Leviticus teems with them. The taboo is the "don't" applied to children—a curb on basic desire for the sake of the community. To break a taboo was to bring dire misfortune upon oneself, and often upon one's family. It could even threaten the whole community and some action would have to be taken to counter the effects of a broken taboo.

Transforming Spells

There are copious examples of injury or transformation of a person, animal, or object. These were nearly always affected by a spell of a given formula. No fewer than 12 chapters of the Egyptian *Book of the Dead* (chapters 77 to 88) are devoted to providing the deceased with words of power, the recital of which was necessary to enable him to transform himself into various animal and human forms.

S. Baring Gould, in his *Book of Folklore* (1913), states that in such cases the consequence of a spell being cast on an individual required him or her to become a beast or a monster with no escape except under conditions difficult to obtain. To this category belong a number of so-called fairy tales that are actually folktales. Wherever the magical art is believed to be all-powerful, one of its greatest achievements is the casting of a spell so as to alter completely the appearance of the person on whom it is cast, so that this individual becomes an animal. One need only recall the story in the *Arabian Nights* of the Calendars and the three noble ladies of Baghdad, in which the wicked sisters are transformed into dogs that have to be thrashed every day. Also of this class are the stories "Beauty and the Beast" and "The Frog Prince."

Procurement Spells

Procurement spells are spells to procure some minor end. Love spells were engraved on metal tables by the **Gnostics** and the magicians of the Middle Ages. Instances of these are to be found in *The Book of the Sacred Magic* of **Abraham the Jew.** Spells were often employed to imprison evil spirits.

Jewish folklore has many opinions and legends relating to this subject, which appear to have derived in a great measure from the Babylonians. The ancient historian Josephus affirmed that it was generally believed by his countrymen that **Solomon** left behind many spells that had the power of terrifying and expelling evil spirits. Some of the old rabbis also described Solomon as an accomplished magician. It is possible that the belief in the power of spells and incantations became general among the Hebrews during the captivity, and that the invention of them was attributed to the wise Solomon, as a more creditable personage than the deities of the Assyrians.

Those fictions acquired currency, not only among the Arabs, Persians, and other Islamic nations, but, in the process of time, also in many Christian communities. They were first adopted by the Gnostics and the dualistic sects in whose beliefs pagan rituals mixed with Jewish and Christian notions. In the Middle Ages they found their way among Catholics too, principally by means of the apocryphal gospels and the hagiography of the saints.

An incident in the life of St. Margaret is typical. This holy virgin, having vanquished an evil spirit who assaulted her, demanded his name. "My name," replied the demon, "is Veltis, and I am one of those whom Solomon, by virtue of his spells, confined in a copper caldron at Babylon, but when the Babylonians, in the hope of finding treasures, dug up the caldron and opened it, we all made our escape. Since that time, our efforts have been directed to the destruction of righteous persons, and I have long been striving to turn thee from the course which thou hast embraced." The reader of the *Arabian Nights' Entertainments* will be immediately reminded of the story of the fisherman. The Oriental origin of many similar legends, e.g., of St. George of Cappadocia, seems equally clear.

Modern Spell Magic

Spells became a large part of popular folk magic, a fact illustrated by the magic of the Pennsylvania Dutch as compiled in *The Long Lost Friend* by John Hohman. This book of magic largely consists of short spells that could be easily learned and just as easily repeated at any appropriate moment. Through the nineteenth century, as Western society reoriented itself around science and technology, spells supposedly became part of the superstitious pre-scientific past. However, the survival of magic into the post-scientific world has been accompanied with a reappraisal of magic in light of its social function.

As magic has been revived in the West, one can note the spread and use of spells, especially among the Wiccans, practitioners of neo-pagan **witchcraft.** Much of the popular Wiccan movement is focused on the improvement of the lives of the adherents and the lives of their friends and family. Low magic is common and accompanies a program that emphasizes psychic training, self-discipline, and the development of new social skills.

In modern Wicca, the emphasis is placed upon positive spells, but there is a place for curses and negative spells. Admonitions surround the use of such spells. Some pagan priestesses speak of a threefold law of return. If one seeks out a spell, and if that spell does not take, it will rebound upon the one who sent it with a triple force.

Sources:

Abbott, John. *The Keys of Power: A Study of Indian Ritual and Belief.* London: Methuen, 1932. Reprint, New Hyde Park, N.Y.: University Books, 1974.

Aima. *Ritual Book of Herbal Spell.* Los Angeles: Hermetic Science Center, 1970.

Budge, E. A. Wallis. *Egyptian Magic.* London: Kegan Paul, 1899.

Campbell, J. G. *Witchcraft and Second Sight in Scottish Highlands and Islands.* Glasgow: Alex, MacLehose, 1902.
Cohen, Daniel. *Curses, Hexes and Spells.* Philadelphia: Lippincott, 1974.
De Pascale, Marc. *The Book of Spells.* New York: Taplinger, 1971.
González-Wippler, Migene. *The Complete Book of Spells, Ceremonies, and Magic.* St. Paul: Llewellyn Publications, 1978.
Graves, Samuel R. [Osirus]. *Potions and Spells of Witchcraft.* San Francisco: JBT Marketing, 1970.
Grimm, Macob. *Teutonic Mythology.* 4 vols. London: Bell, 1880–88.
Heim, Richard, ed. *Incantamenta Magica Graeca Latina.* Leipzig: Teubner, 1893.
Hohman, John George. *The Long Lost Friend.* Harrisburg, Pa., 1850.
Holroyd, Stuart. *Magic, Words, and Numbers.* London: Aldus Books; Garden City, N.Y.: Doubleday, 1975.
Leek, Sybil. *Book of Curses.* Englewood Cliffs, N.J.: Prentice-Hall, 1975.
———. *Cast Your Own Spell.* New York: Bee-Line Books, 1970.
MacKenzie, William, ed. *Gaelic Incantations, Charms and Blessings of the Hebrides.* Inverness, Scotland, 1895.
Malbrough, Ray T. *Charms, Spells, and Formulas.* St. Paul: Llewellyn Publications, 1987.
Maple, Eric. *Incantations and Words of Power.* New York: Samuel Weiser, 1974.
Martello, Leo. *Curses in Verses.* New York: Hero Press, 1971.
Mickaharic, Draja. *A Century of Spells.* York Beach, Maine: Samuel Weiser, 1988.
Morrison, Sarah Lyddon. *The Modern Witch's Spellbook.* New York: David McKay, 1971.
Norris, David, and Jacquemine Charrott-Lodwidge. *The Book of Spells.* London: Lorrimer, 1974.
Rose, Donna. *Love Spells.* Hialeah, Fla.: Mi-World Publishing Co., n.d.
Waite, Arthur E. *The Book of Ceremonial Magic.* London: William Rider, 1911. Reprint, New Hyde Park, N.Y.: University Books, 1961. Reprint, New York: Causeway Books, 1973.

Spence, (James) Lewis (Thomas Chalmers) (1874–1955)

Scottish journalist and scholar of the occult who took a particular interest in the **Atlantis** theme. Born November 25, 1874, in Forfarshire, Scotland, he was educated privately and at Edinburgh University before following a journalistic career. He was copy editor of the newspaper *The Scotsman,* (1899–1906), editor of *The Edinburgh Magazine* (1904–05), and copy editor of *The British Weekly* (1906–09). About this time he took to serious study of mythology and folklore, with special reference to Mexico and Central America. He published some important books on the subject, including his own study of *The Popul Vuh,* the sacred book of the ancient Quiché Indians of Maya (1908) and *A Dictionary of Mythology* (1910).

He also published more than 40 other works dealing with mythology, folklore, and the occult, including the *Encyclopaedia of Occultism* (1920) the first comprehensive work of its kind and ultimately one of the primary sources of this *Encyclopedia of Occultism and Parapsychology.*

He contributed articles to the *Hibbert Journal,* the *Glasgow Herald,* and *The Times.* An ardent Scottish nationalist, he contested North Midlothian as a candidate in 1929. He also found time to write romantic poetry. He was a fellow of the Royal Anthropological Institute of Great Britain and Ireland and was vice president of the Scottish Anthropological and Folklore Society. In 1951 he was awarded a royal pension for services to literature.

He is best known, perhaps, for his books exploring the Atlantis myth. He also edited the journal *Atlantis Quarterly* in 1932. His *Magic Arts in Celtic Britain* (1945) was used extensively in the early years of the modern neo-pagan **witchcraft** revival. He died March 3, 1955.

Sources:

Spence, Lewis. *Atlantis in America.* London: E. Benn, 1925. Reprint, Detroit: Singing Tree Press, 1972.
———. *British Fairy Origins.* London: Watts, 1946.
———. *The Fairy Tradition in Britain.* London; New York: Rider, 1948.
———. *The History of Atlantis.* 1926. Reprint, New Hyde Park, N.Y.: University Books, 1968.
———. *The Magic and Mysteries of Mexico.* Philadelphia: David McKay, 1930.
———. *The Occult Causes of the Present War.* N.p., 1940.
———. *The Occult Sciences in Atlantis.* London: Rider, 1943. Reprint, New York: S. Weiser, 1970.
———. *The Problem of Atlantis.* 1924. Reprinted as *Atlantis Discovered.* New York: Causeway Books, 1974.
———. *The Problem of Lemuria.* London: Rider, 1932.
———. *Scottish Ghosts and Goblins.* N.p., 1952.
———. *Second Sight: Its History and Origins.* London; New York: Rider, 1951.
———. *Will Europe Follow Atlantis?* N.p., 1942.

Spheres

Divisions of the spirit world, both in spatial and moral-spiritual senses. The doctrine of spheres, in a literal sense, was integral to the ancient world, and much of occult teachings—astrology, magic, Gnosticism—emerged in such a cosmology. It was retained in the occult culture and has passed into modern theosophical and Spiritualist circles, where it has remained, though the spheres are usually thought of as levels of a multidimensional world.

Spiritualists have developed a doctrine of the spheres based upon the communications of spirits in the nineteenth and twentieth centuries. The information conflicts at many points, and there is no authority to declare for one opinion over another, but there is a general agreement as to the number of spheres. They are seven: (1) Hell, (2) Sphere of Desires, (3) Summerland, (4) Mind, (5) Abstract, (6) Meeting of the Sexes, and (7) Union of the Sexes.

There is some contradiction as to whether the Earth should be considered as the first sphere. It is said that the first sphere is the abode of gross and ignorant spirits. It is gloomy and desolate, replete with sadness and misery. After a realization of their state and the circumstances that cast them into it, the desire for progress and betterment will transfer the spirits into the second sphere where, in a scenery as natural as that on Earth, harmony, love, and kindness help to develop the higher qualities of the soul.

The period of the stay in a particular sphere varies individually. The higher spheres cannot be perceived by spirits in the lower ones. Information on the higher spheres is obtained from visitors descending to lower spheres. Owing to a lack of conception, no adequate description can be conveyed to us. It is also said that beyond the spheres are the heavens of boundless extent. These are the ultimate abodes of the glorified and blessed.

Hudson Tuttle, in his book *Arcana of Spiritualism* (1871), furnishes an interesting exposition of the origin of the spheres. According to Tuttle, the spirit world is built up from atomic emanations. Exhalations from all substances ascend as mist rises from a sheet of water. The spirit world therefore depends on the Earth for its existence and is formed through its refining instrumentality. Without the Earth there could not have been corresponding spirit spheres, actually zones rather than spheres. They are 120 degrees wide; that is, they extend 60 degrees on each side of the equator. If we take the sixtieth parallel of latitude each side of the equator and imagine it projected against the blue dome of the sky, we have the boundaries of these zones.

The first zone, or the innermost one, is 60 miles from the Earth's surface. The next external one is removed from the first by about the same distance. The third is just outside the moon's orbit, or 265,000 miles from the Earth. From the third sphere rise the most sublimated exhalations, which mingle with the emanations of the other planets and form a vast zone around the entire solar system, including even the unknown planets beyond the vast orbit of Neptune (the spirits had yet to inform him of the existence of Pluto).

The first zone is nearly 30 miles in thickness, the second 20, the third but two miles. While the Earth is slowly diminishing, the spheres are gradually increasing. The surface of the zones is diversified with changing scenery. Matter, when it aggregates there, is prone to assume the forms in which it existed below. Hence there are all the forms of life there as on Earth, except those, such as the lowest plants and animals, that cannot exist surrounded by such superior conditions. The scenery is of mountain and plain; river, lake and ocean; and of forest and prairie. It is like Earth with all its imperfections perfected, and its beauties are multiplied.

The first trance reference to spheres in the lineage of modern Spiritualism seems to have been made by **Frederica Hauffe,** the seeress of Prevorst. The second is contained in a letter from **G. P. Billot** to **J. P. F. Deleuze** in 1831. Billot wrote: "They taught that God was a grand Spiritual Sun—life on earth a probation—the spheres, different degrees of comprehensive happiness or states of retributive suffering—each appropriate to the good or evil deeds done on earth. They described the ascending changes open to every soul in proportion to his own efforts to improve."

The first exact dimensions were claimed by J. A. Gridley in his book *Astounding Facts from the Spirit World* (1854). According to his data, the first sphere is 5,000 miles, the sixth 30,000 miles from the Earth's surface.

Diagrams of the spheres were first drawn by Hauffe. Nahum Koons in the Koon loghouse was the second to provide detailed sketches; his information was supplemented by accounts given through the trumpet (see also **Jonathan Koons**).

Robert Hare differed from Gridley and agreed with Hudson Tuttle inasmuch as his communicators put the distance of the nearest sphere as 60 miles from the Earth's surface. But his further distances did not tally with Tuttle's calculations. He placed the sixth sphere within the area of the moon. He was told that the spheres are concentric zones, or circles, of exceedingly refined matter encompassing the Earth like belts or girdles. They have atmospheres of peculiar vital air, soft and balmy. Their surfaces are diversified with an immense variety of picturesque landscapes, with lofty mountain ranges, valleys, rivers, lakes, forests, trees and shrubbery, and flowers of every colour and variety, sending forth grateful emanations.

As flights of unverifiable speculation proceeded, almost every trance description of the spheres asserted something different. Eugene Crowell, in *The Identity of Primitive Christianity with Modern Spiritualism* (2 vols., 1875–79), states that he had received the following figures: the first sphere is within our atmosphere, the second is about 60 miles from the earth, the third about 160, the fourth 310, the fifth 460, the sixth 635, the seventh 865 miles.

Precise information was tendered in **J. Hewat McKenzie**'s *Spirit Intercourse* (1916). The supposed spirit of **William James** was quoted as the authority behind the statements. The disagreement is all too apparent. "The third sphere, the Summer Land, is 1,350 miles from the earth, the fourth 2,850, the fifth 5,050, the sixth 9,450, and the seventh 18,250."

The sustenance of the body in superphysical states is derived from the atmosphere by inhalation in the ordinary act of breathing; the material for clothing and houses is manufactured; there is a union of sexes in a bond of affection, with no offspring; the animals that live there have previously existed on Earth; the spiritual worlds of each planet unite at the seventh sphere; the spheres are built of essences cast off by millions of tons of matter that condense into solid substance and float in space like vast continents, by the operation of centripetal and centrifugal attraction; and the passage from one sphere to the other is effected by gradual refinement of the spiritual body under the effect of the spirit.

An impressive conception of after-death states was disclosed in **Geraldine Cummins**'s *The Road to Immortality* (1932), a book said to be dictated by the spirit of **F. W. H. Myers.** According to the chapter "The Chart of Existence," the journey of the soul takes place through the following stages:

1. The Plane of Matter.
2. Hades or the Intermediate State.
3. The Plane of Illusion.
4. The Plane of Color.
5. The Plane of Flame.
6. The Plane of Light.
7. Out Yonder, Timelessness.

Between each plane or new chapter in experience, there is existence in Hades or in an intermediate state when the soul reviews his past experiences and makes his choice, deciding whether he will go up or down the ladder of consciousness.

Although there is marked disagreement between different accounts of spirit worlds in the afterlife, it will be recalled that this is also characteristic of the eschatology (considerations of the afterlife) of the different Eastern and Western religions.

It has been claimed that spirits who have not become purified and refined and remain tied to earthly desires have been easier to contact and that their communications would be unreliable. Advance spirits would have moved on to more rarified planes of existence. However, that idea seems to be contradicted by the attempts to identify various spirits with advanced beings from the past.

It is interesting to note that many individuals who have experienced **out-of-the-body travel,** especially as part of a **near-death experience,** have reported a remarkable similarity of content in terms both of positive experiences of moving toward a bright light and meeting light beings, as well as negative experiences of a purgatorial realm. These experiences, however, have no relation to the spiritualist doctrine of the spheres.

Sources:

Cummins, Geraldine Dorothy. *The Road to Immortality.* London: I. Nicholson & Watson, 1933.

Tuttle, Hudson. *Arcana of Spiritualism.* N.p., 1871. Reprint, Manchester: The Two Worlds Publishing, 1900; Chicago: J. R. Francis, 1904.

Spider

Various folklore beliefs surround the spider. In England, spiders were known as "money makers." If found on clothing, they were a sign that money was on the way, provided that the spider was not killed. A similar idea prevailed in Polynesia, where a spider dropping down in front of a person was a sign of a present. An American belief is that killing a spider will bring rain.

In folk medicine, a spider was rolled in butter or molasses and swallowed. As a cure for ague, it was tied up and secured on the left arm. A spider was also traditionally used as an **amulet.** The insect was baked and worn around the neck.

The British antiquary Elias Ashmole stated in his *Memoirs* (1717): "I took early in the morning a good dose of elixir, and hung three spiders around my neck, and they drove my ague away. Deo Gratias!"

Robert Burton (1577–1640) stated:

"Being in the country in the vacation time, not many years since, at Lindly in Leicestershire, my father's house, I first observed this amulet of a spider in a nut-shell, wrapped in silk, so applied for an ague by my mother. . . . This I thought most absurd and ridiculous, and I could see no warrant in it . . . till at length, rambling amongst authors, I found this very medicine in Dioscorides, approved by Matthiolus, repeated by Aldrovandus. . . . I began to have a better opinion of it, and to give more credit to amulets, when I saw it in some parties answer to experience."

Spiders were sacred to the ancient Egyptian goddess Maat and are used today as symbolism of a Maatian (feminist) form of **ceremonial magic.**

Spiegelschrift

Writing written backward, from right to left, so as to be read in a mirror. **Automatic writing** is frequently done in this way, and it is said that the ability to produce spiegelschrift is often found where there is a natural tendency to automatism.

Spiral Journey

Spiral Journey, a post-**New Age** networking periodical, serves the greater Seattle area of the state of Washington. Appearing ten times annually, *Spiral Journey* covers **holistic** health, **New Thought** spirituality, and alternatives designed to connect the body, mind, and spirit.

Each issue is built around a set of brief feature articles on various religious and health perspectives dominated by a New Thought positive thinking approach, chosen for their aim to empower and inform. There are also several regular columns, including a question-and-answer column by hypnotherapist Ayal Hurst, and an astrology-tarot column, "Astrocures," by health consultant Donna Pinkston, who is also *Spiral Journey*'s editor and marketing director. The sensitivity to a spectrum of alternative spiritual options is demonstrated in the inclusion of a "Totem of the Month" feature highlighting the symbolic significance of various animals.

Spiral Journey initially appeared in July of 1997, and grew out of the spiritual crisis that its editor, Asara Sharon Briski, had gone through in the mid-1990s. It is published at PMB 6121, 13300 Bothell-Everett Hwy., Mill Creek, WA 98012, and distributed free at a number of bookstores, health food stores, and other businesses in its target area. It is issued monthly, with combined issues in December/January and July/August.

Sources:

Spiral Journey. Mill Creek, Wash., n.d.

SPIRICOM

Apparatus invented by research engineer George W. Meek of the METAscience Foundation as a communication system with the dead. This particular development of an **electronic voice phenomenon** (EVP) involves a frequency modulation system using supplementary audio tones. In contrast to the previously claimed EVP or **Raudive voices** system, which obtained very weak voice signals, usually of a few words spoken at higher than normal speeds, Meek and his associates claimed to have received many hours of sustained conversation at normal speed from the American scientist George Jeffries Mueller, who had died of a heart attack 14 years earlier.

The first announcement of SPIRICOM was made on April 6, 1982, following 11 years of research and development. The system was not entirely mechanical, since, like other electronic devices such as the **black box,** it required the psychic energies of an operator.

In a release published in the journal *New Realities* (vol. 4, no. 6), Meek describes his system of SPIRICOM Mark IV as consisting of three components: a transceiver operating in the 30–130 Mhz range; a special combination of 13 audio frequencies from 21 to 701 cps; and the input of energy from an operator who had certain highly psychic abilities, involving energy apparently outside present knowledge of the electromagnetic system, tentatively called "bioplasmic." The system was developed in conjunction with the MetaScience Foundation at Franklin, North Carolina.

The inventor and his associates made their preliminary announcement in order to encourage other researchers to develop their invention beyond basic stage so that communication with the dead by means of electronic apparatus might become perfected as quickly as possible. No patent rights were filed on the equipment, and both printed and audio explanatory materials were published to facilitate the work of other experimenters. For further information, contact METAscience Foundation, P.O. Box 10749, Minneapolis, MN 55458. (See also **Ashkir-Jobson Trianion; Communigraph; Friedrich Jürgenson; Reflectograph**)

Spirit

A basic concept in the Western religious traditions, in which it is often contrasted to the material aspect of existence. The Hebrew word *ruah* (spirit) originally meant "breath" or "wind," and the association of spirit with breath and wind is also found in the Greek word *pneuma.* In the Christian tradition, biblical interpreters generally argue for one of two views of the spirit. Some see the spirit as synonymous with the soul and as the principle of all life, including the intellectual, moral, and religious, and believe that when the body dies the soul returns to God, who made it. Others tend to see a distinction between the spirit and the soul. They believe the soul (psyche) is the principle of animal life and is possessed by humans and animals alike. The spirit, in contrast, is that which humans possess which is not shared with other animals—a moral and an immortal life, a conscious relationship to God. In this view, the soul and body die, but the spirit survives and goes into God's presence. This latter view has tended to dominate within **Spiritualism.**

The Spirit in Spiritualism

In Spiritualism *spirit* is variously defined as the inmost principle, the divine particle, the vital essence, and the inherent actuating element in life. It is seen as manifesting through its association with protoplasm and dwells in the **astral body,** which Spiritualists identify with the **soul,** the connecting link between the spirit and the physical body.

At death the connection between the spirit and the physical body is severed, and the spirit finds no ordinary means of manifestation. Spirits appear to be cognizant of space, although not conditioned by it. The same applies to time. Past, present, and future cease to exist for the spirit in the earthly sense.

Spiritualists do not see spirits in the role of Peeping Toms, keeping watch on the most private actions of the living, but have concluded that they are partly conscious of the thoughts and emotions directed toward them from the Earth.

They also maintain that spirits cannot hold communion with the living if the mental attitude of the latter is not receptive to spirit communication. In the mid-nineteenth century chemistry professor **Robert Hare** was told by alleged spirits that there were peculiar elementary principles out of which spiritual bodies were constructed that were analogous to material elements; that spirits have bodies, with a circulation and respiratory apparatus; and that they breathe a gaseous or ethereal matter that is also inhaled by men, beasts, and fish.

William Denton a geology professor noted for his research in **psychometry,** wrote: "The vision that can see through brick walls and distinguish objects miles away, does not belong to the body; it must belong to the spirit. Hundreds of times have I had the evidence that the spirit can smell, hear and see, and has powers of locomotion. As the fin in the unhatched fish indicates the water in which he may one day swim, so these powers in man indicate that mighty realm which the spirit is fitted eternally to enjoy."

Sources:

Crawley, A. E. *The Idea of the Soul.* New York: Macmillan, 1909.

De Vesme, Caesar. *A History of Experimental Spiritualism.* 2 vols. London: Rider, 1931.

Driesch, Hans. *History and Theory of Vitalism.* New York: Macmillan, 1914.

Hackforth, R., trans. *Plato's Phaedo.* Cambridge, Mass.: Cambridge University Press, 1955.

Hare, Robert. *Experimental Investigation of the Spirit Manifestations.* New York, 1856.

Heysinger, Isaac. *Spirit and Matter Before the Bar of Modern Science.* London: T. Werner Laurie, 1910.

Hyslop, James H. *Contact With the Other World.* New York: Century, 1919.

King, J. H. *The Supernatural.* 2 vols. London, 1892.

Mead, G. R. S. *The Doctrine of the Subtle Body in Western Tradition.* London: J. M. Watkins, 1919.

———. *Human Personality and Its Survival of Bodily Death.* London: Longmans, Green, 1903. Reprint, New York: Arno Press, 1975.

Tweedale, C. L. *Man's Survival After Death.* London, 1909. Reprint, New York: E. P. Dutton, 1918.

Tylor, E. B. *Primitive Culture.* 2 vols. New York: George Putnam's Sons, 1871.

Spirit and Nature (Magazine)

Bimonthly magazine dealing with the teachings of **Paramahansa Yogananda** and his disciple Swami Kriyananda, who left the **Self-Realization Fellowship** to found Ananda. Address: **Ananda Cooperative Village,** 14618 Tyler Foote Rd., Nevada City, CA 95959. Website: http://www.ananda.org/.

Sources:

Ananda. http://www.ananda.org/. April 14, 2000.

Spirit Children

A Spiritualist explanation for the relatively frequent phenomenon of children reporting invisible playmates. In **Spiritualism,** these are children who have died and, according to accounts of mediums in **trance,** are growing to maturity in an afterlife. Child mediums have often claimed spirit children as their playmates, and mediums have often had a "child" as one of their spirit controls.

Florence Marryat, in her book *There is No Death* (1891), writes of medium **Bessie Williams**'s little girl "Mabel": "I have watched her playing at ball with an invisible child, and have seen the ball thrown, arrested half-way in the air, and then tossed back again as if a living child had been Mab's opponent." According to Marryat, when a still-born baby enters the other side, she is delivered over to the nearest relative of its parent to be named and brought up.

"The nurse of the little Guldenstubbe," writes **Baron Hellenbach** in his book *Birth and Death as a Change of Perception* (1886), "who afterwards became a very celebrated medium, noticed with terror that his playthings moved about by themselves, while the child declared that another child was playing with them."

Sources:

Marryat, Florence. *There is No Death.* London: K Paul, Trench, Trubner, 1891. Reprint, London: Griffith, Farran, 1893.

Spirit Hypothesis

The theory that the intelligence that directs the phenomena of the medium and the séance room is a disembodied spirit. Interest in the possibility of this theory being true and of establishing proof of it energized much of **psychical research** in its first generations. The theory suffered greatly from the discovery that most of the more interesting phenomena was simply the product of **fraud.** Most of contemporary **parapsychology** has redirected itself away from any consideration of the spirit hypothesis and in favor of exploring psychic powers inherent in the individual and the various altered states of consciousness that accompany the exercise of such powers. Some consideration of possible spirit activity remains in the study of **poltergeists** and the **near-death experience.**

As **Spiritualism** developed, the spirit hypothesis stood against various psychological theories of mediumship and the diabolic theories of conservative Christian theologians. The psychological theory reduced the genuine phenomena to mental processes inherent in the mediums themselves and their associates.

Theodore Flournoy was an early champion of the psychological hypothesis:

"The state of passivity, the abdication of the normal personality, the relaxation of voluntary control over the muscular movements, and the ideas—this whole psycho-physiological attitude, where the subject is in a state of expectancy of communicating with the deceased—strongly predisposes him to mental dissociation and a sort of infantile regression, a relapse into an inferior phase of psychic evolution, where his imagination naturally begins to imitate the discarnate, utilising the resources of the subconscious, the emotional complexes, latent memories, instinctive tendencies ordinarily suppressed, etc., for the various roles it plays."

James H. Hyslop summed up the fundamental conditions of the spirit hypothesis as follows: (1) The information acquired must be supernormal, that is, not explicable by normal perception; (2) The incidents must be verifiable memories of the deceased persons and so representative of their personal identity; (3) The incidents must be trivial and specific—not easily, if at all, duplicated in the common experience of others.

William James, in his report of the "Richard Hodgson" spirit **control** of **Leonora Piper** states:

"I myself can perfectly well imagine spirit agency, and find my mind vacillating about it curiously. When I take the phenomena piecemeal, the notion that Mrs. Piper's subliminal self should keep her sitters apart as expertly as she does, remembering its past dealings with each of them so well, not mixing their communications more, and all the while humbugging them so profusely, is quite compatible with what we know of the dreamlife of the hypnotised subjects. . . . But I find that when I ascend from the details to the whole meaning of the phenomenon . . . the notion that such an immense current of experience, complex in so many ways, should spell out absolutely nothing but the word humbug, acquires a character of unlikeness. The notion that so many men and women, in all other respects honest enough, should have this preposterous monkeying self annexed to their personality seems to me so weird that the spirit theory immediately takes on a more probable appearance. The spirits, if spirits there be, must indeed work under incredible complications and falsifications, but at least if they are present some honesty is left in the whole department of the universe which otherwise is run by pure deception. The more I realise the quantitative massiveness of the phenomenon and its complexity, the more incredible it seems to me that in a world all of whose vaster features we are in the habit of considering to be sincere at least, however, brutal, this feature should be wholly constituted on insincerity."

In a chapter called "The Spiritistic Hypothesis" in his book *My Philosophy* (1933), **Sir Oliver Lodge** states:

"My doctrine involves the primary reality of mind in association with whatever physical mechanism it may find available. Matter constitutes only one of these mechanisms, and indeed only constitutes it in a secondary fashion; and by a study limited to matter alone we shall never get the full reality of existence.

I hold that all our actions on matter here and now are conducted through empty space, or rather through the entity which fills space; and that if our activity continues, it must be continued in the same sort of way and through the same sort of etheric mechanism that we already unconsciously utilise now. That in brief terms is the spiritistic hypothesis which I proclaim and work on."

Sources:

Beard, Paul. *Survival of Death: For and Against.* London: Hodder & Stoughton, 1966.

Broad, C. D. *Personal Identity and Survival.* London: Society for Psychical Research, 1968.

Carington, Whately. *The Foundations of Spiritualism.* New York: E. P. Dutton, 1920.

Hart, Hornell. *The Enigma of Survival: The Case for and Against Survival.* Springfield, Ill.: C. C. Thomas, 1959.

Hyslop, James H. *Contact With the Other World: The Latest Evidence as to Communication With the Dead.* New York: Century, 1919.

Jacobson, Nils Olof. *Life Without Death? On Parapsychology, Mysticism and the Question of Survival.* New York: Delacorte Press, 1973. Reprint, London: Turnstone Books, 1974.

Richmond, Kenneth. *Evidence of Identity.* London: G. Bell, 1939.

Rogo, D. Scott. *Welcoming Silence: A Study of Psychical Phenomena and Survival of Death.* New Hyde Park, N.Y.: University Books, 1973.

Salter, W. H. *Zoar; or, The Evidence of Psychical Research Concerning Survival.* London: Sidgwick & Jackson, 1961. Reprint, Arno Press, 1975.

Smith, Susy. *Life Is Forever: Evidence for Survival After Death.* Putnam, 1974.

Spirit Intervention

Spiritualist annals contain a number of accounts of the intervention of spirits to find lost wills, other papers, or objects of importance, or to track down murderers. Boccaccio, in his *Life of Dante,* related that the spectral form of Dante appeared in a dream to his son Jacopo Alighiere, and on the son's inquiry whether he had finished his great poem, the thirteenth canto of which they were unable to find, the spirit took him by the hand and led him to the house and into the room where Dante had been accustomed to sleep and pointed out a blind window covered by matting. On waking, Alighiere found the missing canto, which had not been seen before, in this place.

The philosopher Kant, in his revelations on **Emanuel Swedenborg,** narrated the story of a Madame Marteville, a widow who was asked to pay a debt of her deceased husband. She remembered that the debt was paid but could not find the receipt. During a visit to Swedenborg, Marteville asked the seer if he had known her husband. Swedenborg answered in the negative. Eight days afterward, the spirit of the dead man appeared to the widow in a dream and showed her where she would find a casket of finest workmanship with the receipt and a magnificent pin, which was also lost, inside. She immediately got out of bed, ran to the place indicated, and found the casket and contents.

In the morning, she was hardly awake when Swedenborg was announced. Without having knowledge of her dream Swedenborg told her that during the night he conversed with many spirits, among them her deceased husband who, however, cut short the conversation by saying that he must visit his wife in order to reveal to her the whereabouts of a paper of the highest importance and of a diamond breast pin she thought lost. Swedenborg called to find out whether the spirit had kept his promise.

The **Master of Lindsay,** on being questioned before the committee of the **London Dialectical Society** on July 6, 1869, as to whether he ever obtained any information that could not have been known to the medium or to any present, told the following story:

"A friend of mine was very anxious to find a will of his grandmother, who had been dead 40 years, but could not even find the certificate of her death. I went with him to the Marshall's, and we had a séance; we sat at a table, and soon the raps came; my friend then asked his questions *mentally;* he went over the alphabet himself, or sometimes I did so, not knowing the question. We were told the will had been drawn by a man named William Walker, who lived in Whitechapel; the name of the street, and the number of the house were given. We went to Whitechapel, found the man, and subsequently, through his aid, obtained a copy of the draft; he was quite unknown to us, and had not always lived in the locality, for he had once seen better days. The medium could not possibly have known anything about the matter, and even if she had, her knowledge would have been of no avail, as all the questions were mental ones."

Robert Macnish, in his book *The Philosophy of Sleep* (1830), narrates the court case of R. of Bowland. This man was summoned to pay a sum that his father had already paid. When he was about to pay again, the spirit of his father appeared to him in a dream and informed him that the respective papers were in the hands of M. of Inveresk, near Edinburgh. If he had no recollection of it, he should be reminded of the difference of opinion that he had with the deceased about a Portuguese coin. The reminder was most helpful. With the help of it the old attorney remembered and found the papers.

Gabriel Delanne, in his book *Le Spiritisme devant la Science* (1885), tells the story of a spirit communication given to a descendant of Johann Sebastian Bach by the spirit of an Italian musician named Baldasarini who lived at the court of Henry III of France. The communication led to the discovery of a small strip of paper inside a spinet of 1664 with four lines of verse in the handwriting of Henry III. The authenticity of the writing was proved by comparing the strip with manuscripts in the Imperial Library.

The "Widow's Mite" incident was described by Isaac K. Funk in his book of this title, published in 1904. In February 1903, he heard of a Brooklyn family where every Wednesday evening sittings took place in the presence of a few invited guests. On his third visit, when he was getting reconciled to the notion that the mediumship was a remarkably good case of secondary personality, the **control** "George" asked: "Has anyone here got anything that belonged to Mr. Beecher?"

There was no reply. On his emphatic repetition of the question, Funk replied: "I have in my pocket a letter from the Rev. Dr. Hillis, Mr. Beecher's successor. Is that what you mean?"

The answer was: "No, I am told by a spirit present, John Rakestraw[,] that Mr. Beecher, who is not present, is concerned about an ancient coin, the Widow's Mite. This coin is out of place, and should be returned, and he looks to you, doctor, to return it."

Funk was greatly surprised and asked: "What do you mean by saying that he looks to me to return it? I have no coin of Mrs. Beecher's." The control then explained that he knew nothing about it, except that he was told that the coin was out of place and had been for a number of years and that Beecher had said that Funk could find and return it. The control also added that he was impressed that the coin was in a large iron safe in a drawer under a lot of papers.

Funk then remembered that when he was making the Standard Dictionary, he had borrowed a valuable ancient coin, known as the Widow's Mite, from a close friend of Beecher's. This friend had just died several days before. Funk asked if the coin had been returned. The answer came that it had not.

After Funk instituted a search, the coin was found in his office in a little drawer in his large iron safe under a stack of papers. In later inquiries through the control Funk was told that Beecher was not concerned about the return of the coin. His purpose was to give Funk a test to prove communication between the two worlds.

James H. Hyslop, in his report on the **direct voice** mediumship of Elisabeth Blake of Ohio (*Proceedings* of the American Society for Psychical Research, vol. 7, p. 581), quotes the following case given by L. V. Guthrie, superintendent of the West Virginia Asylum at Huntington, Blake's medical adviser:

"An acquaintance of mine, of prominent family in this end of the State, whose grandfather had been found at the foot of a high bridge with his skull smashed and life extinct, called on Mrs. Blake a few years ago and was not thinking of her grandfather at the time. She was very much surprised to have the spirit of her grandfather tell her that he had not fallen off the bridge while intoxicated, as had been presumed at the time, but that he had been murdered by two men who met him in a buggy and had proceeded to sandbag him, relieve him of his valuables, and throw him over the bridge. The spirit then proceeded to describe minutely the appearance of the two men who had murdered him, and gave such other information that had led to the arrest and conviction of one or both of these individuals."

Spiritism

A general term for the belief that the spirits or souls of the dead communicate with the living through a medium or psychically sensitive individual. The term has been used with two quite different meanings in the twentieth century. In conservative Christian circles it is often used as a derogatory term to describe **Spiritualism** in anticult literature. It is also used as the designation of the followers of the particular Spiritualist teachings of **Allan Kardec** (1804–1869), a French medium who also had immense influence on the development of Spiritualism in Spain, Portugal, and South America (especially **Brazil**). Kardec's thought was distinctive from British and American Spiritualism in the nineteenth century by its advocacy of belief in **reincarnation.**

Prior to his adoption of Spiritualist beliefs in about 1862, Kardec had been an exponent of **animal magnetism** and **phrenology.** He based his new teachings on spirit revelations received through clairvoyants, and so popular were these teachings that they rapidly spread over the Continent. In Britain, however, Spiritism obtained little hold, its only prominent exponent being **Anna Blackwell,** who endeavored without success to establish the doctrine of reincarnation.

Spiritism and Spiritualism should not be confused, since the adherents of each section were opposed to the tenets of the other. Even in France, where Spiritism obtained the strongest footing, there was a distinct Spiritualist party reluctant to accept the doctrine of reincarnation.

Kardec's Spiritism flourished in nineteenth-century France, and is today well established in South America, especially Brazil, where it is estimated that there are now some four million Spiritists. In contemporary South American Spiritism there is a noticeable tendency to blur formal distinctions between Spiritism and Spiritualism, particularly in Brazil, where all kinds of physical phenomena are manifest, including **psychic surgery.** The Spiritism of Kardec discouraged such physical mediumship as materialization in favor of **automatic writing,** believing this to be a more direct and unambiguous contact with departed spirits.

Modern Brazilian Spiritists also make a distinction between ordinary automatic writing (*escrita automotica*), which might involve the medium's own subconscious, and *psicografia* (dictation from a spirit entity).

Sources:

Kardec, Allan. *Experimental Spiritism: The Mediums' Book.* London, 1876.

———. *The Spirits' Book.* London, 1875.

Playfair, Guy Lyon. *The Flying Cow: Research Into Paranormal Phenomena in the World's Most Psychic Country.* London: Souvenir Press, 1975. Reprinted as *The Unknown Power.* New York: Pocket Books, 1975. Reprint, London: Panther paperback, 1977.

Spirit Messenger (Journal)

(Full name: *The Spirit Messenger, and The Star of Truth.*) Started in Springfield, Massachusetts, in 1849, the chief organ of **Andrew Jackson Davis**'s "harmonial philosophy" after the *Univercoelum* journal expired. Rev. R. P. Amber, a Universalist minister, and Apollos Munn were joint editors.

Spirito, Ugo (1896– ?)

Professor of philosophy who wrote on parapsychology. He was born on September 9, 1896, at Arezzo, Italy, and he studied at the University of Rome (LL.B., 1918; Ph.D., 1920). He taught at the University of Pisa (1932–34), the University of Messina (1935), the University of Genoa (1936), and the University of Rome (beginning in 1937).

Spirito developed an interest in parapsychology as it related to his own scholarly discipline, and he wrote several related books. He also attended the First International Conference of Parapsychological Studies in Utrecht, Netherlands, in 1953.

Sources:

Spirito, Ugo. *Il Problematicismo* (Problematicism). Firenze: G. C. Sansoni, 1948.

———. *Scienza e Filosofia* (Science and Philosophy). Firenze: G. C. Sansoni, 1950.

———. *La vita come amore* (Life as Love). N.p., 1953. Reprint, Firenze: G. C. Sansoni, 1970.

———. *La Vita come arte* (Life as Art). N.p., 1941.

———. *La Vita come ricerca* (Life as a Search). 2d ed. Firenze: G. C. Sansoni, 1943.

Spiritoid

Term used by psychical researcher **Emile Boirac** for messages that originate in the subconscious mind and appear in a dramatic and personalized form. It was also used by **Cesare Lombroso** and **Theodore Flournoy.**

Spirit Photography

The production of photographs on which alleged spirit forms are visible. When the plate or film is developed there sometimes appears, in addition to the likeness of the sitters at a **séance,** a shape resembling more or less distinctly the human form, which at the moment of exposure was imperceptible to normal vision.

Beginning in the late nineteenth century, Spiritualists asserted that there were photographs of spirits (the spirits of departed friends and relatives of the sitters) and that the presence of a medium was generally required to facilitate their production. Even though the main evidence in favor of spirit photography rests on recognition of the supposed spirit by the sitter and others, the "astral figure" is often very vague and indistinct, with the head and shoulders enveloped in close-clinging draperies.

The practice of "spirit photography" originated in the United States in the nineteenth century and enjoyed a fitful existence through the 1930s. It was first introduced in 1862 by **William H. Mumler,** a Boston photographer. A Dr. Gardner, of the same city, was photographed by Mumler, and on the plate appeared an image that the sitter identified as his cousin, who had died 12 years before. Gardner published his experience, and the new spirit photography was at once adopted by Spiritualists, who saw in it a means of proving their beliefs. In 1863, however, Gardner discovered that in at least two instances a living model was the subject of Mumler's "spirit" pictures. Although he continued to believe that some of the photographs might be genuine, his exposure of Mumler as fraudulent effectively checked the movement for a time.

After a lapse of six years, Mumler appeared in New York, where the authorities endeavored to prosecute him, but the evidence against him was insufficient to prove fraud, and he was acquitted.

Spirit photography had flourished in the United States for some ten years before it became known in Britain. Samuel Guppy and his wife, **Agnes Guppy-Volckman,** the well-known Spiritualist mediums, endeavored without success to produce spirit photographs in private, and at length called for the assistance of **Frederick A. Hudson,** a professional photographer. A photograph of Guppy revealed a dim, draped "spirit" form.

Hudson speedily became popular, and his studio was as largely patronized as Mumler's had been. He found support from several outside observers. **Thomas Slater,** a London optician, made careful observations of his process without being able to detect any fraud. **John Beattie,** a professional photographer and something of a skeptic, made the following statement concerning Hudson's performances: "They were not made by double exposure, nor by figures projected in space in any way; they were not the result of mirrors; they were not produced by any machinery in the background, behind it, above it, or below it, nor by any contrivance connected with the bath, the camera, or the camera-slide." Trail Taylor, editor of the *British Journal of Photography,* said that "at no time during the preparation, exposure, or development of the pictures was Mr. Hudson within ten feet of the camera or darkroom. Appearances of an abnormal kind did certainly appear on several plates."

Such testimonies as these from the lips of skilled and disinterested witnesses would naturally seem to raise spirit photography to the level of a genuine psychic phenomenon. But a careful analysis of the evidence, such as is given by **Eleanor Sidgwick** in her article "On Spirit Photographs . . ." in the *Proceedings* (no. 8, 1891) of the **Society for Psychical Research** shows how even a trained investigator can be deceived by sleight of hand. And it is notable that Beattie himself afterward pointed out instances of double exposure in Hudson's productions.

In spite of this, Hudson continued to practice, and various Spiritualist magazines continued to lend him their support, with the notable exception of the *Spiritualist,* whose editor, himself a practical photographer, had aided John Beattie in denouncing spirit photography. Another enthusiastic Spiritualist, Enmore Jones, who at first claimed to recognize a dead daughter in one of the pictured "spirits," afterward admitted that he had been mistaken.

Those who had pinned their faith to the genuineness of the photographic manifestations were naturally unwilling to relinquish their belief in what they considered sure proof of the reality of the spirit world, and ingenious explanations were offered to cover the circumstance of the apparent double exposures. The spirit aura, they said, differed from the natural atmosphere in its refracting power, and it was not to be wondered at that objects were sometimes duplicated. And so Hudson retained a considerable measure of popularity.

In 1874 the Paris photographer **Édouard Buguet** crossed over to London and commenced the practice of spirit photography. Many of the purported spirits in his pictures were recognized by his clients, and even when he had been tried by the French government and had admitted deception there were those who refused to regard his confession as spontaneous, inclining to believe that he had been bribed by "Jesuits" to confess to fraud of which he was innocent.

Other spirit photographers were **F. M. Parkes,** a contemporary of Hudson, and **Richard Boursnell,** who produced spirit pictures in London in later years.

The principal evidence in favor of spirit photography is undoubtedly the recognition of the spirits by their friends and relatives, but the unreliable nature of such a test has been seen time and again when a single "spirit" has been claimed by several persons as a near relative.

One of the most prominent defenders of the mediumistic photographers was **W. Stainton Moses** (who wrote under the pseudonym M. A. Oxon), who saw in them the best proof of the reality of Spiritualism. The same view was shared by **Alfred Russel Wallace,** who said (*Arena,* January 1891), "It is that which furnishes, perhaps, the most unassailable demonstration it is possible to obtain of the objective reality of spiritual forms."

Throughout the 1920s and 1930s the whole idea of spirit photography was called into question by psychical researchers. In 1933 Fred Barlow and W. Rampling Rose presented the results of their research to the Society for Psychical Research and indicated that they had been unable to locate any spirit photographs not produced fraudulently. Their opinion has remained the consensus opinion of parapsychologists in the decades since. No set of photographs have been offered in recent decades for serious consideration as genuine spirit images.

"Spirits" are not the only paranormal effects claimed in psychic photography. Many photographs have been produced that allegedly show "spirit writing," some on photographic plates not exposed in a camera (see **Skotograph**). In modern times, **Ted Serios** of Chicago has produced what appear to be "thought pictures" of distant scenes on Polaroid film. The Japanese investigator **Tomobichi Fukurai** used the term **thoughtography** to denote "paranormal" images on photographic materials.

Sources:

Barlow, Fred, and W. Rampling Rose. "Report on an Investigation into Spirit-Photography." *Proceedings* of the Society for Psychical Research 41 (1933): 121–38.

Christopher, Milbourne. *Mediums, Mystics, and the Occult.* New York: Thomas Y. Crowell, 1975.

Coates, James. *Photographing the Invisible: Practical Studies in Supernormal Photography, Script, and Other Allied Phenomena.* London: L. N. Fowler, 1911. Reprint, New York: Arno Press, 1973.

Doyle, Arthur Conan. *The Case for Spirit Photography.* London: Hutchinson, 1922. Reprint, New York: George H. Doran, 1923.

Eisenbud, Jule. *The World of Ted Serios: "Thoughtographic" Studies of an Extraordinary Mind.* New York: William Morrow, 1967.

Fukurai, T. *Clairvoyance and Thoughtography.* London: Rider, 1931. Reprint, New York: Arno Press, 1975.

Glendinning, Andrew. *The Veil Lifted: Modern Developments of Spirit Photography.* London: Whittaker, 1894.

Houghton, Miss [Georgiana]. *Chronicles of the Photographs of Spiritual Beings and Phenomena Invisible to the Material Eye.* London: E. W. Allen, 1882.

Mumler, William H. *Personal Experiences of William H. Mumler in Spirit Photography.* Boston, 1875.

Patrick, C. V. *The Case Against Spirit Photography.* London: Kegan Paul, 1921.

Patterson, Tom. *100 Years of Spirit Photography.* London: Regency Press, 1965.

Permutt, Cyril. *Beyond the Spectrum: A Survey of Supernormal Photography.* Cambridge, England: Patrick Stephens, 1983.

Price, Harry. *Confessions of a Ghost Hunter.* 1936. Reprint, Causeway Books, 1974.

Sidgwick, Mrs. Henry [Eleanor]. "On Spirit Photographs, a reply to Mr. R. A. Wallace." *Proceedings* of the Society for Psychical Research 8 (1891): 268–89.

Stead, Estelle W. *Faces of the Living Dead.* London, 1925.

Stein, Gordon. *Encyclopedia of Hoaxes.* Detroit: Gale Research, 1993.

Wilmot, T. S. *Twenty Photographs of the Risen Dead.* Birmingham, England: Midland Educational, 1894.

"Spirit Teachings" (by "M. A. Oxon")

The famous book written by **W. Stainton Moses** that records the teachings of the "Imperator" group of spirit controls.

The Spirit World (Periodical)

The first Spiritualist periodical in England, published by W. R. Hayden in May 1853. However, only one issue appeared. The title had earlier been used by **La Roy Sunderland,** who changed the name of his American periodical *The Spiritual Philosophy* to *The Spirit World* in 1851.

SpiritQuest

SpiritQuest is an educational program designed to introduce people to the spiritual experiences of Peruvian **shamans** and curanderos (healers) who live in the upper Amazonian area of Peru near the city of Iquitos. A defining part of the SpiritQuest experience is the opportunity to work with shamans who use the consciousness expanding substances in **ayahausca,** an hallucinogenic substance made from the vine of the plant Banisteriopsis Caapi, which is boiled in water along with various other plants. These plants contain different substances identified as **psychedelic drugs.**

The SpiritQuest program was put together by a brother/sister team, Howard E. Lawler and Sanchi Reta Lawler. Howard is a former museum curator trained in biology. Reta is a transpersonal psychologist and student of Zen. Both have many years of association which shamans in both South America and Asia. The pair also heads El Tigre Journeys, a tourist company that facilitates travel to Peru and arranges for small groups to enter into the culture, meet the indigenous religious leaders, and see the sights in a way that is sensitive to the ecology of the region. Founded in 1997, El Tigre has been designed to help enhance and restore the natural resources of eastern Peru through various programs financially supported by tourism. Howard Lawler also heads a nonprofit organization, the International BioPark Foundation, as an environmental organization dedicated to preserving the natural world and promoting an understanding of humanity's interdependent relationship with the natural order. The foundation is working with El Tigre on a number of projects including the development of a living Museum of Western Amazonia along the banks of the Río Momón outside Iquitos.

The SpiritQuest program is focused upon small groups (limited to eight people) who travel to Peru to participate in shamanic workshop retreats. The participants have in the Lawlers experienced guides, but are assured of experiencing shamanic initiations, including ceremonies with ayahuasca, much as they have been performed prior to the arrival of Europeans in the area. The Lawlers facilitate the preparation for the journey and are present to assist people through the cleansing, cathartic, and spiritually expansive moments that may go through, some of which may be temporarily uncomfortable.

SpiritQuest (and the associated organization may be contacted through the Lawlers offices: Reta Lawler, P.O. Box 1704, Boulder, CO 80306-1704 and Howard Lawler, Calle Loreto #337, Iquiitos, Peru. They may also be contacted through the International BioPark Foundation website at http://www.biopark.org/, which has subpages for both SpiritQuest and El Tigre Journeys.

Sources:

International BioPark Foundation. http://www.biopark.org/. June 11, 2000.

Spiritual Advisory Council (SAC)

A **New Age** organization. The Spiritual Advisory Council (SAC) was founded in 1974 in Chicago by Paul V. Johnson and Paul Ericsson, both former national leaders in the Spiritual Frontiers Fellowship (now the **International Spiritual Frontiers Fellowship.**) The council adopted a New Age perspective and built an open fellowship of like-minded people who gathered regularly for national and regional conferences and in small study groups. In 1979 Johnson relocated to Florida and opened the New Age Centre for Alternative Realities in Orlando. Also in 1979, some people who had found their primary spiritual home within the council organized the Church of the Spiritual Advisory Council and saw the first ministers of the new church ordained.

SAC has no creed or dogma but generally operates within a New Age perspective. **Channeling,** both for spiritual contact with the other world and for healing energies, is accepted. SAC publishes the *Outreach Newsletter.* Address: 2933 W. State Rd. 434, Longwood, FL 32279.

The Spiritual Age (Periodical)

Early American periodical serving the cause of **Spiritualism.**

Spiritual Athenaeum

Briefly the headquarters of British Spiritualists in London in 1866. The post of residential secretary was offered to **D. D. Home.** The real intent behind the foundation's offer was to help Home, who was at the time struggling with financial difficulties. When, owing to a change of fortune, Home resigned his post, the institution died a natural death. **John Elliotson** was among those who sat on the council.

Spiritual Churches

The spiritual church movement developed in the early twentieth century among African Americans who had responded to **Spiritualism** and its championing of the cause of universal brotherhood. In spite of its rhetoric, however, too often Spiritualists practiced the same racism so evident in non-Spiritualist circles. By World War I, black leaders began to form their own separate churches, some of which grew into substantial denominations. Among the first to emerge was Leafy Anderson (1887–1927), who in 1913 founded the Eternal Life Christian Spiritualist Association. She moved to New Orleans in 1920, by which time her association had more than ten congregations, and founded a congregation, the first of many spiritual churches in what would become one of the most important centers of the spiritual movement.

Through the 1920s a number of new spiritual churches emerged, beginning in 1922 when the black members of the National Spiritualist Association of Churches were pushed out and formed the national Colored Spiritualist Association of Churches. The next year, in Detroit, Willie Hurley founded the Universal Hagar's Spiritual Church, and in 1925 William Frank Taylor and Leviticus L. Boswell founded the Metropolitan Spiritual Churches of Christ in Kansas City. Also founded in the mid-1920s was the Church of God in David (later the Spiritual Israel Church and Its Army).

The spiritual movement is quite diverse. It mixes Protestantism, Spiritualism, and various elements of popular folk religions. Individual congregations and denominations use different blends of these elements. Leafy Anderson represented the more conservative wing of the movement: she used the Bible and denounced the voudou and popular magic she found among potential members. One the other hand, her student, Mother Catherine Seals, freely incorporated elements of "hoodoo," the popular folk magic of the Southern black community, into her church's rituals.

George Willie Hurley incorporated Masonic elements in the mystery school that became a part of every congregation in his Universal Hagar's Spiritual Church. He also followed **Father Divine**'s example and proclaimed himself God. As Jesus was the God of the Picean Age, so he was the God of the coming Aquarian Age. Hurley was also a pioneer black nationalist and incorporated Ethiopianism into his teachings, identifying black Americans with their African heritage, especially with the land of Emperor Haile Selassie.

The spiritual movement has experienced upheavals as new leaders have appeared on the scene. For example, in 1942, the Metropolitan Spiritual Churches of Christ merged with the Divine Spiritual Churches of the Southwest, making it by far the largest spiritual denomination in the country. Shortly thereafter William Taylor died, and Thomas Watson, formerly the head of the Divine Spiritual Church of the Southwest, was elected to succeed him. However, by that time Clarence Cobbs had arisen as a charismatic leader of a church in Chicago and believed that the church was his to inherit. As a result of the struggle for control between Watson and Cobbs, the church split, with Cobbs inheriting the larger group.

During the last half of the twentieth century, spiritual churches have experienced ups and downs. Both Spiritualist and spiritual churches are more susceptible than most to volatile swings in support for prominent leaders who rise and pass from the scene. While several large denominations remain, many of the young talented mediums have formed independent churches or passed into the **New Age** movement.

Sources:

Baer, Hans A. *The Black Spiritual Movement: A Religious Response to Racism.* Knoxville: University of Tennessee Press, 1984.

Jacobs, Claude F., and Andrew J. Kaslow. *The Spiritual Churches of New Orleans: Origins, Beliefs, and Rituals of an African American Religion.* Knoxville: University of Tennessee Press, 1991.

Murphy, Larry G., J. Gordon Melton, and Gary L. Ward. *Encyclopedia of African American Religions.* New York: Garland Publishing, 1993.

The Spiritual Clarion (Periodical)

One of the first American periodicals serving American **Spiritualism.** It was published in Auburn, New York.

Spiritual Community Guide See New Consciousness Sourcebook

Spiritual Frontiers Fellowship See International Spiritual Frontiers Fellowship

Spiritual Gazette

Monthly publication of the **Spiritualist Association of Great Britain,** including reports on psychic phenomena and events of interest to Spiritualists. Address: 33 Belgrave Sq., London, SW1X 8QL, England.

The Spiritual Herald (Journal)

A short-lived British journal of Swedenborgian Spiritualists published in London from February to July 1856.

Spiritual India and Kundalini (Magazine)

Former quarterly journal published in India of international spiritual and scientific consideration in the study of **kundalini,** the energy believed to reside in human beings related to sexual activity and higher consciousness. The journal is published by the Kundalini Research and Publication Trust, New Delhi. This journal centers round the experience and theories of Hindu teacher **Pandit Gopi Krishna** (1903–1984), an advocate of kundalini who has built a following in the West.

Spiritual Institution

Established by pioneer British Spiritualist **James Burns** at 15 Southampton Row, London, in conjunction with a library dealing with books on **Spiritualism.** The organization oversaw a lending library of several thousand volumes on Spiritualism, psychic phenomena, and related subjects, with a reading room and rooms for séances or experiments connected with Spiritualism.

The organization became a center for Spiritualism in London, providing a regular program of circles, séances, concerts, and other social events; it was an influential meeting place for Spiritualists. The organization has been disbanded.

Spiritualism

A social religious movement founded in the mid-nineteenth century in New York State. According to the definition adopted by the **National Spiritualist Association of Churches,** Spiritualism is

> The Science, Philosophy and Religion of continuous life, based upon the demonstrated fact of communication, by means of mediumship, with those who live in the Spirit World. Spiritualism is a science because it investigates, analyses and classifies facts and manifestations, demonstrated from the spirit side of life. Spiritualism is a philosophy because it studies the laws of nature both on the seen and unseen sides of life and bases its conclusions upon present observed facts. It accepts statements of observed facts of past ages and conclusions drawn therefrom, when sustained by reason and by results of observed facts of the present day. Spiritualism is a religion because it strives to understand and to comply with the Physical, Mental and Spiritual Laws of Nature[,] which are the laws of God.

According to the British medium **W. Stainton Moses,** a Spiritualist is "one who has proven for himself, or has accepted on adequate evidence, the fact that death does not kill the spirit."

Spiritualism centers upon two basic teachings: the continuity of personality after the transition of death, and the possibility of communication between those living on Earth and those who have made the transition to death. Spiritualism teaches that death is a new birth into a spiritual body, the counterpart of the physical, which is gifted with new powers. Spiritualists claim that their beliefs are based upon scientific proof and communication with the surviving personalities of deceased human beings by means of mediumship.

After death, the individual faces neither punishment nor rewards. Individuality, character, and memory survive and undergo no change. Continued progression in the new life rests upon individual fitness. The rapidity of progress is in proportion to the mental and moral faculties acquired in Earth life. Every spirit is left to discover the truth for itself. Evil passions or a sinful life may chain a spirit to the Earth, but the road of endless progress opens up for these as soon as they discover the light. Higher and higher spiritual **spheres** correspond to the state of progress. The gradation is apparently endless. Communion with higher intelligences appears to be available, but the spirits report no particular communion with the deity.

Origins of Spiritualism

Spiritualism in its modern form dates back no further than 1848 and the **Fox sisters.** Its practices can be traced to attempts at spirit communication reaching back to ancient times. Such attempts at communication with both the surviving consciousness of the dead and various orders of spiritual beings, both angelic and demonic, appear in the oldest extant records of cultures worldwide. It has only been in the last few centuries that strong doubts about the possibility of life after death and communication with a spiritual world have arisen.

Spiritualism emerged as a direct counter to such post-Enlightenment doubts, which by the nineteenth century had become the subject of popular debates and literature.

In his 1993 book, *Madame Blavatsky's Baboon,* writer Peter Washington noted that the true momentum for the movement was given full vent in America; but, in fact, its roots sprouted up from people and places all over the world. Washington noted that it seemed to have found a particular following in America for certain reasons. He also said that,

> The seance offers a new version of holy communion, in which faith is replaced by evidence, blood and wine by manifested spirits. It was therefore especially popular among the Protestant sects fo the east coast of the United States, deprived as they usually were of any sensuous fulfillment in their religion and susceptible to any sign of the workings of divine grace, however bizarre. It is no coincidence that Hydesville is in the middle of the notorious 'burned-over' district of New York State, so called because of the extraordinary number of religious fashions that swept through it in the early nineteenth century. Spiritualism blends easily with millenarian Christianity: though most of its messages were trivial, the expectation remained that these were merely a prelude to news of real import from the Other World. Having confirmed its own existence through the Fox girls, that world was now expected to come through with the facts about life after death, immortality, and even the future of mankind.

As Spiritualism formed, it looked to a number of individual occurrences of Spiritualist phenomena and previous movements to show its continuity with the past. For example, many famous outbreaks of an "epidemic" nature, such as that among the **Tremblers of the Cevennes** and the **Convulsionaries of St. Médard,** which to the beholders showed clear indications of demonic possession, had in their symptoms considerable analogy with modern Spiritualism. They were accompanied by spontaneous **trance** or **ecstasy,** lengthy discourses, and **speaking in tongues,** all of which are phenomena to be found in the séance room.

The fluency of speech noted in such outbreaks, especially of persons lacking any formal education, has been equaled, if not surpassed, by the outpourings of the unlearned medium under the influence of a "**control.**" In such historical cases, the conditions were generally ascribed to either angelic or diabolic possession, and most frequently to the latter. Witches were supposed to converse with the Devil, and many aspects of **witchcraft,** notably the part played by persecuted young women and children, show a relationship to **poltergeist** disturbances. These were the connecting link between early forms of **possession** and modern Spiritualism. Cases in which children of morbid tendencies pretended to be the victims of a witch are to be found in many records of witchcraft.

However much it seemed otherwise, still it was the poltergeist who showed affinity to the "control" of the mediumistic circle. For at least the past few centuries, poltergeist disturbances have occurred from time to time. The mischievous spirit's favorite modes of manifesting itself have been similar to those adopted by spirit controls.

Both poltergeists and spirit controls require a "medium," an agent for the production of their phenomena. It is in the immediate presence of the medium that the phenomena generally make their appearance. Both also tend to display personality, even if of an infantile nature in the case of poltergeists. Intelligent communication has often been reported to have occurred by means of raps in phenomena attributed to poltergeists.

A related manifestation also believed to be caused by spirits occurred in the practice of **animal magnetism,** which was said to have originated with the alchemist **Paracelsus,** in favor with the old alchemists. An actual magnet was rarely used, but was regarded as a symbol of the magnetic philosophy. This belief rested on the idea of a force or fluid radiating from the heavenly bodies, human beings, and, indeed, from every substance, animate or inanimate, by means of which all things act upon one another.

While Paracelsus's students were engaged in formulating a magnetic philosophy, there were others. They included the seventeenth-century healer **Valentine Greatrakes,** who cured diseases. He claimed such magnetic power as a divine gift and did not connect it with the ideas of the alchemists. According to Spiritualist thought, these two phases of "magnetism" united and climaxed in the work of **Franz Anton Mesmer,** who published *De planetarium influxu,* in 1776, a treatise on the influence of the planets on the human body. His ideas were essentially those of the magnetic philosophers. His cures equaled those of Greatrakes; but he infused new life into both theory and practice and won for himself the recognition, if not of the learned societies, at least of the general public. He laid the groundwork for the discovery of the induced hypnotic trance. This has considerable significance in Spiritualism.

In 1784 a commission was appointed by the French government to consider magnetism as practiced by Mesmer and his followers. Unfortunately, its report only served to cast discredit on the practice and exclude it from scientific discussion. A detailed account of the trance utterances of a hypnotic subject was given in 1787 in the journals of the Swedish Exegetical and Philanthropic Society. Members of the society inclined to the doctrines of their countryman **Emanuel Swedenborg,** who was the first to identify the "spirits" as the souls of the deceased.

Until the third decade of the nineteenth century, the explanations of **mesmerism** concerned themselves almost entirely with a fluid or force emanating from the mesmerist—and even visible to the eye of a clairvoyant. In 1823, however, Alexandre Bertrand, a Parisian physician, published his *Traité du Somnambulisme.* In 1826 he published the treatise *Du Magnetisme Animal en France,* in which he set forth a relationship between ordinary sleepwalking, **somnambulism** associated with disease, and epidemic ecstasy and advanced the doctrine, now generally accepted, of **suggestion.**

Animal magnetism was by this time receiving a good deal of attention all over Europe. A second French commission appointed in 1825 presented its report in 1831, which, although of no great value, contained a unanimous testimony as to the authenticity of the phenomena. In Germany magnetism was also practiced to a considerable extent, but rationalist explanations of the associated phenomena found some acceptance. There was a class, however, more numerous in Germany than elsewhere, who inclined toward a Spiritualist explanation of mesmeric phenomena. Indeed, the belief in spirit communication had grown up beside magnetism from its conception, in opposition to the theory of a magnetic fluid.

In the earlier phases of "miraculous" healing, the cures were ascribed to the divine gift of the person conducting the session, or the operator, who expelled the evil spirits from the patient. In epidemic cases in religious communities, as well as in individual instances, the spirits were questioned both on personal matters and on abstract theological questions.

In Germany **Justinus Kerner** experimented with **Frederica Hauffe,** "the Seeress of Prevorst," in whose presence physical manifestations took place and who described the condition of the soul after death and the constitution of man—the physical body, the soul, the spirit, and the *nervengeist,* an ethereal body that clothes the soul after death—theories afterward elaborated by Spiritualists. Other German investigators, such as **J. H. Jung** (Jung-Stilling), C. Römer, and Heinrich Werner, recorded the phenomenon of **clairvoyance** in their somnambules. In 1845 **Baron Karl von Reichenbach** published research he claimed demonstrated the existence of an emanation, which he called **od** or odyllic force, radiating from every substance. This effluence allegedly could be seen by clairvoyants and had definite colors and produced a sensation of heat or cold.

Animal magnetism received little attention in England until the third decade of the nineteenth century. In 1828, Richard Chevinix, an Irishman, gave mesmeric demonstrations. **John Elliotson,** of University College Hospital, London, practiced mesmerism with the **O'Key sisters,** who were somnambules, and although he first believed in the magnetic fluid, he afterward became a Spiritualist. In 1843 two journals dealing with the subject—the *Zoist* and the *Phreno-magnet*—were founded. Most of the English mesmerists of the time preferred the magnetist explanation of the phenomena to the notion of spirit agency. Within the Spiritualist community, the so-called "magnetic" phenomena were largely attributed to the agency of the spirits of the deceased.

Spiritualism as a Religious Movement

In responding to the challenge of Enlightenment thinking, Spiritualism became the first of the new "scientific" religions. Adherents talked little of faith. Rather, they asserted that they could prove Spiritualism's central doctrine of **survival** of death through facts, instead of relying on traditions and the revelations of ancient times. They saw Spiritualism as a progressive and evolutionary faith reconciling religion with contemporary science. "Spiritualism," wrote **Sir Arthur Conan Doyle,** "is a religion for those who find themselves outside all religions; while on the contrary it greatly strengthens the faith of those who already possess religious beliefs."

Not long after Spiritualism swept America, it began to take over Europe. According to Washington, "In the wake of failing political revolutions in 1848—the very year of the Hydesville phenomena—it rapidly became part of an 'alternative' synthesis which included vegetarianism, feminism, dress reform, homoeopathy and every variety of social and religious dissent." He noted that when Harriet Beecher Stowe, famed American abolitionist, visited Europe in 1853, the seance was "all the rage."

Early Spiritualists also believed their religion restored primitive Christianity, pointing to inscriptions in the Roman catacombs in which the early Christians spoke of the dead as though they were still living. According to Saint Augustine, in *De cura pro Mortuis,* "The spirits of the dead can be sent to the living and can unveil to them the future which they themselves have learned from other spirits or from angels, or by divine revelation." Not surprisingly, much of the movement's motivation still rested in anti-Catholicisim—not so different from the antagonism many Protestant sects harbored without Spiritualism.

Spiritualists do not believe in an afterlife of unchangeable bliss or eternal damnation. In their perspective, there is no hell with brimstone and flames of fire as some Christians teach. In like measure they deny the existence of devils, a final judgment, and the vicarious atonement. Christ was a great teacher who descended to set an example. "It is our task to do for Christianity what Jesus did for Judaism," said a message received by W. Stainton Moses from the spirits who allegedly spoke through his **automatic writing.** Spiritualists also deny the resurrection of the physical body, as did the hieracites, a sect that flourished in the fourth century: they maintain that it is the soul alone that resurrected.

Spiritualism admits all the truths of morality and religion of all other sects. The moral stance is illustrated in the role of mediums. Spiritualists tend to maintain that those mediums who hold séances and become the direct mouthpieces of the spirits are only supereminently endowed with a faculty common to all humanity—that all men and woman are mediums to some degree, and that all inspiration, whether good or bad, comes from the spirits.

It is in connection with this idea of the universality of mediumship that the effect of Spiritualism on the morals and daily life of its adherents is most clearly seen. The spirits are naturally attracted to those mediums whose qualities resemble their own. Enlightened spirits from the highest spheres seek "high-souled" and earnest mediums through which to express themselves. Mediums who use their divine gifts for ignoble ends are sought by the lowest and wickedest human spirits, or by **elementals,** who do not even reach the human standard of goodness. Indeed, it is claimed that the lower spirits communicate with the living much more readily than do the higher, by reason of a certain gross or material quality that binds them to Earth. As with the full-fledged medium, so with the normal individual; if one is to ensure that the source of inspiration be a high one, one must live in such a way that only the best spirits will control.

In the United States, Spiritualists embraced many socialist ideals, and many resided in the socialist communities of the nineteenth century. The loose, nondogmatic approach also allowed some Spiritualists to embrace a variety of different ideals, such as free love. In England, where habit and tradition were more settled, Spiritualists emphasized its compatibility with Christianity and projected an image of affording a fuller revelation of the Christian religion. In France, **Allan Kardec**'s doctrine of **reincarnation** blended with the doctrines of Spiritualism to produce **Spiritism,** a form of Spiritualism highly alienated from Christianity.

These varied forms of Spiritualism are held together by two central beliefs: that the soul continues after "the great dissolution" (death of the body) and continually progresses and that the freed spirit can communicate with living human beings. The continuity of life after death is, of course, one of Spiritualism's most important tenets. It is not a distinctive one, since most of the world's creeds and religions also affirm such a belief. But Spiritualist ideas concerning the *nature* of the life of the freed soul are unique.

Spiritualists believe that the soul, or spirit, is composed of a sort of attenuated matter inhabiting the body and resembling it in form. On the death of the body the soul withdraws itself, without undergoing any direct change, and for a period remains on the "Earth plane." But the keynote of the spirit world is *progress,* so after a time the spirit proceeds to the lowest "discarnate plane." From that plane they go on to higher and higher planes, gradually evolving into a purer and nobler type. At length it reaches the sphere of pure spirit.

From the comments of mediums speaking in trance, a picture of the spirit domain has been constructed by Spiritualists. It is thought to be a somewhat attenuated version of earthly life, conducted in a highly rarified atmosphere. **Automatic drawings,** purporting to depict spirit scenes, afford a description no less flattering than that gleaned from mediums speaking in trance, although many such drawings appear imaginative rather than factual. From their exalted spheres the spirits are said to be cognizant of the doings of their fellow individuals still on Earth.

The other central belief of Spiritualism is that the spirits communicate with the living—primarily through the agency of mediums—offering their aid and counsel. They can produce in the physical world certain phenomena that transcend known physical laws. Most Spiritualists, in seeking proof of the reality of the creed, have been content with what is described as "subjective" phenomena, including such as trance speaking, automatic writing, clairvoyance.

Spiritualism was enlivened by more or less sensational physical manifestations through an entire period of its history. These found great favor among both believers and psychical researchers. Their success seemed to promise irrefutable proof of the extraordinary nature of Spiritualist phenomena, and they were relatively easy to investigate. They were so intimately connected with **fraud** unfortunately, that any hope for verifying the phenomena disappeared in the first half of the twentieth century.

Manifestation of phenomena therefore occupies a central place in Spiritualism, and the question of the genuineness of claimed phenomena remains of great importance. It is true, of course, that paranormal phenomena are also central to the development of other great religions that have claimed miracles in support of doctrine. Spiritualists point to the Judaeo-Christian Holy Bible as a book full of accounts of "miraculous" phenomena not essentially different from those demonstrated by modern mediums—inspired trance addresses, paranormal healing, apparitions, and prophetic statements. The primary difference is that traditional religions assume a perspective of awe in the presence of the occasional miraculous event, whereas Spiritualists view such events as constant aspects of a mundane world.

The Literature of Spiritualism

There is vast literature on Spiritualism. Many important works from the nineteenth century are long out of print. This literature ranges from mediumistic communications of varied value, including spirit revelations from automatic writing, trance sermons, and **séances,** to personal experiences of investigators and theories of psychical researchers, to histories of Spiritualism and attacks on it.

Books that chart the transition from mesmerism and animal magnetism to Spiritualism are valuable for the information and opinions of the time. **Emma Hardinge Britten**'s *Nineteenth Century Miracles* (1884) and *Modern American Spiritualism* (1869) are full of detailed, hard-to-find information on the events of the period but are written from the viewpoint of a firm believer and worker in the field and are sometimes marred by inaccurate quotations. **Alphonse Cahagnet**'s *The Celestial Telegraph* (2 vols., 1851) and Robert Hare's *Experimental Investigation of the Spirit Manifestations* (1856) are also of special period interest.

Autobiographies of mediums are fascinating and well worth studying for their firsthand subjective viewpoint. A classic work of this kind is **D. D. Home**'s *Incidents in My Life* (1863). Other popular works of this kind are **Estelle Roberts**' *Fifty Years a Medium* (1969) and Doris Stokes's *Voices in My Ear* (1980).

Various histories of Spiritualism are available, but there is no single satisfactory work. It is advisable to study different histories, bearing in mind the commitment of their writers. **Cesar de Vesme**'s *History of Experimental Spiritualism* (2 vols., 1931) is a comprehensive survey of Spiritualist type phenomena in many countries from primitive times on. **William Howitt**'s *The History of the Supernatural* (1863) is useful, if simplistic, in tracing the antecedents of Spiritualism in past ages. E. W. Capron's *Modern Spiritualism: Its Facts and Fanaticism, Its Consistencies and Contradictions* (1855) has special interest as an account of the movement in its early years.

Sir Arthur Conan Doyle's *History of Spiritualism* (2 vols., 1926) is an important review of the background and history of the movement, but non-critical in its presentation. **Frank Podmore**'s *Modern Spiritualism* (2 vols., 1902) is a skeptical review, valuable for its detailed information of early mediumship. J. Arthur Hill's *Spiritualism: Its History, Phenomena and Doctrine* (1918) is useful but fragmentary. A. Campbell Holms's *The Facts of Psychic Science and Philosophy* (1925) is a useful tabulation of the phenomena of Spiritualism but non-critical in treatment.

In the decades since Spiritualism celebrated its centennial in 1948, a variety of scholars, primarily sociologists and historians, have taken a look at the movement and provided valuable additions to the literature. Foremost is J. Stillson Judah's *The History and Philosophy of the Metaphysical Movements in America* (1967), which discusses Spiritualism in the larger context of the movement, from the doctrines of Emanuel Swedenborg to Spiritualism and then to **Theosophy.** An excellent modern survey of nineteenth-century Spiritualism in the United States is provided in Slater Brown's *The Heyday of Spiritualism* (1970); and British Spiritualism is covered in Geoffrey K. Nelson's *Spiritualism and Society* (1969). Hans Bear supplies a most valuable discussion of the very neglected **spiritual churches,** the movement of Spiritualism in the African American community. Lamar Keene, a former Spiritualist, documents the continuance of fake materialization séances in some Spiritualist churches. Keene's volume joins a long list of older but still valuable literature, such as John W. Truesdell's *The Bottom Facts Concerning the Science of Spiritualism* (1884); Julien J. Proskauer's *Spook Crooks! Exposing the Secrets of the Prophet-eers Who Conduct Our Wickedest Industry* (1932); **Harry Houdini**'s *A Magician Among the Spirits* (1924); and the anonymous *Revelations of a Spirit Medium* (1891; reissued by **Harry Price** and **Eric J. Dingwall**).

Sources:

Ancient Wisdom and Secret Sects, "Mysteries of the Unknown." Alexandria, Va.: Time-Life Books, 1996.

Barbanell, Maurice. *Spiritualism Today.* London: Herbert Jenkins, 1969.

Barrett, Sir William F. *On the Threshold of the Unseen: An Examination of the Phenomena of Spiritualism and of the Evidence for Survival After Death.* London: Kegan Paul; New York: E. P. Dutton, 1917.

Bayless, Raymond. *Voices From Beyond.* New Hyde Park, N.Y.: University Books, 1975.

Beard, Paul. *Survival of Death: For and Against.* London: Psychic Press, 1972.

Berger, Arthur S., J.D.; and, Berger, Joyce, M.A. *The Encyclopedia of Parapsychology and Psychical Research.* New York: Paragon House, 1991.

Brandon, Ruth. *The Spiritualists: The Passion for the Occult in the Nineteenth and Twentieth Centuries.* New York: Alfred A. Knopf; London: Weidenfeld & Nicolson, 1983.

Britten, Emma Hardinge. *Modern American Spiritualism: A Twenty Years' Record of the Communion Between Earth and the World of Spirits.* New York, 1870. Reprint, New Hyde Park, N.Y.: University Books, 1970.

———. *Nineteenth Century Miracles; or, Spirits and Their Works in Every Country of the Earth.* London and Manchester: John Heywood, 1884. Reprint, New York: Arno Press, 1976.

Capron, E. W. *Modern Spiritualism: Its Facts and Fanaticisms, Its Consistencies and Contradictions.* Boston, 1855. Reprint, New York: Arno Press, 1976.

Carrington, Hereward. *The Story of Psychic Science.* London: Rider, 1930.

Crookall, Robert. *The Supreme Adventure: Analyses of Psychic Communications.* UK: J. Clarke for Churches' Fellowship for Psychical Study, 1961.

Dearden, Harold. *Devilish But True: The Doctor Looks at Spiritualism.* London: Hutchinson, 1936. Reprint, Boston: Rowan & Littlefield, 1975.

Doyle, Arthur Conan. *The History of Spiritualism.* 2 vols. London: Cassell; York: George H. Doran, 1926. Reprint, New York: Arno Press, 1975.

Ducasse, C. J. *A Critical Examination of the Belief in a Life After Death.* Springfield, Ill.: Charles C. Thomas, 1961.

Findlay, Arthur. *On the Edge of the Etheric; or, Survival After Death Scientifically Explained.* London: Psychic Press, 1931. Reprint, Corgi, 1971.

Garrett, Eileen J. *My Life as a Search for the Meaning of Mediumship.* London: Rider, 1939. Reprint, New York: Arno Press, 1975.

Gauld, Alan. *The Founders of Psychical Research.* London: Routledge & Kegan Paul, 1968. Reprint, New York: Schocken Books, 1973.

———. *Mediumship and Survival: A Century of Investigations.* London: Heinemann, 1982.

Gregory, William. *Animal Magnetism; or, Mesmerism and Its Phenomena.* 2d rev. ed. London: Nichols, 1877. Reprint, New York: Arno Press, 1975.

Hare, Robert. *Experimental Investigation of the Spirit Manifestations.* New York, 1855.

Hart, Hornell. *The Enigma of Survival: The Case For and Against an After Life.* Springfield, Ill.: Charles C. Thomas, 1959.

Haynes, Renee. *The Society for Psychical Research, 1882–1982: A History.* London: Macdonald, 1982.

Hill, J. Arthur. *Spiritualism: Its History, Phenomena and Doctrine.* London: Cassell; New York: George H. Doran, 1918.

Home, Daniel Dunglas. *Incidents in My Life.* London: Longmans, Green, 1863. Reprint, New Hyde Park, N.Y.: University Books, 1972.

Houdini, Harry. *A Magician Among the Spirits.* New York: Harper & Row, 1924. Reprinted as *Houdini: A Magician Among the Spirits.* New York: Arno Press, 1972.

Jackson, Herbert G., Jr. *The Spirit Rappers.* New York: Doubleday, 1972.

Jacobson, Nils Olof. *Life Without Death? On Parapsychology, Mysticism, and the Question of Survival.* New York: Delacorte Press, 1973. Reprint, London: Turnstone Books; New York: Dell, 1974.

Kerr, Howard. *Mediums and Spirit-Rappers and Roaring Radicals.* Urbana, Ill.: University of Illinois Press, 1972.

Lewis, James R. *Encyclopedia of Afterlife Beliefs and Phenomena.* Detroit: Visible Ink Press, 1995.

Lodge, Sir Oliver. *Raymond, or Life and Death; with Examples of the Evidence for Survival of Memory and Affection After Death.* London: Methuen; New York: George H. Doran, 1916.

Maryatt, Florence. *There Is No Death.* London, 1892. Reprint, New York: Causeway Books, 1973.

McCabe, Joseph. *Spiritualism: A Popular History from 1847.* London: Fisher Unwin, 1920.

McHargue, Georgess. *Facts, Frauds, and Phantasms: A Survey of the Spiritualist Movement.* Garden City, N.Y.: Doubleday, 1972.

Meek, George W., and Bertha Harris. *From Séance to Science.* London: Regency Press, 1973.

Mulholland, John. *Beware Familiar Spirits.* London: Charles Scribner's Sons, 1938. Reprint, New York: Arno Press, 1975.

Murchison, Carl, ed. *The Case For and Against Psychical Belief.* Worcester, Mass., 1927. Reprint, Arno Press, 1975.

Myers, F. W. H. *Human Personality and Its Survival of Bodily Death.* 2 vols. London: Longmans, Green, 1903. Reprint, New York: Arno Press, 1975. Abr. ed. New Hyde Park, N.Y.: University Books, 1961.

Olcott, H. S. *People From the Other World.* American Publishing, 1875. Reprint, Rutland, Vt.: Charles W. Tuttle, 1972.

Osty, Eugene. *Supernormal Faculties in Man.* London: Methuen, 1923.

Podmore, Frank. *Modern Spiritualism: A History and a Criticism.* 2 vols. London, 1902. Reprinted as *Mediums of the 19th Century.* New Hyde Park, N.Y.: University Books, 1963.

———. *The Newer Spiritualism.* London: T. Fisher Unwin, 1910. Reprint, New York: Arno Press, 1975.

Price, Harry. *Fifty Years of Psychical Research: A Critical Survey.* London: Longmans, Green, 1939. Reprint, New York: Arno Press, 1975.

Price, Harry, and E. J. Dingwall, eds. *Revelations of a Spirit Medium.* London: Kegan Paul; New York: E. P. Dutton, 1922.

Proskauer, Julien J. *Spook Crooks! Exposing the Secrets of the Prophet-eers Who Conduct Our Wickedest Industry.* New York: A. L. Burt, 1932. Reprint, Ann Arbor, Mich.: Gryphon Books, 1971.

Richet, Charles. *Thirty Years of Psychical Research.* London and New York, 1923. Reprint, New York: Arno Press, 1975.

Sargent, Epes. *The Scientific Basis of Spiritualism.* Boston: Colby & Rich, 1880.

Tabori, Paul. *Companions of the Unseen.* London: H. A. Humphrey, 1968.

———. *Pioneers of the Unseen.* London: Souvenir Press, 1972.

Thomas, John F. *Beyond Normal Cognition: An Evaluative and Methodological Study of the Mental Content of Certain Trance Phenomena.* Boston: Boston Society for Psychical Research, 1973. Reprint, New York: Arno Press, 1975.

———. *Spirit Summonings,* "Mysteries of the Unknown." Alexandria, Va.: Time-Life Books, 1996.

Truesdell, John W. *The Bottom Facts Concerning the Science of Spiritualism.* New York: G. W. Carlton, 1883.

Wallace, Alfred Russel. *On Miracles and Modern Spiritualism.* London, 1875. Rev. ed. New York: Arno Press, 1975.

Washington, Peter. *Madame Blavatsky's Baboon: A History of the Mystics, Mediums, and Misfits Who Brought Spiritualism to America.* New York: Schocken

Spiritualism—France

Animal magnetism, the phenomenon so important and central to Spiritualism, manifested itself in France at a comparatively early period in the movement. From correspondence between **J. P. F. Deleuze** and **G. P. Billot** from the year 1829, it appears that phantom forms and the phenomenon of **apports** were well known in this early age. Deleuze more frankly admitted that his experience was more limited.

Almost the full range of the phenomena of Spiritualism are found in **Baron Du Potet**'s *Journal du Magnétisme,* which records his investigations between 1836 and 1848. His magnetized subjects excelled in **clairvoyance,** trance speaking, **healing, dermography, levitation, fire immunity, telekinesis,** apports, **xenoglossis, prophecy, crystal gazing, materializations,** and descriptions of scenes in the spirit world.

The best early séance records come from **Louis-Alphonse Cahagnet,** the author of *Arcanes de la vie future dévoilés* (1848–54), translated as *The Celestial Telegraph* (1850). He received many evidential communications from departed spirits through his somnambule, Adèle Maginot.

Table turning was introduced into France by **Baron Ludwig von Guldenstubbe** and the **Compte d'Ourches** in 1850 and became an epidemic, as in England. Soon other phenomena followed. The famous direct scripts of Guldenstubbe were obtained in 1856.

In that same year **Allan Kardec**'s book *Le Livre des Esprits* was published, and developments took a radically different route from that in the United States and England. Kardec founded a school of thought called **Spiritism** that was dominated by the idea of a series of compulsory reincarnations. This was the opposing school to Spiritualism, which followed the American and English ideas. Spiritualism was represented in France by **Z. J. Piérart** and *La Revue Spiritualiste,* founded in 1858; Spiritism was championed by Kardec's *La Revue Spirite,* founded in the same year.

Kardec's school eventually prevailed. Piérart, after years of bitter controversy, retired to the country. By 1864 there were ten periodicals published in France: three in Paris, the two already mentioned and *L'Avenir;* four in Bordeaux, which, in 1865, were merged into *L'Union Spirite Bordelaise; La Médium Evangélique,* of Toulouse; *L'Echo d'Outre Tombe,* of Marseilles; and *La Vérité* of Lyons. With the exception of *La Revue Spiritualiste* all represented the school of Kardec.

Kardec and his followers discouraged physical phenomena. Because of that the stimulus for experimental investigators was largely provided by the visits of **D. D. Home,** the **Davenport brothers, Henry Slade, William Eglinton, Frank Herne, Charles Williams, Elizabeth d'Esperance, Florence Cook, Lottie Fowler,** and other famous mediums.

Joseph Maxwell, Camille Flammarion, Eugene Rochas, Paul Joire, Charles Richet, Emile Boirac, Gustav Geley, and **Eugèn Osty** represented psychical research. **Gabriel Delanne** founded the *Revue scientifique et morale du spiritisme.* The first attempt at organized psychical research was La Societé de Psychologie Physiologique and its journal, *La Revue des Sciences Psychiques.*

In 1890 the *Annales des Sciences Psychiques* was founded. It was replaced in 1920 by *La Revue Métapsychique,* the official organ of the Institut Métapsychique. In 1904 the Institut Général Psychologique was established in Paris.

The real benefactor of Spiritism and psychical research arrived during the war in the person of **Jean Meyer,** a rich industrialist. He founded La Maison des Spirits for spiritistic propaganda and the Institut Métapsychique for psychical research. In 1918 the institute was recognized as a public utility. Meyer endowed it with a portion of his fortune. The work it has carried on in experimentation and in demonstration of supernormal phenomena before invited scientists has been of great importance for psychical research in France.

In 1987, due to the general dissatisfaction with the nature of the research there, the **Organisation pour la Recherche en Psyochtronique** was established. Such research has had a difficult time in France due to the university system's refusal of official recognition. Much of the work done there at the end of the twentieth century was done "underground." **Prof. Remy Chauvin** has been one such researcher forced to take his work out of the mainstream due to the overly critical educational establishment.

Sources:

Berger, Arthur S., and Joyce Berger. *The Encyclopedia of Parapsychology and Psychical Research.* New York: Paragon House, 1991.

Cahagnet, Alphonse. *Arcanes de la vie future dévoilés.* 3 vols. 1848–54. Translated as *The Celestial Telegraph; or, Secrets of Life to Come Revealed Through Magnetism.* 2 vols. London, [1850]. Reprint, New York, 1851.

Kardec, Allan. *Le Ciel et L'Enfer ou la justice divine selon le Spiritisme.* 1865. Translated as *Heaven and Hell, or The Divine Justice Vindicated in the Plurality of Existences.* N.p., 1878.

———. *L'Evangile selon le Spiritisme.* 1864. Translated as *The Gospel According to Spiritism.* London: Headquarters Publishing, 1887.

———. *Le Livre des Esprits.* Translated as *The Spirits' Book* by Anna Blackwell. Reprint, São Paulo: Livraria Allan Kardec Editora, 1972.

———. *Le Livre des Mediums.* Translated as *The Book of Mediums* by Emma E. Wood. Reprint, New York: Samuel Weiser, 1970.

Osty, Eugene. *Supernormal Faculties in Man.* London: Methuen, 1923.

Richet, Charles. *Thirty Years of Psychical Research.* New York: Macmillan, 1923.

Spiritualism—Germany

In Germany Spiritualism developed very slowly, despite a rather early history of scattered individuals who conducted paranormal investigations back in the 1830s, most notably Justinus Kerner. Philosopher I. H. von Fichte believed in Spiritualism; Gustav Fechner, the founder of psychophysiology, admitted belief in personal immortality; and Edward von Hartmann, author of *The Philosophy of the Unconscious* (1869), desired to give Spiritualist phenomena a definite place in philosophy. Carl Du Prel, author of *The Philosophy of Mysticism* (2 vols., 1889) delved into the subconscious for explanation and founded the first Spiritualist monthly, *The Sphynx.*

Most of the Spiritualist activity was the work of a foreigner, **Alexander Aksakof,** imperial councilor of Russia, who, owing to Russian censorship, concentrated his work in Germany. In 1874 he began publishing *Psychische Studien,* which continued for many years. Its title was changed in 1926 to *Zeitschrift für Parapsychologie. Spiritualistische Blaetter* was started in 1883.

A great impetus was given to Spiritualism by the visit of the well-known medium **Henry Slade** in 1877. The conversion of **Johann C. E. Zöllner** caused a sensation and was the subject of strong language on the part of other scientists. The visits of such mediums as **William Eglinton, Elizabeth d'Esperance, Annie Fairlamb,** and others kept the interest alive.

Psychical Research

Modern psychical research is best represented by **Baron von Schrenck-Notzing.** His book on the materialization phenomena of **Eva C.,** *Materializations-Phaenomene* (Phenomena of Materialization, 1914), aroused heated scientific controversy. With this work and also the investigation of the mediumship of **Willi Schneider,** he convinced a hundred well-known scientists of the reality of **telekinesis** phenomena and of the existence of the elusive substance called **ectoplasm.** Other important thinkers and researchers included **Hans Driesch, Konstantin Oesterreich,** and **Rudolf Tischner.**

Prewar Germany saw the founding of a society for psychical research and also a medical society for psychical research: the Deutsche Gesellschaft für Wissenschaftliches Okkultismus and the Deutscher Spiritisten Verein. Periodicals included *Zeitschrift für Parapsychologie, Zeitschrift für Metapsychische Forschung, Zeitschrift für Psychisch Forschung, Zeitschrift für Seelenleben, Psyche und die übersinnliche Welt.*

Crucial to the history of post-World War I Germany, were the movements of **Rudolf Steiner,** founder of the **Anthroposophical Society,** and whose philosophy continues to be known today in the United States for the background of the **Waldorf Schools.** When Steiner left the Theosophists, deeming it impossible to create a spiritual science based in Eastern mysticism, he inadvertently became a favorite of Hitler's Reich. Even while living in **Switzerland** during World War II and attempting to maintain neutrality, his Anthroposophy became identified with German war aims. His first evolution might have led the Nazis to believe he was on their side. As Peter Washington noted, in his 1993 book, *Madame Blavatsky's Baboon,* "At first, Steiner shared a common view that something pure and noble might arise out of the conflict between nations; but as the apparently unstoppable carnage became ever more horrifying he modified his instinctive nationalism in favour of a broader perspective. After the war he was ready to support the League of Nations." Yet all through the rise of the Aryan model for purity and perfection, even some of the artistic renderings associated with many of the Christian-based spiritual movements, portrayed Christ, for example, as being more Aryan in features than Jewish. Steiner and his group, Washington commented, were only too willing to make Jesus an honorary German, denying his semitic origins completely, and thus lending credence to the mounting racial tensions.

Since World War II, there has been considerable German activity in the field of parapsychological research with the Lehrstühl für Psychologie und Grenzgebiete de Psychologie at Freiburg University and the independent **Institut für Grenzgebiete der Psychologie und Psychohygiene,** directed by **Hans Bender.** A new direction to Spiritualist beliefs in **survival** was stimulated by the experiments in **electronic voice phenomena** (Raudive voices) of **Friedrich Jürgenson,** who cooperated with the Freiburg Institute.

Despite many efforts, Germany's pursuit of paranormal studies and parapsychology remained rather bleak at the turn of the twenty-first century. Individual research under such people as **Gerd H. Hovelmann, Eberhard Bauer, Walter von Lucadou, Klaus Kornwachs, Ulrich Timm,** and **Hans D. Betz,** while remarkable, has not served to form a collective movement for research. All but one effort to form parapsychological associations failed. The research center, Institut für Grenzgebiete der Psychologie and Psychohygiene, (Institute for Border Areas of Psychology and Mental Hygiene) and the organization, **Wissenschaftliche Gesellschaft zur Forderung der Parapsychologie,** (Scientific Society for the Advancement of Parapsychology) are the only two avenues for study currently in Germany.

Sources:

Bander, Peter. *Voices from the Tapes.* New York: Drake, 1973.

Bender, Hans. *Unser sechster Sinn.* Stuttgart: Wilhelm Goldmann Verlag, 1982.

Berger, Arthur S., and Joyce Berger. *The Encyclopedia of Parapsychology and Psychical Research.* New York: Paragon House, 1991.

Schrenck-Notzing, A. von. *Materialisations-Phaenomene* (Phenomena of Materialization). Munich: Ernst Reinhardt, 1914.

Washington, Peter. *Madame Blavatsky's Baboon: A History of the Mystics, Mediums, and Misfits Who Brought Spiritualism to America.* New York: Schocken Books, 1993.

Spiritualism—Great Britain

Spiritualism was introduced from the United States to England within a few years of its emergence in New York. The transition from **mesmerism** into Spiritualism was effected in Britain under the impetus of visiting American mediums, the first being **Maria B. Hayden,** who arrived in 1852. Her way had been prepared by the publication the previous year of William Gregory's book *Animal Magnetism,* which contains records of supernormal occurrences, and by the accounts published from time to time in the mesmerist journal *Zoist.*

Table turning soon became epidemic in Britain, and society invitations, it is said, were extended to five o'clock tea and table turning. An early controversy arose when prominent scientist Michael Faraday suggested that the table movements were caused by unconscious muscular action. Another theory suggested they resulted from "unconscious cerebration."

Hayden herself was treated with derision by the press and returned to the United States in 1853. Yet, besides acting as forerunner for the great medium **D. D. Home,** she registered important conquests: **Robert Owen,** the veteran socialist; **Robert Chambers,** the publisher; and **Agustus de Morgan,** the famous mathematician. Sir Charles Isham and John Ashburner mostly owed their conversion to a belief in **survival** and communication with the dead to her limited powers. One Mrs. Roberts, a second American medium, and later **Pascal B. Randolph** and **J. R. M. Squire** left comparatively slight impressions.

Without Home, Spiritualism in England would probably have made but little further headway. He was received in the highest society and was visited by famous people of the day. Some of them (including novelist **William Thackeray,** Anthony Trollope, Robert Bell, **Bulwer Lytton,** and Lord Brougham) were said to have been deeply impressed but kept quiet for fear of public ridicule. Some figured in press sensations when they vented their anger for having become associated with Spiritualism before the public (e.g., **Sir David Brewster** and **Robert Browning**). Others, including **William Howitt;** J. Garth Wilkinson; **Lord Adare,** the earl of Dunraven; the **Master of Lindsay,** Nassau Senior; **Cromwell Varley;** and **Alfred Russel Wallace,** braved the scorn of the public.

Home first visited England in 1855 at age 23, having acted as a medium for some four years. He made an impression before returning to America in 1856. During Home's tour in 1855, London solicitor John Rymer and his wife, gathered friends at their home in the suburb of Ealing to experience the medium's gifts. Famed poets **Elizabeth Barrett Browning,** a devotee of the spiritualism movement, and her husband, **Robert Browning,** who disdained spiritualism, managed to receive an invitation to this exclusive gathering. In 1859 medium **Thomas Lake Harris** visited England. As early as 1854, the trance utterances of a medium named "Annie" were recorded by a circle of Swedenborgians presided over by Elihu Rich. The first British professional medium, **Mary Marshall,** began to offer séances, but less successfully than D. D. Home and his American colleagues. British Spiritualists, however, did not seek publicity, but practiced for the most part anonymously.

The phenomena at these séances resembled those in America—playing of instruments by unknown means, **materialization** of hands, table-turning, and so on, but on a less sensational scale. It was not so much these physical manifestations that inspired early British Spiritualists as it was **automatic writing** and **automatic speaking.** Although at first rare, it soon became a feature of séances.

In 1860 a new Spiritualist era commenced and the whole subject came into greater prominence. This enhanced attention was caused by an increase in the number of British mediums and the emigration to Britain of many American mediums, including the stage performers the **Davenport brothers,** who did not claim to be Spiritualists but were hailed as such.

Kate Fox of the original Fox Sisters who caused the whole movement to rise, married and settled in England as Mrs. Jencken. It is said that her child became a writing medium. Thomas Lake Harris, **Emma Hardinge Britten,** and **Cora L. V. Richmond** were remembered for inspirational addresses; **Charles H. Foster** for rather dubious **pellet-reading** and skin-writing phenomena (see **dermography**); the Davenport Brothers for noisy telekinetic demonstrations; **Lottie Fowler** for trance communications and predictions; and **Henry Slade** for **slate-writing** demonstrations.

British mediums were rather slow to arise. Mary Marshall was, for a long time, the only professional medium. In October 1867 the journal *Human Nature* knew of only one more, W. Wallace. The number of private mediums, however, was considerable. **Mrs. Thomas Everitt** was considered the most powerful. **Edward Childs** was also credited with strong powers.

William Howitt, William Wilkinson, and Mrs. Newton Crossland developed as automatists (see **automatism**). Agnes Nichols (later **Agnes Guppy-Volckman**) presented mysterious **apport** phenomena and the first materializations in England. The partners **Frank Herne** and **Charles Williams** produced impressive if suspect phenomena.

Frederick A. Hudson introduced **spirit photography** to London, and others followed in his footsteps. Marvelous things were reported to occur in the séances of **Florence Cook, W. Stainton Moses, William Eglinton, Annie Eva Fay, F. W. Monck, Mary Showers, Arthur Colman, Elizabeth d'Esperance, C. E. Wood, Annie Fairlamb, Cecil Husk,** and **David Duguid.**

Organizational Efforts

Because British mediums were slow to arise, Spiritualism as a movement was delayed until comparatively late. The **Charing Cross Spirit Circle** was the first experimental organization. In July 1857 it was superseded by the London Spiritualistic Union, a year later renamed the London Spiritualist Union, and in 1865 the Association of Progressive Spiritualists in Great Britain was formed. The Spiritual Athenaeum of 1866 was a temporary institution, established mainly to offer D. D. Home a paid position. The first really representative body, the **British National Association of Spiritualists,** was not born until 1873. In 1882 it was renamed the Central Association of Spiritualists and in 1884 the **London Spiritualist Alliance.**

The tardiness in organization was also manifested in the field of Spiritualist periodicals. *The Spirit World,* published by W. R. Hayden during his wife's visit in May 1853, was issued only once. Robert Owen's *The New Existence of Man Upon the Earth,* published in 1854, was spiritual but not Spiritualist. In April 1855 the *Yorkshire Spiritual Telegraph* was established by D. W. Weatherhead in Keighley, the chief provincial center of British Spiritualism. In 1857 it was renamed the *British Spiritual Telegraph* but was discontinued the next year.

Toward the end of 1860 *The Spiritual Magazine* was founded by William Wilkinson and became the leading organ. It ran until 1875. Thomas Shorter and William Wilkinson were the editors for the greater part of its existence, and William Howitt was the chief contributor.

The Spiritual Times ran from 1864 to 1866. In 1867 **James Burns** founded *Human Nature,* a monthly that ran until 1877, and in 1869 he brought out a weekly, *The Medium,* which absorbed the provincial *Daybreak,* founded in 1867, and was continued under the title *The Medium and Daybreak* until 1895.

In 1869 W. H. Harrison's paper *The Spiritualist Newspaper* entered the field. Under the later abbreviated title *The Spiritualist,* held its own until 1881. *The Christian Spiritualist* began its month-long run in 1871. *The Pioneer of Progress* lasted for ten months, appearing weekly from January 1874. In 1878 *Spiritual Notes* was founded and ran until 1881, the year in which *Light* appeared.

Light is the oldest British Spiritualist journal. It was founded by Dawson Rogers and W. Stainton Moses. Later editors included **E. W. Wallis** and **David Gow.** It was the official organ of the London Spiritualist Alliance but is now published quarterly by the **College of Psychic Studies,** London.

The *Proceedings* of the Society for Psychical Research and the society's *Journal* had their inception in 1882. *The Two Worlds* began publication in 1888 at Manchester. It is now the second-oldest Spiritualist journal in Britain. (Address: Headquarters Publishing Co., 5 Alexandria Rd., West Ealing, London W13 ONP.)

Emma Hardinge Britten's *Unseen Universe* ran from 1892 to 1893; **W. T. Stead**'s *Borderland* ran from 1893 to 1897; and, **J. J. Morse**'s *The Spiritual Review* was published from 1900 to 1902. *The Spiritual Quarterly Magazine* was started by the Two Worlds Publishing Company in October 1902. An English edition of the *Annales des Sciences Psychiques* was published between 1905 and 1910 under the title *Annals of Psychic Science.*

In addition to *Light* and *Two Worlds,* the most important of surviving Spiritualist journals is *Psychic News,* founded by Maurice Barbanell in 1932 and now published at 2 Tavistock Chambers, Bloomsbury Way, London, WCIA ILY.

The Rise of Psychical Research

Although Spiritualism arose in the United States, the effort to investigate it started in England. There was plenty to investigate. Mrs. De Morgan, Lord Adare, and Alfred Russel Wallace published the first important books. In 1869 the **London Dialectical Society** delegated a committee to investigate. After its favorable report, which brought the testimonies of many important people before the public, **Sir William Crookes** stepped to the fore and announced an investigation. His findings, which were published in 1871, and later in 1874, simply stupefied the contemporary savants.

E. W. Cox founded the **Psychological Society** of Great Britain in 1875; the British National Association of Spiritualists appointed a research committee in 1878; and the year 1882 witnessed a historic event, the foundation of the **Society for Psychical Research** (SPR).

The development of Spiritualism in Britain has been closely associated with the work of the SPR; but it has often been an uneasy relationship. Indeed, many early Spiritualists claimed that the society's initials really meant "Suppression of Psychical Research." From time to time the skepticism of some members of the SPR has seemed hostile. Still, the society has had a wide range of membership and is not tied to a sponsor's opinion on the genuineness of claimed phenomena.

The SPR was formed in 1882 to investigate psychic phenomena in a scientific and impartial spirit, free from the bias of preconceived ideas. The first president was **Henry Sidgwick,** and the council numbered among its members **Edmund Gurney, Frank Podmore, F. W. H. Myers, William F. Barrett,** Stainton Moses, **Morell Theobald,** George Wild, and Dawson Rogers, the latter four individuals being Spiritualists. However, avowedly Spiritualist membership in the society gradually declined over time.

Other notable presidents of the society were **Balfour Stewart, A. J. Balfour, William James,** Sir William Crookes, **Sir Oliver Lodge,** several of these being among original members of the society.

The initial scope of the SPR was defined by the areas of investigation mandated to six committees: (1) thought transference; (2) hypnotism; (3) Reichenbach phenomena; (4) apparitions; (5) physical (Spiritualist) phenomena; and (6) the history and existing literature on the subject. The scope of the society was further enlarged in later years when a committee headed by **Richard Hodgson** conducted an inquiry into the claimed phenomena of **Theosophy.**

To find alternative explanations for Spiritualist phenomena, members explored psychological theories and studied automatism, hallucinations, and **thought transference.** Some members were also instrumental in detecting a great deal of **fraud** in connection with mediumistic performances, particularly in the field of slate writing.

Many individuals had declared slate writing to be such a simple and straightforward phenomenon that fraud was impossible. But **S. T. Davey,** a member of the SPR, attended séances by the well-known medium William Eglinton and considered them fraudulent. He began to study the rationale for slate writing and emulated Eglinton's phenomena by conjuring methods. He then gave a number of pseudo séances, which Richard Hodgson carefully recorded.

Davey's techniques were so successful that none of the sitters could detect the fraud, even though they had been assured in advance that it was simply a conjuring trick—indeed some Spiritualist sitters refused to believe that the performances were fraudulent. After that, slate writing declined in Spiritualist circles and, like the phenomenon of spirit photography, was largely discredited.

Excellent work was done by the society in collecting evidence relating to apparitions of the dead and the living, reported in the monumental *Human Personality and Its Survival of Bodily Death,* by F. W. H. Myers (2 vols., 1903) and *Phantasms of the Living,* by Myers, Frank Podmore, and Edmund Gurney (2 vols., 1886).

A statistical inquiry on a large scale was undertaken by a committee of the SPR in 1889, and some seventeen thousand cases of **apparitions** were collected. The main objective in taking such a census was to obtain evidence for the workings of **telepathy** in apparitions; to make such evidence of scientific value, the utmost care was taken to ensure the impartiality and responsible character of all who took part in the inquiry. From the results it was concluded that the number of apparitions coinciding with a death or other crisis greatly exceeded the number that could be ascribed to chance alone.

There was much to encourage belief in some "supernormal" agency, especially in the last decade of the nineteenth century. The two mediums whose manifestations led many in Britain, the United States, and Europe to conclude that the spirits of the dead were involved in their phenomena were the Italian medium **Eusapia Palladino** and the American **Leonora Piper.**

In 1885 William James of Harvard began a study of Piper, and he was joined a few years later by Richard Hodgson, who had moved to the United States to be the secretary of the American branch of the SPR. Of all the trance mediums, Piper offered the best evidence for spirit agency. The skeptical Hodgson himself declared his belief that the spirits of the dead spoke through the lips of the medium, and among others who held that fraud would not account for the revelations given by Piper in the trance state were James, Sir Oliver Lodge, F. W. H. Myers, and **James H. Hyslop.**

Frank Podmore, while not admitting any supernormal agency, suggested that telepathy, probably aided by skillful observations and carefully conducted inquiries concerning the affairs of prospective sitters, might help to explain the matter. Eleanor Sidgwick also suggested that Piper probably received telepathic communications from the spirits of the dead and reproduced them in her automatic speaking and writing.

The other medium, Eusapia Palladino, after attracting considerable attention from **Cesare Lombroso, Charles Richet, Camille Flammarion,** and others on the Continent, went to Britain in 1895. Several British scientists, including Lodge and Myers, had already witnessed her powers on the Continent, at Richet's invitation. Lodge, at least, said he was satisfied that no known agency was responsible for the remarkable manifestations of Palladino. The British sittings were held at Cambridge, and because it was proved conclusively that the medium made use of fraud, the majority of the investigators ascribed her "manifestations" entirely to that. Later, in 1898, more séances were held at Paris, and they were so successful that Richet, Myers, and Lodge once more declared themselves satisfied of the genuineness of the phenomena.

Perhaps the most convincing evidence for the working of some paranormal agency, however, was to be found in the famous **cross correspondence** experiments conducted in the early twentieth century. F. W. H. Myers had suggested before he died that if a spirit **control** were to give the same message to two or more mediums, it would go far to establish the independent existence of such control.

On the deaths of Sidgwick (in August 1900) and F. W. H. Myers (in January 1901) it was thought that if mediums were controlled by their spirits some agreement might be looked for in the scripts. The first correspondences were found in scripts of **Rosina Thompson** and a Miss Rawson, the former in London, the latter in the south of France. The Sidgwick control allegedly appeared for the first time to these ladies on the same day, January 11, 1901.

On May 8, 1901, the Myers control appeared in the scripts of both Thompson and Margaret Verrall, and later in those of Piper and others. So remarkable were the correspondences obtained in some cases where seemingly there could not possibly have been collusion between the mediums, that it is difficult to believe that some discarnate intelligence was not responsible for at least some of the scripts.

Toward the end of 1916 a great sensation was caused with the publication by Sir Oliver Lodge of a memoir about his son, Lieutenant Raymond Lodge, who was killed near Ypres in September, 1915, during World War I. The book, titled *Raymond, or Life and Death,* is divided into three parts, the first of which contains a history of the brief life of the subject. The second part details numerous records of sittings, both in the company of mediums and at the table, by Sir Oliver Lodge and members of his family. It was claimed that considerable evidence of the personal **survival** of his son were obtained in these sittings. The third part of the book deals with the scientific material relating to life after death, which is reviewed and summarized in a spirit of great fairness, although a natural bias toward belief in immortality is obvious.

Notwithstanding much useful work by the SPR on the phenomena of Spiritualism, there was frequent antagonism from Spiritualists during the first half-century or so of the society's existence. The pioneer Spiritualist W. T. Stead fulminated against it, and **Sir Arthur Conan Doyle,** after several disputes, resigned his membership as a public protest shortly before his death in 1930. Controversies over the phenomena of "Margery" (American medium **Mina Crandon**) also reached across the Atlantic to involve the society in London.

Meanwhile, many independent research organizations had been formed. In 1920 the **British College of Psychic Science** was founded by prominent Spiritualists **Hewat McKenzie** and his wife Barbara. It was a source for information, advice, and guidance for consultation of reputable mediums and the investigation of psychical phenomena. The McKenzies assisted in the development of the psychic faculties of the medium **Eileen J. Garrett,** who was to become world-famous. Garrett was invited to the United States by the **American Society for Psychical Research** in 1931 and took part in parapsychological investigations with **William McDougall** and **J. B. Rhine.** In 1951 she founded the **Parapsychology Foundation** in New York.

Meanwhile the British College of Psychic Science performed useful work for a number of years, finally closing in 1947. Similar work was carried on by the **College of Psychic Science,** London (not to be confused with the former organization), founded in 1955, which grew from the London Spiritualist Alliance, which in turn was an outgrowth of the British National Association of Spiritualists, founded in 1896.

In 1970 the College of Psychic Science was renamed the **College of Psychic Studies.** It publishes the long-established journal *Light* and maintains an excellent library, organizes lectures, and conducts other activities associated with Spiritualism and psychical research.

The **National Laboratory of Psychical Research** was founded by **Harry Price** in 1925 as an independent research body and conducted investigations with such mediums as **Rudi Schneider, Eleonore Zügun, Stella C.,** and **Helen Duncan.** In 1936 the laboratory, with its library collected by Price, passed to the University of London Council for Psychical Investigation. Although laboratory work ceased, the library remains at the University of London.

Ever since the famous experiments of Sir William Crookes with the mediums Daniel Dunglas Home and Florence Cook beginning in 1871, Spiritualists had hoped that science would validate the phenomena of Spiritualism. The overall trend of psychical research tended to be skeptical and sometimes hostile, however, particularly as careful investigation disclosed mediumistic frauds. The different viewpoints of researchers and Spiritualists were largely irreconcilable, because Spiritualists operated within a framework of religious belief and researchers from a largely agnostic stance.

Some interesting Spiritualist organizations did not survive the passage of time. **Julia's Bureau,** associated with W. T. Stead, was absorbed by the W. T. Stead **Borderland Library** in 1914 but closed in 1936. Other ephemeral groups included the Jewish Society for Psychical Research; the Society for the Study of Supernormal Pictures; the Link Association of Home Circles; and, the Survival League.

Spiritualism Today

The British Spiritualist movement as a whole continues to flourish. The exposure of famous mediums in the past as fraudulent or partially fraudulent proved largely irrelevant to the less-publicized activities of nonprofessional mediums in home circles and churches. The larger Spiritualist organizations are now careful to apply the strictest scrutiny to mediums and to regulate their activities through professional organizations. Any unsatisfactory conduct is firmly controlled, frauds exposed, and only the highest standards of integrity permitted.

As a result, British Spiritualist mediums and public demonstrators of evidence for survival are the most famous in the world. Such personalities as **Doris Stokes** became international figures on television and radio programs as well as in public demonstrations but remained dedicated to the Spiritualist cause and did not become rich. There are now more than four hundred Spiritualist churches in Britain.

Many of the Spiritualist organizations founded in the nineteenth century have continued into modern times, and new organizations have also grown up. The **Marylebone Spiritualist Association,** founded in 1872, became the **Spiritualist Association of Great Britain,** and is claimed to be the largest of its kind in the world. It is located at 33 Belgrave Sq., London, SW1.

The **British Spiritualist Lyceum Union,** founded in 1890, was amalgamated with the **Spiritualists' National Union** (SNU) in 1948. The SNU had been founded in 1891. It is now located at Britten House, Stanstead Hall, Stanstead, Essex, CM24 8UD.

White Eagle Lodge grew from the mediumship of **Grace Cooke.** It was founded in 1936 and includes a publishing trust. It has branches in Edinburgh, Bournemouth, Plymouth, Worthing, and Reading, as well as in New Jersey. Headquarters address: New Lands, Rake, Liss, Hampshire, GU33 7HY.

The **Greater World Christian Spiritualist League** was founded in 1921 around the mediumship of **Winifred Moyes.** It has more than 140 local branches throughout Britain, as well as in a dozen foreign countries. Headquarters address: 3 Landsdowne Rd., Holland Park, London, W11.

Associated with the Spiritualist movement are healers, represented by talented individuals and organizations. One of the most famous was **Harry Edwards,** who died in 1976. He claimed the assistance of spirit helpers and established a healing clinic, which is now carried on by Joan and Ray Branch, whom he had designated as his successors. Edwards had published several books on healing and the magazine *The Spiritual Healer,* which continues publication. The address of the Harry Edwards Spiritual Healing Sanctuary is Burrows Lea, Shere, Guildford, Surrey, GU5 9QG.

The National Federation of Spiritual Healers is located at Shortacres, Churchill, Loughton, Essex. There is also a World Healing Crusade at 476 Lytham Road, Blackpool, Lancashire, and a Churches' Council for Health and Healing at 8–10 Denman St., London, W1.

Spiritualism and the Established Churches

Throughout the history of Spiritualism in Britain the established churches have been largely antagonistic. In 1881 Canon Basil Wilberforce was the partisan of Spiritualism before the Church Congress. The reception was hostile and denunciatory.

The General Assembly of the Church of Scotland was three times petitioned, by the Reverend W. A. Reid, to investigate psychic phenomena. On the first occasion, a committee was appointed, which reported that psychic phenomena did occur. Subsequent appeals, however, resulted in no fresh investigation.

Books have been published by Catholics insisting that Spiritualism is the work of evil spirits. In the period of postwar permissiveness, active opposition declined, and still today there are occasional fulminations from dogmatic clergymen that Spiritualism is the work of the **Devil.** The obsession with themes of possession and **exorcism** during the occult boom of the 1950s and 1960s confused many people.

In 1953 a group of interested clergymen led by Reginald M. Lester founded the **Churches' Fellowship of Psychical and Spiritual Studies,** which investigates paranormal healing, psychic phenomena, and mysticism in a sympathetic manner and publishes the *Quarterly Review.* Address: The Rural Workshop, South Rd., North Somercotes, Nr. Louth, Lincs., U.K. LN11 7PT.

One of the greatest obstacles to Spiritualism was the cruel, archaic legislation under which mediums were persecuted. Mediums found themselves accused under the **witchcraft** laws of 1735 for "pretending to communicate with spirits." Throughout the interwar years mediums were frequently brought into court under provisions of both the Witchcraft Act of 1735 and the Vagrancy Act of 1824. Disguised policewomen, posing as bereaved parents, would approach a medium, begging for some consolatory message. A small sum of money would be offered as a "love offering," and if this was accepted the medium was prosecuted and often fined or imprisoned for up to three months. This punitive legislation was finally repealed in 1951 and replaced with the new Fraudulent Mediums Act, which, although not wholly satisfactory to the Spiritualist community, implicitly acknowledged that there might be genuine mediumship.

The matter was by no means settled at the turn of the twenty-first century. The Spiritualists' National Union recently warned its churches about the possibility of prosecutions under the Vagrancy Act of 1824, which was only partially amended. The act has recently halted plans for a large commercial enterprise to combine fortune-telling with computer technology. This has revived fears that mediums are still not adequately protected by law.

Research organizations that continue to thrive were the **Religious Experience Research Centre,** at Manchester College, Osford; the Brain and Perception Laboratory, at the medical school of the University of Bristol; the **International Institute for the Study of Death,** UK Branch, Hampnett, Northelach; the Parapsychical Laboratory, Downton, Wilshire; and, the **Society for Psychical Research,** London.

Sources:

Berger, Arthur S., and Joyce Berger. *The Encyclopedia of Parapsychology and Psychical Research.* New York: Paragon House, 1991.

Edmunds, Simeon. *Spiritualism: A Critical Survey.* Wellingborough, England: Aquarian Press, 1966.

Hall, Trevor H. *The Spiritualists: The Story of Florence Cook and William Crookes.* London: Gerald Duckworth, 1962. Reprint, New York: Garrett/Helix, 1963.

Medhurst, R. G., comp. *Crookes and the Spirit World: A Collection of Writings by or Concerning the Work of Sir William Crookes.* New York: Taplinger, 1972.

Roberts, Estelle. *Forty Years a Medium.* London: Herbert Jenkins, 1959. Rev. ed. *Fifty Years a Medium.* London: Corgi, 1969.

Stemman, Roy. *One Hundred Years of Spiritualism: The Story of the Spiritualist Association of Great Britain, 1872–1912.* London: SAGB, 1972.

———. *Spirits and Spirit Worlds.* London: Aldus Books, 1975.

Stokes, Doris, and Linda Dearsley. *Voices In My Ear: The Autobiography of a Medium.* London: Futura, 1980.

Time-Life Books. *Spirit Summonings,* Mysteries of the Unknown Series. Alexandria, Va.: Time-Life Books, 1996.

Spiritualism—Italy

In Italy the birth of the Spiritualist movement was largely brought about by French periodicals and developed along the lines of the **Kardec** school. The visit of the famous medium **Daniel Dunglas Home** in 1855 led to the formation of many societies and to the publication of the first Spiritualist journal, *L'Amore del Vero.*

The Kardec school of **Spiritism** greatly affected the development of Italian Spiritualism. Copies of Kardec's books and French Kardecean periodicals circulated freely in Italy. Once introduced, Spiritualism developed rapidly, and by 1870 there were more than a hundred societies in different parts of the country. Both Spiritists and Spiritualists were represented.

Among the prominent organizations were La Società Spirituale di Palermo, formed in 1863. In the same year the first representative Spiritualist organ, *Annali dello Spiritismo,* was started in Turin by Niceforo Filalete (also known as Vincenzo Scarpa). The Magnetic Society of Florence, which had influential members, began its activity about the same time. Baron Seymour Kirkup sent many accounts of activities to the London *Spiritual Magazine.*

In 1873 Baron Guitern de Bozzi founded the Pneumatological Psychological Academy at Florence, where earlier the visit of the British medium **Agnes Guppy-Volckman,** beginning in 1868 and extending to a period of almost three years, left a deep impression. The academy existed only a brief time.

A period of lively psychic activity began in 1872 when Signor Damiani discovered the medium **Eusapia Palladino,** around whom famous scientists gathered for a many years. **G. B. Ermacora,** founder and coeditor of the *Rivista di Studi Psichici,* **Cesare Lombroso, Ernesto Bozzano, Enrico Morselli, Angelo Brofferio, Filippo Bottazzi, Benigno Bianchi,** and many other well-known researchers worked to establish the authenticity of psychic phenomena. A succession of such powerful mediums as **Auguste Politi, Francesco Carancini, Amedee Zuccarini, Lucia Sordi,** and **Linda Gazzera** helped them in their task.

Various organizations were formed, including the Società di Studi Psichici in Rome and the Society for Psychic Studies at Florence. Ernesto Bozzano, a leading psychical researcher, presided over the Italian Spiritualists Association, and a very well-organized society, Circulo Arnaldo Vassallo, was formed in Genoa. It was named after one of the pioneers of the movement in Italy.

The formation of the **Associazione Italiana Scientifica de Metapsichica** (1946) at Milan and the **Centro Italiano de Parapsicologia** (1960) in Naples indicates the revived interest in psychic phenomena after World War II.

Spiritualism made considerable progress in Italy in spite of continual opposition from conservative Catholics, who stigmatized the movement as diabolical. Progress owed much to the open-minded investigations of psychical researchers such as **Angelo Brofferio,** author of *Per lo Spiritismo* (1892), **Ercole Chiaia,** and Ernesto Bozzano, who published a defense of the British medium **W. Stainton Moses.** In 1985 the Archivo de Doucumentazione Storica Della Rocerca Psichica was established in Bologna as a collection of psychological books and research records. The collection was built around the collections of Ernest Bozzano and Gastone de Boni.

According to a poll conducted in 1999, nearly a quarter of Italians believed in magic, fortune-telling, astrology, and spiritualism. They spent a total of one billion lire per year on these interests, according to the survey conducted by **Confesercenti** and the polling institute, SWG. The poll found that 22 percent, or more than 10 million people, believed in mystical practices in a country that counts 70,000 magicians, astrologers, clairvoyants and faith healers. About 2.5 percent of those polled, or 1.2 million, admitted that they had been victims of fraud when they turned to the supernatural to solve the more mundane difficulties of love, health, and work. For a nation whose population has been largely one of practicing Roman Catholics, their church's admonition against such practices apparently was not heeded. "While there is an understandable need for a touch of magic in life. . .action is needed to stamp out abuses, illegal behaviour and fraud widely linked to these practices," noted Confesercenti.

Sources:

Berger, Arthur S., and Joyce Berger. *The Encyclopedia of Parapsychology and Psychical Research.* New York: Paragon House, 1991.

Bottazi, F. *Nelle regioni inesplorate della Biologia Umana.* Rome, 1907.

Bozzano, Ernesto. *Popoli Primitivi e Manifestazioni Supernormali.* Milan: Armenia Editore, 1974.

Brofferio, Angelo. *Per Lo Spiritismo.* 3d ed. Turin, 1903.

Carrington, Hereward. *Eusapia Palladino and Her Phenomena.* New York: B. W. Dodge, 1909.

De Vesme, Cesar. *History of Experimental Spiritualism.* 2 vols. London: Rider, 1931.

Lombroso, Cesare. *After Death—What?* Boston: Small, Maynard, 1909.

Morselli, Enrico. *Psicologia e 'Spiritismo': Impressioni e note Critiche sui fenomeni medianici di Eusapia Palladino.* 2 vols. Turin: Boca, 1908.

Reuters News Service. "Almost a Quarter of Italians Believe in Magic. . ." 13 August 1999.

Spiritualism—Phenomena

Spiritualism emerged in response to the post-Enlightenment attack on supernaturalism, which by the mid-nineteenth century had made a significant impact on the public. As part of a general assault on belief in the existence of a spiritual world, post-Enlightenment thinking had cast particular doubt on **survival** of bodily death. Spiritualists claimed that they had discovered a regular method of making contact with the spiritual world and could establish beyond a reasonable doubt the continuation of life beyond death.

The primary phenomenon of Spiritualism centers on **mediums,** individuals who can, it is believed, establish contact with spirit entities and through whom the spirits speak and act. Mediums seem to have a peculiar sensitivity to the presence of spirit forces and entities. Sometimes that sensitivity reportedly manifests early in life in such childhood experiences as knowing something is going to happen before it does or seeing spirits, sometimes described as invisible playmates. Other mediums grow to adulthood unaware of any psychic sensitivity and discover it quite by accident. For example, what occurs while playing with a **Ouija board.** Several report their sensitivity emerging after an accident to the head. Many have discovered their abilities while associating with Spiritualist friends or participating in a psychic ability development class.

The basic task for mediums is facilitating communication between individuals and their acquaintances in the spirit world. In either **trance** or a waking state, the medium mediates the conversation. When the medium is in a trance state, the spirit entity often speaks directly to an individual using the medium's vocal cords, it is said. When awake, the medium most frequently simply repeats messages from the spirits. Such communications may take place in a private session between the medium and the client, in a **séance,** or in "platform work," in which the medium stands in front of a large audience and gives brief readings to selected members.

Mediumship is thus meant to be a demonstration of the continued existence of persons who used to reside in a body on Earth. The problem, of course, is determining whether what appears to be happening (i.e., a simple conversation between an individual, a medium, and a spirit) is real, an elaborate hoax, or an unconscious charade stemming from the vivid imagination of the medium.

The basic evidence comes from the content of the messages. That is, the voice speaking through the medium often reveals information that only the spirit entity could have known. From a successful session with a medium, sitters often report hearing private details of their lives, possibly relating to incidents shared with the deceased. They note peculiar traits of speech of the entity assumed by the medium or the discovery of a lost object by following the directions given by the spirit. Occasionally spirits offer predictions of things that will happen to the sitter. Spirits speaking through an entranced medium often demonstrate knowledge and erudition apparently not available to the medium when awake.

In the course of a séance or platform work, the entire range of **extrasensory perception** (e.g., **telepathy, psychometry, telekinesis, clairvoyance,** and **precognition**) may occur; in fact, some psychical researchers have suggested that mediumship can be completely explained by ESP.

Mediumistic phenomena also include psychic or spiritual healing. Spiritualist healers generally see their healing work as originating in the work of spirit helpers who work through them. At one end of the healing spectrum is **psychic surgery.** Philippine psychic surgeons became famous with claims of actually opening the body of a patient and under spirit guidance removing unhealthy tissue. A tamer form, found among early American and British healers, involved an entranced medium operating on the **astral body** of the patient. With the patient lying on an operating table, the medium would appear to pantomime an operation several inches above the body. Corrections in this spiritual body double having been made, it was believed that appropriate changes would then occur in the physical body.

More commonly today, however, Spiritualist healers simply reach a rapport with their spirit guides and mediate healing energy from them. Spiritualists point to alleged healings as evidence of the spirit world. Critics, of course, point to similar healings in other contexts having no reference to spirits, and all contemporary research in paranormal healing has been directed toward defining a healing power without reference to any spirit agency. In actions akin to healing, mediums have demonstrated the ability to influence the growth of **plants,** seemingly by passing energy from their body to the plants.

Early in the Spiritualist movement various telekinetic phenomena began to appear. In fact, the initial events from which Spiritualism dates itself were rapping sounds that seemed to manifest some intelligence because they occurred in response to questions put to a supposed spirit. Such **raps** became commonplace over the next decades, as did various other noises, such as paranormal **voices** and **music.**

Among the most common mediumistic phenomena are various forms of automatism: agitation of the body or limbs, **automatic writing, automatic drawing and painting, slate writing,** and **direct writing.** Of these forms, automatic writing is by far the most common. Numerous texts have been produced purportedly by a medium simply allowing his or her hands to be controlled by a spirit.

The most controversial physical phenomena have been those associated with **materialization** and dematerialization. Throughout the early twentieth century a great deal of psychical research was devoted to the study of reported claims of full-body materializations of spirit entities created from a mysterious substance called **ectoplasm.** In séances where such materializations occurred, sitters were often treated to the appearance of **apports,** objects believed to have been dematerialized elsewhere and rematerialized in the séance room. Closely related was the occasional production of **plastics** imprints of fingers, hands, faces, legs, and psychic molds of faces, hands, and legs. Spiritualists have also claimed incidents of **matter passing through matter** and the **transportation** of the human body (i.e., **teleportation**).

Less common has been the alleged production of various **chemical phenomena,** including psychic lights (**luminous phenomena**), **perfumes,** catalytic phenomena, and water. Of these, incidences of **psychic photography,** or more particularly, **spirit photography,** were the most spectacular. The literature also reveals incidents of some **electric phenomena,** including the discharge of electroscopes and phenomena suggesting human radioactivity.

Mediums have also claimed the powers attributed to Indian **fakirs,** such as **fire immunity** and the **levitation** of the human body.

Finally, also reported in séances have been a wide variety of unusual but less evidential phenomena, such as the **movement** of objects without contact (telekinesis), vibratory effects, increase and decrease in weight, and spelling out of messages by **typtology.** Reports of psychophysiological phenomena include change in stature (**elongation,** shrinking or puffing out of the human body); **stigmata;** effects of **personation, transfiguration, obsession,** and trance; loss of weight; nervous drain; the appearance of **auras;** and various **emanations.**

Thermodynamic effects include the frequently reported variations of temperature and the less common reports of increase of heat in apported objects or, in case of penetration of matter through matter, currents of air and psychic **winds.**

Explanations

Although numerous fanciful explanations for mediumistic phenomena have been put forth—including one positing the existence of "planetary spirits" with whom mediums communicated and one theorizing a vast "thought reservoir" fed by human "thought rays"—most twentieth-century psychical researchers have concluded that not only were they not produced by spirit agencies, but were produced by **fraud.** That conclusion was reached after numerous cases of cleverly produced fraud were uncovered and information on how such phenomena could be produced through conjuring became available. The broad acceptance of that appraisal has meant the virtual abandonment by mainstream Spiritualism of physical séances and their survival only on the fringes of the movement. Revelations of fraud have called into question all of the accounts of materializations, apports, and spirit photography produced throughout the first century of Spiritualism.

Spiritualism still adheres to the **spirit hypothesis,** meaning the belief that the intelligence that directs the phenomena of the medium is of a disembodied spirit's. The spirit hypothesis remains the most intriguing of the explanations of such phenomena, and the possibility of finding evidence of the spirit's survival after death still motivates many parapsychologists.

Sources:

Barbanell, Maurice. *This Is Spiritualism.* London: Herbert Jenkins, 1959.

Garrett, Eileen. *Many Voices: The Autobiography of a Medium.* Reprint, Alexandria, Va.: Time-Life, Inc., 1991.

Lewis, James R. *Afterlife Beliefs and Phenomena.* Detroit: Visible Ink Press, 1995.

Spiritualism—United States

On March 31, 1848, Mrs. John Fox of Hydesville, New York, summoned her neighbors to hear strange knockings that were disturbing her family. At this time the Fox household comprised John Fox, his wife, and their two young daughters, Margaretta and Kate, aged 15 and 12 years respectively. On being questioned, the **raps** seemed to manifest signs of intelligence, and it was eventually deciphered from them, it was said, that the disturbing influence was the spirit of a peddler, murdered for the sake of his money by a former resident of the house. It was subsequently claimed in April of that year that the Foxes, while digging in their cellar at the instigation of the spirits, discovered fragments of human hair, teeth, and bones.

The neighbors of the Fox family were deeply impressed by these "revelations" and, by way of a test, questioned the spirits on such matters as the ages of their acquaintances, questions that were answered, apparently, with some correctness. Soon afterward the daughter Margaretta Fox visited her married sister, Mrs. Fish, at Rochester, New York, where the knockings broke out as vigorously as they had at Hydesville. Her sister Catherine visited some friends at Auburn, and there, too, the rappings were heard.

Committee after committee was appointed but could not discover the cause of the sounds or how the answers to mental questions that were posed were correctly given. Some of those who sat with the **Fox sisters** soon found that they had similar powers. So the movement spread. The public had already been prepared for such demonstrations by the spread of the teachings of **Emanuel Swedenborg** and demonstrations of **animal magnetism.** Clairvoyants had also made use of rapping prior to the mediumship of the Fox girls. The induced **trance** had also recently been brought to the notice of the American people by lecturers, the clergy, and others. So, accustomed to departures from orthodoxy in every direction, many found no difficulty in admitting the intervention of good or evil spirits in human affairs, and for those who refused to accept the spirit hypothesis a satisfactory explanation of the phenomena was found in electricity, electromagnetism, or the **od** (odic) force.

The first experimental Spiritualist organization, the New York Circle, was formed in 1851. The New York Conference was established the same year, and the preaching of a new science and faith began to make converts among the notable personalities of the day. Wisconsin governor **N. P. Tallmadge,** abolitionist William Lloyd Garrison, Professors Britten, Wells, Bryant, and Bliss of the University of Pennsylvania, Chief Justice Williams, Judge **John Worth Edmonds,** Professor **Robert Hare,** Professor **James Jay Mapes,** General Bullard, Horace Greeley, James Fenimore Cooper, and William Cullan Bryant were some of the distinguished early converts.

According to an estimate in *Spirit World,* there were 100 **mediums** in New York and 50 to 60 private circles in Philadelphia in 1851. The *North American Review* wrote in April 1855 that the New England Spiritualist Association, which computed the number of Spiritualists in America as nearly two million, did not overstate the facts.

Probably the strangest developments in the early history of American Spiritualism were the **new motor** machine of **John Murray Spear** and the **Mountain Cove Community** of Rev. James Scott and **Thomas Lake Harris.** As time progressed,

Spiritualists struggled with many offshoot movements that claimed justification for such ideas as free love and community ownership of the spirit communications of mediums.

Soon physical phenomena began to supplement the simpler forms of spirit communication. **Table turning** and tilting partially replaced the phenomenon of raps. Playing of musical instruments by invisible means, "direct" spirit writing, bell ringing, **levitation,** and **materialization** of spirit hands were just some of the phenomena witnessed and vouched for by distinguished sitters.

The levitation of the great medium **Daniel Dunglas Home** was recorded at an early stage in his career. **Slate writing** and playing of musical instruments were feats practiced by the alleged spirits that frequented the "spirit room" of **Jonathan Koons** in Dover, Ohio.

At Keokuk, Iowa, in 1854 two mediums spoke in **tongues** identified—on somewhat insufficient data—as "Swiss," Latin, and Indian, and thereafter other mediums practiced trance speaking in foreign tongues, a phenomena known as **xenoglossis.** Recognized foreign tongues included Latin and Greek, French, German, Spanish, Italian, Chinese, and Gaelic, but generally the trance utterances, when they were not in English, were not recognized definitely as any known language, and frequently the "spirits" themselves interpreted the "tongue." Speaking in pseudotongues, or **glossolalia,** was evidently related to the articulate but meaningless fluency of people caught up in a moment of religious ecstasy. There were a few verified cases, however, where persons in a state of exaltation spoke fluently in a language with which they were unfamiliar in their normal state.

Many of the "spirit" writings were signed with the names of great people—particularly Franklin, Swedenborg, Plato, Aristotle, St. John, and St. Paul. Trance lecturing before audiences was also practiced, books of inspirational sayings were published, and poetry and drawings were produced in abundance. These "automatic" productions had a character of their own—often vague, high-sounding, incoherent, and distinctly reminiscent. In cases where they displayed even a fair amount of merit, as in the poems of T. L. Harris, it was pointed out that they were not beyond the capacity of the medium in a normal state. As a rule they had a superficial appearance of intelligence, but on analysis were often found to be devoid of meaning.

Spiritualist Literature

With the spread of the movement, Spiritualist periodicals, most short-lived, sprung up. The *Univercoelum* of 1847 and the *Spirit Messenger,* which succeeded it in 1849, were mouthpieces of the "harmonial" philosophy as articulated by **Andrew Jackson Davis.** A similar paper, *Disclosures from the Interior and Superior Care for Mortals,* was published by Rev. James L. Scott, founder of the Mountain Cove Community, and Thomas Lake Harris. *The Spiritual and Moral Instructor,* by T. S. Hiatt, and *Heat and Light* also came into existence. The first true Spiritualist periodical was issued on July 1850 by former "magnetist" **La Roy Sunderland.** The title, *The Spiritual Philosopher,* was changed a year later to *Spirit World.* In 1852 the *Shekinah* was launched on its short career by S. B. Brittan and Charles Partridge. After 18 months it was absorbed by **Joseph R. Buchanan**'s *Journal of Man.*

The first periodical that could boast of permanence was the *Spiritual Telegraph,* born of a resolution of the New York Conference in 1852. It ran until 1860, when it was absorbed by Andrew Jackson Davis's *The Herald of Progress.*

In 1854 the Society for the Diffusion of Spiritual Knowledge, the first well-organized Spiritualist body, started the *Christian Spiritualist* (1854–57), and the year 1857 witnessed the appearance of *The Banner of Light,* which ran into the 1930s. Other early periodicals were *The Spiritual Clarion, The New Eva, The Light from the Spirit World,* of St. Louis, the *Age of Progress,* and *The Sunbeam.* Later ones included the *Religio-Philosophical Journal,* the *Western Star, The Spiritual Scientist, The American Spiritualist,* the *New England Spiritualist, The Spiritual Age,* and *The Lyceum Banner.*

Trends in the Movement

From the beginning of the movement those who accepted the actuality of the phenomena arrayed themselves into two separate schools, each represented by a considerable body of opinion. The theory of the first was frankly Spiritualistic, and the second tended toward **mesmerism** or animal magnetism under one name or another, with a flavor of contemporary scientific thought. These two schools had their foundation in the early days of animal magnetism, when the more rationalist ideas of the magnetists were pitted against the theological theories of angelic or diabolic possession.

In the United States the hypothetical "force" of the rationalists went by such names as od (odic) force, electromagnetism, and so forth. **Poltergeist** disturbances, occurring from time to time, were ascribed either to spirits or to odic force, as in the case of the **Ashtabula poltergeist.** Asa Mahan, one of the "rationalists," suggested that a medium could read the thoughts of sitters by means of odic force. The protagonists of magnetic theory attributed trance speaking to the subject's own intelligence, but after the birth of American Spiritualism in 1848 a Spiritualist interpretation became more common.

Notwithstanding these conflicting theories, little was done in the way of scientific investigation, with the exception of the experiments conducted by Robert Hare, a professor of chemistry at the University of Pennsylvania, which resulted in Hare's conversion to Spiritualism. His critics denounced him violently, and he was obliged to resign.

Very few exposures of **fraud** were made, partly because the majority of the sitters accepted the phenomena with unquestioning faith, and partly because the techniques with which such detection might be made were not available. The collaboration of skillful, trained, and disinterested investigators, such as those who later applied themselves to the elucidation of parapsychology, was entirely lacking in the early days, and the public was left to form its own conclusions.

Spiritualism in the United States was, from the first, intimately bound up with socialism. It was, in fact, the outgrowth of the same original outlook that produced socialistic communities and occasioned the rise and fall of so many strange religions. Warren Chase, Horace Greeley, T. L. Harris, and other prominent Spiritualists founded such communities, and "inspirational" writings (today called **channeling**) frequently gave directions for their construction.

The Problem of Fraud

American Spiritualism has been characterized by a wide range of phenomena, and there has been a problem distinguishing genuine phenomena from those that are fraudulent. For example, the **Davenport brothers,** who traveled far and wide, advertised Spiritualism by inexplicable noisy demonstrations but most likely were simply very good stage magicians. The medium **Henry Gordon** introduced levitation of the human body, and D. D. Home produced phantom hands that dissolved in the grasp of the sitters. Home's accomplishments remain a mystery. Joseph Rhodes Buchanan discovered **psychometry,** which **William Denton** corroborated in some exciting experiments. **William H. Mumler** accidentally became the first exponent of **spirit photography. Mary Hardy** produced the first paraffin wax molds. **Emma Hardinge Britten,** Nettie Colburn (also known as **Henrietta Sturdevant Maynard**), and Cora Scott (later **Cora L. V. Richmond**) did inspirational speaking, and **Mary J. Hollis** and **Mrs. J. H. Conant** became outstanding trance mediums. The infamous **Henry Slade** was the major exponent of slate writing, and **Charles Foster** led in the art of **pellet reading** and skin writing (**dermography**).

The Fox sisters, who gave the first impetus to modern Spiritualism, were soon eclipsed in power and variety of demonstrations by these and other mediums. But they were also the first who had to bear the brunt of the backlash against Spiritualism, which was soon to come. In the sisters' first university examination, on February 17, 1851, Professors Austin Flint, Charles A. Dee, and C. B. Coventry of Buffalo University, delivered the following verdict on their phenomena: "It is sufficient to state that the muscles inserted into the upper and inner side of the large bone of the leg (the tibia) near the knee joint, are brought into action so as to move the upper surface of the bone just named, laterally upon the lower surface of the thigh bone (the femur), giving rise, in fact, to a partial lateral dislocation. This is effected by an act of the will, without any obvious movements of the limb, occasioning a loud noise[,] and a return of the bone to its place is attended by a second sound."

The revelation by Mrs. Norman Culver of an alleged confession by one of the Fox sisters cast more doubt on their credibility.

Then, in 1857, the editor of *The Boston Courier* offered $500 for the production of genuine phenomena and provided a committee from Harvard University be the umpire. On behalf of the Spiritualists, a Dr. Gardner accepted the challenge. The committee consisted of Professors Pierce, Louis Agassiz, and Horsford of Harvard University, N. B. Gould of the Albany Observatory, the editor of the *Boston Courier,* and a few friends of Gardner's. The mediums were Mrs. Brown (Leah Fox), Kate Fox, J. V. Mansfield, Mrs. Kendrick, George Redman, and the Davenport brothers.

Two days were devoted to the manifestations. They were imperfect and unsatisfactory, and the committee returned a negative verdict, promising also a later report of additional investigations, which, however, was never issued. After the failure of the Cambridge investigation, Gardner extended invitations to the press to attend séances with the same mediums. Several papers published impressive accounts.

The Progress of the Movement

Over the years important records of observations and long experiments were published by E. A. Brackett, **Epes Sargent,** a Dr. Wolfe, Allan Putnam, and Eugene Crowell. An early history of Spiritualism by E. W. Capron, *Modern Spiritualism,* was supplemented by Emma Hardinge Britten's *Modern-American Spiritualism* (1870), outlining 15 years of progress. Many organizations and Spiritualist churches worked for the advancement of the cause. In 1873 the first camp meeting was initiated at Lake Pleasant, Massachusetts. It was quickly followed by others.

The years between 1880 and 1890 witnessed four outstanding events: the report of the **Seybert Commission;** the self-exposure of Margaret and Kate Fox in 1885; the founding of the **American Society for Psychical Research** for systematic and organized psychical research in 1885, with the participation of a group of distinguished scientists; and the discovery of the remarkable mediumship of **Leonora Piper.**

The Seybert Commission was set up by the University of Pennsylvania, which received an endowment of $60,000 from the will of Spiritualist Henry Seybert to investigate Spiritualist phenomena. After issuing a preliminary negative report in 1887, which was widely resented, the committee discontinued the investigation.

The self-exposure of Margaret and Kate Fox did not result in the deathblow to Spiritualism hoped for by anti-Spiritualists, because the motives of the sisters were called into question and their confession was followed a year later by full retraction.

The emergence of psychical research with the founding of an American branch of the **Society for Psychical Research** in 1885 was of far-reaching importance, marking the beginning of regular attention to Spiritualist phenomena. At about the same time **William James** discovered and became intensely interested in Leonora Piper's powers. He wedded his research to that of the new organization and lent it the prestige of his name. **Richard Hodgson** joined James in the Piper investigations and acted as secretary of the American Society for Psychical Research until his death in 1905. The American branch of the society was then dissolved, but its work was quickly resumed by Columbia professor **James H. Hyslop,** who assumed leadership of a reorganized American Society for Psychical Research and conducted its work until his death in 1920.

Other keen and able investigators arose. **Hereward Carrington** established his claim to renown and Hyslop's mantle was placed on the shoulders of **Walter F. Prince.** In the early twentieth century, Piper's earlier role was filled by "Margery" (**Mina Crandon**). The controversy produced by her phenomena, focused in the investigation of the *Scientific American* and of Harvard committees, split the psychical research community and its major organization. Prince and other American Society for Psychical Research leaders withdrew and founded the **Boston Society for Psychic Research** in 1925. The Boston society competed successfully with its New York rival for 15 years until the Margery controversy had died and a merger was worked out.

Spiritualism in the Twentieth Century

The nineteenth century has been called the "heyday of Spiritualism," and the period up to World War I was certainly the time when most attention was paid to it. However, such a designation, coupled with the knowledge of the negative results of so many investigations of the movement, led many to assume that it had largely died out. Such was not the case. In 1893 the National Spiritualist Association, later the **National Spiritualist Association of Churches** (NSAC), began to bring some order to the organizational chaos of state and local associations, provided a united front to respond to other competing groups, such as the **Theosophical Society,** and presented a creed abstracted from spirit teachings.

The NSAC dominated the movement for a generation but in the 1920s began to experience internal discord arising from some mediums' belief in reincarnation. While French Spiritualists had adopted a reincarnationist position, in general British and American mediums were opposed to it. As early as 1924 it became an element of contention, with the withdrawal of Amanda Flowers and the formation of the Independent Spiritualist Association. In 1930 the NSAC passed a strong statement repudiating reincarnation only to have the majority of the New York membership withdraw and reorganize as the **General Assembly of Spiritualists.** The issue would arise again and again.

The twentieth century also saw the emergence of an African American presence in the Spiritualist movement. Some joined the NSAC, but as early as 1913 Leafy Anderson founded the Eternal Life Christian Spiritualist Association. Through the remainder of the decade 11 additional congregations were founded, and in 1920 Anderson moved to New Orleans to pastor the congregation there. In 1922 the NSAC pushed black members out of its fellowship, and they founded the **National Colored Spiritualist Association of Churches.** Over the next decade additional black denominations were founded and began to spread throughout the African American community nationally.

Among the larger Spiritualist churches that appeared over the century were the **Universal Church of the Master** (formed in California in 1908), the International General Assembly of Spiritualists (1936), the National Spiritual Science Center (1941), the Spiritual Episcopal Church (1941), the Universal Spiritualist Association (1956), and the United Spiritualist Church (1967).

Spiritualism seems to have spread slowly and consistently across the United States through the century. However, with the emergence of parapsychology and the refocus of psychical research away from the claims of Spiritualists and toward the laboratory production of **psi** phenomena, Spiritualism was largely forgotten. The last great crusade against it was conducted by the magician **Harry Houdini** in the 1920s. A number of Spiritualist mediums attained some public recognition as psychics but were rarely identified with their churches. One such medium was **Arthur A. Ford,** who first came to public notice when he claimed to have received a message left behind by Houdini at the time of his death. Ford went on to inspire the formation of the Spiritual Frontiers Fellowship (now the **International Spiritual Frontiers Fellowship**), a fellowship of non-Spiritualists who wanted the resources of the psychic world to investigate the religious life. He ended his career with a famous séance on Canadian television for Episcopal bishop **James A. Pike.**

The Pike séance revealed a continuing problem of Spiritualism. Several years after the séance and both Pike's and Ford's death, an examination of Ford's papers revealed that he had faked the séance. Periodically, word of similar fraudulent activity served to substantiate that Spiritualism was itself saturated with fakes and thus should simply be dismissed as a movement of consequence. In 1960, psychical researcher **Andrija Puharich** uncovered the fake materializations going on at Camp Chesterfield. Then, in 1976, Lamar Keene quit his career as a fake medium and offered detailed information about a circle of churches operating what amounted to a confidence scheme to provide a constant stream of phenomena for their members.

Meanwhile, during the same period, Spiritualism had to compete with the revival of occult religion in the **New Age** movement. Integral to the New Age has been mediumship under a new name, "channeling." However, Spiritualism has largely remained aloof from the New Age movement, its adherents not participating to any marked degree.

Sources:

Baer, Hans A. *The Black Spiritual Movement: A Religious Response to Racism.* Knoxville: University of Tennessee Press, 1984.

Brandon, Ruth. *The Spiritualists: The Passion for the Occult in the Nineteenth and Twentieth Centuries.* New York: Alfred A. Knopf; London: Weidenfeld & Nicolson, 1983.

Britten, Emma Hardinge. *Modern American Spiritualism: A Twenty Years' Record of the Communion Between Earth and the World of Spirits.* New York, 1870. Reprint, New Hyde Park, N.Y.: University Books, 1970.

Capron, E. W. *Modern Spiritualism: Its Facts and Fanaticisms, Its Consistencies and Contradictions.* Boston, 1855. Reprint, New York: Arno Press, 1976.

Carrington, Hereward. *The Story of Psychic Science.* London: Rider, 1930.

Carter, Huntley, ed. *Spiritualism: Its Present-day Meaning.* Philadelphia: J. B. Lippincott, 1920.

Centennial Book of Modern Spiritualism in America. Chicago: The National Spiritualist Association of the United States of America, 1948.

Gauld, Alan. *The Founders of Psychical Research.* London: Routledge & Kegan Paul, 1968. Reprint, New York: Schocken Books, 1973.

Hare, Robert. *Experimental Investigation of the Spirit Manifestations.* New York, 1855.

Hart, Hornell. *The Enigma of Survival: The Case For and Against an After Life.* Springfield, Ill.: Charles C. Thomas, 1959.

Home, Daniel Dunglas. *Incidents in My Life.* London: Longmans, Green, 1863. Reprint, New Hyde Park, N.Y.: University Books, 1972.

Houdini, Harry. *A Magician Among the Spirits.* New York: Harper & Row, 1924. Reprinted as *Houdini: A Magician Among the Spirits.* New York: Arno Press, 1972.

Jackson, Herbert G., Jr. *The Spirit Rappers.* New York: Doubleday, 1972.

Jacobson, Nils Olof. *Life Without Death? On Parapsychology, Mysticism and the Question of Survival.* New York: Delacorte Press, 1973. Reprint, London: Turnstone Books, 1974. Reprint, New York: Dell, 1974.

Keene, M. Lamar. *The Psychic Mafia.* New York: St. Martin's, 1976.

Kerr, Howard. *Mediums and Spirit-Rappers and Roaring Radicals.* Urbana, Ill.: University of Illinois Press, 1972.

McHargue, Georgess. *Facts, Frauds, and Phantasms: A Survey of the Spiritualist Movement.* Garden City, N.Y.: Doubleday, 1972.

Pearsall, Ronald. *The Table Rappers.* New York: St. Martin's, 1972.

Podmore, Frank. *Modern Spiritualism: A History and a Criticism.* 2 vols. London, 1902. Reprinted as *Mediums of the 19th Century.* New Hyde Park, N.Y.: University Books, 1963.

Spicer, Henry. *Sights and Sounds: The Mystery of the Day; Comprising an Entire History of the American "Spirit" Manifestations.* London: Thomas Bosworth, 1853.

Tabori, Paul. *Companions of the Unseen.* London: H. A. Humphrey, 1968.

———. *Pioneers of the Unseen.* London: Souvenir Press, 1972.

Spiritual Israel Church and Its Army

The beginnings of the Spiritual Israel Church and Its Army, a prominent spiritual church within the African American community of the United States, are somewhat obscure. It seems to have begun with the absorption of black Jewish ideas by Derk Field, a black Alabama man who founded the Church of God in David. Along the way he met a man named W. D. Dickson, who eventually succeeded him as head of the church. Dickson took the title "King of All Israel." According to the Spiritual Israelites, Field and Dickson restored the teachings of the ancient Israelites. They believe that "Ethiopian" is the national name of black people, and "Israel" is their spiritual name.

The Spiritual Israelites are like other Spiritualist churches in that they value contact with the spirit world and the work of mediums who serve as the pastors of their temples. They believe that they belong to the one true spiritual church, but that the Spirit dwells in all people. They believe in life after death but think that traditional ideas of heaven and hell are mere projections of the limited human mind.

The Spiritual Israelites have adopted a version of the black Jewish myth. They maintain that black people were the first people, humanity having originated in Africa. All of the biblical patriarchs and prophets were black people, but at the time of Jacob and Esau, the sons of Isaac, a division occurred. Jacob is the progenitor of the Ethiopian people and Esau of the Caucasian. Modern Jews are the product of intermarriage between the children of Jacob and Esau.

By the 1980s, the Spiritual Israelites had some 40 temples and missions. There were also several schismatic groups, all of whom carried the word Israel in their title. A number of the congregations are located in the greater Detroit area.

Current address unavailable.

Sources:

Baer, Hans A. "Black Spiritual Israelites in a Small Southern City." *Southern Quarterly* 23, no. 3 (1985): 103–24.

———. *The Black Spiritual Movement: A Religious Response to Racism.* Knoxville: University of Tennessee Press, 1984.

Murphy, Larry G., J. Gordon Melton, and Gary L. Ward. *Encyclopedia of African American Religions.* New York: Garland Publishing, 1993.

The Spiritualist (Periodical)

The name of several Spiritualist periodicals. The first was an influential British weekly, edited by W. H. Harrison (formerly coeditor of **The Spiritual Times,**) and published in London from 1869 until 1881 (originally issued as *The Spiritualist Newspaper*). It was closely associated with the **British National Association of Spiritualists** until 1879.

The name was again used by a monthly journal published in New York and edited by C. P. Christenson, from August

1915 to November 1916. A third periodical called *The Spiritualist* was published monthly in England beginning in 1932 by the **Spiritualist Community,** London. The Community dissolved soon after the start of World War II. *The Spiritualist* was the bimonthly journal of the **Spiritualist Association of Great Britain,** since renamed *The Spiritualist and Spiritual Gazette.*

Spiritualist Association of Great Britain (SAGB)

One of the oldest and largest Spiritualist associations. It grew out of the **Marylebone Spiritualist Association** founded in 1872. The story of the association's early struggles "to propagate spiritual truths in the Marylebone area of London" has been told in an SAGB publication *One Hundred Years of Spiritualism,* which also states that Queen Victoria held several séances after the death of the Prince Consort.

Even the term "Spiritualist" led to many difficulties in the early days of the association, which had to change its name to The Spiritual Evidence Society in order to hire halls. Widespread opposition to Spiritualism was also encouraged by the Witchcraft Act of 1735, which was frequently invoked for police prosecution of mediums.

Four years after the repeal of the Witchcraft Act in 1951, the SAGB moved to its present headquarters where it now provides lectures, demonstrations of clairvoyance, healing clinics, Sunday services, a library, a bookstall, and other facilities for the study and practice of Spiritualism. It also links together "a commonwealth" of Spiritualist churches throughout Britain. Among the prominent mediums associated with the group were **Ursula Roberts** and healer Gordon Turner.

Membership of the association is open to interested members of the public, who are put in touch with their local Spiritualist church. Members may also attend psychic development classes or book sittings with approved mediums. The association publishes a magazine, *The Spiritualist and Spiritual Gazette.* Address: 33 Belgrave Sq., London, SW1X 8QL England.

Sources:

Edmunds, Simeon. *Spiritualism: A Critical Survey.* London: Aquarian Press, 1966.

The Spiritualist Community

British organization, active in the period between the two world wars in presenting religious and educational aspects of **Spiritualism.** It was founded by **Mrs. St. Clair Stobart,** known as "the woman on the black horse," who had led one half of the Serbian Army in their retreat during World War I and was an early member of the **British College of Psychic Science.** She eventually became chairperson of its advisory council and published several books on Spiritualism.

The Community, under the presidency of Spiritualist **Hannen Swaffer,** conducted religious services with speakers, clairvoyant and healing services, and organized instruction groups, also publishing a monthly journal *The Spiritualist* from 1932 onward. The community is no longer active.

Spiritualist Episcopal Church

One of the most important Spiritualist churches in the United States in the mid-twentieth century, the Spiritualist Episcopal Church was founded in 1941 out of the turmoil that had plagued Camp Chesterfield, a central gathering point for Spiritualists in the midwestern United States. The founders included Revs. Clifford Bias and John Bunker of the Independent Spiritualist Association and Robert Chaney of the National Spiritualist Association of Churches. Each of these had experienced some degree of alienation over traditional **Spiritualism**'s emphasis on the phenomena believed to constantly demonstrate and prove the existence of life after death. They wanted to emphasize the teachings and philosophy coming through their **channeling** activity. This new emphasis was welcomed by some, and for many years the church conducted a summer seminary at Camp Chesterfield using the materials produced by Rev. Ivy Hooper.

The church prospered through the mid-1950s, though Chaney departed in 1951 to found Astara. However, in 1956, a morals charge was brought against a prominent leader in the church who was a candidate for a church office. The leadership was split by the candidate's supporters and detractors. The tension affected the church's position at Camp Chesterfield, where the church had its headquarters. Hoping to calm the anger, prevent the divisiveness at the camp from spreading through the whole church, and to dissuade the medium from seeking office, church president Rev. Dorothy Graff Flexer moved the headquarters to Lansing, Michigan. Despite the move, the church split, and Clifford Bias founded the Universal Spiritualist Association. The Spiritualist Episcopal Church's mediums were denied access to Camp Chesterfield. Flexer left the church in 1958 and founded the Church of Metaphysical Christianity.

Formally, the Spiritual Episcopal Church has beliefs very similar to those of the National Spiritualist Association of Churches. **Reincarnation** is denied. However, inspiration is drawn from all of the world's religions and the influence of Buddhism, Rosicrucianism, and Theosophy is evident in the lessons produced for the summer seminary. The present status of the church is unknown.

Sources:

Chaney, Robert G. *"Hear My Prayer."* Eaton Rapids, Mich.: Library, Spiritualist Episcopal Church, 1942.

Development of Mediumship. Dimondale, Mich.: Spiritual Episcopal Church, n.d.

The Spiritualistic Dramatic Society

British society of the 1930s, located in London, which presented plays with a Spiritualist theme to spread knowledge of **Spiritualism** through the channels of dramatic art. The Duchess of Hamilton and Brandon, Ms. Lind-af-Hageby, **Hannen Swaffer,** and Robert McAllen were its patrons.

Spiritualistische Blaetter (Periodical)

Pioneering German Spiritualist periodical of 1883.

Spiritualist Outlook (Magazine)

Monthly publication of the First United Spiritualist Church. It included poetry, inspirational articles, and a directory of affiliated Spiritualist churches.

Spiritualists' National Union

One of the oldest British Spiritualist organizations. It was founded in July 1890 at the suggestion of **Emma Hardinge Britten** and focused attention on **Spiritualism** in Manchester and throughout northern England. In the beginning, it was known as the Spiritualists' National Federation, bringing together a number of leading Spiritualists in Manchester for an annual conference with delegates from other Spiritualist societies to discuss matters of common interest. This annual conference still takes place today.

In October 1901, the Spiritualists' National Union was incorporated under the Companies Acts, taking over the assets, rights, and obligations of the federation in July 1902.

In 1948, the **British Spiritualists' Lyceum Union,** founded in 1890, amalgamated with the SNU, transferring its work of spiritual education for children and young people to that organization. The SNU formulates policy through a National Executive Committee, which delegates certain responsibilities to standing and sub-committees such as Trust Property, Education, Training, and Awards, Publicity and Public Relations and Healing. The SNU also operates the **Arthur Findlay College,** which is based at Stansted Hall in Essex and runs courses on Spiritualist philosophy, religious practice, spiritual healing, and other related subjects.

The SNU delegates local matters to fourteen district councils, with executive committees formed by directly-elected members in the districts. Four hundred Spiritualist churches are affiliated with the SNU, most are in the UK, along with one in the US and several in Australia. The union also maintains a register of National Spiritualist ministers and mediums.

Membership in the union is open to individual Spiritualists as well as to churches and other organizations. The primary aim of the union is to promote the religion and religious philosophy of Spiritualism on the basis of the seven principles:

1. The fatherhood of God
2. The brotherhood of Man
3. The communion of spirits and the ministry of angels
4. The continuous existence of the human soul
5. Personal responsibility
6. Compensation and retribution hereafter for good and evil deeds done on earth
7. Eternal progress open to every human soul.

The Spiritualists' National Union may be contacted at Redwoods, Stansted Hall, Stansted, CM24 8UD. Website: http://www.snu.org.uk.

Sources:

Edmunds, Simeon. *Spiritualism: A Critical Survey.* London: Aquarian Press, 1966.

The Spiritual Magazine

A British Spiritualist monthly (1860–77) founded by William Wilkinson, who jointly edited it with Thomas Shorter. **William Howitt** was its chief contributor. It was the successor to the *British Spiritual Telegraph.*

The Spiritual Messenger (Journal)

British Spiritualist monthly that published a few editions in London in the winter of 1858–59. It was edited by W. Carpenter.

Spiritual Notes (Journal)

Monthly official publication of the **British National Association of Spiritualists,** which flourished from 1878 to 1881.

The Spiritual Philosopher (Periodical)

The first Spiritualist periodical in the United States, founded by **La Roy Sunderland** in 1850 as a monthly, then becoming a weekly, the title changing to *Spirit World* after the first year.

The Spiritual Quarterly Magazine

British periodical of Spiritualism, published by the Two Worlds Publishing Company in Manchester beginning in October 1902. It was edited by Will Phillips and had only a short life.

Spiritual Regeneration Movement Foundation

Founded in 1959 to teach the philosophy of **Transcendental Meditation** (TM) and its technique as developed by **Maharishi Mahesh Yogi.** It is now a section of the World Plan Executive council, the international organization that directs the TM movement from **Switzerland.** Address: Maharishi Mahesh Yogi, 433 South Harvard Blvd., Los Angeles, CA 90020-3402.

Spiritual Research Society

The Spiritual Research Society was an early American **New Age** group founded by Edwin Cain, Sr., and his wife, Nellie Cain. The society can be traced to a psychic development circle that the Cains, both Spiritualists, organized in their home. During these sessions, Nellie began to channel messages purported to be from the **Great White Brotherhood,** the group of advanced beings believed by Theosophists to guide the destiny of the human race. These messages were compiled and published in 1965 as *Gems of Truth from the Masters.* A copy was sent to Merta Mary Parkinson, head of the **Sisters of the Amber.** Parkinson's group was an early representative of the Universal Link, the original New Age organization headquartered in England. As a result a relationship developed between the Cains and British New Agers such as Libbie Pugh.

The Cains were introduced to the prediction that a momentous event would occur near Christmas Day 1967. The day came and went with nothing momentous having occurred. The Cains later explained to the disappointed Link members that the predictions had been fulfilled in a somewhat unexpected manner. They stated that during the years before 1967, human life had been tried and tested at every level. During the 1960s, a visible network of spiritual groups had been established through the Universal Link. The late 1960s was a time to shift the emphasis to the invisible work of spiritual practice, which would spread the spiritual energy in the world. They suggested a program termed the Nuclear Evolution Operation, through which the invisible spiritual light would be radiated to humanity.

Sources:

Cain, Nellie B. *Exploring the Mysteries of Life.* Grand Rapids, Mich.: Spiritual Research Society, 1972.

———. *Gems of Truth from the Masters.* Grand Rapids, Mich.: Spiritual Research Society, 1965.

Spiritual Review (Journal)

British monthly founded by **J. J. Morse** in 1900. It continued until May 1902, when Morse departed from England for an extensive lecture tour to Australia, New Zealand, and the United States.

Spiritual Science Mother Church

The Spiritual Science Mother Church grew out of an interest in **Spiritualism** developed by some Christian Scientists in the early twentieth century. It was organized in 1927 by Mother Julia O. Forrest, a former Christian Science practitioner who had become a Spiritualist, and Dr. Carl H. Pieres. They believed they were dealing scientifically with spiritual matters, and they felt comfortable with the organization of the Christian Science movement, which they used as a model. Forrest became the pastor of the Spiritual Science Mother Church, headquartered in New York, and head of the ecclesiastical council, which administered the church's affairs. She and Pieres also established a Spiritual Science Institute for training ministers.

Spiritual Science is specifically Christian in its belief and affirms a Trinity of God the Father and creator, the virgin-born

Son, and the Holy Spirit. Jesus is seen as the Lord, Master, and dispenser of the law of love. Humans have been given free agency and are traveling a spiritual path that includes many incarnations. Members of the church are expected to demonstrate spiritual realities in this life. Three principal demonstrations are emphasized: preaching, i.e., clairvoyant messages from God about what each member has to do; communications from other realms; and healing through the channeling of healing power. Members are expected to grow in their spiritual life, a process termed soul-unfoldment. Salvation eventually results as a cleansing process through intelligent prayer.

The Spiritual Science Mother Church was headquartered in New York City for many years and by the 1970s had some 40 affiliated congregations. It was headed at that time by Glenn Argoe, who had succeeded Forrest as pastor of the mother church. However, its present status is unknown.

The Spiritual Scientist (Journal)

Nineteenth-century American weekly founded in 1874 in Boston and edited by E. Gerry Brown.

Spiritual Telegraph (Periodical)

American Spiritualist weekly founded by S. B. Brittan and Charles Partridge and published in New York from 1852 to 1860. In 1860 it merged into the *Herald of Progress,* which **Andrew Jackson Davis** founded.

The Spiritual Times (Periodical)

British Spiritualist weekly published in London (1864–66) and edited by J. H. Powell and W. H. Harrison.

Spirituelles Addressbuch (Directory)

Annual publication in German giving comprehensive listings of mystical, spiritual, yoga, and New Age organizations all over Germany. Last known address: PARAM, Verlag Gunther Köch, Kurz Strasse 5, D-2161 Ahlerstedt 1, Germany.

Splitfoot

A facetious name for the Devil, who is traditionally depicted with hooves, sometimes expressed as "Old Splitfoot" or "Mr. Splitfoot."

When the **Fox Sisters** first encountered the mysterious **rappings** at Hydesville, New York, that supposedly heralded the beginnings of **Spiritualism,** the youngest child Cathie reportedly said "Mr. Splitfoot, do as I do" and clapped her hands; the raps immediately repeated her clapping. At first, Cathie thought somebody was tricking her, since it was the day before April Fools' Day.

Spodomancy

Divination by means of the cinders from sacrificial fires.

Spokesman (Newsletter)

Former monthly publication of the Universal Christ Church, headquartered in Los Angles, California. It included inspirational messages, advice to readers, and a directory of affiliated churches.

Spontaneous Human Combustion

The idea that human beings can, quite apart from any outside stimulus, be consumed from an internal heat source so intense as to consume even the bones, but leave the immediate environment relatively unburned, has been a subject of controversy since the nineteenth century. Incidents had been reported since the fifteenth century and became the subject of both public and medical controversy in the 1850s following the use of spontaneous combustion as a means of disposing of a character by popular writer Charles Dickens in his novel *Bleak House.* During the twentieth century, with the continued if sporadic reports of burned bodies, the controversy has been pressed by writers on fortean anomalistic phenomena. In a 1992 book on the subject, Jenny Randles and Peter Hough tracked some 85 cases that had occurred since 1850.

Though some incidents appear to be cases of spontaneous combustion in the ancient literature, the modern string of cases begins with the death of the Italian knight Polonus in 1470. A century and a half later, John Hillard tried to bring the issue before the public in his pamphlet *Fire from Heaven* (1613). The death of Nicole Millet, the wife of an innkeeper in Rheims, France, on February 20, 1725, led to the first court inquiry and ruling. In the middle of the night, Jean Millet awoke smelling fire. He awakened the inn's guests and together they found Nicole's body in the kitchen. All except her skull, a few vertebrae, and her lower extremities had been consumed. Wooden objects close by were untouched. Millet was tried and found guilty of murder, but on appeal the conviction was reversed based on the testimony of a physician who had been staying at the inn that night who concluded that Mme. Millet's death was due to a "visitation of God," that is, an unknown cause. The fact that Mme. Millet had consumed a significant amount of alcohol was seen as possibly causing the fire to start and contributing to its disastrous results. Ever since, alcohol consumption has been associated with the phenomenon.

The first American case of spontaneous combustion was that of Hannah Bradshaw in New York City in 1770; however, the most heralded case has been that of Mary Reeser, a widow residing in St. Petersburg, Florida. Her body was discovered on the morning of July 2, 1951, after her landlady's hand found the doorknob too hot to grasp. She and two men called to assist an entry found Reeser's body, the chair she had been sitting in, and a side table burned, along with a six-foot circle of carpet. The remainder of the room, including a pile of newspapers just outside the circle, remained unaffected. The Reeser case illustrated the essential problem raised by human combustion cases. As those in charge of crematoriums are quite aware, it takes a very high temperature applied over a period of time to consume the human body, especially the bones. Under normal conditions, such a concentration of heat would cause considerable damage in the immediate surrounding area.

In the last two centuries a variety of explanations for spontaneous human combustion have been offered, ranging from the scientific to the paranormal. Some have tied it to **leys,** magnetic irregularities in the Earth, and UFOs. Writing in 1995, Larry Arnold, currently the leading proponent of a paranormal explanation for the phenomenon, was not the first to suggest that the image on the Turin Shroud might have been caused by spontaneous human combustion.

Vincent Gaddis, known for his broad study of anomalous phenomena, suggested a tie to depression and even suicide. Possibly the same forces which, when directed outwardly, produce suicide, might when projected inwardly lead to the burning of the body.

Edinburgh University scientist Dougal Drysdale suggested what he termed a candle-wick theory, noting that the body, which contains a considerable amount of fat, could burn like a candle with great local intensity. This theory is favored by the major spokespersons of the skeptical community, especially Joe Nickell and John F. Fischer, as a part of their crusade to remove any paranormal explanations from anomalous phenomena. While this theory accounts for the consumption of body fats and the body's high water content, its flaw remains in the extremely high temperatures needed even to begin to consume bone material.

Spontaneous human combustion remains a rare phenomenon, and even among those most prone to adopt occult interpretations, few have followed that lead. Several forteans have suggested that like the **Bermuda Triangle,** it may be a constructed problem that brings together cases that are only superficially related. Most have accepted the more telling incidents as unexplained, but view it as a natural mystery whose solving has been delayed due to the paucity of cases, the high level of diversity among cases studied, and the limitations imposed on experimenting on human subjects.

Sources:

Arnold, Larry E. *Ablaze! The Mysterious Fires of Spontaneous Human Combustion.* New York: M. Evans and Co., 1995.

Harrison, Michael. *Fire from Heaven: A Study of Spontaneous Combustion in Human Beings.* London: Sidgwick and Jackson, 1976.

Nickell, Joe, and John F. Fischer. *Mysterious Realms.* Amherst N.Y.: Prometheus Books, 1992.

———. *Secrets of the Supernatural.* Buffalo, N.Y.: Prometheus Books, 1988.

Randles, Jenn, and Peter A. Hough. *Spontaneous Human Combustion.* London: Robert Hale, 1992.

Wilson, Damon. *Spontaneous Combustion: Amazing True Stories of Mysterious Fires.* Sydney: The Book Co., 1997.

Spontaneous Phenomena

Unexpected experiences of **estrasensory perception** (ESP), **psychokinesis** (PK), or other paranormal phenomena in everyday life.

The Spotlight (Magazine)

Published by the Lyceum section of the **National Spiritualist Association of Churches** and directed toward young people. It is published ten times a year and includes poetry, stories, cartoons, along with spiritual lessons. It is published from 1418 Hall SE, Grand Rapids, MI 49506-3960. Website: http://www.nsac.org/.

Sources:

NSAC Lyceum Spotlight. http://www.nsac.org/. March 8, 2000.

SPR See Society for Psychical Research

Sprengel, Anna (ca. 1888)

The mythical Rosicrucian adept and member of the German occult society Die Goldene Dämmerung who is supposed to have given permission to Rosicrucian **William Westcott** to found the Hermetic Order of the **Golden Dawn.** Westcott claimed to have found Sprengel's name and address on a sheet of paper inserted in the pages of a mysterious cipher manuscript bought from a bookstall on Farringdon Road, London, in 1887.

Correspondence exists between Westcott and Sprengel relating to the Golden Dawn, but its authenticity has been questioned, and the cipher manuscript is believed to be a forgery that nevertheless launched an occult society.

Sources:

Howe, Ellic. *The Magicians of the Golden Dawn.* London: Routledge and Kegan Paul, 1972.

King, Francis. *The Rites of Modern Occult Magic.* New York: Macmillan, 1970.

Sprenger, Jakob (1436–1495)

Dominican inquisitor of Cologne, **Germany,** generally associated with **Heinrich Kramer** author of **Malleus Maleficarum,** a sourcebook directing the **witchcraft** persecutions in Europe. Sprenger was born in Basel, **Switzerland,** and became a novice in a Dominican house. He rapidly rose to a responsible position, and in 1468 the Dominican General Chapter ordered him to lecture at the University of Cologne on the sentences of Peter Lombard. He soon became master of theology at the university and was elected prior and regent of studies of the Cologne convent. On June 30, 1480, he was elected dean of the faculty of theology at Cologne University, and a year later he became an inquisitor for the provinces of Mainz, Trèves, and Cologne and traveled extensively throughout these provinces. In 1488, he was elected provincial of the whole German province.

His earlier writings included: *The Paradoxes of John of Westphalia Refuted* (1479) and *The Institution and Approbation of the Confraternity of the Most Holy Rosary, which was first erected at Cologne on 8 September in the year 1475* (1475). This latter work recorded his activities for the Confraternity of the Most Holy Rosary, which brought him praise from leading Dominicans as an apostle of the rosary.

In 1484, at the time the pope released the Inquisition to deal with **witchcraft,** now redefined as Satanism, Sprenger became involved with Heinrich Kramer in trying alleged witches and sorcerers. In the following year, Kramer prepared a treatise on witchcraft (later published as the *Malleus Maleficarum*) that circulated in manuscript. Sprenger then added his name to the finished work, first published in 1486. *Malleus Maleficarum* embodied the new direction in the church's consideration of witches. It became the authoritative manual for inquisitors, judges, and magistrates in dealing with accusations of witchcraft, which multiplied over the next several centuries. Interestingly, the Reformation of the sixteenth century did not slow these accusations, as witchcraft was accepted by Protestants as thoroughly as by Roman Catholics. The book went into some thirty editions between 1486 and 1669, and it was published in French, Italian, and English editions, as well as in German.

Sprenger died December 6, 1495, at Strassbourg, where he was buried.

Spriggs, George (1850–1912)

British **materialization** medium. The first records of his phenomena date from 1877 to 1879. Having discovered his psychic gifts, he became a nonprofessional medium and conducted séances for The Circle of Light in Cardiff, Wales. He had two Indian controls: "Swiftwater" and "Shiwaukee," who was "captured" from the medium **Mary J. Hollis** (also known as Mrs. Billings), with whom Spriggs sat in London.

The unique feature of Spriggs' séances was supposedly that the phantoms that appeared moved at a distance from the medium, walked about the house, went out into the garden in evening light (on one occasion three phantoms did this simultaneously), and sometimes changed into the form of somebody else. These visitors were seen by next-door neighbors, who threatened to call the police for "dealings with the devil."

In November 1880, Spriggs went to Melbourne, Australia. Similar phenomena were reported there: spirits who held out heavy objects, drank water, ate biscuits, and wrote letters to former sitters. After six years, the materializations ceased, but other phenomena remained. Spriggs gave **direct voice** sittings and clairvoyant diagnosis and treatment of diseases.

In 1900, he returned to England, and from 1903 until 1905 he gave free medical advice in the rooms of the **London Spiritualist Alliance.** The **Psycho-Therapeutic Society** was largely formed through his efforts. For years he diagnosed diseases for the society without charge.

Sources:

Berger, Arthur S., and Joyce Berger. *The Encyclopedia of Parapsychology and Psychical Research.* New York: Paragon House, 1991.

Denovan, W. C. D. *The Evidences of Spiritualism.* Melbourne, 1882.

Springheeled Jack

Legendary nineteenth-century British creature who supposedly harassed travelers and terrified women with his giant leaps, vicious behavior, and diabolical appearance. As the legend goes, he successfully eluded capture for many years, evading police and the army, and mocking them with his daring leaps and wild eerie laughter.

Reportedly, he was a large man in a black cloak, and when the cloak was thrown aside, blue and white flames shot from his mouth and his eyes appeared like balls of fire. His hands appeared to be metallic claws, with which he slashed at people or tore their clothing. He was able to leap across high walls and hedges with ease. Sometimes he even knocked or rang at front doors, using his athletic ability to escape after terrifying the occupant of the house. The first report survives from September 1837. A press account from 1838, quoted in Peter Haining's *The Legend and Bizarre Crimes of Springheeled Jack* (1977), notes a typical incidence:

"She returned into the house and brought a candle and handed it to the person, who appeared enveloped in a large cloak, and whom she at first really believed to be a policeman. The instant she had done so, however, he threw off his outer garment, and applying the lighted candle to his breast, presented a more hideous and frightful appearance, and vomitted forth a quantity of blue and white flame from his mouth, and his eyes resembled red balls of fire.

"From the hasty glance which her fright enabled her to get at his person, she observed that he wore a large helmet, and his dress, which appeared to fit him very tight, seemed to her to resemble white oilskin. Without uttering a sentence he darted at her, and catching her partly by the dress and the back part of her neck, placed her head under one of his arms, and commenced tearing her gown with his claws, which she was certain were of some metallic substance.

"She screamed out as loud as she could for assistance, and by considerable exertion got away from him and ran towards the house to get in. Her assailant, however, followed her, and caught her on the steps leading to the hall-door, where he again used considerable violence, tore her neck and arms with his claws, as well as a quantity of hair from her head; but she was at length rescued from his grasp by one of her sisters."

Springheeled Jack is reported to have terrorized many people in London and the provinces with his appearances in 1843, 1845, and sporadically until 1877. He appeared again in 1904. He popped up again in 1953 in Houston, Texas, where his appearance was linked to a UFO sighting.

Some have suggested that the original Springheeled Jack was the eccentric Marquis of Waterford, Henry de la Poer Beresford, who was also Baron Tyrone of Haverfordwest (1811–1859). According to the Reverend Brewer in *The Reader's Handbook* (1899; reprinted Gale Research, 1966):

"The Marquis of Waterford in the early parts of the nineteenth century used to amuse himself by springing on travellers unawares, to terrify them; and from time to time others have followed his silly example. Even so late as 1877–78, an officer in her majesty's service caused much excitement, in the garrisons stationed at Aldershot, Colchester, and elsewhere, by his 'spring-heel' pranks. In Chichester and its neighbourhood the tales told of this adventurer caused quite a little panic, and many nervous people were afraid to venture out after sunset, for fear of being 'sprung' upon. I myself investigated some of the cases reported to me."

The Marquis of Waterford was known to have been responsible for a number of somewhat sadistic pranks, particularly involving offensive behavior to women. But there is no firm evidence that he devised special boots fitted with steel springs or a phosphorescent mask with provision for emitting flames or smoke (as reported by victims and onlookers).

He was, however, reported as having protuberant eyes and also a peculiar ringing laugh. Moreover, a servant gave an account of an encounter with the sinister cloaked figure with fiery eyes and claw-like hands and spoke of an ornate crest on the cloak, with the initial "W" in gold filigree.

If the original Springheeled Jack was the Marquis of Waterford, he outgrew this behavior when he met and married Louisa Stuart in 1842. The Marquis seems to have been benevolent towards the tenants on his Irish estates and like many noblemen of the period spent a good deal of time in sport and hunting. He died while hunting; his horse stumbled and threw him, dislocating his neck.

Springheeled Jack has been considered a supernatural or paranormal being by many people. In her book *Stand and Deliver* (1928), historian Elizabeth Villiers commented:

"A thousand tales were afloat and all lost nothing in the telling. Plenty of people definitely swore they had seen him leap right over the roofs of large houses, the cottages and hayricks were as nothing to him, the mail coaches and post chaises and family barouches were taken in his stride. Then, rather unaccountably, public opinion veered from thinking him a new form of highwayman and declared he was an inventor experimenting with a form of flying machine, while others maintained he was not flesh and blood but a haunting spirit."

After the death of the Marquis of Waterford, reports of Springheeled Jack continued, generated either through legend or a succession of imitators, which led to him being the central character of plays, "penny-dreadful" comic books, and popular thrillers. As late as 1945, a British movie was made about Springheeled Jack titled *The Curse of the Wraydons,* starring actor Tod Slaughter.

The suggestion that Springheeled Jack might have been a creature from outer space was made in an article in *Flying Saucer Review* (May–June, 1961) by J. Vyner. It cited twentieth-century reports from the United States.

An earlier suggestion was made that Springheeled Jack might have been a kangaroo that had escaped from captivity. The numerous reports of a creature breathing flames, molesting women, and laughing eerily indicated characteristics beyond the capacity of a kangaroo.

Sources:

Clark, Jerome. *Encyclopedia of Strange and Unexplained Phenomena.* Detroit: Gale Research, 1993.

Haining, Peter. *The Legend and Bizarre Crimes of Springheeled Jack.* London: Frederick Muller, 1977.

Keel, John A. *Strange Creatures from Time and Space.* Greenwich, Conn.: Fawcett, 1970. Reprint: London: Neville Spearman, 1975.

Vyner, J. "The Mystery of Springheel Jack." *Flying Saucer Review* (May–June, 1961).

Sprinkle, Ronald Leo (1930–)

R. Leo Sprinkle, psychologist and researcher of UFO **contactee** experiences, was born on August 31, 1930, in Rocky Ford, Colorado. He received his bachelor's and master's degrees from the University of Colorado and in 1961 completed his doctorate in counseling psychology at the University of Missouri. After three years in the administrative department at the University of North Dakota, he moved to the University of Wyoming, where he remained until his retirement in 1989.

Sprinkle has traced his interest in UFOs to a sighting he had in 1949. He and his wife also had a sighting in 1956. During the years immediately following the completion of his formal education, he conducted several studies, including an early survey of the members of the **National Investigations Committee on Aerial Phenomena** and an initial study of people who had experienced extraterrestrial encounters, both contactees and abductees. He served as a psychological consultant for the **Condon Report** (1969) on UFOs, which led to further work on several **abduction** cases through the 1970s.

Sprinkle is best known, however, for the annual conferences he has organized for UFO contactees each summer since in 1980. For a number of years, Sprinkle had corresponded with people who had claimed friendly contact with the entities who drove the flying saucers. Unlike most ufologists, he had not dismissed them; in contrast, he had responded to them sympathetically. The conferences, sponsored by the Institute for UFO Contactee Studies, brought contactees to the university and provided an open forum for them to tell their stories in a nonjudgmental environment. As the number of abduction reports increased in the late 1980s, abductees were welcomed to the summer conferences and it was in these conferences that the sharp distinction between the two groups began to disappear.

Eventually, Sprinkle identified himself as a contactee. He also concluded that UFO activity was part of a larger program of what he termed "cosmic consciousness conditioning." The UFO entities, whether one thinks of them as being from outer space or another dimension, are attempting to move humanity into an understanding of themselves as cosmic citizens.

Sources:

Clark, Jerome. "Psychologist-Researcher Dr. R. Leo Sprinkle; Exclusive UFO Report Interview." *UFO Report* 3, no.2 (June 1976): 30–32, 72–76, 78.

Parnell, June O., and R. Leo Sprinkle. "Personality Characteristics of Persons Who Claim UFO Experiences." *Journal of UFO Studies* 2 [new series, 1990]: 45–58.

Sprinkle, R. Leo. "The Significance of UFO Experiences." In David Pursglove, ed. *Zen in the Art of Close Encounter.* Berkeley, Calif.: New Being Project, 1995.

———, ed. *Proceedings of the Rocky Mountain Conference on UFO Investigation.* Laramie: School of Extended Studies, 1980.

The Spunkie

A **goblin** similar to the Scottish **kelpie.** He was popularly believed to be an agent of Satan, and travelers who had lost their way were his special prey. Supposedly, he attracted his victim by means of a light, that looked like a reflection on a window not far away, but as the victim proceeded toward the light, it receded. However, the victim still followed the gleam until the spunkie lured him over a precipice or into a morass.

Sources:

Arrowsmith, Nancy, and George Moose. *A Field Guide to the Little People.* New York: Wallaby, 1977.

Squinting

A popular superstition that a squint was a bad omen. It was said that if you met a squint-eyed person, you should spit three times, to avert bad fortune. The superstition is an old one, and it was referred to in the treatise on **Fascination** (*de Fascino*) published in 1589 by Vairus, prior to the Benedictine Convent of St. Sophia in Benevento, Italy. In this work he stated "Let no servant ever hire himself to a squinting master."

Squire, J. R. M. (ca. 1860)

American medium and editor of the Spiritualist weekly *Banner of Light,* who visited England in 1859. He was introduced into society under the auspices of the medium **D. D. Home,** with whom he frequently held joint sittings. In the same year, the American minister presented Squire at court.

Lockhart Robertson described in the *Spiritual Magazine* (1860) some displays of psychic force in his sitting with Squire. Reportedly, a heavy circular table was tossed in the air and thrown on the bed when the medium placed his left hand on the surface; his other hand was held and his legs were tied to the chair on which he sat. Afterward, the table was twice lifted onto the head of Robertson and the medium.

SRI International

Contract research firm conducting advanced research in physics, electronics, bioengineering, and parapsychology. Originally affiliated with Stanford University, it became an independent organization in 1970. Some parapsychological research was conducted at SRI by **Harold E. Puthoff** and **Russell Targ** from 1973 through the end of the decade concerning psychics **Uri Geller** and **Ingo Swann.** Address: 333 Ravenswood Ave., Menlo Park, CA 94025-3493. Website: http://www.sri.com.

Sources:

Berger, Arthur S., and Joyce Berger. *The Encyclopedia of Parapsychology and Psychical Research.* New York: Paragon House, 1991.

SRI International Home Page. http://www.sri.com/. April 14, 2000.

Targ, Russell, and Harold E. Puthoff. *Mind Reach: Scientists Look at Psychical Research.* New York: Delacorte Press, 1977.

SRU

The SRU, formerly the **Synchronicty Research Unit,** is a foundation founded in the Netherlands by Jeff C. Jacobs, a Dutch engineer and statistician. He brought together a team of researchers that included Scottish parapsychologist Brian Miller, who now resides in the Netherlands, to pursue theoretical speculation on the basis of psychic phenomena and to carry out a directed program of research. During the decade of its existence, research has focused on psi-guided awakenings from sleep and theoretical speculation on the problem of the possible influence of the observer on psychic events (a particular interest of Miller's). With the cutback of research at the University of Utrecht, the SRU has emerged as one of the most productive centers of Dutch psychical research. It may be contacted at P.O. Box 7625, 5601 JP Eindhoven, The Netherlands.

Stafford-Clark, David (1916–)

British consulting physician and authority on psychiatry with interests in parapsychology. He was born March 17, 1916, in Bromley, Kent, England and studied at Guy's Hospital, London, and the University of London (M.D.).

Stafford-Clark was a consulting physician at the Department of Psychological Medicine, Guy's Hospital (1950–74), Bethlem Royal and Maudsley Hospitals, and the Institute of Psychiatry from 1954. He was a member of the Archbishop of Canterbury's Commission of Divine Healing, and attended the Conferences on Parapsychology and Pharmacology in July 1959 at St. Paul de Vence, France. Stafford-Clark has authored a number of books, though none on parapsychology.

Sources:

Pleasants, Helene, ed. *Biographical Dictionary of Parapsychology.* New York: Helix Press, 1964.

Stanford, Rex G(ale) (1938–)

Stanford was born June 21, 1938, in Robstown, Texas, and received both his B.A. (1963) and Ph.D. (1967) in psychology from the University of Texas at Austin. He received Summer

Research Fellowships from the Parapsychology Laboratory at Duke University in 1964, 1965, and 1966. He was a research associate at the **Division of Parapsychology,** Department of Psychiatry, University of Virginia School of Medicine (1968–75). From 1976 through 1980, he directed the center for Parapsychological Research, the research division of the former nonprofit corporation, and the Association for the Understanding of Man (led by his brother, psychic Ray Stanford). Stanford then joined the faculty in psychology at St. John's University, Jamaica, New York, where he currently teaches.

Stanford is especially interested in the development and experimental testing of models for spontaneous psi, the factors involved in **extrasensory perception** (ESP) response, and the basic nature of psi events. He was vice-president (1970–71) and then president (1973) of the **Parapsychological Association.** He also served on the Publication Committee of the **American Society for Psychical Research.** He was a participant in the symposium "Parapsychology (Psi) Processes; Towards a Conceptual Integration" held at the annual convention of the American Psychological Association, Montreal, August 27–31, 1973. Stanford is the author on numerous papers on parapsychological topics.

Sources:

Berger, Arthur S., and Joyce Berger. *The Encyclopedia of Parapsychology and Psychical Research.* New York: Paragon House, 1991.

Stanford, Rex G. "Case Studies, Folklore and Personal Experiences of Investigators: Their Role in Experimental Research." In *Spontaneous Psi, Depth Psychology and Parapsychology,* edited by Betty Shapin and Lisette Coly. New York: Parapsychology Foundation, 1992.

———. "Scientific, Ethical and Clinical Problems in the 'Training' of Psi Ability." In *Research in Parapsychology 1976,* edited by William G. Roll and R. L. Morris. Metuchen, N.J.: Scarecrow Press, 1977.

———. "A Study of the Cause of Low Run-Score Variance." *Journal of Parapsychology* 30 (1966).

Stanford Research Institute See SRI International

Stanislawa P. (ca. 1930)

Polish medium, wife of a Polish officer, and subject of psychical experiments by **Baron Schrenck-Notzing** for research **materialization.** At the age of eighteen, Stanislaw believed she saw the phantom of a friend, Sophie M., at the exact time she died. Soon afterward spontaneous **telekinesis** phenomena developed. After Stanislawa joined a Spiritualist circle, "Sophie M." began to materialize through her and "Sophie" became the medium's permanent attendant, occasionally sharing control with "Adalbert" and a young Polish boy.

In 1911, P. Lebiedzinski, a Polish engineer, began a series of experimental séances that lasted intermittently until 1916. His report, published in the *Revue Métapsychique* (1921, no. 4) was favorable. Schrenck-Notzing's experiments began in 1913. After a few months, Stanislawa's mediumship lapsed and did not return until 1915. In 1906, when Schrenck-Notzing recommenced his séance observations, he became assured that Stanislawa produced flows of **ectoplasm.** Schreneck-Notzing took many photographs.

In 1930, her reputation, based on the early favorable reports, suffered a blow. Stanislawa appeared at the **Institut Métapsychique** shortly after a special automatic registering apparatus for phenomena produced in the dark was installed. She produced nearly blank séances until assured that no registering apparatus would remain in the room.

Eugene Osty suspected that the abortive phenomena noticed in séance was brought about by Stanislawa's secretly freed hand. He decided to attempt to catch her in the act. During a later séance, when Osty heard the objects on the table move, he exploded a secret flashlight and took three stereoscopic photographs. Both the sudden light and the developed photographs showed that Stanislawa's hand was free and manipulating the table.

Osty concluded in the *Revue Métapsychique* (Nov.–Dec. 1930): 1) Stanislawa played a joke on the Institute; 2) her **fraud** was persevering and organized; 3) her procedure consisted of giving the illusion of being restrained while she temporarily disengaged one of her hands from the restraints; and 4) used this procedure to displace objects and show luminous movements. Osty, however, hastened to add that his findings made no attempt to judge the phenomena of Stanislawa that were produced elsewhere.

Stapleton, Ruth Carter (1929–1983)

Evangelist, healer, and sister of U.S. president Jimmy Carter. She was born August 7, 1929, in Plains, Georgia. After two years of the Georgia State College for Women, she married Robert Stapleton, a veterinarian, and they settled in North Carolina. She became the mother of four children.

Her career as a healer dates from her own recovery from periods of deep depression. She combined attendance at group therapy sessions with an interdenominational retreat at a North Carolina hotel and "experienced God as a God of love." Some three months later she attended a second retreat and came in contact with Pentecostalism. She received the baptism of the Holy Spirit in a Pentecostal meeting and experienced its definitive manifestation, speaking in **tongues.**

She subsequently developed her own kind of healing technique, which might be described as a spiritually-based psychotherapy. She combined prayer with a probing of the unhappy memories of the individuals who sought her help. She taught them to recreate painful past experiences in a "guided daydream" in which the figure of Jesus is introduced to neutralize emotional difficulties by love and forgiveness.

In her book *The Gift of Inner Healing* (1976), she describes her work over nine years with various Christian groups. She preached and prayed for Roman Catholics as well as Protestants at her spiritual workshops in over 70 American cities and abroad in Indonesia, Malaysia, Japan, and Britain. She rejected the label of "faith healer," since she claimed God is the healer, but was also involved in more traditional healing of physical ailments by means of prayer.

In 1977, Stapleton hit the headlines when she was instrumental in bringing religious conviction to Larry C. Flynt, editor of the pornographic *Hustler* magazine. On February 8, 1977, Flynt was been found guilty of engaging in organized crime and pandering to obscenity. CBS News producer Joe Wershba introduced Flynt to Stapleton, and after a discussion on religion and sexual repression, Flynt claims a religious conversion was set in motion. According to his own account, Flynt discovered God at 40,000 feet while on a flight from Denver to Houston.

Subsequently, both Stapleton and Flynt appeared together on the *Today* program on November 23, 1977, when Flynt publicly acknowledged that God had entered his life and that henceforth his magazine would introduce a religious element. *Hustler* would be transformed into a religious magazine, and Flynt's multimillion-dollar empire would be turned into a nonprofit religious foundation. At a Pentecostal congregation in Houston, Flynt stated: "I owe every woman in America an apology." Flynt did not carry through, and *Hustler* remains a pornographic publication.

Stapleton was plunged into the spotlight by the election of her brother to the presidency in 1976. Through those years she wrote three more books and continued an active life of traveling and speaking. Then in 1983 she discovered that she had cancer, but refused standard medical treatment, turning instead to a macrobiotic diet, meditation, and reliance on God's healing power. She died September 26, 1983, at Fayetteville, North Carolina.

Sources:

Stapleton, Ruth Carter. *The Experience of Inner Healing.* Waco, Tex.: Word Books, 1977.

———. *The Gift of Inner Healing.* Waco, Tex.: Word Books, 1976.

———. *In His Footsteps.* San Francisco: Harper & Row, 1979.

Star, Ely

Pseudonym of Eugène Jacob (1847–1942), French astrologer and medical charlatan. He was a member of the Ahathoor (or Athoor) Temple of the **Golden Dawn.** He was prosecuted and sentenced for **fraud** in 1914.

Star-Esseenia Temple of Ascension Mastery

The Star-Esseenia Temple of Ascension Mastery is a channeling group that grew out of the intense experience of former **Reiki** healer August Stahr during the 1991 solar eclipse. She has described the experience as a walk-in type experience, but one in which her own higher energy self was the entity that stepped in. At that time she was also told to abandon the Reiki and the related Seichem healing systems, as she would soon be bringing in a new set of fifth-dimensional energies that would be needed to assist in the coming **ascension** of the individuals on the planet. Since that time, Stahr has functioned as a healer, a channel, and Quadrant Commander of the Star Esseenia Division. She concentrates her efforts in the training of people to use these healing modalities in the effort to facilitate planetary ascension. In that effort she has discovered a number of new higher healing energies which she has named and to which she offers attunement.

Stahr has also seen herself as operating in the program developed by Solara of **Starborne Unlimited** around the symbol of 11:11. According to Stahr, 11:11 triggers a precoded response in humans indicating the time of completion or ascension. On January 11, 1992, Solara opened the 11:11 doorway that will remain open until December 31, 2011. The doorway includes 11 gates and levels of consciousness. The journey through the levels of consciousness will move us from the present ways of living in duality to the new way of living as ascended beings.

It is believed that at 11 moments during the period between 1992 and 2011, those on the ascension pathway will collectively experience a common issue (or set of related issues). These issues have been released for the purpose of clearing (removing them). Thus in 1992, at the first gate, financial survival issues were released. Once cleared by a realignment to God, the individual can move on to abundance. The second issues, concerning personal relationships, were released in the summer of 1993. In clearing them, everything not related to Divine Love must be abandoned. The third set of issues relates to the sense of personal power. Stahr has indicated the projected course of issue releasement through the time of the closing of the gate.

As each set of issues has been released, Stahr has developed healing modalities for dealing with them. In 1995, she also initiated the Star Team Mastery Program that would allow people to do their own clearing for ascension with her as the guide, rather than relying on Stahr alone to be their healer/facilitator for the cleansing process. Those who align with the program are initially linked up with a Star Team, a group of spirit beings specially trained for the healing needs of the ascension process. This linkup occurs in private sessions with Stahr over a year; individuals are trained to work with the Star Team and are attuned to the new healing energies with which she has come into contact since 1991. Those who complete the program and begin to work with the Star-Esseenia Technologies constitute the Star-Esseenia Temple.

Stahr has authored a number of self-published books that are used by Star-Esseenia members, including *Reality Maintenance 101* (1993), *Implants and Imprints: A Healer's View of Ascension Clearing* (1996), *Spiritual Discernment, Volume One: Sananda's Heart Initiation* (1996), and *Daily Ascension* (1996). The Star-Esseenia Temple of Ascension Mastery is headquartered at 10064 Oglethorpe Way, Elk Grove, CA 95758. It may be contacted through its website at http://www.star-esseenia.org/.

Sources:

Star-Esseenia Temple of Ascension Mastery. http://www.star-esseenia.org/. February 28, 2000.

Stargate

Stargate is a name Americans came to know in the 1990s, first as the name of a television series concerning a doorway that allowed instantaneous travel between planets in different star systems. Then in 1995, the U.S. government announced that it had been carrying on secret parapsychological research, the last phase of which had been given the name Project STAR GATE. Not as well-known, in 1991 Mark Roberts (1934–), an independent spiritual searcher, found what he had termed the real Stargate, an ancient painting of the constellation **Pleiades** located at the entrance to a cave. He believes the painting to be a presentation of a cosmic-portal. The painting seems to connect decades of studies in archeology of Egypt, an ancient alphabet (Ogham), and ancient symbols of the Pleiades. The portal seems to point toward ancient visitors to Earth. The real Stargate provides a mental doorway to step into a new consciousness where massive amounts of materials may be connected, mysteries of the ancient past solved, and contact with extraterrestrials established.

Roberts grew up in Oklahoma during the Dust Bowl era. He had several experiences, which he now interprets as extraterrestrial contacts, but then interpreted as a call to the ministry. After two years as a Methodist minister, he left to become an archeologist. His life traveling the world on archeological digs allowed him to pursue his search for what he had come to see as the spirituality he believed lay behind and contrasted with the religious establishment.

He also was able to study with Arch Druid Thomas Maughn and Margaret Lumley Brown, an associate of **Dion Fortune,** founder of the **Fraternity of the Inner Light.** In the early 1970s he was led to Dianic Wicca, that form of contemporary **Witchcraft** that most emphasized feminism. He also changed occupation within television. Over the next quarter of a century, he moved from cameraman to stage manager to director in television programming.

Since his discovery of the Stargate, and the announcement of it at a meeting of the **Mutual UFO Network** in 1992, Roberts has invited others to share the Quest, especially those drawn by the keys and symbols pictured on the Stargate. From the contemplation of the Stargate, research during the 1990s reached a set of conclusions that now serves as a base for future development. Roberts believes that Earth has been visited many times, from the distant past to the present, by visitors from the Pleiades and Sirius. The set of actual artifacts denoting Sirius and the Pleiades tie together the archeology of the ancient world with the extraterrestrial presence. That presence had a primarily positive effect. The extraterrestrials made judgments about human behavior and offered positive guidelines for human evolution.

Roberts also believes that the **crop circles** reported around the world in the 1990s are related to extraterrestrials.

The Stargate project can be contacted through the Stargate Internet site at http://home.earthlink.net/~pleiades/.

Sources:

Roberts, Mark. *An Introduction to Dianic Witchcraft.* Dallas, Tex.: The Mother Grove, n.d.

Stargate. http://home.earthlink.net/~pleiades/. April 19, 2000.

Starhawk

Starhawk is the public name of Wiccan priestess Miriam Simos. She is an international spokesperson for neo-paganism, feminist concerns, and social activism. Through the 1970s she studied magic and witchcraft with a succession of prominent teachers, including Sara Cunningham of the Temple of Tiperath, Victor H. Anderson (founder of the Faery tradition), and Zsuzsanna E. Budapest.

In the mid-1970s she founded the Compost Coven and was one of the original signers of the **Covenant of the Goddess** (COG), serving as COG's first officer in 1976–77. She cofounded Reclaiming: A Center for Feminist Spirituality and Counseling in Berkeley, California, for which she served as a director, teacher, and counselor.

In 1979 Starhawk wrote the first of her three books, *The Spiral Dance,* a textbook on **witchcraft** that became one of the most popular introductions to **Wicca** in the 1980s. In the wake of the book's success, Starhawk lectured extensively in both America and Europe. She followed it with *Dreaming in the Dark* (1982) and *Truth or Dare* (1987). During the late 1980s Starhawk figured in the conflict between Catholic priest Matthew Fox and the Roman Catholic Church. Among many complaints, church officials objected to Fox using Starhawk as a faculty member at his Institute in Culture and Creation Spirituality at Holy Names College in Oakland, California. Most recently Fox has left the Roman Catholic Church.

Sources:

Starhawk. *Dreaming in the Dark.* Boston: Beacon Press, 1982.

———. *The Spiral Dance.* San Francisco: Harper & Row, 1979.

———. *Truth or Dare: Encounters of Power, Authority, Mystery.* San Francisco: Harper & Row, 1987.

Statues, Moving

The belief that images of gods, goddesses, and saints might become imbued with divine force and acquire movement is an ancient one, and such miracles have been reported of both Christian and nonChristian images. In the 1980s, the belief was revived in Ireland, where a statue of the Virgin Mary at **Ballinspittle,** County Cork, attracted nationwide interest after claims by many witnesses that they had seen it move.

Moving Statues in Ancient History

Many reports of miraculous statues in pagan times were undoubtedly fraudulent, just as there are known cases of moving statue hoaxes in modern times. It is well known that ancient peoples constructed lifelike images of their gods and goddesses.

Plato and Aristotle stated that the Greek Daedalus was said to have made statues that not only walked but also needed to be tethered at night to prevent them from walking away. Aristotle described a wooden statue of Venus that moved as a result of quicksilver being poured into the interior. Pliny reported that the architect Timochares began using loadstone (magnetized ore) to construct the vaulting in the temple of Arsinoê at Alexandria, to suspended in midair an iron statue inside. Such a levitating statue would have been a great wonder if the plan had succeeded. Procopius described a complex clock that the engineers for the ancient Romans were responsible for having figures of gods and heroes that moved on the hour.

Lucian related how a certain Alexander caused a statue of Aesculapius to speak by using the gullet of a crane to transmit a voice through the mouth of the statue. In the fourth century, Bishop Theophilus described statues at Alexandria that he broke open and discovered to be hollow; they were placed against a wall in such a position that priests could slip behind them and speak.

It was believed that in ancient Egypt there were numerous statues of gods, said to deliver oracles. The *Pymander Asclepios* (attributed to Hermes Trismegistus) asserted the Egyptians "knew how to make gods," i.e., to install deities, angels, or demons in statues, with the power to do good or evil. Although such statues have not survived, it seems probable that they were animated by priests. The archaeologist Gaston Maspéro (1846–1916) stated (*Journal des Debats,* December 21, 1898):

"There were thus obtained genuine terrestrial gods, exact counterparts of the celestial gods, and, as their ambassadors here below, capable of protecting, punishing and instructing men, of sending them dreams and delivering oracles.

"When these idols were addressed, they replied either by gesture or by voice. They would speak and utter the right verdict on any particular questions. They moved their arms and shook their heads to an invariable rhythm. . . . And as they assuredly did nothing of all this by themselves, someone had to do it for them. Indeed, there were priests in the temples whose business it was to attend to these things. Their functions, being anything but secret, were carried out openly, in the sight and to the knowledge of all. They had their appointed places in ceremonies, in processions and the sacerdotal hierarchy; each individual knew that they were the voice or the hand of the god, and that they pulled the string to set his head wagging at the right moment. Consequently this was not one of those pious frauds which the moderns always suspect in like circumstances; no one was ignorant that the divine consultation was brought about by this purely human agency.

"Things being so, one wonders how not only the people but the kings, nobles, and scribes could have confidence in advice thus proffered. . . . The testimony afforded by monuments compels us to acknowledge that it was taken seriously until paganism died a natural death, and that all who played any part in it did so with the utmost respect. They had been brought up from childhood to believe that divine souls animated the statues, to approach these living statues only in the most respectful dread and awe. . . . Their mental attitude was that of the modern-day priest who ascends the altar. No sooner has he donned the sacerdotal garb and repeated the first few sacramental words than he no longer belongs to himself but to the sacrifice he is about to consummate; he knows that at this voice and gesture the elements will change into precious blood and flesh, and he continues unperturbed the work which he is certain he can accomplish."

Such a reverential attitude to manipulating statues, if true, offers an alternative theory to views of either miracle or **fraud.** Similarly, in some societies, **shamans** may invoke divine inspiration by initial trickery, acting out a miraculous situation by conjuring tricks as a preliminary to creating the emotional atmosphere in which heightened consciousness and genuine phenomena may arise.

However, there are also many claims in both ancient and modern times that statues have actually moved independently of humans. In some cases, rival religions did not deny the miracles but asserted that they were demonic, not divine. In analyzing a passage from Hermes Trismegistus concerned with "statues animated by divine association, which do great things, foretell the future and heal diseases," St. Augustine did not dispute the claims, but commented that "this art of binding genii to statues is an ungodly art . . . Instead of serving men, these would-be gods can do nothing, except as devils" (*Civitas Dei,* book 8, chapters 23, 24). The Synod of Laodicea defined idolatry as "the art of invoking demons and incorporating them in statues."

Moving Statues in Modern History

Throughout history, moving statues have tended to be reported at times of civil, political, or religious crisis, in which a breakdown of morale or the imminence of national disaster seemed beyond human aid, inviting divine intervention. In 1524, Italy was overrun by French armies and coping with floods, famine, and plague. During this time, when Rome itself seemed threatened, a statue of the Virgin Mary at Brescia was reported to open and close its eyes and to move its hands, bringing them together and separating them in a gesture of sympathy. Thousands of witnesses attested to the phenomenon, and similar moving statues were reported in other towns. After the crisis, such miracles ceased.

A similar event took place in 1716, when Turkish forces threatened war on Venice. One man claimed that the Virgin Mary had appeared to him in a vision and stated that if enough prayers for souls in purgatory were offered up, the infidels would be defeated. A crowd assembled in front of a statue of the Virgin Mary, and some of those present later declared that the statue opened and closed its eyes to confirm what the visionary had stated. The senate of the city and the local bishop affirmed their belief in the reality of the phenomenon.

Eighty years later, when the French revolutionary forces threatened the Papal States during 1796–97 there were numerous reports of Virgin Mary statues opening and closing their eyes or shedding tears. These miracles were claimed in many churches in Rome and also all over the country. A papal commission examined over nine hundred witnesses and reported favorably on the reality of the phenomena. The manifestations subsided when Napoleon Bonaparte entered the Italian seaport town of Ancona and ordered the statue of the Virgin Mary, which had been one of those reported to move, to be covered up.

In 1870, at Soriano, Calabria, Spain, there were reports of a statue that appeared to move its hand and arm. In 1919, at Limpias, Santander, Spain, pictures of saints were reported to move their eyes or drip blood, some even stepping out of their panels. Hundreds of sworn statements attesting to such miracles were obtained. Many similar incidents were reported in Spain, in 1893 at Campocavallo and on five separate occasions at Rimini between 1850 and 1905. In the latter cases, paintings of saints were said to shed tears.

The reports from Limpias, Spain, were investigated by Professor A. Encinas of Santander University, who compared notes with the scientist E. R. Jaensch. These and similar cases were ascribed to collective hallucination, specifically arising from the psychological phenomenon of eidetic imagery.

In his book *The Mechanism of Thought, Imagery and Hallucination* (1939), J. Rosett commented: "The reports of mystics and of devotees about pictures and statues which moved and spoke like living persons and performed miracles are . . . not necessarily fraudulent. An understanding of the mechanism of attention and its relation to the state of falling asleep, and of the hallucinations associated with that state, offers a rational explanation of such reports."

According to Jaensch in his important study *Eidetic Imagery* (1930):

"Topical perceptual (or eidetic) images are phenomena that take up an intermediate position between sensations and images. Like ordinary physiological after-images, they are always *seen* in the literal sense. They have this property of necessity and under all conditions, and share it with sensations. In other respects they can also exhibit the properties of images (*Vorstellungen*). In those cases in which the imagination has little influence, they are merely modified after-images, deviating from the norm in a definite way, and when that influence is nearly, or completely zero, we can look upon them as slightly intensified after-images. In the other limiting case, when the influence of the imagination is at its maximum, they are ideas that, like after-images, are projected outward and literally *seen.*"

Eidetic imagery has relevance to the visual faculty of artists, who can "see" their subject on the blank paper or canvas. It may also have relevance to the phenomenon of **crystal gazing.** The existence of various explanations for moving statues—deliberate fraud, sacramental or ritualistic manipulation, hallucination through eidetic imagery—offers a number of explanations that must be discarded before any claims of paranormal phenomena can be considered.

It would be wrong to assume that moving statues belong only to earlier history. In 1985, there were numerous reports of statues moving, bleeding, or weeping throughout Ireland. Cases were reported from over thirty localities during a few months of that year. Interestingly enough, no cases were reported from Northern Ireland during this period, although there is a large Catholic population there.

Characteristically, the period was one of cultural, political, and religious unrest. The cultural unease was focused around a 1983 referendum on amending the constitution to protect the rights of unborn children. New legislation liberalizing the availability of contraceptives and the promise of a referendum on the issue of divorce (not permitted by the constitution) had excited conservative protests. All this came to a head with the 1985 judicial inquiry into the case of an infant corpse discovered with stab wounds in Chirciveen.

It was against this background that statues of the Virgin Mary were reported as moving throughout Ireland. It began on February 14, when several children in Asdee, County Kerry, claimed to have seen a statue of the Madonna and child at the parish church of St. Mary open its eyes and move its hands. An eighty-year-old farmer also stated that he saw the Madonna blink three times. Thousands of people visited the church, but there were no further reports.

A few weeks later, children at Ballydesmond, County Cork, stated that they saw a statue move in the local church, but parents ascribed this to their imaginations. A group of tourists at Courtmacsharry, County Cork, claimed to have seen a statue near the town move, but no other movements were reported and the affair died down.

In July, two teenage girls reported seeing movement in a statue of the Virgin Mary in a grotto some 20 feet up on the side of a hill at Ballinspittle. Soon other people reported seeing the statue change expression or move, and large crowds gathered regularly to watch and recite the rosary. Many people claimed to have seen the Virgin's eyes or hands move, or the statue to move back and forth or sway from side to side. Thousands of pilgrims visited the shrine, which became the central focus for stories of statues that moved. Pilgrimages and reports of moving statues persisted for over three months and subsided at the end of October, when vandals smashed the hands and face of the statue with an axe and a hammer.

Meanwhile, throughout August and September, further reports of phenomena associated with the Virgin Mary came from all over the Ireland. In Mitchelstown, County Cork, children stated they had seen black blood flowing from a statue of the Virgin Mary and an apparition of the devil had appeared behind the statue. Many pilgrims gathered, and other young people claimed they saw the statue move. Four teenage girls said a statue at the local Marian shrine spoke to them and called for peace.

In Dunkitt, County Waterford, a statue of the Virgin Mary in a grotto on the main Waterford to Kilkenny road was reported to have been seen moving. Some people claimed the statue breathed and the hands moved from center to right. A local publican and his wife stated the statue shimmered. Thousands of pilgrims visited the grotto.

In Waterford, two young boys stated a statue of the Virgin Mary outside the Mercy Convent School moved its eyes, which were full of tears, and spoke of Pope John Paul II being assassinated. Hundreds of people kept vigil around the statue. At Mooncoin, County Waterford, several youths stated they saw a statue move, and a girl said she saw a tear fall from the right eye of the statue and the left eye open and close. Local people gathered at the site.

In the scores of cases reported from all over the country, it seems the statues *appeared* to move, rather than physically shifting position. Psychologists pointed out that staring at statues in dim light, especially with a glare from an illuminated halo, could result in optical illusions. However, the essential and more elusive aspect of the phenomenon was the religious fervor associated with it, and the feelings of spiritual grace experienced by many individuals.

Staus Poltergeist

Between 1860–62, the village of Staus, on the shores of Lake Lucerne, **Switzerland,** was the scene of a reported case of **poltergeist** haunting. The outbreak occurred in the house of M. Joller, a lawyer and a member of the Swiss national council. The household comprised Joller, his wife, seven children (four boys and three girls), and a maid. One night in the autumn of 1860, the maid was disturbed by a loud rapping on her bed frame that she regarded as an omen of death. Joller ascribed the sounds to the girl's imagination and forbade her to speak about them.

A few weeks later, returning after a short absence, Joller found his family alarmed. The knocks had been repeated in the presence of his wife and daughter. A few days later, the family received news of a friend's death and they imagined this must have been what the raps portended.

The outbreak was renewed in June 1861. This time one of the boys fainted at the apparition of a white, indistinct figure. Supposedly, the children began to see and hear other strange things and a few months later the maid complained that the kitchen was haunted by dim, grey shapes who followed her to her bedroom and sobbed all night in the lumber-room.

In October of the same year, the maid was replaced, the rappings ceased, and the disturbances seemed to be at an end. The disturbances returned in August 1862, during the absence of Joller, his wife, and their eldest son on business. Reportedly, the annoyance was so bad that the children fled from the house into the garden, in spite of their father's threat of punishment.

Later, the poltergeist supposedly began to persecute Joller himself, pursuing him from room to room with loud knocks. Reportedly, items were thrown by invisible hands, locked doors and fastened windows were flung open, and strange music, voices, and the humming of spinning wheels were heard.

In spite of Joller's attempts to conceal these happenings, the news spread abroad and people came to witness the phenomena. Finding no rational hypothesis to fit the circumstances, Joller requested the Commissary Niederberger to come and investigate. Niederberger was unavailable so Father Guardian visited the house and blessed it. Reportedly, this did not stop the disturbances and Guardian suggested an inquiry be made by men of authority.

Joller privately called in several scientists he knew, but they also were unable to find a solution, although various theories of electricity, galvanism, and magnetism were advanced. Other authorities were present while Niederberger and Guardian examined the house without discovering any cause for the disturbances, which had continued unabated.

Later, Joller requested a formal examination by the police, and three police were chosen to investigate. The Joller family left and for six days the police occupied the house. At the end of that period, having neither heard nor seen any sign of the poltergeist, they wrote a report to that effect and left the house.

When the Jollers returned to the house, supposedly the phenomena started again. Joller found it impossible to carry on his business and in October 1862, he left his ancestral home forever. The following spring he found a tenant for the house in Staus, but the poltergeist outbreak was not renewed.

St. Chad (620 C.E.–672 C.E.)

According to the hagiography of the Roman Catholic church, St. Chad was a bishop born in what is now England around 620 C.E. He was the youngest of four brothers, two of whom, Cynebil and Caelin, became priests; the other, Cedd, also became a bishop. He was educated at the monastery at Lindisfarne under St. Aidain, and following the advice of his mentor, he lived close to his people and always traveled on foot. In 664, Cedd was serving as the bishop of East Saxons (London). Making his rounds, he arrived at the monastery of Lastingham where Cynebil lay dying of the plague. When Cedd also became ill, he sent for Chad, who became the new abbot at Lastingham.

Meanwhile, Chad had become the bishop of York. This was at the time when the Roman tradition was replacing the Celtic tradition in the Church in England. Five years after his consecration, the archbishop of Canterbury noted that Chad had an irregularity in his past, as he had been ordained as a priest by two Celtic bishops. He asked Chad to step down, and Chad retired to the monastery at Lastingham. His ordination problem was corrected and he soon assumed duties as bishop of Mercia (Lichfield).

In 672, the plague swept through England again and Chad became ill. At the time, he resided with a small group of monks at the monastery at Lichfield. One day Chad called the brothers together and announced that he would soon leave them and admonished them to live together in peace and observe the rules of their order after his passing. He died later that day, and one of the brothers testified that he had earlier heard angelic singing coming from the oratory where the bishop had been praying. The angels had come to summon Chad to heaven. His death occurred on March 2, 672.

Chad soon became a focus of healing stories, and he was eventually canonized. His relics (bones) were moved on several occasions but placed in a special shrine in the cathedral by the bishop of Lichfield in the fourteenth century. When Henry VIII broke with the Roman Church and outlawed the cult of relics, the bones were removed from the shrine and kept quietly in the homes of loyal Roman Catholics until 1841, when they were placed in the new Roman Catholic Cathedral, which was dedicated to St. Chad, in Birmingham.

Modern scholars have charged that Chad and his brother never existed. They allege that he and his brother Cedd are variants of the Pagan deity Ceadda and emerged as the Roman Catholics gained dominance in the formerly Celtic Pagan area. Ceadda was associated with healing springs, a theme that flowed into the legend around St. Chad. He remains a saint on the Roman calendar, however, and churches are dedicated to him throughout the English-speaking world. There are also several ancient wells in the British Midland dedicated to him.

Sources:

Brewster, H. Pomeroy. *Saints and Festivals of the Christian Church.* New York: Frederick A. Stokes Co., 1904.

Walker, Barbara. *The Woman's Encyclopedia of Myths and Secrets.* San Francisco: Harper, 1983.

St. Clair, David (1932–1991)

Actor, journalist, writer, and lecturer on the occult. He was born on October 2, 1932, in Newton Falls, Ohio. He was educated at Columbia University and the New School for Social Research. He spent five years as a professional actor in summer stock as well as did some television work.

In 1956 he went to Mexico and started to travel by land into Central and South America; he reached Brazil, where he worked full-time for *Time* and *Life* until 1965. Afterward he became a freelance writer and lecturer. He had a strong interest in the occult and investigated local occult practices everywhere he traveled. He made expeditions into the Amazon and Mato Grosso jungles, lived with Indians, and was initiated into voudou temples. St. Clair stated, "I've talked to spirits, communicated with and even photographed a ghost, but the living still interest me more than the dead. I believe in the spirit world, in reincarnation, and in spirit intervention in our lives. I've seen too much of it *not* to believe." His experience became the basis of a number of books.

Sources:

St. Clair, David. *David St. Clair's Lessons in Instant ESP.* Englewood Cliffs, N.J.: Prentice Hall, 1978.

———. *Drum and Candle.* Garden City, N.Y.: Doubleday, 1971.

———. *Psychic Healers.* Garden City, N.Y.: Doubleday, 1974.

———. *The Psychic World of California.* Garden City, N.Y.: Doubleday, 1972.

———. *Watseka: America's Most Extraordinary Case of Possession & Exorcism.* Chicago: Playboy Press; 1977. Distributed by Simon & Schuster.

Stead, William T(homas) (1849–1912)

British editor, journalist, publicist, and champion of **Spiritualism.** He was born July 5, 1849, at Embleton, Northumberland, England, the son of a Congregationalist minister. He was first educated by his father, then attended school in Wakefield.

In 1863, Stead left school to apprentice in a merchant's countinghouse in Newcastle-on-Tyne. At the age of eighteen, he was impressed by the poems of James Russell Lowell and resolved to dedicate his life to helping other people. Throughout his subsequent career as an editor, he campaigned for truth and justice. In 1880, while editing the *Northern Echo* at Darlington, England, he protested against the Bulgarian atrocities. The *Pall Mall Gazette* of London, a pro-Turk paper, unexpectedly changed owners, and he was offered the post of assistant editor. Three years later, he received full control of the paper.

Stead founded the *Review of Reviews* in 1890. His interest in psychic subjects was first demonstrated in the publication (as the Christmas issue of the *Review of Reviews*) of his book *Real Ghost Stories* in 1891. Next year it was followed by *More Ghost Stories.*

In 1892, Stead believed he discovered his ability to receive communications in **automatic writing.** This was the beginning of his psychic activities. Stead claimed proof of survival in the form of a message received through his hands, from Julia Ames. Ames was a journalist acquaintance and editor of *The Woman's Union Signal* of Chicago, who had died shortly before. On March 14, 1893, in an address to members of the **London Spiritualist Alliance,** Stead made his first public confession of faith, narrating the details of his discoveries and early psychic experiences.

Reportedly, a communication from "Julia" suggested he could obtain automatic scripts from living friends as well. He noted,

"I put my hand at the disposal of friends at various degrees of distance, and I found that, although the faculty varied, some friends could write extremely well, imitating at first the style of their own handwriting, sometimes for the first few words until they had more or less established their identity, and then going on to write exactly as they would write an ordinary letter. They would write what they were thinking about—whether they wanted to see me, or where they had been."

In 1893, Stead began publication of *Borderland,* a quarterly psychic magazine that ran until 1897, in which the "Letters from Julia" he had obtained automatically were published for the first time. They were printed in a book in 1897 under the title *After Death.*

Stead was assisted in the editorial work by Miss X. (**Ada Goodrich-Freer,** later Mrs. Hans Spoer). In her notes on the origin of *Borderland* she stated:

"Mr. Stead was as definitely spiritualist as I was definitely an anti-spiritualist. He believed in everybody until they were found out, and often afterwards, and he would seek to introduce into *Borderland* the lucubrations of people at whom as a disciple of Lavater I shuddered."

For the 1893 Christmas issue of *Review of Reviews,* Stead wrote a story entitled "From the Old World to the New," a fiction concerning the dangers of icebergs in the Atlantic Ocean. The story is set on a ship named the *Majestic* with Captain Smith as commander. Reportedly, this is the same Captain Smith who 21 years later goes down with the *Titanic.* The narrative pictures the sinking of the liner and depicts the Atlantic Ocean as a grave.

Stead's eldest son, Willie, died in December 1907. It is believed this incident demonstrated to him the need for consoling the bereaved. Reportedly, "Julia" always urged Stead to establish a "bureau" where free communication with the Beyond should serve inquirers.

Julia's Bureau was opened on April 24, 1909. A small circle of sensitives supposedly chosen by "Julia" herself met every morning at ten at Mowbray House, Norfolk St., London, W.C. Strangers were not admitted to this circle. The sittings were invariably held in broad daylight. **Robert King** was engaged as a special clairaudient and clairvoyant. When he was unable to attend, **Alfred Vout Peters** attended. Records were kept of private sittings. **Psychometry** (divination through material objects) was believed to be successful.

In the three years of its existence about 1,300 sittings were given in the bureau. Its maintenance cost Stead 1,500 pounds a year. Besides King and Peters, Mrs. Wesley Adams and J. J. Vango were employed as psychics.

In addition to "Julia," Stead claimed an influence, calling itself "Catherine II" of Russia, among his communicators. In the *Contemporary Review* for January 1909, under the title "The Arrival of the Slav," an article was published under Stead's name. It contained Catherine's "Manifesto to the Slavs," a singularly prophetic script made up of different Catherine messages obtained through the hands of Stead and his secretary.

Stead's review of **Sir Oliver Lodge**'s book *The Survival of Man* (1909) disclosed an experiment. Supposedly, while writing the review, it occurred to Stead to ask one of Sir Oliver's spirit friends on the other side to write the concluding passage of the review through two automatists, one of whom had read the book and one who had not. There was a distance of 70 miles between the two automatists. The second automatists did not know where the script of the first ended. In his review, Stead concluded the two automatists had performed satisfactorily.

As a result of his article "When the Door Opened" in the *Fortnightly Review,* the *Daily Chronicle* challenged Stead on the eve of general elections to obtain Gladstone's views on the political crisis. He consulted "Julia." Supposedly, she deprecated the attempt but did not forbid it. Accordingly, King listened for a clairaudient communication that seemed to come to Stead as though from a long distance. It was published to ridicule and public derision. Stead himself did not claim that it emanated from the spirit of Gladstone, but thought that it resembled the recorded utterances of Gladstone.

The sequel to this interview was obtained from scripts through a nonprofessional automatist as letters of further explanation. They were not published at the time. But in 1911, Admiral Usborne Moore telephoned Stead and informed him that during a séance in Detroit with the medium **Etta Wriedt,** "Gladstone" purported to speak and ask whether Moore remembered the name of the lady in England through whose hand he had given a message. The voice then gave the correct name. As the story of the "Gladstone" interview sequel was only known to a few, Stead considered this as a good test.

There was a constant dispute between Stead and the **Society for Psychical Research.** "What are known as psychical research methods," wrote Edith K. Harper in her book *Stead, the Man* (1918), "was abhorrent to him. He held them truly unscientific in the most extended meaning of the word. He said he would rather die in the workhouse than believe that anyone would tell him a deliberate falsehood for the mere purpose of deceiving him."

Speaking against the society in admitting evidence of communications from the dead, Stead drew, before the members of the Cosmos Club in 1909, a graphic, imaginary picture of himself, shipwrecked and drowning in the sea and calling frantically for help. He imagined that instead of throwing him a rope the rescuers would shout back: "Who are you? What is your name? 'I am Stead! W. T. Stead! I am drowning here in the sea. Throw me the rope. Be quick!' But instead of throwing me the rope they continue to shout back: 'How do we know you are Stead? Where were you born? Tell us the name of your grandmother.' "

The picture of a sinking ocean liner with its attendant horrors often recurred in Stead's writings. His earliest prediction took the form of a narrative by a survivor in the *Pall Mall Gazette.* It was attended by the following editorial note: "This is exactly what might take place if liners are sent to sea short of boats." Twenty-six years afterwards 1,600 lives were lost on the *Titanic,* due to a shortage of lifeboats, and Stead went down among them.

He was invited to speak at Carnegie Hall, New York, on April 21, 1912, on the subject of world peace. Before his departure on the *Titanic* he wrote to his secretary: "I feel as if something was going to happen, somewhere, or somehow. And that it will be for good . . ."

George Henslow's book *The Proofs of the Truths of Spiritualism* (1919) stated that Archdeacon **Thomas Colley** (who later printed a pamphlet *The Foreordained Wreck of the Titanic*) sent a forecast of the disaster to Stead and received the answer: "I sincerely hope that none of the misfortunes which you seem to think may happen, will happen; but I will keep your letter and will write to you when I come back."

Reportedly, Stead intended to bring Etta Wriedt, the Detroit **direct voice** medium, to England when he returned. Wriedt was waiting for him in New York. The *Titanic* was struck by an iceberg on the night of April 14, 1912. Supposedly, two nights later, "Dr. Sharp," Wriedt's **control,** gave a detailed account of the *Titanic* disaster, assured sitters of Stead's death and gave the names of some who went down with the ship. Reportedly, the following night, three days after his death, Stead himself communicated. Reportedly, his articulation was weak in the beginning but he was understood.

The messages which purported to emanate from Stead through automatic writing, direct voice, **materialization,** and **psychic photography** were summed up by James Coates in his book *Has W. T. Stead Returned?* (1913). Coates concluded the messages had established his identity. There was a W. T. Stead Memorial Society in Britain: c/o Victor Jones, "Rosamund," 7A Seagrave Ave. (Hants.), Hayling Island, PO11 9EU, England.

Sources:

Coates, James. *Has W. T. Stead Returned?* London: L. N. Fowler, 1913.

Harper, Edith K. *Stead, the Man.* London: W. Rider & Son, 1914.

Stead, William T. *After Death.* New York: John Lane, 1907. Reprint, London: Review of Reviews, 1914.

Steen, Douglas (1925–)

Researcher in finance, weather, astropsychology, and parapsychology. Steen was born on July 22, 1925, in Los Angeles, California and studied at the University of California at Los Angeles (M.A., 1951). He served in the United States Navy and as a mathematical physicist on guided missiles for the Northrop Air Corp. (1951–54). In 1954 he became a freelance researcher. He assisted at the Parapsychology Laboratory at Duke University in adapting four sports to dice-throwing for laboratory research in psychokinesis.

Sources:

Berger, Arthur S., and Joyce Berger. *The Encyclopedia of Parapsychology and Psychical Research.* New York: Paragon House, 1991.

Steen, Douglas. "Success with Complex Targets in a PK Baseball Game." *Journal of Parapsychology* (June 1957).

Steiger, Brad (1936–)

Popular writer on **UFOs, reincarnation,** and related paranormal subjects. Steiger was born Eugene E. Olson on February 19, 1936, in Bode, Iowa. He was educated at Luther College (1953–57) and the University of Iowa (1963). From 1957 to 1963 he was a high school English teacher in Clinton, Iowa, and then a literature and creative writing instructor at Luther College, Decorah, Iowa, from 1963 to 1967. In 1965 his first book, *Ghosts, Ghouls and Other Peculiar People,* was published. A series of paperbacks began to appear in 1966, and in 1967 Steiger became a full-time writer and lecturer on paranormal and ufological subjects.

Steiger produced a steady stream of books over the next 25 years (sometimes as many as six a year), and in their entirety they chronicle the whole range of paranormal subjects. He early turned his attention to UFOs with the 1966 *Strangers from the Skies.* He would go on to write more books on the subject than any other person (more than 15 titles). Three of these, *Aquarian Revelations* (1971), *Revelation: The Divine Fire* (1973), and *The Fellowship* (1988) remain important studies of the flying saucer contactee movement. In *Gods of Aquarius: UFOs and the Transformation of Man* (1976), he introduced the concept of "star people," human beings who are tied by some means, usually past lives, to extraterrestrials. Star people have reported contacts with otherworldly individuals who are preparing them for a transition through which humanity must go. *Gods of Aquarius* brought Steiger numerous letters from people claiming to be star people. He produced five books on the topic in the early 1980s.

Steiger had an important role in introducing **Paul Twitchell** and **ECKANKAR** to the American public. He wrote a chapter on Twitchell in an early book and followed it with an entire biographical treatment, *In My Soul I Am Free* (1968).

Throughout the 1970s Steiger manifested a strong interest in American indigenous cultures and produced important and empathetic books on the paranormal world of the Hawaiian Kahuna and of Native Americans. He also documented the careers of a number of prominent psychics, such as **Olof Jonsson** and **Irene Hughes.**

While Steiger has often presented a skeptical view of many of the claims of the people he discusses in his books, the overall result of his experience in the psychic and contactee community has been a belief that some external intelligence has been interacting with humanity in order both to learn about our species and to communicate some basic metaphysical truths.

Sources:

Clark, Jerome. *UFOs in the 1980s.* Vol. 1 of *The UFO Encyclopedia.* Detroit: Apogee Books, 1990.

Melton, J. Gordon, Jerome Clark, and Aidan A. Kelly. *New Age Encyclopedia.* Detroit: Gale Research, 1990.

Steiger, Brad. *Animal Miracles: Inspirational and Heroic True Stories.*

———. *Aquarian Revelations.* New York: Dell, 1971.

———. *Gods of Aquarius: UFOs and the Transformation of Man.* New York: Harcourt Brace Jovanovich, 1976.

———. *Guardian Angels and Spirit Guides: True Accounts of Benevolent Beings from the Other Side.* New York: Signet, 1998.

———. *He Walks with Me: True Encounters with Jesus.* New York: Signet, 1998.

———. *Revelation: The Divine Fire.* Englewood Cliffs, N.J.: Prentice-Hall, 1973.

———. *The Seed.* New York: Berkley Books, 1983.

———. *Shadow World.* New York: Signet, 2000.

———. *The Werewolf Book: The Encyclopedia of Shape-Shifting Beings.* Detroit: Visible Ink Press, 1999.

Steiger, Brad, and Sherry H. Steiger. *Mother Mary Speaks to Us.* n.p.: N A L, 1997.

Steiger, Brad, and Joan Whritenour. *New UFO Breakthrough.* New York: Award, 1968.

Steiner, Rudolf (1861–1925)

Founder of the **Anthroposophical Society.** He was born on February 27, 1861, at Kraljevic, **Austria,** but a year later his parents moved to Vienna. He grew up a Roman Catholic and attended a technical college in Vienna. While in college he attended lectures at the university, where he was attracted to the great German writer **Johann Wolfgang von Goethe.** He did intense study in Goethe's writings, in which he developed an expertise. Because of his technical background and his competence in the subject, he was invited to edit a critical edition of Goethe's scientific writings. Eventually he was offered a position at the Goethe Archives in Weimar.

As a young man Steiner became interested in the occult. He was a member of the **OTO** (Ordo Templi Orientis) for a brief period and in the late 1890s moved to Berlin, where he became affiliated with the **Theosophical Society.** He soon rose to leadership of the German section of the society.

Almost from the beginning Steiner had opposed what he considered a downplaying of Christ in Theosophical teachings. **Theosophy** considers Christ but one member of the vast spiritual hierarchy. His differences were brought to the fore, however, in 1910, with the announcement by international president **Annie Besant** that a young Indian boy was to be the new world savior. To Steiner, and many others who identified themselves as Theosophists, the emergence of **Jiddu Krishnamurti** and the formation of the **Order of the Star of the East** was very clearly an un-Christian statement. Steiner moved to oppose Besant and Krishnamurti by declaring that membership in the German section of the Theosophical Society and the Order of the Star were incompatible. Besant revoked the charter of the German section.

With 55 of the 65 chapters with him, Steiner in 1913 reorganized the membership as the Anthroposophical Society. The name of the organization was taken from a alchemical work by Thomas Vaughn, *Anthroposophia Theomagica.* He created a Gnostic-like theology and during the remaining years of his life wrote voluminously, developing his perspective in every area of life, especially art, education, natural farming, and religion. In 1922 he introduced the Christian Community as a related church structure for those members who wanted more traditional worship.

Steiner died on March 30, 1925, at Dornach, in German-speaking Switzerland. From there the movement was later able to survive the destruction of occultism in **Germany** by the Nazi regime. His movement began to spread internationally in the 1920s and is now represented across Europe and North America.

Sources:

Easton, Stewart. *Rudolf Steiner: Herald of a New Epoch.* Spring Valley, N.Y.: Anthroposophical Press, 1980.

Rittelmeyer, Friedrich. *Rudolf Steiner Enters My Life.* London: George Roberts, 1929.

Steiner, Rudolf. *Christianity as Mystical Fact.* West Nyack, N.Y.: Rudolf Steiner Publications, 1961.

———. *Cosmic Memory.* West Nyack, N.Y.: Rudolf Steiner Publications, 1959.

———. *The Course of My Life.* New York: Anthroposophical Press, 1951.

Wachmuth, Guenther. *The Life and Work of Rudolf Steiner.* New York: Whittier Books, 1955.

Steinschneider, Heinrich

Real name of famous clairvoyant and stage performer **Erik Jan Hanussen** (d. 1933), who established a reputation in Germany during the 1920s and 1930s.

Stella C. (Cranshaw) (ca. 1950)

A London hospital nurse whose mediumship was discovered by psychical researcher **Harry Price** in 1923. Price met Stella C. by chance when they shared a compartment on a train. During a casual conversation on psychical matters it was apparent she had psychic gifts. She gave a series of sittings in Price's **National Laboratory of Psychical Research** in London. **Telekinesis** phenomena were reportedly produced, with changes in temperature that were recorded by a self-registering thermometer. On many occasions, the temperature in the séance room was found to be lower.

Price read a paper on the subject before the Third International Congress for Psychical Research in Paris. It was entitled: "Some Account of the Thermal Variations as Recorded During the Trance State of the Psychic Stella C." The physical phenomena of **raps, movements,** and **levitations** of the table took place under stringent conditions.

Price developed a trick table that has since became famous. This table was a double table, the inner one fitting into a table rim of four legs. The space under the table was barred by strips of wood connecting the legs of the outer table. The inner table had a shelf nearly as large as the top. This shelf was surrounded on the sides by gauze of a fine mesh so that the only access to the space was through a trap door in the table top that was easy to push open from the inside but very difficult to lift from the outside. Supposedly, various musical instruments were placed on the shelf and operators of Stella C. got inside to play the instruments.

Price also developed the telekinetoscope. An electric telegraph key was placed in brass cup and connected to a red light under a hermetically sealed glass shade. A soap bubble was blown over the cup and covered with another glass shade. The red light would flash only by pressing the telegraph key. The instrument was placed on the shelf inside the double table. The telegraph key was repeatedly pressed. The soap bubble, at the end of the séance, was found unbroken.

A shadow apparatus, consisting of a battery and lamp in a metal box with a Zeiss telephoto lens as a projector and a Wratten ruby filter to project a pencil of light on a luminous screen, was employed to supposedly detect the shape of the invisible arms that moved the bell or the trumpet. When the light was switched on, the shadow of the arm appeared on screen.

To quote the result of this experiment in the words of **Eric J. Dingwall:**

"When the red light was switched on under the table I lay down on the floor and looked through the passage towards the luminous screen. From near the medium's foot, which was invisible, I saw an eggshaped body beginning to crawl towards the centre of the floor under the table. It was white and where the light was reflected it appeared opal. To the end nearest the medium was attached a thin white neck, like a piece of macaroni. It advanced towards the centre, and then rapidly withdrew to the shadow."

Stella C. married Leslie Deacon in 1928 and ceased to give sittings. Her last sittings in 1926 and 1928 were attended by scientists such as Julian Huxley, Edward Andrade, and R. J. Tillyard.

Sources:

Tabori, Paul. *Companions of the Unseen.* London: H. A. Humphrey, 1968.

Turner, James, ed. *Stella C. An Account of Some Original Experiments in Psychical Research.* London: Souvenir Press, 1973.

Stella Maris Gnostic Church

The Stella Maris Gnostic Church, one of a number of South American Gnostic sect groups, was founded in 1989 by Rodolfo Perez and former members of the Universal Christian Gnostic Movement. Modern **Gnosticism** had emerged in nineteenth-century Europe, from where it had been transferred to South America early in the twentieth century by **Arnoldo Krumm-Heller** and other occult leaders. The Stella Maris is headquartered in Cartegena, Colombia.

The small group rose out of its obscurity in the larger occult milieu in June of 1999. A month earlier, the mother of one of the young adult members complained to the local authorities about the group and asked them to assist her in removing her daughter from the group. They did not respond. In June, the group went on its annual retreat. The day after the small group (fewer than 100 members) departed for the retreat, Colombian papers carried stories that the group had departed for the Sierra Nevada mountains to meet a spaceship that would take them to another world. The Sierra Nevada has been the focus of UFO reports and many flying saucer buffs believe it to be a place where direct contact with extraterrestrials is possible. The story was given added credence by expectations of crazy actions by different groups as the millennium came to an end.

The story was picked up by international wire services, carried worldwide, and tied to memories of the suicide of the 39 members of **Heaven's Gate.** However, within 24 hours of the story breaking, Perez and several members of the group went on television, denied that they had any interest in flying saucers, and said that they would return to Cartegena as usual when their retreat was over. The retreat was taking place near San Pedro, Colombia, as the media had been informed some weeks previously. *El Tiempo,* the leading daily newspaper, had run the initial story without checking the facts that they had at hand. The follow-up story of the group was carried by the Colombian press, but no follow-up appeared in the English-language media for almost a year when *Fortean Times* finally broke the story of the hoax in its May 2000 issue. Meanwhile, the Stella Maris Gnostic Church returned to its routine life in Cartegena.

Sources:

Murdie, Alan. "The Stella Maris Cult." *Fortean Times* 133 (May 2000): 66.

———. "UFOs, Strange Lights, and Meteorites in Columbia." Posted at http://www.xmo85.dial.pipex.com/colombia.htm. May 10, 2000.

Stella Matutina (Order of the Morning Star)

A temple of the Hermetic Order of the **Golden Dawn,** an offshoot of the outer order that broke with the Golden Dawn's chief **S. L. M. Mathers,** and rejected moving the London temple away from magic toward mysticism. It was founded by R. W. Felkin around 1903. Its members included **Dion Fortune, Israel Regardie, W. B. Yeats** and "E. Nesbit" (pseudonym of Mrs. Bland, author of stories for children). Some of the members of the Stella Matutina founded the healing organization, the Guild of St. Raphael.

Sources:

King, Francis. *The Rites of Modern Occult Magic.* New York: Macmillan, 1970.

Stella Tenebrarum

Stella Tenebrarum (Star of Darkness) is a traditionalist Satanic group that was founded on June 21 (the summer solstice), 1993, in Croatia. On that date, three medallions were struck for the three leaders of the group. Each medallion had an inverted pentagram, and they were made to be placed next to each other, at which time the full group motto was depicted: "Vexilla regis prodeunt inferi fulget Stella Tenebrarum" ("Flag of the king flies through hell, shines the Star of Darkness"). Some of the original members of the group, including one who was killed, served in the Croatian army during the Croatian war for independence.

The Stella Tenebrarum accepts the myth of Satan as the fallen angel who rebelled against the autocratic God of Jewish and Christian traditions. **Satanism** thus stands for the free spirit, rebellion against tyranny, standing for one's own beliefs and not allowing oneself to be forced into accepted norms simply to get along with others.

Satanism offers an active approach to living one's life, and encourages the use of magic to carry out one's ends. Members of Stella Tenebrarum are not opposed to the use of magic both to influence others (as in love spells) or to harm an enemy with curses. They promote the exchange of knowledge of effective curses with other Satanist groups. They also recommend the writings of **Anton LaVey,** founder of the American-based **Church of Satan,** as a means of getting started in magic and Satanism. Unlike most Satanist groups in the LaVey tradition, Stella Tenebrarum is not opposed to animal sacrifice, which it sees as primarily an issue between cultures.

Stella Tenebrarum may be contacted through its Internet site at http://www.geocities.com/Athens/Parthenon/2026/stella.html.

Sources:

Stella Tenebrarum. http://www.geocities.com/Athens/Parthenon/2026/stella.html. May 20, 2000.

Stelle Group

The Stelle Group was founded in Chicago in 1963 by Richard Kieninger, a former student of the **Lemurian Fellowship.** That same year he released an autobiography, *The Ultimate Frontier,* under the pseudonym Eklal Kueshana. The book described Kieninger's occult accomplishments, beginning with his meetings with a Dr. White on Kieninger's twelfth birthday. Originally Stelle members were also required to join and absorb the teachings of the Lemurian Fellowship, a practice that continued until the disruptions of the mid-1970s.

White taught Kieninger about **reincarnation** and suggested that he was both King David and Akhnaton. He gave Kieninger his mission: to found a new nation that was to center on an ideal community, Stelle City, near Kankakee, Illinois. By 1970 there were enough members and capital to purchase land, and Stelle City began to rise out of the surrounding corn fields. Some urgency pervaded the creation of Stelle, as *The Ultimate Frontier* predicted a massive natural catastrophe to be triggered by the alignment of the planets on May 5, 2000. Before that, in 1999, an atomic war would occur, killing 90 percent of the Earth's population.

Stelle grew steadily until 1976, when Kieninger left and formed a second community near Dallas, Texas, called the **Adelphi Organization.** It later was revealed that Kieninger had been expelled from Stelle for having sexual liaisons with several married women in the community. A leadership struggle ensued among the Illinois members after Kieninger's departure. A number, including the entire board of trustees and Kieninger's ex-wife, left the community. Those remaining reconciled with Kieninger. The headquarters of the Stelle group was moved to Texas in 1982, and Kieninger was named "Chairman of the Board for Life." However, by 1986 new problems had emerged, and Kieninger was forced out again.

He resigned and founded another organization, the Builders of the Nation, in Dallas. A short time later he again assumed control of the Adelphi Organization, and the Texas and Illinois groups separated.

As of the mid-1990s, the members of the Stelle Group are concentrating on applying Lemurian philosophy to their daily lives. The group is currently led by Tim Wilhelm. Address: The Stelle Administration Building, Stelle, IL 60919.

Sources:

Kossy, Donna. *Kooks: A Guide to the Outer Limits of Human Belief.* Portland, Ore.: Feral House, 1994.

Kueshana, Eklal [Kieninger, Richard]. *The Ultimate Frontier.* Chicago: Stelle Group, 1963.

Stendek (Journal)

A former Spanish-language publication concerned with **UFOs,** published from 1970–1981.

Sterner, Katherine Schmidt

Founder and president of the California Parapsychology Foundation and editor of *Parapsychology News-Notes* beginning in 1956. Born at Steelton, Pennsylvania, Sterner attended Akron University, Juilliard School (N.Y.), Columbia University, and San Diego City College. She was a public school teacher at in Akron, Ohio during World War II.

Stevens, William Oliver (1878–1955)

Author and educator who wrote on parapsychology. Stevens was born on October 7, 1878, in Rangoon, Burma. Stevens studied at Colby College, Waterville, Maine (B.A., 1899) and Yale University (Ph.D., 1903). He taught English for many years at the United States Naval Academy, Annapolis, Maryland (1905–24), and then successively was the headmaster of Roger Ascham School, White Plains, New York (1924–27); headmaster of Cranbrook School, Bloomfield Hills, Michigan (1927–35); and dean of the School of Literature and Journalism, Oglethorpe University (1936–37).

Out of his interest in parapsychology, Stevens joined the **American Society for Psychical Research.** He wrote many books on naval history and other subjects, including psychic research. He died January 16, 1955.

Sources:

Pleasants, Helene, ed. *Biographical Dictionary of Parapsychology.* New York: Helix Press, 1964.

Stevens, William O. *Beyond the Sunset.* New York: Dodd, Mead, 1944.

———. *Mystery of Dreams.* New York: Dodd, Mead, 1949. Reprint, London: Allen & Unwin, 1950.

———. *Psychics and Common Sense.* New York: Dodd, Mead, 1945.

———. *Unbidden Guests.* N.p., 1945.

Stevenson, Ian (1918–)

Physician, professor of psychiatry, and parapsychologist. His special area of study has been used as evidence for **survival,** and apparent memories of former incarnations. Stevenson was born on October 31, 1918, in Montreal, Quebec, Canada. He studied at McGill University, Montreal (B.S., 1943, M.D., 1944). He held positions at Cornell Medical College (1947–49), Louisiana State University (1949–1957), and the Department of Neurology and Psychiatry, University of Virginia School of Medicine, Charlottesville, Virginia, beginning in 1957.

Stevenson was a charter member of the **Parapsychological Association** and a member of the **American Society for Psychical Research.** He wrote on various issues in parapsychology, but was particularly concerned with evidence supporting the belief of reincarnation. His research and writing concentrated in that area, beginning with his contest winning essay in honor of William James, "The Evidence for Survival from Claimed Memories of Former Incarnations" (1961). His publications include 8 books on parapsychology, 136 articles dealing with medicine, and 70 articles that address parapsychology.

Sources:

Pleasants, Helene, ed. *Biographical Dictionary of Parapsychology.* New York: Helix Press, 1964.

Stevenson, Ian. "An Antagonist's View of Parapsychology. A Review of Professor Hansel's 'ESP: A Scientific Evaluation.'&43" *Journal* of American Society for Psychical Research 61 (July 1967).

———. *Cases of the Reincarnation Type.* 3 vols. Charlottesville: University Press of Virginia, 1975–1983.

———. "A Review & Analysis of Paranormal Experiences Connected with the Sinking of the Titanic." *Journal* of American Society for Psychical Research 54 (1961).

———. *Telepathic Impressions: A Review and Report of Thirty-five New Cases.* Charlottesville: University Press of Virginia, 1970.

———. *Twelve Cases in Lebanon & Turkey.* N.p., 1980.

———. *Twenty Cases Suggestive of Reincarnation.* 2d ed. Charlottesville: University Press of Virginia, 1974.

Stewart, Balfour (1828–1887)

Professor of natural philosophy at Owens College, Manchester, England, who received the Rumford Medal of the Royal Society for his discovery of the law of equality between the absorptive and radiative powers of bodies. He occupied the presidential chair of the **Society for Psychical Research,** London, from 1885 to 1887.

Stewart was born on November 1, 1828, in Edinburgh, Scotland. He was educated in Dundee and the Universities of St. Andrews and Edinburgh. He traveled to Australia, where he acquired a reputation as a physicist. After returning to Britain in 1856, he joined the staff of Kew Observatory, becoming a director in 1859. He also made important scientific contributions in mathematics and radiant heat.

Stewart was interested in the phenomena of the medium **Daniel Douglas Home,** of whom he commented to **Sir William Crookes:**

"Mr. Home possesses great electrobiological power by which he influences those present . . . however susceptible the persons in the room to that assumed influence, it will hardly be contended that Mr. Home biologized the recording instrument."

Stewart coauthored with Professor Tait the anonymously published *The Unseen Universe* (1875), a book that created a stir as the first serious scientific attempt to establish a spiritual view of the universe to oppose the prevailing materialistic one. He died suddenly on December 19, 1887, of a cerebral hemorrhage.

Sources:

Berger, Arthur S., and Joyce Berger. *The Encyclopedia of Parapsychology and Psychical Research.* New York: Paragon House, 1991.

Stewart, Kenneth Malcolm (1916–)

Professor of anthropology who studied **possession** and **shamanism.** He was born on June 16, 1916, in Tecumseh, Nebraska. Stewart completed his college work at the University of California (B.A., 1938, M.A., 1940, Ph.D., 1946). In 1947 he began his long tenure as a professor of anthropology at Arizona State University. Stewart conducted ethnological field work among the Native American Mohave and Pagago tribes of the American Southwest.

Sources:

Pleasants, Helene, ed. *Biographical Dictionary of Parapsychology*. New York: Helix Press, 1964.

Stewart, Kenneth M. "Spirit Possession." *Tomorrow* (spring 1956).

———. "Spirit Possession in Native America." *Southwestern Journal of Anthropology* 2, no. 3 (1946).

Stewart, W(ilber) C(larence) (1936–)

Research assistant and graduate student at Duke University, Durham, North Carolina. Stewart was born on July 22, 1936, in Durham, North Carolina. He studied at Duke University (B.S. electrical engineering, 1958, M.S. electrical engineering, 1960). He is an associate member of the **Parapsychological Association.** He experimented with electrical devices for testing extrasensory perception.

Sources:

Stewart, W. C. "Three New ESP Test Machines and Some Preliminary Results." *Journal of Parapsychology* (March 1959).

Sthenometer

Instrument invented by psychical researcher **Paul Joire** to demonstrate the existence of a nervous force acting externally to the body. In the center of a horizontal dial, marked out in 360 degrees, is a light needle or pointer, usually of straw, balanced by a pivot on a glass support. The device is covered with a glass shade.

When the extended fingers of a hand are at a right angle to the pointer, near the shade without touching it, reportedly, after a few seconds, the pointer moves toward the hand in the majority of cases. This movement extends between fifteen and fifty degrees. Certain substances that had been previously held in the hand also produce this movement. Wood, water, linen, and cardboard appear to store up this nervous energy. Tinfoil, iron, and cotton produce no effect.

The **Society for Psychical Research,** London, and some French scientific groups attributed the movement of the needle to the action of radiating heat rather than psychic force. (See also **Biometer of Baradoc; De Tromelin Cylinder; emanations; exteriorization of sensitivity; Magnetometer**)

Stichomancy

Another term for **bibliomancy** (**divination** through random choice of words in a book).

Stigmata

Marks resembling the wounds of the crucified Christ that appear inexplicably on the limbs and body of certain sensitive individuals, especially Christian mystics. The most common stigmata are marks on a person's hands and feet resembling piercing with nails, sometimes accompanied by bleeding. Other stigmata include the weals of scourging, wounds on the shoulder and side, the bruising of the wrists (where Christ was bound with cords), and marks on the mouth (paralleling the effect of the sponge soaked in vinegar). The most dangerous stigma is the *Ferita* or heart wound, which under normal circumstances can cause death.

There have been hundreds of cases of stigmata over the last two thousand years, many of them on the bodies of women. In spite of some actual or suspected frauds, most of these cases seem genuine, and some individuals bearing stigmata have been canonized or beatified by the Roman Catholic Church. In those cases, the stigmata was one of many criteria used to determine canonization and church authorities have never used belief in stigmatization as a mark of holiness.

Some people believe the Apostle St. Paul was the first stigmatic. He wrote in an epistle: *Ego enim stigmata Domini Jesus in corpore meo porto.* In the first twelve centuries of the history of the church his words were taken figuratively. There were ascetics who had wounds attributed to the teeth and claws of the devil on their body, but it was St. Francis of Assisi (died 1226) from whom the history of stigmatic wounds really dates. He was also reported to have manifested the phenomenon of **bilocation.** He carried the marks of stigmata during the final two years of his life. He fasted all through the 40-day fast of St. Michael and concentrated his thoughts on the Passion of Christ.

Not only was his flesh torn and bleeding at the five places, but

". . . his hands and feet appeared to be pierced through the middle with nails, the heads of which were in the palm of his hands and the soles of his feet; and the points came out again in the back of the hands and the feet, and were turned back and clinched in such a manner that within the bend formed by the reversal of the points a finger could easily be placed as in a ring, and the heads of the nails were found and black. They were the source of constant pain and of the utmost inconvenience. He could walk no more and became exhausted by the suffering and loss of blood. It hastened his premature decease. . . . After the death of Francis . . . a certain cavalier, named Jeronime, who had much doubted and was incredulous concerning them . . . ventured, in the presence of the brethren and many seculars to move about the nails in the hands and feet."

The Reverend F. Fielding-Ould, in his book *Wonders of the Saints* (1919), conjectured that the nails were of some horny material the body is able to naturally develop.

La Bienheureuse Lucie de Narni (1476–1544) carried stigmata for seven years, from 1496 onward. Reportedly, four years after her death, her body was exhumed. It was perfectly preserved and exhaled a sweet scent. The stigmatic wounds on her sides were open and blood flowed from time to time. In 1710 she was again exhumed and the body was found still intact.

The stigmatic wounds of Johnanna della Croce, 1524, appeared every Friday and vanished the following Sunday.

St. Veronique Giuliani, born in 1660, received the crown of thorns at the age of 33. On April 5, 1679, the five wounds developed.

Seventy-five years after the death of St. Francis 30 stigmatic cases were on record, including twenty-five women. Dr. Antoine Imbert-Gourbeyre in his monograph *L'Hypnotisme et la Stigmatisation* (1899) recorded more than 321 cases, and men comprised a seventh of the cases. This number includes the "compatients." and not those instances in which the stigmatic wounds were considered the work of the devil.

The "compatients" or participants did not exhibit the physiological signs of stigmatization in the form of wounds. It is believed to be an inner, psychical experience, noticeable, however, by outsiders as well. For instance, the complexion of Jeanne de Marie-Jesus in the ecstatic state of the Passion became dark and blue, the blood mounted under her nails, bruises appeared on her arms and hands as if left by chains, her forehead and other parts of her body sweated blood.

Of the cases enumerated by Imbert-Gourbeyre, 29 occurred in the nineteenth century. **Catherine Emmerich** (1774–1821) furnished one case. Count Stolberg, the celebrated naturalist, visited her in 1821. We learn from his description that for months the nun of Dolmen ate small portions of an apple, plum or cherry and drank water daily. The thorn wounds on her head opened every Friday morning and later blood flowed continuously from eight wounds on her hands and feet.

Research in the Nineteenth and Twentieth Centuries

Marie-Dominique Lazzari, Marie-Agnes Steiner, Marie de Moerl (1812–68), Crescenzia Nierklutsch, Victorie Courtier (1811–88), Louise Lateau (1858–83), Marie-Julie Jahenny, **Therese Neumann** (died 1962) and **Padre Pio** (died 1968) bring the line of stigmatists to the twentieth century.

Padre Pio (Francesco Forgione of Pietrelcina) was a Capucin monk in the convent of San Giovanni Rotondo. Reportedly, in 1918 bleeding scars pierced his hands and feet and produced appoximately a glassful of blood and water daily. Physicians certified the fact. In 1926 the stigmata of Therese Neumann, of Konnersreuth, developed during Lent. There was no evidence of infection or inflammation and blood flowed freely every Friday from the wounds. She also shed tears of blood.

In some cases the stigmata appear as simple red marks, in others as blister-like wounds oozing blood and lymph. The flow of blood, according to many testimonies, conforms to the supposed position of a body on the cross. The individual bearing stigmata may lie in bed and the blood appears to flow up the toes in defiance of gravity. In the case of Dominique Lazzari, of Tyrol, Lord Shrewsbury testified to this fact. He also referred to the statement of a German physician that the stigmatic could not endure water and was never washed, yet the blood sometimes suddenly disappeared, leaving the stigmatic with clean skin on unsoiled bedding. The wounds were often said to be luminous and to exhale a scent. Supposedly, the wounds never produced pus and after death the entire body frequently became exempt from putrefaction.

During the nineteenth century, physicians investigated some 29 reported cases of stigmatization and were convinced of the honesty of the subjects and the objective reality of the phenomenon.

One difficulty in assessing the strictly Christian spiritual value of stigmatization is due to the perception that some stigmatics have not been especially religious. Moreover similar phenomena have been reported of Islamic ascetics, who appear to have reproduced the wounds received by Muhammed the Prophet in spreading the message of Islam. Experiments with posthypnotic suggestion have shown that burns, blisters, and similar wounds may be produced on the body as a result of strong **suggestion,** and it is possible that some cases of stigmatization resulted from conscious or unconscious selfhypnosis.

Professor **Jean-Martin Charcot** was the first to demonstrate in an experiemnt the role of autosuggestion in stigmatic or borderland phenomena. **Hereward Carrington** in *Psychic Oddities* (1952) cited this case from an original document:

"On the afternoon of May 1st, 1916, I was standing in my hall, preparing to go out, when I saw the knob of my front door slowly turn. I stood still, awaiting developments; gradually the door opened, and I saw a man standing there. As he saw me he quickly closed the door and ran down the stairs and out of the front door. (He was, in fact, a burglar, trying to enter my apartment.) The interesting thing about the experience is this: that during the moment he was standing in the door, although he did not actually move, I had the distinct impression that he had run up the hall and grasped me firmly by the arm, and I was for the moment petrified with fear. The next day my arm was black and blue in the exact spot where I thought he had pinched me; and this mark continued for several days until it finally wore off. I told Dr. Carrington about this two days later when he called, and showed him the mark. Louise W. Kops."

Charles Richet stated that marks of stigmata,

". . . may and do often appear on hysterical persons, bearing predetermined forms and shapes, under the influence either of a strong moral emotion, or of religious delirium. These are facts which have been thoroughly and scientifically established, and they only prove the power of the action of the brain upon the circulatory processes and upon the trophism of the skin."

As a mediumistic phenomenon, it was reported by many experimenters, including **J. Malcolm Bird,** in his book *My Psychic Adventures* (1924). Additionally, the stigmatization of **Eleonore Zügun,** who had strange bites and scratches on her body, was supposedly recorded in the process of invisible production by the camera.

An experience, resembling stigmatization, was mentioned by Richet in a footnote to his book *Thirty Years of Psychical Research* (1923). Supposedly, Count Baschieri placed a handkerchief to his eyes and withdrew it stained with blood. His eyes had sweated blood. He was unable to discover any conjunctional ecchymosis.

Dermography (skin writing) is a phenomenon of the stigmatic class, but there is an essential difference. Reportedly, stigmata last for months, years, or throughout a lifetime, whereas skin writing disappears in a few minutes or a few hours at the most. A kindred phenomenon to stigmatization is the mark of a burn or in rare cases blood left by the touch of phantom hands.

Reportedly, some devout Christians experience stigmatization. Such individuals usually exhibit wounds that bleed on Good Friday, sometimes accompanied by a personal identification with Christ during crucifixion.

The Case of Ethel Chapman

The phenomenon of stigmatization was studied in the case of British subject Ethel Chapman. A victim of multiple sclerosis, Chapman was paralyzed from the waist down. She was unable to hold things in her hands. Chapman was a patient at the Cheshire Home in Britain, where she was interviewed by geriatrician Dr. Colin Powell, who found no indication of depression, neurosis, or psychosis. There was also no indication of the condition known as *dermatitis artifacta,* when subjects scratch or otherwise harm themselves for various reasons. Chapman appeared friendly, mentally stable, and far from gaining any psychological advantage from stigmata, she found it a burden. Various witnesses testified to seeing wounds on Chapman's hands and feet on Good Friday. In a BBC radio interview in 1973, Chapman gave a description of her first vision and sensations in the following words:

"I remember saying quite plainly 'Oh Lord, please show me in some way you're there.' In the early hours of the morning, I thought it was a dream. I felt myself being drawn on to the Cross. I felt the pain of the nails through my hands and through my feet. I could see the crowds, all jeering and shouting and, of course, it was in a foreign language, I don't know what they were saying. I felt myself all the agony and all the pain that the Lord Himself went through. . . ."

Chapman also claimed that on occasions she had been lifted up in the air and smelled supernatural sweet **perfumes** (see also **odor of sanctity**). However, it is believed that sensations of floating often occur in subjects with heightened or mystical consciousness and do not involve any actual physical levitation. Reportedly, in some cases, "astral projection" or **out-of-body** experience may occur in which a subtle body appears to leave the physical body.

Witnesses affirmed seeing fresh blood on Chapman's hands on Good Friday and it is believed that Chapman was unable to inflict the wounds herself due to her paralysis. Neither Chapman nor her medical adviser at the Cheshire Home seemed interested in publicity or cultism. Chapman, like some other stigmatics, seemed to regard the phenomenon as a mark of divine love due to her illness. Word spread about Chapman's stigmata and people wrote asking for her help or healing. She regularly devoted time to prayers on behalf of the afflicted.

The objective aspects of such phenomena as stigmata take second place to the spiritual issues and their resolution. The rationalistic explanation of stigmata seems to be of interest chiefly for any light it may throw on the *way* that the phenomenon works, but it says nothing of the mystery of the function of stigmata in the spiritual life of the subject.

Sources:

Carty, Charles M. *The Two Stigmatists: Padre Pio & Therese Neumann.* Dublin: Veritas, 1956.

Fielding-Ould, Fielding. *The Wonders of the Saints in the Light of Spiritualism.* London: John M. Watkins, 1919.

Siwek, Paul. *The Riddle of Konnersreuth.* Dublin: Browne & Nolan, 1956.

Summers, Montague. *The Physical Phenomena of Mysticism.* London: Rider, 1950.

Thurston, Herbert. *The Physical Phenomena of Mysticism.* London, 1952.

Wilson, Ian. *The Bleeding Mind.* London: Weidenfeld & Nicolson, 1988.

Stiles, Joseph D.

American printer who, in the early days of **Spiritualism,** received through **automatic writing** remarkable prophecies of the impending Civil War. The story was published under the title *Twelve Messages from John Quincy Adams through Joseph D. Stiles* in 1859 by Josiah Brigham. The author had met Stiles in June 1854. The messages were written by Stiles in **trance** from August 1854 until March 1858. They came in John Quincy Adams's handwriting and under his signature.

Stiles also produced other remarkable autographs. One prophecy—"I thus boldly prophesy the dissolution of the American Confederacy, and the destruction of slavery"—was signed "George Washington" with every peculiarity of Washington's difficult signature.

St. Irvyne; or the Rosicrucian

A turgid Gothic novel published in 1811 by Percy Bysshe Shelley under the pseudonym "Gentleman of the University of Oxford." It derives from the genre of Ann Radcliffe (1764–1823) and **Matthew Gregory Lewis** (1775–1881) and may also have been influenced by William Godwin's novel *St. Leon; A Tale of the Sixteenth Century* (1799). It tells the story of a man whose desire for the **elixer of life** leads him to make a compact with the devil. (See also English occult **fiction; Rosicrucians**)

St. John's Crystal Gold

A mysterious and possibly symbolic operation, described by alchemist **Thomas Vaughan** (1622–1666), who wrote under the name **Eugenius Philalethes:**

"In regard of the Ashes of Vegetables, although their weaker exterior Elements expire by violence of the fire, yet their Earth cannot be destroyed, but is Vitrified. The Fusion and Transparency of this substance is occasioned by the Radicall moisture or Seminal water of the Compound. This water resists the fury of the fire, and cannot possibly be vanquished. 'In hac Aquâ' (saith the learned Severine), 'Rosa latet in Hieme.'

"These two principles are never separated; for Nature proceeds not so far in her Dissolutions. When death hath done her worst, there is a Union between these two, and out of them shall God raise us to the last day, and restore us to a spiritual constitution. I do not conceive there shall be a Resurrection of every Species, but rather their Terrestrial parts, together with the element of water (for 'there shall be no more sea'—*Revelations*), shall be united in one mixture with the Earth, and fixed to a pure Diaphanous substance.

"This is St. John's Crystal Gold, a fundamental of the New Jerusalem—so called, not in respect of Colour, but constitution. Their Spirits, I suppose, shall be reduced to their first Limbus, a sphere of pure, ethereal fire, like rich Eternal Tapestry spread under the throne of God." (See also **alchemy**)

St. John's Wort

General term for the plant species *Hypericum.* In classical mythology, the summer solstice was a day dedicated to the sun, and was believed to be a day on which witches held their festivities. St. John's Wort was its symbolic plant. People used to judge from it whether their future would be lucky or unlucky, as it grew they read in its progressive character their future lot. This traditional lore carried over into the Christianera, when this festival period was dedicated to St. John's Wort or root. It became a talisman against evil.

In one of the old Scottish romantic ballads, a young lady falls in love with a demon, who tells her:

Gin you wish to be leman mine [my lover]
Lay aside the St. John's Wort and the vervain.

When hung up on St. John's Day, together with a cross over the door, this plant was supposed to keep out the devil and other evil spirits. To gather the root at sunrise on St. John's Day and to retain it in the house, gave luck to the family in their undertakings, especially in those begun on that day.

St. Joseph of Copertino (1603–1663)

St. Joseph of Copertino, a seventeenth-century Roman Catholic monk, is still remembered for his reported **levitations,** many of which were seen by multiple witnesses. He was born Joseph Dasa on June 17, 1603, in Copertino in Northern Italy into a poor family and spent his youthful years preparing himself for the monastic life. His neighbors were aware of his psychic abilities, though they did not blossom until after he joined the Franciscans and was ordained in 1628.

Various incidents of levitation began to occur without planning or control by Fr. Joseph, and no overall pattern emerged. It was noted that many of his levitations occurred as he was in prayer or engaged in veneration of the Virgin Mary. On one occasion he levitated in front of Pope Urban VIII who saw him hover in the air for several minutes. The pope was merely one among many notables of the era who testified to seeing Joseph in the air. The Duke of Brunswich was even taken into the air with Joseph. While the church built much of its case for being the prime contact point with God from the miraculous occurrences that happen among its members, it was somewhat embarrassed by Joseph's paranormal life. They kept him from the public as much as possible and at one point had him examined by the Inquisition. However, in his later years, he won the support of Pope Urban VIII.

The levitations of Joseph remain baffling and inexplicable. They are difficult to dismiss, having been so thoroughly documented from so many sources. They were not promoted, and the very people who tried to keep Joseph from becoming a public spectacle were among those who left the best records of his activity. They also remain an anomaly, his levitations finding few repetitions in other lives. Several medieval monks were reported to have levitated, including St. Philip of Neri and Francis Loyola, but their examples never approached the quality or quantity of Joseph's. The most famous modern levitator was Spiritualist medium **Daniel Dunglas Home** (1833–1886), who also had several spectacular levitations witnessed by a number of people.

Joseph died in 1663. It would only be some years later when the church reversed its opinion of him and canonized him. His levitations were an essential part of their considerations leading to his beatification. The case against him in the beatification process was conducted by Prosper Labertini, who later as Pope Benedict XIV read the beatification decree. Joseph was canonized in 1767. His feast day was set as September 18.

Sources:

Chambers, Paul. *Paranormal People.* London: Blandford, 1998.

Gauch, Patricia Lee. *The Little Man Who Flew.* New York: Putnam, 1980.

St. Leon: A Tale of the Sixteenth Century

A Gothic novel by William Godwin (1756–1836), first published in 1799. It may have been suggested by stories of the mysterious **Comte de Saint Germain** and the curious book *Her-*

mippus Redivivus; or The Sage's Triumph Over Old Age and the Grave by J. H. Cohausen (1744).

Godwin used this novel to propagate some of the ideas expressed in his work *An Enquiry Concerning Political Justice and its Influence on General Virtue and Happiness* (2 vols., 1793). *St. Leon* sought to show that "boundless wealth, freedom from disease, weakness and death are as nothing in the scale against domestic affection and the charities of private life." (See also **Signor Gualdi;** occult English **fiction; St. Irvyne; or the Rosicrucian**)

Stobart, St. Clair (Mrs. Stobart Greenhalgh) (d. 1954)

Author, playwright, and prominent figure in British Spiritualism. She was founder of the Women's Sick and Wounded Convoy Corps during the Balkan War in 1912–13, when she served with the Bulgarian Red Cross. During World War I she organized hospitals in Belgium and France for St. John's Ambulance Association, was taken prisoner by the Germans, and condemned to be shot as a spy. She survived, and in September 1915 was appointed commander of column, First Serbian English Field Hospital.

She lectured for the British Ministry of Information in Canada and Ireland (1917–18) and was a candidate for the Westminster borough at the London County Council Election of 1913. She was a founder and vice president of the SOS Society and chairman and leader of the **Spiritualist Community,** London, which was concerned with religious and educational aspects of Spiritualism.

She was life patron of the **British College of Psychic Science** and a member of the council of the World Congress of Faiths. She was an active lecturer and campaigner for the alliance between Spiritualism and Christianity. She died December 7, 1954.

Sources:

Stobart, St. Clair. *Ancient Lights.* N.p., 1923.

———. *The Either Or of Spiritualism.* N.p., 1928.

———. *Torchbearers of Spiritualism.* N.p., 1925.

Stoicheomancy

A method of **divination** that is practiced by opening the works of Homer or Virgil and reading as an oracular statement the first verse that presents itself. It is regarded as a form of **rhapsodomancy.**

Stoker, Bram [Abraham] (1847–1912)

Writer of books on occult themes and creator of the deathless vampire **Dracula.** He was born on November 8, 1847, in Dublin, Ireland. Stoker was named Abraham after his father but later preferred the short form "Bram."

He was a sickly child for some years although quite athletic as a young man. Perhaps his brooding childhood first engendered those imaginative horrors that found expression in his great vampire story and other weird thrillers. His mother had told him tales of the **banshee,** the Irish fairy whose terrifying wails announce death in the family, and also of the great cholera plague that had claimed thousands of victims in an Ireland ravaged by starvation and foreign occupation.

Stoker studied at Trinity College, Dublin, and became a member of the college's Philosophical Society, later being elected president. His first essay delivered to the society was titled "Sensationalism in Fiction and Society." He was auditor for the Historical Society and also developed a great interest in theater. At age 19 he was electrified by a performance of the great actor Henry Irving, whose company he later joined as a manager.

Stoker graduated with honors in science in 1870 and spent ten uneventful years as a civil servant at Dublin Castle. His first book was the prosaic but quite useful *The Duties of Clerks of Petty Sessions* (1879). In 1878 he married Florence Balcombe, a beautiful woman who had been on friendly terms with Oscar Wilde.

After a period as part-time drama critic, newspaper editor, and barrister at law, he became acting manager for Henry Irving, accompanying him on his British and American tours. Stoker was a hardworking manager and faithful friend to Irving for 27 years until Irving's death in 1905.

His masterpiece, *Dracula,* was written at odd moments and weekends during a busy career. It owed the name of its basic character to chance conversation with the intrepid Hungarian scholar-explorer **Arminius Vambéry** (1832–1913), who visited Dublin on a lecture tour.

It seems that Vambéry told Stoker about Romanian legends of the bloodthirsty tyrant Prince Vlad Tepes (known as Dracula, or "son of Dracul"). Stoker also researched in libraries in Whitby and London and perfected his knowledge of the background of the Transylvanian countryside, in which he set his fictional count. Some of the weird atmosphere of his story probably derived from the vampire story *Carmilla,* written by another Dubliner, Sheridan Le Fanu, and first published in 1871.

In addition to his immortal *Dracula,* Stoker published other novels and stories: *The Snake's Pass* (1890), *The Watter's Mou'* (1895), *The Shoulder of Shasta* (1895), *Miss Betty* (1898), *The Mystery of the Sea* (1902), *The Jewel of Seven Stars* (1904), *The Man* (1905), *The Gates of Life* (1908), *Lady Athlyne* (1908), *Snowbound* (1908), *The Lady of the Shroud* (1909), and *The Lair of the White Worm* (1911). His volume of short stories *Dracula's Guest* was published posthumously in 1937; the title story was originally a chapter in the manuscript of *Dracula,* deleted to shorten the work. He died April 20, 1912. His greatest work, at least to himself, was his biography of his mentor, *Personal Reminiscences of Henry Irving* (2 vols., 1906). He also wrote an interesting volume called *Famous Impostors* (1910).

Bram Stoker's memory and his association with Gothic literature is kept alive by various societies, notably the Bram Stoker Society (c/o David Lass, Hon. Secretary, Regent House, Trinity College, Dublin, 2, Ireland); the **Dracula Society** (36 Elliston House, 100 Wellington St., London, SE10 QQF, England); The Count Dracula Fan Club (29 Washington Sq. W., New York, NY 10011); and the Transylvanian Society of Dracula (P.O. Box 91611, Santa Barbara, CA 93190–1611). (See also **Fiction, English Occult**)

Sources:

Dalby, Richard. *Bram Stoker: A Bibliography of First Editions.* London, 1983.

Farson, Daniel. *The Man Who Wrote Dracula: A Biography of Bram Stoker.* New York: St. Martin's, 1976.

Ludlam, Harry. *A Biography of Dracula: The Life Story of Bram Stoker.* London: Fireside Press, 1962.

Melton, J. Gordon. *The Vampire Book: The Encyclopedia of the Undead.* Detroit: Visible Ink Press, 1994.

Roth, Phyllis A. *Bram Stoker.* Boston: Twayne, 1982.

Stoker, Bram. *Dracula.* London: Constable, 1897.

———. *Dracula's Guest and Other Weird Stories.* London: George Routledge & Sons, 1914.

Stokes, Doris (1920–1987)

British psychic who established a worldwide reputation for her **clairaudience.** Born Doris Sutton, January 6, 1920, in Grantham, Lincolnshire, she grew up in poverty. Her father was gassed in World War I and retired on a small pension; Doris's mother was obliged to take in laundry work to augment the family income. Her father died while Doris was still in school. She left school at age 14 and became a nurse. During this period she discovered she had psychic abilities, but they remained undeveloped.

At 24, she married John Stokes, an army paratrooper. During World War II, she was officially notified that her husband had been killed in action. Reportedly, her dead father appeared to her, however, and stated that her husband was alive and would return, which he did.

Later Doris had another vision, in which her father appeared again to warn her that her baby son would soon die but that he would take good care of him after death. Although the child was perfectly healthy, he died at the time and date predicted. Subsequently John and Doris attended a local Spiritualist church, where Doris claimed she was told that she would become a medium. She was unwilling at first, but gradually her mediumship developed. It principally took the form of hearing spirit voices.

In her autobiography, *Voices in My Ear* (1980), she describes the problems and temptations of a young medium. She was often worried about losing continuity with the spirit voices and the members of the audience for whom the messages came. She was advised by a visiting medium to use one of the "tricks of the trade" by arriving at the meeting early, listening to what people said to each other, then slipping away and writing down conversations and names, to be used later to keep contact between the spirit voices and the audience.

It seemed like cheating, she said, but at her next meeting Stokes tried it, and it was successful, until in the middle of a communication that had been "helped out" in this way contact with the spirit voice was suddenly broken. She struggled to continue, but dried up and had to break off. After two more spirit communications, her spirit guide, "Ramonov," supposedly told her to go back to the recipient of the message and apologize.

This happened at two meetings, after which Stokes determined never again to help out spirit communications in that way, in spite of the fear she felt at losing contact. After that, she openly admitted it to the audience if she lost contact with the spirit voices and simply tried to reestablish the link. She warned other developing mediums to be brave enough to admit it if no messages were being received. In 1948 her credentials as a bona fide clairaudient were endorsed by the **Spiritualists National Union** in England.

In more than thirty years of mediumship, Stokes attracted large and enthusiastic audiences and also appeared on popular radio and television shows in Australia, New Zealand, and the United States. She often dumbfounded skeptical reporters and presenters by the accuracy of her spirit messages. Her reputation as a Spiritualist superstar was phenomenal. On her Australian tour, she packed the massive Sydney Opera House three nights in a row, and a private plane was chartered to take her from city to city. A television soap opera was postponed to make room for her.

Yet this international fame came only in later life. Prior to the mid-1970s, she had lived in modest circumstances in Lancaster, working as a nurse, or giving her mediumistic services to Spiritualist churches for no more than modest traveling expenses, sometimes giving private consultations for £1 (two or three dollars).

Stokes moved to London and became well known as a clairaudient medium, but she never ceased to be amazed by her growing fame. She made no showbiz concessions but appeared on stage in a simple frock, sitting in an armchair, and speaking to her audience in colloquial language.

Her fame attracted derisive and often hostile criticism from skeptics, but she met controversy head on and would not be bullied. In 1980 she appeared on a British television show with professional magician **James Randi,** who denounced her (without evidence) as a liar and a fake. When Doris challenged Randi to appear with her and prove her a fake, he declined.

In addition to *Voices in My Ear* Doris Stokes wrote several other popular books of reminiscences: *More Voices in My Ear* (1981), *Innocent Voices in My Ear* (1983), *A Host of Voices* (1984), *Whispering Voices* (1985), *Voices of Love* (1986), and *Joyful Voices* (1987). Their combined sales exceeded two million copies. Unfortunately, in her last years, she was quite ill and had to go through several operations. She died May 8, 1987, two weeks after surgery for removal of a brain tumor.

Stokes, Henry Newlin (1859–1942)

Theosophist and editor, born in 1859 at Moorestown, New Jersey. Stokes attended Haverford College (B.S.) and Johns Hopkins University (Ph.D., 1884). He later did postgraduate work in **Germany** and **Switzerland.** He returned to the United States in 1889 and became a chemist for the U.S. Geological Survey. He wrote articles for scientific journals and served a term as president of the Chemical Society of Washington, D.C. He moved to the Bureau of Standards in 1903.

Early in the new century the agnostic Stokes began a search in esoteric philosophy that led him to **Theosophy** and the writings of **Annie Besant.** He joined the **Theosophical Society** in 1903 and the following year also became a member of a small, independent theosophical organization, the Oriental Esoteric (OE) Head Center. The OE had been headquartered in Paris but had a small group in Washington. In 1905 Stokes helped establish the Oriental Esoteric Library as a focal point of occult information in the District. In 1909 he retired from the Bureau of Standards. During this time his former wife spread rumors alleging that he was involved with Anna Marsland, the head of the OE.

Over the next three years he devoted his increased free time to the OE, especially to developing the library, into which he poured much of his own finances. In 1910 he and Marsland broke with the Paris headquarters and established the Oriental Esoteric Society as a separate entity. Then, in 1912, he and Marsland split, and he sued the OE Society for the library, claiming that he had largely built it with his own money. The court agreed and gave him the books. He then aligned the library as an independent but associated organization of the American section of the Theosophical Society.

By 1911 Stokes had begun a periodical, the *O. E. Library Critic,* which became his means of livelihood for the rest of his life. After his break with Marsland he conceived the *Critic* as an independent theosophical periodical serving the larger cause of Theosophy. All was fine for a few years, but in the wake of the founding of the theosophically based **Liberal Catholic Church** in 1916, he turned on the church and especially bishops **Charles W. Leadbeater** and James I. Wedgwood. Stokes attacked Leadbeater for the new teachings he was introducing into the society and condemned the homosexual preferences of Wedgwood. He went on to attack theosophical offshoots such as the **Aquarian Foundation,** the **Arcane School,** and the **I AM Movement.**

Stokes couched his criticism of the new trends in the theosophical movement under the slogan Back to Blavatsky, a phrase he first used in the November 14, 1917 issue of the *Critic.* He lauded the groups and independent lodges that still adhered to the writings of **Helena Petrovna Blavatsky,** the cofounder of the Theosophical Society. He did not leave the international Theosophical Society and is credited with reintroducing Blavatsky's writings to the general membership.

Stokes continued to edit the *Critic* until his death on September 20, 1942.

Sources:

Santucci, James. "H. N. Stokes and the O. E. Library Critic." *Theosophical History* 1, 6 (April 1986): 129–39.

———. "H. N. Stokes' Early Contact with the Theosophical Society." *Theosophical History* 2, 1 (January 1987): 4–22.

Stolisomancy

Divination from the manner in which a person dresses. In ancient Rome the emperor Augustus believed that a military revolt was predicted on the morning of its occurrence when his attendant buckled his right sandal to his left foot.

Stomach, Seeing with the

A phenomenon occasionally observed by the followers of **Franz Anton Mesmer** in their somnambules (hypnotic subjects). In a cataleptic state closely resembling death, the subject would sometimes show no signs of intelligence when questions were directed to the ears, but if the questions were addressed to the pit of the stomach, or sometimes to the fingertips or toes, an answer would be given immediately. Several such cases were recorded by one Dr. Pététin, of Lyons, France, who in 1808 published *Électricité Animale,* and by other mesmerists. Not only hearing, but seeing, tasting, and smelling were apparently performed by the stomach, independent of the sensory organs.

Pététin attributed the phenomenon to "animal electricity" and stated that objects placed on the patient's stomach were not seen when they were wrapped in wax or silk, that is, nonconductors. It was believed that the best way to communicate with a subject in the cataleptic state was for the operator to place his hand on the subject's stomach and address questions to the fingertips of his own free hand.

This **trance** phenomenon, as well as others similar to it, might now be considered to be the result of suggestion or hyperesthesia. (See also **Eyeless Sight; Transposition of the Senses**)

Stonehenge

Ancient prehistoric monument of standing stones located in Wiltshire, England. The name derives from the Old English *hengen* ("hung up"), referring to the horizontal lintel stones. Over the centuries, legend ascribed Stonehenge to Druidic, Roman, and Danish construction, but it is now generally accepted that it dates from Neolithic times and stands as the culmination of the period of megalith construction, remnants of which can be found across the British Isles. It was probably last in use about 1400 B.C.E. Megalithic (large stone) monuments exist in many locations in Europe.

A major step in understanding the use and significance of Stonehenge occurred in the 1960s when it was discovered that the alignment of the stones seems to facilitate the prediction of a variety of astronomical events, such as the summer solstice, and were thus probably related to late Neolithic worship ceremonies.

The Stonehenge site is composed of three distinct elements—an outer circle of local sarsen stones and two inner circles of blue stones from the Prescelly Mountains of Wales, 200 kilometers (125 miles) away. The first and third circles are capped with stone lintels, and the whole construction is encircled by a ditch, inside the bank of which are 56 pits known as the "Aubrey Holes" and a cemetery associated with them.

Isolated outside the stone circles is the Heel stone, over which the sun rises on Midsummer Day (June 24). It is clear that Stonehenge had special astronomical significance, since, in addition to the marking of the summer solstice by the Heel stone, the center of the great circle indicated the orbits of sun and moon, and holes were positioned for posts to mark these orbits. The whole construction indicates remarkable astronomical and mathematical knowledge on the part of the ancient builders. Like the pyramids of ancient Egypt, Stonehenge and similar monuments also involved considerable engineering skill in mining and transporting the huge stones.

Prior to modern archaeological investigations, Stonehenge was surrounded by confusing legends of origin and use. Radiocarbon dating has now established a date of around 2000 B.C.E. for the first monument, the second a few centuries later, and the third about the middle of the second millennium B.C.E. It is possible that the Druids inherited an oral tradition of the significance of Stonehenge and used it for sacred rituals involving sun worship.

Folklore credits such sites with magical power, and they have been associated with witchcraft rites. In France young girls would slide down such ancient stones with bare buttocks in the belief that it would make them fertile.

Early Christian missionaries attempted to absorb or neutralize such occult traditions by building churches inside prehistoric mounds. In medieval times, at the great stone monument at Avebury in southern Britain, there was a ceremony in which a single stone was dislodged and ritually attacked to symbolize the victory of the Christian Church over the Devil. Most sites, including Stonehenge, have also suffered vandalism over the centuries.

Modern Stonehenge

In the 1980s Stonehenge became the center of another strange ritual every midsummer. Thousands of hippies, living a nomadic life in battered automobiles (often unlicensed), reminiscent of the American dust bowl days, descended on the fields surrounding Stonehenge and set up makeshift camps, intending to gain access to Stonehenge to celebrate the summer solstice. But the site has been fenced off with barbed wire and the solstice ceremony restricted to a modern revival Druid organization and no more than six hundred ticket-holding visitors. To prevent the hippies from overrunning the site, farmers annually barricaded paths and byways with trailers and machinery, while hundreds of police stood by in riot gear.

For many years there was a ritual battle between hippies and police. Rocks, bottles, and other objects were thrown, while police with helmets and batons forced back the intruders and arrested many of them. After the summer solstice, the hippies were obliged to retreat to their battered vehicles.

Stonehenge remains one of England's most visited tourist sites in spite of the fence, which prevents visitors from walking among the stones.

Sources:

Burl, Aubrey. *The Stone Circles of the British Isles.* New Haven, Conn.: Yale University Press, 1976.

Chippendale, Christopher. *Stonehenge Complete.* Ithaca, N.Y.: Cornell University Press, 1983.

Hawkins, Gerald. *Stonehenge Decoded.* Garden City, N.Y.: Doubleday, 1965. Reprint, London: Souvenir Press, 1966.

Hitching, Francis. *Earth Magic.* London: Cassell, 1976.

Mitchell, J. *Astro-Archaeology.* London: Thames & Hudson, 1977.

Newham, C. A. *The Astronomical Significance of Stonehenge.* UK: John Blackburn, 1972.

Thom, Alexander. *Megalithic Sites in Britain.* Oxford: Oxford University Press, 1967.

Stowe, John R. (1956–)

John R. Stowe, a spiritual teacher, cofounder of Gay Spirit Visions, and founder of EarthFriends, was born in 1956. He lived a closeted gay existence until 1979, when he began a quest to discover what it meant to live as an aware, spiritually-engaged gay man. As with many gay men, much of that struggle meant dealing with negative self images acquired from growing up in a world that does not accept homosexuality as a legitimate option amid the myriad options from which people can choose.

After coming out, he found employment as a bodyworker/masseur and pursued his spiritual and self-understanding quest through a spectrum of alternative spiritual options from the gay-informed Christianity of Episcopal priest Malcolm

Boyd to channeller **Andrew Ramer.** He eventually decided that people have the right to their own spiritual path and that personal spirituality begins in listening to the inner self. He found bodywork as one tool that assisted the exploration of the inner self, but also found help in Jungian reflections on archetypes. He soon emerged as a spiritual teacher serving the gay community primarily in the Atlanta, Georgia, area.

In 1990, Stowe joined with a small group of friends who had pursued similar spiritual journeys, including Ramer, to found Gay Spirit Visions. The primary program of Gay Spirit Visions is an annual conference where gay men gather to explore alternative spiritual options. The work of the group, which Stowe has described as mutual mentoring, provided the atmosphere for him to develop his focus on the archetypes that led to his book, *Gay Spirit Warrior* (1999). *Gay Spirit Warrior* was written to assist men begin an inner journey and start to experience the reality of the self, both positive and negative. Stowe views archetypes as universal characters that reside in the human consciousness. Each person carries the archetypes developed to a greater or lesser strength. By looking at each archetype successively, and assessing how each manifests in its particularity, one can come to new levels of self-understanding.

In 1984, Stowe had discovered **flower essences,** substances distilled from flowers and other plants by a particular method first discovered by Edward Bach, a British physician. Since Bach's death in the 1930s, the number of flowers processed in the manner he discovered has greatly expanded, especially after the formation of the Flower Essence Society in 1979. Stowe began to make his own flower essences from flowers found in the Southeastern United States and use them in his bodywork sessions. In the mid-1980s he founded EarthFriends to manufacture and sell the essences he had developed. One line of products, Exploring Gayspirit Oils, is marketed primarily to gay men.

Sources:

Nichols, Jack. "Interview with John R. Stowe." *Gay Today* (October 1999).

Stowe, John R. *Gay Spirit Warrior.* Findhorn Press, 1999.

Strange Magazine

Quarterly magazine featuring "all aspects of the inexplicable as it appears in science, art, literature, philosophy, technology, magic, religion and everything else we call reality." It gives special attention to **Fortean phenomena** (i.e., scientifically anomalous phenomena of the kind originally cataloged by **Charles H. Fort**) and includes book reviews and news. Address: P.O. Box 2246, Rockville, MD 20847. The magazine is now accessible on the Internet at http://www.strangemag.com/.

Sources:

Strange Magazine Online. http://www.strangemag.com/. March 8, 2000.

Stratton, F(rederick) J(ohn) M(arrian) (1881–1960)

Professor of astrophysics and a notable member of the **Society for Psychical Research** (SPR), London. He was born on October 16, 1881, in Birmingham, England. He studied at Gonville and Caius College, Cambridge University (B.A., 1904; M.A., 1908). In 1928 he began his long tenure as professor of astrophysics and director of the Solar Physics Observatory, Cambridge (1928–47), with time out during World War II to serve with the Royal Corps of Signals. After the war he became president of Gonville and Caius College (1946–48).

An outstanding scientist of his day, Stratton took a great interest in spontaneous phenomena concerning **psi** and **hauntings,** and his reports appear in the *Journal* of the SPR. He was a member of the SPR for some 60 years and served as president (1953–55) and vice president (1955–60). He was also a charter member of the **Parapsychological Association.** He died September 2, 1960.

Sources:

Pleasants, Helene, ed. *Biographical Dictionary of Parapsychology.* New York: Helix Press, 1964.

Stratton, F. J. M. "Four Modern Ghosts." *Journal* of the Society for Psychical Research 39 (1938).

———. "Psychical Research—A Lifelong Interest." *Proceedings* of the Society for Psychical Research (1953).

Strauch, Inge H(enriette) (1932–)

German parapsychologist and research associate in psychology. She was born on April 4, 1932, in Dresden, Germany, and studied at Freiburg University (M.A. psychology, 1956; Ph.D., 1958). While completing her doctorate she was a research associate at the Institut für Grenzgebiete der Psychologie and Psychohygiene, Freiburg (1956–58), and after graduation she became a research associate for the Department for Border Areas of Psychology at Freiburg University, where she stayed for many years. She served as managing editor of the *Zeitschrift für Parapsychologie und Grenzgebiete der Psychologie* and was an associate member of the **Parapsychological Association.**

Her special interest in dream research resulted in her 1960 paper "Investigations into Various Stages of Dream Recall," which became Report 22 at the 1960 Congress of Deutsche Gesellschaft für Psychologie. During 1961–62 she undertook a study tour in the United States and conducted electroencephalographical research on dreams at New York's Mount Sinai Hospital and electroencephalographical studies of the neurological basis of psychic phenomena at the **Parapsychology Foundation,** New York. She also conducted quantitative research at the **Parapsychology Laboratory** at Duke University.

Sources:

Pleasants, Helene, ed. *Biographical Dictionary of Parapsychology.* New York: Helix Press, 1964.

Strauch, Inge H. "Dreams and Psi in the Laboratory." In *Psi Favorable States of Consciousness,* edited by R. Cavenna. New York: Parapsychology Foundation, 1970.

———. "Medical Aspects of 'Mental' Healing." *International Journal of Parapsychology* 5 (1963).

Strieber, Whitley (1945–)

Best-selling author of fantasy and horror stories, several of which, including *Wolfen* and *The Hunger,* have been adapted as successful movies. In 1987 he completed a nonfiction book, *Communion,* in which he relates his personal experiences in encounters with what he believes to be extraterrestrials. The encounters included an abduction and examination by strange creatures in a flying craft. The response led to two follow-up books on the same theme: *Transformation: The Breakthrough* (1988) and a novel, *Majestic* (1989). All three made the best-seller lists.

Strieber was born on June 13, 1945, in San Antonio, Texas. He was educated at the University of Texas (B.A., 1968) and the London School of Economics and Political Science (certificate, 1968). From 1970 through 1977 he wrote novels while working at an advertising company, becoming account supervisor and vice president.

The idea for his novel *The Wolfen* (1978), later made into a successful movie, is said to have arisen from the experience of encountering a pack of feral dogs while walking through Central Park in New York. His other publications include *Black Magic* (1982), *The Night Church* (1983), *Wolf of Shadows* (1986) (with James W. Kunetka), and *The Consequences of the Twentieth*

Century (1986). His novel *The Hunger* (1981), notable for the very different twist it gave to the **vampire** myth, was made into a movie in 1983. Strieber has also designed games based on various periods of history, including a game about the late Middle Ages entitled "1480: Age of Exploration" and one covering computer games. He has participated in archaeological projects in Central America and has been involved with a scientific group attempting to authenticate the **Turin shroud.**

Soon after the publication of *Communion,* Strieber received more than five hundred letters, many claiming similar experiences of contact by extraterrestrials or other creatures. His experience was further publicized in an article in the *International UFO Reporter* (January/February 1987), in which Strieber characterizes such reports as "visitor experiences."

Strieber eventually came to the conclusion that, in spite of the intrusive nature of the initial abduction experience, the extraterrestrials were a benevolent group. In 1989 he founded the Communion Foundation to assist in establishing a productive relationship with the space beings. Professional psychologists working for the foundation began to catalog similar reports in a database and follow-up studies involving mental and physical tests with selected volunteers were planned.

Strieber immediately ran into conflict with the ufological community, which draws a sharp distinction between the more negative abduction reports and the more positive claims of encounters with **flying saucers,** which are classified as contactee accounts. Strieber's account began to sound more and more like a contactee story of the type that had been written off as either fraudulent or religious hyperbole. In 1991 he closed the Communion Foundation and returned to fiction writing. He reportedly is still interested in the field, however, and has continued having encounters with extraterrestrials.

Sources:

Clark, Jerome. *UFOs in the 1980s.* Vol. 1 of *The UFO Encyclopedia.* Detroit: Apogee Books, 1990.

Conroy, Ed. *Report on "Communion:" An Independent Investigation of and Commentary on Whitley Strieber's "Communion."* New York: William Morrow, 1989.

Strieber, Whitley. *Communion: A True Story.* New York: William Morrow, 1987.

———. *Majestic.* New York: G. P. Putnam's Sons, 1989.

———. *Transformation: The Breakthrough.* New York: William Morrow, 1988.

Striges

In Greek folklore, vampire women with the power to transform themselves into birds of prey or other sinister animals. The striges derived from the Roman *strix,* a night demon, named for the screech owl. It was believed to attack infants and drain their blood. The strix appears across southern Europe, where it is known variously as *strega* (Italy), *striges* (Greece), and *strigoi* (Romania). The striges differed from other **vampire** creatures in that they were thought of as living members of the community rather than the returning dead.

Sources:

Melton, J. Gordon. *The Vampire Book: The Encyclopedia of the Undead.* Detroit: Visible Ink Press, 1994.

Strioporta

Frankish name for a witch. (See also **France**)

Stroboscopes

Devices that create light pulsations at intervals varying from one flash every few seconds to several flashes per second. They have become a familiar part of the atmosphere of excitement at some dance halls and discotheques, but in different situations they have proved of some assistance in inducing hallucinatory experiences, especially when seen with half-open or even closed eyes.

Pierre Janet did pioneering work with stroboscopes. He flashed lights at mental patients and saw some immediate breakthroughs in their health. The strobes work by a process called *entrainment,* in which the brain tends to align itself with the frequency of the flashing light. A beam flashed at the right frequency can induce a more relaxed state and cause the brain to change its frequency.

Sources:

Hooper, Judith, and Dick Teresi. *Would the Buddha Wear a Walkman?* New York: Simon and Schuster, 1990.

Stroking Stones and Images

Cotton Mather (1662–1728) wrote that an Irish American witch produced pain and disease in others by merely wetting her finger with saliva and stroking small images, or sometimes a long, slender stone.

Stromberg, Gustaf (Benjamin) (1882–1962)

Astronomer, lecturer, and author of books on parapsychological subjects. He was born on December 16, 1882, at Gothenburg, Sweden, and studied at the University of Lund, Sweden (Ph.D., 1916). After assisting at the Stockholm Observatory during his school years (1906–13) as World War I began, he moved to the United States to become an astronomer at Mount Wilson Observatory in California, where he remained for the next three decades (1917–46). Above and beyond his astronomical work, he turned his scientific training toward explanations for psychic phenomena. In this endeavor he wrote a number of books and articles. He died January 30, 1962.

Sources:

Stromberg, Gustaf. *Det Eviga Sökandet* (The Eternal Quest). N.p., 1948.

———. *God's Place in Modern Science.* N.p., 1958.

———. *Psychic Phenomena and Modern Science.* N.p., 1957.

———. *The Searchers.* N.p., 1948.

———. *The Soul of the Universe.* N.p., 1940.

Strutt, Arthur Charles (1878–1973)

Vice-admiral of the British navy and for a quarter of a century (1933–58) the treasurer of the **Society for Psychical Research,** London. He was born on October 2, 1878, at Chelmsford, England. He entered the navy in 1892 and was named master of fleet during World War I. He later served as the director of navigation for the Royal Navy (1923–25) and as the naval officer in charge of Dartmouth College. He died in February 1973.

Sources:

Pleasants, Helene, ed. *Biographical Dictionary of Parapsychology.* New York: Helix Press, 1964.

Strutt, John William (3rd Baron Rayleigh) (1842–1919)

Physicist who was president of the **Society for Psychical Research** (SPR), London, 1919. He was born on November 12, 1842, at Witham, Essex, England, and was educated at Trinity College of Cambridge University (fellow, 1866). At the height of his outstanding career he was named Cavendish Professor of Experimental Physics at Cambridge (1879–84) and then professor of natural philosophy at the Royal Institution (1887–1905). He was also the secretary to the Royal Society for a decade (1887–96). In 1904 he received the Nobel Prize in physics for his isolation of argon. In 1908 he was named chancellor of Cambridge.

Lord Rayleigh became interested in psychical research after reading about the investigations of his colleague **Sir William Crookes.** He was present at sittings with **Kate Fox** and **Eusapia Palladino.** He died on June 30, 1919, a short time after delivering his presidential address to the SPR.

Sources:

Strutt, John William. "Presidential Address." *Proceedings* of the Society for Psychical Research 30, no. 77 (1918–19).

Strutt, Robert John (4th Baron Rayleigh) (1875–1947)

Physicist and president of the **Society for Psychical Research** of London from 1937 to 1938. Strutt was born on August 28, 1875, at Witham, Essex, England, the son of **John William Strutt.** He was educated at Eton College and Trinity College, Cambridge, England (B.A. 1897, M.A. 1901), and like his notable father majored in physics. He was variously a fellow of Trinity College (1900–1906), professor of physics at the Imperial College of Science and Technology, Kensington (1908–19), and president of the Royal Institution of Great Britain (1945–47). Financially independent, he was able to create a private laboratory at which he conducted research for much of his life. He published one of the first volumes on radioactivity. Also like his father, Strutt had an intense interest in psychic research, which gave the subject some standing with fellow scientists.

He died December 13, 1947.

Sources:

Berger, Arthur S., and Joyce Berger. *The Encyclopedia of Parapsychology and Psychical Research.* New York: Paragon House, 1991.

Pleasants, Helene, ed. *Biographical Dictionary of Parapsychology.* New York: Helix Press, 1964.

Strutt, Robert John. "A Method of Silhouette Photography by Infra-Red Rays for Use in Mediumistic Investigation." *Proceedings* of the Society for Psychical Research 41, 128 (1932).

———. "The Problem of Physical Phenomena in Connection with Psychical Research." *Proceedings* of the Society for Psychical Research 44, 152 (1938).

———. "The Question of Lights Supposed to Have Been Observed near the Poles of a Magnet." *Proceedings* of the Society for Psychical Research 44, 153 (1938–39).

———. "Some Recollections of Henry Sidgwick." *Proceedings* of the Society for Psychical Research 44, 156 (1936–39).

Stuart, C(harles) E. (1907–1947)

Parapsychologist. He was born on December 5, 1907, in Pennsylvania and later attended Duke University (B.A., 1932; Ph.D., 1941). He became interested in the work of **J. B. Rhine** as an undergraduate at Duke and conducted **ESP** tests on himself and friends. He went on to become a research associate in the Parapsychology Laboratory in 1934, and his doctoral thesis dealt with experimental research in ESP. He was on the laboratory staff at Duke for the rest of his life except for two years at Stanford University (1942–44) as a fellow in psychic research. He took a special interest in psychological conditions and personality factors in relation to ESP, concerning which he wrote several papers. During his many years at the Parapsychology Laboratory he was frequently called upon to answer objections to the methodology of the early ESP experiments. He died March 23, 1947.

Sources:

Berger, Arthur S., and Joyce Berger. *The Encyclopedia of Parapsychology and Psychical Research.* New York: Paragon House, 1991.

Pleasants, Helene, ed. *Biographical Dictionary of Parapsychology.* New York: Helix Press, 1964.

Stuart, C. E. "A Classroom ESP Experiment with the Free Response Method." *Journal of Parapsychology* 9 (1945).

———. "The Effect of Rate of Movement in Card Matching Tests of Extrasensory Perception." *Journal of Parapsychology* 2 (1938).

———. "GESP Experiment with the Free Response Method." *Journal of Parapsychology* 10 (1946).

———. "An Interest Inventory Relation to ESP Scores." *Journal of Parapsychology* 10 (1945).

———. "A Review of Recent Criticisms of ESP Research." *Journal of Parapsychology* 2, no. 3 (1939).

Stuart, C. E., and J. G. Pratt. *A Handbook for Testing Extrasensory Perception.* New York: Farrar and Rinehart, 1937.

Stuart, C. E., J. G. Pratt, J. B. Rhine, B. M. Smith, and J. A. Greenwood. *Extrasensory Perception After Sixty Years.* New York: Henry Holt, 1940. Rev. ed. Boston: Bruce Humphries, 1966.

Student's International Meditation Society (SIMS)

Organization founded in 1965 to promote the **transcendental meditation** technique as taught by **Maharishi Mahesh Yogi.** In the early years of the movement in the United States, SIMS and the Spiritual Regeneration Movement were the two major vehicles for spreading the maharishi's teachings, which were mainly focused on college and university campuses.

In 1972 the maharishi announced the World Plan, an overall strategy for sharing his teachings with the world and making them effective in the reformation of society. From that proposal, the World Plan Executive Council was formed to coordinate the different aspects of the plan. SIMS was continued as one of the five divisions of the executive council. The council had headquarters in Europe as well as the United States. Last known address: P.O. Box 390, Lake Shandelee Rd., Livingston Manor, NY 12758.

Studievereniging voor Psychical Research

The Studievereniging voor Psychical Research (Dutch Society for Psychical Research), the oldest of the Dutch parapsychological research facilities, was founded in 1920 by Gerardus Heymans and I. Zeehandelaar. The organization was soon joined by a young psychology student at the University of Utrecht, **W. H. C. Tenhaeff.** In 1928 Tenhaeff and Paul A. Deitz founded the society's journal, *Tijdschrift voor Parapsychologie.*

The early work of the society focused upon the study of the phenomena generated by the spreading Spiritualist movement in the Netherlands, but over the years laboratory parapsychology found its place in the society's work. Among the impressive research reported by the society was the 1950 study of telepathy in schoolchildren conducted by J. G. Busschbach. Through the remainder of the decade parapsychology gained status in the country, as signaled by the holding of the First International Conference of Parapsychological Studies at Utrecht in 1953 and the establishment of a chair of parapsychology and a Parapsychology Institute at the University of Utrecht that same year.

Tenhaeff was named to the chair in parapsychology and given the directorship of the institute at Utrecht. From that time forward he came to dominate the society and resentment grew over his authoritarian leadership. The tension between Tenhaeff and some of the other leading members culminated in 1960 with the withdrawal of a group led by **George A. M.**

Zorab, who founded the **Nederlandse Vereniging voor Parapsychologie.**

During the 1960s Tenhaeff became famous both in the Netherlands and throughout the West because of his studies of and extraordinary claims for the psychic abilities of **Gerard Croiset,** the psychic who became well known for his work in assisting police to solve crimes, especially cases involving missing persons. Tenhaeff authored many articles and books that initially brought him some acclaim, but as people began to give his work close scrutiny, it was discovered that he had falsified data in a number of cases. During the late 1970s his exaggerations, misrepresentations, and alterations of findings became a major scandal in European parapsychology. Tenhaeff tried to withstand the massive attack by calling the religious to his support and suggesting that Communists were behind the attacks upon him. However, by the time of his death in 1981, he had been rejected by his colleagues.

The Studievereniging voor Psychical Research survived the Tenhaeff scandal and was led by Henri van Praag from 1978–1986. Under his management the Parapsychology Institute was transformed into a private organization that existed independently from the university. In 1986, Douwe Bosga became the institute's director and he was succeeded by Dick Bierman who was appointed in 1991. The institute continues a program of lectures for the public and the publication of its journal, **Tijdschrift voor Parapsychology.** Address: Springweg 7, 3511 VH Utrecht, The Netherlands.

Stukeley, William (1687–1765)

William Stukeley, an antiquarian famous for his research on Stonehenge and related megalithic monuments in Western England, was born in Holbeach, Lincolnshire, England, on November 7, 1687, the son of a lawyer. As a youth, he collected and studied plants, and studied astrology. He entered Bennet College, Cambridge, in 1703 and received his degree in 1708. During his school days he made some notable contributions to the cataloguing of plant life.

After college he studied medicine and opened a medical practice in Lincolnshire in 1710. He moved to London in 1717, and soon became a member of the Royal Society. Meanwhile he continued formal studies in medicine and in 1719 received his medical degree from Cambridge. The following year he was admitted as a fellow to the College of Physicians.

While making his living as a physician, Stukeley also developed a spiritual quest centered upon a recovery of the mysteries from the ancients. He joined a speculative Freemasonry lodge in 1720, hoping to find there the answer to his questions. He also made a number of trips exploring ancient ruins in England, the first result being a book, *Intinerarium Curiosum,* published in 1724. His book on **Stonehenge** appeared in 1740.

Through the 1730s he had accepted the idea first broached by **John Aubrey** in the previous century tying Stonehenge and related stone monuments to ancient **Druidism.** He had read and made notes from Aubrey's unpublished *Monumenta Britannica,* and in 1719 began to make annual visits to study the stone remains in Wiltshire. In 1717 a new Druidic order had emerged in England, and **John Toland** was named its first chief. Stukeley became the second chief following Toland's death in 1722. He took the name Chyndonax and became known to his friends as the Archdruid. His 1740 book on Stonehenge argued that it was of Druid origin, and a later volume made a similar argument for the nearby formation at **Avebury.** While Aubrey had first broached the idea, it was Stukeley who popularized it and gave it substance with his publications.

In 1726 Stukeley moved back to Lincolnshire, where he laid out a temple to the Druids centered on an apple tree covered with mistletoe. His understanding of Druidism was consistent with his understanding of Christianity, and in 1730, he became a priest in the Church of England. In 1734 he published a book, *Paleographia Sacra,* in which he argued that Pagan mythology was derived from the biblical tradition.

He spent the rest of his life as a clergyman, though known for some unorthodox quirks. He is remembered for delaying a church service to allow his congregation to experience an eclipse of the sun and of preaching a sermon after receiving a new set of spectacles from a text in Paul's letter to the Corinthians, "Now we see through a glass darkly." He died on February 25, 1765, in Queen Square, Kent, where he had retired. Among the artifacts he left behind that were sold at auction in 1766 was a wooden model of Stonehenge he had carved.

Sources:

Carr-Gomm, Philip. *The Elements of the Druid Tradition.* Shaftesbury, Dorset, UK: Element, 1991.

Sturdevant, William D(esmond) (1922–)

Professor of art who was active in the field of parapsychology. He was born July 3, 1922, in Des Moines, Iowa. He attended Drake University, Des Moines (B.S. education, 1945; M.S. education, 1947) and following graduation became an art instructor at New Mexico Western College, Silver City (1947–48). He afterward taught at Minnesota State College at Mankato (1948–55); was an art supervisor for the Joliet public schools, Joliet, Illinois (1955–59); and was assistant professor of art at California Western University, San Diego (1959–61). A practitioner as well as a teacher, Sturdevant has works in the permanent collection of the Boston Museum of Fine Arts and has exhibited widely. He made experimental studies concerning extrasensory color perception and from his findings published two monographs. He was a charter associate of the **Parapsychological Association.**

Sources:

Pleasants, Helene, ed. *Biographical Dictionary of Parapsychology.* New York: Helix Press, 1964.

Sturdevant, William D. *Extrasensory Color Perception.* N.p., 1958.

———. *Fluorescent Color Perception and Graphic Response in the Perceptually Impaired Child.* N.p., 1957.

St. Winifred's Well

St. Winifred's Well, a holy healing well in northern Wales (United Kingdom), is a site related to ancient Celtic Christianity that has come back into prominence as a result of the contemporary Celtic revival. The legend of the well goes back to the fifth century C.E. and the movement of Christian hermits into the region. Among those who studied Christianity with the hermits was Winifred, the daughter of a Welsh chieftain. One day she was attacked by another chieftain and refused his advances. In his anger, he cut off her head. Where the severed head fell, a healing spring well gushed forth. Where her blood splattered the moss turned red and began to emit an odor like violets. The head rolled into a nearby chapel where Bueno, one of the hermits, retrieved it, carried it to the body, and prayed over Winifred. She returned to life. At a later date, Bueno blessed the well and promised that all who came to the well would receive an answer to their prayer.

While the story of Winifred and Bueno is set in the fifth century, it can be dated as a legend only to the twelfth century. Since that time the well has been in use as a healing spring and relics believed to belong to Winifred were placed in the church at Shrewsbury. During the Middle Ages, pilgrims would go to Shrewsbury and then to the well. Along the route they passed stones said to have been covered with her blood. The wife of Henry VII built a large building over the well in 1500. However, not long afterwards, the cult of Winifred was disrupted when King Henry VIII, who at one time had visited the well, moved against the monasteries and pilgrimage sites across his land. The stones along the pilgrimage site were scattered and the relics lost. Only a single finger believed to be Winifred's survived and was hidden away in Rome until 1852, when it was sent back to England and divided between Shrewsbury and the well.

When the Church of England replaced the Roman Catholic Church as the official state religion, Winifred's Well remained a focus of Catholicism in England. Pilgrims continued to come to the site and reported healing through the years that Catholicism was officially outlawed in England. When the church was again given legal status in the middle of the nineteenth century, the well immediately became the scene of official pilgrimages. Today, both Anglicans and Catholics utilize the well shrine. The Church of England sponsors an annual pilgrimage for the handicapped. The Catholic priest in the church adjacent to the shrine blesses pilgrims with Winifred's finger relic. Though it is not as famous as **Lourdes,** many healings have been reported from the shrine.

Sources:

Charles-Edwards, T. *Saint Winifrede and Her Well.* London: Catholic Truth Society, 1971.

David, Christopher. *Saint Winifrede's Well.* Slough, UK: Kennion Press, 1969.

Jones, Francis. *The Holy Wells of Wales.* Cardiff: University of Wales, 1992.

Subconscious

A term used by some to describe a segment of the mind below the threshold of consciousness and by others as a collective name for mental phenomena dissociated from those directly or introspectively cognized. **F. W. H. Myers,** an early and prominent psychical researcher, ascribed various **supernormal** faculties to it. During the early twentieth century, theories involving such faculties eliminated for many any need to appeal to spirit agencies. Others, however, pointed to the subconscious as a means to reconcile mental activity with spirit agencies. The subconscious may be—as **J. H. Hyslop** pointed out—the very instrument for receiving and transmitting foreign transcendental stimuli, to which, on favorable occasions, it becomes sensitive.

Subjective Phenomena

"Subjective," as distinguished from "objective," is a classification for mental phenomena that are not capable of objective validation, as in the case of physical phenomena.

Subliminal

A term first used by A. H. Pierce of Harvard University for sensations beneath the threshold of consciousness, too vague to be individually recognized. **F. W. H. Myers** extended the meaning to cover all that takes place beneath the consciousness threshold—sensations, thoughts, and emotions that seldom emerge but form a **consciousness** quite as complex and coherent as the supraliminal one, since they demonstrate processes of mentation and exhibit a continuous chain of memory.

Nevertheless, Myers did not consider the subliminal consciousness a separate self but, together with the supraliminal (normal consciousness) one, a fragment of the larger self revealed through an organism that cannot afford it full manifestation. In this concept he came close to the Hindu Vedanta concepts of *jiva* (individual soul) as part of *atman* (collective soul).

Myers attributed most supernormal psychical phenomena to the subliminal self, but not as a complete explanation or exclusion of the **spirit hypothesis.** On the contrary, his inference was that if our incarnate selves may act in **telepathy** in at least apparent independence of the fleshly body, the presumption is strong that other spirits may exist independently of the body and may affect us in a similar manner.

Myers divided the influence of the subliminal on the supraliminal into three main areas: (1) When the subliminal mentation cooperates with and supplements the supraliminal, without changing the apparent phase of personality, we have genius. (2) When subliminal operations change the apparent phase of personality from the state of waking toward the direction of **trance,** we have hypnotism. (3) When the subliminal mentation forces itself up through the supraliminal, without amalgamation, as in crystal vision, **automatic writing,** and so forth, we have sensory or motor **automatism.**

Subliminal Self

A term formerly used in psychical research to denote that part of the personality is normally beneath the "threshold" (*limen*) separating **consciousness** from unconsciousness. The phrase owed its popularity largely to pioneer researcher **F. W. H. Myers,** who made use of it to explain the psychic phenomena he had observed. The view of Myers was that only a fraction of the human personality, or soul, finds adequate expression through the ordinary cerebral processes, because the brain and physical organism have not yet reached a very advanced stage of evolution. The soul, in short, is like an iceberg, with a fraction of its bulk above water but with a much greater part submerged.

The subliminal self, according to Myers, is in touch with a reservoir of psychical energy, from which it draws forces that influence the physical organism. Thus the inspiration of genius, the exaltation of the perceptive and intellectual faculties in hypnosis, and such exercises as **automatic writing** and talking and **table turning** are caused by great influxes of these psychical forces rather than by any spirit influences.

These hypotheses have been advanced to explain **telepathy** and communication between the living and the dead, as well as **hallucination, automatism,** and all the phenomena of **hypnotism.** But the two former, even if they could be demonstrated, would have to be explained on other grounds, while the others, whose existence is undisputed, are more generally regarded as resulting from cerebral dissociation (i.e., the temporary dislocation of the connecting links between the various neural systems). (See also **Subconscious**)

Subterranean Cities

A persistent myth of modern occultism concerns the existence of societies residing underground. The myth takes many forms, including stories of underground caverns inhabited by malevolent **deros** (dwarfs) and subterranean cities inhabited by the survivors of **Atlantis** or **Lemuria,** or **flying saucer** pilots.

Much of this new mythology stems from the publications of the enterprising **Raymond A. Palmer** in *Amazing Stories, Flying Saucers,* and *Search* magazines. In 1945 Palmer introduced the readers of *Amazing Stories* to the fantasies of **Richard S. Shaver,** with whom Palmer collaborated in producing what were stoutly claimed to be factual "racial memories" of survivors from Atlantis and Lemuria, originally giants but now degenerated into malevolent dwarfs, influencing mankind by secret rays.

Palmer, who helped focus the first excitement about flying saucers in his magazine *Fate* in the spring 1948 issue, later went on to publish articles suggesting that saucers came from an underground world entered through the polar ice caps.

Other sources for subterranean mythology include the writings of **Robert Ernest Dickhoff** and Milinko S. Stevic. In Dickhoff's book *Agharta,* he describes a vast network of underground tunnels radiating from Antarctica with openings in the United States, Brazil, Tibet, and Pacific islands. These underground strongholds are inhabited by descendants of Martians, who colonized the Earth in prehistory.

Stevic, a Yugoslav-born engineer, lectures about the extensive subterranean cities beneath New York, Tokyo, Leningrad, São Paulo, and large areas of the Atlantic Ocean. Survivors of Atlantis reside in this subterranean world, where they have built huge domes of fiberglass. There are millions of inhabitants, who also contribute illegal immigrants to the United States. There are, apparently, secret entrances to the underground world through a number of churches, including, specifically, St. John the Divine at 103rd Street and Amsterdam in New York. Stevic also claims that Adolf Hitler did not die but reached the United States through a secret tunnel and now lives quietly in New Jersey.

In Livingston, Montana, W. C. and **Gladys Hefferlin** also publicized a Rainbow City in the Antarctic, founded two million years ago as the focal point of a network of underground tunnels. Heading the large population in Rainbow City are the Ancient Three, descendants of Martians who exercise a favorable influence on world affairs, in contrast to Shaver's malevolent deros. These powerful mystics of Rainbow City won World War II for the Allies by stopping Rommel in Egypt and halting the Japanese in the Pacific.

Early in this century, Frederick Spencer Oliver (writing as the channel for "Phylos the Tibetan") began to speak of people living inside a hollow Mt. Shasta, in northern California. His initial revelations were later strengthened by the revelations of **Guy W. Ballard,** founder of the **I Am Movement.** In 1934, writing as Godfré Ray King, Ballard published *Unveiled Mysteries,* in which he detailed his encounters with a godlike figure named Master Saint-Germain.

Although based somewhat on traditional fairy lore, notions of demonic realms beneath the Earth, and Asian folklore, accounts of underground worlds have emerged as an integral part of modern occult lore. (See also **Subterranean Crypts and Temples**)

Sources:

Chaney, Earlyne. *Revelations of Things to Come.* Upland, Calif.: Astara, 1982.

Dickhoff, Robert Ernest. *Agharta.* Boston: Bruce Humphries, 1951.

Hefferlin, W. C., and Gladys Hefferlin. *A Description of the Rainbow City from the Hefferlin Manuscript.* Vista, Calif.: Borderland Sciences Research Foundation, n.d.

Ramana Maharshi. *Talks with Sri Ramana Maharshi.* Vol. 1. Tiruvannamalai, India: Sri Ramanasramam, 1957.

Subterranean Crypts and Temples

Subterranean resorts, crypts, and places of worship have always fascinated the human mind. The mysteries of the Egyptians and other peoples were held in underground crypts, possibly to render these ceremonies still more mysterious to ordinary people, perhaps because it was essential to the privacy they required, or possibly to symbolize the exploration of the hidden parts of the self. The caves of Elephanta, the Roman catacombs, and similar subterranean edifices are also well-known examples. There are also several lesser but perhaps more interesting underground meeting places and temples in various parts of the world.

An Underworld City in Central America

The Jesuit priests of the early eighteenth century left descriptions of the palace of Mitla in Central America that leave no doubt that in their time it contained many subterranean chambers, and one especially appears to have surpassed all others in the dreadful uses to which it was put.

Father Torquemada gave the following description of the place:

"When some monks of my order, the Franciscan, passed, preaching and shriving through the province of Zapoteca, whose capital city is Tehuantepec, they came to a village which was called Mictlan, that is, underworld (hell). Besides mentioning the large number of people in the village they told of buildings which were prouder and more magnificent than any which they had hitherto seen in New Spain. Among them was the temple of the evil spirit and living rooms for his demoniacal servants, and among other fine things there was a hall with ornamented panels, which were constructed of stone in a variety of arabesques and other very remarkable designs. There were doorways there, each one of which was built of but three stones, two upright at the sides and one across them, in such a manner that, although these doorways were very high and broad, the stone sufficed for their entire construction. They were so thick and broad that we were assured there were few like them. There was another hall in these buildings, or rectangular temples, which was erected entirely on round stone pillars very high and very thick that two grown men could scarcely encircle them with their arms, nor could one of them reach the finger-tips of the other. These pillars were all in one piece and, it was said, the whole shaft of the pillar measured 5 ells [about 18 feet or 6 meters] from top to bottom, and they were very much like those of the church of Santa Maria Maggiore in Rome, very skillfully made and polished."

Father Burgoa was more explicit with regard to these subterranean chambers:

"There were four chambers above ground and four below. The latter were arranged according to their purpose in such a way that one front chamber served as chapel and sanctuary for the idols, which were placed on a great stone which served as an altar. And for the most important feasts[,] which they celebrated with sacrifices, or at the burial of a king or great lord, the high priest instructed the lesser priests or the subordinate temple officials who served him to prepare the chapel and his vestments and a large quantity of the incense used by them.

"And then he descended with a great retinue, when none of the common people saw him or dared to look in his face, convinced that if they did so they would fall dead to the earth as a punishment for their boldness. And when he entered the chapel they put on him a long white cotton garment made like an alb, and over that a garment shaped like a dalmatic, which was embroidered with pictures of wild beasts and birds; and they put a cap on his head, and on his feet a kind of shoe woven of many-colored feathers.

"And when he had put on these garments he walked with solemn mien and measured step to the altar, bowed low before the idols, renewed the incense, and then in quite unintelligible murmurs he began to converse with these images, these depositories of infernal spirits, and continued in this sort of prayer with hideous grimaces and writhings, uttering inarticulate sounds, which filled all present with fear and terror, till he came out of that diabolical trance and told those standing around the lies and fabrications which the spirit had imparted to him or which he had invented himself.

"When human beings were sacrificed the ceremonies were multiplied, and the assistants of the high priest stretched the victim out upon a large stone, bareing his breast, which they tore open with a great stone knife, while the body writhed in fearful convulsions and they laid the heart bare, ripping it out, and with it the soul, which the devil took, while they carried the heart to the high priest that he might offer it to the idols by holding it to their mouths, among other ceremonies; and the body was thrown into the burial-place of their 'blessed,' as they called them. And if after the sacrifice he felt inclined to detain those who begged any favor he sent them word by the subordinate priests not to leave their houses till their gods were appeased, and he commanded them to do penance meanwhile, to fast and to speak with no woman, so that, until this father of sin had interceded for the absolution of the penitents and had declared the gods appeased they did not dare to cross their threshold.

"The second [underground] chamber was the burial place of these high priests, and third that of the kings of Theozapotlan, whom they brought thither richly dressed in their best attire, feathers, jewels, golden necklaces, and precious stones, placing a shield in their left hand and a javelin in the right, just as they used them in war. And at their burial rites great mourning prevailed; the instruments which were played made mournful sounds; and with loud wailing and continuous sobbing they chanted the life and exploits of their lord until they laid him on the structure which they had prepared for this purpose.

"The last [underground] chamber had a second door at the rear, which led to a dark and gruesome room. This was closed with a stone slab, which occupied the whole entrance. Through this door they threw the bodies of the victims and of the great lords and chieftains who had fallen in battle, and they brought them from the spot where they fell, even when it was very far off, to this burial place; and so great was the barbarous infatuation of these Indians that, in the belief of the happy life which awaited them, many who were oppressed by diseases or hardships begged this infamous priest to accept them as living sacrifices and allow them to enter through that portal and roam about in the dark interior of the mountains, to seek the great feasting places of their forefather. And when anyone obtained this favour the servants of the high priest led him thither with special ceremonies, and after they had allowed him to enter through the small door they rolled the stone before it again and took leave of him, and the unhappy man, wandering in that abyss of darkness, died of hunger and thirst, beginning already in life the pain of his damnation; and on account of this horrible abyss they called this village Liyobaa, The Cavern of Death.

"When later there fell upon these people the light of the Gospel, its servants took much trouble to instruct them to find out whether this error, common to all these nations, still prevailed, and they learned from the stories which had been handed down that all were convinced that this damp cavern extended more than 30 leagues underground, and that its roof was supported by pillars. And there were people, zealous prelates anxious for knowledge, who, in order to convince these ignorant people of their terror, went into this cave accompanied by a large number of people bearing lighted torches and firebrands, and descended several large steps. And they soon came upon many buttresses which formed a kind of street. They had prudently brought a quantity of rope with them to use as a guiding line, that they might not lose themselves in this confusing labyrinth. And the putrefaction and the bad odour and the dampness of the earth were very great and there was also a cold wind which blew out their torches. And after they had gone a short distance, fearing to be overpowered by the stench or to step on poisonous reptiles, of which some had been seen, they resolved to go out again and to completely wall up this back door of hell. The four buildings above ground were the only ones which still remained open, and they had a court and chambers like those underground; and the ruins of these have lasted even to the present day."

The Temple Hill at Jerusalem

The vast subterranean vaults under the temple hill at Jerusalem were probably used as a secret meeting place by the Templars during their occupation of the Holy City, and it was perhaps there that the strange Eastern rites of **Baphomet** that they later affected were first celebrated.

In his book *Recent Discoveries on the Temple Hill* (1884), Rev. James King gives the following account:

"On the occasion of a visit to the Noble Sanctuary, the author had an opportunity of examining the ancient masonry inside the wall at the south-east corner, as well as the vast subterranean vaults popularly known as Solomon's stables. A small doorway, under a little dome at the south-east corner, admits by a flight of steps to a small chamber known as the Mosque of the Cradle of our Lord, from the existence of a hollowed stone which somewhat resembles a cradle, and a tradition that the Virgin Mary remained in this chamber for some time after her purification in the Temple. Passing through the chamber, the spacious vaults, which extend over an acre of ground, are reached. These subterranean substructures consist of one hundred square piers arranged in fifteen rows, each pier being five feet wide and composed of large marginal drafted stones, placed singly over each other. The rows are connected by semicircular arches, the intercolumniations of which range from ten to twenty-three feet. The floor of these vaults is about forty-feet below the Haram Area, and more than a hundred feet above the great foundation corner-stone. They are called Solomon's Stables by the Franks. But the Moslems call the place, Al Masjed al Kadim, that is, The Old Mosque. These vaults were used as stables by the Frank kings and the Knights'Templar, and holes in which rings were fastened can still be traced on some of the piers.

"Since the floor of Solomon's Stables is upwards of a hundred feet above the foundation stone, it seems highly probable that there exists another system of vaults below, for the vast space from the rock upwards is not likely to be filled with solid earth.

"Some allusion seems to be made to these vaults in the writings of Procopius, a Greek historian of the sixth century. He was born at Caesarea, in Palestine, about 500 A.D., and as a young man went to Constantinople, where his eminent talents brought him under the notice of the Emperor Justinian. In 529 A.D. Justinian built a splendid church on the Temple Hill, in honour of the Virgin Mary, and in the writings of Procopius there is a full and detailed account of the edifice. The historian relates that the fourth part of the ground required for the building was wanting towards the south-east; the builders therefore laid their foundations on the sloping ground, and constructed a series of arched vaults, in order to raise the ground to the level of the other parts of the enclosure. This account is eminently descriptive of the subterranean vaults at the south-east portion of the Haram, and, according to [an authority], the stone-work of these vaults certainly belongs to the age of Justinian." (See also **Subterranean Cities**)

Subud

A spiritual movement that has grown up around the Indonesian mystic **Muhammad Subuh,** known as "Bapak" (spiritual father). Beginning in Java, it spread to Europe and elsewhere, after winning support from the **Gurdjieff** disciples at Coombe Springs, England, led by **J. G. Bennett.** Gurdjieff himself had predicted that there would be an Indonesian teacher to bring emotional warmth to his system. Subud gained public recognition in 1959 when the movement held an international congress in England. Soon afterward, the Hungarian actress Eva Bartok was initiated and claimed to be healed from childbirth complications.

The basis of the Subud movement is the **latihan,** an initiation ceremony for newcomers and a spiritual exercise for those already initiated. A "helper" prepares the initiate for "opening" or receptivity to the descent of spiritual energy. This often causes pronounced convulsions, similar to the "shakes" or "jerks" elicited by nineteenth century evangelists at camp meetings, or the onset of **kundalini** energy in traditional Hindu mysticism.

This energy is seen as having a purifying function and reportedly brings intense feelings of peace when there is submission to divine will. Subud has no creed, dogma, rules, or regulations but makes available the experience of the latihan to initiates. Subud groups meet regularly in members' homes or in rented halls. The movement does not advertise or proselytize.

More than 70 North American cities have Subud centers, and there are many in the United Kingdom. Address in North America: Subud USA, 13701 Bel-Red Rd., Ste. B, Bellevue, WA

98005. Address in Great Britain: Subud, 342 Cricklewood Ln., London, NW2 2QH.

Sources:

Barter, J. P. *Towards Subud.* London, 1967.
Bennett, John G. *Concerning Subud.* New Hyde Park, N.Y.: University Books, 1959.
Rofe, Husein. *The Path of Subud.* London: Rider, 1959.
Van Hien, G. *What is Subud?* London: Rider, 1963.

Subuh, Muhammad (1901–1987)

Indonesian mystic whose spiritual mission led to the formation of the movement known as **Subud.** Following some years of searching for spiritual guidance in Sufi and other movements, Subuh had an initiatory experience in 1925 on his twenty-fourth birthday when a sphere of light appeared in the night and seemed to enter his head, filling him with vibrating energy and light. Three years later this strange energy source stopped abruptly, and Subuh continued his everyday life as a government official and married man, while passing through the equivalent stage of the Western mystical "dark night of the soul." On his thirty-second birthday he had an enlightenment revealing his spiritual mission, and he devoted himself to his work.

The name Subud derives from an abbreviation of three words: *susila* (morality in line with divine will), *budhi* (enlightenment in man), and *dharma* (attitude of submission and sincerity toward God). Subuh's own name actually means "sunrise," but he is known to his followers as "Bapak," an affectionate Javanese term meaning "father" often applied to a spiritual teacher.

Prior to 1956 Subud was little known outside Indonesia, but after that it attracted European interest. When Subuh visited the **Gurdjieff** headquarters of Coombe Springs in Britain, its director, **J. G. Bennett,** and followers were won over by his emotional and spiritual vibrancy. During his lifetime, Gurdjieff had made mysterious allusions to a forthcoming Indonesian teacher, and Bennett led many Gurdjieffian students in accepting Subuh as that teacher.

By 1960 interest in the group died out and Subuh returned to Indonesia where he died in 1987.

Sources:

Bennett, John G. *Concerning Subud.* New Hyde Park, N.Y.: University Books, 1959.
Muhammad-Subuh Sumohadiwidjojo. *Susila Budhi Dharma.* Subud Publications International, 1975.

Succubus

A demon who takes the shape of a woman, stealing the vitality of men during sleep. Old rabbinical writings relate the legend of how Adam was visited over a period of 130 years by female demons and had intercourse with demons, spirits, specters, lemurs, and phantoms.

Another legend relates how under the reign of Roger, king of Sicily, a young man was bathing by moonlight and thought he saw someone drowning and hastened to the rescue. Having drawn from the water a beautiful woman, he became enamored of her, married her, and they had a child. Afterward she disappeared mysteriously with her child, which made everyone believe she was a succubus.

In the fifteenth century, the succubus and the male demon, the counterpart **incubus** (which takes the form of a man, to seduce women), were associated with **witchcraft,** and witches were assumed to have intercourse with demons. The historian Hector Boece (1465–1536), in his history of Scotland, related that a very handsome young man was pursued by a female demon, who would pass through his closed door and offer to marry him. He complained to his bishop, who enjoined him to fast, pray, and confess, and as a result the infernal visitor ceased to trouble him.

The witchcraft judge **Pierre de Lancre** (1553–1631) stated that in Egypt an honest blacksmith was occupied in forging during the night when a demon in the shape of a beautiful woman appeared to him. He threw a hot iron in the face of the demon, which at once took flight.

The succubus was generally believed to appear most frequently during sleep, especially in nightmares. Roman Catholic theologian Thomas Aquinas argued for the objective existence of the incubus/succubus and believed that such intercourse could lead to the pregnancy of a woman. Twentieth-century psychology tends to see such creatures as dream symbols of repressed sexual feelings.

Sources:

Jones, Ernest. *On the Nightmare.* New York: Liveright, 1951.
Melton, J. Gordon. *The Vampire Book: The Encyclopedia of the Undead.* 2nd edition. Detroit: Visible Ink Press, 1999.
Robbins, Rossell Hope. *The Encyclopedia of Witchcraft and Demonology.* New York: Crown Publishers, 1959.

Sudre, René (1880– ?)

Scientific writer and parapsychologist. Sudre was born April 19, 1880, at Angoulême, France. He received degrees from Poitiers Academy and the University of Paris.

As a writer and teacher he held a variety of positions between the world wars. He was a scientific commentator for Radiodiffusion Française (1926–40), a writer on psychic research for *Mercure de France* (1925–28), a professor at École des Hautes Etudes Sociales, Paris (1931–40), and a scientific writer for the *Journal des Débats* (1935–40). After the war he worked for the French Ministry of Information, the Foreign Ministry (1945–56), and for the *Revue des Deux Mondes* beginning in 1949. He won a number of awards for his writing.

Sudre experimented in many fields of parapsychology and spent many years attempting to show that **psi** phenomena were a matter for science. He argued for a coherent theoretical approach to psi and believed that the universe was permeated with a creative power that accounted for all psychic phenomena. He believed that the assumptions of **Spiritualism** were erroneous and that all living creatures possessed some extrasensory faculty. He was a corresponding member of the **National Laboratory of Psychical Research,** London University; secretary of French committees for international conferences on psychical research in Copenhagen (1922) and Warsaw (1923); and a member of the **Society for Psychical Research,** London. Besides his own books, he translated into French various books on parapsychology by **William James, Sir William Barrett, J. B. Rhine,** and **T. K. Oesterreich** and contributed numerous articles to such journals as *Psychic Research* (1926–31) and *Revue Métapsychique* (1922–26).

Sources:

Berger, Arthur S., and Joyce Berger. *The Encyclopedia of Parapsychology and Psychical Research.* New York: Paragon House, 1991.
Pleasants, Helene, ed. *Biographical Dictionary of Parapsychology.* New York: Helix Press, 1964.
Sudre, René. *Le Huitième art—Mission de la radio* (The Eighth Art—Mission of Radio). N.p., 1946.
———. *Introduction à la métapsychique humaine* (Introduction to Human Metapsychics). N.p., 1929.
———. "Is the Soul Material?" *Psychic Research* 24 (1930).
———. *La Lutte pour la métapsychique* (The Fight for Parapsychology). N.p., 1928.
———. *Les Nouvelles énigmes de l'univers* (New Enigmas of the Universe). N.p., 1943.

———. *Personnages d'au-delà* (People from the Beyond). N.p., 1945.

———. *Traité de parapsychologie.* 1956. Translated as *Treatise on Parapsychology: Essay on the Scientific Interpretation of the Human Phenomenon Known as the Supernatural.* New York: Citadel Press, 1960.

Sufism

A mystical movement of Islam. The name derives from the woollen clothing (*suf*), worn by Sufis as a token of penitence, similar to the Christian penitent tradition of wearing hair shirts.

In medieval times Sufism was characterized by a complex system of striving for spiritual attainment and divine grace. The spiritual stages involved include conversion, abstinence, renunciation, poverty, patience, trust in God, and contentment; with spiritual states of meditation, nearness to God, love, fear, hope, longing, intimacy, tranquility, contemplation, and certainty. Much of this is analogous to the *yama* and *niyama* of Hindu **yoga.**

There were four orders of Sufis: the Qadiriyya, an orthodox wing emphasizing devotional exercises leading to spiritual experience; the Suhrawardiyya, less orthodox and with a suggestion of pantheism; the Shadhiliyya (widespread in Egypt and North Africa) with intense devotion and utter dependence on God; and the Mevlevi order, founded by the poet Rumi, which developed the special mystical dance of the **dervishes.**

Sufism has influenced religious movements in India, Java, and elsewhere and played a part in the development of such unorthodox prophets as Baha'u'llah of the **Baha'i** faith and the mystic Meher Baba. The major emphasis in Sufism is intense love for God, expressed in the perfection of the soul.

A Western Sufi organization is the Sufi Order (headed by Pir Vilayat Inayat Khan), whose traditions are said to predate Islam and to have become incorporated in it. In 1910 the Sufi Order was established in Europe and the United States through the lectures of Hazrat Pir-o-Murshid Inayat Khan. The order stresses that God is one and that there are no barriers between religions. Address: Sufi Order Secretariat, Box 574, Lebanon Springs, NY 12114. British branch: Barton Farm, Pound Lake, Bradford-on-Avon, Wiltshire, England.

A separate group of the Sufi movement is the Sufi Islamia Ruhaniat Society. Address: The Mentorgarten, 10 Precita Ave., San Francisco, CA 94110.

Another Sufi group is the Sufi Cultural Center in London, established in 1971. It places great emphasis on the mysticism of music, and encourages the teaching of classical Indian music with the more modern adjunct of health foods and alternative healing. (See also **Idries Shah**)

Sources:

Khan, Pir V. *The Message in Our Time: The Life and Teachings of the Sufi Master, Hazrat Inayat Khan.* New York: Harper & Row, 1979.

Shah, Idries. *The Sufis.* London: W. H. Allen, 1964.

———. *The Way of the Sufi.* New York: E. P. Dutton, 1970.

Subhan, John. *Sufism: Its Saints and Shrines.* York Beach, Maine: Samuel Weiser, 1973.

Williams, L. F. R., ed. *Sufi Studies: East and West.* London: Octagon Press, 1974.

Suggestion

Sensitivity of an entranced subject to suggestion is the characteristic and invariable accompaniment of the hypnotic state and is also a distinctive feature of hysteria. Indeed, many scientists gave to **hypnotism** the name "suggestion." An abnormal suggestibility implies some measure of cerebral dissociation. In this state every suggestion advanced by the operator, whether conveyed by word, gesture, or even unconscious glance, operates with abnormal force in the brain of the subject, which becomes relieved from the counterexcitement of other ideas and stimuli.

In the view of psychologist **Pierre Janet,** all suggestibility implies a departure from perfect sanity, but this, although perhaps true in the strictest sense, is somewhat misleading, since all individuals are more or less amenable to suggestion. In hypnotism and hysteria, however, the normal suggestibility is greatly exaggerated, and the suggestion, meeting with no opposition from the recipient's critical or judicial faculties (because there are no other ideas with which to compare it), becomes, for the time, the subject's dominant idea. The suggestion thus accepted has a powerful effect on both mind and body; hence the value of suggestion in certain complaints is incalculable.

The miracles of healing claimed by **Christian Science, New Thought,** and other groups, the efficacy of a pilgrimage to **Lourdes,** the feats of healing **mediums**—all testify to its powerful effect.

Posthypnotic suggestion is the term applied to a suggestion made while the subject is entranced but which is to be carried out after awakening. Sometimes an interval of months may elapse between the utterance of a command and its fulfillment, but almost invariably at the stated time or stipulated stimulus the suggestion is obeyed, the recipient usually being unaware of the source of the impulse.

Autosuggestion does not proceed from any extraneous source, but arises in one's own mind, either spontaneously or from a misconception of existing circumstances, as in the case of a person who is persuaded to drink colored water under the impression that it is poison and exhibits every symptom of poisoning. Autosuggestion may arise spontaneously in **dreams,** the automatic obedience to such suggestion often giving rise to stories of "veridical" dreams.

The outbreaks of religious frenzy or ecstasy that swept Europe in the Middle Ages were examples of the results of mass suggestion (i.e., suggestion made by a crowd, and much more potent than that made by an individual). Cases of so-called collective **hallucination** may have the same cause.

Psychical researchers have been interested in suggestion because it involves abnormal conditions of mind and body. It may be an aspect of **healing by faith,** for suggestion can cause and cure diseases and bad habits, remove inhibitions, mitigate deficiencies of character, stimulate the imagination, vivify the senses, and heighten intellectual powers.

William James described suggestion as "another name for the power of ideas, so far as they prove efficacious over belief and conduct." According to **F. W. H. Myers,** the power is exercised by the **subliminal self.** He defined suggestion as "successful appeal to the subliminal self." It is well known that dreams may be influenced by external stimuli applied to the sleeper, such as whispering in the ear or moving the limbs. Suggestion is also a powerful factor in advertising, particularly in the use of persuasive repetition and "subliminal suggestions" in television commercials.

Sukias

Central American witches.

Sullivan, Erin (1947–)

Erin Sullivan, a notable contemporary Canadian astrologer, was born in Vancouver, British Columbia, on November 9, 1947. She took up the study of **astrology** in her late teens and soon developed a thriving practice. She married and became the mother of two daughters. She also became a popular author, contributing articles to a variety of astrological periodicals. She was among the founders of the Association for Astrological Networking and the Cross Canada Council for the Fraternity of Canadian Astrologers. During the 1980s she had a radio show that originated in Victoria, British Columbia.

In 1989, Sullivan moved from Canada to the United Kingdom. She established a private practice and associated with the **Centre for Psychological Astrology,** for whom she taught classes in London and Zürich, **Switzerland.** She also travels to **Australia** annually to teach. Shortly after moving to London, she succeeded **Howard Sasportas** as editor of the Arkana Astrology series published by Viking-Penguin, and she contributed two of her own works to the series, *Saturn in Transet: Boundaries of the Mind, Body and Soul* (1990) and a second volume offering a psychological reevaluation of the phenomenon of retrograde planets, *Retrograde Planets: Traversing the Inner Landscape* (1992). Retrograde planets were a major problem for pre-modern astrologers, who assumed an earth-centered astronomy. While they moved steadily through the sky on their course, at times they appeared to come to a complete stop and begin to move backward. This unusual action came to be seen as an ill omen. Moving to a post-Copernican astronomy explained retrograde planets as an illusion created by the relative movements of the earth and other planets around the sun. Psychologically considered, retrograde became symbolic of challenges presented to the inner self.

Sources:

Sullivan, Erin. *Retrograde Planets: Traversing the Inner Landscape.* New York: Arkana, 1992.

———. *Saturn in Transet: Boundaries of the Mind, Body and Soul.* New York: Arkana, 1990.

Summerland

The land of bliss of spirits, so named by **Andrew Jackson Davis,** similar to the "Plane of Illusion" described by the claimed spirit of **F. W. H. Myers** in the book *The Road to Immortality* by Geraldine Cummins (1932). Summerland is the Spiritualist equivalent to the Christian heaven.

Summers, Montague (1880–1948)

Author who wrote about occult history and folklore. Alphonsus Joseph-Mary Augustus Montague Summers was born on April 10, 1880, near Bristol, England. He attended a private academy that prepared him to enter Clifton College. In 1899 he entered Trinity College, Oxford, and then went on to Lichfield Theological College to prepare for the Anglican priesthood. He received his B.A. in 1905 and an M.A. the following year. After a brief stay in Italy, in 1908 he was ordained a deacon and assigned to a Church of England congregation in Bath. He later served in Bitton, a suburb of Bristol. Soon after his assignment there, he and another clergyman were accused of homosexual activity. Although acquitted, he left the church and became a Roman Catholic. At some point, he seems to have been ordained as a priest.

Summers served in a parish for a brief period but in 1911 became a teacher. Over the next decades he pursued the life of an independent scholar, which led him to become a respected authority on the literature and drama of the Restoration era and on Gothic literature. His expertise emerged fully in the 1930s with a series of texts—*The Restoration Theatre* (1934), *A Bibliography of Restoration Drama* (1935), *The Gothic Quest: A History of the Gothic Novel* (1938), and *A Gothic Bibliography* (1940).

Summers reached a more popular audience with his interest in the occult and some of the more esoteric areas of folklore. Once he retired from his teaching post in 1925, he devoted his full time to research and writing. His first important book, and possibly still his best known, *A History of Witchcraft and Demonology,* appeared in 1926. It was followed by *Geography of Witchcraft* (1927). He moved on to complete his massive surveys of vampirism: *The Vampire: His Kith and Kin* (1928) and *The Vampire in Europe* (1929). He also edited English editions of *Malleus Maleficarum* (The Witches' Hammer, 1928), *Compendium Maleficarum* (1929), *Demonolatry* (1930), and Reginald Scot's *The Discoverie of Witchcraft* (1930). His occult interests continued with his study of *The Werewolf* (1933) and *Witchcraft and Black Magic* (1946).

Summers wrote as a conservative Catholic who retained pre-Enlightenment views concerning the reality of evil supernaturalism. Such views distracted from his otherwise scholarly perspectives on **witchcraft** and **vampires,** both of which he believed existed.

Summers died August 10, 1948, in England. He wrote an autobiographical study, which was published in 1980 as *The Galanty Show.*

Sources:

Frank, Frederick S. *Montague Summers: A Bibliographical Portrait.* Methuchen, N.J.: Scarecrow Press, 1988.

Jerome, Joseph. *Montague Summers: A Memoir.* London: Cecil and Amerila Woolf, 1965.

Morrow, Feliz. "The Quest for Montague Summers." In *The Vampire: His Kith and Kin,* by Montague Summer. New Hyde Park, N.Y.: University Books, 1960.

Smith, Timothy d'Arch. *A Bibliography of the Works of Montague Summers.* New Hyde Park, N.Y.: University Books, 1964.

Summers, Montague. *The Galanty Show.* London: Cecil Woolf, 1980.

———. *Geography of Witchcraft.* London, 1927.

———. *The Gothic Quest: A History of the Gothic Novel.* 1938. Reprint, London: Fortune Press, 1950.

———. *A History of Demonology and Witchcraft.* New York: Alfred A. Knopf, 1926.

———. *The Vampire: His Kith and Kin.* London: Routledge, Kegan Paul, Trench, Trubner, 1928.

———. *The Werewolf.* London: Kegan Paul, Trench, Trubner, 1933.

Summit Lighthouse See Church Universal and Triumphant

Summons by the Dying

It was once maintained by theologians that if anyone who was unjustly accused or persecuted should, with his dying breath, summon his oppressor to appear before the supreme tribunal, the person thus summoned would die on the day fixed by his innocent victim. Thus the grand master of the **Templars** cited the pope and the king of France to appear before God on a certain date, and as the story goes, both died at the appointed time.

François I, duke of Brittany, hired assassins to murder his brother in 1450. The dying prince summoned his murderer before the highest of all courts, and François shortly expired. Yet another instance is that of Ferdinand IV of Spain, who was summoned by two nobles whom he had condemned unjustly; he died at the end of 30 days.

Many more examples could be quoted to show how firmly rooted was this belief in the power of the dying to avenge their death by supernatural means. Fear, and possibly remorse, acting on the imagination of the guilty person might well cause him to expire at the stated time, and authenticated accounts of death caused by these agents are not unknown. This conclusion is further borne out by the fact that if the condemned man was guilty—that is, if the judge's conscience was clear—the summons had no effect.

An old story tells of Gonzalo of Cordova (1453–1515), who sentenced a soldier to death for sorcery. The soldier exclaimed that he was innocent and summoned Gonzalo to appear before God. "Go, then," said the judge, "and hasten the proceedings.

My brother who is in heaven, will appear for me." Gonzalo did not die at that time, as he believed he had acted justly and had no fear of the consequences of the summons.

Sundari, T(irunelveli) A(vudaippan) (1934–)

School psychologist who has also taken an active interest in parapsychology. She was born on December 25, 1934, at Dindigul, Madras State, India. She studied at Presidency College, Madras (B.A. psychology, 1956) and Madras University (M.A., 1959). After her graduation she went to work as a psychologist for the Government Girls' Approved School and the Vigilance Home, Madras. Her master's thesis was titled "Experimental Studies in Time Perception," and she has attempted to train subjects in precognition. She has also collected data relating to clairvoyance and telepathy.

Sources:

Pleasants, Helene, ed. *Biographical Dictionary of Parapsychology.* New York: Helix Press, 1964.

Sunderland, La Roy (1804–1885)

Methodist minister, abolitionist, and magnetist. Sunderland was born May 18, 1804, in Exeter, Rhode Island. He was apprenticed to a shoemaker. He became converted to Methodism and became a revivalist preacher at the age of 18. He had a reputation as an orator of great power and was prominent in the temperance and antislavery movement, presiding at the meeting in New York in October 1834 when the first Methodist antislavery society was organized. He was a delegate to the first antislavery convention at Cincinnati in 1841 and the World Convention in London in 1843.

In 1833 he withdrew from the ministry and two years later became one of the founders of *Zion's Watchman,* the antislavery periodical for the Methodist abolitionists in New England. He edited the tabloid for the next seven years. In 1842 he joined with a number of his socially active colleagues in withdrawing from the Methodist Episcopal Church and founding the Wesleyan Methodist Church. However, at the same time, he was undergoing a crisis of faith. A noted evangelist, he had come to feel that his abilities were a result of hypnotic powers. He had concluded that conversion was a natural, not a supernatural, action. His line of reasoning led him to the conclusion that religion was a fraud.

In 1842 he founded and also edited the *Magnet* in which he expounded his beliefs in mesmeric power and suggestion. He made a special study of animal magnetism and **mesmerism,** and in 1843 published *Pathetism; With Practical Instructions: Demonstrating the Falsity of the Hitherto Prevalent Assumptions in Regard to What Has Been Called "Mesmerism" and "Neurology," and Illustrating Those Laws Which Induce Somnambulism, Second Sight, Sleep, Dreaming, Trance, and Clairvoyance, with Numerous Facts Tending to Show the Pathology of Monomania, Insanity, Witchcraft, and Various Other Mental or Nervous Phenomena.*

He moved on to support Grahamism, an early school of natural diet, and **Spiritualism.** In 1851, he founded *The Spiritual Philosopher,* the first Spiritualist periodical in America. A year later, the title changed to *The Spirit World.* Although in the first issue he criticized the spirit theory and the evidence adduced on its behalf, he quickly became a believer when his own daughter, Margarette Cooper, became a medium. His enthusiasm cooled somewhat in the following year as a result of a hoax played upon him, and he warned his readers against believing that all the phenomena ascribed to spirit intervention had necessarily an extra-mundane cause, as many might be due to unconscious action on the part of the medium.

Sunderland was also an exponent of **phrenology.** Of special interest is the fact that he sometimes exhibited painless tooth extraction with entranced subjects, and on two occasions even the dentist was hypnotized. Sunderland's ideas were mentioned by **James Braid,** whose term "hypnotism" eventually won general consent.

In 1868, Sunderland's doubts about spirit phenomena returned, and in his book *The Trance and Correlative Phenomena* he states that neither mediums nor spirits have ever been able to show where human actions end and the real spiritual begins in phenomena.

In the last years of his life he became an infidel and advocated atheism. He died in Quincy, Massachusetts, on May 15, 1885, reportedly having a happy end in spite of his disbelief in any afterlife.

Sources:

Sunderland, La Roy. "An Appeal on the Subject of Slavery." *Zion's Watchman* (December 5, 1834).

———. *The Book of Human Nature.* New York: Stearns, 1853.

———. *"Confessions of a Magnitizer" Exposed.* Boston: Redding, 1845.

———. *Ideology.* Boston: J. P. Mendum, 1885–87.

———. *Pathetism; With Practical Instructions: Demonstrating the Falsity of the Hitherto Prevalent Assumptions in Regard to What Has Been Called "Mesmerism" and "Neurology," and Illustrating Those Laws Which Induce Somnambulism, Second Sight, Sleep, Dreaming, Trance, and Clairvoyance, with Numerous Facts Tending to Show the Pathology of Monomania, Insanity, Witchcraft, and Various Other Mental or Nervous Phenomena.* Boston: White and Potter, 1847.

———. *Testimony of God Against Slavery.* Boston: D. K. Hitchcock, 1836.

———. *The Trance.* Chicago: J. Walker, 1868.

Suns Ahman Ishrael—I:A:O: (Organization)

A religious/magic organization drawing upon Mormon traditions. It was founded in 1981 by presiding Patriarch David Asia Israel and four other former members of the **Church of Jesus Christ of Latter-Day Saints.** The group believes that angels continue to visit and deliver messages to humans, and David Israel claims to receive regular revelations in the form of morning and evening oracles.

Besides the Bible and the Book of Mormon, the Suns Ahman Ishrael (SAI) accepts a wide variety of materials as scripture, including ancient apocryphal writings (Gospel of Thomas, Gospel of Philip, Book of Enoch, writings from Nag Hammadi) and modern Mormon revelations (Oracles of Mohonri, The Order of the Sons of Zadok). The group believes in a secret oral tradition passed from Moses to the Essenes, to the Gnostics, and eventually to Joseph Smith Jr. That tradition is believed to be preserved in mystical books such as the *Pistis Sophia* and *Sepher Yetzira.*

A 22-item statement of SAI beliefs posits a heavenly hierarchy consisting of the Heavenly Father and Mother; their son, Jesus Christ; the Holy Spirit; angels and archangels; and ministers of the flame (righteous humans made perfect). Human beings are the literal offspring of the heavenly parents and have come into earthly existence to experience the mystery of mortality. Redemption for humans comes only through surrendering their life to Yeshu-Maria the Christ and subsequently developing a relationship with the heavenly hierarchy in the holy temple ordinances and ritualistic ceremonies. The SAI also follows the Old Testament feasts and holy days.

The SAI is headed by a presiding patriarch and matriarch under whom function (when the organization is at full strength) a first presidency, twelve apostles, seven "arch seventies," and twelve "stake princes." Each stake is headed by twelve high counselmen, a "quorum of seventy," and twelve bishops. The church endorses the practice of polygamy, but also believes in perfect equality of the sexes. Women are accepted into the priesthood on an equal basis with men.

SAI publishes a monthly periodical, *Stone Magazine*. During the 1980s the group developed an international following in England, Norway, Japan, and the Netherlands. Address: Chevrah B'Qor Community, HC 65, Box 535, Canebeds, AZ 86022.

Superet Light Doctrine Church

The Superet Light Doctrine Church is an international religious movement that developed from the spiritual teachings of its founder, Dr. Josephine De Croix Trust (d. 1957), called Mother Trust within the movement. She is described as a Light Scientist who rediscovered Jesus' religion because of a special gift she had to see the light, vibrations, and aura of Jesus' words. According to Mother Trust, she was able to see auras, or the light emanations that psychics claim to see around all objects, from the age of four. As a teenager she developed tuberculosis, at that time an incurable disease, but she claimed she was healed by Jesus, who appeared to her in a vision. When she was a young woman living in New York City, she gained a reputation as a miracle healer. Important for her future teaching work, she discovered while reading the Bible that Jesus' words, and only Jesus' words, shone with a light.

In a later revelation she was given the secret of the Holy Spirit as the Mother God, a doctrine not previously revealed because males looked upon females as little more than breeders. In addition, the Holy Spirit told her, "This is the new name, Superet, which is the everlasting Fire in God's sacred purple Heart."

The Superet Science taught by Mother Trust is the manifestation of God's light through our light atom aura. All substances that possess magnetism, especially all life, have an aura. As an aura scientist, Mother Trust was able to see both the inner (light of the soul) and outer aura. We produce the light atom aura, which is capable of receiving God's light, by developing our inner soul aura. We can then use that light for healing and to become successful in life.

The Superet Light doctrine is presented in the more than 25 books written by Mother Trust and in several sets of lessons. Mother Trust also founded the Prince of Peace Movement, an interreligious peace movement, on Christmas Day 1938 in Bethlehem, the site of the Nativity.

The church has congregations in the United States, Canada, Mexico, Panama, and Nigeria. It issues the biennial *Newsletter of the Superet Brotherhood and Sisterhood*. There are Prince of Peace clubs in the United States, Nigeria, Panama, Mexico, Trinidad, and the Bahamas. It is headquartered at 2516 W. Third St., Los Angeles, CA 90057.

Sources:

Miracle Woman's Secrets. Los Angeles: Superet Press, 1949.

Superet Light Doctrine Ministry. Los Angeles: Superet Press, 1947.

Trust, Josephine C. *Bible Mystery by Superet Light Science*. Los Angeles: Superet Press, 1950.

———. *Superet Light*. Los Angeles: Superet Light Center, 1953.

———. *Superet Light Doctrine*. Los Angeles: Superet Press, 1949.

Super-Extrasensory Perception

Term used by parapsychologists for the hypothesis that some individuals may have unlimited powers of acquiring information from living persons or objects, thus making the conventional Spiritualist explanation of discarnate entities unnecessary.

Supernatural

An occurrence in violation of the known laws of nature. This was a concept that developed as the idea of a law-abiding nature was developed in the Middle Ages. The supernatural realm included both the heavenly world of God and the angels and the world of Satan and demons.

Many leaders of the Enlightenment of the eighteenth century were exponents of Deism, a view that drew a sharp line between the natural and supernatural realms and denied that the two interact. Spiritualism reacted to such a view: it suggested that phenomena that had previously been viewed as supernatural actually happened, and it also suggested that they occurred in accordance with natural laws, laws as yet unknown or undefined by science.

Now, the term "paranormal" is more generally used to describe such extraordinary phenomena.

Supernormal

A term substituted in psychical research for "**supernatural.**" It was coined by **F. W. H. Myers** and is applied to phenomena that are beyond what usually happens—beyond, that is, in the sense of suggesting unknown physical laws. While supernormal phenomena point to new powers, abnormal phenomena indicate the degeneration of powers already acquired. The term "paranormal" is now preferred.

Supersensonics

Term devised by New Age teacher **Christopher Hills** to indicate a science of subtle energy therapeutics, involving **radiesthesia, radionics,** homeopathy, Bach flower remedies, and related fields.

Supreme Council of the Independent Associated Spiritualists

Founded in 1925 as a federation of churches and groups of churches concerned with **Spiritualism.** It participated in research on psychic phenomena, psychic photography, and spiritual healing. It was affiliated with Duke Research Foundation. Last known address: 7230 Fourth St. North, #2304, St. Petersburg, FL 33702.

Survival

The continued possession of personality after the change called **death.** It is a fundamental doctrine of **Spiritualism** that Spiritualist phenomena demonstrate survival, and the investigation of that phenomena has been a major aspect of **psychical research.** The emergence of parapsychology represented, in part, a distinct reorientation of priorities away from survival research.

The basis of survival is the contention that mind can exist independently of the brain, that thought is not the result of changes in the brain, but that these changes (as **William James** suggested in his book *Human Immortality*, 1903) merely coincide with the flow of thought through it. The brain fulfills the role of an instrument of transmission. **Thought transference** and experiments in **telepathy** furnished the first scientific support of this contention.

The **trance** communications received through the mediumship of **Leonora Piper** convinced many famous skeptical investigators that the communicators had survived the change of death. Even **Eleanor Sidgwick** admitted in her brilliant but extremely skeptical study of Piper's phenomena: "Veridical communications are received, some of which, there is good reason to believe, come from the dead, and therefore imply a genuine communicator in the background." (*Proceedings* of the Society for Psychical Research, vol. 28, December 1915, p. 204.)

The arguments for and against survival are mainly centered around the evidential value of such communications. The first and most powerful point of attack is made on the subconscious front. The communicating personality is said to be artificial, a masquerading secondary self, and that supernormal information lies occasionally within the bounds of acquisition of the subconscious mind.

It is also pointed out that many of the communications are erroneous, of a lying nature, uncharacteristic of the dead, and easily obtainable by fraudulent means.

Those who argue for survival deny the sufficiency of subconscious powers as an explanation for communications, pointing to the distinct personalities of the communicators, their greatly differing abilities to communicate, their recognition of old friends, their behavior, temper, memories, and ability to give information outside the mind of everybody present and perhaps of everybody living.

They also point out the inconsistency of the telepathic theory in that it gradually leads to the supposition of a cosmic mind that is tapped by the telepathist, forming thereby a more far-reaching and less justified theory than individual survival. As evidence against telepathy, the results of some **cross-correspondences** and **book** (and newspaper) **tests** are quoted.

Philosophic speculation has often supported the concept of survival. P. G. Tait and **Balfour Stewart** posit in their book, *The Unseen Universe* (1875), that the main realities of the universe are not in matter at all, but in the ether of space. Although the concept of the ether has since been refuted, the enigma of the relationship between matter and consciousness remains, and it is feasible that consciousness continues to survive the death and disintegrating changes of the physical body. This implies that consciousness is a superior system to matter.

According to **Sir Oliver Lodge,** "the marvel is that we are associated with matter at all . . . I used to say that death was an adventure to which we might look forward. So it is; but I believe that really and truly it is earth-life that is the adventure. It is this earth-life that has been the strange and exceptional thing. The wonder is that we ever succeeded in entering a matter body at all. Many fail." (*Phantom Walls,* 1929). In the same book he also considers the possibility of grades of survival, stating:

"Now survival only applies to things that really exist. If there is no individuality, then there is nothing to persist. Whether all human beings have sufficient personality to make their individual persistence likely is a question that may be argued. Whether some of the higher animals have acquired a kind of individuality, a character and wealth of affection which seem worthy of continued existence, may also be argued. There may be many grades of personality, and accordingly there may be many grades of survival."

The subjective experience of **out-of-the-body travel** or **astral projection** is often cited as presumptive evidence that the personality can exist independently of the body.

Sources:

Baird, Alexander T. *One Hundred Cases for Survival After Death.* New York: Bernard Ackerman, 1944.

Beard, Paul. *Survival of Death: For and Against.* London: Hodder and Stoughton, 1966.

Broad, C. D. *Personal Identity and Survival.* London: Society for Psychical Research, 1968.

Crookall, Robert. *Case-Book of Astral Projection, 545–746.* New Hyde Park, N.Y.: University Books, 1972.

Ducasse, C. J. *A Critical Examination of the Belief in a Life After Death.* Springfield, Ill.: Charles C. Thomas, 1961.

Garrett, Eileen J., ed. *Does Man Survive Death?: A Symposium.* New York: Helix Press, 1957.

Hart, Hornell. *The Enigma of Survival: The Case For and Against an After Life.* Springfield, Ill.: Charles C. Thomas, 1959.

Jacobson, Nils Olof. *Life Without Death?: On Parapsychology, Mysticism and the Question of Survival.* New York: Delacorte Press, 1973. Reprint, London: Turnstone Books, 1974.

Myers, F. H. *Human Personality and its Survival of Bodily Death.* 2 vols. London: Longmans, Green, 1903. Reprint, New York: Arno Press, 1975.

Rogo, D. Scott. *Welcoming Silence: A Study of Psychical Phenomena and Survival of Death.* New Hyde Park, N.Y.: University Books, 1973.

Salter, W. H. *Zoar; or, The Evidence of Psychical Research Concerning Survival.* London: Sidgwick & Jackson, 1961.

Saltmarsh, H. F. *Evidence of Personal Survival From Cross Correspondences.* London: G. Bell, 1939.

Smith, Susy. *Life is Forever: Evidence for Survival After Death.* New York: G. P. Putnam's Sons, 1974.

Survival Joint Research Committee Trust

British organization founded in 1963, "exclusively concerned with **survival** of human personality after bodily death." In November 1987, the trust held a one-day E. J. Dingwall Memorial Conference on "Science and Survival." The trust meets regularly to discuss experimental design and conduct experiments, and may be contacted at 47 Mayfield Rd., Hornsey, London, N8 9LL, England.

The Survival League

British organization founded in London by Mrs. C. A. Dawson Scott in October 1929 to affirm the unity of all religions and spread the knowledge of the scientific demonstrability of **survival** after death. The first chairman was Spiritualist author **H. Dennis Bradley.** The Survival League of America was an affiliated organization. The league published *Survival Magazine.* The organization did not survive World War II.

Survival Research Foundation

Incorporated in 1971 by author and psychical researcher **Susy Smith** and attorney Frank C. Tribbe, a long-time leader in the Spiritual Frontiers Fellowship. The foundation engaged in scientific research into anomalous phenomena that lie outside the traditional disciplines of science.

The foundation works in the field of end of life care and support as well as develops protocols designed to communicate with comatose patients to determine their wishes with respect to the withdrawal or withholding of life support. The foundation also promotes a cipher test devised by Arthur S. Berger to help lessen grief during the bereavement process.

The foundation may be reached c/o the current president, Arthur Burger, P.O. Box 63-0026, Miami, Florida 33163-0026.

Swaffer, Hannen (1879–1962)

Journalist, drama critic, author, and publicist for **Spiritualism.** He was born on November 1, 1879, in Lindfield, Sussex, England, and was educated at Stroud Green Grammar School. The family moved to London, where young Swaffer discovered that his neighbor was a journalist; he immediately decided that this would be his profession. Many years later, that neighbor worked for Swaffer on the *Weekly Dispatch.*

Swaffer joined the *Daily Mail* in 1902 and spent a number of years working under Lord Northcliffe, becoming, in succession, news editor, art editor, night editor, and assistant editor of the *Daily Mirror.* He originated a gossip column in the *Daily Sketch* that was soon extensively copied by other newspapers. He also worked on the *Daily Herald* and was drama critic for the *Daily Express.* He was editor of the *Weekly Dispatch,* and later he was editor of *The People.* For many years, "Swaff" was a familiar and eccentric figure in London's Fleet Street, center of the national newspaper offices. He affected somewhat Bohemian dress, as befitted a drama critic, and was popularly known as "The Poet."

He became convinced of **survival** in 1924, through attending **direct voice** sittings with the medium **Gladys Osborne Leonard** in the circle of **H. Dennis Bradley.** These sittings were strongly evidential of the survival of Swaffer's old chief Lord Northcliffe, who had died in 1922. Swaffer published accounts of the séances in *The People* and created a sensation with his book *Northcliffe's Return* (1924).

He became an indefatigable propagandist for Spiritualism, and argued that Spiritualism and socialism were two halves of one great whole. He succeeded **Sir Arthur Conan Doyle** as honorary president of the **Spiritualists' National Union** and the **Spiritualist Community,** and he was connected with other Spiritualist organizations.

In 1932, Swaffer was one of the three cofounders of the well-known British newspaper *Psychic News*—the other two were his accountant Jack Rubens and his friend **Maurice Barbanell** (who was editor for many years). He died January 16, 1962.

Sources:

Driburg, Tom. *"Swaff": The Life and Times of Hannen Swaffer.* London: Macdonald, 1974.

Swaffer, Hannen. *Adventures with Inspiration.* N.p., 1929.

———. *Behind the Scenes.* N.p., 1928.

———. *Hannen Swaffer's Who's Who.* London: Hutchinson, 1929.

———. *Norcliffe's Return.* London: Hutchinson, 1925.

———. *Studies in Psychology.* N.p., 1933.

Swain, Marcia M. (1819–1900)

Voice medium of a **rescue circle** in Buffalo from 1875 to 1900 under the direction of Leander Fisher, a music teacher and medium. Daniel E. Bailey, a wealthy man, took interest in the work and at his death made provision for the support of Swain for the rest of her life. She was never a public medium and did not give séances for money. The activity of the rescue circle was largely devoted to making the dead realize their true condition.

Sources:

Bailey, D. E. *Thoughts from the Inner Life.* Boston, 1886.

Swaminarayan, Shree (1781–1830)

Famous saint of nineteenth-century India, born as Nilakantha at Capaiya, near Ayodhya. He developed a revised form of the traditional *Vishishadvaita* **Vedanta** of Shree Ramanujan and traveled all over India for 30 years with his disciples, initiating a religious revival that had an impact upon the masses in Gujarat, Saurashtra, and Kutch. The movement eradicated violence, drunkenness, and lawlessness among those who responded to it and attracted favorable notice from both the Christian bishop Heber and the British rulers.

Shree Swaminarayan performed miracles and was accepted by his followers as an incarnation of the Divine, the first of a succession of such incarnations, of which His Holiness Shree Pramukh Swami is the current living representative. Modern followers of Shree Swaminarayan number hundreds of thousands, and prior to the expulsion of Asians from Uganda, this faith was widespread among Indian people throughout East Africa. The Swaminarayan faith has a popular following in Great Britain and North America among Asian immigrants.

Sources:

Dave, H. T. *Life and Philosophy of Shree Swaminarayan, 1781–1830.* London: Allen & Unwin, 1974.

Swann, Ingo (1933–)

Prominent American psychic research subject, parapsychologist, and author. Born September 14, 1933, at Telluride, Colorado, he studied at Westminster College, Salt Lake City, Utah, receiving a double bachelor's degree in biology and art. He enlisted in the U.S. Army and served three years in Korea, after which he worked for twelve years at the United Nations Secretariat while pursuing an independent art career.

Swann's active participation in parapsychology research began in 1969 when he was 36 years old. During the next twenty years he worked only in controlled laboratory settings with scientific researchers. Although he lectured widely on the importance of psychic faculties and potentials, he has never publicly demonstrated his abilities. Because of his participation in hundreds of thousands of experimental trials, author Martin Ebon wrote of him as "parapsychology's most tested guinea pig," and *Psychic News* and other media often refer to him as "the scientific psychic."

During the 1950s and 1960s, because of psychic potentials partly evident in childhood, he became actively interested in occult and parapsychological literature and in a variety of novel mind-development programs which took positive approaches to the enhancement of ESP potentials.

Swann early distinguished between *psychic phenomenon* and *psychic mind-dynamic processes.* He especially noticed that while parapsychology researched the existence of paranormal phenomena (such as ESP, telepathy, and psychokinesis), there was little interest in the mental processes involved in producing evidence of them. From this distinction he slowly developed unique theoretical approaches to *process enhancement* of psi perceptions, which was in keeping with ancient descriptions of Siddhis as found in various Eastern Yoga literature and Abraham Maslow's developmental abilitism theories.

In 1970–71 Swann experimented with **Cleve Backster** in attempting to influence plants by mental activity. In 1971–72 psychokinetic experiments involved successfully influencing temperature recorded in a controlled setting devised by parapsychologists **Gertrude Schmeidler** and Larry Lewis at City College, New York. This involved PK effects upon target thermistors (temperature measuring devices) in insulated thermos bottles at a distance of 25 feet from Swann. (For a report, see G. R. Schmeidler, "PK Effects Upon Continuously Recorded Temperature," *Journal* of the American Society for Psychical Research, no. 4, Oct. 1973).

Swann was also the subject of experiments in **out-of-the-body travel,** or psychic perception at a distance. These took place during 1971–73 at the **American Society for Psychical Research.** They involved Swann sitting in a chair and attempting to project his consciousness into sealed boxes on a small platform several feet above his head, in which there was a target symbol completely shielded from view. Swann was monitored by electrodes that would have recorded any movement from the chair.

Under these difficult laboratory conditions, Swann nevertheless scored significant successes in describing the targets. In one test he was actually able to state correctly that a light that should have illuminated the target was inoperative. There was no normal way of ascertaining this fact without opening the box.

In 1972–73, at the American Society for Psychical Research, Swann began suggesting experimental protocols to test for the existence of mind-dynamic processes that would enhance ESP perceptions. Together with Dr. **Karlis Osis,** Dr. Janet Mitchell, and Dr. Gertrude Schmeidler, he coined the term "remote viewing" to describe the experiments in which subjects attempted to view targets at a far distance. His original remote-viewing protocols were later utilized and expanded upon in collaboration with the researchers Dr. **Harold E. Puthoff** and **Russell Targ.** Other laboratories ultimately repeated various kinds of remote-viewing experiments.

Swann's successes on the East Coast attracted the attention of the quantum physicist, H. E. Puthoff, at the Stanford Research Institute, in Menlo Park, California (later renamed SRI International). From late 1973 until 1989 Swann worked principally at SRI's "psychoenergetics project" established by Puthoff to examine important psi faculties (rather than psychic phenomena per se).

One of the first most remarkable experiments involved a successful attempt to influence the stable magnetic field of a super-cooled Josephson junction inside a quark detector (a complex apparatus designed to detect subatomic particles). The apparatus was completely inaccessible, being encased in aluminum and copper containers and buried in five feet of concrete. When Swann mentally visualized the hidden target, significant variations were recorded in sine waves. This PK effect was reported at a conference on quantum physics and parapsychology.

On April 27, 1973, in another extraordinary experiment, Swann "visited" the planet Jupiter in a joint "psychic probe" shared by fellow psychic **Harold Sherman.** Swann's drawings made during the experiment showed a 'ring' of tiny asteroids around the planet which scientists at the time said did not exist. The existence of the ring was later scientifically confirmed in 1979.

From the first experiments, Swann was increasingly considered a very unique test subject because, at the command of the experimenters, he could reproduce and sustain the desired effects over time at a significant rate of success. Throughout the history of parapsychology, other test subjects had been temporarily or spontaneously successful. But these subjects typically suffered from the well-known "decline effect" or "psi-missing effect" which statistically erased the successes, and thus permitted skeptics to believe that the successes were due to some outside factor other than claimed human psi abilities.

Most books and articles written after 1973 about parapsychology and psychic matters refer to Swann's work in some way. Many analysts of science and parapsychology generally concede that his work and the high levels of official sponsorship it obtained gradually influenced positive reevaluations of the validity of psi in human experiencing.

After nineteen years on the cutting edge of psi developments, the "longest run" of any subject on record, Swann retired from full-time research to undertake independent research into the problems and states of consciousness. In final interviews regarding the dimensions of his past work, he stated that the long-term stresses of laboratory work and the constant need to defend the validity of psi faculties and exceptional experiencing had taken their toll. He occasionally accepts invitations to lecture but refuses to talk with the media. In a paper read at the United Nations in March 1994 (entitled "Scientists find the basis for seventeen-plus human senses and perceptions"), he stated that psi faculties and exceptional experiencing are not purely scientific issues. Their discovery and development involve larger social, philosophical, political, and religious problems not amenable to objective research and rational appreciation.

Sources:

Berger, Arthur S., and Joyce Berger. *The Encyclopedia of Parapsychology and Psychical Research.* New York: Paragon House, 1991.

Puthoff, H. E., and Russell Targ. "Physics, Entrophy, and Psychokinesis." In *Proceedings of the Conference on Quantum Physics and Parapsychology, Geneva, August 26–27, 1974.* New York: Parapsychology Foundation, 1975.

Schmeidler, Gertrude R. "PK Effects Upon Continuously Recorded Temperature." *Journal* of the American Society for Psychical Research 4 (October 1973).

Swann, Ingo. *Cosmic Art.* New York: Hawthorn Books, 1975.

———. *Natural ESP: A Layman's Guide to Unlocking the Extra Sensory Power of Your Mind.* New York: Bantam, 1987.

———. *To Kiss Earth Goody-bye.* New York: Hawthorn Books, 1974. Reprint, New York: Laurel/Dell, 1975.

———. *Star Fire.* New York: Dell, 1978.

———. *Your Nostradamus Factor: Accessing Your Innate Ability to See into the Future.* New York: Simon & Schuster, 1993.

Swann, William F(rancis) G(ray) (1884–1962)

Physicist and educator who wrote on parapsychology. He was born on August 29, 1884, at Ironbridge, Shropshire, England. He studied at the Royal College of Science, London; University College; King's College; the University of London; and City and Guilds of London Institute. Swann was an authority on cosmic radiation and atomic structure and was head of the Bartol Research Foundation of Franklin Institute at Swarthmore for 32 years. He had previously taught at the Royal College of Science, London and at the University of Sheffield.

Early in his career he was successively employed as the head of the physical division of the Department of Terrestrial Magnetism at the Carnegie Institute, Washington, D.C.; the University of Minnesota (1918–23); the University of Chicago (1923–24); and Yale University (1924–27). His interest in parapsychology was by way of physics and philosophy. He died January 29, 1962, in Swarthmore, Pennsylvania.

Sources:

Pleasants, Helene, ed. *Biographical Dictionary of Parapsychology.* New York: Helix Press, 1964.

Swann, William F. G. "Is the Universe Planned?" *Journal of the Franklin Institute* (May 1953).

———. "The Known and the Unknown." *Journal of the Franklin Institute* (May 1955).

———. "Nature and the Mind of Man." *Journal of the Franklin Institute* (June 1956).

———. "Reality, Imagery and Fantasy." *Journal of the Franklin Institute* (May 1957).

———. "The Science of Yesterday, Today and Tomorrow." *Journal of the Franklin Institute* (March 1960).

Swastika

One of the most important and widespread symbols in ancient religion, mysticism, and magic is the swastika or *tetraskelion.* Essentially, it is a Greek cross with arms of equal length, each with four arms at right angles, either right-handed (regarded as a male symbol implying good fortune) or left-handed (female symbol). The right-handed form is sometimes known as *gammadion,* i.e., formed from joining four gamma letters.

The swastika is generally regarded as a symbol of the power of the sun, and it may have been derived from a circle divided into four by crossed lines. A variation of the swastika is the *Triskele* ("three-legged") form, often found on Sicilian coins and used as the emblem of the Isle of Man off the coast of Britain.

The swastika dates back to the Neolithic Age, when it was engraved on stone implements, but it has also been found in many cultures—in ancient Britain, Ireland, Mycenae, and Gascony, as well as among the Etruscans, Celts, Hindus, Germanic peoples, Central Asians, and pre-Columbian Americans. The Buddhists regarded it as a *chakra* or wheel of the law; the Tibetans called it *Yun-drun* or path of life. The swastika has traveled from the ancient Greek cities of Troy and Mycenae down to the 9th century in Ireland, as well as to Persia, China, North Africa, and Scandinavia.

Some authorities have interpreted the swastika as a symbol of the deity during the Iron Age, and others have associated it with agriculture, compass points, and the origin of the universe. No doubt this universally diffused symbol has acquired many secondary associations in addition to its main association with the sun wheel.

The name "swastika" derives from a long-established use in India, where the expression *Su-asti* means "Be well," implying auspiciousness and good fortune. Hindu parents mark the symbol on the breast and forehead of a baby, and a swastika formed of ears of wheat is made in the birth chamber. Hindu writers often place a red swastika at the beginning and end of manuscripts; the sign is also marked on floors and paths at weddings. There is a hatha **yoga** sitting position known as "Swatikasana" or the auspicious posture, in which the legs are crossed and the feet rest on opposite thighs.

The use of the swastika as a Nazi symbol may have derived from German scholarship in the field of Hindu folklore and religion, distorted by such pseudo-mystical occultists as **Guido von List,** who originated theories of Germanic and Nordic folklore as early as the 1870s. According to List, the swastika was the symbol of a secret band of initiates called the Armanen or "children of the sun," who flourished in ancient times.

It may also have been reputable scholarly discussions of the Indo-European migrations of ancient peoples and cultures that were perverted to the antisemitic doctrine of an Aryan master-race. Before World War I, the use of the swastika symbol was popular among romantic youth folklore movements like the *Wandervögel.* It was continued by political revolutionaries who had been *Wandervögel* members and by Hitler's National Socialist German Workers' Party in the post-war period.

The Nazi swastika was designed by Friedrich Krohn, formerly a member of the Germanen Order, a secret order founded by followers of Guido von List. Krohn's design was adopted around 1920. Ever since, this ancient Hindu sacred symbol of auspiciousness has become inextricably associated with the perverse doctrines of the German Nazis.

Swawm

Burmese vampires. (See also **Myanmar**)

SWEDEN

Witchcraft

In 1649, Queen Christina banned witch trials, stating that **witchcraft** confessions of women were due to illusions or disorders of health. However, there was an extraordinary outbreak of witchcraft hysteria between 1669 and 1670 at Mora, in Dalecarlia, resulting in the burning of 85 individuals accused of transporting no fewer than 300 children by magical flights to a witches' sabbat on the island of **Blockula.**

On July 5, 1668, the pastor of Elfdale in Dalecarlia stated that Gertrude Svensen, aged 18, had been accused by Eric Ericsen, aged 15, of stealing children for the devil. There followed similar charges. Then in May 1669, King Charles XI appointed a commission to look into the matter and attempt to redeem the accused by prayers rather than punishment or torture. However, the prayers resulted in mass hysteria among the 3,000 people who had assembled. The commissioners claimed to have discovered 70 adult witches, who were all burned, together with 15 children. Lesser sentences were given to 56 other children who were punished by having to run a gauntlet or be lashed with rods.

The witches were said to have carried the children on goats, sticks, and the backs of sleeping men, even flying through windows. One writer recorded that "being asked how they could go with their Bodies through Chimneys and broken panes of Glass, they said, that the Devil did first remove all that might hinder them in their flight, and so they had room enough to go." They assembled for their sabbat in a large meadow, where they feasted, danced, and performed diabolical rituals.

Commenting on the affair, Bishop Francis Hutchinson states in his book *An Historical Essay Concerning Witchcraft* (1718):

"Is it not plain that the people had frightened their children with so many tales, that they could not sleep without dreaming of the devil, and then made the poor women of the town confess what the children said of them."

Other witchcraft persecutions followed, and between 1674 and 1675, individuals were burned or beheaded in three parishes. There was also a witchcraft mania in Stockholm in following years, but when it was discovered that accusations were due to the malice or greed of young informers, Charles XI once again prohibited witchcraft prosecutions.

Spiritualism and Psychical Research

Spiritualism entered Sweden at the end of the nineteenth century and progressed slowly. In the decades following World War I, there was a general apathy, and in some areas a marked hostility to Spiritualism, fortune-telling, and psychic matters.

On March 14, 1931, a bill was presented to the Swedish Parliament with the intention both of regularizing mediumship and legitimizing **psychical research.** It did not succeed and Spiritualism was still actively discouraged. However, there was a revival of interest after World War II.

In spite of the hostility to psychical research, the Sällskapet för Parapsykologisk Forskning was established in Stockholm after World War II. It has carried out valuable experimental work. **Gosta Rodhe,** the president, has now been succeeded by Rolf Evjegärd. The former secretary, **Eva Hellström,** well known as a clairvoyant, was succeeded by Eric Uggla. The society maintains a good research library, has organized lectures and meetings, and has carried out research in psychometry and precognition. Another important experimenter was **Haakon Forwald** (1897–1978) of Ludvika, who in the 1950s began research in psychokinesis. More recently, a branch of the **Churches' Fellowship for Psychic and Spiritualist Studies** was organized, and may be reached c/o Mrs. Eva Lejam, St. Sodergatan 17, Lund.

Sources:

Berger, Arthur S., and Joyce Berger. *The Encyclopedia of Parapsychology and Psychical Research.* New York: Paragon House, 1991.

Robbins, Rossell Hope. *The Encyclopedia of Witchcraft and Demonology.* New York: Crown Publishers, 1959.

Swedenborg, Emanuel (1688–1772)

Swedish seer. He was trained as a scientist and became the country's leading expert in mining and metallurgy. He was also a military engineer, learned astronomer, reputed physicist, zoologist, anatomist, financier, political economist, and biblical student.

He was born January 29, 1688, at Stockholm, son of a professor of theology at Upsala, afterward bishop of Scara. Swedenborg graduated from Upsala University in 1710 and then traveled in England, Holland, France, and Germany, studying natural philosophy. He studied and was influenced by the work of the most famous mathematicians and physicians—Sir Isaac Newton, Flamsteed, Halley, and De Lahire. He made sketches of inventions as varied as a flying machine, a submarine, a rapid-fire gun, an air pump, and a fire engine. He wrote many poems in Latin, and when after five years of study he returned to Sweden, he was appointed assessor of the Royal College of Mines.

Originally known as Swedberg, nobility was bestowed upon him by Queen Ulrica, and he changed his name to Swedenborg. He sat in the House of Nobles, his political utterances having great weight, but his tendencies were distinctly democratic. He busied himself privately in scientific gropings for the explanation of the universe. He published at least two works dealing with cosmology remembered primarily as foreshadowing many scientific facts and ventures of the future. His theories regarding light, cosmic atoms, geology, and physics were distinctly ahead of their time.

In 1734 he published *Prodomus Philosophie Ratiocinantrio de Infinite,* about the relation of the finite to the infinite and of the soul to the body. In this work he sought to establish a definite connection between the two as a means of overcoming the difficulty of their relationship. The spiritual and the divine appeared to him as the supreme study of man. He searched the countries of Europe for the most eminent teachers and the best books dealing with anatomy, for he considered that science the locus of the germ of the knowledge of soul and spirit. Through his anatomical studies he anticipated certain modern views dealing with the functions of the brain.

At the height of his scientific career he resigned his office to devote the rest of his life to spreading spiritual enlightenment, for which he believed himself to have been specially selected by God. He showed signs of psychic power as a child. Even at an early age he could cease breathing for a considerable period and freely enter an altered state of consciousness, possibly **trance.** In his book *Dreams of a Spirit Seer* philosopher **Immanuel Kant** narrates several paranormal experiences from Swedenborg's early life. He had gifts of **clairvoyance.** Kant also investigated and reported as authentic the story that in Gothenburg Swedenborg observed and reported a fire that was raging in Stockholm, 300 miles away.

Swedenborg's real illumination and intercourse with the spiritual world in visions and dreams began in April 1744. He claimed that in a waking state his consciousness wandered in the spirit world and conversed with its inhabitants as freely as with living men.

In later experiences he heard wonderful conversations and sensed the eyes of his spirit were so opened that he could see heavens and hells and converse with angels and spirits. He claimed that God revealed himself to him and told him that he had chosen him to unveil the spiritual sense of the whole Scriptures to man. From that moment, according to Swedenborg, he eschewed worldly knowledge and worked for spiritual ends alone. Through the next three decades, he lived in Sweden, Holland, and London.

After initially reviewing his knowledge of the Hebrew language, Swedenborg began his great works on the interpretation of the Scriptures, which were to dominate the rest of his life. A man of few wants, his life was simplicity itself, his food consisting for the most part of bread, milk, and coffee. He was in the habit of lying in a trance for days, and day and night seemed to have no distinction for him. He regularly conversed with angels in broad daylight, he said. At other times, his wrestlings with evil spirits so terrified his servants that they would seek refuge in the most distant part of the house.

Swedenborg speaks of the nature of his visions and communications with the angels and spirits in his book *Heaven and Hell:*

"Angels speak from the spiritual world, according to inward thought; from wisdom, their speech flows in a tranquil stream, gently and uninterruptedly—they speak only in vowels, the heavenly angels in A and O, the spiritual ones in E and I, for the vowels give tone to the speech, and by the tone the emotion is expressed; the interruptions, on the other hand, correspond with creations of the mind; therefore we prefer, if the subject is lofty, for instance of heaven or God, even in human speech, the vowels U and O, etc. Man, however, is united with heaven by means of the word, and forms thus the link between heaven and earth, between the divine and the natural.

"But when angels speak spiritually with me from heaven, they speak just as intelligently as the man by my side. But if they turn away from man, he hears nothing more whatever, even if they speak close to his ear. It is also remarkable that several angels can speak to a man; they send down a spirit inclined to man, and he thus hears them united."

From his ongoing conversations with the angelic beings, he wrote a number of books. These may be divided into expository books, notably *The Apocalypse Revealed, The Apocalypse Explained,* and *Arcana Celestia;* books of spiritual philosophy, such as *Intercourse between the Soul and the Body, Divine Providence* and *Divine Love and Wisdom;* books dealing with the hierarchy of supernatural spheres, such as *Heaven and Hell* and *The Last Judgment;* and books outlining the teachings of the new church, such as *The New Jerusalem, The True Christian Religion,* and *Canons of the New Church.*

Of these works, his *Divine Love and Wisdom* most succinctly presents his entire religious system. God he regarded as the divine man. Spiritually God consists of infinite love, and corporeally of infinite wisdom. From the divine love, all things draw nourishment. The sun, as we know it, is merely a microcosm of a spiritual sun emanating from the creator. This spiritual sun is the source of nature; but whereas the first is alive, the second is inanimate. There is no connection between the two worlds of nature and spirit unless in similarity of construction. The causes of all things exist in the spiritual sphere and their effects in the natural sphere, and the purpose of all creation is that man may become the image of his creator, and of the cosmos as a whole.

Swedenborg believed that man possesses two vessels or receptacles for the containment of God—the will for divine love, and the understanding for divine wisdom. Before the Fall, the flow of these virtues into the human spirit was perfect, but through the intervention of the forces of evil, and the sins of man himself, it was interrupted. Seeking to restore the connection between himself and man, God came into the world as Man, for if he had ventured on Earth in his unveiled splendor, he would have destroyed the hells through which it was necessary for him to proceed to redeem man, and this he did not wish to do, merely to conquer them.

The unity of God is an essential of Swedenborgian theology, and Swedenborg thoroughly believed that God did not return to his own place without leaving behind him a visible representative of himself in the word of Scripture, which is an eternal tripartite incarnation—natural, spiritual, and celestial. Of this Swedenborg was the apostle. Nothing seemed hidden from him; he claimed to be aware of the appearance and conditions of other worlds, good and evil, heaven and hell, and of the planets. "The life of religion," he stated, "is to accomplish good. . . . The kingdom of heaven is a kingdom of uses."

Central to understanding his system is the doctrine of **correspondences.** There are two realms of created existence, the spiritual, which is real and substantial, and the physical, a mere reflection of the spiritual, according to this doctrine. Everything visible, Swedenborg argued, is the shadow of an appropriate spiritual reality. Between the two realms is an exact correspondence.

The work of explaining the correspondences, said Swedenborg, begins with the Scriptures; hence the prodigious amount of time he devoted to his voluminous Scripture commentaries.

Swedenborg died in London on March 29, 1772, at Prince's Square, in the parish of St. George's in East London, on the very day he had earlier predicted in a letter to Methodist leader John Wesley, who had sought an audience with him. In April 1908 his bones were removed, at the request of the Swedish government, for reburial in Stockholm.

Swedenborg wrote at a time when heretical ideas were taken seriously by state and church officials. To avoid any sanctions for his increasingly divergent ideas he initially published his works without his name. It was not until 1760, with the publication of the *Treatise on Four Doctrines,* that his authorship was acknowledged on the title page. Also, he wrote in Latin and argued that he was writing for the intelligentsia and church leadership and had no intention that his new approach would have a following until judged by his colleagues. Nevertheless, in his later years he found it convenient to reside outside his native land.

In England Swedenborg's ideas found some popular support, and beginning in the 1770s his major works were translated. The Church of the New Jerusalem was founded there in 1774, moving to the United States in 1792 soon after the Revolution.

Sources:

Sigstedt, C. O. *The Swedenborg Epic: The Life and Works of Emanuel Swedenborg.* New York: Bookman Associates, 1952. Reprint, London: Swedenborg Society, 1981.

Swedenborg, Emanuel. *Arcana Coelestia.* 12 vols. New York: Swedenborg Foundation, 1905–1910.

———. *Heaven and Hell.* New York: Swedenborg Foundation, 1979.

———. *The New Jerusalem and Its Heavenly Doctrine.* London: Swedenborg Society, 1938.

———. *On the Divine Love and on the Divine Wisdom.* London: Swedenborg Society, 1963.

———. *The True Christian Religion.* London: Swedenborg Society, 1950.

Woofenden, William Ross. *Swedenborg Researcher's Manual.* Bryn Athyn, Pa.: Swedenborg Scientific Association, 1988.

Swedenborg Foundation Newsletter See Logos

Swedenborg Society

Founded in London, England, in 1810 to translate, print, and publish the works of **Emanuel Swedenborg** (1688–1772). The society organizes meetings and conferences and assists the needs of the **New Church,** which has grown up around Swedenborg's teachings, by keeping Swedenborg's writings in print. The society maintains a reference and lending library, with a reading room, at the London headquarters, 20 Bloomsbury Way, London, WC1A 2TH. Website: http://www.swedenborg.org.uk.

SWITZERLAND

[For material on ancient Switzerland, see the entry on the **Teutons.**]

Witchcraft and Demonology

Switzerland was by no means free from the **witchcraft** manias of Europe. About the year 1400, there were secular trials of people accused of **sorcery,** malevolent **magic,** in the Alps region now constituting southern and western Switzerland. During the same period, the Inquisition was pursuing heretics in neighboring valleys. One of the most active secular judges was Peter of Berne (Peter von Freyerz) in Simmenthal. Jeannette Charles was arrested as a sorceress in Geneva in 1401, and after torture she admitted evoking the **devil.** In Basel, in 1407, various women from well-to-do families were prosecuted for alleged sorcery in love affairs. In 1423, at Nieder-Hauenstein, near Basel, an alleged witch was condemned after a peasant testified that she had ridden on a wolf.

In the Valais area in 1428, the Bishop of Sion headed early systematic persecutions involving torture by secular authorities. Some 200 alleged witches were burned. There were many more tortures and burnings throughout the fifteenth century.

The records of the judge Peter of Berne tell of a witch named Staedelin in Boltingen (Lausanne) who confessed after torture to killing seven unborn babies in one house and preventing births in cattle. Also in Lausanne, certain witches were said to have cooked and eaten their own children, and 13 children were said to have been devoured by witches in Berne. Witches confessed to killing unbaptized children and afterwards digging up the remains and boiling them, making a transmutation ointment from the flesh.

Jakob Sprenger (1436–1495), co-author with **Heinrich Kramer** of the infamous *Malleus Maleficarum,* published in the 1480s, was born in Basel (part of German-speaking Switzerland), where he grew up in a Dominican house. While his main work was in **Germany,** after he was established at the University of Cologne, and his writings became the handbook of the great European witchcraft persecutions, some of which occurred in Switzerland.

The Protestant movement begun in Zürich by Ulrich Zwingli (1484–1531) did not slow the prosecution of witchcraft in Switzerland, indeed, some of the Zwinglians were active propagators of the cause. Typical of such attitudes was the book *Magiologia* by Bartholomäus Anhorn (Basel, 1674) which endorsed the demonology of M. A. Del Rio and others. The last legally executed witch in Switzerland appears to have been Anna Göldi, who was hanged in the Protestant canton of Glarus in 1782.

Demonic Possession

A remnant of the witchcraft persecutions appeared in the nineteenth century in the form of an extraordinary outbreak of paranoia over possible demonic possession. This took place in the parish of Morzine, a beautiful valley of the Savoy near Lake Geneva, during 1860. [The following account is drawn from reports in the *Cornhill Magazine,* London daily journals, the *Revue Spirite* and an article by William Howitt titled 'The Devils of Morzine.'] Morzine was quite remote, and was seldom visited by tourists before 1860. Being shut in by high mountains, and inhabited by a simple, industrious, and pious peasantry, Morzine might have appeared to a casual visitor the very center of health, peace, and good order.

The first appearance of an abnormal visitation was the conduct of a young girl, who, once quiet, modest, and well-conducted, suddenly began to exhibit what her distressed family and friends supposed to be the symptoms of insanity. She ran about in the most singular and aimless way, climbed high trees, scaled walls, and was found perched on roofs and cornices that it seemed impossible for any creature but a squirrel to reach. She soon became wholly intractable, was given to fits of hysteria, violent laughter, passionate weeping, and general aberration from her customary modest behavior.

While her parents were anxiously seeking advice in this dilemma, another and still another of the young girl's ordinary companions were seized with the same malady. In the course of ten days, more than 50 females ranging from seven to fifty years of age were reported as having been seized in this way, and were exhibiting symptoms of the most bewildering mental aberration. The crawling, climbing, leaping, wild singing, furious swearing, and frantic behavior of these women soon found crowds of imitators. Before the tidings of this frightful affliction had passed beyond the district in which it originated, several hundred women and children, and scores of young men, were writhing under the contagion. The seizures were sudden, like the attacks. They seldom lasted long, yet they never seemed to yield to any form of treatment, whether harsh, kind, medical, religious, or persuasive.

The first symptoms of this malady do not seem to have been noted with sufficient attention to justify giving details that could be considered accurate. It was only when the number of the possessed exceeded 2,000 persons and the case attracted multitudes of curious inquirers from all parts of the Continent, that the medical men, priests, and journalists of the time began to keep and publish constant records of the progress of the situation.

One of the strangest features of the case, and the one that most constantly baffled the faculty, was the appearance of rugged health and freedom from all physical disease that distinguished this malady. As a general rule, the victims spoke in hoarse, rough tones unlike their own, used profane language, such as few of them could ever have heard, and imitated the actions of crawling, leaping, climbing animals with ghastly fidelity. Sometimes they would roll their bodies up into balls and distort their limbs beyond the power of the attendant physicians to account for or disentangle.

Many among them reportedly experienced **levitation** in the air, and in a few instances, the women spoke in strange tongues, manifested high conditions of exaltation, described glorious visions, prophesied, gave clairvoyant descriptions of absent persons and distant places, sang hymns, and preached in strains of sublime inspiration. It must be added that these instances were very rare and were only noticeable in the earlier stages of the series of events.

It is almost needless to say that the tidings of what was happening in Morzine attracted multitudes of witnesses, as well as the attention of the learned and philosophic. When the attempts of the medical faculty, the church, and the law had been tried again and again, and all had utterly failed to modify the ever-increasing horrors of this malady, Louis Napoleon, the French emperor, under whose protectorate Morzine was then governed, yielding to the representations of his advisers, actually sent out three military companies to Morzine, charged with strict orders to quell the disturbances "on the authority of the Emperor, or by force if necessary." The result of this high-handed policy was to increase tenfold the violence of the disease and to augment the number of the afflicted, including some of the soldiers themselves, who sank under the contagion they were expected to quench.

The next move of the baffled government was a spiritual one. An army of priests, headed by a venerable bishop, much beloved in his diocese, was dispatched in the company of exorcists at the suggestion of the Archbishop of Paris. This second experiment worked no better than the first. Respectable-looking groups of well-dressed men, women, and children, would pass into the churches in reverent silence and with all the appearance of health and piety, but no sooner was heard the sound of the priest's voice or the notes of the organ, than shrieks, sobbings, and frenzied cries resounded from different parts of the assembly. Anxious fathers and husbands were busy in carrying their distracted relatives into the open air, and whether in the church or the home, every attempt of a sacerdotal character seemed to arouse the mania to heights of fury before unknown.

The time came at length when the old bishop thought of a way to achieve a general victory over the diabolical adversary. He commanded that as many as possible of the afflicted should be gathered together to hear high mass, when he trusted that the solemnity of the occasion would be sufficient to defeat what he evidently believed to be the combined forces of Satan. According to William Howitt, the assemblage in question, which included at least 2,000 of the possessed and a number of spectators, recalled Milton's description of Pandemonium. Children and women were leaping over the seats and benches, clambering up the pillars, and shrieking defiance from pinnacles that scarcely admitted of a foothold for a bird.

The bishop's letter contained one remark that seems to offer a clue to these scenes of horror and madness. He stated, "When in my distress and confusion I accidentally laid my hand on the heads of these unfortunates, I found that the paroxysm instantly subsided, and that however wild and clamorous they may have been before, the parties so touched generally sunk down as it were into a swoon, or deep sleep, and woke up most commonly restored to sanity, and a sense of propriety."

The failure of episcopal influence threw the government back on the help of medical science. One Dr. Constans had published a report in which he held out hopes of a cure if his advice was strictly followed. He was commissioned to do what he could for Morzine. Armed with the powers of a dictator he returned there, and, backed by a fresh detachment of sixty soldiers, a brigade of gendarmes, and a fresh cure, he issued despotic decrees and threatened lunatic asylums and deportation for the convulsed.

He fined any person who accused others of magic, or in any way encouraged the prevalent idea of supernatural evil. He desired the *curé* to preach sermons against the possibility of demonica possession, but this order could not be carried out by even the most obedient priest. The persons affected with fits were dispersed in every direction. Some were sent to asylums and hospitals, and many were simply exiled from Chablais. They were not allowed to revisit except by very special favor. Howitt notes,

"We need not point to the salient facts of our narrative, or discuss the various theories that have been invented to account for them. . . . It is impossible not to see the resemblance of the Morzine epidemic with the demonopathy of the sixteenth century, and the history of the Jansenist and Cevennes convulsionnaires. . . . Some of the facts we have related were often observed in the state of **hypnotism,** or nervous sleep, with which physicians are familiar. The hallucinations of which we have given instances are too common to astonish us. But the likeness of this epidemic to others that have been observed does not account for its symptoms."

Psychical Research and Parapsychology

As early as the mid-nineteenth century, interest in what would later be called **psychical research** emerged in Switzerland, one of the earliest pioneers of research into the paranormal being **Maximilian Perty,** who published studies on occult phenomena and **Spiritualism** from 1856 on. Although originally skeptical of **survival** of personality after death, he later became sympathetic to the concept.

Possibly the most famous Swiss psychical researcher is **Theodore Flournoy** (1854–1920), a psychologist at the University of Geneva who took part in the investigations of the mediumship of **Eusapia Palladino.** However, his enduring fame derived from his important investigation of the famous case of the medium **Hélène Smith,** as recorded in his book *From India to the Planet Mars; A Study of a Case of Somnambulism with Glossolalia* (1900).

While Flournoy operated from French-speaking Geneva, most interest in psychical research came from the German-speaking sections of the country. Other important Swiss investigators include Marc Thury (1822–1905); Eugene Bleuler of Zürich; Georg Sulzer (d. 1929); **Karl E. Muller** (1893–1969); Fanny Hoppe-Moser, who published *Okkultismus, Täuschungen und Tatsachen* (1935), and *Spuk* (1950); Guido Huber (died 1953), who published studies on survival; **Gebhard Frei** (1905–1967), who published a useful bibliography on the psychology of the subconscious; **Peter Ringger,** who founded the first parapsychological society in Switzerland and published works on parapsychology; and Friedrich A. Volman, who specialized in the literature of hauntings.

The great psychologist **Carl Jung** also occupies a special position for his interest in reconciling occult studies with the psychology of the subconscious. Between 1899 and 1900, he experimented with a young medium and submitted a doctoral thesis *On the Psychology and Pathology of the So-Called Occult.* He later cooperated in experiments in **psychokinesis** and **materialization** phenomena with famous mediums. There were a number of paranormal events in his own experience.

There are two major parapsychological societies. The Schweitzer Parapsychologische Gesellschaft Zürich was founded in 1952, with Peter Ringger as president. Six years later, his place was taken by Dr. Hans Naegeli-Osjord. The SPG organizes lecture programs in Zürich, maintains a library, and issues the periodical *Parapress.* It may be contacted c/o Frau N. von Muralt, Weihaldenstrasse 3, CH-8700 Kusnacht. Switzerland.

The Schweizerische Vereinigung für Parapsychologie was founded in Zürich in 1966 and organizes public lectures, discussions, and high school courses in psychical subjects. Under the presidency of Theo Locher, it has conducted investigations into a variety of parapsychological subjects, results of which are published in the biannual *Bulletin für Parapsychologie.* The society many be contacted at Industriestrasse 5, 2555 Brug, Zürich.

Sources:

Berger, Arthur S., and Joyce Berger. *The Encyclopedia of Parapsychology and Psychical Research.* New York: Paragon House, 1991.

Sword of Dyrnwyn

Periodical issued sporadically since 1977 by the Association of Cymmry Wicca and the Church of Y Tylwyth Teg, devoted to Welsh pagan traditions; includes articles on ley lines, astrology, megaliths, magick, ecology, and other occult subjects. It is issued by Camelot Press at PO Box 674884, Marietta, GA 30006-0006. Website: http://www.tylwythteg.com.

Sycomancy

Divination by the leaves of the fig tree. Questions or propositions were written on fig leaves. If the leaf dried quickly after the appeal, it was an evil omen, but it was a good sign if the leaf dried slowly.

Symbolism (Metapsychical)

A term used by psychical researcher **Ernesto Bozzano** in relation to:

". . . cases in which, by subconscious or mediumistic methods, an idea is expressed by means of hallucinatory perceptions, or ideographic representations, or forms of language differing from the ideas to be transmitted, but capable of suggesting them indirectly or conventionally. In other words, there is metapsychical symbolism every time an idea is transmitted by means of representations which are not reproductions."

F. W. H. Myers included one instance of such symbolic communication in his book, *Human Personality and Its Survival of Bodily Death* (1903): A botanical student passing inattentively in front of the glass door of a restaurant thought he saw "Verbascum Thapsus" printed on it. The real word was "Bouillon," and that happens to be the trivial name in French for the plant Verbascum Thapsus. The actual optical perception was thus subliminally transformed.

Symbolism often occurs in occultism, particularly in prophetic dreams, which are sometimes represented in visual or etymological puns. **Sigmund Freud** drew attention to such symbolic imagery in his psychoanalytical theory of dreams. Many psychics find their visions of future events occur in symbolic form. Traditional astrological predictions used to be presented in symbolic pictures called **hieroglyphs.**

Symmes, John Cleves (1780–1829)

Born November 5, 1780, Symmes was a captain in the U.S. Army in the war of 1812–14, nephew of the jurist of the same name. He served with distinction at the battle of Niagara and in the sortie from Fort Erie. He later devoted himself to philosophical pursuits. In 1818, he promulgated his theory that the Earth is a hollow sphere, habitable within, open at the poles to admit light, and containing within it six or seven concentric hollow spheres also open at the poles.

In May 1818, he mailed prominent people in various countries a manifesto of his theories, asking for an expedition to be equipped for exploration at the poles. He lectured widely and his convert James McBride was responsible for the anonymously published *Symmes' Theory of Concentric Spheres; Demonstrating that the Earth is Hollow, Habitable Within, and Widely Open About the Poles,* by A Citizen of the United States (1826). It was not favorably received, but later influenced other hollow Earth theorists.

In 1820, a pseudonymous book by "Captain Seaborn" titled *Symzonia* described a steamship voyage to the south polar opening. The ship goes over the rim and enters the continent of "Symzonia," where the inhabitants live in a socialist utopia. This concept may have influenced Edgar Allan Poe's story "Narrative of Arthur Gordon Pym."

Symmes died May 28, 1829, at the early age of 49, but his theories were revived by his son Americus Vespucius, who published *The Symmes' Theory of Concentric Spheres* (1878).

Sources:

A Citizen of the United States [James McBride]. *Symmes' Theory of Concentric Spheres; Demonstrating that the Earth is Hollow, Habitable Within, and Widely Open About the Poles.* Cincinnati, Ohio: Morgan, Lodge, and Fisher, 1826.

Symmes, Americus, ed. *The Symmes' Theory of Concentric Spheres: Demonstrating that the Earth is Hollow, Habitable Within, and Widely Open about the Poles.* Louisville, Ky.: Bradley and Gilbert, 1878.

Symonds, John (1914–)

British novelist, writer of children's books, and author of important works on occultism. He met **Aleister Crowley** in 1945 and tried to assist publication of his writings in the last two years of Crowley's life. He became Crowley's literary executor, and he is the author of the standard biography of Crowley: *The Great Beast* (1951). He went on to write several books about Crowley—the most recent appeared in 1989—and with **Kenneth Grant** he edited *The Confessions of Aleister Crowley* and Crowley's own book *Magick* (1973). Symonds was a member of the editorial board of *Man, Myth, and Magic* (1970) and wrote other books on occult topics, the most notable being his biography of **Helena Petrovna Blavatsky:** *Madame Blavatsky: Medium and Magician* (1960).

Sources:

Symonds, John. *The Great Beast.* London: MacDonald, 1951. Reprint, St. Albans, England: Mayflower, 1973.

———. *The King of the Shadow Realm.* London: Duckworth, 1989.

———. *Light Over Water.* London: J. Baker for the Unicorn Press, 1963.

———. *The Magic of Aleister Crowley.* London: Frederick Muller, 1958.

———. *Thomas Brown and the Angels.* London: Hutchinson, 1961.

Sympathy

A mutual attraction or identity of feeling between individuals and also animals, the opposite of the reaction of **antipathy.** The term "sympathy" has a special significance in **mesmerism** or **animal magnetism,** where it is used to indicate the rapport between operator and subject, by means of which the operator could influence and control the perceptions of the subject. It has also been suggested that a condition of sympathy might exist between **agent** and **percipient** in **telepathy,** particularly in the transmission of emotions.

Synchronicity

A connecting principle, expressing the linkage of events without a cause-and-effect relationship in time. In addition to the normal cause-and-effect connections observed in nature, there appears to be another principle expressed in the simultaneous arrangement or connection of events. A theory of synchronicity was developed by psychotherapist **Carl G. Jung** and related to certain ESP phenomena. In recent decades the concept has been widely borrowed by occultists in support of their worldview.

As an illustration of this principle, some, such as astrologer Dan Rudhyar, suggest a relationship between astrological positions and events in the life of individual human beings. The human events are not necessarily *caused* by the position of heavenly bodies, only linked in a causal relationship.

Sources:

Jung, Carl G., and W. Pauli. *The Interpretation of Nature and the Psyche.* London, 1955.

Synchronicity Foundation

Synchronicity Foundation, known for its support of an innovative high-tech form of **meditation,** was founded in 1983 by Master Charles, a mystic and former leading disciple of Swami Paramahansa Muktananda (1908–1982), one of the most popular spiritual teachers from India to build a following in the West in the 1970s. He taught a form of **kundalini** yoga. Master Charles was born on March 14, 1945, in Syracuse, New York, and raised in a Roman Catholic family. As a child he began to have mystic and visionary experiences and developed a special devotion to the Virgin Mary. He attended a Roman Catholic high school and at one point considered entering a Roman Catholic order, but became disenchanted with the church as an institution.

As he moved into adulthood, he began to explore the alternative spiritualities, especially Eastern forms, that were flowing into the country at the time. Then in 1970, some friends who had been to India showed him a photo of Swami Muktananda. He had an immediate reaction to the picture. He discovered a copy of *Guru,* Muktananda's autobiographical book, and laid plans to go to India himself. His meeting with Muktananda confirmed the awakening of divine energy he already experienced. He became a disciple and was given the name Arjuna. He eventually became Muktananda's private secretary.

Shortly before his passing in 1982, Muktananda instructed Arjuna to return to the West and create a form of the teachings not bound in an Indian cultural format. Thus, in 1982, Arjuna changed his name to Brother Charles and settled in rural Virginia. He began to attract a few disciples, and as his following grew he founded the Synchronicity Foundation. The name of the foundation grew out of his understanding that meditation is an experience that synchronizes the activity of the two halves of the brain. When the brain is unsynchronized, one experiences the duality of the world. When they are synchronized, one experiences the underlying unity of the Source of all.

Brother Charles (now known as Master Charles) has also considered the scientific advances in the West and the understanding of the role sound played in enhancing the meditation experience. He discovered that certain patterns of sound aid synchronization and developed recordings that could be fed to meditators in headphones. This became the basis of a growing technological approach to spirituality and **mysticism.**

The Synchronicity Foundation is headquartered at P.O. Box 694, Nellyford, VA 22923. It offers a program of retreats and workshops, and a network of Synchronicity centers have emerged around the world. The foundation has an Internet site at http://www.synchronicity.org/.

Sources:

Charles, Master. *The Bliss of Freedom: A Contemporary Mystic's Enlightening Journey.* Malibu, Calif.: Acacia Publishing, 1997.

Synchronicity Foundation Homepage. http://www.synchronicity.org/. June 28, 2000.

Synchronicity Research Unit See **SRU**

Szekely, Edmond Bordeaux (?–1980)

Edmond Bordeaux Szekely, the proponent of a modern spiritual pathway he ascribed to the ancient Essenes, was born in Hungary early in the twentieth century. He was the grandson of the poet Alexander Szekely. His father was the Unitarian bishop of Clug, Transylvania (now in Romania), and his mother was a French Roman Catholic. His primary education was at a parochial school, and as a young man he was sent to study in Rome. There around 1923, in the Vatican Archives, he reportedly discovered the lost gospel written in Aramaic, the language Jesus actually spoke. He also reportedly discovered a Hebrew fragment of the text in Monte Cassino. (Szekely left little information about the manuscripts and no one else has been able to locate them.) Szekely also claimed to have found a copy of the manuscript written in Old Slavonic in Vienna, but again few details have been left concerning the find or its present location.

Szekely published a section of the manuscript in 1937 as the *Gospel of Peace by the Apostle John.* It was later republished as the *Essene Gospel of Peace,* the name by which it is currently best known. Given the vague information on its discovery and the failure in locating the original manuscripts, critics have suggested that the ancient texts never existed and that the *Essene Gospel* is an entirely modern product of Szekely's imagination. In spite of these criticisms, many have found the book of great inspirational value.

Shortly after the publication of the Gospel, Szekely founded several communes in France which attempted to embody its teachings. However, as Hitler rose to power, Szekely left for the Americas. He settled in Tecate, Mexico, south of San Diego, and eventually became a Mexican citizen. He purchased a rural estate and opened the Essene School, built upon the idea that Jesus and the first Christians were Essenes. Here he began to systematically teach his principles for healthy living, which he termed biogenics. Keys to the system were vegetarianism and the use of whole fresh foods. His estate, Rancho la Puerta, became famous as a health spa, attracting many wealthy and famous people.

In 1958 Szekely opened the Golden Door, a health spa in Escondido, California, that became one of the most famous of the era. It was especially favored by Hollywood stars. From his base in the Essene School he founded the International Biogenic Society to perpetuate his health perspective and authored numerous books. He also founded the Academy of Creative Living, which published many of his books, including the second and third installments of the *Essene Gospel of Peace* (1974). He spent the last years of his life in Cartago, Costa Rica, where he died in 1980.

Following his death, his wife continued as head of the International Biogenic Society. It may now be contacted at P.O. Box 849, Nelson, BC, Canada VIL 6A5. A spiritual community emphasizing the Essene teachings was created in 1982 by his colleague Garry White in San Diego, California, as the First Christians' Essene Church (now the **Essene Foundation**), headquartered at 2536 Collier Ave., San Diego, CA 92116. More recently, the Essene New Life Church founded by Rev. Dr. Charles A. Thomas in 1993 is headquartered at 110 Smith St., Ste. A, Mount Shasta, CA 96067-2636. It, and its associated Awareness Institute, is the only group to have a website, to be found at http://www.awarinst.com.

Sources:

Berskov, Per. *Strange Tales About Jesus.* Philadelphia: Fortress Press, 1983.

Szekely, Edmond Bordeaux. *The Gospel of Peace by the Apostle John.* London: C. H. Daniels, 1937. Reprinted as *The Essene Gospel of Peace.* San Diego: Academy of Creative Living, 1971.

———. *The Essene Way, Biogenic Living.* Cartago, Costa Rica: International Biogenic Society, 1978.

———. *Talks.* San Diego: Academy of Creative Living, 1972.

T

Table-turning (or Table-tipping)

A form of psychic phenomena in which a table rotates, tilts, or rises completely off the ground by the mere contact of the fingertips of an individual or group of individuals. In exceptional cases tables have been known to move or even levitate without direct contact. The familiar form of **séance** in table-turning is that in which the sitters place their fingertips on the table; then the table moves without conscious exercise of muscular force. By relating the **raps** or tilts of the table to the alphabet it becomes possible to receive intelligent messages. (See **movement**)

Historical Background

Table-turning is the simplest and oldest form of communication with extraneous intelligences or the subconscious self. In ancient times tables were used for purposes of divination as "mensa divinatoriae." In fourth-century Rome, Ammianus Marcellinus described a table with a slab, engraved with the letters of the alphabet, above which a ring was held, suspended by a thread; by swinging to certain letters, messages were spelled out. Tertullian (ca. 155–ca. 222) appears to have been one of the first who knew of table communications with the unseen world.

Table-turning in modern **Spiritualism** dates from the mid-nineteenth century and seems to have originated in America soon after the **Rochester rappings** of 1848. At that time, there was considerable interest in **animal magnetism** or "electro-biology," stemming from the **mesmerism** of Europe.

Mesmerism established the convention of groups of individuals arranged in a circle with a variously named magnetic fluid linking them. After the phenomena of **rappings** in the presence of the **Fox sisters** became widely known, groups gathered around other individuals who possessed the same ability to generate raps.

Table-turning and rapping spread like an epidemic throughout America and was brought to England by such professional **mediums** as **Maria B. Hayden,** who came to London with a lecturer on electro-biology in 1852. An advantage of table-turning was that it did not require a paid professional medium. Amateur groups could sit round a table and obtain the intelligent rappings which had first been manifest only to specially talented individuals, i.e., mediums.

In 1852 afternoon social invitations to tea and table-turning were common. Table-turning was even more successful in France, with its tradition of mesmerism and animal magnetism. One widespread jest was that people no longer asked after each other's health, but asked instead how the table was. "Thank you, mine turns beautifully, and how goes yours?"

Mesmerists welcomed table-turning as a demonstration of animal magnetism or odic force, while Fundamentalist ecclesiastics denounced it as due to Satanic agency. Scientists and doctors thought that the new craze would be a danger to mental health and a committee was formed to find a non-Spiritualist explanation for the phenomenon. They reported in the *Medical Times and Gazette* on June 11, 1853, that the motion of the table was due to unconscious muscular action.

A few weeks later the great chemist and physicist **Michael Faraday** reported experiments with a simple apparatus to demonstrate that the movements of the table were due to unconscious muscular action of the part of the sitters, who were by implication the automatic authors of the messages claiming to come from the spirit world. Faraday's apparatus consisted of two thin wooden boards with little glass rollers between them. The contraption was whole bound together with rubber bands and so contrived that the slightest lateral pressure on the upper board would cause it to slip a little way over the other. A haystalk or a scrap of paper served to indicate any motion of the upper board over the lower.

The conclusion drawn from these experiments was that when the sitters believed themselves to be pressing downward, they were really pressing obliquely in the direction they expected the table to rotate. Other investigators also held the expectation that the operators had much to do with the motions of the table. **James Braid** pointed out in the appendix to his book *Hypnotic Therapeutics* (1853) that someone generally announced beforehand the direction they expected the table to rotate.

Among the earliest investigators of the phenomenon of table-turning were Count **Agenor De Gasparin** and Prof. **Marc Thury** of Geneva, who held séances and were satisfied that the movements resulted from a force radiating from the operators, to which they gave the name of **ectenic force.**

The public, on the whole, ignored the conclusions of Faraday and others, preferring the more popular Spiritualist explanation or the pseudo-scientific theories of "electro-biology." Other explanations offered included **od** or odic force, galvanism, animal magnetism, and the rotation of the Earth. Revs. G. Sandby and C. H. Townshend claimed to have experienced a feeling of fatigue after a table-turning séance as though they had been hypnotizing someone. They reported a tingling sensation in their fingertips, while Townshend claimed somewhat vaguely that spirit rappings might be caused by a "disengagement of Zoogen (an unidentified force in nature) from the System."

Meanwhile various Evangelical clergymen insisted that table-turning was Satanic. Revs. N. S. Godfrey, E. Gillson, and others held séances in which the "spirit" confessed themselves to be either spirits of worthless persons of evil inclination or devils. Both of the "spirits' " confessions caused the reverent gentlemen to denounce the whole practice of table-turning. One of them purposely mentioned the Faraday experiments, stating that the phenomena "appear to be whatever the investigator supposes them to be"—a saying which aptly characterized his own attitude.

The psychical researcher **Camille Flammarion,** whose exhaustive experiments and scientific attainments gave considerable weight to his opinion, offered an explanation of the various phases of table-turning phenomena. Simple rotation of the table he ascribed to an unconscious impulse given by the operators; other movements of the table while the fingers of the sitters rested upon it were ascribed to similar causes. The tilting of the table on the side furthest away from the operator was explained by muscular action. The vibrations in the wood of the table, its **levitation** under the fingers, or extent, its rotation without contact of the operator's hands, he attributed to a force emanating from the body. In the latter case, the operator was capable of acting at a distance by means of ether-waves. This force, the result of a cerebral disturbance, was greater than that of the muscles, as is seen by the levitation of tables so weighty that the combined muscular strength of the operators would not suffice to lift them.

To the dictating of messages and other intelligent manifestations he gave an origin in this psychic force, which is perhaps identical with Thury's "ectenic force," or "psychode," and which is obedient to the will and desires, or even, in some cases, the subconscious will of the operator. Flammarion did not consider the **spirit hypothesis** necessary.

It is possible that some **fraud** may have crept into the séances investigated by Flammarion, as it has done in so many other cases. There are, of course, those among the most qualified of psychical researcher, who find the hypothesis of unconscious muscular action or deliberate fraud a satisfactory explanation of the phenomena.

The Mechanics of Table-Turning

One common procedure followed by those engaged in table tipping began with those in attendance forming a circle around the table. They placed hands lightly, with fingertips touching, on the leaf, and with lowered lights or in complete darkness, waited for the manifestations. According to reports, if someone with psychic powers was present the table might show signs of animation. The first such sign was often a quivering motion under the sitters' hands; it increased until the table pulsated with a mysterious energy. The wooden surface appeared to some to act as a reservoir of externalized nervous force.

The psychical researcher **Hereward Carrington** said that in his séances with **Eusapia Palladino** the table appeared to be somehow alive like the back of a dog. In one of his stories a similar phenomenon that occurred during the mediumship of medium **D. D. Home** induced Alexander Dumas to fantasize the table as an intelligence itself. The conception of a spirit entering furniture became a favorite idea with French authors afterward.

After the vibratory stage the table might jerk, tilt, stumble about, and eventually become entirely levitated. Apparently, there was believed to be an intelligence behind these movements. If the letters of the alphabet were called over in the dark, the table, by tilting, knocking on the floor, or tapping, indicated certain letters that connectedly spelled out a message, often claiming to come from someone deceased. The intelligence that manifested had personal characteristics. In repeated sittings it was soon noticed by observers that the skill with which the table was manipulated or the eccentricities of its behavior were indications of the presence of the same entity. The strange, stolid, or clumsy behavior of the table immediately denoted that a new visitant was tampering with the contact.

But the table might disclose much more than that. Its motions could express humor, emotion, and personality. It might climb up into the sitter's lap as a mark of affection; it might chase others all over the room in a hostile manner. As an additional means of expression, the table could convey queer impressions by creaking. P. P. Alexander noted in his book *Spiritualism: A Narrative with a Discussion* (1871):

"At a particular stage of the proceedings the table began to make strange undulatory movements, and gave out, as these proceeded, a curious accompaniment of creaking sounds. Mr. Home seemed surprised. 'This is very curious,' he said, 'it is a phenomenon of which I have no experience hitherto.' Presently my friend remarked that movement and sound together—it reminded him of nothing he could think of except a ship in distress, with its timbers straining in a heavy sea. . . . This conclusion being come to . . . the table proceeded to rap out: 'It is David.' Instantly a lady burst into tears, and cried wildly: 'Oh, that must be my poor, dear brother, David, who was lost at sea some time since.' "

When the table moves under contact there is an obvious possibility for the subconscious mind or a secondary **personality** to convey ideas by unconscious muscular pressure of either a medium or the sitters. According to **F. W. H. Myers,**

"The subliminal self, like the telegraphist begins its effort with full knowledge of the alphabet, but with only weak and rude command over our muscular adjustments. It is therefore *a priori* likely that its easiest mode of communication will be through a repetition of simple movements, so arranged as to correspond to letters of the alphabet."

But Myers was inclined to attribute to the subconscious mind the movement of the table without contact as well. "If a table moves when no one is touching it, this is not obviously more likely to have been effected by my deceased grandfather than by myself. We cannot tell how I could move it; but then we cannot tell how he could move it either."

Certainly, there are experiences which bear out this possibility and show how singularly deceptive the interpretation of phenomena may be. George S. Long, an acquaintance of **Richard Hodgson,** narrated in the *Proceedings* of the Society for Psychical Research (vol. 9, p. 65) a strange experience with a chair. Through a young lady he received what was said to be the most convincing test of spirit return:

"First the chair spelt out my name and showed a disposition to get into my lap; then it spelt out 'George, you ought to know me as I am Jim.' But I didn't, and said so. Then without my looking at the board, it spelt out 'Long Island, Jim Rowe' and 'Don't you remember I used to cary you when you were a little fellow,' or words to that effect. I had to acknowledge the truth of it and also to say that as he was an ignorant man he possibly intended 'Cary' for carry. I must own I was puzzled for the moment. To make sure of his power I asked that he count the pickets in the fence. Somehow he could not agree to this, and even the medium objected. As a last resort I asked how long he had been in the spirit land and the answer came, between thirteen and fourteen years. Now to the sequel. First it occurred to me a day or two later, that while all the incidents given were correct the name should have been given as Roe instead of Rowe. Second I was upon Long Island this summer, and the matter coming to my mind I inquired how long Jim Roe had been dead, and was informed he died last Winter; so when I received this test so convincing to the believers the man was not dead."

The material from which the chair or table was made seemed to make no difference once the available power was sufficient to manifest. The reason why a table was used for spirit communication was primarily convenience; it was piece of generally available furniture which allowed contact around it for a large number of people. Some Spiritualists also thought its surface acted as a receptacle for the generated force and compared the space underneath the table to a medium's cabinet, especially if it was surrounded by a deep hanging table cloth. In the early days of Spiritualism, they often used a table with a hole in the middle through which "materialized hands" could be thrust.

Eusapia Palladino insisted on a séance table built entirely of wood. She considered soft pinewood the best to absorb vital magnetism. She allowed no metal in the construction of the table.

The color of the table made no difference. **Joseph Maxwell** found an advantage in covering it with some white material of light texture. He also insisted that the table should, if possible, be fastened with wooden pegs instead of nails since mediums, supposedly, are sometimes extremely sensitive to metals.

It was reported that with a powerful medium the movement of the table could occur at any time and disclose a tremendous force in operation. Thus Gambier Bolton, writing in *Psychic Force* (1904) observed,

"During any meal with Mrs. Elgie Corner [i.e., **Florence Cook**] in one's own house, and whilst she herself is engaged in eating and drinking—both of her hands being visible all the time—the heavy dining table will commence first to quiver, setting all the glasses shaking, and plates, knives, forks and spoons in motion, and then to rock and sway from side to side, occasionally going so far as to tilt up at one end or at one side; and all the time raps and tappings will be heard in the table and in many different parts of the room. Taking a meal with her in a public restaurant is a somewhat serious matter."

In experiments conducted by psychical researcher **Harry Price** with the psychic **Stella C.** in 1923, powerful and rhythmical vibrations of tables were obtained, and on one occasion, after violent movements of a table, it suddenly snapped, the top breaking into two pieces, and the legs breaking off.

Table-Turning and Dowsing

The various theories about the rationale of table-turning parallel those advanced for the phenomena of **dowsing** and **radiesthesia,** where there is meaningful movement of a water-witching rod or a **pendulum** or similar indicator. The actual force moving the indicator is still a matter of controversy.

It is generally assumed that unconscious muscular action or nervous energy plays a significant part, but it is still far from clear how information on underground water, minerals, or buried objects is conveyed to the mind, or from the mind to the indicator.

One of the earliest investigators to link the action of table-turning with **divining rods** or pendulums was the French chemist Michel Eugène Chevreul, in his book *De la baguette divinatoire, du pendule dit ex plorateur et des tables tournantes, au point de vue de l'histoire, de la critique et de la méthode expérimentale* (1854).

In modern times, table-turning is a laborious method of establishing contact with unseen intelligence. **Planchette** and **ouija board** are more satisfactory and faster. Also, while a number of prominent mediums such as Betty White began their career with a ouija board, they quickly moved beyond. Messages obtained by such methods are often misleading or false. Again, the communications received at circles in general tend to reflect the general interest level of the sitters.

Sources:

Barrett, William, and Theodore Besterman. *The Divining-Rod: An Experimental & Psychological Investigation.* London: Methuen, 1926. Reprint, New Hyde Park, N.Y.: University Books, 1968.

Burr, Chauncey. *Knocks for the Knockings.* New York: Burr Brothers, 1851.

Capron, E. W. *Modern Spiritualism: Its Facts and Fanaticisms, Its Consistencies and Contradictions.* Boston: B. Marsh, 1855. Reprint, New York: Arno Press, 1976.

Capron, E. W., and H. D. Barron. *Singular Revelations: Explanation and History of the Mysterious Communion with Spirits.* Auburn, N.Y., 1850.

Chevreul, M. E. *De la baguette divinatoire, du puendule dit explorateur et des tables tournantes, au point de vue du l'histoire, de la critique et de la méthode expérimentale.* Paris, 1854.

Close, F. *The Tester Tested; or Table Moving, Turning, Talking, Not Diabolical: A Review of the Publications of the Rev. Messrs. Godfrey, Gillson, Vincent, and Dibdin.* London and Cheltenham, 1853.

Cowan, Charles. *Thoughts on Satanic Influence, or Modern Spiritualism Considered.* London, 1854.

De Gasparin, Comte Agenor. *Des table tournantes, de surnaturel en général, et des esprits.* Paris, 1854.

De Mirville, Marquis J. E. *Pneumatologie: Des Esprits et de leurs manifestations fluidique devant la science modern.* Paris, 1853.

De Szapary, Comte F. G. *Les tables tournantes.* Paris, 1854.

Dewey, D. M. *History of the Strange Sounds or Rappings Heard in Rochester and Western New York.* Rochester, 1850.

Du Potet de Sennevoy, Baron. *Traité complet de magnétisme animal.* Paris, 1856.

Elliott, Charles W. *Mysteries, or Glimpses of the Supernatural.* New York: Harper, 1852.

Godfrey, Nathaniel S. *Table Turning the Devil's Modern Masterpiece; Being the Result of a Course of Experiments.* U.K.: Thames Ditton, 1853.

Guldenstubbe, Baron L. de. *Pneumatologie positive et expérimentale; La réalité des Espirits et le phenom ene merveilleux de leur écriture directe demontrées.* Paris, 1857.

Hartmann, E. von. *Der Spiritismus.* 1855. English ed. as *Spiritism.* London, n.d.

Hornung, D. *Neue Geheimnisse des Tages durch Geistes Magnetismus.* Leipzig, 1857.

Kerner, Justinus. *Die Somnambülen Tische: Zur Geschichte und Erklärungen dieser Erscheinungen.* Stuttgart, 1853.

Lang, Andrew. *Cock Lane and Common-Sense.* London: Longmans, Green, 1894. Reprint, New York: AMS Press, 1970.

Mahan, Asa. *Modern Mysteries Explained and Exposed.* Boston, 1855.

Mattison, Hiram. *Spirit Rapping Unveiled!* Derby, N.Y., 1853.

Maxwell, Joseph. *Metaphysical Phenomena: Methods and Observations.* London: Duckworth, 1905.

Morgan, R. C. *An Inquiry Into Table Miracles.* Bath and London, 1853.

Page, Charles G. *Psychomancy; Spirit Rappings and Tippings Exposed.* New York, 1853.

Perty, Maximilien. *Die Mystischen Erscheinungen der menschlichen Natur.* 2nd ed., Leipzig and Heidelberg, 1872.

Price, Harry. *Stella C.: An Account of Some Original Experiments in Psychical Research.* Edited by James Turner. London: Souvenir Press, 1973.

Prichard, John. *A Few Sober Words of Table-talk about the Spirits.* Leamington, UK, 1853.

Spicer, Henry. *Facts and Fantasies: A Sequel to "Sights and Sounds."* London, 1853.

Table Turning and Table Talking Considered in Connection with the Dictates of Reason and Common Sense. Bath, UK: S. Gibbs, 1853.

Table Turning by Animal Magnetism Demonstrated. London, 1853.

Tiffany, Joel. *Spiritualism Explained.* New York: Graham & Ellinwood, 1856.

Townsend, C. H. *Mesmerism Proved True.* London, 1854.

Taboo (or **Tabu** or **Tapu**)

A Polynesian word meaning "prohibited" and signifying a prohibition enforced by religious or magical power, which has come to be applied to similar usages among primitive peoples all over the world. It also has parallels in the religious codes of sophisticated societies, as in the early Hebrew term *Kherem* ("set apart" or prohibited), and in the highly developed social etiquette of modern society.

Taboo, or prohibition, was enforced in the cases of sacred things and unclean things. In the first instance, the taboo was placed on the object because of the possession by it of inherent mysterious power. But taboo might be imposed by a chief or priest. It would be used for the protection of important individuals, the safeguarding of the weak, women, children, and slaves from the magical influence of more highly-placed individuals, against danger incurred by handling or coming in contact with corpses, or eating certain foods, and the securing of human beings against the power of supernatural agencies, or the depredations of thieves.

Taboo could be sanctioned by social use or instinct. The violation of a taboo made the offender taboo; taboos, like various kinds of social uncleanliness, were transmissible, but the taboo could be thrown off by magical or purificatory ceremonies. It might last for a short period, or be imposed for eternity.

It may be said that the practice of taboo was instituted through human instinct for human convenience. This applies of course merely to the most simple type of taboo. It was, for example, forbidden to reap or steal the patch of corn dedicated to an agricultural deity, for the simple reason that his wrath would be incurred by so doing. Similarly it was taboo to devour the flesh of the totem animal of the tribe, except in special circumstances with the object of achieving communion with him. It was taboo to interfere in any manner with the affairs of the **shamans** or medicine men, also a type of the imposed taboo for the convenience of a certain caste. It was prohibited to marry a woman of the same totem as oneself, because all the members of a totemic band are supposed to be consanguineous; such a union might incur the wrath of the patron deity. A very strict taboo was put upon the witnessing of certain ritual instruments belonging to some primitive tribes, but this only applied to women and uninitiated men. It was considered a degradation for women to behold sacred implements.

If taboo does not spring directly from the system known as **totemism,** it was strongly influenced by it—that is, many intricate taboos arose from the totemic system. There was also the taboo of the sorcerer; it in effect was merely a spell placed upon a certain object, which makes it become useless to others. Taboo, or its remains, can still be found even in modernized communities. From its use the feeling of reverence for ancient institutions and those who represent them is undoubtedly derived.

Sources:

Frazer, James G. *The Golden Bough.* Vol. 3 of *Taboo and the Perils of the Soul.* New York: Macmillan, 1935.

Ganzfried, Rabbi Solomon. *Code of Jewish Law (Kitzur Schulchan Aruch).* New York: Hebrew Publishing, 1927.

Mead, Margaret. *Inquiry Into the Question of Cultural Stability in Polynesia.* New York: Columbia University, 1928. Reprint, New York: AMS Press, 1981.

Webster, Hutton. *Taboo: A Sociological Study.* Palo Alto, Calif.: Stanford University Press, 1942. Reprint, London: Octagon, 1981.

Tabori, Paul (1908–1974)

Hungarian-born British novelist, journalist, political writer, scriptwriter, and psychical researcher. Some of his books were published under the pseudonyms "Christopher Stevens" and "Paul Tabor." Tabori was born on August 5, 1908, in Budapest, Hungary. He was educated at Kaiser Friedrich Wilhelm University (Ph.D., 1930) and Pazmany Peter University (Doctor of Economics and Political Science). He worked in various journalistic positions in Hungary (1926–1937) and London (1937–1960s). Beginning in the 1920s, Tabori wrote a number of books on various political and other subjects. He lived in the United States for several years as a 1966 visiting professor at Fairleigh Dickinson University (1966) and the City College of New York (1967). He also translated a number of books and authored 32 feature films and over a hundred television films and plays.

On the death of psychical researcher **Harry Price** (1881–1948), Tabori was literary executor for Price and a trustee of the Harry Price Library at London University, England. Subsequently he published a biography, *Harry Price: The Biography of a Ghost Hunter* (1950), the first of several books on psychic topics. He died November 9, 1974.

Sources:

Pleasants, Helene, ed. *Biographical Dictionary of Parapsychology.* New York: Helix Press, 1964.

Tabori, Paul. *Beyond the Senses: A Report on Psychical Research in the Sixties.* N.p., 1971.

———. *Companions of the Unseen.* London: H. A. Humphrey, 1968.

———. *Harry Price: The Biography of a Ghost Hunter.* London: Athenaeum Press, 1950.

Tabori, Paul, and Cornelius Tabori. *My Occult Diary.* 1951. Reprint, New York: Living Books, 1966.

Tabori, Paul, and P. Raphael. *Crime and the Occult.* N.p., 1974.

Tabori, Paul, and Peter Underwood. *The Borley Ghosts.* N.p., 1973.

Tadebtsois

Spirits believed in by the Samoyeds. (See also **Siberia**)

Tadibe

The name for a Samoyed magician. (See also **Siberia**)

Taetzsch, Robert Leonard (1931–)

Statistician, management engineer, and parapsychologist. He was born on July 6, 1931, at Irvington, New Jersey, and studied at the Newark College of Engineering, New Jersey, where he received both a B.S. (mechanical engineering, 1952) and a M.S. degree (engineering, cum laude, 1959). For many years after his graduation he was employed at Union Carbide Plastics.

Out of his interest in **parapsychology,** as an engineer he worked on developing statistical techniques in order to control **psi** phenomena, and the development of systems for transmitting messages by psi processes. Utilizing an IBM 1620 digital computer, he developed a psi communication system based on binary targets and sequential sampling. He was a member of both the **Parapsychologcal Association** and the **American Society for Psychical Research.**

Sources:

Pleasants, Helene, ed. *Biographical Dictionary of Parapsychology.* New York: Helix Press, 1964.

T'ai Chi Ch'uan

A system of ancient Chinese physical movements, designed to build up subtle energy in the body, resulting in spiritual development. For centuries it was a secret taught only to males in certain families, but by the middle of the nineteenth century it was openly taught in Peking.

The roots of T'ai Chi Ch'uan are said to go back to the breathing exercises of Taoist monks in the 2nd century B.C.E. The purported founder of the actual Tai Chi Chuan system was a fifteenth century monk named Chang San-feng.

The yielding, supple philosophy behind T'ai Chi Ch'uan is summarized in the Tao Te Ching:

"A man is born gentle and weak, at his death hard and stiff. Green plants are tender and filled with sap, at their death they are withered and dry. Therefore the stiff and unbending is the disciple of death. The gentle and yielding is the disciple of life. Thus an army without flexibility never wins a battle. A tree that is unbending is easily broken. The hard and strong will fall. The soft and weak will overcome."

In addition to the philosophy there are 37 basic exercises and postures that are repeated with variations, culminating in some 65 or 108 exercises fusing energetic with relaxed movement. During practice, it is important to be concerned with centering the body with **meditation** and relaxation. T'ai Chi Ch'uan is often linked with the study of the **I Ching** to enhance the philosophical aspects of the system.

Although T'ai Chi Ch'uan has been facetiously referred to as "shadow boxing," it often resembles a slow-motion ballet, and has been described as "yoga in movement." Like the asanas of **hatha yoga,** T'ai Chi Ch'uan takes the names of its forms from animals or events occurring in nature: "White Crane Spreads Its Wings," "Meteor Runs After Moon," or "Brush Dust Against the Wind." Both hatha yoga and T'ai Chi exercises encompass focused concentration and special breathing patterns. But while the graceful, flowing movements of T'ai Chi seem to superficially contrast with the asanas, developing forms of yoga movement bring the two regimens closer together.

T'ai Chi has become popular in the United States, as Americans realize the great health benefits of the practice. Most often the elderly do these exercises to regain strength and balance, greatly decreasing their chances of injuries from falls. The slow movements of T'ai Chi make it easy for everyone to practice and still gain health benefits.

Sources:

Cheng, Man-ching. *Tai-Chi.* Berkeley, Calif.: North Atlantic, 1981.

Crompton, Paul. *The T'ai Chi Workbook.* Boston: Shambala Publishing, Inc., 1987.

Da Liu. *T'ai Chi Ch'uan and I Ching.* New York: Harper & Row, 1972.

———. *T'ai Chi Ch'uan and Meditation.* New York: Schocken Books, 1986.

Feng, Gia-Fu and Jane English. *Lao Tsu: Tao Te Ching.* New York: Vintage Books, 1972.

Perfetti, Ron. T'ai Chi Chuan Overview. http://www.maui.net/~taichi4u/overview.html. April 14, 2000.

Smith, Robert W. *Chinese Boxing.* New York: Kodansha, 1981.

T'ai Chi Magazine. http://www.tai-chi.com/. April 17, 2000.

"Tao & Tai Chi." http://www.chebucto.ns.ca/Philosophy/Taichi/tao-chi.html. April 4, 2000.

"The Heaven and Earth Academy of T'ai Chi." http://www.taichinews.com/. April 6, 2000.

Taigheirm

A magical sacrifice of cats to the infernal spirits, formerly practiced in the Highlands and islands of Scotland. It is believed to have been originally a ceremony of sacrifice from the more northern lands to the subterranean gods, which became in Christian times an invocation of infernal spirits. The word *taigheirm* signifies either an armory, or the cry of a cat, according to the sense in which it is used.

An early description of the ceremony, which must be performed with black cats, is given in George C. Horst's *Deuteroscopie* (1830):

"After the cats were dedicated to all the devils, and put into a magico-sympathetic condition by the shameful things done to them, and the agony occasioned them, one of them was at once put upon the spit, and, amid terrific howlings, roasted before a slow fire. The moment that the howls of one tortured cat ceased in death, another was put upon the spit, for a minute of interval must not take place if they would control hell; and this continued for the four entire days and nights. If the exorcist could hold it out still longer, and even till his physical powers were absolutely exhausted, he must do so."

When the horrible rites had been continued for a time, the demons began to appear in the shape of black cats, who mingled their dismal cries with those of the unfortunate sacrifices. At length a cat appeared of larger size and more frightful aspect than the others, and the time had come for the exorcist to make known his demands. Usually he asked for the gift of **second sight,** but other rewards might be asked for and received.

The last *Taigheirm* was said to have been held in Mull about the middle of the seventeenth century. The exorcists were Allan Maclean and his assistant Lachlain Maclean, both of whom received the psychic gift of second sight.

Of this particular ceremony Horst stated:

"The infernal spirits appeared, some in the early progress of the sacrifices in the shape of black cats. The first who appeared during the sacrifice, after they had cast a furious glance at the sacrifices, said—Lachlain Oer, that is, 'Injurer of Cats.' Allan, the chief operator, warned Lachlain, whatever he might see or hear, not to waver, but to keep the spit incessantly turning. At length the cat of monstrous size appeared; and after it had set up a horrible howl, said to Lachlain Oer, that if he did not cease before their largest brother came he would never see the face of God.

"Lachlain answered that he would not cease till he had finished his work if all the devils in hell came. At the end of the fourth day, there sat on the end of the beam in the roof of the barn a black cat with fire—flaming eyes, and there was heard a terrific howl quite across the straits of Mull into Mowen."

By this time, the elder of the two men was quite exhausted and sank down in a swoon, but the younger was sufficiently self-possessed to ask for wealth and prosperity, which both received throughout their lifetime.

Shortly before this, Cameron of Lochiel received at a *taigheirm* a small silver shoe which, put on the foot of a newborn son of his family, would give courage and fortitude to the child. One boy, however, had at his birth a foot too large for the shoe, a defect inherited from his mother, who was not a Cameron. His lack of the magically bestowed courage was apparent at the battle of Sheriffmuir, where he fled before the enemy.

Takata, Hawayo (1900–1980)

Hawayo Takata, the teacher who brought **Reiki** healing to the West, was born on December 23, 1900, to a Japanese family in Hawaii. At the age of 16, she married Saichi Takata. She gave birth to two daughters and she settled into the quiet life as a housewife in the growing Hawaiian Japanese-American community. Following her husband's death in 1930, she sought employment at a nearby plantation. She worked her way up to became the owner's housekeeper and then bookkeeper within a few years.

However, during the early 1930s Takata's health deteriorated. When in 1935 her sister died and it became her duty to travel to Japan to take the news of the death to her parents personally, she used the occasion to seek out some Japanese doctors. She located a surgeon, but just before she was to submit to an operation, she decided against it. Instead, she asked for a referral to an alternative doctor who did not do surgery. As it happened, the sister of the surgeon was a Reiki healer. The doctor referred Takata to Chujiro Hayashi (1878–1941), a former naval officer who had opened a clinic based on Reiki. After four months she was healed.

Takata asked Hayashi to train her as a healer. At first he refused, as she was considered an American. However, her persistence was rewarded, and in the spring of 1936, he included her and several others in a class for basic Reiki training. The following spring she was able to take Reiki Master training, from which she emerged as the 13th and last Reiki Master he initiated.

Shortly after becoming a Master, Takata returned home and opened a small clinic similar to Hayashi's in Kapaa, Hawaii. Hayashi visited at the beginning of 1938, and while in Hawaii named Takata as his successor. A few months later, she took the opportunity to come to the mainland as the translator for a group of Buddhist ministers making a tour of the West Coast. She stayed behind to attend the National College of Drugless Physicians, a naturopathic school in Chicago, Illinois.

Hayashi died in 1941. Meanwhile, in Hawaii, Takata operated quietly through the World War II (1939–45) and postwar years, during which time the Hawaiian Japanese received much of the anger for the bombing of Pearl Harbor.

Takata continued as a Reiki healer in Hawaii for several decades. It was only with her aging without a successor that Takata decided to start teaching others as Reiki healers. More importantly, she opened those teachings to those outside of the Japanese American community. In the fall of 1973 she traveled to Puget Sound to offer a first class on Reiki for mainland students. This class launched her brief public career and introduced the public to the Reiki system. Two years later she took the additional step and for the first time trained a new Reiki Master.

The decision to train Masters became one of her more controversial actions. She concluded that the Master status was a thing of value and that the best way to communicate its worth to Westerners was to charge for it. She asked a fee of $10,000.00 U.S. During the remaining five years of her life, she initiated 22 Masters.

In 1979, the year before she died, she named two of the Masters as Grand Masters, her daughter Phyliss Furumoto and Barbara Ray a healer from Atlanta, Georgia. Takata died on December 11, 1980.

Sources:

Haberly, Helen L. *Reiki: Hawayo Takata's Story.* Olney, Md.: Archedigm Publications, 1997.

Stein, Diane. *Essential Reiki: A Complete Guide to an Ancient Healing Art.* Freedom, Calif.: Crossing Press, 1995.

"Tales of Terror"

Title of an anonymous collection of Gothic style ballads, usually ascribed wrongly to **Matthew Gregory Lewis.** There are actually two books with this title. The first, published in 1799, included three of Lewis's ballads, together with others by Sir Walter Scott and Robert Southey, but does not appear to be compiled by Lewis. The three ballads later appeared in his book *Tales of Wonder* (1801).

A second *Tales of Terror* (1801) is a coarse and grotesque collection that contains parodies of the work of Lewis and others, and does not therefore seem to be compiled by Lewis either. (See also English occult **fiction.**)

Talisman

An inanimate object which is supposed to possess a supernatural capacity of conferring benefits or powers, in contradistinction to the **amulet,** the purpose of which is to ward off evil. Talismans were common in ancient Egypt and Babylon, and have been popular in magical communities to the present. Originally, talismans were usually a disc of metal or stone engraved with astrological or magical figures. In recent centuries, among practitioners of ceremonial **magic,** talismans inscribed in parchment have been favored.

Traditionally, three varieties of talisman have been recognized: 1. The astronomical, having the characters of the heavenly signs or constellations; 2. the magical, with extraordinary figures, occult words, or the names of angels; and 3. the mixed, engraved with celestial signs and barbarous words. To this list Thomas D. Fosbrook, in his *Encyclopedia of Antiquities* (1825), added two others: 4. The *sigilla planetarum,* composed of Hebrew numeral letters, used by astrologers and fortune-tellers and 5. one with Hebrew names and characters.

As an example of the most powerful of the latter may be the sacred name of Jehovah. The famous **tephillin** or phylacteries, used in Jewish devotion, which were bound on the head, the arm, and the hand, may be regarded as talismans. They were the subject of many traditional ceremonies. There is also the **mezazoth** or schedules for doorposts; another article of this description mentioned in the following quotation from the *Talmud:* "Whoever had the tephillin bound to his head and arm, and the tsitsith thrown over his garments, and the mezuza fixed on his door-post, is protected from sin."

On astrological talismans the figure of Mercury, engraved upon silver, which is the corresponding metal, and according to the prescribed rites, gave success in merchandise; that of Mars gave victory to the soldier; that of Venus, beauty, and so of the rest. All such talismans were seen as more powerful during the hour of their planet's ascendency.

Writing of talismans in his book *The Occult Sciences* (1891), A. E. Waite stated:

"1. The Talisman of the Sun must be composed of a pure and fine gold, fashioned into a circular plate, and well polished on either side. A serpentine circle, enclosed by a pentagram must be engraved on the obverse side with a diamond-pointed graving tool. The reverse must bear a human head in the centre of the six-pointed star of Solomon, which shall itself be surrounded with the name of the solar intelligence Pi-Rhé, written in the characters of the Magi. This talisman is supposed to insure to its bearer the goodwill of influential persons. It is a preservative against death by heart disease, syncope, aneurism, and epidemic complaints. It must be composed on a Sunday during the passage of the moon through the first ten degrees of Leo, and when that luminary is in a favourable aspect with Saturn and the Sun. The consecration consists in the exposure of the talisman to the smoke of a perfume composed of cinnamon, incense, saffron, and red sandal, burnt with laurel-wood, and twigs of desiccated heliotrope, in a new chafing-dish, which must be ground into powder and buried in an isolated spot, after the operation is finished. The talisman must be afterwards encased in a satchel of bright yellow silk, which must be fastened on the breast by an interlaced ribbon of the same material, tied in the form of a cross. In all cases the ceremony should be preceded by the conjuration of the Four, to which the reader has already been referred. The form of consecration, accompanied by sprinkling with holy water, may be rendered in the following manner:—

"In the name of Elohim, and by the spirit of the living waters, be thou unto me as a sign of light and a seal of will.

"Presenting it to the smoke of the perfumes:—By the brazen serpent before which fell the serpents of fire, be thou unto me as a sign of light and a seal of will.

"Breathing seven times upon the talisman:—By the firmament and the spirit of the voice, be thou unto me as a sign of light and a seal of will.

"Lastly, when placing some grains of purified earth or salt upon the pentacle:—In the name of the salt of the earth and by virtue of the life eternal, be thou unto me as a sign of light and a seal of will.

"2. The Talisman of the Moon should be composed of a circular and well-polished plate of the purest silver, being of the dimensions of an ordinary medal. The image of a crescent, enclosed in a pentagram, should be graven on the obverse side. On the reverse side, a chalice must be encircled by the duadic seal of Solomon, encompassed by the letters of the lunar genius Pi-Job. This talisman is considered a protection to travellers, and to sojourners in strange lands. It preserves from death by drowning, by epilepsy, by dropsy, by apoplexy, and madness. The danger of a violent end which is predicted by Saturnian aspects in horoscopes of nativity, may be removed by its means. It should be composed on a Monday, when the moon is passing through the first ten degrees of Capricornus or Virgo, and is also well aspected with Saturn. Its consecration consists in exposure to a perfume composed of white sandal, camphor, aloes, amber, and pulverized seed of cucumber, burnt with desiccated stalks of mugwort, moonwort, and ranunculus, in a new earthen chafing-dish, which must be reduced, after the operation, into powder, and buried in a deserted spot. The talisman must be sewn up in a satchel of white silk, and fixed on the breast by a ribbon of the same colour, interlaced and tied in the form of a cross.

"3. The Talisman of Mars must be composed of a well-polished circular plate of the finest iron, and of the dimensions of an ordinary medal. The symbol of a sword in the centre of a pentagram must be engraved on the obverse side. A lion's head surrounded by a six-pointed star must appear on the reverse face, with the letters of the name Erotosi, the planetary genius of Mars, above the outer angles. This talisman passes as a preservative against all combinations of enemies. It averts the chance of death in brawls and battles, in epidemics and fevers, and by corroding ulcers. It also neutralizes the peril of a violent end as a punishment for crime when it is foretold in the horoscope of the nativity.

"This talisman must be composed on a Tuesday, during the passage of the moon through the ten first degrees of Aries or Sagittarius, and when, moreover, it is favourably aspected with Saturn and Mars. The consecration consists in its exposure to the smoke of a perfume composed of dried absinth and rue, burnt in an earthen vessel which has never been previously used, and which must be broken into powder, and buried in a secluded place, when the operation is completed. Finally, the talisman must be sewn up in a satchel of red silk, and fastened on the breast with ribbons of the same material folded and knotted in the form of a cross.

"4. The Talisman of Mercury must be formed of a circular plate of fixed quicksilver, or according to another account of an amalgam of silver, mercury, and pewter, of the dimensions of an ordinary medal, well-polished on both sides. A winged caduceus, having two serpents twining about it, must be engraved in the centre of a pentagram on the obverse side. The other must bear a dog's head within the star of Solomon, the latter being surrounded with the name of the planetary genius, Pi-Hermes, written in the alphabet of the Magi. This talisman must be composed on a Wednesday, when the moon is passing through the ten first degrees of Gemini or Scorpio, and is well aspected with Saturn and Mercury. The consecration consists in its exposure to the smoke of a perfume composed of benzoin, macis, and storax, burnt with the dried stalks of the lily, the narcissus, fumitory, and marjolane, placed in a clay chafing-dish which has never been devoted to any other purpose, and which must, after the completion of the task, be reduced to powder and buried in an undisturbed place. The Talisman of Mercury is judged to be a defence in all species of commerce and business industry. Buried under the ground in a house of commerce, it will draw customers and prosperity. It preserves all who wear it from epilepsy and madness. It averts death by murder and poison; it is a safeguard against the schemes of treason; and it procures prophetic dreams when it is worn on the head during sleep. It is fastened on the breast by a ribbon of purple silk folded and tied in the form of a cross, and the talisman is itself enclosed in a satchel of the same material.

"5. The Talisman of Jupiter must be formed of a circular plate of the purest English pewter, having the dimensions of an ordinary medal, and being highly polished on either side. The image of a four-pointed crown in the centre of a pentagram must be engraved on the obverse side. On the other must be the head of an eagle in the centre of the six-pointed star of Solomon, which must be surrounded by the name of the planetary genius Pi-Zéous, written in the arcane alphabet.

"This talisman must be composed on a Thursday, during the passage of the moon through the first ten degrees of Libra, and when it is also in a favourable aspect with Saturn and Jupiter. The consecration consists in its exposure to the smoke of a perfume composed of incense, ambergris, balm, grain of Paradise, saffron, and macis, which is the second coat of the nutmeg. These must be burnt with wood of the oak, poplar, fig tree, and pomegranate, and placed in a new earthen dish, which must be ground into powder, and buried in a quiet spot, at the end of the ceremony. The talisman must be wrapped in a satchel of sky-blue silk, suspended on the breast by a ribbon of the same material, folded and fastened in the form of a cross.

"The Talisman of Jupiter is held to attract to the wearer the benevolence and sympathy of everyone. It averts anxieties, favours honourable enterprises, and augments well-being in proportion to social condition. It is a protection against unforeseen accidents, and the perils of a violent death when it is threatened by Saturn in the horoscope of nativity. It also preserves from death by affections of the liver, by inflammation of the lungs, and by that cruel affection of the spinal marrow, which is termed *tabes dorsalis* in medicine.

"6. The Talisman of Venus must be formed of a circular plate of purified and well-polished copper. It must be of the ordinary dimensions of a medal, perfectly polished on both its sides. It must bear on the obverse face the letter G inscribed in the alphabet of the Magi, and enclosed in a pentagram. A dove must be engraved on the reverse, in the centre of the six-pointed star, which must be surrounded by the letters which compose the name of the planetary Genius Suroth. This talisman must be composed on a Friday, during the passage of the moon through the first ten degrees of Taurus or Virgo, and when that luminary is well aspected with Saturn and Venus. Its consecration consists in its exposure to the smoke of a perfume composed of violets and roses, burnt with olive wood in a new earthen chafing-dish, which must be ground into powder at the end of the operation and buried in a solitary spot. The talisman must, finally, be sewn up in a satchel of green or rose-coloured silk, which must be fastened on the breast by a band of the same material, folded and tied in the form of a cross.

"The Talisman of Venus is accredited with extraordinary power in cementing the bonds of love and harmony between husbands and wives. It averts from those who wear it the spite and machinations of hatred. It preserves women from the terrible and fatal diseases which are known as cancer. It averts from both men and women all danger of death, to which they may be accidentally or purposely exposed. It counterbalances the unfortunate presages which may appear in the horoscope of the nativity. Its last and most singular quality is its power to change the animosity of an enemy into a love and devotion which will be proof against every temptation, and it rests on the sole condition that such a person should be persuaded to partake of a liquid in which the talisman has been dipped.

"7. The Talisman of Saturn must be composed of a circular plate of refined and purified lead, being of the dimensions of an ordinary medal, elaborately polished. On the obverse side must be engraved with the diamond-pointed tool which is requisite in all these talismanic operations, the image of a sickle enclosed in a pentagram. The reverse side must bear a bull's head, enclosed in the star of Solomon, and surrounded by the mysterious letters which compose, in the alphabet of the Magi, the name of the planetary Genius Tempha. The person who is intended to wear this talisman must engrave it himself, without witnesses, and without taking any one into his confidence.

"This talisman must be composed on a Saturday when the moon is passing through the first ten degrees of Taurus or Capricorn, and is favourably aspected with Saturn. It must be consecrated by exposure to the smoke of a perfume composed of alum, assa-foetida, cammonée, and sulphur, which must be burnt with cypress, the wood of the ash tree, and sprays of black hellebore, in a new earthen chafing-dish, which must be reduced into powder at the end of the performance, and buried in a deserted place. The talisman must, finally, be sewn up in a satchel of black silk and fastened on the breast with a ribbon of the same material, folded and tied in the form of a cross. The Talisman of Saturn was affirmed to be a safeguard against death by apoplexy and cancer, decay in the bones, consumption, dropsy, paralysis, and decline; it was also a preservative against the possibility of being entombed in a trance, against the danger of violent death by secret crime, poison, or ambush. If the head of the army in war-time were to bury the Talisman of Saturn in a place which it was feared might fall into the hands of the enemy, the limit assigned by the presence of the talisman could not be overstepped by the opposing host, which would speedily withdraw in discouragement, or in the face of a determined assault."

Sources:

Beard, Charles R. *Lucks and Talismans: A Chapter of Popular Superstition.* London: Sampson, Low, 1934. Reprint, New York: Blom, 1972.

Budge, E. A. W. *Amulets and Superstitions.* Oxford: Oxford University Press, 1930. Reprinted as *Amulets and Talismans.* New Hyde Park, N.Y.: University Books, 1961.

Fosbrook, Thomas D. *Encyclopedia of Antiquities.* 2 vols. N.p., 1825, 1840.

Lamb, Geoffrey. *Discovering Magic Charms and Talismans.* UK: Shire Publications, 1974.

Lippman, Deborah, and Paul Colin. *Amulets, Charms and Talismans: What They Mean and How to Use Them.* New York: M. Evans, 1974.

Lockhart, J. G. *Curses, Lucks and Talismans.* London: Geoffrey Bles, 1938. Reprint, Detroit: Singing Tree Press, 1971.

Pavitt, W. T., and Kate Pavitt. *The Book of Talismans, Amulets, and Zodiacal Gems.* London: Rider, 1914. Reprint, Detroit: Tower Books, 1971. Reprint, North Hollywood, Calif.: Wilshire Publishing, 1972.

Regardie, Israel. *How to Make and Use Talismans.* London: Aquarian Press; New York: Samuel Weiser, 1972.

Sepharial [W. G. Old]. *The Book of Charms and Talismans.* London: W. Foulsham, 1923. Reprint, New York: Arco, 1971.

Waite, A. E. *The Occult Science.* London: Kegan Paul, Trench, Trubner & Co., 1891.

Talking Mongoose

A celebrated paranormal phenomenon from **Cashen's Gap** on the Isle of Man, United Kingdom. It was investigated by psychical researchers **Harry Price** and **R. S. Lambert** in the 1930s. Named "Gef," the mongoose manifested to the Irving family, and there is some doubt whether it was a real creature or a **poltergeist** phenomenon.

Sources:

Price, Harry, and R. S. Lambert. *The Haunting of Cashen's Gap.* London, 1936.

Tallmadge, Nathaniel Pitcher (1795–1864)

United States senator from 1833–34, governor of Wisconsin from 1844–46, and one of the early converts to **Spiritualism.** His experiences with the **Fox sisters,** recounted in a letter to a friend under the date April 12, 1853, were published in most of the newspapers of the time. He stated that he had received messages in **direct writing** from the spirit of John Calhoun and also witnessed very strong physical manifestations, notably the **levitation** of a table with himself on top of it. He also reported experiences in his own household. His thirteen-year-old daughter, who never touched the piano, began to play classical works and popular airs in **trance.**

In April 1854, a memorial was presented in Congress by James Shields, asking for an inquiry into the truth of Spiritualism. Tallmadge's name topped the list of the 13,000 signatures that were attached. Tallmadge contributed an introduction to *The Healing of the Nations* by **automatic writing medium Charles Linton,** published in 1855 by The Society for the Diffusion of Spiritual Knowledge. He died November 2, 1864.

Sources:

Brown, Slater. *The Heyday of Spiritualism.* New York: Hawthorn Books, 1970.

Jackson, Herbert G., Jr. *The Spirit Rappers.* Garden City, N.Y.: Doubleday, 1972.

Pond, Mariam Buckner. *Time Is Kind; The Story of the Unfortunate Fox Family.* New York: Centennial Press, 1947. Reprinted as *The Unwilling Martyrs.* London: Psychic Book Club, 1947.

The Talmud

From the Hebrew *lamad,* to learn, the *Talmud* is the name of the great code of Jewish civil and canonical law. It is divided into two portions—the *Mishna* and the *Gemara;* the former constitutes the text and the latter is a commentary and supplement. But besides being the basis of a legal code, it is also a collection of Jewish poetry and legend.

The *Mishna* is a development of the laws contained in the Pentateuch. It is divided into six *sedarim* or orders, each containing a number of tractates, which are again divided into *peraqim* or chapters. The *sedarim* are:

(1) *Zeraim,* which deals with agriculture;
(2) *Moed,* with festivals and sacrifices;
(3) *Nashim,* with the law regarding women;
(4) *Nezaqin,* with civil law;
(5) *Qodashim,* with the sacrificial law; and
(6) *Tohoroth* or *Tah,* with purifications.

The *Mishna* is said to have been handed down by Ezra and to be in part the work of Joshua, David, or Solomon, and originally communicated orally by the Deity in the time of Moses.

There are two recensions—the *Talmud* of Jerusalem and the *Talmud* of Babylon. The latter, besides the *sedarim* already mentioned, contains seven additional treatises that are regarded as extra-canonical. The first is supposed to have been finally edited toward the close of the fourth century, and the second by Rabbi Ashi, president of the Academy of Syro in Babylon, sometime in the fourth century. Although revised from time to time before then, both versions have been greatly affected through the interpolation of traditions, and reinterpretations in the light of rabbinical discussions. The rabbinical decisions in the *Mishna* are entitled *helacoth* and the traditional narratives *haggadah.*

The cosmogony of the *Talmud* assumes that the universe has been developed by means of a series of cataclysms—world after world was destroyed until the Creator made the present earth. E. Deutsch, commenting on the Talmuc in the *Quarterly Review,* (1867) noted:

"The *how* of the creation was not mere matter of speculation. The co-operation of angels, whose existence was warranted by Scripture, and a whole hierarchy of whom had been built up under Persian influences, was distinctly denied. In a discussion about the day of their creation, it is agreed on all hands that there were no angels at first, lest men might say, 'Michael spanned out the firmament on the south, and Gabriel to the north.' There is a distinct foreshadowing of the Gnostic Demiurgos—that antique link between the Divine Spirit and the world of matter—to be found in the *Talmud.* What with Plato were the Ideas, with Philo the Logos, with the Kabalists the 'World of Aziluth,' what the Gnostics called more emphatically the wisdom (sophi), or power (dunamis), and Plotinus the nous, that the Talmudical authors call Metation.

"There is a good deal, in the post-captivity *Talmud,* about the Angels, borrowed from the Persian. The Archangels or Angelic princes are seven in number, and their Hebrew names and functions correspond almost exactly to those of their Persian prototypes. There are also hosts of ministering angels, the Persian *Yazatas,* whose functions, besides that of being messengers, were two-fold—to praise God and to be guardians of man. In their first capacity they are daily created by God's breath out of a stream of fire that rolls its waves under the supernal throne. In their second, two of them accompany every man, and for every new good deed man acquires a new guardian angel, who always watches over his steps. When a righteous man dies, three hosts of angels descend from the celestial battlements to meet him. One says (in the words of Scripture), 'He shall go in peace;' the second takes up the strain and says, 'Who has walked in righteousness;' and the third concludes, 'Let him come in peace and rest upon his bed.' In like manner, when the wicked man passes away, three hosts of wicked angels are ready to escort him, but their address is not couched in any spirit of consolation or encouragement."

The *Talmud* is the supreme repository of Jewish moral and spiritual law; it also enshrines a wealth of historical, geographical, philosophical, and poetical traditions. It is one of the great documents of human history and the central focus of Jewish law.

It has been considered by some authorities that a great many of the traditional tales in the *Talmud* have a magical basis, and that magical secrets are contained in them, but this depends entirely upon the interpretation put upon them, and the subject is one which necessitates close study. An English translation of the Jerusalem *Talmud* was published in 1871, and of the Babylonian *Talmud* (35 vols.), 1935–52.

Tamlin, Sarah (ca. 1848)

One of the very early American rapping **mediums,** soon after the famous **Rochester rappings** of the **Fox sisters.** E. W. Capron visited Tamlin and attended one of her **séances** at which **raps** were heard. A table moved in various directions and "was held down to the floor so that it required the whole strength of a man to move it from its position." At that time, the phenomenon of raps spread like a contagion. Harriet Bebee, a girl of sixteen, visited Tamlin and on returning to her own home twenty miles away, the raps broke out again in her presence. And, according to Capron's account, about fifty mediums were soon operating in private circles.

Sources:

Capron, E. W. *Modern Spiritualism: Its Facts and Fanaticisms.* N.p., 1855.

Tanagras, Angelos (1875–ca. 1970)

An admiral in the Greek Navy who took an active interest in **parapsychology.** He was born on May 20, 1875, in Athens, Greece. Through his life he authored a number of books on Greek history and legends.

As a young man he became a corresponding member of the **Society for Psychical Research,** London, as well as various European psychical research societies. He founded and served as the first president (1923 on) of the Hellenic Society for Psychical Research; he edited and contributed to the society's journal, *Psychic Research.* Tanagras organized the Fourth International Congress of Psychic Research in Athens during 1930, when he worked closely with **Hans Driesch** and **Sir Oliver Lodge.**

Tanagras took part in experiments in long distance **telepathy,** collaborating with **Rene Warcollier** in France and **Gardner Murphy** in the United States, as well as experimenters in Italian and British psychic research societies. He studied **psychometry** in Greece, and contributed various articles on parapsychological subjects to different psychical research journals and one book.

Sources:

Tanagras, Angelos. *Destiny and Chance.* N.p., 1934.

Tannhäuser

A medieval German legend about how a minstrel and knight of that name, who passed by the Hörselberg (Hill of Venus) and entered therein in answer to a call. He remained there with an enchantress and lived an unholy life. After a time he grew weary of sin, and longing to return to normal living, forswore the worship of Venus and left her.

He then made a pilgrimage to Rome to ask pardon of the Pope, but when he was told by Urban IV himself that the papal staff would as soon blossom as such a sinner as Tannhäuser be forgiven, he returned to Venus. Three days later, the Pope's staff did actually blossom, and the Pope sent messengers into every country to find the despairing minstrel, but to no purpose. Tannhäuser had disappeared.

The story has a mythological basis that has been overlaid by medieval Christian thought, and the original hero of which has been displaced by a more modern personage, just as the Venus of the existing legend is the mythological Venus only in name. She is really a German earth-goddess, Lady Holda.

Tannhäuser was a *minnesinger* (love-minstrel of the middle of the thirteenth century). He was very popular among the *minnesingers* of that time. The restless and intemperate life he led probably marked him out as the hero of such a legend as has been recounted.

He was the author of many ballads of considerable excellence, which were published in the second part of the *Minnesinger* of Friedrich H. von der Hagen (Leipzig, 1838) and in the sixth volume of Moriz Haupt's *Zeitschrift für deutsches Althertum* (1841). The most authentic version of this legend is given in J. L. Uhland's *Alte hoch und niederdeutsche Volkslieder* (Stuttgart, 1844–45).

Tantra

A science or *sadhana* (spiritual practice) based on a vast collection of religious and **occult** Hindu scriptures that emphasize the *shakti* (energy of the deity), usually called **kundalini,** which comes from the goddess. The scriptures are generally in the form of a dialogue between the god Shiva and his wife Parvati. In treatises where Shiva answers the questions, they are called *agama;* where Parvati answers it is a *nigama.*

The tantra scriptures represent a cumulation of knowledge dating to ancient times. The majority of texts are written in Sanskrit, but are also found in Pali, Prakit, Tibetan, Hindi, and Bengali. They are considered encyclopedias of esoteric wisdom, covering topics such as creation and destruction of the universe, worship of the gods, spiritual disciplines, rituals, occult powers, and meditations. The tantras also discuss the subtle anatomy of the body including the **chakras** (spiritual centers) and the connection paths between them through which the kundalini energy travels. The tantras are also supposed to be specially relevant to *Kali Yuga* (the present age of devolution).

As vast and varied as the scriptures appear, however, they all have one characteristic in common: "an integrative approach to sadhana, with the objective of making the best use of all available resources within and without." Tantra can be considered the **holistic** approach to spiritual practice.

In opposition to traditional Judeo-Christian and aesthetic Eastern practices, Tantra does not seek to sublimate the flesh to the spirit, the physical to the metaphysical. Instead, tantra seeks to reintegrate all aspects of life, to "dissolve boundaries we've created, the separateness, the diconnectedness and become more connected with all of life."

Since the tantra's purpose is to integrate all aspects of life, it is a practice where numerous varieties of sciences can blend: **hatha yoga,** pranayama, medras, rituals, kundalini yoga, nada yoga, **mantra,** yantra, mandala, visualization of deities, alchemy, Aryurveda, and astrology can all comfortably fit within the realm of tantra. But because so many intricate sciences and techniques can be employed, it is usually advised that the tantra is studied under a competent master, who can lead the student through the complex weave of ideas and procedures.

In the West, tantra is often identified with sexuality and sexual practices. Tantric ideas are often used to help individuals and couples transform love making into a more satisfying experience, on the physical, emotional, and spiritual realm. By integrating the male and female aspect of the individual and the couple, tantra is used to raise the sexual union to a reflection of the mystical union between the shiva and shakti aspects of the divine.

A popular knowledge of tantric anatomy came to the West through **Theosophy.** Western scholar **Sir John Woodroffe** (1865–1936) wrote several pioneering books on tantra and translated tantric scriptures under a pseudonym, Arthur Avalon. The various systems of **tantric yoga** based on the tantras have spread in the West through the twentieth century.

Sources:

Avalon, Arthur. *The Serpent Power.* London: Luzac & Co., 1919.

———. *Shakti and Shakta.* 3d ed. Madras, India: Ganesh, 1929.

———. *Tantra of the Great Liberation (Mahanirvana Tantra).* London: Luzac, 1913. Reprint, New York: Dover Publications, 1972.

Chakravarti, Chintaharan. *Tantras: Studies on Their Religion and Literature.* Calcutta, India: Punthi Pustak, 1963.

Feuerstein, Georg. *The Shambala Guide to Yoga.* Boston & London: Shambala, 1996.

Greenwell, Bonnie, Ph.D. *Energies of Transformation.* Valencia, Calif.: Shakti River Press, 1990.

Mookerjee, Ajit. *Tantra Art.* New York: Random House, 1971.

Mookerjee, Ajit, and M. Khanna. *The Tantric Way: Art, Science, Ritual.* New York: Graphic, 1977.

Rawson, Philip. *Tantra: The Indian Cult of Ecstasy.* London: Thames & Hudson, 1974.

Tigunait, Pandit Rajmani "The Living Science of Tantra," *Yoga International* (May 1998): 22-29.

Williams, Stephen. "Tantra: An Introductory Dialogue with Raymont Powers C.T.T." Gentleman's Quarterly, August 1997, http://home.earthlink.net/-raypows/INTERVIEW.HTM.

Tantric Yoga

A system of Hindu yoga which emphasizes the *shakti* (sexual energy) associated with the female principle and usually characterized as **kundalini.**

There are essentially two concentrations of tantric yoga, which can be called the pragmatic and the aesthetic.

The pragmatic level focuses primarily on the sexual act and promotes a sacred style of sexuality which promotes communication, breath, and energy. In concert with the Tantra philosophy, this concentration seeks to enhance the sexual experience through integration of the male and female (shiva/shakti) aspects of each individual, and of the couple together. Hatha yoga (postures), raja yoga (meditation), pranayama (breathing techniques), and other techniques such as coitus reservatus (ejaculation control) and amrita (female ejaculation) are employed to enrich the sexual act. Participants are taught to expand their focus from the second (sexual or *svadhisthana*) chakra to all seven chakras throughout the body. This cultivates sensitivity and kundalini throughout the body, vastly enriching the sexual experience.

The second concentration focuses on raising the kundalini energy to encompass several areas of life, including the sexual. It follows the philosophy of tantra (meaning to weave, to expand, to spread) by integrating all aspects of life. In this concentration there is no separation of the physical from the metaphysical, the female to the male, of the animate to the inanimate, of the spiritual to the corporeal. The corporeal is not seen as a barrier to spiritual growth, as in many Judeo-Christian traditions, but instead as another source of divine energy. "Whatever is in the body is also in the universe."

In addition to these concentrations of tantric yoga there exists a specifically left-hand or **occult** pathway of tantric yoga, known as tantrism, that involves a taboo-breaking ceremony with a female assistant. This form of tantrism tends to oppose ascetic forms of yoga that align spiritual development with the denial of the things of the world. Instead of avoiding those things normally eschewed by a *sanyassin* (a person living the renounced life), the tantric uses those things and converts them into a tool of tantric development. The generally avoided items, called the five "M's" consist of: *Madya* (wine), *Mansa* (flesh), *Matsya* (fish), *Mudra* (a term implying both parched grain and mystic gesture), and *Maithuna* (sexual intercourse). From Hinduism, tantric beliefs and practices passed into Buddhism and became a notable part of Tibetan Buddhism.

Knowledge of tantric yoga began to appear in the West in the early twentieth century within the writings of **Sir John Woodroffe** (who wrote under the pseudonym Arthur Avalon). However, it was not until the 1970s, with the volume of Omar Garrison, that details of the rituals of the left-hand path were written down and published in the West. Subsequently, a number of texts have appeared. A measurable number of modern tantric teachers first became familiar with tantric yoga through Bhagwan Rajneesh (later known as Osho).

Through the twentieth century, a form of sexual occultism usually associated with magician **Aleister Crowley** arose out of Western ceremonial **magic.** Because of the common use of sexual intercourse as a means of spiritual attainment in both tantra and Western **sex magic,** many have assumed that the two are related. As knowledge of the rituals and teaching of each system was made public through the 1980s, however, scholars are now aware that the two practices are quite different in operation and purpose and have very different historical roots.

Although there is acknowledgment between the differences between Western sex magic and tantric yoga, there must exist an understanding that the philosophy of Tantra is missing in most Western tantric yoga. Most often tantric yoga is used as a sort of sexual or marital therapy, which is ultimately missing the goal of enlightenment. News of sexual enhancement advantages has even lured such celebrities as Sting to explore the benefits of tantric yoga.

Besides Western exploitation of tantra there is also controversy surrounding teachers who allegedly take sexual advantage of students. Swami Rama of the Himalayas, for example, faced several allegations of sexual misconduct with his students, prior to his death in 1997. There have been numerous other accounts of sexual improprieties between tantric yoga teachers and their students. These stories act as a reminder of the delicate and often vulnerable relationship that can exist between the spiritual master and the student.

Sources:

Feuerstein, Georg. *The Shambala Guide to Yoga.* Boston & London: Shambala, 1996

Garrison, Omar. *Tantra—The Yoga of Sex.* Causeway, 1973. Reprint, London: Academy Editions, 1974.

Grenager, Suzanne Selby, "One Woman's Case for Gurus," *Yoga Journal* (August 1996): 20-23.

Greenwall, Bonnie, Energies of Transformation, Valencia, Calif.: Shakti River press, 1990

Marques-Riviere, J. *Tantrik Yoga.* London: Rider & Co., 1940.

Mookerjee, Ajit, and M. Khanna. *The Tantric Way: Art, Science, Ritual.* New York: Graphic, 1977.

Mumford, John. [Swami Anandakapila]. *Sexual Occultism.* St. Paul, Minn.: Llewellyn Publications, 1975.

O'Neill, Timothy, "A Fire in the Shadows," *Gnosis,* (Fall 1990): 26-31.

Rajneesh, Bhagwan Shree. *Tantra, Spirituality & Sex.* San Francisco, Calif.: Rainbow Bridge, 1977.

Selby, John. *Kundalini Awakening.* New York: Bantam Books, 1992

Tantra: The Science of Ecstacy. http://www.tantra.com. March 10, 2000.

Vatasyayana. "The Love Teachings of Kama Sutra," The Church of Tantra. http://www.tantra.org/. March 10, 2000.

Williams, Stephen. Tantra: An Introductory Dialogue with Raymond Powers, C.T.T. http://www.home.earthlink.net/-raypows/INTERVIEW.HTM. March 10, 2000.

Yoga Journal Online. http://yogajournal.com/. April 14, 2000.

Tao

Term used in ancient Chinese religious philosophy, signifying "the Way" or pathway of life. The *Tao* is understood as a unity underlying the opposites and diversity of the phenomenal world. *Ching Shen Li* (cosmic energy) is manifest in the duality of *yin* and *yang* (negative and positive), female and male principles in nature. *Yin* and *yang* are also energies in the individual human body and the balancing of these energies is one of the tasks of life. The correct harmony between *yin* and *yang* may be achieved through diet, **meditation,** and a life of truth, simplicity, and tranquillity, identifying with the *Tao* of nature.

Taoism teaches union with the law of the universe through wisdom and detached action. Special techniques of Taoist **yoga** normalize and enhance the flow of vital energy in the human body. This yoga is variously named *K'ai Men* (open door), *Ho Ping* (unity), and *Ho Hsieh* (harmony). *K'ai Men* implies opening the path to the channels of mind, spirit, and body so that they reflect the balance of *yin* and *yang* and a harmony with the energy of the cosmos.

Taoist yoga is very similar to the **kundalini** yoga systems of India, and it is not clear whether such a parallel system originated by direct influence of traveling mystics or by spontaneous rediscovery of basic truths. Both Indian and Chinese yogas are concerned with the control of vital energy, seen as the force behind sexual activity, but which may be diverted into different channels in the body for blissful expansion of consciousness. For centuries the techniques of Chinese yoga were little known in the West; teaching manuals were closely guarded and not translated into Western languages. Teachings were usually transmitted orally from teacher to pupil.

During the twentieth century, and especially since the Chinese Revolution, teachers of Taoism and Chinese yoga have established schools in the United States and published translations of basic Chinese yoga texts. Modern teachers of Chinese yoga include Charles Luk (Lu K'uan Yü) of Hong Kong, who has translated various Chinese Buddhist and yoga texts, and Mantak Chia from Thailand, who studied with Taoist and Buddhist masters and has created a synthesis of their spiritual techniques, in conjunction with classical techniques of **T'ai Chi Ch'uan.** Together with his wife Maneewan Chia, Mantak Chia has been instrumental in establishing Healing Tao Centers in the United States and Europe that offer a basic self-development course of what is termed Taoist Esoteric Yoga.

In distinction to the philosophical esoteric concept of the *Tao,* but growing out of it, **Taoism** as a religious system complete with temples and popular worship, became one of the three major religious systems of China, together with Confucianism and Buddhism.

Sources:

Chang, Chung-Yuan. *Tao; A New Way of Thinking*. New York: Harper & Row, 1975.

Chia, Mantak. *Awaken Healing Energy through the Tao.* New York: Aurora Press, 1983.

Chia, Mantak, and Michael Winn. *Taoist Secrets of Love: Cultivating Male Sexual Energy.* New York: Aurora Press, 1984.

Ch'u Ta-Kao, trans. *Tao Te Ching.* London: Allen & Unwin; New York: Samuel Weiser, 1937.

Lu K'uan Yü. *Taoist Yoga: Alchemy and Immortality.* London: Rider & Co., 1970.

Soo, Chee. *The Chinese Art of K'ai Men.* London: Gordon & Cremonesi, 1977.

Suzuki, D. T., and Paul Carus, trans. *The Canon of Reason and Virtue.* La Salle, Ill.: Open Court, 1913.

Taoism

One of the three major religious systems of ancient **China,** together with Confucianism and Buddhism. Early Taoism derives from the **Tao** ("the road" or "the way") teachings of Lao Tzu. The origins and background of Lao Tzu is uncertain; in fact, most details of his life are legendary. Some sources claim Lao Tzu was said born of poor parents in Tau (Honan) under the Emperor Ting of the Kau dynasty (ca. 605 B.C.E.). Others believe he was a philosopher who became disgusted with the world and became a pessimist, later resigning his position in the Record Department and retiring to a monastery. He also allegedly met and was taught by Gautama Buddha, and held discussions with Confucius. The name, Lao Tzu (meaning "Old Master"), may not be an actual persons name but a pseudonym for the philosophers and teachers who developed Taoism as it is known today.

Lao Tzu's book *Tao-te-Ching* was regarded as a sacred work in North and Central China, but was burned with other writings in 220 B.C.E. It reappeared under the Han dynasty and was reinforced by the teachings of *Chuang Tzu,* another Taoist classic. It is believed to have been the work of a philosopher of the same name. Lao Tzu was the first to formalize Taoism while Chuang-Tzu developed a more philosophical system, metaphysics, and epistemology. Chuang Tzu's teachings of the Tao is considered to be transcendental, while Lao-Tzu's is considered to be a natural form.

Taoism was originally an esoteric philosophy, concerned with the unity underlying the opposites and diversity of the phenomenal world. Taoism taught union with the law of the universe through wisdom and detached action. The union of cosmic and individual energies is reminiscent of the **Vedanta** teachings of **India.**

As central to the Taoist tradition as the concepts of **yin and yang** are the ideas of Tao and Te ("the power"). Like yin, Tao is often identified with the passive (or *wu wei*); because the way is often given preeminence over the power. It is said a real seeker of wisdom knows the power (Te) but seeks the way (Tao). One should not strive for wealth or prestige and that aggression is to be avoided.

As part of the Taoists' practice, followers have incorporated lifestyle rituals, such as vegetarianism, herbal and tactile medicinal approaches, good moral conduct, and the use of appropriate incantations, amulets, and charms. T'ai Chi Ch'uan, with its fusion of energetic and relaxed exercise, has provided a means of increasing and enhancing **ch'i** (or Qi), the vital force of life. The overall goal of Taoists' life is to attain harmony with the Tao. This means one must desire nothing, live simply, and act by not acting. It is a practice where solitude and individualism is cherished and where the "upper classes" of social standing are rejected.

Taoism has also developed its own yoga techniques, which parallel the ancient Hindu system of **kundalini** yoga. These involved control of ch'i, the force believed to stand behind sexual activity, but which could also be diverted into different channels in the body for blissful expansion of consciousness. The circulation of this generative force in the body, aided by breathing techniques, corresponds with Indian yoga techniques involving *pranayama* breathing, and the ascent of kundalini energy through the **chakras** or vital centers of the body. This individual **alchemy** was variously known as *k'ai men* (open door), *ho ping* (unity), or *ho hsieh* (harmony).

The extraordinary parallels between ancient Indian and Chinese Taoism in its various forms and Hinduism (Vedanta and yoga) do not appear to have been documented by historians. The yoga teachings of China descended from teacher to pupil; it is only in recent times that basic texts have been translated into English. There are now teachers of Chinese yoga in Western countries and centers for instruction. There are also many translations with commentaries of the earlier Tao teachings in the *Tao-te-Ching.*

Sources:

Bishop, Peter and Darton, Michael. *The Encyclopedia of World Faiths: An Illustrated Survey of the World's Living Religions.* London: MacDonald and Co., Inc., 1987.

Bynner, Witter, trans. *The Way of Life According to Lao Tzu.* New York: G. P. Putnam's Sons, 1944.

Chang, Chung-Yuan. *Tao: A New Way of Thinking.* New York: Harper & Row, 1975.

Feng, Gia-Fu and English, Jane. *Lao Tsu: Tao Te Ching.* New York: Vintage Books, 1972.

Hendricks, Robert G. *Lao-Tzu: Te-Tao Ching.* New York: The Modern Library, 1993.

Hughes, E. R., ed. and trans. *Chinese Philosophy in Classical Times.* London: J. M. Dent; New York: E. P. Dutton, 1942.

Lu Kuan Yü. *Taoist Yoga: Alchemy and Immortality.* London: Rider & Co., 1970.

Soo, Chee. *The Chinese Art of K'ai Men.* London: Gordon & Cremonesi, 1977.

Taoism Information Page. http://www.clas.ufl.cdu/users/gthursby/taoism/. April 4, 2000.

Watson, Burton, trans. *Chuang Tzu, Basic Writings.* New York: Columbia University Press, 1964.

Weaverville Joss House Temple. http://cal-parks-ca.gov/DISTRICTS/nobuttes/wjhsp/wjhshp127.htm. March 31, 2000.

Targ, Russell (1934–)

Physicist with parapsychological interests. He was born on April 11, 1934, in Chicago, Illinois. He studied at Queens College, New York (B.S., physics, 1954) and completed his graduate study in physics at Columbia University. He worked through the 1960s as a senior physicist (plasma and microwaves) at Technical Research Group, Syosset, Long Island, New York.

In 1972 he entered **Stanford Research Institute** as a senior research physicist, where he collaborated with **Harold E. Puthoff** on parapsychological research. Their work on remote viewing (a form of **clairvoyance**) became well known in 1977 when they published *Mind Reach;* in this publication they argued for the reality of psychical phenomena. Even earlier on, their work had become controversial because of their experiments with **metal-bending** attempted by psychic **Uri Geller.** He and Targ left SRI in 1982 to become partners in Delphi Associates, which attempted to use psychic phenomena for commercial purposes, including predictions of changes in silver prices. He has become president of Bay Research Institute and a staff scientist at Lockheed Research and Development.

Sources:

Berger, Arthur S., and Joyce Berger. *The Encyclopedia of Parapsychology and Psychical Research.* New York: Paragon House, 1991.

Pleasants, Helene, ed. *Biographical Dictionary of Parapsychology.* New York: Helix Press, 1964.

Puthoff, Harold E., and Russell Targ. *Mind-Reach: Scientists Look at Psychic Ability.* New York: Delacorte Press, 1977.

Targ, Russell. *The Mind Race: Understanding and Using Psychic Abilities.* New York: Villard Books, 1984.

Targ, Russel, and Harold E. Puthoff. "ESP Experiments with Uri Geller." In *Research in Parapsychology 1973.* Metuchen, N.J.: Scarecrow Press, 1974.

———. "Information Transmission under Conditions of Sensory Shielding." *Nature* (October 1974).

———. "PK Experiments with Uri Geller and Ingo Swann." In *Research in Parapsychology 1973.* Metuchen, N.J.: Scarecrow Press, 1974.

Targ, Russel, Harold E. Puttoff, and Charles T. Tart. *Mind at Large.* New York: Praeger, 1979.

Target

Term used by parapsychologists to indicate the object (mental or physical) to which a subject attempts to respond paranormally. A mental target would relate to **extrasensory perception,** a physical target to **psychokinesis.**

Tarnas, Richard Theodore (1950–)

Richard Theodore Tarnas, a psychologist and intellectual historian best known for his work with the Esalen Institute, was born on February 21, 1950, in Geneva, Switzerland. His parents were Americans and he grew up in Michigan. His father, a professor of law, encouraged his intellectual pursuits and he completed his high school work at the University of Detroit Preparatory School, operated by the Jesuits. He entered Harvard in 1968 and graduated with an A.B. (cum laude) in 1972. He then entered the doctoral program at Saybrook Institute, the graduate school of psychology in San Francisco, California, and completed his Ph.D. in 1976.

Tarnas was able to travel for several years before settling at Esalen, where he was able to interact with some of the leading minds of the human potentials movement including **Stanislav Grof, James Hillman,** and **Rupert Sheldrake.** In 1979 he became Esalen's director of programs and education. While at Esalen he became known for his work on psychedelic therapy. In 1982 he married Heather Malcolm, a Canadian, and the following year left Esalen to enter private practice and to write. The major product of this period was *The Passion of the Western Mind* (1991), a narrative history of the Western worldview from the ancient Greek to the postmodern.

More recently Tarnas has joined the faculty of the California Institute for Integral Studies in San Francisco, where he became the founding director of the Philosophy, Cosmology, and Consciousness program. The program is indicative of his broad eclectic interests which include the evolution of consciousness, depth psychology, psychedelic research, **astrology,** and **gnosticism.** He has, for example, contributed essays furthering the psychological interpretation of astrology and arguing for the importance of astrology in understanding the evolution of the Western mind.

Sources:

Tarnas, Richard T. *The Passion of the Western Mind.* New York: Harmony Books/Random House, 1991.

———. "The Western Mind at the Threshold." *The Astrotherapy Newsletter* 3, no.4 (November 1990).

Tarot (or Tarots)

French term for a special pack of playing cards popularly used for the purpose of **divination.** These cards enjoyed a boost in popularity as a self-discovery tool of the **New Age** and a development tool among Wiccans and ritual magicians. The derivation of the word *tarot* is still debated. Some suggest that these cards were named because of the *tarotes* on the back, that is, the plain or dotted lines crossing diagonally. Some confirmation of this theory is indicated by the German form of the word, a *tarock-karte* being a card checkered on the back.

Tarot cards form part of an ordinary pack in countries of southern Europe and the name *tarocchi* is given to an Italian game. In its familiar form, the tarot pack consists of a pack of 78 cards, comprising four suits of 14 cards each (the extra court card in each suit being the Cavalier, Knight, or Horseman) and 22 symbolical picture-cards as *atouts* or trumps. The four suits, related to the modern hearts, clubs, diamonds, and spades, are swords, cups, coins, and batons (earlier represented as swords, cups, rings, and wands).

The 22 symbolic cards generally picture the Juggler or Magician, High Priestess or Female Pope, Empress, Emperor, Hierophant or Pope, Lovers, Chariot, Justice, Hermit, Wheel of

Fortune, Strength or Fortitude, Hanged Man, Death, Temperance, Devil, Lightning-struck Tower, Star, Moon, Sun, Last Judgment, Fool, and Universe. These symbolic designs, which vary slightly from pack to pack according to different traditions, are popularly interpreted as follows: Willpower, Science or Knowledge, Action, Realization, Mercy and Beneficence, Trial, Triumph, Justice, Prudence, Fortune, Strength, Sacrifice, Transformation, Combination, Fate, Disruption, Hope, Deception or Error, Earthly Happiness, Renewal, Folly, and Expiation. These interpretations also vary according to different authorities. In addition, the other cards in the pack are considered to have symbolic significance.

There are many different ways of consulting the cards for divination, but they mostly involve laying out the cards after shuffling and interpreting the indications of the major symbolic cards in their relationship to each other.

Origins

Much speculation surrounds the whole question of the origins of the tarot and its relationship to the present-day set of 52 playing cards. It is not difficult to see symbolic interpretations of the 52 pack in its division into four suits, corresponding to the seasons of the year, 52 weeks, and the symbolic rulers of the court cards. Some writers have connected the pack with the ancient Eastern origins of the game of chess, with its comparable king, queen, and knight. However, within the **occult** community, many have looked to an origin in ancient **Egypt.** According to such popular lore, the priests of ancient Egypt invented the tarot cards to represent their secret doctrines and teachings. They escaped the destruction of the Christian era because the book burners did not know what they were. Later, some Egyptians brought them to Rome, and they survived in the courts of the popes and passed to France during the period when the papacy was headquartered in Avignon.

This story of the Egyptian lineage first appeared in the French occult community of the eighteenth century, having been invented by a Protestant minister, Antoine Court de Gébelin (1719–1784). De Gébelin, an occultist and Martinist, had become an early supporter of Franz A. Mesmer's ideas of **animal magnetism** and an amateur Egyptologist. In 1781, well before the Egyptian hieroglyphics had been deciphered, he published an eight-volume tome *Le monde primitif* (1781) with his speculative notions. Tarot cards had existed for several centuries in Europe with no speculation about any mysterious foreign or occult connection. But De Gébelin argued, with little evidence, that the word "tarot" actually meant royal road, a derivation he made from the Egyptian words "ta" or "way" and "tosh" or "royal." It should be noted that no such words have been found in the Egyptian language. Along with his essay on the deck, De Gébelin also published another essay by an anonymous friend, the first to label the cards the "Book of Thoth," Thoth being one name for the Egyptian god Horus.

As a result of widespread reading of *Le monde primitif,* the tarot cards began to be used as divination devices in Paris, though the spread of the practice was slow. It was significant that Francis Barrett did not include any mention of the deck in his 1801 catalog of magical practice, *The Magus.*

The next important step in the establishment of the occult tarot occurred in the mid-nineteenth century when **Éliphas Lévi** encountered a deck during his massive reworking of the magical tradition in light of Mesmerist thought. He identified their magical power with animal magnetism, a theory still popular to the present.

In 1853 Lévi published *Dogma de la haute magie,* in which he first laid out his ideas tying the tarot to the ancient Egyptian teacher **Hermes Trismegistus,** the legendary author of the Hermetic magical writings. He then tied the cards to the Hebrew magical/mystical **Kabala** (which he spelled "Qabalah"). He identified the numbered cards with the ten sephiroth. The court cards represented the stages of human life, and the suits symbolized the tetragarmmaton, the four letters that made up the Hebrew name of God. The 22 trump cards were tied to the 22 letters of the Hebrew alphabet, and all of the Kabbalistic content earlier ascribed to each letter was plowed into the tarot cards.

Lévi used the Marseilles tarot deck, but grew increasingly dissatisfied with it. His early efforts to produce a new deck did not come to fruition, but Lévi did promote his project with an English Mason, **Kenneth Mackenzie** (1833–1886). Mackenzie, as a leader in the **Societas Rosicruciana in Anglia,** taught tarot to the group of men who were to found the Hermetic Order of the **Golden Dawn** (OGD), the organization most responsible for the modern magical revival.

S. L. MacGregor Mathers and his wife, Moina, collaborated on the OGD deck to go along with the order's rituals, most of which he also wrote. He produced one original, which was given to each member as they reached the grade of Adapts Minor, who in turn made their own personal copy. It is this deck that was described by **Aleister Crowley** in his journal, *The Equinox.* It was finally published in 1978.

Possibly the most important deck to date to come out of the OGD was that produced by **Arthur Edward Waite** in collaboration with Pamela Coleman-Smith. It was released in 1910 to accompany Waite's *The Key to the Tarot* (later reissued as *The Pictorial Key to the Tarot*) and went on to become the most popular deck for divinatory purposes in the twentieth century. Paul Foster Case (1884–1954), an OGD member who later founded the Builders of the Adytum, developed a deck, based in large part upon the Waite-Smith cards, in collaboration with Jessie Burns Parks. The deck was published in 1931.

Finally, in 1938, Aleister Crowley (1875–1947), who left the OGD and published many of its secrets, began a collaboration with Freda Harris to embody the thelemic magick of the **Ordo Templi Orientis.** They used both the OGD and Waite-Smith deck, but both the art and concepts went far beyond either. While the original art work was displayed at an art gallery during World War II, and a limited edition of 200 decks appeared in 1944, the Crowley-Harris tarot did not reach the public until it was finally published in 1969 by Samuel Weiser. This deck is the only one to challenge the Waite-Smith deck's popularity.

Gypsy Origins

One hypothesis, which parallelled the idea of Egyptian origins and has likewise been largely disproved, concerned the mysterious **Gypsies.** The idea that the tarot was introduced into Europe by the Gypsies of the Middle Ages was first suggested by an anonymous friend of de Gébelin's in the eighteenth century. It was championed in the next century by J. F. Vaillant, who had lived for many years among the Gypsies and who had been instructed by them in their traditional lore. He tied the word "tarot" to the Hungarian Gypsy *tar* (pack of cards), and claimed that ancient esoteric symbolism found its way throughout Europe through Gypsy migrations. Vaillant incorporated what he had been told in his books *Les Rômes, histoire vraie des vrais Bohémiens* (1857), *La Bible des Bohémiens* (1860), and *La Clef Magique de la Fiction et du Fait* (1863). Vaillant's theory was endorsed by the French writer "Papus" (penname of **Gérald Encausse)** in his book *Le Tarot des Bohémiens: Le plus ancien livre du Monde,* (1899) (English edition as *The Tarot of the Bohemians,* 1919) in which he claimed that the tarot was the absolute key to occult science. Papus notes, "the Gypsy pack of cards is a wonderful book according to Court de Gébelin and Vaillant. This pack, under the names of *Tarot,* Thora, and Rota, has formed the basis of the synthetic teaching of all the ancient nations successively.

The British legal authority De l'Hoste Ranking, writing in 1908, adds:

"I would submit that from internal evidence we may deduce that the *tarots* were introduced by a race speaking an Indian dialect; that the form of the Pope shows they had been long in a country where the orthodox Eastern Church predominated; and the form of head-dress of the king, together with the shape of the eagle on the shield, shows that this was governed by Russian Grand Dukes, who had not yet assumed the Imperial insignia. This seems to me confirmatory of the widespread belief that it is to the Gypsies we are indebted for our knowledge of playing-cards."

In 1865, E. S. Taylor added his support to the same hypothesis in his book *The History of Playing Cards.* However, W. H. Willshire, in his book *A Descriptive Catalogue of Playing and Other Cards in the British Museum* (1876), questioned Taylor's conclusion, on the ground that "whether the Zingari [Gypsies] be of Egyptian or Indian origin, they did not appear in Europe before 1417, when cards had been known for some time." But this objection is nullified by the fact that the presence of Gypsies in Europe is now placed at a date considerably before 1417. There was, for example, a well-established *feudum acinganorum,* or Gypsy barony, in the island of Corfu in the fourteenth century. It is also believed that the Gypsies themselves were originally the ancient *chandala* caste of India.

Coincidental with the occult revival referred to as the New Age movement, the tarot has enjoyed an unprecedented period of popularity. New Agers have seen the tarot as an important additional tool for personal transformation and have interpreted the symbolism as a new map of the subconscious. The New Age approach has spurred the production of a variety of decks that explore different symbolic worlds, offer variant interpretations from the psychological to the Wiccan, and present a broad scope of artistic styles. Traditional tarot cards have gone high-tech, with digital decks for sale on the Internet for those who are curious and willing to spend a few dollars. Some of these digital decks have replaced the customary card suits and symbols (i.e. cups, wands, pentacles, swords, priestesses, magicians) with characters representing modern themes. For example, a "king" in a traditional tarot deck is replaced with a "businessman" in a contemporary deck. These modern versions may attract a broader audience to tarot, however, many will take the practice less seriously than with the more traditional decks.

Sources:

Banzhaf, Hajo. *The Tarot Handbook.* Stamford, Conn.: U.S. Games Systems, Inc., 1993.

Butler, Bill. *Dictionary of the Tarot.* New York: Schocken Books, 1975.

Decker, Ronald. *A Wicked Pack of Cards: The Origins of the Occult Tarot.* New York: St. Martin's Press, 1996.

Douglas, Alfred. *The Tarot: The Origins, Meaning and Uses of the Cards.* New York: Taplinger; London: Gollancz, 1972. Reprint, London: Penguin, 1974.

Falconnier, R. *Les lames hermétiques du tarot divinatoire.* Paris, 1896.

Gettings, Fred. *The Book of Tarot.* London: Paul Hamlyn, 1973.

Huson, Paul. *The Devil's Picture Book: The Compleat Guide to Tarot Cards; Their Origins and Their Usage.* New York: G. P. Putnam's Sons, 1971. Reprint, London: Abacus, 1972.

Hutton, Alice. *The Cards Can't Lie: Prophetic, Educational and Playing-Cards.* London: Jupiter Books, 1979.

Lévi, Éliphas. *La clef des grands mystéres.* Paris, 1861.

MacGregor Mathers, S. L. *The Tarot: Its Occult Signification, Use in Fortune-Telling and Method of Play.* London: George Redway, 1888. Reprint, New York: Gordon Press, 1973.

Ozaniec, Naomi. *The Illustrated Guide to Tarot.* New York: Sterling Publications, 1999.

Papus. *The Tarot of the Bohemians: The Most Ancient Book in the World; The Use of Initiates.* 2nd rev. ed. London: William Rider, 1919.

Thierens, A. E. *The General Book of the Tarot.* London: Rider; Philadelphia: David McKay, 1928. Reprint, Hollywood, Calif.: Newcastle Publishing, 1975.

Waite, A. E. *Pictorial Key to the Tarot.* London: William Rider, 1911. Reprint, New Hyde Park, N.Y.: University Books, 1959. Reprint, Blauvelt, N.Y.: Rudolf Steiner, 1971. Reprint, New York: Causeway Books, 1973.

Tarot Network News

A journal serving the community of tarot card readers, *Tarot Network News* was founded in 1983 by Gary Ross. Ross had anticipated the new burst of enthusiasm for tarot cards largely because of the New Age movement and the neopagan Wicca movement. Throughout the twentieth century the tarot deck designed by Pamela Coleman Smith and **Arthur Edward Waite** and published by Rider & Co. in London (1910) has been the most popular deck. Some alternative decks were based on the Rider-Waite deck, but new designs were increasingly based on different psychologies and worldviews. Several decks adopted Egyptian motifs (including one by Oscar Ichazo, the founder of **Arica**), and others operated from such widely divergent realms as tantrism, the 1960s counterculture, and surrealism.

Whereas Wiccans adopted tarot decks as simply part of their magic worldview, New Agers began to see the tarot as an important tool for personal transformation. Both movements created an environment in which creation of new tarot decks was seen as an important personal exploratory activity, and readers were encouraged to find a deck that suited their individual personality and concept of truth.

Tarot Network News, 12 issues of which had appeared by 1994, reviews new decks as they appear, discusses the meaning of the cards of the major arcana, and celebrates the expansion of the world of tarot cards. The *News* also sponsors the Bay Area Tarot Symposium twice annually. Gary Ross continues as editor of the *News,* which is published by Jack and Rae Hurley. Address: c/o TAROCO, P.O. Box 104, Sausalito, CA 94966.

Sources:

Jensen, K. Frank. "A Decade with Tarot!" *Tarot Network News* 12 (spring 1994): 24–32.

Tart, Charles T(heodore) (1937–)

Psychophysiologist and parapsychologist. He was born on April 29, 1937, in Morrisville, Pennsylvania. He studied for two years at the Massachusetts Institute of Technology (MIT) before moving to the University of North Carolina (B.A., 1960; M.A., 1962; Ph.D., 1963). During his student years he also was a research assistant at the Psychophysiology Laboratory, Department of Psychiatry, Duke University Hospital (1958–60). Following his graduation he became a lecturer at Stanford University (1964–65) and at the University of Virginia, School of Medicine (1965–66). This was prior to joining the faculty at the University of California, Davis in 1966. He is currently a professor of psychology at Davis, and the publisher of a quarterly *The Open Mind.*

Tart's interest in **parapsychology** manifested while a student in North Carolina when he became a frequent visitor at the **Parapsychology Laboratory** at nearby Duke University. He became a member of the **American Society for Psychical Research** and in the 1970s associated with **Russell Targ** and **Harold E. Puthoff** in their research at the Stanford Research Institute. He was elected president of the **Parapsychology Association** in 1977.

Tart's research has ranged across the field of parapsychological concerns and been the subject of numerous papers, but he is possibly most respected for his studies of states of consciousness and transpersonal psychology. This research resulted in two classic volumes *Altered States of Consciousness* (1969) and *Transpersonal Psychologies* (1975). Less known, Tart proposed an instrument for automatic testing of **ESP,** which was constructed at the University of Virginia and named the "ESPATEACHER." It was set up in the Research Laboratory of the American Society for Psychical Research.

Sources:

Berger, Arthur S., and Joyce Berger. *The Encyclopedia of Parapsychology and Psychical Research.* New York: Paragon House, 1991.

Pleasants, Helene, ed. *Biographical Dictionary of Parapsychology.* New York: Helix Press, 1964.

Tart, Charles T., ed. *Altered States of Consciousness: A Book of Readings.* New York: John Wiley & Sons, 1969.

———. *The Application of Learning Theory to Extrasensory Perception.* 1975.

———. *Learning to Use Extrasensory Perception.* 1976.

———. *On Being Stoned: A Psychological Study of Marijuana Intoxication.* Palo Alto, Calif.: Science & Behavior Books, 1971.

———. *Psi, Scientific Studies of the Psychic Realm.* N.p., 1977.

———. *States of Consciousness.* N.p., 1975.

———. *Transpersonal Psychologies.* New York: Harper & Row, 1975.

———. *Waking Up: Overcoming the Obstacles to Human Potential.* N.p., 1986.

Tart, Charles T., and Harold E. Puttoff. *Mind at Large.* New York: Praeger, 1979.

Tarthang Tulku

One of several Tibetan lamas known as a **Tulku** (incarnated being) who brought traditional Tibetan Buddhist teachings to the West in the wake of the Chinese takeover of the country. He came to the United States and settled in the San Francisco Bay area early in 1969, bringing with him his wife and a collection of rare Tibetan sacred texts.

With the help of a small group of students, he soon established the Tibetan Nyingmapa Meditation Center in Berkeley. Nyingmapa is one of four Tibetan Buddhism sects with an ancient tradition. It was founded in the eighth century C.E. by Guru Padmasambhava and Shantirakshita. The literature of Nyingmapa is classified as *Kama* (oral tradition from master to disciple) and *Terma* (secret books originally concealed by Padmasambhava, such as *The Tibetan Book of the Dead.*)

Known generally as *Rinpoche* (precious master), Tarthang Tulku teaches the advanced system of Buddhist doctrine known as *Vajrayana.* It embodies some teachings of **tantra,** but is essentially directed at enhancing degrees of understanding and awareness.

Tasseography

A formal term for the branch of **fortune-telling** of **divination** by **tea leaves.**

Tattvic Yoga

Term for the ancient Hindu science of breath, as expounded in one of the earliest texts presenting Hinduism to the West, *The Science of Breath and the Philosophy of the Tattvas* (1897) by Pandit Rama Prasad. The "breath" referred to is the life-giving breath of Brahman and in it are contained, according to Prasad, the five elementary principles of nature, corresponding to the five senses of man. These principles are known as *tattvas,* and from them the body and the physical world is composed.

The knowledge of the *tattvas* is believed to confer wonderful power and to this end all undertakings must be commenced at times that are known to be propitious for the movements of the *tattvas* or vital currents in the body.

Tavibo

Tavibo, a Native American of the Paiute people, emerged among them around 1869 as a prophet and visionary. He resided in Mason Valley, north of Virginia City, Nevada, in mountainous territory. It was common for the men to go to the mountains to seek vision and revelations from various spirit entities. Whites began to move into the area in the 1860s and the various chiefs and religious leaders among the Paiute were confronted, as had Native people before them, with the problem of losing their land to the new settlers.

Accounts of Tavibo vary, but all agree that he received a new revelation in a set of spiritual visions that offered hope to his contemporaries that the Earth would rise up and consume the whites and the land would be returned to its original state before their arrival. These visions most likely occurred in 1869 or 1870. In possibly the best account, left by a Captain J. M. Lee, an infantry officer on duty in the area in the 1870s, Tavibo had gone into the mountains and had an initial vision in which he was told that the Paiute's situation would be relieved by an earthquake. The Earth would open up and consume the white people. He enlarged upon this prediction in a second vision that suggested that all the humans in the area would be taken into the ground by the quake but that after a short while the Native people would be resurrected.

In a final third revelation, Tavibo said that only those who believed in the prophecy would be resurrected. Unbelievers would join the whites in eternal damnation. Each new revelation brought him some additional followers; however, before he was able to firmly establish his teachings, he died. His movement appeared to die with him and little was heard of it for some two decades. However, in the 1890s, his son **Wokova** emerged as a new prophet, teaching a variation of his father's message and what became popularly known as the Ghost Dance.

Sources:

Mooney, James. "The Ghost-Dance Religion and the Sioux Outbreak of 1890." In the *Fourteenth Annual Report of the Bureau of Ethnology.* Compiled by J. W. Powell. Washington: Government Printing Office, 1896.

Taxil, Leo

Pseudonym of **Gabriel Jogand-Pagès,** a French journalist of the nineteenth century, who sustained a prolonged **occult** hoax alleging devil-worship amongst French Freemasons.

Taylor, Gordon Rattray (1911–1981)

A British author and broadcaster who served as a member of the **Society for Psychical Research,** London (1976–81). He was born in Eastbourne on January 11, 1911, and educated at Radley College, Trinity College, and Cambridge University. He worked as a journalist beginning in 1933 and in 1958 joined the British Broadcasting Company where he wrote and devised science television programs. In 1966 he became a full-time author. He had authored a number of books over his lifetime. Taylor died December, 7, 1981.

Sources:

Pleasants, Helene, ed. *Biographical Dictionary of Parapsychology.* New York: Helix Press, 1964.

Taylor, John (Gerald) (1931–)

Professor of applied mathematics at King's College, London, England, who was the first British scientist to investigate the phenomena of **Uri Geller.** Taylor was born on August 18, 1931, in Hayes, Kent. He won his way into Christ's College, Cambridge at age 16; at 18 he enrolled at Mid-Essex Technical College, where he took his B.Sc. in general science. He completed a three-year mathematics degree course in two years at Cambridge and passed with first class honors. His academic career has included visiting professorships in the United States as well as being Professor of Theoretical Physics at the University of Southampton and a post at King's College, London.

When Uri Geller visited Britain in 1974, Taylor conducted scientific tests of Geller's feats of **metal bending** and interference with a Geiger counter. Taylor also experimented with some of the children and adults who manifested paranormal abilities after seeing Uri Geller's appearances on British television programs. Taylor's interest in such phenomena was not only in its scientific validation, but also in investigation of the way in which such phenomena take place and the nature of the forces involved. He suggested the phenomena may be some low-frequency electromagnetic effect generated by human beings.

Through the 1970s Taylor was regarded as fully endorsing the paranormal metal bending of Uri Geller, but gradually has made more guarded statements; then in 1980 he largely retracted his support for Geller's paranormal talents. In 1974 he noted, "The Geller effect—of metal-bending—is clearly not brought about by fraud. It is so exceptional it presents a crucial challenge to modern science and could even destroy the latter if no explanation became available." Taylor then spent three years of careful investigation of such phenomena as **psychokinesis,** metal bending, and **dowsing,** but could not discover any reasonable scientific explanation or validation that satisfied him. He was particularly concerned to establish whether there is an electromagnetic basis for such phenomena. After failing to find this he did not believe that there was any other explanation that would suffice. Most of his experiments under laboratory conditions were negative; this left him in a skeptical position regarding the validity of claimed phenomena.

In contrast to the endorsement in his first book on **psi,** *Superminds,* he published a paper expressing his doubts in a paper in *Nature* (November 2, 1978) titled "Can Electromagnetism Account for Extra-sensory Phenomena?" He followed this with his book *Science and the Supernatural* (1980) in which he expressed complete skepticism about every aspect of the paranormal. In his final chapter he stated: "We have searched for the supernatural and not found it. In the main, only poor experimentation [including his own], shoddy theory, and human gullibility have been encountered."

Taylor's new position seems to stem from his failure to find an electromagnetic explanation for paranormal phenomena. In his new book he stated: "We therefore have to accept that when science faces up to the supernatural, it is a case of 'electromagnetism or bust.' " In contrast, **John Hasted,** another British scientist who has tested Uri Geller, continues to support the reality of the Geller effect and also believes that there is evidence of an electromagnetic field in the phenomenon.

Sources:

Berger, Arthur S., and Joyce Berger. *The Encyclopedia of Parapsychology and Psychical Research.* New York: Paragon House, 1991.

Taylor, John *The Horizons of Knowledge.* N.p., 1982.

———. *Science and the Supernatural.* New York: E. P. Dutton, 1980.

———. *The Shape of Minds to Come.* N.p., 1971.

———. *Superminds.* London: Macmillan, 1975.

Tea Leaves, Divination by

One of the most popular forms of **fortune-telling,** depending largely upon psychic intuition. After a cup of tea has been poured, without using a tea strainer, the tea is drunk or poured away. The cup should then be shaken well and any remaining liquid drained off in the saucer. The diviner now looks at the pattern of tea leaves in the cup and allows the imagination to play around the shapes suggested by them. They might look like a letter, a heart shape, or a ring. These shapes are then interpreted intuitively or by means of a fairly standard system of symbolism, such as: snake (enmity or falsehood), spade (good fortune through industry), mountain (journey or hindrance), or house (changes, success).

With the popularity of tea bags, **divination** by tea leaves has declined somewhat, but the bags can be opened and placed in a tea-pot and brewed in the old-fashioned way. The system can also be used for coffee grounds. This long established popular form of fortune-telling has been given the formal name of **tasseography.**

Sources:

Fontana, Marjorie A. *Cup of Fortune: A Guide to Tea Leaf Reading.* Wis.: Fantastic, 1979.

Sheridan, Jo. *Teacup Fortune-telling.* London: Mayflower, 1978.

Tears Painted on Shutters

It was mentioned in Thomas Pennant's book *A Tour in Scotland* (1769) that in some parts of Scotland it was the custom, on the death of any person of distinction, to paint on the doors and window-shutters white tadpole-like shapes on a black ground. These were intended to represent tears, and were a sign of general mourning.

Techter, David (1932–)

Museum worker who has written widely on parapsychology. Born October 5, 1932, at Morristown, New Jersey, he studied at Yale University (B.S. geology, 1954). He was an assistant in fossil vertebrates at the Chicago Natural History Museum from 1955 on. He was a member of the American Society for Psychical Research, an associate member of the Parapsychological Association, and an organizer and executive secretary of the Illinois Society for Psychic Research.

He has conducted tests for extrasensory ability with schoolchildren and written many reviews of books on parapsychological subjects.

Sources:

Techter, David. *A Bibliography and Index of Psychic Research and Related Topics for the Year 1962.* Illinois Society for Psychic Research, 1963.

Teesing, H(ubert) P(aul) H(ans) (1907–1973)

Dutch professor of German literature and former president of the **Studievereniging voor Psychical Research** (Dutch Society for Psychical Research). He was born on March 6, 1907, in Amsterdam, the Netherlands. He spent his college career at the University of Groningen (B.A., 1932; M.A., German philology and literature, 1935; Ph.D., 1948). After graduation he became a grammar school teacher of German (1935–52) before assuming a position as a professor of German literature and literary theory at the University of Utrecht in 1952. He died August 19, 1973.

Sources:

Teesing, H. P. H. "Mystiek en Literatuur" (Mysticism and Literature). *Tijdschrift voor Parapsychologie* (1959).

Telekinesis

A term denoting the claimed faculty of moving material objects without contact, presumably by **psychic force.** The movement of objects, without contact or with only limited contact was frequently observed in the **séance** room. Phenomena included **rappings, table-turning, levitations,** the conveyance of **apports,** and other material phenomena. Spiritualists believed these were caused by the intervention of discarnate spirits. Magnetists believed in the existence of some kind of fluidic or energetic emanation as the cause of such movements. Others, discounting those phenomena that were the result of **fraud,** suggested some form of telekinetic theory, which held that all these varied feats are accomplished by the thoughts of **mediums** and sitters, independent of muscular energy, whether direct or indirect.

The term has more recently been supplanted by **psychokinesis** or **PK.**

Telepathy

Term coined by British psychical researcher **F. W. H. Myers** in 1882, as a result of his joint investigation with **Edmund Gurney, Henry Sidgwick,** and **William F. Barrett** into the possibilities of **thought-transference.** It was applied to the researchers' concept of "a coincidence between two persons' thoughts which requires a causal explanation," and it was defined as "transmission of thought independently of the recognized channels of sense."

Though the researchers never implied such a connotation, the public assumed that telepathy was an agency of communication between mind and mind, that it was a mysterious link between conscious and subconscious minds, and that it could be used to select intelligence by which incidents from the memories of persons present and familiar or distant and unknown.

The public concept of telepathy became a rival of the **spirit hypothesis.** This misconception spread so widely that many people considered telepathy to be distinct from thought transference, advancing the following argument:

"In telepathy the transmitter is often unaware that he acts as an agent and the receiver does not consciously prepare himself for the reception. Telepathy cannot be made a subject of experiments, while thought-transference can. Thought-transference is a rudimentary faculty. Telepathy is a well-developed mode of supernormal perception and is usually brought into play by the influence of very strong emotions."

The need for differentiation was acknowledged by the old school of telepathists, too, when they spoke of spontaneous telepathy as distinct from experimental telepathy. **Frank Podmore**—a hardened skeptic—in his *The Newer Spiritualism* (1910) suggests that: "Whilst the attempt to correlate the two kinds of phenomena is perhaps legitimate, we can hardly be justified in making the spontaneous phenomena the basis of a theory of telepathy."

Myers argued that telepathy as a faculty must certainly exist in the universe if the universe contains any disembodied intelligences at all. Prayer could be telepathic communion with higher beings, and the basis of sympathy and antipathy may be telepathy. **Monitions of approach** appear to be telepathic messages. The knowledge of victory or disaster in war that so inexplicably occurred among ancient Greeks may have been telepathically acquired.

Origins of Modern Telepathic Theories

The theory of thought transference is not a new one. Like the theory of gravitation, it is a daughter of **astrology,** but while gravitation is universally accepted by science, telepathy remains a questionable hypothesis for many. However, it is clear how both sprang from astrology, and one may trace the connection between them.

The wise men of ancient times taught that the stars radiated an invisible influence that held them together in their course and that affected men and events on our planet, receiving in turn some subtle emanation from the earth and its inhabitants. From this idea it was but a step to assume that a radiant influence, whether magnetic or otherwise, passed from one human being to another. The doctrine of astral influence was shared by **Paracelsus** and his alchemistic successors until the epoch of Sir Isaac Newton, whose discovery of the law of gravitation brought the age of simplistic astrology to a close.

The possible analogy between the mysterious force binding worlds together and the subtle influence joining mind with mind is obvious. The two are vastly different, however, in that while gravitation may be readily demonstrated and never fails to give definite results, experiments in telepathy cannot be depended upon to succeed uniformly even under the most favorable conditions. Nevertheless, the experiments that have been conducted from time to time have more than justified the public interest in telepathy.

In 1882 the **Society for Psychical Research** (SPR), London, came into being, numbering among its members some of the most distinguished men of the era. Its goal was to elucidate the so-called supernatural phenomena that were exciting so much popular interest and curiosity. Foremost among these was the phenomenon of thought transference.

Viewing their subjects in a purely scientific light, trained in handling of evidence, and resolved to pursue truth with open and unbiased minds, members of the SPR did much to bring a purer and more dignified atmosphere to the study of psychic phenomena. They recognized the untrustworthiness of human nature in general, and the prevalence of **fraud,** even where nothing was to be gained but the gratification of a perverted vanity. Their experiments were conducted under the most rigid conditions, with every precaution taken against conscious or unconscious deception.

Among the most valuable evidence obtained from experimental thought transference was that gleaned by Professor Henry Sidgwick and his wife **Eleanor Sidgwick** from their experiments at Brighton in 1889 to 1891. In this series the percipients—clerks and shop assistants—were hypnotized. Sometimes they were asked to visualize, on a blank card, an image or picture chosen by the agent. At other times, the agent would choose one of a bundle of cards numbered from 10 to 90, and the percipient was required to state the number on the chosen card, which was done correctly in a surprising number of cases.

Curiously enough, the results varied in proportion as the agent and percipient were near or far apart, and were affected by the intervention of a door or even a curtain between the two. This was ascribed to a lack of confidence on the part of the percipient, however, or to such physical causes as fatigue or boredom, rather than to the limited scope of the telepathic principle. On the whole it seems probable that chance alone did not account for the number of correct replies given by the hypnotized subject.

Toward the end of the nineteenth century, criticism was leveled at these experiments by **F. C. C. Hansen** and A. Lehmann, of Copenhagen, who believed that the phenomenon known as "involuntary whispering," combined with hyperesthesia on the part of the percipient, would suffice to produce the results obtained by the Sidgwicks (see *Journal* of the Society for Psychical Research, vol. 9, p. 113).

This suggested explanation has some merit. If hypnotism causes such a refinement of the senses, may not some elements of hyperesthesia linger in the subconscious of the normal individual? If **dreams** contain such unusual examples of deduction, may not the mind in waking moments follow a process of reasoning imperceptible to the higher consciousness?

It seems that the "other self," which is never quite as much in the background as we imagine, sees and hears a thousand things of which we are unconscious and that come to the surface in dreams. There is no reason to suppose that it might not see and hear things too slight to be perceived in a grosser sphere of consciousness, and thus account for some cases of thought transference. On the other hand, there is evidence of telepathy acting at a distance where subconscious whispering and hyperesthesia are obviously out of the question.

Unusual Kinds of Telepathy

An example of audibly received telepathy is recorded in an early issue of the *Proceedings* of the Society for Psychical Research (vol. 1, p. 6): "On September 9, 1848, at the siege of Mooltan, Major-General R_____, C. B., then adjutant of his regiment, was severely wounded, and thought himself to be dying, and requested that his ring be taken off and sent to his wife. At the same time she was in Ferozepore (150 miles distant), lying on her bed between sleeping and waking, and distinctly saw her husband being carried off the field, and heard his voice saying 'Take this ring off my finger and send it to my wife.' " The facts of the case were verified and all the names were obtained by the SPR.

The journalist and pioneer Spiritualist **William T. Stead** often received **automatic writing** from the living. Thinking of a lady with whom he was in such communication more than once, his hand wrote:

"I am very sorry to tell you that I have had a very painful experience of which I am almost ashamed to speak. I left Haslemere at 2:27 P.M. in a second-class carriage, in which there were two ladies and one gentleman. When the train stopped at Godalming, the ladies got out, and I was left alone with the man. After the train started he left his seat and came close to me. I was alarmed, and repelled him. He refused to go away and tried to kiss me. I was furious. We had a struggle. I seized his umbrella and struck him, but it broke, and I was beginning to fear that he would master me, when the train began to slow up before arriving at Guildford Station. He got frightened, let go of me, and before the train reached the platform he jumped out and ran away. I was very much upset. But I have the umbrella."

Stead sent his secretary to the lady with a note that he was very sorry to hear what had happened and added, "Be sure and bring the man's umbrella on Wednesday." She wrote in reply: "I am very sorry you know anything about it. I had made up my mind to tell nobody. I will bring the broken umbrella, but it was my umbrella, not his." The lady's decision not to tell of the painful evidence suggests that a telepathic message may not only be unconscious, but may directly counteract the desire of the conscious mind.

In many instances of **cross-correspondence,** where two or more people receive part of a message that only becomes clear when the parts are placed together, telepathy between the receivers would furnish an alternative to the spirit hypothesis.

The working of telepathy is apparently demonstrated in certain cases of **suggestion.** Hypnotization has been claimed to be effected at a distance. Myers called it telepathic hypnotism.

The Wave Theory

In his presidential address to the British Association for the Advancement of Science in September 1898, **Sir William Crookes** said:

"If telepathy takes place we have two physical facts—the physical change in the brain of A, the suggester, and the analogous change in the brain of B, the recipient of the suggestion. Between these two physical events there must exist a train of physical causes. . . . [and] with every fresh advance in knowledge it is shown that ether vibrations have powers and attributes abundantly equal to any demand— even to the transmission of thought."

He believed that these ether waves were of small amplitude and greater frequency than x-rays and continually passed between human brains, arousing an image in the second brain that is similar to the image in the first.

Damaging to this theory is the fact that the intensity of waves—any waves—diminishes with distance and that the telepathic image may not only be very vivid despite the remoteness of the agent, but that the picture is often modified or symbolical. A dying man may appear to the percipient in a normal state of health. As Myers noted: "Mr. L. dies of heart disease when in the act of lying down undressed in bed. At or about the same time Mr. N. J. S. sees Mr. L. standing beside him with a cheerful air, dressed for walking and with a cane in his hand. One does not see how a system of undulations could have transmuted the physical facts in this way."

In cases of collective reception, an added difficulty is presented. Why should only a few people in a room be sensitive to the waves and other strangers outside the room not at all receptive? Why should a crystal gazer get a telepathic message at the time of his own choosing, when he happens to look into the crystal? How can the pictures in the crystal sometimes be seen by others if they are only produced in his brain through telepathy?

In his book *The Survival of Man* (1909), **Sir Oliver Lodge** asserts that the experimental evidence was not sufficient to substantiate the nonphysical nature of thought transference. He had no doubt of its reality, and as early as 1903 he stated in an interview to the *Pall Mall Magazine*: "What we can take before the Royal Society, and what we can challenge the judgment of the world upon, is Telepathy."

Hereward Carrington suggested that telepathic manifestations may take place through a superconscious mind, that there may be a "mentiferous ether," as some writers have suggested, that carries telepathic waves, and that there is a species of spiritual gravitation uniting life throughout the universe, as physical gravity binds together all matter.

In the 1920s the Italian researcher Prof. F. Cazzamali of the University of Milan conducted experiments that appeared to show that the human brain emits short waves of high frequency under the stress of emotion. In an insulated all-metal room, he carried out a number of experiments inducing, by means of suggestion, an emotional crisis in his subjects. Delicate receivers placed in the room registered cerebral radiation in the form of waves, which were also recorded on photographic plates. The reports were published in the *Revue Métapsychique,* but were severely criticized. The wave theory of telepathy remains unproven, and psychical researchers have now largely discarded it, although a few modern Soviet investigators suggested an electromagnetic theory of telepathy.

Animals and Telepathy

There is some evidence indicating that telepathy is not restricted to humans. Among the better cases of telepathy from animal to man is one furnished by the novelist H. Rider Haggard in the *Journal* of the Society for Psychical Research (October 1904). Mrs. Haggard heard her husband groaning and emitting inarticulate sounds like the moaning of a wounded animal during the night of July 7, 1904. She woke him and her husband told her his dream. It consisted of two distinct parts:

In the first, the novelist only remembered having experienced a sense of grievous oppression, as though he were in danger of suffocation. Between the moment when he heard his wife's voice and that in which he regained full consciousness, the dream became much more vivid. He states: "I saw good old Bob [his dog] lying on his side among brushwood by water. My own personality seemed to me to be arising in some mysterious manner from the body of the dog, who lifted up his head at an unnatural angle against my face. Bob was trying to speak to me, and not being able to make himself understood by sounds, transmitted to my mind in an undefined fashion the knowledge that he was dying."

Bob was found dead four days later, floating in the river, his skull crushed in, and his legs broken. He had been struck by a train on a bridge and thrown into the water. His bloodstained collar was found on the bridge the morning after the dream.

William J. Long, in his book *How Animals Talk* (1922), produces many examples of a telepathic faculty in animals. He notes that if a mother wolf cannot head off a runaway cub because there is too much distance between them, she simply stops quiet, lifts her head high, and looks steadily at the running cub. He will suddenly waver, halt, whirl, and speed back to the pack. The famous case of the **Elberfeld horses** also suggests that telepathy may operate between animals and humans, and Edmund Selous, in his book *Thought Transference—or What?—in Birds* (1931), records many observations on the subject from bird life.

Telepathy vs. Survival

Obviously the role of telepathy is of some importance to any understanding of the paranormal, but those who tried to find in it an all-inclusive solution to paranormal manifestations faced great difficulties. If a telepathic message is followed by motor movements—for instance, the announcement of a death in automatic writing—the question is, Who executes the movements—the subconscious self or the agent who sends the message? Similar uncertainty applies if the reception of a telepathic message is accompanied by telekinetic movements.

Frank Podmore, the author of *Apparitions and Thought Transference* (1894)—which deals with the accumulated evidence for telepathy—became the great exponent of the theory that all apparitions could be explained as "telepathic **hallucinations.**" F. W. H. Myers, on the other hand, was among the first to argue that telepathy was an insufficient explanation for **apparitions.** Being forced to concede that collective perception of phantasmal appearances called for something objective, he worked out a theory of "psychical invasion"—the creation of a "phantasmogenetic" center in the percipients' surroundings.

The theory was midway between telepathic and spirit explanations, and it accounted for many freakish phantasmal manifestations for which no satisfactory solution had yet been offered.

Early in the twentieth century, the problem of whether to admit telepathy could occur in both the living and the dead plagued researchers. Apparitions of the dying border between telepathy with the living and telepathy from the dead. A similar phenomenon that lacks all the conditions for evidence of telepathy is visions of the dead appearing to the dying.

The strain on the telepathic theory grew with instances that made the acquisition of certain knowledge by telepathic process wildly improbable but were easily understood on the basis of the **survival** theory. The question was not only how certain information could have been acquired, but also why it was associated with definite personalities or disclosed in a personified form.

In the *Proceedings* of the Society for Psychical Research (vol. 35, 1926), **S. G. Soal** tells how, in a **séance** with **Blanche Cooper,** a voice came through, claiming to be his deceased brother. As proof of identity the voice told him that a year before in a playhut at home he had buried a lead disk which he would probably find if he dug there. Soal was satisfied that none of his brother's surviving acquaintances knew of the incident, and dug and found the disk.

Nevertheless, he argued that this might have been a case of telepathic transmission in his brother's earthly life, the knowledge having remained latent in his own subconscious mind. If yet another person had figured in the telepathic chain it would have been an example of the so-called three-way telepathy first advanced by **Andrew Lang** in his discussion of the case of the medium **Leonora Piper** (*Proceedings* of the Society for Psychical Research, vol. 15, pp. 48–51).

Hugh J. Browne's book *The Holy Truth* (1876) contains the story of his two sons, who drowned. One, in a communication through the medium **George Spriggs,** told the detailed story of their fatal pleasure cruise and added that his brother's arm had been torn off by a great shark. This information could not have been telepathically conveyed by anyone living, except by the shark, yet it was found to be true. The shark was caught two days later, and a man testified to **Sir Arthur Conan Doyle** that he cut the shark open and found an arm, part of a waistcoat, and a watch, which were identified as belonging to the dead youth. The watch had stopped at the exact hour at which the brothers were engulfed by the sea.

There are many cases on record in which missing wills and other lost property were found through alleged **spirit intervention. F. Bligh Bond**'s in *The Gate of Remembrance* (1920) records an incident in which an entire chapel was found. The Glastonbury Abbey was in ruins; every trace of the Edgar Chapel was lost, and very little was known about its location and precise dimensions. Nevertheless, in automatic writing a series of communications came through, giving detailed information. When excavations were undertaken in 1908, a year after the communications were received, the chapel was found. (For a critical view of this case see G. W. Lambert's "The Quest of Glastonbury" in the *Journal* of the Society for Psychical Research, June 1966).

The personal element puts insurmountable obstacles in the way of telepathic explanation in the following case recorded by the psychical researcher **Ernesto Bozzano** in notes on the July 14, 1928, sitting at **Millesimo Castle,** Italy. An unknown voice, in Genoese dialect, addressed sitter Gino Gibelli, saying, "I am Stefano's father. You must tell my son that I insist on his giving the message to Maria with which I entrusted him. He has not carried out my request in the slightest degree." Signor Gibelli explained that he had been in Genoa a month before. In a séance there the father had communicated with the son and charged him with a message to his mother. Very probably the young man had not dared to carry out this request. Gibelli stated that he had completely forgotten the incident, that it had nothing to do with him personally and did not interest him in the slightest degree. He was not thinking of Stefano's father, whom he did not know in life, and was unaware that the request that the father had made to his son had not been carried out.

Some aspects of spirit communication strongly suggest that telepathy was not the means by which the medium gained knowledge. Telepathy makes no allowance for false or confused information, and it does not explain the communicator's loss of the concept of time, nor the individual style of the different spirit controls (i.e., the biblical manner of "Imperator," or "George Pelham's" impatience as he spoke through Leonora Piper). In spirit communications, names are often spelled inaccurately, giving, for instance, "Margaret" instead of "Maggie." Telepathy cannot reveal coming events, and it cannot explain how the spirits of children, if recently dead, ask for their toys and act childishly, yet behave years later as adults although no such memory of them is retained in any living mind.

If a medium operated by means of telepathy, he would have to be omniscient. There is no need for the supposition of omniscience if a telepathic message may originate as well from the dead as from the living. Once this admission is made one can well understand the futility of the "brain wave" theory. A discarnate spirit has no physical brain. The message must come from the spirit and not from the percipient. If it may come from the spirit as an agent, it may be received by the medium's spirit and transmitted to his brain.

The insufficiency of the telepathic explanation has also been demonstrated by hundreds of strange cross correspondences and newspaper and **book tests.**

Many post-mortem letters have been preserved by the Society for Psychical Research and will not be opened until after a communication revealing their contents comes through a medium after the writer's death. It is unlikely that this evidence will ever be conclusive, since in one instance the content of the letter was revealed, apparently through telepathy, by the medium while the writer was still living. The telepathist may always argue that the contents of the letter were subconsciously transferred into another brain while the writer was preparing it.

As proof of survival, cross correspondences are far more conclusive, since the partial messages coming through several mediums are by themselves nonsensical and can only be explained away by the supposition of a conspiracy between several subconscious minds.

The Arguments of James H. Hyslop

Telepathy became a rival of the spirit theory because, according to **James H. Hyslop,** early twentieth-century head of the **American Society for Psychical Research,** of the word *transmission* in the original definition of telepathy. He preferred to define telepathy as "a coincidence excluding normal perception, between the thoughts of two minds." It was the word transmission, Hyslop said, that gave telepathy the implication that "it is a process exclusively between living people and not permitting the intervention of the dead, if the discarnate exist and can act on the living."

Hyslop's definition permits the employment of the term to describe the action of discarnate as well as incarnate minds. Hyslop further concluded, "We are not entitled to assume the larger meaning of telepathy to be a fact because we are not sure of its limitations. Here is where we have been negligent of the maxims of scientific methods and the legitimate formation of convictions."

"Mediumistic phenomena," he writes in his book *Contact with the Other World* (1919), "too often suggest the action of spirits, to be cited as direct evidence for telepathy. The possibility of spirits and the fact that an incident is appropriate to illustrate the personal identity of a deceased person forbids using it as positive evidence for telepathy. One can only insist that one theory is as good as the other to account for the facts."

About selective telepathy, he argues:

"No evidence has been adduced. . . . and I do not see how it would be possible to adduce such evidence. Every extension of the term beyond coincidences between the mental states of two persons is wholly without warrant. The introduction of the assumption that this coincidence is due to a direct transmission from one living mind to another has never been justified, and as there is no known process whatever associated with the coincidences we are permitted to use the term only in a descriptive, not in an explanatory sense.

"There is no scientific evidence for any of the following conceptions of it: (1) Telepathy as a process of selecting from the contents of the subconscious of any person in the presence of the percipient; (2) Telepathy as a process of selecting from the contents of the mind of some distant person by the percipient and constructing these acquired facts into a complete simulation of a given personality; (3) Telepathy as a process of selecting memories from any living people to impersonate the dead; (4) Telepathy as implying the transmission of the thoughts of all living people to all others individually, with the selection of the necessary facts for impersonation from the present sitter; (5) Telepathy as involving a direct process between agent and percipient; (6) Telepathy as explanatory in any sense whatever, implying any known cause.

"The failures in experiments to read the present active states of the agent and the inability to verify any thoughts outside those states, in the opinion of science is so finite that its very existence is doubted, while the extended hypothesis requires us to believe in its infinity without evidence.

"As a name for facts, with suspended judgment regarding explanation, it is tolerable, but there can be no doubt that spirits explain certain facts, while telepathy explains nothing. At least as a hypothesis, therefore, the spiritistic theory has the priority and the burden of proof rests upon the telepathic theory."

Dr. **Richard Hodgson** similarly concluded in his second report on the Piper phenomena: "Having tried the hypothesis of telepathy from the living for several years, and the spirit hypothesis also for several years, I have no hesitation in affirming with the most absolute assurance that the spirit hypothesis is justified by its fruits, and the other hypothesis is not."

Telepathy—The Result of Spirit Agency?

Hyslop was not averse to the possibility that spirits might furnish the explanation of telepathy between the living. He stated that Myers saw this implication at the very outset of his investigations into telepathy. Hyslop said that only part of the story was told in the report on the experiments of Miss Miles and Miss Ramsden in long-distance telepathy (*Proceedings* of the Society for Psychical Research, vol. 21, pp. 60–93). Miles was an all-round psychic, and in her correspondence with Hyslop she disclosed that she could always tell when her telepathy was successful by the **raps** that she heard. She said she concentrated on the object Ramsden was to perceive until she heard raps. Raps are not telepathic phenomena, however, and carry an entirely different connotation.

Further, Hyslop stated that in communications through the medium Mrs. Willis M. Cleveland (also known as **Mrs. Smead**), the deceased Frank Podmore purported to say that telepathy was actually messages carried by spirits and that they could perform it instantly. Had Smead known Podmore, such a misstatement could not have occurred—Podmore always pressed the theory of telepathy between the living to the exclusion of spirits.

The purported spirit of F. W. H. Myers also made a strange allusion through the medium **Minnie Meserve Soule** ("Mrs. Chenoweth"), saying telepathy "all depended on the carrier." When Hyslop asked for an explanation, the answer was: "Telepathy was always a message carried by the spirits."

A more interesting and elaborate statement reportedly came from the spirit of **Margaret Verrall**:

"I said yesterday that I would write more about the telepathic theory as I now understand it. I am not sure of the passage of thought through space as I was once, and I had begun to question the method by which thought was transferred to brains before I came here, but you will recall that I had some striking instances of what seemed telepathy tapping a reservoir of thought direct, and the necessity for an intervening spirit was uncalled for; but there were other instances when the message was transposed or translated and the interposition of another mind was unquestionably true. I tried many experiments and I think you must know about them. I will say that I found more people involved in my work than I had known and there seemed more reason to believe that I was operated upon than that I operated, in other words, the automatic writing was less mine than I had supposed."

The dividing line between **clairvoyance** and telepathy is vague. The telepathic message may take the form of visual or auditory sensation. If the content indicates future events, clairvoyance should be suspected. Past events may be both telepathic communications and the result of a reading by **psychometry.**

A constructive and evidential resumé of experiments in telepathy is given by **Walter Franklin Prince** in an appendix to the sixteenth *Bulletin* of the Boston Society for Psychical Research, published under the title "The Sinclair Experiments Demonstrating Telepathy" (1932).

Parapsychology and Telepathy

From the 1920s on, psychical researchers in both Great Britain and the United States investigated telepathy through intensive laboratory experiments. Card guessing was a favored testing tool, but it was not until the 1930s, after **J. B. Rhine** popularized the **Zener Cards,** a pack of five simple symbols (star, cross, circle, rectangle, and wavy lines), that statistical evaluation of experiments was simplified.

Using the Zener cards, experimenters attempted to obtain significant quantitative tests under laboratory conditions. In the experiments by C. W. Olliver with playing cards over some twenty thousand trials, a distinction was made between telepathy (between agent and percipient) and clairvoyance (perception without an agent).

In the modern period of parapsychological research, many aspects of telepathy have been investigated, including such questions as expectation, emotional incentives, and dream telepathy, in addition to the completion of many quantitative and qualitative experiments. So far researchers have not summarized their findings in a way that will definitely establish telepathy as a scientific fact, repeatable on demand. There is reasonable evidence that some telepathy has occurred under laboratory conditions, however.

Certain basic problems remain, such as the disparity in telepathic faculty between different percipients, and the problem of assessing spontaneous telepathy. In the former Soviet Union there was considerable interest in telepathy because of its possible practical applications, and experimenters gave special attention to methods of intensifying visualization on the part of the agent sending impressions to a percipient. In the United States researchers like **Andrija Puharich** have experimented with high-speed strobe lights on the closed eyes of subjects in order to heighten telepathic impressions.

Sources:

Braddon, Russell. *The Piddingtons.* London: Werner Laurie, 1950.

Carington, Whately. *Telepathy: An Outline of Its Facts, Theory and Implications.* London: Methuen, 1945. Reprint, New York: Gordon Press, 1972.

Ehrenwald, Jan. *New Dimensions of Deep Analysis; A Study of Telepathy in Interpersonal Relationships.* New York: Grune & Stratton, 1954. Reprint, New York: Arno Press, 1975.

Gurney, Edmund, F. W. H. Myers, and Frank Podmore. *Phantasms of the Living* 2 vols. London: Trubner, 1886. Reprint, Gainesville, Fla.: Scholars' Facsimiles, 1970. Abr. ed., New Hyde Park, N.Y.: University Books, 1962.

Hardy, Aleister, R. Harvie, and Arthur Koestler. *The Challenge of Chance: Experiments and Speculations.* London: Hutchinson, 1973. Reprint, New York: Random House, 1974. Reprint, New York: Vintage Books, 1975.

Hyslop, James H. *Contact With the Other World.* New York: Century, 1919.

Lambert, G. W. "The Quest of Glastonbury." *Journal* of the Society for Psychical Research 43, 728 (June 1966).

Lang, Andrew. *The Making of Religion.* London: Longmans, 1898.

Myers, F. W. H. *Human Personality and Its Survival of Bodily Death.* 2 vols. London: Longmans, Green, 1903. Reprint, New York: Arno Press, 1975. Abr. ed., New Hyde Park, N.Y.: University Books, 1961.

Ostrander, Sheila, and Lynn Schroeder. *Psychic Discoveries Behind the Iron Curtain.* Englewood Cliffs, N.J.: Prentice-Hall, 1970. Reprint, New York: Bantam, 1971. Reprint as *Psi: Psychic Discoveries Behind the Iron Curtain.* London: Abacus 1973.

Parish, Edmund. *Hallucinations and Illusions: A Study of the Fallacies of Perception.* London: Walter Scott Publishing, 1897.

Podmore, Frank. *Apparitions and Thought Transference.* London: Scott; New York: Charles Scribner's Sons, 1895.

———. *The Naturalisation of the Supernatural.* New York: George Putnam's Sons, 1908.

———. *Telepathic Hallucinations: The New View of Ghosts.* London: Milner; New York: Stokes, 1909.

Puharich, Andrija. *Beyond Telepathy.* Garden City, N.Y.: Doubleday, 1952. Reprint, Garden City, N.Y.: Anchor Press, 1973. Reprint, London: Souvenir Press, 1974. Reprint, London: Pan Books, 1975.

Rhine, J. B. *Extrasensory Perception.* Boston: Boston Society for Psychical Research, 1934. Reprint, Boston: Branden, 1964.

Schmeidler, Gertrude R., ed. *Extrasensory Perception.* New York: Atherton, 1969.

Schwarz, Berthold Eric. *Parent-Child Telepathy? Five Hundred and Five Possible Episodes in a Family: A Study of the Telepathy of Everyday Life.* New York: Garrett Publications, 1971.

Sinclair, Upton. *Mental Radio.* The Author, 1930. Rev. ed., Springfield, Ill.: C. C. Thomas, 1962.

Targ, Russell, and Harold Puthoff. *Mind-Reach: Scientists Look at Psychic Ability.* New York: Delacorte, 1977.

Tenhaeff, W. H. C. *Telepathy and Clairvoyance.* Springfield, Ill.: C. C. Thomas, 1972.

Thomas, N. W. *Thought Transference: A Critical & Historical Review of the Evidence for Telepathy.* London: De La More Press, 1905.

Tischner, Rudolf. *Telepathy and Clairvoyance.* New York: Harcourt, Brace, 1925.

Tyrrell, G. N. M. *Science and Psychical Phenomena.* New York: Harper, 1938. Reissued with Tyrrell's book *Apparitions.* New Hyde Park, N.Y.: University Books, 1961.

Ullman, Montague, and Stanley Krippner. *Dream Studies and Telepathy: An Experimental Approach.* New York: Parapsychology Foundation, 1970.

Ullman, Montague, Stanley Krippner, and Alan Vaughan. *Dream Telepathy.* New York: Macmillan; London: Turnstone Books, 1973. Reprint, London: Penguin, 1974.

Vasiliev, L. L. *Experiments in Mental Suggestion.* London: Institute for the Study of Mental Images, 1963.

———. *Studies in Mental Telepathy.* CCM Information Corporation, 1971.

Warcollier, René. *Experimental Telepathy.* Boston: Boston Society for Psychical Research, 1938. Reprint, New York: Arno Press, 1975.

———. *Mind to Mind.* Creative Age Press, 1948. Reprint, New York: Macmillan, 1963.

Wilkins, Sir Hubert, and Harold M. Sherman. *Thoughts through Space: A Remarkable Adventure in the Realm of the Mind.* Hollywood, Calif.: House-Warren, 1951. Reprint, London: Frederick Muller, 1971. Reprint, Greenwich, Conn.: Fawcett, 1973.

Telephone Calls (Paranormal)

The extraordinary claimed phenomenon of telephone calls from the dead, one of a variety of new forms of contact with the dead using modern technology, was raised by parapsychologists **D. Scott Rogo** and Raymond Bayless in their 1979 book *Phone Calls From the Dead.* Their research had been stimulated by a report in the September 1976 *Fate* Magazine from Don B. Owens of Toledo, Ohio, concerning his close friend Lee Epps. They had lived in the same neighborhood for years before Lee moved away and their contact became limited to occasional meetings or telephone calls.

On October 26, 1968 at 10:30 P.M., Don's wife Ethel answered a telephone call and immediately recognized the voice as that of Lee. He said: "Sis, tell Don I'm feeling real bad. Never felt this way before. Tell him to get in touch with me the minute he comes in. It's important, Sis." Ethel tried to ring him back but got no answer; neither did Don when he came in. That evening Don learned that Lee was in a coma in hospital, six blocks from their home and died at 10:30 P.M. It would have been impossible for Lee to have made the call himself in his condition, yet Ethel had immediately recognized his voice.

Although this case was purely anecdotal, without firm supporting evidence, Rogo and Bayless were sufficiently intrigued to follow up the phenomenon of "phone calls from the dead." After collecting a few cases, they wrote an article in the October 1977 issue of *Fate* Magazine titled "Phone Calls from the Dead?" More cases came to hand and led to a two-year investigation of the claimed phenomenon. It proved peculiarly difficult to establish in a manner acceptable to the present standards of **psychical research,** since the accounts dealt with spontaneous events, usually without the opportunity of rigid factual verification. Moreover, it was difficult to rule out coincidental hoaxes. Rogo and Bayless concluded, however, that such paranormal phone calls actually did occur and might even be more common than supposed.

A satisfactory theory to explain such cases presents difficulties. On the face of things, if one grants that mediumistic communication is possible through a **trumpet** at Spiritualist séances, or even by **direct voice,** the use of a telephone earpiece is hardly more far-fetched, but the prior ringing of the telephone announcing a call is another matter. Is there an actual **PK** manipulation of the telephone apparatus, or are the ringing tone and the voices actually in the subject's mind? Many individuals have experienced the hallucination of "phantom bells" when they think they hear a door bell or a telephone ringing but find no one there.

In some of the cases examined by Rogo and Bayless, it seemed that the call was placed in a normal way through an exchange that caused the phone to ring. In other cases the phone calls appeared to be placed through long-distance operators. Some subjects reported hearing the familiar "click" at the end of the call as the communicator apparently hung up. Rogo and Bayless suggested PK-mediated electromagnetic effects and discussed the possible relevance to the related phenomenon of **Raudive voices** or **electronic voice phenomenon.**

Sources:

Rogo, D. Scott, and Raymond Bayless. *Phone Calls From the Dead.* Englewood Cliff, N.J.: Prentice-Hall, 1979.

Teleplasm

An alternative term for **ectoplasm.**

Teleportation

The paranormal transportation of human bodies through closed doors and over a distance is a comparatively rare but still a thoroughly documented occurrence. It is a composite phenomenon fitting between **levitation** (frequently reported) and **apports** (objects which were frequently reported in séances in generations past but which were almost totally fraudulently produced). According to the testimony of the Bible, teleportation is by no means new in human experience. We find in Ezek. 11:1, "Moreover the spirit lifted me up, and brought me unto the East gate of the Lord's house which looketh eastward." Elijah, walking with Elisha, was carried away by a whirlwind. Habakkuk was carried from Judea to Babylon to bring food to Daniel in the lion's den, then carried back to Judea through the air.

In the Acts of the Apostles 5:23, the warders of St. Peter's prison testify: "The prison house we found shut in all safety, and the keepers standing before the doors; but when we opened we found no man within." When St. Philip baptized the Ethiopian, the author of the Acts of the Apostles notes (8:39–40), "And when they were come up out of the water, the spirit of the Lord caught away Philip that the eunuch saw him no more. . . . But Philip was found at Azotus." The distance between Gaza, the scene of the baptism, and Azotus was 30 miles.

Reports of this phenomenon reappeared very early in modern Spiritualism. **J. B. Ferguson** said from his observation of the **Davenport brothers:**

"From as good testimony as I have of any fact that I can accept without personal knowledge, I believe that these young men have been raised into the air to the ceilings of rooms, and have been transported a distance of miles by the same force and intelligence, or intelligent force, that has for 11 years worked in their presence so many marvels."

In England, accounts of transportation were published in the Spiritualist press between 1871 and 1874 of **Agnes Guppy-Volckman, Charles Williams,** and **Frank Herne** (*Spiritual Magazine,* July 1871); of **Lottie Fowler** (*The Spiritualist,* March 15, 1872); and of **F. W. Monck** (*Spiritual Magazine,* 1875), the latter reportedly making an aerial journey from Bristol to Swindon.

Thomas Blyton writes in his reminiscences in *Light* (April 11, 1931):

"I was present on one occasion at a private home séance at Hackney in London, when without warning or preparation, in total darkness, Mr. Frank Herne was suddenly placed in the midst of the sitters; and after recovering from our surprise and resuming the séance, Mr. Herne's overcoat, hat and umbrella were dropped on the table. John King, speaking in the direct voice, explained that his band of spirit people had found an unexpected opportunity to transport Mr. Herne from where he had been with friends, witnessing a theatrical play that evening; on his appearance at Hackney he was in a semi-conscious condition."

Grave suspicion surrounds the mediumship of Herne and Williams, however, the latter being exposed in **fraud** on two occasions. In 1876 Monck was imprisoned after his fake **materializations** were discovered.

Very little evidential value can be attached to the episode in Catherine Berry's *Experiences in Spiritualism* (1876), according to which, at the studio of **Frederick A. Hudson,** the spirit photographer, between the hours of 2 and 5 P.M., in the presence of Frank Herne and herself:

"Mr. Williams was seen to descend from the roof of the studio; he fell on the ground very gently. I do not think he was hurt, but sadly frightened. The spirit 'John King' was rather vexed with him for not obeying a summons to come into the studio, and told Mr. Williams that this putting him through the roof bodily was done as a punishment, and he hoped it would teach him not to disobey in the future. We all went immediately to see if there was an opening in the roof, but there was none, and the boards had all the appearance of not having been disturbed."

Guppy-Volckman's transportation must also be called into question. It occurred on June 3, 1871. There were ten witnesses, including the two fraudulent mediums, Williams and Herne, and eight sitters. It was a sequel to Herne's previous questionable transportation to Guppy-Volckman's house. In answer to a witty expressed wish of a sitter, in a moment of time Guppy-Volckman was apparently carried bodily from her home in Highbury (North London) to the house of Williams on Lamb's Conduit Street (West Central London), a distance of over three miles.

The case was the occasion of much facetious comment in the daily press. *The Echo* printed the only serious report. The story was summed up on the basis of the sitters' written testimony by Abraham Wallace in *Light* (1918, p. 259) as follows:

"Neither door nor window could have been opened without the admission of light. After various phenomena usual in dark séances had taken place someone asked Katie King, one of the controls, to bring something. Another member of the circle observed, in a joking sort of way, 'I wish you would bring Mrs. Guppy.' Upon which a third remarked: 'Good gracious, I hope not, she is one of the biggest women in London.' Katie's voice at once said 'I will, I will, I will.' Then John's voice was heard to exclaim, 'Keep still, can't you?' In an instant somebody called out: 'Good God, there is something on my head' simultaneously with a heavy bump on the table and one or two screams. A match was struck, and there was Mrs. Guppy on the table with the whole of the sitters seated round it closely packed together as they sat at the commencement. Mrs. Guppy appeared to be in a trance, and was perfectly motionless. Great fears were entertained that the shock would be injurious to her. She had one arm over her eyes, and was arrayed in a loose morning gown with a pair of bedroom slippers on, and in a more or less décolleté condition. When telling me the story, Mrs. Volckman very naturally said how much she disliked having been brought in such a state into the presence of strangers. There was a pen in one hand, which was down by her side. From the first mention of bringing her to the time she was on the table three minutes did not elapse. It seems that Mrs. Guppy had a pen in one hand and an account book in the other. She had been making up her weekly accounts and had just written the word 'onions,' the ink still being wet on the page."

After Guppy-Volckman had shaken off the effect of the shock, the séance was continued with her presence. During this part of the séance, her boots, hat, and clothes arrived from her home, as well as lots of flowers. Both Herne and Williams were levitated and disappeared in turns.

After the séance one Mr. Harrison, editor of *The Spiritualist,* together with three of the sitters, offered to escort Guppy-Volckman to her home. Then their inquiries convinced them that Guppy-Volckman was really sitting in the room with Miss Neyland, writing her accounts at the time that one of the séance sitters wished her to be brought. Her husband also bore testimony to the fact that his wife, shortly before her disappearance, had been up to the billiard room where he was playing with a friend. This visitor corroborated his statement.

Regarding this visit of inquiry, **Frank Podmore** states in his book *Modern Spiritualism* (1902):

"They there learnt from Miss Neyland, a friend of Mrs. Guppy's, who had come out as a medium under her auspices, that an hour or two previously she had been sitting with Mrs. Guppy near the fire making up accounts when suddenly looking up she found that her companion had disappeared, leaving a slight haze near the ceiling."

The report of this marvelous phenomenon gave rise to repetitions.

In another case, the authenticity of which is difficult to establish, the subject of transportation was a sitter in Guppy-Volckman's house. His name was Henderson. Ten sitters held the séance on November 2, 1873. Suddenly it was discovered that Henderson broke the séance chain and disappeared. The doors and windows of the room were locked. About the same moment of his disappearance, he was discovered at a distance of a mile and a half in the backyard of the house of his friend, Mr. Stoke. Nine people noticed his sudden arrival. The night was wet. His boots and clothes were "almost" dry.

There is one transportation case associated with **William Eglinton** (also cited as a fraudulent medium). It occurred on March 16, 1878, at Mrs. Makdougall Gregory's house. Two other mediums, **Arthur Colman** and **J. W. Fletcher,** were present with five sitters. One of the sitters suggested that Colman should be taken through the ceiling. Almost immediately Eglinton disappeared. The noise of a violent bump was heard and Eglinton was found in the room above on the floor in a trance.

Several cases were put on record in the first years of the present century. The story of one is recounted in the *Annals of Psychic Science* (vol. 9). The place was San Jose, Costa Rica, the date between 1907 and 1909 and the persons concerned were the children of Buenaventura Corralès. The oldest child, **Ophelia Corralès,** was 18 years old. There were two younger sisters and a brother. Separately and together the children frequently vanished from the séance room, found themselves in the garden and returned, to their great delight, in the same mysterious manner. To quote from the account of Alberto Brenes, a professor at the Law Academy:

"A few minutes passed in absolute silence. Suddenly we heard knocks coming from the pavilion; we turned up the gas and found the children were no longer there. The doors were examined and found to be completely closed. Two persons were deputed to look for the children. When the door of the room was opened they were found standing in a row, talking and laughing at what had taken place.

"They said that they had been brought there, one by one; first little Flora, then Berta, and finally Miguel—their respective ages being seven, twelve and ten years.

"We then asked them how they had been carried and they replied that they had felt a pressure under the arms, then they were lifted up in the air and placed where they were found, but they could not tell us anything more.

"The two investigators then asked the spirits to repeat the translation in the reverse direction; they recommended the children to remain silent where they were, and locking the door, returned to the séance room to give an account of what had happened.

"We resumed the séance after taking the necessary precautions of locking the doors. Then 'Ruiz' came and after recommending all to keep up their spirits, said in a clear and energetic voice: 'Let the children come.' Immediately one of them called out: 'We are here.' The light was turned up and the three children appeared in a line in the same order in which they had been previously found. On this occasion all three had been transported at the same time."

Again, we must add, considerable suspicion surrounds the mediumship of Ophelia Corralès.

Joseph Lapponi, medical officer to Popes Leo XVII and Pius X, recorded in his *Hypnotism and Spiritism* (1906) the case of the **Pansini brothers,** Paul and Alfred, eight and ten years old respectively. They experienced mysterious transportation in a half hour from Ruvo to Molfetta. Another time, at 12:30 P.M., they disappeared from Ruvo and at one o'clock found themselves on a boat at sea near Barletta, making towards Trinitapoli. Once they disappeared from the square of Ruvo and found themselves, ten minutes later, before the house of their uncle Jerome Maggiore in Trani. Several other mysterious flights took place to Gios, Biseglie, Mariotta, and Terlizzi. Once they disappeared in Bishop Berardi's presence while he was discussing these phenomena with their mother. The windows and doors were closed. In another volume, *Spedizione e Spiriti,* the same author told of the flying brothers of Bari who could transfer themselves over a distance of 45 kilometers in 15 minutes.

Henry Llewellyn had a series of sittings with the medium **F. G. F. Craddock** at Burslem, Staffs. The medium sat in a corner of the room from which a door led into a cellar beneath. The cellar door was completely covered with a curtain tacked around the opening, so that any disturbance there would have been at once detected. The curtains were drawn over the medium.

Some time later, the medium was discovered in a cataleptic state suspended horizontally across the top of the curtained corner of the room, with his feet and head lodged on each end of about two inches of boarding. The curtain was opened so that all present could see the sight for themselves, and then closed in the hope that the medium would be put safely on the floor again. Hearing no movement for some time the curtain was opened again, when to the bewilderment of the experimenters it was found that Craddock was gone. The cellar door and its curtain were undisturbed. Shortly afterward they heard someone moving about in the next room; when the door of that room was unlocked, the medium walked out of it with his hands still tied behind him. On another occasion Craddock was found to be missing and was discovered in the bedroom directly over the place in which they were sitting. This case must also be treated with reserve, since Craddock was also exposed in fraud on several occasions.

A report of Willi Reichel's experiences with **C. V. Miller,** the California materialization medium, as given in *Psychische Studien* (January–February 1906) states:

" 'Betsy,' the principal control of Mr. Miller, called Herr Reichel first into the cabinet in order that he might assure himself of the presence of the medium asleep. He examined all again and considers it impossible that the medium could have quitted the cabinet in a normal way; in front of the curtains were seated the 27 persons who formed the circle on that evening, and the windows looked out on a much frequented street. The weather, moreover, was very windy and wet, and it would have been impossible, he says, to open a window without causing a current of air to be felt at once. After about four minutes 'Betsy' told him to go with three other persons to the first floor and Mr. Miller's housekeeper gave them the keys. They found the medium breathing heavily on a chair; they brought him back into the séance room, where he awoke, remembering nothing."

Franz Hartmann, the well-known Theosophist and writer on occultism, employed the term "magical metathesis." In *Occult Review* (July 1906), he quoted the case of a Dr. Z., of Florence, a friend of his, who was reportedly transported from Livorns to Florence (100 kilometers) in 15 minutes and deposited in a closed room.

Stepping into the realm of occult magic, the book of Harry de Windt, *From Paris to New York by Land* (1904), may be cited for an ancient transportation case in which a medicine man, while he was closely watched, disappeared from a tent and was found in an unconscious condition in a tent half a mile away.

The medium **Ada Besinnet** was said to have been several times the subject of transportation, but there is no evidential record of the feat. Reporting on the Polish medium **Franek Kluski** in *Psychic Science* (October 1925, p. 214), one Professor Pawlovski writes:

"The most extraordinary case related to me by the members of the circle is that of Mr. Kluski having been fetched by the apparitions, or disappearing from the sealed and locked séance room. The astonished sitters found him in a rather distant room of the apartment quietly sleeping on a couch. I report the case upon the responsibility of my friends, whom I have no reason to distrust."

Harald Nielsson states in *Light* (November 1, 1919), in an account of his experiences with **Indridi Indridason,** the Icelandic medium:

"We have had on several occasions the experience of matter being brought through matter, and one evening the medium herself was taken through the wall into a room which was locked and in darkness. This sounds incredible, but many things occur in the presence of physical mediums which must seem absurd to men who have not themselves investigated them. But they are nevertheless true."

In *Psychic Research* (March 1930), an account was published by **Harry Price** and H. Kohn of the **poltergeist** persecution of an Indian boy, Damodar Ketkar, of Poona, India. According to Kohn, who was a lecturer in languages at the governmental Deccan College (Bombay University), Poona, the following transportation case occurred in April 1928 during the most violent period of the manifestations:

"At 9:45 A.M. on April 23, my sister says in a letter, the elder boy (his brother, Ramkrishna Bapat) suddenly materialised in front of [her]. . . . He looked bright but amazed, and said 'I have just come from Karjat.' He didn't come through any door. My sister describes the posture of the boy as having been most remarkable. When she looked up from her letter-writing she saw him bending forward; both his arms were hanging away from his sides, and the hands hanging limp—his feet were not touching the floor, as she saw a distinct space between his feet and the threshold. It was precisely the posture of a person who has been gripped round the waist and carried, and therefore makes no effort but is gently dropped at his destination."

This account is unique, as in no other case was the actual arrival of the transported individual seen.

Two accounts of transportation are to be found in the amazing case of **Carlos Mirabelli,** the South American medium. On the basis of the original Portuguese documents, psychical researcher **E. J. Dingwall,** in *Psychic Research* (July 1930), recounts:

". . . the transportation of the medium from the railway station at Luz [São Paolo] to the town of S. Vincente, a distance of some 90 kilometers. The report states that at the time the medium was at the station at Luz in company with a number of people and was intending to travel to Santos. Shortly before the train started he suddenly disappeared to the astonishment of everybody, his presence in S. Vincente being ascertained 15 minutes later by telephone, it being proved that he was met in the town exactly two minutes after his disappearance. . . . On one occasion when the medium had been secured in his armchair by means of various ligatures he vanished utterly from his position, the doors and windows remaining both locked and firmly secured. Five sitters remained in the séance room whilst the rest went in search of the missing man. He was soon discovered in a side room lying in an easy chair and singing to himself."

A well-documented case was the transportation of **Marquis Carlo Centurione Scotto,** at Millesimo Castle, on July 29, 1928. Psychical researcher **Ernesto Bozzano** reported on his investigation of the case in *Luce e Ombra* (September–October 1928). It can be summarized as follows:

During the course of the sitting, the medium Marquis Centurione Scotto exclaimed in a frightened voice: "I can no longer feel my legs!" The gramophone was stopped. An interval of death-like silence followed. The medium was addressed, without answer, then felt for. His place was empty. The sitters turned on the red light. The doors were still securely locked with the key on the inside but the medium had disappeared.

All the rooms of the castle were searched without result. Two and a half hours passed when it occurred to the sitters to ask Gwendolyn Kelley Hack to try and get into communication, through automatic writing, with her spirit guide "Imperator." After several attempts in which the sitters were only told, "Do not be anxious, we are watching and guarding" and that the "medium is asleep," the correct information came through: "Go to the right, then outside. Wall and Gate. He is lying—hay—hay—on soft place." The communication was signed by the cross of "Imperator."

The place indicated a granary in the stable yard. The great entrance door was locked, and the key was not in the lock. They ran back to fetch it and, entering, found a small door that had been previously overlooked. This door was also locked, but the key was in the keyhole on the outside. They opened it with the greatest caution. On a heap of hay and oats, the medium was comfortably lying, immersed in profound sleep. When he first regained consciousness and found himself lying in the stable he feared that he had gone out of his mind and burst into tears.

The authenticity of the phenomenon was unexpectedly confirmed by a message from New York from the spirit guide "Bert Everitt," who, manifesting in a sitting with the medium **George Valiantine,** referred to the Millesimo experiments and stated "that he had helped Cristo d'Angelo [the spirit guide] to carry out the phenomenon of the transport of the medium into the granary." This was received a whole month before a report of the case had been published in Italy or elsewhere.

The marquis himself described his impressions as follows:

"At this instant I could not feel my legs any more, having the impression of going into trance. I asked Fabienne for her hand, which I took willingly to reassure myself. After having taken the hand I felt something descending over my brain and my face—and I felt myself light . . . light . . . light . . . but of such lightness . . . I felt myself as if fainting and I . . . Then I recall nothing more. Nothing, nothing."

Many cases have been reported in the hagiogaphic literature of the transportation of saints, and sometimes their bilocation (simultaneous appearance in different places over a great distance) is noted. (See **Gambier Bolton; Psychic Force**)

Sources:

Begg, Paul. *Into Thin Air: People Who Disappear.* London: David & Charles, 1979.

Fodor, Nandor. *Mind Over Space.* New York: Citadel Press, 1962.

Fort, Charles. *The Books of Charles Fort.* New York: Henry Holt, 1941.

Harrison, Michael. *Vanishings.* London: New English Library, 1981.

Telergy

Term used by psychical researcher **F. W. H. Myers** to denote the force that is manifest in **telepathy** and perhaps in other **supernormal** operations.

Telesomatic

Term used by psychical researcher **Alexander N. Aksakof** for **materialization.**

Telesthesia

Perception from a distance through psychic rapport with the place or environment. It is less than **clairvoyance** since it is restricted to the perception of material things or conditions. The word was coined by psychical researcher **F. W. H. Myers** in 1882 to express sensation at a distance after it was found that the communication between distant persons is not a transference of thought alone, but also of emotion, of motor impulses, and of many impressions not easy to define.

Frequent instances were described during World War I. The experience of a Mrs. Fussey of Wimbledon on November 4, 1914, was typical. At home she suddenly felt in her arm the sharp sting of a wound. She jumped up and cried. There was no trace of an injury. Fussey continued to suffer pain and exclaimed: "Tab [her soldier son] is wounded in the arm. I know it." On the following Monday, confirmation arrived.

Telluric

M. Benedict's term for the **rhabdic force** that presumably moves the **divining rod.**

Tellurism

A name applied by Dietrich G. Kieser (1779–1862) to **animal magnetism.** He was one of the early scientific investigators who supported the reality of the phenomenon and drew attention to its legal aspects. **"Téméraire," Charles** (or **Charles the Bold**) (1433–1477)

Duke of Burgundy (1467–1477) in the fifteenth century. During his reign the state enjoyed its height of political, economic, and cultural power. According to legend, he disappeared after the battle of Morat on June 22, 1477, when he was defeated. It was said by his chroniclers that he was carried off by the devil; others maintained that he had withdrawn to a remote spot and become a hermit.

More sober accounts state, however, that he perished in the battle and that his mutilated body was discovered several days later. Charles was introduced into two novels by Sir Walter Scott—*Quentin Durward* and *Anne of Geirstein.* The latter novel contains an account of the battle of Nancy, before the fatal encounter at Morat.

Temperature Changes

Marked changes of temperature sometimes occur in the séance room, usually a sudden lowering. (See also **Winds**)

Templars

The Knights Templars of the Temple of Solomon were a military order founded by Hugues de Payns of Burgundy and Godeffroi de St. Omer for the purpose of protecting pilgrims journeying to the Holy Land. They were soon joined by other knights; a religious chivalry speedily gathered around this nucleus. Baldwin I, king of Jerusalem, gave them as headquarters a portion of his palace, contiguous to a mosque that tradition asserted was part of the Temple of Solomon, and from this building they took their name.

One of the purposes of the society was to convert and render useful knights of evil living. So many of these entered the order as to bring it under the suspicion of the church, but there is every reason to believe that its founders were instigated by pious motives. The fact that they lived in a condition near poverty, notwithstanding the numerous rich gifts that were showered upon them, is the best evidence of their motivations.

They had properly constituted officials, a grand master, knights, chaplains, sergeants, craftsmen, sensechals, marshals, and commanders. The order had its own clergy, who like other clergy in orders were exempt from the jurisdiction of diocesan rule, and its chapters were held as a rule in secret. The dress of the brotherhood was a white cloak with a red cross for unmarried knights, and a black or brown cloak with a red cross for the others. The discipline was very strict and the food and clothing rough and not abundant.

By the middle of the twelfth century, the new order had firm footing in nearly all the Latin kingdoms of Christendom. Its power grew, and its organization became widespread. It formed a nucleus of the Christian effort against the paganism of the east. Its history may be said to be that of the Crusades. Moreover it became a great trading corporation, the greatest commercial agency between the east and west, and as such amassed immense wealth.

On the fall of the Latin kingdom in Palestine, the Templars were forced to withdraw from that country. Although they continued to harass the Saracen power, they made little headway against it, and in reality appeared to have undertaken commercial pursuits in preference to those of a more warlike character.

The Attack Upon the Templars

When the Temple was at the high point of its power, its success aroused the envy and avarice of Philip IV of France (1285–1314), who commenced a series of attacks upon it. Pope Clement V, who was devoted to Philip's interests, denounced the order for heresy and immorality and gave Philip his chance.

For several generations before this time, rumors had been circulating concerning the secret rites of the Templars, which were assisted by the very strict privacy of their meetings. They were usually held at daybreak with closely-guarded doors. It was alleged that the most horrible blasphemies and indecencies took place at these meetings, that the cross was trampled underfoot and spat upon, that an idol named **Baphomet** (*Baphemetios,* baptism of wisdom) was adored, or even that the devil in the shape of a black cat appeared. Other tales told of the roasting of children, and the smearing of the idol with their burning fat. And even wilder rumors spread through the uneducated populous.

A certain Esquian de Horian pretended to betray the "secret" of the Templars to Philip, and they were denounced to the Inquisition. Jacques de Molay, the grand master, who had been called from Cyprus to France, was arrested with 140 of his brethren in Paris and thrown into prison. A universal arrest of the Templars throughout France followed. The wretched knights were tortured *en masse,* as was usually the case, and confessed to the most grotesque crimes. The most damning confession of all was that of the grand master himself, who said that he had been guilty of denying Christ and spitting upon the cross, but repudiated all charges of immorality in indignant terms.

The process dragged on slowly for more than three years, in consequence of the jealousies that arose among those interested in its prosecution. The pope wished to bring it entirely under the jurisdiction of the church, and to have it decided at Rome. The king, on the other hand, mistrusting the pope, resolved on the destruction of the order so that none but himself should reap advantage from it. He decided it should be judged at Paris under his own personal influence.

The prosecution was directed by his ministers, Nogaret and Enguerrand de Marigny. The Templars asserted their innocence and demanded a fair trial, but they found few advocates who would undertake their defense. They were subjected to hardships and tortures, which forced many of them into confessions dictated to them by their persecutors.

During this interval, the pope's orders were carried into other countries, authorizing the arrest of the Templars and the seizure of their goods. Everywhere the same charges were brought against them. The same means of imprisonment and torture were used to procure their condemnation, although they were not subjected to the same severity as in France.

The Destruction of the Order in France

At length, in the spring of 1316, the grand process was opened in Paris. An immense number of Templars, brought from all parts of the kingdom, underwent a public examination. A long act of accusation was read: they denied Christ (and sometimes they denied expressly all the saints) declaring that he was not God truly but a false prophet and that they had no hope of salvation through him; they always, at their initiation into the order, spat upon the cross, and trod it under foot (they did this especially on Good Friday); they worshiped a certain cat, which sometimes appeared to them in their congregation; they did not believe in any of the sacraments of the church; they took secret oaths which they were bound not to reveal; the brother who officiated at the reception of a new brother kissed the naked body of the latter, often in a very unbecoming manner; each different province of the order had its idol, which was a head, having sometimes three faces, and at others only one, or sometimes a human skull; they worshiped these idols in their chapters and congregations, believing that they had great power; they girt themselves with cords, with which these idols had been superstitiously touched; those who betrayed the secrets of their order, or were disobedient, were thrown into prison and often put to death; they held their chapters secretly and by night, and placed a watch to prevent them from any danger of interruption or discovery; and they believed the grand master alone had the power of absolving them from their sins.

The publication of these charges, and the agitation that had been deliberately fomented, created such horror throughout France that the Templars who died during the process were treated as condemned heretics. Burial in consecrated ground was refused to their remains.

A great number of knights agreed to the general points of the formula of initiation. It seems possible that they denied Christ and spat and trod upon the cross. The alleged words of the denial were "Je reney Deu" or "Je reney Jhesu," repeated thrice. Most of those who confessed having gone through this ceremony declared that they did it with repugnance and spat beside the cross, not on it. The reception took place in a secret room with closed doors; the candidate was compelled to take off part or (in rare instances) all of his garments, and then he was kissed on various parts of the body.

One of the knights examined, Guischard de Marzici, said he remembered the reception of Hugh de Marhaud, of the diocese of Lyons. He saw him being taken into a small room, which was closed up so that no one could see or hear what took place within. After some time, he was let out; he was very pale and looked as though he were troubled and amazed. In conjunction with these strange ceremonies, however, there were others that showed a reverence for the Christian church and its ordinances, a profound faith in Christ, and the consciousness that the partaker of them was entering into a holy vow.

The historian Jules Michelet (1798–1874), who carefully investigated the materials relating to the trial of the Templars, suggested an ingenious explanation for these anomalies. He imagined that the form of reception was borrowed from the figurative mysteries and rites of the early church. The candidate for admission into the order, according to this notion, was first presented as a sinner and renegade; in the example of St. Peter, he denied Christ. This denial was a sort of pantomime, in which the novice expressed his reprobate state by spitting on the cross. The candidate was then stripped of his profane clothing, received through the kiss of the order into a higher state of faith, and re-dressed with the garb of its holiness. Forms like these would be easily misunderstood in the Middle Ages and their original meaning soon forgotten.

Another charge in the accusation of the Templars seems to have been proved by the depositions of witnesses, namely the idol or head which they were said to have worshiped; the real character or meaning of which it was difficult to explain. Many Templars confessed to having seen this idol, but as they described it differently, it must be supposed that it was not in all cases represented under the same form. Some said it was a frightful head, with long beard and sparkling eyes; others said it was a man's skull; some described it as having three faces; some said it was of wood, and others of metal; one witness described it as a painting (*tabula picta*) representing the image of a man (*imago hominis*), and said that when it was shown to him, he was ordered to "adore Christ his creator."

According to some it was a gilt figure, either of wood or metal, while others described it as painted black and white. According to another deposition, the idol had four feet. The one belonging to the order at Paris was said to be a silver head with two faces and a beard. The novices of the order were told to regard this idol as their savior. Deodatus Jaffet, a knight from the south of France, deposed that the person who performed the ceremonies of reception showed him a head or idol. It appeared to have three faces. The person from the ceremonies said, "You must adore this as your savior, and the savior of the order of the Temple," and then Jaffet was made to worship the idol, saying, "Blessed be he who shall save my soul." Cettus Ragonis, a knight received at Rome in a chamber of the palace of the Lateran, gave a somewhat similar account.

Many other witnesses spoke of having seen these heads, which, however, were perhaps not shown to everybody. The greatest number of those who spoke on this subject said they had heard others speak of the head, but that they had never seen it themselves. Many of them declared their disbelief in its existence. A friar minor deposed in England that an English Templar had assured him the order had four principal idols: one at London in the sacristy of the Temple, another at Bristelham, a third at Brueria (Bruern in Lincolnshire), and a fourth beyond the Humber.

Baron von Hammer-Purgstall indicated that Gnosticism was the secret doctrine of the Temple. His important essay *Mysterium Baphometis Revelatum* (The Mystery of Baphomet Revealed) was published in vol. 6 of *Fundgraben des Orients* (Vienna, 1811). The suggestion of Baphomet being related to the rituals of Ophite and Gnostic heresies has some plausibility.

The confessions with regard to the mysterious cat were much rarer and more vague. Some Italian knights confessed that they had been present at a secret meeting of 12 knights held at Brindisi. There a grey cat suddenly appeared among them and they worshiped it. At Nismes, some Templars declared they had been present at a chapter at Montpellier at which the demon appeared to them in the form of a cat and promised them worldly prosperity. They added that they saw devils in the shape of women. An English knight, who was examined at London, deposed that in England they did not adore the cat or the idol to his knowledge, but he had heard it positively stated that they worshiped the cat and the idol in parts beyond the sea. English witnesses deposed to other acts of "idolatry."

Such accounts suggest the witchcraft accounts of the appearance of the devil at what were basically pagan rituals. Agnes Lovecote stated she had heard that at a chapter held in Dineslee (Dynnesley, in Hertfordshire), the devil appeared to the Templars in a monstrous form. It had precious stones for eyes, which shone so bright that they illuminated the whole chapter; the brethren, in succession, kissed him on the posteriors and marked there the form of the cross. She was told that one young man, who refused to go through this ceremony, was thrown into a well, and a great stone was cast upon him.

Another witness, Robert de Folde, said he had heard that 20 years ago, in the same place, the devil came to the chapter once a year. He flew away with one of the knights, whom he took as a sort of tribute. Two others stated that certain Templars confessed to them that at a grand annual assembly in the county of York, the Templars worshiped a calf. All this is mere hearsay, but it shows the popular opinion of the conduct of the order.

A Templar examined in Paris, named Jacques de Treces, said he had been informed that at secret chapters held at midnight, a head appeared to the assembled brethren, and "had a private demon, by whose council he was wise and rich."

The wretched aim of King Philippe was successful. He seized the whole treasure of the temple in France and became rich. Those who ventured to speak in defense of the order were browbeaten and received little attention. Torture was employed to force confessions. Fifty-four Templars who refused to confess were carried to the windmill of St. Antoine, in the suburbs of Paris, and there burned. Many others, among whom was the grand master himself, were subsequently brought to the stake. After having lasted two or three years, the process ended in the condemnation and suppression of the order; its estates were given in some countries to the knights of St. John.

It was in France that the persecution was most cruel. In England, the order was suppressed, but no executions took place. Even in Italy, the severity of the judges was not everywhere the same. In Lombardy and Tuscany the Templars were condemned, while they were acquitted at Ravenna and Bologna. They were also pronounced innocent in Castile; in Arragon they were reduced by force only because they had attempted to resist by force of arms. In Spain and Portugal they only gave up their own order to be admitted into others. The pope was offended at the leniency shown towards Templars in England, Spain, and Germany. The Order of the Temple was finally dissolved and abolished, and its memory branded with disgrace.

Some of the knights were said to have remained together and formed secret societies. The result, however, was much the same everywhere. Convicted of heresy, sorcery, and many other abominations, many of the wretched Templars were punished with death by fire, imprisonment, and their goods reverted to the various crowned heads of Europe. Nearly all of these nobles followed the greedy example of Philip of France.

Jacques de Molay, the grand master, was brought out onto a scaffold erected in front of Notre Dame in Paris and asked to repeat his confession and receive a sentence of perpetual imprisonment. He flared into sudden anger and recanted all he had said, protesting his innocence; he was sentenced to burn. De Molay summoned the pope and the king with his dying breath; he waited to meet them before the bar of Heaven. Both of these dignitaries shortly afterwards died and it remained in the public mind that the outcome of the grand master's **summons** seemed to have proved his innocence.

There is every reason to believe there was some foundation for the charges of heresy made against the Templars. Their intimate connection with the East and the long establishment of the order had in all probability rendered their Christianity not quite so pure as that of Western Europe. Numerous treatises have been written for the purpose of proving or disproving the Temple heresy, to show that it followed the doctrines and rites of the Gnostic Ophites of Islam, that "Baphomet" was merely a corruption of "Mahomet," and it has been collated with various other eastern systems.

Hans Prutz furthered the view of the rejection of Christianity in his book *Geheimlehre und Geheimstatutendes Tempelherren-Ordens* (1879) in favor of a religion based on Gnostic dualism, and at once raised up a host of critics.

But many defenders of the order followed, and it was proved in numerous instances that the confessions wrung from the Templars were the result of extreme torture. In a number of cases they were acquitted in Castile, Aragon, Portugal, and in many German and Italian centers. It has also been shown that the answers of a number of the knights under torture were practically dictated to them. In England, out of 80 Templars examined, only four confessed to the charge of heresy, and of these, two were apostates.

The Templars were also the victims of their own arrogance and commercial success, which excited the avarice their enemies and the superstitious ignorance and hatred of their contemporaries. There has been a steady stream of writings on the Templars, especially in the last two centuries. Contemporary writers on the order have agreed that charges of witchcraft and homosexuality directed against the order were basically lies spread to hide Philip's motives.

Modern Templarism

It has been asserted that on the death of Jacques de Molay, a conspiracy was formed by the surviving Templars. The conspiracy had for its ends the destruction of papacy and the various kingdoms of Europe. This tradition was supposedly handed on through generations of initiates through such societies as the **Illuminati** and the **Freemasons,** who in the end brought about the French Revolution and the downfall of the French throne.

After the French Revolution, people claimed the Templar tradition and founded several neo-Templar organizations that spread through the French-speaking world. In 1805 a Frenchman, Bernard-Raymond Fabré-Palpret, founded a reconstituted Templar order with himself as the head. He also created a gnostic church to compete with Roman Catholicism and consecrated Ferdinand-Francois Chatel as the first bishop. After the death of Fabré-Palpret in 1838, the order split. It developed even more factions in every generation. At present more than 30 operate in France, Switzerland, Belgium, and Quebec. One of these neo-Templar groups, the Solar Temple, became the subject of interest when nearly 50 of its members were murdered in Switzerland in 1994. Apparently they were killed by their leaders, who then killed themselves.

A second neo-Templar tradition began in Germany in the 1890s with the founding of the **OTO,** the Ordo Templi Orientis (or Order of the Eastern Temple), which spread from Germany to German-speaking Switzerland and through **Aleister Crowley** to Great Britain and the United States.

Sources:

Campbell, G. *The Knights Templars, Their Rise and Fall.* London: Duckworth; New York: McBride, 1937.

Charpentier, John. *L'Ordre des Templiers.* Paris: La Colombe, 1945.

Lea, Henry Charles. *A History of the Inquisition of the Middle Ages.* 3 vols. London: Sampson, Low; New York: Harper & Bros., 1888. Reprint, New York: Citadel, 1954.

Lees, B. A. *Records of the Templars in England in the Twelfth Century: The Inquest of 1185 with Illustrative Charters and Documents.* Vol. 9 of *British Academy Records of the Social and Economic History of England and Wales.* Oxford: Oxford University Press, 1935.

Legman, G. *The Guilt of the Templars.* New York: Basic Books, 1966.

Martin, Edward J. *The Trail of the Templars.* London: Allen & Unwin, 1928.

Michelet, Jules. *Le Procès des Templiers.* 2 vols. N.p., 1841–51.

Parker, Thomas W. *The Knights Templars in England.* Tucson: University of Arizona Press, 1963.

Temple Beautiful

Temple Beautiful is a **channeling** group currently headquartered in South Africa. It was founded in the United States by Ilona Linda Day who began to channel **St. Germain** and other of the ascended masters associated with the **Theosophical Society** and the "I Am" Religious Activity. Day passed the leadership of the group to a woman named Phaeryn. In the 1980s, tapes of Day's and Phaeryn's channeled messages were received in South Africa by Mienke Riemens, a resident of Rondebosch, a suburb of Cape Town. Riemens held meetings in her home where she played the tapes for those assembled.

At one point in the early 1990s, Phaeryn visited South Africa and gave a channeled reading to Chris Erasmus, a young man who had joined the group around 1990. During the reading, St. Germain asked Erasmus to be his channel in South Africa. He began channeling in 1994 and has established special contact with St. Germain and Serapis Bey. Prior to joining the group, he had been on a spiritual search that had led him to **transcendental meditation.** Shortly after Erasmus began channeling, the group outgrew the space in the Riemens' home and moved to Erasmus' home. The growth of the work in the late 1990s has led the group to build a separate temple facility.

The Temple Beautiful is organized as a mystery school. It is designed to assist people in making a connection to their higher self and places initiates in a position to receive direct guidance.

Temple Beautiful is located in suburban Cape Town.

Sources:

Erasmus, Chris. "A Mystery School in the Suburbs." *Odyssey* 23, no.4 (August 1999): 10–14.

Temple Church (London)

The Church of the Knights **Templars** in London, consisting of two parts, the Round Church and the Choir. The Round Church (transition Norman) was built in 1185. The Choir (early English style) was finished in 1240.

Hargrave Jennings, in his book *The Rosicrucians, their Rites and Mysteries* (1870), states that the Temple Church in London presents many mythic Rosicrucian figures. One figure signifies the Virgin Mary, and displays the cross as rising like the pole or mast of a ship (*argha*) out of the midst of a crescent moon (*navis biprora*), curved at both ends.

The staff of the grand master of the Templars displayed a curved cross of four splays, or blades, red upon white. The eight-pointed red Buddhist cross was also one of the Templar ensigns.

The church's arches abound with stars with wavy or crooked flames. The altar at the east end of the Temple Church has a cross on a field of wavy stars; to the right is the Decalogue, surmounted by the initials A.O. (alpha and omega); on the left are the monograms of the Saviour, I.C., X.C.; beneath is the Lord's Prayer. The winged horse, or Pegasus, is the badge of the Templars.

The tombs of the Templars, disposed around the circular church in London, are of that early Norman shape called *dos d'ane;* their tops are triangular; the molding passes through the temples and issues out of the mouth and horned skull of a mask. The head at the top is shown in the cover of the tomb. There is much hidden meaning in every curve of these Templar tombs.

Temple of Set

The Temple of Set emerged during the period of internal discord that almost destroyed the **Church of Satan** in the early 1970s. In 1972, **Michael Aquino,** an officer in the U.S. Army and a priest in the church, critiqued the authoritarian leadership of church founder **Anton LaVey** as well as his understanding of Satanism. Claiming LaVey to be an atheist who did not believe in the literal existence of Satan, Aquino left the church. Three years later, in response to Aquino's invocation, Satan appeared under the guise of Set, the ancient Egyptian deity. Set gave Aquino a mandate in the form of a book, *The Book of Coming Forth by Night,* which authorized Aquino to found the Temple of Set as the Church of Satan's successor. The temple is dedicated to Set, the corrupted legends of whom became the basis of the Christian devil.

The temple teaches that the universe is a nonconscious environment possessed of mechanical consequences. However, the deity Set can on occasion violate the laws. Over the millennia, Set has altered the genetic makeup of human beings in order to produce an enhanced nonnatural intelligence. The temple works to identify and develop this enhanced ability in selected individuals. It is governed by a Council of Nine, which appoints the high priest of Set. Members are organized into six initiatory degrees: Setian, Adept, Priest(ess) of Set, Master of the Temple, Magus, and Ipsissimis.

The Temple of Set may be contacted at P.O. Box 470307, San Francisco, CA 94147. It publishes the newsletter *Scroll of Set.* While the work occurs primarily on the individual level, the temple provides a variety of resources for the individual to develop as a Setian.

Sources:

Aquino, Michael A. *The Crystal Tablet of Set.* San Francisco: Temple of Set, 1985.

———. *Temple of Set Reading List XIX.* San Francisco: Temple of Set, 1984.

Scott, Gini Graham. *The Magicians.* New York: Irvington Publishers, 1983.

Temple of the Holy Grail (THG)

The Temple of the Holy Grail (THG) is a small initiatory mystery school based upon the belief that what are now known as the "Grail" mysteries (and hence associated with the cup used by Christ at the Last Supper) existed in Western Europe long before the first century and the advent of Christianity. They were a as a graded path of initiation comparable to the Lam Rim of Tibetan Buddhism. Through the centuries, the mysteries evolved into an esoteric Christian school, the primary work being attributed to the legendary Graalmeister Treverezent in the ninth century C.E. It was later associated with chivalric orders, and the alchemical and Gnostic schools.

The Temple of the Holy Grail began its history at the end of the nineteenth century with a secret English Templar order that possessed an ancient Jewish terra-cotta cup believed to be the true Eucharistic vessel of the Last Supper. The cup was encased in gold, with two ancient silver auxiliary "grails," prepared in 1888 to do the sacred Grail Rites as had been done once each century by the order and its predecessors in the 88th year (88 being a mystical number in the Christian Kabbalah). The rite (a theurgical Eucharist) was performed with the understanding that it would reempower a channel for Divine Blessing upon the planet for the coming century and protect humanity from being overwhelmed by dark forces. However, in 1888, the elderly abbot of the order had some concern that the chalices would be stolen by people who wished to use them for less altruistic magical purposes.

The chalices were secretly transported to London, where the centennial ceremony was to be performed. However, in spite of all precautions, the three chalices were stolen and used for black magical purposes. When the primary chalice was eventually recovered, the gold was melted down, and the pottery cup smashed into the earth. (Later, one of the auxiliary chalices turned up at an antiquities auction in Antioch where it was purchased by the Metropolitan Museum in New York; it is now exhibited as the "Chalice of Antioch" with legends of it having been the **Holy Grail.** The third chalice was never found.)

The actual founding of the Temple of the Holy Grail as it presently exists began in the 1960s with the magical preparation undertaken by a solitary magician. He was not aware of the prior history of the destruction of the Grail and not formally connected with any traditional Grail order. However, through interior guidance, he was led over several years to construct a new chalice using white magical and theurgical preparations. Following that same guidance, in August of 1988 he traveled over 1,000 miles to a sacred site in Canada, where he used the new chalice for a theurgical Eucharist to bless the planet and humanity. Only after this event, which he performed quite unaware of its full implications, did he while returning home hear an interior voice naming him the "Grailmaster." He was unfamiliar with the term. Subsequently, he received teachings telepathically in lucid dreams from a Tibetan Lama that eventually became the First Empowerment of the First Order of THG. Shortly after this, he discovered a written account of the events of 1888. He then began to understand the impulse that led him to prepare the new vessel and conduct the 1988 centennial rite.

Soon after these events, Bishop George Boyer of the Sanctuary of the Gnosis in London contacted the new Grailmaster and transmitted to him all of the documents and information necessary to reestablish and preserve the esoteric European lineages deriving from the Grail tradition. The new Grailmaster subsequently brought forth new initiatory materials (by the process commonly called channeling) and led Bishop Boyer in undergoing them.

The new Grailmaster has also received the authority provided by both the traditional apostolic lineages passed through the Christian bishops over the centuries and newer lineages begun by bishops claiming ordination from occult realms. Various independent bishops have consecrated the new Grailmaster in 18 historical Apostolic and 22 European esoteric lineages. Additionally, the Grailmaster and Temple are Keepers of the True Grail, which is the Divine Royal Blood (San Greal in Christian esoteric tradition, and not to be confused with the Grail Chalice itself). For believers, the Grail is the normally invisible and intangible Divine sacrificial energy that nurtures evolutionary unfoldment in the physical universe and among beings developing in the physical level of existence. The Grail power sanctifies matter, and is identified with the Philosopher's Stone that transforms the lower into the Higher, expands contracted Heart-consciousness, and mediates inspiration, guidance, selfless service, and Divine Love.

The THG exists solely for a small number of individuals wishing to undertake private advanced esoteric training in order to anonymously serve human and planetary evolution. A relationship to the order is offered by invitation to people already ordained or otherwise advanced in recognized groups, or to individuals who, having prepared themselves apart from organizations, manifest a devotion to the spiritual unfoldment of humanity and of the planet. Members of the order proceed through the mysteries it perpetuates, the content of which is not disclosed to nonmembers, in an ordered sequence.

The Temple of the Holy Grail may be contacted through the Grailmaster at P.O. Box 3816, Santa Cruz, CA 95063-3816 or through Bishop George Boyer, Bishop Templar, 53 College Rd., Colliers Wood, London, UK SW19 2BP. Information on the temple may be found at its website: http://www.hometemple.org/.

Sources:

Temple of the Holy Grail. http://www.hometemple.org/. April 4, 2000.

Temple of the People

The Temple of the People formed out of the American **Theosophical Society** in Syracuse, New York, in 1898. The American Theosophists had broken with the international theosophical movement under **William Q. Judge,** who died just a few years later. Judge was succeeded by **Katherine Tingley,** who enjoyed strong but less than universal support. Members of the Syracuse lodge were among those who broke with Tingley and established the independent temple.

The Temple of the People was led by Dr. William H. Dower (1866–1937), known by members as "Red Star," and Francis A. LaDue (1849–1922), known as "Blue Star." The pair channeled the masters of the **Great White Brotherhood,** that group of advanced souls believed by Theosophists to guide the destiny of humankind. They had a special relationship to "Hilarion," the master of the fifth, or red, ray. The channeled sessions were published in the massive book *Theogenesis,* which came to be regarded as the third volume of Madame Blavatsky's magnum opus, *The Secret Doctrine,* Volume 1: *Anthropogenesis,* and Volume 2: *Cosmogenesis.*

Dower outlived LaDue as the leader of the temple and was succeeded by Pearl F. Dower and Harold Forgostein. When Forgostein died in 1990, he was succeeded by Eleanor Shumway, the present guardian-in-chief. The temple may be contacted at Box 7100, Halcyon, CA 93421. It has some 200 members worldwide.

Sources:

Kagan, Paul. *New World Utopias.* Baltimore, Md.: Penguin Books, 1975.

Teachings of the Temple. 3 vols. Halcyon, Calif.: Temple of the People, 1947–85.

Theogenesis. Halcyon, Calif.: Temple of the People, 1981.

Temple of Universal Law

The Temple of Universal Law is a Spiritualist church founded in 1936 by the Rev. Charlotte Bright. Bright was a medium whose spirit guide "Master Nicidemus" was considered to be a member of the **Great White Brotherhood,** that group of evolved disembodied entities who are believed to guide the destiny of the human race. Under the brotherhood's direction, Bright erected a church on Chicago's North Side in 1956. She pastored the church until her death in 1989, when she was succeeded by her son, Rev. Robert E. Martin. Before her death she oversaw the establishment of a second congregation in Wisconsin.

The temple affirms the beliefs of metaphysical Christianity, including a belief in a God who expresses himself as a Trinity; God the Father as the universal law of life that creates, sustains, and progresses to eternal life; Christ as the perfect demonstration of divine mind; the Holy Spirit as the action of divine mind within; the variety of forms of worship; the discovery of spiritual truth in the Bible and all spiritual truths; and the immortality of humans. The church teaches that it is the essential duty of people to look within and begin to awaken the Christ Spirit. As one comes to understand universal law, oneness with God can be attained.

Address: 5030 N. Drake, Chicago, IL 60625.

Tempon-teloris (Ship of the Dead)

Among the Dayaks of Borneo, the ship of the dead, the vessel that carried the souls of the departed in search of the hereafter, was generally represented in the shape of a bird, the hornbill (*rhinoplax vigil*). Accompanying the souls on their journey through the fire-sea were all the stores that had been laid out at the feast of the dead (*trivah*), and all the slaves who had been killed for that purpose. After some chain of events in the fiery sea, the ship of the dead, with Tempon-telon at the helm, reached the golden shores of the blessed.

Some of these beliefs echo the ancient burial rites of **Egypt** as portrayed in the **Book of the Dead.**

Tenaille, Jean (1882–1962)

Engineer who was active in the field of parapsychology. He was born on April 16, 1882, in Paris, France. He followed various occupations through his life: ranching in Canada, importing and managing a department store in Paris, and managing several industrial plants near Amiens, France (1931–39). After World War II he operated as an acoustical engineer. Toward the end of his life he wrote one important book, *Civilisation occidentale* (Western civilization, 1957), awarded the Académie Francaise prize for history in 1958. He contributed several articles to the French parapsychological journal *Revue Métapsychique,* including "A propos des sourciers" (Concerning dowsers, 1932). He died December 31, 1962.

Sources:

Pleasants, Helene, ed. *Biographical Dictionary of Parapsychology.* New York: Helix Press, 1964.

Tenhaeff, W(ilhelm) H(einrich) C(arl) (1894–1981)

Dutch parapsychologist, for some years director of the Parapsychology Institute of the State University of Utrecht, Netherlands (which he founded), now known as Parapsychological Division of the Psychological Laboratory. Tenhaeff was born on January 18, 1894, in Rotterdam, the Netherlands. He studied at the University of Utrecht (Ph.D. psychology, 1933). His doctoral thesis *Paragnosie en infuhlen* was the first on parapsychology in the Netherlands.

Tenhaeff had a long career as a respected parapsychologist. He was a lecturer on psychology (1932–53), lecturer on parapsychology (1933–53), professor of parapsychology, and director of the Parapsychology Institute, University of Utrecht (1953 on). He was founder (1928) and for many years editor (1928 on) of *Tijdschrift voor Parapsychologie,* the journal of the **Studievereniging voor Psychical Research** (the Dutch Society for Psychical Research). He served as secretary (1929–38) of the Dutch Society for Psychical Research prior to World War II and as an advisor afterward. In 1960 a number of leading parapsychologists withdrew from the society due to his autocratic disposition and established the rival **Netherlandse Vereniging voor Parapsychologie.**

Tenhaeff showed an interest in parapsychology from an early age, and conducted investigations and reported on psychometry, clairvoyance, precognition, unorthodox healing, the divining rod, and the structure of personality in sensitives. Through his career he lectured in many countries on parapsychological subjects, published numerous articles in *Tijdschrift voor Parapsychologie* and other journals, and wrote a number of books. In 1945 he commenced a long and detailed investigation of the clairvoyant **Gerard Croiset.** In the years after the 1960 break in the society, people began to look into his extraordinary claims for the psychic abilities of Croiset and discovered that he had been systematically doctoring data in his research. The **fraud** called his whole career into question. Because of his own popularity with the media and public, he was able to hold off the critics for some years, but eventually all of his colleagues acknowledged his fall. Tenhaeff died July 9, 1981, in the Netherlands; no major parapsychological journal carried an obituary.

Sources:

Berger, Arthur S., and Joyce Berger. *The Encyclopedia of Parapsychology and Psychical Research.* New York: Paragon House, 1991.

Hoebens, P. H. "Gerard Croiset and Professor Tenhaeff." In *Science Confronts the Paranormal.* Edited by Kenneth Frazier. Buffalo, N.Y.: Prometheus Books, 1986.

———. "Investigation of the Mozart of 'Psychic Sleuths.'" In *Science Confronts the Paranormal,* edited by Kenneth Frazier. Buffalo, N.Y.: Prometheus Books, 1986.

Tenhaeff, W. H. C. *Beknopte Handleiding der "Psychical Research"* (Short Textbook of Parapsychology). 3 vols. N.p., 1926.

———. *Beschouwingen over Het Gebruik van Paranognosten* (The Use of Sensitives for Police and Other Purposes). Utrecht: Erven J. Bijleveld, 1957.

———. *Telepathie en Helderziendheid.* English edition as *Telepathy and Clairvoyance.* C. Bertelsmann, 1962.

Tenskwatawa (1775–1836)

Tenskwatawa, a Native American prophet of the Shawnee people, was the brother of the famous war chief Tecumseh. He grew up in the shadow of his more famous brother, and was a somewhat alienated soul who did not take part in traditional male activities such as hunting and fishing. At some point he also lost the use of his right eye. He compensated for this physical defect by wearing jewelry from his pierced ears and nose. He did have some oratorical abilities.

He arose out of obscurity in the first decade of the nineteenth century as American settlers moved into traditional Shawnee territory in the Midwest. He had become a medicine man in his brother's tribe and claimed additional status as a prophet after being visited by the Great Spirit in a dream. The new settlers labeled him "The Prophet." People took him seriously after he successfully predicted a solar eclipse in 1806. Especially younger Shawnee were drawn to this new leader and his new religion. He told them to reject white culture and adhere to their traditional ways. He also urged them to follow his example and give up the use of alcohol.

The white settlers, however, were more interested in his broad message that North America was a land that was held in common by all the tribes. Hence, no particular Indian group had the right to sign away its territory to the U. S. Government. It was not theirs to give. Tecumseh accepted the idea and used it to build a confederation of tribes. Meanwhile, Tenskwatawa gathered his most dedicated followers and created a new village called Tippecanoe, at the point where the Wabash and Tippecanoe Rivers met. The settlers called it Prophet's Town. As the movement focused in Tenskwatawa grew, anxiety over Indian resistance to further settlement was focused on Prophet's Town.

In the fall of 1811, Tecumseh headed south to gather the support of additional tribes for his confederacy to resist further white encroachments. Indiana governor William Henry Harrison decided to seize the opportunity and remove the heart of the movement. He sent soldiers to Prophet's Town and in what came to be known as the Battle of Tippecanoe, destroyed the village. Though not a great battle, it was later used by Harrison in his quest for the American presidency. It also led to the downfall of Tenskwatawa. Former residents of Tippecanoe almost killed him, and his influence as a man of magical power and prophetic ability waned from that moment. However, the idea of the confederation of tribes was still very much alive the next year and was used by the British to enroll Indians as allies in the War of 1812.

After the war, Tenskwatawa lived in Canada on a British pension. He returned to the United States in 1926 and attempted to reassert his authority among a group of Shawnee who were being moved from Ohio and eventually settled in Kansas. He died there in 1836.

Sources:

Drake, Benjamin. *The Life of Tecumseh and of His Brother the Prophet.* 1841. Reprint, N.p., 1969.

Tephillin

In Hebrew, *tephillin* means "attachments." They were originally prayer thongs worn by Jews at morning prayer—one on the left arm and another on the head. They came to be regarded as **talismans** and were used in many traditional ceremonies. The **Talmud** states: "Whoever has the *tephillin* bound to his head and arm . . . is protected from sin."

Tephramancy

A mode of **divination** in which sacrificed victims from a fire are used.

Teraphim

These appear to have been ancient images of household gods. They were relatively small in size and easily carried. The teraphim were taken away from Jacob by his daughter Rachel (Gen. 31). They were probably seen as bringers of good luck. They are mentioned throughout the earlier record of Hebrew society, but beginning with the prophet Samuel (I Sam. 15:23) were condemned by association with sorcery and idolatry.

When Josiah conducted his reforms (II Kings. 23:24), the destruction of the teraphim was included among his actions. They were still being used, however, after the period of the Babylonian exile (Zech. 10:2).

Tesla, Nikola (1856–1943)

Eccentric scientific genius whose inventions in the field of electrical apparatus stemmed from inspirations received in extraordinary visions of a paranormal character. Unlike most innovators in the fields of engineering and electricity, his inventions did not require patient experiment and trial-and-error testing of models. The ideas flashed into his mind as working units, complete to the final details of component design and size. For example, as a young student of electrical engineering and physics, at a time when the concept of alternating current was considered a fallacy of the perpetual motion type, he knew that he could solve this problem. After only a few years of consideration of the problem, the complete detailed vision of an alternating current motor using a rotating magnetic field came to him while he gazed at a sunset.

He was born in July 10, 1856, in the village of Similjan in the Austro-Hungarian border area of Lika (now in Slovenia). Even as a boy, he was inventive; at the age of nine he constructed a 16-bug power motor by harnessing June bugs to a thin wooden wheel. He was educated at an elementary school, then had four years at Lower Realschule, Gospic, Lika, which was followed by three years at the Higher Realschule, Carlstadt, Croatia. He graduated in 1873. Tesla was a student for four years at the Polytechnic School, Gratz, Austria, studying mathematics, physics, and mechanics. Afterward he enrolled in philosophy studies for two years at the University of Prague, Bohemia (now the capital of the Czech Republic).

He commenced his career as an inventor in Budapest, Hungary, in 1881. There he constructed a telephone repeater and engaged in various branches of engineering and manufacture. In 1884 he immigrated to the United States, later becoming a naturalized citizen. For nearly a year he worked for inventor Thomas A. Edison, who was impressed by his skill and hard work, but the two men were diametrically opposed in temperament and method. Tesla was a visionary who solved problems in a flash of insight, whereas Edison relied on patient trial-and-error in practical experiments. Tesla insisted on the superiority of alternating current and its applications, whereas Edison believed it a dead end and championed direct current. Tesla parted company with Edison after being promised $50,000 for improving the design and efficiency of dynamos. When Tesla solved the problem and asked for the money, Edison said he was only joking. Tesla immediately resigned.

His salary at the Edison Company had been modest. For the next two years he had a difficult time, but in 1887 he was backed to form the Tesla Electric Company in New York. He was now able to construct the alternating current machines he had visualized earlier.

The Tesla system made it possible to supply electricity economically over distances of hundreds of miles, instead of the short distances of the Edison direct current powerhouses. Tesla's demonstrations made a great impression on another inventor, George Westinghouse of the Westinghouse Electric Company of Pittsburgh. Westinghouse paid Tesla $1 million for rights on his alternating current system, comprising some 40 patents, with a contract additionally stipulating a royalty of a dollar per horsepower.

In attempting to span the continent with an alternating current system, Westinghouse ran into financial difficulties; his own backers insisted that he renounce his royalty contract to Tesla, otherwise they would withdraw support. When Westinghouse explained his difficulty to Tesla, Tesla recalled how Westinghouse had believed in him. In a magnanimous gesture Tesla tore up his contract, thereby sacrificing some $12 million in unpaid royalties.

Tesla went on to invent new apparatus involving original principles. He was responsible for many important innovations: the system of electricity conversion and distribution by oscillatory dischargers, generators of high frequency current; the Tesla coil or transformer, a system of wireless transmission of intelligence; mechanical oscillators and generators of electrical oscillation; research and discoveries in radiation, material streams, and emanations; and high-potential magnifying transmitting. One of his most spectacular achievements was harnessing the water power of Niagara Falls. In 1895 the Westinghouse Electric Company installed a gigantic hydroelectric project, using the Tesla polyphase system of alternating current.

Tesla opened up many important avenues of scientific development and has rarely been properly acknowledged by later historians. His experiments with electromagnetic waves formed the basis of the development of radio. He stated that cosmic rays were responsible for the radioactivity of radium, thorium, and uranium and predicted that other substances would be made radioactive by bombardment. He thus anticipated the basic principles of X-ray apparatus and the electron microscope. In his work with wireless controlled automata he anticipated radio-controlled rocket missiles.

Not surprisingly, he had one or two blind spots. He did not accept for many years that atomic fission would produce energy. He misunderstood the mechanism of vision; he believed that visual images perceived by the brain were returned to the retina of the eye, and might be amplified or projected. However, there was no mistaking his own extraordinary visionary faculty and the discoveries associated with it. In an article titled "Making Your Imagination Work For You," he wrote:

"During my boyhood I had suffered from a peculiar affliction due to the appearance of images, which were often accompanied by strong flashes of light. . . . Then I began to take mental excursions beyond the small world of my actual knowledge. Day and night, in imagination, I went on journeys—saw new places, cities, countries, and all the time I tried hard to make these imaginary things very sharp and clear in my mind.

"This I did constantly until I was 17, when my thoughts turned seriously to invention. Then, to my delight, I found I could *visualize* with the greatest facility. I needed no models, drawings, or experiments. I could picture them all in my head.

"Here, in brief, is my own method: After experiencing a desire to invent a particular thing, I may go on for months or years with the idea in the back of my head. Whenever I feel like it, I roam around in my imagination and think about the problem without any deliberate concentration. This is a period of incubation.

"There follows a period of direct effort. I choose carefully the possible solutions of the problem I am considering, and gradually center my mind on a narrowed field of investigation. Now, when I am deliberately thinking of the problem in its specific features, I may begin to feel that I am going to get the solution. And the wonderful thing is, that if I do feel this way, *then I know I have really solved the problem and shall get what I am after.*

"The feeling is as convincing to me as though I already had solved it. I have come to the conclusion that at this stage the actual solution is in my mind *subconsciously,* though it may be a long time before I am aware of it *consciously.*

"Before I put a sketch on paper, the whole idea is worked out mentally. In my mind I change the construction, make improvements, and even operate the device. Without ever having drawn a sketch I can give the measurements of all parts to workmen, and when completed all these parts will fit, just as certainly as though I had made the actual drawings. It is immaterial to me whether I run my machine in my mind or test it in my shop.

"The inventions I have conceived in this way have always worked. In 30 years there has not been a single exception. My first electric motor, the vacuum tube wireless light, my turbine engine and many other devices have all been developed in exactly this way."

Tesla's friend and biographer John J. O'Neill stated that Tesla "was unquestionably an abnormal individual, and of a type that does have what are known as 'psychic experiences.' He was emphatic in his denial that he ever had experiences of that sort; yet he has related incidents that clearly belong in the psychic category." According to O'Neill, Tesla was fearful that admitting to having psychic experiences might cause him to be misunderstood as supporting **Spiritualism** or theories that something operates in life other than matter and energy.

In his later years, Tesla suffered financial difficulties and was unable to construct some of his most ambitious inventions. He claimed he had discovered an inexhaustible source of energy that could be transmitted anywhere in the world without wires or loss of power. He correctly foresaw that at some future time "it will be possible for nations to fight without armies, ships, or guns by weapons far more terrible, to the destructive action and range of which there is virtually no limit." Tesla is credited with having discovered a protective radiation principle of the kind popularly termed "death ray."

In 1912 he refused the Nobel Prize because it was to be awarded jointly to himself and Thomas A. Edison; instead the award went to the Swedish scientist Gustav Dalen.

In an unpublished article entitled "Man's Greatest Achievement" (cited in O'Neill's biographical *Prodigal Genius,* 1968), Telsa writes:

"Long ago he [the human being] recognized that all perceptible matter comes from a primary substance, or tenuity beyond conception, filling all space, the Akasa or luminiferous ether, which is acted upon by the life-giving Prana or creative force, calling into existence, in never ending cycles, all things and phenomena. . ."

This is the language of Theosophy or Hindu metaphysics. Tesla's states of higher consciousness, achieved by intense concentration and a celibate life, resemble Hindu concepts of cosmic energy in the universe, aroused in the human body under the name of **kundalini** through **yoga** disciplines and **meditation,** resulting in expanded consciousness and access to an infinity of cosmic intelligence.

Tesla died in poverty in New York on January 7, 1943. Soon afterward, FBI operatives opened the safe in his room and took away papers reputedly containing details of a secret invention of possible value in warfare.

Sources:

O'Neill, John J. *Prodigal Genius: The Life of Nikola Tesla.* London: Neville Spearman, 1968. Reprint, London: Granada, 1980.

Peat, David. *In Search of Nikola Tesla.* Bath, England: Ashgrove Press, 1983.

Tesla, Nikola. "Making Your Imagination Work For You." *American Magazine* (April 1921).

Wilson, Colin, ed. *Men of Mystery.* London: W. H. Allen, 1977.

Tetford, William N. (1923–1988)

William N. Tetford, a psychologist and transcriber of the channeled work *A Course in Miracles,* was born in Chicago, Illinois, into a Christian Science family. In 1931, following his older sister's death, the family disassociated themselves from Christian Science and Tetford was raised from that time in a largely secular environment. Several years later he became ill with scarlet fever, and though he survived, he was bedridden for two years with the complications. Tutored during his recovery, once back in school he soon caught up with his classmates and graduated from high school with honors.

He attended DePauw University in Indiana, where he majored in psychology. He graduated in 1944, at the height of World War II (1939–45). Deferred from military action because of his medical record, he took a position at the University of Chicago supervising the buildings at which the atom bomb research was being conducted. The week after the detonation of the first bomb in Japan, understanding the full nature of the project, he resigned.

He returned to psychology by taking a course with Carl Rogers, then on his way to psychological fame with what was termed client-centered therapy, a new form of psychotherapy that allowed the analysis to arise from the patient's growing self-understanding rather than from the more common analysis offered by Freudian systems. He went on to complete his Ph.D. at the University of Chicago in 1949. He held several positions through the 1950s before becoming the director of the Psychology Department at Columbia-Presbyterian Medical Center in New York City in 1958. Within a few weeks, another person with whom he was to be intimately related also joined the staff, **Helen Schucman,** who had just graduated from New York University.

Tetford and Schucman were very different personalities, and their relationship was sporadically filled with anger and hostility. However, in 1965, Tetford suggested that they work on their relationship and attempt to change it. He had been reading metaphysical literature from which he offered the discipline of meditation as a tool to assist them. They began meditating and Schucman began to receive a series of vivid images. Tetford encouraged her to keep a record of whatever she received. However, on October 21, 1965, she heard a voice say to her, "This is a course in miracles. Please take notes." Tetford encouraged her to continue to record what she heard. Schucman recorded what she heard in shorthand. She read it to Tetford, who turned it into typescript.

The result of their collaboration over the next seven years was *A Course in Miracles* (ACIM). During this period, Schucman frequently expressed trepidation over her **channeling** work, but Tetford continually calmed her fears and doubts. It was published in 1975. Tetford, a quiet, somewhat passive man, was uncomfortable being in the public eye and allowed others to operate out front on the dissemination of the books and their teachings. In 1978 he moved to Tiburon, California, where the Foundation for Inner Peace, the corporation assigned the task of publishing the *Course,* had relocated. There he lived a quiet existence using much of his time trying to make the teachings on self-forgiveness real in his life. In 1986, he moved to LaJolla, California, and resided there for the last two years of his life. In the years since his death, his essential role in bringing forth *A Course in Miracles* has been widely recognized.

Sources:

A Course in Miracles. 3 vols. New York: Foundation for Inner Peace, 1975.

Miller, D. Patrick. *The Complete Story of the Course: The History, The People and the Controversies Behind A Course in Miracles.* Berkeley, Calif.: Fearless Books, 1997.

Skutch, Judith. "A Course in Miracles, the Untold Story." Parts 1 & 2. *New Realities* 4, no. 1, 2 (August, September/October 1984): 17–27; 8–15, 78.

Wapnick, Kenneth. *Absence of Felicity: The Story of Helen Schucman and Her Scribing of A Course in Miracles.* Roscoe, N.Y.: Foundation for "A Course in Miracles," 1991.

Teutons

Little can be gleaned from the writings of classical authors on the subject, but manuscripts of the Middle Ages by such writers as Snorri Sturluson and Saemund Sigfússon (The *Eddas*) and Saxo Grammaticus, and such epics or pseudohistories as *The Nibelungenlied,* shed some light on Teutonic magic practice and beliefs.

From these writers one can arrive at several basic conclusions: (1) that **magic** with the Teutons was nonhierophantic, and was not the province of the priesthood, as with the Celtic Druids, for example; (2) that women were its chief conservators; and (3) that it principally resided in the study and elucidation of the runic script. In the same manner as in early **Egypt** it was part and parcel of the ability to decipher the hieroglyphic characters.

It seems that all kinds of people dabbled in the practice of magic, and, to a great extent, **sorcery** was principally the province of women. Perhaps only those who could read the **runes**—that is, those who could read at all—were able to undertake the study of the **occult,** and therefore the unlettered warrior too restless to study was barred from all participation in the subject.

Women in all ranks of life seem to have been addicted to the practice of sorcery, from the queen on the throne to the wise-woman or witch dwelling apart from the community. Thus the mother-in-law of Siegfried bewitches him by a draught, and scores of similar stories could be imagined.

Generally ancient Teutonic magic was not very high; it was greatly hampered by human considerations and much at the mercy of the human element on which it acted and the very human desires that called it forth. In many cases it was rendered useless merely by the cunning of the object upon which it was wreaked. It does not seem to have risen very much above the type of sorcery in vogue among primitive peoples in modern times. It is surprising, with all these weaknesses, how powerful a hold sorcery had upon the popular imagination, which was literally drenched with belief in the supernatural.

Runes

In its various forms—German *rune,* Anglo-Saxon *run,* Icelandic *run*—the word is derived from an old Low German word *raunen* (to cut or to carve), since the runes in ancient times were invariably carved instead of written. It later came to designate the characters themselves.

Comparatively few people were able to decipher the runes, and the elucidation was left to the curious, the ambitious among the females, and the leisured few in general, perhaps including priests and lawmen. Consequently the power to decipher runes was a mysterious gift venerated among ordinary people who believed that the ability to elucidate them meant the reader possessed magic powers. The possessors of this ability maximized it so the belief in their prowess would flourish. A certain amount of patience and natural ability were necessary for mastery of such an intricate script, and the tradition that they were connected with sorcery lingered long in some parts of Iceland.

In later times the word *runes* came to be applied to all the alphabetical systems employed by the Teutonic peoples before the introduction of Christianity. Their origin is obscure; some authorities deny that it is Teutonic and assert that the runes are merely a transformation or adaptation of Greek characters, others that they have a Phoenician or even cuneiform origin.

That they are of non-Teutonic origin is inferred from their strong resemblance to other scripts. It has also been argued that it was unlikely that they could have been invented by the Teutonic race given their state of organization and learning at the time the runes first came into general use.

Runes have been divided into three systems—English, German, and Scandinavian—but the difference between these is merely local. They were not employed in early times for literary purposes, but for inscriptions only. Runes were usually found on stone monuments, weapons, implements, and personal ornaments and furniture. In England, runic inscriptions are found in the north only, where Scandinavian influence was strongest.

The first symbols of the runic alphabet are for the letters *f, ú, th, ó, r,* and *c.* For this reason the order of the runic letters is not called an alphabet but a *futhorc.* The system is symbolic. Thus the first letter pictures the head and horns of an ox, and is called *feoh* after that animal; the second is called *ur,* the word for bull; the third, *thoru* (tree), then *os* (door); *rad* (saddle); and *caen* (torch). The runes were probably derived or evolved from a purely pictorial system in which the figures of the animals or objects stood for the letters of the alphabet.

Since runes were carved, some connection may be possible between the Anglo-Saxon *secgan* (to say), and the Latin word *secare* (to cut), especially since secret signatures were made by merely cutting a chip from a bark manuscript. The old meaning of the word spell was "thin chip or shaving." The Roman historian Tacitus mentioned that in Teutonic **divination,** a rod cut from a fruit-bearing tree was cut into slips, and the slips, having marks on them, were thrown onto a white garment to be taken up with prayer to the gods and interpreted as they were taken. A special use of light cuttings for such fateful cross-readings, or "Virgilian lots," may have given the word spells its particular association with the words of the magician.

Belief in Nature Spirits

Among the lesser figures of mythology who were believed to have direct contact with ancient Teutonic peoples and assist them, or were connected with them in the practice of magic, were the *duergar,* or dwarfs, trolls, undines, nixies, and other spirits. Belief in them was distinctly animistic. The people believed that dwarfs and trolls inhabited the recesses of the mountains, caves, and the underworld. Nixies and undines were said to dwell in the lakes, rivers, pools, and inlets of the sea. In general these were friendly to humans, but objected to more than occasional intercourse with them.

Although not of the class of supernatural beings who obeyed humans in answer to magical summonses, these, especially the dwarfs, often acted as instructors in the arts of magic. Many instances of this are found in tales and romances of early Teutonic origin.

The dwarfs were usually assisted by adventitious aids in their practice of magic, such as belts that endowed the wearer with strength (like that worn by the dwarf **"Laurin"**), shoes for swiftness (analogous to the seven-league boots of folk tale), caps of invisibility, and so forth.

Witchcraft

Witchcraft was much more in favor among the northern Teutons than it was in Germany, and this circumstance has been attributed to their proximity to the Finns, a race notorious for its propensities toward magic. In Norway, Orkney, and Shetland, the practice of sorcery seems to have been almost exclusively in the hands of Finnish women. There is little doubt that the Finns exercised upon the Teutons of Scandinavia the mythic influence of a conquered race; that is, they took full advantage of the terror inspired in their conquerors by an alien and unfamiliar religion and ritual in which magic was an integral element.

The principal activities of Teutonic witchcraft were the raising of storms, the selling of pieces of knotted rope (each knot representing a wind), divination and prophecy, and acquiring invisibility. Since the sea was the element of the people, it became the chief element of the witch of the northern Teutons. Thus in the saga of *Frithjof,* the two sea witches Heyde and Ham ride the storm and are sent by Helgi to raise the tempest that will drown Frithjof. They take the shapes of a bear and a storm-eagle. In the saga of *Grettir the Strong,* a witch-wife, Thurid, sends adrift a magic log that comes to Grettir's island. The log leads to his downfall.

In the north of Scotland, the Teutonic and Celtic systems of magic may be said to have met and fused, but not to have clashed, since their many points of resemblance outweighed their differences.

Animal transformation also played a considerable part in Teutonic magic and witchcraft. In early Germany the witch (*hexe*) seems to have also acquired the characteristics of a **vampire.**

Second Sight

The Teutons seem to have excelled in prophecy and divination; the practice was more widespread among the northern Teutons than the southern. Prophetic utterance was usually induced by ecstasy, but it was not the professional diviner alone who was capable of supernatural vision. Anyone under stress of excitement, and particularly if near death, might become fey (prophetic), and great attention was invariably paid to utterances made while the person was in this condition. (See also **Holland** and **Germany**)

Sources:

Berger, H. A. *Nordische Mythologie.* Zittau & Leipzig, Germany, 1834.

Bugge, E. S. *The Home of the Eddic Poems.* London: David Nutt, 1899.

Elliott, Ralph W. *Runes: An Introduction.* New York: Barnes & Noble, 1971. Reprint, Greenwood Press, 1981.

Golther, W. *Religion und Mythus der Germanen.* Leipzig, 1909.

Grimm, Jacob. *Teutonic Mythology.* 4 vols. London: G. Bell, 1880–1919.

Kauffmann, D. F. *Northern Mythology.* London: Dent, 1903.

Meyer, E. H. *Germanische Mythologie.* Berlin, 1891.

Stephens, George. *The Old-Northern Runic Monuments of Scandinavia and England.* 2 vols. London, 1866–68.

———. *Prof. S. Bugge's "Studies on Northern Mythology" Shortly Examined.* London: Williams & Norgate, 1883.

Wilken, Ernst. *Die Prosaische Edda.* Paderhorn, Germany, 1878.

Texas Monthly UFO Report

A former periodical concerned with the technical aspect of **UFO** investigation for individuals with some scientific background. It also included reports on parapsychological research. It was published at the Texas Scientific Research Center for UFO Studies in Waco.

Thackeray, William Makepeace (1811–1863)

This noted novelist was introduced to the phenomena of **Spiritualism** during a lecture tour in the United States, when he attended a séance with the famous medium **D. D. Home.** He also observed the rapping phenomena of Ann (Leah) Underhill, one of the **Fox sisters.** His sympathetic reaction was described in Underhill's book *The Missing Link in Modern Spiritualism* (1885). This experience and subsequent observations with Home led Thackeray to endorse the sincerity of the anonymous account (written by Robert Bell) "Stranger Than Fiction." It was published in the *Cornhill Magazine* and edited by Thackeray. He was severely criticized for this apparent endorsement of Spiritualism.

However, it seems that, in fact, his attitude was somewhat ambiguous. In a letter to his friends Mrs. Thomas F. Elliot and Kate Perry, he states:

"Yes I have seen the Rappers, and the table moving, and heard the Spirits. The moving of tables is undoubted, the noises and knocks (continual raps following the person who has the gift of eliciting them) some natural unexplained phenomenon but the Spirits is of course dire humbug and imposture. They try to guess at something and hit or miss as may be. 1000 misses for one hit—It is a most dreary and foolish superstition. . . . But the physical manifestations are undoubted—Tables moving lifted up and men even lifted off the ground to the ceiling so some are ready to swear—but though I do not believe in this until I see it; I wouldn't have believed in a table turning 3 weeks ago—and that I have seen and swear to. . . ."

Both Thackeray and his friend **Charles Dickens** had the highest regard for **John Elliotson,** a pioneer of **mesmerism** who was later converted to Spiritualism after initial skepticism. Thackeray based his character "Dr. Goodenough" in *Pendennis* and *The Newcomes* on Elliotson, and dedicated the former novel to him.

Sources:

Goldfarb, Russell M., and Clare R. Goldfarb. *Spiritualism and Nineteenth-Century Letters.* New Brunswick, N.J.: Associated University Presses, 1978.

Underhill, A. Leah. *The Missing Link in Modern Spiritualism.* New York: Thomas R. Knox, 1885. Reprint, New York: Arno Press, 1976.

Thanatology

The formal study of the nature of **death** and dying. Prior to the demarkation of thanatology as a new area of specialization, the study of various aspects of death had been included in psychology and parapsychology. Parapsychological research has concentrated on three human experiences that seem to be part of the death experience: 1) the sensation of floating out of the body; 2) feelings of peace or wholeness; and 3) meetings with someone who has died previously. Studies of what today is called the **near-death experience** have been made by psychical researchers since the nineteenth century, often under the label death-bed experiences.

Significant in defining the new field of thanatology has been the work of physician **Elisabeth Kübler-Ross,** author of the book *On Death and Dying* (1970), whose work began with a concern for the grief process she frequently encountered in counseling with dying patients. Her continued interest led her to questions of survival of death, traditionally an area of psychical studies. She is the founder of **Shanti Nilaya,** a healing and growth center in Virginia. Among the leading centers focused on research in thanatology are the **International Institute for the Study of Death** in Florida and the **International Association for Near-Death Studies.**

Sources:

Kastenbaum, Robert, ed. *Between Life and Death.* New York: Springer Publishing, 1979.

Kübler-Ross, Elisabeth. *On Death and Dying.* New York: Macmillan Co., 1969.

———. *To Live Until We Say Goodbye.* Englewood Cilffs, N.J.: Prentice-Hall, 1978.

Osis, Karlis, and Erlendur Haraldsson. *At the Hour of Death.* New York: Avon Books, 1977.

Ring, Kenneth. *Heading Toward Omega—In Search of the Meaning of the Near-Death Experience.* New York: William Morrow, 1984.

Thau Weza

Burmese wizards, literally "wire-man who works in wire." (See also **Myanmar**)

Thayer, M(ary) B(aker) (ca. 1887)

Well-known professional **apport** and **slate-writing** medium of Boston, who chiefly produced flowers and fruits, sometimes live birds. In the *Banner of Light* (1875) there is an account of a canary apport in answer to a mental request. In the report of the **Seybert Commission,** a slate-writing séance attended by one Professor Fullerton was considered a failure. There was a description of another séance, at which 30 people were present. The Seybert Commission was represented by Drs. Koenig and Leidy.

According to the Leidy's account:

". . . sounds were heard of objects dropping on the table, and from time to time matches were lit and exposed, strewn before the company, cut plants and flowers. These were all of the kind sold at this season by the florists, consisting of a pine bough, fronds of ferns, roses, pinks, tulips, lilies, callas and smilax. At one time there fell on the table a heavy body, which proved to be a living terrapin, at another time there appeared a pigeon which flew about the room. . . . The proprietor of the house declared that the flowers and the other objects brought to view in the séance were not previously in the room, and their appearance could not be explained unless through spiritual agency."

In a footnote to his translation of Adolphe d'Assier's book *Posthumous Humanity* (1887) **Henry S. Olcott** writes:

"While she [Mrs. Thayer] was enclosed in a large bag, sealed closely at her neck, and all possibility of trickery guarded against, I have seen a long table, quite covered with vines, plants and flowers, dropped out of space. I marked a certain leaf of a rare plant in the garden without her knowledge, and the same evening, in response to my mental request, it dropped upon the back of my hand, with which I was at the moment holding the medium's two hands. The above occurred in the dark; but once a tree branch was brought me in full daylight, through her mediumship, in the house of a gentleman whose guest I was."

Due to the nature of her work with apports and slate writing and the fact that her only support came from people such as Olcott, who was never known for his critical approach to such phenomena, Thayer is considered likely to be one of the fraudulent mediums of the era.

Thee Satanic Church

Thee Satanic Church was a small Satanic organization in Chicago during the 1970s. It was formed in 1974 as a breakaway group of **Thee Satanic Church of the Nethilum Rite.** Evelyn Paglini, one of the original founders of the Nethilum Rite group, established Thee Satanic Church, opened an occult book store in Chicago, and began the periodical *Psychic Standard.* The group gradually dropped their Satanic elements, the *Psychic Standard* ceased publication in 1980, and shortly afterwards the church was dissolved.

Thee Satanic Church of the Nethilum Rite

Thee Satanic Church of the Nethilum Rite was founded around 1970 in Chicago by High Priest Terry Taylor and Evelyn Paglini and went public in 1971. The church opposed the Satanisn of **Anton S. LaVey** and the **Church of Satan,** founded in 1966, contending that LaVey did not believe in the actual existence of Satan. In contrast, the Nethilum Rite church taught that Satan was the epitome of God's creation who possessed all of the power and knowledge of the universe. Members of the church sought to acquire as much of Satan's knowledge and power as possible. Magical rituals and psychic development were the primary tools for accessing Satan.

By 1973 the church claimed 538 members. It split in 1974 when Paglini led a group out of the church and founded a rival organization, **Thee Satanic Church.** The Nethilum Rite church ceased to exist in the mid-1970s.

Thee Temple ov Psychick Youth (TOPY)

Thee Temple ov Psychick Youth (TOPY) grew out of the magical philosophical thought of rock musician Genesis P. Orridge, formerly with the band Throbbing Gristle. He wished to explore the possibilities of human potential and saw performance art as a fruitful means for his work. In 1981 he started a new band, Psychic TV, and TOPY. He soon reached the conclusion that humans possessed an infinite potential and were limited only by the restraints imposed upon it. That idea brought him close to one of the major tenets espoused in *The Book of the Law,* the Thelemic magical text that had been received by **Aleister Crowley** in 1904, "The word of sin is restriction." Orridge also began to identify what he was doing with magic.

Orridge identified the human problem as the narrowing of choice by society and the movement of most people into a sleep-like state in which they lose awareness of their vast potential. He believes that religion and politics are vast systems that operate to put people to sleep. Temple members are those who have begun to awaken to their potential and are attempting to explore it even as they become more aware. A first step is coming to grips with one's mortality. Members also seek to discover their True Will (a basic concept of Thelemic Magic) and generally accept the basic Thelemic notion, "Do What thou Will shall be the whole of the Law." TOPY has generally prescribed an intuitive approach to life rather than the following of rules, laws, and regulations.

Integral to living intuitively is sexual expression, which should follow one's wants and desires rather than social mores, according to TOPY. Correlatively, sexual magic is the single best tool for raising the energy need for liberation. TOPY has matured into a ritual magic group that espouses all of the traditional teachings of magic, though in a most modern fashion. Unlike traditional magical orders, there is no initiatory grading system, hierarchical organization, or secret rituals. TOPY is organized as a fellowship of equals with various complementary talents and abilities.

Its egalitarian stance and the constant striving of members to expand their individual potential has contributed to TOPY's instability as an organization. On several occasions it has been reported defunct. However, at least in a minimal way, it has survived. The TOPY North American headquarters is at P.O. Box 1212521, Tacoma, WA 98411-1521. It has a website at http://www.uncarved.demon.co.uk/topy/htm.

Sources:

Burton, Tina. *"Intuitive Magick?": A Study of the Temple ov Psychick Youth, 1981–1989.* Unpublished paper in the American Religions Collection, Davidson Library, University of California—Santa Barbara, 1989.

An Introduction to Thee Temple ov Psychick Youth. Brighton, Sussex, UK: Temple Press Limited, 1989.

Theobald, Morell (1828–1908)

British Spiritualist and author of *Spiritualism at Home* (1884) and *Spirit Workers in the Home Circle* (1887), the latter describing a series of curious psychic manifestations in his home that lasted for many years.

Some of Theobald's family members reportedly possessed psychic gifts—his grandfather and father saw spirits. His own friendship with the author **William Howitt** and family initiated him into writing and mediumship in 1855. The psychic ties were further strengthened by intimacy with Mr. and **Mrs. Thomas Everitt,** and the two families held séances together for many years. Not surprisingly, the loss of three children increased the receptivity of the Theobald family. A sitting following their death led to **rapping** phenomena, which, in the presence of three living children, developed into movements of a heavy dining table and, eventually, intelligent communications.

The book by Theobald's sister titled *Heaven Opened; or, Messages for the Bereaved from Their Little Ones in Glory* (1870) contains records of these experiences. The contact with the beyond was, at this period, threefold—the elder boy fell into **trance** and was controlled by the deceased children and others; Theobald and his wife wrote automatically; and Mrs. Everitt produced **direct voice** manifestations for the family.

The strange phenomena of later years were first heralded during a joint excursion with the Everitt family to Cornwall in 1871. To quote from *Spirit Workers in the Home Circle:*

"As we sat on woodland slopes we had the curious sensations of rapping beneath the solid earth on which we sat. If we took a basket of sandwiches, that was moved about by our sportive invisible friends. At an inn where we stayed with our hamper of provisions we expected the waiter would be scared, for raps resounded on the window, walls and wainscoted panelling, while our hamper was bodily taken off by invisible hands into one corner of the room and there opened and partly unpacked for us."

In 1882 Mary, a new cook, was discovered to have clairvoyant powers. When Tom, the youngest son, complained that his hair was being pulled by invisible beings, Mary saw and described the phantom visitors. Because of her gifts Mary was soon advanced to the standing of a trusted friend of the family. After the maid left, Nellie Theobald and Mary occupied the same bedroom and looked jointly after the household duties.

Morell Theobald employed many tests to verify strange occurrences in the house; he often got up in the middle of the night in an attempt to catch the perpetrators in the act, but he was unsuccessful.

For some time, Theobald resisted every request of competent psychic investigators to take Mary to their own rooms for investigation. In this resolve he was strangely strengthened by spirit advice in **direct writing.** The limited investigation of **Frank Podmore** and Frank S. Hughes of the **Society for Psychical Research** (SPR) was finally allowed to continue in the Theobald home in 1884, and cast considerable doubt on many of the marvelous occurrences, especially on the spirit writings, which appeared in every conceivable place—on the ceiling, on the walls, on locked drawers and receptacles, on marked papers, and came in many languages: old French, Latin, Hebrew, Greek, and Raratongan, among others.

The SPR investigators were never able to witness the actual performance of the various phenomena and found many circumstances that suggested human origin in the spirit writings. The letters were regularly formed and of normal size when they appeared in places accessible to persons of ordinary stature but became straggling and irregular on higher places as if they had been written with a broomstick with a pencil attached. The locked secretaire in which writing was produced was not **fraud**-proof. A piece of paper could easily be slipped in through a crack.

The investigators also contended that the small characters in certain pieces of spirit writing could have been written by anybody with a sharp pencil and patient practice. They found many crude mistakes in the Latin and Greek scripts and discovered finally the facts contained in the communications coming from "Saadi" had been published in an article, "Persian Poetry in the Past" in Part 6 of *Chamber's Repository of Instructive and Amusing Tracts.* It also appeared that "Wamik," who claimed to have been "Saadi's" friend and contemporary poet, was a fictitious entity, the imaginary hero of the poem to which he subscribed his name. In the end it appeared that Mary was the mundane source of much if not all of the phenomena.

The findings of the two investigators were strongly criticized in *Light* (January, February, and March 1885). The editor concluded that the investigation was incomplete and hasty and that fraud could not explain the extraordinarily varied phenomena of the Theobald house.

Morell Theobald admitted that "many of the writings . . . are comparatively feeble compositions" and that he had found the source of the most puzzling pieces of direct writing (i.e., the Lord's Prayer as used in the twelfth century and the Rarantongan Script) in a volume he had given Mary as a Christmas present. He refused to seek a normal explanation to the diversified styles of handwriting, even when the scripts were handed out by Mary herself from the cabinet in which she sat to develop materializations.

There was no better evidence for deep-rooted unshakable faith than Theobald's account of the test undertaken on behalf of the SPR in 1886. He was handed two sealed envelopes by E. T. Bennett, assistant secretary of the SPR, in order to have the hidden contents deciphered by spirit agency. After some weeks, writing was obtained on the outside of the envelopes that proved to be a fairly good counterpart of the inside. Theobald was then handed a third envelope, which was in his careful keeping for some months, according to him "no one in the house besides myself and my wife knowing of its existence."

Again the contents were revealed, but instead of triumph, a very painful accusation was made against the Theobald family: the SPR claimed that all the envelopes had been opened and gummed up again. To make matters worse, the handwriting on all three was identical in character with the well-known scripts.

Theobald believed mischievous and fraudulent spirits had spoiled the tests. He said that the family had broken the essential condition of trust and thereby had opened the door to such evil influences. This conviction of Theobald's was apparently borne out by psychometric readings of the envelopes through a clairvoyant and by many mediumistic communications. One of the readings was obtained through the mediumship of **William Eglinton,** who was on more than one occasion caught in mediumistic fraud. It is a very legitimate inference that the atmosphere of blind faith that pervaded the Theobald family had allowed serious deception.

Sources:

"Alleged 'Physical Phenomena' in the Family of Morell Theobald." *Journal* of the Society for Psychical Research 2 (1886).

Podmore, Frank. *Modern Spiritualism.* London: Methuen, 1902. Reprinted as *Mediums of the Nineteenth Century.* New Hyde Park, N.Y.: University Books, 1963.

"Theologus"

One of the spirit controls of **William Stainton Moses,** "Theologus" was said to be St. John the Divine.

Theomancy

The aspect of the study of the **Kabala** that deals with the mysteries of divine majesty and seeks the sacred names. He (and only males over 40 could engage in this study) who possessed this knowledge knew the future, commanded nature, had full power over angels and demons, and could perform miracles.

The Hasidic masters (*zaddik*) claimed that it was by this means that Moses performed so many marvels; that Joshua was able to stop the sun; that Elias caused fire to fall from heaven and raised the dead; that Daniel closed the mouths of the lions; and that the three youths were not consumed in the furnace. Even today, the leaders of some Hasidic groups are reputed to have mastered at least part of this material and are known for their miracle-working abilities.

Sources:

Dresner, Samuel H. *The Zaddik.* New York: Schrocken Books, 1974.

Rabinowitz, H. *A Guide to Hassidism.* New York: Thomas Yoseloff, 1960.

Theon, M(ax) (1850–1927)

Max Theon, the enigmatic occultist whose work initiated the **Hermetic Brotherhood of Luxor** in the mid-1880s, was born Louis Maximilian Bimstein into a Jewish family in Poland. He appears to have first received knowledge of the occult world in the thriving Hassidic communities of his homeland. As a young man he began to travel the world, but in 1873 settled in England at Saint John's Wood, in the northern section of London. He made his living as a psychic healer and advertised himself in the Spiritual periodicals as able to cure cholera.

In 1882 he began to work with a young Scotsman named Thomas Dalton (1855–1895), later known under his pseudonym, **Thomas H. Burgoyne.** In their three years' association, he awakened Burgoyne's spiritual vision and put him in touch with some preternatural entities, the adepts who were acknowledged as the Interior Circle, the real founders of the Hermetic Brotherhood of Luxor. The brotherhood's existence was announced in 1884 in a small advertisement placed in the back of an English translation of the *Divine Pymander of Hermes Mercurus Trismegistus.* It invited contact with Bimstein under his magical name, Theon. Theon was named Grand Master of the Exterior Circle, the human agents who carried out the instructions of the Interior Circle.

Within a short time Theon retired from any active involvement with the brotherhood, which he left to the care of Burgoyne and the Rev. William Alexander Ayton. He married a medium, Mary Christine Woodroffe Ware. Ware was the founder of the Universal Philosophical Society in London, at which she offered Spiritualist lectures. In 1886 Theon, along with his wife and secretary, Augusta Rolfe, moved to Paris and then in 1888 to Algiers.

His activities in the 1890s are largely unknown, though he probably continued to support himself as a healer and worked with his new wife in perfecting her mediumship. In 1899 he surfaced to write for the *Journal du Magnétism st de la Psychologie* against the philosophy of the French Spiritists led by **Allan Kardec.**

Around the turn of the century Theon reappeared in Tlemcen, Algeria, and in 1901 began to issue a magazine, *Cosmic Philosophy,* whose content seems to have been derived from material channeled by Madame Theon. It ceased publication shortly after her death in 1908. In Algeria he also took students, among whom was Mira Alfassa (1878–1973), who as **Mira Richard** became the student and companion of **Sri Aurobindo Ghose** (1872–1950), the famed Indian spiritual teacher. Known as "The Mother," she ran the Aurobindo Ashram for many years.

Theon passed away in March of 1927 in Algiers.

Sources:

Godwin, Joscelyn. *The Theosophical Enlightenment.* Albany: State University of New York Press, 1994.

———, Christian Chanel, and John P. Deveney. *The Hermetic Brotherhood of Luxor: Initiatic and Historical Documents of an Order of Practical Occultism.* York Beach, Maine: Samuel Weiser, 1995.

Theon, Max. *La Tradition Cosmique.* 6 vols. Paris: Bibliothèque Chacornac/Publicationes Cosmiques, 1903–20.

"Theophilus"

One of the spirit controls of **William Stainton Moses,** "Theophilus" was said to be St. John the Apostle.

Theosophical History (Journal)

A quarterly journal founded by Leslie Price in January 1985 that reports on the historical study of the expansive theosophical movement, including individuals and impulses associated with but not a part of the **Theosophical Society.** The journal has an independent stance and is neutral to various expressions of Theosophy. It seeks to promote the common historical enterprise by Theosophists and non-Theosophists interested in the history of the occult.

The journal seeks to aid historical assessment of such pioneers of Theosophy as **Alice Bailey, Annie Besant, William Quan Judge, J. Krishnamurti, C. W. Leadbeater,** and **G. R. S. Mead.** By arrangement with the **Society for Psychical Research,** London, early issues of the journal carried items from its files on theosophical phenomena.

In 1989 funding became a problem after the death of its prime donor and subsequent difficulties with the Theosophical Publishing House, there was a brief lapse of publication in 1989 until James Santucci, a professor at California State University in Fullerton, California, commenced publication with the January 1990 issue. Santucci built a new editorial board (which includes Price) and continued publication with the same independent stance and high standards as Price originally envisioned.

Theosophical History may be ordered from Dr. James Santucci, Department of Comparitive Religion, P.O. Box 6868, California State University, Fullerton, CA 92834-6868. Website: http://idt.net/~pdeveney/.

Theosophical Society

The major modern organization advocating gnostic-esoteric teachings. The Theosophical Society was founded in New York in 1875 by **Helena Petrovna Blavatsky, Henry Steel Olcott, William Quan Judge,** and others. It grew out of interest in the occult generated previously by the magnetist movement and especially **Spiritualism,** in which both Blavatsky and Olcott had participated. The society proposed a different direction, including attention to a distinct philosophical stance drawn from Eastern teachings.

Both Blavatsky and Olcott were closely concerned with Spiritualist investigations, and they met at the house of the **Eddy brothers** in Vermont. They were also concerned in the claimed phenomena of the mediums **Mr. and Mrs. Nelson Holmes** of Philadelphia, who were accused of cheating. The Holmes partnership involved the alleged manifestation of the spirits **"Katie King"** and **"John King,"** associated with the British medium **Florence Cook.** Blavatsky eventually disowned the Holmes phenomena, but endorsed the reality of the spirit "John King."

In May 1875 Blavatsky and Olcott formed the Miracle Club, which offered an alternative to prevailing scientific materialism, but the organization languished. Soon Olcott began to receive messages through Blavatsky from a mysterious "Brotherhood of Luxor," prototypes of the famous **Mahatma letters** of later years. These messages claimed the support of hidden masters of wisdom in the spreading of truth.

In November 1875 the Theosophical Society was founded with Olcott as president, Blavatsky as corresponding secretary, and Judge (a lawyer) as counsel. There were approximately 20 original members. The term "theosophy" was proposed by Charles Sotheran, a well-known bibliophile and editor of the *American Bibliopolist.* The preamble to the society's bylaws states:

"The Title of the Theosophical Society explains the objects and desires of its founder: they 'seek to obtain knowledge of the nature and attributes of the Supreme Power, and of the higher spirits *by the aid of physical processes.*' In other words, they hope, that by going deeper than modern science has hitherto done, into the esoteric philosophies of ancient times, they may be enabled to obtain, for themselves and other investigators, proof of the existence of an 'Unseen Universe,' the nature of its inhabitants if such there be, and the laws which govern them and their relations with mankind. Whatever may be the private opinions of its members, the society has no dogmas to enforce, no creed to disseminate. It is formed neither as a Spiritualist schism, nor to serve as the foe or friend of any sectarian or philosophic body. Its only axiom is the omnipotence of truth, its only creed a profession of unqualified devotion to its discovery and propaganda. In considering the qualifications of applicants for membership, it knows neither race, sex, color, country nor creed."

The stated objects of the society were "to collect and diffuse a knowledge of the laws which govern the universe." To the society, these laws involved phenomena of a miraculous kind as claimed in the history of occultism, **Rosicrucians,** and other secret orders.

This preoccupation with the miraculous, which has also been the popular focal point in the establishment of great world religions, proved to be the strength as well as the weakness of the society. Over the next two years, there was a shortage of unusual phenomena and the society seemed doomed to failure, many members dropping out.

Meanwhile, Blavatsky was preparing her book *Isis Unveiled,* a compilation and survey of esoteric religious and occult traditions through the ages. This book, together with the amalgamation of the Theosophical Society with the Arya Samaj of Swami Dayananda Saraswati in 1878, stimulated new interest in the society.

In 1879 Blavatsky and Olcott toured **India,** establishing new contacts and developing an aura of the mystic East. India was traditionally associated with the supernormal feats of yogis and the esoteric wisdom of the *Vedas* and **Upanishads.** Although Swami Dayananda proved to be something of a disappointment, due to being a social reformer rather than a repository of the prized miraculous feats of **yoga,** extraordinary events surrounded Blavatsky over the next few years in India and reports on them attracted widespread support for the Theosophical Society.

Olcott's tour of Ceylon and acceptance of Buddhism helped to solidify the society's image as a unifying principle for all religions, though it also succeeded in exciting opposition from Christian missionaries who did not believe that religions could or should be unified.

During 1880–82 there were many letters purportedly from the mysterious *Mahatmas,* or Masters of Wisdom, governing the development of the society, which established headquarters at Adyar, Madras. Although the marvels associated with Blavatsky brought new and important supporters for the society, they also excited opposition and accusations of **fraud,** even from Swami Dayananda, who publicly repudiated Blavatsky and the society in April 1882.

Through the years the Theosophical Society suffered from various dissensions and schisms. Most notable was the controversy over the so-called Mahatma letters, which Blavatsky claimed were supernormally produced messages from Masters or adepts. Accusations from Christian missionaries in India that these letters were fraudulent began in 1884; in the same year **Richard Hodgson** of the **Society for Psychical Research,** Britain, went to the headquarters of the Theosophical Society at Adyar, Madras, to conduct an on-the-spot investigation.

He reported the discovery of a shrine with a false back, used with the connivance of Madame Coulomb, an employee of the society, as a fake mailbox for the letters. The confession of fraud by Coulomb was dismissed by loyal members of the society as part of a Christian plot to discredit Blavatsky and the society. Coulomb's disclosure of the different methods by which the "miracles" were produced and Hodgson's own discovery of various fraudulent events proved more conclusive to most.

Blavatsky left India and settled in England, leaving the society in Olcott's hands. There she drew a group of students, and an internal controversy arose in the society over the establishment of an esoteric section for the study of arcane doctrines and practices. Meanwhile, Blavatsky worked on her massive presentation of theosophical teachings, which finally appeared as *The Secret Doctrine.*

Meanwhile, following the transfer of international headquarters to India, Judge had organized and was leading the American section. After Blavatsky's death in 1891, disputes arose over the production of further Mahatma letters by Judge. These letters supported his claim to take charge of the esoteric section, which Blavatsky had bequeathed to newcomer **Annie Besant.**

While there was a temporary agreement for Besant and Judge to share leadership, tension between Judge and the society leadership outside of the United States continued; in 1895–96 he led the great majority of the American lodges in the establishment of the **Theosophical Society in America** as a separate entity. Judge died a short time later and E. T. Hargrove was elected president of the Theosophical Society in America. But like Blavatsky, Judge had found a talented protege, and **Katherine Tingley**'s abilities were recognized by the membership and she became president of the American society—a post she would hold for the rest of her life. She led in the establishment of a Theosophical community at Point Loma, San Diego, California.

Meanwhile, Annie Besant succeeded Olcott (d. 1907) as president of the international Theosophical Society. A capable orator and administrator, she helped the society and built it into a worldwide organization. While the society was hindered by the scandals attached to Blavatsky, Besant attempted to put that history in the past. However, one of her colleagues, **Charles Webster Leadbeater** who impressed Besant as one possessed of occult abilities, was involved in several scandals that involved some young boys. Eventually he was exiled from India to **Australia,** though not before he and Besant had produced some of the standard theosophical texts. Leadbeater cost the society the considerable support of the scholar **G. R. S. Mead** and some 700 other members in England who left in 1908 and established a rival organization.

Besant adopted, with the aid of Leadbeater, a young Brahmin boy named **Jiddu Krishnamurti,** who they claimed would be the vehicle through whom the future "World Teacher" would manifest. After World War I, as Krishnamurti matured, Besant promoted him and took him on speaking tours around the world. The society's membership peaked in response to his presence and both Besant and the members were devastated in 1929 when he resigned and renounced the role she had assigned him. Krishnamurti went on to become an independent teacher in his own right with a considerable following.

Theosophy's teachings had been given to Blavatsky by a group of exalted masters. Following her death, various people, such as Leadbeater, also claimed to be in spiritual contact. One who made such claims was **Alice A. Bailey,** a member living in southern California. She claimed that she was serving as the amanuensis of Djual Khul, usually called the Tibetan. Her claims eventually led to her separation from the society and the establishment in the 1920s of another offshoot of Theosophy—the **Arcane School.**

In spite of its controversial background, the Theosophical Society itself has had a considerable influence on the spiritual and intellectual life of many individuals in India, Europe, and the United States. Much of the power of the Irish literary renaissance of **William Butler Yeats** and AE (**George Russell**) stems from their association with Theosophy, which also exercised a powerful influence on European occultism.

Perhaps its greatest contribution came during the presidency of Besant, when Theosophy provided the people of India with a feeling of pride in their own cultural and spiritual heritage and participated in the growing wave of nationalism that eventually resulted in the independence of India. Under the auspices of the Theosophical Society, many important Hindu scriptures were translated and published and the library at Adyar contains many rare manuscripts preserved by the society.

The Theosophical Society, with its international headquarters in Adyar, Madras, India, is today a worldwide body perpetuating the basic perspective and teachings of ancient Gnosticism, as promoted by Blavatsky in the 1880s and 1890s. While the society is a significant body in its own right, its influence has been extended through the hundreds of organizations that have taken the basic theosophical worldview and built variations upon it. Theosophy led directly to the founding of the **Liberal Catholic Church,** the **Anthroposophical Society,** the Alice Bailey movement, and the **I Am Movement.** Almost a hundred different organizations, some of which rival the parent Theosophical Society in size, have emerged from these offshoots. Less directly attached to Theosophy, but owing much to its initial impulse, is the modern magical revival whose initial major organizational expression was the Hermetic Order of the **Golden Dawn,** but which has found contemporary expression in the **OTO** and the popular neo-pagan **witchcraft** movement. The single most popular expression of Theosophy has been the

New Age movement of the 1980s, which brought literally millions of people into esoteric studies.

The main theosophical bodies, i.e., those that have a specifically theosophical heritage, are the Theosophical Society (with international lodges and headquarters at Adyar, Madras, India); the Theosophical Society, American Branch (with international headquarters at Altadena, California); and the United Lodge of Theosophists (headquarters in Los Angeles, California). The American affiliate of the international society headquartered in Adyar is the Theosophical Society in America, with headquarters in Wheaton, Illinois on an estate called Olcott; the British affiliate is the Theosophical Society at 50 Gloucester Pl., London, W1H 3HJ, England.

Sources:

Besant, Annie. *The Theosophical Society and H. P. Blavatsky.* London, 1891.

Campbell, Bruce F. *A History of the Theosophical Movement.* Berkeley: University of California Press, 1980.

Christian Literature Society. *Theosophy Exposed; or, Mrs. Besant and Her Guru: Appeal to Educated Hindus.* Madras, India: SPCK Press, 1893.

Coulomb, Madame E. *Some Account of My Intercourse with Madame Blavatsky from 1872 to 1884.* London: Elliot Stock, 1885.

Ellwood, Robert. *Theosophy.* Wheaton, Ill.: Theosophical Publishing House, 1986.

Gomes, Michael. *Theosophy in the Nineteenth Century: An Annotated Bibliography.* New York: Garland Publishing, 1994.

Hare, H. E., and W. L. Hare. *Who Wrote the Mahatma Letters?* London: Williams & Norgate, 1936.

Harrison, Vernon. *H. P. Blavatsky and the SPR.* Pasadena, Calif.: Theosophical University Press, 1997.

Hodgson, Richard. "Personal Investigations, in India, of Theosophical Phenomena." *Proceedings* of the Society for Psychical Research 3 (1885); *Journal* of the Society for Psychical Research 1–2 (1884–1886).

Johnson, Paul. *In Search of the Masters: Behind the Occult Myth.* South Boston: The Author, 1990.

Kingsland, William. *The Real H. P. Blavatsky.* London: John M. Watkins, 1928.

Olcott, H. S. *Old Diary Leaves.* 6 vols. Adyar, Madras, India: Theosophical Publishing House, 1895–1910.

Ransom, Josephine. *A Short History of the Theosophical Society.* Adyar, Madras, India: Theosophical Publishing House, 1938.

Ryan, Charles J. *H. P. Blavatsky and the Theosophical Movement.* Pasadena, Calif.: Theosophical University Press, 1975.

Solovyoff, V. S. *A Modern Priestess of Isis.* London: Longmans, Green, 1895.

Symonds, John. *Madame Blavatsky, Medium and Magician.* London: Odhams Press, 1958.

Waterman, Adlai E. [Walter A. Carrithers]. *Obituary: The "Hodgson Report" on Madame Blavatsky, 1895–1960; Reexamination Discredits the Major Charges Against H. P. Blavatsky.* Adyar, Madras, India: Theosophical Publishing House, 1963.

Williams, Gertrude Marvin. *Priestess of the Occult: Madame Blavatsky.* New York: Alfred A. Knopf, 1946.

Theosophical Society in America

The American affiliate society of the international Theosophical Society, which is headquartered in Adyar, Madras, India. It continues the tradition of Theosophy established in 1875 in New York. The American branch was organized in 1886 but became separate from the international movement in 1895–96. The few American lodges still loyal to the international headquarters in Adyar reorganized and eventually became the dominant segment of the society in the United States.

The society is headquartered in Wheaton, Illinois, where it maintains a library of more that 20,000 volumes and publishes books through the Theosophical Publishing House. It issues a magazine, *Quest.* Headquarters are located at 1926 N. Main St., Wheaton, IL 60187. The American branch of the Esoteric Section is headquartered in a small theosophical community in Ojai, California. The complex also houses a large library as well an educational facility known as the Krotona Institute. Theosophical literature is distributed through Quest bookstores, outlets being located in several cities, including Wheaton and Ojai.

Theosophical Society of Agrippa

The famous occultist and alchemist Agrippa (1486–1535) established in Paris and other centers a secret theosophical society, the rites of admission to which were of a peculiar character.

Agrippa visited London in 1510, and there he established a branch of the order in that city.

Theosophy

Term derived from the Greek *theos* (rod) and *sophia* (wisdom), denoting a philosophical-religious system that claims absolute knowledge of the existence and nature of the deity, and is not to be confused with the later system evolved by the founders of the **Theosophical Society.**

This knowledge, or theosophy, it is claimed, may be obtained by special individual revelation, or through the operation of some higher faculty. It is the transcendent character of the godhead of theosophical systems that differentiates them from the philosophical systems of the speculative or absolute type, which usually proceed deductively from the idea of God. God is conceived in theosophical systems as the transcendent source of being, from whom human beings in their natural state are far removed.

Theosophy is practically another name for speculative **mysticism.** Thus Kabalistic and Neoplatonic conceptions of divine emanations are in reality theosophical, as are the mystical systems of **Jakob Boehme** and Baader.

Theosophy has also come to signify the tenets and teachings of the founders of the Theosophical Society. This society was founded in the United States in 1875 by **Helena Petrovna Blavatsky,** Col. **H. S. Olcott,** and others. Its objectives were to establish a nucleus of the Universal Brotherhood of Humanity, to promote the study of comparative religion and philosophy, and to investigate the mystic powers of life and matter.

The conception of the Universal Brotherhood was based upon the oriental idea of one life—that ultimate oneness underlies all diversity, whether inward or outward. The study of comparative religion had materialized into a definite system of belief, the bounds of which were dogmatically fixed. It was set forth in the theosophical system that all the great religions of the world originated from one supreme source and that they are merely expressions of a central "Wisdom Religion" vouchsafed to various races of the earth in such a manner as is best suited to time and geographical circumstances.

Underlying these was a secret doctrine or esoteric teaching, which, it was stated, had been the possession for ages of certain *Mahatmas,* or adepts, in mysticism and occultism. With these Blavatsky claimed to be in direct communication, and she herself manifested occult phenomena, producing the ringing of astral bells, and so forth.

On several occasions these effects were unmasked as fraudulent, but many people believed that Blavatsky was one of those rare personalities who possess great natural psychic powers, which at times failing her, she augmented by fraudulent methods.

The evidence for the existence of the **Great White Brotherhood** of Mahatmas, the existence of which she asserted, was unfortunately somewhat inconclusive. It rested, for the most part, on the statements of Blavatsky, Olcott, **A. P. Sinnett, Charles W. Leadbeater,** and other committed Theosophists, who claimed to have seen or communicated with them.

With every desire to do justice to these upholders of the theosophical argument, it is necessary to point out that in occult, or pseudo-occult experiences, the question of hallucination enters very largely, and the ecstatic condition may be responsible for subjective appearances that seem real enough to the visionary.

Again, the written communications of the Mahatmas—the **Mahatma letters**—give rise to much doubt. One Mahatma employed the American system of spelling, and this was accounted for by the circumstance that his English had been sophisticated by reading American books. A study of these letters leaves little doubt that their style, script, and purpose were nearer to Blavatsky than to Tibetan or Himalayan hermitages.

The revelations of Blavatsky in her books *Isis Unveiled* (2 vols., 1877) and *The Secret Doctrine* (2 vols., 1888–97) are an extraordinary mixture of Buddhistic, Brahministic, and Kabalistic matter with a basic theme of religious unity and the persistence of occult and miraculous phenomena throughout history.

The Theosophical Society has numbered among its members many persons of high ability, whose statement and exegesis of their faith has placed it upon a much higher level and more definite foundation.

The system was constructed in a manner akin to genius, and evolved on highly intricate lines. It was, to a great extent, pieced together after the death of the original founder of the society, on which event a schism occurred in the Brotherhood through the claims to leadership of **William Q. Judge,** of New York, who died in 1896, and who was followed by **Katherine Tingley,** the founder of the great Theosophical community at Point Loma, California.

Olcott became the leader of the remaining part of the original Theosophical Society in America and India, being assisted in his work by **Annie Besant,** but a more or less independent organization was founded in England.

A brief outline of the tenets of Theosophy may be stated as follows. It posits a rational belief in its views rather than blind faith, and allows for individual differences of opinion. It professes to be a religious philosophy that holds the germs of all others. It has also its aspect as a science—a science of life and of the soul.

The basic teaching is that there are three absolute truths that cannot be lost, but yet may remain silent for lack of speech. (1) The soul of humanity is immortal and its future is the future of the thing, whose growth and splendor has no limit. (2) The principle that gives life dwells in us and without us, is undying and eternally beneficent, is not heard, or seen, or smelt, but is perceived by the man who desires perception. (3) Each individual is his or her own absolute law-giver, the dispenser of glory or gloom to oneself, decreer of one's life, one's reward, one's punishment.

Although Theosophy posits the existence of an absolute, it does not pretend to knowledge of its attributes. In the absolute are innumerable universes and in each universe countless solar systems. Each solar system is the expression of a being called the *Logos,* the Word of God, or the Solar Deity, who permeates it and exists above it and outside it.

Below this Solar Deity are his seven ministers, called Planetary Spirits, whose relation to him is like that of the nerve centers to the brain, so that all his voluntary acts come through him to them. Under them are vast hosts or orders of spiritual beings called *devas,* or angels, who assist in many ways. This world is ruled by a great official who represents the Solar Deity, who is in absolute control of all the evolution that takes place upon this planet. When a new religion is to be founded, this being either comes or sends pupils to institute it.

In the earlier stages of the development of humanity the great officials of the hierarchy are provided from more highly evolved parts of the system, but whenever human beings can be trained to the necessary level of power and wisdom these offices are held by them. They can only be filled by adepts, who in goodness, power, and wisdom are immeasurably greater than ordinary individuals, and have attained the summit of human evolution. These advance until they themselves become of the nature of deities.

There are many degrees and many lines of activity among these, but some of them always remain within touch of the Earth and assist in the spiritual evolution of humanity. This body is called the "Great White Brotherhood." Its members do not dwell together, but live separately apart from the world and are in constant telepathic communication with one another.

Their knowledge of higher forces is so great that they have no necessity for meeting in the physical world, but each dwells in his own country, and their power remains unsuspected among those who live near them. These adepts are willing to take as apprentices those who have resolved to devote themselves utterly to the service of humankind. Blavatsky was presumed to be such an apprentice. One of these masters said: "In order to succeed the pupil must leave his own world and come into ours."

The Theosophical conception of the constitution of the human being is that he or she is in essence a spark of the divine fire belonging to the monadic world. For the purposes of human evolution, this monad manifests itself in lower worlds. Entering the spiritual world it manifests itself there as the triple spirit; one of its three aspects always remains in the spiritual sphere.

The second aspect manifests itself in the intuitional world, and the third in the higher mental world, and these two are collated with intuition and intelligence. These three aspects combined make up the ego, which is individual personality during the human stage of evolution. The way or path towards enlightenment and emancipation is known as **karma.**

The human personality is composed of a complex organization consisting of seven principles, which are united and interdependent, yet divided into certain groups, each capable of maintaining a kind of personality. Each of these principles is composed of its own form of matter and possesses its own laws of time, space, and motion.

The most gross of those, the physical body, is known as *rupa,* which becomes more and more refined until we reach the universal self, *atma,* but the circumstance that determines the individual's powers, tests, and advantages, or in short his or her character, is the karma, which is the sum of bodily, mental, and spiritual growth and is spread over many lives past and future. If in one existence the individual is handicapped by any defect, mental or physical, it may be regarded as the outcome of past delinquencies. This doctrine is common to both Buddhism and Brahminism, from which Theosophy derives.

Returning to concepts of the constitution of the human being, the ego existing in the higher mental world cannot enter the physical world until it has drawn around itself a veil composed of the matter of these spheres, nor can it think in any but an abstract manner without them—its concrete ideas being due to them. Having assumed the astral and physical bodies, it is born as a human being, and having lived out its Earth-life sojourns for a time in the astral world, until it can succeed in throwing off the shackles of the **astral body.**

When that is achieved the individual finds himself or herself living in the mental body. The stay in this sphere is usually a long one—the strength of the mental constitution depending upon the nature of the thoughts to which one has habituated oneself. But he or she is not yet sufficiently developed to proceed to higher planes, and once more descends into the denser physical sphere to again go through the same round. It is only through that descent that a full recognition of the higher worlds is developed in the individual.

In the higher mental world, the permanent vehicle is a causal body, which consists of matter of the first, second, and third sub-divisions of that world. As the ego unfolds one's latent possibilities in the course of one's evolution, this matter is greatly brought into action, but it is only in the perfect individual or adept that it is developed to its fullest extent. In the causal body, none of the possibilities of the grosser bodies can manifest themselves.

The mental body is built up of matter of the four lower subdivisions of the mental world, and expresses the individual's concrete thoughts. Its size and shape are determined by those of the causal vehicle.

While on Earth the personality wears the physical, mental, and astral bodies all at once. It is the astral that connects one with the **astral plane** during sleep or trance. It is easy to see how the doctrine of **reincarnation** arose from this idea. The ego must travel from existence to existence, physical, astral, mental, until it can transcend the mental world and enter the higher spheres

The Theosophical path to the goal of *Nirvana* is derived from Buddhistic teaching, but there are also other elements in it—Kabalistic and Greek. The path is the great work whereby the inner nature of the individual is consciously transformed and developed. A radical alternation must be made in the aims and motives of the ordinary mortal. The path is long and difficult, and as has been said extends over many existences. Morality alone is insufficient to the full awakening of the spiritual faculty, without which progress in the path is impossible. Something incomparably higher is necessary.

The physical and spiritual exercises recommended by Theosophy are those formulated in the Hindu philosophical system known as raja yoga. The most strenuous efforts alone can impel the individual along the path, and thus to mount by the practice of vidya, that higher wisdom that awakens the latent faculties and concentrates effort in the direction of union with the absolute.

The way is described as long and difficult, but as the disciple advances he or she becomes more convinced of ultimate success, by the possession of transcendental faculties that greatly assist in overcoming difficulties. But these must not be sought for their own sake, as to gain knowledge of them for evil purposes is tantamount to the practice of **black magic.** (See also **Kabala**)

Theta (Journal)

Scholarly journal of **parapsychology** published quarterly by the **Psychical Research Foundation.** Its title derives from the initial letter of the Greek word, *Thanatos* (death) and its concern is mainly with research on the problem of **survival** of bodily death. It was edited for many years by **William G. Roll.** *Theta* has been published since 1963. The publication can be reached c/o Dr. Andrew Nichols, P.O. Box 142193, Gainesville, FL 32614-2193.

THG See Temple of the Holy Grail

Thian-ti-hwii

The Heaven and Earth League, an ancient esoteric society in **China,** said to have still been in existence in 1674. The society professed to continue a system of brotherhood derived from ancient customs.

Sources:

Chesneaux, Jean. *Secret Societies in China in the Nineteenth and Twentieth Centuries.* Ann Arbor, Mich.: University of Michigan Press, 1971.

Third Eye

The mystical center behind the forehead between the eyes, which is a focus for Oriental mystical **meditation.** It is known in **yoga** philosophy as the *ajna chakra* (center of command) and its activation or opening through meditation is often the preliminary to activation of other *chakras.* The initial experience of the third eye, the seeming presence of a screen inside the head at the front of the brain, can be had by anyone who simply shuts his eyes and attempts to reach a focus.

The idea of "opening" the third eye is a common one in psychic and metaphysical circles. An interesting variation of the idea is found in the popular book *The Third Eye* (1956) by **T. Lopsang Rampa** (pseudonym of Cyril Hoskins). It states that this *chakra* may be opened by a physical operation. Rampa's story was a hoax and the operation complete fiction. No such operation is featured in Hindu or Tibetan **mysticism** (or any other system of occult thought) and it must be regarded as an imaginative fantasy.

Thomas, C(harles) Drayton (1867–1953)

British clergyman who was an active member of the **Society for Psychical Research,** London, for many years. He was a Council member from 1934–53 and one of the first regular sitters with the medium **Gladys Osborne Leonard.** He reported on her phenomena in the society's *Journal* and *Proceedings.*

He worked with **W. Whateley Carington** in the quantitative study of **trance personalities.** His many articles and several books indicate an interest in **psychical research** as a means of supporting his belief in life after death.

His books include: *Some Evidence for Human Survival* (1922), *Life Beyond Death with Evidence* (1928), *The Mental Phenomena of Spiritualism* (1930), *An Amazing Experiment, Beyond Life's Sunset* (1931), *From Life to Life* (1946), *In the Dawn Beyond Death,* and *Precognition and Human Survival* (1948).

Thomas died July 14, 1953.

Sources:

Allison, L. W. "Obituary: The Reverend C. Drayton Thomas." Journal of the American Society for Psychical Research 48 (1953).

Berger, Arthur S., and Joyce Berger. *The Encyclopedia of Parapsychology and Psychical Research.* New York: Paragon House, 1991.

Thomas, C. Drayton. "The Volume of Byron: A Significant Book Test." *Proceedings* of the Society for Psychical Research 48, 175 (1946–49).

———. "The Word Association Test with Mrs. Osborne Leonard." *Proceedings* of the Society for Psycical Research 43, 141 (1935).

Thomas, John F(rederick) (1874–1940)

Psychologist and educator who studied **parapsychology.** He was born on July 22, 1874, in Parker City, Pennsylvania. He attended the University of Michigan (LL.B., 1898; M.A., 1915) and after a break of two decades, he went to Duke University to pursue a doctoral program (Ph.D., 1935). Thomas was a member of the Michigan Education Association (president in 1940), the National Education Association, Boston Society for Psychic Research, and **Society for Psychical Research,** London.

During much of his career Thomas worked for the Detroit public school system. However, he had been interested in **psychical research** for many years, but did not become actively involved until the 1920s when he sat with the Boston medium **Minnie M. Soule** (also known as "Mrs. Chenoweth"); she produced what he perceived as strong evidence of **survival.** He went on to sit with **Gladys Osborne Leonard** and **Eileen J. Garrett.** Sittings in 1932 formed the subject of his Ph.D. thesis at Duke: *An Evaluative Study of the Mental Content of Certain Trance Phenomena.* This was also the first doctoral thesis dealing with parapsychology and the first of several books and articles he contributed to the field. Thomas died November 21, 1940.

Sources:

Berger, Arthur S., and Joyce Berger. *The Encyclopedia of Parapsychology and Psychical Research.* New York: Paragon House, 1991.

Gibson, Edmond P. "The Ethel Thomas Case." *Tomorrow* (summer 1954).

Pleasants, Helene, ed. *Biographical Dictionary of Parapsychology.* New York: Helix Press, 1964.

Thomas, John F. *Beyond Normal Cognition.* Boston: Boston Society for Psychic Research, 1937. Reprint, New York: Arno Press, 1975.

———. *Case Studies Bearing Upon Survival.* N.p., 1929.

Thomas Aquinas (ca. 1225–1274)

One of the most profound scholars and subtlest logicians of his day. Aquinas was born around 1225 in Roccasecca, Italy. He was educated under the Benedictine Monks of Monte Cassino and in the University of Naples, and entered the Society of Preaching Friars, or Dominicans, at 17 years of age. His mother, indignant that he should take the vow of poverty and thus remove himself from the world for life, employed every means in her power to induce him to change his mind. In order to remove Aquinas from her influence, the friars relocated him from Naples to Terracina, from Terracina to Anagnia, and from Anagnia to Rome.

His mother followed him in all these changes of residence but was not permitted to see him. At length she induced his two elder brothers to seize him by force. They kidnapped him while he was traveling to Paris, where he had been sent to complete his course of instruction, and they carried him off to the castle of Aquino, where he had been born. Here Aquinas was confined for two years, but he found a way to correspond with the superiors of his order, and he finally escaped from a window in the castle.

Aquinas exceeded most men in the severity and strictness of his metaphysical disquisitions and thus acquired the name of "Seraphic Doctor." He was canonized by Pope John XXII in 1323.

Because of his association with **Albertus Magnus,** he shared many legends of magical powers. For example, it was said that because his study was placed in a great thoroughfare where the grooms exercised their horses, Aquinas found it necessary to apply a magical remedy to this nuisance. He made by the laws of magic a small brass horse, which he buried two or three feet underground in the middle of this highway so that horses would no longer pass along the road. The grooms were compelled to choose another place for their daily exercises.

Another legend claimed that Aquinas was offended by the perpetual chattering of an artificial man made of brass, constructed by his tutor Albertus Magnus, and he dashed the automaton to pieces. Aquinas was also supposed to have written some tracts on **alchemy.**

However, his credulity regarding **demonology** and **witchcraft** had an unfortunate influence on witchhunters, and he was later cited as an authority by such writers as **Heinrich Kramer** and **Jakob Sprenger,** authors of the infamous *Malleus Maleficarum.* Although Aquinas did not accept the concept of a pact with the Devil, he endorsed the belief of diabolical association, and the **incubus** and **succubus.** He echoed Albertus Magnus in claiming that when Satan tempted Christ on the mountaintop, he carried Christ on his shoulders, and this belief was used by later witchhunters to endorse the theory of transvection, or magical transport of witches through the air. Aquinas also believed in the power of the **evil eye** used by old women who had an association with the Devil. His argument that heretics should be burned was later used to justify the burning of witches.

It should be stressed that Aquinas's credulity was characteristic of his time, and his theses concerning the Devil reflected the conclusions of theological dogmas of his day. Nevertheless, his discussions were used by later and lesser individuals to justify the witchcraft delusion.

The major works of Aquinas include the *Summa Theologica* and the *Summa contra Gentiles.* His great intellectual and theological achievements have somewhat overshadowed the mystical side of his character, and it should be remembered that he ended his life as a contemplative mystic.

He died March 7, 1274, in Fossanova, Italy.

Sources:

St. Thomas Aquinas and His Legacy. Washington, D.C.: Catholic University of America, 1994.

Stockhammer, Thomas. *Thomas Aquinas Dictionary.* New York: Philosophical Library, 1965.

Thomas the Rhymer (fl. 1220)

Scottish soothsayer (prophet) of the thirteenth century. It is impossible to name the exact birth date of Thomas the Rhymer, who is well known for figuring in a ballad included in Sir Walter Scott's *Minstrelsy of the Scottish Border.*

Thomas is commonly supposed to have lived at the beginning of the thirteenth century, that period being assigned because the name "Thomas Rimor de Ercildun" is appended as witness to a deed, whereby one "Petrus de Haga de Bemersyde" agreed to pay half a stone of wax annually to the Abbot of Melrose, and this "Petrus" has been identified with a person of that name known to have been living about 1220.

Erceldoune or Ercildun is simply the old way of spelling Earlston, a village in the extreme west of Berwickshire, near the line demarking that county from Roxburgh.

It would seem that Thomas held estates in this region, for he is mentioned as a land owner by several early writers, most of whom add that he did not hold his lands from the Crown, but from the Earls of Dunbar. Be that as it may, Thomas probably spent the greater part of his life in and around Earlston, and a ruined tower there, singularly rich in ivy, is still pointed out as having been his home, and bears his name, while in a wall of the village church there is a lichened stone with the inscription:

"Auld Rhymour's Race
Lies in this Place."

According to local tradition, this stone was removed to its present resting place from one in a much older church, long since demolished.

Nor are these things the only relics of the soothsayer, a lovely valley some miles to the west of Earlston being still known as "Rhymer's Glen." It is interesting to recall that the artist J. M. W. Turner painted a watercolor of this place, and no less interesting to remember that Sir Walter Scott, when buying the lands that eventually constituted his estate of Abbotsford, sought eagerly and at last successfully to acquire the glen in question. Naturally he loved it on account of its associations with the shadowy past, and his biographer J. C. Lockhart stated that many of the novelist's happiest times were spent in this romantic place. Lockhart related that the novelist Maria Edgeworth visited it in 1823, and that thenceforth Scott used always to speak of a certain boulder in the glen as the "Edgeworth stone," the writer whom he admired so keenly having rested there. It seems probable, however, that the glen was named "Rhymer's Glen" by Scott himself.

It is thought that Thomas died in 1297, and it is clear that he had achieved a wide fame as a prophet, many references to his skill being found in writers who lived comparatively soon after him. A Harleian manuscript in the British Museum known to have been written before 1320 disclosed the significant phrase, "La Comtesse de Donbar demanda a Thomas de Essedoune quant la guere descoce prendreit fyn," but the lady in question was not a contemporary of the prophet. In Barbour's

Bruce, composed early in the fourteenth century, we find the poet saying:

"Sekerly
I hop Thomas Prophecy
Off Hersildoune sall weryfyd be."

The historian Andrew of Wyntoun in the *Originale Cronykil of Scotland,* also mentions Thomas as a redoubtable prophet, while Walter Bower, the continuator of Fordun's *Scoticronicon,* recounts how once Rhymer was asked by the Earl of Dunbar what another day would bring forth, whereupon he foretold the death of the king, Alexander III, and the very next morning news of his majesty's decease was heard.

Blind Harry's poem *Wallace,* written midway through the fifteenth century, likewise contains an allusion to Thomas's prophesying capacities.

Coming to later times, Sir Thomas Cray, constable of Norham, in his Norman-French *Scalacronica,* compiled during his captivity at Edinburgh Castle in 1555, spoke of the predictions of Merlin, which like those of "Banaster ou de Thomas de Ercildoune . . . furount ditz en figure."

A number of predictions attributed to Thomas the Rhymer are still current, for instance that weird verse Sir Walter Scott made the motto of his novel *The Bride of Lammermuir* and also a saying concerning a family with which, as we have seen, the soothsayer was at one time associated:

"Betide, betide, whate'er betide
There'll aye be Haigs at Bemersyde."

It will be observed that these lines are in poetic meter, yet there is really no sure proof that the soothsayer was a poet. It is usually supposed that he acquired the nickname "Rhymer" because he was a popular minstrel in his day, but the fact remains that "Rymour" had long been a comparatively common surname in Berwickshire, and, while it may have originated with Thomas, the assumption has but slight foundation.

Again, the prophet of Earlston has been credited with a poem on the story of Sir Tristram belonging to the Arthurian cycle of romance, and the Advocate's Library contains a manuscript copy of this probably written as early as 1300. However, while Sir Walter Scott and other authorities believed in this ascription, it is quite likely that the poem is only a paraphrase from some French troubadour.

For generations, however, the Scottish peasantry continued to be influenced by the sayings attributed to "True Thomas," as they named him, as evidenced by the continuing publication of books and chapbook pamphlets containing his prophecies until well into the nineteenth century. For a detailed study, see *The Romance and Prophecies of Thomas Erceldoune,* edited by J. A. H. Murray for the English Text Society, London, 1875.

A beautiful legend credits Thomas with obtaining his prophetic powers after visiting fairyland. The ballad of "Thomas Ryner and the Queen of Elfland" in its various forms is classified as no. 37 of the collection of *English and Scottish Popular Ballads,* edited by Francis James Child, published in five vols., 1882–98.

Thompson, Rosina (1868– ?)

British **trance medium,** whose abilities developed at Frederic W. Thurstan's **Delphic Circle** at Hertford Lodge, Battersea, London. In her early sittings in 1897 and 1898, the records of which in *Light* refer to her as Mrs. T., she exhibited startling physical phenomena, **raps, movements** of objects, **luminous phenomena, elongation of the human body, direct voice, apports,** scents, and **materializations.**

Her physical manifestations were discouraged by **F. W. H. Myers** and she was persuaded to give her services to the **Society for Psychical Research** as a trance medium from 1898 onward. Her chief control was her deceased daughter, Nelly, who had died in infancy. Another communicator of importance was a Mrs. Cartwright, the teacher of the school where Thompson was educated. Her trances were much lighter than those of **Leonora Piper** and occasionally they were scarcely distinguishable from the state of normal wakefulness. Many instances of her paranormal perceptions were recorded in the waking state.

Richard Hodgson, after six sittings, formed an unfavorable opinion of her powers; it was the skeptical **Frank Podmore** who hurried to Thompson's defense. He considered Hodgson's conclusion that Thompson was untrustworthy to go beyond the warrant of the facts. Podmore expressed his opinion in plain words: "I should perhaps add that the supernormal source of much of the information given at Mrs. Thompson's **séances** seems to me to be almost beyond dispute."

The reports of **Frederik van Eeden** contained many curious accounts. The results of Frederik van Eeden were very convincing. He came from Holland with an article of clothing that belonged to a young man who first cut his throat and then shot himself. He obtained dramatic communications, and Thompson spoke in Dutch (a language she did not know) with the young man.

Margaret Verrall had 22 sittings with Thompson. She made statistical calculations and found that out of 238 definite statements referring to things past and present, 33 were false, 64 were unidentified, and 141 (approximately 59 percent) were true. Of these 141 true statements, 51 could not have been ascertained from normal sources. Verrall's general opinion of the controlling personalities was that although their characteristics were not very marked, all bore strong resemblance to the waking Thompson, the voice was hardly to be distinguished from hers, and the words and phrases were such as she herself used in the normal state. She nevertheless, admitted that many personalities bore, for the sitters, the marks of independent individuality.

Myers's belief in **survival** was chiefly founded on experiments with Thompson following the death of his great love, Annie Marshall. He and his friends had 217 sittings, about two thirds of which he personally attended. After Myers's death on January 17, 1901, Thompson, who had previously suspended sittings altogether, gave two sittings to **Sir Oliver Lodge.** In both of them, communications characteristic of Myers were forthcoming. She also took part in the **cross-correspondence** sittings.

Sources:

Berger, Arthur S., and Joyce Berger. *The Encyclopedia of Parapsychology and Psychical Research.* New York: Paragon House, 1991.

Myers, F. W. H. "On the Trance Phenomena of Mrs. Thompson." *Proceedings* of the Society for Psychical Research 17 (1902).

Van Eeden, Frederik. "Account of Sittings with Mrs. Thompson." *Proceedings* of the Society for Psychical Research 17 (1904).

Thompson, William Irwin (1938–)

Author of books analyzing society in the light of contemporary **New Age** movements and founder of **Lindisfarne** Association, a commune based on a "new planetary culture." Thompson was born on July 16, 1938, in Chicago, Illinois. He was educated at Pomona College (B.A., 1962) and Cornell University (M.A., 1964, Ph.D., 1966). He became an assistant professor of humanities at Massachusetts Institute of Technology for several years (1965–68). Afterward, he joined the faculty at York University, Toronto, in 1968 and remained there for many years.

In the 1970s, Thompson began to explore the possibility of a new culture emerging in the light of **occult,** spiritual, and new consciousness movements. In *Passages About Earth* (1974), he analyzed the alternative cultures of Paolo Soleri, H. G. Wells, Werner Heisenberg, Aurelio Peccei and his Club of Rome, the

Integral Yoga of **Sri Aurobindo,** the Institute for World Order and W. Warren Wagar, C. F. von Weizäcker of the Max Planck Institute, and the Kundalini yogi **Pandit Gopi Krishna.** The book contains observation into the nature and impact of various New Age movements and lifestyles of the established technological nation-states.

Thompson was most favorably impressed by the alternative culture of **Findhorn Foundation,** the pioneering Scottish New Age community established by Peter and Eileen Caddy in 1962 as "a training center for the embodiment of universal consciousness in those who recognize their path is one of world service." He also visited the ruins of Lindisfarne, a monastery on Holy Island off the coast of Northumberland, England; it was founded by St. Aidan in 635 C.E. Later, Thompson founded the Lindisfarne Association in Southampton, New York, as an educational community for cultural transformation in a new synthesis.

In Thompson's view, the original Lindisfarne typified a historic clash between esoteric Christianity and ecclesiastical Christianity—between religious experience and religious authority. As with Eileen Caddy's experiments at Findhorn, Thompson's Lindisfarne has great significance as an attempt to extend intellectual theories by practical community work. In such a setting, occultism and higher consciousness movements are integrated into a truly New Age "planetary culture" rather than a counterculture.

Sources:

Thompson, William Irwin. *At the Edge of History.* New York: Harper, 1971.

———. *Coming Into Being: Artifacts and Texts in the Evolution of Consciousness.* New York: St. Martin's Press, 1996.

———. *Evil and World Order.* New York: Harper & Row, 1976.

———. *Gaia 2: Emergence: The New Science of Becoming.* Hudson, N. Y.: Lindisfarne Press, 1991.

———. *Islands Out of Times.* Garden City, N.Y.: Dial Press, 1985.

———. *Passages About Earth: An Exploration of the New Planetary Culture.* New York: Harper & Row, 1973.

Thorogood, Brackett K(irkwood) (1881–1965)

Engineer and educator who wrote on parapsychological subjects. He was born on December 21, 1881, at Cambridge, Massachusetts and educated at the Chauncy Hall School, the Lowell Institute, and the Massachusetts Institute of Technology. In 1922 he became a technical and technological consultant and then beginning in 1938 to 1957 was the director of the Franklin Technical Institute.

Thorogood had more than a passing interest in mediumship and became involved in the latter stages of the controversy over the mediumship of **Mina Crandon** (i.e. **"Margery"**). He also served as a consultant to **American Society for Psychical Research** during the turbulent years of the 1930s. He died November 1965.

Sources:

Pleasants, Helene, ed. *Biographical Dictionary of Parapsychology.* New York: Helix Press, 1964.

Thorogood, Brackett K. "The Margery Mediumship." *Proceedings* of the American Society for Psychical Research 22 (1933).

Thoughtforms

The existence of thoughtforms has been claimed by occultists, especially theosophists. The idea of thought-forms has supplied a realm for some interesting and curious speculations by psychical researchers as they investigated the substance of their designated study. The suggestion of psychical researcher **Sir William F. Barrett** that the operator may so stimulate the mind of the subject that he is able to see the thought-shape in the former's mind is similar to what theosophist **A. P. Sinnett** claimed in his book *The Occult World* (1882): "An adept is able to project into and materialize in the visible world the forms that his imagination has constructed out of inert cosmic matter in the visible world. He does not create anything new, but only utilises and manipulates materials which Nature has in store around him."

And there are other similarities. **James H. Hyslop,** in his book *Psychical Research and The Resurrection* (1908), quoted a curious communication from a private source. The communicator, while commenting on the peculiarities of his spiritual life, stated that he "sometimes saw, for instance, a man reading a book, but when he approached to talk with him he found it was only a thought." Hyslop, however, did not agree with the thought-form theory and suggested that the instance was a case of veridical, or subjective **hallucination** in the spiritual life.

James T. Fields in a lecture on "Fiction and its Eminent Authors," said: "Dickens was at one time so taken possession of by the characters of whom he was writing that they followed him everywhere and would never let him be alone for a moment. He told me that when he was writing *The Old Curiosity Shop* the creatures of his imagination haunted him so that they would neither let him sleep or eat in peace."

Vincent Turvey wrote in his book *The Beginnings of Seership* (1911; 1969) about a discussion that took place between him and a man from Christian Evidence Society on psychic matters. The man insisted that Turvey's psychic gifts were from the devil and prayed that the devils should leave him.

"On lying down in the afternoon in order to rest and meditate, I suddenly saw three or four 'devils' in the room—typical orthodox fiends. Men with goats' legs, cloven hoofs, little horns just over their ears, curly hair, . . . tails and clawlike hands. In colour they were entirely brown, like ordinary brown paper. I candidly profess that I was 'a bit shaken' . . . I pulled myself together and rose into the 'higher state of consciousness.' In this 'state' I was able to see not only their fronts, but also their backs. To my utter astonishment they were all *hollow at the back,* like embossed leather, or the ordinary papier maché mask. Then my guardians caused me to make a sign, say a word, or think a sentence—what I do not know; but directly it was done or said, these forms disintegrated or dissolved and vanished."

Thoughtforms are often perceived in the hypnotic state. Dr. Lindsay Johnson, the celebrated British ophthalmic surgeon, described in the May 21, 1921, issue of the Spiritualist journal *Light* an experiment of Professor Koenig of Berlin, in a Paris hospital at which he assisted. A peasant woman was hypnotized. It was suggested that she saw an imaginary picture on a plain sheet of paper. Twenty identical sheets of paper were produced and a picture was suggested for each; a record was kept of the picture and tiny identification marks added on the back of each sheet. Johnson added five more sheets, shuffled them, and handed them back one after the other to the subject. She described the suggested picture in every case, but saw nothing on Johnson's sheets.

A Russian investigator, Dr. Naum Kotik, made similar experiments in Wiesbaden with a fourteen-year-old girl Sophie and drew the following inference: "Thought is a radiant energy. This energy has physical and psychic properties. It may be called psycho-physical. Originating in the brain, it passes to the extremities of the body. It is transmitted through air with some difficulty, more easily through a metallic conductor and can be fixed on paper."

Koenig's and Kotik's experiments echo the experience of the engineer and psychical researcher **René Warcollier.** One evening, partially waking, he saw a large quadrangular corded package in a yellow packing paper on a chair. He inquired about the package. There was no package on the chair but it had been there some time before as described. If the image of a package can impress a chair it is no more improbable that thoughts may similarly impress a sheet of paper.

Hyppolite Baraduc informed the Academie de Médecine in May 1896 that he had succeeded in photographing thought. He experimented with many people. The subjects placed their hands on a photographic plate in the dark room and were asked to think intently of the object they wished to impress upon the plate. Many curious markings were obtained, some of them representing the features of persons and the outline of objects.

Baraduc also contended that thought photography was possible from a distance. He quoted the case of a Dr. Istrati who promised a friend of his that he would appear on a photographic plate at Bucarest on August 4, 1893, while he slept in Campana. The distance was 300 kilometers. Before closing his eyes, Istrati willed that his image should impress the plate with which his friend went to bed. The result was achieved. The plate showed a luminous spot, in the midst of which the profile of a man could be traced.

Commandant Darget, of Tours, France, obtained several good thought photographs in 1896. His procedure was to gaze attentively at a simple object for a few moments in order to engrave it firmly on the mind, then go into the dark room and (1) place a photographic plate with the glass side against the forehead for a quarter of an hour, mentally picturing the object decided upon and strongly desiring to make an impression on the plate, (2) Place the hand on a plate (or hold the plate in the hand) for a quarter of an hour, operating as before, (3) Put the plate into a developing bath, placing the fingers of one hand on the edge of the plate for ten minutes. There should always be the desire to imprint on the plate the picture of the object which is very strongly thought of.

An interesting case was quoted by James Coates from the November 1895 issue of the *Amateur Photographer*. W. Inglis Rogers, the experimenter, gazed for a minute at a postage stamp and then went into the dark room and gazed at a sensitive plate for twenty minutes. When the plate was developed two images of postage stamps were plainly visible.

Tomobichi Fukurai, a professor of Kohyassan University, carried out important experiments with Ikuko Nagao. If she concentrated on Japanese alphabetical symbols they were found printed on photographic plates.

Walter Franklin Prince reported in the *Journal* of the American Society for Psychical Research (April 1925) the case of the Japanese artist Mikaye. Microscopic symbols were projected by some capillary action from the tip of his brush filled with fluid pigment. The artist simply held the brush downwards and he made a mental image of the intended symbol to a large scale.

In his researches with **Stanislawa Tomczyk, Julien Ochorowicz** was deeply puzzled to find that in several of his radiographs the medium's ring appeared on the finger of her "etheric" hand. This seemed to indicate to him: (1) That there is a kind of link between the organism and the object it wears, (2) That the occult notion that material objects have an **astral body** is not limited to living bodies. The ring, however, did not always appear on the radiographs. Ochorowicz tried to find out whether objects frequently worn by the sensitive were more easily produced on the plate than others. He chose a thimble that she rarely used. The medium suggested that he should himself retain the thimble on the finger of his left hand, holding her with his right hand. "Perhaps," she added, "the thimble will pass from your body on to my finger."

The experiment appeared absurd, but he was willing to try it. He took a plate from his box, marked it, and laid it on the medium's knees. She was seated on his right; with his right hand he held up her left hand about sixteen inches above the plate, the thimble being on the middle finger of his left hand, which he kept behind his left knee. After a minute had elapsed, the medium said that she felt a sort of tingling in the direction of her forearm, where their hands met. She exclaimed: "Oh, how strange. Something is being placed on the tip of my finger . . . I do not know if it is the thimble; I feel something keeps pressing the end of my finger."

When the plate was developed, it showed the hand of the medium, and on the middle finger was what he called, jokingly, "the soul of her thimble." Ochorowicz asked in some bewilderment if the image was a double of the thimble, or was it a photograph of the idea of the thimble. A close examination of the photograph and comparison with the thimble showed that the two corresponded exactly, the one "was a true copy of the other, precise in details and in dimension."

This exactness supported the idea of a direct impression from some object rather than merely a thought-image. The finger supporting the thimble was the palest of all the fingers, probably, as Ochorowicz suggests, because the light by which the radiograph was taken, proceeded from it. He inclined to the conclusion that an etheric hand wearing an etheric thimble produced the image, and that mental desire gave the direction to the light that was necessary in order to make the details of the thimble visible on the plate.

When he proceeded to test his conclusion, however, a strange thing happened. Unknown to the medium, he held in his left hand an Austrian five-crown piece. Presently she exclaimed: "I see behind you a white round object . . . it is the moon." "At the same instant," wrote Ochorowicz, "I saw a faint but distinct light pass near my left hand, which held the coin; it was not round, nor a flash, it was like a little meteor, like a thin ray, lighting up the space round my hand on the side away from the medium." When the plate was developed it showed an image of a full moon.

He considered it evident that this time a photograph of thought obtained the existence of a quasi-physical intermediary, since the image represented the medium's conception of something that existed outside her mind.

The image of the moon was once obtained previous to the experiment. On the night of September 7, 1911, the medium was much impressed by the superb sight of the starry heavens, and particularly by the full moon, which she looked at for some time with admiration. On the following day, instead of the little hand, which was desired, a full moon appeared on the plate against a background of white cloud. The cinematograph representations of the eclipse of the moon on April 17, 1912, showed the image of the moon slightly flattened in the direction of the axis of rotation. This characteristic appeared in the radiograph of September 7. The impression was double and it looked as if the cloud had not been duplicated.

Some have suggested that the psychic extras obtained by spirit photographers may be the thoughts of the sitters (though most now agree that they were more likely the product of fraud). **Hereward Carrington** offered some curious evidence out of his experiences with Mrs. A. E. Deane as did **Frederick Bligh Bond,** who experimented with the same medium. Bond prepared a diagram of four by three squares and made, in one of the twelve squares, a cross of two diagonal lines and drew a small circle over the crossed lines. After he deposited this diagram with the principal of the **British College of Psychic Science,** he went to meet Deane. She drew upon a blackboard a similar diagram and asked for a perfect circle over the center of the two intersecting lines.

The camera was loaded by Carrington and he did the development himself; Deane simply placing her hand during the exposures on the camera top. The first plate showed the diagram alone; the second had a sort of localized fog over the square in question; the third, possessed a circular spot of intense blackness, exactly over the intersection.

In a second trial, Bond hung a small picture frame upon the wall of the studio and asked that an image, the exact character of which he did not specify, might be recorded on the space within the frame. The idea was to preclude any successful pre-exposure of a plate for the purpose of fraud. He obtained a cloud of small size that on the first two plates was not quite rightly centered, but was well within the center of the third plate.

A Mr. Warrick, a manufacturing chemist, repeated the experiments but used no camera, only sheets of paper that he had specially sensitized. By impressing upon Deane the exact nature of the image he wanted, and placing the paper beneath Deane's hands or feet, he obtained circles, squares, triangles, or more complex images. Bond believed that his part in the success was dependent upon a power of mental visualization that he had special opportunities to cultivate.

Sources:

Besant, Annie, and Charles W. Leadbeater. *Thought-Forms: A Record of Clairvoyant Investigations.* Adyar, Madras, India: London Theosophical Publishing House, 1901.

Darget, Commandant. *Exposé des différentes methodes pour l'obtention des photographies fluido-magnétiques et spirites.* Paris, 1909.

Eisenbud, Jule. *The World of Ted Serios: "Thoughtographic Studies of an Extraordinary Mind."* New York: William Morrow, 1967.

Fukurai, Tomobichi. *Clairvoyance and Thoughtography.* London: Rider, 1931. Reprint, New York: Arno Press, 1975.

Joire, Paul. *Psychical and Supernormal Phenomena.* New York: F. A. Stokes, 1916.

Kotie, Naum. *Die Emanation der psycho-physichen Energie.* Wiesbaden, 1908.

Ochorowicz, Julien. *De la suggestion mentale.* N.p., 1887. English edition as *Mental Suggestion.* N.p., 1891.

Schatzman, Morton. *The Story of Ruth.* New York: G. P. Putnam's Sons, 1980.

Thoughtography

Term devised by a Japanese experimenter **Tomobichi Fukurai** for thought photography, the impressing of mental images on photographic plates. His researches were embodied in his book *Clairvoyance and Thoughtography* (1911, English translation 1930). Modern Japanese experimenters now use the term "Nengraphy."

Sources:

Fukurai, Tomobichi. *Clairvoyance and Thoughtography.* London: Rider, 1930. Reprint, New York: Arno Press, 1975.

Thought-Reading

Thought-transference from the reverse aspect. The agent attempts to picture the contents of the subject's mind, i.e., to "read it," instead of impressing it with his own transmitted ideas.

In more modern society, where outbursts of ecstatic frenzy are and were ascribed to "demonic" possession, ecstatics are often credited with the power to read thoughts. Various psychic functionaries were supposed to possess the same faculty. In the religious revivals of the sixteenth century among the so-called **Tremblers of the Cevennes,** for example, thought-reading was one of the minor but very practical miracles that occurred. It was used for the detection of spies who frequently attended the meetings of the proscribed devotees.

In the fifteen century, **Paracelsus** had observed the phenomenon of thought-reading, and it was also reported by early experimenters in **animal magnetism.** More recently, Robert Baxter, a member of the Irvingite congregation, seized with Pentecostal fervor in 1831 and recorded that when he was possessed by tongues he could often read the unspoken thoughts of his hearers. **Sydney and Lesley Piddington** and **Julius and Mrs. Zancig** were two couples who also became well-known for their thought-reading abilities.

Thought-reading may occur through **rapport** with or the positive perception of the ideas existing in another mind. Musical strings furnish an analogy to the first mode. A note struck on one string will be taken up and echoed by another. In cases of mass panic, the sense of fear is communicated to surrounding people who may be ignorant of the original cause of the terror. It is often difficult, however, to differentiate between psychic contagion and the transmission of emotions or ideas by subconsciously perceived signs such as facial expressions and postures.

The advent of **Spiritualism** gave thought-reading a new driving force. It was now the spirits who read the thoughts of the sitters and replied to them with **raps** and **table-turning** messages. Sergeant **E. W. Cox,** an early investigator of the phenomena of Spiritualism, speculated:

"If the Darwinian theory be true, there must have been a time when man had no articulate speech. For intercommunication with his kind he must have then possessed some other faculty than language. Most probably that was what the intercourse of animals is, and the abnormal cases of thought reading that occur among ourselves may be possibly the survival of a faculty which has now almost vanished, because it has gradually fallen into disuse."

The term "thought-reading" is also popularly used for demonstrations by stage performers who actually use subtle codes for apparent telepathic communication, a practice described in a number of books such as Stuart Cumberland's 1888 text, *Thought-Reader's Thoughts.* It is possible that some tricks of stage performers may be similar to methods employed subconsciously by ordinary individuals who appear to manifest thought-reading or telepathic faculty. Some performers can do **muscle reading,** perceiving the subtle muscular movements when holding the hand of a subject or even pick up subconscious whispering. (See **Rev. Edward Irving**)

Sources:

Braddon, Russell. *The Piddingtons.* London: Werner Laurie, 1950.

Cumberland, Stuart [Charles Garner]. *Thought-Reader's Thoughts: Being the Impressions and Confessions of Stuart Cumberland.* London: S. Low, Marston, Searle & Rivington, 1888. Reprint, New York: Arno Press, 1975.

Thought-Transference

This claimed faculty was baptized **telepathy** in 1882 by the **Society for Psychical Research,** London. In the fifteenth century, for example, **Paracelsus** observed, "By the magic power of the will, a person on this side of the ocean may make a person on the other side hear what is said on this side . . . the ethereal body of a man may know what another man thinks at a distance of 100 miles or more."

The Swedish seer **Emanuel Swedenborg** (1688–1772) clearly stated that spiritual or sympathetic states of consciousness conquer time and space. The state of **rapport** discovered by the mesmerists of the nineteenth century demonstrated transference of thoughts and emotions. They sought the mechanism in a "magnetic fluid." Somnambulic (hypnotic **trance**) induced from a distance seemed to indicate direct action between mind and mind. The possibility that this condition might have been brought about by conscious or subconscious suggestion was not immediately apparent.

Many experiments in thought transference were recorded in Germany in the beginning of the nineteenth century. A valuable series was published by Dr. Van Ghert, Secretary of the Royal Mineralogical Society at Jena in the *Archive für den tierischen Magnetismus* and by H. M. Weserman, the Government Assessor and Chief Inspector of Roads in Düsseldorf with his *Der Magnetismus und die allgemeine Weltsprache* (1822).

William F. Barrett read a paper on the subject before the British Association in 1876. Psychical researchers Barrett, **Ed-**

mund Gurney, and **F. W. H. Myers** concluded in 1881 in their first report on thought-transference: "The possibility must not be overlooked that further advances along the lines indicated may, and we believe, will, necessitate a modification of that general view of the relation of mind to matter to which modern science has long been gravitating."

It must be admitted, however, that these experiments were severely criticized for not excluding **fraud.**

In an 1883–84, extensive series of experiments in Liverpool, England, conducted by Malcolm Guthrie and James Birchall with a Miss Ralph and a Miss Edwards, concluded that impressions of objects and sensations of taste and pain were successfully transmitted. **Sir Oliver Lodge** participated in some of these experiments and initiated some original ones at a later period.

The experiments of **Eleanor Sidgwick** and her more famous husband **Henry Sidgwick** in 1889–90 were classic. In thousands of experiments, a high percentage of success was registered in transferring simple images. The increase of distance, however, apparently had a marked effect on the results. According to **Frank Podmore,** only Dr. Gilbert's and Professor Janet's experiments with "Leonie" at Havre in 1885 and 1886 could compare in competence, care, and precision to the results with these. In the latter case, the effect aimed at was the induction of hypnotic sleep.

Clarissa Miles and Hermione Ramsden experimented through an intervening distance of 20-300 miles in transferring complex images and obtaining **cross-correspondence** of thought-transference. The results were carefully noted down; in many cases, an agreement was found between the impressions of the two parties (see the *Journal* of the Society for Psychical Research vol. 12 and 13, and the *Proceedings* vol. 25).

The psychical researcher **Cesare Lombroso** found 12 neuropaths in 20 subjects who registered success in thought-transference experiments. In some cases, transmission was facilitated by alcoholic drinks or coffee stimulating the nerve centers. He assigned great importance to the "hysterical" state and expressed the opinion that the disequilibrium of sensibility in hysterical persons was an essential condition for the production of the phenomena. This is because these individuals imply a greater accumulation of nervous energy in certain points of the cortex of the brain, and a diminution in others. He did not, however, exclude the possible influence of other causes and held, in alluding to transmission of thought in the dying, that the greater accumulation of energy in the cortex during the period just before death may be due to ptomaines that become lodged in it.

In reviewing this theory, Dr. Guiseppe Venzano speculated (*Annals of Psychic Science,* January 1906) that the causes of the accumulation of greater energy in the centers of intelligence must be manifold and diverse and that disequilibrium of sensibility does not constitute more than one among these many causes. He concluded that: (1) Mediumship favored the development of the phenomenon of transmission of thought, (2) In mediumistic **séances,** the thought formulated by the agent may be carried out even by material actions absolutely independent both of the medium and of the experimenters, (3) Under special circumstances, thought may be transmitted to the medium in a séance—even at a considerable distance—from a person outside the séance (telepathy), (4) The unconscious transmission of thought was possible.

In *Proceedings,* of the Society Psychical Research (1918), **Margaret Verrall** reviewed 504 previous experiments in thought-transference. The *Proceedings* (1924) also contained Eleanor Sidgwick's report on the experiments of **Gilbert Murray,** which she considered "perhaps the most important ever brought to the notice of the society both on account of their frequently brilliant success and on account of the eminence of the experimenter." The percipient of these experiments was Murray himself.

On February 16, 1927, V. J. Woolley, research officer of the Society for Psychical Research, arranged interesting experiments through radio. He and the agents were in the society's office, with no means of communication with anyone outside it. Sir Oliver Lodge sat in the broadcasting office at the microphone and directed the radio listeners to record any impressions they were able to form of the objects willed. They were shown three minutes each with an interval of two minutes. The only information given to the listeners was that the first and fourth objects were playing cards of unusual design; second was a Japanese print of a skull with a bird on top; the third was a bunch of three sprays of white lilac; the fifth was of Woolley himself wearing a bowler hat and a grotesque mask. The agents remained in the society's premises through the night without access to a telephone.

The morning mail brought in 24,659 answers. According to Woolley's summary in *Proceedings,* vol. 38 (part 105), the card test gave no evidence of telepathic transmission but the answers disclosed the peculiarity of a strong tendency to choose an ace, especially the ace of spades and that there was a marked preference for odd-numbered cards as against even-numbered ones. Of the third object, five listeners gave a skull as the description of the picture, one adding the interesting detail that it represented a skull in a garden, and a sixth noted a human head. Of these six records, no less than three gave flowers as the third object. Of the last object of the test, five answers gave the impression of Mr. Woolley, 146 of someone present, 236 of someone dressed up or masquerading, 73 of masks or faces, 202 of hats, and 499 of feeling of amusement.

Woolley, however, believed that these numbers in themselves were of little importance as there was no definite chance of expectation with which to compare them. The number of double successes was very small. "There does seem to be an indication of a supernormal faculty," stated Woolley, "on the part of a few of those who took part, though their successes are swamped by the very large mass of failures on the part of others."

The first attempt to link thought-transference with radio was staged in Chicago some years previous to the Society for Psychical Research experiment by **Gardner Murphy** while at Harvard. At a later date he conducted a second similar experiment with the assistance of **J. Malcolm Bird** in Newark. Murphy did not publish a complete record though the Newark tests were reported in the *Scientific American* (June 1924).

Interesting results in thought-transference have been obtained in cross-correspondence experiments. The principle is that two people at a stated time think of something, write it down and post it to find out whether their thoughts corresponded.

Charles Richet outlined the steps for successful experiments in transferring drawings or cards: (1) The agent must be absolutely motionless and have his back turned to the percipient, (2) The choice of the number, the card, or the drawing must be made by pure chance, (3) No result, whether success or failure, should be told to the percipient before the end of the sitting, (4) Not more than twenty trials should be made on any one day, (5) All results, whatever they may be, should be stated in full, (6) The percipient must be unable to see anything, directly or indirectly; it is best that his eyes should be bandaged and his back turned.

It had been found that the success of thought-transmission depended upon the moods and health of the experimenters. This required concentration on the part of the transmitter and passivity of mind on the part of the recipient. It proved helpful if the agent tried to visualize the picture that he or she wished to convey and was best to keep an object before the eye and think of it while trying to transmit its image.

Lodge observed that the transference of drawings was much more distinct when tactual contact was maintained between the agent and the percipient. He discovered as early as 1883 that when two agents are acting, each contributes to the effect; the result is due to both combined. He put down between two agents a double opaque sheet of thick paper with a square drawn on one side and a St. Andrew's cross on the other. Each agent looked on one side without any notion what was on the other. One percipient declared that "the thing won't keep still . . . I seem to see things moving about. . . . First I see a thing up there and then one down there." Finally the percipient drew a square and drew a cross inside from corner to corner saying afterward "I don't know what made me put it inside."

He also attempted to find out what is really transmitted—the idea, or name of the object or the visual impressions. He observed the transmission of irregular drawings was very difficult and that in some cases the idea or name, and not the visual impression at all, was the thing transferred.

Engineer and psychical researcher **René Warcollier** made an interesting table of the comparative facility in transmission. He found the percentage of color transmission 70 percent; of attitudes, 55 percent; drawings, 45 percent; objects, 38 percent; ideas 37 percent; mental images, 10 percent; words and figures 10 percent. Russian experimenter Dr. N. Kotik found that the percentage of successes increased when the agent and percipient were linked by a wire.

Objections to the reality of thought-transference is primarily two-fold: chance and natural parallelism of kindred minds. Stage demonstrations of thought-transference are known to be explained by a secret code. Sometimes, however, more subtle sensitivity may be present. The stage performer **Mrs. Zancig,** for instance, was found by **James Hewat McKenzie** in experiments at the **British College of Psychic Science** to possess a marked gift of **clairvoyance** to the degree of reading passages in closed books.

Sources:

Braddon, Russell. *The Piddingtons.* London: Werner Laurie, 1950.

Gurney, Edmund, F. W. H. Myers, and Frank Podmore. *Phantasms of the Living.* 2 vols. London: Trubner, 1886. Reprint, Gainesville, Fla.: Scholars' Facsimiles, 1970. Abridged edition, New Hyde Park, N.Y.: University Books, 1962.

Myers, F. W. H. *Human Personality and Its Survival of Bodily Death.* 2 vols. London: Longmans, Green, 1903. Reprint, New York: Arno Press, 1975. Abridged Edition, New Hyde Park, N.Y.: University Books, 1961.

Ostrander, Sheila, and Lynn Schroeder. *Psychic Discoveries Behind the Iron Curtain.* Englewood Cliffs, N.J.: Prentice-Hall, 1970. Reprint, New York: Bantam, 1971. Reprinted as *Psi: Psychic Discoveries Behind the Iron Curtain.* London: Abacus 1973.

Podmore, Frank. *Apparitions and Thought Transference.* London: Scott; New York: Charles Scribner's Sons, 1895.

Rhine, J. B. *Extrasensory Perception.* Boston: Boston Society for Psychical Research, 1934. Reprint, Boston: Branden, 1964.

Schmeidler, Gertrude R., ed. *Extrasensory Perception.* New York: Atherton, 1969.

Schwarz, Berthold Eric. *Parent-Child Telepathy: Five Hundred and Five Possible Episodes in a Family; A Study of the Telepathy of Everyday Life.* New York: Garrett Publications, 1971.

Sinclair, Upton. *Mental Radio.* Pasadena, Calif.: The Author, 1930. Revised edition, Springfield, Ill.: C. C. Thomas, 1962.

Thomas, N. W. *Thought Transference: A Critical and Historical Review of the Evidence for Telepathy.* London: De La More Press, 1905.

Warcollier, René. *Experimental Telepathy.* Boston: Boston Society for Psychical Research, 1938. Reprint, New York: Arno Press, 1975.

———. *Mind to Mind.* Creative Age Press, 1948. Reprint, New York: Macmillan, 1963.

Thouless, Robert Henry (1894–1984)

Psychologist, parapsychologist, and president of the **Society for Psychical Research,** London, from 1942–45. He was born July 15, 1894, in Norwich, England. He studied at Cambridge University, England (B.A. hons., 1914; M.A., 1919; Ph.D., 1922). After serving in World War I, he was a lecturer of psychology at Manchester University in 1921 and moved on to Glasgow University in 1926, and the Department of Education, Cambridge University in 1938.

His initial interest in parapsychology began about 1934 and was stimulated by contact with the experimental work of **J. B. Rhine.** After that, parapsychology became a prominent theme for half a century of his life. He published nearly ninety articles and book reviews in the *Journal* and *Proceedings* of the Society for Psychical Research.

Through the years, Thouless conducted many experiments in card-calling, **psychokinesis,** and other areas of parapsychology. He created many of the current terms used in parapsychology out of the realization that some of the original terms, such as "extrasensory perception," carried with them a suggestion of their operation—in this case "perception." He coined the less-committal term "**psi.**" He and his colleague B. P. Weiser also coined the terms "psi Gamma" and "psi Kappa" to replace **ESP** and **PK.**

In distinction to parapsychologists who disparaged the study of spontaneous phenomena, Thouless maintained that it had value in structuring experimental methods:

"The special function of the study of spontaneous cases is to serve as a guide to the problems to be investigated by experimental methods. . . . [The] choice is not between statistics and experiment on the one hand and observation of spontaneous cases on the other. Let us have much more of both. . . . New problems for experimental investigation may be suggested by new observations of spontaneously occurring phenomena."

On the question of **survival,** he proposed a cautious optimism, and about 1948 devised a cipher test of survival which he believed was his most significant contribution to parapsychology. The test used a standard method of encipherment with a secret key passage. It consisted of two coded sequences: INXPH CJKGM JIRPR FBCVY WYWES NOECN SCVHE GYRJQ TEBJM TGXAT TWPNH CNYBC FNXPF LFXRV QWQL and BTYRR OOFLH KCDXK FWPCZ KTADR GFHKA HTYXO ALZUP PYPVF AYMMF SDLR UVUB. The key to the first sequence was a passage of poetry or prose indicated by reference to its title, and the key to the second sequence consisted of two words. The key passage necessary to cipher the test might have been transmitted posthumously as a proof of survival of consciousness. This method obviated the objection that a claimed posthumous communication might be read by clairvoyance if left in a sealed envelope. The Thouless test did not involve any sealed message and only the correct key would solve the enciphered message. In the event of a claimed posthumous message, percipients were asked to contact the Society for Psychical Research so that it might be keyed into the society's computer program to see if it yielded a correct message.

Thouless was an active member of the Society for Psychical Research and served on its council. He was elected president in 1942. In the end he was willing to consider the religious implications of psi and argued that parapsychology pointed to a more interesting world in which God and what has been termed the supernatural play their part. Thouless died at the age of 90 on September 25, 1984.

Sources:

Berger, Arthur S., and Joyce Berger. *The Encyclopedia of Parapsychology and Psychical Research.* New York: Paragon House, 1991.

Pleasants, Helene, ed. *Biographical Dictionary of Parapsychology.* New York: Helix Press, 1964.

Thouless, Robert Henry. *Authority and Freedom.* London: Hodder and Stroughton, 1954.

———. *Experimental Psychical Research.* Baltimore, Md.: Penguin, 1963.

———. *From Anecdote to Experiment in Psychical Research.* London: Routledge & Kegan Paul, 1972.

———. "The Present Position of Experimental Research into Telepathy and Related Phenomena." *Proceedings* of the Society for Psychical Research 47 (1943).

———. "Problems of Design in Parapsychological Experiments." *Journal* of the Society for Psychical Research (1955).

———. "Psychical Research Past and Present." [Myers Memorial Lecture] *Journal* of the Society for Psychical Research (1952).

———. *Straight and Crooked Thinking.* N.p., 1930. Reprinted as *How to Think Straight.* New York: Simon and Schuster, 1939.

3a Visao

3a Visao (3rd Vision) is one of two newsstand periodicals serving the psychic and esoteric community of Portugal. Launched in 1997, it is designed to cover issues in the areas of mysticism, parapsychology, spiritualism, astrology, nonconventional science, and natural medicine. Each issue includes a set of feature articles that cover psychic experiences, esoteric sciences (**astrology, numerology,** etc.), health, and the personal appropriation of esoteric truth (an inner vision). The esoteric community in Portugal, while having a long history, remains relatively small, though it has been bolstered by the influx of immigrants from Asia and the Middle East during the last decades of the twentieth century. The older theosophical and Spiritualist organizations have been joined by groups promoting new religions, Asian healing techniques, and **channeling.** As the great majority of the Portuguese public is unfamiliar with the occult world, many of the articles are presented at an introductory level. While a range of literature available in Portuguese is advertised, the magazine does not include a book review column.

3a Visao is a full-color magazine published by 3a Visao Editores and edited by a man who goes by the single name of Papalus. He is assisted by a staff of writers drawn from the Portuguese-speaking communities in Brazil and India. *3a Visao* also cosponsors events in Portugal aimed at promoting its general area of interest. *3a Visao* may be contacted at its editorial offices at Rua Almirante Cesar Augusto Campos Rodrigues, n.16–13 Esq., 2795 Carnaxide, Portugal.

Sources:

3a Visao. Carnaxide, Portugal, n.d.

3D Nibiruan Council

The 3D Nibiruan Council is one of several **channeling** organizations that, like the **Ashtar Command,** claim contact with a set of extraterrestrial beings. Its earthly presence dates from 1992 and a traumatic experience in the life of a trainer and entrepreneur named Jocelyn. While in the hospital for an abortion, she lost consciousness, and a second personality who called herself Jelaila emerged in her place. The new personality described herself as a **walk-in.** Jelaila assumed the role of mother to Jocelyn's daughter Daniele.

Jelaila describes her pre-embodied life as that of a 9th-dimensional being. When she walked in, she was unaware of her mission but in May 1993 made contact with Devin, the head of the 9D Nibiruan Council. He began training her and awakening her to her role as a channel and voice of the Nibiruan Council on earth.

The Greater Nibiruan Council is seen as the largest council of the Galactic Federation (the interplanetary authority mentioned and described in flying saucer **contactee** literature beginning since the 1950s). It serves as the primary governing arm of the Federation. Among its many duties are supporting Federation emissaries to various planets, developing communications between various planetary beings, and initiating training for potential new members of the Federation (such as Earth).

The Greater Nibiruan Council consists of a set of what are described as dimensional councils, among them beiing the 9D (or ninth dimension) Nibiruan Council. This oldest Council in the Greater Council has the task of coordinating efforts with other councils and with various Spiritual Hierarchies for the evolution of all souls. In particular it has charge of the Earth Grand Experiment. The 9D Nibiruan Council is said to be composed of two royal families, Aln and Avyon, from the Lyra constellation.

The 3D Nibiruan Council has the responsibility of representing the higher councils on Earth and of supplying the 9D tools of Integration to Earthlings. It carries out this function through the publication of books and other materials and the sponsoring of seminars and workshops. the 3D Council was formally organized in 1996 in Kansas City, Missouri, and moved to Los Angeles in 1998. That same year, Jelaila married John Starr. In December 1998, John Starr experienced a walk-in an was replaced by an entity personality named Jehowah, a 9D Council member and brother of Divan who had trained Jelaila.

The Nibiruan Council is one of a spectrum of groups that see the human race preparing for ascension to a higher dimension in the near future and who see a key to that ascension being the recodings of the individual's DNA. It offers training in what is termed the Accelerated DNA Recoding Process. This training among its many benefits, releases painful memories of the past. The Council also offers training in the realization and manifestation on compassion.

A more complete description of the larger Nibiruan Council and a presentation of its program are found on its website at http://www.nibiruancouncil.com/.

Sources:

3D Nibiruan Council. http://www.nibiruancouncil.com/. February 28, 2000.

3HO Foundation

Educational branch of the Sikh Dharma, a Sikh religious group founded by Shri Singh Bhai Sahib Harbhajan Singh Khalsa Yogiji, popularly known as Yogi Bhajan in Los Angeles in the late 1960s. "3HO" means "Healthy, Happy, Holy Organization," and is based on the idea that it is everyone's birthright to obtain these three characteristics. The foundation provides teacher training courses, lectures, and demonstrations in all types of **yoga,** with special emphasis on **kundalini** yoga.

The group is also focused on "the uplift of the dignity and respect of womanhood." Programs such as the *Khalsa Women's Training Camp* and *Young Women's Camp* are specialized to unleash the inner potential of women. Publications include a journal **Prosperity Paths** Address: P.O. Box 2337, Espanola, NM 87532. Website: http://www.3ho.org/.

Sources:

Kundalini Yoga/Sadhana Guidelines. Pomona, Calif.: KRI Publications, 1978.

Healthy Happy Holy Organization. http://www.3ho.org/. March 8, 2000.

Thule Society

German occult society founded in Munich in 1918 by Adam Glauer (1875–1945) who styled himself Rudolf, Freiherr von Sebottendorf. This was an anti-Semitic society that had links with Adolf Hitler through the German Workers' Party (later National Socialist German Workers Party). The activities of the Thule Group were as much political as **occult,** and their sphere of influence included judges, police chiefs, professors, and industrialists.

Dietrich Eckart, a central figure in the Thule Group, also played a prominent part in the committee of the German

Workers' Party and became one of the seven founder members of the Nazi Party. When he died in December 1923, he is reported to have said: "Follow Hitler! He will dance, but it is I who have called the tune! I have initiated him into the 'Secret Doctrine,' opened his centers in vision and given him the means to communicate with the Powers. Do not mourn for me: I shall have influenced history more than any other German."

Sources:

Howe, Ellic. *Urania's Children: The Strange World of the Astrologers.* London, 1967. Reprinted as *Astrology: A Recent History Including the Untold Story of its Role in World War II.* Walker, 1968.

King, Francis. *Satan and Swastika: The Occult and the Nazi Party.* London: Mayflower, 1976.

Ravenscroft, Trevor. *The Spear of Destiny.* London, 1973.

Webb, James. *The Occult Establishment.* LaSalle, Ill.: Open Court Publishing, 1976.

Thurston, Herbert Henry Charles (S. J.) (1856–1939)

Roman Catholic priest, historian, and writer on parapsychological subjects. He was born on November 15, 1856, in London. He was educated at Séminaire St. Malo, France; Mount St. Mary's, Derbyshire, England; Stonyhurst, Lancashire, England; Manresa House, Roehampton; and the University of London. He became a novice in the Society of Jesus in 1874. During his lengthy career he authored over 700 articles, essays, pamphlets, and translations.

In 1919 he joined the **Society for Psychical Research,** London, and was active in its deliberation for the rest of his life. He became one of its most widely read members, which compensated for the fact that as a practicing Roman Catholic he could not attend **séances,** even as an observer. He was particularly interested in **poltergeist** phenomena and **Spiritualism,** and also made a study of miraculous and paranormal events associated with holy people and saints in Roman Catholicism. While his opinions in general represented a minority opinion in parapsychological circles, he was a well-respected scholar.

His books include: *Beauraing and Other Apparitions* (1934), *The Church and Spiritualism* (1933), *Ghosts and Poltergeists* (1953), *The Memory of Our Dead* (1915), *Physical Phenomena of Mysticism* (1955), *Superstition* (1933), and *Surprising Mystics* (1955).

He died November 3, 1939.

Sources:

Berger, Arthur S., and Joyce Berger. *The Encyclopedia of Parapsychology and Psychical Research.* New York: Paragon House, 1991.

Crehan, J. *Father Thurston.* London: Sheed and Ward, 1952.

Pleasants, Helene, ed. *Biographical Dictionary of Parapsychology.* New York: Helix Press, 1964.

Thurston, Herbert. "The Phenomena of Stigmatization." *Proceedings* of the Society for Psychical Research 32, no. 83 (1922).

Thury, Marc (1822–1905)

Swiss psychical researcher, professor of physics and natural history at the University of Geneva, and a pioneer of investigations into **telekinesis** phenomena. In a small pamphlet *Les Tables tournantes* (1855) he reviewed **Count de Gasparin**'s experiments and detailed his own observations with a circle of private friends under test conditions. He was the first exponent of the theory of **ectoplasm.** He named the substance that he believed to be a link between the soul and body "psychode," and the force that manipulated it "**ectenic force.**" This force, he believed, was subject to the will power of the **medium.**

While De Gasparin repudiated **Spiritism** as absurd and contrary to moral truth, Thury contended that while "the known facts are not as yet sufficient for the demonstration of the spirit theory," yet "the absurdity of the belief in the intervention of spirits has not been scientifically demonstrated." He asserted that there may exist in this world wills other than those of man and the animals, wills capable of acting on matter.

Sources:

Pleasants, Helene, ed. *Biographical Dictionary of Parapsychology.* New York: Helix Press, 1964.

Thury, Marc. *Les Tables tournantes.* Geneva, 1855.

TIBET

Historical Background

Tibet is a country with ancient religious and mystical traditions that, over the last two centuries, have become the focus of **occult** legends. The peaceful accumulation of data on Tibet was abruptly altered following the Chinese communist invasion in October 1950, when Tibet lost its independent status. On May 23, 1951, Tibetan leaders were obliged to sign a Sino-Tibetan agreement for "the peaceful liberation of Tibet."

Tibetans had formerly been a separate people with a distinctive language, culture, and religion, but had been in an uneasy relationship with **China** since 1720, when the Manchus entered Tibet to help drive out Mongol invaders and used the situation to become overlords. Over the subsequent period, the acknowledgment of Chinese suzerainty was the price of Tibetan autonomy, but for practical purposes Tibet was an independent state.

The 1950 invasion was justified by the Chinese as necessary in order to destroy inequitable feudalism in Tibet and to bring progress, education, and social justice. In practice, this involved suppression of the Buddhist religion, destruction of monasteries and their libraries, and the public humiliation of priests. Tibet was a theocratic society and any reorganization of its governmental system would necessarily involve the destruction of the power held by the Buddhist religious functionaries.

In all fairness, it must be said that these and other reported violations of human rights were largely paralleled by similar excesses in China itself in the early period of the communist revolution and the upheavals of the Cultural Revolution. Since then, however, the age-old Buddhist religion of Tibet has been largely suppressed and related occult practices replaced by practical socialism and exploitation of Tibetan resources and territory.

Religion and Superstition

Buddhism came to Tibet from India in the eighth century C.E. and it pushed aside the earlier polytheistic and magical religion of the Tibetan people. However, the price of the conquest was the integration of many of the old deities, beliefs, and occult practices into the unique form of Buddhism that emerged in the land. Also moving into Tibet from **India** was a form of Hindu **tantra,** with its emphasis upon the subtle energies of the body and ritualized sex. Strong superstitions, belief in **ghosts,** demons, and **magic** coexisted with deep mystical thought.

The apostle of Buddhism in Tibet was named Padmasambhava and entered the country in the 1740s. As Buddhism developed, it divided into various sects, the degree of acceptance of the local religion being an important differentiating factor. The four main groups are popularly distinguished by the color of the hats their followers wear. The older Red Caps or *Ningmapas,* for example, follow the *Adi-Yoga* or path of the Great Perfection, founded by the guru Padmasambhava, while the Yellow Cap sect or *Gelugpas* follow a Middle Way Buddhism; the Kargyütpas, or Followers of Successive Order (deriving from the great Tibetan saint Milarepa, died 1135, successor of the revered gurus Marpa, Tilopa, and Naropa) follow the way of *Mahamudra* or Great Symbol. As with the various sects of Hindu religious philosophy, with their many subtle emphases, the general overall philosophy of the four groups is the same.

By the fifteenth century a teaching had emerged in Tibet that the heads of all of the many monasteries were bodhisattvas, highly evolved beings who were refraining from entering Nirvana to assist other souls in their spiritual pilgrimage. The monastic rulers, or lamas, thus attained a unique role in Tibetan Buddhism as well as significant political power as temporal rulers.

The present spiritual leader of Tibet, the fourteenth Dalai Lama, who escaped to India in 1959, and the other lamas and their successors, are dedicated to keeping alive the spiritual traditions and the political aspirations to independence of the Tibetan people.

Like his predecessors, the Dalai Lama is claimed as a living incarnation of the Divine Spirit, and was discovered as such by traditional search and testing. When a Dalai Lama (or any lama for that matter) departs from life, priests traditionally conduct a search for his successor through signs and visions. Selected children are tested by their ability to recognize objects belonging to the former Dalai Lama. After identification, the child is brought to the holy city of Lhasa and initiated as a monk in the monastery of the Potala, which becomes a power center of the Divine Spirit, which issues forth from the Dalai Lama over the whole of Tibet. As Tibetan Buddhism has spread to the west and lamas have died in the west, the search for successors has also been conducted in the families of Western converts and several European children have been "identified" as reincarnated lamas.

The title "Dalai Lama" is from a Mongolian term meaning "Wide Ocean," and is not normally used by Tibetans among themselves, who prefer such terms as "Precious Protector" or "Precious Ruler," of *Kundun* (Presence), implying spiritual association. The first Dalai Lama was Tsong Ka-pa, born in Am-do in 1358. His disciples became the Yellow Hat sect, as distinct from the earlier priesthood of the Red Hats.

In addition to the regular monastic disciplines of complex prayer, meditation rites, and regular religious festivals, lamas traveling through Tibet were expected to act as oracles, fortune-tellers, and healers for the ordinary people. Prayer wheels with the mystic mantra "Om mani padme Hum" (Om, The Jewel in the Lotus) and rosaries were in use all over the country, and groups of prayer-flags fluttered around the villages. In the monasteries, *tankas* (complex symbolic mandala banners) became a focus for mystical meditation.

It is not difficult to understand why Lamaism should be permeated with **demonology** in view of the vast and terrifying grandeur of the Tibetan environment, in which the forces of nature appear to have the power of supernatural beings. Belief in magic was once universal.

The Dalai Lama came under attack in 1998 when he publicly announced that Dorje Shugden practices should no longer be performed by any sect of Tibetan Buddhism. Shugden has been regarded as a protector spirit of the Geluk sect, to which the Dalai Lama himself belongs. However, after studying ancient texts and consulting the state oracle, the Dalai Lama is convinced that Shugden is a hungry spirit and therefore incorrect to worship and regard as a protector for the Buddhist. Due to the Dalai Lama's opposing view, he is accused by some Buddhists for being a religious censor. Since the Tibetan culture and religion is thought to be near extinction, the Dalai Lama attempted to set a level of commonality between all sects of Buddhism. The great controversy that resulted from this attempted act of unification, may have also been the cause for the deaths of three monks in the Dalai Lama's inner circle.

Dissent within the Tibetan culture may be the result of the larger issues that still exist between Chinese and the Tibetan government-in-exile. The Chinese government seeks to control, and ultimately squelch, the Tibetan Buddhism religion. Ultimately the set-up of the religious hierarchy may become the demise of the religion itself. The Dalai Lama exists as the highest, top authority, while the Panchen Lama is the second in command, and the Karampa is the third in power. Presently the Panchen Lama, a boy of ten years, will be the one to choose the next Dalai Lama. However, with the aging Dalai Lama living in India, the Panchen Lama is still being held under Chinese supervision. This is a direct example of the Chinese wishing to control the Buddhist chain of command, and influence the continuity of the religion. The Chinese government conducted the search for this present Panchen Lama but the Dalai Lama announced their discovery publicly before ever having met him. The boy has never even been in Dharmsala, India. Thus, the boy has become a political pawn between the Dalai Lama (Tibetan Buddhism) and the Chinese government.

The Karampa, third in command, has been raised to heed the Chinese government as well. However, on December 28, 1999, he made his escape from Tibet to India to be united with the Dalai Lama. The two men met " 'as if a father was meeting his dear son after a long separation' ". The Dalai Lama reported his spirit as clear and strong saying after proper instruction he will be able to make great contributions. The struggle between Tibet and China continues and therefore the outcome of the survival of Tibetan Buddhism.

David-Neel's Psychic Sports

For centuries, Tibet was a forbidden territory to Westerners, and only a handful of Europeans succeeded in penetrating the country, usually in disguise. From 1912 on, an intrepid Frenchwoman, Alexandra David-Neel, began a series of travels through Tibet over fourteen years. She acquired the rank of lama.

An Oriental scholar, David-Neel learned Sanskrit and Tibetan and studied the various forms of Buddhism and Lamaism. She became the first European woman to penetrate the holy city of Lhasa. Although skeptical regarding the supernatural, she gained firsthand experience of Tibetan ghosts and demons and saw the paranormal feats of mystics. In her book *With Mystics and Magicians in Tibet* (1931), she revealed how Tibetan mystics acquired the ability to live naked in zero temperatures by generating a protective body heat (*tumo*), how they learned to float in air and walk on water, and how they brought corpses back to life or created **thoughtforms** that had independent existence.

She described such feats as "psychic sports," acquired by special mind and body training. Amongst such feats was the *lung-gom* training of "inner breathing" and meditation, which enabled an individual to travel at high speed for days and nights without stopping, sometimes with the feet hardly touching the ground. David-Neel herself witnessed a *lung-gom-pa,* or swift traveler. She described the special training necessary for feats of **levitation** and for thought-reading and **telepathy** ("sending thoughts on the wind").

She successfully experimented in the creation of a *tulpa* or phantom thoughtforms. After a period in isolation following special concentration techniques, she claimed that she succeeded in creating a phantom monk, who became a guest in her party, seen and accepted by the others. But in the course of time, this phantom form changed from a fat jolly monk, becoming lean, mocking, and somewhat malignant, and it was necessary for her to concentrate on special techniques to destroy a phantom, which was beginning to take on independent life.

She explained that Tibetans believed that such psychic phenomena were the result of utilizing natural forces by the powers of the mind. Her experiences seem to have been the result of a long and intimate association with Tibet and its peoples in a period when magic and mystery were more common. Few subsequent travelers have reported such remarkable phenomena, and her books survive as a unique record of a Tibet that has largely been destroyed. However, they helped create the image of Tibet as a place where the most successful mastery of the occult arts had been made. The spread of Buddhist masters to the west has done much to offer a more mundane picture of Tibetan life.

Tibetan medicine, the fundamentals virtually unchanged for 2,000 years, is completely intertwined with Tibetan Buddhism, in that they are based on the most essential Buddhist belief, that of **karma.** Thus, unhealthy human actions, such as, greed, hatred, and desire can be the cause of disease. Like karma, disease can be caused from present as well as past actions. Disease is also thought to be caused by an imbalance of the three basic humors of the body—air, bile, and phlegm. Diagnosis consists of three techniques, visual observation, pulse reading, and questioning. Simply put, Tibetan medicine is highly **holistic** in the areas of diagnosis and treatment. Treatments are usually always of the non-invasive variety. Lifestyle changes are recommended, medicines are made of herbs, and "surgery" consists of **acupuncture,** cauterization, hot and cold compresses, hot springs and vapor treatments.

A lot can be learned from Tibetan medicine by Western countries, as it and its practitioners listen and are aware of the individual body, as an extension of religion. The body then exists as only part of the whole scheme of the universe.

It is still too early to predict whether the upheavals of the last half of the twentieth century will involve a permanent loss of spiritual and psychic identity for the Tibetan people. Those many Tibetans who moved into exile have established strong enclaves of traditional Tibetan culture and many people have given of their time, energy, and financial resources to see that the manuscripts and artifacts taken out of the country are preserved.

Sources:

Bernard, Theos. *Land of a Thousand Buddhas.* London: Rider, 1952.

Bromage, Bernard. *Tibetan Yoga.* London: Aquarian Press, 1952.

"A Buddha Busts Out: Inside the Dramatic Escape of a Living Buddha." *Newsweek* 135 (March 6, 2000): 38.

Chang, Garma C. C., trans. *The Hundred Thousand Songs of Milarepa.* 2 vols. New Hyde Park, N.Y.: University Books, 1962.

———. *Teachings of Tibetan Yoga.* New Hyde Park, N.Y.: University Books, 1963.

David-Neel, Alexandra. *My Journey to Lhasa.* London: William Heinemann, 1927.

———. *With Mystics and Magicians in Tibet.* London: John Lane, 1931. Reprinted as *Magic & Mystery in Tibet.* New York: Claude H. Kendall, 1932. Reprint, New Hyde Park, N.Y.: University Books, 1956.

David-Neel, Alexandra, and Lama Yongden. *The Secret Oral Teachings in Tibetan Buddhist Sects.* Calcutta, India: Maha Bodhi Society of India, n.d.

Evans-Wentz, W. Y. *Tibet's Great Yogi Milarepa.* London: Oxford University Press, 1928.

Gore, Donald R. "Tibetan Medicine." *Perspectives in Biology and Medicine* 42 (Winter '99): 270–71.

Harrer, Heinrich. *Return to Tibet.* London: Weinfeld & Nicholson, 1984.

———. *Seven Years in Tibet.* London: Rupert Hart-Davis; New York: E. P. Dutton, 1953.

Klein, Richard. "The World's Youngest Political Prisoner." *The Humanist.* 59 (March 1999): 91.

Tibet and Freedom. The Tibet Society of the United Kingdom, 1961.

Tibetan Government in Exile Official Website. http://www.tibet.com/. June 19, 2000.

Waddell, L. Austine. *Tibetan Buddhism: With Its Mystic Cults, Symbolism and Mythology, and in Its Relation to Indian Buddhism.* London: W. H. Allen, 1895. Reprint, New York: Dover Publications, 1972.

Wilson, Mike. "Schisms, Murder, and Hungry Ghosts in Shangra-La." *Cross Currents* 49 (Spring 1999): 251.

Woodward, Kenneth. "A Scratch in the Teflon Lama." 131 (May 11, 1998): 64.

"The Tibetan"

The Master, known in theosophical circles as Dhwal Khul (under various spellings) who first spoke to **Helena Petrovna Blavatsky,** and in the early twentieth century spoke through **Alice A. Bailey** (1880–1949). Bailey, formerly a member of the **Theosophical Society,** withdrew in the 1920s and established the **Arcane School** in New York.

Tibetan Foundation

The Tibetan Foundation began in June of 1982 when Janet McClure established contact with the Ascended **Master Djwal Khul.** He asked her to assist him in his work of helping people in their own spiritual progress and bringing about the coming **New Age.** Previously she had studied with the Brotherhood of the White Light, from whom she received a doctorate degree, and was happy to join in the work. Djwal Khul is the same master who was originally identified by **Helena Petrovna Blavatsky** (1831–1891) as one of the spiritual hierarchy and later was credited with **channeling** a number of volumes through **Alice A. Bailey** (1880–1949). Bailey generally referred to Djwal Khul as The Tibetan.

While McClure was generally thought of as channeling The Tibetan, she spoke of his overshadowing her. Overshadowing is a special connection by which they became permanently linked. The Tibetan was thought to be anchored in McClure's head. He could speak through her without the necessity of her entering a trance state.

The foundation was established in Youngstown, Arizona, but soon developed affiliate centers in Colorado and California. Once launched on her new endeavor, McClure channeled a considerable amount of material from The Tibetan that was published in a number of booklets. She also began to channel from other beings such as Vywamus and Lenduce. She was among the first of the channels to receive material from both the spiritual hierarchy and the space hierarchy led by **Ashtar.** Receiving from both hierarchies would become common in the 1990s. The channels associated with the foundation would become part of the post-New Age Movement that was focused in the **Sedona Journal of Emergence.**

McClure channeled only eight years before passing away in 1990. However, by that time other channels had become associated with the Tibetan Foundation and had begun to channel the various masters previously channeled by McClure, especially The Tibetan and Vywamus. Light Technology Publishing, the parent company that produces the *Sedona Journal of Emergence,* published many of McClure's volumes of channeled material and keeps them in print at present.

Sources:

Bjorling, Joel. *Channeling: A Bibliographic Exploration.* New York: Garland Publishing, 1992.

McClure, Janet [Vywamus]. *Sanat Kumara: Training a Planetary Logos.* Sedona, Ariz.: Light Technology Publishing, 1989.

———. *Scopes of Dimensions.* Sedona, Ariz.: Light Technology Publishing, 1989.

———. *The Source Adventure.* Sedona, Ariz.: Light Technology Publishing, 1988.

Tii

A Polynesian **vampire.**

Tijdschrift voor Parapsychologie

Major Dutch journal of **parapsychology,** founded and edited for many years by **W. H. C. Tenhaeff** (1894–1981) and more recently edited by Dick J. Bierman. It functions as the journal of both the **Studievereniging voor Psychical Research** (the Dutch Society for Psychical Research) and the Parapsychology Institute. Address: Springweg 7, 3511 VH Utrecht, The Netherlands.

Tillyard, R(obin) J(ohn) (1881–1937)

British psychical researcher and biologist, vice president of the **National Laboratory of Psychical Research** in 1926. He was born in Norwich, England, on January 31, 1881. He was educated at Dover College, and Queen's College, Cambridge University (M.A., Sc.D.). Following his graduation in 1903 he migrated to Australia and taught at the Sydney Grammar School for a decade (1904–13) before becoming a Fellow in Zoology at Sydney University (1914–17) and then a lecturer in zoology in 1917. In 1920 he became Chief Entomologist to the Commonwealth of Australia.

He traveled to England and the United States in the 1920s to sit with mediums, especially **Mina Crandon** (**"Margery"**). This sitting convinced him of **survival** of bodily death. He published his convictions in 1928 in *Nature.* In a "solus" sitting with "Margery" in Boston, he obtained apparent fingerprints of "Walter," the **control.** In his enthusiastic letter to **Sir Oliver Lodge** he stated: "This séance is, for me, the culminating point of all my psychical research; I can now say, if I so desire, *nunc dimittis,* and go on with my own legitimate entomological work." However, there now seems little doubt that this particular phenomenon was fraudulent.

During his association with psychical researcher **Harry Price** at the National Laboratory of Psychical Research, Tillyard also investigated the phenomena of **Eleonore Zügun** and **Stella C.**

In his book *Confessions of a Ghost Hunter* (1936; 1974), Harry Price described a visit to Jeanne Laplace, a French clairvoyant, who gave a remarkable series of correct statements about Tillyard through simply holding a letter from him (without seeing the letter itself). The impressions included the prediction, later fulfilled, that he would die in a railway accident.

Sources:

Berger, Arthur S., and Joyce Berger. *The Encyclopedia of Parapsychology and Psychical Research.* New York: Paragon House, 1991.

Evans, J. W. *The Life and Work of Robin John Tillyard, 1881–1937.* St. Lucia: University of Queensland Press, 1963.

Pleasants, Helene, ed. *Biographical Dictionary of Parapsychology.* New York: Helix Press, 1964.

Tillyard, R. J. "Evidence of Survival of a Human Personality." *Nature* 122 (August 28, 1928).

———. "Science and Psychical Research." *Nature* 118 (1926).

Timaeus of Locri (ca. 400 B.C.E.)

One of the earliest known writers on the doctrines of **magic.** He was a Pythagorean philosopher born in Locri, Italy, and lived ca. 420–380 B.C.E. He is credited with the work *On the Soul of the Universe,* although some historians believe this may be an abridgement of Plato's dialogue of *Timaeus.*

The Timaean theory of God, the Universe, and the World-soul was thus set forth by A. F. Büsching:

"God shaped the eternal unformed matter by imparting to it His being. The inseparable united itself with the separable; the unvarying with the variable; and, moreover, in the harmonic conditions of the Pythagorean system. To comprehend all things better, infinite space was imagined as divided into three portions, which are—the centre, the circumference, and the intermediate space.

"The centre is most distant from the highest God, who inhabits the circumference; the space between the two contains the celestial spheres. When God descended to impart His being, the emanations from Him penetrated the whole of heaven, and filled the same with imperishable bodies. Its power decreased with the distance from the source, and lost itself gradually in our world in minute portions, over which matter was still dominant.

"From this proceeds the continuous change of being and decay below the moon, where the power of matter predominates; from this, also, arise the circular movements of the heaven and the earth, the various rapidities of the stars, and the peculiar motion of the planets. By the union of God with matter, a third being was created. namely, the world-soul, which vitalizes and regulates all things, and occupies the space between the centre and the circumference."

Plato's *Timaeus* also tells the legendary story of the lost drowned continent of **Atlantis.**

Time (in Paranormal Perception)

Time is an element of uncertainty in paranormal functions. Yet we know from hypnotic experiments that the subconscious mind has a remarkable faculty in estimating time. J. Milne Bramwell made classical demonstrations, such as suggesting to a hypnotic subject, Miss A., that at the expiration of 11.470 minutes, she should make a cross on a piece of paper and note the time. Out of 55 similar experiments, 45 were completed successfully.

One would expect that if an entity, communicating through an entranced individual, was either a hypnotic or secondary **personality,** that the entity should demonstrate the same consciousness of time discovered by Bramwell. Such has not been the case. Its surprising absence needs an alternative explanation. Certainly fraudulent production of the entity by the **medium** would explain the lack of time consciousness. Spiritualists have suggested that the odd relationship to time, often manifesting displacements of a day or more, provides additional proof of the presence of extraneous entities in **séances.**

In one instance, "Pelham," a spirit control of **Leonora Piper,** was often asked to go and see what a certain friend was doing at the moment. The account that he gave on his return often contained descriptions that applied to happenings a day after or what he thought a day before.

The psychical researcher **S. G. Soal** received through Blanche Cooper communication from Gordon Davis, a friend who, a few months after, turned up alive. Through the medium, he gave a description of his house. The description was incorrect at the time he turned up but perfectly matched his home a year after.

In clairvoyant perceptions, a similar uncertainty is often noticed. The percipients often do not know whether the visions of events that unfold themselves refer to the past or future. There is a good instance in Quaker history. George Fox cried "Woe to the bloody city of Lichfield" as he passed through it, and discovered later this was not a prophecy but a psychometric sensation of the martyrdoms in a past age. The British investigator **J. W. Dunne** observed a mixture of past and future elements in **dreams,** as described in experiments he conducted.

Sources:

Bramwell, J. Milne. *Hypnotism.* London: G. Richards, 1903.

Dunne, J. W. *An Experiment with Time.* London: A. & C. Black; New York: Macmillan, 1927.

Time Pattern Research Institute

A New York astrological corporation founded May 1967, bringing modern technology to horoscopes. The institute used an IBM 360-30 computer in conjunction with well-known astrologer Katina Theodossiou. The computer's memory banks held twenty-five million items of basic information. Individual horoscopes ran to ten thousand words, including character analysis and future trends, and the company merchandized hundreds of thousands of horoscopes, using department stores as outlets. The service provided by the institute became obsolete as the slew of astrological computers permeated the market. (See also **Astroflash**)

Tingley, Katherine (Augusta Westcott) (1847–1929)

Prominent American Theosophist who founded a Theosophical community at Point Loma, California. Tingley was born on July 6, 1847, at Newburyport, Massachusetts, and was educated at a public school in Newburyport and under a private instructress. She took an early interest in social work before becoming active in the fields of **Spiritualism** and later **Theosophy.** In 1887, she formed the Society of Mercy (concerned with emergency relief work on New York's East Side). At this time she became known as a Spiritualist **medium.**

Through her social work she met theosophist **William Q. Judge,** who made a profound impression on her. With the sponsorship of Judge, one of the co-founders of the **Theosophical Society,** she quickly became an important figure in the American branch.

After the death of **Helena Petrovna Blavatsky** in 1891, Judge led the majority of American Theosophists in a secession from the international society then headed by **Annie Besant** and **Henry S. Olcott.** Judge died in March 1896, and his independent **Theosophical Society in America** stated that he had nominated a successor, referred to in symbolic language as "The Purple Mother." A month later, E. T. Hargrove, then president of the Theosophical Society in America, confirmed that "The Purple Mother" was Katherine Tingley.

Soon afterward, Tingley began a World Crusade for Theosophy, during which she claimed to have encountered a theosophical master in Darjeeling. Upon returning to the United States, she founded the School for the Revival of the Lost Mysteries of Antiquity, at Point Loma, California. She also founded the Universal Brotherhood organization, and after taking charge of the Theosophical Society, she merged it with the Universal Brotherhood. Permanent headquarters were established at Point Loma, San Diego, California, in 1900.

During the Spanish-American War, Katherine Tingley organized the War Relief Corps and established an emergency hospital on Long Island for soldiers wounded in Cuba. In 1899 the International Brotherhood League, a department of the Theosophical Society, undertook relief work in Cuba. Later, Tingley visited Cuba and brought a group of children to Point Loma for education. She was first obliged to prove the financial and moral competence of the society to take charge of the children. She was funded by the U.S. government to establish hospitals in Cuba, and in 1925 was awarded the Medal of Honor of the German Red Cross. In 1924 she established a summer school for children at Visingsoe, Sweden, and in the following year, she opened seven new Theosophical Centers in Europe.

Tingley was editor of *Theosophical Path,* published at Point Loma, as well as other Theosophical magazines in Holland, Germany, and Sweden. She also founded *The New Way,* a monthly magazine for free distribution to prisoners in penitentiaries and jails.

She died July 11, 1929, in Sweden, after an automobile accident in Germany, and was succeeded at the Point Loma community by Dr. Gottfried de Purucker. The community survived until World War II when a combination of financial difficulties and the strategic position of the community's land on the Point Loma peninsula led to its sale. The property is now the site of a college.

Sources:

Greenwalt, Emmett A. *California Utopia: Point Loma, 1897–1942.* San Diego, 1978.

Tingley, Katherine. *The Gods Await.* Point Loma, Calif., 1929.

———. *Theosophy and Some of the Vital Problems of the Day.* N.p., 1915.

———. *Theosophy, The Path of the Mystic.* Point Loma, Calif., 1922. Reprint, Pasadena, Calif.: Theosophical University Press, 1977.

———. *The Voice of the Soul.* Point Loma, Calif., 1928.

———. *The Wine of Life.* Point Loma, Calif.: Woman's International Theosophical League, 1925.

———. *The Wisdom of the Heart: Katherine Tingley Speaks.* Compiled by W. Emmett Small. San Diego, 1978.

Tischner, Rudolf (1879–1961)

Ophthalmologist of Munich, who entered the ranks of leading German psychical researchers in 1919 with the publication of his *Über Telepathie und Hellsehen,* one of the groundworks on the subject (translated into English as *Telepathy and Clairvoyance,* 1925). It was followed in 1920 by a small book on the clairvoyant Ludwig Aub, *Einführung in den Okkultismus and Spiritismus,* and *Monismus und Okkultismus.*

Tischner was also the author of many small monographs and of a large historic work: *Geschichte der okkultistischen Forschung. Von der Antike bis zur Gegenwart* (1924), which was published as the second volume to August F. Ludwig's *Geschichte der okkultistischen Forschung bis zur Gegenwart . . . Mitte des 19 Jahrhunderts.* It is a comprehensive and careful survey of the history of **psychical research.** The **Society for Psychical Research,** London, honored this work by making Tischner a corresponding member. He published a study under the title *Fernfühlen und Mesmerismus,* (1925) which deals with the experiments of **Eugerne Rochas** on the exteriorization of sensibility.

With his research, lectures, and propaganda work Tischner did a great deal for the advancement of psychic science in Germany prior to the disruptions of the Nazi era.

His later books included: *Der Okkultimus als Natur und Geisteswissenschaft* (Occultism as a Natural and Philosophical Science, 1926), *Ergebnisse Okkulter Forschung* (Results of Occult Research, 1950), and *Geschichte der Parapsychologie* (History of Parapsychology, 1960). Tischner was among the first to use the term "extrasensory perception" before it was adopted by **J. B. Rhine.** He died April 24, 1961 at Vierhöfen, Germany.

Sources:

Berger, Arthur S., and Joyce Berger. *The Encyclopedia of Parapsychology and Psychical Research.* New York: Paragon House, 1991.

Tischner, Rudolf. *Franz Anton Mesmer: Leben, Werk und Wirkungen.* Munchen: Verlag der Müncher Drucke, 1928.

———. *Geschichte der okkultistischen Forschung.* Pfülling: Johannes Baum Verlag, 1924.

Tissot, James Joseph Jacques (1836–1902)

Well-known French painter of the life of Christ, chiefly remembered in **Spiritualism** for his mezzotint "Apparition Medianimique," which portrayed his impressions of a **materialization séance** in 1885 with the **medium William Eglinton.** He saw the apparition of his departed fiancée accompanied by "Ernest," the guide of the medium. The painting was acquired by the **London Spiritualist Alliance.**

TM

Initialism for **Transcendental Meditation,** the popular Hindu meditation system taught by **Maharishi Mahesh Yogi.**

Tocquet, Robert (1898– ?)

Professor of chemistry who published books on parapsychology and the occult. He was born on June 5, 1898, in Saint-Oulph (Aube), France. He taught at the Ecole des Travaux Publics and the Ecole d'Anthropologie de Paris. In addition to his many books on chemistry and science, he published *Encyclopédie pour la Jeunesse,* a five volume encyclopedia for young people.

Tocquet had a strong interest in psychology and was a member of the board of the **Institut Métapsychique International.** He authored a number of articles and several books on occult topics. His titles include: *Les Calculateurs prodiges et leurs secrets* (The Magic of Numbers, 1957), *La Médecine se tait* (When Medicine is Silent, 1954), *Phénomès de mediumnité* (Phenomena of Mediumship), *Les Pouvoirs secrets de l'Homme* (The Secret Powers of Man, 1963), and *Tout l'Occultisme dévoilé* (Secrets of the Occult Revealed, 1952.)

Today's Astrologer

Monthly bulletin of the **American Federation of Astrologers** available to members of the federation. The bulletin contains news of classes, lectures, and events connected with the AFA, and substantive articles on various aspects of **astrology** of a professional nature. The headquarters of the federation may be reached at P.O. Box 22040, Tempe, AZ 85285 or through their web site at http://www.astrologers.com.

Token Object

An object associated with the subject, held by the psychic giving a reading. It might be a slip of paper with a name on it, unseen to the psychic, who gives information relative to that named person while holding the paper. It might alternatively be an object that the psychic holds while giving impressions through **psychometry,** i.e., apparently being sensitive to impressions from that object.

Toland, John (1670–1722)

John Toland, first chief of the revived Druid movement in England, was born on November 30, 1670, near Londonderry, Ireland. Originally named Junius Janus, he took the name John to avoid being a butt of jokes by his youthful schoolmates. Though raised a Catholic, he converted to Protestantism as a teenager. Some Irish Protestants saw to his education and eventually sent him to Glasgow. He earned his M.A. at Edinburgh in 1690. He completed his education in Leyden, Holland.

By the early 1690s, he had begun to hold liberal opinions that questioned the orthodoxy of his teachers. In 1696 he published his most famous work, *Christianity not Mysterious,* now considered an early classic of the Deist movement, a movement that not only denied the Christian doctrine of the Trinity, but challenged the idea of God's continued activity in the world. He soon became the subject of sermons denouncing his thought. After the Irish House of Commons voted to burn the book and sent out orders for his arrest, Toland moved to England. He made his living as an editor and writer on a variety of subjects. Though he would often attempt to distance himself from his work, he was never successful, as he basically continued to believe. However, his beliefs would lead in a different direction.

In 1717, a number of delegates from what have been described as Druidic circles across the British Isles and Brittany met in Covent Gardens (London) at the Apple Tree Tavern. There they organized the Mother Grove of a revived Druidic order, a group continuing the ancient Druidic traditions as then understood. Toland was elected the chief of this grove, called Ar Tigh Geatha Gaurdeachus. Toland's own understanding of **Druidism** seemed to have been summarized in his 1720 publication *Pantheisticon,* in which he described a nature-oriented religion. He died two years later on February 11, 1722, at Putney, where he had been living since 1718.

While there were rumors of an earlier Druidic organization, possibly traceable to **John Aubrey,** an early writer on Druidism whom Toland had met in 1694, from Toland's term as the Druidic leader there is an organizational continuity of modern Druidism.

Sources:

Carr-Gomm, Philip. *The Elements of the Druid Tradition.* Shaftesbury, Dorset, UK: Element, 1991.

Toland, John. *Christianity not Mysterious.* N.p., 1696.

———. *Pantheisticon.* Putney, 1720.

Tomczyk, Stanislawa (Mrs. Everard Feilding) (ca. 1920)

Non-professional Polish **medium,** the subject of the experiments of **Julien Ochorowicz** in 1908–9, at Wisla, Poland. Tomczyk was regularly hypnotized by Ochorowicz for therapeutic purposes, when she became controlled by an entity called "Little Stasia." She could produce **movement** of objects without contact (**telekinesis**), stop the movement of a clock in a glass case, and influence a roulette wheel to the extent that the numbers chosen by the medium turned up more often than justified by chance.

Ochorowicz hypothesized that the physical movements were performed by rigid "rays" projecting from the fingers of the medium. The medium's hands were thoroughly examined and washed before each **séance.** A small object, such as a ball, cork, matchbox, or scissors, was placed before her on a table. The medium then placed her fingers about six to eight inches from the sides of the object. The object would move and eventually rise in the air, floating between the medium's fingers on each side.

Sometimes investigators claimed to feel a subtle "thread," but it was a psychic line of force, not a material thread. Ochorowicz stated: "I have felt this thread on my hand, on my face, on my hair. When the medium separates her hands the thread gets thinner and disappears; it gives the same sensation as a spider's web. If it is cut with scissors its continuity is immediately restored . . . it is then seen to be much thinner than an ordinary thread." These observations have a strong resemblance to the **od,** the claimed "odic force" of **Baron Karl von Reichenbach,** which sensitive individuals claimed to see in a darkened room issuing from the fingertips. However, Tomczyk's phenomena took place in good light.

"Little Stasia" was a mischievous entity who played many tricks on the medium. She said herself that she was not the spirit of any dead person. The medium considered her, at first, as her **double.** This was Ochorowicz's opinion, too, until he was shaken in this view by having obtained Little Stasia's photograph, as announced by her, in an empty room with all light excluded, while the medium in a normal condition was with him in an adjoining room.

Theodore Flournoy witnessed a séance in Paris in 1909. It left him "in no doubt as to the reality of simple telekinesis." However, at a later series of séances at Geneva to which, besides Flournoy, Professors Clarapède, Cellerier, Batelli, and Flournoy's son were invited, the expectations of the sitters were not fulfilled.

In 1910, Tomczyk was investigated at the Physical Laboratory in Warsaw by a group of scientists. She produced remarkable physical phenomena under strict test conditions. **Baron Schrenck-Notzing** described the experiments in his *Physikalische Phenomene des Mediumismus,* München, 1920. **Charles Richet** quoted his own observations in his book *Traité de Métapsychique,* (1922) (translated as *Thirty Years of Psychical Research,* 1923).

In 1919, Tomczyk married the distinguished British psychical researcher **F. H. Everard Feilding** (1867–1936), and seems to have discontinued séances.

Sources:

Berger, Arthur S., and Joyce Berger. *The Encyclopedia of Parapsychology and Psychical Research.* New York: Paragon House, 1991.

Feilding, Evarard. "Note on the English Sittings with Miss Tomczyk." *Journal* of the Society for Psychical Research 17 (1915).

Richet, Charles. *Traité de Métapsychique.* N.p., 1922. English edition as *Thirty Years of Psychical Research.* New York: Macmillan, 1923. Reprint, New York: Arno Press, 1975.

Tomga

Familiar spirits among the **Eskimos.**

TOM Religious Foundation

The TOM Religious Foundation is a Spiritualist organization founded in the 1960s by Rev. Ruth Johnson in Velarde, New Mexico. The headquarters were moved to Canon City, Colorado, in 1970, and more recently they moved back to New Mexico. The teachings are based upon Johnson's own study and exploration of her past lives, which are disseminated primarily through correspondence lessons, "Moon Time Studies in Spiritual Culture." These lessons cover subjects familiar to occult students, including psychic development, **dreams, ESP, Atlantis,** the Bible, and what is said to be original Christianity. According to Johnson, God is the divine One, Spirit, or Whole, who knows, loves, and cares for us and manifests that love through divine guidance. Students may pursue ordination and receive charters to establish churches. Address: P.O. Box 52, Chinmayo, NM 87522.

Tongues, Speaking in

Vocalization that sounds like a language but is devoid of semantic meaning or syntax; also known as glossolalia. Glossolalia is a protolanguage based on the everyday spoken language of the person, but lacking enough sounds (vowels and consonants) upon which to build an actual language. Glossolalia often occurs in a religious context, most notably modern **Pentecostalism,** where it appears as a vocalized religious expression.

Glossolalia is to be sharply distinguished from **xenoglossia,** or xenoglossy, the speaking or understanding of a foreign language one does not normally know or recognize. In the Bible, glossolalia is referred to as the tongues of angels (1 Cor. 13:1), possibly suggesting that the unintelligible sounds are an angelic language.

Glossolalia is familiar to most from its association with the birth of Christianity at Pentecost as described in the Christian New Testament (Acts 2), though what in fact is described is an event of xenoglossia. Those listening to the apostles speak were amazed to hear the sermon each in their own language. The more obvious example of glossolalia occurred in the Corinthian church of which Paul spoke when he said, "For he that speaks in a tongue speaks not unto men but unto God; for no man understands, but in the spirit he speaks mysteries" (1 Cor. 14:2).

There are accounts of how the gift of tongues descended on the London congregation of Rev. **Edward Irving** in 1831. Robert Baxter, in his book *Narrative of Facts Characterizing the Supernatural Manifestations in Members of Mr. Irving's Congregation* (London, 1833), gives a narrative of his own experiences:

". . . The power of the Spirit was so great upon me that I was obliged to call out, as in agony, for pardon and forgiveness and for strength to bear a faithful testimony. In these cryings I was, however, at the time conscious of a power of utterance carrying me beyond the natural expression of my feelings. . . . for the space of more than ten minutes I was, as it were, paralysed under a shaking of my limbs, my knees rapping one against the other, and no expression except a sort of convulsive sigh. During this period I had no other consciousness than this bodily emotion, and an inexpressible constraint upon my mind, which although it left me composed and sensible of all I was doing, yet prevented my utterance and gave no distinct impression, beyond a desire to pray for the knowledge of the Lord's will. This increased so much that I was led to fall on my knees and cry in a loud voice 'Speak, Lord, for they servant hearest,' and this I repeated many times, until the same power of the Spirit which I had before felt, came upon me, and I was made to cry out with great vehemence, both of tone and action, that the coming of the Lord should be declared, and the messengers of the Lord should bear it forth upon the mountains and upon the hills, and tell it to the winds, that all the earth should hear it and tremble before the Lord."

The utterances often began in an unknown tongue and then passed into English. As one witness described them, "The tongue invariably preceded, which at first I did not comprehend, because it burst forth with an astonishing and terrible crash, so suddenly and in such short sentences that I seldom recovered from the shock before the English commenced."

The phrases were mostly taken from the Scriptures and repeated again and again. The actual words of the tongues were not recorded. Baxter believed them to be a jargon of sounds. However, the possessed also spoke with extraordinary fluency in languages with which they were but imperfectly acquainted. The utterances were supposedly grandiose both in manner and diction.

In a pamphlet, *Drei Tage in Gros Almerode (Three Days in Great Almerode),* J. Busching, a theological student at Leipzig, Germany, described ten cases of glossolalia at a religious revival in 1907 at Almerode, a small town in Hesse. The phenomena began with a hissing or peculiar gnashing sound. It was said that these sounds were produced when the subject, not wishing to disturb the order of service by interrupting a prayer already commenced, tried to repress the inward impulse acting on the speech organs; but the sounds had to come out, and the momentarily repressed glossolalies only burst forth with increased vigor.

Modern American **Pentecostalism** began in 1901 with the speaking in tongues that occurred at the Bethel Bible School in Topeka, Kansas. While away during the Christmas season of 1900, the school's founder set a task for the students: investigate the "baptism of the Holy Spirit" and discover what, according to the Bible, is the sign(s) of its presence. When he returned on New Year's Eve, he asked what the students had discovered. They replied, "speaking in tongues." Shortly after reaching a consensus on that point, the group retired to the chapel, where they entered a time of prayer. Then, on New Year's Day, 1901, Agnes Osman became the first person in modern times to ask for and receive the gift of the Holy Spirit with the accompanying sign of speaking in tongues.

Usually accompanying speaking in tongues is the additional phenomenon of the "interpretation of tongues," in which a reputed "translation" of the glossolalia is offered. An interpretation of tongues does not always occur even when it is prayed for. When it does occur, the speaker may either envision a written translation or hear it inwardly, or perceive directly the meaning of the foreign words.

Receiving the "baptism of the Holy Spirit" accompanied by speaking in tongues became the distinguishing mark of Pentecostalism. The movement spread from Topeka to Houston, Texas, and then to Los Angeles, California, from where it spread around the world.

Although Pentecostals were denigrated as "Holy Rollers" through much of the twentieth century (see George B. Cutten's *Speaking with Tongues*), in the 1960s Pentecostalism began to spread through the mainline Christian churches first in North America and then in Europe. This new charismatic movement, as it was called, brought a new respectability to Pentecostalism and resulted in the acceptance of Pentecostals into the larger Evangelical movement. It also led to new attention to glossolalia by social and behavioral scientists and historians. While supernatural explanations still dominate among Pentecostal believers, a more mundane perspective has emerged from those who have observed glossolalia widely.

A few detractors put forth the idea, a remnant of religious prejudice from earlier in the century, that glossolalia was a sign of psychopathology. This idea was possibly the first laid to rest as it had no basis in empirical data. In fact, quite the opposite was found to be true, in that Pentecostals seemed to have a higher level of mental health than that of the general population.

Other detractors suggested that glossolalia was simply gibberish; however, linguistic studies, most prominently that of William Samarin, have suggested that it is in fact a very structured speech, easily distinguishable from gibberish or attempts to imitate glossolalia. It is also said to be a protolanguage, highly structured and derived from the everyday language of the speaker.

Its relation to everyday language suggests that it too, like everyday language, is a learned behavior, and experimental data, testing people's ability to learn glossolalia in a nonreligious setting, provides some substantiation of this hypothesis. Others have also suggested that glossolalia is related to altered states of consciousness. Glossolalia is not generally associated with severe alteration of consciousness as in trance or hypnosis, but it seems to involve lightly altered consciousness such as that which occurs in daydreaming.

Historians have noted the widespread appearance of glossolalia in various religious traditions from ancient Greece to modern Spiritualism, although certainly the great majority of recorded cases are in Christianity. Some Christians have countered the obvious implications of cross-cultural studies by arguing that some tongues speaking is simply a ruse by the devil to imitate the actions of the Holy Spirit.

Sources:

Christie-Murray, David. *Voices from the Gods: Speaking in Tongues.* London: Routledge & Kegan Paul, 1978.

Cutten, George B. *Speaking With Tongues: Historically and Psychologically Considered.* New Haven, Conn.: Yale University Press, 1927.

Goodman, Felicitas D. *Speaking in Tongues: A Cross-Cultural Survey of Glossolalia.* Chicago: University of Chicago Press, 1972.

Kelsey, Morton T. *Tongue Speaking: An Experiment in Spiritual Experience.* Garden City, N.Y.: Doubleday, 1968. Reprint, London: Hodder & Stoughton, 1973.

Kildahl, John P. *The Psychology of Speaking in Tongues.* New York: Harper & Row, 1972.

Samarin, William J. *Tongues of Men and of Angels: The Religious Language of Pentecostalism.* New York: Macmillan, 1972.

Spanos, Nicholas O., Wendy P. Cross, Mark Lepage, and Marjorie Coristine. "Glossolalia as Learned behavior: An Experimental Demonstration." *Journal of Abnormal Psychology* 95 (February 1986): 21–23.

Toolemak

Familiar spirits among the **Eskimos.**

TOPY See Thee Temple ov Psychick Youth

Totemism

A form of religious and social organization among tribal peoples that associates groups of persons with particular animals or objects. The term derives from the language and practice of the Ojibway tribe of Native Americans, but the Ojibways' own form of totemism was not typical of the use of the term as adopted by anthropologists. A totemic tribe consists of a number of totem groups, each closely related to a totem, which may be an animal or an inanimate object. That totem is specific for that particular group, thus while every member of the tribe has a characteristic totem, it will differ from those of other totem groups within the same tribes in the same area. Plants are used as totems in some parts of the world, and other totems are sometimes only a token part of an animal (i.e., a buffalo tongue instead of a buffalo).

A totem implies some kinship between the animal or object and the members of the group, sometimes a belief in descent from an animal totem. Masks and images may reinforce this association. Members of a particular totemic group respect the animal or object used as totem, and place a **taboo** on its being destroyed by members of that group, although their taboo does not apply to other members of the tribe.

Totemism is practiced around the world, among Australian aborigines, some African societies, certain North and South American Indian tribes, and among the peoples of Indonesia and Melanesia. Among Australian aborigines, totemism is related to a belief in the constant reincarnation of the spirits of primary animal forms into human beings.

In North America, the totem pole, used by Native American tribes of the Northwest coast of Canada and the United States, is the most widely recognized example of totemism. These poles or pillars are carved and painted with symbolic animals or spirits to represent ancestry or to tell family legends.

Sources:

Durkheim, Emile. *The Elementary Forms of the Religious Life.* Reprint, New York: Collier, 1961.

Frazer, James G. *Totemism and Exogamy.* 4 vols. N.p., 1910.

Freud, Sigmund. *Totem and Taboo.* New York: Random House, 1960.

Tedlock, Dennis. *Teachings from the American Earth: Indian Religion and Philosophy.* New York: Liveright, 1975.

Touches, Psychic

Tactile sensations represent an allied phenomenon to the paranormal **movement** of objects. Spiritualists claim such touches are intentional, just as the movement of objects is characterized by perfect localization; the touch is invariably meant for the one who receives it.

While the objects by which the sitters are touched may be recognized, in psychic contacts the case is different, as there is no apparent material means for their production. If the touches are produced by rods of **ectoplasm,** they may cause an immense variety of sensations according to the manipulation of this substance. The tactile sensation is often announced in advance, affected by psychic lights or luminous structures, and is visible to others.

The effect of the sensation may be as though coming from a soft object, for example, a rubber ball, an animal's paw feathers, gloves, fur, powderpuff, cobwebs, flowers, or fingers. The touch itself may be sharp, soft, dry, wet, clammy, or cold. It may be a tap, a caress, a stroke, a slap, a kick, a prick, a push, a punch, or a kiss. The invisible operator may pull or rumple your hair, she may rub your legs and search your pockets.

In 1905, in the *Annales des Sciences Psychiques,* psychical researcher **Charles Richet** translated a Latin chronicle from 1656 dealing with the phenomena that happened to a young girl named Regina Fischerin of Presbourg, Hungary. The chronicle, which is still part of the records of the Venerable

Chapter in the Archbishopric of Pest, gave report on the apparitions of Jean Clement of Presbourg, who led an evil life. The chronicle contained the following dramatic passages:

"Therefore, fearing that she might be the victim of an illusion, Regina asked of the spirit, if it were truly a spirit, to touch her with its finger. Immediately it touched her right arm and she felt the contact instantly. There appeared immediately a blister, giving her the same sensation of pain as though it had been a burn; moreover, fully to attest the phenomenon, the blister remained upon the skin a long time, and all the servants of the house saw it. Thereafter, desirous to be sure that this was not the work of an evil spirit, Regina demanded as proof that the visitor was a good spirit to make the sign of the cross. 'Here then,' said the phantom 'what you ask!' At once a flaming cross appeared outside the cloak which enveloped the figure, and with this it burned deeply the hand of the young girl, leaving thereon a branded cross which everyone could see. . . .

"A little later this spirit of Jean Clement recalled with remorse a crime which he had committed during his life, declaring that the money which had been secured from this crime was not all spent [this proved afterwards to be true]; that part of it had been used for his subsistence, another part had been otherwise spent, but that some still remained and that this should be restored from the possessions which he had left.

"Regina demanded yet other proofs. Surely the proof of the cross burned on her hand, and on her mantle was sufficiently strong, but it did not suffice for the young woman, who, in order to be absolutely sure that the strange visitant was truly a good spirit, insisted that it should make the same Sign of the Cross on a piece of money. The spirit obeyed, took a coin, threw it on the ground, and snatching a piece of cloth from the girl's hands, threw this upon the coin; then, taking Regina's hand violently in his grasp, scorching her deeply as before, burned thereon through the hand and the linen cloth upon the coin the character of a triple cross. 'Here is a further sign,' said he, and launched forth a flame with so much force that it reached the heart of the young woman, while another jet of flame crossed the entire room and struck the opposite wall. Whereupon Regina fell unconscious. . . .

"This affair seems extraordinary to us; firstly because a cross and an exact form of the hand have been marked in every detail; secondly, because this brand of burning did not extend beyond limits of the marks, though, upon linen material, fire has a tendency to spread. Finally, the right hand which was thus branded in on flesh and cloth, was an exact replica of the right hand of Clement, just as though he had been operating by his own dead physical hand. And the proof of this is that, during life, the tip phalange of Clement's forefinger had been amputated by a surgeon for a disease which was then known as 'Worms' and the absence of the finger-tip is clearly indicated upon the branded hand." (This account can also be found in the English edition of *Annals of Psychical Science,* No. 4, April 1905).

Other chronicles contained similar accounts. In 1908 and 1910 Mrs. Zingarapoli, a Naples lawyer, published a dozen such cases in *Luce e Ombra.* One was recorded from the seventeenth century and the brands or scorch marks of the hands of fire preserved at the Convent St. Claire at Todi. The exhibits in Father V. Jouet's Other World Museum at Rome comprised photographic records of the marks. In another instance in 1853, a spirit left an imprint as if by an iron hand heated red-hot on the door of the convent of the Franciscan nuns of Saint Anne at Foligno. When the grave of the deceased was reopened, the hand was found to fit the scorch marks to perfection.

In **William Howitt**'s *History of the Supernatural* (2 vols., 1863), a story was told of an apparition that appeared to the grandfather and father of a fellow student of **Johann H. Jung.** It stated in part:

"Yet there were circumstances which made the father and son believe that he was far from his purification, for fire streamed from every finger when he became angry at their resistance to his wishes. Still more, when he touched the Bible it smoked, and the marks of his thumb and finger shrivelled up the leather of the binding where he held it, and also the paper where he pointed out the place in the hymn 'From guilt of blood deliver me' was black and singed. The Bible with these marks is preserved in the family, and many creditable persons have seen it and may still see it."

Howitt added:

"The fiery touch of the spirit which induced the father and son to believe it a bad one, modern spiritualists can testify to belong to many spirits. How often have we seen fire streaming even from the finger of a medium? How often have spirits, before shaking hands with you, desired you, at Mr. Home's, to lay your handkerchief over your hand first? How often have you felt the touch of spirit fingers prick as from the sparks of electricity?"

Under the mediumship of the **Rev. William Stainton Moses** there are two instances of somewhat similar character. According to his note dated April 18, 1874, a psychic light touched his fingers, which resulted in the skin being broken up and the joint swollen. Mrs. Speer stated in her account in *Light* that a spirit of low order was responsible for the injury.

In the second instance, W. B., a friend of Stainton Moses, figured he had committed suicide. His portrait appeared on a plate on May 16, 1876, when Moses sat for **spirit photography.** On May 20, Moses woke up in the night and saw the spirit trying to reach him; it struggled with two other spirits. He was inspired with horror and revulsion. The spirit got nearer and stretched out his hand. Moses did not remember any more. In the morning, he found on his forehead an oblong dull red mark in the exact place where his friend wounded himself. The mark was a red discoloration and faded in two or three days.

The psychical researcher **Frank Podmore** quoted a similar case in *Proceedings* of the **Society for Psychical Research** (vol. 10, p. 204). A Miss M. P. was awakened in the night with a jump with a horrible feeling that there was someone in the room. An icy hand pressed against her face. The next moment her sister cried out and complained of a violent burn on her cheek. "The gas having been turned up higher, we saw on one side of her face, a very vivid red mark, which rapidly took the form of a hand, with fingers open."

The psychical researcher **Ernesto Bozzano** analyzed this and many similar cases in the journal *The Seer* (1931) under the title 'Spirit Hands of Flame,' and drew attention to the fact that the elder sister felt an icy sensation and a minute later, apparently by the same hand, her sister was burned. Bozzano asked whether the opposed sensation felt by the two percipients might not be explained by "a rapid change in the ectoplasmic condensation of the phantom hand resulting from a sudden modification of the vibratory tonality. This vibratory tonality, under certain circumstances, seems to be very much more intense either on living or inanimate matter, and as a result, like fire, it would destroy living animal or vegetable tissue."

In a séance with **Heinrich Melzer,** the Dresden **apport** medium, as reported in the June 1906 issue of *Die Ünbersinnliche Welt,* a plant was apported. The sitter, at the very same instant that he received the plant, felt the sensation of burning on the thumb. When the light was switched on, the mark of a burn was clearly seen and a blister formed immediately.

Emma Hardinge Britten in her book *Modern American Spiritualism* (1870), vouched for the following occurrences in the family of a well-known merchant of San Francisco in a séance with the eldest daughter:

"Instantly, and while every eye was fixed upon her, she sank back in her chair in a swoon and there, in the broad glare of the sunlight, appeared on her face, which the moment before was perfectly white and colorless, a large patch of wet, reeking blood, one of her cheeks being marked exactly as if struck with a bloody hand. On approaching the swooning figure, a second patch appeared on the other cheek; and as she stretched out her hand as if to ward off an invisible foe, another wet and reeking stain instantaneously became manifest on its palm.

"The ladies present procured a washbowl and removed the stains from the young woman's face and hand; but though they replaced her in the chair, restored her to consciousness and never for one moment lost sight of her, nor suffered a single movement to escape them, this terrible phenomena was repeated five times in less than an hour."

The house in which this occurred was haunted, and the scene of frightful disturbances at night. The younger children always insisted that these frightful marks were made "by a Spanish girl" who followed their sister about. She had her throat cut. Another apparition who helped to make the marks was their mother whom they represented as reproaching her daughter with an infamous life. The fluid was several times analyzed and found to be human blood. The phenomena lasted for many months. Finally the police interfered and the circles were terminated.

The issue of psychic touches has actually been discussed but it is such an allusive phenomena that little can be concluded from its occurrence. It has been noted that records of such occurrences in modern séances have usually be in conjunction with other fraudulent phenomena such as apports and materializations; the mundane action of a sitter or accomplice in a darkened room could account for the overwhelming psychic touches. A variety of body sensations, from the ordinary to the spectacular, can also be ascribed to actions completely internal to the person him/herself. It can even be argued that some cases of burns and bleeding might be ascribed to autosuggestion (or **hypnotism**).

Tower of London

Ancient British fortress on the east side of the city of London, England, scene of many executions, once used for imprisonment of high-ranking traitors. With its grim history, it is not surprising that various ghosts are associated with it.

The jewelroom at the Tower of London is reported to be haunted and in 1860 there was published in *Notes and Queries* by Edmund Lenthal Swifte, Keeper of the Crown Jewels, an account of a spectral appearance witnessed by himself in the tower. He stated in October 1817, he was having supper with his wife, her sister, and his little boy in the sitting room of the jewel house. Swifte stated:

"I had offered a glass of wine and water to my wife when, on putting it to her lips, she exclaimed, 'Good God! what is that?' I looked up and saw a cylindrical figure like a glass tube, seemingly about the thickness of my arm, and hovering between the ceiling and the table; its contents appeared to be dense fluid, white and pale azure. This lasted about two minutes, when it began to move before my sister-in-law; then, following the oblong side of the table, before my son and myself, passing behind my wife, it paused for a moment over her right shoulder. Instantly crouching down, and with both hands covering her shoulder she shrieked out, 'O Christ! it has seized me!'

"It was ascertained that no optical action from the outside could have produced any manifestation within, and hence the mystery has remained unsolved."

Notes and Queries also reported how "one of the night sentries at the jewel house was alarmed by a figure like a bear issuing from underneath the jewel room door. He thrust at it with his bayonet which stuck in the door. He dropped in a fit and was carried senseless to the guard-room. . . . In another day or two the brave and steady soldier died."

In February 1933, a sentry at the Tower reported seeing the ghostly figure of a woman in white floating toward him. A newspaper report stated: "Confronted by such an apparition, the sentry fled, making his way to the guardroom, greatly unnerved."

On February 12, 1957, a young Welsh Guardsman was on duty, and at 3 A.M. saw a "white shapeless form" forty feet up on the battlements of the Salt Tower. He called for a search party, who found nothing, although another guardsman later admitted to seeing a shapeless white apparition. The time and the date was in conjunction with the execution of Lady Jane Grey, four hundred and three years earlier.

Trance

An altered state of consciousness, either spontaneous or induced, bearing some analogy to the ordinary sleep state, but differing from it in certain marked particulars. Among tribal peoples, trance states have been common since ancient times, used by the **shaman,** medicine man, or other religious practitioners for demonstrations of paranormal knowledge. Such shamans were forerunners of the modern Spiritualist **mediums.**

The term is loosely applied to many varied mental states (e.g., hypnosis, **ecstasy, catalepsy, somnambulism,** certain forms of hysteria, and the mediumistic trance). Sometimes, as in catalepsy, there is a partial suspension of the vital functions; generally, there is insensibility to pain and to any stimulus applied to the sense organs. The main distinguishing feature of the trance is that the subject retains consciousness and gives evidence of intelligence, either his or her own normal intelligence or, as in cases of **possession** and impersonation, some foreign intelligence.

In hypnosis, the subject, although indifferent to sensory stimuli, has been known to exhibit a curious sensitivity to such stimuli applied to the hypnotist's body (see **Community of Sensation**).

In ecstasy, which is frequently allied with **hallucination,** the subject remains in rapt contemplation of some transcendental vision, deaf and blind to the outside world. It was formerly considered to indicate that the soul of the ecstatic was viewing some great event distant in time or place or some person or scene from the celestial sphere. Today such a state is believed to be brought about by intense and sustained emotional concentration on some particular mental image, by means of which hallucination may be induced.

The mediumistic trance is recognized as being similar to hypnosis, for the hypnotic trance, induced many times in the same subject, may become spontaneous. It then strongly resembles the trance of the medium.

Some Spiritualists have objected to the term *trance* being applied when there is no sign of spirit possession. The entranced medium (who seems able to produce this state at will) frequently displays an exaltation of memory (hypermnesia), of the senses (hyperesthesia), and even of the intellectual faculties.

Automatic writing and utterances are generally produced in the trance state and frequently display knowledge the medium does not normally possess, or knowledge that is said to give evidence of **telepathy.** Such were the trance utterances of the medium **Leonora Piper,** whose automatic phenomena in the late nineteenth century provided a wide field for scientific research.

Spiritualists believe these phenomena are caused by spirits of the dead acting through the medium's physical organism, as distinct from ancient ideas that trance personalities were all the result of demonic possession. Moreover, the trance messages of Spiritualist mediums are said to come from the spirits of deceased persons, and this assertion is often supported by the medium's exhibiting the voice, appearance, or known opinions of the dead friend or relative.

Such trance representations supply a large part of the evidence on which the structure of Spiritualism rests. In cases of **fraud,** however, the information concerning the deceased was probably obtained by normal means, or, in some cases, obtained telepathically from the minds of the sitters. While there is some strong evidence for a Spiritualist view, there are also many cases when other explanations seem more appropriate.

Subjective Aspects of Trance

Some light can be shed on the nature of trance from the reports of those who have experienced it. The great medium **D. D. Home,** for example, described his movement into trance before a committee of the **London Dialectical Society** in 1869: "I feel for two or three minutes in a dreamy state, then I become quite dizzy, and then I lose all consciousness. When I awake I find my feet and limbs cold, and it is difficult to restore the circulation. When told of what has taken place during the trance it is quite unpleasant to me, and I ask those present not to tell me at once when I awake. I myself doubt what they tell me."

Lord Adare, who studied Home's mediumship, observed, "The change which takes place in him is very striking; he becomes, as it were, a being of higher type. There is a union of sweetness, tenderness and earnestness in his voice and manner which is very attractive."

W. Stainton Moses, himself a medium, added his observations:

"By degrees Mr. Home's hands and arms began to twitch and move involuntarily. I should say that he has been partly paralysed, drags one of his legs, moves with difficulty, stoops and can endure very little physical exertion. As he passed into the trance state he drew power from the circle by extending his arms to them and mesmerizing himself. All these acts are involuntary. He gradually passed into the trance state, and rose from the table, erect and a different man from what he was. He walked firmly, dashed out his arms and legs with great power and passed round to Mr. Crookes. He mesmerized him, and appeared to draw power from him."

"I feel a cold shivering," stated **Annie Fairlamb,** "a sensation as of water running down my back, noise in my ears, and a feeling as if I were sinking down into the earth; then I lose consciousness."

Leonore Piper noted:

"I feel as if something were passing over my brain, making it numb; a sensation similar to that experienced when I was etherized, only the unpleasant odour of the ether is absent. I feel a little cold, too, not very, just a little, as if a cold breeze passed over me, and people and objects become smaller until they finally disappear; then, I know nothing more until I wake up, when the first thing I am conscious of is bright, a very bright light, and then darkness, such darkness. My hands and arms begin to tingle just as one's foot tingles after it has been 'asleep,' and I see, as if from a great distance, objects and people in the room; but they are very small and very black."

It is interesting to note that when the Seeress of Prevorst (**Frederica Hauffe**) awoke from trance, she said that the persons around her looked so thick and heavy that she could not imagine how they could move.

Objective Aspects of Trance

On awakening from trance, Piper often pronounced names and fragments of sentences that appeared to have been the last impressions on her brain. After that, she resumed conversations at the point where they were broken off before she fell into trance. It is significant to quote from among the mumbled remarks during her return to consciousness, "I came in on a cord, a silver cord." Before she became conscious she heard a snap, sometimes two. They were physiological experiences. She said she heard "sounds like wheels clicking together and then snaps." Similar observations have been made by individuals reporting **out-of-the-body travel** experiences.

Describing the development in Piper's trances, **Sir Oliver Lodge** writes in his book *The Survival of Man* (1909):

"In the old days the going into trance seemed rather a painful process, or at least a process involving muscular effort; there was some amount of contortion of the face and sometimes a slight tearing of the hair; and the same actions accompanied the return of consciousness. Now the trance seems nothing more than an exceptionally heavy sleep, entered into without effort—a sleep with the superficial appearance of that induced by chloroform; and the return to consciousness, though slow and for a time accompanied by confusion, is easy and natural. . . . For half an hour or so after the trance had disappeared the medium continues slightly dazed and only partly herself. . . . A record was also made of the remarks of Mrs. Piper during the period of awaking from trance. . . . part of them nearly always consisted of expressions of admiration for the state of experience she was leaving, and of repulsion—almost disgust—at the commonplace terrestrial surroundings in which she found herself. Even a bright day was described as dingy or dark, and the sitter was stared at in an unrecognising way, and described as a full and ugly person. . . ."

Piper's trances seemed to have three distinct stages—subliminal 1, in which the medium was partly conscious of her surroundings but saw things distorted and grotesque; subliminal 2, in which she was possessed by spirits and lost contact with the material world; and subliminal 3, a deep trance in which the loss of consciousness was complete, the body became anaesthetic, and automatic writing began.

William James found Piper's lips and tongue insensible to pain while she was in trance. **Richard Hodgson** later confirmed this by placing a spoonful of salt in Piper's mouth. He also applied strong ammonia to her nostrils.

James also led what became a series of more intrusive experiments, once making a small incision in Piper's left wrist. During trance the wound did not bleed and no notice was taken of the action. It bled freely afterward and the medium bore the scar for life. In England, Lodge pushed a needle into her hand. At another time, **Charles Richet** inserted a feather into her nostril. Harsh experiments in 1909 resulted in a badly blistered and swollen tongue that caused the medium inconvenience for several days, while another test resulted in numbness and partial paralysis of her right arm for some time afterward. Although these scientific experiments were of great importance, it is obvious that the experimenters overstepped the mark in causing inconvenience and pain to the medium.

The trance of the medium **Eusapia Palladino** was described by Italian researcher **Cesare Lombroso:**

"At the beginning of the trance her voice is hoarse and all the secretions—sweat, tears, even the menstrual secretions are increased. Hyperaesthesia . . . is succeeded by anaesthesia. . . . Reflex movement of the pupils and tendons are lacking. . . . Respiratory movements . . . passing from 18 inspirations to 15 and 12 a minute . . . heartbeats increase from 70 to 90 and even 120. The hands are seized with jerkings and tremors. The joints of the feet and the hands take on movements of flexure or extension, and every little while become rigid.

"The passing from this state to that of active somnambulism is marked by yawns, sobs, perspirations on the forehead, passing of insensible perspiration through the skin of the hands, and strange physiognomic expressions. Now she seems a prey to a kind of anger, expressed by imperious commands and sarcastic and critical phrases, and now to a state of voluptuous erotic ecstasy. In the state of trance she first becomes pale, turning her eyes upward and her sight inward. . . . exhibiting many of the gestures that are frequent in hysterical fits. . . . Toward the end of the trance when the more important phenomena occur, she falls into true convulsions and cries like a woman who is lying-in, or else falls into a profound sleep while from the aperture in the parietal bone in her head there exhales a warm fluid or vapour, sensible to the touch.

"After the séance Eusapia is overcome by morbid sensitiveness, hyperesthesia, photophobia and often by hallucinations and delirium (during which she asks to be watched from harm) and by serious disturbances of the digestion, followed by vomiting if she has eaten before the séance, and finally by true paresis of the legs, on account of which it is necessary for her to be carried and to be undressed by others.

"These disturbances are much aggravated. . . . if she is exposed to unexpected light."

"My eyes ache a good deal after a séance," said Annie Fairlamb, "and generally my lower limbs are thin, sometimes very thin, and usually I feel pain in the left side."

Pioneering researcher **F. W. H. Myers** distinguished between three successive stages in trance. In the first stage the subliminal (subconscious) self obtains control. In the next stage the incarnate spirit, whether or not maintaining control of the whole body, makes excursions into or holds telepathic intercourse with the spiritual world. In the third stage, the body of the medium is controlled by another discarnate spirit.

The first stage is well illustrated by the case of Alabama minister C. B. Sanders, whose trance personality always called itself by the name of "X Y Z," and claimed to represent the incarnate spirit of Rev. Sanders exercising his higher faculties. He spoke of Sanders in his normal state of consciousness as his "casket," but showed no evidence of direct communication with discarnate spirits.

The nineteenth-century histologist Gaëtano Salvioli, investigating hypnosis, noticed for the first time that in trance the flow of blood to the brain is greater than in waking hours, which might account for the greater psychical activity and an increase in muscular excitability.

Theodore Flournoy frequently found complete allochiria, a confusion between the right and left side, with the medium **Hélène Smith.** In trance she would consistently look for her pocket on the left side instead of on the right. If one of her fingers was pricked or pinched behind a screen, it was the corresponding finger on the other hand that was agitated. Allochiria is one of the stigmata of hysteria.

Lombroso also called attention to the fact that Eusapia Palladino, who was usually left-handed in sittings, became right-handed in one séance and fellow researcher **Enrico Morselli** became left-handed. This observation served as confirmation of one doctor's hypothesis of transitory left-handedness in the abnormal state, and the transference to the sitters of the anomalies of the medium. The left-handedness seemed to indicate the increased participation of the right lobe of the brain in mediumistic states.

Morselli measured Palladino's left-handedness in dynamometric figures. He found, after a séance, a diminution of 6 kilograms for the right and 14 for the left hand. The spirits around Leonore Piper always communicated on the left side. The trance, as a rule, began with hissing intakes of breath and ended with deep expirations.

There is a suggestion in this of *pranayama,* the **yoga** system of breathing. "Like the fakirs," wrote Morselli, "when they wish to enter into trance, Eusapia begins to slacken her rate of breathing." The seer **Emanuel Swedenborg** believed that his powers were connected with a system of respiration. He said that in communing with the spirits he hardly breathed for half an hour at a time.

The poet **Gerald Massey,** who published an alternative history of humankind, wrote of his own mystical vision: "You know Swedenborg and Blake claimed a kind of inner breathing. I know that is possible. I have got at times to where I find there needs to be no further need for expiring, it is all inspiration, I consider that consciously or unconsciously we all draw life from the spirit world, just as we shall when we pass into it."

"I have tried to simulate the deep and rapid breathing of Rudi in the trance state," writes psychical researcher Harry Price in his book *Rudi Schneider* (1930). He says: "This breathing has been likened to a steam engine, a tyre being pumped up, etc. Taking off my collar and tie and with my watch in my hand, I found that in six and a quarter minutes I was exhausted and could not continue. I have known Rudi to continue this hard breathing, interspersed with spasms and the usual clonic movements, *for seventy-five minutes without cessation.* And this while being held and in a most uncomfortable position, while, of course, I was quite free."

Trances did not always come at will and occasionally appeared when not desired. In Cambridge, England, at the request of F. W. H. Myers, Piper looked into a crystal before going to bed. She saw nothing but looked exhausted the next morning and said that she thought that she had been entranced during the night. The next time when she went into a trance, her spirit **control** "Phinuit" said that he came and called but no one answered. Piper's trances generally lasted about an hour. On one occasion, in Sir Oliver Lodge's experience, it lasted only for a minute.

The trance, as a rule, is continuous. In the mediumship of **Mrs. J. H. Conant,** much discomfort was caused at an earlier stage by the medium's return to consciousness as soon as the control had left. She had to be entranced again for the next communicator. Each change took about ten minutes. In the case of Rudi Schneider, the trance was similarly intermittent but the same entity, "Olga," remained in control.

To be roused from trance by a materialized spirit is exceptional. The spirit form "Katie King" was said to have roused the medium **Florence Cook** when the time of her farewell arrived and a tearful scene was witnessed between the two. The novelist **Florence Marryat,** who was present at this séance, describes a similar experience with the medium **Mary Showers** in her book *There is No Death* (1891): "The spirit ['Peter'] proceeded to rouse Rosie by shaking her and calling her name, holding me by one hand as he did so. As Miss Showers yawned and woke up from her trance, the hand slipped from mine, and 'Peter' evaporated. When she sat up I said to her gently: 'I am here! Peter had brought me in and was sitting on the mattress by my side till just this moment.' 'Ha, ha!' laughed his voice close to my ear, 'and I'm still here, my dears, though you can't see me.'"

The medium **F. W. Monck** was once apparently awakened by the common consent of the materialized spirit and the sitters. However, controversy surrounds the mediumship of Florence Cook, Mary Showers, and Monck, and these unusual occurrences seem to be but further confirmation of the **fraud** engaged in by the three mediums.

Usually the medium has no remembrance of what has passed in the trance. To all intents and purposes he or she is an entirely distinct being while in that state, with physiological functions totally different from the normal ones. Florence Marryat wrote that the medium **Bessie Williams** ate like a sparrow, and only the simplest things. "Dewdrop" (her **guide**), on the other hand, liked indigestible food and devoured it freely, yet the medium never felt any inconvenience from it.

About 1846 the limbs of Mary Jane, servant girl of a Dr. Larkin of Wrentham, Massachusetts, were, under the spirit influence of a rough sailor, thrown out of joint in several directions in a moment and without pain. Larkin was often obliged to call in the aid of his fellow doctors and two or three strong assistants to replace them. On one occasion the girl's knees and wrists were thrown out of joint twice in a single day. These painful feats were always accompanied by loud laughter and hoarse, profane jokes.

On the testimony of S. W. Turner of Cleveland, Ohio, in December 1847, the *Spiritual Telegraph* reported the peculiar adventure of a medium called William Hume. In a trance state and under the control of "Capt. Kidd," Hume threw himself into the lake to recover a ring and was brought out of the water, still in trance, after swimming for 15 to 20 minutes, without injury to his health.

Trance in Animal Magnetism and Hypnotism

The first surgery on a subject in mesmeric trance was performed in France in April 1829, by M. Cloquet on a Mme. Plantin, a 64-year-old woman who suffered from an ulcerated cancer in the right breast. The operation lasted 10–12 minutes. The patient's pulse and breathing remained unchanged. She was not awakened until two days later. The case was reported to the Section of Surgery of the Academy. In 1836 a Dr. Hamard invited a member of the academy, M. Oudet, to extract a tooth from a somnambulic patient. The operation was a success.

In England the first operation in mesmeric trance took place in 1842, in Nottinghamshire, on James Wombell, whose leg was amputated above the knee. W. Topham, a London barrister, was the mesmerist, and the operation was performed by Squire Ward, M.R.C.S. James Esdaile records a number of similar incidents in his book, *Mesmerism in India* (1846).

There is one instance on record in the mediumship of F. L. H. Willis, who later acquired a medical degree and became professor of materia medica in New York, when not the patient, but the operator was in trance. Controlled by the spirit of "Dr. Mason," Willis successfully performed a difficult operation.

Apart from Swedenborg, the first modern conversation with spirits of the departed through the use of trance was recorded in May 1778 by the Societé Exegetique Philantropique of Stockholm. A 40-year-old woman was controlled in trance by her own infant daughter and another young child of the town, who gave accounts of both their Earth lives and their existence in the spirit world.

The somnambulic state in **mesmerism** was the discovery of the Marquis Chastenet de Puységur. **Franz Anton Mesmer** himself was aware of something unknown in the "magnetic sleep" and warned against deepening it. The use of **animal magnetism** was primarily for healing power, and the possibility of intercourse with spirits was largely avoided. It cropped up as early as 1878 in Tardy de Montravel's writings, but he opposed it. Kaleph Ben-Nathan admitted the possibility in 1793 but contended that spirits with which a somnambule might hold intercourse would be spirits of an inferior order and that magnetists practiced sorcery and divination.

Dr. Alexandre Bertrand recorded the exclamation of his young somnambule: "There are no spirits, they are stories, yet I see them, the proof is perfect." **J. P. F. Deleuze** conceded in 1818 that the phenomena of **clairvoyance** established the spirituality of the soul, but he did not consider spirit intercourse proven by the phenomena of somnambulic trance. In later years, however, under the effect of Dr. **G. P. Billot**'s experiments, he appeared to have changed his belief. Billot's somnambules were mediums in the present-day sense. The spirits who possessed them proclaimed themselves to be their guardian angels and on occasion produced physical phenomena.

Louis-Alphonse Cahagnet recorded fully developed trance communications through the early medium **Adèle Maginot.** Before Cahagnet's appearance, an official acknowledgment of trance took place in 1831 when an investigating commission of the Royal Academy of Medicine reported on the phenomena of animal magnetism and found it genuine and the state of somnambulism, although rare, well authenticated.

In Germany the theory of spiritual intercourse in trance took a quicker hold on the imagination of mesmerists. Jung-Stilling (**J. H. Jung**) founded the school with the theory of the psychic body and its elements, based on the luminiferous ether. **Auguste Müller,** of Carlsruhe, appears to have been the first somnambule whose spirit communications and other phenomena were carefully recorded; Fräulein Römer, the second. Müller was the first interplanetary traveler, making claimed clairvoyant excursions to the moon. The most stirring account of intercourse with the spirit world was the story of the Seeress of Prevorst, Frederica Hauffe, published in 1826 by Dr. Justinus Kerner.

Sources:

Cahagnet, L. A. *The Celestial Telegraph; or, Secrets of the Life to Come Revealed Through Magnetism.* 2 vols. London & New York, 1851. Reprint, New York: Arno Press, 1976.

Dingwall, E. J. *Abnormal Hypnotic Phenomena.* 4 vols. London: Churchill, 1967–68.

Esdaile, James. *Natural and Mesmeric Clairvoyance; With the Practical Application of Mesmerism in Surgery and Medicine.* London, 1852. Reprint, New York: Arno Press, 1975.

Fahnestock, W. B. *Statuvolism, or Artificial Somnambulism.* Chicago, 1871.

Flournoy, Theodore. *From India to the Planet Mars.* New York: Harper & Bros., 1900.

Garrett, Eileen J. *My Life as a Search for the Meaning of Mediumship.* New York: Oquaga; London: Rider, 1939. Reprint, New York: Arno Press, 1975.

Goodman, Felicitas D., Jeanette H. Henney, and Esther Pressel. *Trance, Healing and Hallucination: Three Field Studies in Religious Experience.* Wiley-Interscience, 1974.

Gopi Krishna. *The Biological Basis of Religion and Genius.* New York: Harper & Row, 1972.

Inglis, Brian. *Trance: A Natural History of Altered States of Mind.* London: Grafton, 1989.

Kerner, Justinus. *The Seeress of Prevorst.* London, 1845.

Laski, Marghanita. *Ecstasy.* London: Cresset, 1961.

Salter, W. H. *Trance Mediumship: An Introductory Study of Mrs. Piper and Mrs. Leonard.* London: Society for Psychical Research, 1962.

Spiegel, H., and D. Spiegal. *Trance and Treatment: Clinical Users of Hypnosis.* New York: Basis Books, 1978.

Sunderland, La Roy. *The Trance, and How Introduced.* Boston, 1860.

Wavell, Stewart, Audrey Butt, and Nina Epton. *Trances.* London: Allen & Unwin, 1966.

Trance Personalities

Trance messages claiming to come from the medium's spirit **control** do not always reveal a definite personality. The control often reflects the thoughts and opinions of the **medium** and the sitters, possesses little knowledge that they do not possess, and is an artificial personality. Yet, frequently a trance medium is controlled by a spirit of distinct or distinguished personality, whose education level appears to be more extensive and culture of a much different quality than the medium's and whose ideas and opinions appear independent.

Such spirits are generally given distinguishing names. They may control the medium alternately with other controls. On the other hand, the medium has generally a monopoly of one or more of these spirits, though sometimes one control may seemingly appear to be shared by several mediums.

Among those who may justly be regarded as the common property of dubious mediums are the spirits of certain great men—Virgil, Socrates, Shakespeare, Milton, Benjamin Franklin, Victor Hugo, Swëdenborg, and so on. The messages delivered through their control seldom resemble anything they wrote or said during their lives.

Not all the mediums involved in such counterfeit personalities are frauds; some are self-deluded. Others exhibit the faculty of the subconscious mind to weave fantasies like the characters and incidents of a novelist. Similar artificial personalities sometimes manifest in the claimed **reincarnation** experiences of subjects in hypnotic regression as in the famous "Bridey Murphy" case (see **Morey Bernstein**).

Some trance personalities assume pseudonyms, suggesting the possibility that the personality of everyday life, which is modified from year to year, may suffer radical change after death, losing the distinctive nature that the physical body, memories, and emotions normally reinforce.

Some of the most well-known pseudonymous trance personalities were those of the **Rev. William Stainton Moses**—"Imperator," "Rector," "Mentor," "Prudens," and others. "Imperator" and "Rector" were also among the controls of the medium **Leonora E. Piper** in subsequent years and indeed much of her automatic discourse did not come directly from communicating spirits, but was dictated by them to "Rector." It was suggested, however, by **Sir Oliver Lodge** and other investigators, that Piper's controls were not identical with those of Stainton Moses but were merely masqueraders.

Piper had, however, several interesting trance personalities of her own without borrowing from anybody. One of her earliest controls was "Sebastian Bach;" but before long he gave place to a spirit calling himself "Dr. Phinuit," who was an influence for a considerable time, then succumbing in his turn to George Pelham ("G. P."). Pelham was a young author and journalist who died suddenly in 1892. Soon after his death he supposedly controlled Piper, and indeed gave many striking proofs of his identity. He constantly mentioned intimate details of the affairs of Pelham, recognized his friends, and gave to each their due welcome. He never failed to recognize an acquaintance, or give a greeting to one whom he did not know. Many of Pelham's old friends did not hesitate to recognize in him that which he claimed to be.

Only on one occasion, when asked for the names of two persons who had been associated with him in a certain enterprise, the spirit "G. P." refused, saying that as there was present one who knew the names, his mentioning them would be referred to as **telepathy.** Later, he gave the names—incorrectly. When "G. P." ceased to communicate as the principal control of Piper, his place was taken by "Rector" and "Imperator," as mentioned above.

Another well-known trance medium, **Rosina Thompson,** had as her chief control "Nelly" (a daughter of hers who had died in infancy), a "Mrs. Cartwright," and others. Thompson's controls were said not to have shown any individual characteristics, but to resemble Thompson herself strongly both in voice and manner of speech, although **Margaret Verrall,** one of the sitters, stated that the impersonations gave an impression of separate identity to the sitter. Thompson's early trance utterances were controlled by another band of spirits, with even less individuality than those mentioned.

Frequently mediums and investigators themselves, when reaching the discarnate plane, seem to become controls in their turn. The psychical researchers **F. W. H. Myers, Edmund Gurney, Richard Hodgson,** and **Henry Sidgwick** claimed to speak and write posthumously through many mediums, notably through Piper, Thompson, Verrall, and **Alice K. Fleming** (i.e., Mrs. Holland). Many of the statements made by these controls were correct; some matters revealed were apparently outside the scope of the medium's normal knowledge. At the same time several fatal discrepancies were found to exist between the controls and those they were supposed to represent.

Thus the script produced by Fleming contained grave warnings, claiming to come from Myers, against the medium **Eusapia Palladino** and her physical phenomena, whereas Myers was known to hold opinions favorable to the physical manifestations.

On the whole, such trance personalities show themselves influenced by the personality of the medium. In cases where the latter was acquainted with the control, the trance personality was proportionately strong. When there was no personal acquaintance, it was often of a neutral tint, and sometimes bad guesses were made, as when Fleming represented the Gurney control as of a harsh and almost discourteous temperament.

But such instances must not be taken as impeaching the medium's good faith. Instances in which the trance personality is patently the product of the medium's own consciousness do not in themselves suggest that there is any intentional deception. In some of the most definite cases, there is evidence suggesting the operation of a discarnate intelligence, evidence that has proved convincing to careful investigators.

Among the most important pieces of evidence in evaluating the separate existence of trance personalities as spirit entities is the case of **"Philip."** In 1972–73, members of the Toronto Society for Psychical Research, Canada, deliberately created an artificial séance entity named "Philip," with a history, personal characteristics, and an appearance decided upon by the group in a quite mundane manner. Sitting as in a séance, the experimenters soon obtained raps from the séance table and communications from "Philip." It seems that in many instances, a spirit control may simply be a convention of **personality.** In other cases, however, convincing evidence of true personality survival has been established.

Sources:

Broad, C. D. *Personal Identity and Survival.* London: Society for Psychical Research, 1968.

Carington, Whately. *The Foundations of Spiritualism.* New York: E. P. Dutton, 1920.

Ducasse, C. J. *A Critical Examination of the Belief in a Life After Death.* Springfield, Ill.: C. C. Thomas, 1961.

Garrett, Eileen J. *My Life as a Search for the Meaning of Mediumship.* New York: Oquaga; London: Rider & Co., 1939.

Hart, Hornell. *The Enigma of Survival: The Case For and Against an After Life.* Springfield, Ill.: C. C. Thomas, 1959.

M. A. (Oxon) [W. Stainton Moses]. *Spirit Identity.* London, 1879.

Myers, F. W. H. *Human Personality and Its Survival of Bodily Death.* 2 vols. London: Longmans, Green, 1903.

Owen, Iris M., and Margaret Sparrow. *Conjuring Up Philip.* New York: Harper & Row, 1976.

Penelhum, Terence. *Survival and Disembodied Existence.* New York, Humanities Press, 1970.

Richmond, Kenneth. *Evidence of Identity.* London: G. Bell, 1939.

Salter, W. H. *Trance Mediumship: An Introductory Study of Mrs. Piper and Mrs. Leonard.* London: Society for Psychical Research, 1962.

Transcendental Meditation (TM)

A popular Hindu meditation technique first taught in the West by **Maharishi Mahesh Yogi,** an Allahabad University physics graduate who, in the 1940s and 1950s studied among monks in the Himalayas. Emerging with his teachings in 1958, the Maharishi's transcendental meditation spread across the United States and Europe by the mid-1960s. Due largely to the endorsements of celebrities such as the Beatles, Jane Fonda, and Mia Farrow, TM became one of the first forms of Eastern meditative practices to receive widespread media attention in the West. Essentially, TM is a streamlined form of the ancient Hindu initiation of bestowing a **mantra,** or sacred Sanskrit word or phrase, for the pupil to meditate upon for a short period each day.

A number of personal and social benefits have been claimed as a result of meditating. In fact, the movement has cited 508 individual scientific studies conducted since the 1970s, measuring psychological and physiological differences between meditators and non-meditators. The reports laud the physical and mental benefits of transcendental meditation, citing increased creativity, broader comprehension, improved perception, lowered blood pressure, reduced anxiety, and decreased medical visits among the meditators.

In 1977, studies such as those conducted by Fales and Markovsky at the University of Iowa question the validity of claims made by TM studies. Particularly, the analysis examines the phenomenon known as the Maharishi Effect, which asserts the effect advanced TM meditators can exercise over the social serenity of local communities. The scientific work on TM has been criticized within the academic community for methodological flaws, vague definitions, and loose statistical controls. It has been argued that the effects attributed to TM are the same effects produced by any number of yogic and meditative techniques; this places TM in the context of goals and results of traditional **meditation.**

The TM movement has also been criticized for lifting the time-honored Hindu practice from its religious context, mass producing it as a contemplative quick-fix for western consumers. Critics have argued that TM is disjointed from the Hindu **mysticism** from which it emerged, as well as from the other great world religions that have emphasized the need for patient and continuing self-purification through spiritual disciplines in order to give integrity to spiritual growth or eventual transcendental consciousness.

Traditional Hindu mysticism regards meditation as a later stage in the program of continuing spiritual discipline, and passive meditation is considered secondary to active meditation in quality and results. Moreover *mantra-diksha,* or initiation, is not normally given until the aspirant has proven his or her fitness to engage in meditation. Hinduism also reserves its highest transcendental experiences for those who have properly fulfilled their social and religious obligations.

Criticisms aside, the five million TM participants (as asserted by the program) seem to attest to the everyday value of TM as a simple, natural means of relaxation and a feeling of well-being. The method has received worldwide endorsement at every level of society, including support from politicians, scientists, doctors, and members of the general public. Many have brought TM to the pragmatic world of business, asserting its positive affects on productivity, job satisfaction, and employee health in the workplace.

Sources:

Akins, W. R., and George Nurnberg. *How to Meditate Without Attending a TM Class.* New York: Crown, 1976.

Bloomfield, Harold M., Michael Peter Cain, and Dennis T. Jaffe. *TM: Discovering Inner Energy and Overcoming Stress.* New York: Delacorte Press, 1975.

Chopra, Deepak, M.D. *Creating Health.* Boston: Houghton Mifflin Co., 1987.

Fales, Evan and Markovsky, Barry. "Evaluating Heterodox Theories." University of Iowa 1997. http://www.trancenet.org/. March 28, 2000.

Forem, Jack. *Transcendental Meditation.* New York: E. P. Dutton, 1974.

Hemingway, Patricia D. *Transcendental Meditation Primer.* Philadelphia: McKay, 1975.

Kory, Robert B. *The Transcendental Medication Program for Business People.* New York: American Management Association, 1976.

Maharishi Mahesh Yogi. *Meditations of Maharishi Mahesh Yogi.* New York: Bantam, 1973.

Orme-Johnson, David W., and John T. Farrows, eds. *Scientific Research on the Transcendental Meditation Program. Collected Papers 1.* Seelisberg, Switzerland: Maharishi European Research University Press, 1977.

Kanellakos, Demetri P., and Jerome S. Lukas. *Psychobiology of Transcendental Meditation: A Literature Review.* W. A. Benjamin, 1974.

Scott, R. D. *Transcendental Misconceptions.* San Diego: Beta Books, 1978.

The Transcendental Meditation Program. http://www.tm.org/. March 28, 2000.

Transfiguration

The metamorphic power ascribed to certain **mediums** to assume facial or bodily characteristics of deceased people for their representation. The phenomenon was described in detail in the account of William J. Erwood in *The National Spiritualist,* at a **séance** in 1931 with a Mrs. Bullock, a Chicago medium. In the light, which showed every movement of the medium, he claimed to have seen more than fifty faces in an hour and a half.

He writes:

"It was as though the medium's face were of plastic material being rapidly molded from one form to another by some master worker in plastics. Oriental faces, Indians, calm, dignified, serious, spiritual, in short, almost every type of face was depicted during the most unusual séance. One of the most striking was the impersonation of a paralysed girl whom I had known in the States. The medium's entire body, as well as face, was twisted out of all semblance of its normal state, to depict the condition of this victim of paralysis."

H. Dennis Bradley, in his book *The Wisdom of the Gods* (1925), described an experience with the medium Mrs. Scales:

"Gradually the whole of the expression of the medium's face changed completely. It was a transformation. Whilst the outline remained, the eyes and the expression became beautiful . . . At first is was only with very great difficulty that the first few words were articulated. It was as if they were produced with considerable effort. Within a little while, however, the power strengthened considerably, and the spirit of my sister was able to assume complete control. It was my sister. It was her spirit, using the organism of another physical body, and speaking to me in her own voice."

Joseph Maxwell vouched for the following case of transfiguration in sleep, narrated by one of his colleagues in the magistracy:

"On January 1, 1903, my father began to feel the first attacks of the painful disease from which he died after six months of terrible suffering . . . I watched him as he slept, and was not long in noticing that his physiognomy gradually assumed an aspect which was not his own. I finally observed that his face bore a striking resemblance to that of my mother. It was as though the mask of her face was placed over his own. My father had no eyebrows for a long time, and I noticed above his closed eyes the very marked black eyebrows which my mother had retained to the last. The eyelids, the nose, the mouth, were those of my mother. . . . My father wore his moustache and a pointed, but rather short beard. This beard and moustache, which I saw, helped, contrary to what might have been expected, in forming the features of my mother. The appearance lasted for ten or twelve minutes; then it gradually disappeared, and my father resumed his habitual physiognomy. Five minutes later he awoke, and I immediately asked him if he had not been dreaming, especially about his wife. He answered in the negative."

The phenomenon was witnessed by a woman servant who came into the room while it lasted. She was told: "Jeanne, look at Monsieur sleeping!" She cried out, "Oh, how he resembles poor Madame. It is striking, it is quite extraordinary!"

In the experiences of **Allan Kardec,** founder of French **Spiritism,** there was an extraordinary case of a young girl of fifteen whose metamorphic power extended to the duplication of the stature, mass, and weight of deceased persons, especially of her brother. Kardec recorded that another metamorphic meduim, a Ms. Krooke, saw one evening her own face changed. She observed a thick black beard and by it her son-in-law recognized his dead father. A little later, her face changed into that of an old woman with white hair. She preserved her consciousness in the meantime, yet felt through her entire body a prickling like that of a galvanic battery. No such miracles are recorded in modern experience.

Transfiguration is most often reported as occurring in séances in conjunction with **materializations.** It involves grave risks for the medium, but no records of any harm have been reported. There is an observation based on several accounts including an experiment at the **British College of Psychic Science,** a Spiritualist organization, with the medium **Ada Besinnet** in 1921. A light was flashed on a face that was illuminated by a spirit lamp. The medium was leaning over the table and illuminated her own face with light held in her hand. The light quickly vanished, as did the white drapery which draped over her head. When awakened, she was in **trance** and complained of great pain in the pit of her stomach; for three days she was shaken with muscular contractions.

There are some past experiences on record of the disappearance of the medium during materialization. In such cases, Spiritualist argue, the entire bodily substance of the medium is believed to have been withdrawn for the purpose of building up phantom bodies. Such occurrences are also known as transfigurations. More rational approaches to the séance have ascribed more mundane causes to such occurrences.

Henry S. Olcott and **John Newbrough** experienced transfigurations with the medium **Elizabeth J. Compton.** While phantoms were parading in front of the sitters before the **cabinet,** she vanished from the chair into which she was tied in such a way that the least effort to face herself would have given her away. Not only had her body vanished, but the fastenings, threads, wax-ends, seals, and nails as well. Yet something must have been left in the chair, for Olcott was strictly forbidden to touch the chair when he was allowed to go into the cabinet.

Where was the medium? According to Olcott and Newbrough, she was transfigured into the phantom bodies. Many of the phantoms were recognized as departed relatives and divulged intimate knowledge of the lives of their relations. If they were seized, and they were sometimes, they resolved into Compton and always rendered her ill.

In 1890 **Alexander N. Aksakof** had a similar experience with the medium **Elizabeth d'Esperance,** at a séance in Gothenburg. While the phantom "Yolande" was outside the cabinet, he slipped his arm through the curtains and felt for the medium's chair. He found it empty; at the same time his hand was flung aside. At the very moment "Yolande" returned into the cabinet, the séance came to an abrupt end and the medium was discovered on her chair in her red dress ("Yolande" was in white).

Through **automatic writing,** Aksakof, who did not tell of his part in the sudden disturbance, was told by "Walter," d'Esperance's **control,** that if the contribution of the circle was insufficient there might not be enough left of the medium to be visible; the clairvoyant may still see the body, but in reality there might not be much more in her place than her organs of sense. In such cases, a simple touch may do the medium serious injury.

When Aksakof asked what would happen if in such a case he should pull the band of cloth which encircled the medium's waist, whether it would not cut her body in two, the answer was yes. D'Esperance summed up her only sensations in this sentence: "I felt as I were empty inside."

The existence of transfigurations is questionable at best, and like many of the physical phenomena with which it was associated, reports of its occurrence have become quite rare. Most psychical researchers regard it with skepticism, suggesting that its primary occurrences in séances were fraudulently produced. Reported cases have been rare and it is unsatisfactory to attempt to assess them long after the event.

Sources:

Aksakof, Alexander. *A Case of Partial Dematerialization of the Body of a Medium.* Boston, 1898.

Holms, A. Campbell. *The Facts of Psychic Science.* 1925. Reprint, New Hyde Park, N.Y.: University Books, 1969.

Transition

Spiritualist term for death, used to emphasize survival of personality after death. Another term sometimes used is "promotion."

Transmutation of the Body

The aim of spiritual **alchemy**—to restore a human being to the fundemental condition of grace, strength, perfection, beauty, and physical immortality. Dedicated alchemists over the ages labored to discover the secret of the **elixir of life,** which occultists believed would achieve this renewal of youth, and grant immortality. Endless recipes for this medicine have been given, and some alchemists honestly believed they had attained it, but it still has not been proven.

Sources:

Atwood, Mary Anne. *Suggestive Inquiry Into the Hermetic Mystery.* London, 1850. Reprint, Belfast, Ireland, 1918. Reprint, New York: Julian Press, 1960.

Redgrove, H. Stanley. *Alchemy: Ancient and Modern.* London, 1911. Reprint, New Hyde Park, N.Y.: University Books, 1969.

Transportation

Alternative term for the claimed phenomenon of **teleportation,** the paranormal movement of human bodies through closed doors and over a distance.

Transposition of the Senses

An extraordinary phenomenon, first reported by Tardy de Montravel. In his *Essai sur la Theorie du Somnambulisme Magnetique* (1785), he described how in his half-waking **trance** he could see with the "pit of his stomach." In 1808, Dr. Pététin reported in his book, *Electricité Animale* (1808), that he found the senses of taste, smell, and hearing also wandering from the pit of the stomach to the tip of the fingers and of the toes. Since then many similar cases have been recorded, especially with hysterical subjects.

Cesare Lombroso carefully observed the phenomenon of **eyeless sight.** C. S. was a young girl who lost the power of vision, but as a compensation she "saw" with the same degree of acuteness at the point of the nose and the left lobe of the ear. Her sense of smell was transposed under the chin and later to the back of the foot. (See also **Stomach, Seeing with the**)

Transvection

Term used to indicate the claim of witches flying through the air on a broomstick, but also on a distaff, a shovel, or an animal. The term was originally used in a religious sense for the **transportation** of saints, such as St. Joseph of Copertinn. There were some seventy aerial flights claimed, but from the sixteenth century onward the flight of witches was also described as transvection.

The flight of witches was achieved with a magical flying ointment. However, if the witches heard the sound of church bells while flying to the **Sabbat,** they might be grounded. It is likely that the special ointments used to assist transvection may have had a hallucinatory effect, giving the illusion of traveling through the air. Such ointments could have produced experiences akin to **astral projection** or **out-of-the-body travel.**

Transylvanian Society of Dracula

The Transylvanian Society of Dracula emerged at the end of the 1990s as the largest **vampire**-interest organization in the world. It was founded in the early 1990s by a group of writers, Romanian scholars, tourist experts, and others interested in **Dracula** and vampire folklore in Romania and initially announced its existence through the sponsorship of the World Dracula Congress in 1995. Taking the lead was Nicolae Paduraru, formerly with the Romanian Ministry of Tourism. During that conference both an American and a Canadian chapter were established by **J. Gordon Melton** and Elizabeth Miller respectively, and a short time later an Italian chapter was founded by Massimo Introvigne. Each is a scholar in vampire studies and the author of multiple titles in the field.

The Canadian and American chapters joined with the Count Dracula Fan Club to sponsor Dracula 97, the centennial celebration of the publication of the novel *Dracula,* that brought some 100 scholars and more than 600 participants to Los Angeles, California, August 14–17, 1997. For three years, the two chapters cosponsored *The Transylvanian Journal* (1996–98). Currently, the Canadian chapter issues a newsletter,

The Borgo Post, and an annual *Journal of Dracula Studies.* It has an extensive Internet site at http://www.ucs.mun.ca/~emiller/. The American chapter has issued a set of monographs including a detailed bibliography of the English-language editions of *Dracula.* The Italian chapter has an Internet site (in Italian) at http://www.cesnur.org/dracula.htm.

The Romanian chapter sponsors an annual symposium in the Borgo Pass in May of each year. The original novel *Dracula* opens in May as Jonathan Harker travels to Borgo Pass to meet the Count. In May 2000, the society is sponsoring a much larger event, Dracula 2000, which will include a number of international scholars in Dracula and vampire studies.

The international headquarters of the Transylvanian Society of Dracula is at 47 Primaverii Blvd., Bucharest 1, Romania. The Canadian chapter is at P.O. Box 23240, Churchill P.O., St. John's, NF, Canada A1B 4J9; the American chapter at P.O. Box 91611, Santa Barbara, CA 93190-1611; and the Italian chapter at Via Bertola 86, 10122 Torino, Italy.

Sources:

Introvigne, Massimo. *La stripe de Dracula: Indagine sul vampirismpo dall'antichita ai nostro giorni.* Milan: Arnoldo Mondadari Editore, 1997.

Melton, J. Gordon. *The Vampire Book: The Encyclopedia of the Undead.* 2nd ed. Detroit: Visible Ink Press, 1999.

———. *The Vampire Gallery.* Detroit: Visible Ink Press, 1998.

———. *VideoHound's Vampires on Video.* Detroit: Visible Ink Press, 1996.

Miller, Elizabeth. *Dracula: Sense and Nonsense.* Westcliff-on-Sea, UK: Desert Island Books, 1998.

———. *Dracula: The Shade and the Shadow.* Westcliff-on-Sea, UK: Desert Island Books, 1998.

———. *Reflection on Dracula: Ten Essays.* White Rock, B.C.: Transylvanian Press, 1997.

TREAT See Treatment and Research of Experienced Anomalous Trauma

Treatment and Research of Experienced Anomalous Trauma (TREAT)

A center focusing on UFO (unidentified flying object) abduction phenomena, TREAT was founded in 1989 by psychiatrist Rima E. Laibow. It held its first conference May 12–14, 1989, at Fairfield University in Connecticut. Laibow has suggested that such "abductions," which she considers "experienced anomalous trauma," are the result of an unknown factor, possibly one outside the realm of conventional psychological explanation. However, even though the cause remains unknown, it is possible to treat the effects (symptoms) which are themselves well known.

Although Laibow initially maintained a friendly relationship with ufologists, for whom abduction phenomena had emerged as a major issue of research, tension soon developed. Laibow broke with leading abduction spokespersons Budd Hopkins and David M. Jacobs and removed them from participation in TREAT. She also disagreed with other ufologists by asserting the dominant role of mental health professionals, as opposed to a cooperative (essentially equal) role between psychologists and ufologists.

In spite of the problems, TREAT has continued to function. It holds annual meetings in the United States, paralleled by a series of regional meetings in Europe and Russia. Such meetings between professionals and interested parties are intended to create a nexus of collaborators and colleagues worldwide to further research and investigate UFO and parapsychological phenomena. Address: 13 Summit Terr., Dobbs Ferry, NY 10522.

Sources:

Clark, Jerome. *UFOs in the 1980s: The UFO Encyclopedia, Volume I.* Detroit: Apogee Books, 1990.

Laibow, Rima E. "Dual Victims: The Abused and the Abducted." *International UFO Reporter* 14, 3 (May/June 1989): 4–9.

Tree Ghosts

Tree spirits of the Indian subcontinent were among the many mythological spirit entities described by William Crooke in his book *Religion and Folklore of Northern India* (1926).

"These tree ghosts are, it is needless to say, very numerous. Hence most local shrines are constructed under trees; and in one particular tree, the Bira, the jungle tribes of Mirzapur locate Bagheswar, the tiger godling, one of their most dreaded deities. In the Konkan, according to Mr. Campbell, the medium or Bhagat who becomes possessed is called *Jhad,* or 'tree,' apparently because he is a favourite dwelling-place for spirits.

"In the Dakkhin it is believed that the spirit of the pregnant woman of Churel lives in a tree, and the Abors and Padams of East Bengal believe that spirits in trees kidnap children. Many of these tree spirits appear in the folk-tales. Thus, Devadatta worshipped a tree which one day suddenly split in two and a nymph appeared who invited him to go inside the tree. In there was a heavenly palace of jewels and Vidyatprabha, the maiden daughter of the king of the Yakshas [supernatural beings]; in another story the mendicant heard inside a tree the Yaksha joking with his wife."

Sources:

Crooke, William. *Religion and Folklore of Northern India.* Humphrey, Milford: Oxford University Press, 1926.

The Tree of Life, and The Tree of the Knowledge of Good and Evil

Two of the trees said to have been planted by God in the Garden of Eden (Gen. 2:17; 3:24). They were believed by St. Ambrose to be of mystical significance. The former is understood to be the manifestation of God, and the latter of the worldly wisdom to which our human nature is too apt to incline.

Tremblers of the Cevennes

A Protestant caste of convulsionaries, who during the sixteenth century grew in numbers from their center in the Cevennes (south of Lyon, France), over almost the whole of Germany. They possessed many points of resemblance with cases of **obsession and possession,** and are said to have been insensible to thrusts and blows with pointed sticks and iron bars, as well as to the oppression of great weights. They had visions, communicated with good and evil spirits, and are said to have performed many miraculous cures similar to the apostolic miracles. They made use of modes of treatment called *grandes secours* or *secours meurtriers,* which were authenticated by the reports of eyewitnesses and by judicial documents.

Although they were belabored by the strongest men with heavy pieces of wood and bars of iron weighing at least thirty pounds, they complained of no injury, but experienced a sensation of pleasure. They also were covered with boards, on which as many as twenty men stood without its being painful to them. The Tremblers even bore as many as a hundred blows with a twenty pound weight, alternately applied to the breast and the stomach with such force that the room trembled; they begged the blows might be laid on harder, as light ones only increased their sufferings. It seemed only when the power of these blows had penetrated to the most vital parts that they experienced real relief.

Joseph Ennemoser explained this insensibility to pain by stating that in his experience:

". . . spasmodic convulsions maintain themselves against outward attempts, and even the greatest violence, with almost superhuman strength, without injury to the patient, as has often been observed in young girls and women, where anyone might have almost been induced to believe in supernatural influence. The tension of the muscles increases in power with the insensibility of the power, so that no outward force is equal to it; and when it is attempted to check the paroxysm with force, it gains in intensity, and according to some observers not less psychical than physical. . . . I have observed the same manifestations in children, in Catholics, Protestants and Jews, without the least variation, on which account I consider it to be nothing more than an immense abnormal and inharmonic *lusus naturoe.*" (See also **Convulsionaries of St. Médard**)

Sources:

Ennemoser, Joseph. *The History of Magic.* 2 vols., 1854. Reprint, New Hyde Park, N.Y.: University Books, 1960.

Trench, (William) Brinsley Le Poer (1911–1995)

Distinguished British authority on **UFOs.** He is the 8th Earl of Clancarty and a member of the House of Lords, where he introduced a serious debate on UFOs January 18, 1979. This was a historic occasion—the first on which this subject had been discussed by the British Parliament.

Born September 18, 1911, Trench is the fifth son of the fifth Earl of Clancarty and of Mary Gwatkin. He was educated at Nautical College, Pangbourne. His interest in UFOs extends over thirty years. After World War II, he noticed many reports of UFO sightings and began to collect press cuttings on the subject. Through a meeting with **Desmond Leslie,** he was encouraged to attend a lecture on flying saucers at Battersea Polytechnic, London.

Trench, Derek Dempster (aviation correspondent of the British newspaper *Daily Express*), and other interested individuals founded a company named Flying Saucer Service Ltd. and commenced publication of a magazine *Flying Saucer Review.* The first edition appeared in spring 1955 with Derek Dempster as editor, followed by Trench in September 1956, then in September 1959 by Waveney Girvan. When Girvan died, the magazine was edited by Charles Bowen. After 25 years of publication, this remains the first authoritative British publication on the subject of UFOs. It is now included in the House of Lords library.

In 1967, Trench founded Contact International, a worldwide UFO organization with members in 37 different countries. His interest led to his writing a variety of books including some which moved from ufology to a consideration of the **ancient astronaut** hypothesis.

He died May 18, 1995.

Sources:

Trench, Brinsley Le Poer. *The Eternal Subject.* London: Souvenir, 1973.

———. *The Flying Saucer Story.* London: Neville Spearman, 1966.

———. *Forgotten Heritage.* London: Neville Spearman, 1964.

———. *Men Among Mankind.* London: Neville Spearman, 1962.

———. *Operation Earth.* London: Neville Spearman, 1969.

———. *Secret of the Ages: UFOs From Inside the Earth.* London: Souvenir Press, 1974.

———. *The Sky People.* London: Neville Spearman, 1960.

Who's Who 1996. New York: St. Martin's Press, 1996.

Trent, A. G. (1789–1850)

Pseudonym of philologist and author **Richard Garnett,** assistant keeper of printed books at the British Museum Library. He used this alias for his writings on **astrology,** at a time in which his professional reputation might have suffered if it had been known that he was actively interested in such a subject.

Trevelyan, Sir George (Lowthian) (1906–1996)

Fourth Baronet, born November 5, 1906, eldest son of the Rt. Hon. Sir C. P. Trevelyan who was Minister of Education in Ramsay MacDonald's first Labour Government in Britain. Sir George grew up with a background of liberal politics and progressive thought. He was educated at Sidcot School and at Trinity College, Cambridge. He also worked as an artist-craftsman with Peter Waals workshops 1930–1.

For four years (1932–36), he trained and worked in the Alexander Technique, the psychophysical healing system developed by F. M. Alexander. Then until World War II, he taught at Gordonstown School and Abinger Hill School. During the war, he was a Home Guard Training Captain and following the war taught at No. 1 Army College, Newbattle Abbey (1945–47). On retirement for the Army, he became principal of Attingham Park, the Shropshire Adult College, where he did pioneering work in the teaching of spiritual knowledge as adult education.

On his retirement in 1971, he founded the **Wrekin Trust,** one of the pioneering **New Age** organizations, concerned with dissolving the barriers between science and religion. The trust held important conferences on science in relation to **mysticism,** with papers from such distinguished individuals as Prof. Glen W. Schaefer, Prof. Joscelyn Godwin, and Pir Vilayat Inayat Khan. These conferences provided a nexus of early New Age networks. As the new age developed Trevelyan authored a number of books reflecting on the growing vision and offering the movement his mature insights.

He died February 7, 1996.

Sources:

Tarne, Ingham. "A Little Lower Than the Angels. . . and Crowned with Glory." *Meditation* 3, no. 4 (Fall 1988): 24–28.

Trevelyan, George. *The Active Eye in Architecture.* N.p., 1977.

———. *Operation Redemption.* Wellingborough, Northamptonshire, England: Turnstone Press, 1981.

———. *A Vision of the Aquarian Age.* London: Stillpoint, 1984.

Trevelyan, George, and Edward Marchett. *Twelve Seats at the Round Table.* Jersey: Neville Spearman, 1976.

Trévisan, Bernard of (1406–1490)

Italian alchemist seeking to discover the **philosophers' stone.** Trévisan began at an early age to spend large sums of money on the pursuit.

Trévisan was born at Padua. His father was a doctor of medicine, so it is probable that Bernard received his initial training in science at home. At the age of fourteen he devoted himself to **alchemy.** He read the works of Eastern philosophers Gerber and **Rhasis.** Trévisan augmented his learning with the writings of Sacrobosco and Rupecissa. He engaged in a long course of reading and praying.

Trévisan heard that Henry, a German priest, had succeeded in creating the philosophers' stone. He went to Germany, accompanied by other alchemists. Henry claimed he would disclose all if they would supply a certain sum of money to procure the necessary tools and materials. After Henry proved **fraud** Trévisan decided to abandon his search. However, he visited Spain, Great Britain, Holland, and France, trying in each of these countries to learn more about creating the philosophers' stone. Eventually he went to **Egypt,** Persia, and Palestine and subsequently travelled in **Greece.**

Ultimately Trévisan found himself impoverished and was forced to sell his parental estates. He retired to the Island of Rhodes and met a priest who knew something of science. Trévisan proposed they should start fresh experiments together. The cleric agreed to help, so the pair borrowed a large sum of money to purchase the necessary paraphernalia. The two found some success.

It is belived that Trévisan was at least partly responsible for an octavo volume published in 1643, *Le Bernard d'Alchmague, cum Bernard Treveso,* while he is commonly credited with another work titled *La Philosophic Naturelle des Metaux.* In this latter work he insists on the necessity of **meditation** by the scientist who would create the philosophers' stone.

Bernard of Trévisan is often confused with two other individuals—Bernardo Trevisano (1652–1720), a Venetian devoted to languages, mathematics, philosophy, and painting, and Bernardinus Trivisanus (1506–1583), who studied arts and medicine at Padua and became professor of logic and medical theory.

Triad Group

Nonprofit organization founded by author **Whitley Strieber** to catalog and study "visitor experiences"—claims of contacts with extraterrestrials or other creatures. The project followed Strieber's claimed experiences detailed in his book *Communion* (1987). After the formation of the organization, rather than joining his cause, many believers in unidentified flying objects claimed Streiber was an amatuer. After several years, he dissolved the group.

Triad Society

An ancient esoteric society of China. The candidate was taken to a dark room by two members to kneel before the president. He was given a living cock and a knife and took an oath to assist his brethren in any emergency, even at the risk of his life. He then cut off the head of the cock, mingled its blood with his own, and the three assisting individuals added some of their own blood.

After being warned that death is the punishment should he divulge the secrets of the society, he was initiated and given the triad signs of recognition. For example, a member had to lift any object with three fingers only. This society, originally altruistic, later became political.

Various Triad societies were revived in Hong Kong to operate criminal extortion and protection rackets. Cinema protection was a specialty of these gangs and usually involved Triad members being employed as ushers, ticket-sellers, or submanagers.

Financial operations involve magic numerals, symbolic of the particular Triad society. For example, protection money may be demanded in sums relating to the figure 8, the lower half of the Chinese character *Hung,* used by some Triad societies. The numeral 3 denotes heaven, earth, and man. The word Triad originally was used as a mystical symbol.

In the 1970s, the Triad racketeering operations in Hong Kong resulted in the publication of a police manual, *Triad Societies of Hong Kong,* restricted to police personnel. In 1976, the Triad societies spread their operations to Britain, where cities like Birmingham, Bristol, Liverpool, Portsmouth, Southampton, Manchester, and London with large Chinese populations could be victimized. Triad protection rackets even operate in the West End cinemas and clubs of London, where vicious fights have been reported involving meat cleavers.

A muscleman in the Shing Wo Triad is known as "426," a numerical symbol for "Red stick" or "enforcer." In some British cities, the protection racket is being partially reduced by closing down illegal gambling clubs where Triad members meet or convert their funds.

Sources:

Chesneaux, Jean. *Secret Societies in China in the Nineteenth and Twentieth Centuries.* Ann Arbor: University of Michigan Press, 1971.

Triangles (Network)

Network funded by the Lucis Trust, formed to propagate the teachings of **Alice A. Bailey** (1880–1949), former Theosophist who founded her own **Arcane School.**

The Triangles Program was inaugurated in 1937 by Bailey in which she called upon people to form groups of three who would daily unite to channel spiritual energy to the world. Address: 120 Wall St., 24th Fl., New York, NY 10005. British headquarters are at Ste. 54, 3 Whitehall Ct., London, SW1A 2EF, England. Website: http://www.lucistrust.org/.

Trilite Seminars

Trilite Seminars is a Canadian channeling organization built around the activity of a walk-in personality named Shaari. Prior to 1989, she had been a professional in computer graphics who was also a trance medium who led personal growth workshops. That year she was in a car accident. During her period of recovery, she decided that she had completed her life work and requested that she end her incarnation. However, rather than let her body die, she offered it for the use of someone else. That someone came to be known as Shaari.

According to Shaari, she is a commander in the Star Command, which she has worked with for more than 750 years. She had an unusual birth as a Pleiadian/Arcturan hybrid. She was not born of normal parents but created as a result of action by a Pleiadian and Arcturan council. In her early years, she traveled the universe studying various cultures. She had a family with her husband Mishar.

During what on Earth was the 1980s, she had traveled to the planet Ur to assist the development of consciousness of a primitive life form. On the return journey, she stopped at the **Ashtar Command** headquarters near Earth. This area is under the command of Veyares and operates under the strict directives of **Ashtar,** the Star Command, and the Intergalactic Council of Twelve. While here, she was offered the opportunity to assist in the leap of consciousness of Earth and humanity by consciously integrating into another life form. The Earth mission was to last 30 years, at the conclusion of which she would take over the post currently held by Veyares.

Shaari channels Abraham, a member of the Light Brotherhood and Intergalactic Cmmand, as well as Malaya, a feminine consciousness. Together she and these two entities form the triad for which her organization is named. These two entities had previously been channeled by the person whose body she took over. The Trilite organization offers seminars and retreats, and Shaari channels in private sessions for individuals. Several times a year she leads travel seminars to power spots in order to provide a focus for the healing of the planet.

Trilite is headquartered at P.O. Box 22040, Brentwood Bay, BC, Canada, V0S lR0. It does not have a website, but information can be found on the Internet at http://members.spiritweb.org/Spirit/et-journey.htm.

Sources:

Trilite Seminars. http://members.spiritweb.org/Spirit/et-journey.htm. February 28, 2000.

Trintzius, Rene (1898–1953)

A writer and unorthodox healer, born July 29, 1898, at Rouen, France. He became a novelist and playwright and wrote biographical studies of Rousseau, Charlotte Corday, Jacques Cazotte, and John Law. His books include: *L'Astrologie à la portée de tous* (Astrology for All), *Lisez dans vos mains* (Palmistry), *La Magie a-t-elle raison* (Is Magic on the Right Lines?), *Les Guérisons supranormales* (Supernormal Cures), *Les Pouvoirs inconnus de l'Homme* (Man's Unknown Powers), *La Voyance et ses supports* (Clairvoyance and Its Supports), and *Au seuil du Monde invisible* (On the Threshold of the Invisible World). He died in 1953.

Triskaidekaphobia Illuminatus Society

A defunct organization founded in 1984 concerned with superstitions about the number 13. Membership was comprised of individuals who believed the number 13 had the ability to affect the balance of world power and political structure through the "Illuminati" (persons who are or who claim to be unusually enlightened). The society sought to isolate seemingly unconnected events caused by the numerical forces inherent in the number 13, correlate the meanings of these events, and develop solutions and strategies.

The society promoted the organization of illuminated task forces for the elimination of Triskaidekaphobia (fear of the number 13) from society. It operated a think tank, bestowed an annual award for contributions concerning the "power" of the number 13, and maintained an archive collection of media clippings and videotapes from television shows. The society published *The 13th Illuminated Stratum* newsletter (two to five per year); *Thirteen,* an editorial report issued at irregular intervals; and *Fear to Feel: the Illuminated Network of 13 Concealed Phantoms,* a book. The society disbanded around 1990.

Trithemius (Johann) (1462–1519)

Alchemist and magician. The son of a German vine grower named Heidenberg, he received his Latin name from Trittenheim, a village in the electorate of Trêves, where he was born. He lost his father when he was a year old, and his mother remarried.

Trithemius worked all day in the vineyards and studied at night. He read whatever books he could beg or borrow. With his share of the patrimony bequeathed by his father, Trithemius went to Trêves, entered as student at the university, and assumed the name of Trithemius.

By the age of 20, Trithemius had acquired the reputation of a scholar. In the winter of 1482, he left Trêves and returned to Trittenheim to visit his mother.

On arriving at Spanheim, Trithemius found the roads impassable due to snow. He went to a neighboring Benedictine monastery. There he stayed for several days. He liked the monastery and voluntarily took the monastic vows and retired from the world. In the course of two years, he was elected abbot and devoted himself to the repair and improvement of the monastery.

After 21 years as abbot, the monks elected another abbot. Trithemius left Spanheim and wandered from place to place, until finally elected abbot of St. James of Wurzburg, where he died in 1519.

Trithemius devised a shorthand called *stenoganographia,* stigmatized as a Kabalistic and necromantic writing, concealing his most fearful, occult secrets. He wrote a treatise on the subject, another on the supposed administration of the world by its guardian angels, translated into English in 1647 by the astrologer **William Lilly.** He wrote a third book on **geomancy,** or divination by means of lines and circles on the ground, a fourth upon sorcery, and a fifth on **alchemy.** In his work on sorcery, Trithemius made an early mention of the popular story of **Faust,** and recorded his experiences with the spirit named Hudekin.

Reportedly, Trithemius gave the Emperor Maximilian a vision of his deceased wife, the beautiful Mary of Burgundy. Reputedly he defrayed the expenses of his monastic establishment at Spanheim by resources obtained from the **philosophers' stone.**

Sources:

Seligmann, Kurt. *The History of Magic.* New York: Pantheon Books, 1948. Reprinted as *Magic, Supernaturalism and Religion.* New York: Pantheon Books, 1971.

Trivah

Among the Dayaks of Borneo, the trivah, or feast of the dead, was celebrated after a death had taken place. A panel containing a representation of the **tempon-teloris** (ship of the dead) was generally set up at the trivah, and sacrifices of fowls were offered to it. It was believed that until the trivah had been celebrated, the souls were unable to reach the golden shores. (See also **Book of the Dead; Egypt**)

Trollope, Thomas Adolphus (1810–1892)

British novelist, author on travel, biography, history and frequent investigator of the medium **D. D. Home.** In 1855, Trollope opposed Sir David Brewster when the latter published a denial of having witnessed Home's psychic phenomena.

Eight years later, in a letter to *The Athenaeum* (April 1863), Trollope testified to "having seen and felt physical facts, wholly and utterly inexplicable, as I believe, by any known and generally received physical laws. I unhesitatingly reject the theory which considers such facts to be produced by means familiar to the best professors of legerdemain."

The report by a committee of the **London Dialectical Society** contained his written testimony on an **apport** of jonquil flowers through the mediumship of **Agnes Guppy-Volckman** in his own home in Florence, Italy.

Tromp, S(olco) W(alie) (1909–1983)

Geophysicist, director of the Bioclimatological Research Center, Leiden, Netherlands, and writer on parapsychological subjects. Tromp was born on March 9, 1909, at Djarkarta, Indonesia. He moved to Europe for his education and earned his Ph.D. at the University of Leiden in geology in 1932.

After military service (1932–33), Tromp was a field geologist for oil companies in Indonesia and Egypt from 1933 to 1940. During World War II, he worked as an advisor on oil explorations for the Turkish Government (1940–43) and then joined his country's war effort as the director of economic warfare, Netherlands Army (1943–45). After the war he held a variety of positions as an economic geologist. Related to his geological interests, Tromp specialized in the study of phenomena connected with **dowsing** (water divining) about which he wrote several articles and books. He died March 17, 1983, in the Netherlands.

Sources:

Pleasants, Helene, ed. *Biographical Dictionary of Parapsychology.* New York: Helix Press, 1964.

Tromp, S. W. *Dowsing and Science.* N.p., 1950.

———. "First Report on Experiments Concerning the Influence of Variations in the Strength of the Magnetic Field on Muscular Contraction." *Dutch Journal of Parapsychology* (January 1947).

———. *Fundamental Principles of Psychical Physics.* N.p., 1952.

———. "The Problem of the Possible Influence of Dowsing Zones on the Health of Men." *Dutch Journal of Parapsychology* (November 1948).

———. *Psychical Physics.* N.p., 1949.

Tron, Giorgio (1884–1963)

Italian physician who studied parapsychology. Tron was born on September 12, 1884, in Turin, Italy. He studied at the University of Pavia (M.D., 1910; teaching diploma in hygiene, 1924). He was staff doctor at the Hospital for Infectious Diseases, Milan (1915–26), hygiene officer at Milan (1927–38), and director of the Instituto Sieroterapico Italiano, Naples (1940–53). Tron was a member of the Società Italiana di Parapsicologia and served as the society's secretary (1955–59).

In addition to his writings on medical subjects, Tron contributed articles to the *Bulletin of the Società Italiana di Parapsicologia.* He also wrote a chapter on unorthodox healing in the book *Studia Parapsychologica* (1956) and on physical mediumistic phenomena in *Nuovi Problemi di Metapsichica* (1953). He died February 5, 1963, in Rome.

Sources:

Pleasants, Helene, ed. *Biographical Dictionary of Parapsychology.* New York: Helix Press, 1964.

Trophonios

Trophonios, a legendary Greek hero who was eventually considered a god-like being, was credited with building the original temple housing the Oracle at **Delphi.** At a later date, the Oracle at Delphi is said to have ordered the building of an oracle site to be established at Lebadea (known today as the town of Livadia) dedicated to Trophonios. The site would become one of the prominent oracular centers in ancient Greece, and accounts of it survive in the writings of Pausanius.

Those who consulted the oracle at Labadea followed a pattern common in the ancient world. They took up residence at the center for several days, during which they offered sacrifices of various animals. Following the sacrifices, soothsayers were present to read the entrails of the animals (a practice termed **extispicy**), specifically determining if Trophonios would receive the inquirer graciously or not. The night before entering the cave where the god dwelled, the person would receive a bath and was anointed with olive oil. The priests then took him to water springs where the water of forgetfulness (for the loss of memory of all that was past) and the water of memory (to recall all that would be seen) were consumed. It is believed that these waters contained doses of hallucinogenic drugs.

The inquirer was taken to the entrance of the cave and supplied with a ladder by which he went down into a room. In the floor was a small opening through which the person entered into the actual oracle space. Here the person had both visionary experiences and encounters with the deity (possibly one of the priests acting as a **medium**). Upon his return, the person was seated on the Throne of Memory and questioned as to what had been seen or heard.

The site of the Trophonion oracle is well known, though modern explorers of the area have been unable to locate the entrance to the caves used for **divination** in ancient times. Some believe that a complex of interconnected caves exist in the area.

Sources:

Pausanius. *Guide to Greece.* Translated by Peter Levi. Harmondsworth, UK: Penguin, 1971.

Temple, Robert K. G. *Conversations with Eternity: Ancient Man's Attempt to Know the Future.* London: Rider, 1984.

True Black Magic, Book of the

A **grimoire** (manual of **ceremonial magic**) that is an adapted version of the **Key of Solomon the King.**

True World Order (TWO)

Movement started by **Swami Vishnudevananda,** disciple of the late **Swami Sivananda** of Rishikesh, India, and believer in **hatha yoga.**

TWO is dedicated to promoting world peace and understanding, good health, and happiness through yoga harmony and a vegetarian diet. For information: International Sivananda Yoga Vedanta Center, 673 8th Ave., Val Morin, Quebec, Canada J0T 2R0.

Trumpet

A funnel-shaped device of cardboard, aluminum, or other lightweight material used at Spiritualist séances for the manifestation of **direct voice** communication from spirits. **Jonathan Koons,** the nineteenth-century American farmer medium, appears to have been the first to use a trumpet.

Spiritualists have suggested the trumpet serves as a condenser of psychic energy and increases the volume of the spirit voice. Reportedly, weak or inexperienced spirits often have to use the trumpet. It is seldom necessary for a spirit **guide.** Some mediums also wet the trumpet with water, in the belief this facilitates the phenomena.

The trumpet is usually coated with a marking of luminous paint. Supposedly at séances in dark rooms the trumpet is seen levitating when there is sufficient psychic force and moving around the circle, conveying personal messages to individual sitters.

Reportedly as a safeguard against **fraud,** psychical researchers have devised techniques and apparatus to attempt to exclude the possibility of a medium employing ventriloquism in producing voices ostensibly from the trumpet. One method is to fill the medium's mouth with water. During the investigation of the medium **Mina Crandon** (better known as "Margery"), Mark Richardson of Boston invented a "Voice Control Machine."

The American direct voice medium **Elizabeth Blake** used a double trumpet with a saucer-shaped extension at the small end to be placed on the ear of the sitter and on her own. Another trumpet, the "Shastaphone," was developed through a psychic communication in Australia, but does not appear to have been widely used.

Trungpa Rinpoche, Chogyam (1940–1987)

Throughout the nineteenth and twentieth centuries, teachers of the **occult** have portrayed **Tibet** as an outpost of the highest occult wisdom. However, it was not until after the Chinese invasion of Tibet in 1959 that Tibetan teachers arrived in the West, making firsthand encounters with Tibetan Buddhism available to more than a few adventurous explorers. Among the first to arrive was Chogyam Trungpa, the eleventh Trungpa Tulku. He was born in February 1929 in Geje, Tibet. Designated the reincarnation of a famous lama as an infant, he was raised in a monastery and trained in Tibetan Buddhism. He fled Tibet at the time of the invasion, and in 1963 received a Spaulding grant to attend Oxford University. While in England he wrote his autobiography, *Born in Tibet* (1966), and established a center in Scotland.

In 1970 Trungpa renounced his monastic vows to marry. He moved to the United States that same year and founded Karme Choling, a seed center of what would grow into Vajradhatu, an international fellowship of his students. He presented his version of Tibetan Buddhism in a number of books, including *Mudra* (1972); *Cutting through Spiritual Materialism* (1973); *Visual Dharma, the Buddhist Art of Tibet* (1975); *The Dawn of Tantra* (1975), with Herbert Gunther; and *The Myth of Freedom* (1976). He found ready acceptance among one segment of people who appreciated his total dedication to his spiritual teachings and his simultaneous ability to enjoy life, manifested through his love of alcohol and women. He was also a patron of the arts, especially poetry, and founded a school, Naropa Institute, which offers an alternative curriculum with college-level instruction. The institute has taught the likes of Allen Ginsberg and **Ram Dass.**

Trungpa possibly became best known for his denunciation of "spiritual materialism," manifest in the spiritual seekers of alternative religions who seemed preoccupied with collecting as many varied spiritual experiences as possible. Such seekers never settle down long enough to have their search rewarded with real insight, he said.

In 1981 Trungpa expanded his teachings to Canada, where he established a community in Halifax. He died at these Canadian headquarters April 4, 1987 of cardiac arrest and respiratory failure. He was succeeded by Osel Tendzin, his chief disciple.

Sources:

Clark, Tom. *The Great Naropa Poetry Wars.* Santa Barbara, Calif.: Cadmus Editions, 1980.

Fields, Rick. *How the Swans Came to the Lake: A Narrative History of Buddhism in America.* Boulder, Colo.: Shambhala, 1981.

Queen, Edward L., Stephen R Prothero, and Gardiner H Shattuck. "Chogyam Trungpa," *Encyclopedia of American Religious History.* 2 vols. New York: Facts on File, 1996.

The Tibetan Book of the Dead. Translated and with a commentary by Francesca Fremantle and Chogyam Trungpa. Berkeley, Calif.: Shambhala, 1973.

Truth Journal

Publication of the **Center for Spiritual Awareness** (CSA), a kriya yoga organization developed from the teachings of Swami **Paramahansa Yogananda** and headed by Roy Eugene Davis. CSA may be contacted at P.O. Box 7, Lakemount, GA 30552-0001. The center's website is http://www.csa-davis.org/.

Sources:

Center for Spiritual Awareness. http://www.csa-davis.org/. March 8, 2000.

Truzzi, Marcello (1935–)

Contemporary sociologist and scholar of parapsychology and the occult. Truzzi was born on September 6, 1935, in Copenhagen, Denmark. He attended Florida State University (B.A., 1957), the University of Florida (M.A., 1962), and Cornell University (Ph.D., 1970). He taught at several universities before settling permanently in the sociology department at Eastern Michigan University, Ypsilanti. He chaired the department for 12 years (1974–86).

Born into a prominent circus family, Truzzi has interests encompassing folklore, stage magic, the history of science, popular culture, and parapsychology. He has been most identified with anomalous phenomena and coined the term *amnomolistics* to designate the field of study.

In 1972 Truzzi began to issue a small newsletter, *Explorations,* renamed *The Zetetic* two years later. In 1976 *The Zetetic* was offered to the **Committee for the Scientific Investigation of Claims of the Paranormal,** cofounded by Truzzi, as its official publication. Within a short time, Truzzi, who viewed himself as a true skeptic, found himself in conflict with the majority of the committee members. As a skeptic, he expressed his doubts about unproven claims and withheld judgement pending definitive evidence. The majority of the committee proved themselves to be debunkers who opposed all discussion of the paranormal. Truzzi broke with the committee when it was discovered that members had falsified data that tended to support **Michel Gauquelin**'s views on **astrology.**

After separating from the committee, Truzzi founded the Center for Scientific Anomalies Research and began a new periodical, the *Zetetic Scholar.* He edited the *Zetetic Scholar* for a decade (1978–87). Besides his more conventional books on sociology, Truzzi has ventured into the sociology of witchcraft and the occult and cowritten (with Arthur Lyons) the definitive text on the use of occult powers in solving crimes, *The Blue Sense: Psychic Detectives and Crime* (1991).

Sources:

Clark, Jerome. *Encyclopedia of Strange and Unexplained Phenomena.* Detroit: Gale Research, 1993.

Clark, Jerome, and J. Gordon Melton. "The Crusade Against the Paranormal." *Fate* pt. 1, 32, 9 (September 1979): 70–76; pt. 2, 32, 10 (October 1979): 87–94.

Lyons, Arthur, and Marcello Truzzi. *The Blue Sense: Psychic Detectives and Crime.* New York: Mysterious Press/Warner Books, 1991.

Truzzi, Marcello. *Cauldron Cookery: An Authentic Guide for Coven Connoisseurs.* New York: Meredith, 1969.

———. "The Occult Revival as Popular Culture: Some Random Observations on the Old and Nouveau Witch." *Sociological Quarterly* 13 (Winter 1972): 16–34.

———. *Where Witchcraft Lives.* London: Aquarian Press, 1962.

The Tsitsith

An article of Jewish religious apparel, the fringe or tassels attached to the outer garment, which are believed to be endowed with talismanic properties. In modern times, the fringe has survived in the praying shawl named *talith* and in a garment worn on the chest. A sentence in the Talmud states: "Whoever has the tephillin bound to his head and arm, and the tsitsith thrown over his garments . . . is protected from sin." (See also **Tephillin**)

Tubby, Gertrude Ogden (1878–1967)

Teacher, author, and psychic researcher. Born June 18, 1878, at Kingston on Hudson, New York, Tubby studied at Smith College, Northampton, Massachusetts (B.S., 1902). In 1907 she became the special research assistant to **James H. Hyslop,** then president of the **American Society for Psychical Research** (ASPR) and remained in that position for the rest of Hyslop's life. The society split in 1925, with dissident members forming the **Boston Society for Psychic Research.** Tubby, who had control of Hyslop's papers, continued to work for the ASPR as a secretary and as editor of its *Journal* until 1924. However, after a dispute with the leadership of the society she refused to give them the Hyslop collection for their archives. Eventually she turned that material over to the Spiritual Frontiers Fellowship (now the **International Spiritual Frontiers Fellowship**).

Also, as a result of working as Hyslop's assistant, Tubby investigated a wide range of psychic phenomena, including **mediumship, telepathy, clairvoyance, psychokinesis,** and **survival.** After his death, she collected communications apparently from him from various mediums. These messages are discussed in the book *James H. Hyslop—X, His Book* (1929). She also published the book *Psychics and Mediums, A Handbook for Students* (1935; British ed. 1938), as well as various articles in the *Journal* and *Proceedings* of the ASPR.

She died July 1967.

Tulku

Term for a Tibetan entity recognized in a present incarnation. Tibetan Buddhism teaches that highly evolved individuals become spiritually liberated by abandoning the sense of ego or separate identity, but the spiritual forces comprising such an individual may still elect to be reborn for the benefit of other people. It is believed they are only illusory manifestations sustained by the sense of ego.

Traditional tests exist for the identification of tulkus, especially in the case of the Dalai Lama. Other contemporary tulkus include **Chogyam Trungpa** (1939–1987), author of the book *Born in Tibet* (London, 1966) and **Tarthang Tulku,** both popularly known by their disciples as "Rinpoche," a title meaning "precious master."

Tulpa

Tibetan term for a phantom form generated by mental concentration. In her book *With Mystics and Magicians in Tibet* (1931), Alexandra David-Neel describes how she created a tulpa of a monk, who supposedly became a recognizable member of her party during a journey. Reportedly in the course of time this phantom took on an independent life of its own. David-Neel claimed it took six months of intense concentration to dissolve this phantom.

A tulpa may also double as the magician who created it, employed for protective purposes by appearing instead of its creator. A tulpa should be distinguished from a **tulku,** which is either the reincarnation of a saintly individual or the incarnation of a non-human entity, such as a god, demon, or fairy.

Sources:

David-Neel, Alexandra. *Initiations and Initiates in Tibet.* London, 1932. Reprint, New Hyde Park, N.Y.: University Books, 1959.

———. *The Secret Oral Tradition in Tibetan Buddhist Sects.* San Francisco: City Lights, 1964. Reprint, Calcutta: Maha Bodhi Society of India, 1971.

———. *With Mystics and Magicians in Tibet.* 1931. Rev. ed. as *Magic and Mystery in Tibet.* New Hyde Park, N.Y.: University Books, 1956. Reprint, New York: Dover Publications, 1971.

Tumah

According to the **Kabala,** the term refers to physical or moral uncleanness. The latter is divided into three main divisions—idolatry, murder, and immorality. Sin has rendered humanity imperfect, but also affected the whole of nature, even to the sphere of angels and the divinity. In physical uncleanness, there is a coarser and subtler form. The latter causes a dimness in the soul felt by those who are nearest to sacred things. Organic matter that comes into contact with the human body is more liable to tumah than remoter things. The human corpse is more unclean than lower animals, because its more complex nature involves more decay.

Tumo

The mystical practice from **Tibet** of generating bodily heat, so that a hermit may spend winter naked in a cave amid snow and freezing temperatures at an altitude between 11,000 and 18,000 feet. Adepts have supposedly distinguished various types of tumo: exoteric arises spontaneously in the course of mystical raptures; esoteric keeps a hermit comfortable on a snowy hill; and mystic produces experiences of paradisiacal bliss.

According to Alexandra David-Neel, tumo "is also the subtle fire with which warms the generative fluid and drives the energy in it, till it runs all over the body along the subtle channels." This has some similarity to the Hindu teachings of the nature of **kundalini** energy—possibly aroused in subtle physical channels, related to the energy of sexual activity, and productive of either heat or cold in the body.

Sources:

David-Neel, Alexandra. *Initiations and Initiates in Tibet.* London, 1932. Reprint, New Hyde Park, N.Y.: University Books, 1959.

———. *The Secret Oral Tradition in Tibetan Buddhist Sects.* San Francisco: City Lights, 1964. Reprint, Calcutta: Maha Bodhi Society of India, 1971.

———. *With Mystics & Magicians in Tibet.* 1931. Rev. ed. as *Magic and Mystery in Tibet.* New Hyde Park, N.Y.: University Books, 1956. Reprint, New York: Dover Publications, 1971.

Tunisa

Burmese diviners. (See also **Myanmar**)

Turin Shroud

A relic housed in a chapel in Turin (or Turino), Italy, and believed by some to be the shroud in which Jesus was wrapped after his crucifixion. In the accounts of Jesus' burial in the Christian New Testament, the earliest of which appears in the Gospel of Mark 15:46, it is noted, "And he [Joseph of Arimathea] brought fine linen, and took him [Jesus] down and wrapped him in the linen, and laid him in a sepulchre which was hewn out of a rock. . . ." There is no record of the survival of that burial cloth for the next five centuries. Then about 570 C.E., a pilgrim reported that it was kept in a monastery by the river Jordan. In 670 C.E. the French bishop Arculph, returning from a pilgrimage to Jerusalem, was shipwrecked on the coast of Scotland and traveled to a monastery on the island of Iona. Here he said he had seen the shroud and been allowed to kiss it.

Subsequent references are made to a surviving shroud by the Venerable Bede, St. Willibald, St. John Damascene, and the Emperor Baldwin. In 1284, Robert de Clari, chronicler of the Fourth Crusade, described the triumphant entry of Crusaders into Constantinople and mentioned the monastery of Lady St. Mary of the Blachernes, in which a cloth claiming to be the shroud was kept. In the Middle Ages some 40 different shrouds were claimed to be the one in which Christ was buried. At this time there also existed a variety of similar relics, including tears from Jesus, milk from the Virgin Mary, thorns from the crown of thorns worn by Jesus, and enough pieces of the cross to make a number of different such instruments of execution. The reformation of the church concerning such superstitions began in earnest in the sixteenth century and continued in subsequent centuries.

Nothing is known of the particular piece of cloth known as the Shroud of Turin until its appearance in the church of Lirey, Troyes, France, during the fourteenth century. At the time between 1353 and 1356, the shroud was placed in a small wooden church at Lirey by Geoffrey de Charny, Lord of Lirey, but exhibition of the relic aroused opposition from Henry of Poitiers, Bishop of Troyes. Many years later, in 1389, the Lord of Lirey's son (Geoffrey II) obtained permission to exhibit the shroud, but Henry's successor as bishop of Troyes, Pierre d'Arcis, objected most strenuously.

In a statement to the Avignon Pope Clement VII, he complained that the exhibition was not for devotion, but for monetary gain, and that the relic was a forgery, "a certain cloth cunningly painted, upon which by clever sleight of hand was depicted the twofold image of one man, that is to say the back and the front, [the canons at Lirey] falsely declaring and pretending that this was the actual shroud in which our Saviour Jesus Christ was enfolded in the tomb." D'Arcis claimed that Henry of Poitiers, 30 years earlier, after "diligent inquiry and examination" had established that the shroud had been "cunningly painted, the truth being attested by the artist . . . that it was a work of human skill and not miraculously wrought . . ." and that the first exhibition by Geoffrey's father had been prohibited.

Meanwhile, however, Geoffrey's widow had married Aymon of Geneva, who had ecclesiastical influence with Pope Clement, and the prohibition was bypassed, much to the anger of d'Arcis, hence his complaint in 1389. Pope Clement resolved the matter by declaring that Geoffrey II could continue exhibiting the shroud provided that it was always stated that it was only "a figure or representation" of Christ's cloth, and that d'Arcis must keep silence in the matter under pain of excommunication.

This affair has often been revived as "proof" that the shroud was a forgery, but the accusations of d'Arcis were never proved, and the original campaign against the genuineness of the shroud had started on the somewhat flimsy grounds that if such a cloth imprinted with an image of Jesus Christ had really existed, it would have been mentioned in the Gospels, and that the exhibition at Lirey was all part of a plot to hire persons for pretended miracles of healing. The statement that diligent inquiry had revealed a cunning artist remains unconvincing, since the artist was never named or punished.

After the death of Geoffrey II, his widow Margaret claimed that the relic had only been loaned to Lirey by her grandfather, but she was eventually obliged to give it up.

In 1452, it passed into the keeping of the Duke of Savoy. In 1532 it was kept in the sacristy of Sainte Chappelle, France, where it was nearly destroyed in a fire. It was then taken to the monastery of St. Clair where it was patched by nuns. It was brought to Saint Charles Borromeo in Turin, Italy, in 1578, and for more than four centuries remained the property of the ruling House of Savoy from which came the kings of Italy. It was exhibited annually until it was feared that frequent handling might damage it. By the end of the nineteenth century it was exhibited only on very special occasions.

In 1946, Umberto II, former king of Italy and the owner of the shroud, was exiled. He settled in Portugal and in the ensuing years, the Catholic Church, in the person of the archbishop of Turin, became its custodian. In 1978 it was disclosed that Umberto was leaving the shroud to the Pope, an event that occurred in 1983 with Umberto's passing. Italy did not challenge the will or claim the shroud for itself. Since that time, the Roman Catholic Church has had the power to respond directly to pressure to have the shroud definitively tested by modern scientific methods.

Description of the Shroud

The shroud always had vague markings indicating the outlines of a body, but these took on a special significance only at the end of the nineteenth century. Modern interest in the shroud dates from 1898, when Secundo Pia obtained permission to photograph it for the first time and discovered that his negative plate revealed a perfect image of a noble and majestic face with forehead wounds suggesting a crown of thorns, and a body with wounds in the hands and side.

The supposition is that in some unknown way, emanations from the body laid in the shroud reacted with the spices used for burial in such a way as to cause an image on the cloth, rather like a photographic negative. Although the shroud had been venerated for centuries, nobody had formerly realized that the markings might be more revealing than supposed. Pia's negative plate showed a *positive picture,* virtually a full-length photograph of the occupant of the shroud.

The publication of Pia's negative caused great excitement, and led to a scientific investigation by Paul Vignon, professor of Biology at the Institut Catholique in Paris. With his coworker Yves Delage he presented his findings, favorable to the authenticity of the shroud, to the French Academy of Science. The collaboration was a strange one, since Delage was an agnostic and Vignon a Catholic. Since then, the shroud has received increased attention and scholarship, and Vatican experts spent some years studying and verifying historical documents connected with it.

On September 6, 1936, Pope Pius XI offered his opinion of the cloth, "These are the images of the Divine Redeemer. We might say they are the most beautiful, most moving and dearest we can imagine."

The name **sindonology** has been given to studies of the shroud, and in 1939 the first Sindonological Congress was held in Turin. The Centro Internazionale di Sindonologia was created, drawing upon the highest academic, scientific, and ecclesiastical authorities.

In August 1978, the Holy Shroud was publicly exhibited again in the Cathedral of Turin, Italy. Because Turin had been a flashpoint for Red Brigade terrorism, special precautions were taken to protect the relic. In addition to extra police protection, the shroud itself was housed in a special display case with bulletproof glass. Archbishop Anastasio Ballestrero of Turin insisted that the shroud not be the subject of any form of commercialism, and the cost of the new protective case was born by a Turin exposition fund launched in the United States.

In October 1978, at the end of the exposition, a special Shroud Congress was held in Turin and attended by scientists from around the world. Advanced techniques of image analysis were discussed, including infra-red photography, photomicrography, high contrast photography, X-ray fluorescence, radiographic examination, and carbon dating.

Unfortunately much of the scientific analysis and discussion resulted in controversy and confusion. Many issues were hotly debated, such as whether the amount of iron oxide on the shroud indicated genuine bloodstains or artistic pigment. The main issue of dating the shroud was delayed through the reluctance of the authorities to permit destruction of a sample piece of the material for carbon dating. For a presentation of scientific views for and against the authenticity of the shroud, see the book *The Image on the Shroud* by H. David Sox (1981) and more recently *The Mysterious Shroud* by Ian Wilson (1986).

A significant breakthrough in the study of the shroud occurred in early 1987, when Pope John Paul II finally approved a plan to test fragments of the cloth in laboratories for radiocarbon content. Tests had been scheduled to begin in 1986, but were halted at the last minute by the Bishop of Turin.

Three major laboratories—in Switzerland, the United States, and Britain—were involved in these carbon-14 dating tests. Three other institutions were involved in statistical analysis of the results of tests, which included scientific controls using pieces of linen from known sources, ancient and modern. These included fragments of medieval cloth and a specimen from ancient Egypt, as well as modern cloth. The scientists involved did not know which cloth they were being provided with for testing until the results were correlated by the British Museum Research Laboratory and evaluated at the Vatican in Rome.

Edward Hall, of the Research Laboratory for Archaeology and Art at Oxford University, England, was one of the scientists involved in testing. He used an Accelerator Mass Spectrometer, generating a charge of two million volts. This massive new tool for radio-carbon dating is said to have influenced the Vatican decision to go ahead with the tests on actual fragments of the Turin Shroud. Earlier apparatus would have required the destruction of a sample about the size of a pocket handkerchief, whereas the new machine required a sample of only about a quarter of an inch.

In a report by Pearson Phillips in *The Times,* London, (April 15, 1987), Hall was quoted as stating: "If we get a medieval dating then we shall know it is a forgery and we can relax and forget the whole business. Although there will still be a mystery about how anyone in medieval times could have produced such a complex and effective fraud." Hall assumed an agnostic viewpoint, stating: "My view of Christ as a historical individual is that he was obviously a powerful personality. I suppose it is possible that, in some way we do not currently fully understand, some kind of impression from him was transferred to the shroud. But if we produce a carbon date around the start of the first century A.D., the fat will really be in the fire. As a scientist, I would then find it difficult to dismiss the shroud's authenticity."

An official report on October 13, 1988, revealed that the three laboratories in Oxford, Zürich, and Arizona had independently carbon dated the cloth fragments as medieval, and not from the time of Jesus Christ. There was close agreement on the possible dates, giving an estimated span of circa 1260–1390. For most skeptics, this established once and for all that the shroud was a medieval forgery.

Die-hard believers in the authenticity of the shroud either questioned the accuracy of the scientific evidence or propounded fantastic theories to account for the dating of the cloth, e.g., that the image was formed by a burst of divine radiant energy that somehow altered the texture of the cloth.

The close concurrence in dating of three independent scientific laboratories, with the best and most accurate apparatus, cannot be dismissed lightly. The normal margin of error in carbon dating is considered to be about 100 years either way.

It is unlikely that these tests can resolve the enigma of the shroud. Critics of the carbon testing have noted that scientific tests of any kind sometimes overlook anomalies revealed by later research. In the case of the dating of the shroud, there is no reason to doubt the good faith and accuracy of reputable scientific laboratories, but it is good to remember that the centuries-old shroud has been through many vicissitudes, and we are dealing with minute fragments of material.

In 1532, for example, when the shroud was kept in a silver casket at the church of Sainte Chappelle in Chambery, France, a fire broke out in the sacristy, melting drops of silver, which fell on the shroud and burned through folds in the cloth. In 1534, the burns on the cloth were patched by nuns at the monastery of St. Clair. The shroud has also suffered damp stains, and may have been washed or cleaned with oil at some time. Could the samples tested for carbon dating have been contaminated with threads or solutions from the later history of the shroud?

Moreover, carbon dating, accurate or misleading, cannot explain the extraordinary and awe-inspiring character of the image on the shroud as disclosed by the camera negative of Secondo Pia in 1898. There are no apparent brush marks, and other theories of production of the marks, however ingenious, hardly do justice to the beauty and accuracy of the icon. Common sense suggests that even a medieval forger of genius would be unlikely to have the prescience to produce a perfect and noble image *in negative*. What the pilgrims of that period in an out-of-the-way French district would surely have expected to see would have been a stylized rudimentary positive image, more like the icons in stained glass windows or the paintings in churches.

Dr. Robert Otlet, of the Atomic Energy Research Establishment at Harwell, had hoped that his famous laboratory would be included in the carbon dating tests, and later commented: "It is most unfortunate—entirely unnecessary when you put the amount of material to be taken in context. It will lead to a result which will be wide open to criticism and sadly will not be seen as definitive." It is clear that the story of the shroud has not come to an end. True believers in its authenticity have found ways to ignore and question the carbon dating evidence, while many fully accept the carbon dating results as conclusive.

Sources:

Barnes, Arthur Stapylton. *The Holy Shroud of Turin.* London: Burns Oates & Washbourne, 1934.

Heller, John H. *Report on the Shroud of Turin.* Boston: Houghton Mifflin, 1983.

Nickell, Joe. *Inquest on the Shroud of Turin.* Buffalo, N.Y.: Prometheus Press, 1983.

Reban, John. *Inquest on Jesus Christ.* London: Leslie Frewin, 1967.

Rinaldi, Peter M. *The Man in the Shroud.* New York: Vantage Press, 1972. Reprint, London: Futura, 1974. Reprinted as *It Is The Lord: A Study of the Shroud of Christ.* New York: Warner, 1973.

Sox, H. David. *The Image on the Shroud: Is the Turin Shroud a Forgery?* London: Unwin, 1981.

———. *The Shroud Unmasked; Uncovering the Greatest Forgery of All Time.* Basingstoke, England: Lamp Press, 1988.

Stein, Gordon. *Encyclopedia of Hoaxes.* Detroit: Gale Research, 1993.

Vignon, Paul. *The Shroud of Christ.* London: Constable, 1902. Reprint, New Hyde Park, N.Y.: University Books, 1970.

Walsh, John. *The Mysterious Shroud.* Garden City, N.Y.: Doubleday, 1986.

———. *The Shroud.* London: W. H. Allen, 1964.

Wilson, Ian. *The Turin Shroud.* London: Gollancz, 1978.

Wuenschel, Edward. *Self-Portrait of Christ.* New York: Esopus, 1954.

Zugibe, Frederick T. *The Cross and the Shroud: a Medical Inquiry into the Crucifixion.* New York: Paragon House Publishers, 1988.

Turner, Ann

A nineteenth-century English reputed witch. (See also **England**)

Turner, M(alcolm) E(lijah) (1929–)

Biometrician who experimented in the field of parapsychology. Turner was born on May 27, 1929, in Atlanta, Georgia. He studied at Duke University (B.A., 1952) and North Carolina State College (M.S. experimental statistics, 1955; Ph.D., 1959). After graduation he joined the faculty at the Medical College of Virginia. He joined the faculty of Emory University, Atlanta, Georgia, in 1963.

In the field of parapsychology, Turner experimented in model-building and statistical inference. He collaborated with Ann B. Turner and Elizabeth McMahan in experiments relating to the effects of time and distance on card-calling. Turner also worked with **Karlis Osis** on experiments in **extrasensory perception** over distance and developed a statistical model to evaluate ESP over spatial distances.

Sources:

Pleasants, Helene, ed. *Biographical Dictionary of Parapsychology.* New York: Helix Press, 1964.

Osis, Karlis, and M. E. Turner. "Distance and ESP: A Transcontinental Experiment." *Proceedings* of the American Society for Psychical Research 27 (1968).

Osis, Karlis, M. E. Turner, and M. L. Carlson. "ESP Over Distance: Research on the ESP Channel." *Journal* of the American Society for Psychical Research 65 (1971).

Turoff, Stephen

Contemporary British spiritual healer who practices **psychic surgery.** His healing is through an entity claimed to be "Dr. Joseph Kahn," whose healing resembles that of Philippine healers. At times, a real scalpel is manipulated; at other times, an invisible syringe or other apparatus is involved.

Purported healings effected through Turoff's mediumship include cases of fibroids in the womb, infected lungs, and liver tumor. "Dr. Kahn" is said to be one of a team of 18 spirit helpers. Turoff has demonstrated his healing before members of the **Noah's Ark Society for Physical Mediumship.**

Turquoise

A number of ancient beliefs surround this stone. **J. B. Van Helmont** stated: "Whoever wears a Turquoise, so that it, or its gold-setting touches the skin, may fall from any height; and the stone attracts to itself the whole force of the blow, so that it cracks, and the person is safe."

Medieval writers stated that turquoise became paler if its owner was ill, lost color entirely at his or her death, but recovered color when placed upon the finger of a new and healthy owner. It was believed to be a good **amulet** for preventing accidents to horsemen or becoming tired. Another belief was that turquoise moved itself when any danger threatened its possessor. Turquoise originally came from Persia, where it would sometimes be engraved with a motto or a verse from the Koran. The stone was also prized by Native American healers.

Turvey, Vincent Newton (1873–1912)

A British seer who refused to be classified as a medium since he was never entranced or controlled, did not develop his gifts (which he was born with), functioned not by mental passivity but mental activity, and instead of being controlled was able to control others, as a spirit might. Supposedly Turvey saw phantoms as a child. One such experience was a vision of his father while singing in church as a choir boy; the father died at the same time three hundred miles away. At the age of ten Turvey lost his visionary faculty.

Turvey studied engineering. In 1902, while engaged in his profession, he suffered a serious accident. For many years, he lived alone in his garden, in a tent, and spent ten or twelve hours a day reading, writing, and meditating on occult things.

The result is described in his own words:

"After forty thousand hours on one topic, I think I can claim to be, in a small way, a yogi. My illness and my meditation have produced, or awakened, my psychic gifts; and all the Yoga, Vedic and Gnostic teachings which I now read (and much more besides) seem to be familiar to me. I seem to have evolved them in my own mind, during meditation from a sort of 'memory.' In fact I often pitch a book away and say 'Why, I know all this,' and yet I had not read it before. Many Eastern forms come and argue with me, and, of course, I learn from them; but they do not come to teach me as a guru would. They come 'to help you to teach yourself in this present life.' In a word, I am 'Self-taught'; but I owe a great deal to Eastern forms, many of whom visit me and give tests of their identity by talking to me in their own languages; and I get the messages translated."

Turvey affiliated with **Spiritualism.** The Bournemouth Society of Spiritualists, of which he was vice president from 1908, gave demonstrations of clairvoyance at the end of their Sunday service. Turvey announced from the platform the presence of spirit visitors before the service was over, so that those who recognized them could stay for a closer communion.

Supposedly these spirits came to Turvey days before and impressed their appearance on his mind. Once a visitor appeared by the side of his bed, which was only a few inches from the wall. Turvey wrote: "Sometimes, they will come at dead of night and wake me up; at other times they will come when I am alone in the tent in my garden, or in my drawing room, or, what is still more obliging of them, they will look in while passing when I have earthly visitors with me who can bear witness that I described the visitants to them, before I went to the hall!"

Turvey's 1911 book records his experiences in long-distance **clairvoyance, out-of-the-body travel, predictions,** spirit seeing, and a variation of clairvoyance he termed "**phonevoyance.**" A voucher was printed in the book by four men who testified to having inspected the original documents and controlled their reproduction. The journalist and Spiritualist **W. T. Stead,** declared "Mr. Turvey is a man of truth, that his testimony is trustworthy evidence as to what is within his own knowledge, and that the witnesses' letters which are held for the scrutiny of inquirers are the genuine epistles of credible witnesses."

Sources:

Turvey, Vincent Newton. *The Beginnings of Seership.* 1911. Reprint, New Hyde Park, N.Y.: University Books, 1969.

Tutankhamen Curse

On November 26, 1922, in the Valley of the Kings, the tomb of Tutankhamen, the boy king of **Egypt,** was discovered. After three thousand years, four burial chambers were uncovered with nearly five thousand objects of gold, alabaster, lapis lazuli, and onyx, in addition to the mummy of the king and his gold mask. These treasures have expanded modern understanding of the art, life, religion, and history of ancient Egypt.

Two men were responsible for this discovery—Howard Carter, a British painter-archaeologist, and George E. S. M. Herbert, fifth Earl of Carnarvon. A few weeks after the excavation, Lord Carnarvon died suddenly, and this event, together with the deaths of various other individuals associated with the Tutankhamen tomb, started the story of a "Curse of the Pharaohs." One writer claimed the curse was responsible for the lives of some three dozen scientists, archaeologists, and scholars.

Who Was Tutankhamen?

It has been claimed that Tutankhamen was a great king because his tomb contained such treasures. Others have suggested he was the pharaoh of Exodus and it was his wife, Ankhesenpa-Aten, who found Moses in the bulrushes and raised him. In fact, both claims are incorrect. Tutankhamen reigned during the Eighteenth Dynasty of the New Kingdom. He was a boy of nine when he came to the throne and his reign lasted nine years, from about 1334 to 1325 B.C.E. He was not the ruler of Egypt during the exodus described in the Bible.

It is believed Tutankhamen's name was originally Tutankhaten ("perfect life of Aten"). He married Ankhesenpa-Aten when a child. He wife was a daughter of King Amenhotep IV (1372–1334 B.C.E.) who had earlier attempted to supplant the god Amun by the Aten, in the process changing his name to Akhenaten ("pleasing to the Aten"). At that time, the priests of Amun had more power than the ruler, so as Akhenaten he reinforced his rule and suppressed worship of Amun.

During the reign of Tutankhamen, the priesthoods dissolved by Akhenaten were partially reinstated and new images installed in temples. However, in giving pride to Amun, there was no attempt to destroy the worship of Aten, only a displacement of Aten's former status as principal or sole god. Many of the treasures from the tomb of Tutankhamen indicate tolerance toward former gods. One inscription on a golden throne calls Tutankhamen "image of Ra, beloved of the gods," and a cabinet inscription states "eldest son of Aten in heaven." The memory of Akhenaten is also preserved in tomb objects such as a box bearing the name of Akhenaten, and an artist's palette that belonged to Akhenaten's eldest daughter Meritaten.

Tutankhamen died before a grand burial tomb could be prepared. Its importance lies in its contents—chariot bodies, state chairs, gilded couches, royal apparel, trinkets, cosmetics, statues, alabaster vessels, even food, and the golden mask of Tutankhamen himself. Most of the other royal tombs had been ravaged by robbers over the centuries.

The Excavators

Credit for discovery of the tomb was given to Howard Carter. Born May 9, 1873, in Swaffham, Norfolk, England, he was the son of a watercolor painter. At the age of 17, he was hired by Percy E. Newberry of the Egyptian Museum of Antiquities to work at the British Museum, London, to make finished drawings of Egyptian inscriptions. Carter later became assistant to Sir William Flinders Petrie, an Egyptologist, traveling in Egypt and recording in watercolors the paintings and inscriptions in temples.

In 1899, at the age of 25, Carter became inspector of monuments in Upper Egypt and Nubia, employed by the Antiquities Service, which was then administered by the French authorities. In 1904, Britain and France partitioned North Africa, the French assuming control of Morocco, and the British of Egypt. But French rights in archaeology continued, and authorization to excavate tombs required the investigator be accompanied by an inspector of antiquities and share the finds with the Antiquities Service on behalf of the Egyptians.

While Carter was an inspector of monuments, he worked for several seasons excavating the Valley of the Kings with American millionaire Theodore M. Davis. After opposition from the Egyptians, the French, and the newspapers, Carter lost his position as an inspector in 1903 due to an incident in a tomb at Saqqara.

For a time, Carter sold watercolor paintings to tourists and made paintings for Theodore Davis. In 1907, he stated working for the amateur archaeologist Carnarvon. George Edward Stanhope Molyneux Herbert became fifth Earl of Carnarvon on the death of his father in 1890. After an automobile accident he was advised by physicians to avoid the damp English winter and spent a year in Egypt, where he first became attracted to archaeological excavation.

The joint explorations of Carnarvon and Carter began in the winter of 1907–08, with excavations in the Valley of Der al-Bahari in Western Thebes. In 1910–11, they discovered an unfinished temple of Hatshepsut and other remains. In 1911–12, new ground was broken with excavations of Xois near the Nile delta. It was thought by 1922 that there were no more royal tombs in the Valley of Kings, but Carter persisted, and in December 1922 discovered the tomb of Tutankhamen.

On November 6, Carter sent a telegram to Carnarvon in England: "AT LAST HAVE MADE WONDERFUL DISCOVERY IN VALLEY. A MAGNIFICENT TOMB WITH SEALS INTACT. RE-COVERED SAME FOR YOUR ARRIVAL. CONGRATULATIONS." Carnarvon went to Egypt and 20 days later the entrance to the tomb was finally excavated and Carter entered, accompanied by Carnarvon, Lady Evelyn Herbert (Carnarvon's sister), and an assistant.

On February 17, 1923, Carter and Carnarvon entered the main burial chamber of Tutankhamen and found a wall of gold. The work of describing, classifying, and removing the shrine contents, including the mummy of the pharaoh himself, could not take place for another season. There were also disputes between Carter and the Egyptian authorities, notably with the Frenchman Pierre Lacau, appointed head of the Antiquities Service in Cairo in 1917. These disputes concerned the ownership of the antiquities in the Tutankhamen tomb—Carnarvon and Carter claiming rights to a proportion of them and Lacau maintaining all the contents were the property of the Antiquities Service and the Cairo Museum.

In March 1933, Carnarvon and Evelyn left for Cairo so that Carnarvon could negotiate for a "proper division" of the tomb antiquities. However, Carnarvon did not live to see the conclusion of the dispute or even the removal of the golden funerary mask of the Tutankhamen mummy. In April, he became seriously ill after his razor nicked a mosquito bite. Infection set in, followed by pneumonia. He died on April 6. The newspapers printed a story that he was a victim of the "Curse of the Pharaohs."

The Legend of the Curse of the Pharaohs

Curses were certainly known in ancient Egypt, usually invoking the wrath of the gods against those seeking to embezzle funds for guards, occasionally against thieves. Many tombs were robbed by grave robbers over the centuries. An inscription of the Fifth Dynasty of the Old Kingdom, made over five thousand years ago, reads: "As for any people who shall take possession of this tomb as their mortuary property or shall do any evil thing to it, judgment shall be had with them by the great God."

In his book *The Curse of the Pharaohs* (1975), Philipp Vandenberg states there were 22 other "mysterious" deaths of individuals associated with the tomb. The American archaeologist Arthur Mace, who had assisted Carter in opening the tomb, suffered from exhaustion after the death of Carnarvon and fell into a deep coma, dying in the same hotel as Carnarvon. George J. Gould, son of the financier, visited the tomb and died the next day after a high fever ascribed to bubonic plague. Joel Wood, a British industrialist who visited the tomb, died of a high fever on the ship carrying him back to England. Archibald Douglas Reid, a radiologist who worked on the Tutankhamen mummy, suffered from weakness, and died after returning to England.

Other fatalities associated with the tomb included a Professor Winlock, a Professor Foucraft, and archaeologists Garry Davies, Edward Harkness, and Douglas Derry. Carnarvon's wife, Lady Alimina, died in 1929, apparently from an insect bite, and Carter's secretary Richard Bethell died the same year with a circulatory collapse. When Bethell's father heard the news, he committed suicide, and reportedly his hearse ran over a boy on the way to the cemetery.

Vandenberg further claimed Carter had found a clay tablet in the antechamber with an inscription that Alan Gardiner deciphered as "Death will slay with his wings whoever disturbs the peace of the pharaoh." However, such a tablet was never cataloged and there is no trace of it.

One newspaper reported there was a hieroglyphic curse on the door of the inner shrine: "They who enter this sacred tomb shall swift be visited by wings of death," but this story is a fabrication. Similarly another report cited an inscription on the mud base of a candle that stated: "It is I who hinder the sand from choking the secret chamber. I am for the protection of the deceased and I will kill all those who cross this threshold," but the last phrase was another invention.

"The Curse of the Pharaohs" became a newspaper topic for many years and every death of an individual even distantly associated with the tomb long after the excavation was solemnly recorded as another victim of the curse.

Some of these claims were remote. They included the friend of a tourist who had entered the burial chamber; the friend was knocked down by a Cairo taxicab. An associate curator of Egyptology at the British Museum in London died peacefully in his bed, while an Egyptologist in France died of old age—both were reported as curse victims. A workman in the British Museum was said to have died suddenly while labeling objects from the tomb—although the British Museum did not have any of the Egyptian antiquities. For some time, such stories panicked collectors of Egyptian antiquities, who hurriedly donated their souvenirs to museums.

Carnarvon's son was interviewed on NBC Television in New York on July 14, 1977, and questioned about the "curse." Carnarvon's son stated he "neither believed it nor disbelieved it," but added that he would "not accept a million pounds to enter the tomb of Tutankhamen in the Valley of the Kings." A New York *Daily News* report claimed that the same evening, the younger Lord Carnarvon was attending a dinner in an apartment high above Manhattan and looked out over the city and saw all the lights flicker and black out. After candles were lit, he said to his hosts: "It is again the curse of Tutankhamen." However, Carter lived for 17 years after his great discovery, dying March 2, 1939, in his mid-sixties.

For decades, relics of Tutankhamen remained in the Cairo Museum, limited by space, and many objects were not even displayed. In June 1974, President Richard M. Nixon visited Egypt, where President Anwar Sadat suggested an exhibition of the masterpieces of Tutankhamen in the United States could affirm the friendly accord and goodwill between the two nations.

The subject of "King Tut's Curse" has been raised from time to time and still has believers. The term is also used by travelers in the Middle East to describe the hazard of diarrhea, also known in Mexico as "Montezuma's Revenge."

Sources:

Budge, E. A. W. *Tutankhamen: Amenism, Atenism and Egyptian Monotheism.* London: M. Hopkinson, 1923. Reprint, New York: Bell Publishing, 1979.

Carter, Howard. *The Tomb of Tut-ankh-Amen.* 3 vols. London: Cassell, 1923–33. Reprint, New York: Cooper Square Publishers, 1963.

Gilber, Katherine S., with Joan K. Holt and Sara Hudson, eds. *Treasures of Tutankhamen.* Catalog of an Exhibition between 1976 and 1979. New York: Ballantine Books; New York: Metropolitan Museum of Art, 1976.

Herbert, G. E. S. M. (5th Earl of Carnarvon), and Howard Carter. *Five Years' Explorations at Thebes, 1907–1911.* London: H. Frowde, 1912.

Hoving, Thomas. *Tutankhamen: The Untold Story.* New York: Simon & Schuster; London: Hamish Hamilton, 1978.

Stein, Gordon. *Encyclopedia of Hoaxes.* Detroit: Gale Research, 1993.

Vandenberg, Philipp. *Der Fluch der Pharaonen.* Scherz Verlag, 1973. English edition as *The Curse of the Pharaohs.* Philadelphia: J. B. Lippincott, 1975.

———. *Der Vergessene Pharao.* C. Bertelsmann Verlag, 1978. English edition as *The Golden Pharaoh.* New York: Macmillan; London: Hodder & Stoughton, 1980.

Wynne, Barry. *Behind the Mask of Tutankhamen.* New York: Taplinger, 1973.

Tuttle, Hudson (1836–1910)

American seer of the early days of **Spiritualism.** Tuttle was born October 4, 1836, in Berlin Heights, Ohio, and spent his early years in a wilderness on the southern shores of Lake Erie. His father's house was the headquarters for itinerant Unitarian preachers and the atmosphere was burdened with dogmatic disputations. As a result young Tuttle became at an early age skeptical of organized religion.

Tuttle attended his first Spiritualist séance at the home of a retired Congregational minister who had heard of the **Rochester rappings** and called in a few friends for an experiment. Tuttle fell into **trance** and wrote spirit messages automatically. Simultaneously with his **automatic writing, raps** developed and the table moved. The séances were free. The communicators, in hours of seclusion, were his teachers. "It was my only source of knowledge," he wrote in the preface to his book *Arcana of Spiritualism* (1871), "for I had access to few books. I had attended school eleven months in all, six of which were at a district school, and five at a small academy."

In 1857, he married Emma Rood, writer, lecturer on education, composer of songs, and a frequent contributor to the Spiritualist press.

The first article Tuttle published was on prayer in *The Spiritual Telegraph.* He often wrote and rewrote a script several times before the communicator would declare the result satisfactory. He began writing a story founded on spirit life. It was entitled *Scenes in the Spirit World* (1855). In England it was published under the title *Life in Two Spheres* (1895). After completing it, he began a scientific work, *Arcana of Nature.*

His impression was that the French naturalist Lamarck and Alexander von Humboldt, along with other intelligences, were associated in the production of the book. But he knew nothing of these great minds. He was only entering his eighteenth year. When the book was completed, his spirit guides declared it to be unsatisfactory and demanded the destruction of the script. Reluctantly he burned the large bulk of the manuscript and started again.

For two years, the remaining manuscript lay on his table and he made some correction or addition to it nearly every day. The engravings in both volumes were made by the same influences that wrote the book. He claimed no merit for himself and said: "Mine has been the task of an amanuensis, writing that which has been given to me. I claim no honour, except honestly and faithfully attempting to perform my part of the task."

Arcana of Nature, two volumes, published 1860–63, was certainly a remarkable book for the time. It was quoted by F. C. L. Büchner in his own book *Force and Matter* (1864) to strengthen his materialistic position, while Charles Darwin in the *Descent of Man* quoted statements from Tuttle's later *Origin and Antiquity of Physical Man.* Both Büchner and Darwin were unaware that the book was produced by an uneducated farm boy.

The spirit controls were good educators. But Tuttle never gave up his modest life as a farmer and breeder of horses in Berlin Heights, Ohio. The spirit influences did not come to Tuttle at all times. He said:

"Sometimes I have prolific periods, and again, I go over a deserted country. For days, weeks, even months, I feel forsaken and alone. The very fountains of thought seem dried up. No incitement can compel me to write, or if I attempt to do so it is worthless, or worse, unreliable. It sometimes seems to me that I have never written anything of value, and I am sure I never can again. At the same time, when I study it, this experience is one of the most convincing tests that some superior intelligence comes into my life."

He died December 15, 1910, in Berlin Heights, Ohio.

Sources:

Tuttle, Hudson. *Career of Religious Ideas.* New York: D. M. Bennett, 1878.

———. *Career of the Christ—Idea in History.* Boston: Adams, 1870.

———. *Career of the God—Idea in History.* Boston: Adams, 1869.

———. *Ethics of Spiritualism.* Chicago: Religio-Philosophical Publishing, 1878.

———. *Mediumship and Its Laws.* Chicago: Progressive Thinker Publishing, 1900.

———. *Philosophy of Spirit and the Spirit World.* London: H. A. Copley; Berlin Heights, Ohio: H. Tuttle, 1896.

———. *Religion of Man and Ethics of Science.* New York: M. L. Holbrook, 1890.

———. *Studies in Outlying Fields of Psychic Science.* New York: M. L. Holbrook, 1889.

Tuttle, Hudson, and Emma Rood Tuttle. *Stories from Beyond the Borderland.* Berlin Heights, Ohio: Tuttle Publsihing, 1910.

Twain, Mark (1835–1910)

Pseudonym of author **Samuel Langhorne Clemens.** Throughout his life, the great humorist and observer of the world around him often reflected upon the psychic and metaphysical events of which he was aware. In 1880 he wrote an article on "mental telegraphy" that related a personal experience of **telepathy.** He also had a vivid premonitory dream of the death of his brother Henry. Twain was an early and long-term member of the **Society for Psychical Research,** London.

After his death, various posthumous **communications** and writings were claimed. In 1917, the story *Jap Herron* was published in New York, purporting to come from the discarnate Mark Twain, as received by Emily Grant Hutchings and Lola V. Hays. Hutchings, the recorder of the *Patience Worth* material of **Pearl Lenore Curran** of St. Louis, was herself an author who greatly admired Mark Twain. She had a keen sense of somewhat similar humor and a strong tinge of melancholy like Mark Twain's. She had strongly wished him to communicate through her. All this furnished an ideal condition for subconscious production.

James H. Hyslop resolved the problem by interesting cross-reference experiments. The two women received the communications through the **ouija board;** the presence of both of them was necessary to operate it. They were brought by Hyslop to Boston. He gave each woman, at separate times, five sittings with the medium "Mrs. Chenoweth" (see **Minnie M. Soule**). But he did not admit them to the **séance** room until "Mrs. Chenoweth," who knew nothing of them, went into trance, and he made them sit behind her where they could not be seen.

Instead of the usual family relatives, Mark Twain purported to communicate with each of them. He used many of the same expressions that came through the ouija board, mentioned incidents in his life to prove his identity, described what he was doing through the women, and revealed the password that he gave to Hyslop in a St. Louis sitting.

"The outcome of the experiments," concluded Hyslop in the *Journal* of the American Society for Psychical Research (July 1917), "is that there is abundant evidence that Mark Twain is behind the work connected with his name, though the student of psychology would probably find abundant evidence that it was colored more or less by the mind through which it came." The conclusion also applied to *Brent Roberts,* another posthumous Mark Twain novel that the two women received.

In Hyslop's *Contact with the Other World* (1919), a long chapter was devoted to other evidential **spirit** communications from Mark Twain.

Sources:

Paine, Albert Bigelow. *Mark Twain.* 3 vols. N.p., 1912.

Tweedale, Charles L(akeman) (d. 1944)

Prominent British writer on **Spiritualism.** He was educated at Durham University, England, and became the Church of England vicar of Weston, Otley, Yorkshire. A talented and versatile man, he was an astronomer, musician, and inventor. He published books on astronomy and discovered a comet. He was also a close friend of psychic photographer **William Hope,** whom he defended against hostile criticism. He died June 29, 1944.

Sources:

Tweedale, Charles L. *Man's Survival After Death.* N.p., 1909.
———. *News From the Next World.* N.p., 1940.

Tweedale, Violet (1862–1936)

British novelist, granddaughter of author **Robert Chambers,** and a convinced Spiritualist. She attended séances with Lord Haldane, **Arthur Balfour,** and his brother **James Balfour.** W. E. Gladstone held sittings in her house. Most of her experiences came through the mediumships of **Charles Williams** and **Cecil Husk.**

She was a powerful witness in the famous trial when trance speaker **Meurig Morris** sued the *Daily Mail* for libel in 1932. In addition to many poems and novels, she published over 30 books on Spiritualist subjects. She died December 10, 1936.

Sources:

Tweedale, Violet. *The Cosmic Christ.* N.p., 1930.
———. *Ghosts I Have Seen.* N.p., 1920.
———. *Mellow Sheaves.* N.p., 1927.
———. *Phantoms of the Dawn.* N.p., 1924.

Twigg, Ena (1914–ca. 1984)

Well-known British medium. Born in Kent, England, January 6, 1914, she was a member of a psychic family in which the parents and other children had sensitive ability. She played with spirit children at the age of seven and at 14 predicted the death of her father. Her psychic gifts disturbed her marriage to Harry Twigg.

After a serious illness, spirit visitors assured her that she would be restored to health; when she was eventually healed she made a decision to devote her life to helping other people. She became a member of the **Marylebone Spiritualist Association** and in due course opened her own healing clinic.

Sources:

Twigg, Ena, with Ruth Hagy Brod. *Ena Twigg: Medium.* New York: Hawthorn Books, 1972. Reprint, London: W. H. Allen, 1973.

Twins

It has long been believed that there is a special relationship between identical twins, a belief that has become the subject of contemporary research from a variety of approaches. Research has suggested that there are startling correspondences between twins' temperaments, personalities, lifestyles, and even sensitivity to names.

In 1979, the University of Minnesota began a study of identical twins in which twins separated for years were investigated and subjected to medical and psychological tests. The results of nine identical twin studies, involving over 15,000 questions, demonstrated affinities between the subjects.

For example, unknown to each other, Jim Spring and Jim Lewis were raised in different Ohio towns. Both married and divorced women named Linda and chose women named Betty as second wives. Each of the two Jims named his son James Allan and had a favorite dog named Toy. Both twins had remarkable similarities in medical profiles, including identical blood pressures and sleep and heartbeat patterns. Both also suddenly put on 10 pounds at the same time in their lives. At the age of 18, both Jim twins suffered similar syndromes of intermittent migraine headaches. Their drinking and smoking habits were also identical, and both chewed their fingernails.

Another pair of identical twins, Jack and Oscar, were raised apart with completely different backgrounds. Jack was brought up as an American Jew by his father after his parents separated; the mother took Oscar back to Germany (where she had been born) where he was raised as a Catholic, later joining the Nazi Youth party. In adult life, Jack ran a store in San Diego, while Oscar became a factory supervisor in Germany. But both men wore wire-rimmed eyeglasses and mustaches and two-pocket shirts with epaulets. Both were absentminded and had other matching idiosyncracies, such as storing rubber bands on their wrists.

Bridget and Dorothy were identical British twins who were raised apart after being separated soon after birth, yet when they met in 1941, each wore two bracelets on one wrist, and a watch and bracelet on the other. Each sister also wore seven rings. Each twin had married and had a family of a boy and a girl. The sons had been christened Richard Andrew and Andrew Richard, while the daughters were Karen Louise and Catherine Louise.

Many such identical twins share IQ and psychological profiles, as well as EEG tracings. It is not yet clear whether the coincidences derive from some kind of psychic bonding or simply indicate some manifestation of inheritance. It should be noted that astrologers have investigated twins, with ambiguous results to date, with the idea of verifying and informing astrology.

Sources:

Watson, Peter. *Twins: An Investigation Into the Strange Coincidences in the Lives of Separated Twins.* London: Hutchinson, 1981.

Twitchell, (John) Paul (ca. 1918–1971)

Founder of the **ECKANKAR,** a spiritual movement teaching the "ancient science of soul travel." ECKANKAR is derived from the Radhasoami religion of the Punjab area of India. Twitchell was born in Paducah, Kentucky, around 1918. He joined the navy during World War II and then pursued a career as a journalist and the life of spiritual seeking after the war.

His spiritual search led him to the Church of Absolute Monism, a Hindu offshoot of the Self-Revelation Fellowship. He became editor of the church's periodical, *The Mystic Cross,* but came into conflict with the church's founder, Swami Premananda, in 1955. Shortly after leaving, he became a disciple of Kirpal Singh, a teacher in the Radhasoami tradition and head of the Ruhani Satsang. He also became involved with the recently founded **Church of Scientology.**

In 1964 Twitchell and his wife, Gail Atkinson, moved to San Francisco, where he became an independent Radhasoami teacher, and the following year founded ECKANKAR and announced that he was the Living ECK Master. He claimed that he had originally heard of soul travel from his foster father, who learned about it from an Indian holy man, Sudar Singh, originally from Allahabad, whom Twitchell later met in Paris, France. He further claimed that he had been taught soul travel by a mysterious Tibetan master named Rebazar Tarzs, who first appeared to Twitchell in 1944 while Twitchell was serving on a U.S. Navy vessel in the Pacific. He visited India after World War II and upon returning to the United States began writing books allegedly dictated by Rebazar Tarzs.

Twitchell authored a number of books in the years after the founding of ECKANKAR. He died unexpectedly on September 17, 1971, by which time ECKANKAR had become a successful new religion. He was succeeded by Darwin Gross as the new Living ECK Master.

During the 1980s **David Christopher Lane** made serious charges of plagiarism against Twitchell. He suggested that Twitchell not only took his basic teachings from the Radhasoami tradition but also plagiarized lengthy passages from the books of several prominent authors. Lane's well-documented charges caused much dissension within the movement and a reappraisal of Twitchell's career.

Sources:

Lane, David Christopher. *The Making of a Spiritual Movement.* Del Mar, Calif.: Del Mar Press, 1983.

Simpson, Patti. *Paulji: A Memoir.* Menlo Park, Calif.: ECKANKAR, 1985.

Steiger, Brad. *In My Soul I Am Free.* New York: Lancer Books, 1968.

Twitchell, Paul. *The Tiger's Fang.* New York: Lancer Books, 1969.

TWO See True World Order

Two Worlds (Magazine)

Spiritualist monthly magazine, founded in 1887 as a weekly newspaper in Manchester, England, by **Emma Hardinge Britten.** (Another weekly paper under the same title was started in London in 1858 at the beginning of the movement in England but lasted for only a brief period.) It was, for many years, the voice of Spiritualists in the north of England (the movement being dominated at the time by the London centers). It was edited for some time by **Ernest W. Oaten.** Beginning in the 1930s it had as its major rival *Psychic News,* the newspaper edited by **Maurice Barbanell** in London. However, in 1960 the editorial offices of the two periodicals were united, *Two Worlds* was transformed into a monthly magazine, and Barbanell edited both until his death in 1981. Tony Ortzen is the current editor. Address: 7 The Leather Market, Weston St., London, SE1 3ER England. Website: http://www.users.globalnet.co.uk/~tortzen/.

Sources:

Edmunds, Simeon. *Spiritualism: A Critical Survey.* London: Aquarian Press, 1966.

Two Worlds. http://www.users.globalnet.co.uk/~tortzen/. March 8, 2000.

Tyl, Noel (1936–)

American astrologer, born in West Chester, Pennsylvania, on December 31, 1936. Tyl attended Harvard University and received his B.A. in psychology in 1958. He worked in business for more than a decade before becoming a writer-astrologer in 1970. He developed a relationship with **Llewellyn Publications,** a leading publisher of **astrology** literature, which, beginning in 1973 with *Horoscope Construction,* released a 12-volume series entitled *The Principles and Practice of Astrology.* The series largely established his reputation in the field. Through the 1980s he edited *Astrology Today,* Llewellyn's astrology magazine.

In addition to operating as a consulting astrologer, Tyl has continued to write. Additional titles include *The Horoscope as Identity* (1974), *The Missing Moon* (1979), and *Holistic Astrology: The Analysis of Inner and Outer Environments* (1980). He has worked to redefine astrology as a psychological counseling practice.

Sources:

Tyl, Noel. *Holistic Astrology: The Analysis of Inner and Outer Environments.* McLean, Va.: TAI Books, 1980.

———. *The Horoscope as Identity.* St. Paul: Llewellyn Publications, 1974.

———. *The Missing Moon.* St. Paul: Llewellyn Publications, 1979.

Typtology

The science of communicating with spirits by means of **raps,** various codes being arranged for the purpose. The sitters may read the alphabet aloud, or slowly pass a pencil down a printed alphabet, and the rappings will indicate letters that form a message or an answer to some question. One rap may be made to mean "yes," two "no," and so on. Some relationship seems to exist between such rapping and the use of the **divining rod** and **pendulum** in **dowsing.**

Tyromancy (or Tiromancy)

An old form of **divination** based on interpretations from cheese. Unfortunately, the method does not appear to have been recorded.

Tyrrell, G(eorge) N(ugent) M(erle) (1879–1952)

Mathematician and parapsychologist. He was a member of the council of the **Society for Psychical Research** (SPR), London (1940–52), and was elected its president in 1945. Born in 1879, he was educated at Haileybury School, Seafield Engineering College, and London University (where he attained degrees in physics and mathematics). A pioneer in the study of wireless telegraphy, Tyrrell worked under Guglielmo Marconi. He served in the British Army during World War I.

Tyrrell joined the SPR in 1908. After conducting a series of experiments in **telepathy** and **precognition** with Gertrude Johnson, he devoted himself exclusively to psychical research. He undertook further experiments with Johnson in 1924, using quantitative methods, and invented mechanical devices to randomize selection and scoring. His apparatus, unfortunately, was destroyed during an air raid in World War II, and in the years after the war he concentrated on the theoretical and philosophical aspects of extrasensory perception. Out of this period came possibly his single most important volume, *Apparitions* (1953), cited for its clarity in integrating data. He died October 29, 1952.

Sources:

Berger, Arthur S., and Joyce Berger. *The Encyclopedia of Parapsychology and Psychical Research.* New York: Paragon House, 1991.

Pleasants, Helene, ed. *Biographical Dictionary of Parapsychology.* New York: Helix Press, 1964.

Salter, W. H., G. W. Fisk, and Harry H. Price. "G. N. M. Tyrrell and His Contributions to Psychical Research." *Journal* of the Society for Psychical Research 37 (1953).

Tyrrell, George N. M. *Apparitions.* London: Society for Psychical Research, 1953. Reprinted in *Science and Psychical Phenomena and Apparitions.* New Hyde Park, N.Y.: University Books, 1961.

———. "Further Research in Extrasensory Perception." *Proceedings* of the Society for Psychical Research 44, no. 147 (1936–37).

———. *Grades of Significance.* N.p., 1930.

———. *Homo Faber.* N.p., 1951.

———. *The Nature of Human Personality.* London: Allen & Unwin, 1954.

———. *The Personality of Man.* Harmondsworth, UK: Penguin Books, 1947.

———. "Presidential Address." *Proceedings* of the Society for Psychical Research 47, no. 171 (1945).

———. *Science and Psychical Phenomena.* London, 1938. Reprinted in *Science and Psychical Phenomena and Apparitions.* New Hyde Park, N.Y.: University Books, 1961.

U

U.S. Psychotronics Association

Founded in 1975 for persons interested in the study of psychotronics, "the science of mind-body-environment relationships, concerned with the interactions of matter, energy and consciousness," psychic phenomena, free energy systems, **radionics,** and alternative health methodologies.

It provides a forum for the exchange of current research developments in psychotronics; seeks to maintain high standards of ethical, humanitarian, and scientific practices in the study and application of psychotronics; promotes standardization in investigation, testing, reporting, and evaluation of **psychotronics;** and preserves the history of the field.

The association promotes continuing education and training of members, presents members' views to the government, the public and other organizations, bestows research awards, and makes available cassette recordings of conference lectures. Research areas include: anti-gravity, agri-radionics, free energy, psychic detectors, psychic instrumentation (hardware types), radionics, and tesla waves. It publishes a quarterly newsletter and can be contacted at PO Box 45, Elkhorn, WI 53121. Website: http://www.elknet.net/uspa.

Übersinnliche Welt, Die (Journal)

Former German Spiritualist monthly, founded in 1893. It changed into a biweekly in 1902 and merged with *Psyche* under the title *Psyche und die Übersinnliche Welt.*

Udumbara (Center)

Alternative name for the **Minnesota Zen Meditation Center** and also the title of their biannual periodical.

UFO See Unidentified Flying Objects and the Occult

UFOCAT

Computerized files of reports of **UFO**s and related material, maintained by the **Center for UFO Studies** and Dr. Donald A. Johnson. UFOCAT99 contains over 109,000 UFO reports and related information, which may be retrieved by date, geographic location, and special features. The files are available at minimum cost to serious researchers. Inquiries concerning UFOCAT should be directed to the **J. Allen Hynek Center for UFO Studies,** 2457 W. Peterson Ave., Chicago, IL 60659.

The UFO Examiner (Journal)

Former quarterly publication of Private UFO Investigations, a group concerned with UFO reports and international sightings, headquartered in Hazelton, Iowa.

UFOIN See UFO Information Network

UFO Information Network (UFOIN)

Name adopted in the late 1970s by the Page Research Library. It published a newsletter, which merged with *Ohio Sky Watcher* in 1979 to become *UFO Ohio.* UFOIN, which existed only a few years, collected and collated information on UFOs and other Fortean phenomena. It was headquartered in Rome, Ohio.

UFO Information Retrieval Center

Founded in 1966 to collect, analyze, publish, and disseminate information on reports of unidentified flying objects and related anomalies. The center compiles statistics, conducts research programs, maintains a library and an on-line data base, runs children's and students' services, and gives referrals. From time to time it publishes *Reference for Outstanding UFO Sighting Reports.* Address: 3131 W. Cochise Dr., No. 158, Phoenix, AZ 85051-9501.

UFO Investigator (Newsletter)

Longtime monthly newsletter of **National Investigations Committee on Aerial Phenomena.** It was discontinued in 1980, a short time before the organization folded.

UFO Magazine

UFO Magazine, the primary English-language UFO newsstand periodical as the twenty-first century begins, was founded in 1985 as a quarterly California UFO periodical, but quickly moved to national prominence as the abduction phenomenon renewed public interest in extraterrestrial explanations of UFOs. Editor Vicki Ecker also demonstrated both a knowledge of the field and a genuine interest in reporting the news. Several other newsstand periodicals, since defunct, played to outlandish and sensational accounts of UFOs and **contactees,** and were not above fabricating stories to fill space. The magazine has adopted an objective approach that is nevertheless sympathetic to the ufological enterprise.

Each issue of *UFO Magazine* is built around a half-dozen or more feature articles that highlight spectacular sightings, interview celebrities concerning their views on UFOs, focus on issues of government involvement in (and cover-up of) UFO research, debate controversies within the ufological community, and inform readers on various related topics such as time travel or conspiracy theories. The magazine covers more prominent UFO conventions, especially those on America's West Coast, and provides a synopsis of presentations and pictures of participants. Regular columns review new UFO books, highlight prominent websites, and provide contact information on UFO organizations.

In the late 1990s, the magazine launched its own website at http://www.ufomag.com/. It provides space for timely items of interest, guest opinions, an archive of past articles from the magazine, and editorials by Ecker, her husband Don Ecker, the magazine's research director, and publisher William J. Birnes. Also, Peter Robbins continues his timely surveys of other UFO-related websites in a regular page on the *UFO Magazine* website. *UFO Magazine* may be contacted at 5455 Centinela Ave., Los Angeles, CA 90066.

Sources:

UFO Magazine. Los Angeles, California. n.d.

UFO Magazine. http://www.ufomag.com/. June 10, 2000.

UFO Magazine New Bulletin

Former quarterly publication reporting UFO sightings, with critical analyses, published in Cleveland, Ohio.

UFO Nachrichten (Journal)

German bimonthly publication concerned with **UFOs**. Last known address: Karl L. Veit, Deutsche UFO-Studiengesellschaft, Ventla-Verlag, Postfach 13185, 6200 Wiesbaden 13, Germany.

UFO Newsclipping Service

Monthly publication that reproduces North American and other newspaper reports of UFOs and other related unexplained phenomena. It may be ordered from 2 Caney Valley Dr., Plumerville, AR 72127-8725.

UFO-Nyt (Journal)

Danish-language quarterly periodical dealing with unidentified flying objects. It is published by Skandinavisk UFO Information, Postbox 6, DK-2820, Gentofte, Denmark. Website: http://www.ufo.dk.

UFO Quebec (Periodical)

Bilingual (French and English) Canadian quarterly concerned with **UFOs**. Last known address: Claude McDuff, BP 53, Dollard-des-Ormeaux, PQ Canada H9G 2H5.

UFO Reporter (Journal)

Former bimonthly publication reporting UFO sightings and related events, published in La Mesa, California.

UFO Research Newsletter

Former monthly journal edited by Gordon I. R. Lore from Los Angeles, California.

Uhland, Ludwig (1787–1862)

Famous German poet who figured posthumously in an interesting lawsuit in Berlin over ownership of a holograph parchment **apport** obtained in a séance with Else Arnheim in 1920. The medium, in trance, described the presence of Ludwig Uhland. There appeared in her hands, which were tightly clasped by a well-known German author, a yellowed piece of parchment with two short verses scrawled on it, signed: "Uhland, 1920."

The handwriting was pronounced identical to that of Uhland's, the parchment was of his era, and the verses were in genuine Uhland style. A **clairvoyant,** to whom Uhland's handwriting and the parchment were shown, declared after touching both papers that they were written by the same hand but that a long interval had elapsed between the writing of them.

The German author whose hand had encircled the medium's when the parchment appeared claimed the paper. Since witnesses stated that it had been thrust into the medium's hand, the court decided that the parchment belonged to the medium.

UHSC See Universal Hagar's Spiritual Church

Ullman, Montague (1916–)

Psychiatrist, parapsychologist, and trustee of the **American Society for Psychical Research.** He was born on September 9, 1916, in New York City and studied at the City College of New York (B.S., 1935), New York University College of Medicine (M.D., 1938), and New York Medical College (1948). After graduation, he joined the psychoanalytic faculty of New York Medical College (1950–62). Having encountered psi events in his counseling work, he began to work with **Gardner Murphy** in exploring **ESP** experimentally. With Murphy and **Laura Dale,** he helped establish the medical section of the ASPR. The section lasted until 1953.

That same year, the **REM** (or rapid eye movement) stage of sleep was discovered. Ullman soon had the idea of using REM sleep in a controlled experiment in telepathy. With funds provided by the Parapsychology Foundation, Ullman, **Karlis Osis,** and **E. Douglas Dean** carried out the initial experiments. Murphy then arranged for a large grant for the establishment of the famous **Dream Laboratory** at Maimonides Hospital in New York City. Ullman became its initial director and an associate professor of psychiatry at Downstate Medical Center, State University of New York. The work of the dream laboratory produced some striking results, leading Ullman to conclude that altered states of consciousness, such as dreaming, were associated with ESP.

In 1966 Ullman was elected president of the **Parapsychological Association.** He is the author of numerous papers and several books, the most important for parapsychology being his work on dream telepathy.

Sources:

Ullman, Montague. "On the Occurrence of Telepathic Dreams." *Journal* of the American Society for Psychical Research (April 1959).

Ullman, Montague, and Roberto Cavanna, eds. *Proceedings of an International Conference on Hypnosis, Drugs, Dreams and Psi: Psi and Altered States of Consciousness.* New York: Parapsychology Foundation, 1968.

Ullman, Montague, and Stanley Krippner. *Dream Studies and Telepathy: An Experimental Approach.* New York: Parapsychology Foundation, 1970.

Ullman, Montague, Stanley Krippner, and Alan Vaughan. *Dream Telepathy.* 1979. Reprint, Los Angeles: J. P. Tarcher, 1985.

Ullman, Montague, and Nan Zimmerman. *Working with Dreams.* London: Hutchinson, 1983.

Umbanda

A contemporary Afro-Brazilian religion. Like **Santeria,** it is basically a possession religion in which members assume the form of deities both for worship and magic. It was founded in 1920, at a time when a wave of anti-European feelings was sweeping through the country, fanned by the inspiration of a young man, Zélio de Moraes, by an alleged Indian spirit. Among the initial leaders were former Spiritist mediums who became known for receiving spirits of *caboclos,* Brazilian Indians, and *pretos velhos,* former African slaves.

Umbanda's stronghold is Rio de Janeiro and the surrounding area in the south of Brazil. Worship is lively with much clapping, singing, and dancing.

Sources:

Brown, Diana DeGroat. *Umbanda: Religion and Politics in Urban Brazil.* Ann Arbor, Mich.: UMI Press, 1986.

Hess, David J. *Samba in the Night: Spiritism in Brazil.* New York: Columbia University Press, 1994.

St. Clair, David. *Drum and Candle.* Garden City, N.Y.: Doubleday; London: Macdonald, 1971.

Ummo Hoax

Ummo is a planet that reputedly circles the star Iumma located some 14.6 light-years from Earth. Knowledge of this planet and the associated star emerged in 1965 through Spanish **contactee** Fernando Sesma, president of the Society of the Friends of Space, headquartered in Madrid. In 1967 Sesma let it be known that a spacecraft would appear near the city on the evening of June 1. Contact with the Ummites was quite different. Sesma had neither direct physical contact nor telepathic contact. Instead he was contacted via the mail or by telephone. He had received several lengthy documents in typescript that included descriptions of Ummo and insights into a variety of scientific, psychological, technological, and socio-political issues.

The messages from Ummo intersected with a series of UFO sightings that began on February 6, 1966. Several people saw the saucer near Alauche, Spain, and one, José Luis Jordan Peña, drew a sketch and reported it to the newspapers. The saucer was distinguished by a peculiar symbol. A second sighting occurred on June 1, 1967, at which time pictures were taken. One picture showed the same symbol Jordan had reported the previous year. Copies of the pictures were recovered by a Madrid newspaper photographer from an anonymous source. Adding to the mystery, a flyer signed with the name Henri Dagousset was circulated, suggesting that the 1967 UFO had left behind some small cylinders and asking anyone who found one to make contact through the general post office. One of these was sent anonymously to UFO author Marius Leuget. Inside the object was a piece of paper with the mysterious symbol.

In the days after the announcement of Sesma's contact with the Ummites others began to report intriguing but anonymous contacts with people who also claimed to be from Ummo. In the meantime the lengthy messages from the Ummites continued to appear. By 1983 the number had grown to some 6,700.

While written from a knowledgeable standpoint, the Ummo communications were always troubling because of their lack of a means of independently verifying that they were from Ummites. None of those who wrote and circulated the documents allowed any direct contact. In addition, none of the other people who claimed contact were ever located. Then, the U.S.-based Ground Saucer Watch examined the pictures of the Ummo symbol and determined that they were taken of a small object held close to the camera. The saucer appeared to be an eight-inch plate with the symbol painted on it in ink.

In spite of the finding concerning the photographs and the lack of independent verification of either the sightings or the documents, the latter have been published in both English and Spanish. The Ummo material has subsequently been integrated into the large body of flying saucer contactee material and several websites have been placed on the Internet, including one detailing the Ummite philosophy at http://perso.wanadoo.fr/ummo.textes-essentiels/anglais/a016.htm (as of December 1999).

Sources:

Ribera, Antonio. *Ufo Contact from Planet Ummo: The Incredible Truth.* 2 vols. Tucson, Ariz.: UFO Books, n.d.

Sesma, Fernando. *Otro Planeta Habitado, Ummo.* Madrid, Spain: Editorial Grafica Espejo, 1967.

Vallee, Jaques. *Revelations: Alien Contact and Human Deception.* New York: Ballantine Books, 1991.

Underhill, Leah

Married name of Leah Fox, the eldest of the famous **Fox sisters,** who launched American **Spiritualism.** She became Mrs. Underhill by her third marriage. She published the book *The Missing Link in Modern Spiritualism* (1885; reprinted 1976).

Understanding Cults and Spiritual Movements (Research Publication Series)

A short-lived research journal published three times a year in the 1980s and designed to analyze critically new religious groups and their leaders. **David Christopher Lane,** its editor, defined its goals:

"With the continuing growth of new spiritual movements, it is imperative for both the scholar and the seeker to be able to discriminate between groups which are fraudulent and manipulative and those which are genuine and beneficial. The failure to do so has troublesome consequences: witness Jim Jones and Jonestown. What is necessary, therefore, in the examination of religion and its mystical claims—be they old and traditional like Roman Catholicism or new and emerging like Eckankar—with unbridled rational scrutiny. That is, the opportunity to fully investigate every facet about the particular spiritual movement: from the biography of its founder, the history of its organization, the value of its teachings, to the practical application of its techniques, etc.

"*Understanding Cults and Spiritual Movements* is . . . interested in promoting rational inquiries into the entire cult phenomenon. Editorially, it does not hold to any particular religious doctrine, nor does it have any church affiliation. Thus, in this way, it is an open system of study primarily concerned with documented appraisements which help in developing a keen sense of critical discrimination."

Lane established a high standard of scholarly reporting and investigation. Lane has become a leading authority on the history of the **Radhasoami** spiritual movement, and much of the emphasis of *Understanding Cults and Spiritual Movements* was directed to an examination of the new religions that emerged out of that tradition. Most of the writings originally published in the 1980s have been republished as a book, *Exposing Cults.* Lane now teaches in Los Angeles.

Sources:

Lane, David Christopher. *Exposing Cults: When the Skeptical Mind Confronts the Mystical.* New York: Garland Publishing, 1994.

Understanding Magazine

Journal published into the 1980s by Daniel W. Fry, author of the book *White Sands Incident* (1954), in which he claimed contact with a **UFO.** *Understanding* explored the metaphysical ideas that grew out of Fry's claimed contacts. It was the organ of World Understanding, the religious group Fry founded to promote his perspective.

Underwood, Peter (1923–)

British writer on occultism and psychical investigation. He has also written on the cinema. He is a member of the **Society**

for Psychical Research, the vice president of the Unitarian Society for Psychical Studies, and a former member of the Research Committee of the Psychic Research Organization.

Underwood took part in investigations into a **haunting,** conducted worldwide tests in **telepathy** and ESP, and has compiled comprehensive files of hauntings in the British Isles. He has been president and chairman of the **Ghost Club** for many years. He has written a number of books, has lectured extensively on psychic matters, and made several hundred television appearances and radio broadcasts. His interests have reached far beyond ghosts and hauntings to include horror movies, **vampires,** and the occult in general.

Sources:

Underwood, Peter. *The Complete Book of Dowsing and Divining.* London: Rider, 1980.

———. *Dictionary of the Supernatural.* 1978. Reprinted as *Dictionary of the Occult of Supernatural.* London: Harrap, 1978.

———. *A Gazetteer of British Ghosts.* New York: Walker, 1975.

———. *A Gazetteer of Scottish and Irish Ghosts.* New York: Bell, 1985.

———. *Ghosts and How to See Them.* North Pomfret, Vt.: Trafalgar Square, 1995.

———. *Haunted London.* N.p., 1973.

———. *Hauntings; New Light on the Greatest True Ghost Stories of the World.* London: Dent, 1977.

———. *No Common Task: The Autobiography of a Ghost Hunter.* N.p., 1983.

———. *The Vampire's Bedside Companion.* London: Frewin, 1975.

Unguents

General term for ointments used in anointing ceremonies in various religions from Christianity to **witchcraft.** There are many kinds of magical unguents, each with its peculiar properties. Christians ascribed these compounds to the devil, who they believed invented them in order to harm the human race. According to medieval mythology, for example, one such unguent was composed of human (or even baby) fat and was said to be used by witches to enable them to fly through the air.

Many old recipes exist for unguents to induce sleep or visions, and these unguents were made from various obscure ingredients. Some of them are described in *Des Science Occultes* by Eusèbe Salverte (1829).

Sources:

Robbins, Rossell Hope. *The Encyclopedia of Witchcraft and Demonology.* New York: Crown Publishers, 1959.

Unidentified Flying Objects and the Occult

UFOs entered popular consciousness as "flying saucers"—the name an anonymous wire-service reporter gave to the silvery discs Americans were reporting by the thousands in the last week of June 1947. At 3 P.M. on June 24 private pilot Kenneth Arnold, passing over Mount Rainier, Washington, spotted nine shiny disc-shaped objects flying in formation at what he conservatively estimated to be 1200 mph. The worldwide publicity resulting from his sighting, plus the other sightings that came in its immediate wake, brought the UFO age into being.

Since then UFOs have been the focus of furious controversy. Many dispute their existence, claiming that unexplained reports exist only because of inadequate investigation or insufficient data. Proponents counter that some of the best cases have withstood the most thorough scrutiny. The debate that began in earnest in 1947 continues, with essentially the same arguments being recycled endlessly.

Early Reports of UFOs

The UFO phenomenon did not spring abruptly into being one summer afternoon in 1947. In fact, the first UFO book, **Charles Fort**'s *The Book of the Damned,* was published in 1919. An eccentric social critic and keen satirist, Fort collected accounts of anomalous physical phenomena, including extraordinary aerial objects, and poked fun at scientists' sometimes labored efforts to account for them in prosaic terms. In *The Book of the Damned* and two subsequent books, *New Lands* (1923) and *Lo!* (1931), he theorized that visitors from other worlds are observing Earth.

Although it is often claimed that the phenomenon has been part of human history for many centuries, reports of anything resembling modern UFOs do not appear in print until the early decades of the nineteenth century. UFOs, in other words, seem to be a product of the modern age. In the twentieth century UFOs were called, successively, "airships," "foo fighters," and "ghost rockets" before "flying saucers" and (starting in the late 1940s, in U.S. Air Force memos), "unidentified flying objects" and (in the early 1950s) "UFOs."

Postwar UFO Investigations

Between 1947 and 1969 the U.S. Air Force ran three successive public UFO projects. The first was code-named Sign, followed by Grudge (1949–52) and Blue Book (1952–69). A faction within Project Sign concluded by mid-1948 that UFOs were extraterrestrial spacecraft, but air force Chief of Staff Gen. Hoyt S. Vandenberg rejected its report. Reorganized as Grudge, the project took a pronounced anti-UFO line. Except for a period between 1951 and 1953, when Capt. Edward J. Ruppelt, neither pro- nor anti-UFO but committed to open-minded inquiry, directed the project (renamed Blue Book in March 1952), Air Force UFO investigations sought to debunk sightings and to explain them, if not always persuasively, as arising from misidentifications and hoaxes.

In 1966 the Air Force entered into a contract with the University of Colorado ostensibly to conduct an independent investigation under the leadership of physicist **Edward U. Condon** but in fact to find a way of ridding itself of its UFO albatross. The Condon committee, as it was called informally, soon became embroiled in controversy as Condon's view, which echoed the Air Force's in dismissing UFOs as nonsense, were known. Released in January 1969, the **Condon Report** (formally titled *Scientific Study of Unidentified Flying Objects*) declared the phenomenon nonexistent and further research pointless. The National Academy of Sciences endorsed the report's conclusions, and in December 1969 the Air Force cited them when it announced it was closing Blue Book. To many it appeared as if the UFO controversy had ended.

Yet the Condon Report had its critics, including University of Arizona atmospheric physicist James E. McDonald and Northwestern University astronomer (and longtime Blue Book consultant) **J. Allen Hynek,** who pointedly observed that fully one-third of the cases in the report were listed as unsolved. They also contended that even some of the "explained" cases had been inadequately accounted for. In November 1970 a UFO subcommittee of the American Institute of Aeronautics and Astronautics, explicitly rejecting Condon's conclusions, remarked on the "small residue of well-documented but unexplainable cases which form the hard core of the UFO controversy." Hynek's 1972 book *The UFO Experience* argued for renewed inquiry into what he thought might prove to be "not merely the next small step in the march of science but a mighty and totally unexpected quantum leap."

A wave of sightings in the fall of 1973 served to revive popular interest. By the 1980s much of the fascination focused on abduction stories, reported in such widely read books as Budd Hopkins's *Missing Time* (1981) and **Whitley Strieber**'s *Communion* (1987), and on alleged official cover-ups of UFO secrets, including the crash of an unidentified object near Roswell, New Mexico in 1947. In 1994 the Air Force acknowledged its coverup of the so-called Roswell incident but said authorities at the time had been trying to conceal a classified project, Mogul, in which balloons were sent aloft to monitor possible Soviet nuclear tests. Three years later, in a follow-up study, it theorized that the humanoid bodies associated with the crash were "anthropomorphic test dummies that were carried aloft by U.S. Air Force high altitude balloons for scientific research"—though such tests had not commenced until six years later.

Though polls have consistently found that a significant plurality of Americans "believe" in UFOs, the scientific establishment continues to treat the phenomenon as illegitimate. In the fall of 1997, however, an international panel of scientists met in Tarrytown, New York, to examine a body of UFO evidence, mostly cases involving physical evidence, presented by a small group of ufologists. The panel's report, released in June 1998, cautiously stated that "unexplained observations" exist—though it distanced itself from extraterrestrial theories—and that further evidence of the best cases is worth science's time.

Nonetheless, UFOs remain a fringe subject. Most scientific investigations of the phenomenon since the Condon period have been conducted by individuals acting on their own or in concert with such civilian groups as the **J. Allen Hynek Center for UFO Studies** (CUFOS), the **Mutual UFO Network,** and the **Fund for UFO Research.** CUFOS, founded by Hynek in 1973 (Hynek died in 1986), publishes the *Journal of UFO Studies,* the one refereed scientific journal devoted exclusively to the subject.

Schism: Science vs. the Occult

The controversy about UFOs and their meaning has generated innumerable books, scientific papers, popular articles, specialist periodicals in many languages, and Internet websites. Much of this writing, especially in mainstream magazines, newspapers, and journals, has been from a skeptical perspective. Active UFO proponents worldwide probably number no more than several thousand, and they range from the intellectually careful to the wildly credulous. The literature they have produced since the 1940s documents a variety of approaches to the questions raised by UFO reports.

Early on, active proponents divided themselves into two camps. The first, who in the 1950s started calling themselves "ufologists," held a relatively conservative view. In their reading of the phenomenon, UFOs were unexplained occurrences that merited conscientious study. Scientific procedures and logical analysis of the evidence would eventually yield a solution, which probably would validate the notion of extraterrestrial visitation. Ufologists thought communication with UFO intelligences might occur in the future but rejected claims that such contacts were already taking place.

The second camp consisted of individuals sometimes called "saucerians." Saucerians typically were enthusiasts of occultism and the paranormal. Many had backgrounds as active Theosophists, Spiritualists, or followers of other esoteric doctrines. Some believed—even before the Arnold sighting put flying saucers on the world stage—that contact with otherworldly beings not only was possible but already had been accomplished. Such beings, who lived on other planets, in the spirit realm, or in the astral world (or all of these), were on the whole advanced and benevolent, concerned about the fate of the lowly, violent human race and engaged in efforts to guide our spiritual evolution in positive directions. Believers also acknowledged, however, that evil space and spirit entities, operating in concert with terrestrial allies, sought to exert malevolent influences over life on Earth.

Charles Fort's books, especially the collective omnibus *The Books of Charles Fort* (1941), influenced many individuals who would go on to become ufologists. If Fort had alerted them to reports of unusual aerial phenomena, he had also piqued their interest in other mysteries of the physical world: **falls** from the sky, monsters, archaeological anomalies, and more. The **Fortean Society** continued to collect and chronicle accounts of "Fortean phenomena" after Fort's death. In the early UFO age a few ufological theorists, most notably Morris K. Jessup (in *The Case for the UFO,* [1955], and *The Expanding Case for the UFO,* [1957]), sought a sort of unified field theory of anomalistics. Jessup wrote that spillage from "celestial hydroponic tanks" in alien spacecraft causes falls of fish, frogs, and other organic matter, and in his view archaeological evidence indicates that earth once housed an advanced civilization which has now returned to its ancestral home in flying saucers.

Both ufologists and saucerians read **Fate** magazine, the first issue (Spring 1948) of which featured a long article by Kenneth Arnold. A digest-sized pulp quarterly which went bimonthly in 1949 and then monthly in 1952, Fate became the only national magazine to cover UFOs on a regular basis. It also reported on Fortean occurrences. Its main interest, however, was the psychic. Even ufologists who initially had no particular interest in such matters could not help being exposed to material on **ghosts, poltergeists, ESP,** and **psychokinesis.**

The most important early saucerian theorist was California occultist N. Meade Layne, founder of the **Borderland Sciences Research Foundation.** To Layne, who tied the old occult idea of an "etheric world" to the new phenomenon of flying saucers, UFOs were "ether ships." They and their occupants, the "ethereans," come from a fourth dimension of existence or atomic vibration. They enter our realm by lowering their vibratory rates. Their realm exists as an etheric counterpart of our universe. Its inhabitants are also our ethereal counterparts, but they are far more advanced than we are. In the Borderland publication *Round Robin* and in his book *The Ether Ship and Its Solution* (1950), Layne brings forth an eclectic mix of **Theosophy,** Swedenborgianism, **Spiritualism,** and Fortean events. Much of the material came from San Diego medium **Mark Probert,** who channeled teachings from alleged discarnates, among them the 500,000-year-old Himalayan philosopher Yada Di' Shi'ite.

Saucerians embraced Layne's ideas, and favorite Layne phrases such as "mat" (materialization) and "demat" (dematerialization) quickly entered their vocabulary. To southern California's contactee subculture, which arose in the early 1950s in the wake of claimed contacts (physical and telepathic) with space people by **George Adamski, George Van Tassel,** and others, Layne was an intellectual hero. To ufologists, who despised the contactees and all they stood for, he was just another crackpot. Yet a modified version of his idea, called the 4D (fourth-dimensional) theory, found favor among some ufologists. Here science fiction, another important influence on first-generation ufologists, was at least as much an inspiration as watered-down Borderland doctrine.

Generally speaking, ufologists and saucerians existed in separate universes, the former as would-be (and sometimes actual) scientists, the latter as more or less open occultists. In the 1960s, however, the lines began to blur, and occultism became a major force in ufology. Before then, ufologists had assumed that they were dealing with a reasonably straightforward issue. As they saw it, the UFO phenomenon consisted of credible observations of anomalous lights and structured objects in the sky. A number of prominent ufologists went further and included reports of humanoid occupants (later called "close encounters of the third kind") in their definition of the phenomenon. Unlike the golden-haired, angelic "space brothers" of contactee lore, these entities were both uncommunicative and strange enough—alien—to frighten those who encountered them. Such reports were consistent with the conservative version of the extraterrestrial hypothesis ufologists championed.

By the mid-1960s, however, new developments challenged ufology's dominant view that UFOs are space visitors. For one thing, UFO encounters seemed to be getting weirder. Persons of ostensible sanity and sincerity claimed to have been abducted into UFOs and communicated with their crews, who gave odd, conflicting accounts of themselves, their motives, and their origins. Monstrous creatures showed up in areas where UFOs were being seen. UFO witnesses sometimes complained of postsighting visits by odd-looking, dark-suited individuals like the menacing "men in black" in saucerian literature. Some close-encounter percipients told investigators of poltergeistlike infestations in their homes.

Ultraterrestrials: A Malevolent Genesis

Many of these claims seemed incompatible with extraterrestrial theories, which started to fall out of favor in some circles of ufology. The principal figure in this revisionist ufology, at least initially, was writer **John A. Keel,** whose investigations in New York, West Virginia, and Ohio elicited scores of incredible tales that could not be shrugged off as the creations of lunatics and charlatans. On the other hand, these were extraordinary claims without extraordinary—or even ordinary—proof. Someone more cautious would have hesitated to use such material, which existed only in testimony (admittedly, for all its fantastic qualities, at times *compelling* testimony), to construct a phantasmagorical explanatory scheme. Brash and opinionated, Keel had no such reluctance.

Keel credited Layne with having "worked it all out in the early 1950s;" unfortunately, Keel added, "nobody would listen to him." But ufologists, Forteans, and psychic enthusiasts were listening to Keel, whose writing and pronouncements excoriated traditional ufology as the domain of "buffs" who lacked the courage, the imagination, or even the mental health to face the truth. The truth according to Keel was that "ultraterrestrials" from the "superspectrum" (Keel's term for the etheric realm) are entering our world and doing terrible things to us. "We are biochemical robots helplessly controlled by forces that can scramble our brains, destroy our memories and use us in any way they see fit," he wrote. "They have been doing it to us forever." Here he parted radically from Layne, who believed the ethereans to be largely benevolent.

To Keel the contact claims loved by saucerians were not the hoaxes suspected by ufologists; they were actual experiences, but not the sort contactees thought they were. According to Keel, "The quasi-angels of Biblical times have become magnificent spacemen. The demons, devils, and false angels were recognized as liars and plunderers by early man. These same impostors now appear as long-haired Venusians."

He holds that *Homo sapiens* came into existence because of a war waged between ultraterrestrial factions. One faction took on human form so that it could more easily communicate with Neanderthals, whom this ultraterrestrial group wanted to enlist in its "physical army." An unintended consequence of this assumption of physical form was erotic desire. Sexual intercourse between the ultraterrestrials and the protohuman Neanderthals created the modern human race. As Keel tells the tale in *Our Haunted Planet* (1971), "This produced strange responses in [the offspring's] materialized nervous system. Emotions were born. Frequencies were changed. The direct control of the superintelligence was driven from their bodies. They were trapped on Earth, unable to ascend the electromagnetic scale and reenter their etheric world. With the loss of control they became animals, albeit highly intelligent animals."

The other ultraterrestrials continue to torment us, their former adversaries, and effectively control the world, manipulating our social, political, scientific, and religious beliefs, creating all paranormal phenomena and destroying the lives of individual human beings who interact with them.

Jacques Vallee and Magicland

A more restrained, erudite occult ufology is expressed in a series of books by an equally influential theorist, **Jacques Vallee.** A French American educated in astronomy and computer science (with a Ph.D. in the latter), Vallee worked at Northwestern University with Allen Hynek in the mid-1960s. His first two books, *Anatomy of a Phenomenon* (1965) and *Challenge to Science* (1966, with Janine Vallee), were hailed as seminal works of scientific UFO literature. But soon Vallee's thoughts had gone elsewhere, back to an early fascination with the esoteric. In *Passport to Magonia* (1969) Vallee holds that UFOs are a modern manifestation of a supernatural otherworld long ago known as Magonia ("Magicland," according to one controversial translation), whose inhabitants other ages experienced as angels, demons, and fairies.

Passport was misread by some as an effort to depict the UFO phenomenon as a modern folklore (folklore here being equated with delusion). More careful reading reveals Vallee's true meaning: an unknowable "other intelligence" plays to human dreams and manifests accordingly; it manipulates human consciousness and seeks to affect human affairs. Though Vallee sees nothing inherently evil in this, his idea is strikingly like Keel's.

If Vallee at first looked less paranoid than Keel, elements of paranoia would show up soon enough. In such subsequent books as *Messengers of Deception* (1979) and *Revelations* (1991), Vallee speculates that a shadowy human group, intent on manipulating societal consciousness (for reasons Vallee never explains), may be producing fraudulent UFO encounters and paranormal occurrences. It is even conceivable, Vallee hints, that this group has some kind of link with Magonia itself. This group or the UFO phenomenon or both—again Vallee is unclear—comprise a "control system" which communicates with us on a subliminal level, employing a symbolic language of "metalogic" as well as a "schedule of reinforcement." In his view, "UFOs can never be analyzed or conceived because they are the means through which man's concepts are being rearranged."

In time, Vallee persuaded his friend and onetime mentor Hynek that the quest for nuts-and-bolts extraterrestrial UFOs was doomed to certain failure. Particularly in his later years, Hynek's pronouncements took on an increasingly occultish coloration, even to the extent of references to the **astral world** and to **elementals.** While such talk provided ammunition for his critics and made many of Hynek's friends and colleagues uncomfortable, it also reflected a longtime, privately held interest in the occult.

Journalism on the Fringe

Under Charles Bowen's editorship *Flying Saucer Review* (*FSR*), published in England, carried some of the best ufological writing of the 1960s and became for a time the world's most influential UFO magazine. Two or three years into Bowen's stewardship, *FSR*'s contents turned more and more to extraordinary claims and extreme speculations. Eventually, as Bowen's health began to fail, Gordon Creighton—temperamentally much like Keel—assumed de facto (then, in 1982, actual) editorship. Sober material continued to appear, but increasingly Creighton's openly supernaturalist approach dominated the pages of *FSR.* According to Creighton, the **jinn,** the demonic spirits of Middle Eastern mythology, are the cause of UFO, Fortean, and paranormal phenomena, and they are doing all manner of harm to the human race. Among other atrocious acts they are responsible for the AIDS epidemic. (Comparable views figure in the writings of Salvador Freixedo, sometimes called the Latin American John Keel, and of California ufologist Ann Druffel.)

By 1984 Creighton's extremism had so alienated more conservative ufologists that one of them, John Rimmer, was led to observe, "No journal espousing the bizarre beliefs that are now emanating from [*FSR*'s] pages can be considered worthy to be the literary flagship of British ufology. From now on, it seems, it will be of interest largely to paranoid cultists, conspiracy-mongers, and students of fringe literature." *FSR*'s readership and influence have declined markedly during Creighton's tenure.

More UFO Theories

Not all proponents of occult ufology and anomalistics went as far as Creighton, but the notion that UFOs and other strange phenomena may be related, and all the product of paranormal forces, continued to have a wide appeal. Two popular British writers, Janet and Colin Bord, argued the case for a unified paranormal theory in a number of books. In *Alien Animals* (1981) they chronicle worldwide reports of anomalous creatures. All such reports, in their view, "have features in common which suggest they are all aspects of a single phenomenon, together with UFOs and other weird apparitions." These otherworldly entities may feed on electrical power and "earth energies."

Another theorist in what may be termed the paracryptozoological school, the late F. W. Holiday (author of *The Dragon and the Disc,* 1973), held that all through history good and evil entities have fought for the soul of the human race. To the ancients the disc represented the benevolent forces, the dragon the destructive ones, and the two have a sort of symbiotic relationship. Creatures such as the **Loch Ness Monster** are dragons in the literal sense—supernatural and evil. Discs, of course, are flying saucers. On June 2, 1973, accompanied by Holiday, the Rev. Dr. Donald Omand exorcised Loch Ness and subsequently other British and European lakes in which serpent-like beasts traditionally are believed to dwell.

Parapsychologist **D. Scott Rogo** offered a different sort of paranormal theory to explain UFO and Fortean occurrences. They are, he wrote, the product of mass psychic energy. If the psychokinetic energy emanated by the unconscious of a single individual can produce something so dramatic as a poltergeist, what might the psychokinesis of the entire human race produce? Rogo speculated in *The Haunted Universe* (1977) that "our entire culture may be projecting UFOs psychically" in response to our "needs and expectations."

Psychologist Michael Grosso calls these psychokinetically generated entities "psychoterrestrials." Their function is to affect the evolution of human consciousness, specifically to break down modern humanity's excessive focus on materialism and rationalism. Grosso borrows here from the prominent Swiss psychologist-philosopher **Carl G. Jung** who, in *Flying Saucers: A Modern Myth of Things Seen in the Skies* (1959), characterizes the appearance of UFOs as indicative of "psychic change . . . which may be expected when the spring-point enters Aquarius." According to Grosso the UFO image inspires fantasies and dreams and, more profoundly, draws archetypal material from deep within the collective unconscious. Symbolically the disc shape of the flying saucer represents psychic wholeness, a resolution of the conflict between rational (conscious) thought and intuitive (unconscious) feeling.

To Jung, however, the notion of a "materialized psychism"—Grosso's "psychoterrestrial"—"opens a bottomless void under our feet" and "surpasses our comprehension." It is absurd to propose that "psychic projections throw back a radar echo." Since some UFOs seem to do just that, Jung wrote it is more probable that the "appearance of real objects affords an opportunity for mythological projections." These "real objects" may be spacecraft whose presence only now is being noticed because our "earthly existence feels threatened [and] unconscious contents have projected themselves on these inexplicable heavenly phenomena and given them a significance they in no way deserve."

But in Grosso's more radical version of Jung's hypothesis, psychic projections do show up on radar. "If UFOs are mythic constructs," he writes, "it is not surprising that their physical effects fit the UFO construct. To look like real spaceships, they obligingly affect radar." Psychoterrestrials also manifest as religious visions, monsters, men in black, angels, and more—all "forces of rebirth" in the service of the consciousness transformation that will save us from otherwise certain self-destruction.

Unlike Jung, but in common with Grosso and other occult-oriented theorists, folklorist Peter M. Rojcewicz rejects extraterrestrial UFOs in favor of the psychoterrestrials Grosso describes. "In the narrative accounts born of the ongoing human interaction with other worldliness," he writes in *The Boundaries of Orthodoxy* (1984), "we see the articulation over time of a mental argument, both for a more cooperative and harmonious existence on the one hand, and on the other, [for] a transcendent dimension of human will and imagination." Rojcewicz defines "UFO phenomenon" as virtually any sort of encounter with paranormal entities. He argues, "The 'UFO Phenomenon,' so Other, so here and now, reveals to us ourselves triggered by the intensity of unanswered longing and passionate collective desire."

As UFO abduction stories came into prominence in the 1980s, they inspired a new round of both extraterrestrial and occult hypotheses. Among proponents of the latter, Grosso, Rojcewicz, and Dennis Stillings quickly identified the abducting entities as psychoterrestrials, while Whitley Strieber, **Kenneth Ring** (*The Omega Project,* 1992), and John E. Mack (*Abduction,* 1994) believed them to be genuine otherworldly supernatural intelligences bent on human betterment. In this view, abduction experiences were a variety of contact claim. The aliens may be odder-looking than the ones who figure in classic contact tales, and they may not come from outer space, and their methods may be bizarre and even cruel in the short term, but their mission is the same.

Not all ufologists have embraced occultism. Indeed, occult ufology reached its peak in the 1970s, and by the turn of the century, with Keel and Vallee growing less active and publishing little, it was no longer a significant element of mainstream ufology. Meantime, extraterrestrial theories underwent something of a revival.

Just as significantly, by the late 1970s and early 1980s some disillusioned proponents of paranormal ufology had radically altered the occult model in a way that made it possible for them to deal with extreme experiential claims without also having to embrace unverifiable supernatural explanatory schemes. Thus was born the "psychosocial" school, which proposed what were represented as psychological solutions to entity encounters. Though these solutions were themselves often speculative, they were certainly not occult-based; yet they borrowed ideas from Vallee, Grosso, and Rojcewicz, especially the relationship between alleged human needs and encounter experiences. Essentially the psychosociologists disagreed with the occults on only one point, albeit a crucial one: they did not believe dreams and visions could have physical properties.

Over time the psychosocial approach has evolved into more conventionally defined skepticism. It is more popular in Britain and the European continent than in the United States. Criticisms of occult ufology within the UFO literature have focused on its speculative nature and unfalsifiability. Beyond that, Keel and Vallee have been accused of using dubious material, including rumors and claims later exposed as hoaxes, to argue their cases. Critics have also objected that the evidence linking UFOs to other anomalous and paranormal manifestations is slight. In the *Journal of UFO Studies* Thomas E. Bullard writes of Rojcewicz and others:

"Claims about reality demand proof on the same terms that we treat other scientific claims. What do we find instead? The phenomenological theories of alternate realities handicap themselves with a well-nigh fatal combination of poor comparative methodology and unsound structural components, and no algebra of apologetics can transform these two minuses into a plus. Speculations about the psychoid properties of archetypes will not explain the physical effects of UFOs. If those physical effects are genuine, then prove to me first that archetypes exist and can have physical effects, or I will look for simpler and more direct solutions elsewhere. Using one unproven theory to support another is just a more sophisticated tautology, more verbose but ultimately no more informative about the physical world than identifying a bald man as hairless. In one sense this tack is even less informative. It clouds the basic questions with confusing masses of theory, distracting participants in the dialogue to talk only about theories and forget the real issues. The very proliferation of phenomenological theories with no way to sort out the right from the wrong simply underscores the danger that we may become more deeply mired in sophistry than the Athenian Academy."

Another critic complained (in *International UFO Reporter,* January/February 1994) that occult theories turn the UFO argument on its head. The extreme experiential claims on which occult ufologists have been fixated comprise the least compelling evidence for the existence of UFOs. The best evidence—in the form of radar trackings, landing traces, photographs—suggests that at least some UFOs may be technological devices. The extreme claims, even when related by apparently sincere persons, amount only to stories. He went on:

"The fantastic entities described—fairies, merfolk, Blessed Virgins, apparitions of all kinds—do not bless us with physical evidence or even coherent pictures of themselves, their behaviors, and their missions. Of such things we can say only that experiences of them are possible, but the question of whether these experiences are *events* is another matter altogether. If events—in other words, occurrences amenable to incorporation into consensus acceptance via traditional methods of scientific documentation—they would force us to reinvent the world, and they would give us real reason to believe fourth dimensions, ethereal realms, superspectrums, and Magonias are more than words without meaning or attempts to redefine God. Nothing we have seen so far calls on us to embark on so daring an undertaking."

Meanwhile, the saucerian movement, which in its present form began in 1952 with contactees Adamski and Van Tassel, goes on. The flamboyant figures of the early years, often suspected (and often with reason) of conscious charlatanry, are gone, but channelers and visionaries in the thousands still claim to commune with space and extradimensional personalities. An enormous literature of contactee lore and philosophy circulates in books and newsletters and now on the Internet.

Sources

Bord, Janet, and Colin Bord. *Alien Animals.* Harrisburg, Pa.: Stackpole Books, 1981.

Bullard, Thomas E. "Fresh Air, or Air Castles in Folklore Theories?" *Journal of UFO Studies* 4 (n.s., 1992): 165–73.

Clark, Jerome. *The UFO Encyclopedia, Second Edition: The Phenomenon from the Beginning.* 2 vols. Detroit: Omnigraphics, 1998.

———. "Wagging the Dog." *International UFO Reporter* 19, 1 (January/February 1994): 3, 22–24.

Gillmor, Daniel S., ed. *Scientific Study of Unidentified Flying Objects.* New York: Bantam Books, 1969.

Grosso, Michael. *Frontiers of the Soul: Exploring Psychic Evolution.* Wheaton, Ill.: Quest Books, 1992.

Holiday, F. W. *The Dragon and the Disc: An Investigation Into the Totally Fantastic.* New York: W. W. Norton, 1973.

Jacobs, David M. *The UFO Controversy in America.* Bloomington: Indiana University Press, 1975.

Jung, C. G. *Flying Saucers: A Modern Myth of Things Seen in the Skies.* New York: Harcourt, Brace, 1959.

Keel, John A. *The Eighth Tower.* New York: Saturday Review Press, 1975.

———. *Our Haunted Planet.* Greenwich, Conn.: Fawcett Publications, 1971.

———. *UFOs: Operation Trojan Horse.* New York: G. P. Putnam's Sons, 1970.

Layne, N. Meade. *The Ether Ship and Its Solution.* Vista, Calif.: Borderland Sciences Research Associates, 1950.

Mack, John E. *Abduction: Human Encounters with Aliens.* New York: Charles Scribner's Sons, 1994.

Reeve, Bryant, and Helen Reeve. *Flying Saucer Pilgrimage.* Amherst, Wis.: Amherst Press, 1957.

Ring, Kenneth. *The Omega Project: Near-Death Experiences, UFO Encounters, and Mind at Large.* New York: William Morrow, 1992.

Rojcewicz, Peter M. "The Boundaries of Orthodoxy: A Folklore Look at the UFO Phenomenon." 2 vols. Philadelphia: University of Pennsylvania, Ph.D. dissertation, 1984.

Rogo, D. Scott. *The Haunted Universe: A Psychic Look at Miracles, UFOs and Mysteries of Nature.* New York: New American Library, 1977.

Stillings, Dennis, ed. *Cyberbiological Studies of the Imaginal Component in the UFO Contact Experience.* St. Paul, Minn.: Archaeus Project, 1989.

Stupple, David M. "Historical Links Between the Occult and Flying Saucers." *Journal of UFO Studies* 5 (n.s., 1994): 93–108.

Sturrock, Peter A. *The UFO Enigma: A New Review of the Physical Evidence.* New York: Warner Books, 1999.

Vallee, Jacques. *Messengers of Deception: UFO Contacts and Cults.* Berkeley, Calif.: And/Or Press, 1979.

———. *Passport to Magonia: From Folklore to Flying Saucers.* Chicago: Henry Regnery, 1969.

———. *Revelations: Alien Contact and Human Deception.* New York: Ballantine Books, 1991.

Unification Church

A religious movement founded in 1954 in Korea by Rev. **Sun Myung Moon,** a South Korean engineer. His family had converted to the Presbyterian Church, and in 1935 he had a vision of Jesus, who reportedly told him to complete Jesus' unfinished work. He began to collect followers as early as 1944 into the Broad Sea Church. In 1946 he began a six-year stint in a North Korean prison camp. After his release, he made his way to Pusan, South Korea, where he eventually founded his church. Its basic teachings were written down in the *Divine Principle,* first published in 1957.

The first missionaries of the church were sent to Japan, where they had their greatest success. Members moved to the United States in 1959, and the first centers were begun in Eugene, Oregon, and Washington, D.C. Moon moved to the United States in 1971. Soon established were a headquarters in Manhattan, a seminary in Barrytown, New York, and Moon's residence in Irvington, New York.

Unification thought is based on a unique understanding of the concepts of Creation, the Fall, and Restoration. The principle of Creation asserts that God created the world and by that act became known. The world, reflecting God's nature, has two expressions, as Sung Sang (internal, invisible) and Hyung Sang (external, visible). It also is expressed as male and female. In the first set of expressions, one sees the relationship of spiritual and material; the second reveals what is traditionally known as yin and yang, the masculine and feminine. God created out of his inner nature, his heart of love. The purpose of creation is to experience the joy that comes from loving.

The Fall came about from Adam and Eve's failure to realize God's purpose in creation. The Fall placed Satan in control of creation. God has been trying to restore his primal intention ever since. The Bible is an account of God's various restoration attempts.

The principle of Restoration delineates the conditions necessary for the reestablishment of God's intention. The plan involves both God's sending of one sinless man and the response of a free and responsible humankind. The Messiah was to be born as a substantial, physical being, an example of the ideal person. He was also to take a bride and realize the ideal family and thus become the True Parent. Through the True Parent, God will implant love in the hearts of all who follow him. He will also show them how to accomplish the true purpose in life.

Throughout the 1970s the Unification Church (full name: The Holy Spirit Association for the Unification of World Christianity) became one of the more controversial of the new religions. Because of its intense indoctrination, it was labeled a "cult" by many parents of the primarily youthful converts. Many were offended by the church's policy concerning sex and marriage. New members spent at least seven years in celibacy, after which Moon selected a spouse for them. Most marriage partners were drawn from a different country or race. Following their engagement, couples were married in mass weddings, the most recent of which occurred in 1995.

The church spawned a number of organizations, some evangelistic arms and others designed to carry out social policies. The church also made friends with many scholars and intellectuals. Most of the church's programs are now organized into two structures, the International Cultural Foundation and the International Religious Foundation. The former has sponsored possibly the most successful program involving nonchurch members, the International Conference on the Unity of the Sciences.

The church has spread internationally and is active in over 150 countries. It has approximately five thousand members in the United States but counts members in the hundreds of thousands worldwide. Address: HSA-UWC, 4 W. 43rd St., New York, NY 10036. Website: http://www.unification.org/.

Sources:

Barker, Eileen. *The Making of a Moonie.* Oxford: Basil Blackwell, 1984.

Biermans, John T. *The Odyssey of New Religious Movements.* New York: Edwin Mellon, 1986.

Divine Principle. New York: Holy Spirit Association for the Unification of World Christianity, 1973.

Outline of the Principle, Level 4. New York: Holy Spirit Association for the Unification of World Christianity, 1980.

The Unification Church. http://www.unification.org/. March 8, 2000.

Union Esperitista Cristiana de Filipinas, Inc.

The Spiritualist church to which many of the psychic surgeons in the Philippines belong.

Current address unavailable.

Union Spirite Bordelaise (Journal)

Nineteenth-century Spiritist journal, published in Bordeaux, France, incorporating other journals.

Union Spirite Française

French Spiritualist organization, active in the 1930s, founded by Léon Chevreuil, its president, and **Jean Meyer,** its vice president. It published *Le Bulletin de l'Union Spirite Francaise* from its headquarters at the *Maison des Spirities,* 8 Rue Copernic, Paris, a center founded by Jean Meyer.

United Lodge of Theosophists

The United Lodge of Theosophists is an independent theosophical organization founded in 1909 by Robert Crosbie (1849–1919). Crosbie belonged to the theosophical community created by **Katherine Tingley** at Point Loma, San Diego, California, in the early 1900s. Before long he argued that the community had lost its direction as originally established. He moved to Los Angeles, opened the United Lodge, and founded a publishing facility, the Theosophy Company. The first issue of *Theosophy Magazine* appeared in 1912.

Among the people attracted to the United Lodge was B. P. Wadia, an Indian who had held a high position in the **Theosophical Society.** Wadia eventually succeeded Crosbie as head of the lodge and is credited with turning it into an international organization. More recently a leadership role was assumed by Rhagavan N. Iyer, now a retired professor of political science at the University of California, Santa Barbara. With his wife, Nandini, Iyer heads the lodge's Santa Barbara group and founded Concord Press, which has developed an extensive publishing program of theosophical and related materials.

The United Lodge of Theosophists has no formal membership but there are some 11 lodges in the United States and 11 more in other countries. Along with the magazine *Theosophy,* the group publishes the monthly, *The Theosophical Movement,* and the bimonthly, *Vidya.* Address: 245 W. 33rd St., Los Angeles, CA 90007. Website: http://www.ult.org/.

Sources:

Crosbie, Robert. *Answers to Questions on the Ocean of Theosophy.* Los Angeles: Theosophy, 1937.

———. *The Friendly Philosopher.* Los Angeles: Theosophy, 1934.

The Theosophical Movement, 1875–1950. Los Angeles: Cunningham Press, 1951.

United Lodge of Theosophists. http://www.ult.org/. March 8, 2000.

United Lodge of Theosophists: Its Mission and Its Future. Los Angeles: Theosophy, n.d.

United Metropolitan Spiritual Churches of Christ

The United Metropolitan Spiritual Churches of Christ were founded in 1945 by Bishop Thomas Watson, but date to the earliest days of the spiritual church movement in New Orleans. The spiritual movement, the name assumed by many African American Spiritualist churches in the early twentieth century, was brought to New Orleans by Rev. Leafy Anderson in 1921. The popular leader of the Eternal Life Christian Spiritualist Association attracted many African Americans who were interested in psychic phenomena and mediumship. Among them was Thomas Watson. In 1929, two years after Anderson's death, Watson withdrew from his association and founded the St. Joseph Helping Hand Church in a New Orleans suburb. This independent congregation grew by the addition of affiliated congregations into the St. Joseph Helping Hand Missionary Association (1934) and the Divine Spiritual Church of the Southwest (1935).

In 1936 Watson was elected senior bishop of the church. Among his major decisions for the new church was a rejection of his own heritage with Anderson. In 1940, having concluded that women should not be ordained ministers, he removed all of the women mediums and pastors, many of whom left the church. Then in 1942 Watson led his church into a merger with the Metropolitan Spiritual Churches of Christ to form the United Spiritual Churches of Christ. When William F. Taylor, the former president of the Metropolitan Churches, died shortly after the merger, Watson was selected to succeed him. However, Watson immediately ran into a conflict with Clarence Cobbs, who also thought he should be president of the United Spiritual Churches.

The conflict grew over the next three years and eventually Cobbs forced Watson out of office and became the new president. With his following, Watson withdrew and reorganized his following into the United Metropolitan Spiritual Churches of Christ. There is no difference in belief and practice between the two churches, and the area of disagreement was purely administrative.

Current address unavailable.

Sources:

Jacobs, Claude F., and Andrew J. Kaslow. *The Spiritual Churches of New Orleans: Origins, Beliefs, and Rituals of an African American Religion.* Knoxville: University of Tennessee Press, 1991.

Murphy, Larry G., J. Gordon Melton, and Gary L. Ward. *Encyclopedia of African American Religions.* New York: Garland Publishing, 1993.

United Spiritualist Church

The United Spiritualist Church was founded in 1967 by Rev. Floyd Humble, Edwin Potter, and Howard Mangan. Humble had earlier served a variety of independent Spiritualist congregations. The church affirms belief in **Spiritualism** and mediumship, both spiritual and physical, and the example of Jesus as a teacher, healer, and prophet. Humans are immortal and will bring the kingdom of God to Earth as they develop their spiritual sides.

The United Spiritualist Church differs from most Spiritualist churches by its development of a centralized form of government. Most Spiritualists have been organized into very loose fellowships of autonomous congregations. The United Church is headed by a presidency consisting of a president, first adviser-secretary, and second adviser-treasurer. They oversee the board of governors, which in turn guides the boards of publication, education, and church extension and missions. The board of governors is elected by the general conference. The church publishes a periodical, the *Spiritual Outlook.* Address: 813 W. 165th Pl., Gardena, CA 90247.

Sources:

Humble, Floyd. *Bible Lessons.* Gardena, Calif.: United Spiritualist Church, 1969.

Unity-and-Diversity World Council

An international coordinating body devoted to linking metaphysical and **New Age** groups. It was originally formed as the **International Cooperation Council,** and it has been led for three decades by its coordinator Leland Stewart. The council seeks to coordinate cultural and religious organizations that, in their own ways, "foster the emergence of a new universal person and a civilization based on unity in diversity among all peoples." Formed to propagate ideals of unity during International Cooperation Year, it was voted into being in 1965 by the General Assembly of the United Nations. The Unity-and-Diversity World Council continues its work of publicizing the aims and ideas of humanitarian groups that bring together the methods and discoveries of modern science with the insights of religion, philosophy, and the arts. Much of this synthesis is concerned with developing areas of awareness in human consciousness and unorthodox healing techniques.

In its early period, the council took part in a New Age Institute directed toward public and private education. A World-View Exploration Seminar, formed in spring 1969, grew out of the Fifth Annual International Cooperation Festival, composed primarily of professionals from the fields of science, religion, art, education, and philosophy, who met on the campus of the California State College at Los Angeles to explore "the meaning of the new universal person and the world civilization."

In place of the magazine *The Cooperator,* the Unity-and-Diversity Council now issues the monthly newsletter *Spectrum* and also publishes a *World Directory* of affiliated organizations from its headquarters at 5521 Grosvenor Blvd., Ste. 22, Los Angeles, CA 90066-6915.

Univercoelum (Journal)

Early Spiritualist periodical started by **Andrew Jackson Davis** in December 1847, in New York, for "the establishment of a universal system of Truth, the Reform and Reorganization of Society." It ran for a year and a half before being absorbed in July 1849 by W. M. Channing's *The Present Age.*

Univercolian (Magazine)

Quarterly publication growing out of former **Pyramid Guide Newsletter,** concerned with earth mysteries, featuring articles on such subjects as Easter Island, Stonehenge, Atlantis, UFOs, and energy centers. Its mailing address is P.O. Box 292, Dalton, MA 01226.

Universal Balm

An elixir sought by alchemists that was supposed to be a remedy for every malady and would even bring the dead back to life. (See also **elixir of life**)

Universal Christ Church

The Universal Christ Church is a small fellowship of Spiritualist congregations in Southern California. It was founded in 1970 by Rev. Anthony Benik and was unique in its acceptance of an element of ritualism in its worship. It operates out of a Spiritualist perspective and **reincarnation** is accepted. Most of the churches are in the Los Angeles area, but there is one large congregation reported in Australia. In the 1970s there were five congregations in the greater Los Angeles area, but recent attempts to contact the church have failed. Its present status is unknown.

Universal Church of the Master

The Universal Church of the Master, one of the largest Spiritualist churches in the United States, especially on the West Coast, was founded in 1908 in Los Angeles by Dr. B. J. Fitzgerald (d. 1966) and others. The church was incorporated in 1918 and during its first generation was largely confined to congregations on the West Coast. Fitzgerald was the author of the church's basic textbook, *A New Text of Spiritual Philosophy and Religion.* In 1930 the church's headquarters moved to Oakland, California, and then in 1966 to San Jose. The church was headed for many years by Birdie Peterson, who passed away in 1994.

The church has a statement of faith that affirms the fatherhood of God and the brotherhood of man; the necessity of living in harmony with nature; life after death; communication [through mediumship] with the unseen world; the Golden Rule; individual responsibility; the continual possibility of improvement; prophecy; and the eternal progress of the soul. The implication of the emphasis on the laws of nature defies any supernaturalism in the communication with the dead or other psychic phenomena. The church also suggests the use of *The Aquarian Gospel of Jesus the Christ,* a channeled work by Levi Dowling, as a source for teachings.

In the 1980s it had over 300 associated congregations. The church is headquartered at 501 Washington St., Santa Clara, CA 95050.

Sources:

Dowling, Levi. *The Aquarian Gospel of Jesus the Christ.* Los Angeles: Leo W. Dowling, 1925.

Fitzgerald, B. J. *A New Text of Spiritual Philosophy and Religion.* San Jose, Calif.: Universal Church of the Master, 1954.

Universal Faithists of Kosmon

The Universal Faithists of Kosmon is one of several groups founded by believers in the authority of *Oahspe: A New Age Bible.* **Oahspe** was channeled by **John Ballou Newbrough** (1828–1891) and published in 1882. The first convention of Faithists, held in 1883, planned the formation of a community in New Mexico called Shalam. Initially successful, it was destroyed by a flu epidemic, which took many of its leaders, including Newbrough.

The Faithist cause has been kept alive by a variety of independent groups, the Universal Faithists among the oldest of the several presently existing organizations. It has assumed responsibility for preserving Faithist communication. The movement has had some alignment with the **New Age** movement, since *Oahspe* was originally described as a "New Age" Bible. It describes the evolution of the human race into the Kosmon Era, a time of worldwide peace and joy.

The Universal Faithists publish the periodical *Kosmon Voice.* The organization may be contacted at the Oahspe Information Service, Messilla, New Mexico 88046-0891.

Sources:

Dennon, Jim. *Newbrough and Oahspe.* Kingman, Ariz.: Faithist Journal, 1975.

———. *The Oahspe Story.* Kingman, Ariz.: Faithist Journal, 1975.

Stowes, K. D. *The Land of Shalam: Children's Land.* Evansville, Ind.: Molinet Print Shop, n.d.

Universal Hagar's Spiritual Church (UHSC)

The Universal Hagar's Spiritual Church (UHSC), a Spiritualist church operating primarily among African Americans, was founded in 1923 in Detroit, Michigan, by **George Willie Hurley** (1884–1943). Hurley moved to Detroit from Georgia in 1891 and affiliated with Triumph the Church and Kingdom of God in Christ and rose to become the leader of the church in Michigan. A short time later he became involved with the esoteric, left his position in 1920 to join a Spiritualist church, and three years later founded his own church. In 1924 he established the School of Mediumship and Psychology, and as new congregations developed, each also had a school attached to it. Hurley conceived of the school as a branch of the Great School of the Prophets, which he believed to be the school Jesus attended during the 18 years between his appearance in the temple in Jerusalem and the beginning of his public ministry at the age of 30.

UHSC was one of the main bodies spreading **Spiritualism** through the African American community in the twentieth century. Like other spiritual churches, (spiritual was the name adopted by Spiritualism in the black community), UHSC altered traditional Spiritualism by blending Catholic ritual, Holiness preaching, and elements of the folk magic culture or **voudou.** Hurley also drew upon Ethiopianism, a belief that identified black people (Ethiopians) with the ancient Israelites; **astrology;** and insights from *The Aquarian Gospel of Jesus Christ,* a channeled book that purports to tell of Jesus' lost years. Unlike many spiritual leaders, Hurley took a strong stand on social issues and was an early supporter of Franklin D. Roosevelt.

The church planted congregations across the Northeast and Midwest during Hurley's lifetime. As the church expanded, Hurley acquired an increasingly grandiose self-understanding. He told his followers that his carnal flesh had been transformed into the flesh of Christ and that he had become the "God" of this Aquarian Age, just as Jesus had been the God of the previous Piscean Age. Since Hurley's death, the UHSC has been led by Prince Thomas Surbacher, Mother Mary Hatchett, Prince Alfred Bailey, and Rev. G. Latimer, Hurley's daughter. Hurley welcomed women to the ministry, and they have always been well represented on the Wiseman's Board, the church's ruling structure. State directors are called princes, a term taken over from Triumph the Church and Kingdom of God in Christ. In recent years the church has spread into the Southwest and California.

Current address unavailable.

Sources:

Baer, Hans A. *The Black Spiritual Movement: A Religious Response to Racism.* Knoxville: University of Tennessee Press, 1984.

Universal Harmony Foundation

The Universal Harmony Foundation is a Spiritualist church founded in New York in 1942 as the Universal Psychic Science Association. The founders, Revs. Helene Gerling and J. Bertram Gerling, were both prominent mediums at **Lily Dale,** the Spiritualist camp near Rochester, New York. Association headquarters were soon moved to Saint Petersburg, Florida. Helene Gerling wrote several books and a set of correspondence lessons and also opened a seminary for training mediums, through which students could receive ordination and charters for churches. Ordained positions include ministers, healers, missionaries, and teachers.

The church strives for a universal philosophy and draws insight from revelation and the teachings of all religions and prophets. Church belief is premised upon the religious and scientific demonstration of the talents and powers of the Living Spirit, that is, mediumship. The foundation affirms the fatherhood of God, the brotherhood of man, the eternalness of life, the power of prayer, spiritual healing, the reality of the psychic, soul growth as the purpose of life, and that the way of life is fraternal service.

Helene Gerling led the foundation for almost a half century. She retired in 1988 and was succeeded by Rev. Nancy Castillo. Castillo pastors the mother church, and members are encouraged to join it and support it in an annual free-will offering. The church issues the magazine *Spiritual Digest.* Address: c/o Rev. Nancy Castillo, 5903 Seminole Blvd., Seminole, FL 33542.

Sources:

Gerling, Helene. *Healthy Intuitive Development.* New York: Exposition Press, 1971.

Universal Life—The Inner Religion

Universal Life—The Inner Religion began in 1977 to spread the message of contemporary German channel Gabriele Wittek (b. 1930). In 1975, according to Wittek, the same spirit of Christ who had been present in Jesus of Nazareth stepped into her life and chose her as his prophetic instrument for this generation. He disclosed his intention to lead his children back to their eternal home and to build the kingdom of God on Earth. Wittek organized the Homebringing Mission of Jesus Christ, the original name of the new religion.

Wittek, a Wurzburg housewife, received an awakening experience in 1970 when she saw the spirit of her deceased mother. Convinced of "**survival** of bodily death," she began visiting a local medium, then operated as a channel herself for several years before going public with the messages she was receiving. Wittek emphasized the indwelling kingdom of God and taught a method of going within to open the kingdom and experience God in one's innermost being. She advised people to learn to live God's laws as expressed in the Ten Commandments and the Sermon on the Mount.

The mission operated for seven years, and in 1984 was superseded by Universal Life—The Inner Religion. Wittek now taught that, given the contact with God, it was possible to put the Sermon on the Mount into operation immediately. She encouraged those formerly associated with the mission to form businesses that would operate on the principles of the Sermon on the Mount. Toward the end of the decade, a school based on the same principles was opened.

During these years, the mission-turned-religion spread across Europe and into North and South America. By the early 1990s, the teachings had been translated into ten languages, and over 130 Inner-Spirit-of-Christ churches opened. Universal Life publishes the periodical *Christ State-International* and may be contacted through its world headquarters, Universelles Leben, Postfach 5643, 8700 Wurzburg, Germany. In the United States the address is Box 3579, New Haven, CT 06525.

Sources:

The Christian Mystery School. Pelham, N.H.: Homebringing Mission of Jesus Christ, 1983.

The Divine Mystical Method of Instruction of the Homebringing Mission of Jesus Christ. Pelham, N.H.: Homebringing Mission of Jesus Christ, 1980.

A Formerly Spiritually Unknown Person on the Path to God: The Course of Life of the Prophetess in the Homebringing Mission of Jesus Christ. Pelham, N.H.: Homebringing Mission of Jesus Christ, 1980.

Universal Religion of America

The Universal Religion of America was a Spiritualist movement founded in 1958 in Kenosha, Wisconsin, by the Rev. Marnie Koski. Koski was formerly a minister with the Spiritual Science Mother Church. She was known by the members of her church as Soraya ("Solar Ray") as a result of the channeled messages she receives from Jesus.

During the 1960s, Koski left the Kenosha congregations under the leadership of her students and moved to Florida, first to Rockledge and then to Merritt Island. The Universal Religion had some 500 members in its two centers. Last known address: Christ Universal Church, 295 North Tropical Trail, Merritt Island, FL 32952.

Sources:

Koski, Marie. *Personal Talks with Jesus.* Washington, DC: ES-Press, 1979.

Universal Spiritualist Association

The Universal Spiritualist Association is an association of Spiritualist churches and clergy. It was originally founded in 1956 by Clifford Bias to issue credentials for Camp Chesterfield, which housed the seminary where many Spiritualist ministers and healers were trained and licensed. Until 1956, the Spiritualist Episcopal Church was in charge of the seminary. At that point the leaders of the new association, mostly former Spiritualist Episcopalians, assumed the administrative and faculty roles at the Chesterfield school, an arrangement that was cordial until 1970, when a dispute erupted between the camp and the association. The school reverted to the control of the Chesterfield staff, and the Universal Spiritualist Association conducted its own seminary. In 1985 the association moved to the Maple Grove Spiritual Retreat near Pendleton, Indiana, and opened the Institute for Holistic Studies. In 1993 the association moved headquarters once again to the Universal Institute for Holistic Studies at Ball State University, Muncie, Indiana.

The Universal Spiritualist Association provides limited demonstrations of the physical phenomena of spiritualism for their institute registrants and candidates for the clergy, primarily for lack of demand.

Clifford Bias served as first president of the association until his death in 1986. He organized the Ancient Mystical Order of Seekers, the esoteric society for the association's ministers and more serious lay students. Bias' successor was Warren Smith, who retired in 1990. The association is presently led by T. Ernest Nichols. The president heads the association's general board, which charters churches and licenses ministers. A board of regents oversees the Institute for Holistic Studies. Both boards are elected at the annual membership-at-large meeting.

In 1990 the association reported 512 members in 14 churches, including one in Windsor, Ontario, Canada. It publishes the magazine *Banner of Light,* and may be contacted at the Universal Institute for Holistic Studies, 4905 W. University Ave., Muncie, IN 47304-3460. Website: http://www.spiritualism.org.

Sources:

Bias, Clifford. *The Way Back.* York Beach, Maine: Samuel Weiser, 1985.

Universal Spiritualist Manual. Universal Administration, Muncie, Ind.: Universal Spiritualist Association, n.d.

Wallace, Austin D. *Thistle Presents Prince Nikeritis.* Eaton Rapids, Mich.: Transcendental Science Publications, 1905.

Universe Quarterly

Former quarterly journal of the Vortex Institute of Fairbanks, Alaska, concerned with spiritual life in Alaska, self-growth techniques, and meditation.

Universities (Occult)

In many works on the occult sciences, allusions are made to schools and universities and the instruction of those who were drawn to them. The idea for such schools derived from the philosophical schools and academies of the ancient Greek teachers. In the early Christian era, **Gnosticism** was taught in such schools. Since that discipline was centered upon *gnosis* or knowledge, a school (rather than a temple or church) was the natural form that its group life assumed.

While a few similar schools might have existed in the Dark Ages, the idea of such institutions was largely a myth used to credential otherwise informally and self-taught occultists or to refer to the places where alchemists and occultists quietly gathered to consult with each other. It was the practice of those on the faculties of the universities and those who operated independently to draw students around them, and professors of the occult sciences were no different.

There is no doubt that during the Middle Ages many lecturers taught **alchemy** and kindred subjects at great universities. Thus **Paracelsus** lectured on alchemy at the University of Basel, and he was preceded and followed there and elsewhere by others who taught that and other occult arts.

Louis Figuier, in his book *L'alchimie et les alchimistes* (1854), alluded to a school in Paris frequented by alchemists that he himself attended in the middle of the nineteenth century. The school—an ordinary chemical laboratory during the day—became in the evening a center of the most elaborate alchemical study, where Figuier met alchemical students, visionary and practical.

The novelist Balzac alludes to an occult school in the story "The Secret of Ruggier," which he placed at the time of Catherine de Medici. He stated: "At this epoch the occult sciences were cultivated with an ardour which put to shame the incredulous spirit of our century. . . . The universal protection accorded to these sciences by the ruling sovereigns of the times was quite remarkable."

He goes on to say that at the beginning of the sixteenth century, Ruggier was a member of a secret university for the study of the occult sciences, where astrologers, alchemists, and others studied several branches of hidden knowledge. Balzac gives no details as to its locality, or as to the exact nature of its curriculum.

The College of Augurs in Rome and the Calmecac of ancient Mexico are distinct examples of institutions for the study of divination, and in this connection, the House of Wisdom of the Ismaelite sect at Cairo, Egypt, may be mentioned.

Helena Petrovna Blavatsky insisted that a great "school" of illuminated occult adepts flourished in Tibet, but nobody except herself and her immediate friends ever saw them or had any dealings with them. Prior to 1959, Tibet was the home of a large number of monasteries that were also the schools of Tibetan Buddhism and its esoteric practices.

Instructional centers for people who studied the occultism integral to Hinduism, Buddhism, and other Asian systems did exist (and continue to exist) across Asia. These centers, remote and mysterious prior to the transportation and communications revolution of the twentieth century, took on a mythical character in the occult literature of the nineteenth century. Those associated with these Asian schools were rumored to have extraordinary occult prowess.

In the nineteenth and twentieth centuries attempts have been made to recreate these ancient occult schools. For example, the School for the Discovery of the Lost Secrets of Antiquity flourished for a generation in San Diego, California. It was founded by **Katherine Tingley** late in the nineteenth century and taught Theosophy. A decade earlier, Blavatsky founded the Esoteric Section of the Theosophical Society, an organization carried on by Theosophists associated with the **Theosophical Society.**

One modern equivalent of ancient occult universities are the secret magical orders, such as the Hermetic Order of the **Golden Dawn,** where occult and mystical subjects are taught to students, with grades of advancement. Many such orders, based in part on a format adopted from **Freemasonry,** exist.

One outstanding attempt to recreate the ancient Gnostic schools, with an intense course in esoteric training, is Ramtha's School of Enlightenment in Yelm, Washington, opened in 1988 by JZ Knight. Ramtha, a channeled entity, instructs students through the entranced Knight.

University Books, Inc.

One of the most influential imprints in occult publishing from the 1950s on. The corporation was founded by **Felix Morrow,** who played a major role in the modern occult revival by reprinting rare and important scholarly works of occultism and mysticism that had long been unavailable.

In addition to being sold to libraries, the books reached a large general public through the Mystic Arts Book Club. The spokespersons of the occult revival of the 1960s and 1970s drew heavily from these texts. In 1966, the company was absorbed by Lyle Stuart, Inc., which continued occult publishing under the Citadel Press imprint.

University of London Council for Psychical Investigation

A reorganization of the **National Laboratory of Psychical Research,** which had been founded by psychical researcher **Harry Price** in 1926. The National Laboratory passed under the direction of the University of London Council on June 6, 1934. At that date the organization was still at the National Laboratory address, but by the end of 1936 the large library assembled by Price was moved to University College, London.

Later the National Laboratory's séance room and laboratory equipment were transferred to the administrative offices of the University Council, but all experimentation ceased with the outbreak of World War II. After the death of Harry Price in 1948, the library was bequeathed to the University of London.

A short-title catalogue of the library was issued as volume 1, number 2 of the **Proceedings of the National Laboratory of Psychical Research,** and a supplement was issued as the first bulletin of the University of London Council for Psychical Investigation. A second publication was issued by the University of London Council as *Bulletin II, A Report on Two Experimental Fire-Walks; Bulletin III, Preliminary Studies of a Vaudeville Telepathist.*

Last known address: University of London, Senate House, Male St., London.

University of the Trees

An experimental **New Age** school community for world change through consciousness research and related spiritual development. The main thrust of teaching was directed towards self-discovery and creative individual change, and in addition to community life courses, teaching was also maintained through correspondence with students all over the world. Courses were wide-ranging, including art, literature, environmental studies, changing, transpersonal awareness, alternative energy systems, health and yoga, healing, history and neurology of consciousness, philosophy, mysticism, radiational physics, and what is termed "supersensonics" (which includes **radiesthesia, dowsing, pyramid** research, and psychotronics).

The university granted degrees in consciousness research, but aimed to provide students with methods of study that deepen their inner awareness. The term "the Trees" denoted the nerve dendrites in the brain, and the "Tree of Life" of the nervous system that can combine with knowledge to enhance direct perception of truth.

The community was founded in 1973 and grew out of the teachings of **Christopher Hills,** a New Age teacher, researcher, and yogi who directs the work of the university. Associated with the university is a **Research Institute for Supersensonic Healing Energies.** Last known address: P.O. Box 644, 13151 Pine St., Boulder Creek, CA 95006.

The Unknown (Magazine)

Former British monthly magazine "exploring strange phenomena." The first issue, published July 1985, included discussions at a popular level of spontaneous combustion, ley lines, wolf children, lost civilizations, sea serpents, alchemy, and the Fatima apparitions.

The Unknown World (Journal)

Occult and metaphysical journal founded by James Elliott and edited by **Arthur Edward Waite** (1857–1942). Eleven issues appeared from August 1894 to June 1895. It was devoted to "The Occult Sciences, Magic, Mystical Philosophy, Alchemy, Hermetic Archaeology, and the Hidden Problems of Science, Literature, Speculation and History."

Sources:

Gilbert, R. A. *A. E. Waite: A Bibliography.* Wellingsborough, Northamptonshire, England: Aquarian Press, 1983.

Unknown Worlds (Newsletter)

Bimonthly newsletter reporting strange phenomena of a Fortean kind. It was published by World Investigators of Strange Phenomena. Last known address: Rte. 2, Box 159, Vina, AL 35593.

Upanishads

The *Upanishads,* literally teachings received while sitting at the feet of a master, are a set of writings produced in the first millennium B.C.E. in India, which had been the most important in defining the general perspective of that set of religions generally referred to as Hinduism. Transmitted to the West in the nineteenth century, they became a major source for contemporary belief in karma and **reincarnation,** and through **Theosophy** were integrated into the teaching of Western occult thought.

The first era of Indian thought was built around the *Vedas,* writings which suggest that India's ancient culture was built around the celebration of nature, the activity of the deities in the world, and the propitiation of the gods in acts of devotion, temple sacrifice, and the following of rules. The *Upanishads* represent a radical shift in perspective that developed around 1000 B.C.E. The authors of the *Upanishads* launched a search for the unifying reality behind the visible universe.

There are 13 Principle *Upanishads,* which summarize the whole of the teachings, and numerous lesser supportive documents. They critique the *Vedas* and are often referred to as the Vedanta, or "end of the *Vedas*." Rather than outward acts of temple worship, the *Upanishads* call for an inward search for the ultimate principle of reality (called Brahman) and a mystical union with that principle. Brahman is the source of the visible world that goes through a continuous process of being created, sustained, and destroyed. Brahman is hidden by maya (illusion), that aspect of the world that conceals reality from us.

The essential mystical insight offered by the *Upanishads* is the identification of Brahman with Atman. Atman is the essential core of the individual self. The implication is that to reach the inner essence of oneself is to discover ultimate reality. It is upon this identification that disciplines of concentration and **meditation** and ultimately the practice of **yoga** are based.

According to the *Upanishads,* individuals are trapped in maya. Lost in maya, we face a continuous series of incarnations, the exact nature of any incarnation being the result of the consequences of actions in prior lives (karma). To escape maya one must focus upon reality, the yogic path being the ideal process for pursuing that focus. It is also recognized that such a focus can lead to selfishness. To prevent such an error, the *Upanishads* recommend the cultivation of virtues such as detachment and self-control, and call for the performance of one's social duties.

The *Upanishads* now exist in several translations in English and other Western languages, though the 1879 translation by world religions scholar Max Müller was the important early one which built support for Indian perspectives in the West. In 1893, **Swami Vivekananda** brought the teachings of the **Vedanta** to the West and established it throughout the Vedanta Societies that grew out of his work. Through the twentieth century, numerous commentaries on the *Upanishads* were published and circulated by the many Indian religions operating in the West. Equally important, insights from the *Upanishads,* freed from the texts, have permeated Western esoteric and metaphysical groups through which they have been popularized among a public unaware of their origin.

Sources:

Beidler, William. *The Vision of the Self in Early Vedanta.* Delhi: Motilal Barnarsidass, 1975.

Radhakrishnan, Sarvepalli. *The Principal Upanishads.* New York: Harper and Brothers, 1953.

Uphoff, Walter (1913–1998)

Professor of economics who has also written and lectured extensively in the field of parapsychology. He was born February 28, 1913, in Sheboygan County, Wisconsin, and studied at the University of Wisconsin (B.S., 1934; Ph.D., 1935). In 1938 he married Mary Jo Weiler, who co-authored some of his writings on parapsychology. He worked in business for many years before joining the faculty of the University of Minnesota in 1951. He moved to the University of Colorado in 1961. He retired in 1976 and until his death pursued the interest in psychical research that he developed during his student days.

Uphoff and his wife founded the New Frontiers Center and he served as its president. He was a member of the **American Society for Psychical Research, International Spiritual Frontiers Fellowship,** and the **Society for Psychical Research,** London. He was a board member of **ESP Research Associates Foundation** and a member of the former Academy of Parapsychology and Medicine. One of Uphoff's books concerns the early experiments with **Masuaki Kiyota,** the **metal-bending** psychic who later admitted that he had fraudulently accomplished his remarkable PK effects. Uphoff died September 26, 1998.

Sources:

Uphoff, Walter, and Mary Jo Uphoff. *Mind Over Matter: Implications of Masuaki Kiyota's PK-Feats with Metal and Film.* Oregon, Wis.: New Frontiers Center, 1980.

———. *New Psychic Frontiers: Your Key to New Worlds.* Gerrard's Cross, U.K.: Colin Smyth, 1975.

The Upright Man

In the sixteenth century, the vagabonds and beggars of Britain were organized into unions with rules and grades. Of these grades, the order of the "Upright Man" seems to have had some special significance and authority, and it is believed by some authorities to have descended from the folk adherents of paganism, the "Old Religion," or **witchcraft.**

Ura

A Babylonian spirit. (See also **Babylonia**)

Uranian Astrology

Uranian astrology is an innovative system of **astrology** developed early in the twentieth century by Friedrich Sieggrün (1877–1951) and **Alfred Witte** (1878–1943), two pioneers of the contemporary astrological revival. The system is sometimes referred to as the Hamburg School, a reference to Witte's main teaching centre in Germany.

The Uranian system was distinguished from traditional astrology at several points. First, traditional astrology bases many of its interpretations of the chart on the angles formed between planets in the charts. Important relationships or aspects are formed when planets are apart as 0° (conjunction), 30° (semisextile), 45° (semisquare), 60° (sextile), 90°(square), 120° (trine), and 180° (opposition). There are also a set of lesser aspects. Some aspects have traditionally been regarded as beneficent and others as more malevolent. These latter, now termed the hard aspects, include the square, semisquare, and opposition. The Uranian system emphasized the role of hard aspects.

Second, the Uranian system introduced the idea of midpoints to astrological interpretation. As the name implies, a midpoint is a spot halfway between any two planets pictured on the horoscope. The midpoint is the place where the combined energies of the two planets manifest. The two planets and their midpoint form a planetary picture. The calculation of said midpoints requires an additional level of mathematical skill by the astrologer drawing up the chart, a fact that limited the spread of the Uranian approach.

Third, the most questionable aspect of the Uranian system was the introduction of hypothetical planets to the chart. Prior to the advent of space travel and the development of various means of verifying the existence of otherwise unknown planets, the existence of different as yet undiscovered planets was proposed. Such speculation was encouraged by the discovery of Uranus and Neptune and heralded the discovery of Pluto (1930) and **Chiron** (1977), a comet originally believed to be a planet.

Uranian astrology was unique in suggesting the existence of no less than eight hypothetical planets that were given the names Cupido, Hades, Zeus, Kronos, Apollon, Admetos, Vulcanos, and Poseidon. Each of these planets was assigned its particular role in the chart.

Uranian astrology enjoyed its greatest success in German-speaking countries during the first half of the twentieth century. It also gave birth to **cosmobiology,** an astrological system started by **Reinhold Ebertin,** one of Witte's students. It has had little success outside of German-speaking countries, though Witte's most important book, *Rules for Planetary Pictures,* was published in an English edition in 1939. Also, modern advances in astronomy made the addition of hypothetical planets to the horoscope an increasingly dubious endeavor.

Sources:

Brau, Jean-Louis, Helean Weaver, and Allan Edwards. *Larousse Encyclopedia of Astrology.* New York: New American Library, 1982.

Holden, James H., and Robert A. Hughes. *Astrological Pioneers of America.* Tempe, Ariz.: American Federation of Astrologers, 1988.

URANTIA

A lengthy nineteenth-century channeled message published in *The URANTIA Book* (1955). It explains that the true name of Earth is Urantia and that we are part of the universe of Nebadon, or the larger universe of Orvonton, whose central committee of Uversa dictated the work. The book presents its own unique view of human origins, including the precursors of Adam and Eve and a claimed more accurate version of the life and teaching of Jesus (said to have been really Michael of Nebadon, one of the myriad sons of the Eternal Son). The miracles are given largely natural explanations.

The book owes its publication to William S. Sadler (1875–1969), former Seventh-Day Adventist minister, who served as a surgeon in Adventist hospitals before leaving the movement. Although skeptical of psychic phenomena, he became involved with the Urantia writings, which proceeded from an unnamed individual who "became a clearing house for the coming and going of alleged extraplanetary personalities." These channeled communications were first studied in the 1920s by a group of individuals named The Forum. The URANTIA Foundation was formed in 1950 in Chicago, Illinois, and published *The URANTIA Book* five years later. The foundation promotes the study of the book and sponsors study groups of interested people. It is located at 533 Diversey Pkwy., Chicago, IL 60614, and publishes the *URANTIAN NEWS . . . from URANTIA Foundation.*

Sources:

Gardner, Martin. "The Great URANTIA Mystery." *The Skeptical Inquirer* 14, no. 2 (winter 1990).

Myers, Martin W. *Unity, Not Uniformity.* Chicago: URANTIA Foundation, 1973.

The URANTIA Book. Chicago: URANTIA Foundation, 1955.

URANTIA Brotherhood Association

The URANTIA Brotherhood Association was founded in 1989 to continue the work of the URANTIA Brotherhood, founded in 1955. That year people attracted to the teachings of *The URANTIA Book,* a large volume of channeled material first published in 1955, organized to nurture their learning experience. Over the years the URANTIA Brotherhood formed a number of groups around the country. They operated in harmony with the URANTIA Foundation, the corporation established in 1950 to publish and hold the copyrights and trademarks associated with the book. However, in 1989 the brotherhood and the foundation had an irreconcilable disagreement, and the foundation withdrew the use of the name **URANTIA** and the associated symbols from the brotherhood. Committed to the book, the brotherhood reorganized as the Fifth Epochal Fellowship. Those students still in relation to the foundation organized a new structure, the URANTIA Brotherhood Association. It may be contacted at 529 W. Wrightwood Ave., Chicago, IL 60614. Website: http://urantiabook.org/.

Sources:

Special Report to the Readers of THE URANTIA BOOK: URANTIA Foundation Ends Its Relationship with the Former URANTIA Brotherhood. Chicago: URANTIA Foundation, 1990.

The URANTIA Book. Chicago: URANTIA Foundation, 1955.

Urban, Hubert Josef (1904–)

Professor of neuropsychiatry who investigated areas of parapsychology. He was born on June 4, 1904, in Linz, Austria. He studied at the University of Vienna (B.A., 1923; M.D., 1929). He pursued post-graduate studies at several locations and in 1938 became a professor of neuropsychiatry at the University of Innsbruck, Austria. Urban took special interest in telepathy, **clairvoyance,** and mediumship as related to psychiatry, and studied the question of extrasensory ability before and after shock treatment or narcoanalysis. Between 1948 and 1958, he made visits to India to conduct field work in psychiatry, which allowed observation and research on spontaneous psi phenomena. He published articles on connections between psi, psychiatry, and medicine in various journals.

Sources:

Pleasants, Helene, ed. *Biographical Dictionary of Parapsychology.* New York: Helix Press, 1964.

Urim and Thummim

Literally "lights and perfections," a means of **divination** employed by the ancient Hebrews. The objects were placed on a breastplate, which bore the names of the twelve tribes of Israel, that was worn over the heart of the high priest when he went before the Lord (Ex. 28:30). It was believed to consist of a species of casting lots.

The use of Urim and Thummim was not for determining questions concerning individuals, only for questions of national import. Answers were usually given in a brief fashion, yes or no, or the designation of one tribe out of the twelve. There is no mention of the Urim and Thummim after the time of King David. Their form and method of use is uncertain, but from passages in the Hebrew Bible, it seems probable that they were used somewhat like dice to cast lots (I Sam. 10:19–22 and 14:37–42).

The Urim and Thummin reappeared in the nineteenth century in the form of two divining stones possessed by Joseph Smith, Jr., prophet and founder of the **Church of Jesus Christ of Latter-day Saints,** whose followers are commonly called Mormons. Smith used the stones to "translate" the *Book of Mormon* from what was claimed to be golden tablets with writing in a reformed Egyptian text.

Urine

Urine has long been credited with magical and medicinal properties. It has been featured in **black magic** rituals. It has been mixed with wine, herbs, or oils; used as an ointment and in pills; employed in **amulets, talismans,** and **charms**; and used in aphrodisiacs and fertility potions.

Medicinally, urine has unusual properties. It contains ammonia, which can neutralize acids, and is usually free from bacteria, thus has disinfectant properties. Women have drunk urine from their husbands to speed up childbirth or have been given their own urine to relieve hysteria. Male urine contains androsterone, a male hormone, and it has long been believed that drinking one's own urine improves health and virility. Moraji Desai, former prime minister of India, openly admitted to drinking a small quantity of his own urine each morning for health reasons.

USSR See RUSSIA

Usui, Mikao (1865–1926)

Mikao Usui, the creator of the **Reiki** system of healing, a Japanese healing discipline that became a global phenomena during the years of the New Age Movement, was born on August 15, 1865, in Yago, Yamgata district, Gifu Prefecture, Japan. As a young man he married Sadako Suzuki, with whom he fathered two children. For a while he was associated with a Japanese Spiritualist group, Rei Jyutsu Kai, whose headquarters was west of Kyoto at the base of Kurama Kai, a holy mountain. However, he spent most of his life as a Buddhist. He completed the study and reflection that led to his creation of Reiki in 1914. Then, following a mystical experience he had while meditating on Kurama, he was led to found an organization, Usui Reiki Ryoho Gakkai, to disseminate the teachings and practice of Reiki.

Reiki, a Japanese word roughly translated as "universal energy," is a healing system based upon the subtle energy system (variously called **qi,** chi, or ki) within the human body as developed in Taoist China. It is the same system that underlies **acupuncture,** and pictures energy flowing through the body vertically from the head downward through a set of channels or meridians. The Reiki system teaches a method of attuning to the energy and assisting its flow in the body of the patient.

After developing Reiki, Usui worked in a poorer section of Kyoto for several years, but around 1921 moved to the Harajaju section of Tokyo. There he set up a school/clinic. His students would move into the school and work with Usui until they had learned the system, though occasionally he traveled to other parts of the country to teach. Anticipating a practice later popularized in the New Age Movement, Usui is remembered as using crystals in his healing work. He taught the Reiki system to some 2,000 students, several of whom opened clinics and centers around the country. Usui also wrote a brief handbook which included a description of Reiki healing (though without mentioning any of the particulars of the method), the answers to some frequently asked questions, and some poems composed by the emperor designed to advise people on a worthy life.

Usui died on March 9, 1926, of a stroke. He was buried at Saihoji Temple, a traditional Buddhist temple in a Tokyo suburb. Leadership of Usui Reiki Ryoho Gakkai was passed to a Mr. Ushida, and continues to the present. Among his last students was Dr. Chujiro Hayashi, a retired naval officer. He in turn taught Ms. **Hawayo Takata,** a Japanese-American who had traveled to Japan in the mid-1930s to seek help for her failing health. Hayashi named her his successor. Toward the end of her life, she initiated the first non-Japanese into Reiki and through the Reiki Masters she initiated, Reiki became a global phenomenon.

Sources:

Petter, Frank Arjava. *Reiki Fire.* Twin Lakes, Wis.: Lotus Light Publications, 1997.

———. *Reiki: The Legacy of Dr. Usui.* Twin Lakes, Wis.: Lotus Light Publications, 1998.

V

Valentine, Basil

This German adept in alchemical philosophy is commonly supposed to have been born at Mayence toward the close of the fourteenth century. As a young man he became a Roman Catholic priest and entered the Abbey of St. Peter, at Erfurt. He eventually became its prior, but otherwise very little is known concerning him, and even the date of his death is not known. His very existence is believed to be mythical by some authorities.

He appears to have been a very modest person, for according to Olaus Borrichius, the author of *De Ortu et Progressu Chemioe,* Valentine hid all the manuscripts of his writings inside one of the pillars of the Abbey Church where they might have remained for an indefinite period, but they were discovered during a thunderstorm, when a flash of lightning dislodged them from their curious hiding place. Valentine's reluctance for his work to be known may have been prompted by fear of the Inquisition discovering his researches in **alchemy.**

Valentine's works in alchemy certainly mark him as a very shrewd man and a capable scientist. Unlike much other medieval literature, his treatises were not all in Latin, some of them being in high Dutch and others in German. Prominent among those in his own language is *The Triumphal Chariot of Antimony,* first published at Leipzig in 1624. In this work, Valentine extolled antimony as an excellent medicine. The volume also embodies a lengthy metrical treatise on the **philosophers' stone,** the writer contending that whoever should discover and use this must do charitable deeds, mortify the flesh, and pray without ceasing. Among the alchemist's further writings are *Apocalypsis Chymica, De Microcosmo degue Magno Mundi Mysterio et Medecina Hominis* and *Practica unà cum duodecim Clavibus et Appendice.* All these were originally published in Germany at the beginning of the seventeenth century, and various passages in them demonstrate that the author understood the distillation of brandy and was acquainted with the method of obtaining hydrochloric acid from saltwater. Reverting to his faith in antimony, he has been credited with having been the first to extract this from sulphuret.

Valiantine, George (ca. 1874– ?)

Controversial **direct voice** medium of Williamsport, New York. He was a small manufacturer when at the age of 43 his mediumship was discovered by accident. At a hotel where he was staying he heard distinct raps on the door. No physical agency could be detected and he was deeply puzzled. A lady acquaintance who was familiar with **Spiritualism** later persuaded him to hold a séance.

The result was surprising. His deceased brother-in-law, Bert Everett, claimed to be present and rapped out that the spirits for a long time had been trying to attract Valiantine's attention. "Everett" then instructed Valiantine to make a **cabinet.** One evening, the medium went into trance and "Bert Everett" appeared in a materialized form. But direct voice communications became the chief feature of the séances as Valiantine's organism appeared to lend itself to this manifestation. "Bert Everett" found assistants in other controls: "Dr. Barnett," who often gave medical prescriptions, "Hawk Chief" and "Kokum," two Native Americans with booming voices and "Black Foot," another Native American, the last usually speaking in deep tones from the center of the floor.

In 1923 *The Scientific American* of New York offered a prize of $2,500 for the production of genuine physical phenomena. Valiantine was one of the mediums tested. **Gardner Murphy** of Columbia University and Kenneth Andrews of the *New York World* visited him at Wilkes-Barre for two preliminary sittings. Both sittings were successful and they returned with an initial favorable impression. Thereupon Valiantine came to New York.

During his first two séances before the committee of *The Scientific American,* eight distinct spirits manifested and spoke to the sitters. For the third séance, an electrical control apparatus had been secretly fixed to the medium's chair. It was meant to disclose to observers in another room whether the medium left his chair during the séance, under the cover of darkness, to reach for the trumpet. The apparatus did not register the medium's full weight for fifteen seconds on one occasion and from 1–14 seconds on other occasions.

For this reason, although the voices admittedly came from high in the air and carried on prolonged conversations, the result, in the report published in the July 1923 issue of *The Scientific American,* was ruled out as evidence. Over the construction of the report, which conveyed the impression that Valiantine was actually caught in fraud, a controversy arose between psychical researcher **J. Malcolm Bird** and British author **H. Dennis Bradley,** who pointed out the weaknesses of the report and its important admissions, which, however, were not sufficiently emphasized.

On several occasions, Bradley vigorously defended Valiantine. He met him at Arlena Towers, Ramsey, New York, in the home of Joseph de Wyckoff, a wealthy American financier who had been in close association with Valiantine for some years.

In November 1923, Wyckoff received long scripts from Valiantine which Valiantine said he had obtained through **direct writing** in his home. They were signed by "Everett" and "Dr. Barnett," and referred to a project involving an expedition to Guiana. Wyckoff discovered by chance that Valiantine's handwriting showed striking resemblance to the spirit scripts and took them to a handwriting expert who pronounced them identical. Wyckoff showed the report to Valiantine. He insisted that he did not do the writings. A test séance was arranged at his own house at Williamsport. Valiantine, at his request, was tied up. The séance was a failure. Wyckoff thereupon broke off his relations with Valiantine.

Not long afterwards, Wyckoff went to Europe. He met Bradley, who convinced him, by showing indirect evidence that he obtained in sittings with **Gladys Osborne Leonard,** that his evaluation of the Valiantine communications was unjust. Thereupon Wyckoff cabled to Valiantine from Europe and invited him to come and join him. Valiantine arrived in February

1924 and gave séances almost daily for five weeks in Bradley's home.

In the presence of more than fifty prominent people, over one hundred different spirit voices manifested and carried on long conversations in Russian, German, Spanish and even in idiomatic Welsh. Caradoc Evans, the Welsh novelist, spoke with his father's spirit in Cardiganshire Welsh.

But the seeds of suspicion had been sown. Wyckoff soon leveled a second charge against Valiantine, which grew out of a sitting in the St. Regis Hotel in New York on April 19, 1924. When the sitting was closed by the address of "Dr. Barnett," it was revealed that the trumpet had fallen sideways between Valiantine's legs, with the small end against the edge of the chair. As the medium was setting it upright, Wyckoff struck a match and scolded him for his action. Moreover, as Malcolm Bird pointed out in a letter to *Light,* "examination of the trumpet developed the facts that it was quite warm at the point where a human hand would naturally and conveniently grasp it, and that the mouthpiece was damp."

Bradley answered that this is exactly what would happen with independent voice phenomena. In his own séances, in which a luminous trumpet was seen sailing about the room, at the finish the inside was found moist, according to Bradley, for the simple reason that it is necessary for a spirit to materialize the vocal organs and breathe in order to produce its voice.

The following year, Valiantine paid another visit to England. In March 1925, he gave two test sittings before the **Society for Psychical Research** at Tavistock Square. Five words were spoken at the first, none at the second. They were considered blank.

Following this failure, Una, Lady Troubridge and Miss Radcliffe Hall of the society attended some sittings in Bradley's house. Later they were joined by Dr. V. J. Woolley, research officer of the society. Eleven distinct and individual voices were heard. Woolley agreed that he heard them and could not account for them. He was also satisfied that the movement of the luminous trumpet in the air was supernormal. Shortly afterward **E. J. Dingwall,** in company with Dr. Woolley, the other research officer of the society, obtained voices in daylight inside Valiantine's trumpet.

In his reports published in the *Journal* of the SPR (vol. 26, pp. 70–71; vol. 27, p. 170) and the *Proceedings* (vol. 36, pp. 52–53), Woolley wrote of these experiences and stated:

"Both of us heard raps which seemed similar to those she [Lady Troubridge] has described, but as I wish only to deal in this account with evidential utterances I do not propose to consider them in further detail. Both of us also heard whispering sounds, apparently in the trumpet, at times when we were convinced that Mr. Valiantine's lips were entirely closed, and I was able also to distinguish the words 'Father Woolley,' but nothing further."

The Coming of Confucius

But the most important phase of Valiantine's mediumship was yet to come. Strange languages were heard in séances in New York, and it was decided to test their nature by inviting a scholar. Dr. **Neville Whymant,** an authority on Chinese history, philosophy, and ancient literature, who happened to be in New York, was requested by Judge and Mrs. Cannon to come to a séance. He was slightly amused, but accepted. To quote from his notes:

"Suddenly, out of the darkness was heard a weird, crackling, broken little sound, which at once carried my mind straight back to China. It was the sound of a flute, rather poorly played, such as can be heard in the streets of the Celestial Land but nowhere else. Then followed in a low, but very audible voice the words 'K'ung-fu T'Zu.' Few persons, except Chinese, could pronounce the name correctly as the sounds cannot be represented in English letters. The idea that it might be Confucius himself never occurred to me. I had imagined that it might be somebody desirous of discussing the life and philosophy of the great Chinese teacher."

When, however, correct personal information was given, Whymant decided to test the matter. He said: "There is among your writings a passage written wrongly; should it not read thus?" At this point, Whymant began to quote as far as he knew, that is to say, to about the end of the first line. At once the words were taken out of his mouth, and the whole passage was recited in Chinese, exactly as it is recorded in the standard works of reference. After a pause of about fifteen seconds, the passage was again repeated, this time with certain alterations which gave it a new meaning. "Thus read," said the voice, "does not its meaning become plain?" Previous to the voice of "Confucius," Whymant heard a Sicilian chant and conversed with one of the controls, "Cristo d'Angelo," in Italian.

At the next séance at which Whymant was present, after having been absent through illness, "Confucius" again manifested and, omitting all ceremonious expressions, referred to Whymant's indisposition, saying "the weed of sickness was growing beside thy door." This metaphor was used in ancient Chinese literature but it is no longer current in the language. Nor was the dialect in which "Confucius" spoke any longer used in the Chinese Empire.

There are only about twelve Chinese sounds of which it can be definitely said that it was known how the Chinese of Confucius' time would have pronounced them. The voice which claimed to be that of Confucius used these archaic sounds correctly. Moreover, there were at that time only about six Chinese scholars in the world whose knowledge would have been equal to the one displayed by the direct voice. None of them was in America at the time.

In 1927, when Valiantine paid a third visit to England further tests of importance took place. Countess Ahlefeldt-Laurvig brought an ancient Chinese shell to a sitting in the apartment of Lord Charles Hope. At the top of the shell, circular folds ended in a small hollow mouthpiece. In China the shell was used as a horn and blown on occasion. The sitters tried it but could produce no sound whatsoever. Yet at one period during the sitting, from high up in the room, the shell horn was blown, and the peculiar notes were rendered in the correct Chinese fashion.

But the most important Chinese test tried was in making a phonograph record of the voice of "Confucius." The attempt was successful. The voice of "Confucius," (who died in 479 B.C.E.) was recorded in 1927 in London. It has curious flute-like tones, which rise and fall, and sometimes break into a peculiar sing-song tone. Whymant could only interpret a few sentences because the voice was faint and became blurred in the recording. But he recognized a number of the peculiar intonations. He could gather the meaning of the recorded speech by the tonal values. The voice was identical with the one he heard in America.

From H. Dennis Bradley's summary of this strange occurrence it is interesting to quote:

"I have heard the K'ung-fu T'ze voice speaking on two or three occasions in archaic Chinese. I have also heard the same voice with its peculiar intonation, speaking to me personally in English. The voice has spoken slowly, but with quite beautiful cadences. It possessed an extraordinary dignity."

New Controversies

In his books *Towards the Stars* (1942) and *The Wisdom of the Gods* (1925), Bradley published many important accounts of sittings with Valiantine. On several occasions he heard Valiantine speak simultaneously with the voices. He listened to the voices of the controls of Valiantine in séances with other mediums and heard "Feda," the control of Gladys Osborne Leonard, and "Cristo d'Angelo," who later associated himself with the **Marquis Centurione Scotto,** speak through Valiantine.

Including the 1927 period, Bradley conducted over a hundred experiments of which he deemed 95 percent successful.

This high percentage of success was undoubtedly partly due to the powerful direct voice mediumship which Bradley and his wife themselves developed after the first sittings with Valiantine in New York. But the physical manifestation was only part of the evidence. Bradley observed of Valiantine in his book . . . *And After* (1931),

"He is a man of instinctive good manners but it is essential to state that he is semi-illiterate. He possesses no scholastic education whatever, beyond the ordinary simplicities; he is ill-versed in general conversation and ideas. I mention these facts because many of the communications which have been made in the direct voice under his mediumship have been brilliant in their expressions and culture."

On April 26, 1929, Valiantine arrived for the fourth time in England from America. He spent one day with Bradley and then left with the Bradleys for Berlin. The sittings were held in a Ms. von Dirksen's house. Bradley considered them comparatively poor in result. Some members of the Berlin Occult Society, for which the séances had been arranged, subsequently claimed imposture and supported their assertions by referring to Bradley's and Valiantine's refusal to permit strict control. These charges were published five months afterward by Dr. Kroner in the *Zeitschrift für Parapsychologie.* Kroner attended only three of the sittings. Two lady sitters made direct allegations of fraudulent movements on Valiantine's part. However, no definite proof of having caught Valiantine in fraud was brought forward.

In May 1929, Valiantine gave a series of séances at the house of the Marquis Centurione Scotto in Genoa. One of the sittings, held in the presence of psychical researcher **Ernesto Bozzano,** was rigorously controlled. Valiantine was fastened to his chair and an adhesive bandage secured over his mouth. The knots were sealed, the doors were locked.

The results were excellent. The enthusiasm, however, was soon marred by a charge made by Rossi and Scotto. Rossi claimed to have distinctly felt Valiantine in one of their sittings lean forward and speak into the trumpet. He also said that Castellani caught hold of Mrs. Bradley's hand which was touching the back of his (Castellani's) head. Both of them were furiously indignant and left immediately. Castellani later withdrew his allegation against Mrs. Bradley and Rossi also became wavering. (These allegations charged the Bradleys with being Valiantine's accomplices. Evidence that such was the case would be forthcoming.)

As Bradley pointed out there was a truly bizarre aspect in the situation:

"The Marquis Centurione Scotto, Mr. Rossi and Madame Rossi, unknown before to me or to Valiantine, visit me in England in 1927. The Marquis, to his astonishment, speaks to his [dead] son in Italian. The Marquis and Mrs. Rossi then develop voice mediumship entirely from, and because of, their meeting and initiation with Valiantine. Valiantine then, in 1929, visits them in Italy and is accused of being a fraud. The poet is right when he declares 'It is a mad world.'"

In 1931, Valiantine was again invited to England. This visit ended on a tragic note. Bradley asked him to devote six evenings to experiments for psychic imprints (molds). Striking previous successes were recorded in the book *The Wisdom of the Gods.* Since then, famous people whom Bradley knew had died and their original left and right hand imprints were in the possession of palmistry authority **Noel Jaquin.** Scientifically, therefore, the experiments held potential promise. The claimed spirits of **Sir Arthur Conan Doyle,** Lord Dewar, and Sir Henry Segrave all apparently complied with Bradley's eager request, but the plastic substance used in the séances, unknown to Valiantine, was chemically prepared. A stain was found on Valiantine's elbow and expert examination disclosed that the spirit thumbprint of "Sir Arthur Conan Doyle" was exactly similar to the print of Valiantine's big toe on his right foot, a spirit thumbprint of "Lord Dewar" to that of Valiantine's left big toe, a spirit fingerprint of "Sir Henry Segrave" to the print of Valiantine's middle finger and another spirit impression to that of Valiantine's elbow.

Ex-Chief Detective Inspector Bell, the head of the fingerprint department at New Scotland Yard, declared that in a court of law the resemblance would be sufficient to hang a man charged with murder. According to Bradley, when Valiantine was confronted with this evidence, he broke down completely and sobbed. He would not, however, admit fraud. His only answer to questions was: "I cannot understand it."

Bradley believed that the rapid accumulation of money and fame as a professional medium did not have a beneficial effect upon Valiantine's character. He found that he had progressively changed, becoming a conceited and arrogant man. Yet "his reason for attempting these imprint frauds will remain incomprehensible. He received no money from me, and for him to imagine that in the presence of imprint experts he could commit palpable fraud and escape detection was a sign of sheer lunacy."

Besides Valiantine, his controls were also compromised, as on the night, just near the end of the sitting, when "Bert Everett" spoke in his usual shrill tones, announcing that an imprint had been made which was excellent. Mr. X., with whom Valiantine stayed during the visit, obtained the fingerprint of "Walter Stinson," control of the American medium **Mina Crandon** (known as "Margery"). This print was identified by Noel Jacquin as identical to that of the middle finger of Valiantine's left hand.

After the exposure, Valiantine gave twelve séances to Dr. Vivian. The report stated that while two voices were speaking, Valiantine was simultaneously heard to draw the attention of the sitters to the two voices. Surgeon Admiral Nimmo had two sittings in daylight. The voice that he heard to come distinctly from within the trumpet gave intelligent and evidential communication. In the presence of a second doctor, the voices were heard again, speaking distinctly and intelligently. During the phenomena, the doctors kept Valiantine's face under acute observation but they did not discover any movement whatever on it.

The experiences of Whymant with the voice of "Confucius" came before the Society for Psychical Research in 1927. Whymant delivered a lecture, played the phonograph record of the voice, and submitted his account of twelve séances. No action was taken. Thereupon the records were the subject of a book by Whymant, published in 1931 under the title *Psychic Adventures in New York.* In *Proceedings* of the Society for Psychical Research (vol. 40, pt. 125), the report of Lord Charles Hope on his sittings in 1927 concluded: "I was disappointed at the lack of evidence for survival which the voices had given me. I was left uncertain whether Valiantine was a genuine medium or not." (For other cases of imprints and molds, see **plastics.**)

Sources:

Bradley, H. Dennis. . . . *And After.* London: T. Werner Laurie, 1931.

———. *Towards the Stars.* London: T. Werner Laurie, 1924.

———. *The Wisdom of the Gods.* London: T. Werner Laurie, 1925.

Whymant, Neville. *Psychic Adventures in New York.* London: Morley & Mitchell, 1931.

Valiente, Doreen (1922–1999)

Doreen Valiente, poetess and one of the founders of modern Wicca, was born on January 4, 1922, in London, England. During World War II (1939–45) she married a soldier who had been wounded fighting for the Free French and had been sent to England to recuperate from his wounds. Her rise out of obscurity began in 1952 when she was introduced to **Gerald B. Gardner,** who was in the process of creating a new Goddess-oriented religion that he called **Witchcraft.** Following her initiation into the Craft, she worked with Gardner to perfect the rituals he had assembled. Among her most important contributions was a poetic piece called "The Charge to the Goddess." After four years with Gardner, she left to become the priestess of her own coven, and in 1962 authored her first book, a small volume describing the new Wicca religion. In 1964 she accepted a second Witchcraft initiation from Robert Cochrane.

Valiente worked quietly through the 1960s but became an object of controversy in the 1970s as Wicca emerged as a popular counterculture religion and various researchers began to explore the literary origins of the Pagan rituals. This controversy grew in the 1980s after Gardner's papers were sold to Ripley's Believe It or Not. The papers indicated that Gardner had not inherited the Witchcraft rituals, but had created them with the assistance of various people, especially Valiente.

Valiente began to emerge into her own in the 1970s when she wrote a set of popular books on Witchcraft, *An ABC of Witchcraft Past and Present* (1973), *Natural Magic* (1975), and *Witchcraft for Tomorrow* (1978). Then, as the controversy on Gardner heated up, and speculations concerning her own role in the development of the Gardnerian rituals were rife, she published her account of the story confirming much of what had been said about the discontinuity of Gardner's work with any folk survivals of the Craft from previous centuries. At the same time, she documented one of the major aspects of Gardner's story, that he had been initiated into Witchcraft in 1939 by a woman named Dorothy Clutterbuck. Some had speculated that Clutterbuck had never existed. Valiente tracked her birth and death records and found a copy of her will. All of this material was included in her most important book, *The Rebirth of Witchcraft* (1989). Besides being a significant contribution to modern religious history, the book established her place in the creation of modern Wicca.

During the last decade of her life, Valiente was widely acknowledged as a matriarch within the Wiccan community internationally though she lived quietly and made few public appearances. She died on September 1, 1999.

Sources:

Valiente, Doreen. *An ABC of Witchcraft Past and Present.* New York: St. Martin's Press, 1973.

———. *Natural Magic.* New York: St. Martin's Press, 1975.

———. *The Rebirth of Witchcraft.* Custer, Wash.: Phoenix Publishing, 1989.

———. *Where Witchcraft Lives.* London: Aquarian Press, 1962.

———. *Witchcraft for Tomorrow.* New York: St. Martin's Press, 1978.

Valkhoff, Marius (1905– ?)

Professor of Romance studies who investigated areas of parapsychology. He was born on January 7, 1905, at Zwolle, the Netherlands. He studied at the University of Amsterdam (D.Litt., 1931), taught at Amsterdam University for many years (1932–1950), and then moved to South Africa to become head of the Department of Romance Studies and a professor of French at the University of Witwatersrand, Johannesburg, South Africa. In South Africa he became chair of the South African Society for Psychical Research and published various articles on parapsychology in *Tijdschrift voor Parapsychologie* and various publications of the South African Society for Psychical Research. He experimented with **psychokinesis** and with drug-induced states related to **extrasensory perception.**

Sources:

Pleasants, Helene, ed. *Biographical Dictionary of Parapsychology.* New York: Helix Press, 1964.

Vallee, Jacques Francis (1939–)

French scientist and authority on **Unidentified Flying Objects.** He was born September 24, 1939, in Pontoise, France and attended the Sorbonne (B.S. mathematics, 1959), Lille University (M.S. astrophysics, 1961), and Northwestern University (Ph.D. computer science, 1967). He organized a computer company in northern California, and became a member of the editorial board of *Telecommunications Policy.*

While at Northwestern he became an associate of J. Allen Hynek and authored two important works in ufology, *Anatomy of a Phenomenon* (1965) and *Challenge to Science: The UFO Enigma* (1966). Vallee was quickly hailed as one of the most important theorists in the field and was said to be the original of the character "Lacombe" in Steven Spielberg's popular movie *Close Encounters of the Third Kind.*

Several years later, Vallee released *Passport to Magonia* (1969) in which he directed attention to the similarity of UFO reports to folklore. This volume was followed by others in the 1970s which tied some of his speculations concerning the nonphysical nature of UFOs to political conspiracy theories and occultism. *The Invisible College* (1975) and *Messengers of Deceit* (1979) largely marginalized Vallee in the ufological community. There he remained through most of the 1980s, but he returned to the center with *Confrontations* (1990), an account of investigations of UFO-related deaths and various physical evidence cases.

Sources:

Hynek, J. Allen and Jacques Vallee. *The Edge of Reality.* Chicago: Regnery, 1975.

Vallee, Jacques. *Anatomy of a Phenomenon: Unidentified Objects in Space, A Scientific Appraisal.* Chicago: Henry Regnery, 1965.

———. *The Invisible College.* New York: E. P. Dutton, 1975.

———. *Messengers of Deception.* Berkeley, Calif.: And/Or Press, 1979.

———. *Passport to Magonia.* Chicago: Henry Regnery, 1969. Reprint, Chicago: Contemporary Books, 1993.

———. *UFO Chronicles of the Soviet Union.* New York: Ballantine, 1992.

Vallee, Jacques, and Janine Vallee. *Challenge to Science; The UFO Enigma.* Chicago: Henry Regnery, 1966.

Vambéry, Arminius (1832–1913)

Hungarian historian and world traveler who may have communicated to author **Bram Stoker** the facts and legends concerning the real **Prince Dracula** (Vlad V), who supplied the inspiration for Stoker's famous occult thriller. Stoker and Vambéry met at the Beefsteak Club on April 30, 1890, after a performance of Henry Irving in the play *The Dead Heart,* and also two years later at Trinity College, Dublin, where Vambéry was presented with an honorary degree.

Sources:

Adler, Lory, and Richard Dalby. *The Dervish of Windsor Castle.* London: Bachman & Turner, 1979.

Melton, J. Gordon. *The Vampire Book: An Encyclopedia of the Undead.* Detroit: Gale Research, 1994.

Vambéry, Arminius. *The Story of My Struggles: The Memoirs of Arminius Vambéry.* 2 vols. New York, 1904; London: T. F. Unwin, 1905.

Vampire

Russian *vampir,* South Russian *upuir,* probably from the root *pi,* to drain, with the prefix *va,* or *av.* A dead person who returns in spirit form from the grave for the purpose of sucking the blood of living persons, or a living sorcerer who takes a special form for destructive purpose. *Webster's International Dictio-*

nary defines a vampire as "a blood-sucking ghost or reanimated body of a dead person; a soul or re-animated body of a dead person believed to come from the grave and wander about by night sucking the blood of persons asleep, causing their death."

The belief in vampires is an ancient one. It was found in ancient **India, Babylonia, Greece,** and for a time accepted by early Christians. The conception of the vampire was common among Slavonic peoples, especially in the Balkan countries and in Hungary, Bohemia, Moravia, and Silesia.

In these territories from 1730 to 1735, there was a claimed epidemic of vampirism, but it was by no means confined there. In Russia and the Ukraine it was believed that vampires were generally wizards or sorcerers, but in Bulgaria and Serbia it was thought that any corpse over which a cat or a dog jumped or over which a bird flew was liable to become a vampire. In Greece, a vampire was known as a *broncolaia* or *bourkabakos,* which was identified with the Slavonic name for **"werewolf,"** *vlkodlak,* or *vukodlak.* The vampire, too, was often supposed to steal the heart of his victim and to roast it over a slow fire, thus causing interminable amorous longings.

Marks of Vampirism

Vampirism is said to be epidemic in character: where one instance is discovered it is almost invariably followed by several others. It is believed that the victim of a vampire pines away and dies and becomes in turn a vampire after death, and so duly infects others.

After the disinterment of a suspected vampire, various well-known signs are looked for by experienced persons. Thus, if several holes about the breadth of a man's finger are observed in the soil above the grave, the vampire character of its occupant may be suspected. The corpse is usually found with wide-open eyes, ruddy, life-like complexion and lips, a general appearance of freshness, and shows no signs of corruption.

It may also be found that the hair and nails have grown as in life. On the throat, two small livid marks may be observed. The coffin is also very often full of blood, the body has a swollen and gorged appearance, and the shroud is frequently half-devoured. The blood contained in the veins of the corpse is found, on examination, to be in a fluid condition as in life, and the limbs are pliant and have none of the rigidity of death.

Examples of Vampirism

Many tales of vampirism have been recorded. Charles Ferdinand de Schertz, in his work *Magia Posthuma,* printed at Olmutz in 1706, related several stories of apparitions of this sort.

One, among others, was of a herdsman of the village of Blow near the town of Kadam in Bohemia, who visited several persons who all died within eight days.

At last, the inhabitants of Blow dug up the herdsman's body and fixed it in the ground with a stake driven through it. The man, even in this condition, laughed at the action of the people about him and told them they were very obliging to furnish him with a stick with which to defend himself.

The same night, he extricated himself from the stake, frightened several persons by appearing to them, and caused the deaths of many more individuals. He was then delivered into the hands of the hangman, who put him into a cart in order to burn him outside the town. As they went along, the carcass shrieked in the most hideous manner and moved as if it were alive, and upon being again run through with a stake, it gave a loud cry, and a great quantity of fresh blood issued from the wound. At last, the body was burned to ashes.

Augustine Calmet, in his *Dissertation on Vampires* appended to his *Dissertation upon the Apparitions of Angels, Demons, and Ghosts* (English translation, 1759), gave several instances of vampirism:

"It is now about fifteen years since a soldier, who was quartered in the house of a Haidamack peasant, upon the frontiers of Hungary, saw, as he was at the table with his landlord, a stranger come in and sit down by them. The master of the house and the rest of the company were strangely terrified, but the soldier knew not what to make of it. The next day the peasant died, and, upon the soldier's enquiring into the meaning of it, he was told that it was his landlord's father who had been dead and buried above ten years that came and sat down at table, and gave his son notice of his death.

"The soldier soon propagated the story through his regiment, and by this means it reached the general officers, who commissioned the count de Cabreras . . . to make an exact enquiry into the fact. The count, attended by several officers, a surgeon, and a notary, came to the house, and took the deposition of all the family, who unanimously swore that the spectre was the landlord's father, and that all the soldier had said was strictly true. The same was also attested by all the inhabitants of the village.

"In consequence of this the body of the spectre was dug up, and found to be in the same state as if it has been but just dead. . . . The count de Cabreras ordered its head to be cut off, and the corpse to be buried again. He then proceeded to take depositions against other spectres of the same sort, and particularly against a man who had been dead above thirty years, and had made his appearance there several times in his own house at meal-time. At his first visit he had fastened upon the neck of his own brother, and sucked his blood; at his second, he had treated one of his children in the same manner; and the third time, he fastened upon a servant of the family, and all three died upon the spot.

"Upon this evidence, the count gave orders that he should be dug up, and being found, like the first, with his blood in a fluid state, as if he had been alive, a great nail was drove through his temples, and he was buried again. The count ordered a third to be burnt, who had been dead above sixteen years, and was found guilty of murdering two of his own children by sucking their blood.

"The gentleman who acquainted me with all these particulars, had them from the count de Cabreras himself, at Fribourg in Brisgau, in the year 1730."

Other cases alluded to by Calmet are as follows:

"In the part of Hungary . . . on the other side of the Tibiscus, . . . the people named *Heydukes* have a notion that there are dead persons, called by them *vampires,* which suck the blood of the living, so as to make them fall away visibly to skin and bones, while the carcasses themselves, like leeches, are filled with blood to such a degree that it comes out at all the apertures of their body. This notion has lately been confirmed by several facts.

"About five years ago, an Heyduke, named Arnold Paul, an inhabitant of Medreiga, was killed by a cart full of hay that fell upon him. About thirty days after his death, four persons died suddenly, with all the symptoms usually attending those who are killed by *vampires.* It was then remembered that this Arnold Paul had frequently told a story of his having been tormented by a Turkish *vampire,* in the neighbourhood of Cassova, upon the borders of Turkish Servia (for the notion is that those who have been passive *vampires* in their life-time become active ones after death; or, in other words, that those who have had their blood sucked become suckers in their turn) but that he had been cured by eating some of the earth upon the *vampire's* grave, and by rubbing himself with his blood. This precaution, however, did not hinder him from being guilty himself after his death; for, upon digging up his corpse forty days after his burial, he was found to have all the marks of an arch-vampire. His body was fresh and ruddy, his hair, beard, and nails were grown, and his veins were full of fluid blood, which ran from all parts of his body upon the shroud that he was buried in. The *hadnagy,* or bailiff of the village, who was present at the digging up of the corpse, and was very expert in the whole business of vampirism, ordered a sharp stake to be drove quite through the body of the deceased, and to let it pass through his heart, which is attended with a hideous cry from the carcass, as if it had been alive. This ceremony being performed, they cut off the head, and burnt the body to ashes. After this, they proceeded in the same manner with the four other persons that died of vampirism, lest they also should be troublesome. But all these executions could not hinder this dreadful prodigy from appearing again last year, at the distance of five years from its first breaking out. In the space of three months, seventeen persons of different ages and sexes died of vampirism, some without any previous illness, and others after languishing two or three days. Among others, it was said, that a girl, named Stanoska, . . . went to bed in perfect health, but awoke in the middle of the night, trembling, and crying out that the son of the Heyduke Millo, who died about nine weeks before, had almost strangled her while she was asleep. From that time she fell into a languishing state, and died at three days' end. Her evidence against Millo's son was looked upon as a proof of his being a *vampire,* and, upon digging up his body, he was found to be such.

"At the consultation of the principal inhabitants of the place, . . . it was considered how it was possible that the plague of vampirism should break out afresh, after the precautions that had been taken some years before: and, at last, it was found out that the original offender, Arnold Paul, had not only destroyed the four persons mentioned above, but had killed several beasts, which the late *vampires,* and particularly the son of Millo, had fed upon. Upon this foundation a resolution was taken to dig up all the persons that had died within a certain time. Out of forty were found seventeen, with all the evident tokens of vampirism; and they had all stakes drove through their hearts, their heads cut off, their bodies burnt, and their ashes thrown into the river."

Methods of Extirpation

The commonest methods of extirpation of vampires are beheading the suspected corpse, taking out the heart, impaling the corpse with a white-thorn stake (in Russia an aspen), and burning it. Sometimes more than one or all of these precautions is taken.

Instances are on record where the graves of as many as thirty or forty persons have been disturbed during the course of an epidemic of suspected vampirism and their occupants impaled or beheaded.

Persons who dread the visits or attacks of a vampire sleep with a wreath made of garlic round the neck, as garlic is supposed to be especially obnoxious to the vampire.

When impaled, the vampire is usually said to emit a dreadful cry, but it has been pointed out that intestinal gas may be forced through the throat by the entry of the stake into the body, and that this may account for the sound.

The method of discovering a vampire's grave in Serbia was to place a virgin boy upon a coal-black stallion which had never served a mare and to mark the spot that the horse refused to pass. An officer quartered in Wallachia wrote to Calmet, giving him an instance of this method.

A Bulgarian belief was that a wizard or sorcerer may entrap a vampire by placing some food for which the vampire has a partiality in a bottle. When the vampire enters in the shape of fluff, the sorcerer can seal up the flask and throw it into the fire.

Scientific Views of Vampirism

The British custom of piercing a suicide's body with a stake would appear to be a remnant of the belief in vampirism. Such beliefs were also to be seen in the Polynesian *tii,* the Malayan *hantu penyardin* (a dog-headed water demon), and the *kephn* of the Karens, which devoured human souls.

The English anthropologist E. B. Tylor considered vampires to be "causes conceived in spiritual form to account for specific facts of wasting disease." The Russian folklorist Alexander N. Afansyev regarded them as thunder gods and spirits of the storm, who sleep during winter in cloud coffins and rise again in spring.

Calmet's difficulty in accepting vampires was that he could not understand how a spirit could leave its grave and return there with matter in the form of blood, leaving no evidence that the surface of the earth above the grave had been stirred. But this view might be combated by the theory of the precipitation of matter.

In modern times, it is easy to understand how individuals in an unrecognized condition of cataleptic trance might have been prematurely buried alive and upon regaining consciousness have struggled to escape their horrible plight. Their bodies would have exhibited many of the signs associated with vampires.

It is now also generally known that some individuals suffer from a morbid fascination with human blood, and it would have been easy in the past to associate such unnatural appetite with vampirism. The infamous Countess Elizabeth Bathory of Transylvania (d. 1614) was reputed to have murdered nearly 700 young women in the belief that their blood would keep her young.

No doubt the observed activities of the various types of vampire bats (*Desmodus Rufus, Didemus Yungi, Diphylla Caudata, Desmodus Rotunda*) in sucking blood from cattle and horses have helped to spread legends of vampires. The vampire bat drinks 20 ccs of blood per day and has been known to attack human beings. It also spreads rabies, thus enhancing stories of a vampire plague.

Psychic Theories of Vampires

Some individuals seem to have the ability to draw some kind of psychic energy from others. Every stage performer or public speaker is aware of the rapport which exists between performer and audience, and many have become expert at gaining confidence and power through some instinctive techniques of centralizing and transforming psychic or nervous energy.

The common experience of **out-of-the-body travel** or **astral projection** has sometimes been associated with visits to other individuals, as well as contacts with frightening **elementals** on the astral plane. Some occultists appear to have mastered techniques by which they can astrally project, and visit their victims while asleep and drain their vitality from them.

During the nineteenth century, the French Spiritualist **Z. J. Piérart** attempted to reconcile the theory of premature burial with astral projection by those who died after being buried alive. He wrote:

"Poor dead cataleptics, buried as if really dead in cold and dry spots where morbid causes are incapable of effecting the destruction of their bodies, the astral spirit enveloping itself with a fluidic ethereal body, is prompted to quit the precincts of its tomb and to exercise on living bodies acts peculiar to physical life, especially that of nutrition, the result of which, by a mysterious link between soul and body which spiritualistic science will some day explain, is forwarded to the material body lying still within the tomb, and the latter is thus helped to perpetuate its vital existence."

Adolphe d'Assier, in his book *Posthumous Humanity* (1887), admitted that the body of the vampire may be dead but the spirit earthbound and obsessed with the idea that the physical body must be saved from dissolution. Consequently the dense astral body feeds on human victims and, by some mysterious process, conveys the blood into the tomb.

Both speculations furnish explanations of the attestation of numerous ancient chronicles that fresh blood was found in the exhumed and uncorrupted body of dead people suspected of vampirism.

Following the occult boom of the 1950s, **Bram Stoker**'s powerful but much neglected masterpiece *Dracula* was taken up again, examined by critics and found to be as full of vitality as during Stoker's own lifetime. Almost by contagion, it has generated a plethora of horror movies, plays, and other vampire thrillers.

In Britain, the **Dracula Society,** with its general interest in Gothic themes, pioneered tourist expeditions to Transylvania, and in Stoker's Ireland, a Bram Stoker Society was founded to honor a much neglected Irishman. Through the 1980s and 1990s, the most active organization was the Count Dracula Fan Club, headquartered in New York City. However, in 1999, the club announced its closing.

Much of the interest in vampires has also been carried by fan clubs that have grown out of television series. "Dark Shadows" fandom, from the 1960s, had retained its vitality for over 30 years and still attracts 400-600 members to its annual meeting. Another set of fan clubs sprung up from "Forever Knight," the series featuring a vampire policeman from Toronto. As the century ended, vampire fandom received an unexpected boost from the successful series, "Buffy the Vampire Slayer."

In the 1990s, interest in vampires shifted largely to the Internet where thousands of sites cover all aspects of the vampire world. Over 2000 sites alone were devoted just to the "Buffy the Vampire Slayer" show in 1999. *Vampire Junction,* formerly a fan magazine, was one of the first to make the transition to the Internet and emerged as one of the most complete guides to vampires. (See also **Dracula; Magia Posthuma; Monsters**)

Sources:

Auerbach, Nina. *Our Vampires, Ourselves.* Chicago: University of Chicago Press, 1995.

Barber, Paul. *Vampires, Burial, & Death: Folklore & Reality.* New Haven, Conn.: Yale University Press, 1988.

Burton, Sir Richard. *Vikram and the Vampire, or Tales of Hindu Devilry.* London: Tilston & Edwards, 1832. Reprint, New York: Dover Publications, 1969.

Calmet, Augustine. *Dissertations Upon the Apparitions of Angels, Demons, and Ghosts, and Concerning . . . Vampires.* Paris: De Burel'aine, 1746. Reprint, London, 1759.

———. *The Phantom World; or, The History and Philosophy of Spirits, Apparitions, & Co.* 2 vols. London: Richard Bentley, 1850; Philadelphia: A. Hart, 1850.

De Schertz, Charles F. *Magia Posthuma.* Olmutz, 1706.

Dresser, Norine. *American Vampires: Fans, Victims & Practitioners.* New York: W. W. Norton, 1989.

Dundas, Alan. *The Vampire: A Casebook.* Madison: University of Wisconsin Press, 1998.

Ennemoser, Joseph. *The History of Magic.* 2 vols. 1854. Reprint, New York: University Books, 1970.

Frayling, Christopher, ed. *Vampyres: From Lord Byron to Count Dracula.* London: Faber and Faber, 1991.

Glut, Donald F. *The Dracula Book.* Metuchen, N.J.: Scarecrow Press, 1975.

Harenburg, Johann C. *Von Vampyren.* N.p., 1739.

Hartmann, Franz. *Premature Burial.* London: Swann Sonnenschein, 1896.

Hertz, Wilhelm. *Der Werwolf.* Stuttgart, 1862.

Introvigne, Massimo. *La stripe de Dracula: Indagine sul vampirismpo dall'antichita ai nostro giorni.* Milan: Arnoldo Mondadari Editore, 1997.

Mackenzie, Andrew. *Dracula Country.* London: Arthur Barker, 1977.

Marigny, Jean. *Vampires: Restless Creatures of the Night.* New York: Abrams, 1994.

McNally, Raymond T. *Dracula Was a Woman.* New York: McGraw-Hill, 1983.

McNally, Raymond T., and Radu Florescu. *In Search of Dracula: A True History of Dracula and Vampire Legends.* New York: New York Graphic Society, 1972. Boston: Houghton Mifflin, 1994.

Mannhardt, W. *Über Vampirismus.* (see vol. 4 of *Zeitschrift für Deutsche Mythologie und Sittenkunde*) Göttingen, 1858.

Masters, Anthony. *The Natural History of the Vampire.* London: Ruper Hart-Davis, 1972; London: Mayflower 1974.

Melton, J. Gordon. *The Vampire Book: The Encyclopedia of the Undead.* 2nd edition. Detroit: Visible Ink Press, 1999.

———. *The Vampire Gallery.* Detroit: Visible Ink Press, 1998.

———. *Video Hound's Vampires on Video.* Detroit, Visible Ink Press, 1996.

Miller, Elizabeth. *Dracula: Sense and Nonsense.* Westcliffe-on-Sea, UK: Desert Island Books, 1998.

———. *Dracula: The Shade and the Shadow.* Westcliffe-on-Sea, UK: Desert Island Books, 1998.

———. *Reflection on Dracula: Ten Essays.* White Rock, BC: Transylvanian Press, 1997.

Perkowski, Jan I., ed. *Vampires of the Slavs.* Cambridge, Mass.: Slavica Press, 1976.

Ralston, W. R. S. *Russian Folk Tales.* London: Smith, Elder, 1873.

———. *The Songs of the Russian People.* London, 1872. Reprint, New York: Haskell House, 1970.

Ranfft, Michael. *De Masticatione Mortuorum in Tumulis.* Leipzig, 1728.

Rickles, Laurence A. *The Vampire Lectures.* Minneapolis: University of Minnesota Press, 1999.

Rohr, Philip. *De Masticatione Mortuorum.* N.p., 1679.

Ronay, Gabriel. *The Dracula Myth.* London: W. H. Auden, 1972; London: Pan 1975.

Roth, Phyllis A. *Bram Stoker.* Boston: Twayne, 1982.

Senf, Carol A. *The Vampire in Nineteenth-Century English Literature.* Bowling Green, Ohio: Bowling Green State University Popular Press, 1988.

Shepard, Leslie. *The Dracula Book of Great Vampire Stories.* New York: Citadel, 1977.

Summers, Montague. *The Vampire, His Kith and Kin.* London: Kegan, Paul, 1928; New York: University Books, 1960.

———. *The Vampire in Europe.* London: Kegan, Paul, 1929; New York: University Books, 1962.

Thompson, R. Campbell. *The Devils and Evil Spirits of Babylonia.* 2 vols. London, 1903–04.

Underwood, Peter. *The Vampire's Bedside Companion: The Amazing World of Vampires in Fact and Fiction.* London: Leslie Frewin, 1972.

Wright, Dudley. *The Book of Vampires.* 2d ed. London, 1924; Causeway Books, 1973.

Zopfius, Johan Heinrich. *Dissertatio de Vampiris Seruiensibus.* Halle, 1733.

Vampire Information Exchange

Vampire interest group founded by Eric Held and Dorothy Nixon in 1978. In 1979 they began a newsletter which Held has continued over the years as Nixon moved on to other interests. Held has also published an annual Calendar of Vampire Events and a bibliography of vampire books for its members. For information on membership, write to Eric Held, Dir., P.O. Box 290328, Brooklyn, NY 11229-0328.

Sources:

Held, Eric. *The Vampire Bibliography of Fiction and Nonfiction.* Brooklyn, N.Y.: Vampire Information Exchange, 1992.

———. *1993 Calendar of Vampire Events.* Brooklyn, N.Y.: Vampire Information Exchange, 1992.

Melton, J. Gordon. *The Vampire Book: An Encyclopedia of the Undead.* 2nd edition. Detroit: Gale Research, 1999.

The Vampire Journal

Former publication devoted to the subject of **vampires** that served as the organ of the now defunct Dracula and Company, a vampire interest group headquartered in the New Orleans suburb of Metairie, Louisiana.

Vampire Quarterly (Magazine)

Magazine devoted to the subject of **vampires** formerly published from Toms River, New Jersey.

Vampire Studies

Founded in Chicago in 1977 as the Vampire Studies Society by Martin V. Riccardo, the organization was the first vampire fan club to use the word "vampire" in its name (there had previously been several organizations built around Dracula). For several years the society published a *Journal of Vampirism.* The word "society" was dropped in 1990 and Vampire Studies now exists as a correspondence network and information clearinghouse for people interested in all aspects of vampire lore. Those interested may contact Riccardo at P.O. Box 151, Berwyn, IL 60402-0151.

Sources:

"The Lure of Martin V. Riccardo." Special issue of *The Vampire Information Exchange Newsletter* 53 (April 1991).

Melton, J. Gordon. *The Vampire Book: An Encyclopedia of the Undead.* 2nd edition. Detroit: Gale Research, 1999.

Riccardo, Martin V. *Liquid Dreams of Vampires.* St. Paul: Llewellyn Publications, 1997.

———. *The Lure of the Vampire.* Chicago: Adams Press, 1983.

———. *Vampires Unearthed.* New York: Garland, 1983.

Van Bruhesen, Peter (d. 1571)

A Dutch doctor and astrologer who died at Bruges. He published in that town in 1550 a *Grand and Perpetual Almanack* in which he scrupulously indicated by the tenets of judicial **astrology** the correct days for bathing, shaving, haircutting, and so forth. The work caused offense to a certain magistrate of Bruges, a barber by profession, with the result that there appeared against Bruhesen's volume another *Grand and Perpetual Almanack,* with the flippant subtitle *a scourge for empirics and charlatans.* This squib was published by a rival doctor François Rapaert, but Peter Haschaerts, a surgeon and protagonist of astrological science, warmly defended Bruhesen in his *Astrological Buckler.*

Van Busschbach, J(ohan) G(eorge) (1896–1974)

Dutch Inspector of Schools who was winner of the first McDougall Award for Distinguished Research in Parapsychology for his work in investigating ESP between teachers and pupils in American schools. Van Busschbach was born July 3, 1896, in Amsterdam. He was a primary school teacher (1916–21), teacher in psychology (1927–39), director of training school for teachers (1940–49), and inspector of schools, Amsterdam, (1944–61). He was a charter member of the **Parapsychological Association,** a council member of the Parapsychologisch Onderzoek (Amsterdam Foundation for Parapsychological Studies), and a member of the Studievereniging voor Psychical Research (Netherlands Society for Parapsychology).

Sources:

Berger, Arthur S., and Joyce Berger. *The Encyclopedia of Parapsychology and Psychical Research.* New York: Paragon House, 1991.

Pleasants, Helene, ed. *Biographical Dictionary of Parapsychology.* New York: Helix Press, 1964.

Van Busschbach, J. G. "A Further Report on an Investigation of ESP in School Children." *Journal of Parapsychology* 19 (1955).

———. "An Investigation of ESP Between Teacher and Pupils in American Schools." *Journal of Parapsychology* 20 (June 1956).

———. "An Investigation of Extrasensory Perception in School Children." *Journal of Parapsychology* 17 (1953).

Van de Castle, Robert L(eon) (1927–)

Clinical psychologist and parapsychologist. He was born on November 16, 1927, at Rochester, New York, and studied at Syracuse University (B.A., 1951), the University of Missouri (M.A., 1953), and the University of North Carolina (Ph.D., 1959). While in North Carolina he was a research associate at the Parapsychology Laboratory at Duke University (1954–55). Following graduation in 1959 he joined the faculty in psychology at the University of Denver where he remained until he became the director of the Sleep and Dream Laboratory at the University of Virginia in 1967. He is now a psychologist at the Blue Ridge Hospital in Charlottesville, Virginia.

While in Denver he did research with members of the Cuna tribe as part of research on whether people from a nontechnological society would score significantly on **ESP** tests. He went on to conduct dream research with Calvin Itall at the Institute of Dream Research in Miami, publishing a joint work *The Content Analysis of Dreams* (1966). He also studied personality correlates in extrasensory perception and **psychokinesis,** and conducted experiments relating psychological tests to extrasensory ability, on grants from the Parapsychology Foundation.

He was a charter member of the **Parapsychological Association,** since 1969 a council member, and was elected its president in 1970.

Sources:

Berger, Arthur S., and Joyce Berger. *The Encyclopedia of Parapsychology and Psychical Research.* New York: Paragon House, 1991.

Pleasants, Helene, ed. *Biographical Dictionary of Parapsychology.* New York: Helix Press, 1964.

Van de Castle, Robert L. "Development and Validation of a Perceptual Maturity Scale Using Figure Preferences." *Journal of Consultative Psychology* 29 (1965).

———. "An Exploratory Study of Some Personality Correlates Associated with PK Performance." *Journal* of the American Society for Psychical Research 52 (1958).

———. "The Facilitation of ESP Through Hypnosis." *American Journal of Clinical & Experimental Hypnosis* 12 (1969).

———. "An Investigation of Psi Abilities Among the Cuna Indians of Panama." *Journal of Parapsychology* 38 (June 1974).

———. *Our Dreaming Mind.* New York: Ballantine, 1995.

———. "Psi Abilities in Primitive Groups." *Proceedings* of the Parapsychological Association 7 (1970).

Vandermeulen Spirit Indicator

One of various devices invented to facilitate communication with spirits through mechanical means. It consisted of two glass prisms—one plain, the other resinous—fixed face-to-face on a board. Between them hung a very light triangle of wire. The prisms were connected to the positive and negative poles of a dry bell battery.

If the hanging triangle swung out and touched the positive wire, the circuit was closed and the bell rang. The spirits were expected to generate electricity in the prisms. If this was done, the hanging triangle wired to the negative pole would be repelled by the negative prism and attracted to the positive wire. The bell would ring, which was taken as an indication that a spirit desired to communicate, and the observers would rush to the **ouija board** to obtain the message.

The young inventor died in 1930 before his apparatus could be tested properly, but it was revived by a Mr. Rutot, a Belgian professor and a member of the Royal Academy of Sciences. Rutot claimed that by means of the apparatus he had been able to contact the dead inventor. The apparatus, which came to be known as **Rutot's Spirit Indicator,** was described in *Revue Métapsychique* (May–June, 1930, p. 256), and Rutot's own experiences were published in the *Bulletin du Conseil de Recherches Métapsychiques de Belgique* (July 1930). An English-language description of the apparatus, with detailed instructions for construction, was published by Robert J. Strong in his book *Spiritual Engineering* (1931).

For a detailed report of tests, with photographs, see the chapter "Rutot's Triangles" in *Laboratory Investigations into Psychic Phenomena* by Hereward Carrington (n.d.). It was not possible for Carrington to confirm the "instrumental communication with the dead" claimed by Rutot. Mechanical faults were not ruled out, and it was suggested that Rutot's claimed results may have been due to experimenters with mediumistic or telekinetic powers. (See also **electronic voice phenomenon**)

Van Eeden, Frederik (1860–1932)

Dutch physician, author, and poet, who was also actively interested in psychiatry and psychical research and was acquainted with **Frederic William Henry Myers.** He conducted important research with the non-professional British medium **Rosina Thompson** and also made valuable contributions to the study of dreams. He coined the term **"lucid dreams"** to denote dreams in which the sleeper is aware of dreaming, i.e., some degree of waking consciousness persists in the dream state, often a preliminary to **out-of-the-body** (OOB) experiences. He appears to have had some OOB experience himself, since he described it in one of his novels (*The Bride of Dreams,* 1918). He also obtained **cross-correspondences** between his own dreams and the trance utterances of "Nelly," Thompson's control, while Van Eeden was in Holland and Thompson in England.

Sources:

Pleasants, Helene, ed. *Biographical Dictionary of Parapsychology*. New York: Helix Press, 1964.

Van Eeden, Frederik. "A Study of Dreams." *Proceedings* of the Society for Psychical Research 26 (1913).

Vanga

The unenrolled members of the Ndembo secret society of the Lower Congo. (See **Ndembo**)

Van Gelder Kunz, Dora (1904–1999)

American psychic and leader in the **Theosophical Society.** She was born on April 28, 1904, in Java, where she grew up on her father's sugar plantation. Here she saw and communed with **fairies,** unaware that this was a special psychic faculty. At the age of eleven, she left Java for Australia, where she studied with an Anglican priest who also possessed unusual psychic abilities. At the age of twenty-two, she married an American and moved to the United States, where she became president of a corporation concerned with teaching materials, while her husband became head of an educational foundation.

Van Gelder had never been a professional paid medium nor publicized her psychic abilities but instead worked unobtrusively with physicians on difficult cases for diagnostic and healing purposes. She showed a natural ability to see the psychic energy patterns in human beings and their relationship to conditions of health and disease. She also claimed the unusual ability of being able to predict specific illness, sometimes as early as eighteen months in advance.

She said she never lost her ability to commune with fairy life. When she was a young woman she wrote about her fairy experiences. This early manuscript was revised and published as *The Real World of Fairies* (1977). She stated that fairy life is still apparent, but becoming less evident with the growing pollution of cities and urban life. She even reported seeing fairies in Central Park, New York.

Van Gelder Kunz died on August 25, 1999.

Sources:

Van Gelder, Dora. *The Real World of Fairies.* Wheaton, Ill.: Theosophical Publishing House, 1977.

Van Helmont, Jean Baptiste (1577–1644)

Belgian physician, chemist, and physiologist, whose research was associated with occult theories. He was born to an aristocratic family in Brussels. Studying at Louvain, he attained early distinction in mathematics, lecturing on physics at the age of 17. Before he was 22, he had read Hippocrates and the Greek and Arabian authors, had become eminent in the doctrines of Aristotle and Galen, and had practiced medicine, according to Vopiscus and Plempius.

In the year 1599, he received his Ph.D. in medicine. After this, he spent some years in the practice of medicine, but meeting a follower of **Paracelsus,** he became interested in the theories of chemical medicine to such a degree that he retired to the castle of Vilvorde, near Brussels, to spend the rest of his life in the study of experimental chemistry, on which he wrote various treatises, becoming famous throughout Europe for his scientific knowledge.

He revolutionized medicine as known in his day, turning aside from the theories of Galen and the Arabs, and creating an epoch in the history of physiology, being the first to recognize the functions of the stomach and its relation to the other organs of the body.

Van Helmont's many and varied experiments led him to deal with aerial fluids, to which he gave the name of gas—carbonic acid gas being his discovery—and it is said that without him the chemistry of steel in all probability would have been unknown to science.

Van Helmont is remembered as an alchemist more than a scientist. **Alchemy,** with its visions of the **elixir of life** and the **philosophers' stone,** presented itself to him as another field of experiment and research. Although he never pretended to the art of making the transmuting powder, he testified his belief in the **transmutation** of metals, claiming to have seen the experiment performed many times.

Among other things he became a firm believer in mineral and human magnetism, anticipating **Franz Anton Mesmer** in almost the very terms of the later exponent of the theory, and basing his argument on the observed sympathy or antagonism that seems to spontaneously arise between individuals and the influence exerted by a firm will over a weak imagination.

In 1609, he retired to Vilvorde, near Brussels, and devoted himself to medical practice and chemical experiments. He declined to leave his retirement, although his fame brought him flattering invitations and offers from the Emperor and the Elector Palatine. Almost unknown to his neighbors, he attended anyone stricken by illness without accepting any fees for his services.

His published writings included: *De Magnetica Vulnerum naturali et Legitima Curatione* (1621), *De aquis Leondiensibus medicatis* (1624), *Opuscula Medica inaudita* (1641), and *Febrium doctrina inaudita* (1642). Some of these were translated into Dutch, French, and German. English translations of his tracts include: *A Ternary of Paradoxes; The Magnetick Cure of Wounds, The Nativity of Tartar in Wine, The Image of God in Man* (1650), and *Deliramenta Catarrhi: or the Incongruities, Impossibilities and Absurdities couched under the vulgar opinion of Defluxions* (1650).

He died December 30, 1644.

Van Hoof, Mary Ann (1909–1984)

Mary Ann Van Hoof, who reported **apparitions of the Virgin Mary** at **Necedah,** Wisconsin, for a quarter of a century beginning in 1949, was born Mary Ann Bieder on July 31, 1909, in Philadelphia, Pennsylvania. She grew up in Kenosha County, Wisconsin, in a German-speaking family and attended school only through the eighth grade. As a young woman she married Godfried Van Hoof, and together they had eight children. They moved to Necedah, Wisconsin, in 1942.

Van Hoof had her initial brief apparition of the Virgin on November 12, 1949, which happened to be the anniversary of the last apparition of a set of appearances by the Virgin that had occurred the previous year in Lipa, Philippines. The following spring, beginning on April 7 (Good Friday), Van Hoof experienced a set of apparitions that called for a large shrine to be established for Marian devotion. Subsequent apparitions occurred on May 28 (Pentecost Sunday), May 29 and 30, and June 6 (Trinity Sunday). By the time of the June apparition, many had heard of Van Hoof seeing the Virgin, and a large crowd gathered. With the announcement that Mary would return on August 15 (marked by Roman Catholics as the feast day of the Assumption of Mary into heaven) and October 1 (the feast day honoring the rosary), the story became news and articles began to appear in newspapers throughout the Midwest.

In the meantime, the local Roman Catholic priest became aware of the apparitions and sent an initial report to his bishop in La Crosse, Wisconsin. The bishop issued an initial statement decrying any sensationalism associated with the apparitions and launched a study of Van Hoof's claims. Van Hoof believed the apparition told her the American Catholics must rededicate themselves to prayer and peity, or the Korean War would be the beginning of the end for America. She also indicated that the Soviets would invade the United States and Alaska would be "the first stepping stone." Prior to the August apparition, the diocesan paper called them into question. In spite of many bishops discouraging the faithful from attending, crowds estimated in the tens of thousands were present for the last two apparitions of 1950. Over the next few years the apparitions continued, and not only did people travel long distances to be present, but several hundred relocated their residence to Necedah. An organization emerged and the shrine that began at the location of the apparitions grew into a set of related shrines.

In 1955 the bishop gave a more definitive ruling. He suggested that Van Hoof's claims to supernatural visitation were false and prohibited all religious worship at the shrine, now named after Mary's appearance as the Shrine of Our Lady of the Holy Rosary, Mediatrix of Peace. Van Hoof and her supporters were disappointed but continued in hope of a reversal of the ruling. Reminiscent of the apparition of **Catherine Labouré** in 1830, in 1957 Van Hoof was shown the design of a medal for the unity of church, home, and school, which was later struck and distributed.

Finally, in 1975, the bishop of La Crosse placed Van Hoof and her followers under an interdict, one step short of excommunication. They were denied access to all sacraments except confession. The interdict did not stop work at the shrine. Two years later Van Hoof announced plans to build a large sanctuary on her property, which she had inherited when her husband died in 1960.

In 1979, the final break with the Roman Catholic Church came as Van Hoof developed a relationship with Edward Michael Stehlik, the archbishop of a small independent church, the American National Catholic Church. She also pushed ahead with plans to build a home for infants and organized an order of nuns. Stehlik consecrated the shrine, which had grown into a sizable place of pilgrimage, but two years later Stehlik left the shrine. He denounced Van Hoof as a fraud and returned to the Roman Catholic Church. The scandal accompanying Stehlik's departure hurt Van Hoof, but did not affect many who had come to support her apparitions. Her visions of the Virgin continued, the work of the shrine grew, and several books appeared with texts of the apparitions and accounts of Van Hoof by her supporters.

In 1978, Van Hoof married Raymond Hirt. By this time, a pattern of pilgrimages to the shrine on the anniversaries of the 1950 apparitions had been established. Van Hoof died on March 18, 1984. She was buried at the shrine her visions inspired.

Sources:

Revelations and Messages as Given to Mary Ann Van Hoof. 2 vols. Necedah, Wis.: For My God and My Country, Inc., 1971, 1978.

Swan, Henry. *My Work at Necedah.* 4 vols. Necedah, Wis.: For My God and My Country, Inc., 1959.

Van Peursen, C(ornelis) A(nthonie) (1920–)

Dutch professor of philosophy who has written on parapsychology. He was born July 8, 1920, at Rotterdam, Netherlands. His educational career was interrupted by World War II but he completed his doctorate in 1948 at the University of Leiden. After several years with the Netherlands Committee for the United Nations Educational, Scientific, and Cultural Organization (UNESCO) (1948–50), he taught successively at the University of Utrecht (1950–53), the University of Groningen (1953–60), and, since 1960, at the University of Leiden. He has shown an interest in psychical research and was a member of the editorial board of a Dutch parapsychology journal.

Sources:

Pleasants, Helene, ed. *Biographical Dictionary of Parapsychology.* New York: Helix Press, 1964.

Van Peursen, C. A. *Body, Soul, Spirit: A Survey of the Body-Mind Problem.* Translated by Hubert H. Hoskins. New York: Oxford University Press, 1966.

———. "Parapsychologie en Wijsgerige Bezinning" (Parapsychology and philosophical reflection). *Tijdschrift voor Parapsychologie* 1–3 (1959).

———. *The Strategy of Culture.* n.p.: North-Holland Publishing, 1974.

Van Praagh, James (ca. 1960–)

James Van Praagh, a Spiritualist **medium** and author of two best-selling books on his experiences with psychic reality, was born into a Catholic family in Bayside, New York, around 1960. As a youth he attended Sacred Heart School. Responding to his mother's wish that he become a priest, he entered a junior seminary, Eymard Preparatory School in Hyde Park, New York. He stayed only one year, having concluded that neither the priesthood nor the Roman Catholic Church were for him. He completed his high school years in a public school.

As a child, Van Praagh had a variety of psychic experiences. One in particular stood out. At the age of eight, he had a vision of a giant hand above his bed one evening. He interpreted it as the Hand of God and from that time forward his belief in God never wavered. Also, on the first anniversary of singer Janis Joplin's death he tried to contact her. Sitting before a candle, he called her spirit to manifest and immediately afterward the flame bent in a most unusual manner.

In 1978 Van Praagh left New York to attend San Francisco State University, where he majored in broadcasting. He hoped for a career in Hollywood as a screenwriter. Following his graduation in 1982, he moved to Los Angeles and took a menial job as he began working his way up. A colleague at his workplace invited him to visit Spiritualist medium Brian Hurst, who told him that one day he would also be a medium. He was intrigued enough with the prediction that he began to pick up books on psychic development and find ways to hone his skills. Within a year he was regularly receiving calls from friends and acquaintances asking him for advice.

Within a short time, he was spending so much of his time doing readings for people who valued his talents that he was forced to make a choice to either drop his spiritual work or his plans for a Hollywood career. He chose to continue with his spirit contact and soon emerged as a Spiritualist medium. Over the years he gave private readings, conducted many development classes, and traveled frequently. He founded Spiritual Horizons in Los Angeles to coordinate his activities.

In 1997, Van Praagh took a step upward with the publication of his first book, *Talking to Heaven.* The book became a best-seller and he became a public personality as a result of the subsequent radio and television appearances. It was followed by a sequel, *Reaching to Heaven* (1999), which also became a best-seller. Both books recount some of his more successful experiences of spirit contact, discuss the view of the universe they suggest, and offer means for individuals to develop their own **clairvoyance** and mediumistic abilities.

Sources:

Van Praagh, James. *Reaching to Heaven: A Spiritual Journey through Life and Death.* New York: E. P. Dutton, 1999.

———. *Talking to Heaven: A Medium's Message on Life After Death.* New York: E. P. Dutton, 1997.

Van Tassel, George W. (1910–1978)

Early **flying saucer** contactee and author of the pioneering flying saucer volume *I Rode in a Flying Saucer* (1952). As people responded to his claims of extraterrestrial contact and other **contactees** emerged, Van Tassel organized the **Giant Rock Space Convention,** held annually at Giant Rock Airport, near Yucca Valley, California. Van Tassel was proprietor of the airport and had some background in aeronautics.

Van Tassel was born on March 11, 1910, in Jefferson, Ohio. He went into aviation as a young man and worked for both Howard Hughes and Lockheed. He moved to the desert in 1947 where he opened a restaurant, an airport, and a dude ranch. In 1952 he began to receive psychic messages from extraterrestrials, primarily from a group of people who made up what was called the Ashtar Command. The Ashtar Command operated very much like the **Masters** of theosophical traditions, but were seen as authorities in this solar system.

Over the years Van Tassel claimed to have continued contact with the Ashtar Command telepathically. He often went into a trance in his circle of friends and communicated messages allegedly from **UFO** entities. Such communications were published in his journal, *Proceedings of the College of Universal Wisdom,* and became the basis for future books.

He constructed a round domed building called an "Integraton" at Giant Rock, based on instructions from his outer space contacts. The Integraton was designed to assist the development of antigravity and time travel. The Integraton was never finished.

Van Tassel also published *Into this World and Out Again; a modern proof of the origin of humanity and its retrogression from the original creation of man. Verified by the Holy Bible. Revelations received through thought communication* (1956).

Van Tassel died February 9, 1978, after a sudden heart attack. The work of completing the Integraton was continued by an associate designated as successor by Van Tassel in 1977 and the building was later purchased by the Christology Church, P.O. Box 4648, San Diego, CA 92104. The work of his **College of Universal Wisdom** was continued by Van Tassel's widow, Doris Van Tassell.

Sources:

Barker, Gray. *Gray Barker at Giant Rock.* Clarksburg, W.V.: Saucerian Publications, 1976.

Clark, Jerome. *The Emergence of a Phenomenon: UFOs from the Beginning through 1959. The UFO Encyclopedia.* Vol. 2. Detroit: Omnigraphics, 1992.

Van Tassel, George. *The Council of Seven Lights.* Los Angeles: DeVorss & Company, 1958.

———. *I Rode in a Flying Saucer.* Los Angeles: New Age Publishing, 1952.

Van Vuurde, Wilhelm (1909– ?)

Wilhelm van Vuurde, a famous subject of parapsychological research, was born and grew up in the Netherlands. As a young man he attempted to escape the coming war by migrating to South Africa, but wound up a prisoner of the Japanese. While a prisoner he suffered from extreme malnutrition and lost some of his sight. After the war he settled in South Africa.

Van Vuurde believed he had a talent for wakening himself at any unknown and randomly chosen times. He developed an experiment to test himself using two clocks, one of which would be set before he went to sleep at an unknown position and the other set to run but with a string that could be pulled to stop the clock upon awakening. The next morning the two clocks could be checked to see if the times coincided. He tested himself over 200 times between 1951 and 1954 and published a report on his effort in 1956. As a result of his claim, A. E. H. Bleksley of the **South African Society for Psychical Research** conducted a series of experiments between 1959 and 1967, which produced a spectacular level of positive results. During the 1980s van Vuurde moved back to the Netherlands and has most recently been involved in a new set of experiments with Jeff C. Jacobs of the Sychronicity Research Unit. Van Vuurde has thus emerged as one of a very few subjects who have been able consistently to produce positive results over a long period of time in repeated experiments.

Sources:

Bleksley, A. E. H. "An Experiment of Long-Distance ESP During Sleep." *Journal of Parapsychology* 27 (1963): 1.

Jacobs, Jeff C. "Psi-Guided Awakening from Sleep 1: The Original Experiments of W. Van Vuurde." *Journal* of the Society for Psychical Research 53 (1985): 159.

Van Vuurde, Wilhelm. "ESP During Sleep." *Journal* of the Society for Psychical Research 38 (1956): 282.

Vardøgr

A psychic **double** or forerunner that appears in advance to announce the arrival of an individual. Sometimes it may manifest simply as familiar sounds associated with the individual concerned. Occasionally it may appear to the individual himself or herself, as in the celebrated experience of the great German poet **Johann Goethe,** who met his double on the road to Drusenheim dressed in a garment which Goethe was to wear by accident eight years later on the same route. Little has been published on the curious phenomenon of the vardøgr apart from an article in 1917 by Wiers Jensen, editor of the *Norwegian Journal of Psychical Research.*

Varley, Cromwell Fleetwood (1828–1883)

Renowned Spiritualist and consulting electrician of the Atlantic Telegraph Company and the Electric and International Telegraph Company. He was born at Kentish Town, London, April 6, 1828, and named after two of his ancestors, Oliver Cromwell and General Fleetwood. He was educated in South London, and went on to study telegraphy, joining the Electric and International Telegraph Company in 1846.

He was first attracted to **Spiritualism** in 1850. He investigated the hypothesis that table rapping was the result of an electric force and demonstrated that this hypothesis was altogether unfounded. In later years, he had many curious psychic experiences, discovered that he possessed mesmeric healing power, and effected cures on his wife. She in turn had clairvoyant **visions** and spells of **trance** in which she foretold the exact course of her illness. After the birth of a son, Varley was one night aroused by three tremendous **raps.** He felt impelled to go into his wife's room, where he found the nurse intoxicated and his wife rigid and in a cataleptic state.

He later made the acquaintance of the famous medium **Daniel Dunglas Home.** Narrating his experiences before the committee of the **London Dialectical Society** in 1869, he concluded:

"Still, I was too astonished to be able to feel satisfied. Fortunately, when I got home, a circumstance occurred which got rid of the element of doubt. While alone in the drawing room, thinking intently on what I had witnessed, there were raps. The next morning I received a letter from Mr. Home, in which he said 'When alone in your room last night you heard sounds. I am so pleased.' He stated the spirits had told him they followed me, and were enabled to produce sounds. I have the letter in my possession now, to show that imagination had nothing to do with the matter."

Varley gave account of other personal occurrences. In the winter of 1864, at Beckenham Kent, he was awakened during the night by raps. His wife was lying by his side in trance and he saw the transparent phantom of a man in military dress in the air. He asked him, through the voice of his wife, to deliver a message to his brother in Birmingham.

Varley also had other curious experiences. In a dream state, he saw and heard the **double** of his sister-in-law. Next morning she confirmed everything by narrating her own dream experience. At another time, having accidentally chloroformed himself, he had vivid **out-of-the-body** experiences which were similarly confirmed by his wife. In 1860, at Halifax, his double, anxious to wake his physical self, made him dream of a bomb explosion; when the shock woke him he found the scene outside his window exactly corresponding to what his double saw.

In New York, he made the acquaintance of several mediums and conducted experiments in the home of C. F. Livermore, the banker, with the famous medium Kate Fox of the **Fox Sisters.** His efforts to find the laws that govern the physical phenomena of Spiritualism were fruitless. He began to suspect that powers other than electricity and magnetism were at work. On the basis of his varied experiences he was led to believe "that we are not our bodies; that when we die we exist just as much as before, and that under certain conditions we are able to hold communications with those on earth; but I also believe that many of the phenomena are often caused by the spirits of those whose bodies are present."

When **Sir William Crookes** started his famous investigation into the phenomena of Spiritualism, Varley assisted him in devising means of electric control. For his outspoken stand he was subject to abuse from the skeptical W. B. Carpenter who, in the October 1871 *Quarterly Review,* assured readers that there were grave doubts of his scientific ability and that these misgivings of the learned world had kept Varley out of the Royal Society. At the time of this attack, Varley had been a fellow of the Royal Society for more than three months.

In addition to his researches in Spiritualism, Varley was renowned for his important part in the successful laying of the first Atlantic cable. He died at Bexley Heath, Kent, September 2, 1883.

Varma, Devendra P. (1923–1994)

Leading authority on the Gothic novel and author and editor of over two hundred books on the subject. Dr. Varma was born on October 17, 1923, in northeastern India, on the borders of the Himalayan Mountains. He has been a professor of English in Katmandu, Nepal, and also taught at the University of Damascus in Syria and in Cairo. For many years he taught English at Dalhousie University in Halifax, Nova Scotia, specializing in the Gothic romance.

He had taken a particular interest in the study of the **vampire** and discussed the subject in his introduction to the three-volume reprint of *Varney the Vampire* by James Malcolm Rymer (often mistakenly attributed to Thomas Prest), a mid-nineteenth-century vampire novel. In 1973, he traveled to Castle Dracula in Transylvania to investigate the background of Bram Stoker's famous novel *Dracula,* first published in 1897.

Varma had kept in close touch with such Hollywood directors of horror movies as Curtis Harrington, Frank Cunningham, Walter Doughty, and Forrest Ackermann and was friends with such actors as Christopher Lee and Vincent Price. He edited the seven volumes of the "horrid novels" mentioned in Jane Austen's *Northanger Abbey,* the Gothic Studies and Dissertations Series in 36 volumes, and three series of *Gothic Novels* reprinted by Arno Press (including *The Complete Works of Sheridan LeFanu)* in 52 volumes. In 1977, he was awarded the Queen's Silver Jubilee Medal in Britain for his contributions to education and the arts.

Vsarma died in 1994.

Sources:

Varma, Devendra. "The Genesis of Dracula: a Re-Visit." In Peter Underwood, ed. *The Vampire's Bedside Companion.* London: Leslie Frewin, 1975.

———. *The Gothic Flame.* London: Arthur Barker, 1957.

———. *The History of the Gothic Novel in England.* N.p., 1957.

———. "The Vampire in Legend, Lore, and Literature." Introduction to *Varney the Vampyre; or, the Feast of Blood.* New York: Arno Press, 1970.

———, ed. *Voices from the Vaults: Authentic Tales of Vampires and Ghosts.* Toronto: Key Porter Books, 1987.

Vasiliev, Leonid Leonidovich (1891–1966)

Soviet physiologist and parapsychologist. Born in Russia, he graduated from Petersburg University in 1914. He was a teacher of biological sciences at Ufa, Bashkir (1914–21), head of the Physiology Department, Bekhterev Brain Institute, Leningrad (1921–38), and a professor of physiology at Leningrad University from 1943 onward. Vasiliev pioneered parapsychology in the Soviet Union, and helped to establish the first parapsychology laboratory at Leningrad (now St. Petersburg). His work is both contemporaneous with and of equal quality as that of **J. B. Rhine.** He began by attempting to replicate some of the experiments of Pierre Janet, the nineteenth-century French psychologist. His spectacular success gave parapsychology some recognition in the highly politicized atmosphere of Stalinist Russia. He first developed a "politically correct" hypothesis of the material basis of telepathy, but his experiments to establish his theory proved quite the opposite. Financial support was withdrawn and Vasiliev's work was not published until the 1960s, after Stalin's death.

Sources:

Berger, Arthur S., and Joyce Berger. *The Encyclopedia of Parapsychology and Psychical Research.* New York: Paragon House, 1991.

Ebon, Martin, ed. *Psychic Discoveries by the Russians.* New York: Parapsychology Foundation, 1963; New York: New American Library, 1971.

Pleasants, Helene, ed. *Biographical Dictionary of Parapsychology.* New York: Helix Press, 1964.

Vasiliev, Leonid L. *Experiments in Distant Influence.* London: Wildwood House, 1976; New York: Dutton, 1976.

———. *Experiments in Mental Suggestion.* Church Crookham, Hampshire, U.K.: Study of Mental Images Publications, 1963.

———. *Mysterious Manifestations of the Human Psyche.* 1959. Reprinted as: *Mysterious Phenomena of the Human Psyche.* New Hyde Park, N.Y.: University Books, 1965.

Vassago

According to the *Lemegeton* (Book of the Spirits), a famous work attributed to King Solomon, Vassago was one of the seventy-two spirits to be conjured up by magical evocation. Vassago is described as a prince in the hierarchy of genii, favored by those who would know the unknown; he could tell of the future and find anything lost or stolen. As with other princes among the spirits, Vassago could be conjured into a mystical triangle, but kings and emperors among the spirits could be conjured into a magical crystal. (See also **crystal gazing**)

Vasse, Christine M(aria) Piot (1922–)

Teacher who has written on parapsychology. Born December 8, 1922, in Salouel, France, Vasse received her college degree (B.A.) in 1941 and was a charter member of the **Parapsychological Association.**

She experimented in extrasensory perception with children, and studied teacher-student relationships in these tests. She collaborated with her husband on experiments involving dice placement and also plant growth. She is co-author of various articles with her husband **Paul M. Vasse,** and translator of French the *Handbook of Tests in Parapsychology* by **Betty Humphrey Nicols.**

Sources:

Pleasants, Helene, ed. *Biographical Dictionary of Parapsychology.* New York: Helix Press, 1964.

Vasse, Paul M. and Christine M. Vasse. "Comparison of Two Subjects in PK." *Journal of Parapsychology* (December 1951).

———. "ESP Test with French First-Grade School Children." *Journal of Parapsychology* (September 1958).

———. "Plant Growing Experiments." *Revue Métapsychique* (April–June 1948).

Vasse, Paul M(arie) (1910– ?)

Physician who experimented in areas of parapsychology. He was born February 17, 1910, at Amiens, France, studied at the University of Paris (B.A., 1928; M.D., 1936), and was a charter member of the **Parapsychological Association** and the *Ordre des Medécins.* In collaboration with his wife, **Christine M. Vasse,** Vasse conducted experiments in dice placement and in the growth of plants and lectured on his results at the Institut Métapsychique.

Sources:

Pleasants, Helene, ed. *Biographical Dictionary of Parapsychology.* New York: Helix Press, 1964.

Vasse, Paul M. and Christine M. Vasse. "Comparison of Two Subjects in PK." *Journal of Parapsychology* (December 1951).

———. "ESP Test with French First-Grade School Children." *Journal of Parapsychology* (September 1958).

———. "Plant Growing Experiments." *Revue Métapsychique* (April–June 1948).

"Vates"

One of the spirit controls of **William Stainton Moses.** "Vates" was an assistant to the control **"Imperator,"** said to have been the prophet Daniel.

Vaughan, Alan (1936–)

Author, editor, and psychic who has written widely on psychical and parapsychological topics. He was born on December 28, 1936, in Akron, Ohio, and studied at the University of Akron (A.B., 1958), Rutgers University (1958–59), the New School for Social Research (1966–67), and the University of Freiburg (1967–68). He held several editing jobs before going to work for *Psychic* magazine (later *New Realities*) in 1969. He was the editor of *Psychic* for five years (1972–77). From 1978 onward he was president of New Ways of Consciousness Foundation, San Francisco. He also started a Los Angeles-based computer software company called Mind Technology Systems.

Vaughan has worked in parapsychology, especially with the Dream Laboratory at Maimonides Hospital, and he is an associate member of the **Parapsychological Association.** He is also a psychic, having begun his development in Europe in the 1960s. In 1983 he began channelling an entity named "Li Sung" who claimed to be an ancient Chinese healer and herbalist. Vaughan reflected upon his unusual dual life:

"The transition from a skeptical science textbook editor to a parapsychologist and practicing psychic was a painful one. I had to give up the cherished idea of traditional science to discover the more important underlying realities of consciousness and its psychic effects. The research leading to *Patterns of Prophecy* opened up my own prophetic talent, and enabled me to teach others how to develop their latent psi gifts. . . . Each of us has a unique consciousness and a unique task in life. We also have unique problems to solve. But only *our* consciousness has the answers to *our* problems. Your inner self has the wisdom of the universe locked up within it. By finding the key to unlock that wisdom, you will enrich your life."

Sources:

Berger, Arthur S., and Joyce Berger. *The Encyclopedia of Parapsychology and Psychical Research.* New York: Paragon House, 1991.

Vaughan. Alan. *The Edge of Tomorrow.* New York: Coward, McGann, 1982.

———. *Incredible Coincidence: The Baffling World of Synchronicity.* New York: Lippencott, 1979.

———. *Patterns of Prophecy.* New York: Hawthorn Books, 1973.

Ullman, Montague, Stanley Krippner, and Alan Vaughan. *Dream Telepathy.* N.p., 1973.

Vaughan, Alan, and James Bolem. *Psychics.* New York: Harper & Row, 1972.

Vaughan, Diana

The mythical figure in a famous nineteenth-century occult hoax initiated by **Leo Taxil,** pseudonym of **Gabriel Jogand-Pagés,** a French journalist. From 1885 to 1886, Taxil published a sensational story that one branch of **Freemasonry** was following a form of **devil-worship** called Palladianism, of which Diana Vaughan was the High Priestess. Allegedly, she was the descendent of the seventeenth-century alchemist **Thomas Vaughan.**

These revelations synchronized with Roman Catholic opposition to Freemasonry (based upon their support of democratic trends in nineteenth-century Europe) and were profitable for Taxil. Diana Vaughan was supposed to have repented to her Satanist background and embraced the Catholic Church. Her memoirs were read with satisfaction by the pope himself.

An announcement appeared that she would appear at a press conference on Easter Monday 1897. Instead, Taxil appeared and calmly revealed his hoax, stating that he was merely anxious to see how far he could dupe the church. News of this deception was badly received, for the plot had lasted three or four years, and Taxil had to be smuggled away under police protection. In Britain, the hoax was exposed by occult scholar **Arthur Edward Waite** in his book *Devil Worship in France* (1896).

Sources:

Waite, Arthur Edward. *Devil Worship in France; or, The Question of Lucifer: A Record of Things Seen and Heard in the Secret Societies According to the Evidence of Initiates.* London, George Redway, 1896.

Vaughan, Thomas (1622–1666)

British alchemist and poet, who wrote under the pseudonym **Eugenius Philalethes.** He was born April 17, 1622, at Newton, Breconshire, the younger twin brother of poet Henry Vaughan. He matriculated at Oxford and entered Jesus College, Oxford University, becoming a fellow of his college. In 1640, at the age of eighteen, he received the living [i.e., the income as parish priest] of St. Bridget's [Church of England], Breconshire, and on February 18, 1642, the B.A. degree. He was a royalist during the Civil War and in 1658 was accused of "drunkenness, swearing, and incontinency, being no preacher," and deprived of the living of St. Bridget's. However, this may have been no more than high spirits. He became a devoted student of chemistry, following his research both in Oxford and London, under the patronage of Sir Robert Murray. He died February 27, 1666, at the rectory of Albury, Oxfordshire, allegedly from inhalation of fumes of mercury, upon which he was experimenting.

Vaughan was an ardent follower of **Cornelius Agrippa,** to whom, as he stated, "he acknowledged that, next to God, he owed all that he had." He claimed to be a philosopher of nature rather than a vulgar alchemist. In one of his manuscripts he recorded strange dreams of premonitions that he had experienced and prayed for forgiveness of past errors, including former revels and drunkenness. Although he published a translation of a Rosicrucian work with a preface by himself, he explicitly stated that he was not a member of any such fraternity. Under the pseudonym of Eugenius Philalethes, he published a number of books including: *Anthroposophia Theomagica,* with *Anima Magica* (London, 1650; Amsterdam, 1704; and in German, Leipzig, 1749); *Magia Adamica; or the Antiquities of Magic* (London, 1650, 1656; Amsterdam, 1704, in German), *Lumen de Lumine* (London, 1651; Hof, 1750, in German), *Aula Lucis; or the House of Light* (London, 1652), *Euphrates; or the Waters of the East* (London, 1655, Stockholm & Hamburg, 1689, in German), and *The Chymists Key to shut, and to open; or the True Doctrine of Corruption and Generation* (London, 1657). He contributed verses for Thomas Powell's *Elementa Opticæ* (1651), for the English translation of Cornelius Agrippa's *Three Books of Occult Philosophy* (1651), and William Cartwright's *Comedies* (1651). A collection of his Latin verses was included at the end of Henry Vaughan's *Thalia Rediviva* (1678).

Vaughan was falsely identified with the mystical writer "**Eirenæus Philalethes**" through the **Diana Vaughan** writings of **Leo Taxil** (pseudonym of **Gabriel Jogand-Pagès**), who also popularized a false legend of a pact between him and Satan.

Vaulderie

A term indicating connection with Satanic powers, so called from Robinet de Vaulx, a hermit, one of the first persons accused of the crime. In 1453, the Prior of St. Germain-en-Laye, Guillaume de l'Allive, a doctor of theology, was accused of Vaulderie, and sentenced to perpetual imprisonment. Six years later there was burned at Lille a hermit named Alphonse, who preached heterodox doctrines. During the fifteenth century, many accusations of "witchcraft" were directed against those who followed the heretical sect of the Waldenses or Vaudois.

Such were the preludes of a persecution which, in the following year, the Vicar of the Inquisition, administrator of the Diocese of Arras, seconded by the Count d'Etampes, Governor of Artois, directed at first against loose women, but afterwards against citizens, magistrates, knights, and especially the wealthy.

The procedures against the accused had almost always for their basis some accusation of sorcery (i.e., malevolent magic). Most of the unhappy creatures confessed to having attended the Witch's **Sabbat,** and the strange revelations wrung from them by torture gave some idea of the ceremonies that, according to the popular tradition, were enacted in the lurid festivals presided over by Satan.

The following are some extracts from the judgment pronounced at Arras in 1460 upon five women, a painter, a poet nicknamed "an abbé of little sense" and aged about seventy, and several others, who all perished in the flames kindled by barbarous ignorance and fed by a cruel superstition:

"And the said Inquisition did say and declare, that those hereinunder named had been guilty of Vaulderie in manner following, that is to say:—'That when they wished to go to the said Vaulderie, they, with an ointment given to them by the devil, anointed a small wooden rod and their palms and their hands; then they put the wand between their legs, and soon they flew wherever they wished to go, over fair cities, woods and streams; and the devil carried them to the place where they should hold their assembly, and in this place they found others, and tables placed, loaded with wines and viands; and there they found a demon in the form of a goat, a dog, an ape, or sometimes a man; and they made their oblation and homage to the said demon, and adored him, and yielded up to him their souls, and all, or at least some portion of their bodies; then, with burning candles in their hands, they kissed the rear of the goat-devil. . . . [Here the Inquisitor becomes untranslatable].

". . . . And this homage done, they trod and trampled upon the Cross, and befouled it with their spittle, in contempt of Jesus Christ, and the Holy Trinity, then turned their backs towards heaven and the firmament in contempt of God. And after they had all eaten and drunk well, they had carnal intercourse all together, and even the devil assumed the guise of man and woman, and had intercourse with both sexes. And many other crimes, most filthy and detestable, they committed, as much against God as against nature, which the said Inquisitor did not dare to name, that innocent ears might not be told of such villainous enormites.'"

The eagerness displayed by the inquisitor and his acolytes so excited the public indignation that at the close of the year 1460 the judges did not dare any longer to condemn to death the unfortunate wretches accused. It was said that the persecution was only for the purpose of depriving them of their property. As in the case of many great wrongs, a reaction set in favor of justice.

Thirty years later, when the country of Artois had been reunited to the Crown, the Parliament of Paris declared, on May 20, 1491, that these trials were "abusive, void, and falsely made" and condemned the heirs of the duke of Burgundy and the principal judges to an amend of 500 Parisian livres, to be distributed to a reparation among the heirs of the victims. The events as Arras stand behind the formal change of attitude toward **witchcraft** made by the Roman Catholic Church in 1484 in that it was redefined as Satanism. (See also **Sabbat; Witchcraft**)

Sources:

Robbins, Russell Hope. *The Encyclopedia of Witchcraft and Demonology.* New York: Crown Publishers, 1959.

Russell, Jeffrey Burton. *Witchcraft in the Middle Ages.* Ithaca, N.Y.: Cornell University Press, 1972.

Vay, Baroness Adelma (1840–1924)

Authoress, medium, and pioneer of **Spiritualism** in Hungary. Her powers, inherited from her mother, the Countess Teleki, later Duchess Solm, first blossomed in 1865. She became clairvoyant; wrote, spoke and drew in trance; had the prophetic gift; and was credited with many cures. In 1873, with her husband, she formed the Hungarian Spiritualist Association of which they became the first presidents. Her books included: *Spirit, Force and Matter* (1869), *Studies on the Spirit World* (1874), *From My Life* (1900), and *Pictures from the Beyond* (1905).

Vedanta

Vedanta is the highest teaching of the *Vedas,* (*veda* means knowledge), the ancient Sanskrit scriptures of India. There are four *Vedas:* the *Rig-Veda,* the *Yajur-Veda,* the *Sama-Veda,* and the *Artharva-Veda,* which are comprised of hymns, ritual texts, and philosophical treaties that are regarded as divine revelation. Vedanta is considered one of the six *darshanas* (viewpoints) of orthodox Hinduism. However, it is not simply a formal instruction but a revelatory experience of transcendental consciousness.

In 1893, **Swami Vivekananda** appeared "like an Eastern comet in the Western spiritual sky" and made a startling appearance at the Parliament of Religions at the Chicago World's Fair. With him, he brought news of **yoga** and Vedanta; since then, yoga has taken solid root in the Western soil, with an estimated 2 million participants outside India. Vedanta, on the other hand, has remained relatively unknown.

The *Vedas,* completed between 1500–500 B.C.E, were originally an oral tradition, later codified in scriptures called the **Upanishads** (meaning nearness to wisdom). Of the 108 *Upanishads,* created between 900–500 B.C.E., some ten out of twelve books are regarded as the principle ones. The Vedanta, like the New Testament of the Bible, not only serves as the end of the *Upanishads* but the culmination of the scriptures.

Hindu scriptures differ from the sacred writings of other religions as they go beyond faith in particular deities (regarded as legal fictions, useful only at certain stages in life) to awareness of an Absolute, beyond time, space and causality. It is said the Vedanta's two main themes are humanity's true nature as divine, and this divinity as the aim of human life. The ideas of the Vedanta also introduce and reflect the traditional yogic paths.

There are three perspectives of Vedanta: One is dualistic (*dvaita*), the second is nondualistic (*advaita*), while the third is qualified nondualistic (*vishishtadvaita*). The advaita perspective proclaims there are no individual souls, but all are unified. It is called nondualistic because "it acknowledge[s] only one Spirit, a single underlying reality beyond which nothing else could possibly exist."

Sources:

Advaita Vedanta. http://www.advaita-vedanta.org/. March 1, 2000.

Introduction to Vedanta. http://www.geocities.com/Rodeo Drive/1415/veda.html. March 30, 2000.

Johnsen, Linda. "Tantra & Classical Yoga." *Yoga International* (September 1997): 22–29.

Nikhilananda, Swami. *The Upanishads.* 4 vols. London: Phoenix House, 1951–59; New York: Ramakrishna-Vivekananda Center, 1975–1979.

Torwesten, Hans. *Vedanta: Heart of Hinduism.* New York: Grove Weidenfield, 1985.

Vedanta Societies

American Vedanta Societies stem from the visit to the United States by **Swami Vivekananda** in 1893, when he lectured on Hinduism at the World Parliament of Religions held in Chicago. The Swami founded the Vedanta Society of New York in 1896, followed by the Vedanta Society of San Francisco in 1900.

Swami Vivekananda became the foremost interpreter of Yoga and Hinduism in Western countries, basing his teachings on the inspiration of his master **Sri Ramakrishna.**

Vedanta comprises the supreme wisdom of the *Vedas,* the ancient Sanskrit scriptures of India, together with the **Upanishads,** which derived from them. This wisdom is manifest as a revelatory experience after following spiritual disciplines (such as the various forms of **yoga**) in conjunction with scripture study under the guidance of a qualified *guru* or teacher.

There are now some sixteen Vedanta Centres in the United States which form branches of the Ramakrishna Order of India. Addresses: Vedanta Society of Northern California, 2323 Vallejo St., San Francisco, CA 94123; Vedanta Society of Southern California, 1946 Vedanta Pl., Hollywood, CA 90068. There are also Vedanta Centre/Ananda Ashrama communities providing spiritual retreats in both Massachusetts and Southern California. Addresses: Vedanta Centre, 130 Beechwood St., Cohasset, MA 02025; Ananda Ashrama, 5301 Pennsylvania Ave., CA 91214.

Vedic Astrology

Astrologers in India trace their art to the fifth millennium B.C.E. though a new shape was given to ancient astrological speculations by **Parashara Muni** around 1500 B.C.E. He is one of the first astrologers in the world known to have actually cast horoscopes, the personal birth charts for individuals. He also is known to have had a special interest in the application of **astrology** to health and longevity concerns. He wrote several books, the most important being the *Brihat Parashara Hora Shastra,* and composed hymns to the several planetary deities.

Muni's work was expanded by Ranavira, who lived during the same era. Ranavira, who also operated as a clairvoyant seer, concentrated on the astrological correlated to compatible personal relationships, female astrology, and psychological astrology. Ranavira appears to be the fountainhead of Indian astrology's continued interest in applying astrology to predicting successful marriages.

Astrology emerged in the context of the Vedas, the ancient holy writings of the Indian people, which through the Vedic hymns offered a positive worldview oriented to nature and the pastoral agricultural life. Astrology, also called *Joytisha* (meaning of the shining world of light), complemented this worldview in its attempt to shine the divine light on the individual's life. As a teacher, astrological knowledge attempted to dispel the darkness of illusion and assist the person to understand the purpose of the soul's present incarnation.

The birth chart pictures the consequences or karma that the person brings into this incarnation (Indians believing that the soul reincarnates in a series of embodied existences either as humans or animals). While at times, as in Western astrology, astrological interpretation has fallen into a fatalistic mode, contemporary Vedic astrologers, drawing on the optimistic spirit of the Vedic literature, specifically eschew such a view. They emphasize that the natal chart offers a picture of karmic influences but also shows indicative rather than deterministic forces active in the person's life.

The Vedic birth chart differs from the traditional Western horoscope in several ways. Most importantly, Indian astrologers use what is termed the sidereal **zodiac** rather than the topical zodiac. The sidereal zodiac is based upon the actual positions of the 12 signs of the zodiac in the sky. The topical zodiac is based upon the position of the Sun as it rises at the spring equinox. Over the years, that point (called O° Aires) shifts slightly year by year, one aspect of the phenomenon known as the procession of the equinoxes. Over the centuries, the two zodiacs have developed a difference of 23°, enough to throw most planets into an adjacent sign. Vedic astrologers cast a chart based upon the moment of birth (defined as the moment of the first cry of the newborn).

The most important elements in the individuals' charts are the planets, which were in ancient times identified with lesser deities. Planets are termed *graha,* that which possesses a person, hence the planets are seen as symbolic of the illusions (*maya*) of earthly existence that obscure the individual's divine nature. Each planet has acquired a set of associations and its particular placement in the chart indicates a variety of strengths and weaknesses. Generally, only the ancient visible planets are utilized by Vedic astrologers and thus one will not find Uranus, Neptune, or Pluto, not to mention the asteroids or hypothetical planets that occasionally appear as elements in Western horoscopes.

Besides the signs, planets, and houses that both Indian and Western astrology share, Vedic astrology also includes a unique set of divisions placed on the birth chart, the planetary periods. Vedic astrology not only divides the zodiac into the 12 signs, but it also divides it into 27 lunar mansions roughly defined by the movement of the Moon around the earth every 27 days. The planetary periods relate to the lunar mansions very much as houses relate to the traditional signs. The planetary periods are of varying lengths as they are related to the different planets. The place of the newborn in the cycle of periods is determined by the position of the Moon in the natal chart. The recognition of these periods provides Indian astrologers with an additional level of interpretation of the person's life not available to traditional Western practitioners.

The Western appropriation of Vedic astrology began early in the twentieth century but did not become prominent until the migration of large numbers of Indians to the West after World War II (1939–45) and the contemporaneous turn Eastward by numerous young spiritual seekers. The flux through which Western astrology has passed in the last decades of the twentieth century, during which time every aspect and boundary of traditional Western astrology was challenged, provided openings for the introduction of Vedic astrology. Many Westerners found it more appealing than the dominant system and a growing number of books explaining the system have been published in the West. Also, materials published in India have become freely circulated through the English-speaking world. During the 1990s, annual conventions of Vedic astrologers were held in North America.

Sources:

Braha, James T. *Ancient Hindu Astrology for the Modern Western Astrology.* Hollywood, Calif.: Hermetician Press, 1986.

Cameron, Barbara. *Predictive Planetary Periods: The Hindu Dasa.* Tempe, Ariz.: American Federation of Astrologers, 1984.

DeLuce, Robert. *Constellational Astrology: According to the Hindu System.* Los Angeles: DeLuce Publishing, 1963.

Vehm-Gerichte

A secret tribunal that during the Middle Ages, exercised a peculiar jurisdiction in **Germany** and especially in Westphalia. Its origin is uncertain. The sessions were often held in secret, and the uninitiated were forbidden to attend them on pain of death. Various stories have been circulated concerning the group, but these have been discounted by modern research. Far from dabbling in the occult, these courts frequently punished persons convicted of **witchcraft** and sorcery (malevolent magic).

Veleda (ca. 70 C.E.)

A prophetess among the ancient Germans, of whom the historian Tacitus stated:

"She exercises a great authority, for women have been held here from the most ancient times to be prophetic, and, by excessive superstition, as divine. The fame of Veleda stood on the very highest elevation, for she foretold to the Germans a prosperous issue, but to the legions their destruction! Veleda dwelt upon a high tower, whence messengers were dispatched bearing her oracular counsels to those who sought them; but she herself was rarely seen, and none was allowed to approach her. Cercalis is said to have secretly begged her to let the Romans have better success in war. In the reign of the Emperor Vespasian she was honored as a goddess."

Veleda predicted the success of Claudius Civilis in the Batavian revolt against Rome (69–70 C.E.) and the fall of the Roman Empire.

Velikovsky, Immanuel (1895–1979)

Psychoanalyst and cosmologist who emerged as a major defender of catastrophism, the idea that the earth's history and prehistory have been distorted by significant catastrophies. Catastrophism stands over against uniformitarianism, the dominant postulate of geologic sciences that the earth has developed slowly by long-term processes which are still occurring and observable. About the time of the prophet Moses in 1500 B.C.E., a comet from the planet Jupiter is supposed to have collided with Mars, formed the planet Venus, and shifted the orbit of the earth, displacing oceans and reversing the earth's poles.

Velikovsky was born on June 10, 1895, at Vitebsk, Russia. He attended the Medvednikov Gymnasium in Moscow, graduating with full honors. After a short period of study at Montpellier, France, he traveled in Palestine, then started pre-medical studies in natural science at Edinburgh, Scotland, in 1914. On the outbreak of World War I, he enrolled in the Free University in Moscow, studying law and ancient history. In 1915 he took up medical studies again at the University of Moscow and received his medical diploma in 1921. He moved to Berlin, where together with Prof. Heinrich Loewe he founded and published *Scripta Universitatis*, a series of scholarly volumes contributed by Jewish scholars in various countries. Velikovsky also met Albert Einstein, who edited the mathematical-physical volumes.

Velikovsky then moved to Palestine, where he practiced as a physician for fifteen years. He then spent some time in New York researching a study of Freud's own dreams and the relationship of Freud's thought to such figures as Oedipus, Akhnaton and Moses, but in the course of his researches, he became intrigued by the suggestion that there might have been a catastrophe at the time of the Exodus of the Israelites from Egypt.

A new book began to develop, under the title *Ages in Chaos*, followed by a further manuscript, *Worlds in Collision*. The latter work was published in 1950 and created a storm in the scientific world, and the original publisher felt compelled to drop the book. The extraordinary campaign of suppression is fully documented in Alfred de Grazia's book *The Velikovsky Affair; the Warfare of Science and Scientism* (University Books, 1966). Diehard and intolerant scientists were later infuriated when various hypotheses of Velikovsky, originally sneered at as "unscientific" and inaccurate, were eventually proved correct. Velikovsky correctly predicted the existence of geomagnetic planetary fields, the negative electrical charge of the sun, the high temperature of Venus, the existence of hydrocarbon clouds surrounding Venus, and emission of radio sounds from Jupiter—all vindicated by space probes and other recent scientific developments. (At the same time, of course, many other ideas proved completely false).

Velikovsky developed a small but loyal following in the scientific community and a large public response. Two journals, including the *S. I. S. Review* published by the **Society for Interdisciplinary Studies,** appeared in the 1970s to expand the discussion of his ideas, though support has noticeably declined since his death on November 17, 1979 in Princeton, New Jersey. During his lifetime, his ideas were attacked vigorously by many of the same writers who attacked psychic research. Carl Sagan penned the most definitive refutation of Velikovsky's ideas.

Sources:

Gardner, Martin. *Fads and Fallacies in the Name of Science.* New York: Dover Publications, 1957.

Velikovsky, Immanuel. *Ages in Chaos.* Garden City, N.Y.: Doubleday, 1952.

———. *Earth in Upheaval.* Garden City, N.Y.: Doubleday, 1955.

———. *Oedipus and Akhnaton: Myth and History.* Garden City, N.Y.: Doubleday, 1960.

———. *Peoples of the Sea.* N.p., 1977.

Veltis

An evil spirit who assaulted St. Margaret of Cortona (died 1297), but was overcome by her. On being asked by St. Margaret who he was and whence he came, he replied:

"My name is Veltis, and I am one of those whom Solomon by virtue of his spells, confined in a copper cauldron at Babylon, but when the Babylonians, in the hope of finding treasure dug up the cauldron and opened it, we all made our escape. Since that time our efforts have been directed to the destruction of righteous persons, and I have long been striving to turn thee from the course thou hast embraced."

Verdelet

Said to be a demon of the second order, master of ceremonies at the infernal court. He was charged with the transport of witches to the **Sabbat.** He took the names of "Master Persil," "Sante-Buisson," and other names of a pleasant sound, so as to entice women into his snares.

Verdun, Michel (d. 1521)

A self-confessed **werewolf,** burned at Besançon, France, in 1521 together with his accomplice Pierre Burgot. They had stated that they had stripped naked and anointed themselves with a certain **unguent,** after which they changed shape and became werewolves, hunting and attacking children and adults. Verdun was discovered after attacking a traveler who wounded him while in animal form. Following the trail of the wounded creature, the traveler discovered Verdun, who had returned to human form, with his wife bathing the wound.

Sources:

Summers, Montague. *The Werewolf.* London, 1933. Reprint, New York: University Books, 1966.

La Vérité (Journal)

Nineteenth-century Spiritualist journal published in Lyons, France.

Verograph

One of various modern devices for experimenting with aura-electronics or kirlian photography. It is small enough to be conveniently portable.

Veronica

A religious term for a cloth bearing the likeness of Jesus imprinted miraculously. The term was coined by St. Gregory of Tours (538–594 C.E.), deriving from the Greek *icon* (image) and Latin *vera* (true).

The story of veronica is that a woman of rank, living in the Via Dolorosa, broke through the procession of Jesus' crucifixion when it stopped for Simon of Cyrene to assist in carrying the cross. The woman, usually named as Seraphia (sometimes called Veronica), wiped the face of Jesus with a cloth, and the miraculous portrait became impressed from the blood and sweat. Other versions of the story claim that the woman simply handed the cloth to Jesus, who wiped his own face and returned the cloth. A detailed and highly circumstantial version of the incident was given by **Anne Catherine Emmerich** (see **Germany**) when in an ecstatic trance.

A claimed veronica was placed in a marble coffer on the altar of a chapel attached to St. Peter's in Rome during the period of Sixtus V, but it was moved in 1440 and is said to be deposited in the Vatican. Another cloth with a similar miraculous portrait was presented by two Fathers to the seventh synod of Nice, C.E. 787. Such miraculous likenesses not made by people are also known as **Acheropites.**

In 1813, when a vault was opened in St. George's Chapel, Windsor, England, one of the coffins, believed to be that of Charles I, was opened and a portrait found on the grave cloth which had wrapped the body. The myth which surrounds the **Turin Shroud** is quite similar to that of the veronicas.

Verrall, Arthur Woollgar (1851–1912)

Classical scholar, husband of the psychical researcher and medium **Margaret de Gaudrion Verrall,** and father of **Helen Verrall Salter,** the wife of **W. H. Salter.** After his death he was one of the purported communicators in the famous "**cross-correspondence**" tests of the **Society for Psychical Research,** London, in which wife and daughter participated by producing automatic scripts.

Verrall was born on February 5, 1851, in Brighton, England. He studied at Wellington College and Trinity College, Cambridge University, (B.A., 1873; M.A., 1874). He lectured at Trinity, where he became First King Edward VII Professor of English Literature in 1911. He died June 18, 1912.

Verrall, Margaret de Gaudrion Merrifield (1859–1916)

Prominent British psychical researcher, medium and lecturer in classics at Newnham College. She was born December 21, 1859, at Brighton, England, and educated at Newnham College, Cambridge University. She married A. W. Verrall, the well-known classical scholar, in 1882.

Verrall joined the **Society for Psychical Research,** London, in 1889. She wrote a number of papers for the *Proceedings* at the request of **Frederic William Henry Myers,** held sittings with the medium **Leonora S. Piper** when she visited England, and was elected to the Council in 1901.

Eventually she developed psychic powers herself and in 1901 through **automatic writing** obtained the first significant results after the death of Myers. Afterwards she produced hundreds of scripts which often contained matter of paranormal interest. In 1906, she published an analysis of her own scripts in the society's *Proceedings* which formed the starting point of a serious study in **cross-correspondence.**

Sir Oliver Lodge paid the following tribute to Verrall in his book *The Survival of Man* (1909):

"The fame of Mrs. Piper has spread into all lands, and I should think the fame of Mrs. Verrall also. In these recent cases of automatism the society has been singularly fortunate, for in the one we have a medium who has been under strict supervision and competent management for the greater part of her psychical life; and in the other we have one of the sanest and acutest of our own investigators, fortunately endowed with some power herself, some power of acting as translator or interpreter between the psychical and the physical worlds."

After years of experiments and testing, Verrall concluded:

"It cannot be denied that the 'communicator' of the Piper sittings and of my own scripts presents a consistent personality dramatically resembling that of the person he claims to be. I entirely acquiesce in this judgment. . . . The boundary between the two states—the known and the unknown—is still substantial, but it is wearing thin in places; . . . and we are at liberty, not indeed to announce any definite conclusion, but to adopt as a working hypothesis the ancient doctrine of a possible intercourse of intelligence between the material and some other, perhaps ethereal order of existence."

She died July 2, 1916, at Cambridge. Her daughter Helen married **W. H. Salter,** another prominent psychical researcher.

Versailles Adventure

One of the most famous psychic experiences reported at the beginning of the twentieth century. In August 1901, two English ladies, C. A. E. Moberly and E. F. Jourdain, took an afternoon walk in the Gardens of Versailles, France, and found themselves transported to the Trianon of 1789, complete with buildings and other people of the period. They described their experience with much corroborative detail in their 1911 book *An Adventure.* In the first edition their identity was concealed by the names "Miss Morison" and "Miss Lamont."

The book went into many editions and generated much controversy, coinciding with rising British interest in psychic phenomena through the work of the **Society for Psychical Research,** London. In spite of many subsequent attempts to discredit the writers, the adventure still stands as a unique experience.

Sources:

Flew, Antony G. N. *A New Approach to Psychical Research.* London: Watts, 1953.

Gibbons, M. E., and A. O. Gibbons. *The Trianon Adventure.* London: Museum Press, 1958.

Iremonger, Lucille. *The Ghosts of Versailles.* London: Faber & Faber, 1957.

Mackenzie, Andrew. *The Unexplained: Some Strange Cases of Psychical Research.* London: A. Barker, 1953. Reprint, New York: Abelard, 1968.

Moberly, C. A. E., and E. F. Jourdain. *An Adventure.* London: Faber & Faber, 1911.

Olivier, Edith. *Four Victorian Ladies of Wiltshire.* London: Faber & Faber, 1945.

Parrott, Ian. *The Music of "An Adventure."* London: Regency Press, 1966.

"Richard's Garden Revisited." *Journal* of the Society for Psychical Research 41, 712 (June 1962).

Sturge-Whiting, J. R. *The Mystery of Versailles: A Complete Solution.* London: Rider, 1938.

Vervain

A sacred herb used to cleanse the table of Zeus before a feast in ancient Greece. In Rome it was also strewn on the altars of Jupiter, and water containing vervain was also sprinkled in houses to cast out evil spirits.

Among the Druids particularly it was employed in connection with many forms of superstition. They gathered it at daybreak, before the sun had risen. Later sorcerers followed the same usage, and demonologists believed that in order to evoke demons it was necessary to be crowned with vervain.

During the Crusades it was believed that when the nails were driven into the hands of Christ, vervain sprang upon Calvary.

The old herbalists recommended vervain to ease childbirth, and for jaundice, dropsy, gout, worms, stomach complaints, wound healing, ulcers and piles. Native Americans used vervain to cure menstrual disorders.

Vestigia (Organization)

Founded in 1976, with membership that consisted of scientists, engineers, technicians, and interested individuals, to investigate and conduct research into unexplained anamolous scientific phenomena of the kind usually associated with **Charles Fort.** Members are trained in investigative techniques and supply speakers to universities and organizations. The name of the group is the Latin word for "investigate," which, in itself, means footprint.

The group sponsored charitable programs, maintained a library and biographical archives, compiled statistics, and offered computerized services. It had committees on photography and technical matters, and divisions on aerial phenomena, biological matters, earth sciences, and parapsychology, as well as published an annual newsletter. Last known address: 56 Brookwood Rd., Stanhope, NJ 07874.

Vett, Carl Christian (1871–1956)

Danish agriculturalist and author, who played a leading part in organizing international cooperation and spread of information in the field of parapsychology. He was born September 25, 1871, in Aarhus, Denmark. Vett became a director of textile companies in Scandinavia. During World War I he was a diplomatic courier and cultural advisor to the Danish Ministry of Education on museum acquisitions. He was also a pioneer of biodynamic agricultural methods.

Vett was intensely interested in psychical research as a proper scientific study, and it was largely through his efforts that the First International Congress on Psychic Research was held in Copenhagen in 1921, with researchers from fifteen different countries. He became general secretary of a permanent committee for the organization of later international congresses of this kind, held at Warsaw (1923), Paris (1927), Athens (1930), and Oslo (1935). A tribute was paid to his work at the First International Conference of Parapsychological Studies held in Utrecht, Netherlands, in 1953. In the years after World War II, Vett lectured and wrote on parapsychological topics. He died February 1, 1956, in Rome, Italy.

Sources:

Vett, Carl Christian. "Memoirs of Psychic Research." *Tomorrow,* 3, 4 (Summer 1955).

Victoria, Queen (1819–1901)

Queen of England, Scotland and Ireland (1837–1901), Empress of India (1876–1901), who presided over the great days of the British Empire. She was known to be sympathetic to **Spiritualism,** and to have held séances with Prince Albert and other individuals. She approved of the book *Our Life After Death* by medium **Robert James Lees** and was said to have used Lees as a personal medium. Her belief in the possibility of communication between the spirit world and the living is illustrated by an entry in her journal commenting on the story that Princess Feodora, when at the point of death, had talked about a beloved child who had died earlier: "Surely at the approach of death the veil is raised and such pure spirits are allowed to see a glimpse of those dear ones waiting for them."

A short time before the death of Prince Albert, he had told the Queen: "We don't know in what state we shall meet again, but that we shall recognize each other and be together in eternity I am perfectly certain." After Albert's death, Victoria relied heavily on the companionship of her personal servant, the rough Highlander **John Brown.** Rumors suggested both that he was her lover and that together they participated in Spiritualist séances. After his death in 1883, the Queen erected a statue to him at Balmoral.

The Queen's Prime Minister **W. E. Gladstone** was also sympathetic to psychical research and was an early member of the **Society for Psychical Research,** London. He once summoned the famous palmist "**Cheiro**" to explain his theories and also sat with the medium **William Eglinton.**

Sources:

Underwood, Peter. *Queen Victoria's Other World.* London: Harrap, 1986.

Vidya

In **Theosophy,** the knowledge by which man on the **Path** of Life can discern the true from the false and so direct his efforts correctly by means of the mental faculties which he has learned to use. It is the antithesis of *avidya* (ignorance). Both terms are borrowed from Hindu religious philosophy.

Viedma

A Russian name for a witch. (See **Slavs**)

Vila

Vili were nymphs who frequented the forests at the bases of the Eastern Alps. According to popular belief, they could be seen traversing glades, mounted on stags, or driving from peak to peak on chariots of clouds. Old Serbian ballads tell how Marko, the great hero of ancient Serbia, was joined in a bond of brotherhood with a *Vila*, who showed to him the secrets of the future. At that period, Serbia was a mighty nation, extending from the Alps to the Black Sea, from the Danube to the Adriatic.

Vinchon, Jean (1884– ?)

French neuropsychiatrist who published books in areas of parapsychology. He was born on June 21, 1884, in the Department of the Somme, France. He received his M.D. in 1911 at Paris. He was successively the medical director of the Neuropsychiatric Center of the French Army of the East during World War I (1917–18), director of the clinic of Paris Medical School between the wars, and director of Army Neuropsychiatric Center, Paris Region as World War II began (1939–40). He then became a neuropsychiatrist at the War Veterans Ministry and a neuropsychiatric consultant at Hôpital de le Pitié.

Through most of his career Vinchon had a lively interest in psychic phenomena. He was a member and, for a period, president of the **Institut Métapsychique.** He authored several books growing out of his broad interests.

Sources:

Vinchon, Jean. *L'Art et la Folie* (Art and Insanity). Paris: Stock, Delamain et Boutelleau, 1950.

———. *La Magie du dessin: Du griffonage automatique au dessin thérapeutique* (The Magic Drawing: From Automatic Scribbling to Therapeutic Drawing). N.p., 1959.

———. *Mesmer et son secret* (Mesmer and His Secret). Toulouse Privat, 1936.

Vinchon, Jean, and Maurice Garçon. *Le Diable.* 1928. English ed. as *The Devil.* London, 1929. Reprint, New York: E. P. Dutton, 1930.

Vintras, Eugène (1807–1875)

A Normandy peasant of great devoutness, who in the year 1839 was nominated by a strange sect named the Saviours of Louis XVII as a fitting successor to their prophet Thomas Martin who had just died. The sect believed that the child of Louis XVII and Marie Antoinette did not die in prison and would be restored to the throne of France. The Saviours addressed a letter to the pretended Louis XVII and arranged that it should fall into the hands of Vintras. It abounded in good promises for the reign to come and in mystical expressions calculated to attract the attention of a naive excitable character as they believed Vintras to be. Later, in a letter, Vintras himself described the manner in which this communication reached him as follows:

"Towards nine o'clock I was occupied in writing, when there was a knock at the door of the room in which I sat, and supposing that it was a workman who came on business, I said rather brusquely, 'Come in.' Much to my astonishment, in place of the expected workman, I saw an old man in rags. I asked merely what he wanted. He answered with much tranquility, 'Don't disturb yourself, Pierre Michel.' Now, these names are never used in addressing me, for I am known everywhere as Eugène, and even in signing documents I do not make use of my first names. I was conscious of a certain emotion at the old man's answer, and this increased when he said: 'I am utterly tired, and wherever I appear they treat me with disdain, or as a thief.' The words alarmed me considerably, though they were spoken in a saddened and even a woeful tone. I arose and placed a ten sous piece in his hand, saying, 'I do not take you for that, my good man,' and while speaking I made him understand that I wished to see him out. He received it in silence but turned his back with a pained air. No sooner had he set foot on the last step than I shut the door and locked it. I did not hear him go down, so I called a workman and told him to come up to my room. Under some business pretext, I was wishing him to search with me all the possible places which might conceal my old man, whom I had not seen go out. The workman came accordingly. I left the room in his company, again locking my door. I hunted through all the nooks and corners, but saw nothing.

"I was about to enter the factory when I heard on a sudden the bell ringing for mass, and felt glad that, notwithstanding the disturbance, I could assist at the sacred ceremony. I ran back to my room to obtain a prayer book and, on the table where I had been writing, I found a letter addressed to Mme. de Generès in London; it was written and signed by M. Paul de Montfleury of Caen, and embodied a refutation of heresy, together with a profession of orthodox faith. The address notwithstanding, this letter was intended to place before the Duke of Normandy the most important truths of our holy Catholic, Apostolic and Roman religion. On the document was laid the ten sous piece which I had given to the old man."

Vintras immediately concluded that the bringer of the letter was a messenger from heaven and became devoted to the cause of Louis XVII. He became a visionary. He had bloody sweats, he saw hearts painted with his own blood appear on hosts, accompanied by inscriptions in his own spelling. Many believed him a prophet and followed him, among them several priests, who alleged that they partook of his occult vision. Doctors analyzed the fluid which flowed from the hosts and certified it to be human blood. While his enemies referred these miracles to the devil, a small band regarded Vintras as a new Christ.

But one follower named Gozzoli published scandalous accounts of his activities, alleging that horrible obscenities and sacrilegious masses took place in their private chapel at Tilly-sur-seules. The unspeakable abominations alluded to were contained in a pamphlet entitled *Le Prophète Vintras* (1851). The sect was formally condemned by the pope, and in response Vintras designated himself sovereign Pontiff.

He was arrested on a charge of exploiting his followers for money, tried at Caen, and sentenced to five years' imprisonment. When freed in 1845, he went to England and in London resumed his leadership role. In the relative freedom provided in England, he carried on the group's affairs for some time and eventually returned to France and settled in Lyons.

Sources:

Waite, Arthur E. *Studies in Mysticism.* London: Hodder and Stoughton, 1906.

Vishnu Devananda, Swami (1927–1993)

Disciple of the late **Swami Sivananda,** teacher of **hatha yoga,** and founder-president of the **Sivananda Yoga Vedanta Centers,** with branches in Canada, the United States, and Europe. He was born Swamy Kuttan Nair, on December 31, 1927, in Kerala, India. He became a school teacher at the age of 17, then later joined the Indian Army in which he served for two years. By chance he read a pamphlet by Swami Sivananda which emphasized the importance of studying the Hindu scripture *Bhagavad-Gita.* He did so and felt a strong impulse to visit the Sivananda Ashram. In 1946, while on army leave, he went to Rishikesh and became a disciple of Sivananda's. He decided to leave his family and become a renunciate. He was initiated, settled at the ashram, and became the professor of hatha yoga at the affiliated Yoga Vedanta Forest Academy.

At the suggestion of his guru, he undertook a tour of India, demonstrating hatha yoga *asanas* (positions) and training many hundreds of individuals. In 1957, he undertook a world tour, spending two years traveling throughout the U.S. and eventually settling in Canada, where he founded a Sivananda Yoga Vedanta Center. Of the several students of Sivanada operating in North America, he is the one recognized by the Divine Life Society, the Sivananda organization in India.

He became the first yoga instructor to obtain a pilot's license and flew a private "peace plane" decorated by artist Peter Max to such disturbed areas of the world as Northern Ireland, West Pakistan and the Suez Canal, dropping peace leaflets. He established yoga centers in twenty-five communities, including a large yoga camp in Quebec, Canada, and another in the Bahamas. He also founded **True World Order,** an organization dedicated to yoga harmony, health, peace, and vegetarianism. International headquarters of the Sivananda Yoga Ashram is at 673 8th Ave., Val Morin, PQ, Canada J0T 2R0.

Swami Sivananda died of kidney failure in 1993.

Sources:

Vishnu Devananda, Swami. *The Complete Illustrated Book of Yoga.* Julian Press, 1960.

———. *Meditation and Mantras.* New York: OM Lotus Publishing, 1978.

———. *The Sivananda Upanishad.* New York: OM Lotus Publishing, 1987.

Vision (Ocular and Inner)

Ocular vision is the perception of material objects in accordance with optical laws from a definite point in space. Difficult to classify are those rare cases when the sense of sight is transposed and the subject "sees" with his elbows, forehead, fingertips or stomach, since it is not clear what mechanism of vision is involved.

Inner vision is independent of space, objective existence, and, seemingly, optical laws. The simplest type of inner vision is presented by memory images, waking dreams, and images of imagination. The latter type may attain such an intensity as to emerge spontaneously and reach the pitch of **hallucination.**

Hallucination is the widest extent of inner vision. **Dreams** represent the primary type. They are hallucinations of low intensity. Generally, hallucinations appear to conform to all factors of ocular vision—space, optical laws, objectivity. The images appear externalized in space.

Indeed, objectivity in some cases of hallucinations may be more than an appearance, as some believe that a camera may register an apparition when outwardly nothing is visible and the vision must have taken place internally (see **psychic photography**). A still stronger proof of objectivity is furnished by cases of veridical visions in which the perception is afterward found to be a true visual representation of incidents taking place at a distance.

On the other hand, no objectivity is discoverable in degenerative hallucinations, the dogs and snakes of the drunkard, the scarlet fire of the epileptic, or the visions of the psychotic.

Inner vision may be developed empirically in **crystal gazing** and afford fruitful study for the determination of what elements are externalized from the subconscious mind of the scryer or of discarnate intelligences. Visions may also be distinguished as either spontaneous or induced. (See also **Transposition of the Senses.**)

Vision Magazine

Vision Magazine, self-described as a "Catalyst for Conscious Living," is a **New Age** networking tabloid serving San Diego and the surrounding counties in Southern California. Similar to other networking magazines, it attempts to keep readers informed of events and services in the constantly changing post-New Age scene. It seeks to offer a model for a more conscious, peaceful, and healthful world.

Each issue carries a series of short articles that highlight individuals and groups who are active in San Diego or who are visiting the area to put on special programming. Articles are organized so as to present the spectrum of reader interest from natural health to **astrology** and food. There are also one or two feature articles, often interviews conducted by one of the editors with leading figures in the national metaphysical or holistic health world.

Vision Magazine functions as a means for New Age practitioners to reach potential clients, and each issue devotes a significant amount of space to advertisements that inform readers where they may contact an astrologer, a **meditation** teacher, a hypnotist, a **qigong** teacher, or a spiritual community. Ads are selected from those organizations deemed to provide tools that are inspirational, solve problems, and provide dialogue on health, the environment, and the future course of society. The bulk of the ads are grouped into a "Monthly Calendar" and a "Community Resource Directory." The advertising supports the magazine, which is distributed freely throughout Southern California.

Vision Magazine began in 1994 and is published monthly from its headquarters at 4452 Park Blvd., Ste. 211, San Diego, CA 92116. It is edited by Sydney Murray and Kendall Klug. *Vision Magazine* has also extended itself into the Internet with a site found at http://www.visionmagazine.com/. Unlike most similar sites, however, *Vision*'s editors have moved to transform their Internet presence into an extension of the networking services offered by the magazine rather than simply an Internet description of the magazine.

Sources:

Vision Magazine. San Diego, Calif., n.d.

Vision Magazine. http://visionmagazine.com/. March 15, 2000.

Visions

Term derived from Latin *visus,* past participle of *videre,* to see, indicating the appearance to human beings of supernatural persons or scenes. Of great frequency in early and medieval times, and among primitive or semi-civilized races, visions seem to have decreased proportionately with the advance of learning and enlightenment. Thus, among the Greeks and Romans of the classic period, they were comparatively rare, although visions of demons or gods were occasionally seen. On the other hand, among Oriental races, the seeing of visions was a common occurrence, and these visions took more varied shapes.

In medieval Europe, visions were almost commonplace, and directions were given by the church to enable men to distinguish visions of divine origin from false delusions which were either self-generated or the work of the demons and/or the devil.

Visions may be roughly divided into two classes—those which are spontaneous and those which are induced. The great majority belong to the latter class.

In 1854, Joseph Ennemoser, in his work *The History of Magic,* enumerated causative factors in the appearance of visions to an individual: (1) a sensitive organism and delicate constitution; (2) a religious education and ascetic life (fasting, penance, etc.); (3) narcotics—opium, wine, incense, narcotic salves (witch-salves); (4) delirium, monomania; and/or (5) fear and expectation, preparatory words, songs, and prayers.

Among the visions induced by prayer and fasting and the severe self-discipline of the religious ascetic, must be included many historical or traditional instances—the visions of St.

Francis of Assisi, St. Anthony, St. Bernard Ignatius, St. Catherine of Siena, St. Hildegarde, and Joan of Arc. It may be noted that the convent has often been the special haunt of religious visions. A wave of **apparitions of the Virgin Mary** began in France early in the nineteenth century and several hundred incidents have been reported in the intervening decades to the present time. (See **Garabandal; Medjugorje**)

But the most potent means for the induction of visionary appearances are those discovered and used by indigenous people around the world. Over the ages people have indulged in narcotic substances, especially those with hallucinogenic properties, from opium and hashish to peyote. They have also used a variety of spiritual, psychic, and physical disciplines. Thus some fakirs, yogis, and other practitioners have been known to gaze for hours at a time at one object or remain for months in practically the same position, or practice various mortifications of the body, so that they may fall at length into a visionary state. Another ancient method of inducing visionary experience was staring into a shiny object such as a crystal or magic mirror.

The narcotic salves with which some anoint themselves are said to be similar to the witch **unguents** used in the Middle Ages, which induced in the witch the hallucination that she was flying through the air on a goat or a broomstick. Opium is also said to produce a sensation of flying, as well as visions of celestial delight. Alcoholic intoxication can induce visions of a more negative nature, most notably of insects or animals, as those who have experienced delirium can attest. Nitrogen may have a similar effect. The vapors rising from the ground in some places, or those found in certain caverns, are said to exercise an influence similar to that of narcotics.

Native Americans practiced external methods of inducing visions—solitude, fasting, and the use of salves or ointments. The vision quest was a popular activity of young men in many tribes. In some African, West Indian, and Arabic countries certain dances produced altered conferences, helping participants toward the desired visionary **ecstasy.** Rhythmic and repetitive music also assisted this process.

Spontaneous Visions

Spontaneous visions, although less common, are yet sufficiently numerous to merit attention here. The difficulty is, of course, to know just how far "fear and expectation" may have operated to induce the vision. In many cases, as in that of the seer **Emanuel Swedenborg,** the visions may have commenced as "visions of the night," hardly to be distinguished from dreams, and so from vision of an "internal" nature to clearly externalized apparitions. Swedenborg himself declared that when seeing visions of the latter class he used his senses exactly as when awake, dwelling with the spirits as a spirit, but able to return to his body when he pleased. The artist **Benvenuto Cellini,** like Swedenborg, had a number of spontaneous visions, though little of the same positive results.

Visions are by no means confined to the sense of sight. Taste, hearing, smelling, and touch may all be experienced in a vision. Joan of Arc, for instance, heard voices encouraging her to be the deliverer of her country. Examples may be drawn from the Hebrew Bible, as the case of the child Samuel in the temple (I Sam. 3:4), and instances could be multiplied from all ages and all times.

The visions of John Pordage (1607–1681) and the "Philadelphia Society," or, as they called themselves later, the "Angelic Brethren," a British organization stemming from the mysticism of **Jakob Boehme** in 1651, were noteworthy in this respect because they included the taste of "brimstone, salt, and soot." In the presence of the "Angelic Brethren," pictures were drawn on the windowpanes by invisible hands and were seen to move about.

Physiological explanations of visions have, from the earliest times, been offered. Plato observed:

"The eye is the organ of a fire which does not burn but gives a mild light. The rays proceeding from the eye meet those of the outward light. With the departure of the outward light the inner also becomes less active; all inward movements become calmer and less disturbed; and should any more prominent influences have remained they become in various points where they congregate, so many pictures of the fancy."

Democritus held that visions and dreams are passing shapes, ideal forms proceeding from other beings. Of deathbed visions Plutarch said:

"It is not probable that in death the soul gains new powers which it was not before possessed of when the heart was confined within the chains of the body; but it is much more probable that these powers were always in being, though dimmed and clogged by the body; and the soul is only then able to practise them when the corporeal bonds are loosened, and the drooping limbs and stagnating juices no longer oppress it."

The Spiritualist theory of visions can hardly be called a physiological one, save insofar as spirit may be regarded as refined matter. An old theory of visionary ecstasy on these lines was that the soul left the body and proceeded to celestial spheres, where it remained in contemplation of divine scenes and persons.

In modern times, the idea of the soul as an entity distinct from the physical body has been studied under the name of **out-of-the-body travel.** Stemming from this concept is the modern study of **near-death experiences,** in which individuals regarded as clinically dead have been revived and have described visionary experiences (see **death**).

Similar to this was the doctrine of Swedenborg, whose spirit, he believed, could commune with discarnate spirits (the souls of the dead) as one of themselves. To this may be traced the doctrines of modern **Spiritualism,** which thus regarded visions as actual spirits or spirit scenes, visible to the ecstatic or entranced subject whose spirit was projected to discarnate planes.

The question whether or not visions are contagious has been much disputed. It has been said that such appearances may be transferred from one person to another by the laying on of hands. In the case of those Scottish seers who claimed **second sight,** such a transference may take place even by accidental contact with the seer. The vision of the second person is, however, less distinct than that of the original seer.

The same idea prevailed with regard to the visions of "magnetized" patients in the days of **animal magnetism.** Insofar as these may be identified with the collective hallucinations of the hypnotic state, there is no definite scientific evidence to prove their existence.

Visions occur to people of all cultures and all states and positions. They come to the irreligious and educated, and by no means have they been confined to the ignorant or the superstitious. Many men of genius have been subject to visionary appearance. While Raphael was trying to paint the Madonna, she appeared to him in a vision. The famous composition known as the "Devil's Sonata" was said to have been dictated to Tartini by the devil himself. **Johann Wolfgang von Goethe** also had visions. **William Blake**'s portraits of the Patriarchs were done from visionary beings which appeared to him in the night. There have been a number of such instances.

Sources:

Barrett, Sir William. *Death Bed Visions.* London: Methuen, 1926.

Besterman, Theodore. *Crystal-Gazing: A Study in the History, Distribution, Theory and Practice of Scrying.* London: William Rider, 1924. Reprint, New Hyde Park, N.Y.: University Books, 1965.

Fielding-Ould, Fielding. *The Wonders of the Saints in the Light of Spiritualism.* London: John M. Watkins, 1919.

Halifax, Joan. *Shamanic Voices: A Survey of Visionary Narratives.* New York: E. P. Dutton, 1979.

Hall, Manly P. *Visions and Metaphysical Experiences.* Los Angeles: Philosophical Research Society, n.d.

Huxley, Aldous. *The Doors of Perception.* London: Chatto & Windus, 1954. Reprint, New York: Harper & Row, 1970.

Klonsky, Milton. *William Blake: The Seer and His Visions.* New York: Crown Publishers, 1977.

Lewis, David. *The Life of S. Teresa of Jesus.* London, 1970.

Muldoon, Sylvan J., and Hereward Carrington. *The Projection of the Astral Body.* London: Rider, 1929.

Pordage, John. *Truth Appearing Through the Clouds of Undeserved Scandal.* N.p., 1655.

Ring, Kenneth. *Life at Death; A Scientific Investigation of the Near-Death Experience.* New York: William Morrow, 1980.

Visions (Magazine)

Monthly publication containing articles on psychic phenomena, energy fields, and unorthodox healing. It was published by the American National Institute for Psychical Research. Last known address: 11222 La Cienega Blvd., Inglewood, CA 90304.

Visitants

Another term for spirit **apparitions.**

Vitality

Vitality is a name given that force or principle possessed by living things. In the case of human beings, controversy has long raged between those who interpret vitality mechanistically as the energy derived from food and oxygen intake and those who support theories of vitalism, a doctrine that the origin and phenomena of life derive from a vital principle as distinct from a purely chemical or physical force.

Vitalists argue that the mechanistic view appears inadequate as a matter of everyday experience, since there are limits to the vitality obtainable from oxidation of food and air. At a certain point of eating and breathing one becomes tired, and it is impossible to regain vitality without rest and sleep. Exactly what happens in the sleep state to enhance vitality is still not entirely clear. It does appear, however, that the human body is not simply an internal combustion machine, but rather an energy *transforming* machine. Contrary to the energy combustion view is the fact that fasting may often enhance vitality rather than deplete it.

The mind also has a profound effect on the vital condition of the body, as, vitalists further suggest, is clear from one's attitude to life, as well as the special phenomena of hypnosis and the profound effects which are possible through **meditation** techniques. It would seem that subtle processes are involved in energy transformation of food and air and the relationship of such transformation to the psychic life of human beings and their mental activities, states of consciousness, and sociological and spiritual aspirations.

Various great religions posit the existence of an individual soul as an essential principle of a human being, influenced by the physical and mental life as well as by environment and food intake, but independent from the physical body and surviving it after death. Spiritualists and psychical researchers have offered evidence for such survival, while materialists have argued that the phenomena presented as evidence of such apparent survival may be nothing more than mental artifacts. However, even this latter view also predicates mental life as capable of existing in a form almost as subtle as that of the claimed soul.

From a subjective point of view, the experience of **out-of-the-body travel** or **astral projection** has usually carried an overwhelming awareness of individuality as distinct from the body, which it apparently leaves, and for many individuals the experience has been one of deep religious conviction. **J. Sylvan Muldoon,** a pioneer writer on the subject, has argued in the light of his out-of-the-body experiences that the sleep state is a condition of vitality transfer between a "soul body" and the physical body, drawing upon some subtle life force outside the body.

Such a view is similar to the Polynesian concept of **mana** and the Hindu concept of **prana,** a subtle principle in the air and in food that is transformed into **kundalini,** energy in the body. A proportion of *kundalini* remains static in the body, but may become dynamic in sexual activity. It may also be diverted to subtle centers in the body through the spinal column by the practice of meditation in conjunction with the psycho-physical effects of purification of the mind and emotions, traditionally through self-purification and ethical living. Ancient Hindu treatises on *prana* have described at length the atomic structure of matter and its connection with the subtle currents of *prana* operating in the universe generally, as well as modified in the individual human being.

Sources:

Carrington, Hereward. *Vitality, Fasting and Nutrition.* New York: Rebman, 1908.

Crookall, Robert. *During Sleep: The Possibility of "Co-Operation" Between the Living and the Dead.* New Hyde Park, N.Y.: University Books, 1974.

Gopi, Krishna. *The Biological Basis of Religion and Genius.* New York: Harper & Row, 1972.

Hollander, Bernard. *In Search of the Soul and the Mechanism of Thought, Emotion, and Conduct.* 2 vols. London: Kegan Paul; New York: E. P. Dutton, 1920.

LeShan, Lawrence L. *The Medium, The Mystic and The Physicist.* New York: Viking; London: Turnstone Books, 1974.

Muldoon, Sylvan J., and Hereward Carrington. *The Projection of the Astral Body.* London: Rider, 1920.

Rama Prasad. *The Science of Breath and the Philosophy of Tattvas . . . Nature's Finer Forces.* 3rd rev. ed., Adhyr, Madras, India: Theosophical Publishing Society, 1897.

Wheeler, L. Richmond. *Vitalism: Its History and Validity.* London: Witherby, 1939.

Vitality (Magazine)

Vitality, the primary **New Age** networking periodical serving Toronto and surrounding communities in Ontario, Canada, emerged in the 1980s and during the 1990s grew into a substantive bimonthly magazine with more than 100 pages per issue. *Vitality* began as a self-described "wellness journal" primarily as an organ of the holistic health community and through the mid-1990s concentrated its attention on natural foods, herbs, nutrition, alternative psychologies, various body work therapies, and related other forms of drugless and noninvasive healing treatments. However, as the decade progressed, while the holistic health emphasis remains, the attention of the magazine grew to encompass all of the psychic and spiritual concerns of the post-New Age.

Vitality sees itself as an information organ. Each issue highlights the organizations and events that constitute holistic health and the New Age. As with most networking magazines, it is built around the advertisements placed by organizations that sponsor events and individuals who offer services to the public. Four times a year, *Vitality* publishes a pullout supplement, the "Vitality Resource Directory," in which coming events and major holistic organizations are listed.

Each issue carries a set of feature articles, the majority on health issues. There are also a set of columns that treat **astrology,** New Age lifestyles, and meetings and gatherings in the Toronto area. *Vitality* sees its purpose as providing an antidote to the world situation by offering a positive vision of the New Age of wholeness and health for body and soul.

Vitality is distributed as a free magazine in metaphysical and health food stores in Ontario, but subscriptions for home delivery may be obtained at 356 Dupont St., Toronto, ON Canada M5R 1V9.

Sources:

Vitality. Toronto, Ontario, Canada, n.d.

Vivekananda, Swami (1863–1902)

Hindu monk who became the leading interpreter of Yoga and Hinduism in the West; founder of the Ramakrishna Mission. Born as Narendra Nath Dutt in Calcutta in a Bengali family, January 12, 1863, he was educated at a Christian College in Calcutta. Here he was much impressed by the analytic and scientific methods of Westerners. For a time, Narendra was influenced by the Brahmo Samaj movement, but its rationalistic spirit did not altogether satisfy him.

When eighteen years old, he first met his spiritual teacher **Sri Ramakrishna,** who was much impressed by the boy's beautiful singing. Within a couple of years, Narendra was won over by the deep spiritual realization of Sri Ramakrishna and became his follower.

He made a number of visits to Sri Ramakrishna at Dakshineswar, but after the death of his father he was obliged to take charge of family affairs and got a job in an attorney's office. Eventually he persuaded Sri Ramakrishna to use his spiritual powers to ensure that his mother and brothers would never lack food and clothing, then renounced his worldly life.

Sri Ramakrishna died in 1886 and Narendra adopted the name Vivekananda in 1893, when he sailed from Bombay on May 31 to attend the Parliament of Religions held in Chicago in connection with the World's Fair.

In his opening address he caused tumultuous applause by commencing "Sisters and Brothers of America," and thereafter his simple trenchant style and his grasp of both Hindu and Christian beliefs won over many audiences. His book on *Raja Yoga* attracted the attention and respect of such enlightened thinkers as **William James** and Leo Tolstoy. Vivekananda lectured throughout Chicago, Detroit, Boston and New York for two years, then visited England, where he also aroused great enthusiasm, before returning to Calcutta in 1897.

Back in India, he took up the cause of ordinary people with realism as well as spiritual insight, stating: "The great national sin is the neglect of the masses and that is one of the causes of our downfall. No amount of politics would be of any avail until the masses of India are once more well educated and well cared for."

Soon afterwards he established the Ramakrishna Mission for training young monks and preachers. In June 1899, he made a second journey to the West, but by now his strength was giving out. He spent some time in California, which was congenial to his health and his teachings, and in December 1900 returned to India, where he passed away July 4, 1902, in Behur Monastery.

Today there are Ramakrishna Vedanta Centers in a number of countries, and the books of Swami Vivekananda remain one of the best and clearest introductions to Hindu spiritual teachings and yoga. These books are constantly reprinted, and include such popular works as *Jnana Yoga, Raja Yoga, Bhakti Yoga,* and *Karma Yoga.* His *Collected Works* covers eight volumes. The standard biography is by Swami Nikhilananda: *Swami Vivekananda; A Biography,* Adraita Ashram, Calcutta, India, 1975.

Vjestica

A name for a witch among the **Slavs.**

Voices (Paranormal)

Paranormal voices may be objective or subjective. The latter category is covered by **clairaudience.** The former is on the borderline of **apparitions,** as in the biblical statement: "And he fell to the earth, and heard a voice saying unto him: Saul, Saul, why persecutest thou me? . . . And the men which journeyed with him stood speechless, hearing a voice, but seeing no man." (Acts 9:4, 7).

According to Eusebius, a spirit voice was heard by the crowds at the martyrdom of Bishop Polycarp: "Be brave, Oh Polycarp." St. Francis, praying in a little ruined church, heard a voice from the painted wooden crucifix before which he knelt: "Francis, seest thou not that my house is being destroyed? Go, therefore, and repair it for me."

Joan of Arc was started on her mission by voices. "A very bright cloud appeared to her and out of the cloud came a voice." The sentence of death was based on admission of her monitary voices. She heard them first at thirteen years of age. They came mainly when she was awake, but also roused her sometimes from sleep. They were not always intelligible. She believed in them implicitly. The predictions of the voices were mainly fulfilled: the siege of Orleans was raised, Charles VII was crowned at Rheims and Joan was wounded, all as foretold. The preacher George Fox stated in his *Journal:*

"When my troubles and torments were great, when all my hopes in men were gone so that I had nothing outwardly to help me, nor could I tell what to do, then, O then, I heard a voice which said: 'There is one, even Jesus Christ, that can speak to thy condition.' When I heard it my heart did leap for joy."

Dr. Edwin Ash, in his book *Faith and Suggestion* (1912), described the case of Dorothy Kerin, who, after a long illness and on the point of death, suddenly heard a voice say "Dorothy." She woke up and saw the bed enveloped in light and a beautiful woman holding an Annunciation lily in her hand, saying "Dorothy, you are quite well," putting the stress on "quite." She became instantly well. For her own account, see Dorothy Kerin's book *The Living Touch* (1919).

There are various types of clairaudience. As a conscious subjective phenomenon, many writers, from Socrates onward, have claimed that their works were dictated by an inner voice. In **automatic writing,** psychics and Spiritualist mediums are usually unaware what is being written through their hands. Many Spiritualist mediums go into trance and apparently transmit messages from the spirits of the dead through their own vocal organs, sometimes with the tones and mannerisms of the deceased, but often only an approximation. **Inspirational speakers,** or channelers, also occasionally speak with the voices of spirit entities, while at other time employing their own vocal mannerisms with only the message being dictated by inner inspiration.

In the case of a clairvoyant, images of the deceased are perceived and described by the mediums, sometimes in conjunction with clairaudient messages. Both **clairvoyance** and clairaudience are classed as mental phenomena, involving **extrasensory perception.** In such cases, the voices may be paranormal in origin, but not in manifestation, and sometimes they may be more reasonably credited to unconscious mental activity.

Much controversy has surrounded the phenomenon of "**direct voice**" in Spiritualist séances, where spirits are claimed to speak independently of the medium, either through a **trumpet** or through a "voice box" built up from **ectoplasm** drawn from the medium. Both the use of trumpets and the idea of ectoplasm have been largely abandoned.

In line with modern technological developments, a new type of paranormal vocal phenomenon has emerged—"**Raudive voices,**" or "**electronic voice phenomenon.**" It is claimed that messages, often individual words or phrases apparently from deceased individuals, have appeared paranormally on audiotape recordings. In spite of much research, the evidence is ambiguous, as some apparent successes might be due to a mediumistic power of the investigator, rather than to some susceptibility of audiorecording to communications from deceased individuals.

A variant phenomenon which has been reported anecdotally in modern times is the "electronic visual (or video) phenomenon," in which it is believed that paranormal images have appeared on videotape recordings. Much research remains to be done before such claims can be validated.

Sources:

Ellis, David. *The Mediumship of the Tape Recorder.* Pulborough, U.K.: D. J. Ellis, 1978.

Lang, Andrew. *The Valet's Tragedy and Other Studies.* London: Longmans Green, 1903.

Raudive, Konstantin. *Breakthrough: An Amazing Experiment in Electronic Communication with the Dead.* Gerrards Cross, UK: Colin Smythe; New York: Taplinger, 1971. Reprint, New York: Lancer Books, 1973.

Smith, Hester Travers. *Voices from the Void.* London: William Rider, 1919.

Stokes, Doris. *Voices in My Ear.* London: Futura, 1981.

Swaffer, Hannen. *Adventures with Inspiration.* London: Kennerly, Morely and Mitchell, 1929.

Volguine, Alexandre (1903–1976)

Prominent French astrologer. In 1937 he founded *Les Cahiers Astrologiques,* a forum of French astrological research, which he edited until his death in 1976. He wrote a number of works on **astrology,** some of which have now been published in English translation.

Sources:

Volguine, Alexandre. *Lunar Astrology.* New York: ASI Publishers, 1974.

———. *The Ruler of the Nativity.* New York: ASI Publishers, 1973.

———. *The Technique of Solar Returns.* New York: ASI Publishers, 1976.

Vollhardt, Maria (Frau Rudloff) (ca. 1925)

A physical medium whom Dr. F. Schwab, author of *Teleplasma und Telekinese* (Berlin, 1923) made the subject of searching studies for two years. Vollhardt, the wife of an official in the Berlin Postal Ministry, produced **telekinesis** (movements of objects at a distance), **levitations, apports, ectoplasm** and **stigmata** phenomena of a baffling character.

In his book *My Psychic Adventures* (1924), psychical researcher **J. Malcolm Bird** wrote of having seen a quantity of irritated-looking puncture wounds, some actually bleeding, appear in a rough square pattern on the medium's hand. The only suggestion he could make for normal duplication was a battery of three or four forks or a section of nutmeg grater. The mystery of how such wounds were produced deepened when the sitters declared that they had seen on Vollhardt's hand a small object, the shape of a bird's beak, or claw. They put a pot full of farina on the table and asked for an imprint. They got it—in the shape of a chicken's foot.

Once the medium's hand was stigmatized across the hand of one of the sitters who was controlling her. At each puncture, the medium gave a sharp cry of pain. She stated that she felt as though an electric current had entered at the skin and passed through the body.

Schwab observed the phenomenon some fifty times outside the séance room in good light. When he made photographs with a stereoscopic camera he got a picture of a sort of claw of several branches, poised upon the perfectly controlled hand of the medium. He believed it was a materialized symbol of the medium's subconscious notion of oppression and torture.

In 1925, Vollhardt figured in court proceedings. At a séance given to a number of scientists and doctors, her arms, linked up in the orthodox manner, were found, on the lights being turned up, encircled by two massive rings. Albert Moll refused to believe in the penetration of **matter passing through matter** and later declared in a book that the medium must have had the rings concealed under her sleeves. The medium retorted with libel proceedings and offered to demonstrate her powers before the Bench. The offer came to nothing as Moll insisted that the demonstration should be done in daylight.

Degner testified on behalf of Vollhardt. The court found Moll guilty of calumny, but acquitted him as his statement was made "in defense of justified interests." The medium appealed against the acquittal and lost her case. Prof. Busch testified that the apports produced were fraudulently introduced by the medium while in a "semi-conscious condition."

Sources:

Bird, J. Malcolm. *My Psychic Adventures.* New York: Scientific American Publishing, 1924.

Volometer

An instrument invented by Dr. Sydney Alrutz (1868–1925) of Uppsala University, Sweden, to measure **will** as a dynamic power.

Von Däniken, Erich (1935–)

Swiss writer whose 1969 book, **Chariots of the Gods,** gave focus to a wave of popular interest in the idea that in ancient times the earth was visited by **extraterrestrials** whose presence is documented in a variety of archeological remains. Born in Zofingen, Switzerland, April 14, 1935, he was brought up in a conservative Roman Catholic setting at St. Michel College in Fribourg. At an early age von Däniken was fascinated by "inconsistencies" between religious doctrine and the accounts of mysterious events in the Bible. After leaving school, he took various jobs in hotels, and this seasonal work left him with spare time that he spent in traveling and reading. He visited South America, Russia and Egypt, seeing firsthand many of the monuments of the ancient past.

In his reading, he was particularly impressed by the biblical account of Ezekiel's fiery wheel and by Sumerian accounts of the coming of the Sun God in the ancient epic of *Gilgamesh.* Von Däniken began to evolve a theory of sky-borne gods in vehicles resembling accounts of **flying saucers,** built around the religious legends and myths of ancient civilizations. With the advent of American and Soviet space travel, such theories became much more plausible to many people.

In 1961, von Däniken started publishing articles about his theories and by 1966 had prepared a book, *Erinnerungen an die Zukunft,* which was published in Germany and serialized in the Swiss newspaper *Die Weltwoche.* This book was translated into English and published in England in 1969 and in the United States the following year under the title *Chariots of the Gods?* Von Däniken's introduction stated:

"I claim that our forefathers received visits from the universe in [the] remote past. Even though I do not know who these extraterrestrial intelligences were or from which planet they came, I nevertheless proclaim that these 'strangers' annihilated part of mankind existing at the time and produced a new, perhaps the first *homo sapiens.*"

As evidence, von Däniken cited accounts of cosmic battles in ancient legends and inscriptions suggestive of space travel. In later books he supported his theories by further legends, traveler's tales and photographs of ancient religious inscriptions.

Critics jumped upon von Däniken's facile interpretations such as his claims that Mayan temple figures and inscriptions represent spacemen at the controls of their vehicles. Such interpretations pulled odd artifacts out of their cultural context, revealed a significant misunderstanding of ancient cultural motifs, and falsely assumed that "ancient" astronauts would employ "twentieth-century" technology and design.

More crucial to his credibility, however, von Däniken admitted to falsifying his presentation. In an interview on the PBS

Nova science program on television in 1978, he confessed that he had not really explored an artifact-filled cave in South America as claimed in his book *The Gold of the Gods* (1973). In fact the artifacts were brass, not gold. He admitted:

"No that did not happen, but I think when somebody writes books in my style and in my sense, which are not scientific books, we call it in German 'Sachbucher.' It's a kind of popular book but it's not science fiction, though all the facts do exist but with other interpretations. Then an author is allowed to use effects. So some little things like this are not really important because they do not touch the facts . . ."

This astonishing defense of falsehood in order to strengthen a romantic interpretation of facts necessarily casts doubt on Von Däniken's theories. Von Däniken has not appeared perturbed by adverse criticism from scholars and scientists. He believes that his unconventional interpretations of mythology and archaeology will be generally accepted in the course of time.

Von Däniken has found his strongest support in the writings of Zecharia Sitchin. His theories have been debunked by Ronald Story and Clifford Wilson. In light of the intense criticism the idea of ancient astronauts received in the late 1970s, the wave of interest in the idea subsided and new books on the subject have become quite rare.

Sources:

Sitchin, Zecharia. *The 12th Planet.* New York: Stein and Day, 1976.

———. *The Wars of Gods and Men.* New York: Avon, 1985.

Story, Ronald D. *The Space-Gods Revealed.* New York: Harper & Row, 1976; Barnes & Noble, 1978.

Von Däniken, Erich. *According to the Evidence: My Proof of Man's Extraterrestrial Origin.* London: Souvenir, 1977.

———. *Chariots of the Gods?* London: Souvenir Press, 1969. Reprint, New York: G. P. Putnam's Sons, 1970.

———. *The Gods and Their Grand Design: the Eighth Wonder of the World.* London: Souvenir, 1984.

———. *The Gold of the Gods.* London: Souvenir Press, 1973.

———. *In Search of Ancient Gods; My Pictorial Evidence for the Impossible.* London: Souvenir Press, 1974.

Wilson, Clifford. *Crash Go the Chariots.* New York: Lancer, 1972.

Voudou

The African-based religion of Haiti. Voudou can be traced to the first Africans brought to Haiti in the sixteenth century. However, it was during the years of French acquisition of land in Haiti that the bulk of African people were brought to the island. Between 1664 and 1830 some 1,650,000 Africans arrived in Haiti. The dominant group came from Dahomey, and the Dahomean religion became the most important element in the emergence of Voudou.

The Africans brought with them beliefs found throughout West Africa, including a belief in a supreme deity or divine power. In Haiti that deity came to be known as le Bon Diei (the Good God). This deity had largely withdrawn from human affairs, but under him were a number of greater and lesser deities. Among the major deities were Legba, Erzulie, and Damballah. The lesser deities (*loas*) are numerous, and are of two varieties, those of African origin (the Rada) and those of Haitian origin (Pétro). Many of the African deities, especially those tied to local sites, did not survive the Atlantic crossing, and they were replaced with new local deities. The name Pétro derived, according to oral tradition, from a man named Don Pédro who introduced a distinctive dance into Haitian religion.

The plantation owners in Haiti attempted to impose Catholicism on the slave population. One of the means by which Voudou survived was in the identification of the loas with various Catholic saints. Thus Legba was identified with Saint Anthony, Erzulie with the Virgin Mary, and Damballah with Saint Patrick. Damballah is pictured as a snake, and, as in Ireland, there are practically no snakes in Haiti. Hence the association with St. Patrick.

Voudou worship and practice is conducted by male (*oungan*) and female (*manbo*) priests. They operate out of a worship center called *ounfo.* In the center of the ounfo is a *peristil,* a pole that usually has a representation of Damballah coiled around it. Worship includes honoring the deities (which may involve the sacrifice of various animals), lively dancing with drum accompaniment, and the possession of priests or others in attendance by loas.

Like all West African religion, Voudou includes the practice of **magic.** Voudou has a particularly bad image, even among other African-based religions, as the home to much **sorcery** (malevolent magic), even to the extent of the calling forth of **zombies,** dead people brought back to life to handle menial labor in the fields.

The image of evil attached to Voudou in the popular imagination seems to have begun with what is known as the Affaire de Bizoton. On December 27, 1863, a little girl of the town of Bizoton was kidnapped and used in a sinister cannibalistic ritual. Eventually the perpetrators were caught, tried, and convicted. While the actions of the people who had killed the girl were offensive to all, in the popular press, especially the foreign press, the actions of the murderers were identified with the Voudou community. Besides the gruesome stories printed at the time, in the 1880s a volume on Haiti by Sir Spenser St. John describes the incident in vivid detail and uses it in a diatribe against Voudou. His work has been followed by a variety of writings, varying from the academic to the journalistic to the merely exploitive, that point a self-righteous finger at Voudou adherents.

There is, of course, an element of magic, even of black magic in Voudou, but it operates quite differently than outsiders have usually presented it. Besides the oungans and manbos, there are *bocors* (sorcerers), and *caplatas* (lesser magical functionaries). Most magic is used to ward off evil. Charms ward off the **evil eye** and various loas are seen as the cause of the different ills people suffer. Magic will be applied to discover the loa responsible and the means of getting the loa to go away. There are also accounts of evil spirits, creatures such as **vampires** and **werewolves.**

During the eighteenth century, the ruling class did not take particular notice of Voudou. They tended to identify it with the nocturnal gatherings most notable for dancing. The dancing drums, however, served as a communication system across Haiti, and in 1804 they became the means of organizing a massive and successful revolt. Haitians were able to pull off the revolution without the aid of a great leader because they were united by their religious beliefs. Those beliefs, including the protection of the loas, allowed them to rise against the better-armed rulers.

The use of Voudou in this revolt led the first black ruler of Haiti to oppose it. Later rulers embraced Voudou, most notably Jean-Claude Duvalier, who promoted his own image as a great Voudou magician and his use of Voudou priests in his militia.

Voudou was brought to the United States in 1804 and the years following the Haitian revolt. It spread through the black population of New Orleans and the surrounding countryside. It found its most famous practitioner in Marie Laveau in the mid-nineteenth century. Legal measures were taken to curb its power in the years prior to the Civil War, but they merely drove the practice underground. It survives today, both in a public mode accessible to tourists and as a semisecret religious community. In the 1920s it provided inspiration for the development of African American Spiritualism and the Spiritual Church movement.

Sources:

Bisnauth, Dale. *History of Religion in the Caribbean.* Kingston, Jamaica: Kingston Publishers, 1989.

David, Wade. *The Serpent and the Rainbow.* New York: Warner, 1985.

Denning, Melita, and Osborne Phillips. *Voudou Fire: The Living Reality of Mystical Religion.* St. Paul: Llewellyn Publications, 1979.

Deren, Maya. *Divine Horsemen: The Voodoo Gods of Haiti.* New York: Chelsea House, 1970.

Leyburn, James G. *The Haitian People.* New Haven, Conn.: Yale University Press, 1966.

Selden, Rodman. *Spirits of the Night.* Dallas: Spring, 1992.

Vril

A word invented by **Edward Bulwer Lytton,** famous novelist, politican and occultist, to describe a kind of psychic energy. It was featured in his book *Vril: Power of the Coming Race* (1871), which told how "Vril" enabled a race to reach a high degree of civilization and develop a Utopian society without poverty, inequality, or war. Lytton himself had some connections with occultism and received the magician **Éliphas Lévi** at his house. The idea of Vril was very much in tune with ideas of magical power that Lytton had previously espoused in his books and which continue to be used by occultists to the present time. In prewar Germany there was a Vril Society founded in Berlin.

Sources:

Lytton, Edward Bulwer. *Vril: Power of the Coming Race.* Edinburgh; London: W. Blackwood and Sons, 1871.

W

WADL See **Witches Anti-Defamation League**

Wafer (in Devil Worship)

The sacred wafer used in the Christian Eucharist is frequently cited as a prized item in **devil worship** for purposes of profanation. When Satanism was invented in the late fifteenth century by Roman Catholic inquisitors, no phenomenon existed which could be called Satanism. The inquisitors envisioned Satanism as a reversal of Christianity, the devil being the opposite of God. Devil worship, then, would be a reversal of Christian rituals, primarily the Roman Catholic Mass. Thus a Satanist would speak the Lord's prayer in reverse. The idea of a cult that parodied and profaned Christianity was in all likelihood built out of incidents in which different individuals, over the centuries, actually performed individual sacrilegious acts.

It was rumored that Satanists would attempt to obtain consecrated hosts or wafers from the chalice of a church altar to be profaned in some manner. Sometimes, a turnip was said to be colored black and used to imitate a host wafer.

The practice of Satanism was recorded in the memory and documents of the Christian Church in the West but no actual incident of devil worship occurred until the time of Louis XIV of France, although it was alleged that in the house of the Irish sorcerer, **Dame Alice Kyteler,** a wafer of sacramental bread was found bearing the name of the Devil.

Sources:

Robbins, Rossell Hope. *The Encyclopedia of Witchcraft and Demonology.* New York: Crown Publilshers, 1959.

Wagner, Edward A. (1906–1982)

Journalist and astrologer, born in Philadelphia on November 15, 1906. As a youth he moved with his family to Cleveland, Ohio, where he finished high school. In 1924 he went to work for the *Cleveland Press.* He emerged from obscurity to become an assistant to **Harry Houdini** in the exposure of Spiritualist frauds and charlatans. Houdini died in 1926 and Wagner turned his attention to **astrology** with the idea of publishing a Houdini-like exposé. In order to carry out that task, Wagner immersed himself in the subject, learning to cast horoscope charts and interpret them. In the process he was converted to a belief in astrology, and rather than write an exposé, he became a professional astrologer. He affiliated with the **Rosicrucian Fellowship** and eventually moved to Oceanside, California, as the fellowship's assistant superintendent of publications.

In the early 1930s Wagner established a business in Los Angeles and for two years published the *National Astrological Journal* (1933–35). In 1936 he began a nationally syndicated column, "Your Daily Forecast," which continued until the general discontinuance of astrological columns during World War II (a voluntary gesture of the journalistic and astrological community due to Hitler's use of astrology). Wagner served in the army during the war. In 1946 he established a weather forecasting business, but also became the editor-in-chief for Dell Publishing Company (1946–73). Dell published, amid its many astrological publications, *Horoscope* magazine. In 1973 Wagner was named consulting executive editor of *Horoscope,* and he was named editor emeritus in 1975. He died in May of 1982.

Sources:

Holden, James H., and Robert A. Hughes. *Astrological Pioneers of America.* Tempe, Ariz.: American Federation of Astrologers, 1988.

Waite, Arthur Edward (1857–1942)

A British scholar and historian of occultism and mysticism. Waite was born on October 2, 1857, in Brooklyn, New York, and brought to London, England, by his family when he was an infant. He was educated in Roman Catholic schools. As a boy, he cherished an affection for "penny dreadfuls," the romantic popular pulp literature of the day.

Waite grew up during the first European renaissance of occultism which stretched from the end of the nineteenth century to the outbreak of World War I, and his personal friends included **Arthur Machen** and **Ralph Shirley.** He also met **William Butler Yeats, Helena Petrovna Blavatsky, Annie Besant, Rudolf Steiner, Wynn Westcott, Algernon Blackwood,** and **Aleister Crowley.**

Waite regularly contributed to Shirley's *Occult Review,* and for some twenty years he edited anonymously its monthly "Review of Periodical Literature." During this period he acquired a knowledge of the major current developments in occultism all over the world.

He was also a Freemason and authority on Masonic writings. He was responsible for the first British publication of many important occult and mystical texts. He translated and publicized the writings of occultist **Éliphas Lévi** (Alphonse Louis Constant).

In 1891 Waite joined the Hermetic Order of the **Golden Dawn** but quit in less than a year believing his time was better spent studying and translating alchemical texts. He developed a negative attitude toward all magical ritual and believed that rituals differed primarily in the amount of black magic they contained.

Waite became a devoted mystic and in the wake of the collapse of the Golden Dawn in 1915, he founded the Fellowship of the Rosy Cross. He believed that suitably constructed rituals, which he endeavored to write, that had a dramatic form but were of a religious (devotional) rather than magical (manipulative) format, could assist the mystical quest.

Waite was involved in the transition from the first to the second generation of the occult revival. He was a productive occult writer and produced some historical texts and translations. Because he critiqued the magical endeavor, he was disliked and denegrated by occultists, and orthodox mystics distrusted him because of his association with the occult. Recovery of his work has been assisted by the efforts of Robert Gilbert, who has produced a biography and a bibliography of his writings.

Through the twentieth century, Waite was known for his work with Pamela Coleman-Smith in the production of a deck of tarot cards (the Waite deck) and his commentary on the tarot, *The Key to the Tarot* (1910). Both the deck and the book remain popular in spite of the numerous new divinatory tarot decks that have been produced in the late twentieth century as expressions of the Wiccan and **New Age** movements.

Waite died May 19, 1942.

Sources:

Gilbert, Robert A. *A. E. Waite: A Bibliography.* Wellingborough, Northamptonshire, England: Aquarian Press, 1983.

———. *A. E. Waite: Magician of Many Parts.* Wellingborough, Northamptonshire, England: Crucible, Thorsons, 1987.

Waite, Arthur E. *Azoth; or, The Star in the East.* London: Theosophical Publishing Society, 1893.

———. *The Book of Black Magic and of Pacts.* London: George Redway, 1898. Revised as *The Book of Ceremonial Magic.* London: William Rider, 1911.

———. *The Brotherhood of the Rosy Cross.* London: William Rider & Sons, 1924.

———. *The Hidden Church of the Holy Grail.* London: Rebman, 1909.

———. *The Key to the Tarot.* London: William Rider, 1910.

———. *The Occult Sciences.* London: George Redway, 1891. Reprint, Secacus, N.J.: University Books, 1974.

———. *The Pictorial Key to the Tarot.* London: William Rider, 1911.

———. *The Real History of the Rosicrucians.* London: George Redway, 1887.

———. *Shadows of Life and Thought.* London: Selwyn and Blount, 1938.

———. *Studies in Mysticism and Certain Aspects of the Secret Tradition.* London: Hodder and Stoughton, 1906.

Waldensians

The name of a proto-Protestant Christian sect that arose in the south of France late in the twelfth century C.E. Peter Waldo, a prosperous merchant from Lyon, appeared about 1170 as a wandering preacher. He soon built a substantial following in the same region in which the heretical **Albigensians** had their centers. However, the Waldensians were a Bible-centered, theologically orthodox group. The Albigensians had adopted a **Gnostic** religious system that rested somewhat upon that of Manichaeism, with its extreme dualism (a belief that God and evil exist as two equal and opposing forces) and severe asceticism. Waldo's complaints were against much of the undisciplined behavior of priests, and a number of "unbiblical" practices such as pilgrimages, worship of saints, and church wealth, all of which arose as items on the agenda of protestants in the sixteenth century.

Waldensianism's adherents were divided into two classes: "Christ's paupers," who left their secular lives behind; and the "friends" who accepted Waldo's teachings but remained in their secular lives. This division was similar to the two levels of membership among the **Cathari.** As the movement spread to Italy and Germany, it was carried by wandering preachers who went out in pairs.

After a generation in which the church attempted to win them back to the fold, the Waldensians began to experience persecution about the second decade of the thirteenth century. A number were burned in southern France and Germany, but in Italy they were able to survive by retreating into the Alpine mountain valleys. The group survived primarily in Italy, where they aligned themselves to the sixteenth-century reformation. In the last half of the twentieth century, they emerged as a recognized group in Italy and the Methodist Church of Italy recently merged with them.

During the Middle Ages the spokespersons of the Roman church believed that, like the Albigenses, the Waldensians had a diabolical element in their religion, and from time to time they were classed with the various secret societies that sprang up in medieval Europe, such as the **Templars** and the **Rosicrucians.** Although the Waldensians possessed an internal doctrine and disciple accepted by the inner core of adherents, their beliefs and practices were more of an ethical nature and were in no manner associated with the occult or magic.

Sources:

Westin, Gunnar. *The Free Church through the Ages.* Nashville, Tenn.: Broadman, 1958.

Walder, Phileas

A Swiss Lutheran minister who became an occultist and Spiritualist, and a friend of French occultist **Éliphas Lévi.** In the anti-clerical hoax of Léo Taxil (**Gabriel Jogand-Pagès**), Walder and Miss Sophia Walder were represented as associates of Freemason **Albert Pike** in the rites of **devil worship** in Charleston, South Carolina. In reality, Walder was an earnest Freemason and mystic.

WALES

Wales shares with other Celtic countries an ancient mythology and traditional lore, although much of this was suppressed with the spread of Christianity from the fifth century on, and a succession of conquests by Romans, Normans, and English. Many of the enchanted stories of the **King Arthur** cycle are also found in Welsh tradition.

In the seventeenth century, Puritanism took a firm hold, and the spread of Methodism in the eighteenth century further worked to eradicate traditions of magic, although the religious revivals of the late nineteenth century had a wild, almost Pagan flavor about them and were accompanied by the appearance of various forms of paranormal phenomena.

Ancient Traditions

One of the great sources of Welsh legends is the **Mabinogion,** dating from medieval times, containing stories for oral recitation by bards in the halls of the ancient princes of Wales. Typical motifs in these tales are supernatural birth, visits to the Other World, and magic shape-changing. Rhiannon, the wife of Pwyll, possessed marvelous birds that came from the Unseen World, and their singing held warriors spellbound for 80 years. In another story, Lvevelys helps his brother Lludd to eradicate three plagues that have devastated Britain—the Coranians, a strange race whose knowledge is infinite and who hear everything uttered, even the softest whisper; a horrifying shriek that penetrates every house on a May evening, caused by the battle between two dragons; and a great giant who carries off all the food from the king's palace.

A well-known story is that of the birth of Taliesin, chief of the bards of the west. The hero, Gwion Bach, goes to the Land under Waves at the bottom of Lake Bala in North Wales. There he finds the giant Tegid the Bald and his wife Ceridwen, goddess of poetry and knowledge. Ceridwen owns an immense cauldron in which she brews a mixture of science and inspiration, with the aid of her books of magic. This great brew has to simmer for a year and a day, and she sets the blind man Morda to keep the fire going and Gwion to stir the brew. It is to yield three magical drops.

Toward the end of the year, as Ceridwen is picking herbs and making incantations, three drops of the brew spurt out of the cauldron and fall upon Gwion Bach's finger. With the sudden heat on his finger, he puts it into his mouth to cool, whereupon the three drops instantly give him knowledge and meaning of all things, and he becomes aware that he must guard against Ceridwen's cunning, so he flees to his own land. Meanwhile the cauldron bursts and the rest of the brew is a black poison that overflows into the waters, poisoning the horses of Gwyddno Garanhir.

Ceridwen seizes a billet of wood and strikes blind Morda on the head, but he declares that he is innocent and that it is the fault of Gwion Bach. She runs in pursuit of Gwion, but he sees her coming and changes himself into a hare. She changes herself into a greyhound and follows him. He runs toward a river and becomes a fish, but she, in the form of an otter, chases him under the water, so he must turn himself into a bird. She becomes a hawk and gives him no rest in the sky. Just as she is going to swoop on him, he sees a heap of winnowed wheat on the floor of a barn, so he drops among the wheat and turns himself into one of the grains. She turns herself into a black hen, scratches at the wheat and swallows him.

She carries him for nine months and is delivered of him, but cannot kill him because of his beauty, so she wraps him in a leather bag and casts him into the sea to the mercy of God. He is carried into the weir of Gwyddno Garanhir and found by Prince Elphin, who has come to catch fish in his net. Elphin renames him Taliesin, which can mean "beautiful brow" or "great value."

Druids

Wales is also considered a center for the cult of the Druids (brought by the **Celts**), who came into Wales as early as 200 B.C.E. They were said to practice human sacrifice, although it has also been claimed that the victims were criminals. They also employed methods of **divination.**

The Druids are thought to have come from ancient Gaul, where they were suppressed in the Roman Conquest as a rival source of power and prestige. The historian **Pliny the Elder** recorded their association with the mistletoe plant in their sacred rites.

He also mentioned a mysterious object used by the Druids, which he named the "serpent's egg." It was roughly the size and shape of a small apple, and it was said that a mass of hissing serpents threw this egg into the air. If it could be caught in a white cloak before touching the ground, it would convey powers of magic to the possessor, such as the ability to float against a river current, and success in legal undertakings.

Witchcraft and Demonology

Sir Dafydd Llwyd, who lived in Cardiganshire in the reign of Charles II, had studied **black magic** at Oxford. He practiced as a physician and was famous for his wonderful cures, but his skill was owed to a **familiar** spirit or demon that he kept locked up in a book of spells. One day, the story is told, he accidently left this **grimoire** behind and sent his pageboy home to fetch it, commanding him to on no account open it. Like most lads the boy could not resist being inquisitive; he lifted the cover and turned over the leaves, with their weird inscriptions.

Suddenly there came forth a huge demon who frowned and in a hoarse grumbling voice asked to be set to work. In spite of his terror, the boy had the wit to say, "Fetch me some stones out of the River Wye." In a few moments, stones and pebbles began hurtling through the air, when Sir Dafydd, aware that something was wrong, came hurrying back and conjured the spirit back into the book before any serious harm could be done.

As early as the twelfth century, Christian priests in Wales were warned about letting the Eucharistic Host get into the hands of magicians and witches, who might secretly slip it out of their mouths and hide it in a handkerchief or glove. In 1582 the wife of Edward Jones was called upon to prove to the satisfaction of the archdeacon of Lewes "that she did eat the Communion bread and put yt not in hir glove."

As late as the opening years of the eighteenth century, two old dames were said to have attended the morning service at Llanddewi Brefi Church to partake of Holy Communion, but instead of eating it like the other communicants, they kept it in their mouths and went out. Then they walked round the church nine times, and at the ninth circuit the Devil came out of the church wall in the form of a frog, to whom they gave the Host from their mouths, and by doing this, sold themselves to Satan and became witches.

There are many stories about Dr. John Harries (1785–1839), a celebrated Welsh physician and seer of Cërt-y-Cadno, Carmarthenshire, who was said to possess a great book of magic, which was kept locked to prevent any ignorant person from letting loose its powerful influences. Harries boasted of his knowledge of future and distant events, imparted to him by familiar spirits.

Belief in witchcraft persisted into the twentieth century in Wales, but it concerned "white witches" who cast useful spells and horoscopes, or averted evil events. In 1933 there was a wise man in Llangwrig, Montgomeryshire, who was famous throughout Wales for breaking the spells of witches. He kept his book of divination and an almanac in a rosewood casket.

In November 1936 a correspondent in *John O'London's Weekly* stated that "even now belief in witchcraft in the upper parts of the Wye Valley is not quite extinct." In the following month, another correspondent stated: "When we lived in a small village in Montgomeryshire some years ago we found a widespread belief in witchcraft among the farmers of the district." If the cattle became sick, farmers visited the wise man to find out who had bewitched their beasts. If two farmers had a serious quarrel, one of them went to the wise man to obtain a charm to injure his neighbor.

Phenomena at Religious Revivals

Welsh preaching is celebrated for its fervor, and the traditional **hwyl** or peroration of a sermon is said to have magic effects. During the nineteenth century, there were reports of mysterious **luminous phenomena** associated with revivalism, and such accounts were given again in 1904 and 1905 during the inspired revival campaigns of Mary Jones of Egryn. Jones was a happily married peasant woman with a family, when in December 1904 she received beatific visions instructing her to undertake the work of religious revival that had earlier been the mission of the preacher Evan Roberts in Glamorgan.

The first night of Jones' mission was marked by the appearance of a mysterious star and various lights. She herself reported seeing "a circle of small stars, encompassing a cross of diamond stars, and on this cross at times the draped figure of the Saviour." The strange luminous phenomena were witnessed by other individuals. A skeptical businessman was driving her home one evening from a meeting, and prayed that he might be accorded a sign if she was indeed a divinely ordained preacher. Immediately there appeared above the road, in front of the car, a misty star. As the man gazed a luminous cross was formed inside it, sparkling with diamonds, and upon this was a draped figure with bowed head.

On another occasion, Jones herself reported seeing the Devil, who first appeared in the figure of a man, but when she started singing revival hymns, suddenly stopped, turned on her and became transformed into an enormous black dog. She prayed for strength, and the dog rushed growling into a hillock.

The star and the light were seen by many people from the first day of Jones' mission. The star seemed to rest above particular houses where converts later came to the meetings. It also followed her on her journeys. On her trip to Criccieth, for example, the lights were witnessed by the people with her. At Bryncrug, a few miles inland from Towyn, the gallery of the chapel was flooded during the service by the mysterious light. After the service, the light, in the form of a ball of fire casting its rays down to earth, was seen by a party of young quarrymen. Overtaking the light, which had stopped, they knelt down in the middle of the road and held a prayer meeting, bathed in the unearthly light.

Some of these lights and their movements are reminiscent of many modern accounts of **UFOs**.

The Gardnerian Revival

In the last generation, growing out of the initial work of **Gerald B. Gardner** (the witch of the Isle of Man), a new neopagan witchcraft or Wicca movement spread from England through the British Isles, the lands of the commonwealth, and the United States. As the movement grew and broke into numerous segments, there arose a number who attached themselves to Welsh witchcraft traditions. Among the early covens in the northeastern United States in the 1970s were the New York Coven of Welsh Traditional Witchcraft and the New England Coven of Welsh Traditional Witchcraft, which supplemented their Gardnerian rituals with material from folkloric, archeological, and anthropological texts on Wales. Several significant groups—the most notable possibly the Church and School of Wicca (Box 1502, New Bern, NC 28560) and the Cymry Wicca (Box 4196, Athens, GA 30605)—claim to draw on Welsh traditions. In addition, many modern witches, drawing on the **Mabinogion,** have chosen such names as Ceridwen and Taliesin as their religious names.

Sources:

Adler, Margot. *Drawing Down the Moon.* Boston, Mass.: Beacon Press, 1987.

Charlton, I. W. *The Revival in Wales.* London, 1905. (Pamphlet)

Graves, Robert. *The White Goddess.* London: Faber & Faber, 1948.

Guest, Lady Charlotte, trans. *The Mabinogion: From the Llyfr Coch o Hergest.* 3 vols. London, 1948.

Jones, Edmund. *A Relation of Ghosts and Apparitions Which Commonly Appear in the Principality of Wales.* Bristol, England: 1767.

Jones, T. Gwynn. *Welsh Folklore and Folk Customs.* London: Methuen, 1930.

Morgan, J. V. *The Welsh Religious Revival, 1904–05.* London: Chapman & Hall, 1909.

Walker, Kenneth Macfarlane (1882–1966)

Surgeon and author of books relating to parapsychology and mysticism. Walker was born in 1882 in London, England. He studied at Cambridge University (M.A., M.B., Ch.B.), the Royal College of Surgeons, and the International College of Surgeons. He was a captain in the Royal Army Medical Corps during World War I (1915–19) and later a consulting surgeon at London hospitals.

As an adult Walker was introduced to the writings and work of **Georgei I. Gurdjieff,** a mystic. In England he studied with Maurice Nicoll and **P. D. Ouspensky.** He visited Gurdjieff in France in 1948–49 (a visit described in a 1952 article). He wrote both autobiographically of his time as a Gurdjieff student and about his philosophical conclusions. By the time of his death, January 25, 1966, he was a well-known exponent of Gurdjieff's perspective.

Sources:

Driscoll, J. Walter. *Gurdjieff: An Annotated Bibliography.* New York: Garland Publishing, 1985.

Walker, Kenneth. *Diagnosis of Man.* Harmondsworth, U.K.: Penguin Books, 1942.

———. *I Talk of Dreams.* London: Jonathan Cape, 1946.

———. *The Making of Man.* London: Routledge & Kegan Paul, 1963.

———. *Meaning and Purpose.* London: Jonathan Cape, 1944.

———. *A Study of Gurdjieff's Teachings.* London: Jonathan Cape, 1957.

———. *The Unconscious Mind.* London: Rider, 1961. Reprinted as *The Extra-sensory Mind.* New York: Emerson, 1961.

———. *Venture with Ideas.* London: Jonathan Cape, 1951.

Walker, Roland (1907–1993)

Professor of biology who wrote on parapsychology. Walker was born on February 8, 1907, at Stellenbosch, South Africa. He studied at Oberlin College, Ohio (B.A., 1928; M.A., 1929) and Yale University (Ph.D., 1934). Following his graduation he began a long tenure in the biology department at Rennselaer Polytechnic Institute, Troy, New York. Walker developed a side interest in parapsychology and operated from a critical perspective. The primary product of that interest was an essay critical of fellow biologist **J. B. Rhine**'s understanding of **extrasensory perception** (ESP) and **psychokinesis** (PK). He died July 30, 1993.

Sources:

Walker, Roland. "Parapsychology and Dualism." *Scientific Monthly* (July 1954).

Walker, Thane (ca. 1890– ?)

Founder (with Phez Kahlil) of the **Prosperos,** a group stemming from the philosophy of mystic **G. I. Gurdjieff.** Walker was born in Nowaway County, Missouri. He claimed to have been one of America's first psychologists and to have been imprisoned in a Nazi concentration camp after writing the article "I Saw Hitler Make Black Magic." He was a Marine Corps officer and entertained American troops in Japan during the occupation in World War II.

As a former pupil of Gurdjieff, Walker became a Gurdjieff-style figure, teaching students through stories and disorienting activities, but also drawing upon Freudian and Jungian psychology and occult and astrological traditions. Walker believed students should wake from the misleading reality of everyday sensory experience and limited personality to a wider reality.

The Prosperos group was founded in Florida in 1956, but the organization has since moved its headquarters to California and reported some 3,000 members at the end of the 1980s.

Sources:

Melton, J. Gordon. *Encyclopedia of American Religions.* Detroit: Gale Research, 1992.

Walker, William

British spirit photographer, a member of the **Crewe Circle** associated with **William Hope.** Walker was the first to perform **psychic photography** on which spirit "extras" appeared in full color.

Walk-ins

In 1979 popular **New Age** author **Ruth Montgomery** identified an unknown phenomenon that had occurred to a variety of unrelated individuals. They reported that the soul originally inhabiting their body had vacated it so that another could "walk in" and take over. Montgomery wrote about walk-ins in her book, *Strangers Among Us* (1979), suggesting that at times people with otherwise perfectly healthy bodies no longer wished to live. If they were allowed to leave, the people would turn over their physically sound bodies to some advanced (though as yet unperfected) soul. In a subsequent book, *Threshold to Tomorrow* (1983), Montgomery related some 17 case histories of walk-ins, including New Age leaders Dick Sutphen and **Carol Parrish-Harra.**

The background of a person claiming to be a walk-in often contains a traumatic, even life-threatening, event through which the person passed to a new, transformed life. Some individuals suffered a medical crisis, often to the point of clinical death and revival. Others reached the conclusion that they simply no longer wanted to live. Because the new personality emerging after the crisis retains the memory of the previous personality, some observers have suggested more mundane explanations of the walk-in experience, including a dramatic reintegration of a previously fragmented personality. The experience of walk-ins has also been compared to near-death experiences, which have led to similar life transformations, though without the feeling of being a different person.

Montgomery claims she received the concept of walk-ins from her "guides," a group of evolved entities from whom Montgomery had channeled material for many years. According to her guides, many of the world's leading figures have been walk-ins, including Moses, Joseph, and Jesus of Nazareth. More recent leaders include Muhammad, Christopher Columbus, Abraham Lincoln, Joseph Smith Jr., **Mary Baker Eddy,** and many of the founders of the American nation, notably George Washington, Alexander Hamilton, Benjamin Franklin, Thomas Jefferson, James Madison, and Abigail Adams.

None of the outstanding people from history identified by Montgomery as walk-ins left any hint of having experienced anything similar to the experiences of contemporary walk-ins. Montgomery believed the public nature of the contemporary phenomenon is related to the approaching New Age, which she believed would be initiated by a polar shift in the year 1999. In the past, walk-ins have not identified themselves as such, but in the light of the events of 1999, they need to know of each other so they can locate each other as the leaders who will build the new golden age.

Among the more interesting of the contemporary walk-ins is the couple who heads the **Extraterrestrial Earth Mission.** Over the last decade they have claimed to be inhabited by a series of extraterrestrial metaphysical teachers. In 1986, John, a metaphysical teacher in Seattle, Washington, abandoned his body to a personality known as "Avinash." Later that year he met another walk-in, then named "Arthea." During the next eight years Avinash would also depart and be succeeded by persons known as "Aktivar," "Alarius," "Savizar," and "ZaviRah." At the same time Arthea was followed by "Akria," "Polaria," "Silarra," and "Ziva'rah." There is every expectation that further walk-in teachers will appear in the future.

Sources:

Montgomery, Ruth. *Strangers Among Us: Enlightened Beings from a World to Come.* New York: Coward, McGann & Geohegan, 1979.

———. *Threshold to Tomorrow.* New York: G. P. Putnam's Sons, 1983.

Parrish-Harra, Carol W. *Messengers of Hope.* Marina del Rey, Calif.: DeVorss, 1983.

Zuromski, Paul. "Dick Sutphen." *Body, Mind, Spirit* (September/October 1987): 14–18.

Wallace, Alfred Russel (1823–1913)

British naturalist, codiscoverer with Charles Darwin of the principles of biological evolution. Wallace was a philosophical skeptic, a materialist. His experience of Spiritualist phenomena overcame his skepticism.

In the preface to his book *On Miracles and Modern Spiritualism* (1874) Wallace writes:

"They compelled me to accept them, as facts, long before I could accept the spiritual explanation of them: there was at that time 'no place in my fabric of thought into which it could be fitted.' (Argument of Dr. Carpenter). By slow degrees a place was made."

Wallace was led to believe 1) in the existence of numerous preternatural intelligences of various grades and 2) that some of these intelligences, although usually invisible and intangible to us, can and do act on matter, and do influence our minds. It was by the latter doctrine that he accounted for some of the residual phenomena in his work *Contributions to the Theory of Natural Selection* (1870).

Wallace was born on January 8, 1823, at Usk, Monmouthshire. After leaving school he worked as a land surveyor and architect. Around 1840 his interest in botany began and he started a herbarium. In 1845, he was an English teacher at the Collegiate School, Leicester, where he met H. W. Bates, who influenced him to collect and study beetles.

In 1848, they commenced a joint naturalist expedition to the River Amazon. On the return journey, most of Wallace's collection was destroyed in a fire on the ship, but his book *A Narrative of Travels on the Amazon and Rio Negro* appeared in 1853. He next traveled in the Malay Archipelago, and his large insect collections passed to Oxford University and the British Museum.

In February 1858, during a severe attack of fever, he was thinking about Malthus' *Essay on Population* when, to quote his own words: "There suddenly flashed upon me the idea of the survival of the fittest." He drafted a theory which he posted to Charles Darwin a few days later. By coincidence, Wallace's paper was virtually an abstract of Darwin's own theory, written in 1842.

Wallace's earliest experiences relating to Spiritualism dated from 1844 when he was a schoolmaster in Leicester. Influenced by a lecture given by Spencer Hall on **mesmerism,** he tried similar experiments. Later, during twelve years of tropical wanderings in which he was occupied in the study of natural history, he heard occasionally of **table-turning** and spirit **rapping.** He decided to investigate them on his return.

His first opportunity came on July 22, 1865, in the house of a friend. After more than a dozen sittings he became satisfied that "there is an unknown power developed from the bodies of a number of persons placed in connection by sitting round a table with all their hands on it."

The next stage of his inquiry began in September 1865 and was devoted to the physical and mental phenomena of **Mary Marshall.** In broad daylight, Wallace observed **levitation,** movement of objects without contact (**telekinesis**), and the alteration of weight. Although unknown to Marshall, the place name "Para," where Wallace's brother died, his name and that of the last friend who saw him were spelled out. Messages came spelled backwards, through **direct writing.**

Impressed by these occurrences, Wallace investigated in his own home with the help of a medium. Phenomena were obtained and from November 1866 onward, Wallace had the opportunity to watch mediumship of **Agnes Guppy-Volckman** develop. A stout woman, she was lifted noiselessly on the top of the table while sitting in her chair, with five or six persons close around her. Musical sounds were heard without the presence of instruments. A German guest, a stranger, sang several songs and the strains of this music accompanied her throughout.

Guppy-Volckman supposedly had the ability to **apport** flowers and fruit. In midwinter, after she sat for four hours in a small, warm, gas-lighted room in the Wallace home, a quantity of flowers appeared upon a bare table—anemones, tulips, chrysanthemums, Chinese primroses, and several ferns. Wallace stated: "All were absolutely fresh as if just gathered from a conservatory. They were covered with a fine cold dew. Not a petal was crumpled or broken, not the most delicate point or pinnule of the ferns was out of place."

Wallace stated that the phenomenon was repeated afterward hundreds of times. The flowers sometimes arrived in large quantities. They were often brought on request, fruits as well as flowers. A friend of Wallace asked for a sunflower, and one six feet high fell on the table, with a large mass of earth about its roots.

The naturalist formed a committee of the **London Dialectical Society** in 1869 and witnessed, under test conditions, a variety of telekinetic phenomena. When the possibility of **spirit photography** was for the first time demonstrated in England in the studio of **Frederick A. Hudson,** Wallace was anxious to test this new phenomenon. Sitting with Guppy-Volckman he obtained a communication by **raps** that his mother would try to appear on Hudson's photographic plate.

He sat three times, choosing his own position, and found a male figure with a short sword on the first photographic plate, and a female figure on the two other plates. Reportedly, both of the latter images resembled his mother, and the second plate was unlike any known photograph previously taken of her. Under a magnifying glass, supposedly this second picture disclosed a special feature of his mother's face.

In view of these experiences and the large amount of testimony in the literature of Spiritualism to similar occurrences, Wallace declared it was his opinion that the phenomena of Spiritualism did not require further confirmation. "They are proved, quite as well as any facts are proved in other sciences."

His later attitude was in accordance with this conviction. He never missed an opportunity to test psychic phenomena. He made several attempts to convince the pillars of scientific skepticism and started by inviting W. B. Carpenter to attend some sittings in his own home. Carpenter came one evening. Raps were heard, and these were repeated, sounding, at request, in any part of the table. Carpenter sat still and made no comment. He never returned to Wallace's home.

The same thing happened with his colleague John Tyndall, another scientific skeptic. Wallace had sent Thomas Henry Huxley his paper "The Scientific Aspect of the Supernatural," which was later included in *On Miracles and Modern Spiritualism.* Huxley responded to Wallace, "I am neither shocked nor disposed to issue a commission of lunacy against you. It may be true, for anything that I know to the contrary, but really I cannot get up interest in the subject." G. H. Lewes accepted an invitation to the Wallace home but never went.

Between 1870 and 1880, Wallace had many opportunities to witness interesting phenomena in the houses of various friends. Through a member of his own family, **automatic writing** was received in his own home, purporting to come from his deceased brother William and containing many predictions which were later fulfilled.

In 1874, Wallace was asked by the *Fortnightly Review* to write an article on Spiritualism. It appeared under the title "A Defence of Modern Spiritualism" and also later in *On Miracles and Modern Spiritualism,* first published in 1875. The volume also included two new chapters on the nature and purport of **apparitions.** Later editions would be enlarged with accounts of the author's further personal experiences in séances with **Katie Cook, W. Haxby, Francis Ward Monck, William Eglinton,** and others. During much of the rest of his life, Wallace found himself defending mediums, who were increasingly seen as frauds. His defense would lead to a lively discussion with **Eleanor Sidgwick** in the *Journal* of the Society for Psychical Research in 1888.

Wallace defended **Henry Slade** and gave evidence of the genuineness of his phenomena at the trial in Bow Street Police Court, London, in 1876. In the same year, by casting his vote as president of the anthropological subcommittee of the British Association for the Advancement of Science he made possible the presentation of **William F. Barrett**'s paper on Spiritualism.

In the years 1886–87, during a lecture tour of America, Wallace stayed for some time in three centers of Spiritualism—Boston, Washington and San Francisco. He attended **materialization** séances with a medium named Ross, and when it was rumored that she was caught in **fraud** he testified on her behalf in a letter to the *Banner of Light.*

In Washington, in the company of Elliot Coues, General Lippitt and D. Lyman, Wallace had remarkable experiences with the medium **Pierre L. O. A. Keeler,** and he sat in San Francisco at an outstanding **slate-writing** séance with **Fred P. Evans** in which writing was produced in five different colors and, on his impromptu suggestion, six crayon drawings were precipitated on six pieces of paper placed between a pair of slates, some of the drawings having personal relevance.

In later years, Wallace did not encounter much Spiritualist phenomena but he remained true to his convictions up to the end of his busy life. In 1910, he received the Order of Merit for his scientific researches, however, because of his advocacy of Spiritualism, his scientific contributions were largely ignored and have remained unheralded. He died at Broadstone, Dorset, on November 7, 1913.

Sources:

Berger, Arthur S., and Joyce Berger. *The Encyclopedia of Parapsychology and Psychical Research.* New York: Paragon House, 1991.

Pleasants, Helene, ed. *Biographical Dictionary of Parapsychology.* New York: Helix Press, 1964.

Wallace, Alfred Russell. "Correspondence." *Journal* of the Society for Psychical Research 16 (1898).

———. *My Life: An Autobiography.* 2 vols. New York: Harper & Brothers, 1906.

———. *On Miracles and Modern Spiritualism: Three Essays.* London: James Burns, 1975.

Wallis, E. W. (1848–1914)

British trance medium, inspirational speaker, healer, lecturer, and author. "Lightheart," the spirit of a South American Indian, claimed responsibility for his mediumistic development. "Standard Bearer," "Leader," and "Tom Joyce" were others of his well-known controls.

Assisted by his wife, also a notable psychic, Wallis did propaganda work for many decades. He assisted **Emma H. Britten** in starting the journal *The Two Worlds* in Manchester, which he edited until 1899. In that year he came to London and became editor of *Light,* a position he held until his death.

As a medium, his wife did not enter deep trance. She could hear the words she spoke but reportedly could not prevent herself from saying them. Her mediumship began at the age of eighteen in 1872. A young Spanish Indian girl, "Veina Goree," was her first control. From 1875 onward, she gave inspirational addresses at the Spiritual Institution founded by **James Burns.** While speaking there, she was suddenly controlled by "Morambo," an African slave who died in South America.

Wallis produced physical phenomena for many years. His wife was associated with the **London Spiritualist Alliance** and answered questions on **Spiritualism** in afternoon meetings.

Walsch, Neal Donald (1943–)

Neal Donald Walsch, the channel for receiving the material in a three-volume best-selling metaphysical book, *Conversations with God,* was born and raised in Milwaukee, Wisconsin. He grew up in a Roman Catholic family and for a while considered the priesthood. Instead, he went to work at a local radio station and for the next 30 years worked in a variety of jobs that took him around the United States. He also married multiple times.

At the end of the 1980s he was in Ashland, Oregon, and went to work as a talk show host. Fired from one job, he landed a job at KOPE and became known locally as a radio personality under his public name, Bob White. In 1992 he experienced a period of frustration and depression. He was, in part, upset that the success in life that he had hoped for had alluded him. He fell back on a technique that had worked for him in the past. He composed a letter in which he poured out all of his anger in a series of questions. Previously, he would address such letters to individuals with whom he had problems. This time, he decided to direct the letter to God. As he finished the letter, he received an answer. Words formed in his mind and he wrote them down. God asked if Walsch wanted answers to his questions or was merely venting. He responded that he was venting but in fact wanted answers to the questions.

Thus began a dialogue with God that would last over the next three years. Walsch would pose questions and God would reply. Walsch wrote the answers out in longhand. This process has traditionally been called **automatic writing,** and has more recently been seen as a variety of **channeling.** As the material was received, an initial batch of it was compiled as volume one of *Conversations with God* and published in 1995. It quickly became a best-seller and remained on the *New York Times* list for 91 weeks, and was subsequently translated into 27 languages. Volume two appeared in 1997 and it too reached the best-seller list. Volume three appeared in 1998.

As the response to the volumes grew Walsch founded **ReCreation,** an organization to put the idea of the books into action. ReCreation now sponsors a full range of lectures, workshops, retreats, and seminars across the United States and abroad. Beginning in the year 2000, it is organizing an annual Empowerment Week that includes a training session for leaders who wish to expand the work. Walsch also created the CWG in Action program to establish local centers for the work.

Walsch resides in Ashland and continues to lead ReCreation, which may be contacted at PMB #1150, 1257 Siskiyou Blvd., Ashland, OR 97520. His Internet site is at http://www.conversationswithgod.org/.

Sources:

Varble, Bill. "Former Rogue Valley Radio Host Finds Success in Conversations with God." *Mail Tribune* (Ashland, Ore.) (September 14, 1997).

Walsch, Neal Donald. *Conversations with God I, II, III.* Charlottesville, Va.: Hampton Roads Publishing, 1995, 1997, 1998.

"Walter"

The claimed spirit **control** of the medium **Mina Stinson Crandon,** popularly known as "Margery," the name used by those who investigated her early in the twentieth century. "Walter" was identified with Walter Stinson, the medium's brother, who had died in a railway accident in 1911 at the age of 28. He manifested at a séance for the first time during his sister's visit to a clairvoyant. "Walter" furnished proofs of personal identity and took charge of Crandon's sittings.

"Walter" was described as a spirit communicator, active, having a keen sense of humor, showing no pretence of saintliness, and, on occasions, swore and cursed. He was supposedly highly intelligent and full of energy and curiosity. He never pretended to know whether he could accomplish something new, but was always ready to try and was gratified at his own achievements.

Supposedly, "Walter" gave the impression that he himself was learning about conditions while giving a demonstration. "I don't give a damn about convincing the public or anyone. You have no idea why I am here," he said once.

Reportedly, "Walter" often threatened the sitters: "When this is done I am going away, and I shan't come back. My crowd came here because we liked you people, and you kept us here working at this damned thing." However, he never kept this threat. It is believed the satisfaction that his increasing dexterity gave him in producing high-grade psychic phenomena was enough to bind him to the "Margery" circle.

He introduced many new features into the experiments, provided **cross correspondences,** and gave his fingerprints (see **plastics**). These fingerprints were later found to be those of another living individual, prompting accusations that Crandon's mediumship was partly or wholly fraudulent.

"Walter" was also manifested at **Glen Hamilton**'s circle in Winnipeg, being the chief control of the medium "Mary M."

Sources:

Bird, J. Malcolm. *'Margery' the Medium.* New York: Maynard, 1925.

Tietze, Thomas R. *Margery.* New York: Harper & Row, 1973.

Walter, W(illiam) Grey (1910–1977)

Physiologist with special interests in the study of the neurophysiological correlates of such paranormal states as hypnosis, sleep, trance, and hallucination. Walter was born on February 19, 1910, in Kansas City, Missouri. He studied at Cambridge University (B.A., 1931, M.A., 1935; D.Sc., 1947). He was director of the Physiological Department at Burden Neurological Institute, Bristol, England, from 1939 onward, founder of the EEG Society, and the editor of *EEG Journal.* He wrote a number of books, the most famous being *The Living Brain* (1953), which was translated into several foreign languages. He died May 6, 1977.

Sources:

Pleasants, Helene, ed. *Biographical Dictionary of Parapsychology.* New York: Helix Press, 1964.

Walter, W. Grey. *The Living Brain.* New York: Norton, 1953.

———. "The Neurophysiological Aspects of Hallucination and Illusory Experience." *Proceedings* of the Society for Psychical Research.

Walther, Gerda (1897–1977)

Psychical researcher and author. She was born on March 18, 1897, at Nordrach-Colonie, Baden, Germany. As a child she discovered she could communicate telepathically with both the living and the dead. She studied at Ludwig Maximilians University, Munich, Germany (Ph.D. summa cum laude, 1921).

In 1927, she became scientific secretary to **Baron Albert von Schrenck-Notzing,** the German psychic researcher, and assisted his investigations of the mediums **Willi and Rudi Schneider.** After Schrenck-Notzing's death, she edited his manuscripts for publication. She continued her contributions to the field over the years by writing numerous reviews of European books on psychical research for English-language journals. During 1941 in Germany, her research in parapsychology resulted in a short period of imprisonment under the Hitler regime.

Sources:

Berger, Arthur S., and Joyce Berger. *The Encyclopedia of Parapsychology and Psychical Research.* New York: Paragon House, 1991.

Pleasants, Helene, ed. *Biographical Dictionary of Parapsychology.* New York: Helix Press, 1964.

Walther, Gerda. *Zum anderen Ufer.* Remagen: Otto Reichl, 1960.

The Wandering Jew

A medieval German legend that takes several forms. Although writers and details differ, the essential features of the narratives that have been handed down to us are basically the same.

The legend is that as Christ was being dragged on his way to Calvary, he passed the house of a Jew and stopped there, being weary under the weight of his cross. The Jew, however, inspired by the mob, would not allow him to rest there and drove him on. Jesus, looking at him, said, "I shall stand and rest, but thou shalt go till the last day." The Jew was compelled to wander over the Earth until this prophecy was fulfilled.

The legend of the Wandering Jew is regarded as the epic of the Semite people in the Middle Ages. Unfortunately it has often become a vehicle for crude anti-Semitic propaganda and persecution.

In some parts of Germany, the Wandering Jew theme has been identified with the wild huntsman myth, while in several French districts that mythical character is regarded as the wind of the night. This legend was treated in literary fashion by Eugène Sue in his novel *Le Juif errant* (10 vols., 1844–45) and by the British author George Croly in his novel *Salathiel; A Story of the Past, The Present and The Future* (1829). Something of the same atmosphere also pervades the legend of the **Flying Dutchman.**

Sources:

Barring-Gould, Sabine. *Curious Myths of the Middle Ages.* 1866–68. New Hyde Park, N.Y.: University Books, 1967.

Wang, Chung Yu (1880–1958)

Metallurgist, with interests in various aspects of parapsychology. Born in 1880 in Hong Kong, Wang studied at Queens College and Peiyang University and came to the United States for graduate work at the University of California and Columbia University (M.A. mining and geology). He was a member of the American Society for Psychical Research. He died August 30, 1958, in New York City.

Sources:

Wang, Chung Yu. "China's Unwanted Heritage." *Tomorrow* (Autumn 1955).

Wannein Nat

A Burmese evil spirit. (See also **MYANMAR**)

Warcollier, René (1881–1962)

Chemical engineer, author, parapsychologist, and president of the Institut Métapsychique International, Paris (1951–62). He was born on April 8, 1881, at Ormonville-la-Rogue, France. He studied at Ecole Nationale Supérieure de Chimie, Paris (Ch.E., 1903).

He became interested in psychical research, especially in **telepathy,** in the 1920s and collaborated with such experimenters as **Cesar de Vesme** and **Eugene Osty** on investigations of **clairvoyance** and related phenomena. He oversaw the European end of an experiment in telepathy jointly conducted with **Gardner Murphy.** He was affiliated with the Institut Métapsychique, served as its treasurer (1929–38), and edited the *Revue Métapsychique* for two years (1938–40) until the beginning of World War II. He died May 23, 1962, in Paris, France.

Sources:

Warcollier, René. *Experimental Telepathy.* London: George Allen & Unwin, 1939. Reprint, New York: Arno Press, 1975.

———. *Experiments in Telepathy.* New York: Harper & Brothers, 1938.

———. "Fifty Years of Telepathy." *Tomorrow* (summer 1961).

———. *Mind to Mind.* New York: Collier Books, 1963.

Warcollier, René, and Edmond Duchatel. *Les Miracles de la Volonté* (Miracles of the Will). N.p., 1912.

Ward, Arthur Henry (Sarsfield) (1883–1959)

Author who wrote under the pseudonym "Sax Rohmer" and created the celebrated fictional character Dr. Fu-Manchu. Ward was also a student of the occult. Born of Irish Catholic parents in Birmingham, England, on February 15, 1883, Ward had no formal schooling until the age of nine, when he attended a day school in London. As a youth, Ward stopped attending Mass and became an agnostic. His first job was as a bank clerk in London, after which he worked briefly as a newspaper reporter. He started writing short stories at the age of twenty and first used the pseudonym "Sax Rohmer" in 1912. He also wrote some successful songs for music hall comedians George Robey and Little Tich.

His famous character Fu-Manchu was based on reports of a Chinese master criminal operating an international opium racket, and the atmosphere of Limehouse, London's Chinatown district, provided local color. The first Fu-Manchu book was published in 1913, but Rohmer did not immediately settle down to developing his character. Instead, he spent much time on his nonfiction study *The Romance of Sorcery* (first published London, 1914; E. P. Dutton, 1915). The book brought a letter from illusionist **Harry Houdini,** who soon afterward became a friend.

Rohmer is said to have become a member of the Hermetic society the **Golden Dawn** and may also have belonged to a Rosicrucian order. However, his occult interests were eventually overshadowed by the success of his Fu-Manchu books. In 1929, Paramount Pictures first brought the character to the screen with *The Mysterious Dr. Fu-Manchu,* starring Warner Oland and Jean Arthur. Rohmer died June 1, 1959.

Sources:

Rohmer, Sax. *The Romance of Sorcery.* London, 1914. Reprint, New York: E. P. Dutton, 1915. Reprint, New York: Causeway, 1973.

Warminster UFO News

Monthly publication through the 1970s of the **British UFO Society,** dealing with news and sightings in the Warminster district of Britain, where hundreds of local residents have reported **UFO** phenomena since the 1960s.

Warner, Abby

An illiterate American orphan girl who was instrumental in arousing lively interest in **Spiritualism** in Ohio soon after the phenomenon of the **Rochester Rappings.** Mrs. Kellogg of Massillon, in whose house Warner performed domestic services, discovered that **raps** were produced in the girl's presence. Soon she was able to move into a **trance** state, and the uneducated girl, who at eighteen could only read printed characters, wrote with both hands at the same time on different subjects, while a third communication was spelled out by raps.

Reports of the séances began to be widely circulated. Abel Underhill, a physician, took the girl into his family for medical treatment and wrote her history. The occurrences at St. Timothy's Church on Christmas Eve, 1851, put her in the limelight. Supposedly, unusually powerful raps resounded in the church in her presence and attracted the attention of the whole assembly. The minister asked that "those knockings might cease." Instead, they increased in vehemence.

Warner was arrested on a charge of disturbing a religious meeting and brought before a public tribunal. The trial commenced on December 27 and lasted for three days. As "not a single witness could be found who could swear that they perceived the slightest movement in the accused party; on the contrary, when closely examined, those who professed to have scrutinized the action of the spirit rapper narrowly were compelled to admit that they could not detect the least perceptible motion, even of her dress, at the times when the knocks were most numerous and emphatic," the defendant was discharged.

Following the acquittal, Underhill announced an investigation by a selected committee, under stringent test conditions, of the medium's physical and mental phenomena. Four séances were held. The committee believed the phenomena wholly unaccountable and genuine evidences of an occult and intelligent force outside the medium.

Warner, Lucien (Hynes) (1900–1963)

Psychologist and opinion analyst who conducted surveys in parapsychology. He was born on September 9, 1900, at Irvington, New York. He studied at Oberlin College (B.A., 1922) and Columbia University (Ph.D., 1927). After graduation he held a variety of research positions prior to becoming a professor of biology and psychology at Claremont Men's College and Graduate School, Claremont, California, in 1948. He is most remembered in parapsychological circles for the 1938, 1952, and 1955 surveys he conducted among psychologists to ascertain attitudes to extrasensory perception. His reports were published in the *Journal of Parapsychology* (vol.2, 1938; vol.16, 1952; vol.19, 1955). He died in 1963 in Las Vegas, Nevada.

Wartime Occult Phenomena (World War I)

The emergence of **Spiritualism** heightened interest in the separations and deaths caused by war. Thus it was not surprising that a number of stories of supernatural events should have crystallized around the international circumstances of World War I. Perhaps the most striking of these was the alleged vision of the **Angels of Mons.** The first account was the story in the *London Evening News* of September 14, 1915, by writer **Arthur Machen** describing a statement by an officer who had been in the retreat from Mons. This officer saw a large body of horsemen who later vanished. Machen suggested that they were the spirits of the English bowmen who had fought at Agincourt.

Although this story was fiction, it stimulated corroborative reports of phantom armies. The most significant of these were repeated by a Red Cross nurse, Phylis Campbell, who claimed to have heard several different stories of phantom soldiers. In his book *On the Side of the Angels* (1915), Harold Begbie repeated the claims that soldiers saw a vision of angels during the retreat from Mons and gives the narrative of a soldier, who states that an officer came up to him "in a state of great anxiety" and pointed out to him a ". . . strange light which seemed to be quite distinctly outlined and was not a reflection of the moon, nor were there any clouds in the neighbourhood. The light became brighter and I could see quite distinctly three shapes, one in the centre having what looked like outspread wings. The other two were not so large, but were quite plainly distinct from the centre one. They appeared to have a long, loose-hanging garment of a golden tint and they were above the German line facing us. We stood watching them for about three-quarters of an hour."

All the men in the battalion who saw this, with the exception of five, were killed. Begbie went on to say that a nurse told him that a dying soldier spoke to her of the reluctance of the Germans to attack the British line, "because of the thousands of troops behind us." It is believed this man had heard these claims from German prisoners and believed in the ghostly nature of those supporting hosts.

Ralph Shirley published a pamphlet titled *Prophecies and Omens of the Great War* (1914; 1915) dealing with various oracular utterances on the struggle.

Stories were also common in the early period of the war regarding the appearance of saintly and protective figures resembling the patrons of the several allied countries. Thus the English were convinced that in certain engagements they had seen the figure of Saint George mounted on a white charger and the French were equally sure that the figure in question was either Saint Denis or Joan of Arc. Wounded men in base hospitals asked for medallions or coins on which the likenesses of these saints were impressed in order to verify the statements they made.

Sources:

Brown, Raymond Lemment. *The Phantom Soldiers.* New York: Drake, 1975.

Machen, Arthur. *The Angels of Mons: The Bowman and Other Legends.* New York: G. P. Putnam's Sons, 1915.

Stein, Gordon. *Encyclopedia of Hoaxes.* Detroit: Gale Research, 1993.

Warts

Small skin lesions on face, fingers, or elbows, and sometimes on the genitals, caused by a virus, as distinct from **moles,** which are birthmarks. The general medical term for a wart is *verruca,* but warts on the genitals or around the anus are known as *condylomae,* or venereal warts.

Warts often appear and disappear without any obvious cause, and this characteristic tended to reinforce belief in many old folk cures or wart-charming. In eastern Massachusetts, central New York, and parts of England, it used to be believed that warts could be removed by rubbing them with spittle. Other widespread superstitions about warts:

To cure warts, wash hands in the moon's rays in a dry metal basin, saying:

I wash my hands in this thy dish,
O man in the moon, do grant my wish
And come and take away this!

Water taken from a gravestone and rubbed on warts will cure them.

Striking warts with an undertaker's hammer will cure them.

To remove warts from the hand, watch for a funeral procession to pass and as it goes by, say secretly: "I do sincerely hope that these warts will pass off my hands as that body decays in the ground."

If a person steals an egg and secretly buries it in the ground, his or her warts will disappear when the egg decays.

Pick up an old marrow bone, touch it to your warts, walk off, throw it behind you, and don't look back.

If you take as many pins as you have warts and give them to someone else, your warts will be transferred to the other person.

Take as many pebbles as you have warts and touch each wart with a pebble, then wrap the stones in cloth or paper and throw them away in the roadway. Whoever picks up the parcel of pebbles will get your warts, and you will lose them.

Take a piece of string and tie as many knots in it as there are warts and lay the string under a stone. Whoever treads on the stone will be attached to the warts.

Such superstitions are often very ancient. **Pliny** (23–79 C.E.) recommended that warts be touched with chick peas on the first day of the moon, and that the peas then be wrapped in cloth and thrown away behind you. The pebble charm was known to Marcellus of Bordeaux in the fourth century, and it is cited in his book *De Mendicamentis.*

Apart from natural remission, it is possible that many wart cures worked through a process analagous to selfhypnosis. Other wart remedies were of a pseudomedical nature, such as rubbing warts with milkweed, or the fluid from grasshoppers, or the fresh blood of mice. Modern medical remedies involve treating warts with a substance that dissolves the hard layer and cauterizes the remainder, which is then scraped off.

During the witchcraft manias of the sixteenth and seventeenth centuries, warts and moles were considered "devil's marks" if they did not bleed when pricked.

Washington Research Center and Parapsychology Group

The Washington Research Center and Parapsychology Group was founded in 1982 by Russian-American parapsychologist Larissa Vilenskaya (b. 1948). Vilenskaya had been involved in parapsychological research throughout the 1970s at the Research Institute of General and Pedagogical Psychology of the USSR Academy of Sciences. She moved to the United States in 1981. The center published a journal, *Psi Research,* which made an effort at informing an English-speaking audience of research being conducted in Russia, Eastern Europe, and China.

The center also became identified with the firewalking movement. Vilenskaya became interested in firewalking and conducted numerous events teaching attendees to experiment with the practice. Last known address: 484B Washington St. #317, San Francisco, CA 93940.

Wasserman, Gerhard Dietrich (1919–)

University lecturer in applied mathematics who experimented in the field of parapsychology. Wasserman was born December 12, 1919, at Leipzig, Germany. He studied at Queen Mary College, University of London (B.Sc. hons. math. 1942, Ph.D. quantum mechanics, 1946). In 1948 he began a tenure as an instructor in applied mathematics at King's College Newcastle-upon-Tyne, Durham University.

In the field of parapsychology he has taken special interest in the construction of theoretical models for psi phenomena. His article "An Outline of a Field Theory of Organismic Form and Behavior" was published in a Ciba Foundation symposium on **extrasensory perception.**

Sources:

Pleasants, Helene, ed. *Biographical Dictionary of Parapsychology.* New York: Helix Press, 1964.

Wasson, R(obert) Gordon (1898–1986)

Journalist and writer who argued for "ethno-mycology," the claimed relationship of wild **mushrooms** (especially hallucinogenic varieties) to various human cultures throughout history. Wasson was born on September 22, 1898, at Great Falls, Montana. He studied at the Columbia School of Journalism, and in 1926 he married Valentina Pavlovna Guercken, who shared his research in ethno-mycology.

Wasson worked as a reporter through the 1920s before becoming a prominent banker for the Guaranty Company of New York (1928–34) and later the Morgan Guaranty Trust Company. In the 1950s Wasson and his wife conducted field research in Mexico, studying firsthand the sacred mushroom ceremonies of the Mazatec Indians. Their record album *Mushroom Ceremony of the Mazatec Indians of Mexico* (Folkways Records, New York, 1957) was the first documented recording of its kind. Wasson's researches influenced the psychedelic revolution of the 1960s.

Wasson concluded that the **"soma"** mentioned in the literature of ancient India was in fact the *amanita muscaria* mushroom. He suggested that Hindu mysticism arose from its priests' intoxication from this mushroom, considered to be the elixir of immortality. This line of speculation was followed up by John M. Allegro in his book *The Sacred Mushroom and the Cross* (1970), which suggested the crucifixion story of Jesus was a myth, symbolic of the ecstasy of a drug cult. More recently it has been revived approvingly in the journal *ReVision* (vol. 10, no. 4, Spring 1988), together with the suggestion that *amaita muscaria* was the forbidden fruit from the tree in the Garden of Eden in the Old Testament story. Wasson's research found little approval in the scholarly world. He died December 23, 1986.

Sources:

Wasson, R. Gordon. *Persephone's Quest: Entheogens and the Origins of Religion.* New Haven: Yale University Press, 1986.

———. *Soma: Divine Mushrooms of Immortality.* The Hague: Mouton, 1968. Reprint, New York: Harcourt Brace, 1971.

———. *The Wondrous Mushroom: Mycolatry in MesoAmerica.* New York: McGraw, 1980.

Wasson, R. Gordon, and Valentina Pavlovna Wasson. *Mushrooms, Russia, and History.* New York: Pantheon, 1957.

Waterfall Astrological Directory

An annual reference work for individuals involved in **astrology** formerly published by Tony Waterfall of Vancouver, British Columbia.

Watkins, Geoffrey (1896–1981)

Proprietor and later director of **Watkins Book Shop,** a major London bookstore dealing in the literature (both new and used) of the occult, alternative religous traditions, and esoteric philosophy since 1894, when Watkins' father John M. Watkins founded the company at the instigation of Theosophist **Helena Petrovna Blavatsky.** The bookshop has long been a meeting place for leading personalities in such subjects as metaphysics, mystical and hermetic studies, oriental and comparative religion, parapsychology, astrology, and the occult. John Watkins was a close friend of Blavatsky, who was cofounder of the Theosophical Society. **Carl G. Jung, Aldous Huxley, William Butler Yeats,** and magician **Aleister Crowley** were frequent visitors to the shop. Crowley was reputed to have caused thousands of books in the store to vanish and reappear by his occult powers, but, like other stories about Crowley and invisibility, this apocryphal story retains its element of tongue-in-cheek humor.

Watkins, who carried on his father's tradition in the bookshop, was born June 7, 1896. He attended a private school in Heidelberg, Germany. Known to close friends as "Wattie" or "Nigel," he was employed by British Intelligence in both World Wars. In World War I, his duties included interrogation of German officers who were prisoners of war. In World War II, he was concerned with the distribution of top-secret documents to appropriate government departments.

One of his closest friends was **Christmas Humphreys,** who was president of the Buddhist Society for many years and author of numerous books on Buddhism and Eastern philosophy. Humphreys acknowledged Watkins' valuable assistance in the preface to his book **Concentration and Meditation** (1935).

Watkins took over running the bookshop when his father became blind. During his tenure running the bookshop international visitors most remembered him as a spiritual guide rather than a bookseller. Though specializing in selling occult books, he disliked the word "occultism" because of its perjorative connotations. His own special interests lay elsewhere, in depth psychology and the spiritual wisdom commonly called the "perennial philosophy," a term popularized by Aldous Huxley in his book of that name.

Kathleen Raine stated in an obituary in *Temonos* (no.2, 1982):

"Geoffrey Watkins was far more than a bookseller; indeed he was perhaps the only bookseller who made a practice of advising customers (many of whom were, or became, his friends) against purchasing books which he thought unsuitable for their particular interests, or too valuable to be entrusted to ignorant hands. . . . As to his courtesy, he welcomed his customers as his guests, assuming that we were seekers for wisdom, and meeting each of us at the level of our learning (or our ignorance) as he was well able to do. He seemed always to have time to listen. When we left, he saw us to the door of his shop like a courteous host."

Repotedly, Watkins had an encyclopedic knowledge of books and was well-informed on all aspects of the groups, societies, and individuals in the fields of mysticism and occultism. He gave valuable information to many individuals who later became famous. Kathleen Raine, who has since published many works of poetry, literary criticism, and philosophy, acknowledged the help Watkins gave her in her special studies on Thomas Taylor the Platonist. **Alan Watts** also paid tribute in his autobiography *In My Own Way* (1972):

"Nigel [Geoffrey Watkins] runs the most magical bookshop in the world, and is the most unobstrusively enlightened person

I have ever known. . . . Nigel not only became my bibliographer on Buddhism, comparative religion, and mysticism, but also my most trusted adviser on the various gurus, pandits, and psychotherapists then flourishing in London. . . . In the Watkins bookshop one would expect at any moment, to come across a Mahatma or a high Lama visiting England on a secret mission to feel out academically accredited professors. Instead of giving lectures and holding seminars, he simply tells you what to read. . . . He never tries to convert anyone to a system. He is what the Japanese would call a *buji-nin;* a man without affectations, who has also compassion and clarity of mind."

With the death of Watkins, many regular customers at the bookshop felt they had lost a true friend and wise guide. Meanwhile, the bookshop started by his father continues to flourish.

Watkins Book Shop

Long established British bookshop specializing in occultism, mysticism, comparative religion, parapsychology, esoteric psychology, and related topics, founded by John M. Watkins in 1894. Watkins was a friend of **Helena Petrovna Blavatsky** and other leading occult figures of the late nineteenth and early twentieth centuries. The shop in Cecil Court, Charing Cross Road, London, was a meeting place for such famous and varied individuals as **A. E. Waite, William Butler Yeats** and **Aleister Crowley.** Watkins also published texts in the fields of occultism and mysticism. After his death, the business was carried on by his son **Geoffrey Watkins** (1896–1981).

All through the prewar occult boom of the 1920s and 1930s and the more recent occult explosion of the 1960s, the Watkins Book Shop has been a central focus of occultism, with a strong emphasis on mysticism and Eastern religion. After the death of Watkins, the company went through various changes of title, including Stuart & Watkins (associated with Stuart & Robinson), but retained its essential character, as familiar to British students of occultism and mysticism as the **Weiser Bookshop** in New York.

In April 1984, the company became firmly linked with the Weiser Bookshop through the formation of Watkins Books Ltd., with directors Donald Weiser and Henry Suzuki of Samuel Weiser, Inc., and Valerie Chris of Robert Chris Bookseller (also in Cecil Court). Formerly a general literary book shop, Robert Chris is now a leading supplier of books on health and alternative medicine. Both Weiser and Watkins remain important book shops but with the growth of the field, the proliferation of alternative bookshops, and the passing of shops like Watkins into the hands of other owners, they have lost their unique place in the occult/alternative religious community.

The Watseka Wonder

A story told in a pamphlet by physician E. W. Stevens, *The Watseka Wonder,* which details a most intriguing case of continued spirit control. In 1865, at the age of nineteen, a girl named Mary Roff who was mentally ill died in Watseka, Illinois. Thirteen years later, another Watseka girl, Lurancy Vennum, almost a stranger to the Roff family, became similarly afflicted. Stevens diagnosed her case as an **obsession.** In the hypnotic state, Vennum confirmed the diagnosis.

Stevens suggested that she try to induce a good spirit to control her. She answered that several spirits were about who would be willing. "There is one who was called Mary Roff." The father of Mary Roff was present, and he approved the idea. "Mary Roff" was asked to control Vennum. Supposedly she did so.

Reportedly, on February 1, 1878, she possessed Lurancy's body and remained in possession for 16 weeks in an almost unbroken continuity. As soon as she appeared, she took over Vennum's body and behaved like Mary Roff. She did not know Vennum's parents, went "home," and recognized every old object in the Roff house. She continued where she had left off over 13 years before. She exhibited paranormal faculties during this time, gave proofs of **clairvoyance,** made **predictions,** had **out-of-body** experiences in trance, and described her astral journeys on her return to consciousness.

On May 21, 1878, she supposedly left in tears from her Roff parents and all of her friends, fell into trance, and awoke as Lurancy Vennum again. The new Vennum was mentally and physically reestablished. It is believed Vennum had been watched over for a time by "Mary Roff," who came back occasionally in trance. Three and a half years later, Vennum married and when her first baby came "Mary Roff" put her into trance to save her the pains of childbirth. "Mary Roff" never appeared to anyone at Watseka, except through Vennum's body. She never materialized independently.

The psychical researcher **Richard Hodgson** investigated the case on behalf of the **American Society for Psychical Research** and concluded:

"I have no doubt that the incidents occurred substantially as described in the narrative by Dr. Stevens, and in my view the only other interpretation of the case—besides the spiritistic—that seems at all plausible, is that which has been put forward as the alternative to the spiritistic theory to account for the trance communications of Mrs. Piper, and similar cases, viz., secondary personality with supernormal powers. It would be difficult to disprove this hypothesis in the case of the Watseka Wonder, owing to the comparative meagreness of the record and the probable abundance of 'suggestion' in the environment, and any conclusion that we may reach would probably be determined largely by our convictions concerning other cases. My personal opinion is that the 'Watseka Wonder' case belongs in the main manifestations to the spiritistic category."

The evidence obtained by Hodgson was published in the *Religio-Philosophical Journal* (Chicago, December 20, 1890), and his account was verified by J. Bundy, the *Religio-Philosophical Journal*'s editor. A detailed report also appeared in *The Spiritualist* (September & October 1878).

Sources:

Anderson, Rodger J. "The Watseka Wonder: A Critical Reevaluation." *Theta* 8, no. 4 (1980).

Myers, F. W. H. *Human Personality and Its Survival of Bodily Death.* 2 vols. London: Longmans, Green, 1903.

Stevens, E. W. *The Watseka Wonder.* Chicago, 1879.

Watson, Lyall (1939–)

Zoologist and archaeologist whose book *Supernature* attempted to bridge the gap between science and the occult. Watson was born April 12, 1939, in Johannesburg, South Africa. He was educated at the University of Witwatersrand (B.S., 1958), the University of Natal (M.S., 1959), and the University of London, England (Ph.D., 1963). Through the 1960s he was director of the Zoological Gardens of Johannesburg, South Africa (1964–65), produced documentary films for the British Broadcasting Corporation, London (1966–67), and was an expedition leader and researcher in Antarctica, the Amazon River area, Seychelles, and Indonesia (1968–72). In 1967 he founded the life science consultancy Biologic of London, and in the 1970s he wrote a number of books. Three further books followed themes first developed in *Supernature: The Romeo Error* (1974), *Gifts of Unknown Things* (1976), and *Lifetide: The Biology of The Unconscious* (1979).

Lifetide had an important effect within the emerging **New Age** movement. In two pages it told the story of four scientists studying monkeys in islands off the coast of Japan. The scientists left food for the monkeys. In 1953 they observed an older monkey wash the sand and grit from a potato. She then seemed to teach the other monkeys the same procedure. Gradualy the practice spread to the other monkeys in the group. Watson stated:

"In the autumn of that year [1958] an unspecified number of monkeys on [the island of] Kosima were washing sweet potatoes in the sea. . . . Let us say, for argument's sake, that the number of monkeys was ninety-nine and that at eleven o'clock on Tuesday morning one further convert was added to the fold in the usual way. But the addition of the hundreth monkey apparently carried the number across some sort of threshold, pushing it through a kind of critical mass, because by that evening almost everyone was doing it. Not only that, but the habit seems to have jumped natural barriers and to have appeared spontaneously, like glycerine crystals in sealed laboratory jars, in colonies on other islands and on the mainland in a troupe of Takasakiyama."

What became known as the "hundreth monkey" myth would be seized upon by New Age spokespersons who were seeking to explain to people how relatively small groups would be capable of bringing New Age consciousness to a public generally apathetic to their concerns. It was believed if only a critical number of people accepted the consciousness, it would, as if by magic or atomic explosion, spread suddenly to everyone.

Given the jumps in such an argument, Watson was soon attacked on the factual basis of the story. Psychologist Maureen O'Hara and psychic-critic Ron Amundson both challenged the story and forced Watson to admit that it was in essence fiction. By that time, however, it had become a widely discussed issue in the New Age movement and author Ken Keyes had printed and distributed over 300,000 copies of a book, *The Hundreth Monkey* (1982).

Sources:

Keyes, Ken. *The Hundreth Monkey.* Coos Bay, Ore.: Vision Books, 1982.

Melton, J. Gordon. *New Age Encyclopedia.* Detroit: Gale Research, 1990.

Watson, Lyall. *Dark Nature: A Natural History of Evil.* New York: HarperCollins, 1995.

———. *Gifts of Unknown Things.* New York: Simon and Schuster, 1976.

———. *Lifetide: The Biology of The Unconscious.* New York: Simon and Schuster, 1979.

———. *The Romeo Error: A Matter of Life and Death.* Garden City, N.Y.: Anchor Press, 1975.

———. *Supernature.* Garden City, N.Y.: Anchor Press, 1973.

Watson, Thomas (1898–1985)

Thomas Watson, a pioneer spiritual church leader and medium, was raised in New Orleans and attended Xavier University, a school founded to serve the African American community, and Texas Christian University. He became a schoolteacher after graduation. He was in New Orleans at the time Leafy Anderson brought the spiritual movement to the city. He joined Anderson's Eternal Life Christian Spiritual Association and emerged as a leader. He left the association in 1929, two years after Anderson's death, and founded an independent congregation, St. Joseph Helping Hand Church in Algiers, a New Orleans suburb.

Over the next five years similar congregations were founded and affiliated with Watson's work. These were formally organized into the St. Joseph Helping Hand Missionary Association in 1934. Following Anderson's emphasis, the new association retained a strong attachment to traditional Christian affirmations, unlike other Spiritual churches, which had discarded most Christian distinctions. The next year the association reorganized into the Divine Spiritual Churches of the Southwest. This church adopted a strong hierarchial structure and named Watson as its senior bishop. Bessie S. Johnson was named as his junior bishop. During the late 1930s Watson reconsidered his opinions on women ministers, and in 1940 he demoted Smith to Reverend Mother Superior, a non-ministerial position common in many black churches. The change led to a schism, and those members who supported the women pastors and mediums left.

In 1942 Watson led his church into a merger with the Metropolitan Spiritual Churches of Christ to form the United Spiritual Churches of Christ. Shortly after the merger, the leader of the Metropolitan Spiritual Churches of Christ, William Taylor, died, and Watson was named his successor. However, he immediately ran into conflict with Clarence Cobbs, a prominent medium from Chicago. The conflict led to a schism in 1945. Watson departed with his following and organized the United Metropolitan Spiritual Churches of Christ. He led the churches until his death on November 12, 1985, when he was succeeded by his son, Bishop Aubrey Watson.

Sources:

Jacobs, Claude F., and Andrew J. Kaslow. *The Spiritual Churches of New Orleans: Origins, Beliefs, and Rituals of an African American Religion.* Knoxville: University of Tennessee Press, 1991.

Murphy, Larry G., J. Gordon Melton, and Gary L. Ward. *Encyclopedia of African American Religions.* New York: Garland Publishing, 1993.

Watts, Alan (Wilson) (1915–1973)

British-born American philosopher, teacher of Zen Buddhism, and pioneer popularizer of Eastern philosophy in the United States. Watts was born January 6, 1915, in Chislehurst, Kent, England. He came to the United States in 1938, and he was naturalized in 1943. The same year he moved to the United States he married the daughter of Ruth Fuller Everett (who was involved with the First Zen Institute of America). Even as a youth he had been interested in Eastern religions in general and Zen Buddhism in particular. However, Watts studied for the priesthood and after completing his course at Seabury-Western Theological Seminary, he was ordained in the Episcopal Church in 1944. He remained in Evanston, Illinois, and pursued a master of sacred theology degree (1948) at Seabury while serving as a chaplain at Northwestern University (adjacent to the Seabury campus) for six years (1944–50).

In 1950 Watts divorced, resigned from the priesthood, and entered a year of seclusion. In 1951 he moved to California as an instructor at the American Academy of Asian Studies (1951–57). He gained some degree of fame in 1957 with the positive response to his book, *The Way of Zen* (1957), which became a book introducing Zen to a public eager for Eastern wisdom. Over the next fifteen years he wrote numerous books presenting his personal appropriation of Buddhism. As a lecturer, from 1956 onward he traveled to universities across the continent. He directed the *Eastern Wisdom and Modern Life* series on station KQED, San Francisco (1959–60).

In 1962 some of those who had gathered around him as students founded the Society for Comparative Philosophy as a vehicle for his teaching. He died November 16, 1973.

Sources:

Melton, J. Gordon. *Religious Leaders of America.* Detroit: Gale Research, 1991.

Stuart, David. *Alan Watts.* Radnor, Pa.: Chilton Book, 1976.

Watts, Alan. *The Book on the Taboo Against Knowing Who You Are.* New York: Vintage Books, 1966.

———. *The Early Writings of Alan Watts.* Edited by John Snelling. Berkeley, Calif.: Celestial Arts, 1987.

———. *The Essential Alan Watts.* Berkeley, Calif.: Celestial Arts, 1977.

———. *In My Own Way: An Autobiography, 1915–1945.* New York: Pantheon Books, 1972.

———. *Psychotherapy, East and West.* New York: Ballantine Books, 1961.

———. *The Spirit of Zen.* New York: Grove Press, 1958.

———. *The Way of Zen.* New York: Pantheon Books, 1968.

Wayland Smith

A character in German mythological romance, father of Weltich, whom he trained in the art of warfare and sent to the Court of Dietrich in Bern. Wayland Smith gave the sword Miming to Weltich and told him of a **mermaid** to whom he was to apply when in difficulty.

Wayland Smith is also referred to in the Sigfried story as in company with another metalsmith named Mimi when Sigfried joins the smithy. His workmanship is praised in the Beowulf saga and he is mentioned there and elsewhere as a maker of impregnable armor. He is the supernatural smith of the Teutonic peoples and comparable to the gods Vulcan and Hephaistos in Roman and Greek mythology.

Weatherhead, Leslie (Dixon) (1893–1976)

British Methodist minister interested in aspects of parapsychology. Weatherhead was born on October 14, 1893, in London. He studied at the University of Manchester (M.A., 1926) and Richmond College, and he later received his doctorate at the University of London (1950). He served as a chaplain to British troops during World War I, ministered at the English Church in Madras, India, after the war (1918–22), and served several appointments prior to becoming the pastor of City Temple, the large Methodist church in London, in 1936.

Weatherhead wrote a number of notable books over the years, including a frequently reprinted early text on God and the problem of evil. As an adult, he became interested in psychic phenomena and wrote a series of books that ran from a pioneering text in pastoral psychology to more controversial texts within the Christian community on such topics as reincarnation. He died January 5, 1976.

Sources:

Weatherhead, Leslie. *After Death.* London: J. Clarke, 1923.

———. *Psychology, Religion, and Healing.* Rev. ed. London: Hodder and Stoughton, 1952.

———. *The Resurrection of Christ in the Light of Modern Science and Psychical Research.* London: Hodder and Stoughton, 1959.

Webb, James (C. N.) (1946–1980)

Scottish author who conducted historical surveys of the occult. Webb was born in 1946 in Edinburgh, Scotland. He was educated at Harrow and Trinity College, Cambridge University. He spent some years as a ghostwriter, television producer and trainer, and schoolmaster, but in 1969 became a full-time writer.

He was advisory editor of *The Occult,* a series of thirty-three reprints chosen to illustrate the origins and development of modern occultism, as well as *Perspectives in Psychical Research,* a series of 34 books (both for Arno Press, New York, 1976) and contributed to *Man, Myth and Magic* (Marshall Cavendish, 1970), and *Encyclopedia of the Unexplained* (McGraw-Hill, 1974).

Webb's major contribution, however, came from the special study he conducted of the historical and cultural background of Western occultism, with special reference to its relationship with extremist political movements. This research resulted in three major books: *The Occult Underground* (1974; British title *The Flight from Reason,* 1971), *The Occult Establishment* (1976), and *The Harmonious Circle* (1980). Along the way he also edited several volumes, including *The Quest Anthology* (1976), *The Subliminal Consciousness* (selections from writings by Frederic W. H. Myers in *Proceedings* of the Society for Psychical Research, London, 1976), and *The Mediums and the Conjurers* (anthology of writings by J. N. Maskelyne, G. Smith-Buck, and George Sexton, 1976).

The scholarly surveys by Webb of the ideas and personalities preceding the occult revival of the 1960s and 1970s constitute an overview of the problem of the twentieth century as a battleground between reason and unreason. He started his writings with a somewhat skeptical viewpoint, but in the course of time experienced unusual visions and insights, sometimes associated with hallucinations and nervous breakdowns. He died May 9, 1980, in Scotland.

Sources:

Collin-Smith, Joyce. "A Precognitive Dream: James Webb." *Light* (summer 1982).

Webb, James. *The Harmonious Circle.* New York: G. P. Putnam's Sons, 1980.

———. *The Occult Establishment.* LaSalle, Ill.: Open Court Press, 1976.

———. *The Occult Underground.* LaSalle, Ill.: Open Court Press, 1974. Reprinted as *The Flight from Reason.* 1971.

Wilson, Colin. "James Webb and the Occult." *Light* (summer 1982).

Webber, Jack (1907–1940)

Jack Webber was a prominent physical medium who in his few years greatly impressed his fellow Spiritualists with his abilities. Webber lacked formal education and had been a miner in Wales who was brought to **Spiritualism** by his wife. He attended a home circle and discovered his own mediumistic abilities. He acquired several spirit controls, the most famous being an Irish spirit named Paddy. He began with table tipping and soon afterwards experienced the **levitation** of objects, including the famous trumpets which spirits reportedly used as a megaphone-like device. He also became a healer. As he developed, those attending his seances reported hearing spirit voices, both coming through the trumpets and independent of them. They also saw objects move and levitate.

Through the 1930s Webber traveled at an increasing pace and during the last two years of the decade was widely heralded in the Spiritualist press for the phenomena he produced. While not formally investigated, he was the object of attention of several skeptical journalists who reported favorably on what they had witnessed. He worked in a darkened room, but without a cabinet. He was frequently tied to his chair with wire. Among his more spectacular feats was the production of ectoplasm in the form of light rods that were used to levitate objects and the movement of objects from distant places ostensibly through solid walls. At one point a recording was made of Paddy and of a second spirit guide singing a duet.

While Webber was touted in the Spiritualist press and many leading Spiritualists from **Maurice Barbanell** to **Harry Edwards** voiced their support of his work, skeptics accused him of fraud, and today most, even in the larger psychic community, would deny that the abilities Webber reportedly demonstrated exist. Though never exposed as a fraud, his career has to be seen in the light of the many mediums caught in fraud doing exactly the same acts attributed to Webber.

Webber died in 1940 at the age of 33. Within weeks, various mediums, including **Bertha Harris** and Harold Evans, reported that they had heard from him from the spirit world. Harry Edwards penned his biography.

Sources:

Barbanell, Maurice. *This Is Spiritualism.* London: Spiritualist Press, 1959.

Edwards, Harry. *The Mediumship of Jack Webber.* London: Rider & Co., 1940.

Weeping Statues

Through the 1980s and 1990s, a profusion of reports of statues and icons weeping tears emanated from Roman Catholic and Eastern Orthodox settings. These reports came from around the world, including Asia and Africa. One of the more spectacular reports came from an icon at St. George's Antiochean Orthodox Church in Cicero, Illinois, a suburb of Chicago. In the spring of 1994, tears began to flow from an icon picturing the Virgin Mary and the baby Jesus. The tears originated at the eyes of the Virgin. As word spread concerning the occurrence, thousands of people came to see the phenomenon. Ultimately, Metropolitan Philip, the head of the Antiochean Church, visited and pronounced the phenomenon miraculous.

While the number of reports of weeping statues and icons have multiplied in the last decades of the twentieth century, in part a function of media interest, similar events have been recorded since the sixteenth century. An account has survived from 1527 of a statue that wept just prior to the sacking of Rome. In 1719, a statue of St. Lucy wept in the town of **Syracuse** on the island of Sicily. Syracuse appears to be the originating point of modern accounts of weeping statues as it was the site in 1953 of a widely reported incident. The eyes of a statue of the Virgin Mary given to a newly wedded couple began to produce a substance which upon analysis proved to be the same as human tears. The story of the statue was widely disseminated through Roman Catholic circles. The incident has been analyzed from both a parapsychological perspective (as a poltergeist phenomenon) and a skeptical (as a hoax) viewpoint.

Possibly the most spectacular modern incident of a weeping statue occurrence is **Akita,** Japan, where from 1975 to 1981, a statue of the Virgin Mary was seen to weep on more than 100 separate occasions. Sister Agnes, a nun, also experienced the stigmata, three apparitions of the Virgin Mary, and locutions from an angelic being. The statue not only wept, but had previously sweated what upon analysis proved to be human sweat, and bled human blood. The incident in Akita demonstrated the close connection between weeping statues and icons and **bleeding statues** and icons. Some of the reports of weeping icons concern the weeping of blood, the production of a red substance coming from the eyes.

In 1996, an icon on the Church of the Nativity in Bethlehem, Israel, began to weep tears of blood, a phenomenon seen by many of both Christian and Muslim persuasion. In this case, the eyes on the icon were also reported to have winked at the people viewing it. One skeptical journalist, Stephanie Nolen, a Canadian and lapsed Catholic, reported seeing both the red tears and the wink.

Investigators of such incidents have generally sought initially to rule out the obvious, hoaxes and natural phenomena (for example, a leak above the statue or icon). Enough hoaxes have been uncovered, even among people with reputations for piety and honesty, that an extended search for mundane explanations and the hesitancy of church officials to promote phenomena such as weeping statues except in the rarest of cases is justified. Once obvious natural causes are ruled out, a search is launched for various mundane explanations such as might be provided by the particular substance from which the weeping object was made. Beyond the natural explanation, parapsychologists have offered psychic explanations and skeptics have reached for any possible explanation, in the end suggesting hoaxing as the most widespread cause. Unfortunately, in most cases, especially from Third World countries, no adequate investigation has been done.

Sources:

Nickell, Joe. *Looking for a Miracle.* Amherst, N.Y.: Prometheus Press, 1998.

Rogo, Scott. *Miracles: A Parascientific Inquiry into Wondrous Phenomena.* New York: Dial Press, 1982.

Wege—Zur Synthese von Natur und Mensch (Magazine)

A bimonthly German-language, **New Age** publication. Each issue included articles, a program of mystical/spiritual activities in the Frankfurt area, and listings of New Age organizations. Last known address: Aviva, Kobachstr. 12, D-6000 Frankfurt 50 FN, Germany.

Weiant, C(larence) W(olsey) (1897–1986)

Anthropologist and chiropractor with interests in parapsychology. Weiant was born on November 30, 1987, at West Haverstraw, New York. He studied at the School of General Studies, Columbia University (B.S., 1937), pursued graduate work in 1937 at the Instituto de Filosofia y Letras, Mexico City, and finished a doctorate at Columbia University (1943). He lectured in the Department of Sociology and Anthropology at Hunter College, New York (1943–51). He became a chiropractor and was associated with the Chiropractic Institute of New York. He retired as its dean in 1963.

Weiant was interested in **clairvoyance,** mediumship, **reincarnation,** and **survival** theories. He translated the book *Lo Sagrado entre los Primitivos y la Parapsicologia* (The Sacred Among Primitive Peoples, and Parapsychology), by Juan Rogers, and contributed to *Tomorrow* magazine. He died in October of 1986.

Sources:

Pleasants, Helene, ed. *Biographical Dictionary of Parapsychology.* New York: Helix Press, 1964.

Weiant, C. W. "Parapsychology and Anthropology." *Manas* 13 (1960).

Weinberger, Julius (1893–1978)

Radio engineer who wrote on parapsychology. Weinberger was born on July 22, 1893, in New York City and studied at the City College of New York (B.S., 1913). He worked 42 years for the Radio Corporation of America (RCA) in various positions (1916–1958). He wrote numerous aricles in his chosen field, but also delved into parapsychology and reflected upon a variety of issues. He died in June of 1978.

Sources:

Pleasants, Helene, ed. *Biographical Dictionary of Parapsychology.* New York: Helix Press, 1964.

Weinberger, Julius. "On Apparatus Communication with Discarnate Persons." *International Journal of Parapsychology* 3, no. 1 (winter 1961).

———. "A Physicist Looks at Spiritual Healing." *Laymen's Movement Review* 1, no. 5 (1958); 2, no. 1 (1959).

———. "A Physicist Looks at Survival." *Tomorrow* (autumn 1956).

———. "Some Findings of Experimental Psychical Research." *Proceedings of the Seminar on Decline of Material* (November 1956).

Weingarten, Henry

American astrologer, executive secretary of the **National Astrological Society** (1974–) and editor of *NASO Journal.* He has lectured extensively on **astrology** and taught at the NASO School of Astrology in New York.

Sources:

Weingarten, Henry. *A Modern Introduction to Astrology.* New York: ASI Publishers, 1974.

———. *Principles of Synastry.* New York: ASI Publishers, 1978.

———. *The Study of Astrology.* 3 vols. New York: ASI Publishers, 1977.

Weiser Bookshop

Occult bookstore in the United States through most of the twentieth century, the New York equivalent of London's **Watkins Book Shop** or **Atlantis Bookshop,** patronized by occultists and students of the occult. Weiser's was located at 117 4th Ave., then in a large rambling store at 845 Broadway, and in the 1960s it moved to 740 Broadway. Founded by Samuel Weiser, it was taken over by his son Donald in the 1960s. The store has in each of its locations been known for its large antiquarian occult stock as well as a comprehensive selection of new volumes. Its regular catalogs, issued through the 1950s, of new and old occult books have since become useful bibliographical records.

In the 1980s the store moved again, this time to 132 E. 24th St. (between Park Avenue and Lexington), New York, NY 10010. It slowly adapted to **New Age** emphases and responded to the competition supplied by the emergence of many esoteric bookstores both in New York and around the country. It was one of the more significant retail specialty shops in North America.

In April 1984, Donald Weiser and Henry Suzuki of Samuel Weiser, Inc., became directors (with Valerie Chris, England) of the famous Watkins Book Shop in Cecil Court, Charing Cross Road, London. Samuel Weisers, Inc. is an affiliated publishing company specializing in occult titles. The bookshop is now closed.

Weisman, Kenneth E(arl) (1930–   )

Teacher who has been active in the field of parapsychology. Weisman was born on November 16, 1930, in Chicago, Illinois. He served in the United States Army from 1951 to 1954, and he then studied at Bradley University, Peoria, Illinois (B.S. biology, 1958). He began a teaching career in the Peoria, Illinois, public school system.

Weisman conducted experiments among school children to correlate **clairvoyant** ability with class grades, sex, achievement test ratings and teacher attitude toward pupils.

Sources:

Pleasants, Helene, ed. *Biographical Dictionary of Parapsychology.* New York: Helix Press, 1964.

Weiss, Claude J. (1941–   )

Claude J. Weiss, a prominent Swiss astrologer, was born on May 6, 1941, in Basel, Switzerland. He attended the Swiss Institute of Technology, where he earned an engineering degree with a specialization in agronomy. He later spent two years in India, and during his stay, in 1967, was introduced to **astrology.** He studied astrology over the next decade and became a full-time professional in 1977. The following year he created Astrodata, a calculation and interpretation service for astrological delineations that is now the largest in Continental Europe. He continues to serve as its president.

Weiss has emerged as one of the leading European voices calling for the psychological interpretation of astrology, and he has been a particular devotee of transactional analysis and Jungian psychology. He has emphasized the role of free will and individual choice in light of the insights of astrology. He authored a widely used two-volume work on horoscope interpretation and a specialized study of the effects of the planet Pluto.

Through the 1980s and 1990s, Weiss became a dominant voice in the German-speaking astrological community. He is a popular lecturer, has written a number of books, and edits a periodical, *Astrologie Heute.* He has helped organize four world astrological congresses and has served as president of the Swiss Astrological Association. He has also become known as a master of mundane astrology, the astrology that deals with the larger political fates of people and nations. His office is in Wettswil, near Zürich.

Sources:

Weiss, Claude J. *Astrologie: Eine Wissenschaft von Raum und Zeit.* Wettswil, Switzerland: The Author, 1967.

———. *Horoskopanalyse.* 2 vols. Wettswil, Switzerland: Edition Astrodata, 1992.

———, and Verena Bachmann. *Pluto: Das Eritische und Dämonische.* Wettswil, Switzerland: Edition Astrodata, 1991.

WEL

Initialism for *Welt-Eis-Lehre* (Cosmic Ice Theory), a cult built around the eccentric theories of Austrian engineer **Hans Hörbiger,** author of *Glazial-Kosmogonie* (1912). These theories involved a complex system of "cosmic ice" that generated stellar systems in which smaller planets become moons and are captured by larger planets. According to Hörbiger, Earth's present moon is coated with ice 140 miles thick and is now moving towards Earth with a spiral motion.

After Hörbiger's death, his theories were further developed by the British mythologist Hans Schindler Bellamy in his book *Moons, Myths, and Man* (1936). The WEL cult combined such theories with Nazi political philosophy and anti-Semitism. The character of the WEL is indicated by statements such as:

"Our Nordic ancestors grew strong in ice and snow; belief in the World Ice is consequently the natural heritage of Nordic Man. . . . Just as it needed a child of Austrian Culture— Hitler!—to put the Jewish politicians in their place, so it needed an Austrian to cleanse the world of Jewish science."

Sources:

Bellamy, Hans Schindler. *Moons, Myths, and Man.* London: Faber & Faber, 1949.

Hörbiger, Hans. *Glazial-Kosmogonie.* N.p., 1912.

Wellman, Adele

Former executive secretary of the **American Society for Psychical Research.** He was born in Brooklyn, New York.

Wendigo (or Windigo)

A creature of the forests featured in the mythology of many North American and Canadian native peoples. Algonquin tribes believe that a hunter lost in the bush without food may become a Wendigo, seeking other human beings in order to eat their flesh. Members of the Ojibwa tribe use the term "Windigo" to denote a ferocious ogre who will take away children if they do not behave properly.

A powerful horror story called *The Wendigo* was written by novelist **Algernon Blackwood** (1869–1951). It was first published in *The Lost Valley and Other Stories,* London, 1910. It was probably drawn from legends encountered by the author during his own travels in the Canadian backwoods.

In 1982 John Colombo assembled a comprehensive compilation of accounts (both traditional and modern) on the Wendigo. He observed:

"Windigo has been described as the phantom of hunger which stalks the forests of the north in search of lone Indians, halfbreeds, or white men to consume. It may take the form of a cannibalistic Indian who breathes flames. Or it may assume the guise of a supernatural spirit with a heart of ice that flies through the night skies in search of a victim to satisfy its craving for human flesh. Like the vampire, it feasts on flesh and blood. Like the werewolf, it shape-changes at will."

Colombo lists some 37 variant forms of the word "Windigo" or "Wendigo" and states that the first appearance of the word in print appears to be in an account by the French traveler Bacqueville de la Potherie in 1722, when it appeared as "Onaouientagos." The word derives from the Algonquian Indian root *witiku* meaning "evil spirit" or "cannibal." Legends of the

Wendigo are current among the Algoquian tribes in the Northwest Territories of Canada and the northern regions of Quebec, Ontario, Manitoba, Saskatchewan, and Alberta.

The Wendigo is said to inhabit a large territory bounded by the Atlantic Ocean in the east, the Arctic Ocean in the north, and the Rocky Mountains in the west. According to Algonquian belief, a human being may "turn Windigo" through an act of cannibalism, being in the presence of the demon, or the sorcery of a shaman. Such transformation has much in common with legends of the **vampire** and **werewolf.**

Sources:

Colombo, John R., ed. *Windigo: An Anthology of Facts and Fantastic Fiction.* Lincoln: University of Nebraska Press, 1982.

Wenzl, Aloys (1887– ?)

Philosopher active in the field of parapsychology. He was born on January 25, 1887, in Munich, Germany, and studied at the University of Munich (Ph.D., 1912). He was a lecturer in philosophy and psychology at the University of Munich (1926–38), but was discharged on ideological grounds during the Nazi regime. He returned to his position as professor of philosophy at the University of Munich in 1946. He retired with emeritus status in the early 1960s.

Wenzl took an interest in **clairvoyance** and **psychokinesis,** and he attended the International Conference on Philosophy and Parapsychology at St. Paul de Vence, France, held in 1954. He was the author of a number of books, several of which considered parapsychological questions.

Sources:

Pleasants, Helene, ed. *Biographical Dictionary of Parapsychology.* New York: Helix Press, 1964.

Wenzl, Aloys. *Philosophische Grenzfragen der Naturwissenchaften* (Philosophical Border Problems of the Natural Sciences). N.p., 1956.

———. *Unsterblichkeit* (Immorality). Bern: A. Francke, 1951.

Wereide, Thorstein (1882– ?)

Norwegian physicist and parapsychologist. He was born on March 9, 1882, at Nordfjord, Norway. He studied at the University of Oslo (B.A., 1910; Ph.D., 1914). He joined the staff of the University of Oslo as a physicist in the Medical College following World War I and remained there throughout his long career.

In 1919 he was among the cofounders of the Norwegian Society for Psychical Research. In 1926 he became editor of *Psykisk Tidsskrift,* the society's journal (1926–39), and the following year was elected president of the NSPR. He was a delegate to the international psychical research congresses at Copenhagen (1920), Warsaw (1923), Paris (1927), and Athens (1930) and president of the International Congress of Psychical Research held in Oslo in 1935. Having survived World War II, he was also able to attend the International Conference on Parapsychological Studies at Utrecht in 1953 and the International Conference on Spontaneous Phenomena at Cambridge, England, 1955.

His investigations covered mediumship, materialization, and multiple personality phenomena. He made a special study of the Norwegian medium Ingeborg Koeber and the multiple personalities of Hungarian **Lujza Ignath.** Among his many writings, several were translated into English for *Tomorrow* magazine.

Sources:

Pleasants, Helene, ed. *Biographical Dictionary of Parapsychology.* New York: Helix Press, 1964.

Scarabaeus [Thorstein Wereide]. *Mysteriesamfund* (Mystery Societies). N.p., 1948.

Wereide, Thorstein. *Byggesamfund* (Building Societies). N.p., 1956.

———. "Medium or Murderess." *Tomorrow* (winter 1957).

———. *Menneskets Metafysikk* (The Metaphysics of Man). N.p., 1953.

———. "Norway's Human Doubles." *Tomorrow* (winter 1955).

Werewolf

A human temporarily or permanently transformed into a wolf, from the Anglo-Saxon *wer* (man) and *wulf* (wolf). It is a term used in the phenomenon of **lycanthropy,** which in ancient and medieval times was of very frequent occurrence. It was in Europe, where the wolf was one of the largest carnivorous animals, that the superstition became prevalent. Similar tales in other countries usually introduced bears, tigers, leopards, or other animals.

Origins

The belief in werewolves may be a relic of early cannibalism. Communities of semicivilized people would begin to shun those who devoured human flesh, ostracizing them and classifying them as wild beasts. The idea that they had something in common with animals would grow, and the concept that they were able to transform themselves into veritable animals would likely arise.

More likely, however, the belief derives from early ritual practices in the Balkan area. For example, the Dacians, an ancient people who had the wolf as their totem animal, annually turned their young men into wolves during a ritual in which they wore wolf skins and imitated the animal. The wolf was much respected in the area as a hunter. The ritual transformation into a wolf survives today in the Greek word *vrkolaka* (and its Slavic equivalents), derived from the old Slavic word for wolf-pelt, though the term is now applied to a form of **vampire.** It has been suggested that as the people settled into an agricultural life, the wolf lost its positive associations and became the outlaw animal many still consider it today. Thus the *vrkolaka* became the werewolf. *Werewolf* itself is an Old English term meaning shape-shifter, probably derived from older Germanic roots.

The oldest account of a man changing into a wolf came from Greek writings. Lycaon (from whom the term *lycanthropy* is derived) was changed into a wolf by Zeus, whom the unfortunate Lycaon had displeased.

The Nature of the Werewolf

There were two kinds of werewolves: voluntary and involuntary. The voluntary were, as has been said, persons who, because of their taste for human flesh, had withdrawn from association with other people.

They possessed a reputation for the magic power to transform themselves into the animal shape at will. This they effected by merely disrobing—by taking off a girdle made of human skin, or putting on a belt of wolf skin, obviously a substitute for an entire wolf skin. There were also cases in which they donned the entire skin. In other instances, the body was rubbed with a magic ointment, or water was drunk from a wolf's footprint. The brains of the animal were also eaten. Olaus Magnus (1490–1558) stated that "the werewolves of Livonia drained a cup of beer on initiation, and repeated certain magic words."

In order to throw off the wolf shape, the animal girdle was removed, or else the magician merely muttered a certain formula. In some instances, the transformation was supposed to be the work of Satan.

The superstition regarding werewolves seems to have been exceedingly prevalent in France during the sixteenth century, as is evidenced by numerous trials, in some of which murder and cannibalism took place. Self-hallucination may have accounted for some of these cases, the supposed werewolves admitting that they had transformed themselves and had slain numerous persons, but at the beginning of the seventeenth century such confessions were not believed. Self-hallucination does not cover a number of cases in which werewolves were seen by witnesses, however. In Teutonic and Slavonic countries, men of learning complained that werewolves did more damage than real criminals, and a regular "college" or institution for the practice of the art of animal transformation was attributed to them.

Involuntary werewolves were often said to be persons transformed into animals because of the commission of sin, and condemned to pass a certain number of years in that form. Certain saints were said to metamorphose sinners into wolves. In Armenia it was thought that sinful women were condemned to pass seven years in the form of a wolf. To such a woman a demon appeared, bringing a wolf skin. He commanded her to don it, and from that moment she became a wolf, with all the nature of a wild beast, devouring her own children and those of strangers; wandering at night, undeterred by locks, bolts, or bars; returning only in the morning to resume her human form.

French romance literature often mentions werewolves, and there are complete romances on the theme, such as the *Lais du Bisclavret* of Marie de France and the *Guillaume de Palerne* (known as *William and the Werewolf*) of the twelfth century. However, in such romances the werewolf was the innocent victim of magic, rather than a dangerous cannibal.

Many werewolves were said to be innocent persons suffering through the witchcraft of others. To regain their true form it was necessary for them to kneel in one spot for a hundred years, to lose three drops of blood, to be hailed as a werewolf, to have the sign of the cross made on their bodies, to be addressed thrice by their baptismal names, or to be struck thrice on the forehead with a knife.

According to Donat de Hautemer, quoted by Simon Goulart (1543–1628), "There are some lycanthropes who are so dominated by their melancholy humour that they really believe themselves to be transformed into wolves. This malady . . . is a sort of melancholy, of a black and dismal nature. Those who are attacked by it leave their homes in the months of February, imitate wolves in almost every particular, and wander all night long among the cemeteries and sepulchres, so that one may observe a marvelous change in the mind and disposition, and, above all in the depraved imagination, of the lycanthrope. The memory, however, is still vigorous, as I have remarked in one of these lycanthropic melancholiacs whom we call *werewolves.* For one who was well acquainted with me was one day seized with his affliction, and on meeting him I withdrew a little, fearing that he might injure me. He, having glanced at me for a moment, passed on followed by a crowd of people. On his shoulder he carried the entire leg and thigh of a corpse. Having received careful medical treatment, he was cured of this malady. On meeting me on another occasion he asked me if I had not been afraid when he met me at such and such a place, which made me think that his memory was not hurt by the vehemence of his disease, though his imagination was so greatly damaged."

Guillaume de Brabant, in the narrative of Wier, repeated by Goulart, writes in his *History* that a certain sensible man was so tormented by the evil spirit that at a particular season of the year he would think himself a ravening wolf and would run through the woods, caves, and deserts chasing little children. It was said that this man was often found running in the deserts like a man out of his mind, and that at last by the grace of God he came to himself and was healed. Job Fincel, in the book *On Miracles,* relates that a villager near Paule in the year 1541 believed himself to be a wolf and assaulted several men in the fields, killing some. Captured at last, though not without great difficulty, he strongly affirmed that he was a wolf, and that the only way in which he differed from other wolves was that they wore their hairy coats on the outside, while he wore his between his skin and his flesh. Certain persons, more inhuman and wolfish than he, wished to test the truth of this story, and gashed his arms and legs severely. Learning of their mistake and of the innocence of the melancholiac, they passed him on to the surgeons, in whose hands he died some days later.

Those afflicted with lycanthropy are pale, with dark and haggard eyes, seeing only with difficulty; the tongue is dry, and the sufferer very thirsty.

Speaking of lycanthropy, Gaspar Peucer (1525–1602) stated the following:

"As for me I had formerly regarded as ridiculous and fabulous the stories I had often heard concerning the transformation of men into wolves; but I have learnt from reliable sources, and from the testimony of trustworthy witnesses, that such things are not at all doubtful or incredible, since they tell of such transformations taking place twelve days after Christmas in Livonia and the adjacent countries; as they have been proved to be true by the confessions of those who have been imprisoned and tortured for such crimes.

"Here is the manner in which it is done. Immediately after Christmas day is past, a lame boy goes round the country calling these slaves of the devil, of which there are a great number, and enjoining them to follow him. If they procrastinate or go too slowly, there immediately appears a tall man with a whip whose thongs are made of iron chains, with which he urges them onwards, and sometimes lashes the poor wretches so cruelly, that the marks of the whip remain on their bodies till long afterwards, and cause them the greatest pain. As soon as they have set out on their road, they are all changed into wolves. . . .

"They travel in thousands, having for their conductor the bearer of the whip, after whom they march. When they reach the fields, they rush upon the cattle they find there, tearing and carrying away all they can, and doing much other damage; but they are not permitted to touch or wound persons. When they approach any rivers, their guide separates the waters with his whip, so that they seem to open up and leave a dry space by which to cross. At the end of twelve days the whole band scatters, and everyone returns to his home, having regained his own proper form. This transformation, they say, comes about in this wise. The victims fall suddenly on the ground as though they were taken with sudden illness, and remain motionless and extended like corpses, deprived of all feeling, for they neither stir, nor move from one place to another, nor are in any wise transformed into wolves, thus resembling carrion, for although they are rolled or shaken, they give no sign of life."

Jean Bodin (1529–1596) related several cases of lycanthropy and of men changed into beasts, including the following:

"Pierre Mamot, in a little treatise he has written on sorcerers, says that he has observed this changing of men into wolves, he being in Savoy at the time. Henry of Cologne in his treatise *de Lamiis* regards the transformation as beyond doubt. And Ulrich in a little book dedicated to the emperor Sigismund, writes of the dispute before the emperor, and says that it was agreed, both on the ground of reason, and of the experience of innumerable examples, that such transformation was a fact; and he adds that he himself had seen a lycanthrope at Constance, who was accused, convicted, condemned, and finally executed after his confession. And several books published in Germany say that one of the greatest kings of Christendom, who is not long dead, and who had the reputation of being one of the greatest sorcerers in the world, often changed into a wolf.

"I remember that the attorney-general of the King, Bourdin, has narrated to me another which was sent to him from the Low Countries, with the whole trial signed by the judge and the clerks, of a wolf, which was struck by an arrow on the thigh, and afterwards found himself in bed, with the arrow (which he had torn out), on regaining his human shape, and the arrow was recognised by him who had fired it—the time and place testified by the confession of the person.

"Garnier, tried and condemned by the parliament of Dole, being in the shape of a *werewolf,* caught a girl of ten or twelve years in a vineyard of Chastenoy, a quarter of a league from Dole, and having slain her with his teeth and claw-like hands, he ate part of her flesh and carried the rest to his wife. A month later, in the same form, he took another girl, and would have eaten her also, had he not, as he himself confessed, been prevented by three persons who happened to be passing by; and a fortnight after he strangled a boy of ten in the vineyard of Gredisans, and ate his flesh; and in the form of a man and not of a wolf, he killed another boy of twelve or thirteen years in a wood of the village of Porouse with the intention of eating him, but was again prevented. He was condemned to be burnt, and the sentence was executed.

"At the parliament of Bezançon, the accused were Pierre Burgot and Michel Verdun, who confessed to having renounced God, and sworn to serve the devil. And Michel Verdun led Burgot to the Bard du Chastel Charlon where everyone carried a candle of green wax which shone with a blue flame. There they danced and offered sacrifices to the devil. Then after being anointed they were turned into wolves, running with incredible swiftness, then they were changed again into men, and suddenly transformed back to wolves, when they enjoyed the society of female wolves as much as they had done that of their wives. They confessed also that Burgot had killed a boy of seven years with his wolf-claws and teeth, intending to eat him, but the peasants gave chase, and prevented him. Burgot and Verdun had eaten four girls between them; and they had caused people to die by the touch of a certain power."

Some cases of lycanthropy may have been a cover for a perverse appetite for drinking blood or eating human flesh, but it is also possible that there were cases of psychic transformations, in which the astral double of a lycanthrope was projected in the form of a beast, similar to other stories of witches and wizards attacking their victims in an astral form.

Modern attempts to understand the werewolf have opted for a psychological approach, one exception being Robert Eisler, who has explained it in terms of the cycles of human violence that have been a part of social existence since time began. Richard Noll has gathered a variety of reports of modern werewolves, whom psychologists see as people under the delusion that s/he has been transformed into an animal.

Another aspect of lycanthropy is the Romulus and Remus theme of abandoned children reared by wolves. One classic case of such "feral children," as they are termed, is that of the two wolf girls of Midnapore, India, who were rescued by the Reverend J. A. L. Singh in 1942. This case is discussed in detail by Charles Maclean in his book *The Wolf Children* (1978). (See also **Vampire**)

Werewolf Fiction

In the middle of the nineteenth century, as other forms of modern horror fiction were emerging, three werewolf novels appeared: *Hughes the Wer-wolf,* by Sutherland Mnzies (a serial published in installment in the 1850s); *The Wolf-Leader* (1857); and *Wagner the Wehrwolf,* by George W. M. Reynold (1857). The latter is considered the fountainhead of modern werewolf fiction, and it was not until 1934 that another noteworthy werewolf novel was published.

Guy Endore's *The Werewolf of Paris* was bought by Universal Studios, who wanted to produce a cinematic version. The screenplay changes the location of the movie, which appeared in 1935 as *The Werewolf of London.* The story was inspired by the true story of Francis Bertrand, a French noncommissioned officer who in 1848 was convicted of breaking into several Paris graveyards, and consuming the flesh of several recently buried bodies. His ghoulish activity was transformed into the story of Bertrand Caullet, the son born as a result of a brief affair between his mother and a priest. He discovered that he was a werewolf when shot with a silver bullet. (The now-standard association of werewolves and silver is derived from a Scottish belief in the efficacy of silver in killing witches.)

The Werewolf of London was followed by its more famous sequel, *The Wolf Man,* starring Lon Chaney, Jr. Chaney reappeared in several movies with other Universal monsters, but made his next notable appearance in the 1961 remake, *The Curse of the Werewolf.* The werewolf became a television star as a character in the early 1960s in the vampire television soap opera *Dark Shadows.*

Since the 1970s the werewolf has become an integral part of a horror genre that has grown spectacularly. While not approaching the popularity of the vampire, new werewolf novels have appeared annually and some, such as Whitney Streiber's *Wolfen* have become popular movies. Gary Brandner's *The Howling* led to no less than five sequels, most of which were made into movies. The lycanthropy/shape-shifting theme also was prominent in movies like the *Cat People,* which features a woman able to transform into a panther.

Sources:

Baring-Gould, Sabine. *The Book of Were-Wolves.* London, 1965; New York: Causeway Books, 1973.

Cooper, Basil. *The Werewolf in Legend, Fact and Art.* New York: St. Martin's Press, 1977.

Douglas, Adam. *The Beast Within: Man, Myths and Werewolves.* London: Chapmans, 1992. Reprint. London: Orion, 1993.

Dunn, Charles W. *The Foundling and the Werewolf: A Literary-Historical Study of Guillaume de Palerne.* Toronto: University of Toronto Press, 1960.

Eisler, Robert. *Man into Wolf: An Anthropological Interpretation of Sadism, Masochism, and Lycanthropy.* Santa Barbara, Calif.: Ross Erikson, 1978.

Gesell, Arnold. *Wolf-Child and Human Child.* London: Harper/Methuen, 1941.

Hamel, Frank. *Human Animals.* London, 1915. University Books, 1969.

Kaigh, Frederick. *Witchcraft & Magic of Africa.* London: Richard Lesley, 1947.

Maclean, Charles. *The Wolf Children.* Hill & Wang, 1978.

Noll, Richard. *Vampires, Werewolves, and Demons.* New York: Brunner/Mazel, 1992.

O'Donnell, Elliott. *Werewolves.* London, 1912. Rev. ed. New York: Wholesale Book Corp., 1972.

Summers, Montague. *The Werewolf.* London, 1933. University Books, 1966.

Woodward, Ian. *The Werewolf Delusion.* London & New York: Paddington Press, 1979.

Weschcke, Carl Llewellyn (1930–)

Prominent American astrologer, occultist, publisher, and owner-president of **Llewellyn Publications,** St. Paul, Minnesota, originally founded as Llewellyn Publishing Company by **Llewellyn George** in 1905 in Portland, Oregon. Weschcke was born on September 10, 1930, in St. Paul, Minnesota. He was educated at the St. Paul Academy; the Babson Institute, Wellesley Hills, Massachusetts; and the University of Minnesota.

He purchased the Llewellyn Publishing Company of Los Angeles, California, in 1960 and moved the business to St. Paul, Minnesota. For a number of years the Llewellyn enterprise also included Gnostica, a large retail bookstore housed in a 12,000-square-foot former mortuary in St. Paul. In addition to publishing a number of popular occult books, Llewellyn also issued **Gnostica** magazine (now superseded by Llewellyn's *New Worlds of Mind and Spirit*) and **Astrology Now** magazine (discontinued). Among the company's prominent publications are the annual *Moon Sign Book* (established by Llewellyn George in 1905) and *Daily Planetary Guide.* It is now one of the largest wholesale dealers in occult books and products in the United States.

Weschcke was editor-in-chief of *Gnostica* magazine, and his own writings included articles on lunar astrology, gardening, **tantra,** and **witchcraft.** He is a practicing witch and has chaired the Council of American Witches. In addition to many appearances on radio and television interview programs, he was responsible for a half-hour commercial television program on Halloween and prepared a videotape on witchcraft for the University of Wisconsin.

Sources:

Weschcke, Carl L. *The Occult Renaissance.* St. Paul, Minn.: Llewellyn Publishing, 1972.

———. *The Science of Feeling Fine.* St. Paul, Minn.: Chester-Kent, 1954.

West, D(onald) J(ames) (1924–)

Psychiatrist and parapsychologist. He was born on June 9, 1924, in Liverpool, England, and studied at Liverpool University (M.B., Ch.B., 1947; M.D., 1958). He did postgraduate work at London University (D.P.M., 1952) and Cambridge University, England (M.A., 1960). For many years he was the director of the Cambridge University Institute of Criminology. After his retirement in 1984, he was named professor emeritus of clinical criminology research.

He has been a long-time member of the **Society for Psychical Research,** London, having joined when he was only 17. He later served as its research officer (1947–49) and on two occasions as president (1963–65). With **G. W. Fisk** he carried out a set of experiments designed to show the effects of the experimenter on the results of ESP tests. In 1958 he and Fisk won the William McDougall Award for Distinguished Research in Parapsychology. He wrote a book on **Lourdes,** notable for its conclusion that miracles have not been proven to have occurred at the famous shrine. West has played an important part in British laboratory experiments in **extrasensory perception.**

Sources:

Berger, Arthur S., and Joyce Berger. *The Encyclopedia of Parapsychology and Psychical Research.* New York: Paragon House, 1991.

Pleasants, Helene, ed. *Biographical Dictionary of Parapsychology.* New York: Helix Press, 1964.

West, Donald J. *Eleven Lourdes Miracles.* London: Duckworth, 1957.

———. "The Identity of 'Jack the Ripper.' " *Journal* of the Society for Psychical Research 35 (1949).

———. *Psychical Research Today.* London: Duckworth, 1956.

———. "Psychokinetic Experiments with a Single Subject." *Parapsychology Newsletter* (November–December 1957).

West, Donald J., and G. W. Fisk. "ESP and Mood: Report of a 'Mass' Experiment with Clock Cards." *Journal* of the Society for Psychical Research 38 (1956).

Westcar Papyrus

An Egyptian papyrus dating from the eighteenth century B.C.E. devoted chiefly to tales of magic and enchantment. The beginning and ending are missing, yet much of the subject matter has survived.

Alfred Wiedemann, in his book *Popular Literature of Ancient Egypt* (1902), describes these tales of magic and enchantment as follows:

"The papyrus tells how Kheops—the king whom notices of Greek writers have made universally famous as the builder of the Great Pyramid of Gizeh—commands stories of magic to be told to him. The first of these, of which the conclusion only remains, is supposed to have occurred in the reign of King T'eser of the Third Dynasty. The next, which is complete, belongs to the reign of Nebka, a somewhat earlier king.

"In those days it came to the ears of a great nobleman that his faithless wife was in the habit of meeting her lover by the side of a lake. Being skilled in magic he modelled a crocodile in wax and ordered one of his servants to cast it into the water. It was immediately transformed into a real crocodile and devoured the lover. Seven days later the king was walking by the lake with his friend the nobleman, when at the command of the latter the crocodile came to the shore and laid its victim at their feet. The king shuddered at the sight of the monster but at the touch of its maker it became once more a mere figure of wax. Then the whole astonishing story was told to the king, who thereupon granted the crocodile permission to take away that which was its own. The creature plunged into the depths of the lake and disappeared with the adulterer, while the guilty wife was burnt to death and her ashes were scattered in the stream.

"A tale of enchantment follows, the scene of which is laid during the reign of King Sneferu, the predecessor of Kheops. The king was one day taking his pleasure on a lake in a boat rowed by twenty beautiful maidens, when one of the girls dropped a malachite ornament into the water. The king promised to give her another in its stead, but this did not content her, for she wanted her own jewel and no other. A magician was summoned who repeated a spell by the might of which he piled one half of the lake on the top of the other, so that the water, which at first was twelve ells deep in the middle of the lake, now stood twenty-four ells high. The jewel, found lying in the mud in the dry portion of the lake, was restored to its owner; and the magician having once more mumbled his spell the water returned to its former place.

"When Kheops had listened for some time with much interest to the accounts of the strange events that had transpired in the days of his predecessors, then stepped forward Prince Horduduf, who is really known to us from the song in the tomb-temple of King Antef as renowned for his wisdom. He told the king that all marvels were not things of the past but that even then there was living a magician named Deda, who was one hundred and ten years old, and consumed every day five hundred loaves, a side of beef, and a hundred jars of beer.

"Kheops was so much interested that he sent the prince to escort the magician to his presence. Deda obeyed the royal summons and performed his chief feat before the king. This consisted in decapitating a goose, a duck, and an ox, and charming the heads back again on to the bodies so that the creatures lived and breathed as before. Kheops fell into talk with the magician, who told him that the wife of a priest in Sakhebu was awaiting the birth of three sons, children of the god Ra, who should one day sit on the throne of Egypt. Deda sought to allay the king's natural distress at this information by prophesying that only after the reigns of his son and grandson should the power fall into the hands of the descendants of the Sun-god. But Kheops was not to be consoled; he inquired into the details of the story and announced that he would himself travel to Sakhebu, no doubt with the ultimate intention of finding an opportunity to put out of the way the pretenders to his throne.

"The scene of the sequel is laid in Sakhebu. The birth and infancy of the three children are described in detail, and all sorts of marvelous incidents are represented as influencing their fate. The gods cared for the safety of the little ones. A maid to whom the secret was known being enraged by a severe punishment inflicted upon her, threatened to betray all to Kheops. Her own brother beat her, and when she went down to the water she was carried off by a crocodile. Here the papyrus ceases, but it is possible to a certain extent to restore the conclusion. The names of the three children of Ra show that they stand for the first three kings of the Fifth Dynasty, the family that followed the house of Kheops. The papyrus must therefore have told how the boys escaped all the snares laid for their lives and in due time ascended the throne for which they were destined." (See also **Egypt**)

Sources:

Budge, E. A. W. *Egyptian Magic.* London: Kegan, Paul, 1899.

Maspero, G. *Les contes populaires de l'Egypte ancienne.* Paris, 1881.

Wiedemann, A. *Popular Literature of Ancient Egypt.* London: David Nutt, 1902.

Westcott, William Wynn (1848–1925)

Prominent British occultist and one of the founders of the **Hermetic Order of the Golden Dawn.** He was born in December 1848 at Leamington, Warwickshire, England. He lost both parents before the age of ten and was adopted by Richard Westcott Martyn, an uncle who was a surgeon by profession. Westcott was educated at the Queen Elizabeth Grammar School at Kingston-upon-Thames, London, and studied medicine at University College, London.

He qualified as a physician in 1871 and became a partner in his uncle's practice in Somerset. He also joined a Masonic lodge in Crewkerne. After 1879, he moved to Hendon, where he pursued studies in occultism for two years. About 1880, he became a leading member of the **Societas Rosicruciana in Anglia** (Rosicrucian Society of England), an occult society open only to master masons. A year later he was appointed deputy coroner and later coroner for northeast London, and he wrote a number of articles for the Medical Directory. During this period, his occultism remained a closely guarded secret.

In 1887, he acquired an old manuscript written in code, said to have been bought from a bookstall in Farringdon Road, London. In the pages of the manuscript was a sheet of paper with the name and address of a **Fraulein Sprengel,** a Rosicrucian adept living in Germany. Westcott deciphered the manuscript, which contained fragments of mystical rituals.

These rituals were expanded by Westcott's occultist friend **S. L. MacGregor Mathers,** also a member of the Societas Rosicruciana in Anglia. Westcott thereupon corresponded with Sprengel, who authorized him to found an English branch of the German occult society Die Goldene Dämmerung. Westcott, Mathers, and **W. R. Woodman** thereupon founded the Isis-Urania temple of the Hermetic Order of the Golden Dawn in 1888. Westcott's occult motto in the order was *Sapere Aude* (Dare to Be Wise).

This is the official story of the foundation of the famous Golden Dawn order, but there is strong reason to suppose that the manuscript may have been the invention of Westcott or his associates and that Sprengel never existed. Correspondence with her has been produced, but many students of occultism doubt its genuineness. For all that, the Golden Dawn attracted some of the most eminent talents of its day, including poet **William Butler Yeats,** until it eventually degenerated into undignified squabbles, expulsions, resignations, and complex fragmentation.

Westcott had retired from the Golden Dawn by around 1897, possibly because of pressure relating to his official status as a coroner. He continued to be a member of the Rosicrucian Society, and, after the death of Woodman in 1891, he became supreme magus. Through the 1890s he published a number of books and pamphlets. In his later years, he moved to Durban, South Africa, where he became vice president of two Theosophical Society lodges. He died June 30, 1925.

Westcott is not only known for his work with the Golden Dawn, he wrote books on the **Kabbalah** and translated work of **Eliphas Levi.**

Sources:

Gilbert, R. A., ed. *The Magical Mason: Forgotten Hermetic Writings of William Wynn Westcott.* Wellingborough, Northamptonshire, England: Aquarian Press, 1983.

Howe, Ellie. *The Magicians of the Golden Dawn.* London: Routledge and Kegan Paul, 1972.

King, Francis. *The Rites of Modern Occult Magic.* New York: Macmillan, 1970.

Westcott, Wynn. *Aesch Mezareph, or Purifying Fire.* N.p., 1894.

———. *The Chaldean Oracles of Zoroaster.* London: Theosophical Publishing Society, 1895.

———. *Egyptian Magic.* London: Theosophical Publishing Society, 1896.

———. *Numbers: Their Occult Power and Mystic Virtue.* 1890. Reprint, London: Theosophical Publishing Society, 1911.

———. *The Pymander of Hermes.* N.p., 1894.

———. *Rosicrucians, Their History and Aims.* N.p., 1894.

———. *The Science of Alchymy.* N.p., 1893.

———. *Sepher Yetzirah, the Book of Formation.* London, Theosophical Publishing Society, 1893. Rev. ed. Gillette, N.J.: Heptangle Books, 1987.

———. *Somnium Scipionis.* N.p., 1894.

West Indies

The importation of Africans into the Caribbean area as slaves began in the sixteenth century but expanded greatly after 1640 when the islands became a major source of sugar and workers were needed for the plantations. Most of these people came from the various tribes along the coast of West Africa from present-day Senegal to Nigeria. The white planters looked upon Africans with disdain and developed the opinion that they had no religious life, that they were at best bearers of a set of heathenish superstitions. Such was not the case. While a few of the Africans were Muslims, the majority were followers of the West African religious system, which with relatively minor alterations from tribe to tribe pervaded the area from which the slaves were taken.

The West African system acknowledged a supreme divine power but found its more personalized expression in the various deities responsible for the harmonious operation of the natural world. In the West Indies the major deities included Shango, Ogun, and Eshu (in Trinidad) and Legba, Erzulie, and Damballah (in Haiti). The Haitian deities (*loas*) were of two varieties: those of African origin (Rada) and those of Haitian origin (Pétro). Rites were constructed for both.

There was also a belief in fate, which to a large extent determined the course and eventual destiny of the individual. A person's future could be seen through divinatory practices. Also, by propitiating the messenger to the Gods, who carried words of the individual's fate, that fate could be altered to one more favorable. The religion was led by priests and priestesses (variously termed in the different islands), who performed the rites for the higher deities; medicine men, who dealt with lower evil spirits (the cause of disease and harm to individuals); and sorcerers, who were supposed to attack tribal enemies but sometimes, for a price, attacked individuals with their magical powers. The sorcerer (*obayifo*) worked clandestinely at night. People wore **amulets** to protect themselves. The priest supplied the amulets and often worked to counter the effects of the sorcerer.

In Africa, this religion permeated tribal life. Religious practice included *obeah* (**magic**), "possession" of certain people by the deities (similar to mediumship), and communication with and guidance from ancestor spirits.

In the New World, such religion was at best distasteful to the European understanding; it was often despised by the ruling elite. However, some of the planters did not hesitate to make use of obeah to manage the workers. To prevent theft of crops, for instance, they sometimes adorned trees around the edge of a banana or orange grove with miniature coffins, old bones, bottles of dirty water, and other obeah objects. Then the workers would not enter and steal. As late as 1908, a case of obeah was reported in a Jamaican journal:

"The *cause célèbre* at Half-way Tree Court, Jamaica, recently, was the case of Rex V. Charles Donaldson for unlawfully practicing Obeah. Robert Robinson, who stated that he was a laborer living at Trench Pen, in the parish of St. Andrew, stated that on Tuesday, the 8th ult., he was sitting down outside the May Pen cemetery on the Spanish Town Road. He was on his way from work, and had a white handkerchief tied around his head. He was feeling sick, and that led him to sit down. While there sitting the prisoner came to him. He did not know the man before, but he began by asking him what was the matter. Witness replied, 'I am well sick.' The prisoner said, 'No, you are not sick; you have two ghosts on you—one creole and one coolie.' Witness told the prisoner to go away and was left. He next saw prisoner on Wednesday 9th. He came to him at Bumper Hall, where he was working, and he said to him, 'Man, how you find me here?' 'Oh,' replied the prisoner, 'if a man is in hell self I can find him; I come for you to give me the job?' Witness then inquired, 'What job?' and accused told him he wanted to 'take off the two ghosts.' He would do it for £25, and he 'killed' for any sum from £25 to £50. He had worked for all classes—white, black, coolie, Chinese, etc. Witness said he did not give him any 'good consent' at the time, but reported the matter after the accused left to Clark and Wright, two witnesses in the case. Clark told him he must not scare the man but go home. On Thursday, the 10th, the defendant came to him at his yard at French Pen. The accused told him he would come back to him to take off the ghost. He also told him to get a bottle of rum and 5s. He (witness) consented to the arrangement. The defendant began by taking off his jacket. He then opened his 'brief bag' and took out a piece of chalk. The accused then made three marks on the table and took out a phial and a white stone. The phial contained some stuff which appeared like quicksilver. He arrayed his paraphernalia on the table. They consisted of a large whisky bottle with some yellow stuff, a candle, a pack of cards, a looking-glass, three cigarette pictures, a pocket knife, etc. The accused also took out a whistle which he sounded, and then placed the cards on the table. He then asked for the 5s. which was given to him. He placed the coins on the cards around a lighted candle. The pint of rum which he (witness) had brought was on the table and prisoner poured some of it into a pan. He went outside and sprinkled the rum at the four corners of the house. Accused came back in and said, 'Papa! papa! your case is very bad! There are two ghosts outside. The creole is bad, but the coolie is rather worse. But if he is made out of hell I will catch him.' The prisoner then began to blow his whistle in a very funny way—a way in which he had never heard a whistle blown before. He also began to speak in an unknown tongue and to call up the ghosts."

[The following dialogue is taken from court proceedings regarding the case.]

Mr. Lake—"Aren't there a lot of you people who believe that ghosts can harm and molest you?"

Witness—"No, I am not one."

Mr. Lake—"Did you not tell him that a duppy [Jamaican ghost] struck you on your back and you heard voices calling you?"

Witness—"He told me so."[Continuing, witness said he had seen all sorts of ghosts at all different times and of different kinds also].

Mr. Lake—"Of all different sexes, man and woman?"

Witness—"Yes; any man who can see ghosts will know a man ghost from a woman ghost."

While it empowered those who practiced it, African religion had to be practiced undercover, and as a result it underwent some changes. For example, it took on an overlay of Christianity of whatever variety was dominant on the plantation. In Haiti, **Voudou** resulted from obeah's association with French Catholicism. In Cuba and Puerto Rico, Santeria emerged its mixing with Spanish Catholicism. In Brazil, **Macumba** is a result of its mixing with Portuguese Catholicism.

African-based religions gained significant favor in the West Indies because of their role underlying the various rebellions by which the slaves gained their freedom. Today, they survive in competition with the dominant Catholicism or Anglicanism. They are reemerging despite several centuries of negative writing by outsiders.

African-derived Caribbean religion entered the United States at the time of the Haitian slave rebellion in 1908 and in the years to follow. Voudou eventually became established in New Orleans and the surrounding countryside. During the twentieth century, and especially as immigration laws have eased during the last generation, numerous people have moved to America from the Caribbean, carrying their faiths with them.

Sources:

Bisnauth, Dale. *History of Religion in the Caribbean.* Kingston, Jamaica: Kingston Publishers, 1989.

Denning, Melita, and Osborne Phillips. *Voudoun Fire: The Living Reality of Mystical Religion.* St. Paul, Minn.: Llewellyn Publications, 1979.

Deren, Maya. *Divine Horsemen: The Voodoo Gods of Haiti.* New York: Chelsea House, 1970.

Westlake, Aubrey T(homas) (1893–1985)

Prominent British authority on **radiesthesia,** alternative medical therapies, and **holistic** health. Born in 1893, in Redhill, Surrey, he was educated at the Quaker Sidcot school, and he trained in medicine at Birmingham and Cambridge universities and St. Bartholomew's Hospital, London. He entered general practice in Bermondsey, London. In 1938, he and his family moved to the family estate at Fordingbridge, Hampshire, where Westlake continued the private practice of medicine.

He also spent many years investigating a wide range of alternative studies beyond the purely physical parameters of orthodox medical science, such as the Bach flower remedies, medical **dowsing,** radiesthesia, **radionics,** the odic force of **Baron von Reichenbach,** the **orgone** energy of **Wilhelm Reich, Huna,** homeopathy, and anthroposophical medicine. In 1956, he formed a study group with several associates, investigating the use of radiesthesia techniques in healing patients at a distance.

The wide range of his inquiries is demonstrated in his important paper "Vis Medicatrix Naturae," given at the Scientific and Technical Congress of Radionics and Radiesthesia, London, May 16, 1950. He published a number of important articles and a major work, *The Pattern of Health* (1961).

He was a founding member of the Soil Association, an active member of the Medical Society for the Study of Radiesthesia, an honorary fellow of the Radionic Association, an honorary life vice president of the **British Society of Dowsers,** and president of the Psionic Medical Society. He died at the age of 92 in Fordingbridge, on October 30, 1985.

Westwood, Horace (1884–1956)

Unitarian minister who wrote on parapsychology. He was born on August 17, 1884, at Wakefield, England. He became an ordained minister of the Methodist Episcopal Church in 1906 and pastored at Sault Ste. Marie, Michigan (1906–08). Then in 1910 he joined the Unitarian Church and was pastor successively at the First Unitarian Church, Youngstown, Ohio (1910–12); All Soul's Church, Winnipeg, Manitoba, Canada (1912–19); and First Church, Toledo, Ohio (1919–27). He was minister at large for the Unitarian Church (1927–33) and for the First Unitarian Church, Berkeley, California (1934–45).

He studied psychic research for a number of years and described his personal attitudes in his book *There Is a Psychic World* (1949). He died December 24, 1956.

Sources:

Westwood, Horace. *Apostle of Darkness and Prophet of Light.* N.p., 1939.

———. *This Do and Live.* N.p., 1938.

Weyer, Johan (also known as John Wier or Wierus) (1515–1588)

Protestant physician and demonologist, born in Basel, Switzerland, who compiled an inventory of devils published in 1568, in which he estimated that the **devil**'s kingdom consisted of an army of 7,405,926 devils and demons, organized in 1,111 divisions of 6,666 each. During the Reformation, this total was raised by the Lutherans, who calculated that the true figure was 2,665,866,746,664 devils.

However, in his major work *De Praestigiis Daemonum et Incantationibus ac Veneficiis* (Basel, 1568), Weyer denounced witch hunters for extracting confessions under torture, pointing out that extreme hardships would force even the most innocent to confess themselves guilty. Weyer offered a voice of reason, claiming mental disease rather than demonic possession. Unfortunately his book went unheeded and heavily criticized.

For a summary of Weyer's comprehensive book, see H. C. Lea, *Materials Toward a History of Witchcraft.* (See also **demonology**)

Sources:

Lea, H. C. *Materials Toward a History of Witchcraft.* Edited by Arthur C. Howland. 3 vols. Philadelphia, University of Pennsylvania Press, 1939. Reprint, New York: T. Yoseloff, 1957.

Weyer, Johannes. *Witches, Devils and Doctors in the Renaissance: Johann Weyer, De Praestigiis.* Edited by George Mora. Binghamton, N.Y.: Medieval & Renaissance Texts & Studies, 1991.

Weza

Burmese sorcerers. (See also **MYANMAR**)

WFLK Fountain of the World

Hindu-based religious community centered in the San Fernando Valley of southern California. The WFLK Fountain of the World was founded by Francis H. Pencovic (1911–58). He grew up in Utah but became known in 1932 under his religious name, Krishna Venta. As Krishna Venta he claimed that he had been sent from heaven to work among the American Indians. He was believed to be the latest in a series of "saviours" who had come to assist humankind. The lineage included Adam, Enoch, Methuselah, Noah, Abraham, Moses, Elijah, Jesus, and more recently Abraham Lincoln and Joseph Smith, Jr., (the founder of the **Church of Jesus Christ of Latter-day Saints**).

Krishna Venta established his followers on land in Box Canyon in the San Fernando Valley. They lived communally, a practical step in their gaining a unity of mind and spirit, and attempted to put into practice the four cardinal virtues taught by Krishna Venta: Wisdom, Faith, Love, and Knowledge (WFLK), from which the group took its name. The members became well known in the area for their outstanding work in the periodic and dangerous fires that afflict the area.

The organization was traumatized in 1958 when Krishna Venta was assassinated by two former members who complained that he had debauched their spouses. They set off a dynamite explosion in the group's headquarters on December 10, 1958, killing themselves, Krishna Venta, and seven other members. Krishna Venta's wife, Mother Ruth Pencovic, took over leadership of the group and led the group through the 1970s. It was formally dissolved in the early 1980s.

Sources:

Mathison, Richard. *Faiths, Cults, and Sects of America.* Indianapolis, Ind.: Bobbs-Merrill, 1960.

Ormont, Roger. *Love Cults & Faith Healers.* New York: Ballantine Books, 1961.

Wheatley, Dennis (Yates) (1897–1977)

British author of many fictional works on occult themes, born on January 8, 1897, and described by a British newspaper writer as "the greatest adventure-writer of our time." Wheatley wrote stories about **black magic** and **witchcraft** during the 1930s.

Although Wheatley was essentially a popular writer with a prodigious output, many of his occult thrillers have retained their appeal over several decades and are constantly reprinted; some, such as *To the Devil—a Daughter* (1953), have been filmed, others translated into 27 different languages. A versatile individual, Wheatley traveled in 56 countries, became proprietor of a wine merchant business, was a member of Churchill's War Cabinet Secret Planning Committee, and invented (with J. G. Links) the Crime Dossier Murder series of fictional stories in the form of complete police files with clues and reports. Born January 8, 1897, in London, England, he was educated at Dulwich College (1911) and privately in Germany. Upon the death of his father in 1926 he became sole owner of a wine company. He served in the British Army in World War I from 1914 to 1919, becoming second lieutenant. After the war he became the director of various companies.

From 1940 to 1941, Wheatley toured England as a member of Sir John Anderson's panel of voluntary speakers on National Service. In 1945 he was a wing commander serving on Sir Winston Churchill's staff, and he worked for three years in offices of the War Cabinet. He was awarded the United States Bronze Star. He was a fellow of the Royal Society of Literature and the Royal Society of Arts.

Wheatley also edited the Dennis Wheatley Library of the Occult, a series of reprints of significant occult books by other writers. His nonfiction volume, *The Devil and All His Works* (1971), reproduced much of the popular fiction about witches and Satanists. He died November 11, 1977.

Wheatley, J(ames) M(elville) O(wen) (1924–)

Assistant professor of philosophy, active in the field of parapsychology. He was born February 29, 1924, at Guelph, Ontario, Canada. He studied at the University of New Brunswick (B.S., 1947; M.A., 1949) and the University of Toronto (Ph.D. philosophy, 1957). He joined the faculty of the University of Toronto and taught there for many years.

Wheatley has taken special interest in the philosophy of parapsychology, the question of **survival,** quantitative research in **extrasensory perception, psychokinesis,** and epistemological aspects of psi. He worked with **Karlis Osis** in an exploratory study among college students concerning clairvoyance scores in card reading. He was an associate member of the **Parapsychological Association.**

Sources:

Pleasants, Helene, ed. *Biographical Dictionary of Parapsychology.* New York: Helix Press, 1964.

Wheatley, J. M. O. "Implications for Philosophy." In *Philosophical Dimensions of Parapsychology.* Edited by H. L. Edge. Springfield, Ill.: Charles Thomas, 1976.

Whistling

Various superstitions are connected with whistling. It has long been considered unlucky for women to whistle. It was unlucky for sailors to whistle aboard ship, because it was thought that doing so might raise a wind. It was also considered unlucky for miners to whistle in a mine, since this might be followed by an explosion.

A more recent superstition is that whistling in a theater or its dressing rooms may cause a play to fail.

White, Rhea A(melia) (1931–)

Prominent American parapsychologist. Born May 6, 1931, in Utica, New York, she studied at Pennsylvania State University (B.A., 1953). After graduation she spent four years as a research fellow at the **Parapsychology Laboratory,** Duke University (1958), became a research assistant at the Foundation for Integral Research (1959), and worked as a research and editorial associate at the **American Society for Psychical Research** (1959–63).

She was a charter member of the **Parapsychological Association** and held the offices of secretary (1958, 1962), council member (1958, 1960–63), and president (1984). She was the director of information of the American Society for Psychical Research beginning in 1965. She published a series of bibliographical articles for the successive editions of *Advances in Parapsychological Research,* and was editor of the Parapsychological Association's *Research in Parapsychology* from 1981–1985. She also edited *Theta* for the Psychical Research Foundation from 1981–1986. Her background in library science led to the first of a series of bibliographical publications with her 1973 *Parapsychology: Sources of Information.*

In 1981 she founded the Parapsychology Sources of Information Center, an organization with bibliographical control over the vast and ever-growing body of parapsychological and related material. The Psi-Line Database System was the first computerized database of the literature on psychical research and parapsychology. The center publishes *Parapsychology Abstracts International,* providing brief summaries of periodical literature from English, Spanish, Dutch, Portuguese, Italian, German, French, Polish, Japanese, and Russian researchers. The center's other important publications include bibliographies on specific paranormal topics and reading lists for students, the general public, and specialists. In 1992 White published *Parapsychology: New Sources of Information* and in 1994, with Michael Murphy, she wrote *In the Zone: Transcendent Experience in Sports.*

White also has direct involvement in parapsychological research, and quite apart form her bibliographical work, she has published on a wide variety of topics. Address: EHE Network, 414 Rockledge Rd., New Bern, NC 28562. Website: http://www.ehe.org.

Sources:

Anderson, Margaret L., and Rhea A. White. "A Survey of Work on ESP and Teacher-Pupil Attitudes." *Journal of Parapsychology* 22, no. 4 (1958).

Berger, Arthur S., and Joyce Berger. *The Encyclopedia of Parapsychology and Psychical Research.* New York: Paragon House, 1991.

Murphy, Gardner, and Rhea White. *Challenge of Psychical Research: A Primer of Parapsychology.* New York: Harper & Row, 1961.

Murphy, Michael, and Rhea A. White. *The Psychic Side of Sports.* Reading, Mass.: Addison-Wesley, 1978.

Pleasants, Helene, ed. *Biographical Dictionary of Parapsychology.* New York: Helix Press, 1964.

White, Rhea. "Comparison of Old and New Methods of Response to Targets in ESP Experiments." *Journal* of the American Society for Psychical Research 58 (1964): 21–56.

———. "Depth Perspectives and Experimental Parapsychology." *International Journal of Parapsychology* 2, no. 2 (1960).

———. "ESP Score Level in Relation to Students' Attitudes Toward Teacher-Agents Acting Simultaneously." *Journal of Parapsychology* 22, no. 1 (1958).

———. "The Relationship Between Changes in Student Attitude and ESP Scoring." *Journal of Parapsychology* 22, no. 3 1958.

White, Rhea, and Laura A. Dale. *Parapsychology: Sources of Information.* Metuchen, N.J.: Scarecrow Press, 1973.

White, Stewart Edward (1873–1946)

Author who published a number of books of "channeled" material. Born March 12, 1873, in Grand Rapids, Michigan, he studied at the University of Michigan (Ph.D., 1895; M.A., 1903). In 1904 he married Elizabeth (Betty) Grant, and they settled in California where he became well known as an author of many books, articles, and short stories dealing with his experiences around the state in mining and lumber camps, and on exploration trips.

In 1922 he and Betty met a couple known in the literature as Joan and Darby. Several years earlier the couple had been playing with a Ouija board and made contact with a spirit entity, "Stephen," who became the source for a book they published in 1920 as *Our Unseen Guest.* Joan had become a full **trance** medium. Betty eventually followed a similar course and also became a **medium** in contact with a group of entities called simply "the Invisibles." Betty channeled numerous sessions with them. In 1937, after many years of quietly working with a very small group, Stewart told the story of Betty's development and repeated the basic teachings of "the Invisibles" in what has become a classic work in the field, *The Betty Book.* White believed that these messages embodied a valuable philosophy and religious interpretation for daily life. Enough readers agreed and a second "Betty" book was issued in 1939 as *Across the Unknown.*

Betty died in 1939, and in the months after her death, White received communication he believed to be from her through Joan. These were gathered into a book, *The Unobstructed Universe* (1940), which proved the most popular volume in the series and remains in print.

The continued response, possibly accelerated by the war, led to a number of further books. *The Road I Know* (1942) was an anthology of further selections from the material Betty had channeled. *Anchors to Windward* (1943) was a philosophical treatment of the Betty material. *The Stars Are Still There* (1946) grew out of specific questions sent to White during the war. *With Folded Wings* (1947), the last in the Betty book series, was published posthumously.

White died September 18, 1946, at Hillsborough, California. After his death, two manuscripts remained, both reflective of White's own development as a medium. One, *The Job of Living,* was published in 1948; the other, *The Gaelic Manuscripts,* was never published, though it circulated among White enthusiasts in mimeographed form.

Sources:

Joan and Darby. *Our Unseen Guest.* New York: Harper & Brothers, 1920.

Melton, J. Gordon. *The Betty Book Literature of Stewart Edward White.* Evanston, Ill.: The author, 1971.

White, Stewart Edward. *Across the Unknown.* N.p., n.d.

———. *Anchors to Windward.* N.p., 1943.

———. *The Betty Book.* N.p., 1939.

———. *The Road I Know.* N.p., 1942.

———. *The Stars Are Still There.* N.p., 1946.

———. *The Unobstructed Universe.* N.p., 1940.

———. *With Folded Wings.* N.p., 1947.

White Brotherhood

The White Brotherhood, a Bulgarian occult order with roots in Rosicrucianism, was founded in 1900 by **Peter Konstantinov Deunov** (1864–1944), known more popularly by his spiritual name, Beinsa Douno. Douno was raised in the Bulgarian Orthodox Church and at one time thought of being a monk. However, he became a school teacher and then traveled to the United States, where he received a seminary degree in religion and one in medicine. Shortly after his return to Bulgaria, he began a period of seclusion during which time, in 1897, he had an initiatory experience that he described as the Spirit of God descending upon him. He emerged from the experience as The Master and began to take students. He organized the White Brotherhood with his first three students, whom he called to the first of what would become an annual meeting in August of 1900. He also began to write books out of his own mystical experiences.

Douno traveled widely through Bulgaria, and the organization grew through the first decade of the new century. By 1914 Douno was ready to relocate his base of activity to Sofia, the capital. However, his presence in the country's center also called the attention of the government and the closely aligned Orthodox church to his work. Various efforts were made to suppress the movement. Members were arrested and meetings were broken up. In 1922 Douno was excommunicated from the Bulgarian church. However, the movement persisted, and in 1926 a new headquarters was opened in Izfreva, not far from Sofia. A complex of buildings, including a publishing center, soon sprang up.

Among the popular elements of his teachings, paneurhythmy, a set of exercises set to music, was introduced in 1934. Two years later, the first group of the White Brotherhood was brought together in Paris, and other followers emerged in Latvia and Estonia. However, the positive upward course of the movement was brought to a halt by World War II (1939–45) and the changes in the political situation following the war. Douno died only a few weeks after the Soviet Army took control of Bulgaria in 1944.

After the war, the brotherhood reorganized under a council and moved to pick up the work as before. The first major sign of trouble came in 1948 when the headquarters property was nationalized. As a realization of the new hostile environment grew, steps were taken to preserve Douno's writings. A series of suppressive acts culminated in the leveling of the headquarters community in 1970. However, by this time work had been developed in Western Europe and the United States, and manuscripts had found their way throughout Europe and were being translated. In the meantime, Michael Aivanhov, who in 1937 had been sent to take charge of the work in Paris, founded his own movement continuing Douno's teachings in a separate organization, now known as the **Universal Great Brotherhood.**

Douno saw his work as continuing the true spirituality of Christianity and a modern transmission of the eternal religion of Christ. He thought of the White Brotherhood as continuing the Church of St. John as opposed to the official church, the Church of St. Peter.

The White Brotherhood survived as a small movement in the West, and was able to revive in Bulgaria as soon as the political changes at the beginning of the 1990s brought a new level of religious freedom to the country. It was officially recognized in November of 1990. A periodical was reinstituted in 1991. The rebuilding of a White Brotherhood community and an educational center in Sofia began in 1995.

Today the brotherhood exists as a vital international organization with international headquarters in Sofia and North American headquarters at Telesma-Evida Publishing, P.O. Box 174, Ahuntsic, Montreal, PQ Canada H2L 3N7. It has an expansive Internet presence at http://www.vega.bg/~beinsa_douno/.

Sources:

Douno, Beinsa. *The Master Speaks: The Word of the Great White Brotherhood.* Los Angeles: Sunrise Press & Books, 1970.

———. *Reminiscences: Talks with the Master.* Los Angeles: Sunrise Press, 1968.

———. *The Teachings of Beinsa Douno: Pearls of Love.* Glasgow: Beyond the Rising Sun Publications, n.d.

White Dove's Message

White Dove's Message is a quarterly magazine that features the channeled messages of Zavena White Dove, the name adopted by a medium now residing in Wichita, Kansas. The name White Dove was given to her as a child by angelic beings she came to know as her playmates. The little angels told her they were from Gabriel, her guardian angel. They also prophesied that she would one day become a messenger of the Spirit and would experience three confirmatory events that would designate the time that she was to start using her "rightful" name. Two of these events occurred in the late 1980s when she received messages from two Native American guides, one an Apache and one a Cheyenne. The third occurred two years later in a vision of the Indian hierarchy that confirmed the time had come. Since that time she has been known as White Dove. An associated near-death experience confirmed that she had a special mission to fulfill.

In 1997, she was given the additional name Zavena during an initiation ceremony where it was revealed that she was now a Cosmic Inter-galactic Server. She began using her full name on September 21, 1997. She brings messages from a spectrum of beings including her Native American guide, Silver Eagle, a light being, Firefly, and ascended master **Kuthumi.** She is also a Reiki Master and teaches **Reiki** healing.

White Dove's Message was launched in 1993 as a monthly, but in 1999 became a quarterly publication. At about the same time, White Dove began her Internet presence and posts a daily message for interested readers. The Internet site is at http://www.whitedovemsg.com/. Much of the emphasis in White Dove's communication concerns the handling of the ongoing and even accelerated changes in the lives of people involved in the post-New Age spiritual community.

White Dove's Message may be contacted at P.O. Box 781792, Wichita, KS 67278-1792.

Sources:

White Dove's Message. http://www.whitedovemsg.com/. June 10, 2000.

White Eagle Lodge

British Spiritualist organization founded in 1934, arising from the mediumship of **Grace Cooke** (d. 1979), assisted by her husband Ivan Cooke, and presenting the teachings channeled from her Native American spirit guide, "White Eagle." These teachings present "a way of life which is gentle and in harmony with the laws of life," involving the belief that "God, the eternal spirit, is both Father and Mother, and that the Son—the Cosmic Christ—is also the light which shines in every human heart."

Cooke worked for many years as a medium primarily with the Stead Borderland Library in London. Then in 1930 she was contacted by a member of the Polaire Brotherhood in France, who informed her that **Arthur Conan Doyle,** an author and Spiritualist, had chosen her as the medium through which he wished to speak from the other side. She was also given a six-pointed star as a symbol for new work.

The lodge teaches that there is a unity that runs through all forms of life, visible and invisible, including the fairy and angelic kingdoms. White Eagle spoke of five Cosmic Laws: (1) **reincarnation**—the soul may return to earth many times until it has mastered all the lessons it must learn; (2) cause and effect—the belief in the law of **karma** (i.e., "as you sow, so you will reap"); (3) opportunity—every experience in life is an opportunity for an individual to become more Godlike and everyone is placed in exactly the right conditions needed "to learn lessons and give service"; (4) correspondence—the belief that "as above, so below." The microcosm is part of the macrocosm. We are cells of the cosmos, just as our bodies, in turn, are made up of cells, with the same laws applying at all levels; (5) equilibrium and balance—the law connected to karma, described as "the law of compensation." It claims that no action can continue indefinitely, but will travel just as far before a reaction pulls things back to normal. Human joy and sorrow follow this law (i.e., extremes of emotion will eventually cause a reaction that pulls the soul back to normal).

The physical body is considered the outer garment of the soul, which includes subtler bodies of emotions and thoughts, and the spirit that is the heart of the soul and is known as the "Christ Spirit," or real self. Spiritual healing involves concentrating divine power on the soul of the sick person to dissolve the disharmony causing the sickness. In "absent healing," six healers sit as a group, sending out "rays of spiritual light." In lone healing, 36 healers combine meditative healing from their own homes. In contact healing, there is a laying on of hands at special lodge services. The lodge also propagates "spiritual communion," a pure form of meditation.

Membership in the lodge is in three stages—ordinary membership, progressing to "outer brother," and eventually to "inner brother." The lodge publishes a bimonthly magazine, *Stella Polaris,* which includes White Eagle teachings, answers to readers' questions and general articles on healing and meditation.

The lodge is headquartered at New Lands, Rake, Liss, Hampshire, GU33 7HY, England, and has a major center at 9 St. Mary Abbot's Pl., Kensington, London, W8 6L5, England. There are also branches throughout the British Isles. The movement spread to the United States in the 1950s and is headquartered at St. John's Retreat Center, P.O. Box 930, Montgomery, TX 77356. Website: http://www.saintjohns.org/.

Sources:

Cooke, Grace, ed. *The Illuminated Ones.* Liss, England: White Eagle Publishing Trust, 1966.

Cooke, Ivan, ed. *The Return of Arthur Conan Doyle.* Liss, England: White Eagle Publishing Trust, 1956.

Lind, Ingrid. *The White Eagle Inheritance.* Wellingborough, England: Turnstone Press, 1984.

The Story of the White Eagle Lodge. Liss, England: White Eagle Publishing Trust, 1986.

Whiteman, J(oseph) H(ilary) M(ichael) (1906– ?)

Mathematician and writer on religion, science, and parapsychology. He was born on November 2, 1906. He attended Highgate School, London; Gonville and Caius College, Cambridge; and the University of Cape Town (Ph.D. and M.Mus.). He joined the faculty of mathematics at the University of Cape Town and remained there for many years (1939–71). He was named emeritus professor of mathematics in 1972. Also an accomplished musician, he published some 100 articles on music in the journal *South African Music Teacher,* and he also contributed to various symposia on music.

Whiteman experienced **out-of-the-body travel,** prompting his interest in parapsychology. He has described these experiences in several of his books and articles. From a scientific perspective, he has also argued that the new post-quantum physics will provide a new worldview that has a place for parapsychology and psychic phenomena. He has contributed numerous papers on parapsychology and related subjects to various publications. He received the Valkhoff Medallion from the South African Society for Psychical Research for his contributions to the field.

Sources:

Berger, Arthur S., and Joyce Berger. *The Encyclopedia of Parapsychology and Psychical Research.* New York: Paragon House, 1991.

Pleasants, Helene, ed. *Biographical Dictionary of Parapsychology.* New York: Helix Press, 1964.

Whiteman, J. H. M. *The Mystical Life: An Outline of Its Nature and Teachings from the Evidence of Direct Experience.* London: Faber & Faber, 1961.

———. "The Mystical Way, and Habitualizing of Mystical States." In *Handbook of States of Consciousness.* Edited by B. Wolman and Montague Ullman. New York: Van Nostrand Reinhold, 1986.

———. "Parapsychology and Physics." In *Handbook of Parapsychology.* Edited by B. Wolman. New York: Van Nostrand Reinhold, 1977.

———. "The Process of Separation and Return in Experiences Fully 'Out of the Body.' " *Proceedings* of the Society for Psychical Research 50 (1956).

Whiteman, Michael. *Philosophy of Space and Time and the Inner Constitution of Nature: A Phenomenological Study.* London: Allen & Unwin; New York: Humanities Pub., 1967.

White Order of Thule

The White Order of Thule describes itself as a loose alignment of Aryan minds, hearts, and souls working together for the Cause, that is, the revitalization of the culture-soul of the European people. It is modeled upon the idea of an ancient mystery school that facilitates its members' acquisition of a higher state of consciousness, though it is not a mystery school itself, merely an esoteric brotherhood. The order emerged in the late 1990s when its leader, Nathan Pett, posted information about the group on the Internet.

Thule is the mythical site of the origin of the Aryan race. It is believed that the Aryans have become disunited and need to be called to a new unity to face the challenges of the future. To accomplish this task, the order has acquired the knowledge of the mystery schools of the Hermetic alchemical traditions that it is now offering to the Aryan people. The practical work of the order includes **meditation,** the use of imagery, and rituals designed to initiate changes in the inner self leading to an expansion of consciousness. Higher consciousness moves the individual past self-consciousness to the level of intuition where direct knowledge of the answers to life's questions is perceived and a vision of Truth seen. The teachings do not replace activism in the cause of racial advancement but are a means of empowering the individual engaged in active work.

The order teaches the Hermetic tradition in a planned course of study that begins with Hermetic philosophy and Jungian psychology, especially the concept of archetypes. Specific archetypes will become the focus of attention and the subject of pathworking, the foundation of the order's esoteric practices. The basic curriculum also includes instruction in Pagan mythology, genealogy, and **astrology.** The order teaches that the deities of Norse Paganism represent in essence the creative/destructive forces of the cosmos. Students are also advised to supplement their study with additional readings, including the writings of Adolf Hitler, Freidrich Nietsche, Julius Evola, and Oswald Spengler.

The order may be contacted at Box 1473, Deer Park, WA 99006. It publishes a quarterly periodical, *Crossing the Abyss.* Its Web presence may be accessed at http://www.thulean.org/. The order came to public attention in August of 1999 when it held a ceremony on Whitbey Island, Washington, near the site where Robert Mathews had been killed in a shootout with the FBI. Mathews led The Order, a controversial racialist group in the early 1980s tied to a series of violent crimes.

Sources:

White Order of Thule. http://www.thulean.org/. May 5, 2000.

White Sands Incident

Title of a book by Daniel Fry published in 1954, claiming that the author saw a **flying saucer** land at the White Sands Proving Ground in New Mexico and took a trip in it. Fry has importance in UFO history for being among the first to claim to have traveled in a UFO.

White Temple Church

The White Temple Church is the ecclesiastical organization associated with the **Brotherhood of the White Temple,** an occult school headquartered in Sedalia, Colorado. The church emphasizes the "Original Gnostic Teachings of Jesus," the occult beliefs that members of the brotherhood believe Jesus passed on to humankind. The White Temple Church may be contacted c/o the Brotherhood of the White Temple, PO Box 966, Castle Rock, CO 80104.

Whittlesey, John R. B. (1927–)

Data processing analyst who experimented in areas of parapsychology. He was born on July 21, 1927, in Los Angeles, California. He studied at the California Institute of Technology (B.S. physics, 1948; M.S. astronomy, 1950), the University of North Carolina (1951–54), and the Graduate School of Religion, University of Southern California (1960–61). He served with the United States Army (1954–56) and then joined the faculty at the University of California at Los Angeles as a data analyst in 1957.

Whittlesey has taken a special interest in computer statistics and probability as related to **ESP** and ESP in its relationship to religion and mystical experience. He designed an experiment in the use of the chemical LSD and analyzed data in its relation to extrasensory perception, working with several psychiatrists. He also designed and built an electronic device for experimental testing of precognition, using non-verbal responses from subjects influenced by drugs. He is coauthor of various papers on LSD experiences read before the American Psychiatric Association and the California State Psychological Association.

Sources:

Pleasants, Helene, ed. *Biographical Dictionary of Parapsychology.* New York: Helix Press, 1964.

Whittlesey, John R. B. "Further Comments on Causality." *Journal of Parapsychology* 17 (September 1953).

———. "Some Comments Apropos of Pooling." *Journal of Parapsychology* 23 (June 1959).

———. "Some Curious ESP Results in Terms of Variance." *Journal of Parapsychology* 24 (September 1960).

Whole Again Research Guide

Comprehensive annual directory and resource guide (superseding and incorporating **Guide to Psi Periodicals**), several editions of which appeared in the 1980s. First published 1982, it was edited by Tim Ryan and Rae Jappinen and had nearly 30 contributors, including Elizabeth M. Werner (of *Guide to Psi Periodicals* and other publications) and **Elisabeth Kübler-Ross.** The *Guide* covered alternative technologies and therapies, **New Age** teachings, psychic studies, spiritual growth, **yoga, UFOs,** nature religions, environmental issues, minority rights, as well as media—magazines, newspapers, journals, newsletters, sourcebooks, directories, and bibliographies. It was issued by SourceNet in Santa Barbara, California.

Whole Life

New Age networking journal serving New York City and the northeast with news of current events in holistic health, macrobiotics, ecology, spiritual growth, **yoga, gurus,** and **mysticism.** It features a national calendar of events and personalities, as well as directory information. Last known address: Whole Life Enterprises, P.O. Box 2058, New York, NY 10159. *Whole Life* also created *Whole Life Times,* a similar networking journal serving Southern California. *Whole Life Times* is currently an independent venture that sponsors annual New Life expositions in several locations on the West Coast from its headquarters at P.O. Box 1187, Malibu, CA 90265. Website: http://www.wholelifetimes.com/.

Whole Life Expo (Fair)

Annual **New Age** exposition featuring leading spokespeople and organizations in the fields of health, fitness, education, social action, science, the environment, **yoga,** spiritual growth, and related topics. Address: Whole Life Expo, National Headquarters, 803 Fourth St., Suite 7, San Rafael, CA 94901. Information on upcoming expositions can be found at http://www.wholelifeexpos.com/.

Whole Life Times

Whole Life Times is one of the more prominent networking journals to emerge in the 1980s to serve the growing **New Age** Movement. The possibilities of networking as a means of organizing without the burdensome hierarchies of pyramidal structures was placed before New Agers in 1982 by Jessica Lipnack and Jeffrey Stamps in their best-selling book, *Networking: The First Report and Directory.* Periodicals supplying addresses, phone numbers, and announcements of coming events and gatherings initially appeared in the major metropolitan complexes. In the Northeast, *Whole Life* served New York and Boston, but soon developed a section including Los Angeles. *Whole Life* evolved into two editions, one based in New York and one in Los Angeles. By the end of the decade, these had become independent publications with the Los Angeles edition taking the name *Whole Life Times.*

Whole Life Times follows a model pioneered by **Common Ground,** the original networking periodical serving the San Francisco Bay area. It is an oversized magazine built around a set of advertisements organized topically into a directory. Groups and events are arranged under such topics as astrology, beauty and personal care, healing and health centers, psychology and counseling, schools and instruction, and spirit and transformation. Each issue also includes an additional supply of display ads, the advertisements paying the cost of the magazine, which is distributed through health food and metaphysical bookstores without charge.

Also included in each issue is a set of feature articles about issues and personalities of interest to the continuing post-New Age community. These range from issues of health and personal spiritual and psychic development to profiles of channelers and psychic counselors. Additional content is supplied with news coverage and columns.

Whole Life Times is the largest circulating of the regional networking periodicals in the United States. It also organizes the **Whole Life Expo** held annually in the Los Angeles area. Publishing offices of the *Whole Life Times* may be contacted at P.O. Box 1187, Malibu, CA 90265. Its website is at http://www.wholelifetimes.com/.

Sources:

Whole Life Times. http://www.wholelifetimes.com/. February 28, 2000.

Whole Life Times. Malibu, Calif., n.d.

The Whole Person

The Whole Person—Calendar of Events in Southern California is one of several magazines dedicated to networking within the metaphysical/psychic/spiritual community in the greater Los Angeles area. *The Whole Person* is devoted entirely to announcements of upcoming events and has no feature articles, news columns, or book reviews. Over half of the content of any issue is given over to display advertisements. It is designed entirely to serve individuals looking for activities to attend of a spiritual and metaphysical nature, from yoga classes to lectures by visiting teachers.

The Whole Person is published monthly and built around two extensive lists of want-ad-type announcements of events. The initial list provides basic information on events (including location, registration, and sponsor) occurring on each day of the month (with three to four pages devoted to each day). A second list provides information on ongoing events, primarily weekly gatherings held by metaphysical or Eastern spirituality groups on a continuing basis. These announcements are solicited monthly and published without cost to the person or group submitting them.

Readers may subscribe to *The Whole Person* for home delivery, but the overwhelming percentage of copies is distributed monthly to stores in the areas covered by the announcements and given away free. The many advertisements pay the cost of the publication. From a small newsletter in the 1980s, *The Whole Person* has grown into a large magazine of more than 100 pages per issue. It may be ordered from *The Whole Person,* P.O. Box 2398, Santa Barbara, CA 93102. It is assembled by Leslie Snyder and a small staff.

Sources:

The Whole Person. Santa Barbara, Calif., n.d.

Whymant, (A.) Neville (John) (1894– ?)

Author and editor who investigated the phenomena of the medium **George Valiantine.** He was born on September 4, 1894, at Rothwell, England, and studied at Oxford University (Ph.D.). After World War I he served as a professor of Oriental literature and philosophy at the Universities of Tokyo and Peking. He became an editor and journalist in 1926 and eventually became editor of *The Indian Nation* in the 1930s. He was advisor to the embassy of the Republic of China in London from 1947 to 1950.

In addition to various books on China and the Chinese, he published *Psychical Research in China* (1925), dealing with sand painting and "ghost photographs," and *Psychic Adventures in New York* (1928). Whymant was present at séances with the medium George Valiantine, who produced messages in ancient Chinese languages. A report of the phenomena was published in the *Journal* of the American Society for Psychical Research (April 1928).

Sources:

Pleasants, Helene, ed. *Biographical Dictionary of Parapsychology.* New York: Helix Press, 1964.

WICA See Witchcraft International Craft Association

WICA Newsletter

Early newsletter serving the Wiccan and neo-pagan community as it emerged as a national network in the 1970s. Its editor, Leo Martello, a former Spiritualist medium, wrote a number of books detailing the practice of contemporary witches. Martello heads Witchcraft International Craft Associates in New York City.

Wicca

The first world religion to originate in England, Wicca represents a new religious expression inspired by pre-Christian ethnic and tribal religions. The word *wiccan* as a plural for witch was used in Old English; its singular forms were feminine *wicce* with the masculine form as *wicca.* Pronounced with hard C's instead of the former "witch-a," the term Wicca was adopted by Gerald Gardner and other English Witches in the 1940s to distinguish their life-affirming and fertility-based Pagan religion from **Satanism** or individual sorcery.

Although Wiccan writers are prolific, Wicca has no sacred texts as such to guide belief and practice. Most Wiccans view the Divine as dual (male/female) or plural, accept the idea of reincarnation, and see the natural world as a manifestation of divine force rather than as something created by a transcendent god. Attunement of the self to natural cycles through seasonal rituals is Wicca's central public religious practice.

Wicca as a religion has no central authority nor organization, although various umbrella groups such as the **Covenant of the Goddess** in North America and the Pagan Federation in the United Kingdom include many individuals and groups. The primary organization remains the coven, ideally numbering thirteen persons but in actuality often comprised of fewer. Because of Wicca's rapid growth, however, some adherents now seek more formal organizational plans and credentialing of leaders (priests and priestesses), a trend resisted by those Witches who hold individual and small-group practice and experience to be primary. Wiccans often identify with a particular "tradition"—a school of teaching or an initiatory lineage—but the boundaries between traditions are loosely drawn, and new traditions are constantly being created.

Estimates of the number of Wiccans in North America in 2000 ranged from 300,000 to the low millions. Sociological studies of Wicca show its followers as tending to be younger and better-educated than the population overall.

Wiccan Church of Canada

The Wiccan Church of Canada is one of the pioneering organizations of the modern **Witchcraft** movement in Canada. It was founded by two Wiccan priests, Tamara James and Richard F. James, who had their initial contacts with Neo-Paganism while in California in 1977. They moved to Toronto two years later, where they founded the Wiccan Church of Canada and opened an occult store that catered to Pagans and witches. By 1983 the community had grown to the point that an initial regional Pagan festival could be held. In 1984 the first of several covens formed within the church.

It is the belief of the church that many of the important ultimate questions of life are unanswerable. Humans cannot know about the origin of the universe, the reality of life after death, or the mechanics of the miraculous. Thus, the religious answers that are given to such questions carry a large element of subjectivity. They must be held with some reserve and must not become the basis of intolerance and judgmental attitudes toward those who believe differently. Morality also falls into the same category. It is a human creation. However, the church believes that society has a right to organize and pass laws that protect individuals from violence and the land from outside forces.

Its ignorance asserted, the church believes that the universe is self-aware, and that elements of that awareness have been differentiated as the deities. The number of deities is unknown. Awareness is genderless and individual deities may be either male or female. There is also an ordering among the deities and it is proper to speak of the greater and lesser deities. The Wiccan church follows primarily a European format with worship centered upon the eight annual festivals common to Pagans and also the small coven gatherings at the new and full moon (**esbats**). The church also has its own rituals to designate important moments in the life cycle, from the naming ceremony for the new born (wiccaning) to the passing from this incarnation (funeral). It performs both weddings and handpartings (for couples that are separating).

All of the priests and priestesses of the church constitute a ruling Priesthood Council. Their job is to train members and any new priests. The church is headquartered at 109 Vaughn Rd., Toronto, ON, Canada M6C 2L9. Most of its several hundred members reside in Ontario. Its webpage may be found at http://www.wcc.on.ca/.

Sources:

Hopman, Ellen Evert, and Lawrence Bond. *People of the Earth: The New Pagans Speak Out.* Rochester, Vt.: Destiny Books, 1996.

James, Richard. *The WIC-CAN Handbook.* Toronto: Wiccan Church of Canada, 1987.

Rabinovotch, Shelley Tsivia. "The Institutionalization of the Wicca in Ontario via the Wiccan Church of Canada." Unpublished paper in the American Religion Collection, Davidson Library, University of California—Santa Barbara, 1991.

Wickland, Carl August (1861–1945)

Physician, psychiatrist, and Spiritualist who spent more than three decades researching and experimenting with the application of Spiritualist techniques to assist those suffering from mental illnesses. Wickland was born on February 14, 1861, in Leiden, Sweden. He qualified as a physician at Dunham Medical College, Chicago, Illinois, later becoming a medical advisor for the National Psychological Institute, Los Angeles.

He claimed that discarnate spirits caused some phases of mental illness in the living, and his book *Thirty Years Among the Dead* (1924) reports his experiences. Using the services of his wife as a medium, he operated what amounted to a **rescue circle** dealing with what Spiritualists describe as earth-bound entities who attach themselves to unsuspecting individuals. Their work in diagnosing and treating mental patients believed to be possessed by spirit entities had much in common with that of **Titus Bull.** Mrs. Wickland died in March 1937; Carl Wickland died November 13, 1945.

Widdershins

Widdershins, a Pagan periodical that serves the northwest Pagan and Wiccan community, is a tabloid newspaper distributed without cost in the states of Washington and Oregon. It is unique, as most Pagan publications have attempted to transform from informal newsletters into newsstand magazines. In contrast, *Widdershins* has adopted a popular format that has proved successful in the **New Age** community.

Each issue of *Widdershins* includes several longer articles of interest to Neo-Pagans, with special attention to themes that are common to all of the variety within the larger world of contemporary Paganism and **Witchcraft.** The publication also attempts to introduce non-Pagan readers with the essentials of Pagan spirituality and practice, while emphasizing those concerns of common interest with the larger New Age community such as ecology, attention to the changing seasons, and feminism.

Neo-Pagans, still a miniscule minority largely invisible within the larger culture, also have a need for communication among its far-flung groups, the covens and groves, most of whom meet in private homes.

Widdershins carries notices of pubic Pagan events and of individuals and groups that are open to contact. Advertising carries notices of Pagan business, especially stores that carry Pagan and Wiccan books and supplies (candles, incense, and ritual implements).

Widdershins is published eight times annually, its appearance following the eight major Pagan festivals that are spread evenly throughout the year. It is published by Emerald City/Silver Moon Productions, 12345 Lake City Way NE, Ste. 268, Seattle, WA 98125. While distributed free throughout the Seattle and Portland metropolitan regions, it is also available by subscription for delivery to individual addresses. It maintains a Web presence at http://www.widdershins.org/. As many Pagans still do not feel comfortable with identifying themselves openly, most of the editors and writers for *Widdershins* are listed by their first names only.

Sources:

Widdershins. Seattle, Wash., n.d.

Widdershins. http://www.widdershins.org/. May 1, 2000.

Wiesinger, Alois (1885–1955)

Abbot of the Cistercian Order who was active in the field of parapsychology. He was born on June 3, 1885, at Magdalenaberg, Upper Austria. Ordained in 1909, he received his doctorate in theology in 1912 at the University of Innsbruck. He taught philosophy for five years (1912–17) and then became abbot of the Cistercian Monastery, Schlierbach, when World War I was beginning. During his lengthy career as abbot, he took a great interest in such parapsychological phenomena as **poltergeists** and **materialization.**

In addition to his writings on Christianity, he was editor-publisher of the journal *Glaube und Erkenntnis* (Journal for Christian Parapsychology) and author of *Okkulte Phanomene im Lichte der Theologie* (Occult Phenomena from the Theological Point of View, 1948). He died January 3, 1955, at Schlierbach, Upper Austria. The German periodical *Die Vergorgene Welt* published a tribute to his lasting contributions as a parapsychologist.

Sources:

Pleasants, Helene, ed. *Biographical Dictionary of Parapsychology.* New York: Helix Press, 1964.

Wiesinger, Alois. "Wie Stellt Sich der Katholik zu den okkulten Erscheinungen?" (The attitude of the Catholic toward occult phenomena). *Neue Wissenschaft* (1953).

Wilber, Ken

Psychologist and writer on mysticism and transpersonal consciousness. He was one of the pioneers of transpersonal psychology, and his early volume, *The Spectrum of Consciousness* (1977), is considered one of its classic statements. For several years, he was editor-in-chief of the journal **ReVision,** prior to its acquisition by Heldref Publications.

Wilber has taken a special interest in the study of new religious movements in the light of transpersonal psychology, arguing for a non-reductionistic approach that is rooted in a transcendental structuralism and takes into account the various stages of human evolution, which culminates in God-realization. Wilber is a Buddhist but hailed the mystic **Da Free John** as a **New Age** avatar. In the 1980s he became the general editor of the New Science Library, published by Random House.

Sources:

Anthony, Dick, Bruce Ecker, and Ken Wilber. *Spiritual Choices: The Problem of Recognizing Authentic Paths to Inner Transformation.* New York: Paragon House Publishers, 1987.

Wilber, Ken. *Eye to Eye: The Quest for the New Paradigm.* Garden City, N.Y.: Anchor/Doubleday, 1983.

———. *No Boundary: Eastern and Western Approaches to Personal Growth.* Los Angeles: Center Publications, 1979.

———. *A Sociable God: A Brief Introduction to a Transcendental Sociology.* New York: McGraw-Hill, 1982.

———. *Up From Eden: A Transpersonal View of Human Evolution.* Garden City, N. Y.: Anchor Press/Doubleday, 1981.

Wilber, Ken, Jack Engler, and Daniel P. Brown. *Transformation of Consciousness: Conventional and Contemplative Perspectives on Development.* Boston: New Science Library, 1986.

Wild-Women

In German folklore the *Seligen Fräulein* were a species of nature spirits. An early account is provided by Thomas Keightley in his book *The Fairy Mythology* (1850):

"The Wilde Frauen or Wild-women of Germany bear a very strong resemblance to the Elle-maids of Scandinavia. Like them they are beautiful, have fine flowing hair, live within hills, and only appear singly or in the society of each other. They partake of the piety of character we find among the German Dwarfs.

"The celebrated Wunderberg, or Underberg, on the great moor near Salzburg, is the chief haunt of the Wild-women. The Wunderberg is said to be quite hollow, and supplied with stately palaces, churches, monasteries, gardens, and springs of gold and silver. Its inhabitants, besides the Wild-women, are little men, who have charge of the treasures it contains, and who at midnight report to Salzburg to perform their devotions in the cathedral; giants, who used to come to the Church of Grödich and exhort the people to lead a godly and pious life; and the great emperor Charles V., with golden crown and sceptre, attended by knights and lords."

Keightley continues:

"The inhabitants of the village of Grödich and the peasantry of the neighbourhood assert that frequently, about the year 1753, the Wild-women used to come out of the Wunderberg to the boys and girls that were keeping the cattle near the hole within Glanegg, and give them bread to eat.

"The Wild-women used frequently to come to where the people were reaping. They came down eagerly in the morning, and in the evening, when the people left off work, they went back into the Wunderburg without partaking of the supper.

"It once happened near this hill, that a little boy was sitting on a horse which his father had tethered on the headland of the field. Then came the Wild-women out of the hill and wanted to take away the boy by force. But the father, who was well acquainted with the secrets of this hill, and what used to occur there, without any dread hasted up to the women and took the boy from them, with these words: 'What makes you presume to come so often out of the hill, and now to take away my child with you? What do you want to do with him?' The Wild-women answered: 'He will be better with us, and have better care taken of him than at home. We shall be very fond of the boy, and he will meet with no injury.' But the father would not let the boy out of his hands, and the Wild-women went away weeping bitterly.

"One time the Wild-women came out of the Wunderberg, near the place called the Kugelmill, which is prettily situated on the side of this hill, and took away a boy who was keeping cattle. This boy, whom every one knew, was seen about a year after by some wood-cutters, in a green dress, and sitting on a block of this hill. Next day they took his parents with them, intending to search the hill for him, but they all went about it to no purpose, for the boy never appeared any more." (See also **Fairies**)

Sources:

Arrowsmith, Nancy, and George Moorse. *A Field Guide to the Little People.* New York: Wallaby Books, 1977.

Will

Will, a basic category in philosophy, emerged in the nineteenth century as a concern of psychical research, as attempts were made to prove that human will was a dynamic energy. The earliest experimental apparatus was constructed by M. E. Savary d'Odiardy. An investigation of the instrument by the **Society for Psychical Research,** London (*Proceedings,* vol. 8, p. 249) dismissed his claims.

Another instrument was designed by Sydney Alrutz, of the University of Uppsala, Sweden. He called it a **volometer** or "will board." It comprised a small board resting on knife-edged pegs. The longer and heavier end was supported by means of a string attached to a letter scale and held the board in horizontal position. In this position the scale registered a pressure of five ounces. If the short end was depressed, the long end rose and the letter scale showed a decrease of weight.

The task put before the subjects of Alrutz's experiment was to fix their attention on the long end and will its depression. In a number of cases, 40–100 grams of pressure was thus obtained. Among those who attempted the experiment were many members of the Sixth Psychological Congress at Geneva in August, 1909.

Theodore Flournoy wrote after his own test:

"I was able to prove conclusively, after three trials, and under conditions precluding all possibility of fraud or illusion, that the will of these ladies, concentrated upon a certain material object, with a desire to produce a movement in it, ended by producing this movement as if by means of a fluid or an invisible force obeying their mental command."

While these results were impressive, the experiment was flawed by severe methodological vagueness. The experiment demonstrated an unusual effect, but said nothing about the agency involved in causing the change. It could just as easily been an experiment to demonstrate "mesmeric fluid" or ectoplasmic emanations. The intrusion of concepts of "will" have been discarded by parapsychologists in the twentieth century.

Willett, Mrs.

Pseudonym of medium **Winifred Margaret Serocold Coombe-Tennant.**

William Rufus (William II of England) (ca. 1056–1100)

Son of William the Conqueror, and tyrant of England in the eleventh century. Much disliked, particularly by priests and monks, whom he reduced to extreme poverty, he became the subject of a devilish legend after his welcomed death.

One day when he was out hunting in the year 1100 (the 44th year of his life, the 13th of his reign), he was assassinated by an arrow launched by an unknown assailant. According to the legend, while Rufus was drawing his last breath, the Comte de Comonailles, who had been separated from the hunt, saw a shaggy black goat carrying off a mangled human form, pierced by an arrow. The Comte ordered the goat to halt, asked who he was, and tried to find out where he was going. The goat responded that he was the Devil and was carrying William Rufus off to be judged, condemned for his tyranny, and forced to accompany him (the Devil) to his abode.

Williams, Bessie

Late nineteenth-century British clairvoyant, **trance** and healing medium, later also known under her married names as Mrs. Fitzgerald and Mrs. Russell Davies. Her spirit **control,** "Dewdrop," claimed to be a Native American girl and played all the tricks of a mischievous secondary personality on the medium, such as controlling her in an omnibus and talking loudly in a foreign language until the other passengers thought that they were riding with a lunatic.

For a long time, Williams assisted a well-known spiritualist healer known as Dr. Mack in diagnosing medical conditions. She gave her services free. As she took on all the symptoms of the illnesses diagnosed, her failing health compelled her, after a while, to give up this pursuit. W. T. Stead thought highly of the medium's powers and included articles by her on the subject of haunted houses in his journal *Borderland.*

Sources:

Marryat, Florence. *The Spirit World.* New York: C. B. Reed, 1894.

———. *There Is No Death.* New York: Lovell, Coryell, 1891.

———, ed. *The Clairvoyance of Bessie Williams. Related by Herself.* N.p., 1893.

Williams, Charles

British **materialization** medium, claiming the spirit **control "John King,"** who worked from 1871 on in partnership with fellow medium **Frank Herne.** They gave public séances at 61 Lamb's Conduit St., in west central London. The first was held under the patronage of the medium **Agnes Guppy-Volckman.** The famous **transportation** of Guppy-Volckman occurred at one of these séances.

Williams often sat with **W. Stainton Moses,** but the results were always very meager. Moses was in doubt about the authenticity of Williams' mediumship and asked his controls for information. They were reluctant to give it. Catherine Berry's book *Experiences in Spiritualism* (1876) and A. Smedley's *Some Reminiscences* (1900) contained enthusiastic accounts, but **fraud** was often suspected and, in at least one case, glaringly proved.

In Paris, at a séance on May 14, 1874, an attempt was made to seize "John King." He eluded capture and left a piece of drapery behind, the further history of which is not known. The medium was found in his seat. The search of his person revealed nothing suspicious.

In 1878, the research committee of the **British National Association of Spiritualists** constructed a **cabinet** with an automatic recording apparatus. An observer sat in another cabinet with a lighted lamp. In one sitting with Williams, a spirit form appeared, sometimes ten or twelve feet from the cabinet. These appearances corresponded with fluctuations recorded by the self-registering apparatus. The maximum loss of weight amounted to 100 pounds. There was no weight in the cabinet that could have been fixed on the weighing platform. **Frank Podmore** suggested that the medium need only have fastened the suspended cabinet to the floor by a gimlet or a piece of string, but that seemed insufficient to explain fully the extreme variations in weight.

However, a few months after this experiment, in a Spiritualist circle in Amsterdam, Williams and his fellow medium **A. Rita** were exposed. "Charlie," a materialized spirit, was seized and found to be Rita. Many handkerchiefs, a bottle of phosphorized oil, several yards of very dirty white muslin, a false black beard with brown silk ribbon, and other paraphernalia were found on the persons of the two mediums.

The exposure did not stop a subsequent visit to Russia, where Professor Boutlerof and **Alexander Aksakof** (a strong believer in Spiritualist phenomena) had what they considered convincing experiences. In a note to Boutlerof's account of the visit in *Psychische Studien,* Aksakof added:

"I can testify to having received the confirmation of the appearance of John King from Mr. Crookes in his own house, Mrs. Crookes' hand being on William's shoulder while he was asleep behind the curtain; also that in the house of Mrs. MacDougall Gregory, the curtain behind which Williams was placed was in a niche almost hermetically sealed; and that John King appeared above the table, round which the company were assembled in front of the curtain."

Williams, Mrs. M. A.

American **materialization** medium. **Florence Marryat,** who sat with her in a public séance in New York without being introduced, described in her book *There is No Death* (1892) the appearance of her daughter (also named Florence), exactly the way she had seen her in Europe under the mediumships of **Florence Cook, Arthur Colman, Charles Williams,** and **William Eglinton.** Another familiar apparition was "Joey," Eglinton's spirit **control.** Altogether 40 different materializations were witnessed that evening.

In 1894, Williams was the guest of the Duchess of Pomar in Paris. Paul Leymarie, the son of the editor of *La Revue Spirite,* slipped behind the curtain during the séance and grasped the spirit. When the lights came up Williams was found in flesh-colored tights and the whole apparatus of her fraudulent spirit puppet show was discovered in the cabinet.

Williamson, Cecil H.

British occultist who claimed the power to conjure spirits by ritual **magic.** He was a graduate of Malvern College and spent some time as a tobacco planter in Rhodesia. During World War II he was in the British Intelligence Service. An expert on **witchcraft,** he is proprietor of a museum of magic and witchcraft known as the Witches' House, situated in the small Cornish village of Bocastle, England, near Tintagel. The museum was originally based at Bourton-on-the-Water in the Cotswold countryside, but closed about 1966. Williamson was formerly an associate and friend of witchcraft revivalist **Gerald B. Gardner,** who also ran a **Museum of Magic and Witchcraft** on the Isle of Man.

Williamson, George Evans (1887– ?)

A businessman active in South African parapsychology. He was born on January 14, 1887, at Malvern, England. He studied at Rugby School (1900–05) and Cambridge University (M.A., LL.B., 1908). He served in the British Army during World War I (1914–18) and then became a businessman in England (1918–39). He moved to South Africa as World War II began and lived there for the rest of his life. He was a founding member and president for some years of the Cape Town Psychic Club and Library, and a fellow of the **College of Psychic Science,** London.

Sources:

Pleasants, Helene, ed. *Biographical Dictionary of Parapsychology.* New York: Helix Press, 1964.

Williamson, George Hunt (1926–1986)

George Hunt Williamson, a metaphysical teacher, **flying saucer** contactee, and bishop, was born on December 9, 1926, in Chicago, Illinois. As a youth Williamson had a variety of psychic experiences capped by a vivid **out-of-body experience** in his late teens which aroused his interest in the occult. He attended college and studied anthropology, though he never attained the advanced degrees he later claimed. In 1951 he read *The Flying Saucers Are Real* by Donald Keyhoe and became interested in UFOs. Thus it was that in 1952, he and his wife, Betty, then living in Prescott, Arizona, met another couple interested in the saucers, Alfred and Betty Bailey. One evening the four experimented with **automatic writing** and received a message purportedly from an extraterrestrial, Nah-9 of Solar X Group. In subsequent communications, he and other extraterrestrials warned of a nuclear blast about to occur on Earth. The ongoing messages received by the small group later became the basis of a 1954 book, *The Saucers Speak!*

His involvement in contact with the space entities led Williamson to **George Adamski,** and he, his wife, and the Baileys began to commute to Southern California to attend Adamski's lectures. Adamski channeled messages from his space contacts, one of which heralded an imminent face-to-face contact. That contact occurred on November 20, 1952, when the Williamsons, the Baileys, Adamski, and two of his associates met at Blythe, California, and headed into the nearby desert. Here Adamski would have his meeting with Orthon, which the rest looked upon from some distance. After Adamski told his story to the press, the Williamsons moved near Adamski's residence at Palomar, but soon parted company over Adamski's public stance against channeling.

Following the publication of *The Saucers Speak!,* Williamson was briefly associated with fellow **contactee** Dick Miller at the

Telonic Research Center, but soon moved to Peru. There, under the name Brother Philip, he founded the Brotherhood of the Seven Rays, an occult community that attracted not only other contactees, but many of a theosophical inclination. This was Williamson's most productive period as a writer. He authored *Secret of the Andes* (as Brother Philip) (1958), *Secret Places of the Lion* (1958), *UFOs Confidential* (with John McCoy) (1958), and *Road in the Sky* (1959), and a volume he had written earlier, *Other Tongues—Other Flesh,* was also published (1957). He was the first to call attention to the Nasca lines as a possible artifact related to extraterrestrials.

By 1958 the Peruvian experiment had come to an end, and Williamson spent the next years touring the world and lecturing to contactee-oriented audiences. However, by the early 1960s he disappeared from the flying saucer world. In fact, in 1969 he legally changed his name to Michael D'Obenovic, asserting that this was the real name of his Serbian-American family prior to their migrating to America. Also, in 1971, he was ordained as a priest in the Liberal Catholic Church by Archbishop Gerrit Munik and became the priest of a small congregation in Cornville, California. Early in the 1970s he left the Liberal Catholic Church and in 1974 was consecrated as a bishop by John Marion Stanley of the Orthodox Church of the East. He was consecrated a second time in 1977 by Albert R. Coady of the Eastern Catholic Syro-Chaldean Archdiocese of North America, like Stanley's church, a small independent Orthodox jurisdiction. Both jurisdictions were aligned with the Charismatic Movement and believed in the experience of **glossolalia** or speaking-in-tongues.

D'Obenovic had reasserted his Orthodox heritage, but did not agree with the Charismatic emphasis of his consecrators, and a short time after his second consecration, he found a new independent jurisdiction, the Holy Apostolic Catholic Church Syro-Chaldean Diocese of Santa Barbara and Central California. By this time he was pastoring a small parish in Santa Barbara, California. During these years Williamson rarely associated with the flying saucer community though he gave a few conservative lectures on UFOs as D'Obenovic. He died in 1986, and his church dissolved shortly thereafter. A friend who was a member of the church in Santa Barbara subsequently authored a brief biography.

Sources:

Griffin, John. *Visitants.* Santa Barbara, Calif.: The Author, 1989.

Robinson, John J. "George Hunt Williamson—Revisited." *Saucer News* 10, no. 3 (September 1963): 9–10.

Ward, Gary L. *Independent Bishops: An International Directory.* Detroit: Apogee, 1990.

Williamson, George Hunt. *Other Tongues—Other Flesh.* Amherst, Wis.: Amherst Press, 1957.

———. *Road in the Sky.* London: Neville Spearman, 1959.

———. *The Saucers Speak.* London: Neville Spearman, 1963.

———. (under pseudonym Brother Philip). *Secret of the Andes.* Clarksburg, W.Va.: Sucerian Books, 1958.

———. *Secret Places of the Lion.* Amherst, Wis.: Amherst Press, 1958.

Williamson, Marianne (1953–)

Marianne Williamson, a popular metaphysical teacher of the channeled text *A Course in Miracles* (ACIM), was born in Houston, Texas, the daughter of a prominent Jewish lawyer who specialized in immigration law. Her father, Alan Vishnevetsky, had changed the family name when he moved to the United States from his birthplace in Russia. In her youth, she was influenced more by leftist politics than spirituality. She attended Pomona College for two years (1970–72), but found herself rudderless through the next years of her life. In 1977, while living in New York City and trying to develop a singing career, she first encountered *A Course in Miracles.* Though initially put off by its Christian references, the following year she volunteered at the **Foundation for Inner Peace,** the corporation set up to publish the books and disseminate the teachings, and assisted in its move to Tiburon, California.

Williamson moved back to Houston in 1979, and she married a businessman. The marriage soon ended in divorce. Her first attempt to appropriate the teachings of the *Course* led her into a lengthy spiritual crisis which she termed a "dark night of the soul." She eventually found her way to a psychiatrist who was also a student of the ACIM, and attributes his help in getting her through this difficult period. She finally reached the point where she invited God into her life and in essence began her life anew. In 1983 she moved to Southern California. She took a secretarial job with the **Philosophical Research Society** in Hollywood, and soon became the weekly lecturer on *A Course in Miracles.*

Articulate, attractive, and entertaining, Williamson soon outgrew the facilities at the society, and went out on her own. She drew large audiences in both Los Angeles and New York, and discovered that she had a special appeal among gay males who had been affected by the AIDS epidemic. Her recognition of her gay audience led her to found the Center for Living, a combination hospice/cultural center for people with catastrophic illnesses. Centers were opened in both Los Angeles and New York. She spent a considerable amount of her time raising financial resources for the center.

Williamson attained a new level of fame beginning in 1991 when the newsstand magazine *Vanity Fair* published a feature article on her. Then she officiated at the wedding of Liz Taylor and Larry Fortensky. When her first book, *A Return to Love,* appeared early in 1992, Oprah Winfry invited her on the show and endorsed the volume, copies of which she distributed to the audience that day. Williamson was a national celebrity, her fame reaching far beyond that previously attained by ACIM. In the meantime, dissension had emerged at the two centers. She eventually withdrew from an active administrative role and in the mid-1990s moved to Santa Barbara for several years before relocating to New York.

While being attacked in the press for what were considered by some as personality flaws, Williamson continued to write popular spiritual texts including *A Woman's Worth* and *Illuminata.* Still drawing large audiences for her presentations, she remains the single most popular interpreter of *A Course in Miracles.*

Sources:

Bennetts, Leslie. "Marianne's Faithful." *Vanity Fair* (June 1991).

Miller, D. Patrick. *The Complete Story of the Course: The History, the People and the Controversies Behind A Course in Miracles.* Berkeley, Calif.: Fearless Books, 1997.

Oumano, Elena. *Marianne Williamson: Her Life, Her Message, Her Miracles.* New York: St. Martin's Press, 1992.

Willington Mill

A famous British haunted house. The story of the mill was reported in an early issue of the *Journal* of the Society for Psychical Research (vol. 5) in the 1880s. It was owned by a Mr. Proctor, who was quite used to the ghosts. The following extracts give some idea of the manifestations:

"When two of Mrs. Proctor's sisters were staying at the Mill on a visit their bed was suddenly violently shaken, the curtains hoisted up all round to their tester, and then as rapidly let down again, and this again in rapid succession. The curtains were taken off the next night, with the result that they both saw a female figure, of mysterious substance and of a greyish-blue hue, come out of the wall at the head of the bed and lean over them. They both saw it distinctly. They saw it come out of and go back again into the wall. . . . Mrs. Davidson's sister-in-law had a curious experience on one occasion. One evening she was putting one of the bedrooms aright, and, looking towards the dressing table, saw what she supposed was a white towel lying on the ground. She went to pick it up, but imagine her surprise when she found that it rose up, and went behind the dressing table over the top, down on the floor across the room, disappearing under the door, and was heard to descend the stairs with a heavy step! The noise which it made in doing so was distinctly heard by Mr. Proctor and others in the house."

The old mill foreman once saw a bald-headed, luminous figure at a window. The body was brilliant, diffusing radiance, then it turned bluish and gradually faded from the top down. One of the little girls living in the house said on one occasion: "There is a lady sitting on the bed in Mamma's bedroom. She has eyeholes but no eyes, and she looked so hard at me."

It was the opinion of Andrew Lang that the noises and apparitions at Willington Mill were a stimulus to the novelist **Edward Bulwer Lytton** in writing his famous supernatural story *The Haunted and the Haunters.*

Sources:

Armitage, Harold. *The Haunted and the Haunters by Lord Lytton, With an Introduction; and an Account of the Haunted House at Willington.* London: Simpkin, Marshall, 1925.

Willis, F. L. H.

Instructor in medicine at a New York college, who, as a student, was forced out of the Divinity School at Harvard University in 1857, largely because of his developing mediumship. He came from a respected family in Cambridge, Massachusetts, and was a good speaker and improvisor of poetry. While studying at divinity school, he was discovered to be a strong physical medium, and as a result of charges brought against him by a Professor Eustis, he was expelled. He was charged with simulating spiritual phenomena at Harvard, although the authenticity of the phenomena were attested by the famous author and reformer Thomas Wentworth Higginson.

Willis was observed producing **apports, direct writing,** and direct **music.** He was levitated on several occasions and possessed gifts of **healing.** Once, while in trance and controlled by the spirit of a "Dr. Mason," he performed a difficult operation on a female patient. He achieved this feat prior to his medical studies.

Willis was known to **Epes Sargent,** author of *The Scientific Basis of Spiritualism* (1880), who included in this book extracts from a letter written by Willis in May 1879 regarding his **materialization** of spirit hands. Willis wrote:

"It is 23 years ago that these materializations of hands occurred. . . . On one occasion a gentleman present drew a knife from his pocket with a long, keen blade, and taking no one into his counsel, watching his opportunity, pierced with a violent blow one of the psychic hands. The medium [Willis] uttered a shriek of pain. The sensation was precisely as if the knife had passed through his hand. The gentleman sprang to his feet exultant, thinking he had made a most triumphant exposé of trickery, and fully expected to find the medium's hand pierced and bleeding. To his utter chagrin and amazement there was no trace of a scratch even upon either hand of the medium; and yet to him the sensation was precisely as if the knife had passed through muscle and tendon, and the sensation of pain and soreness remained for hours."

This account of early materialization of spirit hands, long before the days of **Eusapia Palladino** and other physical mediums, is of special interest for its claim that violence to pseudopodic **ectoplasm** reacts painfully upon the medium.

Willis described events in his life during a lecture at the Spiritual Institute in London in 1869, published in *The Spiritual Magazine* (1870, p. 193) and in *Human Nature* (1869, p. 573).

Sources:

Britten, Emma Hardinge. *Modern American Spiritualism.* New York: The author, 1870.

Willow Tree

Many superstitions have been connected with the willow ever since, according to the authorized version of the English Bible, the Israelites were said to have hung their harps on willow trees (Psalms 137:2). The weeping willow is said to have drooped its branches since the time of the captivity of the Jews in Babylon, in sympathy with this circumstance.

The common willow was once popularly believed to be under the protection of the devil, and it was said that if any person were to cast a knot upon a young willow, sit under the tree, and renounce his or her baptism, the devil would confer upon that person supernatural power. It was believed in Bulgaria that a fever would depart if you ran around a willow tree three times at sunset, crying "The fever shall take thee and the sun shall warm me."

Wilson, Cedric W(illiam) M(alcolm) (1925–)

Lecturer in pharmacology who has written on parapsychology. He was born on November 23, 1925, in Edinburgh, Scotland. He studied at the University of Edinburgh (B.S., 1947; M.C., Ch.B., 1949; Ph.D., 1954; M.D., 1958). He had a distinguished medical career, and in 1955 he became a lecturer in pharmacology and general therapeutics at the University of Liverpool. In addition to his articles on medical and pharmacological subjects, he has contributed to the *Journal of Parapsychology* and the *International Journal for Parapsychology.* Wilson also conducted experiments on the telepathic control of automatic responses and the influence of drugs on such responses.

Sources:

Pleasants, Helene, ed. *Biographical Dictionary of Parapsychology.* New York: Helix Press, 1964.

Wilson, Colin (Henry) (1931–)

Popular British novelist and writer on occultism who attracted worldwide attention with his first book, *The Outsider.* He was born on June 26, 1931, in Leicester, England. He was educated at the Gateway School, Leicester, and worked at a great variety of jobs before becoming a writer. In 1947 he was employed by a wool company, and he subsequently worked as a laboratory assistant at a secondary technical school (1947–48) and as a tax collector (1947–49). He spent time in Germany and France, and while in Paris he worked on *Merlin* and *Paris Review.* Wilson was writer-in-residence at Hollins College, Virginia (1966–67) and now resides in Cornwall, England.

While preparing his first book *The Outsider* (1956), Wilson researched at public libraries, slept outdoors, and wrote in coffee houses. The book was an instant success, and the term "outsider" passed into common use as a romantic way to denote a type of brilliant misfit capable of surveying life in an original way. Assuming that role himself, Wilson has shown originality in his other writings, and in recent years he has achieved the status of an authority on popular occultism for his many writings and reviews in that subject area. His major study *The Occult* (1971) is a substantive survey of the emerging occult community at the beginning of the 1970s. He has produced several books annually through the 1980s to the present. He has continued to reflect upon the world of psychic experience, the occult, and alternative spirituality. His novel, *The Space Vampires* (1975), was turned into a movie.

Sources:

Wilson, Colin. *Beyond the Outsider.* Boston: Houghton, Mifflin, 1965.

———. *Enigmas and Mysteries.* Garden City, N.Y.: Doubleday, 1976.

———. *The Essential Colin Wilson.* London: Harrap, 1985.

———. *The Geller Phenomena.* London: Aldus Books, 1976.

———. *Mysterious Powers.* Reprinted in the United States as *They Had Strange Powers.* Garden City, N.Y.: Doubleday, 1975.

———. *The Occult.* London: Hodder & Stoughton; New York: Random House, 1971.

———. *The Unexplained.* Lake Oswego, Ore.: Lost Pleiade Press, 1975.

Wilson, Colin, and John Grant, eds. *Directory of Possibilities.* Exeter, England: Webb & Bower, 1981.

Wilson, Graham (1940–)

New consciousness entrepreneur who organized the international annual **Mind-Body-Spirit Festivals** held in England in the 1970s. Born in Yorkshire, England, he spent his preschool years on a farm. After World War II his family returned to London, where Wilson attended Wandsworth Grammar School, studying advanced level zoology and botany and investigating the writing of **Rudolph Steiner** and other occult mystics in his spare time. He was also active in sports and became a London Youth Athletics champion for the half-mile and cross country events at the age of 18. He played rugby and soccer as well as squash, and he took a great interest in the "peak" experiences of athletes.

After a varied business career, Wilson teamed up with Terry Ellis in 1976 to hire an exhibition hall in London and present the first Festival for Mind and Body, drawing upon his own knowledge of mystical and spiritual philosophies and athletic experiences. He put all his own money into the venture, which was presented in April 1977 in London. It was a success and led to successive annual festivals in Britain, Australia, and the United States. He later launched the UK's first Psychics and Mystics Fayres and the UK's first holistic health clinic, the London Natural Health Clinic.

In organizing these festivals, Wilson and his associates provided a regular focal point for **New Age** and mystical activities, and he himself believes that "you can use the best of the commercial world to allow in a spiritual flow in such a way that the final product has quality and integrity."

Wilson, James (fl. 18th century)

Through the seventeenth century, **astrology** enjoyed broad support in the West, though it had come under attack by Protestant church leaders and from the same skeptical voices that had taken the lead in denouncing the witchcraft hysteria. In the eighteenth century it suffered greatly from the new scientific worldview and appeared to be on its way to disappearing completely. However, in the early nineteenth century, as part of the general post-scientific occult revival, astrology also experienced a rebirth. At the fountainhead of that revival in the English-speaking world was James Wilson.

Little is known of this astrologer who worked during the early decades of the nineteenth century except that he published what became the seminal work from which modern astrology would develop. *The Dictionary of Astrology,* a comprehensive new astrology textbook, appeared in 1819. Wilson had made an extensive study of the teachings accumulated by astrologers over the centuries and rejected everything for which he could find no evidence. He paid particular attention to horary astrology, a branch of astrology that assumes that whenever a question is asked, the answer is reflected in the patterns of the planets at that particular moment. The following year Wilson released a new set of astrological tables, the charts of planetary positions needed by the astrologer to construct a horoscope. Later in the decade he would publish a new edition of Ptolomy's *Tetrabiblos,* the book from which all Western astrology derives.

Wilson's *Dictionary* went through several editions and was periodically reprinted throughout the century. It would influence several generations of British astrologers until replaced by the writings of **William J. Simmonite** and **Raphael** (**Robert Cross Smith**). It was regularly quoted by **Luke Broughton,** the founder of contemporary American astrology.

Sources:

Holden, James H., and Robert A. Hughes. *Astrological Pioneers of America.* Tempe, Ariz.: American Federation of Astrologers, 1988.

McCaffery, Ellen. *Astrology: Its History and Influence in the Western World.* New York: Charles Scribner's Sons, 1942.

Wilson, James. *Dictionary of Astrology.* London: W. Hughes, 1819. Reprint, New York: Samuel Weiser, 1969.

———. *A New and Complete Set of Astrological Tables.* London: W. W. Hughes, 1920.

Wilson, John C.

Pseudonym of **Felix Morrow,** pioneer publisher of **occult** and metaphysical books under the imprint of **University Books, Inc.**

Wilson, Percy (1893– ?)

Electronics and acoustics consultant and Spiritualist leader who also wrote on psychical subjects. He was born on March 8, 1893, in Halofax, Yorkshire, England. He attended Oxford (M.A., 1918). He became the technical editor of *The Gramophone* magazine in 1924 and later head of the Roads Department, Ministry of Transport, London (1938–49). He was also chairman of Psychic Press and a consultant in electronics and acoustics.

He was president of the **Spiritualists' National Union** (1950–53), member of the **Society for Psychical Research,** London, and vice president of the **College of Psychic Science,** London. He was author of the books *Modern Gramophones* (1929) and *The Gramophone Handbook* (1957), and he also published a number of articles on physical and trance mediumship, **clairvoyance, clairaudience,** and **healing** in the Spiritualist periodicals *Two Worlds, Psychic News* and *Light.*

Wilson, Richard (1926–)

Physics professor who was active in the field of parapsychology. He was born on April 29, 1926, in London, England. He studied at Oxford University (M.S., Ph.D.). He began his teaching career as a research lecturer at Christ Church, Oxford (1948–53). He spent two years in the United States before returning to Oxford for two years (1953–55), and then moved to the United States as a professor at Harvard University.

A corresponding member of the **Society for Psychical Research,** London, Wilson devised a random number selector for extrasensory perception.

Sources:

Pleasants, Helene, ed. *Biographical Dictionary of Parapsychology.* New York: Helix Press, 1964.

Wilson, Richard. "A Random Number Selector." *Proceedings* of the American Society for Psychical Research 48 (1946–49).

Winds (Paranormal)

Paranormal breezes, currents of air, and cooling temperatures are frequently reported séance room phenomena, as well as being traditionally associated with the subjective effects of **hauntings.** It is an open question whether such temperature changes serve a direct purpose or are only by-products.

Such thermic manifestations are a great convenience both for the sitters and the medium, who sometimes report excessive perspiration. One the other hand, **Celestine Sanders,** a New York medium, used to feel so unnaturally cold during her séances that she enveloped herself in many coverings and shawls to counteract the effect. It is difficult to allot the parts that the sitters and the medium play in the phenomenon. Sometimes the source seems to be the medium.

The spouting fountain of air that psychical researcher **Cesare Lombroso** discussed in his account of séances with **Eusapia Palladino** issued from a depression on the medium's forehead. **Hereward Carrington** noticed that after a good séance the breeze was strong, and after a poor one it was altogether lacking. Yet the breeze was not generally an after-séance effect. It usually preceded and heralded strong physical phenomena.

The chilly feeling that accompanies apparitions may be the result of a sudden drop in the temperature. All those who saw the apparition of a wooden cross in a certain haunted house felt unnaturally cold.

"Walter," the spirit **control** of the medium **Mina S. Crandon** ("Margery"), said that cold breezes and drops in temperature were the result of some psychic emanation from the sitters' brains. "Walter" found immense pleasure in using the thermometer as an indicator of the physical conditions confronting him. He said that if he looked at it and it was steady, he used "Margery" alone, and if it was going down, he used the sitters' brains as well. If he used "Margery" alone no cold breezes or drops in temperature were produced.

"Walter's" statement contains nothing new for Spiritualists. A control of the famous medium **D. D. Home** said more than a half a century earlier: "It is through your brains that the atmosphere we make use of is thrown off." **Lord Adare,** in a séance with Home, heard the sound of a great wind. "We also felt the wind strongly," he wrote "the moaning, rushing sound was the most weird thing I ever heard."

Prior to the Spiritualist era, the seer **Emanuel Swedenborg** also encountered the phenomenon. He wrote in his *Spiritual Diary:*

"A spirit is compared to the wind (John iii, 8); hence it is that spirits have come to me both now, and very frequently before, with wind, which I felt in the face; yea, it also moved the flame of the candle, and likewise papers; the wind was cold, and indeed most frequently when I raised my right arm, which I wondered at, the cause of which I do not yet know."

The same experience has been recorded with many physical mediums. **Sir William Crookes** wrote in *Researches into the Phenomena of Spiritualism* (1874):

"These movements, and indeed, I may say the same of every kind of phenomenon, are generally preceded by a peculiar cold air, sometimes amounting to a decided wind. I have had sheets of paper blown about by it, and a thermometer lowered several degrees. On some occasions I have not detected any actual movement of the air, but the cold has been so intense that I could only compare it to that felt when the hand has been within a few inches of frozen mercury."

In the experiments at the **Millesimo Castle** with the **Marquis Centurione Scotto,** the psychical researcher **Ernesto Bozzano** recorded:

"On the evening of July 7, 1928, the heat was very oppressive . . . we happened to mention this disadvantage, and immediately blasts of unusually strong, icy air were felt by us all. . . . There was a continual change in the direction from which these air currents came; sometimes they descended from the ceiling, then we felt them in front of us, or at our side, or blowing from behind us; sometimes they were like small whirlwinds. It felt as though several electric fans were working in the centre, outside and above the circle."

In the next séance, the phenomenon was repeated and perfected:

"Almost immediately we felt strong blasts of icy air which rapidly increased in force, giving one the impression of a powerful supernormal electric fan which periodically wafted its pleasant, cooling currents of air over the sitters. . . . These currents were so strong that our hair waved in the wind, and men's coats, and the lace on the ladies' dresses were blown about."

Bozzano added that not the slightest sound accompanied the production of this phenomenon. The breezes sometimes brought down the temperature of the séance room by as much as 20 degrees.

George Henslow described the sensations of the sitters of **T. d'Aute Hooper** of Birmingham, England, as of that of "an intensely cold dew or mist, as though a vapour of methylated spirit were floating about the room." While **apports** were being produced, "the sitters felt as if they were sitting up to their knees in cold water."

Measuring Temperature Differences

The psychical researcher **Harry Price** established a definite connection between the phenomenon of **telekinesis** and the drop in temperature. In his experiments with the medium **Stella C.** at the **National Laboratory of Psychical Research** he noticed a maximum drop of 20.5 degrees Fahrenheit. At the close of the séance the temperature was again normal. The medium's temperature was always higher at the end of the sitting, but she herself always complained of feeling cold. The rapidity of her pulse beats was always accompanied in the trance by a pronounced coldness in the extremities.

In the "Margery" séances, a maximum-and-minimum thermometer was employed to measure the temperature. In one case the initial temperature dropped from 68 to 42, a difference of 26 degrees. After the breezes had been blowing for a while "Margery" often complained of feeling as though cobwebs were on her face.

General experience regarding the nature of the cold breezes was curiously contradicted in an address by the British clairvoyant **Robert King** (*Light,* April 25, 1903). He stated that the peculiar cold air of the séance room is not a wind,

". . . it does not move things. I have watched pieces of paper placed on the table when these cold airs have been playing around. If a wind of that intensity had been blowing, the paper would have been moved, so I rather incline to the opinion that this phenomenon is due to a difference in pressure caused by abstraction of etheric matter from the sitters."

Sources:

Hack, Gwendolyn Kelley. *Modern Psychic Mysteries.* London: Rider, 1929.

Windsor Castle

One of the largest inhabited castles in the world. Windsor Castle, in Berkshire, England, is one of the royal residences and headquarters of the Order of the Garter. It is frequently cited as a **haunted house,** filled with numerous notable specters. Queen Elizabeth, Henry VIII, Charles I, and some of the Georges have all been reputed to haunt the castle, and Herne the Hunter is also said to roam the twelve-acre Great Park.

In February 1897, Lieutenant Carr Glynn of the Grenadier Guards was sitting in the library reading in the twilight when he heard the rustle of a silken dress and, looking up, saw the ghost of Queen Elizabeth I glide across the room. He buckled on his sword and reported the matter. The story attracted the attention of the country for some weeks. Sir Richard Holmes and his assistants kept watch for many nights, but the ghost did not reappear.

On another occasion, a housemaid in St. John's Tower thought she saw a ghost. She was so frightened that she became ill and had to be sent home. In 1908, a sentry discharged five rounds of ball cartridge at a figure that appeared on the terrace, which he declared was a specter.

A famous ghost is that of Sir George Villiers, father of the Duke of Buckingham in the reign of James I. Herne the Hunter, who is said to lead a wild hunt in the park, was immortalized in W. Harrison Ainsworth's novel *Windsor Castle* (1843).

Today, Windsor Castle is open daily except when used for royal visits. There are historic treasures in the state apartments, including period furniture, fittings, paintings and suits of armor. The castle also houses Queen Mary's Dolls' House, which is a popular exhibit.

Wingfield, Kate (d. 1927)

British non-commercial medium, the "Miss A." of whom psychical researcher **F. W. H. Myers** wrote enthusiastically in *Proceedings* of the **Society for Psychical Research** (vol. 8, 498–516; vol. 9, 73–92) and in his book *Human Personality and Its Survival of Bodily Death* (1903). Wingfield was also the "Miss Rawson" of **J. G. Piddington**'s report in *Proceedings* of the SPR (vol. 18) on **cross correspondence** with Rosina Thompson.

Her identity was eventually revealed by Sir Lawrence J. Jones, president of the society in 1928, in his presidential address in *Proceedings* (vol. 38). He told the story of a series of sittings that he and his wife had with her in the years 1900 and 1901, when her **clairvoyance** and **automatic writing** developed into **trance** mediumship. He observed many physical phenomena: **raps,** table tilting, movement of objects (**telekinesis**) and **apports.** In one instance, three tiny unset turquoises were brought as apports.

But it was the trance speaking phase of Wingfield's mediumship that convinced Jones of **survival.** Deceased relatives proved their identity and on several occasions their living daughter came through as a communicator.

Among the medium's **controls** was an entity "Semirus," who claimed to have been a doctor in ancient Egypt. Once a sitter desired some information from him. "Semirus" did not come. Later in the day he came through in automatic writing and explained that he heard the call, but was unable to come as he was assisting in a new operation. The operation was successful. On inquiry the story of the operation was found to be true. "Semirus" could report on patients at a great distance with incredible rapidity. Someone asked for information about the health of his aunt. "Semirus" went away and came back to say that the aunt was dead. The sitter hurried away and to his relief found his aunt alive. But he suddenly realized that he had given, by mistake, the address of a neighbor's house to the spirit control. A day or two later, a funeral took place there.

Wingfield's sittings were primarily **rescue circles.** The controls aided many spirits by pointing out the errors of their ways. She ceased holding sittings in 1901, as her family objected that she become known as a trance medium. The automatic writings that came through her hand were published in two books.

Sources:

Wingfield, Kate. *Guidance from Beyond.* N.p., 1923.

———. *More Guidance from Beyond.* N.p., 1925.

Wirdig's Magnetic Sympathy

A theory of magnetic attraction and repugnance formulated by Tenzel Wirdig, professor at Rostock, who published his *Tenzelius Wirdig, Nova medicina spirituum* in 1673. Wirdig believed that everything in the universe possessed a soul, and that the Earth itself was merely a larger animal. Between the souls of things in accordance with each other there was a "magnetic sympathy" and a perpetual antipathy existed between those of an uncongenial nature. To this sympathy and antipathy Wirdig gave the name **magnetism.** He stated:

"Out of this relationship of sympathy and antipathy arises a constant movement in the whole world, and in all its parts, and an uninterrupted communion between heaven and earth, which produces universal harmony. The stars whose emanations consist merely of fire and spirits, have an undeniable influence on earthly bodies; and their influence on man demonstrates itself by life, movement, and warmth, those things without which he cannot live. The influence of the stars is the strongest at birth. The newborn child inhales this influence, and on whose first breath frequently his whole constitution depends, nay, even his whole life."

Wisconsin Phalanx

A Spiritualist community, based upon the doctrines of communalist Francois Fourier, founded by **Warren Chase** in 1844. Chase had settled in Southport, Wisconsin, in 1838, and with his wife and child, he lived there for a time in poverty. At length, however, their circumstances improved and Chase attained to a position of civic honor in Southport. During this time he studied **mesmerism** and socialism with the aid of a few periodicals such as **La Roy Sunderland**'s *Magnet* and the *New York Tribune,* and he was filled with the idea of founding a community where his ideals of social order and harmony might be carried out.

With the aid of his friends, he formed such a community. Each member had a share of 25 dollars. The chosen settlement—near the town of Ripon—was christened "Ceresco," in honor of Ceres, the Roman goddess of agriculture. For six years the Wisconsin Phalanx flourished, with Chase acting as its leader and ruling spirit.

But dissension arose, and in 1850 the community was dissolved. When its affairs were closed, a considerable profit fell to its members. In all, it was one of the more successful Spiritualist communes of the time. (See also **Apostolic Circle; Mountain Cove Community**)

Sources:

Noyes, John Humphery. *History of American Socialisms.* 1870. Reprinted as *Strange Cults and Utopias of 19th-Century America.* New York: Dover Publications, 1966.

Wissenschaftliche Gesellschaft zur Förderung der Parapsychologie

The Wissenschaftliche Gesellschaft zur Förderung der Parapsychologie (Scientific Society for the Advancement of Parapsychology), founded in 1981 by Eberhard Bauer, Walter von Lucadou, and German researchers interested in parapsychology, sponsors and promotes research in universities and similar research institutions. Psychical research had been stamped out in Germany during the Nazi regime and faced a difficult period of recovery after World War II. Several attempts to found parapsychological associations have failed, but this society succeeded in a unique way and through the 1980s was able to secure a membership, among whom were a number of professors in leading German schools. Last known address: Abteilung für Psychologie und Grenzgebiete der Psychologie, Albert-Ludwigs-Universität, Freiburg i. Br., Belforrstrasse 16, 7800 Freiburg i. Br., Germany.

Witch Balls

Decorative items made of glass or metal, used as ornaments and to avert ill fortune or witchcraft. These appear to date from the eighteenth century. One variety favored by antique collectors and occultists is that manufactured in Nailsea, near Bristol, England. These balls are full of swirling colors.

Witchcraft

The word "witchcraft" derives from the Saxon *wicca,* sometimes translated as "wise person" but more accurately derived from an Indo-European root, "weik," that produced words in various Western languages related to magic, religion, and **divination.** Currently, the word is used to designate a variety of very different but vaguely related phenomena including, but not limited to, (1) the magical/religious practitioners in a variety of third world pre-industrial societies; (2) the **Satanism** described in the anti-witchcraft books beginning in the late fifteenth century in Europe; (3) the Neopagan followers of **Wicca,** the religion started by **Gerald B. Gardner** in the 1940s; and (4) individuals (primarily female) who are reputed to have psychic abilities.

Interpretations of Historic Witchcraft

Throughout the nineteenth and twentieth centuries, the figure of the European witch was interpreted and reinterpreted in numerous ways, depending on the orientations of the scholars involved. They described her (typically) as variously an anti-social practitioner of malevolent magic; as a pro-social healer, midwife, and magician condemned by churches and universities; as a victim of mental illness or of accidental poisoning by mind-altering plants; or as a deliberate user of mind-altering plants who sought a shamanic "soul flight." She was either the follower of a Satanic religion developed in opposition to Christianity, or she was the inheritor of pre-Christian Paganism. She was supported by her neighbors, or she was the unfortunate scapegoat for social tensions, a lonely victim with no family to protect her. These different pictures of the typical witch of the Burning Times or the Great Hunt (both terms for the persecutions that peaked in the sixteenth and seventeenth centuries) in turn reflect the sympathies of the writers, whether pro or anti-Catholic, socially rebellious, socially conservative, feminist, or Neopagan. These different perspectives on historical European witchcraft have also influenced what is today called Neopagan Witchcraft, a new religious movement.

Since the mid-1970s, historians have more closely examined the court records of witch trials in various European countries (and in North American colonies). They have studied the verdicts, punishments, social status of accused witches, lists of goods confiscated from the accused, and other evidence. In one notable case, scholarly re-examination of older work revealed a major forgery, a portion of Etienne Leon de Lamothe-Langon's *Histoire de l'Inquisition en France* (History of the French Inquisition), written in 1829. Lamothe-Langon's description of huge 14th-century witch trials with hundreds of executions in the South of France turned out to be complete inventions by the writer—who had also written a profitable series of "gothic" horror novels with titles like *The Monastery of the Black Friars.*

Today, informed estimates of the total deaths in central and western Europe range from 40,000 to 50,000, much lower than the millions once claimed. Contrary to the picture created by writers such as Lamothe-Langon, the Inquisition (an arm of the Roman Catholic Church created in 1246 to combat heresy) did not execute many witches; secular courts were more likely to condemn accused witches than were church courts. As many or more accused witches were executed in Protestant lands as in Catholic countries, and the witch trials did not peak until 1550-1650, a period that historians describe as "early modern" rather than "medieval."

During the early Middle Ages, Church writers were more likely to insist that witchcraft was a delusion and that priests should discourage their congregations from believing that anyone could cast spells or fly through the air in the entourage of a Pagan deity. The famous *Canon Episcopi,* publicized in the tenth century but possibly of earlier date, stated that it was heretical to believe in witchcraft, not to practice it. This ecclesiastical legal document, like others of its kind, urged bishops and priests to combat the practice of sorcery, but also suggested that people who believed that they were witches were deluded by the Devil. Another set of church ordinances from the late eighth century demanded the death penalty not for the witch, but for the person who murdered an alleged witch—again, because believing in witches was a Pagan superstition.

After the Black Death swept Europe in the 1340s, mysteriously killing thousands of people, Europeans were more likely to accept conspiracy theories involving enemies of Christianity, defined variously as heretics, Muslims, Jews or possibly witches. Officers of the Inquisition now began to expand their scope from Christian dissenters and heretics, such as Cathars and Waldensians, to people who supposedly had chosen to follow a diabolical anti-Christian religion (rather than a lingering Paganism). New manuals for witch-hunters appeared, such as the infamous *Malleus Maleficarum,* or "Hammer of Witches," a book that although authored by Dominican monks was used and reprinted equally by Protestant witch-hunters in Germany and England. By the sixteenth century, the witches' sabbat was regarded by authorities as a parody of the Christian Sabbath, the worshipful aspect of a religion which was a distorted image of true religion, i.e., Christianity. According to the records, the sabbat was generally held in some wild and solitary spot, often in the midst of forests or on the heights of mountains, at a great distance from the residence of most of the visitors. (The use of the word "sabbat," clearly derived from the Jewish Sabbath, indicates the way in which medieval and early modern Christians tended to blur distinctions between all perceived enemies of Christianity, whether Jews, Muslims, Pagans, or perceived sorcerers and witches.)

The witches themselves told a story—usually after torture—of taking off their clothes and anointing their bodies with a special **unguent** or ointment. They then strode across a stick, or any similar article, and, muttering a charm, were carried through the air to the place of meeting in an incredible short space of time. Sometimes the stick was to be anointed as well as the witch. They generally left the house by the window or by the chimney, which perhaps suggests survival of the custom of an earth-dwelling people. Sometimes the witch went out by the door, and there found a demon in the shape of a goat, or at times of some other animal, who carried her away on his back, and brought her home again after the meeting was dissolved.

In the confessions extorted from them, the witches bore testimony to the truth of all these details, but those who judged them, and who wrote upon the subject, asserted that they had many other independent proofs in corroboration.

Powers of Witches

In the eyes of the populace, the powers of witches were numerous. The most peculiar of these were: The ability to blight by means of the **evil eye,** the sale of winds to sailors, power over animals, and the power of witches to transform themselves into animal shapes.

Witches were also believed to possess the power of making themselves invisible, by means of a magic ointment supplied to them by the Devil, and of harming others by thrusting nails into a waxen image representing them.

New research has shown that witch trials were more likely to occur in areas of political instability and religious conflict. Hence both **Germany** and **Switzerland,** each a patchwork of small political entities and divided between Catholics and Protestants, witnessed more witch trials than did **France** or **Spain.** In late seventeenth-century Spain, after an outbreak of witchcraft accusations in the Basque region (shared with France), a lawyer for the Spanish Inquisition convinced its supreme council not to prosecute. Instead, the council ordered an "Edict of Silence" forbidding further discussion of witchcraft. In that Spanish case and others, local secular authorities went around the Catholic Church and appealed to the king for the right to try witches. The king agreed with their request and accused witches began to be sentenced until the Inquisition stopped the process on the grounds that this was church business only.

By the eighteenth century, however, fewer educated Europeans believed in spell-casting, witches flying through the sky, or other typical accusations of the Great Hunt. Thinkers of the Enlightenment such as Voltaire (1694–1778) had denounced the witch trials as the product of religious bigotry, whether Catholic or Protestant, supported by superstitious monarchs across Europe. They hoped that new, more rational attitudes would produce societies where such events could not occur.

In America, the Salem witch trials of the 1690s were similarly seen as the product of a repressive Puritan church struggling to hold onto power. Nineteenth-century American historian George Bancroft's *History of the United States* used the Salem trials to condemn Puritan "superstition," as did the poet and editor James Russell Lowell. As part of the nineteenth-century struggle for authority between science and religion, the witchcraft trials were entered into evidence as examples of the excesses of religion. This view tended to overlook the fact that secular courts were as likely or more likely to execute accused witches than were religious courts, producing the slightly skewed stereotype of "medieval" witches being hauled before the "Inquisition."

The Witch as Romantic Rebel

This anti-clerical view of the medieval and early modern witch as the victim of superstitious churchmen was strengthened by a new nineteenth-century view of the witch as a Romantic rebel or outlaw—an idea which partly underlies the new religion of Neopagan Witchcraft. It connects with the romanticization of medieval life (and of rural nineteenth-century life) by writers such as Sir Walter Scott and Thomas Hardy, both of whom described fictional "cunning women" or solitary rural witches in their novels. A leading proponent of this new Romantic view of witches was the French writer Jules Michelet, a fervent anti-Catholic and anti-monarchist, who produced numerous books of history, natural history, and social reform. Advocating a turn from Christianity to worship of a Great Mother Goddess such as Isis, Michelet held that women were morally superior to men, and that their persecution as witches in former centuries was an attack by the elites on both the rights of women and the working classes. Michelet took the position of the *Malleus Maleficarum* that women were innately drawn to witchcraft and made a positive good of it. Medieval witchcraft, he declared in his 1862 book *La Sorcière,* had been an egalitarian rural religion led by female priestesses—a view which was to resonate with later maverick writers on witchcraft such as Charles Leland and Margaret Murray. Had the witches worshipped Satan, as their accusers claimed? Indeed they had, Michelet wrote, for "Satan" was merely the god of fertility and the patron deity of those persons condemned by kings and bishops and their henchmen. Although he did little actual research for *La Sorcière,* Michelet succeed in introducing ideas that would be taken up by later generations of non-academic writers and by unconventional academics. One was the idea that witches were healers and midwives persecuted by a male-dominated medical establishment; another was that the persecuted witches represented traces of a secret Pagan religion.

Michelet's advocacy of a Mother Goddess religion helped reinforce a new current in nineteenth-century scholarship: that there had once been a universal matriarchal period of goddess-worship, later buried by a patriarchal Paganism typified by the well-known Greco-Roman pantheon: Jupiter/Zeus, Hera/Juno, and so on. The notion of a universal ancient matriarchy appealed to thinkers as different as Karl Marx and Sigmund Freud, both of whom incorporated parts of it in their theories of communism and psychoanalysis respectively. It also influenced the first wave of women's rights advocates, such as the American feminist Matilda Joslyn Gage, who published her own version of the anti-clerical witch trials in 1893, *Women, Church, and State.* Basing her research largely on Michelet, Gage produced a figure of nine million victims of the Burning Times, a figure which although wildly inflated continues to be repeated by some persons today.

Witches, Drugs, and Shamans

As the nineteenth century closed, two interpretations of the medieval and early modern witchcraft period were gaining adherents. One interpretation, suggested above, held that the persecuted witches were leaders and followers of an underground pre-Christian religion. The second, somewhat related to the first, was that at least some of the accused practiced an underground form of European shamanism, utilizing an ancient tradition of entheogenic plants such as *Amanita* mushrooms and members of the solanaceous plant genus such as henbane, mandrake, belladonna, and datura.

During the height of the Great Hunt, the fifteenth and sixteenth centuries, some lawyers and physicians had made their own tests of the **unguents** or "flying ointments" seized from accused witches, attempting to learn their compositions and effects. At the time, these men were advancing a counter-argument to the witch-hunters' position that the witches worshiped Satan. No, said such men as Andrés Laguna, physician to Pope Julius III, the witches were merely "wretched ones," deluded by drugs, who "firmly believe that they have done in a waking state all of that which they dreamt while sleeping."

Theologian Nicholas Remy, writing at the height of the trials, in the late 1500s, made numerous references to witches smearing their bodies with oils and ointments, noting, "Now if witches, after being aroused from an 'iron' sleep, tell of things they have seen in places so far distant as compared with the short period of their sleep, the only conclusion is that has been some unsubstantial journal like that of the soul."

In an account published in 1555, Laguna described one of his experiments, using "a jar half-filled with a certain green unguent" confiscated from some accused witches, which he believed was prepared with "cold" herbs such as henbane or mandrake. He took the mixture to another city, where he gave it to the wife of the public hangman. This woman suffered from insomnia, lying awake with worry because she thought her husband was unfaithful to her.

"On being anointed," Laguna wrote, "she suddenly slept such a profound sleep, with her eyes open like a rabbit, that I could not imagine how to wake her. By every means possible, with strong ligatures and rubbing her extremities, with effusions of oil of costus-root and officinal spurge, with fumes and smoke in her nostrils, and finally with cupping glasses, I so hurried her that at the end of thirty-six hours she regained her senses and memory: although the first words she spoke were: 'Why do you wake me at such an inopportune time? I was surrounded by all the pleasures and delights of the world.' And casting her eyes on her husband (who was there all stinking of hanged men), she said to him, smiling: 'Knavish one, know that I have made you a cuckold, and with a lover younger and better than you,' and she said many other and very strange things."

Such experiments led Laguna and some of his contemporaries, including some clergy, to a conclusion that the theologians and demonologists were wrong: the flights through the air, feasts and orgies, encounters with Satan and other fantastic experiences reported by (or tortured out of) the accused witches were really the results of using psychedelic drugs.

These earlier accounts of experiments with witches' unguents led to new experiments using old recipes in the late nineteenth and twentieth centuries. Karl Kiesewetter, a German scholar of the occult, reported dreams of flying after reproducing some of the old ointments; his later experiments were fatal. The pharmacologist Gustav Schenk wrote in *The Book of Poisons* that he experienced the sensations of flying through the clouds after breathing the smoke of burning henbane seeds. As interest in entheogenic or psychedelic drugs increased in the 1950s and 1960s, anthropologists such as Michael Harner returned to the older writings about "flying ointments" in order to suggest that European witches took part in shamanic "soul flights," projecting their consciousness into other realms of existence even while their physical bodies appeared to sleep. If parallel with the shamanism reported from other cultures around the world, these soul-journeys might be attempted to gain a cure for a sick person, for knowledge or simply for the experience.

Some of the same herbs, such as datura, have been traditionally used in India both for religious purposes, pleasure, and as poisons. Likewise, the fly agaric mushroom, *Amanita muscaria,* has been proposed as the source of *soma,* the drink of the gods in the ancient Hindu scriptures. Unlike the peyote and *ayahuasca* of the New World, plants such as henbane, datura or fly agaric can be fatally poisonous—they continue to claim victims today. Therefore, if sixteenth-century witches such as Laguna's indeed were using them, they likely were heirs to an underground tradition of safe preparation and use, although we do not know what form such a shamanic tradition might have taken.

Witchcraft as "The Old Religion"

The identity and motives of the witches and their accusers continue to be re-interpreted. In the period from 1890 to 1930, however, one interpretation of the trials not only blossomed but produced a genuine new religion. That was the theory that the witches followed an underground pre-Christian religion. Even though most modern scholars reject the notion, it contributed to the birth of today's fast-growing Neopagan Witchcraft.

Charles Godfrey Leland, an American lawyer, political journalist, and folklore scholar who lived a number of years in the Italian city of Florence, produced three books in the 1890s arguing that some Italian peasants, through their innate religious conservatism, maintained not only a pre-Christian but a pre-Roman religion, dating to the days of the ancient Etruscan culture. Camouflaged with Catholic saints' names and other details, this hidden "Old Religion" maintained its own deities, creation stories, prayers, and rituals, Leland wrote, describing these surviving bits of Paganism as "something more than a sorcery and something less than a faith." His most influential book, *Aradia: or the Gospel of the Witches,* published in 1899, synthesized traditional legends with material gathered for him by a woman known as Maddalena or Margherita (her surname may have been Talenti) and translated from local dialects into standard Italian, which Leland spoke and wrote moderately well. Aradia, which Leland claims was originally a Semitic goddess name, is described as the daughter of Diana, goddess of darkness, and Lucifer, god of light. Aradia comes to earth, and in the style of Michelet, teaches her ceremonies to outlaws and outcasts, as well as the secrets of poisoning corrupt feudal lords. What remains problematic about *Aradia* is the source of Leland's witchcraft gospel. Is it genuine, or did Maddalena herself concoct it to please her wealthy American patron, or did Leland shape it from a body of genuine invocations, stories, and folk practices?

Twenty years after Leland's work, the English archaeologist Margaret Murray (1862–1963) developed her own version of the "Old Religion" through her reading of witch-trial records from the British Isles and France. A recognized Egyptologist, Murray turned her attention to the witch-cult problem while World War I prevented her from working in Egypt. Her 1921 book *The Witch Cult in Western Europe* and its two successors laid out an apparently clear picture of the Old Religion. Even though that picture has largely been refuted by more recent historians such as Russell Hope Robbins, Elliot Rose, L'Estrange Ewen, and Ronald Hutton, its evocative power threatened to overwhelm the former academically accepted idea of the medieval and early modern witches as victims of bigotry, social stresses, and mob psychology. Many followers of modern Witchcraft continue to accept large portions of Murray's version of earlier witchcraft.

In essence, her version was this. The "witch cult" was a pre-Christian religion centered on a fertility god (somewhat parallel to the Greek Pan), whom Christian theologians deliberately confused with their Devil in order to persecute the witches. This god was often depicted with horns, and a man portrayed and embodied him during group rituals. (Murray had much less to say about goddesses than did Leland.) Covens of witches, ideally consisting of thirteen persons, grouped together at four major holidays—Candlemas, around 1 February; May Day; Lammas, around 1 August; and All Hallows or Hallowe'en. These large-group meetings, with their feasting and fertility rituals, alternated with smaller meetings ("esbats") for spell-casting and other local witch business.

In medieval England, Murray claimed, the Old Religion had been protected by the Plantagenet dynasty of kings, beginning with William the Conqueror in 1066. These were "sacred kings" who had to die as sacrificial victims or else find a substitute after they had reigned for seven years, or a multiple of seven years. Murray held that the murder in 1170 of the archbishop of Canterbury, Thomas à Becket (later made a saint), supposedly at the orders of King Henry II, his longtime friend, was actually the substitution of a voluntary victim for the king himself. Murray also maintained that the French mystical warrior maiden Joan of Arc (1412–1431) was in fact a priestess of the Old Religion. This underground religion, in Murray's view, permeated medieval society, and its followers left traces in the carvings on Christian churches and in folklore.

Murray's views were almost immediately attacked by historians who pointed out that she manipulated evidence, lifted quotations from witch-trial records out of context, and ignored evidence that did not fit her theory. But her picture of the "Old Religion" was embraced by many folklorists, occultists, and all those who wanted to believe that British rural life retained traces of ancient Paganism, even after 1500 years of Christianity.

Neopagan Witchcraft

Neopagan Witchcraft is the only worldwide religion to have begun in England. Its apparent birth date lies between 1939 and 1951, when the Witchcraft Act of 1735 was repealed by Parliament and reports about people claiming to follow the religion of Witchcraft began appearing in British newspapers. Contemporary Witchcraft appears to have multiple parents, and historians of religion continue to debate who exactly was present at its creation, for no solid evidence exists of a religious continuity with pre-Christian Paganism. This new religion of Witchcraft (usually capitalized it differentiate from definitions 1, 2, and 4 above) has grown rapidly in all English-speaking countries and in Western Europe, aided by its compatibility with the feminist and environmental movements. It is often referred to as Wicca, although some Neopagan Witches limit that term to the "tradition" founded by Gerald Gardner (see below), and as "The Craft," a term borrowed from Freemasonry along with certain aspects of Masonic ritual.

The most public figure associated with the new religion of Witchcraft was Gerald Gardner (1884–1964). Gardner spent most of his adult life in Britain's Asian colonies, owning and managing tea plantations and later working for the colonial customs service in Malaya. He and his wife retired to England in 1936. During his time in Asia, his lifelong interest in magic and the supernatural led him both to the Masonic order and to visits with Buddhists priests, tribal shamans, spiritualists, and any other practitioners he chanced across.

In 1949 Gardner published an adventure novel, *High Magic's Aid,* set in the Middle Ages and incorporating much ceremonial magic. He claimed that he had met members of a surviving witches' coven shortly before World War II, operating under the cover of the Rosicrucian Theatre at Christchurch, Hampshire, and headed by a wealthy widow. He had been accepted into the group, which performed a magical ritual during the summer of 1940 to stop the threatened German invasion of England (thus identifying the Witches with the patriotic soul of Great Britain). In 1954 his nonfiction book *Witchcraft Today* was published, which he wrote in the voice of a sympathetic outsider describing the modern continuation of an ancient fertility religion. Margaret Murray supplied an approving introduction.

Subsequent research suggests that it is more likely that Gardner and a female companion whose Craft name was Dafo, plus possibly other individuals, actually began the coven. They drew inspiration for their practices from ceremonial magic, from Classical Pagan religions, and from British folklore. What Gardner in 1954 described as "Wica" or cult of the "wise people" contained "no crucifixes, inverted or otherwise, no sermons, mock or otherwise, and no absolution or [eucharistic] hosts save for the cake and wine. . . . There is no praise or homage to the Devil, no liturgy, evil or otherwise, nothing is said backwards, and there are no gestures with the left hand; in fact with the exception that it is a religious service and all religious services resemble one another, the rites are not in any way an imitation of anything I have ever seen."

In other words, Gardner denied the reality of "Burning Times" witchcraft with its pacts with the Devil and parodies of Christian ritual. For this he substituted a Murray-style "Old Religion," in which the "Devil" was merely the ritual leader with his crown of stag's horns—and often a nobleman in disguise. Witchcraft, he alleged, had come down from the Stone Age as a fertility religion that honored the "God of death and what comes after" (in other words, rest and reincarnation) and the Great Mother Goddess of nature, love, and pleasure.

These new Witches celebrated a cycle of eight festivals a year—the solstices and equinoxes and the four cross-quarter days between them: Lugnasadh or Lammas (Loaf-Mass) at the beginning of August, a harvest festival; Samhain (Hallowe'en) a festival honoring the ancestors; Brigid or Oimelc, at the beginning of February, a feast of creativity and new beginnings; and Beltane, at the beginning of May, celebrating the new growing season. New Moons and full Moons were times of magic-working as opposed to the celebration and attunement of the seasonal festivals.

They worshipped in the nude, a practice indeed claimed of medieval witches. Gardner and his first associations were "naturists," people who advocated sunbathing for better health, and he and his first associates purchased land next to a naturist club north of London. While many Neopagan Witches today wear either ritual robes or other clothing, those who continue to meet nude or "skyclad" claim that the practice erases social distinctions, helps them to overcome the fear of aging and death, and makes magic-working easier.

Other common practices include the creation of a temporary sacred space, the circle, usually marked by candles, which may be drawn indoors or out, but which is erased at the conclusion of a ceremony. Most Neopagan Witchcraft rituals involve the use of a sacred knife, the *athame,* symbolizing the God, and a chalice symbolizing the Goddess.

Coven leadership typically lies with the high priestess ("high" because all experienced Witches are considered to be priests and priestesses themselves) who may or may not have a permanent male partner. This combination of female leadership and a powerful feminine image of deity has drawn many women to the Craft, which they see as a religion that values and sacralizes their bodies, their cycles, their ability to nurture as well as their rage and anger against other male-dominated religions.

Gardner's coven produced a number of offshoots in Britain in the 1950s and 1960s. In addition, other Witches came forth who claimed (sometimes falsely) to have no connection with his coven but rather to represent independent traditions of Witchcraft. These included Alex Sanders (1926–1988), Robert Cochrane (d. 1966) and Sybil Leek, who emigrated to the United States in 1965, where she continued to write books on occult topics and to lecture on Witchcraft.

Two more British Witches of Gardner's lineage, Ray and Rosemary Buckland, moved to Long Island, New York, in the mid-1960s and many American and Canadian "Gardnerian" Witches trace their initiatory lineage to them.

Meanwhile, modern Pagan religions were being developed independently in the United States and elsewhere during the 1960s, including Feraferia in Los Angeles, The Church of All Worlds in St. Louis, and others. However, as more books about Witchcraft were being published, including an edition of the basic Gardnerian ritual manual, the **Book of Shadows,** in 1973, followers of these new movements tended to adopt many of the key characteristics of Gardner's tradition—or else to define themselves in opposition to it. Those saying that they followed some other form of Witchcraft often cast it in ethnic terms such as Italian or Scottish. Other forms of Witchcraft include women-only groups (often called "Dianic" Witchcraft) and male-only groups, including the Radical Faeries.

By the 1980s, most elders and leaders in Witchcraft began to distance themselves from claims of an unbroken pre-Christian religious tradition, saying instead that their practices were inspired by ancient Paganism but adapted to the present times. Whether known as Wicca or Witchcraft, this new religious movement grew steadily from the 1970s to the present, typically among people in their twenties and thirties. The Cold War expansion of the American military provided one means, as Wiccan personnel shuttled between the United States, Europe, and elsewhere. Neopagan Witchcraft is now found throughout the English-speaking world and parts of Europe, particularly Germany, the Netherlands, and Scandinavia.

The historian Ronald Hutton describes these common characteristics of the "protean and ecclectic" varieties of Neopagan Witchcraft: They "aim to draw out and enhance divinity within human beings, abolish the traditional Western distinction between religion and magic, [are] a mystery religion or a set of mystery religions [and their essence lies] in the creative performance of ritual."

Estimates of total membership in North America range into the low millions, but since covens are fluid and ever-changing (and since not all Witches belong to covens), an accurate count is impossible. While Witchcraft has no sacred scriptures, modern Witches have produced dozens of books on the practice of their religion. Notable authors, besides those named, include Stewart and Janet Farrar, **Starhawk,** Scott Cunningham, Vivianne Crowley, Marion Weinstein, Margot Adler, Evan John Jones, and Michael Howard.

In the early 1970s, two organizations, the Church and School of Wicca and the Council of American Witches, began holding conventions for their members and other interested people in American hotels. By 1980, outdoor festivals began at campgrounds across the United States, beginning in the Midwest and spreading to both coasts, the South, and the Rocky Mountains. These provide a venue for the exchange of songs, ritual formats, and the merchandising of clothing, jewelry, and other artifacts of the Pagan lifestyle.

Sources:

Adler, Margot. *Drawing Down the Moon: Witches, Druids, Goddess-Worshippers, and Other Pagans in America Today.* Boston: Beacon, 1979, 1981.

Buckland, Raymond. *Buckland's Complete Book of Witchcraft.* St. Paul: Llewellyn Publications, 1986.

Crowley, Vivianne. *Wicca.* London: Thorsons, 1996.

Ewen, C. l'Estrange. *Witch Hunting and Witch Trials.* London: Kegan Paul, 1929.

Farrar, Stewart. *What Witches Do: The Modern Coven Revealed.* New York: Coward, McGann, & Geoghegan, 1973..

Gardner, Gerald B. *Witchcraft Today.* London: Rider & Co., 1954.

Ginzburg, Carlo. *Ecstasies: Deciphering the Witches' Sabbath.* New York: Penguin Books, 1991.

———. *Night Battles: Witchcraft & Agrarian Cults in the Sixteenth and Seventeenth Centuries.* New York: Penguin, 1983.

Glanvill, Joseph. *Saducismus Triumphatus.* London, 1681.

Hutton, Ronald. *The Stations of the Sun: A History of the Ritual Year in Britain.* Oxford: Oxford University Press, 1996.

———. *The Triumph of the Moon: A History of Modern Pagan Witchcraft.* Oxford: Oxford University Press, 1999.

Jones, Evan John and Chas S. Clifton. *Sacred Mask, Sacred Dance.* St. Paul: Llewellyn, 1997.

Jones, Evan John and Doreen Valiente. *Witchcraft: A Tradition Renewed.* Custer, Wash.: Phoenix, 1990.

Lea, Henry Charles. *Materials Towards a History of Witchcraft.* 3 vols. Philadelphia: University of Pennsylvania Press, 1939.

Leland, Charles G. *Aradia: or the Gospel of the Witches.* London: David Nutt, 1899.

Lewis, James R., ed. *Magical Religion and Modern Witchcraft.* Albany: State University of New York Press, 1996.

Luhrman, T. M. *Persuasions of the Witch's Craft.* Cambridge, Mass.: Harvard University Press, 1989.

Melton, J. Gordon, and Isotta Poggi. *Magic, Witchcraft, and Paganism in America: A Bibliography.* New York: Garland Publishing, 1992.

Michelet, Jules. *The Sorceress: A Study in Middle Age Superstition.* Paris, 1904. Reprint, London: Imperial Press, 1905. Reprint as: *Satanism and Witchcraft.* Wehman, 1939.

Murray, Margaret A. *The Witch-Cult in Western Europe.* Oxford: Oxford University Press, 1921.

Notestein, Wallace. *A History of Witchcraft in England from 1558 to 1718.* American Historical Association, 1911.

Orion, Loretta. *Never Again the Burning Times: Paganism Revived.* Prospect Heights, Ill.: Waveland, 1995.

Remy, Nicolas. *Demonolatry.* 1595. Edited by Montague Summers. London: John Rodker, 1930. Reprint, New Hyde Park, N.Y.: University Books, 1974.

Rose, Elliot. *A Razor for a Goat.* Toronto: University of Toronto Press, 1962.

Scot, Reginald. *Discoverie of Witchcraft.* London, 1584. Reprint, New York: Dover Publications, 1974.

Sprenger, Jakob, and Heinrich Kramer. *Malleus Maleficarum.* 1486. Translated and edited by Montague Summers. London: John Rodker, 1928.

Starhawk. *The Spiral Dance.* San Francisco: Harper, 1979.

Valiente, Doreen. *An ABC of Witchcraft Past and Present.* London: Robert Hale, 1973. Reprint, New York: St. Martin's Press, 1974.

———. *The Rebirth of Witchcraft.* London: Robert Hale, 1989.

Witchcraft Digest: Voice of the Old Religion

A short-lived supplement to the *WICA Newsletter.* It was edited by **Leo Louis Martello** and published by Witchcraft International Craft Association in New York City in the 1970s. Only a few issued appeared.

Witchcraft International Craft Association (WICA)

An early neopagan **witchcraft** organization founded in 1970 as the outward expression of the Sicilian Strege Wiccan tradition in America. WICA is led by Dr. **Leo Louis Martello,** who was a Spiritualist minister in New York City and was also known as a hypnotist and graphologist. Martello stepped into the spotlight within the Wiccan community through his authorship of one of the first widely recognized texts presenting modern post-Gardnerian witchcraft to the public, *Witchcraft: The Old Religion* (1973). He argued effectively that witches were people from all walks of life "who practice the pre-Judeo-Christian, Pagan religion." They were not Satanists and did not believe in the Devil, he said; their main deities were Mother Goddess and Horned God, and they were nature worshipers.

Martello also founded the Witches Antidefamation League (WADL) "to educate the public, counteract false accusations, take legal steps, obtain IRS recognition, paid legal holidays (such as Halloween) for members, fight distortion and discrimination, sponsor seminars across the country, hold regular festivals." In 1970 WICA and WADL, backed by the American Civil Liberties Union, sued the New York Parks Department for discrimination when refused a permit for their "witch-in," and won, the first such victory for witches in the history of the world.

The teachings of the Strege have never been revealed, though much of their lives and thought were written about by Charles B. Leland in his book *Aradia.* Diana is recognized as the major deity and the goddess of witches. During the 1970s Martello published the *Witchcraft Digest* and the *WICA Newsletter.* Books representative of the Strege are published through Hero Press. Last known address: 153 W. 80 St., Ste. 1B, New York, NY 10024.

Sources:

Martello, Leo Louis. *Weird Ways of Witchcraft.* New York: HC Publishers, 1969.

———. *What It Means to Be a Witch.* New York: The Author, 1975.

———. *Witchcraft: The Old Religion.* Secaucus, N.J.: University Books, 1973.

Witches Anti-Defamation League (WADL)

An early organization in the contemporary neo-pagan **witchcraft** movement founded by **Leo Louis Martello.** It was designed ". . . to educate the public, counteract false accusations, take legal steps, obtain IRS recognition, paid legal holidays (such as Halloween) for members, fight distortions, hold regular festivals."

Neo-pagan witches claim that they are descendants of the pagan religions that held sway in Europe prior to the forced conversion of the population to Christianity. They do not believe in the Devil or practice **Satanism.** This view was presented in Martello's book, *Witchcraft: The Old Religion.*

WADL functioned through the 1970s and was superseded by other similar organizations including the Aquarian Anti-Defamation League (1980s) and the presently existing Witches' League for Public Awareness.

Witches' Cradle

During the witchcraft persecutions in Europe, inquisitors were said to have sometimes put an accused witch in a bag, which was then strung up over the limb of a tree and set swinging. When witches learned about this punishment they experimented with it themselves and found that the **sensory deprivation** or confusion of senses it caused induced hallucinatory experiences. A similar technique has long been used by shamans and dervishes and is sometimes known as "dervish dangling." It involves being suspended by a rope tied around the waist.

Modern researchers have followed up on this insight and developed, among other devices, the ASCID (Altered States of Consciousness Induction Device). The ASCID was devised by **Robert Masters** and **Jean Houston** of the **Foundation for Mind Research.** This technological-age witches' cradle is a metal swing in which the subject stands while blindfolded and wearing earplugs. The motion of the swing exaggerates the slightest movement of the occupant. Profoundly altered states of consciousness involving hallucinatory visions and sensations often take place within 20 minutes.

Witte, Alfred (1878–1941)

German astrologer and founder of the Hamburg school of astrological interpretation. Witte was born in Hamburg, Germany, on March 2, 1878. As a young man, he worked for the city of Hamburg and then served in the German army during World War I. By the time the war started he had become interested in **astrology** and pursued his speculations while soldiering. He discovered a certain moving point in the zodiac that he found helpful in interpreting charts and he hypothesized the existence of a trans-Neptunian planet which he call Cupido. Such a planet would be discovered in 1930 and named Pluto.

After the War, Witte gathered a group of astrologers, especially Friedrich Sieggrün (1877–1951), to assist in developing his insights. The results were an innovative system of astrology that came to be known as Uranian Astrology or the Hamburg School, after Witte's hometown. As the system developed, Witte postulated first three additional planets, named Hades, Zeus, and Kronos, and then four additional imaginary planets. Criticism of the additional planets, unknown to anyone except Witte and his associates, was balanced by the good reports of satisfied clients.

Witte also introduced the idea of midpoints, another imaginary addition to the horoscope. As the name implies, a midpoint is a point halfway between any two planets in the chart. The combined influences of the two planets are evident at the midpoint. This combined influence is activated by planets in the present transiting the midpoint. The two planets and their midpoint together made a planetary picture and the various planetary pictures become an important element in chart interpretation.

The Hamburg School, as the Witte-Sieggrün system of interpretation was called, created a controversy in Germany for its challenge to traditional methods of astrological interpretation. Witte defended the system, for which he claimed outstanding results not provided by more traditional charts in several books, beginning with *Regelwerk für Planetenbilder* (1928).

Witte's system never gained support outside Germany and did not reemerge from the Nazi suppression of astrology in the late 1930s. It is remembered today primarily through cosmobiology, the system developed by **Reinhold Ebertin,** one of Witte's students. The Hamburg school was championed by Hermann Lefeldt after the war. Lefeldt published both a revised German edition of Witte's book and an English translation.

The progress of Uranian astrology stopped by Witte's suicide in Hamburg on August 2, 1941, a death possibly related to the rise of Nazism and the resulting suppression of astrology in Germany.

Sources:

Brau, Jean-Louis, Helean Weaver, and Allan Edwards. *Larousse Encyclopedia of Astrology.* New York: New American Library, 1982.

Holden, James H., and Robert A. Hughes. *Astrological Pioneers of America.* Tempe, Ariz.: American Federation of Astrologers, 1988.

Witte, Alfred. *Regelwerk für Planetbilder.* 3d ed. Hamburg: Witte Verlag, 1935. Translated by Richard Svehla as *Rules for Planetary Pictures.* Hamburg: Witte Verlag, 1939.

Witte, Alfred, and Herman Lefeldt. *Rules for Planetary Pictures.* Translated by Kurt Knupfer. Hamburg: L. Rudolph (Witte Verlag), 1974.

The Wolf

Among the ancient Romans, there were many tales in which the wolf figured as a good or evil omen. A wolf running to the right with his mouth full was a sign of great joy. If a wolf escaped unhurt after he had entered a Roman camp, it was regarded as a sign of the army's defeat, and the terrible result of the second Punic war was said to have been foretold when a wolf carried off the sword of a sentinel.

Plutarch related the story of a wolf who ate the landmarks of a proposed new settlement in Libya and thus stopped its colonization, but later another wolf, which had stolen a burnt sacrifice, led his pursuers to the place where they later settled. It is said that a wolf ran off with Hiero's slate when he was a schoolboy, and this was regarded as a sign of his future greatness.

The peasants of Sweden used to avoid speaking of a wolf by name but called it "grey one" or "old grey"; speaking its name was seen as unlucky.

The wolf is featured in Roman mythology in the story of Romulus and Remus, and throughout history there have been stories of feral children—orphans reared by wolves. For a modern case, see Charles Maclean, *The Wolf Children* (1978). As the **werewolf** the wolf was the most popular animal mentioned in accounts of **lycanthropy.**

Wolfsohn, Alfred (1896–1962)

German singing teacher who ran a school of psychophysical vocal development in England during the 1940s and 1950s and revived legends of the occult power of sound. During World War I he served in the trenches and suffered a breakdown; he was haunted by the sound of a voice calling for help. When the Nazis came to power, he was deeply impressed by the evil power associated with the voice of Adolf Hitler, which was amplified over street corners and the great square at Nuremberg and moved people to destructive acts of folly, hatred, ambition, and unspeakable cruelty.

Wolfsohn played a significant role in the life of artist Charlotte Salomon, and he features in her posthumous autobiography *Leben oder Theater* (1981). Wolfsohn had been engaged by Salomon's stepmother, opera singer Paula Lindberg. Salomon, a German Jew, was murdered in the Auschwitz extermination camp by the Nazis, but her paintings and prose had been left with a doctor in France before she was arrested. Salomon's book has been compared with *The Diary of Anne Frank,* and it was the basis of the film *Charlotte* by Dutch director Frans Weisz.

Before he escaped from Germany to serve with the British forces, Wolfsohn had the idea that it must be possible for the voice to have positive power. He also believed that ordinary men and women have potentialities seldom seen, but when placed under stress, they could achieve feats of physical endurance, run faster, see further, shout louder, or bear pain in a way they had not believed possible. Wolfsohn became a kind of voice doctor, working to restore fine and beautiful tones to singers suffering from fear or overstrain and also developing a kind of psychotherapy around the vocal possibilities of ordinary individuals.

In his studio in London, England, he experimented to prove that the conventional musical classifications of male and female voices from bass to soprano were artificial divisions, and that any normal human male or female could develop the whole range in a single voice and in the process discover heightened consciousness. Wolfsohn demonstrated a range of eight octaves in male and female voices, old and young. His pupils figured in the *Guinness Book of Records* after demonstrating phenomenal vocal range.

Wolfsohn's work has been described as a spontaneous revival of what is known as *surat shabd yoga* (the yoga of sound vibration), as taught by the Radhasoami Sat Sang and other spiritual teachers such as **Swami Nadabrahmananda** of **Swami Sivananda**'s Divine Life Society. After Wolfsohn's death, some members of his group carried on under his pupil Roy Hart, and a film was made of their remarkable *sprechstimme* performances. The group tended to concentrate on a new application of extended vocal range in theater rather than in musical sound. Roy Hart also died soon afterward, in 1975, but the members of his group have carried on his work.

The only extant record of the work of Wolfsohn's pupils is the album *Vox Humana* issued by Folkways Records, New York, in 1956. Former pupils of Wolfsohn who adapted his techniques to theater under Roy Hart as the Roy Hart Theatre Group can be reached at Chateau de Malerargues, Thoiras, Aduze 30140, France. The therapeutic aspect of Wolfsohn's work has been carried on by Derek Gale at the Gale Centre for Creative Therapy.

Wood, C. E. (1854– ?)

British **materialization** medium. She was born in October 1854. In 1873, at the age of 18, she was employed, with **Annie Fairlamb,** as an official medium by the Newcastle Spiritual Evidence Society. Fairlamb was a year younger. Both mediums apparently demonstrated **telekinesis.** Wood had shown the first signs of psychic power a year before at a meeting of the society to which she had been taken by her father, a mechanic. She stayed with the society for three years.

In 1874, partial materializations were obtained. Over the next few years there were some outstanding phenomena reported. For example, T. B. Barkas, a prominent Newcastle investigator, wrote in the *Medium and Daybreak* (May 4, 1877):

"I have seen, through the mediumship of Miss Wood, in a private house, living forms walk from the curtained recess, which it was utterly impossible for her to simulate. I have seen children, women and men of various ages, walk forth under her mediumship. I have seen a materialised form and the medium at the same time. I have had through her mediumship a child-like form standing beside me for about half an hour together; the child has placed its arms around my neck and permitted me at the same time to place my arm around her neck, and has laid its cheek against mine, breathed upon my face, and, in fact, caressed me precisely as a child would do its parent or guardian. This was not in darkness but in light, and in the presence of professors and fellows of one of the leading universities in the kingdom. I have, under these conditions, and after having handled the psychic form, seen it gradually vanish or dematerialise and become invisible in the middle of the room."

Barkas also remarked that "she is subject to strange controls, which there is some difficulty in banishing."

Alfred Smedley, in *Some Reminiscences* (1900), also reported on séances with Wood. While the medium was enclosed in a wire cage her phantom "Bennie" left excellent paraffin wax molds of his foot. In front of the sitters, he dipped his foot into the hot dish of paraffin and cold water, then put his left leg across his right knee, tapped the mold, dematerialized his leg, and, when the mold was free, handed it to Mr. Adshead. In the same séance, another left leg mold was obtained from "Maggie," Wood's deceased sister. On measurement it was found to be one inch less in length and one and three quarter inches less in breadth than Wood's foot.

In 1878, **Henry Sidgwick** engaged her for séances at Cambridge University and at the house of **Arthur Balfour. F. W. H. Myers** and **Edmund Gurney** were among the investigators. **Alfred Russel Wallace** wrote in his book *My Life* (2 vols., 1905) that Myers showed him several books full of notes on these séances and described to him the test that they applied. They tied the wrists of the medium securely with tape, leaving two long ends that they tacked down to the floor, covered with sealing wax, and sealed. As the medium lay on a mattress on the bare floor, the light was sufficient to see phantom figures of children and adults issuing from the cabinet. The tapes, knots, and seals were found afterward to be untampered with.

On the chance objection that the medium might provide herself with tape, tacks, wax, and seal, they varied the color of the sealing wax and the pattern of the seal and also employed a hammock that, by means of pulleys, was put on a weighing machine. Nevertheless, the phenomena occurred as before. Myers had never published these experiences.

Morell Theobald (at one time involved in a massive fraudulent mediumship scandal) in his book *Spirit Workers in the Home Circle* (1887) had some moving if nonevidential observations of Wood. "Pocka," a "vivacious coloured little sprite about three feet high" not only came out of the cabinet, but "went to my wife who was sitting 4 or 5 feet from the cabinet, took her hand, and as my wife leaned downwards she put her tiny arms round her neck and kissed her. Crossing over the room she took my hands, then my daughter's and afterwards my daughter-in-law's hands, fondled them a bit, and retired to the cabinet."

However, like most materialization mediums who operated for any length of time, Wood was caught in **fraud.** In the mid-1870s, for example, the materialized form was seized and found to be the medium, after which Wood opined "that she was an unconscious instrument temporarily in the hands of an evil power." In 1882 Wood was exposed in Peterborough by spirit grabbing. "Pocka," her Indian child **control,** was found to be the medium on her knees, partially undressed and covered with muslin, which she attempted to conceal about her person.

Sources:

Smedley, Alfred, and T. P. Barkas. *Some Reminiscences of Alfred Smedley . . . also an Account of Miss Wood's Mediumship.* London: "Light," 1900.

Woodhull, Victoria Claflin (1838–1927)

American Spiritualist, social reformer, and feminist. Born September 23, 1838, in Homer, Licking County, Ohio, she traveled with a medicine show when only a child, giving demonstrations of fortune-telling and Spiritualist séances together with her younger sister Tennessee (1846–1923). Victoria married Canning Woodhull, a physician, before she was 16, was divorced in 1864, and later remarried twice.

In 1868 the sisters moved to New York City where they met Cornelius Vanderbilt, who was interested in Spiritualism. Vanderbilt installed them in a stock-brokerage office as Woodhull, Claflin & Company, where the "Lady Brokers" made considerable profits. From this enterprise they founded the journal *Woodhull and Claflin's Weekly* in 1870. This publication advocated equal rights for women, free love, and other feminist issues.

In 1871, Victoria Woodhull spoke on women's rights before the House Judiciary Committee and became a prominent leader in the cause of women's suffrage. In 1872 she was the first woman to be nominated for the presidency, sponsored by the Equal Rights Party. Although she did not expect to be elected, she and her sister publicized their cause and attracted much attention by attempting to vote.

The February 2, 1872, issue of their *Weekly* contained a sensational story alleging intimacy between Henry Ward Beecher and the wife of Theodore Tilton. This scandal was reported largely to discredit Beecher's sisters, who had attacked the *Weekly*'s stand on free love. In the event, Beecher went on a trial for adultery, but was exonerated. Interestingly enough the *Weekly* was the first periodical in the United States to publish the *Communist Manifesto.*

In 1877, the sisters moved to England, where they continued to publicize women's rights. Victoria Woodhull married a wealthy London banker and became well known for charitable work. With her daughter, Zula Maud Woodhull, Woodhull published *Humanitarian* magazine from 1892 to 1910. She died in England June 10, 1927.

Sources:

Brough, James. *The Vixens.* New York: Simon and Schuster, 1980.

Melton, J. Gordon. *Religious Leaders of America.* Detroit: Gale Research, 1991.

Woodhull, Victoria. *Garden of Eden: Allegorical Meaning Revealed.* London: The author, 1889.

———. *Humanitarian Government.* London: The author, 1892.

———. *Stirpiculture; or, the Scientific Propagation of the Human Race.* London: The author, 1888.

Woodhull, Victoria, and Tennessee Claflin. *The Human Body the Temple of God.* London, 1890.

Woodman, William Robert (1828–1891)

British physician. Woodman was a member of the **Societas Rosicruciana in Anglia** and one of the founders (with **W. W. Westcott** and **S. L. M. Mathers**) of the magic society the Hermetic Order of the **Golden Dawn.**

Woodman was a student of **Kabala,** Egyptian antiquities, **Gnosticism,** and Platonism. In 1867 he became secretary of the Rosicrucian Society and in 1878 was supreme magus. His magic motto in the Golden Dawn was "Vincit Omnia Veritas" (Truth rules all).

Sources:

King, Francis. *The Rites of Modern Occult Magic.* New York: Macmillan, 1970.

Woodroffe, Sir John (1865–1936)

The pioneering scholar of the beliefs and practices of the **Tantra,** a group of religious and occult Hindu scriptures emphasizing the female energy known as **kundalini.** He was born December 15, 1865, the eldest son of J. T. Woodroffe, advocate general of Bengal, India. He was educated at Woburn Park School and Oxford University, England, where he took classes in jurisprudence.

He was called to the bar in 1889, and a year later he was enrolled as an advocate of the Calcutta High Court. He became a fellow of Calcutta University and was appointed Tagore Law Professor. In collaboration with Ameer Ali he published the widely used textbook *Civil Procedure in British India.*

In 1902 he became standing counsel to the government of India, and in 1904 he was raised to the High Court bench, where he served for a number of years before being appointed chief justice in 1915. Upon his retirement he became a reader in Indian law at Oxford University. He died at Beausoleil (Alpes Maritimes) on January 16, 1936, at the age of 70.

In addition to his official duties, he spent many years translating some then little-known Hindu scriptures and in the study of Hindu culture. These were published under the pseudonym "Arthur Avalon." They provided many Western scholars with their initial entre into a major, if minority, perspective in Indian religion. Even under a pseudonym, however, he had to cover the discussion of the Tantrics' sexual practices with indirect allusions. He also published several volumes of *Tantrik Texts.*

Sources:

Avalon, Arthur [Sir John Woodroffe]. *The Garland of Letters: Studies in the Mantra Shastra.* 1922. Reprint, Madras: Ganesh, 1963.

———. *The Great Liberation (Mahanirvana Tantra).* Madras: Ganesh, 1927.

———. *Hymns to the Goddess.* London: Luzac, 1913.

———. *The Serpent Power.* 1918. Reprint, New York: Dover Publications, 1974.

Woodruff, Joseph L(eroy) (1913–1988)

Professor of psychology active in the field of parapsychology. He was born October 8, 1913, in Galesburg, Illinois. He studied at Tarkio College, Missouri (B.A., 1936) and Duke University (M.A., 1939; Ph.D., 1941). While at Duke, Woodruff, in conjunction with **Joseph G. Pratt,** conducted one of the most famous **ESP** tests, still generally considered one of the best ever carried out in parapsychology.

In 1946 he began a lengthy tenure teaching psychology at the City College of New York. For some years Woodruff conducted quantitative research in extrasensory perception, with particular reference to the relationship between certain subjective aspects of card-calling and success in calling. In 1959 he became the secretary of the board of trustees of the **American Society for Psychical Research.** He was also a charter member of the **Parapsychological Association.** He died July 23, 1988.

Sources:

Berger, Arthur S., and Joyce Berger. *The Encyclopedia of Parapsychology and Psychical Research.* New York: Paragon House, 1991.

Pleasants, Helene, ed. *Biographical Dictionary of Parapsychology.* New York: Helix Press, 1964.

Woodruff, J. L. "Some Basic Problems for Parapsychological Research." *Journal of Parapsychology* 12 (1948).

Woodruff, J. L., and Laura A. Dale. "ESP Function and the Psychogalvanic Response." *Journal* of the American Society for Psychical Research 46 (1952).

———. "The Psychokinetic Effect: Further ASPR Experiments." *Journal* of the American Society for Psychical Research 41 (1947).

———. "Subject and Experimenter Attitudes in Relation to ESP Scoring." *Journal* of the American Society for Psychical Research 44 (1950).

Woodruff, J. L., and J. G. Pratt. "Size of Stimulus Symbols in Extrasensory Perception." *Journal of Parapsychology* 3 (1939).

Woodruff, Maurice (1916–1973)

Famous **clairvoyant** whose American television shows attracted a large audience. His syndicated column reached nearly fifty million people and at the height of his career he was receiving 5,000 letters a week from individuals seeking advice. He had a reputation for highly accurate predictions made under any conditions, without special atmosphere or restrictions. He forecast the end of the Vietnam War, the death of President John F. Kennedy, and many other important world events. He died from a heart attack January 28, 1973, while in Singapore.

Worcester, Constance Rulison (1896–1986)

Daughter of Episcopal minister and psychical researcher Elwood Worcester. She was born July 25, 1896, in Bethlehem, Pennsylvania. She attended Bryn Mawr College (1915–17) and Radcliffe College, Cambridge, Massachusetts (B.A., 1921). She worked with **James H. Hyslop** and **Walter Franklin Prince** on the study of spontaneous parapsychological phenomena during the 1920s and 1930s and later with **Gardner Murphy** and **J. B. Rhine.** She died in August of 1986.

Worcester, Elwood (1862–1940)

Episcopal clergyman, psychical researcher, and founder of the Emmanuel movement, which pioneered medicine and psychotherapy in conjunction with spiritual guidance for individuals with physical, mental, and nervous problems. Through **James H. Hyslop** he became interested in psychical research, and he was a founder of the **Boston Society for Psychic Research,** of which he was president from 1925 until his death.

Worcester was born on May 16, 1862, in Massillon, Ohio. He studied at Columbia College, New York (B.A., 1886), General Theological Seminary, New York (1887), and Leipzig University (Ph.D., 1889). He was ordained in 1891. He served as rector at St. Stephen's Church, Philadelphia (1896–1904) prior to his quarter of a century at Emmanuel Episcopal Church in Boston

(1904–29). While at Emmanuel he began to work with a group of pioneering psychotherapists, including Joseph H. Pratt, Richard C. Cabot, and Isador H. Ciriat. Out of their collaboration emerged the Emmanuel movement, one of the early spiritual healing movements in mainline Protestantism (later superseded by the Order of St. Luke).

In the mid 1920s, Worcester became associated with the group within the **American Society for Psychical Research** (ASPR) that believed that medium **Mina Crandon** was a fake. They left the organization and founded the Boston Society for Psychic Research in 1925. Worcester retired a few years later but continued to serve as the society's president almost until the time it was reincorporated into the ASPR.

Worcester wrote a number of books, including several titles with Samuel McComb, who was for many years the associate rector at Emmanuel. He died July 19, 1940, at Kennebunkport, Maine.

Sources:

Melton, J. Gordon. *Religious Leaders of America.* Detroit: Gale Research, 1991.

Worcester, Elwood. *Allies of Religion.* Boston: Marshall Jones, 1929.

———. *The Christian Religion as a Healing Power.* New York: Moffat, Yard, 1909.

———. *Life's Adventure.* New York: Charles Scribner's Sons, 1932.

Worcester, Elwood, and Samuel McComb. *Body, Mind and Spirit.* Boston: Marshall Jones, 1931.

Worcester, Elwood, Samuel McComb, and Isador Ciriat. *Religion and Medicine.* New York: Moffat, Yard, 1908.

World Congress of Faiths

Interfaith organization founded in 1936 by British explorer, soldier, and mystic **Sir Francis Younghusband** (1863–1942). The congress is dedicated to the work of reconciliation between different world faiths and the removal of intolerance and exclusivism, to ". . . instill a spirit of fellowship among mankind through religion, and . . . to revitalise all that is highest in man's spiritual being."

The congress combines dissemination of knowledge of world religions with the building of friendly relationships between them. It encourages interreligious understanding through personal contacts and frank dialogue and believes that all great religions have much to learn from each other.

The congress arranges lectures, debates, visits to religious centers, "All Faith Services," and annual conferences. Speakers from different faiths give talks at schools and colleges. A journal, *World Faiths Encounter,* includes news of activities, book reviews, and articles of religious interest, and a newsletter, *One Family,* is published regularly. Although there are branches in Kent, Bath, and Bristol, the congress headquarters are located at 2 Market St., Oxford OX1 3EF England. Website: http://www.interfaith-center.org/wcf/.

Sources:

World Congress of Faiths. http://www.interfaith-center.org/wcf/. March 8, 2000.

World Goodwill

An organization founded in 1932 to apply the teachings of former Theosophist **Alice A. Bailey** (1880–1949) in the social context, specifically to improve human relations in the world. Bailey founded the **Arcane School** to propagate the theosophical teachings that came through her channelings from the Tibetan Master. World Goodwill extends the work of the Arcane School by mobilizing the constructive power of goodwill in society to dealing with problems throughout the world.

The organization supports the work of the United Nations and is recognized as an accredited nongovernmental organization. As such, it provides advice and assistance to individuals and groups concerned with world service projects. One of its activities has been the formation of **triangles,** a linkage of individuals who employ constructive thought in a daily meditation of groups of three, invoking "the energies of light and goodwill" in a "network of light."

The energies are visualized as circulating through three points of a triangle, connecting with other triangles. This network carries the "great invocation" or universal prayer, forming "a channel for the downpouring of light and love into the body of humanity."

World Goodwill is associated with *Lucis Trust,* which is located at 120 Wall St., 24th Fl., New York, NY 10005. It also has subsidiary offices at 3 Whitehall Ct., Ste. 54, London SW1A 2EF, England, and also in Geneva. Website: http://www.lucistrust.org/.

Sources:

Sinclair, John E. *The Alice Bailey Inheritance.* Wellingborough, England: Turnstone Press, 1984.

World Goodwill. http://www.lucistrust.org/. March 8, 2000.

World League of Illuminati

In 1880, **Theodor Reuss,** a druggist, singer, and student of the esoteric, launched an attempt to reactivate the **Illuminati,** the order originally founded by Adam Weishaupt (1748–1830) in 1776 and destroyed in 1785. The first lodge was opened in Munich, Germany. The Berlin lodge opened in 1895, and soon afterwards Reuss met an actor named Leopold Engel (1858–1931). They became involved in several activities, including the founding of the German section of the **Theosophical Society.** Engel was interested in all things psychic, and practiced mesmerism and naturopathic healing. Like Reuss, he also had the idea of reviving the Illuminati and had himself founded the World League of Illuminati in 1893. In 1896 he joined Ruess' Order of Illuminati and in 1899, they formally merged the two organizations.

On March 12, 1901, Reuss, Engel, and a group of their order members met and drafted a document that was backdated to the first day of the new century, January 1, 1900. It reestablished the then-dormant Munich lodge and asserted the order's authority to found Masonic lodges. Reuss was affirmed as the order's master. The founding of the new Munich lodge was duly announced as a regular Masonic lodge open to master Masons. Masons objected that it was merely an offshoot of the Illuminati and not Masonic. Reuss simply severed its connection with the Order of Illuminati. As a result, he and Engel quarreled. They patched up their relationship for a while, but in 1902 went their separate ways.

Actually, Reuss was losing his interest in the Illuminati. He renewed a relationship with **Karl Kellner** and began the process that would lead to the founding of the **Ordo Templi Orientis** (OTO). In the meantime, Engel reestablished the World League of the Illuminati and issued a new set of regulations at the beginning of 1903. Three years later, he issued a manifesto in the form of a history of the order. He took extra pains to separate his position from that of Reuss, now operating under the OTO banner.

The World League survived through the 1930s and drew on a variety of Masonic and Rosicrucian sources. Engel died on October 8, 1931. He was succeeded by Julius Meyer. Then on September 22, 1934, the League was closed down by the Gestapo, and much of its material confiscated. Work of the order was immediately transferred to the regional groups. As early as 1896, Engel had opened a group in Austria and a Swiss group was founded in 1929. A Polish group opened in 1937, but as with the Austrian group, it was closed after the Nazi takeover of the country. Only the Swiss group under Karl Brodbeck operated through World War II (1939–45).

Meyer was able to revive what was now known as the Illuminaten Orden (IO) after the war. He charged Maximillian Haitz with the task of reassembling the archive that the Gestapo seized, which he was partially able to accomplish. Eduard Korbel revived the IO in **Austria.** Following Brodbeck's death in 1955, Hermann Joseph Metzger (1919–1990) assumed leadership of the Swiss IO. That same year, P. Kirchvogel emerged as the new international leader of the World League, Julius Meyer having died in 1953. In 1963 Kirchvogel passed that office to Metzger.

Metzger had already begun work on a master vision that included the uniting of a various Magical/occult lineages/activities in his person. In 1947 he had taken over a publishing house, Psychosophische Gesellschaft, following the death of its owner. In 1957 he had become a bishop, and then in 1960, the patriarch of the Gnostic Catholic Church, a church that traces its history to the **apparition of the Virgin Mary** and subsequent consecration to the bishopric of **Jules-Benoit Doinel** (1842–1902). Metzger had also joined the Ordo Templi Orientis, the order cofounded by Reuss and passed to magician **Aleister Crowley.** In 1963, Crowley's successor as Outer Head of the Order, **Karl Johannes Germer** (1885–1962), died. Metzger held an election of the German-speaking leadership and in 1963 proclaimed himself the new Outer Head.

The World League was merged into what Metzger called the Ordo Illuminatorum (OI). The work of the new OI includes 13 degrees that borrow material from all of the different organizations over which Metzger had attained control. The 13th degree was the administrative degree for the international leaders, including the Aeropagus of the Illuminati.

Sources:

Anson, Peter. *Bishops at Large.* London: Faber and Faber, 1964.

Koenig, Peter R. "Illuminati and Templars." http://cyberlink.ch/koenig/illumin.htm. April 21, 2000.

Worlds Beyond (Fund)

A special appeal fund of the **National Spiritualist Association of Churches** to promote knowledge of **Spiritualism** on radio and television. Formerly titled "Satellite Séances," this fund is based upon the idea that mass media provides:

". . . an opportunity to show to the world the true facts about 'life after death' and 'communication.' Even now, many outside organizations are stimulating their forces to counter-censor or attempt to head off these facts. . . . Those in spirit are anxious for us to open wide the door between the two worlds of life. All we have to do is present the facts in the true light. . . . The time is now for unification of world Spiritualism. The time is now for Spiritualists to step forward confidently and face the 21st century. The time is now for Worlds Beyond. Once these programs are on the air they can attract the support they need to continue through direct appeals to viewers."

The NSAC Worlds Beyond fund can be contacted at P.O. Box 128, Cassadaga, FL 32706.

Worlds, Planes, or Spheres (in Theosophy)

According to the teachings of **Theosophy,** deriving in part from esoteric Hinduism, the universe is divided into seven planes. Beginning with the one closest to God, they are referred to as the divine, *adi;* monadic, *anutadaka;* spiritual, *nirvana;* intuitional, *buddhi;* mental, *manas;* astral, *kama;* and physical, *sthula.* These worlds are not physically separate in the manner that planets appear to be, but interpenetrate, and their differences depend on the relative density of the matter that composes them and the consequent difference in the rates at which the matter of each world vibrates.

Except for the physical world (the densest), our knowledge of them, so far as it extends, is dependent on **clairvoyance.** The more exalted the vision of the clairvoyant, the higher the world his or her vision can pierce. Each world has its appropriate inhabitants, clothed in appropriate bodies, and possessing appropriate states of consciousness.

According to theosophical belief, the two highest worlds, the divine and the monadic, are at present incapable of attainment by human powers, and the remaining five are attainable in greater or lesser degree. The **monad** (soul), for the purpose of gathering experience, finds it necessary to pass downward into the material sphere. When it has taken possession of the spiritual, intuitional, and higher mental worlds, it may be looked on as a soul embodying will, intuition, and intellect, continuing eternally the same entity, never altering except by reason of increasing development, and hence being immortal.

These worlds, however, do not afford sufficient scope to the monad and it presses still further down into matter, through the lower mental, and into the astral and physical worlds. The bodies with which it is there clothed form its personality and this personality suffers death and is renewed at each fresh incarnation, a process generally called **reincarnation.** At the death of the physical body, the ego has merely cast aside a garment and continues to live in the next higher world, the astral.

At the death of the **astral body** another garment is cast aside, the ego is cleared of all appendages and is as it was before its descent into denser matter, having returned to the mental, the heavenly world. The ego finds itself somewhat strange in this situation, owing to insufficient development, and it again descends into matter as before. This round is completed again and again, and each time the ego returns with a fresh store of experience and knowledge, which strengthens and perfects the mental body.

When at last this process is complete, this body in turn is cast aside and the ego is clothed with its causal body. Again it finds itself strange and the cycle of descent into matter begins again and continues until the causal body has been fully developed. The two remaining worlds are imperfectly known, but the intuitional, as its name indicates, is that where the ego's vision is quickened to see things as they really are, and in the spiritual world the divine and the human become unified and the divine purpose is fulfilled. (See also **Evolution of Life; Logos; Spheres**)

World Union Journal

Bimonthly journal of the World Union Community propagating the teachings of **Sri Aurobindo** and the ideal of human unity. Last known address: World Union International, Pondicherry 2, India 605002.

Worrall, Ambrose Alexander (1899–1972)

Engineer and spiritual healer. He was born on January 18, 1899, at Barrow-in-Furness, Lancashire, England. He studied mechanical engineering. In 1928 he married **Olga Nathalie Ripich Worrall.** For 30 years (1924–64) he was employed by the Martin Company, Baltimore, Maryland, and worked as a consultant for various firms in the years after his retirement.

He and his wife worked quietly as spiritual healers for many years, but their work gained a wider audience after the founding of the Spiritual Frontiers Fellowship (now the **International Spiritual Frontiers Fellowship)** in the 1950s. They became leaders in the organization. They also contributed to the annual seminars on spiritual healing held by the Laymen's Movement, Wainwright House, Rye, New York. Worrall's interests included **clairvoyance, clairaudience, clairsentience, psychokinesis, psychometry,** and theories of **survival.** He lectured widely on **ESP** and spiritual healing at colleges, churches, and other associations and published several pamphlets on spiritual healing and related subjects. He died on February 2, 1972.

Sources:

Worrall, Ambrose A. *The Gift of Healing.* Baltimore, Md.: The Author, 1961.

———. *The Philosophy and Methodology of Healing.* Baltimore, Md.: The Author, 1961.

Worrall, Ambrose A. and Olga Worrall. *Basic Principles of Spiritual Healing.* Evanston, Ill.: Spiritual Frontiers Fellowship, 1969.

———. *Explore Your Psychic World.* New York: Harper & Row, 1970.

———. *The Gift of Healing: A Personal Story of Spiritual Therapy.* New York: Harper & Row, 1965.

Worrall, Olga Nathalie Ripich (1906–1985)

Spiritual healer and associate director of New Life Clinic, Mount Washington Methodist Church, Baltimore, Maryland. She was born on November 30, 1906, in Cleveland, Ohio. In 1928 she married **Ambrose Alexander Worrall** and the two of them worked together for many years as healers. For many years prior to their marriage she healed the sick through a psychic talent that had manifested itself when she was eight. In addition to human beings, she healed cats, dogs, horses, chickens, and plants. In the 1950s, the Worralls associated with the newly-founded Spiritual Frontiers Fellowship (now the **International Spiritual Frontiers Fellowship**), and for many years they were among the fellowship's leading speakers and resource people.

Her special gift was of great interest to physicians, some of whom were her patients. One physician who sought her aid was John Cerutti, who had suffered from severe back pain for many years. Cerutti's experience with the healer was so profound that his wife Edwina, originally a skeptic, was won over and eventually published a book about the healer: *Olga Worrall, Mystic with the Healing Hands* (1975). Following her husband's death in 1972, Worrall continued to be active within the new wave of interest in alternative healing and during the 1970s became one of the most famous healers in the United States. In spite of her fame, she continued to focus her healing work in daily prayer sessions and with the New Life Clinic.

Worrall was also interested in the work of parapsychologists and on one occasion noted, "Since I am gifted in psychic abilities such as clairvoyance, etc. and spiritual healing, I am interested in the scientific research approach into parapsychological demonstrations motivated by personal experiences, especially in the areas of proving immortality and spiritual healing."

Worrall wrote a number of pamphlets explaining her methods of prayer and healing and coauthored several books with her husband. She died January 9, 1985, in Baltimore, Maryland.

Sources:

Cerutti, Edwina. *Olga Worrall, Mystic with the Healing Hands.* New York: Harper & Row, 1975.

Worrall, Ambrose, and Olga Worrall. *Basic Principles of Spiritual Healing.* Evanston, Ill.: Spiritual Frontiers Fellowship, 1969.

———. *Explore Your Psychic World.* New York: Harper & Row, 1970.

———. *The Gift of Healing: A Personal Story of Spiritual Therapy.* New York: Harper & Row, 1965.

Worrall, Olga. *How to Start a Healing Service.* Chicago, Ill.: Inner Creations, 1947.

Wortcunning

Anglo-Saxon term for knowledge of the medical and occult properties of plants. (See also **Cunning**)

Wraith

The apparition or **double** of a living person, generally supposed to be an omen of death. The wraith closely resembles its prototype in the flesh, even to details of dress. There are accounts of people seeing their own wraith, and among those who were warned of approaching death in this way are said to be Queen Elizabeth I, the poet Percy Bysshe Shelley, and Catherine of Russia. The latter, seeing her double seated upon the throne, ordered her guards to fire upon it.

But wraiths of others may appear to one or more persons. Lord Balcarres of Scotland saw the wraith of his friend "Bonnie Dundee" at the moment when the latter fell at the Battle of Killiecrankie, and the poet Ben Jonson saw his eldest son's double when the original was dying of the plague.

The belief in the wraith flourishes in Europe, and in different parts of Britain it goes under different names, such as "waff," "swarth," "task," and "fye." Variants are the Irish "**fetch,**" and the Welsh "lledrith."

In Scotland it was believed that the wraith of one about to die might be seen wrapped in a shroud. The higher the shroud reached, the nearer was the approach of death.

Something analogous to wraith-seeing comes within the scope of modern psychical science, and the **apparition** is explained in various ways, as an **astral projection** or an emanation from the person of its living prototype.

A well-known case is that of the Birkbeck Ghost, when three children witnessed the apparition of their mother shortly before her death. This instance, reported in *Proceedings* of the Society for Psychical Research (vol. 1, 1882, pp. 121–122), is noteworthy because Mrs. Birkbeck was conscious before she died of having spent the time with her children. (See also **J. W. Goethe; Vardøgr**)

Wrekin Trust

British based **New Age** organization, "concerned with the spiritual nature of Man and the Universe. It was not affiliated to any particular doctrine or dogma, did not offer any one way to 'the truth' and helps people find the disciplines most suited to them. After more than 12 years of pioneering courses and conferences on the holistic world view and introductory approaches to various disciplines, the Trust offered in addition, a curriculum for ongoing spiritual training. The inspiration was derived from the medieval concept of the University, which was concerned to find and orchestrate methods and systems of knowledge leading to union with the One, as the term 'Universus,' turned to the One, reveals."

The trust was founded by **Sir George Trevelyan** in 1971 and was especially concerned with dissolving the barriers between science and religion. The trust had been honored with the Right Livelihood Award, known as the "Alternative Nobel Prize," given in Stockholm for "Work forming an essential contribution to making life more whole, healing the planet, and uplifting humanity."

The trust organized important conferences on science and mysticism, with papers from Glen W. Schaefer, Joscelyn Godwin, and Pir Vilayat Inayat Khan. Last known address: Runnings Park, Croft Bank, West Malvern, Worcestershire WR14 4BP, England.

Sources:

Trevelyan, George A. *A Vision of the Aquarian Age.* London: Stillpoint, 1984.

Wriedt, Etta (ca. 1859–1942)

American professional **direct voice** medium who charged a nominal fee of one dollar for a successful séance. She never sat in a **cabinet,** did not pass into **trance,** and often joined in the conversation of the voices with the visitors.

Admiral Usborne Moore, author of *The Voices* (1913), heard three voices talking at once, one in each ear, and one through the **trumpet.** Wriedt only spoke English, but the voices knew no linguistic limitation. On occasion Dutch, French, Spanish, Norwegian, and Arabic were heard.

Wriedt's spirit **control** was an entity called "Dr. John Sharp," who claimed that he was born in Glasgow, Scotland, in the eighteenth century, lived most of his life in the United States as an apothecary farmer, and died in Evansville, Indiana. He took great care of the medium—often at the nervous or psychic expense of the sitters. Moore found the strain on his system so great while sitting with the medium in Detroit that he did not recover his normal health until more than six weeks later.

Wriedt paid five visits to England. She came the first time in 1911, at the age of 51, on the invitation of **W. T. Stead,** and held séances at **Julia's Bureau.** In 1912 and 1913, the arrangements for her visits were made by Moore, and in 1915 and 1919 she sat chiefly in Rothesay, Scotland.

E. K. Harper, W. T. Stead's secretary, recorded nearly 200 sittings with Wriedt. She often heard the direct voice in daylight. There were other features to the séance, such as luminous forms gliding about the room in the darkness. Sometimes dogs materialized and barked.

The spirit control **"John King"** claimed responsibility for the physical phenomena in England. Flowers were taken from vases and placed in the hands of sitters in the dark in different parts of the room. Invisible fingers touched the sitters and rapped by the trumpet to urge a hesitating person to answer promptly when spoken to. Luminous discs were seen to move inside the circle. The sitters were often sprinkled with drops of water, felt wafts of cool air, and saw heavy objects displaced.

From the spirit world, "W. T. Stead," who died in the *Titanic* tragedy, frequently communicated and gave many particulars of his passing over. He said that he was struck on the head when the *Titanic* sank and never felt the actual sensation of drowning.

Wriedt could clairvoyantly read names "written up," as she put it, in the dark. Once a name met with no recognition. Suddenly "John King's" voice broke the silence: "You had better clear out, my friend, nobody knows you." Moore was greeted by the voice of "Grayfeather," the Native American control of the medium **J. B. Jonson** of Detroit, who had never manifested before through Wriedt.

The psychical researcher **William F. Barrett** heard voices simultaneously with Wriedt. "Professor Henry Sidgwick" came through. Barrett stated:

"Mrs. Wriedt doubtless had heard his name, but he died before she visited England, and I doubt if she, or many others who knew him by name, were aware that he stammered badly. So I asked the voice 'Are you all right now?' not referring to his stammering. Immediately the voice replied 'You mean the impediment in my speech, but I do not stutter now' . . . I went to Mrs. Wriedt's séances in a somewhat skeptical spirit, but I came to the conclusion that she is a genuine and remarkable medium, and has given abundant proof to others besides myself that the voices and the contents of the messages given are wholly beyond the range of trickery or collusion."

Chedo Miyatovich, a Serbian diplomat and member of several learned societies, sat with Wriedt in the company of a Croatian lawyer friend, H. Hinkovitch, who had just arrived in London. Voices of deceased friends and relatives spoke to them in Serbian, Croatian, and at a later séance in German when Margarette Selenka of Germany was present.

An attempt to discredit Wriedt's phenomena was made in *Christiania* in August 1912, by one Professor Birkenhead and state chemist L. Schmelck. They averred that the noises in the trumpet were caused by lycopodium, a mildly inflammable powder used by druggists to coat pills. Other chemists held the report up to ridicule, and it became known that Birkenhead was extremely deaf and could not judge voices at all.

Wriedt died in Detroit, Michigan, September 13, 1942.

Wyllie, Edward (1848–1911)

Spirit photographer. He was psychic from his childhood, which was spent in Calcutta. He served in the Maori War in New Zealand with the rank of captain and settled in California in 1886 as a photographer. Spots and lights threatened to ruin his business until a lady, who had heard of **spirit photography,** examined his plates and suggested this explanation.

The Pasadena [California] Society for Psychical Research investigated the case on November 27, 1900, in Los Angeles. Their report stated: "As a committee we have no theory, and testify only to that which we do know. Individually we differ as to probable causes, but unanimously agree concerning the palpable facts." The committee promised $25 to any Los Angeles photographer who by trick or skill could produce similar results under similar conditions.

The early scene of Wyllie's psychic photography was Sycamore Grove, near Los Angeles. He had to move from there as the psychic "extras" obtained were dissolute-looking men and women. It was suggested as an explanation that about 50 years earlier the place had been the scene of wild orgies. The authorities stamped them out, but the evil influences apparently clung to the place.

Wyllie was accused by P. A. Jensen in *The Progressive Thinker* of producing his spirit faces by superimposing a prepared negative. The basis of the charge was that a suspicious negative had been found in a house where Wyllie had been. But according to James Coates in *Photographing the Invisible* (1911), Jensen had not been able to produce a single case where the negative in question had been used.

Another charge was raised by a Dr. Woillard. He said that Wyllie, for a fee, taught him how to take spirit pictures. His method was to hold in the hollow of his arched hand a photo prepared with luminous paint, and to keep it over plates in the darkroom previous to exposure. He said that he found two such miniatures prepared with India ink and luminous paint and also that Wyllie had confessed.

As well as being a spirit photographer, Wyllie was credited with powers of **psychometry.** He could obtain photographic "extras" through the influence of objects. James Coates sent him locks of his and his wife's hair. Two human heads were obtained on a photograph and one was recognized as Mrs. Coates' grandmother. It was as a result of this experiment that Wyllie was invited to England. Coates gave the following summary of his experiments:

"About 60 percent of the photographs taken exhibited psychic extras, and 25 percent of these were identified as those of departed persons. To all the subjects Mr. Wyllie was a complete stranger, and of the origins of the psychic extras or portraits he could have no knowledge; and except in the cases where flowers—roses and lilies—were produced there was a marked absence of symbolism in the photographs taken."

X

Xavier, Francisco Candido (1910–   )

Famous Brazilian Spiritist medium. (**Spiritism,** the Brazilian form of Spiritualism, stems from the teachings of French Spiritist **Allan Kardec.**) Known throughout Brazil as "Chico Xavier" (pronounced *Sheeko Shaveer*), he was born April 2, 1910, in the town of Pedro Leopoldo in the central state of Minas Gerais. He was one of a family of nine children. His mother died when he was only five, but Chico saw her materialize after her death, and during his period at primary school three years later, he became accustomed to hearing voices and sensing spirit presences.

He won an honorable mention for an essay contest with an entry that appeared to be dictated to him by a spirit form. On being challenged to produce another "spirit essay," he went straight to the blackboard and started writing a profound statement on the theme suggested, after which the teacher recommended he stop talking about spirit voices and pray on conventional Catholic lines.

He became a practicing medium in 1927 soon after one of his sisters was cured of apparent possession through the efforts of a healing medium. The whole Xavier family became Spiritists, and the medium's wife, Carmen Perácio, founded an evangelical Spiritist center, where Xavier manifested an ability for **automatic writing.** At one of these sessions, Perácio had a vision of a priestly spirit, "Emmanuel," who became Xavier's spirit guide thereafter. Xavier's mediumship continued in the form of automatic writing from spirit dictation.

Although nearly blind in one eye through most of his life and with only a rudimentary primary education, Xavier produced a prodigious number of books recognizably in the style of hundreds of deceased Brazilian and Portuguese authors whose works he had never had the opportunity to study.

In addition, he visited invalids in the district and undertook voluntary social work at his Pedro Leopoldo Spiritist Center at Uberaba. Hundreds of visitors came to this center for a personal message delivered by Xavier in trance, with instructions on individual problems, whether spiritual or medical. He has written some 130 books, of which over 3,000,000 copies have been sold in 415 editions. Some of these books have been translated into Spanish, French, Japanese, Esperanto, and English.

His book *Evolucão em dois mundos* (*Evolution in Two Worlds,* 1959) was written in collaboration with Dr. Waldo Vieira, who lived 250 miles away. The chapters were written alternately in uniform style and continuity, and the work took only forty days. It contained scientific concepts beyond the medium's understanding, suggesting to many that such information does not come from the medium's subconscious. Brazilian Spiritists follow Allan Kardec in clearly distinguishing between *escrita automatica* (automatic writing involving the medium's subconscious) and *psiografia* (involving a spirit entity).

In spite of the enormous popularity of his prodigious literary output, Xavier never accepted payment for any of his books and even disclaimed personal credit by the phrase "dictated by the spirit of–" on the title page.

He left Brazil only on two occasions. In 1965 and 1966 he made brief trips to Spiritualist centers abroad and a pilgrimage to the tomb of Allan Kardec in Paris, France. He appeared on Brazilian television programs, but remained a modest, sincere individual who devoted his psychic gift to the service of mankind. He was made an honorary citizen of São Paulo in 1973, and was similarly honored by other cities and towns in Brazil, including Rio de Janeiro, Uberada, Campinas, and São Bernardo. In 1977, the government of Brazil endorsed Xavier's half century as a medium by issuing a postage stamp in his honor. This official recognition of Spiritism is unique to Brazil; the government has also issued postage stamps honoring Allan Kardec and his teachings.

Sources:

Xavier, Francisco Candido. *Christian Agenda.* London: Regency Press, 1970.

———. *The World of the Spirit.* New York: Philosophical Library, n.d.

Xenoglossy

Speaking in a language unknown to the speaker in the normal waking state. It is different from what is commonly called glossolalia, or **speaking in tongues,** a form of vocalized religious experience characteristic of some religious movements, such as **Pentecostalism.** It has been compared with **automatic writing,** writing in a language unknown to the writer.

Speaking in an unknown language is perhaps a far more impressive phenomenon than writing in it. Subconscious visual memory may account for occasional reproduction of foreign sentences, but the explanation becomes more difficult if the problem of intonation is added, since it necessitates an auditive memory, the subconscious retention of fragments of strange languages actually heard somewhere at some time.

In medieval times speaking in foreign languages was one of the four principal signs of the presence of a demon. The belief was bound to have its subconscious effect. The Ursuline nuns of **Loudon** (according to their earliest historian in *La Véritable Histoire des Diables de Loudun, par un Témoin, â Poitiers,* 1634) spoke Latin, Greek, Turkish, Spanish, and a Native American tongue and confessed to having been obsessed by the devil.

In later religious revivals, the outbreak was a sign of celestial inspiration. The recitals of the refugees from the Cévennes, reported in *Le Théâtre Sacré des Cevennes,* by M. Misson (London, 1707) contains numerous accounts of the gift among unlettered Camisard (French Protestant) adults and infants, who spoke French in the purest diction (see also **Tremblers of the Cevennes**). The phenomenon was also noted among the **Convulsionaries of St. Medard** in 1730.

It is interesting to note that the psychical researcher **F. W. H. Myers** did not believe in the phenomenon. He said that he knew of only a few instances when a few words, fragments of a language, came through the medium—some Italian and Hawaiian words in Leonora Piper's utterances and a few Kaffir and Chinese words through another medium, a Ms. Browne. "We have no modern case, no case later than the half-mythical Miracles of the Cevennes, where such utterance has proved to be other than gibberish."

Apparently Myers ruled out or was unaware of many early cases, among them the testimony of Judge **John W. Edmonds.** His daughter, Laura Edmonds, was the first medium in modern **Spiritualism** reportedly with a gift for xenoglossy. Supposedly, foreign sitters could converse through her with spirits in their native language, even if it was a country as remote as Greece or Poland. Judge Edmonds wrote in a letter dated October 27, 1857:

"One evening when some 12 or 15 persons were in my parlor, Mr. E. D. Green, an artist of this city, was shown in, accompanied by a gentleman whom he introduced as Mr. Evangelides, of Greece. He spoke broken English, but Greek fluently. Ere long, a spirit spoke to him through Laura, in English, and said so many things to him that he identified him as a friend who had died at his house a few years before but of whom none of us had ever heard. Occasionally, through Laura, the spirit would speak a word or a sentence in Greek, until Mr. E. inquired if he could be understood if he spoke in Greek. The residue of the conversation, for more than an hour, was, on his part, entirely in Greek, and on hers sometimes in Greek and sometimes in English. At times Laura would not understand what was the idea conveyed, either by her or him. At other times she would understand him, though he spoke in Greek, and herself when uttering Greek words. . . .

"One day my daughter and niece came into my library and began a conversation with me in Spanish, one speaking a part of a sentence and the other the residue. They were influenced, as I found, by a spirit of a person whom I had known when in Central America, and reference was made to many things which had occurred to me there, of which I knew they were as ignorant as they were of Spanish. . . . Laura has spoken to me in Indian, in the Chippewa and Menomonie tongues. I knew the language, because I had been two years in the Indian country."

According to the book *Modern American Spiritualism,* by **Emma Hardinge Britten** (1870), in addition to Laura Edmonds, the gift was demonstrated at an early period by Jenny Keyes, who sang in trance in Italian and Spanish, and by a Mrs. Shepherd, Mrs. Gilbert Sweet, a Miss Inman, a Mrs. Tucker, Susan Hoyt, **A. D. Ruggles,** and several others whose names she was not permitted to make public. They frequently spoke in Spanish, Danish, Italian, Hebrew, Greek, Malay, Chinese, and Indian.

In 1859, 19 people testified in the *Banner of Light* to 34 cases of persons who occasionally spoke or wrote in tongues. **J. J. Mapes** and Governor **Nathaniel P. Tallmadge** bore witness to numerous instances in which uneducated mediums conversed with strangers in the streets in various foreign languages.

A decade later, a Mr. Lowenthal testified in England before the Committee of the **London Dialectical Society:** "I am frequently made to speak the language of another nation. I believe it to be an Indian language. My mouth utters sounds that I do not understand and which have no meaning to me. I think it is the language of some North American tribe. It is a soliloquy, and I get an impression on the brain, an idea that it means so and so. A voice articulate but not audible conveys a meaning to me. I have been among the Indians a great deal, and it sounds to me like their language."

Archdeacon **Thomas Colley** wrote of having heard the "Mahedi," a materialized Egyptian in the mediumship of **Francis W. Monck** (who knew no English), speak in that language under the control of Monck's regular guide, "Samuel." This appears to be the only instance on record where a claimed materialized individual was used as an automatic instrument by another spirit.

The Italian medium **Alfredo Pansini,** who, with his brother Paolo, was the subject of reported bodily transportation (see **teleportation**) by mediumistic power, spoke in a sort of hypnotic trance at the age of seven, in French, Latin, and Greek, and recited several cantos of the *Divina Commedia.* On one occasion, according to accounts, he spoke successively in twelve different voices. **Frederik van Eeden** recorded in the *Proceedings* of the Society of Psychical Research (vol. 17, 1901, pp. 59, 75) a Dutch conversation with a deceased friend through the medium Rosina Thompson:

"During a few minutes . . . I felt absolutely as if I were speaking to my friend myself. I spoke Dutch and got immediate and correct answers. The expression of satisfaction and gratification in face and gesture, when we seem to understand one another was too vivid to be acted. Quite unexpected Dutch words were pronounced, details were given which were far from my mind, some of which, as that about my father's uncle in a former sitting, I had never known, and found to be true only on inquiry afterwards."

Many German Orientalists testified that when the stigmatic subject **Thérèse Neumann** relived the Passion of Christ, she spoke in ancient Aramaic. The weakness of the case is that the phrases she used exist in print with translations in modern languages.

The *New York Evening Post* reported on November 10, 1930, the case of a four-year-old girl at Warsaw. Although the parents of Marie Skotnicki spoke only Polish, she developed the extraordinary habit of talking to herself in a foreign tongue that no one about her could understand but was later established to be pure Gaelic. It is important to add that her great-grandfather came from the Island of Lewis in the Scottish Hebrides.

In *The Two Worlds* (March 31, 1933), F. H. Wood wrote of the medium Rosemary and "Lady Nona," her ancient Egyptian **control:** "The fact is now established beyond disproof that over 140 Egyptian word-phrases which were in common use when the great Temple of Luxor in Egypt was built, have been spoken fluently through an English girl who normally knows nothing about the ancient tongue." Howard Hulme of Brighton, Sussex, the translator of the Egyptian phrases, after a preliminary test by mail which resulted in an unexpected but correct Egyptian answer, had also heard Lady Nona speak. After an amazing dialogue in the dead tongue of the pyramid builders, "Nona cleared up many points of pronunciation, gave her own earth name and explained the full meaning of some of her previous language tests."

In the early 1980s, Dr. William H. Kautz also announced a computer-based project at the Research Center for Applied Intuition (of which he is founder and director) involving the preparation of a translation and lexicon of the Rosemary Egyptian language text, to be studied in conjunction with all relevant publications relating to Egyptian language of the Eighteenth Dynasty, and a reconstitution of vocal Egyptian of the same period. The lexicon was to be compared with written Egyptian language and also with the reconstitution of the spoken form.

The medium **Etta Wriedt** reportedly spoke in many unknown tongues, and no stranger inflection could be imagined than the archaic Chinese that the voice of "Confucius" used in speaking through the medium **George Valiantine** to **Neville Whymant,** the renowned Oriental scholar. Whymant heard 14 languages spoken in 12 séances, and the strangest of all was the speech that came to him in fluent classical Chinese: "Greetings, O son of learning, and reader of strange books," and gave a complete new reading of poems and of the analects of Confucius, over which learned scholars have differed for centuries. Whymant's book *Psychic Adventures in New York* (1931) is among the most convincing twentieth-century records of xenoglossia.

Spirit Languages—The Primeval Tongue

The appearance of xenoglossy is not restricted to languages known to the people present when the words are spoken. On occasion, such vocalizations may turn out to be pure gibberish, or possibly attempts at a subconscious creation of a new language. Often they seem to be instances of glossolalia. An example of the latter was reported by **William James** in an article, "A Case of Psychic Automation . . .," published in the *Proceedings* of the Society of Psychical Research, vol. 12, 1896. Albert Le Baron (a pseudonym), an American journalist at a Spiritualist camp, spoke automatically in an unknown tongue. Fragments of the discourse were written down by himself, others were spoken into a phonograph in the presence of both James and **Richard Hodgson.** The following is a specimen: "Te rumete tau. Ilee lete leele luto scele. Impe re scele lee luto. Onko keere scete tere lute. Ombo te scele to bere te kure. Sinte lute sinte Kuru. Orumo imbo impe rute scelete. Singe, singe, singe eru. Imba, Imba, Imba."

The medium went on to supply the translation, "The old word! I love the old word of the heavens! The love of the heavens is emperor. The love of the darkness is slavery. The heavens are wise, the heavens are true, the heavens are sure. The love of the earth is past. The King now rules in the heavens."

Some spirit languages were allegedly extremely condensed. Psychical researcher **Frank Podmore,** for instance, reported that the phrase "Ki-e-lou-cou-ze-ta" required no less than 45 words to furnish an adequate translation in English. This relative difference in the number of words spoken and translation is again typical of glossolalia.

A Primeval Language?

The primeval language and the claimed "Martian" languages (see **Hélène Smith**) present the most interesting problems. The primeval or nature language has been described as the inner language of the soul, the universal tongue of men before the Fall, of which Hebrew is a corrupted form. In origin it is the language of the angels, of which the seer **Emanuel Swedenborg** writes in his book *The True Christian Religion* as follows:

"There is a universal language, proper to all angels and spirits, which has nothing in common with any language spoken in the world. Every man, after death, uses this language, for it is implanted in every one from creation; and therefore throughout the whole spiritual world all can understand one another. I have frequently heard this language and, having compared it with languages in the world, have found that it has not the slightest resemblance to any of them; it differs from them in this fundamental respect, that every letter of every word has a particular meaning."

In his book *Heaven and Hell,* Swedenborg further states: "Writing in the inmost heaven consists of various inflected and circumflected forms and the inflections and circumflections are according to the form of heaven. By these the angels express the arcana of their wisdom, many of which cannot be uttered by words; and, what is wonderful, the angels are skilled in such writing without being taught, for it is implanted in them like their speech . . . and therefore this writing is heavenly writing, which is not taught, but inherent, because all extensions of the thoughts and affections of the angels, and thus all communication of their intelligence and wisdom, proceeds according to the form of heaven, and hence their writing also flows into that form. I have been told that the most ancient people on this earth wrote in the same manner before the invention of letters, and that it was transferred into the letters of the Hebrew language which in ancient times were all inflected. Not one of them had the square form in use at this day; and hence it is that the very dots, iotas and minutest parts of the word contain heavenly arcana and things Divine."

The first record of the existence of a primeval language seems to be in the experiments of Elizabethan magician **John Dee** (1527–1608). The next, apart from Swedenborg's insights, was in the visions of the Seeress of Prevorst (**Frederica Hauffe**), which were confirmed by a somnambule patient of Heinrich Werner's a few years later and cited in Werner's book *Die Schutzgeister, oder Merkwürdige Blicke zweier Seherinnen in die Geisterwelt* (Stuttgart, 1839).

In Dee's notes, the invocation of the spirits was given in the "primeval language." It was accompanied by a word-for-word translation. The properties of this ancient tongue, claimed to be that which Adam employed and the angels speak, are singular, according to Dee: "Every letter signifieth the member of the substance whereof is speaketh: every word signifieth the quiddity of the substance . . . signifying substantially the thing that is spoken of in the centre of his Creator, whereby even as the mind of man moveth at an ordered speech, and is easily persuaded in things that are true, so are the creatures of God stirred up in themselves, when they hear the words wherewithal they were nursed and brought forth . . . the creatures of God understand you not. You are not of their Cities: you are become enemies, because you are separated from Him that governeth the City, by ignorance. . . . Men in his Creation, being made innocent was also authorised and made partaker of the Power and Spirit of God, whereby he did know all things under his Creation, and spoke of them properly, naming them as they were."

In plain language, this apparently means that the original speech bore an organic relation to the outer world, that each name expressed the properties of the thing spoken of, and that the utterances of that name had a compelling power over that creature. This has analogues in the mystical traditions of the Hebrew **shemhamphorash,** the secret name of God, and the mystical traditions connected with Hindu mantras.

In his book *The Seeress of Prevorst* (1845), Justinus Kerner writes:

"In her sleep-walking state, Mrs. H. frequently spoke in a language unknown to us, which seemed to bear some resemblance to the Eastern tongues. She said that this language was the one which Jacob spoke, and that it was natural to her and to all men. It was very sonorous, and as she was perfectly consistent in her use of it, those who were much about her gradually grew to understand it. She said, by it only could she fully express her innermost feelings; and that, when she had to express these in German, she was obliged first to translate them from this language. It was not from her head, but from her epigastric region that it proceeded. She knew nothing of it when she was awake. The names of things in this language, she told us, expressed their properties and quality. Philologists discovered in it a resemblance to the Coptic Arabic and Hebrew: for example, the word 'Elschaddai,' which she often used for God, signifies, in Hebrew, the self-sufficient, or all-powerful. The word 'dalmachan' appears to be Arabic, and 'Bianachli' signifies in Hebrew: I am sighing, or in sighs.

"Here follow a few of the words of this inner language, and their interpretations: 'Handacadi,' physician: 'alentana,' lady; 'chlann,' glass; 'schmado,' moon; 'nohin,' no; 'mochiane,' nightingale; 'bianna fina,' many coloured flowers; 'moy', how; 'toi,' what; 'optini poga,' thou must sleep; 'mo li arato,' I rest, etc.

"The written characters of this language were always connected with numbers. She said that words with numbers had a much deeper and more comprehensive signification than without. She often said, in her sleep-walking state, that the ghosts spoke this language; for although spirits could read the thoughts, the soul, to which this language belonged, took it with it when it went above; because the soul formed an ethereal body for the spirit."

Further on Kerner adds:

"With respect to the inner language, the Seherin [Seeress] said, that one word of it frequently expressed more than whole lines of ordinary language; and that, after death, in one single symbol or character of it, man would read his whole life. It is constantly observed that persons in a sleep-walking state, and those who are deep in the inner-life, find it impossible to express what they feel in ordinary language. Another somnambule used often to say to me, when she could not express herself 'Can no one speak to me in the language of nature?'

"The Seherin observed by Mayers said, that to man, in the magnetic state, all nature was disclosed, spiritual and material; but that there were certain things which could not be well expressed in words, and thus arose apparent inconsistencies and errors. In the archives of animal magnetism, an example is given of this peculiar speech; the resemblance of which to the eastern languages doubtless arises from its being a remnant of the early language of mankind. Thus, sleep-walkers cannot easily recall the names of persons and things, and they cast away all conventionalities of speech. Mayers' Seherin says, that as the eyes and ears of man are deteriorated by the fall, so he has lost in a great degree the language of his sensations; but it still exists in us, and would be found, more or less, if sought for. Every sensation or perception has its proper figure or sign and this we can no longer express.

"In order to describe these perceptions, Mrs. H. constructed figures which she called her 'sun sphere,' her 'life sphere' and so forth.

"Many instances proved how perfect her memory for this inner language was. On bringing her the lithograph of what she had written a year before, she objected that there was a dot too much over one of the signs; and on referring to the copy which I had by me, I found she was right. She had no copy herself."

Heinrich Werner in his book *Die Schutzgeister oder Merkwürdige Blicke Zweier Seherinen in die Geisterwelt* (1839), gave a dissertation on the inner language, traces of which he found in the babbling of children, and stated that in rare states of exaltation the inner spirit can recover the lost vocabulary.

With the advent of modern Spiritualism, the idea of the primeval tongue faded out. Nor did spirit languages hold out for long. **Camilla Crosland** was one of the last of its recorders in Britain. In her book *Light in the Valley* (1857) she writes:

"Three years ago a young lady, a medium whom I shall designate The Rose was taught by spirits, directly communicating with her, three spirit languages; that is to say, she was taught the meaning of certain characters and inflections, which are quite distinct, so far as I have been able to ascertain, from any known languages ancient or modern. . . . Introduced last autumn to another medium, a young lady whom we have been instructed to call Comfort, The Rose discovered that her new acquaintance wrote by spirit power the first-taught of these mystic languages. . . . Subsequently five other mediums, all personally known to me, have developed as writers of the first spirit language; and one of them, an author of repute and M.A. of the University of Oxford, has also on two or three occasions written in the second of the spirit languages, the characters of which seem mainly composed of dots."

The universal language of Swedenborg, according to Crosland, developed dialects. Unfortunately the sample of spirit writing in *Light in the Valley* is the plainest scribble and no evidence whatever was introduced to show how the identity, if any, was established among the strange ornaments of spiral and shell forms, with dots and scroll-like ciphers adorning the spirit drawing illustrations.

Writing in Tongues

Writing xenoglossic script is a comparatively frequent phenomenon. According to Richard Hodgson, "the chief difficulty, apparently, in getting another language written by the hand is that strange words tend to be written phonetically unless they are thought out slowly letter by letter. The medium **William Eglinton,** caught in fraudulent activity on several occasions, produced messages in a séance with the statesman Gladstone in Spanish, French, and Greek in direct writing. He did not know Spanish or Greek. An apparition at a séance held by **Elizabeth d'Esperance,** calling herself "Nepenthes," wrote in classic Greek in Professor L.'s notebook, "I am Nepenthes, thy friend. When thy soul is oppressed by overmuch pain, call on me, Nepenthes, and I will speedily come to assuage thy trouble."

According to **Charles Richet,** Mrs. X. (Laura Finch), a young woman of thirty, "wrote long sentences in Greek, with some errors, that clearly show mental vision of one or more Greek books. After much research . . . I was able to discover the book from which Mrs. X. had drawn most of the long Greek sentences that she had written in my presence. The book is not to be found in Paris except in the National Library—the Greco-French and Franco-Greek dictionary by Byzantios and Coromelas. As it is a dictionary of modern Greek, it is not in use in any school."

Richet further stated that Mrs. X. wrote some twenty lines of Greek with about 8 percent of small errors, that she was looking into space as if she were copying from the text of a language unknown to her of which she saw the characters without knowing their meaning, and that Mrs. X. knew no Greek at all and could not understand the sentences that appeared before her mental vision.

Several other examples of this phenomenon are to be found in Florizel von Reuter's books, *Psychic Experiences of a Musician* (1928) and *The Consoling Angel* (1930). The Chinese **cross-correspondences** of **Mina Crandon** (known as "Margery" in the literature) furnish especially striking instances.

Recent Research

The emergence of the charismatic movement in the 1970s led to a revival of claims that the glossolalia commonly experienced in Pentecostal services was in fact xenoglossy. To bolster this argument anecdotal accounts of xenoglossy in church services and on the mission field were reprinted. However, rather thorough research largely laid these claims to rest.

The most impressive reported incidents of xenoglossy were collected in *Unlearned Language: New Studies in Xenoglossy,* by psychical researcher **Ian Stevenson,** more known for his research on cases of **reincarnation.** Additionally, through the 1970s and into the 1980s, he supposedly recorded some cases of speaking an unlearned language that he had witnessed. He also noted that the publication of his first book on the subject brought numerous reports that, while interesting, were poorly documented.

Sources:

Bozzano, Ernesto. *Polyglot Mediumship (Xenoglossy).* London: Rider, 1932.

Flournoy, Theodor. *From India to the Planet Mars.* New York: Harper, 1900.

Kautz, William H. "The Rosemary Case of Alleged Egyptian Xenoglossy." *Theta* 10, 2 (summer 1982).

Lombard, Emile. *De la Glossolalie chez les Premiers Chrétiens et des Phénomènes Similaires.* Lausanne, Switzerland: Bridel, 1910.

Stevenson, Ian. *Unlearned Language: New Studies in Xenoglossy.* Charlottesville: University of Virginia Press, 1984.

———. *Xenoglossy: A Review and Report of a Case.* Charlottesville: University of Virginia Press, 1974.

Wood, F. H. *After Thirty Centuries.* London: Rider, 1935.

———. *This Egyptian Miracle.* London: Rider, 1940. Rev. ed. London: J. M. Watkins, 1955.

Xibalba

The Hades of the Kiche (or Quiché) Indians of Central America. (See **Mexico and Central America**)

Xylomancy

Divination by means of wood, practiced particularly in Slavonia. It was the art of reading omens from the position of small pieces of dry wood found in one's path. Presages of future events were also drawn from the arrangement of logs in the fireplace and from the manner in which they burned.

Y

Yadachi

A Mongolian weather changer. (See also **Siberia**)

Yadageri

The science of inducing rain and snow by means of enchantment. (See also **Siberia**)

Yaksha (or Jak)

A kind of Hindu supernatural being, usually inoffensive, but sometimes troublesome. Yakshas seem to have been somewhat analogous to the **fairies** of other countries.

According to W. Crooke, author of *Religion and Folklore of Northern India* (1926),

"The *Jak* is the modern representative of the *Yaksha,* who in better times was the attendant of Kuvera, the god of wealth, in which duty he was assisted by the Guhyaka. The character of the *Yaksha* is not very certain. He was called Punay-janas, 'the good people,' but he sometimes appears as an imp of evil. In the folk-tales, it must be admitted, the *Yakshas* have an equivocal reputation. In one story the female, or *Yakshini,* bewilders travellers at night, makes horns grow on their foreheads, and finally devours them; in another the *Yakshas* have, like the *Churel,* feet turned the wrong way and squinting eyes; in a third they separate the hero from the heroine because he failed to make due offerings to them on his wedding day. On the other hand, in a fourth tale the **Yakshini** is described as possessed of heavenly beauty; she appears again when a sacrifice is made in a cemetery to get her into the hero's power, as a heavenly maiden beautifully adorned, seated in a chariot of gold surrounded by lovely girls; and lastly, a Brahman meets some Buddhist ascetics, performs the *Uposhana* vow, and would have become a god, had it not been that a wicked man compelled him by force to take food in the evening, and so he was reborn as a *Guhyaka.*

"In the modern folk-lore of Kashmir, the *Yaksha* has turned into the *Yech* or *Yach,* a humorous, though powerful, sprite in the shape of a civet cat of a dark colour, with a white cap on his head. This small cap is one of the marks of the Irish fairies, and the *Incubones* of Italy wear caps, 'the symbols of their hidden, secret natures.' The feet of the *Yech* are so small as to be almost invisible, and it squeaks in a feline way. It can assume any shape, and if its white cap can be secured, it becomes the servant of the possessor, and the white cap makes him invisible.

"In the *Vishnu Purana* we read that Vishnu created the *Yakshas* as beings emaciate with hunger, of hideous aspect, and with big beards, and that from their habit of crying for food they were so named. By the Buddhists they were regarded as benignant spirits. One of them acts as sort of chorus in the *Meghaduta* or 'Cloud of Messenger' of Kalidasa. Yet we read of the *Yaka Alawaka,* who, according to the Buddhist legend, used to live in a Banyan tree, and slay any one who approached it; while in Ceylon they are represented as demons whom Buddha destroyed. In later Hinduism they are generally of fair repute, and one of them was appointed by Indra to be the attendant of the Jaina Saint Mahavira."

Sources:

Crooke, William. *Religion and Folklore of Northern India.* Humphrey Milford: Oxford University Press, 1926.

Yantra

Hindu mystical diagram, often inscribed on copper. Divine energy is invoked into the *yantra* by special prayers. The *yantra* is clearly a precursor of the magic diagrams of Western occultists, although in India it was used in a religious rather than an **occult** context.

Yarker, John (1833–1913)

British Freemason and occultist, active in Manchester, England. He was initiated as a Mason at the age of 21 in the Lodge of Integrity, Manchester, October 25, 1854, becoming master of this lodge in 1857. He became the first worshipful master of the Fidelity Lodge of Mark Masters. At the age of 23, he was installed a Knight Templar in the Jerusalem Conclave on July 11, 1856. There followed various Masonic honors, and in 1864 he was appointed Masonic Grand Constable of England. He also traveled extensively, visiting the United States, the West Indies, and Cuba. At a time of Masonic renaissance, he revived many rites and promoted a number of rites on his own, probably more for vanity than profit. These included the Rites of Sat B'Hai, Swedenborg, Mizraim, and the Ancient and Primitive Rite. The latter was later associated with magicians **Theodor Reuss** and **Aleister Crowley.**

Yarker was thus associated with the fringe Masonic secret orders that preceded the establishment of the **OTO** and the Hermetic Order of the **Golden Dawn.** The OTO originated in a charter from Yarker to the German occultists Joshua Klein, **Franz Hartmann,** and Theodore Reuss, licensing them to set up in Berlin a Grand Lodge of the Masonic rite of Mizraim and Memphis. By 1904, occultist Karl Kellner was also involved. The August Order of Light, developed by Maurice Portman, was passed to Yarker circa 1890, who amalgamated it with rituals from his Sat B'Hai Rite.

Yarker published a number of Masonic works and also an abridged translation of **Louis-Alphonse Cahagnet**'s *Magie Magnétique* under the title *Magnetic Magic* (1898). His most well-known work is *The Arcane Schools; A Review of Their Origin and Antiquity; with a General History of Freemasonry* (1909). He also edited a periodical, *The Kneph* (1881–95), concerned with Masonic matters. He died on March 30, 1913.

Yasodhara Ashram

A spiritual retreat and study center founded in Canada in 1962 by German-born **Swami Sivananda Radha,** a disciple of the late **Swami Sivananda** Saraswati of Rishikesh, Himalayas,

India. The Yasodhara Ashram is situated in a picturesque rural location and includes residential buildings, a guest lodge, prayer rooms, bookstore, office, and a Temple of Divine Light.

In addition to the ashram residents, facilities are offered for temporary residents to follow teaching programs in courses and workshops dealing with Eastern spiritual teachings and Western techniques for self-development. A yoga teachers course is also organized. The ashram publishes the journal *Ascent* four times a year and issues tape and disc recordings concerned with **meditation, mantras** and **kundalini** yoga. Address: Yasodhara Ashram, Box 9, Kootenay Bay, British Columbia, Canada VOB 1XO. Website: http://www.yasodhara.org.

Yauhahu

A spirit believed to cause diseases among Indians of British Guiana.

Yeats, W(illiam) B(utler) (1865–1939)

Famous Irish poet, playwright, and mystic. He was born at Sandymount, near Dublin, Ireland, on June 13, 1865. His father John Yeats was a talented portrait painter. William's brother Jack Butler Yeats was also an artist, and his sisters Elizabeth and Lily assisted in the establishment of the Dun Emer (later Cuala) Press.

Much of Yeat's childhood was spent in London, where he attended the Godolphin School, Hammersmith, but he also spent time in Dublin and County Sligo, in Western Ireland. At the age of fifteen, he attended Erasmus Smith School, Dublin, then studied art for three years, turning to literature at the age of 21. His first book, a play titled *Mosada,* was published in 1886. It was followed by two books of poems, *The Wanderings of Oisin* (1889) and *The Wind Among the Reeds* (1899). In 1888, he edited a collection titled *Fairy and Folk Tales of the Irish Peasantry,* which included some of his fairy verse. He became one of the leading figures in the Irish literary renaissance.

In London he was a founder of the Rhymers' Club and friend of Ernest Rhys, Ernest Dowson, Lionel Johnson, William Morris, W. E. Henley, and Arthur Symons. In Ireland, he was associated with J. M. Synge, "AE" (**George W. Russell**), Douglas Hyde, George Moore, and Lady Gregory. He helped to establish the Irish Literary Theatre in 1899 (later the Abbey Theatre). His poems and plays have become world famous. He was a member of the Irish Senate from 1922 to 1928 and received the Nobel Prize for Literature in 1923.

The **occult** and mystical side of his life and work received less publicity than his literary work, yet he believed that his poetry owed much to his occult studies. In 1892, he wrote: "If I had not made magic my constant study I could not have written a single word of my Blake book, nor would *The Countess Kathleen* have ever come to exist. The mystical life is the centre of all that I do and all that I think and all that I write."

His interest in the writings of Theosophists led to the formation of the **Hermetic Society,** Dublin, and he presided over its first meeting on June 16, 1885. While in London at the end of 1888, he joined the Esoteric Section of the **Theosophical Society.** In 1890, he joined the pioneering magical society, the Hermetic Order of the **Golden Dawn,** taking the magical motto "Demon Est Deus Inversus," (DEDI) and continued to be associated with the Golden Dawn over some thirty years. In April 1900, he clashed with **Aleister Crowley,** also an order member, in a leadership crisis.

Yeats' book *Ideas of Good and Evil* (1903) contains studies of the mystic element in Blake and Shelley and another essay is titled "The Body of the Father Christian Rosencrux." Another essay titled "Magic" commences: "I believe in the practice and philosophy of what we have agreed to call magic, and what I must call the evocation of spirits, though I do not know what they are, in the power of creating magic illusions, in the visions of truth in the depths of the minds when the eyes are closed."

After his declaration, he related how once an acquaintance of his, gathering together a small party in a darkened room, held a mace over "a tablet of many coloured squares," at the time repeating "a form of words," and immediately Yeats found that his "imagination began to move itself and to bring before me vivid images. . . ." It was **S. L. MacGregor Mathers** of the Golden Dawn, states Yeats, "who convinced me that images well up before the mind's eye from a deeper source than conscious or subconscious memory."

In a lecture on "Psychic Phenomena" before the Dublin Society for Psychical Research (reported in the Dublin *Daily Express,* November 1913), he spoke of most amazing experiences during his investigation, which lasted for many years, and declared that so far as he was concerned, the controversy about the meaning of psychic phenomena was closed. But he was not "converted," in the true sense of the word, since he was a born believer, and he had never seriously doubted the existence of the soul or of God.

Yeats and Spiritualism

Lecturing on "Ghosts and Dreams" before the **London Spiritualist Alliance** in April 1914, he gave another clear account of his beliefs and experiences. In his book *Per Amica Silentia Lunae* (1918), he spoke as a poet and mystic in dealing with some of the deeper issues of **Spiritualism.**

In 1917, he married Georgia Hyde Lees and discovered that his wife was a **medium** and capable of **automatic writing.** In 1934, Yeats wrote a one-act play "The Words Upon the Window-Pane" built around a Spiritualist séance at which the spirit of Jonathan Swift communicated.

He showed considerable courage in making known some of his occult beliefs, although he did not publicize his Golden Dawn connections.

His mystical inclinations, stimulated by the Hindu religious philosophy of the Theosophical Society that had also attracted fellow poet "AE," continued to develop. When in his sixties, he became friendly with the Hindu monk **Swami Shri Purohit** and wrote introductions to the Swami's autobiography *An Indian Monk* (Macmillan, London, 1932) and his translation of the book by the Swami's guru titled *The Holy Mountain* (Faber, London, 1934). In 1935, the Swami published a translation of the *Bhagaved-Gita* under the title *The Geeta; The Gospel of the Lord Shri Krishna* (Faber, London), which he dedicated "To my friend William Butler Yeats" on the poet's seventieth birthday. In the same year, the Swami also published a translation of the *Mandukya Upanishad,* for which Yeats provided a perceptive introduction. He had planned to travel to India to assist the Swami in translating the ten principal Upanishads, but eventually the work was completed by the two friends at Majorca in 1936.

Yeats died January 28, 1939, in the town of Roquebrune, overlooking Monaco, and was buried in the cemetery there until nine years later, when his remains were transferred to the churchyard of Drumcliffe, near Sligo.

Sources:

Harper, George Mills. *Yeats and the Occult.* London: Macmillan, 1975.

———. *Yeats' Golden Dawn.* London: Macmillan, 1974. Reprint, Wellingborough, England: Aquarian Press, 1979.

Yeats, William Butler. *Autobiography.* New York: Macmillan, 1938.

———. *Memoirs.* New York: Macmillan, 1973.

———. *Mythologies.* New York: Macmillan, 1959.

Yeats-Brown, Francis (Charles Clayton) (1886–1944)

British soldier, author, and early popularizer of **yoga** in Western countries. He was born at Genoa, Italy, August 15,

1886, the son of the British consul-general in that city. He was educated at Harrow-on-the-Hill and Sandhurst, England. He was second lieutenant in the king's Royal Rifle Corps at Bareilly, India, in 1906; posted to 17th Cavalry, Indian Army in 1907; and adjutant in 1913. He served in France with 5th Lancers and in Mesopotamia with the Royal Flying Corps (DFC). He was imprisoned in Turkey in November 1915 but escaped in 1918. He retired on pension in 1925. From 1926 to 1928 he was editor of the British journal *The Spectator.*

He published several books, the most famous of which was *Bengal Lancer* (1930), based on his nineteen years in India and his intense interest in yoga. The book became a best-seller and was translated into Italian, Spanish, German, Danish, Norwegian, Swedish, and Romanian. It attracted worldwide interest in the subject of yoga. A film version of the book under the title "Lives of a Bengal Lancer" was produced in 1935, starring Gary Cooper, Franchot Tone, and Richard Cromwell.

Yeats-Brown also published *Yoga Explained* (1937), a pioneering yoga text. In spite of his great interest in yoga philosophy he remained a Christian throughout his life. His other books include *Caught by the Turks* (1919), *Golden Horn* (1932), *Escape: A Book of Escapes of All Kinds* (1933), *Dogs of War* (1934), *Lancer at Large* (1937), *European Jungle* (1939), *Indian Pageant* (1942), and *Martial India* (1945).

During the 1930s, Yeats-Brown was a news correspondent in Germany and expressed admiration for Hitler, whom he compared with Gandhi and T. E. Lawrence. It seems likely that this unfortunate judgment stemmed from Yeats-Brown's enthusiasm for German physical fitness and military precision and that he never really understood the real implications of Nazi philosophy and ambitions.

From 1943 to 1944 Yeats-Brown served in the British Army, touring the Indian and Burmese war fronts.

He died in London, December 19, 1944.

Yerger, Eloise Barrangon (1915–)

American writer who also conducted parapsychology experiments to investigate teacher-pupil attitudes and **clairvoyance** test results among students in fifth, sixth, and seventh-grade levels. She was born on January 16, 1915, at Northampton, Massachusetts. She studied at Smith College (B.A.) and in 1935 became a freelance writer. She was a member of the **Parapsychological Association** and the **American Society for Psychical Research.**

Yes! Bookshop

A **New Age** bookstore founded in Washington, D.C., in 1972 by Cris Popenhoe. The bookshop covers every aspect of New Age concern, spiritual development, and positive **occult** teachings. Popenhoe is convinced of the basic New Age belief that positive social and political change is desirable and such change necessitates individual transformation. She published an excellent annotated bibliography (which doubled as a bookshop catalog): *Books for Inner Development* (1976), revised as *Inner Development; the Yes! Bookshop Guide* (1979), with eleven supplements in the early 1980s. In 1977 she also did a similar work on healing books, entitled simply *Wellness.*

Sources:

Popenhoe, Cris. *Books for Inner Development/The Yes! Guide.* Washington, D.C.: Yes! Bookshop, 1976. Revised as *Inner Development; the Yes! Bookshop Guide.* Washington, D.C.: Yes! Bookshop, 1979. Supplements 1–11. 1982–83.

———. *Wellness.* Washington, D.C.: Yes! Bookshop, 1977.

Yeti

Also known as the "abominable snowman," the yeti is the mysterious humanoid creature reported by Western sources as early as 1832 as living in the Himalayan Mountains. It became well known following several expeditions to the area in the 1950s. In 1960 Sir Edmund Hillary, who conquered Everest, called further attention to the yeti in his attempts to debunk them. The Soviet Ministry of Culture established a group of "cryptozoologists" to locate the yeti, according to a report of January 9, 1988, by *Tass,* the Soviet press agency. The agency stated that nearly one hundred sightings had been collated by Zhanna Kofman of Moscow.

Sources:

Clark, Jerome. *Encyclopedia of Strange and Unexplained Phenomena.* Detroit: Gale Research, 1993.

Sanderson, Ivan. *Abominable Snowmen: Legend Come to Life.* Philadelphia, Pa: Chilton Books, 1961.

Yezidis

A dualistic religious group operating among the Kurds in northern Iraq and the neighboring lands of Syria, Turkey, and Iran. Their religion probably goes back to the Manicheans but has borrowed heavily from the Shiite Muslims. The Yezidis call themselves the Dawasin or Dasnayye. The term Yezidi was originally probably a name of derision. It refers to a Caliph Yezid who in 680 C.E. ordered the death of al-Husayn, the grandson of the Prophet Mohammed. The Shiite hold al-Husayn in special reverence, for they claim to derive their authority from him. Others have suggested that the word is derived from the Persian word *ized* (for angel, deity), and would mean "worshippers of God." They are also derogatorily referred to by their neighbors as "devil-worshippers." The Yezidi community is centered upon the tomb of Shaykh Adi ibn Musafir at Llish in the district of Mosul.

The Yezidi faith is quite eclectic, drawing upon Christian (baptism, breaking of bread, drinking of wine), Jewish (dietary restrictions), Muslim (fasts, circumcision, pilgrimages), Sufi (reverence for Shaykhs, secrecy, ecstatic experiences), and Sabeansist (**reincarnation**) traditions. They believe that they were children of the seed of Adam (but not of Eve). Thus, they believe themselves different from the rest of humanity, who are derived from both Adam and Eve. They try to remain separate and no outsider may join them. One must be born a Yezidi.

A dominant symbol among them is the peacock, a symbol of the seven angels who cooperated in the creation of the world. The peacock angel is their euphemism for evil. They believe evil is a part of the divinity, along with good. Thus they are more properly seen as dualists rather than devil worshippers. The Yezidis also consider Christ an angel in human form, and Mohammed as a prophet with Abraham and others.

Sources:

Drower, E. S. *Peacock Angel.* London: John Murray, 1941.

Empson, R. H. *The Cult of the Peacock Angel.* N.p., 1928.

Guest, John S. *Survival Among the Kurds: A History of the Yezidis.* London: Kegan Paul International, 1993.

———. *The Yezidis.* London: KPI, 1987.

Nau, Abbé F. "Recueil de textes et de documents sur les Yézidis." *ROC* 2, no. 10 (1915–17).

Seabrook, William B. *Adventures in Arabia among the Bedouins Druses Whirling Dervishes & Yezidee Devil-worshipers.* New York, 1927.

Yin and Yang

According to ancient Chinese philosophy, the dual principles of nature. *Yin* signifies earth, passive, negative, female, yielding, weak, or dark; *yang* signifies heaven, active, positive, male, strong, or light. These principles are manifest throughout nature and in the human body. They relate to mental, physical, and spiritual structure and are affected by food, drink, action, and inaction. The balance of *yin* and *yang* in the individual, nature, and the cosmos is symbolized by a circle separated by an "S" shape, one half of the circle dark and the other light. This has something in common with the ancient Greek alchemical symbol of a serpent or dragon eating its tail, known as **Ouroboros.**

The *yin-yang* symbol represents unity and duality, a universal dual monism. It is also inherent in the ancient Chinese system of **divination** of the **I Ching** (Book of Changes). It is basic to the teachings of **Taoism,** as embodied in the classic work *Tao-te-Ching* (Book of the Right Way) of the philosopher Lao Tzu.

In modern times, the *yin* and *yang* principles are a vital part of the revived system of diet known as macrobiotics, where health and mental and spiritual balance are developed by the correct proportions of *yin* and *yang* foods, properly prepared. (See also **China; Tao**)

Sources:

Legge, James, trans. *The I Ching.* New York: Dover Publications, 1963.

Y-Kim (or I Ching), Book of

A Chinese mystical book attributed to the Emperor Fo-Hi and ascribed to the year 3468 B.C.E. It consists of ten chapters and was stated by **Éliphas Lévi** in his *History of Magic* to be a complement and an appendix to the Kabalistic *Zohar,* the record of the utterances of Rabbi Simeon Ben Jochai. The *Zohar,* according to Lévi, explains universal equilibrium, and the *Y-Kim* is the hieroglyphic and ciphered demonstration thereof.

The key to the *Y-Kim* is the pentacle known as the Trigrams of Fo-Hi. In the *Vay-Ky* of Leon-Tao-Yuen, composed in the Som Dynasty (about eleventh century), it was recounted that the Emperor Fo-Hi was one day seated on the banks of a river, deep in **meditation,** when to him there appeared an animal having the parts of both a horse and a dragon.

Its back was covered with scales, on each of which shone the mystic Trigrammic symbol. The animal initiated the just and righteous Fo-Hi into universal science. Numbering its scales, he combined the Trigrams in such a manner that there arose in his mind a synthesis of sciences compared and united with one another through the harmonies of nature. From this synthesis sprang the tables of the *Y-Kim.*

According to Éliphas Lévi, the numbers of Fo-Hi are identical with those of the **Kabala,** and his **pentacle** is similar to that of **Solomon.** His tables are in correspondence with the subject matter of the *Sephir Yesirah* and the *Zohar.* The whole is a commentary upon the Absolute that is concealed from the profane, concluded Lévi.

Since Lévi's time, much scholarship has been expended on the symbolism and mystical significance of this important work under its more generally expressed title of **I Ching.**

Sources:

Legge, James, trans. *The I Ching.* New York: Dover Publications, 1963.

Lévi, Éliphas. *The History of Magic.* London: W. Rider & Son, 1913. Reprint, New York: Samuel Weiser, 1970.

Yoga

General term for various spiritual disciplines in Hinduism. The word "yoga" implies "yoking" (as with oxen to the ox-cart) or "union," expressing the linking of man with divine reality. This union is a transcendental experience beyond the plane of words and ideas and has to be achieved by release from the limiting fields of physical, emotional, mental, and intellectual experience. This requires purification at all levels and according to Hindu belief might take many lifetimes, but sincere exertions in one birth should bear fruit in the next.

Yoga's widespread introduction to the West is thought to have begun with Swami Vivekananda's yoga presentation at the Parliament of Religions in Chicago, 1893. Influential twentieth century yogis since then have included **Ramana Maharshi,** Indra Devi, Selvarajan Yesudian, **Swami Sivananda,** Sri Yogendra, and **Maharishi Mahesh Yogi,** of the Transcendental Meditation movement. In the 1960s and 1970s, Richard Hittleman and Lilias Folan (of *Lilias, Yoga, and You*) brought yoga to the American mainstream through television. Yoga's popularity is also due to endorsements from celebrities such as Sting and Madonna. Yoga's allure as a stress reliever has also helped the practice to gain popularity with Americans who try to regain control over their hectic lifestyles. It is estimated that more than two million people throughout the world practice some discipline of yoga.

The existence of many spiritual disciplines and practices in India allowed for a multitude of forms and beliefs. Most religious systems are aligned to one or more forms of yoga, though most commonly they will emphasize one of the traditional spiritual paths. Some would judge the adoption of a particular spiritual path to be linked to age, occupation, personality, or a particular interest in life.

The six principle branches of yoga are:

Bhakti Yoga

Bhakti yoga is the path of love and devotion. An individual with an emotional temperament can transform those emotions, to be absorbed in spiritual service instead of being attached to physical or sensory gratification. Love can be centered on a familiar form of God, a great saint, or some great task in life. In bhakti yoga, the whole universe, whether animate or inanimate, is seen as permeated by divinity. *Bhakti* (meaning loving devotion) is the practice of self-surrender for the purpose of identifying with the source of love, the higher self.

The Hare Krishna, which became notable in the West in the last generation, follow a form of Hinduism that emphasizes this type of yoga.

Hatha Yoga

Hatha yoga is known as the path of inner power. It is the science of physical exercises most familiar to Westerners. In hatha yoga the mind, body, and spirit are linked, and the purification of the body is intended to enhance mental and spiritual development, balance, and harmony. Good physical health, however, is an essential prerequisite to the strenuous disciplines of this yoga system.

Hatha yoga consists of a number of *asanas,* or physical postures, that develop flexibility in associated muscle groups throughout the body, and favorably affect the tone of veins and arteries. They are also believed to improve the function of the ductless glands through persistent gentle pressure. In Patanjali's system, *asana* was chiefly directed to the achievement of a firm cross-legged sitting position for **meditation.** Other yoga authorities, however, have elaborated the stages of Patanjali yoga to meet the requirements of different temperaments, so that they may be harmonized.

The *asanas* differ from Western gymnastics in that they feature static postures instead of active movements, though some asanas are linked sequentially. There are theoretically some 8,400,000 *asanas,* of which 84 are said to be the best and 32 the most useful for good health. These are named after animals, geometic structures, mountains, or plants. An *asana* is considered to be mastered when the yogi can maintain the position without strain for three hours. *Asanas* may be supplemented by special symbolic gestures and positions called *mudras.*

Various cleansing techniques, called *kriyas,* of the nasal passages, throat, stomach, and bowels can be practiced in conjunction with *asanas. Pranayama,* breathing exercises, are also employed to arouse **kundalini** or vital energy. Some systems focus upon the arousal of kundalini as the central spiritual discipline.

Hatha yoga had largely died out in India but was revived in the nineteenth century in Maharashtra, western India, from whence it radiated out into the world during the twentieth century.

Jnana or Sankya Yoga

Jnana yoga is the path of knowledge, science, and wisdom. This begins with fine distinctions that may be evolved from careful observation; study and experiment; combining knowledge with the ability to reflect, meditate, and develop intuition. It is the way of transcendent knowledge, and is geared for those prone to intellectual curiosity, reason, and analysis.

Karma Yoga

Karma yoga is the science of **karma** or selfless action. Karma yoga teaches the student that all actions have inescapable consequences, some producing immediate results, others delayed results, and some bearing fruit in future lives. Emphasis is placed on altruistic actions that purify the individual soul and release it from petty desires. In karma yoga, actions are spiritualized by dedicating them to selfless service and divine will. Karma yoga calls for union with God through right action, and service for service sake, without regard for accomplishment or glory or attribution.

Mantra Yoga

Mantra yoga is the path of sacred sound. It is the science of sound vibration, prayer, and hermetic utterance. According to Hindu mystical belief, the world evolved from the essence of sound, through the diversity and intricacy of vibration and utterance.

One of the most sacred **mantra**s is the three-syllabled OM or **AUM,** origin of the universe, comparable with the Hebrew Shemhamphorash and the creative Word of God in the Gospel of John. The reading of Hindu scriptures is both begun and ended with the sacred sound AUM.

Raja Yoga

Raja Yoga is the path of stillness, whose goal is to quiet the mind through meditation to create a state of focused, unbroken concentration. It is also known as the path of spiritual science, particularly suitable for those of a more abstract or metaphysical temperament. This path combines religious study with refinement of all levels of the individual, culminating in transcendental awareness. Raja yoga is the summation of all other yogas. Ancient textbooks of hatha yoga emphasize that it should only be practiced in conjunction with raja yoga.

Other yoga paths are usually derivatives of the principle six. They include:

Asparsha Yoga

This is the yoga of non-contact. A form of jnana yoga, asparsha seeks reintegration through non-touching, avoiding all forms of contact with others.

Astanga Yoga

Astanga yoga is often known as the path of Patanjali. The sage Patanjali (ca. 200 B.C.E.) taught a comprehensive yoga system that became a spiritual school unto itself. According to Patanjali, in order to experience true reality one must transcend the body and mind. In his *Yoga Sutras* he outlined the following special stages:

yama and *niyama*–ethical restraints and moral observations.
asana–physical postures.
pranayama–breathing exercises. This uses various cleansing techniques of the nasal passages, throat, stomach, and bowels; it is used to enhance the pranayama.
pratyahara–sense withdrawal.
dharana–concentration.
dhyana–meditation.
samadhi–superconsciousness.

Japa Yoga

A branch of mantra yoga, *japa* (meaning recitation) yoga emphasizes repetition of prayers, hymns and sacred syllables.

Kundalini Yoga

Utilizing hatha yoga and mantra yoga techniques to arouse kundalini, or divine creative energy. This path focuses on the arousal of kundalini as the central focus of spiritual exercise. Whether kundalini rising occurs because of the exercises or on its own accord remains a matter of debate.

Kriya Yoga

Based on teachings of Paramhansa Yogananda, author of *Autobiography of a Yogi.* Kriya yoga stresses the path to Eternal Tranquility, emphasizing the stillness of sensory input.

Laya Yoga

Laya yoga is the yoga of absorption. It underscores absorption in meditation, merging the mind and breath in the divine. In this practice the yogi immerses himself in the universe, becoming a part of the universal body.

Siddha Yoga

This path is based on the teachings of Swami Muktananda. *Siddha* (meaning guru) yoga emphasizes the intervention and guidance of a teacher to raise kundalini.

Tantric Yoga

A derivative of karma and bhakti yogas, tantric yoga is associated with arousal of sexual energy and its conversion into **kundalini,** or creative energy. It is the human reflection of the divine union between the male (*shiva*) and female (*shakti*) as aspects of the divine. It is concerned with techniques and disciplines intended to transform the sexual act into a kundalini-raising experience.

Tantric yoga has often been implicated as an arena for sexual abuses in the West. Less-than-enlightened yogis have been entangled in clandestine affairs with students, later forced to step down from the position of spiritual leader.

Yantra Yoga

Yantra yoga is a form of jnana yoga, in which meditation is accomplished through contemplation of a geometric figure.

No single pathway of yoga is regarded as an alternative to another, and many of the paths intertwine and intersect, as a means of purifying and harmonizing individual temperaments. An intellectual person might profitably concentrate on bhakti yoga or karma yoga; an emotional temperamented one might benefit from jnana yoga and hatha yoga. Likewise, the practice of hatha yoga without proper actions, devotion, and ethical codes might be harmful or result simply in gymnastics without spiritual development.

Sources:

Bernard, Theos. *Hatha Yoga.* London: Rider, 1950. Reprint, New York: Samuel Weiser, 1970.

Bhagavadgita of The Song Divine. Gorakhpur, India: Gita Press, 1943.

Danielou, Alain. *Yoga: The Method of Re-Integration.* London: Christopher Johnson, 1949. Reprint, New Hyde Park, N.Y.: University Books, 1956.

Dvivedi, M. N., trans. *The Yoga-Sutras of Patanjali.* Adyar, Madras, India: Theosophical Publishing House, 1890.

Feuerstein, Georg. *The Shambala Guide to Yoga.* Boston: Shambala Publications, Inc., 1996.

———. "A Short History of Yoga." Yoga Research and Education Center 1999. http://www.yrec.org/.

Giri, Swami Satyeswarananda. "Original Kriya Yoga at a Glance." SpiritWeb 1992. http://www.spiritweb.org/. April 20, 2000.

Gopi Krishna. *The Awakening of Kundalini.* New York: E. P. Dutton, 1975.

The Secret of Yoga. New York: Harper & Row, 1972.

Grupta, Yogi. *Yoga and Long Life.* New York: Dodd, Mead and Co., 1958.

Isherwood, Christopher, and Swami Prabhavananda, trans. *The Bhagavad Gita: The Song of God.* Hollywood, Calif.: Marcel Road, 1944.

Iyengar, B. K. S. *Light of Yoga.* New York: Schrocken Books, 1966.

Keutzer, Kurt and Narayan Prakash. "The Lineage of Swami Shivom Tirth." SpiritWeb 1996. http://www.spiritweb.org/. April 20, 2000.

Majumdar, S. M. *Introduction to Yoga Principles and Practices.* New Hyde Park, N.Y.: University Books, 1964. Reprint, Secacus, N.J.: Citadel Press, 1976.

Melton, J. Gordon. *New Age Encyclopedia.* Detroit: Gale Research, 1990.

Mishra, Rammurti. *Fundamentals of Yoga.* New York: Lancer Books, 1969.

Radhakrishnan, S., trans. *Bhagavad Gita.* London: Allen & Unwin, 1948.

Radha, Swami Sivananda. *Hatha Yoga: the Hidden Language.* Boston: Timeless Books, 1989.

Rosen, Richard, "Georg Feuerstein on Reviving Yoga Research." *Yoga International* (July 1999): 36–43.

The Sounds of Yoga-Vedanta; Documentary of Life in an Indian Ashram. New York: Folkways Records, Long-playing record album FR 8970.

Vishnudevananda, Swami. *The Complete Illustrated Book of Yoga.* New York: Bell Publishing, 1960. Reprint, New York: Pocket Books, 1971.

Wood, Ernest. *Yoga.* London, 1959. Reprint, Baltimore, Md.: Penguin, 1962.

"Yoga Paths." SpiritWeb 2000. http://www.spiritweb.org/. April 20, 2000.

Yogananda, Paramhansa. *Autobiography of a Yogi.* Los Angeles: Self-Realization Fellowship Publishers, 1972.

Yoga International

Quarterly magazine devoted to **yoga, meditation,** philosophy, **psychology,** and holistic living. Formerly called *Dawn,* Yoga International is the official organ of the **Himalayan International Institute of Yoga Science and Philosophy.** Address: R.R. 1, Box 400, Honesdale, PA 18431.

Yoga Journal

Monthly journal of California Yoga Teachers Association, dealing with various aspects of (primarily hatha) **yoga,** nutrition, and health. Lists annually an international directory of yoga teachers and centers. Address: P.O. Box 469088, Escondido, CA 92046-9088. Website: http://www.yogajournal.com/.

Sources:

Yoga Journal. http://www.yogajournal.com/. March 8, 2000.

Yoga Life (Magazine)

Illustrated magazine and organ of the **International Sivananda Yoga Vedanta Centers,** with articles on hatha **yoga, meditation,** and related topics. It includes information on branch activities of the affiliated centers. It is issued from the group's headquarters at 673 8th Ave., Val Morin, Quebec, Canada J0T 2R0. Website: http://www.sivananda.org/.

Sources:

Sivananda Yoga "Om" Page. http://www.sivananda.org/. March 27, 2000.

Yoga-Mimamsa Journal

Indian journal founded in 1935 devoted to the serious study of hatha **yoga** and pranayama, with papers describing medical and scientific researches as well as popular aspects. Edited by **Swami Kaivalyadhama,** a noted authority on yoga. The journal commenced publication in 1935 and describes activities at the Kaivalyadhama SMYM Samiti, India. It is issued from the Yoga-Mimamsa Office, 117 Valvan, Lonavla 410 403, India.

Yogananda, Paramahansa (1893–1952)

An early Indian spiritual teacher who visited and taught in Western countries and who founded the **Self-Realization Fellowship.** Yogananda was born Mukunda Lal Ghosh in Gorakpur, near Calcutta, on January 5, 1893. He manifested psychic powers as a child. As a youth he was fascinated by the holy men of India and visited many of them. Shortly after graduating from high school, he was initiated by Swami Yukteswar in the spiritual lineage of Swami Babaji, a legendary Himalayan master. He graduated from college in 1914. While in college he took the vows of a sannyasin, to live the renounced life, and was given his religious name, Yogananda, meaning the bliss (ananda) of **yoga.**

Yukteswar encouraged Yogananda to come to the West, and he traveled to Boston in 1920, ostensibly to speak at a conference, where he taught a system of yoga deriving basically from the classic text *Yoga Sutras of Patanjali.* He also developed his own variety of kriya yoga, involving withdrawal of life energy from outward affairs to inner spiritual centers (basically a form of **kundalini** yoga).

Yogananda remained in the United States after the 1920 conference and several years later founded the Yogoda Satsang, which was incorporated in 1935 as the Self-Realization Fellowship. He wrote books and a correspondence course that attracted a number of pupils to him. He laid great emphasis on the reconciliation of Hinduism with Christian teachings and established the "Church of All Religions."

Yogananda passed into *mahasamadhi* (the great sleep of death) in 1952, but his body is said to have remained free from decay for 20 years afterward. Among his last accomplishments was the writing of his *Autobiography of a Yogi* (1946), which was widely influential in attracting Americans to Eastern religion. He was also the teacher of Donald Walters, founder of the Ananda Church of Self-Realization, and Roy Eugene Davis, now head of the Church of the Christian Spiritual Alliance.

Sources:

Yogananda, Swami Paramahansa. *Autobiography of a Yogi.* New York: Philosophical Library, 1946.

———. *The Divine Romance.* Los Angeles: Self-Realization Fellowship, 1986.

———. *Metaphysical Meditation.* Los Angeles: Self-Realization Fellowship, 1960.

———. *The Science of Religion.* Los Angeles: Yogoda Sat-Sanga Society of America, 1928.

———. *Whispers of Eternity.* Los Angeles: Self-Realization Publishing House, 1944.

Yoga Research Foundation, Inc.

Founded in 1962 as the Sanatan Dharma Mandir in Puerto Rico by **Swami Jyotirmayananda.** The headquarters moved to suburban Miami in 1969 as the International Yoga Society. It adopted its present name in the 1980s. Swami Jyotirmayananda is a disciple of **Swami Sivananda Saraswati.** He has been assisted by Swami Lalitananda (Leonora Rego), vice president of the foundation.

The foundation publishes books, cassettes, and study courses on **yoga** and Hindu philosophy, and a monthly magazine called *International Yoga Guide.* Swami Jyotirmayananda is an authority on the little-known Hindu scripture *Yoga-Vasishtha Maharamayana,* upon which he comments regularly in the magazine. He has lectured widely, participated in Spanish/English radio programs, and appeared on television.

Branches of the Yoga Research Foundation exist throughout the world. Swami Jyotirmayananda's ashram in Loni, near New Delhi, India, publishes the Hindi Journal *Yogajali,* as well as numerous Hindi translations of Swami Jyotirmayananda's books. Ashram members assist those in need through a medical clinic, and also further the education of children through the Bal Divya Jyoti Public School.

Devotees of Swami Jyotirmayananda have turned his ancestral home of Ananda Bhavan in Dumari (Bihar, India) into a spiritual center. The project provides the village of Dumari Buzurg with a school for children, library, satsang hall, and technical workshop. Women are taught hygiene, nutrition, and home economics. The project is designed to affect the economic, ethical, cultural, and spiritual life of the village.

The foundation is an international organization, dedicated to "elevating the consciousness, alleviating suffering and enriching the lives of all humanity" through integral yoga (Sivananda's system integrating hatha yoga with the four major traditional yogas: raja, bhakti, karma, and jnana), providing "a basis for upgrading the cultural growth of humanity while bringing about a worldwide level of social and religious harmony." Regular classes teaching yoga, Vedanta, and Indian philosophy are conducted from the center. A Yoga Research Foundation catalog of books and cassettes, and subscriptions to the *International Yoga Guide* can be obtained by writing to 6111 SW 74th Ave., South Miami, FL 33143. Website: http://www.yrf.org/.

Sources:

Yoga Research Foundation Home Page. http://www.yrf.org/. March 8, 2000.

Yoga Society of San Francisco

Organization founded in 1972 by Shri Brahmananda Sarasvati that offers classes in **yoga, meditation,** massage therapy, and teacher training courses. Its headquarters are located at 2872 Folsom St., San Francisco, CA 94110. Website: http://www.artnetwork.com/healing/yoga/.

Sources:

Yoga Society of San Francisco. http://www.artnetwork.com/healing/yoga/. March 8, 2000.

Yoga Today (Magazine)

Comprehensive monthly magazine dealing with all aspects of **yoga** as seen from a British and European viewpoint. Typical articles covered interviews with yogis, sidelights on yoga teaching and practitioners, and health and diet. Special features included book reviews and worldwide news coverage. Last known address: Yoga Today Ltd., 21 Caburn Crescent, Lewes, East Sussex, BN7 INR, England.

"Yolande"

The spirit of a young Arabian girl of 15, materialized through the mediumship of **Elizabeth d'Esperance** (1885–1919). Yolande appeared to manifest as an independent entity and was photographed, like the equally famous **"Katie King"** of the medium **Florence Cook.**

'You' and ESP (Newsletter)

Monthly newsletter issued by the Temple of the Inner Flame, headed by Carol Ann Liaros, concerned with such psychic activities as Fingertip Vision (also known as **eyeless sight**) and alternative medical treatments. Last known address: 3329 Niagara Falls Blvd., North Tonawanda, NY 14120

Younghusband, Sir Francis (Edward) (1863–1942)

British explorer, soldier, author, and mystic. Born at Murree, India, May 31, 1863, he was educated at Clifton and Sandhurst, England. He joined the British army in 1882.

From 1886 to 1887 he traveled across central Asia from Peking to Yarkand and on to India, crossing the Karakoram Range by the Muztagh Pass. He discovered the Aghil Mountains and showed that the Great Karakoram was the water divide between India and Turkistan. On later explorations beyond the Karakoram he was able to trace the river Shaksgam to its junction with the Yarkand, and explored the Pamirs. During his period in the 1st Dragoon Guards, Younghusband held the rank of captain.

In 1890 he transferred to the Indian political department and served in northwest frontier stations. He visited South Africa in 1896. He was a special correspondent for *The Times* newspaper, London, in the Chitral Expedition in 1895 and a political agent in Haraoti and Tonk in 1898. While residing in India, he was the British Commissioner to Tibet (1902–04). He led the British mission to Lhasa, culminating in the Anglo-Tibetan Treaty of September 7, 1904. For this he was honored by the decoration of Knight Commander of the Indian Empire. He was one of the first modern British explorers to investigate the almost legendary territory of Tibet and enter the mysterious city of Lhasa, long fabled by Theosophists and others as the center of mysterious adepts and Masters. While he discovered no secret **occult** forces, he did develop a sympathetic consideration of Eastern religions and an appreciation of their spirituality.

In 1905 he returned to England, where he became Rede lecturer at Cambridge University before traveling to Kashmir as Resident. He was honored as Knight Commander of the Star of India in 1917. After his retirement in 1919, he became chairman of the Royal Geographical Society, who had awarded him their gold medal in 1891. He also formed and was chairman of the Mount Everest Committee.

Younghusband typified the best of the old-style British patriots of the British Empire period. He was an excellent and courageous soldier and explorer, yet deeply sympathetic to the aspirations and spiritual ideals of other peoples. He recognized the need for self-government in India. His book *Modern Mystics* (1935; reissued University Books, 1970) expressed his sympathy with the spirituality of different religions and his belief in an underlying unity. In 1936 he founded the **World Congress of Faiths.** His books include: *But in Our Lives* (1926), *The Heart of Nature* (1921), *India and Tibet* (1910), *Within* (1912), *The World Congress of Faith* (1938), and *World Fellowship of Faiths* (1935).

He died at Lytchett Minster, near Poole, Britain, on July 31, 1942.

Sources:

Samuel, Herbert L. *Man of the Spirit: Sir Francis Younghusband.* London, 1953.

Seaver, George F. *Francis Younghusband: Explorer and Mystic.* London, 1952.

Your Astrology (Journal)

Quarterly journal that includes monthly and daily guides for all signs, with articles on **astrology** for lay readers. Last known address: Charlton Publications, Inc., Charlton Building, Derby, CT 06418.

Yowie

Australian equivalent of the **yeti,** or "Abominable Snowman." The first account of the yowie appeared in 1835 when a Mr. Holman said of his trip to the subcontinent, "The natives are greatly terrified by the sight of a person in a mask calling him 'devil' or Yah-hoo, which signifies evil spirit." By 1840, Australian scientists were debating whether or not the yahoo was an imaginary being or a real, but rare, species. By the 1880s European settlers began to report seeing something that resembled a huge monkey or baboon. Through the first half of the twentieth century occasional reports appeared, almost all from New South Wales and Queensland. Along the way, "yahoo" became "yowie."

A new set of reports arose in the 1970s following the sighting of some large (too large to be a human), humanlike tracks by an Australian Air Force surveying team on Sentinel Mountain. In the late 1970s Rex Gilroy founded the Yowie Research Center and now claims over 3,000 sightings.

The yowie has been integrated into the field of cryptozoology, but remains one of the more doubtful creatures under consideration. Australia has no naturally occurring primates other than humans. The major champion of the yowie's existence is Graham C. Joyner, who has argued that it is a bear-like marsupial.

Sources:

Clark, Jerome. *Encyclopedia of Strange and Unexplained Phenomena.* Detroit: Gale Research, 1993.

Joyner, Graham. *The Hairy Man of Southeastern Australia.* Canberra: National Library of Australia, 1977.

———. "Scientific Discovery and the Place of the Yahoo in Australian Zoological History." *Cryptozoology* 9 (1990): 41–51.

"Yram" (1884–1917)

Pseudonym of Dr. Marcel Louis Forhan, pioneer French experimenter and writer on **astral projection,** i.e., **out-of-the-body travel.** Forhan was born on November 17, 1884, at Corbell, France. About 1911 he became a member of the **Theosophical Society** and investigated psychic phenomena and hypnotism.

About this time he had his first experience of astral projection and developed an awareness of higher worlds. It is claimed that he was able to travel astrally from China, where he lived for some years, to France, where he had friends and relatives. His experience of invisible worlds is related in his book *L'Evolution dans les mondes supérieures.* He died in China on October 1, 1917.

Sources:

Yram [Marcel Louis Forhan]. *Le Medecine de l'Ame.* English edition as *Practical Astral Projection.* London, 1935. Reprint, New York: Samuel Weiser, 1966.

Z

Zabulon

Name of a demon said to have possessed a lay sister among the community of nuns at **Loudun,** France, in 1633.

Zacaire, Denis (b. 1510)

This French alchemist is chiefly remembered for his book, *Opuscule Tres-Excellent de la Philosophie naturelle des Metaux* (published 1567). This includes a preface written by Zacaire in his lifetime, giving some account of his life.

As a young man Zacaire studied at Bordeaux under an alchemist and subsequently at Toulouse, intending to become a lawyer. He soon became more interested in **alchemy** than in legal affairs. In 1535, on his father's death, he came into possession of some money. He thereupon decided to try and multiply it by artificial means. Associating himself with an abbé who was considered a great adept in gold-making, Zacaire had soon disposed of the bulk of his patrimony, but far from the charlatan's futile experiments disillusioning him, they encouraged him.

In 1539, he went to Paris, where he made the acquaintance of many renowned alchemists. From one of them, he learned the precious secret, and thereupon he hastened to the court of Antoine d'Albert, the king of Navarre, offering to make gold if the requisite materials were supplied.

The king was deeply interested and promised a reward of no less than four thousand crowns in the event of the researches proving fruitful, but unfortunately Zacaire's vaunted skill failed him, and he retired discomfited to Toulouse. Here he became friendly with a certain priest, who advised him strongly to renounce his quest and study natural science instead. Zacaire went off to Paris once more, intending to act in accordance with his counsel. But after a little while, he was deep in the study of alchemy again, running experiments and studying closely the writings of **Raymond Lully** and **Arnold de Villanova.**

According to his own account, on Easter day of 1550, he succeeded in converting a large quantity of quicksilver into gold. Then, some time after this alleged triumph, he left France to travel in Switzerland and lived for a while at Lausanne. Later on he wandered to Germany, and there he died.

There is a story that he married before setting out to travel through Germany, but on reaching Cologne, he was murdered in his sleep by his servant, who escaped with his wife and his store of transmuting powder. The story of Zacaire's life was told in verse by De Delle, court poet of Emperor Rudolph II (1552–1622), who took a great interest in alchemy, chemistry, and **astrology.**

Zacaire's *Opuscule* was published originally at Antwerp and repeatedly reprinted. It won the honor of being translated into Latin.

Sources:

Davis, T. L. "The Autobiography of Denis Zacaire: An Account of an Alchemist's Life in the Sixteenth Century." *Isis* 8, 2 (1926).

Zacornu

A tree in the Islamic hell that has for fruit the heads of devils.

Zadkiel

Pseudonym of **Richard James Morrison** (1795–1874), one of the pioneer British astrologers of the nineteenth century. He was born in London, England, on June 15, 1795. He joined the navy when only eleven and eventually rose to the rank of lieutenant by the time of his retirement in 1817. He developed an interest in **astrology** in the 1820s and became a friend of Robert Cross Smith ("Raphael") who published *Raphael's Astronomical Ephemeris.* Morrison modeled his own successful *Zadkiel's Almanac,* begun in 1836, on Smith's work. Morrison calculated horoscopes for the Prince Consort and the Princess Royal that were gratefully accepted, but Queen Victoria later expressed concern about predictions for the Prince Consort, possibly because they were so accurate as to cause some disquiet.

Morrison's name made reference to one of the angels in the Jewish rabbinical legend of the celestial hierarchies. He was the ruler of Jupiter. Through him pass grace, goodness, mercy, piety, and munificence, and he bestows clemency, benevolence, and justice on all.

Sources:

Lewis, James R. *Astrology Encyclopedia.* Detroit: Visible Ink Press, 1994.

Morrison, R. J. *An Introduction to Astrology by William Lilly.* 1835. Reprint, Hollywood, Calif.: Newcastle, 1972.

Zaebos

Said to be grand count of the infernal regions. He appears in the shape of a handsome soldier mounted on a crocodile. His head is adorned with a ducal coronet. He is of a gentle disposition.

Zagam

Said to be grand king and president of the infernal regions. He appears as a bull with the wings of a griffin. He changes water into wine, blood into oil, the fool into a wise man, lead into silver, and copper into gold. Thirty legions obey him.

Zahuris (or Zahories)

French people who had traveled in Spain frequently had curious tales to tell concerning the *Zahuris*—people who were so keen-sighted that they could see streams of water and veins of metal hidden in the earth and could indicate the whereabouts of buried treasure and the bodies of murdered persons.

Explanations were offered on natural lines. It was said that these men knew where water was to be found by the vapors arising at such spots, and that they were able to trace mines of gold, silver, and copper by the particular herbs growing in their neighborhood. But to the Spaniards, such explanations were unsatisfactory; they persisted in believing that the *Zahuris* were gifted with supernatural faculties, that they were in rapport with demons, and that, if they wished, they could, without any physical aid, read thoughts and discover secrets that were as a sealed book to the grosser senses of ordinary mortals. The *Zahuris* were said to have red eyes, and in order to be a *Zahuri* it was necessary to have been born on a Good Friday.

Zain, C. C.

Pseudonym of **Elbert Benjamine** (1882–1951), astrologer and occultist. He was born December 12, 1882, in Iowa. As a young man he became associated with an **occult** organization, the Hermetic Brotherhood of Luxor, which presented itself as the outer court of the Brotherhood of Light, a group of spiritual masters equivalent to the **Great White Brotherhood.** In 1907 Benjamine became one of the Hermetic Brotherhood's three leaders. He was asked by the other two leaders to write a series of lessons in occult wisdom. He began to write in 1914. The lessons, published under the pen name C. C. Zain, appeared in 21 volumes, each dealing with one area of occult knowledge.

While Benjamine was writing, the Hermetic Brotherhood was discontinued, and in 1932 Benjamine founded the **Church of Light** as a new outer court for the Brotherhood of Light. Benjamine died November 18, 1951, and was succeeded by Edward Doane as president of the church.

Sources:

"The Founders of the Church of Light." *Church of Light Quarterly* 45, no. 1 (February 1970): 1–2.

Zain, C. C. [Elbert Benjamine]. *Brotherhood of Light Lessons.* 21 vols. Los Angeles: Church of Light, 1922–1932.

Zancig, Julius (1857–1929) and Agnes

Famous Danish **thought-reading** couple, whose mentalist demonstrations at the London Alhambra in Britain fooled many people, caused much public excitement, and led to a minor scientific controversy. Mrs. Zancig could correctly name any article, number, or word at which her husband cast a glance. The *Daily Mail* arranged a series of tests in their offices on November 30, 1906, and published the conclusion that the performance was the result of true **telepathy.** The *Daily Chronicle* differed and considered a clever code system sufficient explanation. The questions and answers were registered by a phonograph record. Nothing was discovered.

The psychical researcher **W. W. Baggally** conducted some experiments. He concluded that although the alleged transmission of thought might possibly depend on a code or codes that he was unable to unravel, the performance was of such a nature that it was worthy of serious scientific examination.

The **Society for Psychical Research,** London, investigated on January 18, 1907. The result was not published. However, it appeared sufficiently favorable for some of the members present to subsequently form an official committee to carry on further tests. The report stated:

"While we are of opinion that the records of experiments in telepathy made by the SPR and others raise a presumption for the existence of such a faculty at least strong enough to entitle it to serious scientific attention, the most hopeful results hitherto obtained have not been in any way comparable as regards accuracy and precision with those produced by Mr. and Madame Zancig. . . . Those who have only witnessed the public theatre performances, clever and perplexing as these are, will not appreciate how hard it is to offer any plausible explanation of their *modus operandi.*"

The Zancigs claimed telepathy as an explanation, and Mrs. Zancig had well-developed **clairvoyant** faculties. At the Spiritualist **British College of Psychic Science,** London, she successfully passed book-reading tests.

Magician Will Goldston was among the first to publicize the Zancigs' method of operation. His book *Sensational Tales of Mystery Men* (1929) spoke of their mentalism from the inside knowledge of a practitioner of stage magic:

"The pair worked on a very complicated and intricate code. There was never any question of thought transference in the act. By framing his question in a certain manner Julius was able to convey to his wife exactly what sort of object or design had been handed to him. Long and continual practice had brought their scheme as near perfection as is humanly possible. On several occasions confederates were placed in the audience and at such times the effects seemed nothing short of miraculous. All their various tests were cunningly faked and their methods were so thorough that detection was an absolute impossibility to the layman."

In his book *Rudi Schneider* (1930), the psychical researcher **Harry Price** expanded upon Goldston's observations: "The Zancigs' performance took years of study to perfect, and several hours practice daily were needed to keep the performers in good form. I have the Zancigs' codes in my library and know the hard work that both Mr. Julius Zancig and his wife put into their 'act,' a matter which I have discussed with Mr. Zancig himself."

Just when the Zancigs were at the pinnacle of their career Agnes died in 1916. Julius tried to continue the act with several other people, but never to the same effect.

"Zanoni"

Title of an **occult** novel by **Bulwer Lytton.** (See also **Fiction, English Occult**)

Zapan

According to demonologist **Johan Weyer,** one of the kings of Hell.

Sources:

Weyer, Johannes. *Witches, Devils and Doctors in the Renaissance: Johann Weyer, De Praestigiis.* Ed. George Mora. Binghamton, N.Y.: Medieval & Renaissance Texts & Studies, 1991.

Zazen

Term used in **Zen** Buddhism to indicate the sitting position for **meditation,** which usually takes place in the *Zen-do* or meditation hall in Zen monasteries. The meditation position is known as *dhyanasana.* It resembles the "lotus" position of **hatha yoga** known as *padmasana,* but the hands have a precise positioning integral to the very different method and goal of Zen meditation.

ZCLA Journal

Former periodical concerned with past and present writings of **Zen** masters on the subject of Zen Buddhism. Some of the contents include material not previously translated into Western languages. It was published three times a year by the Zen Center of Los Angeles and has in recent years been superseded by a new periodical, *The Ten Directions.*

Zedekias (fl. ninth century C.E.)

Said to have been a Jewish physician of the ninth century who was in great favor with the Emperor Charles the Bald. Zedekias had a reputation as a Kabbalist and wizard and was said to have eaten a whole load of hay, together with the driver and horses, in the presence of the emperor's court. On another occasion he supposedly flew around in the air.

Zedekias was mentioned by the **Abbé de Montfaucon de Villars** in his book *Comte de Gabalis* (1670). According to de Villars, Zedekias was anxious to show the world that **elementary spirits** really existed and advised the sylphs to show themselves in the air to everyone:

"These beings were seen in the Air in human form, sometimes in battle array marching in good order, halting under arms, or encamped beneath magnificent tents. Sometimes on wonderfully constructed aerial ships, whose flying squadrons roved at the will of the Zephyrs. What happened? . . . The people straightway believed that sorcerers had taken possession of the Air for the purpose of raising tempests and bringing hail upon their crops. . . . The Emperors believed it as well; and this ridiculous chimera went so far that the wise Charlemagne, and after him Louis the Débonnaire, imposed grievous penalties upon all these supposed Tyrants of the Air. You may see an account of this in the first chapter of the Capitularies of these two Emperors."

Zeernebooch

A dark god, monarch of the empire of the dead among the ancient Germans.

Zeitoun

Zeitoun, a suburb of Cairo, Egypt, was the site from 1968 to 1971 of some of the most spectacular sets of **apparitions of the Virgin Mary.** She was seen not just by a few children as in most of the reported apparitions in the last two centuries, but by thousands of Christians, Jews, and Muslims alike. However, it is also the case that the sightings appeared at a Coptic church, rather than a Roman Catholic one, and that very little interest in the apparitions has been demonstrated by Catholic authorities.

The apparitions began on the evening of April 2, 1968. Two men, both Muslims, working in a garage across from the Coptic Church of St. Mary in Zeitoun, saw what they first thought was a nun standing on top of the central dome of the church's roof. Their initial thought was that she was about to commit suicide by leaping off the dome. One went to get the priest and one an emergency squad. Others began to gather, attracted by the confusion. The woman on the dome rose to her feet and was revealed as a being encompassed in brilliant light. A woman in the crowd shouted out that it was the Virgin. Several objects that appeared to be luminous birds fluttered around the lady. One of the workmen who had originally seen the figure had a wounded hand and was scheduled for surgery the next morning. When he reported to the hospital, the doctors discovered his hand had been healed.

The object on the church roof, soon believed by many to be the Virgin, faded from sight after a while. It would be another week before it reappeared. After that, the appearances varied. For periods they would occur every night. Sometimes they would be brief, and on occasion last as long as six or seven hours. Most of the time she was alone. On occasion she had a child in her arms or appeared with figures believed to be St. Joseph and Jesus as a lad of 12. As many as 250,000 people crowded the streets around the church and witnessed the Virgin's appearances. Eventually, a number of pictures of the phenomena were taken. The last apparition occurred on May 29, 1971, at which pictures were taken.

The Coptic Church has made much of the apparitions and of the many healings reported because of them. Stories of healing have continued to the present. Because of the context, no inquiry by the Roman Catholic Church of the kind that has accompanied reported apparitions in Europe has been made. However, the Coptic patriarch did order an inquiry and the general information and complaints department of the Egyptian government made an inquiry and report. During the apparitions, Fr. Jerome Palmer, an American Benedictine monk, went to Egypt and wrote one of the first accounts of the phenomena by a Westerner. They have also become the subject of ecumenical discussions between the Coptic patriarch and the pope.

To date, no critical studies of the phenomena have appeared. These sightings differ greatly from the more traditional reported encounters with the Virgin that have been limited to only a few people. They also involve the sighting of an object that had enough solidity that it could be seen and photographed. While no hint of fraud has appeared in the literature about the phenomena, one must not rule out the possibility that the sightings were staged, though the hows and whys are unknown.

Sources:

Johnson, Francis. *When Millions Saw Mary.* Chulmleigh, Devon, UK: Augustine Publishing, 1980.

Palmer, Jerome. *Our Lady Returns to Egypt.* San Bernardino, Calif.: Culligan Book Co., 1969.

Zeitschrift für Metapsychische Forschung

Monthly psychical research magazine, established in 1930, and published through the decade in connection with the Institute für Metapsychische Forschung, by Dr. Christop Schroeder, in Berlin, Germany.

Zeitschrift für Parapsichologie

A monthly German periodical of **psychical research,** originally founded by **Alexander Aksakof** in 1874 under the title *Psychische Studien.* The new title was assumed in 1925 and continued through 1934. Aksakof had originally hoped to publish a Spiritualist journal in his native tongue of Russian, but was prevented by the power of the Orthodox Church. His journal was issued in German from Leipzig.

Zeitschrift für Parapsychologie und Grenzgebiete der Psychologie (Journal)

Journal of Parapsychology and Border Areas of Psychology, published by the **Institut für Grenzgebiete der Psychologie** (Institute for Border Areas of Psychology). Articles in the journal frequently are accompanied with summaries in English. Address: Eichhalde 12, D-7800 Freiburg in Br., Germany.

Zen (or Ch'an)

One of the few traditional forms of instant enlightenment in Oriental religions. However, Zen normally demands a long preliminary period of monastic life and spiritual discipline culminating in the somewhat surrealist techniques that give instant *satori,* or enlightenment.

Zen is a special branch of Mahayana Buddhist school (which dominates Buddhism in China, Korea, and Japan), dating from 520 C.E. when Bodhi-Dharma (d. 534 C.E.) went from India to China with a mission later codified in the maxims: "a special transmission outside the scriptures; no dependence upon words and letters; direct pointing at the soul of man; seeing into one's nature; and the attainment of Buddhahood." Zen was later divided into two main schools, called Rinzai and Soto in Japan.

Rinzai Zen depends very much upon sudden or startling paradoxes, embodied in *koans,* mystical riddles such as "Empty-handed I come, carrying a spade." Modern interest in Zen often misunderstands the nature of such riddles, where the verbal factor is merely a trigger to intensify stress in the pupil, and as a result many Westerners tend to treat Zen as a kind of intellectual exercise. In practice, however, such paradoxes were the culmination of a more formal monastic training emphasizing traditional spiritual values. The disciple would be fully extended on all levels of his nature—physically, in the everyday hard work of the monastery; mentally, in the assimilation of spiritual teaching; and emotionally, in the sudden clash of unconventional techniques used in Zen.

The koans merely accentuated an intolerable pressure at all levels, culminating in the sudden flash of enlightenment by transcendence on a higher, spiritual plane. (See also **ZCLA Journal; Zazen; Zen Studies Society**)

Sources:

Humphreys, Christmas. *Zen Buddhism.* London: Heinemann, 1949. Reprint, New York: Macmillan, 1967.

Suzuki, D. T. *Manual of Zen Buddhism.* New York: Grove Press, 1960.

———. *Zen Buddhism: Selected Writings of D. T. Suzuki.* Edited by William Barrett. New York: Doubleday/Anchor, 1956.

Zener Cards

A pack of twenty-five cards bearing simple symbols in groups of five of a kind: star, circle, square, cross, and waves, used in **parapsychology** in testing extrasensory faculty under laboratory conditions. The use of the Zener card pack dates from the work of **J. B. Rhine** in the Department of Psychology at Duke University, North Carolina, from 1927 onward, first reported in Rhine's *Extrasensory Perception,* published 1934 by the **Boston Society for Psychic Research.**

Prior to the work of Rhine, ordinary playing cards had been used in testing telepathy, notably by **Margaret Verrall** between 1890 and 1895. Significant tests were carried out in Britain by Ina Jephson and other members of the **Society for Psychical Research** beginning in 1924.

The Zener card pack was devised by Karl Zener (1903–1963) of the psychology faculty at Duke University as a means of avoiding preferences for individual playing cards during tests and in order to facilitate evaluation of test scores. Having concluded that parapsychology as pursued by Rhine was a threat to the psychology department, Zener later turned against Rhine and joined with some colleagues in an attempt to have him removed from his faculty position.

Two problems developed with the Zener cards. First, while they were designed to be more emotionally neutral than traditional playing cards, in fact, they used some highly charged emotional symbols, such as the star, a prominent symbol in many religions. Second, in the early printings, the ink bled through and the symbol was clearly visible on the back of the card. This later problem was immediately corrected when discovered.

Sources:

Berger, Arthur S., and Joyce Berger. *The Encyclopedia of Parapsychology and Psychical Research.* New York: Paragon House, 1991.

Jephson, Ina. "Evidence for Clairvoyance in Card-Guessing: A Report on Some Recent Experiments." *Proceedings* of the Society for Psychical Research 38: 223–271, and 39: 375–414.

Jephson, Ina, S. G. Soal, and Theodore Besterman. "Report on a Series of Experiments in Clairvoyance (conducted at a distance)." *Proceedings* of the Society for Psychical Research 39 (1928).

Sanger, C. P. "Analysis of Mrs. Verrall's Card Experiments." *Proceedings* of the Society for Psychical Research 2, no. 28 (1895).

Zen Studies Society

American lay organization for the study of traditional **Zen** meditation inspired by the presence of D. T. Suzuki in New York City in 1956. Upon the death of its founder Clifton Cane in 1962, it became inactive for a few years but was reactivated when some of the students met Eido Tai Shimano, a Zen master who agreed to move to New York and lead the work. Emphasis in the reorganized society shifted from study to practice, and branches soon developed in Philadelphia and Washington, D.C.

Associated with the society is the Dai Bosatsu Zendo Kongo-ji, in the Catskill Mountains, that is open to lay people for full-time Zen practice with daily meditation, study, work, and community life. The society publishes *The Newsletter of the Zen Studies Society,* a semi-annual newsletter and writings of Shimano. The society can be contacted at HCR 1 Box 171, Livingston Manor, NY 12758-9402. Website: http://www.zenstudies.org/.

Sources:

Shimano, Eido. *Golden Wind.* Tokyo: Japan Publications, 1979.

Shimano, Eido, ed. *Like a Dream, Like a Fantasy.* Tokyo: Japan Publications, 1978.

The Zen Studies Society. http://www.zenstudies.org/. March 8, 2000.

Zepar

Said to be the grand duke of the infernal empire, possibly identical with Vepar, or Separ. Nevertheless, under the name of Zepar he had the form of a warrior. He cast men into evil passions. Twenty-eight legions obeyed him.

Zeroid

Term used by some ufologists to denote creatures or animals that may exist and live in space. As yet, no positive evidence exists for their reality. To date reports are limited to the likes of the account in the *Weekly World News,* for October 1, 1985, that "a herd of space animals, the size and shape of the Goodyear blimp, grazed for three hours on cattle pastures near the remote Argentine ranching settlement of Villa Iruya."

Zetetic Scholar

A journal of academic research into **occultism, cryptozoology,** and related fields founded by **Marcello Truzzi** of the Department of Sociology at Eastern Michigan University. Originally titled *Explorations,* the title was changed after the second volume to avoid confusion with the Explorations Institute in Berkeley, California.

"Zetetic" derives from the Greek philosophical school of Pyrrho (365–275 B.C.E.) and indicates extreme skepticism. *Zetetic Journal* circulated to serious academics researching occultism and to organizations and individuals in the field. It contained critical notes and news of current events and personalities in occultism, a who's who in occult research, and valuable lists of books and articles in the fields of occultism and **parapsychology.** The *Zetetic* was given to the **Committee for the Scientific Investigation of the Claims of the Paranormal.** However, in 1977 Truzzi had a disagreement with the committee leadership over their handling of a research project in which false data was published in an attempt to refute **astrology.**

Truzzi disassociated himself from the committee and announced publication of *Zetetic Scholar* as an independent scientific review. The first issue appeared in 1978. In the meantime, beginning with the Fall/Winter issue, the committee continued its journal under a new name, *The Skeptical Inquirer.* Truzzi continued the *Zetetic Scholar* through the 1980s, some 15 issues appearing. *The Skeptical Inquirer* continues as the organ of the Committee for the Scientific Investigation of Claims of the Paranormal.

Zhong Gong

Zhong Gong, founded in China in 1988, is one of the most popular of the **qigong** groups operating in the Peoples Republic of China through the 1990s. By the end of the decade it was estimated to have 20 million followers. However, in 1999, in the wake of the crackdown on the **Falun Gong** group, it was also singled out for repressive measures. The Chinese government declared that the meditation-exercise sect was an "evil cult."

Zhong Gong, the China Health Care and Wisdom Enhancement Gong, was founded by Zhang Hongbao (b. 1955) during the heyday of government support for qigong. In spite of its operating apart from the officially sanctioned National Qigong Association, Zhong Gong speedily spread across the country. It was also favorably mentioned in the official press. Its training school in Shaanxi Province had over 2,000 students. Reportedly, the country's president, Jiang Zemin, had sought out a Zhong Gong Master to treat his arthritis and back pain.

Zhang Hongbao taught a traditional form of qigong that emphasized the use of exercises and **meditation** as a means of stimulating **qi** energy. Such energy, once properly flowing through the body, would bring health and enhanced mental functioning.

Through the 1990s, the group had some minor run-ins with authorities and became known as an independent organization apart from government control, though no ideological elements appeared to contradict government authority (as with Falun Gong). However, in December of 1999, police closed the Zhong Gong training facility in Shaanxi. Then in January of 2000, the leader of the group in Zhejiang Province was sentenced to two years for the Chinese equivalent of practicing medicine without a license, a charge potentially placing all qigong groups at risk. The government has charged that following qigong has been accompanied with admonitions to stop seeing medical doctors.

In the wake of the move against Zhong Gong, the government announced broad changes in regulations dealing with qigong groups specifying how they must be organized and what teachings they may espouse. The ongoing issues concerning Zhong Gong and other qigong groups are being covered in the press and monitored by various human rights groups.

Sources:

Eckholm, Erik. "China Imprisons a Leader of Healing-by-Meditation Society." *New York Times* (January 20, 2000).

Ziazaa

A mysterious fabled black and white stone. It was said to render its possessor litigious and cause terrible visions.

Zierold, Maria Reyes

A Mexican **sensitive** who was the subject of experiments by **Gustav Pagenstecher** (1855–1942) from about 1919 onward. Zierold was a housewife whom Pagenstecher treated for insomnia by means of hypnosis. To his surprise, Zierold manifested psychometric ability while in hypnotic trance.

A medical committee in Mexico City also examined Zierold's abilities and reported that the phenomena seemed genuinely paranormal. In 1921 **Walter Franklin Prince,** then principal research officer of the **American Society for Psychical Research** visited Mexico to observe Pagenstecher's experiments and to conduct his own. He reached similar conclusions.

Sources:

Pagenstecher, Gustav. *Die Geheimnisse der Psychometrie oder Hellsehen in die Vergangenheit* (Secrets of Psychometry or Clairvoyance into the Past). N.p., 1928.

———. "Notable Psychometrist." *Journal* of the American Society for Psychical Research 14 (1920).

———. "Past Events Seership." *Proceedings* of the American Society for Psychical Research 16 (January 1922).

Prince, Walter Franklin. "Psychometric Experiments with Maria Reyes de Z." *Journal* of the American Society for Psychical Research 16 (January 1922).

———. "Psychometric Experiments with Maria Reyes de Z." *Proceedings* of the American Society for Psychical Research 15 (1921).

Tyrell, G. N. M. *The Personality of Man: New Facts and Their Significance.* U.K.: Penguin Books, 1947.

Ziito (fl. fourteenth century)

One of the most remarkable magicians that history has left record of. He was a sorcerer at the court of King Wenceslaus of Bohemia (afterward emperor of Germany) toward the end of the fourteenth century. Among his more famous exploits was one chronicled by Janus Dubravius, bishop of Olmutz, in his *Historiae Regni Boiemiae* (History of Bohemia, 1552). On the occasion of the marriage of Wenceslaus with Sophia, daughter of the elector Palatine of Bavaria, the elector, knowing his son-in-law's liking for juggling and magical exhibitions, brought a number of morris dancers, jugglers, and other entertainers. When they came forward to give their exhibition Ziito remained unobtrusively among the spectators. He was not entirely unnoticed, however, for his remarkable appearance drew the attention of those about him. His oddest feature was his mouth, which reportedly stretched from ear to ear.

After watching the magicians for some time in silence, Ziito appeared to become exasperated at the halting way in which the tricks were carried through, and going up to the principal magician, he taunted him with incompetency. The rival professor hotly defended his performance, and a discussion ensued that was ended at last when Ziito allegedly swallowed his opponent, just as he stood, leaving only his shoes, which he said were dirty and unfit for consumption.

After this extraordinary feat, he retired for a little while to a closet, from which he shortly emerged, leading the rival magician by the hand. He then gave a performance of his own which put the former exhibition entirely to shame. He changed himself into many different shapes, taking the form of first one person and then another, none of whom bore any resemblance either to himself or to each other.

In a car drawn by barn-door fowls, he kept pace with the king's carriage. When the guests were assembled at dinner, he played a multitude of elfish tricks on them.

Indeed, he was at all times an exceedingly mischievous creature, as is shown by another story told of him. Pretending to be in want of money, and apparently casting about anxiously for the means of obtaining some, he at length took a handful of corn and made it look like thirty fat hogs. These he took to Michael, a rich but very mean dealer. The latter purchased them after some haggling, but was warned not to let them drink at the river. The warning was disregarded, the hogs drank, and they were turned into grains of corn.

The enraged dealer went in search of Ziito, whom he found in a vintner's shop. In vain Michael shouted and stamped. The magician took no notice, but seemed to be in a fit of abstraction. Eventually the dealer, beside himself, seized Ziito's foot and pulled it as hard as he could. To his dismay, the foot and leg came right off, while Ziito screamed lustily and hauled Michael before the judge, where the two presented their complaints. What the decision was, history does not relate, but it is unlikely that the ingenious Ziito came off worse.

Zikr

A Sufi term meaning "remembrance," indicating the constant awareness of divine consciousness in humanity. In **Sufism,**

Zikr takes the form of a specific ritual to bring individuals into a higher state of consciousness. The practice of zikr varies considerably from group to group, but its most famous form, as practiced by some Turkish Sufis, involves circular movements of the group members who came to be known as whirling **dervishes.**

Zitko, John Howard (1911–)

John Howard Zitko, **New Age** lecturer and founder of the World University, a center for alternative education, was born in Milwaukee, Wisconsin, on October 26, 1911. He attended the University of Wisconsin in Milwaukee and the University of California in Los Angeles, and received a Doctor of Divinity degree from Golden State University.

Zitko was cofounder of the Lemurian Fellowship established in Chicago, Illinois, in 1936 and edited its early book, *The Earth Dweller Returns* (1940), reputedly a sequel to the nineteenth-century channeled text, *A Dweller on Two Planets* (1899), by Phylos the Tibetan (through Frederick William Oliver). The movement of the fellowship to rural California in 1941 encouraged Zitko's move to the West Coast. He served as the minister of the Temple of the Jeweled Cross in Hollywood for four years (1942–46). During this time he conceived of the idea of a World University, and on December 21, 1946, founded the World University Roundtable as a parent corporation to develop the idea and raise funds. He later served a brief tenure as pastor of the Church of the Abundant Life in Huntington Park, California (1956–59).

Over the years the concept of the World University was undergirded with the idea of promoting world peace through world education. Finally, in 1967, the World University was founded in Tucson, Arizona, to offer nontraditional, experiential, and tutorial learning with an emphasis on world order studies, environmental concerns, and human potential knowledge. It is headquartered from its campus, now located in Benson, Arizona, but functions primarily through its many small affiliated schools located around the world. It has pulled together a faculty of independent scholars who are intellectually aligned with the nontraditional curriculum supported by the university. Among its American affiliates is the Aum Esoteric Study Center headed by Robert Hieronimous in Baltimore, Maryland.

Though concentrating on the university's development, through the years Zitko has remained active with the Lemurian Fellowship and in 1981 was named its vice president. His 1947 book, *Streamers of Light from the New World,* had heralded many New Age themes, and as the New Age Movement emerged, he authored several books that embodied the alternative perspective on education and life represented by the university: *New Age Tantra Yoga* (1974) and *World University Insights with the Future in Mind* (1980). These books resonated with the movement of the 1980s and Zitko became a popular New Age lecturer and teacher.

Sources:

Zitko, Howard J. *New Age Tantra Yoga.* Benson, Ariz.: World University, 1974.

———. *World University Insights with the Future in Mind.* Benson, Ariz.: World University, 1980.

Zizaa

A fabulous precious stone, said to produce marvelous dreams for those who looked at it before sleeping. An illustration of it appears in *Hortus Sanitatis* by Johannis de Cuba, Strasbourg (ca. 1483).

Zizis

The name that modern Jews give to their phylacteries.

Zlokobinca

Among the **Slavs,** name for a witch, meaning "evil dealer."

Zoaphite

According to the seventeenth-century traveler Jan Struys, a zoaphite was a species of cucumber that fed on neighboring plants. Its fruit had the form of a lamb, with the head, feet, and tail of that animal distinctly apparent, and it is thus called, in the language of the country, *Canaret,* or *Conarer,* signifying a lamb. Struys described this plant in his book *Drie aanmerkelijke en seer rampspoedige* (1676), translated as *The Voyages and Travels of Jan Struys* (1684).

Its skin was covered with a white down. The ancient Tartars thought a great deal of it and most of them kept it carefully in their houses, where Jan Struys says he saw it several times.

It grew on a stalk about three feet in height, to which it was attached by a sort of tendril. On this tendril it could move about and turn and bend toward the herbs on which it fed, and without which it soon dried up and withered. Wolves loved it, devouring it with avidity, because, reportedly, it tasted like the flesh of a lamb. The author added that he had been assured that it had bones, flesh, and blood, thus being known in its native country as zoaphite, or animal plant.

Zodiac

The zodiac, literally the circle of animals, is constituted by the 12 stellar constellations through which the Sun appears to pass in its annual movement through the heavens. The 12 constellations form a belt across the night sky some 8 to 9 degrees on either side of the solar orbit. The Moon and the planets of this solar system also move within that belt. The path of the Sun is called the ecliptic as eclipses occur when the Moon's orbit crosses the Sun's path.

The idea of a zodiac is relatively complex, and long-term observation of planetary motion is quite possible without it. The idea of naming the various constellations in the sky for gods and animals is ancient; the singling out of the 12 constellations that constitute the zodiac goes back at least to the second millennium B.C.E. in ancient Mesopotamia. The zodiac as it appears in modern **astrology** was certainly in use by the sixth century B.C.E. Each culture gave the constellations of the zodiac different names, the modern Western zodiac being derived from the Greeks. The designation of 12 constellations, a worldwide phenomenon, relates to the division of the year by the Moon's 12 complete orbits through the zodiac in each solar year.

In modern astrology, two different zodiacs are popularly recognized. The sidereal zodiac reflects the actual location of the constellations in the night sky. Practitioners of **Vedic astrology** use this zodiac. The position of the constellations relative to the beginning of the years shifts slightly each year due to the phenomenon known as the **procession of the equinoxes.** Most Western astrologers use the tropical zodiac as defined by **Ptolemy** in the second century C.E. According to Ptolemy, the astrological year would begin each spring **equinox** and it would assume that the sun was at 0 degrees Aries. Due to the progression of the equinoxes, the sun at the spring equinox is close to 0 degrees Pisces. Much of the symbolism of the signs of the zodiac in Western astrology is tied to the seasons of the year. That symbolism would be lost with the acceptance of the sidereal zodiac.

The 12 signs of the zodiac are: Aries, Taurus, Gemini, Cancer, Leo, Libra, Scorpio, Sagittarius, Capricorn, Aquarius, and Pisces. (See also **Astrological Houses; Astrological Planets; Astrological Signs; Astrology**)

Sources:

Brau, Jean Louis, Helen Weaver, and Allen Edwards. *Laurouse Encyclopedia of Astrology.* New York: New American Library, 1980.

Cirlot, J. E. *A Dictionary of Symbols.* New York: Philosophical Library, 1971.

McCaffery, Ellen. *Astrology: Its History and Influence in the Western World.* New York: Charles Scribner's Sons, 1942.

The Zoist (Journal)

The journal of medical mesmerists in Britain during the mid-nineteenth century. It was under the direction of Dr. John Elliotson and was published from 1843 to 1856. The popular side of **mesmerism** was represented by *The Phreno-Magnet,* another periodical started at the same time and edited by Spencer T. Hall.

"Zolar"

Pseudonym of successful astrologer **Bruce King.**

Zöllner, Johann C. F. (1834–1882)

Professor of physics and **astronomy** at the University of Leipzig, remembered most for his speculative work, *The Nature of the Comets,* which attracted the attention of the intellectual world in view of the many original ideas he advanced. He also engaged in **psychical research** beginning with an investigation of the phenomena of the medium **Henry Slade.** His subsequent book, *Transcendental Physics* (1880), rendered his name famous in the annals of psychical research and subjected him to persecution, contempt, and ridicule from the scientific fraternity. He is considered a somewhat naive investigator unable to detect the **fraud** perpetuated on him by a series of physical mediums.

His experiments began in December 1877. He was assisted by William Edward Weber, a professor of physics; W. Scheibner, a professor of mathematics; and Gustave Theodore Fechner, a professor of physics who, to quote Zöllner's words, became "perfectly convinced of the reality of the observed facts, altogether excluding imposture or prestidigation." Professor Fichte, of Stuttgart, and Professor Ulrici, of Halle, also endorsed the experiments that were further supported by an affidavit of Bellachine, the conjurer at the court of Berlin.

The evidential value of the investigation was somewhat weakened by Zöllner's insistence on the theory of fourth dimension as an explanation. Of the theory itself, the astronomer G. V. Schiaparelli wrote in a letter to **Camille Flammarion:**

"It is the most ingenious and probable that can be imagined. According to this theory, mediumistic phenomena would lose their mystic or mystifying character and would pass into the domain of ordinary physics and physiology. They would lead to a very considerable extension of the sciences, an extension such that their author would deserve to be placed side by side with Galileo and Newton. Unfortunately, these experiments of Zöllner were made with a medium of poor reputation."

Zöllner, after his sittings with Slade, had further interesting experiences with **Elizabeth d'Esperance.** In March 1880, Baron von Hoffmann engaged the medium **William Eglinton** to give twenty-five sittings to Zöllner. He was very satisfied with the result and intended to write another book on his experiences. He died before he could do it.

The report of the skeptical **Seybert Commission** quoted testimonies from Scheibner, Fechner, and some others that Zöllner, at the time of his experiments, was of unsound mind. As he filled his chair up to the moment of his sudden death, this charge cannot be seriously supported. In his book *Birth and Death as a Change of Form of Perception* (1886), **Baron Lazar De Baczolay Hellenbach** wrote that Zöllner "was in his last days deeply wounded and embittered by the treatment of his colleagues, whose assaults he took too much to heart. Zöllner, however, was in perfect possession of his intellect till his last breath."

When the report of the Seybert Commission was made public, anti-Spiritualists, like popular atheist writer Joseph McCabe, seized upon the remarks about Zöllner and wrote of him as "elderly and purblind." **Dr. Isaac Kauffmann Funk,** the New York publisher and psychical investigator, wrote to Leipzig and received from Dr. Karl Bücher, the Rector Magnificus of the University of Leipzig, a letter, dated November 7, 1903, that "information received from Zöllner's colleagues states that during his entire studies at the university here, until his death, he was of sound mind; moreover, in the best of health. The cause of his death was a hemorrhage of the brain on the morning of April 26, 1882, while he was at breakfast with his mother, and from which he died shortly after."

Sources:

Berger, Arthur S., and Joyce Berger. *The Encyclopedia of Parapsychology and Psychical Research.* New York: Paragon House, 1991.

Inglis, Brian. *The Paranormal: An Encyclopedia of Psychic Phenomena.* London: Granada, 1985.

Zöllner, Johann C. F. *Transcendental Physics.* Trans. C. C. Massey. London: W. H. Harrison, 1882.

Zombies

In Haitian **voudou** superstition, a zombie is a dead body revived by magic to act as a soulless robot. In recent years stories of zombies have spread throughout Western countries in Hollywood horror films about the walking dead. According to the folk tradition, the *houngans,* or voudou priests, are said to dig up corpses and reanimate them by magic rituals. Another way of creating a zombie is to feed the victim a preparation that stupefies the soul, leaving the body a living corpse.

To cure a zombie, it is said one should give it saltwater to drink. Special burial techniques are sometimes used to prevent corpses from being used as zombies. The corpse may be buried face down and its mouth filled with earth; sometimes the lips are sewn together, presumably to prevent the soul from leaving by the mouth. A somewhat naive custom is to strew handfuls of sesame seed on the grave (a common practice in eastern Europe to entertain vampires), so that the spirit of the deceased will always be occupied in counting the seeds.

Firsthand accounts of zombies have continued into the late twentieth century. Author Alfred Métraux stated that six months after the death of a friend he saw that friend as a zombie at the house of a houngan. Harvard ethnobiologist Wade Davis, who visited Haiti in 1982, succeeded in penetrating the secret societies and understanding and documenting the voudoo culture. He has suggested that certain powerful drugs might be capable of influencing centers in the brain concerned with conscious control. A person given such drugs would appear dead, would be buried alive, and revived several days later. They would then be given hallucinogens and forced into a new life as an unpaid laborer.

Davis' theories were recently validated by an expedition to Haiti that was the subject of a remarkable BBC television program presented by John Tusa in 1984. In interviews with houngans, the secret of creating zombies was disclosed. A poisonous substance from the puffer fish (*Diodon hystrix*) is carefully prepared by the houngan and administered to the victim, who thereafter appears dead and is buried. He is exhumed by the houngan and used as a zombie. The poison stupefies certain brain centers.

The poison was analyzed by Leon Roizy, professor of neurobiology at Columbia University, and identified as tetrodotoxin, found in the puffer fish, the exquisitely dangerous gourmet dish of Japanese Fugu, requiring skillful preparation by experienced chefs in order to avoid poisoning the diner.

When eaten sliced raw (*sashimi*), the flesh is relatively safe, but among eaters of the partly cooked dish known as *chiri*, which includes toxic cooked livers, there are over a hundred deaths annually.

Sources:

Davis, Wade. *The Serpent and the Rainbow.* New York: Simon & Schuster, 1985.

Zoomancy

A system of **divination** based on the appearances and behavior of animals.

Zorab, George A(vetoom) M(arterus) (1898–1990)

Author and parapsychologist. He was born on January 11, 1898, at Surabaya, Java. His family sent him to the Netherlands for his education. He encountered **Spiritualism** when only twelve years old and was interested in psychic phenomena from then on. He was also grateful to Spiritualists for relieving him of his fear of death. He became an active Spiritualist as a young man and edited several Spiritualist periodicals. He joined the Studieverening voor Psychical Research (Dutch Society for Psychical Research) and beginning in 1932, he experimented in **parapsychology** with a concentration on spontaneous paranormal phenomena and quantitative experiments in **extrasensory perception** with psychotics. In 1938 he joined the **Society for Psychical Research,** London. He published his first book in 1940, by which time he had concluded that the spirit hypothesis was only weakly supported and the evidence for survival questionable.

After the war Zorab emerged as an active parapsychologist. He chaired the International Committee for the Study of Spontaneous Paranormal Phenomena, The Hague; was a secretary for the First International Conference on Parapsychological Studies in Utrecht, the Netherlands, in 1953; and participated in the Conference on Spontaneous Paranormal Phenomena at Cambridge, England, in 1955, and the International Conference on Psychology and Parapsychology at Royaumont, France, in 1956.

He was named honorary secretary of the Dutch Society for Psychical Research (1945–57) and directed the **Parapsychology Foundation**'s European Research Center at St. Paul de Vence, France. In 1960 he was selected to become a member of the Council of the Parapsychology Association, a position which he refused. He did accept, however, the Perrott-Warwick Studentship in Psychical Research for 1968/1969. He was the European review editor of the *Indian Journal of Parapsychology*, contributed many articles to *Tijdschrift voor Parapsychologie* and other parapsychological journals, and wrote a number of books. Zorab remained active in the field of parapsychology until 1987, due to failing health. He died July 4, 1990.

Sources:

Berger, Arthur S., and Joyce Berger. *The Encyclopedia of Parapsychology and Psychical Research.* New York: Paragon House, 1991.

Pleasants, Helene, ed. *Biographical Dictionary of Parapsychology.* New York: Helix Press, 1964.

Snel, F. W. J. J., ed. *In Honour of G. A. M. Zorab.* Amsterdam: Verenining voor Parapsychologie, 1986.

Zorab, George A. M. *Bibliography of Parapsychology.* Parapsychology Foundation, 1957.

———. "A Case for Survival." *Journal* of the Society for Psychical Research 31 (1946).

———. *D. D. Home, il Medium.* Milan, 1976.

———. "ESP Experiments with Psychotics." *Journal* of the Society for Psychical Research 39 (1957).

———. "A Further Comparative Analysis of Some Poltergeist Phenomena Cases from Continental Europe." *Journal* of the American Society for Psychical Research 58 (1964).

———. *De Jacht op het Spiritistisch Bewijs* (In Quest of Proof for Survival). The Hague: Boucher, 1940.

———. *Katie King: Donna o Fantasma.* Milan: Armenia Editore, 1980.

———. *Magnetiseurs en Wondergenezers* (Magnetism and Miracle Healers). N.p., 1952.

———. *De Opstandingsverhalen in het Licht de Parapsychologie* (The Resurrection Narratives in the Light of Parapsychology). N.p., 1949.

———. *Parapsychologie* (Parapsychology). N.p., 1958.

———. *Proscopie, Het Raadsel der Toekomst* (Precognition, the Riddle of the Future). N.p., 1953.

———. *Wichelroede en Aardstralen* (The Divining Rod and Earthrays). N.p., 1950.

———. *Wonderen der Parapsychologie* (Wonders of Parapsychology). N.p., 1954.

Zorab, George A. M., P. A. Dietz, and K. H. E. de Jong. *Parapsychologische Woordentolk* (A parapsychological dictionary). N.p., 1956.

Zos Kia Cultus

The system of magic developed by occult artist **Austin Osmond Spare,** involving a complete symbolism of form, sound, desire, and will, deriving from sexual energy. Zos was not only Spare's magic name but also a symbol of the body as a whole, which could project desires and modify the world of matter. The primary practitioner of the system in the United States is Michael Bertiaux, head of the Monastery of the Seven Rays.

Sources:

Grant, Kenneth. *Cults of the Shadow.* New York: Samuel Wiser, 1976.

Zschokke, (Johannes) Heinrich (Daniel) (1771–1848)

German-Swiss writer, actor, and pastor, born at Magdeburg, March 22, 1771. He was educated at Frankfurt-on-Oder, where he studied theology, philosophy, and jurisprudence. He encountered difficulties with authorities on account of his pronounced political opinions, but eventually concentrated on writing plays and Gothic romances influenced by Sir Walter Scott. His romance *Abaeillino, der grosse Bandit* was produced in 1794 and had an enormous success, being dramatized the following year. It was adapted by the English writer Matthew Gregory Lewis as *The Bravo of Venice* in 1804 and greatly influenced themes in Gothic romance. Zschokke died at Aarau June 27, 1848.

Zuccarini, Amedee (ca. 1907)

Italian, non-professional medium of Bologna who exhibited the ability to perform **levitation,** which was studied in great detail by Dr. L. Patrizi, professor of physiology at the University of Modena, and Professor Creste Murani of the Milan Polytechnic. (*Annales des Sciences Psychiques*, vol. 17, pp. 528–549). For an English language account, see *Annals of Psychical Science* (vol. 6, no. 34, 1907, pp. 303–306). Flashlight photographs showed him up in the air without support. Zuccarini had two **trance** personalities, a deceased brother and a doctor who had died in 1600.

Zügun, Eleonore (1914–)

A Romanian peasant girl, born in 1914 at Talpa, Romania, the subject of **poltergeist** persecution and the phenomena of **stigmata.** Her experiences filled her neighbors with dread. When the phenomena appeared, about 1925, the peasants attributed them to Dracu, the devil, an idea the girl accepted. She was incarcerated in an asylum.

The Countess Wassilko-Serecki and her friends heard of the strange case, rescued the girl, and took her to Vienna. The countess published an article and a book about the young girl. The British psychical researcher **Harry Price** visited Vienna in May 1926 and reported on the phenomena surrounding Zügun in the *Journal* of the **American Society for Psychical Research** (August 1926). He found the phenomena genuine. On Price's invitation, the countess and her protégée then came to London for an investigation at the **National Laboratory of Psychical Research.** The case was reported in the NLPR *Proceedings* (vol. 1, part 1, January 1927) and widely discussed in the press.

Capt. Seton-Karr testified on October 19, 1926: "I was present on October 5, when the so-called stigmatic markings appeared on the face, arms and forehead of Eleonore Zügun under conditions which absolutely precluded the possibility of Eleonore producing them by scratching or other normal means. The marks were photographed in my presence."

The report of the National Laboratory of Psychical Research, after describing various telekinetic and **apport** phenomena, concluded on the stigmata as follows:

"There is not the slightest doubt that our careful experiments, made under ideal scientific conditions, have proved that:

"(a) Stigmatic markings appeared spontaneously in various parts of Eleonore's body;

"(b) That Eleonore was not consciously responsible for the production of the marks;

"(c) That under scientific test conditions movements of small objects without physical contact undoubtedly took place. The experimenters, unless they are bereft of all human perceptions, cannot possibly come to any other conclusions.

"What has happened to Eleonore is apparently this: During her early childhood when the so-called 'poltergeist' phenomena became first apparent, the simple peasants threatened her so often with *Dracu* (the Devil) and what he would do to her that her subconscious mind became obsessed with the idea of whippings, bitings, etc., which the ignorant peasants said would be her lot at the hands—or teeth—of *Dracu.* Remove the *Dracu* complex and the girl would probably be troubled no further with stigmatic markings.

"If we have discovered the cause of the 'stigmata' I am afraid we cannot lay claim to having unraveled the mystery of the telekinetic movements of the coins, etc. We have merely proved that they happen."

Toward the end of her fourteenth year, at the approach of the menses, Zügun completely lost her psychic powers.

Sources:

Price, Harry. "Some Account of the Poltergeist Phenomena of Eleonore Zügun." *Journal* of the American Society for Psychical Research (August 1926).

Wassilko-Serecki, The Countess. "Observations on Eleonore Zügun." *Journal* of the American Society for Psychical Research (September/October 1925).

———. *Der Spuk von Talpa.* München, 1926.

Zwaan Rays

An hypothesized energy field demonstrated by N. Zwaan, Dutch delegate to the International Spiritualist Federation Congress in London in 1948. The Zwaan Rays were supposed to be capable of stimulating the psychic senses into activity. Subsequently the Spirit Electronic Communication Society was founded in Manchester, England, on September 10, 1949, and an apparatus was developed that claimed to improve the Zwaan effect. (See also **Ashkir-Jobson Trianion**)

Sources:

Dyne, Mark. *Electronic Communication for the Spiritual Emancipation of the People.* Rev. ed., Manchester, England: The Spirit Electronic Communication Society, 1954.

Internet Resources

This section, organized by subject, contains information on organizations specializing in occultism, parapsychology, New Age, Theosophy, holistic healing, etc. Every effort has been made to provide the most current sites available. All sites were active at the time this edition went to press.

ACUPRESSURE

Acupressure.org
http://www.acupressure.org/
British Columbia Acupressure Therapist's Association
http://www.islandnet.com/~bcata/

ACUPUNCTURE

Acupuncture Canada
http://www.acupuncture.ca/
Acupuncture.com
http://www.Acupuncture.com/
American Association of Oriental Medicine
http://www.aaom.org/
The British Medical Acupuncture Society
http://www.medical-acupuncture.co.uk/
National Certification Commission for Acupuncture and Oriental Medicine
http://www.nccaom.org/

ADAMSKI FOUNDATION

GAF International/Adamski Foundation
http://www.gafintl-adamski.com/html/GAFpg1.htm

THE AETHERIUS SOCIETY

The Aetherius Society
http://www.aetherius.org/

ALCHEMY

Alchemy Lab
http://www.alchemylab.com/
The Alchemy Web Site and Virtual Library
http://www.levity.com/alchemy/
The Hermetic Alchemical Order of the QBLH
http://www.qblh.org/
Hermetic Alchemy
http://www.mension.com/pikealcm.htm
Mensionization Complimentation
http://www.mension.com/#math
White Order of Thule
http://www.thulean.org/

AMERICAN MUSEUM OF MAGIC

American Museum of Magic
http://www.marshallmi.org/tours/virtual/magic.html

AMERICAN SOCIETY FOR PSYCHICAL RESEARCH

American Society for Psychical Research
http://www.aspr.com/

AMULETS

Arabic Folk Medicine and Magic: 20th Century Amulets from the Kelsey Museum of Archaeology
http://www.si.umich.edu/CHICO/Archives/amulets/home.html

ANCIENT ASTRONAUT SOCIETY

Ancient Astronaut Society (German)
http://home.t-online.de/home/astronautik/aas.htm

ANCIENT MYSTERIES

Ancient Mysteries
http://www.ancientweb.com/
Atlantis Rising Online
http://atlantisrising.com/
Mysterious Places
http://www.mysteriousplaces.com/

ANCIENT MYSTICAL ORDER ROSAE CRUCIS (AMORC)

Ancient Mystical Order Rosae Crucis
http://www.amorc.org/
Rosicrucian Park
http://www.rosicrucian.org/

ANCIENT WISDOM

Lemurian Fellowship
http://www.lemurian.org/
Universal Life–The Inner Religion
http://www.universelles-leben.org/

ANGELS

Angel Therapy
http://www.angeltherapy.com/

ANTHROPOSOPHICAL SOCIETY

Anthroposophic Press
http://www.anthropress.org/
Anthroposophical Society in America
http://www.anthroposophy.org/

AROMATHERAPY

Aromatherapy
http://www.naturalland.com/pcv/ar/arom.htm
Aromatherapy Center Home Page
http://www.madison-avenue.com/aroma/aroma01.htm
International Federation of Aromatherapists
http://www.ifa.org.au/index.htm
National Association for Holistic Aromatherapy
http://www.naha.org/

ARTHURIAN STUDIES

Arthuriana
http://dc.smu.edu/Arthuriana/
Arthurian Legends
http://www.ncsa.uiuc.edu/Edu/RSE/RSEblue/arthur/artidu.html
Arthurian Resources
http://www.users.globalnet.co.uk/~tomgreen/Arthuriana.htm
The Camelot Project
http://www.kingarthur.co.uk/
The Cardiff Arthurian Society
http://www.cf.ac.uk/uwcc/archi/howshall/arthurm/
The Oxford Arthurian Society
http://users.ox.ac.uk/~arthsoc/
Pendragon Society
http://www.pendragon.mcmail.com/index.htm

ASTROLOGY

American Federation of Astrologers
http://www.astrologers.com/
Astro Communications Services
http://www.astrocom.com/
The Astrological Journal
http://www.astrologer.com/aanet/journal.html
Astrological Magazine
http://www.personal.vsnl.com/astromag/
Astrology and Numerology (The Basics)
http://astrology-numerology.com/astrology.html
Astrotalk
http://www.astrologysoftware.com/
Free Online Chart Calculation
http://alabe.com/freechart/

Friends of Astrology
http://www.toonland.com/astro/index.html
Online College of Astrology
http://www.astrocollege.com/library/index.html
Project Hindsight (Origins of Ancient Astrology)
http://www.projecthindsight%2Dtghp.com/
Sabian Assembly
http:// www.sabian.org/

AUROVILLE

Auroville Homepage
http://www.auroville.org/

AYURVEDA

Ayurvedic Foundations
http://www.ayur.com/
Ayurvedic Health Center
http://www.ayurvedic.org/
Ayurvedic Institute
http://www.ayurveda.com/

BACH CENTRE

Bachových kvìtových esencích (Czech Republic)
http://www.bachovy-esence.cz/
Dr. Edward Bach Centre
http://www.bachcentre.com/
Instituto Dr. Edward Bach (Brazil)
http://www.institutobach.com.br/

BERMUDA TRIANGLE

Bermuda Triangle Information (Navy)
http://www.history.navy.mil/faqs/faq8-1.htm
Bermuda Triangle Theories/Stories
http://www.gms.ocps.k12.fl.us/student/bt/bt/home.html

BIG FOOT

Big Foot Central
http://www.suresite.com/wa/b/bigfoot/
Big Foot Fact or Fantasy
http://www.netcomuk.co.uk/~rfthomas/bigfoot.html
The Bigfoot Field Researchers Organization
http://www.moneymaker.org/BFRR/
Big Foot Sightings
http://www.suresite.com/oh/b/buckeyebigfo/
Big Foot Sounds
http://www.angelfire.com/wa/sasquatchsearch/page7.html
North America's Great Ape: Sasquatch
http://www.island.net/~johnb/
Sasquatch Society
http://members.aol.com/ParaPsi/OSSS.htm
Shadowland's Big Foot Page
http://www.serve.com/shadows/bf.htm

BIOFEEDBACK

Association for Applied Psychophysiology and Biofeedback
http://www.aapb.org/
Biofeedback Foundation of Europe
http://www.bfe.org/
Biofeedback Network
http://www.biofeedback.net/
Feedback Institute, Ltd. and EEG-Biofeedback Institute
http://www.eeg-bfb-i.cz
Society for Neuronal Regulation
http://www.snr-jnt.org/

BLAVATSKY, HELENA PETROVNA

Die Theosophische Gesellschaft
http://www.theosophie.de/
Blavatsky Net
http://www.blavatsky.net/
Helena Blavatsky
http://www.helena-blavatsky.de/
The Theosophical Society International
http://www.theosociety.org/
Theosophical Society in America
http://www.theosophical.org/
The Theosophical Society in Australia
http://www.austheos.org.au/

BODY WORK

American Chiropractic Association
http://www.amerchiro.org/
American Massage Therapy Association
http://www.amtamassage.org/
Feldenkrais Guild of North America
http://www.feldenkrais.com/
Massage Magazine
http://www.massagemag.com/index.html
Ortho-Bionomy
http://www.ortho-bionomy.org/
Reflexology: A Better Way to Health
http://www.ozemail.com.au/~sharonc/index.html
Reflexology Association of America
http://www.reflexology-usa.org/

BUCKLAND, RAYMOND

Ray Buckland's Home Page
http://www.geocities.com/SoHo/Workshop/6650/

BUDDHISM, TIBETAN

Kagyu Dharma
http://www.kagyu.com
Tibetan Government in Exile's Official Web Site
http://www.tibet.com/

CAO DAI

Cao Dai
http://www.caodai.org/

CHANNELING

Society of Novus Spiritus
http://www.sylvia.org/novusdoc.htm

CLAIRVOYANCE

Berkeley Psychic Institute
http://www.berkeleypsychic.com/
The Spiritual Development Resource
http://www.gettingthru.org/ascend.html

A COURSE IN MIRACLES

A Course in Miracles
http://www.miraclecenter.org/
Foundation for A Course in Miracles
http://facim.org/
Joseph Plan Foundation
http://www.josephplan.org/

CROP CIRCLES

Centre for Crop Circles Studies
http://www.cropcircleconnector.com/anasazi/cccs97.html
The Cereologist
http://www.abel.net.uk/~sayer
Crop Circle Central
http://www.paradigmshift.com/
The Crop Circle Connector
http://www.cropcircleconnector.com/anasazi/connect.html
Crop Circle Researchers
http://www.cropcircleresearch.com/resources/

CRYPTOZOOLOGY

The British Columbia Scientific Cryptozoology Club
http://www.ultranet.ca/bcscc/
Centre for Fortean Zoology
http://www.eclipse.co.uk/cfz/
International Society of Cryptozoology
http://www.izoo.org/isc/
Loren Coleman's Cryptozoology Page
http://www.lorencoleman.com/
Virtual Institute of Cryptozoology (English Version)
http://perso.wanadoo.fr/cryptozoo/welcome.htm

DEMONOLOGY

Demonology
http://www.djmcadam.com/demons.htm

DIVINATION

ANAM (divining)
http://homepage.tinet.ie/~diviner/
Glossary of Divination
http://home.rmci.net/idahopyro/2000.htm

DOWSING

American Society of Dowsers
http://dowsers.new-hampshire.net/
British Society of Dowsers
http://www.dowsers.demon.co.uk/
Canadian Society of Dowsers
http://www.angelfire.com/on/dowsers/
Canadian Society of Dowsing
http://users.uniserve.com/~questers/

DREAMS, STUDY OF

Association for the Study of Dreams
http://www.asdreams.org/
Dream Dictionary
http://www.dreamloverinc.com/Dictionary2.htm
DreamGate
http://www.dreamgate.com/
Lucidity Association
http://www.sawka.com/spiritwatch
The Lucidity Institute (Dream Control)
http://www.lucidity.com/
The Quantitative Study of Dreams
http://psych.ucsc.edu/dreams/

DRUIDISM

The British Druid Order
http://www.druidorder.demon.co.uk/index.htm

Henge of Keltria
http://www.keltria.org/
The Insular Order of Druids
http://www.insular.demon.co.uk/druids.htm
Introduction to Druids
http://www.geocities.com/Athens/2519/druids.html
The Order of Bard, Ovates and Druids
http://www.druidry.org/index.shtml

ECKANKAR

ECKANKAR
http://www.eckankar.org/
ECKANKAR i Norge og Danmark
http://www.eckankar.no/
Eckankar in Australia
http://www.eckankar.org.au/
ECKANKAR Netherlands
http://www.eckankar.nl/
ECKANKAR Oesterich
http://members.eunet.at/eckankar/
ECKANKAR in Ontario
http://www.eckankar-ont.org/

ELECTRONIC VOICE PHENOMENON (EVP)

Alphaland Biographies
http://www.alphaland.com/biogs.htm
The American Association of Electronic Voice Phenomena
http://www.hibrichan.com/evpfiles/AAEVP.html
Electronic Voice Phenomenon Internet Center
http://www.hibrichan.com/evpfiles/evp.html
International Ghost Hunters Society
http://www.ghostweb.com/evp.html
Reincarnation Electronic Voice Phenomenon
http://home.earthlink.net/~iwonder/evp.htm
World ITC
http://www.worlditc.org/
Verein für Tonbandstimmenforschung (VfT) e.V.
http://www.vtf.de/

EXORCISM

Exorcism-links
http://alapadre.net/exorcism.html
New Definitions for Exorcisms in the Catholic Church
http://www.smh.com.au/news/9901/28/text/national4.html
A Simple Exorcism for Priests and Laity
http://www.truecatholic.org/exorcismsimple.htm

FAIRIES

The Cottingley Fairies
http://www.lhup.edu/~dsimanek/cooper.htm
Fairy Encyclopedia
http://www2.cybercities.com/c/cattis/
Fairy Legends (Cornish)
http://www.gandolf.com/cornwall/fairies/index.shtml
Guide to Irish Fairies
http://www.irelandseye.com/animation/intro.html

FALSE MEMORY SYNDROME

False Memory Syndrome Foundation
http://www.fmsfonline.org/

FENG SHUI

American Feng Shui Institute
http://www.amfengshui.com/
Feng Shui Institute of America
http://www.windwater.com/
Feng Shui Institute of New Zealand
http://www.fengshui.co.nz/
Feng Shui Society (England)
http://www.fengshuisociety.org.uk/

FOLKLORE AND MYTHS

American Folklore Society
http://afsnet.org/
Baltic Institute of Folklore
http://haldjas.folklore.ee/BIF/bhome.htm
Lilith Myth
http://ccat.sas.upenn.edu/~humm/Topics/Lilith/

FORTEAN PHENOMENA

Fortean Times
http://www.forteantimes.com/
International Fortean Organization
http://research.umbc.edu/~frizzell/info

GEOMANCY

Geomancy-Online
http://www.3dglobe.com/on/
Geopathic Information Site Project
http://www.geo.org/
Labyrinthina
http://www.flinet.com/~labyrinthina/index.htm
Mid-Atlantic Geomancy
http://www.geomancy.org/

GHOSTS

The Anomolist
http://www.anomalist.com/
Fate Magazine
http://www.fatemag.com/
Ghost Research Society
http://www.ghostresearch.org

GLOSSOLALIA

Glossolalia and I Corinthians 14 (Lecture)
http://www.apologetique.org/en/rticles/neomontanism/BDG_glossolalia_en.htm
Speaking in Tongues (Religious View)
http://www.religioustolerance.org/tongues.htm

GOLDEN DAWN

Alchemy: The Black Art
http://members.aol.com/frateral/alchemy.html
Builders of Adytum
http://www.bota.org
Hermatic Order of the Golden Dawn
http://www.hermeticgoldendawn.org/index.shtml
Hermetic Order of the Morning Star International
http://www.Golden-Dawn.org/
London Lodge of the Oxford Golden Dawn Occult Society
http://www.lawbright.com/logdos/
The Order of the Thelemic Golden Dawn
http://www.tgd.org/
Ra-Hoor-Khuit Network
http://www.rahoorkhuit.net/
Sovereign and Military Order of the Temple of Jerusalem (International)
http://www.osmth.org/index.html

GNOMES

Encyclopedia Mythica
http://www.pantheon.org/
Gnome Encyclopedia
http://www2.cybercities.com/c/cattis/
Gnomes
http://users.erols.com/michaelmyrick/index.html

GNOSTIC STUDIES

Gnostic Alachemical Church of Typhon-Christ
http://www.geocities.com/Area51/Stargate/7770/.
Gnostic Network
http://trufax.org/menu/gnostic.html
Gnostic Order of Christ
http://www.gnostic.net/
The Gnostic Society
http://home.sol.no/~noetic/hotlist/gnosis.htm
Immaculate Heart Servants of Mary
http://www.Gnostic.net/ihsm/
The Path of Gnostic Light
http://www.mnsi.net/~miskovic/pglvx.htm

GRAPHOLOGY

The British Academy of Graphology
http://www.graphology.co.uk/
The British Institute of Graphologists
http://www.britishgraphology.org/

GRIMOIRES

The Grimoires Page
http://www.magitech.com/~grimoires/

HAUNTINGS

H.O.P.E.
http://www.haunt.net/
L.I.F.E. Foundation
http://www.paranormalhelp.com/paranormalhelp/story.htm
Stories of Ghosts and Hauntings
http://theshadowlands.net/ghost/

HINDUISM

Hinduism Today Online
http://www.hinduism-today.com/

HOLISTIC

Alphabiotics
http://www.alphabiotics.com/

HOMEOPATHY

British Institute of Homeopathy (Canada)
http://www.homeopathy.com/
Homeopathy: Modern Medicine
http://www.indiaspace.com/homeopathy

Institute for Traditional Medicine
http://www.itmonline.org/
National Center for Homeopathy
http://www.healthy.net/nch

HYPNOTISM

Alchemy Institute of Healing
http://www.alchemyinstitute.com/
Holistic World: Hypnotism
http://www.holisticworld.com/Health_and_Wellness/
Hypnoforum
http://www.hypnoforum.com/
Hypnotherapy
http://www.hypnotherapy.com/

I CHING

Bio-Ching
http://www.teleport.com/~biosching/
Mensionization Complimentation
http://www.mension.com/#ching

KABBALAH

Hermetic Kabbalah
http://www.digital-brilliance.com/kab/
Kabbalah Home Page
http://kabbalah-web.org/
Mensionization Complimentation
http://www.mension.com/#kabb
The Online Qabalah
http://www.brokentoy.com/qabalah/
Soul Songs
http://www.soulcongs.com/

KUNDALINI

3HO Organization
http://www.3ho.org/
International Kundalini Yoga Teachers Association
http://www.kundaliniyoga.com/
Kundalini Resource Center
http://hmt.com/kundalini/index1.html
SpiritWeb
http://www.spiritweb.org/Spirit/kundalini.html

LOCH NESS MONSTER

Legend of Nessie
http://www.myspace.co.uk/nessie/
Loch Ness Exhibition
http://www.lochness.co.uk/centre/index.html
Loch Ness Fan Club
http://www.lochness.co.uk/fan_club/index.html
Loch Ness Information
http://www.ochaye.co.uk/
Loch Ness Investigation
http://www.dickraynor.co.uk/
Loch Ness Mystery
http://ourworld.compuserve.com/homepages/lesj/ness.htm
Loch Ness Politics
http://parascope.com/articles/slips/fs26_1.htm
Nessie on the Net: Official Website
http://www.lochness.co.uk/

MAGICAL ORDERS

Servants of the Light
http://servantsofthelight.org/
Servants of the Star and the Snake
http://www.wild.au/sss/index.html

MEGALITHS

Andy Burnham's Page
http://easyweb.easynet.co.uk/~aburnham/
The Center for Archaeoastrology
http://www.wam.umd.edu/~tlaloc/archastro/cfaindex.html
Gungywamp Society
http://www.goudsward.com/gungywamp/
Megalithic Pages
http://members.aol.com/janbily/index.htm

METAPHYSICAL STUDIES

The Australian College of Metaphysical Studies
http://www.ica.org.au/4.html
Banyen Books & Sound
http://www.banyen.com/
College of Metaphysical Studies
http://www.cms.edu/faq.html
The Institute for Advanced Metaphysical Studies
http://www.psychicstudy.com/home.html
International Association of Metaphysicians
http://www.iammall.com/

MOUNT SHASTA

The Official Website of Mount Shasta
http://www.mtshasta.com/homepage.html

MYSTICISM

D.O.M.E., the Inner Guide Meditation Center
http://www.dome-igm.com/
Kabbalah and Jewish Mysticism
http://www.jewfaq.org/kabbalah.htm
The Mysticism Resources Page
http://www.clas.ufl.edu/users/gthursby/mys/
Mysticism in World Religions
http://www.digiserve.com/mystic/
Temple of the Holy Grail
http://www.hometemple.org/

NEAR-DEATH STUDIES

International Association for Near-Death Studies
http://www.iands.org/

NECROMANCY

Necromancy Institute
http://www.diginomicon.org/

NEW AGE

Affiliated New Thought Network
http://www.newthought.org/
Altered States of Consciousness
http://www.ascc.org/
Association for Holotropic Breathwork International
http://www.breathwork.com/
Association for the Alignment of Past Life Experience
http://www.aaple.com/
Astral Projection Home Page
http://www.tanega.com/astral/astral.html
Bodhi Tree
http://www.bodhitree.com/
Children of Light
http://www.childrenoflight.com/
Crystals (Healing power)
http://www.netcomuk.co.uk/~asclepus/HealingCrystalsMenu.htm
ESP Test
http://www.sterba.com/esp/
Heaven's Gate
http://www5.zdnet.com/yil/higher/heavensgate/index.html
Horizon Magazine
http://www.horizonsmagazine.com/
I AM America
http://www.iamamerica.com/
In Light Times
http://www.inlighttimes.com/
Martinus Institute of Spiritual Science
http://www.martinus.dk/
The Messenger
http://www.themessenger.cc/
Mind Travel Plus
http://www.execpc.com/~mholmes/index.html
New Age OnLine Australia
http://www.newage.com.au/
New Age Web Works
http://www.newageinfo.com/res/welcome.htm
New Age World Religious and Scientific Research Foundation
http://www.joshuatreevillage.com/
New Dimensions Broadcasting Network
http://www.newdimensions.org/
NewHeavenNewEarth
http://www.nhne.com/
The New Times
http://www.newtimes.org/
Nexus
http://www.nexusmagazine.com/
Psi Explorer-Telepathy
http://www.psiexplorer.com/TELEPTH3.HTM
Royal Priest Research
http://www.royalpriest.com/
Synchronicity Foundation
http://www.synchronicity.org/
World Wide Mind Network
http://www.ozemail.com.au/~lisadev/ctsite.htm

OUIJA BOARDS

Online Ouija Board
http://www.math.unh.edu/~black/cgi-bin/spirit.cgi
Museum of Talking Boards
http://members.tripod.com/~Ouija_/index.html

PAGANISM

American Vinland Association
http://www.freyasfolk.org/
Angelseaxisce Ealdriht Webpage
http://www.geocities.com/Athens/Delphi/6909/
Ar nDraiocht Fein
http://www.adf.org/homepage.shtml
Artemisian Order
http://www.artemisian.org/sanct.html
Asatru Alliance
http://eagle.webpipe.net
Asatru Folk Assembly
http://www.runestone.org/
The Baltic Romuva
http://www.romuva.lt/

The Celtic Traditionalist Order of Druids
http://www.goodnet.com/~merlyn/ctodmain.htm
Church of All Worlds
http://www.caw.org/
Church of the Iron Oak
http://www.ironoak.org/
Circle Sancturary
http://www.circlesanctuary.org/
Covenant of Unitarian Universalist Pagans
http://www.cuups.org/html/intro.html
Covenant of the Goddess
http://www.cog.org/
Crossroads Lyceum/Fellowship of Isis
http://members.aol.com/isislyceum/file.html
Green Egg
http://www.greenegg.org/
IMBAS
http://www.imbas.org/
The "New" Paganism.org
http://www.paganism.org/
Nova Roma
http://novaroma.org/
The Order of the Crystal Moon
http://members.aol.com/CrystalOrd/CrystalO.htm
Pagan Community Council of Ohio
http://www.netwalk.com/~pcco/
Pagan Educational Network
http://www.bloomington.in.us/~pen/welcome.html
The Pagan Federation (Europe)
http://www.paganfed.demon.co.uk/
Rainbow Wind
http://users.aol.com/RainboWind/rbwintr.htm
Ring of Thoth
http://asatru.knotwork.com/troth/index.html
The Stele Home Page of The Omphalos
http://www.cs.utk.edu/~mclennan/OM/
White Dove's Message
http://www.whitedovemsg.com/
Widdershins
http://www.widdershins.org/

PALMISTRY

The Palmistry Center
http://www.palmistry.com/

PARAPSYCHOLOGY

Anomalous Cognition Section, University of Amsterdam
http://www.psy.uva.nl/pn/res/ANOMALOUSCOGNITION/anamol.shtml
Atlantis Rising
http://www.atlantisrising.com/
Borderland Sciences Research Foundation
http://www.borderlands.com/
Exceptional Human Experience Network
http://www.ehe.org/
Explore Parapsychology
http://www.mdani.demon.co.uk/para/parapsy.htm
Instituto de Estudios Parapsichologicos
http://www.healthclub.fortunecity.com/hockey/91/mainieri.html
International Society for the Study of Subtle Energies and Energy Medicine
http://www.issseem.org/
International Society of Life Information Science
http://wwwsoc.nacsis.ac.jp/islis/
Japanese Society for Parapsychology
http://wwwsoc.nacsis.ac.jp/jspp2/
Journal of Scientific Exploration
http://www.jse.com/
Koestler Parapsychology Unit
http://moebius.psy.ed.ac.uk/
MetaScience Foundation
http://www.metascience.com/
The Monroe Institute
http://www.monroeinstitute.org/
Occultopedia
http://members.tripod.com/occultopedia/Paranormal_Psychic.htm
Occult Sciences and Parapsychology
http://www.nypl.org/research/chss/grd/resguides/occult.html
Office of Paranormal Investigations
http://www.mindreader.com/
Ordo Stellae et Serpente
http://members.aol.com/Yechidah37/ossintro.html.
Paranormal Page
http://www.cisnet.com/jimlilko/paranorm.htm
Parapsychology Foundation
http://www.parapsychology.org/
Parapsychology Index (Planet Click)
http://www.planetclick.com/navcat.mpl?categoryID=1000000000008090
Parapsychology Support Group
http://www2.southwind.net/~rmoon/psg/psg.html
The Perrott-Warrick Research Unit
http://phoenix.herts.ac.uk/PWRU/hmpage.html
Princeton Engineering Anomalies Research
http://www.princeton.edu/~pear/index.html
Psychokinesis (PK)
http://www.themystica.com/mystica/articles/p/psychokinesis_pk.html
Rhine Research Center
http://www.rhine.org/
Student Parapsychology Society
http://www.chelt.ac.uk/su/sps/

PSYCHIC RESEARCH

Association for Research and Enlightenment
http://www.are-cayce.com/
Australasian Society for Psychical Research
http://www.ozemail.com.au/~amilani/ufo.html
Barbara Brennan School of Healing
http://www.barbarabrennan.com/
Central Premonitions Registry
http://clever.net/yaron/precog/
College of Psychic Studies
http://www.psychic-studies.org.uk/
Consciousness Research Laboratory
http://www.psiresearch.org/
Foundation for Inner Peace
http://www.acim.org/
Mind-Matter Unification Project
http://www.tcm.phy.cam.ac.uk/~bdj10/mm/top.html
Society for Psychical Research
http://moebius.psy.ed.ac.uk/~spr/

PSYCHOKINESIS

The RetroPsychoKinesis Project (Experiments Online)
http://www.fourmilab.ch/rpkp/

PYRAMIDS

Egypt State Information Service
http://www.sis.gov.eg/
Nova Online–Pyramids
http://www.pbs.org/wgbh/nova/pyramid/
Pyramids Index
http://www.crystalinks.com/pyramids.html

RANDI, JAMES

James Randi Educational Foundation
http://www.randi.org/

REIKI

American Reiki Master Associtation
http://www.atlantic.net/~arma/
The Canadian Reiki Association
http://www.cordscanada.com/cra/homepage.htm
The International Center for Reiki Training
http://www.reiki.org/
The Radiance Technique International Association, Inc. (TRTIA)
http://www.trtia.org
Reiki Pages by Light and Adonea
http://www.angelfire.com/az/SpiritMatters/

RELIGIOUS TOLERANCE

Religious Tolerance Organization
http://www.religioustolerance.org/

SANTO DAIME

The Eclectic Center of the Universal Flowing Light
http://www.santodaime.org/

SATANISM

The Anton Szandor LaVey Page
http://hem.passagen.se/baphomet/
Australian Satanic Council
http://www.satanic.org.au/
The Church of Satan
http://www.churchofsatan.com/
The First Satanic Church
http://www.satanicchurch.com/
The Official Temple of Set World Wide Web Page
http://www.xeper.org/
The Satanic Society
http://www.thesatanicsociety.net/
Stella Tenebrarum
http://www.geocities.com/Athens/Parthenon/2026/stella.html
Temple of Set Australia
http://www.viper.net.au/~lwild/infernus.html

SCIENTOLOGY

Church of Scientology
http://www.scientology.org/scn_home.htm

SECRET SOCIETIES

DeMolay International
http://www.demolay.org/home/index.shtml
The Freemasonry Network
http://www.freemasonry.net/
The Grand Lodge of Minnesota Ancient and Accepted Free Masons
http://www.mn-mason.org/
Knights Templar
http://www.knightstemplar.org/
Lectorium Rosicrucianum
http:///www.lectoriumrosicrucianum.org/
Official Website of the Ancient and Mystical Order Rosae Crucis
http://www.amorc.org/
The Rosicrucian Archive
http://www.crcsite.org/

SHAMANISM

Ayahuasca Home Page
http://www.ayahuasca.com/
Center for Shamanism and Consciousness Studies
http://www.csacs.org/
Council on Spiritual Practices
http://www.csp.org/
Dance of the Deer Foundation
http://www.shamanism.com/
Drugs and Shamanism
http://www.drugtext.org/psychedelics/inglis.htm
The Foundation for Shamanic Studies
http://www.shamanism.org/
The Institute for Contemporary Shamanic Studies
http://www.icss.org/
Sacha Runa
http://www.sacharuna.com/
Shamanic Dimensions Network
http://www.shamanicdimensions.net/
Student Pagan Association
http://www.uark.edu/studorg/stpa/index2.html
Where the Eagles Fly
http://www.siberianshamanism.com/

SHINTO

International Shinto Foundation
http://shinto.org/menu.html

SKEPTICS

PhiladelphiaAssociation for Critical Thinking
http://www.voicenet.com/~eric/phact/
Skeptic Dictionary
http://dcn.davis.ca.us/~btcarrol/skeptic/
Skeptics Society
http://www.skeptic.com/

SPIRITUALISM

The Attunement Guild
http://www.attunement.org/
Beneficent Spiritual Center Uniao do Vegetel
http://www.udv.org.br/udvpag01-ing.htm
Center for Studies on New Religions (CESNUR)
http://www.cesnur.org/
Church of Revelation
http://www.astralphysicsschool.com/
Community of the Beloved Disciple
http://www.emissaryoflight.com/
Ecclesia Gnostica Alba. http://www.newciv.org/ncn/ega.html.
The Emissaries of Divine Light
http://www.emissaries.org/
First Spiritual Temple
http://www.fst.org/
Foundation Church of the New Birth
http://www.divinelove.org/
Great School of Natural Science
http://school-of-natsci.org/
Greater World Christian Spiritualist Association
http://www.greaterworld.com/
Gurdjieff Studies Group
http://www3.mistral.co.uk/gsg/index.html
Harmony Grove Spiritualist Association
http://www2.4dcomm.com/hgchurch/indexm.htm
The Institute of Spiritualist Mediums
http://www.ism.org.uk/
Morris Pratt Institute
http://www.morrispratt.org/
National Spiritualist Association of Churches
http://www.nsac.org/
New Age On-Line Australia
http://www.newage.com.au./library/spiritualism.html
Noah's Ark Society for Physical Mediumship
http://home.clara.net/noahsark/
Society of the Inner Light
http://www.innerlight.org.uk/
Spiritualists' National Union
http://www.snu.org.uk/
The Swedenborgian Church
http://www.swedenborg.org/
Universal Spiritualist Association
http://www.spiritualism.org/
White Eagle Lodge
http://www.saintjohns.org/

STIGMATA

The Catholic Encyclopedia: Stigmata
http://www.knight.org/advent/cathen/14294b.htm
Mystical World Wide Web: Stigmata
http://www.mystical-www.co.uk/stigmata.htm
Padre Pio's Stigmata
http://www.padrepio.com/pp-stig.html

SWEDENBORG

General Church of the New Jerusalem
http://www.newchurch.org/
The Swedenborg Association
http://www.swedenborg.net/
Swedenborg Foundation
http://www.swedenborg.com/
The Swedenborg Lending Library And Enquiry Centre Sydney, Australia
http://www.swedenborg.com.au/~sllandec/sllandec.html
Swedenborg Society
http://www.swedenborg.org.uk/
Swedenborg Society (Hawaii)
http://www.soc.hawaii.edu/~leonj/leonj/leonpsy/instructor/swedenborg.html

TAOISM

Center for Traditional Taoist Studies
http://www.tao.org/
Confucianism and Taoism Digital Text Resources
http://www.human.toyogakuen-u.ac.jp/~acmuller/contaolink.htm
Foundation of Tao
http://www.padrak.com/tao/
The Taoist Restoration Society (TRS)
http://www.taorestore.org/
Translation of Lao-tze's "Tao Te Ching"
http://www.utm.edu/research/iep/text/tao/tao.htm
Universal Society of the Integral Way
http://www.usiw.org/

TAROT

American Tarot Association
http://www.ata-tarot.com/
International Tarot Society
http://www.geocities.com/Athens/Ithaca/3772/

THEOSOPHY

Blavatsky Net
http://www.blavatsky.net/
Logia Unidad de la Sección Mexicana de la Sociedad Teosófica
http://planet.com.mx/~unidad/index.htm
Magyar Teozófiai Társulat
http://globenet.globenet.hu/teozofia/
Order of Napunsakäs in the West
http://www.wild.au/sss/index.html
Sadra Islamic Philosophy Research Institute (SIPRIn)
http://www.mullasadra.org/
Theosophische Loge "Hermes Trismegistos"
http://members.aol.com/HermesTris/index.htm
Theosophy
http://www.spiritweb.org/Spirit/theosophy.html
Theosophical History
http://idt.net/~pdeveney/
Theosophy Library Online
http://theosophy.org/home.htm
Theosophy(Magazine)
http://theosophycompany.org/febcon.html
The Theosophical Society in Iceland (Adyar)
http://www.itn.is/~theosoph/english/index.html
Theosophical Society (International Headquarters)
http://www.theosociety.org/
Theosophical Society-Denmark
http://home6.inet.tele.dk/hansens/TSmenu_index_uk.htm
Theosophical Society in America
http://www.theosophical.org/
Theosophical Society in Australia
http://www.austheos.org.au/
Theosophical Society in New Zealand
http://www.theosophy.org.nz/
The Theosophical Society in Norway
http://www.theosophical.org/norway.html
Theosophical Society in the Philippines
http://www.sequel.net/peace/tspweb.htm
Theosophy World
http://www.theosophy.net/tw.html

The United Lodge of Theosophists
http://www.ult.org/

THOUGHTFORMS

Healing Thoughtforms
http://www.tsl.org/teachings/h_thoughtforms/thoughtforms.html
Thoughtforms and Spirits
http://www3.sympatico.ca/morgaine/magick6.html

T'AI CHI CH'UAN

Chinese Tai Chi Chuan Association of Canada
http://www.wuji.com/ChineseTaiChiAssociation/
International Taoist Tai Chi Society
http://www.taoist.org/
Taoist Tai Chi Society of Western Australia
www.taoist.org.au/

UFOS

The Association for the Study of Anomalous Phenomena
http://dialspace.dial.pipex.com/town/square/ee65/research/info6.htm
The Black Vault-Freedom of Information Act Documents
http://www.blackvault.com/Main/Sector_1/sector_1.html
Citizens Against UFO Secrecy
http://caus.org/
Computer UFO Newsletter
http://www.ufo.it/
Fortean Times Online
http://www.forteantimes.com/
Fund for UFO Research
http://www.fufor.org/
International Society for UFO Research
http://www.isur.com/
Lia Light
http://www.lialight.com/
The Mutual UFO Network
http://www.rutgers.edu/~mcgrew/MUFON/
National Investigations Committee on UFOs
http://www.nicufo.org/
Saucer Smear
http://www.martiansgohome.com/smear/
Scandinavian UFO Information
http://www.ufo.dk/
Turkish UfO and Paranormal Org
http://members.tripod.com/~ufolojist/default.html
UFO Cases
http://ourworld.compuserve.com:80/homepages/AndyPage/famousuf.htm
UFO Magazine
http://www.ufomag.com/
UFO Net Global
http://www.v-j-enterprises.com/ufointro.html
UFO Online
http://www.ufo.it/english/ufo1.htm
UFO Text Files
http://www.textfiles.com/ufo/

VAMPIRES

Bram Sroker's Dracula Online (Book)
http://www.literature.org/authors/stoker-bram/dracula/index.html
The Dracula Society
http://www.cix.co.uk/~blackie/the_dracula_soc.html
Highgate Vampire Society
http://home.wxs.nl/~intrvamp/hvsoc.htm
London Vampire Group
http://www.vein-europe.demon.co.uk/welcomep/lvg/lvg.htm
Lord Ruthven Assembly
http://ebbs.english.vt.edu/LRA/
New Jersey Association of Real Vampires
http://www.angelfire.com/nj/njarv/main.html
Temple of the Vampire
http://pw1.netcom.com/~temple/home.html
Transylvanian Society of Dracula (Canadian Chapter)
http://www.chebucto.ns.ca/Recreation/TSD/tsdhompg.html
Vampire Directory
http://www.sanguinarius.org/cgi-bin/links/pages/

VOUDOU

Caribbean Religion Center
http://www.nando.net/prof/caribe/caribbean.religions.html
The Temple of Yehwe
http://www.vodou.org/
Voudou (Voodoo) Encyclopedia
http://www.arcana.com/voodoo/
African Dahomean Vodoun
http://www.mamiwata.com/index.html
World History Archives
http://www.hartford-hwp.com/archives/43a/index-i.html

WEREWOLVES

Legend of the Werewolf (Lycanthropy)
http://www.crystalinks.com/werewolves.html
Lycanthrope Resources by and for Lycanthropes
http://www.lycanthrope.org:4242/
The Werewolf Page
http://www.rscreations.com/werewolf/#
Werewolf Terms
http://www.geocities.com/RainForest/Vines/1801/glossary.htm

WICCAN (WITCHCRAFT, WHITE MAGICK. . .)

Alliance of Solitary Practitioners
http://www.witchcraft.net/ASP/
The Aquarian Tabernacle Church
http://www.AquaTabCh.org/
Burning Times
http://www.amasterpiece.com/BurningTimes/
The Burning Times by Catala
http://www.silvermoon.net/catala/burning/times.htm
Covenant of the Goddess
http://www.cog.org/
Modern Witchcraft
http://www.bloomington.in.us/~pen/mwcraft.html
Religious Rights
http://www.landmarknet.net/wicca/rights.htm
Sword of Dyrnwyn
http://www.tylwythteg.com
The Total Wiccan Resources
http://www.geocities.com/Athens/Delphi/5452/
Trinity Magick
http://www.vermontel.net/~trinity/trinity/
Wiccan Church of Canada
http://www.wcc.on.ca/
Wiccan Magic
http://www.wiccanmagic.com/
WiccaNet
http://www.wiccanet.com/
Wiccan/Pagan Resources
http://www.pagansunite.com/index.shtml
The Wiccan Pagan Times
http://www.twpt.com/home.htm
The Witches' League for Public Awareness
http://www.celticcrow.com/
The Witches' Voice
http://www.witchvox.com/

YETI

Ancient Myths
http://www.otherplane.com/am/amyeti.htm
Yeti
http://www.serve.com/shadows/yeti.htm
Yeti Information
http://home.istar.ca/~yeti/yeti%20info.html

YOGA

Ananda Ashram
http://www.anandaashram.org/
Ananda Church of Self-Realization
http://www.ananda.org/
American Yoga Association
http://members.aol.com/amyogaassn/
Dhyanyoga Centers
http://www.dyc.org/
Himalayan International Institute of Yoga Science and Philosophy of the U.S.A
http://www.himalayaninstitute.org/
The Institute for Consciousness Research
http://www.stn.net/icr/icr.html
Integral Yoga International
http://www.yogaville.org/
International Sivananda Yoga Vedanta Centers
http://www.sivananda.org/
International Society for Krishna Consciousness
http://www.iskcon.com/
Online Yoga Resource
http://www.santosha.com/
Overview of Different Yoga Paths
http://www.spiritweb.org/Spirit/yoga.html
Self-Realization Fellowship
http://www.yogananda-srf.org/
Self-Realization Meditation Healing Centres
http://www.selfrealizationcentres.org.
Sivananda Yoga "Om" Page
http://www.sivananda.org/
Vendanta Society of Southern California
http://www.vedanta.org/
Yasodhara Ashram
http://www.yasodhara.org/
Yoga Research and Education Center
http://www.yrec.org/
Yogananda Self-Realization Fellowship
http://www.yogananda-srf.org/

ZEN BUDDHISM

Zen Buddhism Virtual Library

General Bibliography

A. Square [E. A. Abbott]. *Flatland: A Romance of Many Dimensions.* 1884. 6th ed. New York: Dover Publications, 1953.

Abayakoon, Cyrus D. F. *Astro-Palmistry: Signs and Seals of the Hand.* New York: ASI Publishers, 1975.

———. *Rahu Pimma [and] Yama Kalaya.* Delhi, India, ca. 1957.

Abbott, David P. *Behind the Scenes with the Mediums.* Chicago: Open Court; London: Kegan Paul, 1909.

———. *Spirit Portrait Mystery . . . Its Final Solution.* Chicago: Open Court Publishing, 1913.

———. *The History of a Strange Case.* Chicago: Open Court Publishing, 1908.

———. *The Revelations of a Spirit Medium.* St. Paul, Minn.: Farrington, 1891. Rev. ed., edited by Harry Price and E. J. Dingwall. London: Kegan Paul, 1922.

Abbott, G. F. *Macedonian Folklore.* Chicago: Argonaut, Inc., 1909.

Abbott, John. *The Keys of Power: A Study of Indian Ritual and Belief.* London: Methuen, 1932. Reprint, New Hyde Park, N.Y.: University Books, 1974.

Abd-ru-shin [Oskar E. Bernhardt]. *Awake! Selected Lectures.* Vomperberg, Austria: Maria Bernhardt Publishing, n.d.

———. *In the Light of Truth.* 3 vols. Vomperberg, Austria: Maria Bernhardt Publishing, 1954.

Abelson, Joshua. *Jewish Mysticism: An Introduction to Kabbalah.* New York: Sepher-Hermon Press, 1981.

Abercromby, John. *The Pre- and Proto-historic Finns.* 2 vols. N.p., 1898.

Abhedananda, Swami. *Doctrine of Karma: A Study in the Philosophy and Practice of Work.* Calcutta: Ramakrishna Vedanta Math, 1965.

Abrams, Albert. *Human Energy.* San Francisco: The Author, 1914.

———. *New Concepts in Diagnosis and Treatment.* San Francisco: Physico-Clinical, 1922.

Academy of Parapsychology and Medicine. *The Dimensions of Healing: A Symposium.* Palo Alto, Calif.: The Author, 1972.

Academy of Traditional Chinese Medicine. *An Outline of Chinese Acupuncture.* New York: Pergamon Press, 1975; Peking: Foreign Language Press, 1975.

Achad, Frater. *Ancient Mystical White Brotherhood.* 4th edition revised. Great Seal Press Publisher, 1991.

Achad, Frater. *XXXI Hymns to the Star Goddess.* Chicago: Will Ransom, 1923. Reprint, Kenilworth, Ill.: Ordo Adeptorum Invisiblum, 1983.

Achad, Frater [Charles Stansfeld Jones]. *The Anatomy of the Body of God: Being the Supreme Revelation of Cosmic Consciousness.* Chicago: Collegium ad Spiritum Sanctum, 1925. Reprint, New York: Samuel Weiser, 1969.

———. *Chalice of Ecstacy.* Chicago: Yogi Publication Society, 1923.

———. *Liber 31.* San Francisco: Level Press, 1974.

———. *Q.B.L. or the Bride's Reception.* N.p.: The Author, 1922.

Achad, Frater [George Graham Price]. *Ancient Mystical White Brotherhood.* Lakemont, Ga.: CSA Press, 1971.

———. *Melchizedek Truth Principles.* Phoenix, Ariz.: Lockhart Research Foundation, 1963.

Achterberg, Jeanne. *Imagery in Healing: Shamanism and Modern Medicine.* Boston: Shambhala, 1985.

Ackernecht, Erwin H. "Psychopathology, Primitive Medicine and Primitive Culture," *Bulletin of the History of Medicine* 14, no. 1 (1943): 30–67.

Adams, Evangeline. *Astrology for Everyone: What It Is and How It Works.* New York: Dodd, Mead, 1931.

———. *Astrology: Your Place among the Stars.* New York: Dodd, Mead, 1930.

———. *Astrology: Your Place in the Sun.* New York: Dodd, Mead, 1928.

———. *The Bowl of Heaven.* New York: Dodd, Mead, 1926.

Adams, Rovert. *New Times Network: Groups Centers for Personal Growth.* London: Routledge & Kegan Paul, 1982.

Adams, W. H. Davenport. *Witch, Warlock, and Magician: Historical Sketches of Magic and Witchcraft in England and Scotland.* London and New York, 1889. Reprint, Detroit: Gale Research, 1973.

Adamski, George. *Cosmic Philosophy.* Freeman, S.D.: Pine Hill Press, 1961.

———. *Flying Saucer Farewell.* 1961. Reprint, *Behind the Flying Saucer Mystery.* New York: Paperback Library, 1967.

———. *Inside the Space Ships.* 1955. Reprint, *Inside the Flying Saucers.* New York: Paperback Library, 1967.

———. *Wisdom of the Masters of the Far East.* N.p.: Royal Order of Tibet, 1936.

Adare, Viscount. *Experiences in Spiritualism with D. D. Home.* UK: Privately printed, 1869. Reprint, London: Society for Psychical Research, 1924.

Addey, John. *Astrology Reborn.* Tempe, Ariz.: American Federation of Astrologers, 1972.

———. *Harmonic Anthology.* Tempe, Ariz.: American Federation of Astrologers, 1976.

———. *Harmonics in Astrology.* Romford: L. N. Fowler, 1976.

———. *Selected Writings.* Tempe, Ariz.: American Federation of Astrologers, 1976.

Adkin, Clare E. *Brother Benjamin: A History of the Israelite House of David.* Berrien Springs, Mich.: Andrews University Press, 1990.

Adler, Janet. "Arching Backward, and, a Cross-cultural Study of Mysticism as the Context for a Phenomenological Study: Arching Backward," *Dissertation Abstracts International* 53, no. 9-A (March 1993): 3246.

Adler, Lory, and Richard Dalby. *The Dervish of Windsor Castle.* London: Bachman & Turner, 1979.

Adler, Margo. *Buckland's Complete Book of Witchcraft.* St. Paul, Minn.: Llewellyn Publications, 1986.

———. *Doors to Other Worlds.* St. Paul, Minn.: Llewellyn Books, 1993.

———. *Drawing Down the Moon: Witches, Druids, Goddess-Worshippers, and Other Pagans in America Today.* 2nd ed. Boston: Beacon Press, 1986.

Advances in Parapsychological Research. Jefferson, N.C.: McFarland & Co. Inc. Publishers, 1997.

AE [George Russell]. *The Candle of Vision.* London: Macmillan, 1919. Reprint, New Hyde Park, N.Y.: University Books, 1965.

———. *The Interpreters.* New York: Macmillian, 1922.

———]. *Homeward: Songs of the Way.* Portland, Maine: T. B. Mosher, 1895.

———. *Song and Its Foundations.* New York: Macmillian, 1932.

Agrippa, Henry. *Three Books of Occult Philosophy.* London: Chthonois Books, n.d.

Agrippa, Henry Cornelius. *The Philosophy of Natural Magic.* London, 1651. Reprint, New Hyde Park, N.Y.: University Books, 1974.

Agrippa von Nettesheim, H. C. *Three Books of Occult Philosophy or Magic.* New York: Samuel Weiser, 1971.

Aima. *Ritual Book of Herbal Spell.* Los Angeles: Hermetic Science Center, 1970.

Ainsworth, William Harrison. *The Lancashire Witches: A Romance of Pendle Forest.* London: George Routledge, 1878.

Akiba ben Joseph Rabbi. *The Book of Formation.* (Sepher Yetzirah). London: William Rider, 1923.

Akins, W. R., and George Nurnberg. *How to Meditate Without Attending a TM Class.* New York: Crown, 1976.

Aksakof, A. N. *Animisme et Spiritisme.* Reprint, Paris, 1985. English ed. as: *Animism and Spiritism.* Leipzig: Oswald Meats, 1890.

Aksakof, Alexander. *A Case of Partial Dematerialization of the Body of a Medium.* Boston, 1898.

Al-Arabi, Ibn. *Sufis of Andalucia.* Berkeley: University of California Press, 1971.

Al-Biruni. *The Book of Instruction in the Elements of the Art of Astrology.* Translated by R. Ramsey Wright. London: Luzac, 1934.

———. *The Chronologies of Ancient Nations.* Translated by Edward Sachau. London: W. H. Allen, 1879.

Albertson, Charles C. *Death & Afterwards.* N.p., 1906. Kila, Mont.: Kessinger Publishing Co., 1998.

Albertus, Frater. *The Alchemist of the Rocky Mountains.* Salt Lake City, Utah: Paracelsus Research Society, 1976.

———. *The Alchemist's Handbook: Manual for Practical Laboratory Alchemy.* Rev. ed. New York: Samuel Weiser, 1974.

Albertus Magnus. *The Book of Secrets of Albertus Magnus: Also, A Book of the Marvels of the World.* Edited by M. R. Best and F. H. Brightman. Oxford: Clarendon Press, 1973.

Alcock, James E. *Science and Supernature: A Critical Appraisal of Parapsychology.* Buffalo, N.Y.: Prometheus Books, 1990.

Alexander, Marc. *Haunted Houses You May Visit.* London: Sphere Books, 1982.

Alexander, Patrick P. *Spiritualism: A Narrative with a Discussion.* Edinburgh, Scotland, 1871.

Alexander, Rolf. *The Power of the Mind: The System of Creative Realism.* London, 1955.

"Alleged Mediumship of F. Herne." *Proceedings of the Society for Psyhical Research* 7; *Journal of the Society for Psychical Research* 10.

"Alleged Mediumship of W. Haxby." *Proceedings of the Society for Psychical Research* 4.

"Alleged 'Physical Phenomena' in the Family of Morell Theobald." *Journal of the Society for Psychical Research* 2 (1886).

Allegro, John M. *The Sacred Mushroom and the Cross.* London: Hodder & Stoughton, 1970; Garden City, N.Y.: Doubleday, 1970.

Allen, A. A. *Bound to Lose, Bound to Win.* Garden City, N.Y.: Doubleday, 1970.

Allen, Christopher, and Steuart Campbell. "Flying Saucer from Moore's?" *Magonia,* 23 (July 1986): 15–18.

Allen, Garth [Donald Bradley]. *Taking the Kid Gloves Off Astrology.* Tucson, Ariz.: Clancy Publications, 1975.

Allen, James. *As a Man Thinketh.* 1890. Reprint, Philadelphia: David O. McKay, n.d.

———. *By-Ways of Blessedness.* Libertyville, Ill.: Sheldon University Press, 1909.

———. *From Poverty to Power.* New York: R. F. Fenno, 1907.

———. *The Life Triumphant.* Libertyville, Ill.: Sheldon University Press, 1908.

Allen, M. R. *Male Cults and Secret Initiation in Melanesia.* Melbourne, Australia: Melbourne University Press, 1967.

Allen, Paul M. *A Christian Rosenkreutz Anthology.* Blauvelt, N.Y.: Rudolf Steiner Publications, 1968.

Alli, Antero, et al. *All Rites Reversed: Ritual Technology for Self-Initiation.* Boulder, Colo.: Vigilantero Press, 1987.

Allingham, Cedric [Patrick Moore]. *Flying Saucer from Mars.* London: Frederick Muller, 1954.

Allison, L. W. "In Memory of Waldemar B. Kaempffert." *Journal* of the American Society for Psychical Research 51 (1957).

———. "Obituary: The Reverend C. Drayton Thomas." *Journal* of the American Society for Psychical Research 48 (1953).

Allison, Lydia W. "The American Society for Psychical Research: a Brief History." *SPR Proceedings* 52, no. 1 (1958).

———. *Leonard and Soule Experiments in Psychical Research.* Boston: Boston Society for Psychical Research, 1929.

———. "Proxy Sittings with Mrs. Leonard." *SPR Proceedings* 42 (1934).

———. "Telepathy or Association." *SPR Proceedings* 35 (1941).

Almarez, Anita Ford. *Simple Introduction to the Ancient Science of Gnosis.* Chicago: Gnostic Association, n.d.

Alper, Frank. *Exploring Atlantis.* 3 vols. Farmingdale, N.Y.: Coleman Publishing, 1982.

Alvarado, Carlos S. "ESP and Altered States of Consciousness: An Overview of Conceptual and Research Trends," *Journal of Parapsychology* 62, no. 1 (March 1998): 27–63.

Alvarado, C. S. "The Life and Work of an Italian Psychical Researcher; A Review of Ernesto Bozzano: La Vite a l'Opera by Giovanni Iannuzzo." *Journal* of the American Society for Psychical Research 81 (1987): 37.

Aly, Lucile Folse. *John G. Neihardt: A Critical Biography.* Amsterdam: Radopi, 1977.

Amadou, Robert. *La Parapsychologie: Essai historique et critique.* Paris: Editions Denoel, 1954.

———. *Les Grands Mediums.* Paris: Editions Denoel, 1957.

Amber, Reuben. *Color Therapy.* New York: ASI Publishers, 1980.

Ambrose, G., and G. Newbold. *A Handbook of Medical Hypnosis.* 4th ed. New York: Macmillan, 1980.

American Rosae Crucis. Kila, Mont.: Kessinger Publishing Co., 1998.

Anandamayi, Ma Sri. *Matri Vani.* 2 vols. Varnasi, India: Shree Shree Annandamayee Charitable Society, 1977.

———. *Sad Vani.* Calcutta, India: Shree Shree Anandamayi Charitable Society, 1981.

Anandamurti, Shrii Shrii. *The Great Universe: Discourses on Society.* Los Altos, Calif.: Ananda Marga Publishers, 1971.

Anandamurti, Shrii [P.R. Sarkar]. *The Spiritual Philosophy of Shrii Anandamurti.* Denver: Ananda Marga Publications, 1981.

Ananthanarayan, N. *From Man to God-Man.* New Delhi: The Author, 1970.

Anderson, Margaret L. "The Use of Fantasy in Testing for Extrasensory Perception." *Journal* of the ASPR, 60 (1966): 150.

Anderson, Margaret L., and R. A. McConnell. "Fantasy Testing for ESP in a Fourth and Fifth Grade Class." *Journal of Psychology* 52 (1961): 491.

Anderson, Mary. *Palmistry—Your Destiny In Your Hands.* London: Aquarian Press, 1973.

Anderson, R. I. "The Mediumship of Geraldine Cummins." *Theta* 11, no. 3 (Autumn 1983).

Anderson, Roger I. "Cahagnet's Contribution to Psychical Research." *Theta* 12, no. 4 (1983): 74.

———. "Channeling." *Journal of Religion and Psychical Research* 19 (1988): 5.

———. "Contemporary Survival Research: A Critical Review." *Parapsychology Review* 12 (1981): 5.

———. "Reincarnation: Can Christianity Accommodate It?" *Journal of Religion and Psychical Research* 9 (1985): 189.

———. "Swedenborg on the Modus Operandi of Spirit Communication." *Parapsychology Review* 13 (1982): 6.

Anderson, Walter Truett. *The Upstart Spring: Esalen & the American Awakening*. Reading, Mass.: Addison-Wesley, 1983.

Anderson, Roger I. "The Watseka Wonder: A Critical Re-evaluation." *Theta*, 8, no. 4 (1980).

Andrade, Hernani Guimàraes. *A material psi*. Matao: Clarim, 1972.

———. *Novos rumos à experimentacao espiritica*. São Paulo: Livraria Batuira, 1960.

———. *Parapsicologia experimental*. São Paulo: Calvario, 1967.

———. *A teorià corpuscular do espirito*. São Paulo: The Author, 1958.

Andrews, Edward Deming. *The People Called Shakers: A Search for the Perfect Society*. New York: Oxford University Press, 1953.

Andrews, H. T. *An Introduction to the Apocryphal Books of the Old and New Testament*. Grand Rapids, Mich.: Baker Book House, 1964.

Andrews, Lynn V. *Star Woman*. New York: Warner Books, 1986.

Andrews, Richard. *The Truth behind the Legends of Mount Shasta*. New York: Carlton Press, 1976.

Anesaki, Masaharu. *History of Japanese Religion*. London: Kegan Paul, 1930.

Angeles, Peter A. *The Problem of God; A Short Introduction*. Buffalo, N.Y.: Prometheus Books, 1981.

Angoff, Allan. *Eileen Garrett and the World Beyond the Senses*. New York: William Morrow, 1974.

Angoff, Allan, ed. *Parapsychology and the Sciences*. New York: Parapsychology Foundation, 1972.

———. *Parapsychology Today: A Geographic View*. New York: Parapsychology Foundation, 1971.

———. *The Psychic Force: Essays in Modern Psychical Research from the International Journal of Parapsychology*. New York: G. P. Putnam's Sons, 1970.

Angoff, Allan, and Betty Shapin, eds. *Proceedings of an International Conference: A Century of Psychical Research*. New York: Parapsychology Foundation, 1971.

Angoff, Allan, and Diana Barth, eds. *Parapsychology and Anthropology*. New York: Parapsychology Foundation, 1973.

Angstadt, L. Jean, and Rhea White. "Student Performance in Two Classroom GESP Experiment with Two Students-Agents Acting Simultaneously." *Journal* of the ASPR 57 (1963): 32.

Angus, Samuel. *The Mystery Religions and Christianity*. London: John Murray, 1928. Reprint, New York: Dover, 1975.

Anisimov, A. F. "Cosmological Concept of the Peoples of the North." In *Studies in Siberian Shamanism*. Edited by Henry N. Michael. Toronto: University of Toronto Press, 1963.

———. "The Shaman's Tent of the Evenks and the Origin of the Shamanistic Rite." In *Studies in Siberian Shamanism*. Edited by Henry N. Michael. Toronto: University of Toronto Press, 1963.

Anson, Jay. *The Amityville Horror: A True Story*. Englewood Cliffs, N.J.: Prentice Hall, 1977. Reprint, New York: Pocket Books, 1991.

Anson, Peter F. *Bishops at Large*. London: Faber & Faber, 1965.

Anthony, Dick, Bruce Ecker, and Ken Wilber. *Spiritual Choices: The Problem of Recognizing Authentic Paths to Inner Transformation*. New York: Paragon House Publishers, 1987.

Apostol, Andrei. "Dowsing and Earthquake Prediction," *PSI Research* 4, no. 3–4 (September–December 1985): 212–218.

———. "Dowsing in Geology: An Experience from Romania," *PSI Research* 4, no. 3–4 (September–December 1985): 199–211.

Apuleius. *The Golden Ass*. Translated by Adlington. London: William Heineman, 1935.

Aquino, Michael A. *The Crystal Tablet of Set*. San Francisco: Temple of Set, 1985.

———. *Temple of Set Reading List XIX*. San Francisco: Temple of Set, 1984.

Aranza, Jacob. *Backward Masking Unmasked*. Shreveport, La.: Huntington House, 1983.

Arden, Harvey. *Dreamkeepers: A Spirit-Journey into Australia*. New York: HarperCollins, 1994.

Arden, Nickey. *The Spirits Speak: One Woman's Journey into the African Spirit World of the Sangomas*. New York: Henry Holt, 1996.

Armitage, Harold. *The Haunted and the Haunters by Lord Lytton, With an Introduction; and an Account of the Haunted House at Willington*. London: Simpkin, Marshall, 1925.

Armor, Reginald C. *Ernest Holmes: The Man*. Los Angeles: Science of Mind Publications, 1977.

Arnold, Kenneth, and Ray Palmer. *The Coming of the Saucers: A Documentary Report on Sky Objects that Have Mystified the World*. Boise, Idaho; Amherst, Wisc.: The Authors, 1952.

Arnold, Larry, and Sandy Nevius. *The Reiki Handbook*. Harrisburg, Pa.: PSI Press, 1982.

Arnold, Paul. *Histoire des Rose-Crois*. Paris, 1934.

Arrowsmith, Nancy, and George Moorse. *A Field Guide to the Little People*. New York: Wallaby Books, 1977.

Artemidorus. *The Interpretation of Dreams: Oneirocritica*. Translated by Robert White. Park Ridge, N.J.: Noyes Press, 1975.

Arundale, Francesca. *Idea of Rebirth Including a Translation of an Essay on Reincarnation by Karl Heckl*. N.p., 1890. Reprint, Kila, Mont.: Kessinger Publishing Co., 1998.

Arundale, George S. *Fragment of Autobiography*. Adyar, Madras, India: Kalaksetra, 1940.

———. *Kundalini: An Occult Experience*. Adyar, Madras, India: Theosophical Publishing House, 1938.

———. *Lotus Fire*. Adyar, Madras, India: Theosophical Publishing House, 1939.

———. *Thoughts on "At the Feet of the Master."* Adyar, Madras, India: Theosophical Publishing House, 1919.

———. *You*. Madras, India: Theosophical Publishing House, 1938. Reprint, Wheaton, Ill.: Theosophical Publishing House, 1973.

Arya, Ushbarbudh. *God*. Honesdale, Pa.: Himalayan International Institute, 1979.

Ashburner, John. *Philosophy of Animal Magnetism and Spiritualism*. London, 1867.

Ashcroft-Nowicki, Dolores. *Building a Temple*. Quigleys of Jersey, UK: SOL Publications, 1974.

———. *First Steps in Ritual*. Wellingborough, England: Aquarian Press, 1982.

———. *Highways of the Mind*. Wellingborough, England: Aquarian Press, 1987.

———. *The Shining Paths*. Wellingborough, England: Aquarian Press, 1983.

———. *The Tree of Ecstacy: An Advanced Manual of Sexual Magic*. Wellingborough, England: Aquarian Press, 1991.

Ashdown, A. J. "The Communigraph and Other Early Psychic Aids for Communications." *The Psychic Researcher* supplements 2 and 3 (1975).

Ashe, Geoffrey. *The Quest for Arthur's Britain*. London, 1968.

Asher, Maxine. *Ancient Energy: Key to the Universe*. New York: Harper & Row, 1979.

Ashley, Leonard R. *The Complete Book of the Devil's Disciples*. New York: Barricade Books, Inc., 1996.

Ashley, Mike. *Who's Who in Horror and Fantasy Fiction*. London: Elm Tree Books, 1977.

Ashton, John. *The Devil in Britain and America*. London, 1896. Reprint, Detroit: Gale Research, 1974.

Assagioli, Roberto. *The Act of Will*. New York: Viking Penguin, 1973.

———. *Parapsychological Faculties and Psychological Disturbances*. London: Medical Society for Study of Radiesthesia, 1958.

———. *Psychosynthesis: A Manual of Principles and Techniques*. Rev. ed. New York: Viking/Penguin, 1971.

Astrological Research & Reference Encyclopedia. 2 vols. Los Angeles: Church of Light, 1972.

Astronomy and Elementary Philosophy, Translated from the Latin of Placidus de Titus. London: W. Justins, 1789.

Atack, Jon. *A Piece of Blue Sky: Scientology, Dianetics, and L. Ron Hubbard Exposed*. New York: Lyle Stuart, 1990.

Atkins, John. *Arthur Koestler*. N.p., 1956.

Atkins, Susan, with Bob Slosser. *Child of Satan, Child of God.* Plainfield, N.J.: Logos International, 1977. Reprint, London: Hodder & Stoughton, 1978.

Atkinson, Jane Monnig. *The Art and Politics of Wana Shamanship.* Berkeley: University of California Press, 1989.

Atkinson, R. C. J. *Stonehenge.* London: Pelican Books, 1960.

Atkinson, William Walker. *The Law of New Thought: A Study of Fundamental Principles and Their Application.* Chicago: Psychic Research, 1902.

———. *The New Thought: Its History and Principles; or, the Message of New Thought.* Holyoke, Mass.: Elizabeth Towne, 1915.

———. *Thought Force: In Business and Everyday Life.* 1900. 18th ed. New York: Sydney Flower, 1903.

Atreya, B. L. *An Introduction to Parapsychology.* Banaras, India: International Standard Publications, 1957.

Attar, Farid al-Din. *Muslim Saints and Mystics.* Translated by A. J. Arberry. Chicago: University of Chicago Press, 1966.

Atwater, P. M. H. *Coming Back to Life: The After Effects of the Near-death Experience.* New York: Dodd, Mead, 1988.

———. "The Magic of Perelandra." *East–West* (August 1986).

Atwood, Mary Anne. *A Suggestive Inquiry Into the Hermetic Mystery.* London, 1850. Rev. ed. Belfast, 1918. Reprint, New York: Julian Press, 1960; New York: Ayer Publishing Co. Inc., 1976.

Aubourg, Michel. *Haiti prehistorique.* Port-au-Prince, Haiti: Editiones Panorama, n.d. [1966?].

———. *Le Mouvement folklorique en Haiti.* Port-au-Prince, Haiti: Imprimerie de l'Etat, 1952.

Aubrun, R. G. *Péladan.* Paris: Sansot, 1904.

Augustine of Hippo. *Confessions of St. Augustine.* Edited by Francis J. Sheed. New York: Sheed, 1943.

Augustine, Saint. *Immortality of the Soul.* Reprinted in the Fathers of the Church series, vol. 4. Washington, D.C.: Catholic University of America Press, 1973.

Augustine, St. *Confessions.* N.p., n.d.

Aurobindo, Sri. *Sri Aurobindo Centenary Library.* 50 vols. Pondicherry, India: Sri Aurobindo Library Press, 1970–72.

Auroville. Pondicherry, India: Sri Auroville Society, n.d.

Austin, Mary. *Acupuncture Therapy.* 2nd ed. New York: ASI Publishers, 1972.

Autobiography of Mr. Bradlaugh: A Page of His Life. London: Watts, 1873.

Automobile Association of Great Britain. *Haunts and Hauntings.* Basingstoke, England: Publications Division of the Association, 1974.

Avalon, Arthur [Sir John Woodroffe]. *The Garland of Letters: Studies in the Mantra Shastra.* 1922. Reprint, Madras: Ganesh, 1963.

———. *The Great Liberation (Mahanirvana Tantra).* Madras, India: Ganesh, 1927.

———. *Hymns to the Goddess.* London: Luzac, 1913.

———. *The Serpent Power.* 1918. Reprint, Madras, India: Ganesh, 1924; 1950; New York: Dover Publications, 1974.

Avalon, Arthur. *Shakti and Shakta.* 3d ed. Madras, India: Ganesh, 1929.

———. *Tantra of the Great Liberation (Mahanirvana Tantra).* London: Luzac, 1913. Reprint, New York: Dover Publications, 1972.

Aylesworth, Thomas. *Astrology and Foretelling the Future; A Concise Guide.* Danbury, Conn.: Watts, 1973.

Baba, Meher. *Discourses.* Myrtle Beach, S.C.: Sheriar Press, 1987.

———. *God Speaks.* New York: Dodd, Mead, 1973.

Bach, Edward. *Heal Thyself.* London: C. W. Daniel, 1931.

———. *The Twelve Healers and Other Remedies: A Simple Herbal Treatment.* 3d ed. London: C. W. Daniel, 1936.

———. *Illusions: The Adventures of a Reluctant Messiah.* New York: Delacorte Press, 1977.

———. *Jonathan Livingston Seagull.* New York: Macmillan, 1970.

———. *One: A Novel.* New York: William Morrow, 1988.

Bach, Edward, and F. J. Wheeler. *The Bach Flower Remedies.* New Canaan, Conn.: Keats, 1977.

Bäckman, Louise, and Äke Hultkrantz. *Studies in Lapp Shamanism.* Stockholm Studies in Comparative Religion, vol. 16. Stockholm: Almqvist & Wiksell International, 1978.

Backster, Cleve. "Evidence of a Primary Perception in Plant Life." *International Journal of Parapsychology* 10 (1968): 329–48.

Bacon, Roger. *Roger Bacon's Philosophy of Nature: A Critical Edition.* Oxford: Clarendon Press, 1983.

———. *The Mirror of Alchemy.* London, 1597. Reprint, Los Angeles: Press of the Pegacycle Lady, 1975.

———. *The Opus Majus of Roger Bacon.* 2 vols. Philadelphia: University of Pennsylvania Press, 1928.

Baer, Hans A. *The Black Spiritual Movement: A Religious Response to Racism.* Knoxville, Tenn.: University of Tennessee Press, 1984.

———. "Black Spiritual Israelites in a Small Southern City." *Southern Quarterly* 23, no. 3 (1985): 103–24.

Baer, Randall, and Vicki Baer. *The Crystal Connection: A Guidebook for Personal and Planetary Ascension.* New York: Harper & Row, 1986.

Baggally, W. W. "Some Sittings with Carancini." *Journal of the Society for Psychical Research* 14 (June 1910). Reprinted in Everard Feilding, *Sittings with Eusapio Palladino and Other Studies.* New Hyde Park, N.Y.: University Books, 1963.

Baggally, W. W., Everard Fielding, and Hereward Carrington. "Report on a Series of Sittings with Eusapia Palladino." *Proceedingsof the Society for Psychical Research,* 23 (1909): 309.

Bagger, E. S. *Psycho-Graphology.* London; New York: G. P. Putnam's & Sons, 1924.

Bagnall, Oscar. *The Origin and Properties of the Human Aura.* London, 1937. Rev. ed. New Hyde Park, N.Y.: University Books, 1970.

Bahadur, Krishna Prakash. *The Wisdom of Saankhya.* New Delhi, India: Sterling, 1978.

Bahr, Donald M., Juan Gregorio, et al. *Piman Shamanism and Staying Sickness (Kácim Múmkidag).* Tucson, Ariz.: University of Arizona Press, 1974.

Bailey, Alice A. *The Unfinished Autobiography of Alice A. Bailey.* New York: Lucis Publishing, 1951.

———. *Works.* New York: Lucis Publishing, New York, various dates.

Bailey, D. E. *Thoughts from the Inner Life.* Boston: Colby & Rich, 1886.

Bailey, Wilson G. *No, Not Dead, They Live.* Camden, N.J.: I. F. Huntzinger, 1923.

Bainbridge, William S. "Biorhythms: Evaluating a Pseudoscience." *Skeptical Inquirer* (spring/summer 1978): 41–56.

Bainbridge, William Sims, and Daniel H. Jackson. "The Rise and Fall of Transcendental Meditation." In *The Future of Religion.* Edited by Rodney Stark and William Sims Bainbridge. Berkeley: University of California Press, 1985.

Baird, A. T. *Richard Hodgson: The Story of a Psychical Researcher and His Times.* London: Psychic Press, 1949.

Baird, Alexander T. *One Hundred Cases for Survival After Death.* New York: Bernard Ackerman, 1944.

Baird, George W. *Great American Masons.* Kila, Mont.: Kessinger Publishing, 1992.

Baker, John R. "The Old Woman and Her Gifts: Pharmacological Bases of the Chumash Use of Datura," *Curare* 17, no. 2 (1994): 253–276.

Baldrick, Chris. *In Frankenstein's Shadow: Myth, Monstrosity, and Nineteenth-Century Writing.* Oxford: Oxford University Press, 1987.

Balfour, Arthur James. *Chapters of Autobiography.* London: Cassell, 1930.

———. *The Foundations of Belief.* 8th ed. London: Longmans, Green, 1906.

———. *Science, Religions, and Reality.* London: Sheldon Press, 1925.

———. *Theism and Humanism.* London: Hodder & Stoughton, 1915.

Balfour, G. W. "A Study of the Psychological Aspects of Mrs. Willett's Mediumship." *Proceedings of the Society for Psychical Research* 43 (1935): 43.

Balfour, Gerald W. "The Ear of Dionysius: Further Scripts Affording Evidence of Personal Survival." *Proceedings of the Society for Psychical Research* 29, no. 74 (1916–18).

———. "Some Recent Scripts Affording Evidence of Personal Survival." *Proceedings of the Society for Psychical Research* 27, no. 69 (1915).

Balick, Michael J., Elaine Elisabetsky, and Sarah A. Laird, eds. *Medicinal Resources of the Tropical Forest. Biodiversity and its Importance to Human Health.* New York: Columbia University Press, 1996.

Balleline, G. R. *Past Finding Out: The Tragic Story of Joanna Southcott and Her Successors.* New York: Macmillan, 1957.

Ballou, Adin. *Autobiography of Adin Ballou, 1803–1890.* Lowell, Mass.: Vox Populi Press, 1896. Reprint, Philadelphia: Porcupine Press, 1975.

———. *Practical Christian Socialism.* New York: Fowler and Wells, 1854. Reprint, New York: AMS Press, 1974.

———. *Primitive Christianity and its Corruptions.* 3 vols. 1870–1900.

Balyoz, Harold. *Three Remarkable Women.* Flagstaff, Ariz.: Altai Publishers, 1986.

Balyuzi, H. M. *The Bab: The Herald of the Day of Days.* Oxford: G. Ronald, 1973.

Balzer, Marjorie Mandelstam. "Doctors or Deceivers? The Siberian Khanty Shaman and Soviet Medicine." In *The Anthropology of Medicine. From Culture to Method.* Edited by Lola Romanucci-Ross, Daniel Moerman, and Laurence Tancredi. South Hadley, Mass.: Bergin & Garvey Publishers, 1983.

Balzer, Marjorie Mandelstam, ed. *Shamanic Worlds. Rituals and Lore of Siberia and Central Asia.* Armonk, N.Y.: M. E. Sharp, 1997.

———. *Shamanism: Soviet Studies of Traditional Religion in Siberia and Central Asia. Translated from Russian.* Armonk, N.Y.: M. E. Sharpe, 1990.

Bander, Peter. *Carry On Talking: How Dead are the Voices?* Colin Smythe, 1972. Reprinted as *Voices from the Tapes: Recordings from the Other World.* New York: Drake Publishers, 1973.

———. *The Prophecies of St. Malachy.* Gerrards Cross, England: Colin Smythe, 1969.

Banerjee, H. N., and W. C. Oursler. *Lives Unlimited: Reincarnation East and West.* Garden City, N.Y.: Doubleday, 1974.

[Bangs Sisters]. *The Bangs Sisters' Manifesto to the World.* Chicago, 1909.

Baraduc, Hippolyte. *L'Âme humaine.* (The Human Soul). Paris, 1896.

———. *Les Vibrations de la Vitalité Humaine.* Paris, 1904.

Barbanell, Maurice. *Across the Gulf.* N.p., 1940.

———. *He Walks in Two Worlds: The Story of John Myers, Psychic Photographer, Healer and Philanthropist.* London: n.p., 1964.

———. *Parish the Healer.* London: Psychic Book Club, 1938.

———. *Spiritualism Today.* London: Herbert Jenkins, 1969.

———. *This Is Spiritualism.* London: Herbert Jenkins, 1959.

———. *The Trumpet Shall Sound.* London, Psychic Press, 1933.

———. *Where There is a Will.* N.p., 1962.

Barbanell, Sylvia, ed. *Silver Birch Speak. . . .* London: Psychic Book Club, 1949.

Barbault, Armand. *Gold of a Thousand Mornings.* London: Neville Spearman, 1975.

Barbault, André. *De la Psychanalyses de l'Astrologie.* Paris: Editions du Seuil, 1961.

———. *Les Astres et l'historie.* Paris: J.-J. Pauvert, 1967.

———. *Traité pratique d'Astrologie.* Paris, 1961.

Barber, Paul. *Vampires, Burial, & Death: Folklore & Reality.* New Haven, Conn.: Yale University Press, 1988.

Barber, Richard, and Anne Riches. *A Dictionary of Fabulous Beasts.* New York: Walker, 1971.

Barber, Theodore Zenophon. *Hypnosis: A Scientific Approach.* New York: Psychological Dimensions, 1976.

Barclay, Glen St. John. *Anatomy of Horror: The Masters of Occult Fiction.* London: Weidenfeld & Nicolson, 1978.

Barclay, Glen. *Mind over Matter: Beyond the Bounds of Nature.* London: Arthur Barker, 1973. Reprint, London: Pan, 1975.

Barett, Francis. *The Magus.* London: Lackington, Allen, 1801. Reprint, New Hyde Park, N.Y.: University Books, 1967.

Barrett, S. A. "Pomo Bear Doctors," *University of California Publications in American Archaeology and Ethnology,* Vol. 12, no. 11. Berkeley: University of California Press, 1917.

———. "Ceremonies of the Pomo Indians." *University of California Publications in American Archaeology and Ethnology.* Vol. 12. Berkeley: University of California Press, 1917.

Barham, A. "Dr. W. J. Crawford: His Work and Legacy in Psychokinesis." *Journal of the Society for Psychical Research* 55 (1988): 113.

Baring-Gould, S. *A Book of Folk-Lore.* London, [1913].

———. *Curiosities of Olden Times.* London: J. T. Hayes, 1869.

———. *Devonshire Characters and Strange Events.* Rev. ed., London: John Lane, 1926.

———. "The Terrestrial Paradise." In *Curious Myths of the Middle Ages.* 1872. Reprint, New Hyde Park, N.Y.: University Books, 1967.

Baring-Gould, Sabine. *The Book of Were-Wolves.* London, 1865. Reprint, New York: Causeway Books, 1973; Detroit: Omnigraphics, Inc., 1989.

Barkas, Thomas P. *Outlines of Ten Years' Investigations into the Phenomena of Modern Spiritualism.* London, 1862.

Barker, A. T. *Collected Writings.* 14 vols. Wheaton, Ill.: Theosophical Publishing House, 1950–87.

Barker, A. Trevor, ed. *The Mahatma Letters to A. P. Sennett from the Mahatams M. & K.H.* London: T. Fisher Unwin, 1923. 3rd rev. ed. Adyar, Madras, India: Theosophical Publishing House, 1962.

Barker, Eileen. *The Making of a Moonie.* Oxford, England: Basil Blackwell, 1984.

———. *New Religious Movements: A Practical Introduction.* London: HMSO, 1989.

Barker, Elsa. *War Letters from the Living Dead Man.* London: W. Rider & Son, 1915.

Barker, Gray. *The Book of Adamski.* Clarksburg, W. Va.: Saucerian Publications, 1965.

———. *Gray Barker at Giant Rock.* Clarksburg, W. Va.: Saucerian Publications, 1976.

———. *The Silver Bridge.* Clarksburg, W. Va.: Saucerian Books, 1970.

———. *The Strange Case of Dr. M. K. Jessup.* Clarksburg, W. Va.: Saucerian Books, 1962.

———. *They Knew Too Much About Flying Saucers.* New York: University Books, 1956.

Barker, Gray, ed. *Bender Mystery Confirmed.* Clarksburg, W. Va.: Saucerian Books, 1962.

———. *MIB: The Secret Terror Among Us.* Jane Lew, W. Va.: New Age Press, 1983.

———. *They Knew Too Much about Flying Saucers.* Clarksburg, W. Va.: Saucerian Press, 1962. Reprint, New York: Tower, 1967.

Barker, J. C. *Scared to Death; An Examination of Fear, Its Causes and Effects.* London: Muller, 1958. Reprint, New York: Dell, 1969.

Barlow, Fred, and W. Rampling Rose. "Report on an Investigation into Spirit-Photography." *Proceedings of the Society for Psychical Research* 41 (1933): 121–38.

Barlow, Sita, et al. *Sri Swami Satchidananda: Apostle of Peace.* Yogaville, Va.: Integral Yoga Publications, 1986.

Barnard, G. William. "William James and the Origins of Mystical Experience." In *The Innate Capacity: Mysticism, Psychology, and Philosophy.* New York: Oxford University Press, 1998.

Barnes, Arthur Stapylton. *The Holy Shroud of Turin.* London: Burns Oates & Washbourne, 1934.

Barnes, Michael. *Draumkvaede.* Oslo, 1974.

Baroja, Julio Caro. *The World of the Witches.* Chicago: University of Chicago Press, 1961.

Barr, Sir James. *Abrams' Methods of Diagnosis and Treatment.* London, 1925.

Barrat, Rodford. *Elements of Numerology.* UK: Element Books, Inc., 1997.

Barrett, Francis. *The Lives of the Alchemystical Philosophers.* 1815. Rev. ed. as *Alchemists Through the Ages.* Blauvelt, N.Y.: Rudolf Steiner Publications, 1970.

———. *The Magus: A Complete System of Occult Philosophy.* London, 1801. Reprint, New Hyde Park, N.Y.: University Books, 1967.

Barrett, Harrison D. *The Life and Work of Cora L. V. Richmond.* Chicago: Hack & Anderson Printers, 1895.

Barrett, J. O. *The Spiritual Pilgrim: A Biography of James M. Peebles.* Boston: William White, 1872.

Barrett, Sir William F. *Death-Bed Visions.* London: Methuen, 1926. Reprint, Wellingborough, England: Aquarian Press, 1986.

———. *The Divining Rod.* New Hyde Park, N.Y.: University Books, 1968.

———. *On the Threshold of a New World.* London: Kegan Paul, 1908. Revised as *On the Threshold of the Unseen: An Examination of the Phenomena of Spiritualism and of the Evidence for Survival After Death.* New York: E. P. Dutton, 1971.

———. *On the Threshold of the Unseen (1917).* Reprint, Kila, Mont.: Kessinger Publishing Co. 1998.

———. "Poltergeists, Old and New." *Proceedings of the Society for Psychical Research* 25, no. 64 (August 1911).

———. *Psychical Research.* New York: H. Holt, [1911].

———. "Some Reminiscences of Fifty Years of Psychical Research," *Proceedings of the Society for Psychical Research* 34 (1924).

Barrett, William, and Theodore Besterman. *The Divining Rod: An Experimental and Psychological Investigation.* London, 1926. Reprint, New Hyde Park, N.Y.: University Books, 1968.

Barring-Gould, Sabine. *Curiosities of Olden Times.* London, J. T. Hayes, 1895.

———. *Curious Myths of the Middle Ages.* 1866–68. New Hyde Park, N.Y.: University Books, 1967.

Barrington, Mary Rose. "The Kluski Hands," *Journal of the Society for Psychical Research* 59, no. 834 (January 1994): 347-351.

Barrows, David Prescott. *The Ethno-Botany of the Coahuilla Indians of Southern California.* Chicago: University of Chicago Press, 1900.

Barruel, Augustin. *Memoirs Illustrating the History of Jacobinism.* 4 vols., London, 1797.

Barstow, Anne Llewellyn. *Joan of Arc: Heretic, Mystic, Shaman.* Lewiston, N.Y.: Edwin Mellen Press, 1986.

Barter, J. P. *Towards Subud.* London, 1967.

Bartholin, Thomas. *Acta Medica & Philosophical Hafniensia Ann. 1671 & 1672.* Copenhagen, 1673.

Bartlett, George C. *The Salem Seer.* New York, 1891.

Bartlett, Robert. *Trial by Fire and Water: The Medieval Judicial Order.* Oxford: Clarendon, 1988.

Bartley, William Warren. *Werner Erhard: The Transformation of a Man, the Founding of est.* New York: C. N. Potter, 1978.

Barton, Blanche. *The Church of Satan.* Hell's Kitchen Productions, Inc., 1990.

Barton, Blanche. *The Secret Life of a Satanist: The Authorized Biography of Anton LaVey.* Los Angeles: Feral House, 1990.

Barton, Michael X. *Rainbow City and The Inner Earth Story.* Los Angeles: Futura Press, 1960. Reprint, Clarksburg, W. Va.: Saucerian Press, 1969.

Barzini, Luigi. *Nel mondo dei Misteri con Eusapia Palladino.* Milan, 1907.

Basgöz, Ilhan. "Dream Motif in Turkish Folk Stories and Shamanistic Initiation," *Asian Folklore Studies,* no. 1 (1966): 1–18.

Basham, Don. *A Manual for Spiritual Warfare.* Greensburg, Pa.: Manna Books, 1974.

Bashir, Mir. *Your Past, Your Present, and Your Future Through the Art of Hand Analysis.* Garden City, N.Y.: Doubleday, 1974.

Basil, Robert, ed. *Not Necessarily the New Age.* Buffalo, N.Y.: Prometheus Books, 1988.

Baskin, Wade. *Dictionary of Satanism.* New York: Philosophical Library, 1972.

Basset, W. *Wanderships.* Chicago, 1917.

Bassett, F. S. *Legends and Traditions of the Sea and Sailors.* Chicago & New York: Belford, Clarke, 1886.

Bastide, Roger. *The African Religions of Brazil.* Baltimore, Md.: Johns Hopkins Press, 1978.

Bataille, Dr. [Gabriel Jogand-Pagès]. *Le Diable du XIXe Siècle.* Paris, 1892.

———. *Memoire à l' Adresse des Members du Congrès de Trent.* N.p., 1897.

Bataille, Georges. *Procès de Gilles de Rais.* Paris, 1959.

Batcheldor, Kenneth. "Contributions to the Theory of PK Induction from Sitter-Group Work." *Journal* of the American Society for Psychical Research 78 (1984).

———. "Notes on the Elusiveness Problem in Relation to a Radical View of Paranormality." *Journal* of the American Society for Psychical Research 88 (April 1994).

———. "Report on a Case of Table-Levitation and Associated Phenomena." *Journal of the Society for Psychical Research* 43 (1966).

Batcheldor, Kenneth, and D. W. Hunt. "Some Experiments in Psychokinesis." *Journal of the Society for Psychical Research* 43 (1966).

Bates, Paul A., ed. *Faust: Sources, Works, Criticism.* New York: Harcourt, Brace, and World, 1968.

Battersby, H. F. Prevost. *Man Outside Himself.* London, 1942. Reprint, New Hyde Park, N.Y.: University Books, 1969.

Baudelaire, Charles. *Artificial Paradise: On Hashish & Wine as Means of Expanding Individuality.* New York: McGraw-Hill, 1971.

Bauer, Eberhard. "Criticism and Controversies in Parapsychology." *European Journal of Parapsychology* 5 (1984): 141.

Baugnet, Michael. Introduction to *Primum Mobile. . . .* by Placidus de Titis. Translated by John Cooper. London: Davis and Dickson, 1814.

Baumann, Elwood David. *Bigfoot: America's Abominable Snowman.* New York: Franklin Watts, 1976. Reprint, New York: Dell, 1976.

Baumard, Claire. *Leon Denis intime.* N.p., n.d.

Baumbach, Emily. *Michael's Cast of Characters.* Orinda, Calif.: Affinity Press, 1989.

Baur, F. N. *A Short and Faithful Description of the Remarkable Occurrences and . . . Conduct of . . . Prince Alexander of Hohenlohe.* N.p., 1822.

Bauval, Robert, and Adrian Gilbert. *The Orion Mystery.* London: Heinemann, 1994.

Baxter, Robert. *A Narrative of Facts Characterising the Supernatural Manifestations in the Members of Mr. Irving's Congregation, and Other Individuals in England and Scotland, and formerly in the Writer Himself.* London, 1833.

Bayless, Raymond. *Voices From Beyond.* New Hyde Park, N.Y.: University Books, 1975.

Baynes, C. F., and R. Wilhelm, trans. *The I Ching or Book of Changes.* Princeton, N.J.: Princeton University Press, 1967.

Beal, James B. "The Formerly 'Supernatural': Electrical and Psi Fields in Medical Anthropology." In *Extrasensory Ecology: Parapsychology & Anthropology,* edited by E. K. Long. Metuchen, N.J.: Scarecrow Press, 1977.

Beard, Charles R. *Lucks and Talismans: A Chapter of Popular Superstition.* London: Sampson, Low, 1934. Reprint, New York: Blom, 1972.

Beard, George Miller. *The Study of Trance, Muscle Reading and Allied Nervous Phenomena.* New York: n.p., 1882.

Beard, Paul. *Survival of Death: For and Against.* London: Hodder and Stoughton, 1966. Reprint, London: Psychic Press, 1972.

Beasley, Norman. *The Cross and the Crown.* Boston: Little, Brown, 1952.

Beasse, Pierre. *A New and Rational Treatise of Dowsing according to the methods of Physical Radiesthesia.* France, 1941.

Beaumont, John. *An Historical, Physiological & Theological Treatise of Spirits, Apparitions, Witchcraft & Other Magical Practices.* London, 1750.

Becker, Carl B. "Extrasensory Perception, Near-Death Experiences, and the Limits of Scientific Knowledge," *Journal of Near-Death Studies* 9, no. 1 (Fall 1990): 11–20.

Becker, Robert O. *Cross Currents.* New York: Quill, 1985.

———. *The Body Electric.* Los Angeles: J. P. Tarcher, 1990. Distributed by St. Martin's Press.

Bedell, Clyde. *Concordex to the URANTIA Book.* Leguna Hills, Calif.: The Author, 1980.

Beebe, Tom. *Who's Who in New Thought.* Lakemount, Ga.: CSA Press, 1977.

Begg, Paul. *Into Thin Air: People Who Disappear.* North Pomfret, Vt.: David & Charles, 1979.

"Behind the Scenes of Oki Yoga." *East West Journal* 15, no. 9 (September 1985).

Behringer, Wolfgang. *Witchcraft Persecutions in Bavaria.* New York: Cambridge University Press, 1998.

Belden, L. W. *Somnambulism: The Extraordinary Case of J. C. Rider, the Springfield Somnambulist.* London, 1834.

Belfage, Sally. *Flowers of Emptiness.* New York: Dial Press, 1981.

Bell, Charles Bailey, and Harriet Parks Miller. *Bell Witch of Tennessee.* Reprint, Nashville, Tenn.: C. Elder, 1972.

Bell, H. Idris. *Cults and Creeds in Graeco-Roman Egypt.* Liverpool, England: Liverpool University Press, 1957.

Bell, Hesketh J. *Obeah: Witchcraft in the West Indies.* London: Sampson, Low & Co., 1889.

Bellamy, Hans Schindler. *Moons, Myths, and Man.* London: Faber & Faber, 1949.

Bellot, Hugh H. L. *Temple of the Inner Temple.* N.p., 1914. Kila, Mont.: Kessinger Publishing Co., 1999.

Beloff, John. *The Existence of Mind.* London: MacGibbon, 1962. Reprint, New York: Citadel, 1965.

———. *The Importance of Psychical Research.* London: Society for Psychical Research, 1988.

———. *Parapsychology: The Way Ahead.* Turnbridge Wells, UK: Institute for Cultural Research, 1974.

———. *Psychological Sciences: A Review of Modern Psychology.* New York: Barnes & Noble, 1974.

Beloff, John, ed. *New Directions in Parapsychology.* London: Paul Elek (Scientific Books), 1974. Reprint, Metuchen, N.J.: Scarecrow Press, 1975.

Bem, D. J. and Honorton, C. "Does psi exist? Replicable evidence for an anomalous process of information transfer," *Psychological Bulletin,* 115 (1994): 4–18.

Bender, Hans. "Modern Poltergeist Research—A Plea for an Unprejudiced Approach." In *New Directions in Parapsychology,* edited by John Beloff. London: Paul Elek (Scientific Books), 1974. Reprint, Metuchen, N.J.: Scarecrow Press, 1975.

Bender, Hans. "New Developments in Poltergeist Research." *Proceedings of the Parapsychological Association* 6 (1969): 81.

Bender, Hans. *Unser sechster Sinn.* Stuttgart: Wilhelm Goldmann Verlag, 1982.

Bendit, L. J., and Phoebe Bendit. *Living Together Again.* London, Gramol Publications, 1946.

Bendit, Laurence J. *The Mirror of Life and Death.* Adyar, Madras, India: Theosophical Publishing House, 1965.

———. *Self Knowledge: A Yoga for the West.* Wheaton, Ill.: Theosophical Publishing House, 1967.

Bendit, Laurence J., and Phoebe D. Bendit. *Man Incarnate.* N.p., 1957. Reprinted as *The Etheric Body of Man.* Wheaton, Ill.: Theosophical Publishing House, 1977.

———. *This Transforming Mind.* Wheaton, Ill.: Theosophical Publishing House, 1970.

Bendit, Phoebe. *Man's Latent Powers.* London, Faber and Faber, 1938.

Bendit, Phoebe. *The Psychic Child or Oversensitive Child.* N.p., 1955.

Bendit, Phoebe, and Laurence J. Bendit. *The Psychic Sense.* London: Faber and Faber, 1943.

———. *This World and That.* London: Faber and Faber, 1950.

Benedikt, M. *Ruten- und Pendel-lehre.* Vienna; Leipzig, 1917.

Benham, W. G. *Laws of Scientific Hand Reading.* Rev. ed. New York: G. P. Putnam's Sons, 1928. Reprinted as *The Benham Book of Palmistry.* North Hollywood, Calif.: Newcastle, 1988.

Benitez, Fernando. *In the Magic Land of Peyote.* Austin: University of Texas Press, 1975. Reprint, New York: Warner Books, 1975.

Benjamine, Elbert. *Astrological Lore of All Ages.* Chicago: Aries Press, 1945.

———. *Beginner's Horoscope Maker.* Chicago: Aries Press, 1940.

———. *Stellar Dietetics.* Chicago: Aries Press, 1942.

Bennett, Allan. *The Wisdom of the Aryas.* London, 1923.

Bennett, E. T. *Apparitions and Haunted Houses: A Survey of Evidence.* London: Faber & Faber, 1939. Ann Arbor, Mich.: Gryphon Books, 1971.

Bennett, Ernest. *Apollonius; or, The Future of Psychical Research.* N.p., 1927.

———. *Apparitions and Haunted Houses.* London: Faber and Faber, 1939.

———. *Christianity and Paganism in the Fourth and Fifth Centuries.* London: Rivingtons, 1900.

———. *The Downfall of the Dervishes.* New York: Negro University Press, 1969.

Bennett, J. G. *Gurdjieff: Making a New World.* New York: Harper & Row, 1974.

———. *Gurdjieff, A Very Great Enigma: Three Lectures.* New York: Samuel Weiser, 1973.

———. *Concerning Subud.* New Hyde Park, N.Y.: University Books, 1959.

Bennett, John. *Creative Thinking.* Sherbourne, UK: Coombe Springs Press, 1964.

———. *Enneagram Studies.* York Beach, Maine: Samuel Weiser, 1983.

———. *Spiritual Psychology.* Lakemont, Ga.: CSA Press, 1974.

———. *Witness.* New York: Dharma Book Co., 1962.

Bennett, John G., with Thakur Lal Manandhar. *Long Pilgrimage: The Life and Teaching of Sri Govinananda Bharati known as the Shivapuri Baba.* London: Hodder & Stoughton, 1965.

Bennett, John Godolphin. *Gurdjieff: Making a New World.* New York: Harper & Row, 1974.

———. *Is There Life on Earth?—An Introduction to Gurdjieff.* New York: Stonehill, 1973. 1st Bennett Books ed., Santa Fe, N.Mex.: Bennett Books, 1989.

Bension, Ariel. *The Zohar in Moslem and Christian Spain.* New York: Sepher-Hermon Press, 1932.

Benson, E. F. *The Horror Horn, and Other Stories.* Edited by Alexis Lykiard. London: Panther, 1974.

———. *More Spook Stories.* London: Hutchinson, 1934.

———. *The Room in the Tower, and Other Stories.* London: Mills & Boon, 1912.

———. *Spook Stories.* London: Hutchinson, 1928.

———. *Visible and Invisible.* London: Hutchinson, 1923.

Bentley, Edmund. *Far Horizon: A Biography of Hester Dowden, Medium and Psychic Investigator.* London: Rider & Co., 1951.

Benwell, G., and A. Waugh. *The Sea Enchantress: The Tale of the Mermaid and Her Kin.* London: Hutchinson, 1961.

Beowulf. Edited by F. Klaeber. Boston, 1950.

Beowulf. Translated by John R. Clarke. Rev. ed. New York: C. L. Wrenn, 1954.

Bercovici, Konrad. *The Story of the Gypsies.* Cosmopolitan Book Corp., 1928. Reprint, Detroit: Gale Research, 1974.

Berdecio, R., and S. Appelbaum, eds. *Posada's Popular Mexican Prints.* New York: Dover, 1972.

Berendt, Heinz C. "A New Israeli Metal-Bender (with Film)." In *Research in Parapsychology, 1982.* Edited by William Roll, John Beloff, and Rhea W. White. Metuchen, N.J.: Scarecrow Press, 1983.

———. *Parapsychology: The World beyond Our Five Senses.* N.p., 1966.

Berg, Charles. *The Unconscious Significance of Hair.* London: Allen & Unwin, 1951.

Berger, Arthur S. *Aristocracy of the Dead.* Jefferson, N.C.: McFarland, 1987.

Berger, Arthur S. *Evidence of Life after Death: A Casebook for the Tough-Minded.* Springfield, Ill.: Charles C. Thomas, 1988.

———. *Lives and Letters in American Parapsychology: A Biographical History, 1850–1987.* Jefferson, N.C.: McFarland, 1988.

Berger, Arthur S. and Joyce Berger. *The Encyclopedia of Parapsychology and Psychical Research.* New York: Paragon House, 1991.

———. *Encyclopedia of Parapsychology & Psychical Research.* New York: Marlowe & Co., 1994.

Berger, Arthur S., F. E. Gurney, and F. W. H. Myers. *Phantasms of the Living.* 2 vols. London: Trubner, 1986.

Berger, H. A. *Nordische Mythologie.* Zittau & Leipzig, Germany, 1834.

Berger, Helen A. *Witchcraft and the Domination of Women: A Reexamination of the English Witch Trials.* New York: New York University Press, 1983.

Berger, Ruth. *The Secret Is in the Rainbow: Aura Interrelationships.* Clearwater, Fla.: Beau Geste, 1979.

Bergier, Jacques. *Extraterrestrial Visitations from Prehistoric Times to the Present.* Chicago: Henry Regnery, 1973. Reprinted as *Mysteries of the Earth: The Hidden World of the Extra-Terrestrials.* London: Sidgwick and Jackson, 1974.

Bergier, Jacques. *Secret Doors of the Earth.* Chicago: Henry Regnery, 1975.

Bergier, Jacques, and INFO editors. *Extraterrestrial Intervention: The Evidence.* Chicago: Henry Regnery, 1974.

Bergman, Jerry. *Can the Living Talk with the Dead? A Clear Explanation of Spiritism.* Brooklyn, N.Y.: International Bible Students, 1920.

———. *Jehovah's Witnesses and Kindred Groups: A Historical Compendium and Bibliography.* New York: Garland Publishing, 1984.

Bergson, Henri. *Creative Evolution.* New York: Modern Library, 1944.

———. *The World of Dreams.* New York: Philosophical Library, 1958.

Berke, Joseph H. "Psychoanalysis and Kabbalah," *Psychoanalytic Review* 83, no. 6 (December 1996): 849–863.

Berlitz, Charles. *Mysteries from Forgotten Worlds.* Garden City, N.Y.: Doubleday, 1972.

———. *World of Strange Phenomena.* New York: Wynwood Press, 1988.

Berlitz, Charles F. *The Dragon's Triangle.* New York: Wynwood Press, 1989.

Berlitz, Charles, and J. M. Valentine. *Without a Trace: New Information from the Triangle.* Garden City, N.Y.: Doubleday, 1977.

Berlitz, Charles, and J. Manson Valentine. *The Bermuda Triangle.* Garden City, N.Y.: Doubleday, 1974.

———. *Doomsday 1999 A.D.* Garden City, N.Y. Doubleday, 1981.

Berlitz, Charles, and William L. Moore. *The Roswell Incident.* New York: Grosset & Dunlap, 1980.

Berlitz, Charles, and William Moore. *The Philadelphia Experiment: Project Invisibility.* N.p., 1979.

Berman, David. "Papal Visit Resurrects Ireland's Knock Legend." *The Freethinker* (October 1979). Reprinted in *The British and Irish Skeptic* 1, no. 1 (January/February 1987).

The Bermuda Triangle: An Annotated Bibliography. Buffalo, N.Y.: Buffalo and Erie County Public Library Librarians Association and Buffalo and Erie County Library, 1975.

Bernard, Pierre. *In Re Fifth Veda. International Journal of the Tantrik Order.* New York: Tantrik Order in America, [1909].

Bernard, Theos. *Hatha Yoga.* New York: Columbia University Press, 1944. Reprint, London, 1950; New York: Samuel Weiser, 1970.

———. *Heaven Lies Within Us.* New York: Scribner's Sons, Ltd., 1939.

———. *Hindu Philosophy.* New York: Philosophical Library, 1947.

———. *Land of a Thousand Buddhas.* London: Rider, 1952.

———. *Philosophical Foundations of India.* London: Rider, 1945.

———. *A Simplified Grammar of the Literary Tibetan Language.* Santa Barbara, Calif.: Tibetan Text Society, 1946.

Bernheim, H. *Hypnosis and Suggestion in Psychotherapy: A Treatise on the Nature and Uses of Hypnotism.* London, 1888. Reprint, New Hyde Park, N.Y.: University Books, 1964.

Bernstein, Alan E. *The Formation of Hell: Death and Retribution in the Ancient and Early Christian Worlds.* Ithaca, N.Y.: Cornell University Press, 1993.

Bernstein, Jay H. *Spirits Captured in Stone. Shamanism and Traditional Medicine among the Taman of Borneo.* Boulder, Colo.; London: Lynne Reinner, 1997.

Bernstein, Morey. *The Search for Bridey Murphy.* Garden City, N.Y.: Doubleday, 1956.

Berry, Catherine. *Experiences in Spiritualism.* London, 1876.

Bersterman, Theodore, and Sir William Barrett. *The Divining Rod: An Experimental and Psychological Investigation.* 1926. Reprint. New Hyde Park, N.Y.: University Books, 1968.

Bertrand, A. *Traité du Somnambulisme.* Paris, 1824.

Besant Annie. *The Ancient Wisdom.* 1897. Reprint, Wheaton, Ill.: Theosophical Press, 1928.

———. *Annie Besant: An Autobiography.* London, 1893.

———. *Autobiographical Sketches.* London: Freethought Publishing, 1885.

———. *Charles Bradlaugh: A Character Sketch.* Adyar, Madras, India: Theosophical Publishing House, 1941.

———. *H. P. Blavatsky and the Masters of Wisdom.* London, 1907.

———. *My Path to Atheism.* London, 1877.

———. *The Seven Principles of Man.* 1892. Reprint, New York: London & Bernes; Theosophical Publishing Society, 1904.

———. *The Theosophical Society and H. P. Blavatsky.* London, 1891.

———. *Why I became a Theosophist.* London: Theosphical Publishing Society, 1891.

Besant, Annie, and Charles W. Leadbeater. *Thought-Forms: A Record of Clairvoyant Investigations.* Adyar, Madras, India: London Theosophical Publishing House, 1901.

Besterman, Theodore. *A Bibliography of Annie Besant.* London: Theosophical Society in England, 1924.

———. *Collected Papers on the Paranormal.* New York, Garrett Publications, 1968.

———. *Crystal Gazing: A Study in the History, Distribution, Theory and Practice of Scrying.* London: William Rider, 1924. Reprint, New Hyde Park, N.Y.: University Books, 1965.

———. *Dictionary of Theosophy.* London: Theosophical Publishing House, 1927.

———. *The Mind of Annie Besant.* London: Theosophical Publishing House, 1927.

———. *Mrs. Annie Besant: A Modern Prophet.* London: Kegan Paul, Trench, Trubner, 1934.

———. *Water Divining: New Facts & Theories.* London: Methuen, 1938.

Beth, Rae. *The Wiccan Path.* Freedom, Calif.: The Crossing Press Inc., 1995.

Betty, L. Stafford. "The Kern City Poltergeist: A Case Severely Straining the Living Agent Hypothesis," *Journal of the Society for Psychical Research* 52, no. 798 (October 1984): 345–364.

Bevan, Edwyn Robert. *Holy Images; An Inquiry Into Idolatry and Image—Worship in Ancient Paganism and in Christianity.* London: George Allen, 1940.

Beyerl, Paul V. *Wiccan Reader.* Palm Springs, Calif.: International Guild of Advanced Sciences Research Society, 1994.

Bhagavadgita of The Song Divine. Gorakhpur, India: Gita Press, 1943.

Bharati, Agehananda. *The Light at the Center: Context and Pretext of Modern Mysticism.* Santa Barbara, Calif.: Ross-Erickson, 1976.

———. *The Ochre Robe.* Garden City, N.Y.: Doubleday, 1970.

———. "Separate Realities: Sense and (Mostly) Nonsense in Parapsychology." In *Extrasensory Ecology: Parapsychology and Anthropology.* Edited by Joseph K. Long. Metuchen, N.J.: Scarecrow Press, 1977.

———. *The Tantric Tradition.* London: Rider, 1965.

Bias, Clifford. *The Way Back.* York Beach, Maine: Samuel Weiser, 1985.

Bierce, Ambrose. *Devils Dictionary.* N.p., 1841, 1913. Reprint, New York: Oxford University Press, Inc., 1999.

Biermans, John T. *The Odyssey of New Religious Movements.* New York: Edwin Mellon, 1986.

Bigelow, John. *Mystery of Sleep.* London: Unwin; New York: Harper, 1903. N.p., 1905. Reprint, Kila, Mont.: Kessinger Publishing Co., 1998.

Binet, Alfred, and Charles Féré. *Animal Magnetism.* London: Kegan Paul, 1887.

Binns, Ronald. *The Loch Ness Mystery Solved.* Buffalo, N.Y.: Prometheus Books; London: Star (W. H. Allen),, 1984.

Biographical Sketch of Gabriel Green. Northridge, Calif.: Amalgamated Flying Saucer Clubs of America, 1974.

Bird, Christopher. *The Diving Hand: The 500 Year-Old Mystery of Dowsing.* New York: E. P. Dutton, 1979.

Bird, J. Malcolm. *Margery the Medium.* Boston: Small, Maynard, 1925.

———. *My Psychic Adventures.* New York: Scientific American Publishing, 1924.

———. *'Margery' the Medium.* New York: Maynard, 1925.

Birkhead, Edith. *The Tale of Terror: A Study of the Gothic Romance.* London: Constable, 1921.

Birks, Walter. *The Treasure of Montsagur: A Study of the Cathar Heresy and the Nature of the Cathar Secret.* UK: Crucible, 1987.

Bisnauth, Dale. *History of Religion in the Caribbean.* Kingston, Jamaica: Kingston Publishers, 1989.

Bisson, Juliette A. *Les Phénomènes dits de Matérialisations.* Paris, 1914.

Bittle, William G. *James Nayler, 1618–1660: The Quaker Indicted by Parliament.* Richmond, Ind.: Friends United Press, 1986.

Black Hawk. *Autobiography.* St. Louis, Mo.: The Author, 1882.

Black, David. *Ekstasy: Out-of-the-Body Experiences.* Indianapolis: Bobbs-Merrill; Macmillan Publishing Co. Inc., 1975.

Black, George F. *A Calendar of Cases of Witchcraft in Scotland 1510–1727.* New York: New York Public Library, 1938.

———. *A Gypsy Bibliography.* London: Gypsy Lore Society, 1914. Reprint, Ann Arbor, Mich.: Gryphon Books, 1971.

The Black Pullet: Science of Talismanic Magic. New York: Samuel Weiser, 1972.

Blackmore, Susan J. *Adventures of a Parapsychologist.* Buffalo, N.Y.: Prometheus Books, 1986.

———. *Beyond the Body: An Investigation of Out-of-the-Body Experiences.* London: Heineman, 1981.

———. "Down the Tunnel." *British and Irish Skeptic* 3, no. 3 (May/June 1989).

———. "The Elusive Open Mind: Ten Years of Negative Research in Parapsychology." *The Skeptical Inquirer* 9, no. 3 (spring 1987).

———. *Parapsychology and Out-of-the-Body Experience.* London: Society for Psychical Research; Hove, England: Transpersonal Books, 1978.

———. "A Psychological Theory of the OBE." In *Research in Parapsychology 1984.* Edited by Rhea A. White and Jerry Solfvin. N.p., 1985.

———. "A Report of a Visit to Carl Sargent's Laboratory." *Journal of the Society for Psychical Research* 54, no. 808 (July 1987).

Blackmore, Susan J. and Frances Chamberlain. "ESP and Thought Concordance in Twins: A Method of Comparison," *Journal of the Society for Psychical Research* 59, no. 831 (April 1993): 89–96.

Blackmore, Susan J., and John Harris. "OBEs and Perceptual Distortions in Schizophrenic Patients and Students." In *Research in Parapsychology 1982.* Edited by William G. Roll, John Beloff, and Rhea A. White. 1983.

Blackwood, Algernon. *Best Ghost Stories of Algernon Blackwood.* Edited by E. F. Bleiler. New York: Dover Publications, 1973.

———. *Episodes before Thirty.* New York: E. P. Dutton, 1924.

———. *The Human Chord.* London: Macmillan, 1910.

———. *Tales of the Supernatural.* Woodbridge, England: Boydell Press, 1983.

———. *Tales of Terror and Darkness.* London; New York: Spring Books, 1977. Distributed by Transatlantic Arts.

———. *The Willows, and Other Queer Tales.* 1934.

Blakney, Raymond B. *Meister Eckhart: A Modern Translation.* New York: Harper, 1941.

Blanchard, Robert. *Ancient Grimoire of Dark Magick.* Palm Springs, Calif.: International Guild of Advanced Sciences Research Society, 1993.

———. *Witchcraft Grimoire.* Palm Springs, Calif.: International Guild of Advanced Sciences Research Society, 1993.

Blatty, William Peter. *The Exorcist.* New York: Harper & Row, 1971.

Blavatsky, Helena P. *From the Caves and Jungles of Hindustan.* London: Theosophical Publishing Society, 1892.

———. *Isis Unveiled.* 2 vols. New York: J. W. Bouton, 1877.

———. *The Key to Theosophy.* Pasadena, Calif.: Theosophical University Press, 1972.

———. *Letters of H. P. Blavatsky to A. P. Sinnett.* Edited by A. T. Barker. London: T. Fisher Unwin, 1925.

———. "Psychic and Noetic Action." In *Studies in Occultism.* Boston: New England Theosophical Corp., 1895.

———. *The Secret Doctrine.* 2 vols. London: Theosophical Publishing House, 1889. Reprint, London: Thesophical Publishing House, 1928.

———. *Theosophical Glossary.* New York: Theosophical Publishing House, 1892.

Bleibtreu-ehrenberg, G. "Homosexualität und Transvestition im Schamanismus," *Anthropos,* Vol. 65 (1970).

Bleksley, A. E. H. "An Experiment of Long-Distance ESP During Sleep." *Journal of Parapsychology* 27 (1963): 1.

Bliss, Douglas Percy, ed. *The Devil in Scotland.* London: Alexander MacLehose, 1937.

Bloch, Chayim. *Der Prager Golem.* Translated by Harry Schneiderman as *The Golem: Legends of the Ghetto of Prague.* Vienna, 1925.

Block, Marguerite Beck. *The New Church in the New World.* New York: Henry Holt, 1932.

Blofeld, John. *Beyond the Gods.* New York: E. P. Dutton, 1974.

———. *Bodhisattva of Compassion: The Mystical Tradition of KuaYin.* Boulder, Colo.: Shambhala, 1977.

———. *The Jewel in the Lotus: An Outline of Present-Day Buddhism in China.* London: Sidgwick & Jackson, 1948.

———. *Mahayana Buddhism in Southeast Asia.* Singapore: Asia Pacific Press, 1971.

———. *Mantras: Sacred Words of Power.* New York: E. P. Dutton, 1977.

———. *The Secret and Sublime.* New York: E. P. Dutton, 1973.

———. *Tantric Mysticism of Tibet: A Practical Guide.* New York: Dutton, 1970. Reprinted as *The Way of Power.* London: Allen & Unwin, 1970.

———. *The Wheel of Life.* London: Rider, 1959. Rev. ed. Boulder, Colo.: Shambhala, 1972.

Blofeld, John, trans. *I Ching: The Book of Changes.* New York: E. P. Dutton, 1968.

Bloomfield, Harold M., Michael Peter Cain, and Dennis T. Jaffe. *TM: Discovering Inner Energy and Overcoming Stress.* New York: Delacorte Press, 1975.

Blum, Ralph. *The Book of Runes.* New York: St. Martin's Press, 1984.

———. *Rune Play.* New York: St. Martin's Press, 1985.

Blythe, Henry. *The Three Lives of Naomi Henry.* London: Frederick Muller, 1956.

Boadella, David. *Wilhelm Reich: the Evolution of His Work.* Chicago: Henry Regnery, 1973.

Bodin, Jean. *De la démonomania des sorciers.* Paris, 1580.

Bock, Carl. *The Head-Hunters of Borneo. A Narrative of Travel up the Mahakkam and down the Barito; also, Journeyings in Sumatra.* London: Sampson Low, Marston, Searle & Rivington, 1881. Reprint, Singapore; Oxford: Oxford University Press, 1985.

The Bodhisattva Doctrine in Buddhism. Waterloo, ON, Canada: Canadian Corporation for Studies in Religion, Wilfrid Laurier University Press, 1981.

Boehme, J. *Aurora.* London: John M. Watkins, 1960.

———. *The Confession of Jacob Boehme.* New York: Harper, 1954.

———. *The Life and Doctrines of Jacob Boehme.* New York: McCoy Publishing, 1929.

———. *Mysterium Magnum.* London: John M. Watkins, 1965.

———. *The Signature of All Things.* London: James Clarke, 1969.

———. *Six Theosophic Points.* Lansing: University of Michigan State Press, 1970.

———. *The Three Principles of the Divine Essence.* Jacksonville, Fla.: Yoga Publication Society, 1909.

———. *The Way to Christ.* New York: Paulist Press, 1978.

Bogoraz, Waldemar G. "The Chukchee." *Memoirs of the American Museum of Natural History.* Vol. 16. New York: G. E. Stechert, 1904.

Boguet, Henri. *Discours des sorciers.* Translated as *Examen of Witches.* New York: Barnes & Noble, 1971.

Bohn, Erich. *Der Fall Rothe.* Breslau, 1901.

Boirac, Emile. *L'Avenir des sciences psychiques.* Paris, 1917. Translated as *The Psychology of the Future.* London, 1918.

———. *La Psychologie Inconnue; Introduction et contribution à l'étude expérimentale des sciences psychiques.* Paris, 1908. English edition as *Psychic Science: An Introduction and Contribution to the Experimental Study of Psychical Phenomena.* London, 1918.

Bois, Jules. *Le Petites Religions de Paris.* Paris, 1894.

———. *Le Satanisme et la Magie.* Paris, 1895.

Boisserie, P. J. *Lourdes.* Paris, 1891.

Bolen, J. G. "Interview: Shafica Karagulla." *Psychic* 4, no. 6 (1973).

Bolshakoff, Serge. *Russian Nonconformity.* Philadelphia: Westminster Press, 1950. Reprint, New York: AMS Press, 1973.

Bolton, Brett, ed. *Edgar Cayce Speaks.* New York: Avon, 1969.

Bolton, Brett L. *The Secret Powers of Plants.* New York: Berkley, 1974. Reprint, London: Abacus, 1974.

Bolton, Gambier. *A Book of Beasts and Birds.* London: G. Newnes, Ltd., 1903.

———. *Ghosts in Solid Form.* London: W. Rider and Son, Ltd., 1919.

———. *Psychic Force: An Experimental Investigation.* London, 1904.

Bond, Frederick Bligh. "Athanasia." *Journal* of the American Society for Psychical Research (January–May 1929).

———. *The Company of Avalon.* Oxford: B. H. Blackwell, 1924.

———. *The Glastonbury Scripts.* 9 vols. Glastonbury, England: Abbot's Leigh, n.d.

———. *Gate of Remembrance (1918).* Oxford: B. H. Blackwell, 1918. Kila, Mont.: Kessinger Publishing Co., 1999.

Bond, Frederick Bligh, and Thomas Simcox Lea. *Gematria: A Preliminary Investigation of the Cabala.* Wellingborough, England: Thorsons, 1977.

Bonewits, P. E. I. *Authentic Thaumaturgy.* Albany, Calif.: The CHAOSium, 1978.

———. *Druid Chronicles (Evolved).* Berkeley, Calif.: Berkeley Drunemetron Press, 1976.

———. *Real Magic.* Coward, McCann & Geoghegan, 1971. Rev. ed. Berkeley, Calif.: Creative Arts Book Co., 1979.

Bonewitz, Ra. *Cosmic Crystals: Crystal Consciousness and the New Age.* Van Nuys, Calif: Newcastle Publishing, 1983.

Bonner, Hypatia Bradlaugh, and J. M. Robertson. *Charles Bradlaugh: His Life and Work.* London, 1898.

Bonner, Saniel. *The Divine Emergence of the World: Teacher: The Realization, the Revelation and the Revealing Ordeal of Heart Master Da Love-Ananda.* Clearlake, Calif.: Dawn Horse Press, 1990.

The Bonseigneur Rituals a Collection of 18th Century Ecossais Rituals. Kila, Mont.: Kessinger Publishing Co., 1998.

The Book of Shadows and Substance. Owlexandrian Multimedia/Hermetic Educational Institute, n.d.

The Book of the Dead. Translated by E. A. Wallis Budge. New Hyde Park, N.Y.: University Books, 1960.

The Book of the Sacred Magic of Abra-Melin the Mage. Translated by S. L. MacGregor-Mathers. 1898. Reprint, Chicago: de Laurence, 1932. Reprint, New York: Causeway Books, 1974.

"Books and Reports on Leonard Mediumship." *Psychic Science* 16, no. 4 (January 1938).

Boone, J. Allen. *Kinship with All Life.* New York: Harper & Brothers, 1954.

Bord, J. *Astral Projection.* New York: Samuel Weiser Inc., 1981.

Bord, Janet. *Ghosts.* Newton Abbot, England: David & Charles, 1974.

Bord, Janet, and Colin Bord. *Alien Animals.* Harrisburg, Pa.: Stackpole Books, 1981.

———. *The Bigfoot Casebook.* Harrisburg, Pa.: Stackpole Books, 1982.

Borges, Jorge Luis, with Margarita Guerrero. *The Book of Imaginary Beings.* Translated by Norman Thomas de Giovanni. New York: E. P. Dutton, 1970.

Borrow, George. *Lavengro; the Scholar, the Gypsy, the Priest.* 3 vols. London, 1851.

———. *The Romany Rye.* London, 1957.

Bose, J. C. *Growth and Tropic Movements of Plants.* London/New York: Longmans, Green and Co., 1929.

———. *Motor Mechanisms of Plants.* London/New York: Longmans, Green and Co., 1928.

———. *The Nervous Mechanism of Plants.* London/New York: Longmans, Green and Co., 1926.

———. *The Physiology of the Ascent of Sap.* London/New York: Longmans, Green and Co., 1923.

———. *The Physiology of Photosynthesis.* London/New York: Longmans, Green and Co., 1924.

———. *Plant Autographs & Their Revelations.* Washington, 1915. Reprint, London: Longmans Green, 1927.

———. *Plant Response as a Means of Physiological Investigation.* London/New York: Longmans, Green and Co., 1906.

———. *Researches in Irritability of Plants.* London/New York: Longmans Green and Co., 1913.

———. *Response in the Living and Non-Living.* London/New York: Longmans, Green and Co., 1902.

Bosman, Leonard. *The Meaning and Philosophy of Numbers.* 1932. Reprint, London: Rider, 1974.

Boswell, Charles. "The Great Fume and Fuss over the Omnipotent Oom." *True* (January 1965): 31–33, 86–91.

Bottazi, F. *Nelle regioni inesplorate della Biologia Umana.* Rome, 1907.

Bouché-Leclercq, A. *Histoire de la divination dans l'antiquité.* Paris, 1879. Reprint, New York: Ayer Publishing Co. Inc., 1975.

Bouissou, Michaël. *The Life of a Sensitive.* London: Sidgwick & Jackson, 1955.

Bounds, E. M. *Power Through Prayer.* London, 1912. Reprint, Chicago: Moody Press, 1979.

Boutet, Frederic. *Dictionnaire des Sciences Occultes.* New York: French & European Publications, Inc., 1993.

Bowen, Sandra, F. R. Nick Nocerino, and Joshua Shapiro. *Mysteries of the Crystal Skulls Revealed.* Pacifica, Calif.: Aquarian Networking, 1887. Revised edition, 1988.

Boyd, Doug. *Swami.* New York: Random House, 1976.

Boyer, Paul and Stephen Nissenbaum. *Salem-Village Witchcraft.* Belmont, Calif.: Wadsworth Publishing, 1972. Boston: Northeastern University Press, 1993.

Boyer, Paul, and Stephen Nissenbaum. *Salem Possessed.* Cambridge, Mass.: Harvard University Press, 1974.

Boyle, Robert. *Works.* 5 vols. London, 1744. Rev. ed. 6 vols. London, 1772.

Bozzano, Ernesto. "Animals and Psychic Perceptions." *Annals of Psychic Science* (August 1905).

———. *Dei Fenomeni d'Infestazione.* Rome, 1919.

———. *Phénomènes Psychiques au Moment de la Mort.* Paris, 1923.

———. *Polyglot Mediumship (Xenoglossy).* London: Rider, 1932.

———. *Popoli Primitivi e Manifestazioni Supernormali.* Milan: Armenia Editore, 1974.

Bracelin, L. L. *Gerald Gardner: Witch.* London: Octagon Press, 1960.

Brackett, E. A. *Materialized Apparitions.* Boston: Colby & Rich, 1886; William Rider, n.d.

Braddon, Russell. *The Piddingtons.* London: T. Werner Laurie, 1950.

Braden, Charles S. *Spirits in Rebellion.* Dallas, Tex.: Southern Methodist University Press, 1963.

———. *These Also Believe.* New York: Macmillan, 1949.

Bradford, David T. "Neuropsychology of Swedenborg's Visions," *Perceptual & Motor Skills* 88, no. 2 (April 1999): 377–383.

Bradley, Don. *Freemasonry in the Twenty-First Century.* Phoenix, Ariz.: Native Planet Publishing, 1995.

———. *Picking Winners.* St. Paul, Minn.: Llewellyn Publications, 1954.

———. *Profession and Birthdate.* Los Angeles: Llewellyn Publications, 1950.

———. *Stock Market Predictions.* Los Angeles: Llewellyn Foundation for Astrological Research, 1950.

Bradley, H. Dennis. . . . *And After.* London: T. Werner Laurie, 1931.

———. *Towards the Stars.* London: T. Werner Laurie, 1924.

———. *The Wisdom of the Gods.* London: T. Werner Laurie, 1925.

Braid, James. *Magic, Witchcraft, Animal Magnetism, Hypnotism, and Electro-Biology.* London: John Churchill, 1852.

———. *Neurpnology; Or, The Rationale of Nervous Sleep.* London, 1843. Reprint, New York: Ayer Publishing Co. Inc., 1975.

———. *Neurypnology.* 1843. Reprinted as *Braid on Hypnotism: The Beginnings of Modern Hypnosis.* New York: Julian Press, 1960.

———. *Observations on J. C. Colquhoun's History of "Magic, Witchcraft, and Animal Magnetism."* Manchester, England: J. T. Parkes, 1852.

———. *Observations on the Nature and Treatment of Certain Forms of Paralysis.* London: T. Richards, 1855.

———. *Observations on Trance; or, Human Hibernation.* London: J. Churchill 1850.

———. *The Physiology of Fascination, and the Critics Criticised.* Manchester, England: Grant and Co., 1855.

———. *The Power of the Mind Over the Body.* 1846.

Brailsford, Mabel Richmond. *A Quaker from Cromwell's Army: James Nayler.* London: Swathmore Press, 1927.

Bramwell, J. M. *Hypnotism: Its History, Practice, and Theory.* London, 1903.

Bramwell, J. Milne. *Hypnotism and Treatment by Suggestion.* London: Cassell, 1909. Reprint, New York: Da Capo Press, Inc., 1982.

Branch, Ramus. *Harry Edwards: The Life Story of the Great Healer.* Burrows Lea, Guildford, Surrey, UK: Healer Publishing, 1982.

Brand, John. *Observations on Popular Antiquities.* 2 vols. London, 1813.

———. *Popular Antiquities.* 1849. Reprint, London: J. R. Smith, 1870.

Brandon, Ruth. *The Spiritualists: The Passion for the Occult in the Nineteenth and Twentieth Centuries.* New York: Alfred A. Knopf; London: Weidenfeld & Nicolson, 1983.

Branston, Brian. *Gods of the North.* London: Thames & Hudson, 1955.

Brau, Jean-Louis, Helen Weaver, and Allan Edmands, eds. *Larousse Encyclopedia of Astrology.* New York: New American Library, 1982.

Braun, Kirk. *The Unwelcome Society.* West Linn, Ore.: Scout Creek Press, 1984.

Breasted, J. H. *Religion and Thought in Ancient Egypt.* London: Hodder & Stoughton, 1912.

Breasted, James. *A History of Egypt: From the Earliest Times to the Persian Conquest.* New York: Charles S. Scribner's Sons, 1919.

Brehier, Emile. *The Philosophy of Plotinus.* Chicago: University of Chicago Press, 1958.

Brett, William H. *The Indian Tribes of Guiana.* London, 1868.

Bridges, John Henry. *The Life and Work of Roger Bacon.* 1914. Reprint, Merrick, N.Y.: Richwood, 1976.

"Bridey Murphy—Fact, Fraud, or Fancy?" Special issue of *Tomorrow* 4, no. 4 (summer 1956).

A Brief account of Mr. Valentine Greatrakes, and divers of the strange cures by him lately Performed; written by himself in a letter addressed to the Honourable Robert Boyle Esq. London, 1666. Reprint, Dublin: Samuel Dancer, 1688.

A Brief History of the Fund for UFO Research. Washington, D.C.: Fund for UFO Research, n.d.

Brier, Robert. *Precognition and the Philosophy of Science; An Essay on Backward Causation.* New York: Humanities Press, 1973.

Briggs, Katharine M. *The Anatomy of Puck: An Examination of Fairy Beliefs Among Shakespeare's Contemporaries and Successors.* London: Routledge & Kegan Paul, 1959.

———. *A Dictionary of British Folktales in the English Language.* 4 vols. Bloomington: Indiana University Press, 1970–71.

———. *A Dictionary of Fairies.* London: Penguin Books, 1976. Reprinted as *An Encyclopedia of Fairies, Hobgoblins, Brownies, Bogies, and Other Supernatural Creatures.* New York: Pantheon Books, 1976.

———. *The Fairies in English Tradition and Literature.* 1967. Reprinted as *The Fairies in Tradition and Literature.* London: Routledge and Kegan Paul, 1967.

———. *Folktales of England.* Chicago: University of Chicago Press, 1965.

———. *The Personnel of Fairyland: A Short Account of the Fairy People of Great Britain for Those Who Tell Stories to Children.* 1953. Reprint, Detroit: Singing Tree Press, 1971; Detroit: Gale Research, Inc., 1971.

———. *The Vanishing People: A Study of Traditional Fairy Beliefs.* London: B. T. Batsford, 1978.

Brightman, Edgar S. *The Problem of God.* New York: Abingdon Press, 1930.

Brinton, Daniel G. *The Myths of the New World.* Leypoldt and Holt, 1868.

Brinton, Howard H. *The Mystic Will: Based on a Study of the Philosophy of Jacob Boehme.* New York: Macmillan, 1930.

[Britten, Emma Hardinge.] *Art Magic.* Boston, 1875. Reprint, Chicago: Progressive Thinker Publishing House, 1898.

———. *Ghost Land; or, Researches into the Mysteries of Occultism.* Chicago: Progressive Thinker Publishing House, 1897.

Britten, Emma Hardinge. *Modern American Spiritualism: A Twenty Years' Record of the Communion Between Earth and the World of Spirits.* London, 1869. Reprint, New Hyde Park, N.Y.: University Books, 1970.

———. *Nineteenth Century Miracles; or, Spirits and Their Works in Every Country of the Earth.* London and Manchester: John Heywood, 1884. Reprint, North Stratford, N.H.: Ayer Publishers, Inc., 1976.

Bro, Harmon Hartzell. *Begin a New Life: The Approach of Edgar Cayce.* New York: Harper & Row, 1971.

———. *Dreams in a Life of Prayer: The Approach of Edgar Cayce.* New York: Paperback Library, 1970.

———. *Edgar Cayce on Dreams.* New York: Castle Books, 1968.

———. *Edgar Cayce on Religion and Psychic Experience.* New York: Paperback Library, 1970.

———. *High Play; Turning on Without Drugs.* New York: Coward-McCann, 1970.

———. *A Seer Out of Season: The Life of Edgar Cayce.* New York: New American Library, 1989.

Broad, C. D. "Immanuel Kant and Psychical Research." *Proceedings of the Society for Psychical Research* 49 (1950).

———. *Lectures on Psychical Research, Incorporating the Perrott Lectures Given in Cambridge University in 1939 and 1960.* New York: Humanities Press, 1962.

———.*The Mind and Its Place in Nature.* London: Routledge and Kegan Paul, 1925.

———. *Perception, Physics, and Reality: An Inquiry into the Information that Physical Science Can Supply about the Real.* 1914.

———. *Personal Identity and Survival.* London: Society for Psychical Research, 1968.

———. *Religion, Philosophy, and Psychical Research.* London: Routledge and Kegan Paul, 1953.

Broch, Harald B. " 'Crazy Women are Performing in Sombali: A Possession-Trance Ritual on Bonerate, Indonesia," *Ethos* 13, no. 3 (Fall 1985): 262–282,

Brodie-Innes, J. W. *Scottish Witchcraft Trials.* London: Chiswick Press, 1891.

Broekman, Marcel. *The Complete Encyclopaedia of Practical Palmistry.* Englewood, N.J.: Prentice-Hall, 1972. Reprint, London: Mayflower, 1975.

Brofferio, Angelo. *Per Lo Spiritismo.* 3d ed. Turin, 1903.

Bromage, Bernard. *Tibetan Yoga.* London: Aquarian Press, 1952.

Bromley, David G., and Larry D. Shinn, eds. *Krishna Consciousness in the West.* Lewisburg: Bucknell University Press, 1989.

Bronson, Bertrand Harris. *The Traditional Tunes of the Child Ballads.* 4 vols. Princeton, N.J.: Princeton University Press, 1959–72.

Bronson, Matthew. "When As-If Becomes As-Is: the Spontaneous Initiation of a Brazilian Spiritist Medium," *Anthropology of Consciousness,* 3, nos. 1–2 (1992): 9–16.

Brooked-Smith, Coin. "Data-tape Recorded Experimental PK Phenomena." *Journal of the Society for Psychical Research* 47 (1973).

Brooks, C. Harry. *The Practice of Autosuggestion by the Method of Emile Coué.* New York: Dodd, Mead, 1922.

Brooks, Louise McNamara. *Early History of Divine Science.* Denver: First Divine Science Church, 1963.

Brooks, Nona L. *Mysteries.* Denver: The Author, 1924.

———. *The Prayer that Never Fails.* Denver: The Author, 1935.

———. *Short Lessons in Divine Science.* Denver: The Author, 1928.

Brooks, Pat. *Out! In the Name of Jesus.* Carol Stream, Ill.: Creation House, 1972.

Brother Francis [Ralph F. Raymond]. *The Universal Link Concept.* Los Angeles: Universal Link Heart Center, 1968.

Brough, James. *The Vixens.* New York: Simon and Schuster, 1980.

Brown, Diana DeGroat. *Umbanda: Religion and Politics in Urban Brazil.* Ann Arbor, Mich.: UMI Press, 1986.

Brown, John P. *The Darvishes; or Oriental Spiritualism.* London, 1927. Rev. ed., London: Frank Cass, 1968.

Brown, Michael F. "Dark Side of the Shaman," *Natural History* (November, 1989): 8–10.

Brown, Raymond Lemment. *The Phantom Soldiers.* New York: Drake, 1975.

Brown, Rosemary. *Immortals at My Elbow.* London: Bachman & Turner, 1974. Reprinted as *Immortals by My Side.* Chicago: Henry Regnery, 1975.

———. *Unfinished Symphonies: Voices from the Beyond.* London, 1971. Reprint, New York: William Morrow, 1971.

Brown, Slater. *The Heyday of Spiritualism.* New York: Hawthorn Books, 1970.

Brown, William. *Mind and Personality.* College Park, Md.: McGrath, 1927.

———. *Mind, Medicine, and Metaphysics; The Philosophy of a Physician.* London: Oxford University Press, 1936.

———. *Psychological Methods of Healing; An Introduction to Psychotherapy.* London: University of London Press, Ltd., 1938.

———. *Science and Personality.* New Haven, Conn.: Yale University Press, 1929. Reprint, College Park, Md.: McGrath, 1972.

———. *Suggestion and Mental Analysis.* New York: Doran, 1922.

Brown, William A. *The Life of Prayer in a World of Science.* London: Hodder & Stoughton, 1927.

Browning, Elizabeth Barrett. *Letters to her Sister, 1846–1859.* Edited by Laura Huxley. London: John Murray, 1929. Reprint, New York: E. P. Dutton, 1930.

Browning, Norma Lee. *The Psychic World of Peter Hurkos.* Garden City, N.Y.: Doubleday, 1970.

Browning, Robert. *Dramatis Personae.* London: Chapman and Hall, 1864.

Browning, Vivienne. *My Browning Family Album.* London: Springwood Books, 1979.

Brownson, Orestes Augustus. *The Spirit-Rapper.* Boston: Little, Brown, 1854.

Brudal, Paul J. "PSI-forskning og psykologi som vitenskap. En oversiktsartikkel om de seneste 20 ars utvikling innen PSI-forskning" (PSI Research and Psychology as a Science), *Tidsskrift for Norsk Psykologforening* 21, no. 6 (June 1984): 302–309.

Bruce, Henry Addington Bayley. *Historic Ghosts and Ghost Hunters.* New York: Moffat, Yard, 1908.

———. *Riddle of Personality.* New York: Moffat, Yard, 1915.

———. *Scientific Mental Healing.* Boston, Little, Brown, 1911.

Bruce, James Douglas. *The Evolution of Arthurian Romance, From the Beginnings Down to the Year 1300.* Baltimore, Md.: Johns Hopkins University Press, 1923.

Brugger, Peter and Alfred T. Baumann. "Repetition Avoidance in Responses to Imaginary Questions: The Effect of Respondents' Belief in ESP," *Psychological Reports* 75, no. 2 (October 1994): 883–893.

Brugmans, H. J. F. W., G. Heymans, and A. Weinberg. "Some Experiments in Telepathy Performed in the Psychological Institute of the University of Groningen." *Compte-Rendu du Premier Congrés International de Recherches Phychiques.* 1921.

Brundage, James A. *Law, Sex and Christian Society in the Medieval Europe.* Chicago: University of Chicago Press, 1987.

Bruner, Carlos A. "Otra nota sobre parapsicologia: sobre el significado del termino" (Another Note on Parapsychology: Concerning the Meaning of the Term), *Revista Mexicana de Psicologia* 2, no. 2 (July-December 1985): 165–167.

Brunner, S. *Aus dem Nachlasse des Furstein Aloysius von Hehenlohe.* Regensburg: G. J. Manz, 1851.

Brunton, Paul. *A Message from Arunchala.* 1936. Reprint, New York: Samuel Weiser, 1971.

———. *A Search in Secret Egypt.* London, 1935. Reprint, New York: Samuel Weiser, 1970.

Brunton, Ron. *The Abandoned Narcotic: Kava and Cultural Instability in Melanesia.* Cambridge; New York: Cambridge University Press, 1989.

Bry, Adelaide. *est, Erhard Seminars Training: 60 Hours That Transform Your Life.* New York: Avon, 1976.

Bryant, Jacob. *A New System; or an Analysis of Ancient Mythology.* 3 vols. 1776. Reprint, New York: Garland, 1979.

Brynes, Steven. *Wicca Course.* Palm Springs, Calif.: International Guild of Advanced Sciences Research Society, 1994.

Bubba Free John [Franklin Jones]. *No Remedy.* Lower Lake, Calif.: Dawn Horse Press, 1976.

Buber, Martin. *Tales of the Hasidim: The Early Masters.* London: Thames & Hudson, 1956. Reprint, New York: Schocken, 1961.

———. *The Legend of the Baal-Shem.* New York: Schocken Books, 1955.

Buchanan, J. Rhodes. *Manual of Psychometry: The Dawn of a New Civilization.* Boston: Dudley M. Holman, 1885.

Bucke, Richard Maurice. *Cosmic Consciousness: A Study in the Evolution of the Human Mind.* Innes & Sons, 1910. Reprint, New Hyde Park, N.Y.: University Books, 1961; New York: Citadel Press, 1970.

———. *Richard Maurice Bucke, Medical Mystic: Letters of Dr. Bucke to Walt Whitman and His Friends.* Detroit: Wayne State University Press, 1977.

Buckland, Ray. *Ray Buckland's Magic Cauldron.* Lakeville, Minn.: Galde Press, Inc., 1995.

———. *Scottish Witchcraft.* St. Paul, Minn.: Llewellyn Publications, 1999.

———. *Witchcraft: Ancient and Modern.* New York: H. C. Publishers, 1970.

———. *Witchcraft from the Inside.* St. Paul, Minn.: Llewellyn Publications, 1999.

Budapest, Zsuzsanna E. *The Feminist Book of Lights and Shadows.* Venice, Calif.: Luna Publications, 1976.

———. *The Grandmother of Time.* San Francisco: Harper & Row, 1989.

———. *The Holy Book of Women's Mysteries.* Los Angeles: Susan B. Anthony Coven Number One, 1979.

Budge, E. A. Wallis. *Amulets and Superstitions.* Oxford: Oxford University Press, 1930. Reprinted as *Amulets and Talismans.* New Hyde Park, N.Y.: University Books, 1961.

———. *The Book of the Dead.* London, 1898. Reprint, New York: Dover, 1967; New York: Causeway, 1974.

———. *Egyptian Magic.* London: Kegan Paul, 1899.

———. *The Gods of the Egyptians.* 2 vols. London, 1898.

———. *A History of Egypt.* 8 vols. London, 1902. 4 vols. Reprint, The Netherlands: Anthropological Publications, n.d.

———. *The Mummy.* London, 1925.

———. *Tutankhamen: Amenism, Atenism and Egyptian Monotheism.* London: M. Hopkinson, 1923. Reprint, New York: Bell Publishing, 1979.

Buess, Lynn M. *Numerology for the New Age.* Marina del Rey, Calif.: DeVorss, 1978.

Bugge, E. S. *The Home of the Eddic Poems.* London: David Nutt, 1899.

Bugliosi, Vincent, with Curt Gentry. *Helter Skelter.* New York: W. W. Norton, 1972. Reprint, New York: Bantam, 1975.

Bulkeley, Kelly. *Visions of the Night: Dreams, Religion, and Psychology.* Albany.: State University of New York Press, 1999.

Bulkley, Patricia. "Pre-Death Dreams and Visions: A Study of Their Religious Significance," *Dissertation Abstracts International Section A: Humanities & Social Sciences* 56, no. 11-A (May 1996): 4434.

Bull, K. T. "Mrs. Piper—A Study." *Harper's Bazaar* 33 (1900).

Bull, Titus. "Mental Obsession and the Latent Faculty." *Journal* of the American Society for Psychical Research 32 (1938): 260.

———. "Resistance to Metaphysical Science." *Journal* of the American Society for Psychical Research 17 (1927): 645.

Bullard, Thomas E. "Fresh Air, or Air Castles in Folklore Theories?" *Journal of UFO Studies,* 4 (1992): 165–73.

———. *On Stolen Time: A Summary of a Comparative Study of the UFO Abduction Mystery.* Bloomington, Ind.: The Author, 1987.

Bunger, Fred S., and Hans N. Von Koerber. *A New Light Shines Out of the Present Darkness.* Philadelphia: Dorrance, 1971.

Bunker, Dusty. *Numerology and Your Future.* Rockport, Mass.: Para Research, 1980.

Bunson, Matthew E. *The Vampire Encyclopedia.* New York: Crown Publishing Group, Inc., 1993.

Burgoyne, Thomas H. *Celestial Dynamics.* Denver: Astro-Philosophical Publishing, 1896.

———. *The Language of the Stars.* Denver: Astro-Philosophical Publishing, 1892.

———. *Light of Egypt: The Science of the Soul and the Stars.* Albuquerque, N.Mex.: Sun Publishing, 1980.

Burkan, Tolly. *Guiding Yourself into a Spiritual Reality.* Twin Harte, Calif.: Reunion Press, 1983.

Burke, O. M. *Among the Dervishes.* New York: E. P. Dutton, 1973.

Burkert, Walter. *Ancient Mystery Cults.* Cambridge, Mass.: Harvard University Press, 1987.

Burl, Aubrey. *Prehistoric Astronomy and Ritual.* Aylesbury, Bucks, England: Shire Publications, 1983.

———. *The Stone Circles of the British Isles.* New Haven, Conn.: Yale University Press, 1976.

Burland, C. A. *The Arts of the Alchemists.* London, 1967.

Burleson, Donald R. *Lovecraft: Disturbing the Universe.* Lexington: University Press of Kentucky, 1990.

Burman, Edward. *The Assassins.* Wellingborough, UK: Crucible, 1987.

Burnham, Kenneth E. *God Comes to America.* Boston: Lambeth Press, 1979.

Burr, Chauncey. *Knocks for the Knockings.* New York: Burr Brothers, 1851.

Burr, Harold S. *The Fields of Life.* New York: Ballantine, 1973.

Burridge, Kennelm. *Mambu.* New York: Harper Torchbook, 1978.

Burt, Cyril. *Psychology and Psychical Research.* London: Society for Psychical Research, 1968.

Burton, Jean. *Heyday of a Wizard: Daniel Home the Medium.* London: George G. Harrap, 1948.

Burton, Maurice. *The Sixth Sense of Animals.* New York: Taplinger, 1973; London: Dent, 1973.

Burton, Sir Richard. *Vikram and the Vampire, or Tales of Hindu Devilry.* London: Tilston & Edwards, 1832. Reprint, New York: Dover Publications, 1969.

Butler, Bill. *Dictionary of the Tarot.* New York: Schocken Books, 1975.

Butler, Christopher. *Number Symbolism.* London: Routledge and Kegan Paul, 1970.

Butler, Walter E. *Apprenticed to Magic.* 1962. Reprint. Wellingborough, England: Aquarian Press, 1990.

———. *How to Develop Clairvoyance.* New York: Samuel Weiser, 1971.

———. *How to Develop Psychometry.* London: Aquarian Press; New York: Samuel Weiser, 1971.

———. *How to Read the Aura, Practice Psychometry, Telepathy, and Clairvoyance.* New York: Warner Destiny Books, 1978. Rochester, Vt.: Inner Traditions International, Limited, 1998.

———. *An Introduction to Telepathy.* 1975.

———. *Magic: Its Ritual, Power, and Purpose.* London: Aquarian Press, 1952.

———. *The Magician: His Training and Work.* London: The Aquarian Press, 1959. Reprint, North Hollywood, Calif.: Wilshire Book, 1959.

Butt, Audrey. "The Shaman's Legal Role," *Revista do Museu Paulista, Nova Série,* Vol. 16 (1965–66).

Butt, G. Baseden. *Life of Madame Blavatsky.* London: Rider, 1926.

Bynner, Witter, trans. *The Way of Life According to Lao Tzu.* New York: G. P. Putnam's Sons, 1944.

Byrd, Anita. *Handwriting Analysis: A Guide to Personality.* New York: Arco, 1982.

Byrne, Peter. *The Search for Big Foot: Monster, Myth or Man?* Washington, D.C.: Acropolis Books, 1975. Reprint, New York: Pocket Books, 1976.

Cabaniss, Allen. *Charlemagne.* New York: Twayne Publishers, 1972.

Cadbury, H. J. *George Fox's "Book of Miracles."* Cambridge, Mass.: Cambridge University Press, 1948.

Caddy, Eileen. *The Dawn of Change.* Forres, Scotland: Findhorn Publications, 1979.

———. *The Spirit of Findhorn.* New York: Harper & Row, 1976. Reprint, London: L. N. Fowler, 1977.

Cadoret, Remi J. "An Exploratory Experiment: Continuous EEG Recoding During Clairvoyant Card Tests." *Journal of Parapsychology* 28 (1964).

———. "Effect of Novelty in Test Conditions on ESP Performance." *Journal of Parapsychology* 16 (1952).

Cadoret, Remi J., and J. Fahler. "ESP Card Tests of College Students With and Without Hypnosis." *Journal of Parapsychology* 22 (1958).

Cadoret, Remi J., and J. G. Pratt. "The Consistent Missing Effect in ESP." *Journal of Parapsychology* 14 (1950).

Cadwallader, M. E. *Hydesville in History.* Chicago: Progressive Thinker Publishing House, 1922.

Cahagnet, Louis-Alphonse. *The Celestial Telegraph; Or, Secrets of the Life to Come Revealed Through Magnetism.* London, 1850. Reprint, New York: Ayer Publishing Co. Inc., 1976.

———. *Magnátisme arcanes de la vie future devoile.* Paris, 1848. Translated as *The Celestial Telegraph.* 2 vols. New York, 1851.

———. *Magnátisme: Encyclopédie magnétique spiritualiste.* N.p., 1861.

———. *Sanctuaire au Spiritualisme.* Paris, 1850. Translated as *The Sanctuary of Spiritualism: A Study of the Human Soul and of Its Relation with the Universe through Somnambulism and Ecstasy.* N.p., 1851.

———. *Thérapeutique du magnétisme et du Somnambulisme appropriée aux maladies les plus communes.* N.p., 1883.

Cain, Nellie B. *Exploring the Mysteries of Life.* Grand Rapids, Mich.: Spiritual Research Society, 1972.

———. *Gems of Truth from the Masters.* Grand Rapids, Mich.: Spiritual Research Society, 1965.

Caine, Mary. *The Glastonbury Zodiac: Key to the Mysteries of Britain.* Torquay, England: Grael Communications, 1978.

Calder-Marshall, Arthur. *The Magic of My Youth.* N.p., 1951.

Calef, Robert. *More Wonders of the Invisible World; or, The Wonders of the Invisible World Display'd in Five Parts.* London, 1700.

Calmet, Augustine. *Dissertations Upon the Apparitions of Angels, Demons, and Ghosts, and Concerning . . . Vampires.* Paris: De Burel'aine, 1746. Reprint, London, 1759.

———. *The Phantom World; or, The History and Philosophy of Spirits, Apparitions, & Co.* 2 vols. London: Richard Bentley, 1850; Philadelphia: A. Hart, 1850.

———. *Dissertations sur les apparitions, des anges, des démons et des esprits, et sur les revenants et vampires de Hongrie, de Boheme, de Moravie et de Silésie.* Rev. ed. Paris, 1751. Reprinted as *The Phantom World.* 2 vols. London: Richard Bentley, 1850.

———. *Treatise on Vampires & Revenants: The Phantom World.* Brighton, Sussex, England: Desert Island Books, 1995. Digot, A. *Notice biographique et littéraire sur Dom Augustin Calmet.* Nancy, France, 1860.

Cambridge Buddhist Association. Cambridge, Mass.: Cambridge Buddhist Association, 1960.

Cameron, Charles. *Who Is Guru Maharaj Ji?* New York: Bantam Books, 1973.

Cameron, David. *Who Is Guru Maharaj Ji?* New York: Ballantine Books, 1973.

Cameron, Verne L. *Aquavideo; Locating Underground Water.* Santa Barbara, Calif.: El Cariso, 1970.

———. *Map Dowsing.* Santa Barbara, Calif.: El Cariso, 1971.

———. *Oil Locating.* Santa Barbara, Calif.: El Cariso, 1971.

Campbell, Alan Tornmaid. *To Square with Genesis. Causal Statements and Shamanic Ideas in Wayapi.* Iowa City: University of Iowa Press, 1989.

Campbell, Bruce F. *A History of the Theosophical Movement.* Berkeley: University of California Press, 1980.

Campbell, Elizabeth Montgomery, and David Solomon. *The Search for Morag.* London: Tom Stacey, 1972.

Campbell, G. *The Knights Templars, Their Rise and Fall.* London: Duckworth; New York: McBride, 1937.

Campbell, J. G. *Witchcraft and Second Sight in Scottish Highlands and Islands.* Glasgow: Alex, MacLehose, 1902.

Campbell, John F. *Popular Tales of the West Highlands, Orally Collected.* 4 vols. Edinburgh, 1860–62. Rev. ed.: London and Paisley: Alexander Gardner, 1890–93. Reprint, Detroit: Singing Tree Press, 1969.

Campbell, John L., and Trevor H. Hall. *Strange Things: The Story of Fr. Allan McDonald, Ada Goodrich Freer, and the Society for Psychical Research's Enquiry into Highland Second Sight.* London: Routledge & Kegan Paul, 1968.

Campbell, John W., Jr. "Psionic Machine-Type One." *Astounding Science Fiction* (June 1956).

Campbell, Joseph. *The Hero With a Thousand Faces.* New York: Pantheon, 1949.

———. *Historical Atlas of World Mythologies.* 2 vols. New York: Harper, 1983–88.

———. *The Masks of God.* 6 vols. New York: Viking, 1959–68.

———. *Myths to Live By.* New York: Viking, 1972.

Campbell, Steuart Campbell. *The Loch Ness Monster: The Evidence.* Wellingborough, England: Aquarian Press, 1986.

Canada, Steve. *Crop Circles: The Theory That Works.* The Author, 1998.

———. *Crop Circles: A Vocabulary of the Symbols.* The Author, 1998.

———. *Crop Circles: Interplanetary Communication Begins.* The Author, 1997.

———. *Crop Circles: Returning Rulers from Biblical Planet Olam.* The Author, 1998.

———. *Crop Circles & Isis, "Mistress of the Great Pyramid" at Giza.* The Author, 1997.

———. *Crop Circles. . .The End of Time.* The Author, 1996.

Candragomin. *Difficult Beginnings: Three Works on the Bodhisattva Path.* Boston: Shambhala, 1985.

Cannell, J. C. *The Secrets of Houdini.* London, 1931. Reprint, Detroit: Gale Research, 1976.

Cannon, Alexander. *Hypnotism, Suggestion & Faith-Healing.* 1932.

———. *The Invisible Influence.* New York: E. P. Dutton, 1934.

———. *The Power of Karma.* N.p., 1936.

———. *Powers That Be.* New York: E. P. Dutton, 1935.

———. *The Science of Hypnotism.* N.p., 1936.

———. *Sleeping Through Space.* N.p., 1938.

———. "Some Hypnotic Secrets." *The British Journal of Medical Hypnotism* 1, 1 (1949).

Cannon, Walter B. "Voodoo Death," *American Anthropologist,* 44 (1942): 169–181.

Capp, Bernard. *Astrology and the Popular Press: English Almanacs 1500–1800.* London: Faber & Faber, 1979.

Capron, E. W. *Modern Spiritualism: Its Facts and Fanaticisms, Its Consistencies and Contradictions.* Boston: B. Marsh, 1855. Reprint, New York: Ayer Publishing Co. Inc., 1976.

Capron, E. W., and H. D. Barron. *Singular Revelations: Explanation and History of the Mysterious Communion with Spirits.* Auburn, N.Y., 1850.

Carden, Karen W., and Robert W. Pelton. *The Persecuted Prophets: The Story of the Frenzied Snake Handlers.* New York: A. S. Barnes; London: Thomas Yoseloff, 1976.

Carey, Ken. *Notes to My Children: A Simplified Metaphysics.* Kansas City, Mo.: Uni-Sun, 1984.

———. *Return of the Bird Tribes.* Kansas City, Mo.: Uni-Sun, 1988.

———. *Terra Christa: The Global Spiritual Awakening.* Kansas City, Mo.: Uni-Sun, 1985.

———. *Vision.* Kansas City, Mo.: Uni-Sun, 1985.

Carey, Ken [Raphael]. *The Starseed Transmissions: An Extraterrestrial Report.* Kansas City, Mo.: Uni-Sun, 1982.

Carington, Walter Whately. *The Death of Materialism.* N.p., 1932.

———. *The Foundations of Spiritualism.* New York: E. P. Dutton, 1920.

———. *Matter, Mind and Meaning.* Completed by H. H. Price. London: Methuen, 1949.

———. "The Quantitative Study of Trance Personalities." *Proceedings of the Society for Psychical Research.* Part 1, 42 (1934): 173. Part 2, 43 (1935): 319. Part 3, 44 (1937): 189.

———. *Telepathy: An Outline of its Fact, Theory and Implications.* London: Methuen, 1945. Reprint, New York: Gordon Press, 1972.

———. *A Theory of the Mechanism of Survival.* N.p., 1920.

Carmichael, Alexander. *Carmina Gadelica, Hymns and Incantations.* 2 vols. 1900. 2nd ed. 5 vols. Edinburgh & London, 1928–54.

Carmona, Michel. *Les Diables de Loudun: Sorcellerie et politique sous Richelieu.* Paris: Fayard, 1988.

Caron, M., and Serge Hutin. *Les Alchimistes.* 1959. Translated as *The Alchemists.* New York: Grove Press, 1961.

Carpenter, James C. "The Early Parapsychological Contributions," *Journal of Parapsychology* 57, no. 1 (March 1993): 25–37.

Carr, John Dickson. *The Life of Sir Arthur Conan Doyle.* London: John Murray, 1949.

Carrel, Alexis. *Man the Unknown.* New York: Harper & Brothers, 1935.

———. *Reflections on Life.* New York: Hawthorn, 1953.

———. *Voyage to Lourdes.* New York: Harper & Brothers, 1950.

Carrié, Abbé. *L'hydroscopographie et métalloscopogragie, ou l'art de découvrir les sources et les gisement metallifers au moyen de l'é lectromagnétisme.* Saintes, France, 1863.

Carrington, Hereward. *The American Séances with Eusapia Palladino.* New York: Helix Press, 1954.

———. *The Case for Psychic Survival.* New York: Citadel Press, 1957.

———. *Eusapia Palladino and Her Phenomena.* New York: B. E. Dodge, London: T. Werner Laurie, 1909.

———. "An Examination and Analysis of the Evidence for 'Dematerialization' as Demonstrated in Mons. Aksakof's Book." *Proceedings of the American Society for Psychical Research* (March 1907).

———. *Higher Psychical Development.* London: Kegan Paul, 1920. Reprint, New York: Dodd, Mead, 1924.

———. *The Invisible World.* New York: The Beechhurst Press; B. Ackerman Inc., 1946.

———. *Loaves and Fishes.* New York: Charles Scribner's Sons, 1935.

———. *Modern Psychic Phenomena.* New York: Dodd, Mead, 1919.

———. *The Physical Phenomena of Spiritualism: Fraudulent and Genuine.* Boston, Small; London: T. Werner Laurie, 1907. Reprint, New York: Dodd, Mead, 1920.

———. *Problems of Psychical Research & Theories in the Realm of the Supernormal.* N.p., 1921. Kila, Mont.: Kessinger Publishing Co., 1998.

———. "Psychical Phenomena Among Primitive Peoples." *Psychic Research* (October 1930).

———. *Psychic Science and Survival.* Manchester, England: Two Worlds Publishing; New York: American Psychical Institute, 1939.

———. *The Story of Psychic Science.* London: Rider, 1930. Reprint, New York: Ives Washburn, 1931.

———. *True Ghost Stories.* London, [1933].

———. *Vitality, Fasting and Nutrition.* New York: Rebman, 1908.

———. *Your Psychic Powers and How to Develop Them.* New York: American Universities Publishing, 1920. Reprint, New York: Causeway, 1973.

Carrington, Hereward, and J. Meader. *Death, Its Causes & Phenomena.* London, 1911.

Carrington, Hereward, and Nandor Fodor. *Haunted People: Story of the Poltergeist Down the Centuries.* New York: E. P. Dutton, New American Library, 1951. Reprinted as *The Story of the Poltergeist Down the Centuries.* London: Rider, 1953.

Carrington, Hereward, and Sylvan J. Muldoon. *The Phenomena of Astral Projection.* London: Rider, 1951.

———. *The Projection of the Astral Body.* 1929. Reprint, New York: Samuel Weiser, 1970.

Carrithers, Walter A., Jr. "Madam Blavatsky: One of the World's Great Jokers." *Journal* of the American Society for Psychical Research 56 (July 1962).

———. *The Truth about Madame Blavatsky: An Open Letter to the Author of the Priestess of the Occult.* Covina, Calif.: Theosophical University Press, 1947.

Carrol, F. *The Prayer of the Early Christians.* London: Burns & Oates, 1930.

Carter, C. E. O. *An Introduction to Political Astrology.* London: L. N. Fowler, 1951.

———. *Astrological Aspects.* London: L. N. Fowler, 1930.

———. *The Encyclopedia of Astrology.* London: Theosophical Publishing House, 1924.

———. *The Principles of Astrology.* London: Theosophical Publishing House, 1925.

———. *The Zodiac and the Soul.* London: Theosophical Publishing House, 1928.

Carter, Howard. *The Tomb of Tut-ankh-Amen.* 3 vols. London: Cassell, 1923–33. Reprint, New York: Cooper Square Publishers, 1963.

Carter, Huntley, ed. *Spiritualism: Its Present-day Meaning.* Philadelphia: J. B. Lippincott, 1920.

Carter, Lin. *Lovecraft: A Look Behind the Cthulhu Mythos.* New York: Ballantine Books, 1972.

Carter, Mary Ellen, and William McGarey. *Edgar Cayce on Healing.* New York: Warner, 1972.

Cartwright, Rosalind D. *Night Life: Explorations in Dreaming.* Englewood, N.J.: Prentice-Hall, 1977.

Carty, Charles M. *The Two Stigmatists: Padre Pio & Therese Neumann.* Dublin: Veritas, 1956.

Carus, Paul. *Chinese Astrology.* LaSalle, Ill.: Open Court, 1907.

———. *History of the Devil and the Idea of Evil.* LaSalle, Ill.: Open Court Publishing, 1974. Reprint, Bell Publishing, 1974.

———. *Karma: A Study of Buddhist Ethics.* La Salle, Ill.: Open Court, 1894.

———. *The Soul of Man.* Chicago: Open Court, 1900.

"The Cases of Mr. Moss and Mr. Munnings." *Journal of the Society for Psychical Research* 23 (1926).

Casewit, Curtis. *Graphology Handbook.* Rockport, Mass.: Para Research, 1980.

Cassirer, Manfred. "ESP in Post-Medieval Witchcraft," *Journal of the Society for Psychical Research* 55, no. 815 (April 1989): 350–359.

———. "Helen Victoria Duncan: A Reassessment." *Journal of the Society for Psychical Research* 53, 801 (October 1985).

Cassoli, Piero. "Parapsychology in Italy Today." In *Parapsychology Today: A Geographical View.* Edited by Allan Angoff and Betty Shapin. New York: Parapsychology Foundation, 1971.

Castaneda, Carlos. *The Eagle's Gift.* New York: Simon & Schuster, 1981.

———. *Journey to Ixtlan: The Lessons of Don Juan.* New York: Simon & Schuster, 1972.

———. *The Power of Silence: Further Lessons of Don Juan.* New York: Simon & Schuster, 1987.

———. *The Second Ring of Power.* New York: Simon & Schuster, 1977.

———. *A Separate Reality: Further Conversations with Don Juan.* New York: Simon & Schuster, 1971. Reprint, New York: Pocket Books, 1991.

———. *Tales of Power.* New York: Simon & Schuster, 1974.

———. *The Teachings of Don Juan: A Yaqui Way of Knowledge.* Berkeley: University of California Press, 1998.

Cauzons, Theodore de. *La Magie et la Sorcellerie en France.* 4 vols. Paris, 1900.

Cavanna, Roberto, and Emilio Servadio. *ESP Experiments with LSD 25 and Psilocybin.* New York: Parapsychology Foundation, 1964.

Cavanna, Roberto, and Montague Ullman, eds. *Psi and Altered States of Consciousness.* New York: Parapsychology Foundation, 1968.

Cavanna, Roberto, ed. *Psi Favorable States of Consciousness.* New York: Parapsychology Foundation, 1970.

Cavendish, Richard. *The Black Arts.* New York: G. P. Putnam's Sons, 1967.

Cayce, Edgar. *Atlantis: Fact or Fiction.* Virginia Beach, Va.: ARE Press, 1962.

———. *Auras.* Virginia Beach, Va.: ARE Press, 1970.

———. *Edgar Cayce on Atlantis.* New York: Paperback Library, 1968. New York: Warner Books, Inc., 1999.

———. *The Edgar Cayce Reader.* 2 vols. New York: Paperback Library, 1969.

Cayce, Hugh Lynn. *Earth Changes Update.* Virginia Beach, Va.: ARE Press, 1980.

———. *Faces of Fear.* New York: Berkeley Books, 1980.

———. *The Jesus I Knew.* Virginia Beach, Va.: ARE Press, 1984.

———. *Venture Inward.* New York: Paperback Library, 1966.

Cazotte, Jacques. *Le Diable.* Paris: B. Grasset, 1921. Translated as *The Devil in Love.* London: Consortium, 1993.

Cellini, Benvenuto. *Autobiography.* New York: Dodd, Mead, 1961.

Centennial Book of Modern Spiritualism in America. Chicago: The National Spiritualist Association of the United States of America, 1948.

The Centennial Memorial of Modern Spiritualism Records, 1848–1948. Lily Dale, N.Y.: National Spiritualist Association of the U.S.A., 1988.

Cerney, J. V. *Acupressure: Acupuncture without Needles.* West Nyack, N.Y.: Parker Publishing, 1974. Reprint, Upper Saddle River, N.J.: Prentice Hall Press, 1998.

Cerutti, Edwina. *Olga Worrall, Mystic with the Healing Hands.* New York: Harper & Row, 1975.

Cerve, Wishar S. [H. Spencer Lewis]. *Lemuria: The Lost Continent of the Pacific.* San Jose, Calif.: Supreme Grand Lodge, AMORC, 1931.

Ch'u Ta-Kao, trans. *Tao Te Ching.* London: Allen & Unwin; New York: Samuel Weiser, 1937.

Chakravarti, Chintaharan. *Tantras: Studies on Their Religion and Literature.* Calcutta, India: Punthi Pustak, 1963.

Chamberlin, E. R. *Antichrist and the Millennium.* New York: E. P. Dutton, 1975.

Chambers, Howard V. *Dowsing, Water Witches & Divining Rods for the Millions.* Los Angeles: Sherbourne Press, 1969.

———. *Phrenology.* Sherbourne, 1968.

Chambers, Robert. *Domestic Annals of Scotland from the Reformation to the Revolution.* 2 vols. Edinburgh, 1858.

———. *Testimony: Its Posture in the Scientific World.* N.p., 1959.

———. *Traditions of Edinburgh.* N.p., 1825.

Chan, Chen Chi. "Tibetan Phantasies." *Tomorrow* 6, 2 (spring 1958).

Chan, Pedro. *Finger Acupressure.* New York: Ballantine Books, 1975.

Chancellor, P. *Handbook of the Bach Flower Remedies.* London: C. W. Daniel, 1971.

Chandrasekhar, Sripati. *"A Dirty Filthy Book."* Berkeley: University of California Press, 1981.

Chaney, Earlyne. *Beyond Tomorrow.* Upland, Calif.: Astara, 1985.

———. *Remembering.* Los Angeles: Astara's Library of Mystical Classics, 1974.

———. *Revelations of Things to Come.* Upland, Calif.: Astara, 1982.

———. *Secrets from Mount Shasta.* Anaheim, Calif.: Stockton Trade Press, 1953.

Chaney, Earlyne, and William L. Messick. *Kundalini and the Third Eye.* Upland, Calif.: Astara's Library of Mystical Classics, 1980.

Chaney, Robert. *Mysticism: The Journey Within.* Upland, Calif.: Astara's Library of Mystical Classics, 1979.

———. *The Inner Way.* Los Angeles: De Vorss, 1962.

Chaney, Robert G. *"Hear My Prayer."* Eaton Rapids, Mich.: Library, Spiritualist Episcopal Church, 1942.

Chaney, Robert Galen. *Mediums and the Development of Mediumship.* Michigan: Psychic Books, 1946. Reprint, Freeport, N.Y.: Books for Libraries, 1972.

Chang, Chung-Yuan. *Tao: A New Way of Thinking.* New York: Harper & Row, 1975.

Chang, Garma Chen-Chi. *Esoteric Teachings of the Tibetan Tantra.* Lausanne, Switzerland: Falcon's Wing Press, 1961.

———. *Teachings of Tibetan Yoga.* New Hyde Park, N.Y.: University Books, 1963.

———. "Tibetan Phantasies." *Tomorrow* 6, 2 (Spring 1958): 13–16.

Chang, Garma Chen-Chi, ed. *The Hundred Thousand Songs of Milarepa.* New Hyde Park, N.Y.: University Books, 1962. Reprint, Boulder, Colo: Shambhala, 1977.

Chapman, Janine. *Quest for Dion Fortune.* York Beach, Maine: Samuel Weiser, 1993.

Chapman, Robert. *Unidentified Flying Objects.* London: Arthur Barker, 1969.

Charcot, Jean Martin. *Lectures on the Diseases of the Nervous System.* London, 1881. Reprint, New York: Hafner, 1962.

———. *Les demoniaques dans l'art.* Paris, 1887. Reprint, Amsterdam: B. M. Israel, 1972.

Charet, F. X. *Spiritualism and the Foundations of C. G. Jung's Psychology.* Albany: State University of New York Press, 1993.

Chari, C. T. K. "The Challenge of Psi; New Horizons of Scientific Research." *Journal of Parapsychology* 38 (1974).

———. "Regurgitation, Mediumship, and Yoga." *Journal of the Society for Psychical Research* 47 (1973).

Charles, R. H. *A Critical History of the Doctrine of a Future Life in Israel, in Judaism and in Christianity.* London, 1899. Reprinted as *Eschatology, The Doctrine of a Future Life in Israel, in Judaism, and in Christianity: A Critical History.* New York: Schocken Books, 1963.

Charles, R. H., ed. *The Book of Enoch [Ethiopic text].* London: Society for Promoting Christian Knowledge, 1917.

Charlton, I. W. *The Revival in Wales.* London, 1905. (Pamphlet)

Charpentier, John. *L'Ordre des Templiers.* Paris: La Colombe, 1945.

Charpentier, Louis. *The Mysteries of Chartres Cathedral.* London: Research into Lost Knowledge Organization, 1972. Reprint, New York: Avon, 1972.

Charroux, Robert. *The Mysteries of the Andes.* New York: Avon, 1977.

Chase, Warren. *Forty Years on the Spiritual Rostrum.* Boston, 1888.

———. *The Life Line of the Lone One, an Autobiography of the World's Child.* Boston: B. Marsh, 1857.

Chee Soo. *Chinese Yoga: The Chinese Art of K'ai Men.* London: Gordon & Cremonesi, 1977.

Cheek, David B. "Pre- & Peri-Natal: Are Telepathy, Clairvoyance and "Hearing" Possible in Utero? Suggestive Evidence as Revealed During Hypnotic Age-Regression Studies of Prenatal Memory," *Psychology Journal* 7, no. 2: Winter 1992: 125–137.

Cheek, David B., and Leslie M. LeCron. *Clinical Hypnotherapy.* New York: Grine & Stratton, 1968.

Cheetham, Erika. *The Prophecies of Nostradamus.* New York: G. P. Putnam's Sons, 1972. Reprint, London: Neville Spearman, 1973; London: Corgi, 1975.

Cheiro [Count Louis Hamon]. *The Book of Numbers.* London, 1926. Revised as *Cheiro's Book of Numbers.* London: Barrie & Jenkins, 1978.

———. *Cheiro's Complete Palmistry.* New Hyde Park, N.Y.: University Books, 1968. Reprint, New York: Dell, 1969.

———. *Cheiro's Guide to the Hand.* London: Nichols, 1900. Reprint, London: Corgi, 1975.

———. *Cheiro's Language of the Hand; A Complete Practical Work on the Science of Cheirognomy and Cheiromancy.* 28th ed. London: H. Jenkins, 1949. Reprint, London: Corgi, 1975.

———. *Cheiro's Memoirs: The Reminiscences of a Society Palmist.* London: William Rider, 1912.

———. *Cheiro's Year Book.* Rev. ed., London: London Publishing, 1930.

———. *Mysteries and Romances of the World's Greatest Occultists.* London: Herbert Jenkins, 1935.

———. *You and Your Hand.* Garden City, N.Y.: Doubleday, Doran, 1931.

———. *You and Your Star.* Los Angeles: London Publishing; London: Herbert Jenkins, 1926.

Cheney, Sheldon. *Men Who Have Walked with God.* New York: Alfred A. Knopf, 1968. Reprint, New York: Dell, 1974.

Cheng, Man-ching. *Tai-Chi.* Berkeley, Calif.: North Atlantic, 1981.

Cherryh, C. J. *Rusalka.* New York: Ballantine Books, 1989.

Chesi, Gert. *Faith Healers in the Philippines.* Austria: Perlinger Verlag, 1981.

Chesneaux, Jean. *Secret Societies in China in the Nineteenth and Twentieth Centuries.* Ann Arbor, Mich.: University of Michigan Press, 1971.

Chestnut, V. K. "Plants Used by the Indians of Mendocino County, California." *Contributions of U.S. National Herbarium,* Vol. 7, no. 3. Washington (D.C.), 1902.

Chevalier, J. C. *Experiments in Spiritualism; or, The Adjuration of Spirits, by a late member of Mr. Home's Spiritual Athenaeum.* London, 1867.

Chevreul, M. E. *De la baguette divinatoire, du puendule dit explorateur et des tables tournantes, au point de vue du l'histoire, de la critique et de la méthode expérimentale.* Paris, 1854.

Chia, Mantak. *Awaken Healing Energy Through the Tao: The Taoist Secret of Circulating Internal Power.* New York: Aurora Press, 1983.

———. *Awaken Healing Energy through the Tao.* New York: Aurora Press, 1983.

———. *Iron Shirt Chi Kung I.* Huntington, N.Y.: Healing Tao Books, 1986.

Chia, Mantak, and Maneewan Chia. *Healing Love Through the Tao: Cultivating Female Sexual Energy.* Huntington, N.Y.: Healing Tao Books, 1986.

Chia, Mantak, and Michael Winn. *Taoist Secrets of Love: Cultivating Male Sexual Energy.* New York: Aurora Press, 1984.

Chidananda, Swami. *Destiny of Man.* Shivanandanagar, India: Divine Life Society, 1989.

———. *Forest Academy Lectures on Yoga.* Rishikish, India: The Author, 1960.

———. *Path to Blessedness.* Shivanandanagar, India: Divine Life Society, 1975.

———. *The Philosophy, Psychology, and Practice of Yoga.* Shivanandanagar, India: Divine Life Society, 1984.

———. *Truth that Liberates.* Shivanandanagar, India: Divine Life Society, 1993.

A Child at School [Samuel Guppy]. *Mary Jane: or Spiritualism Chemically Explained.* London: John King, 1863.

Child, Francis J. *The English and Scottish Popular Ballads.* 5 vols. Boston, 1882–98. Reprint, Folklore Press; Pageant Book, 1957.

Child, I. L. "Psychology and anomalous observations: The question of ESP in dreams." *American Psychologist,* 40, (1985): 1219–30.

Ching-nan, Lee, and R. Figueroa. *Techniques of Self-Defense.* New York: A. S. Barnes, 1963.

Chinmoy, Sri. *Arise! Awake! Thoughts of a Yogi.* New York: F. Fell, 1972.

———. *Astrology: The Supernatural and the Beyond.* Hollis, N.Y.: Vishma Press,1973.

———. *Death and Reincarnation: Eternity's Voyage.* Jamaica, N.Y.: Agni Press, 1974.

———. *Mother India's Light-house.* San Francisco: Shi Chinmoy Center, n.d.

———. *The Seeker's Mind.* Jamaica, N.Y.: Agni Press, 1978.

Chippendale, Christopher. *Stonehenge Complete.* Ithaca, N.Y.: Cornell University Press, 1983.

Chkashige, Masumi. *Oriental Alchemy.* New York: Samuel Weiser, 1936.

Chnaiderman, Miriam. "O processo psicanalitico: A experiencia mistica e mitica na passagem do sagrado ao tragico" (The Psychoanalytic Process: The Mystical and Mythical Experiences in the Passage from the Sacred to the Tragic Dimension), *Percurso: Revista de Psicanalise* 6, 11[2] (1993): 19–24.

Cholmondely-Pennell, H. *"Bringing it to Book": Facts of Slate-Writing through Mr. W. Eglinton.* London, 1884.

Chorvinsky, Mark. "The Mary F. Morgawr Photographs Investigation." *Strange Magazine* 8 (Fall 1991): 8–9, 11, 46–48.

———. "The Shiels-Related Fairy Photos." *Strange Magazine* 9 (spring/summer 1992): 24–25, 60.

Chrétien de Troyes. *Le Conte del Graal (Perceval).* Edited by Félix Lecoy. Paris: Champion, 1973.

Christensen, Alice, and David Rankin. *The Light of Yoga Society Beginner's Manual.* Cleveland Heights, Ohio: Om Ram Productions, 1972. Revised edition as: Christensen, Alice. *The American Yoga Association Beginner's Manual.* New York: Simon & Schuster, 1987.

Christian Literature Society. *Theosophy Exposed; or, Mrs. Besant and Her Guru: Appeal to Educated Hindus.* Madras, India: SPCK Press, 1893.

The Christian Mystery School. Pelham, N.H.: Homebringing Mission of Jesus Christ, 1983.

Christian Science: A Sourcebook of Contemporary Materials. Boston: Christian Science Publishing Society, 1990.

Christian, Paul [Jean Baptiste Pitois]. *Historie de la Magie, du monde Surnaturel et de la fatalité a travers les Temps et les Peuples.* 1870. Translated by Ross Nichols as *The History and Practice of Magic.* New York: Citadel Press, 1969. Reprint, Kila, Mont.: Kessinger Publishing, 1994.

The Christic Teachings. Quakertown, Pa.: Church of Illumination, 1955.

Christie-Murray, David. *Voices from the Gods: Speaking in Tongues.* London: Routledge & Kegan Paul, 1978.

Christmas, Henry. *The Cradle of the Twin Giants, Science and History.* 2 vols. London, 1849.

Christopher, Milbourne. *ESP, Seers and Psychics.* New York: Thomas Y. Crowell, 1970.

———. *Houdini: The Untold Story.* New York: Thomas Y. Crowell, 1969. Reprint, New York: Pocket Books, 1970.

———. *The Illustrated History of Magic.* New York: Thomas Y. Crowell, 1973. Reprint, London: Robert Hale, 1975.

———. *Mediums, Mystics & The Occult.* New York: Thomas Y. Crowell, 1975.

———. *Panorama of Magic.* New York: Dover Publications, 1962.

———. *Search for the Soul: An Insider's Report on the Continuing Quest by Psychics and Scientists for Evidence of Life After Death.* New York: Thomas Y. Crowell, 1979.

Ch'u, Yuan. *The Nine Songs: A Study of Shamanism in Ancient China.* London: George Allen and Unwin, 1955.

Churchward, James. *Children of Mu.* New York: Ives Washburn, 1931.

———. *Cosmic Forces of Mu.* New York: Ives Washburn, 1935.

———. *The Lost Continent of Mu: The Motherland of Man.* New York: Ives Washburn, 1926.

———. *The Sacred Symbols of Mu.* New York: Ives Washburn, 1933.

Cirlot, J. E. *A Dictionary of Symbols.* New York: Dorset Press, 1991.

A Citizen of the United States [James McBride]. *Symmes' Theory of Concentric Spheres; Demonstrating that the Earth is Hollow, Habitable Within, and Widely Open About the Poles.* Cincinnati, Ohio: Morgan, Lodge, and Fisher, 1826.

Clarie, Thomas C. *Occult Bibliography: An Annotated List of Books Published in English, 1971 through 1975.* Metuchen, N.J.: Scarecrow Press, 1978.

———. *Occult/Paranormal Bibliography: An Annotated List of Books Published in English, 1976 through 1981.* Metuchen, N.J.: Scarecrow Press, 1984.

Clark, Doug. *Earthquake—1982: When the Planets Align—(Syzygy).* Garden Grove, Calif.: Lyfe Production Publications, 1976.

Clark, Jerome. *Encyclopedia of Strange and Unexplained Phenomena.* Detroit: Gale Research, 1993.

———. *The Emergence of a Phenomenon: UFOs from the Beginning through 1959. The UFO Encyclopedia. Volume 2.* Detroit: Omnigraphics, 1992.

———. "Life in a Pyramid." *Fate* 36, no. 6 (June 1983): 38–44.

———. "The Thickets of Magonia." *International UFO Reporter* 15, 1 (January/February 1990): 4–11.

———. *The UFO Encyclopedia. I, UFOs in the 1980s.* Detroit: Apogee Books, 1990.

———. *UFOs in the 1980s. The UFO Encyclopedia. Volume 1.* Detroit: Apogee Books, 1990.

———. "Wagging the Dog." *International UFO Reporter* 19, 1 (January/February 1994): 3, 22–24.

Clark, Jerome, and J. Gordon Melton. "The Crusade Against the Paranormal." Parts 1 and 2. *Fate* 32, 9 (September 1979): 70–76; 32, 10 (October 1979): 87–94.

Clark, Linda. *The Ancient Art of Color Therapy.* Old Greenwich, Conn.: Devin-Adair, 1975.

Clark, Richard J., S.J. *The Holy Coat of Treves.* London, 1892.

Clark, Tom. *The Great Naropa Poetry Wars.* Santa Barbara, Calif.: Cadmus Editions, 1980.

Clark, Walter Houston. *The Oxford Group; Its History and Significance.* New York: Bookman Associates, 1951.

———. *The Psychology of Religion; An Introduction to Religious Experience and Behavior.* New York: Macmillan, 1958.

———. *Religious Experience; Its Nature and Functioning in the Human Psyche.* Springfield, Ill.: Charles Thomas, 1973.

Clark, Walter Houston, and M. H. Malony, J. Daane, and A. R. Tippett. *Chemical Ecstasy; Psychedelic Drugs and Religion.* New York: Sheed and Ward, 1969.

Clarke, Ada. *Memoirs of the Wesley Family.* 4th ed. London: W. Tegg, 1860.

Clarke, Arthur C. *Ascent to Orbit: A Scientific Autobiography.* New York: John Wiley, 1984.

———. *The Ghost from the Great Banks.* London: V. Gollancz, 1990.

———. *Profiles of the Future: An Inquiry into the Limits of the Possible.* New York: Holt Rinehart, and Winston, 1984.

Clarke, Edward H. *Visions: A Study of False Sight.* Boston, 1878.

Clayton, Rev. George. *Angelology; Agency & Ministry of Holy Angels.* New York, 1851.

Cleather, Alice L. *H. P. Blavatsky: A Great Betrayal.* Calcutta: Thacker, Spink, 1922.

Clébert, Jean-Paul. *The Gypsies.* London: Vista Books, 1963. Reprint, Harmondsworth, Middlesex, UK: Penguin Books, 1967.

Clemens, Samuel Langhorne. *The Writings of Mark Twain.* New York: Harpers, 1907.

Clifford, Hugh. *In Court and Kampong.* London: Grant Richards, 1897.

———. *Studies in Brown Humanity.* London: Grant Richards, 1898.

Clissold, Augustus. *The Prophetic Spirit in its Relation to Wisdom and Madness.* London, 1870.

Clodd, Clara M. *The Ageless Wisdom of Life.* Adyar, Madras, India: Theosophical Publishing House, 1956.

Close, F. *The Tester Tested; or Table Moving, Turning, Talking, Not Diabolical: A Review of the Publications of the Rev. Messrs. Godfrey, Gillson, Vincent, and Dibdin.* London and Cheltenham, 1853.

Clulee, Nicholas H. *John Dee's Natural Philosophy: Between Science and Religion.* New York: Routledge, 1988.

Clymer, R. Swinburne. *The Age of Treason.* Quakertown, Pa.: Humanitarian Society, 1959.

Clymer, R. Swinburne. *The Book of Rosicrucie.* 3 Vols. Quakertown, Penn: Philosophical Publishing, 1946–49.

———. *Christisis.* Quakertown, Pa.: Philosophical Publishing, 1945.

———. *A Compendium of Occult Law.* Quakertown, Pa.: Philosophical Publishing, 1938.

———. *Diet: A Key to Health.* Quakertown, Pa.: Humanitarian Society, 1930.

———. *The Fraternitas Rosae Crucis.* Quakertown, Pa.: Philosophical Publishing, 1929.

———. *The Interpretation of St. John.* Quakertown, Pa.: Philosophical Publishing, 1953.

———. *The Rose Cross Order.* Allentown, Pa.: Philosophical Publishing, 1916.

———. *The Rosicrucian Fraternity in America.* 2 vols. Quakertown, Pa.: Rosicrucian Foundation, 1935.

———. *The Rosy Cross: Its Teachings.* Quakertown, Pa.: Beverly Hall, 1965.

———. *The Way to Happiness.* Quakertown, Pa.: Humanitarian Society, 1920.

Coates, Austin. *Numerology.* London: Frederick Muller, 1974. Reprint, London: Mayflower, 1978.

Coates, James. *Has W. T. Stead Returned?* London: L. N. Fowler, 1913.

———. *Photographing the Invisible: Practical Studies in Supernormal Photography, Script, and Other Allied Phenomena.* London: L. N. Fowler, 1911. Reprint, North Stratford, N.H.: Ayer Publishing, 1973.

Cobbe, Frances Power. *The Peak in Darien.* London, 1882.

Cockayne, T. O. *Leechdoms, Wortcunning, and Starcraft.* 2 vols. London, 1864–1866. Reprint, London: Holland Press, 1968.

Codrington, R. H. *The Melanesians: Studies in Their Anthropology and Folk-lore.* Oxford: Clarendon Press, 1891.

Cohen, D. *Sleep and Dreaming: Origins, Nature and Functions.* New York: Pergamon Press, 1981.

Cohen, Daniel. *Curses, Hexes and Spells.* Philadelphia: Lippincott, 1974.

———. *The Encyclopedia of Ghosts.* New York: Avon Books, 1991.

———. *The Encyclopedia of Monsters.* New York: Avon Books, 1991.

———. *Encyclopedia of the Strange.* New York: Dodd, Mead, 1985.

Cohen, Shaye J. D. *From the Maccabees to the Mishnah.* Philadelphia: Westminster Press, 1987.

Cohn, Norman. *Europe's Inner Demons.* New York: Basic Books, Inc., 1975.

Cohn, Shari A. "A Survey on Scottish Second Sight." In *Research in Parapsychology, 1993: Abstracts and Papers from the Thirty-sixth Annual Convention of the Parapsychological Association, 1993.* Lanham, Md.: Scarecrow Press, Inc., 1998.

Coil, Henry. *Coil's Masonic Encyclopedia.* Richmond, Va.: Macoy Publishing, 1961.

———. *Freemasonry Through Six Centuries.* 2 vols. Richmond, Va.: Macoy Publishing, 1961.

Colby, Benjamin N., and Lore M. Colby. *The Daykeeper. The Life and Discourse of an Ixil Diviner.* Cambridge, Mass.: Harvard University Press, 1981.

Cole, J. A. Abayomi. *Astrological Geomancy in Africa.* London, 1898.

Coleridge, Samuel Taylor. *Selected Poems.* London: Oxford University Press, 1965.

Colinon, Maurice. *Faux prophètes et sectes d'aujourd'hui.* N.p., 1953.

———. *Guide de la France religieuse et mystique.* Paris: Tchou, 1969.

———. *Le Phénomène des sectes au 20ème siècle.* N.p., 1959.

———. *Les Guérisseurs.* N.p., 1957.

Colley, Thomas. *Confessions of a Medium.* London, 1882.

———. *Sermons of Spiritualism.* London, 1907.

Collin-Smith, Joyce. "A Precognitive Dream: James Webb." *Light* (summer 1982).

Collins, Doris. *A Woman of Spirit.* London: Panther Books, 1983.

Collins, Mabel. *The Awakening.* London: Theosophical Publishing Society, 1906.

———. *The Blossom and the Fruit: The True Story of a Black Magician.* New York: Theosophical Publishing Society, 1888.

———. *A Cry from Afar.* London: Theosophical Publishing Society, 1905.

———. *The Idyll of the White Lotus.* Adyar, Madras, India: Theosophical Publishing House, 1885.

———. *Light on the Path.* Boston: Occult Publishing, 1884.

———. *Through the Gates of Gold.* London: J. M. Watkins, 1887.

Collins, Rodney. *The Theory of Celestial Influence.* London: Stuart & Watkins, 1955.

Colombo, John Robert. *Abracadabra.* Toronto: McClelland and Stewart, 1967.

———. *Colombo's Book of Marvels.* N.p., 1979.

———. *Extraordinary Experiences: Personal Accounts of the Paranormal in Canada.* Willowdale, ON, Canada: Hounslow Press, 1989.

———. *Mysterious Canada.* N.p., 1988.

Colombo, John Robert, ed. *Windigo: An Anthology of Facts and Fantastic Fiction.* Lincoln: University of Nebraska Press, 1982.

Colquhoun, Ithell. *The Sword of Wisdom: MacGregor Mathers and The Golden Dawn.* New York: G. P. Putnam's Sons, 1975.

Colquhoun, John C. *An History of Magic, Witchcraft & Animal Magnetism.* 2 vols. N.p., 1851.

———. *Report of the Experiments on Animal Magnetism; Made By a Committee of the Medical Section of the French Royal Academy of Sciences . . . 1831.* Edinburgh, 1833. Reprint, New York: Ayer Publishing Co. Inc., 1975.

Colville, Frederick V. "Notes on the Plants Used by the Klamath Indians of Oregon." *Contributions of U.S. National Herbarium,* Vol. 5, no. 2. Washington (D.C.), 1897.

Coly, Lisette, and Rhea A.White, eds. *Women and Parapsychology.* New York: Parapsychology Foundation, Inc., 1994.

Comenius, John A. *Orbis Pictus.* N.p., 1887. Reprint, Kila, Mont.: Kessinger Publishing Co. 1999.

Comstock, Christine Mason. "Selected Rorschach Scores in Spiritualist Mediums," *Dissertation Abstracts International: Section B: The Sciences & Engineering* 57, no. 10-B (April 1997): 6563.

Condon, Edward U. *Scientific Study of Unidentified Flying Objects.* Springfield, Va.: National Technical Information Service, 1968. Reprint, New York: E. P. Dutton, 1970.

———. "UFOs I Have Loved and Lost." *Bulletin of the Atomic Scientists* (December 1969).

Condron, Barbara. *Kundalini Rising: Mastering Creative Energies.* Windyville, Mo.: SOM, 1992.

Congdon, M. H., J. Hain, and Ian Stevenson. "A Case of Multiple Personality Illustrating the Transition from Role-Playing." *Journal of Nervous and Mental Disease* 132 (1961).

Conlan, Barnett D. *Nicholas Roerich: A Master of the Mountains.* Liberty, Ind.: Flamma, Association for Advancement of Culture, 1938.

Connell, R., and Geraldine Cummins. *Perceptive Healing.* London: Psychic Book Club, 1945.

Connor, W. R. *Roman Augury and Etruscan Divination.* New York: Ayer Publishing Co. Inc., 1976.

Conroy, Ed. *Report on "Communion": An Independent Investigation of and Commentary on Whitley Strieber's "Communion."* New York: William Morrow, 1989.

Constable, T. J. "Orgone Energy Engineering through the Cloudbuster." In John White and Stanley Krippner, eds. *Future Science.* Garden City, N.Y.: Doubleday, 1977.

Conway, Moncure D. *Demonology and Devil-Lore.* 2 vols. London: Chatto & Windus, 1879.

Conybeare, F. C., ed. *The Key of Truth.* London, 1898.

Cooke, Grace. *The Illumined Ones.* Liss, Hampshire, England: White Eagle Publishing Trust, 1966.

———. *The New Mediumship.* Liss, Hampshire, England: White Eagle Publishing Trust, 1965.

———. *Sun-Men of the Americas.* Liss, Hampshire, England: White Eagle Publishing Trust, 1975.

Cooke, Ivan, ed. *The Return of Arthur Conan Doyle.* Liss, England: White Eagle Publishing Trust, 1956.

Cooper, Basil. *The Werewolf in Legend, Fact and Art.* New York: St. Martin's Press, 1977.

Cooper, Irving Steiger. *Ceremonies of the Liberal Catholic Church.* Los Angeles: St. Alban Press, 1924.

———. *Methods of Psychic Development.* Adyar, Madras, India: Theosophical Publishing House, 1912.

———. *The Secret of Happiness.* Chicago: Theosophical Publishing House, 1925.

———. *Theosophy Simplified.* Wheaton, Ill.: Theosophical Publishing House, 1928.

Cooper, Irving Steiger, and Willi Kowa. *The Pendulum: Operational Practice and Theory.* Haywards Heath, UK: Academic Publications, 1978.

Cooper, Joe. *The Case of the Cottingley Fairies.* London: Robert Hale, 1990.

Cooper, Robert. *Spiritual Experiences, Including Seven Months with the Brothers Davenport.* London: Heywood & Co., 1867.

Cooper, Wendy. *Hair: Sex Society Symbolism.* London: Aldus Book, 1971.

Cooper, William M. [James Glass Bertram]. *Flagellation and the Flagellants: A History of the Rod in All Continents from the Earliest Period to the Present Time.* London, 1868. Rev. ed. Paris: C. Carrington, 1900.

Cooper-Oakley, Isabel. *The Compte St. Germain.* Milan, Italy: Liberia Editrice del Dr. G. Sulli-Rao, 1912.

———. *The Comte de Saint-Germain.* New York: S. Weiser, 1970.

———. *Mystical Traditions.* Milan, Italy: Liberia Editrice del Dr. G. Sulli-Rao, 1909.

———. *Traces of a Hidden Tradition in Masonry and Medieval Mysticism.* London: Theosophical Publishing Society, 1900.

Coopland, G. W. *Nicole Oresme and the Astrologers; A Study of His "Livre de Divinacions."* Liverpool, UK: University Press of Liverpool, 1952.

Coover, J. E. *Experiments in Psychical Research at Leland Stanford Junior University.* Palo Alto, Calif.: Stanford University, 1917. Reprint, North Stratford, N.H.: Ayer Publishing, 1975.

Copestake, David R. and H. Newton Malony. "Adverse Effects of Charismatic Experiences: A Reconsideration," *Journal of Psychology & Christianity* 12, no. 3 (Fall 1993): 236–244.

Corbett, Cynthia L. *Power Trips.* Santa Fe, N.Mex.: Timewindow Publications, 1988.

Cordovero, Moses ben Jacob. *Moses Cordovero's Introduction to Kabbalah: An Annotated Translation of His Or na'errav.* New York: Michael Sharaf Publishing Trust of the Yeshiva University Press, 1994. (Originally published sixteenth century.)

Corey, Kathleen. *Rev. Amanda C. Flower.* Holly, Mich.: The Author, n.d.

Corliss, William R., ed. *Handbook of Unusual Natural Phenomena.* Glen Arm, Md.: Sourcebook Project, 1977.

———. *Tornados, Dark Days, Anomalous Precipitation, and Related Weather Phenomena: A Catalog of Geophysical Anomalies.* Glen Arm, Md.: The Sourcebook Project, 1983.

Cornell, A. D. "An Experiment in Apparitional Observation and Findings." *Journal* of the Society for Pyschical Research 40 (1959): 120.

Cornell, James C., Jr., and John Surowiecki. *The Pulse of the Planet: A State of the Earth Report from the Smithsonian Institution Center for Short-lived Phenomena.* Harmony Books, 1972.

Corradi Musi, C. "Shamanism from East to West." *Bibliotheca Shamanistica.* Vol. 4. Budapest: Akadémiai Kiadó, 1997.

Corydon, Bent, and L. Ron Hubbard, Jr. *L. Ron Hubbard: Messiah or Madman?* New York: Lyle Stuart, 1987.

Cosmic Awareness Speaks. Vol. 1. Olympia, Wash.: Servants of Awareness, n.d. Vols. 2–3. Olympia, Wash.: Cosmic Awareness Communications, 1977, 1983.

Cosmic Law and the World Today. London: Atlanteans, 1967.

Costello, Peter. *In Search of Lake Monsters.* New York: Coward, McCann & Geohegan, 1974. Reprint, London: Panther, 1975.

Cott-MacPhail, Carolyn. *Choices and Connections: The First Catalog of the Global Family.* Boulder, Colo.: Human Potential Resources, 1987.

Cottrell, Alan P., ed. *Goethe's Faust: Seven Essays.* Chapel Hill, N.C.: University of North Carolina Press, 1976.

Coué, Emile. *My Method, Including American Impressions.* Garden City, N.Y.: Doubleday, Page, 1923.

———. *Self Mastery through Conscious Autosuggestion.* New York: American Library Service, 1922.

Coulomb, Madame E. *Some Account of My Intercourse with Madame Blavatsky from 1872 to 1884.* London: Elliot Stock, 1885.

The Count Dracula Fan Club Handbook. New York: Count Dracula Fan Club, 1992.

Courmes, D. A. *A Theosophical Question Book.* Translated from the French by Elin Salzer and Harry Banbery. Adyar, Madras, India: Theosophist Office, 1898.

Covell, Alan Carter. *Ecstasy: Shamanism in Korea.* Elizabeth, N.J.: Hollym International, 1983.

———. *Folk Art and Magic: Shamanism in Korea.* Seoul: Hollym Corp., 1986.

Coville, W. J. *Light and Color.* New York: McCoy Publishing and Masonic Supplies, 1914.

———. *Spiritual Science of Health and Healing.* Chicago: Garden City Publishing, 1888.

———. *Spiritual Therapeutics; or, Divine Science.* Chicago: Educator Publishing, 1914.

———. *Studies in Theosophy.* Boston: Colby & Rich, 1890.

———. *Universal Spiritualism.* New York: R. F. Fenno, 1906.

Cowan, Charles. *Thoughts on Satanic Influence, or Modern Spiritualism Considered.* London, 1854.

Cox, Edward W. *The Mechanism of Man: An Answer to the Question "What Am I?"* London: Longman, 1876.

———. *Spiritualism Answered by Science.* London, 1871.

———. *What Am I?: A Popular Introduction to Mental Philosophy and Psychology.* London: Longman, 1974.

Cox, Katharine. *Haunted Royalties.* London: W. Rider, 1916.

Cox, William E. "The Effects of PK on the Placement of Falling Objects." *Journal of Parapsychology* 15 (1951): 40–48.

———. *Mentalis and Magicians: Some Conclusive Arguments about a Modern Problem.* Singapore: Stamford College Press, 1972.

———. "Precognition and Intervention." *Journal* of the American Society for Psychical Research 50 (1956): 47–58.

———. "Some Extremely Significant Scores Produced by Recurrent PK (RPK)," *Journal of the Society for Psychical Research* 58, no. 829 (October 1992): 353–362.

Cox, William S. "An Experiment in Extra-Sensory Perception." *Journal of Experimental Psychology* 19 (1936): 429–37.

Coyne, William D. *Our Lady of Knock.* New York: Catholic Book Publishing, 1948.

Crabb, Riley Hansard. *An Attempt at Cosmic Fellowship.* Vista, Calif.: Borderland Science Research Foundation, 1964.

Crabtree, Adam. *Animal Magnetism, Early Hypnotism, and Psychical Research, 1766–1925: An Annotated Bibliography.* White Plains, N.Y.: Kraus International Publications, 1988.

Crasilneck, Harold B. *Clinical Hypnosis: Principles and Applications.* Orlando: Grune & Stratton, 1985.

Cravalho, Mark Andrew. "An Invisible Universe of Evil: Supernatural Malevolence and Personal Experience Among Amazon Peasants," *Dissertation Abstracts International Section A: Humanities & Social Sciences* 55, no. 3-A (1994): 622.

Crawford, E. F. *Experiment in Psychic Science.* N.p., 1919.

———. *The Psychic Structures in the Goligher Circle.* New York: E. P. Dutton & Co., 1921.

———. *The Reality of Psychic Phenomena.* London: J. M. Watkins, 1919.

Crawford, W. J. *Experiments in Psychic Science.* London: John M. Watkins, 1919. New York: E. P. Dutton, 1919.

———. *Experiments in Psychical Science: Levitation, "Contact," and the "Direct Voice."* London: John M. Watkins, 1919.

———. *The Psychic Structures at the Goligher Circle.* London: John M. Watkins, 1921.

———. *The Reality of Psychic Phenomena: Raps, Levitations, etc.* 2nd ed. London: John M. Watkins, 1919.

Crawley, A. E. *The Idea of the Soul.* New York: Macmillan, 1909.

Crehan, J. *Father Thurston.* London: Sheed and Ward, 1952.

Crehore, John D. *Mental Telepathy: Radiesthesia or Radesia, Our Sixth Sense.* Cleveland, Ohio: J. E. Johnson, 1956.

Creme, Benjamin. *Maitreya's Mission.* Amsterdam, The Netherlands: Share International, 1986.

———. *Messages from Maitreya the Christ.* 2 Vols. London: Tara Press, 1980.

———. *The Reappearance of the Christ and the Masters of Wisdom.* London: Tara Press, 1980.

———. *Transmission: A Meditation for the New Age.* North Hollywood, Calif.: Tara Center, 1983.

Crenshaw, James. *Telephone between Two Worlds.* Los Angeles: DeVorss, 1950.

Crile, George. *The Phenomena of Life: A Radio-Electric Interpretation.* London: William Heinemann, 1936.

Crombie, I. M. *Plato: The Midwife's Apprentice.* London: Routledge & Kegan Paul, 1964.

Crookall, Robert. *Case-Book of Astral Projection, 545–746.* New Hyde Park, N.Y.: University Books, 1972.

———. *During Sleep: The Possibility of "Co-Operation" Between the Living and the Dead.* New Hyde Park, N.Y.: University Books, 1974.

———. *During Sleep: the Possibility of "Cooperation."* London: Theosophical Publishing House, 1964.

———. *Ecstasy: The Release of the Soul from the Body.* Moradabad, India: Darshand International, 1975.

———. *Interpretation of Cosmic & Mystical Experiences.* London: James Clarke, 1969.

———. *More Astral Projections.* London: Aquarian Press, 1964.

———. *Out-of-the-Body Experiences and Survival.* UK: World Fellowship Press, 1970.

———. *Out-of-the-Body Experiences: A Fourth Analysis.* New Hyde Park, N.Y.: University Books, 1970. Secaucus, N.J.: Carol Publishing Group, 1992.

———. *The Study and Practice of Astral Projection.* London: Aquarian Press, 1961. Reprint, New Hyde Park, N.Y.: University Books, 1966.

———. *The Supreme Adventure: Analyses of Psychic Communications.* UK: J. Clarke for Churches' Fellowship for Psychical Study, 1961.

———. *The Techniques of Astral Projection: Denouement After Fifty Years.* London: Aquarian Press, 1964.

Crooke, William. *The Popular Religion and Folk-Lore of Northern India.* Allahabad, India: Government Press, 1894. Reprint, 2 vols. London: A. Constable, 1896.

———. *Religion and Folklore of Northern India.* Humphrey Milford: Oxford University Press, 1926.

———. "Address by the President." *Proceedings of the Society for Psychical Research* 12 (1896): 338.

———. "Notes of an Enquiry into the Phenomena Called Spiritual." *Quarterly Journal of Science* (January 1874).

———. *Research in the Phenomena of Spiritualism.* London: J. Burns, 1874. Reprint, London and Manchester, 1926.

———. "Some Further Experiments on Psychic Force." *Quarterly Journal of Science* (October 1, 1871).

———. "Spiritualism Viewed by the Light of Modern Science." *Quarterly Journal of Science* 7 (July 1870).

Crop Circles: Harbingers of World Change. Santa Rosa, Calif.: Atrium Publishers Group, 1995.

Crosbie, Robert. *Answers to Questions on the Ocean of Theosophy.* Los Angeles: Theosophy, 1937.

———. *The Friendly Philosopher.* Los Angeles: Theosophy, 1934.

Crosland, Newton. *Apparitions.* London, 1873. N.p., 1957.

Cross, Frank Moore. *The Ancient Library of Qumran.* Minneapolis, Minn.: Fortress Press, 1995.

[Crosse, Cornelia A. H.] *Memorials, Scientific and Literary, of Andrew Crosse, the Electrician.* London: Longman, 1857.

Crossley, Alan Ernest. *The Story of Helen Duncan, Materialization Medium.* UK: Stockwell, 1975.

Crow, W. B. *A History of Magic, Witchcraft & Occultism.* London: Aquarian Press, 1968. Reprint, London: Abacus, 1972.

Crow, W. B. *Precious Stones.* New York: Samuel Weiser, 1968.

Crowe, Catherine. *Ghosts and Family Legends.* London, 1859.

———. *The Night Side of Nature; or, Ghosts and Ghost Seers.* N.p., 1848. Reprint, Folcroft, Pa., 1976; Philadelphia: R. West, 1978.

Crowell, Eugene. *Identity of Primitive Christianity and Modern Spiritualism.* 2 vols. 1875–79.

Crowley, Aleister. "The Book of the High Magick that as Worked by Frater O.S.V. 6-5 and Frater L. T. 2-9: The Paris Working." *The Equinox* (Nashville, Tenn.) 5, 4 (1981): 171–228.

———. *The Book of Thoth: A Short Essay on the Tarot of the Egyptians.* New York: Samuel Weiser, 1974.

———. *The Confessions of Aleister Crowley.* Edited by John Symnonds and Kenneth Grant. New York: Hill and Wang, 1969. Reprint, New York: Viking Penguin, 1989.

———. *De Arte Magica.* San Francisco: Level Press, [1974].

———. *Eight Lectures on Yoga.* 1938. Reprint, Phoenix, Ariz.: Falcon Press, 1985.

———. *The Holy Books of Thelema.* York Beach, Maine: Samuel Weiser, 1983.

———. *The Law Is for All.* Edited by Israel Regardie. St. Paul, Minn.: Llewellyn Publications, 1975.

———. *Magical Diaries of Aleister Crowley.* Edited by John Symonds and Kenneth Grant. Montreal: Next Step Publications, 1972.

———. *The Magical Record of the Beast 666.* Edited by John Symonds and Kenneth Grant. Montreal: Next Step Publications, 1972.

———. *Magick in Theory and Practice.* 4 vols. Paris, 1929. Reprint, New York: Castle Books, 1965; St. Paul, Minn.: Llewellyn Publications, 1989.

———. *Magick without Tears.* St. Paul, Minn.: Llewellyn Publications, 1973.

———. *The Secret Rituals of the O.T.O.* New York: Samuel Weiser, 1973.

———. 777. London: Walter Scott Publishing, 1909. Revised as 777 *Revised.* London: Neptune Press, 1952.

———. *The Vision and the Voice.* Dallas, Tex.: Sangreal Foundation, 1972.

[Crowley, Aleister] The Master Therion. *Magick in Theory and Practice.* Paris, 1929. Reprint, New York: Castle Books, n.d. Rev. ed. *Magick.* Edited by John Symonds and Kenneth Grant. London: Routledge & Kegan Paul, 1973. Reprint, New York: Samuel Weiser, 1974.

Crumbaugh, James C. "A Scientific Critique of Parapsychology." *Behavior Psychology* 2 (September–October 1966).

"CSAR: Statement of Goals." *Zetetic Scholar* 12/13 (1987): 205–06.

Cuddon, Eric. *Hypnosis: its Meaning and Practice.* N.p., 1938.

Culling, Louis, ed. *A Manual of Sex Magick.* St. Paul, Minn.: Llewellyn Publications, 1971.

Culpepper, Nicolas. *Culpepper's English Physician and Herbal Remedies.* North Hollywood, Calif.: Wilshire, 1971.

Cumberland, Stuart [Charles Garner]. *Thought-Reader's Thoughts: Being the Impressions and Confessions of Stuart Cumberland.* London: S. Low, Marston, Searle & Rivington, 1888. Reprint, New York: Ayer Publishing Co. Inc., 1975.

Cummings, Richard. *Alchemists: Fathers of Practical Chemistry.* New York: David O. McKay, 1966.

Cummins, Geraldine. *Beyond Human Personality.* London: Psychic Press, 1935. Revised edition, 1952.

———. *The Fate of Colonel Fawett.* London, 1955.

———. *The Road to Immortality.* London: Ivor Nicholson & Watson, 1933.

———. *Swan on a Black Sea: A Study in Automatic Writing: The Cummins-Willett Scripts.* London: Routledge & Kegan Paul, 1965. Reprint, New York: Samuel Weiser, 1970.

———. *Travelers in Eternity.* Compiled by E. B. Gibbs. London: Psychic Press, 1984.

———. *Unseen Adventures.* London: Rider, 1951.

Cumont, F. V. M. *Mysteries of Mithra.* London: Kegan Paul; Chicago: Open Court, 1910.

Cumont, Franz. *The Mysteries of Mithra.* LaSalle, Ill.: Open Court Publishing, 1903. Reprint, New York: Dover Publications, 1956.

Cunningham, Janet B. "A Phenomenological Study of Post-Modern Transpersonal and Spiritual Experiences with Quantitative survey and Case Study Interviews," *Dissertation Abstracts International: Section B: The Sciences & Engineering,* 58, no. 8-B (February 1998): 4481.

Cunningham, Scott. *Cunningham's Encyclopedia of Magical Herbs.* St. Paul, Minn.: Llewellyn Publications, 1985.

Cunninghame, Graham R. B. *A Brazilian Mystic: Being the Life and Miracles of Antonio Conselheiro.* London: Heineman, 1920. Reprint, Freeport, N.Y.: Books for Libraries Press, 1971.

Cupron, E. W. *Modern Spiritualism: Its Facts and Fanaticisms.* Boston: B. Marsh; New York: Partridge and Brittan, 1855.

Curnow, W. Leslie. "Spirits in the Flesh." *Psychic Science* (January 1927).

Currie, Ian. *You Cannot Die: The Incredible Findings of a Century of Research on Death.* New York: Methuen; London: Hamlyn, 1978.

Curry, Patrick. "Research on the Mars Effect." *Zetetic Scholar* 9 (1982): 34–52.

Curtin, Jeremiah. *Tales of the Fairies and of the Ghost World, Collected from Oral Tradition in Southwest Munster.* London: D. Nutt, 1895. Reprint, Dublin: Talbot Press, 1974.

Curtis, James. *Rustlings in the Golden City.* Ballard, 1894.

Curtis, James T. and John P. Wilson. "Sensation-Seeking and ESP Test Performance: A Preliminary Investigation," *Journal of the Society for Psychical Research* 62, no. 848 (July 1997): 1–21.

Curtiss, Harriette Augusta, and Homer Curtiss. *The Key of Destiny.* New York: E. P. Dutton, 1991.

———. *Letters from the Teacher.* 2 vols. Hollywood, Calif.: Curtiss Philosophic, 1918.

———. *The Message of Aquaria.* San Francisco: Curtiss Philosophic, 1921.

———. *The Voice of Isis.* Washington, D.C.: Curtiss Philosophic, 1935.

Cuthbert, Arthur A. *The Life and World Work of Thomas Lake Harris, Written from Direct Personal Knowledge.* Glasgow, Scotland, 1908.

Cutten, George B. *Speaking With Tongues: Historically and Psychologically Considered.* New Haven, Conn.: Yale University Press, 1927.

Czaplicka, Maria Antonina. *Aboriginal Siberia: A Study in Social Anthropology.* London: Oxford University Press, 1914.

D'Albe, E. E. Fournier. *The Goligher Circle: May to August, 1921.* London: John M. Watkins, 1922.

———. *The Life of Sir William Crookes.* London: T. F. Unwin Ltd., 1923.

D'Andrade, Hugh. *Charles Fillmore: Herald of the New Age.* New York: Harper & Row, 1974.

D'Esperance, Elizabeth. *Shadow Land or Light From the Other Side.* London: George Redway, 1897.

Da Free John [Franklin Jones]. *The Dawn Horse Testament.* San Rafael, Calif.: Dawn Horse Press, 1985.

Da Liu. *T'ai Chi Ch'uan and I Ching.* New York: Harper & Row, 1972. Reprint, Toronto: HarperCollins Publishers, 1978.

Da Love-Ananda. *The Holy Jumping Off Place.* San Rafael, Calif.: Dawn Horse Press, 1986.

Dalton, Kathy and Paul Stevens. "Geomagnetism and the Edinburgh Automated Ganzfeld," *European Journal of Parapsychology* 12 (1996): 23–34.

Daim, W. *Der Mann, der Hitler die Ideen gab* (The man who gave Hitler the ideas). München: Isar Verlag, 1958.

Dalby, Richard. *Bram Stoker: A Bibliography of First Editions.* London, 1983.

Dale, Laura A., and Gardner Murphy. *Challenge of Psychical Research: A Primer of Parapsychology.* New York: Harper & Row, 1966.

Dale, Laura A., and Rhea A. White. *Parapsychology: Sources of Information.* Metuchen, N.J.: Scarecrow Press, 1973.

Dallas, Helen A. *Across the Barrier.* N.p., 1913.

———. *Human Survival and Its Implications.* N.p., 1930.

———. *Leaves from a Psychic Notebook.* N.p., 1927.

———. *Mors Janus Vitae? A Discussion of Certain Communications Purporting to be from Frederic W. H. Myers.* London: William Rider and Son, 1910.

———. *The Nurseries of Heaven.* N.p., 1920.

———. *Objections to Spiritualism Answered.* Manchester, England: Two Worlds Publishing, 1916.

———. *The Victory that Overcometh.* N.p., 1901.

Dallimore, Arnold A. *Forerunner of the Charismatic Movement: The Life of Edward Irving.* Chicago: Moody Press, 1983.

Dallway, James. *Constantinople Ancient and Modern.* N.p., 1797.

Dalton, J. G. *The Boston Ephemeris.* Boston: Occult Publishing, 1898.

———. *The Sixteen Principal Stars.* Boston: Occult Publishing, 1898.

———. *The Spherical Basis of Astrology.* Boston: Arena Publishing, 1893.

Dane, Victor. *Naked Ascetic.* N.p., 1933.

Danemarie, J. *The Mystery of Stigmata from Catherine Emmerich to Theresa Neumann.* N.p., 1934.

Danforth, Loring M. *Firewalking and Religious Healing: The Anastenaria of Greece and the American Firewalking Movement.* Princeton, N.J.: Princeton University Press, 1989.

Danielou, Alain. *The Ragas of Northern Indian Music.* London: Barrie & Rockliff, 1968.

———. *Yoga: The Method of Re-Integration.* London: Christopher Johnson, 1949. Reprint, New Hyde Park, N.Y.: University Books, 1955.

Daraul, Arbon. *A History of Secret Societies.* New York: Citadel Press, 1962.

———. *Secret Societies, Yesterday and Today.* London: Fernhill Housen, 1961. Reprinted as *A History of Secret Societies.* New York: Citadel, 1961.

Darget, Commandant. *Exposé des différentes methodes pour l'obtention des photographies fluido-magnétiques et spirites.* Paris, 1909.

Darnton, Robert. *Mesmerism and the End of the Enlightenment in France.* Cambridge, Mass.: Harvard University Press, 1968.

Das, Ghagavan. *The Science of Social Organisation; or, The Laws of Manu in the Light of Atma-Vidya.* 2 vols. Rev. ed. Adyar, Madras, India: Theosophical Publishing House, 1932.

Dass, Baba Ram. *Be Here Now.* San Cristobal, N.Mex.: Lama Foundation, 1971.

Dave, H. T. *Life and Philosophy of Shree Swaminarayan, 1781–1830.* London: Allen & Unwin, 1974.

Davenport, Reuben Briggs. *The Death Blow to Spiritualism.* New York: G. W. Dillingham, 1888.

Davey, John, ed. *Work Arising from the Life of Rudolf Steiner.* London: R. Steiner Press, 1975.

Davey, S. T. "Spurious Mediumship." *Journal of the Society for Psychical Research* 3 (1888): 199–207.

David, Wade. *The Serpent and the Rainbow.* New York: Warner, 1985.

David-Neel, Alexandra. *Buddhism: Its Doctrines and Its Methods.* New York: St. Martin's, 1939. Reprint, London: Bodley Head, 1977.

———. *Initiations and Initiates in Tibet.* London, 1932. Reprint, New Hyde Park, N.Y.: University Books, 1959.

———. *Magic and Mystery in Tibet.* Rev. ed., New Hyde Park, N.Y.: University Books, 1956. Reprint, New York: Dover Publications, 1971.

———. *My Journey to Lhasa.* London: William Heinemann, 1927.

———. *The Secret Oral Tradition in Tibetan Buddhist Sects.* San Francisco: City Lights, 1964. Reprint, Calcutta: Maha Bodhi Society of India, 1971.

———. *With Mystics and Magicians in Tibet.* London: John Lane, 1931. Reprinted as *Magic & Mystery in Tibet.* New York: Claude H. Kendall, 1932. Reprint, New Hyde Park, N.Y.: University Books, 1956.

David-Neel, Alexandra, and Lama Yongden. *The Secret Oral Teachings in Tibetan Buddhist Sects.* Calcutta, India: Maha Bodhi Society of India, n.d.

Davidson, David. *The Great Pyramid: Its Divine Message.* London, 1924.

Davidson, Gustav. *A Dictionary of Angels: Including the Fallen Angels.* New York: Free Press, 1967.

Davidson, Thomas. *Philosophy of Goethe's Faust.* Boston, 1906. Reprint, Haskell, 1969.

———. *Rowan Tree and Red Thread.* Edinburgh: Oliver and Boyd, 1949.

Davies, John D. *Phrenology, Fad and Science: A Nineteenth Century American Crusade.* Archon, 1955. Reprint, Shoe String, 1971.

Davies, Lady Eleanor. *Great Britains Visitation.* London, 1645.

———. *Of Times and Seasons, Their Mystery.* London, 1651.

———. *The Revelation Interpreted.* London, 1645.

Davis, Andrew Jackson. *Answers to Ever-Recurring Questions from People: A Sequel to the Penetralia.* Boston: Banner of Light Publishing, 1862.

———. *Beyond the Valley; A Sequel to the Magic Staff: An Autobiography.* Boston: Colby & Rich, 1885.

———. *The Diakka, and Earthly Victims.* Boston: Colby & Rich, 1880. Reprint. New York, 1873; Las Vegas, Nev., 1996.

———. *The Great Harmonia.* New York: J. S. Redfield, Fowler & Wells, 1853.

———. *The Harmonial Philosophy: A Compendium and Digest of the Works of Andrew Jackson Davis.* London: Rider, 1917.

———. *The Magic Staff: An Autobiography of Andrew Jackson Davis.* New York, 1857.

General Bibliography

———. *Penetralia: Being Harmonial Answers to Important Questions.* Boston: Bela Marsh, 1858.

Davis, Charles [Dorothy Flexer]. *A New Way of Life.* Sarasota, Fla.: Church of Metaphysical Christianity, 1989.

———. *Spirit Speaks.* Sarasota, Fla.: Church of Metaphysical Christianity, 1988.

Davis, Eugene Roy. *An Easy Guide to Meditation.* Lakemont, Ga.: CSA Press, 1978.

———. *God Has Given Us Every Good Thing.* Lakemont, Ga.: CSA Press, 1986.

Davis, Eugene Roy. *The Path of Soul Liberation.* Lakemont, Ga.: CSA Press, 1975.

———. *The Teachings of the Masters of Perfection.* Lakemont, Ga.: CSA Press, 1979.

Davis, F. Hadland. *Myths and Legends of Japan.* London: Harrap, 1912.

Davis, James. "Comments on the Levy Affair." In *Research in Parapsychology 1974.* Metuchen, N.J.: Scarecrow Press, 1975.

Davis, Mikol, and Earle Lune. *Rainbows of Life: The Promise of Kirlian Photography.* New York: Harper & Row, 1978.

Davis, T. L. "The Autobiography of Denis Zacaire: An Account of an Alchemist's Life in the Sixteenth Century." *Isis* 8, 2 (1926).

Davis, Wade. *The Serpent and the Rainbow.* New York: Simon & Schuster, 1985.

Davy, Kitty. *Love Alone Prevails.* Myrtle Beach, S.C.: Sheriar Press, 1981.

Day, Langston & G. De la Warr. *New Worlds Beyond the Atom.* London, 1956.

Dayal, Har. *The Bodhisattva Doctrine in Buddhist Sanskrit Literature.* Delhi, India: Motilal Banarsidass, 1970.

De Becker, R. *The Meaning of Dreams.* London, 1968.

De Camp, L. Sprague. *The Ancient Engineers.* Garden City, N.Y.: Doubleday, 1960. Reprint, New York: Ballantine Books, 1974.

———. *Lovecraft: A Biography.* Garden City, N.Y.: Doubleday, 1975.

De Camp, L. Sprague, ed. *Al Azif (The Necronomicon).* Philadelphia: Owlswoch, 1973.

de Carvalho, Andre Percia. "Purported Spontaneous Psi Events and Psychodynamics: The Emergence of the 'System of Integrated Factors.' " *Journal of the Society for Psychical Research* 60, no. 839 (April 1995): 229–239.

De Charms, George. *The Distinctiveness of the New Church.* Bryn Athyn, Pa.: Academy Book Room, 1962.

De Cressac Bachelerie, Bertrande. *Démonstrations experimentales de la télépathie* (Experimental demonstrations of telepathy). N.p., 1946.

———. *Etudes sur la télépathie des sensations* (Studies on the telepathy of sensations). N.p., 1954.

———. *Etudes sur la voyance* (Studies in clairvoyance). N.p., 1942.

———. *La Métapsychique devant la science* (Parapsychology in relation to science). N.p., 1948.

———. *Le Miracle, illusion ou réalite* (The miracle, illusion or reality). N.p., 1961.

———. *Mise en évidence de l'effet psychocinétique* (Revelation of the psychokinetic effect). N.p., 1960.

De Cressac Bachelerie, Bertrande, and Marige George Chevalier. *La Métapsychique—probleme crucial* (Parapsychology: a crucial problem). N.p., 1960.

De Fontenay, Guillaume. *Apropos d'Eusapia Palladino.* Paris, 1898.

De France, Henry. *The Elements of Dowsing.* London: G. Bell, 1971. Reprint, Albuquerque, N.Mex.: Transatlantic Arts, Inc., 1979.

De Gasparin, Comte Agenor. *Des table tournantes, de surnaturel en général, et des esprits.* Paris, 1854.

De Giustino, David. *Conquest of Mind: Phrenology and Victorian Social Thought.* London: Croom Helm; Totowa, N.J.: Rowman & Littlefield, 1975.

De Givry, Grillot. *Witchcraft, Magic & Alchemy.* London, 1931. Reprinted as *Illustrated Anthology of Sorcery, Magic & Alchemy.* New York: Causeway, 1973.

De Hartmann, Thomas. *Our Life with Gurdjieff.* New York: Penguin, 1972. Rev. ed. San Francisco: Harper & Row, 1983.

De Jubainville, H. d'Arbois. *Les Droides et les dieux celtiques à forme d'animaux.* Paris, 1906.

De Laurence, L. W. *Clairvoyance & Thought-Transference, Auto Trance & Spiritualism, Psychometry & Telepathy.* Kila, Mont.: Kessinger Publishing Co., 1994.

De la Warr, George, with Langston Day. *New Worlds Beyond the Atom.* London: Vincent Stewart Publishers, 1956.

De Martino, Ernesto. *La Terra del Rimorso* (The land of remorse). N.p., 1961.

———. *Morte e Pianto rituale nel Mondo antico* (Death and ritual dirge in the ancient world). N.p., 1958.

———. *Sud e Magia* (South Italy and magic). 2nd ed. Milan: Feltrinelli, 1971.

De Mille, Richard. *Castaneda's Journey: The Power and the Allegory.* Santa Barbara, Calif.: Capra Press, 1976.

———. *The Don Juan Papers.* Santa Barbara, Calif.: Ross-Erikson, 1980.

De Mirville, Marquis J. E. *Pneumatologie: Des Esprits et de leurs manifestations fluidique devant la science modern.* Paris, 1853.

De Morgan, Augustus. *A Budget of Paradoxes.* Chicago: Open Court Publishing, 1915. Reprinted as *The Encyclopedia of Eccentrics.* La Salle, Ill.: Open Court Publishing, 1974.

De Morgan, Sophia Elizabeth. *Three Score Years and Ten; Reminiscences of the Late Sophia Elizabeth De Morgan.* London: R. Bentley, 1895.

De Morogues, Baron. *Observations sur le fluide organo-électrique.* Paris, 1854.

De Pascale, Marc. *The Book of Spells.* New York: Taplinger, 1971.

De Rola, Stanislaw K. *Alchemy: The Secret Art.* Bounty Books/Crown, 1973. Reprint, London: Thames & Hudson, 1973.

De Saint Pierre, Michel. *The Remarkable Cure of Ars: The Life and Achievement of St. John Marie Vianney.* Garden City, N.Y.: Doubleday, 1963.

De Schertz, Charles F. *Magia Posthuma.* Olmutz, 1706.

De Szapary, Comte F. G. *Les tables tournantes.* Paris, 1854.

De Tonquedec, Joseph. *Introduction a l'étude du merveilleux et du miracle* (Introduction to the study of the marvelous and the miracle). N.p., n.d.

———. *La Critique de la connaissance* (Criticism of knowledge). N.p., n.d.

———. *La Notion de Verite dans la "Philosophie Nouvelle"* (The concept of truth in the "new philosophy"). N.p., n.d.

———. *La Philosophie de la natur* (Philosophy of nature). N.p., n.d.

———. *Maladies neuveuses ou mentales et manifestations diaboliques* (Nervous or mental diseases and diabolical manifestations). N.p., n.d.

———. *Merveilleux métapsychique et miracle Chrétien* (The marvelous in parapsychology and the Christian miracle). N.p., n.d.

De Troyes, Chrétien. *Arthurian Romances (Erec and Enide; Cligés; Yvain; Lancelot).* London, 1914.

De Vallemont, Abbe. *La physique occulte, ou Traité de la baguette divinatoire.* Paris, 1693.

De Vesme, Caesar. *A History of Experimental Spiritualism.* 2 vols. London: Rider, 1931.

De Villars, l'Abbé de Montfaucon. *Comte de Gabalis.* London: Printed for B. M., Printer to the Cabalistical Society of the Sages, at the Sign of the Rosy-Crucian, 1670. Reprint, Paris, 1670; London: Old Bourne Press, 1913; New York: Macoy Publishing and Masonic Supply, 1922; London: Methuen, 1941.

De Zirkoff, Boris, comp. "General Bibliography with Selected Biographical Notes." In *Collected Writings.* Vol XII. by H. P. Blavatsky. Wheaton, Ill.: Theosophical Publishing House, 1980.

Deacon, R. *John Dee: Scientist, Astrologer & Secret Agent to Elizabeth.* London: Frederick Muller, 1968.

Dean, E. Douglas, John Mihalasky, Sheila Ostrander, and Lynn Schroeder. *Executive ESP.* Englewood Cliffs, N.J.: Prentice-Hall, 1974.

———. *The Mystery of Healing: Still a Mystery after 60,000 Years.* New York: Search, 1987.

Dean, G. *Recent Advances in Natal Astrology.* Cowes, England: The Author, 1977.

Dearden, Harold. *Devilish But True: The Doctor Looks at Spiritualism.* London: Hutchinson, 1936. Reprint, Boston: Rowan & Littlefield, 1975.

Decker, Larry R. "Beliefs, Post-Traumatic Stress Disorder, and Mysticism," *Journal of Humanistic Psychology* 33, no. 4 (1993): 15–32.

Decuypere, J. M. "Channelling—Sick or Scientific?," *Journal of the Society for Psychical Research* 63, no. 856 (July 1999): 193–202.

Dee, John. *The Hieroglyphic Monad.* Translated by J. W. Hamilton Jones. London, 1847.

———. *A True and Faithful Relation of What Passed for Many Years Between Dr. John Dee . . . and Some Spirits. . . .* London, 1659. Reprint, Askin, 1974.

Defano, M. M. *The Living Prophets.* New York: Dell, 1972.

[Defoe, Daniel]. *An Essay on the History & Reality of Apparitions.* London, 1727.

Deguchi, Onisaburo. *Memoirs.* Japan: Kameoka, 1957.

Del Rio, Martin Antoine. *Disquisitionum Magicarum Libri Sex.* Moguntiae: Typis Joannis Albini, 1600.

Delacour, J. B. [Hanns Kurth]. *Glimpses of the Beyond.* New York: Delacorte Press, 1974.

Delanne, Gabriel. *Evidence for a Future Life.* London: Philip Wellby/New York: G. P. Putnam's Sons, 1904.

———. *L' Ame est Immortelle.* N.p., 1904.

———. *L'Evolution Animique.* N.p., 1897.

———. *Le Phenom Agene Spirite.* N.p., 1894.

———. *Le Spiritisme devant la Science.* N.p., 1895.

———. *Les Apparitions Materialisées des Vivants et des Morts.* Paris, 1911.

———. *Récherches sur la Mediumnité.* N.p., 1896.

Deleuze, Jean P. F. *Défense du Magnétisme.* N.p., 1819.

———. *Histoire Critique du Magnétisme.* N.p., 1813–19.

———. *Mémoire sur la Faculté de Prevision.* N.p., 1836.

———. *Practical Instruction in Animal Magnetism.* Providence, R.I.: B. Cranston, 1837. Rev. ed. New York: Samuel R. Wells, 1846. Reprint, New York: Da Capo Press, Inc., 1982.

Delfano, M. M. *The Living Prophets.* New York: Dell, 1972.

Delgado, Pat, and Colin Andrews. *Circular Evidence: A Detailed Investigation of the Flattened Swirled Crop Phenomenon.* London: Bloomsbury Publications, 1989.

Delgado, Pat, and Colin Andrews. *Crop Circles: The Latest Evidence.* London: Bloomsbury Publications, 1990.

DeLouise, Joseph, and Tom Valentine. *Psychic Mission.* Chicago: Henry Regnery, 1971.

Demarest, Donald, and Coley Taylor. *The Dark Virgin: The Book of Our Lady of Guadalupe.* Freeport, Maine: Coley Taylor, 1956.

Dement, William C. *Some Must Watch While Some Must Sleep: Exploring the World of Sleep.* Stanford, Calif.: Stanford Alumni Association, 1972. Reprint, San Francisco: San Francisco Book, 1976; New York: Norton, 1978.

DeMille, Richard. *Castaneda's Journey; The Power and the Allegory.* Santa Barbara, Calif.: Capra Press, 1976.

DeMille, Richard, ed. *Don Juan Papers: Further Castaneda Controversies.* Santa Barbara, Calif.: Ross-Erickson, 1980. Reprint, Belmont, Calif.: Wadsworth, 1990.

Demos, John Putnam. *Entertaining Satan: Witchcraft and the Culture of Early New England.* New York: Oxford University Press, 1982.

Dempsey, T. *The Delphic Oracles.* Oxford: B. H. Blackwell, 1918.

Dendy, W. C. *Philosophy of Mystery.* London, 1841.

Denis, Leon. *d'Apres la Mort.* N.p., n.d.

———. *Dans l'Invisible (Spiritisme et Mediumnité).* N.p., n.d.

———. *Genie Celtique, et le Monde Invisible.* N.p., n.d.

———. *Jeanne d'Arc Medium: L'Au-delà et la Survivance de l'Etré, La Grande Énigme.* Translated as *The Mystery of Joan of Arc.* New York: E. P. Dutton, 1925.

Denning, Melita, and Osborne Phillips. *The Magical Philosophy.* 5 vols. St. Paul, Minn.: Llewellyn Publications, 1974–81.

Denning, Melita, and Osborne Phillips. *The Magick of Sex.* St. Paul, Minn.: Llewellyn Publications, 1982.

———. *The Magick of Tarot.* St. Paul, Minn.: Llewellyn Publications, 1983.

———. *Voudou Fire: The Living Reality of Mystical Religion.* St. Paul, Minn.: Llewellyn Publications, 1979.

Dennon, Jim. *Newbrough and Oahspe.* Kingman, Ariz.: Faithist Journal, 1975.

———. *The Oahspe Story.* Kingman, Ariz.: Faithist Journal, 1975.

Denovan, W. C. D. *Evidences of Spiritualism.* Melbourne, 1882.

Denson, Alan. *Printed writings of George W. Russell (AE): A Bibliography.* London: Northwestern University Press, 1961.

Dentan, Robert. *The Samai: A Non-Violent People of Malaya.* New York: Holt, Rinehart and Winston, 1968.

Denton, Jim. *Dr. Newbrough and Oahspe.* Kingman, Ariz.: Faithist Journal, 1975.

———. *The Oahspe Story.* Kingman, Ariz.: Faithist Journal, 1975.

Denton, William. *Our Planet, Its Past and Future; or, Lectures on Geology.* Wellesley, Mass.: Denton Publishing, 1868.

Denton, William. *The Soul of Things: Psychometric Experiments for Re-living History.* 1863. Reprint, Wellingborough, Northampton, England: Aquarian Press, 1988.

Denton, William, and Elizabeth Denton. *Nature's Secrets, or Psychometric Researches.* London: Houston & Wright, 1863.

Deren, Maya. *Divine Horsemen: The Voodoo Gods of Haiti.* New York: Chelsea House, 1970.

Derleth, August. *H.P.L.: A Memoir.* Ben Abramson, 1945.

Derrey, Francois. *The Earth is Alive.* London: Arlington Books, 1968.

Desbarolles, A. *Les Mysteres de la Main.* Paris, 1860.

Desjarlais, Robert R. *Body and Emotion: The Aesthetics of Illness and Healing in the Nepal Himalayas.* Philadelphia: University of Pennsylvania Press, 1992.

Desmond, Shaw. *Healing: Psychic and Divine.* London: Rider, 1956. Reprinted as *The Power of Faith Healing.* New York: Award Books, 1969.

———. *Ragnarok.* N.p., 1926.

———. *Reincarnation for Everyman.* N.p., 1939.

———. *Spiritualism?* N.p., 1941.

———. *We Do Not Die.* N.p., 1934.

———. *You Can Speak With Your Dead.* N.p., 1941.

Desroche, Henri. *The American Shakers.* Amherst, Mass.: University of Massachusetts Press, 1971.

Dessoir, Max. *Aesthetics and the Theory of Art.* Detroit: Wayne State University Press, 1970.

———. *Das Ich, der Traum, der Tod.* N.p., 1947.

———. "Die Parapsychologie, Eine Entgegnung auf den Artikel 'Der Prophet.'&43" *Sphinx* (June 1889): 341–44. Reprinted as "Parapsychology, A Response to the Article 'The Prophet.'&43" *Journal of the Society for Psychical Research* 53, 802 (January 1986).

———. *Die Rede als Kunst.* N.p., 1948.

———. *Einleitung in die Philosophie.* N.p., 1946.

———. "Experiments in Muscle Reading and Thought-Transference." *Proceedings of the Society for Psychical Research* 4, 10 (1886–87).

———. *Psychologische Briefe.* N.p., 1948.

Deutsch, Richard. *Exorcism: Possession or Obsession?* Foreword by Christopher Neil-Smith. London: Bachman & Turner, 1975.

Deutch, Yvonne, ed., and F. Strachan, comp. *Fortune Tellers.* London, 1976. Reprint, New York: Black Watch, 1974.

Development of Mediumship. Dimondale, Mich.: Spiritual Episcopal Church, n.d.

Devereux, George. "Bridey Murphy, a Psychoanalytic View." *Tomorrow* (Summer 1956).

———. "Primitive Psychiatry." *Bulletin of the History of Medicine,* 8 (1940–1942): 1194–1213; 11 (1940–1942): 522–542.

Devereux, George, ed. *Psychoanalysis and the Occult.* New York: International Universities Press, 1953.

Devi, Indra. *Forever Young, Forever Healthy.* New York: Prentice-Hall, 1954.

———. *Renew Your Life through Yoga.* Englewood Cliffs, N.J.: Prentice-Hall, 1963.

———. *Yoga for Americans.* Englewood Cliffs, N.J.: Prentice-Hall, 1959.

———. *Yoga—the Technique of Health and Happiness.* Kitabistan, India, 1948.

Devotional Somnium; or a Collection of Prayers and Exhortations Uttered by Rachel Baker . . . During her Abstracted and Unconscious State. New York, 1815.

Dewey, D. M. *History of the Strange Sounds or Rappings Heard in Rochester and Western New York.* Rochester, 1850.

Dexter, T. F. *Fire Worship in Britain.* Edmonds, Wash.: Holmes Publishing Group, 1995.

Diamond, E. *The Science of Dreams.* London, 1962.

Dickhoff, Robert Ernest. *Agharta.* Boston: Bruce Humphries, 1951. Reprint, Mokelumne Hill, Calif.: Health Research, 1964.

———. *Behold . . . the Venus Garuda.* New York: The Author, 1968.

———. *The Eternal Fountain.* Boston: Bruce Humphries, 1947.

Didi-Huberman, Georges, and J. M. Charcot. *Invention de l'hysterie: Charcot et l'iconographia photographiqe de la Salpetriere.* Paris: Macula, 1982.

Digby, George. *Symbol and Image in William Blake.* Oxford: Oxford University Press, 1957.

The Dimensions of Healing: A Symposium. Los Altos, Calif.: Academy of Parapsychology and Medicine, 1972.

Dingle, Edwin John. *Abnormal Hypnotic Phenomena.* 4 vols. London: Churchill, 1967–68.

———. *Borderlands of Eternity.* Los Angeles: Institute of Mentalphysics, 1939.

———. *Breathing Your Way to Youth.* Los Angeles: Institute of Mentalphysics, [1931].

———. *The Critic's Dilemma: Further Comments on Some Nineteenth Century Investigations.* Dewsbury, England: The Author, 1966.

———. "An Experiment with Polish Medium Stefan Ossowiecki." *Journal of the Society for Psychical Research* 21 (1924).

———. "The Need for Responsibility in Parapsychology." In *A Skeptic's Handbook of Parapsychology,* edited by Paul Kurtz. Buffalo, N.Y.: Prometheus Books, 1985.

———. *Some Human Oddities.* London: Home & Van Thal, 1947. Reprint, New Hyde Park, N.Y.: University Books, 1962.

———. *The Voice of the Logos.* Los Angeles: Econolith Press, 1951.

Dingwall, E. J., K. M. Goldney, and Trevor H. Hall. *The Haunting of Borley Rectory.* London: Duckworth, 1955.

———. "The Haunting of Borley Rectory; A Critical Survey of the Evidence." *Proceedings of the Society for Psychical Research* 51 (1956).

Dingwall, Eric J. *Ghosts and Spirits of the Ancient World.* London: Kegan, Paul, 1930.

———. *Some Human Oddities.* London, 1947. Reprint, New Hyde Park, N.Y.: University Books, 1962.

———. *Very Peculiar People: Portrait Studies in the Queer, the Abnormal and the Uncanny.* London: Rider, 1950. Reprint, New Hyde Park, N.Y.: University Books, 1962.

Dingwall, E. J. and Harry Price, eds. *Revelations of a Spirit Medium.* London: Kegan Paul, 1925.

Dingwall, Eric J., and John Langdon-Davies. *The Unknown—Is It Nearer?* New York: New American Library, 1956.

Dingwall, Eric J., and Trevor H. Hall. *Four Modern Ghosts.* London, 1958.

Dinsdale, Tim. *Loch Ness Monster.* London: Routledge & Kegan Paul, 1961.

———. *The Story of the Loch Ness Monster.* London, 1973.

Diószegi, Vilmos "The Origin of the Evenki Shamanic Instruments (Stick, Knout) of Transbaikalia," *Acta Ethnographica,* 17, nos. 3–4 (1968): 265–311.

———. "Problems of Mongolian Shamanism," *Acta Ethnographica.* 10 nos. 1–2 (1961): 195–206.

Diószegi, Vilmos, and Mihály Hoppál, eds. "Folk Beliefs and Shamanistic Traditions in Siberia." In *Bibliotheca Shamanistica.* Vol. 3. Budapest: Akadémiai Kiadó, 1996.

———. "Shamanism in Siberia." In *Bibliotheca Shamanistica* Vol. 2. Budapest: Akadémiai Kiadó, 1996.

Directory of Activities and Services. New York: Rudolf Steiner Information Center, n.d.

DiStasi, Lawrence. *Mal Occhio (Evil Eye): The Underside Vision.* San Francisco: North Point Press, 1981.

The Divine Mystical Method of Instruction of the Homebringing Mission of Jesus Christ. Pelham, N.H.: Homebringing Mission of Jesus Christ, 1980.

Divine Life Society. *An Apostle of India's Spiritual Culture: Souvenir Released on the Auspices of the Sixtieth Birthday Anniversary of H.H. Sri Swami Chidaananda.* Shivanandanagar, India: Divine Life Society, 1976.

Divine Principle. New York: Holy Spirit Association for the Unification of World Christianity, 1973.

Divine, Mother. *The Peace Mission Movement.* Philadelphia: Imperial Press, 1982.

Dixon, Roland B. "Some Shamans of Northern California," *Journal of American Folklore.* 17 (1904): 23–27.

DK [through Alice A. Bailey]. *Serving Humanity.* New York: Lucis Trust, 1972.

———. *The Soul, The Quality of Life: From the Writings of the Tibetan Teacher (Djwhal Khul).* New York: Lucis Trust, 1972.

Doane, Doris Chase. *Astrological Rulerships.* Redondo Beach, Calif.: Foundation for Scientific Spiritual Understanding, 1970.

———. *Astrology as a Business.* Tempe, Ariz.: American Federation of Astrologers, 1986.

———. *Astrology: Thirty Years of Research.* Los Angeles: Church of Light, 1956.

———. *Horoscopes of the Presidents.* Hollywood, Calif.: Professional Astrologers, 1971.

Doane, T. W. "The Creation and Fall of Man." In *Bible Myths and Their Parallels in Other Religions.* 1884. Reprint, New Hyde Park, N.Y.: University Books, 1971.

Dobbs, Betty Jo T. *Foundations of Newton's Alchemy; or, The Hunting of the Greene Lyon.* Cambridge, Mass.: Cambridge University Press, 1975.

Doberer, Kurt K. *The Goldmakers: Ten Thousand Years of Alchemy.* Westport, Conn.: Greenwood, 1948.

Dobinson, George. "The Gurdjieff Enigma," *Journal of the Society for Psychical Research* 61, no. 844 (July 1996): 152–155.

Dobkin De Rios, Marlene. *Hallucinogens: Cross-Cultural Perspectives.* Albuquerque: University of New Mexico Press, 1984. Reprint, Garden City Park, N.Y.: Avery Publishing Group, 1990.

———. *Amazon Healer: The Life and Times of an Urban Shaman.* Bridport, Dorset: Prism Press/Garden City Park, N.Y.: Avery Publishing Group, 1992.

Dobkin De Rios, Marlene, ed. "Special issue on Shamanism and Altered States of Consciousness," *Journal of Psychoactive Drugs.* 21, no. 1 (1989).

Dodds, Eric R. *The Greeks and the Irrational.* Berkeley: University of California Press, 1951.

———. *Missing Persons: An Autobiography.* Oxford: Clearendon Press, 1977.

———. "Supernormal Phenomena in Classical Antiquity." *Proceedings of the Society for Psychical Research* 55 (1971): 189.

———. "Why I Do Not Believe in Survival." *Proceedings of the Society for Psychical Research* 42 (1934): 147.

Dole, Arthur A. and Michael D. Langone. "Strongly Held Views about the New Age: Critics Versus Experts," *Cultic Studies Journal* 11, no. 1 (1994): 1–28.

Dommeyer, Frederick C. *Body, Mind and Death.* N.p., 1965.

Dommeyer, Frederick C., ed. *Current Philosophical Issues: Essays in Honor of Curt John Ducasse.* N.p., 1966.

———. "Some Ostensibly Precognitive Dreams." *Journal of the Society for Psychical Research* (July 1955).

Donnelly, Ignatius. *Atlantis: The Antediluvian World.* New York: Harper's, 1882. Rev. ed., edited by Egerton Sykes. New York: Gramercy, 1949.

———. *The Great Cryptogram: Francis Bacon's Cipher in the So-called Shakespeare Plays.* Chicago: R. S. Peale, 1888.

———. *Ragnarok: The Age of Fire and Gravel.* New York: Harper's, 1883. Reprinted as *The Destruction of Atlantis: Ragnarok.* Blauvelt, N.Y.: Rudolf Steiner Publications, 1971.

Donnelly, Morwinna. *Founding the Life Divine.* Lower Lake, Calif.: Dawn Horse Press, 1976.

Donovan, James M. "Charisma, Empathy, and the Experience of Telepathy," *Journal of Indian Psychology* 10, no. 1-2 (January-July 1992): 11–26.

Dooley, Anne. *Every Wall a Door.* London: Abelard-Schuman, 1973. Reprint, Bergenfield, N.J.: E. P. Dutton, 1974.

Doore, Gary, ed. *Shaman's Path: Healing, Personal Growth, and Empowerment.* Boston: Shamabala, 1988.

Dorato, M. *Gli ultimi papi e la fine del mondo nelle grandi profezie.* Rome: n.p., 1950.

Doreal, Maurice. *Maitreya: Lord of the World.* Sedalia, Colo.: Brotherhood of the White Temple, n.d.

———. *Man and the Mystic Universe.* Denver: Brotherhood of the White Temple, n.d.

———. *Personal Experiences among the Masters and Great Adepts in Tibet.* Sedalia, Colo.: Brotherhood of the White Temple, n.d.

———. *Secret Teachings of the Himalayan Gurus.* Denver: Brotherhood of the White Temple, n.d.

Doresse, Jean. *The Secret Books of the Egyptian Gnostics.* London: Hollis and Carter, 1960. Reprint, New York: AMS Press, 1972.

Doten, Elizabeth. *Poems of Progress.* Boston: White & Co., 1871.

Doughty, Oswald. *Perturbed Spirit: The Life and Personality of Samuel Taylor Coleridge.* Rutherford, N.J.: Fairleigh Dickinson University Press, 1981.

Douglas, Adam. *The Beast Within: Man, Myths and Werewolves.* London: Chapmans, 1992. Reprint. London: Orion, 1993.

Douglas, Alfred. *Extra Sensory Powers: A Century of Psychical Research.* Woodstock, N.Y.: Overlook Press, 1977.

———. *The Tarot: The Origins, Meaning and Uses of the Cards.* New York: Taplinger; London: Gollancz, 1972. Reprint, London: Penguin, 1974.

Doumato, Lamia. *Imhotep.* Monticello, Ill.: Vance Bibliographies, 1981.

Dourley, John. "The Innate Capacity: Jung and the Mystical Imperative." In *The Innate Capacity: Mysticism, Psychology, and Philosophy.* New York: Oxford University Press, 1998.

Dow, James. *The Shaman's Touch : Otomí Indian symbolic healing.* Salt Lake City: University of Utah Press, 1986.

Dowden, Hester. *Psychic Messages from Oscar Wilde.* London: T. Werner Laurie, 1923.

———. *Voices from the Void.* London: Rider & Co., 1919.

Dowding, Lady Muriel. *Beauty—not the Beast.* St. Helier, Jersey: Neville Spearman, 1980. Reprinted as *The Psychic Life of Muriel, The Lady Dowding: An Autobiography.* Wheaton, Ill.: Theosophical Publishing House, 1981.

Dowling, Levi. *The Aquarian Gospel of Jesus the Christ.* Los Angeles: Leo W. Dowling, 1925.

Dowling, Lord. *The Dark Star.* London: Museum Press, 1951.

———. *Lychgate: The Entrance to the Path.* N.p., 1945.

———. *Many Mansions.* London: Rider, 1943.

"Dowsing in the Soviet Union." *PSI Research* 5, no. 1-2 (March-June 1986): 34–38.

Doyle, Arthur Conan. *The Case for Spirit Photography.* London: Hutchinson, 1922. Reprint, New York: George H. Doran, 1923.

———. *The Coming of the Fairies.* London: Hodder & Stoughton, 1922. 2nd ed., rev. and enl. London: Psychic Press, 1928. Reprint, New York: Samuel Weiser, 1972.

———. *The Edge of the Unknown.* N.p., 1930.

———. *The History of Spiritualism.* New York: Charles H. Doran; London: Cassele, 1926. Reprint, Stratford, N. H.: Ayer Co. Publishing, Inc., 1979.

———. *Letters to the Press.* Edited by John M. Gibson and Richard L. Green. Iowa City: University of Iowa Press, 1986.

———. *Wanderings of a Spiritualist.* New York: G. H. Doran;London: Hodder & Stoughton, 1921. Reprint, Berkeley, Calif.: Ronin Publishing, 1988.

Doyle, J. *Miracles Said to Have Been Wrought by the Prince Hohenlohe.* N.p., 1823.

Dresner, Samuel H. *The Zaddik.* New York: Schrocken Books, 1974.

Dresser, Horatio W. *History of the New Thought Movement.* New York: Thomas Y. Crowell, 1919.

———. *The Spirit of New Thought.* New York: Thomas Y. Crowell, 1917.

Dresser, Norine. *American Vampires: Fans, Victims & Practitioners.* New York: W. W. Norton, 1989.

Driburg, Tom. *"Swaff": The Life and Times of Hannen Swaffer.* London: Macdonald, 1974.

Driesch, Hans A. E. *Alltagraetsel des Seelenlebens Psychical Research* (Everyday Enigmas of the Mind). N.p., 1938.

———. *The Crisis in Psychology.* N.p., 1925.

———. *History and Theory of Vitalism.* New York: Macmillan, 1914.

———. *Leib und Seele.* (Body and Mind). N.p., 1916.

———. *Parapsychologie, die Wissenschaft von den "occulten" Erscheingen* (Parapsychology, Science of "Occult" Phenomena). N.p., 1932.

———. *Psychical Research: The Science of the Supernormal.* London: G. Bell, 1933. Reprint, New York: Ayer Publishing Co. Inc., 1975.

Driscoll, J. Walter. *Gurdjieff: An Annotated Bibliography.* New York: Garland Publishing, 1985.

Drouet, Bessie C. *Station Astral.* New York: G. P. Putnam's Sons, 1932.

Drower, E. S. *Peacock Angel.* London: John Murray, 1941.

Drown, Ruth, ed. *The Forty-Nine Degrees: The Road to Divine Truth.* New York: Greenwich Book Publishers, 1957.

Drummond, Andrew L. *Edward Irving and His Circle.* London: J. Clarke, 1937.

Drury, Nevill. *The Elements of Shamanism.* Dorset: Elements Books, 1989. UK: Element Books, Inc., 1997.

Drury, Nevill, and Gregory Tillett. *Other Temples/Other Gods: The Occult in Australia.* Sydney: Hodder & Stoughton, 1982.

Drury, Nevill, and Stephen Skinner. *The Search for Abraxas.* London: Neville Spearman, 1972.

Du Potet de Sennevoy, Baron. *Cours de magnétisme animal.* N.p., 1834. 1840.

———. *Discours sur le magnétisme animal.* N.p., 1833.

———. *Essai sur l'enseignement philosophique du magnétisme.* N.p., 1845.

———. *Exposé des expériences sur le magnétisme animal.* N.p., 1821.

———. *La Magie dévoilée ou principes des sciences occultes.* 1852. Translated as *Magnetism and Magic.* Edited by A. H. E. Lee. London, 1927.

———. *Le magnétisme animal opposéà la médecine, mémoire pour servir a l'histoire du magnétisme en France et en Angleterre.* N.p., 1840.

———. *Manuel de l'é tudiant magnétiseur ou nouvelle instruction pratique du magnétisme fondée sur 30 anné es d'observations.* N.p., 1846.

———. *Traité complet de magnétisme animal.* Paris, 1856.

Du Prel, Carl. *Die Magie als Naturwissenschaft.* Leipzig: M. Altmann, 1912.

Du Vignois, Elisée. *Notre histoire racontée à l'avance par Nostradamus.* Paris, 1910.

Dubrin, Stanley, and J. Keenan. *Acupuncture and Your Health.* Chatsworth, Calif.: Books for Better Living, 1974.

Ducasse, C. J. *A Critical Examination of the Belief in a Life After Death.* Springfield, Ill.: Charles C. Thomas, 1961, 1974.

———. *Nature, Mind and Death.* LaSalle, Ill.: Open Court Publishing, 1951.

———. *Paranormal Phenomena, Science, and Life After Death.* New York: Parapsychology Foundation, 1969.

Duce, Ivy Oneida. *How a Master Works.* Walnut Creek, Calif.: Sufism Reoriented, 1971.

Duchesneau, Louise. *The Voice of the Muse.* Frankfurt, Germany: P. Lang, 1986.

Duguid, David. *Hafed, Prince of Persia; his Experiences in Earth Life, being Spirit Communications Received Through Mr. David Duguid, the Glasgow Trance Speaking Medium, with an Appendix, containing Communications from the Spirit Artists Ruisdael and Steen, illustrated by Facsimiles of Forty-Five Drawings and Writings, the Direct Work of the Spirits.* London: James Burn, Glasgow: Nisbet, 1876.

Duke, H. H. *The Holy Angels: Their Nature & Employments.* London, 1875.

Dukes, Eugene D. *Magic & Witchcraft in the Dark Ages.* Lanham, Md.: University Press of America, 1996.

Dukes, Paul. *Come Hammer, Come Sickle.* N.p., 1947.

———. *Red Dusk and the Morrow.* N.p., 1922.

———. *The Unending Quest.* London, 1950.

———. *The Yoga of Health, Youth and Joy.* N.p., 1960.

———. *Yoga for the Western World.* N.p., 1953.

Duncan, Malcolm C. *Duncan's Masonic Ritual and Monitor.* New York: McKay, 1976.

Dunn, Charles W. *The Foundling and the Werewolf: A Literary-Historical Study of Guillaume de Palerne.* Toronto: University of Toronto Press, 1960.

Dunne, J. W. *An Experiment with Time.* London: A. & C. Black; New York: Macmillan, 1927. Reprint, New York: Hillary, 1958.

Dunne, John J. *Haunted Ireland: Her Romantic and Mysterious Ghosts.* Belfast: Appletree Press, 1977.

Dunninger, Joseph. *Inside the Medium's Cabinet.* New York: David Kemp, 1924.

Dunraven, Windham Thomas Wyndham-Quin. *Experiences in Spiritualism with Mr. D. D. Home.* N.p., 1871. Reprint, Glasgow: R. Maclehose & Co. Ltd., 1924; New York: Ayer Publishing Co. Inc., 1976.

Dunwich, Gerina. *Everyday Wicca.* Secaucus, N.J.: Carol Publishing Group, 1997.

———. *Wiccan Prophecy.* Secaucus, N.J.: Carol Publishing Group, 1997.

Duplessis, Yvonne. "Dermo-optical Sensitivity and Perception." *International Journal of Biosocial Research* 7, no. 2 (1985).

DuPlessis, Yvonne. "Differences between ESP of the Blind and Dermo-Optical Perception." *International Journal of Paraphysics* 10, no. 3 (1976): 51–60.

DuPoteat, Jules. *Magnetism and Magic.* New York: F. Stokes, n.d.

Durdin-Robertson. *The Goddesses of Chaldea, Syria and Egypt.* Enniscorthy, Eire: Cesara Publications, 1975.

Durkheim, Emile. *The Elementary Forms of the Religious Life.* New York: Collier, 1961.

Durville, (Marie-François) Hector. *Almanach spirite et magnétique illustre pour 1893.* N.p., 1893.

———. *Bibliographie du Magnétisme et des Sciences Occultes.* N.p., 1895.

———. *Le Fantôme des Vivants, Anatomie et physiologie de l'âme; Recherches expérimentales sur le dé doublement du corps de l'homme.* N.p., 1909.

———. *Le Magnétisme considéré comme agent lumineux.* N.p., 1896.

———. *Le magnétisme des animaux; Zootherapie (Polarité des animaux morts et vivants; Zoothérapie, Biothérapie, etc.).* N.p., 1896.

———. *Le Magnétisme humain considéré comme agent physique.* N.p., 1890.

———. *Le massage et le magnétisme menacés par les médecins; le proces Moureux à Angers; necessite d'un amendement a la loi du 30 Nov. 1892, sur l'exercice de la médecine.* N.p., 1897.

———. *Le Massage et le magnétisme sous l'empire de la loi du 30 Nov. 1892, sur l'exercice de la médecine; Règlement statutaire de l'Ecole pratique de Magnétisme et de Massage: statuts du syndicate des Masseurs et Magnétiseurs de Paris.* N.p., 1894.

———. *Lois physiques du magnétisme; Polarité humaine; Traité expérimental et thérapeutique de magnetisme.* N.p., 1886.

———. *Magnétisme personnel; Education de la Pensée—Développement de la Volonté—Pourêtre heureux, fort, bien portant et réussir en tout.* N.p., 1905.

———. *Pour combattre la surdité, les bourdonnements, l'otite, etc. . . . par le magnétisme.* N.p., 1906.

———. *Pour combattre les maladies par suggestion et auto-suggestion, se débarrasser de ses mauvaises habitudes, prendre de l'Energie et de la Confiance en soi, dominer les autres, et éviter leurs suggestions.* N.p., 1896.

———. *Pour combattres les maladies par l'application del'aimant.* N.p., 1906.

Durville, Henri, and Andre Durville, eds. *Les Trucs de la Prestidigitation dévoilés.* A series of 17 titles reprinted from *Revue du Psychisme expérimental* and *Journal du Magnétisme* 1911–1914.

Durville, Henri, ed. *Cours de magnétisme personnel.* N.p., 1933.

———. *La Magie divine.* N.p., 1930.

———. *Mystères initatiques.* N.p., 1929.

———. *1er Congres international de Psychologie expérimentale.* N.p., 1910.

———. *2e Congres international de Psychologie expérimentale, La Science secrete.* N.p., 1923.

Duvall, Piere [Rémy Chauvin], and E. Montredon [Jean Mayer]. "A PK Experiment with Mice." *Journal of Parapsychology* 32 (1968): 153.

———. "Further Psi Experiments with Mice." *Journal of Parapsychology* 32 (1968): 260.

Dvivedi, M. N., trans. *The Yoga-Sutras of Patanjali.* Adyar, Madras, India: Theosophical Publishing House, 1890.

———. *The Yoga-Sutras of Patanjali.* London: Theosophical Publishing House, 1890.

Dwyer, Walter W. *The Churches' Handbook for Spiritual Healing.* 9th ed. New York: Ascension Press, 1965.

Dyer, T. F. Thiselton. *The Ghost World.* London: Ward & Downey, 1893.

Dykshoorn, M. B. *My Passport Says Clairvoyant.* New York: Hawthorn, 1974. N.p.: Jove Publications, Inc., 1978.

Dyne, Mark. *Electronic Communication for the Spiritual Emancipation of the People.* Rev. ed., Manchester, England: The Spirit Electronic Communication Society, 1954.

Earll, Tony [Raymond Buckland]. *Mu Revealed.* New York: Paperback Library, 1970.

Easlea, Brian. *Witch-hunting, Magic and the New Philosophy 1450–1750.* Atlantic Highlands, N.J.: Humanities, 1980.

Easton, Steward C. *The Era of Charlemagne.* New York: Van Nostrand, 1961.

———. *Roger Bacon and His Search for a Universal Science.* Westport, Conn.: Greenwood Press, 1970.

———. *Rudolf Steiner: Herald of a New Epoch.* Spring Valley, N.Y.: Anthroposophical Press, 1980.

Easwaran, Eknath. *The Mantram Handbook.* London: Routledge & Kegan Paul, 1978.

Ebertine, Reinhold. *Applied Cosmobiology.* Aalen, Germany: Ebertin Verlag, 1972.

———. *Combination of Solar Influences.* Aalen, Germany: Ebertin Verlag, 1972.

Ebon, Martin. *Communicating with the Dead.* New York: New American Library, 1968.

———. *The Evidence for Life After Death.* New York: New American Library, 1977.

———. *Prophecy in Our Time.* New York: New American Library, 1969. Reprint, London: Alhambra, 1971.

———. *Psychic Discoveries by the Russians.* New York: Parapsychology Foundation, 1963. Reprint, New York: New American Library, 1971.

———. *Psychic Warfare: Threat or Illusion?* New York: McGraw-Hill, 1983.

———. *The Signet Handbook of Parapsychology.* New York: New American Library, 1978.

———. *The Soviet Propaganda Machine.* New York: McGraw-Hill, 1987.

———. *They Knew the Unknown.* New York: New American Library, 1971.

———. *True Experiences in Exotic ESP.* New York: New American Library, 1968.

———. *True Experiences with Ghosts.* New York: New American Llibrary, 1968.

———. *True Experiences in Prophecy.* New York: New American Library, 1967.

———. *True Experiences in Telepathy.* New York: New American Library, 1967.

———. *What's New in ESP.* New York: New American Library, 1976.

Ebon, Martin, ed. *Exorcism: Fact Not Fiction.* New York: New American Library, 1974.

———. *Miracles.* New York: New American Library, 1981.

———. *Psychic Discoveries by the Russians.* New York: Parapsychology Foundation, 1963; New York: New American Library, 1971.

Eckartshausen, Karl von. *The Cloud upon the Sanctuary.* Translated by Isabel de Steiger. Introduction by Arthur E. Waite. London: Philip Wellby, 1903.

Ecroyd, H. R. "A Strange Adventure in Switzerland." *The Quest* 21, 1 (October 1939).

Eddison, E. R. *The Worm Ouroboros.* New York: E. P. Dutton, 1952.

Eddy, Mary Baker. *Church Manual of the First Church of Christ, Scientist, in Boston, Mass.* Boston: Trustees Under the Will of Mary Baker Eddy, 1908.

———. *Poetical Works.* Boston: Trustees Under the Will of Mary Baker Eddy, 1936.

———. *Prose Works.* Boston: Trustees Under the Will of Mary Baker Eddy, 1925.

———. *Science and Health with Key to the Scriptures.* Boston: Trustees Under the Will of Mary Baker Eddy, 1906.

Edelstein, Emma Jeanette Levy. *Asclepius: a Collection and Interpretation of the Testimonies.* New York: Ayer Publishing Co. Inc., 1975.

Eden, Jerome. *Animal Magnetism and the Life Energy.* Hicksville, N.Y.: Exposition Press, 1974.

———. *The Desert Makers: A Study of the Creation of Deserts in Man, His Atmosphere and Planet.* N.p.: PPCC, 1981.

———. *Do Not Disturb: The Emotional Plague in Education.* Valdez, Ala.: Eden Press, 1959.

———. *Orgone Energy—The Answer to Atomic Suicide.* N.p., 1972.

———. *Planet in Trouble—The UFO Assault on Earth.* Hicksville, N.Y.: Exposition Press, 1973.

———. *Suffer the Children.* New York, 1959.

———. *View From Eden—Talks to Students of Orgonomy.* N.p., 1976.

Eden, Jerome, trans. *Memoir of F. A. Mesmer, Doctor of Medicine, on His Discoveries, 1799.* Mount Vernon, N.Y.: Eden Press, 1957.

Edge, H. L., J. Morris, J. Palmer, and J. H. Rush. *Foundations of Parapsychology: Exploring the Boundaries of Human Capabilities.* London: Routledge & Kegan Paul, 1986.

Editors of *Psychic Magazine. Psychics.* New York: Harper & Row, 1972.

Edmonds, Simeon. *ESP: Extrasensory Perception.* London: Aquarian Press, 1965. Reprint, North Hollywood, Calif.: Wilshire Book, 1972.

———. *Hypnosis: Key to Psychic Powers.* London: Aquarian Press, 1968.

———. *Hypnotism and Psychic Phenomena.* Hollywood, Calif.: Wilshire, n.d.

———. *Hypnotism and the Supernormal.* Hollywood, Calif.: Wilshire Book Co., 1968.

———. *The Psychic Power of Hypnosis.* New York: Samuel Weiser, 1968.

———. *Spiritualism: a Critical Survey.* London: Aquarian Press, 1966.

Edwards, David. *Dare to Make Magic.* London: Regal Press, 1971.

Edwards, Frank. *Flying Saucers Here and Now.* New York: Lyle Stuart, 1967.

———. *Flying Saucers—Serious Business.* New York: Lyle Stuart, 1966.

———. *My First Ten Million Sponsors.* New York: Ballantine Books, 1956.

———. *Strange World.* New York: Lyle Stuart, 1964.

———. *Stranger Than Science.* New York: Lyle Stuart, 1959.

———. *Strangest of All.* Secaucus, N.J.: Citadel Press, 1958.

Edwards, Gillian. *Hobgoblin and Sweet Puck: Fairy Names and Natures.* London: Geoffrey Bles, 1974.

Edwards, Harry. *The Evidence for Spirit Healing.* London: Spiritualist Press, 1952.

———. *The Healing Intelligence.* New York: Taplinger, 1971.

———. *A Guide to the Understanding and Practice of Spiritual Healing.* Surrey, England: Spiritual Healing Sanctuary, 1974.

———. *The Science of Spirit Healing.* London: Rider and Co., 1945.

———. *Spirit Healing.* London: Herbert Jenkins, 1960.

———. *Thirty Years a Spiritual Healer.* London: Herbert Jenkins; Surrey, England: Spiritual Healing Sanctuary, 1968.

———. *The Truth about Spiritual Healing.* London: Spiritualist Press, 1956.

Edwards, Owen Dudley. *The Quest for Sherlock Holmes, A Biographical Study of Arthur Conan Doyle.* Edinburgh: Mainstream Publishing, 1983.

Eek, Sven, and Boris de Zirkoff. *William Quan Judge: Theosophical Pioneer.* Wheaton, Ill.: Theosophical Publishing House, 1969.

Eells, Charles P. *Life and Times of Apollonius of Tyana, Rendered into English from the Greek of Philostratus the Elder.* Stanford, Calif.: Stanford University Press, 1923.

Eglinton, John. *A Memoir of AE: George William Russell.* London: Macmillian, 1937.

Ehrenwald, Jan. *Anatomy of Genius: Split Brains and Global Minds.* New York: Human Sciences Press, 1984.

———. "An Autobiographical Fragment." In *Men and Women of Parapsychology,* edited by R. Pilkington. Jefferson, N.C.: McFarland, 1987.

———. *The ESP Experience: A Psychiatric Validation.* New York: Basic Books, 1978.

———. *The History of Psychotherapy: From Healing Magic to Encounter.* New York: J. Aronson, 1976.

———. *New Dimensions of Deep Analysis; A Study of Telepathy in Interpersonal Relationships.* New York: Grune & Stratton, 1954. Reprint, New York: Ayer Publishing Co. Inc., 1975.

———. *Psychotherapy, Myth and Method.* New York: Grune & Stratton, 1966.

———. *Telepathy and Medical Psychology.* New York: W. W. Norton, 1948.

Eigen, Michael. *The Psychoanalytic Mystic.* Binghamton, N.Y.: ESF Publishers, 1998.

Eikerenkoetter, Frederick. *Reverend Ike's Secrets of Health, Happiness, and Prosperity—For You.* New York: Reverend Ike Prayer Tower, n.d.

Eisen, William. *Agasha, Master of Wisdom.* Marina del Rey, Calif.: DeVorss, 1977.

———. *The English Cabala.* 2 vols. Marina del Rey, Calif.: DeVorss, 1980–82.

Eisen, William, ed. *The Agashan Discourse.* Marina del Rey, Calif.: DeVorss, 1978.

Eisenbud, Jule. "On Ted Serios' Alleged 'Confession.' " *Journal of the American Society for Psychical Research* 69 (1975).

Eisenbud, Jule. *Paranormal Foreknowledge: Problems and Perplexities.* New York: Human Sciences Press, 1982.

———. "Paranormal Photography." In *Handbook of Parapsychology,* edited by B. B. Wolman. New York: Van Nostrand Reinhold, 1977.

Eisenbud, Jule. *Psi and Psychoanalysis.* New York: Grune & Stratton, 1970.

———. "Psychic Photography and Thoughtography." In *Psychic Exploration: A Challenge for Science,* edited by Edgar D. Mitchell and John White. New York: Putnam, 1974.

———. "Some Investigations of Claims of PK Effects on Metal: The Denver Experiments." *Journal* of the American Society for Psychical Research 76 (1982).

———. *The World of Ted Serios: "Thoughtographic" Studies of an Extraordinary Mind.* 2d ed. Jefferson, N.C.: McFarland, 1989.

Eisler, Robert. *Man into Wolf: An Anthropological Interpretation of Sadism, Masochism, and Lycanthropy.* Santa Barbara, Calif.: Ross Erikson, 1978.

Eisler, Robert. *The Royal Art of Astrology.* London: Herbert Joseph, 1946.

Eitel, E. J. *Feng-shui: The Rudiments of Natural Science in China.* Bristol, England: Pentacle Books, 1979.

El Morya [through Mark L. Prophet]. *Light From Heavenly Lanterns.* Colorado Springs, Colo.: Summit Lighthouse, 1973.

———. [through Mark L. Prophet and Elizabeth Clare Prophet]. *Morya the Darjeeling Masters Speaks to His Chelas on the Quest for the Holy Grail.* Los Angeles: Summit University, 1973.

Elbe, Louis. *Future Life in the Light of Ancient Wisdom & Modern Science.* N.p., 1906. Reprint, Kila, Mont.: Kessinger Publishing Co. 1998.

Eliade, Mircea. *De Zalmoxis à Genghis Khan.* 1970. Translated as *Zalmoxis, the Vanishing God.* Chicago: University of Chicago Press, 1972.

———. *The Forge and the Crucible; The Origins and Structures of Alchemy.* New York: Harper & Row, 1956. London, 1962.

———. *Forgerons et Alchimistes.* Flammarion, 1956. Translated as *The Forge and the Crucible.* New York: Harper & Brothers, 1962. Reprint. Chicago: University of Chicago Press, 1979.

———. *Le Yoga: Immortalité et liberté.* 1954. Translated as *Yoga: Immortality and Freedom.* New York: Pantheon Books, 1958.

———. "1907 to 1937: Journey East, Journey West." In *Autobiography.* Vol. 1. San Francisco: Harper & Row, 1981.

———. *Occultism, Witchcraft and Cultural Fashion: Essays in Comparative Religion.* Chicago: University of Chicago Press, 1976.

———. *Patanjali et le Yoga.* 1962. Translated as *Patanjali and Yoga.* New York: Funk and Wagnall's, 1969.

———. *Rites and Symbols of Initiation: The Mysteries of Birth & Rebirth.* New York: Harper Torchbooks, 1968.

———. "Shamanism: An Overview." *Encyclopedia of Religion*. Vol. 13. New York: Macmillan Publishing Co./London: Collier Macmillan, 1987.

———. "Shamanism." In *Ancient Religions*. Edited by Vergilius Ferm. New York: Citadel Press, 1965.

———. *Shamanism: Archaic Techniques of Ecstasy*. Princeton, N.J.: Princeton University Press, 1964.

———. *Two Tales of the Occult*. New York: Herder and Herder, 1970.

Eliade, Mircea., ed. *Encyclopedia of Religion*. 16 vols. New York: Macmillian, 1987.

Elkin, A. P. *Aboriginal Men of High Degree*. 2nd edition. New York: St. Martin's Press, 1978. Rochester, Vt.: Inner Traditions International, Ltd.,1993.

Elliotson, John. *Human Physiology*. London, 1840.

Elliott, Charles W. *Mysteries, or Glimpses of the Supernatural*. New York: Harper, 1852.

Elliott, G. Maurice. *The Psychic Life of Jesus*. 1938. Reprint, New York: London Press, 1974.

———. *Spiritualism in the Old Testament*. London: The Psychic Book Club, 1940.

Elliott, Ralph W. *Runes: An Introduction*. New York: Barnes & Noble, 1971. Reprint, Greenwood Press, 1981.

Ellis, Arthur J. *The Divining Rod: A History of Water Witching, with a Bibliography*. Washington, 1917; 1938.

Ellis, D. J. *The Mediumship of the Tape Recorder*. Pulborough, England: The Author, 1978.

Ellis, Havelock. *The World of Dreams*. Boston: Houghton Mifflin Co., 1922. Reprint, Detroit: Gale Research, 1976.

Ellis, Ida. *Planchette and Automatic Writing*. Blackpool, UK, 1904.

———. *Thoughts on Psychometry*. Blackpool, UK, 1899.

Ellis, Keith. *Prediction and Prophecy*. London: Wayland, 1973.

Ellwood, Gracia Fay. *Psychic Visits to the Past: An Exploration of Retrocognition*. New York: New American Library, 1971.

Ellwood, Robert S., Jr. *Alternative Altars: Unconventional and Eastern Spirituality in America*. Chicago: University of Chicago Press, 1979.

———. *Religious and Spiritual Groups in Modern America*. Englewood Cliffs, N.J.: Prentice-Hall, 1973.

———. *Theosophy*. Wheaton, Ill.: Theosophical Publishing House, 1986.

Elworthy, F. T. *The Evil Eye*. London, 1894. Reprint, New York: Julian Press, 1958.

Emboden, William A. "The Sacred Journey in Dynastic Egypt: Shamanistic Trance in the Context of the Narcotic Water Lily and the Mandrake," *Journal of Psychoactive Drugs*. 21 (1989): 61–75.

———. "Transcultural Use of Narcotic Water Lilies in Ancient Egyptian and Maya Drug Ritual," *Journal of Ethnopharmacology*. 3, no. 1 (1981): 39–83.

Emboden, William A., and Marlene Dobkin De Rios. "Mayan-Egyptian Uses of Water Lilies (Nymphaceae) in Shamanic Ritual Drug Use." In *Folk Medicine and Herbal Healing*. Edited by George G. Meyer, Kenneth Blum, and John G. Cull. Springfield, Ill.: Charles C. Thomas, 1981.

Emerick, Abraham J. *Obeah and Duppyism in Jamaica*. Woodstock, N.Y.: privately printed, 1915.

Emmerich, Anne Catherine. *The Dolorous Passion of Our Lord Jesus Christ*. Springfield, Ill.: Templegate, 1951.

———. *Leben der Heil, Jungfrau Maria*. Munich: Literarisch-artistische Anstalt, 1852. Translated as *The Life of the Blessed Virgin Mary* by Michael Paliret. Springfield, Ill.: Templegate, 1954.

Emmons, Nuel. *Manson in His Own Words*. New York: Grove Press, 1986.

Empson, R. H. *The Cult of the Peacock Angel*. N.p., 1928.

Endersby, Victor. *Hall of Magic Mirrors*. New York: Carlton Press, 1969.

Endicott, Kirk. Batek. *Negrito Religion. The World View of a Hunting and Gathering People of Peninsular Malaysia*. Oxford: The Clarendon Press, 1979.

Endore, Guy. *King of Paris*. New York: Pocket Books, 1958.

Engelbrecht, Johann. *The Divine Visions of Johann Engelbrecht*. 2 vols. Northampton, England, 1780.

Eniatos. *Mirabilis Annus; or, The Year of Prodigies and Wonders; Being a Collection of Several Signs That Have Been Seen in the Heavens, in the Earth, and in the Waters, Together with Many Remarkable Accidents and Judgments . . . Within the Space of One Year Last Past*. London, 1661.

Ennemoser, Joseph. *The History of Magic*. 2 vols., 1854. Reprint, New Hyde Park, N.Y.: University Books, 1960.

———. *The History of the Supernatural*. Translated by William Howitt. 2 vols. 1854. Reprint, New Hyde Park, N.Y.: University Books, 1970.

The Equinox. 5, nos. 10–4. New York: Samuel Weiser, 1975–1981.

The Equinox. 1, nos. 1–10. London, 1909–1913. Reprint, New York: Samuel Weiser, 1972.

The Equinox. 3, no. 1. Detroit: Universal Publishing, 1919. Reprint, New York: Samuel Weiser, 1972.

The Equinox of the God. London: Ordo Templi Orientis, 1936. .

Erdman, David, ed. *The Illuminated Blake*. Garden City, N.Y.: Doubleday, 1974.

Ericson, Eric. *The World, The Flesh, and the Devil: A Biographical Dictionary of Witches*. New York: Mayflower Books, 1981.

Ermacora, Giovanni B. *I fatti spiritici e le ipotesi affrettate* (Spiritistic facts and hasty hypotheses). Padua, Italy, 1892.

Erman, Adolf. *Life in Ancient Egypt*. London, 1894. Reprint, New York: Dover, 1971.

Ernst, Bernard M. L., and Hereward Carrington. *Houdini and Conan Doyle: The Story of a Strange Friendship*. Albert and Charles Boni, 1932. London: Hutchinson, 1933.

Erskine, Alex. *A Hypnotist's Casebook*. London: Rider, 1932.

Erskine, Steuart *Memoirs of Edward, Eighth Earl of Sandwich, 1839–1916*. London, N.p., 1919.

Esdaile, James. *Mesmerism in India and its Practical Application to Surgery and Medicine*. 1846. Reprint, Chicago: Psychic Research, 1902.

———. *Mesmerism in India*. 1850. Reprinted as *Hypnosis in Medicine and Surgery*. New York: Institute for Research in Hypnosis Publication Press, 1957.

———. *Natural and Mesmeric Clairvoyance; With the Practical Application of Mesmerism in Surgery and Medicine*. London: H. Bailliere, 1852. Reprint, New York: Ayer Publishing Co. Inc., 1975.

Essays in Honor of Gilbert Murray. Freeport, N.Y.: Books for Libraries Press, 1972.

Estabrooks, George H. *Hypnosis: Current Problems*. New York: Harper, 1962.

———. *Hypnotism*. New York: Dutton, 1957.

———. *Man, Mechanical Misfit*. New York: Macmillan, 1941.

———. *Spiritism*. New York: Dutton, 1947.

Estabrooks, George H., and Nancy Gross. *The Future of the Human Mind*. New York: Dutton, 1961.

Estabrooks, George H., and Richard Lockbridge. *Death in the Mind*. New York: Dutton, 1947.

Estes, J. Worth. *Dictionary of Protopharmacology: Therapeutic Practices, 1700–1850*. Canton, Mass.: Science History Publications, 1990.

Estrade, J. B. *The Appearances of the Blessed Virgin Mary at the Grotto of Lourdes: Personal Souvenirs of an Eyewitness*. London: Art & Book Co., 1912.

Evans, Christopher. *Cults of Unreason*. New York: Farrar, Straus & Giroux, 1973. Reprint, London: Harrap, 1974; New York: Dell, 1975.

———. *Cybernetics*. Baltimore, Md.: University Park Press, 1968.

———. *The Mighty Micro*. London: Gollancz, 1979.

———. *Psychology: A Dictionary of the Mind, Brain, and Behavior*. London: Arrow Books, 1978.

———. *Understanding Yourself*. New York: A & W Visual Library, 1977.

Evans, Colin. *The New Waite's Compendium of Natal Astrology*. 1917. Revised by Brain E. F. Gardener. York Beach, Maine: Samuel Weiser, 1971.

[Evans, Frederick W.]. *Autobiography of a Shaker*. Mount Lebanon, N.Y., 1869.

Evans, Frederick W. *Shakers and Shakerism*. New York, 1859.

Evans, Henry Ridgeley. *The Old and New Magic.* Chicago: Open Court Publishing, 1909.

Evans, Hilary. *Alternate States of Consciousness: Unself, Otherself, and Superself.* Wellingborough, Northampton, England: Aquarian Press, 1989.

———. *Gods, Spirits, Cosmic Guardians.* Wellingborough, Northampton, England: Aquarian Press, 1987.

———. *Intrusions: Society and the Paranormal.* London and Boston: Routledge & Kegan Paul, 1982.

———. *UFO's 1947–1987: The 40-year Search for an Explanation.* London: Fortean Times, 1987.

———. *Visions, Apparitions, Alien Visitors.* Wellingborough, Northampton, England: Aquarian Press, 1984.

Evans, Hilary, and John Spencer, eds. *Phenomena: Forty Years of Flying Saucers.* New York: Avon Books, 1989.

Evans, I. H. N. *The Religion of the Tempasuk Dusuns of North Borneo.* Cambridge, Mass.: Cambridge University Press, 1953.

Evans, J. W. *The Life and Work of Robin John Tillyard, 1881–1937.* St. Lucia: University of Queensland Press, 1963.

Evans, John W. "Conan Doyle Still Lives." *American Weekly,* November 2, 1952.

———. "Haunted by the Ghost of Bernard Shaw." *American Weekly,* June 7, 1953.

———. "Patrice Munsel's Neon Ghost." *American Weekly,* November 8, 1953.

———. "The Phantom Model." *American Weekly,* April 4, 1954.

———. "When the Clocks Stood Still." *American Weekly,* June 13, 1954.

Evans-Pritchard, E. E. *Witchcraft, Oracles, and Magic among the Azande.* Oxford: The Clarendon Press, 1937.

Evans, W. H. *Constructive Spiritualism.* Manchester, England: Two Worlds, 1917.

———. *Modern Spiritualism.* Rochdale, England: British Spiritualists' Lyceum Union, 1923.

Evans, Warren Felt. *The Divine Law of Cure.* Boston: H. H. Carter, 1881.

———. *Esoteric Christianity and Mental Therapeutics.* Boston: H. H. Carter & Karick, 1886.

———. *The Mental Cure.* Boston: Colby & Rich, 1869.

———. *Mental Medicine.* Boston: H. H. Carter, 1873.

———. *The Primitive Mind Cure.* Boston: H. H. Carter & Karrick, 1885.

———. *Soul and Body.* Boston: H. H. Carter, 1876.

Evans-Wentz, W. Y. *The Fairy-Faith in Celtic Countries.* Oxford: Oxford University Press, 1911. Reprint, New Hyde Park, N.Y.: University Books, 1966; New York: Lemma, 1973.

———. *The Tibetan Book of the Dead.* 1927. Reprint, London: Oxford University Press, 1957.

———. *The Tibetan Book of the Great Liberation.* New York: Oxford University Press, 1954.

———. *Tibet's Great Yogi . . . Milarepa.* 2d ed. London: Oxford University Press, 1969.

———. *Tibetan Yoga and Secret Doctrines; or, Seven Books of Wisdom of the Great Path.* 2d ed. London: Oxford University Press, 1958.

Ewen, Cecil L'Estrange. *Witch Hunting and Witch Trials.* London, 1929.

———. *Witchcraft and Demonism.* London, 1933.

"Exposure of Mr. Eldred." *Journal of the Society for Psychical Research* 12: 242–52.

"Exposures of Mr. Craddock." *Journal of the Society for Psychical Research* 12.

Eyries, Jean Baptiste. *Fantasmagoriana, or Collection of the Histories of Apparitions, Spectres, Ghosts, etc.* Paris: F. Schoell, 1812.

Eysenck, Hans J. *Astrology: Science or Superstition?* London: Maurice Temple Smith, 1982.

———. *Handbook of Abnormal Psychology: An Experimental Approach.* New York: Basic Books, 1961.

———. "Personality and Extrasensory Perception." *Journal of the Society for Psychical Research* 44 (1967).

———. *Sense and Nonsense in Psychology.* London: Penguin, 1957.

Eysenck, Hans J., and C. Sargent. *Explaining the Unexplained.* London: Weidenfield and Nicholson, 1982.

———. *Know Your Own PSI-IQ.* New York: World Almanac Publications, 1983.

Fagan, Cyril. *Astrological Origins.* St. Paul, Minn.: Llewellyn Publications, 1971.

———. *Fixed Zodiac Ephemeris for 1948.* Washington, D.C.: National Astrological Library, 1948.

———. *Zodiacs Old and New.* Los Angeles: Llewellyn Publications, 1950.

Fagan, Myron. *A Brief History of the Illuminati.* Lansing, Ill.: H.B.C., 1978.

Fahler, Jarl I. "ESP Card Tests With and Without Hypnosis." *Journal of Parapsychology* 21 (1957).

Fahler, Jarl I., and H. H. J. Keil. "Nina S. Kulagina: A Strong Case for PK Involving Directly Observable Movements of Objects Recorded on Cine Film." *Research in Parapsychology, 1974.* Edited by J. D. Morris, William G. Roll, and R. L. Morris. Metuchen, N.J.: Scarecrow Press, 1975.

Fahler, Jarl I., and Karlis Osis. "Checking for Awareness of Hits in a Precognition Experiment with Hypnotized Subjects." *Journal* of the American Society for Psychical Research 60 (1966).

Fahler, Jarl I., and R. J. Cadoret. "ESP Card Tests of College Students With and Without Hypnosis." *Journal of Parapsychology* 22 (1958).

Fahnestock, W. B. *Statuvolism: Artificial Somnambulism.* Chicago: Religio-Philosophical Publishing House, 1871.

Fahsel, K. *Konnersreuth: Le mystère des stigmatisés.* N.p., 1933.

Fairbanks, K. "Le Cas Spirite de Dickens." *Arch. de Psychol.* T.I. (June 1892).

Fairfax, Edward. *Daemonologia: A Discourse on Witchcraft.* Harrogate, England: R. Ackrill, 1882. Reprint, New York: Barnes & Noble, 1971.

Fairley, John. *Arthur Clarks' World of Strange Powers.* New York: G. P. Putnam's Sons, 1984.

Faizi, Gloria. *The Baha'i Faith: An Introduction.* New Delhi, India: Baha'i Publishing Trust, 1988.

Falcomer, Marco T. *An Introduction to Modern Spiritualism.* [Venice], 1895.

———. *Phenomenography.* Paris, 1903.

Falconnier, R. *Les lames hermétiques du tarot divinatoire.* Paris, 1896.

Fanthorpe, Patricia, and Lionel Fanthorpe. *The Holy Grail Revealed: The Real Secret of Rennes-le-Château.* North Hollywood, Calif.: Newcastle Pub. Co., 1982.

Faraday, Ann. *Dream Power.* New York: Coward, McCann & Geoghegan, 1972. Reprint, New York: Berkeley, 1973.

Farmer, John S. *'Twixt Two Worlds: A Narrative of the Life and Work of William Eglinton.* London: The Psychological Press, 1886.

Farrar, Janet, and Stewart Farrar. *Eight Sabbats for Witches.* London: Robert Hale, 1981.

Farrar, Stewart. *What Witches Do.* New York: Coward, McCann & Geoghegan; London: Peter Davies, 1971. Reprint. Custer, Wash.: Phoenix Publishing, Inc., 1983.

Farson, Daniel. *The Man Who Wrote Dracula: A Biography of Bram Stoker.* New York: St. Martin's, 1976.

Farson, Daniel, and Angus Hall. *Mysterious Monsters.* London: Aldus Books, 1978.

Farzan, Massud. *The Tale of the Reed Pipe.* New York: E. P. Dutton, 1974.

Fassbender, Pantaleon. "Parapsychology and the Neurosciences: A Computer-based Content Analysis of Abstracts in the Database 'Medline' from 1975 to 1995," *Perceptual & Motor Skills* 84, no. 2 (April 1997): 452–454.

Fast, Francis R. *The Houdini Messages: The Facts Concerning the Messages Received Through the Mediumship of Arthur Ford.* New York: The Author, 1929.

Faw, Duane L., comp. *The Paramony.* Malibu, Calif.: The Author, 1986.

Fawcett, Lawrence, and Barry J. Greenwood. *Clear Intent: The Government Coverup of the UFO Experience.* Englewood Cliffs, N.J.: Prentice-Hall, 1984.

Fay, Charles Eden. *Mary Celeste: The Odyssey of an Abandoned Ship.* Salem, Mass.: Peabody Museum, 1942.

Federman, Reinhold. *The Royal Road of Alchemy.* New York: Chilton, 1969.

Feilding, Evarard. "Note on the English Sittings with Miss Tomczyk." *Journal of the Society for Psychical Research* 17 (1915).

———. *Sittings with Eusapia Palladino and Other Studies.* New Hyde Park, N.Y.: University Books, 1963.

Feilding, F. E., W. W. Baggally, and Hereward Carrington. "Report on a Series of Sittings with Eusapia Palladino." *Proceedings of the Society for Psychical Research* 23, no. 59 (1909); 25, no. 62 (1911).

Feldenkrais, Moshe. *Higher Judo.* New York: Warner, 1952.

Fenwick, Sherida. *Getting It: The Psychology of est.* Philadelphia: J. P. Lippencott, 1976.

Ferguson, Ian. *Philosophy of Witchcraft.* Kila, Mont.: Kessinger Publishing Co., 1998.

Ferguson, J. *Bibliotheca Chemica; a Bibliography of Books on Alchemy, Chemistry and Pharmaceutics.* 2 vols. London, 1954.

Ferguson, J. B. *Supramundane Facts of the Life of Rev. J. B. Ferguson.* London, 1865.

Ferguson, Jesse Babcock. *Spirit Communion: A Record of Communications from the Spirit Spheres.* Nashville, Tenn., 1854.

Ferguson, John. *An Illustrated Encyclopaedia of Mysticism and The Mystery Religions.* London: Thames & Hudson, 1976.

———. *Witchcraft Literature of Scotland.* Edinburgh: Edinburgh Bibliographical Society Papers, 1899.

Ferguson, Marilyn. *The Aquarian Conspiracy: Personal and Social Transformation in Our Time.* New York: St. Martin's Press, 1980. Los Angeles: J. P. Tarcher/Houghton Mifflin; New York: Putnam Publishing Group, 1987.

———. *The Frontiers of Mind Research.* New York: Taplinger, 1973.

Fernandez, James W. *Bwiti. An Ethnography of the Religious Imagination in Africa.* Princeton, N.J.: Princeton University Press, 1982.

Fernández, José S. *Application of the Statistical Method to the Study of Cryptesthetic Phenomena.* N.p., 1942.

———. *Clairvoyance and Probability.* N.p., 1941.

———. *Experimental Parapsychology.* N.p., 1953.

———. *A Mathematical Preface to the Study of ESP.* N.p., 1949.

———. *Parapsychology and the Existence of the Soul.* N.p., 1959.

———. *Philosophical and Scientific Bases for Survival and Reincarnation.* N.p., 1957.

———. *The Photoelectric Cell and Perception of the Spiritual World.* N.p., 1932.

Ferreiro, Alberto and Jeffrey B. Russell. *The Devil, Heresy, & Witchcraft in the Middle Ages.* Boston: Brill Academic Publishers, Inc., 1998.

Ferro, Robert, and Michael Gromley. *Atlantis: The Autobiography of a Search.* New York: Bell Publishing, 1970.

Ferry, David. *Gilgamesh: a New Rendering into English Verse.* New York: Farrar, Straus and Giroux, 1992.

Festinger, Leon, Henry W. Riecken, and Stanley Schachter. *When Prophecy Fails.* New York: Harper & Row, 1956.

Feuchtwanger, E. J. *Gladstone.* Blasingtoke, UK: Macmillan, 1989.

Field, Geoffrey G. *Evangelist of Race: The Germanic Vision of Houston Stewart Chamberlain.* New York: Columbia University Press, 1981.

Field, Sidney. *Krishnamurti: The Reluctant Messiah.* New York: Paragon House, 1989.

Fielding, Charles, and Clark Collins. *The Story of Dion Fortune.* York Beach, Maine: Samuel Weiser, 1985.

Fielding, H. *The Soul of a People.* London: n.p., 1902.

Fielding-Ould, Fielding. *The Wonders of the Saints in the Light of Spiritualism.* London: John M. Watkins, 1919.

Fields, Rick. *How the Swans Came to the Lake: A Narrative History of Buddhism in America.* Boulder, Colo.: Shambhala, 1981.

Figuier, Louis. *L'Alchimie et les Achimistes.* Paris, 1856.

———. *The Day After Death, or, Our Future Life, According to Science.* London: R. Bentley, 1874.

Fillmore, Charles S. *Christian Healing: Science of Being.* Kansas City, Mo.: Unity School of Christianity, 1909.

———. *Jesus Christ Heals.* Kansas City, Mo.: Unity School of Christianity, 1931.

———. *Metaphysical Bible Dictionary.* Kansas City, Mo.: Unity School of Christianity, 1931.

———. *Prosperity.* Kansas City, Mo.: Unity School of Christianity, 1936.

———. *The Twelve Powers of Man.* Lee's Summit, Mo.: Unity School of Christianity, 1930, 1955.

Fillmore, Charles, and Cora Fillmore. *Teach Us to Pray.* New York: Seabury Press, 1976.

Fillmore, Myrtle. *How to Let God Help You.* Lee's Summit, Mo.: Unity School of Christianity, 1956.

———. *The Letters of Myrtle Fillmore.* Kansas City, Mo.: Unity School of Christianity, 1936.

Fincher, Susanne F. *Creating Mandalas.* Boston: Shambhala Publications, Inc., 1991.

Findhorn Community. *Faces of Findhorn.* Forres, Scotland: Findhorn Publications, 1980.

———. *The Findhorn Garden.* New York: Harper & Row, 1975.

Findlay, Arthur J. *On the Edge of the Etheric; or, Survival After Death Scientifically Explained.* London: Psychic Press, 1931. Reprint, Corgi, 1971.

———. *The Curse of Ignorance.* 2 vols. London, 1947.

———. *An Investigation of Psychic Phenomena.* London, 1924.

———. *Looking Back: the Autobiography of a Spiritualist.* London: Psychic Press, 1955.

———. *On the Edge of the Etheric.* London: Psychic Press, 1931.

———. *The Psychic Stream.* London, 1939.

———. *The Rock of Truth, or Spiritualism, the Coming World Religion.* London: Rider, 1933.

———. *The Unfolding Universe.* London, 1935.

———. *The Way of Life* London, 1953.

Fiore, Edith. *You Have Been Here Before: A Psychologist Looks at Past Lives.* New York: Coward, McCann & Geoghegan, 1978.

Firebrace, R. C., and Lucien Landau. "The Delawarr Camera." *Light: A Journal of Psychic Science* 77, no. 3430 (March 1937).

Fischer, Oskar. *Experimente mit Raffael Schermann. Ein Beitrag zum Problem der Graphologie, Telepathie und des Hellsehens.* N.p., 1924.

Fisher, B. Aubrey. "Leadership as Medium: Treating Complexity in Group Communication Research," *Small Group Behavior* 16, no. 2 (May 1985): 167–196. Fisher, Joe. *The Case for Reincarnation.* New York: Bantam, 1985.

Fisk, George W. "How Primitive is ESP?" *Tomorrow* (spring 1957).

———. "We Card-Guessers." *Tomorrow* (winter 1957).

Fisk, George W., and Donald J. West. "Psychokinetic Experiments with a Single Subject." *Parapsychology Newsletter.* November–December 1957.

Fitzgerald, B. J. *A New Text of Spiritual Philosophy and Religion.* San Jose, Calif.: Universal Church of the Master, 1954.

Fitzgerald, Randall. *The Complete Book of Extraterrestrial Encounters.* New York: Collier, 1979.

Fitzsimons, Raymund. *Death and the Magician: The Mystery of Houdini.* London: Hamish Hamilton, 1980.

Flaherty, Gloria. *Shamanism and the Eighteenth Century.* Princeton, N.J.: Princeton University Press, 1992.

Flambert, Paul [Paul Choisnard]. *Etude nouvelle sur l'héré dité.* Paris, 1903.

———. *Influence astrale.* Paris, 1901.

———. *Langage astral.* Paris, 1903.

Flammarion, Camille. *Death and Its Mystery.* 3 vols. London: Century, 1921–23.

———. *Haunted Houses.* Paris, 1924. Reprint, New York: Appleton, 1924. Reprint, Detroit: Gale Research, 1971.

———. *Mysterious Psychic Forces.* Boston: Small, Maynard, London: T. Fisher Unwin, 1907.

———. "The Unknown of Yesterday and the Truth of Tomorrow." *Journal of the Society for Psychical Research* 29 (1935).

Flammarion, Cesar. *After Death—What?* London: T. Fisher Unwin, 1909.

Flammonde, Paris. *The Mystic Healers.* New York: Stein & Day, 1974.

Fleckles, Elliott V. *Willie Speaks Out: The Psychic World of Abraham Lincoln.* St. Paul, Minn.: Llewellyn Publications, 1974.

Flew, Antony, G. N., ed. *Body, Mind and Death.* New York: Macmillan, 1964.

———. There a Case for Disembodied Spirit?" *Journal* of the American Society for Psychical Research 66 (1972).

———. *Logic of Mortality.* Oxford: Blackwell, 1987.

———. *A New Approach to Psychical Research.* London: C. A. Watts, 1953.

Flier, Len. "Demystifying Mysticism: Finding a Developmental Relationship Between Different Ways of Knowing," *Journal of Transpersonal Psychology* 27, no. 2 (1995): 131–152.

Flinn, H. C. *Spiritualism Among the Shakers.* East Canterbury, N.H., 1899.

Flint, Leslie. *Voices in the Dark: My Life as a Medium.* New York: Bobbs-Merrill, 1971.

Florescu, Radu & Raymond T. McNally. *Dracula: A Biography of Vlad the Impaler 1391–1476.* New York: Hawthorn Books, 1973.

Florescu, Radu. *In Search of Frankenstein.* New York: New York Graphic Society, 1975.

Flournoy, Theodore. *From India to the Planet Mars.* New York: Harper, 1900. Reprint, New Hyde Park, N.Y.: University Books, 1963. Reprint, New Jersey: Princeton University Press, 1994.

———. *Des Indes à la Planète Mars.* English ed. as *From India to the Planet Mars: A Study of a Case of Somnambulism with Glossolalia.* New York: Harper, 1900. Reprint, New Hyde Park, N.Y.: University Books, 1963.

———. *Esprits et Médiums, Mélanges de Métapsychique et de Psychologie.* Geneva: Libraire Kundig, 1911. Translated by Hereward Carrington and abridged as *Spiritism and Psychology.* New York: Harper & Brothers, 1911.

———. *The Philosophy of William James.* Freeport, N.Y.: Books for Libraries Press, 1969.

Flowers, S. Edred. *Fire and Ice: Magical Teachings of Germany's Greatest Secret Occult Order.* St. Paul, Minn.: Llewellyn Publications, 1990.

Flowers, Stephen E. *Runes and Magic: Magical Formulaic Elements in the Older Runic Tradition.* New York: Kang, 1986.

Fludd, Robert. *Medicina Catholica.* Frankfurt: William Fitzer, 1629.

———. *Monochordum Mundi Symphoniacum.* Frankfurt, 1622.

———. *Philosophia Mosaica, in quâ sapientia et scientia Creationis explicantur.* Gouda: Peter Rammazen, 1638. Translated as *Mosaicall Philosophy.* London: Humphrey Moseley, 1659.

———. *Tractatus Apologeticus integritatem Societatis de Rosae Cruce defendans.* Leiden: Gottfried Basson, 1617.

———. *Veritatis Proscenium.* Frankfurt: Johann Theodore de Bry, 1621.

Fodor, Nandor. *Between Two Worlds.* New York: Paperback Library, 1964.

———. *Encyclopedia of Psychic Science.* London: Arthurs Press, 1934.

———. *Freud, Jung, and Occultism.* New Hyde Park, N.Y.: University Books, 1971.

———. *The Haunted Mind: A Psychoanalyst Looks at the Supernatural.* Helix Press, New York, 1959.

———. *Mind Over Space.* New York: Citadel Press, 1962.

———. *New Approaches to Dream Interpretation.* New York, 1951. Reprint, New Hyde Park, N.Y.: University Books, 1951.

———. *On the Trail of the Poltergeist.* New York: Citadel, 1958. Reprint, London: Arco Publications, 1959.

———. *These Mysterious People.* London: Rider, 1936.

———. *The Unaccountable.* New York: Award Books, 1968.

Fodor, Nandor, and Hereward Carrington. *Haunted People.* New York: Dutton, 1951.

———. *The Story of the Poltergeist down the Centuries.* London: Rider, 1953.

Fontaine, Jean de la. *La Fontaine des Amoureux de Science.* Paris, 1561.

———. *La Fontaine Perilleuse.* Paris, 1572.

Fontana, Marjorie A. *Cup of Fortune: A Guide to Tea Leaf Reading.* Wisc.: Fantastic, 1979.

Fontenrose, Joseph. *Python: A Study of Delphic Myth and Its Origins.* Berkeley: University of California Press, 1959.

Ford, Arthur. *The Life Beyond Death.* New York: G. P. Putnam's Sons, 1971.

———. *Nothing So Strange.* New York: Harper, 1958.

———. *Spiritual Vibrations.* New York: H.P.B. Publishers, 1926.

———. *Unknown But Known.* New York: Harper, 1968.

Ford, Arthur, and Margueritte Harmon Bro. *Nothing So Strange.* New York: Harper & Row, 1958.

Ford, J. Massyngberde. *The Pentecostal Experience.* Paramus, N.J.: Paulist Press, 1970.

Forem, Jack. *Transcendental Meditation.* New York: E. P. Dutton, 1974.

Forman, Robert K. C. "What does mysticism have to teach us about consciousness?" *Journal of Consciousness Studies* 5, no. 2 (1998): 185–201.

A Formerly Spiritually Unknown Person on the Path to God: The Course of Life of the Prophetess in the Homebringing Mission of Jesus Christ. Pelham, N.H.: Homebringing Mission of Jesus Christ, 1980.

Fornell, Earl. *The Unhappy Medium: Spiritualism and the Life of Margaret Fox.* Austin, Tex., 1964.

Forry, Steven Earl. *Hideous Progenies: Dramatizations of Frankenstein from Mary Shelley to the Present.* Philadelphia: University of Pennsylvania Press, 1990.

Fort, Charles. *The Books of Charles Fort.* New York: Henry Holt, 1941. Reprinted as *The Complete Books of Charles Fort.* New York: Dover Publications, 1974.

———. *The Outcast Manufacturers.* B. W. Dodge, 1909.

Fortune, Dion. *Applied Magic.* New York: Samuel Weiser, 1962.

———. *The Esoteric Orders and Their Work.* London: Rider, 1929. Reprint, St. Paul, Minn.: Llewellyn Publications, 1971.

———. *The Mystical Qabalah.* London: Ernest Benn, 1935.

———. *Psychic Self-Defence.* London: Rider, 1930.

Fortune, Dion. *Sane Occultism.* London: Rider, 1929.

———. *The Secrets of Dr. Traverner.* London: Noel Douglas, 1926.

———. *The Training and Work of an Initiate.* London: Rider, 1930. Reprint, New York: Samuel Weiser, 1972.

———. *The Winged Bull.* London: Williams & Norgate, 1935.

Forwald, Haakon G. "An Approach to Instrumental Investigation of Psychokinesis." *Journal of Parapsychology* (1954).

———. "Experiments with Alternating PK Placement and Control Tests." *Journal of Parapsychology* (1955).

———. "A Further Study of the PK Placement Effect." *Journal of Parapsychology* 16 (1952).

———. *Mind, Matter, and Gravitation: a Theoretical and Experimental Study.* New York: Parapsychological Foundation, 1969.

———. "A Study of Psychokinesis in its Relation to Physical Conditions." *Journal of Parapsychology* 19 (1955).

Forwald, Haakon G., and Joseph G. Pratt. "Confirmation of the PK Placement Effect." *Journal of Parapsychology* 22 (March 1958).

Fosbrook, Thomas D. *Encyclopedia of Antiquities.* 2 vols. N.p., 1825, 1840.

Fosdick, Sara. *Nicholas Roerich.* New York: Nicholas Roerich Museum, 1964.

Foster, Esther B. "General Extrasensory Perception with a Group of Fourth and Fifth Grade Retarded Children." *Journal of Parapsychology* 2 (1937).

———. "A Re-examination of Dr. Soal's Clairvoyance Data." *Journal of Parapsychology* 20 (1956).

Foster, Esther B., and J. G. Pratt. "Displacement in ESP Card Tests in Relation to Hits and Misses." *Journal of Parapsychology* 14 (1950).

Foster, Esther B., and Karlis Osis. "Multiple Aspect Targets in Tests of ESP." *Journal of Parapsychology* 16 (1952).

———. "A Test of ESP in Cats." *Journal of Parapsychology* 17 (1953).

Foundation for Research on the Nature of Man. "Joseph A. Greenwood, 1906–1988." *Foundation for Research on the Nature of Man Bulletin* 37 (Spring 1988).

"The Founders of the Church of Light.' " *Church of Light Quarterly* 45, no. 1 (February 1970): 1–2.

Fournier d'Albe, E. E. *The Life of Sir William Crookes, O.M., F.R.S.* London: T. F. Unwin, 1923.

Fournier, D'Albe. *New Light on Immortality.* London, 1908.

Fourrey, René. *The Curé D'Ars.* London: Burns & Oates, 1959.

Fowler, Raymond. *MUFON Field Investigator's Manual.* 3d ed. Seguin, Tex.: Mutual UFO Network, 1983.

———. *UFOs, Interplanetary Visitors.* New York: Exposition, 1974.

Fox, George. *Journal.* Edited by John L. Nickalls. Cambridge, Mass.: Cambridge University Press, 1952.

Fox, Marietta N., and Kenneth Bates. "An Experimental Study of ESP Capacity in Mental Patients." *Journal of Parapsychology* (December 1951).

Fox, Oliver [Hugh G. Callaway]. *Astral Projection.* London, 1939. Reprint, New Hyde Park, N.Y.: University Books, 1962. Reprint, Secaucus, N.J.: Carol Publishing Group, 1974.

Fox, Samuel J. *Hell in Jewish Literature.* Wheeling, Ill.: Whitehall, 1969.

Franck, Adolphe. *The Kabbalah.* New Hyde Park, N.Y.: University Books, 1967. Reprint, New York: Citadel, 1979.

Franck, Sebastian. *Paradoxa.* Jena, Germany: E. Diederichs, 1909.

Frank, Eduard. *Gustav Meyrink.* Budingen-Gettenbach, Germany: Avalun Verlag, 1957.

Frank, Frederick S. *Montague Summers: A Bibliographical Portrait.* Methuchen, N.J.: Scarecrow Press, 1988.

Frank, Henry. *Psychic Phenomena Science & Immortality.* N.p., 1916.

Frankau, Gilbert, ed. *Mesmerism by Doctor Mesmer (1779): Being the First Translation of Mesmer's Historic "Mémoire sur la dé couverte du Magnétisme Animal" to appear in English.* London: Macdonald, 1948.

Franklin, Benjamin, and others. *Animal Magnetism: Report of Dr. Franklin and Other Commissioners.* Philadelphia: H. Perkins, 1837.

Franklin, J. H. *The Rebuilding of King Solomon's Temple.* N.p., 1910. Reprint, Kila, Mont.: Kessinger Publishing Co., 1998.

Franklin, T. Bedford. *Radiations.* London, 1949.

Franklyn, Julian. *A Survey of the Occult.* London, 1935. Reprinted as *A Dictionary of the Occult.* New York: Causeway Books, 1973.

———. *Death by Enchantment.* New York: G. P. Putnam's Sons, 1971.

Franz, Marie-Louise von. *On Divination and Synchronicity: The Psychology of Meaningful Chance.* Toronto: Inner City Books, 1980.

Fraser-Harris, David. *The Great Design: Order and Progress in Nature.* New York: Macmillan, 1934.

Frater Achad [Charles Stansfeld Jones]. *Crystal Vision Through Crystal Gazing.* Chicago: Yogi Publication Society, 1923.

Frayling, Christopher. *Vampyres: From Lord Byron to Count Dracula.* London: Faber and Faber, 1991.

Frazer, James G. "The Golden Bough." In *Taboo and the Perils of the Soul.* Vol. 3. New York: Macmillan, 1935.

———. *Totemism and Exogamy.* 4 vols. N.p., 1910.

Freedland, Nat. *The Occult Explosion.* New York: G. P. Putnam's Sons, 1972. Reprint, London: Michael Joseph, 1972.

Freeland, L. S. "Pomo Doctors and Poisoners." *University of California Publications in American Archaeology and Ethnology,* Vol. 20, no. 4. Berkeley: University of California Press, 1923.

Freeman, Paul. "A festival for the Dead in Japan," *Transcultural Psychiatry* 35, no. 4 (December 1998): 551–555.

Frei, Gebhard. "Die Heutige Situation in der Parapsychologie" (The Present Situation of Parapsychology). *Neue Wissenchaft.* N.p., n.d.

———. "Psychologie, Parapsychologie and Weltanschaung." *Schweizer Rundschau.* N.p., 1946.

Freidel, David, Linda Schele, and Joy Parker. *Maya Cosmos: Three Thousand Years on the Shaman's Path.* New York: William Morrow, 1993.

French, Peter J. *John Dee: The World of an Elizabethan Magus.* London: Routledge & Kegan Paul, 1972.

Freud, Sigmund. *The Interpretation of Dreams.* London, 1942.

———. *Studies in Parapsychology.* Edited by Philip Rieff. New York: Collier Books, 1963.

Freudenberg, Gideon G. *Robert Owen: Educator of the People.* Tel Aviv, Israel: Dvir, 1970.

Freudenberg, Karl. *Natural Weapons: A Manual of Karate, Judo, and Jujitsu Techniques.* New York: A. S. Barnes, 1962.

Frick, Harvey Lee. *Apostate Physician.* New York: House of Field, 1937.

Friedenhain, Paula. *Write and Reveal: Interpretation of Handwriting.* London, 1959.

Friedlander, Ira. *The Whirling Dervishes.* New York: Macmillan, 1975.

Fripp, Peter. *The Mystic Philosophy of Sant Mat.* London: Neville Spearman, 1964.

Fritscher, John. *Popular Witchcraft: Straight from the Witch's Mouth.* Bowling Green, Ohio: Bowling Green University Popular Press, 1972.

"Fritz." *Where Are the Dead?* London, 1873.

Froud, Brian, and Alan Lee. *Faeries.* London: Souvenir Press, 1978. Reprint, New York: Bantam Books, 1979. Reprint, London: Pan Books, 1979.

Fry, Daniel. *Alan's Message: To Men of Earth.* Los Angeles: New Age Publishing, 1954.

———. *Atoms, Galaxies, and Understanding.* El Monte, Calif.: Understanding Publishing, 1960.

———. *Can God Fill Teeth? The Real Facts Behind the Miracle Ministry of Evangelist Willard Fuller.* Lakemont, Ga.: CSA, 1970.

———. *The Curve of Development.* Lakemont, Ga.: CSA, 1965.

———. *White Sands Incident.* Los Angeles: New Age Publishing, 1954.

Fu, Chung. *Evolution of Man.* San Francisco: Circle of Inner Truth, 1973.

Fujimoto, Rindo. *The Way of Zazen.* Cambridge, Mass.: Cambridge Buddhist Association, 1969.

Fukurai, T. *Clairvoyance and Thoughtography.* London: Rider, 1931. Reprint, North Stratford, N.H.: Ayer Co. Publishers, Inc., 1975.

Fuller, Jean Overton. *Blavatsky and Her Teachers: An Investigative Biography.* London: East-West Publications/Theosophical Publishing House, 1988.

———. *Madeleine: The Story of Noor Inayat Kahn.* London: Gollancz, 1952. Reprinted as *Noor-un-nisa Inayat Kahn (Madeleine).* Rotterdam: East-West Publications, 1971.

———. *The Magical Dilemma of Victor Neuburg.* London: W. H. Allen, 1965.

Fuller, John F. *The Secret Wisdom of the Qabalah.* London, 1937.

———. *The Star in the West.* London: Walter Scott Publishing, 1907. Reprint, Mokelumne Hill, Calif.: Health Research, 1969.

———. *Yoga: A Study of the Mystical Philosophy of the Brahmins and Buddhists.* London, 1925.

Fuller, John G. *Arigó, Surgeon of the Rusty Knife.* New York: Thomas Y. Crowell, 1972. Reprint, London: Panther, 1975.

———. *The Great Soul Trial.* New York: Macmillan, 1969.

Fuller, John R. *Arigó: Surgeon of the Rusty Knife.* New York: Thomas Y. Crowell, 1974.

Fuller, Robert C. *Mesmerism and the American Cure of Souls.* Philadelphia: University of Pennsylvania Press, 1982.

Fülop-Miller, René. *Rasputin; The Holy Devil.* New York: Viking Press, 1928.

Funck-Brentano, Frantz. *Cagliostro and Company.* London, 1900.

Funk, Isaac K. *The Next Step in Evolution; The Present Step.* London/New York: Funk & Wagnalls, 1902.

———. *The Psychic Riddle.* London/New York: Funk & Wagnalls, 1907.

———. *The Widow's Mite and other Psychic Phenomena.* London/New York: Funk & Wagnalls, 1904.

Furnivall, F. J., ed. *The History of the Holy Grail . . . from the French Prose of Sires R. de Borron.* London: Early English Text Society, 1874.

Furst, Peter T. (editor) *Flesh of the Gods: The Ritual Use of Hallucinogens.* New York: Praeger, 1972.

———. *Hallucinogens and Culture.* Navato, Calif.: Chandler & Sharp, 1976. 1982.

Fytche, A. *Burma, Past & Present.* 2 vols. London: n.p., 1878.

G'Zell, Otter. *Gaia: A New Look at Life on Earth.* London: Oxford University Press, 1979.

———. "Theogenesis: The Birth of the Goddess." *Green Egg* 21, 81 (May 1, 1988): 4–7, 27.

Gabory, Emile. *Alias Bluebeard.* New York: Brewer & Warren, 1930.

Gach, Michael Reed. *Acu-yoga: Self Help Techniques.* Tokyo: Japan Publications, 1981.

Gaddis, Vincent H. *Mysterious Fires and Lights.* New York: McKay, 1967.

Gaddis, Vincent, and Margaret Gaddis. *The Strange World of Animals and Pets.* 1970. Reprint, New York: Pocket Books, 1971.

Gaillard, Lady Zoe. *A New Conception of Love.* London, 1934.

———. *Sir Vincent Caillard Speaks from the Spirit World.* London, 1932.

Galanopoulos, A. G., and E. Bacon. *Atlantis.* London: Nelson, 1969.

Galbreath, Robert C. "Arthur Edward Waite, Occult Scholar and Christian Mystic: A Chronological Bibliography." *Bulletin of Bibliography* 30, no. 2 (April–June 1973).

———. "History of Modern Occultism: A Bibliographical Survey." *Journal of Popular Culture* 5, no. 3 (winter 1971).

Galbreath, Robert C., ed. *The Occult: Studies and Evaluations.* Bowling Green, Ohio: Bowling Green University Popular Press, 1972.

Gall, Edward. *Mysticism Throughout the Ages.* London: Rider, 1934.

Gall, Franz J. *On the Functions of the Brain and of Each of Its Parts: with Observations on the Possibility of Determining the Instincts, Propensities and Talents, or the Moral and Intellectual Dispositions of Men and Animals, by the Configuration of the Brain and Head.* 6 vols. Boston, 1835.

Gallup, George, Jr., with William Proctor. *Adventures in Immortality.* New York: McGraw-Hill, 1982. London: Souvenir Press, 1983.

Galston, Arthur W., and Clifford L. Slayman. "Plant Sensitivity and Sensation." In *Science and the Paranormal: Probing the Evidence of the Supernatural.* Edited by George O. Abell and Barry Singer. New York: Charles Scribner's Sons, 1981.

Galton, Francis. *Hereditary Genius.* London, 1869. Reprint, London: Watts, 1950.

Gambhrananda, Swami. *History of the Ramakrishna Math and Mission.* Calcutta, India: Advaita Ashraam, 1957.

Ganzfried, Rabbi Solomon. *Code of Jewish Law (Kitzur Schulchan Aruch).* New York: Hebrew Publishing, 1927.

Gardner, F. Leigh. *Bibliotheca Rosicruciana.* Edmonds, Wash.: Holmes Publishing Group, 1992.

———. *A Catalogue Raisonne of Works on the Occult Sciences.* Vol. 1 of the *Rosicrucian Books.* Privately printed, 1923.

Gardiner, John. *The New Age Cult in South Africa.* Cape Town: Stuikhof, 1991.

Gardner, Edward L. *Fairies: The Cottingley Photographs and Their Sequel.* London: Theosophical Publishing House, 1945.

Gardner, Gerald. *A Goddess Arrives.* London: A. W. Stockwell, 1948.

———. *Meaning of Witchcraft.* London: Aquarian Press, 1959.

Gardner, Gerald. *Witchcraft Today.* London: Rider, 1954.

Gardner, Hugh. *The Children of Prosperity.* New York: St. Martin's Press, 1978.

Gardner, Marshall B. *A Journey to the Earth's Interior; or, Have the Poles Really Been Discovered?* Aurora, Ill.: The Author, 1913.

Gardner, Martin. *Fads and Fallacies in the Name of Science.* New York: Dover Publications, 1957.

———."The Great URANTIA Mystery." *The Skeptical Inquirer* 14, no. 2 (winter 1990).

———. *How Not to Test a Psychic: Ten Years of Remarkable Experiments with Renowned Psychic Pavel Stepanek.* Buffalo, N.Y.: Prometheus Books, 1989.

———.*In the Name of Science.* New York: George Putnam's Sons, 1952. Reprinted as *Fads and Fallacies in the Name of Science.* New York: Dover Publications, 1957.

———. *New Age Notes of a Fringe Watcher.* Buffalo, N.Y.: Prometheus Books, 1988.

———. "Notes of a Fringe-Watcher: The False Memory Syndrome." *Skeptical Inquirer* 17 (summer 1993).

———. *Science, God, Bad, and Bogus.* Buffalo, N.Y.: Prometheus Books, 1981.

———. "The Tragedies of False Memories: The Accused Are Striking Back, But Grave Injustices Have Been Done." *Skeptical Inquirer* 18 (fall 1994).

Garfield, Patricia L. *Creative Dreaming.* New York: Simon & Schuster, 1974.

Garinet, Jules. *Histoire de la Magie en France.* Paris, 1818.

Garland, Hamlin. *Forty Years of Psychic Research.* New York: Macmillan, 1936.

———. *The Shadow World.* New York, 1908.

Garrett, Clarke. *Spirit Possession and Popular Religion: From the Camisards to the Shakers.* Baltimore, Md.: Johns Hopkins University Press, 1987.

Garrett, Eileen J. *Adventures in the Supernormal: A Personal Memoir.* New York: Garrett/Helix, 1949. Reprint, New York: Paperback Library, 1968.

———. *Awareness.* New York: Creative Age Press, 1941.

———. *Does Man Survive Death?* New York: Helix Press, 1957.

———. *Life is the Healer.* Philadelphia: Dorrance, 1957.

———. *Many Voices: The Autobiography of a Medium.* 1968. Reprint, New York: Dell, 1969.

———. *My Life As a Search for the Meaning of Mediumship.* New York: Oquaga Press, 1938. Reprint, London: Rider, 1939. Reprint, New York: Ayer Publishing Co. Inc., 1975.

———. *The Sense and Nonsense of Prophecy.* New York: Farrar, Straus & Giroux, 1950. Reprint, New York: Berkley, 1968.

———. *Telepathy: In Search of a Lost Faculty.* New York: Creative Age Press, 1945.

Garrett, Eileen J., ed. *Beyond the Five Senses.* Philadelphia: J. B. Lippincott, 1957.

———. *Does Man Survive Death?: A Symposium.* New York: Helix Press, 1957.

Garrison, Omar V. *Encyclopedia of Prophecy.* New York: Citadel, 1979.

———. *Tantra—The Yoga of Sex.* New York: Causeway, 1973. Reprint, London: Academy Editions, 1974.

Garver, Will. *Brother of the Third Degree.* Halcyon, Calif.: Halcyon Temple Press, 1929.

Garvin, Richard. *The Crystal Skull.* Garden City, N.Y.: Doubleday, 1973. Reprint, New York: Pocket Books, 1974.

Gaster, M. *Conjurations & the Ancient Mysteries.* Kila, Mont.: Kessinger Publishing Co., 1999.

Gaster, Moses. *The Origin of the Kabbala.* New York: Gordon Press Publishers, 1976.

Gates, Robert J. *The Awntyrs off Arthure at the Terne Wathelyne: A Critical Edition.* Philadelphia: University of Pennsylvania Press, 1969.

Gauld, Alan. *The Founder of Psychical Research.* New York: Schrocken Books/London: Routledge & Kegan Paul, 1968. Reprint, New York: Schocken Books, 1973.

———. *Mediumship and Survival: A Century of Investigations.* London: Heinemann, 1982.

Gauld, Alan, and A. D. Cornell. *Poltergeists.* London: Routledge & Kegan Paul, 1979.

Gauld, Alan, and J. D. Shotter. *Human Action and its Psychological Investigation.* Boston and London: Routledge & Kegan Paul, 1977.

Gauquelin, Michel. *The Cosmic Clocks: From Astrology to a Modern Science.* Chicago: Henry Regnery, 1967. Reprint, New York: Avon, 1969.

———. *Cosmic Influences on Human Behavior; the Planetary Factors in Personality.* New York: Stein & Day, 1973. Rev. ed. New York: ASI Publishers, 1978.

———. *Dreams and Illusions of Astrology.* Buffalo, N.Y.: Prometheus Books, 1979. Reprint, London: Glover & Blair, 1980.

———. *How Atmospheric Conditions Affect Your Health.* New York: Stein and Day, 1971.

———. *Scientific Basis of Astrology: Myth or Reality?* New York: Stein and Day, 1969. London: P. Davies; Lanham, Md.: Madison Books, Inc., 1970.

Gauquelin, Michel, and Françoise Guaquelin. *The Mars Effect and Sports Champions: A New Replication.* Paris: Laboratorie d'études des relations entre rhythmes cosmiques et psychophysiologiques, 1979.

Gay, Susan E. *John William Fletcher, Clairvoyant.* London, 1883.

Geddes, Patrick. *The Life and Work of Sir Jagadis C. Bose.* London/New York: Longmans, Green and Co., 1920.

Gelberg, Steven, ed. *Hare Krishna, Hare Krishna.* New York: Grove Press, 1983.

Geley, Gustave. *Clairvoyance & Materialisation.* London: T. F. Unwin Ltd./New York: George Doran, 1927. North Stratford, N. H.: Ayer Co. Publishers, Inc., 1975.

———. *De l'Inconscient au Conscient.* Paris: F. Alcan, 1919. Translated as *From the Unconscious to the Conscious.* New York and London: Harper & Brothers, 1921.

———. *L'Etre Subconscient.* Paris: Editions Pygmalion, 1899.

———. *From the Unconscious to the Conscious.* London: William Collins, 1920.

———. *Materialisation and Clairvoyance.* London, 1927.

———. "Une sensationelle expérience de M. Stephan Ossowiecki au Congrès de Varsovie." *Revue Métapsychique* (September-October 1923).

Geller, Uri. *My Story.* New York: Praeger, 1975.

Geller, Uri, and Guy Lyon Playfair. *The Geller Effect.* London: Jonathan Cape, 1986.

Gems and Stones: Based on the Edgar Cayce Readings. Virginia Beach, Va.: Association for Research and Enlightenment, 1960.

General Assembly of Spiritualists, State of New York. New York: Flying Saucer News, n.d.

General Church of the New Jerusalem. *The General Church of the New Jerusalem: A Handbook of General Information.* Bryn Athyn, Pa.: General Church Publication Committee, 1965.

———. *Liturgy and Hymnal.* Bryn Athyn, Pa.: General Church Publication Committee, 1966.

Gennep, Arnold Van. "De l'emploi du mot 'chamanisme.' " *Revue de l'Histoire des Religions,* Vol 47, no. 1 (24e année 1903): 51–57.

George, Llewellyn. *The A to Z Horoscope Delineator.* Portland, Ore.: Portland School of Astrology, 1910.

———. *Astrology: What It Is and What It Is Not.* Los Angeles: Llewellyn Publishing, 1931.

———. *How Planets Affect People.* Los Angeles: Llewellyn Publishing, 1921.

———. *The New A to Z Horoscope Maker and Delineator.* Rev. ed. St. Paul, Minn.: Llwellyn Publications, 1987.

———. *Practical Astrology for Everyone.* Portland, Ore.: Portland School of Astrology Bulletina Publishing, 1911.

———. *The Student's Chart Reader.* Portland, Ore.: Portland School of Astrology Bulletina Press, 1912.

Gerber, H. *Léo Taxil's Palladismus-Roman. Oder Die "Enthüllungen" Dr. Battaille's, Margiotta's and "Miss Vaughan's" Über Freimaureri kritisch beleuchtet.* Berlin, 1897.

Gerhardie, William A. *Memoirs of a Polyglot.* London: Macdonald, 1973.

———. *The Memoirs of Satan.* Garden City, N.Y.: Doubleday, Doran, 1933.

———. *Resurrection.* London: Macdonald, 1973.

Gerling, Helene. *Healthy Intuitive Development.* New York: Exposition Press, 1971.

Gerloff, Hans. *The Crisis in Parapsychology: Stagnation or Progress?* Tittmoning, Obb., Germany: W. Pustet, 1965.

———. *Das Medium Carlos Mirabelli: Eine kirtische Untersuchung* (The Medium Carlos Mirabelli: An Investigation.) N.p., 1960.

Gerloff, Hans. *Die Heilungen von Lourdes im Lichte der Parapsychologie* (The Healings at Lourdes in the Light of Parapsychology). Budingen-Geltenbach: Verlag Welt und Wissen, 1959.

———. *Materialisation: Die Phantome von Kopenhagen* (Materialization: The Phantoms of Copenhagen). N.p., 1956.

Germain, Saint, through Guy W. Ballard. *The "I AM" Discourses.* Chicago: Saint Germain Press, 1935.

Germain, Walter. *The Magic Power of Your Mind.* New York: Hawthorn Books, 1956.

Gerson, Lloyd P. *Plotinus.* London: Routledge, 1994.

Gervaso, Roberto. *Cagliostro: A Biography.* London, 1974.

Gervis, Pearce. *Naked They Pray.* London: Cassell, 1956.

Gesell, Arnold. *Wolf-Child and Human Child.* London: Harper/Methuen, 1941.

Gestefeld, Ursula N. *The Builder and the Plan.* Chicago: Exodus Publishing, 1901.

———. *Jesuitism in Christian Science.* Chicago: The Author, 1888.

———. *The Science of the Christ.* Chicago: The Author, 1889.

———. *A Statement of Christian Science.* Chicago The Author, 1888.

Gettings, Fred. *Dictionary of Occult, Hermetic and Alchemical Sigils.* London: Routledge & Kegan Paul, 1981.

———. *The Book of Tarot.* London: Paul Hamlyn, 1973.

Ghadiali, Dinshah P. *Spectro-Chrome Metry Encyclopedia.* 3 vols. Malaga, N.J.: Spectro-Chrome Institute, 1933.

Ghalioungui, Paul. *The House of Life: Magic and Medical Sciences in Ancient Egypt.* Rev. ed., New York: Wittenborn, 1975.

Ghirardelli, Cornelio. *Cefalogia fisonomica divisa in dieci Doche, dove conforme a'documenti d'Aristotile, e d'altri filosofi naturali. . . .* Bologna, Italy, 1630.

Ghirardelli, Cornelio. *Compendio della cefalogia fisonomica; nella quale si contiene cento sonetti di diversi eccellenti posti sopra cento teste humane.* Bologna, Italy, 1673.

Gibbons, M. E., and A. O. Gibbons. *The Trianon Adventure.* London: Museum Press, 1958.

Gibbons, Walter. *The Tragedy of the Heavens.* N.p., 1930.

Gibier, Paul. *Le Spiritisme (Fakirisme occidental).* Paris: C. Doin, 1887.

———. *Physiologie transcendentale: Analyse des choses.* 1890. Translated as *Psychism: Analysis of Things Existing.* N.p., 1890.

Gibran, Kahlil. *A. E. Waite: Magician of Many Parts.* Wellingborough, England: Aquarian Press, 1987.

———. *Beloved Prophet: The Love Letters of Kahhil Gibran and Mary Haskell and her Private Journal.* New York: Alfred A. Knopf, 1972.

———. *Earth Gods.* New York: Alfred A. Knopf, 1931.

———. *Gibran: A Self-Portrait.* New York: Citadel, 1959.

———. *The Golden Dawn Companion.* Wellingborough, England: Aquarian Press, 1986.

———. *The Golden Dawn: Twilight of the Magicians.* Wellingborough, England: Aquarian Press, 1983.

———. *Jesus the Son of Man.* New York: Alfred A. Knopf, 1956.

———. *The Prophet.* New York: Alfred A. Knopf, 1923.

———. *Sand and Foam.* New York: Alfred A. Knopf, 1926.

———. *Wisdom of Kahlil Gibran.* New York: Philosophical Library, 1966.

Gibran, Kahlil. [Edward Dunning]. *Selected Masonic Writings of A. E. Waite.* Wellingborough, England: Aquarian Press, 1988.

Gibran, Kahlil., ed. *The Sorcerer and His Apprentice: Hermetic Writings of S. L. McGregor Mathers & J. W. Brodie Innes.* Wellingborough, England: Aquarian Press, 1983.

Gibson, Edmond P. "The Ethel Thomas Case." *Tomorrow* (summer 1954).

Gibson, Ian. *The English Vice: Beating, Sex, and Shame in Victorian England and After.* London: Duckworth, 1978.

Gibson, John. *Monsters of the Sea: Legendary and Authentic.* London: T. Nelson & Sons, 1887.

Gibson, W. B., and L. K. Gibson. *The Complete Illustrated Book of Divination and Prophecy.* Garden City, N.Y.: Doubleday, 1973. Reprint, London: Souvenir Press, 1974.

Gibson, Walter B. *The Georgia Magnet.* St. Louis, 1922.

Gilber, Katherine S., with Joan K. Holt and Sara Hudson, eds. *Treasures of Tutankhamen.* Catalog of an Exhibition between 1976 and 1979. New York: Ballantine Books; New York: Metropolitan Museum of Art, 1976.

Gilberg, R. "How to Recognize a Shaman among Other Religious Specialists," In *Shamanism in Eurasia.* Edited by Mihály Hoppál. Göttingen, 1984.

Gilbert, Mostyn. "J. Fraser Nicol: An Appreciation of His Dedication to Psychical Research." *Journal of the Society for Psychical Research* 56, no. 818 (January 1990).

Gilbert, Robert A. *A. E. Waite: A Bibliography.* Wellingborough, England: Aquarian Press, 1983.

———. *A. E. Waite: Magician of Many Parts.* Wellingborough, Northamptonshire, England: Crucible, Thorsons, 1987.

———. *The Golden Dawn: Twilight of the Magicians.* Wellingborough, England: Aquarian Press, 1983.

———. *The Sorcerer and His Apprentice: Unknown Hermetic Writings of S. L. MacGregor Mathers and J. W. Brodie-Innes.* Wellingborough, England: Aquarian Press, 1983.

Gilbert, R. A., ed. *The Magical Mason: Forgotten Hermetic Writings of William Wynn Westcott.* Wellingborough, Northamptonshire, England: Aquarian Press, 1983.

Gilbert, Robert A., and Michael A. Cox, eds. *The Oxford Book of English Ghost Stories.* Oxford: Oxford University Press; New York: Oxford University Press, 1989.

Gilbert, Robert A., and W. N. Birks. *The Treasure of Montsegur.* Crucible, 1987.

Gill, Derek L. T. *Quest: The Life of Elisabeth Kübler-Ross.* New York: Harper & Row, 1980.

Gillespie, William H. "Extrasensory Elements in Dream Interpretation." *Psychoanalysis and the Occult.* Edited by George Devereaux. New York: International Universities Press, 1953.

Ginsburg, Christian D. *The Essenes: Their History and Doctrines.* London: Routledge and Kegan Paul, 1863.

———. *The Kabbalah* (with *The Essenes*). London: Routledge, 1863. Reprint, New York: Samuel Weiser, 1970.

Giraldus Cambrensis. *The Historical Works of Giraldus Cambrensis, Containing the Topography of Ireland, and The History of the Conquest of Ireland.* Translated by R. C. Hoare. London: Bohn's Antiquarian Library, 1847.

Gissurarson, Loftur R., and Erlendur Haraldsson. "The Icelandic Physical Medium Indridi Indridason." *Proceedings of the Society for Psychical Research* 57, 214 (January 1989).

Gittelson, Bernard. *Bio-Rhythms: A Personal Science.* New York: Warner Books, 1977.

Glanvill, Joseph. *Sadicismus Triumphatus.* London: Printed for J. Collins and S. Lownds, 1681.

Glasenapp, Helmuth von. *The Doctrine of Kerman in Jain Philosophy.* Bombay: Bai Vojibai Jivanial Panalal Charity Fund, 1942.

Glaskin, G. M. *A Door to Eternity: Proving the Christos Experience.* London: Wildwood House, 1979.

———. *Windows of the Mind; Discovering Your Past and Future Lives Through Massage and Mental Exercise.* New York: Delacorte Press, New York, 1974. Reprinted as *Windows of the Mind: The Christos Experiment.* London: Wildwood House, 1974.

———. *Worlds Within: Probing The Christos Experience.* London: Wildwood House, 1976. Reprint, London: Arrow, 1978.

Gleadow, Rupert. *Magic and Divination.* London: Ryerson Press, 1941. Reprint, Wakefield, England: EP Publishing, 1976

Glendinning, Andrew. *The Veil Lifted: Modern Developments of Spirit Photography.* London: Whittaker, 1894.

Glenn, Jerome Clayton. *Linking the Future: Findhorn, Auroville, Arcosanti.* Cambridge, Mass.: Center on Technology and Society, 1979.

Glut, Donald F. *The Dracula Book.* Metuchen, N.J.: Scarecrow Press, 1975.

———. *The Frankenstein Catalog.* Jefferson, N.C.: McFarland, 1984.

Goblet D'Alviella, E. F. *Lectures on the Origin and Growth of the Conception of God.* London, 1892. Reprint, New York: AMS Press, 1982.

Globus, Gordon, Ken Wilber, Fritjof Capra, Charles D. Laughlin, Jr., John McManus; Jon Shearer, and Kenneth Ring. "Science, Technology, and Transcendence." In *Paths Beyond Ego: The Transpersonal Vision.* Los Angeles: Perigee Books/Jeremy P. Tarcher, Inc., 1993.

Godfrey, Nathaniel S. *Table Turning the Devil's Modern Masterpiece; Being the Result of a Course of Experiments.* UK: Thames Ditton, 1853.

Godwin, John. *Occult America.* Garden City, N.Y.: Doubleday, 1972.

Godwin, Joscelyn, Christian Chanel, and John P. Deveney. *The Hermetic Brotherhood of Luxor.* New York: Samuel Weiser Inc., 1995.

Godwin, Joscelyn. *Robert Fludd: Hermetic Philosopher and Surveyor of Two Worlds.* Boulder, Colo.: Shambhala, 1979.

Goethe, Johann Wolfgang von. *The Autobiography of Johann Wolfgang von Goethe.* 2 vols. Chicago: University of Chicago Press, 1975.

Gold, Gari. *Crystal Energy.* Chicago: Contemporary Books, 1987.

Gol'dberg, I. M. "On Whether Tactile Sensitivity Can Be Improved by Exercise." *Soviet Psychology and Psychiatry* 2, no. 1 (1963).

Goldenstubbe, Baron Ludwig von, and J. von Guldenstubbe. *La Morale Universelle.* 1863.

Goldfarb, Russell M., and Clare R. Goldfarb. *Spiritualism and Nineteenth-Century Letters.* New Brunswick, N.J.: Associated University Presses, 1978.

Goldney, Mrs. A. P., Mrs. H. Richard, and others. "Photographs of Jumping Model Imitating Levitation." *Proceedings of the Society for Psychic Research* 45, no. 158.

Goldsmith, Margaret L. *Franz Anton Mesmer: The History of an Idea.* Garden City, N.Y.: Doubleday, 1934. Reprint, London: Arthur Barker, 1934.

Goldston, Will. *Secrets of Famous Illusionists.* London: Long, 1933.

Golson, K. K. *Presidents Are People.* New York: Carlton Press, 1964.

Golther, W. *Religion und Mythus der Germanen.* Leipzig, 1909.

Gomes, Michael. *The Dawning of the Theosophical Movement.* Wheaton, Ill.: Theosophical Publishing House, 1987.

———. *Theosophy in the Nineteenth Century: An Annotated Bibliography.* New York: Garland Publishing, 1994.

Gomme, G. L. *Ethnology in Folklore.* New York: D. Appleton, 1892.

Gonzalez, Conchita, and Harry Daley. *Miracle at Garabandal: The Story of Mysterious Apparitions in Spain and a Message for the Whole World.* Garden City, N.Y.: Doubleday, 1983.

Gonzalez-Quevado, Oscar. *A Face Oculta da Mente.* São Paulo, Brazil: Edicos Loyola, 1967.

———. *As Forcas Fisicas da Mente.* São Paulo, Brazil: Edicos Loyola, 1968.

Gonzàlez-Wippler, Migene. *The Complete Book of Spells, Ceremonies, and Magic.* St. Paul, Minn.: Llewellyn Publications, 1978.

Goodavage, Joseph F. *Astrology: The Space Age Science.* Englewood Cliffs, N.J.: Prentice-Hall, 1965. Reprint, New York: New American Library, 1966.

———. *The Comet Kohoutek.* New York: Pinnacle Books, 1974.

———. *Our Threatened Planet.* New York: Simon and Schuster, 1978.

———. *Seven by Seven.* New York: New American Library, 1978.

———. *Storm on the Sun.* New York: New American Library, 1979.

———. *Write Your Own Horoscope.* New York: New American Library, 1969.

Goodman, Felicitas D. *Ecstasy, Ritual, and Alternate Reality. Religion in a Pluralistic World.* Bloomington: Indiana University Press, 1988.

———. *Speaking in Tongues: A Cross-Cultural Survey of Glossolalia.* Chicago: University of Chicago Press, 1972.

———. *Where the Spirits Ride the Wind: Trance Journeys and Other Ecstatic Experiences.* Bloomington: Indiana University Press, 1990.

Goodman, Felicitas D., Jeannette H. Henney, and Esther Pressel. *Trance, Healing, and Hallucination: Three Field Studies in Religious Experience.* New York: John Wiley & Sons, 1974.

Goodman, Jeffrey. *Psychic Archeology: Time Machine to the Past.* New York: Berkley Publishing, 1977.

Goodman, Jordan, Paul Lovejoy, and Andrew Sherratt, eds. *Consuming Habits: Drugs in History and Anthropology.* London: Routledge, 1995.

Goodman, Linda. *Linda Goodman's Love Signs: A New Approach to the Human Heart.* New York: Harper, 1978.

———. *Sun Signs.* New York: Taplinger, 1968. Reprinted as *Linda Goodman's Sun Signs.* New York: Bantam Books, 1971.

———. *Venus Trines at Midnight.* New York: Taplinger, 1970.

Goodrich-Freer, Ada. *Arabs in Tent and Town.* London: Seeley, Service, & Co. Int., 1924.

———. *Essays in Psychical Research.* 2nd ed., London: G. Redway, 1899.

———. *Inner Jerusalem.* New York: E. P. Dutton, 1904.

———. *Outer Isles.* London: A. Constable, 1902.

Goodrich-Freer, Ada, and John, Marquess of Bute. *The Alleged Haunting of B. House.* London: G. Redway, 1899.

Goodrick-Clarke, Nicholas. *The Occult Roots of Nazism.* New York: New York University Press, 1992.

Goodwin, Jean, Sally Hill, and Reina Attias. "Historical and Folk Techniques of Exorcism: Applications to the Treatment of Dissociative Disorders," *Dissociation: Progress in the Dissociative Disorders* 3, no. 2 (June 1990): 94–101.

Gopalacharlu, S. E. *An Introduction to the Mantra Sastra.* Adyar, Madras, India: Theosophical Publishing House, 1934.

Gopi Krishna, Pandit. *The Biological Basis of Religion and Genius.* New York: Harper & Row, 1972.

Gopi Krishna. *Biblical Prophecy for the 20th Century.* Toronto: Kundalini Research Institute of Canada, 1979.

———. *Kundalini for the New Age: Selected Writings.* Edited by Gene Kieffer. New York: Bantam, 1988.

———. *Kundalini: The Evolutionary Energy in Man.* New Dehli: Ramadhar and Hopman, 1967. Reprint, Boulder, Colo.: Shambala, 1970.

———. *Living with Kundalini: The Autobiography of Gopi Krishna.* Boston: Shambhala, 1993.

———. *The Secret of Yoga.* New York: Harper & Row, 1972.

———. *The Shape of Events to Come.* New Delhi: Kundalini Research and Publication Trust, 1979.

Gordon, James S. *The Golden Guru.* Lexington, Mass.: Stephen Greene Press, 1986.

Gordon, Mrs. M. M. *The Home Life of Sir David Brewster.* Edinburgh, Scotland, 1869, 1870.

Goswami, Satsvarupa dasa. *Srila Prabhupada-lilamrta.* 6 vols. Los Angeles: Bhaktivedanta Book Trust, 1980–83.

Gottshalk, Stephen. *The Emergence of Christian Science in American Religious Life.* Berkeley: University of California Press, 1973.

Gould, Charles. *Mythical Monsters.* London, 1886. Reprint, Detroit: Singing Tree Press, 1969.

Gould, R. F. *History of Freemasonry.* 5 vols. Rev. ed. London: Caxton, 1931.

Gould, Rupert T. *The Case for the Sea-Serpent.* London: Philip Allan, 1930. Reprint, Detroit: Singing Tree Press, 1969.

———. *The Loch Ness Monster.* London, 1934. Reprint, New Hyde Park, N.Y.: University Books, 1969.

———. *The Loch Ness Monster and Others.* London: Geoffrey Bles; New York: Citadel Press, 1976.

———. *Oddities: A Book of Unexplained Facts.* London, 1928. Reprint, New Hyde Park, N.Y.: University Books, 1965

———. *The Stargazer Talks.* London, 1944. Reprinted as *More Oddities and Enigmas.* New Hyde Park, N.Y.: University Books, 1973.

The Government UFO Collection: A Collection of UFO Documents from the Government of the USA and Canada. Mount Rainier, Md.: Fund for UFO Research, 1981–85.

Grad, Bernard. "Healing by the Laying on of Hands: Review of Experiments and Implications." *Pastoral Psychology* 21 (September 1970): 206.

———. "Paranormal Healing and Life Energy." *American Society for Psychical Research Newsletter* 7 (1981).

Grad, Bernard. "Some Biological Effects of the 'Laying on of Hands': A Review of Experiments with Animals and Plants." *Journal* of the American Society for Psychical Research 59 (1965).

———. "A Telekinetic Effect on Plant Growth." *International Journal of Parapsychology* 3 (1961); 5 (1963).

Grad, Bernard, Remi J. Cadoret, and G. I. Paul. "The Influence of an Unorthodox Method of Treatment on Wound Healing in Mice." *International Journal of Parapsychology* 3, no. 2 (1961).

Grady, Brian and Kate Miriam Loewenthal. "Features Associated with Speaking in Tongues (Glossolalia)," *British Journal of Medical Psychology* 70, no. 2 (June 1997): 185–191. Graef, Hilda. *The Case of Thé rèse Neumann.* Westminister, Md.: Newman Press, 1951.

Grand Orient [A. E. Waite]. *Complete Manual of Occult Divination.* 2 vols. Reprint, New Hyde Park, N.Y.: University Books, 1972.

Grant, Douglas. *The Cock Lane Ghost.* New York: Macmillan; St. Martin's Press, 1965.

Grant, Ernest. *Astrological America.* Washington, D.C.: National Astrological Library, 1949.

———. *Ephemeris for the Year 1776.* Washington, D.C.: National Astrological Library, 1944.

———. *Tables of Diurnal Planetary Motion.* Washington, D.C.: National Astrological Library, 1948.

Grant, Ernest, and Catherine T. Grant. *Grant Textbook Series.* 4 vols. Washington, D.C.: National Astrological Library, n.d.

Grant, Joan. *Eyes of Horus.* London: Methuen, 1942. New York: Ayer Publishing Co. Inc., 1980.

———. *Far Memory.* Reprinted as *Time Out of Mind, A Lot to Remember.* New York: Ayer Publishing Co. Inc., 1980.

———. *Life as Carola.* London: Methuen & Co. Ltd., 1939; New York & London: Harper & Brothers, 1940; New York: Ayer Publishing Co. Inc., 1980.

———. *Lord of the Horizon.* London: Methuen & Co. Ltd., 1943.

———. *Return to Elysium.* New York: Ayer Publishing Co. Inc., 1980.

———. *So Moses Was Born.* London: Methuen, 1952; New York: Ayer Publishing Co. Inc., 1980.

———. *Winged Pharaoh.* New York: Harper & Brothers, 1938.

Grant, Kenneth. *Aleister Crowley and the Hidden God.* London: Muller, 1973.

———. *Cults of the Shadow.* London: Frederick Muller, 1975. Reprint, New York: Samuel Weiser, 1976.

———. *Images of Austin Osman Spare.* London: Frederick Muller, 1975.

———. *The Magical Revival.* New York: Samuel Weiser, 1972.

———. *Nightside of Eden.* London: Frederick Muller, 1977.

———. *Outside the Circles of Time.* London: Frederick Muller, 1980.

Gratton-Guinness, Ivor. *Psychical Research: A Guide to Its History, Principles & Practices.* London: Aquarian Press, 1982.

Graves, Kersey. *The World's Sixteen Crucified Saviors.* Boston, Mass., 1875. Reprint, New Hyde Park, N.Y.: University Books, 1971.

Graves, Robert. *The White Goddess.* London: Faber & Faber, 1948.

Graves, Robert, and Raphael Patai. *Hebrew Myths: The Book of Genesis.* Garden City, N.Y.: Doubleday, 1964.

Graves, Samuel R. [Osirus]. *Potions and Spells of Witchcraft.* San Francisco: JBT Marketing, 1970.

Graves, Tom. *Elements of Pendulum Dowsing.* UK: Element Books, Inc., 1997.

Gray, Isa. *From Materialisation to Healing.* London: Regency Press, 1973.

Gray, Ronald D. *Goethe, the Alchemist: A Study of Alchemical Symbolism in Goethe's Literary & Scientific Works.* Cambridge, Mass.: Cambridge University Press, 1952. Reprint, New York: AMS Press, 1979.

Gray, William G. *Qabalistic Concepts.* New York: Samuel Weiser Inc., 1997.

Great White Brotherhood. *The Books of Azrael: Teachings.* Santa Barbara, Calif.: J. F. Rowney Press, n.d.

The Greater Key of Solomon. Translated by S. L. MacGregor Mathers. London: George Redway, 1888. Reprint, Chicago: De Laurence, 1914. Reprint, London: Routledge & Kegan Paul, 1972.

Greatrakes, Valintine. *A Brief Account of Mr. V. Greatrakes and Divers of the Strange Cures by Him Performed, Written by Himself.* London, 1666.

———. *Val. Greatrakes, Esq., of Waterford, in the Kingdom of Ireland, Famous for Curing Several Diseases and Distempers by the Stroak of His Hand Only.* London: The Author, 1660.

Greed, John A. *Glastonbury Tales.* Bristol, England: St. Trillo Publications, 1975.

Green, Andrew M. *Ghost Hunting: A Practical Guide.* London: Garnstone Press, 1973.

Green, Celia E. *The Decline and Fall of Science.* London: Hamilton, 1976.

———. *The Human Evasion.* London: Hamilton, 1969.

Green, Celia E. *Lucid Dreams.* London: Hamish Hamilton; Oxford: Institute of Psychophysical Research, 1968.

———. *Out-of-the-Body Experiences.* Oxford: Institute of Psychophysical Research, 1968. Reprint, New York: Ballantine Books, 1973.

———. "Report on the Spontaneous Cases Enquiry." *Proceedings of the Society for Psychical Research* 53, no. 191 (November 1960).

Green, Celia, and Charles McGreery. *Apparitions.* London: Hamish Hamilton; New York: State Mutual Book, 1977.

Green, Edward C. "Mystical Black Power: The Calling to Diviner-Mediumship in Southern Africa." In *Women as Healers: Cross-Cultural Perspectives.* New Brunswick, N.J.: Rutgers University Press, 1989.

Green, Elmer. "Biofeedback for Mind-Body Self-Regulation: Healing and Creativity." In *The Varieties of Healing Experience: Exploring Psychic Phenomena and Healing.* Los Altos, Calif.: Academy of Parapsychology and Medicine, 1971.

———. "How to Make Use of the Field of Mind Theory." In *The Dimensions of Healing: A Symposium.* Los Altos, Calif.: Academy of Parapsychology and Medicine, 1972.

Green, Gabriel, and Warren Smith. *Let's Face the Facts about Flying Saucers.* New York: Popular Library, 1967.

Green, Landis Knight. *The Astrologer's Manual: Modern Insights into an Ancient Art.* Sebastopol, Calif.: CRCS Publications, 1975.

Green, Marian, ed. *Quest List of Esoteric Sources.* London: Quest, 1984.

Green, Miranda J. *Dictionary of Celtic Myth and Legend.* London: Thames and Hudson, 1992.

Green, Peter. *Heal, My Son! The Amazing Story of John Cain.* London: Van Duren, 1977.

Greenbank, Richard K. "Allegedly Prophetic Dreams in Psychotherapeutic Treatment." *International Journal of Parapsychology* (Summer 1960).

———. "Communication of Suicidal Thoughts." *Canadian Psychiatric Association Journal* (July 1957).

———. "My Wolf." *Journal of Abnormal and Social Psychology* (May 1957).

———. "Unexplained Mental Phenomena Regarding Suicide." *Journal of Nervous and Mental Diseases* (January 1957).

Greenberg, David, Eliezer Witztum, and Jacob T. Buchbinder. "Mysticism and Psychosis: The Fate of Ben Zoma," *British Journal of Medical Psychology* 65, no. 3 (September 1992): 223–235.

Greene, Barbara, and W. Gollancz. *God of a Hundred Names.* London: Gollancz, 1962.

Greenfield, Robert. *The Spiritual Supermarket.* New York: Saturday Review Press/E. P. Dutton, 1975.

Greenfield, Sidney M. "Legacies from the Past and Transitions to a "Healed" Future in Brazilian Spiritist Therapy," *Anthropologica* 35, no. 1 (1993): 23–38.

Greenhouse, Herbert B. *Astral Journey: Evidence for Out-of-the-Body Experiences from Socrates to the ESP Laboratory.* Garden City, N.Y.: Doubleday, 1975.

Greenhouse, Herbert B. *Premonitions: A Leap Into the Future.* London: Turnstone Press, 1972. Reprint, London: Pan, 1975.

Greenwalt, Emmett A. *California Utopia: Point Loma, 1897–1942.* San Diego, Calif., 1978.

Greenwood, Joseph A. "Analysis of a Large Chance Control Series of ESP Data." *Journal of Parapsychology* 2 (1938).

———. "A Co-Variation Statistic." *Journal of Parapsychology* 3 (1939).

———. "An Empirical Investigation of Some Sampling Problems." *Journal of Parapsychology* 2 (1938).

———. "Mathematical Techniques Used in ESP Research." *Journal of Parapsychology* 1 (1937).

———. "A Reply to Dr. Feller's Critique." *Journal of Parapsychology* 4 (1940).

———. "Some Mathematical Problems for Future Consideration Suggested by ESP Research." *Journal of Parapsychology* 3 (1939).

———. "Variance of the ESP Call Series." *Journal of Parapsychology* 2 (1938).

Greenwood, Joseph A., and C. E. Stuart. "Review of Criticisms of the Mathematical Evaluation of ESP Data." *Journal of Parapsychology* 1 (1937).

Gregory, Anita. "London Experiments with Matthew Manning." *Proceedings of the Society for Psychical Research* 56 (1982).

———. "Psychical Research as a Social Activity." *Journal of the Society for Psychical Research* 51 (1981).

———. *The Strange Case of Rudi Schneider.* Metuchen, N.J.: Scarecrow Press, 1985.

Gregory, Lady. *Visions and Beliefs in the West of Ireland.* 2 vols. New York: George Putnam's Sons, 1920. Reprint, UK: Colin Smythe, 1970.

Gregory, William. *Animal Magnetism: Mesmerism and its Phenomena.* 2d rev. ed. London: Nichols, 1877. London, 1884, 1909. Reprint, New Stratford, N.H.: Ayer Co. Publishing Inc., 1975.

Greville, T. N. E. "Exact Probabilities for the Matching Hypothesis." *Journal of Parapsychology* 2 (1938).

———. "A Method of Evaluating the Reinforcement Effect." *Journal of Parapsychology* 15 (1951).

———. "On Multiple Matching with One Variable Deck." *Annals of Mathematical Statistics* 15 (1944): 432–34.

———. "A Reappraisal of the Mathematical Evaluation of the Reinforcement Effect." *Journal of Parapsychology* 18 (1954).

———. "A Summary of Mathematical Advances Bearing on ESP." *Journal of Parapsychology* 3 (1939).

———.. "A Survey and Appraisal of the Statistical Methods Used in Parapsychological Research." *Journal of Parapsychology* 13 (1949).

Grey, E. Howard. *Visions, Previsions and Miracles in Modern Times.* London: L. N. Fowler, 1915.

Gribbin, John R. *Beyond the Jupiter Effect.* London: MacDonald, 1983.

———. *The Jupiter Effect.* New York: Walker, 1974. Revised as *The Jupiter Effect Reconsidered.* New York: Vintage, 1982.

Gribbin, John R., and Stephen H. Plageman. *The Jupiter Effect.* New York: Vintage Books, 1975.

Grierson, Francis [Jesse Shepard]. *Abraham Lincoln: The Practical Mystic.* New York: John Lane, 1918.

———. *The Celtic Temperament and Other Essays.* London: John Lane, 1913.

———. *Modern Mysticism and Other Essays.* London: G. Allen, 1899.

Griffin, David Ray. *Parapsychology, Philosophy, and Spirituality: A Postmodern Exploration.* Albany: State University of New York Press, 1997.

Griffin, William, ed. *Endtime: The Doomsday Catalog.* New York: Macmillan, 1979.

Grillet, Claudius. *Victor Hugo Spirite.* Paris, 1929.

Grim, John A. *The Shaman: Patterns of Siberian and Ojibway Healing.* Norman: University of Oklahoma Press, 1983.

Grim, William E. *The Faust Legend in Music and Literature.* Lewiston, N.Y.: Edwin Mellen Press, 1988.

Grimassi, Raven. *The Wiccan Mysteries.* St. Paul, Minn.: Llewellyn Publications, 1999.

———. *Ways of the Strega–Italian Witchcraft.* St. Paul, Minn.: Llewellyn Publications, 1999.

Grimm, Jacob. *Teutonic Mythology.* 4 vols. London: G. Bell, 1880–1919.

The Grimoire of Raphael. Edited by Fra. Zarathustra [Nelson White]. Pasadena, Calif.: The Technology Group, 1987.

Gross, Don H. *The Case for Spiritual Healing.* New York: T. Nelson, 1958.

———. "Kathryn Kuhlman: Another Point of View." *The Pittsburgher* (October–December 1954).

———. "Prayer That Heals." *Religion in Life* (Spring 1955).

———. "Spiritual Healing and the Archbishop's Commission." *International Journal of Parapsychology* (Autumn 1959).

Gross, Loren E. *Charles Fort, the Fortean Society, and Unidentified Flying Objects.* Fremont, Calif.: The Author, 1976.

Grossi, Ralph. *Reliving Reincarnation Through Hypnosis.* Smithtown, N.Y.: Exposition Press, 1975.

Grosso, Michael. *Frontiers of the Soul: Exploring Psychic Evolution.* Wheaton, Ill.: Quest Books, 1992.

———. "Padre Pio and the Paranormal." *Christian Parapsychologist* 4, no. 7 (1982).

Grubb, W. Barbrook. *An Unknown People in an Unknown Land.* London, 1911.

Gruber, Karl. *Okkultismus und Biologie.* Munich, 1930.

———. *Parapsychologische Erkenntnisse.* Munich, 1925.

Gruess, Edmond G. *The Ouija Board: Doorway to the Occult.* Chicago: Moody Press, 1975.

Grüber, Karl. *Parapsychologische Erkenntnisse.* München: Drei Masken Verlag, 1925.

Grumbine, J. C. F. *Clairaudience.* Boston: Order of the White Rose, 1911.

———. *Melchizedek; or, The Secret Doctrine of the Bible.* Boston: Order of the White Rose, 1919.

Grünewald, Fritz. *Physikalisch-Mediumis-tische Untersuchungen.* N.p., 1920.

Grupta, Yogi. *Yoga and Long Life.* New York: Dodd, Mead and Co., 1958.

Guaita, Stanislas de. *Essais des sciences maudites.* Paris: Carré, 1885.

———. *La Serpent de la genese.* 2 Vols. Paris: Chamuel, 1891, 1897.

Guest, John S. *Survival Among the Kurds: A History of the Yezidis.* London: Kegan Paul International, 1993.

———. *The Yezidis.* London: KPI, 1987.

Guest, Lady Charlotte, trans. *The Mabinogion: From the Llyfr Coch o Hergest.* 3 vols. London, 1948.

Guiley, Rosemary Ellen. *The Encyclopedia of Witches and Witchcraft.* New York: Facts on File, 1989. 2nd ed., New York: Facts on File, 1999.

Guirdham, Arthur. *The Cathars & Reincarnation.* London: Neville Spearman, 1960. Reprint, London, 1970. Reprint, Theosophical Publishing House, 1978. Reprint, Wellingborough, England: Turnstone Press, 1982.

———. *Christ and Freud.* London: Allen & Unwin, 1959.

———. *Cosmic Factors in Disease.* London: Duckworth, 1963.

———. *A Foot in Both Worlds: A Doctor's Autobiography of Psychic Experience.* [St. Helier] Jersey, Spearman, 1973.

———. *The Great Heresy.* St. Helier: Neville Spearman, 1977.

———. *Obsession: Psychic Forces and Evil in the Causation of Disease.* London: Neville Spearman, 1972.

Gulat-Wellenburg, W. von et al. *Der Physikalische Mediumismus.* Berlin: Ullstein, 1925.

Guldenstubbe, Baron L. de. *Pneumatologie positive et expérimentale; La réalité des Espirits et le phenom ene merveilleux de leur écriture directe demontrés.* Paris, 1857.

———. *Pensés d'Outre-Tombe.* 1858.

Guppy, Samuel. *Mary Jane; or Spiritualism chemically explained, with Spirit Drawings.* London, 1863.

Gurdjieff, G. I. *All and Everything.* New York: Harcourt, Brace, 1950. Reprint, New York: E. P. Dutton, 1963.

———. *Meetings With Remarkable Men.* New York: E. P. Dutton, 1964.

———. *Views From the Real World: Early Talks in Moscow, Essentuku, Tiflis, Berlin, London, Paris, New York, Chicago as Recollected by His Pupils.* New York: Triangle Editions; London: Routledge & Kegan Paul, 1973.

Gurney, Edmund. "Account of Some Experiments in Mesmerism." *Proceedings of the Society for Psychical Research* 2, no. 6 (1884).

———. "Hallucinations." *Proceedings of the Society for Psychical Research* 3, no. 8 (1885).

———. "Hypnotism and Telepathy." *Proceedings of the Society for Psychical Research* 5, no. 12 (1888–89).

———. "Peculiarities of Certain Post-Hypnotic States." *Proceedings of the Society for Psychical Research* 4, no. 11 (1886–87).

———. *The Power of Sound.* London: Smith, Elder, 1880. Reprint, New York: Basic Books, 1966.

———. "The Problems of Hypnotism." *Proceedings of the Society for Psychical Research* 2, no. 7 (1884).

———. "Recent Experiments in Hypnotism." *Proceedings of the Society for Psychical Research* 5, no. 12 (1888–89).

———. "Some Higher Aspects of Mesmerism." *Proceedings of the Society for Psychical Research* 3, no. 10 (1885).

———. "Stages of Hypnotic Memory." *Proceedings of the Society for Psychical Research* 4, no. 11 (1886–87).

———. "The Stages of Hypnotism." *Proceedings of the Society for Psychical Research* 2 (1884).

———. *Tertium Quid: Chapters on Various Disputed Questions.* London, K. Paul, Trench & Co., 1887.

Gurney, Edmund, F. W. H. Myers, and Frank Podmore. *Phantasms of the Living.* 2 vols. London, 1886. Rev. ed. New Hyde Park, N.Y.: University Books, 1962. Reprint, Delmar, N.Y.: Scholars Facsimiles and Reprints, 1970.

Gurudas. *Flower Essences.* Albuquerque, N.Mex.: Brotherhood of Life, 1983.

Gurudas. *Gem Elixirs and Vibrational Healing.* 2 vols. Boulder, Colo.: Cassandra Press, 1985–86.

Guyon, Jeanne Marie. *Autobiography of Madame Guyon.* St. Louis, Mo.: B. Herder, 1897.

A Gypsy Queen. *Zingara Fortune Teller.* Philadelphia: David McKay, 1901.

Haas, George C. O. *The Key to Enrichment of Life.* N.p., 1949.

———. "The New Orientation of Science." *IS* 23 (1960).

Hack, Gwendolyn Kelley. *Modern Psychic Mysteries at Millesimo Castle Italy.* London: Rider, 1929.

———. *Venetian Voices.* London, 1937.

Hackethorn, Charles William. *The Secret Societies of All Ages and Countries.* 2 vols. Reprint, New Hyde Park, N.Y.: University Books, 1965.

———. *The Secret Societies of All Ages and Countries.* London: Redway, 1897. Reprint, New Hyde Park, N.Y.: University Books, 1966.

Hackett, Rosalind I. J. "New Age Trends in Nigeria: Ancestral and or Alien Religion?" In *Perspectives on the New Age,* edited by James R. Lewis and J. Gordon Melton. Albany: State University of New York Press, 1992.

———. *Religion in Calabar: The Religious Life and History of a Nigerian Town.* Berlin: Mouton de Gruyter, 1989.

Hackforth, R., trans. *Plato's Phaedo.* Cambridge, Mass.: Cambridge University Press, 1955.

Haddock, Joseph W. *Somnolism and Psycheism; Or, The Science of the Soul and the Phenomena of Nervation as Revealed by Vital Magnetism or Mesmerism.* London, 1851. Reprint, New York: Ayer Publishing Co. Inc., 1975.

Hadot, Pierre. *Plotinus; or, The Simplicity of Vision.* Chicago: University of Chicago Press, 1993.

Hagio, Shigeki. "An Experiment to Explore Psi in the Human Associative Process." In *Research in Parapsychology, 1993: Abstracts and Papers from the Thirty-sixth Annual Convention of the Parapsychological Association, 1993.* Lanham, Md.: Scarecrow Press, Inc., 1998.

Haines, Frederick H. *The Book of Spiritual Wisdom.* N.p., 1928.

———. *A Lamp to the Feet.* N.p., 1928.

———. *Locusts and Wild Honey.* N.p., 1928.

———. *Thus Saith Celphra.* N.p., 1928.

———. *A Voice from Heaven.* Watford, England: Pure Thought Press, [1932].

Haining, Peter. *Ghosts: The Illustrated History.* London: Sidgwick & Jackson, 1974. Reprint, New York: Macmillan, 1975.

———. *The Legend and Bizarre Crimes of Springheeled Jack.* London: Frederick Muller, 1977.

———. *The Leprechaun's Kingdom.* London: Souvenir Press, 1979.

———. *The Man Who Was Frankenstein.* London: Frederick Muller, 1979.

Hale, Anthony S. and Narsimha R. Pinninti. "Exorcism-Resistant Ghost Possession Treated with Clopenthixol. *British Journal of Psychiatry* 165, no. 3 (September 1994): 386–388.

Halevi, Z'ev Ben Shimon. *Adam and the Kabbalistic Tree.* London: Rider, 1974.

———. *An Introduction to the Cabala—Tree of Life.* New York: Samuel Weiser, 1972. New York: Samuel Weiser Inc., 1991.

———. *A Kabbalistic Universe.* New York: Samuel Weiser Inc., 1999.

Halifax, Joan. *Shaman: The Wounded Healer.* New York: Thames and Hudson, 1982.

———. *Shamanic Voices: A Survey of Visionary Narratives.* New York: E. P. Dutton, 1979.

Hall, Elizabeth. *Possible Impossibilities: A Look at Parapsychology.* Boston: Houghton Mifflin, 1977.

Hall, James. *Sangoma: My Odyssey into the Spirit World of Africa.* New York: Tarcher/Putnam, 1994.

Hall, James A. *Hypnosis: A Jungian Perspective.* New York: Guilford Press, 1989.

———. "The Works of J. B. Rhine: Implications for Religion." *Journal of Parapsychology* (1981).

Hall, James A., and H. B. Crasilneck. "Physiological Changes Associated with Hypnosis." *International Journal of Clinical and Experimental Hypnosis* 7, no. 1 (January 1959).

Hall, John R. *Gone from the Promised Land: Jonestown in American Cultural History.* New Brunswick, N.J.: Transaction, 1987.

Hall, Manly P. *An Encyclopedic Outline of Masonic, Hermetic, Qabbalistic and Rosicrucian Symbolical Philosophy.* Los Angeles: Philosophical Research Society, 1928.

———. *Astrological Keywords.* 1958. Reprint, Savage, Md.: Littlefield Adams Quality Paperbacks, 1975.

———. *Lost Keys of Freemasonry.* Richmond, Va.: Macoy Publishing, 1923.

———. *Growing Up with Grandmother.* Los Angeles: Philosophical Research Society, 1985.

———. *The Little World of PRS.* Los Angeles: Philosophical Research Society, 1982.

———. *Reincarnation: The Cycle of Necessity.* Los Angeles: Philosophical Research Society, 1942.

———. *The Search for Harry Price.* Dallas: Southwest Book Services, 1978.

———. *Secret Teachings of All Ages.* Hollywood, Calif.: Philosophical Research Society, 1962. Rev. ed. 1977.

———. *Self-Unfoldment by Disciplines of Realization.* Los Angeles: Philosophical Research Society, 1945.

———. *The Spiritualists.* 1962. Reprinted as *The Medium and the Scientist.* Buffalo, N.Y.: Prometheus Books, 1984.

———. *The Strange Case of Edmund Gurney.* London: Duckworth, 1964.

———. *Visions and Metaphysical Experiences.* Los Angeles: Philosophical Research Society, n.d.

Hall, Manly Palmer, ed. "The Harrison Case." *Proceedings of the American Society for Psychical Research* 13 (1919).

Hall, Prescott F. "Experiments with Mrs. Caton." *Proceedings of the American Society for Psychical Research* 8 (1914).

Hall, Radcliffe, and (Una) Lady Troubridge. "On a series of Sittings with Mrs. Osborne Leonard." *Proceedings of the Society for Psychic Research* 30.

Hall, Richard. "Major Donald E. Keyhoe: An Appreciation." *MUFON UFO Journal* (February 1989): 12–13.

———. *The UFO Evidence.* Washington, D.C.: National Investigations Committee on Aerial Phenomena, 1964.

Hall, Trevor. *Florence Cook & William Crookes: A Footnote to an Enquiry.* London: Tomorrow Publications, 1963.

———. *The Enigma of Daniel Home.* Buffalo, N.Y.: Prometheus Books, 1984.

———. *Florence Cook & William Crookes: A Footnote to an Enquiry.* London: Tomorrow Publications Ltd., 1963.

———. *New Light on Old Ghosts.* London: G. Duckworth, 1965.

———. *The Spiritualist: The Story of Florence Cook and William Crookes.* London: Duckworth, 1962. New York: Helix Press, 1963. Reprinted as *The Medium and the Scientist: The Story of Florence Cook and William Crookes.* Buffalo, N.Y.: Prometheus Books, 1984.

———. *The Strange Case of Edmund Gurney.* London: Duckworth, 1964.

Hall, Trevor H., and E. J. Dingwall. *Four Modern Ghosts.* London: Duckworth, 1958.

Hall, Trevor H., E. J. Dingwall, and K. M. Goldney. *The Haunting of Borley Rectory.* London: Duckworth, 1956.

Hall, Trevor H., and J. L. Campbell. *Strange Things.* London: Routledge & Kegan Paul, 1968.

Hallam, Jack. *The Ghost Tour: A Guidebook to Haunted Houses Within Easy Reach of London.* London: Wolfe Publishing, 1967.

Halliday, W. R. *Greek Divination: A Study of Methods and Principles.* London: Macmillan, 1913. Reprint, Chicago: Argonaut, 1967.

Halliwell, J. O., ed. *The Private Diary of Dr. John Dee, and the Catalogue of His Library of Manuscripts.* London: Camden Society, 1842.

Halliwell-Phillipps, J. O. *Nursery Rhymes and Nursery Tales of England.* London, 1853.

Halloween and Other Festivals of Death and Life. Knoxville: University of Tennessee Press, 1994.

Halperin, Daniel Tzvi. "Dancing at the edge of Chaos: An Ethnography of Wildness and Ceremony in an Afro-Brazilian Possession Religion," *Dissertation Abstracts International Section A: Humanities & Social Sciences* 56, no. 9-A (March 1996): 3632.

Halperin, David A. "The Appeal of the Impossible and the Efflorescence of the Unbelievable: A Psychoanalytic Perspective on Cults and Occultism," *Cultic Studies Journal* 9, no. 2 (1992): 190–205.

Halpin, Marjorie, and Michael M. Ames, eds. *Manlike Monsters on Trial: Early Records and Modern Evidence.* Vancouver, B.C.: University of British Columbia Press, 1980.

Hamel, Frank. *Human Animals.* London, 1915. Reprint, New Hyde Park, N.Y.: University Books, 1969.

Hamilton, Margaret L. *Is Survival a Fact? Studies of Deep-Trance Automatic Scripts.* London, 1969.

Hamilton, T. Glen. *Intention and Survival: Psychical Research Studies and Bearing of Intentional Acts by Trance Personalities on the Problem of Human Survival.* Toronto: Macmillan, 1942. Rev. ed. London: Regency Press, 1977.

———. "A Lecture to the British Medical Association." *Psychic Science* 9, no. 4 (January 1931).

———. "The Mary M. Teleplasm of Oct. 27, 1929." *Psychic Science* 10, no. 4 (January 1932).

———. "Teleplasmic Phenomena in Winnipeg." *Psychic Science* 8, no. 3 (1929); 8, no. 4 (January 1930); 9, no. 2 (July 1930).

Hammond, Sally. *We Are All Healers.* New York: Harper & Row, 1973. Reprint, New York: Ballantine, 1974.

Hand, Robert. *Essays on Astrology.* Rockport, Mass.: Para Research, 1982.

———. *Horoscope Symbols.* Rockport, Mass.: Para Research, 1981.

———. *Planets in Composite.* Rockport, Mass.: Para Research, 1975.

———. *Planets in Transit.* Rockport, Mass.: Para Research, 1976.

———. *Planets in Youth.* Rockport, Mass.: Para Research, 1977.

Handbook of the Lord's New Church Which Is Nova Hierosolyma. Bryn Athyn, Pa.: Lord's New Church Which Is Nova Hierosolyma, 1985.

Hanish, O. Z. A. *Health and Breath Culture.* Chicago: Sun Worshipper Publishing, 1902.

———. *Inner Studies.* Mokelumne Hill, Calif.: Health Research, 1963.

———. *Mazdaznan: What It Teaches.* Los Angeles: Mazdaznan Press, 1969.

———. *The Philosophy of Mazdaznan.* Los Angeles: Mazdaznan Press, 1960.

Hankey, Muriel A. *James Hewat McKenzie, Pioneer of Psychical Research.* London: Aquarian Press, 1963.

Hanna, Ralph. *The Awntyrs off Arthure: An Edition Based on Bodleian Library MS. Douce 324.* Manchester, UK: Manchester University Press, 1974.

Hansel, C. E. M. *ESP: A Scientific Evaluation.* New York: Charles Scribner's Sons, 1966. Rev. ed. as *ESP and Parapsychology: A Critical Re-evaluation.* Buffalo, N.Y.: Prometheus, 1980.

———. "A Critical Analysis of the Pearce-Pratt Experiment." *Journal of Parapsychology* (June 1961).

———. "A Critical Analysis of the Pratt-Woodruff Experiment." *Journal of Parapsychology* (June 1961).

———. "A Critical Review of the Experiments on Mr. Basil Shackleton and Mrs. Gloria Stewart." *Proceedings of the Society for Psychical Research* (May 1960).

———. "Experimental Evidence for Extrasensory Perception." *Nature* (1959–60).

———. "Experiments on Telepathy." *New Scientist* (February 1959).

———. "Experiments on Telepathy in Children: A Reply to Sir Cyril Burt." *British Journal of Statistical Psychology* (November 1960).

Hansel, C. E. M. and David Loye. "Has Science Discredited ESP?" In *Taking Sides: Clashing Views on Controversial Psychological Issues* 7th ed. Guilford, Conn.: Dushkin Publishing Group, 1992.

Hansen, Chadwick. *Witchcraft at Salem.* New York: George Braziller, 1969. Reprint, New York: New American Library, 1970.

Hansen, F. C. C., and Alfred Lehmann. "Über unwilkürliches Flüstern: Eine kritische und experimentelle Untersuchung der sogenannten Gedankenübertragung." *Philosophische Studien* 11, no. 4 (1895).

Hansen, George P. "CSICOP and the Skeptics: An Overview," *Journal of the American Society for Psychical Research* 86, no. 1 (January 1992): 19–63.

Hansen, Joseph. *Zauberwahn, Inquisition und Hexenprozess in Mittalalter und die Entstehung der grossen Hexenverfolgung.* Munich/ Leipzig: R. Oldenbourg, 1900. Reprint, Aalen: Scientiia, 1983.

Hanson, Virginia, ed. *Karma: The Universal Law of Harmony.* Wheaton, Ill.: Theosophical Publishing House, 1975.

Hanussen, Erik Jan. *Meine Lebenslinie.* Berlin, 1930.

Haraldsson, Erlendur. "Are Religiosity and Belief in an Afterlife Better Predictors of ESP Performance than Belief in Psychic Phenomena?," *Journal of Parapsychology* 57, no. 3 (September 1993): 259–273.

———. *Miracles Are My Visiting Cards: An Investigative Report on Psychic Phenomena Associated with Sri Sathya Sai Baba.* 1978. Reprinted as *Modern Miracles.* New York: Fawcett Columbine, 1988.

———. "Representative National Surveys of Psychic Phenomena: Iceland, Great Britain, Sweden, USA and Gallup's Multinational Survey." *Journal of the Society for Psychical Research* 53, no. 801.

———. "The Sai Baba Enigma." In *Miracles,* edited by Martin Ebon. New York: New American Library, 1981.

Haraldsson, Erlendur, and L. R. Gissurarson. "The Icelandic Medium Indridi Indridason." *Proceedings of the Society for Psychical Research* 57 (1989).

Harary, Keith, and Patricia Weintraub. *The Creative Sleep Program.* New York: St. Martin's Press, 1989.

———. *The Erotic Fulfillment Program.* New York: St. Martin's Press, 1990.

———. *The Free Flight Program.* New York: St. Martin's Press, 1989.

———. *Have an Out-of-Body Experience in 30 Days.* New York: St. Martin's Press, 1990.

Harary, Stuart Blue [Keith Harary]. "A Personal Perspective on Out-of-Body Experiences." In *Mind Beyond the Body: The Mystery of ESP Projection,* edited by D. Scott Rogo. New York: Penguin Books, 1978.

Harder, Michael. *Way of the Shaman: A Guide to Power and Healing.* New York: Bantam Books, 1982.

Harding, Douglas E. *On Having No Head.* 1971. Reprint, Boston: Arkana, 1986.

———. *The Hierarchy of Heaven and Earth.* Gainesville, Fla.: University of Florida Press, 1979.

Hardy, Alister C., Arthur Koestler, and Robert Harvie. *The Challenge of Chance: A Mass Experiment in Telepathy and Its Outcome.* New York: Random House, 1974.

Hardy, Sir Alister. "Biology and Psychical Research." *Proceedings of the Society for Psychical Research* 50, no. 183 (1953).

———. *The Biology of God.* London: Jonathan Cape, 1975.

———. *The Divine Flame.* London: Collins, 1966.

———. *The Living Stream: A Restatement of Evolution Theory and its Relation to the Spirit of Man.* London: Collins, 1965.

———. *The Spiritual Nature of Man.* Oxford: Clarendon, 1979.

———. "Telepathy and Evolutionary Theory." *Journal of the Society for Psychical Research* 35 (1950).

Hardy, Sir Alister, R. Harvie, and Arthur Koestler. *The Challenge of Chance: Experiments and Speculations.* London: Hutchinson, 1973. Reprint, New York: Random House, 1974. Reprint, New York: Vintage Books, 1975.

Hare, H. E., and W. L. Hare. *Who Wrote the Mahatma Letters?* London: Williams & Norgate, 1936.

Hare, Robert. *Experimental Investigation of the Spirit Manifestations.* New York: Partridge & Britten, 1855. Reprint, Elk Grove, Wisc.: Sycamore Press, 1963.

Harenburg, Johann C. *Von Vampyren.* N.p., 1739.

Hargrove, Robert A. *est: Making Life Work.* New York: Delacorte Press, 1976.

Hark, Ann. *Hex Marks the Spot in Pennsylvania Dutch Country.* Philadelphia: J. B. Lippincott, 1938.

Harland, Marion. *Where Ghosts Walk (1913).* Kila, Mont.: Kessinger Publishing Co., 1998.

Harley, Gail. "Emma Curtis Hopkins: 'Forgotten Founder' of New Thought." Ph.D. diss., Florida State University, 1991.

Harley, Trevor A. "Psi Missing in a Dream Clairvoyance Experiment," *Journal of the Society for Psychical Research* 56, no. 817 (October 1989): 1–7.

Harley, Trevor, and Gerald Matthews. "Cheating, Psi, and the Appliance of Science: A Reply to Blackmore." *Journal of the Society for Psychical Research* 54, no. 808 (July 1987).

Harner, Michael J. *The Way of the Shaman.* 3rd edition. San Francisco: Harper & Row, 1990.

Harner, Micheal J., ed. *Hallucinogens and Shamanism.* London: Oxford University Press, 1981.

Harper, Charles G. *Haunted Houses: Tales of the Supernatural with Some Account of Hereditary Curses and Family Legends.* London: Cecil Palmer, 1927. Reprint, Detroit: Gale Research, 1971.

Harper, Edith K. *Stead, the Man.* London: W. Rider & Son, 1914.

Harper, George Mills. *Yeats' Golden Dawn.* London: Macmillan; Wellingsborough, Northamptonshire, UK: Aquarian Press, 1974. Reprint, Wellingborough, England: Aquarian Press, 1979. Reprinted as *Yeats' Golden Dawn: The Influence of the Hermetic Order of the Golden Dawn on the Life and Art of W. B. Yeats.* San Bernadino, Calif.: Borgo Press, 1988.

Harrell, David Edwin, Jr. *All Things Are Possible With God.* Bloomington: Indiana University Press, 1975.

Harrer, Heinrich. *Return to Tibet.* London: Weinfeld & Nicholson, 1984.

Harrer, Heinrich. *Seven Years in Tibet.* London: Rupert Hart-Davis; New York: E. P. Dutton, 1953.

Harriman, Sarah. *The Book of Ginseng.* New York: Pyramid Books, 1975.

Harris, Errol E. *The Foundations of Metaphysics in Science.* Atlantic Highlands, N.J.: Humanities Press International, Inc., 1992.

Harris, John W. *Inferences from Haunted Houses and Haunted Men.* London, 1901.

Harris, Melvin. *Jack the Ripper: The Bloody Truth.* London: Columbus Books, 1987.

———. *Sorry, You've Been Duped!* London: Weidenfeld and Nicolson, 1986.

Harris, Thomas Lake. *Arcana of Christianity: Celestial Sense of the Divine Word.* 2 vols. New York, 1858.

———. *Brotherhood of the New Life: Its Fact, Law, Method, and Purpose.* Fountain Grove, Calif.: Fountain Grove Press, 1891.

———. *An Epic of the Starry Heaven.* New York: Partridge & Britten, 1854.

———. *A Lyric of the Golden Age.* New York: Partridge & Britten, 1856.

———. *The New Republic.* Santa Rosa, Calif.: Fountain Grove Press, 1891.

Harrison, Jane E. *Prolegmena to the Study of Greek Religion.* Cambridge, Mass.: Cambridge University Press, 1922.

Harrison, John F. C. *Quest for the New World.* New York: Charles Scribner's Sons, 1969.

Harrison, Michael. *Fire From Heaven.* London, 1976. Reprint, New York: Methuen, 1977. Rev. ed. London: Pan, 1977.

———. *Vanishings.* London: New English Library, 1981.

Harrison, Vernon. *H. P. Blavatsky & the SPR.* Pasadena, Calif.: Theosophical University Press, 1997

———. " 'J'Accuse: An Examination of the Hodgson Report of 1885." *Journal of the Society for Psychical Research* 53 (April 1986).

Harrison, William H. *Mother Shipton Investigated.* Reprint, London: The Author, 1881.

Hart, Hornell N. "ESP Projection: Spontaneous Cases and the Experimental Method." *Journal* of the American Society for Psychical Research (1954).

———. *Living Religion.* New York: Abingdon Press, 1937.

———. "The Psychic Fifth Dimension." *Journal* of the American Society for Psychical Research (1953).

———. "Psychical Research and the Methods of Science." *Journal* of the American Society for Psychical Research (1957).

———. "Six Theories About Apparitions." *Proceedings of the Society for Psychical Research* (May 1956).

———. *Skeptic's Quest.* New York: Macmillan, 1938.

———. *Toward a New Philosophical Basis for Parapsychological Phenomena.* New York: Parapsychological Foundation, 1965.

Hart, Hornell. *The Enigma of Survival: The Case For and Against an After Life.* Springfield, Ill.: Charles Thomas, 1959.

———. "Visions and Apparitions Collectively and Reciprocally Received." *Proceedings of the Society for Psychical Research* (May 1933).

———. *Your Share of God: Spiritual Power for Life Fulfillment.* Englewood Cliffs, N.J.: Prentice Hall, 1958.

Hart, Ralph. *Doctors Pronounced Me Dead in Dallas.* Detroit: The Author, n.d.

Harte, Richard. *Hypnotism and the Doctors. I. Mesmer/De Puységur.* London: L. N. Fowler, 1902.

Hartland, Edwin, W. *The Science of Fairy Tales: An Enquiry Into Fairy Mythology.* London, 1891. Reprint, Detroit: Singing Tree Press, 1968.

Hartlaub, Gustav Friedrich. *The Inexplicable: Study of the Magic World View.* N.p., 1951.

———. *Magic of the Mirror.* N.p., 1950.

———. *The Philosopher's Stone: Character and Image of Alchemy.* N.p., 1959.

Hartman, William C. *Who's Who in Occultism, New Thought, Psychicism, and Spiritualism.* Jamaica, N.Y.: Occult Press, 1927.

Hartmann, Eduard von. *Der Spiritismus.* Translated by C. C. Massey as *Spiritism.* London: Psychological Press, 1885.

Hartmann, Franz. *An Adventure Among the Rosicrucians.* Boston: Occult Publishing, 1887.

———. *Geomancy: The Art of Divining by Punctuation According to Cornelius Agrippa and Others.* London: William Rider & Son, 1913.

———. *In the Pronaos of the Temple of Wisdom.* London: Theosophical Society, 1890. Reprint, Chicago: Aries Press, 1941.

———. *The Life and Doctrines of Jacob Boehme.* New York: McCoy Publishing, 1929.

———. *Life and Doctrines of Paracelsus.* N.p., 1891.

———. *The Life and Teachings of Paracelsus.* London: George Redway, 1887. Reprinted with *The Prophecies of Paracelsus.* Blauvely, N.Y.: Rudolf Steiner, 1973.

———. *The Life of Philippus Theophrastus Bombast of Hohenheim Known by the Name of Paracelsus and of the Substance of his Teachings.* London: George Redway, 1887; Retd. with: *The Prophecies of Paracelsus; Occult Symbols and Magic Figures.* Blauvelt, N.Y.: Rudolf Steiner Publications, 1973.

———. *Magic White and Black; or, The Science of Finite and Infinite Life.* London: George Redway, 1886. Reprint, New York: University Books, 1970.

———. *Occult Science in Medicine.* N.p., 1893.

———. *Premature Burial.* London: Swann Sonnenschein, 1896.

———. *The Principles of Astrological Geomancy.* Boston: Occult Publishing, 1889. Reprint, Mokulumne Hill, Calif.: Health Research, 1965.

———. *Report of Observations During a Nine Months' Stay at the Headquarters of the Theosophical Society at Adyar (Madras), India.* Madras, India: Scottish Press, 1884.

Harvey, Youngsook Kim. *Six Korean Women: The Socialization of Shamans.* St. Paul, Minn.: West Publishing Co., 1979.

Hashimoto, M. *Japanese Acupuncture.* New York: Liveright Publishing, 1968; London: Thursons, 1966.

Hasted, John B. *The Metal-benders.* London: Routledge & Kegan Paul, 1981.

Hasted, John B., David Bohm, Edward W. Bastin, and Brendan O'Regan. "Experiments on Psychokinetic Phenomena." In *The Geller Papers: Scientific Observations on the Paranormal Powers of Uri Geller,* edited by Charles Panati. Boston: Houghton Mifflin, 1976.

Hasted, John B., David Robertson, and Ernesto Spinelli. "Recording of Sudden Paranormal Changes of Body Weight." In *Research in Parapsychology 1982.* Eds. W. G. Roll, John Beloff, and Rhea A. White. Metuchen, N.J.: Scarecrow Press, 1983.

Hastings, A. C. "Expectancy Set and 'Poltergeist' Phenomena." *ETC* 18, no. 3 (October 1961).

Hastings, A. C., and Stanley Krippner. "Poltergeist Phenomena and Expectancy Set." *Northwestern Tri-Quarterly* 3, no. 3 (Spring 1961).

Hastings, A. C., James Fadiman, and James B. Gordon. *Health for the Whole Person.* Boulder, Colo.: Westview Press, 1980.

Hastings, Arthur. "Psi and the Phenomena of Channeling." In *Research in Parapsychology 1989: Abstracts and Papers from the Thirty-second Annual Convention of the Parapsychological Association, 1989.* Metuchen, N.J.: Scarecrow Press, Inc., 1990.

Hastings, James, ed. *Encyclopaedia of Religion and Ethics.* 12 vols. Edinburgh: James Clark, 1908.

Hatcher, William S., and J. Douglas Martin. *The Baha'i Faith.* San Francisco: Harper & Row, 1984.

Hawi, Khalil. *Kahlil Gibran: His Background, Character, and Works.* Beirut, 1963.

Hawken, Paul. *The Magic of Findhorn.* New York: Harper & Row, 1975.

Hawkins, Gerald. *Stonehenge Decoded.* Garden City, N.Y.: Doubleday, 1965. Reprint, London: Souvenir Press, 1966.

Hay, George, ed. *The Necronomicon: The Book of Dead Names.* UK: Neville Spearman, 1978. Reprint, London: Corgi, 1980.

Hayek, Max. *Der Schriftdeuter Raffael Schermann.* N.p., 1921.

Hayes, Linda J. "Understanding Mysticism," *Psychological Record* 47, no. 4 (Fall 1970): 573–596.

Haynes, Renée. *The Hidden Springs: An Enquiry into Extra-Sensory Perception.* London: Hollis and Carter, 1961. Rev. ed. Boston: Little, Brown, 1973.

———. *Philosopher King: The Humanist Pope Benedict XIV.* London: Weidenfeld & Nicolson, 1970.

———. "Pope Benedict XIV and Parapsychology," *Parapsychology Review* 20, no. 5 (September-October 1989): 6–8.

———. *The Seeing Eye, The Seeing I: Perception, Sensory and Extra-Sensory.* New York: St. Martin's Press, 1976.

———. *The Society for Psychical Research: A History 1882–1982.* London: McDonald, 1982.

Haywood, H. I. *The Newly Made Mason.* Richmond, Va.: Macoy Publishing, 1948.

Hazard, T. R. *Eleven Days in Moravia.* N.p., n.d.

Hazelrigg, John. *Astrosophia: Being Metaphysical Astrology.* New York: The Author, 1915.

———. *Astrosophical Principles.* New York: Hermetic Publishing, 1917.

———. *Fundamentals of Hermetic Science: Being the Bona Fides of Astrology.* New York: Hermetic Publishing, 1925.

———. *Metaphysical Astrology.* New York: Metaphysical Publishing, 1900.

———. *The Sun Book; or, the Philosopher's Vade Mecum.* New York: Hermetic Publishing, 1916.

Head, Joseph, ed. *Reincarnation in World Thought: A Living Study of Reincarnation in All Ages.* New York: Julian Press, 1967.

Head, Joseph, and S. L. Cranston, eds. *Reincarnation: An East-West Anthology.* New York: Julian Press, 1961. Reprint, Wheaton, Ill.: Theosophical Publishing House, 1968. Rev. ed. *Reincarnation: The Phoenix Fire Mystery, an East-West Dialogue on Death and Rebirth.* New York: Julian Press/Crown Publishers, 1977.

Heard, Gerald. *Is Another World Watching?* New York: Harpers, 1951.

———. *Training for the Life of the Spirit.* Hankins, N.Y.: Strength Books, 1975. Distributed by Steiner Books.

Hearn, Lafcadio. *Kokoro: Hints & Echoes of Japanese Inner Life.* Boston: Houghton Mifflin, 1906.

Hearne, Keith M. "A Dream-Telepathy Study Using a Home 'Dream Machine'," *Journal of the Society for Psychical Research* 54, no. 807 (April 1987): 139–142.

———. "A Nationwide Mass Dream-Telepathy Experiment," *Journal of the Society for Psychical Research* 55, no. 814 (January 1989): 271–274.

Hearne, Keith M. T. "'Lucid' Dreams and ESP: An Initial Experiment Using One Subject." *Journal* of the Society for Psychic Research 51, no. 787 (1981).

Hearnshaw, L. S. *Cyril Burt, Psychologist.* London: Hodder and Stoughton, 1979.

Heath, Frederick W. "The Story of Mr. Isaacs' Life." *Occult Review* (October 1912).

Heckethorn, Charles. *The Secret Societies of all Ages and Countries.* 2 vols. 1897. Revised ed., N.p., 1965.

Hedayetullah, Muhammed. *Kabir: The Apostle of Hindu Muslim Unity.* Delhi, India: Motilal Banarsidass, 1977.

Hedgepath, William, and Dennis Stock. *The Alternative.* New York: Macmillan, 1970.

Heehs, Peter. "Genius, Mysticism, and Madness," *Psychohistory Review* 26, no. 1 (Fall 1997): 45–75.

Hefferlin, W. C., and Gladys Hefferlin. *A Description of the Rainbow City from the Hefferlin Manuscript.* Vista, Calif.: Borderland Sciences Research Foundation, n.d.

Heidrick, Bill. *Magick and Qaballah.* Berkeley, Calif.: Ordo Templi Orientis, 1980.

Heim, Richard, ed. *Incantamenta Magica Graeca Latina.* Leipzig: Teubner, 1893.

Heim, Roger, and R. B. Wasson. *Les champignons hallucinogens du Mexique.* Paris: Editions du Museum National d'Histoire Naturelle, 1958.

———. *Les champignons toxiques et hallucinogens.* Paris: Boubee, 1978.

Heindel, Augusta Foss. *The Birth of the Rosicrucian Fellowship.* Oceanside, Calif.: Rosicrucian Fellowship, n.d.

Heindel, Max. *Rosicrucian Cosmo-Conception.* Oceanside, Calif.: Rosicrucian Fellowship, 1909, 1937.

———. *The Rosicrucian Mysteries.* Oceanside, Calif.: Rosicrucian Fellowship, 1911.

———. *The Rosicrucian Philosophy, Questions and Answers.* Oceanside, Calif.: Rosicrucian Fellowship, 1922.

———. *Simplified Scientific Astrology.* Oceanside, Calif.: Rosicrucian Fellowship, 1928.

Heindel, Mrs. Max [Augusta Foss]. *The Birth of the Rosicrucian Fellowship.* Oceanside, Calif.: Rosicrucian Fellowship, n.d.

Heinze, Ruth-Inge. "Life Patterns of Women Active in Parapsychology." In *Women and Parapsychology.* New York: Parapsychology Foundation, Inc., 1994.

Heinze, Ruth-Inge. *Trance and Healing in Southeast Asia Today.* Bangkok: White Lotus Co./Berkeley: Independent Scholars of Asia, 1988.

Heinze, Ruth-Inge, et al. *Shamans of the 20th Century: With Contributions by Charlotte Berney [et al.].* New York: Irvington, 1991.

Heline, Corinne. *Color and Music in the New Age.* La Canada, Calif.: New Age Press, 1964.

———. *Healing and Regeneration through Color.* Santa Barbara, Calif.: J. F. Rowney Press, 1943.

———. *New Age Bible Interpretation.* 7 vols. Los Angeles: New Age Press, 1938–54.

Heline, Theodore. *America's Destiny: A New Order of the Ages.* Oceanside, Calif.: New Age Press, 1941.

Hellenbach, Baron. *Eine Philosophie des Gesunden Menschenverstandes.* N.p., 1876.

Heller, John H. *Report on the Shroud of Turin.* Boston: Houghton Mifflin, 1983.

Hellström, Eva Backström. "Collection of Spontaneous Cases." *Journal of the Society for Psychical Research* 43.

———. "Precognition of Girls Dancing." *Journal of the Society for Psychical Research* 41; 44.

Hemingway, Patricia D. *Transcendental Meditation Primer.* Philadelphia: McKay, 1975.

Henderson, William. *Notes on the Folk-lore of the Northern Counties, and the Borders.* London, 1866. Reprint, London: Folk-Lore Society, 1879.

Hendry, Allan. *The UFO Handbook: A Guide to Investigating, Evaluating, and Reporting UFO Sightings.* Garden City, N.Y.: Doubleday, 1979.

Henkel, Linda A. and Gertrude R. Schmeidler, eds. *Research in Parapsychology 1990: Abstracts and Papers from the Thirty-third Annual Convention of the Parapsychological Association, 1990.* Metuchen, N.J.: Scarecrow Press, Inc., 1992.

Herron, William Joseph. "A Questionnaire Study Comparing Mystical Experience among Zen, Yoga, Christian, and Non-Spiritual Groups," *Dissertation Abstracts International* 54, no. 4-B (October 1993): 2179.

Henry Stubbe: The Miraculous Conformist; or an account of Several Marvailous Cures performed by Mr. Valentine Greatarick. Oxford, England, 1666.

Henry, T. Shekleton. *Spookland: A Record of Research and Experiment in the Much Talked of Realm of Mystery.* Chicago, 1902.

Henslow, George. *The Proofs of the Truths of Spiritualism.* London: K. Paul, Trench, Trubner; New York: E. P. Dutton, 1919.

———. *The Religion of the Spirit World.* Chicago: Marlow Press, 1920.

Henslow, George, and D. J. D'Aute Hooper. *Spirit Psychometry.* London: W. Rider, 1914.

Henson, Dale S. *Encyclopedia Magica.* Lake Geneva, Wisc.: T S R, Inc., 1995.

Herbelot, Barthélemy d'. *Bibliotheque Oriental.* Paris, 1697.

Herbert, G. E. S. M. (5th Earl of Carnarvon), and Howard Carter. *Five Years' Explorations at Thebes, 1907–1911.* London: H. Frowde, 1912.

Hermannsson, H. *Catalogue of Runic Literature Forming Part of the Icelandic Collection at Cornell University.* Ithaca, N.Y.: Cornell University Press, 1918.

Hermes, Trismegistus. *The Divine Pymander.* Translated by Dr. Everard. London: Theosophical Publishing Society, 1894.

The Hermetic and Alchemical Writings of Aureolus Philippus Theophrastus Bombast, of Hohenheim, called Paracelsus the Great. 2 vols. Edited by Arthur E. Waite. London: James Elliott, 1894. Reprint, New Hyde Park, N.Y.: University Books, 1967.

———. *Hermetica.* Edited by Brian Copenhaver. Cambridge, Mass.: Cambridge University Press, 1992.

———. *Hermetica.* Edited by Walter Scott. Vol. 1. Oxford: Oxford University Press, 1924. Reprint, Boston: Shambhala, 1985.

Hermes, Trismegistus. *Theological and Philosophical Works.* Edited by J. D. Chambers. 2 vols. Edinburgh: T. and T. Clark, 1882.

Herodotus. *The Histories of Herodotus of Halicarnassus.* London: Oxford University Press, 1962.

Hertz, Wilhelm. *Der Werwolf.* Stuttgart, 1862.

Hess, David J. "Parapsychology in Brazil: Relations with Non-Brazilian Researchers and the Context of Brazilian Culture," *European Journal of Parapsychology* 8 (1990–1991): 51–56.

———. *Samba in the Night: Spiritism in Brazil.* New York: Columbia University Press, 1994.

Hesse, Herman. *Siddhartha.* New York: New Directions, 1951.

Hettinger, John. *Exploring the Ultra-Perceptive Faculty.* London: Rider, 1941.

———. *Telepathy and Spiritualism.* London: Rider, 1952.

———. *The Ultra-Perceptive Faculty.* London: Rider, 1938.

Heuvelmans, Bernard. "The Birth and Early History of Cryptozoology." *Cryptozoology* 3 (1984): 1–30.

———. *On the Track of Unknown Animals.* New York: Hill and Wang, 1958. Rev. ed. 1965. Reprint, London: Paladin Books, 1970.

———. *In the Wake of the Sea Serpents.* London: Rupert Hart-Davis/New York: Hill and Wang, 1968.

———. "What Is Cryptozoology?" *Cryptozoology* 1 (Winter 1982): 1–12.

Hewit, S. C. *Messages from the Superior State.* Boston: B. Marsh, 1853.

Heydon, John. *Eugenius Theodidactus.* London, 1655.

Heymans, Gerardus. "Psychische Monismus und 'Psychical Research.'" In *Zeitschrift für Psychologie.* Leipzig: J. A. Barth, 1912.

Heymans, Gerardus, Henry J. F. W. Brugmans, and A. Weinberg. "Une communication sur des expériences télépathiques au laboratorie de psychologie a Groningue." In *Compte Rendu Officiel du Primier Congres International des Recherches Psychiques.* Copenhagen, 1922.

Heysinger, Isaac. *Spirit and Matter Before the Bar of Modern Science.* London: T. Werner Laurie, 1910.

Heywood, Rosalind. *Beyond the Reach of Sense: An Inquiry into Extra-Sensory Perception.* New York: E. P. Dutton, 1961.

———. *ESP: A Personal Memoir.* London: Chatto & Windus, 1964. Reprint, New York: E. P. Dutton, 1964.

———. "G. W. Fisk and ESP." *Journal of the Society for Psychical Research* 47 (1973).

———. *The Infinite Hive.* London: Chatto & Windus, 1964. Reprinted as *ESP: A Personal Memoir.* New York: E. P. Dutton, 1972.

———. "Mrs. Gladys Osborne Leonard: A Biographical Tribute." *Journal* of the Society for Psychic Research 45 (1969).

———. "Notes on the Mediumship of Geraldine Cummins." *Journal of the Society for Psychical Research* 45, 746 (December 1970).

———. *The Sixth Sense: An Enquiry into Extrasensory Perception.* London: Chatto & Windus, 1959. Reprint, London: Pan Books, 1971. Reprinted as *Beyond the Reach of Sense.* New York: E. P. Dutton, 1974.

Hibbert, Samuel. *Sketches of the Philosophy of Apparitions.* Edinburgh, 1825.

Hickman, Irene. *I Knew Patience Worth.* Sacramento, Calif., The Author, 1971.

Higgins, Godfrey. *Anacalypsis, An Attempt to Draw Aside the Veil of the Saitic Isis; or An Inquiry into the Origin of Languages, Nations and Religions.* 2 vols. London, 1933, 1936. Reprint, New Hyde Park, N.Y.: University Books, 1965.

Higgins, Paul Lambourne, ed. *Frontiers of the Spirit.* Minneapolis: T. S. Denison, 1976.

Hilarion, Master [through Maurice B. Cooke]. *The Nature of Reality.* Toronto: Marcus Books, 1978.

Hill, Douglas. *Fortune Telling.* London: Hamlyn, 1972.

Hill, J. Arthur. *Emerson and His Philosophy.* 1919. Reprint, Folcroft, Pa.: Folcroft Library Editions, 1971.

———. *From Agnosticism to Belief.* London: Methuen, 1924.

———. *Man Is a Spirit.* New York: George H. Doran, 1918.

———. *New Evidences in Psychical Research.* London: W. Rider and Son, 1911.

———. *Psychical Investigations.* New York: George H. Doran, 1917.

———. *Psychical Miscellanea.* New York: Harcourt, Brace and Howe, 1919.

———. *Psychical Science and Religious Belief.* London: Rider, 1929.

———. *Religion and Modern Psychology.* N.p., 1911.

———. *Spiritualism and Psychical Research.* London: T. C. and E. C. Jack; New York: Dodge Publishing, 1913.

———. *Spiritualism: Its History, Phenomena and Doctrine.* London: Cassell; New York: George H. Doran, 1919.

Hill, J. Arthur, ed. *Letters from Sir Oliver Lodge.* London: Cassell, 1932.

Hillman, James. *A Blue Fire: Selected Writings.* New York: Harper & Row, 1989.

———. *The Dream and the Underworld.* New York: Harper & Row, 1979.

———. *Emotion: A Comprehensive Phenomenology of Theories and their Meanings for Therapy.* 1960. Reprint, Evanston, Ill.: Northwestern University Press, 1961.

———. *The Feeling of Function.* N.p., 1971.

———. *Insearch: Psychology and Religion.* New York: Charles Scribner's Sons, 1967.

———. *Loose Ends.* Dallas: Springhill Publications, 1975.

———. *The Myth of Analysis.* Evanston, Ill.: Northwestern University Press, 1972.

———. *Pan and The Nightmare.* New York: Spring Publications, 1972.

———. *Re-visioning Psychology.* New York: Harper & Row, 1975.

———. *Suicide and The Soul.* New York: Harper and Row, 1964.

Hills, Christopher. *The Christ Book.* Boulder Creek, Calif.: University of the Trees, 1980.

———. *Christ Yoga of Peace: Proposal for a World Peace Center.* 1970. Rev. ed. as *Universal Government by Nature's Laws.* N.p., 1978.

———. *Creative Conflict.* Boulder Creek, Calif: University of the Trees, 1980.

———. *Exploring Inner Space.* Boulder Creek, Calif.: University of the Trees, 1978.

———. *The Golden Egg.* Boulder Creek, Calif.: University of the Trees, 1979.

———. *Nuclear Evolution: A Guide to Cosmic Enlightenment.* London: Centre Community Publications; n.d.: Dr. Hills Technologies, 1968.

———. *Rays from the Capstone.* Boulder Creek, Calif.: University of the Trees, 1976.

———. *Rejuvenating the Body Through Fasting With Spirulina Plankton.* Boulder Creek, Calif.: University of the Trees, 1980.

———. *The Secrets of Spirulina.* Boulder Creek, Calif.: University of the Trees, 1980.

Hilsenrad, Zalman Aryeh, comp. *The Baal Shem Tov: His Birth and Early Manhood.* Brooklyn, N.Y.: Kehot Publication Society, 1967.

Hindley, Charles. *Curiosities of Street Literature.* 1871. London: The Broadsheet King, 1966.

Hine, Robert V. *California's Utopian Colonies.* New Haven, Conn.: Yale University Press, 1966.

Hines, Donald M. *Magic in the Mountains: The Yakima Shaman Power and Practice.* Issaquah, Wash.: Great Eagle Publishing, 1993.

Hinton, C. H. *The Fourth Dimension.* London: G. Allen & Unwin, 1934.

———. *Scientific Romances.* London, 1886.

Hints on Sitting With Mediums. London: Society for Psychical Research, 1965.

Hippisley-Coxe, A. D. *Haunted Britain: A Guide to Supernatural Sites Frequented by Ghosts, Witches, Poltergeists & Other Mysterious Beings.* London: Hutchinson; New York: McGraw Hill, 1973. Reprint, London: Pan, 1975.

Hipskind, Judith. *Palmistry: The Whole View.* St. Paul, Minn.: Llewellyn Publications, 1977.

Historie des diables de Loudun. N.p., 1839.

Histoire nouvelle et remarquable de l'esprit d'une femme qui c'est apparue au Faubourg Saint-Marcel après qu'elle a demeué cinq ans entiers ensevelie; elle a parlé a son mari, lui a commandé de faire prier pour elle, ayant commencé de parler le mardi II Decembre, 1618. Paris, 1618.

History of Flagellation Among All Nations. New York: Medical Publishing, 1903.

Hitchcock, C. A. *Remarks Upon Alchemy and the Alchemists.* Boston: Crosby, Nichols, 1857. Reprint, New York: Ayer Publishing Co. Inc., 1976.

Hitching, Francis. *Earth Magic.* London: Cassell, 1976.

———. *Pendulum: The Psi Connection.* London: Fontana, 1977.

Hittleman, Richard L. *Richard Hittleman's Yoga for Total Fitness.* New York: Bantam Books, 1983.

Hobana, Ion, and J. Weverbergh. *Unidentified Flying Objects from Behind the Iron Curtain.* London: Souvenir Press, 1974. Reprint, London: Corgi, 1975.

Hocart, A. M. *Kingship.* London: Humphrey Milford, 1927.

Hockley, Frederick. *The Rosicrucian Seer: Magical Writings of Frederick Hockley.* Wellingborough, England: Aquarian Press, 1986.

Hodges, Edward Lewi. *Be Healed. . . A Remedy That Never Fails.* San Diego, Calif.: Christian Fellowship Organization, 1949.

Hodges, Edward Lewi. *Teachings of the Secret Order of the Christian Brotherhood.* Santa Barbara, Calif.: J. F. Rowney Press, 1938.

———. *Wealth and Riches by Divine Right.* San Diego, Calif.: Christian Fellowship Organization, 1945.

Hodgson, B. H. "On the Mammalia of Nepal." *Journal of the Asiatic Society of Bengal* 1 (1832).

Hodgson, Richard. "An Account of Personal Investigations in India, and Discussion of the Authorship of the 'Koot Hoomi' Letters." *Proceedings of the Society for Psychical Research* 3 (1885).

———. "Mr. Davey's Imitations by Conjuring of Phenomena Sometimes Attributed to Spirit Agency." *Proceedings of the Society for Psychical Research* 8, 22 (1892): 253–310.

———. "Personal Investigations, in India, of Theosophical Phenomena." *Proceedings of the Society for Psychical Research* 3 (1885); *Journal of the Society for Psychical Research* 1–2 (1884–1886).

———. "Report on Phenomena Connected with Theosophy." *Proceedings of the Society for Psychical Research* 3 (1885).

Hodgson, Richard, and S. J. Davey. "The Possibilities of Malobservation and Lapse of Memory from a Practical Point of View." *Proceedings of the Society for Psychical Research* 4 (1887).

Hodson, Geoffrey. *The Kingdom of Faerie.* London, 1927.

———. *The Science of Seership.* London, 1920.

Hoebens, Piet Hein. "Croiset and Professor Tenhaeff: Discrepancies in Claims of Clairvoyance." *Zetetic Scholar* 6, no. 2 (Winter 1981–82): 32–40.

———. "Gerard Croiset and Professor Tenhaeff." In *Science Confronts the Paranormal.* Edited by Kenneth Frazier. Buffalo, N.Y.: Prometheus Books, 1986.

———. "Investigation of the Mozart of 'Psychic Sleuths.'" In *Science Confronts the Paranormal,* edited by Kenneth Frazier. Buffalo, N.Y.: Prometheus Books, 1986.

———. "The Mystery Men From Holland." *Zetetic Scholar* 8 (July 1981); 9 (March 1982); 10 (December 1982).

———. "The Mystery Men From Holland, I: Peter Hurkos' Dutch Cases." *Zetetic Scholar* 8 (July 1981).

———. "The Mystery Men From Holland, III: The Man Whose Passport Says Clairvoyant." *Zetetic Scholar* 10 (December 1982).

Hoene-Wronski, Jozef Maria. *Hoene-Wronski: Une philosopie de la creation.* Paris: Seghers, 1970.

Hoerschelmann, Dorothee von. "Religious Meaning of the Samoan Kava Ceremony," *Anthropos,* Vol. 90 (1995): 193–195.

Hoffer, Abram, and Humphrey Osmond. *Megavitamin Therapy: In Reply to the American Psychiatric Association Task Force Report on Megavitamins and Orthomolecular Psychiatry.* Regina, Sask., Canada: Canadian Schizophrenia Foundation, 1976.

Hoffman, Enid. *Huna, A Beginner's Guide.* Rockport, Mass.: ParaResearch, 1976.

Hogarth, Hyun-Key Kim. "Kut: Happiness through Reciprocity." In *Bibliotheca Shamanistica.* Vol. 7. Budapest: Akadémiai Kiadó, 1998.

Hogue, John. *Nostradamus and the Millennium.* Garden City, N.Y.: Doubleday, 1987.

Hohenwarter, Peter. "The Experiments of Astro-Physicist Dr. Alois Gatterer, S. J., with Maria Silbert." *Vergorgene Welt* 2, no. 3 (1957).

———. "Germany's Leading Parapsychologist: The 100th Anniversary of Schrenck-Notzing's Birth." *Vergorgene Welt.* 3–5 (1959).

———. "Hauntings at Schwarzach in the Voralberg Region." *Neue Wissenschaft* (July 1954).

———. "Our Experiments with Maria Silbert." *Schweizer Rundschau* (February 1954).

———. "Should We Study Parapsychology?" *Der Seelsorger* (March 1958).

Hohman, Johann George. *Der lange vernorgene Freund.* Reading, Pa., 1819. English edition as *The Long Lost Friend.* N.p., 1820. Reprint, Harrisburg, Pa., 1850.

Holden, James H., and Robert A. Hughes. *Astrological Pioneers of America.* Tempe, Ariz.: American Federation of Astrologers, 1988.

Holden, Ralph William. *The Elements of House Division.* Essex, UK: L. N. Fowler, 1977.

Hole, Christina. *Witchcraft in England.* New York: Charles Scribner's Sons, 1947.

Holiday, F. W. *The Dragon and the DiS.C.: An Investigation Into the Totally Fantastic.* New York: W. W. Norton, 1973.

Holistic Health Directory and Resource Guide, 1994–1995. Watertown, Mass.: New Age Journal, 1994.

Hollander, Bernard. *In Search of the Soul and the Mechanism of Thought, Emotion, and Conduct.* 2 vols. London: Kegan Paul; New York: E. P. Dutton, 1920.

Hollen, Henry. *Clairaudient Transmission.* Hollywood, Calif.: Keats Publications, 1931.

Hollenback, Jess B. *Mysticism.* University Park, Pa.: Pennsylvania State University Press, 1996.

Holloway, Emory. "Walt Whitman's Visit to the Shakers; With Whitman's Notebook Containing his Description and Observations of the Shaker Group at Mt. Lebanon." *The Colophon* 1 (spring 1930).

Holloway, Gilbert N. *Let the Heart Speak.* Los Angeles: DeVorss, 1951.

———. *New Ways of Unfoldment.* Deming, N.Mex.: New Age Truth Publications, n.d.

———. *The Way Up.* Deming, N.Mex.: New Age Church of Truth, 1975.

Holloway, Jean. *Hamlin Garland, a Biography.* Austin, Tex.: University of Texas Press, 1960.

Holloway, Mark. *Heavens on Earth: Utopian Communities in America, 1680–1880.* London: Turnstile Press, 1951.

Holm, Nils G. "Sunden's Role Theory and Glossolalia," *Journal for the Scientific Study of Religion* 26, no. 3 (September 1987): 383–389.

Holm, Nils G., ed. "Religious Ecstasy: Based on Papers read at the Symposium on Religious Ecstasy held at Abo, Finland, on the 26th–28th of August, 1981," In *Scripta Instituti Donneriani Aboensis,* Vol. 11. Stockholm: Distributed by Almqvist & Wiksell International, 1982.

Holmberg, Uno. *Finno-Ugric, Siberian Mythology.* (The Mythology of All Races, Vol. IV). New York: Cooper Square, 1964.

Holmes, Donald. *The Illuminati Conspiracy.* Los Angeles: Falcon Press, 1987.

Holmes, E. G. A. *Albigensian or Catharist Heresy.* London: William & Norgate, 1925.

Holmes, Ernest S. *How to Use the Science of Mind.* New York: Dodd, Mead, 1948.

———. *The Science of Mind.* 1925. Rev. ed. New York: R. M. McBride, 1938.

———. *This Thing Called Life.* Los Angeles: Institute of Religious Science and Philosophy, 1943.

———. *What Religious Science Teaches.* Los Angeles: Church of Religious Science, 1944.

Holmes, Fenwicke L. *Ernest Holmes: His Life and Times.* New York: Dodd, Mead, 1970.

Holms, A. Campbell. *The Facts of Psychic Science and Philosophy Collated and Discussed.* London, 1925. Reprint, New Hyde Park, N.Y.: University Books, 1969.

———. *The Fundamental Facts of Spiritualism.* Indianapolis: Stow Memorial Foundation, n.d.

Hoppál, Mihály, ed. *Shamanism in Eurasia.* Göttingen, 1984.

———. "Shamanism. Selected Writings of Vilmos Diószegi." In *Bibliotheca Shamanistica.* Vol. 6. Budapest: Akadémiai Kiadó, 1998.

Hoppál, Mihály, and Keith D. Howard, eds. "Shamans and Cultures." In *ISTOR Books.* Vol. 5. Budapest: Akadémiai Kiadó, 1993.

Hoppál, Mihály and Otto J. von Sadovszky, eds. "Shamanism: Past and Present." In. *ISTOR Books.* 2 vols. Budapest: Akadémiai Kiadó, 1989.

Holroyd, Stuart. *Magic, Words, and Numbers.* London: Aldus Books; Garden City, N.Y.: Doubleday, 1975.

Holt, Henry. *Calmire.* New York: Macmillan, 1892.

———. *Garrulities of an Octogenarian Editor.* Boston: Houghton Mifflin, 1923.

———. *Man and Man.* N.p., 1892. Reprint, 1905.

———. *On the Cosmic Relations.* 1914. Rev. ed. as *The Cosmic Relations and Immortality.* Boston: Houghton Mifflin, 1919.

Holzer, Hans. *Applied Astrology.* London: L. N. Fowler, 1953.

———. *Born Again: The Truth about Reincarnation.* Garden City, N.Y.: Doubleday, 1970. Reprint, London: Bailey Bros. & Swinfen, 1975.

———. *The Directory of the Occult.* Chicago: Henry Regnery, 1974.

———. *Elvis Speaks from the Beyond and other Celebrity Ghost Stories.* New York: Dorset Press, 1993.

———. *The Great British Ghost Hunt.* Boston: G. K. Hall, 1975.

———. *Hans Holzer's Haunted Houses: A Pictorial Register of the World's Most Interesting Ghost Houses.* New York: Crown, 1971.

———. *The Modern Textbook of Astrology.* Rev. ed., London: L. N. Fowler, 1967.

———. *The New Pagans.* Garden City, N.Y.: Doubleday, 1972.

———. *Pagans and Witches.* New York: Manor Books, 1979.

———. *The Prophets Speak.* Indianapolis, Ind.: Bobbs-Merrill, 1971.

———. *The Truth about Witchcraft.* Garden City, N.Y.: Doubleday, 1969.

———. *Wicca: The Way of the Witches.* New York: Manor Books, 1979.

Home, D. D. *Incidents in My Life.* London: Longman, Green, 1863. 2nd series. New York: A. K. Butts, 1874. Reprint, New Hyde Park, N.Y.: University Books, 1972.

Homes, Ronald. *Witchcraft in British History.* London: Muller, 1974.

Hone, Margaret. *Modern Textbook of Astrology.* London: Fowler, 1951.

Honorton, Charles. "Has Science Developed the Competence to Confront Claims of the Paranormal?" In *Research in Parapsychology 1975,* edited by J. D. Morris, W. G. Roll, and R. L. Morris. New York: Parapsychological Association, 1976.

———. "Meta-Analysis of Psi Ganzfeld Research: A Response to Hyman." *Journal of Parapsychology* 49 (1985): 59.

———. "Psi-Mediated Imagery and Ideation in an Experimental Procedure for Regulating Perceptual Input." *Journal* of the American Society for Psychical Research 68 (1974).

———. "Separation of High- and Low-Scoring ESP Subjects Through Hypnotic Preparation." *Journal of Parapsychology* 28 (1964).

———. "Significant Factors in Hypnotically-Induced Clairvoyant Dreams." *Journal* of the American Society for Psychical Research 66 (1972).

———. "State of Awareness Factors in Psi Activation." *Journal* of the American Society for Psychical Research 68 (1974).

Honorton, Charles, Diane C. Ferrari, and Daryl J. Bem. "Extraversion and ESP Performance: A Meta-Analysis and a New Confirmation," *Journal of Parapsychology* 62, no. 3 (September 1998): 255–276.

Hood, Ralph W., Jr. "The Empirical Study of Mysticism." In *The Psychology of Religion: Theoretical Approaches.* Boulder, Colo.: Westview Press, 1997.

Hood, Ralph W., Ronald J. Morris, and P. J. Watson. "Further Factor Analysis of Hood's Mysticism Scale," *Psychological Reports* 73, no. 3, Pt. 2 (December 1993): 1176–1178.

Hooper, Judith, and Dick Teresi. *Would a Buddha Wear a Walkman?* New York: Simon & Schuster, 1990.

[Hooper, T. D'Aute]. *Spirit Psychometry and Trance Communications by Unseen Agencies.* London: Rider, 1914.

Hopkins, Budd. *Intruders: The Incredible Visitations at Copley Woods.* New York: Random House, 1987.

———. *Missing Time: A Documented Study of UFO Abductions.* New York: Richard Marek, 1981.

Hopkins, Emma Curtis. *Class Lessons, 1888.* Marina del Rey, Calif.: DeVorss, 1977.

———. *High Mysticism.* Cornwall Bridge, Conn.: High Watch Fellowship, n.d.

———. *Scientific Christian Mental Practice.* Cornwall Bridge, Conn.: High Watch Fellowship, 1958.

Hopkinson, Tom, and Dorothy Hopkinson. *Much Silence.* New York: Dodd, Mead, 1975.

Hörbiger, Hans. *Glazial-Kosmogonie.* N.p., 1912.

Hövelman, G. H. "Neglected Figures in the History of Parapsychology. I. Some General Reflections." In *Liber Amicorum in Honoue of G. A. M. Zorab,* edited by F. W. J. J. Snel. Amsterdam: Nederlander Vereniging voor Parapsychologie, 1986.

Hornung, D. *Neue Geheimnisse des Tages durch Geistes Magnetismus.* Leipzig, 1857.

Hornung, Erik. *Conceptions of God in Ancient Egypt.* Ithaca, N.Y.: Cornell University Press, 1982.

Hose, Charles, and William McDougall. *The Pagan Tribes of Borneo.* 2 vols. London: Macmillan, 1912.

Houdini, Harry. *A Magician Among the Spirits.* New York: Harper & Brothers, 1924. Reprinted as *Houdini: A Magician Among the Spirits.* New York: Ayer Publishing Co. Inc., 1972.

———. *The Right Way to Do Wrong.* Boston: H. Houdini, 1906.

———. *The Unmasking of Robert Houdin.* New York: Publishers Printing, 1908.

Houghton, Miss [Georgiana]. *Chronicles of the Photographs of Spiritual Beings and Phenomena Invisible to the Material Eye.* London: E. W. Allen, 1882.

Hounam, Peter, and Andrew Hogg. *Secret Cult.* London: Lion, 1984.

Houston, Jean. *Lifeforce: The Psycho-historical Recovery of the Self.* New York: Delacorte Press, 1989.

———. *The Search for the Beloved: Journeys in Sacred Psychology.* Los Angeles: Jeremy P. Tarcher, 1987.

Houston, Jean, and Robert E. L. Masters. *Listening to the Body.* New York: Delacorte Press, 1978.

———. *Mind Games: The Guide to Inner Space.* New York: Viking, 1972.

———. *The Varieties of Psychedelic Experience.* New York: Holt, Rinehart and Winston, 1966.

Hoving, Thomas. *Tutankhamen: The Untold Story.* New York: Simon & Schuster; London: Hamish Hamilton, 1978.

Howard, Michael. *The Magic of Runes.* New York: Samuel Weiser, 1980.

Howard-Gordon, Francis. *Glastonbury: Maker of Myths.* Glastonbury, England: Gothic Image, 1982.

Howe, Ellic. *The Magicians of the Golden Dawn.* London: Routledge and Kegan Paul, 1972.

———. *Urania's Children: The Strange World of the Astrologers.* London: William Kimber, 1967. Rev. ed. as *Astrology and Psychological Warfare During World War II.* London, 1972. Reprinted as *Astrology: A Recent History Including the Untold Story of Its Role in World War II.* New York: Walker, 1968.

Howe, Ellic, ed. *The Alchemist of the Golden Dawn: The Letters of the Revd W. A. Ayton to F. L. Gardner and Others, 1886–1905.* Wellingborough, England: Aquarian Press, 1985.

Howitt, William. *The History of the Supernatural in All Ages and Nations and in All Churches, Christian and Pagan, Demonstrating a Universal Faith.* Philadelphia: J. B. Lippincott, 1863. Reprinted as *The History of Magic.* New Hyde Park, N.Y.: University Books, 1970.

———. *Homes and Haunts of the Most Eminent British Poets.* New York: Harper & Brothers, 1847.

Howitt-Watts, Mrs. *Pioneers of the Spiritual Reform.* London: Psychological Press Association, 1883.

Hua-Ching Ni. *Internal Alchemy.* Santa Monica, Calif.: SevenStar Communications Group, 1993.

Huard, Pierre, and Ming Wong. *Oriental Methods of Mental & Physical Fitness: The Complete Book of Meditation, Kinesiotherapy & Martial Arts in China, India & Japan.* New York: Funk & Wagnall, 1971.

Hubbard, L. Ron. *The Book Introducing the E-meter.* Los Angeles: Church of Scientology of California, 1975.

———. *The Book of E-meter Drills.* Compiled by Mary Sue Hubbard. Los Angeles: Church of Scientology of California, 1965.

———. *Dianetics 55!* Los Angeles: Publications Organization, 1954.

———. *Dianetics: The Modern Science of Mental Health.* New York: Hermitage House, 1950.

———. *E-Meter Essentials.* Los Angeles: Church of Scientology of California, 1975.

———. *Handbook for Preclears.* Los Angeles: Publications Organization, 1951.

———. *Science of Survival.* Los Angeles: Publications Organization, 1951.

———. *Scientology: A New Slant on Life.* Los Angeles: Publications Organization, United States, 1965.

———. *Scientology: The Fundamentals of Thought.* Los Angeles: Publications Organization, 1956.

———. *Self-Analysis.* Los Angeles: Publications Organization, 1951.

———. *Understanding the E-Meter.* Los Angeles: Bridge Publications, 1981.

———. *You Have Lived Before This life?* Los Angeles: Publications Organization, 1977.

Hubbell, Walter. *The Great Amherst Mystery.* New York, 1888.

Huber, Peter Alfred. *Arthur Koestler, Das Literarische Werk.* Zürich: Fretz & Wasmuth, 1962.

Huby, Pamela M. C. "Case of Xenoglossy." *Journal of the Society for Psychical Research* 44.

———. "Effects of Centrally Acting Drugs on ESP Ability." *Journal of the Society for Psychical Research* 41.

———. "New Evidence About 'Rose Morton.'&43" *Journal of the Society for Psychical Research* 45.

Huck, Gwendolyn K. *Modern Psychic Mysteries: Millesimo Castle, Italy.* London, 1929.

Hudson, Thomson Jay. *Divine Pedigree of Man.* Chicago: A. C. McClure, 1900.

———. *Evolution of the Soul and Other Essays.* Chicago: A. C. McClure, 1904.

———. *The Law of Psychic Phenomena: A Working Hypothesis for the Systematic Study of the Vast Potential of Man's Mind.* New York: G. P. Putnam's Sons, 1894. Reprint, Chicago: Hudson-Cohan, 1970. Reprint, New York: Weiser, 1972.

———. *Scientific Demonstration of the Future Life.* Chicago: A. C. McClure, 1896.

Huebner, Louise. *Magic Sleep.* Kansas City, Mo.: Springbok Editions, 1972.

———. *Magical Creatures.* Kansas City, Mo.: Springbok Editions, 1972.

———. *Never Strike a Happy Medium.* Los Angeles: Nash Publishing, 1971.

———. *Power through Witchcraft.* Los Angeles: Nash Publishing, 1969. Reprint, New York: Bantam Books, 1972.

———. *Your Lucky Numbers.* Kansas City, Mo.: Springbok Editions, 1972.

Hughes, E. R., ed. and trans. *Chinese Philosophy in Classical Times.* London: J. M. Dent; New York: E. P. Dutton, 1942.

Hughes, Irene. *ESPecially Irene: A Guide to Psychic Awareness.* Blauvelt, N.Y.: Rudolph Steiner Publications, 1972.

———. *Know Your Future Today.* New York: Paperback Library, 1970.

Huhm, Halla Pai. *Kut: Korean Shamanist Rituals.* Elizabeth, N.J.: Hollym International, n.d.

Hull, C. L. *Hypnosis and Suggestibility: An Experimental Approach.* New York: Century Psychology Service, 1933.

Hull, Daniel. *Moses Hull.* Wellesley, Mass.: Maugus Printing, 1907.

Hultkrantz, ¤'c5ke. "A Definition of Shamanism," *Temenos.* 9 (1973): 25–37.

———. "Ecological and Phenomenological Aspects of Shamanism." In *Shamanism in Siberia.* Edited by Vilmos Diószegi and Mihály Hoppál. Budapest, 1978.

———. "The Meaning of Ecstasy in Shamanism." *Tribal Epistemologies* Aldershot: Avebury/Ashgate Publishing, 1998.

———. "The Shaman and the Medicine-Man," *Social Science & Medicine.* 20, no. 5 (1985): 511–515.

———. *Shamanic Healing and Ritual Drama. Health and Medicine in Native North American Religious Tradition.* New York: Crossroads, 1992.

———. *The Religions of the American Indians.* Berkeley: University of California Press, 1979.

Humbard, Rex. *Prayer With Power.* Grand Rapids, Mich.: Baker Books, n.d.

Humble, Floyd. *Bible Lessons.* Gardena, Calif.: United Spiritualist Church, 1969.

Hume, Lyn. *Witchcraft & Paganism in Australia.*Melbourne, Austrailia: Melbourne University Press, 1997.

Humpfner, Winfried G. *L'Interpretazione di Fenomeni Metapsichici; ovvero, L'Anima in Metapsichica, in Psicologia, ecc.* (The Interpretation of Metapsychical Phenomena; or, The Soul in Metapsychics, Psychology, etc.). N.p., 1951.

Humphrey, Caroline, and Urgunge Onon. "Shamans and Elders: Experience, Knowledge, and Power among the Daur Mongols." In *Oxford Studies in Social and Cultural Anthropology.* New York: Oxford University Press, 1996.

Humphrey, Elizabeth. *Handbook of Tests in Parapsychology.* Durham, N.C.: Parapsychology Laboratory, 1948.

———. "Simultaneous High and Low Aim in PK Tests." *Journal of Parapsychology* 11 (1947).

Humphreys, Christmas. *Zen Buddhism.* London: Heinemann, 1949. Reprint, New York: Macmillan, 1967.

———. *An Outline of Buddhism.* Honolulu: Hongwanji Buddhist Temple, 1929.

Hunt, H. Ernest. *A Book of Auto-Suggestion.* N.p., 1923.

———. *Essentials and Symbols of the Buddhist Faith.* Honolulu: The Author, 1955.

———. *Gleanings from Soto-Zen.* Honolulu: The Author, 1953.

———. *Hidden Self and Its Mental Processes.* London: W. Rider and Son, 1921.

———. *Manual of Hypnotism.* London: W. Rider, 1917.

———. *Nerve Control.* N.p., 1923.

———. *Self Training.* Philadelphia: D. McKay, 1918.

———. *Spirit and Music.* N.p., 1922.

———. *Spiritualism For the Enquirer.* N.p., 1931.

———. *Why We Survive.* N.p., 1928.

Hunt, Roland. *The Seven Keys to Colour Healing.* Ashington, England: C. W. Daniel, 1954.

Hunter, Jennifer. *21st Century Wicca.* Secaucus, N.J.: Carol Publishing Group,1997.

Hunter, Louise. *Buddhism in Hawaii.* Honolulu: University of Hawaii Press, 1971.

Hurkos, Peter. *Psychic.* London: Arthur Baker, 1962.

———. *Psychic: The Story of Peter Hurkos.* London: Arthur Barker, 1961.

Hurst, Lulu. *Lulu Hurst Writes Her Autobiography.* Rome, Ga., 1897.

Huson, Paul. *The Devil's Picture Book: The Compleat Guide to Tarot Cards; Their Origins and Their Usage.* New York: G. P. Putnam's Sons, 1971. Reprint, London: Abacus, 1972.

Hutchins, Jane. *Discovering Mermaids and Monsters.* Shire Publications, 1968.

Hutchinson, H. *Dreams and their Meanings.* London, 1901.

Hutin, Serge. *A History of Alchemy.* New York: Walker, 1963. Reprint, New York: Tower Books, n.d.

———. *Histoire des Rose-Croix* (History of the Rosicrucians). Paris: G. Nizet, 1955.

———. *Histoire mondiale des sociétés secrétes* (World History of Secret Societies). N.p., 1959.

———. *Les Civilisations inconnues* (Unknown Civilizations). N.p., 1961.

———. *Les Disciples anglais de Jacob Boehme.* Paris; n.p., 1960.

———. *Les Francs-Macons* (The Freemasons). Paris: Editions du Seuil, 1960.

———. *Voyages vers Ailleurs* (Travels to Elsewhere). Paris: Fayard, 1962.

Hutton, Alice. *The Cards Can't Lie: Prophetic, Educational and Playing-Cards.* London: Jupiter Books, 1979.

Hutton, Bernard. *Healing Hands.* London: W. H. Allen, 1966.

Hutton, Christopher M. and John E. Joseph. "Back to Blavatsky: The Impact of Theosophy on Modern Linguistics," *Language & Communication* 18, no. 3 (July 1998): 181–204.

Huxley, Aldous. *Aldous Huxley's Hearst Essays.* New York: Garland Publishing, 1994.

———. *The Devils of Loudon.* London: Chatto & Windus, 1952. Reprint, New York: Harper & Row, 1971.

———. *The Doors of Perception.* London: Chatto & Windus, 1954. Reprint, New York: Harper & Row, 1970.

———. *Heaven and Hell.* New York: Harper/London: Chatto & Windus, 1956.

———. *Island.* London: Chatto & Windus, 1962.

———. *Moksha: Writings on Psychedelics and the Visionary Experience.* New York: Stonehill, 1977.

Huxley, Francis. *The Way of the Sacred.* Garden City, N.Y.: Doubleday, 1974. Reprint, New York: Dell, 1976.

Huysmans, J. K. *Là-Bas.* 1891. Translated as *Down There: A Study in Satanism.* New Hyde Park, N.Y.: University Books, 1958.

———. *Down There (La-Bas): A Study in Satanism.* Translated by Keene Willis. New Hyde Park, N.Y.: University Books, 1958.

Hyatt, Christopher and James Wasserman. *Inside Secret Societies.* Glendale, Ariz.: New Falcon Publications, 1997.

Hyman, Ray. "Evaluation of the Program on Anomalous Mental Phenomena," *Journal of Parapsychology* 59, no. 4 (December 1995): 321–351.

Hyman, Ray. "The Ganzfeld Psi Experiment: A Critical Appraisal." *Journal of Parapsychology* 49 (1985): 3.

Hymenaeus Beta, Caliph [Grady McMurtry]. "Introduction: Culture vs. Cult." *Equinox* 3, 10 (1986): 9–12.

———. *Tao Teh King.* London: Askin Publishers; New York: Samuel Weiser, 1976.

Hymenaeus Beta, comp. *The Equinox* 3, no. 10. New York: Thelema Publications, 1986.

Hynek, J. Allen. *The Hynek UFO Report.* New York: Dell, 1977.

———. *The UFO Experience: A Scientific Inquiry.* Chicago: Henry Regnery, 1972. N.p.:Marlowe and Co., 1999.

Hynek, J. Allen, and Jacques Vallee. *The Edge of Reality: A Progress Report on Unidentified Flying Objects.* Chicago: Henry Regnery, 1975.

Hynek, R. W. *Konnersreuth: A Medical and Psychological Study of the Case of Teresa Neumann.* N.p., 1932.

Hyslop, George H. "An Instance of Apparent Spontaneous Telepathy." *Journal* of the American Society for Psychical Research (April 1948).

Hyslop, George H. "The Biological Approach to Psychic Phenomena." *Journal* of the American Society for Psychical Research (April 1942).

———. "Certain Problems of Psychic Research." *Journal* of the American Society for Psychical Research (August 1930).

———. "James H. Hyslop: His Contribution to Psychical Research." *Journal* of the American Society for Psychical Research (October 1950).

———. "Report of the Questionnaire Committee." *Journal* of the American Society for Psychical Research (November 1930).

Hyslop, James H. *Borderland of Psychical Research.* London: G. P. Putnam's Sons, 1906.

———. *Contact With the Other World: The Latest Evidence as to Communication with the Dead.* New York: Century, 1919. Reprint, Finch Press, 1972.

———. *Enigmas of Psychical Research.* New York: G. P. Putnam's Sons/Boston: H. B. Turner, 1906.

———. *Life After Death: Problems of the Future Life and Its Nature.* New York: E. P. Dutton, 1918.

———. "Professor Newcomb and Occultism." *Journal* of the American Society for Psychical Research 5 (1909).

———. *Psychical Research and Survival.* London: G. Bell and Sons, 1913.

———. *Psychical Research and the Nature of Life After Death.* Albuquerque, N.Mex.: American Institute for Psychological Research, 1980.

———. *Psychical Research and the Resurrection.* Boston: Small, Maynard, 1908.

———. "Replies to Mr. Carrington's Criticism of M. Aksakof." *Proceedings of the American Society Psychical Research* N.d.

———. *Science and a Future Life.* London: G. P. Putnam's Sons, 1906.

"I Was Cured by Ghost of Elvis." *Sun* (January 24, 1995).

Ichazo, Oscar. *The Human Process for Enlightenment and Freedom.* New York: Arica Institute, 1976.

Imoda, Enrico. "The Action of Eusapia Palladino on the Electroscope." *Annals of Psychical Science* 7, 44/45, (August–September 1908).

———. *Fotographie di fantasma.* Turin, 1912.

"In Memoriam: Professor C. D. Broad, 1887–1971." *Journal* of the SPR 46 (1971): 107.

Ince, R. B. *Franz Anton Mesmer.* London: William Rider, 1920.

Inengar, B. K. S. *Light on Yoga.* New York: Schocken Books, 1966.

Inge, William Ralph. *Christian Mysticism.* London: Methuen, 1899.

Ingenito, Marcia Gervase, ed. *National New Age Yellow Pages.* Fullerton, Calif.: National New Age Yellow Pages, 1987. Rev. ed. Fullerton, Calif.: Highgate House, 1988.

Inglis, Brian. *Fringe Medicine.* 1964. Reprinted as *The Case for Unorthodox Medicine.* New York: Berkeley, 1969.

———. *The Hidden Power.* London: Jonathan Cape, 1986.

———. *Natural and Supernatural: A History of the Paranormal from Earliest Times to 1914.* London: Hodder & Stoughton, 1977.

———. *Natural Medicine.* London: Collins, 1979.

———. *The Paranormal: An Encyclopedia of Psychic Phenomena.* London: Granada, 1985.

———. *Science and Parascience: A History of the Paranormal, 1914–1939.* London: Hodder & Stoughton, 1984.

———. "Sir William Barrett (1844–1925)." *Journal of the Society for Psychical Research* 55 (1988): 16.

———. *Trance: A Natural History of Altered States of Mind.* London: Grafton, 1989.

Inglis, Brian, and Ruth West. *The Alternative Health Guide.* New York: Alfred A. Knopf, 1983.

Ingoldsby, Thomas. *The Ingoldsby Legends or Mirth and Marvels.* London: R. Bentley, 1840.

Ingram, John H. *Haunted Houses and Family Traditions of Great Britain.* London, 1884.

Ingram, M. V. *An Authenticated History of the Famous Bell Witch.* Clarksville, Tenn.: W. P. Titus, 1894.

The International Psychic Register. Edited by Donald McQuaid. 3 vols. Erie, Pa.: Ornion Press, 1977, 1978, and 1979.

"Interview: Penny Torres on Mafu." *Life Times* 1, no. 2 (winter 1986–87): 74–79.

"Interview: Thelma S. Moss." *Psychic* 1, no. 1 (1970).

Interviews with Oscar Ichazo. New York: Arica Institute Press, 1982.

Introductory Study Course in Theosophy. Wheaton, Ill.: Theosophical Society of America, 1967.

Iremonger, Lucille. *The Ghosts of Versailles.* London: Faber & Faber, 1957.

Irvine, Doreen. *From Witchcraft to Christ.* London: Concordia Press, 1973.

Irwin, Harvey J. "Charles Bailey: A Biographical Study of the Australian Apport Medium." *Journal of the Society for Psychical Research* 54 (1987): 97.

———. *Flight of Mind: A Psychological Study of the Out-of-Body Experience.* Metuchen, N.J.: Scarecrow Press, 1985.

———. *An Introduction to Parapsychology.* Pittsburgh: R. A. McConnell, 1983.

———. "Parapsychology in Australia," *Journal of the American Society for Psychical Research* 82, no. 4 (October 1988): 319–338.

Irwin, H. J. *Psi and the Mind: An Information Processing Approach.* Metuchen, N.J.: Scarecrow Press, 1979.

———. "A Study of Paranormal Belief, Psychological Adjustment, and Fantasy Proneness," *Journal of the American Society for Psychical Research* 85, no. 4 (October 1991): 317–331.

Isherwood, Christopher. *Ramakrishna and His Disciples,* New York: Simon & Schuster, 1965.

Isherwood, Christopher, and Swami Prabhavananda, trans. *The Bhagavad Gita: The Song of God.* Hollywood, Calif.: Marcel Road, 1944.

Ivanova, Barbara. *The Golden Chalice.* Edited by M. Mir and L. Vilenskaya. San Francisco: H. S. Dakin, 1986.

———. "Reincarnation and Healing." *Psi Research* 5, 1,2 (March/June 1986).

———. "Some Experiments on Healing Processes." *International Journal of Paraphysics* 19, 5,6 (1985).

Iverson, Jeffrey. *More Lives Than One?* London: Souvenir Press, 1976. Reprint, London: Pan, 1967.

Iyangar, Yogi Srinivasa. *Hatha-Yoga-Pradipika of Svatmarama Svamin.* Adyar, Madras, India: Theosophical Publishing House, 1933.

Iyengar, B. K. S. *Light of Yoga.* New York: Schrocken Books, 1966.

Jabir ibn Hayyan. *The Works of Geber.* London: Printed for William Cooper, 1686.

Jack, Alex. *The New Age Dictionary.* Brookline Village, Mass.: Kanthaka Press, 1976.

Jacks, L. P. *All Men Are Ghosts.* London: Williams & Norgate, 1913.

———. *The Confessions of an Octogenarian.* N.p., 1942.

———. *The Inner Sentinel.* New York; London: Harper & Brothers, 1930.

———. "Dramatic Dreams, an Unexplored Field for Psychical Research." *Journal of the Society for Psychical Research* 17 (1915).

———. *Elemental Religion.* New York: Harper, 1934.

———. *My American Friends.* London: Constable & Co. Ltd, 1933; New York: Macmillian, 1933.

———. *My Neighbour the Universe.* N.p., 1928.

———. *Near the Brink.* London: Allen & Unwin, 1955.

———. "Presidential Address: The Theory of Survival in the Light of Its Context." *Proceedings of the Society for Psychical Research* 29 (1918).

Jackson, Herbert G., Jr. *The Spirit Rappers.* Garden City, N.Y.: Doubleday, 1972.

Jackson, Nigel. *The Compleat Vampyre.* Edmonds, Wash.: Holmes Publishing Group, 1995.

Jacob, August Henri. *L'Hygiène naturelle, ou l'art de consevèr sa santé et de se gué rir soi-même.* Paris, 1868.

Jacob, August Henri. *Les Pensées du Zouave Jacob.* Paris, 1868.

———. *Poisons et contre-Poisons dévoilés.* Paris, 1874.

Jacobi, Jolande S. *Case Studies in Counselling and Psychotherapy.* N.p., 1959.

———. *Die Psychologie von C. G. Jung.* New Haven, Conn.: Yale University Press, 1943.

———. *Komplex, Archetypus, Symbol in der Psychologie von C. G. Jung.* Zürich: Rascher, 1957; London: Routledge & Paul, 1959.

———. *Paracelsus.* Wien: P. Neff, 1951.

———. *Vom Bilderreich der Seele.* Zürich: Rascher, 1940.

———. *The Way of Individuation.* London: Hodder & Stoughton, 1967.

Jacobi, Jolande S., ed. *Man and His Symbols.* Garden City, N.Y.: Doubleday, 1964.

Jacobs, Claude F., and Andrew J. Kaslow. *The Spiritual Churches of New Orleans: Origins, Beliefs, and Rituals of an African American Religion.* Knoxville: University of Tennessee Press, 1991.

Jacobs, David M. *The UFO Controversy in America.* Bloomington: Indiana University Press, 1975. Reprint, New York: New American Library, 1976.

———. "J. Allen Hynek and the UFO Phenomenon." *International UFO Reporter* 11, no. 3 (May/June 1986): 4–8, 23.

Jacobs, Jeff C. "Psi-Guided Awakening from Sleep 1: The Original Experiments of W. Van Vuurde." *Journal of the Society for Psychical Research* 53 (1985): 159.

Jacobson, Nils Olof. *Life Without Death? On Parapsychology, Mysticism and the Question of Survival.* New York: Delacorte Press, 1973. Reprint, London: Turnstone Books, 1974.

———. *Life Without Death? On Parapsychology, Mysticism and the Question of Survival.* New York: Delacorte Press, 1973. Reprint, London: Turnstone Books, 1974. Reprint, New York: Dell, 1974.

Jacobson, Nils Olof and Jens A. Tellefsen. "Dowsing Along the Psi Track: A Novel Procedure for Studying Unusual Perception," *Journal of the Society for Psychical Research* 59, no. 834 (January 1994): 321–339.

Jacobson, Wendy S. *The Companion to "The Mystery of Edwin Drood."* London: Allen & Unwin, 1986.

Jacoby, H. J. *Analysis of Handwriting.* London: Allen & Unwin, 1929.

Jacoby, Mario. *The Longing for Paradise: Psychological Perspectives on an Archetype.* Boston: Sigo Press, 1985.

Jacolliot, Louis. *Occult Science in India and Among the Ancients.* London: William Rider, 1919.

Jaffé, Aniela. *Apparitions and Precognition: A Study From the Point of View of C. G. Jung's Analytical Psychology.* New Hyde Park, N.Y.: University Books, 1963. Reprint, New York: Harper & Row, 1971.

———. *From the Life and Work of C. G. Jung.* New York: Harper & Row, 1971.

———. *The Myth of Meaning.* New York: Putnam, 1971.

———. "The Psychic World of C. G. Jung." *Tomorrow* (spring 1961).

Jahagirdar, Keshav Tatacharya, and Edwin C. May. "From Where Does the Kum-Kum Come? A Materialization Attempt." In *Research in Parapsychology 1975,* edited by J. D. Morris, W. G. Roll, and R. L. Morris. New York: Parapsychological Association, 1976.

Jahn, R. G. "The Persistent Paradox of Psychic Phenomena: An Engineering Perspective," *Proceedings of the IEEE.* 70 (1982):136–170.

Jahn, R. G. and Dunne, B. J. "On the Quantum Mechanics of Consciousness, With Application to Anomalous Phenomena," *Foundations of Physics.* 16, (1986): 721–772.

Jahoda, G. *The Psychology of Superstition.* London, 1969. Reprint, Baltimore, Md.: Penguin, 1971. Reprint, New York: J. Aronson, 1974.

Jahoda, Gustav. *White Man: A Study of the Attitudes of Africans to Europeans Before Independence.* London; New York: Oxford University Press, 1961.

Jal, A. *Scènes de la vie maritime.* Paris, 1830.

James, I. *Daemonologie.* Edinburgh, 1597. Reprint, London, 1603. Reprint, London: John Lane/New York: E. P. Dutton, 1924. New York: De Capo Press, 1969. Macdougall, Norman. *James IV.* Edinburgh: John Donald Publishers, 1989.

James, Paul. *California Superquake, 1975–77: Scientists, Cayce, Psychics Speak.* New York: Exposition Press, 1974.

James, R. L. L. *The Church and Bodily Healing.* Essex, England: C. W. Daniel, 1929.

James, William. *Essays in Psychical Research.* Cambridge, Mass.: Harvard University Press, 1986.

———. *Letters of William James and Theodore Flournoy.* Edited by R. C. Le Clair. Madison, Wisc.: University of Wisconsin Press, 1966.

———. "Report on Mrs. Piper's Hodgson Control." *Proceedings of the Society for Psychical Research* 23 (1909).

———. *The Varieties of Religious Experience.* London: Longmans Green, 1902. Reprint, New Hyde Park, N.Y.: University Books, 1963.

———. *The Will to Believe and Human Immortality.* New York: Dover Publications, n.d.

———. *William James on Psychical Research.* Edited by Gardner Murphy and Robert O. Ballou. New York: Viking Press, 1960.

Janet, Pierre. "La psychologie de la croyance et le mysticisme" (The Psychology of Belief and Mysticism), *Bulletin de Psychologie* 47, no. 414 (January-February 1993–94): 143–155.

Jaquin, Noel. *The Hand and Disease.* N.p., 1926.

———. *The Hand of Man: A Practical Treatise of the Science of Hand Reading.* London: Faber & Faber, 1933.

———. *Hand-reading Made Easy.* N.p., 1928.

———. *The Human Hand.* London: Rockliff, 1956.

———. *It's in Your Hands: The Secrets of the Human Hand.* New York: R. M. McBride & Co., 1941.

———. *Man's Revealing Hand.* London: Routledge, 1934.

———. *Scientific Palmistry.* London: C. Palmer, 1925.

———. *The Signature of Time.* London: Faber & Faber Ltd., 1940.

———. *The Theory of Metaphysical Influence: A Study of Human Attunements, Perception, Intelligence and Motivation.* N.p., 1958.

Jarman, Archie. "High Jinks on a Low Level." *Tomorrow* 2, no. 2. Reprinted in *Spiritualism: A Critical Survey,* by Simeon Edmunds. London: Aquarian Press, 1966.

———. "Physical Phenomena: Fraud or Frontier?" *Tomorrow* (autumn 1960).

———. "Unsolved Animal Mysteries." *Tomorrow* (spring 1960).

Jarricot, Jean. *Pendule et Médecine* (Pendulum and Medicine). Paris: G. Doin, 1949.

———. *Radiesthesie* (Radiesthesia). N.p., 1958.

Jast, L. Stanley. *Reincarnation and Karma.* Secaucus, N.J.: Castle Books, 1955.

Jastrow, Joseph. *Error and Eccentricity in Human Belief.* New York: Dover Publications, 1962.

———. *Fact and Fable in Psychology.* Boston; New York: Houghton, Mifflin & Co., 1900.

———. *Freud, His Dream and Sex Theories.* Cleveland, Ohio; New York: The World Publishing Co., 1943.

———. *The House That Freud Built.* New York: Greenberg, 1932.

———. *The Psychology of Conviction.* Boston; New York: Houghton, Mifflin & Co., 1918.

———. *Time Relations of Mental Phenomena.* N.p., 1890.

———. *Wish and Wisdom.* New York; London: D. Appleton-Century Co. Inc., 1935.

Jastrow, Joseph., ed. *The Story of Error.* N.p., 1936.

Jastrow, Morris. *Aspects of Religious Belief and Practice in Babylonia & Assyria.* New York: G. P. Putnam's Sons, 1911.

Jayakar, Pupul. *Krishnamurti: A Biography.* San Francisco: Harper & Row, 1986.

Jayne, Charles. *A New Dimension in Astrology.* New York: Astrological Bureau, 1975.

———. *The Technique of Rectification.* New York: Astrological Bureau, 1972.

———. *The Unknown Planets.* New York: Astrological Bureau, 1974.

Jefferson, William. *The Story of Maharishi.* New York: Pocket Books, 1976.

Jenkins, Elizabeth. *The Shadow and the Light: A Defence of Daniel Dunglas Home, the Medium.* London: Hamish Hamilton, 1982.

Jennings, Hargrave. *The Rosicrucians: Their Rites and Mysteries.* 3rd ed. 2 vols. London: J. Nimmo, 1887.

Jensen, Bernard. *Tony: The Miraculous Spiritual Healer at Work.* Escondido, Calif.: The Author, [1966].

Jensen, K. Frank. "A Decade with Tarot!" *Tarot Network News* 12 (spring 1994): 24–32.

Jephson, Ina. "A Behaviourist Experiment in Clairvoyance." *Proceedings of the Society for Psychical Research* 128, no. 41 (January 1933).

———. "Evidence for Clairvoyance in Card-Guessing: A Report on Some Recent Experiments." *Proceedings of the Society for Psychical Research* (December 1928): 38: 223–271, and 39: 375–414.

Jephson, Ina, S. G. Soal, and Theodore Besterman. "Report on a Series of Experiments in Clairvoyance." *Proceedings of the Society for Psychical Research* 118, no. 39 (April 1931).

Jerome, Joseph. *Montague Summers: A Memoir.* London: Cecil and Amerila Woolf, 1965.

Jessen-Schardebøl, E. J. *Afhandling om de Norske Finners og Lappers Hedenske Religion.* N.p., 1765.

Jinarajadasa, C. *The Early Teachings of the Masters, 1881–1883.* Chicago: Theosophical Press, 1925. Kila, Mont.: Kessinger Publishing Co., 1996.

Jinarajadasa, C., ed. *The K. H. Letters to C. W. Leadbeater.* Adyar, Madras, India: Theosophical Publishing House, 1941.

———. *Letters from the Masters of Wisdom.* 2 vols. Adyar, Madras India: Theosophical Publishing House, 1919.

———. *The Story of the Mahatma Letters.* Adyar, Madras, India: Theosophical Publishing House, 1946.

Joan and Darby. *Our Unseen Guest.* New York: Harper & Brothers, 1920.

John of Ruysbroeck. *Adornment of the Spiritual Marriage.* Translated by P. Synschenk. London, 1916.

Johns, June. *King of the Witches: The World of Alex Sanders.* London, 1969. Reprint, London: Pan, 1971.

Johnson, Alice. "Mrs. Henry Sidgwick's Work in Psychical Research." *Proceedings of the Society for Psychical Research* (1936–37).

———. "The Education of the Sitter." *Proceedings of the Society for Psychical Research* (1908–09).

———. "On the Automatic Writing of Mrs. Holland." *Proceedings of the Society for Psychical Research* 21 (1908).

———. "Report of Some Recent Sittings for Physical Phenomena in America." *Proceedings of the Society for Psychical Research* (1908–09).

———. "Second Report on Mrs. Holland's Script." *Proceedings of the Society for Psychical Research* 24 (1910).

———. "Supplementary Notes on Mrs. Holland's Scripts." *Proceedings of the Society for Psychical Research* 22 (1909).

———. "Third Report on Mrs. Holland's Scripts." *Proceedings of the Society for Psychical Research* 25 (1911).

Johnson, Fred H. *The Anatomy of Hallucinations.* Chicago: Nelson Hall, 1978.

Johnson, K. Paul. *The Masters Revealed: Madam Blavatsky and the Myth of the Great White Lodge.* Albany: State University of New York Press, 1994.

Johnson, Kendall. *The Living Aura: Radiation Field Photography and the Kirlian Effect.* New York: Hawthorn Books, 1976.

Johnson, Kenneth. *Slavic Sorcery.* St. Paul, Minn.: Llewellyn Publications, 1999.

Johnson, Paul. *In Search of the Masters: Behind the Occult Myth.* South Boston: The Author, 1990.

Johnson, Raynor C. *The Imprisoned Splendour.* New York: Harper & Brothers, 1953.

———. *Nurslings of Immortality.* London: Hodder & Stoughton, 1957.

———. *Psychical Research.* New York: Philosophical Library, 1955.

———. *The Spiritual Path.* New York: Harper & Brothers, 1971.

———. *Watcher on the Hills.* New York: Harper & Brothers, 1959.

Johnston, Francis M. *The Wonder of Guadalupe.* Rockford, Ill.: TAN, 1981.

Joire, Paul. *Précis historique et pratique de Neuro-Hypnologie.* Paris, 1892.

———. *Psychical and Supernormal Phenomena.* London: William Rider & Son/New York: F. A. Stokes, 1916.

———. *Traité de Graphologie scientifique.* N.p., 1906.

———. *Traité de l'Hypnotisme expérimental et thérapeutique.* N.p., 1908.

Jolly, W. P. *Sir Oliver Lodge.* New Jersey: Fairleigh Dickinson University Press, 1975.

Jones, David. *Visions of Time.* Wheaton, Ill.: Theosophical Publishing House (Quest), 1979.

Jones, E. Michael. *Medjugorje: The Untold Story.* South Bend, Ind.: Fidelity Press, 1988.

Jones, Edmund. *A Relation of Ghosts and Apparitions Which Commonly Appear in the Principality of Wales.* Bristol, England: 1767.

Jones, Ernest. *On the Nightmare.* New York: Liveright Publishing, 1951.

Jones, Franklin. *The Method of the Siddhas.* Los Angeles: Dawn Horse Press, 1973.

Jones, Franklin [Heart Master Da Love Ananda]. *Dawn Horse Testament.* San Rafael, Calif.: Dawn Horse Press, 1985.

———. *The Heart's Shout.* Clearlake, Calif.: Dawn Horse Press, 1993.

———. *The Knee of Listening.* Los Angeles: Dawn Horse Press, 1972.

Jones, Franklin [Heart Master Da Love Ananda]. [Da Avabhasa]. *Free Daism: The Eternal, Ancient, and New Religion of God-Realization.* Clearlake, Calif.: Dawn Horse Press, 1992.

Jones, Kelvin I. *Conan Doyle and the Spirits: The Spiritualist Career of Sir Arthur Conan Doyle.* Wellingborough, England: Aquarian Press, 1989.

Jones, Marc Edmund. *Essentials of Astrological Analysis.* Stanwood, Wash.: Sabian Publishing Society, 1970.

———. *How to Live With the Stars.* Wheaton, Ill.: Theosophical Publishing House, 1976.

———. *Key Truths of Occult Philosophy.* Los Angeles: J. F. Rowney Press, 1925.

———. *Occult Philosophy: An Introduction.* Stanwood, Wash.: Sabian Publishing Society, 1971.

———. *The Ritual of Living.* Los Angeles: J. F. Rowney Press, 1930. Rev. ed. *The Sabian Manual: A Ritual for Living.* New York: Sabian Publishing Society, 1957.

———. *The Sabian Book.* Stanwood, Wash.: Sabian Publishing Society, 1973.

———. *Scope of Astrological Prediction.* Stanwood, Wash.: Sabian Publishing Society, 1969.

Jones, Richard H. *Mysticism Examined: Philosophical Inquiries into Mysticism.* Albany: State University of New York Press, 1993.

Jones, Richard M. *The New Psychology of Dreaming.* New York: Grune & Stratton, 1970.

Jones, Rufus Matthew. *Studies in Mystical Religion.* N.p., 1909. Reprint, New York: Russell & Russell, 1970.

Jones, T. Gwynn. *Welsh Folklore and Folk Customs.* London: Methuen, 1930.

Jones, William. *Credulities Past and Present.* London: Chatto & Windus, 1880. Reprint, Detroit: Singing Tree Press, 1967.

Jong, K. H. "The Trumpet Medium Mrs. Harris." *Journal of the Society for Psychical Research* 16 (1914).

Jonte-Pace, Diane. "The Swami and the Rorschach: Spiritual Practice, Religious Experience, and Perception." *The Innate Capacity: Mysticism, Psychology, and Philosophy.* New York: Oxford University Press, 1998.

Jordan, Pacual. *Verdrängung and Komplementarität* (Repression and Complementarity). N.p., 1951.

———. "New Trends in Physics and Their Relation to Parapsychology." *Parapsychology Foundation Newsletter* (July–August 1955).

Jourdan, Jean-Pierre. "Near-Death and Transcendental Experiences: Neurophysiological Correlates of Mystical Traditions," *Journal of Near-Death Studies* 12, no. 3 (Spring 1994): 177–200.

Journal of the Alchemical Society 3 vols., London, 1913–15.

Journal of Ethnopharmacology: An Interdisciplinary Journal Devoted to Bioscientific Research on Indigenous Drugs. 1, (1947).

Joyner, Graham. *The Hairy Man of Southeastern Australia.* Canberra: National Library of Australia, 1977.

———. "Scientific Discovery and the Place of the Yahoo in Australian Zoological History." *Cryptozoology* 9 (1990): 41–51.

Judah, J. Stillson. *The History and Philosophy of the Metaphysical Movement in America.* Philadelphia: Westminster Press, 1967.

Judge, William Q. *Echoes of the Orient.* 2 vols. San Diego, Calif.: Point Loma Publications, 1975, 1980.

———. *The Ocean of Theosophy.* Reprint, Point Loma, Calif.: Theosophical University Press, 1974.

Judith, Anodea. *Neo-Paganism.* St. Paul, Minn.: Llewellyn Publications, 1999.

———. *Wheels of Life: A User's Guide to the Chakra System.* St. Paul, Minn.: Llewellyn Publications, 1987.

Judy, Dwight H. "Transpersonal Psychology: Roots in Christian Mysticism." In *Textbook of Transpersonal Psychiatry and Psychology.* New York: Basicbooks, Inc., 1996.

Jules-Bois, A. H. "Charles Richet: Father of Metaphysics." *Journal of the American Society for Psychical Research* 30 (1936).

Jung, Carl G. *Alchemical Studies.* Vol. 13. *Collected Works.* Princeton, N.J.: Princeton University Press, 1967.

———. *Archetypes and the Collective Unconscious.* Vol. 9. *Collected Works.* Princeton, N.J.: Princeton University Press, 1959.

———. *Flying Saucers: A Modern Myth of Things Seen in the Skies.* New York: Harcourt, Brace, 1959.

———. *Jung on Synchronicity & the Paranormal.* Princeton, N.J.: Princeton University Press, 1875. Reprint, 1961, 1998.

———. *Psychology and Alchemy.* Volume 12 of the *Collected Works.* Princeton, N.J.: Princeton University Press, 1968.

———. *Sychronicity: An Acausal Connecting Principle.* London: Ark Paperbacks, 1985.

Jung, Carl G., and W. Pauli. *The Interpretation of Nature and the Psyche.* London, 1955.

Jung, Johann Heinrich. *Heinrich Stilling.* Translated by S. Jackson. 1835–36. 2nd ed. 1843. Abridged ed., edited by R. O. Moon. N.p., 1886.

Jung on Synchronicity & the Paranormal. New York: Routledge, 1998.

Jürgenson, Friedrich. *Rösterna från Rymden* (Voices From Space). Sweden, 1964. German edition as *Sprechfunk mit Verstorbenen.* Freiburg i. Br.: Herman Bauer, 1967.

Juste, Michael [Michael Houghton]. *Escape, and Other Verse.* Leeds, 1924.

———. *Many Brightnesses, and Other Verse.* London, 1954.

———. *Shoot—and Be Damned.* London, 1935.

———. *The White Brother.* London, 1927.

Jyotir Maya Nanda, Swami. *The Way to Liberation.* Miami, Fla.: Swami Lalitananda, 1976.

———. *Waking, Dream, and Sleep.* Miami, Fla.: Yoga Research Foundation, 1974.

———. *Yoga Can Change Your Life.* Miami, Fla.: International Yoga Society, 1975.

———. *Yoga in Life.* Miami, Fla.: The Author, 1973.

———. *Yoga Vasistha.* Miami, Fla.: Yoga Research Society, 1977.

The Kabbala Unveiled. New York: Krishna Press, 1973.

Kabir. *One Hundred Poems of Kabir.* Translated by Rabinadrath Tagore. London, 1915.

Kaempffert, Waldemar B. *Explorations in Science.* N.p., 1953.

———. *Invention and Society.* Chicago: American Library Association, 1930.

———. *Science Today and Tomorrow.* New York: Viking Press, 1945.

Kagan, Paul. *New World Utopias.* Baltimore, Md.: Penguin Books, 1975.

Kahn, S. David. "Ave Atque Vale: Gardner Murphy." *Journal* of the American Society for Psychical Research 74 (1980).

———. "The Enigma of Psi: A Challenge for Scientific Method." *Journal* of the American Society for Psychical Research (July 1962).

———. "Extrasensory Perception and Friendly Interpersonal Relations." In *Explorations in Altruistic Love and Behavior,* edited by Pitirim A. Sorokin. N.p., 1950.

———. "A Mechanical Scoring Technique for Testing GESP [General Extrasensory Perception]." *Journal of Parapsychology* 13, no. 3 (1949).

———. "Studies in Extrasensory Perception: Experiments Utilizing an Electronic Scoring Device."*Proceedings of the American Society for Psychical Research* 25 (October 1952).

Kaigh, Frederick. *Witchcraft and Magic of Africa.* London: Richard Lesley, 1947.

Kakar, Sudhir. "Ramakrishna and the Mystical Experience," *Annual of Psychoanalysis* 20 (1992): 215–234.

———. *Shamans, Mystics, and Doctors: A Psychological Inquiry into India and Its Healing Traditions.* New York: Knopf, 1982.

Kalé, Shrikrishna Vasudeo. "Parapsychology and Science." *Indian Journal of Parapsychology* 1, no. 2 (1959).

———. "Parapsychology and Science." *Indian Journal of Parapsychology* 2, no. 1 (1961).

Kalisch, Isidor, trans. *Sepher Yezirah.* New York, 1877. Reprint, San Jose, Calif.: Rosicrucian Press, 1950. Reprint, N. Hollywood, Calif.: Symbols and Signs, n.d.

Kalweit, Holger. *Dreamtime & Inner Space: The World of the Shaman.* (Translated from German). Boston: Shambhala, 1988.

———. *Shamans, Healers, and Medicine Men.* (Translated from German). Boston: Shambhala, 1992.

Kamiya, Joe. "Conscious Control of Brain Waves." *Psychology Today* 1, no. 11 (April 1968).

Kane, Beverley, Jean Millay, and Dean Harold Brown, eds. *Silver Threads: 25 Years of Parapsychology Research.* Westport, Conn.: Praeger Publishers/Greenwood Publishing Group, Inc., 1993.

Kane, Elisha. *Arctic Explorations in Search of Sir John Franklin.* London: T. Nelson, 1885.

Kane, Margaret Fox. *The Love-Life of Dr. Kane.* New York, 1865.

Kanellakos, Demetri P., and Jerome S. Lukas. *Psychobiology of Transcendental Meditation: A Literature Review.* W. A. Benjamin, 1974.

Kant, Immanuel. *Träume eines Geistersehers erläutert durch die Träume der Metaphysik.* 1766. Translated as *Dreams of a Spirit-Seer.* N.p., 1900.

Kao, James. *Chinese Divination.* Smithtown, N.Y.: Exposition Press, 1980.

Kaplan, Aryeh. *Chassidic Masters: History, Biography, and Thought.* New York: Maznaim Publishing, 1984.

Kaplan, Fred. *Dickens and Mesmerism: The Hidden Springs of Fiction.* Princeton, N.J.: Princeton University Press, 1975.

Kaplan, R. W. "The Sacred Mushroom in Scandinavia," *Man* 10, no. 1 (1975): 72–79.

Kappers, Jan. "ESP Status in 1966." *International Journal of Neuropsychiatry* (September–October 1966).

———. "The Investigation of Spontaneous Cases." *Tijdschrift voor Parapsychologie* (1954).

———. "Is It Possible to Induce ESP with Psilocybine? An Exploratory Investigation." *International Journal of Neuropsychiatry* 2, no. 5 (1966).

Karadja, Mary. *Esoteric Meaning of the Seven Sacraments.* N.p., 1910.

———. *Etincelles* (French epigrams). N.p., 1890.

———. *King Solomon: A Mystic Drama.* N.p., 1912.

———. *Towards the Light.* New York: Dodd, Mead, 1909.

Karagulla, Shafica. *Breakthrough to Creativity: Your Higher Sense Perception.* Santa Monica, Calif.: DeVorss, 1967.

Karcher, Janet. *The Way to Cassadaga: A Look at Spiritualism, Its Roots, and Beliefs, and Cassadaga, Florida.* Daltona, Fla: J. Hutchinson Productions, 1980.

Karcher, Stephen. *The Encyclopedia of Divination.* UK: Element Books, Inc., 1997.

Kardec, Allan. *Collection of Selected Prayers.* New York: Stadium, 1975.

———. *Experimental Spiritism: The Mediums' Book.* London, 1876.

———. *Heaven and Hell.* Translated by Anna Blackwell. 1878.

———. *L'Evangile selon le Spiritisme.* 1864. Translated as *The Gospel According to Spiritism.* London: Headquarters Publishing, 1887.

———. *Le Ciel et L'Enfer ou la justice divine selon le Spiritisme.* 1865. Translated as *Heaven and Hell, or The Divine Justice Vindicated in the Plurality of Existences.* N.p., 1878.

———. *Le Livre des Esprits.* Translated as *The Spirits' Book* by Anna Blackwell. 1875. Reprint, São Paulo: Lake-Livraria Allan Kardec Editora, 1972.

———. *Le Livre des Mediums.* Translated as *The Book of Mediums* by Emma E. Wood. Reprint, New York: Samuel Weiser, 1970.

———. *The Mediums' Book.* Translated by Anna Blackwell. London, 1876. Reprint. New York: Samuel Weiser, 1970.

———. *Spiritualist Philosophy; The Spirits' Book.* London, 1893. Reprint, New York: Ayer Publishing Co. Inc., 1976.

Kardec, Allan [H. L. D. Rivail]. *The Book of Spirits.* N.p., 1893.

Karunaratne, K. P. *Olcott Commemoration Volume.* Ceylon: Olcott Commemoration Society, 1967.

———. *Olcott's Contribution to the Buddhist Renaissance.* Colombo, Sri Lanka: Publication Division, Ministry of Cultural Affairs, 1980.

Kast, Verena. *Joy, Inspiration, and Hope.* College Station, Tex.: Texas A & M University Press, 1991.

Kastenbaum, Robert, ed. *Between Life and Death.* New York: Springer Publishing, 1979.

Katchen, Martin H. and David K. Sakheim. *Out of Darkness: Exploring Satanism and Ritual Abuse.* New York: Lexington Books/ Macmillan, Inc., 1992.

Katz, Richard. "The Painful Ecstasy of Healing," *Psychology Today* (December 1976): 81–86.

Katz, Richard, Megan Biesele, and Verna St. Denis. *Healing Makes Our Hearts Happy: Spirituality and Cultural Transformation among the Kalahari Jul'hoansi.* Rochester, Vt.: Inner Traditions, 1998.

Kauffmann, D. F. *Northern Mythology.* London: Dent, 1903.

Kautz, William H. "The Rosemary Case of Alleged Egyptian Xenoglossy." *Theta* 10, 2 (summer 1982).

Kautz, William H., and Melanie Branon. *Channeling: The Intuitive Connection.* San Francisco: Harper & Row, 1987.

Kay, Frank E. *Kabir and His Followers.* London, 1931.

Keating, Laurence J. *The Great Mary Celeste Hoax: A Famous Sea Mystery Exposed.* London: Heath-Cranton, 1929.

Keel, John A. *Disneyland of the Gods.* New York: Amok Press, 1988.

———. *The Eighth Tower.* New York: New American Library/ New York: Saturday Review Press/E. P. Dutton, 1975.

———. *Jadoo.* London, 1958.

———. *The Mothman Prophecies: An Investigation Into the Mysterious American Visits of the Infamous Feathery Garuda.* New York: Saturday Review Press/Dutton, 1975. Reprint, New York: New American Library, 1976. Reprinted as *Visitors From Space: The Astonishing True Story of the Mothman Prophecies.* St. Albans, England: Panther, 1976.

———. *Our Haunted Planet.* Greenwich, Conn.: Fawcett Gold Medal, 1977.

———. *Strange Creatures from Time and Space.* Greenwich, Conn.: Fawcett, 1970. Reprint: London: Neville Spearman, 1975.

———. *UFOs: Operation Trojan Horse.* New York: G. P. Putnam's Sons, 1970.

———. *Why UFOs?* New York: Manor Books, 1978.

Keene, M. Lamar. *The Psychic Mafia.* New York: St. Martin's Press, 1976. Buffalo, N.Y.: Prometheus Books, 1997.

Keil, Jürgen. *Gaither Pratt: A Life for Parapsychology.* Jefferson, N.C.: McFarland, 1987.

Keil, Jürgen, and J. Gaither Pratt. "First Hand Observations of Nina S. Kulagina Suggestive of PK on Static Objects." *Journal of the American Society for Psychical Research* 67 (1973).

Keil, Jürgen, Montague Ullman, and J. Gaither Pratt. "Directly Observable Voluntary PK Effects." *Proceedings of the Society for Psychical Research* 56 (1976).

Keller, Franz. *Amazon and Madeira Rivers.* London, 1874.

Kellock, Harold. *Houdini: His Life-Story.* New York: Harcourt, Brace, 1928.

Kelly, Aidan A. *Crafting the Art of Magic: A History of Modern Witchcraft, 1939–1964.* St. Paul, Minn.: Llewellyn Publications, 1991.

Kelly, Henry Ansgar. *The Devil, Demonology, and Witchcraft.* Garden City, N.Y.: Doubleday, 1974.

Kelsey, Denys, and Joan Grant. *Many Lifetimes.* Garden City, N.Y.: Doubleday, 1967.

Kelsey, Morton T. *God, Dreams, and Revelation: A Christian Interpretation of Dreams.* Minneapolis, Minn.: Augsburg Publishing House, 1974.

———. *Tongue Speaking: An Experiment in Spiritual Experience.* Garden City, N.Y.: Doubleday, 1968. Reprint, London: Hodder & Stoughton, 1973.

Kelzer, Kenneth. *The Sun and the Shadow: My Experiment with Lucid Dreaming.* Virginia Beach, Va.: A.R.E. Press, 1987.

Kenawell, William W. *The Quest at Glastonbury: A Biographical Study of Frederick Bligh Bond.* New York: Helix Press/Garrett Publications, 1965.

Kendall, Laurel. *Shamans, Housewives, and Other Restless Spirits: Women in Korean Ritual Life.* Honolulu, Hawaii: University of Hawaii Press, 1992.

Kendrick, Tertius T. C. *The Kako-daemon or The Cavern of Anti-Paros.* London, 1825.

Kenin-Lopsan, M. B.,ed. "Shamanic Songs and Myths of Tuva," In *ISTOR Books,* vol. 7 (joint publication with the International Society for Trans-Oceanic Research, Los Angeles). Budapest: Akadémiai Kiadó, 1997.

Kenmore, Dallas. *The Nature of Genius.* Westport, Conn.: Greenwood Press, 1972.

Kennard, Nina H. *Lafcadio Hearn, His Life and Work.* New York: D. Appleton and Co., 1912.

Kennedy, Patrick. *Legendary Fictions of the Irish Celt.* 1866. Reprint, Detroit: Singing Tree Press, 1968.

Kennett, Frances. *History of Perfume.* London: Harrap, 1975.

Kenton, Warren. *Astrology: The Celestial Mirror.* London: Thames & Hudson, 1974.

Kerins, Deborah, ed. *The Spinner of Tales: A Collection of Stories as Told by Ramtha.* Yelm, Wash.: New Horizon Publishing, 1991.

Kerner, Justinus. *Die Seherin von Prevorst.* 1829. Abridged and translated as *The Seeress of Prevorst.* London, 1845. Reprint, Stuttgart: J. F. Steinkopf, 1963.

———. *Die Somnambülen Tische: Zur Geschichte und Erklärungen dieser Erscheinungen.* Stuttgart, 1853.

Kerner, Justinus. *The Seeress of Prevorst.* London, 1845.

Kerr, Howard. *Mediums and Spirit-Rappers and Roaring Radicals.* Urbana, Ill.: University of Illinois Press, 1972.

Keyes, Ken. *The Hundreth Monkey.* Coos Bay, Ore.: Vision Books, 1982.

Keyhoe, Donald E. *Aliens From Space: The Real Story of Unidentified Flying Objects.* Garden City, N.Y.: Doubleday, 1973.

Keyhoe, Donald E. *The Flying Saucer Conspiracy.* New York: Henry Holt, 1955.

———. *The Flying Saucers Are Real.* New York: Fawcett Publications, 1950.

———. *Flying Saucers from Outer Space.* New York: Henry Holt, 1953.

———. *Flying Saucers: Top Secret.* New York: G. P. Putnam's Sons, 1960.

Keynes, Geoffrey, ed. *Blake: Complete Writings.* Oxford: Oxford University Press, 1974.

Khérumian, Raphaël. "Essai d'interprétation des expériences de Soal et Goldney" (Interpretative Essay on the Experiments of Soal and Goldney). *Revue Métapsychique* 8 (1949).

———. "Introduction à l'étude de la connaissance parapsychologique" (Introduction to the Study of Parapsychology Knowledge). *Revue Métapsychique* 1–3 (1948).

———. "Les propriétés groupales des organismes et la parapsychologie" (The Group Properties of Organisms and Parapsychology). *Revue Métapsychique* 10 (1950).

———. "Procédés mécaniques pour faciliter les transmissions télépathiques" (Mechanical Procedures to Facilitate Telepathic Messages). *Revue Métapsychique* 26 (1953).

———. "A propos de l'hypothèse cryptesthétique" (Regarding the Cryptesthetic Hypothesis). *Revue Métapsychique* 1, no. 2 (1955).

———. "Réflexions sur l'état actuel et les perspectives de la parapsychologie" (Remarks on the Present Status and the Future of Parapsychology). *Revue Métapsychique* 2, nos. 8, 9 (1958–59).

Khalsa, Parmatma Singh, ed. *Spiritual Community Guide No. 4,* California: Spiritual Community Publications, 1979.

Khan, Pir V. *The Message in Our Time: The Life and Teachings of the Sufi Master, Hazrat Inayat Khan.* New York: Harper & Row, 1979.

Khilji, Anjum. "Behind the Veil: Muslim Women's Contributions to Parapsychology." In *Women and Parapsychology.* New York: Parapsychology Foundation, Inc., 1994.

Kieckhefer, Richard. *European Witch Trials: Their Foundations in Popular and Learned Culture 1300–1500.* Berkeley: University of California Press, 1976.

Kieffer, Gene. "An Appeal for Common Sense." *SFF Newsletter* [Spiritual Frontiers Fellowship] (October 1988).

———. "It's Not the Soma that the Brahmans Know!" *SFF Newsletter* [Spiritual Frontiers Fellowship] (September 1988).

———. "*ReVision* Revisits the Sacred Mushroom." *SFF Newsletter* [Spiritual Frontiers Fellowship] (August 1988).

Kieffer, Gene, ed. *Kundalini for the New Age: Selected Writings of Gopi Krishna.* New York: Bantam Books, 1988.

Kiev, Ari, ed. *Magic, Faith, and Healing: Studies in Primitive Psychiatry Today.* New York: The Free Press, [1964] 1969.

Kildahl, John P. *The Psychology of Speaking in Tongues.* New York: Harper & Row, 1972.

Kilner, Walter J. *The Human Atmosphere.* London, 1911. Reprinted as *The Human Aura.* New Hyde Park, N.Y.: University Books, 1965.

———. *The Human Aura.* 1911. Reprint, New Hyde Park, N.Y.: University Books, 1965.

Kilpatrick, Jack F., and Anna G. Kilpatrick. "A Notebook of a Cherokee Shaman." *Smithsonian Contributions to Anthropology* 2, no. 6 (1970): 83–125.

Kindermann, Henny. *Lola; or, The Thought and Speech of Animals.* New York: E. P. Dutton, 1923.

Kindersley, Nathaniel E. *Specimens of Hindoo Literature.* N.p., 1794.

King, F. *Astral Projection Magic & Alchemy.* New York: Samuel Weiser Inc., 1981.

King, Francis. *Astral Projection, Ritual Magic & Alchemy: Being Hitherto Unpublished Gold Dawn Material.* London: Neville Spearman, 1971.

———. *The Holy Books of Thelema.* York Beach, Maine: Samuel Weiser, 1988.

———. *Magic: The Western Tradition.* London: Thames & Hudson, 1975.

———. *The Magical World of Aleister Crowley.* New York: Coward, McCann & Geoghegan, 1978.

———. *O.T.O. System Outline.* San Francisco, Calif.: Stellar Vision, 1981.

———. *The Rites of Modern Occult Magic.* New York: Macmillan, 1970.

———. *Ritual Magic in England: 1887 to the Present Day.* London: Neville Spearman, 1970. Reprinted as *The Rites of Modern Occult Magic.* New York: Macmillan, 1971.

———. *Satan and Swastika: The Occult and the Nazi Party.* London: Mayflower, 1976.

———. *Sexuality, Magic & Perversion.* London: Neville Spearman, 1971. Reprint, New York: Citadel Press, 1972.

———. *Wisdom From Afar.* London: Aldus Books, 1975.

King, Francis, ed. *Sexuality, Magic, and Perversion.* Secaucus, N.J.: Citadel Press, 1972.

King, Francis, ed. *The Secret Rituals of the O.T.O.* New York: Samuel Weiser, 1973.

King, Francis, and Isabel Sutherland. *The Rebirth of Magic.* London: Corgi, 1982.

King, Francis, and Stephen Skinner. *Techniques of High Magic.* New York: Destiny Books, 1980.

King, George. *The Practices of Aetherius.* Hollywood, Calif.: Aetherius Society, 1964.

———. *The Nine Freedoms.* Los Angeles: Aetherius Society, 1963.

———. *The Twelve Blessings.* London: Aetherius Press, 1958.

———. *You Are Responsible.* London: Aetherius Press, 1961.

King, Godfre Ray [Guy W. Ballard]. *The "I AM" Discourses.* Chicago: St. Germain Press, 1935.

———. *The Magic Presence.* Chicago: St. Germain Press, 1935.

———. *Unveiled Mysteries.* Chicago: Saint Germain Press, 1982.

King, J. H. *The Supernatural.* 2 vols. London, 1892.

King, James. *William Blake: His Life.* London: Weidenfeld and Nicolson, 1991.

King, Noel Q. *African Cosmos: An Introduction to Religion in Africa.* Belmont, Calif.: Wadsworth, 1986.

King, Serge. *Kahuna Healing.* Wheaton, Ill.: Theosophical Publishing House, 1983.

———. *Mastering Your Hidden Self.* Wheaton, Ill.: Theosophical Publishing House, 1983.

———. *Urban Shaman.* New York: Simon & Schuster, 1990.

Kingsford, Anna B. and Edward Maitland. *Clothed with the Sun (1889).* London: John M. Watkins, 1889. Kila, Mont.: Kessinger Publishing Co., 1999.

———. *The Perfect Way; or, The Finding of Christ.* London, 1882. Rev. ed. London, 1887. Reprint, Mokelumne Hill, Calif.: Health Research, 1972. Reprint, Boston: Esoteric Book Co., 1988.

———. *The Story of Anna Kingsford and Edward Maitland and of the New Gospel of Interpretation.* Birmingham, England: Ruskin Press, 1905.

———. *The Virgin of the World.* 1885. Reprint, Minneapolis, Minn.: Wizard's Bookshelf, 1977.

Kingsland, William. *The Real H. P. Blavatsky.* London: John M. Watkins/ Theosophical Publishing House, 1928.

Kingsley, Charles. *The Heroes.* 1856. Reprint, New York: Dutton, 1963.

Kirban, Salem. *666.* Huntingdon Valley, Pa.: Salem Kirban, 1970.

Kirk, Ella Boyce. *My Pilgrimage to Coué.* New York: American Library Service, 1922.

Kirk, Robert. *The Secret Commonwealth of Elves, Fauns, and Fairies.* 1691. Reprint, Edinburgh, 1815. Reprint, London: D. Nutt, 1893. Reprint, Stirling, Scotland: Eaneas Mackay, 1933.

Kister, D. A. "Korean Shamanistic Ritual," *Bibliotheca Shamanistica,* vol. 5. Budapest: Akadémiai Kiadó, 1998.

Kittredge, George Lyman. *Witchcraft in Old and New England.* Cambridge, Mass.: Harvard University Press, 1929. Reprint, New York: Atheneum, 1972.

Klemp, Harold. *The Book of ECK Wisdom.* Illuminated Way Publishing, Inc., 1986. Reprint, Minneapolis, Minn.: Ecankar, 1987.

———. *Soul Travelers of the Far Country.* Minneapolis, Minn.: ECKANKAR, 1987.

Kleps, Art. *Millbrook: The True Story of the Early Years of the Psychedelic Revolution.* Oakland, Calif.: Bench Press, 1977.

Klibanv. A. I. *History of Religious Sectarianism in Russia (1860s–1917).* Oxford: Pergamon Press, 1982.

Klimo, Jon. *Channeling: Investigations on Receiving Information from Paranormal Sources.* Los Angeles: Jeremy P. Tarcher, 1967.

Klinckowstroem, Graf Carl von. *Bibliographie der Wünschelrute* (Bibliography of the Divining Rod). N.p., 1911.

———. *Die Zauberkunst* (The Art of Magic). N.p., 1954.

———. *Virgula divina. Ein Beitrag zur Geschichte der Wünschelrute.* Berlin, 1910.

———. *Yogi-Künste* (Yogic Arts). N.p., 1922.

Klinckowstroem, Graf Carl von, and Rudolph von Maltzahn. *Handbuch der Wünschelrute* (Handbook of the Divining Rod). München; Berlin: R. Oldenbourg, 1931.

Klinckowstroem, Graf Carl von, W. von Gulat-Wellenburg, and Hans Rosenbusch. *Der Physikalische Mediumismus* (Physical Mediumship). N.p., 1925.

Klineman, George, and Sherman Butler. *The Cult That Died.* New York: G. P. Putnam's Sons, 1980.

Klonsky, Milton. *William Blake: The Seer and His Visions.* New York: Crown Publishers, 1977.

Kloppenburg, Boaventura. *A Maçonario no Brasil* (Masonry in Brazil). 4th ed. N.p., 1961.

———. *Nossas Supersticoes* (Our Superstitions). N.p., 1959.

———. *O Espiritismo no Brasil* (Spiritism in Brazil). Petropolis: Editoria Vozes, 1964.

———. *O Reencarnacionismo no Brasil* (Reincarnationism in Brazil). Petropolis: Editoria Vozes, 1961.

———. *Pastoral Practice and the Paranormal.* Translated by Paul Burns. Chicago: Franciscan Herald Press, 1979.

Kneale, Martha Hurst. "Is Psychical Research Relevant to Philosophy?" *Proceedings, Aristotelian Society.* Supplementary volume 24 (1950).

———. "Time and Psychical Research." *Proceedings of Four Conferences of Parapsychological Studies* (1957).

Knibb, Michael A. *The Qumran Community.* Cambridge, Mass.: Cambridge University Press, 1987.

Knight, Alfred E. *Amentet: An Account of the Gods, Amulets and Scarabs of the Ancient Egyptians.* London: Longmans, Green, 1915.

Knight, Damon. *Charles Fort, Prophet of the Unexplained.* Garden City, N.Y.: Doubleday, 1970.

Knight, David C., ed. *The ESP Reader.* New York: Grosset & Dunlap, 1969.

Knight, G. Norman, and F. Smyth. *The Pocket History of Freemasonry.* London: Fred K. Muller, 1977.

Knight, Gareth. *The Practice of Ritual Magic.* Toddington, England: Helios Book Service, 1969. Reprint, New York: Samuel Weiser, 1976.

Knight, JZ. *A State of Mind: My Story.* New York: Warner Books, 1987.

Knight, Richard Payne. *A Discourse on the Worship of Priapus.* 1786. Reprint, Secaucus, N.J.: University Books, 1974.

Knight, Stephen. *The Brotherhood: The Secret World of the Freemasons.* New York: Stein & Day, 1984.

Knopf, A. Adolphus. *A Reminiscence of and a Promise to Professor James Hervey Hyslop.* New York: The Author, 1921.

Knott, Kim. *My Sweet Lord.* Wellingsborough, England: Aquarian Press, 1986.

Knowles, Elsie A. G. "Report on an Experiment Concerning the Influence of Mind Over Matter." *Journal of Parapsychology* 13, no. 3 (September 1949).

———. "Report on the Susceptibility of Manually Operated Random Selector to Psi Dexterity." *Journal of Parapsychology* 16, no. 1 (March 1952).

Knowles, Frederick W. "ESP Today." *Corrective Psychiatry and Journal of Special Therapy* 12, no. 2 (March 1966).

———. "Psychic Healing in Organic Disease." *Journal* of the American Society for Psychical Research 50, no. 3 (July 1956).

———. "Rat Experiments and Mesmerism." *Journal* of the American Society for Psychical Research 53, no. 2 (April 1959).

———. "Some Investigations into Psychic Healing." *Journal* of the American Society for Psychical Research 48, no. 1 (January 1954).

Knudtson, Peter H. "Flora, Shaman of the Wintu," *Natural History* 84 (May 1975): 6–17.

Koch, Walter A. *Astrologische Farbenlehre* (Astrological Science of Colors). N.p., 1930.

———. *Deine Farbe—Dein Charakter* (Your Color—Your Character). N.p., 1953.

———. *Die Seele der Edelsteine* (The Psyche of Precious Stones). N.p., 1934.

———. *Dr. Korsch und Die Astrologie* (Dr. Korsch and Astrology). N.p., 1956.

———. *Innenmensch und Außenmensch* (Man: Introversion and Extraversion). N.p., 1956.

———. *Prophetie und Astrologische Prognose* (Prophecy and Astrological Prediction). N.p., 1954.

———. *Psychologische Farbenlehre* (Psychological Science of Colors). C. Marhold, 1931.

———. *Regiomontanus und das Häusersystem des Geburtsortes* (Regiomontanus and the System of Houses of Birthplaces). N.p., 1960.

Koestler, Arthur. *The Ghost in the Machine.* New York: Macmillan, 1968.

———. *The Lotus and the Robot.* London: Hutchinson, 1960.

———. *The Roots of Coincidence.* London: Hutchinson, 1972.

———. *The Yogi and the Commissar.* New York: Macmillan, 1946.

Kohler, Kaufmann. *Heaven and Hell in Comparative Literature.* Folcroft, Pa., 1923.

Kolakowski, Leszek. *Bergson.* Oxford: Oxford University Press, 1989.

Konraad, Sandor. *Numerology: Key to the Tarot.* Rockport, Mass.: Para Research, 1983.

Kooy, J. M. J. "Introspectief Onderzoek naar Het Dunne-Effect" (Introspective Investigation of the Dunne-Effect). *Tijdschrift voor Parapsychologie* 6, no. 3 (March 1934).

———. "Paragnosie en Kansrekening" (Extrasensory Perception and the Calculus of Probability). *Tijdschrift voor Parapsychologie* 7, no. 3 (March 1935).

———. "Reply to Dr. Chari." *Journal of Parapsychology* 22, no. 1 (March 1958).

———. "Space, Time and Consciousness." *Journal of Parapsychology* 21, no. 4 (December 1957).

———. "Tijd, Ruimte en Paragnosie" (Time, Space and Extrasensory Perception). *Tijdschrift voor Parapsychologie* 15, nos. 3–4, (May–July 1947).

Kors, Alan C. *Witchcraft in Europe 1100–1700: A Documentary History.* Philadelphia: University of Pennsylvania Press, 1972.

Koski, Marie. *Personal Talks with Jesus.* Washington, D.C.: ESPress, 1979.

Kossy, Donna. *Kooks: A Guide to the Outer Limits of Human Belief.* Portland, Ore.: Feral House, 1994.

Kotie, Naum. *Die Emanation der psychophysichen Energie.* Wiesbaden, 1908.

Kovech, F. J., and R. W. Shahan, eds. *Albert the Great: Commemorative Essays.* Norman, Okla.: University of Oklahoma Press, 1980.

Kozminsky, Isidore. *Numbers, Their Meaning and Magic.* New York: G. P. Putnam's Sons, 1927.

Krader, Lawrence. "Shamanism: Theory and History in Buryat Society." Vilmos Diószegi and Mihály Hoppál, eds., In *Shamanism in Siberia.* Bibliotheca Uralica 1. Budapest: Akadémiai Kiadó, 1978: 21-45.

Kraft, Robert A., and George W. E. Nickelsburg. *Early Judaism and Its Modern Interpreters.* Philadelphia: Fortress Press, 1986.

Kral, Josef. *Das Heisse Eisen: Das Außersinnliche als Wissenschaft und Glaube* (The Hot Iron: The Paranormal as Science and Faith). Berlin: Verlag Harmonie, 1962.

———. *Der Neue Gottesbeweis: Parapsychologie, Mystik, Unsterblichkeit* (New Proof of God: Parapsychology, Mysticism, Immortality). N.p., 1956.

———. *Die Irrelehre vom Zufall und Schicksal im Lichte der Wissenschaften und des Glaubens* (The Heresy of Coincidence and Fate in the Light of Science and Faith). N.p., 1953.

Kraljevic, Svetozar. *Apparitions of Our Lady of Medjugorje (1981–1983).* Chicago: Franciscan Herald Press, 1984.

Krall, Karl. *Denkende Tiere.* Leipzig, 1912.

Kramer, Samuel N. *From the Tablets of Sumer.* Falcon's Wing, 1956.

———. *Gilgamesh and the Huluppu-tree: A Reconstructed Sumerian Text.* Chicago: University of Chicago Press, 1938.

Krammer, Heinrich, and James Sprenger. *The Malleus Maleficarum (Witches Hammer).* Translated by Montague Summers, 1928. Reprint, New York: Dover Publications, 1971.

Kreskin [George J. Kresge, Jr.]. *The Amazing World of Kreskin.* New York: Random House, 1973.

Krieger, Delores. "Healing by the Laying-On of Hands as a Facilitator of Bioenergetic Change: The Response of In-Vivo Human Hemoglobin." *Psychoenergetic Systems* 1 (1976): 121.

———. "Therapeutic Touch: The Imprimatur of Nursing." *American Journal of Nursing* 75, no. 5 (May 1875): 784–87.

Krippner, Stanley. *Dreamworking: How to Use Your Dreams for Creative Problem Solving.* Buffalo, N.Y.: Bearly Ltd., 1988.

———. *Human Possibilities: Mind Exploration in the USSR and Eastern Europe.* Garden City, N.Y.: Anchor Press/Doubleday, 1980.

———. *Psychoenergetic Systems: The Interaction of Consciousness, Energy, and Matter.* New York: Gordon and Breach Science Publishers, 1979.

———. "The Shaman as Healer and Psychotherapist," *Voices* (Winter 1992): 12–23.

———. *Song of the Siren: A Parapsychological Odyssey.* New York: Harper & Row, 1975.

———. "The Use of Dreams in Shamanic Traditions," Mihály Hoppál and Otto J. von Sadovszky eds., In *Shamanism: Past and Present.* 2 vols. ISTOR Books. Budapest: Ethnographic Institute, 198: 381-391.

Krippner, Stanley, and A. Villoldo. *The Realms of Healing.* Millbrae, Calif.: Celestial Arts, 1976.

Krippner, Stanley, and Daniel Rubin. *Galaxies of Life: The Human Aura in Acupuncture and Kirlian Photography.* Gordon & Breach, 1973. Reprinted as *The Kirlian Aura: Photographing the Galaxies of Life.* Garden City, N.Y.: Doubleday Anchor, 1974. Reprinted as *Energies of Consciousness: Exploration in Acupuncture, Auras, and Kirlian Photography.* New York: Interface, 1976.

Krippner, Stanley, and Patrick Welch. *Spiritual Dimensions of Healing: From Native Shamanism to Contemporary Health Care.* New York: Irvington Publishers, 1992.

Krippner, Stanley, and Sidney Cohen. *LSD Into the Eighties.* N.p., 1981.

Krippner, Stanley, and Susan Marie Powers, eds. *Broken Images, Broken Selves: Dissociative Narratives in Clinical Practice.* Washington D.C.: Brunner/Mazel, 1997.

Krishnamurti, Jiddu. *The Awakening of Intelligence.* New York: Harper & Row, 1973.

———. *The First and Last Freedom.* London: V. Gollancz, 1954.

———. *Life Ahead.* London: V. Gollancz, 1963.

———. *The Only Revolution.* London: V. Gollancz, 1970.

Krishnananda, Swami. *Swami Sivananda and the Spiritual Renaissance.* Sivanandanagar, India: Sivananda Literature Research Institute, 1959.

Kriyananda, Swami. *The Book of Bhrigu.* San Francisco: Hansa Publications, 1967.

Kroeber, Alfred L. "The Religion of the Indians of California," *University of California Publications in American Archaeology and Ethnology* (University of California Press) 1907.

Krohn, Sven I., and Ake Tollet. *Jälleenlöydetty sielu: Kekusteluja parapsykologiasta* (Soul Rediscovered: Dialogues Concerning Parapsychology). N.p., 1936.

Kselman, Thomas A. *Miracles and Prophecies in Nineteenth-Century France.* New Brunswick, N.J.: Rutgers University Press, 1983.

Ksenofontov, G. V. *Legends of the Siberian Shamans.* Munich, 1955.

———. *Legiendy i rasskazy o szamanach u Jakutov, Buriat i Tungusov* (Legends and Tales of Shamans among the Yakuts, Buryats, and Tungus) Moscow: Izdatel'stwo Bezbozhnik, 1930.

Kübler-Ross, Elisabeth. *AIDS: The Ultimate Challenge.* New York: Macmillan, 1987.

———. *Coping With Death and Dying.* Edited by John T. Chirban. Lanham, Md.: University Press of America, 1985.

———. *Death: The Final Stage of Growth.* Englewood Cliffs, N.J.: Prentice-Hall, 1975.

———. *Living with Death and Dying.* New York: Macmillan, 1981.

———. *On Death and Dying.* New York: Macmillan Co., 1969.

———. *Questions & Answers on Death & Dying.* New York: Macmillan, 1974.

———. *To Live Until We Say Good-Bye.* Englewood Cliffs, N.J.: Prentice-Hall, 1978.

Kueshana, Eklal [Kieninger, Richard]. *The Ultimate Frontier.* Chicago: Stelle Group, 1963.

Kuhlig, Kathryn. *Spiritualist Lyceum Manual.* Milwaukee, Wisc.: National Spiritualist Association of Churches, 1962.

Kuhlman, Kathryn. *I Believe in Miracles.* New York: Prentice-Hall, 1962.

———. *Nothing Is Impossible With God.* Englewood Cliffs, N.J.: Prentice-Hall, 1974.

Kulagina, V. V. "Nina S. Kulagina." *Journal of Paraphysics* 5 (1971).

Kundalini Yoga/Sadhana Guidelines. Pomona, Calif.: KRI Publications, 1978.

Kurdsen, Stephen. *Graphology: The New Science.* Washington, D.C.: Acropolis Books, 1971.

Kurtz, Paul. *The Transcendental Temptation: A Critique of Religion and the Paranormal.* Buffalo, N.Y.: Prometheus Books, 1991.

Kurtz, Paul, ed. *A Skeptic's Handbook of Parapsychology.* Buffalo, N.Y.: Prometheus Books, 1985.

Kusche, Lawrence David. *The Bermuda Triangle Mystery—Solved.* New York: Harper & Row, 1975.

———. *The Disappearance of Flight 19.* New York: Harper & Row, 1980.

Kusche, Lawrence David, and Deborah K. Blouin. *Bermuda Triangle Bibliography.* Tempe, Ariz.: Arizona State University Library, 1974.

Kutscher, M. L., et al., eds. *A Comprehensive Bibliography of the Thanatology Literature.* New York: Irvington Publications, 1975.

Kuvalayananda, Swami. *Asanas.* Lonavla (C.R.), India: Yoga-Mimamsa Office. Reprinted as *Popular Yoga Asanas.* Rutland, Vt.: C. E. Tuttle, 1972.

———. *Popular Yoga Asanas.* Rutland, Vt.: C. E. Tuttle, 1972.

———. *Pranayama.* Lonavla (C.R.), India: Yoga-Mimamsa Office. Reprint, Bombay: Popular Prakashan, 1966.

Kvanvig, Jonathan L. *The Problem of Hell.* New York: Oxford University Press, 1993.

Kydd, Ronald A. N. *Charismatic Gifts in the Early Church.* Peabody, Mass.: Hendrickson Publishers, 1984.

———. *Dogme de la haute magie.* N.p., 1854.

———. *Histoire de la magie.* Translated as *The History of Magic.* 1860. Trans. by Arthur Edward Waite. London: W. Rider, 1913. Reprint, New York: Samuel Weiser, 1971.

———. *La Clef des grands mystères.* Translated as *The Key of the Mysteries.* 1861. Trans. by Aleister Crowley. London: Rider, 1959. Reprint, New York: Samuel Weiser, 1970.

———. *The Magical Ritual of the Regnum Sanctum.* New York: Samuel Weiser, 1970.

———. *The Mysteries of Magic: A Digest of the Writings of Éliphas Lévi.* Trans. by Arthur Edward Waite. 1886. Reprint, New Hyde Park, N.Y.: University Books, 1974.

———. *The Paradox of the Highest Science.* Adyar, Madras, India: Theosophical Publishing House. Reprint, Mokelumne Hill, Calif.: Health Research, 1969. Reprint, Kila, Mont.: Kessinger Publishing Co., 1993.

———. *Rituel de la haute magie.* N.p., 1856.

———. *Transcendental Magic.* Translation of *Dogme de la haute magie* and *Rituel de la haute magie.* Translated by Arthur Edward Waite. London: George Redway, 1896. Reprint, New York: Samuel Weiser, 1972.

L'Ecuyer, Michele. "Mafu." *Life Times* 1, no. 2 (winter 1986–87): 80–82.

L'Estrange, Ewen C. *Witch Hunting and Witch Trials: The Indictments for Witchcraft from the Records of 1373 Assizes Held for the Home Circuit, A.D. 1559–1736.* London: Kegan Paul, 1929.

La Barre, Weston. *The Ghost Dance: The Origins of Religion.* Garden City, N.Y.: Doubleday, 1971. London: George Allen & Unwin, 1972.

———. "Hallucinogens and the Shamanic Origins of Religion." In *Flesh of the Gods: The Ritual Use of Hallucinogens.* Peter T. Furst, ed. (London: George Allen & Unwin, 1972), 261–278.

———. "Old and New World Narcotics: A Statistical Question and an Ethnological Reply," *Economic Botany* 24 (1970): 368–373.

———. *The Peyote Cult.* New York: Schocken Books, 1969.

———. *They Shall Take up Serpents.* New York: Schocken Books, 1969.

LaBerge, Steven. *Lucid Dreaming: The Power of Being Awake and Aware in Your Dreams.* Los Angeles: Jeremy P. Tarcher, 1987.

Lacarrière, Jacques. *The Gnostics.* London: Owen, 1977. Reprint, San Francisco: City Lights, 1989.

Lacy, Norris J. *The Arthurian Encyclopedia.* New York: Garland Publishing, Inc., 1986. Revised ed. *The New Arthurian Encyclopedia.* New York: Garland Publishing, Inc., 1995.

Laibow, Rima E. "Dual Victims: The Abused and the Abducted." *International UFO Reporter* 14, 3 (May/June 1989): 4–9.

Laing, David. *Select Remains of the Ancient Popular Poetry of Scotland.* Edinburgh: Balfour & Clarke, 1822.

Laing, Lloyd Robert. *Celtic Britain and Ireland, A.D. 200–800: The Myth of the Dark Ages.* Dublin, Ireland: Irish Academic Press, 1990.

Lair, Pierre. *Essai sur les combustions humaine, produites par l' abus des liqueurs spiritueses.* Paris, 1808.

Lamb, Geoffrey. *Discovering Magic Charms and Talismans.* UK: Shire Publications, 1974.

Lambert, G. W. "Antoine Richard's Garden." *Journal of the Society for Psychical Research* 37 (July–October 1953, March–April 1954); 41 (June 1962).

———. "The Dieppe Raid Case." *Journal of the Society for Psychical Research* 35 (May–June 1952).

———. "Poltergeists: A Psychical Theory." *Journal of the Society for Psychical Research* 38 (June 1955).

———. "The Quest of Glastonbury." *Journal of the Society for Psychical Research* 43, 728 (June 1966).

Lambert, Ricahrd Stanton. *Areil and all His Quality.* London: V. Gollancz Ltd., 1940.

———. *Exploring the Supernatural.* London: A. Barker, 1955.

Lambert, Rudolf. "Dr. Geley's Report on the Medium Eva C." *Journal of the Society for Psychical Research* 37, no. 682 (November 1954).

Lancaster, John B. "A GESP Experiment with a Dual (Color-Symbol) Target." *Journal of Parapsychology* (December 1959).

Lancelin, Charles. *Comment on meurt, comment on nait.* Paris: H. Durville, 1912.

———. *Histoire mythique de Shatan: de la légende au dogme.* N.p., 1903.

———. *L'ame hume: etudes expérimentales de psycho-physiologie.* Paris: H. Durville, 1921.

———. *L'humanité posthume et le monde angélique.* N.p., n.d.

———. *L'occultisme et la science.* Paris: J. Meyer, 1926.

———. *L'occultisme et la vie.* Paris: Editions Adyar, 1928.

———. *La fraude dans la production des phénomès mediumiques.* N.p., 1912.

———. *La réincarnation.* N.p., n.d.

———. *La sorcellerie des campagnes.* N.p., 1923.

———. *La vie posthume.* Paris: H. Durville, 1922.

———. *Méthode de dédoublement personnel.* N.p., 1913.

———. *Qu'est-ce l'âme?* N.p., n.d.

Landau, Lucian. "Radionics: General Considerations." *Journal of the British Society of Dowsers* (September 1958).

Landau, Ron. *God Is My Adventure.* London: Ivor Nicholson & Watson, 1935.

———. *The Philosophy of Ibn 'Arabi.* London: Allen and Unwin, 1959.

Lane, C. *Life and Bibliography of Joanna Southcott.* London, 1912.

Lane, David Christopher. *Exposing Cults: When the Skeptical Mind Confronts the Mystical.* New York: Garland Publishing, 1994.

Lane, David Christopher. *Fate* (June 1982).

———. *The Making of a Spiritual Movement.* Del Mar, Calif.: Del Mar Press, 1983.

———. *The Radhasoami Tradition: A Critical History of Guru Successorship.* New York: Garland Publishing, 1992.

Lang, Andrew. *The Book of Dreams & Ghosts.* London, 1898. Reprint, New York: Causeway, 1974. Reprint, San Bernardino, Calif.: Borgo Press, 1980.

———. *Cock Lane and Common Sense.* London: Longmans, Green, 1894. Reprint, New York: AMS Press, 1970.

———. "The Fire Walk." *Proceedings of the Society for Psychical Research* 15, p. 36.

———. *Historical Mysteries.* London: Smith, Elder, 1904.

———. *Magic and Religion.* 1901. Reprint, New York: Greenwood Press, 1969.

———. *The Maid of France, Being the Story of the Life and Death of Jeanne d'Arc.* London: Longmans, Green, 1908.

———. *The Making of Religion.* 1898. Reprint, New York: AMS Press, 1968.

———. *The Valet's Tragedy and Other Studies.* London: Longmans Green, 1903.

Lang, Johannes. *Die Hohlwelttheorie.* Franfurt am Main, Germany: Goethe Verlag, 1938.

Langdon, Jean Matteson, and Gerhard Baer, eds. *Portals of Power: Shamanism in South America.* Albuquerque: University of New Mexico Press, 1992.

Langguth, A. J. *Macumba: White & Black Magic in Brazil.* New York: Harper and Row, 1975.

Lantis, Margaret. *Alaskan Eskimo Ceremonialism: Monographs of the American Ethnological Society.* New York: J. J. Augustin Publisher, 1947.

Laoux, Gaston. *Dictionnaire Hermetique.* Paris, 1695.

Lapidus. *In Pursuit of Gold: Alchemy in Theory and Practice.* London: Neville Spearman, 1976.

Lapponi, Joseph. *Hypnotism and Spiritism.* New York: Longmans, Green, and Co., 1907.

Larcher, Hubert. "Perspectives parapsychochimiques: La Drogue" (Parapsychochemical Outlook: Narcotics). *La Tour St. Jacques* 1 (1960).

———. "Prodiges sanguins après la mort' (Wonders of the Blood after Death). *Revue Métapsychique* (Sept.–Oct. 1953; Nov.–Dec. 1953).

———. "Towards a Science of Healing." *Proceedings of Four Conferences on Parapsychological Studies* (1957).

———. "Trois cas extraordinaires d'oncorruption de la chair" (Three Remarkable Cases of Lack of Decay of Flesh). *Revue Métapsychique* (March–April 1954).

Larsen, David. "Society Flatly Denies Global Theory." *Los Angeles Times,* May 15, 1978.

Laski, Marghanita. *Ecstasy.* London: Cresset, 1961.

The Last Incarnation. Malibu, Calif.: Lakshmi Publications, 1983.

Latham, M. W. *The Elizabethan Fairies.* New York: Columbia University Press, 1931.

Latourette, K. C. *The Chinese: Their History & Culture.* 2 vols. New York: Macmillan, 1934.

Laufer, Berthold. "Origin of the Word Shaman," *American Anthropologist,* vol. 19 (1917): 361–371.

Laurence, Richard, trans. *The Book of Enoch the Prophet . . . from an Ethiopian Manuscript.* London: Kegan Paul, Tench, 1883.

Laurentin, René, and Henri Joyeux. *Scientific & Medical Studies on the Apparitions at Medjugorje.* Dublin: Veritas, 1987.

Laurentin, René, and L. Rupcic. *Is the Virgin Mary Appearing at Medjugorje?* Washington, D.C.: Word Among Us Press, 1984.

Laurentin, René, L. Rupcic, and René Lejeune. *Messages and Teachings of Mary at Medjugorje.* Milford, Ohio: The Riehle Foundation, 1988.

Laver, James. *Nostradamus, or the Future Foretold.* London: Collins, 1942. Reprint, UK: Penguin Books, 1952. Reprint, London: George Mann, 1973.

LaVey, Anton. *The Compleat Witch; or, What to Do When Virtue Fails.* New York: Dodd, Mead, 1971.

———. *The Satanic Bible.* Seacaucus, N.J.: University Books, 1969. Reprint. New York: Avon Books, 1976.

———. *The Satanic Rituals.* Secaucus, N.J.: University Books, 1972. Buccaneer Books, Inc., 1991.

———. *The Satanic Witch.* Los Angeles: Feral House, 1989.

Law, William. *The Absolute Unlawfulness of the Stage Entertainment Fully Demonstrated.* Reprint, New York: Garland Publishing, 1973.

———. *The Grounds and Reason of Christian Regeneration.* Philadelphia: Andrew Bradford, 1741.

———. *A Practical Treatise upon Christian Perfection.* Newcastle upon Tyne: J. Gooding, 1743.

———. *A Serious Call to a Devout and Holy Life, Adapted to the State and Condition of All Orders of Christians.* London: W. Innys, 1732.

———. *The Spirit of Love.* London: W. Innys and J. Richardson, 1752.

———. *The Spirit of Prayer.* London: W. Innys, 1750.

———. *The Works.* Brockenhurst: G. Moreton, 1892–93.

Lawrence, Brother. *The Practice of the Presence of God.* London, 1691.

Lawrence, Jodi. *Alpha Brain Waves.* New York: Avon, 1972.

Lawrence, Peter. *Road Belong Cargo.* Melbourne, Australia: Melbourne University Press, 1964.

Lawson, Donna. *Brothers and Sisters All Over This Land: America's First Communes.* New York: Praeger Publishers, 1972.

Lawson, John Cuthbert. *Modern Greek Folklore and Ancient Greek Religion.* 1910. Reprint, New Hyde Park, N.Y.: University Books, 1964.

Lawton, George. *The Drama of Life after Death.* New York: H. Holt, 1932.

Layne, Meade. *The Coming of the Guardians.* 5th ed. Vista, Calif.: Borderland Sciences Research Foundation, 1964.

———. *The Ether Ship and Its Solution.* Vista, Calif.: Borderland Sciences Research Associates, 1950.

Le Bon, Gustave. *The Crowd: A Study of the Popular Mind.* London: T. Fisher Unwin, 1896.

Le Forestier, René. *La Franc-maconnerie occultiste au XVIII siecle et l'ordre des Elus Coens.* Paris: Dorbon, 1928.

Le Grand Grimoire, ou l'art de commander les esprits célestes. Paris, 1845.

Le Malefan, Pascal. "Pierre Janet, le spiritisme et les delires spirites" (Pierre Janet: Spiritualism and Spiritualistic Deliria), *Evolution Psychiatrique* 58, no. 2 (April-June 1993): 445–452.

Le Pelletier, Anatole. *Les Oracles de Michel de Nostredame.* 2 vols. Paris, 1867.

Le Plongeon, Augustus. *Queen Moo and the Egyptian Sphinx.* London; New York: The Author, 1896. 2nd ed. Reprint, Las Vegas, Nev.: Health Research, 1996.

Le Probleme de l'Etre et de la Destinée: Christianisme et Spiritisme. Translated as *Christianity & Spiritualism.* London, [1904].

Le Vert, Liberte E., ed. *The Prophecies and Enigmas of Nostradamus.* Glen Rock, N.J.: Firebell Books, 1979.

Lea, H. C. *Léo Taxil and Diana Vaughan.* Paris, 1901.

———. *Léo Taxil, Diana Vaughan et l'Eglise romaine.* Paris, 1901.

———. *Materials Toward a History of Witchcraft.* Edited by Arthur C. Howland. 3 vols. Philadelphia, University of Pennsylvania Press,1939. Reprint, New York: T. Yoseloff, 1957.

Lea, Henry Charles. *A History of the Inquisition of the Middle Ages.* 3 vols. London: Sampson, Low; New York: Harper & Bros., 1888. Reprint, New York: Citadel, 1954.

———. *History of the Inquisition in Spain.* New York and London, 1906.

Leadbeater, C. W. *The Chakras.* Wheaton, Ill.: Theosophical Publishing House, 1972.

———. *Clairvoyance (1903).* Kila, Mont.: Kessinger Publishing Co., 1999.

———. *The Hidden Side of Christian Festivals.* Los Angeles: St. Alban Press, 1920.

———. *The Hidden Side of Things.* 1913. Reprint, London: 1968. Abridged reprint, Adyar, Madras, India: Theosophical Publishing House, 1974.

———. *The Lives of Alcyone: A Clairvoyant Investigation.* 2 vols. N.p., 1924.

———. *Man Visible & Invisible.* Reprint, London: Theosophical Publishing House, 1920. Kila, Mont.: Kessinger Publishing Co., 1998.

———. *Man, Whence, How, and Whither.* 1913. Reprint, Wheaton, Ill.: Theosophical Press, n.d.

———. *The Masters and the Path.* Chicago: Theosophical Press, 1925. Wheaton, Ill.: Theosophical Publishing House, 1985. Reprint, Kila, Mont.: Kessinger Publishing Co. Inc. Reprint, Las Vegas, Nev.: Health Research, 1998.

———. *Occult Chemistry, Clairvoyant Observations.* N.p., 1919.

———. *Outline of Theosophy.* Chicago: Theosophical Book Concern, 1903.

———. *The Science of the Sacraments.* Los Angeles: St. Alban Press, 1920.

———. *Talks on the Path of Occultism.* Vol. 1: *At the Feet of the Master.* 1926. Vol. 2: *The Voice of the Silence.* Adyar, Madras, India: Theosophical Publishing House, 1947.

———. *A Textbook of Theosophy.* Adyar, Madras, India: Theosophical Publishing House, 1956.

———. *Thought-Forms: A Record of Clairvoyant Investigation.* London: Theosophical Publishing House, 1948.

———. *The Astral Plane.* London: Theosophical Publishing House, 1915.

Leadbeater, C. W., and Annie Besant. *Light on the Path.* N.p., 1926.

Leaf, Horace. *Ahmed's Daughter.* N.p., 1933.

———. *Death Cannot Kill.* N.p., 1967.

———. *Psychology and Development of Mediumship.* London: Rider, 1923.

———. *Under the Southern Cross.* N.p., 1923.

———. *What is this Spiritualism?* New York: G. H. Doran, 1919.

———. *What Mediumship Is.* London: Psychic Press, 1938. Reprint, London: Spiritualist Press, 1976.

Leary, Timothy. *Changing My Mind Among Others: Lifetime Writings.* Englewood Cliffs, N.J.: Prentice-Hall, 1982.

———. *Flashbacks: An Autobiography.* Los Angeles: J. P. Tarcher, 1983.

———. *High Priest.* New York: World Publishing, 1968.

———. *Politics of Ecstasy.* New York: G. P. Putnam's Sons, 1968.

———. *Psychedelic Prayers after the Tao te ching.* New Hyde Park, N.Y.: University Books, 1966.

———. *The Psychedelic Experience.* New Hyde Park, N.Y.: University Books, 1964.

Leary, Timothy, Robert Wilson, and George A. Koopman. *Neuropolitics: The Sociobiology of Human Metamorphosis.* Los Angeles: Starseed/Peace Press, 1977.

Lebot, Vincent, Mark Merlin, and Lamont Lindstrom. *Kava: The Pacific Drug.* New Haven, Conn.: Yale University Press, 1992.

LeClair, R. C. *The Letters of William James and Theodore Flournoy.* Madison, Wisc.: University of Wisconsin Press, 1966.

Lecour, Paul. *Hellénisme et Christianisme* (Hellenism and Christianity). Bordeaux: Editions Bierre, 1943.

———. *Le Septième sens* (The Seventh sense). N.p., n.d.

———. *Ma Vie mystique* (My mystical life). N.p., n.d.

———. *Saint Paul et les mystères Chrétiens* (St. Paul and the Christian mysteries). N.p., n.d.

LeCron, Leslie M. *Experimental Hypnosis.* New York: Macmillan, 1952.

———. "The Paranormal in Hypnosis." *Tomorrow* magazine (spring 1955).

———. *Self-Hypnosis: The Technique and Its Daily Use in Daily Living.* Englewood Cliffs, N.J.: Prentice-Hall, 1964.

———. *Techniques of Hypnotherapy.* New York: Julian Press, 1962.

LeCron, Leslie M., and Jean Bordeaux. *Hypnotism Today.* New York: Grune & Stratton, 1964.

Ledezma, Eugenio and Ramon Monroig. "Parapsychology in Mexico," *Journal of the American Society for Psychical Research* 91, no. 2 (April 1997): 122–132.

Leduc, Dr. Stéphane. *Théorie Physicochimique de la Vie et Générations Spontanées.* Translated as *The Mechanism of Life.* London: William Heinemann, 1911.

Lee, Dal. *Dictionary of Astrology.* New York: Coronet Communications/Paperback Library, 1968.

———. *How to Use and Understand Astrological Predictive Systems.* New York: Astro Books, 1939.

———. *Understanding the Occult.* New York: Paperback Library, 1969.

Lee, Gloria. *The Changing Conditions of Your World!* Palos Verdes Estates, Calif.: Cosmon Research Foundation, 1962.

———. *Why We Are Here!* Palos Verdes Estates, Calif.: Cosmon Research Foundation, 1959.

Lee, Jung Young. *Korean Shamanistic Rituals.* New York: Mouton, 1981.

Leek, Sybil. *Astrology and Love.* New York: Berkley, 1977.

———. *The Best of Sybil Leek.* New York: Popular Library, 1974.

———. *Book of Curses.* Englewood Cliffs, N.J.: Prentice-Hall, 1975.

———. *Cast Your Own Spell.* New York: Pinnacle Books, 1970.

———. *The Complete Art of Witchcraft.* New York: World Publishing, 1971.

———. *Diary of a Witch.* Englewood Cliffs, N.J.: Prentice-Hall, 1968.

———. *Reincarnation: The Second Chance.* New York: Stein & Day, 1974. Reprint, New York: Bantam, 1975.

———. *A Shop in the High Street.* New York: David McKay, 1962.

———. *Sybil Leek's Book of Curses.* Englewood Cliffs, N.J.: Prentice-Hall, 1975.

———. *Sybil Leek's Book of Fortune Telling.* New York: Collier, 1969.

Lees, B. A. *Records of the Templars in England in the Twelfth Century: The Inquest of 1185 with Illustrative Charters and Documents.* Vol. 9 of *British Academy Records of the Social and Economic History of England and Wales.* Oxford: Oxford University Press, 1935.

Lees, Robert J. *The Car of Phoebus: An Astral Bridegroom.* N.p., 1909.

———. *The Gate of Heaven.* N.p., n.d.

———. *The Heretic.* N.p., 1901.

———. *The Life Elysian.* N.p., 1905.

———. "My Books: How They Were Written." *Occult Review* (December 1931).

———. *Through the Mists.* London: W. Rider & Sons Ltd., 1910.

Lefebure, Francis. *Expériences initiatiques.* 3 vols. N.p., 1954, 1956, 1959.

———. *Les Homologies; architecture cosmique ou, La Lumière secrète de l'Asie devant la science modern* (Homologies; or, The Secret Light of Asia in Relation to Modern Science). Paris: Editions Aryana, 1950.

Lefort, Rafael. *The Teachers of Gurdjieff.* New York: Samuel Weiser, 1973.

Legge, Francis. *Forerunners and Rivals of Christianity from 330* B.C. *to 330* A.D. 2 vols. 1915. Reprint, New Hyde Park, N.Y.: University Books, 1964.

Legge, James, trans. *I Ching; Book of Changes.* N.p., 1899. Reprint, New York: Dover Publications, 1963. Reprint, New Hyde Park, N.Y.: University Books, 1964. Reprint, New York: Causeway, 1973.

Legman, G. *The Guilt of the Templars.* New York: Basic Books, 1966.

Lehner, Ernest, and J. Lehner. *Picture Book of Devils, Demons, and Witchcraft.* New York: Dover Publications, 1972.

Lehrer, Ernst, and Johanna Ernst. *Folklore and Odysseys of Food and Medicinal Plants.* New York: Tutor Publishing, 1962.

Leland, Charles Godfrey. *The Alternate Sex; or, The Female Intellect in Man, and the Masculine in Woman.* London: P. Wellby, 1904.

———. *Aradia; or, The Gospel of the Witches.* 1899. Reprint, New York: Hero Press, 1971. Reprint, New York: Samuel Weiser, 1974.

———. *A Dictionary of Slang, Jargon, and Cant.* London: Ballantyne Press, 1889. Reprint, Detroit: Gale Research, 1967.

———. *The English Gypsies and their Language.* New York: Hurd and Houghton, 1872. Reprint, Detroit: Gale Research, 1968.

———. *The Gypsies.* Boston: Houghton, Mifflin, 1882.

———. *Memoirs.* 1893. Reprint, Detroit: Gale Research, 1968.

———. *The Mystic Will.* New York: Hero Publishers, 1972.

Leland, Charles Godfrey, and Albert Barrére. *Gypsy Sorcery and Fortune-Telling.* London: T. Fisher Unwin, 1891. Reprint, New Hyde Park, N.Y.: University Books, 1963. Reprint, New York: Dover Publications, 1971.

Lellenberg, Jon L. *The Quest for Sir Arthur Conan Doyle.* Carbondale: Southern Illinois University Press, 1987.

Lemegeton; Clavicula Salomonis: or, The Complete Lesser Key of Solomon the King. Edited by Nelson White and Anne White. Pasadena, Calif.: The Technology Group, 1979.

The Lemurian Scribe. *Let It Be Resolved.* Milwaukee, Wisc.: Lemurian Press, 1940.

Lenglet, Dufresnoy N. *Histoire de la Philosophie Hermetique.* 2 vols. Paris, 1792.

Lenormant, Francois. *Chaldean Magic: Its Origin & Development.* London: Samuel Bagster, [1877].

Lenz, Frederick. *Life Times.* New York: Fawcett Crest, 1979.

Leo, Alan. *Astrology for All.* 2 vols. London: Modern Astrology Office, 1921.

———. *Casting the Horoscope.* London: Modern Astrology Office, 1912. Reprint, London: Fowler, 1969.

———. *The Horoscope and How to Read It.* N.p., 1902.

———. *How to Judge a Nativity.* 2 vols. 1904. Reprint, London: Modern Astrology Office, 1928.

———. *Practical Astrology.* Philadelphia: David McCay, n.d.

Leo, Bessie. *The Life and Works of Alan Leo.* N.p., 1919.

Leonard, Gladys Osborn. *My Life in Two Worlds.* London: Cassell, 1931.

Leonard, Maurice. *Battling Bertha; The Biography of Bertha Harris.* London: Regency Press, 1975.

———. *Medium: The Biography of Jessie Nason.* London: Regency Press, 1974.

Leonard, William J. *The Pioneer Apostle of Mental Science: A Sketch of the Life and Work of Rev. Warren Felt Evans, M.D.* N.p.: The Author, n.d.

Leoni, Edgar. *Nostradamus and His Prophecies.* New York: 1961.

Leroy, Oliver. *Les hommes salamandres: Recherches et réflexions sur l'incombustibilité du corps humain.* Paris, 1932.

———. *Levitation.* London: Burns, Oates, 1928.

Leroy, Olivier-Gilbert. "Apparitions de Sainte Thé rèse de Jésus" (Apparitions of Saint Theresa of Jesus). *Revue d'Ascétique et de Mystique* 134 (1958).

———. "Examen des témoignages sur la lévitation extatique chez Sainte Thérèse de Jésus" (Study of the Testimony on Ecstatic Levitation of Saint Theresa). *Revue d'Ascétique et de Mystique* 131 (1937).

———. "La Pénètration des consciences chez Sainte Thérèse de Jésus" (The Penetration of Consciousness in Saint Theresa of Jesus). *Revue d'Ascétique et de Mystique* 136 (1958).

———. *La Raison primitive* (Primitive Reason). N.p., 1926.

———. *Les Hommes-Salamandres* (The Salamander Men). N.p., 1931.

———. *Sainte Jeanne d'Arc, Les Voix* (The Voices of St. Joan of Arc). N.p., 1956.

LeShan, Lawrence. *Alternative Realities.* New York: M. Evans, 1976.

———. *Einstein's Space and Van Gogh's Sky: Physical Reality and Beyond.* New York: Macmillan, 1982.

———. *From Newton to EAP: Parapsychology and the Challenge of Modern Science.* Wellingborough, England: Turnstone Press, 1984.

———. *How to Meditate: A Guide to Self-Discovery.* New York: Bantam Books, 1975.

———. *The Medium, the Mystic, and the Physicist.* 1974. Reprint, New York: Viking; London: Turnstone Books, 1974. Reprinted as *Clairvoyant Reality: Toward a General Theory of the Paranormal.* Wellingborough, England: Turnstone Press, 1980.

———. *The Psychology of War: Comprehending Its Mystique and Its Madness.* Chicago: Noble Press, 1992.

Leslie, Desmond. *The Amazing Mr. Lutterworth: A Novel.* London: Allan Wingate, 1958.

———. "Leslie Strikes Back." *Nexus* 1, nos. 2–5 (May 1955): 7–8; *Saucer News* 2, nos. 2–6 (June/July 1955): 7–8.

———. "Obituary: George Adamski." *Flying Saucer Review* 11, no. 4 (July/August 1965): 18–19.

Leslie, Desmond, and George Adamski. *Flying Saucers Have Landed.* New York: British Book/ London: Werner Laurie, 1953. Rev. London: Neville Spearman, 1970.

The Lesser Key of Solomon/Göetia/The Book of Evil Spirits. Chicago: De Laurence, 1916.

Letbridge, T. C. *The Power of the Pendulum.* London: Routledge & Kegan Paul, 1976.

Letort, Ellen. "The Frauds of Mediums." *Annals of Psychic Science* 3, no. 6 (1906).

Leuschner, Wolfgang. "Ueber ein telepathisches Phaenomen" (A Telepathic Phenomenon), *Psyche: Zeitschrift fuer Psychoanalyse und ihre Anwendungen* 43, no. 5 (May 1989): 415–428.

Levack, Brian P. *Possession & Exorcism.* New York: Garland Publishing, Inc., 1992.

———. *Witchcraft, Women and Society.* New York: Garland, 1992.

Levack, Brian, ed. *Witchcraft in the Ancient World and the Middle Ages.* New York:Garland 1992.

Leventhal, Herbert. *In the Shadow of the Enlightenment: Occultism and Renaissance Science in Eighteenth Century America.* New York: State University of New York Press, 1976.

Lévi, Éliphas. *The Book of Splendors.* New York: Samuel Weiser, 1973.

Levin, Ira. *Rosemary's Baby.* New York: Random House, 1967.

Levin, Jeffrey S. " 'Age Differences in Mystical Experience: Erratum," *Gerontologist* 33, no. 5: (October 1993).

Levine, Robert M. *Vale of Tears: Revisiting the Canudos Massacre in Northeastern Brazil.* Berkeley: University of California Press, 1992.

Levy, Walter J., Jr. "Possible PK by Rats to Receive Pleasurable Brain Stimulation." In *Research in Parapsychology 1973.* Metuchen, N.J.: Scarecrow Press, 1974.

Levy, Walter J., Jr., and James Davis. "A Potential Animal Model for Parapsychological Interaction between Organisms." *Research in Parapsychology 1973.* Metuchen, N.J.: Scarecrow Press, 1974.

Levy, Walter J., Jr., Brian Artley, Al Mayor, and Carol Williams. "The Use of an Activity Wheel Based Testing Cage in Small Rodent Precognition Work." In *Research in Parapsychology 1973.* Metuchen, N.J.: Scarecrow Press, 1974.

Lewes, George H. *The Life of Goethe.* London, 1864. Reprint, Norwood Editions, 1979.

Lewi, Grant. *Astrology for the Millions.* Garden City, N.Y.: N.p., 1940.

———. *Heaven Knows What.* New York: Doubleday, 1935.

———. *Your Greatest Strength.* New York, N.p., 1946.

Lewin, L. *Phantastica, Narcotic and Stimulating Drugs.* New York: E. P. Dutton, 1964.

Lewis, Arthur H. *Hex.* New York: Pocket Books, 1972.

Lewis, Bernard. *The Assassins: A Radical Sect in Islam.* London: Al Saqi, 1985.

Lewis, David. *The Life of S. Teresa of Jesus.* London, 1970.

Lewis, E. E. *A Report of the Mysterious Noises Heard in the House of Mr. John D. Fox.* Canandaigua, N.Y.: The Author, 1848.

Lewis, H. Spencer. *Mansions of the Soul.* San Jose, Calif.: Rosicrucian Press, 1930.

———. *Rosicrucian Manual.* San Jose, Calif.: Rosicrucian Press, 1941.

———. *Rosicrucian Principles for the Home and Business.* San Jose, Calif.: Supreme Grand Lodge of AMORC, 1929.

———. *Rosicrucian Questions and Answers with Complete History.* San Jose, Calif.: Supreme Grand Lodge of AMORC, 1929.

———. *Rosicrucian Questions and Answers.* San Jose, Calif.: Supreme Grand Lodge of the AMORC, 1969.

———. *Self Mastery and Fate with the Cycles of Life.* San Jose, Calif.: Supreme Grand Lodge of AMORC, 1929.

Lewis, I. M. *Ecstatic Religion: A Study in Shamanism and Spirit Possession.* London: Routledge, 1989.

———. "What is Shaman," *Folk* vol. 23 (1981): 25–35.

Lewis, James R. *The Astrology Encyclopedia.* Detroit: Gale Research, 1994.

———. *The Dream Encyclopedia.* Detroit: Gale Research, Inc., 1995.

Lewis, James R., and J. Gordon Melton, eds. *Church Universal and Triumphant in Scholarly Perspective.* Stanford, Calif.: Center for Academic Publications, 1994.

———. *Perspectives on the New Age.* Albany: State University Press of New York, 1992.

———. *Sex, Slander, and Salvation.* Goleta, Calif.: Center for Academic Publication, 1994.

Lewis, Lionel. *St. Joseph of Arimathea at Glastonbury.* London: James Clarke, 1955.

Lewis, Matthew Gregory. *Journal of a West Indian Proprietor.* London: J. Murray, 1861. Reprint, New York: Negro University Press, 1961.

Lewis, Mrs. J. *The Awakening in Wales.* London: Marshall; New York: Revell, 1905.

Lewis, Ralph M. *Behold the Sign.* San Jose, Calif.: Supreme Grand Lodge of the AMORC, 1944.

———. *The Conscious Interlude.* San Jose, Calif.: Supreme Grand Lodge of the AMORC, 1957.

———. *The Sanctuary of the Self.* San Jose, Calif.: Supreme Grand Lodge of the AMORC, 1948.

———. *Yesterday Has Much to Tell.* San Jose, Calif.: Supreme Grand Lodge of the AMORC, 1973.

Lewis-Williams, J. D. and T. A. Dowson. "The Signs of All Times: Entoptic Phenomena in Upper Palaeolithic Art," *Current Anthropology* vol. 29, no. 2 (1988): 201–245.

Leyburn, James G. *The Haitian People.* New Haven, Conn.: Yale University Press, 1966.

Lhermitte, Jacques Jean. *Le Cerveau et la pensée* (The Brain and Thought). 1951.

———. *Le Probléme des miracles.* N.p., 1956.

———. *Les Hallucinations.* N.p., 1951.

———. *Les Reves* (Dreams). N.p., 1942.

———. *Mystiques et faux mystiques* (Mystics and False Mystics). N.p., 1952.

———. *Psychopathologie de la vision.* N.p., 1942.

———. *Vrais et faux possédés.* (True and False Possession). New York: Hawthorn Books, 1956.

Liébeault, A. A. *Du sommeil et des etats analogues.* Paris, 1886.

Lietaer, Hugo and Jozef Corveleyn. "Psychoanalytical Interpretation of the Demoniacal Possession and the Mystical Development of Sister Jeanne des Anges from Loudun (1605–1665)," *International Journal for the Psychology of Religion* 5, no. 4 (1995): 259–276.

The Life of a Karmi-Yogi. Malaga, N.J.: American Vegan Society, 1973.

Lillie, Arthur. *Mme. Blavatsky and Her Theosophy.* London: Swan Sonnonschein, 1895.

Lilly, J. *Man and Dolphin.* Garden City, N.Y.: Doubleday, 1961.

Lilly, William. *The History of Lilly's Life and Times.* N.p., 1715.

Lincoln, J. S. *The Dream in Primitive Cultures.* London, 1935. Reprint, Academic Press, 1970.

Lind, Ingrid. *The White Eagle Inheritance.* Wellingborough, Northamptonshire, England: Turnstone Press, 1984.

Lindsay, Gordon. *William Branham, A Man Sent From God.* Dallas, Tex.: Voice of Healing Publishing, 1950.

Lipnack, Jessica, and Jeffrey Stamps. *The Networking Book: People Connecting with People.* New York: Methuen; London: Routledge & Kegan Paul, 1986.

Lippman, Deborah, and Paul Colin. *Amulets, Charms and Talismans: What They Mean and How to Use Them.* New York: M. Evans, 1974.

———. *How to Make Amulets, Charms, and Talismans.* New York: M. Evans, 1974.

Lipski, Alexander. *Life and Teachings of Sri Anandamayi Ma.* Delhi, India: Motilial Banaridass, 1977.

Little, A. G. *Roger Bacon Essays.* Oxford: Clarendon Press, 1914.

Littlefield, Charles W. *"M. M. M."—Man, Minerals and Masters.* Los Angeles: DeVorss, 1937.

The Liturgy of the Liberal Catholic Church. London: St. Alban Press, 1983.

Litvag, Irving. *Singer in the Shadows: The Strange Story of Patience Worth.* Macmillan, 1972; New York: Popular Library, 1973.

Liu, Da. *I Ching Coin Prediction.* New York: Harper & Row, 1975.

Livsey, Clara. *The Manson Women: A Family Portrait.* New York: Richard Merek Publishers, 1980.

Llorente, J. A. *History of the Inquisition of Spain.* 1826.

Lobb, John. *Talks with the Dead.* N.p., 1906.

———. *Uncle Tom's Story of His Life.* N.p., 1877.

Lockhart, J. G. *Curses, Lucks and Talismans.* London: Geoffrey Bles, 1938. Reprint, Detroit: Singing Tree Press, 1971.

Lockwood, W. M. *Continuity of Life a Cosmic Truth.* N.p., 1902. Kila, Mont.: Kessinger Publishing Co. 1998.

Lodge, Sir Oliver. *Christopher: A Study in Human Personality.* New York: George H. Doran, 1919.

———. *Conviction of Survival.* N.p., 1930.

———. *Letters from Sir Oliver Lodge.* Edited by J. A. Hill. London: Cassell, 1932.

Lodge, Sir Oliver. *Past Years.* London: Hodder and Stoughton, 1931.

———. *Raymond Revised.* N.p., 1922.

———. *Raymond, or Life and Death; with Examples of the Evidence for Survival of Memory and Affection After Death.* London: Methuen; New York: George H. Doran, 1916.

———. *The Reality of a Spiritual World.* N.p., 1930.

———. *The Substance of Faith Allied with Sciences.* London: Methuen, 1915.

———. *Survival of Man.* London: Methuen, 1909.

———. *Why I Believe in Personal Immortality.* Garden City, N.Y.: Doubleday, Doran, 1929.

Loehr, Franklin. *Death with Understanding.* Grand Island, Fla.: Religious Research Press, 1987.

———. *The Power of Prayer on Plants.* Garden City, N.Y.: Doubleday, 1959. Reprint, New York: New American Library, 1969.

———. *Psychography: A Method of Self Discovery.* Grand Island, Fla.: Religious Research Press, 1990.

———. *Science, Religion, and the Development of Religion as a Science.* Grand Island, Fla.: Gnosticours, 1983.

Logan, Daniel. *America Bewitched: The Rise of Black Magic and Spiritism.* New York: William Morrow, 1973.

———. *Do You Have ESP?* N.p., 1970.

———. *The Reluctant Prophet.* Garden City, N.Y.: Doubleday, 1968.

———. *Vibrations.* N.p., 1976.

———. *Your Eastern Star.* N.p., 1972.

Lomaxe, Paul R. *What Do Spiritualists Believe?* New York: General Assembly of Spiritualists, 1943.

Lombard, Emile. *De la Glossolalie chez les Premiers Chrétiens et des Phénomènes Similaires.* Lausanne, Switzerland: Bridel, 1910.

Lombroso, Cesare. *After Death—What?* Boston: Small, Maynard/ Cambridge, Mass.: Small Maynard/ London: T. Fisher Unwin, 1909.

———. *The Man of Genius.* London: Scott, 1891.

London Dialectical Society. *Report on Spiritualism: Together with the Evidence Oral and Written.* London: Longmans, Green, Reader & Dyer, 1871. Reprint, London: J. Burns, 1873. London: Longmans, Green, Reader & Dyer, 1971. Reprint, North Stratford, N. H.: Ayer Publishing Co. Press, 1976.

Long, Frank Belknap. *Howard Phillips Lovecraft: Dreamer on the Nightside.* Sauk City, Wisc.: Arkham House, 1975.

Long, Max Freedom. *Growing Into Light.* Vista, Calif.: Huna Research Publications, 1955.

———. *Introduction to Huna.* Sedona, Ariz.: Esoteric Publications, 1975.

———. *Recovering the Ancient Magic.* London, 1936. Reprint, Cape Girardeau, Mo.: Huna Press, 1978.

———. *The Secret Science at Work.* Vista, Calif.: Huna Research Publications, 1953.

———. *The Secret Science Behind Miracles.* Kosmon Press, 1948. Reprint, Vista, Calif.: Huna Research Publications, 1954.

Loomis, Roger Sherman. *The Grail: From Celtic Myth to Christian Symbol.* Cardiff: University of Wales Press, 1963.

Loomis, Roger Sherman, ed. *Arthurian Literature in the Middle Ages.* Oxford: Clarendon Press, 1959.

Lörber, Jakob. *The Three-Days-Scene at the Temple of Jerusalem.* Bietigheim, Germany: Neu-Salems-Society, 1932.

Lord's New Church Which Is Nova Hierosalyma. *Handbook of the Lord's New Church Which Is Nova Hierosolyma.* Bryn Athyn, Pa.: The Author, 1985.

Lord-Drake, Maud. *Psychic Light: The Continuity of Law and Life.* Kansas City, Mo.: Frank T. Riley, 1904.

Lorenz, Konrad. *King Solomon's Ring.* New York: Time, 1962.

Lorenzen, Coral E. *The Great Flying Saucer Hoax: The UFO Facts and Their Interpretation.* New York: William Frederick Press, 1962. Rev.: *Flying Saucers: The Startling Evidence of Invasion from Outer Space.* New York: New American Library, 1966.

Lorenzen, Coral, and Jim Lorenzen. *Abducted! Confrontations with Beings from Outer Space.* New York: Berkley, 1977.

———. *Encounters with UFO Occupants.* New York: Berkley, 1976.

———. *UFOs: The Whole Story.* New York: New American Library, 1969.

———.*UFOs Over the Americas.* New York: New American Library, 1968.

Lorenzen, David N. *Kabir Legendas and Ananta-das's Kabir Parachai.* Albany: State University of New York Press, 1991.

Lovecraft, Howard Phillips. *At the Mountains and Other Novels.* Sauk City, Wisc.: Arkham House, 1964.

———. *Collected Poems.* Sauk City, Wisc.: Arkham House, 1963.

———. *The Dunwich Horror and Others.* Sauk City, Wisc.: Arkham House, 1963.

———. *Haunter of the Dark, and Other Tales of Horror.* London: Gollancz, 1950.

———. *Supernatural Horror in Literature.* New York: B. Abramson, 1945.

Lovland, Paul. "An Experiment Proposed to Test Exchange of Mental Entropy in Telepathy," *Journal of Indian Psychology* 15, no. 1-2 (January-July 1997): 31–43.

Lowell, Percival. *Occult Japan.* Boston: Houghton Mifflin, 1895.

Loweman, Emily. *Egoland.* London, 1932.

Lowengard, Manfred. *How to Analyze Your Handwriting.* London: Marshall Cavendish, 1975.

Lowery, T. L. *The End of the World.* Cleveland, Tenn.: Lowery Publications, 1969.

Lozowick, Lee. *The Alchemy of Transformation.* Prescott, Ariz.: Hohm Press, 1996.

Lu K'uan Yü. *Taoist Yoga: Alchemy and Immortality.* London: Rider & Co., 1970.

Lubeck, Walter. *Complete Reiki Handbook.* Westerville, Ohio: Lotus Press, 1994.

Lubow, Robert. *The War Animals.* Garden City, N.Y.: Doubleday, 1977.

Luce, Gaston. *Leon Denis l'apotre du spiritisme, sa vie, son oeuvre.* N.p., n.d.

Luce, Gay Gaer. *Biological Rhythms in Psychiatry and Medicine.* Washington, D.C.: National Institute of Mental Health, 1970. Reprinted as *Biological Rhythms in Human and Animal Physiology.* New York: Dover Books, 1971.

———. *Body Time: Physiological Rhythms and Social Stress.* New York: Pantheon Books, 1971.

Luce, Gay Gaer, and J. Segal. *Sleep.* New York: Coward, McCann, 1966.

Ludlam, Harry. *A Biography of Dracula: The Life Story of Bram Stoker.* London: Fireside Press, 1962.

Ludwig, J. K., ed. *Philosophy and Parapsychology.* Buffalo, N.Y.: Promethus Books, 1978.

Luk, Charles. *Ch'an and Zen Teachings.* Series 1, 2 & 3. London: Rider, 1960–62.

———. *Practical Buddhism.* London: Rider, 1971.

———. *Taoist Yoga, Alchemy, and Immortality.* London: Rider, 1970 New York: Samuel Weiser, 1973.

———. *The Secrets of Chinese Meditation.* London: Rider, 1964.

———. *The Vimalakirti Nirdesa Sutra.* Berkeley, Calif.: Shambhala, 1972.

Lunan, Duncan. *Man and the Stars.* London: Souvenir Press, 1974. Reprinted as *Interstellar Contact; Communication with Other Intelligences in the Universe.* Chicago: Henry Regnery, 1975.

Lundahl, Craig R. "Near-Death Visions of Unborn Children: Indications of a Pre-Earth Life," *Journal of Near-Death Studies* 11, no. 2 (Winter 1992): 123–128.

Lupton, Thomas. *A Thousand Notable Things.* London, 1660.

"The Lure of Martin V. Riccardo." Special issue of *The Vampire Information Exchange Newsletter* 53 (April 1991).

Lutoslawski, Wincenty. *Pre-Existence and Reincarnation.* N.p., 1928.

———. *The Knowledge of Reality.* N.p., 1930.

———. *The World of Souls.* N.p., 1924.

Lutyens, Emily. *Candles in the Sun.* Philadelphia: Lippincott, 1957.

———. *Krishnamurti, The Years of Awakening.* New York: Farrar, Straus, & Giroux, 1975.

———. *Krishnamurti, The Years of Fulfillment.* London: J. Murray, 1983.

Luzzatto, Moses. *General Principles of the Kabbalah.* New York: Research Center of Kabbalah, 1970.

Lyons, Arthur. *Satan Wants You: The Cult of Devil Worship in America.* New York: Dodd, Mead; London: Rupert Hart-Davies, 1970. London: Hart-Davis, 1971. New York: Mysterious Press, 1988. New York: Warner Books, Inc., 1989.

Lyons, Arthur, and Marcello Truzzi. *Blue Sense: Psychic Detectives and Crime.* New York: Mysterious Press; New York: Warner Books, 1991.

Lysaght, Patricia. *The Banshee.* Dublin, 1986.

Lyttelton, Edith. *The Faculty of Communion.* N.p., 1925.

———. *Our Superconscious Mind.* London, 1931.

———. *Some Cases of Prediction.* London: Bell, 1938. Pleasants, Helene, ed. *Biographical Dictionary of Parapsychology.* New York: Helix Press, 1964.

Lytton, Bulwar. *The Coming Race.* London: George Routledge & Sons, 1877.

———. *Complete Works.* New York: Thomas Y. Crowell, n.d.

———. *A Strange Story.* Mobile, Ala.: S. H. Goetzel, 1863. Frequently reprinted.

Lytton, Edward Bulwer. *Vril: Power of the Coming Race.* Edinburgh; London: W. Blackwood and Sons, 1871.

———. *Zanoni.* London: Saunders & Otley, 1842. Reprinted as *Zanoni: A Rosicrucian Tale.* Blauvelt, N.Y.: Rudolf Steiner Publications, 1971.

———. "Proofs for Reincarnation." *Psychic News* (October/November 1960).

———. *Reincarnation Based on Facts.* London: Psychic Press, 1970.

———. "Spiritualist Doctrine." *Tomorrow.* (Autumn 1960).

M. A. (Oxon) [W. Stainton Moses]. *More Spirit Teachings.* Manchester, England: Two Worlds Publishing, 1942.

———. *Spirit Identity.* London, 1879.

The Mabinogion. London: J. M. Dent, 1949.

Maby, J. Cecil, and T. B. Franklin. *The Physics of the Divining Rod.* London: G. Bell and Sons, 1939.

Mac Manus, D. A. *The Middle Kingdom: The Faerie World of Ireland.* London: Max Parrish, 1959.

MacCullough, John A. *The Harrowing of Hell: A Comparative Study of an Early Christian Doctrine.* London: T. & T. Clark, 1930. Reprint, New York: AMS Press, 1981.

Macdonald, Malcolm. *Borneo People.* New York: Alfred P. Knopf, 1958.

MacDowall, M. W. *Epics and Romances of the Middle Ages.* London: S. Sonnenschein, 1896.

Macedo, Nertan. *Antonio Conselheiro.* N.p.: Graf Record, 1969.

Macgregor, Alexander. *Highland Superstitions Connected with the Druids, Fairies, Witchcraft, Second-Sight, Hallowe'en, Sacred Wells and Lochs.* Stirling, Scotland: Eaneas Mackay, 1922.

———. *Highland Superstitions.* Eneas Mackay, 1901.

———. *The Prophecies of the Brahan Seer.* Inverness, 1896. Reprint, Stirling, Scotland: Eaneas Mackay, 1935. Reprint, London: Constable, 1977.

MacGregor, Helen, and Margaret V. Underhill. *The Psychic Faculties and Their Development.* London: LSA Publications, 1930.

MacGregor Mathers, S. L. *The Tarot: Its Occult Signification, Use in Fortune-Telling and Method of Play.* London: George Redway, 1888. Reprint, New York: Gordon Press, 1973.

Machen, Arthur. *The Angel of Mons: The Bowmen and Other Legends of the War.* New York: G. P. Putnam's Sons, 1915.

———. *The Great God Pan.* 1894. Reprint, London: M. Secker, 1926.

———. *The Great Return.* London: Faith Press, 1915.

———. *The Hill of Dreams.* 1907. Reprint, New York: Dover, 1986.

———. *The House of Souls.* 1906. Reprint, Freeport, N.Y.: Books for Libraries Press, 1971.

———. *The Terror.* 1917. Reprint, New York: W. W. Norton, 1965.

Mack, John E. *Abduction: Human Encounters with Aliens.* New York: Charles Scribner's Sons, 1994.

Mackal, Roy Paul. *The Monster of Loch Ness.* Chicago: Swallow Press, 1976.

———. *Searching for Hidden Animals.* Garden City, N.Y.: Doubleday, 1980.

Mackay, Charles. *Memoirs of Extraordinary Popular Delusions.* London: Richard Bentley, 1841. Reprint, New York: Farrar, Strauss & Giroux, 1932. Reprinted as *Extraordinary Popular Delusions and the Madness of Crowds.* Wells, Vt.: Fraser Publishing, 1963.

Mackenzie, Alexander. *The Prophecies of the Brahan Seer Doinneach Odhar Fiosaiche.* Stirling, Scotland: Eneas Mackay, 1935. Rev. ed., Golspie, Scotland: Sutherland Press, 1970. Reprint, London: Constable, 1977.

MacKenzie, Andrew. *Apparitions and Ghosts.* London: Barker, 1971. Reprint, New York: Popular Library, 1972.

———. *Dracula Country.* London: Arthur Barker, 1977.

———. *Hauntings and Apparitions.* London: Heinemann, 1982.

———. *The Riddle of the Future: A Modern Study of Precognition.* London: Barker, 1974. Reprint, New York: Taplinger, 1975.

———. *The Unexplained; Some Strange Cases of Psychical Research.* London, 1966. Reprint, New York: Popular Library, 1970.

Mackenzie, Kenneth. *Royal Masonic Cyclopaedia.* 1877. Reprint, New York: Sterling Publishing, 1987.

MacKenzie, Norman, ed. *Secret Societies.* London: Aldus Books; New York: Collier Books, 1967.

Mackenzie, William. "Les Experiences de Genes avec le medium Erto." *Revue Métaphysique* (November–December 1922).

MacKenzie, William, ed. *Gaelic Incantations, Charms and Blessings of the Hebrides.* Inverness, Scotland, 1895.

Mackey, Albert Gallatin. *Encyclopedia of Freemasonry.* 1874. Reprint, Chicago: Masonic History, 1927.

———. *Mackey's Revised Encyclopedia of Freemasonry.* Richmond, Va.: Macoy Publishing, 1909.

Mackey, Albert G., and Rob Morris. *Lights & Shadows of the Mystic Tie* N.p., 1889. Kila, Mont.: Kessinger Publishing Co., 1999.

Maclagan, Robert Craig. *The Evil Eye in the Western Highlands.* London: David Nutt, 1902. Reprint, UK: E. P. Publishing, 1972. Reprint, Norwood, Pa.: Norwood Editions, 1973.

MacLaglan, R. C. *The Evil Eye in the Western Highlands.* London: David Nutt, 1902.

MacLaine, Shirley. *Dancing in the Light.* New York: Bantam Books, 1985.

———. *Don't Fall Off the Mountain.* New York: W. W. Norton, 1970.

———. *It's All in the Playing.* New York: Bantam Books, 1987.

———. *Out on a Limb.* New York: Bantam Books, 1983. Reprint, London: Elm Tree Books; Hamish Hamilton, 1983.

———. *You Can Get There from Here.* New York: W. W. Norton, 1975.

Maclean, Charles. *The Wolf Children.* Hill & Wang, 1977.

MacLean, Dorothy. *To Hear the Angels Sing.* Middleton, Wisc.: Lorian Press, 1980.

MacLean, John P. *Bibliography of Shaker Literature.* 1905. Reprint, Burt Franklin, 1971.

MacLeod, Fiona. *The Divine Adventure.* Portland, Maine: T. B. Mosher, 1903.

———. *The Dominion of Dreams.* New York: F. A. Stokes, 1900.

———. *Green Fire.* N.p., 1896.

———. *The Immortal Hour.* Portland, Maine: T. B. Mosher, 1907.

———. *The Mountain Lovers.* N.p., 1895.

———. *Pharais.* Chicago: Stone & Kimball, 1895.

———. *The Sin-Eater.* New York: Duffield, 1910.

———. *The Washer of the Ford.* New York: Stone & Kimball, 1896.

———. *Winged Destiny.* New York: Dufdfield, 1910.

MacLeod, Nicholas A. *Scottish Witchcraft.* St. Ives, England: James Pike, 1975.

Macmillan, W. J. *The Reluctant Healer.* London: Victor Gollancz, 1952.

MacNaghten, Hugh. *Emile Coué: the Man and his Work.* New York: Dodd, Mead, 1922.

MacPhilpin, John. *The Apparitions and Miracles at Knock, also Official Depositons of the Eye-Witnesses.* Tuam, Ireland, 1880. 2d ed. Dublin: M. H. Gill & Son, 1894.

Macrae, Norman, ed. *Highland Second-Sight: With Prophecies of Conneach Odhar of Petty.* Dingwall, Scotland: G. Souter, 1908. Reprint, Norwood, Pa., 1972.

MacRithie, David. *Shelta: The Cairds' Language. Transactions* of Gaelic Society of Inverness 24 (1904).

MacRobert, Russell G. "Current Attitudes of American Neuropsychiatrists towards Parapsychology." *Journal of Parapsychology* (November 1948).

———. "Hallucinations of the Sane." *Journal of Insurance Medicine* 5, no. 3 (1950).

———. "Psychiatry and Intuition." *Journal of Insurance Medicine* 4, no. 3 (1949).

———. "Science Studies Intuition." *Tomorrow* (May 1950).

———. "When Is Healing 'Psychic'?" *Tomorrow* (spring 1955).

———. "Where Is Bridey Murphy?" *Tomorrow* (spring 1956).

Maeterlinck, Maurice. *The Great Secret.* London: Methuen, 1922. Reprint, New York: University Books, 1969.

———. *L'Ornemant des Noces Spirituelles, de Ruysbroeck l'admirable.* English ed. as: *Ruysbroeck and the Mystics with Selections fron Ruysbroeck.* N.p., 1894.

———. *Ruysbroeck and the Mystics.* London, 1908.

———. *The Unknown Guest.* London, 1914. Reprint, New Hyde Park, N.Y.: University Books, 1975.

Mager, Henri. *Water Diviners and Their Methods.* London, 1931.

Magre, Maurice. *The Return of the Magi.* London: P. Allen, 1931.

Mahan, Asa. *Modern Mysteries Explained and Exposed.* Boston, 1855.

Mahararj Ji, Guru. *The Living Master.* Denver: Divine Light Mission, 1978.

Maharishi Mahesh Yogi. *Meditations of Maharishi Mahesh Yogi.* New York: Bantam, 1973.

———. *The Science of Being and Art of Living.* London: International SRM Publications, 1966.

Maher, Michaeleen, and Gertrude Schmeidler. "Confirmation of a Family's Report of an Apparition." In *Research in Parapsychology 1974.* Edited by J. D. Morris, W. G. Roll, and R. L. Morris. Metuchen, N.J.: Scarecrow Press, 1975.

Maisyuk, Alexander. "This Mysterious Clairvoyance: An Experiment in Moscow." *PSI Research* 5, no. 1-2 (March-June 1986): 4–10.

Maitland, Edward. *Anna Kingsford: Her Life, Letters, Diary.* London, 1896.

———. *The Story of Anna Kingsford and Edward Maitland and of the New Gospel of Interpretation.* Birmingham, England: Ruskin Press, 1905.

Majumdar, S. M. *Introduction to Yoga Principles and Practices.* New Hyde Park, N.Y.: University Books, 1964. Reprint, Secacus, N.J.: Citadel Press, 1976.

Malbrough, Ray T. *Charms, Spells, and Formulas.* St. Paul, Minn.: Llewellyn Publications, 1987.

Malo, Henry. *Life of Delphine Gray.* N.p., 1925.

Maloney, Clarence, ed. *The Evil Eye.* New York: Columbia University Press, 1976.

Malony, H. Newton and A. Adams Lovekin. *Glossolalia.* New York: Oxford University Press, Inc., 1985.

Maltwood, Katherine E. *A Guide to Glastonbury's Temple of the Stars.* London, 1929.

Manas, John H. *Divination: Ancient and Modern.* New York: Pythagoran Society, 1947.

Manchen-Helfen, Otto. *The World of the Huns: Studies in Their History and Culture.* Berkeley: University of California Press, 1973.

Mangan, Gordon Lavelle. "Evidence of Displacement in a Precognitive Test." *Journal of Parapsychology* (March 1955).

———. "An ESP Experiment with Dual-Aspect Targets Involving One Trial Day." *Journal of Parapsychology* (December 1957).

———. "How Legitimate Are the Claims for ESP?" *Australian Journal of Psychology* (September 1959).

———. "Parapsychology: A Science for Psychical Research?" *Queen's Quarterly* (spring 1958).

———. "A PK Experiment with Thirty Dice Released for High and Low Face Targets." *Journal of Parapsychology* (December 1954).

———. *A Review of Published Research on the Relationship of Some Personality Variables to ESP Scoring Level.* New York: Parapsychology Foundation, 1958.

Mangan, Gordon Lavelle, and L. C. Wilbur. "The Relation of PK Object and Throwing Surface in Placement Tests." *Journal of Parapsychology* 20 (1956); 21, (1957).

Maning, F. E. *Old New Zealand.* London: R. Bentley, 1884. Reprint, Auckland: Whitcombe & Tombs, 1922.

Manisis: The Interpretation of the Divine Law for the Manistic Dispensation. Quakertown, Pa.: Beverley Hall, 1955.

Mann, Felix. *Acupuncture.* New York: Random House, 1963; London: W. Heinemann Medical Books, 1962.

Mann, William Edward. *Orgone, Reich and Eros.* New York: Simon and Schuster, 1973.

Mannhardt, W. *Über Vampirismus.* (see vol. 4 of *Zeitschrift für Deutsche Mythologie und Sittenkunde*), Göttingen, 1858.

Manning, Alcie G. *Helping Yourself with the Power of Gnostic Magic.* West Nyack, N.Y.: Parker Publishing, 1979.

———. *Helping Yourself with White Witchcraft.* West Nyack, N.Y.: Parker Publishing, 1972.

Manning, Matthew. *In the Mind of Millions.* London: W. H. Allen, 1977.

———. *The Link: Matthew Manning's Own Story of His Extraordinary Psychic Gifts.* London: Corgi, 1975. Reprint, New York: Holt, Rinehart & Winston, 1975.

———. *The Link: The Extraordinary Gifts of a Teenage Psychic.* UK: Colin Smythe, 1974. Reprint, New York: Holt, Rinehart, 1975.

———. *The Strangers.* London: W. H. Allen, 1978.

Mannix, Daniel P. *The Hell Fire Club.* New York: Ballantine Books, 1959.

Manuel, David. *Like a Mighty River.* Orleans, Mass: Rock Harbor Press, 1977.

Manvell, Roger. *The Trial of Annie Besant and Charles Bradlaugh.* London: Elek/Pemberton, 1976.

Maple, Eric. *The Complete Book of Witchcraft and Demonology: Witches, Devils, and Ghosts in Western Civilization.* South Brunswick, N.J.: A. S. Barnes, 1966.

———. *The Dark World of Witches.* London: Robert Hale; New York: A. S. Barnes, 1962. Also reprinted with two other Eric Maple books in one volume as *The Complete Book of Witchcraft and Demonology.* New York: A. S. Barnes, 1964.

———. *Deadly Magic.* Wellingborough, England: Thursons, 1976.

———. *The Domain of Devils.* London: R. Hale, 1966.

———. *Incantations and Words of Power.* New York: Samuel Weiser, 1974.

———. *Magic, Medicine, and Quakery.* London: R. Hale, 1968.

———. *The Realm of Ghosts.* New York: A.S. Barnes, 1964.

———. *Superstition and the Superstitious.* London and New York: W.H. Allen, 1971.

———. *Witchcraft: The Story of Man's Quest for Psychic Power.* London: Octopus Books, 1973.

Marabini, Enrico. "Esperienze di Telepatia collectiva eseguite nella Citta' di Bologna" (Experiments in Mass Telepathy in Bologna). *Metapsichica* 1 (1954).

———. "Esperienze trienneli di lettura della mano con una sensitiva Bolognese: Maria Guardini" (Three Years of Experiments in Hand-reading with the Sensitive Maria Guardini of Bologna). *Parapsicologia di Minerva Medica* (June 1957).

———. "Il Comportamento paranormale in rapporto a stati neuro-endocrini" (Paranormal Behavior in Connection with Neuro-Endocrinological Conditions). *Parapsicologia di Minerva Medica* (November 1957).

———. "Il Metodo scientifico in parapsicologia" (Scientific Method in Parapsychology). *Bulletin of the Italian Society for Parapsychology* (July–December 1957).

———. "La Psi e'stata dimonstrata sperimentalmente?" (Has Psi Been Experimentally Demonstrated?). *Bulletin of the Italian Society for Parapsychology* (July–December 1959).

———. "La Telapatia" (Telepathy). *Metapsichica* 1–4 (1953).

———. "Problemi parapsicologici e psicosomatica" (Parapsychological Problems and Psychosomatics). *Medicina psicosomatics* 1, no. 2 (1957).

———. "Proposta di una modifica al test di Stuart per la Chiaroveggenza" (Proposal of a Modification of the Stuart Test for Clairvoyance). *Metapsichica* 3 (1954).

———. "Sogno paragnosico" (Paragnostic Dreams). *Parapsicologia di Minerva Medica* (June 1957).

———. "Una Nuova ESP?" *Bulletin of the Italian Society for Parapsychology* (January–June 1959).

Marbewick, Betty. "The Soal-Goldney Experiments with Basil Shackleton: New Evidence of Data Manipulation." *Proceedings of the Society for Psychical Research* 56, no. 211 (May 1978).

Marchand, A. *The Facts of Lourdes and the Medical Bureau.* London: Burns Oates & Wasbourne, 1924.

Marcuse, Irene. *The Key to Handwriting Analysis.* New York: R. M. McBride, 1959.

Margiotta, D. *Souvenirs d'un Trente-Troisieme. Adriano Lemmi, chef supreme des francsmaçons.* Paris, 1896.

Marglis, Nadia. *Joan of Arc in History, Literature, and Film: A Select Bibliography.* New York: Garland Publishing, 1990.

Marion, Frederick. *In My Mind's Eye.* London: Rider, 1949.

Marks, David F. "Investigating the Paranormal," *Nature* 320, no. 6058 (March 1986): 119–124.

Marques-Riviere, J. *Tantrik Yoga.* London: Rider & Co., 1940.

Marricks, William S. *Edward Irving: The Forgotten Giant.* East Peoria, Ill.: Scribe's Chamber Publications, 1983.

Marryat, Florence. *The Spirit World.* New York: C. B. Reed, 1894.

———. *There is No Death.* New York: John W. Lovell/ London: K Paul, Trench, Trubner, 1891. Reprint, London: Griffith, Farran, 1893. Reprint, New York: Causeway Books, 1973.

Marryat, Florence, ed. *The Clairvoyance of Bessie Williams. Related by Herself.* N.p., 1893.

Mars, Louis. *The Crisis of Possession in Voudou.* Port-au-Prince, Haiti: State Printing, 1946. Rev. ed. Reed, Cannon and Johnson, 1977.

Mars, Louis, and G. Devereux. "Haitian Voudou and the Revitalization of the Nightmare." *Psychoanlytic Review* 38, no. 4 (1951).

Marshall, Charles. "The Mahatma Letters: A Syntactic Investigation into the Possibility of 'Forgery' by Helena Petrovna Blavatsky, a 19th Century Russian Occultist." *Viewpoint Aquarius* 96 (October 1980).

Martel, Roy. *The Mysterious Power of Linda Martel.* Guernsey, Channel Islands: Toucan Press, 1973.

Martello, Leo Louis. *Curses in Verses.* New York: Hero Press, 1971.

———. *Weird Ways of Witchcraft.* New York: HC Publishers, 1969.

———. *What It Means to Be a Witch.* New York: The Author, 1975.

———. *Witchcraft: The Old Religion.* Secaucus, N.J.: University Books, 1973.

Martensen, H. L. *Jacob Boehme.* Rockliff, 1949.

Martin, Charles Rochelle. "Mystical Experience and Mental Health: Three Perspectives," *Dissertation Abstracts International: Section B: The Sciences & Engineering* 55, no. 7-B (January 1995): 2999.

Martin, Dorothy R. "An Analysis of a Second Series of 25,000 Trials." *Journal of Parapsychology* 2 (1938).

———. "Chance and Extra-Chance Results in Card Matching." *Journal of Parapsychology* 1 (1937).

———. "A Review of All University of Colorado Experiments." *Journal of Parapsychology* 4 (1940).

Martin, Dorothy R., and F. P. Stribic. *The Immortality of Living Beings.* Copenhagen, Denmark: Martinus Institute, 1970.

Martin, Dorothy R., and F. P. Stribic. "Studies in Extrasensory Perception: An Analysis of 25,000 Trials." *Journal of Parapsychology* 2 (1938).

Martin, Edward J. *The Trail of the Templars.* London: Allen & Unwin, 1928.

Martin, Katherine. "The Voice of Lazaris." *New Realities* 7, no. 6 (July/August 1987).

Martin, William. "This Man Says He's the Divine Sweetheart of the Universe." *Esquire* (June 1974): 76–78, 140–43.

Martinez-Taboas, Alfonso. "A Case of Spirit Possession and Glossolalia," *Culture, Medicine & Psychiatry* 23(3) (September 1999): 333–348.

Martinez-Taboas, Alfonso and Margarita Francia. "The Feilding Report, Wiseman's Critique and Scientific Reporting," *Journal of the Society for Psychical Research* 59, no. 831 (April 1993): 120–129.

Martinus. *The Principle of Reincarnation.* Copenhagen, Denmark: Martinus Institute, 1938.

———. *The Road to Initiation.* Copenhagen, Denmark: Martinus Institute, 1957.

Marx, C. W. *The Devil's Rights & the Redemption in the Literature of Medieval England.* Rochester, N.Y.: Boydell & Brewer, Inc., 1995.

Maryatt, Florence. *There Is No Death.* London, 1892. Reprint, New York: Causeway Books, 1973.

Maryona [Helen Spitler]. *Light of the Universe.* 2 vols. Tiffin, Ohio: The Light of the Universe, 1965, 1976.

———. *Mini-Manual for Light Bearers.* Tiffin, Ohio: Light of the Universe, 1987.

Maskarinec, Gregory Gabriel. *The Rulings of the Night: An Ethnography of Nepalese Shaman Oral Texts.* Madison: University of Wisconsin Press, 1995.

Maskelyne, John N. *The Magnetic Lady; or, a Human Magnet Demagnetised.* Bristol, 1892.

———. *Modern Spiritualism: A Short Account of Its Rise and Progress, with Some Exposures of So-Called Spirit Media.* London: F. Warne, 1876.

———. *The Fraud of Modern "Theosophy" Exposed.* London: G. Routledge, 1913.

Masks of Dionysus. Ithaca, N.Y.: Cornell University Press, 1993.

Maspero, G. *Les contes populaires de l'Egypte ancienne.* Paris, 1881.

Massey, Gerald. *Ancient Egypt, the Light of the World.* 2 vols. London, 1907. Reprint, New York: Samuel Weiser, 1974.

———. *A Book of the Beginnings.* 2 vols. London, 1881. Reprint, New Hyde Park, N.Y.: University Books, 1974.

———. *The Natural Genesis.* 2 vols. London: n.p., 1883.

Masters, Anthony. *The Natural History of the Vampire.* London: Ruper Hart-Davis, 1972; London: Mayflower 1974.

Masters, Robert E. L. *Eros and Evil: The Sexual Psychopathology of Witchcraft.* New York: Julian Press, 1962.

———. *Forbidden Sexual Behavior and Morality.* New York: Julian Press, 1962.

———. *The Homosexual Revolution: A Challenging Exposé of the Social and Political Directions of a Minority Group.* New York: Julian Press, 1962.

Masters, Robert E. L., and Jean Houston. *Listening to the Body.* New York, Delacorte Press, 1978.

———. *Mind Games: The Guide to Inner Space.* New York: Viking, 1972.

Masters, Robert V. *Complete Book of Karate and Self-Defense.* New York: Sterling, 1974.

Masters, R. E. L., and Jean Houston. *The Varieties of Psychedelic Experience.* New York: Holt, Rinehart & Winston, 1966. Reprint, London: Anthony Blond; New York: Dell, 1967.

Mata, Sri Daya. *Only Love.* Los Angeles: Self-Realization Fellowship, 1976.

Materialy z Konfernecji Parapsychologó w '94. Warsaw: Polskie Towarzystwo Psychotroniczne, 1994.

Mather, Cotton. *Memorable Provinces, Relating to Witchcraft and Possessions.* Boston, 1689.

———. *Wonders of the Invisible World.* Boston: Benjamin Harris, 1693. Reprint, Amherst, Wisc.: Amherst Press, 1980. Reprint, n.p.: Reprint Services Corporation, 1999.

Mather, Increase. *Cases of Conscience Concerning Evil Spirits.* Boston, 1693.

———. *Essay for the Recording of Illustrious Provinces.* Boston, 1684.

Mathers, S. L. MacGregor. *Astral Projection, Ritual Magic, and Alchemy.* Rochester, Vt.: Destiny Books, 1987.

———. *The Kabbalah Unveiled.* 1907. Reprint, London: Routledge and Kegan Paul, 1926. 2nd edition reprint. Life Science Institute, 1991.

Mathers, S. L. MacGregor, ed. *The Key of Solomon the King.* London: George Redway, 1908. Reprint, London: Routledge and Kegan Paul, 1972. Reprint, York Beach, Maine: Samuel Weiser, Inc., 1985. N.p.: The Book Tree, 1999.

Mathers, S. L. MacGregor, trans. *The Book of the Sacred Magic of Abra-Melin the Mage.* 1898. Reprint, Chicago: De Laurence, 1932. Reprint, New York: Causeway Books, 1974.

Mathison, Richard. *Faiths, Cults, and Sects of America.* Indianapolis, Ind.: Bobbs-Merrill, 1960.

Matlock, James G. "Leonora or Leonore? A Note on Mrs. Piper's First Name." *Journal* of the American Society for Psychical Research 82, no. 3 (July 1988).

———. "Records of the Parapsychology Laboratory: An Inventory of the Collection in the Duke University Library," *Journal of Parapsychology* 55, 3 (September 1991): 301–314.

Matsumoto, Teruo. *Acupuncture for Physicians.* Springfield, Ill.: Thomas, 1974.

Matter, A. J. *Saint-Martin, le philosophe inconnu.* Paris, 1862.

Matthews, Ronald. *English Messiahs.* London: Methuen, 1936.

Mattison, Hiram. *Spirit Rapping Unveiled!* Derby, N.Y., 1853.

Maurina-Raudive, Zenta, ed. *Konstantin Raudive zum Gedaechtnis.* München: Maximilian Dietrich Verlag, 1975.

Maury, Marguerite. *How to Dowse: Experimental and Practical Radiasthesia.* London: G. Bell and Sons, 1953.

Maxfield, Melinda. "The Journey of the Drum," *ReVision* vol. 16, no. 4 (Spring 1994): 157–163.

Maxwell, J. *Metapsychical Phenomena: Methods and Observations.* London: Duckworth, 1905.

Maxwell, Joseph. *La Divination.* Paris: E. Flammarion, 1927.

———. *La Magie.* Paris: E. Flammarion, 1922.

———. *Les Phénomènes psychiques* (Metapsychical Phenomena). London: Duckworth, 1905.

———. *Metaphysical Phenomena.* New York: G. P. Putnam's Sons; London: Duckworth, 1905.

May, Antoinette. *Haunted Ladies.* San Francisco: Chronicle Books, 1975.

Mayer, G., V. Neissner, P. Schwarzmayr, and K. Meier-Ewert. "Schlafentzug bei Somnambulismus. Auswirkung auf Arousals, Tiefschlaf und Schlafstadienwechsel" (Sleepwalking in somnambulism. Effect of arousals, deep sleep and sleep-stage shifts), *Nervenarzt* 69, no. 6 (June 1998): 495–501.

Maynard, Henrietta S. *Was Abraham Lincoln a Spiritualist?* Philadelphia.: R. C. Hartranft, 1891. Reprint, London: Psychic Book Club, 1917.

Mayne, Alan James. "The Promotion of Research." *Journal of the Society for Psychical Research* 42 (1963).

Mayo, Jeff. *The Planets and Human Behavior.* 1972. Reprint, Reno, Nev.: CRCS Publications, 1985.

McAnally, D. R., Jr. *Irish Wonders: The Ghosts, Giants, Pookas, Demons, Leprechawns, Banshees, Fairies, Witches, Widows, Old Maids and Other Marvels of the Emerald Isle.* Boston: Houghton Mifflin, 1888. Reprint, Detroit: Grand River Books, 1971.

McBirnie, William S. *Anti-Christ.* Dallas, Tex.: International Prison Ministry, 1978.

McCabe, Joseph. *Spiritualism: A Popular History from 1847.* London: Fisher Unwin, 1920.

McCarthy, C. W. *Rigid Tests of the Occult.* Melbourne, Australia: Stephens, 1904.

McCearney, James. *Arthur Conan Doyle.* Paris: La Table Ronde, 1988.

McClenon, James. "Parapsychology in Japan," *Parapsychology Review* 20, no. 4 (July 1989): 13–15.

McCloy, J. F., and Ray Miller, Jr. *The Jersey Devil.* Newark, Del.: Middle Atlantic Press, 1976.

McClure, Kevin. *The Evidence for Visions of the Virgin Mary.* Wellingborough, England: Aquarian Press, 1983.

McConnell, Robert A. *Encounters with Parapsychology.* Pittsburgh, Pa.: The Author, 1982.

———. *ESP Curriculum Guide.* New York: Simon & Schuster, 1971.

———. *An Introduction to Parapsychology in the Context of Science.* Pittsburgh, Pa.: The Author, 1983.

———. *Parapsychology and Self-Deception in Science.* Pittsburgh, Pa.: The Author, 1982.

———. *Parapsychology in Retrospect: My Search for the Unicorn.* Pittsburgh, Pa.: The Author, 1987.

McConnell, Robert A., and Gertrude Schmeidler. *ESP and Personality Patterns.* New Haven, Conn.: Yale University Press, 1958.

McCormick, Donald. *The Hell-Fire Club.* London: Jarrolds Publishers, 1958. Reprint, London: Sphere Books, 1975.

McCoy, Edain. *Inside a Witches' Coven.* St. Paul, Minn.: Llewellyn Publications, 1997.

McCreery, Charles. *Science, Philosophy, and ESP.* London: Faber & Faber, 1967. Reprint, Hamden, Conn.: Archon Books, 1968.

McCulloch, Joseph. *The Trumpet Shall Sound.* London, M. Joseph, Ltd., 1944.

McDermott, Robert, ed. *The Essential Aurobindo.* New York: Schrocken Books, 1973.

———. *Six Pillars.* Chambersburg, Pa.: Wilson Books, 1974.

McDougall, William. *Body and Mind: A History and Defense of Animism.* London: Methuen, 1911.

———. "The Case of Sally Beauchamp." *Proceedings of the Society of Psychical Research* 19–20 (1905–07).

———. "Further Observations on the 'Margery' Case." *Journal of the American Society for Psychical Research* 19 (1925).

———. "The Margery Mediumship." *Psyche* 26 (1926).

———. *Modern Materialism and Emergent Evolution.* New York: D. Van Nostrand, 1929.

———. "The Need for Psychical Research." *Harvard Graduate Magazine.* Reprinted in *ASPR Journal* 17 (1923).

———. *The Riddle of Life.* London: Methuen, 1938.

McEvers, Joan. *The Houses: Power Places of the Horoscope.* St. Paul, Minn.: Llwellyn Publications, 1991.

———. *Planets: The Astrological Tools.* St. Paul, Minn.: Llwellyn Publications, 1989.

McGarey, William. *Acupuncture and Body Energies.* Phoenix, Ariz.: Gabriel Press, 1974.

McGinn, Bernard. *The Growth of Mysticism.* New York: Crossroad Publishing Co., 1996.

McGregor, Pedro. *Jesus of the Spirits.* New York: Stein & Day, 1966.

———. *Moon and Two Mountains.* London, 1966.

McHargue, Georgess. *Facts, Frauds, and Phantasms: A Survey of the Spiritualist Movement.* Garden City, N.Y.: Doubleday, 1972.

McIntosh, Christopher. *The Astrologers and Their Creed: An Historical Outline.* New York: Frederick A. Praeger, 1969.

———. *The Devil's Bookshelf.* Wellingborough, England: Aquarian Press, 1985.

———. *Éliphas Lévi and the French Occult Revival.* New York: Samuel Weiser, 1972.

———. *The Rosicrucians.* New York: Samuel Weiser Inc., 1997.

———. *The Rosy Cross Unveiled: The History, Mythology, and Rituals of an Occult Order.* Wellingborough, England: Aquarian Press, 1980.

McKenna, Terrence. "Hallucinogenic Mushrooms and Evolution," *ReVision* vol. 10 (1988): 51–57.

McLean, Dorothy. *To Hear the Angels Sing.* Middleton, Wisc.: Lorian Press, 1980.

McMahan, Elizabeth Anne. "An Experiment in Pure Telepathy." *Journal of Parapsychology* 10 (1946).

———. "PK Experiments with Two-Sided Objects." *Journal of Parapsychology* 9 (1945).

McMahan, Elizabeth Anne, and E. K. Bates. "Report of Further Marchesi Experiments." *Journal of Parapsychology* 18 (1954).

McMahan, Elizabeth Anne, and J. B. Rhine. "Extrasensory Perception of Cards in an Unknown Location." *Journal of Parapsychology* 12 (1948).

———. "A Review of the Evidence for Dowsing." *Journal of Parapsychology* 11 (1947).

———. "A Second Zagreb-Durham ESP Experiment." *Journal of Parapsychology* 11 (1947).

McNally, Raymond T. *Dracula Was a Woman.* New York: McGraw-Hill, 1983.

McNally, Raymont T., and Radu Florescu. *In Search of Dracula: A True History of Dracula and Vampire Legends.* New York: New York Graphic Society, 1972. Rev. ed. Boston: Houghton Mifflin, 1994.

McNutt, Dan J. *The Eighteenth-Century Gothic Novel: An Annotated Bibliography of Criticism and Selected Texts.* New York: Garland Publishing, 1975.

———. *Apollonius of Tyana: The Philosopher-Reformer of the First Century A.D.* 1901. Reprint, New Hyde Park, N.Y.: University Books, 1966.

———. *Did Jesus Live 100 B.C.?* 1903. Reprint, New Hyde Park, N.Y.: University Books, 1968.

———. *The Doctrine of the Subtle Body.* London: John M. Watkins, 1919. Reprint, Wheaton, Ill.: Theosophical Publishing House, 1967.

———. *Echoes from the Gnosis.* 1907. Reprint, Hastings, E. Sussex, England: Chthonius Books, 1987.

———. *Essay Written as a Preface to a New Edition of T. Taylor's "Select Works of Plotinus."* London: Theosophical Publishing Society, 1895.

———. *Fragments of a Faith Forgotten.* 1900. Reprint, New Hyde Park, N.Y.: University Books, 1960.

———. *Human Personality and Its Survival of Bodily Death.* London: Longmans, Green, 1903. Reprint, New York: Ayer Publishing Co. Inc., 1975.

———. *Pistis Sophia: A Gnostic Miscellany.* London, 1921. Reprint, New Hyde Park, N.Y.: University Books, 1974.

———. *Simon Magus.* London: Theosophical Publishing Society, 1892.

Mead, G. R. S., ed. *Thrice-Greatest Hermes.* 3 vols. London: J. M. Watkins, 1964.

Mead, Margaret. *Inquiry Into the Question of Cultural Stability in Polynesia.* New York: Columbia University, 1928. Reprint, New York: AMS Press, 1981.

Meade, Marion. *Madame Blavatsky: The Woman Behind the Myth.* New York: G. P. Putnam's Sons, 1980.

Meaden, George Terence. *The Circles Effect and its Mysteries.* Bradford-on-Avon, England: Artetech Publishing, 1989.

———. *Circles from the Sky.* London: Souvenir Press, 1991.

Medeiros, Earl C. *The Complete History and Philosophy of Kung Fu.* Rutland, Vt.: Charles Tuttle, 1975.

Medhurst, R. G. "On the Origin of the 'Prepared Random Numbers' Used in the Shackleton Experiments." *Journal of the Society for Psychical Research* 46 (March 1971).

Medhurst, R. G., contr. *Crookes and the Spirit World.*Marlboro, N.J.: Taplinger Publishing Co. Inc.; London: Souvenir Press, 1972.

Medhurst, R. G., and K. M. Godney. "William Crookes and the Physical Phenomena of Mediumship." *Proceedings of the Society for Psychical Research* 54, 195 (March 1964).

A Medium [Ed Lunt]. *Mysteries of the Séance.* Boston: Lunt Brothers, 1905.

"Mediumship of Mr. C. Bailey." *Journal of the Society for Psychical Research* 12 (1905): 77, 109.

Meehl, Paul E., and M. J. Scriven. "Compatibility of Science and ESP." *Science* 123 (1956).

Meehl, Paul E., H. R. Klann, and K. H. Breimeter. *What, Then, Is Man?* N.p., 1958.

Meek, George W., and Bertha Harris. *From Séance to Science.* London: Regency Press, 1973.

Meerloo, Joost A. M. "The Biology of Time." *Tomorrow* (winter 1954).

———. *Hidden Communion.* New York: Garrett Publications, 1964.

———. "Man's Ecstatic Healing." *Tijdschrift voor Parapsychologie* 27 (1959).

———. *The Rape of the Mind: The Psychology of Thought Control, Menticide, and Brainwashing.* N.p., 1956.

———. "Telepathy and Foreknowledge." In *Proceedings of the First International Conference on Parapsychology.* Utrecht, 1953.

———. "Telepathy as a Form of Archaic Communication." *Psychiatric Quarterly* 23 (1949).

———. *Unobtrusive Communication.* Assen, The Netherlands: Van Gorcum, 1964.

Mehrabian, Albert, Catherine A. Stefl, and Melissa Mullen. "Emotional Thinking in the Adult: Individual Differences in Mysticism and Globality-Differentiation," *Imagination, Cognition & Personality* 16, no. 4 (1997): 325–355.

———. *Ancient Incubation and Modern Psychotherapy.* Evanston, Ill.: Northwestern University Press, 1968.

———. "C. G. Jung's Concept of Synchronicity." In *Proceedings of the First International Conference of Parapsychological Studies* (1955).

———. "Jung's 'Meaningful Coincidence.' " *Tomorrow* (spring 1954).

———. "Projection, Transference, and Subject-Object Relation." In *Proceedings of the International Symposium on Psychology and Parapsychology* (1957).

———. "Psychological Background of So-Called Spontaneous Phenomena." In *Proceedings of the Conference on Spontaneous Phenomena* (1957).

Mellor, Alec. *Our Separated Brethren: The Freemasons.* London: George G. Harp, 1964.

Melton, J. Gordon. *The Betty Book Literature of Stewart Edward White.* Evanston, Ill.: The Author, 1971.

———. "Comet Kouhotek: Fizzle of the Century." *Fate* 27, no. 5 (May 1974): 58–64.

———. "The Contactees: a Survey." In *The Spectrum of UFO Research: Proceedings of the Second UFO Conference.* Chicago: Center for UFO Studies, 1975.

———. *A Directory of Religious Bodies in the United States.* New York: Garland Publishing, 1977.

———. *Encyclopedia of American Religions.* Detroit: Gale Group, 1998.

———. *Encyclopedic Handbook of Cults in America.* New York: Garland Publishing, 1986. Rev. ed. 1992.

———. "A History of the New Age Movement." In *Not Necessarily the New Age.* Edited by Robert Basil. Buffalo, N.Y.: Prometheus Press, 1988.

———. *New Age Encyclopedia.* Detroit: Gale Research, 1990.

———. *New Thought: A Reader.* Santa Barbara, Calif.: Institute for the Study of American Religion, 1990.

———. *Paganism, Magic, and Witchcraft.* New York: Garland Publishing, 1982.

———. "Pascal Beverly Randolph: America's Pioneer Occultist." In *Le Défi Magique,* edited by Jean Baptiste Martin and Francois Laplantine. Lyon, France: Presses Universitaires de Lyon, 1994.

———. *A Reader's Guide to the Church's Ministry of Healing.* Independence, Mo.: Academy of Religion and Psychical Research, 1977.

———. *Religious Leaders of America.* 2d ed. Detroit: Gale Group, 1999.

———. "The Revival of Astrology in the United States." In *Religious Movements: Genesis, Exodus, and Numbers.* Edited by Rodney Stark. New York: Paragon House Publishers, 1985.

———. "Toward a History of Magical Religion in the United States." *Listening* 9, no. 3 (autumn 1974): 112–33.

———. *The Vampire Book: An Encyclopedia of the Undead.* Detroit: Gale Research, 1994.

———. *The Ways of Meditation.* Evanston, Ill.: Stellium Press, 1974.

Melton, J. Gordon, and George M. Eberhart. *The Flying Saucer Contactee Movement: 1950–1990.* Santa Barbara, Calif.: Santa Barbara Centre for Humanistic Studies, 1990.

Melton, J. Gordon, and Isotta Poggi. *Magic, Witchcraft, and Paganism in America: A Bibliography.* New York: Garland Publishing, 1992.

Melton, J. Gordon, and James R. Lewis, eds. *Perspectives on the New Age.* Albany: State University of New York Press, 1992.

Melton, J. Gordon, and Robert L. Moore. *The Cult Experience.* New York: Pilgrim Press, 1982.

Melton, J. Gordon, ed. *The Peoples Temple and Jim Jones: Broadening Our Perspectives.* New York: Garland, 1990.

Melton, J. Gordon, Jerome Clark, and Aidan A. Kelly. *New Age Encyclopedia.* Detroit: Gale Research, 1990.

Meltzer, David, ed. *The Secret Garden: An Anthology of the Kabbalah.* New York: Seabury Press, 1976.

Melville, John. *Crystal-Gazing and The Wonders of Clairvoyance.* London: Nichols, 1897. Reprinted as *Crystal Gazing and Clairvoyance.* Wellingborough, England: Aquarium Press, 1979.

Meng-Koehler, Heinrich O. "Parapsychologie, Psychohygiene, and Aerztliche Fortbildung" (Parapsychology, Mental Hygiene and Medical Training). *Hippokrates* (1954).

———. "Wunderheilungen" (Miracles of Healing). *Hippokrates* (1954).

Merchant, Francis. *A.E.: An Irish Promethean.* Columbia, S.C.: Benedict College Press, 1954.

Meredith, Dennis L. *Search at Loch Ness: The Expedition of the New York Times and The Academy of Applied Science.* New York: Quadrangle/New York Times Book Co., 1977.

Merkur, Daniel. *Becoming Half Hidden: Shamanism and Initiation among the Inuit.* New York: Garland, 1992.

———. *Gnosis: An Esoteric Tradition of Mystical Visions and Unions.* Albany: State University of New York Press, 1993.

Mermet, Abbe. *Principles & Practice of Radiesthesie.* London, 1967.

Merrell-Wolff, Franklin. *Pathways through to Space: A Personal Record of Transformation in Consciousness.* New York: Warner Books, 1976.

———. *The Philosophy of Consciousness without an Object.* New York: Julian Press, 1973.

Merry, Eleanor. *The Dream Song of Olaf Asteson.* England: New Knowledge Books, 1961.

Mesmer, F. A. *Memoir of F. A. Mesmer, Doctor of Medicine, On His Discoveries, 1799.* Translated by Jerome Eden. Mount Vernon, N.Y.: Eden Press, 1957.

———. *Mesmerism by Doctor Mesmer (1779), Being the First Translation of Mesmer's Historic "Memoire sur la découverte du Magnétism Animal" to Appear in English.* London: Macdonald, 1948.

Messent, Peter B., ed. *Literature of the Occult.* Englewood Cliffs, N.J.: Prentice-Hall, 1971.

Messmer, Joseph, and Sigismund Waitz. *A Visit to the Stimatized Seer: Therese Neumann.* Chicago: John P. Dalriden, 1929.

Metcalf, Peter. *A Borneo Journey into Death: Berawan Eschatology from Its Rituals.* Philadelphia: University of Pennsylvania Press, 1982.

Metzner, Ralph. "Mushrooms and the Mind." In *Psychedelics: The Use and Implications of Hallucinogenic Drugs.* Edited by B. Aaronson and H. Osmond. London: Hogarth Press, 1971.

Metzner, Ralph, et al. *The Well of Remembrance: Rediscovering the Earth Wisdom Myths of Northern Europe.* Boston: Shambhala, 1994.

Meurger, Michel, with Claude Gagnon. *Lake Monster Traditions: A Cross Cultural Analysis.* London: Fortean Tomes, 1988.

Mew, James. *Traditional Aspects of Hell.* London: Swan, Sonnenschein, 1903. Reprint, Detroit: Gale Research, 1971.

Meyer, Donald. *The Positive Thinkers.* New York: Doubleday, 1965.

Meyer, E. H. *Germanische Mythologie.* Berlin, 1891.

Meyrink, Gustav [G. Meyer]. *The Golem.* London, 1928. Reprint, New York, 1964.

Miall, A. M. *Complete Fortune Telling.* Greenberg, 1950. Reprint, Hackensack, N.J.: Wehman, 1962.

Michael, Henry N., ed. *Studies in Siberian Shamanism: Translations from Russian Sources,* vol. 4. Arctic Institute of North America, Toronto: University of Toronto Press, 1963.

———. *Studies in Siberian Ethnogenesis. Anthropology of the North.* Trans. from Russian Sources, No. 2. Arctic Institute of North America, Toronto: University of Toronto Press, 1962.

Michelet, Jules. *Le Procès des Templiers.* 2 vols. N.p., 1841–51.

———. *The Sorceress.* London, 1905. Reprinted as *Satanism and Witchcraft: A Study in Medieval Superstition.* New York: Dell, 1971. Reprint, New York: Citadel Press, 1973.

Michell, John. *New Light on the Ancient Mystery of Glastonbury.* Glastonbury, England: Gothic Images Publications, 1990.

———. *The View over Atlantis.* Rev. ed. London: Abacus, 1976.

Michell, John, and Robert J. M. Rickard. *Living Wonders: Mysteries and Curiosities of the Animal World.* New York: Thames and Hudson, 1982.

———. *Phenomena: A Book of Miracles.* London: Thames and Hudson, 1977. Reprint, New York: Pantheon Books, 1977.

———. *Phenomena: A Book of Wonders.* London: Thames and Hudson, 1977. Reprint, New York: Pantheon Books, 1977.

Mickaharic, Draja. *A Century of Spells.* York Beach, Maine: Samuel Weiser, 1988.

Mikhailowski, V. M."Shamanism in Siberia and European Russia: Being the Second Part of Shamanstvo." Translated from Russian by Oliver Wardrop. *Journal of the Royal Anthropological Institute* 24 (1894): 62–100, 126–158.

Mickler, Michael L. *The Unification Church in America: A Bibliography and Research Guide.* New York: Garland, 1987.

Middleton, Jessie A. *The White Ghost Book.* London: Cassell, 1918.

Millard, Joseph. *Edgar Cayce.* Greenwich, Conn.: Fawcett, 1967.

Miller, Albert J., and M. J. Acrí. *Death: A Bibliographical Guide.* Metuchen, N.J.: Scarecrow Press, 1977.

Miller, C. Leslie. *All About Angels: The Other Side of the Spirit World.* Glendale: G/L Regal Books, 1973.

Miller, Don Ethan. *Bodymind: The Whole Person Health Book.* Englewood Cliffs, N.J.: Prentice-Hall, 1974.

Miller, Hugh. *Scenes and Legends in the North of Scotland.* Nimmo, 1834.

Miller, Paul. *Born to Heal.* London: Spiritualist Press, 1948.

Miller, R. Dewitt. *The Man Who Lived Forever.* N.p., 1956.

———. *Reincarnation.* N.p., 1956.

Miller, R. DeWitt, and Ellora F. Miller. *Forgotten Mysteries.* Chicago: Cloud Inc., 1947.

———. *You Do Take It with You.* New York: Citadel Press, 1955.

Miller, Russell. *Bare-Faced Messiah: The True Story of L. Ron Hubbard* New York: Henry Holt; London: Michael Joseph, 1987.

Miller, Stuart. *Hot Springs.* New York: Viking Press, 1971.

Miller, Timothy. *American Communes, 1860–1960: A Bibliography.* New York: Garland Publishing, 1990.

Mills, Joy. *100 Years of Theosophy: A History of the Theosophical Society in America.* Wheaton, Ill.: Theosophical Publishing House, 1987.

Mills, Watson E. *A Theological-Exegetical Approach to Glossolalia.* Lanham, Md.: University Press of America, 1985

Milne, Hugh. *Bhagwan: The God That Failed.* New York: St. Martin's Press, 1986. Reprint, London: Sphere Books, 1987.

Milne, J. Bramwell. *Hypnotism: Its History, Practice, and Theory.* London, 1903.

Milovsky, Akexander S. "Tubiakou's Spirit Flight," *Natural History* (July,1992): 34–41.

Milton, Julie. "A Meta-Analysis of Waking State of Consciousness, Free-Response ESP Studies." In *Research in Parapsychology, 1993: Abstracts and Papers from the Thirty-sixth Annual Convention of the Parapsychological Association, 1993.* Lanham, Md.: Scarecrow Press, Inc., 1998.

Milton, Julie and Richard Wiseman. *Guidelines for Extrasensory Perception Research.* Hertfordshire UK: University of Hertfordshire Press, 1997.

The Mind, Meditation, and Healing. London: Atlanteans, 1972.

Miracle Woman's Secrets. Los Angeles: Superet Press, 1949.

Mironov, N. D., and S. M. Shirokogoroff. "Sramana-Shaman: Etymology of the Word 'Shaman,' " *Journal of the Royal Asiatic Society (North-China Branch, Shanghai)* 55 (1924): 105–130.

Miscellaneous Masonic Documents. Kila, Mont.: Kessinger Publishing Co., 1998.

Misegades, Charles. *Know Your Number.* Marina Del Rey, Calif.: DeVorss, 1980.

Mishra, Rammurti. *Dynamics of Yoga-Mudras and Five Successive Suggestions for Meditation.* Pleasant Valley, N.Y.: Kriya Press, 1967.

———. *Fundamentals of Yoga.* New York: Lancer Books, 1969. Reprint, *Yoga Sutras: The Textbook of Yoga Psychology.* New York, 1973.

———. *Isha Upanishad.* Dayton, Ohio: Yoga Society of Dayton, 1962.

Mishra, Shri Ramamurti. *Self Analysis and Self Knowledge.* Lakemont, Ga.: CSA Press, 1977.

Mitchell, Edgar D., ed. *Psychic Exploration: A Challenge for Science.* Edited by John White. New York: G. P. Putnam's Sons, 1974.

Mitchell, G. W. *X + Y = Z; or the Sleeping Preacher of North Alabama.* New York, 1876. Reprint, Owens Cross Roads, Ala.: Drake Publications, 1981.

Mitchell, J. *Astro-Archaeology.* London: Thames & Hudson, 1977.

Mitchell, John, and Robert J. M. Rickard. *Phenomena: A Book of Wonders.* N.p., 1977.

Mitchell, T. W. "The Appreciation of Time by Somnambules." *Proceedings of the Society for Psychical Research* (1908–09).

———. *Medical Psychology and Psychical Research.* London: Methuen, 1922.

———. *Psychology and the Sciences.* Edited by William Brown. London: A & C Black Ltd., 1924.

———. *The Psychology of Medicine.* New York: R. M. McBride, 1922.

———. "Psychotherapy and Psychoanalysis." *Proceedings of the Society for Psychial Research* (1912–13).

———. "A Study in Hysteria and Multiple Personality." *Proceedings of the Society for Psychial Research* (1912–13).

Mitchell-Hedges, F. A. *Danger My Ally.* Boston: Little-Brown, 1955.

Mitland, Edward. *The Story of Anna Kingsford and Edward Maitland and of the New Gospel of Interpretation.* Birmingham, England: Ruskin Press, 1905.

Moberly, C. A. E., and E. F. Jourdain. *An Adventure.* London: Faber & Faber, 1911.

Moll, Albert. *Hypnotism.* London: Walter Scott Publishing, 1909. Reprint, New York: Da Capo Press, Inc., 1982.

Molloy, J. Fitzgerald. *The Romance of Royalty.* London, 1904.

Monroe, Robert A. *Journeys Out of the Body.* Garden City, N.Y.: Doubleday, 1971.

Montague, Nell St. John. *Revelations of a Society Clairvoyante.* London, 1926.

Monter, E. William. *European Witchcraft.* New York: Wiley 1969.

Montgomery, Ruth. *Born to Heal.* New York: Coward, McCann & Geochegan, 1973.

———. *Companions Along the Way.* New York: Coward, McCann & Geochegan, 1974.

———. *A Gift of Prophecy: The Phenomenal Jeane Dixon.* New York: William Morrow, 1965.

———. *Here and Hereafter.* New York: Coward, McCann & Geochegan, 1966.

———. *A Search for the Truth.* New York: William Morrow, 1967.

———. *Strangers Among Us: Enlightened Beings from a World to Come.* New York: Coward, McGann & Geochegan, 1979.

———. *Threshold to Tomorrow.* New York: G. P. Putnam's Sons, 1983.

———. *The World Before.* New York: Coward, McCann & Geochegan, 1976.

———. *A World Beyond.* New York: Coward, McCann & Geochegan, 1971.

Moody, Raymond A., Jr. *Reflections on Life After Life.* Covington, Ga.: Mockingbird Books, 1975. Reprint, Mechanicsburg, Pa.: Stackpole Books, 1977. N.p.: R. Bemis Publishing, Ltd., 1981. New York: Macmillan Library Reference, 1982. New York: Bantam, 1984.

Mookerjee, Ajit. *Tantra Art.* New York: Random House, 1971.

Mookerjee, Ajit, and M. Khanna. *The Tantric Way: Art, Science, Ritual.* New York: Graphic, 1977.

Moon, Mary. *Ogopogo: The Okanagan Mystery.* London: David & Charles, 1977.

Moon, Sun Myung. *Christianity in Crisis: New Hope.* New York: HSA-UWC, 1974.

———. *A Prophet Speaks Today.* New York: HSA-UWC, 1975.

Mooney, James. "The Ghost-Dance Religion." In *Annual Report of Bureau of American Ethnology.* 14, 2, (1893).

———. "The Ghost-Dance Religion," part 2, *Fourteenth Report of the Bureau of American Ethnology* Washington D.C.: Smithsonian Institution, 1897.

Moore, Clara Sophia Bloomfield. *Keely and His Discoveries.* London, 1893. Reprint, New Hyde Park, N.Y.: University Books, 1972.

Moore, Edward. *Bealings Bells.* Woodbridge, England, 1841.

Moore, Gerun. *Numbers Will Tell.* London: Barker; New York: Grossett & Dunlap, 1973.

Moore, J. D. "A Medium Appearing in a Materialized Form." *Facts* 6 (March 1887).

Moore, Mary-Margaret. *From the Heart of a Gentle Brother.* Taos, N.Mex.: High Mesa Press, 1987.

———. *I Come as a Brother: A Remembrance of Illusions.* Taos, N.Mex.: High Mesa Publishing, 1984.

Moore, R. Laurence. *In Search of White Crows.* New York: Oxford University Press, 1977.

Moore, Rebecca, ed. *New Religious Movements, Mass Suicide, and Peoples Temple: Scholarly Perspectives on a Tragedy.* New York: Edwin Mellen Press, 1989.

Moore, W. Usborne. *Glimpses of the Next State (The Education of an Agnostic).* London: Watts, 1911.

———. *The Voices.* London, 1913.

Moore, William L., and Charles Berlitz. *The Philadelphia Experiment.* New York: Grosset & Dunlap, 1979.

Moretti, Girolamo M. *The Saints Through Their Handwriting.* New York: Macmillan, 1964.

Morfill, W. R., trans. *The Book of the Secrets of Enoch.* Oxford, England: Clarendon Press, 1896.

Morgan, Harry T. *Chinese Symbols and Superstitions.* P. D. and Ione Perkins, 1942. Reprint, Detroit: Gale Research, 1972.

Morgan, J. V. *The Welsh Religious Revival, 1904–05.* London: Chapman & Hall, 1909.

Morgan, R. C. *An Inquiry Into Table Miracles.* Bath and London, 1853.

Morin, Jean-Baptiste. *Astrologia Gallica.* The Hague, Netherlands, 1661.

Morley, H. *Jerome Cardan.* London, 1854.

The Morley-Martin Experiments. BSRA booklet No. 1. San Diego, Calif.: Borderland Sciences Research Associates, 1948.

Morrill, Sibley. *Ambrose Bierce, F. A. Mitchell-Hedges and the Crystal Skull.* San Francisco: Cadleon Press, 1972.

Morris, R. L., S. B. Harry, J. Janis, J. Hartwell, and William G. Roll. "Studies of Communication during Out-of-body Experiences." *Journal of the American Society for Psychical Research* 72 (1978).

Morris, Robert L. "The Amityville Horror." *The Skeptical Inquirer* Vol. 2, no. 2 (Spring/Summer 1978): 95–102.

———. "Biology and Psychical Research." Edited by Gertrude R. Schmeidler. In *Parapsychology: Its Relation to Physics, Biology Psychology, and Psychiatry.* N.p., 1976.

———. "Obtaining Non-Random Entry Points: A Complex Psi Process." In *Parapsychology Today.* Edited by J. B. Rhine and R. Brier. New York: Citadel Press, 1968.

———. "PK on a Bio-Electrical System." In *Parapsychology Today.* Edited by J. B. Rhine and R. Brier. New York: Citadel Press, 1968.

———. "The Psychobiology of Psi." In *Psychic Exploration.* Edited by E. D. Mitchell. New York: G. P. Putnam's Sons, 1974.

———. "Some New Techniques in Animal Psi Research." *Journal of Parapsychology* 31 (December 1967).

Morrison, R. J. *An Introduction to Astrology by William Lilly, being the whole of that Celebrated Author's Rules for the Practice of Horory Astology . . .* London, 1835. Reprint, Hollywood, Calif.: Newcastle Publishing, 1972.

Morrison, Sarah Lyddon. *The Modern Witch's Spellbook.* New York: David McKay, 1971.

Morrison, Tony. *Pathways to the Gods: The Mystery of the Andes Lines.* London: Granada Publishing, 1980.

Morrow, Feliz. "The Quest for Montague Summers." In *The Vampire: His Kith and Kin,* by Montague Summer. New Hyde Park, N.Y.: University Books, 1960.

Morse, J. J. *Leaves From My Life: A Narrative of Personal Experiences in the Career of a Servant of the Spirits.* N.p., 1877.

Morse, Louise. *The Living Water.* Richardson, Tex.: Morse Fellowship, 1970.

Morselli, Enrico. *I fenomei telepatici e le allucinazioni veridiche.* N.p., 1897.

———. *Psicologia e 'Spiritismo': Impressioni e note Critiche sui fenomeni medianici di Eusapia Palladino.* 2 vols. Turin: Boca, 1908.

Moseley, James W. "Peruvian Desert Map for Saucers?" *Fate* 8, no. 10 (October 1055): 28–33.

Moses, W. Stainton. *Direct Spirit Writing (Psychography).* London, 1878. Reprint, London: Psychic Book Club, 1952.

———. *Spirit Identity.* London: London Spiritualist Alliance, Ltd., 1908.

———. *Spirit Teachings.* London, 1883. Reprint, North Stratford, N. H.: Ayer Co. Publishers, 1976.

Moss, Peter. *Ghost Over Britain.* UK: Elm Tree Books, 1977.

Moss, Thelma. *The Body Electric: A Personal Journey into the Mysteries of Parapsychological Research, Bioenergy, and Kirlian Photography.* London: Granada, 1981.

———. "ESP Effects in 'Artists' Contrasted with Non-Artists." *Journal of Parapsychology* 33 (1969).

Motoyama, Hiroshi, and Rande Brown. *Science and the Evolution of Consciousness: Chakras, Ki, and Psi.* Brookline, Mass.: Autumn Press, 1978.

Motta, Marcelo. *Letter to a Brazilian Mason.* Nashville, Tenn.: Troll Publishing, 1980.

———. *Manifesto.* Nashville, Tenn.: Society Ordo Templi Orientis in America, 1978.

———. *The Political Aims of the O.T.O.* Nashville, Tenn.: Ordo Templi Orientis in America, 1980.

———. *Thelemic Political Morality.* Nashville, Tenn.: Society Ordo Templi Orientis in America, 1978.

Motzki, Harald. "Shamanismus als Problem religionswissenschaftlicher Terminologie". In *Arbeitsmaterialien zur Religionsgeschichte* vol. 2, Köln, 1977.

Moum, Margaret R. *Guidebook to the Aquarian Gospel of Jesus the Christ.* Washington, D.C.: ESPress, 1974.

Muhaiyadden, Guru Bawa, Shaikh. *God, His Prophets, and His Children.* Philadelphia: Fellowship Press, 1978.

———. *Guidebook.* 2 vols. Philadelphia: Fellowship Press, 1976.

———. *Mata Veeram, or the Forces of Illusion.* York Beach, Maine: Samuel Weiser, 1982.

———. *Truth and Light.* Philadelphia: Guru Bawa Fellowship of Philadelphia, 1974.

Muhammad ibn Umail al-Tamini. *Three Arabic Treatises on Alchemy.* Calcutta: Asiatic Society of Bengal, 1933.

Muhammad-Subuh Sumohadiwidjojo. *Susila Budhi Dharma.* Subud Publications International, 1975.

Mühl, Anita M. *Automatic Writing: An Approach to the Unconscious.* Steinkopff, 1930. Reprint, New York: Helix Press, 1964.

Muktananda, Swami. *Guru.* New York: Harper & Row, 1971.

———. *In the Company of a Siddha: Interviews and Conversations with Swami Muktananda.* Ganeshpuri, India: Gurudev Siddha Peth, 1981.

———. *Kundalini: The Secret of Life.* South Fallsburg, N.Y.: SYDA Foundation, 1979.

———. *The Perfect Relationship: The Guru and the Disciple.* South Fallsburg, N.Y.: SYDA Foundation, 1980.

———. *Play of Consciousness.* New York: Harper & Row, 1974.

———. *Satsang with Baba.* Oakland, Calif.: S.T.D.A., 1975.

Mulacz, Peter. "Eleonore Zugun: The Re-evaluation of a Historic RSPK Case," *Journal of Parapsychology* 63, no. 1 (March 1999): 15–45.

Muldoon, Sylvan, and Hereward Carrington. *The Case for Astral Projection.* 1936. Reprint, Chicago: Aries Press, 1946.

———. *The Phenomena of Astral Projection.* London, 1951. Santa Fe, N.Mex.: Sun Publishing Co., 1981.

———. *The Projection of the Astral Body.* London, 1929. Reprint, New York: Samuel Weiser, 1967.

Mulford, Prentice. *Life by Land and Sea.* New York: F. J. Needham, 1889.

———. *Thought Forces.* London: G. Bell & Sons, 1913.

———. *Your Forces and How to Use Them.* 6 vols. White Cross Library. New York: F. J. Needham, 1887–92.

Mulholland, John. *Beware Familiar Spirits.* London: Charles Scribner's Sons, 1938. Reprint, New York: Ayer Publishing Co. Inc., 1975.

Muller, Brigitte and Gunther H. Horst. *A Complete Book of Reiki Healing.* Mendocino, Calif.: LifeRhythm, 1995.

Müller, Karl E. "Aspects of Astral Projection." Introduction for F. C. Sculthorp. *Excursions to the Spirit World.* London: n.p., 1962.

Mullin, Albert A. "Some Apologies by a Cyberneticist." *Journal of Parapsychology* 23, no. 4 (1959).

Mullins, John. *The Divining Rod and Its Results in Discovery of Springs.* N.p., 1880.

Mumford, John. [Swami Anandakapila]. *Sexual Occultism.* St. Paul, Minn.: Llewellyn Publications, 1975.

Mumford, Linda Anne. "An Expanded Psychological Understanding of Religious Glossolalia among Women," *Dissertation Abstracts International: Section B: The Sciences & Engineering* 56, no. 4-B (October 1995): 2386.

Mumford, Stan. *Himalayan Dialogue: Tibetan Lamas and Gurung Shamans in Nepal.* Madison: University of Wisconsin Press, 1989.

Mumler, William H. *Personal Experiences of William H. Mumler in Spirit Photography.* Boston, 1875.

Mundle, C. W. K. "The Experimental Evidence for Precognition and Psychokinesis." *Proceedings of the Society for Psychical Research* 49 (July 1950).

———. "Is Psychical Research Relevant to Philosophy?" *Proceedings, Aristotelian Society* Supplemental Vol. 24 (1950).

———. "Philosophical Implications of ESP Phenomena." In *Encyclopedia of Philosophy.* Edited by P. Edwards. N.p. 1967.

———. "Professor Rhine's Views on Psychokinesis." *Mind* (July 1950).

———. "Selectivity in Extrasensory Perception." *Journal of the Society for Psychical Research* (March 1951).

———. "Some Philosophical Perspectives for Parapsychology." *Journal of Parapsychology* (December 1952).

Murchison, Carl A., ed. *The Case For and Against Psychical Belief.* Worcester, Mass.: Clark University, 1927. Reprint, New York: Ayer Publishing Co. Inc., 1975.

Murphet, Howard. *Hammer on the Mountain: Life of Henry Steel Olcott, 1832–1907.* Wheaton, Ill.: Theosophical Publishing House, 1972.

———. *Sai Baba Avatar.* London, Frederick Muller, 1979.

———. *Sai Baba, Man of Miracles.* Levittown, N.Y.: Transatlantic Arts, 1972.

Murphy, Gardner. "Difficulties Confronting the Survival Hypothesis." *Journal of the American Society for Psychical Research* 39 (April 1945).

———. *Historical Introduction to Modern Psychology.* New York: Harcourt, Brace and World, 1925.

———. *Human Potentialities.* New York: Basic Books, 1958.

———. *In the Minds of Men.* New York: Basic Books, 1953.

———. *Personality.* New York: Harper & Row, 1947.

———. "Psychical Research and Personality." *Journal of the American Society for Psychical Research* (January 1950).

———. *There Is More Beyond: Selected Papers of Gardner Murphy.* Jefferson, N.C.: McFarland, 1989.

———. *Three Papers on the Survival Problem.* New York: American Society for Psychical Research, 1945.

———. "Triumphs and Defeats in the Study of Mediumship." *Journal of the American Society for Psychical Research* 52 (October 1957).

———. "W. Wately Carington: In Memoriam." *Journal of the American Society for Psychical Research* 41 (1947): 123.

Murphy, Gardner, and Rhea White. *Challenge of Psychical Research: A Primer of Parapsychology.* New York: Harper & Row, 1961.

Murphy, Gardner, and Robert Ballou. *William James and Psychical Research.* New York: Viking Press, 1960.

Murphy, Larry G., J. Gordon Melton, and Gary L. Ward. *Encyclopedia of African American Religions.* New York: Garland Publishing, 1993.

Murphy, Michael, and Rhea White. *The Psychic Side of Sports.* Reading, Mass.: Addison-Wesley, 1978.

Murphy, Robert F. "Mundurucú Religion." In *American Archaeology and Ethnology* (University of California Press) 49, no. 1 (1958): 1–154.

Murray, Gilbert. *Gilbert Murray: An Unfinished Autobiography.* London: Allen and Unwin, 1960.

Murray, Margaret A. *My First Hundred Years.* London: William Kimber, 1963.

———. *The Witch-cult in Western Europe: A Study in Anthropology.* Oxford: Clarendon Press, 1921.

Murray, Muz. *Seeking the Master: A Guide to the Ashrams of India.* London: Neville Spearman, 1980.

Musès, Charles A. "Aspects of Some Crucial Problems in Biological and Medical Cybernetics." In Norbert Wiener and J. P. Schade, eds. *Progress in Bio-Cybernetics.* Vol. 2. 1975.

———. *East-West Fire; Schopenhauer's Optimism and the Lankavatara Sutra: An Excursion toward the Common Ground between Oriental and Western Religion.* London: J. M. Watkins, 1955.

———. *Esoteric Teachings of the Tibetan Tantra.* Falcon's Wing Press, 1961.

———. *An Evaluation of Relativity Theory after a Half-Century.* 1953.

———. *Illumination of Jacob Boehme: The Work of Dionysius Andreas Freher.* 1951.

———. "The Limits of Consciousness." *Journal for the Study of Consciousness* 1 (1968).

———. *Prismatic Voices; An International Anthology of Distinctive New Poets.* 1958.

———. "Psychotronic Quantum Theory; A Proposal for Understanding Mass/Space/Time/Consciousness Transductions in Terms of a Radically Extended Quantum Theory." *Proceedings of International Association for Psychotronic Research,* 1975.

———. "The Politics of Psi: Acculturation and Hypnosis." In *Extrasensory Ecology,* edited by Joseph K. Long. Metuchen, N.J.: Scarecrow Press, 1977.

Musès, Charles A., and A. M. Young, eds. *Consciousness and Reality; the Human Pivot Point.* New York: Outerbridge & Lazard, 1972.

Musso, J. Ricardo. *En los Límites de la Psicología: Desde el Espiritismo hasta la Parapsicología* (On the Frontiers of Psychology: From Spiritualism to Parapsychology). N.p., 1954.

———. "Il Movimiento Parapsicologico in Argentina" (The Parapsychology Movement in Argentina). *International Review of Parapsychology* (1956).

———. "Parapsychology in Argentina." *Parapsychology Today: A Geographic View.* Edited by Allan Angoff and Betty Shapin. New York: Parapsychology Foundation, 1973.

Musso, J. Ricardo, and M. Granero. "An ESP Drawing Experiment with a High-Scoring Subject." *Journal of Parapsychology* 37 (1973).

Myerhoff, Barbara G. *Peyote Hunt: The Sacred Journey of the Huichol Indians.* Ithaca, N.Y.: Cornell University Press, 1974.

Myers, Arthur Thomas. "Report on a Alleged Physical Phenomenon." *Proceedings of the Society for Psychical Research* 3, no. 9 (1885).

Myers, Arthur Thomas, and F. W. H. Myers. "Mind-Cure, Faith-Cure, and the Miracles of Lourdes." *Proceedings of the Society for Psychical Research* 9, no. 24 (1893).

Myers, F. W. H. *Human Personality and its Survival of Bodily Death.* 2 vols. London: Longmans, Green, 1903. Abridged edition, New Hyde Park, N.Y.: University Books, 1961.

———. "On the Trance Phenomena of Mrs. Thompson." *Proceedings of the Society for Psychical Research* 17 (1902).

———. *Science and a Future Life: With Other Essays.* London: Macmillan, 1901.

Myers, F. W. H., Edmund Gurney, and Frank Podmore. *Phantasms of the Living.* London: Trubner, 1886.

Myers, Martin W. *Unity, Not Uniformity.* Chicago: URANTIA Foundation, 1973.

Mylonas, George E. *Eleusis and the Eleusian Mysteries.* Princeton, N.J.: Princeton University Press, 1961.

Mystic Helper, The. *The Evolution of the Universe, or, Creation According to Science.* Los Angeles: Cosmos Publishing, 1924.

Nada-Yolanda [Pauline Sharper]. *Mark-Age Period and Program.* MiaMich.: Mark-Age Metacenter, 1970.

Nagorka, Diane S. *Spirit as Life Force.* Washington, D.C.: ESPress, 1983.

Nakayama, M. *Dynamic Karate.* Cedar Knolls, N.J. Wehman, 1966.

Namikoshi, Tokujiro. *Shiatsu.* Tokyo: Japan Publications, 1969.

Nanking Army Ear Acupuncture Team. *Ear Acupuncture: A Chinese Medical Report.* Emmaus, Pa.: Rodale Press, 1974.

Napier, John. *Bigfoot: The Sasquatch and Yeti in Myth and Reality.* London: Jonathan Cape, 1972. Reprint, New York: E. P. Dutton, 1973. Reprint, London: Abacus, 1976.

Napier, James. *Folklore, or Superstitious Beliefs in the West of Scotland, within this Century.* Paisley, Scotland, 1879.

Narayana, Har, trans. *The Vedic Philosophy; or, An Exposition of the Sacred and Mysterious Monosyllable AUM; The Mandukya Upanishad.* Bombay, 1895.

Narayananda, Swami. *The Primal Power in Man of the Kundalini Shakti.* Risikesh, India: N. K. Prasad, 1950.

Nash, C. S. "Checking Success and the Relationship of Personality Traits to ESP." *Journal of the American Society for Psychical Research* 52 (1958).

———. "Experiments in Plant Growth." *International Journal of Parapsychology* (autumn 1959).

———. "Report on the Second Annual Convention of the Parapsychological Association." *Newsletter, Parapsychology Foundation* (September–October 1959).

Nash, C. S. "A Test of Adding Extrasensorially Perceived Digits." *Journal of Parapsychology* 23 (1959).

Nash, Carroll B. "Can Precognition Occur Diametrically?" *Journal of Parapsychology* 27 (1963).

———. *Parapsychology: The Science of Psiology.* Springfield, Ill.: Charles C. Thomas, 1986.

———. "Psi and Probability Theory." *Science* 120 (1954).

———. "Psychokinesis Reconsidered." *Journal of Parapsychology* 45 (1951).

———. *Science of Psi: ESP and PK.* Springfield, Ill.: Charles C. Thomas, 1978.

Nash, Carroll B. "The Unorthodox Science of Parapsychology." *International Journal of Parapsychology* 1 (1959).

Nash, Carroll B., and C. S. Nash. "An Exploratory Analysis for Displacement in PK." *Journal of the American Society for Psychical Research* 50 (1956).

———. "Relation Between ESP Scoring and Minnesota Multiphasic Personality Inventory." *Journal of the American Society for Psychical Research* 60 (1960).

Nash, Carrol B., and M. G. Durkin. "Correlation Between ESP and Religious Value." *Journal of Parapsychology* 22 (1958).

The National Spiritualist Association of United States of America. *One Hundredth Anniversary of Modern Spiritualism.* Chicago: The Author, 1948.

Nau, Abbé F. "Recueil de textes et de documents sur les Yézidis." *ROC* 2, no. 10 (1915–17).

Nauman, St. Elmo, Jr. *Exorcism Through the Ages.* New York: Philosophical Library, 1974.

Naylor, P. I. H. *Astrology: A Fascinating History.* N. Hollywood, Calif.: Wilshire Book Co. 1970.

Naylor, William, ed. *Silver Birch Anthology.* London: Psychic Book Club, 1955.

Neale, Hazel. *Powerful Is the Light.* Denver: Divine Science College, 1945.

Neame, Alan. *The Happening at Lourdes.* London: Hodder & Stoughton, 1968.

Needleman, Jacob. *The New Religions.* Garden City, N.Y.: Doubleday, 1970.

Neff, H. Richard. *Psychic Phenomena and Religion: ESP, Prayer, Healing, Survival.* Philadelphia: Westminster Press, 1971.

Neihardt, John G. *All Is But a Beginning.* New York: Harcourt, Brace, Jovanovich, 1972.

———. *Patterns and Coincidents: A Sequel to All Is but a Beginning.* Columbia: University of Missouri Press, 1978.

———. *The Sixth Grandfather: Black Elk's Teachings given to John G. Neihardt.* Lincoln: University of Nebraska Press, 1984.

———. *When the Tree Flowered: The Fictional Biography of Eagle Voice, a Sioux Indian.* Lincoln: University of Nebraska Press, 1970.

Neil-Smith, Christopher. *The Exorcist and the Possessed: The Truth about Exorcism.* Cornwall, England: James Pike, 1974. Reprint, New York: Pinnacle Books, 1974.

Neimark, Anne E. *With This Gift: The Story of Edgar Cayce.* New York: William Morrow, 1978.

Neoplatonism and Gnosticism. Albany: State University of New York Press, 1992.

Nepomnyashchikh, I. A. " 'Biofields,' 'Geofields' and Dowsing," *PSI Research* 4, no. 3-4 (September-December 1985): 195–199.

Nesfeld-Cookson, Bernard. *William Blake: Prophet of Universal Brotherhood.* UK: Crucible, 1987.

Nester, Marian L. "New Methods of Parapsychology." *Tomorrow* 9, no. 4 (1961).

Nethercot, A. H. *The First Five Lives of Annie Besant.* Chicago: University of Chicago Press, 1961.

———. *The Last Four Lives of Annie Besant.* Chicago: University of Chicago Press, 1963.

———. *The Road to Trye: A Study of the History, Background, and Purposes of Coleridge's "Christabel."* Chicago: University of Chicago Press, 1939. Reprint, New York: Russell & Russell, 1962.

Neuburg, Victor E. *Vickybird: A Memoir by His Son.* London: The Polytechnic of North London, 1983.

The New Age Resources Directory. Fullerton, Calif.: Goddess Press, 1994.

The New Consciousness Sourcebook, #5. Berkeley, Calif.: Spiritual Community Publications, 1982. Rev. ed. Pomona, Calif.: Arcline, 1985.

New Pilgrims of the Spirit. Boston: Beacon Press, 1921.

Newbold, William R. *The Cipher of Roger Bacon.* Philadelphia, Pa.: University of Pennsylvania Press, 1928.

———. "Subconscious Reasoning." *Proceedings of the Society for Psychical Research* 12 (1896).

Newbrough, John Balllou. *Oahspe.* New York; London: Oahspe Publishing Association, 1882. Reprint, Los Angeles: Essenes of Kosmon, 1950.

Newcomb, Simon. *Reminiscences of an Astronomer.* Boston: Houghton, Mifflin, 1903.

Newham, C. A. *The Astronomical Significance of Stonehenge.* UK: John Blackburn, 1972.

Newhouse, Flower A. *Natives of Eternity.* Vista, Calif.: The Author, 1950.

Ni, Hua-Ching. *The Subtle Universal Law and the Integral Way of Life.* Malibu, Calif.: Shrine of the Eternal Breath of Tao, 1979.

Niblo. *The Complete Palmist.* 1900. Reprint, North Hollywood, Calif.: Newcastle, 1982.

Nichol, Francis D. *The Midnight Cry.* Washington, D.C.: Review & Herald Publishing Association, 1944.

Nicholas Roerich, 1874–1947. New York: Nicholas Roerich Museum, 1974.

Nichols, T. L. *A Biography of the Brothers Davenport.* London, 1864.

———. *Supramundane Facts in the Life of the Rev. J. B. Ferguson.* London, 1865.

Nicholson, Shirley, ed. *Shamanism: An Expanded View of Reality.* Wheaton, Ill: Theosophical Publishing House, 1987.

Nickell, Joe. *Inquest on the Shroud of Turin.* Buffalo, N.Y.: Prometheus Press, 1983.

Nickell, Joe, and John F. Fischer. *Secrets of the Supernatural: Investigating the World's Occult Mysteries.* Buffalo, N.Y.: Prometheus Press, 1988.

Nicol, J. Fraser. "The Founders of the Society for Psychical Research." *Proceedings of the Society for Psychical Research* 55 (1972).

———. "The Fox Sisters and the Development of Spiritualism." *Journal of the Society for Psychical Research* 34 (1948).

———. "The Silences of Mr. Trevor Hall." *International Journal of Parapsychology* 1, no. 1 (1966).

Nicola, John T. *Diabolical Possession and Exorcism.* Rockford, Ill.: TAN Books, 1974.

Nicolai, Christoph Friedrich. "An Account of the Apparition of Several Phantoms." *The German Museum* (1800).

Nicolas, Jean. *La verge de Jacob, ou l'art de trouver les trésors les sources, les limites, les métaux, les mines, les minéraux et autres cachées, par l'usage du baton fourché.* Lyons, France, 1693. Translated as *Jacob's Rod.* London: Thomas Welton, 1875.

Nicoll, Maurice. *Dream Psychology.* Oxford: Henry Frowde, 1917.

———. *Living Time and the Integration of Life.* London: Vincent Stuart, 1952.

———. *The Mark (On the Symbolism of Various Passages from the Bible).* London: Watkins, 1954.

———. *The New Man: An Interpretation of Some Parables and Miracles of Christ.* London: Start & Richard, 1950.

———. *Psychological Commentaries on the Teaching of G. I. Gurdjieff and P. D. Ouspensky.* 5 vols. London: Vincent Stuart, 1954, 1964, 1966.

Nielsen, Einer. *Solid Proofs of Survival.* Translated by Helmi Krohn. London: Psychic Book Club, 1950.

Nielsen, Greg, and Joseph Polansky. *Pendulum Power: A Mystery You Can See, A Power you Can Feel.* New York: Destiny Books, 1977; Wellingborough, UK: Excalibur, 1981.

Nielsen, Winnifred M. "An Exploratory Study in Precognition." *Journal of Parapsychology* (March 1956).

———. "Mental States Associated with Precognition." *Journal of Parapsychology* (June 1956).

Nieuwenhuis, A. W. "Principles of Indian Medicine in American Ethnology and Their Psychological Significance," *Janus* 28 (1924): 305–356.

Nightingale, Michael. *The Healing Power of Acupuncture.* New York: Javalin Books, 1986.

Nikhilananda, Swami. *The Upanishads.* 4 vols. London: Phoenix House, 1951–59; New York: Ramakrishna-Vivekananda Center,1975–1979.

Nikhilananda, Swami, trans. *Mandukya Upanishad.* Chicago: Vedanta Press, 1972.

Niklewski, Guenter. "Esoterik: Zeitgeist oder Zeitwende?" (Esotericism: Spirit of the Time or a Tendency of the Time?), *Analytische Psychologie* 22, no. 3 (October 1991): 174–190. Nilsson, Martin P. *The Dionysian Mysteries of the Hellenistic and Roman Age.* Lund, Sweden: C. W. K. Gleerup, 1957.

Nizida. *The Astral Light.* London: Theosophical Publishing House, 1889. Reprint, Talent, Ore.: Eastern School Press, 1983.

Nolen, William. *Healing: A Doctor in Search of a Miracle.* New York: Random House, 1975.

Noll, Richard. "Shamanism and Schizophrenia: A State-specific Approach to the Schizophrenia Metaphor of Shamanic States," *American Ethnologist* 10, no. 3 (1983): 443–459.

———. *Vampires, Werewolves, and Demons: Twentieth Century Reports in the Psychiatric Literature.* New York: Brunner/Mazel, Inc., 1992.

Nomad, Ali. *Cosmic Consciousness.* Chicago, 1913.

Nordon, Pierre. *Conan Doyle.* London: John Murray, 1966.

Nordquist, Ted A. *Ananda Cooperative Village.* Upsala, Sweden: Borgstroms Tyckeri Ab, 1978.

Norris, David, and Jacquemine Charrott-Lodwidge. *The Book of Spells.* London: Lorrimer, 1974.

Northage, Ivy. *The Mechanics of Mediumship.* London: Spiritualist Association of Great Britain, 1973.

Norton, Robert. *The Willow in the Tempest: A Brief History of the Liberal Catholic Church in the United States, 1817–1942.* Ojai, Calif.: St. Alban Press, 1990.

Notestein, Wallace. *A History of Witchcraft in England from 1558 to 1718.* Washington, 1911. Reprint, New York: Russel & Russel, 1965.

Noyes, John Humphrey. *Strange Cults & Utopias of 19th Century America.* 1870. Reprinted as *History of American Socialisms.* New York: Dover Publications, 1966.

Noyes, Ralph. *The Crop Circle Enigma.* Santa Rosa, Calif.: Atrium Publishers Group, 1995.

Nu'aymah, Mikha'il. *Kahlil Gibran: A Biography.* New York: Quartet, 1988.

Nutt, Alfred. *Studies on the Legend of the Holy Grail.* London: Folklore Society, 1888. Reprint, New York: Cooper Square Publishers, 1965.

"Obituary and Tributes to Mrs. E. W. Allison." *Journal of the ASPR* vol. 53 (1959): 81.

O'Brien, Elmer. *Varieties of Mystical Experience.* New York: Holt, Rinehart, and Winston, 1964.

O'Carroll, Michael. *Medjugorje: Facts, Documents, Theology.* Dublin: Veritas, 1986.

O'Donnell, Elliott. *Animal Ghosts.* London, 1913.

———. *The Banshee.* London: Sands, 1920.

———. *Byways of Ghostland.* London, 1911.

———. *Confessions of a Ghost Hunter.* London, 1928.

———. *Family Ghosts & Ghostly Phenomena.* London: Philip Allan, 1933.

———. *Ghostly Phenomena.* London, n.d.

———. *Ghosts Helpful & Harmful.* London, 1924.

———. *Haunted Places in England.* London: Sands, 1919.

———. *Strange Disappearances.* London, 1927. Reprint, New Hyde Park, N.Y.: University Books, 1972.

———. *Werewolves.* London, 1912. Rev. ed. New York: Wholesale Book Corp., 1972.

O'Keefe, Daniel Lawrence. *Stolen Lightning: The Social Theory of Magic.* New York: Continuum, 1982.

O'Kennedy, Rev. R. *Book of the Holy Angels.* London, 1887.

O'Neill, John J. *Prodigal Genius: The Life of Nikola Tesla.* London: Neville Spearman, 1968. Reprint, London: Granada, 1980.

O'Regan, Vivienne. *The Pillar of Isis.* London: Aquarian Press, 1993.

Ochorowicz, Julien. *De la suggestion mentale.* Paris, 1887. English edition as *Mental Suggestion.*New York: The Humbolt Publishing, 1891.

———. *La Questione della frode negli Esperimenti coll' Eusapia Palladino.* Milan, 1896.

———. *Mediumistic Phenomena.* N.p., 1913.

———. *Psychology and Medicine.* N.p., 1916.

———. *Psychology, Pedagogics, and Ethics.* N.p., 1917.

Octavia. [Helen Exeter]. *Healing for All: The "Joanna Southcott Healing."* London: Panacea Society, 1925.

Oesterreich, Maria. *Traugott Konstantin Oesterreich—Lebenswerk und Lebensschicksal.* N.p., 1954.

Oesterreich, T. K. *Die Bessessenheit.* English ed. as *Possession: Demoniacal and Other among Primitive Races, in Antiquity, the Middle Ages, and Modern Times.* Translated by D. Ibberson. New Hyde Park, N.Y.: University Books, 1966.

———. *Occultism and Modern Science.* New York: McBride, 1923.

———. *Occultism of the Present Day.* London, 1922.

———. *Possession, Demoniacal and Other.* London: Kegan Paul; New York: R. R. Smith, 1930. Reprint, New Hyde Park, N.Y.: University Books, 1966. Reprinted as *Possession and Exorcism.* New York: Causeway Books, 1974. N.p.: Brown Book Co., 1984.

Offner, C. B., and H. van Straelen. *Modern Japanese Religions.* Leyden, The Netherlands: E. J. Brill, 1963.

Ogden, Tom. *Wizards & Sorcerers.* New York: Facts on File, 1998.

Ohashi, Wataru. *Do It Yourself Shiatsu.* New York: ASI Publishing, 1976.

Ohlmarks, ¤'c5ke. *Studien zum Problem des Schamanismus.* Lund-Kopenhagen, 1939.

Olcott, Henry Steel. *Old Diary Leaves.* 4 vols. Reprinted as *Inside the Occult: The True Story of Madame H. P. Blavatsky.* Philadephia: Running Press, 1995.

———. *People from the Other World.* Hartford, Conn.: American Publishing Co., 1875. Reprint, Rutland, Vt.: Charles E. Tuttle, 1972.

Old, Walter [Sepahrial]. *The Book of Charms and Talismans.* N.p., 1974.

———. *Book of the Crystal and the Seer.* N.p., 1897.

———. *Book of the Simple Way of Laotze.* N.p., 1904.

———. *The Kabala of Numbers.* 2 vols. N.p., 1913. Revised ed., 1928.

———. *A Manual of Occultism.* N.p., 1910.

———. *Prognostic Astronomy.* N.p., 1901.

———. *Second Sight.* N.p., 1911.

———. *What Is Theosophy?* N.p., 1891.

Oliver, Ian P. *Buddhism in Britain.* London: Rider, 1979.

Oliver, Rev. George. *The History of Initiation, in Twelve Lectures; comprising a Detailed Account of the Rites & Ceremonies, Doctrines and Discipline, of all the Secret and Mysterious Institutions of the Ancient World.* London: Richard Spencer, 1829. Rev. ed. 1841.

Olivier, Edith. *Four Victorian Ladies of Wiltshire.* London: Faber & Faber, 1945.

Olson, Alan M., ed. *Disguises of the Demonic: Contemporary Perspectives on the Power of Evil.* New York: Association Press, 1975.

Olson, Carl. *The Book of the Goddess, Past and Present.* Philadelphia: J. P. Lippincott, 1983.

Oman, J. Campbell. *Cults, Customs & Superstitions of India.* London: T. Fisher Unwin, 1908.

———. *The Mystics, Ascetics and Saints of India.* London: T. Fisher Unwin, 1903.

Omez, Reginald. *Psychical Phenomena.* Translated by René e Haynes. New York: Hawthorn, 1958.

Omkarananda, Swami. *In Sivananda Literature.* Rishikesh, India: Sivananda Literature Research Institute, 1960.

"On the Experiments of Brugmans, Heymans, and Weinberg." *European Journal of Parapsychology* 2 (1978): 247.

Oosthuizen, Gehardus C. "The 'Newness' of the New Age in South Africa and Reactions to It." In *Perspectives on the New Age,* edited by James R. Lewis and J. Gordon Melton. Albany: State University of New York Press, 1992.

Oram, Arthur T. "An Experiment with Random Numbers." *Journal of the Society for Psychical Research* (1954) 37; (1955) 38.

Ormand, Ron, and Gill Ormond. *Into the Strange Unknown.* Hollywood, Calif.: Esoteric Foundation, 1959. Reprinted as *Religious Mysteries of the Orient.* New York: A. S. Barnes, 1976.

Orme-Johnson, David W., and John T. Farrows, eds. *Scientific Research on the Transcendental Meditation Program: Collected Papers, I.* Seelisberg, Switzerland: Maharishi European Research University Press, 1977.

Ormont, Arthur. *Love Cults & Faith Healers.* New York: Ballantine Books, 1961.

Osborn, Arthur W. *The Axis and the Rim: The Quest for Reality in a Modern Setting.* London: V. Stuart, 1963.

———. *The Cosmic Womb: An Interpretation of Man's Relationship to the Infinite.* Wheaton, Ill.: Theosophical Publishing House, 1969.

———. *The Expansion of Awareness: One Man's Search for Meaning in Living.* Wheaton, Ill.: Theosophical Publishing House, 1967.

———. *The Future Is Now: The Significance of Precognition.* New Hyde Park, N.Y.: University Books, 1962. Wheaton, Ill.: Theosophical Publishing House, 1967.

———. *The Meaning of Personal Existence in the Light of Paranormal Phenomena: The Doctrine of Reincarnation & Mystical States of Consciousness.* London: Sidgwick and Jackson, 1966.

———. *Occultism, Christian Science and Healing.* 1926.

———. *Superphysical: A Review of the Evidence for Continued Existence, Reincarnation, and Mystical States of Consciousness.* Rev. ed. New York: Barnes & Noble; London: Frederick Muller, 1974.

———. *What Am I Living For?* 1974.

Osborn, Edward Collet. "The Woman in Brown, an Investigation of an Apparition." *Journal of the Society for Psychical Research* (1939).

Osborn, Edward Collet, and C. C. Evans. "An Experiment in the Electro-Encephalography of Mediumistic Trance." *Journal of the Society for Psychical Research* (1952).

Osborne, Arthur. *The Incredible Sai Baba.* New Delhi: Orient Longmans, 1957.

———. *Ramana Maharshi and the Path of Self-Knowledge.* New York: Samuel Weiser, 1970.

Osborne, Arthur., ed. *The Teachings of Ramana Maharshi.* 1963. Reprint, New York: Samuel Weiser, 1978.

Osis, Karlis. "ESP Tests at Long and Short Distances." *Journal of Parapsychology* 20, 2 (1956).

———. "Out-of-the-Body Research at the ASPR." *ASPR Newsletter* 22 (1974),

———. "A Test of the Relationship Between ESP and PK." *Journal of Parapsychology* 17, 4 (1953).

———. "What Did The Dying See?" *ASPR Newsletter* 24 (1975).

Osis, Karlis, and Erlendur Haraldsson. *At the Hour of Death.* New York: Avon Books, 1977. Rev. ed.: New York: Hasting House, 1986.

———. "Deathbed Observations by Physicians and Nurses: A Cross-cultural Survey." In *Signet Handbook of Parapsychology,* edited by Martin Ebon. New York: New American Library, 1978.

Osis, Karlis, and M. E. Turner. "Distance and ESP: A Transcontinental Experiment." *Proceedings of the American Society for Psychical Research* 27 (1968).

Osis, Karlis, M. E. Turner, and M. L. Carlson. "ESP Over Distance: Research on the ESP Channel." *Journal of the American Society for Psychical Research* 65 (1971).

Osmond, Humphrey. "A Call for Imaginative Theory." *International Journal of Parapsychology* (Autumn 1959).

Osmond, Humphrey, and Abram Hoffer. *The Chemical Basis of Clinical Psychiatry.* Springfield, Ill.: Thomas, 1960.

———. *The Hallucinogens.* New York: Academic Press, 1967.

Osmond, Humphrey, and Bernard Aaronson. *Psychedelics: The Uses and Implications of Hallucinogenic Drugs.* Garden City, N.Y.: Doubleday, 1970. Cambridge, Mass.: Schenkman, 1971.

Osmond, Humphrey, H. Yaker, and F. Cheek. *The Future of Time: Man's Temporal Environment.* Garden City, N.Y.: Doubleday, 1971.

Osmont, Anne. *Envoutements et exorcisms à travers le ages* (Sorcery and Exorcism Through the Ages) N.p., 1954.

———. *Le Mouvement Symboliste* (The Symbolist Movement). Paris: Maison du livre, 1917.

———. *Le Rythme Créateur de forces et de formes* (The Creative Rhythm of Forces .and Forms). Paris: Les Editions de Champselysees, 1942.

Ossendowski, Ferdinand. *Beasts, Men, and Gods.* New York: E. P. Dutton, 1922.

Ostrander, Sheila, and Lynn Schroeder. *Handbook of Psi Discoveries.* New York: G. P. Putnam's Sons, 1974. Reprint, New York: Berkeley Publishing, 1975. Reprint, London: Abacus, 1977.

———. *Psychic Discoveries Behind the Iron Curtain.* Englewood Cliffs, N.J.: Prentice-Hall, 1970. Reprint, New York: Bantam, 1971. Reprinted as *Psi: Psychic Discoveries Behind the Iron Curtain.* London: Abacus 1973.

Ostow, Mortimer. *Ultimate Intimacy: The Psychodynamics of Jewish Mysticism.* Madison, Conn.: International Universities Press, Inc., 1995.

Osty, Eugene. "Un Homme doué de connaissance paranormale: M. Ludwig Kahn." *Revue Métapsychique* (March–April, May–June, 1925).

———. *Une Facultéde connaissance Supra-Normal.* (Super Normal Faculties in Man). Paris: Felix Alcan, 1926.

———. *Supernormal Faculties in Man: An Experimental Study.* London: Methuen, 1923.

Osty, Marcel. "Eugene Osty: Pioneer Researcher." *Tomorrow.* 7, 1 (1959).

Otani, Soji. "The Aim of Parapsychology." *Journal of Psychical Research and Spiritualism* (1955).

———. "The Method of ESP Card Testing." *Journal of Psychical Research and Spiritualism* (1951).

———. "Past and Present Situation of Parapsychology in Japan." In *Parapsychology Today: A Geographic View.* Edited by Allan Angoff and Betty Shapin. New York: Parapsychology Foundation, 1973.

———. "Relations of Mental Set and Change of Skin Resistance to ESP Scores." *Journal of Parapsychology* (1955).

———. "Studies on the Influence of Mental and Physiological Conditions Upon ESP Function." *Journal of the Department of Liberal Arts* (Defense Academy) (1959).

———. "A Survey of Public Opinion on Psychical Phenomena" *Journal of Psychical Research and Spiritualism* (1951).

Ott, Jonathan. *Ayahuasca Analogues: Pangaean Entheogens.* Kennewick, Wash.: Natural Products Co., [1994] 1995.

———. *Hallucinogenic Plants of North America.* Berkeley, Calif.: Wingbow Press, [1976] 1979.

———. *The Age of Entheogens & The Angels' Dictionary.* Kennewick, Wash.: Natural Products Co., 1995.

———. *Pharmacotheon: Entheogenic Drugs, Their Plant Sources and History,* 2nd ed. (Kennewick, Wash.: Natural Products Co., 1996).

Oudemans, A. C. *The Loch Ness Animal.* Leyden, 1934.

Ousby, W. J. *A Complete Course of Auto-Hypnosis—Self Hypnotism and Auto-Suggestion.* London & Durban, 1950.

———. *Methods of Inducing and Using Hypnosis.* London, 1951.

———. *The Theory and Practice of Hypnotism.* London, 1967.

Ouseley, S. G. J. *The Science of the Auras.* London: L. N. Fowler, 1970.

Ouspensky, P. D. *The Fourth Way.* New York: Alfred A. Knopf, 1953.

———. *A New Model of the Universe.* New York: Alfred A. Knopf, 1931.

———. *In Search of the Miraculous.* New York: Harcourt, Brace, 1949.

———. *Tertium Organum; the Third Canon of Thought; a Key to the Enigmas of the World.* Rochester, N.Y.: Manas Press, 1920.

Outline of the Principle, Level 4. New York: Holy Spirit Association for the Unification of World Christianity, 1980.

Ouvaroff, M. *Essay on the Mysteries of Eleusis.* London: Rodwell & Martin, 1817.

Oved, Yaacov. *Two Hundred Years of American Communes.* New Brunswick, N.J.: Transaction Publications, 1993.

Owen, A. R. G. *Can We Explain the Poltergeist?* New York: Garrett Publications; New York: Helix Press, 1964.

———. *Hysteria, Hypnosis, and Healing.* 1971.

———. *Psychic Mysteries of Canada.* New York: Harper & Row, 1975.

Owen, A.R.G. and J. Whitton. "Proceedings of the First Canadian Conference on Psychokinesis." *New Horizons* (1975).

Owen, A. R. G., J. P. Rindge, and W. Cook. "An Investigation of Psychic Photography with the Beilleux Family." *New Horizons* (1972).

Owen, G. Vale. *Problems Which Perplex (Mainly Psychic) Explained by Question & Answer.* N.p., 1890. Kila, Mont.: Kessinger Publishing Co., 1998.

Owen, George Vale. *Facts and the Future Life.* London: Hutchinson & Co., 1922.

———. *How Spirits Communicate.* N.p., n.d.

———. *Jesus the Christ.* N.p., 1929.

———. *The Life Beyond the Veil.* 5 vols. London: Greater World Association, 1926.

———. *What Happens After Death.* London: Hutchinson & Co., 1924.

Owen, George Vale, and H. A. Dallas. *The Nurseries of Heaven.* (1920).

Owen, Iris M., and Margaret Sparrow. *Conjuring Up Philip; An Adventure in Psychokinesis.* New York: Harper and Row, 1976.

Owen, Iris M., and P. Mitchell. "The Alleged Haunting of Borley Rectory." *Journal of the Society for Psychical Research* 50 (1979).

Owen, J. J. *Psychography: Marvelous Manifestations of Psychic Power Given Through The Mediumship of Fred P. Evans.* San Francisco, 1893.

Owen, Robert Dale. *The Debatable Land Between this World and the Next.* London: Trubner, 1871.

———. *Footfalls on the Boundaries of Another World.* Philadelphia: J. B. Lippincott, 1860.

———. *The Life of Robert Owen.* 2 vols. Hamden, Conn.: Archon Books, 1966.

———. *Threading My Way; Twenty-Seven Years of Autobiography.* 1874. Reprint, New York: A. M. Kelley, 1967.

Owens, Ted. *Flying Saucer Intelligences Speak: A Message to the American People from the Flying Saucer Intelligences.* New Brunswick, N.J.: Interplanetary News Service, [1966].

———. *How to Contact Space People.* Clarksburg, W.Va.: Saucerian Books, 1969.

Oxley, William. *Angelic Revelations.* 5 vols. N.p., 1885.

———. *Modern Messiahs and Wonder Workers.* London: Trubner, 1889.

Oxon, M. A. [Stainton Moses]. *Higher Aspects of Spiritualism.* N.p., 1880.

———. *Psychography; or, A Treatise on the Objective Forms of Psychic or Spiritual Phenomena.* N.p., 1878. Reprinted as *Direct Spirit Writing.* N.p., 1952.

Ozanne, Charles. "A Layman Looks at Psychical Research." *Journal of the American Society for Psychical Research* (April 1942).

———. "Significance of "Non-Evidential" Material in Psychical Research." *Hibbert Journal* (October 1913).

———. *La decadence esrhétique*. Paris: Dalou, 1888.

———. *Le Vice supreme*. Paris: Labrairie de la Presse, Laurens, 1886.

Padgett, James E. *True Gospel Revealed Anew by Jesus*. 4 vols. Washington, D.C.: Foundation Church of the New Birth, 1958–72.

Pagal Baba. *Temple of the Phallic King: The Mind of India; Yogis, Swamis, Sufis, and Avataras*. New York: Simon & Schuster, 1973.

Page, Charles G. *Psychomancy; Spirit Rappings and Tippings Exposed*. New York, 1853.

Pagel, Walter. *Paracelsus: An Introduction to Philosophical Medicine in the Era of the Renaissance*. New York: Karger, 1982.

Pagenstecher, Gustav. *Die Geheimnisse der Psychometrie oder Hellsehen in die Vergangenheit* (Secrets of Psychometry or Clairvoyance into the Past). N.p., 1928.

———. "A Notable Psychometrist." *Journal of the American Society for Psychical Research* 14 (1920).

———. "Past Events Seership." *Proceedings of the American Society for Psychical Research* 16 (January 1922).

Paine, Albert Bigelow. *Mark Twain*. 3 vols. N.p., 1912.

Paley, John. "Satanist Abuse and Alien Abduction: A Comparative Analysis Theorizing Temporal Lobe Activity as a Possible Connection Between Anomalous Memories," *British Journal of Social Work* 27, no. 1 (February 1997): 43–70.

Pallas Athena and the Master Hilarion Speak. Part I: The Master Hilarion. Kings Park, N.Y.: Bridge to Freedom, 1975.

Palmer, Edward, "Plants Used by the Indians of the United States," *American Naturalist* 12 (1878): 593–606, 646–655.

Palmer, John. "Explorations with the Perceptual ESP Test," *Journal of Parapsychology* 58, no. 2 (June 1994): 115–147.

———. "External Psi Influence on ESP Task Performance," *Journal of Parapsychology* 60, no. 3 (September 1996): 193–210.

———. *The Perceptual ESP Test in a Religious Context. Research in Parapsychology, 1993: Abstracts and Papers from the Thirty-sixth Annual Convention of the Parapsychological Association, 1993*. Lanham, Md.: Scarecrow Press, Inc., 1998.

Palmer, Philip M., and Robert P. More. *Sources of the Faust Tradition from Simon Magus to Lessing*. Oxford: Oxford University Press, 1936. Reprint, New York: Haskell House, 1965.

Palmer, Ray. "Invitation to Adventure." *The Hidden World* A-1 (Spring 1961): 4–14.

Palos, Stephan. *The Chinese Art of Healing*. New York: Herderand Herder, 1971.

Pan, Shinhwan. "A Psychological Study of Divine and Parental Images of Korean Protestant Glossolalists in Comparison to Nonglossolalists," *Dissertation Abstracts International Section A: Humanities & Social Sciences* 56, no. 12-A (June 1996): 4816.

Panacea Society. *Transactions of the Panacea Society with the Archbishops and Bishops of the Church of England with Reference to Joanna Southcott*. London: Panacea Society, 1935.

Panati, Charles, ed. *The Geller Papers: Scientific Observations on the Paranormal Powers of Uri Geller*. Boston: Houghton Mifflin, 1976.

Pancoast, S. *The Kabbala: or True Science of Light*. Kila, Mont.: Kessinger Publishing Co., 1992.

Pandit, Madhav Pundalik. *Traditions in Mysticism*. New Delhi, India: Sterling, 1987.

Paper, J., "From Shaman to Mystic in Ojibwa Religion," *Studies in Religion* no. 2 (1980): 185–199.

Papish, Mary, and Daniel Papish. *We Are Servants of Master M*. Ojai, Calif.: Hanuman Publications, 1973.

Papus. *Le tarot divinatoire* (The divinatory tarot). 1909. Reprint, Paris: Dangles, 1969.

———. *The Qabalah*. New York: Samuel Weiser, 1977.

———. *Traité élémentaire de science occulte* (Elementary treatise on occult science). 10th ed. Paris: A. Michel, 1926.

———. *Traité méthodique de magie pratique* (Systematic treatise on practical magic). 1924. Reprint, Paris: Dangles, 1969.

Papus [G. Encausse]. *Le Diable et l'occultisme*. Paris, 1895.

Papusérard Encausse. *Le tarot des bohémiens*. 1889. Revised edition as *The Tarot of the Bohemians*. Translated by A. P. Morton. Edited by A. E. Waite. London: Rider & Son, 1910.

Paracelsus. *The Archidoxes of Magic*. Translated by Robert Turner. London, 1656. Reprint, New York: Samuel Weiser, 1975.

Paranjpe, A. C. "Parapsychology and Patanjali's Yoga," *Journal of Indian Psychology* 4, no. 2 (July 1985): 13–20.

Parapsychology, New Age & the Occult: A Source Encyclopedia. Teeswater, ON, Canada: Reference Press International, 1994.

Parchment, S. R. *Ancient Operative Masonry*. San Francisco: San Francisco Center—Rosicrucian Fellowship, 1930. Life Science Institute, 1991.

———. *Astrology, Mundane and Spiritual*. San Francisco: Anthroposophical Rosicrucian League, 1933.

———. *The Just Law of Compensation*. San Francisco: San Francisco Center—Rosicrucian Fellowship, 1932.

———. *Steps to Self-Mastery*. Oceanside, Calif.: Fellowship Press, 1927.

Parfitt, Will, and A. Drylie. *A Crowley Cross-Index*. Avon, England: ZRO, 1976.

Parish, Edmund. *Hallucinations and Illusions: A Study of the Fallacies of Perception*. London: Walter Scott Publishing, 1897.

Parke, Herbert W. *Greek Oracles*. London: Hutchinson, 1967.

———. *Oracles of Zeus*. Oxford: Blackwell, 1967.

Parke, Herbert W., and Donals Ernest Wilson Wormell. *The Delphic Oracles*. Oxford: Blackwell, 1956.

Parker, Gail. *Mind Cure in New England*. Hanover, N.H.: University Press of New England, 1973.

Parker, Thomas W. *The Knights Templars in England*. Tucson: University of Arizona Press, 1963.

Parot, Francoise. "Psychology Experiments: Spiritism at the Sorbonne," *Journal of the History of the Behavioral Sciences* 29, no. 1 (January 1993): 22–28.

Parrinder, Geoffrey. *African Traditional Religion*. Westport, Conn.: Greenwood Press, 1962. Reprint, London: Sheldon Press, 1974. Reprint, New York: Harper, 1977.

Parrish-Harra, Carol W. *A New Age Handbook on Death and Dying*. Marina del Rey, Calif.: DeVorss, 1982.

———. *Messengers of Hope*. Black Mountain, N.C.: New Age Press; Marina del Rey, Calif.: DeVors; Tahleqhuah, Okla.: Sparrow Hawk Press, 1983.

Parrott, Ian. *The Music of "An Adventure."* London: Regency Press, 1966.

Parsons, Denys. "Attempts to Detect Clairvoyance and Telepathy with a Mechanical Device." *Proceedings of the Society for Psychical Research* 48 (1946).

———. "Cloud Busting: A Claim Investigated." *Journal of the Society for Psychical Research* 38, 690 (December 1956).

———. "Experiments on PK with Inclined Plane and Rotating Cage." *Proceedings of the Society for Psychical Research* 47 (1945).

———. "A Nonexistent Building Located." *Journal of the Society for Psychical Research* 41 (July 1962).

———. "On the Need for Caution in Assessing Mediumistic Material." *Proceedings of the Society for Psychical Research* 48 (1949).

Parsons, William B. *The Enigma of the Oceanic Feeling: Revisioning the Psychoanalytic Theory of Mysticism*. New York: Oxford University Press, 1999.

Partanen, Jorma, "A Description of Buriat Shamanism" (translation of Text No. VIII in Pozdneyev's Mongolian Chrestomathy), *Journal de la Société Finno-Ougrienne* vol. 51 (1941–42).

Partner, Peter. *The Murdered Magicians: The Templars and their Myth*. Oxford: Oxford University Press, 1981. Reprint, N.p.: Crucible, 1987.

Pasche, Francis. "Freud et la mystique" (Freud and mysticism), *Revue Francaise de Psychanalyse* 59, no. 1 (January-March 1995): 27–39.

Pasqually, Martines de. *Traité de la réintegration des etres*. Paris: Chacorac, 1899.

Patai, Raphael. *The Hebrew Goddess*. New York: Ktav Publishing House, n.d.

Patanjali. *The Yoga-Sutras of Patanjali*. Translated by M. N. Dvidedi. Adyar, Madras, India: Theosophical Publishing House, 1890.

Patanjali, Bhagwan Shree. *Aphorisms of Yoga.* London: Faber, 1938.

Pater, Thomas. *Miraculus Abstinence: A Study of the Extraordinary Mystical Phenomena.* Washington, D.C.: Catholic University of Medica, 1946.

Pathways to Wholeness: A Healing Guide. Berkeley, Calif.: Clear Light Publications, 1975.

Patrick, C. V. *The Case Against Spirit Photography.* London: Kegan Paul, 1921.

Patterson, Tom. *100 Years of Spirit Photography.* London: Regency Press, 1965.

Patton, William P. *Prayer and Its Answers.* New York, 1885.

Pauwels, Louis, and Jacques Bergier. *Der Planet der unmöglichen Möglichkeiten.* Bern: Scherz Verlag, 1968. English edition as *Impossible Possibilities.* New York: Stein and Day, 1971.

———. *The Eternal Man.* London: Souvenir, 1972.

———. *Impossible Possibilities.* New York: Stein and Day, 1971.

———. *Le Matin des magiciens.* Paris: Editions Gallimard, 1960. Translated as *The Dawn of Magic.* London: Anthony Gibbs and Phillips, 1963. Reprinted as *The Morning of the Magicians.* New York: Stein and Day, 1964.

Pauwels, Louis. *Gurdjieff.* New York: Samuel Weiser, 1972.

Pavitt, William T., and Kate Pavitt. *The Book of Talismans, Amulets, and Zodiacal Gems.* London: Rider, 1914. Reprint, Detroit: Tower Books, 1971. Reprint, North Hollywood, Calif.: Wilshire Publishing, 1972.

Pealian, Gerhard. *Nicholas Roerich.* Agoura, Calif.: Aquarian Education Group, 1974.

Pearce-Higgins, John D. *Life, Death and Psychical Research: Studies on Behalf of the Churches' Fellowship for Psychical and Spiritual Studies.* London: Rider, 1973.

Pearsall, Ronald. *Table-Rappers.* London: Joseph, 1972. Reprint, New York: St. Martin's Press, 1972.

Pearson, E. Norman. *Space, Time and Self.* Adyar, Madras, India: Theosophical Publishing House, 1957.

Pearson, Hesketh. *Conan Doyle, His Life and Art.* London: Methuen, 1943.

Peat, David. *In Search of Nikola Tesla.* Bath, England: Ashgrove Press, 1983.

Peatman, John G., and Eugene L. Hartley, eds. *Festschrift for Gardner Murphy.* N.p., 1960.

Pechlin, J. N. *Observationes Physico-Medicae.* Hamburg, Germany, 1691.

Pederson-Krag, Geraldine H. "Telepathy and Repression." *Psychoanalytic Quarterly* 16 (1947).

Pedlar, Kit. *Quest for Gaia.* UK: Sovereign Press, 1979.

Peebles, James M. *Around the World: or, Travels in Polynesia, China, India, Arabia, Egypt, Syria.* Boston: Colby & Rich, 1875.

———. *Celebration of the Fiftieth Anniversary of Modern Spiritualism at Its Birthplace.* Battle Creek, Mich.: The Author, 1898.

———. *The Demonism of the Ages, Spirit Obsessions So Common in Spiritism, Oriental and Occidental Occultism.* Battle Creek, Mich.: Peebles Medical Institute, 1904.

———. *Five Journeys around the World: or, Travels in the Pacific Islands, New Zealand, Australia, Ceylon, India, Egypt and Other Oriental Countries.* Los Angeles: Peebles Publishing, 1910.

———. *Seers of the Ages.* 1869. Reprint, Chicago: Progressive Thinker, 1905.

Peebles, James M., Helen Densmore, and W. J. Colville. *Reincarnation; or the Doctrine of "Soul's" Successive Embodiment.* Battle Creek, Mich.: Peebles Medical Institute, 1904.

Peek, Philip M., ed. *African Divination Systems.* Bloomington: Indiana University Press, 1991.

Peel, Edgar. *The Trials of the Lancashire Witches: A Study of Seventeenth-Century Witchcraft.* Nelson, England: Hendon Publishing, 1985.

Peel, Robert. *Mary Baker Eddy.* 3 vols. New York: Holt Rinehart & Winston, 1971.

Peiris, William. *The Western Contribution to Buddhism.* Delhi, India: Motilal Banarsidass, 1953.

Péladan, Joséphin. *Comment on devient mage.* Paris, 1892.

Pelletier, Joseph A. *The Queen of Peace Visits Medjugorje.* Worchester, Mass.: Assumption, 1985.

Pelletier, Kenneth R. *Mind as Healer/Mind as Slayer: A Holistic Approach to Preventing Stress Disorder.* New York: Delta, 1977.

Pelletier, Robert A. *God Speaks at Garabandal.* Worcester, Mass.: Assumption, 1970.

———. *The Sun Dances at Garabandal.* Worcester, Mass.: Assumption, 1973.

Pelton, Robert W. *Ancient Secrets of Fortune-Telling.* South Brunswick, N.J.: A. S. Barnes, 1976.

Penelhum, Terence. *Survival and Disembodied Existence.* New York: Humanities Press, 1970.

Peng, Therese (Chu-Kiaw). "Meditation and Psycho-Spiritual Transformation: A Phenomenological Study of Ch'an (Zen) Buddhism and Christian Mysticism," *Dissertation Abstracts International: Section B: The Sciences & Engineering* 54, no. 11-B (1994): 5928.

Pennant, Thomas. *A Tour in Scotland and Voyage to the Hebrides, MDCCLXXII.* 1774. Reprint, Chester, UK: J. Monk, 1969.

Pennell, Elizabeth. *Charles Godfrey Leland.* Boston: Houghton, Mifflin, 1906.

Pennick, Nigel. *Geomancy.* Cambridge, Conn.: Cokayne Publishing, 1973.

———. *Oracle of Geomancy.* Edmonds, Wash.: Holmes Publishing Group, 1995.

Percival, Harold W. *Democracy Is Self-Government.* New York: Word Publishing, 1952.

———. *Man and Woman and Child.* New York: Word Publishing, 1951.

———. *Masonry and Its Symbols.* New York: Word Publishing, 1952.

———. *Thinking of Destiny.* New York: Word Publishing, 1946.

Pereira, Jose, ed. *Hindu Theology: A Reader.* Garden City, N.Y.: Image Books, 1976.

Perkins, Lynn F. *The Masters as New Age Mentors.* Lakemont, Ga.: CSA Press, 296.

Perkins, Mary, and Philip Hainsworth. *The Baha'i Faith.* London: Ward Lock Educational, 1980.

Permutt, Cyril. *Beyond the Spectrum: A Survey of Supernormal Photography.* Cambridge, England: Patrick Stephens, 1983.

Perovsky-Petrovo-Solovovo, Count. "My Experiments with S. F. Sambor." *Journal of the Society for Psychical Research* 30 (1937).

———. "On the Production of Spurious 'Spirit Raps.' " *Journal of the Society for Psychical Research* 6 (1893).

Perriman, A. E. *Broadcasting From Beyond.* London, 1952.

Perriman, Florence. *Secrets of a Famous Clairvoyante.* London, 1936.

Perry, Lewis. "Adin Ballou's Hopedale Community and the Theology of Anti-slavery." *Church History* 39 (September 1970): 372–389.

Perry, Michael C. *Crisis for Confirmation.* N.p., 1967.

———. *The Eastern Enigma.* N.p., 1959.

———. *Meet the Prayer Book.* N.p., 1963.

———. "A New View of the Resurrection." *Tomorrow* (Summer 1954).

———. "Parapsychology in Apologetics." *Church Quarterly Review* (January 1959).

———. *The Pattern of Matins & Evensong.* N.p., 1961.

———. *The Resurrection of Man.* N.p., 1975.

———. *Sharing in One Bread.* N.p., 1980.

Perry, Nicholas, and Loreto Echeverria. *Under the Heel of Mary.* London: Routledge, 1988.

Persinger, Michael A. "Striking EEG Profiles from Single Episodes of Glossolalia and Transcendental Meditation," *Perceptual & Motor Skills* 58, no. 1 (February 1984): 127–133.

———. "Subjective Telepathic Experiences, Geomagnetic Activity and the ELF Hypothesis: II. Stimulus Features and Neural Detection," *PSI Research* 4, no. 2 (June 1985): 4–23.

Persinger, Michael A. and George B. Schaut. "Geomagnetic Factors in Subjective Telepathic, Precognitive, and Postmortem Experiences," *Journal of the American Society for Psychical Research* 82, no. 3 (July 1988): 217–235.

Perty, Maximilien. *Die Mystischen Erscheinungen der menschlichen Natur.* 2nd ed., Leipzig and Heidelberg, 1872.

Peschel, Lisa. *The Runes.* St. Paul, Minn.: Llewellyn Publications, 1989.

Peters, Edward. *Inquisition.* New York: Free Press, 1988.

———. *The Magician, the Witch, and the Law.* Philadelphia: University of Pennsylvania Press, 1978.

Peters, Larry. *Ecstasy and Healing in Nepal: An Ethnopsychiatric Study of Tamang Shamanism.* Malibu, Calif.: Undena Publications, 1981.

Peters, Larry G. and Douglas Price-Williams. "Towards an Experiential Analysis of Shamanism," *American Ethnologist* vol. 7: 397–418.

Petitot, Émile. *Les Grands Esquimaux.* N.p., 1887.

Petitpierre, Dom Robert. *Exorcism: The Findings of a Commission Convened by the Bishop of Exeter.* London: Society for Promoting Christian Knowledge, 1972.

Pettigrew, T. J. *On Superstitions connected with the History and Practice of Medicine and Surgery.* N.p., 1844.

———. *Superstitions Connected with Medicine or Surgery.* N.p., 1844.

Pettiward, Cynthia. *The Case for Possession.* UK: Colin Smythe, 1975.

Petuchowski, Jacob J., ed. *Understanding Jewish Prayer.* New York: Ktav Publications, 1972.

Pfeifer, Samuel. "Belief in Demons and Exorcism in Psychiatric Patients in Switzerland," *British Journal of Medical Psychology* 67, no. 3 (September 1994): 247–258.

Pfungst, Oskar. *Clever Hans (The Horse of Mr. Von Osten): A Contribution to Experimental Animal and Human Psychology.* New York, 1911. Reprint, New York: Holt, Rinehart & Winston, 1965.

Philalethes, Eirenaeus. *Enarratio methodica trium Gebri medicinarum.* N.p., 1678.

———. *Introitus apertus ad occlusum Regis Palatium.* N.p., 1667.

———. *The Marrow of Alchemy.* N.p., 1654.

———. *Ripley Reviv'd; or an Exposition upon Sir George Ripley's Hermetico-Poetical Works.* 5 vols. London: T. Ratcliff and N. Thompson, 1677–78.

———. *Tractatus tres: (i) Metallorum Metamorphosis; (ii) Brevis Manuductio ad Rubinum Coelestem; (iii) Fons Chymicae Veritatis.* N.p., 1678; 1694.

Phillips, G. Ragland. *Brigantia: A Mysteriography.* London: Routledge & Kegan Paul, 1976.

Philostratus. *The Life of Apollonius of Tyana.* Translated by F. C. Conybeare. London: Macmillan, 1912.

Philpott, Kent. *Manual of Demonology and the Occult.* Grand Rapids, Mich.: Zondervan, 1973.

Phylos the Tibetan. *An Earth Dweller Returns.* Milwaukee, Wisc.: Lemurian Press, 1940.

Pick, Bernhard. *The Cabala.* LaSalle, Ill.: Open Court Publishing, 1903.

Pickering, Edward Charles. "Possibility of Errors in Scientific Researches, Due to Thought-Transference." *Proceedings of the American Society for Psychical Research* 1 (1885).

Pickering, Edward Charles, and J. M. Peirce. "Discussion of Returns in Response to Circular No. 4." *Proceedings of the American Society for Psychical Research* 1 (July 1885).

Piddington, John George. "Cross Correspondences of a Gallic Type." *Proceedings of the Society for Psychical Research* 29, 72 (1916).

———. "Presidential Address." *Proceedings of the Society for Psychical Research* 34, 89 (1924).

———. "A Reply to Sir Oliver Lodge's Note." *Proceedings of the Society for Psychical Research* 30, 77 (1918).

Piddington, John George. "A Series of Concordant Automatisms." *Proceedings of the Society for Psychical Research* 22, 57 (1908).

Piddington, John George, and Eleanor Sidgwick. "Note on Mrs. Piper's Hodgson-Control in England." *Proceedings of the Society for Psychical Research* 23, 58 (1909).

Piedra, Carlos Aguilar. *Religión y Magia entre los Indios de Costa Rica de origen sureño*, 3rd ed. (La Paz: Editorial de la Universidad de Costa Rica, 1986).

Pienaar, Domenick C., and Karlis Osis. "ESP Over Seventy-Five Hundred Miles." *Journal of Parapsychology* 20, no. 4 (1956).

Pierce, Henry W. *Science Looks at ESP.* New York: New American Library, 1970.

Pike, Albert. *Morals & Dogma of the Ancient & Accepted Rite of Freemasonry.* Kila, Mont.: Kessinger Publishing Co., 1992.

Pike, Richard. *Life's Borderland and Beyond.* London, n.d.

A Pilgrim's Guide to Planet Earth: A Traveler's Handbook and New Age Directory. San Rafael, Calif.: Spiritual Community Publications, 1981.

Pincock, Jenny O'Hara. *Trails of Truth.* London, 1930.

Piper, Alta C. *The Life and Work of Mrs. Piper.* London: Kegan Paul/ K. Paul, Trench, Trubner, & Co. Ltd., 1929.

Pitcairn, Theodore. *The Book Sealed with Seven Seals.* Bryn Athyn, Pa.: Cathedral Book Room, 1927.

———. *My Lord and My God.* New York: Exposition Press, 1967.

Placidus de Titus. *Astronomy and Elementary Philosophy.* Translated by Manoah Sibley. London: W. Justins, 1789.

———. *A Collection of Thirty Remarkable Nativities.* Translated by Manoah Sibley. London: W. Justins, 1789.

Playfair, Guy Lyon. *The Flying Cow: Research Into Paranormal Phenomena in the World's Most Psychic Country.* London: Souvenir Press, 1975. Reprinted as *The Unknown Power.* New York: Pocket Books, 1975. Reprint, London: Panther paperback, 1977.

———. "Identical Twins and Telepathy," *Journal of the Society for Psychical Research* 63, no. 854 (January 1999): 86–98.

———. *The Indefinite Boundary.* London: Souvenir Press, 1976.

———. *This House is Haunted; An Investigation of the Enfield Poltergeist* London: Souvenir Press, 1980.

———. *The Unknown Power.* 1975. Reprinted as *The Flying Cow.* London: Souvenir Press, 1975.

Pleasants, Helene, ed. *Biographical Dictionary of Parapsychology.* New York: Helix Press, 1964.

Plinth, August. *Principles of Levitation.* New York: White Sun Prees, 1970.

Plotinus Amid Gnostics and Christians: Papers Presented at a Plotinus Symposium held at the Free University, Amsterdam, on January 25, 1984. Amsterdam: Free University Press, 1984.

Plotkin, Mark J. *Tales of a Shaman's Apprentice: An Ethnobotanist Searches for New Medicines in the Amazon Rain Forest.* New York: Viking, 1993.

Plummer, George Winslow. *The Art of Rosicrucian Healing.* New York: Society of Rosicrucians, 1947.

———. *Consciously Creating Circumstances.* New York: Society of Rosicrucians, 1939.

———. *This House is Haunted; An Investigation of the Enfield Poltergeist* London: Souvenir Press, 1980. *Principles and Practices for Rosicrucians.* New York: Society of Rosicrucians, 1947, 1978.

Pococke, Edward. *India in Greece.* London: J. J. Griffin & Co., 1852.

Podmore, Frank. *Apparitions & Thought-Transference: An Examination of the Evidence for Telepathy.* New York: G. P. Putnam's Sons, 1894. New York: Charles Scribner's Sons, 1895; London: Walter Scott Publishing, 1896.

———. *Biography of Robert Owen.* London: Hutchinson, 1906.

———. *Mesmerism and Christian Science.* Philadelphia: G. W. Jacobs; London: Metheun, 1909.

———. *Modern Spiritualism.* 2 vols. London, 1902. Reprinted as *Mediums of the Nineteenth Century.* 2 vols. New Hyde Park, N.Y.: University Books, 1963.

———. *The Naturalisation of the Supernatural.* New York: George Putnam's Sons, 1908.

———. *The Newer Spiritualism.* London: T. Fisher Unwin, 1910. Reprint, New York: Henry Holt, 1911; New York: Ayer Publishing Co. Inc., 1975.

———. *Studies in Psychical Research.* London: Kegan Paul, Trench, Tubner; New York: G. P. Putnam's and Son, 1897. Reprint, New York: Ayer Publishing Co. Inc., 1975.

———. *Telepathic Hallucinations: The New View of Ghosts.* London: Milner; New York: Stokes, 1909.

Podolsky, Edward. *Music Therapy.* New York: Philosophical Library, 1954.

The Poetic Edda. Oxford: Clarendon Press, 1969.

Pohl, Hans Ludwig. "Investigation of the PK-Effect." *Journal of Parapsychology* 24, no. 3 (September 1930).

Polidori, John, et al. *The Count Dracula Fan Club Book of Vampire Stories.* Chicago: Adams Press, 1980.

Pollack, Jack Harrison. *Croiset the Clairvoyant.* Garden City, N.Y.: Doubleday, 1964. Reprint, New York: Bantam Books, 1965.

Pollock, James S. *Dead and Gone.* London, 1874.

Poloma, Margaret M. *The Charismatic Movement: Is There a New Pentecost?* Boston, Mass: Twayne Publishers, 1982.

Poncé, Charles. *Kabblah: An Introduction and Illumination for the World Today.* San Francisco: Straight Arrow Books, 1973.

Pond, Mariam Buckner. *Time Is Kind: The Story of the Unfortunate Fox Family.* New York: Centennial Press, 1947. Reprinted as *The Unwilling Martyrs.* London: Psychic Book Club, 1947.

Poortman, J. J. *De Grondparadox.* N.p., 1961.

———. *Drei Vorträge Über Philosophie und Parapsychologie.* N.p., 1939.

———. "The Feeling of Being Stared At." *Journal of the Society for Psychical Research* (1959).

———. "Henri Bergson and Parapsychology." *Tijdschrift voor Parapsychologie* N.p., 1941.

———. "Mysterious Words." *Tijdschrift voor Parapsychologie.* N.p., 1939, 1940.

———. *Occult Motives in Literature.* N.p., 1937.

———. "Psychophysical Parallelism or Interactionism?" *Journal of the American Society for Psychical Research* (1937).

———. *Variaties op een en meer Themata* (Collected Essays on Philosophy, Parapsychology and Theosophy). N.p., 1947.

Pope, Alexander. *The Rape of the Lock.* N.p., 1821. Reprint, London: Methuen, 1941.

Pope, Dorothy H. "The Search for ESP in Animals." *Tomorrow* (Summer 1953).

Pope, Dorothy H., and J. G. Pratt. "The ESP Controversy." *Journal of Parapsychology* (September 1942).

———. "Five Years of the Journal of Parapsychology." *Journal of Parapsychology* (March 1942).

Pope, Joya. *The World According to Michael.* San Mateo, Calif.: Sage Publications, 1987.

Pope-Hennessy, John Wyndham. *Cellini.* New York: Abbeville Press, 1985.

Pope Jr., Harrison G., "Tabernanthe Iboga: An African Narcotic Plant of Social Importance," *Economic Botany* vol. 23 (1969): 174–184.

Popenhoe, Cris. *Books for Inner Development/ The Yes! Guide.* Washington, D.C.: Yes! Bookshop, 1976. Revised as *Inner Development; the Yes! Bookshop Guide.* Washington, D.C.: Yes! Bookshop, 1979. Supplements 1–11. 1982–83.

———. *Wellness.* Washington, D.C.: Yes! Bookshop, 1977.

Pordage, John. *Truth Appearing Through the Clouds of Undeserved Scandal.* N.p., 1655.

Porteous, Alexander. *Forest Folklore, Mythology, and Romance.* London: George Allen & Unwin, 1928.

Porter, Katherine H. *Through a Glass Darkly: Spiritualism in the Browning Circle.* Lawrence: University of Kansas Press, 1958.

Post, Eric. *Communication with the Beyond: A Practical Handbook of Spiritualism.* New York: Atlantic Publishing, 1946.

Potapov, L. P., "O szamanskom jazykie u altaje-sajanskich narodow". In *Istoriko-kulturnyje kontakty narodow altajskoj jazykowoj obscznosti.* Moscow, 1986: 56–57 [in Russian].

Powell, A. E. *The Etheric Double.* 1926. Reprint, Wheaton, Ill.: Theosophical Publishing House, 1969.

Powell, Arthur E. *The Astral Body and Other Astral Phenomena.* London: Theosophical Publishing House, 1927. Kila, Mont.: Kessinger Publishing Co., 1998.

Powell, Ellis T. *The Essentials of Self-Government.* N.p., 1909.

———. *The Mechanism of the City.* London: P. S. King & Son, 1910.

———. *The Practical Affairs of Life.* N.p., 1918.

———. *The Psychic Element of the New Testament.* N.p, n.d.

Powell, Kenneth F., R. A. McConnell, and Ruth J. Snowden. "Wishing With Dice." *Journal of Experimental Psychology* 50 (1955).

Powell, T. G. E. *The Celts.* New York: F. A. Praeger, 1958.

Poynton, J. C. "Making Sense of PSI: Whiteman's Multilevel Ontology," *Journal of the Society for Psychical Research* 59, no. 835 (April 1994): 401–412.

Prabhavananda, Swami, with Frederick Manchester. *The Spiritual Heritage of India.* Garden City, N.Y.: Doubleday, 1963.

Prabhupada, A. C. Bhaktivedanta Swami. *Bhagavad-Gita As It Is.* New York: Bhaktivedanta Book Trust, 1972.

———. *KRSHA: The Supreme Personality of Godhead.* 3 vols. New York: Bhaktivedanta Book Trust, 1970.

———. *The Nectar of Devotion.* Los Angeles: Bhaktivedanta Book Trust, 1970.

———. *Teachings of Lord Chaitanya.* Los Angeles: Bhaktivedanta Book Trust, 1974.

———. *Teachings of Lord Kapila: The Son of Devahuti.* New York: Bhaktivedanta Book Trust, 1977.

Practical Psychomancy & Crystal Gazing. Santa Fe, N.Mex.: Sun Publishing Co., 1997.

Pradhan, Rao Bahadur M. W. *Shri Sai Baba of Shirdi: A Glimpse of Indian Spirituality.* Bandra, India: R. A. Turkhud, n.d.

Prasad, Rama. *The Science of Breath and the Philosophy of the Tattvas . . . Nature's Finer Forces.* London: Theosophical Publishing Society, 1897.

———. *The Science of Breath and the Philosophy of the Tattvas, Translated from the Sanskrit, with Introductory and Explanatory Essays on Nature's Finer Forces.* London: Theosophical Publishing House, 1887.

Pratt, J. G. "A Decade of Research with a Selected Subject." *Proceedings of American Society for Psychical Research* (1973).

———. *ESP Research Today: A Study of Developments in Parapsychology Since 1960.* Metuchen, N.J.: Scarecrow Press, 1973.

———. *On the Evaluation of Verbal Material in Parapsychology.* New York: Parapsychology Foundation, 1969.

———. *Parapsychology: An Insider's View of ESP.* Metuchen, N.J.: Scarecrow Press, 1977.

———. *The Psychic Realm.* New York: Random House, 1975.

———. "A Review of Kahn's 'Studies in Extrasensory Perception.'&43" *Journal of Parapsychology* 17 (1953).

Pratt, J. G., with Champe Ransom. "Exploratory Observations of the Movement of Static Objects Without the Apparent Use of Known Physical Energies by Nina S. Kulagina." *Proceedings of the Parapsychological Association* 8 (1971).

———. "Extrasensory Perception or Extraordinary Sensory Perception?" *Journal of American Society for Psychical Research* 66 (1972).

Preliminary Report of the Commission Appointed by the University of Pennsylvania to Investigate Modern Spiritualism. Philadelphia: J. B. Lippincott, 1887.

Preliminary Studies of a Vaudeville Telepathist. Bulletin III. London: London Council for Psychical Investigation, 1937.

Presman, A. S. *Electromagnetic Fields and Life.* New York: Plenum Press, 1970.

Pressing, R. G., comp. *Houdini Unmasked.* Lily Dale, N.Y.: Dale News, 1947.

Preston, William. *Illustrations of Masonry.* London, 1775.

Price, E. Alan, Marius Valkhoff, and J. H. Van Der Merwe. *Parapsychology and Modern Science.* South African Society for Psychical Research, 1958.

Price, George R. "Apology to Rhine and Soal." *Science* 175 (1972).

———. "Science and the Supernatural." *Science* 122 (August 26, 1955).

———. "Where Is the Definitive Experiment?" *Science* (January 6, 1956).

Price, Harry. *Confessions of a Ghost Hunter.* New York: G. P. Putnam's Sons, 1936. Reprint, New York: Causeway Books, 1974.

———. *The End of Borley Rectory.* London: George G. Harrap, 1946.

———. *Fifty Years of Psychical Research: A Critical Study.* London: Longmans, Green, 1939. Reprint, New York: Ayer Publishing Co. Inc., 1975.

———. *Leaves From a Psychist's Case-Book.* London: Gollancz, 1933.

———. *"The Most Haunted House in England": Ten Years' Investigation of Borley Rectory.* London: Longmans, Green, 1940.

———. *Poltergeist Over England.* London: Country Life, 1945.

———. *Regurgitation and the Duncan Mediumship.* Council at the Rooms of the National Laboratory of Psychical Research, London, 1931.

———. *Rudi Schneider; A Scientific Examination of his Mediumship.* London: Methuen, 1930.

———. "Same Account of the Poltergeist Phenomena of Eleonore Zügun." *Journal of the American Society for Psychical Research* (August 1926).

———. *Search for Truth: My Life for Psychical Research.* London: Collins, 1942.

———. *Stella C.: An Account of Some Original Experiments in Psychical Research.* Edited by James Turner. London: Souvenir Press, 1973.

Price, Harry, and R. S. Lambert. *The Haunting of Cashen's Gap.* London, 1936.

Price, Harry, and E. J. Dingwall, eds. *Revelations of a Spirit Medium.* London: Kegan Paul, Trench, Trubner, 1922; New York: E. P. Dutton, 1922.

Price, Henry H. *Belief.* Gifford Lectures, 1969.

———. *Essays in the Philosophy of Religion.* Oxford: Claredon Press, 1972.

———. "Haunting and the 'Psychic Ether' Hypothesis" *Proceedings of the Society for Psychical Research* (vol. 45, 1939).

———. *Hume's Theory of the External World.* Oxford: Claredon Press, 1940. Reprint, Greenwood Press, 1981.

———. *Perception* (1932; 1973).

———. "Psychical Research and Human Personality." *Hibbert Journal* (January 1949).

———. "Some Philosophical Questions About Telepathy and Clairvoyance." *Philosophy* (October 1940). Reprint in: J. M. O. Wheatley and H. L. Edge, eds. *Philosophical Dimensions of Parapsychology.* Springfield, Ill.: Charles C. Thomas, 1976.

———. "Survival and the Idea of Another World." *Proceedings of the Society for Psychical Research* 50 (January 1953).

———. *Thinking and Experience.* Cambridge, Mass.: Harvard University Press; London; New York: Hutchinsons University Library, 1953.

Price, Vincent, and V. B. Price. *Monsters.* New York: Grosset & Dunlap, 1981.

Price-Mars, Jean. "Africa in the Americas." *Tomorrow* (Autumn 1954).

Prichard, John. *A Few Sober Words of Table-talk about the Spirits.* Leamington, UK, 1853.

Prieditis, Arthur A. *Fate of the Nations.* London: Neville Spearman; St. Paul, Minn.: Llewellyn Publications, 1973.

Priestley, J. B. *Man and Time.* London, 1964. Reprint, New York: Dell, 1971.

Priestley, Joseph. *Original Letters by the Rev. John Wesley and his Friends.* Birmingham, England, 1791.

Prince, Morton. "A Contribution to the Study of Hysteria." *Proceedings of the Society for Psychical Research* 14 (1899).

———. "The Development and Genealogy of the Misses Beauchamp." *Proceedings of the Society for Psychical Research* 15 (1900–01).

———. *The Disassociation of a Personality.* 1905. Reprint, Oxford: Oxford University Press, 1978.

———. *The Nature of Mind and Human Automatism.* Philadelphia: J. B. Lippincott, 1885.

Prince, Raymond, ed., "Issue on Shamans and Endorphins," *Ethos* 10, no. 4 (1982): 299–423.

Prince, Walter F. *Noted Witnesses for Psychic Occurrences.* Boston: Boston Society for Psychic Research, 1928. Reprint, New Hyde Park, N.Y.: University Books, 1963.

———. "A Survey of American Slate Writing Mediumship." *Proceedings of the American Society for Psychical Research* 15 (1921).

———. "Supplementary Report on the Keeler-Lee Photographs." *Proceedings of the American Society for Psychical Research* 12 (1919).

———. *The Psychic in the House.* Boston: Boston Society for Psychical Research, 1926.

———. *Two Old Cases Reviewed.* Boston: Boston Society for Psychical Research, n.d.

Prince, Walter Franklin. *The Case of Patience Worth: A Critical Study of Certain Unusual Phenomena.* Boston: Society for Psychical Research, 1927; New Hyde Park, N.Y.: University Books, 1964.

———. *The Enchanted Boundary: Being a Survey of Negative Reactions to Claims of Psychic Phenomena, 1820–1930.* Boston: Boston Society for Psychic Research, 1930. Reprint, North Stratford, N. H.: Ayer Co. Publishers, Inc., 1975.

———. *Leonard and Soule Experiments.* Boston: Boston Society for Psychical Research, 1929.

———. "Psychometric Experiments with Maria Reyes de Z." *Journal of the American Society for Psychical Research* 16 (January 1922).

———. "Psychometric Experiments with Maria Reyes de Z." *Proceedings of the American Society for Psychical Research* 15 (1921).

———. "Psychometrical Experiments with Señora Maria Reyes de Z." *ASPR Journal* 16 (January 1922).

———. "Psychometrical Experiments with Senora Maria Reyes de Z." *Proceedings of the American Society for Psychical Research* 15 (1921).

———. *The Sinclair Experiments Demonstrating Telepathy.* Boston: Boston Society for Psychic Research, n.d.

Prinz, Armin., "Initiation of Shamans of the Azande," *Yearbook for Ethnomedicine and the Study of Consciousness (Jahrbuch für Ethnomedizin und Bewusstseinsforschung)* vol. 3 (1994): 133–144.

Pritchett, W. Douglas. *The Children of God, Family of Love: An Annotated Bibliography.* New York: Garland Publications, 1985.

Probert, Mark. *Excerpts from the Mark Probert Séances: 1950 Series.* 3 vols. San Diego, Calif.: Inner Circle Press, 1950.

———. *The Magic Bag.* San Diego, Calif.: Inner Circle Kethra E'Da Foundation, 1963.

The Problem of Pure Consciousness: Mysticism and Philosophy. New York: Oxford University Press, 1990.

Proceedings of the Scientific and Technical Congress of Radionics and Radiesthesia London May 16–18, 1950, London, n.d.

Proctor, Russell F. "The Rhetorical Functions of Christian Glossolalia," *Journal of Psychology & Christianity* 9, no. 3 (Fall 1990): 27–34.

Progoff, Ira. *The Image of an Oracle: A Report on Research into the Mediumship of Eileen Garrett.* New York: Helix Press, 1964.

Progroff, Ira, ed. *The Cloud of Unknowing.* N.p., 1957.

———. *Death and Rebirth of Psychology.* N.p., 1956.

———. *Depth Psychology and Modern Man.* N.p., 1959.

———. *Jung's Psychology and Its Social Meaning.* N.p., 1953.

———. "Parapsychology in Modern Thinking." *International Journal of Parapsychology* 1, 1 (Summer 1959).

———. *The Practice of Process Meditation.* N.p., 1980.

———. *The Symbolic and the Real.* N.p., 1963.

———. "Transformation of Jewish Mysticism." *International Journal of Parapsychology* 2, 2 (Autumn 1960).

Prophet, Elizabeth Clare. *The Great White Brotherhood in the Culture, History and Religion of America.* Los Angeles: Summit University Press, 1983.

———. *Saint Germain on Prophecy.* Livingston, Mont.: Summit University Press, 1986.

Prophet, Mark L., and Elizabeth Clare Prophet. *Climb the Highest Mountain.* Colorado Springs, Colo.: Summit Lighthouse, 1972.

———. *The Lost Teachings of Jesus.* 2 vols. Livingston, Mont.: Summit University Press, 1986.

———. *Saint Germain on Alchemy.* Livingston, N.Y.: Summit University Press, 1962.

Proskauer, Julien J. *Spook Crooks! Exposing the Secrets of the Prophet-eers Who Conduct Our Wickedest Industry.* New York: A. L. Burt, 1932. Reprint, Ann Arbor, Mich.: Gryphon Books, 1971.

Prosnick, Kevin P. "Claims of Near-Death Experiences, Gestalt Resistance Processes, and Measures of Optimal Functioning," *Journal of Near-Death Studies* 18, no. 1 (Fall 1999): 27–34.

Pryse, F. N., ed. *The Fame and Confession of the Fraternity of R:C: Commonly of the Rosie Cross . . . by Eugenius Philalethes . . . now reprinted in facsimile together with an Introduction, Notes and a Translation of the letter of Adam Haselmeyer.* Societas Rosicruciana in Anglia, 1923.

Pryse, James Morgan. *The Apocalypse Unsealed.* Los Angeles: The Author, 1931.

———. *Reincarnation in the New Testament.* New York: Theosophical Publishing Co. of New York, 1900.

———. *The Restored New Testament.* Los Angeles: The Author, 1914.

———. *The Sermon on the Mount.* New York: Theosophical Society, 1904.

Psychic magazine, editors of. *Psychics.* New York: Harper & Row, 1972.

"Psychokinetic Metal-bending." *Psi News,* Bulletin of the Parapsychological Association 4, 1.

Ptolemy, Claudius. *The Quadripatite, or Four Books.* Translated by J. Whalley. Edited by Manoah Sibley and J. Browne. London, 1786.

Puharich, Andrija. *Beyond Telepathy.* Garden City, N.Y.: Doubleday, 1952. Reprint, Garden City, N.Y.: Anchor Press, 1973. Reprint, London: Souvenir Press, 1974. Reprint, London: Pan Books, 1975.

———. *The Sacred Mushroom: Key to the Door of Eternity.* Garden City, N.Y.: Doubleday, 1959.

———. *Time No Longer.* N.p., 1980.

———. *Uri: A Journal of the Mystery of Uri Geller.* Garden City, N.Y.: Doubleday, 1974.

Puharich, Andrija, and Harold E. Puthoff. *The Iceland Papers.* Amherst, Wisc.: Essentia Research Associates, 1979.

Pullar, Philippa. *The Shortest Journey.* London: Hamish Hamilton, 1981.

Pullen, Philip. *Index to the Divine and Spiritual Writings of Joanna Southcott.* Ashford, England: Clock House Press, 1921.

Purohit, Swami Shri. *The Geeta: The Gospel of the Lord Shri Krishna.* London: Faber & Faber, 1935.

Pursel, Jach. *Lazaris Interviews.* 2 vols. Beverly Hills, Calif.: Concept Synergy, 1988.

———. *Lazaris: The Sacred Journey; You and Your Higher Self.* Beverly Hills, Calif.: Concept Synergy, 1987.

Purucker, Gottfried de. *Dialogues with G. de Purucker.* 3 vols. Covina, Calif.: Theosophical University Press, 1948.

———. *The Esoteric Tradition.* 2 vols. Point Loma, Calif.: Theosophical University Press, 1935.

———. *Fundamentals of Esoteric Philosophy.* London: Rider, 1932.

———. *Questions We All Ask.* 4 vols. Covina, Calif.: Theosophical University Press, 1930–31.

Puryear, Herbert B. *The Edgar Cayce Primer.* New York: Bantam Books, 1982.

———. *A Prophet in His Own Country.* New York: William Morrow, 1974.

Puthoff, Harold E., and Russell Targ. "ESP Experiments with Uri Geller" In J. D. Morris, W. G. Roll, and R. L. Morris, eds. *Research in Parapsychology 1973.* Metuchen, N.J.: Scarecrow Press, 1974.

———. "Information Transmission under Conditions of Sensory Shielding." *Nature* (October 1974).

———. *Mind-Reach: Scientists Look at Psychic Ability.* New York: Delacorte Press, 1977.

———. "A Perceptual Channel for Information Transfer over Kilometer Distances: Historical Perspective and Recent Research." *Proceedings, Institute of Electrical and Electronics Engineers* 64 (1975).

———. "Physics, Entrophy, and Psychokinesis." In *Proceedings of the Conference on Quantum Physics and Parapsychology, Geneva, August 26–27, 1974.* New York: Parapsychology Foundation, 1975.

———. "PK Experiments with Uri Geller and Ingo Swann." In J. D. Morris, W. G. Roll, and R. L. Morris, eds. *Research in Parapsychology 1973.* Metuchen, N.J.: Scarecrow Press, 1974.

———. "Remote Viewing of Natural Targets." In J. D. Morris, W. G. Roll, and R. L. Morris, eds. *Research in Parapsychology 1974.* Metuchen, N.J.: Scarecrow Press, 1975.

———. "Replication Study on the Remote Viewing of Natural Targets." In J. D. Morris, W. G. Roll, and R. L. Morris, eds. *Research in Parapsychology 1975.* Metuchen, N.J.: Scarecrow Press, 1976.

Putnam, Allen. *Bible Marvel Workers.* Boston, 1876.

Putnam, Allen, comp. *Biography of Mrs. J. H. Conant.* Boston: W. White and Co., 1873.

———. *Flashes of Light from the Spirit-Land.* Boston: William White, 1872.

The Q Directory. London: Aquariana, 1978–79. Rev. ed. London: Pallas Aquariana, 1980–81.

Quebedeaux, Richard. *The New Charismatics: The Origins, Development and Significance of Neo-Pentecostalism.* Garden City, N.Y.: Doubleday, 1976.

Quigley, Joan. *What Does Joan Say? My Seven Years as White House Astrologer to Nancy and Ronald Reagan.* New York: Birch Lane Press, 1990.

Quinan, Clarence., "The American Medicine-man and the Asiatic Shaman: A Comparison," *Annals of Medical History* vol. 10 (1938): 508–533.

Quimby, Phineas P. *The Complete Writings.* Edited by Ervin Seale. 3 vols. Marina del Rey, Calif.: DeVorss, 1987.

———. *The Quimby Manuscripts.* Edited by Horatio Dresser. New York: Thomas Y. Crowell, 1919. Reprint, New York: Julian Press, 1961.

Qvarnstrom, S. Birger. *Parapskologi Resultat och Perspecktiv* (Parapsychology—Results and Perspectives). N.p., 1959.

Ra Un Nefer Amen [R. A. Straughn]. *Black Man's Guide to a Spiritual Union.* Bronx, N.Y.: Oracle of Thoth, 1981.

———. *Meditation Techniques of the Kabalists, Vedantins, and Taoists.* Bronx, N.Y.: Maat Publishing, 1976.

———. *The Oracle of Thoth: The Kabalistical Tarot.* Bronx, N.Y.: Oracle of Thoth, 1977.

———. *The Realization of Neter Nu.* Brooklyn, N.Y.: Maat Publishing, 1975.

Rabinowitz, H. *A Guide to Hassidism.* New York: Thomas Yoseloff, 1960.

Radha, Swami Sivananda. *Gods Who Walk the Rainbow.* Porthill, Idaho: Timeless Books, 1981.

———. *Hatha Yoga, Hidden Language.* Porthill, Idaho: Timeless Books, 1987.

———. *Kundalini Yoga for the West.* Spokane, Wash.: Timeless Books, 1978.

———. *Mantras, Words of Power.* Porthill, Idaho: Timeless Books, 1980.

———. *Radha, Diary of a Woman's Search.* Porthill, Idaho: Timeless Books, 1981.

Radhakrishnan, S., trans. *Bhagavad Gita.* London: Allen & Unwin, 1948.

Radhasoami Satsang Beas and its Teachings. Beas, India: Radha Soami Satsang, n.d.

Radin, D. I. "On Complexity and Pragmatism," *Journal of Scientific Exploration* 8, no. 4 (1994): 523–534.

———. "Searching for "Signatures" in Anomalous Human-Machine Interaction Research: A Neural Network Approach. *Journal of Scientific Exploration* vol. 3 (1989): 185–200.

Radin, D. I. & Nelson, R. D., "Evidence for Consciousness-Related Anomalies in Random Physical Systems," *Foundations of Physics* 19 (1989): 1499–1514.

Radionic Therapy (leaflet). Oxford, England: Delawarr Laboratories, 1953.

Rael [Claude Vorilhon]. *Sensual Meditation.* Tokyo: AOM Corporation, 1986.

———. *Space Aliens Took Me to Their Planet.* Liechtenstein: Foundation pour l'Accueil des Elohim, 1978.

———. *Welcome Our Fathers from Space: They Created Humanity in Their Laboratories.* Tokyo: AOM, 1986.

Raffé, W. G. *Art and Labour.* N.p., 1927.

———. *The Control of the Mind.* N.p., 1934.

———. *Graphic Design.* London, Chapman and Hall, Ltd., 1927.

———. *Poems in Black & White.* N.p., 1922.

Rahn, Otto. *Invisible Radiations of Organisms.* Berlin, 1936.

Raine, Kathleen. *From Blake to "A Vision."* Dublin: Dolman Press, 1979.

———. *William Blake.* Westport, Conn.: Praeger, 1971.

Rajneesh: The Most Dangerous Man Since Jesus Christ. Zürich, Switzerland: Rebel Publishing House, 1983.

Rajneesh, Bhagwan Shree. *The Great Challenge: A Rajneesh Reader.* New York: Grove Press, 1982.

———. *I Am the Gate.* New York: Harper & Row, 1977.

———. *The Orange Book.* Rajneeshpuram, Ore.: Rajneesh Foundation, 1983.

———. *Tantra, Spirituality, and Sex.* San Francisco, Calif.: Rainbow Bridge, 1977.

Raknes, Ola. *Wilhelm Reich and Orgonomy.* New York: St. Martin's Press, 1970.

Rakoczi, Basil Ivan. *Foreseeing the Future.* New York: Harper & Row, 1973.

Ralston, W. R. S. *Russian Folk Tales.* London: Smith, Elder, 1873. Reprint, New York: Ayer Publishing Co. Inc., 1977.

———. *The Songs of the Russian People.* London, 1872. Reprint, New York: Haskell House, 1970.

Ram Dass, Baba [Richard Alpert]. *Be Here Now.* Christobal, N.Mex.: Lama Foundation, 1972.

———. *Grist for the Mill.* Santa Cruz, Calif.: Unity Press, 1977.

———. *Journey to Awakening.* New York: Bantam Books, 1976.

———. *The Only Dance There Is.* New York: Aronson, 1976.

Rama Prasad. *The Science of Breath and the Philosophy of Tattvas . . . Nature's Finer Forces.* 3rd rev. ed., Adhyr, Madras, India: Theosophical Publishing Society, 1897.

Rama [Frederic Lenz]. *The Wheel of Dharma.* Malibu, Calif.: Lakshmi Publications, 1982.

Rama, Swami. *Lectures on Yoga.* Arlington Heights, Ill.: Himalayan International Institute of Yoga Science and Philosophy, 1972.

———. *Living with the Himalayan Masters: Spiritual Experiences of Swami Rama.* Edited by Swami Ajaya [Allan Weinstein]. Honesdale, Pa.: Himalayan Institute, 1978.

Rama, Swami. *Path of Fire and Light.* Honesdale, Pa.: Himalayan International Institute of Yoga Science and Philosophy, 1986.

———. *A Practical Guide to Holistic Health.* Honesdale, Pa.: Himalayan International Institute of Yoga Science and Philosophy, 1978.

Rama, Swami, Rudolph, and Swami Ajaya. *Yoga and Psychotherapy.* Glenview, Ill.: Himalayan Institute, 1976.

Ramacharacka, Swami [William Walker Atkinson]. *Advanced Course in Yogi Philosophy and Oriental Occultism.* Chicago: Yogi Publication Society, 1904.

———. *Hatha Yoga.* Chicago: Yogi Publication Society, 1932.

———. *The Hindu-Yogi System of Breath.* Chicago: Yogi Publication Society, 1904.

———. *Raja Yoga, or Mental Development.* Chicago: Yogi Publication, 1905.

———. *The Spirit of the Upanishads; or, The Aphorisms of the Wise.* Chicago: Yogi Publication Society, 1936.

Ramakrishna, Sri. *The Gospel of Ramakrishna.* Boston: Beacon Press, 1947.

Raman, B. V. *Astrology and Modern Thought.* 5th ed. Bangalore, India: Raman Publications, 1965.

———. *Hindu Predictive Astrology.* Bangalore: Raman Publications, 1938.

———. *A Manual of Hindu Astrology.* Bangalore: Raman Publications, 1935.

———. *Notable Horoscopes.* Bangalore: Raman Publications, 1956.

Ramana Maharshi. *The Collected Works of Ramana Maharshi.* 20 vols. London: Rider, 1970.

———. *Talks with Sri Ramana Maharshi.* Vol. 1. Tiruvannamalai, India: Sri Ramanasramam, 1957.

Ramge, Sebastian. *An Introduction to the Writings of St. Teresa.* Chicago: Henry Regnery, 1963.

Rampa, T. Lopsang [Cyril Henry Hoskins]. *As It Was!* N.p., 1976.

———. *Beyond the Tenth.* N.p., 1969.

———. *Candlelight.* N.p., 1974.

———. *Cave of the Ancients.* N.p., 1963.

———. *The Hermit.* N.p., 1971.

———. *Living With the Lama.* N.p., 1964.

———.. *My Visit to Venus.* N.p., 1966.

———. *The Rampa Story.* London: Souvenir Press, 1960.

———. *The Saffron Robe.* N.p., 1964.

———. *The Thirteenth Candle.* N.p., 1972.

———. *Wisdom of the Ancients.* N.p., 1965.

———. *You—Forever.* N.p., 1965.

Ramtha (The White Book). Edited by Steven Lee Weinberg, with Randall Weischedel, Sue Ann Fazio, and Carol Wright. Eastsound, Wash.: Sovereignty, 1986.

Ramtha (as channeled by JZ Knight). *The Ancient Schools of Wisdom.* Transcribed by Diane Munoz. Yelm, Wash.: Diane Munoz, 1992.

Ramtha (as channeled by JZ Knight). *I Am Ramtha.* Edited by Cindy Black, Richard Cohn, Greg Simmons, and Wes Walt. Portland, Ore.: Beyond Words Publishing, 1986.

Ramtha's School of Enlightenment: The American Gnostic School. Yelm, Wash.: JZK, 1994.

Ranaghan, Kevin, and Dorothy Ranaghan. *Catholic Pentecostals.* New York: Paulist Press, 1969.

Randall, Edward Caleb. *The Dead Have Never Died.* New York: A. A. Knopf, 1917. London, 1918.

———. *Frontiers of the After Life.* New York: A. A. Knopf, 1922.

———. *Future of Man.* Buffalo, N.Y.: O. Ulbrich, 1908.

———. *Life's Progression.* Buffalo, N.Y.: H. B. Brown, 1906.

———. *The Living Dead.* N.p., 1927.

———. *Told In The After Life.* N.p., 1925.

Randall, John L. "Biological Aspects of Psi." In John Beloff, ed. *New Directions in Parapsychology.* London, 1974; Metuchen, N.J.: Scarecrow Press, 1975.

———. "A New Science of Life: The Hypothesis of Formative Causation." *Journal of the Society for Psychical Research* 51, 1981.

———. *Parapsychology and the Nature of Life.* New York: Harper & Row, 1975.

———. "Psi Phenomena and Biological Theory." *Journal of the Society for Psychical Research* 46, 1971. Reprint in Rhea A. White's *Surveys in Parapsychology.* N.p., 1976.

———. *Psychokinesis; A Study of Paranormal Forces Through the Ages.* N.p., 1982.

———. *Tests for Extrasensory Perception & Psychokinesis.* N.p., 1980.

Randall, Tom M. "Belief in the Paranormal Declines: 1977–1987," *Psychological Reports* 66, no. 3, Pt. 2 (June 1990): 1347–1351.

Randi, James. *The Faith Healers.* Buffalo, N.Y.: Prometheus Books, 1987.

———. *Flim-Flam! Psychics, ESP, Unicorns & Other Delusions.* Buffalo, N.Y.: Prometheus Books, 1982.

———. *The Magic of Uri Geller.* New York: Ballantine Books, 1975. Reprinted as *The Truth About Uri Geller.* Buffalo, N.Y.: Prometheus Books, 1982.

———. *The Mask of Nostradamus.* Buffalo, N.Y.: Prometheus Books, 1993.

———. "Project Alpha Experiment." In Kenneth Frazier, ed. *Science Confronts the Paranormal.* Buffalo, N.Y.: Prometheus Books, 1986.

———. *The Truth about Uri Geller.* Buffalo, N.Y.: Prometheus Books, 1982.

Randles, Jenny. *Abduction: Over 200 Documented UFO Kidnappings Investigated.* London: Robert Hale, 1988.

———. *The UFO Conspiracy: The First Forty Years.* Poole, England: Blandford Press, 1987.

———. *UFO Reality: A Critical Look at the Physical Evidence.* London: Robert Hale, 1983.

Randles, Jenny and Peter Hough. *The Complete Book of UFOs.* New York: Sterling Publishing Co. Inc., 1996.

Randles, Jenny, and Paul Fuller. *Crop Circles: A Mystery Solved.* London: Robert Hale, 1990.

———. *The Controversy of the Circles.* London: British UFO Research Association, 1989.

Randles, Jenny, and Peter Warrington. *UFOs; A British Viewpoint.* N.p., 1979.

Randolph, Paschal Beverly. *After Death: The Disembodiment of Man.* 4th ed. Toledo, Ohio: Randolph Publishing, 1886.

———. *The Davenport Brothers.* Boston, 1869.

———. *Dealings with the Dead.* 1861. Reprinted as *Soul! The Soul World: The Homes of the Dead.* Quakertown, Pa.: Confederation of Initiates, 1932.

———. *Eulis! The History of Love.* Toledo, Ohio: Randolph Publishing, 1874.

———. *Magia Sexualis.* Paris: R. Telin, 1931. Published in English as *Sexual Magic.* Translated by Robert North. New York: Magickal Childe Publishing, 1988.

———. *Pre-Adamic Man.* Reprint, Toledo, Ohio: Randolph Publishing, 1888.

———. *Ravalette, Rosicrucian's Story.* 1863. Reprint, Quakertown, Pa.: Philosophical Publishing, 1939.

———. *The Unveiling; or, What I Think of Spiritualism.* Newburyport, Mass.: The Author, 1860.

Ranfft, Michael. *De Masticatione Mortuorum in Tumulis.* Leipzig, 1728.

Ransom, Champe. "Recent Criticisms of Parapsychology: A Review." *Journal of American Society for Psychical Research* 65 (1971).

Ransom, Josephine. *A Short History of the Theosophical Society.* Adyar, Madra, India: Theosophical Publishing House, 1938.

Rao, B. Suryanarain. *Compendium of Astrology.* Bagalore: Raman Publications, n.d.

———. *Strijataka, or Female Horoscopy.* Bangalore: Raman Publications, 1933.

Rao, K. Ramakrishna. *The Basic Experiments in Parapsychology.* Jefferson, N.C.: McFarland, 1984.

———. "A Consideration of Some Theories in Parapsychology." *Journal of Parapsychology* (March 1961).

———. *Experimental Parapsychology: A Review and Interpretation.* Springfield, Ill.: Charles C. Thomas, 1966.

———. *Gandhi and Pragmatism.* Calcutta & Oxford, N.p., 1968.

———. *J. B. Rhine: On the Frontiers of Science.* Jefferson, N.C.: McFarland, 1982.

———. *Mystic Awareness.* Mysore, India, 1972.

———. *Psi Cognition.* India: Tagore Publishing House, 1957.

———. "Vedanta and the Modus Operandi of Paranormal Cognition." *Philosophical Quarterly* 1955.

Rao, K. Ramakrishna, and J. Palmer. "The Anomaly Called Psi: Recent Research and Criticism," *Behavioral and Brain Sciences* 10 (1987): 539–551.

Rao, K. Ramakrishna, and K. S. Murty. *Current Trends in Indian Thought.* New Delhi, 1972.

Rao, K. Ramakrishna, and P. Sailaja. *Experimental Studies of the Differential Effect in Life Setting.* N.p., 1972.

Raphaell, Katrina. *Crystal Enlightenment: The Transforming Properties of Crystals and Healing Stones.* Sante Fe, N.Mex.: Aurora Press, 1985.

———. *Crystal Healing: The Therapeutic Application of Crystals and Stones.* Santa Fe, N.Mex.: Aurora Press, 1987.

Rappoport, Angelo S. *Superstitions of Sailors.* London: Stanley Paul, 1928. Reprint, Ann Arbor, Mich.: Gryphon Books, 1971.

Raskin, Paula B. "Kevin Ryerson." *Pychic Guide* 4, no. 4 (March–April 1986): 16–21.

Rasmussen, Susan J., "Spirit Possession and Personhood Among the Kel Ewey Tuareg," *Cambridge Studies in Social and Cultural Anthropology* vol. 94 (New York: Cambridge University Press, 1995).

Rasputina, Maria. *My Father.* London: McClelland/Cassell, 1934. Reprint, New Hyde Park, N.Y.: University Books, 1970.

Ratcliff, A. J. J. *A History of Dreams.* London, 1913.

Rätsch, Christian, ed. *Chactun. Die Götter der Maya. Quellentexte, Darstellung und Wörterbuch [Chactun. The Gods of the Maya. Original Texts, Commentaries and Word Book].* 2nd edition. München: Eugen Diederichs Verlag, 1994.

———. *Gateway to Inner Space: A Festschrift in Honor of Albert Hofmann. [Sacred Plants, Mysticism, and Psychotherapy]* Bridport, Dorset: Prism Press/ Garden City Park, N.Y.: Avery Publishing Group, 1989.

———. *Indianische Heilkräuter. Tradition und Anwendung. Ein Pflanzenlexikon [Indian Sacred Plants. Tradition and Use. A Plant Dictionary].* München: Eugen Diederichs Verlag, 1996.

Rätsch, Christian, and K'ayum Ma'ax, eds. *Ein Kosmos im Regenwald. Mythen und Visionen der Lakadonen-Indianer [A Cosmos in the Rainforest. Myths and Visions of the Lacandon Indians].* 2nd edition. München: Eugen Diederichs Verlag, 1994

Ratte, Rena J. "Three Exploratory Studies of ESP in a Game Situation." *Journal of Parapsychology* 25 (1961).

Ratte, Rena J., and Frances M. Greene. "An Exploratory Investigation of PK in a Game Situation." *Journal of Parapsychology* (1960).

Rauchlen, Johannes. *On the Art of the Kabbalah.* Translated by Martin Goodman and Sarah Goodman. New York: Abaris Books, 1983.

Raudive, Konstantin. *Sprechfunk mit Vesterbenen.* Freiburg I Br., Germany: Herman Bauer, 1967. Translated as *Breakthrough: An Amazing Experiment in Electronic Communication with the Dead.* Gerrards Cross, UK: Colin Smythe; New York: Japlinger, 1971. Reprint, New York: Lancer Books, 1973.

———. *Unhörbares Wird Hörbar* (The Inaudible Made Audible). N.p., 1968. English edition as *Breakthrough: An Amazing Experiment in Electronic Communication with the Dead.* Translated by Peter Bander. New York: Taplinger, 1971.

Rauscher, William V. *The Spiritual Frontier.* Garden City, N.Y.: Doubleday, 1975.

Ravenscroft, Trevor. *The Spear of Destiny.* London: Spearman, 1972. Reprint, New York: Putnam, 1973.

Rawcliffe, D. N. *Illusions and Delusions of the Supernatural and Occult.* Rev. ed. New York: Dover Publications, 1959.

Rawson, Philip. *Tantra: The Indian Cult of Ecstasy.* London: Thames & Hudson, 1974.

Ray, Barbara Weber. *The Reiki Factor.* St. Petersburg, Fla.: Radiance Associates, 1983. Radiance Associates, 1989.

Ray, Barbara Weber, and Nonnie Green, eds. *The Official Reiki Handbook.* Atlanta, Ga.: The American-International Reiki Association, 1982.

"Ray Palmer Dies." *Fate* 30, no. 12 (December 1977): 53.

Rayleigh, Lord. "Presidential Address." *Proceedings of the Society for Psychical Research* 30, 70 (1918–1919).

Read, J. *Prelude to Chemistry.* London, 1936. Reprint, Cambridge, Mass.: MIT Press, 1957.

Reagan, Nancy. *My Turn: The Memoirs of Nancy Reagan.* New York: Random House, 1989.

Reban, John. *Inquest on Jesus Christ.* London: Leslie Frewin, 1967.

Recinos, Adri àn, Delia Goetz, and Sylvanus G. Morley, trans. and eds. *Popul Vuh: The Sacred Book of the Ancient Quiché Maya.* London: William Hodge, 1951.

Redgrove, H. Stanley. *Alchemy: Ancient and Modern.* London: Rider, 1922. Reprint, New Hyde Park, N.Y.: University Books, 1969.

———. *Bygone Beliefs: Being a Series of Excursions in the Byways of Thought.* London: Rider, 1920. Reprinted as *Magic & Mysticism: Studies in Bygone Beliefs.* New Hyde Park, N.Y.: University Books, 1971.

———. *A Mathematical Theory of Spirit.* London: Rider, 1912.

Redgrove, H. Stanley, and I. M. L. Redgrove. *Joseph Glanvill and Psychical Research in the Seventeenth Century.* London: William Rider & Son, 1921.

Reece, Richard. *A Correct Statement of the Circumstances that Attended the Last Illness and Death of Mrs. Southcott.* London, 1815.

Reed, Donald. *The Vampire on the Screen.* Inglewood, Calif.: Wagon & Star Publishers, 1965.

Reed, Graham. *The Psychology of Anomalous Experience.* Boston: Houghton Mifflin, 1974.

Reed, Henry. *Edgar Cayce on Channeling Your Higher Self.* New York: Warner Books, Inc., 1999.

Reed, T. J. *Goethe.* Oxford: Oxford University Press, 1984.

Reeve, Bryant, and Helen Reeve. *Flying Saucer Pilgrimage.* Amherst, Wisc.: Amherst Press, 1957.

Regan, Donald. *For the Record.* San Diego: Harcourt Brace Jovanovich, 1988.

Regardie, Israel. *The Art and Meaning of Magic.* Dallas, Tex.: Sangreal Foundation, 1964.

———. *Enochian Dictionary.* Dallas, Tex.: Sangreal Foundation, 1971.

———. *The Eye in the Triangle.* St. Paul, Minn.: Llewellyn Publications, 1970.

———. *A Garden of Pomegranates.* London: Rider, 1936. Reprint, St. Paul, Minn.: Llewellyn Publications, 1970. 3rd ed., Revised, St. Paul, Minn.: Llewellyn Publications, 1999.

———. *The Golden Dawn.* 4 vols. Chicago: Aries Press, 1937–40. Revised ed., St. Paul, Minn: Llewellyn Publications, 1969. Reprint, St. Paul, Minn.: Llewellyn Publications, 1986.

———. *How to Make and Use Talismans.* London: Aquarian Press; New York: Samuel Weiser, 1972.

———. *Middle Pillar.* Chicago: Aries Press, 1938. Rev. ed. St. Paul, Minn.: Llewellyn Publications, 1971.

———. *My Rosicrucian Adventure.* Chicago: Aries Press, 1936. Reprint, St. Paul, Minn.: Llewellyn Publications, 1971.

———. *The Philosopher's Stone.* St. Paul, Minn.: Llewellyn Publications, 1958.

———. *What You Should Know about the Golden Dawn.* Glendale, Ariz.: New Falcon Publications, 1993.

Reginald, Robert. *Science Fiction and Fantasy Literature, 1975–1991.* Detroit: Gale Research, 1992.

Réginald-Omez, Fr. O. P. *Psychical Phenomena.* London: Burns & Oates, 1959.

Reich, Ilse Ollendorff. *Wilhelm Reich: a Personal Biography.* New York: St. Martin's Press, 1969.

Reich, Peter. *A Book of Dreams.* New York: Harper & Row, 1973.

Reich, Wilhelm. *Character Analysis.* New York: Orgone Institute Press, 1949. Reprint, New York: Farrar, Straus & Giroux, 1961.

———. *The Discovery of the Orgone.* 2 vols. New York: Orgone Institute Press, n.d.

———. *The Discovery of the Orgone.* Vol. 1. In *The Function of the Orgasm; Sex-economic Problems of Biological Energy.* New York: Orgone Institute Press, 1942.

———. *The Discovery of the Orgone.* Vol. 2. In *The Cancer Biopathy.* New York: Orgone Institute Press, 1948.

———. *The Function of the Orgasm: Sex-Economic Problems of Biological Energy.* New York: Orgone Institute Press, 1942. Reprint, New York: Farra, Straus and Giroux, 1973.

———. *The Mass Psychology of Fascism.* New York: Orgone Institute Press, 1946.

———. *The Orgone Energy Accumulator.* New York: Orgone Institute Press, n.d.

———. *Selected Writings: An Introduction to Orgonomy.* New York: Farrar, Straus, and Giroux, 1973.

Reichel-Dolmatoff, Gérardo. *Amazonian Cosmos: The Sexual and Religious Symbolism of the Tukano Indians.* Chicago: University of Chicago Press, 1971.

———. *The Shaman and the Jaguar: A Study of Narcotic Drugs among the Indians of Colombia.* Philadelphia: Temple University Press, 1975.

———. *Yurupari: Studies of an Amazonian Foundation Myth.* Cambridge, Mass.: Harvard University Center for the Study of World Religions, 1995.

Reichel, Willie. *Occult Experiences.* N.p., 1906.

Reichenbach, Bruce R. *The Law of Karma: A Philosophical Study.* London: Macmillan, 1990.

Reichenbach, Karl von. *Aphorismen Über Sensitivität und Od.* French ed. as *Le Fluide des Magnétiseurs.* Edited by Albert De Rochas. N.p., 1891.

———. *Der sensitive Mensch und sein Verhalten zum Ode* (The sensitive man and his relation to od). 2 vols. Stuttgart and Tübingen, 1854–55.

———. *L'Exteriorisation de la motricité.* N.p., 1896.

———. *L'Exteriorisation de la Sensibilité.* N.p., 1895.

———. *Les états profonds de l'hypnose.* N.p., 1892.

———. *Les états Superficiels de l'hypnose.* N.p., 1898.

———. *Les effleuves odique; L'envoutement; Les frontières de la science.* N.p., 1902.

———. *Letters on Od and Magnetism.* Translated by F. D. O'Byrne. London: Hutchinson, 1926. Reprinted as *The Odic Force; Letters on Od and Magnetism.* New Hyde Park, N.Y.: University Books, 1968.

———. *Physico-Physiological Researches on the Dynamics of Magnetism, Electricity, Heat, Light, Crystallization, and Chemism, in their Relations to Vital Force.* Translated by H. John Ashburner. London: H. Baillière, 1851.

———. *Researches on Magnetism, Electricity, Heat, Light, Crystallization, and Chemical Attraction in their Relations to the Vital Force.* Translated by William Gregory. London, 1850. Reprint, New Hyde Park, N.Y.: University Books, 1974.

Reid, Lori. *Elements of Handreading.* UK: Element Books Inc., 1997.

Reifler, Sam. *I Ching: A New Interpretation for Modern Times.* New York: Bantam, 1974.

Reinert, Duane F. and Kenneth R. Stifler. "Hood's Mysticism Scale Revisited: A Factor-Analytic Replication," *Journal for the Scientific Study of Religion* 32, no. 4 (December 1993): 383–388.

Reinhard, Aime. *Justinus Kerner und das Kernerhaus zu Weinsberg.* Tübingen, Germany, 1862.

Reiser, Oliver L. *This Holyest Erthe: The Glastonbury Zodiac and King Arthur's Camelot.* Bedford, England: Perennial Books, 1976.

Reiss, Edmund, Louise Horner Reiss, and Beverly Taylor. *Arthurian Legend and Literature: An Annotated Bibliography.* New York: Garland Publishing, 1984.

Reiterman, Tom. *Raven.* New York: E. P. Dutton, 1982.

Rejdak, Z. "Nina Kulagina's Mind Over Matter." *Psychic* 2, no. 4 (June 1971).

Rele, Vasant G. *The Mysterious Kundalini: The Physical Basis of the "Kundalini (Hatha) Yoga" in Terms of Western Anatomy and Physiology.* Rev. ed. Bombay, India: D. B. Taraporevala, 1950.

Remarkable Sermons of Rachel Baker and Pious Ejaculations Delivered During Sleep Taken Down in Shorthand. London, 1815.

Remy, Nicolas. *Demonolatry.* 1595. Reprint, New Hyde Park, N.Y.: University Books, 1974.

Renfrew, Sita Paulickpulle. *A Buddhist Guide for Laymen.* Cambridge, Mass.: Cambridge Buddhist Association, 1963.

"Report of the Census of Hallucinations." *Proceedings of the Society for Psychical Research* 10 (1894): 25.

Report on Spiritualism of the Committee of the London Dialectical Society. London: Longmans, Green, Reader, & Dyer, 1871. Reprint, New York: Ayer Publishing Co. Inc., 1976.

Research in Parapsychology. N.p., 1993. Reprint, Lanham, Md.: Scarecrow Press, Inc., 1998.

Reuter, Florizel von. *A Musician's Talks with Unseen Friends.* London: Rider, 1931.

Rex Nemorensis [Charles Cardell]. *Witch.* London: Privately published, 1964.

Reynolds, Aidan, and William Charlton. *Arthur Machen: A Short Account of His Life and Work.* London, 1963.

Rhine, J. B. *Extra-sensory Perception.* Boston: Boston Society for Psychical Research, 1934. Rev. ed. Boston: Branden, 1964.

———. "History of Experimental Studies." In *Handbook of Parapsychology,* edited by B. Wolman. New York: Van Nostrand Rhinhold, 1977.

———. "An Investigation of a 'Mind-Reading' Horse." *Journal of Abnormal and Social Psychology* 23 (1929).

———. *New Frontiers of the Mind.* New York: Farrar and Rinehart, 1939.

———. *New World of the Mind.* New York: William Sloane Associates, 1953.

———. *The Reach of the Mind.* New York: William Sloane Associates, 1947.

Rhine, J. B. and Associates. *Parapsychology from Duke to FRNM.* Durham, N.C.: Parapsychology Press, 1965.

Rhine, J. B., and J. G. Pratt. *Parapsychology, Frontier Science of the Mind.* N.p., 1957.

Rhine, J. B., and R. Brier. *Parapsychology Today.* New York: Citadel Press, 1968.

Rhine, J. B., J. G. Pratt, Charles E. Stuart, Burke M. Smith, and Joseph A. Greenwood. *Extrasensory Perception After Sixty Years; a Critical Evaluation.* New York: Henry Holt, 1940. Reprint, Boston: Bruce Humphries, 1960. Reprint, Boston: Branden, 1966.

Rhine, J. B., ed. *Progress in Parapsychology.* Durham, N.C.: Parapsychology Press, 1971.

Rhine, Louisa E. *ESP in Life and Lab: Tracing Hidden Channels.* New York: Macmillan, 1967.

———. *Hidden Channels of the Mind.* New York: William Sloane, 1961. London, 1962. Reprint, New York: Apollo, 1966. Reprint, Alexandria, Va.: Time-Life, Inc., 1990.

———. *The Invisible Picture.* Jefferson, N.C.: McFarland, 1981.

———. *Mind Over Matter: Psychokinesis.* New York: Macmillan, 1970. Reprint, New York: Collier, 1972.

———. *Psi: What Is It?* New York: Harper & Row, 1975.

———. *Something Hidden.* Jefferson, N.C.: McFarland, 1983.

Rhinehart, Keith Milton. *Soul Mates and Twin Rays.* Seattle, Wash.: Aquarian Foundation, 1972.

Rhodes, H. T. F. *The Satanic Mass.* London, 1954. Reprint, London: Arrow, 1964.

———. *The Satanic Mass.* New York: Citadel, 1955. Reprint, London, 1973.

Rhys, John. *Celtic Britain.* London, 1882.

Rhys, Sir John. *Studies in the Arthurian Legend.* Oxford: Clarendon Press, 1891.

Riccardo, Martin V. *The Lure of the Vampire.* Chicago Adams Press, 1983.

———. *Vampires Unearthed.* New York: Garland, 1983.

Rice, Edward. *John Frum He Come.* Garden City, N.Y.: Doubleday, 1974.

Richards, John Thomas. *SORRAT: A History of the Neihardt Psychokinesis Experiments, 1961–1981.* Metuchen, N.J.: Scarecrow Press, 1982.

Richards, M. C. *Toward Wholeness: Rudolf Steiner Education in America.* Middletown, Conn.: Wesleyan University Press, 1980.

"Richard's Garden Revisited." *Journal of the Society for Psychical Research* 41, 712 (June 1962).

Richardson, Alan. *Priestess: The Life and Magic of Dion Fortune.* Wellingborough, England: Aquarian Press, 1987.

Richardson, J. E. *Great Known (1928).* Kila, Mont.: Kessinger Publishing Co., 1999.

———. *The Great Message.* Great School of Natural Science, 1950.

———. *The Great Work.* Chicago: Indo-American, 1907.

———. *Who Answers Prayer?* Great School of Natural Science, 1954.

Richardson, James T., Joel Best, and David G. Bromley. *The Satanism Scare.* New York: Aldine de Gruyter, 1991.

Richardson, Katherine W. *Salem Witchcraft Trials.* Salem, Mass.: Peabody Essex Museum, 1997.

Richeport, Madeleine M. "The Interface Between Multiple Personality, Spirit Mediumship, and Hypnosis." *American Journal of Clinical Hypnosis* 34, no. 3 (January 1992): 168–177.

Richet, Charles. *Thirty Years of Psychical Research.* New York: Macmillan, 1923. Reprint, New York: Ayer Publishing Co. Inc., 1975.

———. *Notre Sixième Sens.* N.p., 1927. English ed. as *Our Sixth Sense.* N.p., 1929.

———. *Traité de Métapsychique.* N.p., 1922. English edition as *Thirty Years of Psychical Research: Being a Treatise on Metaphysics.* New York: Macmillan; London: W. Collins Sons, 1923. Reprint, New York: Ayer Publishing Co. Inc., 1975.

Richmond, A. B. *What I Saw at Cassadaga Lake; A Review of the Seybert Commissioners' Report.* N.p., 1888.

Richmond, Cora L. V. *Discourses Through the Mediumship of Mrs. Cora L. V. Tappan.* Boston: Colby & Rich, 1876. Reprint, London, N.p., 1878.

———. *My Experiments While out of the Body and My Return after Many Days.* Boston: Christopher Press, 1915.

———. *Psychosophy.* Chicago: The Author, 1888. Reprint, Chicago: Regan Printing House, 1915.

———. *The Soul in Human Embodiment.* Chicago: Spiritualist Publishing, 1887.

Richmond, Kenneth F. *Evidence of Identity.* London: G. Bell, 1939.

———. "Preliminary Studies of the Recorded Leonard Material." *Proceedings of the Society for Psychical Research* (1936).

Richmond, Zoe. *Evidence of Purpose.* N.p., 1938.

Rickard, Robert J. M., and Richard Kelly. *Photographs of the Unknown.* London: Book Club Associates, 1980.

Ridge, Martin. *Ignatius Donnelly: The Portrait of a Politician.* Chicago: University of Chicago Press, 1962.

Rinaldi, Peter M. *The Man in the Shroud.* New York: Vantage Press, 1972. Reprint, London: Futura, 1974. Reprinted as *It Is The Lord: A Study of the Shroud of Christ.* New York: Warner, 1973.

Ring, Kenneth. *Heading Toward Omega: In Search of the Meaning of the Near-Death Experience.* New York: William Morrow, 1984.

———. *Life at Death: A Scientific Investigation of the Near-Death Experience.* New York: William Morrow, 1980.

———. *The Omega Project: Near-Death Experiences, UFO Encounters, and Mind at Large.* New York: William Morrow, 1992.

Ringger, Peter. *Das Problem der Besessenheit* (The Problem of Possession). N.p., 1953.

———. *Das Weltbild der Parapsychologie* (The World View of Parapsychology). N.p., 1959.

———. *Parapsychologie: Die Wissenschaft des Okkulten* (Parapsychology: The Science of the Occult). N.p., 1957. Reprint, Zürich; Stuttgart: Werner Classen, 1972.

Ripinsky-Naxon, Michael. "Hallucinogens, Shamanism, and the Cultural Process: Symbolic Archaeology and Dialectics," *Anthropos* 84 (1989): 219–224.

———. "Psychoactivity and Shamanic States of Consciousness," *Yearbook for Ethnomedicine and the Study of Consciousness (Jahrbuch für Ethnomedizin und Bewusstseinsforschung)* vol. 4 (1995): 35–43.

———. "Cognition, Symbolization, and the Beginnings of Shamanism," *Journal of Prehistoric Religion* vol. 9 (1995): 43–54.

———. "Evolution, Cognition, and the Origins of Shamanism." In *Welten des Bewusstseins [Worlds of Consciousness].* Edited by Christian Scharfetter and Christian Rätsch. vol. 9, Berlin: VWB-Verlag für Wissenschaft und Bildung, 1998.

———. "Maya Cosmovision and Shamanistic Symbolism," *Journal of Prehistoric Religion* vol. 7 (1993): 49–61.

———. "Psychoactivity and Shamanic States of Consciousness," *Yearbook for Ethnomedicine and the Study of Consciousness (Jahrbuch für Ethnomedizin und Bewusstseinsforschung)* vol. 4 (1995): 35–43.

———. *Shamanism in Siberia and Central Asia,* review of *Shamanism: Soviet Studies of Traditional Religion in Siberia and Central Asia,* by Marjorie M. Balzer, ed., *Anthropology of Consciousness* 4 (1993): 15–16.

———. "Shamanism: Religion or Rite?" *Journal of Prehistoric Religion* vol. 6 (1992): 37–44.

———. "Shamanistic Knowledge and Cosmology." In *Tribal Epistemologies.* Edited by Helmut Wautischer. Aldershot: Avebury/Ashgate Publishing, 1998.

———. *The Nature of Shamanism: Substance and Function of a Religious Metaphor.* Albany: State University of New York Press, 1993.

Ripley Revived, or an Exposition upon George Ripley's Hermetico-Poetical Works. London, 1978.

Ripley, George. *The Compound of Alchemie.* N.p., 1591.

———. *Medulla Alchimioe.* N.p., n.d.

———. *The Treatise of Mercury.* N.p., n.d.

Rist, J. M. *Plotinus: The Road to Reality.* Cambridge, Mass.: Cambridge University Press, 1967.

Ritley, Mary. *Invitation to a Hungry Feast.* Santa Monica, Calif.: The Prosperos Inner Space Center, 1970.

Ritson, Joseph. *Fairy Tales, Now First Collected: To Which Are Prefixed Two Dissertations: 1. On Pygmies; 2. On Fairies.* London, 1831.

Rittelmeyer, Friedrich. *Rudolf Steiner Enters My Life.* London: George Roberts, 1929.

Roach, William, ed. *The Didot Perceval.* Philadelphia: University of Pennsylvania Press, 1941.

Roach, Marilynne K. *In the Days of the Salem Witchcraft Trials.* New York: Ticknor & Fields, 1996.

Robinson, Lyle W. *Edgar Cayce's Story of the Origin & Destiny of Man.* New York: Berkley Publishing Group, 1985.

Robbins, Anne Manning. *Both Sides of the Veil: A Personal Experience.* Boston: Sherman & French, 1909.

Robbins, Rossell Hope. *The Encyclopedia of Witchcraft and Demonology.* New York: Crown Publilshers, 1959.

Roberts, C. E. Bechhofer, ed. *The Trial of Mrs. Duncan.* London, 1945.

Roberts, Estelle. *Fifty Years a Medium.* London, 1959. Reprint, New York: Avon, 1972. Reprint, London: Corgi, 1975.

———. *Forty Years a Medium.* London: Herbert Jenkins, 1959. Revised as *Fifty Years a Medium.* London: Corgi Books, 1969.

Roberts, Henry C. *The Complete Prophecies of Nostradamus.* New York, 1947.

Roberts, Jane. *Adventures in Consciousness: An Introduction to Aspect Psychology.* Englewood Cliffs, N.J.: Prentice-Hall, 1975.

———. *Dreams, "Evolution," and Value Fulfillment; A Seth Book.* 2 vols. Englewood Cliffs, N.J.: Prentice-Hall, 1986.

———. *The God of Jane: A Psychic Manifesto.* Englewood Cliffs, N.J.: Prentice-Hall, 1981.

———. *How to Develop Your ESP Power.* New York: Frederick Fell, 1966. Reprinted as *The Coming of Seth.* New York: Pocket Books, 1976.

———. *Seth Speaks:The Eternal Validity of the Soul.* Englewood Cliffs, N.J.: Prentice Hall, 1972.

———. *Seth, Dreams and Projection of Consciousness.* Walpole: N. H., Stillpoint Publishing, 1986.

———. *The Nature of Personal Reality: A Seth Book.* Englewood Cliffs, N.J.: Prentice-Hall, 1974.

———. *The Seth Material.* Englewood Cliffs, N.J.: Prentice-Hall, 1970.

Roberts, Kenneth. *Henry Gross and His Dowsing Rod.* Garden City, N.Y.: Doubleday, 1952.

Roberts, Marie. *British Poets and Secret Societies.* Totowa, N.J.: Barnes & Noble, 1986.

Roberts, Oral. *My Story.* Tulsa, Okla.: Oral Roberts Evangelistic Association, 1961.

Roberts, Thomas B. and Robert N. Jesse. "Recollections of the Good Friday Experiment: An Interview with Huston Smith," *Journal of Transpersonal Psychology* 29, no. 2 (1997): 99–104.

Roberts, Ursula. *The Mystery of the Human Aura.* London: Spiritualist Association of Great Britain, 1972.

Robertson, Olivia. *The Call of Isis.* Enniscorthy, Eire: Cesara Publications, 1975.

———. *The College of Isis Manual.* Enniscorthy, Eire: Cesara Publications, n.d.

———. *Dea: Rites and Mysteries of the Goddess.* Enniscorthy, Eire: Cesara Publications, 1975.

———. *Handbook of the Fellowship of Isis.* Enniscorthy, Eire: Cesara Publications, n.d.

———. *The Isis Wedding Rite.* Enniscorthy, Eire: Cesara Publications, 1975.

———. *Ordination of a Priestess.* Enniscorthy, Eire: Cesara Publications, n.d.

———. *Rite of Rebirth.* Enniscorthy, Eire: Cesara Publications, 1977.

Robertson, Olivia, and Lord Strathloch. *The Fellowship of Isis Directory for 1980.* Enniscorthy, Eire: Cesara Publications, 1979.

Robertson, R. Macdonald. *Selected Highland Folktales.* North Pomfret, Vt.: David and Charles, 1977.

Robertson, Sandy. *The Aleister Crowley Scrapbook.* York Beach, Maine: Samuel Weiser, 1988.

Robinson, Douglas. *American Apocalypses: The Image of the End of the World in American Literature.* Baltimore, Md.: Johns Hopkins University Press, 1985.

Rochas, Albert de. *L'Extériorisation de la Motricité.* Paris, 1906.

Rochas, Eugene. *Les Vies Successives.* N.p., 1911.

Rochas, Eugene A. A. *L'Exteriorisation de la Motricité.* 1896. Reprint, N.p., 1899.

Rochas, Eugene Albert de. *La Science des Philosophes et l'Art des Thaumaturges dans l'Antiquité.* N.p., 1882.

———. *Suspension de la Vie.* N.p., 1913.

———. *Les Forces non définies.* Paris: Masson, 1887.

———. *Les Sentiments, la Musique et le Geste; Les Vies Successives.* N.p., 1911.

———. *Receuil de documents relatifs à la levitation du corps humain.* N.p., 1897.

Rochester Knockings! Discovery and Explanation of the Source of the Phenomena Generally Known as the Rochester Knockings. Buffalo, N.Y., 1851.

Rockwell, Theodore, Robert Rockwell, and W. Teed Rockwell. "Irrational Rationalists: A Critique of the Humanists' Crusade Against Parapsychology." *Journal of the American Society for Psychical Research* 72 (January 1971): 23–34.

Rodegast, Pat, and Judith Stanton. *Emmanuel's Book: A Manual for Living Comfortably in the Cosmos.* New York: Some Friends of Emmanuel, 1985.

Rodway, Howard. *The Psychic Directory: A Comprehensive Guide to Practicing Psychics in the UK* London: Futura/Macdonald, 1984.

Roerich, Helena. *Fiery World.* 2 vols. New York: Agni Yoga Press, 1943.

———. *Hierarchy.* 3d ed. New York: Agni Yoga Press, 1947.

———. *Infinity.* 2 vols. New York: Agni Yoga Press, 1956, 1957.

———. *Leaves of Morya's Garden.* 2 vols. New York: Agni Yoga Press, 1952, 1953.

———. *Letters of Helena Roerich.* New York: Agni Yoga Press, 1954, 1967.

Roerich, Nicholas. *Adamant.* New York: Corona Mundi, 1922.

———. *Flame in Chalice.* New York: Nicholas Roerich Museum, 1929.

———. *Heart of Asia.* New York: Atlas Publishing, 1929.

———. *Realm of Light.* New York: Nicholas Roerich Museum, 1931.

Rofé, Husein. *Path of Subud.* London: Rider & Co., 1959.

Rogers, E. C. *Philosophy of Mysterious Agents, Human and Mundane.* Boston, 1853.

Rogers, Spencer L., "Shaman and Medicineman," *Ciba Symposia* 4, no. 1 (1942): 1202–1224.

———. *The Shaman: His Symbol and His Healing Power.* Springfield, Ill: Charles C. Thomas, 1982.

Rogo, D. Scott.. "ESP in the Ganzfeld: An Exploration of Parameters." In *Research in Parapsychology 1975,* edited by J. D. Morris, W. G. Roll, and R. L. Morris. Metuchen, N.J.: Scarecrow Press, 1976.

———. *An Experience of Phantoms.* New York: Taplinger, 1974.

———. ' "Free Response Ganzfeld Experiments With a Selected Subject." In *Research in Parapsychology 1975,* edited by J. D. Morris, W. G. Roll, and R. L. Morris. Metuchen, N.J.: Scarecrow Press, 1976.

———.*The Haunted Universe.* New York: New American Library, 1977.

———. "In-depth Analysis of the Vampire Legend." *Fate* 21, no. 9 (September 1968): 77.

———. *Leaving the Body: A Complete Guide to Astral Projection.* Englewood Cliffs, N.J.: Prentice-Hall, 1983.

———. *Methods and Models for Education in Parapsychology.* N.p., 1973.

———. *Minds and Motion.* New York: Taplinger, 1978.

———. *Mind Beyond the Body: The Mystery of ESP Projection.* New York: Penguin, 1978.

———. *Miracles: A Parascientific Inquiry Into Wondrous Phenomena.* New York: Dell Press, 1982. Reprinted as *Miracles: A Parascientific Exploration Into Wondrous Phenomena.* Dallas, Tex.: Aquarian Press, 1991.

———. *Nad: A Study of Some Unusual "Other World" Experiences.* 2 vols. New Hyde Park, N.Y.: University Books, 1970, 1972.

———. *Parapsychology: A Century of Inquiry.* New York: Dell, 1975.

———. *The Poltergeist Experience.* New York: Penguin, 1979.

———. *Welcoming Silence.* New Hyde Park, N.Y.: University Books, 1973.

Rogo, D. Scott, and Raymond Bayless. *Phone Calls From the Dead.* Englewood Cliff, N.J.: Prentice-Hall, 1979.

Rohmer, Sax. *The Romance of Sorcery.* London, 1914. Reprint, New York: E. P. Dutton, 1915. Reprint, New York: Causeway, 1973.

Rohr, Philip. *De Masticatione Mortuorum.* N.p., 1679.

Rojcewicz, Peter M. "The Boundaries of Orthodoxy: A Folkloric Look at the UFO Phenomenon." 2 vols. Philadelphia: University of Pennsylvania. Ph.D. dissertation, 1984.

———. "The 'Men in Black' Experience and Tradition: Analogues with the Traditional Devil Hypothesis." *Journal of American Folklore* 100 (April/June 1987): 148–60.

Roll, W. G., R. L. Morris, and J. D. Morris, eds. *Research in Parapsychology 1975.* Metuchen, N.J.: Scarecrow Press, 1976.

———. *Research in Parapsychology 1974.* Metuchen, N.J.: Scarecrow Press, 1975.

———. *Research in Parapsychology 1973.* Metuchen, N.J.: Scarecrow Press, 1974.

———. *Research in Parapsychology 1972.* Metuchen, N.J.: Scarecrow Press, 1973.

Roll, William G. "ESP and Memory." In *Philosophical Dimensions of Parapsychology,* edited by J. M. O. Wheatley and H. L. Edge. Springfield, Ill.: Charles C. Thomas, 1976.

———. *The Poltergeist.* New York: New American Library; Garden City, N.Y.: Doubleday 1972. Reprint: Methuchen, N.J.: Scarecrow Press, 1976.

Rollins, Hyder E., ed. *The Pack of Autolycus or Strange and Terrible News of Ghosts, Apparitions, Monstrous Births, Showers of Wheat, Judgments of God, and other Prodigious and Fearful Happenings as told in Broadside Ballads of the Years 1624–1693.* Cambridge, Mass.: Harvard University Press, 1927.

Romains, Jules [Louis Farigoule]. *Vision Extra-Rétinienne.* 1920. Translated by C. K. Ogden as *Eyeless Sight: A Study of Extra-Retinal Vision and the Paroptic Sense.* New York: G. P. Putnam's Sons, 1924. Reprint, New York: Citadel Press; Secaucus, N. J.: Carol Publishing Group, 1978.

Romanucci-Ross, Lola, Daniel Moerman, and Laurence Tancredi, eds. *The Anthropology of Medicine: From Culture to Method.* South Hadley, Mass.: Bergin & Garvey Publishers, 1983.

Romer, C. *Ausführliche historische Darstellung einer höchst merkwürdigen Somnambule.* Stuttgart, 1821.

Rommel, Kenneth M. *Operation Animal Mutilation.* Report of the District Attorney, First Judicial District, State of New Mexico. Sante Fe, N.Mex.: District Attorney, 1980.

Ronay, Gabriel. *The Dracula Myth.* London: W. H. Auden, 1972; London: Pan 1975.

Roney-Dougal, S. M. and Guenther Vogl. "Some Speculations on the Effect of Geomagnetism on the Pineal Gland," *Journal of the Society for Psychical Research* 59, no. 830 (January 1993): 1–15.

Rosaldo, Renato. *The Ilongot Headhunting 1883–1974: A Study in History and Society.* Stanford, Calif.: Stanford University Press, 1980.

Rose, Donna. *Love Spells.* Hialeah, Fla.: Mi-World Publishing Co., n.d.

Rose, Elliot. *A Razor for a Goat: A Discussion of Certain Problems in the History of Witchcraft and Diabolism.* Toronto: University of Toronto Press, 1989.

Rose, Louis. *Faith Healing.* London: Victor Gollancz, 1968.

Rose, Ronald. "Australia's Medicine Men." *Tomorrow* (spring 1954).

———. "Crisis Telepathy in Australia." *Tomorrow* (winter 1957).

———. "Experiments in ESP and PK with Aboriginal Subjects." *Journal of Parapsychology* (September 1952).

———. *Living Magic: The Realities Underlying the Psychical Practices and Beliefs of Australian Aborigines.* New York: Rand McNally, 1956. Reprint as *Primitive Psychic Power; the Realities Underlying the Psychical Practices and Beliefs of Australian Aborigines.* New York: New American Library, 1968.

———. *South Seas Magic.* London: R. Hale, 1959.

Roseman, Bernard. *The Peyote Story.* North Hollywood, Calif.: Wilshire Book, 1963.

Rosenbohm, Alexandra, "Halluzinogene Drogen im Schamanismus: Mythos und Ritual im Kulturellen Vergleich," *Marburger Studien zur Völkerkunde* vol. 8, Berlin: Dietrich Reimer Verlag, 1991.

Rosenkruz, Sergius. *Rosikrucinism.* Los Angeles: The Author, 1915.

Rosenthal, Franz. *The Herb: Hashish Versus Medieval Muslim Society.* Leiden: E. J. Brill, 1971.

Rosenthal, Robert. *Experimenter Effects in Behavioral Research.* New York: Appleton-Century-Crofts, 1966.

Rosher, Grace. *Beyond the Horizon.* London, 1961.

The Rosicrucian Manual. San Jose, Calif.: Rosicrucian Press, 1952.

Ross, Anne. *Pagan Celtic Britain.* London: Routledge and Kegan Paul, 1967.

Rossbach, Sarah. *Feng Shui: The Chinese Art of Placement.* New York: E. P. Dutton, 1983.

Roth, Phyllis A. *Bram Stoker.* Boston: Twayne, 1982.

Rothschild, Friedrich S. "Biosemiotische Analyse der Verwandschaft zwischen Parapsychologie und Physik" (Biosemiotic Analysis of the Relation Between Parapsychology and Physics), *Dynamische Psychiatrie* 21, no. 1-2 (1988): 96–109.

Row, M. C. Nanjunda. *Cosmic Consciousness, or the Vedantic Idea of Realisation of Muktu in the Light of Modern Psychology.* Madras, India, 1910.

Rowdon, Maurice. *The Talking Dogs.* New York: Macmillan, 1978.

Rowley, Harold H. *Prophecy and Religion in Ancient China and Israel.* New York: Harper, 1956.

Royce, Josiah. "Report of the Committee on Phantasm and Presentiments." *Proceedings of the American Society for Psychical Research* 1, 3 (December 1877); 1, 4 (March 1889).

———. *William James and Other Essays on the Philosophy of Life.* N.p., 1911. Reprint, Freeport, N.Y.: Books for Libraries Press, 1969.

Rubens, Donna, Darina Gyurkovics and Karol Hornacek. "The Cultural Production of Bioterapia: Psychic Healing and the Natural Medicine Movement in Slovakia," *Social Science & Medicine* 41, no. 9 November 1995: 1261–1271.

Rucker, Rudy von Bitter. *The Fourth Dimension: Toward a Geometry of Higher Reality.* Boston: Houghton-Mifflin, 1984.

Rudhyar, Dane. *The Astrological Houses: The Spectrum of Individual Experience.* Garden City, N.Y.: Doubleday, 1972.

———. *The Astrology of Personality: A Reformulation of Astrological Concepts and Ideals, in Terms of Contemporary Psychology and Philosophy.* New York: Lucis Publishing, 1936.

———. *The Astrology of Transformation: A Multilevel Approach.* Wheaton, Ill.: Theosophical Publishing House, 1980.

———. *From Humanistic to Transpersonal Astrology.* Palo Alto, Calif.: Seed Center, 1975.

———. *Occult Preparations for the New Age.* Wheaton, Ill.: Theosophical Publishing House, 1975.

———. *Person-centered Astrology.* Lakemont, Ga.: CSA Press, 1972.

———. *The Planetarization of Consciousness.* New York: Harper, 1972.

———. *Rhythm of Wholeness: A Total Affirmation of Being.* Wheaton, Ill.: Theosophical Publishing House, 1983.

Rudolph, Erwin Paul. *William Law.* Boston: Twayne, 1980.

Rudwin, Maximilian J. *The Devil in Legend and Literature.* LaSalle, Ill.: Open Court Publishing, 1973.

Runyon, Carroll. *The Original Cypher Manuscript of the Golden Dawn.* St. Paul, Minn.: Llewellyn Publications, 1996.

Rush, J. H. "Parapsychology: Some Personal Observations." In *Men and Women of Parapsychology.* Edited by R. Pilkington. Jefferson, N.C.: McFarland, 1987.

———. "Some Considerations as to a Physical Basis of Extrasensory Perception." *Journal of Parapsychology* (1943).

———. "A Reciprocal Distance GESP Test with Drawings." *Journal of Parapsychology* (1949).

Russ, Charles. "An Instrument Which is Set in Motion by Vision." *The Lancet* (July 3, 1931).

Russell, Charles Taze. *Unseen Spirits—Do They Help Us? or, Do They Harm Us?* Brooklyn, N.Y.: Watchtower Bible and Tract Society, 1978.

———. *What Do the Scriptures Say about "Survival of Death?"* Brooklyn, N.Y.: Watchtower Bible and Tract Society, 1955.

———. *What Say the Scriptures about Spiritism?* Brooklyn, N.Y.: Watchtower Bible and Tract Society, 1897.

Russell, Edmund. " 'Mr. Isaacs' of Simla." *Occult Review* (March 1917).

Russell, Eric Frank. *Great World Mysteries.* London, 1957.

Russell, Jeffrey Burton. *The Devil: Perceptions of Evil from Antiquity to Primitive Christianity.* Ithaca, N.Y.: Cornell University Press, 1977.

———. *Lucifer: The Devil in the Middle Ages.* Ithaca, N.Y.: Cornell University Press, 1984.

———. *Satan: The Early Christian Tradition.* Ithaca, N.Y.: Cornell University Press, 1981.

———. *Witchcraft in the Middle Ages.* Ithaca, N.Y.: Cornell University Press, 1972.

Russell, Rick Frank. *The Best of Eric Frank Russell.* Edited by Alan Dean Foster. New York: Del Rey, 1978.

———. *Sinister Barrier.* Reading, Pa.: Fantasy Press, 1948.

Rutherford, Ward. *Shamanism: The Foundations of Magic.* Wellingborough: Aquarian Press, 1986.

Rutter, J. O. N. *Human Electricity: The Means of Its Development.* London: Parker, 1854.

Rutter, Owen. *The Pagans of North Borneo.* London: Hutchinson, 1929.

Ryan, Charles J. *H. P. Blavatsky and the Theosophical Movement.* Pasadena, Calif.: Theosophical University Press, 1975.

Rymer, J. Snaith. "Spirit Manifestations." A lecture presented in London, 1857.

Rynne, Catherine. *Knock 1879–1979.* Dublin: Veritas Publications, 1979.

Ryzl, Milan. "Training the Psi Faculty by Hypnosis." *Journal of the Society for Psychical Research* 41 (1962).

Ryzl, Milan, and J. Bekoff. "Loss of Stability of ESP Performance in a High-Scoring Subject." *Journal of Parapsychology* 29 (1965).

Ryzl, Milan, and J. G. Pratt. "The Focusing of ESP Upon Particular Targets." *Journal of Parapsychology* 27 (1963).

———."A Further Confirmation of Stabilized ESP Performance in a Selected Subject." *Journal of Parapsychology* 27 (1963).

———. "A Repeated-Calling ESP Test with Sealed Cards." *Journal of Parapsychology* 27 (1963).

Ryzl, Milan, and J. T. Barendregt, P. R. Barkema, and Jan Kappers. "An ESP Experiment in Prague." *Journal of Parapsychology* 29 (1965).

Sabin, Katharine C. *ESP and Dream Analysis.* Chicago: Henry Regnery, 1974.

Sabine, William Henry Waldo. *A Prophecy Concerning the Swedish Monarchy.* N.p., 1968.

———. "Is There a Case for Retrocognition?" *Journal of the American Society for Psychical Research* 44 (April 1950): 43–64. Reprint as *Surveys in Parapsychology.* Edited by Rhea A. White. 1976.

Sachse, Julius F. *The German Pietists of Provencial Pennsylvania.* Philadelphia, 1895. Reprint, New York: AMS Press, 1970.

Sadoul, Jacques. *Alchemists and Gold.* New York: G. P. Putnam's Sons, 1972. Reprint, London: Neville Spearman, 1972.

Sage, M. *Mrs. Piper and the Society for Psychical Research.* London, 1903; New York, Scott-Thaw, 1904.

Sahagun, Bernardino de. *Historia de la Conquista de Mexico.* Mexico, 1829.

Saint Germain. *Violet Fire: The Torch of Freedom's Holy Light.* Portland, Ore.: Universariun Foundation, 1983.

Saint-Germain, Comte C. de. *The Practice of Palmistry for Professional Purposes.* 2 vols. 1897–98. Reprint, Hollywood, Calif.: Newcastle, 1973.

Saller, K. F. "Die Parapsychologie vom Standpunkt des Anthropologen" (Parapsychology from the anthropologist's point of view). *Die Heilkunst* 68, no. 7 (1955).

Salter, Helen. "Evidence for Telepathy." *Journal of the American Society for Psychical Research* (1951).

———. "The History of George Valiantine." *Proceedings of the Society for Psychical Research* (1931).

———. "Some Experiments with a New Automatist." *Proceedings of the Society for Psychical Research* (1918).

———. "Some Observations on Scripts of the SPR Group of Automatists." *Journal of the American Society for Psychical Research* (1951).

Salter, W. H. "F. W. H. Myers' Posthumous Message." *Proceedings of the Society for Psychical Research* 52 (1958).

———. *Ghosts & Apparitions.* London: G. Bell & Sons, 1938.

———. "J. G. Piddington and His Work on the Cross-Correspondence 'Scripts.'" *Journal of the Society for Psychical Research* 36 (1952).

———. *Trance Mediumship: An Introductory Study of Mrs. Piper and Mrs. Leonard.* London: Society for Psychical Research, 1950. Rev. ed. London: Society for Psychical Research, 1962.

———. *Zoar; or, The Evidence of Psychical Research Concerning Survival.* London: Sidgwick & Jackson, 1961. Reprint, Ayer Publishing Co. Inc., 1975.

Salter, W. H., G. W. Fisk, and Harry H. Price. "G. N. M. Tyrrell and His Contributions to Psychical Research." *Journal of the Society for Psychical Research* 37 (1953).

Salter, William H. "An Experiment in Pseudo-Scripts." *Proceedings of the Society for Psychical Research* 36, no. 103 (1927).

———. *The Society for Psychical Research; An Outline of Its History.* London: Society for Psychical Research, 1948.

———. "Some Automatic Scripts Purported to be Inspired by Margaret Veley." *Proceedings of the Society for Psychical Research* 38, no. 110 (1928–29).

———. *Trance Mediumship: An Introductory Study of Mrs. Piper and Mrs. Leonard.* London: Society for Psychical Research, 1950.

Saltmarsh, H. F., and S. G. Soal. "A Method of Estimating the Supernormal Content of Mediumistic Communications." *Proceedings of the Society for Psychical Research* 39, no. 114 (1930).

Saltmarsh, Herbert Francis. "Ambiguity in the Question of Survival." *Proceedings on the Society for Psychical Research* 46, no. 165 (1941).

———. *Evidence of Personal Survival from Cross Correspondences.* London: G. Bell & Son, 1938. Reprint, New York: Ayer Publishing Co. Inc., 1975.

———. *Foreknowledge.* London: G. Bell & Sons, 1938. Reprint, New York: Ayer Publishing Co. Inc., 1975.

———. "Is Proof of Survival Possible?" *Proceedings of the Society for Psychical Research* 40, no. 122 (1931–32).

———. "Report on the Investigation of Some Sittings with Mrs. Warren Elliott." *Proceedings on the Society for Psychical Research* 39, no. 112 (1930).

Salverte, Eusèbe. *Des sciences occultes.* Paris, 1834.

Samarin, William J. *Tongues of Men and of Angels: The Religious Language of Pentecostalism.* New York: Macmillan, 1972.

Samorini, Giorgio. "La Religión Buiti y la Planta Psicoactiva Tabernanthe Iboga. África Ecuatorial," In *Plantas, Chamanismo y Estados de Consciencia* Barcelona: Los Libros de la Liebre de Marzo (1994): 177–195.

———. "The Oldest Representations of Hallucinogenic Mushrooms in the World (Sahara Desert, 9000-7000 B.P.)," *Integration: Journal for Mind-Moving Plants and Culture* nos. 2 & 4 (1992): 69–78.

———. "Sciamanismo, funghi psicotropi e stati alterati di coscienza: un rapporto da chiarire," *Bollettino del Centro Camuno di Studi Preistorici* vol. 25–26 (1990): 147–150.

———. "Sulla presenza di piante e funghi allucinogenu in Valcamonica," *Bollettino del Centro Camuno di Studi Preistorici* vol. 24 (1988): 132–136.

Sampath, Ursula. *Kaspar Hauser: A Modern Metaphor.* Columbia, S.C.: Camden House, 1991.

Samuel, Geoffrey. *Civilized Shamans: Buddhism in Tibetan Societies* Washington D.C.: Smithsonian Institution Press, 1993.

Samuel, Herbert L. *Man of the Spirit: Sir Francis Younghusband.* London, 1953.

Samuels, Mike. *Seeing With the Mind's Eye: The History, Techniques, and Uses of Visualization.* New York: Bookworks; Random House, 1975.

Sananda, as recorded by Sister Thedra. *I, the Lord God Says Unto Them.* Mt. Shasta, Calif.: Association of Sananda and Sanat Kumara, [1954].

Sanchez, Regina. "Empathy, Diversity, and Telepathy in Mother/Daughter Dyads: An Empirical Investigation Utilizing Rogers' Conceptual Framework," *Scholarly Inquiry for Nursing Practice* 3, no. 1 (Spring 1989): 29–44.

[Sanders, Alexander]. *The Alex Sanders Lectures.* New York: Magickal Childe Publishing, 1980. Rev. ed. 1982.

Sanders, Ed. *The Family.* New York: E. P. Dutton, 1971. Reprint, New York: Avon, 1972.

Sanderson, Ivan T. *Abominable Snowmen: Legend Comes to Life.* New York: Chilton, 1961. Abridged ed., New York: Pyramid Publications, 1968.

———. *Investigating the Unexplained.* Englewood Cliffs, N.J.: Prentice-Hall, 1972.

———. *Invisible Residents: A Disquisition Upon Certain Matters Maritime, and the Possibility of Intelligent Life Under the Waters of This Earth.* New York: World Publishing, 1970.

———. *More "Things."* New York: Pyramid Books, 1969.

———. *"Things."* New York: Pyramid Books, 1967.

———. *Uninvited Visitors; A Biologist Looks at UFO's.* New York: Cowles, 1967.

Sandwich, The Earl of [Edward George Henry Montague]. *My Experiences in Spiritual Healing.* London, N.p., 1915.

Sandwith, George, and Helen Sandwith. *Research in Fiji, Tonga & Samoa.* Surrey, England: Omega Press, 1954.

Sanger, C. P. "Analysis of Mrs. Verrall's Card Experiments." *Proceedings of the Society for Psychical Research* 2, no. 28 (1895).

Santucci, James. "H. N. Stokes and the O. E. Library Critic." *Theosophical History* 1, 6 (April 1986): 129–39.

———. "H. N. Stokes' Early Contact with the Theosophical Society." *Theosophical History* 2, 1 (January 1987): 4–22.

Sanyal, J. M., trans. *The Srimad Bhagavatam.* 2 Vols., New Delhi, India: Munshiram Manocharlal, 1973.

Sargant, William. *The Mind Possessed: A Physiology of Possession, Mysticism & Faith Healing.* London: Heinemann, 1973. Reprint, Philadelphia: J. B. Lippincott, 1974.

Sargent, Epes. *Planchette; or, The Despair of Science.* Boston: Roberts Brothers, 1869.

———. *The Proof Palpable of Immortality.* Boston: n.p., 1876. Boston: Colby & Rich, 1881. Reprint, Boston: Banner of Light Publishing, 1901.

———. *The Scientific Basis of Spiritualism.* Boston: Colby & Rich, 1880. Rev. ed. Boston: Banner of Light Publishing, 1891.

Sarkar, P. R. *Ideas and Ideology.* Calcutta, India: Ananda Marga Pracaraka Research, 1967. Calcutta, India: Acarya Pranavananda Avadhuta, 1978.

Sasche, Julius F. *The German Pietists of Provincial Pennsylvania.* Philadelphia, 1895.

Satchakrananda, Yogi. *Coming and Going: The Mother's Drama.* Deming, N.Mex.: Raj-Yoga Math & Retreat, 1975.

———. *Thomas Merton's Dharma.* Deming, N.Mex.: Raj-Yoga Math & Retreat, 1986.

Satchidananda, Sri Swami. *A Decade of Service.* Pomfret Center, Conn.: Satchidananda Ashram-Yogaville, 1976.

———. *Integral Hatha Yoga.* New York: Holt, Rinehart & Winston, 1970. New York: Henry Holt and Co. Inc.; Buckingham, Va.: Integral Yoga Publications, 1995.

Satchidananda, Swami. *Beyond Words.* New York: Holt, Rinehart and Winston, 1977.

———. *The Glory of Sannyasa.* Pomfret Center, Conn.: Integral Yoga Institute, 1975.

Satchidananda, Swami, et al. *Living Yoga: The Value of Yoga in Today's Life.* New York: Gordon and Beach Science Publishers, 1977.

———. *Sri Satchtheidananda: A Decade of Service.* Pomfret Center, Conn.: Satchidananda Ashram–Yogaville, 1976.

Saunders, David R., and R. Roger Hawkins. *UFOs? Yes! Where the Condon Committee Went Wrong.* New York: World, 1968. Reprint, New York: New American Library, 1968.

Savage, Minot J. *Can Telepathy Explain?* New York; London: G. P. Putnam's & Sons, 1902; 1903.

———. *Immortality.* N.p., 1906.

———. *Life Beyond Death.* New York; London: G. P. Putnam's & Sons, 1899; 1902; 1903.

Savile, Bourchier W. *Apparitions; A Book of Facts.* London, 1874.

Savizar and Silarra. *Conscious Channeling.* Sedona, Ariz.: Earth Mission, 1989.

———. *Extraterrestrial Earth Mission. Book I: The Awakening.* Sedona, Ariz.: Earth Mission, 1989.

———. *The Superconscious Technique.* Sedona, Ariz.: Earth Mission, 1989.

Scarabaeus [Thorstein Wereide]. *Mysteriesamfund* (Mystery Societies). N.p., 1948.

Scarborough, Dorothy. *The Supernatural in Modern English Fiction.* New York: G. P. Putnam's Sons, 1917.

Scarre, Geoffrey F. *Witchcraft Magic-16th & 17th C.* London: Macmillan Publishers, Limited, 1996.

Schadewald, Robert. "Biorhythms: A Critical Look at Critical Days." *Fate* (February 1979): 75–80.

Schaefer, Hans. "Ist die Existenz Parapsychologischer Phènomene Bewiesen?" (Have Parapsychological Phenomena Been Proved?) *Münchner Medizinische Wochenschrift* 99 (1957).

———. "Parapsychologie." *Arztliche Praxis* 3, no. 48 (1951).

———. "Telepathie und Hellshehen" (Telepathy and Clairvoyance). *Die Umschau* 52 (1952).

Schang, F. C. *Visiting Cards of Celebrities.* Paris: Gale Research, 1973.

Schärer, Hans. *Ngaju Religion: The Conception of God among a South Borneo People.* Translated by Rodney Needham from the 1946 German edition. The Hague: Martinus Nijhoff, 1963.

Schatzman, Morton. *The Story of Ruth.* London: Duckworth; New York: G. P. Putnam's Sons, 1980.

Schaut, George B. and Michael A. Persinger. "Subjective Telepathic Experiences, Geomagnetic Activity and the ELF Hypothesis: I. Data Analyses," *PSI Research* 4, no. 1 (March 1985): 4–20.

Schaya, Leo. *The Universal Meaning of the Kabbalah.* Baltimore, Md.: Penguin Books, 1973.

Schepis, Giovanni. "I 'Poteri magici' e l'Uomo Normale" ("Magical powers" and the normal man). *Ulisse* (October 1948).

———. "La Esplorazione delle Percezioni Extra-Sensoriali col Metodo Statistico" (Exploring extrasensory perception by statistical methods). *Notiziario di Metapsichica* (March 1949).

———. "La Parapsicologia in Italia e la scienza ufficiale: Anno Zero" (Parapsychology in Italy and official science: The year zero). *Studies and Problems of Parapsychology* (1961).

———. "Questioni di Metodo in Parapsicologia" (Questions of method in parapsychology). *Revista de Parapsicologia* (April–June 1955).

———. "Un Nuovo Campo di Applicazione del Metodo Statistico: Lo Studio dell' effetto detto di ESP" (A new field for the application of statistical methods: The study of so-called extrasensory perception). *Proceedings,* Societ à Italiana di Demografia e Statistica (1947).

Scherer, Wallace B. "Spontaneity as a Factor in ESP." *Journal of Parapsychology* (June 1948).

Schiller, F. C. S. "On Some Philosophical Assumptions in the Investigation of the Problem of a Future Life." *Proceedings of the Society for Psychical Research* 15 (1900).

———. "Philosophy, Science, and Psychical Research. A Presidential Address." *Proceedings of the Society for Psychical Research* 27 (1914).

———. *Problems of Belief.* London: Hodder & Stoughton; New York: George H. Doran, 1924. Reprint, New York: AMS Press, 1980.

———. "The Progress of Psychical Research." *Fortnightly Review* 77 (1905).

———. *Psychology and Logic in Psychology and the Sciences.* N.p., 1924.

———. *The Riddle of the Sphinx.* N.p., 1891. Reprint, New York: Greenwood Press, 1968. Reprint, Freeport, N.Y.: Books for Libraries Press, 1970.

———. *Studies in Humanism.* N.p., 1907. Reprint, Freeport, N.Y.: Books for Libraries Press, 1969. Reprint;, Westport, Conn.: Greenwood Press, 1970.

———. *Tantalus, or the Future of Man.* N.p., 1924. London: K. Paul, Trnch, Trubner & Co.; New York: E. P. Dutton, 1924.

Schilliro, Cristina. "Reimmaginando Jung: Un percorso interiore tra i sogni e le visioni descritti nell'autobiografia" (Reinventing Jung: A Spiritual Journey among the Dreams and Visions Described in His Autobiography), *Giornale Storico di Psicologia Dinamica* 18, no. 36 (June 1994): 67–83.

Schmeidler, Gertrude. *ESP in Relation to Rorschach Test Evaluation.* New York: Parapsychology Foundation, 1960.

———. *Extrasensory Perception.* New York: Atherton Press, 1969.

———. *Parapsychology and Psychology; Matches and Mismatches.* Jefferson, N.C.: McFarland, 1988.

———. *Parapsychology; Its Relation to Physics, Biology, Psychology, and Psychiatry.* Metuchen, N.J.: Scarecrow Press, 1976.

———. "Separating the Sheep from the Goats." *Journal of the American Society for Psychical Research* (1945).

———. "Some Lines About Gardner Murphy, the Psychologist's Parapsychologist." *Parapsychology Review* (July–August, 1976).

Schmeidler, Gertrude, and R. A. McConnell. *ESP and Personality Patterns.* New Haven, Conn.: Yale University Press, 1958.

Schmeidler, Gertrude R. "PK Effects Upon Continuously Recorded Temperature." *Journal of the American Society for Psychical Research* 4 (October 1973).

———. *Extrasensory Perception.* New York: Atherton, 1969.

Schmidt, Helmut. "Clairvoyance Tests with a Machine." *Journal of Parapsychology* 33 (1969).

———. "PK Effects on Pre-Recorded Targets." *Journal of the American Society for Psychical Research* 70 (1976).

———. "PK Experiments with Animals as Subjects." *Journal of Parapsychology* 34 (1970).

———. "A PK Test with Electronic Equipment." *Journal of Parapsychology* 34 (1970).

———. "PK Tests with a High Speed Random Number Generator." *Journal of Parapsychology* 37 (1973).

———. "Precognition of a Quantum Process." *Journal of Parapsychology* 33 (1969).

Schmöger, Carl E. *The Life of Anna Catherine Emmerick.* 2 vols. Los Angeles: Maria Regina Guild, 1968.

Schneider, Herbert Wallace. *A Prophet and a Pilgrim, Being the Incredible History of Thomas Lake Harris and Laurence Oliphant: Their Sexual Mysticisms and Utopian Communities.* New York: Columbia University Press, 1942.

Schoenholtz, Larry. *New Directions in the I Ching: The Yellow River Legacy.* New Hyde Park, N.Y.: University Books, 1975.

Scholem, Gershom. *Kabbalah.* New York: Quadrangle, 1974.

———. *On the Kabbalah and Its Symbolism.* New York: Schocken, 1960. New York: Schocken Books, 1965. New York: Schocken Books, Inc., 1969. Reprint, New York: Schocken Books, Inc., 1996.

Scholem, Gershom., ed. *Zohar—The Book of Splendor: Basic Readings from the Kabbalah.* New York: Schocken, 1963.

Schouten, Sybo A. "An Overview of Quantitatively Evaluated Studies with Mediums and Psychics." *Journal of the American Society for Psychical Research* 88, no. 3 (July 1994): 221–254.

Schrenck-Notzing, Albert von. *Die Traumtanzerin Magdeleine C.* Stuttgart, 1904.

———. *Materialisationspaenomene.* Munich: Ernst Reinhart, 1914. Translated as *Phenomena of Materialisation: A Contribution to the Investigation of Mediumistic Teleplastics.* London, 1923. Reprint, North Stratford, N. H.: Ayer Publishing Co., 1975.

Schrenck-Notzing, Baron A. von. *Phenomena of Materialisation: A Contribution to the Investigation of Mediumistic Teleplastics.* London and New York, 1920. Reprint, New York: Ayer Publishing Co. Inc., 1975.

Schrodter, Willy. *History of Energy Transference.* New York: Samuel Weiser Inc., 1999.

Schueler, Betty, and Gerald J. Schueler. *Enochian Magick.* St. Paul, Minn.: Llewellyn Publications, 1999.

Schueler, Gerald J. *An Advanced Guide to Enochian Magic: A Complete Manual for Angelic Magic.* St. Paul, Minn.: Llewellyn Publications, 1987.

———. *Enochian Magic: A Practical Manual.* St. Paul, Minn.: Llewellyn Publications, 1985.

———. *Enochian Physics: The Structure of the Magical Universe.* St. Paul, Minn.: Llewellyn Publications, 1988.

Schul, Bill. *The Psychic Power of Animals.* Greenwich, Conn.: Fawcett, 1977.

Schul, Bill, and Ed Pettit. *The Secret Power of Pyramids.* Greenwich, Conn.: Fawcett, 1975.

Schulman, Arnold. *Baba.* New York: Viking Press, 1971.

Schultes, Richard E., and Albert Hofmann. *Plants of the Gods: Origins of Hallucinogenic Use.* London: Hutchinson, 1979/New York: McGraw-Hill, 1980. [Reprinted: Rochester, Vt.: Healing Arts Press, 1992]

Schultes, Richard Evans. "An Overview of Hallucinogens in the Western Hemisphere." In *Flesh of the Gods: The Ritual Use of Hallucinogens.* P. T. Furst, ed., (New York: Praeger, 1972).

Schultz, Ted. *The Fringes of Reason: A Whole Earth Catalog.* New York: Harmony Books, 1989.

Schulz-Weider, Willy. "Shamanism." *Encyclopedia of World Art* vol. 13. (New York: McGraw-Hill, 1967).

Schwab, Gustav. *Gods and Heroes: Myths and Epics of Ancient Greece.* New York: Pantheon Books, 1946.

Schwartz, Emanual K. "The Psychodynamics of Spontaneous Psi Experiences." *Journal of the American Society for Psychical Research* 46 (1952).

———. "The Study of Spontaneous Psi Experiences." *Journal of the American Society for Psychical Research* 43 (1949).

Schwarz, Berthold Eric. *Parent-Child Telepathy: Five Hundred and Five Possible Episodes in a Family; A Study of the Telepathy of Everyday Life.* New York: Garrett Publications, 1971.

Schweitzer, Darrell. *The Dream Quest of H. P. Lovecraft.* San Bernardino, Calif.: Borgo Press, 1978.

Scoresby, William. *Journal of a Voyage to Australia for Magnetical Research.* London: Longman, Green, Longman, & Roberts, 1859.

———. *Magnetical Investigations.* 2 vols. London: Longman, Brown, Green, and Longmans, 1844–52.

———. *Zoistic Magnetism.* London: Longman, Brown, Green, and Longmans, 1849.

Scot, Reginald. *The Discoverie of Witchcraft.* 1584. Reprint, New York: Dover Publications, 1972.

Scott, Christopher S. O. "Experimental Object-Reading: A Critical Review of the Work of Dr. J. Hettinger." *Proceedings of the Society for Psychical Research* (November 1959).

———. "Fresh Light on the Shackleton Experiments." *Proceedings of the Society for Psychical Research* 56 (1974).

———. "G. Spencer Brown and Probability: A Critique." *Journal of the Society for Psychical Research* (June 1958).

———. "Models for Psi." *Proceedings of the Society for Psychical Research* (October 1961).

Scott, Cyril. *The Adept of Galilee.* N.p., 1920.

———. *Bone of Contention* N.p., 1969.

———. *The Christian Paradox.* N.p., 1942.

———. *The Initiate in the Dark Cycle.* N.p., 1932; 1977. Reprint, York Beach, Maine: Samuel Weiser, 1991.

———. *Memoirs, Entitled My Years of Indiscretion.* N.p., 1924.

———. *Music: Its Secret Influence Throughout the Ages.* 6th ed. London: Rider, 1956.

———. *An Outline of Modern Occultism.* New York: E. P. Dutton, 1935. Reprint, New York: Dutton, 1950.

———. *The Vision of the Nazarene.* N.p., 1933.

Scott, G. Laughton. *"The Abrams Treatment" in Practice: An Investigation.* London: Bless, 1925.

Scott, Gini Graham. *The Magicians.* New York: Irvington Publishers, 1983.

Scott, Peter. "Naming the Loch Ness Monster." *Nature* (December 11, 1975).

Scott, R. D. *Transcendental Misconceptions.* San Diego, Calif.: Beta Books, 1978.

Scott, Sir Walter. *Letters on Demonology and Witchcraft.* London J. Murray, 1830. Reprint, New York, 1831. Reprint, New York: Citadel Press, 1970.

Scott-Elliott, W. *The Story of Atlantis.* London: Theosophical Publishing House, 1896.

Scriven, Michael John. "Modern Experiments in Telepathy." *Philosophical Review* (April 1956).

———. "New Experimental Designs for Psi Research." *Journal of the Society for Psychical Research* (June 1956).

———. "Randomness and the Causal Order." *Analysis* (October 1956).

———. "Some Theoretical Possibilities in Psi Research." *Journal of the Society for Psychical Research* (June 1957).

Seabrook, William Buehler. *Adventures in Arabia.* New York, 1927. New York, Blue Ribbon Books, 1930. Reprint, New York: Marlowe and Co., 1994. Reprinted as *Adventures in Arabia Among the Bedouins Druses Whirling Dervishes & Yezidee Devil-Worshipers.* St. Paul, Minn.: Paragon House Publishers, 1991.

———. *Jungle Ways.* N.p., 1931.

———. *No Hiding Place.* Philadelphia; New York: J. B. Lippencott, 1942.

———. *These Foreigners.* New York: Harcourt, Brace & Co., 1938.

———. *The White Monk of Timbuctoo.* New York: Harcourt, Brace & Co., 1934.

———. *Witchcraft: Its Power in the World Today.* New York: Harcourt, Brace & Co., 1940.

Seafield, Frank. *The Literature & Curiosities of Dreams.* 2nd ed. London, 1877.

"A Searcher After Truth." *The Rappers; or, the Mysteries, Fallacies, and Absurdities of Spirit Rapping, Table-Tipping and Entrancement.* Long, N.Y., 1854.

Seaver, George F. *Francis Younghusband: Explorer and Mystic.* London, 1952.

Sebald, Hans. *Witch-Children: From Salem Witch-Hunts to Modern Courtrooms.* Amherst, N.Y.: Prometheus Books, 1995.

The Secrets of the Invisible World Laid Open, or an Universal History of Apparitions, Sacred & Profane. London, 1770.

Sédir, Paul. *Initiations.* London: Regency Press, 1967.

Seeing Casteneda: Reaction to the "Don Juan" Writings of Carlos Castaneda. New York: G. P. Putnam & Sons, 1976.

Seiss, Joseph. *The Great Pyramid: A Miracle in Stone.* Blauvelt, N.Y.: Multimedia (Steiner Books), 1972.

Selden, Rodman. *Spirits of the Night.* Dallas, Tex.: Spring, 1992.

Selections from the Writings of the Bab. Comp. Habib Taherzadeh. Haifa, Israel: Bahai World Center, 1976.

Self, Jane. *60 Minutes and the Assassination of Werner Erhard: How America's Top Rated Television Show Was Used in an Attempt to Destroy a Man Who Was Making a Difference.* Houston, Tex.: Breakthru Publishing, 1992.

Self-Realization Fellowship Highlights. Los Angeles: Self-Realization Fellowship, 1980.

Self-Realization Fellowship Manual of Services. Los Angeles: Self-Realization Fellowship, 1965.

Seligman, Kurt. *The History of Magic.* New York: Pantheon Books, 1948. Reprined as: *Magic, Supernaturalism and Religion.* New York: Pantheon Books, 1971.

Selous, Edmund. *Thought-Transference (or What?) in Birds.* London: Constable & Co. Ltd., 1931.

A Sender of Words: Essays in Honor of John G. Neihardt. Salt Lake City, Utah: Howe Brothers, 1984.

Sepharial [W. G. Old]. *The Book of Charms and Talismans.* London: W. Foulsham, 1923. Reprint, New York: Arco Books, 1969. Reprint, New York: Arco, 1971. Reprinted as *Sepharial's Book of Charms and Talismans.* Garden City Park, N.Y.: Avery Publishing Group, 1991. Santa Fe, N.Mex.: Sun Publishing Co., 1992.

———. *How to Read the Crystal.* London, 1922.

———. *The Kabala of Numbers.* 2 vols. London, 1913. New York: MacKay, 1928. Reprint, San Bernadino, Calif.: Borgo Press, 1980.

Series A: Professional Notabilities. 6 vols. Paris: Laboratoire d'Etude des Relations entre Rythmes Cosmiques et Psychophysiologiques, 1970–71.

Series B: Heredity Experiments. 6 vols. Paris: Laboratoire d'Etude des Relations entre Rythmes Cosmiques et Psychophysiologiques, 1970–71.

Series C: Psychological Monographs. 5 vols. Paris: Laboratoire d'Etude des Relations entre Rythmes Cosmiques et Psychophysiologiques, 1972–77.

Series D: Scientific Documents. 10 vols. Paris: Laboratoire d'Etude des Relations entre Rythmes Cosmiques et Psychophysiologiques, 1976–82.

Serio, Harry L. "Mysticism and Ministry: A Descriptive Inquiry into the Varieties of Mystical Experiences among United Church of Christ People in Berks County, Pennsylvania," *Dissertation Abstracts International* 53, no. 7-A (January 1993): 2410.

Serling, Rod. *More Stories From the Twilight Zone.* New York: Bantam Books, 1961.

———. *Night Gallery.* New York: Dember Books, 1987. Distributed by W. W. Norton.

———. *Night Gallery Two.* Toronto; New York: Bantam Books, 1972.

———. *Patterns.* New York: Simon & Schuster, 1957.

———. *Stories from the Twilight Zone.* N.p., 1960. Reprint, New York; Toronto: Bantam Books, 1986.

Servadio, Emilio. "Freud et la Parapsychologie." *Revue Francaise de Psychoanalyse* 3 (1956).

———. "Le conditionnement transferentiel et contre-transférentiel des événements 'psi' au cours de l'analyse" (Transference and counter-transference conditioning of 'psi' events during analysis). *Acta Psychotherapeutica* (1955).

———. "Mysticism and Parapsychology," *Parapsychology Review* 17, no. 3 (May-June 1986): 1–5.

———. "The 'Normal' and the 'Paranormal' Dream." *International Journal of Parapsychology* (1962).

———. "A Presumptively Telepathic-Precognitive Dream During Analysis." *International Journal of Psycho-Analysis* 1 (1955).

———. "Psychoanalyse and Telepathie" (Psychoanalysis and telepathy). *Imago* 4 (1935). Reprinted in *Psychoanalysis and the Occult,* edited by 1953 George Devereux.

———. "Transference and Thought-Transference." *International Journal of Psycho-Analysis* 4, no. 5 (1956).

Servier, Jean H. "Geomancy, Clairvoyance and Initiation." *La Tour Saint-Jacques* (September–December 1956). Reprinted in the *Proceedings of Four Conferences of Parapsychology* (1957).

———. *L'Homme et l'Invisible.* Paris: R. Laffonto, 1964.

———. *Les Partes de l'Année.* Paris: R. Laffonto, 1962.

Settanni, Harry. *The Philosophical Foundations of Paranormal Phenomena.* Lanham, Md.: University Press of America, 1992.

Sevric, Ivo. *The Hidden Side of Medjugorje.* Saint Francois du Lac, Canada: Psilog, 1989.

Seward, A. F. *The Art of Crystal Gazing or Secrets of the Crystal Revealed.* Chicago: A. F. Seward, 1873.

Sewell, Dan. "Snake Handlers Put Bite into Religion." *Santa Barbara News-Press* (May 1,1995).

Sewell, May W. *Neither Dead nor Sleeping.* London, 1921.

Seymour, Richard B., and David E. Smith. *Guide to Psychoactive Drugs: An Up-to-the-Minute Reference to Mind-Altering Substances.* New York: Harrington Park Press, 1987.

Sexton, George. *Spirit Mediums and Conjurers.* London, 1873.

Seymour, Percy. *The Scientific Basis of Astrology.* New York: St. Martin's, 1992.

Seymour, St. John. *Irish Witchcraft and Demonology.* 1913. Reprint, New York: Causeway Books, 1973.

Seymour, St. John D. and Harry L. Neligan. *True Irish Ghost Stories.* London: Oxford University Press, 1915. Reprint, New York: Causeway Books, 1974.

Shackley, Myra. *Wildmen: Yeti, Sasquatch and the Neanderthal Enigma.* London: Thames & Hudson, 1983.

Shah, Idries. *The Exploits of the Incomparable Mulla Nasrudin.* London: Cape, 1966. Reprint, New York: Simon & Schuster, 1967.

———. *Learning How to Learn; Psychology and Spirituality in the Sufi Way.* London: Octagon Press, 1978. San Francisco: Harper & Row, 1981.

———. *Oriental Magic.* London; New York: Rider, 1956. Reprint, New York: Penguin Arkana, 1993.

———. *Reflections.* London: Zenith Books; Octagon Press, 1968. Reprint, Baltimore, Md.: Penguin Books, 1972.

———. *The Secret Lore of Magic.* London: Frederick Muller, 1957. Reprint, New York: Citadel Press, 1957. Reprint, Atlantic Highlands, N. J.: Humanities Press International, 1965. Secaucus, N. J.: Carol Publishing Group, 1970. Reprint, London: Abacus, 1972.

———. *Special Problems in the Study of Sufi Ideas.* London: London Society for Understanding Fundamental Ideas, 1966. Reprint, London: Octagon Press, 1974.

———. *The Sufis.* New York: Anchor Books, 1940. Reprint, London: W. H. Allen, 1964. Reprint, London: Cape, 1969.

———. *Tales of the Dervishes.* London: Cape, 1967. Reprint, New York, Dutton, 1969.

———. *Way of the Sufi.* London: Cape, 1968. Reprint, New York: Dutton, 1969. Reprint, New York: E. P. Dutton, 1970.

Shah, Idries, trans. *The Subtleties of the Inimitable Mulla Nasrudin.* New York: Dutton; London: Cape, 1973.

Shah, Sayed Idries. *The Secret Lore of Magic: Books of the Sorcerers.* London: Frederick Muller, 1957.

Shapiro, Dolores J. "Symbolic Fluids: The World of Spirit Mediums in Brazilian Possession Groups," *Dissertation Abstracts International* 53, no. 3-A (September 1992): 867–868.

Sharaf, Myron. *Fury on Earth: A Biography of Wilhelm Reich.* New York: St. Martin's Press, 1983.

Sharma, I. C. *Cayce, Karma and Reincarnation.* Wheaton, Ill.: Theosophical Publishing House, 1975.

Sharon, Douglas. Wizard of the Four Winds. A Shaman's Story. New York: The Free Press, 1978.

Sharp, Arthur F. *The Spirit Saith.* London: H. H. Greaves, n.d.

Sharp, William. *Earth's Voices.* N.p., 1884.

Sharp, Lesley A. "Exorcists, Psychiatrists, and the Problems of Possession in Northwest Madagascar," *Social Science & Medicine* 38, no. 4 (February 1994): 525–54.

Sharp, William. *Flower o' the Vine.* N.p., 1894.

———. *Human Inheritance.* N.p., 1882.

———. *Life of D. G. Rossetts.* N.p., 1882.

Sharpe, Charles Kirkpatrick. *Historical Account of the Belief in Witchcraft in Scotland.* N.p., 1819.

Shaver, Richard. "I Remember Lemuria." *Amazing Stories* March 1945. Reprinted in *The Hidden World* A–1 (Spring 1961): 52–134.

Sheargold, Richard K. "The Ghost of Twenty-Nine Megacycles." *Journal of the Society for Psychical Research* 53 (1986).

———. *Hints on Receiving the Voice Phenomenon.* N.p., 1973.

———. "The Occultism of Occultism." *Journal of the Society for Psychical Research* 45 (1970).

Sheba, Lady. *The Book of Shadows.* St. Paul, Minn.: Llewellyn Publications, 1973.

Sheldrake, Rupert. *A New Science of Life: the Hypotehsis of Formative Causation.* London: Blond & Briggs; Los Angeles: J. P. Tarcher, 1981.

———. *The Presence of the Past.* New York: New York Times Books, 1988.

———. *The Presence of the Past: Morphic Resonance and the Habits of Nature.* New York: Vintage Books, 1989.

Shelton, Harriet M. *Abraham Lincoln Returns.* New York: Evans Publishing, 1957.

Shepard, Jess F. G. "How I Became a Musical Medium." *Medium* (May 6, 1970).

Shepard, Les. *The Dracula Book of Great Vampire Stories.* New York: Citadel Press, 1981.

———. *How to Protect Yourself Against Black Magic and Witchcraft.* New York: Citadel Press, 1978.

———. *The History of Street Literature.* Detroit: Singing Tree Press, 1973.

———. "People and Weather." *Orgonomic Functionalism* 2, no. 4 (July 1955).

Sherfan, Andrew Dib. *Kahlil Gibran: The Nature of Love.* New York: Philosophical Library, 1971.

Sheridan, Jo. *Teacup Fortune-telling.* London: Mayflower, 1978.

Sherman, Harold. *Adventures in Thinking.* Master Publications, 1956.

———. *How to Foresee and Control Your Future.* Greenwich, Conn.: Fawcett; New York: Information, Inc., 1970. New York: Fawcett Book Group, 1986.

———. *How to Know What to Believe.* Greenwich, Conn.: Fawcett, 1976.

———. *How to Make ESP Work for You.* Los Angeles: DeVorss; Greenwich, Conn.: Fawcett, 1964. New York: Fawcett Book Group, 1997.

———. *How to Picture What You Want.* New York: Fawcett, 1978.

———. *How to Turn Failure into Success.* Englewood Cliffs, N.J.: Prentice-Hall, 1958.

———. *How to Use the Power of Prayer.* New York: C. & R. Anthony, 1959. Reprint, Unity Village, Mo.: Unity Books, 1985.

———. *Know Your Own Mind.* New York: G. & R. Anthony, 1953.

———. *TNT—The Power Within You.* Englewood Cliffs, N.J.: Prentice-Hall, 1959.

———. *Wonder Healers of the Philippines.* Los Angeles: DeVorss, 1966. Reprint, London: Psychic Press, 1967.

———. *You Can Communicate with the Unseen World.* New York: Fawcett, 1974.

———. *You Live After Death.* New York: C. R. Anthony, 1949. New York: Fawcett Book Group, 1987.

———. *Your Key to Happiness.* New York: G. P. Putnam's Sons, 1935. Reprint, Greenwich, Conn.: Fawcett, 1964. Reprint, New Canaan, Conn.: Mulvey Books, 1990.

———. *Your Power to Heal.* New York: Harper & Row, 1972.

———. *"Wonder" Healers of the Philippines.* London: Psychic Press, 1967.

Sherman, Harold, and Sir Hubert Wilkins. *Thought through Space.* Greenwich, Conn.: Fawcett, 1972.

Sherwin, Byron L. *The Golem Legend: Origins and Implications.* Lanham, Md.: University Press of America, 1985.

Shi Kun. "Shamanic Practices in Southwest China: Comparative Perspectives of the Minorities," *Temenos* vol. 24 (1988): 121–135.

Shields, Tony. *Entertaining With "ESP."* UK: David & Charles, 1974.

Shimano, Eido. *Golden Wind.* Tokyo: Japan Publications, 1979.

———. "Notable Psychometrist." *Journal of the American Society for Psychical Research* 14 (1920).

———. "Past Events Seership." *Proceedings of the American Society for Psychical Research* 16 (January 1922).

Shimano, Eido, ed. *Like a Dream, Like a Fantasy.* Tokyo: Japan Publications, 1978.

Shin, Gosung. *Zen Teachings of Emptiness.* Washington, D.C.: American Zen College Press, 1982.

Shindler, M. D. *A Southerner Among the Spirits.* Memphis, Tenn., 1877.

Shirley, Ralph. *The Mystery of the Human Double.* London, 1938. Reprint, New Hyde Park, N.Y.: University Books, 1965.

———. *The New God, and Other Essays.* N.p., 1911.

———. *Occultists and Mystics of All Ages.* London: W. Rider & Son, 1920.

———. *The Problem of Rebirth.* N.p., 1936.

———. *A Short Life of Abraham Lincoln.* New York: Funk & Wagnalls; London: W. Rider & Son, 1919.

Shirokogoroff, Sergei M. "General Theory of Shamanism among the Tungus," *Journal of the Royal Asiatic Society, North-China Branch* vol. 62 (1923):.123–183.

———. *Psychomental Complex of the Tungus.* London: Kegan Paul, Trench, Trubner, 1935. [Reprinted: New York: AMS, 1980].

Shorter, Alan W. *The Egyptian Gods.* London: Routledge & Kegan Paul, 1937. Reprint. 1981.

Shuffey, Sandi L. *Reiki.* UK: Hodder & Stoughton, Limited, 1998.

Sidgwick, Eleanor. "Discussion of the Trance Phenomena of Mrs. Piper." *Proceedings of the Society for Psychical Research* (1899).

———. "An Examination of Book-Tests Obtained in Sittings with Mrs. Osborne Leonard." *Proceedings of the Society for Psychical Research* (1921).

———. "Hindrances and Complications in Telepathic Communication." *Proceedings of the Society for Psychical Research* (1923).

———. "History of the SPR." *Proceedings of the Society for Psychical Research* (1932–33)

———. "Phantasms of the Dead." *Proceedings of the Society for Psychical Research* (1885).

———. "The Physical Phenomena of Spiritualism." *Proceedings of the Society for Psychical Research* (1886).

———. "Report on Further Experiments in Thought-Transference Carried Out by Professor Gilbert Murray, LL.D, Litt.D." *Proceedings of the Society for Psychical Research* 34 (1924).

Sidgwick, Henry. "Canons of Evidence in Psychical Research." *Proceedings of the Society for Psychical Research* (1888–90).

———. "Disinterested Deception." *Journal* 6 (1894).

Sidgwick, Henry, A. Johnson, F. W. H. Myers, Frank Podmore, and Eleanor Sidgwick. "Report on the Census of Hallucinations." *Proceedings of the Society for Psychical Research* 10 (1894).

Sidgwick, Mrs. Henry [Eleanor]. "On Spirit Photographs, a reply to Mr. R. A. Wallace." *Proceedings of the Society for Psychical Research* 8 (1891): 268–89.

Siegal, Taggart, and D. Conquer Good. *Between Two Worlds: The Hmong Shaman in America.* N.p., n.d., video.

Siemon, Fred. *Ghost Story Index: An Author-Title Index to More than 2,200 Stories of Ghosts, Horrors, and the Macabre Appearing in 190 Books and Anthologies.* San Jose, Calif.: Library Research Associates, 1967. Reprint, Denver: Opar Press, 1973.

Sieroszewski, Waclaw, "The Yakuts: Abrigded from the Russian of Sieroshevski by W. G. Summer," *Journal of the Royal Anthropological Institute of Great Britain and Ireland* vol. 31, London (1901): 65–110.

Sighart, J. *Albert the Great.* London: Washbourne, 1876.

Sigstedt, C. O. *The Swedenborg Epic: The Life and Works of Emanuel Swedenborg.* New York: Bookman Associates, 1952. Reprint, London: Swedenborg Society, 1981.

Sikes, Wirt. *British Goblins.* London, 1880. Reprint, Wakefield, England: EP Publishing, 1973.

Silananda, U. *An Introduction to the Law of Karma.* Berkeley, Calif.: Dharmachakka Meditation Center, 1990.

Silberer, Herbert. *The Hidden Symbolism of Alchemy and the Occult Arts.* New York: Dover Books, 1971. Reprint, Magnolia, Mass.: Peter Smith, 1972.

Silver Birch. *More Philosophy of Silver Birch.* Compiled by Tony Ortzen. London: Spiritualist Press, 1979.

Silver, Ednah C. *Sketches of the New Church in America.* Boston: Massachusetts New Church Union, 1920.

Silverman, David. *Reading Castaneda: A Prologue to the Social Sciences.* London: Routledge & Kegan Paul, 1975.

Simmonite, W. J. *The Celestial Philosopher.* 2d ed. London: Simpkin, Marshall, 1847.

———. *Medical Botany, or Herbal Guide to Health.* London: Simpkin, Marshall, [1848].

———. *The Prognostic Astronomer, or Horary Astrology.* London: Simpkin, Marshall, 1851.

———. *Prognostications on Revolutions or Solar Figures.* London: Simpkin, Marshall, 1845.

Simon, ed. *The Necronomicon.* New York: Schlangekraft/Barnes Graphics, 1877. Reprint, New York: Avon Books, 1977.

———. *Necronomicon Spellbook.* New York: Magickal Childe, 1986.

Simon, Marcel. *Jewish Sects at the Time of Jesus.* Philadelphia: Fortress Press, 1967.

Simpson, Eve. *The Faith Healer: Deliverance Evangelism in North America.* St. Louis, Mo.: Concordia, 1977. Reprint, New York: Pyramid, 1977.

Simpson, M. A. *Death and Grief: A Critically Annotated Bibliography & Source Book of Thanatology and Terminal Care.* New York: Plenum, 1979.

Simpson, Patti. *Paulji: A Memoir.* Menlo Park, Calif.: ECKANKAR, 1985.

Simson, Eve. *The Faith Healer: Deliverance Evangelism in North America.* Concordia/Pyramid, 1977.

Sinclair, George. *Satan's Invisible World Discovered.* Edinburgh, 1685. Reprint, Edinburgh: Thomas G. Stevenson, 1865.

Sinclair, John R. *The Alice Bailey Inheritance.* Wellingsborough, England: Turnstone Press, 1984.

Sinclair, Upton. *The Autobiography of Upton Sinclair.* N.p., 1962.

———. *Mental Radio: Does it Work, and How?* Pasadena, Calif.: The Author, 1930. Rev. ed., Springfield, Ill.: C. C. Thomas, 1962.

Sinel, Joseph. *The Sixth Sense.* London: T. W. Laurie, 1927.

Singh, Charan. *Light on San Mat.* Beas, India: Radha Soami Satsang, Beas, 1958.

Singh, Joseph Amrito Lal. *Wolf-children and Feral Man.* Hamden, Conn.: Archon Books, 1965.

Sinnett, A. P. *The Autobiography of Alfred Percy Sinnett.* London: Theosophical History Centre, 1986.

———. *Early Days of Theosophy in Europe.* London: Theosophical Publishing House, 1922.

———. *Esoteric Buddhism.* London: Trubner, 1883.

———. *The Growth of the Soul: A Sequel to "Esoteric Buddhism."* London: Theosophical Publishing Society, 1896.

———. *Incidents in the Life of Madame Blavatsky: Compiled from Information Supplied by Her Relatives and Friends.* London: George Redway, 1886. Reprint, Kila, Mont.: Kessinger Publishing Co., 1996.

———. *The Mahatma Letters to A. P. Sinnett.* Edited by A. T. Barker. London: T. Fisher Unwin, 1924.

———. *The Occult World.* London: Trubner, 1881.

———. *The "Occult World Phenomena," and the Society for Psychical Research.* London: George Redway, 1886.

———. *The Rationale of Mesmerism.* Boston: Houghton, Mifflin, 1892.

Sioborg, N. H. *Tympanum Schamanico-lapponicum.* N.p., 1808.

Sitchin, Zecharia. *The Stairway to Heaven.* New York: Avon, 1980.

———. *The Twelfth Planet.* New York: Avon, 1978. Reprint, Santa Fe, N.Mex.: Bear and Co., 1991.

———. *The Wars of Gods and Men.* New York: Avon, 1985.

Sitamma, M. and P. V. Krishna Rao. "Three gunas and cognitive characteristics: A Study of Memory and Extrasensory Perception," *Journal of the Indian Academy of Applied Psychology* 21, no. 2 (July 1995): 185–191.

Sitwell, Sacheverell. *Poltergeist.* London: Faber & Faber, 1940.

Sivananda, Swami. *Autobiography of Swami Sivananda.* Shivanandanagar, India: Divine Life Society, 1983.

———. *Music as Yoga.* Sivananda Nagar, India: Yoga-Vedanta Forest University, 1956.

———. *Practical Lessons in Yoga.* Sivanandanagar, India: Divine Life Society, 1978.

———. *Practice of Karma Yoga.* Sivanandanagar: Divine Life Society, 1980.

———. *Sadhana.* Sivanandanagar: Divine Life Society, 1967.

———. *Science of Yoga.* 18 vols. Durban, South Africa: Sivananda Press, 1977.

The Sivananda Yoga Center. *The Sivananda Companion to Yoga.* New York: Simon & Schuster, 1983.

Sivin, Nathan. *Chinese Alchemy.* Cambridge, Mass.: Harvard University Press, 1968.

Siwek, Paul. *The Riddle of Konnersreuth.* Milwaukee, Wisc.: Bruce Publishing, 1953; Dublin: Browne & Nolan, 1956.

Skeat, Walter William. *Malay Magic: An Introduction to the Folklore and Popular Religion of the Malay Peninsula.* London, 1900. [Reprinted: New York: Benjamin Blom, 1972].

Skia, Persona. *O.A.I. Manifesto: Origin, History, Organization.* Kenilworth, Ill.: Ordo Adeptorum Invisiblum, 1982.

Skinner, Joseph. *State of Peru.* London, 1805.

Skinner, Stephen. *The Living Earth Manual of Feng-shui: Chinese Geomancy.* London: Routledge & Kegan Paul, 1982.

———. *The Oracle of Geomancy.* London: Routledge & Kegan Paul, 1977.

———. *Terrestrial Astrology: Divination by Geomancy.* London: Routledge & Kegan Paul, 1980.

Sklar, Dusty. *Gods and Beasts: The Nazis and the Occult.* New York: Thomas Y. Crowell, 1977.

Slack, Charles W. *Timothy Leary, the Madness of the Sixties, and Me.* New York: Peter H. Wyden, 1974.

Sladek, John. *The New Apocrypha: A Guide to Strange Sciences & Occult Beliefs.* New York: Stein and Day, 1974.

Slater, John. "Memories." *National Spiritualist* (September 1926).

Slattery, Charles L. *Gift of Immortality.* N.p., 1916. Reprint, Kila, Mont.: Kessinger Publishing Co., 1998.

Small, John. *Select Remains of the Ancient Popular and Romance Poetry of Scotland.* London: W. Blackwood & Sons, 1885.

Smedley, Alfred, and T. P. Barkas. *Some Reminiscences of Alfred Smedley . . . also an Account of Miss Wood's Mediumship.* London: "Light," 1900.

Smedley, Edward, W. C. Taylor, Henry Thompson, and Elihu Rich. *The Occult Sciences.* London and Glasgow: Richard Griffin, 1855.

Smith, A. Robert. *Hugh Lynn Cayce: About My Father's Business.* Norfolk, Va.: Donning, 1988.

Smith, Alson Jesse. *Faith to Live By.* Garden City, N.Y.: Doubleday, 1949.

———. *Immortality: The Scientific Evidence.* N.p., 1954.

———. *Psychic Source Book.* New York: Creative Age Press, 1951.

———. *Religion and the New Psychology*. Garden City, N.Y.: Doubleday, 1951.

Smith, Anson J. "Walter Franklin Prince." *Tomorrow* (Summer 1955).

Smith, Charles A. "Dowsing in the Desert: A Critical Essay and Manual on the Dynamics of Sexism for Men," *Dissertation Abstracts International* 51, no. 4-B (October 1990): 2118.

Smith, Eleanor Touhey. *Psychic People*. New York: William Morrow, 1968.

Smith, Hester Travers. *Voices from the Void*. London: William Rider, 1919.

Smith, Jody Brant. *The Image of Guadalupe: Myth or Miracle?* Garden City, N.Y.: Doubleday, 1983. Reprinted as *The Guadalupe Enigma: Myth or Miracle?* London: Souvenir Press, 1983.

Smith, Robert A. *Hugh Lynn Cayce: About My Father's Business*. Norfolk, Va.: Donning, 1988.

Smith, Robert W. *Chinese Boxing*. New York: Kodansha, 1981.

Smith, Roy O. *Incarnation and Reincarnation*. Los Angeles: Religious Research Press, 1975.

Smith, Susan M. "Psychics and Mediums: The Role of Religion and Belief in Rationalizing Paranormal Phenomena," *Dissertation Abstracts International* 50, no. 5-B (November 1989): 2141–2142.

Smith, Susy. *The Book of James*. New York: Putnam, 1974.

———. *The Conversion of a Psychic*. Garden City, N.Y.: Doubleday, 1978.

———. *Confessions of a Psychic*. New York: Macmillan; London: Collier-Macmillan, 1971.

———. *The Enigma of Out-of-body-Travel*. Garrell Publications, 1965. Reprint, New York: Helix, 1968. Reprint, New York: New American Library, 1968.

———. *ESP*. New York: Pyramid Books, 1962.

———. *ESP and Hypnosis*. New York: Macmillan, 1973.

———. *ESP for the Millions*. Los Angeles: Sherbourne Press, 1965.

———. *Ghosts Around the House*. New York: World Publishing, 1970. Reprint, Pocket Books, 1971.

———. *Haunted Houses for the Million*. New York: Bell Publishing; Los Angeles: Sherbourne Press, 1967.

———. *Life is Forever: Evidence for Survival After Death*. New York: G. P. Putnam's Sons, 1974.

———. *The Mediumship of Mrs. Leonard*. New Hyde Park, N.Y.: University Books, 1964.

———. *More ESP for the Millions*. Los Angeles: Sherbourne Press, 1969.

———. *Out-of-Body Experiences for the Millions*. New York: Dell, 1968.

———. *Prominent American Ghosts*. New York: World Publishing, 1967.

———. *Reincarnation*. N.p., 1969.

———. *She Spoke to the Dead*. New York: Award Books, 1972.

———. *A Supernatural Primer for the Millions*. Los Angeles: Sherbourne Press, 1966.

———. *Today's Witches*. Englewood Cliffs, N.J.: Prentice-Hall, 1970.

Smith, Timothy d'Arch. *A Bibliography of the Works of Montague Summers*. New Hyde Park, N.Y.: University Books, 1964.

S.M.R.D., Frater, et al. *The Secret Workings of the Golden Dawn: Book "T" the Tarot*. Cheltenham, England: Helios Book Service, 1967.

Smyth, Charles Piazzi. *Our Inheritance in the Great Pyramid*. London, 1864.

Smythies, J. R., ed. *Science and ESP*. London: Routledge & K. Paul: 1922. New York: Humanities Press, 1967.

Smythies, John Raymond, and Arthur Koestler, ed. *Beyond Reductionism: New Perspectives in the Science of Life*. London: Hitchinson, 1969. Reprint, New York: Macmillian, 1970; London: Hutchinson, 1972.

Snel, F. W. J. J., ed. *In Honour of G. A. M. Zorab*. Amsterdam: Verenining voor Parapsychologie, 1986.

Snell, Joy. *The Ministry of Angels*. London, 1918.

Snowdon, Ruth J., R. A. MacConnell, and K. F. Powell. "Wishing with Dice." *Journal of Experimental Psychology* 50 (October 1955).

Soal, S. G. "Experiments in Supernormal Perception at a Distance." *Proceedings of the Society for Psychical Research* 123 (1932).

———. "Fresh Light on Card Guessing." *Proceedings of the Society for Psychical Research* 46 (1940).

———. "Note on the 'Oscar Wilde' Script." *Journal of the Society for Psychical Research* (July 1926).

———. "A Report on Some Communications Received Through Mrs. Blanche Cooper." *Proceedings of the Society for Psychical Research* 35 (December 1925).

Soal, S. G., and F. Bateman. *Modern Experiments in Telepathy*. New Haven, Conn.: Yale University Press, 1954.

Soal, S. G., and H. T. Bowden. *The Mind Readers*. London: Faber and Faber, 1959.

Soal, S. G., and J. G. Pratt. "ESP Performance and Target Sequence." *Journal of Parapsychology* (September 1951).

———. "Some Relations Between Call Sequence and ESP Performance." *Journal of Parapsychology* (September 1952).

Soal, S. G., and K. M. Goldney. "Experiments in Precognitive Telepathy." *Proceedings of the Society for Psychical Research* 47 (1943).

Sochevanov, Nikolai. "The Influence of Certain Factors on the Intensity of the Biophysical Effect," *PSI Research* 3, no. 1 (March 1984): 16–20.

Solfvin, J., W. G. Roll, and E. F. Kelly. "A Psychophysical Study of Mediumistic Communications." In *Research in Parapsychology, 1976,* edited by J. D. Morris, W. G. Roll, and R. L. Morris. Metuchen, N.J.: Scarecrow Press, 1977.

Solomon, P., and others eds. *Sensory Deprivation*. Cambridge, Mass.: Harvard University, 1961.

Solomon, Shirl. *How to Really Know Yourself Through Your Handwriting*. New York: Taplinger, 1974. Reprint, London: Coronet, 1975.

Solovyoff, V. S. *A Modern Priestess of Isis*. London: Longmans, Green, 1895.

Soo, Chee. *The Chinese Art of K'ai Men*. London: Gordon & Cremonesi, 1977.

Sourcebook 1994. Watertown, Mass.: New Age Journal, 1994.

The Sounds of Yoga-Vedanta; Documentary of Life in an Indian Ashram. New York: Folkways Records, Long-playing record album FR 8970.

"The South African Society for Psychical Research.' " *Journal of the Psychical Research Society* 40 (1959): 43.

Southcott, J. *The Book of Wonders, Marvelous and True*. 5 parts. London, 1813–14.

———. *The Divine Writings of Joanna Southcott*. 2 vols. Bolton, England, 1931.

———. *Prophecies: A Warning to the Whole World from the Sealed Prophecies of Joanna Southcott*. 2 parts. London, 1803.

———. *The Strange Effects of Faith; with Remarkable Prophecies*. 2 parts. Exeter, England, 1801–2. With three "*Continuations*." 1802–3.

Sox, H. David. *The Image on the Shroud: Is the Turin Shroud a Forgery?* London: Unwin, 1981.

———. *The Shroud Unmasked; Uncovering the Greatest Forgery of All Time*. Basingstoke, England: Lamp Press, 1988.

Spangler, David. *Channeling and the New Age*. Issaquah, Wash.: Morningtown Press, 1988.

———. *Conversations with John*. Elgin, Ill.: Lorian Press, 1980.

———. *Emergence: The Rebirth of the Sacred*. New York: Delta, 1980.

———. *Explorations: Emerging Aspects of the New Culture*. Forres, Scotland: Findhorn Publications, 1980.

———. *Revelation: The Birth of a New Age*. San Francisco: Rainbow Bridge, 1976.

———. *Towards a Planetary Vision*. Forres, Scotland: Findhorn Publications, 1977.

Spanos, Nicholas. "Hypnosis, Demonic Possession, and Multiple Personality: Strategic Enactments and Disavowals of Responsibility for Actions." In *Altered States of Consciousness and Mental Health: A Cross-Cultural Perspective*. Newbury Park, Calif.: Sage Publications, Inc., 1989.

Spanos, Nicholas, Wendy P. Cross, Mark Lepage, and Marjorie Coristine. "Glossolalia as Learned behavior: An Experimental Demonstration." *Journal of Abnormal Psychology* 95 (February 1986): 21–23.

Spare, Austin Osman. *A Book of Automatic Drawing.* London: Catalpa Press, 1972.

———. *The Book of Pleasure (Self-Love): The Psychology of Ecstasy.* London: Cooperative Printing Society Limited, 1913. Reprint, Montreal: 93 Publishing, 1975.

———. *The Focus of Life.* London: The Author, 1921.

Sparkes, Barry H. "Playing with the Devil: Adolescent Involvement with the Occult, Black Magic, Witchcraft, and the Satanic to Manage Feelings of Despair," *Dissertation Abstracts International* 50, no. 12-B, Pt.1 (June 1990): 5904–5905.

"Special Ralph M. Lewis Memorial Issue." *Rosicrucian Digest* (1987).

Special Report to the Readers of THE URANTIA BOOK: URANTIA Foundation Ends Its Relationship with the Former URANTIA Brotherhood. Chicago: URANTIA Foundation, 1990.

Speeth, Katherine Riodan. *The Gurdjieff Work.* Berkeley, Calif: And/Or Press, 1976. Rev. ed., Los Angeles: Jeremy P. Tarcher, 1989.

Spence, Lewis. *Atlantis in America.* London: Ernest Benn, 1925. Reprint, Detroit: Singing Tree Press, 1972.

———. *British Fairy Origins.* London: Watts, 1946.

———. *The Civilization of Ancient Mexico.* London, 1911.

———. *The Fairy Tradition in Britain.* London; New York: Rider, 1948.

———. *The Gods of Mexico.* London: Fisher, Unwin, 1913.

———. *The History of Atlantis.* 1926. Reprint, New Hyde Park, N.Y.: University Books, 1968.

———. *The Magic and Mysteries of Mexico.* London: Rider; Philadelphia: David McKay, 1930.

———. *Magical Arts in Celtic Britain.* London: Rider, n.d.

———. *Mysteries of Egypt.* London, 1929. Reprint, Baluvelt, N.Y.: Multimedia (Steiner Books), 1972.

———. *Myths and Legends of Babylonia & Assyria.* London, 1916. Reprint, Detroit: Gale Research, 1975.

———. *The Myths of Mexico and Peru.* London: Harrap, 1913.

———. *The Occult Causes of the Present War.* N.p., 1940.

———. *The Occult Sciences in Atlantis.* London: Rider, 1943. Reprint, New York: S. Weiser, 1970.

———. *The Popul Vuh: The Mythic & Heroic Sagas of the Kichés of Central America.* London: David Nutt, 1908.

———. *The Problem of Atlantis.* London: Rider, 1924. Reprinted as *Atlantis Discovered.* New York: Causeway Books, 1974.

———. *The Problem of Lemuria.* London: Rider, 1932.

———. *Scottish Ghosts and Goblins.* N.p., 1952.

———. *Second Sight: Its History and Origins.* London; New York: Rider, 1951.

———. *Will Europe Follow Atlantis?* N.p., 1942.

Sperling, Harry, and Maurice Simon, trans. *The Zohar.* 5 vols. New York: Rebecca Bennet Publishing, n.d.

Spicer, Henry. *Facts and Fantasies: A Sequel to "Sights and Sounds."* London, 1853.

———. *Sights and Sounds: The Mystery of the Day; Comprising an Entire History of the American "Spirit" Manifestations.* London: Thomas Bosworth, 1853.

Spiegel, H., and D. Spiegal. *Trance and Treatment: Clinical Users of Hypnosis.* New York: Basis Books, 1978.

Spirit Evolution. London: Atlanteans, 1976.

Spirit Teachings. 1898. Reprint, London: Spiritualist Press, 1949.

Spirito, Ugo. *Il Problematicismo* (Problematicism). Firenze: G. C. Sansoni, 1948.

———. *La vita come amore* (Life as Love). N.p., 1953. Reprint, Firenze: G. C. Sansoni, 1970.

———. *La Vita come arte* (Life as Art). N.p., 1941.

———. *La Vita come ricerca* (Life as a Search). 2d ed. Firenze: G. C. Sansoni, 1943.

———. *Scienza e Filosofia* (Science and Philosophy). Firenze: G. C. Sansoni, 1950.

Spiritual Frontiers Fellowship. *Christianity and the Paranormal.* Independence, Mo. The Author, 1986.

The Spiritual Philosophy of Shrii Shrii Anandamurti. Denver: Ananda Marga Publications, 1981.

Spiritual Unfoldment and Psychic Development through Inner Light Consciousness. Atlanta, Ga.: Fellowship of the Inner Light, n.d.

Spiro, Melford E. *Burmese Supernaturalism.* Englewood Cliffs, N.J.: Prentice-Hall, 1967.

Spraggett, Allen. *Kathryn Kuhlman: The Woman Who Believes in Miracles.* New York: Thomas Y. Crowell, 1970. Reprint, New York: New American Library, 1971.

Spraggett, Allen, with William V. Rauscher. *Arthur Ford: The Man Who Talked with the Dead.* New York: New American Library, 1973.

Sprenger, Jakob, and Heinrich Kramer. *Malleus Maleficarum.* Edited by Montague Summers. London, 1928.

Squire, Charles. *Mythology of the Ancient Britons.* London, 1905.

St. Aubyn, Lorna, ed. *Healing.* London: Heineman, 1983.

St. Clair, David. *David St. Clair's Lessons in Instant ESP.* Englewood Cliffs, N.J.: Prentice Hall, 1978.

———. *Drum and Candle.* Garden City, N.Y.: Doubleday; London: Macdonald, 1971.

———. *Psychic Healers.* Garden City, N.Y.: Doubleday, 1974. Rev. ed. New York: Bantam, 1979.

———. *The Psychic World of California.* Garden City, N.Y.: Doubleday, 1972.

———. *Watseka: America's Most Extraordinary Case of Possession & Exorcism.* Chicago: Playboy Press; 1977. Distributed by Simon & Schuster.

St. Thomas Aquinas and His Legacy. Washington, D.C.: Catholic University of America, 1994.

Staff, V. S. *Remembered on Waking; Concerning Psychic & Spiritual Dreams & Theories of Dreaming.* Crowborough, UK: V. S. Staff, 1975.

Stamp, Tom, and Cordelia Stamp. *William Scoresby, Arctic Scientist.* Whitby, UK: Whitby Press, 1975.

Stanford, Rex G. "Case Studies, Folklore and Personal Experiences of Investigators: Their Role in Experimental Research." In *Spontaneous Psi, Depth Psychology and Parapsychology,* edited by Betty Shapin and Lisette Coly. New York: Parapsychology Foundation, 1992.

———. "Scientific, Ethical and Clinical Problems in the 'Training' of Psi Ability." In *Research in Parapsychology 1976,* edited by William G. Roll and R. L. Morris. Metuchen, N.J.: Scarecrow Press, 1977.

———. "A Study of the Cause of Low Run-Score Variance." *Journal of Parapsychology* 30 (1966).

Stanford, Rex G., and Gary Thompson. "Unconscious Psi-mediated Instrumental Response and its Relation to Conscious ESP Performance." In W. G. Roll, R. L. Morris, and J. D. Morris, eds. *Research in Parapsychology 1973* Metuchen, N.J.: Scarecrow Press, 1974.

Stanford, Rex G., and Peter Rust. "Psi-mediated Helping Behavior: Experimental Paradigm and Initial Results." In J. D. Morris, W. G. Roll, and R. L. Morris, eds. *Research in Parapsychology 1976* Metuchen, N.J.: Scarecrow Press, 1977.

Stanford, Rex G., R. Zennhausern, A. Taylor, and M. Dwyer. "Psychokinesis as a Psi-mediated Instrumental Response." *Journal of the American Society for Psychical Research* 69 (1975).

Stanhope, Earl. *Tracts Relative to Caspar Hauser.* London: James S. Hodson, 1836.

Stanton, Horace. *Telepathy of the Celestial World.* New York, 1913.

Stanway, Andrew. *Alternative Medicine.* New York: Penguin, 1982.

Stapleton, Ruth Carter. *The Experience of Inner Healing.* Waco, Tex.: Word Books, 1977.

———. *The Gift of Inner Healing.* Waco, Tex.: Word Books, 1976.

———. *In His Footsteps.* San Francisco: Harper & Row, 1979.

Starhawk. *Dreaming in the Dark.* Boston: Beacon Press, 1982.

———. *The Spiral Dance.* San Francisco: Harper & Row, 1979.

Starhawk. *Truth or Dare: Encounters of Power, Authority, Mystery.* San Francisco: Harper & Row, 1987.

Stark, Erwin E. *A History of Dowsing and Energy Relationships.* North Hollywood, Calif.: BAC, 1978.

Starkey, Marion L. *The Devil in Massachusetts.* New York: Time, 1949. Reprint, Garden City, N.Y.: Doubleday, 1952.

Starkie, Walter. *Raggle Taggle; Adventures With a Fiddle in Hungary and Roumania.* London, 1933.

Stavert, Geoffrey. *A Study in Southsea.* Portsmouth, England: Milestone Publications, 1987.

Stead, Christiane. *The Power of Holistic Aromatherapy.* Poole, England: Javalin Books, 1986.

Stead, Estelle W. *Faces of the Living Dead.* London, 1925.

Stead, William T. *After Death.* New York: John Lane, 1907. Reprint, London: Review of Reviews, 1914.

———. *Letters from Julia; or Light from the Borderland: A Series of Messages as to the Life Beyond the Grave Received by Automatic Writing.* London, 1897.

———. *Real Ghost Stories.* London, 1891. Reprinted as *Borderland: A Casebook of True Supernatural Stories.* New Hyde Park, N.Y.: University Books, 1970.

———. *Real Ghost Stories.* London, 1892. Rev. ed. 1897. Reprinted as *Borderland: A Casebook of True Supernatural Stories.* New Hyde Park, N.Y.: University Books, 1970.

Stearn, Jess. *The Power of Alpha-Thinking: Miracle of the Mind.* New York: William Morrow, 1976. Reprint, New York: New American Library, 1977.

Steckling, Fred. *We Discovered Alien Bases on the Moon.* Vista, Calif.: GAF International Publishers, 1981.

———. *Why Are We Here?* New York: Vantage Press, 1969.

Steen, Douglas. "Success with Complex Targets in a PK Baseball Game." *Journal of Parapsychology* (June 1957).

Stegall, C., and C. C. Harwood. *The Modern Tongues and Healing Movement.* Western Bible Institute, n.d.

Steiger, Brad. *Aquarian Revelations.* New York: Dell, 1971.

———. *Astral Projection.* Rockport, Mass.: Para Research, 1982.

———. *Gods of Aquarius: UFOs and the Transformation of Man.* New York: Harcourt Brace Jovanovich, 1976.

———. *Guardian Angels & Spirit Guides.* New York: NAL/Dutton, 1999.

———. *In My Soul I Am Free.* New York: Lancer Books, 1968.

———. *Irene Hughes on Psychic Safari.* New York: Warner Paperback Library, 1972.

———. *Kahuna Magic.* Rockport, Mass.: Para Research, 1971.

———. *The Psychic Feats of Olof Jonsson.* New York: Popular Library, 1971.

———. *Revelation: The Divine Fire.* Englewood Cliffs, N.J.: Prentice-Hall, 1973.

———. *The Seed.* New York: Berkley Books, 1983.

———. *Strange Disappearances.* New York: Magnum Books, 1972.

Steiger, Brad, and Joan Whritenour. *New UFO Breakthrough: The Allende Letters.* New York: Award Books, 1968.

Stein, Diane. *The Women's Spirituality Book.* St. Paul, Minn.: Llewellyn Publications, 1987.

Stein, Gordon. "The Amazing Medium Mirabelli." *Fate* 44, 3 (March 1991): 86–95.

———. *Encyclopedia of Hoaxes.* Detroit: Gale Research, 1993.

Stein, Sandra Kovacs. *Instant Numerology: Charting Your Road Map to the Future.* New York: Harper & Row, 1979.

Steinbach, Marten. *Medical Palmistry: Health & Character in the Hand.* New Hyde Park, N.Y.: University Books, 1975. Reprint, New York: New American Library, 1976.

Steiner, Johannes. *Thérèse Neumann: A Portrait Based on Authentic Accounts, Journals, and Documents.* Staten Island, N.Y.: Alba House, 1967.

Steiner, Robert A. "Exposing the Faith-Healers." *The Skeptical Inquirer* 11, 1 (fall 1986).

Steiner, Rudolf. *Christianity as Mystical Fact.* West Nyack, N.Y.: Rudolf Steiner Publications, 1961.

———. *Clairvoyance.* N.p., 1861, 1925. Reprint, New York: Krishna Press, 1973.

———. *Cosmic Memory: Prehistory of Earth and Man.* West Nyack, N.Y.: Rudolf Steiner Publications, 1959. Reprint, West Nyack, N.Y.: Paperback Library, 1968.

———. *The Course of My Life.* New York: Anthroposophical Press, 1951.

———. *Goethe's Conception of the World.* Reprint, Brooklyn: Haskell, 1972.

———. *Knowledge of the Higher Worlds: How Is It Achieved?.* 1923. Rev. ed., London: R. Steiner Press, 1969.

———. *The Lord's Prayer.* London: Anthroposophic Press, n.d.

———. *Reincarnation and Immortality.* New York: Harper & Row, 1980.

———. *The Story of My Life.* London: Anthroposophical Publishing, 1928; New York: Anthroposophic Press, 1928.

———. *The Theory of Knowledge Implicit in Goethe's World Conception.* Hudson, N.Y.: Anthroposophic Press, 1978.

Steinkamp, Fiona, Julie Milton, and Robert L. Morris. "A Meta-Analysis of Forced-Choice Experiments Comparing Clairvoyance and Precognition." *Journal of Parapsychology* 62, no. 3 (September 1998): 193–218.

Stekert, Ellen. "The Snake Handling Sect of Harlan County, Kentucky: Its Influences on Folk Tradition." *Southern Folklore Quarterly* 27 (December 1963).

Stelle, Robert D. *The Sun Rises.* Ramona, Calif.: Lemurian Fellowship, 1952.

Stemman, Roy. *Medium Rare: The Psychic Life of Ena Twigg.* London: Spiritualist Association of Great Britain, 1971.

———. *One Hundred Years of Spiritualism: The Story of the Spiritualist Association of Great Britain, 1872–1912.* London: SAGB, 1972.

———. *Spirits and Spirit Worlds.* London: Aldus Books, 1975. Reprint, Garden City, N.Y.: Doubleday, 1976.

Stephens, George. *Prof. S. Bugge's "Studies on Northern Mythology" Shortly Examined.* London: Williams & Norgate, 1883.

———. *The Old-Northern Runic Monuments of Scandinavia and England.* 2 vols. London, 1866–68.

Stern, Jess. *The Power of Alpha Thinking: Miracle of the Mind.* New York: William Morrow, 1976.

Stern, Madeleine B. *Heads and Headlines: The Phrenological Fowlers.* Norman: University of Oklahoma Press, 1971.

Stevens, E. W. *The Watseka Wonder.* Chicago: Religion-Philosophical Journal, 1879.

Stevens, Jose, and Simon Warwick-Smith. *Essence and Personality: The Michael Handbook.* Orinda, Calif.: Warwick Press, 1987.

Stevens, Paul. "Remote Psychokinesis," *European Journal of Parapsychology* 14 (1998–1999): 68–79.

Stevens, William O. *Beyond the Sunset.* New York: Dodd, Mead, 1944.

———. *Mystery of Dreams.* New York: Dodd, Mead, 1949. Reprint, London: Allen & Unwin, 1950.

———. *Psychics and Common Sense.* New York: Dodd, Mead, 1945.

———. *Unbidden Guests.* N.p., 1945.

Stevenson, Ian. "An Antagonist's View of Parapsychology. A Review of Professor Hansel's 'ESP: A Scientific Evaluation.'" *Journal of American Society for Psychical Research* 61 (July 1967).

———. *Cases of the Reincarnation Type.* 4 vols. Charlottesville: University of Virginia Press, 1975, 1977, 1980, 1983.

———. "A Communicator Unknown to Medium and Sitter." *Journal of the American Society for Psychical Research* 64 (1970).

———. "A Review & Analysis of Paranormal Experiences Connected with the Sinking of the Titanic." *Journal of American Society for Psychical Research* 54 (1961).

———. *Telepathic Impressions: A Review and Report of Thirty-five New Cases.* Charlottesville: University Press of Virginia, 1970.

———. *Twelve Cases in Lebanon & Turkey.* N.p., 1980.

———. *Twenty Cases Suggestive of Reincarnation.* 2d ed. Charlottesville: University Press of Virginia, 1974.

———. *Unlearned Language: New Studies in Xenoglossy.* Charlottesville: University of Virginia Press, 1984.

———. *Xenoglossy: A Review and Report of a Case.* Charlottesville: University of Virginia Press, 1974.

Stewart, Basil. *The Mystery of the Great Pyramid: Traditions Concerning It and Its Connection with the Egyptian Book of the Dead.* London, 1929.

Stewart, James R. "Cattle Mutilations: An Episode of Collective Delusion." *The Zetetic* 1, 2 (Spring–Summer 1977): 55–66.

Stewart, Kenneth M. "Spirit Possession." *Tomorrow* (spring 1956).

———. "Spirit Possession in Native America." *Southwestern Journal of Anthropology* 2, no. 3 (1946).

Stewart, R. J. *UnderWorld Initiation: A Journey Towards Psychic Transformation.* Wellingborough, England: Aquarian Press, 1985.

Stewart, W. C. "Three New ESP Test Machines and Some Preliminary Results." *Journal of Parapsychology* (March 1959).

Stifler, Kenneth R., Joanne Greer, William Sneck, and Robert Dovenmuehle. "An Empirical Investigation of the Discriminability of Reported Mystical Experiences among Religious Contemplatives, Psychotic Inpatients, and Normal Adults," *Journal for the Scientific Study of Religion* 32, no. 4 (December 1993): 366–372.

Stillings, Dennis, ed. *Cyberbiological Studies of the Imaginal Component in the UFO Contact Experience.* St. Paul, Minn.: Archaeus Project, 1989.

Stillman, John M. *Theophrastus Bombast von Hohenheim called Paracelsus; his Personality and Influence as Physician, Chemist and Reformer.* LaSalle, Ill.: Open Court Publishing, 1920.

Stobart, St. Clair. *Ancient Lights.* N.p., 1923.

———. *The Either Or of Spiritualism.* N.p., 1928.

———. *Torchbearers of Spiritualism.* N.p., 1925.

Stockhammer, Thomas. *Thomas Aquinas Dictionary.* New York: Philosophical Library, 1965.

Stockman, Robert H. *The Baha'i Faith in America: Origins, 1892–1900.* Wilmette, Ill.: Baha'i Publishing Trust, 1985.

Stockwell, Shelley L. *Automatic Writing & Hieroscripting.* Rancho Palos Verdes, Calif.: Creativity Unlimited Press, 1996.

Stockton, Bayard. *Catapult: The Biography of Robert A. Monroe.* Norfolk, Va.: Donning, 1989.

Stoker, Bram. *Dracula.* London: Constable, 1897.

———. *Dracula's Guest and Other Weird Stories.* London: George Routledge & Sons, 1914.

Stokes, Doris. *Voices in My Ear: The Autobiography of a Medium.* London: Futura, 1981. Thorndike, Maine: G. K. Hall and Co., 1989.

Stones, Bones and Skin. Ritual and Shamanistic Art. Toronto: The Society for Art Publications, 1977.

Storr, Anthony. *The School of Genius.* London: A. Deutsch, 1988.

The Story of Aetherius Society. Hollywood, Calif.: Aetherius Society, n.d.

The Story of the Lotus Ashram. Miami, Fla.: Lotus Ashram, n.d.

The Story of the White Eagle Lodge. Liss, England: White Eagle Publishing Trust, 1986.

Story, Francis, and Nyanaponika Thera. *Rebirth as Doctrine and Experience.* Kandy, Sri Lanka: Buddhist Publication Society, 1975.

Story, Ronald D. *The Space-Gods Revealed.* New York: Harper & Row, 1976; Barnes & Noble, 1978.

———. "Von Däniken's Golden Gods." *The Zetetic* 2, no. 1 (1977).

———. *The Space Gods Revealed: A Close Look at Erich von Däniken.* New York: Harper and Row, 1976.

Stoudt, J. J. *Sunrise to Eternity.* Philadelphia: University of Pennsylvania, 1957.

Stowes, K. D. *The Land of Shalam: Children's Land.* Evansville, Ind.: Frank Molinet Print Shop, n.d.

Strachan, Françoise. *Casting Out the Devils.* London: Aquarian Press, 1972.

Stratton, F. J. M. "Four Modern Ghosts." *Journal of the Society for Psychical Research* 39 (1938).

———. "Psychical Research—A Lifelong Interest." *Proceedings of the Society for Psychical Research* (1953).

Strauch, Inge H. "Dreams and Psi in the Laboratory." In *Psi Favorable States of Consciousness,* edited by R. Cavenna. New York: Parapsychology Foundation, 1970.

Strauch, Inge H. "Medical Aspects of 'Mental' Healing." *International Journal of Parapsychology* 5 (1963).

Street, Noel. *Karma: Your Whispering Wisdom.* Fabens, Tex.: Lotus Ashram, 1978.

———. *Reincarnation: One Life—Many Births.* Fabens, Tex.: Lotus Ashram, 1978.

Strelley, Kate. *The Ultimate Gate.* San Francisco: Harper & Row, 1987.

Strieber, Whitley. *Communion: A True Story.* New York: William Morrow, 1987.

———. *Majestic.* New York: G. P. Putnam's Sons, 1989.

———. *Transformation: The Breakthrough.* New York: William Morrow, 1988.

Stromberg, Gustaf. *Det Eviga Sökandet* (The Eternal Quest). N.p., 1948.

———. *God's Place in Modern Science.* N.p., 1958.

———. *Psychic Phenomena and Modern Science.* N.p., 1957.

———. *The Searchers.* N.p., 1948.

———. *The Soul of the Universe.* N.p., 1940.

Strommenburg, Aaders Gabriel. *A Prophecy Concerning the Swedish Monarchy As It was Related in 1809.* New York: Colburn & Tegg, 1968.

———. *Second Sight in Daily Life.* New York: Coward-McCann, 1949.

Strutt, John William. "Presidential Address." *Proceedings of the Society for Psychical Research* 30, no. 77 (1918–19).

Strutt, Robert John. "A Method of Silhouette Photography by Infra-Red Rays for Use in Mediumistic Investigation." *Proceedings of the Society for Psychical Research* 41, 128 (1932).

———. "The Problem of Physical Phenomena in Connection with Psychical Research." *Proceedings of the Society for Psychical Research* 44, 152 (1938).

———. "The Question of Lights Supposed to Have Been Observed near the Poles of a Magnet." *Proceedings of the Society for Psychical Research* 44, 153 (1938–39).

———. "Some Recollections of Henry Sidgwick." *Proceedings of the Society for Psychical Research* 44, 156 (1936–39).

Stuart, C. E. "A Classroom ESP Experiment with the Free Response Method." *Journal of Parapsychology* 9 (1945).

———. "The Effect of Rate of Movement in Card Matching Tests of Extrasensory Perception." *Journal of Parapsychology* 2 (1938).

———. "GESP Experiment with the Free Response Method." *Journal of Parapsychology* 10 (1946).

———. "An Interest Inventory Relation to ESP Scores." *Journal of Parapsychology* 10 (1945).

———. "A Review of Recent Criticisms of ESP Research." *Journal of Parapsychology* 2, no. 3 (1939).

Stuart, C. E., and J. G. Pratt. *A Handbook for Testing Extrasensory Perception.* New York: Farrar and Rinehart, 1937.

Stuart, C. E., J. G. Pratt, J. B. Rhine, B. M. Smith, and J. A. Greenwood. *Extrasensory Perception After Sixty Years.* New York: Henry Holt, 1940. Rev. ed. Boston: Bruce Humphries, 1966.

Stuart, Charles. "An Analysis to Determine a Test Predictive of Extra-chance Scoring in Card-calling Tests." *Journal of Parapsychology* vol. 5 (1941).

———."An Interest Inventory Relation to ESP Scores." *Journal of Parapsychology* vol. 10 (1946).

Stuart, David. *Alan Watts.* Radnor, Pa.: Chilton Book, 1976.

Stupple, David W. "Historical Links Between the Occult and Flying Saucers." *Journal of UFO Studies,* 5 (1994): 93–108.

Sturdevant, William D. *Extrasensory Color Perception.* N.p., 1958.

———. *Fluorescent Color Perception and Graphic Response in the Perceptually Impaired Child.* N.p., 1957.

Sturge-Whiting, J. R. *The Mystery of Versailles: A Complete Solution.* London: Rider, 1938.

Subhan, John. *Sufism: Its Saints and Shrines.* York Beach, Maine: Samuel Weiser, 1973.

Sudre, R. "The Ideas of Hans Driesch." *Journal of the American Society for Psychical Research* 20 (1926).

Sudre, René. "The Case of Victor Hugo and the Collective Psychism." *Psychic Research* 23 (1971).

———. *Introduction à la métapsychique humaine* (Introduction to Human Metapsychics). N.p., 1929.

———. "Is the Soul Material?" *Psychic Research* 24 (1930).

———. *La Lutte pour la métapsychique* (The Fight for Parapsychology). N.p., 1928.

———. *Le Huitième art—Mission de la radio* (The Eighth Art—Mission of Radio). N.p., 1946.

———. *Les Nouvelles énigmes de l'univers* (New Enigmas of the Universe). N.p., 1943.

———. *Personnages d'au-delà* (People from the Beyond). N.p., 1945.

———. *Traité de parapsychologie.* 1956. Translated as *Treatise on Parapsychology: Essay on the Scientific Interpretation of the Human Phenomenon Known as the Supernatural.* New York: Citadel Press, 1960.

Sudre, Rene. "The Life and Works of Schrenck-Notzing." *Psychic Research* 23 (1929).

Sugden, E. H. "Note on Muscle Reading." *Proceedings of the Society for Psychical Research* 1, 4 (1882–83).

Sullivan, Jack, ed. *The Penguin Encyclopedia of Horror and the Supernatural.* New York: Viking Press, 1986.

Summers, Montague. *Geography of Witchcraft.* London, 1927.

———. *A Gothic Bibliography.* London: Fortune Press, 1940.

———. *The Gothic Quest: A History of the Gothic Novel.* 1938. Reprint, London: Fortune Press, 1950.

———. *The Gallantry Show.* London: Cecil Woolf, 1980.

———. *The Geography of Witchcraft.* London, 1927. Reprint, New Hyde Park, N.Y.: University Books, 1958.

———. *A History of Demonology and Witchcraft.* New York: Alfred A. Knopf, 1926.

———. *The Physical Phenomena of Mysticism.* London: Rider, 1950.

———. *A Popular History of Witchcraft.* New York: Causeway Books, 1973.

———. *The Vampire: His Kith and Kin.* London: Routledge, Kegan Paul, Trench, Trubner, 1928. Reprint, New York: University Books, 1960.

———. *The Vampire in Europe.* London:Routledge, Kegan Paul, Trench, Trubner, 1929; New York: University Books, 1962.

———. *Witchcraft and Black Magic.* London: Rider, 1946. Reprint, New York: Causeway Books, 1974.

———. *The Werewolf.* London, Kegan Paul, Trench, Trubner, 1933. Reprint, New Hyde Park, N.Y.: University Books, 1966.

Sun Bear. *Path of Power.* Spokane, Wash.: Bear Tribe Publishing, 1983.

Sunderland, La Roy. "An Appeal on the Subject of Slavery." *Zion's Watchman* (December 5, 1834).

———. *The Book of Human Nature.* New York: Stearns, 1853.

———. *"Confessions of a Magnitizer" Exposed.* Boston: Redding, 1845.

———. *Ideology.* Boston: J. P. Mendum, 1885–87.

———. *Pathetism; With Practical Instructions: Demonstrating the Falsity of the Hitherto Prevalent Assumptions in Regard to What Has Been Called "Mesmerism" and "Neurology," and Illustrating Those Laws Which Induce Somnambulism, Second Sight, Sleep, Dreaming, Trance, and Clairvoyance, with Numerous Facts Tending to Show the Pathology of Monomania, Insanity, Witchcraft, and Various Other Mental or Nervous Phenomena.* Boston: White and Potter, 1847.

———. *Testimony of God Against Slavery.* Boston: D. K. Hitchcock, 1836.

———. *The Trance.* Chicago: J. Walker, 1868.

———. *Trance and Correlative Phenomena.* Chicago: J. Walker, 1868.

———. *The Trance, and How Introduced.* Boston, 1860.

Superet Light Doctrine Ministry. Los Angeles: Superet Press, 1947.

Suster, Gerald. *The Legacy of the Beast.* York Beach, Maine: Samuel Weiser, 1989.

Sutherland, Elizabeth. *Ravens and Black Rain: The Story of Highland Second Sight.* London: Constable, 1986.

Sutherland, Gail Hinich. *The Disguises of the Demon: The Development of the Yaksa in Hinduism and Buddhism.* Albany: State University of New York Press, 1991.

Sutphen, Dick. *Sedona: Psychic Energy Vortexes.* Malibu, Calif.: Valley of the Sun Publishing, 1986.

Suzuki, D. T. *Manual of Zen Buddhism.* New York: Grove Press, 1960.

———. *Zen Buddhism: Selected Writings of D. T. Suzuki.* Edited by William Barrett. New York: Doubleday/Anchor, 1956.

Suzuki, D. T., and Paul Carus, trans. *The Canon of Reason and Virtue.* La Salle, Ill.: Open Court, 1913.

Swaffer, Hannen. *Adventures with Inspiration.* London: Kennerly, Morely and Mitchell, 1929.

———. *Behind the Scenes.* N.p., 1928.

———. *Hannen Swaffer's Who's Who.* London: Hutchinson, 1929.

———. *Norcliffe's Return.* London: Hutchinson, 1925.

———. *Studies in Psychology.* N.p., 1933.

Swainson, William P. *Thomas Lake Harris and His Occult Teaching.* London: William Rider & Son, 1922.

Swami Ramacharaka [William Walker Atkinson]. *Fourteen Lessons in Yogi Philosophy and Oriental Occultism.* Chicago: Yogi Publication Society, 1903.

———. *Reincarnation and the Law of Karma.* Yogi Publication Society, 1908.

Swann, Ingo. *Cosmic Art.* New York: Hawthorn Books, 1975.

———. *Natural ESP: A Layman's Guide to Unlocking the Extra Sensory Power of Your Mind.* New York: Bantam, 1987.

———. *Star Fire.* New York: Dell, 1978.

———. *To Kiss Earth Goody-bye.* New York: Hawthorn Books, 1974. Reprint, New York: Laurel/Dell, 1975.

———. *Your Nostradamus Factor: Accessing Your Innate Ability to See into the Future.* New York: Simon & Schuster, 1993.

Swann, William F. G. "Is the Universe Planned?" *Journal of the Franklin Institute* (May 1953).

———. "The Known and the Unknown." *Journal of the Franklin Institute* (May 1955).

———. "Nature and the Mind of Man." *Journal of the Franklin Institute* (June 1956).

———. "Reality, Imagery and Fantasy." *Journal of the Franklin Institute* (May 1957).

———. "The Science of Yesterday, Today and Tomorrow." *Journal of the Franklin Institute* (March 1960).

Swedenborg, Emanuel. *Arcana Coelestia.* 12 vols. New York: Swedenborg Foundation, 1905–1910.

———. *Divine Love and Wisdom.* New York: Swedenborg Foundation, n.d.

———. *Earths in Our Solar System Which Are Called Planets, and Earths in the Starry Heaven, Their Inhabitants, and the Spirits and Angels There.* London: Swedenborg Society, 1860. Frequently reprinted.

———. *Earths in Planets & in Starry Heavens: Inhabitants, Spirits & Angels.* London, 1758.

———. *Heaven and Hell.* 1758. Reprint, New York: E. P. Dutton, 1931. Reprint: Swedenborg Foundation, 1979.

———. *On the Divine Love and on the Divine Wisdom.* London: Swedenborg Society, 1963.

———. *The New Jerusalem and Its Heavenly Doctrine.* London: Swedenborg Society, 1938.

———. *The True Christian Religion.* London: Swedenborg Society, 1950.

Swettenham, Sir Frank A. *Malay Sketches.* London: John Lane, 1895.

Swihart, Altman K. *Since Mrs. Eddy.* New York: Henry Holt, 1931.

Swindoll, Charles R. *Tongues.* Insight for Living, 1935, 1998. Reprint, Grand Rapids, Mich.: Zondervan Publishing House, 1995.

The Sword Book of Honourius the Magician. Translated and edited by Daniel J. Driscoll. Gilette, N.J.: Heptangle Books, 1977.

Sykes, Pat. *You Don't Know John Cain?* London: Van Duren, 1980.

Sylvestre, Ralph E. *Gambols with the Ghosts: Mind Reading, Spiritualistic Effects, Mental and Psychical Phenomena, and Horoscopy.* Chicago: privately printed, 1901.

Symmes, Americus, ed. *The Symmes' Theory of Concentric Spheres: Demonstrating that the Earth is Hollow, Habitable Within, and Widely Open about the Poles.* Louisville, Ky.: Bradley and Gilbert, 1878.

Symonds, J. A. *The Life of Benvenuto Cellini.* 2 vols. London, 1888.

Symonds, John. *The Great Beast.* London: MacDonald, 1971. Reprint, St. Albans, England: Mayflower, 1973.

———. *The King of the Shadow Realm.* London: Duckworth, 1989.

———. *Light Over Water.* London: J. Baker for the Unicorn Press, 1963.

———. *Madame Blavatsky, Medium and Magician.* London: Odhams Press, 1958.

———. *The Magic of Aleister Crowley.* London: Frederick Muller, 1958.

———. *Thomas Brown and the Angels.* London: Hutchinson, 1961.

Symonds, John, and Kenneth Grant. *The Confessions of Aleister Crowley.* New York: Hill & Wang, 1969.

Synan, Vincent, ed. *Aspects of Pentecostal-Charismatic Origins.* Plainfield, N.J.: Losgos International, 1975.

Table Turning and Table Talking Considered in Connection with the Dictates of Reason and Common Sense. Bath, UK: S. Gibbs, 1853.

Table Turning by Animal Magnetism Demonstrated. London, 1853.

Tabori, Paul. *Beyond the Senses: A Report on Psychical Research in the Sixties.* N.p., 1971.

———. *Companions of the Unseen.* London: H. A. Humphrey, 1968. Reprint, London: Souvenir Press, 1972.

———. *Crime and the Occult.* N.p., 1974.

———. *Harry Price: The Biography of a Ghost-Hunter.* London: Athenaenum Press, 1930.

———. *Pioneers of the Unseen.* London: Souvenir Press, 1972.

Tabori, Paul, and Cornelius Tabori. *My Occult Diary.* London, 1951. Reprint, New York: Living Books, 1966.

Tabori, Paul, and P. Raphael. *Crime and the Occult.* N.p., 1974.

Tabori, Paul, and Peter Underwood. *The Borley Ghosts.* N.p., 1973.

———. *The Ghosts of Borley: Annals of the Haunted Rectory.* Newton Abbot, UK: David and Charles, 1973.

Tadblavananda, Avadhuta Archrya. *Glimpses of Prout Philosophy.* Copenhagen, Denmark: Central Proutish Publications, 1981.

Tanagras, A. *Psychophysical Elements in Parapsychological Transactions.* New York: Parapsychology Institute, 1967.

Tanagras, Angelos. *Destiny and Chance.* N.p., 1934.

Tapley, Charles Sutherland. *Rebecca Nurse.* Boston: Marshall Jones, 1930.

Targ, Russell. *The Mind Race: Understanding and Using Psychic Abilities.* New York: Villard Books, 1984.

Targ, Russel, and Harold E. Puthoff. "ESP Experiments with Uri Geller." In *Research in Parapsychology 1973.* Metuchen, N.J.: Scarecrow Press, 1974.

———. "Information Transmission under Conditions of Sensory Shielding." *Nature* (October 1974).

———. *Mind Reach: Scientists Look at Psychical Research.* New York: Delacorte Press, 1977.

———. "PK Experiments with Uri Geller and Ingo Swann." In *Research in Parapsychology 1973.* Metuchen, N.J.: Scarecrow Press, 1974.

Targ, Russel, Harold E. Puttoff, and Charles T. Tart. *Mind at Large.* New York: Praeger, 1979.

Targ, Russell, and Keith Harary. *The Mind Race: Understanding and Using Psychic Abilities.* New York: Villard Books, 1984.

Tarne, Ingham. "A Little Lower Than the Angels. . . and Crowned with Glory." *Meditation* 3, no. 4 (Fall 1988): 24–28.

Tarostar. *A Book of Shadows.* New Brunswick, N.J.: Inner Light Publications,1987.

Tart, Charles T. *Altered States of Consciousness.* Garden City, N.Y.: Anchor/Doubleday, 1972.

———. "Firewalk." *Parapsychology Review* 18, no. 3 (May–June 1987).

———. *States of Consciousness.* New York: E. P. Dutton, 1975.

Tart, Charles T., and Harold E. Puttoff. *Mind at Large.* New York: Praeger, 1979.

Tart, Charles T., ed. *Altered States of Consciousness: A Book of Readings.* New York: John Wiley & Sons, 1969.

———. *The Application of Learning Theory to Extrasensory Perception.* 1975.

———. *Learning to Use Extrasensory Perception.* 1976.

———. *On Being Stoned: A Psychological Study of Marijuana Intoxication.* Palo Alto, Calif.: Science & Behavior Books, 1971.

———. *Psi, Scientific Studies of the Psychic Realm.* N.p., 1977.

———. *States of Consciousness.* N.p., 1975.

———. *Transpersonal Psychologies.* New York: Harper & Row, 1975.

———. *Waking Up: Overcoming the Obstacles to Human Potential.* N.p., 1986.

Tasso, Torquato. *Jerusalem Delivered.* Rutherford, N.J.: Fairleigh Dickinson University Press, 1970.

Taussig, Michael. *Shamanism, Colonialism, and the Wild Man: A Study in Terror and Healing.* Chicago: University of Chicago Press, 1987.

Tautriadelta [Roslyn D'Onston]. "A Modern Magician: An Autobiography. By a Pupil of Lord Lytton." *Borderland* 3, no. 2 (April 1896).

Taves, Ernest H. "Communion with the Imagination." *The Skeptical Inquirer* 12, 1 (Fall 1987).

Taylor, John *The Horizons of Knowledge.* N.p., 1982.

———. "A New Theory for ESP," *Journal of the Society for Psychical Research* 62, no. 851 (April 1998): 289–310.

———. *Science and the Supernatural.* New York: E. P. Dutton, 1980.

———. *The Shape of Minds to Come.* N.p., 1971.

———. *Superminds: A Scientist Looks at the Paranormal.* London: Macmillan, 1975; New York: Viking Press, 1975; New York: Warner Books, 1975.

Taylor, Michael Brooks. " 'Try the Spirits': Shaker Responses to Supernaturalism." *Journal of Religious Studies* 7 (fall 1979): 30–38.

Taylor, Peggy. "Life at the Leading Edge: A New Age Interview with Marilyn Ferguson." *New Age* 8, no. 1 (August 1982): 30–35, 52–53.

Taylor, Sascha. *Glanvill: The Uses and Abuses of Skepticism.* New York: Pergamon Press, 1981.

Taylor, W. G. Langworthy. *Katie Fox, Epoch-making Medium and the Making of the Fox-Taylor Record.* Boston: Bruce, 1933.

Taylor, W. S. *Morton Prince and Abnormal Psychology.* New York; London: D. Appleton & Co., 1928.

Taylor, Wayne. *Pillars of Light.* Columbus, N.Mex.: The Author, 1965.

Teachings of the Temple. 3 vols. Halcyon, Calif.: Temple of the People, 1947–85.

Teahan, John F. "Warren Felt Evans and Mental Healing: Romantic Idealism and Practical Metaphysics in Nineteenth-Century America." *Church History* 48, no. 1 (March 1979): 63–80.

Techter, David. *A Bibliography and Index of Psychic Research and Related Topics for the Year 1962.* Illinois Society for Psychic Research, 1963.

Tedlock, Dennis. *The Mayan Book of the Dawn of Life.* trans. & comm. Popol Vuh. Rev. ed. New York: Touchstone/Simon & Schuster, 1996.

Teed, Cyrus Reed. *The Cellular Cosmogony; or, the Earth, a Concave Sphere.* Chicago: Guiding Star, 1899.

Teesing, H. P. H. "Mystiek en Literatuur" (Mysticism and Literature). *Tijdschrift voor Parapsychologie* (1959).

Teitze, Thomas. *Margery.* New York: Harper & Row, 1973.

Temple Messages. Halcyon, Calif.: Temple of the People, 1983.

Temple, Robert K. G. *The Sirius Mystery.* Folkstone, Kent, England: Bailey Brothers and Swinfen, 1972.

Temple, Sir Richard C. *The Thirtyseven Nats (Burmese Animism).* London: n.p., 1906.

Tenhaeff, W. H. C. *Beknopte Handleiding der "Psychical Research"* (Short Textbook of Parapsychology). 3 vols. N.p., 1926.

———. *Beschouwingen over Het Gebruik van Paranognosten* (The Use of Sensitives for Police and Other Purposes). Utrecht: Erven J. Bijleveld, 1957.

———. *Paranormal Healing Powers.* Olten, 1957.

———. "Psychoscopic Experiments on Behalf of the Police." *Conference Report No. 41.* Paper presented at the First International Conference of Parapsychological Studies, Utrecht, Holland, 1953.

———. *Telepathie en Helderziendheid.* English edition as *Telepathy and Clairvoyance.* C. Bertelsmann, 1962. Springfield, Ill.: C. C. Thomas, 1973.

Tenyi, Tamas and Matyas Trixler. "A magikus befolyasoltsag es a demonikus megszallottsag pszichopatologiai vonatkozasairol ciganyok szkizofren pszichozisaiban" (Delusions of Magical Influence and Demoniacal Possession in Gypsy Patients with the Diagnosis of Schizophrenia), *Psychiatria Hungarica* 7, no. 2 (April 1992): 167–173.

Teresa of Avila, St. *The Interior Castle.* Translated by Kieran Kavanaugh and Oyilio Rodriguez. New York: Paulist Press, 1979.

Tesla, Nikola. "Making Your Imagination Work For You." *American Magazine* (April 1921).

Thalbourne, Michael A. "Belief in the Validity of Horoscopes as Related to the Sheep-Goat Effect," *Journal of Parapsychology* 56, no. 2 (June 1992): 163–168.

———. "Personality Characteristics of Students Who Believe Themselves to be Psychic," *Journal of the Society for Psychical Research* 63, no. 856 (July 1999): 203–212.

———. "The Sheep-Goat Variable and Mystical Experience: Their Relationship and Their Levels in a Special Population," *European Journal of Parapsychology* 14 (1998–1999): 80–88.

Thedra. *Excerts of Prophecies from Other Planets Concerning Our Earth.* Mt. Shasta, Calif.: Association of Sananda and Sanat Kumara, [1956].

———. *Mine Intercome Messages from the Realms of Light.* Sedona, Ariz.: Association of Sananda and Sanat Kumara, [1990].

Theobald, Morell. *Spirit Workers in the Home Circle.* Boston: Colby & Rich, 1887.

Theodorowicz, Jose. *Mystical Phenomena in the Life of Therese Neumann.* St. Louis, Mo.: B. Herder, 1940.

Theogenesis. Halcyon, Calif.: Temple of the People, 1981.

Theories of Hypnosis: Current Models and Perspectives. New York: Guilford Press, 1991.

The Theosophical Movement, 1875–1950. Los Angeles: Cunningham Press, 1951.

Theresa, St. *The Interior Castle.* London: Baker, 1921.

Thierens, A. E. *Astrology in Mesopotamian Culture.* Leiden: E. J. Brill, 1935.

———. *The General Book of the Tarot.* London: Rider; Philadelphia: David McKay, 1928. Reprint, Hollywood, Calif.: Newcastle Publishing, 1975.

Thigpen, C. H., and H. Cleckley. *The Three Faces of Eve.* New York: McGraw-Hill, 1957.

Thirty Years Work: The Books of Alice Bailey and the Tibetan Master Djwhal Khul. New York: Lucis Publishing, n.d.

This House is Haunted: The True Story of a Poltergeist. London: Souvenir Press, 1980.

Thom, Alexander. *Megalithic Lunar Observatories.* Oxford: Oxford University Press, 1971.

———. *Megalithic Sites in Britain.* Oxford: Oxford University Press, 1967.

Thomas, C. Drayton. *Life beyond Death with Evidence.* N.p., 1928.

———. "A New Hypothesis Concerning Trance-Communications." *Proceedings of the Society for Psychical Research* 48 (May 1947).

Thomas, C. Drayton. *Some Recent Evidence for Human Survival.* London: William Collins, 1922.

———. "The Volume of Byron: A Significant Book Test." *Proceedings of the Society for Psychical Research* 48, 175 (1946–49).

———. "The Word Association Test with Mrs. Osborne Leonard." *Proceedings of the Society for Psychical Research* 43, 141 (1935).

Thomas, John F. *Beyond Normal Cognition: An Evaluative and Methodological Study of the Mental Content of Certain Trance Phenomena.* Boston: Boston Society for Psychical Research, 1973. Reprint, Ann Arbor, Mich.: University Microfilms, n.d. Reprint, New York: Ayer Publishing Co. Inc., 1975.

———. *Case Studies Bearing on Survival.* Boston: Boston Society for Psychical Research, 1929.

Thomas, Keith. *Religion and the Decline of Magic.* New York: Charles Scribner's Sons, 1971.

Thomas, L. "Late-Life Effect of Early Mystical Experiences: A Cross-Cultural Comparison," *Journal of Aging Studies* 11, no. 2 (Summer 1997): 155–169.

Thomas, N. W. *Thought Transference: A Critical and Historical Review of the Evidence for Telepathy.* London: De La More Press, 1905.

Thomas, Nicholas, and Caroline Humphrey, eds. *Shamanism, History, and the State.* Ann Arbor: University of Michigan Press, 1994.

Thomas, Northcote W. *Crystal Gazing: Its History and Practice, with a Discussion of the Evidence for Telepathic Scrying.* London: Alexander Moring (The De La More Press), 1905.

Thommen, George. *Is This Your Day?* New York: Award, 1964.

Thompson, C. J. S. *The Hand of Destiny.* London, 1932. Reprint, Detroit: Singing Tree Press, 1970.

———. *Magic and Healing.* London: Rider, 1947. Reprint, Detroit: Gale Research, 1973.

———. *The Mysteries and Secrets of Magic.* London: Allen Lane, 1927. Reprint, Causeway, 1973.

———. *The Mystery and Lore of Apparitions.* London: Shaylor, 1930. Reprint, Detroit: Gale Research, 1975.

———. *The Mystery and Lore of Monsters.* London, 1930. Reprint, New Hyde Park, N.Y.: University Books, 1968. New York: Citadel Press, 1970.

———. *The Mystery and Lure of Perfume.* London: J. Lane; Detroit: Singing Tree Press, 1969.

———. *The Mystery and Romance of Astrology.* London, 1929. Reprint, Detroit: Singing Tree Press, 1969. Reprint, New York: Causeway, 1973.

———. *The Mystic Mandrake.* 1934. Reprint, New Hyde Park, N.Y.: University Books, 1968.

Thompson, Charles J. *Alchemy: Source of Chemistry & Medicine.* London, 1897. Reprint, Sentry Press, 1974.

Thompson, Francis. *The Supernatural Highland.* London: Robert Hale, 1976.

Thompson, Richard Campbell. *Devils & Evil Spirits of Babylonia* 2 vols. London: Luzac, 1903–04.

———. *Semitic Magic.* London: Luzac, 1908.

Thompson, Richard Lowe. *The History of the Devil.* New York: Harcourt, Brace, 1929.

Thompson, William Irwin. *The American Replacement of Nature: The Everyday Acts and Outrageous Evolution of Economic Life.* Garden City, N.Y.: Doubleday, 1991.

———. *Evil and World Order.* New York: Harper & Row, 1976.

———. *Islands Out of Times.* Garden City, N.Y.: Dial Press, 1985.

———. *Passages About Earth: An Exploration of the New Planetary Culture.* New York: Harper & Row, 1975. N.p.: HarperTrade; Toronto: Harper Collins Publishing, Inc., 1980.

———. *Reimagination of the World: A Critique of the New Age, Science, and Popular Culture.* Santa Fe, N.Mex.: Bear, 1991.

Thomsen, Harry. *The New Religions of Japan.* Rutland, Vt.: Charles E. Tuttle, 1963.

Thorndike, Lynn. *History of Magic and Experimental Science.* Vol. 3. New York: Columbia University Press, 1923–58.

Thorogood, Brackett K. "The Margery Mediumship." *Proceedings of the American Society for Psychical Research* 22 (1933).

Thorsson, Edred. *Futjhark: A Handbook of Rune Magic.* York Beach, Maine: Samuel Weiser, 1984.

———. *Teutonic Magick.* St. Paul, Minn.: Llewellyn Publications, 1999.

Thouless, Robert Henry. *Authority and Freedom.* London: Hodder and Stroughton, 1954.

———. *Experimental Psychical Research.* Baltimore, Md.: Penguin, 1963.

———. "Crookes and Cook." *Journal of the Society for Psychical Research* 42 (1963).

———. "Dr. Rhine's Recent Experiments in Telepathy and Clairvoyance and a Reconsideration of J. E. Coover's Conclusions on Telepathy." *Proceedings of the Society for Psychical Research* 43 (1935): 24.

———. *From Anecdote to Experiment in Psychical Research.* London: Routledge & Kegan Paul, 1972.

———. "The Present Position of Experimental Research into Telepathy and Related Phenomena." *Proceedings of the Society for Psychical Research* 47 (1943).

———. "Problems of Design in Parapsychological Experiments." *Journal of the Society for Psychical Research* (1955).

———. "Psychical Research Past and Present." [Myers Memorial Lecture] *Journal of the Society for Psychical Research* (1952).

———. *Straight and Crooked Thinking.* N.p., 1930. Reprinted as *How to Think Straight.* New York: Simon and Schuster, 1939.

Thurston, Herbert. *Surprising Mystics.* London: Burns & Oates, 1955.

———. *Ghosts and Poltergeists.* Chicago: Henry Regnery, 1954.

———. "The Phenomena of Stigmatization." *Proceedings of the Society for Psychical Research* 32, no. 83 (1922).

———. *The Physical Phenomena of Mysticism.* London: Burns & Oates, 1952. Reprint, Chicago: Henry Regnery, 1953.

Thury, Marc. *Les Tables tournantes.* Geneva, 1855.

Tibet and Freedom. The Tibet Society of the United Kingdom, 1961.

The Tibetan Book of the Dead. Translated and with a commentary by Francesca Fremantle and Chogyam Trungpa. Berkeley, Calif.: Shambhala, 1973.

"The Tibetan Lama Hoax.'" *Tomorrow* 9, 2 (spring 1958).

Tiertze, Thomas R. *Margery.* New York: Harper & Row, 1973.

Tiffany, Joel. *Spiritualism Explained.* New York: Graham & Ellinwood, 1856.

Tiller, William A. "Radionics, Radiesthesia and Physics." In *The Varieties of Healing Experience.* Palo Alto, Calif.: Academy of Paraspsychology & Medicine, 1971.

Tillett, Gregory. *The Elder Brother: A Biography of Charles Webster Leadbeater.* London: Routledge & Kegan Paul, 1982.

Tillyard, R. J. "Evidence of Survival of a Human Personality." *Nature* 122 (August 28, 1928).

———. "Science and Psychical Research." *Nature* 118 (1926).

Timmons, Beverly, and Joe Kamiya. "The Psychology and Physiology of Meditation and Related Phenomena." *Journal of Transpersonal Psychology* 1 (1970).

Timms, Moira. *Prophecies and Predictions: Everyone's Guide to the Coming Changes.* Santa Cruz, Calif.: Unity Press, 1981.

Tingley, Katherine. *Theosophy and Some of the Vital Problems of the Day.* N.p., 1915.

———. *Theosophy, The Path of the Mystic.* Point Loma, Calif., 1922. Reprint, Pasadena, Calif.: Theosophical University Press, 1977.

———. *The Gods Await.* Point Loma, Calif., 1929.

———. *The Voice of the Soul.* Point Loma, Calif., 1928.

———. *The Wine of Life.* Point Loma, Calif.: Woman's International Theosophical League, 1925.

———. *The Wisdom of the Heart: Katherine Tingley Speaks.* Compiled by W. Emmett Small. San Diego, Calif., 1978.

Tinterow, Maurice M. *Foundations of Hypnosis: From Mesmer to Freud.* Springfield, Ill.: Chas. C. Thomas, 1970.

Tischner, Rudolf. *Franz Anton Mesmer: Leben, Werk und Wirkungen.* Munchen: Verlag der Müncher Drucke, 1928.

———. *Geschichte der okkultistischen Forschung.* Pfülling: Johannes Baum Verlag, 1924.

———. *Geschichte der Parapsychologie.* Titmoning (Pustet), 1960.

———. *Telepathy and Clairvoyance.* New York: Harcourt, Brace, 1925.

Tisserand, Robert. *Aromatherapy.* 1977. Reprint, London: Mayflower, 1979.

Tobacyk, Jerome, Mark J. Miller, Patsy Murphy, and Thomas Mitchell. "Comparisons of Paranormal Beliefs of Black and White University Students from the Southern United States," *Psychological Reports* 63, no. 2 (October 1988): 492–494.

Tohei, Koichi. *The Book of Ki: Coordinating Mind and Body in Daily Life.* San Francisco: Japan Publications, 1978.

———. *This is Aikido.* Tokyo: Japan Publications, 1975.

Tóibín, Colm, ed. *Seeing is Believing.* Ireland: Pilgrim Press, 1985.

Toksvig, Signe. *Emmanuel Swedenborg, Scientist and Mystic.* New Haven, Conn.: Yale University Press, 1948.

Tolaas, Jon. "The Puzzle of Psychic Dreams." In *Dreamtime and Dreamwork: Decoding the Language of the Night.* Los Angeles: Jeremy P. Tarcher, Inc., 1990.

Tompkins, Peter. *Mysteries of the Mexican Pyramids.* New York: Harper & Row, 1976.

———. *Secrets of the Great Pyramid.* New York: Harper & Row, 1971.

Tompkins, Peter, and Christopher Bird. *The Secret Life of Plants.* New York: Harper & Row, 1973. Reprint, New York: Avon, 1974.

Tonner, W. "The Genius of Francis Grierson." *Trend* (March 1914).

Torné-Chiavigny, H. *L'Histoire prédite et jugée par Nostradamus.* 3 vols. Bordeaux, 1860–62.

Torrens, Robert George. *The Inner Teachings of the Golden Dawn.* London: Neville Spearman, 1969.

———. *Secret Rituals of the Golden Dawn.* Wellingborough, England: Aquarian Press, 1973.

Torrenti, Raymond E. "Analyzing the Transcendent: Psychotherapists and Their Mystical Experiences," *Dissertation Abstracts International: Section B: The Sciences & Engineering* 56, no. 9-B (March 1996): 5187.

Torres, Penny [Mafu]. *Reflections on Yeshua Ben Joseph.* Vacaville, Calif.: Mafu Seminars, 1989.

———. *And What Be God?* Vacaville, Calif.: Mafu Seminars, 1989.

Toth, Max, and Greg Nielsen. *Pyramid Power.* London: Freeway, 1974. Reprint, New York: Warner Books, 1976.

Toulmin [Crosland], Camilla. *Light in the Valley: My Experiences in Spiritualism.* London; New York: G. Routledge & Co., 1957.

Towers, Eric. *Dashwood: The Man and the Myth.* UK: Crucible, 1986.

Townsend, C. H. *Mesmerism Proved True.* London, 1854.

Townshend, Chauncy Hare. *Facts in Mesmerism, with Reasons for a Dispassionate Inquiry into It.* London, 1844.

Transcendental Physics: An Account of Experimental Investigations from the Scientific Treatises of Johann Carl Friedrich Zöllner. Translated by Charles C. Massey. London: W. H. Harrison, 1882. Reprint, New York: Ayer Publishing Co. Inc., 1976.

Tregortha, John. *News from the Invisible World.* UK: Burslem, 1808.

Treharne, R. F. *The Glastonbury Legends.* London, 1967.

Trench, Brinsley Le Poer. *The Eternal Subject.* London: Souvenir, 1973.

———. *The Flying Saucer Story.* London: Neville Spearman, 1966.

———. *Forgotten Heritage.* London: Neville Spearman, 1964.

———. *Men Among Mankind.* London: Neville Spearman, 1962.

———. *Operation Earth.* London: Neville Spearman, 1969.

———. *Secret of the Ages: UFOs From Inside the Earth.* London: Souvenir Press, 1974.

———. *The Sky People.* London: Neville Spearman, 1960.

Trethewy, A. W. *The "Controls" of Stainton Moses.* London, 1923.

Trevelyan, George. *The Active Eye in Architecture.* N.p., 1977.

———. *Operation Redemption.* Wellingborough, Northamptionshire, England: Turnstone Press, 1981.

———. *A Vision of the Aquarian Age.* London: Stillpoint, 1984.

Trevelyan, George, and Edward Marchett. *Twelve Seats at the Round Table.* Jersey: Neville Spearman, 1976.

Trevino, Rick. *Revelations & Spiritual Enlightenment of Yahwism.* Palm Springs, Calif.: International Guild of Advanced Sciences Research Society, 1993.

Trigg, E. B. *Gypsy Demons and Divinities: The Magical and Supernatural Practices of the Gypsies.* Secaucus, N.J.: Citadel Press, 1973. Reprint, London: Sheldon Press, 1975.

Trine, Ralph Waldo. *In Tune With the Infinite.* New York: Thomas Y. Crowell, 1897.

Trochu, Francis. *Saint Bernadette Soubirous, 1844–1879.* London: Longmans, 1957.

———. *The Curé D'Ars.* London: Burns & Oates, 1936. Reprint, Westminster, Md.: Newman Press, 1950.

———. *The Insight of the Cure D'Ars.* London: Burns Oates & Washburn, 1934.

Tromp, S. W. *Dowsing and Science.* N.p., 1950.

———. "First Report on Experiments Concerning the Influence of Variations in the Strength of the Magnetic Field on Muscular Contraction." *Dutch Journal of Parapsychology* (January 1947).

———. *Fundamental Principles of Psychical Physics.* N.p., 1952.

———. *Physical Physics; A Scientific Analysis of Dowsing, Radiesthesia, and Kindred Divining Phenomena.* New York: Elsevier, 1949.

———. "The Problem of the Possible Influence of Dowsing Zones on the Health of Men." *Dutch Journal of Parapsychology* (November 1948).

Troop, Martin. *Mary Shelley's Monster.* Houghton Mifflin, 1977.

Trouncer, Margaret. *Miser of Souls.* London: Hutchinson, 1959.

Troward, Thomas. *The Edinburgh Lectures on Mental Science.* London, 1904.

———. *The Hidden Power and Other Papers on Mental Science.* New York: Dodd, Mead, 1917.

Trowbridge, W. R. H. *Cagliostro: The Splendour and Misery of a Master of Magic.* London, 1910. Reprinted as *Cagliostro: Savant or Scoundrel?* New York: Gordon Press, 1975. Reprinted as *Cagliostro: Maligned Freemason and Rosicrucian.* Kila, Mont.: Kessinger Publishing, 1992.

True & Faithful Relation of What Passed for Many Years Between Dr. John Dee & Some Spirits. N.p., 1659. Reprint, Kila, Mont.: Kessinger Publishing Co., 1999. Truesdell, J. W. *The Bottom Facts Concerning the Science of Spiritualism.* New York: G. W. Carleton, 1883.

Truesdell, J. W. *Bottom Facts of Spiritualism.* New York, 1883.

Trust, Josephine C. *Bible Mystery by Superet Light Science.* Los Angeles: Superet Press, 1950.

———. *Superet Light.* Los Angeles: Superet Light Center, 1953.

———. *Superet Light Doctrine.* Los Angeles: Superet Press, 1949.

Truthseeker, A. *The Planchette Mystery: Being a Candid Inquiry Into the Nature, Origin, Import, and Tendencies of Modern Signs and Wonders.* New York: Samuel R. Wells, 1870.

Truzzi, Marcelo. "A Bibliography on Fire-Walking." *Zetetic Scholar* 11 (1983): 105–07.

———. *Cauldron Cookery: An Authentic Guide for Coven Connoisseurs.* New York: Meredith, 1969.

———. "The Occult Revival as Popular Culture: Some Random Observations on the Old and Nouveau Witch." *Sociological Quarterly* 13 (Winter 1972): 16–34.

———. *Where Witchcraft Lives.* London: Aquarian Press, 1962.

Tubby, Gertrude Ogden. *James Hysop X—His Book.* York, Pa.: York Printing, 1929.

———. *Psychics and Mediums.* Boston: Marshall Jones, 1935.

Tucci, Giuseppe. *The Theory and Practice of the Mandala.* London: n.p., 1961.

Tucker, Rob. *Recovery From Cults: Help For Victims of Psychological and Spiritual Abuse.* New York: W. W. Norton & Co. Inc., 1993.

Tuckett, Ivor L. *The Evidence for the Supernatural.* London, 1911.

Tugwell, Simon. *Human Immortality and Redemption.* London: Darton, Longman, & Todd, 1990.

Tuke, W. H. *Sleep-walking and Hypnotism.* Philadelphia: Blakiston; London: Churchill, 1884.

Turnbull, Grace, ed. *The Essence of Plotinus.* New York: Greenwood Press, 1934.

Turner, Edith. "The Reality of Spirits," *ReVision,* 15, no. 1 (Summer 1992): 28–32.

Turner, James, ed. *Stella C. An Account of Some Original Experiments in Psychical Research.* London: Souvenir Press, 1973.

Turner, Robert. *Elizabethan Magic.* Londmead, Dorset, England: Element Books, 1989.

Turner, Robert, and David Edwards. *The Outer Court.* Woverhampton, UK: Order of the Cubic Stone, 1968.

Turnbull, Coulson. *The Solar Logos or Studies in Arcane Mysticism.* Santa Fe, N.Mex.: Sun Publishing Co., 1997.

Turvey, Vincent N. *The Beginnings of Seership.* London, 1911. Reprint, New Hyde Park, N.Y.: University Books, 1969.

Tuttle, Hudson. *Arcana of Spiritualism.* N.p., 1871. Reprint, Manchester: The Two Worlds Publishing, 1900; Chicago: J. R. Francis, 1904.

———. *Career of the Christ—Idea in History.* Boston: Adams, 1870.

———. *Career of the God—Idea in History.* Boston: Adams, 1869.

———. *Career of Religious Ideas.* New York: D. M. Bennett, 1878.

———. *Ethics of Spiritualism.* Chicago: Religio-Philosophical Publishing, 1878.

———. *Mediumship and Its Laws.* Chicago: Progressive Thinker Publishing, 1900.

———. *Philosophy of Spirit and the Spirit World.* London: H. A. Copley; Berlin Heights, Ohio: H. Tuttle, 1896.

———. *Religion of Man and Ethics of Science.* New York: M. L. Holbrook, 1890.

———. *Studies in Outlying Fields of Psychic Science.* New York: M. L. Holbrook, 1889.

Tuttle, Hudson, and Emma Rood Tuttle. *Stories from Beyond the Borderland.* Berlin Heights, Ohio: Tuttle Publsihing, 1910.

Tweedale, Charles L. *Man's Survival After Death.* London: Psychic Book Club, 1909. Reprint, New York: E. P. Dutton, 1918.

———. *News From the Next World.* N.p., 1940.

Tweedale, Violet. *The Cosmic Christ.* N.p., 1930.

———. *Ghosts I Have Seen and Other Psychic Experiences.* New York: Frederick A. Stokes, 1919. London, 1920. Reprint, Las Vegas, Nev.: Health Research Inc., 1996.

———. *Mellow Sheaves.* N.p., 1927.

———. *Phantoms of the Dawn.* N.p., 1924.

Twigg, Ena, with Ruth Hagy Brod. *Ena Twigg: Medium.* New York: Hawthorn Books, 1972. Reprint, London: W. H. Allen, 1973.

Twitchell, Paul. *All about ECK.* Las Vegas, Nev.: Illuminated Way Press, 1969.

———. *ECKANKAR, the Key to Secret Worlds.* New York: Lancer Books, 1969.

———. *The Tiger's Fang.* New York: Lancer Books, 1969.

Tyl, Noel. *Holistic Astrology: The Analysis of Inner and Outer Environments.* McLean, Va.: TAI Books, 1980.

———. *The Horoscope as Identity.* St. Paul, Minn.: Llewellyn Publications, 1974.

———. *The Missing Moon.* St. Paul, Minn.: Llewellyn Publications, 1979.

Tylor, E. B. *Primitive Culture.* 2 vols. London: John Murray, 1871.

Tyndall, John. *Fragments of Science for Unscientific People.* New York: Appleton, 1872.

Tyrrell, George N. M. *Apparitions.* London, 1953. Reissued in one volume with Tyrrell's *Science & Psychical Phenomena.* New Hyde Park, N.Y.: University Books, 1961. Reprint, London: Society for Psychical Research, 1973.

———. "Further Research in Extrasensory Perception." *Proceedings of the Society for Psychical Research* 44, no. 147 (1936–37).

———. *Grades of Significance.* N.p., 1930.

———. *Homo Faber.* N.p., 1951.

———. *The Nature of Human Personality.* London: Allen & Unwin, 1954.

———. *The Personality of Man: New Facts and Their Significance.* Harmondsworth, UK: Penguin Books, 1947.

Tyrrell, George N. M. "Presidential Address." *Proceedings of the Society for Psychical Research* 47, no. 171 (1945).

———, George N. M. *Science and Psychical Phenomena.* London, 1938. Reprinted in *Science and Psychical Phenomena and Apparitions.* New Hyde Park, N.Y.: University Books, 1961.

Tyson, Donald. *Rune Magic.* St. Paul, Minn.: Llewellyn Publications, 1989.

Uban, Sujan Singh. *The Gurus of India.* London: Fine Books (Oriental)/New Delhi, India: Sterling Publishers, 1977.

Ulansey, David. *The Origins of the Mithraic Mysteries: Cosmology and Salvation in the Ancient World.* New York: Oxford University Press, 1989.

Ullman, Montague. "On the Occurrence of Telepathic Dreams." *Journal of the American Society for Psychical Research* (April 1959).

———. *The Varieties of Dream Experience: Expanding Our Ways of Working with Dreams.* New York: Continuum, 1987.

Ullman, Montague, and Nan Zimmerman. *Working with Dreams.* London: Hutchinson, 1983.

Ullman, Montague, and Roberto Cavanna, eds. *Proceedings of an International Conference on Hypnosis, Drugs, Dreams and Psi: Psi and Altered States of Consciousness.* New York: Parapsychology Foundation, 1968.

Ullman, Montague, and Stanley Krippner. *Dream Studies and Telepathy: An Experimental Approach.* New York: Parapsychology Foundation, 1970.

Ullman, Montague, Stanley Krippner, and Alan Vaughan. *Dream Telepathy.* New York: Macmillan; London: Turnstone Books, 1973. Reprint, London: Penguin, 1974. Reprint, Los Angeles: J. P. Tarcher, 1985. Rev. ed. Jefferson, N.C.: McFarland, 1989.

Underhill, A. Leah. *The Missing Link in Modern Spiritualism.* New York: Thomas R. Knox, 1885. Reprint, New York: Ayer Publishing Co. Inc., 1976.

Underhill, Evelyn. *The Mystic Way: A Psychological Study in Christian Origins.* London and New York, 1913.

———. *Mysticism: A Study in the Nature and Development of Man's Spiritual Consciousness.* London: Metheun, 1911.

Underwood, Guy. *Patterns of the Past.* London: Museum Press, 1969.

Underwood, Peter. *The Complete Book of Dowsing and Divining.* London: Rider, 1980.

———. *Dictionary of the Supernatural.* 1978. Reprinted as *Dictionary of the Occult of Supernatural.* London: Harrap, 1978.

———. *Gazetteer of British Ghosts.*

———. *Gazetteer of Scottish and Irish Ghosts.* London: Souvenir Press; New York: Walker, 1975. New York: Bell, 1985.

———. *Haunted London.* N.p., 1973.

———. *Hauntings; New Light on the Greatest True Ghost Stories of the World.* London: Dent, 1977.

———. *No Common Task: The Autobiography of a Ghost Hunter.* N.p., 1983.

———. *The Vampire's Bedside Companion: The Amazing World of Vampires in Fact and Fiction.* London: Leslie Frewin, 1972.

Underwood, Peter, and Leonard Wilder. *Lives to Remember: A Case Book on Reincarnation.* London: Robert Hale, 1975.

United Lodge of Theosophists: Its Mission and Its Future. Los Angeles: Theosophy, n.d.

United States Army. *Index-Catalogue of the Library of the Surgeon-General's Office.* Washington, D.C., 1882.

Universal Spiritualist Manual. Manor Grove, Ind.: Universal Spiritualist Church, n.d.

Upham, Charles W. *Salem Witchcraft with an Account of Salem Village and a History of Opinion on Witchcraft and Kindred Subjects.* 2 Vols. Boston, 1867. Reprint, New York: Ungar, 1959.

Uphoff, Walter, and Mary Jo Uphoff. *Mind Over Matter: Implications of Masuaki Kiyota's PK Feats with Metal and Film.* Oregon, Wisc.: New Frontiers Center, 1980. Reprint, UK: Colin Smythe, 1980.

———. *New Psychic Frontiers: Your Key to New Worlds.* Gerrard's Cross, UK: Colin Smyth, 1975.

The URANTIA Book. Chicago: URANTIA Foundation, 1955.

Usha, S.I. and Satwant Pasricha. "Claims of Paranormal Experiences: A Survey of Psi and Psi-Related Experiences," *NIMHANS Journal* 7, no. 2 (July 1989): 143–150.

Utts, Jessica., "Replication and Meta-Analysis in Parapsychology," *Statistical Science* 6 (1991): 363–378.

———. "Response to Ray Hyman's Report Evaluation of the Program on Anomalous Mental Phenomena'," *Journal of Parapsychology* 59, no. 4 (December 1995): 353–356.

Valentine, Basil. *Triumphal Chariot of Antimony.* London, 1656.

Valentine, Tom. *Psychic Surgery.* Chicago: Henry Regnery, 1974.

Valiente, Doreen. *An ABC of Witchcraft Past and Present.* New York: St. Martin's Press; London: Macmillan, 1973.

———. *The Rebirth of Witchcraft.* London: Robert Hale, 1989.

Vallee, Jacques. *Anatomy of a Phenomenon: Unidentified Objects in Space, A Scientific Appraisal.* Chicago: Henry Regnery, 1965.

———. *The Invisible College.* New York: E. P. Dutton, 1975.

———. *Messengers of Deception: UFO Contacts and Cults.* Berkeley, Calif.: And/Or Press, 1979.

———. *Passport to Magonia: On UFOs, Folklore, and Parallel Worlds.* Chicago: Henry Regnery, 1969. Reprint, Chicago: Contemporary Books, 1993.

———. *Revelations: Alien Contact and Human Deception.* New York: Ballantine Books, 1991.

Vallee, Jacques, and Janine Vallee. *Challenge to Science; The UFO Enigma.* Chicago: Henry Regnery, 1966.

Vambéry, Arminius. *The Story of My Struggles: The Memoirs of Arminius Vambéry.* 2 vols. New York, 1904; London: T. F. Unwin, 1905.

Van Busschbach, J. G. "A Further Report on an Investigation of ESP in School Children." *Journal of Parapsychology* 19 (1955).

———. "An Investigation of ESP Between Teacher and Pupils in American Schools." *Journal of Parapsychology* 20 (June 1956).

———. "An Investigation of Extrasensory Perception in School Children." *Journal of Parapsychology* 17 (1953).

Van de Castle, Robert L. "Development and Validation of a Perceptual Maturity Scale Using Figure Preferences." *Journal of Consultative Psychology* 29 (1965).

———. "An Exploratory Study of Some Personality Correlates Associated with PK Performance." *Journal* of the American Society for Psychical Research 52 (1958).

———. "The Facilitation of ESP Through Hypnosis." *American Journal of Clinical & Experimental Hypnosis* 12 (1969).

———. "An Investigation of Psi Abilities Among the Cuna Indians of Panama." *Journal of Parapsychology* 38 (June 1974).

———. "Psi Abilities in Primitive Groups." *Proceedings of the Parapsychological Association* 7 (1970).

Van Deusen, Glyndon G. *Horace Greeley: Nineteenth-Century Crusader.* Philadelphia: University of Pennsylvania Press, 1953.

Van Eeden, Frederik. "Account of Sittings with Mrs. Thompson." *Proceedings of the Society for Psychical Research* 17 (1904).

———. "A Study of Dreams." *Proceedings of the Society for Psychical Research* 26 (1913).

Van Gelder, Dora. *The Real World of Fairies.* Wheaton, Ill.: Theosophical Publishing House, 1999.

Van Hien, Gordon. *What is Subud?* London: Rider, 1963. Revised, 1968.

Van Lysebeth, Andre. *Pranayama.* London: Mandala Books, 1979.

Van Over, Raymond. *ESP & the Clairvoyants.* New York: Award Books, Happauge, 1970.

———. *Total Meditation.* New York: Collier Books, 1978.

Van Peursen, C. A. "Parapsychologie en Wijsgerige Bezinning" (Parapsychology and philosophical reflection). *Tijdschrift voor Parapsychologie* 1–3 (1959).

Van Rijckenborgh, Jan. *The Coming New Man.* Haarlem, The Netherlands: Rozekruis-Pers, 1957.

———. *Elementary Philosophy of the Modern Rosecross.* Haarlem, The Netherlands: Rozekruis-Pers, 1961.

Van Tassell, George. *The Council of Seven Lights.* Los Angeles: DeVorss & Co., 1958.

———. *I Rode in a Flying Saucer.* Los Angeles: New Age Publishing, 1952.

Van Valer, Nola. *My Meeting with the Masters of Mount Shasta.* Mount Shasta, Calif.: Radiant School, 1982.

Van Vuurde, Wilhelm. "ESP During Sleep." *Journal of the Society for Psychical Research* 38 (1956): 282.

Vandenberg, Philipp. *Der Fluch der Pharaonen.* Scherz Verlag, 1973. English edition as *The Curse of the Pharaohs.* Philadelphia: J. B. Lippincott, 1975.

Vandenberg, Philipp. *Der Vergessene Pharao.* C. Bertelsmann Verlag, 1978. English edition as *The Golden Pharaoh.* New York: Macmillan; London: Hodder & Stoughton, 1980.

Vanscyoc, Linda Jane. "Knowing the Mystical: The Melchizedek Mystery School, Transpersonal Psychology, and Therapy," *Dissertation Abstracts International: Section B: The Sciences & Engineering* 57, no. 11-B (May 1997): 7240.

The Varieties of the Healing Experience. Los Altos, Calif.: Academy of Parapsychology and Medicine, 1971.

Varma, Devendra. "The Genesis of Dracula: a Re-Visit." In Peter Underwood, ed. *The Vampire's Bedside Companion.* London: Leslie Frewin, 1975.

———. *The Gothic Flame.* London: Arthur Barker, 1957.

———. *The History of the Gothic Novel in England.* N.p., 1957.

———. "The Vampire in Legend, Lore, and Literature." Introduction to *Varney the Vampyre; or, the Feast of Blood.* New York: Ayer Publishing Co. Inc., 1970.

Varma, Devendra., ed. *Voices from the Vaults: Authentic Tales of Vampires and Ghosts.* Toronto: Key Porter Books, 1987.

Varvoglis, Mario. " 'Anglo-Saxon' vs. 'Latin' Parapsychology: Behind the Communication Barrier," *European Journal of Parapsychologists* 8 (1990–1991): 41–50.

Varro, Marcus Terrentius. *De Lingua Latina.* Translated as *On the Latin Language.* Cambridge, Mass.: Harvard University Press, 1958.

Vasiliev, Leonid. L. *Experiments in Mental Suggestion.* London: Institute for the Study of Mental Images, 1963.

———. *Experiments in Distant Influence.* London: Wildwood House, 1976; New York: Dutton, 1976.

———. *Mysterious Manifestations of the Human Psyche.* 1959. Reprinted as: *Mysterious Phenomena of the Human Psyche.* New Hyde Park, N.Y.: University Books, 1965.

———. *Studies in Mental Telepathy.* CCM Information Corporation, 1971.

Vasilescu, Eugen and Elena Vasilescu. "The Mechanism of Telepathy," *Journal of the Society for Psychical Research* 61, no. 845 (October 1996): 211-220.

Vasse, Paul M. and Christine M. Vasse. "Comparison of Two Subjects in PK." *Journal of Parapsychology* (December 1951).

———. "ESP Test with French First-Grade School Children." *Journal of Parapsychology* (September 1958).

———. "Plant Growing Experiments." *Revue Métapsychique* (April–June 1948).

Vaughn, Alan. "Channeling." *New Realities* 3, no. 3 (January/February 1987).

———. *The Edge of Tomorrow.* New York: Coward, McGann, 1982.

———. *Incredible Coincidence: The Baffling World of Synchronicity.* New York: Lippencott, 1979.

———. *Patterns of Prophecy.* New York: Hawthorn Books, 1973. Reprint, London: Turnstone, 1974.

Vaughan, Alan, and James Bolem. *Psychics.* New York: Harper & Row, 1972.

Vaughan, Diana [Gabriel Jogand-Paqés]. *Mémoires d'une Ex-Palladiste, parfaite Initié, Indépendante.* Paris, 1895–97.

Velikovsky, Immanuel. *Ages in Chaos.* Garden City, N.Y.: Doubleday, 1952.

———. *Earth in Upheaval.* Garden City, N.Y.: Doubleday, 1955.

———. *Oedipus and Akhnaton: Myth and History.* Garden City, N.Y.: Doubleday, 1960.

———. *Peoples of the Sea.* N.p., 1977.

———. *Worlds in Collision.* Garden City, N.Y.: Doubleday, 1950.

Ventimiglia, Mark. *Wiccan Prayer Book.* Secaucus, N.J.: Carol Publishing Group, 1999.

Verax [J. J. Garth Wilkinson]. *Evenings with Mr. Hume and the Spirits.* Keighley, England, 1855.

Verity. *The Going and the Glory.* Auckland, New Zealand: Heralds of the New Age, 1966.

Vermaseren, M. J. *Mithras, The Secret God.* London: Chatto & Windus, 1963.

Verner, A. *Practical Psychometry* (pamphlet). Blackpool, England, 1903.

Vett, Carl Christian. "Memoirs of Psychic Research." *Tomorrow,* 3, 4 (Summer 1955).

Victoria, Queen. *Leaves from the Journal of Our Life in the Highlands.* Smith, Elder, 1868.

Viereborne, A. *Life of James Riley.* Akron, Ohio: Werner, 1911.

Vignon, Paul. *The Shroud of Christ.* London: Constable, 1902. Reprint, New Hyde Park, N.Y.: University Books, 1970.

Vinchon, Jean. *L'Art et la Folie* (Art and Insanity). Paris: Stock, Delamain et Boutelleau, 1950.

———. *La Magie du dessin: Du griffonage automatique au dessin thérapeutique* (The Magic Drawing: From Automatic Scribbling to Therapeutic Drawing). N.p., 1959.

———. *Mesmer et son secret* (Mesmer and His Secret). Toulouse Privat, 1936.

Vinchon, Jean, and Maurice Garçon. *Le Diable.* 1928. English ed. as *The Devil.* London, 1929. Reprint, New York: E. P. Dutton, 1930.

Vishnu-Devananda, Swami. *The Complete Illustrated Book of Yoga.* New York: Julian Press, 1960. Reprint, New York: Pocket Books, 1971.

———. *Meditation and Mantras.* New York: OM Lotus Publishing, 1978.

———. *The Sivananda Upanishad.* New York: OM Lotus Publishing, 1987.

Vitebsky, Piers. *The Shaman.* Boston: Little, Brown, 1995.

Vogel-Jorgensen, T. *Rasputin: Prophet, Libertine, Plotter.* London: T. Fisher Unwin, 1917. Reprint, New Hyde Park, N.Y.: University Books, 1970.

Vogt, Evon Z., and Ray Hyman. *Water Witching, U.S.A.* 2nd ed. Chicago: University of Chicago Press, 1979.

Voldben, A. *After Nostradamus.* London: Neville Spearman, 1973. Reprint, New York: Citadel, 1974.

Volguine, Alexandre. *Lunar Astrology.* New York: ASI Publishers, 1974.

———. *The Ruler of the Nativity.* New York: ASI Publishers, 1973.

———. *The Technique of Solar Returns.* New York: ASI Publishers, 1976.

Volin, Michael, and Nancy Phelan. *Yoga Breathing.* N.p.: Information Inc., 1966.

Von Däniken, Erich. *According to the Evidence: My Proof of Man's Extraterrestrial Origin.* London: Souvenir, 1977.

———. *Chariots of the Gods?: Unsolved Mysteries of the Past.* New York: G. P. Putnam's Sons, 1960. Reprint, New York: G. P. Putnam's Sons, 1970.

———. *The Gods and Their Grand Design: the Eighth Wonder of the World.* London: Souvenir, 1984.

———. *The Gold of the Gods.* London: Souvenir Press, 1973.

———. *In Search of Ancient Gods; My Pictorial Evidence for the Impossible.* London: Souvenir Press, 1974.

Von Franz, Marie-Louise. *Alchemical Active Imagination.* Boston: Shambhala Publications, Inc., 1997.

Von Görres, J. J. *Die Christliche Mystik.* 5 vols. Regensburg & Landshut, 1836–42.

Von Lama, Frederick. *Thérèsa Neumann, une stigmatisée de nos jours.* N.p., 1928.

Voohris, Harold V. B. *Masonic Rosicrucian Societies.* New York: Press of Henry Emmerson, 1958.

———. *Masonic Organizations and Allied Orders and Degrees.* N.p.: Press of Henry Emmerson, 1952.

Vyasdev, Brahmachari Swami. *Science of Soul (Atma Vijnana).* Gangotri, India: Yoga Niketan Trust, 1964.

Vyner, J. "The Mystery of Springheel Jack." *Flying Saucer Review* (May–June, 1961).

Wachmeister, Countess Constance. *Reminiscences of H. P. Blavatsky and the Secret Doctrine.* London: Theosophical Publishing Society, 1893.

Wachmuth, Guenther. *The Life and Work of Rudolf Steiner.* New York: Whittier Books, 1955.

Waddell, L. Austine. *Tibetan Buddhism: With Its Mystic Cults, Symbolism and Mythology, and in Its Relation to Indian Buddhism.* London: W. H. Allen, 1895. Reprint, New York: Dover Publications, 1972.

Wade, Alsa Madison. *At the Shrine of the Master.* Philadelphia, Pa.: Dorrance, 1953.

Wagner, Henry O., comp. *A Treasure Chest of Wisdom.* Denver: H. O. Wagner, 1967.

Wagner, Melinda Boiler. *Metaphysics in Midwestern America.* Columbus: Ohio State University Press, 1983.

Waida, Manabu, "Problems of Central Asian and Siberian Shamanism," *Numen* 30 (1983): 215–239.

Waite, Arthur Edward. *The Alchemical Writings of Edward Kelly.* New York: Samuel Weiser, 1973.

———. *Azoth, or the Star in the East.* London, 1893. Reprint, New Hyde Park, N.Y.: University Books, 1973.

———. *The Book of Black Magic and of Pacts.* London: George Redway, 1898. Reprinted as *The Book of Ceremonial Magic.* London: William Rider & Sons, 1911. Reprint, New Hyde Park, N.Y.: University Books, 1961. Reprint, New York: Bell Publishing, 1969. Reprinted as *The Book of Black Magic and Ceremonial Magic.* New York: Causeway Books, 1973.

———. *Book of Mystery & Vision.* N.p., 1902. Reprint, Kila, Mont.: Kessinger Publishing Co., 1999.

———. *The Brotherhood of the Rosy Cross.* London: Rider, 1924.

———. *Devil Worship in France.* London, 1896.

———. *Fludd & Freemasonry.* Edmonds, Wash.: Holmes Publishing Group, 1994.

———. *Hermetic Papers of A. E. Waite.* Edited by R. A. Gilbert. Wellingborough, England: Aquarian Press, 1987.

———. *The Hidden Church of the Holy Grail.* London: Rebman, 1909.

———. *The Holy Grail: The Galahad Quest in the Arthurian Literature.* London: J. M. Watkins, 1921. Reprint, New Hyde Park, N.Y.: University Books, 1961.

———. *The Holy Kabbalah.* New Hyde Park, N.Y.: University Books, 1960. New York: Citadel, 1976.

———. *The Key to the Tarot.* London: William Rider, 1910.

———. *Lamps of Western Mysticism.* London: Kegan Paul; New York: Alfred A. Knopf, 1923. Reprint, Blauvelt, N.Y.: Multimedia, 1973.

———. *The Life of Louis Claude de Saint-Martin, The Unknown Philosopher.* London: Philip Welby, 1901.

———. *Lives of the Alchemical Philosophers.* London: George Redway, 1888. Reprinted as *Alchemists through the Ages.* Blauvelt, N.Y.: Rudolf Steiner Publications, 1970.

———. *A New Encyclopedia of Freemasonry.* 2 vols. London: William Rider; New York: David McKay, 1921. Reprint, New Hyde Park, N.Y.: University Books, 1970. Reprint, New York: Weatherwane, 1971.

———. *The Occult Science.* London: Kegan Paul, Trench, Trubner & Co., 1891. Reprint, Secaucus, N.J.: University Books, 1974.

———. "Papus: A Biographical Note." *Occult Review* 25 (January 1917): 34–36.

———. *Pictorial Key to the Tarot.* London: William Rider, 1911. Reprint, New Hyde Park, N.Y.: University Books, 1959. Reprint, Blauvelt, N.Y.: Rudolf Steiner, 1971. Reprint, New York: Causeway Books, 1973.

———. *Raymond Lully, Illuminated Doctor, Alchemist, and Christian Mystic.* London, 1922. Reprint, London, 1939. Reprint, New York: David McKay, 1940.

———. *The Real History of the Rosicrucians.* London: George Redway, 1887. Reprint, Blauvelt, N.Y.: Steiner Books, 1977. Revised as *The Brotherhood of the Rosy Cross.* London: William Rider & Son, 1924. Reprint, New Hyde Park, N.Y.: University Books, 1961.

———. *Saint-Martin, The French Mystic, and the Story of Modern Martinism.* London: William Rider & Son, 1922.

———. *The Secret Tradition in Alchemy.* Kegan Paul, London, Alfred A. Knopf, 1926. Reprint, New York: S. Weiser, 1969.

———. *The Secret Tradition in Freemasonry.* London, Rider, 1937. Reprint, New York: S. Weiser, 1969.

———. *Shadows of Life and Thought.* London: Selwyn and Blount, 1938.

———. *Studies in Mysticism and Certain Aspects of the Secret Tradition.* London: Hodder and Stoughton, 1906.

———. *The Unknown Philosopher: Louis Claude de St. Martin.* Blauvelt, N.Y.: Rudolf Steiner Publications, 1970.

Waite, Arthur Edward, ed. *The Hermetical & Alchemical Writings of Paracelsus.* 2 vols., London, 1894. Reprint, New Hyde Park, N.Y.: University Books, 1967.

———. *The Works of Thomas Vaughan, Mystic and Alchemist.* London, 1919. Reprint, New Hyde Park, N.Y.: University Books, 1968.

Wajda, Laszlo, "Zur Phaseologischen Stellung des Schamanismus," *Ural-Altaische Jahrbücher (Gedenkband Julius V. Farkas)* 31 (1959): 456–485.

Wakefield, Walter, and Austin P. Evans. *Heresies of the High Middle Ages.* New York, 1969.

Walker, Barbara. *The Woman's Encyclopedia of Myths and Secrets.* San Francisco: Harper & Row, 1983.

Walker, D. P. *Spiritual and Demonic Magic: From Ficino to Camperella.* South Bend, Ind.: University of Notre Dame Press, 1975.

Walker, Daniel E. *Witchcraft and Sorcery of the American Native Peoples.* Moscow, Idaho: University of Idaho Press, 1989.

Walker, Daniel P. *Decline of Hell: Seventeenth Century Discussions of Eternal Torment.* London: Routledge, 1964.

Walker, George B. *Beyond the Body: The Human Double and the Astral Planes.* London/Boston: George Benjamin Walker, 1974.

Walker, Kenneth. *Diagnosis of Man.* Harmondsworth, UK: Penguin Books, 1942.

———. *I Talk of Dreams.* London: Jonathan Cape, 1946.

———. *The Making of Man.* London: Routledge & Kegan Paul, 1963.

———. *Meaning and Purpose.* London: Jonathan Cape, 1944.

———. *A Study of Gurdjieff's Teachings.* London: Jonathan Cape, 1957.

———. *The Unconscious Mind.* London: Rider, 1961. Reprinted as *The Extrasensory Mind.* New York: Emerson, 1961.

———. *Venture with Ideas.* London: Jonathan Cape, 1951.

Walker, Roland. "Parapsychology and Dualism." *Scientific Monthly* (July 1954).

Walker, Sheila S. *Ceremonial Spirit Possession in Africa and Afro-Americana.* Leiden, Netherlands: E. J. Brill; New York: Humanities Press, 1972.

Wall, J. Charles. *Devils.* London, 1904. Reprint, Detroit: Singing Tree Press, 1968.

Wallace, Alfred Russell. "Correspondence." *Journal of the Society for Psychical Research* 16 (1898).

———. *My Life: A Record of Events and Opinions.* London: Chapman & Hall, 1902.

———. *My Life: An Autobiography.* 2 vols. London: Chapman & Hall, 1905; New York: Harper & Brothers, 1906.

———. *On Miracles and Modern Spiritualism.* London, 1875. Rev. ed. North Stratford, N.H.: Ayer Co. Publishing Inc., 1975.

Wallace, Austin D. *Thistle Presents Prince Nikeritis.* Eaton Rapids, Mich.: Transcendental Science Publications, 1905.

Wallis, E. W. and M. H. Wallis. *Guide to Mediumship & Psychical Unfoldment.* 3 vols. London, 1903. Life Science Institute, 1991.

Wallis, Roy. *The Road to Total Freedom.* New York: Columbia University Press, 1976.

Walraven, Boudewijn C. A. "Korean Shamanism," *Numen* 30 (1983): 240–264.

———. *Songs of the Shaman: The Ritual Chants of the Korean Mudang.* London: Kegan Paul International, 1994.

Walsh, John. *The Mysterious Shroud.* Garden City, N.Y.: Doubleday, 1986.

———. *The Shroud.* London: W. H. Allen, 1964.

Walsh, Michael. *The Apparition at Knock.* Tuam: St Jarlath's College, 1959.

Walsh, Roger N. *The Spirit of Shamanism.* Los Angeles: Jeremy P. Tarcher, 1990.

Warman, Edward B. *Clairvoyance & Clairaudience: Premonitions & Impressions.* Santa Fe, N.Mex.: Sun Publishing Co., 1995.

Wasson, R. Gordon. *Soma: Divine Mushroom of Immortality.* New York: Harcourt Brace Jovanovich, 1969.

———. "What Was the Soma of the Aryans?" In *Flesh of the Gods: the Ritual Use of Hallucinogens.* P. T. Furst, ed. (New York: Praeger, 1972): 201–213.

Wasson, R. Gordon, Albert Hofmann, and Carl A. P. Ruck. *The Road to Eleusis: Unveiling the Secret of the Mysteries.* New York: Harcourt Brace Jovanovich, 1978.

Wasson, R. Gordon and Valentina P. Wasson. *Mushrooms, Russia and History.* New York: Pantheon Books, 1957.

Wasson, R. Gordon, Stella Kramrisch, Jonathan Ott, and Carl A. P. Ruck. *Persephone's Quest: Entheogens and the Origins of Religion.* New Haven, Conn.: Yale University Press, 1988.

Walter Franklin Prince: A Tribute to His Memory. Boston: Boston Society for Psychical Research, 1935.

Walter, J. Donald [Kriyananda]. *Cities of Light.* Nevada City, Calif.: Crystal Clarity Publishers, 1987.

———. *Cooperative Communities: How to Start Them and Why.* Nevada City, Calif.: Ananda Publications, 1968.

———. *Crises in Modern Thought.* Nevada City, Calif.: Ananda Publications, 1972.

———. *The Path.* Nevada City, Calif.: Ananda Publications, 1977.

Walter, W. Grey. *The Living Brain.* New York: Norton, 1953.

———. *The Neurophysiological Aspects of Hallucinations and Illusory Experience.* London: Society for Psychical Research, 1963.

———. "The Neurophysiological Aspects of Hallucination and Illusory Experience." *Proceedings of the Society for Psychical Research.*

Walther, Gerda. *Zum anderen Ufer.* Remagen: Otto Reichl, 1960.

Walton, Bruce, ed. *Mount Shasta: Home of the Ancients.* Mokelume Hill, Calif.: Health Research, 1985.

Walton, Bruce A. *A Guide to the Inner Earth.* W.Va.: New Age Books, 1983.

Wambach, Helen. *Reliving Past Lives: The Evidence Under Hypnosis.* New York: Harper & Row, 1978.

Wang, Chung Yu. "China's Unwanted Heritage." *Tomorrow* (autumn 1955).

Wang, Robert. *An Introduction of the Golden Dawn Tarot.* New York: Samuel Weiser, 1978.

Wang, Robert, and Chris Zalewski. *Z-Five: Secret Teachings of the Golden Dawn.* St. Paul, Minn.: Llewellyn Publications, 1991.

Warcollier, René. "Fifty Years of Telepathy." *Tomorrow* (summer 1961).

———. *Experimental Telepathy.* Boston: Boston Society for Psychical Research, 1938. Reprint, London: George Allen & Unwin, 1939. Reprint, New York: Ayer Publishing Co. Inc., 1975.

———. *Mind to Mind.* Creative Age Press, 1948. Reprint, New York: Macmillan, 1963.

———. *Mind to Mind.* New York: Collier Books, 1963.

Warcollier, René, and Edmond Duchatel. *Les Miracles de la Volonté* (Miracles of the Will). N.p., 1912.

Ward, Charles A. *Oracles of Nostradamus.* London, 1891. Reprint, N.Y.: Modern Library, 1942.

Ward, Gary L. *Independent Bishops: An Independent Directory.* Detroit: Apogee Books, 1990.

Warner, H. J. *The Albigensian Heresy.* 2 vols. London: SPCK, 1922–28.

Wassen, Ralph, ed. *Yada Speaks.* San Diego, Calif.: Kethra E'Da Foundation, 1985.

Wassilko-Serecki, The Countess. *Der Spuk von Talpa.* München, 1926.

———. "Observations on Eleonore Zügun." *Journal of the American Society for Psychical Research* (September/October 1925).

Wasson, R. Gordon. *Mushrooms, Russia, and History.* New York: Pantheon, 1957.

———. *Persephone's Quest: Entheogens and the Origins of Religion.* New Haven, Conn.: Yale University Press, 1986.

———. *Soma: Divine Mushroom of Immortality.* The Hague: Mouton, 1968. Reprint, New York: Harcourt Brace, 1972.

Waterman, Adlai E. [Walter A. Carrithers] *Obituary: The "Hodgson Report" on Madame Blavatsky, 1885–1960.* Adyar, Madras, India: Theosophical Publishing House, 1963.

———. [Walter A. Carrithers]. *Obituary: The "Hodgson Report" on Madame Blavatsky, 1895–1960; Re-examination Discredits the Major Charges Against H. P. Blavatsky.* Adyar, Madras, India: Theosophical Publishing House, 1963.

Wates, L.G., "Indian Medicine Men," *Overland Monthly* 2nd Ser., 28 (1896): 171–182.

Water Witching U. S. A. Westerville, Ohio: National Ground Water Association, 1986.

Waters, W. G. *Jerome Cardan.* London, 1898.

Watkins, Alfred. *The Old Straight Track.* 1925. Reprint, London: Garnstone Press, 1970.

Watkins, Allen. *Alfred Watkins of Hereford: His Life and Pioneer Work in the Three Worlds of Archaeology, Photography, and Flour Milling, 1855–1935.* England: Privately printed, 1961.

———. *The Ley Hunter's Manual: A Guide to Early Tracks.* 1927. Reprint, Wellingborough, England: Aquarian Press, 1983.

———. *The Old Straight Track.* London: Methuen, 1925. Reprint, London: Sphere Books, 1974.

Watkins, Susan. *Conversations with Seth. The Story of Jane Roberts's ESP Class.* 2 vols. Englewood Cliffs, N.J.: Prentice-Hall, 1980–81.

Watson, Burton, trans. *Chuang Tzu, Basic Writings.* New York: Columbia University Press, 1964.

Watson, Lyall. *Gifts of Unknown Things.* New York: Simon and Schuster, 1976.

———. *Lifetide: The Biology of The Unconscious.* New York: Simon and Schuster, 1979.

———. *The Romeo Error: A Matter of Life and Death.* Garden City, N.Y.: Anchor Press, 1975.

———. *Supernature.* Garden City, N.Y.: Anchor Press, 1973.

Watson, Peter. *Twins: An Investigation Into the Strange Coincidences in the Lives of Separated Twins.* London: Hutchinson, 1981.

Watson, Simone. *The Cult of Our Lady of Guadalupe: A Historical Study.* Collegeville, Minn.: Liturgical Press, 1964.

Watt, Caroline A. "What Makes a Good Psi Target? Three Studies of Forced-Choice ESP Varying Target Emotionality and Complexity." *Journal of Parapsychology* 60, no. 1 (March 1996): 25–42.

Watt, Caroline A. and Robert L. Morris. "The Relationships among Performance on a Prototype Indicator of Perceptual Defence/Vigilance, Personality, and Extrasensory Perception," *Personality & Individual Differences* 19, no. 5 (November 1995): 635–648.

Watt, William W. *Shilling Shockers of the Gothic School: A Study of Chapbook Gothic Romances.* Cambridge, Mass.: Harvard University Press, 1932.

Watts, Alan. *The Book on the Taboo Against Knowing Who You Are.* New York: Vintage Books, 1966.

———. *The Early Writings of Alan Watts.* Edited by John Snelling. Berkeley, Calif.: Celestial Arts, 1987.

———. *The Essential Alan Watts.* Berkeley, Calif.: Celestial Arts, 1977.

———. *In My Own Way: An Autobiography, 1915–1945.* New York: Pantheon Books, 1972.

———. *Psychotherapy, East and West.* New York: Ballantine Books, 1961.

———. *The Spirit of Zen.* New York: Grove Press, 1958.

———. *The Way of Zen.* New York: Pantheon Books, 1968.

Wavell, Stewart, Audrey Butt, and Nina Epton. *Trances.* London: Allen & Unwin, 1966.

The Way of the Rosecross in Our Times. Haarlem, The Netherlands: Rozekruis-Pers, 1978.

Wayland, Bruce, and Shirley Wayland. *Steps to Dowsing Power.* Howell, Mich.: Life Force Press, 1976.

Weatherhead, Leslie. *After Death.* London: J. Clarke, 1923.

———. *Psychology, Religion, and Healing.* Rev. ed. London: Hodder and Stoughton, 1952.

———. *The Resurrection of Christ in the Light of Modern Science and Psychical Research.* London: Hodder and Stoughton, 1959.

Weaver, Herbert. *Divining, the Primary Sense: Unfamiliar Radiation in Nature, Art, and Science.* London: Routledge & Kegan Paul, 1978.

Webb, James. *The Flight from Reason.* London: Macdonald, 1971. Reprinted as *The Occult Underground.* LaSalle, Ill.: Open Court, 1974.

———. *The Harmonious Circle: The Lives and Work of G. I. Gurdjieff, P. D. Ouspensky, and Their Followers.* New York: G. P. Putnam's Sons, 1980.

———. *The Occult Establishment.* LaSalle, Ill.: Open Court Publishing, 1976.

Webberly, Rob, ed. *Astride the Two Cultures: Arthur Koestler at 70.* London: Hutchingson, 1975.

Webster, Charles. *From Paracelsus to Newton: Magic and the Making of Modern Science.* Cambridge, Mass.: Cambridge University Press, 1982.

Webster, Hutton. *Taboo: A Sociological Study.* Palo Alto, Calif.: Stanford University Press, 1942. Reprint, London: Octagon, 1981.

Wedgwood, James Ingall. *The Beginning of the Liberal Catholic Church.* Lakewood, N.J.: Ubique, 1967.

Wedgwood, J. I. *Varieties of Psychism.* N.p., 1914. Reprint, Kila, Mont.: Kessinger Publishing Co., 1998.

Weeks, N. *The Medical Discoveries of Edward Bach.* London: C. W. Daniel, 1940.

Weems, Lela Louise. "Religiosity and Religious Attitudes as They Relate to Mysticism and Sexual Permissiveness," *Dissertation Abstracts International: Section B: The Sciences & Engineering* 59, no. 8-B (February 1999): 4524.

Weiant, C. W. "Parapsychology and Anthropology." *Manas* 13 (1960).

Weigle, Marta. *Brothers of Light, Brothers of Blood: The Penitentes of the Southwest.* Albuquerque: University of New Mexico Press, 1976.

Weinberger, Julius. "On Apparatus Communication with Discarnate Persons." *International Journal of Parapsychology* 3, no. 1 (winter 1961).

———. "A Physicist Looks at Spiritual Healing." *Laymen's Movement Review* 1, no. 5 (1958); 2, no. 1 (1959).

———. "A Physicist Looks at Survival." *Tomorrow* (autumn 1956).

———. "Some Findings of Experimental Psychical Research." *Proceedings of the Seminar on Decline of Material* (November 1956).

Weiner, Sita. *Swami Satchidananda.* New York: Bantam Books, 1972.

Weingarten, Henry. *A Modern Introduction to Astrology.* New York: ASI Publishers, 1974.

———. *Principles of Synastry.* New York: ASI Publishers, 1978.

———. *The Study of Astrology.* 3 vols. New York: ASI Publishers, 1977.

Weingarten, Henry, comp. *The NASO International Astrological Directory.* New York: National Astrological Society, 1977–78. Rev. ed. 1980–81.

Weinhold, Arnold. *Seven Lectures on Somnambulism.* Edinburgh, Scotland, 1845.

Weisberg, Irving. "The Converging Influences of Sigmund Freud, Melanie Klein and the Bhagavad-Gita: W. R. Bion," *International Journal of Communicative Psychoanalysis & Psychotherapy* 9, no. 1 (1994): 19–23.

Weisbrot, Robert. *Father Divine and the Struggle for Racial Equality.* Urbana: University of Illinois Press, 1983.

Weiss, Jane. *Reflections by Anoah.* Austin, Tex.: Planetary Light Association, 1986.

Wellard, James. *Lost Worlds of Africa.* New York: E. P. Dutton, 1967.

Wells, Samuel R. *How to Read Character: A New Illustrated Handbook of Phrenology and Physiognomy.* New York: Samuel R. Wells, 1871. Reprint, Rutland, Conn.: C. E. Tuttle, 1971.

Weltmer, S. A. *Telepathy & Thought Transference (1902).* Kila, Mont.: Kessinger Publishing Co., 1998.

Wendell, Leilah. *The Book of Azrael.* New York: Westgate Press, 1988.

Wenzl, Aloys. *Philosophische Grenzfragen der Naturwissenchaften* (Philosophical Border Problems of the Natural Sciences). N.p., 1956.

Wenzl, Aloys. *Unsterblichkeit* (Immorality). Bern: A. Francke, 1951.

Weor, Samuel Aun Weor. *Manual of Practical Magic.* Los Angeles: Gnostic Association, 1988.

———. *Manual of Revolutionary Psychology.* Los Angeles: Gnostic Association, 1987.

———. *The Perfect Matrimony.* New York: Adonai Editorial, 1980.

Wereide, Thorstein. *Byggesamfund* (Building Societies). N.p., 1956.

———. "Medium or Murderess." *Tomorrow* (winter 1957).

———. *Menneskets Metafysikk* (The Metaphysics of Man). N.p., 1953.

———. "Norway's Human Doubles." *Tomorrow* 3, no. 2 (winter 1955).

Werner, Elizabeth, ed. *Directory of Psychic Sciences Periodicals.* Burbank, Calif.: Inner-Space Interpreters Services, 1973.

Wernli, Hans J. *Biorhythm: A Scientific Exploration into the Life Cycles of the Individual.* New York: Crown, 1961.

Weschcke, Carl Llewellyn. *The Science of Feeling Fine.* St. Paul, Minn.: Chester-Kent, 1954.

Weschcke, Carl Llewellyn, and Stan Baker. *The Truth About Astrology.* St. Paul, Minn.: Llewellyn Publications, 1989.

West, Donald J. *Eleven Lourdes Miracles.* London: Duckworth, 1957; New York: Helix Press, 1957.

———. "The Identity of 'Jack the Ripper.' " *Journal of the Society for Psychical Research* 35 (1949).

———. *Psychical Research Today.* London: Duckworth, 1956.

———. "Psychokinetic Experiments with a Single Subject." *Parapsychology Newsletter* (November–December 1957).

West, Donald J., and G. W. Fisk. "ESP and Mood: Report of a 'Mass' Experiment with Clock Cards." *Journal of the Society for Psychical Research* 38 (1956).

West, Sylvester A. *TK and the Great Work in America.* Chicago: The Author, 1918.

Westbrook, A. and O. Ratti. *Aikido and the Dynamic Sphere.* Rutland, Vt.: Charles Tuttle, 1970.

Westcott, G. H. *Kabir and the Kabir Panth.* Calcutta: Varanasi Bhartiya Publishing House, 1974.

Westcott, W. W. *Numbers: Their Occult Power and Mystic Virtue.* London: Theosophical Publishing House, 1890. Reprint, 1974. Reprint, London: Theosophical Publishing Society, 1911. Reprint, Kila, Mont.: Kessinger Publishing Co., 1993. 2nd ed., Reprint, Las Vegas, Nev.: Health Research, 1996.

Westcott, William W. *An Introduction to the Study of the Kabalah.* New York: Allied Publications, n.d.

Westcott, Wynn. *Aesch Mezareph, or Purifying Fire.* N.p., 1894.

———. *The Chaldean Oracles of Zoroaster.* London: Theosophical Publishing Society, 1895.

———. *Egyptian Magic.* London: Theosophical Publishing Society, 1896.

———. *The Pymander of Hermes.* N.p., 1894.

———. *Rosicrucians, Their History and Aims.* N.p., 1894.

———. *The Science of Alchymy.* N.p., 1893.

———. *Sepher Yetzirah, the Book of Formation.* London, Theosophical Publishing Society, 1893. Rev. ed. Gillette, N.J.: Heptangle Books, 1987.

———. *Somnium Scipionis.* N.p., 1894.

Westen, Robin. *Channelers: A New Age Directory.* New York: Perigee Books (Putnam), 1988.

Westin, Gunnar. *The Free Church through the Ages.* Nashville, Tenn.: Broadman, 1958.

Weston, Jessie L. *From Ritual to Romance.* Cambridge, Mass.: Cambridge University Press, 1920. Reprint, Garden City, N.Y.: Doubleday Anchor, 1957.

———. *The Quest of the Holy Grail.* London: G. Bell & Sons, 1913; London: Frank Cass, London, 1964.

Westwood, Horace. *Apostle of Darkness and Prophet of Light.* N.p., 1939.

———. *This Do and Live.* N.p., 1938.

Wethered, V. D. *A Radiesthetic Approach to Health and Homeopathy, or Health and the Pendulum.* London: British Society of Dowsers, 1950.

Weyer, Johannes. *Witches, Devils and Doctors in the Renaissance: Johann Weyer, De Praestigiis.* Edited by George Mora. Binghamton, N.Y.: Medieval & Renaissance Texts & Studies, 1991.

What Is Scientology? Los Angeles: Bridge Publications, 1992.

Wheatley, J. M. O. "Implications for Philosophy." In *Philosophical Dimensions of Parapsychology.* Edited by H. L. Edge. Springfield, Ill.: Charles Thomas, 1976.

Wheeler, Francis J. *The Bach Remedies Repertory.* London: C. W. Daniel, 1952.

Wheeler, L. Richmond. *Vitalism: Its History and Validity.* London: Witherby, 1939.

Whitaker, Thomas D. *A History of The Original Parish of Whalley.* London, 1818.

White Eagle. *The Path of the Soul: The Great Initiations of Every Man.* Liss, UK: White Eagle Publishing Trust, 1959.

White, Carolyn. *A History of Irish Fairies.* Cork, Ireland: Mercier Press, 1976.

White, Elijah. *Exorcism as a Christian Ministry.* New York: Morehouse-Barlow, 1975.

White, John. *Everything You Want to Know about TM, Including How to Do It.* New York: Pocket Books, 1976.

White, John, ed. *The Highest State of Consciousness.* Garden City, N.Y.: Anchor/Doubleday, 1972.

White, K. D. and M. R. Grimmer. "Psychics and ESP: Across the Enchanted Boundary?" *Australian Psychologist* 25, no. 2 (July 1990): 210–214.

White, Rhea. "Comparison of Old and New Methods of Response to Targets in ESP Experiments." *Journal of the American Society for Psychical Research* 58 (1964): 21–56.

———. "Depth Perspectives and Experimental Parapsychology." *International Journal of Parapsychology* 2, no. 2 (1960).

———. "ESP Score Level in Relation to Students' Attitudes Toward Teacher-Agents Acting Simultaneously." *Journal of Parapsychology* 22, no. 1 (1958).

———. "The Relationship Between Changes in Student Attitude and ESP Scoring."*Journal of Parapsychology* 22, no. 3 1958.

———. "A Survey of Work on ESP and Teacher-Pupil Attitudes." *Journal of Parapsychology* 22, no. 4 (1958).

———. "A Select Bibliography of Books on Parapsychology, 1985–1988." In *Advances in Parapsychological Research.* Vol. 6. Jefferson, N.C.: Mcfarland & Co. Inc., 1990.

———. "Suggestions for Exploring and Recording the Inscape of Psi Researchers," *European Journal of Parapsychology* 13 (1997): 96–109.

White, Rhea A., and Laura A. Dale. *Parapsychology: Sources of Information.* Metheun, N.J.: Scarecrow Press, 1973.

White, Ruth, and Mary Swainson. *Gildas Communicates; The Story and the Scripts.* London: Spearman, 1971.

White, Stewart Edward. *Across the Unknown.* N.p., n.d.

———. *Anchors to Windward.* N.p., 1943.

———. *The Betty Book.* New York: E. P. Dutton, 1930. Reprint, New York: E. P. Dutton, 1937. Reprint, New York: E. P. Dutton, 1939.

———. *The Road I Know.* N.p., 1942.

———. *The Stars Are Still There.* N.p., 1946.

———. *The Unobstructed Universe.* N.p., 1940.

———. *With Folded Wings.* N.p., 1947.

White, Terence H. *The Once and Future King.* London: Collins, 1958.

Whiteman, J. H. M. "Dream and Dreamlike States seen as kinds of Possession: Implications for Mediumship, ESP and Survival," *Journal of the Society for Psychical Research* 62, no. 852 (July 1998): 407–416.

———. *The Mystical Life: An Outline of Its Nature and Teachings from the Evidence of Direct Experience.* London: Faber & Faber, 1961.

———. "The Mystical Way, and Habitualizing of Mystical States." In *Handbook of States of Consciousness.* Edited by B. Wolman and Montague Ullman. New York: Van Nostrand Reinhold, 1986.

———. "Parapsychology and Physics." In *Handbook of Parapsychology.* Edited by B. Wolman. New York: Van Nostrand Reinhold, 1977.

———. "The Process of Separation and Return in Experiences Fully 'Out of the Body.' " *Proceedings of the Society for Psychical Research* 50 (1956).

Whiteman, Michael. *Philosophy of Space and Time and the Inner Constitution of Nature: A Phenomenological Study.* London: Allen & Unwin; New York: Humanities Pub., 1967.

Whiting, Beatrice Blyth, "Paiute Sorcery," *Viking Fund Publications in Anthropology* no. 15. New York: Viking Fund, 1950.

Whiting, Lilian. "The Spiritualistic Camp-Meetings in the United States." *Annals of Psychical Science* (January 1907).

Whitman, John. *The Psychic Power of Plants.* New York: New American Library, 1974. Reprint, London: W. H. Allen, 1974.

Whitten, Ivah Bergh. *What Color Means to You.* Ashington, England: C. W. Daniel, 1932.

Whittlesey, John R. B. "Further Comments on Causality." *Journal of Parapsychology* 17 (September 1953).

———. "Some Comments Apropos of Pooling." *Journal of Parapsychology* 23 (June 1959).

———. "Some Curious ESP Results in Terms of Variance." *Journal of Parapsychology* 24 (September 1960).

Whymant, Neville. *Psychic Adventures in New York.* London: Morley & Mitchell, 1931.

Wickland, Carl. *Thirty Years Among the Dead.* Los Angeles, 1924.

Wickwar, J. W. *The Ghost World.* London, n.d.

Wiedemann, A. *Popular Literature of Ancient Egypt.* London: David Nutt, 1902.

Wiertz, Antoine Joseph. *Antoine Wiertz, 1806–1865.* Paris: J. Damase, 1974.

Wiesel, Elie. *The Golem: The Story of a Legend.* New York: Summit Books, 1983.

Wiesinger, Alois. "Wie Stellt Sich der Katholik zu den okkulten Erscheinungen?" (The Attitude of the Catholic Toward Occult Phenomena). *Neue Wissenschaft* (1953).

Wilber, Ken. *Eye to Eye: The Quest for the New Paradigm.* Garden City, N.Y.: Anchor/Doubleday, 1983.

———. *No Boundary: Eastern and Western Approaches to Personal Growth.* Los Angeles: Center Publications, 1979.

———. *A Sociable God: A Brief Introduction to a Transcendental Sociology.* New York: McGraw-Hill, 1982.

———. *Up From Eden: A Transpersonal View of Human Evolution.* Garden City, New York: Anchor Press/Doubleday, 1981.

Wilber, Ken, Jack Engler, and Daniel P. Brown. *Transformation of Consciousness: Conventional and Contemplative Perspectives on Development.* Boston: New Science Library, 1986.

Wilbert, Johannes. *Tobacco and Shamanism in South America.* New Haven, Conn.: Yale University Press, 1987.

Wilcock, John. *A Guide to Occult Britain: The Quest for Magic in Pagan Britain.* London: Sidgwick & Jackson, 1976.

Wilczewski, Janusz, Zbigniew Szczerba, and Barbara Szbicka, eds. *Materialy z Konferencji Parapsychologow '94.* Warsaw: Polskie Towarzystwo Psychotroniczne, 1994.

Wilder, Franklin. *Good News for Martha Wesley.* Hicksville, N.Y.: Exposition Press, 1976.

Wilgus, Neal. *The Illuminoids.* New York: New American Library, 1989.

Wilhelm, Hans. *Your Chinese Horoscope.* New York: Avon, 1980.

Wilhelm, James J., and Laila Zamuelis Gross, eds. *The Romance of Arthur.* New York: Garland Publishing, 1984.

Wilhelm, Richard, and C. G. Jung. *The Secret of the Golden Flower: A Chinese Book of Life.* Rev. ed. New York: Harcourt, Brace, 1962. Reprint, New York: Causeway Books, 1975.

Wilke, Joanne. *William Blake's Epic: Imagination Unbound.* London: Croom Helm, 1986.

Wilken, Ernst. *Die Prosaische Edda.* Paderhorn, Germany, 1878.

Wilkins, Eithne. *The Rose-Garden Game.* London: Victor Gallancz, 1969.

Wilkins, Sir Hubert, and Harold M. Sherman. *Thoughts through Space: A Remarkable Adventure in the Realm of the Mind.* Hollywood, Calif.: House-Warren, 1951. Reprint, London: Frederick Muller, 1971. Reprint, Greenwich, Conn.: Fawcett, 1973.

Wilks, Washington. *Edward Irving: An Ecclesiastical and Literary Biography.* London, 1854.

Willey, Raymond C. *Modern Dowsing.* Cottonwood, Ariz.: Esoteric Publications, 1976.

Williams, George H. *The Radical Reformation.* Philadelphia: Westminster Press, 1962.

Williams, Gertrude Marvin. *Priestess of the Occult: Madame Blavatsky.* New York: Alfred A. Knopf, 1946.

Williams, Henry L. *Life of John Brown. . . . for 30 Years Personal Attendant of . . . The Queen.* London: E. Smith, 1883.

Williams, Joseph J. *Voodoos and Obeahs; Phases of West Indian Witchcraft.* New York: Dial Press, 1933.

Williams, L. F. R., ed. *Sufi Studies: East and West.* London: Octagon Press, 1974.

Williams, Mary. *Glastonbury: A Study in Patterns.* Hammersmith, England: Research into Lost Knowledge Organization, 1969.

Williams, Richard N., Carl B. Taylor, and Wayne J. Hintze. "The Influence of Religious Orientation on Belief in Science, Religion, and the Paranormal," *Journal of Psychology & Theology* 17, no. 4 (Winter 1989): 352–359.

Williams, Thomas A. *Eliphas Levi: Master of Occultism.* University, Ala.: University of Alabama Press, 1975.

Williams, Thomas Rhys. *The Dusun, A North Borneo Society: Case Studies in Cultural Anthropology* New York: Holt, Rinehart and Winston, 1965.

Williams, William F. *Encyclopedia of Pseudoscience.* New York: Facts on File, 1999.

Williamson, Roger Andrew. "Houston Stewart Chamberlain: A Study of the Man and His Ideas, 1855–1927." Ph.D diss., University of California-Santa Barbara, 1973.

Williamson, Tom, and Liz Bellamy. *Ley Lines in Question.* Kingwood, England: World's Work, 1983.

Willis, Tony. *The Runic Workbook.* New York: Sterling Publishers, 1986.

Wilmot, T. S. *Twenty Photographs of the Risen Dead.* Birmingham, England: Midland Educational, 1894.

Wilson, Clifford. *Crash Go the Chariots: An Alternative to "Chariots of the God."* New York: Lancer Books, 1972.

Wilson, Colin. *Beyond the Outsider.* Boston: Houghton, Mifflin, 1965.

———. *Enigmas and Mysteries.* Garden City, N.Y.: Doubleday, 1976.

———. *The Essential Colin Wilson.* London: Harrap, 1985.

———. *The Geller Phenomena.* London: Aldus Books, 1976.

———. *Guidance from Beyond.* N.p., 1923.

———. "James Webb and the Occult." *Light* (summer 1982).

———. *More Guidance from Beyond.* N.p., 1925.

———. *Mysteries: An Investigation into the Occult, the Paranormal, and the Supernatural.* New York: G. P. Putnam's Sons, 1978.

———. *Mysterious Powers.* Reprinted in the United States as *They Had Strange Powers.* Garden City, N.Y.: Doubleday, 1975.

———. *The Occult: A History.* London: Hodder & Stoughton; New York: Random House, 1971. Reprint, New York: Vintage Books, 1973. Reprint, London: Mayflower, 1973.

———. *Poltergeist: A Study in Destructive Haunting.* London: Hodder & Stoughton, 1981. New York: Putnam Publishing Group, 1982.

———. *Rasputin and the Fall of the Romanovs.* London: Arthur Barker, 1964.

———. *Strange Powers.* New York: Random House, 1973.

———. *The Unexplained.* Lake Oswego, Ore.: Lost Pleiade Press, 1975.

Wilson, Colin, ed. *Men of Mystery.* London: W. H. Allen, 1977.

Wilson, Colin, and John Grant, eds. *Directory of Possibilities.* Exeter, England: Webb & Bower, 1981.

Wilson, Ian. *The After Death Experience.* London: Sidgwick & Jackson, 1987.

———. *The Bleeding Mind.* London: Weidenfeld & Nicolson, 1988.

———. *Mind out of Time? Reincarnation Claims Investigated.* London: Gollancz, 1981. Revised as *Reincarnation?* Baltimore, Md.: Penguin Books, 1982.

———. *The Turin Shroud.* London: Gollancz, 1978.

Wilson, Joyce. *The Complete Book of Palmistry.* New York: Bantam Books, 1971.

Wilson, Mona. *The Life of William Blake.* London: Oxford University Press, 1971.

Wilson, Richard. "A Random Number Selector." *Proceedings of the American Society for Psychical Research* 48 (1946–49).

Wilson, Robert Anton. *Cosmic Trigger: Final Secret of the Illuminati.* Berkeley, Calif.: And/Or Press, 1977.

———. *The Illuminati Papers.* Berkeley, Calif.: And/Or Press, 1980.

———. *Illuminatus!* 3 vols. New York: Dell, 1975.

———. *Masks of the Illuminati.* New York: Timescape, 1981.

———. *The New Inquisition: Irrational Rationalism and the Citadel of Science.* Las Vegas, Nev.: Falcon Press, 1986.

Wilson, Thomas. *Blue-Beard: A Contribution to History & Folk-Lore.* London, 1899. Reprint, New York: B. Blom, 1971. Reprint, New York: Ayer Publishing Co. Inc., 1981.

Wincup, Gregory. *Rediscovering the I Ching.* Garden City, N.Y.: Doubleday, 1986.

Winer, Richard. *From the Devil's Triangle to the Devil's Jaw.* New York: Bantam Books, 1977.

———. *The Devil's Triangle.* New York: Bantam Books, 1974.

———. *The Devil's Triangle 2.* New York: Bantam Books, 1975.

Wingo, E. Ortha. *The Story of the Huna Work.* Cape Girardeau, Mo.: Huna Research, 1981.

Winkelman, Michael. "A Cross-Cultural Study of Shamanistic Healers," *Journal of Psychoactive Drugs* 21, no. 1 (January–March 1989): 17–24.

Winkelman, Michael James, "Shamans, Priests and Witches: A Cross-Cultural Study of Magico-Religious Practitioners." *Arizona State University Anthropological Research Papers* no. 44. Tempe: Anthropology Department, Arizona State University, 1993.

Winkler, Gershon. *The Golem of Prague.* New York: Judaica Press, 1980.

Winsbro, Bonnie C. "Supernatural Forces: Belief, Difference, and Power in Contemporary Works by Ethnic Women," *Dissertation Abstracts International* 53, no. 8-A (February 1993): 2819.

Winstedt, R. *The Malays: A Cultural History.* London: Routledge, 1950.

Winzeler, Robert L., ed. "The Seen and the Unseen: Shamanism, Mediumship and Possession in Borneo," *Borneo Research Council Monograph Series* vol. 2. Williamsburg, Va.: Borneo Research Council, Inc., 1993.

Wirth, Oswald. *Stanislas de Guaita, souvenirs de son secrétare.* Paris: Editions du Symbolisme, 1935.

The Wisdom of Silver Birch. London: Psychic Book Club, 1944.

The Wisdom of White Eagle. Liss, Hampshire, England: White Eagle Publishing Trust, 1967.

Wisdom Workshop Lessons. 12 vols. Los Angeles: Fellowship of Universal Guidance, n.d.

Wiseman, Richard, John Beloff, and Robert L. Morris. "Testing the ESP Claims of SORRAT," *Journal of the Society for Psychical Research* 58, no. 829 (October 1992): 363–377.

Witchell, Nicholas. *The Loch Ness Story.* London, 1974. Rev. ed. London: Penguin Books, 1975.

Witherspoon, Thomas E. *Myrtle Fillmore, Mother of Unity.* Unity Village, Mo.: Unity Books, 1977.

Witte, Alfred. *Regelwerk für Planetbilder.* 3d ed. Hamburg: Witte Verlag, 1935. Translated by Richard Svehla as *Rules for Planetary Pictures.* Hamburg: Witte Verlag, 1939.

Witte, Alfred, and Herman Lefeldt. *Rules for Planetary Pictures.* Translated by Kurt Knupfer. Hamburg: L. Rudolph (Witte Verlag), 1974.

Witte, Karl Heinz. "Das 'Unbewusste': Die 'mystische' Seite des Rationalen?" (The 'unconscious': The Mystic Aspect of Rationality?), *Zeitschrift fuer Individualpsychologie* 23, no. 4 (1998): 356–374.

Wittemans, Frank. *The Golden Rosicrucians.* Edmonds, Wash.: Holmes Publishing Group, 1994.

Wittkower, E. D., "Trance and Possession States," *International Journal of Social Psychiatry* 16, no. 2 (1970): 153–160.

Wohlberg, J., "Haoma-Soma in the World of Ancient Greece," *Journal of Psychoactive Drugs* 22, no. 3 (1990): 333–342.

Wolf, Laibl. *Practical Kabbala.* New York: Crown Publishing Group, Inc., 1999.

Wolf, Leonard. *The Annotated Dracula.* New York: Clarkson N. Potter, 1975.

———. *Bluebeard: The Life & Crimes of Gilles de Rais.* New York: Crown, 1980.

Wolf-Gumpold, Kaethe. *William Blake: Painter, Poet, Visionary: An Attempt at and Introduction to his Life and Work.* London: Rudolf Steiner Press, 1969.

Wolfe, Burton H. *The Devil's Avenger.* New York: Avon Books, 1974.

Wolfe, N. B. *Startling Facts in Modern Spiritualism.* Cincinnati, Ohio: The Author, 1874. Reprint, Chicago: Religio-Philosophical Publishing House, 1875.

Wolff, Charlotte. *The Human Hand.* London: Methuen, 1942.

Wollgast, Siegfried. *Der deutsche Pantheismus im 16. Jahrhundert.* Berlin: Deutscher Verlag der Wissenschaften, 1972.

Wolman, Benjamin B., ed. *Handbook of Parapsychology.* New York: Van Nostrand Reinhold, 1977. Reprint, Jefferson, N.C.: McFarland, 1986.

The Wonderful History of Virgilius The Sorcerer of Rome. London: Daure Nutt, 1893.

Wood, Ernest. *Yoga.* London, 1959. Reprint, Baltimore, Md.: Penguin, 1962.

Wood, F. H. *After Thirty Centuries.* London: Rider, 1935.

———. *This Egyptian Miracle.* London: Rider, 1940. Rev. ed. London: J. M. Watkins, 1955.

Wood, Thomas E. *The Mandukya Upanishad and the Agama Shastra: An Investigation into the Meaning of the Vedanta.* Honolulu: University of Hawaii Press, 1990.

Woodhouse, Barbara. *Talking to Animals.* Croxley Green, England: Campions, 1970.

Woodhull, Victoria. *Garden of Eden: Allegorical Meaning Revealed.* London: The Author, 1889.

———. *Humanitarian Government.* London: The author, 1892.

———. *Stirpiculture; or, the Scientific Propagation of the Human Race.* London: The Author, 1888.

Woodhull, Victoria, and Tennessee Claflin. *The Human Body the Temple of God.* London, 1890.

Woodroffe, Sir John. *The Garland of Letters (Varnamala): Studies in the Mantra-Shastra.* Madras, India: Ganesh, 1951.

———. *Sakti and Sakta.* Madras, India: Ganesh, 1918.

Woodruff, J. L. "Some Basic Problems for Parapsychological Research." *Journal of Parapsychology* 12 (1948).

Woodruff, J. L., and J. G. Pratt. "Size of Stimulus Symbols in Extrasensory Perception." *Journal of Parapsychology* 3 (1939).

Woodruff, J. L., and Laura A. Dale. "ESP Function and the Psychogalvanic Response." *Journal of the American Society for Psychical Research* 46 (1952).

———. "The Psychokinetic Effect: Further ASPR Experiments." *Journal of the American Society for Psychical Research* 41 (1947).

———. "Subject and Experimenter Attitudes in Relation to ESP Scoring." *Journal of the American Society for Psychical Research* 44 (1950).

Woods, William H. *History of the Devil.* London, 1973, New York: G. P. Putnam's Sons, 1974.

Woodward, Ian. *The Werewolf Delusion.* London & New York: Paddington Press, 1979.

Woodward, Mary Ann. *Edgar Cayce's Story of Karma.* New York: Coward-McCann, 1971.

Woofenden, William Ross. *Swedenborg Researcher's Manual.* Bryn Athyn, Pa.: Swedenborg Scientific Association, 1988.

Worcester, Elwood. *Allies of Religion.* Boston: Marshall Jones, 1929.

———. *The Christian Religion as a Healing Power.* New York: Moffat, Yard, 1909.

———. *Life's Adventure.* New York: Charles Scribner's Sons, 1932.

Worcester, Elwood, and Samuel McComb. *Body, Mind and Spirit.* Boston: Marshall Jones, 1931.

Worcester, Elwood, Samuel McComb, and Isador Ciriat. *Religion and Medicine.* New York: Moffat, Yard, 1908.

Worcester, William L. *Lessons in Correspondence.* 1892. Reprinted as *The Language of Parable: A Key to the Bible.* New York: Swedenborg Foundation, 1984.

Worrall, Ambrose A. *The Gift of Healing.* Baltimore, Md.: The Author, 1961.

———. *The Philosophy and Methodology of Healing.* Baltimore, Md.: The Author, 1961.

Worrall, Ambrose A. and Olga Worrall. *Basic Principles of Spiritual Healing.* Evanston, Ill.: Spiritual Frontiers Fellowship, 1969.

———. *Explore Your Psychic World.* New York: Harper & Row, 1970.

———. *The Gift of Healing: A Personal Story of Spiritual Therapy.* New York: Harper & Row, 1965.

Worrall, Olga. *How to Start a Healing Service.* Chicago: Inner Creations, 1947.

Worsley, Peter. *The Trumpet Shall Sound.* New York: Schocken Books, 1962.

Worth, Patience." *Hope Trueblood.* New York: Henry Holt, 1918.

———. *Light from Beyond: Poems of Patience Worth.* Compiled by Herman Behr. New York: Patience Worth Publishing, 1923.

Worth, Patience." *The Pot upon the Wheel.* New York: Patience Worth Publishing, 1916. Reprint, St. Louis, Mo.: Dorset Press, 1921.

———." *The Sorry Tale.* New York: Henry Holt, 1917.

Wraxall, Lascelles. *Remarkable Adventurers and Unrevealed Mysteries.* 2 vols. London, 1863.

Wright, Dudley. *The Epworth Phenomena.* London: William Rider & Son, 1917.

———. *Vampires & Vampirism.* London, 1914. Reprinted as *The Book of Vampires.* New York: Causeway, 1973.

Wright, Machaelle S. *Behaving As If the God in All Life Mattered.* N.p., 1983.

———. *The Perelandra Garden Workbook.* N.p., 1987.

Wright, Peggy A. "The Nature of the Shamanic State of Consciousness: A Review," *Journal of Psychoactive Drugs* 21, no. 1 (January-March 1989): 25–33.

Wright, Thomas. *Narratives of Sorcery and Magic.* 2 vols. London: R. Bentley, 1851. Reprinted as *Narratives of Sorcery and Magic from the Most Authentic Sources.* Detroit: Omnigraphics, Inc., 2000.

Wright, Thomas, ed. *A Contemporary Narrative of the Proceedings Against Dame Alice Kyteler.* 1843. Reprint, New York: AMS Press, 1968.

Wuenschel, Edward. *Self-Portrait of Christ.* New York: Esopus, 1954.

Wyckoff, James. *Franz Anton Mesmer.* Englewood Cliffs, N.J.: Prentice-Hall, 1975.

Wydenbruck, Nora. *Doctor Mesmer.* London: John Westhouse, 1947.

Wyman, Walker D. *Witching for Water, Oil, Pipes, and Precious Minerals.* River Falls: University of Wisconsin Press, 1977.

Wyndham, Horace. *Mr. Sludge: The Medium.* London: G. Bles, 1937.

Wynn [Sidney K. Bennett]. *Astrology, Science of Prediction.* Los Angeles: Wynn Publishing, 1945.

———*Astrology, Your Path to Success.* Philadelphia: David McKay, 1938.

———. *The Key Cycle.* 1931. Reprint, Tempe, Ariz.: American Federation of Astrologers, 1970.

Wynne, Barry. *Behind the Mask of Tutankhamen.* New York: Taplinger, 1973.

Wynne-Tyson, Esmé. *Mithras, the Fellow in the Cap.* London: Rider, 1968.

X, Miss [Ada Goodrich-Freer]. *Essays in Psychical Research.* London: George Redway, 1899.

X, Miss [Ada Goodrich-Freer], and John, Marquess of Bute. *The Alleged Haunting of B. House.* London, 1899. Rev. ed. 1900.

Xavier, Francisco Candido. *Christian Agenda.* London: Regency Press, 1970.

———. *The World of the Spirit.* New York: Philosophical Library, n.d.

"Xenes." *Joanna Southcott and Her Box.* London: W. Foulsham, 1927.

Yang, C. K. *Religion in Chinese Society.* Berkeley: University of California Press, 1961.

Yarbro, Chelsea Quinn. *Messages from Michael.* Chicago: Playboy Press, 1979.

———. *Michael's People.* New York: Berkeley Books, 1988.

———. *More Messages from Michael.* New York: Berkeley Books, 1986.

———. *The Vampire Stories of Chelsea Quinn Yarbro.* White Rock, B.C.: Transylvania Press, 1994.

Yarker, John. *The Arcane Schools: A Review of Their Origin and Antiquity; With a General History of Freemasonry.* Belfast: William Tait, 1909.

Yaryan, Homer T. "An Investigator's Experience of Materialization Phenomena." *Psychic Science* (October 1926).

Yates, Frances A. *The Rosicrucian Enlightenment.* London: Routledge & Kegan Paul, 1972.

Yatiswarananda, Swami. *Universal Prayers.* 6th ed. Hollywood, Calif.: Vedanta Press, 1963.

Yearbook of the American Academy of Astrologians. 2 vols. New York: Hermetic Publishing, 1917, 1918.

Yearsley, Macleod. *The Folklore of Fairy-Tale.* London: Watts, 1924. Reprint, Detroit: Singing Tree Press, 1968.

Yeats, W. B., ed. *Fairy and Folk Tales of the Irish Peasantry.* London: Walter Scott Publishing, 1888. Reprint, New York: Grosset & Dunlap, 1957.

Yeats, William Butler. *Autobiography.* New York: Macmillan, 1938.

———. *Is the R. R. et A. C. to Remain a Magical Order?* Privately printed, 1901.

———. *Memoirs.* New York: Macmillan, 1973.

———. *Mythologies.* New York: Macmillan, 1959.

Yeats-Brown, F. *Bengal Lancer.* London: V. Gollancz Ltd., 1930. Reprinted as *The Life of a Bengal Lancer.* New York: Viking Press: 1931.

Yellowtail, Thomas. *Yellowtail: Crow Medicine Man and Sun Dance Chief. An Autobiography, as told to Michael Oren Fitzgerald.* Norman: University of Oklahoma Press, 1991.

Yogananda, Swami Paramahansa. *Autobiography of a Yogi.* New York: Philosophical Library, 1946. Reprint, Los Angeles: Self-Realization Fellowship, 1971.

———. *Descriptive Outlines of Yogoda.* Los Angeles: Yogoda Satsang Society, 1928.

———. *The Divine Romance.* Los Angeles: Self-Realization Fellowship, 1986.

———. *Metaphysical Meditation.* Los Angeles: Self-Realization Fellowship, 1960.

———. *The Science of Religion.* Los Angeles: Yogoda Sat-Sanga Society of America, 1928.

———. *Whispers of Eternity.* Los Angeles: Self-Realization Publishing House, 1944.

Yogashakti Saraswati, Ma. *Prayers and Poems from Mother's Heart.* Melbourne, Fla.: Yogashakti Mission, 1976.

———. *Shree Shree Narayana Vrata Katha.* Melbourne, Fla.: Yogashakti Mission, n.d.

———. *Yoog Vashishtha.* Gondia, India: Yogashakti Mission, [1970].

Yost, Casper S. *Patience Worth; A Psychic Mystery.* New York: Henry Holt, 1916. Reprint, London: Skeffington, 1919.

Yost, G. W. N. *Blavatsky's Posthumous Memoirs.* Boston: Joseph M. Wade, 1896.

Young, Barbara. *This Man from Lebanon: A Study of Kahlil Gibran.* New York: Alfred A. Knopf, n.d.

Young, Frank W. *Initiation Ceremonies: A Cross-Cultural Study of Status Dramatization.* Bobbs-Merrill, 1965.

Young, James Harvey. *The Medical Messiahs.* Princeton N.J.: Princeton University Press, 1967.

Younghusband, Sir Francis. *The Living Universe.* London: John Murray, 1933.

———. *Modern Mystic.* London: John Murray, 1935. Reprint, New Hyde Park, N.Y.: University Books, 1970.

Youngson, Jeanne, and Shelley Leigh Hunt, ed. *Do Vampires Exist? A Special Report from Dracula World Enterprises.* New York: Dracula World Enterprises, 1993.

Youngson, Jeanne, ed. *A Child's Garden of Vampires.* Chicago: Adams Press, 1980.

———. *The Count Dracula Book of Classic Vampire Tales.* Chicago: Adams Press, 1981.

Yram [Marcel L. Forham]. *Le Medecin de l'Ame'.* Translated as *Practical Astral Projection.* London, 1935. Reprint, New York: Samuel Weiser, 1966.

———. *Le Medecine de l'Ame.* English edition as *Practical Astral Projection.* London, 1935. Reprint, New York: Samuel Weiser, 1966.

Zacharias, Paul. *Insights into the Beyond.* New York: Swedenborg Publishing Association, n.d.

Zaehner, R. C. *Hindu and Muslim Mysticism.* London: Athlone Press, 1960.

———. *Mysticism; Sacred & Profane.* London: Clarendon Press, 1957. Reprint, London: Galaxy Book; Oxford University Press, 1961.

Zain, C. C. *Ancient Masonry.* Los Angeles: Church of Light Press, 1998.

———. *Cosmic Alchemy.* Los Angeles: Church of Light Press, 1997.

———. *Natural Alchemy.* Los Angeles: Church of Light Press, 1997.

Zain, C. C. [Elbert Benjamine]. *Brotherhood of Light Lessons.* 21 vols. Los Angeles: Church of Light, 1922–1932.

Zalewski, Pat and Christine Zalewski. *The Equinox & Solstice Ceremonies of the Golden Dawn.* St. Paul, Minn.: Llewellyn Publications, 1992.

Zalewski, Patrick J. *Golden Dawn Enochian Magic.* St. Paul, Minn.: Llewellyn Publications, 1990.

———. *Secret Inner Order Rituals of the Golden Dawn.* Phoenix, Ariz.: Falcon Press, 1988.

Zenor, Richard. *Maggie Answers You.* San Diego: Philip J. Hastings, 1965.

Zetznerus, L., ed. *Theatrum Chimicum.* 6 vols. Strasbourg, France, 1659–61.

Zha, Leping and Tron McConnell. "Parapsychology in the People's Republic of China: 1979–1989," *Journal of the American Society for Psychical Research* 85, no. 2 (April 1991): 119–143.

Zingaropoli, F. *Case Infestate degli Spiriti.* Naples, 1907.

Zinsstag & Timothy Good. *George Adamski: The Untold Story.* Beckenham, UK: Ceit Publications, 1983.

Zitko, Howard John. *The Lemurian Theochristic Conception.* N.p., n.d.

Zolar [Bruce King]. *Black Magic.* New York: Arco Publishing, 1972.

———. *Dreams and Your Horoscope.* New York: Zolar Publishing, 1970.

———. *The Encyclopedia of Ancient and Forbidden Knowledge.* Los Angeles: Nash, 1970.

———. *Fortune Telling with Cards, Palmistry.* New York: Arco Publishing, 1973.

———. *History of Astrology.* New York: Arco Publishing, 1972.

———. *It's All in the Stars.* New York: Zolar Publishing, 1962.

———. *Nature's Mysteries.* New York: Arco Publishing, 1972.

———. *Sex and the Zodiac.* New York: Zolar Publishing, 1971.

Zolar Staff. *Encyclopedia of Signs, Omens & Superstitions.* Secaucus, N.J.: Carol Publishing Group, 1995.

Zöllner, J. C. F. *Transcendental Physics.* London, 1880. Reprint, Boston: Colby and Rich, 1881. Reprint, North Stratford, N.H.: Ayer Co. Publishers, Inc., 1976. Reprint, Las Vegas, Nev.: Health Research; Kila, Mont.: Kessinger Publishing Co., 1996.

Zopfius, Johan Heinrich. *Dissertatio de Vampiris Seruiensibus.* Halle, 1733.

Zorab, George A. M. *Bibliography of Parapsychology.* Parapsychology Foundation, 1957.

———. "A Case for Survival." *Journal of the Society for Psychical Research* 31 (1946).

———. *D. D. Home, il Medium.* Milan, 1976.

———. *De Jacht op het Spiritistisch Bewijs* (In Quest of Proof for Survival). The Hague: Boucher, 1940.

———. *De Opstandingsverhalen in het Licht de Parapsychologie* (The Resurrection Narratives in the Light of Parapsychology). N.p., 1949.

———. "ESP Experiments with Psychotics." *Journal of the Society for Psychical Research* 39 (1957).

———. "A Further Comparative Analysis of Some Poltergeist Phenomena Cases from Continental Europe." *Journal of the American Society for Psychical Research* 58 (1964).

———. *Katie King: Donna o Fantasma.* Milan: Armenia Editore, 1980.

———. *Magnetiseurs en Wondergenezers* (Magnetism and Miracle Healers). N.p., 1952.

———. *Parapsychologie* (Parapsychology). N.p., 1958.

———. *Proscopie, Het Raadsel der Toekomst* (Precognition, the Riddle of the Future). N.p., 1953.

———. *Wichelroede en Aardstralen* (The Divining Rod and Earthrays). N.p., 1950.

———. *Wonderen der Parapsychologie* (Wonders of Parapsychology). N.p., 1954.

Zorab, George A. M., P. A. Dietz, and K. H. E. de Jong. *Parapsychologische Woordentolk* (A parapsychological dictionary). N.p., 1956.

Zubeck, John P., ed. *Sensory Deprivation: Fifteen Years of Research.* Appleton-Century-Crofts, 1969.

Zugibe, Frederick T. *The Cross and the Shroud: a Medical Inquiry into the Crucifixion.* New York: Paragon House Publishers, 1988.

Zuromski, Paul. "A Conversation with Charles Thomas Cayce." *Psychic Guide* (September–November 1984): 14–19.

———. "Dick Sutphen." *Body, Mind, Spirit* (September/October 1987): 14–18.

Zymonidas, A. *The Problems of Mediumship.* London: Kegan Paul, 1920.

General Index

General Index

B

C

D

E

General Index

G

H

General Index

I

J

K

L

M

General Index

General Index

N

O

General Index

General Index

S

T

U

W

X

Y

Z